THE CONTINUUM

Encyclopedia of
CHILDREN'S
LITERATURE

BERNICE E. CULLINAN
and DIANE G. PERSON, Editors

A Giniger Book

CONTINUUM

NEW YORK • LONDON

2001

The Continuum International Publishing Group Inc
370 Lexington Avenue, New York, NY 10017

The Continuum International Publishing Group Ltd
The Tower Building, 11 York Road, London SE1 7NX

The K. S. Giniger Company, Inc., Publishers
250 West 57th Street
New York, NY 10107

Printed in the United States of America

Library of Congress Cataloging-in-Publication Data

The Continuum encyclopedia of children's literature / Bernice E. Cullinan and Diane G.
Person, editors.
p.   cm.
"A Giniger book."
Includes bibliographical references and index.
ISBN 0-8264-1271-8 (hardcover : alk. paper)
1. Children's literature—Encyclopedias.   2. Children's
literature—Bio-bibliography—Dictionaries.   I. Title: Encyclopedia of children's literature.
II. Cullinan, Bernice E.   III. Person, Diane Goetz.

PN1008.5.C66 2001
809′.89282′03—dc21
00-059036

THE CONTINUUM

Encyclopedia of

CHILDREN'S
LITERATURE

Dedicated to

Jamison Webb Ellinger, Trisha Carley, Jason R. Ream, Kali Brooke Ream
B.E.C.

Yonatan David Rechtman, Liya Naomi Rechtman, My Special Angel
D.G.P.

Board of Advisers

Guide to Topical Articles

List of Author-and-Illustrator Photographs

1. Verna Aardema
2. Alma Flor Ada
3. David Adler
4. Arnold Adoff
5. Janet and Allan Ahlberg
6. Aliki
7. Hans Christian Andersen
8. Anno Mitsumasa
9. Isaac Asimov
10. Avi
11. Natalie Babbitt
12. Byron Barton
13. Byrd Baylor
14. John Bellairs
15. Judy Blume
16. Bruce Brooks
17. Marcia Brown
18. Margaret Wise Brown
19. Joseph Bruchac
20. Eve Bunting
21. Betsy Byars
22. Eric Carle
23. Beverly Cleary
24. Joanna Cole
25. Barbara Cooney
26. Susan Cooper
27. Robert Cormier
28. Joy Cowley
29. Donald Crews
30. Roald Dahl
31. Tomie dePaola
32. Leo and Diane Dillon
33. Walt Disney
34. Lois Ehlert
35. Paul Fleischman
36. Mem Fox
37. Paula Fox
38. Russell Freedman
39. Jean Fritz
40. Wanda Gag
41. Jean Craighead George
42. Gail Gibbons
43. James Cross Giblin
44. Patricia Reilly Giff
45. Nikki Giovanni
46. Paul Goble
47. Eloise Greenfield
48. Robert A. Heinlein
49. Kevin Henkes
50. S. E. Hinton
51. Lillian Hoban
52. Tana Hoban
53. Lee Bennett Hopkins
54. Langston Hughes
55. Mollie Hunter
56. Johanna Hurwitz
57. Pat Hutchins
58. Trina Schart Hyman
59. Ezra Jack Keats
60. Eric A. Kimmel
61. E. L. Konigsburg
62. Karla Kuskin
63. Patricia Lauber
64. Madeleine L'Engle
65. Julius Lester
66. C. S. Lewis
67. Astrid Lindgren
68. Leo Lionni
69. Jean Little
70. Myra Cohn Livingston
71. Anita Lobel
72. Arnold Lobel

73. Lois Lowry
74. David Macaulay
75. Margaret Mahy
76. Patricia MacLachlan
77. Jan Mark
78. James Marshall
79. John Marsden
80. Ann M. Martin
81. Robert McCloskey
82. Bruce McMillan
83. Emily Arnold McCully
84. Fredrick and Patricia McKissack
85. Milton Meltzer
86. Eve Merriam
87. A. A. Milne
88. Jim Murphy
89. Walter Dean Myers
90. Sheldon Oberman
91. Scott O'Dell
92. Katherine Paterson
93. Gary Paulsen
94. Philippa Pearce
95. Jerry Pinkney
96. Patricia Polacco
97. Beatrix Potter
98. Jack Prelutsky
99. Margret and H. A. Rey
100. Faith Ringgold
101. J. K. Rowling
102. Cynthia Rylant
103. Allen Say
104. Jon Scieszka
105. Lane Smith and Jon Scieszka
106. Maurice Sendak
107. Dr. Seuss (Theodor Geisel)
108. Ernest H. Shepard
109. Seymour Simon
110. Isaac Bashevis Singer
111. Elizabeth George Speare
112. John Steptoe
113. James Stevenson
114. Mildred Taylor
115. J. R. R. Tolkien
116. Michael O. Tunnell
117. Chris Van Allsburg
118. Jules Verne
119. Cynthia Voigt
120. Martin Waddell
121. Rosemary Wells
122. E. B. White
123. Laura Ingalls Wilder
124. Garth Williams
125. Don and Audrey Wood
126. Laurence Yep
127. Jane Yolen
128. Ed Young
129. Paul O. Zelinsky
130. Paul Zindel

Author-and-Illustrator-Photo Credits

Alma Flor Ada courtesy Simon and Schuster
Children's Publishing
David Adler courtesy Scholastic
Arnold Adoff courtesy HarperCollinsPublishers
Children's Books
Janet and Allan Ahlberg courtesy Penguin
Putnam Books for Young Readers
Aliki by Val Lambros courtesy
HarperCollinsPublishers Children's Books
Anno Mitsumasa courtesy
HarperCollinsPublishers Children's Books
Isaac Asimov: Literarische Agentur Utoprop/Jan
Kay Klein
Avi courtesy Orchard Books
Natalie Babbitt courtesy Farrar, Straus and
Giroux
Byron Barton courtesy HarperCollinsPublishers
Children's Books
Byrd Baylor courtesy Simon and Schuster
Children's Publishing
John Bellairs courtesy Penguin Putnam Books for
Young Readers
Judy Blume courtesy Orchard Books
Bruce Brooks courtesy HarperCollinsPublishers
Children's Books
Marcia Brown courtesy Simon and Schuster
Children's Publishing
Margaret Wise Brown by Consuelo Kanaga
courtesy HarperCollinsPublishers Children's
Books
Joseph Bruchac courtesy
HarperCollinsPublishers Children's Books
Eve Bunting courtesy Clarion Books
Betsy Byars courtesy Penguin Putnam Books for
Young Readers
Eric Carle by Sigrid Estrada courtesy Penguin
Putnam Books for Young Readers
Beverly Cleary by Alan McEwen, 1999, courtesy
HarperCollinsPublishers Children's Books
Barbara Cooney courtesy Penguin Putnam Books
for Young Readers
Susan Cooper courtesy Simon and Schuster
Children's Publishing
Robert Cormier by Beth Bergman, courtesy
Random House Children's Books

Joy Cowley courtesy Boyds Mills Press
Donald Crews by Nina Crews courtesy
HarperCollinsPublishers Children's Books
Roald Dahl courtesy Penguin Putnam Books for
Young Readers
Tomie dePaola Copyright Jon Gilbert Fox
courtesy Penguin Putnam Books for Young
Readers
Walt Disney courtesy Hyperion
Lois Ehlert courtesy HarperCollinsPublishers
Children's Books
Paul Fleischman by Becky Mojica courtesy
HarperCollinsPublishers Children's Books
Mem Fox by Randy Larcombe courtesy Harcourt
Brace
Paula Fox courtesy Orchard Books
Russell Freedman courtesy Clarion Books
Jean Fritz courtesy Penguin Putnam Books for
Young Readers
Jean Craighead George by Ellan Young
Photography courtesy
HarperCollinsPublishers Children's Books
Gail Gibbons courtesy Holiday House, Inc.
James Cross Giblin by Miriam Berkley courtesy
HarperCollinsPublishers Children's Books
Patricia Reilly Giff by Tornbery Associates
courtesy of Random House Children's Books
Paul Goble courtesy Orchard Books
Patricia Reilly by Tornberg Associates, Giff
courtesy of Random House Children's Books
Eloise Greenfield courtesy
HarperCollinsPublishers Children's Books
Robert A. Heinlein: Literarische Agentur
Utoprop/Jay Kay Klein
Kevin Henkes courtesy HarperCollinsPublishers
Children's Books
Lillian Hoban courtesy HarperCollinsPublishers
Children's Books
Tana Hoban courtesy HarperCollinsPublishers
Children's Books
Lee Bennett Hopkins courtesy Boyds Mills Press
Mollie Hunter courtesy HarperCollinsPublishers
Children's Books
Pat Hutchins by Laurence Hutchins courtesy
HarperCollinsPublishers Children's Books

Trina Schart Hyman courtesy Holiday House, Inc.

Eric A. Kimmel courtesy Holiday House, Inc.

E. L. Konigsburg courtesy Simon and Schuster Children's Publishing

Karla Kuskin by Piper Productions

Madeleine L'Engle courtesy Farrar, Straus and Giroux

Leo Lionni courtesy of Random House Children's Books

Julius Lester by Milian Sabatini

C. S. Lewis © HarperCollins Publishers

Astrid Lindgren courtesy Penguin Putnam Books for Young Readers

Jean Little courtesy HarperCollinsPublishers Children's Books

Myra Cohn Livingston courtesy Scholastic, Inc.

Anita Lobel courtesy HarperCollinsPublishers Children's Books

Arnold Lobel by Van Williams courtesy HarperCollinsPublishers Children's Books

Lois Lowry by Amanda Smith courtesy Clarion Books

David Macaulay courtesy Clarion Books

Margaret Mahy by Vanessa Hamilton courtesy Penguin Putnam Books for Young Readers

Patricia MacLachlan by Judy B. Messer

Jan Mark courtesy HarperCollinsPublishers Children's Books

John Marsden courtesy Clarion Books

Ann M. Martin by Susan Richman courtesy Scholastic, Inc.

Robert McCloskey by Mary Velthoven courtesy Penguin Putnam Books for Young Readers

Bruce McMillan courtesy Clarion Books

Emily Arnold McCully by Tom Bloom

Fredrick and Patricia McKissack by Alan Mills © 1998

Milton Meltzer by Catherine Norer

Eve Merriam by Bachrach

A. A. Milne courtesy Penguin Putnam Books for Young Readers

Jim Murphy courtesy Clarion Books

Walter Dean Myers by Constance Myers courtesy HarperCollinsPublishers Children's Books

Sheldon Oberman courtesy Boyds Mills Press

Scott O'Dell courtesy Clarion Books

Katherine Paterson by Samantha Loomis Paterson

Gary Paulsen courtesy Simon and Schuster Children's Publishing

Philippa Pearce courtesy HarperCollinsPublishers Children's Books

Patricia Polacco courtesy Penguin Putnam Books for Young Readers

Beatrix Potter Copyright © Frederick Warne and Company courtesy Penguin Putnam Books for Young Readers

Jack Prelutsky courtesy HarperCollinsPublishers Children's Books

Margret and H. A. Rey courtesy Clarion Books

Faith Ringgold courtesy of Random House Children's Books

J. K. Rowling Courtesy Scholastic, Inc.

Allen Say courtesy Clarion Books

Jon Scieszka by Brian Smale courtesy Penguin Putnam Books for Young Readers

Lane Smith and Jon Scieszka by Brian Smale

Ernest H. Shepard courtesy Penguin Putnam Books for Young Readers

Seymour Simon by Billy Cunningham courtesy HarperCollinsPublishers Children's Books

Isaac Bashevis Singer © 1991, Jerry Bauer, courtesy Farrar, Straus and Giroux

Elizabeth George Speare courtesy Clarion Books

John Steptoe by James Ropiequet Schmidt courtesy HarperCollinsPublishers Children's Books

James Stevenson courtesy HarperCollinsPublishers Children's Books

J. R. R. Tolkien by Roger Hill

Michael O. Tunnell courtesy Holiday House, Inc.

Chris Van Allsburg courtesy Clarion Books

Jules Verne: Deutsche Staatsbibliothek Berlin/ Grambow

Cynthia Voigt by Walter Voigt courtesy Simon and Schuster Children's Publishing

Martin Waddell by Terry Brown courtesy Candlewick Press

Rosemary Wells courtesy Penguin Putnam Books for Young Readers

E. B. White by Donald E. Johnson

Garth Williams Copyright © 1992 H. D. Potter

Don and Audrey Wood courtesy Harcourt Brace

Laurence Yep by K. Yep

Jane Yolen courtesy Boyds Mills Press

Ed Young courtesy Penguin Putnam Books for Young Readers

Paul O. Zelinsky courtesy Penguin Putnam Books for Young Readers

Introduction

Literature written especially for children's pleasure is a relatively recent phenomenon. John Newbery first published books for children to enjoy but, like other children's books of their day, they were intended for instruction in socially acceptable behavior. The Industrial Revolution allowed middle-class children, no longer working, more opportunity to read. As child labor decreased and child reading increased, a literature written especially for them began to grow. This early literature first appeared in England; it nurtured the imagination and encouraged the dissolution of child labor. Books such as George MacDonald's *At the Back of the North Wind* (1871) and Charles Kingsley's *The Water Babies* (1863) dealt with a make-believe world alongside a realistic one. These and other books represented the prevailing notion that people should write for children strictly for their enjoyment rather than for their instruction or moral development. They appeared with Lewis Carroll's *Alice's Adventures in Wonderland* (1865) and were soon reprinted in English–speaking countries throughout the world. They are still read by children who delight in a book written just for pleasure. Many of the books children adopted as their own were actually written for adults, such as Robert Louis Stevenson's *Treasure Island* (1883), Johann David Wyss's *The Swiss Family Robinson; or, The Shipwreck of the Swiss Minister and His Family* (1812–14), and *Adventures of Huckleberry Finn* (1884) by Mark Twain. The successful publication of *Alice's Adventures in Wonderland* encouraged other writers of fantasy and realistic novels. Louisa May Alcott published *Little Women* in two volumes in 1888 and 1889, respectively. In 1898, Ernest Thompson Seton published *Wild Animals I Have Known* in Canada. Mrs. Ambrose Moore published *Fairyland* in New Zealand in 1909. In 1918, May Gibbs published *Snugglepot and Cuddlepie* in Australia.

When the first laws restricting child labor were enacted and public-school attendance was made available, more children could read and, consequently, the quantity of books published for them increased rapidly. At the same time, new technology helped reduce publishing costs. Public libraries created separate children's rooms and storytelling hours were established. The generosity of charitable individuals, notably Andrew Carnegie, made books available to vast numbers of children. In 1918, Macmillan in the United States established a separate department for children. Other publishers including those in England followed. The purpose of early publications for children was to instill community values in them and to socialize them in the ways of their elders. Over the past one hundred fifty years or so, this approach changed to reflect a broad spectrum of values from a wide range of cultures. Children have now been introduced to the lives of other children living amid political turmoil, social upheaval, and alternate lifestyles. Today, children's books reflect the variety of topics and extensive genres available to adults.

The need to recognize quality in children's literature became apparent to leaders in the field. In the United States the Newbery Medal, named for a British bookseller, was established in 1922 to honor excellence in the text of children's books. The Caldecott Medal, named for a British illustrator, was established in 1938 to identify outstanding illustration in children's literature. The Carnegie Medal for outstanding work was established in the United Kingdom in 1938 and the Kate Greenaway Award for illustration was established in 1955. The Canadian Library Association's Children's Book of the Year has been given annually since 1947 and the Amelia Frances Howard-Gibbon Award, recognizing illustration, since 1971. New Zealand established the Esther Glen Award in 1945 for the most distinguished contribution to children's literature by a citizen and Australia established the Children's Book of the Year Awards in 1946 for literary merit. Award programs have grown to include specific genres, such as the National Council of Teachers of English Orbis Pictus Award, established in 1990 for informational books, and the NCTE Award for Poetry for Children.

THE WORK

The Continuum Encyclopedia of Children's Literature is intended as a comprehensive single-volume reference source describing the development and current trends in children's literature throughout the world. Because of its genesis, there is an emphasis on the English–speaking countries and/or works appearing in English translation. To our knowledge, no other reference book in any language is its equivalent. The work contains 97 topical entries and some 1,200 biographical entries on authors and illustrators of books for children and young adults, which include biographical data and critical discussion of their work. We include entries for authors and illustrators who publish specifically for children as well as those whose work has been embraced by children and young adults. We also acknowledge books written for a young audience that cross over to adult audiences. So-called crossovers has become an especially important category among librarians who increasingly face budgetary constraints. The result of this trend is the establishment of a separate children's book best-seller list in the *New York Times,* as well as a column devoted to crossovers in one library journal, *Booklist.*

As noted, we primarily considered material appearing in English that has found a place in the hearts of children. The full study of children's literature includes a study of genres, forms, development, awards, authors, and illustrators. It encompasses work over the course of time, across national boundaries, and through the changing definitions of childhood. Traditional genres including fairy tales, adventure stories, and oral storytelling are discussed along with groundbreaking new modalities such as Internet resources, websites for children, and technology and communications.

Five years in the making, this *Encyclopedia* is intended for use by scholars, teachers, librarians, parents, and children. It represents the collaborative work of a distinguished international board of advisers and contributors.

BASES OF SELECTION

The selection of authors and illustrators for inclusion in the *Encyclopedia* is based on an evaluation of an author's or illustrator's significant contribution to the field regardless of the amount of work written or published. Working with the board of advisers from the library and teaching professions as well as the professional literature, a recommended list of authors and illustrators was assembled. As a reading specialist, a children's librarian, and as educators, we ultimately used our professional judgment; final responsibility for inclusion and exclusion rests with us. We try to stay abreast of all the current journals as contributors and readers, and are active in professional organizations. Consideration has also been given to the selections children have made over the years. The entries represent their choices as well. Children usually have unfailingly good taste in discovering books that they love to read. Their instincts often make for enduring classics.

Despite the breadth of the *Encyclopedia,* it is inevitable when working with authors and illustrators representing five continents and a nearly one hundred-fifty-year time frame that authors and illustrators significant to children's literature will have been omitted. Efforts to be as comprehensive as possible resulted in inclusion of such authors and illustrators in topical entries whenever possible. We have closely followed trends—such as comic books and graphic novels, and the latest artists—without succumbing to trendiness for its own sake.

ENTRIES—ORGANIZATION AND DATA

Topical entries appear in appropriate alphabetical sequence with cross-references to related entries. All cross-references to other authors, illustrators, and related topics are included where appropriate within the text entry. When an author, illustrator, or topic is cited in another entry, the last name (or topic) is in SMALL-CAPITAL LETTERS the first time it appears.

Individual author and illustrator entries are usually organized in five parts: full name with date and place of birth and death (where applicable) followed by brief biographical information with critical discussion and highlights of the author or illustrator's major work as well as notable achievements. By and large, we do not attempt critical interpretation or pass judgment on the literary or artistic value of an author's or illustrator's work. A list of significant awards appears next, followed by a list, or select list, of further works. Entries conclude with bibliographical materials used to write the entry. For many entries, particularly where the individual has a limited body of published work, few bibliographical sources are available. Working with our contributors, we have searched available print and online sources. In many cases, especially for recently published authors and illustrators, only a single source of bibliographic data is available. We have used that source and attempted to confirm the material with the respective publishers.

ABBREVIATIONS, CROSS-REFERENCES, AND PSEUDONYMS

Author-and-illustrator entries are arranged alphabetically by last name. Authors and illustrators best known by their pseudonyms are entered this way, with an appropriate cross-reference.

CONTRIBUTORS

The contributors represent a broad range of authors as well as library and university professionals in the field from across the United States, Canada, and other English–speaking countries. Many topical entries were prepared by notable authorities. Each author-and-illustrator entry or topical article appears over the name of the individual contributor or joint contributors.

ACKNOWLEDGMENTS

We wish to express our appreciation to all those individuals who helped make this book possible. The suggestions of our distinguished international board of advisers helped us focus on, and identify, the figures most worthy of biographical entries. The board unfailingly recommended knowledgeable scholars to research and write the entries.

We are grateful for the vision of Kenneth S. Giniger, who recognized the need for a comprehensive volume and encouraged us to develop this *Encyclopedia.* Our editor, Evander Lomke, provided editorial wisdom and was accessible at all times by fax, E-mail, and telephone, as well as through encounters and meetings with Stanley Person. Our copy editor, Bruce Cassiday, patiently read and recommended elegant revisions. Thanks are also due Russell Wolinsky and William E. Jerman for proofreading services; to Steven R. Serafin for editorial help; to Donna Ryan for indexing. We would like to recognize Martin Gomez, Executive Director, and Evan Kingsley, Deputy Director, of the Brooklyn Public Library who put the full resources of the Youth Division at our service. Martin Dooley, Pepi Brooks, Barbara Genco, Helen Hurwitz, Susan Levy, Vandana Ranjan, Amy

Sears, Mary Ann Sekely, and Paul Smaldone were extremely helpful. The Port Washington Public Library staff, Carey Ayres, Rachel Fox, Lucy Salerno, and Joni Simon, provided valuable resources. The Donnell Branch of the New York Public Library, especially John Peters, was an important source for tracking down and verifying information. Marjorie Glassman faithfully helped us meet deadlines and stay in touch with our contributors. Angie Orsino kept careful track of our contributors and their entries. Louis Valentino provided encouragement with his coffee, office supplies, and conference table. We thank the Writer's Group: Ann Lovett, who read and reviewed entries; Ginnie Schroder, Marilyn Scala, Joie Hinden, and Deborah Wooten who listened to ideas, wrote entries, and made valuable recommendations; Martin Lipsitt, who advised on the dust jacket. We also thank owners of copyrighted artwork for their generosity.

Finally, we could not have done this without our families. Our love and thanks go to our children and grandchildren. Special thanks go to Marguerite Ellinger and Hara Person who became contributors as well as manuscript editors and proofreaders when called upon. Thanks to Yigal Rechtman, who provided technical support, computer literacy, and assurance that no, the manuscript has not disappeared. More special thanks to Stanley Person, who lived with papers on the kitchen table, provided encouragement, a central switchboard, meeting room, and cheerfully transported manuscript over the last few years. We further thank our children, Marguerite and James Webb Ellinger, Hara Person and Yigal Rechtman, Janie and Alan Carley, Jennifer Person and Craig Lieberman. They provided support and love at the right times. We both agree that working on this project has been a challenging but ultimately rewarding venture that strengthened the bonds of family and friendship.

B. E. C.

D. G. P.

THE CONTINUUM

Encyclopedia of

CHILDREN'S
LITERATURE

AARDEMA, Verna

Author, b. 6 June 1911, New Era, Michigan; d. 11 May 2000, Fort Myers, Florida

A.'s love of STORYTELLING began when her mother would read stories to A. and her eight siblings. A. would often sit behind her brothers and sisters so they could not see her crying if the story was sad. The first book she owned and cherished as a child was *Hans Christian ANDERSEN's Fairy Tales.* It contained her favorite story, "The Little Mermaid," a tale with a sad ending that would bring her to tears just before bedtime. A. called her favorite place to spend time the "secret room," a cedar swamp cave hidden behind her house where she imagined and wrote her first stories. When she was eleven, she showed her mother a poem she had written; her mother bestowed one of the highest accolades upon A. by saying, "Why, Verna, you're going to be a writer just like my Grandpa Vander Ven." From then on, A. would escape to her secret room to write stories and to avoid washing dishes.

A. wrote for the school newspaper while she attended high school. At Michigan State College (now University) she took all of the writing courses they offered. She began her writing career as a staff correspondent for *The Muskegan Chronicle.* A.'s first book resulted from stories she created to coax her young daughter to eat. The first tale published was a so-called AFRICAN feeding story entitled *Tales from the Story Hat* (1960), a result of her longtime interest in African legends and folktales. Since then, A. has written over twenty-five books that are based on folktales from around the world, especially Africa.

A. is regarded as one of the best storytellers in the United States. This is because of her meticulous attention to detail, her ability to preserve the culture from which her stories originate, and her knowledge of the techniques of the oral tradition. Because A. retold folktales, she often began with authentic tales she heard from African immigrants. After hearing the stories, she tried to find them in print, and then create her own version of the tales based on her research. *This for That: A Tonga Tale,* (1997) has been criticized by reviewers for using Westernized stereotypes of Africans, a rare exception in her work.

In contrast, *Why Mosquitoes Buzz in People's Ears: A West African Tale* (1975) has been heralded by many as A.'s best work. This humorous book is based on a West African folktale regarding the origin of the buzzing sound mosquitoes make. The myth is retold by several different animals throughout the book, who each have their own version of the story. This leads to misunderstanding and further miscommunication, which teaches readers the importance of cause and effect. Young readers are captivated by A.'s use of onomatopoeia, such as her description of the iguana who "went off mek, mek, mek, through the reeds." This allows readers to become engaged with the text instead of just reading the words on the page.

Play with words can also be found in *Misoso: Once upon a Time Tales from Africa* (1994). The book contains twelve different African folktales intended to be read aloud. Once again, A. uses rhythm, repetition, and cadence to encourage listeners to chant along. These stories also contain HUMOR and vivid imagery to pique readers' imaginations.

Several of A.'s books such as *Anansi Does the Impossible* (1997) and *Misoso: Once upon a Time Tales from Africa,* include glossaries and dictionaries to aid readers in learning more about the culture discussed in the text. This is where A.'s attention to detail is realized. It not only preserves the history and culture of people, but it also introduces new readers to the history and customs of that particular part of the world.

AWARDS: Children's Book Showcase Award (1974) for *Behind the Back of the Mountain: Black Folktales from Southern Africa.* National Parenting Publications Award and the *Redbook* Children's Picture Book Award (1991) for *Borrequita and the Coyote;* ALA CALDECOTT MEDAL (1976) for *Why Mosquitoes Buzz in People's Ears.* AMERICAN LIBRARY ASSOCIATION Notable Book and Booklist Editors' Choice (1991) for *Traveling to Tondo: A Tale of Nkundo of Zaire*

FURTHER WORKS: *Otwe,* 1960; *The Na of Wa,* 1960; *The Sky-God Stories,* 1960; *More Tales from the Story Hat,* 1966; *Tales for the Third Ear,* 1969; *Who's in Rabbit's House?,* 1977; *Ji-Nongo-Nongo,* 1978; *The Riddle of the Drum: A Tale from Tizapan, Mexico,* 1979; *Half-a-Ball-of-Kenki: An Ashanti Tale,* 1979; *Bringing the Rain to Kapiti Plain,* 1981; *What's so Funny, Ketu?,* 1982; *The Vingananee and the Tree Toad: A Liberian Tale,* 1983; *Oh, Kojo! How Could You!,* 1984; *Bimwili and the Zimwi,* 1985; *Princess Gorilla and a New Kind of Water,* 1988; *Rabbit Makes a Monkey of Lion,* 1989; *Pedro and the Padre,* 1991; *Borreguita and the Coyote,* 1991; *Anansi Finds a Fool,* 1992; *Koi and the Kola Nuts: A Tale from Liberia,* 1999

BIBLIOGRAPHY: A., V. *A Bookworm Who Hatched,* 1992; the *Horn Book* magazine, 1998; *Kirkus Reviews,* 1994, 1996; *Something about the Author,* vol. 68, 1992

DENISE P. BEASLEY

AASENG, Nathan
Author, b. 7 July 1953, Park Rapids, Minnesota

When A. set out to become a writer he had no intention of writing for a juvenile audience. However, he soon discovered that he had a voice and perspective that appealed to that particular age group. A. writes SPORTS STORIES for youngsters that profile these heroes. However, he has also tried to write about those heroes in ways that are realistic and that keep them in perspective. A. has also done sports fiction, including *A Winning Season for the Braves,* 1982, which is based on his own early endeavors in athletics. Most of A.'s sports titles have been selected as Children's Choice award titles.

A.'s collective biographies focus on twentieth-century inventors who have contributed to the advance of technology and the eradication of disease. Titles such as *Better Mousetraps: Product Improvements That Led to Success* (1990) are characterized by A.'s emphasis on the human aspect of each inventor and the impact of the invention on the social history of the times.

FURTHER WORKS: *Baseball: You Are the Manager,* 1983; *Football's Most Controversial Calls,* 1986; *Baseball: It's Your Team,* 1985; *Football, It's Your Team,* 1985; *Disease Fighters,* 1987; *Inventors,* 1988; *Rejects,* 1989

MICHAEL O'LAUGHLIN

ABOLAFIA, Yossi
Author, illustrator, animator, b. 4 June 1944, Tiberias, Israel

Born and reared in Israel, A. began taking drawing seriously while in high school on an Israeli kibbutz. After studying graphic design at the Bezalel Art Academy, he drew ILLUSTRATIONS and cartoons for an army news magazine and later as an animator and cartoonist for the Israel Television Authority. His work eventually brought him to North America where he began to illustrate other people's stories. Some award-winning books that Abolafia has illustrated include Barbara Ann PORTE's *Harry's Mom* (1985), Jack PRELUTSKY's *My Parents Think I'm Sleeping* (1985), and Miriam CHAIKIN's *Aviva's Piano* (1986).

FURTHER WORKS: Self-Illustrated: *My Three Uncles,* 1985; *A Fish for Mrs. Gardenia,* 1988; *Fox Tale,* 1989; Illustrator: Jack Prelutsky, *It's Valentine's Day,* 1983; Barbara Ann Porte, *Harry Gets an Uncle,* 1991; Meir Shalev, *My Father Always Embarrasses Me,* 1990

BIBLIOGRAPHY: *Something about the Author,* vol. 60, 1990

MARY ARIAIL BROUGHTON

ACHEBE, Chinua
Author, poet, b. 15 November 1930; Ogidi, Nigeria, Africa

Born in a small village in eastern Nigeria where his father taught at a church missionary school, A. studied medicine and literature at the University of Ibadan. He then worked for the Nigerian Broadcasting Corporation in Lagos as director of external broadcasting before becoming a professor of literature at the University of Nigeria at Nsukka. In the United States he has taught at the Universities of Massachusetts and Connecticut. His first novel, *Things Fall Apart* (1958), a classic that has sold over two million copies, recounts the effects of colonialism on the residents of a small village early in the twentieth century, and the struggle to retain traditions as experienced by Okonkwo, a leading member of the Obi tribe. Writing in English, A. effectively describes the universal influence of traditional ways and religious superstition on people as they live through changing times. He has received many international AWARDS and honors including a fellowship from the Modern Language Association of America (MLA) and the Commonwealth POETRY Prize in 1972 for *Beware Soul Brother.*

FURTHER WORKS: *A Man of the People,* 1966; *AFRICAN Short Stories,* A. and C.L. Innes, eds., 1985

BIBLIOGRAPHY: Cott, Jonathan, *Pipers at the Gates of Dawn: The Wisdom of Children's Literature,* 1983

DIANE G. PERSON

ACKERMAN, Karen
Author, b. 9 October 1951, Cincinnati, Ohio

A. came to writing for children from a career as a poet and dramatist. In addition to writing for stage and film, she studied heraldic script, pottery and other aspects of materials culture. Historical events and stressful family circumstances often inform the plots of A.'s stories which feature young children who are well-connected to caring and realistic relatives. Events in the real world are presented in terms that are accessible to young readers and influence, while not intruding upon, the personal stories of A.'s fictional characters. Some of A.'s PICTURE BOOK texts are written in rhyme, such as *Flannery Row* (1986), which combines a recounting of the alphabet with a sea captain's farewell to his children.

Family ties are strong in A.'s stories. *Song and Dance Man* (1988) is the story of a former vaudeville actor who is still quite capable of entertaining his grandchildren with his old soft-shoe routine. *The Tin Heart* (1990) and *When Mama Retires* (1992) depict American family life during wartime. In the former, two children wear a symbolic heart divided into halves to represent their friendship although the Civil War pits their fathers against each other. In the second, a mother changes from the work of homemaker to a job as a riveter in a war plant during World War II. A.'s novel *The Night Crossing* (1994) recounts a Jewish family's escape in 1938 from Austria to a safe haven in Switzerland.

Social issues are made relevant and accessible in A.'s work. *By the Dawn's Early Light* (1994), a picture book, features a contemporary mother who works the night shift. As a single parent, she and her children must rely on help from her own mother to care for the family and to keep them safe. *The Leaves of October* (1991), a novel, considers the issue of homelessness, presenting life through the eyes of a nine-year-old girl who has been deserted by her mother and brought to a homeless shelter by her unemployed father. A. delivers these socially accurate stories as simple truths that include evidence of parental warmth and awareness of the child's need to sense security is attainable.

A.'s picture book texts provide psychologically sound, historically revealing stories in which literary merit is not compromised by the implicit messages that familial love is the greatest treasure. Her novels for children present realistic problems that require sensitivity on the parts of both the children and the adults within the story.

AWARDS: 1989 CALDECOTT MEDAL for *Song and Dance Man* (illustrated by Stephen GAMMELL); 1989 Society of Midland Authors Fiction Award

FURTHER WORKS: *Araminta's Paint Box,* 1990; *Movable Mabeline,* 1990; *The Banshee,* 1990; *The Broken Boy,* 1991; *This Old House,* 1992; *I Know a Place,* 1992; *The Sleeping Porch,* 1995

FRANCISCA GOLDSMITH

ADA, Alma Flor

Writer, professor, b. 3 January 1938, Camaguey, Cuba

Daughter of a professor and a teacher, A. is a graduate of Universidad Central de Madrid, (1959); Pontificia Universidad Catolica del Peru, M.A., 1963, Ph.D., 1965; Harvard University, postdoctoral study, 1965–67. A. worked as an instructor and head of the Spanish Department, was a Fulbright Scholar, taught at Emory University, became an associate professor of romance language, professor of language and codirector of the Institute for Bilingual Bicultural Studies. She has also served as a member of the selection committee for Fulbright Overseas Fellowship Program, chair of the National Seminar on Bilingual Education, National Policy Conference on Bilingual Education and the International Congress of Children's Literature in Spanish. A. has been a consultant to publishing houses and a visiting professor at the University of Guam, and the University of Texas, El Paso. A. has participated in the development of a number of reading series for children and translated numerous texts from English to Spanish. Currently, she is a professor of MULTICULTURAL education at the University of San Francisco, California.

A. grew up in Cuba on the outskirts of Camaguey in a big old house whose front door led to the street but whose back door led to a garden filled with fruit trees, flowers, and animals. A.'s grandmother was an excellent storyteller; she and other members of her extended family were always available to tell A. stories, to participate in garden activities, and to listen to her adventures. A. says "I was always trying to make sense of the world around me and continually asking questions: Why were so many people poor? What did ants do inside their anthills? But I also spent many hours lost in the world of books. Almost all the books I read as a child were TRANSLATIONS from other languages, so it isn't surprising that as I grew up I began to translate many books from English into Spanish."

A.'s career goals were formed early. She says, "As a young child I could not accept the fact that we had to read such boring textbooks while my wonderful storybooks awaited at home. I made a firm commitment while in the fourth grade to devote my life to producing schoolbooks that would be fun to read. I am having a lot of fun doing just that." A. says "I feel I'm very fortunate to be able to do in life just what I love to do: write and teach. To see the books I have written in the hands of any child is one of the greatest joys I can think of. To see them in the little hands of my grandchildren is a gift beyond belief."

A.'s early writings were written and published in Spanish. More recently her publications appear in separate Spanish and English editions, or in bilingual versions, as in *Gathering the Sun: An Alphabet in Spanish and English* (1997) and *The Christmas Tree* (1997). A.'s publications are based on a solid foundation and knowledge of FOLKLORE. For example, *The Malachite Palace* (1998) is a traditionally inspired FAIRY TALE involving a princess whose family feels she is too delicate to play with the neighborhood children. A. also writes about Hispanic children who face discrimination as in *My Name Is Maria Isabel* (1993). She has written stories using the technique of a series of letters between characters: *Dear Peter Rabbit* (1994), and *Yours Truly, Goldilocks* (1998).

A. writes in nearly every genre. Some of her books are retellings of folklore: *The Rooster Who Went to His Uncle's Wedding* (1993, 1998), and *The Lizard and the Sun* (1997). She writes POETRY: *Abecedario de los animales* (1998), *Cancion de todos los ninos del mundo, Gathering the Sun* (1997). She writes autobiography: videotapes *Writing from the Heart* and *Meeting an Author; Where the Flame Trees Bloom* (1994) and *Under the Royal Palms: A Childhood in Cuba* (1998). She writes real-life stories set in Mexico: *El Vuelo de los colibries* (1995) and *El manto de plumas* (n.d.). A. is an excellent example of a writer who both understands and produces high-quality multicultural literature. She has examined cultural issues and addresses them in her writing for children.

AWARDS: The Christopher Award, American Booksellers Association Pick of the Lists, and the NCSS/CBC Notable Book in the Field of Social Studies (1991) for *The Gold Coin;* ABA Pick of the List and Aesop Award Accolade (1995) for *Medio-Pollito/Half Chicken;* Parent's Choice Honor Award, (1997) for *Dear Peter Rabbit;*

NCSS/CBC Notable Book in the Field of Social Studies (1996) for *My Name Is Isabel;* Pura Belpre Honor Book (1997) for *Gathering the Sun: An ABC in Spanish and English;* American Booksellers Association Pick of the Lists (1997) for *The Rooster Who Went to His Uncle's Wedding*

FURTHER WORKS: *The Gold Coin,* 1991; *Mediopolliato/Half Chicken,* 1995; *Moneda de oro,* 1991; *My Name Is Maria Isabel,* 1996; *Dear Peter Rabbit,* 1997; *Yours Truly, Goldilocks,* 1998; *The Malachite Palace,* 1997

BIBLIOGRAPHY: Ada, Alma Flor. *Under the Royal Palms: A Childhood in Cuba,* 1998. Ada, Alma Flor. *Where the Flame Trees Bloom* (1994); *Contemporary Authors Online,* www.galenet.com/servlet/GLD

BERNICE E. CULLINAN

ADAMS, Adrienne

Author, illustrator b. 8 February 1906, Fort Smith, Arizona

An illustrator of more than fifty children's books, A. has for many decades delighted children with her colorful illustrations. Known primarily for her skillfully crafted art, A. also authored award-winning PICTURE BOOKS like *The Easter Egg Artists* (1976), winner of the Irma Simonton Black Award, Bank Street College. In this story, Orson Abbot, a young rabbit, has parents who are Easter-egg artists. However, Orson is more interested in using Easter-egg designs to paint other things like the car and household items. When he decides to paint an Ostrich egg, it becomes a great success. *The Easter Egg Artists* is a creative blend of artistic design, HUMOR, and self-discovery that showcases A.'s talent with the medium of pastel ILLUSTRATION. Orson Abbot reappeared in two more adventures, *The Christmas Party* (1978) and *The Great Valentine's Day Balloon Race* (1980). Philosophically, A. believed that "a book cannot succeed unless little children love it and wear out its cover and pages. . . ." A's artistic contributions, as illustrator for numerous authors, far outnumber her independent efforts. A. and her husband collaborated on many books: e.g., *Ponies of Mykillengi* (1966), *Two Hundred Rabbits* (1968), *Mr. Biddle and the Birds* (1971), *Izzard* (1973), *The Halloween Party* (1974), and *Arion and the Dolphins* (1978). In *Two Hundred Rabbits,* A. transports the reader to another time and place, using double-page watercolor landscapes

to create a bucolic setting where a boy is aided by a rabbit in an effort to please a king. In *Houses from the Sea* (1959), an identification book on seashells, A. creates beautifully delicate watercolor illustrations. A.'s illustrations also appeared in several works by Rumer GODDEN, including *Impunity Jane* (1954); *The Fairy Doll* (1956); *Mouse House* (1957); *The Story of Holly and Ivy* (1958); and *Candy Floss* (1960). In addition, A. has illustrated classic folktales from the Brothers GRIMM, such as *The Shoemaker and the Elves* (1960); *Snow White and Red Rose* (1964), *Jorinda and Joringel* (1968); *Hansel and Gretel* (1975), and Andrew LANG, adapter, *The Twelve Dancing Princesses* (1966), as well as two of Hans Christian ANDERSEN'S FAIRY TALES, *Thumbelina* (1961) and *The Ugly Duckling* (1965).

AWARDS: CALDECOTT MEDAL Honor Book (1960) for *Houses from the Sea,* and (1962) for *The Day We Saw the Sun Come Up* (both books by Alice Goudey); Lewis CARROLL Shelf Award, (1962) for *Thumbelina; Boston Globe–Horn Book* Illustration Honor, 1968, *Jorinda and Joringel;* Rutgers University College of Library Sciences, (1973) for Contributions to Children's Literature

FURTHER WORKS: *The Summer Is Magic* with Patricia Gordon, 1952; *The Light in the Tower* with Patricia Gordon, 1957; *Where Does Everyone Go?* with Aileen FISHER, 1961; *Favorite Fairy Tales Told in Scotland* with Virginia HAVILAND, 1963; *In the Middle of the Night* with Aileen Fisher, 1965; *Poetry of the Earth,* an illustrated collection of poems compiled by ADAMS, 1972; *The River Bank* (from Kenneth GRAHAME's *The Wind in the Willows*), 1977; *The Wounded Duck* with Peter Barnhart, 1979; *A Halloween Happening* 1981

ANDREW KANTAR

ADAMS, Richard (George)

Author, b. 9 May 1920, Newbury, Berkshire, England

The beloved children's FANTASY novel *Watership Down* (1972) appears to have been written for children, but often surprises readers to know that it was originally published for adults. A. first told the story to his children at bedtime, but when he wrote down the story at their bidding it was rejected by many publishers before being printed for adults by Rex Collins in 1972 and reprinted by Penguin (juvenile) in 1974, winning the Guardian Award and the CARNEGIE MEDAL. *Wa-*

tership Down's release as an animated film by Avco Embassy in 1978 also reinforced the connection to children as an audience.

How this graduate of Worster College, Oxford (M.A., 1972), became one of the best known writers of ANIMAL fantasy is a story of hard government work. A. served in the British army during World War II, and then in the Home Service following the war. Working his way up to assistant secretary in the Department of the Environment in 1968, A. only became a full-time writer in 1974 after the success of his story about rabbit society and the encroachment of humanity on animals' habitats.

Although A. does not recognize the distinction between juvenile and adult writing, he has written several books that are appropriate for, and have been well-received by, older children and adolescents. *Shardik* (1974), a fantasy in which society worships a giant bear (Shardik), continues A.'s legacy of being able to accurately describe the behavior of animals and to provide them with personality without inflicting them with anthropomorphism. Like *Shardik* and *Watership Down*, *The Plague Dogs* (1977), A.'s third novel revolves around animal experiences within the human world, this time taking on the dangerous life of animals used in scientific experimentation.

While all of these books were read by YOUNG ADULTS and deemed appropriate for their reading, some of A.'s books have been seen as more adult, including his first novel with human characters, *The Girl in the Swing* (1980). Made into a film in 1989, *The Girl in the Swing* is a psychological ghost story and a wide departure from his earlier writing. *Maia* (1985) a high-fantasy novel revolving around humans, might be seen as the connection between this human novel and his animal fantasy.

In *Traveller* (1988), A. returns to his animal characters, this time the horse of Robert E. Lee. Traveller sees the events of the American Civil War and filters them, naturally, through his perspective. A.'s ability to take on so many animals' perspectives, and make them palatable to humans, has secured his niche in children's literature. A. lives and writes in Hampshire, England.

FURTHER WORKS: (with Max Hooper): *Nature through the Seasons,* 1975; *Tales from Watership Down,* 1976; *The Unbroken Web: Stories and Fables,* 1980

BIBLIOGRAPHY: *Major Authors and Illustrators for Children and Young Adults,* 1993; Kirkpatrick, D. L., (ed.), *Twentieth Century Children's Writers,* 1978

GWYNNE ELLEN ASH

ADLER, C. S. (Carole Schwerdtfeger)
Author, b. 23 February 1932, Long Island, New York

A former English teacher, A. writes novels and short stories for adolescents because she considers them the most interesting people around. A.'s writing is often personal; she writes about emotional problems and family relationships. She eschews global concerns such as nuclear war; rather, she writes about issues that children often face in their everyday lives, such as child abuse or latchkey homes. A significant number of A.'s books contain elements of magic such as her first published work, *The Magic of the Glits* (1979), a recipient of several AWARDS. A.'s writing is generally full of optimism; she hopes that when adolescents read her work, they will find ways of dealing with life that they had not thought of before.

AWARDS: 1979, Golden Kite Award for *The Magic of the Glits;* 1983, AMERICAN LIBRARY ASSOCIATION Best YOUNG ADULT Books of the Year for *The Shell Lady's Daughter*

FURTHER WORKS: *Carly's Buck* 1981; *With Westie and the Tin Man,* 1985; *Always and Forever Friends,* 1988; *The Cat That Was Left Behind,* 1981; *Daddy's Climbing Tree,* 1993; *One Sister Too Many,* 1999

BIBLIOGRAPHY: *Something about the Author,* vol. 63, 1991

MARY ARIAIL BROUGHTON

ADLER, David
Author, b. 10 April 1947, New York City

A., author of mysteries, ADVENTURE STORIES, riddle books, and BIOGRAPHIES, is successful, prolific, and versatile. He is well known for his riddle books, biographies, mystery SERIES, and PICTURE BOOKS. A. acknowledges that because of the numerous genres he writes in, he is able to vary his work every day, "from doing research on a nonfiction book to writing fiction to creating a silly riddle or poem." During 1997, ten of A.'s books were released by five different publishers. The author's success is evident in the many AWARDS his works have received and the wide distribution of his books. His works have been translated into Chinese, Danish, Dutch, German, Hebrew, Japanese, Spanish, Swedish, and colloquial British speech. Some of his books have also been published in Braille.

A. grew up in New York City, the second of six children. As a child, he and his siblings spent every Friday afternoon visiting the library and every Friday night reading books. Although his favorite books were biographies, baseball stories, and mysteries, he did not plan to become a writer. He thought he would become a baseball player or a United States senator. In college, he majored in economics and graduated from Queens College in New York in 1968. In 1971, he received a master's degree in marketing from New York University. A. worked as a financial writer, cartoonist, math teacher, arts and crafts teacher, and waiter before becoming a children's author. It was his young nephew who gave A. the inspiration to write his first book when the child asked him a long series of questions. A. wrote some of the questions and his answers in his journal, these entries eventually led to his first book, *A Little at a Time* (1976), the award-winning story of a small boy going for a walk to a museum with his grandfather.

Since then, A. has written over 150 fiction and nonfiction books in various genres, including several MYSTERY series. His first fictional detective was Cam Jansen, a red-haired girl who uses her photographic memory to help her solve mysteries. The books also feature her timid friend, Eric Sheldon, who helps her solve crimes as they attempt to unravel clues. In addition, A. writes mysteries about Houdini Foster, a young magician. In each of these books, the main character performs a magic trick that gets him involved in a mystery. At the end of the book, the author includes instructions so the reader can try the magic tricks. Other mystery series include the Jeffrey's Ghost ADVENTURE series, the Fourth Floor Twins adventure series, and the T. F. Benson mystery series.

A. has written several books that deal with Jewish culture and the HOLOCAUST. His award-winning nonfiction work, *We Remember the Holocaust* (1989), contains historical commentary, photos, and recollections from survivors of the concentration camps in World War II. *Hiding from the Nazis* (1997) is the true story of a Jewish child placed with a Christian family in Dutch farm country. A. has also published *A Picture Book of Jewish Holidays* (1981), an AMERICAN LIBRARY ASSOCIATION Notable Book, *Jewish Holiday Fun* (1987), and *The Kids' Catalog of Jewish Holidays* (1996). *The Number on My Grandfather's Arm* (1987) received the Sydney TAYLOR Book Award as one of the best Jewish children's books of the year by the Association of Jewish Libraries.

The author's versatility as a writer is further illustrated in his many picture-book biographies, several of which have won awards. Among his acclaimed books in this genre is *Our Golda: The Story of Golda Meir* (1984), an Outstanding Social Studies Book for Children and the Carter G. Woodson Award Honor Book citation by the National Council for the Social Studies. His *Thomas Jefferson: Father of Our Democracy* (1987) was a 1988 Children's Books of the Year of the Child Study Book Committee. And his *A Picture Book of Martin Luther King, Jr.* (1989), was a Children's Book Council Outstanding Social Studies Book for Children and received a citation for one of the best books of the year by the Society of School Librarians International. A. notes that books in this format are difficult to write because the history surrounding the character must be woven into the story in a small amount of space while keeping the book focused on the life of the subject.

A. notes that his ideas come from his experiences and people he has known. For example, A. recalls that the inspiration for *I Know I'm a Witch* (1988) came from an incident in his youth when a neighbor's boy convinced him that a jar of brown liquid was a magic potion. When his son Michael was eight years old, he read the first three chapters of A.'s *Benny, Benny, Baseball Nut* (1987) and recognized himself as a character in the manuscript.

FURTHER WORKS: PICTURE BOOKS: *Bunny Rabbit Rebus,* 1983; *Happy Hanukkah Rebus,* 1989; *The Rabbit and His Driver,* 1993; *One Yellow Daffodil,* 1993; BIOGRAPHY: *A Picture Book of Abraham Lincoln,* 1989; *Jackie Robinson: He Was the First,* 1989; *A Picture Book of Anne Frank,* 1993; Puzzle/Riddle Books: *A Teacher on Roller Skates* and Other School Riddles, 1989; Easy Math Puzzles, 1997; Nonfiction: Amazing Magnets, 1983; Breathe In, Breathe Out: All About Your Lungs, 1991; Fraction Fun, 1997; Shape up: Making Shapes, Eating Polygons, 1998

BIBLIOGRAPHY: Lewis, V. "David A.," Instructor, vol. 105, i.3, 1995; Major Authors and Illustrators for Children and YOUNG ADULTS: A Selection of Sketches from Something about the Author, vol. 1, 1993; McElmeel, S.; 100 Most Popular Children's Authors, 1999; Sixth Book of Junior Authors and Illustrators, 1989

MARY ARIAIL BROUGHTON

ADOFF, Arnold

Author, poet, anthologist, b. 16 July 1935, New York City

A. is one of the first writers to portray black subjects accurately and consistently in a mode that conveys universalism. Born in New York City, he grew up in a neighborhood of mixed working-class residents. A. was the son of a pharmacist, a Polish immigrant. His family environment was rich in literature, music, causes for social justice and strong Jewish influence. All genres of reading material were readily available except the comics, which his grandmother prohibited. Conversation, expression of views, and declamation were invited and common in their everyday lives. A. started college at Columbia University School of Pharmacy, but left to study literature and history at The City College of New York. He received a B.A. in 1956 and continued in graduate studies at Columbia University from 1956 to 1958. Ten years later, he attended the New School for Social Research from 1965 to 1967. The fusion of these studies led to careers in teaching, anthropology, in literary agentry, and eventually writing.

A. is recognized for his ability to communicate intimate relationships of family and friends in his writings while not adhering to strict traditional usage of capitalization and punctuation. Myriad tones and moods are represented in his idiosyncratic style, which he believes promotes movement and the rhythm of POETRY.

In addition to A.'s obvious values of family, other life experiences that have impacted his writings occurred as he taught in Harlem and on Manhattan's Upper West Side. He began collecting

AFRICAN AMERICAN LITERATURE for his students because no appropriate anthologies seemed to exist. He wanted to expose his students to good literature written by and about blacks; at the same time, he was learning from his students' lives. He married award-winning children's writer Virginia HAMILTON in 1960. They have two children (now grown) who inspired him to write Black Is Brown Is Tan (1973), which deals with an interracial family, one of the first PICTURE BOOKS to do so. Critics from various opinions all applaud A.'s depth of emotions and rhythm of verse; however, some consider his unusual format of broken words and lines as more of a hindrance than an enhancement to understanding the meaning. In spite of this response, A. reacts by explaining that his experimentation with style encourages young readers to open their minds and souls to challenges; it helps them see the world in a new way.

A. writes passionately about families, friends, foods, seasons, and sounds. His goal is to give young readers the earliest possible exposure to quality MULTICULTURAL LITERATURE in the hope of filling the gap between races and adequate representation in literature. He reminisces regrettably that he went through all his studies, high school through graduate school, without being exposed to one single piece of literature by an African American writer. He has changed this with his numerous anthologies of black authors for younger and older readers. In 1992, A. joined other writers in The Center for Multicultural Children's Literature in its effort to advise and promote unpublished, talented authors and illustrators of color.

A.'s sense of involvement and caring for young readers can be felt in his works. His first book published for children, MA nDA LA (1971), graced by the watercolor ILLUSTRATIONS of Emily Arnold MCCULLY, is a story poem using singsong sounds based on the native language to tell the story of AFRICAN family life in a small village. For his anthology It Is the Poem Singing into Your Eyes (1971), over six thousand submissions from young poets nationwide were received for only one hundred selections. The intensity of this endeavor is evident in the suggestion for the title from one correspondent who stated that a poem "truly does sing into your eyes and then on into your mind and soul." Another one of the young contributors to this volume would later become a Pulitzer Prize winning playwright, August Wilson.

AWARDS: Children's Books of the Year citation, Child Study Association of America (1968) for *I Am the Darker Brother,* (1969) for *City in All Directions,* (1986) for *Sports Pages;* Notable Children's Trade Book citation, National Council for the Social Studies/CHILDREN'S BOOK COUNCIL (1974) for *My Back Me: A Beginning Book of Black Poetry.* Art Books for Children Award for *MA nDA LA,* 1975. Books for the Teen Age citation, New York Public Library (1980), (1981), (1982), all for *It Is the Poem Singing into Your Eyes.* CORETTA SCOTT KING AWARDS Honor Book (1983) and Jane Addams Children's Book Award special recognition (1983) for *All the Colors of the Race.* NATIONAL COUNCIL OF TEACHERS OF ENGLISH Award in Excellence in Poetry (1988)

FURTHER WORKS: Nonfiction: *Malcolm X,* 1970; *Make a Circle Keep Us In: Poems for a Good Day,* 1975; *Big Sister Tells Me That I'm Black,* 1976; *Eats,* 1979; *OUTside/INside Poems,* 1981; *Sports Page,* 1986; *Chocolate Dreams,* 1988; *Hard to Be Six,* 1990; *In for Winter, Out for Spring,* 1991; *Street Music: City Poems,* 1995; *Slow Dance Heart Breaks Blues,* 1995; *Love Letters,* 1997; Edited anthologies: *Celebrations: A New Anthology of Black American Poetry,* 1977

BIBLIOGRAPHY: HOPKINS, Lee Bennett, *Pauses: Autobiographical Reflections of 101 Creators of Children's Books,* 1995; *Children's Literature Review,* vol. 7, 1984; Gary, Kelli, "The Center for Multicultural Children's Literature," *Writer,* July 1994, vol. 107, i. 7; Kiefer, Barbara, selector, *Getting to Know You: Profiles of Children's Authors Featured in Language Arts, 1985–90,* 1991; Phelan, Carolyn, "Two Poets," *Book Links,* July 1994, vol. 3, i. 6; *Something about the Author,* vol. 96, 1998

NANCY HORTON

ADVENTURE STORIES

Whereas many of the books and stories written for children in the early 1800s were didactic, written primarily to promote moral virtues, the nineteenth century heralded the publication of a new breed of books embraced by young readers. *Little Women* (1868) and other novels by Louisa May ALCOTT were eagerly accepted by children who responded to their realistic and often entertaining portrayals of family life, as were Mary Mapes DODGE's *Hans Brinker; or, The Silver Skates* (1865), Johanna SPYRI's *Heidi* (1884), and

Sara Crewe (1888) as well as later novels by Frances Hodgson BURNETT.

Contemporary with these lifelike FAMILY STORIES were adventure tales that offered young readers the same relief from didacticism. Early in the century, children read A. written primarily for adults, such as *The Swiss Family Robinson* (1814) by Johann David WYSS, *Ivanhoe* (1820) and other novels by Sir Walter Scott, *The Last of the Mohicans* (1826) and other Leatherstocking tales by James Fenimore Cooper, and *Two Years before the Mast* (1840) by Richard Henry Dana. The latter half of the century was marked by the popularity of the "dime novel," formulaic SERIES of literarily undistinguished adventures by writers such as American Horatio Alger and BRITISH–born Oliver Optic (the pen name of William Adams), and Harry Castlemon (pseudonym of Charles Austin Fosdick).

Contemporary to these REALISTIC adventure tales were SCIENCE FICTION adventures by Jules VERNE as translated from the French, including *Twenty Thousand Leagues under the Sea* (1869). ANIMAL adventures by British writers Anna SEWELL (*Black Beauty,* 1877) and Rudyard KIPLING (*The Jungle Books,* 1894–95), and the publication of Ernest Thompson SETON's *Wild Animals I Have Known* (1898) in addition to his later realistic animal adventures helped define another related emerging genre, namely, the animal adventure story.

The British publication of *Treasure Island* (1883) by Robert Louis STEVENSON was a benchmark, a well-written realistic adventure tale with exciting plot and well-drawn characters that was written primarily for children rather than for adults. In the United States, the 1876 publication of *The Adventures of Tom Sawyer* and the 1884 appearance of *Adventures of Huckleberry Finn* by Mark TWAIN also offered young readers stories about children like themselves.

As the twentieth century dawned, the market for children's adventure stories grew. Spurred by the nineteenth-century popularity of adventure series, Edward STRATEMEYER established a syndicate of writers that produced a host of long-lived adventure series, including The Rover Boys (1899–1926) and Tom Swift (1910–41). Eventually, the Stratemeyer focus shifted from pure adventure to mystery–adventures such as The

Hardy Boys (1927–) and Nancy Drew (1930–) series.

During this same time period, several British writers published modern FANTASY adventures that became well-loved on both sides of the Atlantic. Hugh LOFTING's Doctor Dolittle books (1920–28) chronicled the adventures of an adventurous physician who communicated with a host of anthropomorphized animals. A. A. MILNE recounted the fantasy adventures of his son Christopher Robin and his toy-animal playmates in the Hundred Acre Wood in *Winnie-the-Pooh* (1926) and three later books. Arthur RANSOME wrote *Swallows and Amazons* (1930) and eleven other books describing the imaginative adventures of the Walker children.

Adventure stories set in fantasy worlds took on new depths with the 1938 publication of J. R. R. TOLKIEN's first Middle-Earth adventure *The Hobbit* and its sequel, *The Lord of the Rings* trilogy (1954–55). Tolkien's friend and fellow Oxford don, C. S. LEWIS, created the fantasy world Narnia in his seven-volume series beginning with the 1950 publication of *The Lion, the Witch, and the Wardrobe.* Contemporary British fantasy writers Susan COOPER and J. K. ROWLING, along with U.S. authors Lloyd ALEXANDER, Robin MCKIN-LEY, and Ursula K. LE GUIN, continue the tradition of Tolkien and Lewis, offering children well-written adventures set wholly, or in part, in fantastic worlds.

Joan AIKEN, British–born daughter of American poet Conrad Aiken, is well-known for imaginary historical adventures set in an England that never was. Suspenseful tales of the supernatural by writers such as Natalie BABBITT and André NORTON, and the dragon fantasies of Anne MC-CAFFREY and Patricia Wrede, are other outstanding examples of the blending of adventure and fantasy. Virginia HAMILTON's Justice trilogy (1978–81) and Madeleine L'ENGLE's Time Fantasy series about the Murry family (1962–) are science fiction adventures.

Realistic adventure stories for children dominated a large share of the children's literature market during the twentieth century. A look back at NEWBERY MEDAL winners reveals many award-winning adventure stories, ranging from the 1929 winner *Trumpeter of Krakow* by Eric KELLY or the 1941 winner, *Call It Courage,* by Armstrong

SPERRY to more recent award-winning adventure tales such as the 1987 winner *The Whipping Boy* by Sid FLEISCHMAN, the 1990 winner *Number the Stars* by Lois LOWRY, the 1999 winner *Holes* by Louis SACHAR, or the 2000 winner *Bud, Not Buddy* by Christopher Paul CURTIS. As this list of award-winners reflects, both historic and modern-day adventurers make up the body of realistic adventure fiction for children that are currently available.

Since the days of Daniel DEFOE's *The Life and Strange Surprizing* [sic] *Adventures of Robinson Crusoe* (1719), stories of survival against the elements have appealed to the imaginations of adventure-seeking readers of all ages, and children's literature is rich with SURVIVAL STORIES. Some are set in the past, including fictionalized accounts of true-life survival tales such as Elizabeth George SPEARE's account of a boy on his own in colonial Maine in *Sign of the Beaver* (1983) or Scott O'DELL's *Island of the Blue Dolphins* (1960), about a nineteenth-century Indian girl who spent eighteen years living alone on an island off the California coast, or fictional survival stories like that of a young girl who finds herself in the middle of a nineteenth-century shipboard mutiny in *The True Confessions of Charlotte Doyle* (1990) by AVI.

Other survival stories are set in modern times, such as Jean Craighead GEORGE's *Julie of the Wolves* (1972), in which a young Eskimo girl survives on the frozen tundra by joining a wolf pack, Scott O'Dell's *Black Star, Bright Dawn* (1988), which is about a young Eskimo girl who runs the 1,197-mile Iditarod sled race, or Gary PAULSEN's *Hatchet* (1987) and its sequels, about a young boy stranded alone in the Canadian wilderness. Each of these authors has written other outstanding adventure stories.

Modern-day survival adventures may require the courage to face tough odds other than the natural elements. In E. L. KONIGSBURG's *From the Mixed-up Files of Mrs. Basil E. Frankweiler* (1987), two young suburbanites run away to Manhattan, drawing on their ingenuity to survive by hiding in the Metropolitan Museum of Art. In a less light-hearted vein, Felice HOLMAN's *Slake's Limbo* (1986) tells the story of a homeless orphan who survives in the New York City subway system until a repair crew destroys his "home" and he must find a new way to survive. Equally compelling is Cynthia VOIGT's *Homecoming* (1981), in which four siblings are in an emotional as well as geographic journey to find a new home when they are abandoned by their mentally ill mother.

Historical or contemporary, stories of adventure and survival have a powerful appeal to pre-adolescents preparing themselves for their own journeys toward independence. These stories, like adventure stories in general, command a wide readership when they offer both exciting action and fast-moving plots combined with the quintessential elements of all good fiction: namely well-drawn characters, believable settings, and meaningful themes.

DIANE L. CHAPMAN

AFANASYEV, Aleksandr N.

Folklorist, b. 1826, Voronegh Province, Central Russia; d. 1871

A teller of Russian folk and FAIRY TALES, A.'s thirst for Russian legend, folktales and history led him to write down and publish over six hundred Russian fairy and folk tales. He was born into a large family and educated by local parish priests and a local college teacher. Although his education was inadequate he loved reading; his persistent study efforts were rewarded when he passed the rigorous examinations for admission to Moscow University's law school. He graduated with honors but his interest was in writing.

Called the Russian GRIMM, A. published eight volumes titled *Russian Popular Fairy Tales* between 1855 and 1863 and translated in 1945. *Russian Folk Legends* (1859) was translated as *Russian Folk Tales* in 1915. *Foma the Terrible: A Russian Folktale,* was published in 1919 and again in 1970. *Ivan Korovavich: The Son of the Cow* was published in Scotland in 1982. Readers meet well-known traditional Russian folk characters in A.'s stories such as Baba Yaga, a witch who lives in a house set on chicken legs and lures children much like the witch in Hansel and Gretel; the mischievous Firebird; the villainous Koshchey; and the Deathless and the Cinderella-like Vasilisa the Beautiful. "Beyond the thrice-nine land, in the thrice-ten kingdom" that A. writes about are places found specifically in Russian tales. Arthur RANSOME's adaptation of *The Fool of the World and the Flying Ship,* based on

A.'s version, illustrated by Uri SHULEVITZ, won the CALDECOTT MEDAL in 1969.

FURTHER WORKS: *Soldier and Tsar in the Forest* (Uri Shulevitz, illus), 1972; *Old Peter's Russian Tales* (Arthur Ransome, tr.), 1975; *Russian Fairy Tales,* 1976; *Flying Ship: A Russian Folk-tale,* 1997

BIBLIOGRAPHY: *Fiction, FOLKLORE, Fantasy and POETRY for Children, 1876–1985,* vol. 1, 1986; Silvey, Anita, ed., *Children's Books and Their Creators,* 1995

IRVYN C. GILBERTSON

AFRICAN AMERICAN LITERATURE

African American literature has been shaped by African American authors and illustrators as well as others whose writing includes depictions of blacks. Violet Harris (1997), authority on African American literature, states: "We are in the midst of a renaissance and an aesthetic revolution in children's literature depicting Blacks" (p. 44). Harris attributes the enlightenment to the increasing excellence and variety in African American literature rather than an increase in the number of publications by and about blacks. A brief look at the history, trends, and themes in this literature help explain Harris's statement.

Children's literature depicting blacks has existed for well over 150 years. Until the mid 1900s, however, most of that literature was highly stereotypical—the bandanna-wearing fat mammy and the kinky-haired, thick-lipped "funny" boy (Huck, Hepler, and Hickman, 1989). Two early African American writers, Langston HUGHES and Arna BONTEMPS, received critical acclaim for their combined and separate efforts. They collaborated on *Popo and Fifina: Children of Haiti* (1932), which was subsequently published in several languages. Bontemps received a NEWBERY MEDAL for *Story of the Negro* (1949). The work of Langston Hughes continues to be republished and enjoyed today. *The Dreamkeeper and Other Poems* (1932; 1994), *The Block* (1995), and *Black Misery* (1969; 1994) have been republished with new illustrations.

During the 1960s, a new breed of black authors emerged who began to capture the complexity and diversity within the African American community. Among the most prominent were Virginia HAMILTON, Mildred TAYLOR, Walter

Dean MYERS, Eloise GREENFIELD, Lucille CLIF-TON, Tom FEELINGS, and John STEPTOE. These writers pointed the way for others such as Sharon Bell MATHIS, Alice CHILDRESS, Rosa GUY, James HASKINS, Patricia MCKISSACK, June JORDAN and even more recent writers such as Angela JOHN-SON, Christopher Paul CURTIS, Irene Smalls, Belinda Rochelle, Faith RINGGOLD, and Gloria, Andrea Davis, and Brian PINKNEY. As the number of outstanding works continues to grow so does an ever-expanding and multifaceted view of African American life.

One notable example is the first collection of stories about an African American character in the Pleasant Company's *The American Girls' Collection, Meet Addy* (1993), and its sequels, by Connie Porter. Angela Johnson's children's books, which include *Toning the Sweep* (1993) is set in the western United States with a grandmother figure who has grown dreadlocks. Elizabeth Fitzgerald Howard has written deeply moving stories about middle-class African Americans such as *Aunt Flossie's Hats (And Crab Cakes Later)* (1991).

Visual artists within the tradition of African American literature have made outstanding contributions to children's literature as a whole. Award-winning picture book artists include Jerry PINKNEY, Ashley BRYAN, George FORD, James RANSOME, Tom FEELINGS, Jan Spivey GILCHRIST, John Steptoe, E. B. LEWIS, and Floyd COOPER. Such illustrators help artists see words in specific contexts, and their legacy continues with artists such as Brian PINKNEY, son of Jerry PINKNEY, and Javaka Steptoe, son of John STEPTOE. Other celebrated illustrators include Pat CUMMINGS, Carole BYARD, Cheryl Hannah, and Will CLAY.

Over the years, several themes have remained constant in African American literature. Stories about families are prevalent. Young children, their parents, grandparents, aunts, uncles, and cousins, are often included in the extended family portrayed in the story line. Older family members are frequently found telling stories to younger members and stories within stories appear. This device is used to teach children about their culture. A story might be told about some incident in the family history or as a way of sharing the heritage of the broader African American community. Stories and poems are used to help so-cialize children toward gaining a sense of pride in themselves, in their families, and in the broader community. These stories have a universal quality as well, since the messages and values they contain are shared by many cultures and many groups.

Many issues affecting blacks as members of a minority community are reflected in the literature about them. For example, the segregation of blacks was evident in books such as *Araminta* (Eva Knox Evans, 1935) and the photographic essay *Tobey* (Stella Sharpe, 1939). Racial prejudice was openly discussed for the first time in Jesse Jackson's *Call Me Charley* (1945) and Marguerite DE ANGELI's *Bright April* (1946). *Two Is a Team* (Jerrold and Lorraine BEIM, 1945) received considerable attention, since it was one of the first books to depict a black and white child playing together. More recently, black writers have included interracial friendships in their books. In *My Friend Jacob* (Lucille CLIFTON, 1980) Jacob is white, friend Sam is black. In *The Boy Who Didn't Believe in Spring* (Clifton, 1973) Tony is white as well. In both books, however, Lucille CLIFTON makes it clear that the black child is the leader.

In Nancy LARRICK's 1965 study of five thousand children's books published from 1962–1964 she found that only 349, or 7 percent, included any black characters, and of this 7 percent almost 60 percent were set outside the United States or before World War II. Occurring at the time of the civil rights movement, this study helped to influence trade as well as textbook publishers. During the late 1960s and 1970s there was an increase in the number of books with black characters, but the 1980s saw a steady decline. Estimates for the 1990s differ somewhat but not a great deal. Currently about 5,000 children's books are published annually but only about 2 percent (about 100 books) contain people of color. Even though the percentages are small, there are more books that reflect African American heritage than any other cultural group.

Many professionals are concerned that even the limited gains will worsen if the multicultural movement falters. They believe that mainstream publishers practice condescension and that people of European ancestry have the license to continue telling the stories of people of color. This has led African American INDEPENDENT PUB-LISHERS such as Johnson Publications and Haki Madhubuti's Third World Press to expand the tradition of including children's literature in their programs. The development of Afrocentric children's literature is a recent priority of Kassahun Checole's Africa World Press. Other notable African American PUBLISHERS of children's books include Wade and Cheryl Hudson's Just Us Books and Glen Thompson's Black Butterfly Press/Readers and Writers.

BIBLIOGRAPHY: Andrews, W., Foster, F., and Harris, T. (eds.) (1997), *The Oxford Companion to African-American Literature.* Cullinan, B. and Galda, L. (1994), *Literature and the Child.* Harris, V. (1997), *Sharing Multiethnic Literature in Grades K–8.* Harris, V. (1982). *Teaching MULTI-CULTURAL LITERATURE* in Grades K–8. Huck, C., Hepler, S., and Hickman, C. (1989), *Children's Literature in the Elementary School.* Larrick, N. (1965), "All-White World of Children's Books," *Saturday Review.* September 11. Sims, R. (1985), *Shadow and Substance*

DOROTHY S. STRICKLAND
AND MICHAEL R. STRICKLAND

AFRICAN LITERATURE

Postcolonial Africa is experiencing many political, economic, cultural, and educational transitions. One of the most profound is the expansion of child literacy efforts. The pride of nationalism and the struggle for survival as autonomous nations has increased the pressure for universal education of African children. More children are attending school and educators are attempting to respond.

Accompanying this movement is the growing demand for appropriate children's literature to support school curricula. The growth of nationalism in the second half of the twentieth century parallels a turning away from European, mostly English, fiction to children's books set in Africa. African political leaders and educators believe that books for youth should be set in one of the fifty-three African countries; they call for literature to enhance national pride by respectfully presenting the many peoples, lands, values, and customs of a diverse continent.

African writers are being challenged to provide the bulk of this literature for children. At a 1987 Pan-African conference, reknowned Nigerian author Chinua ACHEBE (*Things Fall Apart,* 1958) called on African authors and illustrators to create quality books for African youth. In his keynote address on "Children's Literature in Africa," Achebe challenged serious African writers to save African children from the "beautifully packaged poisons" that are imported children's books by making a commitment to write at least two children's stories each. Encouraging them to draw from oral traditions, he continued, "Africa has an infinite treasury for those writers who want [to] and can exploit it." He was quick not to be restrictive, stating that there was room for entirely new creations. Achebe suggested that the oral tradition can be construed to yield contemporary meanings and recommended the publication of "simple and inexpensive booklets."

This call for local authorship of children's books is intertwined with the establishment of the indigenous publishing of African materials. Similar to other industries, book publishing in Africa struggles for balance on the shifting grounds of political reform and economic restructuring. Moving away from European traditions and influences, book publishers in Africa strive for their own autonomy. An example in Kenya is illustrative of this change. Longman Kenya Limited was established in 1965 as a sales and marketing outlet for Longview in England. By the 1980s, it had developed into a full publishing house. In 1994, Longman Group of the United Kingdom divested fully from their Kenya subsidiary and Longhorn Limited, a wholly Kenyan-owned publishing house was established. This change of ownership shifted the responsibility for publishing decisions entirely to management in Nairobi. As of 1998, one-third of the publishers in Kenya are locally owned and operated. They produce textbooks as well as children's literature both in English and local languages.

The competition in the publishing industry is intense both internally and from foreign publishers. The national government publishers tend to control the market in many African countries. In Kenya, the two government-owned publishers, Jomo Kenyatta and the Kenya Literature Bureau, dominate the school textbook market. Competition is intense from the multinational publishers who can provide high-quality materials at lower prices than the indigenous publishers. The hopes for local publishers to provide quality children's books to support literacy efforts and the struggle to survive economically is reflected in a local expression: "The publishing house is located between the cathedral and the stock market."

Children's PICTURE BOOKS published by both indigenous publishers and international companies reflect this spirit of national pride. Invited by a local publisher to visit the Great Zimbabwe ruins and create a children's book, Ghanaian author and artist Meshack Asare traveled to the 700-year-old ruins in central Zimbabwe. The result was *Chipo and the Bird on the Hill: A Tale of Ancient Zimbabwe* (Zimbabwe Publishing House, 1984). Written and illustrated by Asare, it tells the story of Chipo and Dambudzo who search for the big stone bird that guided their ancestors across the veld to the stone structure on the hill. Zimbabwe means "stone house" and the pride in these ancient ruins led to renaming the country in 1981.

A similar sense of national pride infuses *The Day Gogo Went to Vote—April 1994* (1996) published in the U.S. Elinor Batezat Sisulu relates the story of Thembi and her great-grandmother who votes for the first time in South Africa's presidential elections. Gogo is the oldest voter in her township and her pride in being able to vote and elation in Nelson Mandela's victory are evident in the text as well as in Sharon Wilson's illustrations. Distributed in both England and the United States, this book uses names and colloquial expressions from the Xhosa and Zulu dialects spoken in Soweto, South Africa.

Language is a major challenge for African book publishers. Many languages are spoken in each country. South Africa has eleven official languages, Kenya has over forty languages and dialects and a second language policy that mandates that all children study English and Kiswahili, both of which are second languages for most Kenyans. Should publishers offer books in a child's native language or in English, which is the language of record in most public schools? ACHEBE's response to this language issue is that "people should be allowed to write in the language they are most at home in." Young readers should have access to books in the language they best understand.

One solution to the language issue is to have children's PICTURE BOOKS include text in multiple languages. The Early Learning Resource Unit in South Africa publishes a series of "simple and inexpensive booklets" that feature color photographs with accompanying text in four local languages. Two versions of each title are published; one edition is in Xhosa, English, Afrikaans, and Tswana and the second edition is in N. Sotho, English, Zulu, and Sotho. One series features concept books such as *Knock! Knock!* (1996), which allows the reader to knock on several doors in South Africa and visit families showcasing the diversity of South African culture. The Keteka series features the daily lives of children in the community. *Mhlanguli* (1998) uses color photography to present the activities in Mhlanguli's day in the Khayelitsha community.

Language and other issues were discussed at the Indaba (conference) at the 1998 Zimbabwe International Book Fair. The theme, "Children and Books," attracted authors, publishers, and educators from Africa, Europe, and the United States. In addition to the economic issues surrounding the publishing of children's books, the major focus was the need to develop a "reading culture" for African children and families. Books and reading have not been part of many indigenous cultures in Africa but stories and the oral tradition have. Suggestions for creating and sustaining a reading culture include building on Africa's rich oral tradition in book publishing, encouraging recreational reading in schools, improving adult literacy, and employing literature promotion efforts.

Successes in African children's book publishing were celebrated at the Indaba and Book Fair in Zimbabwe. Publishers in many countries have formed supportive professional associations such as the Publishers Association of Tanzania, the Uganda Publishers Association and Booksellers Association, and the Kenya Publishers Association. Individual efforts were spotlighted, such as the outreach to the international market by Jacaranda publishers in Kenya. A new publisher in Uganda, Fountain Publishers, recently initiated Our Heritage series, which features local books based on Ugandan FOLKLORE and ANIMAL STORIES, previously part of the oral tradition. The intent is to encourage partnerships, identify local managerial talent, and to copublish continues.

Niki DALY, a successful South African author and illustrator of children's picture books, was featured at the 1998 Indaba and Book Fair in Zimbabwe. His award-winning popular picture books have demonstrated the quality of local efforts and have added new perspectives and diversity to African children's literature. *Not So Fast Songolo* (1986), published in the U.S., relates the story of Malusi and his granny on a shopping trip from their village into the city. Other books by Daly published in Africa take the reader into African cities, adding perspective to African children's books, which are mostly set in rural areas. *Ashraf of Africa* (1990) features a boy who lives in the city and only sees the wild animals of Africa in the children's books he borrows from the library. *Mama, Papa and Baby Joe* (1991) features a Dr. SEUSS-like humorous rhyme about a family's day in an African city.

African children's book publishing has increased in the past decade and many feel confident that it will survive economic shifts and encourage a reading culture—and find its permanent address between the stock market and the cathedral.

PAUL GREGORIO

AGEE, Jon
Author, illustrator, b. 19 April, 1960, Philadelphia, Pennsylvania

A. started producing books while attending Cooper Union School of Art in New York City. His first book, *If Snow Falls* (1982), is told entirely through expressive watercolors. Since then he has written and illustrated more than a dozen books that demonstrate his stylistic range. He successfully combines cleverness, HUMOR, and artistic ability to appeal to readers both young and old. *The Incredible Painting of Felix Clousseau* (1988) employs all three elements by poking fun at the eccentricities of the art world. A. is well known for his books that feature word games. *Go Hang a Salami! I'm a Lasagna Hog!* (1992), *So Many Dynamos!* (1994), and *Sit on a Potato Pan, Otis* (1999) are written with palindromes, spelling the same word when read from either direction. *Who Ordered the Jumbo Shrimp?* (1998) introduces oxymorons, pairs of contradictory

words, to young readers. A book of anagrams entitled *Elvis Lives* was published in 2000. Several collaborations: *Flapstick* (1993), *The Toy Box!* (1989), and *Dishes All Done* (1989) feature lift-up flaps to involve the reader.

AWARDS: *READING RAINBOW* selection (1985) for *Ludlow Laughs;* AMERICAN LIBRARY ASSOCIATION and Book Review Notable Book (1988) for *The Incredible Painting of Felix Clousseau. New York Times* Best Illustrated Children's Book (1996) for *Dimitri the Astronaut*

FURTHER WORKS: *Ellsworth,* 1989; *The Return of Freddy Legrand,* 1992; Illustrator: *The Halloween House,* 1997; *Mean Margaret,* 1997; *Mr. Lee,* 1995; Playwright and lyricist for *B.O.T.C.H.,* 1991; *Flies in the Soup,* 1995

BIBLIOGRAPHY: "Jon A. Children's Book Festival": http://www.lib.usm.edu/~degrum/agee.html; *Seventh Book of Junior Authors and Illustrators,* 1999; Dunleavey, M. P. Review of *Mean Margaret, New York Times* Book Review, Nov. 16, 1997, p. 34; Review of *Dimitri the Astronaut, New York Times Book Review,* Mar. 2, 1997, 25

BARBARA L. BATTLES

AHLBERG, Allan and Janet
Allan. Author, b. 5 June 1938, England; Janet (Hall). Illustrator, b. 21 October 1944, Huddersfield, England; d. 15 November 1994, Leicester, England

The A.s met and married as students at Sunderland College (Great Britain), a marriage that soon extended to their work, where A.A. wrote the text and J. A. created the pictures. Together, the A.s, who saw themselves as PICTURE BOOK "makers," became a well-regarded and most prolific team. Their first book, *Here Are the Brick Street Boys* (1975), launched the five-book Brick Street Boys series, comic-strip style, EASY-TO-READ picture books for beginning readers. The stories have received much critical acclaim because of their HUMOR, amusing pictures, and, perhaps most noteworthy, the skillful union of text and illustrations. One of their creative and innovative books, *The Jolly Postman; or, Other People's Letters* (1986), sold over one million copies and enjoyed much critical acclaim. An imaginative text sets the scene for humorous FANTASY. The readers follow a bicycling postman on his route as he delivers letters and postcards to FAIRY-TALE characters (e.g., Goldilocks writes an apology to the three bears or the giant gets a postcard from Jack who is busy spending all the giant's loot). The book itself contains actual letters that are found inside envelopes for children to remove and read. Later, the A.s came out with *The Jolly Christmas Postman,* which was awarded Great Britain's KATE GREENAWAY MEDAL for ILLUSTRATION (1991). An earlier work and winner of the 1978 Greenaway Medal, *Each Peach Pear Plum: An "I Spy" Story* (1978), also utilizes folktale and MOTHER GOOSE characters (e.g., Tom Thumb, Jack and Jill, Mother Hubbard, Little Bo Peep, and Cinderella). The I Spy game format encourages children to spot hidden characters found in ornately designed pastel watercolor illustrations. In *Burglar Bill* (1977), Bill steals silly things like a toothbrush or a can of beans; however, when the tables are turned and he becomes the victim, he opts for an honest life.

The A.s make books that are fun for children, and like the folktales of which they are so clearly fond, the stories have happy endings, transporting their readers to a simpler world.

AWARDS: Kate Greenaway Medal (1978) for *Each Peach Pear Plum* and (1991) for *The Jolly Christmas Postman.* Kurt Maschler Award (1986) for *The Jolly Postman; or, Other People's Letters.* INTERNATIONAL BOARD ON BOOKS FOR YOUNG PEOPLE (1980) for *Each Peach Pear Plum.* AMERICAN LIBRARY ASSOCIATION Notable Book (1981) for *Peek-a-Boo!* and (1983) for *The Baby Catalogue.* Commendation, Library Association (U.K.) for *Burglar Bill* (1977); Best Books of the Year Award, *School Library Journal* (1981), and Silver Paint Brush Award (Holland, 1988), both for *Funnybones;* Notable Children's Book Committee of the Association for Library Service to Children (1981), and Best Book for Babies Award, *Parents'* magazine (1985), both for *Peek-A-Boo!;* Best Books of the Year Award, *School Library Journal* (1983), Children's Books of the Year Award, Library of Congress (1983), Teacher's Choice Award, NCTE (1983), Notable Children's Book Committee of the Association for Library Service to Children (1983), all for *The Baby's Catalogue;* and Emil/Kurt Maschler Award, Book Trust (Great Britain), commendation, Library Association (Great Britain), Golden Key (Holland, 1988), Prix du Livre pour la Jeunesse (Young People's Book Prize, France), all for *The Jolly Postman;* Signal POETRY Award (1990) for *Heard It in the Playground*

FURTHER WORKS: *A Place to Play; Sam the Referee* (both Brick Street Boys series, 1975); *Fred's Dream; The Great Marathon Football Match* (both Brick Street Boys series, 1976); *The Old Joke Book,* 1976; *Jeremiah in the Dark Woods,* 1977; *Mr. Biff the Boxer, Peek-a-Boo!,* 1980; *Mrs. Wobble the Waitress* (both Wacky Families series, 1982); *The Ha Ha Bonk Book,* 1982; *Ready Teddy Go; Which Witch* (both Daisychains verse series, 1983); *Yum Yum; Playmates* (Both Slot Book series, 1984); *Starting School,* 1988; books by AA.: *The Giant Baby,* 1994; *Mysteries of Zigomar,* 1997; *Monkey Do!,* 1998; *Bravest Bear Ever,* 1999; *My Brother's Ghost,* 2001

ANDREW KANTAR

AIKEN, Joan (Delano)

Author, b. 4 September 1924, Rye, Sussex, England

A., one of the more popular and prolific novelists for children, has long been recognized as a highly accomplished writer whose novels, short stories, and POETRY span a spectrum that includes tales of horror and MYSTERY, as well as humorous ANIMAL STORIES. Critics have noted that A.'s keen sense of DRAMA and suspense, inventive plots, colorful and humorous characters, and extraordinary imagination are reminiscent of Charles DICKENS, who most certainly served as an inspiration. Growing up in a literary household, A. decided very early that she wanted to be a writer, reading the works of her favorites: Rudyard KIPLING, Walter DE LA MARE, E. NESBIT, and Frances Hodgson BURNETT. Her father was the American-born poet Conrad Aiken. By the time A. was a teenager, she began to publish poems and stories. Her first publications for children, *All You've Ever Wanted* (1953) and *More Than You Bargained For* (1955), represented collected stories that she had told to her two children. Although A. has authored more than fifty works for children and more than twenty works for adults, she is probably best known for her gothic FANTASY series of novels, set in an imaginary nineteenth-century Britain under the fictitious Tudor-Stuart reigns of James III and Richard IV, both of whom are threatened by partisans of the House of Hanover. The first of these novels, *The Wolves of Willoughby Chase* (1962), is the story of two girls, Bonnie Willoughby-Green and her orphan cousin Sylvis Green, who attempt to save Bonnie's father's estate from the sinister governess Miss

Slighcarp. The girls endure hardships and face many dangers, including a pack of wolves that surrounds the English estate. Although the characters are not carefully drawn and are more caricatures (e.g., Miss Slighcarp) than real people, the story is powered by a swiftly moving, melodramatic plot that concentrates on action rather than description. *The Wolves of Willoughby Chase* was followed by *Black Hearts in Battersea* (1964), *Night Birds on Nantucket* (1966), *The Whispering Mountain* (1969), *The Cuckoo Tree* (1971), *The Stolen Lake* (1981), and *Dido and Pa* (1986). Only the first three are in chronological sequence, sharing some of the same characters, but all are part of the same English historical-fantasy setting. In *The Whispering Mountain,* we begin to observe A.'s fascination with unusual vocabulary and strange dialect, as well as the rhythm of language. Her ear for language is perhaps nowhere more evident than in *The Stolen Lake,* where A., according to some, is "at the height of her powers."

Many of A.'s works have been adapted to film and television, including a BBC-TV adaptation (1978) of her collection of humorous fantasy stories entitled, *Armitage, Armitage, Fly Away Home* (1968); a film adaptation of *The Wolves of Willoughby Chase* (1988, Atlantic/Zenith); and several BBC adaptations of one of A.'s most humorous and popular characters, Mortimer the talking raven, who appears in many of her animal stories.

A. maintains that writing for children should not be a full-time job, arguing that some of the best-loved work for children by Dickens, Kipling, William Blake, Hans Christian ANDERSEN, and Lewis CARROLL was informed by a broader knowledge derived from outside professional interests, adding that "they wrote, when they did write for children, purely for love. And that is the way children's writing should be done; it should not be done for any other reason."

AWARDS: Lewis Carroll Shelf Award (1965) for *The Wolves of Willoughby Chase;* Edgar Allan Poe Award (1973) for *Night Fall* (1969, England)

FURTHER WORKS: *A Necklace of Raindrops and Other Stories,* (1969); *Tales of Arabel's Raven,* 1974; *The Skin Spinners: Poems,* (1976); *Go Saddle the Sea,* (1977); *Arabel and Mortimer* (1980, a collection); *The Shadow Guests,* 1980; *Bridle the Wind* (1983, sequel to *Go Saddle the Sea*); *Mortimer's Cross* (1983, a collection)

ANDREW KANTAR

ALCOCK, Vivien
Author, b. 23 September 1924, Worthing, England

A. is the author of several novels that combine action, MYSTERY, and FANTASY. Especially popular with teenage readers in England, she has been widely praised for her ability to create intriguing tales of suspense while involving credible characters who appeal to the emotions and experiences of her readers. All of A.'s novels contain elements of fantasy and the supernatural. Several of her works, including her first book, *The Haunting of Cassie Palmer,* have been adapted and broadcast on television in England.

AWARDS: ALA Notable Book of the Year citation for *The Cuckoo Sister* (1985); ALA Notable Book of the Year citation for *The Monster Garden* (1988). *Horn Book* Honor List citation (1983) for *Travelers by Night* and Notable Book of the Year citation)

FURTHER WORKS: *The Stonewalkers,* 1980; *The Sylvia Game: A Novel of the Supernatural,* 1982; *Travelers by Night,* 1982; *The Cuckoo Year,* 1984; *The Monster Garden,* 1987; *The Trial of Anna Cotman,* 1990

BIBLIOGRAPHY: *Something about the Author,* vol. 76, 1994; Townsend, John Rose, *A Sense of Story: Essays on Contemporary Writers for Children,* 1973

MARY ARIAIL BROUGHTON

ALCOTT, Louisa May
Author, b. 29 November 1832, Germantown, Philadelphia, Pennsylvania; d. 6 March 1888, Boston, Massachusetts

The daughter of Amos Bronson and Abba May A., Louisa and her three sisters were surrounded by a strong intellectual and family environment. Living most of her life in the Boston/Concord area of New England, including a brief stint on her father's failed experimental commune (Fruitlands), A. grew up in the company of some of America's literary giants, most notably Ralph Waldo Emerson and Henry David Thoreau. Bronson Alcott, a well-known educator, philosopher, and social experimenter, was a highly principled individualist, and Abba was a brilliant, practical, hard-working, loving mother with a strong sense of family and a marvelous sense of humor. Together, they created a home and family that were the inspiration for A.'s *Little Women* (1868–69) and her other memorable domestic stories of the March family. These CLASSIC, much-loved tales of filial love and loyalty, security and friendship, laughter and tragedy are recognized as the first American works of domestic realism, a genre that would spawn such works as Laura Ingalls WILDER's Little House books and Sydney TAYLOR's *All-of-a-Kind Family*. *Little Women,* A.'s most famous work, is the episodic story of the four March sisters, Meg (sixteen), Jo (fifteen), Beth (thirteen), and Amy (twelve) and is set in the Boston area during the Civil War. One reason why generations of girls have loved these characters is because each is an individual with her own unique personality—Meg is very pretty and clothes conscious; Jo, a tomboy, wants to be a famous writer (Louisa May's autobiographical counterpart); Beth is a shy child with musical talent; and Amy is artistic but a little spoiled. The family is of modest means and includes the father who is living away, serving in the war as a Union chaplain; the mother ("marmee"); and an Irish servant, Hannah. Originally published in two parts, part 1 (1869), contains the favorite scenes, such as the Christmas episode in which the four sisters take what little money they have and use it to buy presents for their mother and then bring breakfast over to a poor family, the Hummels. In another memorable episode (part 1), while at a party, Jo meets the young Theodore Laurence, or "Laurie," with whom she ends up developing a close friendship (in part 2 he proposes marriage but Jo refuses). In response to the great success of *Little Women,* the sequel, part 2 (known in the U.K. as *Good Wives),* was published the following year (1869). Probably the most touching episode in this volume was the death of Beth. Sequels to *Little Women* continued with *Little Men: Life at Plumfield with Jo's Boys* (1871) and *Jo's Boys and How They Turned Out* (1886). A. also published two other FAMILY novels, *Eight Cousins* (1875) and its sequel, *Rose in Bloom* (1876). Her first successful book, *Hospital Sketches* (1863), was based upon letters she wrote home during her experiences as a Civil War nurse at Union Hospi-

tal in Georgetown (Washington, D.C.). Although her longer works were far more successful, A. published short fiction, including serialized works in *St. Nicholas (Under the Lilacs* [1878]; *Jack and Jill* [1880]), as well as thrillers with an abolitionist theme in *The Atlantic Monthly* and *Commonwealth.* In his journals, nearly thirty years before A. wrote her novels, Bronson acknowledged the dearth of good juvenile literature. Didactic, moralistic tales abounded, but until A. came along with her simple, yet moving episodic stories, American children had no literature that depicted relationships that were infused with the strength that comes from the warmth and love of family. A. shared her birthdate with her father; his death preceded hers by two days.

FURTHER WORKS: *An Old Fashioned Girl,* 1870; Aunt Jo's Scrap-Bag (six volumes), 1872–82; *A Garland for Girls,* 1888

BIBLIOGRAPHY: Cheney, E., ed., *Louisa May A.: Her Life, Letters, and Journals,* 1889; MEIGS, Cornelia, *Invincible Louisa: The Story of the Author of "Little Women"* 1993; Saxon, Martha, *Louisa May: A Modern Biography of Louisa May A.,* 1977; Stern, Madeleine B., *Louisa May A.,* 1950

ANDREW KANTAR

ALDERSON, Brian
Literary critic and writer, b. Date unknown 1930, Great Britain

First becoming well known as a critic of British children's books, more recently A. is known for his lecturing in the field of children's literature, becoming Senior Lecturer (on Children's Literature and the Book Trade) in the School of Librarianship at the Polytechnic of North London, now the University of North London. A. was appointed as the Children's Books Editor of *The Times* in 1976, where he still serves as the children's book consultant. He has edited and reissued several CLASSIC books for children, including two of Andrew LANG's fairy books and a new TRANSLATION of the stories from GRIMM (1978). *Cakes and Custard* (1974), an anthology of rhymes for children, was published in 1974. Most recently he is a contributor to the *Horn Book* magazine.

FURTHER WORKS: Editor: *Sing a Song for Sixpence: The English PICTURE BOOK Traditions and*

Randolph CALDECOTT, 1987; *The Helen* OXEN-
BURY *Nursery Rhyme Book,* 1990; *Moonfleet,*
1993; *Ezra Jack* KEATS: *Artist and Picture-Book
Maker,* 1994; *The Arabian Nights; or, Tales Told
by Scheherazade during a Thousand Nights and
One Night,* 1995; *The Treasures of Childhood,*
1995; *The Water-Babies* (Charles KINGSLEY, au.;
A., ed.), 1995; *The Swan's Stories,* 1997; *Tale of
the Turnip,* 1998

SANDRA IMDIEKE

ALDIS, Dorothy (Keeley)

Author, b. 13 March 1896, Chicago, Illinois; d. 4
July 1996, Place unknown

Born in turn-of-the-century Chicago to James
Keeley, a newspaperman, and his wife Gertrude,
A. attended a private school and later was a student at Smith College for two years. Afterward
A. embarked on a successful career as a novelist
and poet, publishing more than thirty books of
fiction and POETRY for children. Perhaps best
known for her poetry, A. has been recognized as
one of the first American poets to celebrate the
experiences of childhood. Her popularity can be
attributed to her superb sense of HUMOR, acute
understanding of children's feelings, and an appreciation for the everyday things that children
do. Her first four books of poems were combined
and published in *All Together* (1952), a collection
that demonstrates A.'s sensitivity to the feelings
of children in poems like "Bad" and "Alone."
Using the simple verse form in her poem "I Can
Do It," A. transforms an everyday experience
(brushing teeth) into a childhood accomplishment. Her popular narrative poem "Hiding" is
often pantomimed by children as they re-enact
the playful story of two parents pretending to
look for their hiding child. A.'s short stories and
poems were found in such magazines as *The New
Yorker, Harper's,* and *Ladies Home Journal.* In
addition, she was widely anthologized, and her
poetry appeared in school books and teaching
aids. Her literary contributions earned her the
Children's Reading Round Table Award, 1966–
67, for "outstanding service by an individual in
the course of children's literature over a long period of time." A.'s *Nothing Is Impossible: The
Story of Beatrix* POTTER (1969), a BIOGRAPHY for
children in the middle grades, has been praised
for its simplicity of style and effective use of pri-

mary source material, such as Potter's journal entries and letters.

FURTHER WORKS: *Everything and Anything*
(1925); *Murder in a Hay Stack,* (1930); *Magic
City,* (1933); *Cindy,* 1942; *Poor Susan,* 1942;
Dark Summers, 1947; *Lucky Year,* 1952; *The Boy
Who Cared,* 1956; *Ride the Wild Waves,* 1958;
Hello Day, 1959; *The Secret Place: Anthology,*
1962; *Is Anybody Hungry?,* 1964

BIBLIOGRAPHY: Kunitz, S, and H. Haycraft, eds.,
Junior Book of Authors, 1951

ANDREW KANTAR

ALDRIDGE, James

Author, b. 10 July 1918, White Hills, Victoria,
Australia

A. began writing fiction for YOUNG ADULTS after
completing his career as a journalist and author
of adult international suspense novels. His novels
comment on questions that humanity has always
sought answers to, including: how do people live
together in harmony, and what is the perfect political and social climate for a community?

   In order to answer these moral, political, and
social questions, A. created the fictional town of
St. Helen, Australia, to use in his stories. He cre-
ated a series of novels that describe heroic, un-
usual, and mysterious characters who overcome
great obstacles in his books: *The True Story of
Lili Stubeck* (1984), *The True Story of Spit Mac-
Phee* (1986), and *The True Story of Lola MacKel-
lar* (1992), all set in St. Helen. Critics consider
A. one of the most prolific authors of AUSTRA-
LIAN horse stories, which include: *A Sporting
Proposition* (a.k.a., *Ride a Wild Pony*) (1973);
The Marvelous Mongolian (1974); and *The Bro-
ken Saddle* (1983), which are all set during the
Great Depression.

BIBLIOGRAPHY: *Something about the Author,* vol.
87, 1996

DENISE P. BEASLEY

ALEXANDER, Lloyd

Author, b. 30 January 1924, Philadelphia, Pennsylvania

A. has gained critical and popular recognition as
an author of FANTASY novels for children and
YOUNG ADULTS. His devotion to the written word
developed early as he read his way through what-

ever books he found stored in his family's house. Although he planned, at fifteen, to become a poet, he graduated from high school the next year without the prospect of attending college and without any realistic ideas about earning a living. In the following year, he tried a few college courses while working as a bank messenger but found the course work provided too little challenge to maintain his interest.

A. joined the army to seek adventure as the United States had entered World War II. Eventually, he was sent to Wales. There, his boyhood love of Arthurian legend was reawakened and he felt newly inspired by the countryside and the local language. Later in the war, he was transferred to France and was mustered out, at the war's end, in Paris. He studied for a while at the Sorbonne, met his wife and returned with her and their daughter to the outskirts of Philadelphia.

During the next few years A. earned a living in advertising, as a cartoonist, as a translator, and as a trade publication editor. A.'s hopes of becoming a published author seemed to him to be dwindling. Just as he had decided to walk away from that long-held aspiration, an adult novel he'd written was accepted for publication.

A.'s first book for children, *Border Hawk: August Bondi* (1958) won the Isaac Siegel Memorial Juvenile Award in 1959, for its portrayal of a Jewish abolitionist who was an associate of John Brown. The *Black Cauldron* (1965) was a NEW-BERY MEDAL Honor Book. *The High King* (1968) won the Newbery Medal in 1969. *The Marvelous Misadventures of Sebastian* (1970) won the National Book Award in 1971. *The First Two Lives of Lukas-Kasha* (1978) won both the Silver Pencil Award, in 1981, and the Austrian Children's Book Award, in 1984. *Westmark* (1981) earned the American Book Award in 1982. A.'s work has earned four Parents' Choice Awards, each in the year of the book's publication: *The Kestrel* (1982), *The Beggar Queen* (1984), *The Illyrian Adventure* (1986), and *The Fortune-tellers* (1992). In 1984, A. was honored with the Golden Cat Award (Sweden's Sjoestrands Foerlag), for excellence in children's literature. The Catholic Library Association's Regina Medal went to A. in 1986, and the Church and Synagogue Library Association Award was awarded to him in 1987. Several of A.'s books have been nominated for the Na-

tional Book Award and his works are included in many citations of "best books" by both professional groups and literary publications.

Following two juvenile biographies, A. turned to his first love: historically based fantasy. *Time Cat: The Remarkable Journeys of Jason and Gareth* (1963), published in England as *Nine Lives,* is the tale of a boy and a cat who find themselves visiting nine cultures in nine historic moments. Critics note that A. has researched time and place well, so that the adventures are accurate in detail.

A. sustained a much longer fantasy, the Prydain Chronicles, in a five-volume SERIES that begins with *The Book of the Three* (1964). Inspired by the Welsh lore comprising the Mabinogion, A. created his own mythic hero, Taran, whose quest continues through *The Black Cauldron, The Castle of Llyr* (1966), *Taran Wanderer* (1967) and *The High King.*

In A.'s second series, the Westmark Trilogy, politics, rather than magic, precipitate the evolving events. *Westmark, The Kestrel,* and *The Beggar Queen* comprise an exploration of revolution, corrupt leadership, and war. The Westmark Trilogy provides compelling characters and adventures, but it also engages readers in the ethical considerations these actors and their actions raise.

A.'s third series is more lighthearted, but nonetheless substantive, this time for the historical accuracy underpinning the Vesper Holly Adventures. Here a girl, rather than a boy, is the central character. Vesper Holly enjoys a variety of international escapades during the 1870s, in *The Illyrian Adventure, The El Dorado Adventure* (1987), *The Drackenberg Adventure* (1988), *The Jedera Adventure* (1989), and *The Philadelphia Adventure* (1990).

In addition to the series A. has authored for middle-grade and older readers, he has provided younger children with fantasy stories, including *Coll and His White Pig* (1965), *The Truthful Harp* (1967), and *The Foundling and Other Tales of Prydain* (1973), all of which are set in the Prydain fantasy world. The *Marvelous Misadventures of Sebastian* is set in a country that seems to foreshadow A.'s invention of Westmark, although the story is lighthearted and concerned with beauty rather than politics.

A. has demonstrated facility within the context of PICTURE BOOKS as well as lengthier texts. *The*

King's Fountain (1971), illustrated by Ezra Jack KEATS, is a fairy-tale-like story in which a king must consider the needs of his people in addition to his own desires. *The Fortune-Tellers* (1992), illustrated by Trina Schart HYMAN, set in Cameroon, gives very young readers a taste for the magic and adventure for which A.'s novels are noted.

In addition to his remarkable ability to invent fantasy worlds and his success in portraying seemingly inexhaustible ADVENTURES, critics laud A. for offering children access to issues of moral significance. This has been demonstrated in his biographies, novels, and picture books, in each of which he has reported upon or created characters who must consider the ramifications of conditions as they are and then act so as to render the most good and the least harm.

FURTHER WORKS: *The Four Donkeys,* 1972; *The Cat Who Wished to Be a Man,* 1973; *The Town Cats and Other Tales,* 1977; *The Remarkable Journey of Prince Jen,* 1991; *The Arkadians,* 1995; *The Iron Ring,* 1997

BIBLIOGRAPHY: *Contemporary Authors, New Revision Series,* vol. 55, 1997; HOPKINS, Lee Bennett, *Pauses: Autobiographical Reflections of 101 Creators of Children's Books,* 1995; *Something about the Author,* vol. 49, 1987, and vol. 81, 1995; Tunnell, M. *The Prydain Companion,* 1989

FRANCISCA GOLDSMITH

ALEXANDER, Martha G.

Author, illustrator, b. 25 May 1920, Augusta, Georgia

Art teacher, freelance artist, and creator of more than twenty-five PICTURE BOOKS of her own, as well as providing the illustrations for several more, A. has immersed herself in the arts since childhood. While growing up, her artistic talent manifested itself in a variety of ways, including dollmaking, ceramics, mosaics, and collages, murals, and clothing design. However, it was not until midlife that she discovered picture book ILLUSTRATION, recognizing that this would be her true passion, the artistic expression she had been searching for. A. studied at the Cincinnati Academy of Fine Arts, and later moved to New York with her two teenage children where she tried to earn a living as a freelance magazine illustrator. Her formal artistic schooling enabled her to ap-

preciate the ability of artists like Marc Chagall and Paul Klee to create playful images that could convey entire stories without words. A. has noted that, as an illustrator, she takes "great pride in telling as much of the story as I can without text, but rather through gestures and expressions." One of A.'s most popular efforts is found in the *Blackboard Bear* (1969) and its sequels (*And My Mean Old Mother Will Be Sorry* [1969]; *Blackboard Bear* [1969]; *I Sure Am Glad to See You, Blackboard Bear* [1976]; and *We're in Big Trouble, Blackboard Bear* [1980]). *Blackboard Bear,* a *New York Times* Notable Book and the first book in the series, is a story of a little boy who, after being rejected by some older boys, goes home and draws a big bear on his blackboard. When he takes the fantasy bear out for a neighborhood stroll, all the boys want a chance to walk or ride him, giving the child a satisfying opportunity to be in control of the situation. Using words sparingly, A. tells the story through illustrations that have been praised by critics as ingenious, imaginative, and eloquent. A. uses family experiences as a creative stimulus for her work; for example, sibling rivalry in *Nobody Asked Me if I Wanted a Baby Sister* (1971) and *When the Baby Comes I'm Moving Out* (1979) can be traced to A.'s young granddaughter's apprehension about getting a new baby sister. Sibling and parental frustration are conveyed in the humorous *Jeremy Isn't Hungry* (1978), written by Barbara Williams. In this story, a little boy attempts unsuccessfully to feed his baby brother while mother moves about at a frenetic pace, trying to get dressed for a school program. A. connects with her readers through humorous stories that present very real emotions. She maintains that her experiences as a mother, grandmother, and great-grandmother help her to stay in touch with her young audience.

AWARDS: Christopher Award (1974) for *I'll Protect You from the Jungle Beasts*

FURTHER WORKS: *Big Sister and Little Sister,* with Charlotte ZOLOTOW, 1955; *Maybe a Monster,* 1968; *Out! Out! Out!,* 1968; *You,* with Louis UNTERMEYER, 1969; *We Never Get to Do Anything,* (1970); *I'll Be the Horse if You'll Play with Me,* 1975; *Mandy's Grandmother,* with Liesel Moak Skorpen, and *Marty McGee's Space Lab,* 1981; *Even That Moose Won't Listen to Me,*

1988; *My Outrageous Friend Charlie*, 1988; *Where Does the Sky End, Grandpa?*, 1992

ANDREW KANTAR

ALEXANDER, Sue
Author, b. 20 August 1933, Tucson, Arizona

Born to a mother who was an avid reader, A. became an early reader herself, and has woven her love of books and STORYTELLING into all aspects of her life. As a young child, she discovered that she could make friends by telling stories to them, leaving them hanging on the end so that they would come back for more. She intended to turn her storytelling skill into a career in journalism, but found that her creative tendency would not match the objectivity necessary for a journalist. She changed her major to psychology, but left college before graduating. Her mother's death in 1967 caused her to devote herself to her writing and she soon began to write stories for children. Her first successes came in publishing stories in children's magazines and her leadership role in the SOCIETY OF CHILDREN'S BOOK WRITERS AND ILLUSTRATORS. Because of A.'s participation in SCBWI, many authors and publishers became involved in the organization and its activities. A. remains one of SCBWI's most enthusiastic and prominent members. Her first published book, *Small Plays for You and a Friend* (1973), is based on skits she created as a child. Her highly acclaimed *Nadia the Willful* (1983) was based on the death of her brother, yet to give her the distance that enabled her to write about this subject, she set the book in the culture of the Bedouins. Throughout her career, A. has taught courses in PICTURE BOOK writing, and has remained active in professional writers organizations.

A. has written on subjects such as plays for children, FANTASY stories about witches and goblins, nonfiction, and REALISTIC FICTION set within and outside of the United States. In all of her work, A. has drawn from her childhood experiences, whether as an imaginative inventor of plays and skits or as a lonely child seeking friendship.

AWARDS: Dorothy C. McKenzie Award, Southern California Council of Literature for *Children and Young People* (1980): distinguished contribution to the field of children's literature. Society of Children's Book Writers Golden Kite Honor Plaque (1980). Notable Children's Book in the Field of Social Studies (1982), for *Finding Your First Job*. Establishment of the Sue A. Service and Encouragement Award, Society of Children's Book Writers and Illustrators

FURTHER WORKS: *Witch, Goblin and Sometimes Ghost*, 1976; *World Famous Muriel*, 1985; *Lila on the Landing*, 1987; *Sara's City*, 1995; *What's Wrong Now, Millicent?*, 1996; *One More Time, Mama*, 1999

BIBLIOGRAPHY: Roginski, James W., *Behind the Covers: Interviews with Authors and Illustrators of Books for Children and YOUNG ADULTS*, vol. 2, 1989

SANDRA IMDIEKE

ALGER, Leclaire Gowens
(See NIC LEODHAS, Sorche)

ALIKI, (Liacouras Brandenberg)
Author, illustrator, visual artist, b. 3 September 1929, Wildwood Crest, New Jersey

Publishing under her first name only, A. writes children's INFORMATION and fiction PICTURE BOOKS. A. grew up in Philadelphia, where her kindergarten teacher first recognized her artistic abilities. A. began drawing in her preschool years and continued to attend weekend art classes as well as study piano. In 1951, A. graduated from the Philadelphia Museum School of Art (now the Philadelphia College of Art) and went to work as a commercial artist in a department store. A. started her own greeting-card company, and taught classes in art and ceramics before traveling to Europe to paint and sketch. A. and her husband lived in Switzerland for three years before returning to the United States. Her first book, *The Story of William Tell* (1960), was inspired by A.'s years in Switzerland.

A. writes fiction in response to events she and members of her family experience. *Three Gold Pieces: A Greek Folk Tale* (1967) and *The Eggs: A Greek Folk Tale* (1969) are based on her Greek heritage that she discovered while traveling through that country. *At Mary Bloom's* (1976) was written after her daughter's visit to a neighbor. Her self-illustrated nonfiction is often written in response to A.'s own curiosity about a subject. A. says she does a tremendous amount of research before she writes so that readers have a detailed and accurate presentation of the subject.

1. VERNA AARDEMA

2. ALMA FLOR ADA

3. DAVID ADLER

4. ARNOLD ADOFF

5. JANET AND ALLAN AHLBERG

6. ALIKI

This is evident in *The King's Day: Louis XIV of France* (1989), where lavish, colorful ILLUSTRATIONS reflect the grandeur of the French court, and multiple texts tell the story on several levels.

A. writes about a variety of subjects that interest her including BIOGRAPHY, science and fiction. She is noted for clear, EASY-TO-READ texts accompanied by finely detailed illustrations appropriate to the content. A. is also noted for the many titles she has written for the Let's Read-and-Find-Out Science series edited by Franklyn M. BRANLEY. Many of the titles have been revised and reissued since their first publication. *Dinosaurs Are Different* (1985) offers text with further explanations provided in comic-style balloon insets. The detailed illustrations done in ink and watercolor allow children to compare dinosaurs with things they know in their contemporary environment. Critics have praised both A.'s illustrations and her writing, noting that her work is attractive, informative, and entertaining.

AWARDS: American Institute of Graphic Arts for the Children's Book Show (1976) and Children's Book Council (1977) for *At Mary Bloom's*. New York Academy of Sciences Children's Science Book Award (1977) for *Corn Is Maize: The Gift of the Indians*. Dutch Children's Book Council Silver Pencil Award (1981) for *Mummies Made in Egypt*. Prix du Livre pour Enfants (Geneva) (1987) for *Feelings*. New York Academy of Sciences Children's Science Book Award (1977) for *Corn Is Maize*. Drexel University/Free Library of Philadelphia citation, 1991, in recognition of outstanding contributions in the field of literature

FURTHER WORKS: *The Story of Johnny Appleseed,* 1963; *The Story of William Penn,* 1964; *Fossils Tell of Long Ago,* 1972, 1990; *Go Tell Aunt Rhody,* 1974, 1996; *Digging up Dinosaurs,* 1981; *A Medieval Feast,* 1983; *How a Book Is Made,* 1986; *Communication,* 1993; *Gods and Goddesses of Olympus,* 1994; *All by Myself,* 2000

BIBLIOGRAPHY: Cianciolo, Patricia J., *Picture Books for Children,* 3rd ed., 1990; HOPKINS, Lee Bennett, *Pauses: Autobiographical Reflections of 101 Creators of Children's Books,* 1995; *Something about the Author,* vol. 75, 1994

CRAIG LIEBERMAN

ALLARD, Harry G., Jr.
Author, b. 27 January 1928, Evanston, Illinois

The author of two very popular children's SERIES, The Stupids and the Miss Nelson books, A. believed that sharing the same birthday as Lewis CARROLL was a good omen. A Yale-educated French professor, A. has spent his career teaching at Salem State College (Massachusetts). He grew up in the Chicago area and received his bachelor's degree in art from Northwestern University. While serving in the U.S. Army Signal Corps, A. lived in Korea and Japan and later spent four years in Paris where he worked as a legal translator and taught English in the Berlitz language school. His first children's book, *The Stupids Step Out* (1974), was inspired by the art of James MARSHALL, the illustrator with whom A. would successfully collaborate on many books. Admitting that he hates anything with a message, A. asserts, "with the Stupids there is no message at all. They just seem to do what they want to." Two books about the Stupids followed (also illustrated by Marshall): *The Stupids Have a Ball* (1978) and *The Stupids Die* (1981). A.'s simple and rhythmic text and eccentric, wacky characters are nicely complemented by Marshall's humorously informal ILLUSTRATIONS. The release of *Miss Nelson Is Missing!* (1977) represented the beginning of another series collaboration between A. and Marshall that would prove highly popular. In this PICTURE BOOK, kind-hearted Miss Nelson's ill-mannered students come to appreciate her after suffering terribly under the harsh rule of the horrible and nasty substitute, Miss Viola Swamp. *Miss Nelson Is Missing!,* a runner-up for the 1977 Edgar Allan Poe Award, was followed by *Miss Nelson Is Back* (1982) and *Miss Nelson Has a Field Day* (1985), featuring a return engagement for Miss Viola Swamp as a hard-nosed coach. Some of A.'s works have also been adapted to film, television, and filmstrips. *It's So Nice to Have a Wolf around the House* (illustrated by Marshall, 1977), was made into a full-length cartoon feature (1978) and received an Academy Award nomination for best-animated film; *Miss Nelson Is Missing!* became a motion picture (1979) and a filmstrip (1984); *Miss Nelson Is Back* was featured on television's READING RAINBOW (1983); and *I Will Not Go to Market Today* (illustrated by Marshall, 1979) was adapted to five filmstrips (1984). A.'s passion for language is also evinced by his German-to-English TRANSLATIONS for children (*A Hamster's Journey* [1976], written in German by Luis Murschetz;

Three Is Company [1980], written in German and illustrated by Friedrich Karl Waechter; and *May I Stay!* [1978], FAIRY TALE adapted and translated from the German, illustrated by F. S. Fitzgerald).

AWARDS: *New York Times* Best Illustrated Children's Books of the Year (1975) for *The Tutti-Frutti Case* (James Marshall, illus.). Children's Book Showcase (1975) for *The Stupids Step Out.* American Institute of Graphic Arts Book Show (1980) for *I Will Not Go To Market Today*

FURTHER WORKS: *The Tutti-Frutti Case: Starring the Four Doctors of Goodge* (illustrated by Marshall), 1975; *Crash Helmet* (illustrated by Jean-Claude Suares), 1977; *Bumps in the Night* (illustrated by Marshall), 1979; *The Cactus Flower Bakery,* 1991; *The Hummingbirds' Day,* 1991

ANDREW KANTAR

AMERICAN LIBRARY ASSOCIATION

The American Library Association (ALA), founded in 1876, is the oldest, largest, and most influential library association in the world, with approximately 57,000 members, primarily librarians, but also trustees, publishers, and other library supporters. The association represents all types of libraries—public, school, academic, state, and special libraries serving persons in government, commerce, armed services, hospitals, prisons, and other institutions. Its mission is to serve as the voice of America's libraries and the people who depend on them. The goals of ALA are to promote the highest quality library and information services and to protect public access to information. ALA upholds America's right to a free and open information society with the highest quality of information services.

ALA has influenced the course of America's libraries since 1876, when early library luminaries such as Melvil Dewey and Justin Winsor issued a call to librarians to form a professional organization. Melvil Dewey was one of the founders, the first treasurer and secretary, and the organization's fifth president. The first meeting was held in Philadelphia with ninety men and thirteen women who came from as far away as Chicago and England. ALA has been a leader in promoting and developing library information services via a broad-based program of legislative advocacy, professional education, publishing, awards, and public awareness.

The ALA has its headquarters in Chicago and maintains another office in Washington, D.C. The association, governed by a 175-member council, has an executive board, made up of elected officers and eight council members. The executive board is responsible for the management of the association, subject to review by the council. The association is served by a staff of 275 and administered by an executive director. ALA is organized by a divisional structure that focuses on specific types of libraries or library service: American Association of School Librarians (AASL); Association for Library Service to Children (ALSC); Public Library Association (PLA); Young Adult Library Services Association (YALSA), among others.

The ALA parent organization as well as its various divisions publishes journals, books, newspapers, and pamphlets. These include *American Libraries, Journal of Youth Services in Libraries, Booklist,* and *Book Links.* Recent publications include ALSC's *Born to Read: How to Raise a Reader; The Newbery and Caldecott Awards: A Guide to the Medal and Honor Books;* STORYTELLING *with Puppets* (Champlin); *Leading Kids to Books through Puppets* (Feller, Bauer); *America as Story: Historical Fiction for Middle and Secondary Schools* (Coffey and Howard); *Building a Special Collection of Children's Literature* (Jones, ALSC); *The Frugal Youth Cybrarian: Bargain Computing for Kids* (Ross); *Sizzling Summer Reading Programs for Young Adults* (Kan, YALSA); *Storytimes for Two-Year Olds* (Nichols, Sears).

ALA presents more than a hundred awards and medals, grants, and scholarships, many for books for children and young adults. Among the best known, the NEWBERY MEDAL recognizes superior quality in text and the CALDECOTT MEDAL recognizes superior quality in illustrations. The Batchelder Award is given to a publisher for an outstanding translation of a children's book from another language to English. The LAURA INGALLS WILDER AWARD is given every three years for the entire body of a writer's work considered good enough to sit on the same shelf as the Wilder books. The Pura BELPRÉ Award, named for the first Latina librarian at the New York Public Library, is presented biennially to a Latino/Latina author and illustrator who affirms and celebrates the Latino/Latina cultural experience in an outstanding children's book. The Newbery, Caldecott, Batchelder, and the Laura Ingalls WILDER Awards are administered by ALSC, Association for Library Service to Children. The CORETTA SCOTT KING Award, administered by ALSC and the Social Responsibilities Round Table, is given in two categories. One award is given to a black author and one to a black illustrator whose books are considered "outstanding, inspirational and educational contributions to literature." The Pura Belpré Award, cosponsored by ALSC and REFORMA, is intended to promote library services to Spanish speaking children. An ALSC committee annually chooses a list of ALA Notable Books for Children. A Young Adult Library Services Association (YALSA) committee chooses a list of the Best Books for Young Adults. First granted in 2000, the Michael L. Printz Award is given by YALSA for a book that exemplifies literary excellence in young adult literature. ALA awards and booklists are intended to stimulate achievement in library science and publishing. Citations recognize excellence in every field from school media center programs to library architecture to public relations.

National Library Week is an annual observance held each April to encourage library use and support. Each year a theme, such as "Kids Connect @ the Library," is selected. ALA sponsors Library Card Sign-Up Month each year as a reminder that a library card is the most important school supply of all. Libraries host special programs encouraging parents and children to explore the world with a library card. The ALA, American Booksellers Association and other groups designate one week each September as Banned Books Week—Celebrating the Freedom to Read. Banned Books Week commemorates the freedom to read and the First Amendment, which specifies that "Congress shall make no law abridging the freedom of speech or of the press." An annual list of "Books Some People Consider Dangerous" is published in conjunction with the observance. The Young Adult Library Services Association, a division of the American Library Association, sponsors a Teen Read Week in partnership with the National Education Association. A sample theme: "Read for the fun of it." School Library Media Month is sponsored annually by

the American Association of School Librarians, a division of the American Library Association. This annual observance is a time to celebrate the special contribution of the nation's school libraries and school librarians. The theme for School Library Media Month is the same as for National Library Week.

ALA holds two conferences each year: a midwinter business meeting in January at which time Newbery, Caldecott, and other awards are announced and a general annual conference in June. Approximately 20,000 libraries attend the annual conference. Programs include exhibits, displays, guest speakers, award presentations, lectures, panel discussions, workshops, and debates.

LINDA K. WALLACE

AMERICAN (UNITED STATES) LITERATURE BEFORE 1900

Colonial American children had too few books that they could call their own and the demand for children's literature was not great. In general, few people could afford to own many books. The book that is recognized as the first children's PICTURE BOOK in the English language is John Amos COMENIUS's *Orbis Sensualium Pictus*. It was translated from the original Czech by Charles Hoole in 1659. Engravings depicted many everyday objects that were numbered and described below the drawing in Latin and in English.

Books were so costly in Colonial America that a hornbook was used for early lessons as an inexpensive substitute. Hornbooks were not actual books but small wooden paddles, about three inches by five inches, on which a lesson sheet containing the alphabet, combinations of letters, and the Lord's Prayer was pasted and covered with transparent horn. Peddlers, or chapmen, also sold small inexpensive booklets that were appealing to children and related the adventures of such characters as Robin Hood, Jack the Giant Killer, and Dick Whittington.

Such fantasies were not acceptable for Puritan children, however. In seventeenth century New England many of the first books intended for children focused on death and eternal damnation. Examples include John Cotton's *Milk for Babes, Drawn out of the Breasts of Both Testaments* published in Boston in 1646, and books from England such as James Janeway's *Token for Children,* which appeared about 1671. Puritan ideals made rather gloomy reading for children. The *New England Primer,* published about 1690 in Boston by Benjamin Harris, was a very popular book intended for Puritan children. It contained stories about Christian martyrs, the alphabet, and rules for behavior. John Bunyan's *Pilgrim's Progress,* although intended for adults when published in 1678, was popular with children as was Bunyan's *A Book for Boys and Girls; or, Country Rhimes for Children* published in 1686. This book became known by the more popular title of *Divine Emblems* after Bunyan's death. Other adult titles that children took as their own were Daniel DEFOE's *Robinson Crusoe* in 1719 and *Gulliver's Travels* in 1726 by Jonathan SWIFT.

Most books for children in America continued to be imported from England; the same titles were popular in both countries. Robert Samber's 1729 translation into English from the French of Charles PERRAULT's *Stories and Tales of Past Times with Morals; or, Tales of MOTHER GOOSE* included such classics of childhood as Little Red Riding Hood, Sleeping Beauty, Puss-in-Boots, and Cinderella. No nursery rhymes were included although it was probably the first publication using the term "Mother Goose."

Americans were slow to develop their own literature for children but their production of religious works for the young was plentiful. *A New Gift for Children* was published by D. Fowle in Boston in 1756 and is generally considered the first American story book for children. It included ten stories and appears crude next to English publications of that time.

John NEWBERY was one of the first publishers to acknowledge a market for children's books; his popular titles include *A Little Pretty Pocket-Book Intended for the Instruction and Amusement of Little Master Tommy and Pretty Miss Polly* in 1744. He is also credited with publishing what is considered the first work of fiction for children, *The History of Little Goody Two-Shoes,* which may have been written by Oliver Goldsmith in 1765; all were reprinted frequently in America. Hugh Gaine, a New York publisher, was the first American to print an abridged edition of *Robinson Crusoe* for children in 1774, copying Newbery's printing style meticulously. The founder

of the American Antiquarian Society in Worcester, Massachusetts, Isaiah Thomas, imitated Newbery's Lilliputian Library even to faithfully copying his illustrations, text, and style of binding. In 1785 he reproduced Newbery's earlier 1760 *Mother Goose's Melody* with slight alterations and original woodcuts. Thomas's 1878 edition of Newbery's *A Little Pretty Pocket-Book* used Newbery's exact text and woodcuts. Many of Thomas's children's books were illustrated with original American woodcuts by John and Thomas Bewick who set the standard for woodcut engraving.

The constant moralizing of many early books for children was broken with the publication in the nineteenth century of *Grimm's Fairy Tales,* first translated and published in Great Britain in two volumes as *German Popular Stories* in 1823 and 1826.

Denmark's Hans Christian ANDERSEN wrote *Fairy Tales and Stories* (1835), which was translated into English in 1846. These works allowed children to use their imaginations as they were entertained by kings and queens, elves and fairies and talking beasts. The popularity of these tales remains to this day.

Laughter became part of children's books with Edward LEAR's *Book of Nonsense,* a collection of limericks and line drawings published in 1846. The 1865 publication of *Alice's Adventures in Wonderland* by Lewis CARROLL, the pseudonym of Charles Lutwidge Dodgson, a mathematics don at Oxford, combined nonsense and FANTASY as did its sequel, *Through the Looking Glass* (1872). Illustrators like John TENNIEL who worked closely with Lewis Carroll became significant as well, although most pictures in books were in black and white.

Edmund Evans, an English printer, was one of the first to publish full color books for children at a reasonable price. Nursery rhymes such as *Sing a Song of Sixpence* and *The House That Jack Built* were illustrated by Walter CRANE and published in the 1860s and 1870s. Kate GREENAWAY's charmingly dressed children and flowers had great popularity toward the end of the nineteenth century and the third artist in the Evans stable, Randolph CALDECOTT, is a name well-known in America as it is the CALDECOTT MEDAL that is given annually to an illustrator for the most distinguished picture book for children. Caldecott's illustrations were notable for their humorous action. Among his most famous is *The Diverting History of John Gilpin,* which was illustrated by Caldecott in 1878. Many of these books were imported and sold in America with great success.

As the second half of the nineteenth century continued, children in America began to see works of realistic fiction written by Americans. *Little Women* by Louisa May ALCOTT, published in two volumes in 1888 and 1889, told about the lives of four New England sisters facing and conquering life in their own inimitable but socially acceptable way. Mark TWAIN, the pseudonym for Samuel L. Clemens, took realism a bit further by peopling his books with characters involved in murder, alcoholism, and grave robbery in *The Adventures of Tom Sawyer,* published in 1876 and its sequel, *Adventures of Huckleberry Finn,* in 1884. Children's literature in America had certainly changed since the times of the Puritans and *Milk for Babes.*

DONARITA VOCCA

AMERICAN (UNITED STATES) LITERATURE, 1900–1945

The early 1900s catapulted American children's literature from mere recognition to literary and commercial success in its own right. The initiation of children's rooms in public libraries fostered interest in children's literature in the late 1800s and helped forge an identity separate from literature written for older readers and the general population. In the first half of the twentieth century several salient events promoted recognition and acceptance of children's literature. However, American authors continued to add to the national identity and creation of an identifiable American character rather than follow the European tradition and version of FANTASY and FAIRY TALES exclusively. One of the first examples of this change is L. Frank BAUM's *The Wonderful Wizard of Oz* (1900). Previously established patterns of realism and presentation of everyday folk were evident; yet the author stretched the readers' minds with his "other world" fantasy of Oz. Baum's totally American characters established a publishing phenomenon that remained a commercial record until the mid-1960s.

The prominence of the protagonist's inventiveness coupled with the appreciation of place, family, and friends also prevailed in Kate Douglas WIGGIN's *Rebecca of Sunnybrook Farm* (1903). It continued through the forties with other publications such as the Little House books by Laura Ingalls WILDER, the first published in 1932. The emphasis on daily life proved to be a departure from traditional European themes in children's books. Work was central to everyday activities of Americans; thereby creating events in the life an American child. The presentation of this daily life was peculiar at that time and specific to American children's literature. It unleashed great energy and optimism, which became the signature of the country's children's literature. America's new FOLKLORE departed from previous old world folklore prevalent in Wanda GAG's *Millions of Cats* (1928) to the new, more American style in Virginia Lee BURTON's *Mike Mulligan and His Steam Shovel* (1939) and Robert MCCLOSKEY's *Make Way for Ducklings* (1941). Also unique to American children's literature was a new sense of HUMOR and style as well as the great hope of America as exhibited in the stories and illustrations of Robert LAWSON, including the *Story of Ferdinand* (1936), *Ben and Me* (1939), and *Rabbit Hill* (1944).

Other significant events supported the prominence of children's literature in America. During the late teens and early 1920s, publishing companies created separate children's departments and began to promote children's recommended-book lists. The first NEWBERY MEDAL was given in 1922, the *Horn Book* magazine appeared in 1924, and the first CALDECOTT MEDAL followed in 1938. During this period, the appearance of books that studied American children's literature validated it as a worthwhile field of study. Two of these works included A. S. W. Rosenbach's *Early American Books* (1933) and Jacob Blanck's *Peter Parley to Penrod: A Biographical Description of the Best-Loved American Juvenile Books* (1938). The AWARDS, acceptance speeches and press coverage aided in the further recognition of the importance of children's literature. Although interest waned somewhat during the Great Depression years, eventually the momentum was regained and continued to strengthen. During the first decades of the twentieth century, the importance of

Edward STRATEMEYER's establishment of the Stratemeyer Literary Syndicate was evident. The Syndicate developed and marketed over sixty-five juvenile series through several decades, with the first widely recognized of these being the Bobbsey Twins in 1904 and continuing with the Hardy Boys and Nancy Drew SERIES.

Significant and critical to the diversity of a nation is the inclusion of literature for, by, and about minority cultures. Previously white authors' attempts to present other cultures resulted in exaggerations of dialect and ILLUSTRATIONS that negated their value. The entry of AFRICAN AMERICAN writers into mainstream children's literature began in the late 1920s to the early 1930s. It would be decades before other minorities would be represented in a significant way. Before the 1920s, African American authors had depended on small religious publishing houses or small black publishing companies. Langston HUGHES and Arna BONTEMPS are credited with the accomplishment of prominent publication as they coordinated efforts to produce a significant number of works for children. In 1932, Macmillan published Hughes's and Bontemps's *Popo and Fifina* illustrated by the critically acclaimed African American artist E. Simms Campbell. The two authors followed with *You Can't Pet a Possum* (1937), *Sad-Faced Boy* (1937), *Golden Slippers* (1941), and *The Fast Sooner Hound* (1942). Hughes continued to publish for children and Bontemps is frequently referred to as the father of contemporary African American children's literature.

The presence of literature for adolescents and YOUNG ADULTS increased in prominence from the early to the mid-1900s. In 1911, the NATIONAL COUNCIL OF TEACHERS OF ENGLISH met to study and discuss the primary purposes of high schools. With this conference came the recognized need for a list of books for home and class reading recommending the inclusion of present-day works (published no earlier than ten years previously) in addition to "old" classics. Dora V. Smith, University of Minnesota, taught the first course on teaching adolescent literature, another marker for the growing advancement of YOUNG ADULT LITERATURE. Accessibility was greatly increased with the appearance of pulp magazines, COMIC BOOKS AND GRAPHIC NOVELS, Big-Little

Books, Little Blue Books, and the Stratemeyer series. In 1903, Street and Smith published the *Popular* magazine, known for its specialized interests of detective, love, Western, SPORTS, and sea stories that had high appeal to readers who were not yet adults. Although judged harshly by critics, the popularity of the comic book and comic strip genre was evident with characters like Superman. By 1941, the publication and popularity of comic books increased to over 160 comic-book titles monthly, selling more than 12 million copies. Less influential, but still widely read were the Big-Little Books (the first one, *The Adventures of Dick Tracy,* 1932), published by Whitman with cardboard covers and varying sizes. They sold for ten cents and featured popular comic strip characters, movie actors or characters created for movies. In addition, the impact of the highly debated Little Blue Books by Emanuel Haldeman-Julius was profound in that multitudes of Americans who had little formal education were afforded access to books that covered a variety of controversial subjects and writings, but cost only pennies. (See also MINIATURE BOOKS)

Several works were published prior to 1950 that are viewed as instrumental to later developments in the field. Hendrik Willem VAN LOON's Newbery winner *The Story of Mankind* (1921) served as a model for later INFORMATION BOOKS. N. C. Wyeth's art in STEVENSON's *Treasure Island* (1911) was an early example of illustrations that extend the text rather than solely reproduce what the text describes. And John R. TUNIS is considered the forefather of the genre of young adult sports fiction for his attention to detail, description, and authenticity in *The Kid from Tompkinsville* (1940) and *All-American* (1942).

The first half of the twentieth century provided the momentum on which children's literature thrived in later years. The recognition, and the paths that were paved seemed monumental at the time. They proved to be stepping stones for a much faster pace of development for later decades in the proliferation and validation of American children's literature.

BIBLIOGRAPHY: "American Children Literature: Background and Bibliography," *American Studies International,* 1992; Bishop, Rudine Sims, "Books from Parallel Cultures: Let Our Rejoicing Rise," the *Horn Book* magazine, Sept./Oct., 1994;

Egoff, Sheila A., *Worlds Within: Children's Fantasy from the Middle Ages to Today,* 1988; Meyer, Susan E., *A Treasury of the Great Children's Book Illustrators,* 1983; Silvey, Anita, *Children's Books and Their Creators,* 1995; Townsend, John Rowe, *Written for Children,* 1983

NANCY HORTON

AMERICAN (UNITED STATES) LITERATURE, 1945–60

The middle of the twentieth century (1945–60) was a time in which children's literature made great strides, not so much as markers in themselves, but as turning points for later developments.

Robert HEINLEIN created the first American children's SCIENCE FICTION with his *Rocket Ship Galileo* (1947). Science fiction of this era began to provide readers with stories of good versus evil. The genre also reflected society's concerns about race relations and communism in a format available to young readers. Authors Andre NORTON and Arthur C. CLARKE helped catapult this genre to great popularity.

Daily life stories abounded with Beverly CLEARY's *Henry Huggins* (1950) and *Henry and Ribsy* (1954), literature written exclusively for early elementary age readers. *Charlotte's Web* (1952) by E. B. WHITE exemplified readers' engagement with the DRAMA and FANTASY of daily life. And Alice DALGLIESH's *Courage of Sarah Noble* (1954) exemplifies a family's support and a child's need for discovery.

The writer Jesse Jackson advanced the quality of AFRICAN AMERICAN LITERATURE immensely with *Call Me Charley* (1945) and its sequel *Anchor Man* (1947). By the late 1950s, Lorenz GRAHAM's nine-year mission to publish *South Town* (1958) was finally successful. Other cultures would remain under- or unrepresented. An early book dealing with the issue of growing up Chinese in America during the 1930s was *Fifth Chinese Daughter* (Jade Snow Wong, 1950). This issue would not be addressed in this manner again for more than twenty-five years. REALISM took a strong hold in stories beginning as early as the midfifties with Meindert DE JONG's *House of Sixty Fathers* (1956), a story that explores issues of Japanese-occupied China.

Interest in the past swelled in America and produced historical novels, period stories, and IN-FORMATIONAL BOOKS. Unlike previous publications based on personal experiences, *The Witch of Blackbird Pond* (1958) by Elizabeth George SPEARE revealed a great amount of detailed research to support America's drive for freedom in the newfound country, while Marguerite DE ANGELI gave us *The Door in the Wall* (1949), based on thirteenth century England.

Teachers and parents become more involved in children's literature. For teachers, one of the most respected sources was May Hill Arbuthnot's *Children and Books* (1947). Nancy LARRICK's *A Parent's Guide to Children's Reading* (1958) was one of the first to advise and guide parents in their involvement with their children's reading, including use of library, book lists of varied genres, and integration with other media. Bibliotherapy was established by the 1950s, resulting in teachers extending their suggestions of titles, thereby increasing the number of titles read.

A new area that would capture audiences was the intense interest in providing material for early readers, or lap listeners, and their parents. The classic *Goodnight Moon* (1947) by Margaret Wise BROWN paved the way for preschool audiences. Dr. SEUSS's *Cat in the Hat* (1957) and Else Holmelund MINARIK's *Little Bear* (1957) with Maurice SENDAK's ILLUSTRATIONS opened a new world of entertainment combining pictures and text using wordplay to introduce children to fantasy books called EASY READERS. Significant to the genre of POETRY was David MCCORD's *Far and Few* (1952). McCord was one of the first to create a body of poetry intended exclusively for children. His inventive rhythms and sound effects engaged children in American poetry.

The nature of the books being read by adolescents was changing. Along with the presence of YOUNG ADULT LITERATURE came criticism of the works. Literary criticism began to appear in the *English Journal* in the early 1950s, citing recommended authors, novels, and points of consideration for teacher selection of novels. Junior novels were being written with the special interests of this age group in mind. Subject matter with which teens could identify included Henry Gregor Felsen's *Hot Rod* (1952), *Street Rod* (1953), and *Crash Club* (1958); however, few authors wrote of issues that concerned teens. Mary STOLZ wrote some of the most sophisticated novels in the 1950s including her first *To Tell Your Love* (1950) and *Pray Love, Remember* (1954). Still, teens reached for reading material that included more mature themes, ones still ignored by most junior novels. They began to read novels intended for adult audiences; the reading habits of teenagers would be changed forever. The coming-of-age themes and social issues raised in several books were welcomed by teenagers and later came to be considered young adult novels. J. D. SALINGER's *Catcher in the Rye* (1951), William Golding's *The Lord of the Flies* (1955), and John Knowles's *A Separate Peace* (1959) were among the most popular.

Before the 1950s, art in children's books was dominated by Europeans living in America. The 1950s was deemed the Golden Age of Picture Books. PICTURE BOOKS provided readers with a new format of broad HUMOR and short but strong story lines. Change was imminent at this time. Maurice Sendak's art in *Kenny's Window* (1956) and *A Hole Is to Dig* (KRAUSS, 1952) was black and white which was typical of the technology of the era but a breakthrough in having the illustrations extend the text; they paved the way for the changes seen in decades to come.

The late 1940s and the 1950s brought several changes to children's literature: the Golden Age of picture books, the proliferation and acceptance of realism and science fiction, and the advent of easy readers for early exposure to literature for young children. Additionally, the 1950s would be the last decade that children's publishing could be described as mostly peaceful and quiet. The need for economic and societal change in America would be reflected in children's literature in the coming decades.

BIBLIOGRAPHY: "American Children Literature: Background and Bibliography," *American Studies International,* April 1992; Bishop, Rudine Sims, "Books from Parallel Culture: Let Our Rejoicing Rise," *Horn Book* magazine, Sept./Oct., 1994; Donelson, Kenneth L. and Alleen Pace Nilsen, *Literature for Today's Young Adults.* 1980; Egoff, Sheila A., *Worlds within: Children's Fantasy from the Middle Ages to Today,* 1988; Meyer, Susan E., *A Treasury of the Great Children's Book Illustrators,* 1983; Silvey, Anita, ed. *Children's Books and Their Creators,* 1995; Townsend, John Rowe, *Written for Children,* 1983

NANCY HORTON

AMERICAN (UNITED STATES) LITERATURE: CONTEMPORARY

(At the time of writing this essay, Lauren Wohl was Library and Education Marketing Director at Hyperion Books for Children. She has worked in children's book publishing for thirty years. From her unique point of view she writes, "In this article, I present a number of snapshots of the children's book publishing industry taken over the last thirty years with a very particular camera. This is not a picture of the literature created over these years, but rather of the business of publishing as it responded to challenges and changes in the marketplace.")

They were golden years—the late sixties and early seventies—the first years of my career in children's book publishing. E. L. KONIGSBURG, Maurice SENDAK, Scott O'DELL, Leo LIONNI, Zilpha Keatley SNYDER, Ezra Jack KEATS, and Lloyd ALEXANDER (to name only a few) were at their heights. Wonderful books were being published—books that would matter in the lives of children.

But that was not the only reason the era was golden. Federal funding was what made those years glisten. Funding for libraries—primarily school libraries—for staffing and for books to fill their shelves created a demand for children's books that was unprecedented. And the recognition of the importance of libraries—and therefore of books—in the education of our children brought a prestige to the field that before had only been dreamed of.

School libraries, whose primary purpose is to support curriculum, needed fiction and nonfiction titles in the sciences, the social studies, and math, and publishers responded with ever-increasing numbers of books to meet these new demands. Changes in both society at large and in the classroom required that books reflect the ethnic diversity of the country; in the 1970s we began to see more books by and for AFRICAN AMERICANS, ASIAN AMERICANS, and LATINAS/OS. The role of women in society was freshly examined, and children's books reflected those changes, too, with stories featuring active heroines and histories and biographies revealing the contributions of women throughout our past.

During the 1970s, for many trade book publishing houses, schools, and libraries were the source of most of their children's book sales. But slowly, the funding began to dry up: public library hours were cut back; dollars for new books for school libraries diminished; many librarians lost their jobs. These were difficult times for children's book PUBLISHERS, who had to put on the brakes and shift gears all at once.

There were some bright spots, however. Early childhood programs received a lot of attention. Publishers recognized that very young children needed books, too. Many publishers began to develop board books and very simple PICTURE BOOKS for babies, toddlers, and preschoolers. Other publishers mined their backlists for books that met these needs, and they repackaged or re-promoted them with this new audience in mind.

Another gleam of hope was the children's-only bookstores—at first just a handful, but with time, more and more. Many of these independent shops were owned and run by former librarians and teachers who brought to the retail environment their passion for quality and their zeal to bring books and children together. They happily handsold each book. At the same time, chain bookstores, most located in shopping malls, were growing fast. These stores, with their limited shelf space for children's books and their limited selling staffs needed books that were self-selling: glitzy covers, brand-name authors, apparent value for the dollar. Both the independents and the chains had their greatest successes with picture books. They made terrific baby gifts, birthday gifts, holiday presents. Fiction for older readers—middle graders and young adults—sold primarily in paperback. In this period, publishers responded to these market trends with larger picture book lists and increased numbers of paperbacks.

Among those paperbacks, a mini-phenomenon occurred: romance series for preteen and teen-aged girls. Each series followed the light romantic adventures of a specific group of adolescents in one particular town. Girls couldn't get enough, and one series spawned another, then another. Booksellers could not be happier: kids were coming to their stores to buy the latest title on a regular basis. Chains expanded the space given to children's and young adult books; independents

hoped to use the readers' love of the series to lead them to other, perhaps more literary, books.

For younger children, PBS's READING RAINBOW series caused a small revolution of its own. Books featured on the shows—picture books—were suddenly in great demand by parents. Bookstores and nontraditional book outlets (like toy stores, drug stores, mass merchants) made room for books that proudly wore their *Reading Rainbow* stickers. And, contrary to industry wisdom of the past that held that picture-book readers were too young to handle paperbacks, *these* picture books sold best in paperback editions.

Things were looking up for children's books, and then, one more dramatic change occurred: whole language. Teachers who adopted the whole language philosophy were committed to providing their students with a literature-rich classroom—to putting books at the center of every lesson. Many abandoned basals and textbooks altogether, replacing them with individual titles and with multiple copies of trade books.

Teachers—all those teachers—shopped for books for their students everywhere, and, it seemed that everyone everywhere made room for children's books. Parents, too, encouraged by their children's teachers, became more enthusiastic buyers of books. And children themselves asked for more books, recognized authors and artists, and knew the kind of books they enjoyed. At this point, for most children's book publishers, retailers (including book clubs and book fairs and a wide range of premium sales) represented the greatest percentage of their children's book sales.

Onto this very fertile field, the book superstore emerged. These huge, comfortable, coffee-serving, woody, cozy-chair stores have large children's book departments that feature many special events (the kinds of programs previously limited to independent stores) to attract families. What they lack in knowledgeable sales people and readers' guidance services, they compensate for in enormous inventories.

Superstores cut into sales of their own sister chain stores, and the mall-based chains began closing as free-standing superstores opened nearby. Superstores also hurt the sales at independent book shops—both general stores and children's only stores. Many independents dug in, offering additional services, increased hours, and discounts. But for many, the competition was insurmountable, and stores began to close.

Publishers responded to this change by looking harder for those elusive big hits and tending less to the midlist and the literary books. Superstores could sell media tie-in books very well, and publishers licensed many characters, movies, and television shows for picture books, chapter books, and middle-grade fiction. Popular series—from friendship stories to horror tales—are also easy for the superstores. Just line 'em up, spine out, and let the kids themselves find the books they're up to. Even nonfiction series—large, photographic volumes treating specific subjects of interest to children—are easy for the superstores to merchandise and sell. Individual titles—works of singular imagination and art—do not find their strongest homes in superstores.

But throughout all the changes, such books continued to be published. And although library sales were flat or falling, the profession strongly supported such books. The awards library and teacher organizations continuously bestowed on outstanding children's books encouraged writers and artists and publishers. Literacy efforts supported by two different White House administrations as well as efforts of private businesses also kept open a place for fine fiction, nonfiction, and picture books. Caring editors nurtured talent—whatever else the market required.

Today, we see a turn-around in funding for libraries. School libraries, in recent years serving as the home of technology, are getting new funds to fill those bookshelves again. Children's public librarians are returning to book-related services while still managing additional technology services for their young patrons. Young adult librarians are in demand as the children of baby boomers reach middle grades.

And, while whole language is losing some ground to phonics and other skills-driven reading-teaching methods, teachers are reluctant to abandon the books they have grown to love over the last decade. They will use children's literature to make the learning of skills worth the effort.

Those independent bookstores that have survived the turmoil of the chains and superstores and warehouse clubs continue to thrive and to match a book and a child—one to one—every day.

In these days, children's book sales are more balanced than before. Most are on the retail side,

but a strong and growing percentage are to schools, libraries, and early childhood centers. Children's book lists are more diverse than ever—and on them we can find many books that are golden, books that will matter in the lives of children long into the future.

LAUREN L. WOHL

ANAYA, Rudolfo
Author, b. 30 October 1937, Santa Rosa, New Mexico

A. grew up in a Spanish-speaking home with strong Mexican American traditions and says that learning English at school was burdensome; until he started school he thought the whole world spoke English. Now professor emeritus, A. entered the University of New Mexico in 1958 and was soon enchanted with words and literature. In an effort to capture the experiences and exuberance of his community, he started writing POETRY and stories. His first novel, for adults, *Bless Me Ultima* (1972) was written over the course of seven years and includes much autobiographical material. A. continues to write for adults as he pursues a child audience as well and is active in the burgeoning Chicano Movement in art and literature. He believes that children need to see themselves and their culture reflected in the books they read while people outside the community need to be able to look into the Mexican American community and learn about their culture.

In *The Farolitos of Christmas* (1995) A. tells a warm FAMILY STORY about preserving Christmas traditions in a small Mexican American community during World War II. Spanish words are smoothly incorporated into the English text and a glossary is provided. A. won the 1999 Tomas Rivera Mexican-American Children's Award for *My Land Sings*.

FURTHER WORKS: *The Farolitos of Christmas* (play), 1987; *Zia Summer*, 1995; *Maya's Children: The Story of La Llorona* (1997); *Farolitos for Abuelo*, 1998; *My Land Sings: Stories from the Rio Grande*, 1999; *Roadrunner's Dance*, 2000

DIANE G. PERSON

ANCONA, George
Photographer, author, b. 4 December 1929, New York City

Although he worked as a television art director for NBC, a fashion photographer, and independent filmmaker, A. is probably best known for his artistic and imaginative photo essays for children. His photographs have appeared in more than seventy-five books for children, over one-third of which he also authored. Remembering what he found fascinating as a child, some of A.'s work focuses on giants at work (e.g., *Freighters* [1985]; *Monsters on Wheels* [1974]; *Monsters Movers* [1984]. In keeping with his interest in the workplace, A.'s titles also include job-centered themes and some unusual careers (e.g., *Teamwork: A Picture Essay about Crews and Teams at Work,* [1983]); *Riverkeeper* (1990); *Man and Mustang* (1992); *Stone Cutters, Carvers and the Cathedral* (1995). A.'s diverse literary repertoire also reflects his bilingual upbringing and Mexican heritage (e.g., *Fiesta U.S.A.* [1993]; *Pablo Remembers: The Fiesta of the Day of the Dead* [1993]; *Ser util* [1993; the text appears in Spanish and English on facing pages]; *The Pinata Maker/ El Pinatero* [1994]; *Ricardo's Day/El Dia de Ricardo* [1994]). His creative approach to photographic ILLUSTRATION is evidenced by the award-winning and popular Handtalk series. These four books utilize sign language to show how children communicate by signing. In *Handtalk Zoo* (with Mary Beth Miller and Remy CHARLIP, 1989), for example, A.'s photographs convey the hand motions of signing children as they identify zoo animals. Another anatomical focus is evidenced by A.'s interesting black-and-white photographs in *Faces* (1970), written by Barbara Brenner. Varying the distance from his subject, A. makes us take notice of facial features and qualities we may not often think about. A. has also collaborated with authors of books dealing with physically challenged adults and children (*Finding a Way: Living with Exceptional Brothers and Sisters,* with Maxine Rosenberg, 1988; and *Mom Can't See Me,* with Sally Hobart Alexander, 1990).

AWARDS: 1975 and 1988 Nonfiction Youngster Honor, Science Book Awards, New York Academy of Sciences for *Handtalk: An ABC of Finger Spelling and Sign Language* (with Remy CHARLIP and Mary Beth Miller) and 1988 for *Turtle Watch,* respectively; 1980 Golden Kite Award (Society of Children's Book Writers and Illustrators for *Finding Your First Job* (with Sue ALEXANDER); 1986 ALA Notable Book for *Sheepdog;* 1987 *New York Times* Best Illustrated Children's Books of the Year Citation, 1987, for *Handtalk*

Birthday: A Number and Story Book in Sign Language (with Charlip and Miller); and many other AWARDS

FILM WORK: In addition to his highly regarded children's books, A. has also written filmscripts for *Sesame Street* (*Doctor* and *Dentist*) and films for children (e.g., *Faces* and *The River*). (See *READING RAINBOW* AND CHILDREN'S LITERATURE ON TELEVISION.) A.'s success is due in part to his acute awareness of what interests children. His eclectic interests, reflected by the breadth and versatility of his numerous titles, help to energize children's curiosity about diverse topics, such as animals, babies, giant machinery, unusual occupations, and cultural excursions to faraway places (e.g., a Brazillian sea turtle expedition in *Turtle Watch* or a trip to a banana plantation in Honduras in *Bananas: From Manola to Margie*)

FURTHER WORKS FOR CHILDREN: *Bodies,* (with Barbara Brenner), 1973; *And What Do You Do?* 1975; *I Feel: A* PICTURE BOOK *of Emotions* 1977; *It's a Baby!* 1979; *Dancing Is . . .* 1981; *Being Adopted* (with Maxine Rosenberg) 1984; *Helping Out,* 1985; *Spanish Pioneers of the Southwest* (with Joan Anderson), 1989; *My Camera,* 1992; *Powwow,* 1993; *The Golden Lion Tamarin Comes Home,* 1994

ANDREW KANTAR

ANDERSEN, Hans Christian

Author, b. 2 April 1805, Odense, Denmark; d. 4 August 1875, Rolighed, Denmark

As an author of stories loved by all generations, A. is often acclaimed as the foremost writer of FAIRY TALES in literary history. His masterful STORYTELLING ability, drawing from a wealth of FOLKLORE, wove his curiosity, imagination, life experiences, and vision of humanity into universal tales. While autobiographical elements of these tales have been easily identified, A. also shared his keen insight into the everyday riches of life often overlooked as well as the greed, pride, and envy he recognized within society.

As the son of a shoemaker and washerwoman, A.'s early life was filled with poverty and struggles. At the age of eleven he worked in a cloth factory, a tobacco factory, and as an assistant shoemaker. Growing up with unusual family members could have easily fed his imagination—a superstitious mother, a mildly insane grandfather, and a grandmother who worked in an insane asylum. It was when accompanying this grandmother that he heard the tales from the poor women of the town who were working nearby the asylum. These tales, he felt, were as rich as those of the *Thousand and One Nights.* His father was also a source of encouragement as he nurtured his son's imagination through reading and acting out stories with dolls. His father died, however, when A. was about eleven years old. With the hope of being a performer, A. left school at the age of fourteen and spent three years in Copenhagen trying to become an actor, including studying voice. Although he was not successful in these endeavors, the support of his friends and A.'s perseverance and determination that he could achieve fame motivated him to return to school. Having met Jonas Collin through a friend, A. received a royal grant through this theater director. A. then returned to school at age seventeen and studied for six years before his focus turned to a literary career. His first book, *A Journey on Foot from Copenhagen to the Eastern Point of Amager* (1829), was followed by *Love on St. Nicholas Church Tower* (1829) as well as some POETRY; all were successful.

During his youth, A. fell in love with numerous women including Jenny Lind and Louise Collin, the daughter of A.'s benefactor who had become a father figure to him. These women were the inspiration for his poetry as well as models for characters in his tales. However, A. never married and was distraught at times over his lack of success in this area of his life. As he traveled about Europe he continued writing, although his work was not considered as good as his first book. While living in Italy, he wrote his best long work, *The Improvisatore* (1835), a recreation of his own life set in Italy.

The year 1835 was also significant because A.'s first collection of fairy tales, *Eventyr,* was published. Of the four stories included in this volume, three were tales he had heard as a child. These included "The Tinderbox," "Little Claus and Big Claus," "The Princess and the Pea," and one with an original plot, "Little Ida's Flowers." However, A.'s retellings were not done to preserve the historical and cultural significance of the tales; rather, they were his stories to create allegories representing his ideals about life. The language A. used in these Wonder Stories, the closest phrase one can use to translate *Eventyr,* was conversational. "I seize an idea for older

people," he wrote, "and then tell it to the young ones, while remembering that father and mother are listening and must have something to think about." For this reason many of the first reactions to the tales were negative as the colloquial style was much too unsophisticated for adults and the stories were not didactic enough for children. Others, however, realized the genius in the stories. Soon A. knew that not only were they an "outlet for his message to the world" but that they "commanded his greatest audience and could bring him the international fame he sought."

A.'s second collection (1836) included "Thumbelina," "The Naughty Boy," and "The Traveling Companion." "The Little Mermaid" and "The Emperor's New Clothes" were in the third collection. The list of successes continued each year until his death with stories that have both happy endings as well as those that reflected the hardships he knew as a child. Subtle HUMOR is found frequently within his tales, although it is often lost in TRANSLATION. His language has been described by literary critics as poetic and polished in these tales, which scholars also describe as having "depth of experience and clarity in expression." Autobiography, satire, and response to critics were found within the two hundred tales published during his career. These tales also contain some of the most memorable child characters in children's literature. A.'s biographer states that "he is the hero, who triumphs over poverty, persecution and plain stupidity, and who sometimes, in reversal of the facts, marries the princess ('Clodpoll') or scorns her ('The Swineherd')." He is an old poet who is shot by Cupid in "The Naughty Boy." In "The Little Mermaid," Louise Collin is the prince while he is the mermaid. Other loves are found in "Sweethearts" and in "The Steadfast Tin Soldier." Jenny Lind and A. are together in "The Nightingale." Tales such as "The Ugly Duckling" and "The Fir Tree" reflect his life as well as respond to critics.

A. also wrote other novels and plays in addition to his autobiography *Mit Livs Eventyr* (1855). At this time he had achieved his ambition, had become internationally known, and had developed a mutual admiration and friendship with Charles DICKENS. He continued writing in a variety of genres and was honored by his hometown, which made him an honorary citizen. Despite failing health, he celebrated his seventieth birthday in 1875 with tributes and festivities and died later that year. Just as in "The Ugly Duckling," the snubbed signet becomes a beautiful swan, so A. became the pride of Denmark and its international literary representative. . . . He is usually recognized today as "a consummate storyteller who distilled his vision of humanity into a simple format that can be universally appreciated."

AWARDS: A. received grants from the King of Denmark, 1833–35, for travel. He was made an Honorary Danish Councillor of State and an Honorary Citizen of Odense

FURTHER WORKS: Translated collections: *Wonderful Stories for Children* (Mary Howitt, trans.), 1835–37, 2nd series 1838, 3rd series 1845; *Danish Fairy Legends and Tales* (C. Peachey, trans.), 1st ed. 1846; *A Danish Story-book* (C. Boner, trans.), 1846; *A Poet's Day Dreams* (A. S. Bushby, trans.), 1853; *Fairy Tales of Hans A.,* 1899; *Four Tales from Hans A.,* 1935; *The Complete A.* (J. Hersholt, ed., trans.), 1952; *Hans Christian A.: The Complete Fairy Tales and Stories,* 1974; Single stories: "The Story Teller and Other Fairy Tales," 1850; "The Ice Maiden," 1863; "What the Moon Saw and Other Stories," 1866; "The Snow Queen," 1883; "Little Thumb," 1883; "The Real Princess," 1932; "Thumbelina," 1939; "The Little Match Girl," 1944; "The Emperor's New Clothes," 1949; *"The Princess and the Pea" and Other Famous Stories,* 1962

BIBLIOGRAPHY: *Children's Literature Review,* vol. 6, 1984. Gronbech, B. *Hans Christian A.* 1980; Spink, Reginal. *Hans Christian A. and His World,* 1972

JANELLE B. MATHIS

ANDERSON, C. W. (Clarence William)
Author, illustrator, b. 12 April 1891, Wahoo, Nebraska; d. 26 March 1971

A. developed an early interest in horses—he especially loved to draw them. Although A. considered himself an artist, his experience and research with horses resulted in at least thirty fiction books involving horses and at least twenty nonfiction books about horses. A. often based his stories on real people and horses. For example, A.'s first horse, Bobcat, plays a role in many of his stories. *Billy and Blaze* (1936) is the first and best known

story in a popular SERIES of books A. wrote about a boy and his horse.

FURTHER WORKS: *And So to Bed,* 1935; *Blaze and the Forest Fire,* 1938, rpt. 1992; *Salute,* 1940; *High Courage,* 1941; *Big Red,* 1943; *Head up, Heels Down,* 1944; *Bobcat,* 1949; *Horseshow,* 1951; *Blaze and Thunderbolt,* 1955; *The Horse of Hurricane Hill,* 1956; *Blaze and the Mountain Lion,* 1959; *Bred to Run,* 1960; *A Filly for Joan,* 1960; *Blaze and the Indian Cave,* 1964; *Blaze Finds Forgotten Roads,* 1970

BIBLIOGRAPHY: Chevalier, T., ed., *Twentieth Century Children's Writers,* 1989; *Something about the Author,* vol. 11, 1977

JODI PILGRIM

ANGLUND, Joan Walsh
Author, illustrator, b. 3 January 1926, Hinsdale, Illinois

A.'s characteristic children, drawn with no noses or mouths, evolved out of her constant observation of children, her own and others, in an attempt to capture their essence and thus the essence of childhood. As a part of these observations, she wrote her first book, *A Friend Is Someone Who Likes You* (1958/1983), while watching children at play at a local playground. A.'s images of children appear in greeting cards, dolls, and numerous commercial products; they are sometimes called "precious."

FURTHER WORKS: *Childhood Is a Time of Innocence,* 1964; *Christmas Is a Time of Giving,* 1961; *The Joan Walsh Anglund Storybook,* 1978; *Love is a Special Way of Feeling,* 1960; *Memories of the Heart,* 1984; *Morning Is a Little Child,* 1969

BIBLIOGRAPHY: *Third Book of Junior Authors,* 1972

GWYNNE ELLEN ASH

ANGELL, Judie
Author, b. 10 July 1937, New York City

A. has written REALISTIC FICTION for preteens and adolescents for more than twenty years. Her early novels for YOUNG ADULTS often feature protagonists who are experiencing transitions in their lives. In addition, the novels explore many of the common issues that young readers encounter. Later in her career, A. began writing novels of a darker nature under the pen name of Fran Arrick. In these books for older teens, the author deals with more serious issues such as suicide, AIDS, prostitution, rape, and mental illness. In the 1992 novel, *What You Don't Know Can Kill You,* the main character's sister becomes infected with HIV, and her boyfriend, who had an affair with another girl, commits suicide. In the 1980s, the author began a series of lighter novels for middle-school readers under the pen name of Maggie Twohill. All of A.'s works reflect the author's respect for the strength and resiliency of young people.

FURTHER WORKS: *In Summertime It's Tuffy,* 1977; *The Buffalo Nickel Blues Band,* 1982; *Tunnel Vision; One-Way to Ansonia,* 1995

BIBLIOGRAPHY: *Something about the Author,* vol. 78, 1995

MARY ARIAIL BROUGHTON

ANGELOU, Maya

Author, poet, playwright, b. 4 April, 1928, St. Louis, Missouri

Besides writing POETRY, plays, and musical scores, as well as performing in theater, A. is well known for *I Know Why the Caged Bird Sings* (1970), her first book in a series of five autobiographies that describe her childhood, adolescence, and young adulthood. At three years of age, A. was sent to be reared by her grandmother in segregated Stamps, Arkansas, until she was sent back to her mother in 1936. She stopped talking at the age of eight after being raped by her mother's boyfriend. Sent back to live with her grandmother, A. gradually regained her speech and confidence. She has become a leading literary voice of the AFRICAN AMERICAN community. A frequent lecturer, A. became a professor of American Studies at Wake Forest University in 1981.

I Know Why the Caged Bird Sings portrays A.'s life as an African American in the South during the 1930s–Depression era. Although Mera, the five-year-old in this book, cannot speak, she is a keen observer of the racial politics and division around her. Throughout her writing, her ability as a poet translates into rich, textured prose. Her early observational skills continue through the other books in the series, as well as through her poetry and later prose.

A. writes, "All my work, my life, everything is about survival. All my work is meant to say,

'You may encounter many defeats, but you must not be defeated.' In fact, the encountering may be the very experience which creates the vitality and the power to endure."

AWARDS: Nominated for National Book Award, 1970, for *I Know Why the Caged Bird Sings;* Pulitzer Prize nominations in 1972 for *Just Give Me a Cool Drink of Water 'fore I Die* (1971); Tony Award nomination 1973 for her performance in *Look Away;* and in 1977 for her performance in *Roots;* several honorary degrees including degrees from Smith College, 1975, and Lawrence University, 1976

FURTHER WORKS: *Gather Together in My Name,* 1974; *Singin' and Swingin and Gettin' Merry like Christmas,* 1976; *The Heart of a Woman,* 1981; *All God's Children Need Traveling Shoes,* 1986; "On the Pulse of Morning" (presidential-inaugural poem), 1993

BIBLIOGRAPHY: Tate, Claudia, *Black Women Writers at Work,* 1983

SANDRA IMDIEKE

ANIMAL STORIES

Throughout the history of children's literature animals play a significant role. They entertain, touch hearts, help readers identify with emotions, values, and relationships, and inform about the interdependency of the natural world. Initially, animal stories were shared orally in the form of fairy stories, bestiaries and fables—some of the earliest forms of written children's literature. In the mid-eighteenth century, as the market for children's literature developed, animal stories were often a focus, such as John NEWBERY's *Goody Two-Shoes* (1765) in which the main character is helped by her animal friends. Most of the books written at this time were satires on human behavior, moral lessons for children, and lessons about cruelty to animals. Often animals talked and related their own tales. Humorous POETRY about animals also began to appear, such as the verses of MOTHER GOOSE in contrast to the presentation of animals in the woodcuts of the *New England Primer.* Joseph JACOBS began retelling folktales for children and the early 1800s also found the GRIMM Brothers' tales being transcribed from the oral tradition although originally these were not intended for children.

In the latter part of the nineteenth century, such significant works as Anna SEWELL's *Black*

Beauty (1877), which spoke against cruelty to animals, and KIPLING's *Jungle Books* (1894 and 1895), a true ADVENTURE STORY, began their reigns of popularity. *A Dog of Flanders and Other Stories* (1872) by Marie Louise de la Ramee is considered the first modern dog story. *Fables from Uncle Remus* (1880) by Joel Chandler HARRIS, and *The Wind in the Willows* (1908) by Kenneth GRAHAME are considered classics.

Early in the twentieth century Beatrix POTTER told her wonderful tale of *Peter Rabbit* (1902) and Leslie BROOKE published humorous animal verse in *The Golden Goose Book* (1905). As the century progressed, A. A. MILNE gave readers *Winnie the Pooh* (1926), Wanda GAG created the classic *Millions of Cats* (1928) and the first CALDECOTT MEDAL was given to *Animals of the Bible* (1937) by Dorothy P. LATHROP.

During the mid-twentieth century authors tried to present realistically the lives of animals in fiction and INFORMATIONAL BOOKS. Books from this period that continue to be widely read are *The Yearling* (Marjorie Kinnan RAWLINGS, 1938), and *My Friend Flicka* (Mary O'Hara, 1941). *Smoky, the Cowhorse* (W. JAMES, 1926), the NEWBERY MEDAL winner, told of the cruel mistreatment of a beloved Western horse. *Bambi* (Felix SALTEN) was translated in 1926 from the German and although it was fiction, it was based on scientific fact. Eric KNIGHT's *Lassie Come Home* (1940) and the horse stories of Marguerite HENRY have been favorites of readers since their publication. In addition to these works of fiction, writers such as Addison Webb (*White Birds Island* [1948]) and Wilfred Bronson (*Children of the Sea* [1940]) recreated the beauty of nature in text for children. Theodore Waldece, in *The White Panther* (1941) and Harold McCracken, in *The Last of the Sea Otters* (1942), among others, shared their personal outdoor life experiences through telling their animal stories.

As animal stories continued to be respected and loved, the second half of the twentieth century began with such well-remembered titles as *The Incredible Journey* (Sheila BURNFORD, 1960) and *Where the Red Fern Grows* (Wilson RAWLS, 1961)—both touching readers' hearts for decades. In England, *Watership Down* (Richard ADAMS, 1972), an epic tale in which rabbits are the main characters, is considered one of the best animal fantasies ever written.

Contemporary children's literature is rich with authentic accounts of animal life in information books and REALISTIC FICTION. The books of Seymour SIMON, Gail GIBBONS and Jean Craighead GEORGE, among many others, use a diversity of art forms and research approaches to inform young readers about the natural life of a variety of animals.

Animal stories are also the vehicle for many social issues that are embedded in children's literature. Environmental issues, such as accounts involving endangered species, are the focus of both informational and fiction books, as in *And Then There Was One: The Mysteries of Extinction* (Marjorie FACKLAM, 1990) and *Prince William* (Gloria and Ted RAND, 1992) about efforts to save wildlife after the Alaskan oil spill. Issues of animal abuse appearing in such books as *Pole Dog* (T. Seymour, 1993), or *A Dog like Jack* (DiSalvo Ryan, 1999) often contain the endorsement of organizations and people concerned with the humane treatment of animals. In *Speak!* (Michael ROSEN, ed., 1993), noted children's illustrators write about their pets and illustrate their story; proceeds from the books go to animal shelters.

Animals are often central characters in stories that involve human issues. *Shiloh* (Phyllis NAYLOR), the 1992 NEWBERY MEDAL WINNER, is about a young boy's developing integrity and the decisions he must make, choosing between the truth and responsibility he feels for an abused dog. *Smoky Night,* Eve BUNTING's 1995 CALDECOTT winner, illustrated by David DIAZ, uses the rescue of two cats as the vehicle to improve relationships between diverse ethnic families. A cat also helps create a bond between a young African American boy and an elderly Jewish woman in *Mrs. Katz and Tush* (Patricia POLACCO, 1992). Dealing with death is often contemplated through the death of an animal. *The Tenth Good Thing about Barney* (Judith Viorst, 1971) offers a way for children to deal with the finality of death and the ongoing cycle of life. *The Old Dog* by Charlotte ZOLOTOW was reissued in 1995 with James RANSOME's illustrations. This, along with *I'll Always Love You* (Hans Wilhelm, 1989) and *Bonesy and Isabel* (Michael Rosen, 1995), tell of the loss of pets and represent different ways to deal with that loss. Adventure stories in which the protagonist is faced with survival, such as *Julie of the Wolves* (1972) and *My Side of the Mountain* (1988) both by Jean Craighead GEORGE, contain authentic depictions of wildlife that contributes to the characters' coming of age experiences.

Many examples of FOLKLORE dealing with animals are still collected and written as children's literature, such as *The Mightiest Heart* (1999) by Lynn Cullen, a Welsh legend about a dog's faithfulness. This is especially true as writers try to capture the lore of many diverse cultures. Folklore from various cultures uses animals extensively, portraying them as tricksters or telling a tale about some aspect of the natural world occurred. This is particularly so with NATIVE AMERICAN stories. Michael J. Caduto and Joseph BRUCHAC have recorded many of these in their collection, *Keepers of the Earth* (1991). Paul GOBLE is another noted author who writes about buffalo, horses, and other animals of the plains area as told by the Plains Indians. Additionally, modern variants of familiar tales, as *The True Story of the Three Pigs as Told by A. Wolf* (1996) by Jon SCIESZKA, continue to use animals albeit in different contexts as a spoof on folklore.

Anthropomorphism, or giving human qualities to animals, is found frequently in FANTASY. Kevin HENKES has created mice characters with life experiences familiar to children in *Julius, the Baby of the World* (1990), *Lilly's Purple Plastic Purse* (1996), and *Owen* (1993) who wants to take his blanket to school. *Officer Buckle and Gloria,* a 1995 Caldecott Medal winner, by Peggy RATHMANN, is one of several humorous animal books by this author. Other well-known writers who have written numerous books with animals behaving like humans include Bernard WABER, *Lyle, Lyle Crocodile* (1965); William STEIG, *Sylvester and the Magic Pebble* (1979); Leo LIONNI, *Matthew's Dream* (1991); Alexandra DAY, *Good Dog, Carl* (1985); David MCPHAIL, *Pig Pig Grows Up,* (1980); Rosemary WELLS, *Noisy Nora* (1973); Arnold LOBEL, *Frog and Toad Together* (1972), Jane Breskin ZALBEN's series about the bear, Beni; and Margaret Wise BROWN's classic PICTURE BOOK, *Goodnight Moon* (1947).

The genre of poetry also includes animal books. Barbara ESBENSEN's *Words with Wrinkled Knees* (1986), Myra Cohn LIVINGSTON's *Cat Poems* (1987) and *Dog Poems,* (1990), Lee Bennett HOPKINS's *Dinosaurs* (1987), Nancy LARRICK's *Cats Are Cats* (1988) provide rich word images of animal behavior and life. Dr. SEUSS, of course, with his nonsensical use of rhyme and rhythm will always be remembered for his unique depiction of animals in fantasy, such as *The Cat in the Hat* (1957).

Animals stories reflect everyday life. They create pictures and patterns from the past and present to inform, touch hearts, and suggest the significance of animals for all readers.

JANELLE B. MATHIS

ANNO, Mitsumasa

Author, illustrator, b. 20 March 1926, Tsuwano, Japan

A. grew up in the small isolated town of Tsuwano, Japan; nestled in a valley surrounded by mountains. A.'s dream, as a young boy was to explore the world outside of Tsuwano, and this dream came true when he attended high school in another town far away. There he began focusing his studies on art and drawing, and he continued his passion for mathematics. In 1948, he graduated from Yamaguchi Teacher Training College, and began teaching elementary school in Tokyo. While teaching, his own students taught A. how children perceive the world differently from adults, which would ultimately help him in his career as a writer for children.

A.'s first two PICTURE BOOKS, *Topsy-Turvies: Pictures to Stretch the Imagination,* (1970) and *Upside Downers: More Pictures to Stretch the Imagination* (1971), used ILLUSTRATIONS that show different images when observed from different angles or directions. The stated purpose of the books was to stimulate the imaginations of young people in order to "keep us magically human."

A. has also created several other books based on mathematical concepts such as *A.'s Counting Book* (1977), which shows how mathematical relationships occur all around us. This wordless book depicts the growth of a village and its surrounding countryside during a twelve-month period. In *Anno's Mysterious Multiplying Jar* (1983) the author uses simple text and beautiful artistry to introduce the mathematical concept of factorials. This book moves the reader from the concrete world of mathematics to the abstract by using a visual format. A.'s later work, *A.'s Magic Seeds* (1994), continues his interest in mathematical principles as he questions and probes the reader with mathematical games included within his beautiful artwork.

A.'s Alphabet; An Adventure in Imagination (1975) is another innovative book, which includes wood grain letters that are framed by borders containing objects that begin with that letter. His son, Masaichiro, helped illustrate a second interesting alphabet book, *A.'s Magical ABC: An Anamorphic Alphabet* (1980), in which the corresponding pictures are viewed through a reflective cylinder.

Among A.'s most acclaimed books are those referred to as "journey" books. These are wordless picture books that document A.'s travels through various parts of the world. The first of these books, *A.'s Journey* (1978), takes the reader on a tour of northern Europe, including such places as Scandinavia, Germany, and England. A. has included some of Europe's famous landscapes, geographical locations, people, and architecture in these illustrations, which helps readers connect to those things they may have heard about in the past. For instance, he includes a picture of Beethoven peering out a window at people passing by and playing in the streets of a European village.

A. also created journey books for other places he visited including *A.'s Italy* (1979), *A.'s Britain* (1982), and *A.'s USA* (1983). In *A.'s USA,* he depicts such places as New York City filled with a parade of people dispersed among its skyscrapers. This book also contains illustrations of scenes from famous American films such as *Gone With the Wind,* and *Shane.* In addition to the people and FOLKLORE, he includes famous historical, geographical, and architectural sites including the Alamo, Independence Hall in Philadelphia, plantations, cornfields, and the Capitol Building in Washington, D.C. Using the watercolor and ink technique, he blends the present with the past to capture the beauty of the United States. A. creates these journey books as wordless picture books to allow readers to invent stories for the characters, and to show all who look at the books what the people are doing, thinking,

and feeling, whether they speak the same language or not.

In addition to creating picture books, A. displays his paintings and graphic art in galleries and museums throughout several countries including the United States, Japan, Canada, and Great Britain. He has also created several interactive CD-ROMs including *A.'s Math Games* (1994) and *A.'s Learning Games* (1994).

AWARDS: *New York Times* Best Illustrated Children's Books of the Year and AMERICAN LIBRARY ASSOCIATION Notable Book (1970) for *Topsy-Turvies: Pictures to Stretch the Imagination.* American Institute of Graphics Fifty Books of the Year citation (1974). *Boston Globe–Horn Book* Award (1975), *New York Times* Best Illustrated Books of the Year (1975), ALA Notable Book (1975), Christopher Award (1975) for *A.'s Alphabet: An Adventure in Imagination.* ALA Notable Book (1979), for *A.'s Journey* and for *The King's Flower.* *New York Times* Best Illustrated Books of the Year (1982) for *A.'s Britain;* ALA Notable Book (1982) for *A.'s Counting House;* Hans Christian ANDERSEN Medal, 1984

FURTHER WORKS: *Dr. A.'s Magical Midnight Circus,* 1972; *A.'s Animals,* 1979; *A.'s Medieval World,* 1980; *A.'s Counting House,* 1982; *A.'s Flea Market,* 1984; *All in a Day,* 1986; *A.'s Peekaboo,* 1987; *A.'s Sundial,* 1987; *A.'s Math Games,* 1987; *A.'s Faces,* 1988; *In Shadowland,* 1988; *A.'s Aesop: A Book of Fables by Aesop and Mr. Fox,* 1989; *A.'s Masks,* 1989; *A.'s Math Games II,* 1989; *A.'s Math Games III,* 1991; *A.'s Counting Book Big Book,* 1992

BIBLIOGRAPHY: A., Mitsumasa. *The Unique World of Mitsumasa A.: Selected Works (1968–77);* 1980; *Booklist,* April 1985; the *Horn Book* magazine, 1990, 1995; Keifer, Barbara, selector, *Getting to Know You: Profiles of Children's Authors Featured in Language Arts, 1985–90,* 1991; *Something about the Author,* vol. 77, 1994

DENISE P. BEASLEY

ARCHAMBAULT, John

Author, poet, storyteller, b. Date unknown, Pasadena, California

Since the mid-1980's, when A. studied at the University of California, Riverside, he has collaborated with Bill MARTIN, Jr., in creating books for children ages four and up. Because of the poetic language and energetic rhythms, their books are particularly suitable for reading aloud to children. For example, their popular alphabet book, *Chicka*

Chicka Boom Boom (Lois EHLERT, illus., 1989) features an unforgettable beat that invites children of all ages to join the letters as they race to the top of the coconut tree. Many of A. and Martin's books are illustrated by Ted RAND, who first joined the two authors with his ILLUSTRATIONS of the award-winning *The Ghost-eye Tree* (1985). A later work by the trio, *Knots on a Counting Rope* (1987), was acclaimed by both the public and critics, as it was named a Notable Children's Trade Book in the field of Social Studies by the CHILDREN'S BOOK COUNCIL and National Council on the Social Studies. A. has also written books on his own, including *Counting Sheep* (1989) and *The Birth of a Whale* (1996).

FURTHER WORKS: (With Bill Martin, Jr.): Little Seashore Books series; *Barn Dance*, 1986, *Here Are My Hands* 1998

MARY ARIAIL BROUGHTON

ARDIZZONE, Edward

Author, illustrator, b. 10 October 1900, Haiphong, French Indochina (now Vietnam); d. 8 November 1979, London, England

A.'s childhood began in the Far East, but the major portion of his boyhood was spent growing up in England from the age of five. Often lonely since his father continued to work in the Far East and his mother frequently traveled, A. discovered an interest in painting and sketching. Much of his childhood was spent at boarding school or with a cousin exploring the docks of his seaside home. A. first began employment as a clerk, but soon turned his hobby of sketching and painting into a career when an inheritance gave him the independence to pursue art full time. He married and had three children whom he credits for the encouragement and inspiration for his first children's book, *Little Tim and the Brave Sea Captain* (1936). This book led to several more in the popular Little Tim series.

A. was a self-taught artist. He wrote and illustrated twenty books for children, edited and illustrated two classic FAIRY TALE collections, and illustrated over a hundred books for other authors of adult and children's literature. He uses watercolor and pen-and-ink for his ILLUSTRATIONS, which have been described as full of movement

yet understated, leaving room for the viewer's imagination.

His respect for children is reflected in his conviction that illustrators should not draw down for children but rather up, creating the quality of work as one would for exhibition. His first book for children, *Little Tim and the Brave Sea Captain,* began as a story he told to entertain his children. After many tellings and revisions, and with the help of his children's suggestions, he felt he had a story other children would enjoy. A. later reflected that this STORYTELLING process would yield the type of story best suited to an adult reading the story out loud to a child.

AWARDS: KATE GREENAWAY MEDAL (1956) for *Tim All Alone.* (First Greenaway Medal). *New York Times* Best Illustrated Children's Books of the Year (1962) for *The Island of Fish in the Trees* (Eva-Lis Wuorio, author), (1973) for *Tim's Last Voyage,* (1980) for *A Child's Christmas In Wales* (Dylan Thomas, author)

FURTHER WORKS: Written and illustrated: *Nicholas and the Fast Moving Diesel* (1947); *Tim and Charlotte* (1951); *Tim in Danger* (1953); *Johnny the Clockmaker* (1960); *Tim and Ginger* (1965); *Tim to the Lighthouse* (1968); illustrated: *A Child's Christmas in Wales* by Dylan Thomas (1980); *Dick Whittington,* retold by Kathleen Lines (1970)

BIBLIOGRAPHY: Edward A., *Young A.: An Autobiographical Fragment,* Macmillan, 1971

SANDRA IMDIEKE

ARMSTRONG, William

Author, educator, b. 14 September 1914, Lexington, Virginia; d. 11 April 1999, Kent, Connecticut

A. became deeply interested in the regional history of the Shenandoah region during his boyhood there. During his freshman year at Augusta Military Academy, he was accused of plagiarizing a story he composed for a class assignment. While the accusations caused him to give up a creative writing career for years afterward, he was successful in his studies, graduating from Hampden-Sydney College cum laude in 1936. He became a history teacher at Kent School (Connecticut) in 1945, and began writing about education ten years later. Finally in 1970, he was struck by the need to return to imaginative writing and authored *Sounder,* which won the NEWBERY MEDAL that year. This novel draws on A.'s memories of a story heard in his own boyhood, his love of dogs, and his understanding of the aloneness children feel. *Sounder* was followed by a few more novels for children as well as nonfiction works. The theme of aloneness pervades much of A.'s writing, as does the subject of dogs. He preferred teaching history and working at crafts like carpentry to creative writing.

FURTHER WORKS: *Barefoot in the Grass: The Story of Grandma Moses,* 1970; *The MacLeod Place,* 1972; *Tales of Tawny and Dingo,* 1979

BIBLIOGRAPHY: HOPKINS, Lee Bennett, *Pauses: Autobiographical Reflections of 101 Creators of Children's Books,* 1995; *Something about the Author,* vol. 4, 1973; *Third Book of Junior Authors,* 1972

FRANCISCA GOLDSMITH

ARNOLD, Caroline
Author, b. 16 May 1944, Pittsburgh, Pennsylvania

Best known for her books about science and nature, A. has written many books that invite children to learn about the fascinating world of ordinary and exotic animals. Often collaborating with photographer Richard Hewitt, A. describes the lives and habitats of animals from around the world. Her concern for human responsibility for animal survival is apparent in her books, *Saving the Peregrine Falcon* (1985) and *On the Brink of Extinction: The California Condor* (1993). Although her books include many facts and statistics, A. writes in ways that even very young children can easily understand. Several of her books have been cited by regional organizations for the quality of their INFORMATIONAL contents.

FURTHER WORKS: *Animals That Migrate,* 1982; *Dinosaur Mountain: Graveyard of the Past,* 1989; *Pets without Homes,* 1983; *Baby Whale Rescue,* 1999

MARY ARIAIL BROUGHTON

ARNOSKY, Jim
Author and illustrator, b. 1 September 1946, New York City

A. has combined his passion for art with his enthusiasm and interest in nature to become a popular children's book author and illustrator. He began his adult career as a draftsman in Philadel-phia, but then altered his career direction and became a freelance illustrator and writer. His first book for children, *I Was Born in a Tree and Raised by Bees* (1977), introduced readers to his signature character and mouthpiece, Crinkleroot, a knowledgeable woodsman. His books about how to draw what one observes from nature were the basis for the 1987 Public Television (see *READING RAINBOW* AND CHILDREN'S LITERATURE ON TELEVISION) series *Drawing from Nature.* He has also published wordless books, such as *Nathaniel* (1978) and *Mouse Numbers and Letters* (1982), the latter a concept book.

In addition to illustrating the nature found in nearby bogs, fields, woods, and streams, A. lives the life of a naturalist. Underlying the how-to style of his books, whether on fly-fishing, drawing from nature, or noticing and identifying wildlife, is his respect and reverence for animals in nature. He helps readers see nature through the eyes of an artist. A.'s watercolor and black-and-white line ILLUSTRATIONS have been described as humorous and whimsical, while realistically and accurately portraying the natural environment and its occupants. When writing, A.'s sparse text contains an anecdotal style that invites the reader to enter the world of the naturalist.

The reader is introduced to nature through the eyes of A.'s popular character, Crinkleroot, whom A. admits is himself. A. commented that "Crinkleroot is a vehicle I use to express the teacher and father in me. He is an old grandfatherly woodsman who knows endless wonders about the natural world and teaches them to his readers through activities they can join in."

AWARDS: Outstanding Science Book Award, American Association of Science Teachers, 1978 for *Possum Baby; Crinkleroot's Book of Animal Tracks and Wildlife Signs* and *Moose Baby* were named outstanding science books of 1979 by the National Science Teachers Association and the CHILDREN'S BOOK COUNCIL; the Christopher Award and the New York Academy of Sciences Children's Science Book Honorable Mention, both in 1983 for *Drawing from Nature;* 1991 Eva L. Gordon Award given by the American Nature Study Society, for his contributions to children's science literature

FURTHER WORKS (SELECT): *Freshwater Fish and Fishing,* 1982; *I See Animals Hiding,* 1995; *Every Autumn Comes the Bear,* 1996; *Animal Tracker*

(Jim A.'s Nature Notebooks), 1977; *Crinkleroot's Guide to Knowing Animal Habitats,* 1997

BIBLIOGRAPHY: "The Moon in My Net," the *Horn Book* magazine, September-October 1989

SANDRA IMDIEKE

ARTZYBASHEFF, Boris
Author and illustrator, b. 25 May 1899, Kharkov, Ukraine, Russia; d. 16 July 1965, Place unknown

A. immigrated to the United States in 1919 and became one of the most popular illustrators of the twentieth century. Best known for his many cover illustrations for *Time* and *Life* magazines, he also illustrated some fifty books, several of which he wrote. One book he illustrated—Dhan Gopal Mukerji's *Gayneck, the Story of a Pigeon*—was awarded the NEWBERY MEDAL in 1928. *The Seven Simeons* (1937) was A.'s interpretation of an old Russian folktale; his accompanying line drawings subtly complement the humorous text.

AWARDS: CALDECOTT MEDAL Honor Book (1938) for *Seven Simeons*

FURTHER WORKS: *Fairy Shoemaker and Other Fairy Poems,* 1928; *Poor Shaydullah,* 1931

MARY ARIAIL BROUGHTON

ARUEGO, José
Author, illustrator, b. 9 August 1932, Manila, Philippines

A. was born in Manila into a family of lawyers and politicians. However, his early interests ran to COMIC BOOKS and his pet animals, which included dogs, cats, chickens, roosters, pigeons, frogs, tadpoles, ducks, and pigs. He followed the family tradition and earned a law degree from the University of the Philippines in 1955. After an unsuccessful three-month career he enrolled in the Parsons School of Design in New York City, where he developed an interest in line drawing. His first work as an artist was freelance cartooning, and his first book for children was *The King and His Friends* (1968), a FANTASY with animals. Although A.'s first book was not a success, it drew publishers' attention to his skill as an artist. *We Hide, You Seek* (1979), a book about camouflage that instructs and entertains, was one of his first truly successful books.

Many of his most popular books have been collaborations with such authors as Robert KRAUS (*Whose Mouse Are You* [1970] and *Leo the Late Bloomer* [1973], and illustrator Ariane DEWEY *Little Louie the Baby Bloomer* [1988]). A.'s combination of HUMOR and sensitivity in the pen-and-ink drawings of funny animals have become his trademark. His texts contain few words, allowing the ILLUSTRATION to advance the story significantly. Critics have credited his wide appeal to the universality of his themes, his deep understanding of human nature, and his positive outlook on life. Technically, he is lauded for his simple yet detailed line drawings and for his use of color, whether the brilliant and bold splashes in *Leo the Late Bloomer* or the pale pastels and subtle tones in other works.

AWARDS: *New York Times* Best Illustrated Children's Books of the Year (1971) for *Look What I Can Do.* AMERICAN LIBRARY ASSOCIATION Notable Book (1970) for *Whose Mouse Are You?* (1972), *Milton the Early Riser* (1974), *Mushroom in the Rain,* and *We Hide, You Seek* (1979)

FURTHER WORKS: *Good Night* (Elizabeth COATSWORTH, author), 1972; *We Hide, You Seek,* 1979; *Rockabye Crocodile,* 1988; With Robert Kraus, author, and Ariane Dewey, co-illustrator: *Milton the Early Riser,* 1974; *Oliver,* 1973; *Come out and Play, Little Mouse* 1987

BIBLIOGRAPHY: Appel, Ida J., and Marion P. Turkish, "Profile: The Magic Work of José A.: *Language Arts,* May 1997, pp. 585–90. *Fourth Book of Junior Authors and Illustrators,* 1978

SANDRA IMDIEKE

ASBJORNSEN, Peter Christen
Folklorist, b. 15 January 1812, Christiania (now Oslo), Norway; d. 1 September 1885, Christiania (Oslo), Norway

(See MOE, Jørgen Engebretsen)

ASCH, Frank
Author, illustrator, b. 6 August 1946, Somerville, New Jersey

Following his formal education at Pratt Institute and Cooper Union, A., a Montessori teacher, taught school in India and New Jersey. With his wife he later produced and performed with a children's theater troupe called The Bellybuttons. Inspired as a writer by Maurice SENDAK and E. B.

WHITE, A.'s PICTURE BOOKS focus on themes of self-discovery, peace, love, nature, and imagination. Simplistically designed, the popular Bear books, beginning with *Moon Bear* (1978), explore human concerns such as memory, love, and loss. A. also writes POETRY and juvenile novels that focus in areas such as SCIENCE FICTION and ecology. A. has won numerous AWARDS including the Soviet National Book Award for his collaborative book, *Here Comes the Cat* (1989) with Vladimir Vagin.

FURTHER WORKS: *George's Store,* 1968; *The Blue Balloon,* 1971; *Rebecka,* 1972; *Popcorn,* 1979; *Happy Birthday, Moon,* 1982; *Oats and Wild Apples,* 1988; *Journey to Terezor,* 1989; *The Alphabet Zoo,* 1989; *Sawgrass Poems: A View of the Everglades,* 1996; *Cactus Poems,* 1998; *Ziggy Piggy and the Three Little Pigs,* 1998; *Good Night, Baby Bear,* 1998

BIBLIOGRAPHY: A., Frank. *Frank A.: One Man Show,* 1997; *Fourth Book of Junior Authors and Illustrators,* 1978; *Something about the Author,* vol. 102, 1999; *Twentieth Century Children's Writers,* 4th ed., 1995

JANELLE B. MATHIS

ASHABRANNER, Brent

Author, b. 3 November 1921; Shawnee, Oklahoma

A. is most noted for his nonfiction writing about contemporary social issues. His first attempt at writing was a story based on a Robert Louis STEVENSON novel when A. was eleven. Although the story was not a success, from that point on A. continued to love writing. His later experience as a Peace Corps director took him around the world and provided rich material and perspective for his highly acclaimed nonfiction books for children. His earliest books were written in collaboration with colleague Russell Davis. A. writes about contemporary youth from around the world, as in *Gavriel and Jemal: Two Boys of Jerusalem* (1984), as well as young people in the United States, in *To Live in Two Worlds: American Indian Youth Today* (1984). He also writes about the history of American landmarks, such as *A Grateful Nation* (1990), the history of the Arlington National Cemetery, and *Always to Remember: The Story of the Vietnam Veterans Memorial* (1988). In 1990 A. wrote his memoir, which traced his childhood growing up in the Great Depres-

sion through his 1960s experiences in the Peace Corps in *The Times of My Life: A Memoir* (1990).

A. states his respect for the capacity of young readers, a quality that is evidenced in the literature he writes by saying: "I write mostly about rather complex social issues and problems; finding ways to make these subjects interesting and understandable to young readers is a challenging task I never tire of. I firmly believe that we do our most important reading when we are young; to try to engage young minds on worthwhile subjects is a great satisfaction."

AWARDS: Christopher Award (1988) for *Into a Strange Land!: Unaccompanied Refugee Youth in America.* Notable Children's Trade Book in the Field of Social Studies and AMERICAN LIBRARY ASSOCIATION Notable Book (1983) for *The New Americans: Changing Patterns in U.S. Immigration.* Notable Children's Trade Book in the Field of Social Studies (1984), ALA Best Book for YOUNG ADULTS (1984) and Carter G. Woodson Book Award (1985) for *To Live in Two Worlds: American Indian Youth Today.* ALA Notable Book (1986) for *Children of the Maya: A Guatemalan Indian Odyssey.* ALA Notable Book and ALA Best Book for Young Adults (1988) for *Always to Remember: The Story of the Vietnam Veterans Memorial*

FURTHER WORKS: *Morning Star, Black Sun: The Northern Cheyenne Indians and American's Energy Crisis,* 1982; *Dark Harvest: Migrant Farmworkers in America,* 1985; *The Vanishing Border: A Photographic Journey along Our Frontier with Mexico,* 1987; *Still a Nation of Immigrants,* 1993; *A Strange and Distant Shore: Indians of the Great Plains in Exile,* 1996; *The Choctaw Code,* 1997

BIBLIOGRAPHY: Abrahamson, Richard F., and Betty Carter, *From Delight to Wisdom: Nonfiction for Young Adults,* 1990

SANDRA IMDIEKE

ASHE, Geoffrey (Thomas)

Author, b. 29 March 1923, London, England

A., author of books for children and YOUNG ADULTS, developed a strong interest in the legends of King Arthur. Not only did he write several books reflecting this interest, he served on the Camelot Research Committee. A. writes nonfiction books on a variety of other topics as well, and has done archaeological excavations in search of the historic Camelot.

FURTHER WORKS: *The Tale of the Tub: A Survey of the Art of Bathing through the Ages*, 1950; *King Arthur's Avalon*, 1957; *Gandhi*, 1968; *All about King Arthur* (1969, pub. in the U.S. as *King Arthur in Fact and Legend*, 1971); *Camelot and the Vision of Albion*, 1971; *The Arthurian Encyclopedia* (assoc. ed.), 1986; *New Arthurian Encyclopedia*, 1990; *King Arthur: The Dream of a Golden Age*, 1990; *King Arthur in Fact and Legend*, 1971; *Atlantis: Lost Lands, Ancient Wisdom*, 1992

BIBLIOGRAPHY: *Booklist*, May 15, 1972; *Something about the Author*, vol. 17, 1979

JODI PILGRIM

ASIAN AND ASIAN AMERICAN LITERATURE

The history of children's literature representing Asian Americans is relatively short and the percentage of books that focus on Asian Americans is particularly small in comparison to the percentage of Asians in the population. In general, books focused on Asian Americans published prior to the 1970s were written by non–Asians and often contained numerous stereotypes. Illustrations in books of this period commonly included "Fu Manchu mustaches, short-straight-cereal-bowl haircuts, buck teeth, myopic vision, and clothing that were cruelly and offensively indicative of ancient ways." Portrayals included garishly yellow-skinned people with eyes so slanted that eyeballs were not visible, and they strongly suggested that "all Asians look alike." Unfortunately, such books continue to be available in libraries and through other sources.

Toward the end of the 1980s a trend began that continues today. More Asian American authors began publishing books based on their personal experiences; Sook Nyul Choi, Lensey NAMIOKA and Huynh Quang Nhuong and Yoko Kawashima Watkins joined established writers such as Allen SAY, Yoshiko UCHIDA, Ed YOUNG, and Laurence YEP. Also at this time, heightened sensitivity toward the importance of diversity in American society and, in particular, the need for MULTICULTURAL points of view in educational curriculum and materials, supported the depiction of a variety of lifestyles and individual experiences within each cultural group. This demand for culturally sensitive and authentic material meant that authors, illustrators, and EDITORS became increasingly sensitive to the need for creating accurate portrayals of Asian cultures. Also major publishing houses began actively recruiting more Asians to write and illustrate stories based on their own experiences, as well as requiring non–Asian authors and illustrators to be particularly sensitive to accurate portrayals of cultures, particularly when it was outside their own experiences.

Several small presses established during the 1980s continue today to provide a strong commitment to publishing children's literature that authentically illuminates various ethnic experiences. One such company is Children's Book Press, specializing in bilingual Asian books in Korean, Vietnamese, Khmer (Cambodia), and Hmong (Laos). They publish folktales as well as original Asian American stories. Another publisher with such a commitment is Kane/Miller whose books depict the uniqueness of various cultures. A few of their titles are also published bilingually. Lee and Low publishes multicultural books exclusively, and many reflect Asian American experiences. Polychrome's books also focus on Asian American experiences. In addition, there are niche companies that publish only a single Asian culture.

Asian and Asian American cultures are very diverse, yet they are often clustered and referred to as one cultural conglomerate. When it comes to literature, it is important to distinguish between Asian literature and Asian American literature. Asian literature is set entirely in Asian countries. Asian American literature originates in America and is about the unique ethnic experiences of Asian Americans. In Asian American literature, Asian traditions sometimes take on a uniquely American flavor. Although it is necessary to understand the origin of the cultural heritage, it is equally important to understand how that culture has been maintained and changed in an American context.

A problem in Asian American literature exists when "outsiders" create books without having sufficient personal experience in a culture. Often stereotyped images based on generic understanding of "Asia" mix various elements of distinctly different Asian cultures. For example, a text that is supposedly set in one culture may contain illustrations of clothing from another, along with buildings or backgrounds from yet others. Such books perpetuate the stereotype of Asia as a single conglomerate culture.

Cultural authenticity is achieved by including rich details that naturally reflect nuances of the particular culture. "Insiders" who have been reared within a cultural group understand these details. Others acquire their understanding of a cultural group through extensive research and first-hand experience in the culture.

As recently as 1990 a study conducted on the "Perceptions of Asian Americans" indicates that misinformed images still abound and that books contribute to the formulation of these images. This, then, reinforces the need for books that transmit a culturally authentic view. Multiple perspectives and multidimensional images of cultural groups are necessary in order to avoid further development of stereotypes. Most of all, it is important to remember that how we interact with others of differing cultures is determined by what we believe to be true about them.

The 1990 U.S. Census showed that Asian Americans claimed a variety of countries as their point of origin: China, Philippines, Japan, India, Korea, Vietnam, Hawaii, Samoa, and Guam. It is true that all are Asian countries; however, it is necessary to understand the distinctions among cultures. Depictions of generically Asian experiences wash these distinctions away and assimilate them into a confused image in such a way that even natives of Asian countries are often unable to identify whether a book is supposed to represent their own country.

In some books identified by various sources as "Asian American," the only thing Asian American about the book is the inclusion of characters who are identified as being generically Asian American. No details help determine what Asian culture the character belongs to, and no information that illuminates an Asian experience is included. It is also important to remember that having an Asian author or illustrator does not necessarily mean the book can be classified as Asian.

A disproportionately high percentage of books identified as Asian/Asian American can be classified as FOLKLORE. INFORMATIONAL BOOKS tend to be parts of series published for the school market,

although some books of history exist. A few books of poetry have been published. As for fiction, there are many more historical fiction than contemporary ones. FANTASY is seldom found, and SCIENCE FICTION is nonexistent. There continues to be a need for more books representing the Asian American experience.

No one book can give a complete depiction of Asians or Asian Americans. This means that one needs to read a variety of books. For example, to gain insight into Japan and Japanese American cultures, one should read a range such as the following: Folktales like Katherine PATERSON's translation of Momoko Ishi's *The Tongue-Cut Sparrow* (1982) offer readers an example of traditional Japanese tales that generations have shared. Historical fiction novels such as Lensey Namioka's *Den of the White Fox* (1997) help readers gain a sense of medieval periods in Japanese history when samurais ruled the country. Books like Kazumi Yumoto's *The Friends* (1996) provides readers a glimpse of contemporary Japan. *Journey to Topaz* (Uchida, 1971) is historical fiction describing experiences during World War II Japanese American internment. Informational books such as Tunnell and Chilcoat's *The Children of Topaz* (1996) offer real-life examples of what some of the children did during those years. Allen Say's *The Lost Lake* (1989) depicts a contemporary image of Japanese Americans in which a young boy and his father deepen their relationship during a fishing trip. Books set in contemporary times may help readers understand that Japanese Americans enjoy much of the same experiences as others in the mainstream population. Reading books from a range of genres like these helps readers gain a better sense of the Japanese American culture. Likewise, reading a range of Asian and Asian American literature will help readers understand the breadth and depth of Asian cultures.

BIBLIOGRAPHY: Chu E. and C. V. Schuler "United States"; "Asian Americans" in L. Miller-Lachman, ed., *Our Family, Our Friends, Our World: An Annotated Guide to Significant Multicultural Books for Children and Teenagers* (1992); S. Ting-Tooney. *"Stereotypes and Misperceptions."* In Li, M. H. and P. Li, ed. *Understanding Asian Americans: A Curriculum Resource Guide* (1990)

JUNKO YOKOTA

ASIMOV, Isaac

Author, b. 2 January 1920, Petrovichi, former U.S.S.R; d. 6 April 1992, New York City

A. was brought to the United States in 1923 and became a naturalized citizen in 1928. A.'s degrees, all from Columbia University, are: B.S. 1939, M.A. 1941, Ph.D., 1948, in chemistry.

At a young age, A. tried several times to get a short story published. After twelve rejections, he made his first sale. It was a story entitled "Marooned off Vesta," and was bought by *Amazing Stories*. A.'s first book, *Pebble in the Sky,* was published in January 1950. A. accepted a position on the faculty of Boston University School of Medicine, and achieved the rank of Associate Professor of Biochemistry. He worked on a textbook for medical students and discovered the delights of nonfiction. Gradually his writing devoured more and more of his time until he gave up teaching and continued to write full-time.

When asked about his writing habits, A. said, "I do all my own typing, but I type 90 words a minute and never slow down. The key characteristic is, I suppose, single-mindedness. I type every day, except when the typewriters are kept forcibly out of reach; I start early each day and continue typing till the number of typographical errors reaches an unacceptable concentration. I don't take vacations." A.'s father, owner of a candy store, attributed his success to the stern fashion in which he kept A. from all forms of worthless literature, allowing him to absorb only helpful and invigorating SCIENCE FICTION.

A., considered the world's most prolific science and science fiction writer, published more than 100 books in his first 20 years as a writer. He wrote more than 350 short stories and 400 books; most of his work is science fiction and nonfiction. He enlivens his writing with incidents from his own life and invites readers to share his triumphs and to laugh at his blunders and lack of sophistication. His early interest in science fiction came from reading magazines in his family's candy store. In A.'s first autobiography, *In Memory Yet Green* (1979), he recalls how he was attracted to the glossy covers of science fiction magazines but his father did not allow A. to read them. His father called the early magazines junk and said they were not fit to read. When, in 1929, a new magazine, entitled *Science Wonder Stories,* was published, A. persuaded his father to allow him to read it. From then on he was an avid science fiction fan.

A. was a pioneer in using robots in science fiction. In 1934, he wrote a letter commenting on several stories that had appeared; his letter was published in the magazine *Astounding Stories*. He later wrote a story for the magazine that had become *Astounding Science Fiction*. Because a subway fare cost only ten cents, and postage would cost twelve cents, A. delivered the manuscript to the editor in person.

A. wrote hundreds of nonfiction books for children explaining how electricity works, how we found out about photosynthesis, superconductivity, microwaves, the universe, dinosaurs, germs, computers, lasers, nuclear power, oil, genes, outer space, and solar power, among other topics. He also wrote biographies about Hudson, Columbus, and Magellan. More than a hundred of his books remain in print.

A.'s most impressive SERIES is thought to be the Foundation series. The series started out as short stories in magazines that were collected into a trilogy in the 1950s. The series, written as a future history of a society, established A. as the foremost science fiction writer of his day.

AWARDS: Honored guest Thirteenth World Science Fiction Convention, 1955; Edison Foundation National Mass Media Award, 1958; Blakeslee Award for Nonfiction, 1960; Hugo Award, 1963, for science articles, Hugo Award, 1966, for *Foundation, Foundation and Empire, Second Foundation,* Hugo Award, 1973 for *The Gods Themselves,* 1983 for *Foundation's Edge,* James T. Grady Award, American Chemical Society, 1965; American Association for the Advancement of Science-Westinghouse Award for science writing, 1967; Nebula Award, 1973 and 1977 for "The Bicentennial Man." In 1979, "Nightfall" was chosen the best science fiction story of all time in a Science Fiction Writers of America poll

FURTHER WORKS (SELECT) *How Did We Find out about the Universe?,* 1983; *How Did We Find out about Superconductivity?,* 1988; *How Did We Find out about Microwaves?,* 1989; *How Did We Find out about Photosynthesis?,* 1989; *Complete Science Fair Handbook,* 1990; *Christopher Columbus: Navigator to the New World,* 1991;

Henry Hudson: Arctic Explorer and North American Adventurer, 1991

BERNICE E. CULLINAN

ATWATER, Richard

Author, b. 29 December 1892, Chicago, Illinois; d. 21 August 1948, Downey, Wisconsin

Born Frederick Mund A., the writer legally changed his name to Richard Tupper A. in 1913. A. is best known for his ALA NEWBERY MEDAL Honor Book, *Mr. Popper's Penguins* (1938), a simple, humorous story of a house painter who is given a gift of penguins that he keeps in his refrigerator. A. was not pleased with an early version of the book, but because of a debilitating stroke that he suffered in 1934, he was unable to rewrite it. His wife, Florence, revised portions of the book for him. The work was an immediate success with critics and children upon its publication. *Mr. Popper's Penguins* has been issued as a listening cassette, read-along cassette, record, filmstrip, videocassette, talking book, and in Braille.

AWARDS: AMERICAN LIBRARY ASSOCIATION Newbery Medal Honor Book (1939) for *Mr. Popper's Penguins*

FURTHER WORKS: *Doris and the Trolls,* 1931; *The King's Sneezes* (operetta and Braille); *Rickety Rimes of Riq* (verse; published under pseudonym Riq), 1925

REFERENCE: *Something about the Author,* vol. 66, 1991

MARY ARIAIL BROUGHTON

AUSTRALIAN LITERATURE

The early days of Australian children's literature reflect, as one might expect, the country's colonial beginnings. Many of the first books set in Australia were written as travelers' tales of an exotic country, often by people who had never visited the country. *A Mother's Offering to Her Children* (1841) by a Lady Long Resident in New South Wales (later identified as Charlotte Barton) was the first children's book actually published in Australia, and is written in the form of a children's catechism about the flora, fauna, and indigenous people of the country. Howitt's *A Boy's Adventures in the Wilds of Australia* (1854) is a typical British Empire ADVENTURE STORY of the period, telling yarns of flood, bushfire, and digging for gold, but with a more authentic sense of place than most previous books.

Taming and understanding the "bush" as the Australian landscape came to be known, was to become an important feature of many children's books as late as the 1950s. Bruce's fourteen "Billabong" books published between 1910 and 1942, for example, idealized bush life, which was seen to epitomize the true Australian way of life. The bush inspired many FANTASY stories with illustrators such as Ida Rentoul Outhwaite and Pixie O'Harris presenting a romantic view of the bush with European syle fairies; May Gibbs, however, captured the spirit of the bush creatures in a more robust style in text and ILLUSTRATION in books like *Snugglepot and Cuddlepie* (1918).

The portrayal of Aboriginal peoples and cultures in children's books was problematic for many years, largely reflecting racist attitudes of the times. Fear of, and contempt for, Aboriginal peoples was common, and even when authors were kindly disposed toward Aborigines, as in *The Little Black Princess* (Gunn, 1905) the portrayal of Aboriginal characters was essentially paternalistic. Later books such as *Piccaninny Walkabout* (Poignant, 1957), *Tangara* (Nan Chauncey, 1960), and *The Rocks of Honey* (1960) and others by Patricia WRIGHTSON gave relatively enlightened portrayals of Aboriginal characters. Until comparatively recently Aboriginal people have not been involved in the writing, editing, and publishing of children's books, so it is not surprising that distortions and misappropriation of sensitive materials have been common. In recent years, however, the voices of Aboriginal people themselves are increasingly heard both in retellings of dreaming stories in books such as *Tjarany Roughtail: "The Dreaming of the Roughtail Lizard" and Other Stories Told by the Kukatja* (Green, Tramacchi, Gill, 1993), and in contemporary REALISTIC FICTION such as *Killing Darcy* (Lucashenko, 1998). Several significant Aboriginal illustrators have emerged such as Bancroft, Meeks, Abdulla, and Torres, and there are now Aboriginal publishing houses such as Magabala Books, and Aboriginal editors at other publishers.

From tentative beginnings there is now a strength, vitality, and innovation in Australian children's publishing overall, with many authors and illustrators having acquired an international reputation with their books being published in the U.S., Britain, and Europe as well as in Australia. The author Patricia Wrightson and illustrator Robert INGPEN, for example, won the Hans Christian ANDERSEN Medals in their respective categories in 1986, and the illustrator Bob Graham has won several overseas awards including the UNICEF Illustrators Award in 1994.

Part of the reason for the strong growth of Australian children's publishing has been the CHILDREN'S BOOK COUNCIL of Australia, especially through its annual Book of the Year AWARDS. Each State and Territory has its own Branch, but the Book Awards operate nationally. The Awards are very influential, especially through the Shortlist, which generates more sales than any other book award in Australia, including adult awards. Originally there was only one CBCA Award, but there are now four categories—Book of the Year for Older Readers, Book of the Year for Younger Readers, Picture Book of the Year Award, and the Eve Pownall Award for INFORMATION BOOKS. As each category of the Award has been instituted, the quality of writing, illustrating, and publishing in that category has continued to develop and improve. Debate about the categories is a continuing one as the novels for YOUNG ADULTS often stretch the CENSORSHIP boundaries, and some people complain that short-listed picture books are often for older readers rather than young readers. PUBLISHERS (including individuals) can enter any book they wish for the Awards, which means that judges read and compare all books entered. This system, while arduous for the judges, means that new authors and illustrators are considered as seriously as those who are more established.

Support for the study of children's literature is increasing around the country through research collections such as the Children's Literature Foundation at Dromkeen, at Riddells Creek, Victoria, the Lu Rees Archives in Canberra, and at various State Libraries. The CBCA holds a national biennial conference, and various State Writers Festivals and many other functions promote children's literature for young people, their parents and teachers. There are also several Australian journals related to Children's Literature (see references for further study).

PICTURE BOOKS have been an area of strength in A. children's publishing for some years in terms of text, ILLUSTRATION, and overall design. Just a few of those worthy of note are Jeannie Baker's three-dimensional illustrations in books such as *Where the Forest Meets the Sea* (1997), Pamela Allen's picture books for young children like *Fancy That!* (1988), Ann James's children in *Dog in Cat Out* (Gillian RUBINSTEIN, 1991), *The Midnight Gang* (Margaret Wild, 1996), Gouldthorpe's *Grandad's Gift* (Paul JENNINGS, 1992), Julie VIVAS's swirling watercolors in *Possum Magic* (Mem FOX, 1993), *Let the Celebration Begin* (Margaret Wild, 1991), and Graeme BASE's amazingly detailed illustrations in books like *Animalia* (1986) and *The Eleventh Hour* (1988).

The genre of picture books for older readers has developed significantly over the last decade with such books as the strongly realistic *Way Home* (Libby Hawthorne Hathorn, 1994) winner of the KATE GREENAWAY Award, illustrated by Gregory Rogers, *Wolf* (Margaret Barbalet, 1991) illustrated by Jane Tanner; *The Watertower* (Gary Crew, 1994) and *Caleb* (Crew, 1996) illustrated by Woolman and *The Rabbits* (John MARSDEN, 1998) illustrated by Shaun Tan.

Since the inception of the CBCA award for newly independent readers, this area of publishing has increased markedly. Authors of humorous books like Paul JENNINGS and Morris GLEITZMAN are extremely popular, as are the authors Emily Rodda, Gillian Rubinstein, Elizabeth Honey, and Libby Gleeson. Other authors worthy of note are Gary Disher, Gary Carey, Anna Fienberg, James Moloney, Tim Winton, and Odo Hirsch. Australia's MULTICULTURAL society is gradually being reflected in its children's literature with books like *Onion Tears* (Diane Kidd, 1989), *Looking for Alibrandi* (Melina Marchetta, 1992), and through the illustrations of Tan, Di Wu, and Junko Morimoto.

Novels for young adults by Australian authors often cause controversy because of their subject matter, which may deal with issues such as youth suicide, sibling incest, homosexuality, and homeless children. Nevertheless, authors continue to write realistic and historical fiction fearlessly with names like Gary Crew, Gillian Rubinstein, James Moloney, Ursula Dubosarsky, Hamett, Jenny Pausacker, David Metzenthen, and Mavis Thorpe Clark of particular note. Authors such as

Isobelle Carmody and Christophe Caswell also explore the genre of fantasy writing for older readers with much success.

Australia's authors, illustrators, and publishers have always had to contend with the difficulties of a vast country with a relatively small population. The economic imperatives of the multinational publishers and bookselling chains inevitably affect the Australian market, as do cutbacks in education and library book buying budgets in recent years. Nevertheless, Australian writers, illustrators, and publishers of children's books continue to produce many books of high quality with a freshness of vision that reach out to young readers around the world.

REFERENCES FOR FURTHER STUDY: Bradford, Clare, ed. (1996). *Writing the Australian Child.* Hillel, Margot and Anne Hanzl, compilers (1996). *Celebrate! The Color and Splendor of Australian Children's Literature over Half a Century.* Ringwood, Lees, Stella and Pam McIntyre (1993). *The Oxford Companion to Australian Children's Literature.* Matthews, Stephen (1998). *The Eye of the Soul: Interviews with Seventeen of the Younger Generation of Australians Writing for Children and Young Adults.* Niall, Brenda (1984). *Australia through the Looking-Glass: Children's Fiction 1830–1980.* Saxby, Maurice (1993). The *Proof of the Puddin': Australian Children's Literature 1977–1990.* Saxby, Maurice (1998). *Offered to Children: A History of Australian Children's Literature 1841–1941.* Scobie, Susan (1997). *The Dromkeen Book: Australian Children's Illustrators. Who's Who of Australian Children's Writers* (1996); JOURNALS: *Magpies: Talking about Books for Children. Papers: Explorations into Children's Literature.* School of Literary & Communication Studies, *Reading Time: The Journal of the Children's Book Council of Australia. Viewpoint: On Books for Young Adults.* 3052; WEBSITES: www.ozlit.org

ANNE HANZL

AVERY, Gillian

Author, b. 30 September 1926, Reigate, Surrey, England

A. is the author of numerous children's books set in Victorian Britain. Although she had always worked among writers and worked variously as a reporter, as an encyclopedia staff member, and an editor for the Clarendon Press, she did not publish her first novel, *The Warden's Niece* until 1957. Later republished under the title of *Maria*

Escapes, this remains one of her most popular books. Several of her books, beginning with *The Warden's Niece,* draw on the same cast of characters, usually with different ones featured in each book. The title character, Maria, reappears in *The Italian Spring* (1964) when she visits Italy with her cousin.

Occasionally A. creates a memorable character, such as the unpredictable tutor Copplestone in *The Warden's Niece.* She can always be counted on to provide vivid and faithful details of nineteenth-century British society, for which she has a passion. Not surprisingly, her novels bear the marked influence of DICKENS and Trollope. Other titles in this series include *Trespassers at Charlecote* (1958), *James without Thomas* (1959), and *The Elephant War* (1960) about saving an elephant from being sold to the circus.

Particularly Dickensian in its melodramatic plot and eccentric characters is *A Likely Lad* (1971), a Guardian Award winner, set in industrial Manchester at the turn of the century. This is a classic story of class and family rivalry. The book was a CARNEGIE MEDAL Honor Book and was A.'s last full-length novel for children. After this, she turned to nonfiction, including history for children and literary criticism. She has edited and contributed to several collections of works for children.

AWARDS: Guardian Award and Carnegie Medal Honor Book (1972) for *A Likely Lad*

FURTHER WORKS: *The Elephant War,* 1960; *The Greatest Gresham,* 1962; *To Tame a Sister,* 1961; *Mrs. Ewing,* 1961; *The Italian Spring* 1964, republished in 1993 as *Maria's Italian Spring; Call of the Valley,* 1966

BIBLIOGRAPHY: *British Children's Writers since 1960;* Cott, Jonathan, *Pipers at the Gates of Dawn: The Wisdom of Children's Literature,* 1981; *Dictionary of Literary Biography,* vol. 161: *Something about the Author,* vol. 7, 1975; *Twentieth-Century Children's Writers,* 3rd ed., 1989

DAVID L. RUSSELL

AVI (Wortis)

Author, b. 23 December 1937, New York City

A. has created literature rich in character and captivating plots. He believes that he began his writing career as a reader, learning about the world through all sorts of genres ranging from COMIC

BOOKS, to histories, to science magazines. His parents were academic writers, and thus constantly emphasized the importance of writing. His father, Joseph, was a psychiatrist, and his mother, Helen, a social worker. Although writing was important and A. loved to read, writing did not come easily to him. His path to becoming a writer was filled with teacher's red marks and discouraging comments. Teachers never thought that he would become a writer, let alone a prolific writer of children's literature. In fact, A. was diagnosed with a writing problem called dysgraphia, which caused him to misspell words and reverse letters. After his junior year in high school A.'s parents had him tutored, because according to the school he had not learned to spell or write. The tutor taught him the basics and instilled in him the possibility that he could write. Then in the beginning of his senior year, A. made the decision that he was going to become a writer.

A. received his undergraduate degree from Antioch College in history and theater. He did graduate work at the University of Wisconsin in playwriting. It was through the playwriting experience that A. first began writing seriously. In 1961 he returned to New York and attained a job at the theater collection department of the New York City Public Library. While in that position, he attended Columbia University and received his master's degree in Library Science. He worked for twenty-five years as a librarian, but never lost his desire to become an author. A.'s writing for children began with *his* children. His oldest son would tell him what a story would be about and he would start writing. His first children's book appeared in 1970, titled *Things That Sometimes Happen.*

A.'s novels cover a wide range of topics. He has written in many genres: MYSTERIES, REALISTIC FICTION, children's PICTURE BOOKS, young reader books, and novels for the YOUNG ADULT. A. creates characters that encourage readers to think and evaluate the world in which they live. In *The History of Helpless Harry* (1980), the parents believe that Harry is a helpless small boy, yet in reality he is quite adept at getting out of a tough situation. Emily in *Emily Upham's Revenge* (1978) acts helpless in the beginning of the novel, and in the end shows that she has the strength to do what is right. Whereas in *The True*

Confessions of Charlotte Doyle (1990), Charlotte embarks on a journey across the Atlantic as a proper young lady only to learn that her heart has other plans for her. Through these characters, A. allows readers to realize that they can be what they want to be and do not need to live within the confines of other people's expectations. In *Nothing but the Truth* (1991) the main character is depicted as a hero, standing up for his right as an American, surrounded by people who do not understand him. Phillip helps readers to see that impulsive actions can have unintended implications. Andy in *Wolf Rider* (1986) is propelled by his curiosity to solve the mystery of Zeke's identity while refusing to accept the fact that the encounter was coincidence, still shows a strength of conviction. In *Night Journeys* (1979), Peter discovers the horror of violence and indentured servitude when he becomes involved in a part of a bounty hunt. Regardless of genre, A.'s novels allow the reader to travel with the protagonist on an adventure that includes a compelling story while encouraging the reader to evaluate the world.

A. is well known for his historical fiction novels. He has stated that he sees history as a story. His ability to provide a realistic setting allows the reader to envision the past clearly. *The Fighting Ground* (1984), a novel set during one day of the Revolutionary War, received the Scott O'DELL Historical Fiction Award in 1984. In the *True Confessions of Charlotte Doyle* (1990) the time is the 1800s and Charlotte portrays the true aspects of a lady traveling abroad. The accuracy of the ship design adds realism to this thrilling mystery. Another historical novel, *Night Journeys* (1979), deals with the issue of a young boy struggling with the reality of indentured servitude. The continuation of the novel *Encounter at Easton* (1980) sets the stage for the political and social mores of the time period.

A. also uses the past as a setting to emphasize basic themes. *Emily Upham's Revenge; or, How Deadwood Dick saved the Bankers Niece* (1978) is set in 1875. In this novel A. uses the past to set the tone for the struggle between good and the evil that money can cause. In *The History of Helpless Harry* (1980) the time period allows for a comedy of errors and a sense of trust in other people that is not applicable in today's society.

7. HANS CHRISTIAN ANDERSEN

8. ANNO MITSUMASA

9. ISAAC ASIMOV

10. AVI

The themes are simple, but the setting is key to the realism the story provides.

Young adult readers are often attracted to novels in which the character is in pursuit of truth. A.'s characters seek to find answers in a world that is often confusing, contradicting, and frightening. In *Wolf Rider* (1986) Andy searches for the man who called his house saying that he had killed someone; even though his father and friends tell him to forget about it and to move on, Andy persists. Charlotte in *The True Confessions of Charlotte Doyle* (1990) learns that the truth is not always what we are led to think. John Proud, the protagonist in the *Devil's Race* (1984), searches for the truth about his family's past. Poppy, the young field mouse in *Poppy* (1995), searches for the reason that Mr. Ocax will not allow her family to move to a new farm. Yet, the search for truth is not always in the form of a mystery. In *The History of Helpless Harry* (1980), Harry learns the truth about people; they are deeper than surface appearances. In *Emily Upham's Revenge* (1978) Emily learns that Seth, better known as Deadwood Dick, is a mischievous boy and that the real robber in the bank was her father. Andy, in *Windcatcher* (1991), discovers the truth about the Shallows Bay treasure. A.'s novels provide a wide range of reading experiences. He writes for the young child as well as the young adult emphasizing the basic tendencies of good human character. His novels provide adventure as well as fun for readers of all ages.

AWARDS: British Book Council Best Book of the Year (1973) for *Snail Tale: The Adventures of a Rather Small Snail.* Mystery Writers of America Special Award (1975) for *No More Magic,* (1979) for *Emily Upham's Revenge,* (1983) for *Shadrach's Crossing.* Christopher Book Award (1980) for *Encounter at Easton.* Scott O'Dell Award for Historical Fiction, Bulletin of the Center for Children's Books, and AMERICAN LIBRARY ASSOCIATION Best Books for Young Adults (1984) for *The Fighting Ground.* ALA Best Books for Young Adults citation (1986) for *Wolf Rider: A Tale of Terror.* Library of Congress Best Books of the Year citation for *Something Upstairs* (1989) and *The Man Who Was Poe* (1990). ALA NEWBERY MEDAL Honor Book, Golden Kite Award, Society of Children's Book Writers, ALA Notable Book citation (1990) and *Boston Globe–Horn Book* Award (1991) all for *The True Confes-*

sions of Charlotte Doyle. Newbery Medal Honor Book (1992) for *Nothing but the Truth*

FURTHER WORKS: *Snail Tale: Adventures of a Rather Small Snail,* 1972; *No More Magic,* 1975; *Captain Grey,* 1977; *Man from the Sky,* 1980; *A Place Called Ugly,* 1981; *Who Stole the Wizard of Oz?,* 1981; *Sometimes I Think I Hear My Name,* 1982; *S.O.R. Losers,* 1984; *Devil's Race,* 1987; *Something Upstairs: A Tale of Ghosts,* 1988; *The Man Who Was Poe,* 1989; "*Who Was That Masked Man, Anyway?,*" 1992; *Blue Heron,* 1992; *Judy and Punch,* 1993; *The Barn,* 1994; *Beyond the Western Sea,* 1996; *Tom, Babette and Simon: Three Tales of Transformation,* 1995; *Poppy and Rye,* 1998; *What Do Fish Have to Do with Anything?,* 1997

BIBLIOGRAPHY: Bloom, S. P. and C. M. Mercier. *Presenting A.,* 1997; *Contemporary Authors, New Revision Series,* vol. 42, 1990; *Something about the Author,* vol. 71, 1993

NANCE S. WILSON

AWARDS

Many awards today recognize excellence in children's literature, and most of these began after 1980. *Children's Books: Awards and Prizes* (CHILDREN'S BOOK COUNCIL, 1996), a comprehensive review updated every few years, contains information on approximately 200 awards currently in operation. Some of these are single whereas others are multiple awards, as one given for quality of text and another for ILLUSTRATION, one for each of several age or grade levels (preschool, ages four to eight, ages eight to twelve, ages twelve–up), and one for each book that meets selection criteria. Because of the multiple awards, the approximately 200 listings in the Children's Book Council volume represent more than 350 awards, most of which are based in the United States. The CBC book also lists awards from AUSTRALIA, CANADA, NEW ZEALAND, and the United Kingdom, as well as some of international and multinational scope.

Most awards are given annually; some are presented less frequently. Winners receive certificates, plaques, or some similar recognition; a few awards also include a small monetary gift. However, especially for some of the most prestigious national and international awards, the attendant publicity that leads to an immediate increase in demand for the books is of much greater consequence. For example, winning one of the AMERICAN LIBRARY ASSOCIATION'S CALDECOTT or NEWBERY MEDALS assures heightened interest in winning titles. Following award announcements, winning authors and illustrators are often invited to make presentations at national and international conferences. Though authors, illustrators, and publishers benefit from increased sales, by far the most important outcome is that more children, teachers, librarians, and parents are encouraged to read the books.

The common thread of excellence in children's literature runs through children's book awards. The focus, however, varies from award to award. Some awards are given to books, or to their writers or illustrators, dealing with a given geographic area (as state or region), science, nature, religion, FOLKLORE, plus many others. Recent trends in awards reveal increasing interest in poetry, INFORMATIONAL BOOKS, and books for young people.

A few awards in predominantly English-speaking countries include attention to good literature for children written in minority languages. For example, each year the Canadian Library Association's Book of the Year for Children selects a children's book written in French as well as one in English. In addition to its awards for books written in English, the New Zealand Library and Information Association offers the Te Kura Pounamu Award for excellence in books for children or young adults written in the Maori language.

Among the awards in the United States is one that may be given to a book written in Spanish, another to a book TRANSLATED from another language, and several focusing on children's books written in English that deal with race or ethnicity. The Americus Award for Children's and Young Adult Literature honors books, written in English or Spanish, that treat the lives of LATINOS in an accurate manner. The AFRICAN Studies Association makes its award to books about Africa; the CORETTA SCOTT KING AWARDS are given to a black author and a black illustrator; and the Carter G. Woodson Awards winners are selected from among books dealing with United States race relations or with ethnic minorities. The Mildred L. Batchelder Award goes to an American publisher for an outstanding children's book from another country that has been translated into English.

Various other requirements or restrictions apply to some awards. Writers and/or illustrators often are required to be citizens or residents of the country—or of some state or region of that country. Some awards are also based on the total body of work of a writer or illustrator rather than on a single book.

Awards involving children's choices have increased over the past two decades. As many as forty states in the United States have one or more such awards. Sponsors of the children's choices awards often are one or more statewide organizations, such as a Division of a State Department of Education, a State Council of the INTERNATIONAL READING ASSOCIATION, a State Library Association, a Children's Literature Association, or a college or university. These awards considerably enhance children's interest in and knowledge of good books published for them.

Some selection committees announce winners or winners plus honor books only; others release "shortlists," usually of from four to eight titles from which winners will be selected later. Some awards are announced at about the same time each year. The American Library Association's Caldecott and Newbery Medal winners and honor books are announced at the midwinter meeting of the Association, which comes in late January or early February each year. The (British) Library Association usually releases shortlists for the KATE GREENAWAY and CARNEGIE MEDALS in April or early May, with winners and honor book announcements coming in mid-July. The Children's Book Council of Australia usually publicizes shortlists in April for its PICTURE BOOK of the Year, Book of the Year—Younger Readers, and Book of the Year—Older Readers, with winners and honor books being announced in August each year. The Canadian Library Association, in contrast, varies from year to year on whether shortlists are a part of the award procedures, for its Amelia Frances Howard-Gibbon Award, Book of the Year for Children, and Young Adult Canadian Book Award; winners are usually announced in May.

Award-winning children's books, as a whole, are considered to be among the best books published for young readers. Nevertheless, the book community often discusses the appropriateness of choices. For example, some negative reaction followed the announcement of Melvin Burgess's *Junk* (1996) as winner of the (British) Library Association's 1996 Carnegie Medal. This well-written and realistic portrayal of teenage drug addiction and the painful road through detoxification—with the attendant heartbreak and physical, emotional, and mental problems—was considered by some to be questionable fare for teenage readers. It received wide publicity in *Publishers Weekly* (Feb. 16, 1998, p. 123). The story includes teenage involvement in prostitution, pregnancy, and parenthood in addition to the horrors of drug addiction. Another point of view is that the book will help teenagers to realize that the negative outcomes of drug use far surpass the limited and temporary pleasure it may bring. The book is published in the United States under the title of *Smack* (1998).

The passage of time sometimes sorts out quality rankings. In 1953, when Ann Nolan CLARK's *Secret of the Andes* won the American Library Association's Newbery Medal, one of the honor books was E. B. WHITE's *Charlotte's Web*. *Charlotte's Web* soon became a children's classic and has been widely read and loved by millions of children since 1953; more than ten million copies have been published. The 1953 winner, though of excellent literary quality, has been read by far fewer children.

Announced for 2001 is the PEN/Phyllis Naylor Working Writer Fellowship.

Children's book awards, as a whole, make significant contributions to increasing awareness of good literature on the part of writers, illustrators, publishers, children, and young adults, teachers, librarians, and parents.

BIBLIOGRAPHY: Children's Book Council. *Children's Books: Awards and Prizes.* 1996. Criscoe, Betty L., and Lanasa, Philip J., III. *Award-Winning Books for Children and Young Adults: 1990–1991.* 1992. Jones, Dolores Blythe. *Children's Literature Awards and Winners: A Directory of Prizes, Authors, and Illustrators.* Third Edition. 1994

IRA E. AARON

AWARDS: PUBLISHING TRENDS

(James Cross GIBLIN has sat on both sides of the desk in publishing houses. Here he speaks as a distinguished editor as well as an author of INFORMATIONAL BOOKS giving advice to new writers.)

When I have commented over the years on trends in children's book publishing, I have sometimes said that realistic picture-book stories were in vogue, or that FANTASY novels seemed to be out of favor. But I have never questioned the basics of publishing itself. Books were books, after all, and I assumed they would be published in the same old way as far as one could see into the future.

Not any more. Now, each week brings a raft of new articles about the latest developments in information technology. If you took all these stories at face value, you might think that book publishing as we know it would cease tomorrow, to be replaced by E-books and other forms of electronic transmission. I am convinced change will come, but I do not believe that it will come that soon—or so completely. In the meantime, much can still be gained from studying the trends that are currently at work in the children's book field.

We should get one trend out of the way at the start. In fact, it is much more than a trend: it is a publishing phenomenon. I am speaking, of course, of the Harry Potter success story. If any of you are thinking of trying to latch onto that success by writing a similar fantasy novel, my advice is, "Don't go there." Imitations of successful books almost never succeed on their own.

A more constructive approach would probably be to examine some recent award-winning books, not in order to imitate them, but instead to analyze and learn from them. What qualities made the books stand out from the thousands of other children's titles published in the past year? Do your book ideas or manuscripts embody some of the same qualities? If not, can you see places where you might weave them into your projects so that they will be more attractive to editors and more salable in the marketplace?

For the purposes of this exercise, I selected five major AWARDS for close scrutiny. All of them are given annually. Three of the awards are administered by the AMERICAN LIBRARY ASSOCIATION: the NEWBERY MEDAL for excellence in children's literature; the CALDECOTT MEDAL for children's book ILLUSTRATION; and the new Michael L. Printz Award for excellence in YOUNG

ADULT LITERATURE. The other two are the *Boston Globe–Horn Book* Awards, which are bestowed in three categories: PICTURE BOOKS, fiction, and nonfiction; and the ORBIS PICTUS AWARD, which is presented by the NATIONAL COUNCIL OF TEACHERS OF ENGLISH and is limited to works of nonfiction. With these basic facts, let us take a look at the award books, starting with picture books, and moving on to nonfiction and fiction.

PICTURE BOOKS: Of the eight picture books singled out as winners and honor books, only one had an author who was not the illustrator. And that author was the well-known John Updike. This news will no doubt be distressing to those of you who write picture-book stories, but there is a reason for it and a lesson to be learned.

First the reason. Having worked as editor with many author-illustrators, I know that they usually have a better sense of what can be omitted from the text and shown in the illustrations than a writer working in isolation on the text alone. The result is often a more unified work, with text and pictures flowing together in a harmonious whole.

But there is also a lesson for writers to learn from books by author-illustrators. Take several such books that you particularly admire and break them down spread by spread, studying what the creator conveyed in words and what story points were made exclusively in the illustrations. This exercise should help you to pare down your own picture-book texts and make them more inviting to illustrators. (If you are worried that by doing so, the manuscripts will seem incomplete to editors, you can insert brief descriptions, in parentheses, of the plot twists you think can be depicted in the illustrations.)

Now to the award winners. The Caldecott Medal went to author-illustrator Simms TABACK for his picture book rendition of the old Yiddish folk song, "Joseph Had a Little Overcoat," and two of the four Caldecott Honor Books were also based on classic material: Jerry PINKNEY's new version of Hans Christian ANDERSEN's *The Ugly Duckling*, and Trina Schart HYMAN's interpretation of Updike's *A Child's Calendar*. There's little for writers to learn from these choices beyond the fact that the classics continue to challenge illustrators, just as Shakespeare's plays challenge each new generation of actors. And, of course,

the classic tales have a "presold" appeal in the children's book marketplace.

The other two Caldecott Honor Books present an interesting study in contrasts. David WIESNER's *Sector 7* is a wordless fantasy about a boy, on a class trip to the top of the Empire State Building, who is transported to the laboratory where clouds are made and gets to design some of his own. Wordless picture books are popular with teachers and parents because they invite young viewers to create their own texts. But if they are to work, they must have as strong and clear a story line as a picture book with words.

The one original story among the Caldecott Honor Books is *When Sophie Gets Angry— Really, Really Angry* by Molly BANG. The latter is a prime example of a type of picture book that has come to the fore in recent years. Unlike earlier texts that portrayed young children as sweet-tempered innocents, these stories acknowledge the raging emotions that young children often experience. There is a danger that such stories will seem too purposeful and therapeutic, however. The best of them avoid this pitfall by focusing on a strongly defined character like Sophie, and bringing out the HUMOR in the situation.

The *Boston Globe–Horn Book* Picture Book Awards offer a wider range of choices, all of them strikingly original. The winner, *Henry Hikes to Fitchburg* by first-time author-illustrator D. B. Johnson, is based on a passage from the writings of Henry David Thoreau. Inspired by Aesop's "The Tortoise and the Hare," it tells of the two ways to get to Fitchburg, Massachusetts—the fast way by train, and the slow way by hiking. Guess which way is more rewarding? Johnson adds to the fun of the story by portraying all of the characters as bears.

The two *Boston Globe–Horn Book* Honor Books are equally distinctive. *Buttons* by Brock COLE is a tall tale in the vein of such classics as "The Three Sillies." When a plump old man bursts all his buttons and loses them in the fire, his three daughters set out to find replacements for them. How their attempts fail and finally succeed, results in a rollicking tale. *Buttons* reflects the enduring viability of the classic STORYTELLING patterns, exemplified here by the three daughters and their quest for new buttons. The story is set in the nineteenth century, but similar patterns can be adapted as easily to contemporary material.

A Day, a Dog by Gabrielle Vincent is the third *Boston Globe–Horn Book* winner. It is an experimental, wordless picture book by a Belgian artist, and may be better suited to teenagers and adults than it is to young children. At the outset, a family tosses an unwanted dog out the window of their car, and the rest of the book chronicles the dog's often perilous search for safety and the means for survival. This is the kind of book that its creator has to believe in fiercely and an editor usually has to fight to get published. Picture books of this type may not sell well, but they extend the boundaries of the form.

What generalizations, if any, can be drawn from this assortment of prize-winning picture books? The first and most obvious, applying to these awards and most others, is that there's really no such thing as a "best book." Different award committees often single out different titles for recognition, as was the case with the two committees here. This goes to show that there are many deserving books, and deciding which are the best depends as much if not more on the makeup of the award committee as it does on the books themselves.

The second generalization applies mainly to the original stories. If you want your picture book to receive special attention, you will need to ensure that it has something striking about it, and more than one level of meaning and enjoyment. *Henry Hikes to Fitchburg* is an especially good example of this. At its core is a time-tested lesson, and when combined with a colorful nineteenth-century setting, steady action, gentle humor, and a cast of appealing bears, one is bound to have a story that will catch an editor's eye and evoke a warm response from young readers.

NONFICTION: The nonfiction winners and Honor Books span all age groups, from picture books to books for young adults. The Orbis Pictus Award Honors list included three titles in a picture-book format. They are: *Mapping the World* by Sylvia A. Johnson, which traces the history of cartography from an early Babylonian map incised in clay to contemporary maps developed with satellite and computer technology; *The Snake Scientist* by Sybil Montgomery, with color photos by Nic Bishop, about a Canadian zoologist's research on the red-sided garter snake; and

The Top of the World: Climbing Mount Everest by Steve Johnson, whose subject matter is clearly indicated by its title.

Only the last book, however, is aimed at the picture-book audience in kindergarten through grade three. Following a trend that grows stronger with each publishing season, the other works are designed to appeal to a wide range of readers from ages eight to fourteen. And even the Mount Everest book could, and no doubt will, be enjoyed by older readers.

This nonfiction trend defies the old truism that once children reach the age of eight or so they would not be caught dead reading a picture book. Today's young readers, (see READING RAINBOW AND CHILDREN'S LITERATURE ON TELEVISION) and the Internet (see INTERNET RESOURCES FOR CHILDREN), actually welcome informational books that feature brief, tightly written texts and large illustrations on almost every page. Is this trend a good one? Not necessarily. By its very nature, picture-book nonfiction can convey only a modicum of information on any given topic. But as long as young readers show a preference for it, more and more children's nonfiction titles are likely to be written and produced in a picture-book format.

Autobiography is represented on the nonfiction award roster by three memoirs. The youngest of them, directed toward beginning readers, is *26 Fairmount Avenue*, a CHAPTER BOOK of incidents from his Connecticut childhood by the renowned picture book creator, Tomie DEPAOLA. It is the recipient of a Newbery Honor—the Newbery Committee's only nod to nonfiction in 2000.

The other two memoirs are both for ages eight to twelve. *Through My Eyes* by Ruby Bridges, illustrated with photographs, won the 2000 Orbis Pictus Award. Described as "a slice of living history," it recounts the author's experiences as the first AFRICAN AMERICAN child to integrate a New Orleans elementary school. A third autobiography, *Osceola: Memoirs of a Sharecropper's Daughter*, collected and edited by Alan Govenar, is a *Boston Globe-Horn Book* Honor Book. Arranged in twenty short chapters, this oral history focuses on Osceola Mays as she describes the highs and lows of her life in the small town of Wascom, Texas.

Through My Eyes and *Osceola* are examples of the strong, ongoing interest in children's books that explore the lives of minorities in the United States. All three autobiographies also reflect one of the main thrusts in teaching today—the demand that students seek out primary source material and firsthand accounts to bolster their reports and term papers. So if you have access to such material, either from your own life, or the lives of others in your community, now is certainly the time to make use of it in your writing. And if it concerns the experiences of a minority group, so much the better.

The remaining winner and Honor Books in the nonfiction category are all biographies. *Sir Walter Raleigh and the Quest for El Dorado,* Marc Aronson's in-depth portrait of the Elizabethan adventurer and explorer, is the winner of the 2000 *Boston Globe–Horn Book* Award for nonfiction. It is suitable for upper elementary and young adult readers.

Two other biographies will help to satisfy the continuing demand for MULTICULTURAL material. *Sitting Bull and His World,* a book for young adults by Albert MARRIN, has been named a *Boston Globe–Horn Book* Honor Book. *At Her Majesty's Request: An African Princess in Victorian England* by Walter Dean MEYERS is an Orbis Pictus Honor Book. Written for upper-elementary readers, the latter book tells the little-known story of an African princess who, in the mid-1800s, was presented by her father as a gift to Queen Victoria, who supervised her education and upbringing.

The last BIOGRAPHY on the winners' list is *Clara Schumann—Piano Virtuoso* by a new writer, Susanna Reich. It is the fifth and last Orbis Pictus Honor Book. Directed toward readers in grades four to six, this is another book that relies heavily on primary sources, including Clara's diaries and her letters to her composer/husband Robert. It should be welcomed warmly by all those teachers, librarians, and parents who are seeking biographies of strong, active women. All of the nonfiction winners have certain characteristics in common. Even the books for older readers are heavily illustrated with prints, drawings, maps, and archival photographs which, in most instances, the authors were responsible for obtaining. The books also contain generous amounts of supplementary material at front and back. For example, the biography of Sir Walter

Raleigh has a note to readers, an extensive list of acknowledgments, nineteen pages of endnotes and bibliography, and a complete index. So if one is planning to write a nonfiction book for young readers, do not imagine your work is finished when you get to the last page of the manuscript. In some ways, it is just beginning.

FICTION: The fiction winners and honorees divide in a rather striking way. Those written for the upper elementary audience are either fantasies or works of historical fiction, whereas the novels for young adults are set in today's often harsh and unfeeling world. Does this mean that the award committees think young people can avoid the realities of contemporary life until they become teenagers? To some observers it might seem so.

The Newbery Medal winner, *Bud, Not Buddy,* is Christopher Paul CURTIS's second novel. His first, *The Watsons Go to Birmingham—1963,* was a Newbery Honor Book in 1996. Set in the midwest during the Great Depression, *Bud, Not Buddy* centers on the title character, a ten-year-old boy who runs away from the latest in a string of foster homes and sets out in search of his long-gone bandleader father.

Two of the three Newbery Honor Books are also examples of historical fiction. *Getting Near to Baby,* a first novel by Audrey Coloumbis, takes place in the South of thirty years ago and tells the story of spunky Willa Jo and silent Little Sister. The girls are separated from their distraught mother after their baby sister dies, and sent against their will to live with their bossy Aunt Patty. Jennifer L. Holm's *Our Own May Amelia,* another first novel, centers on twelve-year-old May Amelia Jackson who describes her life as the only girl among seven boys in a Finnish-American family. Along the way, May Amelia offers a vivid picture of pioneer life in Washington state in 1899.

Author Franny Billingsley upholds the fantasy tradition in children's literature with her second novel, *The Folk Keeper,* winner of the *Boston Globe–Horn Book* Award for fiction. In this story, fifteen-year-old Corinna disguises herself as a boy so that she can train to be one of the privileged Keepers, wise men who use their knowledge of the ancient ways to protect the households they guard from evil spirits.

One of the two *Boston Globe–Horn Book*s for fiction is also a fantasy, *King of Shadows* by Susan COOPER, who won the Newbery Medal in 1976 for another fantasy, *The Grey King*. Now she tells the story of a young actor rehearsing the role of Puck in a present-day production of *A Midsummer-Night's Dream* who travels back in time to William Shakespeare's London and meets the great playwright himself.

Taken as a group, the children's fiction winners can provide writers with a number of insights. Whether fantasies or works of historical fiction, they feature well-drawn characters caught up in dramatic situations that evoke strong emotions in readers. Each of them shows a high degree of imagination that makes them stand out from your average run-of-the-mill novel. Not least, the fact that they are almost all by first- and second-book writers should be reassuring to those who wonder if editors are open to beginning writers. From this roundup, it is obvious that they are.

The second and final *Boston Globe–Horn Book* fiction Honor is *145th Street: Short Stories,* a book for young adults by Walter Dean MYERS. This collection of original short stories about life in Harlem today ranges in tone from brash comedy to all-out tragedy. Its success reminds us that the short-story format, which can be read in small doses, is popular with teenagers who often are pressed for time. It should encourage writers comfortable with this format to try their hands at story collections of their own. The book also serves as an excellent introduction to the area of young adult fiction—an area that is generating a great deal of interest at the moment.

No commentator would have been likely to make the last statement five or even ten years ago. At that time, young adult literature was thought in most quarters to be dying, if not already dead. It had been more than twenty years since the field was thriving, marked by the publication of such classic titles as Paul ZINDEL's *The Pigman* (1968) and Robert CORMIER's *The Chocolate War* (1974). By the early 1990s, young adult sales were down and publishers had cut back their young adult lists drastically.

Then a resurgence occurred, fueled by a scaling downward of the age limit for young adult books—now many good readers of twelve and thirteen are devouring young adult literature—coupled with a new willingness on the part of writers and publishers to tackle difficult subject matter. One result has been the establishment by the American Library Association of an award for young adult literature, named in honor of Michael L. Printz, a pioneer young adult librarian in Kansas. The first Printz Award books were announced early in 2000, and all four choices display the new vitality that is apparent throughout the field.

Monster by Walter Dean Myers came out on top—his third win in this batch of awards, which must be a record. *Monster* tells the story of sixteen-year-old Steve, who has been arrested and charged with the murder of a Korean storekeeper. While in jail, Steve writes a screenplay about the incident, interspersed with entries from the journal he keeps. This unique form of storytelling involves readers and makes them ask, "Is Steve guilty. Or is he innocent?"

The three Printz Honor Books are equally compelling. In *Skellig,* a first novel for young people by British writer David Almond, a boy stumbles upon a mysterious figure, the *Skellig* of the title, while investigating a ruined garage near his family's new home. The other two Honor Books explore the complexities of teenage life. John and Marisol, the leading characters in *Hard Love* by Ellen Wittlinger, have a lot in common. Both are concerned about the issue of trust, both have problem parents, and both, as it turns out, like girls. In *Speak* by Laurie Halse Anderson, the heroine, Melinda, remains frustratingly silent for much of the novel, only gradually gaining the courage to reveal that she has been sexually assaulted—and who the attacker is.

Obviously these books are a far cry from the young adult novels of old, where the big moment occurred when the hero gave the heroine her first kiss after bringing her home from the senior prom. Because of this cultural shift, many writers steer completely clear of the young adult field, saying they have no idea what teenage life is like today. But for those who feel they do have a finger on the adolescent pulse, the market for serious young adult fiction has rarely been as strong as it is now.

This wraps up this survey. But you may wonder if I have not omitted something. What about the Harry Potter books? Did they win any awards? No—not from these organizations, and for several good reasons. The Orbis Pictus, as mentioned, is limited to nonfiction, and only American writers are eligible for Newbery Medal consideration. Regarding the *Boston Globe–Horn Book* Award, the judges may have felt that Harry Potter had received enough recognition already. Or perhaps they simply did not think that the Potter books were as well written as the fiction titles they ultimately selected. Award committees often work in mysterious ways.

JAMES CROSS GIBLIN

AYLESWORTH, Jim
Author, b. 21 February 1943, Place unknown

A. was reared in Alabama and Indiana. He attended Miami University where he earned a B.A. degree in 1965. In 1978, he received an M.A. degree from Concordia University in Illinois. A. developed an interest in writing books for children during his twenty-five years of teaching first grade. While teaching, he read hundreds of books to children and found that he wanted to create his own stories. His first book, *Hush Up!* was published in 1980 and was followed by more than twenty books. His writings are characterized by rolling rhymes and language that is fun to read out loud. A.'s tales are often filled with loud sounds, rhythms, and rhymes—elements of stories that children love to hear. Critics have noted that A. is able to make the sounds in his text come alive. For example, his book, *Hanna's Hog* (1988), is filled with loud sounds remembered from his own boyhood on his grandmother's farm in Indiana. In contrast, *Country Crossing* (1991) uses softer sounds to describe a quiet evening in the country.

A. has drawn from various contexts to find subjects and tales that support his enthusiastic use of loud noises, rhythm, and rhyme. *Hush Up!* and *Hanna's Hog* (1988) both emulate FOLKLORE, the latter resembling a trickster tale. Borrowing from nursery rhymes, A. created nonsense versions of familiar lyrics in *The Complete*

Hickory Dickory Dock (1990) and *The Cat and the Fiddle and More* (1992). *My Sister's Rusty Bike* (1996) takes listeners on a rollicking journey to various states where unusual animals and their owners are discovered. The serenity of a quiet evening is created in *Country Crossing* (1991) as the noise of a train breaks the silence. Appealing to both listening and oral language development, A.'s books are a significant contribution to classroom libraries. A. is keenly aware that children are motivated to learn and to read when they experience books that are fun. He has greatly contributed to this category of "fun" books with his creative use of language.

A.'s most widely acclaimed work is *Old Black Fly* (1992), illustrated by Stephen GAMMELL, an alphabet book featuring a pesky fly who lands on various objects in a house. Awards for the book include the Reading Magic Award, *Parenting* magazine; Notable Book for Children, AMERICAN LIBRARY ASSOCIATION, INTERNATIONAL READING ASSOCIATION/CHILDREN'S BOOK COUNCIL Children's Choice Award.

Although A. retired from teaching in 1996, he continues to read to children as he visits schools across America, narrating his stories and inspiring children to read more on their own.

FURTHER WORKS: *Tonight's the Night*, 1981; *Mary's Mirror*, 1982; *Siren in the Night*, 1983; *The Bad Dream*, 1985; *Two Terrible Frights*, 1987; *Mother Halverson's New Cat*, 1989; *Mr. McGill Goes to Town*, 1989; *The Folks in the Valley: A Pennsylvania Dutch ABC*, 1991; *McGraw's Emporium*, 1995; *Wake up Little Children: A Rise and Shine Rhyme*, 1996; *The Gingerbread Man*, 1998; *Through the Night*, 1998; *Jim Aylesworth's Book of Bedtime Stories*, 1998; *One Crow, A Counting Rhyme*, 1988; *My Son John*, 1994; *Teddy Bear Tears*, 1997

BIBLIOGRAPHY: Aylesworth, Jim. "Hanna's Hog." *Book Links*. March, 1996; Illinois Gateway State Library. Accessed July 9, 1999. http://www.sos.state.il.us/depts/library/programs/kids/qu—ia—ja.html; *Something about the Author*, vol. 89, 1997; *Seventh Book of Junior Authors and Illustrators*, 1996

MARY ARIAIL BROUGHTON AND
JANELLE B. MATHIS

B

BABBITT, Natalie

Author, illustrator, b. 28 July 1932, Dayton, Ohio

B. decided as a nine-year-old that she would grow up to become an illustrator. Previous to that, she had considered a career as a pirate and then as a librarian, but when introduced to the illustrations of John TENNIEL, her final decision was made. Her parents shared their appreciation for books, stories, language, and art with her. Their influence has remained with her from childhood and she holds them responsible for her success as an illustrator and a writer.

After graduating from Smith College in 1954, marrying and starting a family, B. observed what the life of a writer entails. Her husband's attempts to write a novel foundered when he could not bear the solitude required for the work of revision. He returned to academic life. B.'s first publication was her ILLUSTRATION work for his children's book, *The Forty-ninth Magician* (1966). Subsequently, she composed her own self-illustrated books of verse for children (*Dick Foote and the Shark,* 1967; *Phoebe's Revolt,* 1968) and illustrated POETRY collections written by Valerie WORTH.

Knee Knock Rise (1970), a self-illustrated tale of a town held captive by its belief in an imaginary beast, was an AMERICAN LIBRARY ASSOCIATION Notable Book (1970) and an ALA NEWBERY MEDAL Honor Book (1971). *The Devil's Storybook* (1974) was an ALA Notable Book and nominated for the National Book Award. *Tuck Everlasting* (1975), B.'s most well-known book,

was an ALA Notable Book, a Christopher Award winner for juvenile fiction (1976), and received citations from the INTERNATIONAL READING ASSOCIATION and the INTERNATIONAL BOARD ON BOOKS FOR YOUNG PEOPLE (both in 1978). *The Eyes of the Amaryllis* (1977) earned a citation as an ALA Notable Book. B. won the George C. Stone Center for Children's Books Award in 1979, and was nominated for the Hans Christian ANDERSEN Medal in 1981.

B.'s illustrations, rendered for the most part and until recently in pen and ink, are crisp and good-natured. Her stories often involve good people who must resolve issues of morality for themselves. Both images and words are presented with simplicity, frankness of feeling, and a style of delivery that would lead one to imagine that the characters and their plights are legendary.

In *Goody Hall* (1971), a gothic mansion withstands the secret lives of its numerous inhabitants, while providing readers with just enough anticipation of chills to be thrilling. B. offers readers a devil who is part trickster and part fool in *The Devil's Storybook* (1974). *Tuck Everlasting* (1975) has become a classic of children's literature. This novel, accessible to middle-grade readers but of equal appeal to adults, recounts the dilemma faced by a young girl who discovers an immortal family. The Tuck family has kept their relative youth by drinking from an enchanted spring and, although the adults in the family have come to perceive the insidious effects of outliving their interests, the teenage son would have their young visitor consider sharing the drink of ever-lasting life.

In her stories for younger readers, B. retains the magic, FANTASY, and symbolism with which she works in her middle-grade stories, but utilizes them toward the end of evoking delight, rather than introspection. *Nellie: A Cat on Her Own* (1989) is a self-illustrated picture book featuring a wooden cat who disports herself with all the feline independence of a fleshly one. B. features her own grandson—as a crown prince—and others of her household, including her dog, in *Bub— The Very Best Thing* (1995). *In Ouch!: A Tale from GRIMM* (1998), B. tells the story of Marco, a commoner who grows up to marry a princess and who is then sent by her father to take three hairs from the devil's head. To critical acclaim, B. combines her work as a reteller with her own talent for imagining the private life of, and inconveniences experienced by, the devil.

B. is conscious of her ability to write for children without being condescending. Her literary critics, too, praise her skill in creating stories that transcend their messages—which are usually quite trenchant—with their grace and wit. Besides fiction and PICTURE BOOKS, B. has edited, along with other notable contemporary children's authors, *The Big Book for Peace* (1991), a volume intended to give children many vantage points on their world through exposure to quality STORY-TELLING and illustrations. B. has also written extensively for literary periodicals.

FURTHER WORKS: *The Search for Delicious,* 1969; *The Something,* 1970; *Herbert Rowbarge,* 1982; *The Devil's Other Storybook,* 1987

BIBLIOGRAPHY: *American Women Writers,* vol. 5, 1994; HOPKINS, Lee Bennett, *Pauses: Autobiographical Reflections of 101 Creators of Children's Books,* 1995; Silvey, Anita, ed., *Children's Books and Their Creators,* 1995; *Something about the Author,* vol. 68, 1992

FRANCISCA GOLDSMITH

BAGNOLD, Enid
Author, playwright, b. 27 October 1889, Rochester, England; d. 31 March 1981, London, England

B. was educated in England and France and studied painting. She was a volunteer nurse in World War I and wrote several books based on her wartime experiences. Although B. wrote many plays

and books for adults, she published only two books for children. Her FAMILY STORY for children, *Alice and Thomas and Jane* (1935), was illustrated by the author with the help of her young daughter, Laurian. The second, *National Velvet,* (England, 1930, United States, 1935), an enduring classic, also has ILLUSTRATIONS by B.'s daughter. Fourteen-year-old Velvet Brown's steadfast determination to enter the horse she has won in a lottery in England's Grand National horse race inspires young readers to pursue their dreams. The book was adapted as a three-act play and produced in London in 1943. The book was also adapted as a major motion picture by Metro-Goldwyn-Mayer and was filmed in 1944. The film starred Elizabeth Taylor as a young horse lover who won England's Grand National race.

FURTHER WORKS: (for adults): *The Chalk Garden.* (Award of Merit Medal, and prize from American Academy of Arts and Letters). *Poor Judas.* (Arts Theater Prize)

BIBLIOGRAPHY: Doyle, Brian, *The Who's Who of Children's Literature,* 1968; *Major Authors and Illustrators for Children and YOUNG ADULTS,* 1993

MARY ARIAIL BROUGHTON

BAILEY, Carolyn Sherwin
Author, b. 25 October 1875, Hoosick Falls, New York; d. 23 December 1961, Place unknown

B. received the NEWBERY MEDAL in 1947 for her story of the handmade doll, *Miss Hickory* (1946) who comes to life. She develops this character with a hickory nut head, as one who is quite spunky and determined to survive. With earthy HUMOR and style, Miss Hickory is able to turn adversity to advantage. B. had an enormous commitment to early American arts and crafts, and her body of work reflects this interest and communicates it to young readers. She was the editor of *American Childhood Magazine.*

FURTHER WORKS: MOTHER GOOSE: *Old Rhymes Reproduced in Connection with Their Veracious History* (Peter Newell, illus). 1905; *What to Do for Uncle Sam,* 1918; *The Enchanted Bugle and Other Stories,* 1920; *The Wonderful Days* (C. B. Falls), 1929; *Tops and Whistles: True Stories of Early American Toys and Children,* 1937; *Pioneer Art in America,* (Grace Paull, illus), 1944; *Finnegan II, His Nine Lives* (Kate SEREDY, illus), 1953; *A Christmas Party,* 1975

BIBLIOGRAPHY: Southern Connecticut State College, New Haven, Library, *The Carolyn Sherwin B. Historical Collection of Children's Books: A Catalogue,* ed. Dorothy R. Davis, New Haven: Southern Connecticut State College, 1966, Davis, Dorothy R., *Carolyn Sherwin B., 1875–1961: Profile and Bibliography,* 1967

KAY E. VANDERGRIFT AND JODI PILGRIM

BAKER, Jeannie

Author, illustrator, artist, b. 2 November 1950, London, England

B. emigrated to Australia in 1975, and currently resides in Sydney. While attending art school in London, B. became obsessed with texture and since 1972 has been developing her distinctive style of "relief collage" that explores sensory experience. The photographic reproductions of her strikingly tactile collage constructions give the illusion of three dimensionality. The intricate detail is painstakingly crafted over several years from preserved natural materials like twigs, leaves, and hair, juxtaposed with such materials as peeled paint and custom-made knitted clothes. B.'s collages can stand alone as art; many are part of public art collections and have been exhibited frequently around the world.

B.'s earliest children's books explore the warm relationships between children and older people as in *Grandfather* (1977) and *Millicent* (1980). She later developed a passionate concern for the natural environment, and her recent books are designed to help raise awareness of the need to halt the unthinking waste and environmental destruction of our planet. These books specifically provide thought-provoking commentary on the devastating changes wrought over time on the unique AUSTRALIAN landscape. *The Story of Rosy Dock* (1995) exposes the desert scourge of an introduced species that threatens to push native species to extinction. *Where the Forest Meets the Sea* (1988 Australian Picture Book of the Year Honor Book) subtly explores the potential destruction of the Daintree rainforest in Queensland with its ghostly images from the past and future. *Window,* (1992 Australian PICTURE BOOK of the Year), offers a sobering, wordless view of the changing landscape over twenty years from one boy's window, from rural tranquility to rampant urban sprawl. B.'s endnote explicitly challenges readers

to make a difference in the conservation of our environment.

AWARDS: AMERICAN LIBRARY ASSOCIATION Notable Book (1984) for *Home in the Sky.* Australian Film Institute Award for Best Australian Animated Film (1988) for *Where the Forest Meets the Sea.* (Australian) Children's Books of the Year Award (1992) for *Window.* IBBY Honor List (1990) for *Where the Forest Meets the Sea*

FURTHER WORKS: *One Hungry Spider,* 1982

BIBLIOGRAPHY: *Children's Literature Review,* vol. 28, 1992; *Seventh Book of Junior Authors and Illustrators,* 1996; *Something about the Author,* vol. 88, 1997

BARBARA TOBIN

BAKER, Keith

Author, illustrator, b. Date unknown 1953; Place unknown

B.'s books for children are recognized for their bold colors and fancy textures. In the counting book, *The Big Fat Hen* (1994), Baker creatively illustrates a familiar children's rhyme, "one two buckle my shoe" by using highly decorated hens and their chicks. In *Hide and Snake* (1991), and *Cat Tricks* (1997), Baker appeals to children's visual imaginations by creating lines or shapes in one picture that turn into something totally different in the next; he creates a spider web that becomes a ship's rigging, and a green feather that transforms to become the ocean. *The Magic Fan* (1989), a MOVABLE BOOK (POP-UP BOOKS), uses fan-shaped pop-up ILLUSTRATIONS that open to reveal a Japanese carpenter's creations. In *The Dove's Letter* (1993), a book quite different from his others, B. tells the story of a dove searching for her owner as she flies from woodsman to farmer, from baker to weaver. *The Dove's Letter* illustrates how each person finds a different meaning in the message the dove carries.

BIBLIOGRAPHY: *Horn Book* Guide Interactive, 1998

DENISE P. BEASLEY

BANG, Molly

Author, illustrator, b. 29 December 1943, Princeton, New Jersey

Known for her illustrations of folktales, B. recalls that ILLUSTRATIONS by Arthur RACKHAM were favorites during her childhood. A writer herself,

B.'s mother also influenced her by encouraging an early love of reading. Later B. would illustrate several of her mother's adapted and translated folktales. Well educated with an undergraduate degree from Wellesley College and master's degrees from the University of Arizona and Harvard University, B. traveled widely. She taught English in Japan and later worked for a health organization illustrating health manuals, utilizing folktales gathered during her travels as part of the illustrations in the manuals. *The Goblins Giggle, and Other Stories* (1973), one of her early books, is typical of her enjoyment of stories of mystery and suspense. Two of her later books, *The Grey Lady and the Strawberry Snatcher,* a wordless book, and *Ten, Nine, Eight,* a counting book, were both CALDECOTT MEDAL Honor Books.

A versatile illustrator, B.'s books reflect her high regard and extensive study of foreign lands, people, and FOLKLORE. She skillfully combines her interest in folklore with her gift at expressing mystery and suspense through writing and illustrations, often using collage, watercolors, pencil, and charcoal. Denise M. Wilms described her illustrative style as a visual jigsaw, a sum of disparate colors, patterns, and spreads of gray that unexpectedly blend.

AWARDS: AMERICAN LIBRARY ASSOCIATION Notable Book Award (1977) for *Wiley and the Hairy Man* and (1980) for *The Grey Lady and the Strawberry Snatcher.* ALA Caldecott Medal Honor Book (1981) for *The Grey Lady and the Strawberry Snatcher* and (1983) for *Ten, Nine, Eight.* KATE GREENAWAY Honor Award (1983) for *Ten, Nine, Eight.* Hans Christian ANDERSEN Award nomination and *Boston Globe–Horn Book* Award for Illustration (both 1988) for *The Paper Crane*

FURTHER WORKS: *Dawn,* 1991; *One Fall Day,* 1994; *Goose,* 1997; *Common Ground: The Water, Earth, and Air We Share,* 1997

BIBLIOGRAPHY: Wilms, Denise M. review of *The Grey Lady and the Strawberry Snatcher, Booklist,* 1980

SANDRA IMDIEKE

BANKS, Lynne Reid
Author, b. 31 July 1929, London, England

Born in London, B. and her mother moved to the Canadian prairies during World War II. She grew up expecting to become an actress, and attended

the Italia Stage School in London in 1946 and the Royal Academy of Dramatic Art in London from 1947 to 1949. B. first acted in English repertory companies from 1949–55, then became a freelance journalist, television news reporter, and writer in London. In 1959, B. wrote her first novel for adults, *The L-Shaped Room,* which was later made into a movie. The success of her book provided the financial resources for her 1962 move to a kibbutz in Israel where she taught English as a second language. She returned to England in 1972. B. recalls feeling guilty for her relative safety in Canada during the war, and she, therefore, felt a great desire to go to Israel. Her first book for children, *One More River* (1973), reflects her experience in Israel through the eyes of a fictional Canadian girl adjusting to life on a kibbutz. From that beginning, B. has become known for her FANTASY books, beginning with *Indian in the Cupboard* (1980).

The popularity of *Indian in the Cupboard* continues, having been made into a motion picture in 1995 despite criticism for the stereotypical portrayal of Little Bull, the toy who comes to life. Several sequels continue the adventures of Omri and Little Bull. In her fantasy writing, B. skillfully draws the reader into the fantasy world with lively detail and description. B. commented that "I especially enjoy writing wish-fulfillment tales for younger children in which real, everyday life coexists with magic."

AWARDS: *New York Times* Notable Book (1981) for *Indian in the Cupboard* and (1986) for *Return of the Indian*

FURTHER WORKS: *The Adventures of King Midas,* 1976; *Return of the Indian,* 1986; *Melusine: A Mystery,* 1988; *The Secret of the Indian,* 1989; *The Mystery of the Cupboard,* 1993; *I, Houdini: The Amazing Story of an Escape-artist Hamster,* 1991

BIBLIOGRAPHY: *Sixth Book of Junior Authors,* 1989

SANDRA IMDIEKE

BANNERMAN, Helen
Author, illustrator, b. 1863 (some sources: 1862), Edinburgh, Scotland; d. 13 October 1946, Edinburgh, Scotland

B. is best known as the creator of *Little Black Sambo* (1899), one of the most beloved and most controversial books in children's literature. Although B. published other books, she is remembered for this one. Much of her childhood was spent in various parts of the British Empire since her father was an army chaplain. After studying abroad, she returned to India in 1889 and married William Bannerman, a doctor in the Indian Medical service. They spent the next thirty years of their marriage in India, where they reared four children.

Although B. was not a professional writer she often made up stories that she told to her children. Legend has it that B. wrote and illustrated *Little Black Sambo* over the course of a two-day train trip to Madras as a way of cheering up her children who had been left at home. The story was a FANTASY about a little INDIAN (EAST) boy who cleverly avoids being eaten by the local tigers who trade his clothing for his life. Clearly this fable about a small protagonist who encounters the jungle alone and survives by his own ingenuity is a most empowering tale. Initially the book was a great success. Like the Beatrix POTTER books, it was made in a size that a child could comfortably hold, had clear bright stylized ILLUSTRATIONS, and short rhythmic sentences with only a phrase or so on each page. However, by the mid–twentieth century, the work was criticized by educators as one that reinforced racist attitudes. It was recalled that the word "Sambo" in history had been used to describe a submissive, childlike AFRICAN AMERICAN. The book was denigrated for its stereotyped caricatured illustrations, degrading names, exaggerated dialect, and primitive jungle settings.

Although B.'s defenders said that it was about India and Indian characters, and there was no intentional racial message, the book was dropped in 1972 by libraries and recommended book lists in the United States and England.

In recent years, new versions of the story have appeared that have eliminated the objectionable elements. An example is *Little Babaji* (1996) by the illustrator Fred MARCELLINO, who cleverly kept B.'s beloved story, but gave all characters authentic Indian names and placed them in an authentic looking Indian setting. The successful team of Julius LESTER, author, and Jerry PINKNEY, illustrator, published *Sam and the Tigers* (1996) another fantasy variation that avoids ob-

jectionable stereotypes while retaining the charm of the original story.

BIBLIOGRAPHY: *Children's Literature Review,* vol. 21; Hay, Elizabeth, *Sambo Sahib,* 1981; *Something about the Author,* vol. 19, 1979

JUDY LIPSITT

BARRACCA, Debra and Sal
Authors. Debra: b. 12 December 1953, New York City; Sal: b. 11 October 1947, Brooklyn, New York

Husband and wife, D.B. and S.B., work not only as children's writers, but also as publishers of children's books; they run their PUBLISHING company, Halcyon Books. Native New Yorkers, the B.s still live in New York City and have based their book, *The Adventures of Taxi Dog* (1990), on a real New York City taxi driver who drives customers around with his dog in the front seat. They continue the adventures of Maxi, the dog, in subsequent books such as *Maxi, the Hero* (1991), *Maxi, the Star* (1993), and *A Taxi Dog Christmas* (1994). In 1996, *The Adventures of Taxi Dog* was translated into a lively rhythmic Spanish edition called *Las Aventuras de Maxi, el Perro Taxista.*

BIBLIOGRAPHY: "Debra B." *Young Readers Catalog,* www.penguinputnam.com/catalog/yreader/authors/4895_biography.html; "Sal B.," www.penguinputnam.com / catalog / yreader / authors/10772_biography.html

DENISE P. BEASLEY

BARRIE, J(ames) M(atthew)
Author, playwright, b. 9 May 1860, Kirriemuir, Forfarshire, Scotland; d. 19 June 1937, London, England

B.'s talent as a writer was evident in his adolescence when, at the age of seventeen, his first play, *Bandolero, the Bandit* (1877), was produced. After graduating from Edinburgh University, he worked as a journalist for the *Nottingham Journal,* published several novels, and wrote successful plays. His first novel, *Better Dead,* was published in 1887. Determined to become a playwright, B. wrote several including *Little Minister* (1891), and *Walker, London* (1892). These plays led him to write the children's classic, *Peter Pan; or, The Boy Who Would Not Grow Up* (1904), about a young boy who does not want to lose the magic of his youth. Peter Pan first appeared in *The Little White Bird* (1902). In it the story of Peter Pan is told to children by a family friend. Influenced by his own love of FANTASY and a friendship that developed with five young brothers, B. created a second story in which Peter Pan was the leader of several children known as *The Lost Boys in Never Never Land. Peter Pan; or, The Boy Who Would Not Grow Up,* won great acclaim when it appeared on the London stage, also in 1904. Praised for its imaginative and delightful depiction of eternal youth, B. was called "the most fashionable playwright of his time." B. created subsequent adaptations based on the main character of Peter Pan including *Peter Pan in Kensington Gardens* (1906), *When Wendy Grew Up* (1908), and *Peter and Wendy* (1911). The little girl, Wendy Darling, and her two brothers share Peter's adventures in these later stories. Originally written and performed as a play, the play itself was published as a book in 1928 as *Peter and Wendy.* It was first released as a silent film in 1924 and as an animated musical film by DISNEY in 1953. A 1950 stage revival featured new music by Leonard Bernstein; the menacing Captain Hook was played by Boris Karloff. B. donated all the profits from his Peter Pan stories to a London children's hospital.

B. authored numerous successful plays in the early 1900s, although his later writing often dealt with adult themes of unhappy marriage and alcoholism. His last significant work was *Mary Rose* (1924), after which depression and a lapse into poor health ended his life. *Peter Pan* continues to be an enduring work of fantasy for both young and old readers and viewers.

BIBLIOGRAPHY: Bingham, Jane M., *Writers for Children: Critical Studies of Major Authors since the Seventeenth Century,* 1988; *Dictionary of Literary Biography,* vol. 141; BRITISH *Children's Writers, 1880–1914,* 1994; *The Oxford Companion to Children's Literature,* 1984; *Twentieth-Century Children's Writers,* 4th ed., 1995

DENISE P. BEASLEY AND JANELLE B. MATHIS

BARRON, T(om) A.
Author, b. 26 March 1952, Unknown location

Reared in Colorado, B. acquired a love of nature, which is reflected in his work. B. graduated from Princeton University and attended Oxford University on a Rhodes scholarship. After spending several years working in the business world, B. made writing his primary focus. He once journeyed across South Asia, writing stories as he traveled. Three of his YOUNG ADULT novels, *Heartlight* (1990), *The Ancient One* (1992), and *The Merlin Effect* (1994), all combine elements of SCIENCE FICTION, FANTASY, and myth with contemporary ADVENTURE and environmental activism. B. is praised for his ability to weave these elements into books that are fun to read. Kate Gordon acts as the heroine in each of these stories.

B.'s Lost Years of Merlin series is based on ancient Celtic legend. The action in the three fantasy quest novels focuses first on Merlin's youth in *The Lost Years of Merlin,* an ALA Best Book for Young Adults selection. The second book, *The Seven Songs of Merlin* (1998), recounts the adventurous escapades of Merlin and Arthur, and, finally, the challenges Merlin faces as a young adult are retold in *The Fires of Merlin,* a 1999 VOYA Best Book of the Year title. While there is an emphasis on action and the spirit of the old Merlin and Arthur legends, B.'s themes deal with the universal quest among young adults for knowledge about the forces of good and evil and how power is used for better or worse to accomplish change in the world.

FURTHER WORKS: *Walk in Wilderness,* 1993; *The Mirror of Merlin,* 1999; *Where Is Grandpa?,* Chris SOENTPIET, illus.), 2000

BIBLIOGRAPHY: *Something about the Author,* vol. 93, 1996

JODI PILGRIM

BARTON, Byron
Author, illustrator, b. 8 September 1930, Pawtucket, Rhode Island

B.'s clear text and bold, bright ILLUSTRATIONS entertain and inform young children and their parents. His nonfiction books help expand the minds of his readers: Children experience traveling into space, assembling bones to reconstruct a dinosaur, and building a house. The sparse text and rhythmic language include enough details to inform, but not so many words as to confuse the very young. B. attributes his early development of creativity to a couple of factors: As a child, B.

benefitted from his father's winter seasonal occupation as a seller of wood and coal; the piles, along with all the nooks and crannies of barns and attics, provided a playground for creativity. The other factor appeared when B., in the fourth grade, moved with his family from Pawtucket, Rhode Island, to California: He was allowed to paint in the back of the classroom in the new school because his classmates were being taught some subjects he had already mastered in his previous school. This extra time to paint and play resulted in his being referred to as "the artist." Also instrumental to his development were all the paint supplies he received as gifts and his exposure to how-to-draw books. Later, B. attended Los Angeles City College from 1948 to 1950. His art education was interrupted when he was drafted into the Army in 1950, and was sent to Korea. He served until 1952. After he left the service, he finished his art education at Chouinard Art Institute from 1953 to 1956. In addition to his career in children's literature, B. worked with Studio 7 in Los Angeles as an illustrator from 1956 to 1957, as a designer with Equitable Life Assurance Company, New York City, from 1957 to 1960, and also with the Columbia Broadcasting System (CBS), in New York City, from 1960 to 1966.

Diversity might best describe B.'s works for children. This diversity is present in artistic style and color, the ethnicity of characters, and the representation of settings and interests. B.'s first publication was a wordless PICTURE BOOK, *Elephant* (1971). Although many of B.'s books do not have lengthy texts, there is an abundance of authentic action. B.'s books are often used in early literacy classrooms to lead children into book-related play and communication. One such example is *Bones, Bones, Dinosaur Bones* (1990), a high-quality nonfiction book for the young. Another example that furthers preschoolers' literacy is *Machines at Work* (1987), one of B.'s many titles referred to as "slice of life stories." B.'s stories encourage interaction and imagination, prompting children to join in, verbally and physically, acting out the drama of people at work. B. creates literature that appears simple and nonthreatening, and yet motivates children to extend the action and adventure. In turn, many readers get their first exposure to career education.

B. also writes fiction to entertain, such as *The Wee Little Woman* (1995), with plenty of repetition and predictability. More variety of style is evident when B. illustrates for other authors. In *Gila Monsters Meet You at the Airport* (1980), by Marjorie Weinman SHARMAT, the illustrator uses earth tones with shadowing and a whimsical touch to represent the setting of the West accurately, as well as the mythical flare of the story. B.'s work has an extraordinary impact on emerging readers.

AWARDS: *New York Herald Tribune* Spring Book Festival Middle Honor (1969) for *A Girl Called Al. New York Times* Best Illustrated Children's Books of the Year (1972) for *Where's Al?* and (1988) for *I Want to Be an Astronaut.* CBC Children's Book Showcase Title (1972) for *The Paper Airplane Book* and (1973) for *Where's Al? Dinosaurs, Dinosaurs* (1989) was awarded the Please Touch Award, Please Touch Museum for Children (1990)

FURTHER WORKS: Self-illustrated: *Applebet Story.* 1973. *Buzz Buzz Buzz.* 1973. *Harry Is a Scaredy-Cat.* 1974. *Wheels.* 1979. *Building a House.* 1981. *Airport.* 1982. *Airplanes.* 1986. *The Three Bears.* (Reteller). 1991. *Big Machines.* 1996. *Tools.* 1996. *Zoo Animals.* 1996. Illustrator only: *The Checker Players.* 1973. *Good Morning, Chick.* 1980. *Truck Song.* 1984. *The Tamarindo Puppy.* 1993. *Little Factory.* 1998

BIBLIOGRAPHY: Dennis, Lisa. "It's Toddler Time . . . Now What?" *School Library Journal.* Feb. 92, vol. 38, i. 2. Rowe, Deborah Wells. "The Literate Potentials of Book-Related Dramatic Play," *Reading Research Quarterly.* Jan.–Mar. 98, vol. 33, i. 1. Silvey, Anita, ed. *Children's Books and Their Creators.* 1995. *Something about the Author,* vol. 9, 1976, and vol. 90, 1997

NANCY HORTON

BASE, Graeme
Author, illustrator, b. 6 April 1958, Amersham, England

Born in England, B. moved to Australia with his family in 1966. His first career was as a graphic designer in the field of advertising, but B. found that occupation unfulfilling. He had the germ of an idea for what he titled a "Fieldguide to Dragons of the World," but a publisher he approached was not interested in that concept. However, the publisher encouraged B. to pursue his illustrating interest; six months later B. returned to the publisher with *My Grandma Lived in Gooligulch* (1983), a poetic and visual portrayal of the fauna of the Australian bush. It took him three years to develop his next book, *Animalia* (1986), an alphabet book that challenges the reader's powers of observation. His later book, *The Discovery of Dragons* (1996), returns to his initial interest in a book about dragons.

B. is known for his sense of HUMOR, his intricate, detailed art work, and his ability to challenge the viewer through illustrative codes, puzzles, and hidden clues. He describes himself as a very happy person with a love of wildlife, which he feels comes across in his work.

He tried illustrating the work of other authors, but found the process too confining, not being able to change the words as he created his art. When describing his creative process, B. stated: "For me, the relationship between text and ILLUSTRATION is the very essence of producing a good picture book. . . . Throughout the whole life of a project I constantly revise the relationship of the two parts, looking for unnecessary duplication of information, mistakes in continuity, and ways of improving what I have come up with to date."

AWARDS: AUSTRALIAN Children's Book Award, CHILDREN'S BOOK COUNCIL of Australia, Picture Book Honor (1987) for *Animalia*. PICTURE BOOKS of the Year (1989) for *The Eleventh Hour: A Curious Mystery*. BOOK DESIGN Award high commendation, Australian Book Publishers' Association (1988) and Young Australian Best Book Award (1989) both for *The Eleventh Hour: A Curious Mystery*

FURTHER WORKS: *The Eleventh Hour,* 1989; *The Sign of the Seahorse,* 1992; *The Discovery of Dragons,* 1996; *The Worst Band in the Universe,* 1999

SANDRA IMDIEKE

BASH, Barbara
Author, illustrator, b. 20 October 1948, Barrington, Illinois

B. found her inspiration for her writing and ILLUSTRATION within the letters of the alphabet, an interest she followed through early illuminated manuscripts. The inspiration for her children's books comes from her experience with the natural world, such as bats streaming out of a cave in Colorado and suggesting *Shadows of Night: The Hidden World of the Little Brown Bat* (1992). It,

as well as *Desert Giant: The World of the Saguaro Cactus* (1988), *Urban Roosts: Where Birds Nest in the City* (1990), and *Ancient Ones: The World of the Old Growth Douglas Fir* (1994), was named an Outstanding Science Trade Book for Children.

FURTHER WORKS: *In the Heart of the Village,* 1996; *Tiger Lillies and Other Beastly Plants* (Elisabeth Ring, author). 1984; *Tree of Life: The World of the African Baobab,* 1989

BIBLIOGRAPHY: *The Seventh Book of Junior Authors and Illustrators,* 1996

GWYNNE ELLEN ASH

BASKIN, Leonard
Illustrator, graphic artist, sculptor, printer, teacher, b. 15 August 1922, New Brunswick, New Jersey; d. 3 June 2000, Northampton, Massachusetts

B. is an internationally known artist and illustrator with works in private and public collections. He studied at Yale, the Academia di Belle Arte, and the Academia de la Grande Chaumiere in Paris. However, one of the great influences on his work was the arrival in postwar New York City of the European expressionists. During this period many figurative artists including B. became particularly interested in the woodcut printing techniques of Germany and Japan. In the late 1950s, figurative artists in the United States had a much wider audience than their abstract colleagues; there was a loyal group of collectors who supported those artists like B. who found representation basic to other visions of life in the postatomic age. In 1961 his bold, lifelike, intensely emotional woodcut *Man of Peace,* won the first prize in the São Paulo Bienal.

In the late 1950s, B. founded the Gehenne Press, which specialized in limited edition prints. From 1953 to 1971 he was a professor of graphic arts at Smith College. B. was an experienced and successful printer and illustrator of adult books when he began doing children's books. His first attempt, *Hosie's Alphabet* (1972), was a CALDECOTT MEDAL Honor Book. B. said that the book was a result of a Baskin family project with his wife and his children—Hosie, Tobias, and Lucretia—who created the whimsical text. Again, they collaborated to produce *Hosie's Aviary* (1979) and *Hosie's Zoo* (1981). B.'s ILLUSTRATIONS for children's books are fanciful and stylized, but realistic, softly outlined watercolor drawings. Besides his family, B. has had many outstanding collaborators such as Ted HUGHES who published with B.: *Moon Whales and Other Moon Poems* (1975) and *Under the North Star* (1981).

AWARDS: AMERICAN LIBRARY ASSOCIATION Caldecott Medal Honor Book (1973) for *Hosie's Alphabet*. *New York Times* Best Illustrated Children's Books of the Year (1972) for *Hosie's Alphabet* and (1983) for *Leonard B.'s Miniature Natural History: First Series*

FURTHER WORKS: *Imps, Demons, Hobgoblins, Witches, Fairies and Elves,* 1984; *Leonard B.'s Miniature Natural History,* 1983; *The Raptors and Other Birds,* 1985

BIBLIOGRAPHY: *Something about the Author,* vol. 27, 1982, and vol. 30, 1983

JUDY LIPSITT

BAUER, Marion Dane
Author, b. 20 November 1938, Oglesby, Illinois

Although her childhood in a small Illinois town was limited in its exploration of her geographical surroundings, B. traveled throughout the world in her imagination, spending considerable time in the town library and daydreaming stories in her mind. Although she always knew that she would be a writer, B. did not consider becoming one seriously until she was a teenager. She received her B.A. from the University of Oklahoma in 1962, and went on to teach high school in Wisconsin and adult education courses in Minnesota, always working with her writing. As an adult and a mother, she realized that her writing needed to be based on reality and informed by dreams. This realization opened her writing to the places and experiences of her growing up years and her young adulthood, the midwest of imagination and reality.

B.'s NEWBERY MEDAL Honor Book, *On My Honor* (1986), explores one of these dream-informed experiences in the Midwest. When she was a teenager, B. had a friend who watched another child drown in a river near their home and went home afraid to admit to the occurrence. This core event, supplemented by her imagination and her own sense of obligation and responsibility,

allowed her to craft a novel that questioned adults' assumptions about the moral lives of children.

Likewise in *Face to Face* (1991) and in *A Question of Trust* (1994), B. continues to explore children's turbulent emotional and moral development, particularly in response to a parents' divorce. In *Face to Face,* Michael learns that his father, whom he rarely sees, indeed has feet of clay and that he has built his father up in an attempt to hurt his mother and to remain disconnected from his stepfather. Like Michael, Brad in *A Question of Trust* harbors denial and anger over his parents' separation. He refuses to speak or to visit his mother, thinking that this will eventually bring her home. Equally angry with his father, he and his younger brother secretly care for a cat against his father's wishes, a betrayal that leads to lying, theft, and danger.

B.'s concern for children's emotional development, awareness, and well-being encouraged her to edit a collection of short stories about gay and lesbian teenagers. *Am I Blue? Coming out from the Silence* (1994) was an attempt to help children respect themselves and others as human beings deserving of love.

In addition to her thought-provoking fiction and novels, B. also writes lighthearted PICTURE BOOKS (*Beyond the Playhouse Wall,* 1997) and edits nonfiction travel guides for children. She has also written and edited two books for children on the craft of writing: *What's Your Story?: A Young Person's Guide to Writing Fiction* (1992) and *Our Stories: A Fiction Workshop for Young Readers* (1996). B. is a former lecturer at the Institute for Children's Literature and a recipient of many state and local AWARDS and honors for *On My Honor, Rain of Fire* (1983), and *Am I Blue?* among others.

AWARDS: AMERICAN LIBRARY ASSOCIATION Newbery Medal Honor Book (1987) for *On My Honor.* KERLAN Award (1996).

FURTHER WORKS: *Alison's Wings,* 1996; *Ghost Eye,* 1992; *Taste of Smoke,* 1993; *When I Go Camping with Grandma,* 1995

BIBLIOGRAPHY: B., M. D. *A Writer's Story, from Life to Fiction,* 1995; *The Fifth Book of Junior Authors and Illustrators,* 1983; *Something about the Author, Autobiography Series,* vol. 9, 1990

GWYNNE ELLEN ASH

BAUM, L(yman) Frank

Author, b. 15 May 1856, Chittenango, New York;
d. 6 May 1919, Hollywood, California

Desiring to write a modern fairy tale without didacticism, cruelty, or terrifying characters, and one set in America, B. created a land of castles, kingdoms, and witches in which unique characters, such as Dorothy Gale, the Lion, the Scarecrow, and the Tin Man looked for happiness. In the *Wizard of Oz* (1900), the first genuine American FANTASY, B. created a tale filled with adventure and problems to be solved. The story was continued in thirteen other books B. wrote as well as twenty-six written by others, chiefly Ruth Plumly Thompson and John R. Neill, after his death.

In the first story, the characters are presented as optimistic and forthright, searching for qualities they already have, evident during the incidents of their journey. Though not didactic, the SERIES champions the prevailing turn-of-the-century ideals of morality, rugged individuality, and isolationist, antiwar attitudes. His characters, in particular women, were strong and independent—very much in the spirit of the American frontier. Like Carl SANDBURG who was a contemporary of B.'s, his characters display humility, an aversion to an elite intellectual stance and a general sense of modesty. The same as most Americans of that era, B.'s characters held antimilitary views and supported rugged individual behaviors in a gently satiric setting. Similar to Sandburg, B. plays with language and enjoys telling puns, making his books as enjoyable to adults as they are to children. Overall, B.'s stories are best remembered for their fantastic incidents, unusual characters, and HUMOR.

Born and reared near Syracuse, New York, B. indulged in many hobbies, such as printing a monthly newspaper, stamp collecting, and poultry breeding. A heart condition restricted his activities, thus allowing his imagination to soar. As his father had obtained a fortune working in the Pennsylvania oil fields in the 1860s, he could financially support B.'s various interests. In 1880, B. became director of several small-town theaters owned by his father. *The Maid of Arran* (1881) was a successful play written to be performed in these theaters. In 1882, he met Maud Gage while on tour with this play and married her. His following plays were not as successful and finally, due to his father's death, his wife's illness, and misfortune with the family business, they decided to move to North Dakota near her family. His efforts at business there failed, and with four sons to support he moved to Chicago where he held various odd jobs before beginning a successful magazine, *The Show Window.*

After hearing B. tell stories to his son based on MOTHER GOOSE, his mother-in-law encouraged him to write the stories and submit them for publication. In 1897, his first children's book, *Mother Goose in Prose,* was published, and along with *Father Goose, His Book* (1899), identified B. as a successful writer for children. *The Wonderful Wizard of Oz* (1900), "the first distinctive attempt to construct a fairy land out of American materials" according to literary critic Edward Wagenknecht, enthralled readers and became a landmark in American literature. In 1902, B. adapted the book into a stage musical for Broadway. With many special effects and dazzling sets, it was a Broadway hit and was performed 293 times. Some changes were made in the plot to accommodate viewers' interests.

In 1904, B. again experienced financial problems and created a sequel to his first Oz book, *The Marvelous Land of Oz.* This sequel contained many theatrical elements in hopes it would be as successfully adapted to theater as his first Oz book. This led to several more books about Oz and although he attempted to end the series in 1910 with *The Emerald City of Oz,* bankruptcy required him to listen to the pleas of his readers and create even more stories of the famous land. He wrote about one Oz book a year from 1914 until his death in 1919. Other writers continued the series for some time after that.

Although B. had written other books for children, many under pen names such as Laura Bancroft, Floyd Akers, Edith Van Dyne, John Estes Cook, Suzanne Metcalf, Schuyler Stanton, and Captain Hugh Fitzgerald, none were as popular as the Oz series. The significance of B.'s work, however, was not fully recognized by critics and educators for several decades. Later critical attention, however, recognized that B., in Allen Eyles words, "was the most celebrated children's author of his time." Numerous adaptations for stage, screen, and text have been created, including the classic 1939 film version starring Judy Garland. The *Wiz* was a stage-musical version of the Wizard with an AFRICAN AMERICAN cast (also released as a film, in 1978), and *Journey Back to Oz* (1974) was an animated version. The characters from the initial tale have been immortalized as the 1939 classic movie is considered one of the most-viewed films ever made.

AWARDS: In 1968, B. received the Lewis CARROLL Shelf Award for *The Wizard of Oz*

FURTHER WORKS: *The Marvelous Land of Oz,* 1904; *Ozma of Oz,* 1907; *Dorothy and the Wizard in Oz,* 1985; *The Road to Oz,* 1909; *The Patchwork Girl of Oz,* 1913; *Tik-Tok of Oz,* 1914; *The Scarecrow of Oz,* 1915; *Rinkitink in Oz,* 1916; *The Lost Princess of Oz,* 1917; *The Tin Woodman of Oz,* 1918; *The Magic of Oz,* 1919; *Glinda of Oz,* 1981; *The Army Alphabet,* 1900; *American FAIRY TALES,* 1901; *Dot and Tot of Merryland,* 1901; *The Life and Adventures of Santa Claus,* 1902; (pseud. Suzanne Metcalf), *Annabel: A Novel for Young Folks,* 1906; (pseud. Captain Hugh Fitzgerald), *Sam Steele's Adventures on Land and Sea,* 1906; *The Sea Fairies,* 1911; (pseud. Floyd Akers), The Boy Fortune Hunters' series (1908–11); (pseud. Laura Bancroft), Twinkle Tales series (1906–11); (pseud. Edith Van Dyne); Aunt Jane's Nieces series (1906–15)

BIBLIOGRAPHY: Bingham, Jane M., ed., *Writers for Children,* 1988; *Children's Literature Review,* vol. 15, 1988; Eyles, Allen. *The World of Oz,* 1985; Wagenknecht, Edward, *Utopia Americana,* 1929

JANELLE B. MATHIS

BAWDEN, Nina (Mary Mabey)
Author, b. 19 January 1925, London, England

B. grew up in London with a younger brother. She began writing when she was young, completing a novel by the time she was eight years old. During World War II, B. and her brother were evacuated from London to safer areas out in the country. They spent time at a mining village in South Wales and later at a farm in Shropshire. B. enjoyed the farm, where she learned to drive a tractor and take care of farm animals as well as to organize a group of Italian prisoners of war who were sent to the farms to work. B.'s experiences later led to two popular novels. *Carrie's War,* told from the grown-up Carrie's point of view, is the story of a brother and sister who are

evacuated from war-torn London during World War II to live with a penny-pinching shopkeeper in Wales. *Peppermint Pig* also focuses on uprooted children. At age seventeen, B. returned to London to finish high school. She earned a Bachelor's degree in 1946 and a Master of Arts degree in 1951 from Somerville College, Oxford. Her areas of study included politics, economics, and philosophy.

B. had been publishing adult books for ten years before her first children's book was written. In response to her own children's request, B. attempted to write for children and received much pleasure from doing so. She published her first children's book with the title *The House of Secrets* (1964). B.'s books are directed toward mature readers; they often have realistic settings with everyday events in the plots.

Although B. writes for both adults and children, she admits she receives more pleasure from writing for children. B.'s work reveals her understanding of her child characters as well as her understanding of her child readers.

AWARDS: CARNEGIE Commendation (1973) and Phoenix Award (1993) for *Carrie's War;* Guardian Award (1976) for *The Peppermint Pig;* Parents' Choice (1982) and Edgar Allan Poe Award (1983) for *Kept in the Dark;* Parents' Choice (1987) for *The Finding* and (1992) for *Humbug;* Booker Prize nomination (1987) for *Circles of Deceit; Parenting*'s Reading Magic Award (1988) for *Henry*

FURTHER WORKS: *Runaway Summer,* 1969, *Squib,* 1971; *Witch's Daughter,* 1991; *Handful of Thieves,* 1991; *White Horse Gang,* 1992; *Real Plato Jones,* 1993; *The Outside Child,* 1994

JODI PILGRIM

BAYLOR, Byrd
Poet, author, b. 28 March 1924, San Antonio, Texas

B. spent her childhood in the Southwest as her father's work on ranches and in mines took the family to Arizona, Texas, and Mexico. She came to know and love the people, land, and animals of this area and developed a somewhat spiritual attitude toward nature and NATIVE AMERICAN culture. From her personal experiences with the Southwest environment, many themes emerged that became the focus of her writing. With lyrical language that comes from the heart, B. celebrates the natural world, spiritual connections to nature, and the people who once dwelled on this land as well as those who still do. She continues to live in a remote area in southern Arizona.

Growing up, B. became intrigued with the culture of the Native Americans who lived in the Southwest desert. As a result, several of her books share the stories she discovered behind petroglyphs. *Before You Came This Way* (1969) describes, through explanations of the various carved figures in rock, what life may have been like in prehistoric times. It also establishes a sense of place through rich descriptions as the author imagines what the canyons and the rugged land may have been like at that time. *When Clay Sings* (1972) continues this archeological insight by explaining the meaning of drawings on ancient pottery. In both, the artistic quality of B.'s language supports the significance of the ancient art she describes. *The Desert Is Theirs* (1975) continues this theme by addressing the relationship of the present desert dwellers with the land. Combining FOLKLORE and fact, B. uses graceful, simple phrases sensitively to describe the care and respect with which these Native Americans regard their land.

Spiritual connections to nature are evident in *Hawk, I'm Your Brother* (1976) in which a young boy attempts to learn to fly by capturing a young hawk. With underlying lessons in freedom, the boy is left with a spiritual bonding to the hawk, even though he cannot fly. *The Other Way to Listen* (1978) also pursues this theme as an older man shares with a young listener how to listen to the world around him. In *The Way to Start a Day* (1978), B. suggests that one begin a day by going outdoors and facing the sun with a gift or blessing as ancient people throughout the world have done. The delicately chosen text in each of these selections is enhanced by the art of Peter PARNALL. His elegant use of color and line established a winning artistic approach to B.'s books as together they have received the CALDECOTT MEDAL twice, as well as many local and state AWARDS.

While each of B.'s books celebrate the environment, certain ones have this as a central theme. *I'm In Charge of Celebrations* (1986) shares in a conversational, though rhythmic style

of poetic narrative, the author's reasons for celebration. The desert wildlife and natural phenomenon become sources for personal celebrations—a reminder to readers everywhere that true celebrations are from the heart and can be very individual in nature. The overall notion that each person can create his own celebrations is shared through the narrator's description of a sunrise, desert creatures, and seasonal changes. *The Table Where Rich People Sit* (1995) celebrates the richness of nature as it is bestowed upon the narrator. It is a source of wealth that belongs to anyone for merely the appreciation and respect they bestow. The main characters try to put a price on each aspect of nature that fills their lives with happiness and discover that they are millionaires. The value lesson within this book is well received with the natural dialogue and sincere attitude of the main character.

B. captures events of childhood from a child's perspective. *Amigo* (1963) tells in rhyming narrative POETRY the story of a young boy who desperately wants a dog. When he decides to adopt a prairie dog, readers discover the prairie dog is also planning to adopt him. *Everybody Needs a Rock* (1974) goes to great lengths to describe the attention needed in choosing a personal rock. *Your Own Best Secret Place* (1979) describes the many places that are special to people including the author's own secret place shared with an unknown inhabitant. She values these personal experiences and being in touch with self.

With words that only can come from one's own experiences with nature, B. shares with readers the joy she has found in the land where she lives. The songs of celebration within her many texts ask to be read aloud as readers of all ages are invited to remember their connections to the natural world.

AWARDS: Caldecott Medal Honor Book and AMERICAN LIBRARY ASSOCIATION Notable Book (1973) for *When Clay Sings;* Caldecott Medal Honor Book, *Boston Globe–Horn Book* Honor Book (1975) for *The Desert Is Theirs;* ALA Notable (1976) for *Everybody Needs a Rock;* Caldecott Medal Honor Book (1976) for *Hawk, I'm Your Brother;* 1979 Caldecott Honor Medal (1979) for *The Way to Start a Day*

FURTHER WORKS: *One Small Blue Bead,* 1965; *Coyote Cry,* 1972; ed., *And It Is Still That Way:*

Legends Told by Arizona Indian Children, 1976; *Your Own Best Secret Place,* 1979; *If You are a Hunter of Fossils,* 1980; *Desert Voices,* 1981

BIBLIOGRAPHY: Kiefer, Barbara, selector, *Getting to Know You: Profiles of Children's Authors Featured in Language Arts,* 1985–90, 1991; *Something About the Author,* vol. 69, 1994; *Children's Literature Review,* vol. 3, 1978

JANELLE B. MATHIS

BEATTY, John and Patricia

Authors. John: b. 24 January 1922, Portland, Oregon; d. 23 March 1975, California. Patricia: b. 26 August 1922, Portland, Oregon; d. 9 July 1991, Riverside, California

P.B. grew up on the northwest coast of the United States. Her father's career as a Coast Guard Commander led the family to many stations located on Indian Reservations. Experiencing NATIVE AMERICAN customs and history helped P.B. gain an interest and empathy that would later evolve in her writing. P.B. entered Reed College during World War II to become a high school teacher. There she met J.B., whom she married in 1950.

P.B. taught English and history in Idaho while J.B. developed a career as a history professor. In 1953 the couple settled in Riverside, California, where P.B. worked in a library and wrote her first book, *Indian Canoemaker* (1960). J.B. and P.B. coauthored their first novel, *At the Seven Stars* (1963), while the family lived in London. A pattern soon developed in which the B.'s published two books per year—one of English historical fiction written jointly and another on American historical themes written by P.B.—until J.B. died in 1975. P.B. continued her writing career.

The B.s' novels required much research. They effectively draw readers into the past. In 1988, Patricia established the John and Patricia Beatty Award through the California Library Association to encourage the writing of children's books about the culture and heritage of California.

AWARDS: *New York Times* One Hundred Outstanding Books for Young People (1963) for *At the Seven Stars.* Commonwealth Club of California Medal for best juvenile by a California author (1965) for *Campion Towers. Horn Book* honor list (1966) for *A Donkey for the King.* Southern California Council on Children's and Young People's Literature Medal (1967) for *The Royal Dirk.* P.B. earned several additional awards. California

Council Medal (1974) for "distinguished body of work" and (1976) for "comprehensive contribution of lasting value to the field of children's literature." Southern California Council on Children's and Young People's Literature Medal for distinguished fiction (1983) for *Jonathan down Under.* Western Writers of America Awards (1984) and (1987). Scott O'DELL award for Historical Fiction (1987) for *Charley Skedaddle*

FURTHER WORKS FOR CHILDREN: *At the Seven Stars,* 1963; *The Queen's Wizard,* 1967; *Witch Dog,* 1968; *Pirate Royal,* 1969; *King's Knight's Pawn,* 1971; *Holdfast,* 1972; *Red Rock over the River,* 1973; *Who Comes to King's Mountain?,* 1975; *By Crumbs, It's Mine!,* 1976; *I Want My Sunday, Stranger!,* 1977; *Wait for Me, Watch for Me, Eula Bee,* 1978; *Lacy Makes a Match,* 1979

BIBLIOGRAPHY: *Something about the Author,* vol. 6, 1974, and vol. 73, 1993

JODI PILGRIM

BEGAY, Shonto

Author, illustrator, b. 7 February 1954, Shonto, Arizona

B., author and illustrator of NATIVE AMERICAN poetry and FOLKLORE, was born into a large Navajo family. His father, a medicine man, and his mother, a rug weaver, along with his aunt and grandparents taught him to revere and love nature and understand that land is sacred. He liked to draw as a child, and among nature's many subjects one of his favorites was horses. The first book he illustrated, *The Mud Pony: A Traditional Skidi Pawnee Tale* (1988), reflects this early fascination. *Ma'ii and Cousin Horned Toad: A Traditional Navajo Story* (1992) came to life for B. when as a child he listened to his grandmother tell the story by firelight. B. has worked in a mixture of watercolor and colored pencils as well as acrylics. His art has been displayed in numerous exhibitions and museums. One especially significant book is *Navajo: Voices and Visions across the Mesa* (1995) in which he celebrates both nature and the everyday life of people he has observed. Eloquent poetic text supported by colorful, realistic ILLUSTRATIONS portrays B.'s personal visions of the Navajo struggles to live both in contemporary society and in the ancient world of cultural traditions with respect for the earth.

FURTHER WORKS: *Native People, Native Ways,* a series of four books written by White Deer of Autumn, 1994

BIBLIOGRAPHY: Giorgis, Cyndi and Janelle Mathis, "Visions and Voices of American Indians in Children's Literature, *New Advocate,* vol. 8, no. 2, 1995; *Seventh Book of Junior Authors and Illustrators,* 1996; Internet Public Library Youth Division; *Ask the Author,* 1997

JANELLE B. MATHIS

BEHN, Harry

Author, b. 24 (25 some sources) September 1898, Yavapai County, Arizona; d. 6 September (4 some sources) 1973, McCabe, Arizona

Although B. wrote many works for adult audiences and was well known for his contributions to the world of film, theater, and radio, he was also dedicated to composing POETRY and stories for children. Much of his work for children reflects his reverence for nature. B. wrote, "Children are accustomed to thinking about the beginnings of things, the creation of beauty, the understanding of plants and animals, of how alive stones and stars and wildflowers are, and how wonderfully different each is from the other." B.'s first book for children was *The Little Hill* (1949), a book of verse that received the Graphics Arts award for BOOK DESIGN. *Cricket Songs* (1964), one of his most popular books, contains haiku and appreciation of nature. After that, he wrote six more poetry books and translated two books of Japanese haiku. He also wrote novels for young readers.

FURTHER WORKS: *All Kinds of Time,* 1950; *Windy Morning,* 1953; *The House beyond the Meadow,* 1955; *The Wizard in the Well,* 1956; *The Two Uncles of Pablo,* 1959; *The Golden Hive,* 1966; *More Cricket Songs,* 1971; *Chrysalis: Concerning Children and Poetry,* 1968

BIBLIOGRAPHY: MEIGS, C., A. T. EATON, E. NESBIT, R. H. Viguers, *A Critical History of Children's Literature,* 1969; 1969; *Something about the Author,* vol. 2, 1971, and vol. 34, 1984

MARY ARIAIL BROUGHTON

BEIM, Jerrold and Lorraine Beim

Jerrold: Author, b. 1910, Newark, New Jersey; d. 2 March 1957; Lorraine: Author, b. 1909, Syracuse, New York; d. 15 June 1951

L.B., best known for her book on infantile paralysis (polio) based on her own rehabilitation from a horse riding accident (*Triumph Clear,* 1946),

began writing with J.B. soon after their marriage. The partnership that began with *The Burro That Had a Name* (1939) continued until L.B.'s death in 1951. Although J.B. and L.B. also wrote individually after their marriage, after L.B.'s death, J.B. began writing under the pseudonym Neil Anderson (*Freckle Face,* 1957).

FURTHER WORKS: *Andy and the School Bus.* 1947, J.B.; *Alice's Family.* 1948, L.B.; *The Little Igloo.* 1941, J.B. and L.B.; *The Shoeshine Boy* 1954, J.B.

REFERENCES: *Fiction, FOLKLORE, FANTASY and POETRY for Children, 1876–1985,* 1986 *Third Junior Book of Authors,* 1951

GWYNNE ELLEN ASH

BELLAIRS, John

Author, b. 17 January 1938, Marshall, Michigan; d. 8 March 1991, Haverhill, Massachusetts

MYSTERY writer B. was born and reared in Marshall, Michigan, a small town with many large, older homes that eventually provided the settings for the first of his three SERIES of mystery novels. B. was the son of a saloon owner and although the family's financial condition was unstable and caused ongoing concern, B. enjoyed a happy youth and was fond of his hometown. He received an A.B. from the University of Notre Dame in 1959 and an M.A. from the University of Chicago in 1960. Upon graduation, he taught English at the College of St. Teresa in Winona, Minnesota, and Shimer College in Mount Carol, Illinois. After traveling to England for six months, he returned to New England. B. continued teaching English at Emmanuel College in Boston and at Merrimack College in North Andover, Massachusetts. In 1980, he moved to Haverhill, Massachusetts, where he wrote full-time for the remainder of his life.

When the author died in 1991, he left behind two unfinished manuscripts and plot outlines for two more novels. B.'s son, Frank, asked Brad Strickland, a friend and fellow mystery writer, to complete the novels. B. completed fourteen mystery novels in his career. His early works were written for an adult audience, although some reviewers have suggested that the books, particularly *The Face in the Frost* (1969), inspired by J. R. R. TOLKIEN's *The Lord of the Rings,* might be more accurately classified for children. Like most of B.'s novels, *The Face in the Frost* combines horror with HUMOR in a FANTASY adventure in which good is pitted against evil. B. is often praised for the skillful way he used humor to brighten the tone of his thrillers. According to writer Brad Strickland, "I was completely swept away upon reading the first paragraph of *The Face in the Frost*, with its irresistible comic tone" (personal correspondence, 30 September 1999). All of B.'s books for children were written in series, and most of his books feature one or more youths coupled with an older character. The protagonists collaborate in fast-paced adventures, usually involving the supernatural and a struggle against the forces of evil. His writing has been praised for its seamless blending of the supernatural and the mundane. Classic horror elements such as ghosts, haunted houses, tombs, skulls, and sorcerers are skillfully paired with realistic, lovable, and amusing characters whose problems are familiar to adolescents.

In addition to pleasing a vast readership of children between the ages of nine and thirteen, B.'s stories have delighted critics. One critic, Marilyn Stasio, wrote, "I have just spent a long rainy weekend buried under a quilt, devouring salty peanuts and a stack of John Bellairs mysteries. It was heaven. Do I hafta get up from the couch and grow up?" B.'s first book was particularly well received. After reading *The House with the Clock in Its Walls,* a reviewer in *Publishers Weekly* wrote, "For devotees of the genre, here's the genuine article, a ghost story guaranteed to raise hackles. . . . B.'s story and Edward GOREY's pictures are satisfyingly frightening."

The author's first book for children, *The House with a Clock in Its Walls* (1973), received a *New York Times* outstanding book citation, and a Michigan Young Readers award nomination. This book was the first of a trilogy set in the town of New Zebedee, Michigan, the fictional counterpart of B.'s hometown of Marshall. Two other books by B. were set in New Zebedee, *The Figure in the Shadows* (1975) and *The Letter, the Witch, and the Ring* (1976). The last three books in the series, *The Ghost in the Mirror* (1993), *The Vengeance of the Witch-Finder* (1993), and *The Doom of the Haunted Opera* (1995), were started by B. and completed by Brad Strickland. A second series contains four books set in Hoosac, Minnesota, a fictional town inspired by Winona, Minnesota, where B. lived in the early 1960s. This series describes the ADVENTURES of Anthony Monday, a gangly youth, and his older librarian friend, Miss Eells. Books in the series include *The Treasure of Alpheus Winterborn* (1978), *The Dark Secret of Weatherend* (1984), *The Lamp from the Warlock's Tomb* (1988), and *The Mansion in the Mist* (1992). The third series, featuring young John Michael Dixon and the likable, eccentric Professor Childermass, is set in Duston Heights, Massachusetts. For the first book in the series, *The Curse of the Blue Figurine* (1983), B. received a Parents' Choice award as well as several child-selected AWARDS. The Duston Heights series contains eight books completed by B. and one book started by B. and completed by Brad Strickland. Five additional books, written entirely by Strickland, feature B.'s characters and settings.

FURTHER WORKS: Books set in Duston Heights, Massachusetts: *The Curse of the Blue Figurine,* 1983; *The Mummy, the Will, and the Crypt,* 1983; *The Spell of the Sorcerer's Skull,* 1984; *The Revenge of the Wizard's Ghost,* 1985; *The Eyes of the Killer Robot,* 1986; *The Trolley to Yesterday,* 1989; *The Chessmen of Doom,* 1989; *The Secret of the Underground Room,* 1990; *The Drum, the Doll, and the Zombie* 1994, completed by Brad Strickland

BIBLIOGRAPHY: *Children's Literature Review,* vol. 37, 1996; McElmeel, S., *100 Most Popular Children's Authors,* 1999; *Something about the Author,* vol. 68, 1992

MARY ARIAIL BROUGHTON

BELPRÉ, Pura
Author, b. 2 February 1903, Cidra, Puerto Rico; d. 1 July 1982, in the United States

B. and four siblings grew up in Puerto Rico listening to stories told by family members. These stories, handed down by word of mouth for generations, sparked her early interest in Puerto Rican FOLKLORE. B. excelled in school. She planned to attend the University of Puerto Rico to become a teacher. These plans changed, however, when her family traveled to New York in the 1920s for B.'s sister Elisa's wedding. B. stayed in New York City, as did many Puerto Ricans during this time period. Ernestine Rose, branch librarian of the East 135th Street branch of the New York Public Library noticed the influx of a Spanish-speaking community and realized the need for a bilingual assistant librarian. She offered Elisa a job but Elisa's husband refused to let her work. Elisa persuaded B. to apply for the position. B. then became the first Hispanic librarian in the New York Public Library system.

B. abhorred the absence of Puerto Rican folktales in the children's collection at the NYPL. She was determined to preserve the rich Puerto Rican folklore she heard as a child for the children of the continental United States. She wrote her first Puerto Rican tale when she enrolled in the Library School of the New York Public Library in 1925. B. shared her love of literature through STORYTELLING, puppet shows, and books. Her first book, *Perez and Martina: A Puerto Rican Folktale,* published in 1932, tells the well-loved traditional story B. remembered from her island childhood of the disastrous courtship of two insects. In 1940, B. presented a professional paper on library work with the Spanish speaking community; she became an influential leader in making folklore available to all children. Some of B.'s outstanding contributions to children's literature included library services outreach work on behalf of Puerto Rican, Spanish–speaking children. She was responsible for expanding Puerto Rican folklore programs, which involved storytelling and puppet theaters. B. wanted to be remembered as the Puerto Rican "Johnny Appleseed" in the United States. The AMERICAN LIBRARY ASSOCIATION established the Pura B. Children's Book Award (1996) to honor an author and illustrator of LATINA/O children's books that portray and affirm an authentic cultural experience in an outstanding work of literature.

AWARDS: Brooklyn Arts Book Citation (1973) *Santiago.* Insituto de Puerto Rico Citation, Bay Area Bilingual League, and the University of San Francisco (1978) honored her for her distinguished contribution in Spanish literature; Mayor's Award of Honor for Arts and Culture, and the Baricus College Professional Award.

FURTHER WORKS: *The Tiger and the Rabbit and Other Tales,* 1946; *Juan Bobo and the Queen's Necklace: A Puerto Rican Folk Tale,* 1962; *Dance of the Animals,* 1972; *Once in Puerto Rico* 1973; *The Rainbow-Colored Horse,* 1978

BIBLIOGRAPHY: *Latina and Latino Voices in Literature: For Children and Teenagers,* 1997; Hernandez-Delgado, Julio L., "Pura Teresa B.: Storyteller and Pioneer Puerto Rican Librarian," *Library Quarterly,* 1992; *Something about the Author,* vol. 30, 1982

JODI PILGRIM

BELTING, Natalia (Maree)
Author, b. 11 July 1915, Oskaloosa, Iowa

B. wrote her first book at the age of six. B. pursued a career writing historical fiction after receiving a bachelor's degree in journalism and her master's and doctoral degrees in history. Her first PICTURE BOOK, *Pierre of Kaskaskia* (1951), and her third book, *In Enemy Hands* (1953), were based on her research on NATIVE AMERICANS and French colonizers in Illinois. Her books *Indy and Mr. Lincoln* (1960), and *Verity Mullens and the Indian* (1960) were also based on similar historical events.

B. used an alternative approach to explain historical events, by reworking historical myths and folktales to make them appropriate for young readers. These collections of myths and folktales, such as *Elves and Ellefolk* (1961), and *The Sun is a Golden Earring* (1962), included myths and ancient folk sayings from around the world. They usually focused on a single theme such as little people, the sun, or other natural phenomena. *The Earth Is on a Fish's Back* (1965) is a collection of creation stories from Asia, the South Pacific, and the Americas.

AWARDS: ALA CALDECOTT MEDAL Honor Book and AMERICAN LIBRARY ASSOCIATION Notable book (1963) for *The Sun Is a Golden Earring*

BIBLIOGRAPHY: DE GRUMMOND REFERENCE COLLECTION; "Natalia Maree B. Papers," McCain Library and Archives, University Libraries, University of Southern Mississippi; http//avatar.lib.usm.edu/~degrum/findaids/belting.htm

DENISE P. BEASLEY

BELTON, Robyn
Illustrator, b. 23 June 1947, Wanganui, New Zealand

B. grew up knowing she could draw and that her family enjoyed her work. Her grandmother "saved the backs of letters for paper for her . . . to draw on." When she was twelve she went to boarding school in Wanganui and used a hard-cover book given her by her grandmother to draw everyone in the dormitory. After going to art school at the insistence of her secondary art school teacher, she knew she wanted to be an illustrator. Her first book, *The Duck in the Gun* (Joy COWLEY, author, 1985) received the NEW ZEALAND Library and Information Association's Russell Clark Award for distinguished ILLUSTRATION. The story of how Duck prevented a war by laying her eggs in the barrel of a huge gun is joyously portrayed in B.'s illustrations. *David's Dad* (1990) received the Choysa Illustrator's Award. *Bow down Shadrach,* with text by Joy Cowley, was named 1992 AIM Children's Book of the Year. *The Bantam and the Soldier* (Jennifer Beck, 1996), New Zealand Post Children's Book for the Year, was selected for the Bologna Book Fair; it presents images of traveling to war in a far-off land as part of the New Zealand experience.

B. uses pen and ink or pencil for outlines and does the pictures in watercolors. She generally works from the beginning of the book to the end, doing the cover and title page last. She was awarded the New Zealand Arts Council Grant in 1995. B. uses imagery from her own life in her books and adds secret messages and background clues for young readers trying to learn words. Her books reflect the quality books published in New Zealand today.

FURTHER WORKS: *Greedy Cat* (Joy Cowley, author), 1983

BIBLIOGRAPHY: Gaskin, C., ed., *PICTURE BOOK Magic,* 1996; New Zealand Book Council, Karen Ross, director, *School Library Journal,* June 1989

IRVYN G. GILBERTSON

BEMELMANS, Ludwig
Author and illustrator, b. 27 April 1898, Austrian Tyrol; d. 1 October 1962, Place unknown

B. was born the son of a Belgian painter, Lambert Bemelmans, and a Bavarian brewer's daughter, Frances Fisher. He arrived in the United States in 1914. Though his career reflected B.'s passion for life, spanning various media—the author of books for children and adults, magazine correspondent, screenwriter, painter, and restaurateur—he found his fame with the literary invention of a schoolgirl named Madeline. B.'s

Madeline series served as an outlet for his childlike ways and his love of painting, in addition to being an important revenue stream: "My greatest inspiration is a low bank balance," B. once admitted.

Born in the Austrian Tyrol, B.'s self-confessed arrested development established itself early. When his parents separated, B. was sent to live with his mother in Regensburg where he shortly flunked out of the city's schools. He was subsequently employed in various hotels owned by an uncle, and after wreaking havoc in all of them, was offered the choice between America and a correctional institution.

B. chose America and sailed into New York City at the age of 16. Eventually landing at the Ritz Hotel, B. found a place to provide him with an education he would have otherwise lacked. This "tankful of fish," as B. proclaimed it, supplied him with an incredible source of material. B. drew caricatures on order pads and menus and honed his ear for language and conversation.

In 1933, a fateful meeting changed the course of his career. May Massee, noted children's book editor at Viking Press, visited B.'s rented studio with a mutual friend. After seeing the murals he had painted to brighten his walls, she encouraged him to apply his skills to children's books. B.'s first book, *Hansi* (1934), was set in the Tyrolean landscape where he grew up, and was followed by three more books for Viking: *Golden Basket* (1936), *Castle* (1937), and *Quito Express* (1938).

B.'s first Madeline tale came out of a trip to Paris, where a bicycle accident landed B. in the hospital. Months later, on a menu in New York City's Pete's Tavern, he inscribed the words about a crack in the hospital ceiling which "had the habit of sometimes looking like a rabbit." Written in rhyming couplets that sing themselves right off the page, the Madeline adventures revolve around twelve identically shaped, blue-coated, yellow-hatted Parisian schoolgirls, their teacher Miss Clavel, and of course, Madeline. Precocious, principled and preternaturally bright, Madeline incorporates characteristics of B.'s daughter, wife, mother and the child he wished he could be. Madeline is ever the bravest and the most troublesome little girl in Paris, surviving tigers, a fall in the Seine, and Pepito, the Bad Hat. Thought by May Massee to be too sophisticated for children, *Madeline* was published in 1939 under the imprint of Simon and Schuster. A successful live-film version composite of the various Madeline stories was released in 1998. It is also a long-running animated television series.

B.'s work continues to attract audiences today. Anthony Mazzola, former art director for *Town and Country* where B. contributed stories, claims B.'s appeal stems from the fact that "he was basically a child. He looked like a cherub and thought in odd, childlike ways." This is especially evident in B.'s whimsical watercolor ILLUSTRATIONS. By addressing his work to children, B. found not only a wide, appreciative audience for his painting, but one that also allowed him his privacy.

B. took his inspiration from real life. The city scapes in *Madeline's Rescue* (1953) came from sketches made on-site in Paris during his brief stint as a bistro owner. And while the story concept came from neighborhood girls suggesting B. write about Madeline and a dog, B. has also said he was motivated by the sight of a long line of schoolgirls passing over the LePont Royal Bridge in Paris. Later, on a menu in the Restaurant Voltaire, B. sketched out the first lines of the story that would win him the CALDECOTT MEDAL in 1954. He turned to the familiar scene of his childhood with the 1954 publication of *The High World* set in the Austrian Alps.

B.'s free-spirited nature led him briefly to Hollywood, then on to living rent-free at the Carlyle Hotel while working on murals for the walls of the Bemelmans Bar. It was this easygoing disposition that also helped garner him acceptance into all classes of society. Not only was B. commissioned by Aristotle Onassis to paint children's rooms onboard his yacht, but just before B.'s death in 1962, he was collaborating with Jacqueline Kennedy on the idea of Madeline in Washington.

"I am conscious," B. wrote to May Massee in October 1960, "that in the matter of Madeline, we are working for all time." B.'s achievements have clearly shown that to be true.

AWARDS: NEWBERY MEDAL (1937) for *The Golden Basket.* Caldecott Medal (1939) for *Madeline.* Caldecott Medal (1954) for *Madeline's Rescue*

FURTHER WORKS: *Sunshine: A Story about the City of New York,* 1950; *Madeline and the Bad Hat,* 1956; *Madeline and the Gypsies,* 1959; *Madeline in London,* 1961; *Marina* 1962; *Madeline's Christmas* (1985, originally published in *McCall's* magazine in 1956); *Madeline in America and Other Holiday Tales* (1999, published posthumously)

BIBLIOGRAPHY: Ferris, Helen, ed., *Young Wings,* 1952; Collins, Amy Fine, "Madeline's Papa." *Vanity Fair,* July 1998, pp. 118–30; Hunt, Peter, ed., 1995 *Children's Literature: An Illustrated History,* 1995; Silvey, Anita, ed., *Children's Books and Their Creators,* 1995

MARGUERITE ELLINGER

BENARY-ISBERT, Margot
Author, b. 2 December 1889, Saarbruken, Germany, d. 27 May 1979, Santa Barbara, California

B. was born and reared in Germany. In 1917, she married Wilheim Benary and the couple moved to his family home in Erfurt where they raised Great Dane dogs, and she wrote short stories and poems for periodicals. The outbreak of World War II and the Russian occupation of Germany forced B. and her family to flee their home in Erfurt and to settle in West Germany where she began writing books for children. Her experiences during the war served as inspiration for her novels, including *The Ark* (1953), *Castle on the Border* (1965), and *Under a Changing Moon* (1964). Her books are set primarily in postwar Germany and depict the physical and psychological hardships of the Germans after the war. B.'s novels serve as a testament to the strength and will of people, especially children, to overcome impossible odds and to rebuild their lives. Her work is known for her realistic characters who show courage and sympathy in the midst of war-ravaged surroundings.

FURTHER WORKS: *Rowan Farm,* 1954; *A Time to Love,* 1962; *The Wicked Enchantment,* 1955; *Blue Mystery,* 1957

MARY ARIAIL BROUGHTON

BENCHLEY, Nathaniel (Goddard)
Author, b. 13 November 1915, Newton, Massachusetts; d. 14 December 1981, Boston, Massachusetts

B. was the son of comic essayist Robert Benchley. His work includes adult novels, children's books, and many contributions to newspapers and periodicals. His writing career resulted in over fifteen adult novels and screenplays and almost two dozen children's books. B.'s children's books contain HUMOR, which he believed to be an important ingredient. Other necessary elements of children's books, according to B., include not talking down to children and suspense.

FURTHER WORKS: *The Benchley Roundup: The Best of Benchley,* (ed.), 1954; *Robert Benchley: A Biography,* 1955; *Red Fox and His Canoe,* 1964; *The Strange Disappearance of Arthur Cluck,* 1967; *Snip. George, the Drummer Boy,* 1977; *Sam the Minuteman,* 1969; *A Ghost Named Fred,* 1968; *Several Tricks of Edgar Dolphin,* 1970; *Small Wolf,* 1972

BIBLIOGRAPHY: *Something about the Author,* vol. 25, 1981, and vol. 28, 1982

JODI PILGRIM

BERENSTAIN, Stanley and Janice

Author and illustrator team, Stanley. b. 29 September 1923, Philadelphia, Pennsylvania, Janice. b. 26 July 1923, Philadelphia, Pennsylvania

Married and always working as a team, the B.s began as cartoonists and creators of greeting cards, calendars, and advertisements. J. and S. met at Philadelphia College of Art and eventually married and worked together as artists while raising two sons. Parenthood and the belief that their own children as well as others needed more humorous books led to their interest in writing books for young children. Coupled with this motivation and encouragement from Theodore Geisel (Dr. SEUSS), the B.s channeled their talents into children's books through the characters of the Berenstain Bears. Their first Beginner Book was *The Big Honey Hunt* (1962). In 1974, the B.s began a SERIES of First Time Books with *The Berenstain Bears' New Baby.* This series depicts a nuclear family and is intended to help children identify with their first-time experiences such as a new baby, going to school, and riding a bicycle. Many books in this series are based on the B.s' own reactions to situations they were encountering. With approximately 200 books in print, the B.s have created numerous series including: Beginner Books; First Time Books, Bright and Early, Family Time Storybooks, Mini-Storybooks, Play Along, Bear Scout, Comic Tale Easy Readers, Young Readers, Big Chapter Books, and

Bilingual Picture Books. In addition, the B.s developed television specials, books on video, and other media. Substantial sales continue to show their popularity. The appeal of humorous situations, the humanlike family of bears, and the craft of rhyming verse as read-alouds provide easy entertainment and have led to a second generation of loyal readers.

AWARDS: INTERNATIONAL READING ASSOCIATION's Children's Choices of 1981 for *The Berenstain Bears and the Missing Dinosaur Bone,* 1982 for *The Berenstain Bears Go to the Doctor* and *The Berenstain Bears Visit the Dentist*

FURTHER WORKS (SELECT): *The Bike Lesson,* 1964; *Inside, Outside, Upside Down,* 1968; *Bears in the Night,* 1971; *The Berenstain Bears and the Spooky Old Tree,* 1978; *The Berenstain Bears Go to School,* 1978; *The Berenstain Bears' Christmas Tree,* 1980; *The Berenstain Bears and the Truth,* 1983; *The Berenstain Bears Learn about Strangers,* 1985; *The Berenstain Bears and the Bermuda Triangle,* 1997 (Syracuse University houses a collection of B. manuscripts)

BIBLIOGRAPHY: Berg, Julie. *A Tribute to The Young at Hearts: The B.s,* 1993

NANCY HORTON

BERGER, Melvin

Author, b. 23 August 1927, Brooklyn, New York

B., author of nonfiction for children, was born and reared in Brooklyn. From an early age, B.'s interests included reading, writing, music, and science, all of which would later influence his work. B. was already writing short stories when he entered high school. After graduating from high school in 1944, B. entered college as an electrical-engineering student. In addition, he took viola lessons and practiced with an orchestra. Although B. did not continue after a year in college, he accepted a position with the New Orleans Philharmonic. He later returned to school at the Eastman School of Music and at Columbia University for a master's degree in music education. While teaching music in Plainview, Long Island, he learned of a strong effort to publish science books for children and YOUNG ADULTS. B.'s first attempt at writing children's books resulted in a work called *Science and Music* (1965), which explains music in scientific terms. His interest in writing developed and he became a specialist in juvenile nonfiction. His early work encompassed science, scientific processes, and music. In the 1970s, B.'s work centered on fundamental science such as *The New Water Book* (1973) and *The New Air Book* (1979). After retiring from teaching in 1979, he expanded his book topics to include subjects such as MYSTERY and SPORTS. Later he and his wife co-authored the Discovery Readers series for children. He developed another SERIES that describes behind-the-scenes views of where and how scientists work in laboratories.

B. has written over two hundred titles for children and young adults. A specialist in the field of nonfiction, B. has often been admired for his effective use of concrete examples and details that enable him to simplify his subjects without trivializing them.

AWARDS: Outstanding Science Trade Books for Children Citations, National Science Teachers Association/ CHILDREN'S BOOK COUNCIL for *Computers* (1973); *The New Water Book* (1978); *Disease Detectives* (1979); *The Stereo Hi-Fi Handbook* (1979); and *Sports Medicine* (1982). Notable Trade Book in the Field of Social Studies Citations for *Consumer Protection Labs* (1975) and *The Story of Folk Music* (1976); Library of Congress Best Children's Books Citation (1964–1978) for *Quasars, Pulsars, and Black Holes in Space*

FURTHER WORKS: *Triumphs of Modern Science,* 1964. *Famous Men of Modern Science, Biography,* 1968; *Atoms,* 1968; *The Violin Book,* 1972; *Why I Cough, Sneeze, Shiver, Hiccup, and Yawn,* 1983; *Whole World in Your Hands: Looking at Maps,* 1993; *Where Did Your Family Come From?,* 1993; *Where Are the Stars during the Day?,* 1993; *Round and Round the Money Goes,* 1993; *How's the Weather?,* 1993; *Oil Spill,* 1994; *Germs Make Me Sick!,* 1995

BIBLIOGRAPHY: *Something about the Author,* vol. 88, 1997

JODI PILGRIM

BERRY, James
Poet, author, b. Date unknown 1925, Jamaica

Born and reared in Jamaica, B. grew up in an impoverished community. B. inherited a rich background in a CARIBBEAN culture that he later shares through his writing. It was not until after B. moved to England in 1948 that he began to write stories depicting life in the West Indies. He published his first work for children, *A Thief in*

the Village and Other Stories, in 1987. These stories consisted of tales set in a rural Jamaican seaside village. B. uses authentic voices in his writing. He values the authentic voice of Caribbeans because language, including dialect and traditional STORYTELLING, plays a central role in the preservation of Caribbean culture. *When I Dance: Poems* (1988) expresses Caribbean life through varying points of view.

B. is recognized as among the first authors to introduce West Indian folktales and realistic stories of Caribbean life to British and American children. He has earned respect as a writer whose works address universal themes while reflecting the native Caribbean heritage.

AWARDS: Grand Prix Smarties Prize (1987) and CORETTA SCOTT KING AWARDS Honor Book (1988) for *A Thief in the Village and Other Stories;* the *Signal* POETRY Award in (1989) for *When I Dance; Boston Globe–Horn Book* Award (1993) for *Ajeemah and His Son*

FURTHER WORKS: *Fractured Circles,* 1979; *The Girls and Yanga Marshall,* 1987; *Spiderman-Anancy,* 1989; *Ajeemeh and His Son,* 1992

BIBLIOGRAPHY: Kirkpatrick, D. L., ed., *Twentieth Century Children's Writers* 1978; Senick, G., ed. *Children's Literature Review,* vol. 22, 1991; *Something about the Author,* vol. 67, 1992

JODI PILGRIM

BESKOW, Elsa Maartman
Author, illustrator, b. 11 February 1874, Stockholm, Sweden; d. 1953, Place unknown

B. wrote and illustrated over thirty books while a drawing instructor at the Anna Whitlock School in Sweden. During her fifty-year career, she received international recognition for simple, cheerful stories and outstanding ILLUSTRATIONS. Her work combined realism and FANTASY in both her stories and pictures, which depicted a happy home atmosphere in the Swedish countryside of the late nineteenth and early twentieth centuries. B. painted scenes in soft-hued watercolors. *Pelle's New Suit* (1930) tells how Pelle grows large while his clothes grow smaller. To help get himself a new suit of clothes Pelle shears the lamb, cooperates to card the wool, spin, and dye it until finally a new suit is woven and tailored for him. At the end, a happy Pelle is shown wearing his new suit thanking the sheep. B.'s books are classics of Swedish literature; they also have a following around the world, appealing to readers looking for children's stories set in an earlier, more traditional time. Many have been translated into English and continue to be available in the United States.

AWARDS: Swedish Library Association (1952) Nils Holgersson Plaque

FURTHER WORKS: *Olle's Ski Trip,* 1928; *Buddy's Adventures in the Blueberry Patch,* 1931

BIBLIOGRAPHY: Arbuthnot, May Hill, *Children and Books,* 1947; *Children's Literature Review,* vol. 17, 1989; *Contemporary Authors Online,* 1999

SUSAN SWORDS STEFFEN

BETTELHEIM, Bruno

Psychologist, theorist, b. 28 August 1903, Vienna, Austria; d. 13 March 1990, Silver Springs, Maryland

Coming of age in Nazi-occupied Austria was difficult for young Jewish psychologist B., as it was for his much-older idol, Sigmund Freud. Freud fled Austria before being imprisoned in a concentration camp, but B. spent time in both Dachau and Buchenwald; it influenced his later writings, his view of the developing psychology of children and adolescents, and subsequently, his recommendations for the use of FAIRY TALES for children and adolescents.

Born in Vienna, B. grew up in the shadow of Freud, even walking out of his way to go by his house. After undergoing psychoanalysis and receiving a Ph.D. in Psychology from the University of Vienna in 1938, B. hoped to become a leader in the field of Freudian psychoanalysis. When Austria became a part of the Third Reich in 1938, he was arrested and sent to Dachau and later to Buchenwald. Using his psychological observations as a way to distance himself from the horrors of the camps, B. tried to remember everything he learned about the effects of terror and dehumanization on the psyche.

When released in 1939, B. immigrated to the United States where he became a research associate in Chicago, Illinois. Later working as a professor at several universities including the University of Chicago, B. published his research based on his experiences in the camps. "Individ-

ual and Mass Behavior in Extreme Situations" described the experiences in concentration camps that remained unknown until 1945, following the liberation of the camps. This piece and his later writings on his World War II experiences, *The Informed Heart* (1960) and *Surviving, and Other Essays* (1979), explore his theory that psychological strength was more essential than physical strength in surviving the ravages of the concentration camps.

Expanding on this theory, B. created a concept of child development that focused on the total environment of children, rather than just their experience at school. In *Love Is Not Enough: The Treatment of Emotionally Disturbed Children* (1950) and *The Empty Fortress: Infantile Autism and the Birth of the Self* (1967), B. explored his Orthogenic School's attempts to influence the education and therapy of children.

The Uses of Enchantment: The Meaning and Importance of Fairy Tales (1976) and *On Learning to Read: The Child's Fascination with Meaning* (1982) brought Freudian theory to children's literature studies. B. called for reading material that stimulated children, particularly a renewed use of fairy and folk tales in the classroom. B. argued that these ancient tales of the struggle between good and evil created a catharsis for children through which they could control their own fears and fantasies. *The Uses of Enchantment* won both the National Book Award and the National Book Critics Circle Award in 1977, firmly creating a place for B. in the history of children's literature criticism. B. established a strong base for choosing stories that are worth the effort of reading.

BIBLIOGRAPHY: Sutton, N., *B.: A Life and a Legacy,* 1996

GWYNNE ELLEN ASH

BIAL, Raymond

Author, photographer, educator, b. 5 November 1948, Danville, Illinois

B. has published more than thirty INFORMATIONAL BOOKS of photographs for children and adults. As a writer and photographer, B. often features rural and small-town subjects. His photoessays appeal to a wide range of readers, including young children, middle readers, and adults.

His nonfiction book, *Corn Belt Harvest* (1991), was selected as Outstanding Science Trade Book for Children, (1991). B is a full-time library director at Parkland College in Champaign, Illinois.

FURTHER WORKS: *Amish Home,* 1993; *Frontier Home,* 1993; *Shaker Home,* 1994; *The Underground Railroad,* 1995; *Portrait of a Farm Family,* 1995; *With Needle and Thread: A Book About Quilts,* 1996; *Mist over the Mountains: Appalachia and Its People,* 1997; *The Strength of These Arms: Life in the Slave Quarters,* 1997; *First Frost* (Kathryn Kerr), 1997

BIBLIOGRAPHY: *Something about the Author,* vol. 76, 1994

MARY ARIAIL BROUGHTON

BIANCO, Margery Williams
Author, translator; b. 22 July 1881, London, England; d. 4 September 1944, New York City

B. was the daughter of a classical scholar who believed that a child should learn to read and education should take place at home until around the age of ten. Therefore, she attended school only a few years. B. read much from her father's library, however, and wrote a novel at seventeen that was published a few years later in England. Books continued to be an important part of her life after she married Francesco Bianco, a dealer in rare books. Living in London, New York, Paris, and Italy, B. continued writing books for adults until her first children's book, *The Velveteen Rabbit; or, How Toys Became Real* (1922) was published. The source of this story was in her own lovingly remembered toys as well as those of her two children. This was the first of many occasions for her to share her own memories, keen insights into writing for children, and her understanding of animals. Her philosophy of the significance of a child's imagination as the child learns about the world around him is reflected in many of her books.

AWARDS: ALA NEWBERY MEDAL Honor book (1937) for *Winterbound*

FURTHER WORKS: *The Little Wooden Doll,* 1925; *The House That Grew Smaller,* 1931; *More about Animals,* 1934; *Other People's Houses,* 1939

BIBLIOGRAPHY: *Junior Book of Authors,* 2nd ed. 1951; Moore, Anne C. and Bertha M. Miller, eds., *Writing and Criticism: A Book for Margery B.,* 1951

JANELLE B. MATHIS

THE BIBLE IN CHILDREN'S LITERATURE

The Bible was the first book printed on Gutenberg's printing press in 1454. Since then, the Bible has been translated into every known language and reprinted more often than any other book. The Bible's rich and diverse literary features appeal to many because it includes MYTHS, LEGENDS, fables, parables, short stories, essays, lyrics, epistles, sermons, orations, proverbs, history, BIOGRAPHY, prophecy, and DRAMA. Since the Bible has been retold more than any other book, it has influenced authors and illustrators of children's literature for centuries. Many children's literary works are written with the assumption that children will already have some knowledge of Biblical history, characters, parables, incidents, poems, and proverbs and can, therefore, better understand the literary work.

The Bible not only offers its contents as food for children's literature but has traditionally been, and still is, used to teach children and adults how to read and write. Lois LOWRY, winner of the NEWBERY MEDAL for *Number the Stars* (1990) and *The Giver* (1994), admits that she learned to read from memorizing Bible verses. Many of Lowry's books, such as *Number the Stars* and *Autumn Street* (1980) bring together both Old and New Testament teachings. In *Number the Stars,* Lowry writes about Protestants smuggling Jews out of Denmark to safety during World War II (1939–45). In *Autumn Street,* a young Pennsylvania girl's father is a medical doctor serving in Europe during World War II.

The Bible as literature is a universal common denominator for people around the world, having earned a rightful position in children's literature regardless of religious affiliation. In a purely secular setting, the Bible is acknowledged as a great work of literature rather than a way of indoctrinating a viewpoint.

The Bible's influence in children's literature can be illustrated in at least four distinct settings: (1) exact Biblical reprints and retellings; (2) Biblical quotes and references used in a story; (3) fictitious stories that are based on or relate to some aspect of the Bible; and (4) the Bible based holidays and other special events.

Exact Biblical reprints and retellings as children's literature in collections or arrangements is the earliest representation in children's literature. Although there have been Biblical stories handed down to children through various retellings for generations, the period of the 1920s to the 1960s has seen the launching of the most publications of "arrangements" of the Bible, specifically the King James version. A need for a readable and more child-friendly version of the Bible prompted this trend in children's literature. These retellings of the Bible, often based on the King James version, have been produced more by illustrators than by writers or theologians. The author's intent is to choose and rearrange sections without altering the actual text; it is accomplished by omitting superfluous passages to that a seamless whole, suitable for children, is created. For example, Helen SEWELL illustrated a selection of stories from the King James text, *A First Bible* (1934). Other examples include *The Little Children's Bible* (1924), *The Older Children's Bible* (1927), edited by Canon Alexander Nairne, Sir Arthur QUILLER-COUCH, and T. R. Glover. Walter DE LA MARE's *Stories from the Bible* (1929) is a collection in which the author transforms the Bible into a more modern comprehensible TRANSLATION while maintaining a Biblical narrative style.

The Bible has also been reviewed in children's literature from social viewpoints. For example, *Miriam's Well: Stories about Women in The Bible* (1989) by Alice Bach and J. Cheryl Exum focuses on the role of women in the Old Testament. Leo and Diane DILLON enrich this collection with stunning illustrations. Present collections of legends and stories of the Bible feature more and more women. In *Be Not Far from Me: The Oldest Love Story* (1998) Eric KIMMEL tells the story of Deborah.

Biblical quotes are sometimes used as part of the text in stories for children. The Bible appears in children's literature when it is quoted in another body of work. As early as 1691 the *New England Primers* were published for use in teaching children to read. They contain Bible-based poetical lines such as: *In Adam's fall / We sinned all. / Thy life to mend / God's Book attend.* Along with this rhyming alphabet, *New England Primers* contained prayers, poems, and verses from the Bible including the Ten Commandments. They

also contained certain spiritually significant historic accounts such as that of Queen Mary's having Mr. John Rogers, minister of the gospel in London, his wife, and their nine children burned at the stake.

Until the 1800s, books produced by the printing press were primarily Bibles and other religious books. Book making and printing was slow and costly. The "good godly" Puritan books continued to fill the minds of children until the nineteenth century with few exceptions.

The Bible's influence permeates children's literature in more subtle but literal ways such as in *Sign of the Beaver* (1983) by Elizabeth George SPEARE. In this NEWBERY MEDAL Honor book set during the 1700s, a young boy named Matt uses the Biblical story about Noah and the flood to teach a NATIVE AMERICAN boy, Attean, to read. After Matt reads the story aloud, Attean explains a similar Native American flood story.

Biblical fictitious tangent stories are on the rise. Authors of these stories merge Biblical heroes, heroines, events, and holidays found in the Bible creatively with fiction. The mix of fiction and actual Bible text varies. Some of these stories do not stray as far from the Bible as others.

Noah has been a popular character to write about in fiction and nonfiction. Peter SPIER's *Noah's Ark,* winner of the 1978 CALDECOTT MEDAL, depicts the flood and all the animals with water color ILLUSTRATIONS. On the other hand Patricia Lee GAUCH's *Noah* (1994) transforms this Bible story into a song. These two examples of Noah stories do not move as far from the actual Bible story as does *Noah's Trees* (1999) by French-born Bijou Le Tord. In this story Le Tord describes Noah's life prior to the flood as a man who had a close relationship with nature and trees. In this story, Noah plants several saplings that he will ultimately save by bringing them aboard the ark.

Imagination links fiction and the Bible in *The Tale of Three Trees: A Traditional Folktale* (1989) retold by Angela E. Hunt. This tale is told from the point of view of three trees and their important destinies when cut down: one became a cradle, the second a ship, and the third a cross. All three items played important roles in the life of Jesus. *The Last Straw* (1998), by Fredrick Thury, is a story told from the point of view of a camel,

Hoshmakaka, whose job was to collect items and carry them to a baby in a manger.

The *Dreamer* (Cynthia RYLANT, 1993), *What a Truly Cool World* (Julius LESTER and Joe Cepeda, 1999) and *You Are Special* (Max Lucado, 1997) are good examples of how God has been portrayed in varying ways in children's literature. In *The Dreamer,* God is depicted as an artist explaining the creation story. While in *What a Truly Cool World,* told in a black story-telling voice, God is shown to be busy making improvements in the world that he created through his wife (Irene God), his secretary (Bruce), and an angel (Shaniqua). *You Are Special* (1997) contains another portrayal of God, this time as a woodcarver lovingly instructing his creations, the Wemmicks, that each one is special just the way he is.

Fiction affects collections of Biblical Children's literature as well as single stories. One example is Rabbi Marc Gellman's *Does God Have a Big Toe?* In this collection Gellman uses the long-held Jewish tradition of telling midrashim, stories about stories in the Bible using HUMOR to involve the reader. Another midrashic telling is Eric A. KIMMEL's *Be Not Far from Me, The Oldest Love Story: Legends from The Bible* (1998), which pulls together the past, present, and future, using Old Testament Biblical heros such as David, Samson, and Deborah. The bold illustrations by David DIAZ offer contrasting colors and shapes that move the reader's eye deeper into the text.

A classic popular series that merges Bible with fantasy to produce a story is C. S. LEWIS's seven-volume work, *The Chronicles of Narnia,* starting with *The Lion, The Witch, and The Wardrobe* (1951). *The Bronze Bow,* by Elizabeth SPEARE, a 1962 NEWBERY MEDAL recipient is based on a Bible verse alluding to a bow that no man can bend with his personal strength but only through divine intervention. *A Fine White Dust* by Cynthia Rylant, a 1987 Newbery Medal Honor recipient, is a fictional account of a young man's experiences with God and the influence of a preacher. Another book, appealing primarily to young girls, is *Are You There God? It's Me, Margaret* by Judy BLUME, depicts an eleven-year-old's daily one-on-one discussions with God and commitment to God's recommendations.

Bible-based themes in children's literature such as holidays and special days include books about Biblically related holidays, special days, and fictitious stories that are extensions of the Bible. There are numerous books about Christmas, Easter, Hanukkah, and other holidays less well-known in the U.S. such as Ramadan. Madeleine L'ENGLE's *The Glorious Impossible* (1990) portrays the miraculous and tragic life of Jesus through dramatic narrative, illustrated by twenty-four paintings from the fourteenth century Italian artist Giotto.

A less dramatic holiday book is *The Legend of the Poinsettia* (1994) by Tomie DEPAOLA, revealing the story behind the poinsettia during Christmas. Walter Wangerin Jr.'s *Mary's First Christmas* unveils the story of Jesus through the eyes of his mother, Mary. A Russian version of Christmas is found in MIKOLAYCAK's *Babushka.* Other stories that include a Christmas theme are *One Wintry Night* (1994) by Ruth Graham Bell, *The Not-So-Wise Man: A Christmas Story* (1999), by Alan McDonald, and *The Christmas Miracle of Jonathan Toomey* (1995) by Susan Wojciechowski.

Hanukkah is celebrated with Karla KUSKIN's *A Great Miracle: A Chanukah Story* (1993), Ruth Heller's *A Picture Book of Hanukkah,* and *Hershel and the Hannukkah Goblins* by Eric Kimmel, a 1990 Caldecott Medal Honor Book. Another book that honors a special day in many religious circles is Maxine Rose Schur's *Day of Delight: A Jewish Sabbath in Ethiopia* (1994). A story that celebrates two December holidays is *Elijah's Angel: A Story for Chanukah and Christmas* (1992) by Michael ROSEN. Eric Kimmel's *Bar Mitzvah: A Jewish Boy's Coming of Age* (1995) celebrates and supports the special day in a young Jewish boy's life.

Other holidays are celebrated in lavishly illustrated PICTURE BOOKS such as Suhaib Ghazi's *Ramadan* (1996). Readers are treated to a month-long family celebration of evening feasts and daily prayers in a mosque while Islamic traditions and customs are explained. In Madhur Jaffray's *Seasons of Splendor: Tales, Myths and Legends of India* (1985) with illustrations by Michael FOREMAN in traditional images and colors of India, the religious significance of Indian festivals and celebrations is related and explained.

The Bible's influence has not been overlooked in poetry. *Poems and Prayers for the Very Young* (1973), selected and illustrated by Martha ALEXANDER, contains poems by famous authors such as "Father, We Thank Thee" by Ralph Waldo Emerson and "Clouds" by Christina G. ROSSETTI. A contemporary collection of poetry is *Absolutely Angels: Poems for Children and Other Believers* (1998) selected by Mary Lou Carney and lovingly illustrated by Viqui Maggio. An exact passage from the Bible is used as children's POETRY in *The Shepard's Son: The Twenty-Third Psalm* (1993), illustrated by Julia Miner. According to *Booklist*'s Spotlight on Religion: Books for Youth one of the top ten favorite religious books purchased is *To Every Thing There Is a Season: Verses from Ecclesiastes* by Leo and Diane DILLON.

BIBLIOGRAPHY: *Booklist,* Spotlight on Religion, October 1999; Cullinan, B. and L. Galda, *Literature and the Child,* 1976; MEIGS, C., E. NESBITT, A. T. EATON and R. H. Viguers, *Children's Literature in the Elementary School,* 1969 *A History of Children's Literature*

DEBORAH A. WOOTEN

BIERHORST, John
Folklorist, b. 2 September 1936, Boston, Massachusetts

B. writes books that focus on the customs, traditions, and stories that NATIVE AMERICANS have passed on for centuries. B.'s first book of Indian tales, *The Fire Plume: Legends of the American Indians* (1979), consisted of seven legends gathered from the husband of a Chippewa. B. eventually became a specialist in the language of the Aztecs. He began work with the Aztec language when he and his wife toured the Museum of Anthropology in Mexico City. An Aztec poem caught B.'s attention. B. traced the source of the poem, and upon finding the manuscript, began translating his first book of Aztec verse. He also published two translated PICTURE BOOKS called *Spirit Child: A Story of the Nativity from the Aztec* (1984) and *Doctor Coyote: A Native American Aesop's "Fables"* (1987). Through the years, B. has chosen a variety of Native American cultures to translate. He has concentrated on the native peoples of South America and produced *Black Rainbow: Legends of the Incas* and *Myths of Ancient Peru* (1976). He extended his research by editing three volumes of myths from Indians in North, South, and Central America. This produced *The Mythology of North America* (1985), *The Mythology of South America* (1988), and *The Mythology of Mexico and Central America* (1990), which include photos, maps, and Indian drawings. B. also studied the Native Americans near his own area to develop *The White Deer and Other Stories Told by the Lenape* (1995). A specialist in the language of Aztecs, B. sees himself not as an author, but primarily as a translator, specializing in the native literature of the Americas.

AWARDS: State Historical Society of Wisconsin Book Award (1975) for *Songs of the Chippewa;* Center for Inter–American Relations Grant (1972) and (1979); National Endowment for the Humanities Grant (1979) and (1986); May Hill Arbuthnot Honor Lecturer, Association for Library Service to Children, AMERICAN LIBRARY ASSOCIATION (1988); American Library Association Notable Book Citations (1971) for *In the Trail of the Wind: American Indian Poems and Ritual Oration;* (1976) for *Black Rainbow: Legends of the Incas and Myths of Ancient Peru;* (1978) for *The Girl Who Married a Ghost: Tales from the North American Indians;* (1979) for *A Cry from the Earth: Music of the North American Indians;* (1982) for *The Whistling Skeleton: American Indian Tales of the Supernatural;* (1983) for *The Sacred Path: Spells, Prayers, and Power Songs of the American Indians;* (1984) for *Spirit Child: A Story of the Nativity;* and (1987) for *The Naked Bear: Folktales of the Iroquois;* the Southwest Book Award (1987) for *Doctor Coyote: A Native American Aesop's Fables*

FURTHER WORKS: *Monkey's Haircut and other Stories Told by the Maya,* 1987; *A Cry from the Earth,* 1992; *Lightning inside You and Other Native American Riddles,* 1992; *The Woman Who Fell From the Sky: The Iroquois Story of Creation,* 1993

BIBLIOGRAPHY: *Something about the Author,* vol. 91, 1997

JODI PILGRIM

BIESTY, Stephen
Illustrator, b. Date unknown, England

Trained as an illustrator, B. has worked full-time illustrating INFORMATIONAL BOOKS for adults and children since 1985. His specialty is drawing historical and architectural ILLUSTRATIONS. His most well-known book, published in 1992, *Ste-*

phen Biesty's Incredible Cross-Sections (Richard Platt, author) features minutely detailed and labeled cut-away illustrations of many diverse structures, from a medieval castle to the Space Shuttle, in a large-format volume ideal for browsing. In *Castle* (1994), life in a medieval castle under siege is visualized in precise cross-section details while readers are given an interactive opportunity to follow along and identify details presented in the text. With texts written by Richard Platt, B. has successfully used this format for several volumes attractive to children and adults. He currently lives in an old converted village hall in Somerset, England.

FURTHER WORKS: *Man-of-War,* 1993; *Incredible Explosions,* 1996; *Incredible Everything,* 1997

BIBLIOGRAPHY: Publisher's biographical information

DIANE G. PERSON

BINCH, Caroline
Illustrator, b. 5 June 1947, Manchester, England

B. remembers being good at drawing and not particularly interested in other academics as she made her way through school. Her interest and talent in drawing eventually helped her in her career as a successful photographer and illustrator. Her work as an illustrator came with the critical success of Mary HOFFMAN's *Amazing Grace* (1991). Her interest in drawing black people stems from her fascination with their culture, which she sees as being much more interesting than her own English working-class background. Although she had illustrated other children's works before *Amazing Grace,* it was that story that earned her a KATE GREENAWAY MEDAL nomination and accolades on both sides of the Atlantic. B. is the illustrator of *Hue Boy* (Rita Mitchell, author), the 1993 Smarties Prize winner in the five years and under category.

FURTHER WORKS: Illustrator: *Billy the Great,* 1992; *Hue Boy,* 1993; *Boundless Grace,* 1995; *Down by the River,* 1996; *Since Dad Left,* 1998; *Starring Grace,* 2000

MICHAEL O'LAUGHLIN

BIOGRAPHY

Biographies and autobiographies, the stories of people's lives, have been a part of children's literature since its beginnings. Earliest collections of biographies instructed children in the right way to behave by describing exemplary lives of heroic individuals. John Foxe's *Book of Martyrs,* translated into English in 1563, was assigned reading for both English and American children for many years thereafter. These grim stories of the uplifting lives of saints, and their torture and death at the hands of their persecutors, were intended to inspire children to live saintly lives. Plutarch's *Lives of the Noble Grecians and Romans,* translated into English for young people by Sir Thomas North in 1579, provided secular role models. Parson Weems's 1808 biography, *The Life of George Washington; With Curious Anecdotes Equally Honorable to Himself and Exemplary to His Young Countrymen,* published nine years after the first president's death, was intended to provide children with a uniquely American role model.

Until well into the 1960s, biographies for children presented great historical figures as people without flaws. These books generally included narration that turned these lives into uplifting stories, providing descriptions of dress, meals, and conversations that may have occurred but are not actually documented. Early winners of the NEWBERY and CALDECOTT MEDALS reflect these tendencies to idealize and fictionalize aspects of their subjects' lives, including Cornelia MEIGS's *Invincible Louisa* (1934) about Louisa May ALCOTT, James H. DAUGHERTY's *Daniel Boone* (1940), and Ingri and Edgar Parin D'AULAIRE's *Abraham Lincoln* (1940).

By the 1970s, biographies for young people began to change. While heroic figures from our past are still very much the subject of contemporary biography, the portraits of these figures are more rounded and honest. Russell FREEDMAN's *Lincoln: A Photobiography* (1987) shows Lincoln's political savvy, the assaults on his decisions by the press, and the pain and stress of his family tragedies alongside the larger tragedy of the Civil War. This portrait of Lincoln, while honest, does not diminish him; Lincoln becomes more heroic because he is more human. Jean FRITZ challenges preconceived notions about heroic figures of the past in books such as her humorous portrait of an American character in *Why Don't You Get a Horse, Sam Adams?* (1982) and her serious consideration of a legendary figure in *The Double Life of Pocahontas* (1983). Using a comfortable style that includes details of life in a given period, she frankly discusses what is actually known about their lives and what is merely legend. F. N. MONJO's brief biographies of Jefferson, Franklin, Lincoln, Teddy Roosevelt, and Mozart, each told from the perspective of a child, also humanize these figures by describing not only their heroic actions, but also the quirks of their personalities and their occasional failures. Like Monjo, authors such as Eloise GREENFIELD with *Mary McLeod Bethune* (1977) began writing brief, illustrated biographies also referred to as STORYOGRAPHIES, suitable for younger readers.

Picture book biographies, in which illustrations coupled with brief text enhance children's understanding of different times and places, have become increasingly popular. Alice and Martin PROVENSEN's Caldecott Medal–winning *The Glorious Flight across the Channel with Louis Bleriot, July 25, 1909* (1983), perfectly captures in pictures and amusing text Papa Bleriot's indomitable spirit in spite of many failed flights. Diane STANLEY and Peter VENNEMA have introduced young readers to other international figures including *Shaka, King of the Zulus* (1988), *Peter the Great* (1988), *The Last Princess: The Story of Princess Ka'iulani Of Hawai'i* (1991), and *Cleopatra* (1994).

Other PICTURE BOOKS highlight the childhood of an interesting figure, including Alan Schroeder's *Ragtime Tumpie* (1989), the story of Josephine Baker's childhood love of dancing, and Barbara COONEY's *Eleanor* (1996), depicting the lonely childhood of Eleanor Roosevelt. Still others build pictures around a significant incident from the subject's life, such as Robert D. SAN SOUCI's *Kate Shelley: Bound for Legend* (1995), the true story of a fifteen-year-old heroine who ran through a terrible storm to stop a train before it crossed a washed-out bridge.

Along with changes in attitudes toward heroes in biographies, books are now written about people whose lives are less well known. These include stories of heroic women such as Deborah Sampson, in Ann MCGOVERN's *The Secret Soldier* (1987), who fought as a soldier in the American Revolution. Heroic children have also made their way into print. The best known among these,

Anne Frank's *The Diary of a Young Girl* (1960), has been followed more recently by *Zlata's Diary: A Child's Life in Sarajevo* (Filipovic, 1994), another powerful portrait of a child living through terrible circumstances.

Biographical coverage of people of diverse ethnic and racial backgrounds has increased, although some of these groups and individuals are better represented than others. Picture-book biographies such as Andrea Davis PINKNEY's *Dear Benjamin Banneker* (1994) and Mary Sciosa's *Bicycle Rider* (1983) capture individual AFRICAN AMERICAN contributions to American culture. Collective biographies such as Russell Freedman's *Indian Chiefs* (1987) and Virginia HAMILTON's *Many Thousand Gone: African-Americans from Slavery to Freedom* (1993) expose young people to different voices from the American past. Diane HOYT-GOLDSMITH's biographies featuring photographs that show contemporary children as they play, work, and participate in cultural events include *Hoang Anh: A Vietnamese-American Boy* (1992) and *Pueblo Storyteller* (1991).

Because biographical coverage has expanded, the tone of these books has changed. Biographies are now more apt to deal with hardships faced by victims of racism. Yoshiko UCHIDA's autobiography *The Invisible Thread* (1991), and Michael O. Tunnell and George W. Chilcoat's *The Children of Topaz* (1996) illustrate this in their portraits of life in the Japanese-American internment camps during World War II. The hardships of poverty are revealed in Jerry Stanley's *Children of the Dustbowl* (1992), a story of discrimination against Okies moving to California during the Depression, and in the contemporary collection, *Voices from the Fields: Children of Migrant Farmers Tell Their Stories* (Atkin, 1993). Illness and death are discussed frankly in Jill KREMENTZ's *How It Feels to Fight for Your Life* (1989), a collection of interviews with critically ill young people.

Biographies of authors and illustrators have increased, perhaps as a result of growing interest in the writing process. Bill PEET's cartoon-filled *Bill Peet: An Autobiography* (1989), Sid FLEISCHMAN's magical *The Abracadabra Kid* (1996), and Betsy BYARS's humorous *The Moon and I* (1991), provide autobiographical insight into the lives, inspirations, and writing processes of well-loved authors. Richard C. Owens's Meet the Author series provides author biographies for middle to late elementary school readers of Jane YOLEN, Cynthia RYLANT, and Lee Bennett HOPKINS among others. Picture-book biographies provide glimpses into creative lives. William Miller's *Zora Neale Hurston and the Chinaberry Tree* (1994) shows Hurston's early fascination with the stories and songs of African American people and Trina Schart HYMAN's *Self-Portrait: Trina Hyman* (1989) shows how family, friends, and personal experiences have influenced her art.

Perhaps the most dramatic change in biography for young people has been in style. Dry, instructive volumes have been replaced with lively narrative and eloquent artwork. Diary and journal entries, letters and other documents, samples of handwriting and personal notes, humorous anecdotes and poetry increase interest in the people about whom these stories are told. Joan BLOS's *The Heroine of the Titanic: A Tale both True and Otherwise of the Life of Molly Brown* (1991) and Myra Cohn LIVINGSTON's *Let Freedom Ring: The Ballad of Martin Luther King* (1992) are written as poetry. Claudia Lewis's *Long Ago in Oregon* (1987) and *Up in the Mountains* (1991) reminisce through poetry about her childhood in Oregon at the time of World War I, while the poems in the collection *In Daddy's Arms I Am Tall: African American Poems Celebrating Fathers,* compiled by Javaka Steptoe (1997), describe the fathers of each of the poets. Biographies have greatly changed since they were seen as uplifting lives for young readers to try to emulate. They now provide more honest portraits of flawed but heroic people, lives of people of color, of women, and children, and of everyday heroes who have lived exemplary lives in spite of difficult circumstances. Contemporary biography attempts to reveal something not only about the life of an individual but also about what it means to be human.

BARBARA CHATTON

BISHOP, Claire Huchet

Storyteller, librarian, author, b. ca. 1899 Brittany, France; d. 11 March 1993, Paris, France

Early in her career, B. was a storyteller in France. She was instrumental in opening France's first children's library, L'Heure Joyeuse, in 1924 and later served as librarian in the New York Public Library. She traveled extensively in the United States as a lecturer and storyteller. Her STORYTELLING led to her career as a children's author, beginning with the TRANSLATION of her story "The Five Chinese Brothers," which she wrote down and published in 1938.

AWARDS: NEWBERY MEDAL Honor Book (1948) for *Pancakes-Paris;* Newbery Medal Honor Book (1954) for *All Alone;* Child Study Bank Street College Children's Book Award (1952) for *Twenty and Ten*

FURTHER WORKS: *French Children's Books for English-Speaking Children,* 1938; *The King's Day,* 1940; *The Man Who Lost His Head,* 1942, 1970; *Augustus,* 1945; *Christopher the Giant,* 1950; *All Alone,* 1953, 1992; *Yeshu, Called Jesus,* 1966; *Mozart: Music Magician,* 1968

BIBLIOGRAPHY: Silvey, A., ed., *Children's Books and Their Creators,* 1995

MARY A. BROUGHTON

BLAKE, Quentin (Saxby)

Author, illustrator, b. 16 December 1932, Sidcup, Kent, England

B. grew up in a middle-class family with little encouragement for his artistic bent until he was at Chiselhurst Grammar School where he met a cartoonist for *Punch.* His first published drawings were in *Punch* and he soon adopted an uninhibited cartoon style as his hallmark. B. studied English at Cambridge and very nearly became a teacher before turning to his heart's desire and becoming a freelance artist. B. continued his artistic studies at Chelsea College of Art, and for many years taught at the Royal College of Art, eventually becoming head of the ILLUSTRATION Department. B. was named Great Britain's first-ever children's laureate (1999), in a two-year appointment designed to draw attention to the world of children's books.

Not content with political satire, B. began seeking other outlets, including illustrating books for other writers, such as Jules VERNE, J. B. S. Haldane, Aristophanes, Lewis CARROLL, Rudyard KIPLING, Hilaire Belloc, and Charles DICKENS. However, his lively line drawings are perfectly suited for children's books and he has illustrated numerous books for Joan AIKEN, Russell HOBAN, and Michael ROSEN, but is perhaps most famous as the illustrator of the works of Roald DAHL, including *The BFG* (1982), *The Witches* (1983), *Matilda* (1988), and the reissued *James and the Giant Peach* (1995).

Early on B. also began writing and illustrating his own children's books. *Patrick,* his first children's book, appeared in 1968. The most famous of his own books is *Mister Magnolia* (1980), which won the KATE GREENAWAY MEDAL. In this nonsense poem about a man with only one shoe, B. manages to extend a sense of the preposterous situation through comical illustrations. The poignancy of *The Story of Dancing Frog* (1984) reveals B.'s keen sensitivity, mingling HUMOR with sadness.

B.'s line illustrations are light, fluid and filled with color, giving them a spritely vitality that is unmistakable. While his illustrations appear to be scribbled lines done in haste, they are carefully thought out images that convey the personalities of the stories' characters and humorously exaggerate facial expressions and inner thoughts. Their casual appearance belies their skillful artistry.

AWARDS: Hans Christian ANDERSEN Award for Illustration (1976). Kate Greenaway Medal for *Mister Magnolia* (1981). Officer of the Order of the British Empire (1988). University of Southern Mississippi Medallion, DE GRUMMOND REFERENCE COLLECTION (1993). First Children's Laureate of Great Britain (1999)

FURTHER WORKS: *The Enormous Crocodile,* 1978, 1993; *Great Piratical Rumbustification and the Librarian and the Robbers,* 1978, 1986; *Magic Finger,* 1995; *McBroom's Wonderful One-Acre Farm: Three Tall Tales,* 1992; *Old Mother Hubbard's Dog Dresses Up,* 1989, 1990; *Zagazoo,* 1999

BIBLIOGRAPHY: *The Oxford Companion to Children's Literature,* 1984; "A Man for All Children," *School Library Journal,* July 1999; *Something about the Author,* vol. 96, 1998

DAVID L. RUSSELL

BLEGVAD, Erik
Illustrator, b. 3 March 1923, Copenhagen, Denmark

B. studied at the School of Arts and Crafts in Copenhagen and then worked at an advertising agency. He has illustrated nearly one hundred books by different authors covering a variety of subjects. He has also illustrated books written by his wife, Lenore. Together they designed a series of nursery rhymes including *Mittens for Kittens* (1974) and *This Little Pig-a-Wig* (1978). In 1978, the *New York Times* chose *This Little Pig-a-Wig: And Other Rhymes about Pigs,* selected by B.'s wife and illustrated by B., as one of its Best Illustrated Children's Books of the Year. B. prefers pen-and-ink drawings and feels that the picture should complement the text.

FURTHER WORKS: *Bedknobs and Broomsticks.* (Mary NORTON, author). 1957. *The Gammage Cup.* (Carol KENDALL, author). 1959. *Mr. Jensen and the Cat.* 1965. *The Tenth Good Thing about Barney.* (Judith VIORST, author). 1971. *The Narrow Passage.* 1973. *Polly's Tiger.* 1974. *May I Visit.* 1976. *Mushroom Center Disaster.* 1974. *The Winter Bear.* 1974. *Self-Portrait: Erik Blegvad.* 1978. *Anna Banana and Me.* 1985

JODI PILGRIM

BLISHEN, Edward
Author, critic, b. 29 April 1920, Whetshone, Middlesex, England; d. 13 December 1996, United Kingdom

Noted for his books of autobiographical fiction, B. kept a diary from the age of fourteen. He used facts from his diary writing and converted them into fiction by renaming his children, his wife, and the town where he lived. Comparing it to a kaleidoscope, he shook up the information and looked at the patterns that came forth. His first book, *Roaring Boys,* was published in 1955. Among other books he published are *This Soft Lot* (1969), *The School That I'd Like* (1969), *Sorry, Dad* (1978), an autobiography, and *The Penny World* (1990). B. won the British Library Association's CARNEGIE MEDAL in 1970 for *The God beneath the Sea* written with Leon GARFIELD, a dramatic retelling from ancient MYTHOLOGY. He received The Society of Authors traveling scholarship in 1979 and the J. R. Ackerly Prize for autobiography in 1981. B. compiled the *Treasury of Stories for Seven Year Olds* (1988) and *The Kingfisher Treasury of Stories for Children* (1992) with his wife Nancy. He was made a Society of Literature Fellow in 1989.

Of his writing B. said, "In the end, I love work with words—jeweller's work—and also the toil of making books—laborer's work."

FURTHER WORKS: *The Golden Shadow* (with Leon Garfield). 1973; *The Oxford Book of POETRY for Children*, ed., 1973

BIBLIOGRAPHY: *Literature Resource Center,* The Gale Group, 1999: http: /www.galenet.com/servlet/ LitRC; *Something about the Author,* vol. 93, 1997

IRVYN G. GILBERTSON

BLOCK, Francesca Lia
Author, b. 3 December 1962, Hollywood, California

Reared in Hollywood, B. was exposed to art and creativity at an early age. Her father was an artist and her mother wrote poetry. B. recalls literature as always being an important part of her life. B. was immersed in books and remembers her mother recording her stories before she herself could write. B. always wanted to be a writer. Growing up in Hollywood, B. frequented the street scene, observing punk costumes and people on the Sunset Strip. One person in a punk costume sparked an idea for her first book, *Weetzie Bat* (1989). B. describes the person as "a punk princess with spiky bleached hair, a pink 1950s prom dress, and cowboy boots." Later, B. discovered a name for the character when she noticed a pink Pinto with a "punk" driver and a license plate reading "Weetzie." B. considered the idea of a character named Weetzie for approximately six years before she put her thoughts into a novel. She worked on the novel while attending college in Berkeley, California. After graduation, B. moved to Los Angeles, took a job in a gallery, and wrote. Four sequels followed *Weetzie Bat,* a book that proved to be popular with YOUNG ADULTS.

Many of B.'s novels take place in big city settings and involve young adult issues such as self-identity, sex, drugs, and rock and roll music. The story of *Weetzie Bat* is set in Los Angeles while *Missing Angel Juan* (1993) takes place in New York City. Each of her stories focuses on a different character growing up in a problematic world. Love and art play a role in what some consider modern FAIRY TALES. According to B., all her work has some relationship to her own personal life.

AWARDS: Shrout Fiction Award, University of California (1986) Emily Chamberlain Cook

POETRY Award (1986); AMERICAN LIBRARY ASSOCIATION Best Books of the Year, *Booklist* Best Books of the 1980s, YASD Best Book Award, and Recommended Books for Reluctant Young Adult Readers (1989) for *Weetzie Bat;* Books for Reluctant Young Adult Readers (1990) for *Witch Baby;* ALA Best Books of the Year Citation, Recommended Books for Reluctant Young Adult Readers, the *New York Times* Best Books, and *Publishers Weekly* Best Fifty Books (1991) for *Cherokee Bat and the Goat Guys; School Library Journal* Best Books of the Year, ALA Recommended Books for Reluctant Young Adult Readers (1993) for *Missing Angel Juan;* ALA Gay, Lesbian, and Bisexual Book Award, ALA Best Books for Young Adults (1996) for *Baby Be-Bop*

FURTHER WORKS: *The Hanged Man,* 1994; *Baby Be-Bop,* 1995; *Girl Goddess #9,* 1997

BIBLIOGRAPHY: *Something about the Author,* vol. 80, 1995

JODI PILGRIM

BLOOM, Lloyd
Illustrator, b. 10 January 1947, New York City

B. grew up in New York City but spent childhood summers in the country. He played in the woods and took walks with his father who taught him the names of the plants and wildlife they saw there. B. began drawing early in life but studied English literature in college. He graduated from Hunter College in 1972, and went on to earn a master's degree in fine arts from Indiana University, Bloomington, in 1975.

B. brings his knowledge and understanding of nature's changing appearances, and also of Jewish life, to bear in much of his ILLUSTRATION work. B. communicates his understanding of the stories he illustrates for Lillie Chaffin (*We Be Warm Till Springtime Comes* [1980]), Mavis JUKES (*Like Jake and Me* [1984]), Patricia MACLACHLAN (*Arthur for the Very First Time* [1987]), Sue ALEXANDER (*Nadia the Willful* [1983]), Dennis Haseley (*Ghost Catcher* [1991]), David ADLER (*One Yellow Daffodil* [1995]), and many other storytellers whose picture-book texts are rooted in specific aspects of American culture or world history. B. sometimes uses soft black and white to create complex and detailed scenes of rituals or woodlands. Other stories inspire his employment of a full-spectrum palette to present life on a Western ranch, in an urban apartment, or as mural-like interpretations of the story. B.'s use of pastels as paint is a unique technique for illustration.

AWARDS: In graduate school, B. earned a Fulbright Scholarship in painting. *Grey Cloud* (1979) was cited by the Friends of American Writers as winner of the Juvenile Merit Award in 1980. *Arthur for the Very First Time* won a 1980 Golden Kite Award from the Society of Children's Book Writers, and appeared on ALA's Notable Books list that year. *Like Jake and Me* (1984) and *A Man Named Thoreau* (1985) were also ALA Notable Books. *Like Jake and Me* by Mavis Jukes was named a NEWBERY MEDAL Honor Book and a *Boston Globe–Horn Book* Honor Book for Illustration, both in 1985. *Poems for Jewish Holidays* by Myra Cohn LIVINGSTON (1986) won the 1987 National Jewish Book Award for Illustration

FURTHER WORKS: ILLUSTRATOR: *Wilkin's Ghost,* 1978; *A Dog's Life: Stories of Champions, Hunters, and Faithful Friends,* 1978; *The Green Book* (Jill PATON WALSH), 1982; *No One Is Going to Nashville* (Mavis Jukes), 1983; *A Man Named Thoreau,* 1985; *Miriam's Tambourine,* 1986; *Yonder* (Tony JOHNSTON), 1988; *Hear O Israel: A Story of the Warsaw Ghetto* (Terry W. Treseder), 1990

BIBLIOGRAPHY: Silvey, Anita, ed., *Children's Books and Their Creators,* 1995; *Sixth Book of Junior Authors and Illustrators,* 1989

FRANCISCA GOLDSMITH

BLOS, Joan Windsor
Author, b. 9 December 1928, New York City

B. was born and reared in New York City in a family of educators; she attended Vassar College and received a master's degree from The City College of New York. She studied physiology, psychoanalytic theory, and children's literature, and combined what she learned about children with her love of books and language, and began to write children's books. She has authored several popular PICTURE BOOKS, including *Old Henry* (1987) the story of an elderly man whose neighbors complain about his rundown property until they drive him away. Her novel, *A Gathering of Days: A New England Girl's Journal, 1830–32* (1979) about a girl growing up in New Hampshire during the nineteenth century, won the 1980 NEWBERY MEDAL. In the book, fourteen-year-old Catherine Hall records the daily events of her life on her family farm in New Hampshire, relating

how she copes with her father's remarriage and the death of her best friend. B. has an international reputation.

AWARDS: Newbery Medal (1980) for *A Gathering of Days: A New England Girl's Journal, 1830–1832.* Society of Midland Authors Award (1992) for *The Heroine of the Titanic: A Tale Both True and Otherwise of the Life of Molly Brown* (1991)

FURTHER WORKS: *Brothers of the Heart: A Story of the Old Northwest 1837–1838,* 1985; *The Grandpa Days,* 1989; *Littie's Circus,* 1989; *Brooklyn Doesn't Rhyme,* 1994; *The Days before Now,* 1994; *Nellie Bly's Monkey: His Remarkable Story in His Own Words,* 1996

BIBLIOGRAPHY: "Joan B., Author," online: http: freenet.buffalo.edu/~acsd/windermere/wbslib/jb/, accessed October 10, 1998; Silvey, Anita, ed., *Children's Books and Their Creators,* 1995; *Something about the Author,* vol. 74, 1992

MARY ARIAIL BROUGHTON

BLUMBERG, Rhoda
Author, b. 14 December 1917, New York City

Author of nonfiction books for young people on a variety of topics ranging from "fun facts" to inventors and explorers, B.'s work reflects her love of history. Often writing from the feminist standpoint as in *Bloomers!* (1993), B. has an incredible ability to make readers think. She never accepts pat answers and often raises a "What if?" concept throughout her work. *Commodore Perry in the Land of the Shogun* (1985), an example of a story in which her obvious love of history pours forth from the pages, was an ALA NEWBERY MEDAL Honor Book in 1986. *The Great American Gold Rush* (1989) provides a realistic picture of the hoards who rushed to the California goldfields from 1848 to 1852 to seek their fortune. Her work is characterized by intense scholarly research and the ability to capture the human beings behind the well-known events.

AWARDS: AMERICAN LIBRARY ASSOCIATION Newbery Medal Honor Book (1986), *Boston Globe–Horn Book* Award for Nonfiction (1985), Golden Kite Award for Nonfiction (1985) for *Commodore Perry in the Land of the Shogun.* The John and Patricia BEATTY Award (1989) for *The Great American Gold Rush*

FURTHER WORKS: *The First Travel Guide to the Moon,* 1980; *The Incredible Journey of Lewis and Clark,* 1987; *The Great American Gold Rush,*

1989; *What's the Deal?: Jefferson, Napoleon, and the Louisiana Purchase,* ed., 1998; *The Remarkable Voyages of Captain Cook,* 1991

BIBLIOGRAPHY: *Sixth Book of Junior Authors,* 1989; *Something about the Author,* vol. 70, 1993

KAY E. VANDERGRIFT AND JODI PILGRIM

BLUME, Judy

Author, b. 12 February 1938, Elizabeth, New Jersey

B. is one of the most well known and controversial authors of children's literature. Children have reached toward her novels to help uncover the difficulties of growing up, while educators and parents have often shied away from them. B.'s novels are controversial because they deal with topics that are difficult for many adults to speak about among themselves, let alone with their children. Her books treat topics of concern for young readers, such as: menstruation (*Are You There God?: It's Me, Margaret,* 1970), nocturnal emissions (*Then Again, Maybe I Won't,* 1971), sibling rivalry (*Tales of a Fourth Grade Nothing,* 1972, *Superfudge,* 1980), divorce (*It's Not the End of the World,* 1972, *Just as Long as We're Together,* 1987), DEATH (*Tiger Eyes,* 1981), friendship (*Here's to You Rachael Robinson,* 1993, *Just as Long as We're Together,* 1987), and moving (*Then Again, Maybe I Won't,* 1971, *Starring Sally J. Freedman as Herself,* 1977). The topics lead to criticism, which stems from a feeling that children do not need to be exposed to these issues through literature. But actually, the blunt attack against these sensitive issues enhances B.'s popularity with readers. Through her novels, the readers learn that they are not alone. Her topics, although controversial, are ones that children discuss among themselves. B. is an active member of the Coalition Against CENSORSHIP.

B.'s novels deal effectively with issues that interest young readers. Through the use of the first person narrator B. initiates an intimate relationship with her protagonist and allows the reader to make a new friend. Her novels are realistic; they read like a child's diary. Her syntax is colloquial, which makes her novels accessible. She presents conversations that readers can envision having or overhearing in the lunchroom.

Realism is the key to B.'s popularity. As in a child's life, the problems are not always solved in B.'s novels. The protagonist learns to understand and cope with the issue at hand. The characters learn how to use their strengths to overcome or deal with adversity. B. leaves her readers predicting and thinking about what the characters will do next. For example, in *Tiger Eyes* (1981), Davey's family decides to return to New Jersey to deal with the death of her father. The reader is left wondering how the family will cope with life once they return home. Questions about life and where it will take the reader are an important part of B.'s novels. She does not present characters that know all the answers; her protagonist must sort through feelings of frustration. They are presented as survivors of real situations.

Some critics have called B.'s novels simplistic but readers say that this is not the case. B.'s novels present issues at the child's level of understanding. As adults we see the difficult issue of divorce as multifaceted. In *It's Not the End of the World* (1972) and *Just as Long as We're Together* (1987) the characters deal with their parents' divorce from a personal perspective. Adults see this as limited, but it represents the view of the child. The popularity of B.'s books is evidence that children do not see her novels as simplistic, but as realistic.

B.'s novels are set in suburban, middle-class neighborhoods. She develops her setting from places that she has lived and experienced. She uses her experiences to help her add realism to her novels. Her novels are universal in the sense that children everywhere deal with tough issues and can relate to the characters. Although setting is an important element, it only helps to create a general background. Most of B.'s novels could occur anywhere.

A common theme in several of B.'s novels is that of moving. The child's lack of control over this traumatic change is key in how they deal with the dilemma. In *Iggie's House* (1970), Winnie's best friend and neighbor moves; the new family becomes central to the entire story. In *Are You There God?: It's Me, Margaret* (1970), Margaret has moved to New Jersey and some of her concerns deal with fitting in and finding new friends. *Then Again, Maybe I Won't* (1971) presents Tony dealing with the stress of changing neighborhoods and social class. B. herself experienced a move to Florida for a year that is portrayed in *Starring Sally J. Freedman as Herself* (1977); it is a time of learning and adapting. As a way of dealing with the death of her father, Davey's family in *Tiger Eyes* (1981) moves from New Jersey to New Mexico. In *Otherwise Known as Sheila the Great* (1972), Sheila has to deal with living at camp for the summer. *Superfudge* has the Hatcher family dealing with a move to support Mr. Hatcher's career. Addressing the unsettling factors children must deal with when they move helps readers to connect to the characters in B.'s novels.

B.'s novels deal with sensitive issues. She chooses to write about these issues; despite having a positive relationship with her family, she could not talk about her concerns. As a child, she loved to read and make up stories inside her head while she was practicing piano, bouncing a ball, or playing with paper dolls. B. started writing when her children were in preschool. She would mentally create stories while washing dishes. These first stories were never accepted for publication. She later returned to her alma mater, New York University, where she took a graduate course on writing children's literature. It was through this class that B.'s success as a writer took off. Her first novel, *The One in the Middle Is the Green Kangaroo* (1969), and *Iggie's House* (1970) were both written through her experience in the writing class. These novels, like all of B.'s novels, have protagonists who are trying to discover their place in the world. B. uses her novels to help give her readers a vehicle to express their concerns.

B.'s novels have been called simplistic as well as profane. Regardless, her popularity with readers contradicts the critics. Children love and understand B.

AWARDS: *New York Times* Best Books (1970) for *Are You There, God?: It's Me, Margaret.* Young Readers Choice Award (1975), West AUSTRALIAN Young Readers' Book Award (1980), United States Army in Europe Kinderbuch Award (1981) for *Tales of a Fourth Grade Nothing.* Numerous awards chosen by children. AMERICAN LIBRARY ASSOCIATION Margaret A. Edwards Award for body of work (1995). Recipient of Carl SANDBURG Freedom to Read Award (1984) Civil Liberties Award, Atlanta American Civil Liberties Union, and John Rock Award (1986) South Australian Youth Media Award for Best Author (1998)

FURTHER WORKS: *Freckle Juice,* 1971; *Deenie,* 1973; *Blubber,* 1974; *The Pain and the Great One,* 1984; *Fudge-a-Mania,* 1990; *The Judy B. Diary,* 1981; *Letters to Judy: What Your Kids Wish They Could Tell You,* 1986; *The Judy B. Memory Book,* 1988; *Places I Never Meant to Be: Stories by Censored Authors,* 2000

BIBLIOGRAPHY: *Contemporary Authors, New Revision Series,* vol. 66, pp. 57–62; *Contemporary Literary Criticism,* vol. 12, pp. 44–48; vol. 30, pp. 20–25; Lee, Betsy, *Judy B.'s Story,* 1981; *Something about the Author* vol. 79, 1992; *Biography Today,* pp. 22–27; Weidt, M. N., *Presenting Judy B.,* 1990

NANCE S. WILSON

BLYTON, Enid

Author, b. 11 August 1897, East Dulwich, London, England; d. 28 November 1968, Hampstead, London, England

One of the most prolific and influential children's book authors in the twentieth century, B. wrote some six hundred books; new editions of her work continue to be produced in Britian and in numerous foreign-language editions throughout the world. The eldest child of a middle-class family, B. was reared in Beckenham, Kent, where as a teen she first developed her interest in becoming a writer. Trained as a teacher, B. taught for a year at the Bickley Park School in Kent, followed by a four-year period as a nursery governess for a family in Surbiton, before devoting herself full-time to writing.

In 1917–18, B. published poems in *Nash's* magazine and contributed as well to several literary and educational journals before publishing "Peronel and His Pot of Glue" (1922) in the weekly *Teachers' World,* which initiated her career as a children's author. Her first book for children, *Child Whispers* (1922), was followed by *Real Fairies: Poems* (1923), both illustrated by Phyllis Chase. At this same time, B. began writing a weekly periodical column for *Teachers' World,* which, in addition to her numerous creative and editorial endeavors, she continued until 1945. Married in 1924 to Hugh Alexander Pollack, B. had already established a reputation for tireless energy and productivity, writing between four and five thousand words a day. She gained increasing recognition with *The Enid Blyton Book of Fairies* (1924), *The Zoo Book* (1925), and *The Book of Brownies* (1926), illustrated by

Ernest Aris and republished in 1964 as *Brownie Tales,* and further enhanced her popularity by extending her readership through *Sunny Stories for Little Folks,* the magazine she edited and produced from 1926 to 1952.

In 1929, B. and her husband moved to "Old Thatch" at Bourne End in Buckinghamshire, west of London, which figured into numerous pieces for B.'s column in *Teachers' World* as did most elements of B.'s life, including her pets and even her children, For B., family and friends often served a literary purpose as characters in her STORYTELLING. This fact was not always a welcomed affiliation as evidenced in her daughter Imogen's critical account of her upbringing in *A Childhood at Green Hedges* (1989). Located in Beaconsfield, just north of Bourne End, "Green Hedges" was the name given to the second home B. would make famous, where in 1938 she moved with her husband and children. Here she established a daily routine that produced a steady stream of books for the remainder of her life. *Adventures of the Wishing Chair* (1937) initiated a highly productive period in B.'s career that produced a number of imaginative stories that evolved into a variety of sequels as well as SERIES. The FANTASY world B. created in *Adventures of the Wishing Well* was continued in works such as *The Enchanted Wood* (1939) and *The Magic Faraway Tree* (1943). *The Secret Island* (1938) produced sequels such as *The Secret of Spiggy Holes* (1940) and *The Secret Mountain* (1941). In 1941, B. published the first book in the Adventurous Four series, and in the following year she published the first book in the Mary Mouse series, which continued until 1964, and the first book in the Famous Five series.

In December 1942, B. and her husband were divorced, and in October of the following year she married Kenneth Darrell Waters, a surgeon who would eventually assume responsibility for managing B.'s business affairs. Throughout the 1940s and 1950s, B. produced book after book and continued to introduce new series, notably the MYSTERY series that began with *The Mystery of Burnt Cottage* (1943), the SCHOOL STORY series that began with *First Term at Malory Towers* (1946), another mystery series that began with *The Rockingdown Mystery* (1949), and the ADVENTURE series that began with *The Secret Seven*

(1949), republished in 1972 as *The Secret Seven and the Mystery of the Empty House.* In 1949, B. was also commissioned by the publishing house of Sampson Low to create a series to be illustrated by the Dutch artist Harmsen Van der Beek that resulted in the numerous Noddy books. Extremely popular with readers, the Noddy books nonetheless received considerable criticism for the negative qualities of B.'s characterization of the boy named Noddy as well as for the suggested racist overtones interspersed throughout the stories.

Although often delegated a minor position as a serious writer for children, B. remains a significant figure in children's literature and continues to be read and appreciated. For many readers, B. came to symbolize the experience of childhood, and her stories provided the means to open the door of wonderment and possibility.

FURTHER WORKS: *Silver and Gold,* 1925; *Tarrydiddle Town,* 1929; *The Red Pixie Book,* 1934; *The Children's Garden,* 1935; *Hedgerow Tales,* 1935; *The Famous Jimmy,* 1936; *The Adventures of Binkle and Flip,* 1938; *Billy-Bob Tales,* 1938; *Mr. Galliano's Circus,* 1938; *Naughty Amelia Jane!,* 1940; *Mr. Meddle's Mischief,* 1940; *The Treasure Hunters,* 1940; *Children of Kidillin,* (as Mary Pollock), 1940; *Three Boys and a Circus* (as Mary Pollock), 1940; *The Adventurous Four,* 1941; *Mary Mouse and the Doll's House,* 1942; *Bimbo and Topsy,* 1943; *John Jolly by the Sea,* 1943; *John Jolly on the Farm,* 1943; *The Boy Next Door,* 1944; *Five Run Away Together,* 1944; *The Island of Adventure* 1944; republished as *Mystery Island,* 1945; *The Mystery of the Disappearing Cat,* 1944; *The Three Golliwogs,* 1944; *The Bad Little Monkey,* 1946; *The Put-em-Rights,* 1946; *Tales of Green Hedges,* 1946; *The House at the Corner,* 1947; *The Mystery of the Missing Necklace,* 1947; *The Adventures of Pip,* 1948; *Little Noddy Goes to Toyland,* 1949; *Humpty Dumpty and Belinda,* 1949; *Those Dreadful Children,* 1949; *Rubbalong Tales,* 1950; *The Ship of Adventure,* 1950; *Here Comes Noddy Again,* 1951; *Noddy and His Car,* 1951; *The Six Bad Boys,* 1951; *Up the Faraway Tree,* 1951; *The Story of My Life,* 1952; *The Mad Teapot,* 1952; *Noddy Goes to School,* 1952; *The Rubadub Mystery,* 1952; *Mr. Tumpy in the Land of Wishes,* 1953; *The Children of Green Meadows,* 1954; *Bobs,* 1955; *Gobbo in the Land of Dreams,* 1955; *Bimbo and Blackie Go Camping,* 1955; *The Troublesome Three,* 1955; *The Birthday Kitten,* 1958; *Bom and the Clown,* 1959; *Adventure of the Strange Ruby,* 1960; *The Mystery of Banshee Towers,* 1961; *The Boy Who Wanted a Dog,*

1963; *Five Are Together Again,* 1963; *Noddy and His Passengers,* 1967; *Adventures on Willow Farm,* 1968; *Once upon a Time,* 1968

BIBLIOGRAPHY: Dixon, B. "The Nice, the Naughty, and the Nasty: The Tiny World of Enid B.," *Children's Literature in Education,* 15 (1974): pp. 43–61; Mullan, B. *The Enid B. Story,* 1987; Ray, S., *The B. Phenomenon: The Controversy Surrounding the World's Most Successful Children's Writer,* 1982; Smallwood, I. *A Childhood at Green Hedges,* 1989; Stoney, B. *Enid B.: A Biography.* 1974

STEVEN R. SERAFIN

BOBER, Natalie S.

Author, anthologist, b. 27 December 1930, New York City

B. spent many years as an educator before beginning to write biographies and collect POETRY for adolescent readers. She drafted her first BIOGRAPHY, *William Wordsworth: The Wandering Poet* (1975) while recovering from a problem with her leg. She received twenty-one rejections before the book was accepted and published, but after its release, the book was named one of the Child Study Association's Best Biographies of the Year. B. wrote her doctoral dissertation on Robert FROST; *A Restless Spirit* (1991) was a natural outgrowth. B. also wrote *Abigail Adams: Witness to a Revolution* (1995), which won the *Boston Globe–Horn Book* Award for nonfiction, *School Library Journal*'s Best Books of 1995 selection, and *Booklist*'s 1995 Editor's Choice selection. B. said that her aim is "to ungrave" her subjects, to bring them alive for young people, and to enable readers to identify with them. B. compiled a collection of poetry that she attributes to developing a sense of wonder and imagination, *Let's Pretend* (1986).

FURTHER WORKS: *Breaking Tradition; The Story of Louise Nevelson,* 1984; *Thomas Jefferson: Man on a Mountain,* 1988; *Marc Chagall: Painter of Dreams,* 1991

BIBLIOGRAPHY: *Something about the Author,* vol. 87, 1996

MARY ARIAIL BROUGHTON

BODECKER, N. M. (Niels Mogens)

Poet, illustrator, b. 13 January 1922, Copenhagen, Denmark; d. 1 February 1988, Hanover, New Hampshire

B. lived with his grandparents while growing up in Denmark and said he was a "late blooming

Victorian" in a letter to editor Robert KRAUS of Windmill Press. He wrote his first book of POETRY while working as an illustrator in the 1940s. After moving to the United States in 1952, he was asked to illustrate Edward EAGER's book *Half Magic* (1954) and began his career as a children's book illustrator. His ILLUSTRATIONS for Eager's books *Knight's Castle* (1984) and *The Time Garden* (1985) were his favorites. *Miss Jaster's Garden* (1992) was a *New York Times* Best Illustrated Children's Book for 1992. He is best known for his children's poetry and nonsense verse, often inspired by his own sons Sandy, Torsten, and Niels, who were sung to sleep in their triple bunks, each with his own special song, by their father each night.

When asked why he wrote for children, B. said, "I have retained strong emotional ties to the childhood condition and need to share my imaginings with a sympathetic audience" (correspondence in THE KERLAN COLLECTION).

He wrote amusingly about children with loose teeth, snowmen with sniffles as the weather warmed at the end of winter, and animals of every species. B. was a master of figurative language whose poetic descriptions of nature revealed his reverence for the world around him. He was recognized by two Christopher Awards. After B.'s death *Water Pennies and Other Poems* (1991), and *Hurry, Hurry, Mary Dear* (1998) illustrated by his close friend Erik BLEGVAD, (1998) were published posthumously.

FURTHER WORKS: ILLUSTRATOR: *Seven-day Magic,* 1962; *Hurry, Hurry, Mary Dear,* 1976, 1998; *It's Raining, Said John Twaining,* 1973; *"Let's Marry, Said the Cherry" and Other Nonsense Poems,* 1980; *Pigeon Cubes and Other Verse,* 1982; *Snowman Sniffles,* 1983

REBECCA RAPPORT

BOND, Felicia

Author, illustrator, b. 18 July 1954, Yokohama, Japan

B. grew up wanting to be an artist. She became interested in illustrating children's books at age twenty-two. Encouraged by her editor, she created *Poinsettia and Her Family* (1980), which began her writing career. She illustrated Laura NUMEROFF's popular books, including *If You Give a Mouse a Cookie* (1985) and *If You Give a Moose a Muffin.* B.'s brightly colored childlike cartoon drawings outlined in black ink capture the zany improbability of Numeroff's "What if?" text.

FURTHER WORKS: Author: *Poinsettia and Her Family,* 1981; *Four Valentines in a Rainstorm,* 1990; *How to Think like a Scientist* (S. Kramer). 1987; *Big Red Barn* (Margaret Wise BROWN), ed. 1989); *Big Green Pocketbook* (C. RANSOME). 1993; *If You Give a Pig a Pancake* (Numeroff). 1998

BIBLIOGRAPHY: *Something about the Author.* vol. 49, 1987

JODI PILGRIM

BOND, Michael
Author, b. 13 January 1926, Newbury, Berkshire, England

B. grew up in Reading, Berkshire, England, spending his time going to the cinema, and building amplifiers and radio sets. At age seventeen B. spent a short three-month stint as a pilot with the Royal Air Force, then transferred to the Army. While stationed in Egypt, B. published his first short story in the magazine *London Opinion.* Later, working as a cameraman for the BBC, he continued writing short stories, radio plays, and articles that were slowly accepted. His first entrance into children's literature began on Christmas Eve 1957 when he spotted a lonely bear in a toy store. He purchased the bear and took it home for his wife. At the time, B. lived near Paddington Station in London and decided that this bear should be named Paddington. One year later, in 1958, B. published *A Bear Called Paddington,* the first of many books that chronicle the lively experiences of the bear from darkest Peru. Peggy Fortnum originally illustrated *Paddington,* with his trademark shabby old hat and duffle coat. Other illustrators have included Barry Macey, Fred Banberry, Barry Wilkinson, and David McKee. The Paddington books have been translated into more than eighteen languages and are enjoyed by children and adults the world over. In addition to the books, Paddington has had his own television show, stage play, film adaptations, and, of course, lovable stuffed toy.

B. enjoys positive reviews from critics who cite his ability to create a character that possesses the lovableness and security of a bear with the human characteristics of a person with the most unfortunate luck in performing regular mundane events. Young readers are enthralled to read about Paddington's adventures at the market, in the kitchen, at the zoo, or many other places he and the Browns, his host family, visit. One of the major reasons for Paddington's success can be attributed to B.'s masterful ability to situate Paddington into everyday human situations that are easily understood by children and yet retain Paddington's animal characteristics. This formula produces enjoyable stories for young readers. B. also introduces children to three other characters: a mouse named Thursday, a lion named Parsley, and a guinea pig named Olga da Polga. Although his three other animal characters were met with positive reviews from readers and were a part of multiple volumes, they do not share the wide appeal of Paddington. Paddington is a timeless character who has thrilled readers for many generations in the past and continues to be just as popular today.

FURTHER WORKS: Thursday SERIES, 1967–74; Parsley series, 1969–76; Olga da Polga series, 1971–83

BIBLIOGRAPHY: *Something about the Author Autobiography Series,* vol. 3, 1987

BERT CROSSLAND

BOND, Nancy (Barbara)
Author, b. 8 January 1945, Bethesda, Maryland

Books were a constant source of pleasure in B.'s life as she was growing up near Concord, Massachusetts. She earned a Bachelor of Arts degree from Mount Holyoke College and attended library school in Wales. B. worked on the promotional staff of a publishing house when she realized that she could earn a living working with children's literature. She found a job as an assistant librarian and spent her days reading, discussing, and recommending books to children. After obtaining her library science degree B. looked for work while beginning her first novel length writing. B. was a library director when *A String in the Harp* (1976) was published and won the INTERNATIONAL READING ASSOCIATION Children's Book Award in 1977. In it she used material from the *Maboginogi* and was recognized as using an authentic Welsh background for her story.

B.'s writing skill enables her to portray sensitive, realistic characters dealing with major changes and conflict often at the blurred edge between reality and fantasy. B.'s books have strong connections to setting—places she knows intimately through living or studying there—and to character: people she learns to know as she writes. *A String in the Harp* grew from a year she spent studying librarianship in Wales. *The Best of Enemies* (1978), set in Concord, the place she grew up, centers around a reenactment of the battle between the British and the colonists at Old North Bridge. *Country of Broken Stone* (1980) is set in modern-day Northumberland, Hadrian's Wall, where a group of students and archaeologists conduct a dig on the site of ancient Roman fort. B. says that once the place is established she begins to get to know the characters and at first it is like meeting strangers. As she continues to write and rewrite the story, the characters reveal themselves to her through their actions and reactions to one another. B.'s sensual and vivid writing about the settings harness historical events, people, and even a supernatural consciousness, that adds to B.'s tightly woven plots and rich prose. B.'s interest in England began after traveling there with her family as a child. She masterfully combines reality with British and Welsh FOLKLORE and settings to explore such dilemmas as accepting responsibility, upholding principles, family breakups, stepfamilies, and death in settings from Wales to Concord, Massachusetts to Hadrian's Wall. B. says that she sometimes finds the theme of a book in retrospect; that is, after finishing a novel she reflects upon what has happened and sees that one of the major themes concerns the deceptiveness of first appearances. B. is truly a scholar who approaches her writing from a depth of knowledge about literature.

AWARDS: NEWBERY MEDAL Honor Book, *Boston Globe–Horn Book* Honor Book, International Reading Association Children's Book Award, and Tir na n-Og Award, Welsh Book Council (1977) for *A String in the Harp; Boston Globe–Horn Book* Honor Book (1981) for *The Voyage Begun; Boston Globe–Honor Book* Honor Book (1984) for *A Place to Come Back To;* Parents' Choice Honor Book (1994) for *Truth to Tell*

FURTHER WORKS: *Another Shore,* 1988

BIBLIOGRAPHY: *Children's Literary Review,* vol. 11, 1986; Hunt, P., ed., *Children's Literature: An Illustrated History,* 1995; Silvey, Anita, ed., *Chil-*

dren's Books and Their Creators, 1995; *Something about the Author,* vol. 82, 1995

CRAIG LIEBERMAN

BOND, Ruskin
Author, b. 19 May 1934, Kasauli, India

The son of British parents, B. grew up in colonial India, and chose to make Mussoorie, in the foothills of the Himalayas, his home after India became an independent country. His dual British and Indian heritage lends depth, complexity, and an ironic stance to his writings. Author of more than sixty books for children and adults—novels, short stories, historical accounts, essays, poems, BIOGRAPHIES, FOLKLORE, and travelogues—B. is a versatile writer who constantly explores the meaning of "home" and belonging. He avoids the stereotypical postcolonial novels of progress or the Enid BLYTON-style ADVENTURES and MYSTERIES that are popular genres in INDIAN (EAST) CHILDREN'S LITERATURE. Instead, a small Himalayan town is the setting for his stories, and the rights of animals, conservation of the Himalayan region, and love and loyalty among people are his themes. There is adventure in his novels *Angry River* (1972), *Flames in the Forest* (1981), *Earthquake* (1984), and *Panther's Moon* (1969), but it is the adventure of the simple hill folk surviving flood, fire, earthquake, or a man-eater panther—or there is adventure in a tiger facing trophy hunters from the city, as in *Tigers Forever* (1983). There is mystery in his stories, but it is in the mystical realm of nature—in its destructive and nurturing manifestations—or in the characters' realization of their spiritual affinity with creation. B.'s simple yet graceful and poetic prose conveys his philosophical approach to life in a manner that children can both comprehend and experience vicariously.

AWARDS: 1957 John Llewellyn Rhys Prize, given to a Commonwealth writer under thirty years; 1992 Sahitya Akademi Award; finalist for 1998 Hans Christian ANDERSEN Author Award; 1999 Padmashree, awarded by the President of India

FURTHER WORKS: *A Flight of Pigeons,* 1980; *Tales and Legends from India,* 1982; *The Cherry Tree,* 1988; *An Island of Trees,* 1992; *The Room on the Roof and Vagrants in the Valley: Two Novels of Adolescence,* rpt. 1993; *The Ruskin Bond*

Children's Omnibus, 1995; *Binya's Blue Umbrella,* 1995

BIBLIOGRAPHY: Khorana, Meena. "In the Lap of the Himalayas." *Writer and Illustrator* 12, no. 2 (Jan.–Mar. 1993): *The Life and Works of Ruskin B.* forthcoming. "The River Is Eternal: Nature Mysticism and Vedanta Philosophy in Ruskin B.'s *Angry River.*" *The Lion and the Unicorn* 19, no. 2 (December 1995): 253–68. "Ruskin B.: A Critical Appreciation." *Writer and Illustrator* 17, no. 4 (July–Sept. 1998): 9–14. "Ruskin B.: Man of the Mountains." *Writer and Illustrator* 17, no. 4 (July–Sept. 1998): 15–18. Singh, Prabhat K., ed. *The Creative Contours of Ruskin B.: An Anthology of Critical Writings.* 1995

MEENA KHORANA

BONSALL, Crosby (Barbara Newell)
(Crosby Newell)

Author, Illustrator, b. 2 January 1921, Queens, New York; d. 10 January 1995, Boston, Massachusetts

As a child, B. expressed her creativity by making paper dolls and creating doodle drawings of dolls; these became important in her life. B. received a scholarship to New York University School of Architecture in sculpture and design; she later enrolled at The American School of Design where she specialized in commercial art. While she worked as a commercial artist, a doll manufacturer noticed a sketch of a doll on her drawing board; he immediately bought the rights to manufacture that doll and other dolls she designed. B.'s children's book career actually began with a group of dolls she designed. She created an entire family of dolls that she used as characters in her first book for children, *The Surprise Party* (1955). B. wrote and illustrated numerous books for beginning readers in an I Can Read format. Many of these books were mysteries involving the exploits of realistic children. The books engage readers who can solve the mysteries by observing the action going on in the background that the characters did not notice. In her early books, B. wrote under the name Crosby Newell. B. created unique characters for her books from simple rag dolls; she wanted the drawings to look like something children thought they might draw. The black-line, finely detailed drawings became identifiable as B.'s individualistic style; her art and strong story lines led to her recognition as an outstanding writer and illustrator. B.'s ILLUSTRA-

TIONS appear primarily in black-and-white or two-color art in most books. Among her greatest contributions are the I Can Read series with recognizable characters involved in intriguing plots; her books draw readers in to help solve the mysteries her characters face.

AWARDS: *New York Times* Best Illustrated Books of the Year (1964) for *I'll Show You Cats,* illustrated by Ylla (pseudonym of Camilla Koffler); National Association of Independent Schools Junior Booklist (1966) for *The Case of the Dumb Bells;* THE KERLAN COLLECTION at the University of Minnesota holds B.'s works; *Horn Book* Honor List (1973) for *Mine's the Best;* CHILDREN'S BOOK COUNCIL/INTERNATIONAL READING ASSOCIATION Children's Choice Selection (1974) for *And I Mean It, Stanley,* (1981) for *Who's Afraid of the Dark?*

FURTHER WORKS: As Crosby Newell: (with George B.): *What Are You Looking At?,* 1954; (with G. B.) *The Helpful Friends,* 1955; *Captain Kangaroo's Book* (illus. Evan Jeffrey), 1958; *Polar Bear Brothers* (illus. Ylla), 1960; *Kippy the Koala* (illus. George Leavens), 1960; *Hurry up, Slowpoke,* 1961; as Crosby Bonsall: *Listen, Listen!,* (illus. Ylla), 1961; *Tell Me Some More* (illus. Fritz Siebel), 1961; *Look Who's Talking* (illus. Ylla), 1962; *Who's a Pest?,* 1962; *The Case of the Hungry Stranger,* 1963; Spanish edition, translated by Pura BELPRÉ as *El caso del forastero hambriento* 1969; *What's Spot?,* 1963; *It's Mine!* 1964; *The Case of the Cat's Meow,* 1965; *Here's Jellybean Reilly* (illus. Ylla), 1966; *Whose Eye Am I?* (illus. Ylla), 1968; *The Case of the Scaredy Cats,* 1971; *The Day I Had to Play with My Sister,* 1972; *Piggle,* 1973; *Twelve Bells for Santa,* 1977; *Good-bye Summer,* Greenwillow, 1979; illustrator: as Crosby Newell; George B., *The Really Truly Treasure Hunt,* 1954; George B., *The Big Joke,* 1955; as Crosby B.: Joan L. Nodset, *Go Away, Dog,* 1963; Phil Ressner, *August Explains,* 1963; Joan Kahn, *Seesaw,* 1964; Ralph Underwood, ed., *Ask Me Another Riddle,* 1964; Oscar Weigle, ed., *Great Big Joke and Riddle Book,* 1970

BIBLIOGRAPHY: Silvey, Anita, ed., *Children's Books and Their Creators,* 1995

CRAIG LIEBERMAN

BONTEMPS, Arna Wendell

Author, b. 13 October 1902, Alexandria, Louisiana; d. 4 June 1973, Nashville, Tennessee

B.'s father took him as a small child from Louisiana to Los Angeles to allow him to grow up apart from discrimination. He had a happy childhood and began to write poetry in college. B. was an important AFRICAN AMERICAN author who depicted the lives and struggles of black Americans. He was part of a talented group of writers who characterized the Harlem Renaissance, the name given to the period from the end of World War I and through the middle of the 1930s–Depression years, during which Black writers produced a sizable body of sophisticated literature in the four prominent genres of fiction, POETRY, DRAMA, and essay. The works of these writers encouraged a new awareness of Black life and culture and stimulated racial pride. B.'s first novel, *God Sends Sunday* (1931), is considered a later work of the Harlem Renaissance. B. also wrote many nonfiction works on Black history for younger readers and edited several anthologies of Black American poetry and FOLKLORE. B's *Story of the Negro* (1948) was named a NEWBERY MEDAL Honor Book in 1949 and received the Jane Addams Children's Book Award in 1956. In it, B. traced the history of his people from earliest times, described the variety of cultures, and portrayed some of the Black leaders.

FURTHER WORKS: *An Anthology of Negro Poetry for Young Readers,* 1958; *The Fast Sooner Hound,* 1942; *Sam Patch, the High, Wide and Handsome Jumper,* 1951; *Chariot in the Sky: A Story of the Jubilee Singers,* 1951; *The Story of George Washington Carver,* 1954; *Lonesome Boy,* 1955; *Hold Fast to Dreams,* 1961; *Famous Negro Athletes,* 1964

BIBLIOGRAPHY: HOPKINS, Lee Bennett, *Pauses: Autobiographical Reflections of 101 Creators of Children's Books,* 1995; *Something about the Author,* vol. 44, 1986
                              MARY ARIAIL BROUGHTON

BOOK CLUBS FOR CHILDREN

Children's book clubs have a relatively recent history in American classrooms and libraries, though they can be traced to earlier events in the U.S. As early as the 1800s, both book clubs and writing clubs were encouraged by magazines for young readers. When newspapers started carrying serials, book clubs were created in factories, especially where children were used to do the repetitive handwork in fairly quiet circumstances. Some Sunday schools that also fed and bathed poor working children introduced book clubs. However, these book clubs had a very different meaning from that used today. Based in democratic principles, these early book clubs largely functioned as a means to provide access to books and literacy for the poor, the illiterate, the uneducated young. Thus, the adult primarily read to the children and led discussions designed to improve the children's aesthetic sensibilities. Children were not expected, nor empowered, to engage in their own meaning making or story interpretations.

In addition to these more formal efforts, spontaneous book clubs certainly were formed by enthusiastic readers over time, in families and communities. Nonetheless, in terms of U.S. classrooms, book clubs as a whole—the concept of children engaging in their own discussion groups—were largely irrelevant to educational goals. The dominant educational philosophy through the early 1900s assumed that it was teachers who held knowledge and their task was to impart that knowledge to their students. Rather than discussion, teachers typically used a pattern of asking a question, identifying the student to answer to the question, and evaluating whether or not the student's response was accurate. These questions often were ones for which the teacher already had an answer in mind, and students' success was measured in terms of how well his or her response matched the one the teacher had been seeking.

Children's book clubs as a pedagogical activity is relatively recent, with different terms used to describe both student-led discussion groups, as well as programs that make central such discussions. Terms used interchangeably or generically to convey students's discussions include readers' conferences, literature circles, literature study groups, and book clubs. These terms take on specific meanings in particular instructional approaches, such as the Raphael's Book Club Program, Daniel's Literature Circles and Hansen's Readers Workshop. Each of these programs can be traced to different educational "roots." For example, Readers Workshop parallels the process writing movement, where students confer about what they have created. In Readers Workshop, students self-select books they think will be interesting, then, upon completion, confer with their peers or their teacher about the books they have read. Literature Circles can be traced to the idea of "cooperative learning" study groups in which students work collaboratively on specific projects or tasks. Roles are assigned such as recorder, moderator, and so forth. In the Literature Circles program, groups of students read a book in common, then meet to discuss the book, taking on the roles assigned to them for the day. Being a Book Club classroom has specific meaning as well. This program traces its roots to sociocultural theory that emphasizes the fundamental importance of language in the development of the mind.

The Book Club Program grows out of three understandings from current educational theory. The first recognizes that language and its use is fundamental to thinking and that what is learned by any individual begins in the social interactions in which he or she engages. The second recognizes the increased importance of literature in reading instruction. The third relates to the need for schools to do more to prepare students to live and work in a diverse, democratic society. Thus Book Club reflects trends over the past decade to change the nature of classroom discourse, provide students with greater opportunities to engage in talk about text, and provides teachers with more guidelines for supporting, not dominating, such discussions.

Within Book Club, four components: community share, reading, writing, and book club interweave to support students' learning to read, respond to, and discuss literature in student-led discussion groups. A typical Book Club session begins and ends with community share. When used to open the Book Club session, this teacher-led, whole-group session is used to introduce students to the language of literature discussion, and to specific skills, strategies, and knowledge they need to read their books effectively, respond individually in writing, and engage in their small-group and whole-class discussions. When used to close the Book Club session, community share emphasizes coming together to share ideas and issues that emerged in students' discussions.

The "reading" component involves students' reading, independently or with support, the book to be discussed in their book clubs. In addition to the selected book, other aspects of the reading component can include thematically related teacher read-alouds, classroom library for sus-

tained silent reading, and guided reading books. The more books that students read related to the Book Club theme, the greater the opportunities for students to make intertextual connections and connections between their reading and their own lives.

The "writing" component involves daily response in students' reading logs, to help prepare for upcoming discussions; and sustained writing that occurs when process writing activities are connected thematically (e.g., similar genre, theme, content, author craft) to the books students are reading and discussing in Book Club.

The fourth component, book club, is the student-led discussion group for which the program was named. Book clubs have four to five students, heterogeneously grouped for reading level, gender, classroom status, verbal abilities, and so forth. Students remain in the same book club throughout a unit (based in one book or a set of thematically connected books). Within their group, they discuss ideas that emerge from their reading, log responses, questions, confusions, and related personal experiences. Within these groups, students develop skills important to life in a diverse, democratic society; listening to each other with respect, building upon each others' ideas, critiquing and debating ideas, and assuming leadership as well as supporting group processes.

Children's book clubs, literature circles, and reader's workshops honor literature that is the basis for instruction. They integrate the literacy curriculum, ground literacy activity in the social interactions among students and between teachers and students, emphasize the relationship between language and thought, and build a sense of community and ownership among teachers and students.

Commercial book clubs developed by publishers offer children opportunities to purchase books regularly, to build a home library. Junior Literary Guild, Scholastic, Troll, and Doubleday illustrate this type of book club. Book clubs have long existed as part of summer and after-school reading programs in public libraries. The federal government supported "Reading is Fundamental" (RIF) initiative in schools and libraries has given away millions of books to children since the 1960s.

BIBLIOGRAPHY: Daniels, H. *Literature Circles: Voice and Choice in the Student-Centered Classroom.* 1994. Goatley, V. J., Brock, C. H., and Raphael, T. E. "Diverse Learners Participating in

Regular Education 'Book Clubs'." *Reading Research Quarterly.* 1995. 352–80. Hansen, J. *When Writers Read.* 1987. McMahon, S. I., Raphael, T. E., with, Goatley, V. J., and Pardo, L. S. (eds.). 1997

TAFFY E. RAPHAEL AND JAMES R. GAVELEK

BOOK CLUBS FOR TEACHERS

The first book club in America was founded in 1629 by Anne Hutchinson, the Puritan founder of the Massachusetts Bay Colony. Always popular, membership increased rapidly after World War II with an emphasis on reading established literary classics. Many organizations such as university alumni associations, public libraries, and religious affiliated organizations sponsor book clubs. Numerous informally organized groups flourish among friends and in civic communities. The popularity of book clubs is enduring.

Teacher Book Clubs, in which teachers meet periodically to discuss pieces of literature, are becoming increasingly more visible in educational communities. These book clubs are usually organized by a group of teachers who choose the titles that the group will read. Titles range from contemporary fiction to INFORMATION texts to children's literature. The primary purpose of these book clubs is to explore literature as a vehicle for understanding one's own literacy and literary processing and the secondary purpose is to provide opportunities for teachers to become acquainted with new authors, new titles, and new themes. Frequently, members of teacher book clubs share ideas with one another about literature instruction and assessment from their classroom experiences.

Typically, teacher book club sessions last from one to three hours and are held in teacher's lounges or in individual members' homes. Group size varies and usually ranges from four to fifteen members. Book club moderators who encourage journal writing in conjunction with discussion are more successful than those who do not use journaling. Further, moderators who follow a list of guidelines are able to keep the discussion more focused and informative than moderators who do not follow guidelines.

Teacher book clubs are successful in helping members understand their own literacy development. One participant commented: "I gained a broader understanding of other cultures" (and) "a respect for other life styles from being a member of this book club." When student teachers read contemporary MULTICULTURAL works, one student commented: "I need to realize and deal with the fact that my students may be coming from a completely different place than I am. I must see that in order to teach them effectively."

Reading and discussing literature helps teachers grow professionally in their understanding of their own literary skills as well as their literature teaching skills. Teachers who work together in literature discussion groups move from not knowing what to talk about to requesting more time for discussion. Teachers who had previous experience with book clubs often sparked the discussion and served as models for teachers who had little experience with discussion.

In several studies of teacher discussion groups about literature, researchers have reported that participants experience many different kinds of personal growth from professional development to feelings of empowerment in curricular decision making. Adults who participate in discussion groups show striking differences between their participation and that of secondary school students. Teachers are far more willing to tolerate ambiguity, and have less need for resolution of conflicting opinions among book club participants than do their students.

As teachers hear one another's life stories in their book clubs, a camaraderie of trust and understanding develops among the members of the group and carries over to other activities at school. Through book clubs, participants are able to reflect on the ways they think, interpret, and respond to various texts and various interpretations. During their discussions teachers are often able to reflect upon issues that are critical to their own professional development, they are empowered through discussion. They also grow in awareness that beliefs can be reflected upon, challenged, and modified. Through listening to one another's reasoning and classroom experiences teachers achieve a broader and often more comprehensive perspective about teaching literature.

Teacher discussion groups are not a new phenomenon; they have long been an effective vehicle for reflection and change. The Philadelphia Teachers' Learning Cooperative; the Teacher

Lore Project; Maitlin and Short's Study Group Experiences all illustrate the power that comes to teachers when they work together, share their expertise and receive support from one another in their efforts to affect positive change within their school communities.

In the preparation of future English/Language Arts teachers, some argue that teachers need to read and talk about many different kinds of texts as they design their own classroom literacy program. Teachers develop new understandings about themselves and the students they teach through the process of reading and talking. Several researchers argue that when teachers from a variety of backgrounds read stories together they better understand how students from different cultural groups interpret stories.

Several teacher development projects have had the transmission of ideas across groups as their primary goal. The Philadelphia Teachers' Learning Cooperative shows that knowledge of one generation of teachers is passed on to another. The Teacher Lore Project captured the discoveries of teachers and their insights enabling them to be shared with other teachers. In book clubs, knowledge flows across generations, across ethnic groups, and between genders as participants interpret stories and construct meaning. Different group members assume the role of expert. Over a period of time all members of the group have the opportunity to provide and receive insights about literature.

REFERENCES: Bealor, S. *Minority Literature Book Groups for Teachers. Reading in Virginia.* 1992. Buchanan, 3 (1991). "Teacher as Learner." *Working in a Community of Teachers.* In T. Shanahan (ed.), *Teacher Thinking-Teacher Knowing—In Literacy and Language Education.* 1992 Dana, N. *Developing an Understanding of the Multicultural Classroom Experiences for the Monocultural Preservice Teacher.* 1991. (Paper presented at the 71st annual meeting of Association of Teacher Educators. Washington, D.C.) Fisher, P. and Shapiro, S. *Teachers' Exploration of Historical Fiction in Literature Discussion Groups.* May, 1991. (Paper presented at the Annual International Reading Association Convention, Orlando, Florida). Flood, J. and Lapp, D. "Teacher Book Clubs: Establishing Literature Discussion Groups for Teachers. *The Reading Teacher.* April, 1994. Flood, J., Lapp, D., Alvarez, D., Rornero, A., Ranck-Buhr, W., Moore, J., Jones, M., Kabildis, C., Lungren, L. (in press). "A Teacher Book Club: A Study of Teachers' and Student Teachers' Participation in a Contemporary Multicultural Fiction Literature Discussion Group." *Research Report.* 1997. Grossman, P. and Shulman, L. (1995). "Knowing, Believing, and the Teaching of English." In T. Shanahan (ed.) *Teacher Thinking. Teacher Knowing—In Literacy and Language Education.* (1992). "Authors of Color: A Multicultural Perspective." *Journal of Reading. 36.* 124–29. Maitlin, M. and Short, K. "How Our Teachers Study Group Sparks Change. *Educational Leadership, 49, 68.* 1991. O'Flahavan, J. F., Erting, L. C., Marks, T. A., Mintz, A. W., & Joyce Wiencek, J. B. *At the Intersection of Mind and Society: Synthesis of Research on School-Based Peer Group Discussion about Text from a Sociocultural Perspective.* (December, 1992). Paper presented at the 42nd Annual Meeting of the National Reading Conference. Rosenblatt, L. M. "Literature—S.O.S." *Language Arts, 68 (7),* 44–448 (1991). Sanacore, J. (1993). *Continuing to Grow as Language Arts Educators: Focusing on the Importance of Study Groups.* Eric Document 352629. Smith, M. W. and Marshall, D. 1992. "Toward an Understanding of the Culture of Practice in the Discussion of Literature: An Analysis of Adult Reading Groups." Unpublished manuscript. Zucanella, D. "Teachers Reading/Readers Teaching: Five Teachers' Personal Approaches to Literature and Their Teaching of Literature." *Research in the Teaching of English.* 1991

JAMES FLOOD AND DIANE LAPP

BOOK DESIGN

Book design contributes to a reader's experience of a book, although most readers are not conscious of it. The goal of book design is to create an object, a book, that functions as an aesthetic whole. Picture-story books most vividly reveal the aesthetics of book design for children.

One basic element of book design is the size of a book. Size may suggest use, for example, a small book that a child holds easily in her own hand, such as Beatrix POTTER's *Peter Rabbit* (1902), is appropriate for intimate one-on-one sharing and offers a different experience from a large book with bold ILLUSTRATION, such as *Lunch* (Denise FLEMING, 1992), that works successfully in a group setting as well as one-on-one.

The shape of a book orients in one of two ways—typically landscape (in which the longer sides of the closed book are the horizontal top and bottom) or portrait (in which the longer sides of the closed book are the vertical left, the spine, and right)—that may enhance the telling of the story. In *The Ox-Cart Man* (Donald HALL, 1979), illustrated by Barbara COONEY, the landscape orientation of the book contributes to the telling of a story, in which a character journeys from the country to town and back, by allowing the traveler to move along the length of the page, emphasizing the length of the journey. In Crockett JOHNSON's *The Carrot Seed* (1945) a portrait orientation gives the pages height and allows the carrot space to grow. A book may be perfectly square or may be die-cut to an irregular shape, suggesting some aspect of the story. Standard sizes and shapes are less costly to produce.

The design of covers sets the mood of the book and is extremely important; it is true that we often choose books by their covers. A story may begin on a cover, as in *The Dead Bird,* by Margaret Wise BROWN, illustrated by Remy CHARLIP (1963), or the cover may present an illustration from the story, as on the cover of *Sylvester and the Magic Pebble* (William STEIG, 1969). The cover of *Pink and Say* (Patricia POLACCO, 1994) shows a moment that "might have been" had the story turned out differently and is suggestive of the themes and characters in the book.

Dust-jacket or cover art is said to "wrap around" when the illustration on the front cover extends to the back, offering the illustrator a chance to depict an expansive scene. Alternatively, a back cover may show a moment from the story that is separate from what is depicted on the cover. Often, back covers feature a small vignette from the book, perhaps a close-up of one character or an important or engaging detail from a scene, which serves as an invitation or teaser to the reader who is examining the book before it is opened. On the back cover of *Tuesday* (David WIESNER, 1991) a small illustration shows a lone grumpy frog levitating on a lily pad beneath the moon. After reading the book, when the book is closed, the reader may experience this same vignette as a snapshot or reminder of the story, as when scenes from a film are shown during the final credits. It is important to note that the cover design for a book's jacket may differ from the design for the actual hardcover of a book and that the cover often offers the first textual information about the book, usually the title, author, and illus-

trator. The display type chosen to present this information is designed to be harmonious with the cover art and with the overall feel of the book.

Dust-jacket flaps typically offer a short summary of the contents of the book as well as biographical information about the author and illustrator. This information, written by marketing staff or sometimes by the author, is called "flap copy." The design of flaps takes into account the end papers (the inside of the front and back covers) against which they are viewed. The careful design of *What a Wonderful World* (George D. Weiss and Bob Thiele, Ashley BRYAN, illus. 1995), is evident in the bright green flaps set against the wide blue end papers, followed by a bold yellow dedication page. The contrasting expanses of color prepare the reader for a lavish rainbow of color in the book's illustrations.

The end papers in a picture story book can assist in setting tone and telling story. In *Hey Al!* (Arthur YORINKS, Richard EGIELSKI, illus., 1986), the front end papers are a dull tan, suggesting Al's dull life; the end papers at the back of the book, however, are bright yellow, reflecting the bright-yellow paint Al uses to add color to his life and his apartment at the end of the story. Often designed by the illustrator, end papers can also function as an extension or commentary on the story. In *Smoky Night* (Eve BUNTING, David DIAZ, illus. 1994), the beautiful collage end papers act as a metaphor for the story. The paper scraps, the flamelike shapes, and the matches, among other objects that comprise the collage, suggest the beauty that can be made and found in a piecing together small bits of life and love that are the remnants of the chaos of the Los Angeles riots.

Front matter, the first few pages of a book, often includes a half-title page, title page, dedication, and copyright information, although some of this information is moved to the end of the book where it is less obtrusive. In some books, the front matter is distinctly separate from the story proper, and contains no illustrations. In other books, illustration may be part of the design of these first few pages, and may begin to tell the story or gently move the reader into the story. In *Grandfather's Journey* (Allen SAY, 1993), a small paper origami boat appears on the title page (and on the back cover) as a symbol of the journey that the boy's grandfather takes in the story.

Like other elements of design, the type font can contribute to the overall experience of story. Choice of font is often so subtle that only "mistakes" call attention to themselves, as when a large, heavy, black, sans serif font works against, rather than with, delicate pale watercolor illustrations. In *Bootsie Barker Bites* (Barbara Bottner, Peggy RATHMANN, illus., 1992), the font chosen for the text has an appropriately sharp, pointy seraph that is particularly noticeable on the "B's" in Bootsie's name. The font chosen for "The Squiggle" (Carol L. Schaefer, P. Morgan, illus., 1996), is satisfyingly squiggly, for the letters look almost as if they could have been shaped by the little girl's swirling red string. The font chosen for *Make Way for Ducklings* (Robert MCCLOSKEY, 1941), has a rounded, ducklike wobble. In McCloskey's book, the brown ink in which the text is printed works well with the monochromatic illustrations and the cream colored paper to suggest the warm brown color of the mama duck and ducklings whose adventures are the subject of his story. The purpose or use of a book—its audience—can influence design decisions as well. In PICTURE BOOKS, the font choice is based on how well the font works with the art, and because an adept, adult reader will probably be reading the book to the child, the inherent readability of the type is seldom a point of disagreement. Reading teachers and special education teachers prefer clear readable text on a plain background: words printed on colored backgrounds are difficult for children with special needs to see—to discriminate. If words are integrated with the art they should stand out clearly. When designing text for books intended for beginning readers, however, a sans-serif font is preferable because it is easier to decode. In picture story books, a variety of font sizes and types are sometimes used in the same book and, like punctuation, they help the reader to hear how the text sounds or should be read, thus adding meaning to the story. So, for example, at the end of *Madeline* (Ludwig BEMELMANS, 1939), the lines of text drift gently toward the right as the font size becomes smaller and smaller with each line, directing the reader to lower her voice as the little girls fall asleep and the story ends.

The placement of text and illustration on a page in relation to one another has to do with page layout. In picture books, along with artistic elements such as line, placement of text, and illustration may guide the eye to move across the page. If type is at the upper left corner of a page, for example, an individual may read text and then move down the page to the illustration, following reading convention. Or, if the text is at the bottom of a page, a reader may look, then read. A child may not concentrate on the words at all but, rather, look at the illustrations while listening to the story, experiencing the event more as cinema. Still, the relation of text and illustration is important as a way that the design of the book influences a reader or listener's experience. In *Lilly's Purple Plastic Purse* (Kevin HENKES, 1996), Lilly apologizes for her misbehavior to her teacher by repeating how "really, really, really" sorry she feels. Lilly is so sorry that the long line of "really"s that starts at the top of the page sweeps down and around and upside down until it finally guides our eye to Lilly, in the bottom right corner, desperately reaching up to offer her teacher her gifts of apology.

The purpose of book design is not to call attention to itself but, foremost, to work harmoniously with text and illustration to create a meaningful whole. Still, some books consciously call attention to design by breaking conventions or focusing on them. *The Stinky Cheese Man and Other Fairly Stupid Fairy Tales* (Jon SCIESZKA, Lane SMITH, illustrator, 1992), is a spoof on classic FAIRY TALE conventions and is an example of effective irreverence toward design convention as well. The pop-up book *A Christmas Alphabet* (Robert SABUDA, 1994) is a stunning example of a book that calls attention to design through its sheer beauty and elegance.

Although many books, such as those in SERIES, are similar in design, most picture books represent the unique collaborative efforts of an author, illustrator, editor, designer, and art director, among others. Thus, each individual book requires the careful attention of those interested in design issues. Where the text breaks on a page, the qualities of the paper on which it is printed, details such as gilding or a ribbon to mark a page, all contribute to the reader's experience of the book. Finally, while it is important to remember that some design decisions may be a function of economics, it is also important to recognize that a simple, small book with black and white illustrations may be just as effective as a large, elaborately produced item.

BIBLIOGRAPHY: Craig, James, W. Bevington, and Susan Meyer, *Designing with Type: A Basic Course in Typography;* Cummins, Julie, ed. *Children's Book Illustration and Design.* vol. 1 (1992). vol. 2, 1998; Harms, Jeanne M., and Lucille Lettow, *Book Design,* part 1, Nov. 1996; part 2, March 1997; part 3, July 1997; part 4, November 1997, in *Book Links;* Scieszka, Jon and Molly Leach (designer). "Design Matters," in *Horn Book* magazine (March/April 1998); Vandergrift, Kay E., *Child and Story: The Literary Connection,* 1986

REBECCA PLATZNER

(See also ILLUSTRATION; PICTURE BOOKS; VISUAL LITERACY)

BOOKS AS FILM

As the role of technology in our lives increases, the world of young people becomes increasingly rich with visual images, movement, and sound. In addition to books, films present many young people with much of their literary experience. For these reasons, film adaptations of children's books play a crucial role in introducing young people to literature. Thus, thoughtfully approaching and analyzing different interpretations and representations in books and film adaptations can encourage young people to think critically and creatively about the elements of story.

Whenever a text is translated from one language to another, some amount of meaning is lost, added, or altered in the translation. The transition from book to film is a unique kind of translation that poses special challenges to filmmakers and viewers alike. Print and film are very different media; while print conveys meaning through words alone, film uses visual images, music, voices, and action to tell a story. Because of these differences, viewers are often inclined to judge a film based on how well it adheres to the book's original story. An effective adaptation requires some changes from the original in order to capture the "spirit and essence" of the story in the film environment.

Filmmakers face the task of applying the special characteristics and possibilities of the film environment and technology in ways that both replicate and enhance the story they seek to tell. Thus, adapting a book to film poses a twofold challenge. The filmmaker must take care not to emphasize the effects of film technology to such an extent that the spirit and meaning of the original story are lost to the medium. At the same time, it is important to take advantage of the distinctive ways that film has of telling a story. An adaptation should not translate the original so literally that the traits of film media are lost, and the story becomes unsuccessful as a film.

In adapting a book into a film, filmmakers face many decisions, including the choice of setting, actors and costumes, technologies and effects, and story alterations. In making these decisions, filmmakers may challenge viewers to consider new contexts or meanings for traditional stories through the use of creative settings, casting, and character depiction, and innovative stylistic elements. Particularly popular are creative adaptations of folk and FAIRY TALES, which can illustrate the universal appeal and applicability of stories across boundaries of time, place, and culture.

The film versions of fairy tales in Davenport Films' from the Brothers GRIMM series are noteworthy for their ability to capture the essence of the original stories while creatively transporting them into a variety of historical periods, locations, and cultures. Some films in the series include: Hansel and Gretel: An Appalachian Version set in the Depression Era; Ashpet: An American Cinderella, set in the rural South during World War II; a Victorian Era rendition of Rapunzel; and Willa: An American Snow White, set in Virginia around 1915, and winner of the AMERICAN LIBRARY ASSOCIATION (ALA) Andrew CARNEGIE MEDAL for Excellence in Children's Video in 1998. Davenport's films expose viewers to classic fairy tales, while at the same time introducing them to elements unique to the culture, time period, and setting that the films reflect. In this way, the films encourage viewers to think creatively about how the stories relate to the lives of people in a diverse range of contexts.

Countless children's books have been recreated as films, and many classic stories for young people, such as *Little Women* (Louisa May ALCOTT, 1868), *The Secret Garden* (Frances Hodgson BURNETT, 1911), *Pinocchio* (Carlo COLLODI, 1883), and *Cinderella* have been adapted into multiple film versions. Each version reflects the unique sensibility of its own time in terms of the themes it emphasizes, stylistic elements, character representation, and/or the technology used to bring the story to the medium. For example, in contrast to its animated version of *Cinderella,* DISNEY's 1997 live-action version featuring Brandy and Whitney Houston represents both a unique multicultural presentation of the fairy tale and a shift in intended audience from very young children to older children, teenagers, and adults. The various versions of *Little Women* (MGM Studios, 1933; MGM Studios, 1949; and Columbia/Tristar Studios, 1994) are another good example of different eras reflecting on a classic piece of literature and presenting it in their own unique way.

In addition, children's literature is full of wonderfully creative features such as magical transformations and animals with human characteristics; these imaginative aspects can present special challenges for filmmakers. The availability of new technologies often results in new film versions of previously adapted stories as well as adaptations of stories never before brought to film. Often adaptations of children's stories provide filmmakers with opportunities to showcase breakthroughs in film technology. For example, as Disney Studios continues to enhance its animation technologies, it also incorporates new strategies, such as the cutting-edge technology that transformed Jonathon Taylor Thomas into Pinocchio in Disney's 1990s live-action version of the classic story. Animatronics allow for realistic depictions of animals talking in Universal Studios' 1995 film adaptation of *Babe* (Dick KINGSMITH, 1985) and in Monterey Home Video's 1999 update of *Animal Farm* (George Orwell, 1945). And E. B. WHITE's classic novel *Stuart Little* (1945), about a mouse adopted into a human family, has been brought to film in a live-action version, using sophisticated computer effects beyond the realm of animatronics.

Moving from the classic to the contemporary, J. K. ROWLING's Harry Potter series, full of magic and action (most notably the famous Quidditch matches, a sport in which players zoom through the air on broomsticks) will also be brought to film using live-action techniques. Dr. SEUSS's *How the Grinch Stole Christmas* (1957) became a major film in 2000. Many other examples are

possible. While technology will certainly play a large part in bringing this magical tale to life through film, the incredible transatlantic appeal of the series, set in England, poses another type of "TRANSLATION" challenge for filmmakers. While the books are published in two slightly different versions, reflecting British and American terminology, the Warner Brothers film will need to bridge the gap between the two cultures. Preserving the far-reaching appeal of the books in the film medium means wrestling with issues of setting, filming location, accent, and many cultural details.

Much debate about the value of film adaptations of children's books and the problems involved in translating books to film centers on the myriad film adaptations created by the Walt Disney Studios. The influence of these films and their marketing tie-ins is tremendous, such that Disney has shaped the visual images of settings, scenes, and characters from classic children's stories like *Snow White, Cinderella, Alice in Wonderland* (Lewis CARROLL, 1865), and *Pinocchio* for generations of people. While Disney's vast appeal allows it to bring its stories to large audiences, the film adaptations Disney produces alter the original text so significantly as to make it difficult to match the original to the film in terms of characters, plot, meaning, and spirit. Thus, Disney's films do not adapt classic stories so much as they refashion the original material into completely new works.

BIBLIOGRAPHY: "Children's Books Go Hollywood." Available at http://www.publishersweekly.com/articles/1990816_79904. asp. October 18, 1999; Davenport, Tom. (1981). "Some Personal Notes on Adapting Folk-Fairy Tales to Film" in Butler, Francelia, ed., *Children's Literature,* 9; Annual of the Modern Language Association Division of Children's Literature and The Children's Literature Association; 107–15. from the Brothers Grimm Series—available at http://www.oz.net/~davfilms/grimmfilms.html. October 29, 1999; Gaffney, Maureen. "Evaluating Attitude: Analyzing Point of View and Tone in Film Adaptations of Literature," in Butler, Francelia, ed., *Children's Literature,* 9. Annual of the Modern Language Association Division of Children's Literature and The Children's Literature Association, pp. 116–25; Gay Carol, "Little Women at the Movies," in Street, Douglas, ed., *Children's Novels and the Movies,* pp. 28–38, 1983. "Harry

Potter Gets the Hollywood Treatment," available at http://www.the-tim/23/timnwsnws01032.html? 2514223, October 18, 1999; Nodelman, Perry, *The Pleasures of Children's Literature,* pp. 53–55, 1992; Vandergrift, Kay, and Jane Anne Hannigan, "Reading Images: Videos in the Library and Classroom," *School Library Journal,* 39 (1), pp. 20–25, 1993

JENNIFER DUNNE

BOOKS FOR THE VERY YOUNG

It is clear that experiences with books in the preschool years can afford lasting benefit for children. Early exposure to books with plenty of time for talk and enjoyment during the shared reading between adult and child appear to be key factors in the child's acquisition of literacy. Margaret Wise BROWN's *Goodnight, Moon,* first published in 1947, has become a staple bedtime book for young children. In recent decades publishers have turned even more attention and resources to producing a variety of books for the youngest child.

Because very young children learn as much through their mouths as through their other senses, many of their first books are made of washable foam-filled cloth pages or constructed with heavy laminated cardboard or plastic pages that will withstand teeth and sticky fingers. These "board books" or cloth books are frequently identification books or "naming books" such as Tana HOBAN's *Is It Red? Is It Yellow? Is It Blue?* (1978). Such books allow a child to point to one picture after another, demanding to know "wha dat?" Often these books have simple narrative lines and reflect the common everyday experiences of children from many cultures as in Helen OXENBURY's Baby Board Books. As part of the interest in books for babies, publishers have reissued well-known nursery classics in board book form or have enlisted well-known illustrators or writers in creating series of baby books.

Young children respond to a book by pointing or labeling, and some books have a kind of "built-in participation" as part of their design. These books have flaps to lift up and peek under, soft flannel to touch, or holes to poke fingers through. Such books may serve as the transition between toys and real books. *Pat the Bunny* by Dorothy Kunhardt has been a bestseller for the very youngest children since 1940. Beginning

with Eric HILL's "lift the flap" stories about the dog "Spot," an increasing number of sophisticated cut-out books and "lift the flap" stories have appeared. Eric CARLE's story of *The Very Hungry Caterpillar* (1981) has holes just the right size for little fingers. In Carle's *The Very Busy Spider* (1985) children are invited to feel the pictures as well as see the pictures. Carle's *The Very Quiet Cricket* (1990), *The Very Lonely Firefly* (1995) and *The Very Clumsy Click Beetle* (1999) have technological support in the form of computer chips that brings each tale to its conclusion. The sounds and lights imbedded in the pages delight and surprise children in these multisensory books.

Participation books for the very young should be sturdily made to meet the demands of inexperienced baby and toddler fingers. "Pop-Up" books (cf. BOOK DESIGN) that have intricate paper engineering allow a variety of movable three-dimensional forms to arise from the book's pages are more suitable for older children.

Wordless books are PICTURE BOOKS in which the story line is told entirely through pictures and offer young children the chance for a different form of participation. Wordless books are helpful in developing some of the skills necessary for reading. Handling the book, turning the pages, beginning at the left-hand side and moving to the right are all skills that give the young child a sense of directionality and the experience of acting like a reader. These books are particularly useful in stimulating language development by encouraging children to take an active part in STORYTELLING. Many of them are laid out in the same sequential style as COMIC BOOKS AND GRAPHIC NOVELS, and have wide appeal to different age levels. As children relate the story, they become aware of beginnings, endings, the sequence of the story, the climax, the actions of the characters—all necessary for learning how a story works, for developing a sense of story. "Reading" or telling what is happening in the pictures in a wordless book also requires specific comprehension skills. In order to help the child tell the story, pictures must show action and sequence clearly so children will not be confused in their tellings.

Wordless picture books cover a range of topics and forms from the simple pleasures of morning and nighttime rituals of a little girl found in

Sunshine (1981) and *Moonlight* (1982) by Jan ORMEROD, to the fantastic adventures of a group of flying frogs in David WIESNER's *Tuesday* (1991). The best wordless books for the very young are books such as Emily MCCULLY's stories of a large mouse family, *Picnic* (1984), *First Snow* (1985), and *School* (1987) or Tomie DEPAOLA's *Pancakes for Breakfast* (1978). These books provide real narratives, with identifiable characters and exciting plots in the context of appealing watercolor illustrations.

Alphabet books are one of the oldest form of book written for children. These books are still directed to helping young children learn the names and shapes of the letters of the English alphabet. In addition, ABC books can also be used for identification or naming, as they provide the young child with large, bright pictures of animals or single objects to look at and talk about. In general, alphabet books for the youngest child should present easily identifiable objects that are clearly presented on a page. Only one or two objects should be shown and it is best to avoid portraying anything that might have several correct names. For example, if a rabbit is presented for "R," the very young child might refer to it as a "bunny."

For the older preschool child more complex alphabet books can serve as a format to present detailed information about a particular subject, as a showcase for an art book, or to create complicated puzzles. Books such as *A Is for Asia* (Cynthia Chi-Lee, 1997) or *V for Vanishing* (Patricia Mullins, 1994) introduce children to important concepts about their world. Other alphabet books such as *Q Is for Duck* (Mary Elting and Michael Folsom) raise important questions about the world of print by focusing on letter sound relationships.

Counting books, like alphabet books, are meant to teach children names and concepts. Ideally, boys and girls should learn to count by playing with real objects. Since time immemorial, however, we have been providing children with counting books, substituting pictures for real objects. Young children can make this transition from the concrete to its visual representation if they first experience the real and the visual illustrations are then clearly presented. In counting books for the youngest child the objects to be counted should stand out clearly on the page. Various groupings of objects should avoid a cluttered, confusing look.

Counting books, too, vary from the very simple to the more complex. They include books that present one-to-one correspondence such as Molly BANG's *Ten. Nine. Eight.* (1983) or books that present simple mathematical concepts as in Donald CREWS's *Ten Black Dots* (1968, 1986). For preschoolers, number stories such as Ann JONAS's *Splash* (1995) or Bruce MCMILLAN's *Eating Fractions* (1991) are fine introductions to mathematical operations. Lloyd Moss's counting book, *Zin! Zin! Zin! A Violin* (1995), introduces young children to musical concepts while *Emeka's Gift: An African Counting Story* (1995) by Ifeoma Onyefulu extends their understanding of scientific or geographical concepts.

We apply the same standards of excellence to all forms of books for the very young that we expect of literary and artistic objects for all ages. Authors and illustrators provide books that delight the eyes, engage the bodies and intrigue the minds of babies, toddlers, and preschoolers; they make it possible for young children to grow into lifelong readers and lovers of books.

BARBARA A. KIEFER

BOSSE, Malcolm
Author, b. 6 May 1933 (1926 some sources), Detroit, Michigan

Living extensively in India, Bangladesh, Burma, Thailand, and other areas in the Pan-Pacific region shaped B.'s settings for both his YOUNG ADULT and adult novels. *Ganesh* (1982, later reprinted as *Ordinary Magic*) follows an American boy who is born and reared in India. Likewise, *Deep Dream of the Rain Forest* (1994) follows a young boy who joins a Bornean tribesman's attempts to help his tribe; it was named an outstanding book for the middle-school reader by Voice of Youth Advocates.

FURTHER WORKS: *The Barrucuda Gang,* 1982; *Captives of Time,* 1987; *Cave beyond Time,* 1980; *The Seventy-nine Squares,* 1979

BIBLIOGRAPHY: *The Fifth Book of Junior Authors and Illustrators,* 1983

GWYNNE ELLEN ASH

BOSTON, Lucy M.

Author, b. 10 December 1892, Southport, Lancashire, England; d. 30 July 1990, Hemingford Grey, Huntingtonshire, England

One of the most engaging British children's authors in the second half of the twentieth century, B. is known primarily for her SERIES of novels with the principal setting of Green Knowe, the fictionalized version of her house in Hemingford Grey. B. introduced the series with the publication in 1954 of *The Children of Green Knowe,* the same year in which she published her first adult novel entitled *Yew Hall,* which together marked the beginning of B.'s literary career. Most remarkable is that B. made her debut at the age of sixty-two.

Born Lucy Maria Wood in the north of England, B. attended boarding school in Sussex and after studying in Paris attended Somerville College, Oxford. She later worked in Paris as a nurse's aide during World War I before returning to England in 1917. B. purchased the twelfth-century house known as the Manor in Hemingford Grey in 1939 where she would live for the remainder of her life.

Drawn to the beauty and complacency of the idyllic Huntingtonshire countryside, B. found solace in the home she restored and cherished, preferring to fill the void of loneliness with a world of her own invention. As a result, she created the character of Toseland or Tolly, who in the first novel in the Green Knowe series, *The Children of Green Knowe,* travels as a seven-year-old to meet his great-grandmother for the first time longing for a family he has never known. During the visit, Tolly comes to experience an intuitive affinity not only for the enchanting house but also for the insightful Mrs. Oldknow, modeled after B. herself. Mrs. Oldknow realizes Tolly's potential and guides him in the process of discovering his self-worth and identity. Merging the past with the present, the story unfolds as a mystery as Tolly learns about the history of the house and his extended family culminating in a sequence of events that enables Tolly to interact with his seventeenth-century ancestors. *The Children of Green Knowe* was illustrated by B.'s son, Peter Boston, who illustrated all of the books in the Green Knowe series and all but two of B.'s works for children.

Tolly reappears in the second novel of the Green Knowe series, *The Chimneys of Green Knowe* (1958), published in the United States as *Treasure of Green Knowe.* Returning to Green Knowe several months after his first visit, Tolly arrives to find his great-grandmother in danger of losing the beloved house. The only means to save Green Knowe is to discover the long-lost family jewels, and Tolly sets out to unravel the mystery. Once again, the house holds the secret, and in searching for the treasure Tolly is drawn into an intricate web of intrigue and adventure. Similar to the previous novel, a supernatural interaction with the past allows Tolly to become part of the family history from which he emerges with a true sense of accomplishment and belonging. In the end, the jewels are found and the house saved, but for Tolly the true reward lies within his personal growth and development.

During the next five years, B. produced three more novels in the series: *The River at Green Knowe* (1959), noteworthy for the absence of both Tolly and Mrs. Oldknow as the house is let for the summer and a new set of children are introduced to the magical qualities of Green Knowe; *A Stranger at Green Knowe* (1961), for which B. received the CARNEGIE MEDAL, and *An Enemy at Green Knowe* (1964), the darkest and most controversial of the Green Knowe novels. Following the publication of *An Enemy of Green Knowe,* B. published a series of shorter works for children as well as a second adult novel, *Persephone* (1969), published in the United States as *Strongholds,* before returning to her most familiar subject with the publication in 1976 of *The Stones of Green Knowe.* In addition, she produced two volumes of memoirs, *Memory in a House* (1973) and *Perverse and Foolish: A Memoir of Childhood and Youth* (1979).

FURTHER WORKS: *The Castle of Yew* (illus. by Marjery Gill). 1965; *The Sea Egg,* 1967; *The House That Grew* (Caroline Heming, illus.). 1969; *The Horned Man; or, Whom Will You Send to Fetch Her Away?,* 1970; *Nothing Said,* 1971; *The Fossil Snake,* 1973; *The Guardians of the House,* 1974

BIBLIOGRAPHY: Blatt, G. "Profile: Lucy M. Boston," *Language Arts,* 60 (February 1983):

pp. 220–25; B., D. ed. *Lucy B. Remembered: Reminiscences Collected by Diana B.* 1994; Cameron, E. *The Green and Burning Tree: On the Writing and Enjoyment of Children's Books,* 1969; Hollindale, P. "Timescape at Hemingford Grey: Lucy B.'s Centenary," *Children's Literature,* 22, 1994, pp. 139–48; Rose, John Rose, *Lucy B.,* 1965; Townsend, John Rose, *A Sense of Story: Essays on Contemporary Writers for Children,* 1973; Stott, J. C., "From Here to Eternity: Aspects of Pastoral in the Green Knowe Series," *Children's Literature.* 11, 1983, pp. 145–55

STEVEN R. SERAFIN

BOUTET DE MONVEL, Maurice (Louis)

Illustrator, b. 16 March 1850, Orleans, France; d. 16 March 1913, Nemours, France

B. was born the oldest of several children in an artistic family. His inclination toward art was encouraged and cultivated especially by his mother. He studied at the Ecole des Beaux-Arts in Paris and won first place in 1878 in a Paris exhibit. B. eventually became an illustrator of children's books although he commented that he did not consider the painting for children to be his serious work, but necessity forced him to do it. Even so, B. is often compared in importance to Kate GREENAWAY and Walter CRANE. He was the illustrator for the French edition of *St. Nicholas,* the children's MAGAZINE, and *Fables of La Fontaine,* 1897.

His best-known work, *Jeanne d'Arc* (1896, U.S. edition 1907) for which he also wrote the text, is characterized by delicate, muted, flattoned colors reminiscent of Japanese art that depict mostly the emotional effect of the story as well as its dramatic events. B.'s concept of an illustrated picture book for children was new and it is still considered one of the most beautiful PICTURE BOOKS ever published. The ILLUSTRATIONS faithfully depict fifteenth-century France, from the colorful pomp-filled ceremony crowning the King, to the solemn scene of Joan praying quietly before she goes into battle, the background illuminated by golden candlelight. Most memorable is the scene of Joan's trial: the blue of her robe in stark contrast to the drab grays of the judge's robes and the walls of the courtroom. With this book, B. established a level of art not seen before in children's books, influencing many illustrators and still highly esteemed in the children's publishing world.

FURTHER WORKS: *Brother of the Birds: A Little History of St. Francis of Assisi,* reissued 1929; *Everybody's St. Francis,* 1912; *Girls and Boys* (Anatole France, author). 1913; *Our Children* (Anatole France, author). 1917; *Joan of Arc,* written and illustrated by Maurice B.; introduction by Gerald Gottlieb, 1980

BIBLIOGRAPHY: Cott, Jonathan, *Pipers at the Gates of Dawn: The Wisdom of Children's Literature,* 1981

MICHAEL O'LAUGHLIN

BOVA, Ben(jamin)

Author, b. 8 November 1932, Philadelphia, Pennsylvania

B. has had a distinguished career writing both science and SCIENCE FICTION. He has worked on both authoring and editing works for young people and adults. B. enjoyed studying science, even as he pursued a degree in journalism and worked as a newspaper editor. His enjoyment came through reading science fiction and the works of scientists written for the general public. This love led him to write in the same style that appealed to him as a reader both in fiction and nonfiction. His first novel for YOUNG ADULTS was *The Star Conquerors* (1959). This novel was soon followed by several others including *The Milky Way Galaxy* (1961), *The Fourth State of Matter* (1971), and *Welcome to Moonbase* (1987), which were all named best science books of the year by the AMERICAN LIBRARY ASSOCIATION.

FURTHER WORKS: *The Uses of Space,* 1965; *The Weathermakers,* 1967; *Escape,* 1970; *Flight of Exiles,* 1972; *As on a Darkling Plain,* 1972; *The Amazing Laser,* 1972; *Man Changes the Weather,* 1973; *Exiled from Earth,* 1974; *Workshops in Space,* 1974; *Ben B., through the Eyes of Wonder: Science Fiction and Science,* 1975; *The Winds of Altair,* 1983

MICHAEL O'LAUGHLIN

BOYLSTON, Helen Dore

Nurse, author, b. 4 April 1895, Portsmouth, New Hampshire; d. 30 September 1984, Place unknown

B. is best known as the author of the Sue Barton, Student Nurse (1936) series for young girls. Having served as a nurse in the British Expeditionary Force during World War I, B. had firsthand experience in the war, and she used her knowledge in her stories. In addition to the Sue Barton series, Boylston wrote an autobiography of her experiences during the war, entitled *Sister: The War Diary of a Nurse* (1927). She also wrote a BIOGRAPHY of Clara Barton called *Clara Barton, Founder of the American Red Cross* (1955), and another series featuring Carol Page. B.'s work had enduring appeal for young readers, and gave rise to many other career SERIES during the 1930s and 1940s.

FURTHER WORKS: *Sue Barton, Student Nurse,* 1936; *Sue Barton, Senior Nurse,* 1937; *Sue Barton, Visiting Nurse,* 1938; *Sue Barton, Rural Nurse,* 1939; *Sue Barton, Superintendent of Nurses,* 1940; *Sue Barton, Neighborhood Nurse,* 1949; *Sue Barton, Staff Nurse,* 1952; *Carol Plays Summer Stock,* 1942; *Carol Goes on the Stage,* 1947; *Carol on Broadway,* 1944; *Carol on Tour,* 1946

BIBLIOGRAPHY: Cornelia MEIGS, et al., *A Critical History of Children's Literature,* 1953, 1969; *Something about the Author,* vol. 23, 1981

MARY ARIAIL BROUGHTON

BRADBURY, Ray
Author, b. 22 August 1920, Waukegan, Illinois

With childhood memories of beastly creatures, ghosts, dead men, and magicians, B. remembers growing up exhilarating in the complexities of his imagination and emotions. His response to these experiences was writing. Before the age of twelve, B. was recording experiences on a toy typewriter and at twelve began writing Martian stories. Other interests found him as a young adolescent broadcasting on a local radio and, following a family move to Los Angeles, spending much of his time at the MGM film studio. Later, he received encouragement from the authors in the Los Angeles Science Fiction League as he pursued his goal of becoming a professional writer. An early philosophy B. shares was ". . . to have a ball, to be joyful, to be loving, and to be explosive." Early stories were accepted in magazines and his first novel, *The Martian Chronicles* (1950), was the result of combining a series of short stories about Mars. This novel was followed by other early successes as *The Illustrated Man* (1951) and his first screenplay, *Moby Dick* (1953).

Fahrenheit 451 (1953) a novel about book burning (CENSORSHIP) was followed by *Dandelion Wine* (1957), a series of autobiographical reflections and searches for meanings behind his childhood experiences. His indulgence in writing novels, short stories, POETRY and plays as he re-created his own life experiences supported his philosophy to write out of his own heartfelt needs.

As a prolific contributor to the literary field, B.'s early love for SCIENCE FICTION resulted in captivating stories for young people as the genre acquired respect in the field. Motivating readers and providing superb examples of literary elements, B. feels he is a chronicler of his time and a teller of cautionary tales. He often writes one thousand to two thousand words a day. His celebration of all life has to offer is seen in his writing. B. continues adding to his legacy with such books as *Quicker Than the Eye* (1996) and *Dogs Think That Every Day* (1997). His books have sold millions of copies.

Originally published in 1955, *Switch on the Night,* a PICTURE BOOK with science fiction overtones, celebrated a child conquering his fear of the night with help from Dark, a character who introduces him to the mesmerizing atmosphere and visual spectacle that appear at night. Reissued in 2000, *Switch on the Night,* illustrated by Leo and Diane DILLON, updates B.'s story by introducing Dark as an AFRICAN AMERICAN girl, providing a contemporary MULTICULTURAL extension that is appropriate to the picture book.

B.'s numerous awards include: The O. Henry Award (1947) for "Homecoming"; Best Author of 1949 Science Fiction and Fantasy Award from the National Institute of Arts and Letters (1954); *New York Times* Best Illustrated Children's Books of the Year (1955) and Boys' Club of America Junior Book Award (1956) for *Switch on the Night;* Science Fiction Hall of Fame by the Science Fiction Writers of Ameria (1970) for "Mars is Heaven!"; Jules VERNE Award (1984); Body of Work Award from PEN (1985); and the Grand Masters Award from Nebula Science Fiction Writers of America (1988).

FURTHER WORKS: *R Is for Rocket,* 1962; *Something Wicked This Way Comes,* 1962; *I Sing the Body Electric,* 1969, reissued 1998; "When Elephants Last in the Dooryards Bloomed," 1973;

The Halloween Tree, 1982, reissued 1988; *Death Is a Lonely Business,* 1985

BIBLIOGRAPHY: B. Ray. "Day of the Bird Man," *American Way,* Jan. 1, 1993; Levy, Mark, interview with Ray B., "People In Books: Creating Something Memorable," *American Bookseller,* Feb. 1997; Numerous news clippings from the *Los Angeles Herald Examiner* and the *San Francisco Examiner*

JANELLE MATHIS

BRANLEY, Franklyn M.

Author, b. 5 June 1915, New Rochelle, New York

B., author of children's science books, began his teaching career in the field of elementary school science in the 1930s. As a relatively new content area for elementary students, B. saw a need and began writing guides for elementary science teachers. This eventually led to a career writing INFORMATIONAL texts, beginning with books that helped children do simple experiments at home, and then writing books on scientific principles, specifically astronomy. B. helped develop the concept of the informational picture book with his science-based PICTURE BOOKS in the 1950s, including *Snow Is Falling* (1963, rev. ed. 1986), and *Flash, Crash, Rumble, and Roll* (Edward EMBERLEY, illus., 1964, rev. 1985) about thunderstorms. In 1956 B. was appointed Associate Astronomer of the American Museum-Hayden Planetarium in New York City. B. has won several AWARDS including Outstanding Science Trade Books for Children for *Star Guide* and *From* Sputnik *to Space Shuttles: Into the New Space Age* (1986). B. also won the Library of Congress Choice Book for *Saturn.*

AWARDS: Eva L. Gordon Award for Children's Science Literature, (1988)

FURTHER WORKS: *Exploring by Satellite,* 1957; *Solar Energy,* 1957; *The Nine Planets,* 1958; *Earthquakes,* 1990; *Keeping Time: From the Beginning and into the 21st Century,* 1993

BIBLIOGRAPHY: *Contemporary Authors,* online, 2000; MEIGS, C., A. T. EATON, E. NESBIT, R. H. Viguers, *A Critical History of Children's Literature.* 1969. *Something about the Author,* vol. 68, 1992

MICHAEL O'LAUGHLIN

BRETT, Jan (Churchill)

Author, illustrator, b. 1 December 1949, Hingham, Massachusetts

B. was born in a seacoast town and has always lived near the sea. She attended Colby-Sawyer College and the Boston Museum of Fine Arts School. She has exhibited both her paintings and illustrations. As a child, B. decided to become an illustrator; she spent many hours reading and drawing. She felt she could enter the pages of beautiful PICTURE BOOKS that she read and now hopes that children can do that with her picture books. B. first illustrated Stephen Krensky's *Woodland Crossings* (1978) and began to realize her dream of becoming a professional artist. She continued to illustrate books for other writers while developing a unique style of incorporating Old World FOLKLORE and motifs into borders framing her art. B.'s books have received attention for her effective use of ILLUSTRATION to further the meaning, symbolism, moral, and action in a story. Her elaborate borders and side panels graphically reveal simultaneous and forthcoming events, or details not presented in the main story line and pictures. Foreshadowing through borders has become a trademark of her work. B. visits many countries of the world where she researches the architecture and costumes native to the residents. She says, "From cave paintings, to Japanese gardens, I study the traditions of the many countries I visit, and use them as a starting point for my children's books." B.'s most successful picture books find their subjects in folklore, FANTASY, holidays, or ANIMAL tales. B. appropriately clothes her characters in traditional folk costumes and fills dramatic backgrounds with tapestries and complex architectural structures. B. prepares extensive materials for teachers and librarians to use with her books.

AWARDS: Parents' Choice Award, Parents' Choice Foundation (1981) Children's Choices (1982) for *Fritz and the Beautiful Horse,* (1988) for *Mother's Day Mice;* INTERNATIONAL READING ASSOCIATION/CHILDREN'S BOOK COUNCIL Children's Choices (1982), *Redbook* magazine Children's Picturebook Award (1985) for *Annie and the Wild Animals.* AMERICAN LIBRARY ASSOCIATION Notable Book (1986) for *The Twelve Days of Christmas,*

(1987) for *Goldilocks and the Three Bears. Parents* magazine Book of the Year (1988) for *Mother's Day Mice* by Eve BUNTING, (1991) for *The Owl and the Pussycat* by Edward LEAR. American Bookseller Pick of the Lists (1988) for *The First Dog,* (1989) for *The Mitten: A Ukranian Folktale,* (1990) for *The Wild Christmas Reindeer,* (1991) for *The Owl and the Pussycat* and *Berlioz the Bear. Booklist* Best Children's Book of the 1980s (1989) for *The Mitten;* New England Book Award for lifetime achievement (1990). *School Library Journal* Best Book of the Year and ALA Notable Book (1991) for *The Owl and the Pussycat.* David MCCORD Children's Literature Citation (1993) for Contribution to Excellence

FURTHER WORKS: Self-Illustrated: *Good Luck Sneakers,* 1981; reteller and illustrator: *Beauty and the Beast,* 1989; illustrator (under name Jan Brett Bowler). *Inside a Sand Castle and Other Secrets,* Mary Louise Cuneo, 1979; *The Secret Clocks: Time Senses of Living Things,* 1979; *St. Patrick's Day* by Eve Bunting, 1980; *Young Melvin and Bulger,* Mark Taylor, 1981; *In the Castle of the Cats,* Betty Boegehold, 1981; *I Can Fly,* Ruth KRAUSS, 1981; *The Valentine Bears,* Eve Bunting, 1983; *Noelle of the Nutcracker,* Pamela Jane, 1986; *Scary, Scary Halloween,* Eve Bunting, 1986; *The Enchanted Book: A Tale from Krakow,* Janina Porazinska, trans. Bozena Smith, 1987; *Happy Birthday, Dear Duck,* Eve Bunting, 1988

BIBLIOGRAPHY: Silvey, A. ed., *Children's Books* and *Their Creators,* 1995; *Something about the Author,* vol. 42, and vol. 71; www.janbrett.com

CRAIG LIEBERMAN

BRIDGERS, Sue Ellen
Author, b. 20 September 1942, Greenville, North Carolina

B. grew up in a small Appalachian village in eastern North Carolina where generations of family from both sides had lived. She attended Eastern Carolina University and graduated from Western Carolina University. Her writing deals with the rural South in ways that resonate with its geographical and emotional spaces. B.'s themes recall both the demands and benefits of family life. Her first novel, *Home before Dark* (1976), received high praise. B. begins a novel, not with plot, but with one or two characters. She believes that characters form the bridge between author and reader. B.'s father, Wayland Louis, is the basis for a character in *Notes for Another Life*

(1981). Her father represents the farmer's spiral into depression. This is an example of the way B. uses autobiographical portraits; she also includes themes of social rejection and the death of her parents. Faced with difficult problems, families band together to save a troubled son or to support a mother's decision to move forward in her career.

B.'s mother supported B.'s private decision in her secondary school years to become a writer. Her mother read to her as a child and taught her the alphabet, not for purposes of writing, but to read. B.'s writing progressed from POETRY, usually about the holidays, to short stories. Her early success gave her the encouragement to try something longer. B. is a firm believer in visions. According to B., her books begin in a visionary moment. She envisions a scene that comes spontaneously with potent images from which she cannot shake free until she writes.

AWARDS: Breadloaf Writer's Fellowship (1976); *Boston Globe–Horn Book* Award, Christopher Award, AMERICAN LIBRARY ASSOCIATION Best Books for YOUNG ADULTS (1980) for *All Together Now;* ALAN Award, Assembly on Literature for Adolescents of the NATIONAL COUNCIL OF TEACHERS OF ENGLISH (1985); Parents' Choice Award, North Carolina Literary and Historical Association Award (1987) for *Permanent Connections*

FURTHER WORKS: *Keeping Christina,* 1993; *Connections: Short Stories by Outstanding Writers for Young Adults* (ed. D. Gallo), 1989; *Our Words, Our Ways: Reading and Writing in North Carolina* (with Sally Bockner, ed., 1995)

BIBLIOGRAPHY: Hipple, Ted. *Presenting Sue Ellen B.,* 1990; *Children's Literature Review,* vol. 18; *Something about the Author,* vol. 90

CRAIG LIEBERMAN

BRIDWELL, Norman
Author, illustrator, b. 15 February 1928, Kokomo, Indiana

B. is a freelance artist and author. He is best known for his popular SERIES of books about Clifford, a big red dog, and the dog's owner, Emily Elizabeth. B. was selected as Author of the Year by the Lucky Book Club/Four-Leaf Clover Award for *Clifford, the Big Red Dog,* first published in 1962. The book also won the Children's Choice Award for best PICTURE BOOK (1987) and the Jeremiah Ludington Memorial Award, Educational Paperback Association (1991). B. has also written and illustrated several delightful and humorous books about witches and monsters, including *The Witch Next Door* (1965), *The Witch's Christmas* (1986), *The Witch's Vacation* (1987), and *Monster Holidays* (1988). B. has illustrated all the books he has written.

FURTHER WORKS: *Clifford's Good Deeds,* 1975; *Clifford Gets a Job,* 1985; *Clifford Takes a Trip,* 1985; *Clifford's Bathtime,* 1991; *Clifford, We Love You,* 1991; *Clifford and the Big Storm,* 1995; *Clifford Barks,* 1996; *Clifford's Sports Day,* 1996; *Clifford's First Valentine's Day,* 1997

BIBLIOGRAPHY: *Something about the author,* vol. 68, 1992

MARY ARIAIL BROUGHTON

BRIGGS, Raymond
Author, illustrator, b. 18 January 1934, London, England

Originally an artist, B. became involved in children's books when he began accepting illustration assignments from publishers. B. has illustrated hundreds of pictures for collections of nursery rhymes and FAIRY TALES. Finding some books unappealing, however, B. tried writing children's books himself; his first attempt was published. B.'s self-illustrated works often contain cartoon-style drawings. *The Snowman* (1978) is a perennially popular wordless picture-book FANTASY done with softly colored pencil drawings, in which a little boy dreams he meets a snowman. B. writes for no particular audience—he simply writes and draws to please himself and his readers.

B.'s PICTURE BOOKS often have multilayered texts and illustrations intended for all age levels. He uses a comic strip format contrasted with stark, impressionist-style illustrations to portray the horrors of nuclear war in *When the Wind Blows* (1982). Contrasting styles of art and his use of color create scenes of devastation caused by nuclear holocaust. Small cartoons, twenty to a page, alternate with full-page drawings of the impending holocaust until B. uses a two-page spread to show the violent white flash of the

blast. His colors gradually fade from bright green of the countryside to bleak tints as characters prepare for doom and then to sickening tones representing radiation poisoning. Though technically a picture book, the audience for *When the Wind Blows* is much broader than the usual picture book, but B.'s ability to use color, facial expression, body language, and other ILLUSTRATION techniques is as apparent here as in his more traditional picture books. *The Tin-Pot Foreign General and the Old Iron Woman* (1985) is a satirical antiwar picture book done in charcoal, based on the events of the Falkland Islands (Islas Malvinas) War. B. uses two distinctive styles of illustration—soft evocatives and sharp metallic caricatures—to represent his powerful antiwar theme.

AWARDS: *Boston Globe–Horn Book* Award for Illustration (1979) for *The Snowman.*

FURTHER WORKS: *The MOTHER GOOSE Treasury* (1966); *Elephant and the Bad Baby.* (E. Vipont, author). 1969; *Jim and the Beanstalk,* 1970; *Father Christmas,* 1973; *Fee Fi Fo Fum: The Mother Goose Treasury,* 1980; *Fungus the Bogeyman* 1982; *When the Wind Blows,* 1982; *The Bear,* 1994

BIBLIOGRAPHY: Cianciolo, Patricia; *Picture Books for Children.* 3rd ed. 1990; Schwarz, Joseph, and Chava Schwarz, *The Picture Book Comes of Age,* 1991; *Something about the Author,* vol. 66, 1991

JODI PILGRIM

BRINK, Carol Ryrie
Author, b. 28 December 1895, Moscow, Idaho; d. 15 August 1981, La Jolla, California

B. was reared in the little country town of Moscow, Idaho. An orphan by the age of eight, she went to live with her grandmother. B. loved to listen to her grandmother's stories about her pioneer life on the Wisconsin frontier. She later recorded these memories in her 1936 NEWBERY MEDAL winning historical fiction novel, *Caddie Woodlawn.* B.'s interest in writing developed in high school as she wrote a number of stories for a magazine. During her college years at the University of Idaho, she worked on the college newspaper as well as other publications. B. attended the University of Idaho for three years, but graduated from the University of California at Berkeley. After graduation, she married Raymond Brink, a college mathematics professor. She chronicled their travels through Europe and their trips on the Seine and Yonne Rivers with their son in her first book, *Anything Can Happen on the River* (1934). *Mademoiselle Misfortune* (1937) was also inspired by their journeys in France and bears an inscription to B.'s daughter.

B. wrote seventeen children's novels as well as novels and poetry for adults, often drawing on the experiences of her family as the subject of her books. She is praised for her understanding of childhood and family life as well as for her knowledge of history. Her work often features characters who were orphaned or motherless. B. felt that the best fiction writing arises out of the emotions, so most of her books begin with a feeling for a person or a place. Her 1937 poem about colonial life in Plymouth Colony, *Goody O'Grumpity,* was reissued in 1994 in a newly illustrated picture-book format.

AWARDS: The story of B.'s grandmother's pioneer childhood, *Caddie Woodlawn,* won the Newbery Medal in 1936 and the Lewis CARROLL Shelf Award in 1959. B. also won the University of Minnesota Irvin KERLAN Award in 1978 for *Four Girls on a Homestead,* which was self-illustrated. She received the Friend of American Writers Award in 1956 for *The Headland.* She was awarded both the McKnight Family Literature Foundation Award (1964) and the National League of American Pen Women Award (1966), for her adult novel *Snow in the River;* which B. claims was close to being an autobiography. Finally, B. earned the Southern California Council on Literature for Children and Young People Award (1966)

FURTHER WORKS: *Baby Island,* 1937; *Magical Melons: Stories about Caddie Woodlawn,* 1944; *Family Grandstand,* 1952; *Family Sabbatical,* 1956; *Andy Buckram's Tin Men,* 1966; *Winter Cottage,* 1968; *Two Are Better Than One,* 1968; *The Bad Times of Irma Baumlein,* 1972; *Louly,* 1974

BIBLIOGRAPHY: *Something about the Author,* vol. 31, 1983; *Children's Literature Review,* vol. 30, 1993; HOPKINS, Lee Bennett, *Pauses: Autobiographical Reflections of 101 Creators of Children's Books,* 1995

JODI PILGRIM

BRITISH LITERATURE

Before the eighteenth century, British children either shared the folktales printed for adults, most widely in chapbook form, or read purely educational or religious material. With literacy rapidly increasing, publishers saw a sales opportunity; John NEWBERY's *A Little Pretty Pocket Book,* and Mary Cooper's *Tom Thumb,* both published in 1744 marked the beginning of the exploitation of a major market.

They also marked the beginning of a hundred-year contest between commercial publishers, who generally blended the educational with the entertaining, and the religious publishers who frowned on folktale and FANTASY. Writers like Sarah TRIMMER (*Fabulous Histories,* 1786, and *The Guardian of Education,* 1802–6), produced endless improving tracts, often with examples of dire punishments for misbehavior. Perhaps the most famous of these books was Mary Martha Sherwood's *The History of the Fairchild Family* (1818 and sequels). There were, of course, exceptions, such as Maria Edgeworth and William Godwin, and as the century progressed, children in the books became more realistic, notably in Catherine Sinclair's *Holiday House* (1839).

With the translation of the GRIMMS' *Household Tales* (1823) and Hans Christian ANDERSEN's *FAIRY TALES* (1846), fairy- and folktales became increasingly popular and were adapted for children. Broadly, writing for children divided between books for boys and books for girls. Captain Marryatt's *Masterman Ready* (1841–42) a riposte to the inaccuracies that he found in the very popular *Swiss Family Robinson* (WYSS, translated 1814) began a tradition of sea and desert-island ADVENTURE STORIES which was soon grafted on to the empire-building stories. In both the "penny dreadfuls" (the successor to the less Puritan strain of the chapbook, and cousin to the American "dime novels") and from mainstream publishers came epics of clean-cut English boys who heroically extended or defended the British Empire. Major writers were R. M. Ballantyne (*The Coral Island,* 1858), W. H. G. Kingston (*Peter the Whaler,* 1851), and G. A. Henty, whose eighty-three books, between 1871 and 1906 covered every aspect of the imperial idea. At home, books for girls by writers like Charlotte YONGE (*The Daisy Chain,* 1856), and "Brenda" (*Froggy's Little Brother,* 1875) emphasized middle-class family values, Christian benevolence and—incidentally—maintained the status quo. Fairy-tale elements found their way into these books:

notable examples are Mrs. MOLESWORTH's *The Cuckoo Clock,* 1876) and Jean INGELOW's *Mopsa the Fairy* (1869).

In the 1860s came a remarkable series of books, products of a rapidly changing world, where British supremacy was being challenged, and attitudes to children were altering as families became smaller and health care and education improved. Charles KINGSLEY's fable *The Water Babies* (1873) led the way with a kaleidoscopic display of social and political philosophy and eccentric opinion under the guise of a moral fantasy. Lewis CARROLL's *Alice's Adventures in Wonderland* (1865) has no claims to moralism, but is an intricate fantasy, laden with intellectual, semantic, and mathematical puzzles and jokes. It portrays Victorian childhood as a world of repression, but, perhaps for the first time, it genuinely empowers the (female) child hero in a land of mad adults with arbitrary powers. George MACDONALD's *The Princess and the Goblin* (1871) combined fairy-tale elements with high religious allegory. Other major figures were Robert Louis STEVENSON, who transformed the sea story into a mature, morally complex fiction with *Treasure Island* (1883), and the transatlantic author, Frances Hodgson BURNETT, who transformed the romantic fiction genre into a subtle discussion of class and gender in *The Secret Garden* (1911).

Two figures overshadow the others. The first is Rudyard KIPLING, who excelled in several genres, including the ANIMAL STORY in *The Jungle Book* (1894), the SCHOOL STORY in *Stalky and Co.* (1899), and the HISTORICAL STORY in *Puck of Pook's Hill* (1906). The second, Edith NESBIT, was instrumental in shifting the tone that authors used toward readers away from the didactic and patronizing tendency of the nineteenth century. She contributed notable series of books, some of which blended fantasy with realism, such as *Five Children and It* (1902), and others that brought a new realism to the Victorian family story, such as *The Treasure Seekers* (1899).

Three other classics, all of which have entered the British national psyche date from this period. Beatrix POTTER's gently ironic Peter Rabbit series (1902 on), like Kenneth GRAHAME's *The Wind in the Willows* (1908), epitomizes a lost rural idyllic world—although there is some doubt as to whether the latter is actually a children's book. J. M. BARRIE's *Peter Pan* (first performed as a play in 1904) is notable for not having a definitive version.

The period between the world wars (1918–39) was marked by retreatism, epitomized in fantasy by A. A. MILNE's *Winnie-the-Pooh* (1926) and P. L. TRAVER's *Mary Poppins* (1934) and in realism by Arthur RANSOME's "Swallows and Amazons" sequence (1934–47), largely set in the English Lake District. Two writers who had huge success after World War II, Enid BLYTON—whose eventual 600-plus books put her at the top of the world bestseller list for children—and J. R. R. TOLKIEN, whose *The Hobbit* (1938) looked forward to the books often voted as books of the century, *The Lord of the Rings* (1954–56) trilogy.

Since 1945, British children's books have boomed, both in quantity and quality. In the 1950s and 1960s, major writers such as Alan GARNER, William MAYNE, Philippa PEARCE, and Jill PATON WALSH established themselves, alongside picture-book writers and illustrators such as Quentin BLAKE, John BURNINGHAM, Helen OXENBURY, and Shirley HUGHES. In the 1970s, partly because of the influence of the U.S.A., the emphasis shifted away from fantasy towards realism, culminating in Melvin Burgess's *Junk* (1997), a very grim book about drug abuse, which won the CARNEGIE MEDAL. By 1997, production had reached over 8,000 titles each year, and although the market is heavily dominated by SERIES BOOKS (such as the imported Point Horror, or the homegrown Animal Ark) the general opinion is that British children's books have never been so healthy in range and quality.

BIBLIOGRAPHY: *The Oxford Companion to Children's Literature.* 1984. Harvey Darton, F. J. *Children's Books in England.* (rev. ed., 1982) Hunt, Peter. *An Introduction to Children's Literature,* 1994. Hunt, Peter. (ed). *Children's Literature: An Illustrated History,* 1995. Townsend, John Rowe. *Written for Children,* 1990; Watkins, Tony, *The Heroic Figure in Children's Pop Culture,* 1998

PETER HUNT

BRITTAIN, William E. (Bill)
Author, b. 16 December 1930, Rochester, New York

B. writes adult mysteries under the pseudonym James Knox, but he is known primarily for his funny, wise, and weird tales for young people. His ability to juxtapose the amazing, the strange, and the gothic, with the funny, the hilarious, and the exaggerated, easily captures readers and takes them along in a series of grand adventurous romps. The four Coven Tree books are the best exemplars of this, and certainly the 1984 NEW-BERY MEDAL Honor book, *The Wish Giver: Three Tales of Coven Tree* is one of his finest. B.'s stories make clear that what we might wish for is not necessarily what we really want. His combination of the humorous and the frightful in a carefully balanced work is experienced by fascinating characters such as Stew Meat of the Coven Tree novels who leads readers through his adventurous literary mazes. B.'s plot twists are clever and he creates mood by the careful presentation of what might be, not necessarily what actually is.

AWARDS: AMERICAN LIBRARY ASSOCIATION Newbery Medal Honor Book (1984) for *The Wish Giver*. Charlie May Simon Children's Book Award (1981–82) for *All the Money in the World*

FURTHER WORKS: *Devil's Donkey*, 1981; *Dr. Dredd's Wagon of Wonders*, 1987; *Professor Popkin's Prodigious Polish*, 1990; *Shape-changer*, 1994

BIBLIOGRAPHY: *Something about the Author*, vol. 7, 1989; Hannigan, Jane Anne, "Bill B.," *Twentieth-Century Children's Writers*, 4th ed., ed. by Laura Standley Berger, 1995; Silvey, Anita, ed., *Children's Books and Their Creators*, 1995

KAY E. VANDERGRIFT

BROOKE, L(eonard) Leslie
Illustrator, author, b. 24 September 1862, Birkenhead, Cheshire, England; d. 1 May 1940, England

B., the son of a Liverpool businessman, was trained in art at the Schools of the Royal Academy in London and was passionate about drawing. His first children's ILLUSTRATIONS were for the girls' stories of Evelyn Everett-Green, 1889, and the stories of Mrs. MOLESWORTH, *The Carved Lions* (1895). It was with the illustrations for An-

drew LANG's *Nursery Rhyme Book* (1897) that he achieved fame, followed by illustrations for Edward LEAR's *The Pelican Chorus* (1899) and *The Jumblies and Other Nonsense Verses* (1900).

In 1903 came the first of his Johnny Crow books, *Johnny Crow's Garden: A PICTURE BOOK*, a work for very young children. The text, by B. himself, is comic doggerel describing the antics of several different animals and was based on stories from B.'s father, to whom the book is dedicated. B.'s lively illustrations, part in color and part in black and white, are reminiscent of Randolph CALDECOTT's, if somewhat more sedate. Some critics even find a touch of the sinister in the faces of many of his animal characters with their humanlike characteristics, though they are generally regarded as friends portrayed with gentle warmth and gentle HUMOR. While B.'s rhymed couplets describe the animals and their behavior, the details in the illustrations really tell the story. In 1960, *Johnny Crow's Garden* received a Lewis CARROLL Shelf Award. The book was followed by two more, *Johnny Crow's Party* (1907) and *Johnny Crow's New Garden* (1935). The books remain popular to this day and are the foundation for his lasting reputation despite the fact that he illustrated some three dozen books, mostly for children.

FURTHER WORKS: The *Story of the Three Little Pigs*, 1904; *The Golden Goose Book*, 1904; *The House in the Wood, and Other Old Fairy Stories* (J. and W. GRIMM, 1909); *Oranges and Lemons: A Nursery Rhyme Book*, 1913

BIBLIOGRAPHY: *Something about the Author*, vol.17, 1979; *The Oxford Companion to Children's Literature*, 1984

DAVID L. RUSSELL

BROOKS, Bruce
Author, b. 23 September 1950, Washington, D.C.

B. spent his childhood and youth moving between his divorced parents' homes in Washington, D.C., and North Carolina, an experience that exposed him to the social pluralism of American culture and that inspired him to play with words and alternative accounts of stories. His early experiences with Northern and Southern approaches to social issues, his frequent status as a new student in school, and the influence of his family's Protestant heritage inform his writings for middle-grade children and YOUNG ADULTS. B. earned a bachelors degree at the University of North Carolina at Chapel Hill (1972) and a masters of fine arts at the University of Iowa (1982).

The Moves Make the Man (1984) was named a notable children's book by the AMERICAN LIBRARY ASSOCIATION in the year of its publication; in 1985, it was named a NEWBERY MEDAL Honor Book. ALA named *Midnight Hour Encores* (1986) a best book for young adults; it earned recognition, in 1987, by the NATIONAL COUNCIL OF TEACHERS OF ENGLISH as a teacher's choice, and, in 1988, the INTERNATIONAL READING ASSOCIATION named it a young adult choice. *Midnight Hour Encores* also became one of ALA's best of the 1980s books for young adults. *No Kidding* (1989) was an ALA best book for young adults. *Everywhere* (1990) was named by ALA as a notable children's book. All of these books have received high praise by various professional and literary publications as well. *What Hearts* was named a Newbery Medal Honor Book in 1993.

From his first published novel, *The Moves Make the Man*, B. has been recognized by critics as opinionated and both brave enough and verbally dexterous enough to provide young readers with literary experiences that make them think and to reconsider what they know. In what could have become an improbable tale in less capable hands, B. shows an interracial friendship between two lonely boys in a Southern town at midcentury. This is not a formula problem novel but a sophisticated and variegated literary work with subplots that include gender roles, race relations, economic and class issues, mental illness, and basketball. B.'s interest in SPORTS STORIES permeates many of his novels, and many of them end ambiguously, as does this first one.

Midnight Hour Encores is somewhat exceptional among B.'s fiction in that he provides a female protagonist, while most of his novels place girls and women in the background. *No Kidding* marked a departure from contemporary realism as B. set this book in the twenty-first century, in a society where alcoholism is endemic. Returning to our current time in *Everywhere,* B. explored such issues as mortality, morality, and spirituality within the confines of a novella-length story.

Asylum for Nightface (1996) offers teenage readers a longer and more nuanced exploration of faith, morals, and the individual's experience of adjusting beliefs with social harmony. Here B. provides a fully worked theology, as it is understood by his protagonist, the son of parents who belatedly discover religious fervor within a cult-like sect. The boy attempts to think and act independently of his parents' beliefs, as well as realize a distance between his spirituality and that of a group of peers who adhere to an exclusive Christianity. B.'s willingness to address the topic of religion and religious expression—an area of keen interest to many teens and one that remains largely absent from contemporary literature published for them—demonstrates his assertion that he wants to continue to attempt new challenges as a writer.

In keeping with his devotion to sports and his primary occupation with male protagonists, B. has provided middle-grade readers with a SERIES featuring an ice-hockey team. The Wolf Bay Wings Sports Series for Boys shows members of the featured hockey team displaying the depth and thoughtfulness with which B. imbues his nonseries characters.

In addition to his fiction, B. has gained repute as a nonfiction writer for children. Most of his nonfiction work addresses topics of natural science, including *On the Wing: The Life of Birds from Feather to Flight* (1989) and *Nature by Design* (1991). However, *Boys Will Be* (1993) is a collection of essays celebrating aspects of boy-ness and boyhood ranging from sweat to reading. This collection has excited some critical discussion on several fronts. B. has been reprimanded for his use of antifemale slang of the type still commonly heard among schoolboys who have not had their feminist consciousnesses yet raised (e.g., "wussie"). That the essays vary in their accessibility to young readers—an intentional variation according to B.'s introduction—also has bothered some reviewers. However, B.'s enthusiasm for books and reading within the natural world of boys is viewed as an antidote to popular wisdom that boys do not care about literature.

B. published his first PICTURE BOOK, *Each a Piece* (1998), to mixed reviews. Admired for his facility with words with which he has created memorable characters and scenes that stimulate readers to think linearly and rationally, B. tries a wholly different approach here, offering a riddle rather than a narrative. This attempt seems to be in keeping with his desire to continue to try new ways of writing a book by writing a new book. In addition to work as a children's writer, B.'s career has included newspaper and magazine reporting, and teaching.

FURTHER WORKS: *Making Sense: Animal Perception and Communication,* 1993; *The Red Wasteland: A Personal Selection of Writings about Nature for Young Readers,* (editor) 1998

BIBLIOGRAPHY: Campbell, P. "Asylum for Nightface." The *Horn Book* magazine July–August 1996; *Contemporary Authors,* vol. 137, 1992; Heppermann, C. "Bruce Brooks on Ice," The *Horn Book* magazine May–June, 1998; Silvey, Anita. ed., *Children's Books and Their Creators,* 1995; *Something about the Author,* vol. 72, 1993

FRANCISCA GOLDSMITH

BROOKS, Gwendolyn

Author, poet, b. 7 June 1917, Topeka, Kansas; d. 3 December 2000, Chicago, Illinois

A highly acclaimed writer of both POETRY and fiction for children and adults, B. became the first AFRICAN AMERICAN to win a Pulitzer Prize in 1950 for her novel *Annie Allen.* B. has served as Illinois's poet laureate and as consultant in poetry to the Library of Congress. She became interested in poetry when she was young and kept a journal for many years of observations and ideas to be developed in poetry. A teacher and mentor of young poets, B. was influenced by relationships with such notable poets as Langston HUGHES and James Weldon Johnson. B. writes in a variety of poetic forms from sonnets and ballads to blues and free verse. Her poetry is characterized by themes of racial injustice, community, and the simultaneous tragedy and joy that marks the lives of poor African Americans.

Bronzeville Boys and Girls (1956), B.'s first book for children, was based on events and people she knew growing up on Chicago's South Side, which is also known as "Bronzeville." It established her as a leading poet for young people. She had written an earlier volume of adult lyric poetry, *Bronzeville* (1945), in a traditional sonnet style. Her poetry expresses the language of ordinary people, urban black women espe-

cially, and uses a conversational tone. Her later poetry is written in free verse.

AWARDS: National Women's Hall of Fame (1988) induction. National Endowment for the Arts (1989) Lifetime Achievement Award

FURTHER WORKS: *Maud Martha, a Novel,* 1953; *The Tiger Who Wore White Gloves; or, What You Are You Are,* 1974

BIBLIOGRAPHY: B., G. *Report from Part One,* 1972; B., G. *Report from Part Two,* 1996; *Dictionary of Literary Biography,* volume 165; *American Poets since World War II,* 1996; Kent, G. E. *A Life of Gwendolyn B.,* 1990; Melhem, D. H. *Gwendolyn B.: Poetry and the Heroic Voice,* 1990; Serafin, S.R., ed., *The Continuum Encyclopedia of American Literature.* 1999; Shaw, Harry B. *Gwendolyn B.,* 1980

JENNIFER E. DUNNE

BROOKS, Martha

Author, b. Date unknown 1944, Ninette, Manitoba, Canada

B. writes YOUNG ADULT short stories and novels from a uniquely teenage point of view, an ability she credits to her daughter's insights. B. has also worked as a creative writing teacher in junior and senior high schools and has written plays, both individually and in collaboration with others. She was reared on the grounds of a tuberculosis sanatorium where her father was a surgeon and her mother a nurse. At an early age B. was aware of the struggle for health and life which took place around her, and was exposed to many people of different backgrounds among the staff. She feels that her unusual background made her a keen student of human behavior; she uses her observations in her writing.

B. uses the first-person narrative effectively in her writing. Her first book, *Paradise Cafe and Other Stories* (1990), contains fourteen stories, each about a different kind of love. The first-person voice brings an immediacy to the telling which allows readers to identify with the joys and sorrows of love, as well as experience its full range of emotions. Although less contemporary in setting (a tuberculosis sanatorium in 1959), *Only a Paper Moon* (1992) conveys the desperation of a sixteen-year-old girl who is trying to cope with her mother's death.

B. feels that life is full of possibilities, and healing and hope are important in her stories, even in the face of reality in the form of addiction, dysfunctional families, love and death. Many teen readers will recognize themselves and their peers in her stories.

AWARDS: INTERNATIONAL BOARD ON BOOKS FOR YOUNG PEOPLE Honor List (1996) for *"Traveling into the Light" and Other Stories*

FURTHER WORKS: *A Hill for Looking,* 1982; *"Traveling into the Light" and Other Stories,* 1994

BIBLIOGRAPHY: Silvey, A., ed., *Children's Books and Their Creators,* 1995

ANITA M. TROUT

BROOKS, Polly Schoyer
Author, b. 11 August 1912, South Orleans, Massachusetts

Best noted for her books about Renaissance and Medieval Europe written with her coauthor Nancy Zissner Walworth (*The World Awakes: The Renaissance in Western Europe,* 1962; *The World of Walls: The Middle Ages in Western Europe,* 1966), B.'s BIOGRAPHY of Eleanor of Aquitaine, *Queen Eleanor, Independent Spirit of the Medieval World: A Biography of Eleanor of Aquitaine* (1983), was named a Notable Book by the AMERICAN LIBRARY ASSOCIATION, An Honor Book in the Nonfiction category of the *Boston Globe-Horn Book* Awards, and a Notable Children's Trade Book in the Field of Social Studies.

FURTHER WORKS: *Beyond Myth: The Story of Joan of Arc,* 1990; *Cleopatra, Goddess of Egypt, Enemy of Rome,* 1995

REFERENCES: *The Seventh Book of Junior Authors and Illustrators,* 1996

GWYNNE ELLEN ASH

BROOKS, Walter R.
Author, b. 9 January 1886, Rome, New York; d. 1958, date and place unknown

B., author of the famous Freddy the Pig books, was orphaned at fifteen. He was then educated at the Mohegan Lake Military Academy in Peekskill, New York, the University of Rochester, and New York's Homeopathic Medical College, which he left without graduating in 1909 to pursue a career in advertising.

It was while working as a publicist for the American Red Cross in Washington, D.C., that he wrote the first Freddy book, *To and Again,* which was published by Alfred A. Knopf in 1927 and reissued in 2000. This droll story of a group of farm animals from upstate New York who decide to vacation in Florida was the first in what would become a SERIES of twenty-five talking animal fantasies starring Freddy the Pig.

Like *The Story of Doctor Dolittle* (Hugh LOFTING) to which it is often compared, *To and Again* is a landmark work in the evolution of American humorous fiction for children. It is ground-breaking in its brisk use of vernacular language, in its respect for the intelligence of its readers, and in its simple and unaffected narrative voice. It is also memorable for introducing one of the great characters of children's literature. Though little more than a featured player at first, Freddy took over center stage in *Freddy the Detective* (1932), the third title in the series, and quickly proved himself to be a pig of many parts: in subsequent titles he would be not only a detective, but also an intrepid traveler, poet, banker, newspaper editor, hot-air balloonist, pilot, politician, pied piper, magician, camper, football player, and more.

In recounting Freddy's respective adventures, B. proved himself a master of humorous devices including inspired wordplay and satire. An amateur linguist, he loved words and playing with their sounds. Indeed, when one of his characters confesses, "I've always had a predilection for this here sesquipedaliainism," it might as well be the author himself talking. His related delight in lampooning long-winded and self-important authority figures, especially politicians (and eagles who "since they are the national bird, have a great sense of their own dignity"), places him squarely in an American tradition that began with the Down East humorists of the 1830s. Finally, his love for inventing comic and archaic-sounding exclamations and regionalisms also derives from this same Yankee tradition.

In addition to their HUMOR and memorable characterizations, the Freddy books brilliantly capture and preserve in their setting the kind of uniquely American rural and small-town world that flourished until the 1950s, a place where friendship is treasured and loyalty is unquestioned. Freddy's friends were often in danger; yet, even if the pig was so frightened that his tail had

11. NATALIE BABBITT

12. BYRON BARTON

13. BYRD BAYLOR

14. JOHN BELLAIRS

15. JUDY BLUME

16. BRUCE BROOKS

come completely uncurled, he gritted his teeth and did whatever was necessary to help.

Aside from the Freddy books, B. published a novel *(Ernestine Takes Over,* 1935) and more than 150 short stories for adults, twenty-five of which feature another talking animal hero, Ed the Horse, the inspiration for *Mr. Ed* the popular television series of the 1960s.

B. is one of the few authors whose enduring work is celebrated by two separate fan clubs: the Friends of Freddy and the Mr. Ed Fan Club.

BIBLIOGRAPHY: *Junior Book of Authors,* 2nd ed., 1951; *Something about the Author,* vol. 17, 1979; *Twentieth Century Children's Writers,* 3rd ed., 1989

MICHAEL CART

BROWN, Marc

Author, illustrator, b. 25 November 1946, Erie, Pennsylvania

Recognized today as the creator of anteater siblings Arthur and D.W., B. began his publishing career as a freelance illustrator. Always devoted to the art of STORYTELLING, B.'s early interest in art was encouraged by his grandmother. At the age of ten, he legally had the spelling of his first name changed out of admiration for Marc Chagall. High school art classes further developed his talent and interest in drawing and painting. He enrolled at the Cleveland Institute of Art, supported by his grandmother and scholarships. After graduating with a bachelor of fine arts (1969), he planned to attend Syracuse University. However, the offer of freelance artwork by Houghton Mifflin publishers altered his career path. B.'s early published art work served to illustrate writings by authors including Isaac ASIMOV, Peter DICKINSON, and Janwillem Van de Wetering.

The Child Study Association of America awarded Children's Book of the Year citations in 1971, 1976, and 1986 for *What Makes the Sun Shine?* (I. ASIMOV, 1970), *One Two Three: An Animal Counting Book* (1976), *The Banza: A Haitian Story* (D. WOLKSTEIN, 1981), *What's So Funny, Ketu?* (adapted by Verna AARDEMA, 1982) and *Hand Rhymes* (1985). B.'s first book about Arthur, *Arthur's Nose* (1976), earned recognition from the CHILDREN'S BOOK COUNCIL and INTERNATIONAL READING ASSOCIATION (1976), as did *Arthur's Eyes* (1979) in 1980, *Arthur's Valentine*

(1980), in 1981, *The True Francine* (1981), *Arthur's Halloween* (1982), and *Arthur Goes to Camp* (1982), all in 1982, and, in 1983, *Arthur's April Fool* (1983). *The True Francine* also earned recognition as Notable by the joint committee of the National Council for Social Studies and the Children's Book Council (1982) as did *Oh, Kojo! How Could You?!* (Aardema, 1984) in 1985. The AMERICAN LIBRARY ASSOCIATION awarded Notable Book citations to *Why the Tides Ebb and Flow* (J. Bowden, 1979), *Dinosaurs Beware!: A Safety Guide* (with S. Krensky, 1982), and *Oh, Kojo! How Could You?! Swamp Monsters* (M. Christian, 1983) was awarded the 1985 Library of Congress Book of the Year citation.

B.'s PICTURE BOOKS about Arthur, Arthur's family, and Arthur's friends present preschool and lower elementary grade readers with humorous but insightful stories rooted in contemporary middle-class suburbia. First told by B. to his older son as bedtime stories, Arthur's continuing adventures are all written and rewritten many times over by B. before he illustrates a final manuscript. Arthur undergoes teasing (*Arthur's Nose*), learns responsibility (*Arthur's Pet Business,* 1990), overcomes stage fright (*Arthur Meets the President,* 1991) and learns to cope with other trials with which youngsters can feel sympathy. His younger, brasher sister, D.W., is featured in several books, including *D.W. Rides Again!* (1993) and *D.W. the Picky Eater* (1997).

While B. populates picture books with anthropomorphic woodland animals, he relies on memories of his own childhood—his family, his teachers—for inspiration when it comes to developing both personalities and plotlines. Inspired to address his sons' lack of table manners, he teamed with Stephen Krensky to produce *Perfect Pigs: An Introduction to Manners* (1983). Here, poor manners stand correction—and the insufferably well-mannered bore who appears throughout the guided tour of what would be better behavior gets a satisfying comeuppance in the end, too.

B. has collaborated with his wife, Laurene Krasny Brown, on several books addressing social and psychological issues facing children in the early grades. *Dinosaurs Divorce: A Guide for Changing Families* (1986) and *Dinosaurs to the Rescue! A Guide to Protecting Our Planet* (1992)

present their titular concerns in a manner that both appeals to and communicates well with the intended audience. The two authors also provide age-appropriate guidance for cultural visits, as in *Visiting the Art Museum* (1986, published in London as *Visiting an Exhibition*) and *Dinosaurs Travel: A Guide for Families on the Go* (1988). *What's the Big Secret?: Talking about Sex with Girls and Boys* (1998) offers families a book to read together in which anatomically correct IL-LUSTRATIONS, as well as cartoons, advance a sensitive and sensible explanatory narrative.

B. prefers drawing and watercolor painting as the media with which he illustrates. In addition to illustrating his own stories and picture books by other authors, he has edited and decorated well-regarded collections of *Finger Rhymes* (1980), *Party Rhymes* (1988), and other collections of POETRY for very young listeners. He has illustrated literary anthologies for somewhat older children and their families, too, including *The Family Read-aloud Christmas Treasury* (A. Low, ed., 1989) and *The Family Read-aloud Holiday Treasury* (Low, ed., 1991).

Most recently, B. has advanced Arthur's literary appeal into the arena of CHAPTER BOOK readers. *Arthur's Mystery Envelope* (1998) and *Arthur and the Scare-Your-Pants-Off Club* (1998) offer beginning independent readers the opportunity to find new—and age-appropriate—ADVEN-TURES with a recognizable and faithful character. The popularity of Arthur and his community has been boosted by B.'s association with the children's television program *READING RAINBOW* and the public-television Arthur SERIES, the merchandising of Arthur-based toys, computer software, and curriculum-support materials. However, B.'s incorporation of HUMOR into stories that provide young readers with social and psychological insight is what assures his books' continuing success.

FURTHER WORKS: *The Iron Lion* (P. DICKINSON, author), 1972; *Moose and Goose*, 1978; *Spooky Riddles*, 1983; *Little Owl: An Eight-fold Buddhist Admonition* (J. Van de Wetering, author), 1978; *Read-Aloud Rhymes for the Very Young.* (Jack PRELUTSKY, ed.) 1986; *Arthur's Tooth*, 1985; *Arthur's Teacher Trouble*, 1986; *Dinosaurs Alive and Well!: A Guide to Good Health*, 1990; *Arthur's Puppy*, 1993; *Scared Silly!: A Book for the Brave—Poems, Riddles, Jokes, Stories, and More*, 1994; *Arthur and the True Francine*, 1996;

Arthur Makes the Team, 1998; *Arthur's TV Trouble*, 1999

BIBLIOGRAPHY: *Something about the Author.* vol. 80, 1995; Silvey, Anita, ed., *Children's Books and Their Creators.* 1995; "King Arthur," *People Weekly*, May 1997

FRANCISCA GOLDSMITH

BROWN, Marcia

Author, illustrator, b. 13 July 1918, Rochester, New York

Acknowledged as one of the most distinguished American women in the field of children's literature, B. is a three-time recipient of the prestigious ALA CALDECOTT MEDAL and six of her books have received the Caldecott Medal Honor Award. In addition, B. has twice been the American nominee for the international Hans Christian ANDER-SEN Award for ILLUSTRATION.

Despite an early interest in becoming an artist, B. attended the New York College for Teachers (now the State University of New York at Albany), earning her B.A. in 1940. Afterward, she taught English and drama on the high school level in Cornwall, New York, before moving to New York City to study art. From 1943 to 1948, B. worked as a children's librarian at the New York Public Library, and during this same period she initiated her own career as a children's author. Her first book, *The Little Carousel* (1946), established B.'s ability to incorporate elegant prose with inventive and stimulating illustration. In the following year, B. published *Stone Soup*, the first of the many folktales she would retell and illustrate in her career and the first of her books to receive a Caldecott Medal Honor Award.

B. continued to pursue her interest in the FOLKLORE of other cultures with the publication of *Henry-Fisherman: A Story of the Virgin Islands* (1949), which earned B. a second Caldecott Medal Honor Award. The simple story of a young boy whose greatest wish is to go fishing with his father is brought to life by the beauty and arrangement of B.'s illustrations. Her next two books, *Dick Whittington and His Cat* (1950) and *Skipper John's Cook* (1951), both of which received Caldecott Medal Honor Awards, were followed by the publication in 1952 of B.'s rendition of Charles PERRAULT's *Puss in Boots*. In the next year, B. illustrated Hans Christian Andersen's

The Steadfast Tin Soldier, translated by M. R. James, for which she received another Caldecott Medal Honor Award. In 1954, B. further enhanced her critical reputation with the publication of her TRANSLATION and illustrations for Perrault's *Cinderalla; or, The Little Glass Slipper,* the first of her works to be awarded the Caldecott Medal.

Following the publication of *The Flying Carpet* (1956), a condensed version of the *Tales of the Arabian Nights* in which B.'s illustrations vividly capture the exotic and magical quality of the text, B. embarked on a new stage in her career, influenced in part by her extended travels in Europe as well as her experimentation with different forms of illustration. Her infatuation with Italy, and in particular the city of Venice, is evident in *Felice* (1958), the story of a stray Venetian cat rescued by a stranger and given both a name and a home. In *Tamarindo!* (1960), set against the vast and colorful landscape of Sicily, B. tells the story of four boys in search of a lost donkey. Simultaneously, B. began to explore the artistic possibilities of colored woodblock printing and used the method to illustrate *Once a Mouse . . .* (1961), the second of B.'s works to be awarded the Caldecott Medal. B. used block printing to illustrate a number of other works, notably *Backbone of the King: The Story of Paka'a and His Son Ku* (1966), a coming-of-age story based on Hawaiian legend, *All Butterflies: An ABC* (1974), chosen as an AMERICAN LIBRARY ASSOCIATION Notable Book, and *The Blue Jackal* (1977), a philosophical lesson similar to *Once a Mouse . . .* based on a tale of INDIA.

In 1979, B. published *Listen to a Shape, Touch Will Tell,* and *Walk with Your Eyes,* a series of works about nature that B. illustrated with her own photographs. Representing a departure for B., the series preceded the publication of B.'s most unique book entitled *Shadow* (1982), an AFRICAN tale based on a poem by Blaise Cendrars. The collage illustrations represented another new departure for B. Despite the criticism by some that B.'s depiction of silhouetted Africans was suggestive of racial overtones, the book was generally considered a masterful achievement and the third of B.'s works to receive the Caldecott Medal. *Lotus Seeds: Children, Pictures and Books* (1986)—a collection of selected speeches and articles and the only work

B. designed specifically for an adult audience—followed.

As an author–illustrator of remarkable versatility and vision, B. has throughout her career created works of visual beauty and innate perception. Crafted with care and precision, her books produce a sense of joy and wonderment of exceptional and enduring quality.

FURTHER WORKS: *The Trail of Courage: A Story of New Amsterdam* (Virginia Cruse Watson, author). 1948; *Anansi, the Spider Man* (Philip M. Sherlock, author). 1954; *The Three Billy Goats Gruff* (Peter Christen ASBJORNSEN and J. E. MOE, retellers). 1957; *Peter Piper's Alphabet: Peter Piper's Practical Principles of Plain and Perfect Pronunciation,* 1959; *The Wild Swans* (Hans Christian Andersen), 1963; *The Neighbors,* 1967; *How, Hippo!,* 1969; *Giselle; or, The Wilis* (Violette Verdy, adapted from Théophile Gautier). 1970; *The Snow Queen* (Hans Christian Andersen). 1972; *The Bun: A Tale from Russia,* 1972

BIBLIOGRAPHY: HOPKINS, Lee Bennett, *Pauses: Autobiographical Reflections of 101 Creators of Children's Books,* 1995; Kent, N., "Marcia B.—Author and Illustrator," *American Artist,* 27, Jan. 1963, pp. 26–31; Loranger, J., "Marcia B.," the *Horn Book* magazine, 59, Aug. 1983, pp. 423–24; Masten, H., "From Caldecott to Caldecott," the *Horn Book* magazine, 38, Aug. 1962, pp. 347–52; *Something about the Author,* vol. 47, 1987

STEVEN R. SERAFIN

BROWN, Margaret Wise

Author, b. 23 May, 1910, Brooklyn, New York; d. 13 November 1952, Nice, France

Best known as the author of *Goodnight Moon* (1947) and *The Runaway Bunny* (1942), B. pioneered in writing stories and poems for the youngest ages. During a brief but many-faceted and brilliant career, she completed more than one hundred PICTURE BOOKS; championed the work of such talented illustrators as Garth WILLIAMS and Clement HURD; persuaded Gertrude Stein to write her now classic children's FANTASY *The World Is Round* (1939); and helped develop the board book and other fresh approaches to bookmaking for very young children. With seemingly boundless energy and imagination, she kept experimenting, always hoping, as she once said, "to write a book simple enough . . . to lift the child for a few moments from his own problems of shoelaces that won't tie and busy parents . . . into the timeless world of story."

B. was born in Brooklyn, New York, and reared in middle-class comfort on suburban Long Island, where she became a keen observer of nature. To her childhood friends she was known as the neighborhood storyteller, good at concocting tall tales and at putting her own words to old tunes like "Dixie."

Always something of a daydreamer, B. had a lackluster student career until, as a young woman in the mid-1930s, she enrolled in graduate courses at one of America's most vibrant centers of early childhood development research—the Bank Street College of Education in New York. Lucy Sprague Mitchell, teacher at Bank Street, pursued the study of children's language development and its relationship to other aspects of the child's emerging self. Intrigued by the playfulness and inventiveness of children's everyday speech, Mitchell asked students to record thousands upon thousands of their linguistic fragments. It was found that children begin to play with sounds long before words have any meaning to them and respond to the rhythm, sound quality, and patterns of sound. At Bank Street, B. observed children, listened to the stories and poems they told, recorded voluminous quantities of speech, and found her own vocation.

The core of the Bank Street philosophy was the belief that children should be made full partners in learning. B. applied this idea in her writings by working in simple, gamelike forms and structures that the young might readily grasp and make their own.

In the Noisy Book series, she encouraged children to listen hard to the sounds and rhythms of their own everyday surroundings and to say and sing them back—the bee's buzz, the jackhammer's rattlings—as loudly as they liked. In *Goodnight Moon,* she invited the young to decide which objects of their world mattered enough to them to be remembered one last time at the end of the day.

B.'s legacy consists of a vast store of writings of incomparable tenderness, sparkling mischief, and poetic piquancy and grace. Best of all, perhaps, her stories and poems are beguilingly openended: in them, the child, not the author, always has the last word.

BIBLIOGRAPHY: Bechtel, Louise Seaman, "Margaret Wise B.: Laureate of the Nursery: *Horn Book* magazine, 1958; Marcus, Leonard S., *Margaret Wise B.: Awakened by the Moon,* 1992; Mitchell, Lucy Sprague, "Margaret Wise B.: 1910–1952," *69 Bank Street,* 19, n.d.

LEONARD S. MARCUS

BROWN, Ruth

Author, illustrator, b. 20 May 1941, Tiverton, England

B. studied at the Birmingham School of Art and the Royal College of Art. She reflects her British heritage in her art, portraying a lavish English countryside and architecture in her ILLUSTRATIONS for children's books. Her first book was published in 1978. She has written and illustrated more than twenty books on her own and has illustrated many books by other writers, including several by the popular veterinarian–author James HERRIOT. B. uses full-color, impressionist-style paintings of the Yorkshire countryside in Herriot's *Blossom Comes Home* (1972, reissued 1988).

B.'s artistic style has a lush, realistic look. She is a master at creating textured, mysterious paintings of an English countryside in which an animal, usually a dog, explores an area. Text is minimal or nonexistent with most of the story told through the illustrations. Sometimes the animal is searching for something; at other times just exploring. Whatever the scene, the beauty and texture of the surroundings are evident.

In *One Stormy Night* (1992) an adorable, winsome puppy pokes around a lovely estate home, its stables, and grounds. The puppy greets each creature he discovers in a friendly manner but does not always receive a similar response. He runs through a churchyard that lies nearby and inside the church finds a sarcophagus atop a grave. He clambers over them and licks the figure's face. The molded figures continue to sleep but the live animals respond in a frightened or unfriendly manner.

In *Our Puppy's Vacation* (1987), a young dog romps along a beach with happy children, screeching gulls, and flopping frogs. The dog splashes incoming waves, digs holes in the sand, and climbs dunes as he truly enjoys his day at the beach. B. captures a joyful moment in a puppy's life.

Toad (1997) looks like a slimy creature covered with warts, but a monster tries to eat him anyway. The monster spits the frog out when he gets a taste of the slippery creature. A subtle message appears when we notice that the endpapers of the book are covered with toad eggs.

Buddy, a kitten, plays *Copycat* (1994) with the animals in his life: a lazy mother cat, a shy baby kitten, and Bessie, a dog who chews on bones. Unfortunately, Buddy tries to chew on bones but a cat's teeth are not made for chewing bones. Buddy's teeth show the wear and tear even after a visit to the veterinarian. B. alternates full and half-page spreads of realistic line-and-wash illustrations to reveal a surprise image as each page is turned. B. has also worked on animated films for the BBC.

FURTHER WORKS: *A Dark, Dark Tale,* 1981; *Alphabet Times Four: An International ABC,* 1991; *Ladybug, Ladybug,* 1992; *The Picnic,* 1993; *If at First You Do Not See,* 1995; *Cry Baby,* 1997; *The Littlest Angel,* 1998; *The Big Sneeze,* 1999; books illustrated by B.: *Christmas Day Kitten* (Herriot, 1986); *Bonny's Big Day* (Herriot) 1991; *Blossom Comes Home* (Herriot), 1993; *The Bear and Mr. Bear* (Frances Thomas), 1995; *Ben's Christmas Carol* (Toby Forward), 1996; *Baba Yaga and the Wise Doll* (Hiawyn Gram), 1998

BIBLIOGRAPHY: Cianciolo, Patricia. *PICTURE BOOKS for Children,* 3rd ed., 1990, and 4th ed., 1997

BERNICE E. CULLINAN

BROWNE, Anthony (Edward Tudor)
Author, illustrator, b. 11 September, 1946, Sheffield, England

B.'s parents ran a pub called the Brinkcliffe Oaks Hotel in Sheffield, England. While he was still quite young they moved to Wyke, near Bradford, where they operated the Red Lion in a fairly rough area in northern England. "I remember my father having to physically boot people out. I was five years old the first time I saw men fighting in a field out back."

He remembered, "I was a kid with terrors—people coming after me, things under the bed, in the wardrobe. We had a lot of dark furniture, which looked very menacing to me." Although he was learning Latin by the age of five, he always knew art was his best subject.

At the age of seven his father began a career as a sales representative and they moved from the pub into "a proper house" in Yorkshire. B.'s father and older brother, Michael, would draw soldiers and B. would draw battles. "I used to fill the page with lots and lots of battles—and lots and lots of little figures with plenty of what would now be called surrealistic jokes. Things like a disembodied head with a speech bubble coming out saying "Aaargh!"

At sixteen he went directly from high school to art college and registered for graphic arts because of the commercial possibilities. His father died three-quarters of the way through his first year. B. had assumed his father would live forever and was unprepared for his death although his father previously had two massive heart attacks. His artwork became morbid as a result. He "found it very difficult to paint anything happy . . . I just couldn't paint a happy picture."

Rejecting graphic design, he investigated other art schools in London, was disappointed, and returned to live in the attic of his mother's home. He found a profession called "medical ILLUSTRATION," put together a portfolio and went for an interview, only to be turned down. He was later hired as an assistant medical artist in Manchester. While surgeons operated, he made drawings that told the story of the operation in pictures.

The next drawing level was greeting cards, but it was difficult to make a "proper living" and his greeting card patron, Gordon Fraser, suggested children's books.

B. is very critical of his first published book, *Through the Magic Mirror* (1976). "It began with images and was linked with words afterward. They should both come together ideally." The book has been reprinted twice since 1976.

Bear Hunt (1979) features a white bear with a red and white polka-dot bow tie walking with a pencil in his hand. Two hunters spy Bear and set out to trap him. Characteristic of B.'s artwork, surrealistic images appear in the illustrations—e.g., the hunter's car has teeth in the grill, plants are wearing white collars and colorful ties, a blob has eyeglasses, fish are swimming through the jungle, and a flower has tennis shoes for leaves. The last page has Bear flying away on a white bird as the flower leaves are laughing. Large simple text and intriguing artwork make this a book to look over again and again.

Hansel and Gretel (1981) received the KATE GREENAWAY MEDAL Commendation from the

British Library Association (1982) and the INTERNATIONAL BOARD ON BOOKS FOR YOUNG PEOPLE Award for illustrations for Great Britain in 1984. This was the first book he illustrated that had been written by someone else and he did it in fifties style, the style of his own childhood. Rooms familiar to children are reflected through mirrors. Several black triangle images recur. The stepmother's fancy toiletries and clothing belie the poverty of the family. Cages and bars underscore a dark side of the story. B. takes the reader on a psychological journey through fears of rejection and feelings of abandonment to the return of safety.

The book that made him famous is *Gorilla* (1983). "Hannah loved Gorillas" begins the book that won the Kate Greenaway Medal (1984); was selected one of the *New York Times* Best Illustrated Children's Books of the Year (1985); designated the *Boston Globe–Horn Book* Honor Book for Illustration; was a Child Study Association of America's Children's Books of the Year (1966); and won the Silver Pencil Award (Netherlands) in 1989. Hannah sits alone on the bare floor in her room watching TV. Where the light shines on the wallpaper, there are butterflies and flowers. Beyond the light an outline of Africa hangs midway up the wall surrounded by shadows of birds, bats, wolves, witches, and creepy crawling things. B. is not sure how *Gorilla* came about, but the gorilla of the story is a warm, kind, loving father image, possibly reminiscent of his own gorilla-like father. The isolation of Hannah could be the separation B. felt when his father died.

The dust-jacket illustration for *Piggybook* (1986) portrays Mrs. Piggott carrying her husband and two sons on her back. The text and illustrations correlate the story of an overworked mother. Weary from doing all the work, Mrs. Piggott leaves home. Subtle changes occur in the house. The doorknob, light socket, and pictures take on pig images. The wallpaper turns from tulips to pigs and a threatening wolf shadow appears outside the window. The transformation is complete when the males take on swine characteristics; an interesting commentary on family life and household chores. Mrs. Piggott returns and chooses to fix the car.

B. illustrated Lewis CARROLL's *Alice's Adventures in Wonderland* (1988) that won the Kurt Maschler/"Emil" Award. A FANTASY well suited

to B.'s style, there are Surrealistic surprises in many of the illustrations such as a gorilla running in the caucus race: an elephant with spectacles; pig in a white shirt, tie, and jacket; and parrot in a fur-trimmed coat and top hat. When Father William balances an eel on his nose, one table leg grows inordinately long. At the Mad Hatter's tea party, there are strange things on the plates such as a frog, an alarm clock, a hat, chocolate-covered teeth, a shoe and snail along with little cakes and sandwiches. Children enjoy looking for inappropriate figures found in the various pictures. It is altogether visually imaginative rendering of a well-loved tale.

Zoo (1992) was awarded the Kate Greenaway Medal in 1992. A family of four: Father, Mother, and two boys go for a trip to the zoo. At the zoo surrealist images appear—e.g., a man in a gray-striped suit with a pig's head and a man with a blue jacket and tan pants sports a lion's tail. A cat woman, small monkey-faced child, man with a coxcomb down the center of his head and egg in an egg holder on his shirt and a man with a banana for a tie are in the crowd watching the orangutan. Full-page brightly colored illustrations outlined in black often alternate with text pages. The gorilla reveals a hint of a smile as he watches "Dad" doing his King Kong impersonation, almost as though he scorns the egotistical authoritative personality. *Zoo* is currently out of print in the United States.

When he writes, B. says he "tunes in to the child I was."

BIBLIOGRAPHY: *Children's Literature Review*, vol. 19, 1990; *Fiction, FOLKLORE, Fantasy and POETRY for Children, 1876–1985*, vols. 1 and 2, 1986; Jones, Delores Blythe, ed., *Children's Literature AWARDS and Winners, Authors and Illustrators*, 3rd ed., 1994; THE KERLAN COLLECTION University of Minnesota; Sketch by Susan M. Reicha, "Anthony (Edward Tudor) Browne," www.galenet.comlservlet1LitRe.Biography + OR + work + overview + OR + topic (accessed Feb. 13, 1999); Silvey, Anita, ed., *Children's Books and Their Creators*, 1995

IRVYN G. GILBERTSON

BRUCE, Mary Grant

Author, b. 1878, Sale, Victoria, Australia; d. 2 July 1958, England

B. grew up in the Australian bush where her father was a surveyor. She first wrote serialized stories in the Australian weekly *Leader,* then went to London in 1913 and wrote for newspapers there. B. wrote for the Australian Imperial Forces during World War I, and wrote children's books as well. B. wrote books such as *Timothy in Bushland* (1912), and *The Stone Axe of Burkamukk* (1922), which introduced readers to the Australian bush, its strange animals, and aboriginal legends. Critics heralded these books for idealizing the lifestyle of the Australian outback.

B.'s most famous books, a collection known as the Billabong books, began with *A Little Bush Maid* (1910), about the Linton family and their adventures. This series reflects the struggles of the Australian people as they survived both a world war and a depression. In the collection, B. chronicles the life of Norah Linton and her family as she grows from a child to a woman. Throughout the series, the family endures natural disasters such as droughts, floods, and bushfires. Several books of the collection include: *Norah of Billabong* (1913), *From Billabong to London* (1915), *Back to Billabong* (1921), *Billabong Adventurers* (1927), *Wings above Billabong* (1935), and *Billabong Riders* (1942).

FURTHER WORKS: *The Happy Traveller,* 1929

BIBLIOGRAPHY: Berger, Laura S., *Twentieth Century Children's Writers,* 4th ed., 1995; *The Oxford Companion to Children's Literature,* 1984

DENISE P. BEASLEY

BRUCHAC, Joseph

Author, storyteller, b. 16 October 1942, Saratoga Springs, New York

One of the best-known storytellers of NATIVE AMERICAN folk and historical lore, B. is himself of Abenaki descent as well as having English and Slovak heritage. He is most influenced, however, by his Native American heritage. B. spent his childhood in upstate New York and was raised by his maternal grandparents. His grandfather was Abenaki Indian; however, as B. shares in *Bowman's Store: A Journey to Myself* (1997), his grandfather never spoke of his ancestry because of the social attitude associated with being Indian prevalent during his grandfather's life. B.'s interest in his Native American culture began when he was a teenager and continued as he studied at Cornell and Syracuse Universities where he re-

ceived his M.F.A. degree. Much of his literary work appeared in anthologies and magazines during the years that followed, and after teaching with his wife in Africa for a few years, B. established the Greenfield Review Press at the home where he had grown up. *Greenfield Review* was a source of MULTICULTURAL poetry by many writers including B. In 1975, B. received a Ph.D. from Union Graduate School and during this same year *Turkey Brother and Other Tales* was published. This collection of Iroquois trickster tales began B.'s search for other stories. Besides devoting his life's work to sharing the Native American experience through stories and poems, B. also shares his heritage through music with a family group, the Dawn Land singers.

B.'s Native American heritage and his interest in its history, culture, and literature are the essence of his writing. He focuses on Native American wisdom, spirituality, relationships with the natural world, and its practical connections to contemporary society. B. sees this culture as alive today, and writes to make readers respectfully aware of the complexity of the Native American experience. His stories are rich combinations of his own heritage and his literary style with which he creates characters with multidimensional attributes interacting within authentic contexts. In *Dawn Land* (1995), for example, B. combines a young warrior's dangerous quest 10,000 years ago with his own understandings of legends, tall tales, and myths. In this first novel, B. re-creates life, mythical yet somewhat realistic, in New England through a detailed account of the young Abenaki hunter's journey to save his homeland.

B.'s many contributions represent various literary genres—POETRY, folktales, contemporary stories and INFORMATIONAL texts. Characterized by thorough research, his work includes Abenaki stories from his own culture as well as both individual stories from other cultures and collections of stories from various tribes about a central theme. *Turtle Meat and Other Stories* (1992) depicts the relationship between the Abenakis and whites in the Adirondack Mountains from the Viking era to the mid-twentieth century. *Dog People: Native Dog Stories* (1994)—a 1995 Parents' Choice Honor title—is also a collection of Abenaki lore. While not claiming to be an expert on each of the many tribes, B.'s meticulous research has provided information and stories representative of other tribes. *The First Strawberries: A Cherokee Story* (1993) is about the origin of strawberries. *A Boy Called "Slow": The True Story of Sitting Bull* (1995) tells of the youth and coming of age of this great Lakota chief. Perhaps most evident of B.'s comprehensive knowledge and insights from research into various tribal stories are his collections representing various tribes' perspectives on one particular theme. *Thirteen Moons on Turtle's Back: A Native American Year of Moons,* a 1992 Notable Children's Book in the Language Arts and INTERNATIONAL READING ASSOCIATION Young Adults and Teachers' Choice, shares thirteen moon legends from different tribes, while *The Earth under Sky Bear's Feet* (1998) contains stories of the living earth. *The Circle of Thanks: Native American Poems and Songs of Thanksgiving* (1996) is a collection of thirteen brief original poems created from traditional songs and prayers. B. collaborated with artist Thomas LOCKER in *Between Earth and Sky: Legends of Native American Sacred Places* (1996) to describe these places in poetry and paintings.

The natural world and man's relationships therein are topics found continuously throughout B.'s work, as in *The Circle of Thanks* (1996), which shows appreciation for many aspects of nature. One particular example connects folktales to environmental teaching. B.'s interest in the natural world combined with Native American wisdom is the focus of *Keepers of the Earth* (1988), *Keepers of the Animals* (1991), *Keepers of Life* (1994), and *Keepers of the Night* (1994). This SERIES of books, created in collaboration with Michael Caduto, provides environmental lesson strategies for the science curriculum based on accompanying folktales. Highlighting the delicate balance between people and nature, as has been observed, these valuable resources bring tradition and humanity's relationship with the environment together. *The Story of the Milky Way* (1995) received the Young Readers Book Award from *Scientific American* magazine.

Meaningful themes such as family, environment, and community resonate in B.'s books, and he realizes that these themes are universal and bridge insights for readers into the Native American culture as readers make personal connections.

A contemporary story, *Fox Song* (1993) sensitively addresses the subjects of accepting death, relationships with the elderly, and acknowledges a literacy that comes from knowing the natural environment. *Eagle Song* (1997) is a novel about a contemporary Native American fourth grade Iroquois boy who is taunted by others in his class. Themes of family, stereotypes, and touching base with one's roots are all found within this novel. B. also frequently uses the universal theme of coming of age. *The Arrow over the Door* (1998), a work of historical fiction, describes an actual incident concerning an Abenaki boy and a Quaker boy during the American Revolution.

B. is considered to be a major voice in Native American STORYTELLING and writing. His own literary style brings life and depth to the culture and people he describes. As author, publisher, and editor of Native American literature, he has significantly impacted the understandings of both Native and non–Native people concerning the rich legacy of Native American heritage.

AWARDS: 1995 AMERICAN LIBRARY ASSOCIATION Notable Children's Book for *A Boy Called "Slow"*; 1996 ALA Notable Children's Book and *Boston Globe-Horn Book* nonfiction honor for *The Boy Who Lived with the Bears: And Other Iroquois Stories,* 1996

FURTHER WORKS FOR CHILDREN: *Flying With the Eagle, Racing the Great Bear,* 1993; *The Girl Who Married the Moon,* 1994; *Children of the Longhouse,* 1996; *Many Nations: An Alphabet of Native America,* 1997; *When the Chenoo Howls: Native American Tales of Terror,* 1998

BIBLIOGRAPHY: B., Joseph, *Bowman's Store,* 1997; Giorgis, Cyndi and Janelle Mathis, "Book Review Sampler: Visions and Voices of American Indians in Children's Literature," *The New Advocate,* vol. 8/2, 1995; *Something about the Author,* vol 89, 1997

JANELLE B. MATHIS

BRUNA, Dick

Author, illustrator, b. 23 August 1927, Utrecht, Netherlands

B. was a quiet, insecure child who began illustrating at age sixteen for the family publishing firm established by his great grandfather. B. attended the Art Academy in Amsterdam for six months. In addition to his children's books, B. has designed book jackets, posters, postage stamps, murals, greeting cards, postcards, and medical information booklets for children. His work has been widely exhibited in the Netherlands and abroad. B. creates books that appeal to children under the age of six. In the early 1950s when B. began creating first books for young children, he was one of the earliest authors to do so.

B.'s main goal in creating a book is the potential aesthetic experience of his readers; he designs books that he likes himself. Some of B.'s books are wordless, while others have sparse text. Written in Dutch, B.'s books have been translated into twenty-eight languages and include FAIRY TALES, original stories, and concept books. Over seventy of B.'s books have been translated into English. The images in B.'s art are simple, often a solid background behind a single character, who looks directly at the reader. Little or no action takes place in the ILLUSTRATIONS, which have flat perspective and are usually done in primary colors. To achieve this simplicity, B. creates many more illustrations than will be used, taking out what seems unnecessary until he achieves the most economical composition possible. He works in brush and poster paints, allowing the brush strokes to show so that children will see the imperfections and understand that the books are made by a real person—just like himself or herself.

AWARDS: Benelux Prize (1960); Silver Medal, City of Utrecht for contribution to the city's cultural enrichment. D. A. Thiemeprize, Netherlands, (1990) Knight of the Order of Orange Nassau

FURTHER WORKS: In the Miffy series: *Miffy,* 1975; *Miffy at the Zoo,* 1975; *Miffy's Birthday,* 1976; *Miffy Goes Flying,* 1976; *Miffy in the Hospital,* 1978; *Miffy at the Seaside,* 1979; *Miffy's Dream,* 1980; *Miffy's Bicycle,* 1984; *Miffy Goes to School,* 1991; *Miffy Goes Outside,* 1997; *Miffy at Play: A Flip Book,* 1998; *Peek-a-Boo, Miffy!: A Flip Book,* 1998; other books: *The Circus,* 1963; *The Egg,* 1964; *B Is for Bear: An A-B-C,* 1971; *I Can Count,* 1975; *I Can Read,* 1975; *Lisa and Lynne,* 1975; *The Little Bird,* 1975; *My Shirt Is White,* 1975; *Snuffy,* 1975; *Snuffy and the Fire,* 1975; *A Story to Tell,* 1975; *I Can Count More,* 1976; *I Can Read More,* 1976; *I Can Read Difficult Words,* 1978; *The Sailor,* 1979; *My Meals,* 1980; *Out and About,* 1980; *I Know about Numbers,* 1981; *I Know More about Numbers,* 1981; *Poppy Pig's Garden,* 1982; *The Orchestra,* 1984; *When I'm Big,* 1984; *Dick B.'s Picture Word Book,* 1989; *Animals,* 1991; *I Know the Shapes,* 1991

BIBLIOGRAPHY: Dohm, J. H., " 'D' is for Dutch—and Dick," *Junior Bookshelf,* August 1967, pp. 225–28; Hunt, Peter, ed., *Children's Literature: An Illustrated History,* 1995; Kingman, L., G. A. Hogarth, and H. Quimby, eds., *Illustrators of Children's Books: 1967–76,* 1978; Kohnstamm, G. A., *The Extra in the Ordinary: Children's Books by Dick B.,* 1979

JANE WEST

BRYAN, Ashley
Author, illustrator, b. 13 July, 1923, New York City

B. knew in kindergarten that art would be his life. He was reared in a tough section of the Bronx, New York, but had the strong support of his family. His ambition to succeed in art led him to Cooper Union, but his studies were interrupted by army service in World War II. He returned to complete his degree and then enrolled at Columbia University to work toward a degree in philosophy. A bookbinding course rekindled his enthusiasm for book-making. He taught art at several schools in the New York area and had opened his own studio when he was approached by Jean Karl, an editor at Atheneum, to illustrate a book, *Moon, for What Do You Wait?* (1967) by Nobel Prize–winning INDIAN (EAST), poet Rabindranath Tagore. This collaboration led to the first book, *The Ox of the Wonderful Horns and Other African Folktales* (1971), of what would become B.'s specialty, retellings of AFRICAN tales. The art of Africa has always had a strong appeal for B. He states that he has always worked to develop a personal style based on the influences of African sculpture, masks, jewelry, textiles, and rock paintings he has studied. B., a versatile artist, uses a variety of techniques and styles for his books ranging from paintings resembling woodcuts for *The Ox of the Wonderful Horns* to actual woodcuts for *Beat the Story-Drum, Pum-Pum* (1980), a brushpainting technique for *The Dancing Granny* (1977), sepia-line drawings for *The Cat's Purr* (1985), and black-and-white illustrations for *Walk Together Children* (1974), volume one of a collection of spirituals.

B. began retelling stories because of his dissatisfaction with the way many African tales were told. He does extensive background research, but makes the stories his own by using elements such as rhythm, alliteration, and interior rhyming to recreate the flavor and feel of the oral tradition. He

127

often fleshes out a story from nothing more than an abbreviated text. Besides his work on books, B. is known for POETRY readings and as a STORY-TELLER. His work creates a wonderful link from the African tradition to all who love stories. B.'s combination of rich, poetic retellings and evocative illustrations has created a body of work which is popular as well as critically praised.

AWARDS: CORETTA SCOTT KING AWARD for ILLUS-TRATION (1981) for *Beat the Story-Drum, Pum-Pum;* Coretta Scott King Honor Books; Lupine Award (1992) for *Sing to the Sun;* Lee Bennett HOPKINS Poetry Award (1993) for *Sing to the Sun;* New England Book Award (1994) for Lifetime Achievement

FURTHER WORKS: *Lion and the Ostrich Chicks and other African Folk Tales,* 1986; *Sh-Ko and His Eight Wicked Brothers,* 1988; *Turtle Knows Your Name,* 1989; *All Night, All Day: A Child's First Book of AFRICAN AMERICAN Spirituals* 1991; *The Story of Lightning and Thunder,* 1993

BIBLIOGRAPHY: HOPKINS, Lee Bennett, *Pauses: Autobiographical Reflections of 101 Creators of Children's Books,* 1995; Silvey, Anita, ed. *Children's Books and Their Creators,* 1995; *Something about the Author,* vol. 72

ANITA M. TROUT

BULLA, Clyde Robert
Author, b. 9 January 1914, King City, Missouri

B., a prolific writer, has written dozens of stories and books for children. He has also written songs and composed music for several song books written by Lois LENSKI. B. writes in a variety of genres, including nonfiction, contemporary fiction, historical fiction, and stories set in various locations around the world. His historical fiction often focuses on NATIVE AMERICANS, as in *Squanto, Friend of the White Man* (1954), *Pocahontas and the Strangers* (1971), and *Conquista!* (1978). Other historical fiction includes *Lincoln's Birthday* (1965), *Washington's Birthday* (1967), *Charlie's House* (1983), and *A Lion to Guard Us* (1981, Notable Children's Trade Book in Social Studies). B.'s stories tend to be simple and easy to read, making them popular with younger readers.

AWARDS: Christopher Award (1972) for *Pocahontas and the Strangers.* Commonwealth Award (1970) for *Jonah and the Great Fish.* George G.

Stone Center for Children's Books Recognition of Merit (1968) for *White Bird*

FURTHER WORKS: *The Donkey Cart,* 1946; *John Billington, Friend of Squanto,* 1956; *The Sword in the Tree,* 1956; *Stories of Favorite Operas,* 1959; *Songs of Mr. Small* (words and pictures by Lois Lenski with music by C. R. B.); *Dexter,* 1973; *Shoeshine Girl,* 1976; *Almost a Hero,* 1981; *A Grain of Wheat,* 1985

BIBLIOGRAPHY: HOPKINS, Lee Bennett, *Pauses: Autobiographical Reflections of 101 Creators of Children's Books,* 1995; *Something about the Author,* vol. 91, 1997

MARY ARIAIL BROUGHTON

BUNTING, Eve (Anne Evelyn Bolton)
Author, b. 19 December 1928, Maghera, Northern Ireland

B. is a prolific and versatile author, writing over 150 books for children from preschoolers to YOUNG ADULTS in a wide variety of genres. She emigrated to the United States in 1960 and became an American citizen. B. was reared in Northern Ireland in a family of readers. She describes her father, a postmaster and merchant, as a rough, country man whose secret passion was poetry. Her earliest memories include sitting on her father's lap in front of the fire and having him read poetry to her. B. did not have aspirations to write herself until her children were nearly grown and she began to wonder what she should do with the rest of her life. She discovered a free writing class at a local community college that provided the impetus for her writing career. Her first book, *The Two Giants* (1972), retold an Irish folktale she wanted American children to know. In the next years, she wrote novels, PICTURE BOOKS, stories for basal reading programs, and nonfiction about sea life. She also wrote SERIES BOOKS such as horse stories, SCIENCE FICTION, ghost stories, and romances, some of which are recognized as having high interest for older students with limited reading skills.

B.'s novels have been selected as favorites by young readers for children's choice AWARDS in numerous states as well as for the INTERNATIONAL READING ASSOCIATION Children's Choice Awards. The books honored include *Karen Kepplewhite is the World's Best Kisser* (1983); *Someone is Hiding on Alcatraz Island* (1984), a suspense novel about young teenagers trying to escape the revenge of a gang; *Sixth Grade Sleepover* (1986), a story of two girls, one of whom is afraid her friends will discover her fear of the dark, and another who is trying to hide the fact that she cannot read; *A Sudden Silence* (1988), in which a teen discovers that the person who caused the DEATH of his younger deaf brother in a hit-and-run accident is the alcoholic mother of his brother's friend; and *Is Anybody There?* (1988), the story of a boy who is dealing with his widowed mother's developing romance and the mystery of disappearing items in their home. In 1997, B. received the thirty-ninth Annual Regina Medal for her overall body of work and in 1993 she received the Southern California Council on Literature for Children and Young People Award for her body of work.

Critics describe B.'s novel plots as well-crafted, fast-paced, enthralling, and suspenseful entertainment but somewhat improbable. Characterization is described as sensitive and realistic, but sometimes shallow. Some critics find the novels didactic in tone and overly obvious in theme, whereas others praise her for showing young people making difficult but good choices, for dealing with contemporary issues, and for writing about topics important to young people.

Although B. continued to write novels into the nineties, picture books have come to dominate her writing. Some of her picture books are happy stories focusing on FAMILY life, celebrations, and making the world a beautiful place: *The Mother's Day Mice* (1986); *The Pumpkin Fair* (1997); and *Flower Garden* (1994).

Increasingly, B.'s picture books have focused on societal problems and difficult events in life and history. The themes often involve change, a reflection of B.'s life. She came from Ireland to the U.S., as noted, but also with her husband and three young children, an experience that has made her empathetic with others whose lives have been uprooted. Her distress about the turmoil in her native Ireland between Catholics and Protestants has made her sensitive to the upheaval caused by prejudice and injustice.

B. often looks at serious issues from the viewpoint of a child who tells the story in the first-person. *Fly Away Home* (1991) describes the life of a homeless boy who lives in a large metropoli-

tan airport with his father, sleeping in waiting rooms and trying to be inconspicuous to avoid being forced to leave the only home they have. *The Wall* (1990) shows a young boy sad but honored to see his grandfather's name on the Vietnam Veterans Memorial. *Smoky Night* (1994), for which the illustrator, David DIAZ won the CALDECOTT MEDAL, shows a child living through an urban riot. In *Cheyenne Again* (1995), a boy is forced to leave his parents and culture to go to a government boarding school where he is taught the white man's ways. *How Many Days to America? A Thanksgiving Story* (1988) tells of a Caribbean family fleeing soldiers in their country, taking a perilous sea journey, and hoping for a new life in the United States.

B.'s books often express a tension between recognizing injustice and coming to personal acceptance. In *So Far from the Sea* (1998), a Japanese-American girl visits her grandfather's grave. She expresses puzzlement and anger about the cruel uprooting her father and his father experienced during World War II when the United States government moved them to an internment camp in the Eastern California desert. Her father, though obviously grieved at the memory, replies, "It is just a thing that happened long years ago. A thing that cannot be changed."

Although the tone of these picture books is somber, they are not without hope. In *Smoky Night* (1994) Daniel, a young boy frightened by the rioting, expresses the hope that after the rioting, people in the community will come to understand that they are alike in more ways than they are different. In *Dandelions* (1995), a pioneer girl tries to transplant a dandelion on the grass roof of their soddie, hoping to remind her depressed mother of their home in the east and bring cheery color to the open grasslands. When the plant begins to wither, the girl is distressed but hopeful for the dandelion and her mother. "It will take time. I can wait."

Most of B.'s serious picture books are intended for children slightly older than the typical picture-book audience. They are not stories with traditional plot development but, rather, simple vignettes that open a window to worlds where people suffer pain with dignity and still have hope for the future. B.'s spare prose and inspirational themes encourage empathy and provide a starting place for discussion on how to make a better world.

AWARDS: Caldecott Medal (1995) for *Smoky Night* (illus. David Diaz); Golden Kite Award (1976) for *One More Flight;* Edgar Allan Poe Award (1993) for *Coffin on a Case*

FURTHER WORKS: *Flower Garden,* 1994; *Turkey for Thanksgiving,* 1991; *Spying on Miss Muller,* 1995; *Going Home,* 1996; *Some Frog!,* 1998

BIBLIOGRAPHY: Phinney, M., *"Eve B.: A* 'Wonderful Happenstance,' " *New Advocate,* 10, pp. 195–202

ADELE GREENLEE

BURCH, Robert Joseph
Author, b. 26 June 1925, Inman, Georgia

B. writes books geared toward children in the middle grades drawn from his own Southern background. He often uses realism in his stories about children from modest families struggling to make ends meet, and they do not have the expected happy endings. *Simon and the Game of Chance* (1970), which deals with infant death and *Queeny Peavy* (1966), the story of a girl's father who is getting out of prison, are two examples. Despite the teasing of classmates, Queenie learns how to cope with their jibes and respond in ways that help her overcome her feelings of inadequacy. A friendly orphan waiting to enter an orphanage, *Skinny* (1964) tries hard, with grace and humor, to please folks who come to Miss Bessie's hotel. He carries bags and hustles to help out wherever he can and is ready to tackle whatever comes his way. Many of B.'s characters use HUMOR to deal with the harsh realities of life. Several of B.'s books have been Junior Literary Guild and Weekly Reader Book Club selections. *Queenie Peavy* won both the Georgia Children's Book Award and the Jane Addams Children's Book Award. *Ida Early Comes over the Mountain* (1980) was adapted by NBC-TV as a television movie.

FURTHER WORKS: *The Whitman Kick,* 1977; *Wilkin's Ghost,* 1978; *Ida Comes Early Over the Mountain,* 1980; *King Kong and Other Poets,* 1986; *Christmas with Ida Early,* 1983

BIBLIOGRAPHY: HOPKINS, Lee Bennett, *Pauses: Autobiographical Reflections of 101 Creators of Children's Books,* 1995; MEIGS, C., A.T. EATON, E. NESBIT, R. H. Viguers. *A Critical History of*

Children's Literature. 1969; *Something about the Author* 1969.

MICHAEL O'LAUGHLIN

BURGESS, (Frank) Gelett
Author, illustrator, b. 30 January 1866, Boston, Massachusetts; d. 18 September 1951, Carmel, California

B. established his career as an author and satirical humorist while editing a literary magazine called *The Lark. The Lark* featured B.'s grotesque illustrations, including his strange pen drawings of creatures he called "goops." The Goops, children with oversized, balloon-shaped heads, are notable for their naughty behavior, which young readers find humorous. Their disastrous behaviors became models for similar tales of admonition intended to instruct through HUMOR and ILLUSTRATION. B. first became famous for a silly poem published in *The Lark* called the "Purple Cow." His third book, *Goops and How to Be Them* (1900), brought B. fame as an American humorist.

FURTHER WORKS: *The Purple Cow,* 1899; *Goops and How to Be Them,* 1900; *The B. Nonsense Book,* 1901; *More Goops and How Not to Be Them: A Manual of Manners for Impolite Infants,* 1903; *Goop Tales Alphabetically Told,* 1904; *The Goop Encyclopedia,* 1916; *Why Be a Goop?,* 1924; *New Goops and How to Know Them,* 1951

BIBLIOGRAPHY: *Something about the Author,* vol. 32, 1983

JODI PILGRIM

BURGESS, Thornton Waldo
Author, b. 14 January 1874, Sandwich, Massachusetts; d. 5 June 1965, Sandwich, Massachusetts

After working as an office boy for Phelps Publishing Company, B. started writing for some of their weekly magazines and then for *Good Housekeeping,* where he became an associate editor.

Although noted for his ANIMAL STORIES and often criticized for running the gamut of anthropomorphism, B. appealed enormously to children in the early part of the twentieth century. Originally written as letters to his young son and then published in *Good Housekeeping, Old Mother West Wind* (1910) used the pattern of Aesop's *Fables* to develop short tales with clearly delineated morals. He created stories for children with details of animal life and habitats in seven volumes.

B. then used the animals in these stories to instruct children in their behavior while evoking a sense of the importance of nature in our lives. Many similar SERIES followed: the Bedtime Story series of twenty volumes was published between 1913 and 1919; the Green Meadow series in four volumes (1918–20); the Green Forest series, four volumes (1921–23). B. wrote a daily nature story for the *Herald Tribune* for forty-five years as well as books for the Boy Scouts.

AWARDS: Chandler Book Talk Reward of Merit in 1963; Northwestern University (1928) honorary doctorate

FURTHER WORKS: *The Adventures of Poor Mrs. Quack,* 1917; *Blacky the Crow,* 1922; *Tales from the Story Teller's House,* 1937; *The Dear Old Briar Patch,* 1947; *Bedtime Stories,* 1959; *Now I Remember* (Autobiography), 1960

BIBLIOGRAPHY: Doyle, Brian. *The Who's Who of Children's Literature,* 1968; Wright, Wayne W. *Thornton Waldo B.: A Descriptive Book Bibliography,* B. Society, 1979

KAY E. VANDERGRIFT

BURKERT, Nancy Ekholm

Artist, b. 16 February 1933, Sterling, Colorado

B. became interested in drawing quite young and describes the PICTURE BOOKS she had as a child as old friends. B. studied art at the Wustum Museum in Racine, Wisconsin, and served as art editor for her high school yearbook. After graduating with a bachelor's degree from the University of Wisconsin, Madison, she earned a master's degree in applied art from the same institution.

B. began her career in children's books by illustrating Roald DAHL's *James and the Giant Peach* (1961); her subsequent book illustrations have been for equally distinguished authors. B. describes her process as one of visualizing the text, or staging a play. She spends a great deal of time researching each subject, bringing together all of the details of dress, landscape, architecture, and figure. B. uses models for the characters she portrays in order to bring individualism to each book. Furthering this, she also has in mind a specific location for the story, and a specific time of year. All of this painstaking work is only the beginning. Once she has these details in place, B. makes drawing after drawing to capture the effect she wants before she transfers the final product to paper and adds color.

B.'s eye for detail and ability to re-create what she sees in her mind have contributed to a small but illustrious body of work. B. brings not only her artistic talent, but also her personal commitment to her work. She has illustrated *Nightingale* (1965) and *The Fir Tree* (1970) by Hans Christian ANDERSEN, both affirmations of the beauty and vulnerability of the natural world. Her illustrations for *The Scroobious Pip* (1968) begun by Edward LEAR and completed by Ogden NASH, are in many ways a roll call of animals that have become extinct since the poem was first written. Her illustrations have received high critical praise; many of the books she has illustrated have been chosen as AMERICAN LIBRARY ASSOCIATION Notable Books. The illustrations for Randall JARRELL's TRANSLATION of *Snow White and the Seven Dwarfs* (1973) received a CALDECOTT MEDAL Honor Citation.

B.'s artwork is the embodiment of what book ILLUSTRATION should be, a wonderful visualization of the scene, enabling the reader to participate fully in the story.

AWARDS: *Boston Globe–Horn Book* Special Award (1990) for *Valentine and Orson.* Caldecott Medal Honor Book Award, 1973 for *Snow White and the Seven Dwarfs*

FURTHER WORKS: Illus. *The Big Goose of the Little White Duck* (Meindert DEJONG), 1963; *Jean-Claude's Island* (Natalie Savage CARLSON), 1963; *A Child's Calendar,* 1965; *Acts of Light: Emily Dickinson Poems,* 1980

BIBLIOGRAPHY: Silvey, Anita, ed., *Children's Books and Their Creators,* 1995

ANITA M. TROUT

BURLEIGH, Robert

Author, illustrator, b. 4 January 1936, Chicago, Illinois

B. writes books that introduce young readers to difficult historical topics. He uses simple language, present tense narration, and staccato text to convey the complexity of the lives of such men as Henry David Thoreau, *A Man Named Thoreau* (1980), Charles Lindbergh, *Flight: The Journey of Charles Lindbergh* (1991), and Admiral Richard Byrd, *Black Whiteness: Admiral Byrd Alone in the Antarctic* (1998). Although easily understood, B.'s language is often described as eloquent as he maintains the integrity of historic occasions and captures the essence of historic figures without distorting their accomplishments. Emotion, intensity, and carefully selected words and sentences recreate for young readers authentic historical events and people, such as in *Flight: The Journey of Charles Lindbergh* for which he received the NCTE ORBIS PICTUS AWARD and *Home Run: The Story of Babe Ruth* (1998). B.'s *Who Said That? Famous Americans Speak* (1997) allows young readers a glimpse into the lives of thirty-three famous Americans and what they had to say. It is a book that offers enormous possibilities for teachers. B.'s book of sports POETRY, *Hoops* (1997), gives readers a sense of anticipation that is usually felt exclusively by players. His writing style presents PICTURE BOOKS, for older readers, with clear historical information that is guaranteed to arouse children's interest in history. B. is also an artist and has produced educational filmstrips and cassettes.

AWARDS: Orbis Pictus Award, NATIONAL COUNCIL OF TEACHERS OF ENGLISH (1992) for *Flight: The Journey of Charles Lindbergh*

FURTHER WORKS: *The Triumph of Mittens: Poems*, 1980; *A Man Named Thoreau*, 1985; *Colonial America*, 1992; *Black Whiteness: Admiral Byrd Alone in the Antarctic*, 1997

BIBLIOGRAPHY: *Bulletin of the Center for Children's Books*, November 1991; *School Library Journal*, October 1991; May 1997; *Something about the Author*, vol. 98, 1998

JANELLE B. MATHIS AND NANCE S. WILSON

BURMAN, Ben Lucien

Author, b. 12 December 1895, Covington, Kentucky; d. 23 November 1984, the Players Club, New York City

B. is best known for his chronicles of life on the Mississippi River. Like Mark TWAIN, B. wrote books for adults that were adopted by young readers. The Catfish Bend stories are among his most popular.

B. worked as a journalist on the *New York World* and as the book review editor of *The Nation*. B. served in World War I and was wounded in France. He also served as a correspondent for

Readers Digest and was stationed with the French troops in North Africa.

B. began his serious writing as a poet and had numerous poems published in magazines. His first book of collected poems, *Children of Noah: Glimpses of Unknown America* (1951), contained an anecdotal, philosophical view of American life along the Mississippi and in the state of Kentucky. B. reinforced the similarities that he perceived among Kentucky mountaineers and Mississippi River folk in his POETRY. The first novel, *Mississippi* (1929), was about life on the big river, illustrated by his young bride Alice Caddy. His second novel, *Steamboat round the Bend* (1933), was made into a movie starring Will Rogers.

B.'s writing reflects a desire to travel and his sensitivity to the regional speech he heard. *Everywhere I Roam* (1949) was filled with regional speech; the story told about the horse-drawn trailer pilgrimage of Captain Asa and his three teenage children. Captain Asa wanted to turn Ula, age 19, Vergil, age 17, and Fernie, age 16, away from jukeboxes, pinball machines, and other distractions of the time. The teenagers enthusiastically tried out ever new gimmick they discovered. *Everywhere I Roam* was also filled with music that B. incorporated. The hill dwellers mirrored other characters that lived along the river. B. stated, "The only people I can write about are those close to the soil and the water." Through his well-developed characters, B. demonstrated his consistent theme that the human spirit is indestructible in a difficult world.

B. and his faithful illustrator, wife Alice Caddy, worked together on seven volumes of the Catfish Bend stories. Among them, *Big River to Cross: Mississippi Life Today* (1940), *High Water at Catfish Bend* (1952), *High Treason at Catfish Bend* (1977), and *Thunderbolt at Catfish Bend* (1984) are favorites. Because of B.'s writing, a historical marker stands at Catfish Bend on the Mississippi River. It states: "Ben Lucien Burman was called 'The New Mark Twain' and 'Mr. Mississippi.' He is author of *Steamboat round the Bend* and *Blow for a Landing* [1938], and is the creator of Catfish Bend. He made America remember its rivers."

BIBLIOGRAPHY: Elwell, Jake, ed., *Ben Lucien B.: Tributes and Mementos*, 1992; personal interview with Kenneth Giniger and Ben Lucien Burman

BERNICE E. CULLINAN

BURNETT, Frances Hodgson
Author, b. 24 November 1849, Manchester, England; d. 29 October 1924, Long Island, New York

B. wrote novels and plays for adult audiences before beginning the career as children's author, for which she is now remembered. *Little Lord Fauntleroy* (1886) was the first children's book to gain the status of international best-seller. Her later children's novels have remained popular with young audiences who have been introduced to them in the form of stage and film productions as well as print.

B.'s youth was filled with both economic and geographic change, from her father's death when she was four to the faltering of the family's business in England due to the American Civil War, through their subsequent transplantation to the United States. While a teenager, B. turned her early interest in writing into prospective financial support by submitting short stories to the popular American magazines of the day. Her talent was recognized quickly and she sold work to *Godey's Lady's Book, Scribner's,* and other periodicals.

Most of B.'s first novels for adults were written in the then-popular realistic style. Her first juvenile novels blended realism with wish fulfillment to offer her reading public distinctly inspiring and cheering accounts of young characters for whom bad situations find great improvement. The main character in *Little Lord Fauntleroy* is rewarded socially and financially for his moral goodness. Another famous B. character, the ostensibly orphaned and maltreated Sara Crewe, appears first in *Sara Crewe; or, What Happened at Miss Minchin's* (1888), and was later reworked into the fuller *A Little Princess: Being the Whole Story of Sara Crewe, Now Told for the First Time* (1905). In these stories, the eponymous heroine moves from riches to rags and despair and back not only to riches but to a restored status of respectability. B. wrote the three-act play *The Little Princess* (1903) from her own story. It was produced in London and in New York City. The story was later filmed several times, with the 1939 production starring child-actress Shirley Temple, and the most recent version released in 1995.

Another of B.'s perennially popular novels is *The Secret Garden* (1911), in which several children discover that, through each other's intercessions, all of their lives can be made not only more tolerable but outright pleasant. As in *A Little Princess,* the children in *The Secret Garden* discover and work with their imaginative powers without B.'s story line moving into the realm of FANTASY. B.'s accurate portrayal of how children grow stronger and better by caring—here, for a garden—as well as by being recipients of care, has earned her acclaim as a historically important figure in the field of juvenile fiction.

B.'s personal life as an adult invited social criticism by those who valued ladylike propriety above intellectual and artistic inquiry. Among her last children's books, *The Lost Prince* (1915) has political themes accessible to the juvenile reader. As with Sara Crewe, the restoration of order relies upon the revelation of the true nature of someone from the past and his distinction from a putative absence of glory. Unlike Sara Crewe and *The Secret Garden,* however, this last of B.'s children's novels slips into sentimentality.

As in her novels and plays, B. invested her shorter works of fiction with moral issues but also with sensual detail and good-humored insight. Her memoir of childhood, *The One I Knew Best of All* (1893), describes her devotion to writing, demonstrating the joy that authorship brought her even in youth.

FURTHER WORKS: *Editha's Burglar: A Story for Children,* 1888; *The Land of Blue Flower,* 1909; *Barty Crusoe and His Man Saturday,* 1909

BIBLIOGRAPHY: Burnett, F., *The One I Knew the Best of All: A Memory of the Mind of a Child,* 1893; *Contemporary Authors,* vol. 136, 1992; Silvey, Anita, ed., *Children's Books and Their Creators,* 1995; *Something about the Author,* vol. 100, 1999; *The Stanford Companion to Victorian Literature,* 1989

FRANCISCA GOLDSMITH

BURNFORD, Sheila
Author, b. 11 May 1918, Scotland; d. 20 April 1984, England

British-born B. made the CANADIAN province of Ontario home following World War II. There her love for the northern wilderness combined with fascination for the relationship among her own three pets to produce *The Incredible Journey* (1961). Translated into twenty languages, B.'s

REALISTIC tale of animal survival won the hearts of children the world over. It was made into a DISNEY Studio film twice, one with the same title in 1963 and a second in 1993 entitled *Homeward Bound.* Although not written as a children's book, *The Incredible Journey* eclipsed the popularity of *Mr. Noah and the Second Flood* (1973), the only one of B's six books written for children.

AWARDS: Canadian Library Association Book of the Year for Children (1963), AMERICAN LIBRARY ASSOCIATION Notable Book (1964), INTERNATIONAL BOARD ON BOOKS FOR YOUNG PEOPLE Honor Book (1964), and Lewis CARROLL Shelf Award (1971) for *The Incredible Journey*

FURTHER WORKS: *Bel Ria,* 1977

BIBLIOGRAPHY: *Fourth Book of Junior Authors and Illustrators,* 1978; publishers' notes; Silvey, Anita, ed., *Children's Books and Their Creators,* 1995; *Something about the Author,* vol. 3, 1972; *Twentieth Century Children's Writers,* 1983

DIANE L. CHAPMAN

BURNINGHAM, John (Mackintosh)

Author, illustrator, b. 27 April 1936, Farnham, Surrey, England

The youngest of three children, B. grew up in England where frequent family moves contributed to an unsteady early education in various boarding schools. At the age of twelve, B. attended A. S. Neill's Summerhill School, a school noted for its liberal teaching methods and noncompulsory lessons. At Summerhill, B. began experimenting with various artistic techniques.

From 1953 to 1955, B. joined The Friends' Ambulance Unit. This alternative to National Military Service allowed him to travel in Israel, Southern Italy, and Scotland and work in hospitals, agriculture, forestry, and do social work. From 1956–59, B. was a student at the Central School of Art and Craft in London and there met his future wife, Helen OXENBURY; renowned author and illustrator of PICTURE BOOKS for babies and preschoolers. They married in 1964, and eventually she, too, began illustrating children's books. Upon leaving Central in 1960, B. worked in a graphics design studio, for the London Transport Commission creating posters, and in Israel on an animated film project. His first book, *Borka: The Goose with No Feathers,* published by Jonathan

Cape in 1963, received the KATE GREENAWAY MEDAL in 1964.

Known for his wry HUMOR and understanding his child audience, B. relies on his inventive and colorful illustrations to relate the story. Exploiting a variety of mediums and often capitalizing on the chasm between a child's imagination and an adult's reality, B. successfully interweaves FANTASY and reality. *Come Away from the Water, Shirley* (1977), *The Shopping Basket* (1980), and *Hey! Get off Our Train* (1989) typify this chasm. In *Come Away from the Water, Shirley,* for example, Shirley's wordless pirate ADVENTURE is rendered in vivid color on the right and juxtaposed with her parents' mundane reproaches in pastel illustrations on the left. In *The Shopping Basket,* Steven outsmarts a bear, monkey, kangaroo, goat, pig, and elephant, only to meet his mother's disapproval that this simple shopping trip has taken too long. Long a favorite, *Mr. Gumpy's Outing* (1970), a mock serious story about a rowing adventure in a boat full of animals and children, was a Kate Greenaway Medal winner. This, like several of B.'s other titles, appeared on the *New York Times* Best Illustrated Children's Books of the Year list.

The range of B.'s repertoire includes the serious—*Granpa* (1984) addresses a grandparent's death; the familiar—the Little Books series focuses on simple aspects of a young child's life; animal fantasies, such as *Trubloff: The Mouse Who Wanted to Play the Balalaika* (1964); and concept books, such as *John Burningham's Colors* (1985). In addition to self-illustrated picture books, B. has illustrated Ian FLEMING's *Chitty-Chitty-Bang-Bang* (1964), Jules VERNE's *Around the World in Eighty Days* (1970), and Kenneth GRAHAME's *The Wind in the Willows* (1983).

AWARDS: Kate Greenaway Medal (1963) for *Borka* and (1970) for *Mr. Gumpy's Outing.* Boston Globe-Horn Book Award (1972) for *Mr. Gumpy's Outing* (ILLUSTRATION)

FURTHER WORKS: *John Burningham's ABC,* 1964; *Harquin: The Fox Who Went down to the Valley,* 1967; *Mr. Gumpy's Motor Car,* 1973; *Would You Rather,* 1978; *Where's Julius?,* 1986; *John Patrick Norman McHennessey: The Boy Who Was Always Late,* 1988; *Harvey Slumfenburger's Christmas Present,* 1993; *Courtney,* 1994

17. MARCIA BROWN

18. MARGARET WISE BROWN

19. JOSEPH BRUCHAC

20. EVE BUNTING

21. BETSY BYARS

BIBLIOGRAPHY: *Something about the Author,* vol. 60, 1990; *Children's Literature Review,* 1985
JUNE M. JACKO

BURTON, Hester (Wood-Hill)
Author, b. 6 December 1913, Beccles, Suffolk, England

Author of eighteen historical novels for children, B. attended Oxford University where she had C. S. LEWIS and J. R. R. TOLKIEN among her professors and earned an honors degree in English literature. She also worked as a part-time elementary school teacher and examiner for public examinations. From 1956 to 1961, she served as an assistant editor for *The Oxford Children's Encyclopedia.* As well as authoring historical novels for children, B. has edited and written the commentary for works about Coleridge, the Wordsworths, and Tennyson, as well as an adult biography about British feminist Barbara Bodichon. Her children's works have been translated into numerous languages. In 1962 she was runner-up for CARNEGIE MEDAL for her book about the Battle of Trafalgar, *Castor's Away!* (1962). She won the prestigious award in 1963 for *Time of Trial* about the British class struggles of the 1800s and freedom of speech. When her bookseller father is imprisoned for publishing pamphlets encouraging citizens to revolt in response to wretched social conditions, a young girl comes to his aid and learns how she can be an effective instrument for change.

AWARDS: Carnegie Medal (1963) for *Time of Trial*

FURTHER WORKS: *In Spite of all Terror,* 1968; *Otmoor Forever,* 1968; *Riders of the Storm,* 1972; *Kate Ryder,* 1975; *To Ravensrigg,* 1977; *Five August Days,* 1981

BIBLIOGRAPHY: *The Oxford Companion to Children's Literature,* 1984; *Something about the Author,* vol. 74, 1993
JANET HILBUN

BUTLER, Dorothy
Author, b. ca. 1925, Auckland, New Zealand

A bookstore owner, and author of books for children and adults, B. is perhaps best known as an advocate of reading with babies and very young children. In *Cushla and Her Books* (1979), B. tells the true story of how her granddaughter, Cushla, a child born with multiple disabilities (see THE DISABLED IN CHILDREN'S AND YOUNG ADULT LITERATURE), blossomed through interaction with books from a very young age. *Babies Need Books* (originally published in 1980; second rev. ed., 1997), which argues for the advantages and necessity of reading to all children from birth, has become a modern classic for those who work with books and young children, and has been adapted for television. B.'s own creative work for children includes stories and POETRY; she has edited anthologies of poetry for children as well.

AWARDS: Eleanor FARJEON Award (1979) for "Outstanding book on a disabled person." AMERICAN LIBRARY ASSOCIATION's Committee for the Year of the Disabled Person Award (1981). May Hill Arbuthnot Honor Lecturer (1982). Anne Carol Moore Spring Lecturer, Lincoln Center, New York (1982)

FURTHER WORKS: *I Will Build You a House: Poems,* 1984; *Higgledy Piggledy Hobbledy Hoy,* 1990

BIBLIOGRAPHY: *Something about the Author,* vol. 73, 1993
REBECCA PLATZNER

BYARD, Carole
Illustrator, b. 22 July 1941, Atlantic City, New Jersey

After many years teaching art as well as exhibiting her own prints, paintings, and sculpture, B. began illustrating children's books in 1971, echoing among other life events her Ford Foundation travel grant to AFRICA. Since then, her work has earned several AWARDS for ILLUSTRATION; in 1978 she won the CORETTA SCOTT KING AWARD for *Africa Dream* (Eloise GREENFIELD, author), and again in 1980 for *Cornrows* (Camille YARBROUGH, author). In 1993, *Working Cotton* (Sherley Anne Williams, author, 1992) was named an ALA CALDECOTT MEDAL Honor Book.

FURTHER WORKS: *The Black Snowman.* (Philip Mendez, author). 1989; *Grandmama's Joy* (Eloise Greenfield, author). 1980; *Willy* (Helen H. King, author). 1971

REFERENCES: *The Seventh Book of Junior Authors and Illustrators,* 1996
GWYNNE ELLEN ASH

BYARS, Betsy

Author, b. 7 August 1928, Charlotte, North
Carolina

B. was reared during the heart of the Great Depression, yet she never experienced poverty. Her
father worked at a cotton mill outside of Charlotte, which allowed B. to live in the city and in
the country; she had the best of both worlds. She
learned to read when she was four. Throughout
her school experience, B. excelled in reading; her
teachers never encouraged her to become a
writer, in fact she was a math major when she
first entered college. Math was not her forte, and
in 1950 she graduated from Queens College with
a B.A. in English.

After her children were of school age B. found
her day empty and thought that she would try
writing. She was certain she could do it and did
not believe it would be as difficult as others had
led her to believe. Her first article appeared in the
Saturday Evening Post. In 1962 her first book,
Clementine, was published. B. had put a lot of her
personality into the book and it was panned; she
was very hurt. She did not risk putting herself
into a book again until 1968 when she published
Midnight Fox. Many of B.'s books grow out of
her personal experiences. She may get an idea for
a book from a newspaper article, a story in her
children's lives, or her own daily interactions.
B.'s books appeal to children and YOUNG ADULTS
because of her ability to create vivid characters
who feel real emotions and have real problems.
B.'s books also appeal because of their subtle
HUMOR.

In 1970, *The Summer of the Swans* won the
NEWBERY MEDAL. When the committee called to
tell B. she had won the medal, she queried,
"What's that?" This novel was drawn from B.'s
experiences with developmentally disabled children (see THE DISABLED IN CHILDREN'S AND
YOUNG ADULT LITERATURE). The protagonist in
the story, Sara, is a typical adolescent struggling
with her self-identity. She is frustrated with a
summer in which she has to spend much of her
time watching her younger brother Charlie who is
developmentally disabled. When Charlie wanders
off and Sara goes in search of him she finds her
brother and begins to understand herself. In this

novel B. vividly presents Sara with the confusion
that overwhelms many adolescents in their search
for self.

B.'s characters allow readers to envision
themselves as the protagonists. Her characters
portray the suffering that is often a part of growing up. In *The Pinballs* (1977), B. presents three
characters in a foster home. Carlie, Harvey, and
Thomas J. have all been abandoned by their parents; they are searching for love and acceptance.
The Cartoonist (1978) presents Alfie as struggling to keep his own identity as an individual
when his older, abusive brother threatens to return home. Alfie does not have a lot of choices
but when he decides to lock himself in the attic,
he learns that he will not always be able to change
his world, but that he must be true to himself.
In *The Animal, the Vegetable, and John D. Jones*
(1982), B. creates vivid characters all searching
for ways to deal with their parents' divorce.
Clara, Deanie, and John D. are presented as individuals in the manner that they choose to deal
with their problems. *Trouble River* (1969) presents Dewey, a young boy, and his grandma escaping Indian attacks on the frontier. As they take
their escape on *Trouble River* they learn to deal
with each other and their fear. In *McMummy*
(1993), Mozie learns about self-respect and respect for nature as he interacts with a beauty pageant contestant and a piece of lettuce. *The Not-
Just-Anybody Family* (1986) presents the Harper
family working to get grandpa out of jail. During
the search, their love of family and identity as a
complete unit is strongly reinforced. Vividly depicted characters searching for the all-elusive understanding of self as they progress in life are
hallmarks of B.'s novels.

B.'s novels often deal with sensitive and controversial topics. In *Summer of the Swans,* she
deals with mental retardation. In *The Pinballs*
(1977), she deals with parental abuse and neglect.
The Cartoonist (1978) deals with school failure
and poverty. *Cracker Jackson* (1985) involves
physical abuse. *The Animal, the Vegetable and
John D. Jones* (1982) has characters who are
forced to accept their parents' lives after divorce.
In *The Cybil War* (1981), B. deals with honesty
and first love.

B.'s use of HUMOR is evident throughout most
of her novels. When characters are struggling in

The Cartoonist, Cracker Jackson, The Cybil War, and *The Pinballs* (1977) there are undertones of humorous situations that help the reader to keep the difficult situation in perspective. In *The Not-Just-Anybody Family* (1986), B. depicts poverty and family tragedy in a humorous setting; in this novel the children actually break in to the jail. In *The Computer Nut* (1984), an alien makes inappropriate jokes adding an interesting twist of humor to the protagonist's lives.

AWARDS: AMERICAN LIBRARY ASSOCIATION Notable Book Award (1969) for *Trouble River*, (1970) for *The Summer of the Swans*, (1972) for *The House of Wings*, (1977) for *The Pinballs*, and (1996) for *My Brother Ant*. Lewis CARROLL Shelf Award (1970) for *The Midnight Fox*. ALA NEWBERY Medal (1971) for *The Summer of the Swans*. Hans Christian ANDERSEN Honor List for Promoting Concern for the Disadvantaged and Handicapped (1979). *School Library Journal* Best Children's Books, (1982) for *The Two-Thousand Pound Goldfish*. Regina Medal, Catholic Library Association (1987) for *The Computer Nut*. Edgan Allan Poe Award, Mystery Writers of America (1992) for *Wanted . . . Mud Blossom*

FURTHER WORKS: *The Dancing Camel,* 1965; *Rama, the Gypsy Cat,* 1966; *The Grobber,* 1967; *Go and Hush the Baby,* 1971; *The House of Wings,* 1972; *After the Goat Man,* 1974; *The Lace Snail,* 1975; *The TV Kid,* 1976; *Good-bye Chicken Little,* 1979; *The Night Swimmers,* 1980 and 1990; *The Glory Girl,* 1983; *The Golly Sisters Go West,* 1986; *The Blossoms Meet the Vulture Lady,* 1986; *The Blossoms and the Green Phantom,* 1987; *Beans on the Roof,* 1988; *The Burning Question of Bingo Brown,* 1988; *Bingo Brown and the Language of Love,* 1988; *Hooray for the Golly Sisters,* 1990; *Bingo Brown, Gypsy Lover,* 1990; *The Seven Treasure Hunts,* 1991; *Bingo Brown's Guide to Romance,* 1992; *Coast to Coast,* 1992; *The Golly Sisters Ride Again,* 1994; *The Dark Stairs: A Herculeah Jones Mystery,* 1994; *Growing up Stories,* 1995; *Tarot Says Beware,* 1995; *My Brother, Ant,* 1996; *Dead Letter,* 1996; *The Joy Boys,* 1996; *Tornado,* 1996; *Ant Plays Bear,* 1997; *Death's Door,* 1997; *The Moon and I,* 1991 and 1996

BIBLIOGRAPHY: HOPKINS, Lee Bennett, *Pauses: Autobiographical Reflections of 101 Creators of Children's Books,* 1995; *Something about the Author,* vol. 46, 1991; *Contemporary Authors, New Revision Series,* vols. 18 and 57

NANCE S. WILSON

CALDECOTT MEDAL

Each year, with the announcement of the winner of the Caldecott Medal for "the artist of the most distinguished American picture book for children" and the Honor Books for that award, comes a wave of excitement throughout the world of children's PICTURE BOOKS. The AWARDS are made by a group of fifteen members of the Association for Library Service to Children, a division of the AMERICAN LIBRARY ASSOCIATION. They are experienced librarians and other experts on children's books, who spend the year preceding the judging examining several thousand picture books on their own. Then, as a committee, they devote several intensive days during ALA's Midwinter Meeting to negotiating before selecting and announcing the winners. Their deliberations and decisions over the years help all of us pay closer attention to the large number of high-quality contenders.

The criteria for selecting the Caldecott Medal—craftsmanship, consistency, coherence with text, and appeal to children up to the age of fourteen—is useful background when responding to any picture book. A picture book is a special sort of illustrated book in which there should be at least parity between the story-telling impact of the words and that of the pictures. The words and the visuals must supplement each other in telling the story—except, of course, in a textless book; in that case, the ILLUSTRATIONS carry the whole weight of the story. Generally, the words produce the body of the story and the pictures create the emotional content, the spirit. There are no mea-suring sticks to tell how many words balance how many pictures. Some Caldecott winners of the past, such as *Animals of the Bible* (1937), the first winner of that award, with text selected by Helen Dean Fish and illustrations by D. P. LATHROP, would be questionable picture books in contemporary terms. That book has a lengthy text, and the drawings that face each text page merely identify the animals described without engaging in the action of the story. So, every year, each new committee decides which books fit its definition of a distinguished picture book.

Looking back over the years the Caldecott Medal has been awarded, and focusing on just the winners, it is clear that these books exemplify many of the general attributes of picture books in subject matter, form, style, and the media used by the artists. They also offer many different avenues of exploration with students, from the most obvious variations in story type and overall appearance of the book to the more subtle changes in the content and images that relate to society's changing concerns and values. For example the texts of early titles reflect a relatively benign world for children, with cozy stories such as Virginia Lee's BURTON's *The Little House* (1942), Leonard WEISGARD's *The Little Island* (1946) by Golden MacDonald—pseudonym of Margaret Wise BROWN—and Robert MCCLOSKEY's emotionally involving *Make Way for Ducklings* (1941) or his more poetic *Time of Wonder* (1957). Rachel FIELD's *Prayer for a Child* (1944) illustrated by Elizabeth Orton JONES might not receive consideration today because of its narrowly

Christian context, although Biblical stories such as Peter SPIER's *Noah's Ark* (1977), or Ruth Robbins' *Baboushka and the Three Kings* (1960), visually set by Nicolas SIDJAKOV to emphasize folkloric qualities in the story, seem appropriate and more universal.

In 1955 the first retelling of a standard FAIRY TALE appears: Marcia BROWN's elegant setting of PERRAULT's *Cinderella* (1954). Then, there was adaptation of Chaucer, *Chanticleer and the Fox* (1958), visualized by Barbara COONEY. Marcia Brown chose to retell an Indian fable, *Once a Mouse. . . .* (1961), and to illustrate it with woodcuts in subtle tones that enhance the mystic sensibilities. The number of retellings increases in the 1970s, with Arlene MOSEL's rendering of *The Funny Little Woman* (1972), set in lively abstract fashion by Blair LENT, and Harve ZEMACH's version of *Duffy and the Devil* (1973), devilishly designed by Margot ZEMACH. Gerald MCDERMOTT's *Arrow to the Sun* (1974), with its powerfully composed double-page spreads, reinforces the magic of the Pueblo culture along with that of this folktale from that tradition. Verna AARDEMA's retelling of *Why Mosquitoes Buzz in People's Ears* (1975), set in stylized scenes by Leo and Diane DILLON, was another folktale winner.

Indeed, well before the recent flood of "MULTICULTURAL" titles, the picture-book folktales of the 1970s provided glimpses into other cultures. The Dillons' winning artwork in *Ashanti to Zulu: African Traditions* (1977), is a notable expression of that genre. Going much further back, precursors of the interest in exploring other cultures is found in Thomas HANDFORTH's *Mei Li* (1938), a picture of life in China in the 1930s, and Marie Hall ETS and Aurora Labastida's *Nine Days to Christmas* (1959), with Ets's illustrations of a young girl's celebration of the Christmas posada in a Mexican town. The 1980s and 1990s have been dominated by original stories, but then in 1998 Paul O. ZELINSKY's Renaissance setting of *Rapunzel* (1997) reminds readers that there can be no single definitive interpretation of any traditional story; there are always fresh insights to be added.

The subjects of picture books are limited only by the imaginations of their creators and the tolerance of their publishers. There is no prescribed form. There have been collections of fables, such as Arnold LOBEL's *Fables* (1980). Many picture-book texts have qualities of poetic prose, but poetry has rarely been found in winners, an exception being the text written by Blaise Cendrars and translated by Marcia Brown for Brown's dramatically illustrated *Shadow* (1982). The great majority of Caldecott Award–winning titles are stories. Some of these are based on history, including Ingri and Edgar Parin D'AULAIRE's *Abraham Lincoln* (1939) and Alice and Martin PROVENSEN's *The Glorious Flight: Across the Channel with Louis Ble'riot* (1983). Others relate personal histories, such as Allen SAY's *Grandfather's Journey* (1993) recalling Say's grandfather's passage from Japan to America.

Although HUMOR is by far the most popular emotion expressed in picture books as a whole, it by no means dominates the Caldecott Medal winners. For every zany *Officer Buckle and Gloria* by Peggy RATHMANN (1995), there are many more serious subjects represented. Chris VAN ALLSBURG's eerie *Jumanji* (1981), Paul GOBLE's stylized treatment of a NATIVE AMERICAN tale, *The Girl Who Loved Wild Horses* (1978), shows children's curiosity and universal human emotions. Eve BUNTING's dark tale of trouble in the Los Angeles riots with David DIAZ's melodramatic visualization of a *Smoky Night* (1994) demonstrates further this wide and powerful emotional range.

The Caldecott Medal is given to the artist, so we must move beyond examination of the subject, format, and message of the text to focus on the art of the illustrator. Technological advances in the past five decades have liberated artists from many of the former limitations on color reproductions. Black or monochrome drawings were frequently used in the first decades that the award was bestowed. *Animals of the Bible, Mei Li,* and Lynd Ward's *The Biggest Bear* (1952) typify titles that were able to exploit the possibilities of those techniques in order to create effective visual stories. With investment in expensive color reproduction during the early years of the Caldecott's history, such art frequently appeared in double-page spreads alternating with spreads containing either black-and-white illustrations, as in Berta and Elmer HADER's *The Big Snow* (1948), or art with black and a single other hue, as in Leo POLITI's *Song of the Swallows* (1949) or Cooney's *Chanticleer and the Fox* (1958).

As methods of accurately replicating the textures and transparencies of the original art have improved, there is no longer a need to separate colors by manually cutting separate stencils for each of the printing inks, a tedious process that artists are glad to avoid. Illustrators are free to produce full-color work at a reasonable cost. Van Allsburg's *Jumanji* appears in black-and-white in 1982 only because that fits the surrealistic aesthetic vision of its creator. The use of laser scanning since the 1970s has led to increasingly handsome color reproduction. We can have the mysteriously ghostly forms in Brown's *Shadow,* the velvety exotic dark tones of Ed YOUNG's *Lon Po Po: A Red-Riding Hood Story from China* (1989), and the glorious color ranges of Zelinsky's *Rapunzel.*

Stylistically, there seems to be a subtle evolution, over the decades, from an open, somewhat simpler representation of our world to a more complex and, at times, darker vision. Looking at the winners arranged along a time line, there is no obvious or abrupt sense of change. It is as if the picture-book world had chosen—until recently—to ignore the major revolutionary movements in the art world proper. It was a surprise, even to the author/illustrator himself, when David MACAULAY's *Black and White* (1990), an inventively illustrated quadripartite story, was chosen. There was also both surprise and controversy when Bunting and Diaz's *Smoky Night* was announced as winner in 1995, due to both the stark realism of the story and the postmodern imagery of the art.

There has been a conservative approach to the awards, perhaps because of the need for a consensus among fifteen people. There has certainly been a great variety demonstrated in the illustration styles over the years, however from Jones's almost saccharine sentimentality in *Prayer for a Child* to David WISNIEWSKI's bold, baroque paper-cut art in *Golem* (1996). Barbara Cooney's overt simplicity in Donald HALL's *Ox Cart Man* (1979) is countered by Trina Schart HYMAN's linear intricacies in Margaret HODGES's *Saint George and the Dragon* (1984). The medal-winning books demonstrate the many possibilities of the wonderful, fanciful picture-book world. Expand the exploration to the many Honor Books, and the range is far wider.

SYLVIA AND KENNETH MARANTZ

(Excerpted and revised from the authors' article in Book Links, *March 1999, pages 9–14)*

(See also BOOK DESIGN; PICTURE BOOKS; PICTURE BOOKS FOR OLDER READERS; VISUAL LITERACY)

CALDECOTT, Randolph (J.)

Illustrator, b. 22 March 1846, Chester, Cheshire, England; d. 12 February 1886, St. Augustine, Florida

C. was born and reared in Chester, England, where from an early age he displayed a talent for drawing. But it was not nurtured by his parents and he eventually began work as a bank clerk. In his free time, he sketched the people and landscapes of Cheshire and Shropshire, and these images would recur in his mature work. In 1867 he moved to Manchester where, in addition to his banking work, he took classes at the Manchester School of Art. Some of his drawings began to sell and in 1872 he moved to London to pursue a full-time art career.

C. published many drawings in periodicals, including *Punch, Harper's,* and *London Society.* His first book contract was for Henry G. Blackburn's *The Harz Mountains: A Tour in Toy Country* (1872) but he gained celebrity with his illustrations of *Old Christmas* (1875) and *Bracebridge Hall* (1876), both excerpted from Washington IRVING's *Sketch Book.* He attracted the attention of the famous engraver Edmund Evans, who invited C. to illustrate a series of children's books. His first efforts were *The House That Jack Built,* (1878) and *The Diverting History of John Gilpin* (1878). This was the beginning of a very successful collaboration and C. illustrated two children's PICTURE BOOKS a year, usually choosing nursery rhymes or light verse as his text. In all, C. illustrated sixteen children's books.

C.'s style bears a striking resemblance to that of Walter CRANE and Kate GREENAWAY, both of whom he knew well. The three of them are generally regarded as the triumvirate of Victorian children's ILLUSTRATION. C. is usually described, however, as livelier than Crane and funnier than Greenaway. C.'s illustrations, which alternate between monochrome and full-color drawings, are indeed characterized by freedom of movement and a witty sense of HUMOR. Through facial expressions, his characters, both human and animal, are imbued with distinctive personalities. A close examination of his pages will be rewarded with delightful comic touches. His fluid lines deftly carry the action from page to page and give a unity seldom found in children's picture books of the day. Perhaps most importantly, he never patronized his child audience nor sentimentalized his drawings.

C. brought a sophistication to children's book illustration it had not previously enjoyed. His books were a commercial success and they brought him considerable fame, and his work was admired by artists such as Vincent Van Gogh and Paul Gauguin. He deeply influenced such illustrators as Beatrix POTTER (whose father owned some original C. drawings) and Maurice SENDAK. C.'s work, particularly its flowing quality, has also been suggested as an inspiration for animated cartoons.

C. married a cousin, Marian Brind, in 1880 but they had no children. C. had suffered rheumatic fever as a child and his health was always precarious. He died in 1886 while on an extended visit to the United States to make drawings of American life for *Graphic*. He is buried in St. Augustine, Florida.

In 1938, the AMERICAN LIBRARY ASSOCIATION, at the urging of Frederic MELCHER, established the CALDECOTT MEDAL in C.'s honor, which is awarded annually "to the artist of the most distinguished American picture book published in the United States during the preceding year." The first Medal was awarded to *Animals of the BIBLE*, illustrated by Dorothy P. LATHROP, text by Helen Dean Fish. One or more Honor Books are typically selected each year.

The medal itself displays a characteristically lively illustration from C.'s *John Gilpin*. The Caldecott Medal is widely regarded as the most prestigious American award for children's picture-book illustration, and the winner's announcement early each year is considered a major publishing event. It is a fitting tribute to this pioneer artist in the field of children's illustration whose influence is still being felt today.

FURTHER WORKS: *The Babes in the Wood* (James Riordan). 1879; *Three Jovial Huntsmen*, 1880; *Sing a Song of Sixpence*, 1880; *The Queen of Hearts*, 1881; *Hey Diddle Diddle, the Cat and the Fiddle* [and] *Baby Bunting*, 1882; *A Frog He Would a-Wooing Go*, 1883; *Jackanapes* (Juliana Horatia Ewing, author). 1884

BIBLIOGRAPHY: Cott, Jonathan, *Pipers At the Gates of Dawn: The Wisdom of Children's Literature*, 1981

DAVID L. RUSSELL

CALVINO, Italo
Author, b. 15 October 1923, Santiago de Las Vegas, Havana, Cuba; d. 19 September 1985, Siena, Italy

Shortly after his birth C. returned to San Remo, Italy, where he later attended public school. C. entered the School of Agriculture at the university of Turin where his father was a distinguished professor until the German occupation during World War II. His parents were abducted by the Germans and C. joined a resistance group in the Maritime Alps. Between 1945 and 1949 he wrote many short stories, thirty of which were collected into a volume published in 1949 as *The Crow Comes Last*.

Italian Folktales (1980) is a collection of two-hundred traditional folktales C. collected from all over Italy, many never before written down. They come from the oral tradition, from memories of stories people heard as children and transcribed by C. He gives his source for each story in an appendix.

IRVYN G. GILBERTSON

CAMERON, Ann
Author, b. 21 October 1943, Rice Lake, Wisconsin

C. began her career by working in the publishing field after graduating from Radcliffe College. In New York, as an editorial assistant at Harcourt Brace Jovanovich, she was able to meet famous authors while she learned to edit books. In 1967, C. decided to start her own writing career with an adult novel, and received a fellowship to work toward her master's degree at the University of Iowa. Becoming discouraged with the problems of finishing her adult novel, C. turned to children's books. *The Seed*, the story of a frightened seed, was published in 1975.

C. returned to New York and worked as a free-lance manuscript reader while continuing to write. Her breakthrough came with *The Stories*

Julian Tells (1981). Julian is a lively, intelligent black boy with a younger brother, Huey, a friend, Gloria, and two loving parents. Julian gets into mischief, discovers new things about himself, and is supported and encouraged by his parents. C.'s ability is well displayed in the episode of the lemon pudding. She introduces the delectable pudding, involves the boys in eating it, and delivers justice and a fitting ending all in one short story. The other stories in the book are equally ordinary in plot and equally engaging because of the charm of the children and loving support of the parents. This successful form is repeated in *More Stories Julian Tells* (1986), *The Story Huey Tells* (1995), and *More Stories Huey Tells* (1997). She has also elaborated on Julian's adventures in three longer stories for beginning readers.

C. feels that the success of her stories is based on the universality of the human experience. Letters from children all over the world support her idea that there are more similarities than differences among people.

Two other books, *The Most Beautiful Place in the World* (1988) and *The Kidnapped Prince* (1955) are based on her experience in Guatemala, where she moved in 1983. *The Kidnapped Prince,* adapted from the 1789 autobiography of Olaudah Equiano, tells the story of an eleven-year-old boy kidnapped from Africa, who served as a slave in England, America, and the West Indies before he managed to buy his freedom. Living in a small mountain town, C. has been able to achieve her goal of experiencing another lifestyle. The stories of C. touch many readers because she has been able to show very individual children from different backgrounds in ways that reveal the humanity of all children.

FURTHER WORKS: *Julian's Glorious Summer* (1987); *Julian, Secret Agent* (1988); *Julian, Dream Doctor* (1990)

BIBLIOGRAPHY: *Something about the Author,* vol. 89, 1997

ANITA M. TROUT

CAMERON, Eleanor

Author, b. 23 March 1912, Winnipeg, Manitoba, Canada; d. 11 October 1996, Monterey, California

C.'s writing life was divided into two quite different periods based on the two SERIES she wrote for children. C. had a long career in libraries and had published an adult novel, *The Unheard Music* (1950), before she wrote the first of what became five books about Mr. Bass. According to C., she wrote *The Wonderful Flight to the Mushroom Planet* (1954) at the instigation of her son David, who wanted a story about two boys and a space ship. As SCIENCE FICTION, they definitely seem more fiction than science to today's children reared on *Star Wars* movies and *Voyager* flights. But these books, the last of which was written in 1967, before the first moon walk, are still enjoyed by children because of the characters of Tyco Bass and his cousin Theodosius.

The second main body of C.'s work for children is the Julia Redfern books. The first, *A Room Made of Windows* (1971), introduces Julia as a strong young girl with a decided ambition—to be a writer. Julia also has to deal with her older brother, her grandmother, and her mother, who wants to marry again. C. stated that the books were autobiographical in that they were based on incidents in her own life. C. took those incidents, translated them through Julia's perspective and created a new reality. Other books in the series, although written later, tell of Julia's life at an earlier age, reversing the usual order of character development.

Although the Mushroom Planet and Julia Redfern books are two distinct bodies of C.'s work, she wrote many other books. *The Court of the Stone Children* (1973), a time FANTASY, is one of the best known. It is set in San Francisco, in a museum where a magical transformation takes place. C. felt that there was a sort of magic in each of her works, whether of imagination, of time, or of science, and she was able to share it with her many readers.

C. gave much thought to what makes good children's books good. The result of her efforts was *The Green and Burning Tree* (1969), which she describes as a combination of her experiences with writing and the principles of art that she could detect in the books she read. C. was one of the inspired writers who cannot only write well, but can also write well about writing. The book and its successor, *The Seed and the Vision* (1993), provide many perceptive essays into the art of writing, and the appreciation of children's books and authors. C. felt that children appreciated a good story and that they appreciated good writing that invokes a mood and a place.

FURTHER WORKS: *Stowaway to the Mushroom Planet* (1956); *Mr. Bass's Planetoid* (1958); *The Terrible Churnadryne* (1959); *A Mystery for Mr. Bass* (1960); *A Spell Is Cast* (1964); *To the Green Mountains* (1975); *Julia and the Hand of God* (1977); *Beyond Silence,* (1980)

BIBLIOGRAPHY: MEIGS, et al. A Critical History of Children's Literature, 1969; Anita Silvey, ed., *Children's Books and Their Creators,* 1995

ANITA M. TROUT

CANADIAN LITERATURE

When people think of Canada, they often think of the Great White North. Consequently, survival, of the chilly kind, is expected to be a major theme in its literature, and, not surprisingly, it still is. Also, being situated next to the overwhelmingly U.S. book market, makes survival a daily way of life in Canada. Fortunately, Canadian children's PUBLISHERS have not only survived but are flourishing.

At the turn of the century, publishing endeavors for children were primarily focused on nature tales. Notable works were Ernest Thompson SETON's *Wild Animals I Have Known* (1898), G. D. Robert's *The Kindred of the Wild* (1902), Marshall Saunders's *Beautiful Joe* (1894) and Grey Owl's (Archibald Belaney) *The Adventures of Sajo and Her Beaver People* (1935). *Anne of Green Gables* (1908) by L. M. MONTGOMERY was the most prominent book of the period and is still one of our most famous and beloved books.

Gradual development of ADVENTURE STORIES evolved until the 1960s when interest in the retelling of Native legends resulted in Christie Harris's *Once upon a Totem* (1963), Robert Ayre's *Sketco the Raven* (1961), Dorothy Reid's *Tales of Nanabozho* (1963), as well as editor William Toye's retellings, illustrated by Elizabeth CLEAVER, of *The Mountain Goats of Temlaham* (1969), *How Summer Came to Canada* (1969), and later, *The Loon's Necklace* (1977).

In the centennial year, 1967, there were only thirty eight children's titles in English in Canada. At the end of the twentieth century, over 400 titles are being published in English and 170 in French. What stimulated this remarkable growth in such a short time? First, credit must be given to

the work of the Canada Council, which provided grants to publishers and to the Canadian Children's Book Centre in Toronto. The Centre is the national resource for the promotion of Canadian books for children and young people. It regularly publishes newsletters and a yearly "Our Choice" catalog, listing the best of the books published. Since its inception in 1976, the Canadian Children's Book Centre has dramatically increased the awareness of teachers, librarians, and bookstore owners. Each November the Centre sponsors the Canadian Children's Book Festival, a nationwide celebration, with visits by authors and illustrators to all ten provinces and three territories.

Thanks to Canada Council grants, there has occurred a rapid expansion of publishing houses for children's books. Besides Toronto, children's publishers are located from St. John's, Newfoundland, to Victoria, British Columbia. These companies give a regional presence to children's literature and allow for more books of local interest to be published. Growth of Canadian children's literature was characterized by an early appreciation of fine art in PICTURE BOOKS. From its beginning, Tundra Books set out to feature the work of fine artists; May Cutler created a line featuring many fine artists: William Kurelek's *A Prairie Boy's Winter* (1973), Sheldon Cohen's *The Hockey Sweater* (Roch Carrier, 1984), Stéphan Poulin's *Have You Seen Josephine?* (1986), Ted HARRISON's *A Northern Alphabet* (1982), and C. J. Taylor's *The Secret of the White Buffalo* (1993). A major turning point occurred in 1984: the first coproduction of picture books with American publishers to increase print runs and cut costs, thus guaranteeing the regular use of four-color printing. Ian WALLACE's *Ching Chiang and the Dragon's Dance* was successfully coproduced with Margaret McElderry Books. This has encouraged the development of Canadian picture books with distinctive artistic styles and a fresh view of life as seen through the eyes of young children: Barbara REID's use of plasticine illustrations in *Have You Seen Birds?* by Joanne Oppenheim (1986), Dayal Kaur KHALSA's vivid, detailed paintings in *Tales of a Gambling Grandma* (1986), Kim LaFave's fresh watercolors in *Amos's Sweater* (Janet LUNN, 1988), and Paulette Bourgeois's growth spurt in *Big Sarah's Little Boots* (1987).

A recent development is the "on-the-street" name recognition of leading writers. Who is number one? Robert MUNSCH! Young children and their parents know his stories by heart, chanting their noisy refrains with great gusto. Much of the appeal of these best-selling books is the hilarious cartoon illustrations by Michael Martchenko: *Paper Bag Princess* (1981), *Thomas's Snowsuit* (1985), *Moira's Birthday* (1987), and *Andrew's Loose Tooth,* 1998. Jean LITTLE, the remarkable writer who is 95 percent blind is widely known for her *Mama's Going to Buy You a Mockingbird* (1984) and the first part of her autobiography, *Little by Little* (1987); Monica HUGHES, Canada's foremost SCIENCE FICTION writer for children is recognized for *The Keeper of the Isis Light* series (1981) and *The Golden Aquarians* (1994). Canadian characters are also becoming recognized widely. One of the most famous, after Anne of Green Gables, is Franklin, a friendly green turtle who has all sorts of adventures, just like the young readers who adore him. Franklin has brought fame to its creators, Paulette Bourgeois and illustrator Brenda Clark; *Franklin in the Dark* (1986), *Franklin Has a Sleepover* (1996) and a bevy of other adventures.

Canadian children's books have taken on a national character. There is a staunch recognition that in all aspects of Canadian life regionalism plays an important part. The influence of the environment can be seen in picture books such as Anne Blades's northern British Columbia forests in *Mary of Mile 18* (1971), Betty Waterton's Pacific coastline in *A Salmon for Simon* (1986), and Yvette Moore's Saskatchewan landscapes in *A Prairie Alphabet* (Jo Bannatyne-Cugnet, 1992). The same is true for novels as evident in the Newfoundland setting of Kevin Major's *Hold Fast,* the Northwest Territories for Farley MOWAT's *Lost in the Barrens* (1977), the Ontario wilderness for William Bell's *Crabbe* (1986) and Tim WYNNE-JONES's *Maestro* (1995), or the Alberta forests in Monica Hughes's *Hunter in the Dark* (1982).

Without doubt there is also a greater awareness of the MULTICULTURAL fabric of Canada. This is shown in picture books such as Richardo Keens-Douglas's *Grandpa's Visit* (1996), Michael Kusugak's *Northern Lights: The Soccer Trails* (1993), Tolowa Mollel's *The Orphan Boy* (1990), Sheldon Oberman's *The Always Prayer Shawl* (1994), and W. D. Valgardson's *Thor* (1994). It can also be seen in Martha BROOKS's *Bone Dance* (1997), when a First Nation's girl and a Metis boy are brought together by a plot of sacred lakeshore land. There is a continuing appreciation and merging of the French presence, as French speaking writers and illustrators from Quebec are published first by English speaking publishers or simultaneously coproduced. This can be seen in Marie Louise Gay's *Angel and the Polar Bear* (1988) and *Rumpelstiltskin* (1997), Rémy Simard's *The Magic Boot* (1995), Sylvie Gaigneault's *Bruno in the Snow* (1994), and Pierrette Dubé's *Sticks and Stones* (1995).

There is an emerging sense of the history of Canada, as gradually we are witnessing a growing awareness of the past: Janet Lunn's time travel back to the time of the U.S. Civil War in *The Root Cellar* (1981), Barbara Smucker's immigration story of a family coming from Russia in *Days of Terror* (1979), Kit PEARSON's wartime arrival of two children in *The Sky Is Falling* (1989), and Paul YEE's Depression setting in Vancouver for *Breakaway* (1995). A part of Canadian culture is being able to laugh at ourselves; we chuckle at Brian DOYLE's *Easy Avenue* (1988), Claire Mackay's collection of *Laughs* (1997), Farley Mowat's *Owls in the Family* (1973), and Gordon KORMAN's *The Chicken Doesn't Skate* (1996).

For Canadian writers, illustrators, and publishers, the most important development is direct sales to the United States; all it takes is fortitude, an American address, and a dedicated marketing sales force. This is most exciting as more publishers are selling their books directly into the larger market, yet editors are keeping authentically Canadian settings and characters so that they do not merge into a melting pot of commonality. Survival is what Canadian children's literature and Canada is all about.

RONALD JOBE

CANNON, Janell
Author, illustrator, b. 3 November 1957, St. Paul, Minnesota

C. has a small body of work, but has already found a format that gives her full scope for both her writing and illustrating talents. C. reports that as a student she drew most frequently with black pens, yet it is the vibrant color in her PICTURE BOOKS that is distinctive. *Stellaluna* (1993) is the story of a young fruit bat who becomes separated from her mother and is raised with a family of birds. Although she adapts well enough, the tension of the story lies in whether she will be reunited with her mother. C. has accurately portrayed the differences between bats and birds and the lifestyle of fruit bats, and included facts about bats at the end of the story. In *Stellaluna,* C. has used muted colors to evoke the night life of bats, and to convey a comforting tone to the search for the bat mother.

She uses this formula again in *Verdi* (1997), the tale of a young python who so loves his yellow striped skin and the speed with which he can zip around the forest, that he determines he will never change. The snake finds out, however, that even though he cannot stop himself from growing or from changing in the way that all pythons do, he can appreciate advantages to the changes. C. again adds facts about snakes at the end of the book. In *Verdi,* C. uses brilliant greens and yellows to portray the lushness of the rain forest, many times in double-page spreads.

C.'s use of HUMOR makes the stories appealing to youngsters. She creates animals that, while true to the facts of nature, give children characteristics with which to identify and empathize. Her pairing of text and artwork is a very successful combination.

FURTHER WORKS: *Trupp: A Fuzzhead Tale,* 1995; *Crickwing,* 2000

BIBLIOGRAPHY: Library of Congress website

ANITA M. TROUT

CARIBBEAN LITERATURE

Children's books set in the Caribbean hold great value for readers interested in discovering the richness of this region. Through the folk literature, historical fiction, poetry, nonfiction books, and contemporary realism of the area, readers can explore the various islands of the Caribbean and experience its cultural diversity. Many stories exist with Caribbean–island settings by authors who grew up on the various islands. But most are written by people from other cultures who capture an authentic flavor of the region.

James BERRY grew up on the island of Jamaica and supplies a true Caribbean flavor to his original stories and retellings of old folktales. Anansi stories were brought to the islands hundreds of years ago by captured AFRICAN slaves. Berry blends African and Caribbean influences in the text of his original Anansi tale, *First Palm Trees: An Anancy Spiderman Story* (1997), in which the greedy Anansi wants to keep the reward the king offers to anyone who causes palm trees to grow in his kingdom rather than sharing his with the spirits who help him. Berry masterfully incorporates information about Anansi's prominent characteristics and images of the Spirits into this beautifully crafted tale that blends elements of African and Caribbean FOLKLORE. In *Don't Leave an Elephant To Go Chase a Bird* (1996), with woodcuts by Anne GRIFALCONI, Berry takes the folktale back to its African roots and unfuses it with a Caribbean flavor reflecting his Jamaican upbringing. Frances TEMPLE also retells an Anancy story with a Jamaican setting in *Tiger Soup: An Anansi Story from Jamaica* (1994). *Ajeemah and His Son* (Berry, 1992) is a historical novel for middle-grade readers that recounts the tragic experience of an African father and his son who are captured in their African homeland in 1807, and transported to Jamaica. There, they are sold to neighboring sugarcane estates. The stories continue through a few generations in which the ex-slaves come to see themselves as Jamaican, not African. Other characters represent various circumstances or situations, making the entire novel an allegory for the African experience in Jamaica.

Monica Gunning, a poet who grew up in Jamaica, captures her early experience in imagery that provides readers with a delicious bit of her Jamaican childhood through two books of verse: *Not a Copper Penny in Me House: Poems from the Caribbean* (1993) and *Under the Breadfruit Tree: Island Poems* (1998). In both collections, Gunning depicts life as experienced by Jamaican children buying fruit from roadside peddlers, watching the John Canoe dancers at Christmastime, and sitting outdoors under the palm trees to learn their school lessons. In addition to the Jamaican landscape, food, and customs, Gunning deftly captures the essence of friends, relatives, and neighbors—their behaviors, idiosyncracies, and philosophies in her poetry. A glossary of words possibly unfamiliar to non–Jamaican readers provides a thoughtful introduction to the terminology and patois.

Lynn Joseph, a native of Trinidad, shares memories of childhood on the island through poems that tell of her brother taking a sea bath, racing snails at noon recess, buying ice cream from the palet man, watching boys play cricket, sipping coconut water and eating coconut jelly, hearing the steel drum playing, and fearing the *jumbi* man. The joyous images evoked by Joseph's words capture the experience of life on a tropical island in *A Coconut Kind of Day: Island Poems* (1990). She continues the celebration of tropical island life in *An Island Christmas* (1992), a jubilant collection of verse written with a touch of dialect. The culture of this South Caribbean island comes shining through with Joseph's upbeat verse that portrays the warmth and joy of the Christmas season minus snow, sleighbells, and warm fireplaces.

Joseph has also written a collection of six stories, *A Wave in Her Pocket: Stories from Trinidad* (1991), based on well-known figures from Trinidad's rich traditional folklore: the Soucouyant, a woman who becomes a ball of fire that sucks people's blood; Ligahoo, a shape-changing medicine man; and Papa Bois, the protector of trees and animals. The stories are told by the narrators Tantie (auntie), who helps take care of all her grandnieces and grandnephews. According to the author's note, almost all families in Trinidad have a tantie who gives mothers advice on child rearing and entertains children during family outings by telling them stories. Her well-loved and readily available stories may make them laugh, scare them, or teach a lesson. These six stories provide a window into indigenous, West African, Spanish, French, and English influences in the islands' folklore. They also show the importance of storytelling and the high regard given to storytellers in the Caribbean. An afterword and glossary provide background for these highly entertaining stories. Six characteristic masterful black-and-white scratchboard ILLUSTRATIONS by Brian PINKNEY clearly capture the content and tone of each of the tales.

Several other authors who also write about the Caribbean. Notable among them is Robert SAN SOUCI, with his retelling of the universal favorite *Cendrillon: A Caribbean Cinderella* (1998). This Caribbean variant of Cinderella is loosely based on the French Creole tale that follows the basic outline of Charles PERRAULT's telling of the tale while incorporating elements of West Indian culture. Here, breadfruit changes into a coach, agoutis into carriage horses, lizards into footmen, a *manicou* into a horseman, and Cendrillon's calico dress becomes blue-velet gown. Brian Pinkney's exquisite illustrations in his signature scratchboard style, subtly echo the humor in the text while capturing the elegance, pathos, and love inherent in the tale.

Maricel Presilla (*Feliz Nochebuena Feliz Navidad: Christmas Feasts of the Hispanic Caribbean,* 1994) and Alma Flor ADA (*Under the Royal Palms, a Childhood in Cuba,* 1998; *Mediopollito/Half Chicken,* 1995) from Camaguey, Cuba, write from the viewpoint of their Cuban heritage. Nicholasa MOHR relies on memories of Puerto Rico in her books *Felita* (1979) and *Song of el Coqui and Other Tales of Puerto Rico/Cancion del Coqui otros cuentos de Puerto Rico* (1995).

Several authors have successfully written about early Caribbean history, telling the story of the Taino and Arawak Indians. Michael DORRIS tells the story of Columbus's arrival and provides a glimpse of what life might have been like on a Caribbean island before the arrival of European explorers and settlers in *Morning Girl* (1992). Francine Jacobs (*The Tainos: The People Who Welcomed Columbus,* 1992) provides ample documentation in a highly readable informational book that begins with a detailed account of the life and culture of the Tainos before the arrival of Columbus in the Bahamas, and continues through the oppression of the Tainos in Haiti and the Dominican Republic through their ultimate disappearance within fifty years. *My Name Is Not Angelica* (Scott ODell, 1989) is set in 1733. This historical novel tells the story of Raisha, renamed Angelica, daughter of an African chieftain sold into slavery and brought to the West Indies. The book tells of her escape and the ensuing slave revolt in dramatic episodes that show the cooperation among slave owners and European governments to quell the uprising.

ELIZABETH A. POE

CARLE, Eric

Illustrator, author, b. 25 June 1929, Syracuse, New York

C. designs his work to serve as a bridge between toy and book, a step he identifies as critical to the child on the verge of entering school. His colorful PICTURE BOOKS utilize collage illustrations, often incorporating elements that invite preschool readers to manipulate or otherwise investigate the text design.

C. spent his own preschool and kindergarten years in the United States, where he was recognized for and encouraged in his artistic expression by his parents and his first teacher. When his family returned to Stuttgart, Germany, in 1935, C. found himself in a far more repressive school environment. The traditional regimentation of the German educational system was augmented by Nazism's rise and the hardships of World War II. From secondary school, C. entered Akademie der bildend Künste, Stuttgart, studying art from 1946 to 1950. Having missed his first home in the U.S. throughout his youth, he returned to New York to begin a career as a graphic designer. In 1967, Bill MARTIN invited him to illustrate *Brown Bear, Brown Bear, What Do You See?* (1967); he quickly made the transition to full-time book ILLUSTRATION and publishing. Twenty five years later, they collaborated on *Polar Bear, Polar Bear, What Do You Hear?* (1992).

C.'s first self-illustrated text, *1, 2, 3, to the Zoo* (1968) won first prize for picture books at the 1970 International Children's Book Fair and the 1970 Deutscher Jugendpreis citation. *The Very Hungry Caterpillar* (1969) earned the American Institute of Graphics Award (1970), Best Children's Books of England citation (1970), Selection du Grand Prix des Treize (France, 1972), and the Nakamori Reader's Prize (Japan, 1975). *Pancakes, Pancakes* (1970) won both the American Institute of Graphic Arts Award and the Child Study Association book list citation in 1970. *Do You Want to Be My Friend?* (1971) earned first prize for picture books at the International Children's Book Fair and the Deutscher Jugendpreis Award, both in 1972; the same year the AMERICAN LIBRARY ASSOCIATION named it a notable book and, in 1973, it earned the Selection du Grand Prix des Treize. *Have You Seen My Cat?* (1973) earned the Selection du Grand Prix des Treize that year. *Do Bears Have Mothers, Too?* (Aileen FISHER, 1973) received a citation from the Bulletin of the Center for Children's Books (1973). *The Very Busy Spider* (1984) was among ALA's Best Books of the 1980s. *Papa, Please Get the Moon for Me* (1986) received special mention by the Young Critics Award, citation at the International Children's Book Fair, and Parents' Choice Award in illustration, all in 1986. C. has earned recognition from various professional societies for his illustration work and has received AWARDS from museums and in art shows.

C. composes collages cut from tissue paper he paints himself in a full spectrum of colors. He cuts and glues the paper to cardboard to create the images, sometimes highlighting aspects with crayon. He photographs the completed collage, the color photograph serving as the illustrated page. With *The Very Hungry Caterpillar,* C. discovered that his own playful use of hole-punching paper could expand the narrative quality of his illustration. In subsequent works, he has manipulated page size, as in *The Grouchy Ladybug* (1977, published in England as *The Bad-Tempered Ladybird*), and used raised surfaces, as in *The Very Busy Spider,* to elaborate on his protagonists' spiderweb-weaving talents.

C.'s greatest appeal is to very young readers and, to that end, many of his titles are reproduced in board and miniature versions. The play with scale often enhances and refreshes the tale, as when *The Mixed-up Chameleon* (1975) and *A House for Hermit Crab* (1988) appeared in miniature editions (1991). These cumulative stories, among others by C., invite prereaders to tell their own versions of the titular characters' depicted changes. *The Very Quiet Cricket* (1990) has been produced in board book form with an embedded sound chip that chirps just like its protagonist, another page-turning invitation to toddlers. *The Long Tail* (1972) and *The Very Long Train* (1972) were produced originally as folding books, their physical layout echoing the dimensions recounted in their narratives. C.'s series, My Very First Library, contains books suitable for those too young for any narrative. *My Very First Book of Colors* (1974), *My Very First Book of Shapes* (1974), *My Very First Book of Motion* (1986), *My Very First*

Book of Sounds (1986), *My Very First Book of Touch* (1986), and others in the series invite caregivers to share the rudimentary but engagingly presented concepts with a lap-sitting audience.

In addition to illustrating his own stories, C. has illustrated narratives by Isaac Bashevis SINGER, (*Why Noah Chose the Dove,* 1974), Norton JUSTER (*Otter Nonsense,* 1982) and Mitsumasa ANNO (*All in a Day,* 1986). He has published collections of traditional tales, newly illustrated with his bright and expansive colors as well, including *Eric C.'s Storybook: Seven Tales by the Brothers GRIMM* (1976) and *Twelve Tales from Aesop* (1980). C.'s books appear in fifteen languages. The Eric C. Museum of Picture Book Art in Amherst, Massachusetts, is dedicated as a repository of picture-book artwork of many artists with permanent displays, workshop facilities for children, and the capacity to offer traveling shows.

FURTHER WORKS: *The Rooster Who Set out to See the World* 1972 (Published in 1987 as *Rooster's Off to See the World*); *Walter the Baker: An Old Story Retold,* 1972; *The Honeybee and the Robber: A Moving Picture Book,* 1981; *Catch the Ball,* 1982; *Eric C.'s Treasury of Classic Stories for Children,* 1988; *You Can Make a Collage: A Very Simple How-To Book,* 1998; *The Very Clumsy Click Beetle,* 1999

BIBLIOGRAPHY: *Contemporary Authors, New Revision Series,* vol. 25, 1989; Silvey, Anita, ed., *Children's Books and Their Creators,* 1995; *Something about the Author,* vol. 65, 1991

FRANCISCA GOLDSMITH

CARLSON, Natalie Savage
Author, b. 3 October 1906, Kernstown, Virginia

Writing in a time when people without homes were referred to as *tramps,* C. was a groundbreaker in terms of novels for children that dealt with less than pretty problems. Her nearly fifty books for young people have won AWARDS and have been popular with children throughout generations. Born to a distiller father and French-Canadian mother in 1906, C. published her first piece of writing in the *Baltimore Sun* at age eight. She grew up listening to Acadian folktales from her mother and her uncle, and she would later use these tales as well as family members as bases for her writing.

C. began writing professionally in the mid-1920s, when it was necessary for her to go to work to help support the family. As a reporter for the *Long Beach Morning Sun,* C. experimented with different writing styles and topics, and following her marriage to a naval officer, she began to have her worldwide travels to write about as well. Reading to her children, who were born in the 1930s, encouraged her to begin to write for children, and in 1952, C. published *The Talking Cat and Other Stories of French Canada,* followed by *Alphonse, That Bearded One* in 1954. These books of FOLKLORE were followed by *Wings against the Wind* (1955), a novel that told the story of a young seagull and his quest for a family; it was named an AMERICAN LIBRARY ASSOCIATION Honor Book.

Following her husband to Paris, C. began her Orpheline series after volunteering at an orphanage in the French capital. *The Happy Orpheline* (1957), a tale of orphans so happy with their home and their friends that they do not want to be adopted, was followed by *A Pet for the Orphelines* (1962), *The Orphelines in the Enchanted Castle* (1964), and *A Grandmother for the Orphelines* (1980).

France also provided the impetus and the setting for C.'s NEWBERY MEDAL Honor Book, *The Family Under the Bridge* (1958). Her tale of a man whose home was Paris's tunnels and streets was a touching and sometimes realistic portrayal of the isolation and hunger of the poor of Paris. *Luigi of the Streets* (1967) explored similar themes in the setting of a poor neighborhood in Marseilles.

This trend toward books that explored society's ills continued upon her return to the United States. *The Empty Schoolhouse* (1965) addressed desegregation, and *Marchers for the Dream* (1969), the Civil Rights Movement, but neither was as well received as *The Family under the Bridge.* However, C. also created lighthearted PICTURE BOOKS such as *Marie Louise and Christophe* (1974) and *Spooky and the Ghost Cat* (1985). For her work, C. was nominated as the United States candidate for the Hans Christian ANDERSEN Award in 1966.

FURTHER WORKS: *Evangeline: Pigeon of Paris* (1960); *The Half-Sisters* (1970); *Hortense: The*

Cow for a Queen (1957); *Spooky and the Witch's Goat* (1989)

BIBLIOGRAPHY: *Major Authors and Illustrators for Children and Young Adults* (1993); Fuller, M., ed. *More Junior Authors* (1963); *Twentieth-Century Children's Writers* (1978)

GWYNNE ELLEN ASH

CARLSTROM, Nancy White

Author, b. 4 August 1948, Washington, Pennsylvania

C. grew up in a household without television. She learned to entertain herself through her rich FANTASY life and reading and writing. Bible stories were among her favorites, and her religious faith continues to be important in her life and her writing. In high school C. was editor of the yearbook and school newspaper and worked in the children's department of the public library. She received a B.A. in education from Wheaton College (1970), then taught school four years before studying children's literature at Harvard Extension and Radcliffe. C. has also owned a children's bookstore and taught in West Africa, the West Indies, and Mexico—settings that appear in her books. In 1981, C. participated in a writers' workshop led by author Jane YOLEN and wrote her first work for children (*Wild, Wild Sunflower Child Anna*, 1987). She began submitting manuscripts to publishers, receiving eighty-two rejections before *Jesse Bear, What Will You Wear?* (1986) was accepted. In 1987, C. moved to Alaska with her family, where she found inspiration for several books.

C. finds her subject matter in events and moments of everyday life. For example, *Jesse Bear, What Will You Wear?*, which spawned the popular *Jesse Bear* series, began as a song she sang when dressing her young son. Her simple, elegant language and gentle stories are well suited for her young audience. The rhythm and cadence in C.'s writing mimic children's natural tendencies to play with words and sounds. The feelings of joy and hope often evoked by C.'s stories arise from her own faith and positive outlook on life.

AWARDS: *Jesse Bear, What Will You Wear?* was a *Booklist* Editor's Choice (1986), and INTERNATIONAL READING ASSOCIATION/CHILDREN'S BOOK COUNCIL Children's Choice (1987). *Wild, Wild Sunflower Child Anna* was an American Book-

sellers Pick of the List and National Council of Teachers of English Notable Book (1987). *Where Does the Night Hide?* was *Parents'* magazine Best Book of 1990. *Blow Me a Kiss, Miss Lilly* was an IRA/CBC Children's Choice and *Booklist* Parents' Choice (1991). *Goodbye Geese* was an NCTE Notable Book (1991)

FURTHER WORKS: In the *Jesse Bear* series: *Better Not Get Wet, Jesse Bear* (1988), *It's about Time, Jesse Bear: And Other Rhymes* (1990), *You're the Best, Jesse Bear* (1991), *How Do You Say It Today, Jesse Bear?* (1992), *Happy Birthday, Jesse Bear!* (1994), *Jesse Bear's Wiggle-Jiggle Jump-Up* (1994), *Let's Count It out, Jesse Bear* (1996), *Jesse Bear's Colors* (1997), *Jesse Bear's Toys* (1997), *Guess Who's Coming, Jesse Bear?* (1998)

OTHER WORKS: *The Moon Came Too* (1987), *Graham Cracker Animals 1-2-3* (1989), *Light: Stories of a Small Bright Kindness* (1990), *Moose in the Garden* (1990), *Where Does the Night Hide?* (1990), *Glory* (1991), *No Nap for Benjamin Badger* (1991), *Northern Lullaby* (1992), *The Snow Speaks* (1992), *Who Gets the Sun Out of Bed?* (1992), *Does God Know How to Tie Shoes?* (1993), *Swim the Silver Sea, Joshie Otter* (1993), *Wishing at Dawn in Summer* (1993), *I Am Christmas* (1995), *Who Said Boo?: Halloween Poems for the Very Young* (1995), *Ten Christmas Sheep* (1996), *I Love You Mama, Anytime of the Year* (1997), *Raven and River* (1997), *Midnight Dance of the Snowshoe Hare* (1998)

BIBLIOGRAPHY: Copeland, J. S., & Copeland, V. L. (1994). *Speaking of Poets 2: More Interviews with Poets Who Write for Children and Young Adults*. McClure, A. A., & Kristo, J. V. (1996). *Books That Invite Talk, Wonder, and Play.*

JANE WEST

CARNEGIE MEDAL

The Carnegie Medal is given for a children's book of outstanding merit written in English and first published in the United Kingdom in the preceding year. The Carnegie Medal has been given annually since 1937 by the British Library Association. Since 1990, the Peters Library Service makes a substantial grant to the Library Association; the grant is matched by the Business Sponsorship Incentive Scheme of the British government to publicize the CARNEGIE MEDAL and the KATE GREENAWAY MEDAL. The Carnegie is comparable to the American NEWBERY MEDAL. Originally limited to titles published in England by

U.K. writers, since 1969 any book written in English and published first or concurrently anywhere in the United Kingdom is eligible. The list of winners represents the date that the book was published. The Medal is presented during the summer of the following year.

1936: *Pigeon Post,* Arthur RANSOME; 1937: *The Family from One End Street,* Eve Garnett; 1938: *The Circus is Coming,* Noel STREATFEILD; 1939: *Radium Woman,* Eleanor Doorly; 1940: *Visitors from London,* Kitty Barne; 1941: *We Couldn't Leave Dinah,* Mary TREADGOLD; 1942: *The Little Grey Men,* BB; 1943: No Award; 1944: *The Wind on the Moon,* Eric Linklater; 1945: No Award; 1946: *The Little White Horse,* Elizabeth Goudge; 1947: *Collected Stories for Children,* Walter DE LA MARE; 1948: *Sea Change,* Richard Armstrong; 1949: *The Story of Your Home,* Agnes Allen; 1950: *The Lark on the Wing,* Elfrida Vipont Foulds; 1951: *The Wool-Pack,* Cynthia HARNETT; 1952: *The Borrowers,* Mary NORTON; 1953: *A Valley Grows Up,* Edward Osmond; 1954: *Knight Crusader,* Ronald Welch; 1955: *The Little Bookroom,* Eleanor FARJEON; 1956: *The Last Battle,* C. S. LEWIS; 1957: *A Grass Rope,* William MAYNE; 1958: *Tom's Midnight Garden,* Philippa PEARCE; 1959: *The Lantern Bearers,* Rosemary SUTCLIFF; 1960: *The Making of Man,* I. W. Cornwall; 1961: *A Stranger at Green Knowe,* Lucy BOSTON; 1962: *The Twelve and the Genii,* Pauline Clarke; 1963: *Time of Trial,* Hester BURTON; 1964: *Nordy Bank,* Sheena Porter; 1965: *The Grange at High Force,* Philip Turner; 1966: No Award; 1967: *The Owl Service,* Alan GARNER; 1968: *The Moon in the Cloud,* Rosemary Harris; 1969: *The Edge of the Cloud,* K. M. PEYTON; 1970: *The God beneath the Sea,* Leon GARFIELD and Edward BLISHEN; 1971: *Josh,* Ivan SOUTHALL; 1972: *Watership Down,* Richard ADAMS; 1973: *The Ghost of Thomas Kempe,* Penelope LIVELY; 1974: *The Stronghold,* Mollie HUNTER; 1975: *The Machine-Gunners,* Robert WESTALL; 1976: *Thunder and Lightnings,* Jan MARK; 1977: *The Turbulent Term of Tyke Tiler,* Gene Kemp; 1978: *The Exeter Blitz,* David Rees; 1979: *Tulku,* Peter DICKINSON; 1980: *City of Gold and Other Stories from the Old Testament,* Peter Dickinson; 1981: *The Scarecrows,* Robert WESTALL; 1982: *The Haunting,* Margaret MAHY; 1983: *Handles,* Jan MARK; 1984: *The Change-over: A Supernatural Romance,* Margaret Mahy; 1985: *Storm,* Kevin CROSSLEY-HOLLAND; 1986: *Granny Was a Buffer Girl,* Berlie DOHERTY; 1987: *The Ghost Drum,* Susan Price; 1988: *A Pack of Lies,* Geraldine MCCAUGHREAN; 1989: *Goggle-Eyes,* Anne FINE; 1990: *Wolf,* Gillian CROSS; 1991: *Dear Nobody,* Berlie Doherty; 1992: *Flour Babies,* Anne Fine; 1993: *Stone Cold,* Robert SWINDELLS; 1994: *Whispers in the Graveyard,* Theresa Bresling; 1997: *River Boy,* Tim Bowler; 1995: *His Dark Materials: Northern Lights,* Philip PULLMAN; 1996: *Junk,* Melvin Burgess; 1997: *Riverboy,* Tim Bowler; 1998: *Skellig,* David Almond; 1999: *Postcards from No Man's Land,* Aidan CHAMBERS

BERNICE E. CULLINAN

CARRICK, Carol and Donald

Authors/illustrators; Carol (Hatfield), b. 20 May 1935, Queens, New York; Donald b. 7 April 1929, Dearborn, Michigan; d. 26 June 1989

Carol and Donald C. have written and/or illustrated over ninety children's PICTURE BOOKS between them of which about half were written by Carol and illustrated by Donald during the course of their twenty-four-year marriage. Both loved to draw as children, and Carol spent hours of her vacation time immersed in library books. Personal inscriptions in books in THE KERLAN COLLECTION indicate that Carol C. was particularly inspired by events in their sons' lives and Donald used the boys as models. In writing *Patrick's Dinosaurs* (1983), Carol had difficulty imagining the immense size of the giant dinosaurs until she saw a huge crane dangling a generator over a rooftop, "like a huge praying mantis." This inspired her to write the book through her son's imagination, in which he transforms large objects in the environment into dinosaurs. In an inscription for *A Rabbit for Easter* (1979), Carol wrote that the rabbit in Paul's kindergarten classroom and their own cat's reaction to a vacationing guinea pig one Christmas inspired the story and paintings. Summering in Vermont and wintering on Martha's Vineyard, they lived a lifestyle that reflected their love of nature and provided them with local resources, such as a nearby lobster hatchery, for researching their topics. Donald was primarily a landscape painter, so Carol often chose topics that would include or focus on the environment (e.g., *Swamp Spring,* 1969). Both perfectionists, together and separately, they researched both text and visuals thoroughly.

While teaching children about nature, pet care, animal behavior, and other science and social studies topics, the Cs. also incorporate themes common to childhood: fears of the unknown, of taking steps toward independence and broadening their world; the pain of learning how to act responsibly; being a social outcast; and the difficulties inherent in learning to be caring and considerate. Donald's realistic illustrations skillfully show the characters' emotional responses through facial expressions and body language, and his beautiful landscapes and detailed settings teach about environments well beyond the scope of the texts.

AWARDS: Their joint productions have earned them over thirty major awards, including the Children's Book of the Year Award from the Library of Congress for *Lost in the Storm* (1974); Outstanding Science Trade Book for children from the National Science Teachers Association and the CHILDREN'S BOOK COUNCIL for *The Blue Lobster* (1975) and *The Crocodiles Still Wait* (1980); and five times chosen by Children's Choice from the INTERNATIONAL READING ASSOCIATION and the Children's Book Council for *The Blue Lobster* (1975), *Sand Tiger Shark* (1978), *Octopus and Paul's Christmas Birthday* (1979), and *The Empty Squirrel* (1982). Donald received additional awards for books he illustrated, including the Christopher Award for *Secrets of a Small Brother* (Margolis, 1985)

FURTHER WORKS: *Bear Mouse* (Freschet, 1973), *The Accident* (1976), *The Washout* (1978), *Some Friend!* (1979), *What a Wimp!* (1979), *Stay Away from Simon!* (1985), *What Happened to Patrick's Dinosaurs?* (1986), *Sleep Out* (1988), *In the Moonlight, Waiting* (1990)

BIBLIOGRAPHY: Kerlan Collection, the University of Minnesota; *Something about the Author,* vol. 63, 1991

MARGARET YATSEVITCH PHINNEY

CARROLL, Lewis (Charles Lutwidge Dodgson)

Author, b. 27 January 1832, Cheshire, England; d. 14 January 1889, Surrey, England

C. is the author of children's FANTASY and POETRY, as well as adult mathematical treatises.

Recognized around the world as the author of *Alice's Adventures in Wonderland* (1865) and *Through the Looking-Glass and What Alice Found There* (1872), C. is considered a genius who liberated juvenile literature from didacticism and over-moralizing. It was written as fantasy for the entertainment of children, with no attempt to instruct them in strict puritanical behavior or to imbue the stories with sentimentality. The publication of *Alice* marked what is generally referred to as the Golden Age of children's literature, a period characterized by its imaginative and purely entertaining works for the young. Both children and adults, however, enjoy C.'s books, which have become classics for all ages and have been translated into more than eighty languages. C. combined his eccentric personality, opinions about Victorian life, and his genuine love of children to become one of the most quoted authors in English along with Shakespeare and the Bible.

As the oldest of eleven children, C., whose real name was Charles Lutwidge Dodgson, grew up entertaining and caring for his siblings. His father, a country pastor, and his gentle, loving mother provided a strict but warm and nurturing home for their active brood where C. was her favorite. A number of humorous and gently satiric family magazines were written and produced under C.'s guidance. C. was sent to a boys' school at the age of twelve, and while his writing was encouraged, he was teased by other students, which, some say, might explain his preference for friendships with young girls. He attended both Rugby and Christ Church College, Oxford, and although he planned to be a clergyman, a stutter precluded this. Ordained a deacon in the Anglican Church, he did preach occasionally but spent most of his life teaching, lecturing in mathematics, excelling in photography, and, of course, writing. One of his first writing efforts was "Jabberwocky," which was an attempt to parody Anglo-Saxon poetry. In December 1854, he was awarded a bachelor of arts degree and around this time began using Lewis C. as his pen name; he adapted it from Charles Lutwidge, his given name. C. continued teaching at Christ Church College for many years during which he also contributed to numerous periodicals as Charles L. Dodgson when writing scientific articles and with the pseudonym Lewis C. when writing poems and stories of a lighter nature.

The Alice books were created during a riverboat ride 4 July 1862, with the college dean's three young daughters: Lorina, Alice, and Edith Liddell. Alice, of whom C. was especially fond, was the model for the resilient, intelligent, and courteous protagonist in these books. The character Alice is wiser after encounters with the foolishness and selfishness of the characters and events in the worlds of her unconscious. At Alice Liddell's request, C. wrote down the story he had told her that afternoon giving it the original title *Alice's Hour in Elfland.* When in 1864 it was published, it became *Alice's Adventures in Wonderland,* and artist Sir John TENNIEL was asked to illustrate it. *Through the Looking Glass* (1872), was also successful. Later, C. combined the two stories and adapted an easier format for younger children called *The Nursery Alice* (1890).

C.'s love for childhood and children was evident in other aspects of his life. His photography, which was known for its excellence, often focused on children. He loved theater and child performers, so it was only natural that in 1876 *Alice in Wonderland* was presented in tableaux form with readings and songs. C. visited hospitals and presented free copies of the Alice books to children there.

C. eventually gave up his position at Christ Church College to devote his full time to writing. *Euclid and his Modern Rivals* (1879) was an elaborate mathematical book with HUMOR. This was the only one of his mathematics books that has been considered of lasting importance, although he wrote numerous others. His later years were spent modestly. He enjoyed telling stories, discussing logic problems, countryside walks, and helping children financially who wished to pursue the theater as well as friends in need. After *The Game of Logic* (1887) was published, C. became ill and died. The many donations from children at his death were used to endow a cot in Children's Hospital in his memory.

Critics have examined C.'s works from various points of view. As a personal work of art, C. combined various aspects of his personality, his opinions of adults, and his feelings toward Alice Liddell through the interactions among unusual characters in his works of fantasy. These charac-

ters—the White Rabbit, the Cheshire Cat, Tweedledum and Tweededee, the Red Queen, and the Mad Hatter—have evolved into universal symbols. The Dodo in *Alice's Adventures in Wonderland* and the White Knight in *Through the Looking-Glass* are regarded as C.'s self-portraits. In addition to considering his works as outlets for his insights and feelings, critics often focus on the literary style of C.'s books and his use of language, verbal wit, parody, and satire.

Following his death, political, philosophical, metaphysical, and psychoanalytic interpretations of his books were published. Despite some criticism regarding the appropriateness of the violent and frightening aspects of the books for children, C. is universally acknowledged as the foremost writer of nonsense verse and prose. Combining mathematical logic skills with the imagination and humor of creative authorship, C. successfully created stories and verses that are still popular today, recognized all over the world, and speak directly to children's imaginations as no other author before or since has been able to do.

AWARDS: C. was honored with the creation of The Lewis Carroll Shelf Award that was presented annually from 1958–80 by the University of Wisconsin to children's books considered worthy to share a shelf with *Alice in Wonderland*

FURTHER WORKS: *Phantasmagoria, and Other Poems,* 1869; *The Hunting of the Snark: An Agony in Eight Fits,* 1876; *Rhyme? And Reason?,* 1883; *A Tangled Tale,* 1885; *Alice's Adventures Underground,* 1886; *Sylvie and Bruno,* 1889; *The Lewis C. Picture Book: A Selection from the Unpublished Writings and Drawing of Lewis C.* (Stuart Dodgson Collingwood, nephew, ed.) 1899; *The Lewis C. Birthday Book* (Christine Herrick, ed). 1905; *Novelty and Romancement: A Story,* 1925; *The Collected Verse of Lewis C.,* 1929; *A Selection from the Letters of Lewis C. to His Child-Friends* (Evelyn Hatch, ed), 1933

BIBLIOGRAPHY: Bingham, June M., ed., *Writers for Children: Critical Studies of Major Authors Since the Seventeenth Century,* 1988; "Charles Lutwidge Dodgson at <http://www.lewiscarroll.org> (accessed March 15, 1999); *Children's Literature Review,* vol. 18, 1989; Cohen, Morton N., *Lewis C.: A Biography.* 1995; Silvey, Anita, ed., *Children's Books and Their Creators,* 1995

JANELLE B. MATHIS

CASELEY, Judith

Author, illustrator, b. 17 October 1951, Rahway, New Jersey

C. received a Bachelor of Fine Arts degree from Syracuse University in 1973, followed by several years painting and exhibiting her work in art galleries in London as well as the United States. She then began to illustrate children's books after her art in *The Garden of Eden* was successfully received in 1982. C. began writing as well as illustrating her own books beginning with *Molly Pink,* published in 1985. She received the New Jersey Writer's Conference Author's Citation in 1986 for *Molly Pink* and *Molly Pink Goes Hiking.* Both these books as well as several others are based on C.'s own childhood experiences. Her characters face typical growing-up experiences such as a desire for a pet, seen in *Mr. Green Peas* (1995), relationships with other family members, as in *When Grandpa Came to Stay* (1986), and *My Sister Celia* (1986) or using the potty chair for the first time in *Annie's Potty* (1990). Gentle HUMOR is evident in all her stories even when broaching a more serious topic such as a child wearing a prosthetic arm in the book *Harry and Wiley and Carrothead* (1991). Children in her books are portrayed as being part of loving families surrounded by supportive, reassuring adults, from grandparents to teachers who help them face the challenges and problems of childhood. C.'s picture-book illustrations are warm, pastel watercolors, often within a framed format.

School-age readers follow the humorous situations faced by the Kane family in the series of books *Hurricane Harry* (1991), *Starring Dorothy Kane* (1992), *Chloe in the Know* (1993), and *Harry and Arney* (1994), highlighting family events such as moving, the first day of school and Mom's newest pregnancy. Other easy readers include *Dear Annie* (1991) and *Jorah's Journal* (1991), both of which quietly model the importance of writing in young characters' lives.

C. also writes REALISTIC FICTION for young adults. In *Kisses,* published in 1990, sixteen-year-old Hannah successfully deals with problems at school, with her parents and with the opposite sex. In *My Father, the Nutcase,* published in 1992, the teenage protagonist and her family must cope with the father's emotional breakdown.

FURTHER WORKS: Self-Illustrated: *Apple Pie and Onions* (1987); *Silly Baby* (1988); *Ada Potato* (1989); *Three Happy Birthdays* (1989); *The Cousins* (1990); *Grandpa's Garden Lunch* (1990); *The Noisemakers* (1992); *Sophie and Sammy's Library Sleepover* (1993); *Mama, Coming and Going* (1994); *Slumber Party!* (1996); *Witch Mama* (1996); *Jorah's Journey* (1997); *Dorothy's Darkest Days* (1997); *Mickey's Class Play* (1997); *Field Day Last Friday* (2000)

LINDA GOLDMAN

CASSEDY, Sylvia

Author, b. 29 January 1930, Brooklyn, New York; d. 6 April 1989, Manhasset, New York

C. is best remembered for her fiction for middle graders, including much-praised works such as *Behind the Attic Wall* (1983) and *M. E. Morton* (1987). The protagonists in her books consist of troubled young girls who are outsiders in one way or another. C. uses FANTASY and daydream as a healing tool for her characters. Entering a fantasy world, C.'s main characters achieve the time and space to use the power of their imaginations to effect meaningful growth, and change, in their lives. Maggie, in *Behind the Attic Wall,* finds solace and the time to sort through her unhappiness by following the voices she hears in the room behind the attic wall in her house. C. accomplishes Maggie's inner journey through the use of perceptive, subtle language and insightful probing dialogue. C. also wrote POETRY books for children including *Roomrimes* (1987) and *Moon-Uncle* (1972). Her poetry is marked by unique use of metaphor and the author's fascination with language.

FURTHER WORKS: *Little Chameleon,* 1966; *In Your Own Words,* 1979; *Lucie Babbidge's House,* 1989; *Zoomrimes: Poems about Things That Go,* 1993

BIBLIOGRAPHY: *Something about the Author,* vol. 77, 1994

JODI PILGRIM

CATALANOTTO, Peter

Illustrator and author, b. 21 March 1959, Atlanta, Georgia

Son of a painter and a printer, with siblings who also aspired to art, C. tells children he has always been an artist. He graduated from Pratt Institute in Brooklyn and supported his passion for art for several years doing odd jobs until a book-jacket painting brought him the offer to illustrate Cynthia RYLANT's *All I See* (1988). Through this project he was fully launched into children's picture-book ILLUSTRATION. It is easier for him to illustrate others' writing than to write his own works. He claims ancestry among the coal miners of Appalachia, to whom he dedicates *My Mama is a Miner* (1994).

C.'s paintings never fail to tell an indispensable part of the story he is illustrating. Using the luminescence of watercolor and dreamy, overlapping, collage-style compositions, C. plays heavily on blending light, shadow, and color to focus and draw the eye first to the figures and focal points highlighted in the text, then to the supporting and supplemental mysteries and actions that enrich the story. For example, in *Who Came Down That Road?* (LYON, 1992), a story about social history and geological evolution, he has translucent figures emerging from the background, and he paints the corners to hint at what went before and what is coming next. The text's quiet, thoughtful meanings are ignited by the paintings. In *A Day at Damp Camp* (Lyon, 1996) C.'s collage-like layering of smaller-upon-larger pictures of the events in a busy day at camp support the one-activity-after-another feel of camp life, moving from clear, focused scenes of concentration to blurred movement as children run on to yet another venture.

C. enjoys working with children in schools. When children ask where his ideas come from he says, " 'What if . . . ?' is a wonderful place to begin an idea. What if I throw my spaghetti in the air? What if I paint the dog blue?" He supports children's efforts with the advice, "You don't have to be good at everything. Do your best and work hard at something you like to do, and you will succeed."

AWARDS: Children's Choice Award of the INTERNATIONAL READING ASSOCIATION and a "Students' Favorite" book Fairfield-Westchester (Connecticut) Children's Reading Project for *All I See* (1989)

FURTHER WORKS (SELECT): *Wasted Space* (Gulley, 1988); *Dylan's Day Out* (1989); *Soda Jerk* (Rylant, 1990); *Mr. Mumble* (1990); *Cecil's Story* (Lyon, 1991); *Christmas Always* (1991); *An Angel for Solomon* (Rylant, 1992); *Dreamplace* (Lyon, 1993); *The Catspring Somersault Fling One-Handed Flip-Flop* (Kiser, 1993); *Dark Cloud Strong Breeze* (Patron, 1994); *The Painter* (1995); *My House Has Stars* (MCDONALD, 1996); *The Rolling Store* (Johnson, 1997); *Circle of Thanks* (Fowler, 1998); *Letter to the Lake* (Swanson, 1998); *Getting Used to the Dark* (Swanson, 1997), *Celebrate: Stories of the Jewish Holidays* (BERGER, 1998)

SOURCES: Personal assessment of books; Silvey, Anita, ed., *Children's Books and the Creators*, 1995; http://www.co.henrico.va.us/schools/short pmp/pta.html;http://www.fsu.umd.edu/projects/clc/html; Library of Congress web catalog

MARGARET YATSEVITCH PHINNEY

CAUDILL, Rebecca

Author, b. 2 February 1899, Harian County, Kentucky; d. 2 October 1985, Urbana, Illinois

Rebecca Caudill is the pen name for Mrs. James S. Ayers. C. is known for the Appalachian settings she describes in her books. Her own experience growing up in Appalachia and her historical research provide the background for her stories. C.'s novels resonate with characters notable for their perseverance, determination and commitment to family. She wrote more than twenty works for older and younger children, including *Tree of Freedom* (1950), a NEWBERY MEDAL Honor Book and *A Pocketful of Cricket* (1965), a 1965 CALDECOTT MEDAL Honor Book illustrated by Evaline NESS. Her novels are set in the hills of Kentucky and Appalachia; they feature sharecroppers and colonial families who personify the enduring qualities of the early pioneers who settled the American frontier.

FURTHER WORKS: *Barrie and Daughter*, 1943; *House of Fifers*, 1954; *Susan Cornish*, 1955; *The Far off Land*, 1964; *A Certain Small Shepherd*, 1965

BIBLIOGRAPHY: MEIGS, C., et al., *A Critical History of Children's Literature*. 1969; *Something about the Author*, vol. 1, 1971, and vol. 44, 1986

JODI PILGRIM

CAUSLEY, Charles

Poet, b. 24 August, 1917, Launceston, Cornwall, England

C.'s writing has been compared to that of A. E. Housman, Thomas Hardy, Rudyard KIPLING and others as celebrating the English oral ballad-style tradition of POETRY, though he writes lyrical verse. Many of his poems are lighthearted and purely nonsensical. Much of it comes from the legends and FOLKLORE of his native Cornwall. C. wanted to be a writer from an early age and actually began his first novel at nine years of age. His movement from prose to poetry began when he watched his father die from exposure to mustard gas. C. regards poetry as "magic" and an opportunity to enlighten readers about the wonder and possibility of what can be, of the places where imagination can take readers. C. has won many poetry AWARDS including the Queen's Gold Medal for Poetry in 1967 and the Charity Randall Citation from the International Poetry Forum in 1991. One of his latest works is a new edition of *Collected Poems* (1975), which includes works written between 1951 and 1975.

AWARDS: Kurt Maschler Award (1987) for *Jack the Treacle Eater* (Charles KEEPING, illus.). Signal Poetry Award (1987) for *Early in the Morning*

FURTHER WORKS: *The Sun Dancing.* Charles Keeping, illus., 1982; *The Hill of the Fairy Calf,* 1976; *The Tail of the Trinosaur,* 1973; *Figgie Hobbin,* 1970; *Figure of 8: Narrative Poems,* 1969

BIBLIOGRAPHY: Hunt, Peter, ed., *Children's Literature: An Illustrated History,* 1995; *The Oxford Companion to Children's Literature,* 1984; *Something about the Author,* vol. 66, 1991

MICHAEL O'LAUGHLIN

CAVANNA, Betty
Author, b. 24 June 1909, Camden, New Jersey

C. has published widely under her own name as well as pseudonyms (Elizabeth Headley and Betsy Allen). With nearly eighty books for children and YOUNG ADULTS, C. is best known for her writings for adolescent girls, writing that concentrates on the difficulties of growing up such as *Going on Sixteen* (1946). C.'s early young adult novels were set in small-town middle America inhabited by middle-class white teens who were concerned about their popularity and finding a date and the perfect dress for the prom. As C.'s writing developed, her novels reflected realistic concerns of young adults. *Jenny Kimura* (1964) sensitively tells the perceptive story of a multiracial teen who has always lived in Tokyo and the cultural hurdles she encounters when her American grandmother invites her to the United States the summer she is sixteen.

In addition to the focus on adolescent girls, C. also wrote the series Around the World Today (including *Arne of Norway,* 1960; *Doug of Australia,* 1965; and *Ali of Egypt,* 1966) as well as juvenile mysteries as Betsy Allen (*The Clue in Blue,* 1948; *The Silver Secret,* 1956).

FURTHER WORKS: *Banner Year,* 1987; *A Girl Can Dream,* 1947; *Puppy Stakes,* 1943; *Spurs for Suzanna,* 1946

REFERENCES: Fuller, M., ed., *Major Junior Authors,* 1963; *Major Authors and Illustrators for Children and Young Adults,* vol. 2, 1993

GWYNNE ELLEN ASH

CAZET, Denys
Author, illustrator, b. 22 March 1938, Oakland, California

Having worked twenty-five years as both a teacher and a library media specialist in elementary schools, C., author and illustrator of PICTURE BOOKS, is well aware of the significance of everyday experiences to children as well as their need for attention. Additionally, most important to his writing are his family memories that are often evident in his books as shared experiences between children and grandparents or extended family. *Big Shoe, Little Shoe* (1984) and *Sunday* (1988) both reflect these relationships. Similarly, the STORYTELLING he remembers as a child has both influenced his writing and is seen reflected in the stories themselves. The majority of C.'s books are anthropomorphic as closely knit animal families handle the serious and nonsensical dilemmas facing children. *Are There Any Questions?* (1992) humorously tells of a field trip while *A Fish in His Pocket* (1987) addresses the role of a young bear cub who feels responsible for a fish's death. C. also demonstrates variety in style of ILLUSTRATION, creating art for both his own books and those of other writers.

FURTHER WORKS: *The Duck with Squeaky Feet,* 1980; *You Make the Angels Cry,* 1983; *Frosted Glass,* 1987; *Never Spit on Your Shoes,* 1990; *I'm Not Sleepy,* 1992; *Nothing at All?* 1994; *Night Lights: Twenty-four Poems to Sleep On,* 1997

BIBLIOGRAPHY: *Something about the Author,* vol. 99, 1999

JANELLE B. MATHIS

CENSORSHIP

In the United States, the word *censorship* epitomizes the conflict between First Amendment freedoms that guarantee the right to read and the belief that children need to be protected from material that may conflict with traditional or parental values. Opponents of censorship consider it an invasion of rights and see those who advocate censorship as self-righteous, irrational individuals with an obsession to protect everyone, especially the young, from reality. An opposing view holds the belief that parents and other citizens have the right to raise objections to the choice of materials available for or used by their own children and the children in their community.

Issues that tend to be grounds for censorship include four broad areas—moral, political, social mores, and religious. Moral objections focus on content areas such as sex, language, and alleged obscenity. Political topics include not only antigovernment sentiments or sentiments supporting opposing governments, but also incitement to riot, treason, or general rebellion against authority. Social mores problem areas are generally considered to be those about which society has strong feelings—abortion, homosexuality, racial stereotypes, for example. Religious-censorship areas include the occult, witchcraft, and the supernatural, as well as heresy and secular humanism. Popular children's books such as Alvin SCHWARTZ's *Scary Stories to Tell in the Dark* (1981), Katherine PATERSON's *Bridge to Terabithia* (1977) and *The Great Gilly Hopkins* (1978), Shel SILVERSTEIN's poetry, Judy BLUME's *Are You There, God? It's Me, Margaret* (1970, 1982) and *Forever* (1975), and Roald DAHL's *The Witches* (1983) and *James and the Giant Peach* (1961) are titles frequently included among the more than 700 books challenged each year in schools and public libraries.

Censorship likely began in Greece about 399 B.C.E. when the Greek state condemned Socrates for denying state approved gods and for corrupting youth. In China about 200 B.C.E., some of the works of Confucius were burned—as well as some of his disciples—in an effort to suppress his beliefs. The Bible was the first book banned in England. In the United States, most legal decisions surrounding censorship issues have dealt with obscenity, usually pertaining to sexual matters. The first court decision, that of Judge Cockburn in 1867, established the precedent that "publishing an obscene book is an offense against the law of the land." This decision remained in effect until 1957 when the Supreme Court decided that sex and obscenity were not necessarily the same thing and that for materials to be considered obscene they must appeal to prurient interests. By 1966 a three-part test for obscenity had evolved that determined that material as a whole must appeal to prurient interests, affront contemporary community standards, and be utterly without redeeming social value. The Supreme Court overruled the test in 1973 when it declared that state laws would establish community standards. As a result of the 1973 ruling, many more school censorship issues now reach the courts.

Censors may include parents, teachers, librarians, school boards, legislative groups, and organized special interest groups. During the last decade, the religious right and fundamental religious groups have been responsible for many of the book challenges and censorship fights. Their fight often centers over a single title in a given community or may be part of a more widespread effort to censor specific predetermined titles from a base list. These and other organizations, though, cannot be held entirely responsible for book challenges. The attacks often come from parents and community members who are distressed and concerned with the general permissiveness of society, political and social events such as school violence and shootings, the rise in teenage pregnancies, the divorce rate, drug use, and their concern with how these issues are portrayed in contemporary children's and adolescent novels. They view the subject matter of some reading materials as a threat to their children's well-being.

Not all censorship is overt. Librarians and teachers often see the issue as not "censorship but selection." As a result, many books containing elements that might be considered controversial in a community—homosexuality, teen pregnancy, violence, the occult, language, racial issues, growing up and other issues of sexuality—are simply not selected for the library or for classroom use. School and district level administrators also may serve as censors, most usually in situations where a book is challenged and they decide to remove it with or without due process, especially when no written book selection policy exists. State and local legislative bodies also serve as censors when they determine that certain topics such as sex education and creationism may not be taught in schools. The issue of filtering the INTERNET has become a major area in which censorship is a governmental issue with many schools and public libraries either being forced to or choosing to limit access to websites to minors because of concern over content. With the AMERICAN LIBRARY ASSOCIATION (ALA) as the lead plaintiff in a suit brought by publishers, internet users and online service providers, the Supreme Court struck down the Communications Decency Act designed to protect children from access to some materials on the Internet through the use of filters.

The ALA, THE NATIONAL COUNCIL OF TEACHERS OF ENGLISH, THE INTERNATIONAL READING ASSOCIATION and other educational bodies all support the ideas of intellectual freedom and the right to read. The ALA has issued a public statement known as the Library Bill of Rights outlining how LIBRARIES should provide access to information and ideas in all forms of media. Objections by parents, patrons, and the public based on personal points of view are not sufficient cause for the removal of materials from libraries, according to the ALA. These organizations suggest that teachers and librarians be prepared to fight censorship by implementing some basic procedures and principles: (1) Develop a selection policy or policy statement that sets criteria for book selection. The criteria should minimally include standards for authority, review sources, and scope of material in both print and nonprint format. (2) Have a policy to handle challenged materials. This policy should have a form for the person challenging the material to fill out that asks for specific complaints and page numbers. A review committee procedure and a time frame for dealing with situations should be a part of the policy. (3) Be familiar with the content of the materials for children and YOUNG ADULTS that are in the library or being read in the classroom. (4) Work to gain community support for freedom to read before censorship becomes an issue. Communicate to the public what goes on in classrooms and libraries and why it goes on.

Censorship will continue to be an issue in the future as children's literature continues to reflect society. The growth of Internet resources and the issue of filtering sites that adults consider inappropriate for children will most likely be at the center of the censorship issue.

BIBLIOGRAPHY: Cline, R., and McBride, W. *A Guide to Literature for Young Adults.* 1983; Donaldson, K. "What to Do When the Censor Comes." *Elementary English,* 51, (3): 403–9; Person, Diane G., "Censorship Issues: Confronting the Sound of Silence," *Journal of Children's Literature,* 24:1, Spring, pp. 118–21, 1998

JANET HILBUN

CHAIKIN, Miriam

Intermediate and young adult novelist, poet, translator, and nonfiction writer, b. 9 December 1928, Jerusalem, Palestine; emigrated to the United States, 1929

Born in Jerusalem and raised in Brooklyn, New York, C. worked in public relations and was a secretary to a U.S. Senator before becoming an editor for a major publishing house in New York. She has traveled extensively and spends part of each year in Israel. She has written both fiction and nonfiction books, many with Jewish themes.

One of C.'s goals in her fiction is to acknowledge children's common, but nevertheless troublesome feelings of isolation and loneliness, and to let them know others have had the same feelings. In *I Should Worry, I Should Care* (1979), her protagonist's family moves and she must deal with feelings of resentment, isolation, and confusion in dealing with the ups and downs and complexities of building new relationships. In *How Yossi Beat the Evil Urge,* C. recognizes the nonacademic, nontraditional singer-dreamer kind of child and provides him or her with an avenue for a valid place in the community, as well as an implicit avenue for adults to adjust their expectations and perceptions of children with different styles of relating to the world. *The Happy Pair* (1972), a collection of three light, humorous stories, focus on the nature and power of love, manifested in very different ways. Another goal, particularly in her later books, is to illuminate and record the history, traditions, and values of the

Jewish people. In an effort to prevent a collective amnesia from setting in, which could allow for recurrences of cultural genocides, *A Nightmare in History* (1987) traces the roots of Nazi anti-Semitism, describes the annihilation plans and procedures, and recognizes the courage it took to survive and assist during that era. On the flyleaf she is quoted, "The inability to comprehend evil on such a scale gives evil an advantage. It allows evil to slip away from memory and be forgotten. It must not be forgotten, or it will come back again. This is my reason for writing this book."

AWARDS: Sydney TAYLOR Body-of-Work Award of the Association of Jewish Libraries

FURTHER WORKS (SELECT): *Ittki Pittki* (1971), *Finders Weepers* (1980), *Joshua in the Promised Land* (1982), *Ask Another Question: The Story and Meaning of Passover* (1985), *Aviva's Piano* (1986), *Yossi Tries to Help God* (1987), *Sound the Shofar: The Story and Meaning of Rosh Hashanah and Yom Kippur* (1986), *Feathers in the Wind* (1989), *Hanukkah* (1990), *Menorahs, Mezuzas, and Other Jewish Symbols* (1990), *Clouds of Glory: Jewish Legends and Stories about Bible Times* (1998)

MARGARET YATSEVITCH PHINNEY

CHALMERS, Mary Eileen
Author, illustrator, b. 16 March 1927, Camden, New Jersey

C. began her career in 1955 by writing and illustrating a series of miniature books for preschool children that focused on human characters and their daily lives: *Come for a Walk with Me* (1955), *A Hat for Mary Jean* (1956), and *Come to the Doctor, Harry* (1977). She also wrote and illustrated a number of fantasies that featured humanlike animals: *George Appleton* (1957), *The Cat Who Liked to Pretend* (1959), and *Easter Parade* (1988). In addition to her own writing, she illustrated books for a number of major children's authors including Ruth KRAUSS, Syd HOFF, Patricia LAUBER, and Russell HOBAN. C.'s fascinating ILLUSTRATIONS were widely praised in a variety of review sources in the late 1950s.

FURTHER WORKS: Author: *Here Comes the Trolley Car*, 1955; *Kevin*, 1957; *Mr. Cat's Wonderful Surprise*, 1961; Illustrator: Ursula Nordstrom, *The Secret Language*, 1960; Marjorie Weinman SHARMAT, *Goodnight Andrew, Goodnight Craig*, 1969; Syd Hoff, *When Will It Snow?*, 1971; Rus-

sell Hoban, *Letitia Rabbit's String Song*, 1973; Stephanie CALMENSON, *Marigold and Grandma on the Town*, 1994

BIBLIOGRAPHY: *Contemporary Authors Online*, 1999; *Something about the Author*, vol. 6, 1974; C. Papers are housed at the DEGRUMMOND REFERENCE COLLECTION; University of Southern Mississippi; http://www.lib.usm.edu/~degrum/findaids/chalmers.htm

SUSAN SWORDS STEFFEN

CHAMBERS, Aidan
Author, b. 27 December 1934, Chester-le-Street, County Durham, England

C. writes with sensitivity and style that promotes intelligence and reflection among young adults. C. studied at Borough Road College, London, England, and married Nancy Harris Lockwood, former editor of *Children's Book News*. Together they founded the British critical journal *Signal*. C. also wrote a *Horn Book* magazine column, "Letter from England," which connected children's literature supporters for twelve years in the seventies and eighties. C. worked as a teacher of drama and English in England, a critic, a lecturer, a producer of children's plays, and a writer of television and radio programs in addition to work in children's literature. C. grew up as an only child, shy, and not too fond of school until he became intensely interested in reading. Eventually, C. developed a keen interest in DRAMA and speaking and decided at age fifteen that he wanted to write fiction. He served in the armed forces and lived for seven years as a monk. He left the order to fulfill his ambition of teaching and writing fiction. C. began publishing young adult novels in the late sixties with *Cycle Smash* (1968). He advocates that children should be allowed their own preferences in reading selections. *Breaktime* (1978) establishes the author as a risk taker who wishes to give voice to adolescence. C. writes about how individual adolescents define themselves with language. His books require introspection and present thought-provoking examination. Sensitive topics are not ignored. This author is not a prolific producer of books, but rather takes his time to develop the characters and problems of the novel. One of C.'s highest credits is that he advanced the belief that children and YOUNG ADULTS should have books written specifically for them and about them.

AWARDS: *Breaktime* was named one the Best Books in 1979 by *School Library Journal. Dance on My Grave* was an ALA Best Book for Young Adults in 1983. Both *The Present Takers* (1997) and *Seal Secret* (1981) won Holland's Silver Pencil Award. C. was the 1986 May Hill Arbuthnot Honor Lecturer, the winner of the Eleanor FARJEON Award, and the first recipient of the Children's Literature Association Award for Literary Criticism

FURTHER WORKS: *Merle* (1968); *Nik: Now I Know* (1987); *The Toll Bridge* (1992); as editor: *Aidan Chamber's Book of Ghosts and Hauntings* (1980); *Shades of Dark* (1984)

BIBLIOGRAPHY: Chambers, Aidan, *Booktalk: Occasional Writing on Literature and Children* (1985)

NANCY HORTON

CHAPTER BOOKS FOR BEGINNING READERS

Simply stated, chapter books for beginning readers are stories with more words and fewer pictures than their younger cousins, the EASY-TO-READS. They are short books written for newly emergent readers to read on their own and look like novels, albeit, mini-novels. They are divided into chapters, hence the name "chapter books." In essence, chapter books are "first novels" for six-to-nine-year-old readers who have gone beyond easy-to-reads, but aren't quite ready for middle-grade novels.

As contrasted to PICTURE BOOKS and easy-to-reads, in chapter books, it is the words that must do the lion's share of the work in captivating the minds and hearts of the readers. What the reader sees, hears, smells, thinks, and feels must be generated primarily by words, not pictures. These added words (usually 2,000 to 5,000 more than easy-to-reads) offer greater opportunities for the writer to develop setting, character, plot, and theme.

How then do chapter books differ from middle grade novels for young readers such as *Cousins* (1990) by Virginia HAMILTON or *The True Confessions of Charlotte Doyle* (1990) by AVI? Obviously, they contain fewer words, are less complex, and usually the youthful protagonists are under the age of ten. These characters must be brought to life "on the fly," as noted author and children's librarian Judy Freeman so aptly puts it. There is no time for nonessential description or

introspection, which most young readers will not tolerate anyway.

Also, because chapter books contain fewer words than novels, their focus is narrower. Instead of a month or year in the life of the protagonist, the time frame is often a week or a day—a single episode stretched into several chapters. For example, although many chapter books contain eight to ten chapters, *The Best Worst Day* (Graves, 1996) takes place in just a day, *No Copycats Allowed!* (Graves, 1998) two days, and *Mystery of the Tooth Gremlin* (Graves, 1997) a whopping four days.

Just as length is a factor, so is print size and number of illustrations. Chapter books are usually around sixty-four pages, but can range anywhere from forty-five to one hundred, depending on page size, width of margins, white space, and size of print. In chapter books, the typeface is larger than in middle-grade novels and there are some illustrations, usually at least one per chapter and sometimes two.

Although the primary audience for chapter books for beginning readers is readers from ages six-to-nine, these first novels can offer pleasurable reading for readers as young as five and as old as eleven. For younger readers there are books such as *Alison's Wings* (Marion Dane BAUER, 1996) and *Edwin and Emily* (S. Williams, 1995); and at the other end of the spectrum, edging closer to the middle-grade novel, are chapter books with strong appeal for older beginning readers—Jerry SPINELLI's *Fourth Grade Rats* (1991), Gary SOTO's *The Skirt* (1992), Paula DANZIGER's *Amber Brown Goes Fourth* (1991), and Patricia MACLACHLAN's NEWBERY MEDAL title, *Sarah, Plain and Tall* (1985), a wonderfully spare and evocative chapter book. And, of course, there are many wonderful chapter books that fall in between—*Wild Willie and King Kyle* (Barbara M. Joosee, 1993), *I Hate Company* (P. J. Peterson, 1994), *Marvin Redpost: Why Pick on Me?* (Louis SACHAR, 1994), *Song Lee in Room B* (S. Kline, 1993), *Second-Grade Friends* (Miriam COHEN, 1993), *Solo Girl* (Andrea Davis PINKNEY, 1997), and *Junie B. Jones and a Little Monkey Business* (Barbara PARK, 1994)—to name only a few.

In large measure, what chapter books do is introduce young readers to the novel genre. Although there are some six, seven, and eight-year-olds who know what novels are because they have heard them read aloud by a parent or a teacher, even for these fortunate ones, reading a sixty-four-page book with chapters on their own is a new adventure. Fortunately, there are many good first novels available, and the numbers are growing. But that has not always been the case.

It was not until the early 1980s, a few years after whole language and literature-based reading proponents had begun stressing the importance of using "authentic literature" as part of the reading curriculum, that chapter books for beginning readers appeared on trade-book publishers' lists. Some of the first chapter books published appeared as a series, such as Patricia Reilly GIFF's *The Beast in Ms. Rooney's Room* (1984)—the first book in Giff's landmark Polk Street School series and David ADLER's mystery adventures starring master sleuth *Cam Jansen* (1982). A few years later, Random House launched its "Stepping Stone Books," which included chapter books such as *Julian's Glorious Summer* (1987) and *Julian, Secret Agent* (1988) both by Ann CAMERON; Little, Brown introduced its "Springboard Books" with Ellen CONFORD's *A Case for Jenny Archer* (1988); and in 1988 Dell brought out the Pee Wee Scout series by Judy DELTON. These chapter books for beginning readers were well-received by teachers, librarians, and parents as well as their intended young readers, who gobbled up stories featuring protagonists their own age dreaming dreams and solving problems similar to their own. This genre fulfills a need for engaging stories that give young readers a voice, first novels that six-to-nine-year olds can read themselves.

The beginning of the next decade saw even more chapter books appearing on publishers' lists. Some were individual titles and not a part of a line or series, such as Kathryn O. Galbraith's *Roommates* (1990), Betsy Duffey's *A Boy in the Doghouse* (1991), and *The Seven Treasure Hunts* (1991) by NEWBERY Medal winner Betsy BYARS. In the early 1990s, with the help of other award-winning authors such as Karen HESSE, Laurence YEP, Daniel PINKWATER, and Jerry Spinelli, the chapter book made additional strides as a literary genre, with more and more reviews appearing in review journals such as *Booklist, Kirkus,* and *School Library Journal.* In 1995, Hyperion

Books for Children launched a chapter book line with the specific intent of acquiring and publishing books that would introduce fledgling readers to the joys of real literature, books with strong characters, engaging plots, and memorable themes, calling on the talents of respected writers such as Marion Dane Bauer, Dick KING-SMITH, Jane Resh THOMAS, Elizabeth Levy, and Kathryn LASKY.

It is encouraging to see that chapter books for beginning readers—that critical link between easy-to-read books and middle-grade novels—have not only an increasingly large following of young readers, but a shelf or two of their own in libraries and bookstores, and a strong foothold on most trade-book publishers' lists.

BONNIE GRAVES

CHARLIP, Remy

Actor, dancer, choreographer, producer, stage director, filmmaker, author, and illustrator, b. 10 January 1929, Brooklyn, New York

C. is a multitalented, extraordinarily gifted artist. He attended Cooper Union, Black Mountain College, and the Juilliard School. He was a choreographer and actor with the original Living Theater Company and for eleven years a director, designer, actor, and dancer at the American Place Theater and Cafe Mama. He was a founding member of the Paper Bag Players and a performer in the first four original productions. He has also been involved in performances at the Joyce Theater, The Barn Opera House, and with Merce Cunningham's Dance Group.

As an author, he has created a variety of acclaimed children's books ranging from simple reading exercises to elaborate word games to visually innovative narratives. His knowledge of theater has made him particularly sensitive of the way to capture an audience with DRAMA and HUMOR. His work encourages children to use their imaginations and to improvise. When he began writing in 1967 with Burton Buprie, a writer, he received an award from the Boys Club of America for *Mother, Mother, I Feel Sick* (1966). In 1969, he received a *New York Times* citation for *Arm in Arm.* The latter also received a prize at the Bologna Book Fair. For *Harlequin and the Gift of Many Colors* (1973) he won the Irma Simonton Black Award from Bank Street

College. In 1975 he won the Children's Science Book award and an award from the New York Academy of Science for *Handtalk*. In 1987 he received a *New York Times* Best Illustrated book citation for *Handtalk Birthday*.

FURTHER WORKS: wrote and illustrated: *Where Is Everybody?* (1957); *Hurray for Me* (1979); *Fortunately* (1964). With Judith Martin's collaboration: *Beans and the Three Angels* (1962); illustrator: *The Dead Bird* (Margaret Wise BROWN; 1958); *What a Fine Day For . . .* (Ruth KRAUSS, 1967); *The Seeing Stick* (Jane YOLEN; 1977), *I Love You* (1989)

BIBLIOGRAPHY: *Children's Literature Review*, vol. 8; Silvey, Anita, ed., *Children's Books and Their Creators*, 1995; *Something about the Author*, vol. 68, 1992

JUDY LIPSITT

CHARLOT, Jean
Illustrator, b. 7 February 1898, Paris, France; d. 20 March 1979, Honolulu, Hawaii

C. was an illustrator, muralist, painter, printmaker, scholar, and college professor. He spent his childhood in Paris and recalled playing with Indian artifacts in the apartment of his Mexican-born grandfather. In 1921, C. moved to Mexico and joined the Mexican muralist movement, which included Diego Rivera. C. also worked in the Yucatan, copying ancient Mayan bas reliefs as a staff artist with the Carnegie Archeological Expedition.

C. is one of the most prominent artists to work in the field of children's books. Although he illustrated collections of Mexican folk tales, C.'s collaboration with author Margaret Wise BROWN resulted in some of his best known children's books. For *A Child's Good Night Book* (1943), a CALDECOTT MEDAL Honor Book, C. used colored, compact soft lithographs that extend the gentle text. In *Two Little Trains* (1949), C. displayed masterful use of line to create action and HUMOR, celebrating his belief in art as STORYTELLING. C.'s ILLUSTRATIONS for two NEWBERY MEDAL books, *The Secret of the Andes* (Ann Nolan CLARK, 1952) and *And Now Miguel* (Joseph KRUMGOLD, 1953), depict the strength of their main characters' personalities and traditional Hispanic cultures.

AWARDS: ALA Caldecott Medal Honor Book (1944) for *A Child's Good Night Book* (Margaret Wise Brown), and (1954), for *When Will the World Be Mine?* (Miriam Schlein, author). ALA Newbery Medal (1953) for *The Secret of the Andes* (Ann Nolan Clark, author) and (1954) for *And Now Miguel* (Joseph Krumgold, author).

FURTHER WORKS: *The Boy Who Could Do Anything and Other Mexican Folk Tales,* 1942. Anita Brenner, author; *The Corn Grows Ripe*, 1956. Dorothy Rhoads, author; By Margaret Wise Brown: *Fox Eyes.* 1951; *A Child's Good Morning* 1952. *Seven Stories about a Cat Named Sneakers* 1955

BIBLIOGRAPHY: Bader, Barbara, *American PICTURE BOOKS from Noah's Ark to the Beast Within,* 1976; *More Junior Authors,* 1963; Silvey, Anita, ed., *Children's Books and Their Creators,* 1995; *Something about the Author,* vol. 8, 1976

KATHIE KRIEGER CERRA

CHASE, Richard
Storyteller, author, folklorist, editor/compiler, b. 15 February, 1904, near Huntsville, Alabama; d. 2 February 1988, Huntsville, Alabama

Educated at Antioch College, C. dedicated his life to collecting and preserving the folk stories and songs of the Appalachian and Great Smoky Mountain regions of the southeastern United States. He organized craft workshops and folk festivals, and lectured in a wide variety of forums to bring attention to the mountaineers' interpretation and evolution of a piece of English- and Celtic-based folk heritage. C.'s adaptations of oral FOLKLORE are written in a comfortable, STORYTELLING, vernacular style that helps place the reader in the homey environment in which folk stories have always been transmitted. Action, high HUMOR, cleverness, determination, and outrageousness characterize the stories and their protagonists, while satisfying outcomes explain the world and provide frameworks for living. An avid storyteller himself, C. tells his readers, in his preface to *Grandfather Tales*, that after reading the stories they should "shut the book and tell 'em."

C. traveled all through Appalachia listening to stories that clearly had their origins in English and Scotch-Irish folklore but had long been adapted to Southern mountain customs and traditions. He particularly enjoyed retelling versions of stories about Jack, an unassuming country boy and his fantastic adventures. In the full cycle of stories C. recorded and presented in *The Jack Tales* (1943) and *Grandfather Tales* (1948), Jack is sometimes a trickster character but always one of the local rural folk. Some people now question his adaptations, which C. first heard from local storytellers R. M. Ward and Council Harmon. It was they who encouraged C. just to tell them orally the way he remembered them, claiming they never told a story the same way twice.

AWARDS: AMERICAN LIBRARY ASSOCIATION Notable book for *Billy Boy,* 1966; Southern California Council on Literature for Children and Young People award for distinguished contribution to the field of folklore for children and young people, 1970; Governor of Virginia recognition, 1972; Los Angeles Renaissance Pleasure Fair recognition, 1973

FURTHER WORKS: *Old Songs and Singing Games* (ed., 1938); *The Jack Tales* (ed., 1943); *Grandfather Tales* (ed., 1948); *Hullabaloo, and Other Singing Folk Games* (comp., 1949); *Jack and the Three Sillies* (1950); *Wicked John and the Devil* (1951); *Complete Tales of Uncle Remus* (Harris. ed., 1955); *Billy Boy* (ed., 1966); *American Folk Tales and Songs* (1971)

BIBLIOGRAPHY: THE KERLAN COLLECTION flyleaves of books; Library of Congress web catalog; http://www.dur.ac.uk/Classics/histos/1997/stadter.html#n13; http://www/virginia/edu.vfh/vfp/keycon.html; *Something about the Author,* vol. 45, 1989, and vol. 64, 1991

MARGARET YATSEVITCH PHINNEY

CHEN, Tony
Author, illustrator, b. 3 January 1929, Kingston, Jamaica

C. immigrated to the United States in 1949. In his long and prolific career, he has worked as a children's book author and illustrator, art director, art instructor, and a painter and sculptor. He has been honored with a number of AWARDS, including the American Institute of Graphic Arts Book Award (1972) and the Society of Illustrators Award of Excellence (1972). C. is most noted for his ILLUSTRATIONS involving animals and nature themes. His work also includes retelling of MULTICULTURAL folktales and Biblical stories. *In the Land of the Small Dragon* (1979), a Vietnamese Cinderella story retold by Ann Nolan CLARK, uses double-page realistic illustrations. C.'s mi-

nutely detailed pictures are done in full color and a black and gray pen-and-ink wash, creating a powerful emotional monochromatic effect.

FURTHER WORKS: *Run, Zebra, Run,* 1972; *Little Koala,* (Suzanne Noguere, coauthor), 1979; *Wild Animals,* 1981; Illustrated by Chen: *Tales from Old China,* (Isabelle Chang), 1969; *Honschi* (Aline Glasgow), 1972; *The Princess and the Admiral* (Charlotte POMERANTZ), 1974; *The Cucumber Stem: Adapted from a Bengali Folktale* (Betsy Bang), 1980. *Black Beauty: The Autobiography of a Horse* (Anna SEWELL), 1986; *The Christmas Story: Based on the Gospels according to Saint Matthew and Saint Luke* (Deborah Hautzig), 1987; *Animals Showing Off* (Jane R. McCauley), 1988; *A Child's First Bible* (Sandol Stoddard), 1990

BIBLIOGRAPHY: Cianciolo, Patricia J., PICTURE BOOKS *for Children.* 3rd ed. 1990; *Contemporary Authors, New Revision Series,* vol. 14, 1985

JENNIFER E. DUNNE

CHERRY, Lynne
Author and illustrator, b. 5 January 1952, Philadelphia, Pennsylvania

Among C.'s first drawing surfaces as a young child were the bodies of her dolls because she liked the feel of a ball-point pen on the rubber. With degrees in art and history, and influenced by artists such as Aubrey Vincent Beardsley, Carl LARSSON, and Maurice SENDAK, she has graced more than three dozen books, more than half of which she has written herself, and almost all of which contain natural history elements, with her loving portrayals of the lush chaos of flora and partially hidden animals in forests and waterways. C.'s love of nature comes from the time she spends in natural settings, which, she says, "have always provided me with places for my thoughts to wander and my imagination to fly." She actively promotes programs and organizations that support environmental education for children, including her position as artist-in-residence at the Smithsonian Environmental Research Center in Maryland.

C. is a long-time environmental preservationist and activist. In a web site letter to her readers (www.geocities.com/Athens/Olympus/1333/kids.htm) she writes, "as well as developing in children an appreciation of nature, I am concerned with instilling in them the importance of working to make the world a better place. One individual can make a difference. . . . To me, democracy means participation. . . . Preserving nature is necessary for the continuation of our species—but nature's beauty also provides food for the soul." As the anteater says in *The Great Kapok Tree,* "What happens tomorrow depends on what you do today."

AWARDS: National Science Teachers Award for *Hidden Messages* (1981); New York Academy of Science Annual Children's Book Award for *The Snail's Spell* (1983); The Alumni Association of the New Jersey Institute of Technology's Award for Outstanding Children's Book Illustrations (1983); *"READING RAINBOW" Review Book,* American Bookseller's "Pick of the Lists" selection, NSTA-CBC Outstanding Trade Book for Children, INTERNATIONAL READING ASSOCIATION Teacher's Choice selection (all 1991) and Iowa Children's Choice Award selection (1990) for *The Great Kapok Tree*

FURTHER WORKS: *Coconut, the Tree of Life* (1976); *Snail Spell* (1982); *When I'm Sleepy* (1985); *Orangutan* (1987); *Snow Leopard* (1987); *Grizzly Bear* (1987); *A River Ran Wild* (1992); *The Dragon and the Unicorn* (1995); *The Armadillo from Amarillo* (1994); *Flute's Journey: The Life of a Wood Thrush* (1997); *The Shaman's Apprentice: A Tale of the Amazon Rain Forest* (1998)

SOURCES: www.geocities.com/Athens/Olympus/ 1333/kids.htm; www.carolhurst.com; *Something about the Author,* vol. 34, pp. 51–52; Personal assessment of books; book flyleaves; Library of Congress web catalog

MARGARET YATSEVITCH PHINNEY

CHESS, Victoria

Author, illustrator, b. 16 November 1939, Chicago, Illinois

After living all over the world, C. now resides in the state of Connecticut, where she grew up. From a young age, she was more motivated to draw than pursue her academic studies. In a career spanning more than thirty years, C. is noted for ILLUSTRATIONS that enhance the story line and characterization with HUMOR. During the 1990s she illustrated a number of books by the poet J. Patrick LEWIS and the Spider Kane mysteries by Mary Pope OSBORNE. Among her AWARDS are the American Institute of Graphic Arts Book Show Award for *Bugs,* 1976 and Par-

ents Choice Awards for *Taking Care of Melvin* (1980), *Tales for the Perfect Child* (1985) and *Slither McCreep and His Brother Joe* (1992).

FURTHER WORKS: Illustrator: *Once around the Block* (Kevin HENKES). 1987; *Ghosts: Ghostly Tales from FOLKLORE* (Alvin SCHWARTZ). 1991; *This for That: A Tonga Tale* (Verna AARDEMA). 1995; *King Long Shanks* (Jane YOLEN), 1997

BIBLIOGRAPHY: *Contemporary Authors,* vol. 107; Cummings, P., ed., 1992; *Talking with Artists; Junior Book of Authors and Illustrators; Something about the Author,* vol. 33, 1983

BARBARA JAINDL

CHILD, Lydia Maria

Author, b. 11 February 1802, Medford, Massachusetts; d. 20 October 1880, Wayland, Massachusetts

C. began her literary career with *Handbook: A Tale of Early Times* (1824), a sentimental novel that portrays the NATIVE AMERICAN Hobomok from the settlement of Salem, as a noble savage. Although the book displays C.'s humanitarian spirit, it also reflects the theory of the inevitable displacement of the American Indian. While C. used a conventional writing style, her themes were quite different from other nineteenth century writers and journalists. Specifically, she addressed the themes of class and race: chattel slavery; white racism; women's rights; life in the cities; and social change. As a female author, C. was unique in having her works published in the public arena, which until then was strictly a male domain. C.'s well-known letters to the *Boston Courier* appear in the volume *Letters from New York* (1845). She edited the first children's monthly in the United States, *Juvenile Miscellany* (1826–34); Sara Josepha HALE's "Mary Had a Little Lamb" first appeared in its pages. C.'s POETRY was simple and childlike, appealing directly to young children. Her best known poem is known variously as "A Boy's Thanksgiving" (1844) and as "Thanksgiving Day"; it is popularly known as "Over the River and through the Woods." *The Little Girl's Own Book* was a collection of short stories that C. published in 1835.

FURTHER WORKS: *Appeal in Favor of That Class of Americans Called Africans,* 1833; *The Rebels; or, Boston before the Revolution,* 1825

PATRICIA JOEL

CHILDREN'S BOOK COUNCIL

The Children's Book Council (CBC), founded in 1919, is a nonprofit trade association of children's book publishers and producers of related literacy materials. The purpose of the CBC is to promote the use and enjoyment of children's trade books and related materials, and to disseminate information about books for young people and trade-book publishing. CBC is the official sponsor of National Children's Book Week. The Council's membership is made up of United States publishers and packagers of trade books for children and young adults, and also producers of book-related materials for children. Proceeds from materials support the Council's literacy efforts. Working with publisher members and outside educational organizations, CBC creates programs, publications, and reading-encouragement materials that promote literacy among young people. Much of the work is accomplished through liaisons with librarians, booksellers, and educators, which bring children and books together by encouraging reading through the creation of strong, quality collections in libraries, classrooms, and bookstores.

Membership in the CBC is open to U.S. children's book publishers, packagers, and producers of related literacy materials. Personal memberships are not available. Interested individuals, organizations, and institutions can be added to the mailing list to receive a biannual newsletter, *CBC Features,* illustrated materials catalogs, and information on other CBC materials and activities. Becoming knowledgeable about CBC is a requisite to becoming informed about children's books.

The CBC examination library of members' books published in the last two years is open to the public. The library also includes selected journals and reference materials. *CBC Features* is a semiannual newsletter of the Council that includes articles on children's books and lists of free materials available from member publishers. Many publications are available to help members achieve their publishing goals and the public to understand the work of the Council in promoting children's literaure such as a *Members List* of CBC, a listing of member publishing companies (including addresses, phone numbers) and a de-

scription of their publication programs; it includes manuscript submission guidelines. An *Illustrator's Guide to Members of the Children's Book Council* lists personnel (including addresses, phone numbers) at CBC-member publishing companies who are responsible for reviewing artwork; includes submission guidelines. Information for writers about children's book publishing with tips on preparing and presenting manuscripts to publishers, including a bibliography is available in *Writing Children's Books.* Information about children's book ILLUSTRATION and children's book publishing for illustrators new to the field, including a bibliography is available in *Illustrating Children's Books. Choosing a Child's Book* contains helpful tips for parents and others on selecting books for children of all ages and includes a bibliography. *75 Authors and Illustrators Everyone Should Know* is a selection to introduce children, and the adults who care for them, to children's book writers and illustrators and their books. It was created by Bernice Cullinan for the 75th anniversary of National Children's Book Week in 1994.

A guide for teachers and program planners, *Inviting Children's Book Authors and Illustrators to Your Community!,* explains how to invite authors and illustrators with names of personnel to contact at CBC member publisers. CALDECOTT and NEWBERY MEDAL Awards Bookmarks, available as single copies or in multiples, contain a list of current and past medalists. *Not Just for Children Anymore!* (publications available online www. cbc.books.org) is an annotated bibliography selected by booksellers of children's books that adults buy for themselves and other adults. *Children's Books Mean Business* is a catalog of recent backlist titles identified as books with strong potential for bookstore sales. *Notable Children's Trade Books in the Field of Social Studies* is a fully annotated annual bibliography, created in cooperation with the National Council of Social Studies. *Outstanding Science Trade Books for Children* is a fully annotated annual bibliography, created in cooperation with the National Science Teachers Association. A guide for publishers interested in publishing Spanish-Language children's books is available in *Publishing Spanish-language Children's Books.*

Since 1919, educators, librarians, booksellers, and families have celebrated National Children's Book Week during the week preceding Thanksgiving. Each year committee members develop a theme to promote reading. They prepare and distribute a National Children's Book Week Kit that includes posters, friezes, streamers, bookmarks with a poem, booklets, and other items.

JOANN SABATINO-FALKENSTEIN

CHILDRESS, Alice

Playwright and novelist, b. 12 October 1920, Charleston, South Carolina; d. 14 August 1994, Queens, New York

Reared in New York from the age of five, C. left high school before graduation. She is better known as an actress and dramatist than as a novelist, but since the 1970s, C. wrote works for young adults. *A Hero Ain't Nothin' but a Sandwich* (1973) was named a Best YOUNG ADULT Book of 1975 by the AMERICAN LIBRARY ASSOCIATION and was nominated for the National Book Award in 1974. *Rainbow Jordan* (1981) received critical acclaim, including honorable mention for the CORETTA SCOTT KING Award in 1982.

As with her writing for adults, C.'s fiction for younger readers concerns such social realities as racism, drug abuse, homosexuality, and poverty. *Hero* concerns a thirteen-year-old heroin addict and is told from multiple perspectives. C. later developed the story into a play and then a film that earned her the Black Filmmakers Hall of Fame's first Paul Robeson Award (1977). *Rainbow Jordan* is the story of a teenager and her foster mother, both of whom assert their dignity in the face of rejection. In *Those Other People* (1989) C. portrays a group of outsiders, each of whom recounts his or her story—of sexual abuse, of racial ostracism, of homosexuality—to give readers a wide-angle view on the issues underlying one event at their school. C.'s dramatic work includes plays for children. *When the Rattlesnake Sounds* (1975) is about the life of Harriet Tubman.

BIBLIOGRAPHY: *Contemporary Authors, New Revision Series,* vol. 50, 1996; *Afro-American Writers after 1955: Dramatists and Prose Writers,* 1985

FRANCISCA GOLDSMITH

CHORAO, Kay

Author, illustrator, poet, compiler, b. 7 January 1936, Elkhart, Indiana

C. grew up in a stable, middle-class, suburban family. She loved to draw as a young child, and creativity in writing and art were strongly encouraged during her early schooling. She studied art through college, then in England, and under the mentorship of N. M. BODEKER and Edward GOREY. Her children and children's interest in general, as well as her own feelings, inspire her writing, and she works to create an appropriate match between text and pictures. C. has written, illustrated and/or compiled at least one book per calendar year, with an average of almost three per year in the twenty-seven years she has been involved with children's literature. About half are her own fiction or POETRY, or are her selections of nursery rhymes, poems, and songs.

Drawing on her own childhood experiences, memories, and feelings, C.'s books address feelings commonly experienced by young children: being different from others and lack of self worth (*A Magic Eye for Ida,* 1973); the anxiety associated with venturing out in a big, intimidating world (*Ralph and the Queen's Bathtub,* 1974); concerns over finding a place in the world; fear of getting lost or of losing things (*Molly's Moe,* 1976, and *Maudie's Umbrella,* 1975); conflicted emotions associated with social relationships (*George Told Kate,* 1987); and fear of powerful, intimidating adults (*The Repair of Mr. Toe,* 1972). She honors unusual styles of living and interacting, helping children recognize that there are multiple ways of being a part of society. A master at illustrating facial expressions and body language, C.'s empathetic and detailed characterizations of animal, FANTASY, and human characters draw children in and help them identify with the characters in the texts: they know they have felt the way C.'s characters look. Her effort is to offer sympathy and understanding, to encourage children to find their own ways of problem solving, and to arouse children's curiosity.

AWARDS: ALA Notable Book and a selection of the Children's Book Showcase and American Institute of Graphic Arts Books Show for *Albert's Toothache* (1974); certificate of excellence,

American Institute of Graphic Arts for *Ralph and the Queen's Bathtub* (1974); Society of Illustrators Certificate of Merit for *Clyde Monster* (1976); the *New York Times* named *Cathedral Mouse* one of the ten best books of the year (1988); Children's Choices of the INTERNATIONAL READING ASSOCIATION and CHILDREN'S BOOK COUNCIL for *Annie and Cousin Precious* (1995). In 1989, *The Good-bye Book,* written by Judith VIORST and illustrated by C., won a Christopher Award

FURTHER WORKS: Written and illustrated by C.: *The Baby's Lap Book* (1977); *Oink and Pearl* (1981); *The Cherry Pie Baby* (1989); *Mother Goose Magic* (1994); *The Christmas Story* (1996); *The Cat's Kids* (1998). Illustrated by C.: *Mama Says There Aren't Any Zombies, Ghosts, Vampires, Creatures, Demons, Monsters, Fiends, Goblins, or Things* (Viorst, 1973); *I'm Terrific* (SHARMAT, 1977); *Kevin's Grandma* (Williams, 1978); *But Not Billy* (ZOLOTOW, 1983), *Pig and Crow* (2000)

MARGARET Y. PHINNEY

CHRISTELOW, Eileen
Author, illustrator, photographer, b. 22 April 1943, Washington, D.C.

Receiving a degree in architecture from the University of Pennsylvania, C. began her career photographing buildings, classrooms, and various places across the United States for magazines and text books. After a move to California and the birth of her daughter, she began to focus on graphic design and ILLUSTRATION. Influenced by her daughter learning to read and often finding topics from her daughter's experiences, C. has created numerous books that are both entertaining and informative. Her delightful animal characters invite readers into realistic stories for young children. *Jerome the Babysitter* (1987) introduces a bright young alligator at his first babysitting job. Dogs are the main characters in the cleverly designed plots of *Five Dog Night* (1993), *Gertrude, the Bulldog Detective* (1992), and *The Robbery at the Diamond Dog Diner* (1988). An important INFORMATIONAL BOOK for young readers and writers is *What Do Authors Do?* (1995). C. has received numerous AWARDS for books she both wrote and illustrated. Additionally, she has illustrated numerous books for other authors.

FURTHER WORKS: *Henry and the Red Stripes,* 1982; *Henry and the Dragon,* 1984; *Five Little Monkeys Story,* 1992; *Five Little Monkeys Jumping on the Bed,* retelling, 1991; *Don't Wake up Mama: Another Five Little Monkeys Story,* 1992; *The Great Pig Escape,* 1994; *Jerome Camps Out,* 1998; *Five Little Monkeys Wash the Car,* 2000

BIBLIOGRAPHY: *Horn Book,* magazine, September–October, pp. 633–34, 1989; *School Library Journal,* p. 66, February 1987; p. 90, June 1992; *Something about the Author,* vol. 90, 1997

JANELLE B. MATHIS

CHRISTOPHER, John (Christopher Samuel Youd)
Author, b. 16 April 1922, Knowsley, Lancashire, England

C. is one pseudonym used by Youd and under which he has written series and stand-alone SCIENCE FICTION for children. C. began writing as a teenager and became a full-time author in 1958. C.'s critics find his work lacking in scientific and technological interest, but C. is more concerned with his characters' sense of self than with their social trappings.

The Tripods Trilogy, comprising *The White Mountains* (1967), *The City of Gold and Lead* (1967) and *The Pool of Fire* (1968), was a Guardian Award runner-up (1969) and earned the George C. Stone Center for Children's Books Recognition of Merit Award (1977). The AMERICAN LIBRARY ASSOCIATION named *The White Mountains* a Notable Book. *The Guardians* (1970) earned C. the Christopher Award, the Guardian Award for children's fiction, and the German Children's Book Prize. *New Found Land* (1983), the second volume of The Fireball Trilogy, won the Parents' Choice Award. C.'s fictional worlds are set in futures that resemble medieval times in many details.

The Sword Trilogy, comprising *The Prince in Waiting* (1970), *Beyond the Burning Lands* (1971), and *The Sword of the Spirits* (1972), presents readers with a future Dark Age brought on by natural disaster. In The Fireball Trilogy, future events parallel prior aspects of history that include the Roman and Aztec Empires. C.'s underlying themes often devolve on choosing between painful freedom and comfortable servitude. C. has written under several other pseudonyms for adults.

FURTHER WORKS: *The Lotus Caves*, 1969; *Empty World*, 1977; *Fireball,* 1981; *Dragon Dance,* 1986; *When the Tripods Came,* 1988

BIBLIOGRAPHY: *Contemporary Authors, New Revision Series* vol. 37, 1992; Townsend, John Rose, *A Sense of Story: Essays on Contemporary Writers for Children,* 1973

FRANCISCA GOLDSMITH

CHRISTOPHER, Matt

Author, b. 16 August 1917, Bath, Pennsylvania; d. 20 September 1997, Charlotte, North Carolina

Matt Christopher, the eldest of nine children of an Italian father and a Hungarian mother, wrote more than 120 SPORTS STORIES, 300 short stories and magazine articles, a one-act play, humorous verses, and a comic-strip adventure. He grew up in upstate New York, near Ithaca. At age eighteen, he won an award in a *Writer's Digest* short story contest, later admitting that they gave 200 awards and his was for 191st place. For many years, he worked at menial jobs, wrote in his free time, and sent out as many as 40 stories at the same time. After high school, he worked a full-time job during the day, played semiprofessional baseball at night, and wrote a 4,000-to-5,000 word detective story every week. He finally sold one for $50. His first book for children was *The Lucky Baseball Bat* (1954, re-issued 1991) and his favorite was *The Kid Who Only Hit Homers* (1972). His characters were sports heroes who overcame handicaps, prejudice, and physical and emotional trauma by trying harder, playing fair, and persevering. He said, "I became a writer because I have always loved to make things starting from practically nothing." He also said, "If I've learned one thing from my writing career, it's this: don't ever let anyone stop you from trying to realize your dreams. Don't ever stop doing what you believe in."

FURTHER WORKS: *Baseball Pals* (1956); *The Basket Court* (1968); *Catch the Pass* (1969); *Desperate Search* (1973); *The Diamond Champ* (1977); *Baseball Flyhawk* (1995); *At the Plate With Mark McGwire* (1999); *The Captain Contest* (1999); *Hat Trick* (2000)

BIBLIOGRAPHY: HOPKINS, Lee Bennett, *Pauses: Autobiographical Reflections of 101 Creators of Children's Books,* 1995

BERNICE E. CULLINAN

CHUKOVSKY, Kornei Ivanovich

Journalist, scholar, critic, translator, author, and poet, b. 31 March 1882, St. Petersburg, Russia; d. 28 October 1969, Russia

Born N. I. Korneichuk, C. was raised in poverty by a proud, hardworking, single mother. She sacrificed enormously to send him and his sister to private school, knowing that was the route to success. Expelled on a pretext of keeping him out of the university track, he became a voracious reader and continued his education on his own. He taught himself English and other subjects from second-hand books. Entranced by the melody of POETRY, he became a translator and a writer, landing a job with a newspaper. He supported himself with his writing for the rest of his life as a literary critic, journalist, editor, translator, and, inspired by his own children, a writer of children's literature, giving him the distinction of being "the first modern Russian writer for children." Although his joyful and highly imaginative children's poems had their roots in Russian literary and folkloric traditions, they were also greatly influenced by English writers like Lewis CARROLL and Edward LEAR. Rich language, lilting rhythm and rhyme, humorous, nonsensical poetry, and rapid-fire stories characterize his work.

C. wrote verse and story poems, fantasies that connect with the lively imaginations and active lives of children. "The world I have shown to children is almost never allowed to rest. . . . Human beings and beasts run pell-mell from page to page through adventures, battles, and feats. . . . This swift tempo corresponds fully to the intellectual needs of children. For children, at the beginning of their existence, are interested least of all in the characteristic features of objects." In her NEWBERY MEDAL acceptance speech, Karen CUSHMAN quoted C.: "The goal of storytellers consists of fostering in the child, at whatever cost, compassion and humaneness—this miraculous ability of man to be disturbed by another being's misfortunes, to feel joy about another being's happiness, to experience another's fate as one's own." For C., writing was the ultimate joy, and writing for children required the capture of childhood joyfulness. In his book, *From Two to Five*

(1963) C. defends the right of children to literature such as nursery rhymes that encourage FANTASY and imagination. The figurative language and the absurd nonsense he wrote delight children and allow them to develop their imaginations and language skills; when children are deprived of FAIRY TALES and imaginative literature they create their own. C. also translated many highly imaginative English-language works, like *Doctor Dolittle* (LOFTING, 1920) into Russian.

AWARDS: Order of Lenin, 1957; PhD, Moscow University, 1957; DLitt, Oxford University, 1962; Lenin Prize for Literary Activities, 1962

FURTHER WORKS: *Wash 'em Clean* (1924/1969 [Felgenhauer]); *Telephone* (1926/1996 [Gambrell]); *Cock-the-Roach* (1927/1981); *FAIRY TALES* (1935/1984); *Doctor Powderpill* (1974 [Rottenberg]); *The Stolen Sun* (1958/1983 [Rottenberg]; *The Silver Crest: My Russian Boyhood* (1961/1976 [Stillman]); *The Muddle* (1976 [Rottenberg])

BIBLIOGRAPHY: www.eduplace.com/rdg/author. cushman/newbery.html; *Horn Book* magazine, 1971; SATA vol. 34, 1984, pp. 53–63; Library of Congress web catalogue: lcweb.loc.gov; Personal assessment of work; Chukovsky, K. *From Two to Five* (Miriam Morton, trans., 1963); Cutt, Jonathan, *Pipers at the Gates of Dawn: The Wisdom of Children's Literature*, 1981 http://www.odessit. com/cgi/lat.cgi/namegal/english/chukovsk.htm

MARGARET YATSEVITCH PHINNEY

CHUTE, Marchette
Author, b. 18 August 1909, Wayzata, Minnesota; d. 8 May 1994, Montclair, New Jersey

C., daughter of a Minnesota pioneering family, focused on British literary characters and became a Fellow of the Royal Society of Arts. Her biographical novels feature classic British authors such as Shakespeare in *Shakespeare of London* (1950); Ben Jonson in *Ben Jonson of Westminster* (1953); and Geoffrey Chaucer in *Geoffrey Chaucer of England* (1946).

Her fictional novels involve realistic characters who live in historical time periods and with whom young readers can identify. For instance, *The Innocent Wayfaring* (1943) tells of the midsummer journey of two young boys as they travel to London during Chaucer's era. In *The Wonderful Winter* (1954), a young nobleman, living in Elizabethan London, runs away from home to join Shakespeare's company of players at the Burbage Theatre. These books give readers a taste of historical fiction, and provide them with information about life in historical England.

C. also wrote several books of POETRY including *Rhymes about Ourselves* (1932), *Rhymes about the Country* (1941), *Rhymes about the City* (1946); and *Around and About* (1957).

FURTHER WORKS: *An Introduction to Shakespeare,* 1951; *Stories from Shakespeare,* 1956

BIBLIOGRAPHY: Kirkpatrick, D. L., ed., *Twentieth Century Children's Writers,* 1983

DENISE P. BEASLEY

CIARDI, John
Poet, b. 24 June 1916, Boston, Massachusetts; d. 30 March 1986, Edison, New Jersey

Scholar, literary critic, translator, and poet, C. grew up poor in Boston's Little Italy, the son of a doting Italian widow who neither spoke much English nor knew how to read. Forced to bridge the territory between two cultures, he was sensitized to both cultural and linguistic differences, accounting in part, perhaps, for his love for and fascination with words. He was also an insatiable reader from early childhood, immersing himself indiscriminately in whatever literature was available. In college, an inspiring writing course and helpful professor set him on his life path as a writer and scholar. He taught English at Harvard and Rutgers, and was the poetry editor for *Saturday Review.* C's contributions to children's poetry began when he wrote poems to entertain nephews and his own children. He once said a publisher's request to write controlled vocabulary poems for beginning readers challenged him to create a book for his daughter, then in kindergarten. They had such fun with the poems that the child learned to read, much to the dismay of her teacher.

C.'s motivation for POETRY IN CHILDREN'S LITERATURE was twofold: (1) to capture the childhood propensity for strong emotional responses to the world in rhythm, rhyme, HUMOR, and imaginative twists of meaning and (2) to keep the child inside himself alive as long as possible. He believed only enjoyable experiences with reading and writing will result in real learning. From visits to schools, he came in touch with children's straightforward eagerness for exploring their world and for engaging with poetry. His poems are lively, upbeat, and delightfully ridiculous. He wrote his poetry for fun, to cultivate joy, pure and simple.

AWARDS: Numerous AWARDS for both scholarly and juvenile work, including the Avery Hopwood Award for poetry (1939), Prix de Rome, American Academy of Arts and Letters, 1956–57, Junior Book Award, Boys' Clubs of America (1962) for *The Man Who Sang the Sillies,* and many honorary doctorates. NATIONAL COUNCIL OF TEACHERS OF ENGLISH Award for Excellence in Poetry, 1982

FURTHER WORKS: *The Reason for the Pelican,* 1959; *I Met a Man,* 1961; *You Read to Me, I'll Read to You,* 1962; *The Wish Tree,* 1962; *John J. Plenty and Fiddler Dan: A New Fable of the Grasshopper and the Ant,* 1963; *You Know Who,* 1964; *The King Who Saved Himself from Being Saved,* 1965; *The Monster Den; or, Look What Happened at My House, and to It,* 1965; *Someone Could Win a Polar Bear,* 1970; *Fast and Slow: Poems for Advanced Children and Beginning Parents,* 1975; *Doodle Soup,* 1985

BIBLIOGRAPHY: Cateura, L. B. (Ed.). *Growing up Italian,* Cifelli, E. M., *John C.: A Biography,* 1997; C., John, *C. Himself,* 1989; Hopkins, Lee Bennett, *Pauses: Autobiographical Reflections of 101 Creators of Children's Books,* 1995; Krickel, E. F., *John C.,* 1980

MARGARET YATSEVITCH PHINNEY

CISNEROS, Sandra
Author, poet, b. 20 December 1954, Chicago, Illinois

C. writes compelling fiction for older YOUNG ADULT readers. Her poetry, periodical entries and novels represent her own heritage and gender: female Chicanos and Latinos. C. received a B.A. from Loyola University of Chicago in 1976 and an M.F.A. from the University of Iowa in 1978. She has been a teacher and counselor at the high school level as well as a teacher and recruiter at the college level. C.'s poetry, fictional stories, and novels stray from the mainstream, yet attract many readers from all groups for their appeal to the emotions. C. feels that her experiences while growing up provide her with a basis for many of her beliefs. These beliefs serve as catalysts for her writings. C. moved back and forth between Chicago and her father's homeland, Mexico City.

She also felt lonely as the only girl of seven children. She threw herself into books. Although shy as a child, she grew into an adult, proud to share her beliefs and political stands. Her purpose in writing is to write the stories that have not been written and present thoughts, ideas and feelings in a new light. The strength in C.'s writing appears to be that it comes from her heart and has begun to fill a gap for a group of people who previously had no spokesperson.

AWARDS: C. was the National Endowment for the Arts fellow in 1982 and 1987. Before Columbus Foundation Award, 1985, for *The House on Mango Street* PEN/West Fiction Award, and Lannan Foundation Award, 1991, for *Woman Hollering Creek and Other Stories*

FURTHER WORKS: *Bad Boys,* 1980; *Hairs: Pelitos,* 1994; *Loose Woman: Poems,* 1994; work in anthologies: *We Are the Stories We Tell: The Best Short Stories by North American Women since 1945,* 1990

BIBLIOGRAPHY: Aranda, Pilar E., "On the Solitary Fate of Being Mexican, Female, Wicked and Thirty-Three: An Interview with Writer Sandra Cisneros," *The Americas Review,* vol. 18, no. 1, p. 64; Mohr, Nicholasa, "The Journey toward a Common Ground: Struggle and Identity of Hispanics in the USA," *The Americas Review,* vol. 18, no. 1, p. 81; Sagel, Jim, "Sandra Cisneros," *Publishers Weekly,* March 29, 1991, vol. 238, no. 15, p. 74

NANCY HORTON

CLAPP, Patricia
Author, playwright, b. 9 June 1912, Boston, Massachusetts; d. Unknown

C., who lived in New Jersey, divided her time between writing books and working in community theater. She did not consider herself a professional writer. Recent works include a history of her community theater and an unpublished autobiography. Because she did not write for financial reasons she was content to wait "for the first flicker of an idea" before she began a book. Her works often involve a good deal of research that allowed her to involve herself deeply in her stories. C., also an adult author, is best known for her acclaimed children's novels including *Constance: A Story of Early Plymouth* (1968), which was a National Book Award runner up; *Witches' Children: A Story of Salem* (1982), which was awarded an AMERICAN LIBRARY ASSOCIATION Best YOUNG ADULT Book citation.

FURTHER WORKS: *I'm Deborah Sampson: A Soldier in the War of the Revolution,* 1977; *The Tamarack Tree: A Novel of the Siege of Vicksburg,* 1986

BIBLIOGRAPHY: *Something about the Author,* vol. 4, 1973

MICHAEL O'LAUGHLIN

CLARK, Ann Nolan
Author, b. 5 December 1896, Las Vegas, New Mexico; d. 13 December 1995, Tucson, Arizona

C. was the author of more than forty children's books that focus on children of American Indian, Hispanic, Finnish, and Vietnamese cultures. Teaching in the schools of the American Southwest Bureau of Indian Affairs in the early- and mid-1900s, C. was aware of the struggles the Pueblo children faced learning a new language and culture. Realizing the need to have their own culture represented in the books they read, C. began writing beginning readers about the Pueblo way of life that included *Little Herder in Spring* (1940), *Little Boy with Three Names: Stories of Taos Pueblo* (1940), and *In My Mother's House* (1941). Her work is characterized by easily translated poetic language, rich cultural heritage, insight into the problems and hopes of diverse people, as well as being noted for bridging cultures. Quite often C. would have children tell her the stories and illustrate the books about their own culture. C. won the 1953 NEWBERY MEDAL for *Secret of the Andes,* a story about young people torn between cultural traditions as young Cusi learns the history of his Inca heredity, how to tend llamas, and the old tribal ways high in the Andes mountains of Peru.

FURTHER WORKS: *There Still Are Buffalo,* 1942; *Santiago,* 1955; *The Desert People,* 1962; *Journey to the People,* 1969; *To Stand against the Wind Viking,* 1978; *In the Land of Small Dragon: A Vietnamese Folktale,* 1979 (with Dang Manh Kha)

BIBLIOGRAPHY: *Children's Literature Review,* vol. 16, 1989; Griese, Arnold A. "Ann Nolan C.—Building Bridges of Cultural Understanding," *Elementary English,* May, 1972

JANELLE B. MATHIS

CLARKE, Arthur C.
Author, b. 16 December 1917, Minehead, Somersetshire, England

C. is considered one of the greatest visionaries and authors of hard SCIENCE FICTION. His optimism in this genre sets him apart from other authors. C. attended King's College, University of London, graduating with a B.A. of Science in physics and math in 1948. His career has included professor, lecturer, underwater explorer and photographer, actor, commentator with Walter Cronkite on Apollo missions, and host of two television series: *Arthur C. Clarke's Mysterious World* (1980) and *Arthur C. Clarke's World of Strange Powers* (John Farley and Simon Welfare, eds., 1984). C. is the author of over eighty books, hundreds of articles, several television series, and screenplays. His work is accented by his interest and participation in scuba diving and his contribution to the invention of satellite technology. He was an explorer in his youth, of the sea, the beach, and futuristic ideas. C. credits his imagination to W. Olaf Stapledon's *Last and First Men* (1931). Reading the book, he says, changed his outlook on the universe and greatly influenced his writing. One of his best known works stems from his work with filmmaker Stanley Kubrick, *2001: A Space Odyssey* (1968). More than twenty years earlier C. had proposed that geosynchronous satellites could be used for global communications. Clearly, C.'s knowledge of science and his uncanny feel for the future, coupled with his talent for writing, catapulted him into recognition shared by few others. As an author of nonfiction and fiction read by adults and young adults, his works have appeared through the span of almost six decades.

AWARDS: C. has received numerous AWARDS in the area of science technology and writing beginning in 1952 for *The Exploration of Space. The Challenge of the Sea* received the Boys' Club of America Junior Book Award in 1961. The American Association for the Advancement of Science recognized C. in 1969 with the Westinghouse Science Writing Award. The AMERICAN LIBRARY ASSOCIATION's Best Books for Young Adults recognized *Rendezvous with Rama* in 1973 and *2001* in 1975

FURTHER WORKS: *Islands in the Sky* (1952); *The Young Traveller in Space* (1954); *Boy beneath the*

Sea (1958); *The First Five Fathoms: A Guide to Underwater Adventure* (1960); *Indian Ocean Adventure* (1961); *2010: Odyssey Two* (1982); *2061: Odyssey Three* (1988); *3001: The Final Odyssey* (1997); *Earthlight* (1998 1955, re-issued)

BIBLIOGRAPHY: *Business Week,* Feb. 24, 1997, issue 3515, p. 123; *Discover,* May 1997, vol. 18 i 5, p. 68; *Popular Mechanics,* May 1996, vol. 13 i 5, p. 24

NANCY HORTON

CLASSIC NOVELS

The field of children's literature thrived during the twentieth century. The classic novel, as one of its art forms, is no exception. It consistently draws children into the world of the imagination through the literary criteria that define it. They are: a well-crafted plot; a sharp, clear setting that gives a sense of place, period, time and feeling; fully developed characterizations; natural dialogue appropriate to the characters; a logically developed theme; and accuracy that lends authenticity to the whole. The adult's goal is to unite a child with a novel exhibiting these characteristics. Generally, children are first led to books demonstrating these attributes by a caring parent, concerned teacher, or knowledgeable librarian. Taste is, after all, an acquired characteristic, not an inherited one.

With the classic novel, the goal, according to Lloyd ALEXANDER, is to place "the right book in the hands of the right child at the right time" to create a dramatic, rewarding encounter—one that may have a significant effect on the child throughout his lifetime. In order to do this, look at the historical background of the classic novel in children's literature.

From roots in the oral tradition of each culture, the novel was transported to the pages of books with the advent of printing in the fifteenth century. The early focus was on adult literature. But as time passed, "Most of those books which we regard as classics of children's literature were written without children in mind and were taken over by them with cheerful disregard of what they could not understand," according to Dr. Henry Steele Commager. They became classics of children's literature; such as, Daniel DEFOE's *Robinson Crusoe* (1719), Jonathan SWIFT's *Gulliver's Travels* (1726), and Robert Louis STEVENSON's *Treasure Island* (1883).

According to Cornelia MEIGS, "the distinct tradition of writing the sort of literature which appealed to children as well as to adults continued to flourish through the Victorian Age and into the twentieth century" inspiring the likes of Robert Louis Stevenson, Rudyard KIPLING, Arthur Conan DOYLE, Kenneth GRAHAME, and Andrew LANG.

Later, in America, this pattern was repeated as titles such as Washington IRVING's "Rip Van Winkle" (1820) and Richard Henry Dana's *Two Years before the Mast* (1840) were adopted by children. Today the readership of classic novels follows a two-way path. Children continue to adopt adult classic novels while adults now read some of the excellent children's novels on topics of interest to them; such as, Katherine PATERSON's *Bridge to Terabithia* (1977), a title frequently used in grief counseling. J. K. ROWLING's *Harry Potter and the Sorcerer's Stone* (1998) and other titles in the series is also read as eagerly by adults as it is by the juvenile population for whom it is intended.

Then, halfway through the nineteenth century, American scenes and American characters appeared fully developed in children's books, with Louisa May ALCOTT's *Little Women* (1869), Samuel CLEMENS's *The Adventures of Tom Sawyer* (1876) and *Adventures of Huckleberry Finn* (1884), and Mary Mapes DODGE's *Hans Brinker and the Silver Skates* (1865). See list below.

The transition into the twentieth century saw Rudyard Kipling's *Jungle Books* (1894, 1895), *Kim* (1901), and *Just So Stories* (1902) and Kenneth GRAHAME's *Wind in the Willows* (1908) captivate children with their elements of FANTASY and adventure. The first quarter of the twentieth century followed this tradition with Hugh LOFTING's *The Story of Doctor Doolittle* (1922) and later P. L. TRAVERS's *Mary Poppins* (1934), J. R. R. TOLKIEN's *The Hobbit* (1937), and Mary NORTON's *The Borrowers* (1951).

The period after World War I saw increased development of a focus on children's literature with the classic novel as the beneficiary. The public library movement, the advancement of Progressive Education and its resulting need to establish school libraries; and youth organizations clamoring for better reading materials for boys and girls, encouraged publishers to establish separate departments for publishing children's books. Children's Book Week, the NEWBERY MEDAL and the CALDECOTT MEDAL were established during this time.

Throughout the early development of American children's literature, Henry Steele Commager insists that "Americans have never believed that childhood was merely a preparation for life; they have insisted, rather, that it was life itself." An emphasis on equality would interest all classes, all parts of the country and all faiths, while at the same time blurring the differences between the sexes. Now, most of the differences between boys and girls stories were erased.

Regional books representing stories of the South, such as Joel Chandler HARRIS's *Uncle Remus Tales* (1880) and of the Midwest with Laura Ingalls WILDER's Little House series were complemented by the invigorating development of an appealing format for children's books embellished with works of art.

After World War II, and throughout the second half of the century, novels for the AFRICAN AMERICAN child appeared with increasing frequency. Titles such as *Sounder* (William ARMSTRONG, 1969), *House of Dies Drear* (Virginia HAMILTON, 1968), and *Roll of Thunder, Hear My Cry* (Mildred TAYLOR, 1976) achieved wide appeal.

During this same period children's novels abounded with HUMOR like Roald DAHL's *Charlie and the Chocolate Factory* (1964) and *James and the Giant Peach* (1961). Assurance, proportion, and a sense of spiritual values appeared in novels such as *Homecoming* (1981) by Cynthia VOIGT and *Charlotte's Web* (1952) by E. B. WHITE.

The field of children's literature has expanded to include all fields of human knowledge and endeavor. The novel then, is an invaluable tool for the parent to share with the child, since findings from current research indicate that reading to children may be the single most significant contribution that parents can make toward their child's success in school. The classic novel is a powerful tool for this purpose.

An event of the 1970s limited children's access, and thus chance for discovery of some delightful novels, on their own. When the U.S. Congress taxed publishers on their unsold inventory at the end of the year, a situation was created that forced publishers to sell that inventory at discounts of 70 percent to 90 percent, and forever

changed the face of children's publishing. As a result, books go out-of-print in twelve to eighteen months. How can a charming tale such as *Pearl's Pirates* by Frank ASCH, ever get the chance to be revered in the same way as *Charlotte's Web* when it went out of print in such a short time, and thus was not readily available in children's departments of libraries and in bookstores? The responsibility of the significant adult in a child's life is more important than ever, as a result of this situation. Also, award-winning books, frequently on booklists, assume a paramount role. At the dawn of the twenty-first century, classic children's novels continue to provide children with the greatest degree of refinement through quality literature.

1700s: *Robinson Crusoe* (1719) by Daniel Defoe; *Gulliver's Travels* (1726) by Jonathan Swift

1800s: *Swiss Family Robinson* (1818) by Johann David Von Wyss; *Heidi* (1880) by Johanna SPYRI; *Oliver Twist* (1838) by Charles DICKENS; *A Christmas Carol* (1843) by Charles Dickens; *David Copperfield* (1850) by Charles Dickens; *A Tale of Two Cities* (1859) by Charles Dickens; *Great Expectations* (1863) by Charles Dickens; "The Legend of Sleepy Hollow" (1864) by Washington Irving; *Alice's Adventures in Wonderland* (1865) by Louis CARROLL; *Hans Brinker and the Silver Skates* (1865) by Mary Mapes DODGE; "Rip Van Winkle" (1870) by Washington Irving; *At the Back of the North Wind* (1871) by George MacDonald; *The Princess and the Goblin* (1872) by George MACDONALD; *Through the Looking-Glass* (1872) by Louis Carroll; *The Adventures of Tom Sawyer* (1876) by Mark Twain (Samuel Langhorne Clemens); *Black Beauty* (1877) by Anna SEWELL; *Five Little Peppers and How They Grew* (1881) by Margaret SIDNEY (Harriet Lothrop); *Prince and the Pauper* (1881) by Mark Twain (Samuel Langhorne Clemens); *The Adventures of Pinocchio* (1883) by C. COLLODI (Carlo Lorenzini); *The Princess and Curdie* (1883) by George MacDonald; *Treasure Island* (1883) by Robert Louis Stevenson; *Adventures of Huckleberry Finn* (1884) by Mark Twain (Samuel Langhorne Clemens); *Around the World in 80 Days* (1874) by Jules VERNE; *Journey to the Center of the Earth* (1874) by Jules Verne; *Twenty Thousand Leagues under the Sea* (1874) by Jules Verne; *The Mysterious Island* (1875) by Jules

Verne; *Kidnapped* (1886) by Robert Louis Stevenson; *Little Lord Fauntleroy* (1886) by Frances Hodgson BURNETT; *The Black Arrow* (1888) by Robert Louis Stevenson; *A Connecticut Yankee in King Arthur's Court* (1889) by Mark Twain (Samuel Langhorne Clemens); *Five Little Peppers Midway* (1890) by Margaret Sidney (Harriet Lothrop); *The Adventures of Sherlock Holmes* (1892) by Arthur Conan DOYLE; *Five Little Peppers Grown Up* (1892) by Margaret Sidney (Harriet Lothrop); *The Jungle Books* (1894) by Rudyard Kipling; *Red Badge of Courage* (1894) by Stephen Crane; *The Second Jungle Book* (1895) by Rudyard Kipling; *The Time Machine* (1895) by Herbert George WELLS; *The Island of Dr. Moreau* (1896) by Herbert George Wells; *The Strange Case of Dr. Jekyll and Mr. Hyde* (1896) by Robert Louis Stevenson; *Captains Courageous* (1897) by Rudyard Kipling; *The Invisible Man* (1897) by Herbert George Wells; *Phronsie Pepper: The Youngest of the Five Little Peppers* (1897) by Margaret Sidney (Harriet Lothrop); *The War of the Worlds* (1898) by Herbert George Wells; *The Stories of Polly Pepper Told to the Five Little Peppers* (1899) by Margaret Sidney (Harriet Lothrop)

1900s: *The Adventures of Joel Pepper* (1900) by Margaret Sidney (Harriet Lothrop); *The Wonderful Wizard of Oz* (1900) by Frank BAUM; *Kim* (1901) by Rudyard Kipling; *Mrs. Wiggs of the Cabbage Patch* (1901) by Alice Hegan Rice; *The Five Little Peppers Abroad* (1902) by Margaret Sidney (Harriet Lothrop); *Just So Stories for Little Children* (1902) by Rudyard Kipling; *Five Little Peppers at School* (1903) by Margaret Sidney (Harriet Lothrop); *Call of the Wild* (1903) by Jack LONDON; *Rebecca of Sunnybrook Farm* (1903) by Kate Douglas WIGGIN; *Five Little Peppers and Their Friends* (1904) by Margaret Sidney (Harriet Lothrop); *Ben Pepper* (1905) by Margaret Sidney (Harriet Lothrop); *A Little Princess* (1905) by Frances Hodgson Burnett; *Five Little Peppers in the Little Brown House* (1907) by Margaret Sidney (Harriet Lothrop); *Anne of Green Gables* (1908) by Lucy Maud MONTGOMERY; *The Wind in the Willows* (1908) by Kenneth GRAHAME; *Anne of Avonlea* (1901) by Lucy Maud Montgomery

1910s: *The Secret Garden* (1911) by Frances Hodgson Burnett; *The Lost Prince* (1915) by Frances Hodgson Burnett; *Our Davie Pepper* (1916) by Margaret Sidney (Harriet Lothrop); *Lad, a Dog* (1919) by Albert Payson TERHUNE

1920s: *The Story of Doctor Dolittle* (1920) by Hugh LOFTING; *The Heart of a Dog* (1921) by Albert Payson Terhune; *Velveteen Rabbit* (1922) by Margery BIANCO; *The Voyage of Doctor Dolittle* (1922) by Hugh Lofting; *The Dark Frigate* (1923) by Charles Boardman Hawes; *Smoky, the Cow Horse* (1926) by Will JAMES; *Winnie the Pooh* (1926) by Alan Alexander MILNE; *Bambi* (1928) by Felix SALTEN (Siegmund Salzmann); *The House at Pooh Corner* (1928) by Alan Alexander Milne; *The Trumpeter of Krakow* (1928) by Eric P. KELLY

1930s: *The Way of a Dog* (1932) by Albert Payson Terhune; *Mary Poppins* (1934) by Pamela Lyndon TRAVERS; *Caddie Woodlawn* (1935) by Carol Ryrie BRINK; *Mary Poppins Comes Back* (1935) by Pamela Lyndon Travers; *National Velvet* (1935) by Enid BAGNOLD; *Roller Skates* (1936) by Ruth Sawyer; *Mr. Popper's Penguins* (1938) by Richard and Florence ATWATER; *The Yearling* (1938) by Marjorie Kinnan RAWLINGS; *B Is for Betsy* (1939) by Carolyn HAYWOOD; *Ben and Me* (1939) by Robert LAWSON

1940s: *Call It Courage* (1940) by Armstrong SPERRY; *Lassie Come Home* (1940) by Eric KNIGHT; *They Were Strong and Good* (1940) by Robert Lawson; *The Moffats* (1941) by Eleanor ESTES; *Johnny Tremain* (1943) by Esther FORBES; *The Little Prince* (1943) by Antoine de SAINT-EXUPÉRY; *Mary Poppins Opens the Door* (1943) by Pamela Lyndon Travers; *The Black Stallion* (1944) by Walter FARLEY; *Rabbit Hill* (1944) by Robert Lawson; *Big Red* (1945) by Jim KJELGAARD; *Stuart Little* (1945) by Elwyn Brooks WHITE; *Strawberry Girl* (1945) by Lois LENSKI; *Eddie and the Fire Engine* (1946) by Carolyn HAYWOOD; *Misty of Chincoteague* (1946) by Marguerite HENRY; *King of the Wind* (1948) by Marguerite Henry; *Sea Star: Orphan of Chincoteague* by Marguerite Henry (1949)

1950s: *Henry Huggins* (1950) by Beverly CLEARY; *Pippi Longstocking* (1950) by Astrid LINDGREN; *All-of-a-Kind Family* (1951) by Sidney TAYLOR; *Ginger Pye* (1951) by Eleanor Estes; *Irish Red, Son of Big Red* (1951) by Jim

KJELGAARD; *Prince Caspian* (1951) by C. S. LEWIS; *Charlotte's Web* (1952) by Ewleyn Brooks White; *Mary Poppins in the Park* (1952) by Pamela Lyndon Travers; *The Voyage of the Dawn Treader* (1952) by C. S. Lewis; *By the Shores of Silver Lake* (1953) by Laura Ingalls WILDER; *The Borrowers* (1953) by Mary NORTON; *Brighty of the Grand Canyon* (1953) by Marguerite Henry; *Justin Morgan Had a Horse* (1953) by Marguerite Henry; *Little House in the Big Woods* (1953) by Laura Ingalls Wilder; *Little House on the Prairie* (1953) by Laura Ingalls Wilder; *The Long Winter* (1953) by Laura Ingalls Wilder; *Mr. Revere and I* (1953) by Robert Lawson; *On the Banks of Plum Creek* (1953) by Laura Ingalls Wilder; *The Silver Chair* (1953) by C. S. Lewis; *The Horse and His Boy* (1954) by C. S. Lewis; *The Wheel on the School* (1954) by Meindert DEJONG; *The Borrowers Afield* (1955) by Mary Norton; *Carry On, Mr. Bowditch* (1955) by Jean Lee LATHAM; *The Magician's Nephew* (1955) by C. S. Lewis; *Captain Kidd's Cat* (1956) by Robert Lawson; *The House of Sixty Fathers* (1956) by Meindert DeJong; *The Last Battle* (1956) by C. S. Lewis; *Pippi Goes on Board* (1956) by Astrid Lindgren; *Black Gold* (1957) by Marguerite Henry; *Rifles for Watie* (1957) by Harold KEITH; *Along Came a Dog* (1958) by Meindert DEJONG; *Basil of Baker Street* (1958) by Eve TITUS; *Henry Reed, Inc.* (1958) by Keith ROBERTSON; *The Luckiest Girl* (1958) by Beverly Cleary; *The Borrowers Afloat* (1959) by Mary Norton; *My Side of the Mountain* (1959) by Jean Craighead GEORGE; *Pippi in the South Seas* (1959) by Astrid Lindgren

1960s: *The Cricket in Times Square* (1960) by George SELDEN; *Island of the Blue Dolphin* (1960) by Scott O'DELL; *Meet the Austins* (1960) by Madeleine L'ENGLE; *The Borrowers Aloft* (1961) by Mary Norton; *Farmer Boy* (1961) by Laura Ingalls Wilder; *James and the Giant Peach* (1961) by Roald DAHL; *The Phantom Toolbooth* (1961) by Norton JUSTER; *Wolves of Willoughby Chase* (1962) by Joan AIKEN; *A Wrinkle in Time* (1962) by Madeleine L'Engle; *The Moon by Night* (1963) by Madeleine L'Engle; *Hariett the Spy* (1964) by Louise FITZHUGH; *Across Five Aprils* (1964) by Irene HUNT; *Charlie and the Chocolate Factory* (1964) by Roald Dahl; *Char-

lie and the Great Glass Elevator* (1964) by Roald Dahl; *Chitty Chitty Bang Bang* (1964) by Ian FLEMING; *Shadow of a Bull* (1964) by Majia WOJCIECHOWSKA; *The Arm of the Starfish* (1965) by Madeleine L'Engle; *The Black Cauldron* (1965) by Lloyd ALEXANDER; *Noonday Friends* (1965) by Mary STOLZ; *Henry Reed's Baby-Sitting Service* (1966) by Keith ROBERTSON; *Up a Road Slowly* (1966) by Irene Hunt; *The Black Pearl* (1967) by Scott O'Dell; *The Egypt Game* (1967) by Zilpha Keatley SNYDER; *From the Mixed-Up Files of Mrs. Basil E. Frankweiler* (1967) by Elaine KONIGSBURG; *Jennifer, Hecate, Macbeth, William McKinley, and Me, Elizabeth* (1967) by Elaine Konigsburg; *The Great Brain* (1967) by John D. FITZGERALD; *Taran Wanderer* (1967) by Lloyd Alexander; *Zeely* (1967) by Virginia HAMILTON; *The House of Dies Drear* (1968) by Virginia Hamilton; *Ramona the Pest* (1968) by Beverly Cleary; *The Pigman* (1968) by Paul ZINDEL; *The Young Unicorns* (1968) by Madeleine L'Engle; *Castle of Llyr* (1969) by Lloyd Alexander; *The High King* (1969) by Lloyd Alexander; *My Darling, My Hamburger* (1969) by Paul Zindel; *Sounder* (1969) by William ARMSTRONG; *Tucker's Countryside* (1969) by George Selden

1970s: *I Know Why the Caged Bird Sings* (1970) by Maya ANGELOU; *The Trumpet of the Swan* (1970) by Elwyn Brooks WHITE; *Basil and the Pygmy Cats* (1971) by Eve Titus; *Cuckoo Tree* (1971) by Joan Aiken; *Mrs. Frisby and the Rats of Nimh* (1971) by Robert C. O'BRIEN; *The Planet of Junior Brown* (1971) by Virginia Hamilton; *A Wind in the Door* (1973) by Madeleine L'Engle; *M. C. Higgins, the Great* (1974) by Virginia Hamilton; *Dominic* (1972) by William STEIG; *Julie of the Wolves* (1972) by Jean Craighead George; *The Dark Is Rising* (1973) by Susan COOPER; *Dragonwings* (1975) by Lawrence YEP; *The Ghost Belonged to Me* (1975) by Richard PECK; *The Grey King* (1975) by Susan Cooper; *The Master Puppeteer* (1975) by Katherine PATERSON; *The Second Mrs. Giaconda* (1975) by Elaine Konigsburg; *Abel's Island* (1976) by William Steig; *Basil in Mexico* (1976) by Eve Titus; *Dragon Slayer* (1976) by Rosemary SUTCLIFF; *Roll of Thunder, Hear My Cry* (1976) by Mildred D. TAYLOR; *Bridge to Terabithia* (1977) by Katherine Paterson; *Silver on the Tree* (1977) by Susan

Cooper; *A Summer to Die* (1977) by Lois LOWRY; *Baker Street Irregular* (1978) by Robert Newman; *Book of Three* (1978) by Lloyd Alexander; *The Great Gilly Hopkins* (1978) by Katherine Paterson; *A Swiftly Tilting Planet* (1978) by Madeleine L'Engle; *Anastasia Krupnik* (1979) by Lois Lowry

1980s: *Indian in the Cupboard* (1980) by Lynn Reid BANKS; *Jacob Have I Loved* (1980) by Katherine Paterson; *A Ring of Endless Light* (1980) by Madeleine L'Engle; *Anastasia Again!* (1981) by Lois Lowry; *Homecoming* (1981) by Cynthia VOIGT; *The Violin-Maker's Gift* (1981) by Donn Kushner; *Dicey's Song* (1982) by Cynthia Voigt; *Dragon's Blood* (1982) by Jane YOLEN; *Chester Cricket's New Home* (1983) by George Selden; *Heart's Blood* (1984) by Jane Yolen; *Agony of Alice* (1985) by Phyllis Reynolds NAYLOR; *Dogsong* (1985) by Gary PAULSEN; *Greenwitch* (1985) by Susan COOPER; *Sarah, Plain and Tall* (1985) by Patricia MACLACHLAN; *A Fine White Dust* (1986) by Cynthia RYLANT; *Many Waters* (1986) by Madeleine L'Engle; *Return of the Indian* (1986) by Lynn Reid Banks; *Up from Jericho Tel* (1986) by Elaine Konigsburg; *The Whipping Boy* (1986) by Sid FLEISCHMAN; *Hatchet* (1987) by Gary Paulsen; *The Old Meadow* (1987) by George Selden; *Rabble Starkey* (1987) by Lois Lowry; *The Serpent Never Sleeps* (1987) by Scott O'Dell; *Matilda* (1988) by Roald Dahl; *Number the Stars* (1989) by Lois Lowry; *The Secret of the Indian* (1989) by Lynn Reid Banks; *The Winter Room* (1989) by Gary Paulsen

1990s: *Maniac Magee* (1990) by Jerry SPINELLI; *The Road to Memphis* (1990) by Mildred D. Taylor; *The Midnight Horse* (1990) by Sid Fleischman; *Shiloh* (1991) by Phyllis Reynolds Naylor; *Stepping on the Cracks* (1991) by Mary Downing HAHN; *Dragon's Boy* (1992) by Jane Yolen; *Drylongso* (1992) by Virginia Hamilton; *Missing May* (1992) by Cynthia Rylant; *Dragon's Gate* (1993) by Lawrence Yep; *The Giver* (1993) by Lois Lowry; *Nightjohn* (1993) by Gary Paulsen; *The Wings of a Falcon* (1993) by Cynthia Voigt; *Little House on Rocky Ridge* (1994) by Robert Lea MacBride; *Little Farm in the Ozarks* (1994) by Robert Lea MacBride; *The Boggart* (1995) by Susan Cooper; *In the Land of the Big Red Apple* (1995) by Roger Lea MacBride; *On the Other Side of the Hill* (1995) by Roger Lea MacBride; *The Boggart and the Monster* (1997) by Susan Cooper; *The Library Card* (1997) by Jerry Spinelli; *Amistad: A Long Road to Freedom* (1998) by Walter Dean MYERS

BIBLIOGRAPHY: Arbuthnot, May Hill, Margaret Mary Clark, Ruth M. Hadlow, and Harrriet G. Long, *Children's Books Too Good To Miss,* 1979; Gillespie, J. and D. Lembo, *Introducing Books: A Guide for the Middle Grades,* 1970; Hodges, M. and S. Steinfirst, *Elva Sophronia Smith's The History of Children's Literature,* 1980; Huber, M. B. *Story and Verse for Children,* 1965; Johnson, E., Carrie E. S., and E. R. Sickels, *Anthology of Children's Literature,* 1947, 1948; Johnson, E., E. R. Sickels, and Frances Clark Sayers, *Anthology of Children's Literature,* 1959; Meigs, Cornelia L., A. Eaton, E. Nesbit, R. H. Viguers, *A Critical History of Children's Literature,* 1953; Russell, William F., *Classics to Read Aloud to Your Children,* 1984; Strouf, J. L. H., *The Literature Teacher's Book of Lists,* 1993; Sutherland, Zena, Betsy Hearne, and Rober Sutton. *The Best in Children's Books: The University of Chicago Guide to Children's Literature, 1985–1990,* 1991

EVA MARIE NESBIT

CLEARY, Beverly

Author, b. 12 April 1916, McMinnville, Oregon

C. lived on a farm in Yamhill, Oregon, until she was old enough to go to school. Yamhill had no public library but C.'s mother arranged for the state library to send books to Yamhill; she set up the books as a library in a room over a bank and served as the librarian. Surrounded by books and with a mother as librarian, C. learned to love books. When C.'s family moved to Portland, she attended elementary school but found that she was in the slowest reading group. She mastered reading by the third grade but she has always had a special sympathy for children with reading problems.

A great deal of C.'s childhood was spent in a library or on the way to or from a library. C.'s school librarian suggested that she should write for children when she grew up. The idea appealed to C.; she decided that she would write the kind of books that she had wanted to read—but could not find—on the library shelves when she was growing up. C. wanted books that were funny and about children like the ones in her neighborhood. Her first writing effort, when she was ten years old, won a two-dollar prize because, C. explains, no one else entered the contest. C. graduated from junior college, Ontario, University of California, Berkeley, and entered the School of Librarianship at the University of Washington, Seattle. In library school she specialized in work with children. C. served as children's librarian in Yakima, Washington, until she married, moved to California, and became the mother of twins. During World War II, C. served as Post Librarian at the Oakland Army Hospital. C. wrote *Henry Huggins* (1950), her first book, when she heard children complain that there were no books about people like them. Most of the books for children were about those who lived in foreign countries and had adventures that could never happen to ordinary children. Henry Huggins, a composite of the boys C. knew as a child, has normal, everyday experiences. Henry finds a stray dog and names him Ribsy; Ribsy would soon have a story told from his point of view as C.'s books became even more popular. Henry's friend Beezus and her little sister Ramona, widen the circle of believable characters who inhabit C.'s stories. Beezus and Ramona act like children who live down the street. C. is a masterful storyteller who sees the HUMOR in simple, childlike adventures. She is talented at developing a character through dialogue and behavior and portrays children as they see themselves.

C. produced other types of stories that also became popular with readers. For example *The Mouse and the Motorcycle* (1965), *Runaway Ralph* (1977), and *Ralph S. Mouse* (1982) feature an extraordinary talking mouse who creates adventures everywhere he goes. C. won the NEWBERY MEDAL for *Dear Mr. Henshaw* (1984), a remarkable story told through Leigh Botts's letters to an author and his diary entries. The story contains pathos, humor, and heartache; it is the first time C. wrote about a child of divorced parents. It is obvious that C.'s work appeals to children; several million copies of her books are in print.

C. writes from her own life experiences. *Mitch and Amy* (1967) comes directly from C.'s experience rearing her twin son and daughter filtered through the author's imagination. Family relationships are frankly explored in language and dialogue familiar to children. Ramona's fear of spelling tests, following in her big sister's footsteps and fear for her family when her father loses his job are familiar situations to children. C. discusses these things with characteristic candor and humor. She depicts the ways family members come together to support each other in crises, to learn and to grow. C. enjoys writing and makes no special effort to be funny. Her irreverently humorous outlook on life has universal appeal to children. They see their own lives reflected in C.'s stories about Ramona, her family, and friends in suburbs and small towns across America.

AWARDS: Laura Ingalls WILDER Award (1975) for body of work. Golden Kite Award (1982) for *Ralph S. Mouse*. AMERICAN LIBRARY ASSOCIATION Newbery Medal Honor Book (1978) for *Ramona and Her Father* and (1982) for *Ramona Quimby, Age 8*. ALA NEWBERY MEDAL (1984), Christopher Award (1984), Friends of Children and Literature Award (1987) for *Dear Mr. Henshaw*. DE GRUMMOND REFERENCE COLLECTION, University of Southern Mississippi Medallion (1982), George C. Stone Center Award (1983) and CHILDREN'S BOOK COUNCIL Honor (1985) for a body of work. Bay Area Reviewer's Award (1988) for *A Girl from Yamhill: A Memoir*. IBBY Honor List (1980) for *Ramona and Her Father*

FURTHER WORKS: *Ellen Tebbits*, 1951; *Otis Spofford*, 1953; *Beezus and Ramona*, 1955; *Ramona the Pest*, 1968; *Socks*, 1973; *Ramona the Brave*, 1975; *Ramona and Her Father*, 1977; *Ramona and Her Mother*, 1979; *Ramona Quimby, Age 8*, 1981; *Ramona Forever*, 1984; *Muggie Maggie*, 1990; *Strider*, 1991; *Ramona's World*, 1999

BIBLIOGRAPHY: C., B., *A Girl from Yamhill: A Memoir*, 1988; C., B., *My Own Two Feet: A Memoir*, 1995; C., B., "The Booklist Interview," *Booklist*, October 15, 1990; C., B., "Newbery Medal Acceptance," the *Horn Book* magazine. August 1984; HOPKINS, Lee Bennett, *Pauses: Autobiographical Reflections of 101 Creators of Children's Books*, 1995; Kovacs, D and J. Preller, *Meet the Authors and Illustrators*, 1991; MEIGS, C. et al., *A Critical History of Children's Literature*, 1969

BERNICE E. CULLINAN

CLEAVER, Elizabeth

Illustrator, b. 19 November 1939, Montreal, Quebec; d. 27 July 1985, Montreal, Quebec

Educated in both Hungary and CANADA, C. received her masters degree from Concordia University in 1980 but had been illustrating children's books since 1968. She combined her love of FOLKLORE and legends with experiences of living and traveling in other countries to produce illustrations that accurately reflected different cultures and countries. *The Miraculous Hind: A Hungarian Legend* (1973) retold by C., included illustrations based on the author's careful research into native Hungarian culture as well as on her years living there as a young person.

She illustrated the Micmac legend *How Summer Came to Canada* (1969) and a Tshimshian story, *The Mountain Goats of Temlaham* (1969), both retold by William Toye, with collage based on NATIVE AMERICAN design motifs. Both these titles received Honor Book citations from the Canadian Association of Childrens' Librarians.

C. wrote and illustrated *Petroucha* (1980), a PICTURE BOOK based on the Stravinsky ballet. She used a layered collage look and bold colors to help reflect a theatrical context for the story. This title won the Parents Choice Award in 1980 and the Canadian Children's Literature Award in 1981, both for ILLUSTRATION.

Fire Stealer (1979), based on an Ojibwa story, used collage pieces to cast a shadow onto the paper behind them to create "a sense of kinetic energy." Use of shadow and the theme of transformation is evident also in her *ABC,* a small alphabet book filled with seemingly random shapes in rainbow colors. Her last book, *The Enchanted Caribou,* published in 1985, reveals again Cleaver's interest in the motif of transformation as Tyya, a doll maker, is changed into a white caribou. She wrote the text for this Inuit legend and illustrated it with photographs of images cast by shadow puppets on a screen.

C. was one of Canada's most well-known children's illustrators. She was noted especially for her unique torn paper collages and considered her use of it "creative play." Her brightly colored, layered collages and black and white linocuts in the *Wind Has Wings: Poems From* Canada (1968) won the first Amelia Frances Howard-Gibbon medal for illustration in 1971. She won the same award in 1978 for *The Loon's Necklace,* a story based on a Tsimshian legend. In 1972 she was a runner-up for the Hans Christian ANDERSEN Award from INTERNATIONAL BOARD ON BOOKS FOR YOUNG PEOPLE. That same year she represented Canada at the International Book Fair in London. Much of her art was presented at international competitions. Her work is on display as part of a permanent exhibition at both the Toronto Public Library and McGill University.

FURTHER WORKS: Illustrated by Cleaver: *Canadian Wonder Tales,* 1974; *Witch of the North: Folktales of Northern Canada,* 1975; *Love and Kisses Heart Book,* 1975

BIBLIOGRAPHY: *School Library Journal,* Jan./Feb. 1986; *Something about the Author,* vol. 23, 1981

LINDA GOLDMAN

CLEAVER, Bill and Vera
Authors, Bill: b. 24 March 1920, Hugo, Oklahoma; d. 20 August 1981, Winter Haven, Florida; Vera: b. 6 January 1919, Virgil, South Dakota; d. 11 August 1992, Winter Haven, Florida

Reared during the Great Depression, the C.s lived through many of the struggles depicted vividly in their works. The result of their writing partnership is known for its grim realism that presents honest portrayals of human nature using authentic dialogue, traditional values, and an abiding respect for education to fight against great odds. Unable to complete their formal education, they taught themselves in public LIBRARIES. Vera did attend schools in Kennebeck, South Dakota, and Perry and Tallahassee, Florida. Bill has said that he is a graduate of the public LIBRARIES of the United States of America. He also served in the U.S. Air Force. During that time Vera worked as a civilian accountant in Tachikawa, Japan and Chaumont, France.

Early in their marriage, the C.s composed over 275 stories for pulp MAGAZINES. Their writing was about children and for adults. Wishing to stretch their creativity and produce writings of more lasting value, they then began to write for children and especially young adult readers. Their work, most often set in Appalachia and other rural settings, was both popular and critically acclaimed. Bill usually generated the ideas, which were then developed in collaboration. He performed the technical research that Vera later incorporated into the writing of the story.

After her husband's death, Vera continued to write similar types of novels that depict young people accepting responsibility beyond their years and coming to terms with maturity. Both regularly contributed stories to periodicals including *McCall's* and *Woman's Day.* Collections of C. manuscripts are at the KERLAN COLLECTION, University of Minnesota, Minneapolis, and at the University of North Carolina, Chapel Hill. In 1974 *Where the Lilies Bloom* was adapted for the screen and filmed by United Artists.

AWARDS: *Ellen Grae* (illustrated by Ellen RASKIN; *Horn Book* Honor List, 1967); *Where the Lilies Bloom* (illustrated by Jim Spanfeller; *Horn Book* Honor List, AMERICAN LIBRARY ASSOCIATION Notable Book, 1970, NEWBERY MEDAL Honor Book, National Book Award nomination, 1969); *Grover* (illustrated by Frederic Marvin; Finalist for the 1971 National Book Award, Children's Book Category, 1970); *Me Too* (ALA Notable Book, *New York Times* outstanding book, 1973); *The Whys and Wherefores of Littabelle Lee,* 1974 National Book Award nomination, Atheneum, (1973); *Dust of the Earth* (Golden Spur Award, Western Writers of America, Lewis CARROLL Shelf award, and *New York Times* outstanding book citation, 1975); *Queen of Hearts* 1979 National Book Award nomination (1978); Vera only: *Sweetly Sings the Donkey* (1986 Children's Choice Award, 1985); *Belle Pruitt* (Junior Library Guild selection, 1988)

FURTHER WORKS: *Lady Ellen Grae* (illustrated by E. Raskin, 1968); *The Mimosa Tree,* (1970); *I Would Rather Be a Turnip* (1971); *The Mock Revolt,* (1971); *Delpha Green and Company* (1972); *Trial Valley* (1977); *A Little Destiny* (1979); *The Kissimmee Kid* (1981); *Hazel Rye* (1983). Vera only: *Sugar Blue* (illustrated by Eric Nones (1984); *Moon Lake Angel* (1987)

BIBLIOGRAPHY: *Authors of Books for Young People,* 2nd edition, 1971; *Contemporary Authors,* volumes 73–76, 1978; *Fourth Book of Junior Authors,* 1978; *Twentieth-Century Children's Writers,* 1978; *Who's Who in America,* 41st edition, 1980. Obituaries: *Publishers Weekly,* September 18, 1981. *Children's Literature Review,* volume 6, 1984. *Twentieth-Century Children's Writers,* 3rd edition, 1989. *Horn Book,* October 1969, April 1970, October 1970, April 1971, October 1971, June 1973, December 1975, June 1979, October 1979; *New York Times Book Review,* May 2, 1971, *Publishers Weekly,* April 16, 1973, March 18, 1974; *Fourth Book of Junior Authors & Illustrators,* 1978. *Something about the Author,* vols. 22, 1981, 27 1982, (obit.), and 76, 1994

CRAIG M. LIEBERMAN

CLEMENS, Samuel Langhorne (pseud. Mark Twain)

Novelist and essayist, b. 30 November 1835, Florida, Missouri; d. 21 April 1910, Redding, Connecticut

C. spent his early years moving from one place to another with his family. At age five, his father died in Hannibal, Missouri, putting an end to C.'s schooling. He became an apprentice to his brother Orion, who ran a country paper called the *Missouri Courier.* C. maintained many different jobs in many places, including a job as an apprentice pilot on the Mississippi River. However, C.'s years in the newspaper business launched his writing career. By 1862, he worked as city editor of the *Enterprise* in Virginia City, Nevada. He wrote under the pseudonym "Mark Twain," which derived from a depth call used by Mississippi River pilots. His early writing included crude humor consisting of hoaxes and tall stories. He became a nationally known humorist after he published "*The Celebrated Jumping Frog of Calaveras County*" in a New York newspaper. Ironically, C. did not think so highly of this piece.

Innocents Abroad, which established C. as a writer, evolved after a tour to the Mediterranean and Palestine. It is during this time that C. met Olivia Langdon, whom he married in 1870. Olivia edited C.'s work very strictly. C. received his M.A. degree in 1888 and his L.L.D. from Yale in 1901 and from the University of Missouri in 1902. Oxford University awarded C. these same degrees in 1907. He was so proud of his gown from Oxford that he wore it to his daughter Clara's wedding.

Much of C.'s work never was published until he was near his death. He is most famous for his juvenile books *The Adventures of Tom Sawyer* (1876) and *Adventures of Huckleberry Finn* (1884). It has been said about C.'s style that he wrote as he talked—for the ear more than for the eye. While perennially popular among young readers, adults discern the author's stinging social commentary as well. *Adventures of Huckleberry Finn* is frequently attacked for C.'s use of racial epithets despite Huck's efforts to help Jim, the runaway slave, escape to freedom.

FURTHER WORKS: *The Celebrated Jumping Frog of Calaveras County and Other Sketches* (1867); *Innocents Abroad* (1869); *Roughing It* (1872); *Mark Twain's Sketches: New and Old* (1875); *The Prince and the Pauper* (1882); *Tom Sawyer Abroad* (1894); *Personal Recollections of Joan of Arc* (1896); *Tom Sawyer: Detective* (1897); *The Man That Corrupted Hadleyburg* (1900); *Mark Twain's Autobiography* (1924)

For a fuller treatment of the life and career of C., see Steven R. Serafin, general editor, *The Continuum Encyclopedia of American Literature* (New York: Continuum, 1999), pp. 198–205.

JODI PILGRIM

CLIFFORD, Eth
Author, b. 15 October 1915, New York City

C., author of children's fiction and nonfiction, began writing at an early age after the death of her father. She found solace in making up stories and having the power to create situations and characters. After getting married and having children, C.'s husband suggested that she write down the stories that she was telling their children at bedtime. C. took her husband's advice and launched her career as a children's author. C.'s *The Rocking Chair Rebellion* (1978) was adapted for film by NBC television and her book, *Red Is Never a Mouse* was a Best Children's Book selection for both *Saturday Review* and the *New York Times* in 1961. *The Remembering Box* (1985) uses gentle prose to recall Joshua's memories of the times he spent with his grandmother. C. uses the device of a memory box to store the boy's reminiscences of things they shared; as he looks at each item, Joshua is helped to remember the special bond he had with his grandmother.

FURTHER WORKS: *Wild One*, 1974; *Help, I'm a Prisoner in the Library*, 1979; *Harvey's Horrible Snake Disaster*, 1984; *I Never Wanted to Be Famous*, 1986; *Summer of the Dancing Horse*, 1991

BIBLIOGRAPHY: *Something about the Author,* vol. 92, 1997

MICHAEL O'LAUGHLIN

CLIFTON, Lucille
Author and poet, b. 27 June 1936, Depew, New York

Reared to prize literacy and the grace of oral language, Thelma Lucille Clifton was the first member of her family to attend college. She lost her scholarship at Howard University by her own self-characterized lack of studying due to her sense of isolation. Although completing her college degree in 1955 at Fredonia State Teachers College in New York, it was there that she began her involvement with others who would encourage her writing, including her future husband.

However, her six children and fifteen years separated this time from the publication of her first book of POETRY for adults, *Good Times* (1969), a book that was cited by the *New York Times* as one of the Ten Best Books of the year. C. also won a National Endowment for the Arts Award that year (and again in 1970 and 1972). Nineteen-seventy also saw C. publishing her first book for children, *The Black ABCs,* a book of alphabet poems. She would soon become one of the premiere writers of children's poetry and fiction, and one of the few authors writing books with AFRICAN AMERICAN protagonists.

Continuing to write her prize-winning adult poetry (being named the Poet Laureate of Maryland in 1979–82, and nominated for the Pulitzer Prize for poetry in 1980 and 1988, and the Lannan Literacy Award for Poetry in 1996), C. began her Everett Anderson series, books of prose poetry that provide glimpses into the life of Everett Anderson, a young African American boy who lives his life with joy, fear, and triumph. *Some of the Days of Everett Anderson* (1970), the first book in the series, gives us the first look at a character whom audiences would follow through his mother's pregnancy (*Everett Anderson's Nine Month Long,* 1978), his mother's possible remarriage (*Everette Anderson's 1, 2, 3,* 1977), and his father's death (*Everett Anderson's Goodbye,* 1983). *Everett Anderson's Goodbye,* the touching story of Everett Anderson's progression through the five psychological stages that Elisabeth Kübler-Ross and others associate with grief (denial, anger, bargaining, depression, and acceptance) in haunting verse, was honored with the CORETTA SCOTT KING AWARD in 1984.

C., who cites her children as an inspiration for her writing, has also written many other books outside of the Everett Anderson series. *My Friend Jacob* (1980) details the relationship between a young African American boy and his white

neighbor with a mental disability (see THE DIS-
ABLED IN CHILDREN'S AND YOUNG ADULT LITER-
ATURE). *Lucky Stone* (1979) is a multigenerational story, deeply entrenched in the oral
tradition that shaped her childhood. C. has also
created more books of poetry for her juvenile
readers including *Dear Creator: A Week of
Poems for Young People and Their Teachers*
(1997).

Possessing honorary degrees from both the
University of Maryland and Towson State University, C. has continued to write her exquisite
poetry for both children and adults. She currently
lives and writes in Maryland, where she is a distinguished professor of Humanities at St. Mary's
College of Maryland.

FURTHER WORKS: *The Boy Who Didn't Believe
in Spring* (1973); *Good, Says Jerome* (1973); *My
Brother Fine with Me* (1975); *Three Wishes*
(1976)

BIBLIOGRAPHY: *Major Authors and Illustrators
for Children and Young Adults* (1993); *The Fifth
Book of Junior Authors and Illustrators* (1983);
Twentieth-Century Children's Writers (1978)

GWYNNE ELLEN ASH

CLIMO, Shirley
Author, b. 25 November 1928, Cleveland Ohio

C.'s childhood was filled with stories—those told
by her mother, herself a children's author, as well
as those she made up to amuse herself. She later
used her STORYTELLING skills as a scriptwriter
for a weekly radio show for children, FAIRYTALE
Theatre which ran from 1949 to 1953. In the late
seventies she wrote travel and HUMOR articles for
adult magazines.

A visit to Cornwall inspired her first book, a
collection of Cornish FOLKLORE called *Piskies,
Spriggans and Other Magical Beings* (1981).
Folklore and legends are the basis of many of
Climo's works. *A Cobweb Christmas* published
in 1982 is a PICTURE BOOK that retells a German
legend explaining the hanging of tinsel on Christmas trees. Climo continues in the "why" genre
with *King of the Birds,* published in 1991. This
title was the first of several joint efforts between
Climo and illustrator Ruth Heller.

Climo is perhaps best known for her picture-
book retellings of Cinderella variants. She has re-

searched hundreds of different versions of the
Cinderella story form around the world. *The
Egyptian Cinderella,* published in 1989, is set in
6th century Egypt and features a Greek slave girl,
Rhodopis, who in fact did live and marry an
Egyptian pharaoh. *The Korean Cinderella* followed in 1993 and was a retelling based on a tale
popular in Korea for centuries. This Cinderella is
aided by a frog, a sparrow and a black ox. Both
these works are illustrated by Ruth Heller. *The
Irish Cinderlad* (1996) includes both a magical
being, this time a bull, and the prerequisite "shoe
test"—in this version, a boot.

Using her research on legends and myths from
around the world, C. wrote *A Treasury of Princesses; Princess Tales from around the World*
(1996) and *A Treasury of Mermaids: Mermaid
Tales from around the World* (1997). *Atalanta's
Race* (1996) and *Stolen Thunder* (1994) are also
picture books based on myths and both are illustrated by Alexander Koshkin. *The Little Red Ant
and the Great Big Crumb* (1995) is a Mexican
tale retold by Climo and based on a fable found
in Spain and France. Spanish words in the text
add a Mexican flavor to this humorous story.

Climo has also written chapter books, *Gopher,
Tanker and the Admiral* (1984) and *T.J.'s Ghost*
(1989) are both ADVENTURE STORIES. *A Month of
Seven Days* (1987) is a historical novel set during
the American Civil War.

Branching out to nonfiction, she wrote three
travel guides for school-age readers illustrated
with photographs by George ANCONA. These are
City!: New York (1990) *City!: San Francisco*
(1990), and *City!: Washington D.C.* (1991). All
include suggestions to young readers for interesting sights to see and things to do.

FURTHER WORKS: *Someone Saw a Spider: Spider
Facts and Folktales,* 1985; *The Match between
the Winds,* 1991

BIBLIOGRAPHY: *Something about the Author,* vol.
77, 1994

LINDA GOLDMAN

CLYMER, Eleanor
Author, b. 7 January 1906, New York City

C. has written books on a variety of topics, concentrating mostly on REALISTIC FICTION. Through
her work she addresses the problems of young

children. Ideas for C.'s books often came from personal sources. For example, her son inspired *Treasure at First Base* (1950) and *Chester* (1954), while her experiences in the city inspired *The Latch-key Club* (1949) and *The Trolley Car Family* (1947). In *My Brother Stevie* (1967), C. describes a young girl's despair as she watches her younger brother slipping into difficulties when he joins a gang of troubled boys. *Luke Was There* (1973) is a spellbinding book about a child and a teacher in a special education class. C. wrote nonfiction for a science SERIES including *The Case of the Missing Link* (1962). She also wrote under the pseudonyms Janet Bell and Elizabeth Kinsey.

FURTHER WORKS: *A Yard for John,* 1943; *The Spider, the Cave, and the Pottery Bowl,* 1971; *The Get-away Car,* 1978; *The Horse in the Attic,* 1983

BIBLIOGRAPHY: *Something about the Author,* vol. 85, 1996

JODI PILGRIM

COATSWORTH, Elizabeth
Poet and storyteller, b. 31 May 1893, Buffalo, New York; d. 31 August 1986, Nobleboro, Maine

By the age of twelve C. traveled with her family to California, Europe, and Egypt. She had lived many years on a farm in Nobleboro, Maine, overlooking a lake at the end of a country road, where many of her novels are set. C. went to Buffalo Seminary and graduated in 1911. She then went on to Vassar College where she attained a bachelor's degree in 1915. C. also attended Radcliffe College. She received her Master of Arts at Columbia University in 1916. After completion of her Master of Arts she traveled with her sister to the Orient. C. began her writing career as a poet, but has achieved recognition as a writer of children's books. The first publications were volumes of adult poetry, *Fox Footprints* (1923); *Atlas and Beyond* (1924); and *Compass Rose* (1929). Stories appeared in *Dial* and *Atlantic Monthly.* In 1927, her first book for children, *The Cat and the Captain,* was written as result of challenge from Louise Seaman Bechtel. The second book for children, *The Cat Who Went to Heaven,* received the NEWBERY MEDAL in 1931 where she was first recognized. This second book was based on Japanese FOLKLORE and telling of an artist and his cat.

Since that time, C. has written over ninety books. Settings include Canada, Egypt, Guatemala, Japan, France, Greenland, and the West Indies, as well as many regions of the United States. It is quite obvious that her travels influenced her writings immensely. She shares with us through her writings the places where she has traveled and what she has experienced in creative and imaginative ways.

C., the perceptive impressionist, did not say much about who she was or about her own works, but her objective for writing was stated as such: "Any book should in some way sharpen the reader's appetite for living, whether the reader be seven or seventy." She also stated that, "An author should write for children about the things which are of sharpest interest to his own imagination." Critics say she is one of the most skillful. They feel that writing so many books for all ages taught her always to write clearly, using the best words for each situation. She is an author who is revered for her brilliant work.

AWARDS: ALA NEWBERY MEDAL, 1931, for *The Cat Who Went to Heaven;* Litt.D., University of Maine, 1955; L.H.D., New England College, 1958; Children's Spring Book Festival Honor Award, 1971, for *Under the Green Willow.* C. was the American candidate for Hans Christian ANDERSEN Medal in 1968, and was one of the runner-ups for this award. *The Cat Who Went to Heaven* is listed by *Horn Book* magazine as one of the thirty children's books every adult should know.

BIBLIOGRAPHY: HOPKINS, Lee Bennett, *Pauses: Autobiographical Reflections of 101 Creators of Children's Books,* 1995; Kuhn, Doris Young (1969); *Elizabeth Coatsworth. Perceptive Impressionist.* Elementary English, 46, 8, 991–1007; *Contemporary Authors,* new revision series, vol. 4

ANNALEE HAMILTON

COBB, Vicki
Author, b. 19 August 1938, New York City

C. believes it is her job to present the world in a manner that is engaging to her readers. She achieves this goal by writing hands-on science books for children as well as by conducting science demonstrations for teachers. C. credits childhood experiences for her hands-on approach to science and her interest in books. She grew up in an environment in which children learned by doing things, which method she still stands by today. C. has been praised for making science fun for children.

FURTHER WORKS: *Science Experiments You Can Eat* (1972); *Bet You Can't! Science Impossibilities to Fool You* (1980, Children's Science Book Award); *The Secret Life of School Supplies* (Washington Irving Children's Book Choice Award for nonfiction); *Lots of Rot* (1981); *Fun & Games: Stories Science Photos Tell*

JODI PILGRIM

COERR, Eleanor
Author, b. 29 May 1922, Kamsack, Saskatchewan, Canada

C. tells fictional stories to children while enlightening them about the lifestyles of children from various parts of the world. C. attended the University of Saskatchewan and graduated from Kadel Airbrush school in 1945, American University in 1969 with a B.A. and University of Maryland with an M.L.S. in 1971. In her career, she has been an editor, writer, lecturer, and librarian. She married Wymberley De Renne Coerr, a diplomat and United States ambassador to South American countries. Always an avid reader, C.'s interest in children's books evolved into writing for children. Her journeys provided her with the opportunities to experience countries in a manner that served as research for her books. She spent nine years in the Orient, which resulted in the writings *Circus Day in Japan* (1958), *The Mystery of the Golden Cat* (1968), and *Twenty-Five Dragons* (1971). She likes to think that she is informing young readers about the real lives of children who live in Asia. Her husband's career afforded her the opportunity to visit Ecuador where she established the first children's library. Two of C.'s most well-known works for children are *Sadako and the Thousand Cranes* (1977) and *Sadako* (1993), a PICTURE BOOK. These works tell the story of Sadako and her battle against the "atom bomb disease." Japanese legend shares the belief that the making of a thousand paper cranes can grant an ill person's wish to recover. C.'s story is about the coming together of a young girl's friends in her struggle to live. The author wrote the story because she felt that telling the story of one little girl would have more of an impact than statistics alone in the bombing of Hiroshima. C. also authored several I Can Read Books

including, *The Big Balloon* (1981), *The Bell Ringer and the Pirates* (1983), and *The Josefina Story Quilt* (1986).

AWARDS: The INTERNATIONAL READING ASSOCIATION and the CHILDREN'S BOOK COUNCIL awarded the Children's Choice Award to *The Big Balloon Race* in 1982. *Sadako and the Thousand Paper Cranes* received the West AUSTRALIA Book Award and OMAR Award in 1982. *The Josefina Story Quilt* was recognized as an ALA *Booklist* Children's Editor's Choice in 1986

FURTHER WORKS: *Biography of a Giant Panda,* (1974); *Biography of Jane Goodall,* (1976); *Twenty-Five Dragons,* (1971); *Chang's Paper Pony,* (1989); *Mieko and the Fifth Treasure,* (1993); *Buffalo Bill and the Pony Express,* (1995)

NANCY HORTON

COHEN, Barbara
Author, b. 15 March 1932 Asbury Park, New Jersey; d. 22 November 1992, Bridgewater, New Jersey

C. graduated from Barnard College and then received a masters degree from Rutgers University in 1957 while teaching high school English. Rearing her family was the main focus of her life until 1972 when her first book was published. *A Carp in the Bathtub,* which dealt with a family's humorous conflict over the fish to be served during the Passover meal, was an instant success and has become a modern classic.

Her own childhood experiences, especially growing up Jewish in America influenced much of her writing. "I understand that everything I write grows out of my own experience. It has nowhere else to come from." The theme of being an outsider is seen in several of Cohen's novels including *The Innkeeper's Daughter,* published in 1979, which also reflects her memories of the years when her own family ran an inn. Young female protagonists who are in one way or another different from their peers, are also found in *Where's Florrie?* (1976); *People like Us,* (1987), and *Seven Daughters and Seven Sons* (1982). Issues of Jewish identity and survival are explored in both her PICTURE BOOKS and novels including *Bitter Herbs* (1976) and *King of the Seventh Grade* (1982), which won the National Jewish Book Award.

Perhaps her most well-known book, *Molly's Pilgrim,* published in 1983, describes the experiences of a young Russian Jew, recently arrived in America and her classroom trials as a modern day "pilgrim." The movie version of this picture book received an Academy Award in 1986 in the short subject category. *Make a Wish Molly,* published in 1993, continues the story of Molly.

Cohen's biblical retellings include *I Am Joseph* (1980), which was an AMERICAN LIBRARY ASSOCIATION Notable Book and *David, A Biography* (1993). This latter work was based on research in history, politics, and archeology and shows a colorful and very human religious leader, whose influence is still reflected in today's culture.

AWARDS: *Unicorns in the Rain* (1980) and *Seven Daughters for Seven Sons* (1982) were named ALA's Best Books for Young Adults. *Thank You Jackie Robinson* (1974) and *Gooseberries to Oranges* (1982) were cited as ALA's Notable Children's Books. Cohen received the Association of Jewish Libraries' Best Picture Book Award for *Yussel's Prayer* (1981) as well as their Sydney TAYLOR Body-of-Work Award. Cohen was inducted into the New Jersey Literary Hall of Fame in 1992

FURTHER WORKS: *The Binding of Issac* (1978); *Fat Jack* (1980); *Lovely Vassillisa* (1980); *Queen for a Day* (1981); *The Demon Who Would Not Die* (1982); *Lovers' Games* (1983); *Here Comes the Purim Players* (1984); *Roses* (1984); *The Secret Grove* (1985); *Coasting* (1985); *Four Canterbury Tales* (1987); *The Christmas Revolution* (1987); *First Fast* (1987); *Headless Roommate* (1987); *The Orphan Game* (1988); *The Donkey's Story* (1988); *People Like Us* (1989); *Tell Us Your Secret* (1989); *The Long Way Home* (1990); *213 Valentines* (1991); *Robin Hood and Little John* (1995); *The Chocolate Wolf* (1996)

LINDA GOLDMAN

COHEN, Daniel
Author, b. 12 March 1936, Chicago, Illinois

C. writes for children and YOUNG ADULTS on a variety of topics that usually deal with the supernatural, extraterrestrials, and other unexplained phenomena. He does not proclaim much of what he writes about to be true in a literal sense. His intent in writing for children is to help them understand the nature of science and the fact that there are indeed many unanswered questions, and in the real world there is often no black or white.

He also writes books that appeal to readers who might not otherwise read for pleasure. This comes naturally to C. who himself was an average student who spent more time watching movies than reading.

FURTHER WORKS: *The World's Most Famous Ghosts,* 1978; *The Encyclopedia of Ghosts,* 1984; *Encyclopedia of the Strange,* 1985; *UFOs—the Third Wave,* 1988; *The Headless Roommate and Other Tales of Terror,* 1980; *Carl Sagan: Superstar Scientist,* 1987

BIBLIOGRAPHY: *Something about the Author,* vol. 70, 1993

MICHAEL O'LAUGHLIN

COHEN, Miriam
Author, b. 14 October 1926, Brooklyn, New York

At seventeen, C. went to Greenwich Village to become an artist—"a painter, a poet, a teller of stories on paper." She learned from her first husband, a photographer, that being an artist was like any other job, you had to work at it every day. She did not put this idea into practice for several years, however.

C. considered writing a children's book about her oldest son's experiences in nursery school following the death of her husband. When she remarried, C. was still not writing but was following the advice she now gives to writing classes. "Keep watching everything . . . Take memory pictures . . . you might need them for a book someday."

When C. began writing and decided her first manuscript was ready to submit, she was living in New York City. C. hand-delivered it to the nearest publisher. The editor she met convinced C. that she was a writer. She suggested C. read as many children's books as she could to help find her own voice so she could produce something unique. Many years and many rewrites later, her first book, *Will I Have a Friend?* (1967) was published. Jim, the main character in this book and several that followed, is a composite of all three of her sons. *Will I Have a Friend?* was C.'s thank you to all the caring teachers who taught her children. This was important to C. because as a young child, she dreaded school. In fact, *The New Teacher* (1972), about a class changing teachers during the year, was originally entitled "The Mean Teacher," about her own first-grade experience.

C. is best known for her school-based PICTURE BOOKS for younger children. Starting with her first book, she has used her scrapbook-like memory to write over twenty-five books about experiences and fears common to all children. Her books are recommended in texts for teacher preparation and by LIBRARIANS as vehicles for talking to children about everything from taking a test *(First Grade Takes a Test,* 1971) to what to do on a museum field trip if you are lost *(Lost in the Museum,* 1979). Her books have stood the test of time as many are still in print from the late 1960s and 1970s. Though the text is simple, the message for children is clear and reassuring. C.'s works are included in THE KERLAN COLLECTION at the University of Minnesota and the DE GRUMMOND REFERENCE COLLECTION at the University of Southern Mississippi. Several of her books have been Junior Literary Guild selections.

FURTHER WORKS: *Born to Dance Samba,* 1984; *Don't Eat Too Much Turkey,* 1996; *Down in the Subway,* 1998; *Jim's Dog Muffin,* 1984; *Mimmy and Sophie Stories,* 1999

BIBLIOGRAPHY: *School Library Journal,* March 1979, p. 120; *Something about the Author,* vol. 29, 1982; *Something about the Author Autobiographical Series,* vol. 2, 1991

SHARON HARTMAN

COLE, Babette
Author and illustrator, b. 10 September 1949, Jersey, Channel Islands, England

C. writes and illustrates for young readers with zany happenings through her words and pictures in an idiosyncratic style that sometimes borders on irreverent and always entertains. C. graduated with honors from Canterbury College of Art with a B.A. in 1974. She grew up with few childhood friends but a fierce love for animals, especially her horse, and the exploration of England's Channels Islands where she lived. She also loved to read, but would rewrite and redraw the books if she did not like the published version. In her youth, she aspired to be a veterinarian but knew she lacked the science background. Before C. began writing and illustrating children's books she supported herself by illustrating greeting cards and books. One of C.'s first children's works was *Nungu and the Hippopotamus* (1978),

one of a trio. The Nungu books are based on myths she heard while living in Africa for nine months. Intense AFRICAN landscapes provide the setting for these funny, yet unlikely occurrences. *The Trouble with Mum* (1984), later published as *The Trouble with Mom* (1984), introduced C.'s engaging ability to exaggerate family relations and happenings with quirky humor. Other works include fractured FAIRY TALES, weird superheroes, and hilarious perspectives of health and body works. Fairy tales include *Princess Smartypants* (1986) and *King Change-a-lot* (1989). The adventures of twisted superheroes are *Tarzanna* (1991) and *Supermoo!* (1992). And *Mommy Laid an Egg!; or, Where Do Babies Come From?* (1993) is an example of how C. presents the humorous side of health topics. Highly productive and always providing a laugh, C.'s works permeate the reading lists of light-hearted literature.

AWARDS: *Nungu and the Hippopotamus* received the Children's Book of the Year, Child Study Association of America in 1980. *Princess Smartypants* was awarded the Kate GREENAWAY MEDAL Commendation in 1986. *Prince Cinders* was also recognized with the Kate Greenaway Medal Commendation in 1987. The Kurt Maschler Award went to *Drop Dead* in 1996. C. also illustrated Kenneth GRAHAME's *The Wind in the Willows Pop-Up Book* (1983), which was selected a New York Public Library's Children Book

FURTHER WORKS: *Basil Brush of the Yard* (1977); *Nungu and the Elephant* (1980); *Nungu and the Crocodile* (1982); *The Trouble with Gran* (1988); *The Trouble with Grandad* (1988); *Three Cheers for Errol!* (1988); *The Silly Book* (1989); *Cupid* (1989); *The Trouble with Uncle* (1992); *Winni Allfours* (1993); *Dr. Dog* (1994); *The Bad Good Manners Book* (1995); illustrator only: *Your Dog* (1975); *Grasshopper and the Unwise Owl* (1979); *Grasshopper and the Poisoned River* (1982); *The Vampire's Holiday,* (1992)

NANCY HORTON

COLE, Brock
Author and illustrator, b. 29 May 1938, Charlotte, Minnesota

After receiving his B.A. from Kenyon College and his Ph.D. from the University of Minnesota, C. taught college English and philosophy until 1975. He then began writing and illustrating children's books full-time. Because he had no formal training as an artist, he studied and learned from the works of major illustrators he admired including Ernest Howard SHEPARD and Maurice SENDAK.

In 1979 he published his first PICTURE BOOK, *The King at the Door,* the story of a king disguised as a beggar, who is rebuffed by all but the lowly chore boy. Like several of Cole's later works, the theme of recognition and being seen for "what we are" is set against a cold unresponsive adult world. *No More Baths* and *Nothing But a Pig,* published in 1980 and 1981 were both written and illustrated by Cole. He received a Parents Choice Award in 1986 for his picture book, *The Giant's Toe,* a spoof of the "Jack and the Beanstalk" tale.

Cole entered the world of young adult novels with *The Goats* in 1987. Misfits thrown purposely together on a small island during summer camp, the two teenage main characters try to survive against cruel peers and irresponsible adults. Cole believes that readers of all ages identify with being isolated and nerdish and wanting to fit in but not being able to. *The Goats* presents a pessimistic view of society and adults in particular; a "fallen world" in which the young protagonists must manuever and survive.

In 1989 Cole published another YOUNG ADULT novel, *Celine,* featuring a teenage girl with an artistic bent and the young boy she befriends. As in *The Goats,* the characters in *Celine* are survivors. Cole writes about young people caught between "innocence and maturity," children who, ready or not, must enter the adult world without much support from the adults around them. Cole paints a less than positive picture of contemporary society, yet his stories end on a hopeful note. Misfit or loner characters don't end up failing. They succeed, with help from each other, while holding onto their openness, sensitivity, HUMOR and hope.

AWARDS: *The Goats* was named an AMERICAN LIBRARY ASSOCIATION (ALA) best book for young adults, ALA Notable Book and a *New York Times* Notable Book in 1987. It also received the Carl Sandburg Award, Friends of Chicago Public Library in 1988.

FURTHER WORKS: written and illustrated by Cole: *The Winter Wren* 1984; *Alpha and the Dirty Baby* 1991; *The Facts Speak for Themselves,* 1998. Il-

lustrated by Cole: *The Indian in the Cupboard* (BANKS) 1980; *Gaffer Sampson's Luck* (Walsh) 1984

BIBLIOGRAPHY: Alderdice, Kit. "Brock Cole: Children Braving an Adult World." *Publishers Weekly,* Feb. 17, 1997; *Children's Literature Review,* vol 18. 1989; McDonnell, Christine. "New Voices, New Visions: Brock Cole." *Horn Book,* Sep./Oct. 1989; *Something about the Author* vol. 72, 1993

LINDA GOLDMAN

COLE, Joanna
Author, b. 11 August 1944, Newark, New Jersey

Best known as a prolific writer of science for young readers, C. always loved the subject of science and the art of making it interesting. As a student she would decorate her reports with humorous additions and drawings. She was always an avid reader and a keeper of diaries. Her father was a great influence in her development as a writer; not because of his writing or reading abilities—he was dyslexic and struggled in that area—but because he was a great storyteller and instilled the value of hard work in his daughter. Although C. wrote regularly, it never occurred to her as a child that she could have a career in writing. She attended the University of Massachusetts at Amherst and Indiana University–Bloomington; she received a B.A. in 1967 from The City College of New York. C. taught school and was an elementary school librarian and editor before she began writing as a professional.

C. piques the interest of young readers by engaging them in the study of science, sometimes in fictional settings as in the Magic School Bus books, which she creates with illustrator Bruce DEGEN. Fictional elements and natural elementary-age dialogue are present in these volumes, but more importantly the facts are presented in an understandable fashion. C. invites her readers to journey along with her as she travels with Ms. Frizzle's class on fantastical field trips. In each book, the magic school bus detours to fictional adventures to precisely, yet simply, explain a particular area of science such as the water system, the earth, human body, ocean floor, and dinosaurs. Through exaggeration of character and the addition of HUMOR, C. succeeds in teaching science while entertaining. Her explanations are impeccable as she accomplishes the task of simplifying technical subjects for young audiences while using cutting-edge research. The popular character of Ms. Frizzle is an exaggeration of one of the author's and the illustrator's former teachers. The Magic School Bus books have been transformed into an animated series on PBS television with C. and Degen as consultants, further catapulting the books' popularity. Other works by C. include nonfiction books such as *Cockroaches* (1971), her first publication, and *My Puppy Is Born* (1973); anthologies including *Anna Banana: 101 Jump Rope Rhymes* (1989) and *The Read-Aloud Treasury* with Stephanie Calmenson (1988); fiction such as *The Clown-Arounds* (1981), which caught the attention of editor Craig Walker and prompted him to approach C. with the idea for Ms. Frizzle and her science class.

C.'s fictional stories are based on folktales and personal experiences. *Bony-Legs* (1983) and *Doctor Change* (1986) are retellings of folktales. *Monster Manners* (1986) is reminiscent of C. and her best childhood friend while *Clown-Arounds* (1981) is based on family occurrences. C.'s subjects for nonfiction stem from her own curiosity and are developed by following her sense of argument, sequencing one idea after another to make sense. C. resides with her family in Connecticut.

AWARDS: Most of C.'s nonfiction science books have been recognized as Outstanding Science Trade Books for Children, National Science Teachers Association/CHILDREN'S BOOK COUNCIL; 1990 Eva L. Gordon Award from the American Nature Study Society, the 1991 *Washington Post*/Children's Book Guild nonfiction award, the David McCord Children's Literature Citation for her body of work. Child Study Association of America's Children's Books of the Year (1971) for *Cockroaches*, (1972) for *Giraffes at Home* and *Twins: The Story of Multiple Births*, (1973) for *My Puppy Is Born* and *Plants in Winter*, (1974) for *Dinosaur Story*, (1975) for *A Calf Is Born*, (1985) for *Large as Life: Nighttime Animals* and *The New Baby at Your House*. Golden Kite Honor citation for nonfiction (1984) for *How You Were Born*. *Boston Globe-Horn Book* Honor Book (1987) for *The Magic School Bus at the Waterworks*

FURTHER WORKS: *A Chick Hatches*. 1976. *Cuts, Breaks, Bruises, and Burns: How Your Body Heals*. 1985. *The Human Body: How We Evolved*. 1987. *The Magic School Bus inside the Human Body*. 1989. *The Magic School Bus on the Ocean Floor*. 1992. *You Can't Smell a Flower with Your Ear!: All About Your Five Senses*. 1994. *How I Was Adopted*. 1995. *The Magic School Bus and the Electric Field Trip*. 1997. *The Magic School Bus Explores the Senses*. 1999. *Fun on the Run: Travel Games and Songs*. 1999. Editor with Stephanie Calmenson: *Pin the Tail on the Donkey and Other Party Games*. 1993. *Six Sick Sheep: One Hundred Tongue Twisters*. 1993. *The Parents TM Book of Toilet Teaching*. 1983. With Calmenson: *Safe from the Start: Your Child's Safety from Birth to Age Five*. 1990

BIBLIOGRAPHY: *Children's Literature Review*, vol. 40, 1996; Cleghorn, Andrea, "Aboard the Magic School Bus," *Publishers Weekly*, January 25, 1991, vol. 238 i. 5; C., Joanna with Wendy Saul, *On the Bus with Joanna C.: A Creative Autobiography* 1996; *Something about the Author*, vol. 81, 1995

NANCY HORTON

COLE, William
Poet, anthologist, b. 20 November, 1919, Staten Island, New York; d. 26 July 2000, New York City

C.'s interest in reading and literature began when he was a teenager and has continued throughout his adult life. He says, "I'm never without something in my pocket to read." Although his formal education ended with high school, a job in a bookstore and a ravenous appetite for knowledge helped to continue his education informally. Cole ran a regimental newspaper while in the army during World War II and after his discharge as a decorated veteran, he went to work for Alfred A. Knopf as a publicity director. During this time, he put together a collection of cartoons from the magazine *Punch* and his career as an anthologist was begun.

Although C. has written and compiled several books for adults, the bulk of his works have been aimed at children. C., the father of four children, had his first children's book *Humorous Poetry for Children* published in 1955. Dozens more anthologies have followed over the course of many years. These collections of poetry have been immensely popular with his young readers; two of them, *I Went to the Animal Fair* (1958), and *Beastly Boys and Ghastly Girls* (1964), have been included in the AMERICAN LIBRARY ASSOCIATION's Notable Books. *Poem Stew* (1983) was a *READING RAINBOW* selection and a Children's Choice winner. C. is a poet in his own right as well, saying that writing poems for children is fun and when writing, he would be as silly as possible. This is reflected in the humorous nature of many of the anthologies he put together.

C. referred to himself as a pack rat, saying "It has been my habit, since I was a teenager, to clip and file away anything from a newspaper or magazine that struck my fancy." When putting together an anthology, whether POETRY, music, or humor, he would first go through his files, then head for the public library and second-hand bookstores searching for materials that would be a good fit. "An anthologist is someone who has a crushing enthusiasm for his subject. An anthology done without enthusiasm is like a TV dinner: frozen, tasteless, and quickly forgotten."

FURTHER WORKS: *Good Dog Poems* (1981); *Poem Stew* (1982); *Oh, What Nonsense!* (1990); *A Zooful of Poems* (1990); *A Zooful of Animals* (1992); *Have I Got Dogs!* (1996)

JENNIFER GERINGER

COLLIER, James Lincoln and Christopher

James Lincoln: Author, b. 27 June 1928, New York City. Christopher: Author, b. 29 January 1930, New York City

The C. brothers bring a family tradition of writing to their collaborations. Many other members of their family also write, but Christopher began as a teacher. He was educated at Clark University and earned graduate degrees from Columbia University. Christopher taught at both junior and senior high schools and as a history professor at Yale, Columbia, and the University of Connecticut. James attended Hamilton College, and then worked as a magazine editor and freelance writer. He has many books, both fiction and nonfiction to his credit, and is particularly noted for the fast pace of his contemporary YOUNG ADULT books.

The first joint effort of the C.s was *My Brother Sam Is Dead* (1974), a NEWBERY MEDAL Honor book. Christopher approached his brother with the idea of a historical fiction work for children. He had already written several books on American history, and felt that many of the history texts for children were too dry. James, a well-known author, was hard to convince, but they eventually worked out a system. Christopher usually starts with a topic and provides the background and his-

torical details. James creates the characters and plot and fleshes out the story. Their collaboration has created a number of highly successful books, many of them set during the Revolutionary War. *My Brother Sam Is Dead* is the story of the Meeker family, farmers in Connecticut when the war starts. Tim is eager to join his brother Sam, who has gone off to fight the British, but his father is against the rebellion. The family story helps readers understand that there are seldom clear-cut right and wrong sides to an issue such as war.

In *The Bloody Country* (1976), the story of the struggle of Connecticut settlers in the Wyoming Valley of Pennsylvania is interwoven with the relationship of young Ben and Joe Mountain, a slave. As the story progresses and Joe's future is in doubt, Ben comes to realize that freedom is something that should belong to all. No matter what the period of history, the C.s combine historic details that lend authenticity to the backgrounds of significant historical events with the personalities and action of a strong plot. The combination has produced many entertaining and enlightening books.

FURTHER WORKS: *The Winter Hero,* 1978; *Jump Ship to Freedom,* 1981; *War Comes to Willie Freeman,* 1983; *Who Is Carrie?,* 1984; *The Clock,* 1992

BIBLIOGRAPHY: Silvey, Anita, ed., *Children's Books and Their Creators,* 1995; *Something about the Author,* vol. 7, 1993

ANITA M. TROUT

COLLODI, Carlo

Author, b. 24 November 1826, Florence, Italy; d. 26 October 1890, Florence, Italy

Born Carlo Lorenzini, C. took his literary pen name from his mother's hometown. He was educated in Florence and entered a seminary, briefly studying for the priesthood before he began a career as a journalist. C. supported the revolutionary cause against Austria and served as a volunteer in 1848, and again in 1859. He founded a newspaper and later a magazine, wrote many educational texts, and translated Perrault's tales, but his real fame comes from a single work, *Le Avventure di Pinocchio* (The adventures of Pinocchio).

C. began writing for children in 1875, declaring that adults were too hard to please. *Giannettino* was created in 1876, but it was not until 1881, when C. was fifty-five, that *Pinocchio* was born. Originally published as a thirty-five chapter serial, it was published in book form in 1883. The story of a puppet boy who spends much of his time running away from and returning to his human father, Gepetto, *Pinocchio* is often rambling and inconsistent, but it is brightened by a wonderfully original premise and a wide range of colorful characters. The adventures are revealing of many children's fantasies and also of their fears, the most prevalent being that of a parent's love being withdrawn. Perhaps one of the reasons for *Pinocchio*'s enduring success is its constant reassurance that no matter what Pinocchio does, Gepetto will continue to love him and search for him. *Pinocchio*'s success as a story did not come during C.'s lifetime. It was translated into English and published in the United States in 1892, and has gone on to be translated into many languages, including Latin.

Variations and adaptations, including films, have been numerous, and have not always been true to the original; even so, they have not succeeded in quashing the spirit that made *Pinocchio* a classic. C. may have been only marginally successful as a writer, but his one true vision of childhood, as evidenced by a puppet, continues to endure.

ANITA M. TROUT

COLMAN, Hila
Author, b. Date unknown, New York City

C.'s books often contain experiences from her childhood. C. began writing for magazines and newspapers to earn a living. She published her first book, *The Big Step,* in 1957. She generally bases her books on people and places she has known. She focuses on an adolescent audience— her characters often confront tough problems at home and with peers. C. has also written under the pseudonym Teresa Crayder.

FURTHER WORKS: *The Girl from Puerto Rico* (1961) (Child Study Association of Americas Wel-Met Children's Book Award); *Mixed-Marriage Daughter* (1968); *Nobody Has to Be a Kid Forever* (1976) (Garden State Children's Book Award from the New Jersey Library Asso-

ciation); *Ethan's Favorite Teacher* (1975) (Junior Literary Guild selection); *Sometimes I Don't Love My Mother* (1977); *The Diary of a Frantic Kid Sister* (1973); *Tell Me No Lies* (1978); *Forgotten Girl* (1990); *The Double Life of Angela Jones* (1988); *Suddenly* (1987); *Weekend Sisters* (1985); *Nobody Told Me What I Need to Know* (1984)

JODI PILGRIM

COLUM, Padraic
Poet, playwright, author, b. 8 December 1881, Longford, Ireland; d. 12 January 1972, Enfield, Connecticut

C. was born in Ireland, but it was not until the age of seven, when his mother, brothers, and sister went to live in County Cavan with his grandmother that he began to hear the stories that are part and parcel of Irish tradition. His father had gone to America to find work, and so the family that was left in Ireland joined a large household that included aunts, uncles, and cousins as well. His education at home included Catholic religion, traditional songs and ballads, and many of the legends and stories of the little people and the early folk of Ireland. His formal education was accomplished at the Glasthule National School until he was sixteen or seventeen. By that time he was living in a suburb of Dublin, his father having returned from America and begun work as a railway station master. His mother died in 1897 and C. spent much time visiting relatives and began writing POETRY.

C. was founder and editor of the *Irish Review* and wrote plays for children. The novel, *A Boy in Eirinn* (1913), reveals what would later be C.'s strength. Many of the chapters are actually recountings of stories told to a boy who has been sent to stay with relatives after the breakup of his family.

In 1914, C. first came to the United States, and began to translate Irish stories into English. At the urging of an editor of the *New York Tribune,* C. submitted one of his stories, and launched a whole new aspect of his writing career. Three of his collections of stories, *The Golden Fleece and the Heroes who Lived before Achilles* (1921), *The Voyagers* (1925), and *The Big Tree of Bunlahy* (1933), were chosen as NEWBERY MEDAL Honor books.

In 1923, C. was invited by the Hawaiian legislature to visit the islands and give shape to their legends. This venture produced two volumes of collected stories for adults, *At the Gateways of the Day* (1924), and *The Bright Islands* (1925). C. continued to produce books for children, including two original works, *The Peep-Show Man* and *The Girl Who Sat by the Ashes* (both 1925). His collections of stories have the strengths of the oral tradition—strong narrative line and strong characters. As he wrote them, the language seems dated now, but C.'s legacy to children's literature is the collection and preservation of a body of stories that can still be enjoyed and that provide a wonderful resource for storytellers.

FURTHER WORKS: *The King of Ireland's Son,* (1916); *The Children Who Followed the Piper,* (1922); *The Fountain of Youth,* (1927)

ANITA M. TROUT

COMENIUS, John Amos

Author, b. 1592, Moravia; d. 1670

With a belief in the possibility of a Utopian society, C. thought that observation through the senses, as one might see in ILLUSTRATION, should precede explanations in words. Therefore, his *Orbis Sensualium Pictus* was a natural way for C. to work with students who could not read as he was restructuring a school in Hungary. *Orbis Pictus: The World Illustrated,* was translated into English in 1658 and is considered the first PICTURE BOOK specifically for children as it contained numerous woodcuts of everyday objects. Having also lived in Poland, England, and Sweden, C., a Moravian bishop, wrote numerous educational books and texts as he worked to reform education. Among these, *Janua Linguarum Reserata* (The gate of languages unlocked, 1631) was highly regarded as an advance in the method of teaching languages. In 1990, the NATIONAL COUNCIL OF TEACHERS OF ENGLISH established the ORBIS PICTUS AWARD for outstanding nonfiction for children.

JANELLE B. MATHIS

COMIC BOOKS AND GRAPHIC NOVELS

Comic books were first published in the 1920s and have developed by a series of creative and technical peaks and valleys. The comic book's nineteenth century ancestors were illustrated books, like German satirist Wilhelm Busch's (1832–1908) *Max und Moritz,* and American newspaper novelty comic strips, like *Little Nemo in Slumberland.* While newspaper strips originated as an appeal to general (adult) readership, comic books targeted younger readers from the start.

Most of the conventions of comic books were developed within the newspaper comic-strip medium: boundaried panels combining text with image, speech balloons, onomatopoeia, and a lexicon of visual puns. The syntactic unit of the comic book (like the comic strip) requires the reader to synthesize text and image, not merely to read the words or study the pictures. An understanding of comics conventions, including speech balloons (however minimally stylized) and thought bubbles, is presupposed on the reader's part. Visual puns, like the bright-idea light bulb, have become standardized as well. Onomatopoeia is used generally in comics: the "squeak" of a new shoe is expressed as are the sounds of superhuman flesh hitting steel with a "kapow." Literacy, then, is required by comic book readers who must decode written language, synthesize new with formerly withheld information, and reason abstractly.

Originally printed on cheap pulp paper and available by mail subscription and at neighborhood stores, comic books have been affordable to middle-class children from the start. Perhaps because of this cheapness and "extracultural" availability, as well as because of the crudeness and fantastic exuberance of so much of the content, comic books received little critical approval by American educators and aesthetes during their first half century. In Japan, however, comic-book lending libraries were institutionalized by the 1930s.

The earliest comic books mined the same veins of HUMOR as contemporary newspaper strips: silly families, rude children and anthropomorphic animals. However, the medium need not be limited to such lowbrow "funnies" and it quickly evolved to support more diverse content. In the 1930s, Americans Jerry Siegel and Joe Schuster created Superman, the first of a host of superheroes introduced through comics to American and international culture. Over the next five decades Batman, Spider-Man, X-Men, and other fantastic fighters of Good moved from comics to film to television and electronic format and back into print. Writers, like Stan Lee, developed into editors employing several artists to work on the same superhero series so that the supply of stories seemed endless. Also from the 1930s and on through the decades, filmmakers like Walt DISNEY produced and distributed comic-book versions of their screen stars' cartoon adventures.

In Belgium, HERGÉ created Tintin, a teenaged-boy adventurer, in 1929. Within a year, Tintin graduated from a weekly comic strip to book-length stories. In 1962, American children were introduced to him when Little, Brown published Hergé's work in a hardcover series. Today, Tintin is a staple of many American children's casual reading collections (and the object of politically correct criticism for his colonialism).

Captain America, first drawn by Jack Kirby, was one of many superheroes and regular heroes invented during World War II. Military daring, civilian intrigue, and patriotism were thematized in comic books in Allied, Axis, and even neutral countries.

After the war, American comic books foundered. Publishers had oversaturated their youthful market with too many creations and too frequent spinoffs of nascent series—jading the youngsters they sought to engage. However, the Japanese comics industry flourished. Osamu Tezuka, as an art school student in 1947, began to develop the cinematically inspired style that, by the 1980s, became recognized internationally as "manga."

In the U.S., the Cold War affected comic book plots. Horror became the newly favored genre of artists and some publishing houses. Warned that comics would tempt youth toward lives of delinquency, socially conservative legislators, educators, and parents threatened to kill the industry. Publishers responded by adopting a Comics Code Authority, averting government CENSORSHIP at the expense of diluting the efforts of those whose creativity might have found a more mature audience than the traditional child reader. Comic books became derivative, offering emasculated superheroes and canonically "safe" literary classics abridged and regurgitated in comic book format. Little Lulu, however, emerged during the 1950s as a genuinely endearing and child-appropriate heroine. And chronically teenaged Archie

began a climb of popularity that did not peak for more than twenty years.

In the 1960s and 1970s, so-called underground comix by R. Crumb and others gained readership among college students. Subject matter and language were directed at "adult" sensibilities. Comic strips were collected in book form for younger (and older) readers. Charles SCHULZ's *Peanuts*—a strip that Schulz announced in December 1999 that he would no longer draw (he died soon thereafter, on February 12, 2000, and the strip no longer features new comics) in which no adult character has ever appeared—was popular in every venue from newspaper to book collection to stage to television screen. Walt Kelly's *Pogo* and Garry B. Trudeau's *Doonesbury* provided readers with near-profound insights when panels appeared in book format, as ongoing stories, rather than chopped up between days in the newspaper.

The 1980s brought the rise of the graphic novel, a more sophisticated and better produced comic book. Graphic novels from many countries treat themes that are standard comic book fare (ADVENTURE, romance, FANTASY) as well as more intellectual and nonfictional ones. Art Spiegelman's Holocaust survival story, *Maus*, won a special Pulitzer Prize in 1992, leading to its appearance on school reading lists. In 2000, Spiegelman and Françoise Mouly edited *Little Lit: Folklore and Fairy Tale Funnies.*

Increasing acceptance of graphics-driven literature by educators and librarians have made comic books available to a wider and more varied audience of readers. Perceptions of comic book aesthetics change with the times and growing sophistication of readers, too. Wendy and Richard Pini's Elfquest series, introduced nearly twenty years ago, is no longer a novelty item but has attained the status of fantasy classic. Jeff Bone's 1990s invention, *Bone*, provides heartwarming family reading fare not popularly associated with comic books.

Changes in society also get comic book treatment. James Robinson's nearly teenaged heroine tries to prove to her father that a girl is too worthy of inheriting his wizard powers *(Leave It to Chance: Shaman's Rain)*. Scott McCloud recapitulates American history and recent politics, through the eyes of an African American seventh grader, in *The New Adventures of Abraham Lincoln.*

At the start of the twenty-first century, Japanese manga is popular with American readers of all ages while *Uncanny X-Men* and *Archie* continuously appear in new adventures at corner stores here and abroad. Comic books have become a broad category of popular literature, outgrowing early perceptions of them as marginal reading material.

BIBLIOGRAPHY: Fleisher, Michael, *The Encyclopedia of Comic Book Heroes,* 1976; Goulart, Ron, *The Comic Book Reader's Companion: An A-to-Z Guide to Everyone's Favorite Art Form,* 1993; Harvey, Robert, *The Art of the Comic Book: An Aesthetic History,* 1996; Horn, Maurice, editor, *The World Encyclopedia of Comics,* 1976; McCloud, Scott, *The New Adventures of Abraham Lincoln,* 1998; n.a., *Understanding Comics: The Invisible Art,* 1993; Peeters, Benoit, *Tintin and the World of Hergé,* 1992; Robinson, James, *Leave It to Chance: Shaman's Rain,* 1997; Schodt, Frederik, *Manga! Manga! The World of Japanese Comics,* 1983; n.a., *Comics Journal: The Magazine of Comics News and Criticism,* 1976

FRANCISCA GOLDSMITH

CONE, Molly (Lamken) (joint pseud., Caroline More)
Author, b. 3 October 1918, Tacoma, Washington

C. grew up in Tacoma, Washington, the middle child among five brothers and sisters. C. remembers always believing she could be anything she wanted to be, and what she wanted to be was a writer. "In my mind, I always was [a writer]. As far back as I can remember, I thought of myself as a writer." C. was the editor of her high school yearbook before she began her formal education, which included a three-year stint at the University of Washington in Seattle. Later, C. went to work as an advertising copywriter where she sold advertising space and wrote copy. Her first stories for children were published in children's MAGAZINES. She began writing her first children's novel, *Only Jane,* in 1953; it was published in 1960. She has since written over forty fiction and nonfiction books for children.

C.'s writing was often inspired by events in her own life. She has gleaned ideas from personal childhood memories, her own children, and even family pets. Her first installment of what would later become a series, *Mishmash* (1962)—the story of a dog and his adventures—was based on the Cone's family dog named Tiny. *Mishmash* was named one of the one hundred outstanding books for young readers by the *New York Times* in 1962. C. has also written works that deal with her own Jewish heritage including: *Hear O Israel* (1972) and *The Mystery of Being Jewish: As Seen in the Lives of Nineteen People* (1989). The Association of Jewish Libraries gave C. the Sydney TAYLOR Book Award in 1972 for her general contributions in the field of Jewish literature for children. C.'s *Only Jane* (1962) was selected by the Library of Congress for magnetic tape for blind readers.

Cone's love of nature, and in particular the environment of her native Washington state, have inspired some of her more recent works. Published by Sierra Club Books for Children, *Come Back, Salmon: How a Group of Dedicated Kids Adopted Pigeon Creek and Brought It Back to Life* (1992) is the true story of a group of elementary school students in Washington who set out to clean a polluted river. C.'s subsequent environmental works include: *Listen to the Trees: Jews and the Earth* (1995) and *Squishy, Misty, Damp and Muddy: The In-between World of Wetlands* (1996).

C.'s rich variety in subject matter and writing style might best be explained by the author's own words: "I find that, old as I am, in a certain sense I have not stopped growing . . . while my intellect is an organ of narrow limitations, my inner world—perhaps it is my world of feeling—expands."

FURTHER WORKS: *Hurry Henrietta* (1966); *Annie Annie* (1969); *About Belonging* (1972); *About Learning* (1972); *Mishmash and the Sauerkraut Mystery* (1974); *Who Knows Ten? Children's Tales of the Ten Commandments* (1997)

BIBLIOGRAPHY: *Something about the Author,* vols. 1, 1971, and vol. 28 1982; *Contemporary Authors,* vol. 4

MICHAEL O'LAUGHLIN

CONFORD, Ellen
Author, b. 20 March 1942, New York City

C. enjoyed writing as early as third grade when her teacher encouraged her attempts at poetry. She developed her skills in high school by writing for the school paper, magazine, and yearbook. After high school, C. continued writing at Hofstra College while she worked as a proofreader and a salesperson. C. wrote her first book for young children when her son was four years of age. *Impossible, Possum* (1971) evolved after a trip to the library where she did not like any of the books she found. She decided she could write better stories than those available. The family of opossums in her first book later appeared in two more of her PICTURE BOOKS, including *Just the Thing, Geraldine* (1974) and *Eugene the Grave* (1978). C. then began to write stories for older children. C.'s characters are mostly contemporary teenagers, especially females, growing up in suburbia. Her books are known for their humorous characters and dialogues.

C. is praised for depicting situations familiar to her audience using an entertaining style based on funny characters and witty dialogue. Many of her themes build optimism and self-esteem, demonstrating to the reader that you should believe in yourself. C. once commented that she writes for children probably because she was a kid who loved to read.

AWARDS: *Impossible, Possum* was recognized as one of the best books of the year by *School Library Journal* in 1971. In 1974, *Just the Thing for Geraldine* was named one of the Children's Books of International Interest. *Me and the Terrible Two* earned recognition as one of the Library of Congress Children's Books of the Year in 1974 while *The Luck of Pokey Bloom* and *Dear Lovey Hart, I Am Desperate* appeared on the list of Child Study Association of America Books of the Year (1975). The AMERICAN LIBRARY ASSOCIATION named *The Alfred G. Graebner Memorial High School Handbook of Rules and Regulations* as one of the Best Books for Young Adults in 1976. *Hail, Hail, Camp Timberwood* won several AWARDS including: the Surrey School Award (1989), Pacific Northwest Young Reader's Choice Award (1981), and the California Young Reader's Medal (1982). *Lenny Kandell, Smart Aleck* was named one of *School Library Journal*'s Best Books of the Year in 1983 in addition to receiving a Parents' Choice Award. *Why Me?* (1985) and *A Royal Pain* (1986) also received Parents' Choice Awards. *If This Is Love, I'll Take Spaghetti* won both the South Carolina Young Adult Book Award in 1986–87 and the South Dakota Prairie Pasque Award in 1989

FURTHER WORKS: *You Never Can Tell* (1984); *A Job for Jenny Archer* (1988); *Jenny Archer to the Rescue* (1990)

BIBLIOGRAPHY: *Something about the Author,* vol. 68, 1992; *Children's Literature Review,* vol. 10, 1986

JODI PILGRIM

CONRAD, Pam

Author, b. 18 June 1947, New York City; d. Jan. 22, 1996, Rockville Centre, New York

C. attended High School of Performing Arts in New York City; attended Hofstra University; B.A. from the New School for Social Research.

C. first started writing when she had the chicken pox in February 1957. Instead of drawing on the pad of paper her mother gave her, she wrote POETRY. Although C. continued to write periodically, her writing career really began in 1979. She lived in Colorado and Texas before returning to her native state of New York. In addition to her fiction books for children and YOUNG ADULTS, C. wrote nonfiction and poetry. As a freelance writer, she wrote essays and articles for journals and newspapers. She taught creative writing at Queens College. C. is perhaps best known for *Prairie Songs* (1985) and *The Tub People* (1989).

C. was a prolific author with a diverse range. She wrote for the very young, for reluctant readers, and for young adults using realism, MYSTERY, FANTASY, contemporary settings, and settings in times past. Her imagination was boundless. She captured ordinary moments and made them memorable and authentic through her characters, settings, and adept use of language. She was a talented, eclectic writer who contributed substantially to the field of children's literature. About writing she said, "I believe that all we write comes *through* us not from us, that we're channels of sorts for hundreds of stories that are floating around in the universe."

AWARDS: C. received numerous AWARDS including the INTERNATIONAL READING ASSOCIATION Children's Book Award, *Booklist* Best of the 80s, AMERICAN LIBRARY ASSOCIATION Best Book for Young Adults, Golden Kite Honor Book, Western Heritage Award, Golden Spur Award, *Boston Globe-Horn Book* Honor Award, Edgar Allan Poe Award for Best Juvenile Mystery, ALA *Booklist* Children's Editors Choice, Notable Children's Trade Book in the Field of Social Studies, *Horn Book* Honor List, Child Study Association of America's Children's Books of the Year, ALA Notable Book, *New York Times* Notable Book, and CHILDREN'S BOOK COUNCIL Children's Choice citation.

FURTHER WORKS: *Animal Lingo* (1995); *Animal Lullabies* (1991); *Call Me Ahnighito* (1995); *Doll Face Has a Party!* (1994); *Holding Me Here* (1986); *I Don't Live Here* (1984); *The Lost Sailor* (1992); *Molly and the Strawberry Day* (1994); *My Daniel* (1989); *Old Man Hoover's Dead Rabbit* (1991); *Our House; The Stories of Levittown* (1995); *Pedro's Journal: A Voyage with Christopher Columbus* (1991); *Prairie Songs* (1985); *Prairie Visions: The Life and Times of Solomon Butcher* (1994); *The Rooster's Gift* (1996); *Staying Nine* (1968); *Stonewords: A Ghost Story* (1990); *Taking the Ferry Home* (1988); *This Mess* (1997); *The Tub Grandfather* (1993); *What I Did for Roman* (1967); *Zoe Rising* (1996)

BIBLIOGRAPHY: *Children's Books in Print,* vol. 1; *Awards, Authors, Illustrators,* 1997; *Children's Literature Review,* vol. 18, 1989; *Something about the Author,* vols. 49, 52, 80, 90, 1987, 1988, 1995, 1997

BONNIE BLUE ROBERTSON

COOLIDGE, Olivia
Author, b. 16 October 1908, London, England

Educated in the classics at Oxford, C. taught school in London before emigrating to the United States. Writing for adolescent readers, C. is known for her books on MYTHOLOGY as well as for her BIOGRAPHIES. She retold many of the famous epic tales from Greek and Roman mythology, such as *Men of Athens* (1962) and *Lives of Famous Romans* (1965). Careful to maintain historical accuracy, C. would often create minor characters and incidents to make an ancient era more meaningful and keep the story moving along. Based on the legend of Agamemnon, *The King of Men* (1966) recounts the youthful adventures of a legendary hero in a novel. With verve and inspiration, C. re-creates daily life in *The Golden Days of Greece* (1968, 1990), describing historical events and the leaders who shaped them.

FURTHER WORKS: *Greek Myths* 1949; *Egyptian Adventures,* 1954; *Roman People,* 1959; *Men of Athens,* 1962; *Lives of Famous Romans,* 1965; *Women's Rights,* 1966; *Marathon Looks on the Sea,* 1967; *Golden Days of Greece,* 1968; *Tom Paine, Revolutionary,* 1969; *Gandhi,* 1971; *Come by Here,* 1976; *The Statesmanship of Abraham Lincoln,* 1976

BIBLIOGRAPHY: *Something about the Author,* vol. 26, 1982

JODI PILGRIM

COOLIDGE, Susan (Sarah Chauncey Woolsey)
Author, b. 29 January 1835, Cleveland, Ohio; d. 9 April 1905, Newport, Rhode Island

As a young child, Sarah Woolsey displayed a love for reading and writing stories. Her writing career began in 1870 when she first published magazine articles. Writing under the pseudonym Susan Coolidge, she published her popular SERIES about the doings of the Carr family in the Katy Did series for children. This collection included the books *What Katy Did* (1873), *What Katy Did at School* (1874), and *What Katy Did Next* (1887). These books became very popular in the U.S. and gained ever greater fame in Great Britain. C. was a prolific author of girls' novels and short story collections, many of which appeared first in *St. Nicholas* magazine. C. also wrote at least sixteen other books for children including several short story collections, such as *Barberry Bush* (1893). She published poetry for adults and edited the correspondence of Jane Austen.

FURTHER WORKS: *Eyebright,* 1879; *A Guernsey Lily,* 1880; *Clover,* 1888; *In the High Valley,* 1890

DENISE P. BEASLEY

COONEY, Barbara
Author, illustrator, b. 6 August 1917, Brooklyn, New York; d. 10 March 2000, Damariscotta, Maine

With over fifty years of contributions to children's literature, C. is acclaimed for both the extensive and intensive qualities of her art. She is admired as a storyteller, author, illustrator, and her creations extend across a variety of genre—FANTASY, BIOGRAPHY, PICTURE BOOKS, fiction, and nonfiction. They appeal to readers of all ages. The intensity of her work is realized in its delicately complex detail, discerningly selected color and design, and authenticity resulting from thorough research.

C. grew up on Long Island, and was influenced artistically during her early years. As a child she was allowed to play with the paints and brushes of her impressionist artist mother. C. frequently spoke of her great-grandfather, a German immigrant, who painted Cigar Store Indians and oil landscapes for a living. C.'s grandmother was allowed to help her father. As a child she loved drawing and once stated in the *Horn Book* magazine that she maintained her artist "soul" despite growing older because of "access to materials and pictures, a minimum of instruction, and a stubborn nature." C. spent summers in Maine with her family and thus began a lifelong love affair with New England. She made her home in Maine until her death. After receiving a degree at Smith College where she studied mainly art history, she joined the Women's Army Corps. She left army service after she married and was expecting a child.

C.'s early art for books focused on children and animals. Her work was done in black and white since color was not economical for publishers. C. says it was not until she was in her forties that the sense of place, now characterizing her books, became of great importance to her. While traveling, she discovered the use of light through photography to provide a means of creating mood. During her career, C. illustrated books for many established authors, such as Louisa May ALCOTT, Edward LEAR. Walter DE LA MARE, Margaret Wise BROWN, Jane YOLEN, Gloria HOUSTON, John BIERHORST and Virginia HAVILAND. As an illustrator, C. worked with the scratchboard technique, line drawings in five-color wash, charcoal, acrylic, and collage. Colorful paintings that often incorporate medieval and folk art, a variety of formats and mediums, and many hidden details and pictures within the ILLUSTRATION characterize her work.

C.'s beginnings as both author and illustrator mainly consisted of retelling familiar stories. *Chanticleer and the Fox* (1959) had its beginnings with C.'s delight in the colorful plummage of a chicken she happened to see in the early evening sunlight. However, it was not until she read the "Nun's Priest Tale" of *The Canterbury Tales* that she had a suitable framework for her chickens. After much research on medieval times, C. created a book that was acclaimed for artistic format as well as retelling of this classic tale. It received the ALA CALDECOTT MEDAL (1959).

C.'s writing and illustration is noted for its authenticity, accomplished through her research, travel, and "living through" each story. The more she traveled to such places as France and Spain

where she illustrated versions of MOTHER GOOSE set in these countries the more connections she felt between her character and the settings. Her *Tortillitas para Mama and Other Nursery Rhymes* was a 1982 Notable Children's Trade Book in the Field of Social Studies. The detail of her work shows her keen artist's eye for new places as seen in *Roxaboxen* (1991). As Anna Newton Porter, her mother-in-law wrote, "There is no separation of her creative life from her everyday domestic activity. That is perhaps because she lives as creatively as she works. The children who run and dance across her pages run and dance across her life . . . If she likes a book, she lives in it while she is illustrating it."

It was only natural that C. made her beloved Maine the focus of several of her books. *Ox-Cart Man* (1979) by Donald HALL is about a nineteenth century New Hampshire farmer who makes the long journey from his inland home to a coastal market. Her art resembles early American primitive wood paintings. C. won a second Caldecott Medal for *Ox-Cart Man*. C. said the three books that followed this one C. says are autobiographical. While C. did not scatter lupines or travel exactly as *Miss Rumphius* (1982), she did include various events and items from her own life within the book. She also gave Miss Rumphius an artist's soul reflecting her own for creating beautiful things. This book has been praised for its wisdom and affirmation of life. *Island Boy* (1988) celebrates the various generations of life as it tells of the life and death of a nineteenth century man living on a remote island in New England. *Hattie and the Wild Waves* (1990) is the story of C.'s mother and her decision to become an artist at the turn of the century. Each book is insightful, has appeal across the generations, and sensitively addresses universalities of life. The characters reflect C.'s own personal characteristics of self-discipline, independence, motivation, and ardent living.

C. enjoyed creating picture-book biographies with American settings. *Eleanor* (1996), C. said, was a significant experience to write and illustrate because she had never written a book that was purely fact-based. C. believed that *Eleanor* was the nicest thing she wrote and spoke to the attention given to truth in each word and sentence. *Eleanor* has a freshness and dignity as do all of

C.'s books. Similarly, each has made the world a better place for those who read them.

AWARDS: AMERICAN LIBRARY ASSOCIATION Caldecott Medal (1959) for *Chanticleer and the Fox,* (1980) for *Ox-Cart Man.* ALA Notable Book (1984) for *Spirit Child.* C. received a medal from Smith College for her body of work in 1976 and a 1992 KERLAN Award for body of work. She was proclaimed an official state treasure of Maine, 1996

FURTHER WORKS: *The Little Juggler: Adapted from a Old French Legend.* 1961. *The Courtship, Merry Marriage, and Feast of Cock Robin and Jenny Wren: To Which Is Added the Doleful Death of Cock Robin.* Adapted. 1965. *Snow White and Rose Red.* Adapted from Jacob and Wilhelm GRIMM. 1965; illustrated by C.: *The Little Fir Tree.* (Margaret Wise Brown). 1954. *A White Heron: A Story of Maine.* (Sarah Orne Jewett). 1963. *Plant Magic.* (Aileen FISHER). 1977. *Spirit Child: A Story of the Nativity.* (John BIERHORST, translator). 1984. *The Year of the Perfect Christmas Tree: An Appalachian Tale.* (Gloria HOUSTON). 1988. *Emily.* (Michael Bedard). 1992. *Only Opal: The Diary of a Young Girl.* (Opal Whiteley, adapted by Jane Boulton). 1994

BIBLIOGRAPHY: *Children's Literature Review.* 1991. C., Barbara. "The Spirit Place." *Children's Literature Association Quarterly.* Winter, 1984–85. C., Barbara. "Caldecott Medal Acceptance." the *Horn Book* magazine. Aug. 1980. Hale, Robert D. "Interview with Barbara C." the *Horn Book* magazine. Jan./Feb. 1994; Hedblad, Alan, ed. Walton, Julie Yates. "Portrait of a First Lady to Be." *Publishers Weekly.* Oct. 14, 1996. McClellan, Constance Reed. "Barbara C." in the *Horn Book* magazine. vol. 56, no. 4, 1980. Porter, Anna N. "Barbara C." the *Horn Book* magazine. vol. 35, i 4, Aug. 1959. *Something about the Author,* vol. 96, 1998; Walton, Julie Yates. "Portrait of a First Lady to Be." *Publishers Weekly.* Oct. 14, 1996

JANELLE B. MATHIS

COONEY, Caroline
Author, b. 10 May Year unknown, Geneva, New York

C. is a popular writer for YOUNG ADULTS. Her novels vary from REALISTIC FICTION to MYSTERY and suspense. Adolescents relate to C.'s books because her novels reflect the viewpoint of young people. In *Both Sides of Time* (1995) Annie Lockwood and Hiram Stratton are teenagers who fall in love despite the hundred years between their births. In *Driver's Ed* (1994), Morgan and

Remy are teenagers who steal a stop sign as a prank. In *Flight #116 Is Down!* (1992), Patrick and Heidi are teenagers who come to the rescue of the survivors of the crash. In *The Face on the Milk Carton* (1990) Janie is a sixteen-year-old girl who discovers that her parents are not really her birth parents.

C. is a master at vivid characterization. In *The Face on the Milk Carton* (1990) her description of Reeve continues throughout the beginning of the novel allowing readers to clarify their visual image of him. In *The Voice on the Radio* (1996), C. uses vivid characterization to help us to learn about Reeve's college roommate. *Twins* (1994) uses characterization skillfully to describe Jon Pear, the true essence of evil. *Both Sides of Time* (1995) characterizes Hiram Stratton's first impressions of Annie Lockwood so clearly that we see how others will view her as she enters the year 1895.

FURTHER WORKS: *The Fire,* 1990; *Operation Homefront,* 1992; *Whatever Happened to Janie?,* 1993; *Out of Time,* 1996; *Among Friends,* 1988; *Emergency Room,* 1994; *Twenty Pageants Later,* 1995; *Flash Fire,* 1996; *Prisoner of Time,* 1998; *Burning Up,* 1999

BIBLIOGRAPHY: Bushman, J. "Flight #116 Is Down!," *English Journal.* vol. 84, no. 4, 84–85, 1992; Donelson, K. "Driver's Ed," *English Journal,* vol. 84 no. 7, p. 98, 1995; *Publishers Weekly,* July 4, 1994; *Something about the Author,* vol. 20, 1995; biography (online) www.norfolk.ne.us/cooney.htm

NANCE S. WILSON

COOPER, Floyd
Author, illustrator, b. 8 January 1956, Tulsa, Oklahoma

C.'s first art experience was at the age of three as he drew a large duck on a piece of Sheetrock while his father added new rooms to their home. Art became an important part of C.'s life as he progressed through school. He received continual praise from art teachers while a student. A graduate of the University of Oklahoma with a degree in fine arts, C. worked for an advertising firm and as an illustrator for Hallmark cards.

C. relies on the power of imagination as he prepares to capture the essence of text in pictures. In *Talking with Artists, Volume One* (1991), C. claims that "atmosphere is everything!" And via his rich-oil paintings, C. invites his viewers along into visual stories, capturing the essence of the characters, their emotions, desires, and expressions. He says that he wants to bring readers into the story, allowing them to "get a sense of the smells, the atmosphere, and the emotions conveyed by the characters." The first book that C. illustrated, *Grandpa's Face* (1988) by Eloise GREENFIELD, was indicative of the artist's prolific future. His work in *Grandpa's Face* foreshadowed and solidified his commitment to create warm, affectionate portraits of generations of AFRICAN AMERICAN families. Although it appears that C. paints his pictures, C. explains his technique and design in the *Horn Book* (vol. 74): "The images are made with an eraser. . . . After coating the paper, board, or canvas with a 'wash' of very thin oil paint or chalk to make a background, the picture is created by erasing the shapes of the lighter areas of the subject or image I wish to make." C.'s unique art process continues to evolve with each new image, evoking the warmth and vitality of readers' lives. C.'s selection of earth tones all within similar hues leads to a full unity of picture and text. This apparent sense of unity seems to be evident in nearly all of C.'s work. Whereas the thrust of his career continues to be ILLUSTRATION, C. has embarked upon combining his illustrating with writing. In a widely acclaimed book, *Coming Home: From the Life of Langston HUGHES* (1994), which is C.'s debut as author and illustrator, he paints a picture with words and illustrations of the life of Langston Hughes, revealing the social dimensions and details of the life of this renowned poet. His eloquent prose and golden images unite to proclaim the significance of Hughes's poetic life.

AWARDS: CORETTA SCOTT KING Illustrator Honor AWARDS (1999) for *I Have Heard of a Land* (Joyce Carol THOMAS), (1995) for *Meet Danitra Brown* (Nikki GRIMES), (1994) for *Brown Honey in Broomwheat Tea* (Joyce Carol Thomas)

FURTHER WORKS: Illustrated: *The Girl Who Loved Caterpillars: A Twelfth-Century Tale from Japan* (Jean MERRILL, 1992); *Gingerbread Days: Poems* (Joyce Carol Thomas, 1995); *Be Good to Eddie Lee* (Virginia Fleming, 1997); *Ma Dear's Apron* (Patricia MCKISSACK, 1997); *Faraway Drums* (Virginia Kroll, 1998); *I Have Heard of a Land* (Joyce Carol Thomas, 1998); *AFRICAN Be-*

ginnings (James HASKINS, 1998); as author & illustrator: *Cumbayah,* (1997)

BIBLIOGRAPHY: Cooper, Floyd, "Studio Views" in *Horn Book,* vol. 74; Cummings, Pat ed., *Talking with Artists,* (vol. 2), 1991; Smith, Henrietta, ed., *The Coretta Scott King Awards Book, 1970–99,* 1999

SHANE RAYBURN

COOPER, Susan
Author, b. 23 May 1935, Burnham, Buckinghamshire, England

C. grew up in England during World War II, which deeply affected her life and her writing. Living just outside of London, she remembers vividly the sound of air-raid sirens, bombs falling and the time spent with her family in air-raid shelters. Her father worked for the Great Western Railway as generations before him had. He hated the office aspect of his job, not the railway itself. He influenced C. through his love for music and drawing. C.'s mother was a teacher and brought POETRY to her children's lives. Three early influences aside from books helped to form C. as a writer: poetry, introduced by her mother; interest in theater with traditional family visits to London Christmas productions; and the BBC–radio dramatizations of books. C. began writing as a young girl. She wrote plays, weekly newspapers, and small books that she also illustrated. She attended an all-girl school, Slough High School, and won a scholarship to Somerville College at Oxford where she received an M.A. in 1956 and was the first woman to edit *Cherwell,* the Oxford newspaper.

After graduation, C. pursued a career in journalism. She was not pleased with the lack of prospects in the major cities; however, she was able to work as a temporary reporter, which gave her experience. She then worked for the *Sunday Times* for seven years. During this time, her superior was author Ian FLEMING. Working as a journalist taught her four lessons that she says contributed to her career as a writer: working with deadlines (she says she still needs them); making her prose tight and vivid; learning to type quickly with four fingers; and adjusting to writing anywhere. Her first fiction writing that sold was a short story entitled "A Proper Sailor's Bird."

In 1963, she married an M.I.T. professor with three children and moved to the United States.

She has lived there ever since, but has continued to use England as settings for her books. She wrote *Mandrake* (1964), an adult science-fiction book, weekly columns about America from the British point of view, and a biography of writer J. B. Priestly. The publication of *Over Sea, under Stone* (1965, 1966) however, catapulted her career toward books for YOUNG ADULTS. In addition to the FANTASY *Over Sea, under Stone*, C. wrote four more books referred to as The Dark Is Rising series, including *The Dark Is Rising* (1973), *Greenwitch* (1973, 1974), *The Grey King* (1974, 1975), and *Silver on the Tree* (1977). These books received numerous AWARDS including the prestigious NEWBERY MEDAL for *The Grey King*.

The author draws on major English and Celtic myths and legends, spinning them into fascinating tales of universal battles between good and evil, including modern characters. Her early memories of living through World War II are intertwined with the traditional substance of myth as a quest to overcome the forces of evil and darkness. C. believes that fantasy engages the reader by going "one stage beyond realism, requiring complete intellectual surrender." She tries to maintain the freshness of the child's vision in her books. With her British settings and stories of myths, she attempts to provide American children with a sense of myth and ritual. She feels that they do not inherit myths and rituals like children from older countries. Her fantasies have been compared to J. R. R. TOLKIEN and C. S. LEWIS, both of whom she heard lecture while in college. In addition to adult fiction and nonfiction and fantasy for young adults, C. penned an autobiographical story in *Dawn of Fear* (1970). Although the protagonist is a boy, C. states that the story is an account of her life as a child in Buckinghamshire during World War II, her first experience with a real-life battle between good and evil. C. always writes for herself and depends on her longtime editor, Margaret McElderry, to tell what age she has written for.

During the early 1980s, C.'s personal and professional life changed. She experienced the loss of her parents, a divorce, and a new direction in her writing. During the next few years, C. would not only succeed as a Broadway playwright and author of television screenplays, she would be instrumental in her associates receiving Emmy and Tony nominations and awards. C. herself won an Emmy nomination for her adaptation of *Foxfire* in which John Denver, Hume Cronyn, and Jessica Tandy starred. C. continued to work with Cronyn and Tandy.

During the 1980s and 1990s, C. returned to writing children's books, including PICTURE BOOKS *Jethro and the Jumbie* (1979) and *Danny and the Kings* (1993). *The Boggart* (1993), which is a modern slant to myth and legend, was followed by its companion book *The Boggart and the Monster* (1997).

In 1996, C. married her longtime friend and writing partner, now widowed, (formerly married to the actress Jessica Tandy) actor Hume Cronyn. They live in Connecticut. She has published a collections of essays on children's literature in *Dreams and Wishes* (1996).

AWARDS: *Boston Globe–Horn Book* Award, CARNEGIE MEDAL runner-up, AMERICAN LIBRARY ASSOCIATION Newbery Medal Honor Book (all 1973) for *The Dark Is Rising*. ALA Newbery Medal, Tir na N'og Award (Wales), Carnegie Medal commendation (all 1974) for *The Grey King*. Tir na N'og Award (1977) for *Silver on the Tree*. Christopher Award, Writer's Guild of America Award, Humanities Prize, and Emmy Award nomination from the Academy of Television Arts and Sciences (all 1984) for "The Dollmaker"; Janusz Korczak Literary Award (1983) for *Seaward*. Writer's Guild of America Award and Emmy Award nomination (1988) for *Foxfire*

FURTHER WORKS: *The Silver Cow: A Welsh Tale*, 1983; *The Selkie Girl*, 1986; *Tam Lin*, 1991; *Seaward*, 1983; *King of Shadows*, 1999

BIBLIOGRAPHY: *Children's Literature Review*, vol. 4; Cooper, Susan. "Fantasy in the Real World," *Horn Book* magazine, May/June 1990, vol. 66, no. 3; Rochman, Hazel. "The *Booklist* Interview: Susan C.." *Booklist*, Sept. 15, 1997, vol. 94, no. 2; *Something about the Author*, vol. 64, 1991; http://missy.shef.ac.uk/~emp94ms/welcome.html

NANCY HORTON

CORBETT, Scott
Author, b. 27 July 1913, Kansas City, Missouri

C. was reared in Kansas City and attended junior college there. C. began writing at this time while working at a branch public library. He contributed to *College Humor* and to the "Post Scripts" page of the *Saturday Evening Post*. In 1934, he graduated with a bachelor's degree in journalism from the University of Missouri. Six years later he married Elizabeth Grosvenor Pierce. Although C. began publishing novels in 1950, he did not publish his first children's book until 1956. At the time his first book was published, his family was living on Cape Cod, which became the setting for several of his stories including *Diamonds are Trouble* (1967) and *The Mystery Man* (1970). Many of C.'s books evolved during trips, including *The Turnabout Trick* (1967), which was written during a trip around the world. In 1957, C.'s family moved from Cape Cod to Providence, Rhode Island, to improve their daughter's high-school education.

C. has written over thirty-five books. He is best known for his Trick series. C. feels his books capture the attention of reluctant readers while his best efforts have included ghost stories of a modern day and age.

AWARDS: C. received the 1962 Edgar Allan Poe Award from the Mystery Writers of America for *Cutlass Island.* He won the Mark TWAIN Award from the Missouri Library Association in 1976 and the Golden Archer Award from the University of Wisconsin in 1978, both for *The Home Run Trick. Bridges* (1978) earned recognition as an ALA Notable book. Nine of C.'s books were chosen as Junior Literary Guild selections

FURTHER WORKS: *Treehouse Island* (1959); *The Lemonade Trick* (1960—Trick series); *Cutlass Island* (1962); *The Limerick Trick* (1964); *The Case of the Gone Goose* (1966); *What Makes a Boat Float* (1970); *The Home Run Trick* (1973); *Bridges* (1978); *The Mysterious Zetabet* (1979); The Great McGoniggle series.

JODI PILGRIM

CORCORAN, Barbara (pseuds. Paige Dixon and Gail Hamilton)
Author, b. 12 April 1911, Hamilton, Massachusetts

When C. wrote her first novel for children, *Sam,* in 1967, she had not planned to do so. *Sam* was meant to be a novel for adults, but when C. told the story of a teenage girl leaving the isolation of her rural Montana home for the first time, her role in children's literature had begun. Prior to this unplanned beginning, C. grew up in the small town of Hamilton, Massachusetts, where her family had lived for decades. A writer even as a child,

she published her first piece in *The Turret* at age twelve.

Continuing her interest in writing, she was the class poet in high school and earned a B.A. in English from Wellesley College in 1933. After college she worked in New Deal programs like the Works Progress Administration Writers Project and followed this service with summer jobs as a stage manager—which prompted C. to ask if she could attend Yale Drama School. Too much for her father's pocketbook, Yale was shelved in place of time working in New York and writing plays, some of which sold. With the coming of World War II, C. added electronics inspector and cryptanalytic aide to her list of experiences.

Moving to California after the war, C. began to work as a researcher for Celebrity Service, and in 1953, wary of the everexpanding Los Angeles area, C. moved to Missoula, Montana, working as a copywriter for a radio station and enrolling in a Masters program at the University of Montana. After receiving her degree in 1955, C. taught English at the University of Kentucky, the Marlborough School, the University of Colorado, and Palomar College. In California, while working at Palomar College, she published *Sam,* and two years later she decided to try to write full-time.

Writing with incredible fecundity, C. published eleven novels in the next five years, causing her publishers to ask her to take a pseudonym to avoid competing with herself. Her first, Paige Dixon, was for a male persona who wrote her nature books as well as some mystery novels; it was soon to be followed by Gail Hamilton, named for a nineteenth century writer from the Hamilton, Massachusetts, area. In 1974, C. published *A Dance to Still Music,* a novel that was based on her own experience with sudden (and in her case temporary) deafness. Also well-received were *Meet Me at Tamerlane's Tomb* (1975), a mystery; *Axe-Time, Sword-Time* (1976), a war novel; and the first novel of the Camp Allegro MYSTERY series, *You're Allegro Dead* (1981). More recent novels have taken on family problems (*Family Secrets,* 1992).

Awarded a National Endowment for the Humanities Fellowship in 1975, C.'s writing has also been acknowledged with Outstanding Science Trade Book for Children Citations (as Paige

Dixon for *The Young Grizzly,* 1974 and *The Summer of the White Goat,* 1977)

FURTHER WORKS: *A Candle to the Devil* (as Gail Hamilton, 1975); *The Clown* (1975); *Me and You and a Dog Named Blue* (1979); *A Row of Tigers* (1969); *Sasha, My Friend* (1969); *Walk My Way* (as Paige Dixon, 1980); *Which Witch Is Which* (1983)

REFERENCES: *American Writers for Children Since 1960: Fiction* (1986); *The Fifth Book of Junior Authors and Illustrators* (1983)

GWYNNE ELLEN ASH

CORMIER, Robert

Author, b. 17 January 1925, Leominster, Massachusetts; d. 26 October 2000, Leominster, Massachusetts

C. attended only one year of postsecondary education before beginning a journalism career. However, it was during that year at Fitchburg State College in which a teacher recognized his skill as a STORYTELLER. After a brief stint writing radio advertisements, C. became a newspaper reporter, experience he credits for sharpening his skill for placing readers of his fiction at the scene of the stories he has to tell. Although C. published three novels for adults between 1960 and 1965, he did not leave the newspaper business (in which he rose from reporter to editor) until 1978.

As a reporter and newspaper columnist, C. earned several local press AWARDS. His first novel marketed for young readers, *The Chocolate War* (1974), was cited that year by the AMERICAN LIBRARY ASSOCIATION as a Best Book for Young Adults. In 1979, the same novel earned the Lewis CARROLL Shelf Award. *I Am the Cheese* (1977) also received ALA's Best Book for Young Adults citation, as did *After the First Death* (1979) and *The Bumblebee Flies Anyway* (1983), each in its year of publication. ALA's Young Adult Services Division Best Book for Young Adults citation went to *Fade* (1988), which was nominated the following year for the World FANTASY Award. ALA's Margaret A. Edwards Award was given to C. in 1991, for *The Chocolate War, I Am the Cheese,* and *After the First Death.* In 1977, he was awarded an honorary Doctor of Letters by Fitchburg State College.

Although C.'s novels and stories feature teenaged protagonists, he writes about young adults and about issues trenchant to that age, rather than for them as a predetermined audience. In C.'s fiction, the struggle between good and evil is realistic and it is often beyond the abilities of the protagonists to maintain goodness, let alone innocence, in the face of institutions and adults who can overwhelm their acts of idealism. C. has been called a political writer but his politics are based on the nature of the adolescent's role and power—or powerlessness—in the world, not on a specific economic or religious system.

In *The Chocolate War,* C. utilized an incident—which in reality led to no dramatic repercussion—from his son's high-school experience to create an engrossing story about power and corruption. The novel revolves around the decision by a high school freshman to go against both school administration and peer pressure, a decision that leads to the protagonist's physical, social, and even moral downfall. So realistic were the characters C. devised in this novel that readers—and he himself—needed to hear what happened to them after the close of the story. *Beyond the Chocolate War* (1985) provides a sequel in response to those questions.

Young protagonists are not only stripped of their innocence in C.'s novels, but sometimes they lose their lives, an unusual occurrence in REALISTIC YOUNG ADULT LITERATURE. In *The Bumblebee Flies Anyway,* the main characters are terminally ill. *After the First Death* explores a hostage situation, based on a real event C. learned about while working as a journalist.

Other news events have gained substantiation in C.'s more recent novels. *We All Fall Down* (1991) begins with a home invasion by teenage boys, one of whom later, and unknowingly, becomes romantically involved with the sister of the girl assaulted during the invasion. This is a classic C. character: a young man who knows absolutely that he has been involved in a great evil and yet is hurt by the repercussions of that evil. He is victim as well as perpetrator and self-conscious of both aspects of his situation, an awareness that can scarcely be contained by any one human being.

The working class French Canadian neighborhood in which C. grew up seems to have provided inspiration for characters in some of his books. In *Heroes* (1998) the events unfold in a small New

England town during World War II, in a neighborhood wanting for real-life heroism. The community's most respected young man goes off to fight in Europe, with no one except his victim and his victim's young boyfriend aware that he has committed a rape. Both this novel and *Tunes for Bears to Dance To* (1992), in which a boy learns the thoroughgoing meaning of anti-Semitism only after perpetrating an evil act against someone who loves him, are brief and stark in their rapid unfolding. Yet, the subtleties of characterization that bring fictional people to life are not missing and the very swiftness of the action makes it all the more compelling a vehicle for C.'s theme: there is evil, not only in the world, but in each of us, and there is hope, as well, the hope that we learn to recognize evil and grow able to counter it.

C. enjoys popularity among teenage readers, especially those who recognize the dichotomy between their minor status and their maturing moral development. The brutality of his plot lines and the uncomfortably realistic plights of his protagonists have invited challenges to C.'s work in spite of his literary artistry. Like his idealistic characters, however, C. continues to do what he can in the very best way that he can, supplying readers with the opportunity to examine universal moral issues through the microcosm of realistic accounts of how his characters have tried to deal with the loss of innocence and the responsibilities that loss implies.

C. has used the pseudonym "John Fitch IV" in some of his newspaper columns and other periodical writings.

AWARDS: 1991 Margaret A. Edwards Award for body of work

FURTHER WORKS: *Eight Plus One* (1980); *In the Middle of the Night* (1995); *Tenderness* (1997)

BIBLIOGRAPHY: Campbell, P. *Presenting Robert Cormier* (1985)

FRANCISCA GOLDSMITH

COURLANDER, Harold

Folklorist, b. 18 September 1908, Indianapolis, Indiana; d. 16 March 1996, Bethesda, Maryland

C. grew up in a culturally diverse neighborhood in Detroit, which he credited with making him aware of how other cultures lived and how people celebrated their unique heritages. After graduating from the University of Michigan in 1931 and doing graduate work at Columbia University, C. tried his hand at farming in Michigan. Working for the U.S. Office of War Information, the Voice of America, and as a press officer for the U.S. Mission to the UN allowed him to travel to India and Africa to pursue his early interest in FOLKLORE and how other cultures maintained their oral traditions. In 1942, after receiving a research grant to study folklore in the Caribbean, his first collection of folktales, *Uncle Bouqui of Haiti,* was published. It was based on previously unpublished oral stories C. gathered from local storytellers in isolated mountain villages. C. was one of the first folklorists to go into the field to listen to the rhythms and language patterns of native storytellers; he quickly became aware of patterns and themes among stories with AFRICAN origins.

C. viewed himself as a narrator, transmitting the cultural heritage and common humanity of specific communities, allowing children and adults to see what is universal in people's behavior despite language differences. He used clear, simple language and imagery, and a straightforward narrative style to make his folktales accessible. He also recorded and published music from his travels, and many adult titles. C. maintained that his African-based folktales are appropriate for all ages because of their universality. In 1977, C. and his publisher, Crown, filed a lawsuit against Alex Haley for plagiarizing portions of C.'s *The African* in Haley's *Roots.* C. won an out-of-court settlement.

AWARDS: Two Guggenheim fellowships (1948 and 1955) enabled him to study African and AFRICAN AMERICAN culture. After traveling to West Africa he published, with George Herzog, *"The Cow-Tail Switch" and other West African Stories,* a 1947 NEWBERY MEDAL Honor Book and *"The Hat-Shaking Dance" and Other Tales from the Gold Coast* (1957) with Albert K. Prempeh, which reflect the oral wisdom and earthy HUMOR of the Ashanti. The stories deal with talking animals and people in universal situations; many feature the trickster character Anansi the spider who assumes a human shape. In 1980 C. was nominated for the Laura Ingalls WILDER Award.

FURTHER WORKS: *"Kantchil's Lime Pit," and Other Stories from Indonesia,* (1950); *The Fire on the Mountain," and Other Ethiopian Stories,* with Wolf Leslau, (1950); *"The Tiger's Whisker,"* and Other Legends from ASIA and the Pacific. 1959; *"Olode the Hunter,"* and Other Tales from Nigeria with Ezekiel A. Eshugbayi (1968); *People of the Short Blue Corn: Tales and Legends of the Hopi Indians* (1970)

BIBLIOGRAPHY: Jaffe. Nina, *A Voice for the People: The Life and Work of Harold Courlander* (1997)

DIANE G. PERSON

COUSINS, Lucy (Elizabeth)
Author, illustrator, b. 10 February 1964, Reading, England

Daughter of parents who studied at the Royal College of Art in London, and an admirer from childhood of children's books, C. received a B.A. in Graphic Design at Brighton College of Art where she studied ILLUSTRATION with a family friend, Raymond BRIGGS. While there, she worked on a promotion for an animal-care facility and discovered she was "a bit afraid of color," an irony, given her current bold use of color. Later, while attending the Royal College of Art, she studied with Quentin BLAKE who recognized her singular talent and took second prize in the Macmillan Prize contest for *Portly's Hat* (1988), followed by a collection of nursery rhymes. With time, C. became comfortable with color, adding her signature black outline. The early prototype for her Maisy character, incorporated into an interactive book, was developed as part of her final degree project for the Royal College of Art resulting in her full launch into children's books.

Aimed at infants and preschoolers, frequently published as board books, C.'s illustrations are simple and vibrant, with large masses of color set off dramatically by black outlines. Her animals and people are cheerful, funny, and active. Wee Willie Winkie flies up a stairway, candle in hand; the little pig dashes "Wee, wee, wee, all the way home," ears forward, legs flying (*Wee Willie Winkie and Other Nursery Rhymes,* 1989); and Noah's joyful smile and raised arms celebrate the arrival of the dove as the colorful animals wait for a landing (*Noah's Ark,* 1993). Simplicity, color, and action are C.'s hallmarks, attracting the eye of the prereading child. Many of her books, particularly the Maisy series, are interactive, allowing the child to lift a flap, pull a lever, or rearrange objects and figures as part of the

reading process. Her publisher writes, "C. has captured the play, curiosity, spirit, and most importantly, the growing independence of a three-year-old." She is quoted as saying, "I draw by heart; I think of what children would like by going back to my own childish instincts." One parent wrote, "Our tornadolike toddler froze when we opened one." C.'s books also contribute to vocabulary and concept development and incidentally affirm activities, interests, habits, and values generally supported in the culture.

AWARDS: Bologna Graphics Prize runner-up (1989); *Parents'* magazine Best Book of the Year, *Parenting* magazine's Best Book of the Year Award; American Bookseller Pick of the Lists; Children's Book of the Month Club Selection; and starred review in Horn Book, all for *Noah's Ark* (1993); Child Magazine's Best Children's Books, for *Maizy's ABC* (1994); Commendation by The National Art Library Illustration Awards, 1996, Victoria and Albert Museum, London for *AZ-AZ's Baby Brother* (1995); and Working Mother Best Books of the Year for *Count with Maisy* (1977)

FURTHER WORKS: *What Can Rabbit Hear?* (1991); *Maisy Goes to School* (1992); *Maisy's Pop-up Playhouse* (1995); *Katy Cat and Beaky Boo* (1996); *Little Miss Muffet and Other Nursery Rhymes* (1997)

BIBLIOGRAPHY: Karen Jameyson's Book 'em Early site: http://family.disney.com/Features/family__ 1997__12/melb/melb127books/melb127books. html; personal assessments of books; Logan, Claudia, "The Fresh Vision of Lucy Cousins," *Publishers Weekly,* March 1, 1991; Library of Congress web catalog; Victoria and Albert Museum website

MARGARET YATSEVITCH PHINNEY

COVILLE, Bruce
Author, b. 16 May 1950, Syracuse, New York

C. is best known for his fast-paced, light reading contributions to juvenile fiction. C.'s novels contain mythic creatures, such as unicorns and dragons, as well as imaginary characters like aliens and ghosts. These creatures combined with ordinary characters create tales of MYSTERY or ADVENTURE and light FANTASY. C.'s wife often illustrates his books, many of which are frequently chosen as children's choices in many states throughout the United States. Primarily an author of fiction, *Prehistoric People* (1990), is C.'s account of early humans through their art, tools, and other artifacts.

With Jane YOLEN, C. has written *Armageddon Summer* (1998), a searing YOUNG ADULT novel about life inside a religious cult preparing for a cataclysmic end-of-the-world event. Using the alternating voices of two teenaged protagonists, C. and Yolen write about the responsibility the teens feel to protect their families, the effects of their dysfunctional families that brought them to the mountaintop, and the teens' perspectives as believer and as cynic.

FURTHER WORKS: *The Foolish Giant,* 1978; *The Ghost in the Big Brass Bed,* 1987; *Jeremy Thatcher, Dragon Hatcher,* 1991; *Monster's Ring,* 1982; *Mostly Michael,* 1987; *Short and Shivery: Thirty Chilling Tales,* 1987; *My Teacher Fried My Brains,* 1991; *Aliens Ate My Homework,* 1993; *Fortune's Journey,* 1995; *My Grandfather's House,* 1996; *The Ghost Wore Gray,* 1999; *Song of the Wanderer,* 1999; A.I. Gang series

JODI PILGRIM

COWCHER, Helen

Author, illustrator, b. 1957, Cheltenham, England

C. writes and illustrates stories for young readers to entertain and teach conservation. Always interested in the environment, C. paints pictures of nature with her words and illustrations. She lives in London, England, and studied at Chelsea Art College. In addition to illustrating children's books, she exhibits her paintings to raise funds for conservation groups. C.'s first book was published in 1988 and is titled *Rain Forest*. Since this first publication, she has continued to write accounts for children to read and learn about the earth, its condition, and its inhabitants. Although C.'s stories are PICTURE BOOKS for young children, she does not oversimplify the problems or solutions of survival and conservation. In *Tigress* (1991), a tigress and her cubs leave their sanctuary and kill domestic animals for food and in turn are threatened by the herdspeople. C. chronicles the event in her richly colored drawings as well as the text. Readers learn about the tigers in a presentation that is layered with concerns not only for the tigers, but for their prey and their predators. Another account of the hunter and the hunted is in C.'s *Jaguar* (1997). The reader views the struggle to achieve a satisfactory coexistence

between humans and nature. The bold color and composition vividly illustrates the setting of Venezuela's Orinoco flood plain.

AWARDS: C.'s *Rain Forest* (1988) is recognized by the National Council of Social Studies as the CHILDREN'S BOOK COUNCIL Notable Children's Trade Book in the Field of Social Studies and the National Science Teachers Association as the Children's Book Council Outstanding Science Trade Book. C. is also a recipient of the John Burroughs award. *Tigress* (1991) received the Parent's Choice award.

FURTHER WORKS: *Antarctica* (1990); *Whistling Thorns* (1993); *La Tigresa* (1993)

NANCY HORTON

COWLEY, Joy

Author, b. 7 August 1936, Levin, New Zealand

C. was educated in New Zealand and published five adult novels and several collections of short stories before she became primarily a writer of children's literature. Several of her early books for children, *The Duck in the Gun* (Robyn BELTON, illus., 1984) and *Salamugundi* (1985) satirized the foolishness of war. *The Terrible Tanisha of Timberditch* (1982) concerned the antics of a warlike Maori monster. Never condescending, C. uses simple language to present serious, thought-provoking themes in many of her books for young readers.

Besides publishing for the public, C. has made a most invaluable contribution to the teaching of reading by creating exceptionally literate Big Books texts for several companies that produce educational read-together SERIES such as The Story Chest Books and The Story Box Books. With C.'s use of HUMOR, rhyme, and rhythm these first reading experiences become magical adventures. Some of her most memorable titles are *Mrs. Wishy-Washy* (1980), which has sold more than 40 million copies and *Greedy Cat* (1988). *In a Dark, Dark Wood* and *One Cold Wet Night.*

Red-eyed Tree Frog (1999) describes, in a few simple words, a hungry tree frog's search for dinner and careful effort to avoid becoming another rain forest creature's dinner. The scientifically accurate, interactive text is readily accessible to three- to five-year-olds and the informative afterword provides easily understood questions young readers ask.

C. writes at her ranch in Marlborough Sounds, New Zealand. Early in her writing career, C. captured a sense of rhythm and melody that make her words easy for stories of this type. C. also writes CHAPTER BOOKS and novels. Her novel *The Silent One* (1981) has been made into a film and shown on the DISNEY Channel.

AWARDS: *Boston Globe–Horn Book* Outstanding PICTURE BOOK (2000) for *Red-eyed Tree Frog*. NEW ZEALAND Russell Clark Award (1996) for *The Cheese Trap*, (1985) for *The Duck in the Gun*. New Zealand AIM Children's Book Awards (1992) for *Bow Down Shadrach* and (1982) for *The Silent One*. New Zealand Commemorative Medal for Service to Children's Literature. The Order of the British Empire. Honorary doctorate of letters, Massey University (1993).

FURTHER WORKS: *What a Mess,* 1982; *Mouse's Bride,* 1995; *Gracias, the Thanksgiving Turkey,* 1996; *Singing down the Rain,* 1997; *Big Moon Tortilla,* 1998; *The Video Shop Sparrow,* 1998; *The Rusty, Trusty Tractor,* 1999; *Agapanthus Hum and the Eyeglasses,* 1999; *Starbright and the Dream Eater,* 2000

BIBLIOGRAPHY: *Children's Literature Review,* vol. 55; Hunt, Peter, ed., *Children's Literature: An Illustrated History,* 1995; *Something about the Author,* vol. 4, 1973, and vol. 90, 1977; *Something about the Author Autobiography Series,* vol. 26; *Twentieth Century Children's Writers*

JUDY LIPSITT

CRAIG, Helen

Author, illustrator, b. 30 August 1934, London, England

C. is best known for her self-illustrated mouse stories such as *A Number of Mice* (1978), *The Mouse House ABC* (1978), and *The Town Mouse and the Country Mouse* (1992), which was shortlisted for Great Britain's Smarties Book Prize in 1992. C. also has illustrated more mice with the Angelina series, authored by Katharine Holabird, *Angelina Ballerina* (1983), *Angelina's Birthday* (1989), and *Angelina's Baby Sister* (1991).

FURTHER WORKS: *Angelina's Ice Skates,* (Katharine Holabird, author), 1993; *I See the Moon and the Moon Sees Me,* 1993; *Helen Craig's Book of Nursery Rhymes,* 1992; *Turnover Tuesday,* (Phyllis Root, author), 1998

REFERENCES: Ward, M. E., D. A. Marquardt, N. Dolan, and D. Eaton, eds., *Authors of Books for Young People,* 1990

GWYNNE ELLEN ASH

CRANE, Sir Walter

Illustrator, b. 15 August 1845, Liverpool, England; d. 15 March 1915, London, England

C. is considered one of the most important of all children's book illustrators and was one of the first to experiment with color in PICTURE BOOKS. His name is associated with Randolph CALDECOTT and Kate GREENAWAY as pioneers in the production of illustrated books for children. He sketched animals as a child and received encouragement to pursue his artistic talents early in his life from his father who was an artist and his father's friends. Private tutoring and self-instruction comprised his education. His first painting was exhibited at the Royal Academy when he was sixteen and a year later he illustrated his first book. Being an apprentice to W. J. Linton, an engraver, gave him the experience and recognition to develop his abilities further. Throughout his life, C. worked as an English designer, painter, and illustrator, director of design at the Manchester School of Art (1893–96) and principal of the Royal Art College of Art (1898–99). By age twenty-five, he was established as an illustrator of children's books and a ceramic designer for Wedgwood. Among the more than forty children's books he illustrated, C.'s most notable works are his illustrations in Nathaniel HAWTHORNE's *A Wonder Book for Girls and Boys* (1892, reissued 1973), Jacob GRIMM's *Household Stories from the Collection of Brothers Grimm* (1882, reissued 1966), and Edmund Spenser's *Faerie Queene* (1894). In addition to illustrating children's and adult books, C. authored textbooks in instruction in design and ILLUSTRATION. C.'s works have been exhibited at Dudley and Grosvenor Galleries, London.

AWARDS: C. received the silver medal in Paris for *The Driver* in 1889 and the gold medal in Munich in 1895 for the *Chariot of the Hours*. He was given the Albert Gold Medal of Society of Arts in 1904 in recognition for promoting popular decorative art and craftsmanship. At the Milan International Exhibition in 1906, he received the gold medal and grand prize.

FURTHER WORKS: *Baby's Own Alphabet* (1874). C. illustrated classic children's verses and stories in the Toy Book (1867–76) and Picture Book (1871–1911) series such as *Buckle My Shoe*

203

(1910), *This Little Pig Went to Market* (1895), *Little Red Riding Hood* (1898), *The Sleeping Beauty* (1914), *Sing a Song of Sixpence* (1909), *Cinderella* (1897), *Old Mother Hubbard* (1913), and *Beauty and the Beast* (1900); *The Baby's Opera,* (1878); *Baby's Bouquet,* (1878); *The Baby's Own Aesop,* (1878); *The Man in the Moon: and Another Tale for Children at Christmastime* (1880); *Reynard the Fox* (1897); *Goody Two Shoes* (1901); *Rumbo Rhymes* (Alfred C. Calmour, author, 1911); "Puss in Boots" and "The Forty" Thieves (1914)

BIBLIOGRAPHY: Doyle, Brian, ed., *The Who's Who of Children's Literature,* (1968); *The Oxford Companion to Children's Literature,* (1984); Egoff, Sheila, *Thursday's Child,* (1981); Hunt, Peter, ed., *Children's Literature: An Illustrated History.* (1995); MEIGS, C., et al., *A Critical History of Children's Literature.* (1969)

NANCY HORTON

CREECH, Sharon
Author, b. 29 July 1945, Cleveland, Ohio

C.'s books are invitations for readers to journey with the writer and characters to see the world outside their own. C. was reared in Ohio and moved to England in 1979 where she met and married the headmaster of an American School in England. They live in Surrey, England, nine months each year and spend summers on Lake Chautauqua in New York with her two grown children, Rob and Karin. C. obtained a Bachelor of Arts degree from Hiram College, Ohio, and a Master of Arts degree from George Mason University, Virginia. She has been an editorial assistant, researcher, and teacher of American and British literature. In addition to children's novels, she has written poems and plays that have been performed off Broadway, and adult novels. Some of her works are published under her married name of Sharon Rigg. Although at one point C. considered herself a poet and writer, it was her father's stroke, his six years of living a mute life, and his subsequent death that set in motion her unsuppressible need to write. Within one year of his death, she had penned three novels. When asked about how and why she wrote her NEW-BERY MEDAL winning novel *Walk Two Moons* (1994), C. shared three memories that served as sources: receiving a gift of leather moccasins on her twelfth birthday while vacationing with her family in Idaho; years later opening a fortune

cookie with the American Indian proverb, "Don't judge a man until you've walked two moons in his moccasins"; and her childhood desire to exaggerate her heritage of Indian culture. But C.'s explanations stop short of answering all the questions about her writing; she prefers to keep some mystery and dreams in the reader's reflections.

AWARDS: C.'s publication of *Walk Two Moons* earned her the 1995 Newbery Medal, the School Library Journal Best Book selection, and the AMERICAN LIBRARY ASSOCIATION Notable Children's Book selection. Earlier in her writing career, she received the Billee Murray Denny Poetry award in 1988 sponsored by Lincoln College in Illinois

FURTHER WORKS: *Absolutely Normal Chaos,* 1995; *Pleasing the Ghost,* 1996; and *Chasing Redbird,* 1997; *Bloomability,* 1998; *Fishing in the Air,* 2000

BIBLIOGRAPHY: www.sharoncreech.com

NANCY HORTON

CRESSWELL, Helen
Author, b. 11 July 1936, Nottingham, England

C. remembers loving to write as young as six or seven. Educated at Nottingham Girls High School, King's College, University of London, she worked as a literary assistant, fashion buyer, and teacher before her marriage. A self-admitted lover of words with immense feelings for place and atmosphere, C. exhibits these qualities in her works and her interests in gardening, walking, philosophy, and collecting antiques. Her characters, settings, and plots are familiar but bigger than life, spun with exaggeration, HUMOR, and unpredictability to entertain and intrigue her readers. C. has written for a range of levels from easy for young readers to rigorous reading for YOUNG ADULTS. Beginning as a writer of poetic fantasies, she varied her writings to depict humor, magic, and mystery. Publication of books, plays, television drama, and stories for readers number over one hundred. Collection or SERIES works include the Bagthorpe Saga, Jumbo Spenser stories, Posey Bates books, and Lizzie Dripping stories. Her characters, while lovable, are often eccentric and usually unpredictable in their behaviors, but always memorable for their fantastic adventures.

AWARDS: *The Piemakers* (1967), runner-up CAR-NEGIE MEDAL and runner-up Guardian Award;

22. ERIC CARLE

23. BEVERLY CLEARY

24. JOANNA COLE

25. BARBARA COONEY

26. SUSAN COOPER

27. ROBERT CORMIER

28. JOY COWLEY

29. DONALD CREWS

The Night-Watchman (1969), *Up the Pier* (1971), and *The Bongleweed* (1973), all runner-up Carnegie Medals; *Absolute Zero: Being the Second Part of the Bagthorpe Saga* (1978), Best Book by Library School Journal, AMERICAN LIBRARY ASSOCIATION Notable Book, and Children's Choice by International Association; *Bagthorpes Unlimited: Being the Third Part of the Bagthorpe Saga* (1978), Children's Choice by IRA and ALA Notable Book

FURTHER WORKS: *Sonya-by-the-Shore* (1960); *The Sea Piper* (1968); *The Signposters* (1968); *The Beachcombers* (1972); *The Winter of the Birds* (1976); *Dear Shrink* (1982); *The Secret World of Polly Flint* (1982); *Classic* FAIRY TALES (1993); as editor; *Moondial* (1987); *The Watchers: A Mystery at Alton Towers* (1994); *Time Out* (1997); *The Little Sea Pony* (1997)

BIBLIOGRAPHY: Egoff, Sheila, *Worlds Within,* 1988; Tomlinson, Carl M., ed., *Children's Books from Other Countries,* 1998; Townsend, John Rose, *A Sense of Story: Essays on Contemporary Writers for Children,* 1973: wwwpuffin.co.uk/living/aut_13

NANCY HORTON

CREWS, Donald

Author, illustrator, b. 30 August 1938, Newark, New Jersey

The third of four children, C. says he has "drawn and sketched for as long as I can remember." Influenced by their mother, all of the children "were . . . involved in art-related projects." Annual trips to Florida to visit his grandparents' small farm gave him the idea for the book *Freight Train* (1978). For three summer months the children watched and counted the long and frequent freight trains passing nearby.

An illustrator and author of PICTURE BOOKS, C. studied in Newark at Arts High School and later, at New York City's Cooper Union for the Advancement of Science and Art. He trained as a designer. C. was drafted and stationed in Germany for eighteen months with the U.S. Army. While there he wrote and illustrated *We Read: A to Z* to add to his portfolio. Published in 1967, it presents abstract concepts that are accessible to young children. Both upper- and lower-case letters appear on the left-hand page along with a word and an explanation of the word: e.g., Bb, bottom: where the green is. The visual representation appears on the right-hand page—A splash of green across the bottom of the page. The bright bold colors appeal to children. *We Read: A to Z* was named one of Fifty Best Illustrated Books of the Year, American Institute of Graphic Arts.

Ten Black Dots (1968) followed. It was redesigned and revised in 1986 using four-color preseparated art: red, yellow, blue, and black. The rhyming text expounds on each of the large dot ILLUSTRATIONS. Using everyday objects that children can recognize C. causes the dots to build to the number ten.

Eclipse: Darkness in Daytime (1973) was chosen as a Children's Book Showcase selection by the CHILDREN'S BOOK COUNCIL (1974). Written by Franklyn M. BRANLEY and illustrated by C., it was revised in 1988. The illustrations clearly present a total solar eclipse along with its effects on animals and ancient peoples.

Freight Train (1978) received a Notable Book citation, AMERICAN LIBRARY ASSOCIATION and was designated a CALDECOTT MEDAL Honor Book (1979). C. says he "works on real things from a piece of experience. The idea is to tell a story on a two-dimensional page. The book must be a moving experience and feel right." The freight train changes size as it moves through tunnels and cities and darkness and daylight until it is "gone." A big book edition was issued in 1993.

Rain by Robert Kalan, and illustrated by C. (1978), was an American Institute of Graphic Arts Book Show selection. The concept of rain is everywhere in this book. The actual word *rain* is used rather than visual raindrops and "rain" descends from the sky across page after page changing color from gray "rain" to blue sky "rain," green grass "rain," and black road "rain," and so forth.

Truck (1980) was chosen a Caldecott Medal Honor Book (1981) and received a Notable Book citation, American Library Association, 1980. A wordless book, *Truck* includes signs for young children to identify and roadways to follow. Done in four halftone separations combined with black line drawings, the reader follows a load of bicycles to their destination. C. uses bright colors and movement to entice children to look at the important places on the page.

C. believes, "If you are going to do a picture book for children it should have some value." *School Bus* (1984) is dedicated: "For the buses, the riders, and the watchers." The book opens with row upon row of yellow school buses facing the reader, ready to go and ends with row upon row of yellow school buses parked with the caption, "home again." A comforting book for young children, especially those who will be going to school for the first time on a school bus.

Harbor (1982) presents a busy active place where motor cruisers, tankers, fire boats, and passenger liners appear. To create the book he cut and pasted wax-backed paper. Colorful images outlined in black are the primary focus with minimal text identifying the activities and objects. It is one of several transportation books C. has done for young children.

Parade (1983) features various participants in a colorful progression viewed by faceless watchers. The cavalcade builds on double-page spreads and moves from right to left so it is coming at the reader as though passing by. Minimal text and the groupings of faceless people make this a book that can be used with children in art creations where they can feature their own parade.

Flying (1986) was chosen as one of the *New York Times* Best Illustrated Children's Books of the Year. Another book in the transportation theme, the words follow the pictures as the two-propeller plane is boarded, takes off in daylight, then flies and lands in darkness. The full-color art was done with gouache paints and an airbrush. Although somewhat outdated with today's jet engines, the book simplifies a plane trip and provides information for children.

In *Bigmama's* (1991), C. returns to the setting of Cottondale, Florida, and his grandparents' farm. The reader sees Big Mama's house, inside and out. Watercolor and gouache paints were used to create the full-color illustrations; the text correlates with the pictures, which are meaningful reminiscences for the author of his childhood. A book takes about a year for C. to do and each book has its own memories for the artist–author. The author's recollections create memories for readers of their own visits to family and grandparents.

FURTHER WORKS: *Bicycle Race,* 1985; *Each Orange Had 8 Slices,* 1992; *Shortcut,* 1992; *Sail Away,* 1995; *Tomorrow's Alphabet,* 1996

BIBLIOGRAPHY: *Best Books for Children: Preschool through Grade 6,* 5th ed. 1994. *Children's Literature AWARDS and Winners, Authors and Il-*lustrators, 3rd ed. 1994. *Children's Literature Review.* 1984. *Fiction, FOLKLORE, FANTASY and POETRY for Children, 1876–1985.* 1986. Lecture by Donald Crews, University of Minnesota, June 19, 1990. Silvey, Anita, ed.; *Children's Books and Their Creators.* 1995; *Something about the Author,* vol. 30, 1983 vol. 32, 1983, and vol. 76 1994

IRVYN GILBERTSON

CRITICAL THEORISTS

Critical theory for children's literature is largely a phenomenon of the last twenty years; it is the result of "children's literature" becoming a university discipline in its own right, and of critical theory breaking down old value structures that regarded children's books as beneath theoretical notice. Previous to that, writing on children's books was largely confined to descriptive surveys (such as John Rowe TOWNSEND's *Written for Children,* 1980), prescriptive or selective criticism (such as Michelle Landsberg's *The World of Children's Books,* 1985), or educational applications (such as Bernice E. Cullinan and Lee Galda's *Children's Literature and the Child,* 1998, 4th ed.). Excellent as these are, they do not find the subject problematic: theory is not required, and concepts of "goodness" and "literature" are applied that do not acknowledge any ambiguity. The fundamental problem for all theorists has been that children's literature "belongs" to different disciplines, with different mindsets and critical standards.

There have been two general movements: the first, to apply theory developed for other kinds of literature to children's literature; this usually involves fascinating negotiations between the relative simplicity of peer-related criticism and the complexity of taking the "child reader" into account; the other, to develop a new theory specifically for children's literature, sometimes modifying existing theory.

Roderick McGillis's *The Nimble Reader* (1996) and Perry Nodelman's *The Pleasures of Children's Literature* (1996), the latter a highly respected text, have been the best attempts to apply theory and to make it accessible. Both emphasize the richness of the literature and the importance of individual readings and reactions. L. Paul's *Reading Otherways* (1998) provides a succinct synthesis of theory for the lay reader, which amounts to a fresh concept of critical reading.

Among more specialist approaches which apply feminist theory to literature are Marjorie Houlihan's *Deconstructing the Hero* (1997), which applies cultural theory, and Murray Knowles and Kirsten Malmkjaer's *Language and Control in Children's Literature* (1996), which applies stylistics and computational linguistics. Tony Watkins (1998) in the U.K. and Mitzi Myers (1997) in the United States, have eloquently advocated a historicist approach. Several studies have incorporated modern critical thinking into historical studies, notably the feminist-historicist approach to "classic" girls' stories by Shirley Foster and Judy Simons in *What Katy Read* (1995). Maria Nikolajeva's *Introduction to the Theory of Children's Literature* (1997) presents a basic review of the whole field.

Aiden CHAMBERS, who extended Rosenblatt's *The Reader, the Text, the Poem* (1978), has been one of the most widely influential theorists; his concern has been specifically with the interaction of the text and the reader. His *The Reader in the Book* developed the work of Wolfgang Iser (*The Implied Reader,* 1974). Chambers's pragmatic theories are collected in *Booktalk* (1985), and in a series of practical explorations of reader response and eliciting reader response, notably in *Tell Me* (1993). Possibly the most dramatic and original blending of contemporary literary— notably feminist—theory has been Lissa Paul's series of articles in the British journal *Signal,* notably "Intimations of Imitations: Mimesis, Fractal Geometry and Children's Literature (1992)."

Among the most recent developments of theory specific to children's books has been Peter Hollindale's *Signs of Childness in Children's Literature* (1997), which attempts to redefine children's literature without using conventional terminology. Peter Hunt's *Criticism, Theory and Children's Literature* (1991), similarly, puts forward the idea of "childist" criticism—reading as far as possible from the point of view of children. In the Yale journal *Children's Literature* the idea of "cross-writing" has been developed by Mitzi Myers and U. C. Knoepflmacher (1997). Picture books, arguably the area that is most original to children's literature, have been theorized by Perris Nodelman (*Words about Pictures,* 1988), Jane

Doonan (*Looking at Pictures in* PICTURE BOOKS, 1993), Victor Watson, and Morag Styles (*Talking Pictures,* 1998), and in the work of David Lewis and Geoff Moss.

One of the most stimulating theoretical incursions into the field, by a scholar only incidentally concerned with children's literature has been Jacqueline Rose's *The Case of Peter Pan or the Impossibility of Children's Literature* (1984). In this, she argues that it is impossible for adults to write for children without in some way violating the child and the adult-child relationship—an unsurprising conclusion given her main text. This thesis was extended by Karin Lesnik-Oberstein in *Children's Literature and the Fictional Child* (1994); she suggests that the "child" in children's book criticism is a misleading abstraction, and that the only way forward for real criticism is through individual psychotherapy. Needless to say, this view has been refuted by pragmatists such as Nodelman and Margaret Meek.

Little has been theorized on race or postcolonialism, although this lack is rapidly being corrected. Certainly the question of ideology has been addressed by Charles Sarland and by Peter Hollindale, whose *Ideology and the Children's Book* (1988) has been widely influential.

Despite these books, much of the children's-book world remains hostile or indifferent to theory. At best, it might well be that theorizing microencounters of book and child may produce a theory that is unique to children's books and that will be influential in the long-term.

BIBLIOGRAPHY: Chambers, A., *Booktalk,* 1985; Chambers, A., *Tell Me, Children, Reading and Talk,* 1993; Cullinan, B. E. and L. Galda, *Children's Literature and the Child,* 4th ed, 1998; Doonan, J., *Looking at Pictures in Picture Books,* 1993; Foster, S. and J. Simons, *What Katy Read,* 1995; Hollindale, P., *Ideology and the Children's Book,* 1988; Hollindale, P., *Signs of Childness in Children's Literature,* 1997; Houlihan, M., *Deconstructing the Hero,* 1997; Hunt, P. *Criticism, Theory, and Children's Literature,* 1991; Knowles, M. and K. Malmkjaer, *Language and Control in Children's Literature,* 1996; Landsberg, M., *The World of Children's Books,* 1985; Lesnik-Oberstein, K. *Children's Literature and the Fictional Child,* 1994; McGillis, R., *The Nimble Reader;* Myers, M. and U. C. Knoepflmacher, " 'Cross-Writing' and the Reconceptualizing of Children's Literature Studies." *Children's Liter-*

ature, 25, 1997. vii–xvii; Paul, L. "Intimations of Imitations: Mimesis, Fractal Geometry, and Children's Literature" in Hunt, P. ed. *Literature for Children,* 1992; Paul, L., *Reading Otherways,* 1998; Nikolajeva, M. *Introduction to the Theory of Children's Literature,* 1887; Nodelman, P. *The Pleasures of Children's Literature,* 1996; Nodelman, P., *Words about Pictures,* 1988; Rose, J. *The Case of Peter Pan; or, The Impossibility of Children's Literature,* 1984; Sarland, C. "Ideology" in P. Hunt, ed. *International Companion of Children's Literature;* Townsend, J. R., *Written for Children,* 1980; Trites, R. S., *Waking Sleeping Beauty,* 1997; Watson, V. and M. Styles, ed. *Talking Pictures.* 1998

PETER HUNT

CROSS, Gillian
Author, b. 24 December 1945, London, England

C. writes to attract the attention of young adults who normally would not be avid readers. She is credited with creating fast-paced stories that include psychological thrillers, historical fiction, and HUMOR. C. grew up reading, writing, and performing for all who would pay attention to her. C.'s education includes a B.A. and M.A. from Somerville College, Oxford, and a doctorate of philosophy from the University of Sussex. In addition to writing, she has worked as a teacher, clerk assistant, and assistant to a Member of Parliament. While in college studying accomplished writers, she became overwhelmed by the complexities of quality writing. She would be almost thirty years old before she finally realized that she could write by focusing on the story she wanted to tell and keeping her target audience in mind rather than all the fine intricacies. It was at this point that she began her works that are considered social realism for YOUNG ADULTS. Although she uses the darker aspects of life, she develops characters who confront their problems and foster happier lives as the result of their decision making. An example of this type of character development exists in *On the Edge* (1984), an Edgar Allan Poe and Whitbread finalist, when a young boy is kidnapped and must struggle to maintain his identity.

AWARDS: C.'s writings have received myriad AWARDS through two decades. In 1982, she received the CARNEGIE MEDAL Highly Commended Book and Guardian Award runner-up for *The Dark behind the Curtain* (1982). *On the Edge* fol-

lowed in the mideighties as an AMERICAN LIBRARY ASSOCIATION Best Book for Young Adults and Notable Book, the Whitbread Award runner-up, and the Edgar Allan Poe runner-up. The publication of *Chartbreak* (1986), titled *Chartbreaker* in the U.S., brought C. the Carnegie commended book in 1986 and an ALA best book for young adults in 1987. The 1988 runnerup Carnegie Medal was *A Map of Nowhere* (1989). *Wolf* was recognized with the Carnegie Medal in 1991. Smarties Prize and the Whitbread Children's Novel Award went to *The Great American Elephant Chase* (1993)

FURTHER WORKS: *The Iron Way,* 1979; *Save Our Schools,* 1981; *The Demon Headmaster,* 1982; *Twin and Super-Twin,* 1990; *New World,* 1994

BIBLIOGRAPHY: Gallo, Donald R., ed., *Speaking for Ourselves Too,* 1993; Hunt, Peter, ed., *Children's Literature: An Illustrated History,* 1995; Tomlinson, Carl M., ed., *Children's Books from Other Countries,* 1998; www.puffin.co.uk/living/aut_14

NANCY HORTON

CROSSLEY-HOLLAND, Kevin
Author, b. 7 February 1941, Mursley, Buckingham, England

C. is an author, editor, and poet who brings ageless tales, myths, and legends to children's literature. He grew up in a musical family playing the viola and incorporated this background into the rhythms of his works. Receiving an M.A. from St. Edmund Hall, Oxford, in 1962, he has worked as an editor, translator, professor, and visiting lecturer in many countries including England, Germany, Iceland, India, and Yugoslavia. He also contributed to radio and television dramas. C.'s focus lies primarily with his ability to bring stories from the far past to the timely interests of contemporary young readers. These retellings feature plots and characters with universal truths about life for modern audiences. His first publication for YOUNG ADULTS was *Havelak the Dane* (1964). He continued his works in Anglo-Saxon stories and added East Anglian tales and medieval novels. Many of his works are adaptations of stories that include haunting tales of witches, dead hands, and ghosts.

AWARDS: Writing AWARDS C. has received include the Arts Council for the best book for children for *The Green Children* in 1966–68, the Francis Williams Award as editor for *The Wildman* in

1977, and the CARNEGIE MEDAL for *Storm* in 1985. As a poet, he received an award for *The Rain-Giver* in 1972, the Poetry Book Society Choice for *The Dream House* in 1976, and the Poetry Book Society Recommendation for *Waterslain and other Poems* in 1986

FURTHER WORKS: *The Sea Stranger* (1973); *The Fire-Brother* (1974); *The Earth-Father* (1976); *The Dead Moon and Other Tales from East Anglia and the Fen Country* (1982); *Beowulf* (1982); *Tales from the Mabinogion* with Gwyn Thomas (1984); *Small-Tooth Dog* (1988); *Under the Sun and Over the Moon* (1989); *Norse Myths* (1993)

BIBLIOGRAPHY: Tomlinson, Carl M., ed., *Children's Books from Other Countries,* 1998; dust-jacket flyleaves

NANCY HORTON

CROSSOVERS: CHILDREN'S BOOKS FOR ADULT READERS

It is certainly not unusual to see a child or a teenager browsing adult books in libraries and bookstores, hunting materials for research or flipping through items on a best-seller rack. The best current example is the Harry Potter SERIES by J. K. ROWLING. However, most adults who scan the juvenile shelves have a child in tow. Even if they happen to be among those enlightened grownups who know that children's literature is not "second class" and that books for young people are often the best place to begin investigations on almost any subject, they usually are not looking for books for themselves. Consequently, they are likely to be missing some tremendous new material.

Dramatic changes in publishing over the last decade have begun to erode traditionally accepted boundaries between children's and adult books. Today, the fact that a book has thirty-two pages, full-color illustrations, and a nine-by-thirteen-inch trim size no longer automatically means "for children only" any more than the presence of a fourteen-year-old protagonist signifies a particular book is a teenage novel. PICTURE BOOKS with campy artwork or complex irony are increasing in number, and a flood of edgy, sophisticated novels for young readers has emerged from juvenile book departments: Australian writer Sonya Harnett's dark novel *Sleeping Dogs* (1995) revolves around sibling incest; Suzanne Fisher STAPLES's *Shabanu* (1989) introduces a young Pakistani woman dealing with cultural conflict and

concepts of loyalty, loss, and feminism; and rape and murder are an integral part of Brock COLE's *The Facts Speak for Themselves* (1997). Substantive, incisive, and stylistically polished, these novels rival much adult fiction in quality; they also have significant adult appeal. Rollicking good fun and thumbing one's nose at stuffy-adult conventions propelled J. K. ROWLING's Harry Potter series to the top of the *New York Times* bestseller charts for months. *Harry Potter and the Sorcerer's Stone* (1998), the story of a reluctant adolescent at a school for witchcraft who finds himself with magic powers, appeared as the number-one seller on both the hardcover and paper back lists simultaneously, with *Harry Potter and the Chamber of Secrets* (1999) and *Harry Potter and the Prisoner of Azkaban* (1999) in the number two and three positions for several weeks. *Harry Potter and the Goblet of Fire* was another publishing phenomenon in mid-2000.

The trick is letting adults know they are out there. Unfortunately, that is not as straightforward as it seems. Publicity and marketing departments for children's and adult books, particularly in larger publishing houses, are frequently separate entities, with different budgets and distinct agendas that leave little room for cross-promotion. And bookstores traditionally follow publisher's leads as to placement of titles: Annette Curtis KLAUSE's werewolf story *Blood and Chocolate* (1997), part smoldering romance, part visceral horror story, part feminist fiction is likely to be found with children's or young adult titles, even though adult FANTASY fans will love it. As Judith Rosen points out in "Breaking the Age Barrier" (*Publishers Weekly,* September 8, 1997): "it sometimes seems that where a book is placed on the bookshelf has less to do with content than with the division that happened to publish it."

Some changes do, however, seem to be taking place. Knopf Books for Young Readers division spent a generous amount on cross-marketing *The Golden Compass* (1996), the first volume in Philip PULLMAN's lush fantasy trilogy. The following year, the CHILDREN'S BOOK COUNCIL, comprising a diverse group of children's booksellers, editors, and publishers, added its voice with the publication of *"Not Just for Children Anymore!"* an annual roundup of children's books likely to attract "the many adults who buy, or are receptive to buying, children's books for themselves." Chosen by a four-member panel of booksellers from submissions made by publishers (who contribute a small fee to cover the costs of producing the pamphlet), the compilation includes a wide variety of children's titles, along with suggestions for presenting and positioning them in stores to capture the adult market. In 1998, HarperCollins juvenile division tried a different tactic. It began repackaging selected young adult titles—among them, Hazel Rochman and Darlene McCampbell's *Leaving Home* (1977), an anthology of stories written by adult-book authors—in sophisticated paperback format, with upscale prices and with covers designed to appeal to adult readers. HarperCollins spokesperson Ginee Seo hangs the idea on the work of popular YA author Francesca Lia BLOCK, whose "postmodern FAIRY TALES" and magic realism have attracted a substantial college-age following and have been mentioned in such popular-press publications as *Spin* magazine and the *Village Voice.*

Unlike publishers and booksellers, librarians have no underlying financial agenda in promoting children's books to adults, but they also frequently lack the resources to alert them to appropriate material. Adult collection development and readers' services librarians may not have ready access to children's and YA reviews or, more importantly, to the books themselves. To address this, *Booklist,* the review publication of the AMERICAN LIBRARY ASSOCIATION, introduced the column "Crossovers" in 1998, its contribution to the blurring of the age barrier in books. A feature appearing twice a year in the Adult Books section of the magazine, it targets children's fiction, nonfiction, and picture-book titles that adult services librarians should know about. Theme, content, format, and design were of equal importance in *Booklist* editors' selections. So was jacket art. Some great books did not make the final cut because the jacket art seemed too juvenile for adults who browse the shelves.

Children's and young adult nonfiction, particularly in the areas of history and biography, provides fertile ground for crossovers. Tom FEELINGS's *The Middle Passage* (1995), for example, is a powerful combination of history and art that reconstructs in dramatic black-and-white paintings the passage of enslaved Africans to the

Americas. All of Russell FREEDMAN's biographies, whether about Crazy Horse, Lincoln, or Martha Graham, have direct adult appeal, too, with excellent photos as well as enough information to satisfy even some discriminating adult readers. And there is a host of fine autobiographies: Anita LOBEL's *No Pretty Pictures: A Child of War* (1998) tells of the well-known picture-book author's dark, terrifying childhood hiding from the Nazis and in the concentration camps, and books such as Beverly CLEARY's *My Own Two Feet* (1995) and Roald DAHL's *Going Solo* (1986) will appeal to any adult with an interest in literary life.

The children's poetry shelf is yet another place for finding bridge books. Palestinian American poet Naomi Shihab NYE has written and edited books for both children and adults. *The Space between Our Footsteps: Poems and Paintings from the Middle East* (1998), which she edited, was published for young people, but grown-ups, including fans of her adult books, will enjoy it and have no problem with the jacket, which is not the least bit childish. And there is nothing juvenile about the strong sturdy poems of well-known Appalachian children's book writer Cynthia RYLANT, which appear in *Something Permanent* (1994) alongside famous photographer Walker Evans's photos of Southern life during the Depression. *War and the Pity of War* (1998) edited by Neil Philip, is another good example. An outstanding collection of poems capturing the bravery and cruelty of conflicts across the world and through history, it includes work by Alfred Lord Tennyson, Rupert Brooke, and other classic and contemporary writers whose work will be familiar to many adult poetry enthusiasts.

Adults can also find some unexpected delights among children's picture books. *The Stinky Cheese Man and Other Fairly Stupid Tales* (1993), written by Jon SCIESZKA and illustrated by Lane SMITH, is a raucous collection of fractured fairy tales that will have adults laughing as hard as children. Every part of the book bears the loving stamp of its creators, whose dry, sometimes dark HUMOR, wordplay, and wacky sophomoric jokes will attract a considerable adult following. Maira KALMAN's picture books are also noted for their rich wordplay. Kalman's art style is elaborate, exciting, and very adult. In *Ooh-La-La: Max in Love* (1991), Max the dog-poet dashes around Paris looking for the love of his life. It is a similar retrohip look that will attract grownup readers to J. Otto Siebold's *Mr. Lunch* books, about a dog who is the Michael Jordan of bird chasers.

Art books like Marc Aronson's *Art Attack* (1998), which plunges readers into the history and culture of the avant-garde movement; short story collections, like Chaim Potok's *Zebra* (1998), comprising stories that originally appeared in magazines for adults; novels like Victor Martinez's a 1996 National Book Award winner *Parrot in the Oven,* an authentic portrayal of Hispanic life in an urban California housing project: there is an enormous range of material available. The idea of books written for one age group having appeal for an entirely different age group certainly is not new. What is different these days is that everyone is starting to pay more attention.

STEPHANIE ZVIRIN

(See also YOUNG ADULT LITERATURE)

CRUTCHER, Chris(topher)
Author, b. 17 July 1946, Cascade, Idaho

C. brings the insight, sensitivity, and awareness he has developed in his child-and-family therapy practice to his fiction writing for YOUNG ADULTS. His REALISTIC novels and short stories all contain characters for whom mental health as well as emotional stability and physical safety are at stake.

After graduating from Eastern Washington State College (now University) in 1968, C. taught at and directed alternative secondary schools for youth who had dropped out, or were in danger of dropping out, before high school graduation. In 1980, he turned from teaching to more therapeutic and investigative activities with children at risk, working for child protective services and then as a family therapist.

C.'s first novel, *Running Loose* (1983), was named a Best Book for Young Adults by the AMERICAN LIBRARY ASSOCIATION that year. *Stotan!* (1986) and *Chinese Handcuffs* (1989) earned the same honor in their respective years of publication. In 2000, C. was honored for his body of work with the Margaret A. Edwards Award, by ALA's Young Adult Library Services Association.

The teenaged protagonists of C.'s novels often come from dysfunctional homes, the details of which are realistically portrayed by the author/therapist who uses evidence from his mental health career to inform his artistic productions. Because of his own lifelong enjoyment of SPORTS, C. also usually includes well-rendered athletic motifs in his fiction. *Stotan!* concerns the rigors of a high school swim team while *The Crazy Horse Electric Game* (1987) is titled for the baseball event that becomes the catalyst for the ensuing action in this novel. The contents of *Athletic Shorts: Six Short Stories* (1991) feature youth engaged in various athletic pursuits.

C. occasionally peoples his later books with characters he has created in earlier ones, as happens in *Ironman* (1995) where the cast of adult characters in the teen protagonist's life include some who first appeared in *Stotan!*

C. provides interventions such as anger-management training classes in the plots he develops and through which his protagonists grow. Like the various sports of which he writes so compellingly, the clinical details of such group-and-individual-therapy situations are realistic and engage young readers as a means of coming to understand how mental health care providers interact with clients and groups. Although reviews of C.'s books often note that his characters are talky, his dialogues impart much in the way of life-skill information as well as character development.

The settings for C.'s fiction are almost all school-based but range among urban, suburban, and rural places, each of which he realizes with subtle accuracy. Characters are multiracial and include those with such diverse characteristics as being gay, exceptionally brilliant, or physically disfigured. Each novel contains a particular ethical issue, among which are racism, ostracism, and suicide. In spite of the grimness that drives most of C.'s plots, including abusive fathers, fatal illness, and running away from home, there is much HUMOR in his narratives, both spoken by his characters and embedded in their interactions.

C. continues to use his writing as a vehicle for exploring the events he uncovers in his mental-health practice. His identity as an author is enmeshed in his work toward the safety and well-being of children in peril both because of circumstances beyond their choosing and because they have not learned how to reflect on healthy possibilities from which to choose.

FURTHER WORKS: *The Deep End,* 1992; *Staying Fat for Sarah Byrnes,* 1993; *Whale Talk,* 2001

BIBLIOGRAPHY: *Contemporary Authors, New Revision Series,* vol. 36, 1992; Davis, Terry, *Presenting Chris C.,* 1997; Silvey, Anita, ed., *Children's Book and Their Creators,* 1995

FRANCISCA GOLDSMITH

CUFFARI, Richard
Illustrator, b. 2 March 1925, Brooklyn, New York

C. began his career working as a painter and illustrator for a variety of art studios. He illustrated a new edition of Kenneth GRAHAME's *The Wind in the Willows* in 1966, which began his stint as an illustrator of children's books. C. noted that his fascination with history and personalities has helped him in his career as a children's illustrator. His personal interests are reflected in his works and hopefully lend a "vitality" that make them appeal to children. C. has stated that he feels it is a privilege to work for children in any capacity.

FURTHER WORKS: *The Winged Colt of Casa Mia* (Betsy BYARS, author). 1973; *Hunter's Stew and Hangtown Fry: What Pioneer America Ate and Why* (Lila PERL, author). 1977; *Perilous Guard* (Elizabeth Marie POPE, author), 1974. *Cartoonist.* Betsy Byars, author), 1978

MICHAEL O'LAUGHLIN

CUMMINGS, Pat
Author, illustrator, b. 9 November 1950, Chicago, Illinois

C. was launched into her art career before the age of eight when, on a military base in Germany, she followed some girls onto a bus and spent an afternoon in a ballet class. Grounded for a lengthy period, she occupied herself drawing ballet dancers, which her friends subsequently bought. Art has been her love and her living ever since. Supported by the positive, constructive attitudes of her parents, C. used her artistic talent to accommodate the always-changing school situations of her mobile military family. Designing art for yearbooks and theater productions allowed her to become part of each new school community in which she found herself. She studied art formally and worked at commercial art jobs, including painting sets, illustrating publicity material, and designing costumes for children's theater. Eventually, inspired by the books her mother read to her as a child, she applied her talent to illustrating children's books. She has also been influenced by other children's book illustrators, most notably Tom FEELINGS, who gave her pointers when she started her first ILLUSTRATION project. C. incorporates the people, places, and events from the many and varied environments and experiences to which she was sensitized as a child. Her closeness to her siblings, the consistent peers of her childhood, also provide topics for her work.

C.'s mission is to help children see that difficult situations and disturbing emotions can be resolved or softened with a positive and willing outlook. She tries to visualize from a child's point of view. Using themes common to children's lives, such as the struggle to be responsible, fear of new situations, disappointment in a parent, and the emotional complexities of sibling relations, she lubricates serious issues with humor and warmth. Childhood experiences with racial exclusion prompted her efforts to emphasize inclusion in both her stories and illustrations. Her pictures are integral to the texts, telling unwritten portions through facial expressions and body postures. Her careful use of color and light enhance the mood of her stories, whether to ease the tension of a difficult emotional situation (*Carousel,* 1994) or enhance the suspense of a scary one (*Storm in the Night,* 1988).

AWARDS: In 1984, C.'s illustrations for *My Mama Needs Me* (WALTER, 1983) earned the CORETTA SCOTT KING AWARD and honorable mentions in 1983 for *Just Us Women* (Caines, 1982) (also a notable book by the NCSS and the CHILDREN'S BOOK COUNCIL, and C.L.O.U.D.S. in 1987). She won the Black Women in Publishing Award in 1988. 1992, her edited collection, *Talking with Artists,* was an AMERICAN LIBRARY ASSOCIATION Notable Book and received the *Boston Globe/ Horn Book* Award for Nonfiction in 1992 and the ORBIS PICTUS AWARD in 1993

FURTHER WORKS: *Good News* (GREENFIELD, 1977), *Fred's First Day* (Warren, 1984); *Jimmy Lee Did It* (1985); *Two and Two Much* (Walter, 1990); *Clean Your Room, Harvey Moon!* (1991); *Petey Moroni's Camp Runamok Diary* (1992); *"C" Is for City* (GRIMES, 1994), *My Aunt Came Back* (1998)

BIBLIOGRAPHY: *Something about the Author,* vol. 42, 1993; Library of Congress website; *Children's Literature Web Guide*

MARGARET YATSEVITCH PHINNEY

CUNNINGHAM, Julia
Author, b. 4 October 1916, Spokane, Washington

Although C. started writing at the age of nine, she did not publish her first book until the age of forty-four. Since 1960, she has published over twenty books including PICTURE BOOKS, juvenile novels, YOUNG ADULT novels, and poetry for adults. A versatile writer, she is as well known for her humanlike animal characters as for her realistic and sometimes violent fiction both contemporary and historical. Many of her books are set in France and frequently feature orphans and urchins as main characters. Her work explores major themes about the meaning of life, the power of love, isolation, and spiritual freedom. She believes that children can understand and respond to sophisticated themes; she prides herself on not speaking down to her readers. *Drop Dead* (1965, James Spanfeller, illustrator) is her most famous and controversial work; it is about a learning-disabled child, and the spelling of the title makes the point. (See the DISABLED IN CHILDREN'S AND YOUNG ADULT LITERATURE.) *Dorp Dead* received AWARDS from the *New York Herald Tribune,* Southern California Council on Literature for Children and Young People, and the Lewis CARROLL Shelf Award.

FURTHER WORKS: *Dear Rat,* 1961; *Maybe, a Mole* (Cyndy SZEKERES, illus), 1974; *Oaf* (Peter SIS, illus). 1986; *The Shadow Heart: Poems,* 1999

AWARDS: Southern California Council on Literature for Children and Young People for a Body of Work (1982). Christopher Award and Lewis Carroll Shelf Award (1978) for *Come to the Edge New York Times* Outstanding Book and NBA finalist (1973) for *The Treasure Is the Rose. New York Times* Outstanding Book (1970) for *Burnish Me Bright*

BIBLIOGRAPHY: HOPKINS, Lee Bennett, *Pauses: Autobiographical Reflections of 101 Creators of Children's Books,* 1995; *Contemporary Authors Online,* 1999; Interview by M. Jerry Weiss in *From Writers to Students,* 1979

SUSAN SWORDS STEFFEN

CURRY, Jane Louise
Author, b. 24 September 1932, East Liverpool, Ohio

C. credits author E. NESBIT for her interest in FANTASY and time travel. Her professions have not been limited to books: she has taught art, stagecraft, English, and writing for various levels. She also has commented on how her Gypsy-like lifestyle on two continents has allowed her the freedom to continue writing. In 1969, *The Change Child* was named an AMERICAN LIBRARY ASSOCIATION Notable Book. Many other of C.'s books have also won AWARDS. *The Daybreakers* (1970) was a Book World's Children's Spring Book Festival Honor Book; *The Watchers* (1975) was chosen a *New York Times* Notable Book; *Poor Tom's Ghost* (1978) and *The Bassumtyte Treasure* (1979) were selected by the Mystery Writers of America. The four Smith children help break up a forgery ring and a burglary in *The Big Smith Snatch* (1989) and *Great Smith House Hustle* (1993). C. provides lots of clues for readers in these suspenseful tales. C. was cited for her "Distinguished Contribution to the Field of Children's Literature" for her body of work from the Southern California Council on Literature for Children and Young People (1979).

FURTHER WORKS: *Back in the Beforetime: Tales of the California Indians,* 1987; *The Christmas Knight,* 1993; *Moon Window,* 1996; *Dark Shade,* 1998; *A Stolen Life,* 1999; *Turtle Island: Tales of the Algonquian Nations,* 1999

BIBLIOGRAPHY: *Contemporary Authors,* vols. 17–18; *Fourth Book of Junior Authors and Illustrators,* 1978; *Something about the Author,* vol. 1, 1971

BARBARA JAINDL

CURTIS, Christopher Paul
Author, b. 10 May 1954, Flint, Michigan

Following a traditional upbringing, in which his father was a chiropodist (podiatrist) and his mother stayed at home, C. entered the University of Michigan in 1971 but left before graduating. Unsure of what he wanted to do, C., the first AFRICAN AMERICAN male author to win the NEWBERY MEDAL, went to work on the assembly line at an automobile plant in 1972. He hated his job attaching doors to car frames and remembers dreaming about working on the assembly line. In his dreams he would imagine his bed moving across the floor to keep up with the steady movement of cars and car parts. He eventually quit the assembly line in 1985 and held a series of jobs he calls uninspiring. C.'s wife remembered the long, detailed letters he wrote to her before their marriage and encouraged him to write a book instead of wasting his time working at jobs he did not like. She encouraged C. to take one year off and concentrate on writing a book.

The Watsons Go to Birmingham—1963 (1995) became his first book. It tells the story of a ten-year-old boy and his family who travel from Flint, Michigan, to visit their grandmother. In Birmingham, Alabama, they get caught up in the events of the 16th Street Baptist Church bombing in which four African American children were killed. Within the context of the story, C. gives information about the migration of Southern African Americans to the industrial North. In 1996 the book was named an AMERICAN LIBRARY ASSOCIATION Newbery Medal Honor Book and a CORETTA SCOTT KING AWARDS Honor Book.

C. has written his family into his second children's book, *Bud, Not Buddy* (1999), about a foster child during the Great Depression who goes in search of Herman E. Caldwell, a jazz musician playing with a group called the Dusky Devastators of the Depression!!!!!!, who he thinks is his father. Bud is befriended by Lefty Lewis, an unemployed Pullman porter, labor organizer, and former pitcher in the Negro Leagues. C.'s maternal grandfather was named Lefty Lewis; he pitched in the Negro Leagues and worked as a Pullman porter. His other grandfather, Herman E. Curtis, a conservatory-trained violinist, also had a jazz band called the Dusky Devastators of the Depression!!!!!! C.'s young daughter wrote the song "Mommy Says No," used in *Bud, Not Buddy,* and owns the copyright to it.

C. writes with warmth and HUMOR for mature readers; he captures the language of the Great Depression and the desperation of a young black child who needs to escape his cruel foster home and find out who he is. C.'s books are coming-of-age stories with universal appeal. *Bud, Not Buddy* is the year 2000 recipient of both the ALA Newbery Medal and the Coretta Scott King Author Award.

BIBLIOGRAPHY: *New York Times,* January 21, 2000, and January 22, 2000, vol. 159, no. 57, 275, and no. 57, 276, pp. E3 and C9

DIANE G. PERSON

CUSHMAN, Karen
Author, b. 4 October 1941, Chicago, Illinois

C. writes historical fiction, developing both setting and characters in detail after conscientious, painstaking research. A move during her childhood and her research-based college degrees proved to be foundations in writing her young adult novels. She graduated from Stanford University with a B.A. in English and Greek, U.S. International University, San Diego with an M.A. in human behavior, and John F. Kennedy University, Orinda, California, with an M.A. in museum studies. C.'s move to California with her family when she was eleven years old provided emotions that would later serve as a foundation for her character Lucy's reaction to life changes in *The Ballad of Lucy Whipple* (1996). C.'s interest in young adult literature began while reading with her daughter. When her daughter progressed to adult novels, C. continued reading YOUNG ADULT LITERATURE because she liked the themes and the characters who were coming of age, learning to accept responsibility, and developing compassion. C. was fifty years old before she wrote her first book. Throughout her adult life, C. had attended writer's conferences in which speakers encouraged only certain popular, marketable topics of the moment and discouraged C.'s own interests, which were historical fiction, diaries, and the Middle Ages. C. got the confidence to put her interests in writing for publication only after hearing an inspirational speech delivered by author Ray BRADBURY. He advised writers to write from the heart. With Bradbury's words, she set out to tell her stories. Three novels later, she was a multiple-award-winning author with the prestigious NEWBERY MEDAL. Her first two novels are set in the medieval world and feature strong adolescent female characters. The first book, *Catherine, Called Birdy* (1994) took her three years to research and write. Her continuing interest in the Middle Ages led her to write her Newbery Medal winner *The Midwife's Apprentice* (1995). Her third book *The Ballad of Lucy Whipple* is a story of a young girl going west with her family during the Gold Rush.

AWARDS: Newbery Medal for *The Midwife's Apprentice* (1995). Her previous publication, *Catherine, Called Birdy* (1994) was cited as a Newbery Metal Honor Book, Carl Sandburg Award for Children's Literature, Golden Kite Aware, *School Library Journal* Best Book, and the Parents' Choice Foundation Ten Best Book list

BIBLIOGRAPHY: www.eduplace.com/rdg/author/cushman; www.ipl.org/youth/AskAuthor/cushmanbio

NANCY HORTON

D

DAHL, Roald

Author, screenwriter, b. 13 September 1916, Llandaff, South Wales; d. 23 November 1990, Oxford, England

Energetic and mischievous as a child, and controversial as an adult, D.'s works entertain young and old in many countries. His father was a Norwegian shipbroker, from near Oslo. His mother was a strong, courageous woman who was determined to provide excellent education for her children, even after their father's death from pneumonia in 1920. D. graduated from British public schools in 1932. Experiences from his childhood schooling provided fodder for later episodes in his modern FAIRY TALES for children. After his education, D. worked for an oil company for the opportunity of traveling to faraway places. In 1939, he joined the Royal Air Force training squadron in Nairobi, Kenya, then fought German forces in the Mediterranean Sea during World War II. He moved to Washington, D.C., in 1942 to work for the British Embassy. It was here that D. wrote his first story for publication, somewhat by chance. Over a lunch interview for the *Saturday Evening Post,* D. made some notes while the interviewer ate. The notes proved to be of high quality and were published under D.'s name with the title "Piece of Cake." They were later published in book format as *Over to You: Ten Stories of Fliers and Flying* (1946). D. continued to be a contributor to anthologies and periodicals including *Colliers, Harper's, Ladies Home Journal, Tomorrow,* and *Town and Country.* Gradually his writing moved from nonfiction to fiction. *The Gremlins* (1943) was his first children's book and although he didn't invent the word for the miniature creatures, he was the first to publish them as characters in a book.

D.'s popularity with his audience has never been questioned; however some critics question his presentation of adult authority figures and minority characters. In D.'s stories for children, cruel, unloving adults dispense harsh treatment and, in return, receive appropriate retribution. James's two cruel, uncaring aunts in *James and the Giant Peach* (1961) are crushed beneath the giant peach, the vehicle in which James escapes their tyranny. D.'s fans defend his style of HUMOR by comparing them to modern fairy tales, stories of children winning in battles with evildoers. The author felt that a writer must cater to the traditional childhood FANTASY that children will prevail in battles with evil adults. D. exaggerates the revolting characteristics of evil and magnifies the sympathetic nature of good characters, he combines fast action, mega-doses of nonsense, engaging word play, and endings in which the good prevail with a vengeance. Adult characters such as Miss Trumbull (*Matilda,* 1988) and Aunt Sponge and Aunt Spiker (*James and the Giant Peach,* 1961) do not succeed in their inhumane treatment of children, much to the delight of readers. D.'s writings are low fantasy, which enables him to integrate fantasy elements in real world settings. Several of his books, including *The B.F.G.* (1982) were illustrated by Quentin BLAKE.

D. reacted to one of the most controversial issues in his books by changing the color of the Oompa-Loompas in *Charlie and the Chocolate Factory* (1964, 1973) He had created them as black and said he never considered that audiences would be offended since he featured them as charming and most of the white child characters in the book as obnoxious and rude. However, beginning with the 1973 edition of the book, the revised characters from the imaginary Loompaland are depicted differently than the originally perceived pygmies from Africa. D.'s critics continue to criticize and his fans continue to praise. He remains one of the most popular creators of children's books of all time.

In addition to D.'s writing achievements, he is credited with the invention of a medical device that he, a mechanical engineer and a neurosurgeon, created. The shunt, known as the Dahl-Wade-Till valve was invented in hopes of helping D.'s son Theo who had suffered head injuries. Although Theo no longer needed the device by the time it was developed, it was widely used by others around the world until newer versions were perfected.

Biographies and autobiographies of D. include, but are not limited to *Boy* (1984) and *Going Solo* (1986), written by the author; *Roald D.* (1992) by West, *Roald D.* (1994) by Treglown. D. devotees can visit a glass elevator much like Charlie's and climb into a giant peach, complete with silkworms and spiders at Roald Dahl's Children's Gallery, an extension of the Buckinghamshire County Museum in Aylesbury. Los Angeles Opera's *Fantastic Mr. Fox* combines D.'s whimsical humor from the book, (*The Fantastic Mr. Fox,* 1970), and artist Gerald Scarfe's talents for another successful venture for D. Among D.'s approving audiences are readers who enjoy disgusting characters and the invitation to enter a fantasy world perhaps not permitted in their real worlds of home and school.

AWARDS: Edgar Allan Poe Awards, Mystery Writers of America, 1954, 1959, and 1980; Nene award (1978) for *Charlie and the Great Glass Elevator. New York Times* Outstanding Books Award (1983), Whitbread Award (1983) and West AUSTRALIAN Award (1986) for *The Witches.* World Fantasy Convention Lifetime Achievement Award. Kurt Maschler Award runner-up (1985) for *The Giraffe and the Pelly and Me. Boston*

Globe–Horn Book Nonfiction Honor Citation (1985) for *Boy: Tales of Childhood.* INTERNATIONAL BOARD ON BOOKS FOR YOUNG PEOPLE AWARDS for Norwegian and German TRANSLATIONS of *The BFG* (1986). Smarties Award (1990) for *Elsio Trot*

FURTHER WORKS: *The Magic Finger,* 1966; *Charlie and the Great Glass Elevator,* 1972; *Danny, The Champion of the World,* 1975; *The Enormous Crocodile,* 1978; *The Twits,* 1981; *George's Marvelous Medicine,* 1981; *The B. F. G.,* 1982; *Roald D.'s Revolting Rhymes,* 1982; *Matilda,* 1988; *Rhyme Stew,* 1989; *The Vicar of Nibbleswicke,* 1992; Screenplays: *Chitty Chitty Bang Bang* (with Ken Hughes), 1969; *Willie Wonka and the Chocolate Factory* (Motion picture based on *Charlie and the Chocolate Factory*), 1971

BIBLIOGRAPHY: *Children's Literature Review,* vol. 41, 1997; D. Roald, *Boy: Tales of Childhood,* 1984; D., Roald, *Going Solo,* 1986; Hitchens, Christopher, "The Grimmest Tales," *Vanity Fair,* vol. 57, no. 50, Jan. 1994; Labi, Nadya, *Time Australia,* 50, Dec. 9, 1996; Scarfe, Gerald, "Slyboots," *The New Yorker,* vol. 74, no. 35, Nov. 1998; Treglown, Jeremy, *Roald D.: A Biography,* 1994; West, Mark I., *Roald D.,* 1992

NANCY HORTON

DALGLIESH, Alice

Author, b. 7 October 1893, Trinidad, British West Indies; d. 11 June 1979, Woodbury, Connecticut

D. began writing when she was six years old, motivated by being read to often by her Scottish father and English mother. From the time she learned to read, she tried to read every book in the house, both child and adult levels. Her seaside surroundings as well as other places she lived during her childhood were reflected in her writings. The gift of a silver pencil from her father became the title of her book *The Silver Pencil* (1944); it was based on her years of growing up in Trinidad and England. At age nineteen she began her training at Pratt Institute in Brooklyn, New York, to be a teacher. She continued her education at Columbia University and received a B.A. in education and an M.A. in English. When she taught kindergarten and elementary students, she learned their likes and dislikes in literature. D. implemented practices in the 1920s and 1930s that preceded their time in the classroom and the literature world: She read aloud to her young students daily and allowed them to make their own choices in the literature they read.

After seventeen years of teaching, D. began her writing career. She wrote over fifty fiction and nonfiction titles, and also became an editor. The PICTURE BOOKS she wrote early in her career reflected her teaching background. In *"The Wooden Farmer,"* and *"The Story of the Jungle Pool"* (1930), she encouraged her young readers to interact with her books by playing along with toy animals. She encouraged interaction in *The Choosing Book* (1932) as the readers helped characters decide which purchases to make as a family. Her INFORMATIONAL BOOKS for young readers held their interest with a balance between information and ILLUSTRATIONS. During her career, D. taught children's literature at Columbia University and served as the first president of the CHILDREN'S BOOK COUNCIL. Working for Scribner's as editor of books for young readers, 1934–60, she is credited with advancing the place of children's literature in the publishing world.

AWARDS: ALA NEWBERY MEDAL Honor Book (1945) for *The Silver Pencil,* (1953) for *The Bears on Hemlock Mountain,* and (1955) for *The Courage of Sarah Noble.* ALA CALDECOTT MEDAL Honor Medal (1955) for *The Thanksgiving Story*

FURTHER WORKS: *The Little Blue Teapot: Sandy Cover Stories,* 1931; *America Travels: The Story of a Hundred Years of Travel in America,* 1933; *Christmas: A Book of Stories New and Old.* (Editor), 1934; *The Little Wooden Farmer,* 1938; *The Columbus Story,* 1955; *The Fourth of July Story,* 1956; *Adam and the Golden Cock,* 1959

NANCY HORTON

DALY, Niki (Nicholas)
Author, illustrator, b. 13 June 1946, Cape Town, South Africa

D. is known for illustrating children's books that depict everyday incidents children encounter. He displays special interest in themes that evolve around children from one to six years old as they play around the home. After establishing a career in London, D.'s family returned to South Africa. There, he wrote and illustrated books that reflect the lives of black children in Africa. *Not So Fast Songololo* (1987), *Charlie's House* (1991), *Papa Lucky's Shadow* (1992), and *All the Magic in the*

World (1993) are included among these books. The apartheid atmosphere in South Africa prompted D. to write books that challenge the propaganda that sets people apart.

AWARDS: Parents' Choice Book Award for Literature, *Horn Book* Honor List, and Katrien Harries Award for ILLUSTRATION, South Africa (1987) for *Not So Fast, Songololo. New York Times* Best Illustrated Children's Books of the Year (1995) for *Why the Sun and Moon Live in the Sky*

FURTHER WORKS: *The Little Girl Who Lived down the Road,* 1978; *Monsters Are like That,* 1985; *Day of the Rainbow* (R. Craft, author), 1989; *Charlie's House,* 1991; *Somewhere in Africa* (I. Mennen and D.), 1992; *One Round Moon and a Star for Me* (I. Mennen, author), 1994; *My Dad,* 1995; *Red Light, Green Light, Mama, and Me,* 1995; *Bravo Zan Angelo!,* 1998

BIBLIOGRAPHY: *Something about the Author,* vol. 78, 1994

JODI PILGRIM

DANZIGER, Paula
Author, b. 18 August, 1944, Washington, D.C.

By second grade D. knew she wanted to be a writer. Although her parents were caring, her father was angry and her mother fearful of the imagined dangers on the farm where they lived. With the support of a local librarian, D. lost herself in books and in the creation of imaginary characters she could control. Her imaginative interpretation of school assignments and her social vulnerability due to weight problems resulted in a dislike of school. Nevertheless, she earned both a B.A. and M.A. from Montclair State College, and in 1967 D. began teaching. She loved junior-high school students who appreciated her creative, flamboyant style. Several summers of mentoring by John CIARDI developed her awareness of literary structures, an acting class taught her about character building, and repeated readings of *The Catcher in the Rye* (SALINGER, 1951) set her free. In 1970, two automobile accidents left her temporarily unable to read or write. During her lengthy recovery, she was encouraged by a therapist to refocus her childhood wish to write by exploring her terrifying feelings of helplessness. The result was the material that eventually resulted in *The Cat Ate My Gymsuit* (1974) and the start of her career as a children's novelist. Both the protagonist, Marcy Lewis, and the teacher, Barbara Finney, represent aspects of D.'s image of herself. She draws on feelings of compassion, vulnerability, and the will to survive that flow from her childhood and teaching experiences and from her highly developed imagination.

Grounded in her memories of a turbulent childhood, her respect for children's feelings, and her acute observations of children's likes and habits, D.'s mission is to acknowledge children's emotional needs and rights. She tries to show children how to survive difficult situations with a sense of HUMOR and compassion. Her characters are caring "outlaws" who cope imaginatively and humorously with difficult parents, teachers, schools, and peer relationships. She wants her books to help children feel less alone, to gain perspective on their place in the world, to provide outlets for emotions, and to nurture gentleness and sensitivity. D. accomplishes this with a sparkling sense of humor. P.'s *Longer Letter Later* (1998), written with Ann MARTIN, is a series of letters between best friends when one of them moves to Ohio. Using humor and insight, the letters continue in *Snail Mail No More* (2000) as the friends grapple with adolescent concerns and challenging family relationships.

AWARDS: From the beginning, D. has been recognized repeatedly by state library and reading associations. Her books received Children's Choice designation from the INTERNATIONAL READING ASSOCIATION and CHILDREN'S BOOK COUNCIL (1979) for *The Pistachio Prescription* (1978), 1980 for *The Cat Ate My Gymsuit* (1974) and *Can You Sue Your Parents for Malpractice?* (1979), 1981 for *There's a Bat in Bunk Five* (1980), and 1983 for *The Divorce Express* (1974).

FURTHER WORKS: *It's an Aardvark-Eat-Turtle World,* 1985; *This Place Has No Atmosphere,* 1986; *Remember Me to Harold Square,* 1987; *Everyone Else's Parents Said Yes,* 1989; *Amber Brown Is Not a Crayon,* 1994, and SERIES. *Make like a Tree and Leave,* 1991; *Earth to Matthew,* 1991; *Not for a Billion Gazillion Dollars,* 1994

BIBLIOGRAPHY: Krull, Kathleen. *Presenting Paula D.,* 1995

MARGARET YATSEVITCH PHINNEY

DAUGHERTY, James
Author, illustrator, b. 1 June 1889, Asheville, North Carolina; d. 21 February, 1974, Place unknown

D. studied art in the U.S. and in Europe. While in London, he read the POETRY of Walt Whitman for the first time. The images that whirled in his head sent him back to the U.S. to paint wall murals in public buildings and illustrate books where his bold, swirling style became his signature. Adult books D. illustrated include Harriet Beecher STOWE's *Uncle Tom's Cabin* (1929); William Shakespeare's *Three Comedies* (1929); Abraham Lincoln's *Gettysburg Address* (1947); *Walt Whitman's America* (1964); and *Henry David Thoreau: A Man for Our Time* (1967).

D.'s first book ILLUSTRATIONS for children were for *Daniel Boone, Wilderness Scout* (1926) by Stewart Edward White. This was familiar territory as one of the fondest memories of D.'s childhood was the picture of his grandfather telling him stories about Daniel Boone and Davy Crockett. *Abe Lincoln Grows Up* (1928) by Carl SANDBURG gave D. another chance to draw a childhood hero. He particularly enjoyed being able to collaborate with Sandburg on this book.

The first book D. wrote and illustrated for children was *Andy and the Lion* (1938); it was his only picture book. Mindful of his young audience as he retold the tale of Androcles, he simplified and enlarged his characters and illustrations. His peers spoke of this marriage between words and pictures as a breakthrough book, "Any who are interested in the picturebook technique . . . will do well to study the subtle nuances that have been worked out on these pages," stated Lynd WARD. ALA's CALDECOTT MEDAL committee agreed, designating *Andy and the Lion* a Caldecott Medal Honor Book (1940). *Gillespie and the Guards* (1957), written by Benjamin Elkin, was D.'s second Caldecott Medal Honor Book.

He won the NEWBERY MEDAL in 1940 for his first CHAPTER BOOK, a BIOGRAPHY, *Daniel Boone.* In discussions of MULTICULTURALISM in children's literature, the book has been cited as stereotyping NATIVE AMERICANS. Others defend it as accurately portraying frontier conditions and pioneer life. Another concern is that D. did not write objective biographies but interpreted events to show his subjects in the best light. Some of his books were part of the Random House/Landmark series, a staple in classrooms across the country in the 1950s and 1960s. *The Landing of the Pilgrims* (1950) and *Trappers and Traders of the Far West* (1952) are examples of his books that enlivened learning about United States history.

AWARDS: AMERICAN LIBRARY ASSOCIATION Newbery Medal Award (1940) for *Daniel Boone;* ALA Caldecott Medal Honor Book (1939) for *Andy and the Lion;* (1957) for *Gillespie and the Guards* (by Benjamin Elkin)

FURTHER WORKS: Author and illustrator: *Poor Richard,* 1941; *Abraham Lincoln,* 1943; *Marcus and Narcissa Whitman: Pioneers of Oregon,* 1953

BIBLIOGRAPHY: Bader, Barbara. *American PICTURE BOOKS from "Noah's Ark" to "The Beast Within."* 1976. HOPKINS, Lee Bennett, *Pauses: Autobiographical Reflections of 101 Creators of Children's Books,* 1995. Huck, Charlotte, *Children's Literature in the Elementary Classroom.* 1979. Silvey, Anita, ed. *Children's Books and Their Creators.* 1995. *Something about the Author,* vol. 13, 1978. Tomlinson, Carl and Carol Lynch-Brown, *Essentials of Children's Literature,* 1996

SHARON HARTMAN

D'AULAIRE, Ingri and Edgar Parin

Illustrator and author team. Ingri: b. 27 December 1904, Kongsberg, Norway; d. 24 October 1980, Wilton, Connecticut; Edgar: b. 30 September 1898, Munich, Germany; d. 1 May 1986, Georgetown, Connecticut

Married and working as a team, the D.s established the picture-book BIOGRAPHY for young readers and brought to life Norwegian folktales, MYTHS, AND LEGENDS. Both artists were exposed to art early in their lives and studied under the tutelage of Hans Hofmann in Munich, where they met and married in 1925. They visited the United States and decided to make it their home, first in New York and then rural Connecticut. Initially, they kept their art careers separate. E.D. specialized in murals, having studied architecture and landscaping, and I.D. painted child portraits. While living in New York, a librarian suggested they collaborate to write a children's book. Capitalizing on their travels to North Africa and the more than two thousand sketches they had made, they wrote *The Magic Rug* in 1931. The D.s then concentrated on Scandinavian subjects. The characters originated from stories and experiences of both their childhoods. Their Norwegian adventures in *Ola* (1932) and *Ola and Blakken and Line, Sine, Trine* (1933, later revised as *The Terrible Troll-Bird* 1976) featured Ola, a fictional character for whom their first son was named.

The D.s' focus then turned to early American heroes with subjects such as Lincoln, Washington, and Franklin. Thorough travel and research went into their books, with E.D. providing the DRAMA and I.D. the HUMOR. Their biographies maintained a regular pattern: large picture-book format; lithographic ILLUSTRATIONS of alternating spreads in black and white, then color, due to the cost and time of color; and lively dialogue that was uncommon in biographies of the period. In 1940, the D.s were awarded the ALA CALDECOTT MEDAL for their picture-book biography *Abraham Lincoln.* For over forty years they provided children with outstanding PICTURE BOOKS, fiction, and nonfiction. They were the first artists to employ color-stone lithography in books for children. This technique was a meticulous, detailed multi-step process done by hand beginning with exact size color drawings before they were transferred to stone. In their later years, the D.s redrew these early illustrations because printers were no longer willing to manage the cumbersome stone slabs required for lithography. Despite the D.s' original doubts about combining their art careers with marriage, their success is evident in four decades of works for children.

AWARDS: AMERICAN LIBRARY ASSOCIATION Caldecott Medal (1940) for *Abraham Lincoln.* Edgar illustrated the ALA NEWBERY MEDAL Honor Book (1933) for *Children of the Soil: A Story of Scandinavia.* The Regina Medal (1970) for their contribution to children's literature

FURTHER WORKS: *George Washington,* 1946; *Benjamin Franklin,* 1950; *Columbus,* 1955; *Norse Gods and Giants,* 1967; *D'Aulaires' Trolls,* 1972

BIBLIOGRAPHY: *Contemporary Authors Online,* www.galenet.com; HOPKINS, Lee Bennett, *Pauses: Autobiographical Reflections of 101 Creators of Children's Books,* 1995; MEIGS, C. et al., *A Critical History of Children's Literature,* rev. ed. 1969

NANCY HORTON

DAY, Alexandra (pseud. Sandra Darling)

Author, illustrator, b. 1941, Cincinnati, Ohio

D. lives in Seattle, Washington, where she owns and operates a studio with her husband, a collaborator on most of her work and co-founder of Blue Lantern Studio and Green Tiger Press. D. is best known for her self-illustrated Carl books, which feature a large, gentle Rottweiler dog and a baby named Madeline. *Good Dog, Carl* (1985), the first of numerous titles, introduces the patient baby-sitter dog who carefully takes his charge on simple adventures to the park, a day-care center, the store and places familiar to preschoolers. The realistic ILLUSTRATIONS done in oils complement the serene, almost wordless, text in each story.

D. has also written and illustrated several Frank and Ernest books featuring the adventures of a bear and elephant with the emphasis on learning the vocabulary of the activities the duo engage in to the accompaniment of bright watercolor illustrations. D.'s illustrations for *The Teddy Bears Picnic* (1983, lyrics by Jimmy Kennedy) won a special mention at the Bologna Book Fair and a Children's Choice Award from the INTERNATIONAL READING ASSOCIATION in 1984.

FURTHER WORKS: *Paddy's Pay-Day.* 1989. *Frank and Ernest Play Ball.* 1990. *Carl's Masquerade.* 1985. *Frank and Ernest on the Road.* 1994.

BIBLIOGRAPHY: *Something about the Author,* vol. 97, 1998

MICHAEL O'LAUGHLIN

DE ANGELI, Marguerite

Author, illustrator, b. 14 March 1889 Lapeer, Michigan; d. 16 June 1987 Philadelphia, Pennsylvania

D. grew up in Michigan and Pennsylvania, attending public schools. Her first adult occupation was singing professionally. Rather than return to her singing career after marrying and rearing her children, D. chose to develop her favorite childhood pastime of drawing. She took drawing lessons while her children were young and developed her talent as an artist as she continued her household and mothering responsibilities. She secured her first commission after only one year. Within a few years she was illustrating and writing her own children's stories. Beginning with *Ted and Nina Go to the Grocery Store* (1935) and *Ted and Nina Have a Happy Rainy Day* (1936), she based her works on her own FAMILY STORIES, FOLKLORE, and travels. She gave children a link to the past and to different cultures with historical fiction written in a style that young readers enjoyed. Her NEWBERY MEDAL winner, *The Door in the Wall* (1949), set in thirteenth-century England

is the tale of a young crippled boy who triumphs over his handicaps. D. believed that a children's book is a composite of reality, imagination, and supposition. The artwork in her books uses several media including oil painting, watercolor, pencil, and pen and ink. Over a fifty-year career, D. published thirty children's books. In 1981 the Marguerite de Angeli Library was dedicated in D.'s birthplace, Lapeer, Michigan.

AWARDS: AMERICAN LIBRARY ASSOCIATION Newbery Medal (1950) for *The Door in the Wall.* Newbery Medal Honor Book (1957) for *Black Fox of Lorne.* ALA CALDECOTT MEDAL Honor Books (1945) for *Yonie Wondernose,* (1945) for *Book of Nursery and MOTHER GOOSE Rhymes.* Lewis CARROLL Shelf Award (1961). The Regina Medal (1968).

FURTHER WORKS: *Henner's Lydia,* 1936; *Copper-Toed Boots,* 1938; *Thee, Hannah,* 1940; *Turkey for Christmas,* 1944; *Bright April,* 1946; *Jared's Island,* 1947; *Fiddlestrings,* 1974; *Whistle for the Crossing,* 1977

BIBLIOGRAPHY: deAngeli, Marguerite, *Butter at the Old Price: The Autobiography of Marguerite de Angeli,* 1971; HOPKINS, Lee Bennett, *Pauses: Autobiographical Reflections of 101 Creators of Children's Books,* 1995

NANCY HORTON

DEATH AND DYING IN CHILDREN'S LITERATURE

Historically, death and dying were not considered appropriate material for children's books. Although folk and FAIRY TALES include all manner of fractured and blended families, the endings generally are "they lived happily ever after." After World War II realism blossomed in children's stories. Child advocates acknowledged that when someone close to a child dies, the child is affected and asks "Why?" Professionals observed children grieving as well as adults. Books were written telling adults how to deal with children's grief and the stages of grief were enumerated, but actual children's books dealing with death were few. In one of the first children's books about death, *The Dead Bird* (Margaret Wise BROWN, 1938), the children have no emotional involvement other than that they are sorry the bird is dead.

A book that deals more directly with children's questions is *When Dinosaurs Die: A Guide to Understanding Death* (Laurene Krasny Brown and Marc BROWN, illus. 1966). First calling attention to what it means to be alive, the author then turns to why someone dies and what it means to be dead. Although informative, a discussion of ways to remember someone is the most hopeful portion of the book.

A book that explores the grieving of a child for a pet that has died is *Jim's Dog Muffins* (1984) by Miriam COHEN. Muffins's death affects Jim's attitude at school and on the playground. His best friend finally helps Jim cry, laugh, and remember Muffins.

Lifetimes: A Beautiful Way to Explain Death to Children (Bryan Mellonie and Robert INGPEN, 1983) explains life and death to the reader. Rather than concentrate on death, we are told about beginnings, endings, and in between living for all living things. Although mentally one can rationalize everyone/everything has a lifetime to live and then eventually death, it does not prepare the person experiencing death for the loss they will feel nor for the fact that not everyone lives a long life.

A realistic book on pet loss is *The Accident* (1976) by Carol CARRICK. The authentic dialogue and reaction of Christopher when his dog Bodger is hit and killed by a truck ring true. Christopher experiences the many stages of grief. *The Tenth Good Thing about Barney* (1971) by Judith VIORST, recounts the death of a pet cat. A grieving boy is helped by his father to understand that death is one phase in the life cycle when he understands that his cat is in the ground, helping new flowers grow.

A book that gently focuses on the loss of a person and the pain is *When Someone Dies* (Greenlee, 1992), a comforting book that compares the separation of death to a person being on a long vacation. It relates the stages of grief to feeling mad inside that you're alone, worry that other people important to you might die also, and sad empty feelings. Suggestions to help heal such as remembering happy times spent together are encouraging.

A classic on death and dying for children is Charlotte ZOLOTOW's *My Grandson Lew* (1974). Lewis is six, his Grandpa died when he was two. Lew relates to his mother the times his Grandpa would come in the night when he called, the scratchiness of his beard, the smell of tobacco from his pipe and a trip to the museum where he saw paintings with bright colors and one with a sky and an ocean. Lew says, "I miss Grandpa." The most revealing portion is the response of Lew's mother: "You never asked for him before." To which Lew replies, "I think about him though." This revelation of Lew's thinking about his Grandpa without his mother realizing it is the crux of children's grieving. Children may quietly revisit grief as they grow without the parent understanding what is actually occurring emotionally and/or psychologically.

A story that addresses dying is *Old Timers: The One That Got Away!* (Noa Schwartz, 1998). Written in rhyme, a boy visits his Grandfather, Papa Joe, and his mother tells him Papa Joe has a sickness in his brain he thinks is Old Timers but finds out it really is al-z-heimer's. He is thankful he had ten years to love his Grandfather and decides one day he will tell Papa Joe's stories to his wife and children. Although the physical separation from Papa Joe has not happened, the story presents the intentional separation that occurs with alzheimer's and it foreshadows the physical.

Old Pig (1995) by Margaret Wild is a happy/sad story about Old Pig and her Granddaughter who have lived together for a long, long time. Old Pig does not get up one morning and Granddaughter worries. She realizes Old Pig is dying. They take a slow walk to feast on the trees, the flowers, the sky, and taste the rain. The last scene is Granddaughter and a white duck watching birds flying. A gentle story that helps prepare children for the loss of a loved one.

Nana Upstairs and Nana Downstairs (1973), a classic, by Tomie DEPAOLA, tells of his Sunday visits to his ninety-four-year-old great-grandmother, Nana Upstairs. One day his mother tells him Nana Upstairs "died last night." Tomie struggles to understand what "died" means. When he sees her empty bed he cries. His emotional distress at the death of Nana Upstairs is softened by viewing a falling star as a kiss from Nana Upstairs. Another star falls when Nana Downstairs dies. Now a grown man, Tomie says "You are both Nana Upstairs" now.

Dorothy Carter brings us an AFRICAN AMERICAN story in *Bye, Mis' Lela* (1998). While her mother works, "Sugar" stays with Mis' Lela. The children going to school wave and are told to "Study your lessons and mind your manners, children." The reply is "Yes, Ma'am, Mis' Lela, bye." One day Mis' Lela dies. When Sugar goes to school she says, "Hi," as she walks by Mis' Lela's house just as though Mis' Lela was saying "Study your lessons, Sugar Plum, and mind your manners." Sugar says, "Yes, Ma'am. Bye, Mis' Lela." Mis' Lela is still very much alive in Sugar's memory.

For older children, the NEWBERY MEDAL winner, *Missing May* (1992) by Cynthia RYLANT, gently walks the reader through the stages of shock, denial, anger, bargaining, depression, and finally acceptance as Summer struggles to deal with the loss of May who had been her mother for six happy years.

A story that deals with the death of a parent is *Everett Anderson's Goodbye* (1983) by Lucille CLIFTON. A CORETTA SCOTT KING AWARD winner, the poetic story expresses a child's grieving as well as the healing that comes with time.

Barbara Joosse's *Lewis and Papa: Adventure on the Santa Fe Trail* (1998) is based on history. In their journey across the desert, water runs out and Papa's favorite ox, Big Red, collapses. To put him out of his misery Papa shoots him and Lewis and Papa cry together at the loss of a friend.

A child's bewilderment at the death of a friend is treated sensitively in Katherine PATERSON's Newbery Medal book, *Bridge to Terabithia* (1977). Jess's confusion and guilt over Leslie's death is difficult for Jess to rationalize on his own and the need for adult intervention is made painstakingly clear. Terabithia, the imaginary world the friends created, provides space for Jess to retreat to while he heals himself and comes to accept his friend's death. Sensitive ILLUSTRATIONS by Donna Diamond evoke Jess's attempt to cope with the tragedy.

Children's books on death and dying are sparse, especially those that deal with the death of a parent or sibling. Explaining what death is, presents facts, but there is small comfort in explanations. When confronted by death, children's needs are expressed in different ways and they process their needs differently. Meaningful acknowledgment of their loss and adult support

sends spoken and unspoken messages and empowers children to recover from the trauma.

BIBLIOGRAPHY: Brown, Laurie Krasny. Marc Brown, illus. *When Dinosaurs Die: A Guide to Understanding Death*. 1996. Brown, Margaret Wise. Remy Charlip, illus. *The Dead Bird*. 1938, 1965. Carrick, Carol. Donald Carrick., illus. *The Accident*. 1976. Carter Dorothy. Harvey Stevenson, illus. *Bye, Mis' Lela*. 1998. Clifton, Lucille. Ann Grifalconi, illus. *Everett Anderson's Goodbye*. 1983. Cohen, Miriam. Lillian Hoban, illus. *Jim's Dog Muffins*. 1984. dePaola, Tomie. *Nana Upstairs & Nana Downstairs*. 1973. Greenlee, Sharon. Bill Drath, illus. *When Someone Dies*. 1992. Joosse, Barbara. Jon Van Zyle, illus. *Lewis and Papa: Adventure on the Santa Fe Trail*. 1998. Mellonie, Bryan and Robert Ingpen. *Lifetimes; A Beautiful Way to Explain Death to Children*. 1953. Paterson, Katherine. *Bridge to Terabithia*. 1977. Rylant, Cynthia. *Missing May*. 1992. Schwartz, Noa, Erica Vipond, illus. *Old Timers— The One that Got Away!* 1998. Viorst, Judith, Erik Blegvad, illus. *The Tenth Good Thing about Barney*. 1971. Wild, Margaret. Ron Brooks, illus. *Old Pig*. 1995. Zolotow, Charlotte. William Pene Du Bois, illus. *My Grandson. Lew* 1974

IRVYN G. GILBERTSON

(See also THE DISABLED IN CHILDREN'S AND YOUNG ADULT LITERATURE and REALISTIC FICTION)

DE BRUNHOFF, Jean and Laurent

Jean: Author, illustrator, b. 9 December 1899, Paris, France; d. 16 October 1937, Switzerland; Laurent: Author, illustrator, b. 30 August 1925, Paris, France

J.deB. introduced Babar to the world of children's literature; his stories remain a classic example of anthropomorphic ANIMAL tales. After enjoying the stories about an elephant that his wife would create for their children, J.deB. decided to create a book for children about this lovable character, *The Story of Babar* (1933). J.deB. created detailed pen and watercolor paintings and cursive text that spread across oversized double-page spreads. Critics applauded his revolutionary style and almost immediately his stories found their way into the hands of children. *The Story of Babar* became an instant success and spread from France to the United States, England, and other European countries. Unfortunately, in 1935, J.deB. was diagnosed with tuberculosis and lived his remaining days in a sanitorium in Switzerland. While fighting this once terminal disease, J.deB. continued to write his stories of Babar via letters to his sons. He completed seven Babar books prior to his death. Critics and readers mourned the loss of J.deB. and what also seemed the loss of Babar.

Nearly ten years after J.deB.'s death, L.deB. decided to continue his father's legacy. L.deB. published *Babar's Cousin: That Rascal Arthur* in 1947 with such enthusiasm that it was as if Babar had never left. Although some critics argued that Babar lost his spirit, distinctiveness, and individuality, Babar was back and L.deB. helped him evolve. L.deB. positioned Babar in contemporary settings and situations. Now, Babar cooks, camps, paints, and gardens. He has been to other planets and many countries, and even started a family. L.deB. also thrust Babar into the realm of teacher as the elephant helped children learn colors, numbers, other languages, and the alphabet. In addition to these developments, Babar entered the commercial world. He is now available in nearly every merchandise form including stuffed animals, lunchboxes, and T-shirts. Babar was featured in his own film, *Babar: The Movie,* in 1989 and has made numerous appearances on television. Babar has even made his presence a matter of debate in academia; critics continue to consider the sociopolitical and historical dimensions of this character. Certainly J.deB. and L.deB. created a character with universal appeal.

AWARDS: *New York Times* Best Illustrated Children's Books of the Year (1956) for *Babar's Fair.* Lewis CARROLL Shelf Award (1959) for *The Story of Babar*

BIBLIOGRAPHY: *Children's Literature Review,* vol. 4, 1982; *Major Authors and Illustrators for Children and Young Adults,* vol. 1, 1993

SHANE RAYBURN

DECLEMENTS, Barthe

Author, b. 8 October 1920, Seattle, Washington

D. attended Western Washington College and earned a B.A. in 1944 and a M.Ed. in 1970, from the University of Washington. She is retired from twenty-five years of teaching and devotes her full time to writing. D. uses her own life experiences as a springboard to the literature she writes for children. These memories seem to shape the action of her books. Not only does D. use her childhood memories as fuel for her writing, she draws heavily upon her career as a teacher and guidance counselor. She recalls writing *I Never Asked You to Understand* (1986) as a direct result of counseling girls in an alternative school who were struggling with issues resulting from sexual abuse. In other books, her characters tackle issues such as being the new kid in school, being overweight, and dealing with the death of a parent. As a ten-year-old student, D. would write story after story. Later, she published a newspaper column and wrote for a magazine while she was a student at the University of Washington. Her work focuses on adolescent issues and reverberates with a liveliness and authenticity of growing up. D. captures authentic adolescent dialogue and the feelings of awkwardness about becoming an adult. D. constructs characters that mirror the same concerns as youth today. She crafts realistic, engaging characters through vivid dialogue and action. Her works guide readers to experience more than just an interesting story; they challenge readers to cry, laugh, grieve, and most of all, to wonder. D. credits her own children and her students with much of the realistic dialogue and the liveliness of the plots in her novels. Her family continues to play an influential role in her career as a writer. In fact, her son, Christopher Greimes, has collaborated with his mother on some of D.'s novels. He first became involved when D. asked him to write Jack's letters in *Seventeen and In-between* (1993). Later Greimes collaborated with D. in writing *Double Trouble* (1997). D.'s books are engaging and continue to be popular picks among children.

AWARDS: INTERNATIONAL READING ASSOCIATION Children's Choice Books (1981) for *Nothing's Fair in Fifth Grade*

FURTHER WORKS: *Monkey See, Monkey Do,* 1990; *The Bite of the Gold Bug,* 1992; *Liar, Liar,* 1998

BIBLIOGRAPHY: *Children's Literature Review,* vol. 23, 1991; *Something about the Author,* vol. 71, 1993

SHANE RAYBURN

DE FELICE, Cynthia
Author, b. 28 December 1951, Philadelphia, Pennsylvania

D. began oral STORYTELLING while working as a school librarian; soon that oral tradition grew into written storytelling through books such as *The Dancing Skeleton* (1989) and *Mule Eggs* (1994). D. tries to base her writing on experiences in her childhood such as *Devil's Bridge* (1992) and *The Light on Hogback Hill* (1993), or on historical events such as *Lostman's River* (1994).

FURTHER WORKS: *The Strange Night Writing of Jessamine Colter,* 1988; *When Grandpa Kissed His Elbow,* 1992

BIBLIOGRAPHY: *The Seventh Book of Junior Authors and Illustrators,* 1996

GWYNNE ELLEN ASH

DEFOE, Daniel
Author, b. 1660, Cripplegate, London, England; d. 26 April 1731, Moorfields, London, England

D., author of possibly 560 books, pamphlets, and journals, first considered entering the ministry; he became a political pamphleteer and was imprisoned for six months. *The Strange and Surprizing* [sic] *Adventures of Robinson Crusoe* (1719), a stirring ADVENTURE STORY, is regarded as the first modern novel. It tells of being shipwrecked on a deserted island and attacked by cannibals before being rescued by a native Crusoe named Friday. *Robinson Crusoe* serves as the quintessential adventure story, beloved by generations of primarily boy readers. Loosely based on one sailor's real-life experience, D. presented the novel as a factual account of those adventures. Johann WYSS's *Swiss Family Robinson* (1812–14) is modeled on D.'s novel and Jean Jacques Rousseau in *Émile* (1762) recommends it as required reading for young boys.

FURTHER WORKS: *The Further Adventures of Robinson Crusoe,* 1719; *Moss Flanders and Colonel Jack,* 1722

BIBLIOGRAPHY: DOYLE, Brian, *The Who's Who of Children's Literature,* 1968; Drabble, Margaret, *The Oxford Companion to English Literature,* 1985

DIANE G. PERSON

DEGEN, Bruce
Author, illustrator, b. 14 June 1945, Brooklyn, New York

D. received a B.F.A. in 1966 from Cooper Union and an M.F.A. in 1975 from Pratt Institute. An experienced artist, D. has shared his talents in various capacities—as an art teacher for the New York City high schools, a teacher of printmaking, calligraphy, and life-drawing, a painter of opera scenery, and a director of a lithography studio in Ein Hod, Israel.

D. always enjoyed books as a child and fondly remembers frequent trips to the library with the joy and excitement of plunging into a new book. D. recalls what he responded to as a child; he attempts to convey that same excitement and wonder through his own work, through characters with which children identify and through humorous adventures in which children delight. The whimsical and FANTASY adventures of characters are exemplified through D.'s self-illustrated work and through his ILLUSTRATIONS for Nancy White CARLSTROM's Jesse Bear books, Jane YOLEN's Commander Toad series, and Joanna COLE's the Magic School Bus series.

The self-illustrated *Jamberry* (1983) and *Sailaway Home* (1996) typify D.'s depiction of animal fantasy. In *Jamberry,* D.'s whimsical, often double-spread, illustrations complement the strong use of rhyme and rhythm in a story where a boy and a bear collect "mountains and fountains" of berries. Like *Jamberry,* D.'s recent *Sailaway Home,* utilizes a rhythmic pattern. Sweeping illustrations rendered in pen and ink, watercolor, color pencil, and gouache reveal the little pig's imaginary adventures and are balanced by illustrations that reveal the security of the pig's home.

D.'s partnership with author Joanna Cole has afforded D. further opportunities for the intermingling of fantasy, reality, and HUMOR. From Ms. Frizzle's outlandish outfits, to Liz, the reptilian class pet, to the quirky children of the Magic School Bus series, D.'s artistic interpretations bring alive often challenging scientific concepts. The books' extensively researched information is balanced through D.'s often humorous illustrations, making accessible to children detailed scientific information.

AWARDS: INTERNATIONAL READING ASSOCIATION and CHILDREN'S BOOK COUNCIL Children's Choices (1982) for *Little Chick's Big Day* and 1985 for *My Mother Didn't Kiss Me Good-Night*

FURTHER WORKS: Self-illustrated: *Aunt Possum and the Pumpkin Man.* 1977. *The Little Witch and the Riddle.* 1980. *Sailaway Home.* 1996. Illustrator: *Commander Toad in Space.* (Yolen). 1980. *Jesse Bear, What Will You Wear?* (Carlstrom). 1986. *Better Not Get Wet, Jesse Bear.* (CARLSTROM). 1988. *If You Were a Writer.* (NIXON). 1988. *The Josefina Story Quilt.* (COERR). 1986. *Mouse's Birthday.* (Yolen). 1993. *Will You Give Me a Dream.* (Nixon). 1994. The Magic School Bus series. (With Joanna Cole)

BIBLIOGRAPHY: Judge, A. (1996), *Sailaway Home* [Review of the book *Sailaway Home*], *Booklist,* 92, 1997; Reisman, A. (producer and director), *Riding the Magic School Bus with Joanna Cole and Bruce Degen,* 1992; *Something about the Author,* vol. 56, 1989; http://www.scholastic.com/MagicSchoolbus/author/index.htm

JUNE M. JACKO

DE GRUMMOND REFERENCE COLLECTION

The de Grummond Children's Literature Collection at the University of Southern Mississippi is one of North America's leading children's literature research centers. It was established in 1966 by Lena Young de Grummond, a retired Louisiana school library supervisor and author of children's books. It was created to preserve the manuscripts and artwork of authors and illustrators of children's and YOUNG ADULT LITERATURE. The collection consists of original manuscripts, artwork, ILLUSTRATIONS, galleys, dummies, correspondence, and fan mail documenting the entire process of creating a work of children's literature. The main focus of the de Grummond Collection is American and BRITISH CHILDREN'S LITERATURE, both historical and contemporary. There are currently 55,000 published children's books as well as notes and documents related to children's literature; six hundred of these items date from between 1530 and 1830 and include an early printed edition of Aesop's fables. Many of these items represent first editions and prize-winning juvenile titles. Since its founding, more than

1,200 authors and illustrators have donated their original source material to the Collection for use by scholars, researchers, other authors and the public, both adults and children. An annual award, the University of Southern Mississippi Medallion, administered by the de Grummond Research Collection, is given to an author or illustrator it selects for an outstanding contribution to the field of children's literature.

There is a large and varied collection of at least 250 children's magazines representing historically significant publications such as *St. Nicholas* magazine and *Girl's Own Paper* to more contemporary titles. All genres are represented from the ever-popular FAIRY TALES, nursery rhymes and alphabet books to children's bibles, etiquette books, grammars, and schoolbooks. There is a special, in-depth collection of more than three hundred Kate GREENAWAY original artworks, especially her almanac illustrations. Other highlights of the de Grummond collection include materials relating to Randolph CALDECOTT and George MACDONALD and pertinent items from 18th and 19th century British publishers. A charming special feature is the Neubert Valentine Collection of more than 650 Victorian valentines consisting of embossed lace paper and multicolored decorative valentines with lace, ribbons, silk flower, and gold and silver filigree.

Many authors are represented in depth with the collection being the depository of Caldecott Medal author–artist, Ezra Jack KEATS's prodigious illustrations and texts. A study of Keats's materials allows viewers to follow his creative processes from his first conceptions for a story based on photos and models to sketches to original paintings while following numerous revisions of the text for a story. Storyboards, book dummies, and full-size canvases are also part of the collection. Stuffed animals, dolls, games and other related items based on characters Keats created are also included in the collection as they are for other authors' characters such as H. A. REY's internationally recognized monkey Curious George.

Use of the collection allows the public to understand how authors and illustrators create their works. The Ezra Jack Keats Foundation Endowment to the de Grummond Collection fosters use of the collection for all types of children's literature research according to Dee Jones, curator of the de Grummond. Established in 1992, the endowment allows a children's literature research scholar to visit the collection and prepare an indepth study of some aspect of the de Grummond's holdings.

Organizing the 55,000-plus items in the de Grummond has been made possible by a two-year Access Grant from the National Endowment for the Humanities, which supported the arrangement and description of many of the most valuable original materials in the collection. One such special aspect is a complete 42-volume set of the Doubleday Book Club for children published between 1957 and 1961. It is not indexed and the early works of such prestigious illustrators as Maurice SENDAK, Ezra Jack KEATS, Barbara COONEY, and Richard SCARRY are now accessible to scholars. The set contains well-known FAIRY TALES and folktales adapted by recognized children's authors, some original pieces, children's classics, and some INFORMATIONAL pieces.

The de Grummond Collection is open to the public, has several websites where virtual exhibits may be visited, and publishes scholarly materials and notecards that help support its work. Parts of the collection are exhibited at the McCain Library and Archives at the university, where all visitors may enjoy them.

BIBLIOGRAPHY: http://www.lib.usm.edu/~degrum

DIANE G. PERSON

DEJONG, Meindert

Author, b. 4 March 1906, Wierum, Netherlands; d. 6 July 1991, Allegan, Michigan

D. spent his early childhood in a tiny fishing village in Holland. He was small for his age and sickly, suffering from pneumonia three times, and near death during one illness. His family moved to Grand Rapids, Michigan, when he was eight, where the family struggled financially and his mother developed diabetes. Poverty, a poor-quality Dutch Christian school, and ridicule by other children typified D.'s first years in America. D. taught in a college in Iowa after graduating from Calvin College in 1928, but he disliked the work. He next tried farming but could not make a living at it. Based on a librarian's encouragement, D. shifted to writing full time for children.

The success of his first book, *The Big Goose and the Little White Duck* (1938), led him to continue to write while he worked for the Federal Writer's Project. His writing became his full-time career, interrupted by military service in China during World War II as a historian.

In his acceptance speech for the Hans Christian ANDERSEN Award, D. reflected on the influence of his early years in Holland. "The dike will still be there, the sea will be there, and the tower. They will be there, because in the mind's eye, in the child's eye of an eight-year-old boy, they are there, strong and eternal, set forever." His ability to communicate and explore the inner consciousness of children has often been noted in reviews and articles about his work. D.'s writing reflects his empathy for outcasts, his ability to tap into his insights of the child's inner mind, and his appreciation for the values found in small communities like that of his childhood in Holland. Whether writing about children or animals, his detailed descriptions of fishing villages, steep roofs, and dikes communicate a Dutch setting to readers, while the experiences of the characters remain universal. D. wrote twenty-seven books for children; many were translated for international publication.

AWARDS: ALA NEWBERY MEDAL (1955) for *The Wheel on the School.* AMERICAN LIBRARY ASSOCIATION Newbery Medal Honor Book (1954) for *Shadrach,* (1954) for *Hurry Home, Candy,* and (1957) for *The House of Sixty Fathers.* International Hans Christian Andersen Award (1962) for his body of work for children, although this award is usually reserved for a single book of fiction; National Book Award in Children's Literature (1969) for *Journey from Peppermint Street*

FURTHER WORKS: *Dirk's Dog Bello,* 1939; *Along Came a Dog,* 1958; *Far out the Long Canal,* 1964

BIBLIOGRAPHY: De Jong, David Cornel, "My Brother Meindert," *Newbery Medal Books: 1922–1955,* 1955; HOPKINS, Lee Bennett, *Pauses: Autobiographical Reflections of 101 Creators of Children's Books,* 1995; Townsend, John Rose, *A Sense of Story: Essays on Contemporary Writers for Children,* 1973; Manuscripts of D. are found in THE KERLAN COLLECTION at the University of Minnesota and at the Central Michigan University Park Library

SANDRA IMDIEKE

DELACRE, LuLu

Author, illustrator, b. 20 December 1957, Rio
Piedras, Puerto Rico.

D. received her fine arts degree from L'Ecole Su-
perieure d'Arts Graphiques in Paris, 1980. She
grew up in Puerto Rico and as a child established
her love of art. Her grandmother provided the atmosphere for D. to pursue her art interest: a bedroom floor and classical recordings. D. recalls
that her grandmother savored each piece of her
early artwork and stacked it in a corner. This
early Puerto Rican experience energized D.'s engagement with art and music. The major thrust of
her work includes rich FOLKLORE and music; the
colorful traditions of a LATINO childhood and a
need for authentic representations of Latin
Americans serve as catalysts for D.'s ILLUSTRA-
TIONS and collaboration with other writers. Many
of her works are available in English and Spanish;
some include both languages.

D. nearly always peppers her collaborative and
individual works with the Spanish language and
usually includes a pronunciation guide and glossary, as in her work with Lucia Gonzalez on *The
Bossy Gallito: A Traditional Cuban Folk Tale*
(1994). She also includes additional information
concerning the evolution of Latin American folktales and their significance within Latino culture.
D. is widely recognized for her illustrated song
books. Two of her bilingual collections, *Arroz
Con Lecho: Popular Songs and Rhymes from
Latin America* (1992) and *Las Navidades: Popular Christmas Songs from Latin America* (1990),
celebrate and depict Latino life through warm watercolor illustrations. Each includes musical arrangements, artist's notes, and bibliographies.
D.'s selections and illustrations work together to
build bridges of understanding among children.

AWARDS: Pura Belprè Honor Book (1994) for *The
Bossy Gallito—El Gallo de Bodas: A Traditional
Cuban Folktale* retold by Lucia M. Gonzales;
Americas Award (1993) for *Vejigante Masquerader*

FURTHER WORKS: *Los Zapaticos De Rose*. (Jose
Marti), 1997. *Senor Cat's Romance: And Other
Favorite Stories from Latin America*. (L. Gonza-
les, reteller). 1997

BIBLIOGRAPHY: *Something about the Author*, vol.
36, 1984

SHANE RAYBURN

DE LA MARE, Walter

Poet, novelist, short story writer, anthologist,
b. 25 April 1873, Charlton, Kent, England; d. 22
June 1956, Twickenham, Middlesex, England

After graduating from St. Paul's Cathedral Choir
School in London at age seventeen, D. went to
work for the statistical department of an international oil company. He remained there eighteen
years while pursuing a literary career on the side.
At thirty-five, he received a government pension
enabling him to devote his life to writing. Spanning over fifty years, his writing career included
POETRY, novels, short stories, anthologies, book
reviews, essays, and plays for children and adults.
His works exemplify the romantic imagination,
evoking an awareness of beauty in ordinary
things, a belief in the fantastic, and a sense of
wonder about life's mysteries.

D.'s first publication, *Songs of Childhood*
(1902) established him as a talented writer of
verse for children. *Peacock Pie* (1913), reissued
with ILLUSTRATIONS by Barbara COONEY (1961)
and a seventy-fifth anniversary edition illustrated
by Louise Brierly in 1989, demonstrated D.'s
mastery of rhythm, rhyme, and alliteration. A
child's view of a haircut is described in "The
Barber": "Gold locks, and black locks / Red
locks, and brown, / Topknot to love-curl / The
hair wisps down; / Straight above the clear eyes, /
Rounded round the ears, / Snip-snap and snick-a-
snick / Clash the Barber's shears." D.'s careful
descriptions of shadowy woods, summer meadows, and moonlit seas create images that stir the
imagination and often leave the reader with a
sense of mystery and unanswered questions. D.'s
characters in his short stories and novels also encounter the mysterious with fantastic creatures,
magical spells, and dreamlike worlds (*The Three
Mulla-Mulgars* [1910], reprinted as *The Three
Royal Monkeys* [1946]; *The Lord Fish,* 1913).

D. edited an enduring anthology, *Come
Hither: A Collection of Rhymes and Poems for
the Young of All Ages* (1923). He retold traditional folk tales in *Told Again* (1927) and Old
Testament narratives in *Stories from the BIBLE*
(1920). His stories, poems, and retellings have
been reprinted in anthologies and in PICTURE
BOOKS such as *The Story of Joseph* (1958) illus-

trated by Edward ARDIZZONE and *Molly Whuppie* (1983) illustrated by E. Le Cain. Many of his works have been issued in multiple editions with revised titles and texts or new formats and illustrations.

AWARDS: CARNEGIE MEDAL (1947) for *Collected Stories for Children.* Champion of Honour (1948). Order of Merit (1953). Honorary degrees from Oxford and Cambridge Universities

FURTHER WORKS: *Rhymes and Verses: Collected Poems for Children,* 1947; *Turnip,* 1992

ADELE GREENLEE

DELESSERT, Etienne

Illustrator, author, b. 4 January 1941, Lausanne, Switzerland

D. shares Bruno BETTELHEIM's idea that traditional tales can provide a psychological catharsis for the reader, so he endeavors to illustrate such stories without their oft-associated saccharine qualities. *La Belle et la Bete—Beauty and the Beast* (1984) is one such example. He is the winner of a Hans Christian ANDERSEN Highly Commended Illustrator Award as well as numerous worldwide honors including the Premerio Europeo Prize in 1977 and a Gold Medal from the Society of Illustrators in 1967, 1972, 1976, and 1978. D. divides his time between Lausanne, Switzerland, and Lakeville, Connecticut.

FURTHER WORKS: *Story Number One for Children Under Three Years of Age* (illus.), 1968; *How the Mouse Was Hit on the Head by a Stone and So Discovered the World,* 1971; *I Hate to Read!* (With R. Marshall), 1992

BIBLIOGRAPHY: Marshall, R., *Etienne D.,* 1992; *Major Authors and Illustrators for Children and YOUNG ADULTS,* 1993; *The Sixth Book of Junior Authors and Illustrators,* 1989

GWYNNE ELLEN ASH

DELTON, Judy

Author, b. 6 May 1931, St. Paul, Minnesota

D., who began writing books for children at the age of thirty-nine, draws heavily from her own troubled childhood as she writes about common problems that confront today's youth. Memories of a strict Catholic upbringing directly influence the stories in books such as her Kitty SERIES, the tales of a fourth-grade girl in a Catholic school.

Other books include the Angel and the Pee Wee Scouts series. She also writes for YOUNG ADULTS, addressing such issues as a mother's new boyfriend, pregnancy, infirm grandparents, and giving up a beloved pet. Among the literary honors D. has received are AMERICAN LIBRARY ASSOCIATION Notable Book Award for *Two Good Friends* (1974) and Junior Literary Guild selections for *Two Good Friends* (1974), *Three Friends Find Spring* (1977), and *Brimhall Turns to Magic* (1979).

FURTHER WORKS: *I'll Never Love Anything Ever Again,* 1985; *Hired Help for Rabbit,* 1988; *Bookworm Buddies,* 1996

BIBLIOGRAPHY: *Something about the Author,* vol. 77, 1994

MARY ARIAIL BROUGHTON

DEMI

Author, illustrator, b. 2 September 1942, Cambridge, Massachusetts

Although D.'s work is diverse in both content and style, she typically draws heavily upon the cultural context of ASIAN peoples. Her retellings and original works are based upon historical accounts and FOLKLORE; she is well-versed in Asian cultures. D.'s accompanying ILLUSTRATIONS are intricately crafted and detailed for the reader's pleasure; readers notice minute details. D.'s artistic technique combines pen-and-ink drawings, watercolor washes, and painting. Throughout her work, whether it is folklore or nonfiction, D.'s prose and illustrations function uniformly to share, reveal, celebrate, and explain various cultural customs of China such as the Chinese New Year in *Happy New Year! Kung-Hsi Fa-Ts'ai!* (1998). In this book, D.'s intricate figures spread across each page as she labels pictures and expresses the joy of the holiday celebrations through her explanations.

D. received a B.A. degree from Immaculate Heart College in 1962 and her M.S. from the University of Baroda in 1963. She did additional graduate study at the China Institute.

D. has written and illustrated biographies for young children. *The Dalai Lama: A Biography of the Tibetan Spiritual and Political Leader* (1998) is "told with respect and devotion, this is an inspirational picture-book BIOGRAPHY of a peacemaker whose self-declared 'true religion is kindness,' " in one reviewer's comment. D. also narrates the life of Siddhartha in *Buddha* (1996). Her careful and meticulous work remains fluid and respectful of diverse experiences throughout the world. Her books represent nearly every genre ranging from POETRY and folklore to nonfiction and biography.

AWARDS: Fulbright fellow, 1962. *New York Times* Best Illustrated Children's Books of the Year (1985) *The Nightingale* (Hans Christian ANDERSEN)

FURTHER WORKS: *Dragon Kites and Dragonflies: A Collection of Chinese Nursery Rhymes,* 1986; *In the Eyes of the Cat: Japanese Poetry for All Seasons* (trans. by Tze-si Huang), 1992; *The Empty Pot,* 1990; *Chingis Khan,* 1991; *Buddah,* 1996

SHANE RAYBURN

DEPAOLA, Tomie
Author, illustrator, b. 15 September 1934, Meriden, Connecticut

A favorite of children and adults alike, dePaola has illustrated, and often also written, more than 200 books, giving the children's literature field a rare combined gift of imaginative stories, realistic PICTURE BOOKS, religious stories, Christmas tales, informational titles, and folktales. Though deP. is often criticized for being too prolific, a close inspection finds versatility and a distinct style to be the significant hallmarks of his work.

One of his most famous books is *Strega Nona: An Old Tale* (1975), an original work often taken for an old folktale, which brought deP. recognition as a CALDECOTT MEDAL Honor Book Award in 1976. Since then, he has beguiled readers with more Strega Nona tales, including *Big Anthony and the Magic Ring* (1979) and *Strega Nona: Her Story* (1998). The chuckle-inducing plots and spry artwork quickly draw in children.

DeP., however, also has a serious side to his writing, which his autobiographical stories demonstrate. *Now One Foot, Now the Other* (1981) deals with aging; *Nana Upstairs and Nana Downstairs* (1973), which he re-illustrated in full color in 1978, is a sensitive rendition of a child's experience with the DEATH of a grandparent; *Oliver Button Is a Sissy* (1970) addresses name calling; and *The Art Lesson* (1989) tells about a student-teacher confrontation. These autobiographical

stories often find HUMOR woven into their plots. In *Tom* (1993), for example, Tommy's Irish grandfather inadvertently gets him in trouble at school, and in *The Baby Sister* (1996) Tommy makes friends with his crabby grandmother while waiting impatiently for a new sibling to be born.

Amusing incidents often pepper his concept books as well, in a genre where amusement is too rarely found. *The Quicksand Book* (1977), while giving concise and factual details about Jungle Girl and her particular dilemma in the sinking mud, tells a funny story. *The Popcorn Book* (1978) and *The Kids' Cat Book* (1979) are patterned in that same tradition.

Stories such as the early *Helga's Dowry* (1977) and the more recent *Bill and Pete Go down the Nile* (1987), also provide a showcase for the author-artist's nimble wit. Simple but clever wordplay is highly evident in the fast-paced Bill and Pete stories, while a more sophisticated *Bonjour, Mr. Satie* (1991), set in the art salons of 1920s Paris, expresses a subtler side to deP.'s joviality.

The more serious side of the author-artist's nature surfaces more clearly, perhaps, in his religious titles. *The Clown of God: An Old Story* (1978); *Francis, The Poor Man of Assisi* (1982); *The Miracles of Jesus* (1987); and *Jingle the Christmas Clown* (1992) are sensitive but not sentimental, thoughtful but not didactic. Some of his folktales also sound a somber note. *The Legend of the Bluebonnet: An Old Tale of Texas* (1983) and *The Legend of the Indian Paintbrush* (1988), both NATIVE AMERICAN tales, and *The Days of the Blackbird* (1997) deal with sacrifice and personal courage. *Bluebonnet,* in which a young girl throws her doll into the fire to help bring rain to her starving people, is particularly compelling.

The retellings of folktales, which have generated some of the most critical attention accorded deP., provide a generous stage for his wide-ranging talents. He has stayed away from the GRIMM, PERRAULT, and ANDERSEN tales, gravitating to stories from the Italian and Irish sides of his heritage. Often he has incorporated his own New England background into his Americana works. His illustrations for Clement C. MOORE's "The Night before Christmas" (1980), Sarah Josepha HALE's *Mary Had a Little Lamb* (1984), and *An Early*

American Christmas (1987) evoke the artist's interest in antique quilts, old houses, and nineteenth-century decorative objects. Concern with authenticity can be seen in the source notes provided, and, in the latter title, which he wrote as well as illustrated, his careful choice of words and dialogue results in a tale that rings true.

This artist counts five major anthologies among his credits. In addition to the popular *Tomie deP.'s MOTHER GOOSE* (1985), he has selected and illustrated collections of Christmas carols, BIBLE stories, nursery tales, and poems. Large and diverse, these collections are all generously and lavishly illustrated with expressive artwork that extends the written words. Perusal of these books shows the selections have been made carefully and thoughtfully, with the attention span and interest of readers and the appeal of the tales and poems clearly in mind.

In 1999, deP. began a new writing venture, creating chapter books for older children. The first, *26 Fairmount Avenue,* a 2000 Caldecott Medal Honor Book and the second, *Here We All Are* (2000) are based on childhood incidents and contain spirited line drawings. As in his autobiographical picture books, these stories, too, emphasize themes of individuality and family relationships in a way that is amusing and appealing to his audience.

The artist uses several ILLUSTRATION styles: sometimes the painterly style found in *Days of the Blackbird* (1997), and other times the coloring-book style, as he calls it, of the Bill and Pete stories. Regardless, his fluid but sure line is masterful, giving quick definition to the images, and his palette is distinctive. Whether employing the muted but warm tones found in *Legend of the Bluebonnet* (1983) or the spicy sun-hot colors in Tony JOHNSTON's *The Tale of Rabbit and Coyote* (1994), deP. carefully considers harmony and balance with the text and their total appearance on the page. These factors play a major role in deP.'s entire design of a picture book. Constantly aware of the constraints of the page, he accommodates the format, page size, and margins, using them to advantage, and the book is the better for it.

Whether original story, autobiographical vignette, folktale, INFORMATIONAL BOOK, or anthology, the books deP. creates are child-centered and inviting. In all, the child deP. once was shines through, captivating readers and enriching the field of children's literature.

AWARDS: ALA NEWBERY MEDAL Honor Book (2000) for *26 Fairmont Avenue.* AMERICAN LIBRARY ASSOCIATION Caldecott Medal Honor Book (1976) for *Strega Nona.* Golden Kite Award (1982) for *Giorgio's Village.* KERLAN Award

BIBLIOGRAPHY: Elleman, B., *Tomie deP.: His Art and His Stories,* 1999; HOPKINS, Lee Bennett, *Pauses: Autobiographical Reflections of 101 Creators of Children's Books,* 1995

BARBARA ELLEMAN

DE REGNIERS, Beatrice Schenk

Author, poet, b. 16 August 1914, Lafayette, Indiana; d. 1 March 2000, Washington, D.C.

This word lover discovered the joy of words at an early age. Her inspirations were nearly all derived from her intense memories of childhood, growing up in Indiana. It was from these memories that she wrote of how children feel: happy, sad, bewildered, angry—the full breadth of human emotions. D., editor of Scholastic's Lucky Book Club, 1961–81, attended the University of Illinois and University of Chicago, and received a M.Ed. degree in 1941 from Winnetka Graduate Teachers College. While she was a student teaching in a nursery school, she conceived *The Giant Story* (1953), her first book. With its publication, D. soon became one of America's most treasured, prolific writers for children. She likes to play with language; her work inevitably rings with rhythm, tempo, pattern, and rhyme. D. wrote in her introduction to *Sing a Song of Popcorn* (1988): "But it seems to me that the full power of a poem . . . can be fully appreciated only if the poem is read aloud." This is certainly true of D.'s works. Her fascination with giants and teeny tiny things reverberates in her many lighthearted PICTURE BOOKS. D.'s Uncle Ben seemed bigger than life to her as she grew up, and she credited him for encouraging her interests. For D., he was a giant of many dimensions. As D. shares significant events in her life, she refers to them as memory pictures. She claimed that memory pictures are better than photographs because they elicit not only sight, but also taste, touch, sound, and smell. She recalled preparing the manuscript for *A Little House of Your Own* (1954): "I would find a rock I could lean against, or a small gathering of trees that was like a private woods for me (a little house of my own). Each day, I wrote carefully, slowly, the sentences that had been taking shape in my head during the past year." D. weaves powerful language in small spaces and directs readers to celebrate everyday, familiar things in unusual ways. For example, in *Something Special* (1985), she tells readers, "if you find a feather, / a little white feather, / a soft and tickly feather, / it's for you." In this same collection, she suggests that we "listen for the little secret sounds" all around us, and tickles our imagination with "If I Were Teeny Tiny." D. is an American legacy in children's literature; she invites her readers to join her in the pure joy of words.

AWARDS: Children's Spring Book Festival Award (1955). *New York Times* Best Illustrated Children's Book (1956) for *Was It a Good Trade?* and (1960) for *The Shadow Book* (I. Gordon, illus.). ALA CALDECOTT MEDAL (1965) for *May I Bring a Friend?* (Beni MONTRESOR, illus). Children's Book Showcase Title, 1973 and 1977

FURTHER WORKS: *What Can You Do with a Shoe?* (Maurice SENDAK, illus.). 1955, 1997; *Little Sister and the Month Brothers*, 1975; *Waiting for Mama*, 1984; *A Week in the Life of Best Friends*, 1986; *The Way I Feel Sometimes*, 1988

BIBLIOGRAPHY: HOPKINS, Lee Bennett, *Pauses: Autobiographical Reflections of 101 Creators of Children's Books*, 1995

SHANE RAYBURN

DERWENT, Lavinia

Author, b. Date unknown, near Jedburgh, Scotland; d. 1989, Glasgow, Scotland

"Can ye no gang awa' and mak'up stories for yoursel', lassie?" So she did. Jessie, the odd-job woman on the farm in the Scottish Borders, "was for many years the most important influence in my life." She had unknowingly started D. off on her writing career. D. pays warm tribute in *A Border Bairn* (1979) to the woman who gave the lonely child a sense of security and fired her imagination. D. was a born storyteller, a warm and vivid personality whose homely tales appeal to adults and children alike. Independence and total self-reliance are traits of her own character that also appear in her children's books. She created a wonderful radio character called Tammy Troot, a little fish who lived in a Scottish burn

with his gran, and used his wits to get himself out of many a scrape. Over 200 episodes were broadcast on the BBC's *Children's Hour*. The MacPherson books, about a spunky wee Glasgow message boy, and her later SERIES about Magnus, a boy on the island of Sula, both solitary children, each have at least one older person in the background on whom they can rely. Magnus—like the author—has a secret talent. He paints the island's wildlife. Two of the Sula books were produced as plays on BBC-TV.

As was the custom in those days, D.'s future was decided for her: she was to keep house for her brother, a newly ordained Minister. Away from her home, only seventeen years old, longing for freedom to write, she coped with running a large, drafty manse, learning to cook and clean, and tending the sick and elderly in the parish. Her brother married and she left the borders for Glasgow, where she started work at Collins, the publishers (now HarperCollins). Finally she was free to lead her own life as she wanted it. She began as a caption writer, graduated to being an editor, and ended up representing her firm on business in Egypt. All this time she was writing stories, articles, radio scripts; she was learning her craft.

D. will probably be best remembered for the seven books about her early life in the borders. Packed full of lively sketches of these times, and ringing with Scottish dialect, they bring to life the people on the farm and the countryside and discuss their hardships. She tells her tales with HUMOR, wit, and above all, with great humanity.

D. was a member of the Society of Authors and International PEN, and served a term as President of their Scottish Centres. Much in demand as a speaker, she also had a career in radio and television. She was a Member of the Order of the British Empire and received her medal from the Queen at Buckingham Palace. The complete archive of her work, including typescripts, is housed in the Mitchell Library, Glasgow, Scotland.

FURTHER WORKS: The MacPherson series. 1960s. *Joseph and the Coat of Many Colors*, 1963; *Sula, Return to Sula, Song of Sula, Sula Symphony* (four vols.), 1976–77; *A Breath of Border Air*, 1975; *Another Breath of Border Air*, 1977; *A Border Bairn*, 1979; *God Bless the Borders*, 1981; *Lady of the Manse*, 1983; *A Mouse in the Manse*, 1985; *Beyond the Borders*, 1988

BIBLIOGRAPHY: Author's personal notes and manuscripts in the archives, Mitchell Library, Glasgow, Scotland

MARY BAXTER

DESIMINI, Lisa
Author, illustrator, b. 21 March 1964, Brooklyn, New York

D. initially intended to work as an illustrator for magazines and newspapers when she completed her education at New York's School of Visual Arts. Instead she was referred to Harper Junior Books and began her career as an illustrator, producing sample works for Ann TURNER's *Heron Street* (1989). D. illustrated many books for various authors before trying her hand at writing. Her first book, *I Am Running Away Today* (1990) was well received and was soon followed by several other works. Her vibrant ILLUSTRATIONS often capture more critical attention than the text as she uses a variety of media to set the mood for her stories.

FURTHER WORKS: *Adelaid and the Night Train* (Liz Rosenberg), 1989; *Housekeeper of the Wind* (Christine Widmon), 1990; *Moose in the Garden* (Nancy CARLSTROM), 1990; *The Thieves' Market* (Dennis Hoseley), 1991; *The Great Peace March* (H. Near), 1993; *Moon Soup*, 1993; *Magic Weaver of Rugs: A Tale of the Navajo* (J. Oughton), 1994; *My House* (an American Booksellers Pick of the List citation), 1994; *Anansi Does the Impossible* (Verena AARDEMA), 1997; *Love Letters* (Arnold ADOFF), 1997; *Tulip Sees America* (Cynthia RYLANT), 1998; *The Sun and the Moon*, 1999; *Feelings*, 2000; *Touch the Poem* (A. ADOFF), 2000

MICHAEL O'LAUGHLIN

DE TREVINO, Elizabeth Borton
Author, b. 2 September 1904, Bakersfield, California

T. is best known for her 1966 NEWBERY MEDAL–winning novel *I, Juan de Pareja*. It is the dramatic story of Spanish painter Diego Velázquez's black slave who became the artist's assistant and loyal friend. *Nacar, the White Deer* (1963), based on historical records, tells of the bond of loyalty and friendship that developed between a shepherd boy and the deer being sent to the King of Spain from the New World in the 1500s. Many of D.'s other writings, *Casilda of the Rising Moon* (1967), *El Guero: A True* ADVENTURE STORY (1989), and *A Carpet of Flowers* (1955) are set in Spain, the American Southwest, and Mexico. Living in her adopted country of Mexico, T. has also published under the name Elizabeth Borton.

AWARDS: AMERICAN LIBRARY ASSOCIATION Newbery Medal (1966) for *I, Juan de Pareja*

FURTHER WORKS: *Pollyanna in Hollywood*, 1931; *Here Is Mexico*, 1970; *Juarez, Man of Law*, 1974

BIBLIOGRAPHY: Colliers, L., and Nakamura, L. *Major Authors and Illustrators for Children and YOUNG ADULTS*, 1993; HOPKINS, Lee Bennett, *Pauses: Autobiographical Reflections of 101 Creators of Children's Books*, 1995; *Third Book of Junior Authors*, 1972; Ward, M. E., D. A. Marquardt, N. Dolan, and D. Eaton, *Authors of Books for Young People*, 1990

GWYNNE ELLEN ASH

DEWEY, Ariane
Author, illustrator, b. 17 August 1937, Chicago, Illinois

D. received a B.A. in art from Sarah Lawrence College in 1959. The major emphasis in D.'s work is lighthearted fun. D. works individually but also collaborates frequently with José ARUEGO. Together, they have crafted a unique style that evokes joy and laughter among readers. D. and Aruego illuminate the text with their trademark watercolor and black-pen ILLUSTRATIONS, creating space for lively engagement with the story. Usually, A. designs the page, draws the sketches, and D. fills in with colorful, often comical watercolor washes. One of D.'s individual works, *Naming Colors* (1995), vividly captures the history and evolution of colors with powerfully compelling illustrations. Her illustrations typically extend the simple text. In *They Thought They Saw Him* (C. Strete, 1996), D. and Aruego create a vivid chameleon who plays hide-and-seek with his pursuers. D.'s retelling of *Pecos Bill* (1983) represents one of the many picture-book editions of tall-tale heroes. In Robert KRAUS's PICTURE BOOKS, D. captures the essence of the baffled mouse. With simple lines and bold colors, A. and D. collaborate with the text to enhance the personalities of Kraus's lovable characters and his universal themes.

FURTHER WORKS: *Dance Away* (George SHANNON), 1982; *Where Are You Going, Little Mouse?* (Robert Kraus). 1989; *April Showers* (George

Shannon). 1995; *Antarctic Antics* (Judy Sierra), 1998

BIBLIOGRAPHY: Silvey, Anita, ed., *Children's Books and Their Creators,* 1995; *Something about the Author,* vol. 7, 1975

SHANE RAYBURN

DEWEY, Jennifer Owings

Author, illustrator, b. 2 October 1941, Chicago, Illinois

D. illustrated books for other authors before writing her first book, *Clem: The Story of a Raven* (1986). Her experiences with wildlife and nature provide the source for her writings and ILLUSTRATIONS. *Wildlife Rescue: The Work of Dr. Kathleen Ramsay* (1994), appearing on the John Burroughs List of Nature Books for Young People, introduces a noted veterinarian at work in the natural environment. Through her animated text and dramatic photographs, D. shows Dr. Ramsay working to rescue and heal injured animals. She brings the same realistic and thorough probing of events to her own autobiography, *Cowgirl Dreams: A Western Childhood* (1995) where she relates her experiences with animals, neighbors, and family growing up on a ranch in New Mexico.

FURTHER WORKS: *Idle Weeds,* 1980; *Living Fossils,* 1982; *The Secret Language of Snow,* 1984; *The Dinosaurs and the Dark Star,* 1985; *Snowflakes,* 1985; *Faces Only a Mother Could Love,* 1996; *Rattlesnake Dance: True Tales, Mysteries, and Rattlesnake Ceremonies,* 1997; *Poison Dart Frogs,* 1998; *Navajo Summer,* 1998

BIBLIOGRAPHY: *Something about the Author,* vol. 103, 1999

JODI PILGRIM

DIAZ, David

Illustrator, b. 1958, Fort Lauderdale, Florida

After attending Fort Lauderdale Art Institute, D. began his art career as a newspaper illustrator, designer, and graphic artist. His unusual talent as a book-cover designer was soon recognized and D. was invited to illustrate Gary SOTO's POETRY, *Neighborhood Odes* (1992); this became his debut in the field. D. was awarded the 1995 CALDECOTT MEDAL for Eve BUNTING's *Smoky Night* (1994), his second illustrated children's book. As he does in *Smoky Night,* D. uses a collage approach where he sets acrylic paintings atop common objects. The adapted media, shaped in unusual ways, works harmoniously to create the intensity of each double-page spread. This unorthodox approach to illustrating children's books brings acclaim.

D.'s ILLUSTRATIONS are not contained or conditioned by a specific format; he has established a distinctive style. D. exudes freedom in his use of artistic style, design, technique, and even font. He uses watercolor, gouache, and acrylics to create what appears as wood carvings atop photographic compositions in *Wilma Unlimited: How Wilma Rudolph Became the World's Fastest Runner* by Kathleen KRULL (1996). This same rich intensity can be found in *December* by Eve BUNTING (1997). D. has illustrated books that tackle sensitive issues of social reality as in Eve MERRIAM's *The Inner City MOTHER GOOSE* (1996) and Eve Bunting's *Going Home* (1996). D. is careful in his manipulation of color to portray race. In an interview in the *Reading Teacher* (1996), D. addresses the issue of character representation in *Smoky Night:* "It just seemed . . . the appropriate way to represent these characters. I tried to use the same color palette throughout on all the different characters so that there's no indication of any ethnic background or nationality." This perspective challenges its readers to enter and engage in the experience of the story as it delicately depicts humanity.

His family is very supportive of D.'s works. In fact, readers find it interesting to note D.'s acknowledgment of his wife's contributions in design and photography, often found within the final pages of his books. D.'s unique style and selection of mixed media serve to extend and transcend the text, authenticate the integrity of the story, and invite readers to pause and escape within the pages of art.

SELECT AWARDS: ALA Caldecott Medal (1995) for *Smoky Night*

FURTHER WORKS: *Going Home* (Eve Bunting). 1996; *Be Not Far from Me: The Oldest Love Story: Legends from the BIBLE* (Eric A. KIMMEL), reteller). 1998; *The Disappearing Alphabet* (Richard Wilbur), 1998; *The Little Scarecrow Boy* (Margaret Wise BROWN). 1998

BIBLIOGRAPHY: Cooper, Ilene, Review in *Booklist,* vol. 94; Krull, Kathleen, Review in the *Horn Book* magazine, vol. 72; Peck, J. and J.

Hendershot. "Conversation with a Winner—David D. talks about *Smoky Night*," *Reading Teacher,* 49, pp. 386–88; *Something about the Author,* vol. 96, 1998

SHANE RAYBURN

DICKENS, Charles

Author, journalist, b. 7 February 1812, Landport, England, d. 9 June 1870, Gad's Hill, England

D. is probably the most celebrated Victorian novelist, and although most of his writing was for adults, he wrote several pieces with children in mind. D.'s Christmas books (1843–48), which included *A Christmas Carol* (1843) and *The Cricket on the Hearth* (1845), *A Child's History of England* (1851-53) and *A Holiday Romance* (1868) were all intended for young audiences. He is best known for his richly descriptive novels filled with satiric social commentary, including *Oliver Twist* (1838), *David Copperfield* (1849–50), *Hard Times* (1854), *A Tale of Two Cities* (1859) and *Great Expectations* (1860–61). Since publication, all these works have been enjoyed by readers of all ages. In 1888, D. was voted the favorite author among boys in a British poll. His novels were staples on school reading lists well into the twentieth century and many remain so today. *A Christmas Carol* is a cultural fixture, resurrected annually in film versions, on television, the stage, and in ever-renewing garb. The name of Ebenezer Scrooge, the mean-spirited central character, has become eponymous for miser, even though Scrooge himself does, in the course of events, find happiness and achieve redemption. Perhaps only *A Child's History of England,* a highly personal and idiosyncratic account, is today considered dated.

BIBLIOGRAPHY: Murray, Brian, *Charles D.,* 1994

DAVID L. RUSSELL

DICKINSON, Peter

Author, b. 16 December 1927, Livingston, Northern Rhodesia (now Zambia)

D. attended Eton College and received a B.A. from King's College, Cambridge, in 1951. D.'s interest in mysteries evolved while he worked as a writer for *Punch,* the London HUMOR magazine. Working at *Punch* for seventeen years, he reviewed crime novels and wondered about writing

his own book. Soon D.'s unrestrained imagination began to structure much of his writing. His mysteries compel readers to suspend disbelief and engage in fantastical, extraordinary events. This prolific writer's works have science fiction elements, twisting normal into not-so-normal events. This power to manipulate reality appeals to adolescents exercising their own imaginations, creating multiple worlds in which to cope with life's difficult issues. His first work for children, *The Weathermonger* (1969), became the beginning of a trilogy including *Heartsease* (1969) and *The Devil's Children* (1970); they were later combined into one book: *The Changes: A Trilogy* (1975). Characters in this trilogy have the power to manipulate the weather and encounter Merlin in their search for answers. The characters are thrust into the Dark Ages as England continues to incur multiple changes. In *Eva* (1989), D. introduces a girl, who after being struck by a car, has her memory transplanted into a chimpanzee. She struggles in her new body and ultimately flees with a group of chimps to a remote island. Naturally this seems impossible, but D.'s craft conjures a believable space in which the events occur. In *Shadow of a Hero* (1994), D. weaves facts from the Balkan conflicts of the 1990s into this story. While much of his work is heavily influenced by politics and history, D. has also written: lighthearted animal fantasies. For example, D. plays with point of view in *Chuck and Danielle* (1996) as Danielle's paranoid, high-strung dog narrates a wildly exuberant tale. It is evident that D. is intrigued and fueled by the power of imagination. In an influential 1986 article, he writes, "The crucial thing about the act of imagination is its self-coherence, the way in which each part fits with all the other parts and by doing so authenticates them." D. achieves this sense of coherency as he develops realistic, fantastical worlds in which characters experience a wide range of emotions. He concludes, "It is imagination which makes us what we are. It is the core of our humanity." D. appeals to a sophisticated audience of YOUNG ADULT readers who find it hard to resist D.'s imaginative invitations; they are pulled into the depth of his scientifically fantastic fictional worlds.

SELECT AWARDS: *Boston Globe-Horn Book Award* (1977) for *Chance, Luck and Destiny.*

CARNEGIE MEDAL (1979) for *Tulku* and (1980) for *City of Gold and Other Stories from the Old Testament.* Guardian Award (1977) for *The Blue Hawk.* Whitbread Award (1979) for *Tulku* and (1990) for *AK.* INTERNATIONAL BOARD ON BOOKS FOR YOUNG PEOPLE Honor List (1982) for *Tulku.* AMERICAN LIBRARY ASSOCIATION Honor Book and ALA Best Book for Young Adults (1989) for *Eva*

FURTHER WORKS: *A Bone from a Dry Sea,* 1993; *Time and the Clock Mice, Etcetera,* 1994; *The Lion Tamer's Daughter and Other Stories,* 1997

BIBLIOGRAPHY: Dickinson, Peter, *Children's Literature Review,* Spring 1986; *Something about the Author,* vol. 95, 1998

SHANE RAYBURN

DILLON, Leo and Diane

Illustrators. Diane: b. 13 March 1933, Glendale, California; Leo: b. 2 March 1933, Brooklyn, New York

Artists Leo and Diane Dillon were born within days of each other on opposite sides of the country. L.D.'s mentor was Ralph Volman, a painter, poet, and friend of his father's who was involved in the Marcus Garvey political movement in the 1930s. L.D. painted for Volman and received encouragement and respect in return. D.D. was initially influenced by her father who knew drafting and explained some simple, yet surprising, artistic rules to her: "If the light was coming from the left, the shadow would be on the right side of the object." She also admired the modern work of fashion illustrator Dorothy Hood. D.D. and L.D. eventually met at Parsons School of Design where they began as competitors, each admiring and worrying about the high quality of the work of the other. Before they fell in love and were married, Leo described their relationship as "not merely competition, it was war. We spent a lot of time and energy trying to prove ourselves to each other." It is this close relationship that continues to define the work they do together.

In their acceptance speech for the 1977 CALDECOTT MEDAL for *Ashanti to Zulu: AFRICAN Traditions* (Musgrove, 1976), L.D. and D.D. explain how they work together to achieve their final illustrations: "We each have our own distinct styles, but when we work together, as we do on all our children's books, we essentially create a third artist. . . . Over the years we have blended our thoughts and styles together to produce art we couldn't have produced separately. In the beginning we worked pretty much by trial and error, but later, working together became automatic, the work passing from one drawing board to the other at different stages."

When trying to decide what the demands of the words meant to their art for *Ashanti to Zulu,* the D.s realized that they needed to do extensive research to create realistic portraits of the life of the twenty-six tribes represented in the book. They needed to know what clothes people wear, where they live, what adornments they prefer, what they eat. Perhaps the Nigerian kano knot used on the corners of the frames on each page not only symbolizes endless searching for that tribe but also endless researching for the artists. As they read and reread the text, they "began to appreciate the grandeur in ordinary living, in what actually exists. It is the intelligence in a person's eyes or the nuances of body language— things shared by all people—that make for real beauty." The golden illustrations of the gentle caresses of one family member to another or the jubilation of a bridal procession or the ceremonies of everyday life are grand in their depictions and intent.

L.D. and D.D. talk and argue and sketch and research as they collaborate to seek perfection in the artwork they produce for each book. They are stylistically versatile. In an interview after winning their first Caldecott Medal for *Why Mosquitoes Buzz in People's Ears* (Verna AARDEMA, reteller 1975), L.D. said, "We've never thought in terms of a kiddie style. Our job is to re-state visually what the words already say, and we use whatever style is appropriate. We don't water down a message for children." D.D. added, "But we do sneak in a little fun whenever we can." The bold, African batik-styled art for *Why Mosquitoes Buzz in People's Ears* perfectly suits both the location and the tone of the book. The HUMOR of rabbit's nervous look as snake approaches or mosquito's punishment on the last page appeals to the child in every reader. Antelope often peers out quixotically from the pages of the book, commenting nonverbally on the story action with his funny, emotive facial expressions.

Though they mainly use watercolor, pastel, and acrylic in their work, the D.s enjoy experimenting with different techniques in many of their books. They have perfected the frisket technique where the basic drawing is done on vellum, which is then cemented to a fine-grained heavier paper. They then cut areas of the drawing from the vellum, applying powdered pastels with a brush and cotton. The pastels are affixed permanently with a clear spray. The bold effect created is like that of woodblock prints. *The Tale of the Mandarin Ducks* (PATERSON, 1990) is stylistically reminiscent of Japanese woodcuts known as ukiyo-e. Heavy black lines outline the figures and contrast with the softened, dusky colors. The dramatic illustrations for *Aida* (Price, 1990) are painted on marbleized paper in strong and dramatic colors, including bright golden gilt, to create an ancient Egyptian effect. The hieroglyphic-inspired borders on all left-side pages give story information while helping to set the mood with the more expansive art on the facing page. Lee Dillon, D.D. and L.D.'s son, created the decorative metal frame used to border each page.

The D.'s have also experimented with other unusual illustrative techniques and materials, from crewel, used on the cover for Carson McCullers's *A Member of the Wedding,* (1946) to plastic and leading made of liquid steel to evoke a stained glass effect on the cover of C. S. LEWIS's *Till We Have Faces,* 1956. Their soft-charcoal artwork appears in Sharon Bell MATHIS's 1976 NEWBERY MEDAL Honor Book *The Hundred Penny Box.* In their book, *To Everything There Is a Season: Verses From Ecclesiastes* (1998), the D.s illustrate the timelessness and universality of the words from Ecclesiastes with their re-creation of art from many ancient cultures using different media. Art representing traditional AUSTRALIAN aboriginal painting is done in gouache on bark paper; gouache is also used for ancient Chinese painting but is painted on silk; Irish artwork is in gouache on brown parchment paper. The artwork in the book is a compilation of all that these artists have discovered during their professional lives. It is a tribute to their quest to create stylistically diverse art of the highest quality. Over many years of working together, the D.s have become one. Theirs is not only a marriage of two individuals, but of two artists as well.

AWARDS: AMERICAN LIBRARY ASSOCIATION Caldecott Medal (1977) for *Ashanti to Zulu* (M. Musgrove). ALA Caldecott Medal Honor Book

(1976) for *Why Mosquitoes Buzz In People's Ears* (V. Aardema). Empires State Award for Excellence in Literature for Children (1992). *Boston Globe–Horn Book* Award for ILLUSTRATION (1992) for *The Tale of the Mandarin Ducks* (K. Paterson). CORETTA SCOTT KING AWARD for Illustration (1991) for *Aida* (Leontyne Price). *New York Times* Best Illustrated Book of the Year (1976) for *Ashanti to Zulu,* (1985) *The People Could Fly,* (1990) *The Tale of the Mandarin Ducks.* INTERNATIONAL BOARD ON BOOKS FOR YOUNG PEOPLE Illustration Award (1986) for *The People Could Fly: American Black Folktales* (V. HAMILTON, author)

FURTHER WORKS: Illus: *Brother to the Wind.* (M. WALTER). 1985: *The People Could Fly.* (V. Hamilton). 1985: *Her Stories: African American Folktales, FAIRY TALES, and True Tales.* (V. Hamilton. 1994: *The Porcelain Cat.* (M. Hearn). 1987: *Wind Child.* (S. Murphy). 1999. *The Girl Who Spun Gold* (V. Hamilton). 2000

BIBLIOGRAPHY: Pamphlet from Blue Sky Press for *The Sorcerer's Apprentice;* pamphlet from Cathcart Galleries, Weston, Connecticut; Cummings, P. ed, *Talking with Artists,* 1992; Diane D., "Leo D.," the *Horn Book* magazine, August 1997, pp. 423–24; Leo and Diane D., *Christian Science Monitor,* May 12, 1976; Leo and Diane D., "Caldecott Award Acceptance," the *Horn Book* magazine, August 1997, pp. 415–21; Leo D., "Diane D.", the *Horn Book* magazine, August 1997, p. 422; *Something about the Author,* vol. 51, 1988

REBECCA RAPPORT

THE DISABLED IN CHILDREN'S AND YOUNG ADULT LITERATURE

Over 35 million citizens of the United States have a physical, cognitive, learning, or health disability. This constitutes approximately 10 percent of the population, which is a fairly consistent percentage throughout the rest of the world. According to the World Health Organization, an impairment is an abnormality or a loss of a mental or physical structure or function. A disability is noted as the inability to perform a function due to the impairment.

Over the past two decades enhancing the classroom environment to promote success for all students has become a legal issue. In 1973, Congress passed the Rehabilitation Act (PL 93–112), which stated that persons with disabilities should be provided with the means "to learn, work and compete on a fair and equal basis." If this was denied, federal funding could be eliminated. In 1975, Congress passed the Education for All Handicapped Children Act (P.L. 94–142), which guaranteed all children an equal education in the "least restrictive environment." This prompted both inclusion and mainstreaming programs for millions of children. If requested, any child with a documented disability could obtain an Individualized Education Plan, or IEP. In 1986, Congress passed the Individuals with Disabilities Education Act (PL 101–476), which amended the 1973 law by extending public educational assistance to any person with a disability from birth to age twenty-one years. In 1990, President George Bush signed the Americans With Disabilities Act.

At the same time children's and young adult literature has responded to the increasing visibility of this special population through the publication of stories featuring characters with a variety of disabilities. Whether legally required to or not, classroom teachers, librarians, and parents look for ways to help all children succeed. A relatively common and inexpensive tool is literature, which can enhance the success of all students by broadening their attitudes and perceptions.

A key purpose of literature is to enable readers to understand better the human experience of self and others. Literature does this vicariously by engaging its readers in the lives, values, and struggles of those who are very different or very similar to themselves. Specifically literature can encourage a healthy attitude toward a given disability by giving readers disabled characters they can identify with and giving an awareness and understanding of a given disability to nondisabled students. Among middle-grade readers literature is highly successful in prompting a positive change in attitude toward disabled individuals.

Books need to be carefully selected so that characters with disabilities are portrayed accurately and realistically. In successful novels, characters with disabilities are treated realistically and respectfully as they face the same problems as their peers. Although the texts are fiction, the facts about the various disabilities are accurate; for the most part, plots are engaging, yet not contrived. The increasing number of books featuring characters with disabilities and special needs is consistent with society's growing awareness of this population. Just as they have moved out of the shadows in public settings and are mainstreamed in regular classrooms, books featuring special needs children and adolescents frequently place them as main characters in stories. Such books are realistic in presenting a population that may incur a change in the disability but no false hope for a cure is offered. A character with spina bifida or a developmental disability is not miraculously restored to perfect health but may show improvement through the efforts of therapy, rehabilitation, or medical intervention. Most of these books are intended for an older audience. The few available picture-book stories deal mainly with a simple level of disability even though these may be traumatic to the picture-book population. Examples of such picture books are Jane Breskin ZALBEN's *Buster Gets Braces* (1992), Amy Hest's *Baby Duck and the Bad Eyeglasses* (1996), Remy CHARLIP and Miller's *Handtalk Birthday* (1987), about the hearing disabled, and Petra MATHERS's *Sophie and Lou* (1991) dealing with such extreme shyness that it becomes an emotional disability. These books offer young children an optimistic outlook on accepting and coping with disability.

Many novels for older readers featuring characters with mental disabilities such as autism, mental retardation, cerebral palsy, and developmental disabilities are told either from the perspective of a relative or through multiple perspectives. The twin sister of an adolescent male is the voice in Nancy Werlin's (1994) *Are You Alone on Purpose?* An older sister describes living with a brother who has cerebral palsy in *Ellen's Case* (Lois Metzger, 1995). Told from the perspective of multiple characters, *Fair Game* (Erika Tamar, 1993) is the story of popular high school athletes who repeatedly sexually assault a pretty, mentally retarded female classmate. In *The Man Who Loved Clowns* (June R. Wood, 1992) and *When Pigs Fly* (Wood, 1995), novels about characters with developmental disabilities, the story is told through the eyes of a niece and a sister, respectively. An older brother of a gifted runner with a developmental disability is the voice readers hear in Matt CHRISTOPHER's (1995) *Fighting Tackle*. The classic NEWBERY MEDAL novel, *Summer of the Swans* (Betsy BYARS, 1970), was one of the first books to present a mentally retarded young boy as a central character in a novel and show the effects of his disability on other members of the family. *The Alfred Summer* (Jan SLEPIAN, 1980) examines the friendship between its two main characters with disabilities. Alfred is developmentally disabled and Lester has cerebral palsy but their friendship with two other neighborhood children is positive and realistically portrayed.

Stories dealing with sensory impairments, such as dyslexia, blindness, or deafness, are often told in the first person. *The Worst Speller in Jr. High* (Caroline Janover, 1995) portrays the frustrations of a seventh grader with dyslexia. Blindness, from birth or contracted in adolescence, is discussed in *Listen for the Fig Tree* (Sharon MATHIS, 1974) and *The Window* (Jeanette Ingold, 1996). Nancy Butt's (1996) *Cheshire Moon* is a sci-fi text about an angry adolescent girl without hearing who is seeking a haven, and John Neufeld's (1996) *Gaps in Stone Walls* is a whodunnit murder mystery set on Martha's Vineyard in the 1880s, where one-fourth of the population is deaf.

Adolescents coping with various types of physical disabilities appear in three novels. A main character suffers from severe physical deformity in *Lizard* (Covington, 1991), in *Staying Fat for Sarah Byrnes* (Chris CRUTCHER, 1993) and in *Under the Mermaid Angel* (Martha A. Moore, 1994). Adolescent novels also deal with the struggle of able-bodied characters who become disabled during adolescence. In *Izzy Willy-Nilly* (Cynthia VOIGT, 1986) the main character loses her leg in a drunk-driving accident, and in *Are You Alone on Purpose?* (Nancy Werlin, 1994) one character's legs become paralyzed from a freak diving accident. An athletic, talented adolescent boy contracts MS and becomes confined to a wheelchair in *Hero of Lesser Causes* (Julie Johnston, 1992).

BIBLIOGRAPHY: Andrews, S. E., "Using Inclusion Literature to Promote Positive Attitudes Toward Disabilities." *Journal of Adolescent and Adult Literacy.* 41.6. pp. 420–26, 1998; Baskin, B. and Harris, K., *Notes from a Different Drummer,* 1977; Dobo, P. J., "Using Literature to Change Attitudes toward the Handicapped." *The Reading Teacher,* pp. 290–92, 1982; Gartner, A., and Joe, T., *Images of the Disabled, Disabling Images,* 1987; Gross, A. L., and Ortiz, L. W., "Using Children's Literature to Facilitate Inclusion in Kindergarten and the Primary Grades," *Young Children,* pp. 32–35, 1994; Heim, A. B., "Beyond the Stereotypes: Characters with Mental Disabilities in Children's Books," *School Library Journal,* pp. 139–42, 1994; Landrum, J. E., "Adolescent Novels Which Feature Characters with Disabilities: An Annotated Bibliography," *Journal of Adolescent and Adult Literary,* 42.4, pp. 284–90, 1998/99; Rosenblatt, L. M., *Literature as Exploration.* 4th ed. 1983; Salende, S. J., and Moe, L., "Modifying Nonhandicapped Students' Attitudes Toward Their Handicapped Peers through Children's Literature," *Journal for Special Education,* 19, pp. 22–27, 1983; Scheer, J., and Groce, N., "Impairment as a Human Constant: Cross-cultural and Historical Perspectives on Variation," *Journal of Social Issues,* 44, pp. 23–37, 1998; Umerlik, A., "Fostering an Understanding of the Disabled through Young Adult Literature," *School Library Media Activities Monthly,* vol. 8, pp. 35–36, 1992

JUDITH E. LANDRUM

DISNEY, ENTERTAINMENT AND PUBLISHING

Walt D., who would revolutionize family entertainment not only in the United States but throughout the world, was born in Chicago, Illinois, on December 5, 1901. He spent his childhood in Missouri, where he attended school and eventually made his earliest attempts with animated films. Moving to California, he began a series combining a live girl with cartoon animals, called the Alice Comedies, which he made for four years, followed by a year of Oswald the Lucky Rabbit cartoons, But, after a dispute with his distributor, he lost the rights to the character, and he had to come up with a new one. That new character was Mickey Mouse. With his chief animator, Ub Iwerks, D. designed the famous mouse and gave him a personality that endeared him to all. *"Steamboat Willie,"* the first Mickey Mouse cartoon to be seen by the public, opened to rave reviews in New York on November 18, 1928. The new character was immediately popular, and a lengthy series of Mickey Mouse cartoons followed.

Not one to rest on his laurels, D. soon began producing, in 1929, another series—the Silly Symphonies—to go with the Mickey series. Beginning with *Flowers and Trees* in 1932, a D. Silly Symphony won the Oscar every year for the rest of the decade. Additional characters joined

Mickey Mouse in the D. cartoons—Minnie Mouse, Donald Duck, Pluto, Goofy.

The first Mickey Mouse book was published in 1930, as was the first Mickey Mouse newspaper comic strip, and COMIC BOOKS followed later. The books and comics, hardly considered fine children's literature, nevertheless often encouraged children to start reading.

In 1934, D. decided to produce the first animated feature film, and turned to a GRIMM'S fairy tale for his source. *Snow White and the Seven Dwarfs* was finished at Christmastime, 1937, and it was a spectacular hit. Now Walt D.'s studio was on a firmer footing.

The next two features, *Pinocchio* and *Fantasia,* were released in 1940. They were technical masterpieces, but their costs were too high for a company losing most of its foreign markets because of the onset of World War II. *Dumbo* was made in 1941 on a very limited budget, but *Bambi,* in 1942, was another expensive film, and caused the studio to retrench.

During the war, D. made two films in South America, *Saludos Amigos* and *The Three Caballeros,* at the request of the State Department. When the war ended, it was difficult for the D. Studio to regain its prewar footing. Several years went by with the release of "package" features—films such as *Make Mine Music* and *Melody Time,* containing groups of short cartoons packaged together.

Nineteen-fifty saw big successes at D.—the first completely live action film and the first based on a well-known book, *Treasure Island,* (Robert Louis STEVENSON), the return to classic animated features with *Cinderella,* and the first D. television show at Christmastime. D. went onto television in a big way in 1954 with the beginning of the *Disneyland* anthology series. This series eventually would run on all three networks and remain on the air for twenty-nine years, making it the longest-running prime-time television series ever. *The Mickey Mouse Club,* one of television's most popular children's series, debuted in 1955—and made stars of a group of talented Mouseketeers.

D. was never satisfied with what he had already accomplished. As his motion pictures and television programs became successful, he felt a desire to branch out. One area that intrigued him

was amusement parks. As a father, he had taken his two young daughters to zoos, carnivals, and playgrounds, but he always ended up sitting on the bench as they rode the merry-go-round and had all the fun. He felt that there should be a park where parents and children could go and have a good time together. This was the genesis of Disneyland. After several years of planning and construction, the new park opened July 17, 1955.

Disneyland was a totally new kind of park. Observers coined the term "theme park," but even that does not seem to do Disneyland justice. It has been used as a pattern for every amusement park built since its opening, becoming internationally famous, and attracting hundreds of millions of visitors.

The 1950s saw the release of the classic *20,000 Leagues under the Sea,* based on Jules VERNE's book, the first in a series of wacky comedies, *The Shaggy Dog,* and a popular TV series about the legendary hero, Zorro. In the 1960s came *Mary Poppins,* perhaps the culmination of all D. had learned during his long movie-making career. But the 1960s also brought the end of an era. Walt D. died on December 15, 1966.

Plans that D. left behind carried the company for a number of years under the supervision of his brother, Roy. *The Jungle Book* (Rudyard KIPLING), in 1967 and *The Aristocats* in 1970 showed that the company could still make animated classics, and *The Love Bug* in 1969 was the highest grossing film of the year. D. got into educational films and materials in a big way with the start of an educational subsidiary in 1969.

After the success of Disneyland, it was only natural for Walt to consider another park on the East Coast. Prior to his death the company purchased land in Florida, and the Walt D. World project, located on some 28,000 acres near Orlando was announced. It opened October 1, 1971. In Florida, the company had the space it lacked in California. Finally there was room to create a destination resort, unencumbered by the urban sprawl that had grown up around Disneyland. It did not take long for Walt D. World to become the premier vacation destination in the world.

The first foreign D. park, Tokyo Disneyland, opened in 1983, and Disneyland Paris followed in 1992. Walt D. World in Orlando, Epcot in

1982, and the D.-MGM Studios in 1989 were followed by D.'s Animal Kingdom in 1998.

Moviemaking also was changing in America in the early 1980s. Audiences were diminishing for the family films that had been the mainstay of the company for many years, and D. was not meeting the competition for films that attracted the huge teenage and adult market. To reverse that trend, D. established a new label, Touchstone Pictures, with the release of *Splash* in 1984.

The company had left network television in 1983 to prepare for the launch of a cable network, The D. Channel, but in 1985 D. began a return to TV with the immensely successful *Golden Girls.* In early 1996, D. completed the acquisition of Capital Cities/ABC. The $19 billion transaction, second largest in U.S. history at this writing, brought the nation's top-TV network at that time to D. Films from the D. library were selected for the syndication market, and some of the classic animated films were released on video cassette. The D. classics soon reached the top of the all-time video best-seller lists.

D. animation began reaching even greater audiences, with *The Little Mermaid* (Hans Christian ANDERSEN), being topped by *Beauty and the Beast,* in turn topped by *Aladdin* and finally by the spectacular hit, *The Lion King. The Lion King* and *Beauty and the Beast* now run on Broadway.

For the first time, D. moved into publishing, forming Hyperion Books, Hyperion Books for Children, and the D. Press, which released books on D. and non-D. subjects. Previously, D. books had been licensed to other publishers. In 1991, D. purchased *Discover* magazine, the leading consumer science monthly.

D. soon moved in retailing, with the D. Stores; sports, with the Mighty Ducks hockey team and a share of the Anaheim Angels major-league baseball club; and cruise ships, with the launch of the *D. Magic.*

For more than seven decades, The Walt D. Company has succeeded in making its name preeminent in the field of family entertainment. From humble beginnings as a cartoon studio in the 1920s to today's megacorporation, it continues its mandate of providing quality entertainment for the entire family.

BIBLIOGRAPHY: Maltin, Leonard, *The D. Films,* 1973, 1984, 1995; Finch, Christopher, *The Art of Walt D.,* 1973, 1975; Thomas, Bob, *Walt D.: An American Original,* 1976, 1994; Green, Katherine & Richard, *The Man behind the Magic; The Story of Walt D.,* 1991; (1991); Thomas, Bob, *Art of Animation: From Mickey Mouse to Hercules,* 1997; Thomas, Frank and Ollie Johnston, *The Illusion of Lift: D. Animation,* 1995; Smith, Dave, *D. A to Z: The Official Encyclopedia,* 1998, (1998); Cotter, Bill, *The Wonderful World of D. Television,* 1997; Watts, Steven, *The Magic Kingdom: Walt D. and the American Way of Life,* 1997; Grant, John, *Encyclopedia of Walt D.'s Animated Characters,* 1998; Thomas, Bob, *Building a Company; Roy O. D. and the Creation of an Entertainment Empire,* 1998

DAVE SMITH

DODD, Lynley

Author, illustrator, b. 5 July 1941, Rotorua, New Zealand

D. began drawing at the age of two. As a child she had her own books and loved A.A. MILNE and all FAIRY TALES. Her hero was Dr. SEUSS because he was "crazy" with his "silly language and the silly pictures." She attended Elam Art School, majoring in sculpture. A writer asked D. for a story idea and she suggested a cat climbing in and out of boxes and dustbins. *My Cat Likes to Hide in Boxes* (1974) received the Esther Glen Medal from the NEW ZEALAND Library Association. *Druscilla* (1981) received the New Zealand Book Award for ILLUSTRATION.

The Hairy Maclary series with its delightful cumulative rhythmic text, began as a drawing on a scrap of paper. In both text and illustrations D. captures the essence of her feline and canine cast of characters. Hairy has acquired the stature of a national icon. *Hairy Maclary from Donaldson's Dairy* (1983), New Zealand Children's PICTURE BOOK of the Year, was written in one afternoon. The next Hairy story is a result of watching a dog carry off a string of bones and wondering if his dog friends would be waiting to share the loot. *Hairy Maclary's Scattercat* (1985) and *Hairy Maclary's Caterwaul Caper* (1987) received the New Zealand Children's Picture Book of the Year Award. D. has received the AIM Children's Picture Book of the Year Award for most of the titles in the Hairy Maclary series.

FURTHER WORKS: *Hairy Maclary's Rumpus at the Vet,* 1989; *Hairy Maclary's Showbusiness,* 1991

BIBLIOGRAPHY: Gaskin, C. ed., *Picture Book Magic,* 1996; *New Zealand Book Council,* Karen Ross, director; *Something about the Author,* vol. 86, 1996

IRVYN G. GILBERTSON

DODGE, Mary Mapes

Author, poet, editor, b. 26 January 1831, New York City; d. 31 August 1905, Catskill Mountains, New York

From the time D.'s *Hans Brinker and the Silver Skates* was published in 1865, it was an immediate success. During the next thirty years there were more than one hundred editions in at least a half-dozen languages. At age twenty-seven, D. became a widow; she turned to writing as a means of supporting herself and her two young sons. She had written only one other book, *Irvington Stories* (1864) set in an earlier United States, when she wrote *Hans Brinker* and received a most prestigious award, the Montyon Library Prize from the French Academy. The popularity of this CLASSIC may be largely attributed to its dramatic family narrative which has Hans and his sister undefeated by their poverty, struggling to aid their ailing father, and at the climax, heroically overcoming all adversity. However, it had a faithful description of Dutch life, and was also a pioneer SPORTS STORY climaxing with a championship skating race.

Although D. published more of her own work, it was as the editor of *St. Nicholas: A Magazine for Boys and Girls* from 1873 to 1888 that she made her greatest contribution to children's literature. This magazine that began with her as editor was to provide reading in the form of well-written stories, POETRY, and nonsense specifically for children. Authors such as Louisa May ALCOTT, Rudyard KIPLING, Frances Hodgson BURNETT, Joel Chandler HARRIS, Sarah Orne Jewett, Mark TWAIN, and E. M. White wrote stories that were first serialized in the magazine. D. published poems by such poets as Whittier and Longfellow. Other sections of the magazine had biographies and how-to articles on the arts and sciences. In 1898 the St. Nicholas League was formed to provide prizes to gifted writers. Ring Lardner, Rosemary and Stephen Vincent Benet, Cornelia Otis Skinner, and Edmund Wilson were some of the winners to have their first works published in *St.*

Nicholas. D. died in 1905, but the magazine continued publication until 1940; it is still the standard by which MAGAZINES FOR CHILDREN are measured.

BIBLIOGRAPHY: DOYLE, B., *Who's Afraid of Children's Literature?,* 1968; Silvey, Anita, ed., *Children's Books and Their Creators,* 1995; *Something about the Author,* vol. 21, 1980, and vol. 100, 1999

JUDY LIPSITT

DODGSON, Charles Lutwidge
(See CARROLL, Lewis)

DOHERTY, Berlie
Author, b. 6 November 1943, Liverpool, England

D. knew she wanted to be a writer by the age of five. She was told bedtime stories every night by her father and decided she wanted to make up stories for people to read. She also remembered the familiarity and comfort of her father typing short stories in the corner of the room. She went to a secondary-level convent school, developed an enthusiasm for studying English and wrote stories that were noticed by an English teacher who introduced her to literature and a lifelong love of reading.

D. received a degree in English from the University of Durham in 1964 and a postgraduate certificate in social science from the University of Liverpool in 1965. She obtained a postgraduate certificate in education from the University of Sheffield (1966). In 1978, D. began teaching school in Sheffield and was motivated to resume writing for young children.

In 1982 her first book, *How Green You Are!* was published. Originally broadcast on radio as a collection of short-story episodes, elements of her own childhood are woven into the background. *White Peak Farm,* a collection of ten interwoven stories that won an award from Television and Film Awards in New York, and *Tilly Mint Tales,* a group of stories about magical dreamlike adventures a little girl has when her baby-sitter falls asleep were published in 1984.

Jess is preparing to go abroad for a year of study and leave Sheffield, England, her hometown in *Granny Was a Buffer Girl* (1986). Three generations of her family gather and reminisce about the joys and trials that connect families and

30. ROALD DAHL

31. TOMIE DEPAOLA

32. LEO AND DIANE DILLON

34. LOIS EHLERT

33. WALT DISNEY

individuals. The book won the CARNEGIE MEDAL, Burnley/National Provincial Children's Book of the Year Award and the *Boston Globe-Horn Book* Honor Award.

Dear Nobody (1991), more structured than most of D.'s writing, won the Carnegie Medal. Dealing with teenage pregnancy, the book is divided into nine chapters, one for each month of Helen's pregnancy as both she and the baby's father journey toward an understanding of what parenthood means.

Known for her memorable characterizations, D.'s advice to aspiring writers is "to write and write and write and to love writing. To write about anything and everything. To keep a notebook, to make writing part of their daily life. . . . To take an idea that they've written about and bring it out again and rework it—never to think of something as being finished."

FURTHER WORKS: *Tough Luck,* 1987, *White Peak Farm,* 1990; *Street Child,* 1994; *Willa and Old Miss Annie,* 1994

BIBLIOGRAPHY: *Children's Literature Review,* vol. 21, 1990; Silvey, A. ed., *Children's Books and Their Creators,* 1995; *Something about the Author,* vol. 72, 1993

IRVYN G. GILBERTSON

DOMANSKA, Janina
Author, illustrator, b. 1913 (date uncertain), Warsaw, Poland

D., an award-winning illustrator in Poland, studied in Italy. She moved to the United States in 1952 and became a citizen in 1964. D. concentrated on illustrating folktales, bringing her own vision to each story she retold and illustrated. In 1972, *If All the Seas Were One Sea* (1971) was named an ALA CALDECOTT MEDAL Honor Book, the culmination of many honors she had received over the years for books such as *The Golden Seed* (1962) and *The Coconut Thieves* (1964). *King Krakus and the Dragon* was one of the *New York Times* Best Illustrated Children's Books of the Year (1979).

FURTHER WORKS: *I Saw a Ship a-Sailing,* 1972; *Marek, the Little Fool,* 1982; *A Was an Angler,* 1991

BIBLIOGRAPHY: Collier, L., and L. Nakamura, *Major Authors and Illustrators for Children and YOUNG ADULTS,* 1993; *Third Book of Junior Au-* *thors,* 1972; Ward, M. E., D. A. Marquardt, N. Dolan, and D. Eaton, *Authors of Books for Young People,* 1990

GWYNNE ELLEN ASH

DONOVAN, John
Author, b. 1928, Lynn, Massachusetts; d. 29 April 1992, New York City

D. was a graduate of William and Mary College and the University of Virginia School of Law. In addition to his career as a writer, D. served as Executive Director of the CHILDREN'S BOOK COUNCIL from 1967 until the time of his death.

D. has been dubbed "a taboo buster" by the British critic and author John Rowe TOWNSEND. In his small but influential body of work, this extraordinary writer proved himself fearless in pushing back the borders of literature for young readers. In developing his signature themes of loneliness and alienation he did not flinch from expletives that were previously deemed off-limits or from dealing frankly with such issues as alcoholism, divorce, sexual experimentation, and death. Most importantly in his 1969 novel, *I'll Get There: It Better Be Worth the Trip,* he became the first author for young adults to deal with the subject of homosexuality. This deeply felt coming of age story deals honestly and, for its time, openly with a sexual encounter between thirteen-year-old protagonist Davy Ross and his best friend Douglas Altschuler. D.'s next novel, *Wild in the World* (1971) was, if anything, even more controversial in its uninflected, matter-of-fact treatment of the deaths of protagonist John Greatly's parents and eleven siblings. In his review the influential critic Paul Heins spoke for most adult observers of the time when he wrote, "one is left wondering why such a book is at all published for children." Three decades later, however, the novel remains powerfully moving and timeless in its celebration of love's capacity for survival in the face of death. Moreover, its understated language is beautiful in its spareness and lends the story the power of parable or allegory. D.'s third novel, *Remove Protective Coating a Little at a Time* (1973) is a more traditional young adult novel. Like *I'll Get There* it is told in the breezy, wry, first-person voice of its protagonist and, in style, is clearly influenced by J. D. SALINGER's *The Catcher in the Rye* (1951). Harry Knight, at

243

fourteen, is emotionally isolated from his wealthy, irresponsible parents. Through his befriending of an elderly bag lady, however, he finds the love and support he is unable to derive from his father and mother. Another senior adult is the protagonist of D.'s fourth title, the PICTURE BOOK *Old James* (1974), a spare story about a man who finds retirement a one-way ticket to loneliness and superfluity until, by chance, he befriends and makes a pet of a housefly. *Family* (1976), D.'s fifth—and final—book for young readers is billed as a novel but is, in fact, a fable. This emotionally involving story of the escape of four apes from an experimental laboratory explores the meaning of connectedness and continuity. Telling the apes' story in one of their voices gives D. the ironic distance necessary to comment on the failings of human society. Though his work has gone into eclipse, he remains a ground-breaking presence in the evolution of YOUNG ADULT LITERATURE.

BIBLIOGRAPHY: *Fifth Book of Junior Authors and Illustrators,* 1983; Townsend, John Rowe, review of *Remove Protective Coating a Little at a Time, New York Times Book Review,* November 4, 1973, pp. 34, 36; *Something about the Author,* vol. 72, 1993; *Contemporary Literary Criticism,* vol. 35, 1995

MICHAEL CART

DORRIS, Michael
Author, b. 30 January 1945, Louisville, Kentucky; d. 11 April 1997, Concord, New Hampshire

D. received a M.Phil. in anthropology from Yale, then served as adjunct professor and Montgomery Fellow in NATIVE AMERICAN Studies at Dartmouth College, where he founded the Native American Studies Program in 1972. He also engaged in anthropological fieldwork in Alaska, NEW ZEALAND, Montana, and South Dakota.

D. was of mixed Native American, Irish, and French ancestry, and this personal intersection of cultures resonates clearly in his compelling writings. He spent much of his life in pursuit of revealing the contributions and importance of Native American heritage and culture, and sought to illuminate and improve the lives of others through his writings. D.'s diverse contributions to the field of literature span ages and genres ranging from his first adult novel, *A Yellow Raft in Blue Water* (1987), and award-winning autobiographical nonfiction for adults, *The Broken Cord: A Father's Story* (1990). This latter book documents his adopted son's lifelong struggle with Fetal Alcohol Syndrome; it won the National Book Award and served as a catalyst for Congress to draft legislation requiring warning labels on alcoholic beverages.

D. entered the field of children's literature in 1992, the year of the five-hundredth anniversary of Christopher Columbus's discovery of America, with the publication of *Morning Girl,* a story of two young Bahamians in 1492. This first work was met with accolades and D. received the Scott O'DELL Award for Historical Fiction in 1993. *Guests* (1996), *Sees behind Trees* (1997), and *The Window* (1997) followed this first novel. D. invites readers to experience the natural world and other cultural worlds with sensitivity and intense engagement. His characters inevitably discover the wonder of familiar things, recognize the essence of humanity, and respond to the unknown with compassion. This was a goal for D.'s life and he hoped his readers might adopt the same goal. D. writes, "Reading anything that moves you, disturbs you, thrills you is a path into the great swirl of humanity, past, present, and future" (D. and Buchwald, 1997, p. 14). Although readers mourn D.'s untimely death, his work remains passionate and influential in the field. Readers will undoubtedly continue to be swept into this "great swirl of humanity" and will surrender, at least momentarily, to the humanely just and provocative writings of D.

FURTHER WORKS: *A Guide to Research in Native American Studies,* 1984; *The Crown of Columbus* (with Louise Erdrich), 1991; *Route Two and Back* (with Erdrich, 1991; *Cloud Chamber,* 1998

BIBLIOGRAPHY: Dorris, Michael, and Emilie Buchwald, eds., *The Most Wonderful Books,* 1997; Silvey, Anita, ed., *Children's Books and Their Creators.* 1995; *Something about the Author,* vol. 75, 1994, vol. 94, 1998

SHANE RAYBURN

DORROS, Arthur
Author, illustrator, b. 19 May 1950, Washington, D.C.

D. once owned thirteen turtles, all named Bobby because they all looked alike. But readers are enthralled by the continually changing face of his books. Growing up in Washington D.C., D. had all kinds of pets and loved reading and drawing. However, he became frustrated with his drawing in elementary school and abandoned it until later in high school when he needed to do animal ILLUSTRATIONS for his biology class. A self-described reader of a book a day until age sixteen, D. did not begin to create books himself until he was twenty-nine.

D. earned a B.A. degree at the University of Wisconsin in 1972, and his teaching credentials at Pacific Oaks College in California in 1979. He worked as a longshoreman, a drafter, and an elementary and junior high school teacher. But it was his work as a builder that led him to become an author, allowing him to record and illustrate the stories he used to entertain the children who watched him remodel houses. Writing and illustrating the mock-legendary story of the invention of pretzels (*Pretzels*, 1981), D. began his varied writing career. *Alligator Shoes* (1982) is a humorous FANTASY of an alligator's search for footwear; it was selected for the PBS series *Reading Rainbow* (see *READING RAINBOW* AND CHILDREN'S LITERATURE ON TELEVISION) in 1986. Further demonstrating his range, D. published *Ant Cities*, his first nonfiction book in 1987. *Ant Cities* was also a *Reading Rainbow* selection, and was named an Outstanding Trade Book in the Sciences.

D. is well known for books that celebrate North and South American and Caribbean (LATINO/A LITERATURE) heritage. Having spent a year in South America and speaking fluent Spanish, D. began to create a collection of bilingual books for U.S. publication. In 1991, *Tonight Is* Carnaval and *Por fin es carnaval* were published with illustrations by Club de Madres Virgenes del Carmen. Sandra Marulanda Dorros, a teacher, translator, and editor, translated D.'s text into Spanish for *Por fin es carnaval*. This text was chosen as a Notable Book in the Field of Social Studies and was named to *Booklist*'s Best of the Year list in 1991.

Tonight Is Carnaval was soon followed by *Abuela* (1991), illustrated by Elisa KLEVEN. The story of Rosalba and her *abuela* (grandmother) was told in the Spanish-English code-switching of bilingual intergenerations. An AMERICAN LIBRARY ASSOCIATION Notable Book, a Parents'

Choice Award, one of *Horn Book*'s Twenty Best Books, and one of the *Boston Globe*'s Twenty-five Best Books, *Abuela* spawned a continuing adventure of Rosalba and her *abuela* in *Isla* (1995). Like *Abuela*, *Isla* is rich in English and Spanish, but was also published in a Spanish edition, *La Isla* (1995), with TRANSLATIONS by Sandra Marulanda Dorros.

FURTHER WORKS: *Elephant Families*, 1994; *Feel the Wind*, 1989; *Radio Man/Don Radio* (Bilingual, trans. S. M. Dorros), 1993; *Rain Forest Secrets*, 1990; *This Is My House*, 1992; *A Tree Is Growing*, 1997; *Ten Go Tango*, 2000

BIBLIOGRAPHY: *Something about the Author*, vol. 78, 1994; *The Seventh Book of Junior Authors and Illustrators*, 1996

GWYNNE ELLEN ASH

DOTLICH, Rebecca Kai

Poet, author, b. 10 July 1951, Indianapolis, Indiana

As a child playing marbles, jumping rope and counting the stars with the kids in her neighborhood, D. was inspired to write POETRY. *Lemonade Sun: And Other Summer Poems* (GILCHRIST, illus., 1998) evokes those childhood memories. In high school, a favorite teacher inspired her to write down her verses and think of herself as a poet, promising her that one day she would be published. Always a reader, D. spent the early years of her marriage rearing children and reading voraciously, just as she had as a child. She is fascinated with language and words and uses verse to express her wonder about nature and living things. *Sweet Dreams of the Wild* (1996) explores the mystery of where and how wild animal babies sleep, using language familiar to young children and their bedtime rituals. Her poems appear frequently in children's MAGAZINES and poetry anthologies. While she admits that finding the right word is sometimes a struggle, D. says that writing poetry is "like putting together a wonderful puzzle or a beautiful patchwork quilt—I'll suddenly discover that the right piece goes there, or there!"

FURTHER WORKS: *What Is Round?*, 1999; *What Is Square?*, 1999; *Away We Go!*, 2000

BIBLIOGRAPHY: Interview by Lee Bennett HOPKINS. *Creative Classroom*, Nov. 1999, p. 36; Website material at: http://.boydsmillspress.com

DIANE G. PERSON

DOWDEN, Anne Ophelia (Todd)

Author, illustrator, b. 17 September 1907, Denver, Colorado

D., whose early writings are under the name Anne Ophelia Todd, began her career at the age of sixteen when her father included some of her illustrations in a scientific book that he published. She went on to become a textile designer, art instructor, and author/illustrator. D. is best known to children for her nature books, particularly books about plants. Her book, *Wild Green Things in the City* (1972) was selected as a Children's Showcase Title for 1963.

FURTHER WORKS: Self-illustrated: *Look at a Flower*. 1963. *State Flowers*. 1963. *This Notable Harvest: A Chronicle of Herbs*. 1979. *The Blossom on the Bough*. 1975. *From Flower to Fruit*. 1984. Illustrator: *Plants of Christmas*. (Hal Borland). 1969. *Shakespeare's Flowers*. (Jessica Kerr). 1969. *Consider the Lilies*. (John and Katherine PATERSON). 1998

BIBLIOGRAPHY: Marquardt, M., D. A. E. Ward, N. Dolan, and D. Eaton, eds., *Authors of Books for Young People*, 3rd ed., 1990; *Something about the Author*, vol. 7, 1975

MARY ARIAIL BROUGHTON

DOYLE, (Sir) Arthur Conan

Author, b. 22 May 1859, Edinburgh, Scotland; d. 7 July 1930, Sussex, England

Because D.'s father, Charles, was a civil servant and his grandfather, John, was a well-known political caricaturist of the day, there were often important visitors in the Doyle home. Most notable was William Makepeace THACKERAY who inspired D.'s first literary efforts. D. was a rapid reader and performed well at the Hodder School and later at the Jesuit college of Stonyhurst. In 1875, D. entered school in Austria and during his one year there started the newspaper *Feldkirch*. The next year D. returned to Scotland to study medicine at Edinburgh University, graduating in 1881. D. practiced medicine in England and later worked as a ship's doctor and a hospital surgeon during the Boer War. In addition to enjoying writing, D. used his writing as a means to supplement his physician's income. While studying at Edinburgh D. met a remarkable man who was to become the inspiration for the character of Sherlock Holmes, master detective of fiction. Joseph Bell was a surgeon at the Edinburgh Infirmary who had the uncanny ability of diagnosing not only the disease but also the occupation and character of his patients. Sherlock Holmes first appeared in *A Study in Scarlet* (1887) in *Beeton's Christmas Annual*. Three more novels featuring Holmes, *The Sign of Four* (1890), *The Hound of the Baskervilles* (1902), and *The Valley of Fear* (1915) along with over fifty short stories were to follow. These tales were enormously popular with adults and children alike. In 1893, D. tried to kill off Sherlock Holmes to focus on what he considered more serious writing, but public outcry demanded Holmes's return. While the Holmes stories were not written with a young audience in mind, they were often republished in editions targeting young readers.

D. was a writer of wide range. His historical novels such as *The White Company* (1891) and SCIENCE FICTION like *The Lost World* (1912) were also well received. In addition, D. wrote domestic comedies, ADVENTURE STORIES, POETRY, and nonfiction. Always interested in psychic matters, D. became focused on spiritualism late in his life. D. spent the last twelve years of his life writing and lecturing on the topic around the world.

In 1902, D. was knighted at Buckingham Palace for his work in war propaganda. D. passed away at the age of seventy due to heart problems. After a memorial service attended by ten thousand people, D. was buried in the rose garden at Windlesham where he often wrote.

FURTHER WORKS: *The Mystery of Cloomber*, 1889; *The Captain of the Polestar and Other Tales*, 1890; *The Parasite*, 1895; *Round the Fire Stories*, 1908; *Tales of Terror and Mystery*, 1922

BIBLIOGRAPHY: Cox, Don Richard, *Arthur Conan D.*, 1985; Riley, Dick and Pam McAllister, *The Bedside, Bathtub and Armchair Companion to Sherlock Holmes*, 1999

DEDE SMALL

DOYLE, Brian

Author, b. 12 August 1935, Ottawa, Ontario, Canada

D. spent his childhood years divided between winters in an ethically divided section of Ottawa, Ontario, and summers north of town in the Gati-

neau Hills, Canada. Both locations figure prominently in his writing. D.'s family ingrained a love
of STORYTELLING within him early in life and he
began writing when he was only ten years old. D.
graduated from Carleton University in 1957 with
a degree in journalism but soon turned to teaching high-school English, a career move that lasted
thirty-three years. As a teacher, D. found that
teenagers can be talented writers. In addition to
helping develop young writers, D. was also very
involved writing and producing school plays. His
vast experiences with young people have led him
to possess great insight and respect for young
adult readers. His novels do not patronize, rather
it is the opinion of many critics that D. writes up
to his readers and not down to them.

D. points out that his writing is separate from
his teaching, noting that his first two novels were,
in fact, written for his own children. *Hey, Dad!*
(1978) was written for his daughter while *You
Can Pick Me up at Peggy's Cove* (1979) was written for his son. D.'s next four novels go back to
his own childhood and the places of his youth.
Up to Low (1982) is set in the Gatineau Hills in
the mid-1900s; with its unique perspective it
looks at a misfit world of adults from the viewpoint of Tommy, a sympathetic teen. *Up to Low*
was the winner of the CANADIAN Library Association's Book of the Year award in 1983. Tommy
is also the narrator of D.'s next novel *Angel
Square* (1984), which takes place in Ottawa's
Lowertown and examines issues of race and bigotry. All of D.'s novels raise substantial issues
and examine serious problems without falling
into the category of the problem novel. Easy answers are never offered, rather problems are acknowledged and realistically dealt with as a part
of life. D.'s next work, *Easy Avenue* (1988), winner of the 1989 Canadian Library Association's
Book of the Year, has been likened to other classics for YOUNG ADULT readers such as SALIN-
GER's *The Catcher in the Rye* (1951). It touches
on homelessness and the disparity between rich
and poor.

D. retired from teaching in 1991 and continues
to write novels with respect for young adults both
as reader and as subject. Among children's fiction writers, D. is considered to be one of the best
known, critically respected, and widely read writers in Canada today. D. was awarded the Vicky

Metcalf Body of Work Award from the Canadian
Authors Association.

AWARDS: INTERNATIONAL BOARD ON BOOKS FOR
YOUNG PEOPLE (1984) for *Je t'Attends a Peggy's
Cove.* Canadian Library Association Book of the
Year (1983) for *Up to Low,* and (1989) for *Easy
Avenue.* Metcalf Award (1991) for the entire body
of his work. Mr. Christie's Book Award (1990)
for *Covered Bridge*

FURTHER WORKS: *Covered Bridge,* 1990; *Spud
Sweetgrass,* 1992; *Uncle Ronald,* 1997

BIBLIOGRAPHY: Contemporary Authors Online:
www.galenet.com; Hunt, Peter, ed., *Children's
Literature: An Illustrated History,* 1995

DEDE SMALL

DOYLE, Richard
Illustrator, b. September 1824, Hyde Park, Lon-
don, England; d. 11 December 1883, London,
England

The son of an Irish political cartoonist and uncle
of Sir Arthur Conan DOYLE, from an early age D.
was instructed in art by his uncle, Michael
Conan, and his father. In 1840, at the age of sixteen his first book of sketches, *The Eglinton Tournament,* a burlesque of the early days of chivalry,
was published. D. had a special gift for painting
processions, historical pageantry, and parades.

In 1843 he joined the staff of *Punch,* a maga-
zine presenting humorous and satirical sketches.
As a regular contributor his features included il-
lustrations, sketches, and decorations; his ILLUS-
TRATION for the cover of *Punch* was used for over
a century. He resigned in 1850 in protest to anti–
Catholic statements appearing in the magazine.
While at *Punch,* he collaborated with John Leech
and others illustrating *The Chimes* (1844), *The
Cricket on the Hearth* (1845), and *The Battle of
Life* (1646), all written by Charles DICKENS.

A new translation of the GRIMM brothers' tales,
*The Fairy Ring: A New Collection of Popular
Tales* (1846) offered new challenges in illustration for D. and the results were superb. This was
followed by *FAIRY TALES from All Nations*
(1849), also extremely well received. *The Enchanted Doll* (1849) preceded John RUSKIN's *The
King of the Golden River: Or, The Black Brothers, Legend of Stiria* (1850), one of the earliest
children's fantasies. D.'s illustrations are synony-
mous with Ruskin's story.

The work that established D.'s reputation was *Manners and Customs of Ye Englyshe Drawn from Ye Quick* (1849). It was a satire on English society and also lamented his own bachelorhood.

His FANTASY masterpiece, illustrations for a poem by William Allingham, appeared—*In Fairyland: A Series of Pictures from the Elf World* (1870). The illustrations revealed the secret fairy world of D.'s imagination; the book is a fine example of Victorian book production. The sixteen color plates with thirty-six illustrations plus pictorial title page were adapted for use with a story specially written by Andrew LANG, *The Princess Nobody: A Tale of Fairyland* (1884). *In Fairyland* was reissued in 1979. D.'s special aptitude for art, attention to detail, and love of pixies, dwarfs, giants, trolls, wood sprites, birds, and butterflies made him an outstanding illustrator of "fairyland" creatures.

FURTHER WORKS: *The Story of Jack and the Giants,* 1851; *Jack the Giant Killer,* 1888; *The Great Sea Serpent; The Doyle Fairy Book,* 1890

BIBLIOGRAPHY: amazon.com: *A Glance: Richard Doyle's Journal,* 1840; http://www.amazon.com/exec/obidos/ASIN/; Chute, J. and J. Grant, eds, *Encyclopedia of Fantasy, Fiction, FOLKLORE, Fantasy and Poetry for Children 1876–1985,* vol. 1, 1986; Hunt, Peter, ed. *Children's Literature: An Illustrated History,* 1995; *Something about the Author,* vol. 21, 1980, vol. 24, 1981, and vol. 31, 1983

IRVYN G. GILBERTSON

DRAGONWAGON, Crescent
Author, b. 25 November 1952, New York City

Born Ellen Zolotow, D. grew up watching her father Maurice, an archaeologist, and her mother Charlotte, a children's author, constantly writing. This early exposure gave D. not only direction, but also insight into the publishing process. D. published her first book, *Rainy Day Together* (1972), under the pseudonym Ellen Parsons before she was twenty. D. had her name legally changed when she married. Not believing that a woman should have to take her husband's name, the couple opted to change both their names legally. Reflecting on it later, D. questions the particular choice of name but she was already published and had established a professional reputation.

One of D.'s early works, *Wind Rose* (1976), is a special book for children about conception and birth. The idea for it evolved from the birth of a friend's child. It was praised for looking at the emotions involved and the reasons couples might want to have a child and not simply addressing how conception, and birth, occur. It was named an Outstanding Science Trade Book for Children in 1976. Another of D.'s works for children, *Home Place* (1990), follows a family hiking through the countryside when they happen upon the remains of an old house, wondering who had lived there. This work earned D. the SOCIETY OF CHILDREN'S BOOK WRITERS AND ILLUSTRATORS Golden Kite Award.

D. tried many times to write a novel but had difficulty in completing one. She approached Paul ZINDEL, a young adult novelist who had in the past worked with other writers. Together they wrote *To Take a Dare* (1982), a novel about adolescent drinking and sex. It was praised for its uncompromising, no-patronizing voice. D.'s second novel, this time a solo work, *The Year It Rained* (1985), also deals with difficult issues in the story of a seventeen-year-old girl who must come to terms with her own mental instability.

D. views herself, first and formost, as a writer, not just a children's writer or a YOUNG ADULT writer. Her other works include adult novels, cookbooks, and POETRY.

AWARDS: CORETTA SCOTT KING AWARDS, illustrator (1987) for *Half a Moon and One Whole Star* (Jerry PINKNEY, illus.). SCBWI Golden Kite Award (1990) for *Home Place*

FURTHER WORKS: *Strawberry Dress Escape* (Lillian HOBAN, illus.), 1975; *I Hate My Brother, Harry* (Dick Gackenbach, illus.), 1983; *Half a Moon and One Whole Star* (Jerry PINKNEY, illus.), 1986; *Alligators and Others, All Year Long* (José ARUEGO, illus.), 1992; *Brass Button* (Susan Paradis, illus.), 1997

DEDE SMALL

DRAMA

Theater, a visual and auditory art, is unlike the visual art of painting. Drama is evanescent; once the performance is over it disappears. This makes writing about theater more difficult than writing about painting, and this is the reason why there are more children's books about art in the museums than about the art created in theaters. Despite this difficulty, authors have recently successfully captured in print the nature of this transitory art form. Sharing such books with children expands their understanding of the varied nature of the arts in general, and of the specific qualities of this art form.

The most common type of book about theater is the fictional story about children performing a play. Often these are humorous. An example is *The Halloween Play* (1999) by Felicia BOND, a reissue of a previously published title, which recounts the adventures of Roger (a mouse) who has a "small but important role." Roger and his classmates practice every day, under their teacher's direction. The night of the performance, the appreciative audience "laughed when they were supposed to." The wordless spread that reveals Roger's part will come as a pleasant surprise to the reader.

Another example of this type is *Mickey's Class Play* (1998) by Judith CASELEY, in which his entire family helps young Mickey, a lower-primary age child, who is to be a duck in the class play. Mickey's ingenuity finally results in a truly unique costume of his own creation.

Other equally fine fiction includes James HOWE's *Pinky and Rex and the School Play* (1998), which like previous books in this Ready-to-Read series features more text on a smaller page, and is divided into short chapters, unlike a PICTURE BOOK. Pinky is the aspiring actor, and persuades his friend to accompany him to the auditions, even though she is reluctant to go. Rex inadvertently finds herself cast as the lead, and this seriously tests their friendship. In the end, Rex performs well, Pinky saves the performance in his role, and the two find they can be friends again.

Most titles deal with plays done at school. The tradition of doing a play at home celebrating the religious heritage of Queen Esther, Mordechai, and King Ahasueras, may be unfamiliar to many children. Roni Schotter's *Purim Play* (1998) shows that theater can happen in many places. The child actors must cope when two regulars become ill, and they discover that the most unlikely person, old Mrs. Teplitzky, can indeed become a convincing evil Haman. This creates an opportunity to talk with children about the theater tradition of understudies who pinch-hit when an emergency occurs.

A second category includes theater biographies; Shakespeare is most often written about. ALIKI's *William Shakespeare and the Globe* (1999), with the author-artist's modestly unassuming art serves to bring to life this unfamiliar time and culture for middle-grade readers. The writing is simple and direct, reporting what is known and acknowledging what is speculation about his life. In addition to the connected text, there are numerous informative captions and small panels with related information. Diane STANLEY and Peter VENNEMA's *Bard of Avon: The Story of William Shakespeare* (1992) tells about the playwright's life against a background setting of the theater and events of the times; the illustrations teem with vignettes of life in the Elizabethan era and at the Globe theater.

In Bruce Koscielniak's *Hear, Hear, Mr. Shakespeare* (1998), the author has constructed a slight imaginary tale of Shakespeare approached in his tranquil garden by a troupe of traveling players to write a new play for them. They are forced indoors by the rain, where he writes while the players kibbitz, until, with the weather clearing, the queen approaches in her coach, also to request a new play. Everyone is happy that the new play will be performed. Endpapers provide a list of Shakespeare's dates and a listing of the plays by period.

Another title, *Shakespeare and Macbeth* (1994) by Stewart Ross, is for middle-school students. Not the play itself but rather the rich array of circumstances relating to its writing and first production, set in the context of theater conventions and cultural customs of the time, form the main focus of this lavishly illustrated book. The writing is direct and engrossing; readers learn facts without being burdened by too much detail. There is even a comparison chart, showing how Shakespeare altered two sources he used in writing this play, making the point that playwrights take liberties in order to come up with more interesting final products.

BIOGRAPHIES of contemporary theater people are also available. *Young, Black and Determined* (1998), by Patricia C. and Frederick L. MCKISSACK, is about Lorraine Hansberry, the first black woman to have a play produced on Broadway (in 1959). *A Raisin in the Sun* won the New York Drama Critics Circle Award as best play of the same year. The authors describe for middle-school readers the advantages Hansberry enjoyed growing up in an intact, relatively affluent family. This was indeed the source of her lifelong concern about the problems of lower-class blacks; much of her writing was concerned with redressing the wrongs committed against the poor. Throughout the text, the McKissacks provide extensive background about the people, the times, and the political movements through which Hansberry lived.

In addition to individual biographies, we also find shorter treatments in composite biographies, like that from David Weitzman's fine series. *Great Lives: Theatre* (1996) is written with the skill and imagination that characterize the entire series. Here, the author draws us into the lives of major dramatists, classic actors, modern playwrights and actors, and uniquely American dramatists. The book provides a long historic look, from Molière (born in 1622), to Luis Miguel Valdez (born in 1940). Each profile averages only ten to fourteen pages, a real advantage in working with middle schoolers unwilling or unable to read longer biographies. Though the condensed form might lead to dull summaries, this never happens. We are drawn into these lives, because these exciting people responded positively to lives often fraught with problems, which they overcame and, in the process, produced memorable art.

A third category of book focuses on the processes involved in the theater. Sometimes this information is presented in a fictionalized format as in Ann Hayes's *Onstage and Backstage at the Night Owl Theatre* (1997), in which an extensive group of animal characters are involved in all the steps in producing a play in a proscenium theater for a paying audience. There is a heavy load of technical names/terms, and processes described, but this never bogs down the action of moving from first auditions to final curtain call, because of the light-handed HUMOR in the illustrations. There is a list of theater words included, but child readers will be able to figure out most of the meanings because Hayes so skillfully embeds them in the context of the language she uses to describe the processes.

The World of Theatre (1995) is a high-energy pastiche, crammed to all four sides of the small shape with so many tidbits of information that repeated viewing/reading is necessary. Utilizing all sorts of bookmaking devices (fold-out pages, movable wheels, pockets containing stickers), this encourages reader interaction. The brief paragraphs are juxtaposed with no connecting threads, and describe Roman theater, Chinese opera, commedia dell'arte, Victor Hugo, and the Sydney Opera House, among other topics. There are a few traditional book elements (a "Words to Know" section and a very compressed time line). But the kinetic presentation continues the approach used in other books in this Voyages of Discovery series, designed to appeal to twenty-first-century readers.

A look at getting into theater is provided by Lisa O'Brien in *Lights, Camera, Action* (1998). In only six brief chapters, as well as an introduction, "So You Want to Be a Star," end matter that includes a note to parents, and a list of resources, the author follows a cartoon character, Johnny, from getting an agent to seeing the finished performance. Page layout is subdivided into small, captioned components, including interviews with real people involved in theater, "Director's Notes" with specific instructions to follow, recurring "Popcorn Quiz" boxes about aspects of film history, and "Action" sections that include acting activities.

A final category of children's books about theater presents retellings or condensations of plays in either play form, or rewritten in connected prose. One example is Marcia Williams's *Tales from Shakespeare* (1998). In an oversized format, Williams presents seven plays, in a multiple-paneled double-spread format including many small drawings (done in watercolor and thin pen line). Excerpts of the original language are included in the art, while beneath each panel is a summary of the action that moves the reader/viewer along. Purists may object to presenting all of *Hamlet* in two double-page spreads, and *A Midsummer-Night's Dream* in three, but there is no doubt that this can serve as an effective introduction to students who would not be interested in approaching a text-only version. The margins are packed with other characters, discussing the main events in the picture panels. Williams's drawings are perfect for students who enjoy poring over small pictures to discover details missed in a first viewing.

Bruce COVILLE shows his skill in recasting long, complex plays into forty-eight-page prose retelling in his *William Shakespeare's "Macbeth"* (1997) and several other books. He smoothly incorporates pieces of the original dialogue into his own prose, condensing action but retaining essential plot elements. The book reads well aloud and could serve as an effective introduction for young audiences. An introduction (for the adult) and Gary Kelley's handsome, darkly brooding full-page art make this even more appealing.

In these, and other examples of the four categories, librarians and teachers can find well-written books that capture the sounds and sights, people, and processes of theater.

BIBLIOGRAPHY: Stewig, John Warren, *Capturing Drama and Theatre on the Page,* in press (2000)

CHILDREN BOOKS CITED: Aliki. *William Shakespeare and the Globe.* 1999; Bond, Felicia. *The Halloween Play,* 1999; Caseley, Judith. *Mickey's Class Play,* 1998; Coville, Bruce. *William Shakespeare's "Macbeth,"* Ill. by Mary Kelley, 1997; Hayes, Ann. *Onstage and Backstage at the Night Owl Theatre,* 1997; Howe, James, *Pinky and Rex and the School Play,* Ill. by Melissa Sweet, 1998; Koscielniak, Bruce. *Hear, Hear, Mr. Shakespeare,* 1998; McKissack, Patricia C., and Frederick L. Young, *Black, and Determined,* 1998; O'Brien, Lisa, *Lights, Camera, Action: Making Movies and TV from the Inside Out,* 1998; Ross, Stewart, *Shakespeare and "MacBeth": The Story behind the Play,* Ill. by Tony Karpinski, 1994; Schotter, Roni, *Purim Play,* Ill. by Marylin Hafner, 1998; Weitzman, David. *Great Lives. Theater,* 1996; Williams, Marcia. *Tales from Shakespeare,* 1998; *The World of Theater,* 1995

JOHN WARREN STEWIG

DRESCHER, Henrik
Author, illustrator, b. 15 December 1955, Denmark

D. was born in Denmark and came to the United States with his family as a young teenager. He was an artist first and then became a writer. He contributed editoral drawings to numerous magazines before being encouraged to write and illustrate a children's book. That first attempt, *The Strange Appearance of Howard Cranebill, Jr.* (1982), was named a *New York Times* Best Illustrated Children's Book. D. is noted for his distinctive ILLUSTRATIONS and is praised for his

unique texts intended to "engage the mind." His stories are notable for their HUMOR and fantastic adventures; they are typically based on places D. has been to in his travels. His colorful, action-filled illustrations with decorative borders mirror the humor and FANTASY of his texts.

In *Whose Furry Nose? Australian Animals You'd Like to Meet* (1987) and *Whose Scaly Tale? African Animals You'd Like to Meet* (1987), D. combines humorous cartoon-style art, a guessing game that first shows a part of each animal, and a short paragraph providing information about little-known species, all in an enjoyable format.

FURTHER WORKS: *Simon's Book,* 1983; *Looking for Santa Claus,* 1984; *Look-alikes,* 1985; *Boy Who Ate Around,* 1994; *Poems of A. Nonny Mouse* (Jack PRELUTSKY, sel.), 1989; *No Plain Pets* (M. Barasch, author), 1991

BIBLIOGRAPHY: *Something about the Author,* vol. 30, 1983

MICHAEL O'LAUGHLIN

DU BOIS, William Pène
Author, illustrator, b. 9 May 1916, Nutley, New Jersey; d. 5 February 1993, Nice, France

Born the son of a painter/art critic father and a children's clothing designer mother, D. was encouraged in his artistic endeavors from an early age. When he was eight, D. moved with his family to France where he attended Lycée Hoche. D. credited his time at this strict school with instilling in him the sense of order and meticulousness that he applied to his craft.

D.'s family returned to the United States when he was fourteen and a few years later he decided to enter Carnegie Technical School of Architecture where he was granted a scholarship. However, D. then sold his first children's book, which he had done as a summer diversion. With the sale of *Elisabeth the Cow Ghost* (1936), D. instead embarked on a new career. By the time D. was twenty-five he had written and illustrated five more books for children. D. entered the armed services, serving with the coast artillery in Bermuda, but continued to write and illustrate while working as a correspondent for *Yank* magazine. Shortly after the war, D. finished what is probably known as his best work, *The Twenty-one Balloons* (1947). Winner of the 1948 NEWBERY MEDAL, *The Twenty-one Balloons* is a FANTASY

251

tale of Professor William Waterman Sherman who, while on a hot-air balloon journey, crashes on the island of Krakatoa. Due to the incredible wealth of diamonds on the island, all the inhabitants have devices that spare them work and provide entertainment. D.'s early fascination with the circus and the work of Jules VERNE are evident in this fanciful story. Indeed, all of D.'s writing and illustrations are marked with an appreciation for eccentricity.

Noted for his illustrations as well as his writing, D. won the CALDECOTT MEDAL Honor Award twice in the 1950s. First for *Bear Party* in 1952, a story of teddy bears at a masquerade party, and then in 1957 for *Lion*, the story of how the lion is created as the king of the beasts. All of D.'s illustrations are meticulously done first in pencil and then painstakingly traced with pen. D. would do only one drawing a day and if not satisfied it was his best work he would tear it up. In many cases, D. would only write the accompanying text after the ILLUSTRATION was done.

The Twenty-one Balloons explores human greed as a theme; D. also turned his attention to the seven deadly sins. *Lazy Tommy Pumpkinhead* (1966) examined laziness, *Pretty Pretty Peggy Moffitt* (1968) looked at self-adoration, and *Call Me Bandicoot* (1970) considered gluttony. D. also illustrated other writers' works, most notably Claire Huchet BISHOP's *Twenty and Ten,* Roald DAHL's *The Magic Finger* (1966), and Charlotte ZOLOTOW's *William's Doll* (1972).

AWARDS: AMERICAN LIBRARY ASSOCIATION Newbery Medal (1948) for *Twenty-One Balloons.* ALA Caldecott Medal Honor Book (1952) for *Bear Party,* and (1957) for *Lion. New York Times* Best Illustrated Children's Books Award (1971) for *Bear Circus,* and (1978) for *The Forbidden Forest*

FURTHER WORKS: *The Great Geppy,* 1940; *Peter Graves,* 1950; *The Giant,* 1954; *Horse in the Camel Suit,* 1967; *Bear Circus,* 1971; *Gentleman Bear,* 1985

DEDE SMALL

DUDER, Tessa
Author, b. 13 November, 1940, Auckland, New Zealand

D. grew up in Auckland and attended the University of Auckland. A reporter for the *Auckland Star* and *Daily Express* out of London, D. moved on to working as a freelance journalist, editor, and novelist. D. has strong feelings about NEW ZEALAND and realized through rearing four daughters that few authors were writing fiction reflecting the way of life unique to New Zealand. Therefore, D. focuses her writing efforts on her home country in both her fiction and nonfiction. Her work is also marked by the presence of strong female characters. D.'s first novel, *Night Race to Kawau* (1982), is a fast-paced sailing adventure that follows a family through an annual boat race. When the father is injured and the mother ill with sea sickness, twelve-year-old Sam must see her family through. This debut novel for young readers was praised for being uncompromisingly REALISTIC. D.'s second novel, *Jellybean* (1985), follows a girl through her up-and-down relationship with her mother who is a professional cellist. Both the feelings of frustration on Jellybean's part and her experiences with music are vividly described.

The Alex Archer Quartet SERIES brought D. the most exposure and popularity. For it, D. drew on her own experiences in competitive swimming, having won New Zealand's national championship in butterfly and medley swimming awards and was New Zealand's first Swimmer of the Year in 1959. The first novel, *Alex* (1987), published in the United States two years later as *In Lane Three, Alex Archer,* centers on a young swimmer and her struggle to make the 1960 New Zealand Olympic swim team. Alex must not only rise to the challenges of her sport but also to the challenges of her personal life when a close friend dies. *Alex* was adapted as a film and released in 1993. In the third novel in the series, *Alessandra: Alex in Rome* (1991) Alex travels to Rome to participate in the Olympic Games and falls in love.

D.'s work has won a number of AWARDS including the New Zealand Library Association Esther Glen award three times as well as the New Zealand Children's Book of the Year in 1988, 1990, and 1993. In addition, D. was named a member of the Order of the British Empire for her services to literature. D. does not plan on writing any more Alex novels, rather she wishes to explore different projects such as monologues for performance, writing for television and theater and discovering her talents as an actor. D. is a founding member of Metaphor, a drama quartet of writers/actors formed in 1993.

AWARDS: New Zealand AIM Children's Book Award (1988) for *Alex*, (1990) for *Alex In Winter*, and (1993) for *Songs for Alex*. Esther Glen Award (1992) for *Alessandra: Alex in Rome*

FURTHER WORKS: *The Book of Auckland*, 1985; *Alex in Winter*, 1988; *Songs for Alex*, 1992; *The Making of Alex: The Movie Journey to Olympia— The Story of the Olympic Games* (with Grant Cole), 1992; *Mercury Beach*, 1997; *Hot Mail*, 2000

BIBLIOGRAPHY: *Bulletin of the Center for Children's Books*, November 1989, p. 54, September 1992, p. 9; Hunt, Peter, ed., *Children's Literature, an Illustrated History*, 1995; *School Library Journal*, September 1992, p. 9; *Twentieth Century Children's Literature*, 3rd ed., 1989

DEDE SMALL

DU JARDIN, Rosamond
Author, b. 22 July 1902, Fairland, Illinois; d. 27 March 1963, Place unknown

In addition to the many short stories and serials that she wrote for popular magazines, such as *Redbook* and *Good Housekeeping*, D. is also remembered for her novels for YOUNG ADULTS. Her stories generally focus on the romantic interests of young girls. They depict a glossy, near-perfect image of life in small-town America in the 1950s, free of any significant problems other than finding a date for the prom. All of her books for teens have been published in other countries, including Holland, Sweden, and Japan.

FURTHER WORKS: *Practically Seventeen*, 1949; *Wait for March*, 1950; *A Man for Marcy*, 1954; *Senior Prom*, 1957; *Wedding in the Family*, 1958; *Someone to Count On*, 1962; *Young and Fair*, 1963

BIBLIOGRAPHY: *Something about the Author*, vol. 2, 1971; Ward, M. E., D. A. Marquardt, N. Dolan, and D. Eaton, eds., *Authors of Books for Young People*, 3rd ed., 1990

MARY ARIAIL BROUGHTON

DULAC, Edmund
Illustrator, b. 22 October 1882, Toulouse, France; d. 25 May 1953, Place unknown

D. began painting at age eight. He produced his first illustrations for a children's story when he began contributing to *Pall Mall* magazine. In ad-

dition to illustrating popular books such as *Stories from the Arabian Nights* (1907), D.'s career as an artist included designing costumes and props for plays, candy boxes, playing cards, and even a stamp for George VI's Coronation. D. was notable for bringing new interpretations to acknowledged classics in lavishly illustrated expensive editions.

FURTHER WORKS: *Wuthering Heights*, 1905; *Jane Eyre*, 1905; *Stories from the Arabian Nights*, 1907; *Lyrics, Pathetic, and Humorous from A to Z*, 1908; *Stories from Hans C. ANDERSEN*. 1911; *The Bells, and Other Poems*, 1912; *Edmund Dulac's Fairy Book: FAIRY TALES of the Allied Nations*, 1916; *Treasure Island*, 1927

BIBLIOGRAPHY: *Something about the Author*, vol. 19, 1980

JODI PILGRIM

DUNCAN, Lois
Author, b. 28 April 1934, Philadelphia, Pennsylvania

D., daughter of well-known magazine photographers Joseph and Lois Steinmetz, grew up in Sarasota, Florida. D. knew very early on that she wanted to be a writer and published her first story at the age of thirteen. While still in high school D. won *Seventeen* magazine's annual short story contest three times. D. attended Duke University for a time and later graduated from the University of New Mexico, where she was an instructor in the department of journalism. As D. matured as a writer her work progressed to full-length manuscripts. Her first full-length novel was *Debutante Hill* (1958). D. returned to writing for magazines, however, in order to support her children. In 1965 she resumed writing YOUNG ADULT novels. One of these novels was *Ransom* (1966), the story of five teenagers kidnapped by their bus driver. It was runner-up for the Edgar Allan Poe Award that year.

D. is the author of over forty books including children's PICTURE BOOKS, young adult suspense novels, adult novels, and POETRY. Her young adult suspense novels are best known, however, and have established a wide readership. These novels are often fast-paced, told in the first person by a female teenager and contain some element of the supernatural. *I Know What You Did Last Summer* (1973), released as a major Hollywood movie in 1997, *Summer of Fear* (1976), *Killing*

Mr. Griffin (1978), and *Don't Look Behind You* (1989) are some of her best known works.

Tragedy struck D.'s family in 1989 when her youngest child, Kaitlyn, was killed in a manner strangely similar to the heroine in *Don't Look behind You,* which had been released only one month earlier. This difficult experience led D. to write the nonfiction work *Who Killed My Daughter?* (1992), which reviewed D.'s own investigation of her daughter's murder including consultations with parapsychologists and psychics. D.'s firsthand experience with the world of psychics also led to her collaboration with William Roll, Ph.D., on *A Journey into the Mysterious World of Psi* (1995), a nonfiction work that introduces teens to the world of parapsychology.

D.'s work, recognized by critics as well as readers, has received several AMERICAN LIBRARY ASSOCIATION Best Books for Young Adult citations, several *New York Times* Best Books for Children citations and young reader AWARDS in sixteen states and three foreign countries. In 1992, D. was named the recipient of the Margaret A. Edwards Award, which honors a living author for a distinguished body of adolescent literature.

FURTHER WORKS: *Gift of Magic* (with Arvis Stewart), 1971; *Stranger with My Face,* 1981; *Chapters: My Growth as a Writer,* 1982; *The Birthday Moon,* (with Susan Davis), 1989; *Magic of Spider Woman* (With Shonto BEGAY), 1996; *Gallows Hill,* 1997

DEDE SMALL

DUVOISIN, Roger

Author, illustrator, b. 28 August 1904, Geneva, Switzerland; d. 30 June 1980, Morristown, New Jersey

D. displayed an early love of drawing and reading and had early artistic role models in his father, an architect, and his godmother, a famous painter of enamels. When D. was fourteen years old he entered College Moderne and Ecole des Arts et Metiers in Geneva. Murals, posters, and stage scenery were D.'s first works but he soon included ceramics. This led to his becoming the manager of a pottery plant in France. D. moved on to designing textiles in Paris and Lyons; a job in textiles brought him to New York in 1927. The firm went bankrupt in 1931 but D. had the good fortune of having a book he had written for his son,

A Little Boy Was Drawing, published in 1932. Wishing to remain in the United States, he became a United States citizen in 1938.

D. created more than forty books and illustrated more than 140 books for children. His work is marked with a true affection for his audience and a strong connection to the abundant imagination of children. D. held that it was only in giving children all their imagination could grasp that guaranteed their complete response to the book. His love of animals led D. to create a number of personable animal characters including Petunia, Donkey-Donkey, Hector Penguin, and Veronica, that enjoy great popularity. Of special note among his illustrations was the Happy Lion series, which was written by his wife, children's author Louise FATIO.

AWARDS: D. was honored with the CALDECOTT MEDAL in 1948 for *White Snow, Bright Snow* by Alvin TRESSELT and a Caldecott Medal Honor Book in 1966 for *Hide and Seek Fog,* also by Alvin Tresselt. His illustrations were included in the 1946 NEWBERY MEDAL Honor Book *Bhimsa, the Dancing Bear* by Christine Weston. His work was chosen seventeen times for the American Institute of Graphic Arts Fifty Best Books of the Year and four times for the *New York Times* Best Illustrated Children's Books of the Year. His contributions to the field of children's literature were recognized by several organizations and institutions. In 1961 D. received the Society of Illustrators Award and five years later was the recipient of the Rutgers Award. In 1968 D. was the runner up for the Hans Christian ANDERSEN Award. D. was awarded the Silver Medallion of the University of Southern Mississippi's DE GRUMMOND COLLECTION in 1971 and in 1976 was honored with the Kerlan Award from the University of Minnesota. His works are included in both THE KERLAN COLLECTION and the de Grummond Collection

FURTHER WORKS: *Donkey-Donkey,* 1933; *They Put out to Sea: The Story of the Map,* 1943; *Petunia,* 1950; *A for Ark,* 1952; *The Happy Lion,* (L. Fatio, author), 1952; *Wake up City* (A. Tresselt), 1957; *Veronica,* 1961; *Hide and Seek Fog* (A. Tresselt, author), 1965; *The Remarkable Egg* (A. Holl), 1968; *The Web in the Grass* (B. Freschet), 1972; *The Crocodile in the Tree,* 1973; *Mr. and Mrs. Button's Wonderful Watchdogs* (Janice UDRY), 1978

BIBLIOGRAPHY: Greene, Ellin, *Roger Duvoisin, 1904–1980; The Art of Children's Books,* 1989; HOPKINS, Lee Bennett, *Pauses: Autobiograph-*

ical Reflections of 101 Creators of Children's Books, 1995

DEDE SMALL

DYGARD, Thomas

Author, b. 10 August 1931, Little Rock Arkansas

A sportswriter and Associated Press journalist, D. is a prolific children's author as well. He is best known for his novels for YOUNG ADULT readers organized around SPORTS themes that emphasize good sportsmanship and cooperation.

Among his books named as Junior Literary Guild selections are *Outside Shooter* (1979) and *Soccer Duel* (1981). D. moved to Tokyo in 1985, where he was named Associated Press bureau chief.

FURTHER WORKS: *The Rookie Arrives,* 1988; *Running Scared,* 1977; *Tournament Upstart,* 1984

BIBLIOGRAPHY: *The Sixth Book of Junior Authors and Illustrators,* 1989; Ward, M. E., D. A. Marquardt, N. Dolan, and D. Eaton, *Authors of Books for Young People,* 1990

GWYNNE ELLEN ASH

EAGER, Edward (McMaken)

Author, b. 1911, Toledo, Ohio; d. 23 October 1964, Place unknown

An author of FANTASY books for upper-elementary children, E. was also a playwright and lyricist. His plays and songs were written for Broadway, as well as for radio and television. Reared in Toledo, he attended school in Maryland and Massachusetts, eventually enrolling at Harvard University. His interest in children's literature probably began with reading stories to his son, Fritz. In 1951, he published his first work for children, a PICTURE BOOK in verse, entitled *Red Head.* However, he is best remembered for his seven fantasy books, the inspiration for which can be traced back to his high regard for E. NESBIT's turn-of-the-century fantasies, which he called "the best children's books, I am quite sure, in the world." After reading these lively fantasies to his son, E. was moved to create his own adventures. In *Half Magic* (1954), E. does not hide his great admiration for the British author when, early on, his four child characters bemoan the fact that they cannot have exciting adventures like the children in Nesbit's books. At that moment, they find a magical coin that grants half wishes, propelling them into imaginative and intriguing situations. As with subsequent books, the children's success depends on their ability to learn the rules of the magic. In this case, since they are granted half wishes, they learn to wish for twice as much. *Half Magic* enjoyed great success, appearing on *Horn Book* magazine's Fanfare list and cited in *Choice* magazine. E.'s next work, *Knight's Castle* (1956), is a time-travel fantasy where children are transported to the time of Ivanhoe. Frequently utilizing a magical object (e.g., a coin, book, sprig of garden thyme) as the springboard for his adventures, E.'s creative, though formulaic, plots are based upon clever and inventive situations, as evidenced by *Seven Day Magic* (1962), another *Choice* selection. In this fantasy, E.'s last book, children come upon a magic library book that enables them to embark on a series of adventures to literary lands. The library book, however, must be returned in seven days. Though popular with children, adults have criticized E.'s work as being too derivative of Nesbit and faulted his child characters as tiresomely pert and his episodic plots as repetitive. Nevertheless, E.'s works have delighted children who, for decades, have appreciated his HUMOR, use of puns, and skillful mix of realism and fantasy.

FURTHER WORKS: *Magic by the Lake,* 1957; *The Time Garden,* 1958; *Magic or Not?,* 1959; *The Well-Wisher,* 1960

BIBLIOGRAPHY: *Children's Literature Review,* vol. 42, 1997; Cameron, Eleanore, *The Green and Burning Tree,* 1969; *Dictionary of Literary Biography,* vol. 22, 1983; *Twentieth Century Children's Writers,* 2nd ed., 1983

ANDREW KANTAR

EASTMAN, P. D.

Author, illustrator, b. 25 November 1909, Amherst, Massachusetts; d. 7 January 1986, Cresskill, New Jersey

E., whose full name was Philip Day Eastman, grew up in Amherst and attended Amherst College before attending the Art School of the National Academy in New York. Prior to World War II, E. worked for Warner Brothers Cartoons and DISNEY Studios. During the war, E. was a member of the Army Signal Corps and produced army orientation films under the direction of Frank Capra. E.'s immediate commanding officer was Theodor Geisel (pseud. Dr. SEUSS), with whom he would later collaborate on *The Cat in the Hat Beginner Book Dictionary by the Cat Himself* (1964).

After the war, E. joined the creative staff at United Productions of America in Hollywood, California. While there E. was one of the creators of "Gerald McBoing Boing," a short film that was the first non–Disney animated movie to win an Academy Award. E. began to freelance in the 1950s and produced educational and commercial animated films. In 1958 E. made the transition to children's books and produced his first book for children, *Sam and the Firefly.* Although E. both illustrated and wrote books for children, he considered himself primarily a writer and felt most successful writing for children. E.'s best known work is the self-illustrated *Are You My Mother?* (1956), which has sold over two million copies. A number of E.'s works have been translated into other languages. He decribed his artistic style as cartoonish and representational; his ILLUSTRATIONS were generally done in black and white with two or three additional colors.

FURTHER WORKS: *Go, Dog, Go!,* 1961; *Snow* (with Roy McKie), 1962; *The Best Nest,* 1968; *Flap Your Wings,* 1969; *Big Dog . . . Little Dog: A Bedtime Story,* 1973; *I'll Teach My Dog 100 Words* (with Michael K. Frith), 1973; *The Alphabet Book,* 1974; *What Time Is It?* 1979

BIBLIOGRAPHY: Contemporary Authors Online, www.galenet.com

DEDE SMALL

EASY-TO-READ BOOKS

"Reading should always begin with the comforting lap, the loved voice, HUMOR and wonder and sadness shared. But the moment young listeners discover their ability to enter a book on their own—that is the moment of true power." That quote by NEWBERY MEDAL Honor Book Author Marion Dane BAUER eloquently captures the essence of the easy-to-read genre books intended for newly emergent readers: those five-to-seven year-olds entering the magical realm of literacy, to read on their own.

Easy-to-read books are relatively brief stories and INFORMATIONAL BOOKS written with the newly emergent reader's skills and interests in mind. They are typically thirty-two to sixty-four pages long and contain anywhere from 200 words, as in Patricia C. MCKISSACK's *Who Is Who* (1983) to around 2,000 words, as in Mary Pope OSBORNE's *Mo to the Rescue* (1985), but most fall into the 700-to-900-word range. Books specifically used for beginning reading instruction—books with a vocabulary selected on the basis of word frequency, books with a vocabulary selected for consistent letter-sound correspondences, and predictable books—are not typically considered easy-to-reads.

Easy-to-read books are written in a language—vocabulary and syntax—familiar to most five-to-seven year-olds. Although many of the words used in easy-to-reads are decodable or easily identifiable by sight for many young readers, for the most part authors of this genre do not use a controlled vocabulary. Instead, as good writers in any genre, they use the words that best express what they want to say. They know their target audience well enough to understand what will and what will not be accessible to young readers, not only with regard to vocabulary, text structure, and concepts, but in terms of concerns and interests, and in reader appeal. As educator Sylvia Ashton-Warner has said, "First books must be made of the stuff of the child himself, whatever and wherever the child."

In addition to age-appropriate language, concepts, and topics, illustrations also play an important role in making these books easy to read. Contrasted to chapter books, which usually have only two or three half-page illustrations per chapter (and, for the most part, are in black and white), most easy-to-reads have illustrations on every page, usually in full color and taking up as much space as the text, sometimes more. If one page has only text, the facing page will often have a full-page ILLUSTRATION. Unlike PICTURE BOOKS, however, in which the illustrations often convey meaning beyond that provided by the text, in easy-to-read books, the illustrations complement the text, providing important visual clues as to text meaning.

As with their older cousins the chapter books, the size of easy-to-reads—typically six by nine inches—gives them the look of "real books." Although sometimes divided into short chapters, what distinguishes easy-to-reads from chapter books—in addition to fewer words and more pictures—is the arrangement of the words on a page. Here are examples of the first page of an easy-to-read book and the first page of a chapter book: From *Mr. Putter and Tabby Bake the Cake* (1994), an easy-to-read text by Cynthia RYLANT—"It was wintertime. Mr. Putter and his fine cat, Tabby, sat at their window every night to watch the snow come down." From *No Copycats Allowed!* (1998), a beginning chapter book by Bonnie Graves—"I'm not going in," Gabrielle Gilbert told Dillon at the door to room six. "It'll be okay. Just watch out for mean Mrs. Dean and do what everyone else does," her big brother told her. Dillon opened the door and gave Gabrielle a little shove into the noisy room.

As you can see in these examples, easy-to-read books have a set line length or number of characters. These individual lines usually represent units of meaning. The child reads and comprehends one unit, then moves on to the next. In chapter books, however, the text scrolls from one line to the next.

Since the mid-1950s—when Crockett JOHNSON came out with *Harold and the Purple Crayon* (1955), Else Holmelund MINARIK introduced *Little Bear* (1957), and Syd HOFF gave readers *Danny and the Dinosaur* (1958)—publishers have been including easy-to-reads in their publishing line-ups. Today, almost every children's publisher has a line of easy-to-reads. HarperCollins has an extensive line of "I Can Read Books," which include both fiction, such as Matt Novack's *Newt* (1998) and nonfiction, such as Millicent E. SELSAM's *From Egg to Chick* (1970). Random House has its Step into Reading Series with easy-to-read titles at many levels,

from books with only a few words to beginning chapter books. Other publishers that have easy-to-read series are Bantam (Bank Street Ready-to-Reads), Dial (Easy-to-Reads), Dutton (Easy Reader), Grosset and Dunlap (All Aboard Reading), Holiday House (Holiday House Readers), Scholastic (Hello Reader), and Viking (Easy-to-Reads)—and the list goes on. Most publishers who do not have a series of easy-to-reads include a few single titles on their list, such as *Beezy Magic* by Megan MCDONALD (Orchard, 1998), *Gus and Grandpa* by Claudia Mills (Farrar, Straus & Giroux, 1997), and *The Mighty Movers* by Sidney Levitt (Hyperion, 1994).

Although easy-to-read books function as stepping stones to reading competence, many are also representative of well-crafted literature. Two excellent examples are Else Holmelund Minarik's *Little Bear* (1957) illustrated by Maurice SENDAK and Arnold LOBEL's CALDECOTT MEDAL Honor Book, *Frog and Toad Are Friends* (1970). Both stories, librarian Constance Vidor wrote, "with their gentle tales of friendship and adventure, have a warm aura that reaches out to encircle readers' hearts." Minarik and Lobel are among two of the first authors to use their talents in this genre, but they have been followed by numerous other fine writers—Clyde Robert BULLA, Betsy BYARS, Lillian HOBAN, Gail GIBBONS, Tomie DEPAOLA, and Cynthia Rylant, to name only a few.

Easy-to-read books play an extremely important role in developing a lifelong love of reading since, although easy-to-reads may not be a child's first introduction to literature, they are often the child's first introduction to the joy of reading on one's own.

BIBLIOGRAPHY: Beck, I. L., "Understanding Beginning Reading: A Journey through Teaching and Research," in J. Osborn and F. Lehr, eds., *Literacy for All* (pp. 22–26), 1998; Brimner, L. D., "The Land of YouCanReadMe: The Easy Read," *Society of Children's Book Writers and Illustrators Bulletin,* May/June, 1992; Vidor, C., "Easy-to-Reads: Strategies & Selections." *Book Links,* pp. 56–60, May 1994

BONNIE GRAVES

ECKERT, Allan
Author, b. 30 January 1931, Buffalo, New York

E., an author of historical and documentary fiction and nonfiction for children, worked a variety of jobs including postman and private detective before settling into writing about nature and history for children. He is often praised for his enthusiasm for the subject areas that he writes about. His own love of nature led him to write books on the topic for adults and for young children. His historical works include both narratives and the Winning of America series. E. has also written for the television series *Wild Kingdom* and received several Pulitzer prize nominations for *The Frontiermen.* In *Incident at Hawk's Hill* (1971), based on a true event, E. combines his interest in nature and history. Ben, an emotionally fragile six-year-old is lost in a snowstorm and survives by being adopted by a wild badger and her family.

AWARDS: ALA NEWBERY MEDAL Honor Book (1972) for *Incident at Hawk's Hill*

FURTHER WORKS: *Blue Jacket: War Chief of Shawnees,* 1969; *That Dark and Bloody River,* 1995; *Return to Hawk's Hill,* 1998

BIBLIOGRAPHY: *Something about the Author,* vol. 91, 1997

MICHAEL O'LAUGHLIN

EDITORS OF NOTE

The job of children's book editor was a relatively late addition to the roster of publishing professions. Not until 1919 did the Macmillan Company name an editor who would devote her energies exclusively to the firm's children's book program. The person selected for the position was Louise Seaman (later Louise Seaman Bechtel), and she became not only the first children's book editor in the United States but also one of the most renowned. In her fifteen-year editorial career, Bechtel published the works of such award-winning authors as Padraic COLUM, Rachel FIELD, and Elizabeth COATSWORTH, and established a model for subsequent children's book editors to follow. In her fifteen-year editorial career, Bechtel's authors won three NEWBERY MEDALS in three successive years, nine Newbery Honor Awards, two CALDECOTT MEDALS and four Caldecott Honor Awards.

After a riding accident forced her to take an early retirement from Macmillan, Bechtel continued to make a contribution to children's literature as an associate editor of *The Horn Book,* as the children's book review editor of the *New York Herald-Tribune,* and as a judge for many graphic arts awards. Her thoughts on children's books and publishing, collected in the volume *Books in Search of Children* (1946), are still pertinent today.

Other pioneer children's book editors established their reputations in the 1920s. The best-known and longest-lasting of them was May Massee. A former teacher and librarian, Massee launched the Doubleday children's book department in 1922, left it to go to The Viking Press in 1933, and headed the children's book program at Viking until 1958. Afterward, in retirement, she continued to work with a number of her longtime authors and illustrators.

In the 1930s and 1940s, books edited by May Massee won many of the most prestigious children's book AWARDS. More important, they became lasting favorites with generation after generation of children. Among these books of Massee's, all published by Viking, are Munro LEAF's *The Story of Ferdinand* (1936), illustrated by Robert LAWSON; Robert MCCLOSKEY's *Make Way for Ducklings* (1941); and Ludwig BEMELMANS's *Madeline* (1939).

Building on the foundations of the pioneers, a new wave of noteworthy children's book editors emerged in the late 1930s and early 1940s. Their efforts would shape the children's book scene through the 1970s, and beyond. One of the most gifted of the newcomers was Ursula Nordstrom, who assumed control of the Harper children's book department in 1940, remained at its helm until 1973, and continued on as editor of her own imprint at Harper until 1980.

Nordstrom took chances on books considered daring in their day, such as Louise FITZHUGH's *Harriet the Spy* and John DONOVAN's *I'll Get There: It Better Be Worth the Trip.* She nurtured Maurice SENDAK's talent and published many of his most popular titles, including the Caldecott Medal winning title *Where the Wild Things Are.* She also conceived the popular I Can Read series, which was inaugurated in 1957 with *Little Bear* by Else Holmelund MINARIK and illustrated by Maurice Sendak.

Nordstrom's counterpart in the nonfiction area was Elizabeth Riley, who was editor-in-chief of children's books at Thomas Y. Crowell from the 1940s through the 1960s. It was Riley who developed the idea for the innovative Let's Read and Find Out series of science PICTURE BOOKS for young children. The books in the series were produced under the supervision of two noted educators, Roma Gans and Franklyn BRANLEY, and were illustrated with inviting color pictures by leading illustrators such as Joseph Low, ALIKI, and Paul GALDONE.

Another outstanding children's book editor of this generation was Margaret K. McElderry, who joined the staff of Harcourt Brace in 1945 after working as a children's librarian at the New York Public Library under the legendary Anne Carroll Moore, and serving with the Office of War Information in London during World War II. In 1972, McElderry left Harcourt to start her own children's book imprint, Margaret K. McElderry Books, at Atheneum Publishers. Twenty-five years later she was still directing the imprint, now located at Simon and Schuster. Throughout her career, McElderry delighted in introducing young American readers to the work of outstanding authors and illustrators from abroad. She also originated many award-winning books by American creators such as Eleanor ESTES, Irene HAAS, Feodor ROJANKOVSKY, and Susan COOPER. Estes's novel, *Ginger Pye,* won the 1952 Newbery Medal; *Finders Keepers,* illustrated by Nicholas MORDVINOFF, and written by William Lipkind, won the 1952 Caldecott Medal. This is the only time an editor's books have won both these prestigious awards in the same year.

Beginning in the late 1950s, a number of male editors entered the children's book field, which up till then had been dominated by women. Walter Lorraine began his career at Houghton Mifflin as a book designer, then went on to discover and develop the talents of David MACAULAY, James MARSHALL, and Chris Van ALLSBURG. James GIBLIN built Clarion Books into an important imprint that published award-winning books like Russell FREEDMAN's *Lincoln.* Richard Jackson earned the reputation of being one of the best fiction editors in the business, inspiring authors such as Judy BLUME, Cynthia RYLANT, and Paula FOX

to reach new heights in their novels for Bradbury and Orchard Books. As editor at Farrar, Straus and Giroux, Steven Roxburgh nurtured the talents of Madeleine L'ENGLE, Natalie BABBITT, and others.

In these same years, a number of talented younger women editors also appeared on the children's book scene. Following a stint at Abingdon Press, Jean Karl founded the Atheneum children's list in 1962 and furthered the careers of many outstanding writers including E. L. KONIGSBURG, Phyllis Reynolds NAYLOR, and Maia WOJCIECHOWSKA. After serving as an editor at Harper, and heading the Macmillan department, Susan Hirschman established Greenwillow Books in 1974. The new list quickly became known for its imaginative picture books by such artists as Tana HOBAN, Donald CREWS, and Kevin HENKES. Hirschman was invited to present the 1998 May Hill Arbuthnot Honor Lecture.

Phyllis Fogelman put Dial Books for Young Readers on the map by publishing outstanding MULTICULTURAL titles by people like Mildred TAYLOR, Julius LESTER, and Leo and Diane DILLON. At Crown and later at Orchard Books, Norma Jean Sawicki helped to develop a new kind of nonfiction photo essay with such writers as Patricia LAUBER and Seymour SIMON. And Dorothy Briley nurtured the talents of John STEPTOE, David WIESNER, Karen CUSHMAN, Jan ORMEROD, and Jim MURPHY in her editorial positions at Lippincott and Lothrop, Lee and Shepard, and later at Clarion.

In the 1980s and 1990s, children's book editors have lost some of the power and freedom their predecessors enjoyed. At many houses, marketing directors now play the key role in deciding which manuscripts will be published. But young editors interested in children's literature continue to enter the field, filled with an ambition to discover and support the path-breaking writers of the future. As they pursue their goal, these editors will be carrying forward the traditions established by the illustrious children's book editors of the past.

JAMES CROSS GIBLIN

(See also PUBLISHERS AND BOOK PUBLISHING IN THE UNITED STATES; PUBLISHERS, INDEPENDENT)

EDMONDS, Walter D.

Author, b. 15 July 1903, Boonville, New York; d. 24 January 1998, Concord, Massachusetts

E. began his career writing adult novels, many of which were first printed in adult magazines, but experienced success as a children's author. His first children's book, *The Matchlock Gun,* won the NEWBERY MEDAL in 1942. It was initially published in *The Saturday Evening Post* as *The Spanish Gun.*

E. got his ideas for stories from many sources, including old newspapers, books, and letters. His historical novels with tightly knit plots and tense, dramatic scenes are frequently set in the Boonville area of northern New York, where he enjoyed his summers. E. maintained that he wanted readers to get a sense of the relation of history to the present day from his books. His work reflects society's view of NATIVE AMERICANS as it was when the books were written; this has caused them to be criticized in the years since.

AWARDS: AMERICAN LIBRARY ASSOCIATION Newbery Medal and ALA Notable Book (1942) for *The Matchlock Gun.* Boys' Clubs of America Award (1944) for *Hound Dog Moses and the Promised Land Wilderness Clearing.* Christopher Award, National Book Award (1976) for *Bert Breen's Barn*

FURTHER WORKS: *Drums along the Mohawk,* 1936; *Cadmus Henry,* 1949; *The Boyds of Black River,* 1953; *Uncle Ben's Whale,* 1955; *Beaver Valley,* 1971

BIBLIOGRAPHY: *Something about the Author,* vol. 27, 1982

JODI PILGRIM

EGIELSKI, Richard

Illustrator, b. 16 July 1952, New York City

E. has illustrated PICTURE BOOKS written by various authors, including multiple collaborations with Pam CONRAD, Miriam CHAIKIN, and Arthur YORINKS. With Yorinks, he produced the 1987 CALDECOTT MEDAL winner *Hey, Al,* the 1986 Bratislava Prize–winner *It Happened in Pinsk,* and a 1980 *School Library Journal* Best Book selection, *Louis the Fish.* E.'s work is characterized by imaginative style and innovative use of color and space.

Born and reared in New York City, E. loved to draw as a child, but did not consider a career as an artist until he enrolled in the city's High School of Art and Design. After graduation he studied painting at Pratt Institute, but found his interest in representational drawing out of step with Pratt's emphasis on abstract expressionism. Transferring to the Parsons School of Design to study commercial ILLUSTRATION, he took a course in picture-book illustration taught by Maurice SENDAK, whom he describes as "the most important teacher I ever had." The quality of Sendak's work and his highly personal artistic style inspired E. to trust the evolution of his own idiosyncratic approach to illustration. Although publishers initially thought E.'s work too sophisticated for children, Sendak introduced him to Arthur Yorinks, a young writer whose texts, like E.'s illustrations, were out of the ordinary. Together the pair developed a successful collaborative process, with Yorinks' initial texts passed back and forth from illustrator to writer until a small-scale storyboard emerged, which was then shared with the publisher. Next, E. completed full-scale watercolors, collaborating with Yorinks over final revisions to produce a picture book that flowed with the desired rhythm.

E.'s publications include three books he has authored as well as illustrated: *Buz* (1995) and *Jazper* (1998), both imaginative forays into the insect world, and a fresh, contemporary retelling of the familiar tale *The Gingerbread Boy* (1997) with New York City as the setting.

AWARDS: *School Library Journal* Best Book citation (1980) for *Louis the Fish.* 1986 Bratislava Prize in Illustration (1986) for *It Happened in Pinsk.* ALA Caldecott Medal (1987) for *Hey, Al.* Society of Illustrators certificates of merit in 1978, 1981, 1984, and 1985.

FURTHER WORKS: By F. N. MONJO: *The Porcelain Pagoda.* 1976. By Pam CONRAD: *The Tub People.* 1989. *The Lost Sailor.* 1992. *The Tub Grandfather.* 1993. By Miriam Chaikin: *I Should Worry, I Should Care.* 1979. *Finders Weepers.* 1980. *Getting Even.* 1982. *Lower! Higher! You're a Liar!* 1984. *Friends Forever.* 1988. By Arthur Yorinks: *Sid and Sol.* 1997. *Bravo, Minsk.* 1988. *Oh, Brother.* 1989. *Ugh.* 1990. *Christmas in July.* 1991. *"Fire! Fire!" Said Mrs. McGuire.* (Bill

MARTIN, Jr., author). 1995. *Perfect Pancakes, if You Please.* (William Wise, author). 1997

BIBLIOGRAPHY: *Major Authors and Illustrators for Children and YOUNG ADULTS.* 1993. Silvey, Anita, ed. *Children's Books and Their Creators.* 1995. *Something about the Author*, vol. 49, 1987

                                    DIANE L. CHAPMAN

EHLERT, Lois

Author, illustrator, b. 9 November 1934, Beaver Dam, Wisconsin

A creator of INFORMATIONAL BOOKS for young children, E. grew up making pictures. Her mother gave her scraps of cloth from sewing and her father gave her wood from woodworking projects. They set up a folding table where E. worked on activities and developed her talents. E. sent some of her work to Layton School of Art in Milwaukee, Wisconsin, and obtained a scholarship. Her table went with her.

In 1957 she graduated from art school, did graphic design and illustrated children's books. Unable to approve the final colors of her printed illustrations, she left PICTURE BOOKS and concentrated on graphic design assignments where she won numerous design AWARDS.

Later, as production of children's books improved, she returned to the field, first illustrating for others and then writing and illustrating her own books. Several have a gardening theme. *Growing Vegetable Soup* (1987) has large type and simple text, offset by bright intense colors, shows planting seeds and their need for water and rain. After harvesting the vegetables, a recipe for making vegetable soup is included.

Planting a Rainbow (1988) received an Outstanding Science Trade Book for Children citation, National Science Teachers Association (1989). E. shows and labels bulbs planted in the fall and seeds and seedlings planted in the spring. Fully blossomed radiant flowers are labeled in a visually attractive book with an unusual rainbow link.

An innovative book, *Color Zoo,* was a CALDECOTT MEDAL Honor Book (1990) and an American Booksellers Pick of the List title. Vividly colored pages with layered geometric cutouts present various animals found in the zoo. This carefully designed concept book presents shapes and colors in a manner accessible to young children; a book that shows remarkable ingenuity in design and inventiveness.

E. likes to cut and paste and *Eating the Alphabet: Fruits and Vegetables from A to Z* (1989) shows her skill. Using collage as a medium she walks the reader through the alphabet from apple to zucchini with an array of colorful fruits and vegetables. She used real models, painted the colors of the models onto different pieces of watercolor paper, let them dry, backed them with rubber cement and cutout shapes. Each upper and lowercase letter is presented in large, black type along with the vegetable–fruit name in upper and lowercase letters. This aids visual discrimination for young children learning the alphabet. A glossary at the back of the book gives readers the country of origin for the fruits and vegetables.

Color Farm (1990) was designated an Outstanding Science Trade Book for Children by the National Science Teachers Association in 1990. Similar to *Color Zoo* in using geometric shapes and bright bold colors, this book features barnyard animals. Each animal is named at the bottom of the page.

A counting book, *Fish Eyes: A Book You Can Count On* (1990) follows the form of *Color Zoo* and *Eating the Alphabet.* Awarded the *New York Times* Best Illustrated Children's Books of the Year (1990), cutout eyes invite children to touch them while they look at one green fish or two jumping fish. Fish in different patterns, shapes, movement and physique appear along with one tiny black fish hidden in each dark blue page to pique interest.

Red Leaf, Yellow Leaf (1991) was awarded the *Boston Globe–Horn Book* (Nonfiction Honor) and *Elizabeth Burr* in 1992. It portrays the growth of a sugar maple seedling as it grows and is transplanted. The book is done in collage, roots, seeds, ribbon, fabric, wire, paper, plastic, cardboard, pencils, watercolors, pens, crayons, and oil pastels. A similar ILLUSTRATION format is used in *Snowballs* (1995).

Circus (1992) was inspired by the annual city of Milwaukee Great Circus Parade and the Circus World Museum in Baraboo, Wisconsin, which houses antique circus wagons. Abstract collage figures perform circus acts. End papers contain multicolored stars on a black background.

When asked about her artwork E. replies: "I realize that I write and draw things I know and care about . . . It takes me a long time to make a book . . . setting down something that might, if I'm lucky, be remembered after I'm gone."

FURTHER WORKS: *Feathers for Lunch*, 1990; *Red Leaf, Yellow Leaf*, 1992

BIBLIOGRAPHY: *Children's Literature Review*, vol. 28, 1992. *Fiction, FOLKLORE, FANTASY and POETRY for Children, 1876–1985*. 1986. Harcourt, Brace and Co. flier. Jones, Delores Blythe, ed. *Children's Literature Awards and Winners: A Directory of Prizes, Authors and Illustrators*. 1994. Silvey, Anita, ed. *Children's Books and Their Creators*. 1995. *Something about the Author*, vol. 35, 1984, and vol. 69, 1992

IRVYN G. GILBERTSON

EHRLICH, Amy
Author, b. 24 July 1942, New York City

Even as a young child, E. wanted to write. Inspired by her love of reading and watching her father write suspense novels and television scripts, E. wrote at a young age; in ninth grade she won a prize in a short story contest. This reputation for talented writing left a lasting impression on E. School was difficult however, and feeling that she never really fit in, E. asked to be sent away to boarding school. E. attended a Quaker boarding school for two years and then attended Bennington College in Vermont. E. left school when she became caught up in the spirit of the sixties. During this time E. lived in communes and worked a wide variety of jobs including fabric colorist, day-care worker, hospital receptionist, and proofreader. While working as a part-time copywriter and editorial assistant, E. was encouraged by a co-worker to try writing a children's book. E. liked the idea but experienced writer's block until some close friends had a child. E. wanted to make a gift of a story for the baby and soon found herself writing a book. Written over the course of one weekend, *Zeke Silver Moon* (1972) was well received; it tells the story of a family and what rearing children was like in the early 1970s.

E. spent some time living in Jamaica but returned to the United States in 1973. E.'s life changed dramatically with the birth of her son. With priorities and focus changed, E. returned to

proofreading and editorial work in New York; she was hired as senior editor at Delacorte Press, a position she held for eight years. During this time, E. continued writing children's books and also produced a number of adaptations of well-known FAIRY TALES.

When her sister became ill, E. moved back to Vermont and took a leave of absence to care for her. E. did not return to editing full-time; she focused instead on her own writing, which had grown to include YOUNG ADULT novels. Inspired by her son's friends, *Where It Stops, Nobody Knows* (1988) is the story of a teenage girl whose mother is constantly on the move, running from life's problems.

FURTHER WORKS: *The Everyday Train* (Martha ALEXANDER, illus.), 1977; *Thumbelina* (Hans Christian ANDERSEN). (Susan JEFFERS, illus.), 1979. *Random House Book of Fairy Tales* (Adapter, Diane GOODE, illus.), 1985; *Leo, Zack, and Emmie Together Again* (Steven KELLOGG, illus.), 1987; *Buck Buck the Chicken* (R.W. Alley, illus.), 1987; *Lucy's Winter Tale* (Troy Howell, illus.), 1991; *The Dark Card*, 1991; *Parents in the Pigpen, Pigs in the Tub* (Steven Kellogg, illus.), 1993

DEDE SMALL

EICHENBERG, Fritz
Illustrator, graphic artist, teacher, b. 24 October 1901, Cologne, Germany; d. 30 November 1990, Peace Dale, Rhode Island

Political displacement of artists from Germany began many years before World War II. Numerous intellectuals and creative artists like E. were forced into exile. Although a mature and successful printmaker in Germany, after E. arrived in the United States, he began, in 1935, to work on the WPA Federal Art Project, which provided work for unemployed artists. There, he participated in the creation of prints and murals for public spaces. Also in 1935, he began teaching woodcut printmaking and wood engraving at The New School in New York City until 1945. After the war, E. taught at Pratt Institute from 1947 to 1972.

By 1936, however, he had begun illustrating, using his characteristic wood engraving techniques in black ink. His style was that of the German Expressionist woodcutters who sought not only to convey the intense emotion that they felt when they carved their forms, but also to retain the character of the wood itself. E. had a most prodigious and celebrated career as an illustrator.

AWARDS: ALA NEWBERY MEDAL Honor Book (1943) for *Have You Seen Tom Thumb?* (Mabel Leigh Hunt, author). ALA CALDECOTT MEDAL Honor Book (1953) for *Ape in a Cape: An Alphabet of Odd Animals. New York Times* Best Illustrated Children's Books of the Year (1982) *Rainbows Are Made* (Carl SANDBURG)

FURTHER WORKS: Illustrator: *Jane Eyre* (Bronte), 1943; *Wuthering Heights,* Bronte, 1943; *Devil and Daniel Webster* (Stephen Vincent Benet), 1945; *Black Beauty* (SEWELL), 1945; *The Peaceable Kingdom and Other Poems* (Elizabeth COATSWORTH), 1958

BIBLIOGRAPHY: *Contemporary Authors, New Revision Series.* vol. 57, 1997; *Something about the Authors,* vol. 9, 1976, and vol. 50, 1988

JUDY LIPSITT

EKOOMIAK, Normee
Author, illustrator, b. 1948, Cape James, Quebec, Canada

E. was born into the Inuit people of Arctic Quebec and grew up experiencing many of the traditional ways of life. He lived in his grandfather's tent of seal skin and was reared by both his immediate and extended family. In 1972 E. began attending George Brown College and later went to the New School of Art. E. has created many paintings and wall hangings that maintain Inuit artistic traditions and ensure that the Arctic he remembers as a child not be forgotten. In *Arctic Memories* (1988), E. combines richly detailed paintings and appliqué with INFORMATIONAL text about traditional Inuit culture and lifestyle. Through both English and Inuit languages, readers learn about Inuit food, shelter, games, families, celebrations, and beliefs. In 1991, *Arctic Memories* was selected by the NATIONAL COUNCIL OF TEACHERS OF ENGLISH as an ORBIS PICTUS AWARD Honor Book. This award is given to recognize outstanding nonfiction for children. E. now lives and works in South Quebec as his North homeland no longer exists.

BIBLIOGRAPHY: Ekoomiak, N. *Arctic Memories,* 1988; Temple, C., M. Martinez, J. Yokota, and A. Naylor. *Children's Books in Children's Hands,* 1998

JANELLE B. MATHIS

ELLIS, Sarah
Author, b. 19 May 1952, Vancouver, British Columbia, Canada

E. received her B.A. from the University of British Columbia in 1973 and returned to earn her M.L.S. in 1975. Three years later E. earned her M.A. from Simmons College. She has worked as a children's librarian in both Toronto and Vancouver. While growing up, E. never thought of becoming a writer; she reflects that she now finds writing in every aspect of her life. The youngest in a family of storytellers, E. says that she had to become a storyteller herself in order to be heard at the dinner table. E.'s work is generally told from the viewpoint of female protagonists who discover through experience the strength and truth in themselves, and their families. E.'s first work, *The Baby Project* (1986), is an honest portrayal of a family in crisis. Published in the United States as *A Family Project* (1988), this debut novel tells the story of Jessica, an eleven-year-old girl. The novel reveals her mixed feelings about the birth of her new sister and the way she and her family must deal with tragedy when the infant dies of sudden infant death syndrome. It was applauded for the realistic yet courageous voice of Jessica and the other well-developed characters in her quirky but lovable family. E.'s second novel, *Next-Door Neighbours* (1989), published in the United States one year later, is told in the strong voice of a minister's daughter. Set in 1957, she befriends a refugee's son and learns about racism and responsibility. *Pick-up Sticks* (1991), E.'s third novel, is the story of a young girl trying to make sense of herself and her world. This novel looks at traditional versus nontraditional families and how real love and support are not necessarily related to the number of adults in the household. In addition to her novels E. is also the author of "News from the North," a regular feature on CANADIAN LITERATURE in the *Horn Book* magazine, and is an occasional lecturer on children's literature.

FURTHER WORKS: *Putting up with Mitchell* (Barbara Wood, illus.), 1989; *Out of the Blue,* 1995; *Back of the Beyond,* 1997

DEDE SMALL

EMBERLEY, Edward, Barbara, and Rebecca

Authors, illustrators. Edward: b. 19 October 1931, Malden, Massachusetts; Barbara: b. 12 December 1932, Chicago, Illinois; Rebecca Anne, Michael: b. Date unknown, 1960

With an interest in art since childhood, E.E. attended Massachusetts School of Art and earned a degree in painting and ILLUSTRATION. Following his graduation, he married Barbara Collins, a student of fashion design whom he met during school. His early employment involved art-related work such as painting signs and specializing in cartoons as a commercial artist. His interest in children's literature actually began in the late 1950s, but it was not until 1961 that his first book, *The Wing on a Flea: A Book about Shapes* (1961), was published. This imaginative book about shapes that can be found all around us was the beginning of an extensive career that spanned various techniques, topics, and genre.

B.E. has collaborated with E.E. on numerous books. She integrated her adaptations of folk songs and tales and nursery rhymes with E.E.'s richly imaginative and often humorous illustrations. The E.s work together on numerous projects.

E.E. not only has the insight of an artist but also of an illustrator who is aware of the overall design of the book. His keen graphic sense and extensive knowledge of production techniques and various art media—woodcuts, pen and ink, and pencil—allow him to make artistic decisions based on consideration of all the practicalities of bookmaking. Critics have complimented his originality in designing books, such as *Ed Emberley's ABC* (1978) in which intricate pictures depict unusual representations of the various letters of the alphabet. An extensive series of drawing books invites readers to enjoy and be successful at drawing many different subjects. E.E.'s deliberate attention to both picture and text, as he sculpts images for readers, makes him a frequently read and well-regarded creator of children's books. In *Drummer Hoff* (1967), E.E. and B.E.'s lively cumulative verse uses bright primary-colored woodcuts and ink to retell a traditional tale. Readying the cannon and firing it off results in a bright explosion of yellow flowers that covers the entire final page.

The creation of children's books evolved into a family interest as daughter Rebecca and son Michael became authors. R.E. wrote and illustrated several books containing both English and Spanish text. *My House, Mi Casa: A Book in Two Languages/Mi Casa: UN Libro En DOS Lenguas* (1990) and *Taking a Walk: A Book in Two Languages? Caminando: UN Libro En DOS Lenguas* (1993) each have brightly colored collage illustrations and explore the names of familiar items in two languages. R.E. has written in other genres as in her urban telling of a familiar tale in *Three Cool Kids* (1998) and *My Mother's Secret Life* (1998). M.E. has written in various genre to include: *Dinosaurs!: A Drawing Book* (1980) and *Ruby* (1990), an innovative version of *Little Red Riding Hood*. M.E. has also illustrated several highly acclaimed children's books that focus on the human body and sexuality including *It's Perfectly Normal* (1994), *Happy Birthday!* (1996), and *It's So Amazing* (1999). M.E. uses simple straightforward prose easily accessible to prepubescent children; cartoon characters and accurate physical details describe human development in sexuality within a sensitive matrix.

AWARDS: Two of the collaborative efforts of E.E. and B.E. have been award winners: ALA CALDECOTT MEDAL (1968) for *Drummer Hoff*. AMERICAN LIBRARY ASSOCIATION Caldecott Medal Honor Book (1967) for *One Wide River to Cross*. E.E.: *New York Times* Best Illustrated Children's Books of the Year (1961) for *The Wing on a Flea*

FURTHER WORKS: (E.E. and B.E.): *Night's Nice.* 1963. *Paul Bunyan.* 1963. *Yankee Doodle.* 1965. *Simon's Song.* 1969. *BASIC Book.* 1985. *Bits and Bytes.* 1985. (E.E.): *The Parade Book.* 1962. *Rosebud.* 1966. *London Bridge Is Falling Down.* 1967. *Green Says Go.* 1968. *Ed Emberley's Drawing Book of Animals.* 1970. *Klippity Klop.* 1974. *Ed Emberley's Amazing Look through Book.* 1979. *Ed Emberley's Big Red Drawing Book.* 1987. *Go Away, Big, Green Monster.* 1993. (R.E.): *City Sounds.* 1989. *Jungle Sounds.* 1989. (M.E.): *Ruby.* 1990. *Present.* 1991. *Welcome Back, Sun.* 1993

BIBLIOGRAPHY: *Children's Literature Review,* vol. 5, 1983; HOPKINS, Lee Bennett, *Pauses: Autobiographical Reflections of 101 Creators of Children's Books,* 1995; Kinsman, Lee, ed. *Newbery and Caldecott Medal Books, 1966–1975,* 1975; *Something about the Author,* vol. 70, 1993, and vol. 80, 1995; *Third Book of Junior Authors,* 1972

JANELLE MATHIS

ENDE, Michael
Author, b. 12 November 1929, Garmisch-Partenkirschen, Germany; d. 29 August 1995, Stuttgart, Germany

E., an author, actor, and film critic, best known by U.S. readers as the author of *The Neverending Story* (1979), was the only child of a Surrealist painter and a physiotherapist. The German Army drafted him in 1945 and in 1947 E. began attending the Otto Flackenberg Drama School. He also wrote scripts for Munich cabarets and reviewed books for German radio. His first book, *Jim Knopf und Lucas der Lokomotivführrher* (Jim Button and Lucas the engine driver), was published in 1960 and its sequel *Jim Knopf und die Wilde 13* (Jim Button and the wild 13) published in 1962, was adapted as a popular German radio and television series.

The Neverending Story, translated into more than thirty languages, remained on the best-seller lists in Germany for more than two years. In this quest novel, Bastian, an unhappy child who loves to read, uses his vivid imagination to transform himself through a series of FANTASY adventures. With the help of his new friends he saves the kingdom of Fantastica. The 1984 film adaptation, presented in both English and German versions, met with box-office success but lukewarm reviews. E. himself was one of the film's harshest critics.

AWARDS: Janusz Korczak Literary Prize (Polish section of the INTERNATIONAL BOARD ON BOOKS FOR YOUNG READERS) (1981) for *The Neverending Story*

FURTHER WORKS: With U.S. publication dates: *Momo,* 1985; *Night of Wishes,* 1992; *Ophelia's Shadow Theater,* 1989

BIBLIOGRAPHY: http://members.aol.com/leah/ende.htm; *Something about the Author,* vol 61, 1990

JANET HILBUN

ENGDAHL, Sylvia
Author, b. 24 November 1933, Los Angeles, California

E. graduated from the University of California at Santa Barbara, then taught fourth grade. While working as a programmer developing computerized air-defense systems, E. realized how much she enjoyed writing technical information. In 1967, at the threshold of space exploration, E. was determined to share her enthusiasm for technological development with young people. She quit her job and began writing full-time. In *Enchantress from the Stars* (1970) and its sequel *The Far Side of Evil* (1971) E. explores civilizations on three planets at different stages of development. The first-person narrative relates Elana's efforts to thwart the destruction of the planet with a medieval culture.

E. continues to write SCIENCE FICTION and non-fiction dealing with scientific issues including a PICTURE BOOK, *Our World Is Earth* (1979). *This Star Shall Abide* (1972) continues E.'s attempts to discuss current issues through speculative fiction.

AWARDS: ALA NEWBERY MEDAL Honor Book (1971) for *Enchantress from the Stars.* Christopher Award (1973) for *This Star Shall Abide*

FURTHER WORKS: *Beyond the Tomorrow Mountains,* 1973; *The Doors of the Universe,* 1981

BIBLIOGRAPHY: *The Fourth Book of Junior Authors,* 1978; *Major Authors and Illustrators for Children and YOUNG ADULTS,* 1993; Silvey, Anita, ed., *Children's Books and Their Creators,* 1995

GWYNNE ELLEN ASH

ENRIGHT, Elizabeth
Author, illustrator, b. 17 September 1909, Oak Park, Illinois; d. 8 June 1968, Wainscott, New York

Although E. was born in the midwest, her family moved to New York City when she was a baby, and E. lived there most of her life. Her father was a cartoonist and her mother a children's book illustrator. E. studied at the Art Students League of New York, continued her art studies in Paris, and returned to study at Parsons School of Design. Her early professional career was that of illustrator, for both magazines and children's books. In the 1930s, she began to write stories to accompany her ILLUSTRATIONS. In 1939, she was awarded the ALA NEWBERY MEDAL for *Thimble Summer,* a novel that drew on memories of an idyllic summer she had spent in Wisconsin as a child. Her SERIES of self-illustrated children's novels about the Melendy family, *The Saturdays*

(1941), *The Four-Story Mistake* (1942), *Then There Were Five* (1944), and *Spiderweb for Two* (1951) were immediately successful and proved to have long-term popularity. *The Saturdays* and *Gone-Away Lake* (1958) were AMERICAN LIBRARY ASSOCIATION Notable Books in their respective years. E.'s adult stories were published in O. Henry Award short story collections and Best American Short Stories annuals.

FURTHER WORKS: *Kintu: A Congo Adventure,* 1935; *Return to Gone-Away,* 1961; *Tatsinda,* 1963

BIBLIOGRAPHY: *Current Biography,* 1947; *Something about the Author,* vol. 9, 1976; *Who Was Who in America,* vol. 5

FRANCISCA GOLDSMITH

ESBENSEN, Barbara Juster
Poet, b. 28 April 1925, Madison, Wisconsin; d. 25 October 1996, St. Paul, Minnesota

E. grew up fascinated with words and while her parents nurtured the artistic talents they recognized in their daughter, the art of language permeated E.'s mind. She shared her first poem with an English teacher, Eulalie Beffel, who introduced her to the poets of the 1920s and 1930s. From the time Beffel told E. she was a writer, the teacher, herself a writer and poet, became E.'s lifelong influence and mentor. While E. focused on art at the University of Wisconsin, in her mind the artistry of words continued to be her great joy.

Just as an artist carefully selects and combines the elements of art, so E. uses words as the elements and plays with them to find the exact combination that enables images to come alive for the reader. Often the sources of her ideas have been images spoken by her children, such as her son remarking about "a celebration of bees," which later became the title poem for the book, *A Celebration of Bees: Helping Children Write POETRY.* 1995. Other titles reflect her careful deliberation of creating fresh, exciting images, such as *Words with Wrinkled Knees* (1986) and *Who Shrunk my Grandmother's House?* (1992).

Aware of the unique invitations that language offers young writers just discovering that words can capture their feelings, E. did not use poetry with rhyme in working with children. She felt rhyme restricts what writers think they can do with language as they focus on the deliberate

search for rhyming words rather than words that express their images.

E.'s artistry of words is also seen in her prose writing. *Ladder to the Sky* (1989), *The Star Maiden* (1988), and *The Great Buffalo Race* (1994) combine E.'s interest in NATIVE AMERICAN legends with her storyteller's ability to create images. Besides these retellings, she published other nonfiction for children that brings nature to life using eloquent imagery.

AWARDS: NATIONAL COUNCIL OF TEACHERS OF ENGLISH Award for Excellence in Poetry for Children (1994) for the entire body of her work. NCTE Teacher's Choice Award (1987) for *Words with Wrinkled Knees,* and (1988) for *The Star Maiden.* Notable Children's Trade Book in the Field of Social Studies from the National Council for Social Studies and the CHILDREN'S BOOK COUNCIL (1989) for *Ladder to the Sky*

FURTHER WORKS: *Swing around the Sun,* 1965; *Cold Stars and Fireflies,* 1984; *Great Northern Diver,* 1990; *Tiger with Wings,* 1991; *Playful Slider,* 1993; *Sponges Are Skeletons,* 1993; *Baby Whales Drink Milk,* 1994; *The Dream Mouse,* 1995; *Dance with Me,* 1995; *Swift as the Wind,* 1996; *The Night Rainbow,* 1998

BIBLIOGRAPHY: E., Barbara J. *Words with Wrinkled Knees* (Commemorative Edition), 1997; Greenlaw, M. Jean. *Language Arts,* vol. 71, 1994; Rasmussen, Jay B., *The Reading Teacher,* vol. 48, no. 3, 1994

JANELLE B. MATHIS

ESTES, Eleanor
Author, illustrator, b. 9 May 1906, West Haven, Connecticut; d. 15 July 1988, Hamden, Connecticut

E. was one of four children in a poor family. After her father died, her mother supported the family as a dressmaker. E. remembered the pleasure of playing in the fields, climbing trees, fishing, and sledding. Her mother often sang, recited poetry, and told folktales and stories about New York City where she had grown up. After high school in 1924, E. became a children's librarian. In 1931, she won a scholarship to attend the library school at Pratt Institute, where she met her husband, a library administrator and professor. E. suffered a bout of tuberculosis in 1934, and began writing *The Moffats* (1941) as she recuperated. She continued as a children's librarian until

The Moffats was published, when she became a full-time writer.

E.'s stories, both REALISTIC FICTION and FANTASY, have been translated into many languages. Though primarily an author, she also illustrated some of her own works, including the 1952 NEWBERY MEDAL winning *Ginger Pye*. E.'s most popular books, those in the Moffat and Pye SERIES, both feature families who live in Cranbury, Connecticut—a fictionalized version of E.'s childhood hometown. The Moffat stories, many illustrated by Louis SLOBODKIN, represent E.'s family in the years 1916–18, with characters based on E. and each of her family members. E.'s FAMILY STORIES, built around everyday events, exude warmth and HUMOR, even when the family is experiencing difficulty. Her descriptions of places are detailed and vivid, her portrayal of children's language and thought realistic. E. credited her years as a children's librarian with helping her develop a keen sense of what children think and what appeals to them. Her goal was to write purely for the enjoyment of children.

AWARDS: AMERICAN LIBRARY ASSOCIATION Newbery Medal (1952) for *Ginger Pye*. ALA Newbery Medal Honor Book (1943) for *The Middle Moffat*, (1944) for *Rufus M.*, and (1945) for *The Hundred Dresses*. Lewis CARROLL Shelf Award (1961) for *The Moffats*. Certificate of Award for Outstanding Contribution to Children's Literature from the New York Association for Supervision and Curriculum Development. Pratt Institute Alumni Medal (1968). Laura Ingalls WILDER Award (1970) nomination

FURTHER WORKS: Self-illustrated: *The Sleeping Giant and Other Stories*, 1948; *A Little Oven*, 1955; *The Moffat Museum*, 1983; Other: *The Sun and the Wind and Mr. Todd* (ill. L. Slobodkin). 1943; *The Coat-Hanger Christmas Tree* (ill. S. Suba). 1973; *The Lost Umbrella of Kim Chu* (ill. J. Ayer). 1978; *The Curious Adventure of Jimmy McGee* (ill. J. O'Brien). 1987; Illustrated by E. ARDIZZONE: *Pinky Pye*, 1958; *The Witch Family*, 1960; *The Alley*, 1967; *Miranda the Great*, 1967; *The Tunnel of Hugsy Goode*, 1972

BIBLIOGRAPHY: Berger, L. S. *Twentieth-Century Children's Writers*. 1995. *Dictionary of Literary Biography*. vol. 22: *American Writers for Children, 1990–1960*. 1983. E., E. Newbery Award Acceptance Paper. 1955. In B. M. Miller and E. W. Field. eds., *Newbery Medal Books: 1922–1955*. HOPKINS, L. B. (1974), *More Books by More People*. *Junior Book of Authors*. Hopkins,

L. B., *Pauses: Autobiographical Reflections of 101 Creators of Children's Books*, 1995; Sayers, F. C. *The Books of Eleanor E.* 1955. Townsend, J. R. *A Sense of Story: Essays on Contemporary Writers for Children*, 1973

JANE WEST

ETS, Marie Hall
Author, b. 16 December 1893, Milwaukee, Wisconsin; d. 1984, Place unknown

E. attributes memories of childhood summers in Wisconsin and her love of watching wild animals as the source for the ANIMAL STORIES *Play with Me* (1955), *Mister Penny* (1935), and *In the Forest* (1944). E.'s artistic abilities were recognized as a child and nurtured; she studied art at the New York School of Fine and Applied Art, and the Art Institute of Chicago. Additionally, she pursued other advanced studies in philanthropic areas at various institutions. Having worked in parts of the United States, Czechoslovakia, and Mexico, her career included social case work and organizing child health services. Family influences in this aspect of her work included her philosopher brother, Everett Wesley Hall, and her great-grandfather John Wesley Carhart, physician, poet, and inventor of the first horseless carriage in the 1870s. However, from 1935 on she focused more on her author–illustrator career.

Although published in the 1960s, *Nine Days to Christmas* is still relevant for readers today and reflects the time E. spent working in Mexico. The book focuses on the wonder of a child as her Mexican village comes alive with Christmas traditions. In a similar sense of the simplicity and wonder of childhood, *In the Forest* (1944) and *Gilberto and the Wind* (1963) celebrates a child's awareness of nature.

AWARDS: *New York Herald Tribune* Children's Book Festival Award (1947) for *Oley, the Sea Monster*. Hans Christian ANDERSEN Award (1956) for *Play with Me*. ALA CALDECOTT MEDAL (1960) for *Nine Days to Christmas*. AMERICAN LIBRARY ASSOCIATION Caldecott Medal Honor Book (1966) for *Just Me*, (1957) for *Mr. Penny's Race Horse*, (1956) for *Play with Me*, (1952) for *Mr. T. W. Anthony Woo*, and (1945) for *In the Forest*

FURTHER WORKS: *The Story of a Baby*, 1939; *My Dog Rinty*, 1946; *Little Old Automobile*, 1948; *Beasts and Nonsense*, 1952; *Another Day*, 1953;

Cow's Party, 1958; *Circus,* 1961; *Automobiles for Mice,* 1964; *Bad Boy, Good Boy,* 1967; *Talking without Words; I Can, Can You?* 1968

BIBLIOGRAPHY: *Major Authors and Illustrators for Children and Young Adults.* 1992; HOPKINS, Lee Bennett, *Pauses: Autobiographical Reflections of 101 Creators of Children's Books,* 1995

JANELLE B. MATHIS

EVSLIN, Bernard

Author, b. 9 April 1922, Philadelphia, Pennsylvania; d. 4 June 1993, Kauai, Hawaii

A documentary film writer and producer, E. was best known for his Monsters of Mythology series, especially *Cerberus* (1987), *Medusa* (1987), and *Antaeus* (1988). His other writings also focus on FOLKLORE and MYTHOLOGY. E.'s retellings of Greek and other myths are noted for the traditional eloquence of the legendary tales in combination with informal idiomatic language. *The Green Hero: Early Adventures of Finn McCool* (1975) was nominated for a National Book Award, and *Hercules* (1986) received a Washington IRVING Children's Book Choice Award.

FURTHER WORKS: *Greeks Bearing Gifts,* 1976; *Gods, Demigods, and Demons: An Encyclopedia of Greek Mythology,* 1988; *Signs and Wonders: Tales from the Old Testament,* 1979

BIBLIOGRAPHY: Hunt, Peter, ed., *Children's Literature, An Illustrated History.* 1995. *New York Times.* June 26, 1993, p. 27. Ward, M. E., D. A. Marquardt, N. Dolan, and D. Eaton. *Authors of Books for Young People,* 1990

GWYNNE ELLEN ASH

F

FABER, Doris
Biographer, b. 29 January 1924, New York City

F. is best known for her numerous BIOGRAPHIES of notable women and men in politics, history, and science. F.'s writing has been praised by critics for its clarity and for her direct, simple style, making her books easily accessible to middle readers and young adults. Awards for juvenile books include *Robert Frost: America's Poet* (1964), a Junior Literary Guild Selection, and *Oh, Lizzie: The Life of Elizabeth Cady Stanton* (1972), a Book World honor book. Among other books by F. are biographies of the lives of Clarence Darrow, Bella Abzug, Harry Truman, Franklin Delano Roosevelt, Dwight Eisenhower, and Margaret Thatcher. F. collaborated with her husband, Harold, on several works, including Martin Luther King, Jr., and *Mahatma Ghandi* (1986). The couple also wrote *Birth of a Nation: The Early Years of the United States* (1989), a book praised for its lively writing style and anecdotal details and for *Nature and the Environment* (1991), a collection featuring biographical accounts of significant environmentalists.

FURTHER WORKS: *Petticoat Politics: How American Women Won the Right to Vote,* 1967. *Love and Rivalry: Three Exceptional Pairs of Sisters,* 1983. *Calamity Jane: Her Life and Legend,* 1992. *Eleanor Roosevelt: First Lady of the World,* 1985

BIBLIOGRAPHY: *Something about the Author.* vol. 78, 1994

MARY ARIAIL BROUGHTON

FACKLAM, Marjorie (Metz)
Author, b. 6 September 1927, Buffalo, New York

F.'s life experiences shaped her unique talent to create books for young readers that explain science while revealing insights that both entertain and elicit curiosity. As a child she was an avid reader and her experiences with books left her longing to be an explorer. During high school and college she worked at the Buffalo Zoo, which provided insights and future materials for children's books. Her B.A. in biology supported her inquiries into various biological topics as she pursued her love of writing. Her first book was *Whistle for Danger* (1962), a fictionalized story of her experiences working in the reptile house at a zoo. *Frozen Snakes and Dinosaur Bones: Exploring a Natural History Museum* (1976) describes behind-the-scenes happenings in a museum. *Wild Animals, Gentle Women* (1978) focuses on the varied jobs of women whose love of ANIMALS has guided their professional choices. In *Partners for Life: The Mysteries of Animal Symbiosis* (1989) F. explains three types of symbiosis involving various creatures. F.'s work has been acknowledged as well researched and organized, exceptionally readable, and representative of multiple perspectives. *The Big Bug Book* (1994), recipient of national, state, regional, and science related AWARDS, invites readers to explore nature study through facts and unique illustrations of exotic, large insects. *School Library Journal*'s Best Book Selection and a William Allen White Award nomination were given to *And Then There Was One: The Mysteries of Extinction* (1990), which discusses threats to extinction throughout time.

F.'s enthusiasm and investigation of not-so-common aspects of animal life become motivating topics for young readers as F. shares her findings in detailed yet conversational narrative. In *Bees Dance and Whales Sing: The Mysteries of Animal Communication* (1992) various animals and insects are described as using sign and body language, scents, voices, ultrasonic sounds, dances, and other means to communicate. Additionally, other topics, such as bioengineering in *Spare Parts for People* (1987), one of numerous books that she collaborated on with her husband, and *The Trouble with Mothers* (1989), a book about the problem of CENSORSHIP, have been the focus of her writing. Her son, as an illustrator, and daughter, as a coauthor, have also collaborated with F.

AWARDS: ALA Notable Book (1994) and American Booksellers Association Pick of the Lists (1994) both for *The Big Bug Book*. The *Boston Globe*'s 25 Best Nonfiction Books selection (1992) for *Bees Dance and Whales Sing: The Mysteries of Animal Communication*

FURTHER WORKS: *So Can I,* 1987; *Do Not Disturb: The Mysteries of Hibernation and Sleep,* 1989; *Kid's World Almanac of Amazing Facts about Numbers, Math, and Money* (with Margaret Thomas), 1992; *Who Harnessed the Horse?: The Story of Animal Domestication,* 1992; *What Does the Crow Know?: The Mysteries of Animal Intelligence,* 1994; *Viruses,* 1994; *Creepy, Crawly Caterpillars,* 1996

BIBLIOGRAPHY: *Booklist,* August 1986; *Publishers Weekly,* May 19, 1989; *School Library Journal,* January 1988, and September 1990; *Something about the Author,* vol. 85, 1996

JANELLE B. MATHIS

FAIRY TALES

Fairy tales, or wonder tales, are narratives out of the folk tradition, set in an indeterminate past and typically including some enchantment or sense of the wondrous. Fairy tales frequently portray a protagonist, endowed with special gifts, who is put to some test of character that culminates in the triumph of goodness over evil, with tangible rewards heaped upon the victor. Traditionally, the tales are formulaic, beginning with expressions such as "Once upon a time," clearly distancing the events from the present (giving the stories an archetypal quality). Happy endings are the norm. Contrary to popular belief, fairy tales were originally told by adults for adults. Their themes are serious, dealing with such fundamental issues as love, hate, jealousy, revenge, loyalty, and sexual awakening. They certainly are among the world's oldest literature; although they remained alive only in the oral tradition for centuries.

Fairy stories belong to that body of communal literature that helped bind early societies together. These tales spoke to the deep-seated fears, anxieties, hopes, and dreams of primitive peoples, and, in that sense, are akin to the other types of folk narrative myths, legends, *pourquoi* tales, and so on. Their ritualistic nature, identified by familiar plot patterns, stylized language, larger-than-life characters, and overt symbolism, served to reinforce cultural values and mores in preliterate societies. Because of the striking similarities of tales around the world (virtually every society has its Cinderella story), some believe that the tales have a common source in the earliest Mesopotamian civilizations—a theory termed *monogenesis.* Others suggest the tales have developed independently in the various societies and attribute their similarities to people the world over having fundamentally the same psychological needs, a theory termed *polygenesis.*

The truth will remain forever a mystery, but we can attribute the countless variations in the tales to their lengthy existence in the oral tradition. This also contributed to their vitality, for each generation felt free to adapt the tale to current social, psychological, or cultural conditions.

Among the earliest written collections of traditional tales were those from the Orient. From India came the *Panchatantra,* dated sometime around the sixth century C.E. This work influenced the *Gesta Ramanorum,* the most popular medieval European story collection, as well as many later storytellers. The famed *Arabian Nights Entertainments* (also known as the *Thousand and One Nights*), including the stories of Aladdin, Ali Baba, and Sinbad the Sailor, dates from about the eighth century C.E. Many of these stories became staples of children's literature from the eighteenth century on, and the recent Walt DISNEY animated adaptations attest to their continued popularity.

Although Chaucer retold a folk story in "The Wife of Bath's Tale," the earliest extensive recording of European folktales is considered to be the *Pentamerone* (published from 1634 to 1636) by the Italian Giambattista Basile. Here are to be found versions of "Beauty and the Beast," "Cinderella," and "Snow White." The Puritans thought fairy tales to be ungodly and thus began the dispute over the tales that continues in some form to the present day. It was, in fact, in the France of Louis XIV that the fairy tale first gained a measure of respectability, with writers such as Mme. Marie-Cathérine D'AULNOY and, most notably, Charles PERRAULT. Mme. d'Aulnoy's *Contes des fees,* published in English in 1699 as *Tales of the Fairys* [sic], seems to have been written largely for the pleasure of French aristocratic ladies. Perrault's *Histoires ou Contes du Temps Passé* (1697), called in a subsequent edition *Contes de Ma Mere l'Oye* or *Tales of MOTHER GOOSE,* contained eight stories and, when introduced into England, began the vogue of fairy tales for children. In the middle of the eighteenth century, still another French woman, Mme. Marie Leprince de Beaumont, writing in England, published a version of "Beauty and the Beast," which soon became a favorite tale of adults and children alike. But it was also at this time that the followers of John Locke and Jacques Rousseau joined the Puritans in their campaign against fairy tales for children because they encouraged superstition and did not contain suitable moral lessons. The didactic writers such as Mrs. Anna Laetitia Barbauld and Mrs. Sarah Kirby TRIMMER, who indignantly attacked the fairy tales, seemed to prevail at the end of the eighteenth century.

But in the beginning of the nineteenth century, German Brothers GRIMM, Jacob and Wilhelm, began their celebrated career as students of folk literature. Their *Kinder und Hausmärchen* (Nursery and household tales), first appeared in 1812 and grew in size with each successive edition, until over 200 European tales eventually were included. The Grimms have been credited with establishing the scientific study of folk literature, and they inspired collectors throughout Europe

who began to assemble the traditional tales of their native lands, most notably ASBJORNSEN and MOE in Norway, Hans Christian ANDERSEN in Denmark, and Andrew LANG in Britain.

The Puritan disdain for fairy stories did little to squelch their popularity. But fairy tales still have their detractors who believe that the stories are potentially harmful to children. Certainly, many of the eighteenth- and nineteenth-century versions—including those specifically assembled for children—contain considerable violence and implied, if not overt, sexuality. Many well-meaning adaptors in the twentieth century sought to bowdlerize the tales, removing what they perceived to be objectionable material. Some critics point to the blatant sexism found in many tales as well as to the celebration of material wealth, the hostility toward stepparents and stepsiblings, the discrimination against the ugly and deformed—all of which have their roots in an earlier cultural tradition. Although the adaptation of fairy tales is actually consistent with their normal historical development, many purists believe these sanitized adaptations destroy the power of the tales, making them both less interesting and meaningful for young audiences. They point out that scant evidence has been produced to show that the stories negatively impact young children, and some researchers, notably Bruno Bettelheim, have argued that the tales, in their earlier forms, at least, significantly aid children in their healthy social and psychological development.

The children themselves have the good sense to ignore the dictums of the pundits and simply turn to the tales for enjoyment—clinging to those that speak to their individual needs and discarding the rest. Certainly from a purely aesthetic point of view, the tales contribute to children's understanding of plot and character development, symbolism, and thematic concepts in literature. The generally fast-paced action, the clearly defined characters, the sharp contrast between good and evil, and the triumph of good in the end all help to explain why children continue to cherish these stories, despite the occasional fears and misgivings of adults. And no one can deny the extraordinary influence that the traditional tales have had on our cultural imagination, for scarcely a book, film, or play exists that does not have its roots in fairy tales of old.

BIBLIOGRAPHY: Bettelheim, Bruno, *The Uses of Enchantment: The Meaning and Importance of Fairy Tales,* 1976; Lüthi, Max, *Once upon a Time: On the Nature of Fairy Tales,* 1976; Thompson, Stith, *The Folktale,* 1951; Warner, Marina, *From the Beast to the Blonde: On Fairy Tales and Their Tellers,* 1994; Zipes, Jack, *Breaking the Magic Spell: Radical Theories of Folk and Fairy Tales,* 1979; *When Dreams Came True: Classical Fairy Tales and Their Tradition,* 1999

DAVID L. RUSSELL

(See also FOLKLORE)

FAMILY STORIES

Stories in which the action and interactions center around the family comprise a significant part of the body of children's literature. Because few families live in isolation, family stories also include relationships and activities with friends and the larger community. Family stories often appeal to children who want to read about children like themselves and events with which they can identify. They can also help children to walk in the shoes of someone whose time, ethnicity, or family situation is different from their own while still experiencing the commonalities of the human experience.

Most characters in children's books are part of a family, but in some books, the home is merely a starting place. In these journey-from-home plots, the focus is often on adventure and action. Family stories, on the other hand, are often quieter stories with an emphasis on relationships and ordinary events.

The early novels often showed strong, happy families who met challenges with courage and love. *Little Women* (1868) served as a prototype for many of the family stories that followed. Meg, Jo, Beth, and Amy invent their own entertainment, deal creativity with poverty, help families in need, cope with sickness and death, and find romance and happiness in families of their own. Laura Ingalls WILDER's *Little House in the Big Woods* (1932) is full of cozy word picture. At night, the lonely winds blow, but inside Laura and Mary are tucked into their trundle beds; Ma knits in the rocking chair; and Pa sings old songs with the firelight glistening on his honey-brown fiddle. In *Caddie Woodlawn* (BRINK, 1935) a lively pioneer girl and her brothers make their own adventures in the Wisconsin woods. In *The Moffits* (ESTES, 1941) the four siblings have simple adventures and misadventures in their Connecticut town. The sisters in Mildred TAYLOR's *All-of-a-Kind Family* (1951) maintain their Jewish traditions and holiday celebrations on New York's Lower East Side.

A few happy, supportive families continued to be seen in contemporary novels, many of which have sequels: Beverly CLEARY's *Ramona the Pest* (1968), Lois LOWRY's *Anastasia Krupnik* (1985), Patricia MACLACHLAN's *Sarah, Plain and Tall* (1985), and Phyllis Reynold NAYLOR's *Shiloh* (1991). Beginning in the 1960s, however, fewer stories with wise, supportive parents appeared. The "new realism" often depicted parents as a major source of children's problems. In *Harriet the Spy* (Louise FITZHUGH, 1964) Harriet, largely ignored by her wealthy, socialite parents, turns to journal writing where she makes caustic observations of nearly everyone. In Katherine PATERSON's *Bridge to Terabithia* (1977), Jess feels alienated from his father who doesn't understand his imaginative, artistic personality. In DANZIGER's *Divorce Express* (1982), Phoebe's life is drastically altered with joint custody arrangements and her parents' new romances. The boy in Paula FOX's *Monkey Island* (1991) lives with his mother in a hotel room until she leaves and never returns. In *Catherine Called Birdy* (Karen CUSHMAN, 1994) a medieval-era young woman keeps a diary lamenting her mother's desire to keep her docile and her father's desire to marry her off to a rich dolt.

The children in unhappy families find a variety of ways to cope. Lauren in Paula Danziger's *Can You Sue Your Parents for Malpractice?* (1979), decides that there is nothing she can do to change her obviously incompetent parents and the best she can do is make sure she does not commit malpractice on herself. In Cynthia VOIGT's *Homecoming* (1991), children abandoned by their mother seek a new home with a grandmother whom they have never known. In Judy BLUME's *Just as Long as We're Together* (1987) Stephanie's parents separate leaving the future of her family life uncertain, but Stephanie feels she can cope as long as her friends are loyal and together.

More recently in children's literature, some of the children of unhappy families have gone beyond coping to coming to understand the problems and motivations of their parents. Brann, in Voigt's *Building Blocks* (1984), comes to understand his silent, passive father by magically visiting the past and meeting his father as a boy. Samantha, in *Walk Two Moons* (Sharon CREECH, 1994), travels with her grandparents following the route taken earlier by her mother. The trip gives Samantha the opportunity to walk in her mother's shoes and come to gradually understand why her mother left home. Billie Joe, in Karen HESSE's *Out of the Dust* (1997), sees the barrenness of the Oklahoma Dust Bowl reflected in her father and the emotional life of the family. The blank verse narration shows her growing awareness of her father's losses and a hope for growth in the future. White's *Belle Prater's Boy* (1996) is a layered story in which cousins, Gypsy and Woodrow, gradually learn of the life struggles that eventually led to the father of one committing suicide and the mother of the other abandoning her family.

Although today's stories more consciously reflect the variety in contemporary family structures, book characters have long had a disproportionate amount of children in nontraditional families. Cinderella lived with a stepmother and stepsisters. Tom Sawyer lived with Aunt Polly and Huck Finn lived on his own, largely ignored by his alcoholic father. Anne of Green Gables is an orphan taken in by an unmarried middle-aged woman and her bachelor farmer brother. Heidi is an orphan taken to live with her grandfather who lives the life of a hermit in a Swiss mountain hut. Orphan stories sometimes provided a plausible way for children to have journey-from-home challenges and adventures that would not be offered a child whose parents provide a safe, protected atmosphere. Bud, Not Buddy (Christopher Paul CURTIS) the 2000 NEWBERY MEDAL title takes an 11-year-old orphan on an episodic journey to find his father during the Great Depression. Bud has only his own inner resources and a note from his mother to sustain him. Other orphan stories show orphans finding love, acceptance, and affirmation in being chosen into new families, a type of story which has parallels with the romance genre.

Families in children's books have become more racially and ethnically diverse in the past decades. Although happy families with wise, supportive parents are in short supply in novels with European-American characters, they are very much in evidence in books focusing on families of color. In some, strong families stand against an unjust society. In Mildred TAYLOR's *Roll of Thunder, Hear My Cry* (1976), the Logan children of rural Mississippi experience the humiliations and tragedies caused by racism in rural Mississippi of the 1930s. The family in *The Watsons Go to Birmingham—1963* (Curtis, 1995) experience the tragedy of the Klansman's bombing of a church were four children were killed. Uchida YOSHIKO's *Journey to Topaz* (1971) tells the story of a Japanese-American family's internment in a desert-relocation camp during World War II.

Other novels and PICTURE BOOKS reflecting America's ethnic groups focus on interactions within the family and more ordinary events. In Faith RINGGOLD's *Tar Beach* (1991), the family enjoys a hot summer evening on the roof of their apartment building having a picnic and lying on blankets looking at the sky and city landscape while dreaming of better times. A new immigrant boy from China in *Yang the Youngest and His Terrible Ear* (NAMIOKA, 1994) wants to play baseball instead of participating in the family musical string quartet. A girl, her mother, and grandmother save for a new, comfortable chair after their belongings are burned in a fire in *A Chair for My Mother* (WILLIAMS, 1982). A nonfiction account, *The Sacred Harvest: Ojibway Wild Rice Gathering* (Regguinti, 1992) depicts contemporary Ojibway children playing video games and learning the traditional ways of harvesting wild rice. Garza's folk-style paintings in *Family Pictures/Cuadros de Familia* (1990) help tell the traditions of a Mexican-American family.

Grandparents and relatives help connect children to their ancestry and extended families and are generally seen in a positive light in children's books. *Nana Upstairs, Nana Downstairs* (DE-PAOLA, 1973) depicts fond memories of Tommie's visits to his Italian grandmother and great-grandmother. A family reunion is a joyous, lively occasion in Cynthia RYLANT's *The Relatives Came* (1985). A grandmother passes on the quilting tradition and captures family memories in *The Patchwork Quilt* (FLOURNOY, 1985). Children learn about events in American and family history as an aunt shows her hats worn for a variety of occasions in *Aunt Flossie Hats (and Crab Cakes Later)* by Elizabeth Fitzgerald Howard (1991). A mother and grandmother give Grace the courage to go after her goals in *Amazing Grace* (HOFFMAN, 1991). Allen SAY tells the story of his grandfather's immigrant experience in *Grandfather's Journey* (1993). A brother and sister can never predict what will happen on their annual trip to visit their extraordinary grandmother in the 1999 NEWBERY MEDAL Honor Book *A Long Way from Chicago* (PECK, 1998).

Family stories are also found in picture books with animal characters. Some have realistic animal characters such as Robert MCCLOSKEY's enduring *Make Way for Ducklings* (1941). Most, however, show animal families with very human problems. *Julius, Baby of the World* (HENKES, 1990) shows Lily coming to terms with a new baby in the family. *Koala Lou* (FOX, 1988) comes to realize that her mother's love is not dependent on her achievement. Parents encourage Francis to settle down for sleep in *Bedtime for Francis* (HOBAN, 1969). Sylvester's family finds they do not need any magic or wishes as long as they are together in *Sylvester and the Magic Pebble* (STEIG, 1969).

Family stories are as varied as families in life, reflecting both our changing society and the universal joys and struggles in family life.

ADELE GREENLEE

FANTASY

All fiction invents the truth; fantasy, a special case of fiction, breaks one or more of the rules that govern "real" life as we ordinarily define it and so invents an altered reality that must be true to rules of its own. Paradoxically, although we know fantasy to be other than real, its chief requirement is credibility. This calls for a special attitude on the reader's part, one that Samuel Taylor Coleridge termed the "willing suspension of disbelief." Yet the real burden for belief rests with the author, who may use many different techniques to engage and convince the reader. Some fantasies, like Philippa PEARCE's *Tom's Midnight Garden* (1958), ground the reader in the familiar, known world before introducing elements that test belief. Meticulous description and

detail bring plausibility to Mary NORTON's tiny characters in *The Borrowers* (1951) and to Sylvia Waugh's life-size rag dolls in *The Mennyms* (1993). A protagonist who at first doubts his own fantastic circumstances provides a point of identification for skeptical readers in stories like Mollie HUNTER's *A Stranger Came Ashore* (1975). Still, some stories plunge their readers into the unknown from the very first sentence, demonstrating Ursula K. LE GUIN's argument that fantasy is "essentially dependent on its language." For in the end, it is the beguiling voice of the storyteller and the unaccountable power of well-chosen words that finally permit the reader's entry into what J. R. R. TOLKIEN called the Secondary World of the story. This focus on language may be one of the reasons why so many books of fantasy have achieved the status of classics in children's literature. Older novels like *Alice in Wonderland* (Lewis CARROLL, 1865) as well as more recent ones like Natalie BABBITT's *Tuck Everlasting* (1975) are read for their masterful prose as well as their enchanting stories.

The origins of fantasy for children are rooted firmly in our oldest stories—in myth, legend, and FOLKLORE. Motifs, characters, and entire plots borrowed from traditional literature grace the pages of many fantasy books today. Lloyd ALEXANDER's *The Iron Ring* (1997) is based in part on the *Ramayana* of India; Brian JACQUES's Redwall series rests on tales of chivalry and adventure from BRITAIN and Europe; Virginia HAMILTON calls up AFRICAN themes and AFRICAN AMERICAN folk heroes in *The Magical Adventures of Pretty Pearl* (1983). Fantasy is valued for the link that it provides to stories of the past, an idea embedded in Jane YOLEN's admonition to "Touch magic, and pass it on."

While fantasy appears in many forms of children's literature (picture books by Maurice SENDAK and poetry by Nancy WILLARD are prime examples), those works most often discussed as fantasy have been published as stories or novels. Some scholars date the rise of modern fantasy from the first half of the nineteenth century, when Hans Christian ANDERSEN used elements of traditional stories in authoring literary tales such as "The Ugly Duckling" and "The Steadfast Tin Soldier." Others find a beginning point in Lewis Carroll's remarkable production some decades later of *Alice's Adventures in Wonderland* and *Through the Looking Glass* (1872), books so full of sly humor and soaring flights of fancy that they set a standard against which some stories are still measured.

The production of memorable fantasies from British authors continued through the late nineteenth and early twentieth centuries with such notable books as *At the Back of the North Wind* (1871), a melancholy and mystical tale by George MACDONALD; *Just So Stories for Little Children* (1902) of Rudyard KIPLING, with their rich language and cunning adaptation of the *pourquoi* folklore tradition; and Kenneth GRAHAME's lyrical *The Wind in the Willows* (1908). Unique characters are another hallmark of lasting fantasies: J. M. BARRIE's *Peter Pan* (1904) is remembered for his desire to be forever a boy; A. A. MILNE's *Winnie the Pooh* (1926) and his toy-animal friends have distinct personalities; P. L. TRAVERS's *Mary Poppins* (1934) possesses magic that lies not so much in her umbrella-powered flight as in her ability to solve all the problems of the nursery. Among the contributions of U.S. writers are an observant traveling doll in Rachel FIELD's *Hitty, Her First Hundred Years* (1929); the Tinman and Cowardly Lion of L. Frank BAUM's *The Wizard of Oz* (1900); and a number of articulate animals, most notably E. B. WHITE's *Stuart Little* (1945) and his wise spider in *Charlotte's Web* (1952).

The term *fantasy* continues to comprise many kinds of stories, variously featuring talking animals, sentient toys, ghosts, magical powers, time travel, and lands of make-believe. In the past half century, however, there has been a growing emphasis on stories of mythic proportions, with the term high fantasy often used for novels with serious, far-reaching themes and grand-scale plots that spill over into several volumes. An early example is J. R. R. TOLKIEN's *The Hobbit* (1937), a novel with stirring adventure, thematic complexity, and a fully realized setting that draws on mythic and legendary sources to evoke a believable world. Many readers find allegorical meanings in C. S. LEWIS's *The Lion, the Witch, and the Wardrobe* (1950) with its six sequels, which constitute the Chronicles of Narnia. Madeleine L'ENGLE's *A Wrinkle in Time* (1962) begins a

sequence of stories that explore connections between philosophy and science. Lloyd ALEXANDER's comic touches engage readers in the heroic Prydain Chronicles, from *The Book of Three* (1964) to *The High King* (1969). In Susan COOPER's *The Dark Is Rising* (1973) and its companion books, a large cast of characters are involved in classic struggles between good and evil. Ursula LE GUIN creates an entire geography and a variety of cultures for her story of a proud boy destined to become Archmage in *A Wizard of Earthsea* (1968) and the books that follow.

Regardless of the way a fantasy might be classified, its themes are likely to reflect real-world issues of the time in which it is written. Not surprisingly, more recent fantasy novels by such authors as Robin MCKINLEY and Patricia Wrede present strong female characters and offer implied or explicit commentary on gender roles. Concerns about the environment and caveats to save the planet are reflected in novels by T. A. BARRON and others. Multiple contemporary issues are explored in the elaborate alternate worlds of Philip PULLMAN's Golden Compass trilogy. In general, fantasy has more power to invent such alternatives than do other kinds of fiction. It is this visionary aspect of fantasy, its power to tweak and nurture the imagination, that is most often mentioned as its chief contribution to readers of all ages.

BIBLIOGRAPHY: Le Guin, U. K., *Steering the Craft,* 1998; Tolkien, J. R. R., "Children and Fairy Stories," in *Tree and Leaf,* 1964; Yolen, J., *Touch Magic,* 1981

JANET HICKMAN

FARJEON, Eleanor

Author, b. 13 February 1881, London, England; d. 5 June 1965, Place unknown

Having grown up amidst the 8,000 books in her father's library, it was only natural that F. continue her love of books by becoming an author herself. As a child she read many sophisticated literary works and began to create original verse. Her family also attended the theater frequently as well as experiencing theatrical influences from her mother and maternal grandfather, the American actor Joseph Jefferson. The four children in her family were creative with imaginative activities filling their nursery life. Influenced by her father's idea that Christmas should be the most glorious of celebrations, F. created *Come Christmas* (1927), which contained some of the most descriptive Christmas poems in children's literature. F. explored various writing forms, but her more than seventy years of writing is most acknowledged for her children's verse, plays, and FANTASY works. *Nursery Rhymes of London Town* (1916) and *Martin Pippin in the Apple Orchard* (1921) began F.'s prolific career. *Martin Pippin,* a fantasy story, was originally written for adults, but its popularity among young girls made it one of her best known works.

F. has been described as the poet who never forgot what it is like to be a child. The liveliness of childhood—dancing, playing, discovering—is found in her POETRY. Rather than observe children, she seemed to describe only what she has always known naturally. Children predominate in much of her writing, which is characterized by a wide variety of verse patterns, winsome use of words, and a child's celebratory joy and love of nature.

AWARDS: F. was the first recipient of the Hans Christian ANDERSEN Award (1956) for *The Little Bookroom.* Library Association of England CARNEGIE MEDAL (1956) for *The Little Bookroom.* F. was awarded the first Regina Medal of Catholic Library Association (1959) made yearly for one's lifetime distinguished dedication to children's literature

FURTHER WORKS: *Singing Games for Children.* 1918. *Gypsy and Ginger.* 1920. *Young Folk and Old.* 1925. *Nuts anu May, a Medley for Children.* 1926. *The Perfect Zoo.* 1929. *Mills of Dreams.* 1930. *King's Barn.* 1930. *Ameliaranne and the Magic Ring.* 1933. *The Old Sailor's Yarn Box.* 1934. *Jim and the Pirates.* 1936. *Granny Gray.* 1939. *Miss Granby's Secret.* 1940. *Dark World of Animals.* 1945. *Poems for Children.* 1951. *The Silver Curlew.* 1953. *Then There Were Three: Being Cherrystones, The Mulberry Bush, The Starry Floor.* 1958. *The Hamish Hamilton Book of Kings.* 1964. *The Hamish Hamilton Book of Queens.* 1965. *The Wonderful Knight.* 1967. *Around the Seasons.* 1969

BIBLIOGRAPHY: McCord, David, "Eleanor F.'s 'Poems for Children,' " the *Horn Book* magazine, 60, 5, pp. 618–20; MEIGS, C. et al., *A Critical History of English Literature,* 1969

JANELLE B. MATHIS

FARLEY, Walter
Author, b. 26 June 1920, Syracuse, New York; d. 10 October 1989, Venice, Florida

Living as he encourages children to do, F. developed his writing abilities and focused on what he loved as an occupation. As a child, F. took advantage of what New York City offered—tennis, skating, and horseback riding and related activities such as polo and racing. Friends' stables in Flushing, New York, where he later lived, provided the setting for *The Black Stallion* (1941) as he explored trails on horseback. At the time his love of horses was unfolding, F.'s desire to write was seen in the numerous stories he created as a teenager. Aware of the lack of stories for horse lovers like himself, F. became Alec, the central character in *The Black Stallion,* as he created this novel that was completed while in a college English class. During his army service in World War II, F. continued to write. When discharged he traveled widely. He also bought a farm in Pennsylvania where he could continue to live with his love of horses through raising and writing about them. His understanding of this majestic animal created a basis for his many stories that are recognized as unique by young readers.

Evidence that he attained success as a novelist is seen in the fact that over 12 million of his books have been sold in sixteen countries. F. treasured the response of children from all over the world in the form of their millions of letters. *The Black Stallion* and *The Black Stallion Returns* (1945) were later made into movies—in 1979 and 1983. Besides entertaining generations of readers with the Black Stallion SERIES, F. provides an example of a writer who authentically lived his dream and shared it with others. F.'s letters to his editor written while creating his novels reveals the ownership and insight that goes into successful writing.

In 1944, F. was awarded the Pacific Northwest Library Association's Young Reader's Choice Award for *The Black Stallion* and in 1948 for *The Black Stallion Returns,* which also was awarded the Boys Club Junior Book Award. Special collections at Columbia University, New York City, house Farley's manuscripts and papers.

FURTHER WORKS: *Larry and the Underseas Raider.* 1942. *Son of the Black Stallion.* 1947. *The Black Stallion and Satan.* 1949. *The Island Stallion's Fury.* 1951. *The Black Stallion Revolts.* 1953. *The Black Stallion's Courage.* 1956. *The Black Stallion's Mystery.* 1957. *The Horse-tamer.* 1959. *Man o' War.* 1962. *The Horse That Swam Away.* 1965. *The Great Dane, Thor.* 1966. *The Black Stallion's Ghost.* 1969. *The Black Stallion Legend.* 1983

BIBLIOGRAPHY: HOPKINS, Lee Bennett, *Pauses: Autobiographical References of 101 Creators of Children's Books,* 1995; *Something about the Author,* vol. 93, 1996

JANELLE B. MATHIS

FARMER, Nancy
Author, storyteller, b. 9 July 1941, Phoenix, Arizona

F. grew up surrounded by STORYTELLERS. She met her husband in Africa, where she also encountered many of the characters, the viewpoints, and the humor that eventually inspired her writing. F. wrote her first book in three hours, then wrote another the next day. Many of her stories, whether REALISTIC FICTION or FANTASIES, are set in Zimbabwe, Africa, and relate the customs and culture found there. *Do You Know Me* (1993), a collection of ten short stories attempting to bridge old tribal ways and modern urban life, includes a glossary of African vocabulary. Several of F.'s books—e.g., *The Ear, the Eye, and the Arm: A Novel* (1994), also set in Africa—is a SCIENCE FICTION story based on political intrigue in the twenty-second century.

AWARDS: ALA NEWBERY MEDAL Honor Book (1995) for *The Ear, the Eye and the Arm: A Novel*

FURTHER WORKS: *Lorelei,* 1987; *Tapiwa's Uncle,* 1993; *The Warm Place,* 1995; *Girl Named Disaster,* 1996; *Runnery Granary,* 1996; *Casey Jones's Fireman: The Story of Sim Webb,* 1998

BIBLIOGRAPHY: *Something about the Author,* vol. 80, 1995

JODI PILGRIM

FARMER, Penelope
Author, b. 14 June 1939, Westerham, Kent, England

F. says that she does not sit down and intentionally write books for children. She simply writes and lets the publishers decide who the best audience for her FANTASIES should be. Many of her books are set in the area of England where she grew up. Some of her characters are based on real people that have been a part of her life, such as Charlotte and Emma, characters in *The Summer Birds* (1962). Her time travel fantasies—*Charlotte Sometimes* (1969) and *A Castle of Bone* (1972)—allow contemporary children to travel backward through time and relive history in imaginative settings while discovering psychological insights about themselves and others. Although F. reports that the life of a writer can be a lonely one, she finds that her other interests of traveling and cinema, to name a few, keep her from complete isolation.

FURTHER WORKS: *Emma in Winter,* 1966; *Seagull,* 1966; *The Runway Train; August the Fourth* (1975). *Daedalus and Icarus,* 1971; *Beginnings: Creation Myths of the World,* 1978; *Standing in the Shadow,* 1984; *Eve, Her Story.* 1988. *Away from Home: A Novel in Ten Episodes.* 1987. *Thicker Than Water.* 1993; *Snakes and Ladders,* 1993; *Penelope.* 1996; *Sisters,* 1999

BIBLIOGRAPHY: *Something about the Author,* vol. 105, 1999

MICHAEL O'LAUGHLIN

FATIO, Louise
Author, b. 18 August 1904, Lausanne, Switzerland

F. began to write children's books after her marriage to Roger DUVOISIN, an award-winning author and illustrator, with whom she collaborated until his death in 1980. The couple created many animal characters, including Veronica, Petunia, Donkey-Donkey, and Hector-Penguin. F. is best known for her Happy Lion series, which was inspired by the true story of a friendly, well-fed lion who had escaped from a circus. Like the *Happy Lion,* most of F.'s stories feature animals as characters who represent various kinds of people.

FURTHER WORKS: *The Happy Lion.* 1954. *The Happy Lion in Africa.* 1955. *A Doll for Maria.* 1957. *The Happy Lion's Treasure.* 1971. *Hector Penguin.* 1973. *Hector and Christina.* 1977. *The Happy Lioness.* 1980

BIBLIOGRAPHY: *Major Authors and Illustrators for Children and Young Adults.* 1993. *Something about the Author,* vol. 6, 1974

MARY ARIAIL BROUGHTON

FEELINGS, Tom
Author, illustrator, b. 19 May 1933

Drawing from his own experiences in both the United States and Africa, F. strives to create IL-LUSTRATIONS that convey the complexity of AFRICAN AMERICAN heritage. As a young artist drawing the faces of people in his New York community, F. realized that dark, somber moods characterized his portraits of adults while children's portraits reflected joy. This led to a trip to Ghana where he sought to discover more about the spirit of his people and to find within his art a balance of both the sorrow and joy of their life experiences. F. collaborated with Muriel Grey Feelings, on several books to introduce AFRICAN language and culture. *Zamani Goes to Market* (1970) describes a day in the life of a young East African boy. *Moja Means One* (1971) uses soft, simple illustrations to portray realistically cultural and geographical details of life in Africa while learning to count in Swahili. *Jambo Means Hello* (1974) introduces readers to Swahili through its alphabet format. This book celebrates life and reflects F.'s personal vision of Africa through its illustrations.

F.'s artistry celebrates the strength, beauty, creativity, and endurance of the African American heritage. This is evident in the powerful illustrations and POETRY in *Soul Looks Back in Wonder* (1993). F. also created a book to help readers sense the horror, depravity, and greed of the tragic journey of enslaved Africans across the Atlantic in *The Middle Passage* (1995). This book contains sixty-four narrative paintings in contrasting tones of black and white to tempera, and reflects the triumph of spirit and beauty despite evil circumstances.

AWARDS: ALA CALDECOTT MEDAL Honor Book (1972) for *Moja Means One: Swahili Counting Book,* and (1975) for *Jambo Means Hello.* ALA NEWBERY MEDAL Honor Book (1969) for *To Be a Slave* (Julius LESTER, author). *Horn Book* magazine Honor list (1972) for *Black Pilgrimage. Horn Book-Boston Globe* Award for Illustration (1974) for *Jambo Means Hello* (Muriel Feelings, author). Children's Book Showcase award (1977) for *From Slave to Abolitionist.* CORETTA SCOTT KING Illustrator AWARD (1979) for *Something on My Mind* (Nikki GRIMES, author), (1994) for *Soul Looks Back in Wonder,* and (1996) for *The Mid-dle Passage.* ALA CORETTA SCOTT KING Illustrator Honor Award (1982) for *Daydreamers* (Eloise GREENFIELD, author). AMERICAN LIBRARY ASSOCIATION Notable Book (1972) for *Black Pilgrimage,* (1979) for *Something on My Mind,* and (1982) for *Daydreamers*

FURTHER WORKS: *Tommy Traveler in the World of Black History.* 1991. *Black Pilgrimage.* 1972. *Tales of Temba: Traditional African Stories.* (Kathleen Artno). 1969. *Swahili Alphabet Book.* (Muriel Feelings). 1974. As Illustrator: *Black Folktales.* (Julius Lester). 1969. *From Slave to Abolitionist: The Life of William Wells Brown.* (Lucille Schulberg Warner). 1976. *Black Child.* (Joyce Carol THOMAS). 1981. *Now Sheba Sings the Song.* (Maya ANGELOU). 1987

BIBLIOGRAPHY: Bishop, Rudine S. "Tom Feelings and *The Middle Passage.*" In *The Horn Book* magazine, vol. 72, no. 4, 1996. Feelings, Tom. "The Artist at Work: Technique and the Artist's Vision." in *The Horn Book* magazine, vol. 61, no. 6, 1985. HOPKINS, Lee Bennett, *Pauses: Autobiographical Reflections of 101 Creators of Children's Books,* 1995

JANELLE B. MATHIS

FENNER, Carol
Author, illustrator, b. 30 September 1929, Almond, New York

F., author of stories for elementary and upper elementary readers, spent her childhood traveling between Brooklyn, New York, and rural Connecticut. F. remembers the pleasure she felt listening to stories told by her aunt, author Phyllis Fenner, and how she was determined to write her own stories. F. uses her childhood experiences and people she knows as fodder for her books about relationships, families under stress, struggles, and success. Her book, *The Skates of Uncle Richard* (1978) tells the universal story of how hard work and determination make Marsha's dream come true when Uncle Richard gives her his old hockey skates. The book was released on videocassette by Children's Television International in 1979. It received the Christopher Medal Library of Congress Book of the Year and the Outstanding Science Trade Book.

AWARDS: CORETTA SCOTT KING Honor AWARD (1979) for *The Skates of Uncle Richard.* ALA NEWBERY MEDAL Honor Book (1996) for *Yolanda's Genius.* Christopher Award (1974) for *Gorilla, Gorilla*

FURTHER WORKS: *Tigers In the Cellar,* 1963; *Christmas Tree on the Mountain,* 1966; *Gorilla, Gorilla* (illus. by Symeon Shimiu), 1973; *Yolanda's Genius,* 1995; *Saving Amelia Earhart; A Summer of Horses,* 1989; *Randall's Wall,* 1991; *The King of Dragons,* 1998

BIBLIOGRAPHY: Smith, H. ed. *The Coretta Scott King Awards Book,* 1990; *Something about the Author.* vol. 90, 1997

MICHAEL O'LAUGHLIN

FIELD, Eugene

Author, b. 3 September 1850, St. Louis, Missouri; d. 4 November 1895, Chicago, Illinois

F. attended Williams College and the University of Missouri before becoming a journalist in Kansas City, Chicago, and Denver. Although a writer of children's novels and BIOGRAPHIES as well, F. is best known for his POETRY. Called the "poet of childhood" his *Poems of Childhood* (1904) and *With Trumpet and Drum* (1892) contained the now classic poems "Little Boy Blue," "Wynken, Blynken, and Nod," and "The Gingham Dog and the Calico Cat." F.'s poems still appear frequently in children's anthologies. He continued working as a literary journalist and editor until his death.

FURTHER WORKS: *The Gingham Dog and the Calico Cat.* (Janet Street, illus), 1990. *Love-Songs of Childhood.* 1894. *The Stars: A Slumber Story.* 1901. *A Little Book of Western Verse.* 1889. *With Trumpet and Drum.* 1892

BIBLIOGRAPHY: Dennis, C. H. *Eugene Field's Creative Year.* 1924. *Major Authors and Illustrators for Children and Young Adults.* 1993. Ward, M. E., D. A. Marquardt, N. Dolan, and D. Eaton. *Authors of Books for Young People.* 1990

GWYNNE ELLEN ASH

FIELD, Rachel (Lyman)

Author, b. 19 September 1894, New York City; d. 15 March 1942, Beverly Hills, California

As a child in Western Massachusetts, F.'s interests in books, POETRY, writing, and theater formed images and impressions from which she created stories, poems, and plays for children. Delighting in the childhood worlds she saw as pointed trees, toadstools, children, and patchwork quilts, she also remembered the importance of islands to her imagination. F. wrote before she read

since she would rather listen to her mother read "real" books than read "infantile" books. This memory is reflected in her writing; she carefully selected interesting vocabulary for children's books that would not lose the spirit of the story. She did not write down to young readers. F. realized that she had a vivid memory for descriptive details; she was known as a master of detail in her writings for children and adults.

F.'s most well-known book is *Hitty, Her First Hundred Years* (1929) for which she received the NEWBERY MEDAL. F. shared the story of discovering Hitty, purchasing a one hundred year old doll, and collaborated with illustrator Dorothy P. LATHROP in creating *Hitty, Her First Hundred Years.* Hitty maintained her amiable character and fixed features while the story evolved around her many experiences. F.'s expertise and love of history helped her tell about people, places, and adventure that brought one hundred years of change to America. One critic called *Hitty* a true juvenile classic written in America. In 1999, Rosemary WELLS and Susan JEFFERS gave Hitty new life with a full-color adaptation and brief fast-paced chapters.

A prolific writer for children, F. was known for her success in creating magical moods and understanding perspectives of childhood. She was able to recreate childhood experiences with a belief in the universal nature of childhood. Her artistic integrity as a writer was always appropriate despite the subject or theme.

F. is perhaps best known in the world of adult literature, as the author of *All This, and Heaven Too* (1938). This national best-seller was a fictional account of her great aunt who, before marrying Reverend Henry Field, was "Mademoiselle D." of Paris, the central figure in a famous murder case. It was adapted in 1940 as a movie starring Bette Davis and Charles Boyer.

AWARDS: Drama League of America prize (1918) for *Rise Up, Jennie Smith* (one-act play for children). ALA NEWBERY MEDAL (1928) for *Hitty: Her First Hundred Years* (the first awarded to a woman). AMERICAN LIBRARY ASSOCIATION Newbery Medal Honor Book (1932) for *Calico Bush.* ALA CALDECOTT MEDAL (1945) for *Prayer for a Child* (Elizabeth Orton JONES, illus)

FURTHER WORKS FOR CHILDREN: *Calico Bush.* 1913. *An Alphabet for Boys and Girls.* 1926. *The*

Magic Pawnshop: A New Year's Eve Fantasy.
1927. *The White Cat and Other French Fairy
Tales.* 1928. *American Folk and Fairy Tales.*
1929. *The Yellow Shop.* 1931. *Hepatica Hawks.*
1932. *God's Pocket: The Story of Captain Samuel
Hadlock, Junior, of Cranberry Isles, Maine.* 1934.
Ave Maria: An Interpretation from Walt DISNEY'*s
"Fantasia."* 1940. *Prayer for a Child.* 1944

BIBLIOGRAPHY: *Something about the Author,* vol.
15, 1979

JANELLE B. MATHIS

FINE, Anne

Author, b. 7 December 1947, Leicester, England

F. grew up in a family of five girls that included
triplets and is intrigued with family relationships.
Her books for primary and middle-grade readers,
as well as those for young adults, heartily reflect
this interest. F. creates insightful descriptions of
family life through unforgettable eccentric characters involved in universal problems and unique
twists of plot. F.'s love of reading and writing
began when she was young. She exhausted the
reading materials in her school and continued exploring her imaginative insights through her own
stories. Her first serious efforts at writing occurred when she had completed college and was
housebound with an infant. Writing flowed for
her at this point as she wrote *The Summer-House
Loon* (1978). As in many of her subsequent
books, this story involves an adolescent with peculiar family circumstances. Often these circumstances require tolerance, acceptance of change
as in divorce, respect for the elderly, or for differences. Frequently, personal growth is a direct result as both family issues and topics of societal
concern are explored with humor and sensitivity.

Besides being recognized for humorously describing plots of family life and creating eccentric
characters, F.'s writing skills lie in her vigorous
prose style, lively dialogue, and a wide range of
HUMOR. As evident in *Alias Madame Doubtfire*
(1988), which was made into the film *Mrs.
Doubtfire* (1993), starring Robin Williams, the
story of a divorced father who disguises himself
as a nanny to be able to see his children regularly,
F. does not ignore the pain of the family problem
for any of her characters. She uses wit and irony
to share triumph over the chaos and confusion of
life's situations. To be able to see the humor in
relationships, especially humor that does not be-
little a sensitive situation is evident in many of

F.'s books. *Step by Wicked Step* (1996) relates the
stories told by five children after they read a Victorian boy's diary telling of his cruel stepfather.
Again F. creates voices and attitudes that humanize the situation for readers.

AWARDS: CARNEGIE MEDAL (1989) for *Goggle
Eyes,* and (1992) for *Flour Babies*. British Book
Awards Children's Author of the Year award
(1990) and (1993). Guardian Award (1990) for
Goggle Eyes. Whitbread Books of the Year
(1993) for *Flour Babies*

FURTHER WORKS: *The Stone Menagerie.* 1980.
The Granny Project. 1983. *Bill's New Frock.*
1989. *A Sudden Puff of Glittering Smoke.* 1989.
The Country Pancake. 1990. *Poor Monty.* 1992.
The Tulip Touch: A Novel. 1997

BIBLIOGRAPHY: *Something about the Author,* vol.
111, 2000

JANELLE B. MATHIS

FINE ARTS

An impressive development in publishing has
been the increase in the number of books for children that deal with the arts. Early books about the
visual arts led the way but books about visual art
and other arts were the exception. Now we have
a plethora of fine books, about visual art, MUSIC,
dance, and theater.

VISUAL arts books, still the most numerous,
fall into three categories. Comprehensive books
about art history draw together the works of several different artists and juxtapose their styles. An
example is the Looking at Paintings SERIES, arranged topically around a subject such as a circus
with paintings by many different artists from different time periods.

An early and still exemplary example of biography is the Art Start series, each focusing on a
single person including brief information about
the life, large, full-color reproductions of art
works, and a simple critical commentary. Another example is the Masters of Art series.

Rather than focus on a single artist's work,
some books instead explore visual perception and
use a variety of artists' works as examples. Books
about color are the most numerous, though less
frequently authors also provide books about other
elements, such as line, and compositional principles.

Another kind of book about visual arts deals
with the materials artists use. The book about
paint and painting in the Voyages of Discovery

series deals in imaginative ways that require child interaction.

Music, dance, and theater, unlike the visual arts, are transitory. Once performed, they disappear (existing only in print or notated form) until they are presented once again. Perhaps because of this ephemeral quality, music—like dance and theater—is less often written about by authors of children's books.

Books about music often feature the instruments of the Western orchestra. A recent interesting development is technology that now makes it possible to include compact discs packaged within the book, so children can hear, as well as read about the music (A. Ganeri, *The Young Person's Guide to the Orchestra,* 1996). Some books about musicians are easy to find; they are part of a series, such as Composers World, clearly labeled as about music. Other series include musicians as part of another organizing group. For example, there is a biography of George Gershwin in the Jewish Biography series. A simple biography of Diana Ross is included in the Women of Our Time series. So in looking for books about music, teachers and LIBRARIANS need to remember that books in seemingly unrelated series topics may also be useful.

Few books deal with theater, though there are some longer biographies of actors. One volume in the "Great Lives" series of group biographies contains over two dozen biographies of important actors from Chekhov to Helen Hayes. Recently there have been simplified retellings of Shakespeare's plays presented in illustrated book format.

There are two major kinds of books about dance. The first are INFORMATIONAL BOOKS, and these often feature full-color photographs about children studying to be dancers. A second kind of book is the retellings of ballet plots, presented in picture book format (M. Fonteyn, *Coppelia,* 1998). The major drawback to books about dance has been excessive feminization. The superb *Dance* (Bill T. Jones and Susan Kuklin, 1998), is a book boys will read. Stark–white backgrounds enhance dramatic photographs of dancer Bill T. Jones.

Cutting across all four of the arts areas, authors explore various genres. We have fiction, nonfiction, BIOGRAPHY, and POETRY. In PICTURE BOOK format, Brown and Brown's fictitious family visits an art museum (*Visiting the Art Museum,* 1986) there seeing art that ranges from an Egyptian mummy to work by Roy Lichtenstein. Some art shows actual reproductions while others are portrayed by the Browns' visual re-creation. There are also occasional longer works of fiction for middle-grade readers in which a major character *is* involved in one of the arts.

Among nonfiction, some books are simply collections of reproductions of paintings, arranged in some way. Lucy Micklethwait's *A Child's Book of Art: Great Pictures, First Words* (1993) is in categories like "Pets" with almost no text. The oversized format and limited number of reproductions on a page result in images large enough to be easily seen.

Among biography series, Portraits of Women Artists for Children are among the finest available. These include black and white photos of the artists, as well as full-page, full-color reproductions of their work. The series includes minority women and those working in fields often overlooked, such as photography.

In addition to series biographies, we also have individual biographies: Jeanette Winter's biography of Georgia O'Keeffe, *My Name Is Georgia* (1997), is an example of a picture-book format; the Zheng Zhensun and Alice Low biography of a young Chinese artist, *A Young Artist* (1991), is an example of a full-length illustrated book. Other artists featured in individual biographies for older readers include such well-known artists as Marc Chagall, but also lesser known artists such as Minnie Evans (an untrained AFRICAN AMERICAN artist whose work is receiving much critical attention).

Authors also write composite biographies (i.e., books including brief biographies of several different people related by topic). An example is Kathleen KRULL's very funny collection *Lives of the Musicians: Good Times, Bad Times and What the Neighbors Thought* (1993). In addition to writing about musicians, she has written about creators in other arts.

Mary O'NEILL, *Hailstones and Halibut Bones* (1961, 1989), put her ideas about color into poetry in books that feature art done especially for the poetry. Another interesting example is original art by Wayne Thiebaud, a contemporary artist of studio paintings, for Katharine Bates's poem "O Beautiful for Spacious Skies" (1994). Some editors put together collections of poetry with selections of museum art to show children that the same idea can be exemplified in words and in visual images.

Books about art can be categorized by level of involvement. Do they engage child readers in the art as spectator (or audience), i.e., learning about the art, or as participant, i.e., actually doing the art? In theater, for example, some books describe the art form, while others actually involve children in doing some aspect of theater.

Some books are a hybrid of this categorization. In *Meet Matisse,* Nelly Munthe (1983) provides information about the work of this artist and why it is important and also involves readers in various activities related to his work. The Let's Investigate Art series is another example that includes both critical commentary about various artwork, as well as suggestions to engage children in making art, or otherwise responding to the artists' works.

There are now many more children's books about the arts than existed even a decade ago: those about the visual arts still predominate while other art forms, especially dance, are underrepresented. Books on these topics do get reviewed but are the subject of feature-length articles in journals less frequently than other topics appear. In addition to writing such books, authors are now creating texts for teachers and librarians about how to use such books. For example, Lea Burroughs (1998) provides a comprehensive list of appropriate titles with a rich variety of practical activities to involve children in experiencing all of the arts through books.

REFERENCES: Burroughs, L. *Introducing Children to the Arts: A Practical Guide for Librarians and Educators,* 1988; "Zing Went the Strings," *School Library Journal* 41(12), 42, 1995; Stewig, J. W., "Making Is Not Enough," *Teacher,* pp. 31–33, fall 1974; Stewig, J. W., "Children, Books, and Theatre," *Youth Theatre Journal* 2(3), pp. 15–17, 1988; Stewig, J. W., *Looking at Picture Books,* 1995; Wilton, S., "Reviewing Art Books: Reflections and Projections," *School Library Journal* 39(1), pp. 34–35, 1993

JOHN W. STEWIG

FINGER, Charles
Author, editor; b. 25 December 1869 Willesden, Sussex, England; d. 7 January 1941 near Fayetteville, Arkansas

From an early age, F. was drawn by the lure of travel and adventure. Leaving his home in England, he traveled to South America, Africa, Mexico, Canada, and the United States. His extensive travels provided a rich source of knowledge that he used in writing more than thirty books of fiction and nonfiction. His book of folktales, *Tales from Silver Lands,* won the NEWBERY MEDAL in 1925, and his historical romance, *Courageous Companions,* won the Longmans Juvenile Fiction Prize in 1929. In his later years, he concentrated on books for younger children. F. successfully used a representation of Elizabethan prose to rewrite and edit *Heroes from Hakluyt* (1928).

FURTHER WORKS: *All's Well.* 1920; *Book of Real Adventures,* 1924; *Bushrangers,* 1924; *Robin Hood and His Merry Men,* 1924; *Tales Worth Telling.* 1927. *David Livingstone: Explorer and Prophet; The Spreading Stain: A Tale for Boys and Men with Boys' Hearts.* 1927; *Courageous Companions,* 1929; *Adventure under Sapphire Skies,* 1931; *Foot-Loose in the West,* 1932; *The Destant Prize,* 1935; *The Yankee Captain in Patagonia*

BIBLIOGRAPHY: *Something about the Author.* vol. 42, 1986. Seymour-Smith, M., and A. C. Kimmens, eds. *World Authors 1900–1950,* 1996

MARY ARIAIL BROUGHTON

FISCHER, Hans Erich
Illustrator, author, b. 6 January 1909 Berne, Switzerland; d. 19 April 1958, Place unknown

F. crafted cleverness and caricature within his drawings, and his *Pitschi* (1953) is a memorable cat story with an exuberance of line in this feline version of "the grass is always greener." F., who studied under artist Paul Klee, illustrated for magazines in Switzerland including *Nebelspalter.* His use of fluid line is a model with brushed color revealing only the essential in the ILLUSTRATION. *Pitschi* was selected as a *New York Times* Best Illustrated Children's Book of the Year in 1953. F. adapted many traditional tales, *Puss in Boots*

(1959) and *The Good-for-Nothings* (1957) and his own stories continue to be released in new editions.

FURTHER WORKS: *The Traveling Musicians: A Story by the Brothers* GRIMM. 1955. *The Bremen Town Musicians: A Tale.* (Anthea Bell, trans.) 1998. *Pitschi, The Kitten Who Always Wanted to Be Something Else. A Sad Story, But One which Ends Well.* 1953. *Pitschi, The Kitten Who Always Wanted to Be Something Else. A Sad Story That Ends Well.* (Marianne Martens, trans.). 1996. *Puss in Boots: A Fairy Tale.* (Anthea Bell, trans.). 1996

BIBLIOGRAPHY: Lee et al. *Illustrators of Children's Books: 1957–1966,* 1968

KAY E. VANDERGRIFT

FISHER, Aileen

Author, poet, b. 9 September 1906, Iron River, Michigan

Growing up on a farm in Michigan, F. speaks to the natural beauty of nature with the love of a poet as well as a naturalist. Her writings reflect the keen observations of a scientist shaped with the love of one who has many life experiences with all that is associated with country life. After working in Chicago to save money for her own portion of a country home, F. purchased a large ranch in Boulder, Colorado, with a friend, Olive Rabe. There she continued to write; she and Rabe collaborated on books including one about Emily Dickinson and her contemporary insights into nature, life, death, and eternity.

From her home near the city of Boulder at the foot of Flagstaff Mountain she has written about ninety books of prose and POETRY for children while enjoying the peacefulness and wildlife of country living. Although she has written in other genres, F. claims that her chief love is writing poetry for children. She wakes early every day and walks her dog. Most of her morning is spent writing; she prefers to use a pencil rather than a keyboard. Her first audience is herself as she creates poems that reflect the joys and delights of her childhood.

F.'s poetry, probably the most significant among her work, is in rhymed short verses or one-poem picture books. Integrating imagination and observation, F. creates moments of wonder concerning the most everyday objects. Her verse

has been a source of inspiration for other authors. Likewise, her INFORMATIONAL BOOKS contain this blending of vivid imagination and research as she writes about nature in both Michigan and the mountains of Colorado.

AWARDS: AMERICAN LIBRARY ASSOCIATION Notable Book of the Year (1960) for *Going Barefoot,* (1961) for *Where Does Everyone Go?,* (1962) for *My Cousin Abe,* (1964) for *Listen Rabbit,* (1965) for *In the Middle of the Night,* and (1966) for *Valley of the Smallest.* Western Writers of America Award for juvenile nonfiction (1967) and Hans Christian ANDERSEN Honor Book (1968) for *Valley of the Smallest.* NATIONAL COUNCIL OF TEACHERS OF ENGLISH award for children's poetry (1978)

FURTHER WORKS: Children's Verse: *The Coffee-Pot Face,* 1933; *Inside a Little House,* 1938; *That's Why,* 1946; *Like Nothing at All,* 1962; *In the Middle of the Night,* 1965; *We Went Looking,* 1968; *Do Bears Have Mothers, Too?,* 1973; *I Stood Upon a Mountain,* 1979; *Rabbits, Rabbits,* 1983; *My First President's Day Book,* 1987; *Wishes,* 1990; *Always Wondering,* 1991; *Out There in Space,* 2000; Juvenile Fiction: *Trapped by the Mountain Storm,* 1949; *Off to the Gold Fields,* 1955; *Fisherman of Galilee,* 1959; *My Cousin Abe,* 1962; *Arbor Day,* 1965; Other Juvenile: *Guess Again!,* 1941; *The Life of Emily Dickinson as Seen through the Eyes of Her Brother Austin,* (Olive Rabe, coauthor), 1965; *Easter,* 1968; *Jeanne d'Arc.* 1970

BIBLIOGRAPHY: *Contemporary Authors, New Revision Series,* vol. 37, 1992; Hopkins, Lee Bennett, *Pauses: Autobiographical Reflections of 101 Creators of Children's Books,* 1995; *Something about the Author,* vol. 73, 1993

JANELLE B. MATHIS

FISHER, Dorothy Canfield

Author, educator, lecturer, b. 17 February 1879, Lawrence, Kansas; d. 9 November 1958, Place unknown

A professor's daughter, born Dorothea Frances Canfield, F. was reared in a family that valued education. She attended The Ohio State University, the Sorbornne, University of Paris, and earned her doctoral degree in Romance languages from Columbia University in 1904. When F.'s first child was a toddler, she visited Maria Montessori's school in Rome and became an advocate for Montessori's educational philosophy of child rearing. F.'s firm grasp of her family heritage with its strong New England values, coupled with her enthusiasm for the Montessori methods, greatly influenced her perspective when she crafted her first children's book, *Understood Betsy* (1917). Innovative for its time, the novel's themes of responsibility and independence are realized through insightful and natural characterization. Elizabeth Ann, a pampered and sickly nine-year-old girl, reared by two prim city-dwelling, midwestern aunts, spends time with relatives on a rural farm in Vermont. Adopting a simple name by story's end, Betsy adjusts to the rigors of country life. She learns to appreciate the wholesome atmosphere while developing an increasing sense of self-reliance and competence. *Understood Betsy* maintains an audience among readers interested in REALISTIC FICTION set in the early twentieth century. The book's emphasis on independent characters freed from the traditional conventions that were often published during that time period ensures its position as a classic in children's literature.

In 1925, F. published a collection of short stories entitled, *Made-to-Order-Stories*. These tales evolved from stories that F. wrote for her ten-year-old son. Jimmy abhorred moralistic and educational stories and enjoyed unconventional plots laced with action. He formulated the unique plot devices for each story. A sack of potatoes, a broken bicycle, a trapped fox, a pony cart, and a house fire were some of the unexpected plot devices that F. developed for the so-called made-to-order-story. This book and others reinforce F.'s respect for children and their capacity to grow freely into mature adults. Her literary career includes nonfiction works for children and adult fiction and nonfiction. Active in humanitarian issues throughout her life, F. was honored by Eleanor Roosevelt as one of the ten most influential women in the United States.

AWARDS: D. Litt. from Middlebury College (1921), Dartmouth College (1922), Williams College (1935), Swarthmore College (1935), Smith College (1954), and others. Delta Kappa Gamma Society Educator's Award (1946). Skinner Award, Women's National Book Association (1951). Sarah Josepha HALE Special Award (1958)

FURTHER WORKS FOR CHILDREN: *Tell Me a Story: A Book of Stories to Tell to Children.* (Tibor Ger-

gely, illus.). 1940. *Nothing Ever Happens and How It Does: Sixteen True Stories.* (With Sarah N. Cleghorn, Esther Boston Bristol, illus.). 1940. *Something Old, Something New: Stories of People Who Are American.* (Mary D. Shipman, illus.). 1949. *Paul Revere and the Minute Men.* (Norma Price, illus.) 1950

BIBLIOGRAPHY: Contemporary Authors Online: www.galenet.com; *Dictionary of Literary Biography,* vol. 9, 1981; *Twentieth-Century Children's Writers,* 3rd. ed., 1990; *Horn Book,* vol. 9, 1981; Serafin, Steven R. ed. *The Continuum Encyclopedia of American Literature,* 1999; Silvey, Anita ed., *Children's Books and Their Creators,* 1995; *Twentieth Century Children's Writers,* 1990; YATES, Elizabeth, *In a Pool: The Widening Circle of Dorothy C.'s Life,* 1958

SHEILA GERATY

FISHER, Leonard Everett
Author, illustrator, b. 24 June 1924, the Bronx, New York

F., a visual artist as well as a literary artist, has written and/or illustrated approximately 300 books for children and adolescents. He received a Bachelor of Fine Arts from Yale University (1949) and Master of FINE ARTS (1950). His talent as a storyteller and artist is evident in his illustrations and writing on a variety of topics in stories, poems, and INFORMATIONAL BOOKS using a variety of perspectives. His work appeals to audiences that vary considerably in age, aptitude, and background knowledge. F. uses visual and literary techniques with conscious skill and imagination to depict images of reality and aspects of the human condition. F.'s artistic excellence is never identical with a simple mirroring of the realities of the human condition; instead, whatever the image of reality depicted in pictures and stories may be, it is an allusion of that reality. The images F. creates are truly works of art because he engages in selective interpretation of the reality to which he alludes. The allusionary images he creates are thoroughly identifiable and believable, yet they are not exactly like life. Indeed, one sees in his illustrations, historical novels, and informational PICTURE BOOKS an elusive magic of transformation or representation of reality.

F. puts three basic requirements into illustrating and writing high quality literary works: heart, intellect, and talent. The philosopher in James

Stephens's *The Crock of Gold* (1912) said, "the head does not hear anything until the heart has listened, and what the heart knows today the head will understand tomorrow." F.'s dramatic picture books, novels, poetry, and informational books are done with heart as well as with intellect and talent. Readers of his books remember and ponder over the unique, sophisticated, and mind-stretching ideas and themes F. introduces to them.

AWARDS: Pulitzer Prize in Painting (1950) for *Coney Island.* American Institute of Graphic Arts (1961) for *Bumpers, Boilers, Hooks and Ladders. New York Times* Best Illustrated Children's Books (1964) for *Casey at the Bat,* by E. L. THAYER. Sydney Taylor Book Award (1980) and National Jewish Book Award (1981) for *A Russian Farewell.* KERLAN Award (1991) for accomplishments in literature. Association for Library Services to Children Arbuthnot Honor Lecturer (1994) for distinguished career as writer and illustrator. Numerous AMERICAN LIBRARY ASSOCIATION Notable Children's Book Awards

FURTHER WORKS: *David and Goliath,* 1993; *Gutenberg,* 1993; *Moses,* 1995; *Stars and Stripes,* 1993; *The White House,* 1989

BIBLIOGRAPHY: Fisher, Leonard Everett, *A Life in Art.* 1997; Stephens, James. *The Crock of Gold* 1912; cited in Ruth Sawyer, 1942, *The Way of the Storyteller*

PATRICIA J. CIANCIOLO

FITZGERALD, John
Author, b. 1907, Utah; d. 21 May 1988, Titusville, Florida

F.'s memories of his Utah childhood impacted his writing for adults as well as his novels for children. His writing career began as a journalist, which led to becoming the foreign feature editor for United Press International. His first novel, written for adults, drew upon memories of his youth in Mormon Utah; this same connection with his childhood served as the material for his first children's book, *The Great Brain* (1967). This first book, plus later titles in the same series, was set in turn of the century Utah, and tells about the exploits of an older brother through the eyes of his younger sibling. Their humorous exploits, the ability of the older brother to turn the tables on the younger one, and their ability to outwit adults are themes that continue in later books in the series. F. received many regional AWARDS

including the Young Readers' Choice Award from Pacific Northwest Library Association (1976) for *Great Brain Reforms* and Surrey School Book of the Year Award (1976) for *Me and My Little Brain.*

FURTHER WORKS: *More Adventures of the Great Brain,* 1969; *The Great Brain at the Academy,* 1972; *The Return of the Great Brain,* 1974; *The Great Brain Does It Again,* 1975; *The Great Brain Is Back.* Published posthumously, 1995

BIBLIOGRAPHY: *Contemporary Authors.* vols. 93–96, 1980

SANDRA IMDIEKE

FITZHUGH, Louise
Author, illustrator, b. 5 October 1928, Memphis, Tennessee; d. 19 November 1974, New Milford, Connecticut

F.'s 1964 publication of *Harriet the Spy* marked a milestone in realistic fiction for children. Her eavesdropping young protagonist, Harriet M. Welsch, was a fictional groundbreaker: shrewd, spoiled, and meddling. Harriet's observations of the people around her, meticulously recorded in the black notebook she always carried, echo the honesty with which F. portrayed Harriet. And like Harriet, F. encountered criticism for that honest portrayal; the book was both praised and denounced at its publication. Today it is recognized as a landmark book heralding a new realism in children's fiction.

Unlike Harriet the New Yorker, F. grew up in Memphis, but shared with Harriet an unhappy childhood as the only child of wealthy parents. After her parents' divorce, F. was reared by her father and educated in private schools, dropping out of college just before graduation and moving to New York City to study art. There she illustrated *Suzuki Beane,* a PICTURE BOOK written by Sandra Scoppettone and published in 1961. After the 1964 publication of *Harriet the Spy,* F. authored a follow-up novel, *The Long Secret* (1965), in which Harriet appears as a secondary character. But Harriet's friend Beth Ellen, protagonist of *The Long Secret,* lacks the strength that F. achieved with Harriet, and the novel did not receive the critical acclaim given *Harriet.* In 1969 F. collaborated a second time with Scoppettone to publish the antiwar picture book *Bang, Bang, You're Dead.*

F. died in 1974, a week before the appearance of her third novel, *Nobody's Family Is Going to Change*. Like her earlier two novels, *Nobody's Family* is marked by nonconformity and peopled by bright, lonely kids whose lives are revealed with honesty and humor. *Nobody's Family* was adapted as *"The Tap Dance Kid,"* an NBC-TV television special in 1978 and an award-winning Broadway musical in 1983. Other posthumous publications include F.'s final novel, *Sport* (1979) and a picture-book SERIES that includes *I Am Five* (1978), *I Am Three* (1982), illustrated by Susanna Natti, and *I Am Four* (1982), illustrated by Susan Bonners.

AWARDS: *New York Times* Outstanding Books of the Year (1964), AMERICAN LIBRARY ASSOCIATION Notable Book (1967), for *Harriet the Spy. New York Times* Best Illustrated Children's Books of the Year (1969) and Brooklyn Art Books for Children winner (1974) for *Bang, Bang, You're Dead. Children's Book Bulletin* (1976) for *Nobody's Family Is Going to Change;* a Broadway adaptation, *The Tap Dance Kid,* was a Tony winner

BIBLIOGRAPHY: *Contemporary Authors, New Revision Series,* 1991; *Something about the Author,* vol. 45, 1986; Anita Silvey, ed., *Children's Books and Their Creators,* 1995

DIANE L. CHAPMAN

FLACK, Marjorie

Author, illustrator, b. 23 October 1897, Greenport, New York; d. 29 August 1958, Greenport, New York

F. wrote and illustrated many notable books for children. Her work has been acclaimed for its simple, clear, humorous style; children find it easy to relate to the familiar situations the author created for her characters. F.'s stories typically show common aspects of growing up, usually featuring the adventures of animal characters.

F. developed a love for STORYTELLING while she was a child, and continued her interest as she studied at the Art Students League in New York City. F.'s first book, *Taktuk: An Arctic Boy* (1928), was a collaboration with Helen Lomen and featured the life of an Eskimo child in Alaska. Two years later, Flack published *Angus and the Ducks,* the first of a popular SERIES about Angus, a young Scottish terrier. Other books

about the dog, including *Angus and the Cat* (1931), *Angus Lost* (1932), and *Topsy and Angus and the Cat* (1935), delighted children, parents, and critics. Readers found the books to be especially good for reading aloud, while critics praised the works for the skillful development of Angus's character as he encountered successive challenges.

F.'s 1933 book, *The Story about Ping,* illustrated by Kurt WIESE, is considered her finest work. The story, set on the Yangtze River in China, tells the story of Ping, a Peking duck who becomes separated from his family and home. Critics praised the book for its HUMOR, charm, characterization, appeal to children, and artistic presentation. Like F.'s other PICTURE BOOKS, *Ping* is memorable for its strongly cadenced, poetic rhythm.

Although F.'s last book was published more than fifty years ago, many of her books are still in print and have remained popular with each new generation. Several have been translated into other languages, including Swedish, Spanish, and Portuguese.

AWARDS: ALA CALDECOTT MEDAL Honor Book (1947) for *Boats on the River* (Jay Hyde Barnum, illus.)

FURTHER WORKS: *All about Town: The Story of a Boy in New York,* 1929; *What to do About Molly* (F. and Karl LARSSON, illus), 1936; *The Adopted Dolphin and the Pirate's Daughter* (with William Rose Benet), 1941; *The New Pet,* 1943; *Away Goes Jonathan Wheeler* (Hilma Larsson, illus.), 1944

BIBLIOGRAPHY: *Something about the Author.* vol. 100, 1999. *Major Authors and Illustrators for Children and Young Adults,* 1993

MARY ARIAIL BROUGHTON

FLEISCHMAN, (Albert) Sid(ney)

Author, b. 16 March 1920, Brooklyn, New York

F., the son of a Russian Jewish immigrant, was born in Brooklyn, New York, and reared in San Diego, California. His parents nurtured his interest in STORYTELLING; among his favorite childhood stories were *Aesop's Fables* and *Robin Hood.* He performed magic as a teenager, and his first published work, at nineteen, was a volume of his original tricks, *Between Cocktails* (1939). After high school, he worked as a traveling magician during vaudeville's waning days, an experience that heightened his awareness of regional dialect and FOLKLORE, which he later used in his writings. F. served in the U.S. Naval Reserve in the Pacific and Asia during World War II. F.'s son, Paul, is a NEWBERY MEDAL winning children's writer, distinguishing F. and Paul as the only father-son team to garner this celebrated award.

After the war, F. attended San Diego State College and wrote pulp fiction for adults, chiefly detective and suspense stories. He served as associate editor of *Point* magazine for two years before taking up writing full time in 1951. His early career was largely devoted to writing for adults and in 1955 he adapted his novel *Blood Alley* for the film of the same name starring John Wayne.

His first children's book, *Mr. Mysterious and Company* (1962), was written for his own children and includes family members as characters. The book was so successful that F. turned to writing children's books almost exclusively. It was followed by *By the Great Horn Spoon!* (1963), *The Ghost in the Noonday Sun* (1965), and *Chancy and the Grand Rascal* (1966), all tall tales set in nineteenth-century America.

McBroom Tells the Truth (1966) was the first of a series of popular tall tales about an Iowa farmer rearing his family of eleven children on a single acre of farmland. McBroom is the heir of such American heroes as Paul Bunyan and Pecos Bill. A second series, for older readers, appeared in 1981, featuring the Bloodhound Gang, a multiethnic team of three junior detectives. Originally written as scripts for Children's Television Workshop's *3-2-1 Contact,* the books are fast-paced and clever. F. ventured into new territory with *The Whipping Boy* (1986), a melodramatic story set in an imaginary kingdom in the unspecified past. It is the story of a prince and a streetwise orphan who change places, recalling Mark TWAIN's *The Prince and the Pauper* (1881). With its messages about human nature, justice, and power, this book contains less slapstick HUMOR and a more serious message than most of F.'s previous children's stories. Still it bears F.'s unmistakable comic touch and sense of adventure and won the Newbery Medal. He later wrote the screenplay, under the pseudonym Max Brindle,

for the 1994 DISNEY production of *The Whipping Boy,* starring George C. Scott.

F. returned to American settings in *The Midnight Horse* (1990), a story combining magic and the tall tale. *Jim Ugly* (1992), a parody of the Wild West, includes thinly veiled oldtime movie stars as characters. And in *The 13th Floor: A Ghost Story* (1995), F. experiments with time travel.

His autobiography for young readers, *The Abracadabra Kid: A Writer's Life* (1996), has been widely acclaimed for its lively, engaging style. F. exudes a quintessentially American quality with his robust humor and tall tales; his works have been translated into at least sixteen languages. F. is noted as one of the champions of humor in children's literature during the latter half of the twentieth century.

FURTHER WORKS: *McBroom and the Big Wind,* 1967; *McBroom's Ear,* 1969; *Jingo Django,* 1971; *McBroom's Zoo,* 1972; *McBroom the Rainmaker,* 1973; *The Ghost on Saturday Night,* 1974; *Humbug Mountain,* 1978; *Jim Bridger's Alarm Clock and Other Tall Tales,* 1978; *The Bloodhound Gang in the Case of the Flying Clock,* 1981; *The Bloodhound Gang in the Case of the Secret Message,* 1981; *The Scarebird,* 1988

AWARDS: ALA NEWBERY MEDAL (1987) for *The Whipping Boy; Boston Globe-Horn Book* Award for Fiction (1979) for *Humbug Mountain*

BIBLIOGRAPHY: *Children's Literature Review.* vol. 15, 1988. *Children's Writers. Something about the Author.* vol. 96, 1998

DAVID L. RUSSELL

FLEISCHMAN, Paul

Author, b. 5 September 1952, Monterey, California

F. has the distinction of being a member of the only father-son team to be NEWBERY MEDAL winners. F.'s writings include a wide range: PICTURE BOOKS, POETRY, suspense stories, and YOUNG ADULT novels. F. grew up in a home filled with literary influences. He was privy to discussions between his father, author Sid FLEISCHMAN, and the stream of successful writers and editors such as Maurice SENDAK and poet Myra Cohn LIVINGSTON who visited the Fleischman home. F. was a quick learner; as a child, he would craft little booklets for his father. These booklets for birthdays and special occasions focused on aspects of his father's writing career.

His melodic use of words and engaging literary devices are attributed to the combination of this literary environment and an intense love of music. F. attended University of California, Berkeley 1970–72 and the University of New Mexico, B.A. 1977. While home from college one day, he asked his father to read a story he had just written. Although his father worried about critiquing a first attempt, he complied and was astonished by the lack of usual flaws of a first-time writer. This story eventually became *The Birthday Tree* (1979), a picture book about a family's bond to an apple tree and its symbolic significance to the young man's well-being. F. possessed the qualities needed to produce successful publications without any formal writing courses. It was assumed that F. had received extensive, structured training from his father, but that was not the case. Aside from the natural authentic influence of his environment, F.'s father coached him in only one area: the power a writer can achieve by cutting a word, sharpening a sentence, polishing a paragraph. The elder F. says that his part in his son's career has been as a spectator. However, there is no question that the author had a natural apprenticeship growing up. Early on, his father had consulted F. and his two sisters for ideas and feedback on works in progress. F. was proud that his father had accepted an idea for the book, *Mr. Mysterious and Company* in which the characters get lost and reappear in a later chapter.

F.'s love for music transforms words into the musical flow of poetry. Always able to hear the sounds in his head, he loves composing and performing music, especially ensemble performance. This led to writing *Joyful Noise: Poems for Two Voices* (1987), a collection of poems intended for reading aloud choral style. His fluid, musical writing style helped him win the Newbery Medal. A companion volume published earlier, *I Am Phoenix: Poems for Two Voices* (1985), was a step in that direction. *Joyful Noise* transports readers to a rhythmical existence of insects, exhibiting their insect characteristics coupled with human personalities. The read-aloud intention of unison and choral style adds to the appeal.

F.'s passion for music is apparent in *Rondo in C* (1988) as he shows how listening to Beethoven's piece evokes various visions from different listeners while the young pianist plays: a man envisioning flying geese, a sentimental evening with family members, or snow falling through a street light. The book reflects, just as music often does for F., different perspectives and different points of views and voices.

Strangely different from his euphonic pieces, F. is a storyteller who captivates readers with his uncanny tales such as *Graven Images: 3 Stories* (1982). F. is able to fascinate readers with psychological and moral issues while unraveling mysteries. F. also writes novels for young adults in different genres. *Bull Run* (1993) is a fictional recreation of the first significant battle in the Civil War. A presentation of vignettes, F. tells the story from diverse perspectives; the fictional characters are representative of the North, South, male, female, black and white. F. moves effortlessly from works of the past to the contemporary. In *Whirligig* (1998) he tells the story of a high school student who learns a lesson in self-respect after accidentally killing another teenager while driving drunk. Once again, the author connects the stories and lives of his characters to create the main character and tell his story. His versatility enables F. to extract a range of emotional responses from his readers.

AWARDS: AMERICAN LIBRARY ASSOCIATION Newbery Medal (1989) and *Boston Globe-Horn Book* Award Honor Book (1988) for *Joyful Noise: Poems for Two Voices.* Golden Kite honor book, Society of Children's Book Writers, and *New York Times* Outstanding book citation (1980) for *Half-a-Moon Inn.* ALA Newbery Medal honor award (1983) for *Graven Images: Three Stories.* Golden Kite honor book, Society of Children's Book Writer, and Parents' Choice Award (1983) for *Path of the Pale Horse. Boston Globe-Horn Book* Award Honor Book and ALA notable book (1990) for *Saturnalia.* Golden Kite Honor Book (1991) for *The Borning Room*

FURTHER WORKS: *The Animal Hedge,* 1983; *The Path of the Pale Horse,* 1983; *Phoebe Danger, Detective, in the Case of the Two-Minute Cough,* 1983; *Finzel the Farsighted,* 1983; *Rear-View Mirrors,* 1986; *Shadow Book,* 1990; *Time Train,* 1991; *Townsend's Warbler,* 1992; *A Fate Totally Worse Than Death,* 1995; *Seedfolks,* 1997; *Dateline: Troy,* 1997; *Westlandia,* 1999

BIBLIOGRAPHY: Fleischman, Sid, *The Abracadabra Kid: A Writer's Life,* 1996; Fleischman, Sid. "Paul Fleischman." in *Horn Book* magazine. July/Aug 1989; *Children's Literature Review,* vol. 20, 1990; *Something about the Author.* vol. 72, 1993; Gallo, Donald, ed., *Speaking for Ourselves, Too,* 1990

NANCY HORTON

FLEMING, Denise
Author, illustrator, b. 31 January 1950, Toledo, Ohio

F. was born in Ohio and attended Kendall College of Art and Design from which she graduated in 1970. She began her career as an illustrator in the 1980s. In addition to illustrating books for Alice Low, Linda Hayward, and Natalie Standiford, she drew licensed characters such as Care Bears and Charmkins. Eventually, F. enrolled in a papermaking class, which led to the development of her own technique of pulp painting. Using cotton rag as the basic material, she beats the fibers to a fine pulp, which are then suspended in water. She adds chemicals and pigments, then uses the pulp like paint, squeezing the mixture from bottles onto the underdrawings of hand-cut stencils. The effect is bold, colorful, and vibrant. The coupling of the collage paintings with simple, rhyming texts makes F.'s work especially appealing to young children. F. claims that her work is a family affair; her husband makes her screens and helps her haul pulp while her daughter serves as a sounding board for new works.

F.'s first self-illustrated book, *In the Tall, Tall Grass* (1991), won numerous honors, including an AMERICAN LIBRARY ASSOCIATION notable book award, *School Library Journal* Best Book citation, and the *Boston-Globe-Horn Book* Award honor book. Inspired by the author's love of gardening and her interest in natural habitats, the book features a young boy as he follows a caterpillar through the grass. A later book, *In the Small, Small Pond* (1993), is written in a similar vein; it takes a close look at the animals in a small pond. *In a Small, Small Pond* was chosen an ALA CALDECOTT MEDAL honor book (1994).

FURTHER WORKS: *Count!,* 1992; *Lunch,* 1992; *Barnyard Banter,* 1994; *Denise F.'s Painting with Paper, Easy Papermaking Fun for the Entire Family,* 1994; *Where Once There Was a Wood,* 1996; *Time to Sleep,* 1997; *Mama Cat Has Three Kittens,* 1998

BIBLIOGRAPHY: "Denise F." Baltimore County Public Library. Biography courtesy of Henry Holt and Company. Accessed June 23, 1999, http://mail.bcpl.lib.md.us/kidspage/fleming.html; *Something about the Author,* vol. 81, 1995; *Seventh Book of Junior Authors and Illustrators,* 1996

MARY ARIAIL BROUGHTON

FLEMING, Ian
Author, b. 28 May 1908, London, England; d. 12 August 1964, Canterbury, England

Educated at Eton and the Royal Military Academy at Sandhurst, F. went on to study at the University of Munich and the University of Switzerland. He was fluent in French and German, as well as English, and worked as a journalist and a stockbroker. F.'s military and journalism careers included both official and unofficial secret-service work on behalf of the British government during World War II. He was awarded the Order of Dannebrog (1945).

Most of F.'s novels are spy thrillers informed by the cold war era in which he wrote them. His character, James Bond, appeared in most of these novels and continues to be a popular movie character in film versions of the novels. F.'s only important novel for children, *Chitty Chitty Bang Bang* (1964), illustrated by John BURNINGHAM, won the Young Reader's Choice Award (1967) and was adapted in 1968 as a popularly acclaimed film by Roald DAHL. Based in part on F.'s memory of a custom-built racing car that gained local fame in Canterbury in 1921, F.'s novel presents the screwball adventures of Commander Pott and his family, especially the Potts's magic automobile that can fly and sail. Both novel and movie were critical successes from the first and continue to attract a wide audience.

F. also wrote for periodicals, including a *Sunday Times of London* column, which he authored under the pseudonym Atticus.

BIBLIOGRAPHY: *Contemporary authors New Revision Series,* 1988; *The Oxford Companion to Children's Literature,* 1984; *The Saint James Guide to Crime and Mystery Writers,* 1996

FRANCISCA GOLDSMITH

FLORIAN, Douglas

Author, illustrator, b. 18 March 1950, New York City

F., the son of an artist, chose art as his own career after winning a coloring contest as a youngster. After doing ILLUSTRATIONS for other authors, F. decided that he, too, wanted to write as well as illustrate children's books. His early works were nonfiction books about nature that generally met with favorable reviews. He followed his nonfiction works with *Beast Feast* (1994), which featured twenty-one original light-hearted poems and humorous illustrations. With the success of *Beast Feast,* F. found his niche writing nonsense verse for children. *A Winter Day* (1987), selected as an Outstanding Science Trade Book for Children, depicts winter by showing, in light verse and appealing illustrations, how a family enjoys an outing on a snowy day.

AWARDS: Reading Magic Award (1986) for *Discovering Seashells.* Parents' Choice Award (1991) for *Auto Mechanic;* Lee Bennett Hopkins POETRY Award (1995) for *Beast Feast!*

FURTHER WORKS: *Bing Bang Boing,* 1994; *Monster Motel: Poems and Paintings,* 1993; *On the Wing: Bird Poems and Paintings,* 1996; *In the Swim: Poems and Paintings,* 1997

BIBLIOGRAPHY: *Something about the Author,* vol. 19, 1980, and vol. 84, 1996

MICHAEL O'LAUGHLIN

FLOURNOY, Valerie

Author, b. 17 April 1952, Camden, New Jersey

Best known for her ALA Notable picture book, *The Patchwork Quilt* (1985) with illustrations by Jerry PINKNEY, and its companion *Tanya's Reunion* (1995), F.'s stories reflect strong themes of family unity and independence within intergenerational AFRICAN AMERICAN families. Her books depict enduring family values in a caring and cooperative family setting. An editor as well as an author, F. has written for young adults in addition to her PICTURE BOOK texts.

AWARDS: CORETTA SCOTT KING AWARD for illustration and Ezra Jack KEATS New Writer Award, and Christopher Award (1986) for *The Patchwork Quilt* (Jerry PINKNEY, illustrator)

FURTHER WORKS: *The Best Time of Day,* 1978; *The Twins Strike Back,* 1980; *Until Summer's End,* 1986; *Celie and the Harvest Fiddler* (With Vanessa FLOURNOY), 1995

BIBLIOGRAPHY: *Something about the Author,* vol. 95, 1998

GWYNNE ELLEN ASH

FOLKLORE

Folklore is the beliefs, customs, legends, and traditions that are handed down, generation after generation, in cultures all over the world. It is as old as our first people and has been passed down through most of history via the oral tradition. Ballads, dances, FAIRY TALES, folktales, legends, myths, nursery rhymes, riddles, songs, and superstitions are all areas that folklore can include.

When folklore began to be considered a serious academic discipline, well over one hundred years ago, scholars were astounded to discover that many tales were surprisingly similar yet the societies from which they came were far removed. There are two theories as to how this is possible. Some researchers believe that all stories began in one ancient culture and as people spread throughout the world, so did the tales. Other scholars believe that traditional literature had beginnings in many places all over the world, and there is actually no connection to the tales other than the similarities of the people who told them. We are all alike, so we tell tales that are alike.

An early collector of tales was a member of the French Academy, Charles PERRAULT, who published *Stories and Tales of Past Times with Morals* in the late seventeenth century, a volume that included "Cinderella," "Puss-in-Boots," and "Sleeping Beauty," tales that he may have heard a servant telling his children.

The Arabian Nights is a collection of tales from Asia and North Africa that was translated into English in the eighteenth century and includes such stories as "Aladdin and the Wonderful Lamp" and "Sinbad the Sailor."

By the early nineteenth century scholars were beginning to take folklore more seriously and Jakob and Wilhelm GRIMM, German linguists and scholars, compiled the first great collection, which became known as *Grimm's Fairy Tales* (1812). Although the Grimms claimed not to have altered the tales that they recorded from the tale tellers, it is almost certain that they did. Nevertheless, the tradition of going to the source was established. *Norwegian Folk Stories* (1852) was the collaborative effort of Peter Christian ASBJORSEN and Jorgen Engebretson MOE in their native country.

In Ireland, Thomas Grofton Croker was an important collector with his *Fairy Legends and Traditions of the South of Ireland.* Robert Chambers was responsible for several volumes about Scotland of which *Popular Rhymes of Scotland* is one of the best known. Joseph JACOBS was a leader among folklorists in England. Andrew LANG, also a native of Scotland, was one of the first folklorists to encompass many cultures in the well-known series that began with *The Blue Fairy Book* published in 1889. Although Hans Christian ANDERSEN of Denmark was not a collector, his original tales may have been inspired by his heritage from stories he heard as a boy. In Russia, Aleksandr Nikolaevich AFANSYEV has been called the "Russian Grimm" for the prodigious amount of work that he produced.

American folklore collectors include Joel Chandler HARRIS who used the dialect and tales of plantation slaves for the *Brer Rabbit* and *Brer Bear* stories. Richard CHASE is noted for his *Grandfather Tales* (1948), collected in Appalachia, based on Scotch-Irish traditions. Richard Dorson collected an enormous amount of American folklore, organized and directed the Folklore Institute, and also did a great deal to raise awareness about folklore as a field of study. A more recent American collector is Jan Harold Brunvald who has published several volumes of urban legends. Joseph BRUCHAC, and several others, have been responsible for preserving many Native American tales.

In the past few decades there have been hundreds of books published complementing the study of MULTICULTURALISM and now folklore from Africa, Asia, Australia, the Middle East, and every corner of our globe can be found and enjoyed.

Of the many kinds of folklore, myths are among the oldest form. Myths answer questions the people have about the world and are considered to be true by the listeners. Many Greek, Roman, AFRICAN, NATIVE AMERICAN, and other myths are concerned with the creation of the earth, the people in it, animals, nature, and death.

Epics are very long stories, about heroes like Odysseus in *The Iliad* and *The Odyssey,* or *King Arthur and His Knights of the Round Table.*

Ballads were often sung by minstrels or recited in dramatic verse; they featured heroes like Robin Hood of Sherwood Forest. The American, Francis James Child, was noted for his extremely important collection *The English and Scottish Popular Ballad.* John and Alan Lomax collected ballads particularly of the mountain people, cowboys, migrant workers, and chain gangs.

Fables use short tales that teach moral lessons. The characters are often talking animals that behave like humans. The most famous collection of fables is *Aesop's Fables,* which were told by a Greek slave of the same name around 600 B.C.E. In the seventeeth century the Frenchman, Jean de la Fontaine, also wrote many well-known fables.

Folktales are actually stories that deal with the beliefs and customs of the ordinary people. They are fictional and often feature talking animals and beasts. Trickster tales are popular folktales in many cultures. Anansi the spider is a well-known trickster from the African tradition, while Coyote is a famous Native American trickster.

Fairy tales often begin with "Once upon a time" and end with "they lived happily ever after." Fairy tales contain elements of magic, utilizing wishes and supernatural creatures with extraordinary powers, such as brownies, elves, fairies, giants, goblins, and pixies. Kings and queens, princes and princesses are also often featured in fairy tales.

Legends and tall tales are closely related. Many legends about people are based on actual people from history, but their stories are often exaggerated. Some famous legendary heroes of America are Davy Crockett, Casey Jones, and John Chapman, who was known as Johnny Appleseed. Religious leaders and saints often have legends told about them, such as Saint George and the Dragon. Many legends concern fantastic creatures that some people feel really exist, such as Scotland's Loch Ness Monster and Bigfoot of the American Northwest. Tall-tale heroes are unique to America and their stories often reflect professions that were practiced in the areas where the stories were heard. Pecos Bill the famous cowboy, Old Stormalong the sailor, and Paul Bunyan the lumberjack are just a few that are well-known.

Whether ballad or legend, fairy tale or folktale, myth or tall tale, epic or fable, folklore gives us an understanding of our place in the world. Told orally, read silently or aloud, viewed on television or at the movie theater, these tales help us to share our dreams and fears as they entertain.

DONARITA VOCCA

(See also FAIRY TALES)

FORBES, Esther
Author, b. 28 June 1891, Westborough, Massachusetts; d. 12 August, 1967, Place unknown

Author of historical fiction and nonfiction, F. is best known for her books, *Paul Revere and the World He Lived In,* which won a Pulitzer Prize for history in 1943 and *Johnny Tremain: A Novel for Young and Old,* which won the NEWBERY MEDAL in 1944. Although *Johnny Tremain* is the only novel F. wrote especially for children, the book helped to introduce readers to her other historical writings.

At the start of the Revolutionary War, Johnny Tremain, a fourteen-year-old apprentice silversmith in Boston, has an accident that forces him to leave work. He meets Samuel Adams, and participates in the Boston Tea Party and the Battle of Lexington. As a witness to the dramatic events of the era, Johnny Tremain considers questions of loyalty and ethics as he grows into maturity. This highly successful work, which features the importance of freedom as its theme, has remained popular with young readers since its introduction and has been used as a supplemental textbook in many history courses.

FURTHER WORKS: *America's Paul Revere,* 1946

BIBLIOGRAPHY: *Major Authors and Illustrators for Children and Young Adults,* 1993

MARY ARIAIL BROUGHTON

FOREMAN, Michael
Author, illustrator, b. 21 March 1938, Lowestoft, England

The prolific F. illustrated many texts by authors Leon GARFIELD, Jean MERRILL, Roald DAHL, Alan GARNER, Terry Jones and others, and wrote sev-

eral dozen that he illustrated himself. The award-winning author-illustrator draws on his world travels as well as life in his native England for ILLUSTRATIONS and story lines. *War Boy: A Country Childhood* (1990), prequel *War Game* (1993), and *After the War Was Over* (1996) are memoirs of F.'s childhood during and after World War II. F. is also creator of animated films for British and Scandinavian television.

AWARDS: British Library Association's KATE GREENAWAY MEDAL for *Sleeping Beauty and Other Favourite Fairy Tales* (1982), *Long Neck and Thunder Foot* (1982), *War Boy: A Country Childhood* (1989); Kate Greenaway Commendations for *The Brothers GRIMM: Popular Folk Tales* (Brian ALDERSON, 1978), *City of Gold and Other Stories from the Old Testament* (Peter DICKENSON, 1980), *Seasons of Splendor: Tales, Myths and Legends of India* (Madhur JAFFREY, 1985); *New York Times* Best Illustrated Children's Books (1990) for *War Boy: A Country Childhood.* IBBY Honor List Illustrator Award and Smarties Grand Prize (1996) for *War Game;* W. H. Smith Illustrations Award (1968–72) for *The Great Sleigh Robbery* (1968) and *Horatio* (1969)

FURTHER WORKS: *Grandfather's Pencil and the Room of Stories,* 1994; *Surprise Surprise,* 1995; *Dad! I Can't Sleep,* 1995; *Seal Surfer,* 1997

BIBLIOGRAPHY: *Contemporary Authors, New Revision Series,* 1998; *Something about the Author,* vol. 73, 1993

DIANE L. CHAPMAN

FORMAN, James D.
Author, b. 12 November 1942, Long Island, New York

F. is an author of historical fiction and SCIENCE FICTION for young adults. Courage, honor, friendship, and strength are passionately shown in F.'s books dealing with the social issues of racism, ecology, and most prominently, war. With a focus on young adults who experience the destruction and futility of war, F. presents war's realities with strong characterizations, complex situations, and authentic facts and language. Characters confront ethical problems, such as in *Ceremony of Innocence* (1970), a true story in which a young brother and sister are executed for opposing the state in World War II Germany. F. recreates the misery of war and the strength of characters who react to situations beyond their control. *Song of Jubilee* (1971) focuses on the negative effects of slavery through the first-person perspective of a plantation slave. F.'s complex plots and strong characters are seen in his science fiction stories, such as *Cry Havoc* (1988). This is a story of the creation of killer dogs through genetic experiment. *Doomsday Plus Twelve* (1984) is a postholocaust story. He has also written several INFORMATIONAL BOOKS suitable for young adolescents dealing with communism, fascism, and Nazism.

FURTHER WORKS: *Ring the Judas Bell*, 1965; *The Traitors*, 1968; *The Survivor*, 1976; *Call Back Yesterday*, 1981; *My Enemy, My Brother*, 1969; *Becca's Story*, 1997

BIBLIOGRAPHY: *Contemporary Literary Criticism*, 1982; *Something about the Author*, vol. 70, 1993

JANELLE B. MATHIS

FOSTER, Genevieve (Stump)

Author, illustrator, b. 13 April 1893, Oswego, New York; d. 30 August 1979, Westport, Connecticut

F. is best known for the use of historical figures in stories and biographies she illustrated herself. Her lively action-filled illustrations complement the events she wrote about in a consistent effort to make history come alive for children. F. disclosed that the history lessons she was taught as a schoolchild only confused her and that she found history even more confusing when she got to college. While working as an illustrator she decided to try and write a book about history that children and their parents could share and enjoy. Her biographies feature the life and events of a single historical figure allowing readers to focus on a single person and the events in the character's lifetime. Through excerpts from letters and diaries, F. used her characters to demonstrate what other events were occurring in the world. The use of original source materials was unusual then; most children's biographies presented historical figures as infallible heroes. During her career, F. published nineteen children's books. Her books, including four NEWBERY MEDAL Honor Books, have been translated into fifteen languages.

AWARDS: ALA Newbery Medal Honor Book (1942) for *George Washington's World*, (1945) for *Abraham Lincoln's World*, (1950) for *George Washington*, and (1953) for *Birthdays of Freedom* (vol. 1)

FURTHER WORKS: *Abraham Lincoln's World: 1809–1865*. 1944; *Augustus Caesar's World*. 1947. *World of Columbus and Sons*, 1965. *Andrew Jackson* 1951; *Birthdays of Freedom*, 1952; *Theodore Roosevelt*, 1954; *The World of Captain John Smith*. 1959. *Year of the Pilgrims; Year of Lincoln*, (1970): *1861*, 1970; *The World of William Penn*, 1973

BIBLIOGRAPHY: MEIGS, C., A. EATON, E. NESBITT, R. H. Viguers, *A Critical History of Children's Literature*, 1969; *Something about the Author*. vol. 2, 1971

JODI PILGRIM

FOX, Mem

Author, b. 5 March 1946, Melbourne, Australia

The relationship between F., children, and children's literature reaches significantly beyond her role as a writer of children's books. Her professional activities have focused on three diverse, yet related efforts: as a writer of children's books, as a writer for teachers, and as a university educator preparing preservice teachers for their work with children. F. worked as a teacher educator for twenty-four years splitting her time between university teaching at Flinders University and her children's author role as she visited schools, spoke at conferences, and continued to write PICTURE BOOKS. She retired from teaching in 1996 to concentrate her time and energies on writing children's books and speaking engagements. This unusual combination of talents, interests, and initiatives positions F. as an impressive influence on children, their literature, and their learning.

In the autobiography, *Dear Mem Fox, I Have Read All Your Books Even the Pathetic Ones and Other Incidents in the Life of a Children's Book Author* (1992), F. describes powerful connections between her life experiences and her writing. Although she was born in AUSTRALIA, F. grew up as a daughter of missionary parents in Zimbabwe. She credits the influence of the Bible's lyrical rhythms for her intense efforts to revise texts to capture the perfect cadence as she writes. F. provides the example of the rhythmic parallels between the first line of *Possum Magic* (1983) and the Biblical story of Ruth. Multiple revisions of *Possum Magic*, her first published children's book, transformed the lengthy original text about a mouse into a 512-word tale of love and magic between two possums, Hush and Grandma Poss. Readers appreciate Grandma Poss's efforts to protect young Hush from danger by making her invisible but also enjoy their bicycle adventure around Australia to find just the right foods to make Hush visible again. *Possum Magic* continues to be the top-selling picture book in Australia and is still available in hardback sixteen years after publication with over one and a half million copies sold internationally.

The poetic rhythm of her father's name inspired F. to write *Wilfrid Gordon McDonald Partridge* (1985) based upon her experiences while visiting her grandfather in a nursing home late in his life. Wilfrid Gordon McDonald Partridge is a young boy with a special friend in the nursing home who also has four names, Miss Nancy Alison Delacourt Cooper. When Wilfrid discovers that Miss Nancy has lost her memory, he diligently works to help her find it through simple, loving gifts that trigger Miss Nancy's recollection of the past. Later, her grandfather's death inspired the writing of *Sophie* (1989/1994) published, with different illustrators, in Australia and the United States. F. celebrates the cycle of life through Sophie's growing relationship with her grandfather until a time when "there was no Grandpa, just emptiness and sadness for a while, till a tiny hand held on to Sophie's and sweetness filled the world, once again." When asked about the intergenerational theme found across a number of her books such as *Shoes from Grandpa* (1992), *Night Noises* (1991), *Guess What?* (1988), *With Love at Christmas* (1992), and *Possum Magic,* F. concluded that her special bond with her grandfather was unique and "almost conspiratorial" and that capturing the essence of this wonderful relationship surely influenced her writing.

F. credits her disappointment in *Possum Magic* receiving second place in the Picture Book of the Year competition as influencing her writing of *Koala Lou* (1988). Eager to gain her mother's love by winning the gum tree climbing contest during the Bush Olympics, Koala is devastated by her loss to Koala Klaws until she returns home to her mother's tender hug and her words, "Koala Lou, I DO love you! I always have, and I always will." F. demonstrates passion for children and

books in her voice as both a writer and speaker at professional meetings. Her messages for educators focus on the contribution of quality writing to children's abilities as readers and the importance of cultivating their passion for reading to ensure that books become significant parts of their daily lives. F. argues that writers must never write down to their young audiences; rather, that quality writing for children must be the very finest to ignite children's desires to be readers. Her professional writings are found in a variety of journals such as the *Journal of Children's Literature, The New Advocate, Language Arts, The Reading Teacher, Australian Journal of Language and Literacy,* and also in her collection of essays on educational issues, *Radical Reflections: Passionate Opinions on Teaching, Learning, and Living* (1993). Further information about her life, interests, and books is available at her web site, www.memfox.net.

AWARDS: *New York Times* One hundred Best Books for Children (1987) for *Wilfred Gordon McDonald Partridge;* Dromkeen Medal (1990) for outstanding services to Children's Literature. Advance Australia Award (1990) for an outstanding contribution to the advancement and enrichment of Australia, its people and its way of life. The Alice Award (1994), presented biennially by the Fellowship of Australian Women Writers to a woman writer, for long-term contribution to the profession and in recognition of an outstanding body of work.

FURTHER WORKS: *Whoever You Are,* 1998; *The Straight Line Wonder,* 1987/1997; *Time for Bed,* 1997; *Boo to a Goose,* 1996; *Feathers and Fools,* 1996; *Zoo-Looking,* 1987/1996; *Hattie and the Fox,* 1988/1995; *Wombat Divine,* 1995; *Tough Boris,* 1994; *Time for Bed,* 1993; *How to Teach Drama to Infants without Really Crying,* 1982

PATRICIA A. SCHARER

FOX, Paula
Author, b. 22 April 1923, New York City

F. is a prolific and critically acclaimed novelist, who writes for both children and adults. The hallmarks of her fiction are the hostile environments in which she sets her solitary, and often lonely, protagonists, and the exquisite use she makes of language. From early childhood, F. lived amidst stories and STORYTELLING. Her father was himself a writer, but she did not live with her parents even as a young child. Her earliest years were spent with a Congregational minister who cared for his invalid mother as well as for little Paula, while F.'s parents traveled. From him F. learned both classical and contemporary tales and gained a sense of the narrative potential history holds. He told her bedtime stories from KIPLING and of the exploits of local Hudson Valley folk during the Revolutionary War. He taught her to read and that her ideas—in spite of her youth—were to be respected.

At the age of six, F. moved to California, where her parents had relocated while her father wrote for the movie industry. A couple of years later, however, she was sent into the care of her grandmother who lived in Cuba. By the time F. returned to the United States three years later, she was bilingual as well as literary. Back in New York, she rediscovered the local public library as her true home, a predictably comforting place in her otherwise itinerant life.

After high school, she continued to study at Columbia University for four years, but left before graduation because she had run out of money. She worked as a teacher, making good use of her bilingual abilities. She taught English to Spanish-speaking children and also worked with emotionally disturbed children. In 1962, she traveled to Greece; she had the time and opportunity to begin her career as an author. *Maurice's Room,* her first book for children, was published in 1966.

Blowfish Live in the Sea (1970), her ninth book, was a finalist in the children's book category of the National Book Award in 1971. In 1972, she earned both a Guggenheim fellowship and an award from the National Institute of Arts and Letters, with a grant from the National Endowment for the Arts following in 1974.

Also in 1974, F. was awarded the ALA NEW-BERY MEDAL for *The Slave Dancer.* This award proved controversial. The title character, a young white boy kidnapped off the streets of New Orleans and placed aboard an Africa-bound slave ship, was ordered to play music while the slaves being brought back to America danced to stay limber and thus suitable for labor. F. presents her characters with moral lives from which they choose how to act within the story's dilemmas, but some critics, including reviewers for Interra-

cial Books for Children and Julius LESTER, took issue with the attitudes toward slavery expressed and assumed by the characters in this novel about the Middle Passage. They saw the novel as excusing the whites who had been part of slave trading while also providing contemporary white readers with the opportunity to feel relieved of any further need to make retribution for the injustices of slavery. F.'s critical defenders, including children's literature scholar Anita Moss, championed F.'s work as exemplary historical fiction that provides children the opportunity to be exposed to real and accurately detailed horrors, an exposure which provides the opportunity to further their own moral development. F. accepted the award with a speech that won over a few of her critics. The *Slave Dancer* has become a classic in the quarter century since its publication.

F.'s character-driven fiction derives its power from her elegantly understated and emotionally acute use of language. Her plots are often complex; the issues she addresses are ones her readers and literary critics recognize as needing the kind of explication excellent fiction can provide for real-life concerns. The loss of parents is explored in *A Place Apart* (1980), in which the protagonist's father dies suddenly, and in *The Eagle Kite* (1995), in which the protagonist has the opportunity to acknowledge his father's affection and remorse during the parent's fatal decline from AIDS. Other issues that find their way into the lives of F.'s characters are alcoholism *(Blowfish Live in the Sea,* 1970), homelessness *(Monkey Island,* 1991), and disillusionment with either parents *(The Moonlight Man,* 1986) or the state *(The King's Falcon,* 1969).

F. has also been successful as an author of adult books. She does not decide upon the age of the audience she hopes to engage when writing any particular book. That becomes clear after the story's completion. In the case of *The King's Falcon,* a historical FANTASY that F. thought would be for children, the readership surprised her: the novel proved to be a cult favorite among anti-Vietnam War college students.

Now a mature writer as well as reader, F. takes her counsel not from critics so much as from those authors she herself admires. James Joyce, Lev Tolstoy, and Flannery O'Connor are among her favorites who inspire her to continue to refine her craft.

AWARDS: Hans Christian ANDERSEN Medal (1978) for the entire body of her work. American Book Award (1983) for *A Place Apart*. AMERICAN LIBRARY ASSOCIATION Newbery Medal Honor Book (1985), IBBY Honor List (1986), and Christopher Medal (1984) for *One-Eyed Cat*. ALA Newbery Medal (1974) for *The Slave Dancer*. F. received a Rockefeller Foundation grant in 1984. *Boston Globe-Horn Book* fiction award (1989) for *The Village by the Sea*. Empire State Award for Excellence in Literature for Young People (1994). University of Southern Mississippi Medallion of the DE GRUMMOND Children's Literature Research Collection (1987).

FURTHER WORKS: *How Many Miles to Babylon?*, 1967; *The Stone-Faced Boy*, 1968; *Good Ethan*, 1973; *The Little Swineherd and Other Tales*, 1978; *Radiance Descending*, 1997

BIBLIOGRAPHY: *Contemporary Authors, New Revision Series*. 1998; *Something about the Author*, vol. 60, 1990; Townsend, J. R. *A Sense of Story: Essays on Contemporary Writers for Children*. 1971

FRANCISCA GOLDSMITH

FRAMPTON, David

Illustrator, b. 4 November 1942, Brooklyn, New York

F.'s woodcuts illustrate children's texts based on Biblical stories and folktales, as well as original tales and nonfiction. After graduating from Rhode Island School of Design, F. earned a Master of Fine Arts degree at Penn State University.

For Karla KUSKIN's history of the city, *Jerusalem Shining Still* (1987), F. produced glowing three-color images of the inhabitants and their activities across 4,000 years. As a fan of Rudyard KIPLING, F. brings freshness to *Just So Stories* (1991) with both color and expressive facial details. Carol CARRICK's *Whaling Days* (1992) has its nonfiction explanations of the preindustrial value of whale products and their attainment greatly expanded by the details in F.'s precise and accurate block prints. *Of Swords and Sorcerers: The Adventures of King Arthur and His Knights*, by Margaret HODGES and Margery Evernden (1993), includes decorations by F. that are reminiscent of Beardsley and other illustrators working several generations earlier. Jim AYLESWORTH's *My Son John* (1994), however, represents a different style for F.; here the block prints carry the bright colors of oil paint and curve toward the cartoonish, just as the author's text riffs on traditional nursery rhyme. F. uses woodcut prints in full color to give a modern look to *Miro in the Kingdom of the Sun* (J. Kurtz, 1996), an Inca folktale retold in a contemporary version. In addition to illustrating books for children, F.'s work has appeared in adult texts, including magazines.

FURTHER WORKS: *Waterway West: The Story of the Erie Canal*. M. Phelan, 1977; *Joshua in the Promised Land*. M. Chaikin, 1982; *Fresh Paint: New Poems by Eve Merriam*, 1986; *Bull Run*. P. FLEISCHMAN, 1993; *When Plague Strikes*. J. GIBLIN. 1995; *Clouds of Glory* Chaikin, 1998

FRANCISCA GOLDSMITH

FRASCONI, Antonio

Illustrator, author, b. 28 April 1919, Buenos Aires, Argentina

F. was born in Argentina to Italian parents who had recently immigrated from Italy, establishing a household where language and culture were both intriguing and frustrating. As a child F. cherished books and painting as well as politics that led to his early works of posters and political caricatures. F. moved to the United States to study art and became interested in woodcuts. These would be the inspiration for his children's book ILLUSTRATIONS. One of the first done in three- and four-color woodcuts for which F. is noted is *See and Say* (1955), a PICTURE BOOK done in four languages selected as a *New York Times* Best Illustrated Children's Books of the Year. He prints each woodcut by hand on an inked block producing stunning yet subtle color effects.

AWARDS: ALA CALDECOTT MEDAL Honor Book (1959) for *The House That Jack Built*. *New York Times* Best Illustrated Children's Books of the Year (1955) for *See and Say*, (1958) for *The House That Jack Built*, and (1961) for *The Snow and the Sun*

FURTHER WORKS: Illustrator: *One Little Room: An Everywhere—Poems of Love* (Myra Cohn LIVINGSTON, editor). 1975; *Beginnings: Creation Myths of the World* (Penelope ARMER, compiler), 1978; *Monkey Puzzle and Other Poems* (Myra Cohn Livingston, ed.). 1984; *Elijah the Slave*. (Isaac Bashevis SINGER). 1970; *If the Owl Calls My Name Again: A Collection of Owl Poems*. (Myra Cohn Livingston, ed.). 1990. *At Christ-*

mastime. (Valerie WORTH). 1992. Author: *Twelve Fables of Aesop.* (American Institute of Graphic Arts 50 Books of the Year). 1954; *Birds from My Homeland* 1958; *The Face of Edgar Allan Poe* 1959; *The Cantilever Rainbow* (Ruth KRAUSS, au., 1965)

BIBLIOGRAPHY: MEIGS, C., A. EATON, E. NESBITT, R. H. VIGUERS. *A Critical History of Children's Literature.* 1969. *Something about the Author.* vol. 53, 1988.

MICHAEL O'LAUGHLIN

FREEDMAN, Russell

Author, b. 11 October 1929, San Francisco, California

F. is the author of informative and engaging nonfiction books for young people with topics that include animal life, BIOGRAPHY, and American history. F.'s parents met in a bookshop where his mother was a clerk and his father a publishing representative for Macmillan. They established a home filled with books and book talk. Authors such as John Steinbeck, William Saroyan, and John MASEFIELD were guests in their San Francisco home. F. has pleasurable memories of his childhood reading. He recalls several foggy summer days curled up reading on a maroon chesterfield sofa that dominated his living room. Hendrik VAN LOON's *The Story of Mankind* (1921) was the first book that gave him a sense of living history.

After college at the University of California at Berkeley and duty with the Second Infantry Division in Korea, F. got a job as a reporter and editor for the Associated Press in San Francisco. He considers that experience as the time when he really learned to write. He wanted to be a part of the New York establishment and took a job there with an advertising agency. He spent three years writing television publicity for such shows as *Kraft Television Theatre, Father Knows Best,* and *The Real McCoys.*

One day he read an article in the *New York Times* that told of a sixteen-year-old blind boy who had invented a Braille typewriter and mentioned that the Braille language had also been invented by a sixteen-year-old. These facts started F. wondering about other young people who had made significant contributions to the world. The result was his first hardcover book, *Famous Teen-agers Who Made History.* The book, published in 1961, stayed in print for nearly twenty years.

F.'s next years as a writer were dominated by animal books beginning with *How Animals Learn* (1969). F. describes his early animal books as solid and substantial, but he began to wonder if anyone read them. He did not want to write a book that was only used for reports. He decided to narrow the scope to a particular kind of animal or a particular kind of animal behavior. He also began using interesting photographs rather than drawings to illustrate his books. The books received generally positive reviews for their effective photographs and their informative, entertaining text.

A change in F.'s writing direction began after he visited a photography exhibit featuring New York City's children of the nineteenth century at the New York Historical Society. F. was impressed by the power of the old photographs that evoked the past in a way that nothing else could. The direct result of that experience was *Immigrant Kids* (1980). He wrote a few more animal books, but his interest in history evoked by the archival photographs led to *Children of the Wild West* (1984), *Cowboys of the Wild West* (1985), and *Indian Chiefs* (1987).

F.'s thirty-fourth book was *Lincoln: A Photobiography.* As a child, F. had read fictionalized, idealized accounts of Lincoln. He had the desire to find a believable human being behind the layers of historical makeup. It was a daunting task to write about a man who had more books written about him than any other American. F. got helpful reading guidance from the owner of the Abraham Lincoln Bookshop in Chicago. He visited Kentucky, Illinois, and Washington, D.C., and found a magic in seeing the places where Lincoln had lived and worked. When F. sat down to write, he found he could visualize the settings such as the walk Lincoln took from his home to his office in Springfield, Illinois, because he had walked the route himself. He was emotionally affected by seeing original Lincoln documents, letters he had written to his wife, court notes, and drafts of speeches with doodles and notes. The result of F.'s research was a more realistic, complex, and interesting Lincoln than previous biographies for children. He included over eighty archival photographs and documents that added information, interest, and visual impact. The biography was awarded the ALA NEWBERY MEDAL, the first non-fiction title to win the award in thirty-two years and INTERNATIONAL BOARD ON BOOKS FOR YOUNG PEOPLE.

F. won two Newbery Medal Honor Book awards for subsequent biographies: *The Wright Brothers and How They Invented the Airplane* (1991) and *Eleanor Roosevelt. A Life of Discovery* (1993). Research on one book often led to interest in another. F. reported falling in love with Eleanor Roosevelt while writing *Franklin Delano Roosevelt* (1990). More well-received books followed including *An Indian Winter* (1992), *Kids at Work: Lewis Hine and the Crusade against Child Labor* (1995), *Life and Times of Crazy Horse* (1996), and *Martha Graham: A Dancer's Life* (1998). F. has been described as a dispassionate writer who presents events and their effects without romanticism or judgments. He uses appropriate detail in focused, uncomplicated prose that vividly recreates the times and makes an emotional impact.

In 1998, F. received the prestigious Laura Ingalls WILDER Award to honor his entire body of writing. A *Horn Book* magazine article that accompanies his acceptance speech quotes F.'s mission in writing for children: "It's a much greater challenge to convey the spirit and essence of a life in a hundred pages than to write a 600 or 800 page 'definitive' tome that includes every known detail about that life. A non-fiction children's book requires concision, selection, judgment, lucidity, unwavering focus, and the artful use of language and STORYTELLING techniques. I regard such books as a specialized and demanding art form."

AWARDS: ALA Newbery Medal (1988) for *Lincoln: A Photobiography*. ALA Newbery Medal Honor Book (1994) for *Eleanor Roosevelt: A Life of Discovery* and (1992) for *The Wright Brothers: How They Invented the Airplane. Boston Globe-Horn Book* Award for nonfiction (1994) for *Eleanor Roosevelt: A Life of Discovery*. Empire State Award for Excellence in Literature for Young People (1993). Golden Kite Award for nonfiction (1991) for *The Wright Brothers: How They Invented the Airplane*, (1993) for *Eleanor Roosevelt: A Life of Discovery*, and (1994) for *Kids at Work: Lewis Hine and the Crusade against Child Labor*. NCTE ORBIS PICTUS AWARD (1991) for *Franklin Delano Roosesvelt*. IBBY Honor List (1990) for *Lincoln: A Photobiography*. Laura Ingalls Wilder Award for a lasting contribution to literature for children (1998)

FURTHER WORDS: *Killer Snakes,* 1982; *Sharks,* 1985; *Farm Babies,* 1981; *Rattlesnakes.* 1984

BIBLIOGRAPHY: *Horn Book* magazine, July/August 1988, pp. 444–56, and July/August 1998, pp. 450–58

ADELE GREENLEE

FREEMAN, Don

Author, illustrator, b. 11 August 1908, San Diego, California; d. 1 February 1978, Place unknown

F. is remembered for his popular self-illustrated books for young readers. F. won several AWARDS for his books, including a CALDECOTT MEDAL Honor Book for *Fly High, Fly Low* (1957) and The Southern California Council on Literature for Children and Young People Award for a significant contribution in the field of ILLUSTRATION for *Come Again, Pelican* (1961). He also illustrated many books for other well-known authors such as William Saroyan, James THURBER, and Richard PECK.

During his youth, F. maintained two passions—drawing pictures and playing his trumpet. After studying for two years at the San Diego School of Fine Arts, he hitchhiked to New York and earned a meager living playing the trumpet at nightclubs. One night he accidentally left his trumpet on the subway, and, unable to afford another one, he turned to drawing as a way of making his living. His artwork eventually appeared in the drama pages of New York newspapers and in *Theater* magazine. His first book for children, *Chuggy and the Blue Caboose* (1951), was written in collaboration with his wife, Lydia. A second book by the couple, *Pet of the Met* (1953), earned them the Book World Spring Book Festival Award.

Among F.'s most popular works is *Corduroy* (1968), the story of a lonely stuffed bear who lives in a department store. He is befriended by a little girl willing to spend her own money to buy him. In this gentle FANTASY about caring and friendship, Lisa's determination prevails; Corduroy gets a loving new home and a new button to hold up his overalls. In a related story, *Beady Bear* (1954), a windup bear gets left behind by a boy and sets out to live in a cave. Several of F.'s works are set in culturally inspiring places. For example, *Pet of the Met* (1953) features a mouse who lives in the Metropolitan Opera House, *Norman the Doorman* (1959) is set in an art museum, and *The Guard Mouse* (1967) takes place at Buckingham Palace.

F. wrote and illustrated dozens of stories for preschool children, many of which remain in print. His works are praised for their simplicity, charm, warmth, and sensitivity. Linda Zuckerman, F.'s editor at Viking Press, recalls, "Don Freeman was an unusually successful creator of children's books which have appeared all over the world in hardcover and paperback, in foreign languages, and on filmstrips and films." Zuckerman also noted that, even though F.'s simple, unpretentious artistic style was never fashionable and that his approach to a PICTURE BOOK never changed with the trends of the times, children all over the world have continued to appreciate and love his stories.

FURTHER WORKS: Self-illustrated: *Mop Top,* 1955, reissued 1970; *Dandelion,* 1964; *The Paper Party,* 1974; *Will's Quill,* 1975; *A Pocket for Corduroy,* 1978; Illustrator: *The Human Comedy* (William Saroyan), 1943; *White Deer,* (James THURBER), 1945; *Monster Night at Grandma's House* (Richard PECK), 1977

BIBLIOGRAPHY: *Children's Literature Review.* vol. 80, (1993). HOPKINS, Lee Bennett, *Pauses: Autobiographical Reflections of 101 Creators of Children's Books,* 1995. *Major Authors and Illustrators for Children and Young Adults,* 1993

MARY ARIAIL BROUGHTON

FRITZ, Jean

Author, b. 16 November 1915, Hankow, China

The daughter of missionaries, F. spent the first thirteen years of her life in tumultuous China. Her autobiography, *Homesick: My Own Story* (1982), reveals young F. who felt out of place in China, longing to live in the America she read about in letters from her grandmother. While living in China, she attended a British school that set the stage for her independence and mild rebellion in an effort to exhibit her loyalty to her home country. Feeling lonely as an only child and listening to her parents' frequent referrals to America, she developed a strong patriotism for America and a need to satisfy her curiosity about it. She also developed a sense of humor with

which to view humanity. This curiosity and her love for writing served as the impetus for many of her books for children. Although F. aspired to be a writer from a young age, her early efforts were met with rejection letters. It was not until she was the mother of young children in a community in New York with no children's department at the local library that she decided to turn her efforts to writing for children. She worked as a volunteer at the library, established a children's section, and made the decision to write for children. F. had received an A.B. from Wheaton College in 1937 and studied children's literature under Jean Betsner at Columbia University. Early in her career, F. worked with textbook publishers writing teacher's manuals and educational and promotional materials.

F.'s childhood experiences were the substance for her beginning writings. Most importantly she kept a journal in which she recorded comments and excerpts from great writings. Eventually the comments evolved into and included personal articulations about her life and the people in it. F. began writing for children in the early 1950s with short stories in *Humpty Dumpty,* drawing from her experiences with her young son and daughter. She then wrote concept books from 1954–57, beginning with *Bunny Hopwell's First Spring* (1954). Also during this time period, F. wrote a picture book *Fish Head* (1954). In 1955, *121 Pudding Street* was published; it stemmed from her early journal entries and characters representative of her son and daughter. This work also exhibits F.'s maturation as a writer. Her first historical fiction novel *The Cabin Faced West* was written in 1958, followed by *Brady* (1960). F. wrote several illustrated biographies about Revolutionary War figures. F.'s biographies entertain children with revelations about famous historical figures from the past not found in most historical accounts. An inviting title, usually in the form of a question (*What's the Big Idea, Ben Franklin?,* 1976) is followed by an equally interesting text. F. wants her readers to experience the human qualities of historical figures. She is extremely accurate in her facts while using her humorous style to present the personality and character of the person in history. Exhaustive research is involved in F.'s attempts to uncover primary sources such as journals, diaries, and letters. Her

35. PAUL FLEISCHMAN

36. MEM FOX

37. PAULA FOX

38. RUSSELL FREEDMAN

39. JEAN FRITZ

books present a fresh look at history for children at a depth that includes the motivations behind decisions in salient events, the nature of human interaction, and a humorous perspective. They are written to be captivating when read aloud. She captures her audiences with intriguing tidbits that present panoramic views of characters to entice the most reluctant students of history. In addition to writing for children, F. writes about children's literature in the following periodicals: *Elementary English, Library Journal, Horn Book,* and *Children's Literature in Education.* She wrote an adult biography *Case for a Revolution: Some American Friends and Enemies, 1728–1814* (1972). She is also a contributor to William Zinsser's *Worlds of Childhood: The Art and Craft of Writing for Children* (1990). F. is a remarkable writer who has the rare ability to couple diligent accuracy with creativity to produce fiction and nonfiction reading for children and young adults.

AWARDS: *New York Times* outstanding book of the year citations (1973) for *And Then What Happened, Paul Revere?,* (1974) for *Why Don't You Get a Horse, Sam Adams?,* (1975) for *Where Was Patrick Henry on the 29th of May?,* (1976) for *What's the Big Idea, Ben Franklin?,* (1981) for *Traitor: The Case of Benedict Arnold,* and (1982) for *Homesick: My Own Story. Boston Globe-Horn Book* honor citation (1973) for *And Then What Happened, Paul Revere?,* (1976) for *Will You Sign Here, John Hancock?,* (1979) for *Stonewall.* Children's Book Guild's Honor Award for Nonfiction (1978) for the "body of her creative writing." ALA NEWBERY MEDAL Honor Book (1983), for *Homesick: My Own Story. Boston Globe–Horn Book* Nonfiction Award (1984) for *The Double Life of Pocahontas,* and (1990) for *The Great Little Madison.* NATIONAL COUNCIL OF TEACHERS OF ENGLISH (NCTE) ORBIS PICTUS AWARD (1990) for *The Great Little Madison.* Laura Ingalls WILDER Award 1986

FURTHER WORKS: *Help Mr. Willy Nilly,* 1954; *Growing Up,* 1956; *The Late Spring,* 1957; *Champion Dog, Prince Tom,* 1958; *How to Read a Rabbit,* 1959; *December Is for Christmas,* 1961; *Tip, Tap, Lion—1,2,3,* (1962); *I, Adam,* 1963; *Magic to Burn,* 1964; *Early Thunder,* 1967; *George Washington's Breakfast,* 1969; *Can't You Make Them Behave, King George?,* 1977; *Brendan the Navigator: A History Mystery about the Discovery of America,* 1979; *Where Do You Think You're Going, Christopher?,* 1980; *China Homecoming,* 1985; *Make Way for Sam Houston,* 1986; *Bully for You, Teddy Roosevelt!,* 1991;

Harriet Beecher Stowe and the Beecher Preachers, 1994; *Around the World in a Hundred Years: From Henry the Navigator to Magellan,* 1994; *The World in 1492,* 1998; *Who's That Stepping on Plymouth Rock?,* 1998

BIBLIOGRAPHY: Ammon, Richard. "Profile: Jean Fritz," *Language Arts.* March, 1983, vol. 60, no. 3, p. 365; *Dictionary of Literary Biography.* vol. 52. Fritz, Jean. *Homesick: My Own Story,* 1982; HOPKINS, Lee Bennett, *Pauses: Autobiographical Reflections of 101 Creators of Children's Books,* 1995

NANCY HORTON

FROST, Arthur Burdett

Illustrator, cartoonist, author, b. 17 January 1851, Philadelphia, Pennsylvania; d. 22 June 1928, California

F. worked first as a lithographer and later took assignments from *Harper's* magazine, drawing pictures of outdoors SPORTS. A year spent studying in London began an association with Lewis CARROLL that eventually led to F.'s illustrating *Rhyme? and Reason?* (1883) and *A Tangled Tale* (1885). Although his comic drawings were quite successful and he published his own book of verse and sketches, *Stuff and Nonsense* (1884), his greatest desire was to be known as a painter. He lived for a while in France in efforts to achieve his goal. He is most recognized for his ILLUSTRATIONS in Joel Chandler HARRIS's *Uncle Remus and His Friends: Old Plantation Stories, Songs, and Ballads* (1892), *Uncle Remus, His Songs and His Sayings: FOLKLORE of the Old Plantation* (1895), *The Tar-Baby, and Other Rhymes of Uncle Remus* (1904), and others.

FURTHER WORKS ILLUSTRATED: *American Notes* (Charles DICKENS), 1870; *The Posthumous Papers of the Pickwick Club* (Charles Dickens), 1879; *Tom Sawyer Abroad* (Mark TWAIN), 1896; *Phantasmagoria and Other Poems* (Lewis Carroll), 1911

BIBLIOGRAPHY: Mahony, Bertha E., et al., *Illustrators of Children's Books: 1744–1945,* 1947; Reed, Henry M. *The A. B. Frost Book,* 1967; *Something about the Author,* vol. 19, 1980

JANELLE B. MATHIS

FROST, Robert

Poet, b. 26 March 1874, San Francisco, California; d. 29 January 1963, Boston, Massachusetts

F. grew up in the the wilds of post-goldrush San Francisco, but his poetry was grounded in his late adolescence and adult life in New England. F. often wrote poetry for his children and although he was not expressly a poet for children, several collections, including *A Swinger of Birches: Poems of Robert Frost for Young People* (1982), reflect his ability to express childlike innocence and wonder. Other collections of his that are accessible to children and have been enjoyed by them include *Come in and Other Poems* (1943) and *You Come Too: Favorite Poems for Young Readers* (1959), still in print and widely read. *Birches,* first published in 1916, is available in several illustrated editions; one outstanding volume

is illustrated by Ed YOUNG. F.'s classic lyric has been issued as a single volume, *Stopping by the Woods on a Snowy Evening* (1978), with softly evocative watercolors by Susan JEFFERS that complement the mood of the poem. His poems are also included in anthologies for children.

FURTHER WORKS: *Birches,* 1988; *Poetry for Young People: Robert Frost.* 1994; *The Runaway,* 1996

BIBLIOGRAPHY: Bober, N. S. *A Restless Spirit: The Story of Robert Frost,* 1981

GWYNNE ELLEN ASH

GAG, Wanda

Author, illustrator, translator, b. 11 March 1893, New Ulm, Minnesota; d. 27 June 1946, New York City

G. was the oldest of seven children born to a Bohemian-American painter and artistic wife. Her mother's family read and told Brothers GRIMM folktales to the children. G.'s father died when she was fifteen, and left the family impoverished. She and the older children sold stories, drawings, and cartoons to the children's section of a newspaper. G. supplemented the family income with greeting cards and birthday books that she sold at the local drugstore and to her teachers. Meanwhile, C. told stories to entertain the younger children in the household.

Her dream was to become an artist like her father, and after graduating from high school in 1912 she completed her studies at Minneapolis Art School. G. was determined to study at the Art Students League of New York on scholarship. She worked in New York City as a commercial artist and lived sparingly, sending money home to her family. She continued to tell stories whenever there were children to entertain.

In New York, she showed her portfolio to publishers, but no one seemed interested. Years went by until an editor at Coward McCann saw G.'s one-woman show and invited her to submit a story. She submitted the manuscript for *Millions of Cats,* an original story. It had the cadence, rhyme scheme, and repetition of traditional German folktales. Asked to illustrate it, G. designed the two pages of the opened book as a whole, termed a double-page spread. The text and ILLUSTRATIONS became an integrated whole unit, just as G. had conceived it. The illustrations reflect and expand on the text, the dust jacket and end papers provide an introduction to the interior contents. The book, an instant success when published in the autumn of 1928, remains in print more than seventy years later. G.'s most popular book, it has been translated into languages from Danish to Ukrainian.

G. wrote PICTURE BOOKS, translated the GRIMMS' folktales, and excerpted her early diaries, all of which she illustrated. Two more picture books illustrated with India ink drawings followed, *The Funny Thing* (1929) and *Snippy and Snappy* (1931); in 1932 they were published as *Wanda Gag's Storybook.* The ABC Bunny, an alphabet book with original lithographs, followed in 1933. G. avoided repetition producing unique stories with new characters each time, yet each related somehow to her life. The old man and woman in *Millions of Cats* could have stepped out of the German community of her childhood. The singular *"Funny Thing"* may have been inspired by the heavy equipment that is seen outdoors in her rural New Jersey neighborhood. In contrast, the mice in *Snippy and Snappy* were twins and most of the illustrations are of interior settings. G.'s last picture book, *Nothing at All* (1941), was about an invisible dog and the artist challenged herself with drawing images for color separation on glass to resemble lithographs. In contrast to many alphabet books of her time, G.'s *The ABC Bunny* told a story about a frightened rabbit running after an apple that fell out of a tree.

In searching published versions of Grimm folktales, G. failed to find a particular story she had heard as a child—about a farmer's wife who trades chores with her husband. Therefore, she wrote it as she remembered hearing it and gave it the title *Gone Is Gone* (1935).

G. translated German folktales for language practice and selected several for a book she illustrated, *Tales from Grimm* (1936). Two years later, *Snow White and the Seven Dwarfs* appeared, after the DISNEY–animated version. Later, two more Grimm editions were published, *Three Gay Tales* (1943) and *More Tales from Grimm* (1947), posthumously.

In 1940, excerpts from G.'s teenage and young adult diaries were published as *Growing Pains.* She'd written with candor during these years about her activities, her observations of people, and her yearning for a career as an artist. The book is an autobiographical coming-of-age story.

There were few AWARDS in G.'s time. *Millions of Cats* and *The ABC Bunny* were ALA NEWBERY MEDAL runner-up titles in 1929 and 1934, now termed Honor Book, before the ALA CALDECOTT MEDAL was initiated. The American Institute of Graphic Arts (AIGA) selected these books as the most outstanding children's books published between 1920 and 1962. *Snow White and the Seven Dwarfs* and *Nothing at All* were selected as Caldecott Medal Honor Books in their respective years. AIGA named *More Tales from Grimm* as one of the best examples of design and typography published between 1945 and 1969.

BIBLIOGRAPHY: *Dictionary of Literary Biography: American Writers for Children, 1900–1960,* vol. 22, 1953; Hoyle, K., *Wanda Gag,* 1994; Scott, A., *Wanda Gag: The Story of an Artist,* 1949; Winnan A. *Wanda Gag: A Catalogue Raisonné of the Prints,* 1993

KAREN NELSON HOYLE

GALDONE, Paul

Illustrator, b. 2 June 1914, Budapest, Hungary; d. 7 November 1986, Nyack, New York

G.'s early years remain shrouded in some mystery, but his childhood was often difficult and he emigrated with his family to the United States when he was about fourteen; he studied art in New York City while working at odd jobs to help support his family. G. worked for Doubleday publishers for a time before setting out on his own as a freelance artist. In time he was able to move his family to a rural home in Rockland County, New York, where he gardened, enjoyed the out-of-doors, and pursued a prolific career in children's book ILLUSTRATION. G. is credited with illustrating some 150 books.

G. was influenced by Arthur RACKHAM and Walter CRANE, and like them illustrated many of the old folktales, some of which he retold himself. His drawings, largely done in pen, ink, and wash, are imbued with a fresh vitality and almost naive charm; they frequently reflect his love of nature. They also exhibit free-flowing strokes and broad humor, bringing a lively, contemporary spirit to the old tales. G. illustrated most of the standard folktale fare, including *The Three Wishes* (1961), *Little Red Riding Hood* (1974), *Cinderella* (1978), *Hansel and Gretel* (1982), and *Three Billy Goats Gruff* (1973) to name just a few.

G. also illustrated books by a great many noted writers. His illustrations for Eve Titus's *Anatole* (1956) and *Anatole and the Cat* (1957) were named ALA CALDECOTT MEDAL Honor Books. He illustrated such classics as Oliver Wendell Holmes's *The Deacon's Masterpiece* (1965) and HAWTHORNE's *Pandora's Box: The Paradise of Children* (1967). He also worked in nonfiction, as in Franklyn M. BRANLEY's *High Sounds, Low Sounds* (1967) or Judith VIORST's *Try It Again, Sam: Safety When You Walk* (1970).

His style is distinctive, and if it is not widely varied, it exudes a spontaneity, almost whimsy, greeting the reader with a liberated, joyous spirit.

AWARDS: AMERICAN LIBRARY ASSOCIATION Caldecott Medal Honor Book (1957) for *Anatole,* and (1958) for *Anatole and the Cat* (both written by Eve Titus).

FURTHER WORKS: *Space Cat.* (Ruthven Todd). 1952. *Hans Brinker.* (Mary Mapes DODGE). 1954. *A Gaggle of Geese.* (Eve MERRIAM). 1960. *Old Mother and Her Dog.* 1960. *The Bremen Town Musicians.* (GRIMM). 1968. *George Washington's Breakfast.* (Jean FRITZ). 1969. *Dance of the Animals: A Puerto Rican Folk Tale.* (Pura BELPRE). 1972. *The Little Girl and the Big Bear.* (Joanna Galdone). 1980

BIBLIOGRAPHY: *The Oxford Companion to Children's Literature.* 1984. HOPKINS, Lee Bennett, *Pauses: Autobiographical Reflections of 101 Creators of Children's Books,* 1995

DAVID L. RUSSELL

GAMMELL, Stephen
Author, illustrator, b. 10 February 1943, Des Moines, Iowa

G. is best known for his picture-book illustrations, frequently using watercolor or black and white drawings in a style portraying energy and humor. His technique is varied, as he sometimes rubs pencil shavings for cloudlike effects in books such as *Where the Buffaloes Begin* (1981) or spatters watercolors for a rain effect in *Come a Tide* (1990). G. developed an interest in art at an early age. He remembers his father, an art editor, bringing home assorted art supplies for G. to explore freely. Upon leaving high school, G. pursued a variety of jobs but did not channel his artistic interest and talent into a career until he received a contract for ILLUSTRATION after showing samples of his work to a publisher in New York. Since that time G. has primarily illustrated other people's stories, writing only a few books himself. He reports that he finds illustrating more rewarding than writing.

G.'s softly shaded colored-pencil drawings in the award-winning *Song and Dance Man* (Karen ACKERMAN, 1988) convey drama, movement, and a loving cross-generational relationship when grandpa takes his grandchildren up to the attic for an old-fashioned vaudeville performance. Rounded shapes and lots of yellow allow readers to visualize the stage with the bright lights focused on grandpa as he performs his "song and dance" act for an enthusiastic audience in this acclaimed PICTURE BOOK. G. used a similar style of soft-toned colored pencils to illustrate *The Relatives Came* (Cynthia RYLANT, 1985). He captures an exuberant family reunion where all the relatives have a rollicking good time that never seems to end.

AWARDS: ALA CALDECOTT Medal (1989) for *Song and Dance Man* (ACKERMAN). ALA Caldecott Medal Honor Book (1982) for *Where the Buffaloes Begin* (Baker), and (1986) for *The Relatives Came* (Rylant). *New York Times* Best Illustrated Children's Books of the Year (1981) for *Where the Buffaloes Begin* (Olaf Baker), and (1985) for *The Relatives Came* (Rylant)

FURTHER WORKS: Self-illus.: *Is That You, Winter?: A Story.* 1997. Illus.: *Thunder at Gettysburg.* (Patricia Lee GAUCH). 1975. *Ghosts.* (Seymour SIMON). 1976. *Scary Stories to Tell in the Dark.* (Alvin SCHWARTZ). 1981. *Old Henry.* (Joan BLOS). 1987. *Airmail to the Moon.* (Tom Birdseye). 1988. *Dancing Tepees: Poems of American Indian Youth.* (Virginia Driving Hawk SNEVE, ed.). 1989. *Will's Mammoth.* (Rafe MARTIN). 1989. *Come a Tide.* (George Ella LYON). 1990. *Old Black Fly.* (Jim AYLESWORTH). 1992. *Monster Mama.* (Liz Rosenberg). 1993

BIBLIOGRAPHY: *Something about the Author,* vol. 81, 1995

SANDRA IMDIEKE

GANTOS, Jack
Author, b. 2 July 1951, Mount Pleasant, Pennsylvania

Best known as author of the Rotten Ralph series, G. traces his writing career back to second grade, when he insisted on having a diary because his older sister had one. Though at first he recorded only facts like the weather or what he had eaten that day, his approach to keeping a journal changed when the family moved to the CARIBBEAN island of Barbados. Restricted to packing only books and diaries for the move, he filled the diary with treasures he could not bear to leave behind—stamps, coins, bottle caps, baseball cards, butterflies—even drilling holes in the book to hold his marble collection. The scrapbook-diary evolved into a journal as G. began to write about the objects stuffed between its pages. G. continues this scrapbook-journal approach to writing today, drawing on written memories and "stuff" pasted into journals to add detail to stories.

In college, G. began a collaboration with art student Nicole RUBEL to produce PICTURE BOOKS. Early attempts to write for children proved frustrating until he followed a teacher's advice to "write about what you know" and focused on the irritating antics of his cat. Rotten Ralph, the misbehaving cat who is always forgiven and who always acts up again, has starred in ten popular titles. G. and Rubel have produced nine other picture books, including *Sleepy Ronald* (1976) about a flop-eared rabbit who cannot stay awake.

Nearly twenty years after the appearance of Rotten Ralph, G. published his first chapter book for older readers, *Heads or Tails: Stories from the Sixth Grade* (1994), drawing on childhood experiences recorded in his journals. Like G., the sixth-grade protagonist in *Heads or Tails* (1994) relies on his diary to cope with the misadventures of life. As a seventh grader in *Jack's Black Book* (1997), he runs into trouble when he attempts to write "the great American novel"; in *Jack's New Power: Stories from a Caribbean Year* (1995) he faces unexpected challenges when his family moves to an island paradise. *Joey Pigza Swallowed the Key,* a 1998 National Book Award nominee, as well as the sequel, *Joey Pigza Loses Control* (2000), explore the trials and tribulations of a hyperactive youngster. Despite G.'s humorous writing *Joey Pigza* presents a sympathetic picture of a child suffering from attention deficit disorder. G. tells the too familiar story of a child trying to come to terms with his out-of-control behavior and the havoc he causes everywhere. Joey is labeled the class clown and is always in trouble despite his best efforts at self-discipline and medication.

AWARDS: AMERICAN LIBRARY ASSOCIATION Best Books for Young Readers (1976–93) for Rotten Ralph series. Parents' Choice (1991) for *Not So Rotten Ralph.* National Book Awards nomination (1998) for *Joey Pigza Swallowed the Key*

FURTHER WORKS: Picture books: *Sleepy Ronald.* 1976. *Rotten Ralph.* 1976. *Rotten Ralph's Show and Tell.* 1989. *Not So Rotten Ralph.* 1994. *Rotten Ralph Feels Rotten.* 1996. *Rotten Ralph's Rotten Romance.* 1997. *Back to School for Rotten Ralph.* 1998, and many others, all illustrated by Nicole Rubel. Chapter books for children: *Jack's Black Box.* 1997. *Joey Pigza Swallowed the Key.* 1998

BIBLIOGRAPHY: AMERICAN BOOKSELLERS ASSOCIATION *Bookweb,* 1999. (http://ww.bookweb.org/newsfeatures/748.html). *Contemporary Authors, New Revision Series.* 1997. *Something about the Author.* vol. 81. 1995

DIANE L. CHAPMAN

GARDEN, Nancy
Author, b. 15 May 1938, Boston, Massachusetts

G. has written more than twenty-five fiction and nonfiction books for children and young adults, beginning with *What Happened in Marston,* published in 1971. Her writing spans several genres,

including FANTASY, MYSTERY, horror, REALISTIC FICTION, and nonfiction. She says that writing different genres allows her to do research for nonfiction, make up puzzles and solve them in her mystery stories, and let the improbable happen in her fantasies because she believes anything is possible. Writing primarily for early adolescent and YOUNG ADULT audiences, G. has tackled difficult issues such as race, drug abuse, suicide, and runaways. Her most controversial and celebrated work, *Annie on My Mind,* won numerous AWARDS, including the 1982 *Booklist* Reviewers' Choice, 1982 AMERICAN LIBRARY ASSOCIATION Best Books, 1983 Best of the Best 1970–83, and 1994 ALA Best Books for Young Adults for the Past Twenty-five Years. The novel tells the story of two teenage girls who fall in love and must deal with the consequences and their own sexuality. In addition, she has written the Fours Crossing Series and the Monster Hunter Series for younger readers as well as editing *Favorite Tales from GRIMM* (1982).

FURTHER WORKS: Nonfiction: *Berlin: City Split in Two.* 1972; *Vampires.* 1973; *Werewolves.* 1973; *Witches.* 1975; *Devils and Demons.* 1976; *Fun with Weather Forecasting.* 1977; Fiction: *What Happened in Marston.* 1972; *Maria's Mountain.* 1981; *Peace, O River.* 1986; *My Sister the Vampire.* 1992

BIBLIOGRAPHY: Gallo, D., ed. *Speaking for Ourselves, Too.* 1993. *Something about the Author.* vol. 75. 1994. Website for Nancy Garden: http://www.bergenstein.com/SCBWI/garden/garden.html; accessed February 2, 1999

MARY ARIAIL BROUGHTON

GARDINER, John Reynolds
Author, b. 6 December 1944, Los Angeles, California

Although gifted with a vivid imagination, G. claims to have had difficulties in school with both reading and writing. However, as an adult he attended a writing class and six years later *Stone Fox* (1980) was published. In this well known and beloved short novel, B. uses easily understood language to tell the story of Willy and his sled dog who enter a dog sled race. Their purpose is to win the prize money in the hope of saving the home Willy shares with his grandfather. As Willy competes against the infamous Stone Fox, an immensely powerful NATIVE AMERICAN, tension and themes of animal faithfulness and compassion for all humanity add to the integrity of the story. Among its AWARDS, *Stone Fox* was chosen a *New York Times* Notable Book in 1989. G. works as a thermal analyst for an aerospace engineering firm in California.

FURTHER WORKS: *Top Secret,* 1985; *General Butterfingers,* 1986; *Alto Secreto,* 1998

BIBLIOGRAPHY: *Something about the Author,* vol. 91, 1991

JANELLE B. MATHIS

GARFIELD, Leon
Author, b. 14 July 1921, Brighton, Sussex, England

G. is renowned for capturing the stories of children from another time in history, whether the story is set in ancient Greece or Shakespeare's England. His interest in writing began in childhood, but writing became his full-time career when his first novel, *Jack Holborn* (1964), originally intended for adults, was reworked for a juvenile audience. Many of his novels take place in the seventeenth and eighteenth centuries; several of them comprise his Apprentices series of twelve short novels and later published as one book, *The Apprentices* (1982). The series is characterized by themes of social injustice, poverty, and a search for personal identity in eighteenth century London.

G. has also written numerous short stories and adaptations of Shakespearean plays. In addition, several novels have been adapted for British television and film. Whether through retelling Greek myths, Bible stories, or in his own historical fiction, G. is praised for vivid and compelling writing and characters. His books always tell an exciting story with special emphasis on justice and moral principles. Loneliness, unhappiness, and moral issues leavened with heroic characters caught up in unfortunate circumstances provide the twists and turns of many of G.'s plots. Often his characters are motivated, as in traditional quest novels, by a search for identity that becomes a convoluted plot device for the main character's adventures. In *Jack Holborn* it is a case of confused identity that sets the scene for a tale of piracy and a trek through the African jungles; in

Devil-in-the-Fog (1966) the young hero is confused as the long-lost son of a dying nobleman. Humor, compassion, and exuberance are also noteworthy elements in many of his stories, especially the characters of Bostock and Harris in *The Night of the Comet* (1979) and *The Strange Affair of Adelaide Harris* (1971). The high quality of his work reflects his respect for the interests of his juvenile audience.

AWARDS: Guardian Award (1967) for *Devil-in-the-Fog.* CARNEGIE MEDAL (1970) for *The God beneath the Sea* (G. and Edward BLISHEN, authors). Children's Book Award, British (1982) for *Fair's Fair.* AMERICAN LIBRARY ASSOCIATION Notable Book (1967) for *Smith,* and (1972) for *The Ghost Downstairs.* Child Study Association of America's Children's Books of the Year (1976) for *The House of Hanover.* Hans Christian ANDERSEN Award nomination in 1981

FURTHER WORKS: *Black Jack.* 1968. *Mister Corbett's Ghost.* 1968. *The Drummer Boy.* 1969. *The God beneath the Sea.* 1970. *The Cloak.* 1977. *Fair's Fair.* 1981. *The King in the Garden.* 1984. *Blewcoat Boy.* 1988. *Shakespeare Stories.* 1991. *Shakespeare Stories II.* 1995

BIBLIOGRAPHY: Carpenter, H. and M. Prichard, ed. *The Oxford Companion to Children's Literature.* 1984. *Something about the Author.* vol. 76. 1994

SANDRA IMDIEKE

GARNER, Alan
Author, b. 17 October 1934, Cheshire, England

G. was a sickly child who spent much of his boyhood confined to house and bed. He attributes his solitary childhood to the consequent development of a rich imagination peopled with interesting characters and lots of physical action. G.'s educational attainment outstripped the experiences of his family even before he entered Oxford University, where he studied archaeology and British mythology. G. left Oxford rather than follow the curriculum of Classical studies. He returned to Cheshire and began to write books of FANTASY that are imbued with local myth and geography. His first books were written before he had heard of TOLKIEN, indicating that similarities between the fantastic creatures of their inventions—including trolls and other anthropomorphic beings—are coincidental. Unlike J. R. R. Tolkien, G.'s tales concern events among humans who happen to stumble underground, rather than end up being contained within the world of mythological races.

G.'s first book, *The Weirdstone of Brisingaman* (1960), features a young brother and sister who happen into a nether world of good and bad elfin beings, a wizard, and a power struggle involving enchanted stones. It won the Lewis CARROLL Shelf Award (1970). Like other sibling adventure stories it features a constant flow of exciting events that is very appealing to children; in G.'s later books there would be less emphasis on plot and more on character development. Its sequel, *The Moon of Gomrath,* was published in 1963.

Elidor (1965), which received a CARNEGIE MEDAL commendation, features another quest by contemporary urban children who become involved in an alternative world and in a quest to overcome the forces of evil with those of good. The Mabinogion, a series of Welsh myths, provides the basis for the ultimate emotional maturity of three adolescents in *The Owl Service* (1967), which won the Carnegie Medal and the Guardian Award in its year of publication and brought G. serious critical acclaim. It is generally considered a book that makes difficult demands on readers and requires an investment in concentration. *A Bag of Moonshine* (1986), in which G. retells folktales, won the 1987 MOTHER GOOSE Award.

The Moon of Gomrath (1963) continues the story begun in *The Weirdstone of Brisingamen.* These two novels are set quite specifically in G.'s Cheshire countryside and are the products of G.'s familiarity with Celtic legend. The pace of these stories is rapid and, at times, confusing in the onslaught of emerging characters and perils. His human characters, unlike his mythical beings, lack much individuation.

The Owl Service proffers a more complex narrative than did G.'s first fantasies. Rather than putting mythic creatures from Welsh lore in the service of a children's story, here a story from Welsh legend—specifically that of doomed lovers from the Mabinogion tale of Lleu Llaw Gyffes—is reenacted, echoing the ancient issues of personal and social identity. G. uses the tragic legend to structure a story of modern social conflict engendered within working-class families in an urban environment and the resulting tensions between the generations. *Red Shift* (1973), also set in G.'s home territory, features several stories linked by the landscape and a Stone Age ax. The book unfolds entirely in dialogue, suggesting to some critics, including Aidan CHAMBERS, that it is beyond the abilities of juvenile readers to comprehend. Other critics note, however, that children can indeed follow the story as G. has rendered it, although they must participate as active readers. G. himself refuses to be categorized as a children's author or otherwise, noting that his books are, essentially, about himself.

In addition to fantasy novels, G. has written collections of stories, again set in his home landscape. *The Stone Book* (1978), *Tom Fobble's Day* (1977), *Granny Reardun* (1978), and *The Aimer Gate* (1979) comprise "The Stone Book Quartet." The stories contained in these appeal to the emotions of the reader, who is carried along with the characters through good and bad times, with the land remaining and the obligation to do one's duty by one's craft the clear message. It was originally conceived for children who were having reading difficulties and is a prose-poem paean to his Cheshire roots and family history of craftsmanship over the course of the last century.

G. also writes plays, both original and based on his own novels and stories, as well as on folktales. These have been produced on stage, radio, and television. *Holly from the Bongs* (1966), a nativity play, has been produced as a musical play with a score by Carnegie Medal winner William MAYNE. It was later produced as an opera and a BBC film. His retellings of folktales appear in *Alan Garner's Book of British FAIRY TALES* (1984), *Jack and the Beanstalk* (1985), and other collections.

FURTHER WORKS: *The Old Man of Mow.* 1970. *The Breadhorse.* 1975. *Alan Garner's Fairy Tales of Gold.* 1980. *The Lad of Gad.* 1980. *Once upon a Time, Though It Wasn't in Your Time, and It Wasn't in My Time, and It Wasn't in Anybody Else's Time.* 1993

BIBLIOGRAPHY: *Contemporary Authors, New Revision Series.* 1998. *Something about the Author.* vol. 69. 1992. Townsend, J. *A Sense of Story: Essays on Contemporary Writers for Children.* 1971

FRANCISCA GOLDSMITH

GATES, Doris

Author, b. 26 November 1901, Mountain View, California; d. 3 September 1987, Carmel, California

G., author of REALISTIC FICTION, was a children's librarian in Fresno, California, for ten years. She also presented a radio story hour and began writing children's books during this period. In 1941 *Blue Willow* was named an ALA NEWBERY MEDAL Honor Book. G. decided to write *Blue Willow* after visiting the homes of migrant children with whom she worked. *Blue Willow* is recognized as one of the first books to focus realistically on a child's life as a migrant worker. Some of G.'s stories focus on diverse cultures such as *Little Vic* (1951), a story about an AFRICAN AMERICAN boy and a horse. This book received the William Allen White Children's Book Award (1954). G. is also known for excellent retellings of Greek myths (1972–76). Her manuscripts are preserved in THE KERLAN COLLECTION at the University of Minnesota.

FURTHER WORKS: *Sarah's Idea.* 1938. *My Brother Mike.* 1948. *Becky and the Bandit.* 1952. *The Elderberry Bush.* 1967. *A Filly for Melinda.* 1984

BIBLIOGRAPHY: Gates, Doris. *A Lengthened Shadow and Along the Road to Kansas.* vol. 34 (12), Kansas State College of Emporia, December 1954. *Something about the Author.* vol. 34. 1984 and vol. 54. 1989. Stott, Jon C. *Twentieth-Century Children's Writers,* 3rd ed. 1989

JANELLE B. MATHIS

GAUCH, Patricia Lee

Author, editor, b. 31 January 1934, Detroit, Michigan

G. was an energetic young child who enjoyed laughing and having a good time. She began writing in college for the student-run newspaper at Miami University, Ohio. After graduating with a degree in English Literature, C. spent a short time at the Louisville, Kentucky, newspaper, before rearing three children. Once her children reached school age G. returned to school to earn a Master's Degree in Teaching from Manhattanville College; she began to teach. She also holds a doctorate in English Literature from Drew University. G. credits her attendance at a writing conference led by Jean FRITZ in developing her skill as a writer for children. Ideas for two of her early children's books, *Grandpa and Me* (1972) and *Christina and the Box* (1971) were influenced by her attendance at the conference. Beginning in 1985, G. began a career in children's publishing. Currently she is vice president and editorial director of Philomel Books.

G. has written over thirty titles ranging from picture-book retellings of legends and folk songs, to historical fiction, and REALISTIC FICTION for readers of all ages. G. is praised for her ability to create sensitive and realistic characters such as Christina Katerina and Tanya. Readers can follow the characters' antics through multiple PICTURE BOOKS such as *Christina Katerina and Fats and the Great Neighborhood War* (1997) and *Tanya and the Magic Wardrobe* (1997). G. also receives critical acclaim for her historical fiction. *Aaron and the Green Mountain Boys* (1972) and *This Time, Tempe Wick* (1974) chronicle the contribution of a boy and a girl to the American Revolution. Reviewers comment on her ability to provide readers with a realistic and humane picture of a very important aspect of American history.

G. also writes realistic fiction for YOUNG ADULTS. In titles such as *The Green of Me* (1978), *The Year the Summer Died* (1985), and *Night Talks* (1983), G. explores issues that young adults face as they mature. Critics praise G.'s ability to develop sensitive and moving stories that capture concerns of the young adult age group. G.'s experience as a mother, teacher at various grade levels, writer and editor allows her to interact with people who contribute to her development as a writer and editor. Her influence is seen in the books she writes for children as well as the editorial guidance she provides for other writers of children's books.

AWARDS: Notable Children's Trade Book in the Field of Social Studies (1974) for *This Time, Tempe Wick*

FURTHER WORKS: Christina Katerina series, 1971–96. Tanya series, 1989–97. *Dragons on the Road.* 1986. *Fridays.* 1979. *The Impossible Major Rogers.* 1977. *Kate Alone.* 1980. *The Little Friar Who Flew.* 1980. *Morelli's Game.* 1981. *Noah.*

1994. *On to Widecombe Fair.* 1978. *Once upon a Dinkelsbeuhl.* 1977. *A Secret House.* 1970. *Thunder at Gettysburg.* 1975. *Uncle Magic.* 1992

BIBLIOGRAPHY: Gallo, Donald R., ed., *Speaking for Ourselves, Too,* 1993; *New York Times Review of Books,* Feb. 17, 1980, and Feb. 8, 1981; *Publishers Weekly,* Nov. 6, 1978; www.penguinputnam.com/catalog/yreader/authors/35_biography.html

BERT CROSSLAND

GEISEL, Theodore Seuss
(See SEUSS, Dr.)

GEISERT, Arthur (Frederick)
Illustrator, author, b. 20 September 1941, Dallas, Texas

G. received a B.S. from Concordia College in Nebraska and a Master of Arts from the University of California–Davis. He also studied art at Chouinard Art Institute, Otis Art Institute, and the Art Institute of Chicago. Trained as a teacher, G. soon discovered that his talents and true interests lay in illustrating children's books. For many years G. produced etchings from his home in Galena, Illinois, while he built two family homes. During this time he continued to submit proposals to publishers of children's books hoping for an acceptance letter. No acceptance letter ever came from numerous proposals. G.'s discovery came through an editor from Houghton Mifflin who spotted his etchings in an exhibition. Living in a rural area had afforded him opportunities to view the countryside and animals of the area. His first book capitalized upon those opportunities. *Pa's Balloon and Other Pig Tales* (1984) is a series of three stories that describe the adventures of a pig family in a hot air balloon. This book allowed G. to fulfill his goal of combining the classic etching style of Piranesi, Rembrandt, and Callott within a humorous story. G. continued his use of pigs in *Pigs from A to Z* (1986), which was named one of the Ten Best Illustrated Children's Books of 1986 by the *New York Times.* Following the success of his two early books, G. turned to the Biblical story of Noah and the Ark; he illustrated this with his etchings. *The Ark* (1988) retells the story of the great flood. G. further elaborated on the Genesis story with the publication of *After the Flood* (1994), which is a story of what happens after the flood when the animals leave

the confines of the Ark. Both books are praised for visually stimulating readers. The publication of *Haystack* (1995) was the first collaboration between G. and Bonnie Geisert. *Haystack* (1995) tells readers about the process of making hay; it explains the cycle, from growing, cutting, and stacking to its use as feed for cattle and other animals who in turn fertilize the land for the next crop of hay. G. and Bonnie G. have also collaborated on a second title, *Prairie Town* (1998).

G. is praised for his ability to combine the classical style of etchings with humorous stories for children. G.'s passion for the etching technique was demonstrated in *The Etcher's Studio* (1997), which gives young readers a glimpse into the etching process and the equipment used in the classical method. Through his ILLUSTRATIONS, G. provides young readers with opportunities for a pleasurable reading experience and an explanation of the classical method of etching.

AWARDS: *New York Times* Best Illustrated Children's Books of the Year (1986) for *Pigs from A to Z; Boston Globe–Horn Book* and Parents Choice Honor Book (1995) for *Haystack*

FURTHER WORKS: Self-Illustrated: *Oink.* 1991. *Pigs from 1 to 10.* 1992. *Oink, Oink.* 1993. *Roman Numerals I to MM: Numberabilia Romana Uno Ad Duo Mila.* 1996. Illustrator: *Aesop and Company: With Scenes from His Life.* (Bader). 1991

BIBLIOGRAPHY: Cianciolo, Patricia J., PICTURE BOOKS for Children, 4th ed., 1997; Silvey, Anita, ed., *Children's Books and Their Creators,* 1995; *Something about the Author,* vol. 23, 1997

BERT CROSSLAND

GEORGE, Jean Craighead
Author, b. 2 July 1919, Washington, D.C.

G. grew up in a family of naturalists on land that her ancestors had settled generations before. On weekends, G. and her family often camped in the woods near their home. These outings provided a good place for her to learn about nature as she climbed trees to study owls, caught frogs, gathered edible plants, made fish hooks from twigs, and rode hay wagons with her twin brothers, John and Frank. Domestic pursuits, such as sewing and canning, bored her, but she was always drawn to the outdoors where she learned about animals and nature.

Whereas G.'s brothers became two of the first falconers in the United States, their younger sister became an author of books about nature and the outdoors. She knew from third grade that she wanted to write and she began by writing poems and short stories. Later, she wrote epic poems, and eventually novels and nonfiction works for children. G. studied science and English at Pennsylvania State University and after graduation became a newspaper reporter.

G.'s first book, *Vulpes, the Red Fox,* was published in 1948. The book was coauthored with John Lothar George, with whom G. wrote several self-illustrated juvenile novels. These books were animal biographies based on G.'s firsthand experiences with wild creatures. The writing partnership proved successful as their 1956 book, *Dipper of Copper Creek,* won the AMERICAN LIBRARY ASSOCIATION's Aurianne Award for best nature writing. In 1957, G.'s first book written on her own, *Hole in the Tree,* was published. Since that time, she has written dozens of fiction and nonfiction works. *My Side of the Mountain* (1959), a survival story about young Sam Gribley, who runs away to the Catskill Mountains to live on his own, won several prestigious AWARDS, including the ALA NEWBERY MEDAL Honor Book and AMERICAN LIBRARY ASSOCIATION Notable Book citation, the International Hans Christian ANDERSEN Award honor list, the Lewis CARROLL Shelf citation, and the George G. Stone Center for Children's Books Award. Reviewers praised the book for its vivid descriptions of animal life, its character development, and its unsentimental celebration of nature and freedom. In a review of the book Zena Sutherland notes, "The thoughts and attitudes he [Sam Gribley] quotes from his diary indicate his maturation and deepening self-perception in a wholly convincing manner."

G.'s most celebrated work, *Julie of the Wolves* (1972), won the Newbery Medal and many other honors. This novel, inspired by a whale watch in Barrow, Alaska, reveals the efforts of Miyax, a thirteen-year-old Eskimo girl who escapes from an arranged marriage and learns to survive on the barren tundra of the Arctic by making friends with a family of wolves. G. is praised for capturing "the subtle nuances of Eskimo life, animal habits, the pain of growing up, and combines these elements into a thrilling adventure which is,

at the same time, a poignant love story," according to one critic. After numerous requests from her readers and more years of studying wolf behavior, George wrote two sequels to the book, *Julie* (1994) and *Julie's Wolf Pack* (1997).

In addition to her novels, G. has written many nonfiction books for children. Her Thirteen Moons series looks at wildlife in the light of the yearly moon cycle. The first three books of the series, *The Moon of the Owls* (1967), *The Moon of the Bears* (1967), and *The Moon of the Salamanders* (1967) trace the hibernation patterns and mating times of three different animals. Other animals in the series include chickadees, fox pups, wolves, moles, wild pigs, winter birds, and others. The books in the series are praised for their accuracy, lyrical writing style, and absence of anthropomorphism. George has also written a One Day juvenile nonfiction series, with books such as *One Day in the Desert* (1983), *One Day in the Prairie* (1986), and *One Day in the Tropical Rain Forest* (1990). The author's success is attributed to her intense research into the subjects she writes about. G. subscribes to many scientific journals and does a great deal of reading and talking to scientists. In addition, she often visits the sites where her works take place. Her visits to various parts of the world have yielded much of the information that she incorporates into her novels and nonfiction writing. On a visit to the Arctic Research Lab in Alaska, G. discovered that wolves have a language of communication and that wolf communities are hierarchically ordered with alpha (first) and beta (second) leaders. She used this information in the three Julie books.

Currently, G. enjoys traveling and coming home to write. She has recently added the dimension of music as she collaborates with award-winning composer, Chris Kubie, to bring the sounds of nature to her works.

FURTHER WORKS: *Coyote in Manhattan.* 1968. *Who Really Killed Cock Robin? An Ecological Mystery.* 1971. *Hook a Fish, Catch a Mountain.* 1975. *The Talking Earth.* 1983. *Shark beneath the Reef.* 1989. *Missing Gator of Gumbo Limbo: An Ecological Mystery.* 1992. *The Tarantula in My Purse.* 1996

BIBLIOGRAPHY: *Children's Literature Review,* vol. 1 (1976); *Major Authors and Illustrators for Children and YOUNG ADULTS: A Selection of*

Sketches from Something About the Author, vol. 3 (1993); HOPKINS, Lee Bennett, *Pauses: Autobiographical Reflections of 101 Creators of Children's Books,* 1995; McElmeel, S. (1999), *100 Most Popular Children's Authors;* http://www/ jeancraigheadgeorge.com/ (Accessed October 10, 1999)

MARY ARIAIL BROUGHTON

GERRARD, Roy

Author, illustrator, b. 25 January 1935, Atherton, Lancashire, England; d. 5 August 1997, Stockport, Cheshire, England

G. is best known for his children's PICTURE BOOKS that feature historical settings and incorporate text written in verse. Most of his work features humorous illustrations inspired in part by the works of Lewis CARROLL and Edward LEAR. G. uses satire in his ILLUSTRATIONS and text that is age appropriate and delightful. Although G. was born and lived in England, one of his best known works is set in the American West. *Rosie and the Rustlers* (1989), told in humorous verse and appropriately silly illustrations, won the Parent's Choice for Picture Book award and was also featured on television's *READING RAINBOW* series.

AWARDS: *New York Times* Best Illustrated Children's Books of the Year (1984) for *Sir Cedric,* and (1998) for *Sir Francis Drake: His Daring Deeds*

FURTHER WORKS: *Croco'mile,* 1994; *The Favershams,* 1983; *Sir Cedric,* 1984; *Rosie and the Rustlers,* 1989; *Mik's Mammoth,* 1990; *Jocasta Carr, Movie Star,* 1992; *The Roman Twins,* 1998

BIBLIOGRAPHY: *Third Book of Junior Authors,* 1972; *Something about the Author,* vol. 90, 1997

MICHAEL O'LAUGHLIN

GERSTEIN, Mordicai

Author, illustrator, b. 24 November 1935, Los Angeles, California

G. expressed an interest in painting and books at an early age. He attended the Chouinard Art Institute and began a successful award-winning twenty-year career as an animator. In 1973 G. began collaborating with author Elizabeth Levy on the Something Queer Is Going On series (1973–94). G. and Levy work closely on each project. Both team members are supportive and offer suggestions on how to improve a book both

textually and visually. In addition to the Something Queer Is Going On series, Levy and G. collaborated on *Dracula Is a Pain in the Neck* (1983) and *Frankenstein Moved in on the Fourth Floor* (1994). During his collaboration with Levy, G. began to experiment with writing some of his own stories. Finally after suggestions from editors and others, G. published *Arnold of the Ducks* (1983), a story about a young boy who is reared by birds. The next year G. adapted a film into a book: *The Room* (1984) is about a group of tenants living in a New York apartment building. During a trip to Europe in the 1960s G. read a portion of the book *The Tibetan Book of the Dead;* this led to a desire to study the ancient text and convey its message to the modern world. In 1987, *The Mountains of Tibet* was published. G. spent a great deal of time researching the text and the appropriate ILLUSTRATIONS. Reviewers call *The Mountains of Tibet* (1987) a classic PICTURE BOOK that should be enjoyed by many. G. has written two books drawn from Biblical stories. *The Shadow of a Flying Bird: A Legend from the Kurdistani Jews* (1994) drawn from a Kurdistani tale retells the story of the death of Moses. *Jonah and the Two Great Fish* (1997) is a retelling of the Old Testament story about the prophet Jonah who is swallowed by a great fish. Both books have been critically acclaimed for their attention to detail and their use of colors.

G. uses a variety of media in his illustrations. An analysis of his work shows that each book has its own look and shape. Critics praise G. for his ability to communicate through his illustrations as well as his ability to show detail and capture the sense of movement.

AWARDS: *New York Times* Best Illustrated Children's Books of the Year (1987) for *The Mountains of Tibet*

FURTHER WORKS: *Follow Me.* 1983. *Prince Sparrow.* 1984. *Roll Over.* 1984. *William Where Are You?* 1985. *Tales of Pan.* 1986. *The Seal Mother.* 1986. *The Sun's Day.* 1989. *Beauty and the Beast.* 1989. *Anytime Mapleson and the Hungry Bears.* (Susan Yard Harris, illus.). 1990. *The New Creatures.* 1991. *The Gigantic Baby.* (Arnie Levin, illus.). 1991. *Guess What?* 1991. *The Story of May.* 1993. *The Giant.* 1995. *Daisy's Garden.* 1995. *Behind the Couch.* 1996. *Bedtime, Everybody.* 1996. *Stop Those Pants.* 1998. Illustrator: *Nice Little Girls.* (Levy). 1974. *There Are*

Rocks in My Socks. (Thomas). 1979. *The Shadow Nose.* (Levy). 1983. *David's First Bicycle.* (Silver). 1983. *The Cataract of Lodore.* (Southey). 1991

BIBLIOGRAPHY: *Booklist,* Jan. 9, 1960, p. 60; Oct. 15, 1995, p. 401; *Bulletin of the Center for Children's Books,* Nov. 1985, July–Aug. 1986, Nov. 1986, Jan. 1988, Apr. 1993; Cianciolo, Patricia J., *Picture Books for Children,* 3rd ed., 1990; the *Horn Book* magazine, 1995, p. 205; *Publishers Weekly,* Apr. 12, 1993, p. 62, May 1, 1995, p. 60; *School Library Journal,* Apr. 1993, p. 96, Sept. 1994, pp. 207–8, May 1, 1995, p. 60

BERT CROSSLAND

GIBBONS, Gail

Author, illustrator, b. 1 August, 1944, Oak Park, Illinois

G. always knew that she wanted to be a writer and an artist. As a child, she enjoyed drawing and making her own books in order to recreate favorite places and things. In college, G. studied graphic design (B.F.A., University of Illinois, 1967) and subsequently worked as a graphic designer at television stations, first in Illinois and later in New York City. As a graphic artist for an NBC children's program, *Take a Giant Step,* she became interested in creating a children's book in response to a question asked by children on the program. Her first book, *Willy and His Wheel Wagon* (1975), a Junior Literary Guild Selection, illustrated the concept of set theory.

G.'s early books demonstrated how to make and do things—e.g., *Things to Make and Do for Halloween* (1976) and *Things to Make and Do for Your Birthday* (1978). Others addressed topics concerning how things work, such as, *Clocks and How They Go* (1979), American Institute of Graphic Arts Award, and *Locks and Keys* (1980), National Science Teachers Association/CHILDREN'S BOOK COUNCIL Award, *The Post Office Book: Mail and How It Moves* (1982), certificate of appreciation from U.S. Postmaster General (1982); and *Cars and How They Go* (Joanna COLE, 1983), an AMERICAN LIBRARY ASSOCIATION Notable Book.

Over the years, G. has continued to develop and expand her work; she has written and illustrated more than one hundred INFORMATIONAL BOOKS for children. Her diverse titles range from *Monarch Butterfly* (1989), *Wolves* (1994), *Soaring with the Wind: The Bald Eagle* (1998), and *The Pumpkin Book* (1999) to *Pirates: Robbers of the High Seas* (1993), *Knights in Shining Armor* (1995), *Behold . . . the Dragons!* (1999), and *Santa Who?* (1999). Many of her books have been featured on television's READING RAINBOW and are staples in primary classrooms throughout the United States. In 1987, she was awarded the *Washington Post*–Children's Book Guild Award for her overall contribution to nonfiction children's literature.

G.'s nonfiction writing is distinctive for its clarity and stimulating style, and for the depth and accuracy of the facts presented. Her illustrations extend the text into a cohesive and engaging informative piece. In *Surrounded by Sea: Life on a New England Fishing Island* (1991), G. portrays island activities throughout the year, beginning in spring. She includes details such as diagrams about how a lobster trap works, and underwater views of different kinds of fishing boats: trawler, scalloper, dragger, long-liner, and seiner. G. anticipates children's questions about life on the island by including information concerning mail delivery, telephone, and ferry service. The book provides a rich, balanced portrait of the rhythms of the seasons on a New England fishing island. *Christmas on an Island* (1994) is about the holiday on this island.

Marshes and Swamps (1998) provides another example of G.'s comprehensive treatment of a topic. G. describes the difference between the two types of wetlands, and then extends the topic by discussing freshwater and saltwater marshes, and freshwater and mangrove swamps. The watercolor and ink illustrations of marshes and swamps are integrated with accurately labeled pictures of the variety of animals and plants that live in these places, demonstrating the ecosystem she defines. The child's relationship to the topic is shown through G.'s depiction of people visiting a swamp, and the inclusion of a map of wetlands readers can visit in the U.S. and Canada.

G.'s versatility is particularly evident in her well-researched informational book about an imaginary topic in *Behold . . . the Dragons!* (1999). She skillfully touches on the origin of myths and stories about dragons within the human psyche and experience, provides the etymology of the word dragon, and then proceeds to describe the five classifications of dragons, as identified by dragontologists: serpent dragons, semidragons, classical dragons, sky dragons, and neodragons. G.'s full-color paintings are appropriately expansive and dramatic, effectively portraying dragons in cultures throughout the world. The result is a fascinating book rich in history, myth, and FOLKLORE.

G.'s style of ILLUSTRATION has evolved in tandem with changes in publishing children's books. Illustrations in her earlier books appear as drawings with three colors of hand-separated art, a less expensive reproductive coloring technique available to book artists at the time. Her later work is in pen and ink and watercolor or gouache paintings, reproduced as camera-separated art. Her illustrations consistently reflect excellence of design, appropriateness with regard to each topic, and attention to accurate detail that inquisitive children demand and enjoy.

G.'s prolific work as an illustrator and author of nonfiction books for children continues with several new titles published each year.

AWARDS: American Institute of Physics Children's Science-Writing Award (1993) for *Stargazers*. AMERICAN LIBRARY ASSOCIATION Notable Book (1985) for *The Milk Makers*

FURTHER WORKS: *New Road!* 1983. *From Path to Highway: The Story of the Boston Post Road.* 1986. *Deadline! From News to Newspaper.* 1987. *Dinosaurs, Dragonflies and Diamonds: All about Natural History Museums.* 1988. *Sunken Treasure.* 1988. *Catch the Wind: All about Kites.* 1989. *Easter.* 1989. *How a House Is Built.* 1990. *Beacons of Light: Lighthouses.* 1990. *Whales.* 1991. *Recycle: A Handbook for Kids.* 1992. *Stargazers.* 1992. *Say Woof! The Day of a Country Veterinarian.* 1992. *Caves and Caverns.* 1993. *The Planets.* 1993. *Puff—Flash—Bang! A Book about Signals.* 1993. *Spiders.* 1993. *Nature's Green Umbrella: Tropical Rain Forests.* 1994. *St. Patrick's Day.* 1994. *Bicycle Book.* 1995. *Cats.* 1996. *Click! A Book about Cameras and Taking Pictures.* 1997. *Gulls—Gulls—Gulls.* 1997. *The Honey Makers.* 1997. *The Moon Book.* 1997. *Penguins!* 1998. *The Art Box.* 1998. *Pigs.* 1999. *Bats.* 1999. *Exploring the Deep, Dark Sea.* 1999

BIBLIOGRAPHY: *Sixth Book of Junior Authors and Illustrators* (1989). Silvey, Anita, ed. *Children's Books and Their Creators.* 1995. *Something about the Author,* vol. 72, 1993. www.gailgibbons.com

KATHIE KRIEGER CERRA

GIBLIN, James Cross
Author, editor, b. 8 July 1933, Cleveland, Ohio

G.'s talent for providing children in the middle grades with nonfiction that is well researched, gracefully organized, and engagingly written has made him popular with readers, literary critics, and other authors. In addition to writing, G. is highly regarded in the field of children's publishing (see PUBLISHERS AND BOOK PUBLISHING IN THE UNITED STATES and PUBLISHERS, INDEPENDENT) as an editor (see EDITORS OF NOTE).

G.'s interest in the world around him has been with him since early childhood. His mother introduced him to the wonder of reading and his own personality invited him to explore the everyday details of urban living. During his high school and college years, G. wrote for his schools' newspapers and their theaters. After earning his bachelors degree at Western Reserve University (now Case Western Reserve University) in 1954, G. completed graduate work at Columbia University, earning a masters of FINE ARTS in 1955. In the years immediately following, he worked as a freelance writer and, by 1959, had become an assistant editor at a publishing house. He moved from publisher to publisher as he rose through the ranks of editing, becoming editor-in-chief of children's publishing at Clarion, in 1967, shortly after its founding. In 1979, he became editor and publisher of Clarion Books.

The Scarecrow Book (coauthored with Dale Ferguson, 1980) was named a Notable Children's Book of the year by the AMERICAN LIBRARY ASSOCIATION. *The Skyscraper Book* (1981) received the same honor the following year. *Chimney Sweeps: Yesterday and Today* (1982) was an ALA Notable Children's Book and Golden Kite Award (1982), and an American Book Award for Children's Nonfiction (1983). *Walls: Defenses throughout History* (1984) won G. a second Golden Kite Award (1984). *The Truth about Santa Claus* (1985) was an ALA Notable Children's Book (1985), as was *Milk: The Fight for Purity* (1986), and *From Hand to Mouth; or, How We Invented Knives, Forks, Spoons, and Chopsticks and the Table Manners to Go with Them* (1987). *Let There Be Light: a Book about Windows* (1988) earned G. his third Golden Kite

Award (1988) and was an ALA Notable Children's Book. Both *The Riddle of the Rosetta Stone: Key to Ancient Egypt* (1990) and *The Truth about Unicorns* (1991) were ALA Notable Children's Books.

G. approaches each topic about which he writes with energetic and well-organized research skills. Included in all his studies of such universal experiences as eating, building walls, and fighting illness, is attention to historical developments in many cultures. G.'s books brim with MULTICULTURAL information that is woven in so tidily and sensitively that the reader attends to and enjoys learning about the universality of the titular subject. G. selects his own illustrations, relying upon photo and other archives that will provide his text with greater clarity rather than simply decorating it. He does not create imagined dialogue in order to move along his narrative, but rather puts historical quotations into service, as well as citing dramatic published accounts and other devices that carry readers along without sacrificing the historical veracity of the text. In writing about time periods and societies with which young readers may have little familiarity, he is careful to include relevant background detail. For instance, in *Be Seated: A Book about Chairs* (1993), G. carefully blends details of construction methods with discussions of Egyptian aesthetics and Medieval economics.

In addition to writing social histories, G. has written about the lives of famous individuals, including *George Washington: A Picture Book Biography* (1992), *Thomas Jefferson: A Picture Book BIOGRAPHY* (1994), and, for older readers, *Charles A. Lindbergh: A Human Hero* (1997). As with his studies of chairs, chimney sweeps, and pasteurization, G. does not fabricate dialogue or repeat unsubstantiated legend in order to tell the stories of historical persons' lives. A very thorough researcher, he looks beyond the first or second interesting account he finds in order to assure corroboration before including any detail in his own work. In the case of *Fireworks, Picnics, and Flags* (1983), this thoroughness kept his book on the history of celebrating the Fourth of July free of apocryphal accounts about the original celebration.

As an editor, G. has worked with many well-known children's and young adult authors, including Marion Dane BAUER, Jan BRETT, Eve BUNTING, Kay CHORAO, Paul GALDONE, Russell FREEDMAN, Jim MURPHY, and Jane YOLEN. Although his own writing is nonfiction, as an editor he works with fiction and PICTURE-BOOK writers. G. also has taught at the City University of New York and writes for juvenile literary magazines.

FURTHER WORKS: *Edith Wilson: The Woman Who Ran the United States.* 1992. *When Plague Strikes: The Black Death, Smallpox, AIDS.* 1995. *The Mystery of the Mammoth Bones: And How It Was Solved.* 1999

BIBLIOGRAPHY: *Contemporary Authors,* vol. 106, 1982; *Somethng about the Author,* vol. 75, 1994; Giblin, J. *Writing Books for Young People,* 1995; Silvey, Anita, ed., *Children's Books and Their Creators,* 1995; "More Than Just the Facts: A Hundred Years of Children's Nonfiction," the *Horn Book* magazine, July–Aug. 2000

FRANCISCA GOLDSMITH

GIFF, Patricia Reilly

Author, b. 26 April 1935, Brooklyn, New York

G. says, "I spent most of my childhood with a book in my hands. I read in bed before the sun was up, then hunched over the breakfast table with my book in my lap. After school, I'd sit in the kitchen, leaning against the warm radiator, dreaming over a story. I read the books my mother had read as a child, the classics, mythology and FAIRY TALES . . . I spent hours at our little library in St. Albans, until at last, I had read every book on the juvenile shelves, and my friend Miss Bailey had to tiptoe into the adult section to find something for me there."

G. graduated from Marymount College in New York and received a Master's Degree in history from St. John's University. G. loved teaching and taught all grades from third through sixth. She received a professional diploma in reading from Hofstra University and taught reading for twenty years. G. also worked as an educational consultant for Dell Yearling and Young Yearling Books.

G. wanted to become a writer since the first time she read a book; in 1979 she announced to her family "I'm going to write a book. I've always wanted to write and now I shall." G. targeted middle-grade readers to try and make them laugh. Her experience with this age group exposed her to children coping with serious problems in school and at home; she hopes her books relieve the tension in their lives and show them they are special, that an adult cares about them.

Fourth Grade Celebrity was published in 1979 along with *The Girl Who Knew It All.* In 1980 *Today Was a Terrible Day, Next Year I'll Be Special* and *Left-Handed Shortstop* were published. In 1981, *Have You Seen Hyacinth Macaw?* and *The Winter Worm Business.*

The first of her lighthearted Kids of the Polk Street School series for ages six to nine, *The Beast in Ms. Rooney's Room,* was published in 1984. It was followed by *Fish Face, The Candy Corn Contest,* and *December Secrets* (all 1984). In *December Secrets* Ms. Rooney, the classroom teacher, has everyone in class pick a secret person for the month of December. They are not required to buy expensive presents, only to be nice or do nice things for their special person. It is a story of friendship, giving rather than receiving, thoughtfulness, and acceptance of others.

The Valentine Star, Lazy Lions, and *Lucky Lambs and Purple Climbing Days* were all published in 1985, as was *Say Cheese.* Using the believable situation of wanting a best friend, G. takes the reader through the problems Emily Arrow encounters as she tries to follow the advice she reads in a book to choose a best friend for herself. All of the books in The Kids of the Polk Street School series have short chapters, a lot of HUMOR and are checked out frequently from libraries. Emily Arrow, the protagonist, learns and grows in each story although the maturity comes in small increments rather than stupendous leaps.

Snaggle Doodles (1985), is named for an expression Emily Arrow uses. Everyone wants to know what it means and where it came from. The theme is group socialization and cooperation as Emily learns empathy for leaders. A subplot is the upcoming wedding of their student teacher. Emily is thrilled when the whole class goes to the wedding and the student teacher whispers "Snaggle Doodles" to Emily.

Sunny Side Up and *Pickle Puss* were published in 1986. The latter involves a library "Fish for a Good Book" reading contest and Emily Arrow is determined to win when challenged by a "sometimes" friend in this story about reading, library cards, cats, friendship, and honesty. *Beast and the*

Halloween Horror and *Emily Arrow Promises to Do Better This Year,* about New Year's resolutions, were published in 1990. Emily resolves to be perfect this year but it does not work. She cannot even spell Tuesday but she learns the most important lesson of all: to keep trying and not to give up.

Monster Rabbit Runs Amuck (1991) features Richard Best or *Beast,* as he calls himself. When Matthew and Beast retrieve the Easter Rabbit for the Spring Assembly it slides off the stage and the head rolls down the aisle. To escape punishment and expulsion Beast runs away from school. Potentially a difficult situation, it is handled lovingly by his sister bringing him back to face the teacher. Covering a range of emotions; fear, guilt, anger, confusion, and worry, the story ends happily.

Wake up, Emily, It's Mother's Day, the last of The Kids of the Polk Street School series, was published in 1991. Emily Arrow is again the protagonist and this time she doesn't know what to get her mother for Mother's Day. Promoting sibling goodwill, classroom cooperation, and everyone helping to make the earth green, G. brings the series to a gentle conclusion. The overriding theme for the entire SERIES is socialization, cooperation, and friendship. Series stories present instantly recognizable characters and settings. The familiar world of the classroom is a popular theme in The Kids of the Polk Street School series. Additional series by G. are Polk Street Specials, The New Kids at the Polk Street School series for ages five to eight, The Polka Dot Private Eye series for ages six to nine, and Friends and Amigos series for ages six to nine. For children ages six to nine there is also The Lincoln Lions Band series and for children ages eight to twelve Meet Abby Jones, Junior Detective series.

The title of another book in The Kids of the Polk Street School series, *In the Dinosaur's Paw* (1984), was selected as the name of G.'s children's bookstore in Fairfield, Connecticut. G. organizes and teaches writing workshops at the store for adults and children. The philosophy of the bookstore is: "We want to make The Dinosaur's Paw a community that brings children and books together. We want to share our love of children's books and writing, and to help others explore the whole world of children's books—from inception to publication." It is a place that welcomes people interested in books and children.

Lily's Crossing (1997) was named an ALA NEWBERY MEDAL Honor Book and a *Boston Globe–Horn Book* Honor Book. The protagonist, Lily, going into sixth grade, is deceitful, inquisitive, stubborn, rebellious, courageous, and a liar. She meets a refugee from Hungary and discovers the hurt and harm lies cause. Lily recognizes her need for a friend and during one summer comes to grips with her lying. The themes of love, friendship, commitment, and honesty are interwoven throughout.

G. says, "I want to see children curled up with books, finding an awareness of themselves . . . I want them to write their own stories . . . I hope to say to all the children I've loved that they are special . . . that all of us are special . . . important just because we are ourselves."

BIBLIOGRAPHY: Bantam Doubleday Dell brochure. DE GRUMMOND RESEARCH COLLECTION, University of Southern Mississippi. Gillespie, John T., and Naden, Corrine, J, (eds). (1994). *Best Books for Children: Preschool through Grade Six,* fifth ed. *Fiction, FOLKLORE, FANTASY and POETRY for Children, 1876–1985.* vol. I & II (1986). THE KERLAN COLLECTION, University of Minnesota. *Something about the Author,* vol. 70 (1993)

IRVYN G. GILBERTSON

GILCHRIST, Jan Spivey

Author, illustrator, b. 15 February 1949, Chicago, Illinois

G. grew up in Chicago within a loving, close-knit family. At an early age G. realized that she had special talents. Her parents, who often took her to museums in the Chicago area, encouraged those talents. On those trips G. recognized the need for a positive depiction of AFRICAN AMERICANS in children's books. After earning art degrees from Eastern Illinois University and Northern Iowa University, G. spent time teaching art in schools. During this time, she continued to draw and paint. G. quickly won praise from critics for her paintings that depicted the positive side of life. G. was first introduced to the world of children's literature through a meeting with author and poet Eloise GREENFIELD. Following the meeting with Greenfield, G. was invited to share her artwork with the editors at Philomel; she was chosen to

illustrate a book of poetry entitled, *Children of Long Ago,* written by Greenfield's mother, Lessie Jones Little. In 1988, the first of many collaborations between Greenfield and G. was published. *Nathaniel Talking* (1988) was well received by the critics; it was awarded a 1990 CORETTA SCOTT KING AWARDS Honor Book. G.'s and Greenfield's collaboration on the book *Night on Neighborhood Street* was also a Coretta Scott King Honor Book in 1992. The successful collaboration between G. and Greenfield has produced over fifteen award-winning books that are commended for a positive portrayal of African American families. G. has collaborated with authors Lucille CLIFTON, *Everett Anderson's Christmas Coming* (1993); Tynia Thomassie, *Mimi's Tutu* (1996); and Sharon Bell MATHIS, *Red Dog, Blue Fly; Football Poems* (1995). G. also illustrated poems by Rebecca DOTLICH in *Lemonade Sun* (1996), which show children at play. *Indigo and Moonlight Gold* (1993) is applauded for its sensitive and moving text and striking illustrations; *Madelia* (1997) is praised for its descriptive text and warm illustrations portraying an African American church service and a loving relationship between a father and daughter.

From an early age, G. possessed the passion for providing African Americans with positive images of themselves and their families in books and paintings. G. continues to fulfill her goal of giving hope to all children who read her books. With illustrations in over thirty books G. provides African American children with positive images of themselves. While G.'s books depict mostly African American children, children from all ethnic groups are able to see the positive side of life and continue to hope.

AWARDS: Coretta Scott King Illustrator Award (1990) for *Nathaniel Talking.* Coretta Scott King Illustrator Honor Award (1992) for *Night on Neighborhood Street.* Painting awards from the National Academic Artists Association and the Du Sable Museum, Purchase Award

FURTHER WORKS: Illustrator: *Big Friend, Little Friend.* (Greenfield). 1991. *First Pink Light.* (Greenfield), 1991. *I Make Music.* (Greenfield). 1991. *My Daddy and I.* (Greenfield). 1991. *My Doll Keshia.* (Greenfield). 1991. *Aaron and Gayla's Alphabet Book.* (Greenfield). 1992. *Lift Every Voice and Sing.* (James W. Johnson). 1993. *William and the Good Old Days.* (Greenfield). 1993.

Waiting for Christmas. (M. Greenfield). 1996. *For the Love of the Game.* (Greenfield). 1997. *Kia Tanisha Drives Her Car.* (Greenfield). 1997. *Easter Parade.* (Greenfield). 1998

BIBLIOGRAPHY: Smith, Henrietta M. *The Coretta Scott King Awards Book, 1970–99*

BERT CROSSLAND

GILSON, Jamie
Author, b. 4 July 1933, Beardstown, Illinois

After graduation from Northwestern University in 1955 with a degree in radio-and-television education, G. began working as an English teacher in a junior high school. She was also a writer and producer for radio and television stations, and a filmscript writer for a major publisher. In addition, G. has been a lecturer and writing workshop teacher to sixth-grade students. G.'s first book arose from her ability to observe humorous things that happen every day. *Harvey, the Beer Can King* (1978) was based on a group of boys in her neighborhood who had an amazing beer can collection. During a field trip with a group of fifth graders G. developed the idea for *Do Bananas Chew Gum?* (1980). One of her best-loved characters is a young boy named Hobie Hanson. Readers meet Hobie and his classmates in *Thirteen Ways to Sink a Sub* (1982), *Hobie Hanson, You're Weird* (1987), *Hobie Hanson: Greatest Hero of the Mall* (1989), and *Sticks and Stones and Skeleton Bones* (1991). G. extends her reading audience with the publication of *You Cheat* (1992), a book directed toward early readers. She continues to write for younger readers with *Itchy Richard* (1991) and *Bug in a Rug* (1998).

While G. has written for younger readers, she is best known for her novels, told in first person, that vividly describe the antics of students in the middle grades. Critics praise her abilities to capture the nuances and idiosyncrasies of children at the preadolescent age. Readers hope that G. will continue her personal involvement with students so that this talented writer will bring more tales to life.

FURTHER WORKS: *Dial Leroi Rupert, D.J.,* 1979; *Can't Catch Me, I'm the Gingerbread Man,* 1981; *4-B Goes Wild,* 1983; *Hello, My Name Is Scrambled Eggs,* 1985; *Double Dog Dare,* 1988; *Soccer Circus,* 1993; *It Goes Eeeeeeeeeeeee!,* 1994; *Wagon Train 911,* 1996

BIBLIOGRAPHY: *Booklist,* Apr. 1, 1993, p. 1431, Apr. 1, 1994, p. 1446; *Bulletin of the Center for Children's Books,* Dec. 1982, p. 67, Oct. 1983, p. 27; *Sixth Book of Junior Authors and Illustrators,* 1989; *School Library Journal,* Sept. 1992, p. 283, June 1993, p. 106, June 1994, p. 100

BERT CROSSLAND

GINSBURG, Mirra
Author, folklorist, b. 1919, Bobruisk, Byelorussia, Russia

G. grew up in a remote village in Russia learning to read and write at an early age. After moving to Latvia and then Canada, G. and her family finally settled in the United States. Her first job was as a translator of great works by classic and new Russian authors. Growing up in Russia introduced her to a rich array of Russian folktales. *The Fox and the Hare* (1969), an adaptation of a Russian folktale, was the first of many wonderful Russian folktales that G. retold for the English-speaking world. G. then published a series of collections of Russian folktales. *Three Rolls and One Doughnut: Fables from Russia* (1970), *The Master of the Winds and Other Tales From Siberia* (1970), *One Trick Too Many: Fox Stories from Russia* (1973), and *The Lazies: Tales of the Peoples of Russia* (1973) were all praised for their wittiness, briskness, and usefulness as STORYTELLING sources. G. called these collections a "labor of love and joy." G. has also experienced success in her PICTURE BOOK adaptations. *The Chick and the Duckling* (1972), *Mushroom in the Rain* (1974), *The Night It Rained Pancakes* (1980), *The King Who Tried to Fry an Egg on His Head* (1994), and *Clay Boy* (1997) all received accolades for their fast pace, talented retellings, general happiness, and overall abilities to attract young readers. In addition to the adaptations from her native Russia, G. has also introduced readers to tales from other cultures.

G. is best known for her abilities to utilize folktales from her native Russia, retelling each in a new and entertaining way for young readers. G. gives young readers the opportunity to enter into worlds of imagination. Through her many titles, G. continually shows her love of language and her overwhelming love of literature and life. The universality of her retellings is evident by the numerous titles of hers that have been translated into other languages.

FURTHER WORKS: *What Kind of Bird Is That?*, 1973; *How the Sun Was Brought Back to the Sky*, 1975; *The Two Greedy Bears*, 1976; *Ookie-Spooky*, 1979; *The Twelve Clever Brothers and Other Fools: Folk Tales from Russia*, 1979; *Where Does the Sun Go at Night?*, 1981; *Kitten from One to Ten*, 1980; *Across the Stream*, 1982; *Four Brave Sailors*, 1987; *The Chinese Mirror*, 1988; *Asleep, Asleep*, 1992; *Merry-Go-Round, Four Stories*, 1992; *The Old Man and His Birds*, 1994; *The King Who Tried to Fry an Egg on His Head*, 1994; *Clay Boy*, 1997; *Two Greedy Bears*, 1998; *The Sun's Asleep Behind the Hill*, 2000

BIBLIOGRAPHY: *Contemporary Authors, New Revision Series*, vol. 54, 1997; *Sixth Book of Junior Authors and Illustrators*, 1989

BERT CROSSLAND

GIOVANNI, Nikki

Poet, b. 7 June 1934, Knoxville, Tennessee

G. grew up in southern Ohio, sharing an assertive nature and love of STORYTELLING with several members of her immediate family. Although she defined herself as a conservative Republican in high school, G. became radicalized during the early days of the Black Revolution, a time that coincided with her first years at Fisk University. Asked to leave Fisk at one point, she eventually returned to graduate, with honors, in 1967. During her years as a university student, G. studied with such AFRICAN AMERICAN literary luminaries as John O. Killens. She also took part in the founding of the local chapter of the Student Non-Violent Coordinating Committee (SNCC) when Black Power was on the organization's agenda.

G. pursued graduate studies in social work at the University of Pennsylvania, funded by a Ford Foundation Grant (1967), and then went to Columbia University's School of Fine Arts. In 1968, funded by a grant from the National Foundation for the Arts, she began her teaching career. She has continued to teach and lecture as well as to build a reputation as a preeminent American poet. Her achievements have earned her many local civic and cultural AWARDS, as well as awards from a variety of media, mostly for her poetry for adults and work with political causes. *My House* (1972) earned her the AMERICAN LIBRARY ASSOCI-ATION's Best Books for Young Adults citation (1973). G. has received twelve honorary doctorates from diverse schools, including the tradition-ally black Wilberforce University (1972) and Smith College (1975). In 1996, G. received the Langston HUGHES Award.

G.'s evolution from girlhood to black revolutionary to teacher to motherhood has been recorded in her poetry. Her books for children celebrate both blackness and the universal joys of childhood. *Spin a Soft Black Song* (1971), published when her son was two, presents young readers with pleasant and engaging verses that relate to their own experiences. *Ego Tripping and Other Poems for Young People* (1973) addresses a young adult audience with more thought-provoking issues. In *Vacation Time: Poems for Children* (1980), G. discloses a romantic side to her understanding of childhood. G.'s own life cycle and the social context in which she lives continues to prompt developments in her poetry. At midlife, she is concerned with images of strong women. The *Genie in the Jar* (1996), written for singer Nina Simone, is a book-length children's poem about one beloved girl's childhood.

As she has for adults, G. has extended her writing and publishing for children, too, beyond poetry. *Shimmy Shimmy Shimmy like My Sister Kate: Looking at the Harlem Renaissance through Poems* (1995) provides high school aged readers with an excellent window on that period of American cultural history. *Grand Mothers: Poems, Reminiscences, and Short Stories about the Keepers of Our Traditions* (1994) seeks to share G.'s enthusiasm for adult authors such as Maxine Hong Kingston and members of a retirement home where G. has taught writing with a YOUNG ADULT audience.

G.'s free-verse poems are energetic, speaking to both the senses and sensibilities of her young readers and listeners. She writes about elements of children's daily lives in a manner that invites readers to share her joy both in the sounds of words and in unexpected turns of wit. G. conveys her black feminist view of history to contemporary young adults in a manner that provides understanding for their present as well as evokes pride in their roots.

FURTHER WORKS: *Knoxville, Tennessee*, 1994; *The Sun Is So Quiet*, 1995

FRANCISCA GOLDSMITH

GIPSON, Fred (Frederick Benjamin Gipson)

Author, b. 7 February 1908, Mason, Texas; d. 14 August 1973, Mason, Texas

G. grew up in the Texas hill country and was highly influenced by his father, whom he considered to be his greatest teacher, about the art and technique of STORYTELLING. As a boy, C. loved the woods and the outdoors, he listened to stories of earlier times in Texas, and he read *Adventures of Huckleberry Finn* and other ADVENTURE STORIES. He later drew upon these early influences in his writing. After college, C. worked as a newspaper reporter; in 1940 he became a freelance writer, producing short stories and articles for magazines, novels, screenplays, and several works for children. *Old Yeller* (1956), his best-known children's book, is a compelling first-person account of fourteen-year-old Travis's adventures with a "big yeller dog" on his family's frontier farm in the Texas hill country of the 1860s. A 1957 ALA NEWBERY MEDAL Honor book, *Old Yeller* was made into a DISNEY movie, for which C. wrote the screenplay. *Savage Sam* (1962) continues Travis's story with Old Yeller's son.

FURTHER WORKS: *The Trail Driving Rooster,* 1955; *Little Arliss,* 1978; *Curly and the Wild Boar,* 1979

BIBLIOGRAPHY: Silvey, Anita, ed., *Children's Books and Their Creators,* 1995; *Third Book of Junior Authors,* 1972

KATHIE KRIEGER CERRA

GLEITZMAN, Morris

Author, b. 9 January 1953, Seaford, Lincolnshire, England

G. spent the first fifteen years of his life in England before emigrating to Australia in 1969. He received a B.A. from Canberra College of Advanced Education in 1974. G. is a multitalented individual with success as an award-winning screenwriter, a newspaper columnist, and an award-winning writer of children's books. G. first became known to Australians as the writer for the popular television show, the *Norman Gunston Show,* and later as the screenwriter for the award-winning film *The Other Facts of Life.* It was awarded the AWGIE Award for Best Original

Children's Film Script in 1985. G's novel, *Two Weeks with the Queen* was successful internationally and has become a stage play performed around the world. This REALISTIC novel won the 1990 Australian Family Award for its balanced portrayal of family life. Newspaper readers can continue to enjoy his semiautobiographical columns each weekend.

G. quickly became a successful children's writer with the publication of *The Other Facts of Life* (1985). In 1991 G. created the ebullient and lovable hero named Keith Shipley. Readers are able to follow the antics of Keith Shipley, who like G., grew up on the south side of London and later emigrated to Australia, through the novels *Misery Guts* (1991), *Worry Warts* (1991), and *Puppy Fat* (1995). These titles have been well accepted by readers and critics. *Misery Guts* received the CHILDREN'S BOOK COUNCIL of Australia Honor Book Award. Another one of G.'s characters is the mute Rowena who must confront her challenges through signs, written notes and actions. Readers can follow Rowena in *Blabber Mouth* (1992) and *Sticky Beak* (1993).

G's approach to writing for children is to use humor to explore highly emotional topics such as divorce, alienation, and physical challenges. In *Belly Flop* (1996) G. uses HUMOR to help Mitch understand his father's steadfast love when bullies are critical of his business methods. Critics praise G. for his ability to present these highly charged issues within a story with chaotic situations and comical dialogue. Children enjoy the work of this wonderfully funny writer and his contribution to AUSTRALIAN LITERATURE.

FURTHER WORKS: *Second Childhood,* 1990; *Poems,* 1990; *Belly Flop,* 1996; *Water Wings,* 1997

BIBLIOGRAPHY: Tomlinson, Carl M., *Children's Books from Other Countries,* 1998; Contemporary Authors Online, 1999 www.galenet.com; www.scils.rutgers.edu/special/Kay/authorg.html

BERT CROSSLAND

GLENN, Mel

Author, poet, teacher, b. 10 May 1943, Zurich, Switzerland

G., whose father was a writer, is a high school English teacher at the same school he attended in Brooklyn, New York. He has written numerous works of YOUNG ADULT LITERATURE based on his experiences in the classroom. G. uses POETRY and fiction to express common adolescent concerns such as loneliness, romantic love, and parental conflict. He wants readers to know they are not alone in their concerns and fears about growing up. G.'s first volume of free verse, *Class Dismissed: High School Poems* (1982), as well as its sequel, *Class Dismissed II: More High School Poems* (1986), is written in first person, with each poem bearing the name of the fictional author. *Class Dismissed* was an ALA Best Books for Young Adults title and received the SOCIETY OF CHILDREN'S BOOK WRITER's Golden Kite Honor Book plaque. Other AWARDS include AMERICAN LIBRARY ASSOCIATION's Best Books for Young Adults for his novel, *My Friend's Got This Problem, Mr. Candler* (1991), and ALA's Top Ten Best Books for Young Adults for *Who Killed Mr. Chippendale? A Mystery in Poems.* Glenn has also written stories for younger readers, such as *Play-by-Play* and *Squeeze Play: A Baseball Story* (1989).

FURTHER WORKS: *Back to Class*, 1988; *One Order to Go*, 1984; *Jump Ball*, 1997; *Foreign Exchange: A Mystery in Poems*, 1999

BIBLIOGRAPHY: Copeland, Jeffrey, *Speaking of Poets*, 1993; *Something about the Author*, vol. 93, 1997

MARY ARIAIL BROUGHTON

GLUBOCK, Shirley
Author, b. 15 June 1933, St. Louis, Missouri

An author of children's books on art and artists, G. likes to introduce children to great art treasures of the world while nurturing an understanding and appreciation of the people and cultures from which these treasures came. When G. attended Washington University in Missouri, she discovered her love of archeology and art history, the seeds of which had been planted in her childhood through visits to art museums and art reproductions in her home. When she became a teacher, she wanted to teach about the great works of art through experience with art as children discussed various artworks at museums. Her later position giving lectures to children at the Metropolitan Museum of Art naturally led to writing books, beginning with *The Art of Ancient Egypt* (1962), helping create experiences with art

and culture for children. *The Art of the Lands in the BIBLE* (1963), *The Art of Ancient Greece* (1963), and *The Art of the North American Indian* (1964) followed.

FURTHER WORKS: *The Art of the Eskimo,* 1964: *The Art of the Old West,* 1971; *The Art of China,* 1973; *The Art of America in Early Twentieth Century,* 1974; *The Art of the Comic Strip,* 1979; *The Young Picasso,* 2000

BIBLIOGRAPHY: HOPKINS, Lee B. *More Books by More People: Interviews with Sixty-five Authors of Books for Children,* 1974; *Something about the Author,* vol. 68, 1992

JANELLE B. MATHIS

GOBLE, Paul
Author, b. 27 September 1933, Haslemere, Surrey, England

G., a foremost interpreter of NATIVE AMERICAN FOLKLORE states, "I have been interested in everything Indian since I can remember. Before television days my mother read the complete works of American naturalist writers Grey Owl and Ernest Thompson SETON to my brother and me. The world they wrote about was so different from the crowded island where I lived." He collected pictures from books and magazines of everything he could find relating to Great Plains Indians and went on searches for stone-age flint instruments in Britain. G. imagined that people who made flint tools were similar to American Indians.

After receiving a copy of George Catlin's book *Notes on the North American Indians* (1848) G. compiled a comprehensive library on Native American culture. He also worked as an industrial designer and teacher. During summer breaks he made trips to the United States with his son Richard, living among the Crow Indians in Montana and the Sioux in South Dakota. He was adopted into the Yakima and Sioux tribes by a great grandson of a famous Sioux war chief, but "it was the books concerning the wisdom of Black Elk which finally determined my life's orientation."

G. reads several versions of the same story and evaluates them before writing the text for his books. He researches the oldest Native American sources he can locate for his stories; many first recorded by ethnologists in 1890–1910. G. emphasizes a widespread belief of Native Americans that there should be a harmonious relationship between nature and man. His tales about *Iktomi,* a pompous trickster, written in a contemporary style, have a gray italicized running commentary along with periodic questions to encourage readers to participate. *Iktomi and the Boulder: A Plains Indian Story* (1988), has side comments, the text, and the words Iktomi mutters. Proud Iktomi gives his blanket to a boulder then takes it back. The boulder chases Iktomi and pins him down. Iktomi lies to enlist help from the animals but no one is strong enough to move the boulder until the angered bats chip it to pieces. The tale offers an explanation about why there are rocks scattered over the Great Plains and why bats have flat faces.

Iktomi and the Berries: A Plains Indian Story (1989) has the same three components; the story, side comments, and the words of Iktomi. Iktomi is angry because he can never find the red berries he sees in the water. He even ties a rope around his neck and anchors it to a large rock, heaves the rock in the water and is dragged to the bottom of the river where he thinks the berries are. After almost drowning he lies on his back and discovers the berries above him. In his anger he beats the bushes until all the berries have fallen off. Today buffalo berries are picked "after the first frosts of fall. They spread cloths under the bushes and beat the branches with sticks, just like Iktomi did."

The Girl Who Loved Wild Horses (1978) was an ALA CALDECOTT MEDAL winner, an AMERICAN LIBRARY ASSOCIATION Notable Book, a *Horn Book* Honor List title and received the Art Books for Children award. It expresses "the Native American rapport with nature" and an underlying theme of the oneness of all creatures. The illustrations accurately depict nineteenth century Plains Indians life with the tepees facing the sun. Based on traditional narratives, a young Native American girl stays with wild horses until she is transformed into one. The transformation is assumed complete when a mare runs with a wild stallion. The closing lines reinforce the transformation belief, "Today, we are still glad to remember that we have relatives among the Horse People."

Ambassador of Honor/Books Across the Sea award from the English-Speaking Union went to *The Gift of the Sacred Dog* (1980). G. creates a pourquoi tale of how horses first came to the Plains people. Although the Spanish conquistadors brought the horse to the American continent, a Native American boy discovers a herd of wild horses and believes it a gift from the Great Spirit to help his hungry people. G. uses a child to link the powers of the Great Spirit with the needs of the people.

Star Boy (1983) tells of a boy born of the Morning Star and an earthly mother. The boy is exiled to earth when his mother harvests a forbidden plant; he bears a scar as a reminder of the Sun's displeasure. When grown, with the support of the Chief's daughter, Star Boy courageously seeks his grandfather, begs forgiveness and asks the scar be removed as a sign of forgiveness. The Sun agrees and promises he will restore health to the sick if the people will build a lodge in honor of the Sun each summer. Thus begins the Blackfeet sacred ritual Sun Dance. It was the Library of Congress Children's Book of the Year, an International Youth Library Choice and received the Ambassador of Honor/Books Across the Sea Award, English-Speaking Union.

Buffalo Woman (1984) was an AMERICAN LIBRARY ASSOCIATION Notable Book, on the *Horn Book* Honor List and received the Ambassador of Honor/Books Across the Sea award, English-Speaking Union. The buffalo send a transfigured buffalo as a wife to an Indian hunter. G. presents the Native American perspective as an Indian brave becomes a buffalo to join his wife when she returns to her people. This transformation tale from the Great Plains tribes shows how closely the lives of the buffalo and the people were intertwined. It was believed that these stories would encourage the buffalo herds to give themselves to the people.

G.'s ILLUSTRATIONS use watercolor figures outlined in ink set against a white background. Human faces are featureless but the pictures correlate with the events of the story so mood and feelings can be visualized. The colorful tepees, clothing, plants and animals provide a detailed record of the Great Plains landscape.

"Love of Indians and love of nature have always been my priorities . . . I [try] to express and paint what I believe to be the Native American rapport with nature . . . I hope that Native Americans approve of the book[s] and feel sympathy for the illustrations. It gives me a warm feeling when Indians respond to my books."

BIBLIOGRAPHY: *Best Books for Children: Preschool through Grade Six*, fifth ed. 1994. *Children's Literature Research.* vol. 21. 1990. *Fiction, FOLKLORE, FANTASY and POETRY for Children, 1876–1986.* vols. 1 and 2. Silvey, A., ed. *Children's Books and Their Creators.* 1995. *Something about the Author.* vol. 25 1981 and vol. 69 1992

IRVYN G. GILBERTSON

GODDEN (Margaret) Rumer

Author, b. 10 December 1907, Sussex, England; d. 8 November 1998, Dumfriesshire, Scotland

A prolific author of novels, short stories, POETRY, and BIOGRAPHIES, G. spent her early years in India where she and her sister Jon amused themselves writing stories. Her experiences in India provide a sumptuous setting for much of her fiction. G.'s two most popular adult novels, both successful classic films, *Black Narcissus* (1939) and *The River* (1946), are notable for their lyrical writing style and sensitive characterizations conveying vivid pictures of life in the Himalayas and Bengal, India.

Her first children's book, *The Doll's House* (1947), is about a family of dolls who long for the freedom and independence of the girls who own them. Many of her two dozen children's books offer themes about issues vital to children such as jealousy, growing up, and becoming independent, told through the characters of dolls. G. expresses the belief that children deserve honesty in their stories as well as well-crafted prose and carefully chosen language, that every word counts and children should not be burdened with long descriptive passages. A winner of many AWARDS for her children's works, G. was awarded the Order of the British Empire in 1993.

FURTHER WORKS: *The Mousewife.* 1951. *Impunity Jane.* 1954. *The Fairy Doll.* 1956. *The Story of Holly and Ivy.* 1958. *Candy Floss.* 1961. *Mr. McFadden's Hallowe'en.* 1975. *Listen to the Nightingale.* 1992. *The Little Chair.* 1996

BIBLIOGRAPHY: Carpenter, H. and M. Prichard. *The Oxford Companion to Children's Literature.*

1984. *New York Times* obituary by Andrew Yarrow November 10, 1998

DIANE G. PERSON

GOFFSTEIN, M(arilyn) B(rooke)

Author, illustrator, b. 20 December 1940, St. Paul, Minnesota

G. is an author and illustrator of children's and adolescent literature. Her work is considered contemporary fables about the pursuit of happiness, as seen in *Goldie, the Dollmaker* (1969) and *Two Piano Tuners* (1970). Her writing is simple as are her pictures and both exhibit creative values and family love. G. began illustrating in black and white but when creating *Natural History* (1979), a book about interdependence and peace within the natural world, she felt the need for color. Among her numerous AWARDS are the ALA CALDECOTT MEDAL Honor Book award for *Fish for Supper* (1976), and a Jane Addams Peace Award special certificate. She also received the *New York Times* Best Illustrated Children's Books of the Year award (1972) for *A Little Schubert* and (1979) for *Natural History* and an AMERICAN LIBRARY ASSOCIATION Notable Award.

FURTHER WORKS: *Across the Sea.* 1968. *An Artist.* 1980. *A Writer.* 1984. *An Actor.* 1987. *A House, A Home.* 1989

BIBLIOGRAPHY: *Children's Literature Review.* 1978. *Fourth Book of Junior Authors and Illustrators.* 1978. Kingman, L., G. A. Hogarth, H. Quimby, compilers, *Illustrators of Children's Books: 1967–1976.* 1978. *Something about the Author.* vol. 70, 1993

JANELLE B. MATHIS

GOLDBERG, Leah

Author, b. 1911, Kovno, Lithuania; d. 1970, Israel

G. first began to write Hebrew verse as a schoolgirl. After receiving her Ph.D. in Semitic Languages at the University of Bonn, she emigrated to Israel, then Palestine, in 1935. This prolific and versatile Hebrew POET, master STORYTELLER, playwright, critic, TRANSLATOR, and teacher became a household name for children and adults alike in modern Israel.

Her language, though symbolic, is simple, refreshing, and direct and holds universal appeal. Her expression is articulate, clearly defined and innovative and shows a finely tuned ear for musicality in language, ingenuous freshness, and a delightful sense of HUMOR. Soon after her arrival in Israel, G. joined the editorial staff of the *Davar* newspaper, and later became the literary editor of *Al Ha-Mishmar.* As a member of the modernist Shlonsky group of poets under the mentorship of Abraham Shlonsky, she published her work in many literary journals. In 1952 she became the head of the Department of Comparative Literature at Hebrew University in Jerusalem, a post she held until her death in 1970.

Although her talent was expressed in several genres, G. is best known for the rapport she created with children through an ongoing dialogue with them, using her own distinctive style, rhythm, and choice of words, her profound understanding of the child's immediate frames of reference, and the fact that she drew her materials from the familiar world of childhood. These all enabled her to communicate with children of all ages.

G. was also a prolific literary critic. She was familiar with the literature of all the major European languages, especially Russian. Her works were translated into Spanish, Korean, and English; she translated ANDERSEN'S FAIRY TALES and stories by Chekhov into Hebrew.

AWARDS: Israel Prize for Literature, awarded posthumously

FURTHER WORKS: *My Friend in Arnon Street.* 1943. *The Song of a Young World.* 1950. *Where Is Pluto?* 1957. *A Flat to Let.* 1959. *The Absent-Minded Guy from Kfar Azar.* 1968. *The Elephant Has a Cold.* 1975. *And All Are Friends.* 1978. *The Story of Three Nuts.* 1980. *Come, Clouds.* 1983. *A Golden Leaf.* 1988. *Dreams of a King.* 1994. *Who Is at the Pavilion?* 1997. Other books include poems in: *Smoke Rings.* 1935. *Green-Eyed Spike.* 1940. *From My Old Home.* 1943. *Samson's Love.* 1952. *Sooner or Later.* 1959. *Collected Poems.* 1970. *Small.* 1981. *In My Beloved Country.* 1997

FURTHER WORKS: (in TRANSLATION): *Light on the Rim of a Cloud.* 1972: *The Cobbler.* 1950: *Selected Poems.* 1976: *Of Bloom.* 1992: *Little Queen of Sheba.* 1959

BIBLIOGRAPHY: *Encyclopedia Judaica.* 1972. Goldberg, L. *Collected Poems.* 1970. Meron, D. *Founding Mothers, Stepsisters.* 1991. Ofek, U. *The Ofek Lexicon for Children's Literature.* 1985

ELANA RECHTMAN

GOMI, Taro
Author, illustrator, b. 20 August 1945, Tokyo, Japan

The winner of several children's book AWARDS in various countries, G. has published over two hundred books in Japan, more than fifteen of which have been translated into English. G. creatively describes ordinary events in a child's life according to how he remembers thinking as a child. The interactive nature of his books combine with his artistically designed ILLUSTRATIONS to create concept books such as *Bus Stops* (1988) or *Seeing, Saying, Doing, Playing: A Big Book of Action Words* (1991), and life situations as found in *First Comes Harry* (1987) or *The Crocodile and the Dentist* (1995), that are especially entertaining. G. is perhaps most recognized for *Everyone Poops* (1993), a book sometimes perceived as not appropriate, which shows pictures of many animals and types of feces.

FURTHER WORKS: *Coco Can't Wait,* 1983; *Spring Is Here,* 1989; *Guess Who?,* 1991; *Who Ate It?,* 1991; *Who Hid It?,* 1992; *Bus Stops,* 1999

BIBLIOGRAPHY: *Something about the Author,* vol. 103, 1999

JANELLE B. MATHIS

GOODALL, John
Author, illustrator, b. 7 June 1908, Heacham, Norfolk, England; d. 3 June 1996, London, England

As a young child, G. showed great interest and talent in drawing and painting. He was encouraged by his parents, who arranged for him to study with some of England's foremost painters. G. also attended the Royal Academy of Art. During World War II, G. served in India and the Far East and continued to paint and exhibit. Upon his return to England, G. continued perfecting his craft and was asked to paint some of the Royal Family. G's first entry into books for children came through his ILLUSTRATIONS for authors like Edith Bland and Susan Dorritt. G. also was given the opportunity to illustrate an edition of Lewis CARROLL's *Alice in Wonderland* (1965). G's desire to write books for his granddaughter began his career as an author and illustrator. *The Adventures of Paddy Pork* (1968) was the first of ten wordless PICTURE BOOKS chronicling the life of Paddy Pork, a gentlemanly Victorian pig. Critics praised G. for his meticulous drawing, attention to detail, and his use of deep rich hues and subtle shadings.

G. expanded his work with the publication of a series of wordless stories set in the Edwardian period. *An Edwardian Summer* (1976) and *An Edwardian Christmas* (1977) were the first of numerous stories that beautifully recreated the lavish and genteel events of Edwardian England.

G. is best known for his wordless picture books in which he utilized the transformation book format technique, which alternates full and half-page illustrations. Lavish, flawlessly rendered watercolors are his trademark. His stories set in the Edwardian period and his SERIES of stories chronicling the social history of England from the Middle Ages to present day help readers better understand the people and culture of bygone eras.

AWARDS: *Boston Globe/Horn Book* Award for Illustration (1968) for *The Adventures of Paddy Pork*. *New York Times* Best Illustrated Children's Books of the Year (1977) for *The Surprise Picnic* and (1982) for *Paddy Goes Traveling*.

FURTHER BOOKS; Self-Illustrated: *Field Mouse House*. 1954. *Dr. Owl's Party*. 1954. *The Ballooning Adventures of Paddy Pork*. 1969. *Shrewbettina's Birthday*. 1971. *Jacko*. 1971. *Kelly*. 1971. *Kelly, Dot and Esmerelda*. 1972. *Paddy's Evening Out*. 1974. *The Surprise Picnic*. 1974. *Creepy Castle*. 1975. *Naughty Nancy the Bad Bridesmaid*. 1975. *An Edwardian Holiday*. 1978. *Story of an English Village*. 1978. *An Edwardian Season*. 1979: *Escapade*. 1980. *Paddy's New Hat*. 1980: *Victorians Abroad*. 1980. *Before the War, 1908–1939: An Autobiography in Pictures*. 1981. *Edwardian Entertainments*. 1981. *Paddy Finds a Job*. 1981. *Shrewbettina Goes to Work*. 1981. *Above and Below Stairs*. 1982. *Lavinia's Cottage*. 1982. *Paddy Goes Traveling*. 1982. *Paddy Pork: Odd Jobs*. 1982. *Paddy under the Water*. 1983. *The Midnight Adventures of Kelly, Dot, and Esmerelda*. 1984. *Naughty Nancy Goes to School*. 1985. *Paddy to the Rescue*. 1985. *Story of a Castle*. 1986. *Story of a High Street*. 1987. *Little Red Riding Hood*. (Adapter), 1988. *Story of a Farm*. 1989. *Story of a Seashore*. 1990. *Puss in Boots*. (Adapter). 1990. *Great Days of a Country House*. 1991

BIBLIOGRAPHY: *Book World*, Oct. 20, 1968; Cianciolo, Patricia J. *Picture Books for Children*, third ed. (1990); Silvey, Anita, ed., *Children's Books and Their Creators* (1995); *Times Literary Supplement*, Apr. 16, 1970

BERT CROSSLAND

GOODE, Diane
Author, illustrator, b. 14 September 1949, New York City

G. grew up in Brooklyn, New York, but spent many summers in her mother's home country of France. In France G. began to develop her love of art. G. received a B.A. in FINE ARTS from Queens College and also attended Les Beaux-Arts in Aix-en-Provence. G. taught for a brief time in the New York Public Schools and the University of California at Los Angeles. G.'s first entrance into the world of children's books came with the opportunity to illustrate Christian Garrison's book *Little Pieces of the West Wind* (1975). G. and Garrison continued to collaborate on *Flim Flam and the Big Cheese* (1976) and *The Dream Eater* (1978). G.'s ILLUSTRATIONS have brought to life the words of established authors like Riki Levinson, with whom she teamed on *Watch the Stars Come Out* (1985) and *I Go with My Family to Grandma's* (1986). She also illustrated *The House Gobbaleen* (1995) by Lloyd ALEXANDER. In the late 1980s G. began to illustrate a SERIES of books about Americana. *The Diane G. Book of American Folk Tales and Songs* (1989), *Diane G.'s Book of Scary Stories and Songs* (1994) and *Diane G.'s American Christmas Songs* (1997) brought new life to well known stories, songs, and traditions.

G. views the process of bookmaking as a collaborative effort among author, illustrator, editor, and art director; each person must have respect for the others. She describes her approach to illustrating as tedious yet exciting. She does numerous sketches for each illustration, each time adding, omitting, enlarging, and reducing until she finally has all the right elements in place. She feels lucky to illustrate children's books and privileged to bring joy and love into the lives of children.

AWARDS: ALA CALDECOTT MEDAL Honor Book (1983) for *When I Was Young in the Mountains* (Cynthia RYLANT, author)

FURTHER WORKS: Illustrator: *The Selchie's Seed*. (Oppenheim). 1975. *Tattercoats*. (Steele). 1976. *Beauty and the Beast*. (de Beaumont). 1978. *The*

Unicorn and the Plow. (Moeri). 1982. *The Fir Tree.* (ANDERSEN). 1983. The *Night before Christmas.* (MOORE). 1983. *Ballet Shoes.* (STREATFEILD). 1991. *The Story of the Nutcracker Ballet.* (HAUTZIG). 1993. *A Child's Garden of Verses.* (STEVENSON). 1998. Self-Illustrated: *I Hear a Noise.* 1988. *Where's Our Mama.* 1991. *Diane Goode's Book of Silly Stories and Songs.* 1992. *The Little Book of Nursery Animals.* 1993. *Mama's Perfect Present.* 1996

BIBLIOGRAPHY: Cianciolo, Patricia, PICTURE BOOKS *for Children,* third ed. (1990) and fourth ed. (1997); Schwarz, Joseph H., *The Picture Book Comes of Age* (1991)

BERT CROSSLAND

GOREY, Edward

Author, illustrator, b. 22 February 1925, Chicago, Illinois; d. 15 April 2000, Hyannis, Massachusetts

As a young child, G. showed a great interest in drawing. His only formal training came through intermittent classes at the Chicago Art Institute. Following a two-year service in the United States Army, G. attended Harvard and received a Bachelor of Arts in French in 1950. G. soon moved to New York and continued to write and work as a staff artist with Doubleday Publishers. G.'s entrance into the world of children's books came with the publication of *The Doubtful Guest* (1957). It tells the story of an uninvited penguin, sporting a scarf and tennis shoes that takes up residence in an Edwardian home. *The Doubtful Guest* introduces G.'s characteristic pen and ink style that he used throughout his career. G. used black-and-white cross-hatched drawings to create eerie effects among the unfortunate children and ill-fated monsters in more than sixty books he illustrated. *The Hapless Child* (1961) focused on a world of unfortunate predicaments and eerie, macabre chaos that became the hallmarks of G.'s books. G.'s distinctive pen and ink drawings and use of angles and perspectives gives life to Florence Parry HEIDE's book *The Shrinking of Treehorn* (1971), a story of a young boy who instead of growing each day, shrinks. C. and Heide continued their collaboration with the publication of *Treehorn's Treasure* (1981), *The Adventures of Treehorn* (1983), and *Treehorn's Wish* (1984). G.'s illustrations can also be seen in Edward LEAR's *The Jumblies* (1968) and *The Dong with the Luminous Nose* (1969).

G. wrote and illustrated more than one hundred books for children and adults, many under pseudonyms that are anagrams of his own name; Ogdred Weary, Eduard Blutig and Mrs. Regera Dowdy are but a few. G. is best known in the children's literature world as a writer and illustrator of sophisticated PICTURE BOOKS that give a unique perspective on everyday life. Though many of his characters encounter unfortunate situations and ultimate demise, young people enjoy entering worlds of dark hallways and overgrown gardens created by this most unusual writer and illustrator.

AWARDS: *New York Times* Best Illustrated Children's Books of the Year Award (1966) for *The Monster Den,* (1969) for *The Dong with the Luminous Nose,* and (1971), *The Shrinking of Treehorn.* AMERICAN LIBRARY ASSOCIATION Notable Book Citation (1971) for *The Shrinking of Treehorn*

FURTHER BOOKS: Self-Illustrated: *The Bug Book.* 1959. *The Wuggly Ump.* 1963. *The Gilded Bat.* 1966. *The Epileptic Bicycle.* 1968. *The Chinese Obelisk: Fourth Alphabet.* 1970. *The Gashlycrumb Tinies.* 1972. *Amphigorey.* 1972. *The Sinking Spell.* 1972. *The Glorious Nosebleed Alphabet.* 1974. *The Water Flowers.* 1982. Illustrator: *The Man Who Sang the Sillies.* (CIARDI). 1961. *You Read to Me, I'll Read to You.* (Ciardi). 1962. *The King Who Saved Himself from Being Saved.* (Ciardi). 1965. *Brer Rabbit and His Tricks.* (Rees). 1967. *Sam and Emma.* (Nelsen). 1971. *The House with a Clock in Its Walls.* (BELLAIRS). 1973. *Red Riding Hood.* (DE REGNIERS). 1972. *The Case of the Blue Figurine.* (Bellairs). 1983

BIBLIOGRAPHY: *Dictionary of Literary Biography,* vol. 1, 1977; Gurey, E., *The Betrayed Confidence,* 1992; *New York Times Review of Books,* Nov. 6, 1983; *New York Times* obituary, April 16, 17, 2000; *Publishers Weekly,* Nov. 26, 1982

BERT CROSSLAND

GRAHAM, Lorenz Bell

Author, b. 27 January 1902, New Orleans, Louisiana; d. 11 September 1989, West Covina, California

G., author of PICTURE BOOKS and YOUNG ADULT novels, was the son an AFRICAN AMERICAN Methodist minister whose work required the family to move from the Northern U.S. to the South. The positive perspective on integration G. had gained in the north changed when he was attacked by a white boy in his new Southern hometown—an experience that would later parallel that of the protagonist in G.'s Town series of young adult novels. Graham attended UCLA, but left during his third year to teach in a Liberian mission school. Upon his return to the United States, G. completed his undergraduate education at Virginia Union University and did postgraduate studies in social work at New York University and Columbia University. G.'s experiences in Liberia and additional travels in Africa inspired him to want to create books for young people that would accurately depict AFRICAN life and culture. He found, however, that publishers in the 1920s feared that the public would not buy books depicting African people and experiences so different from the popular images of that time. Discouraged, G. stopped writing and pursued a career in social work. His first book was published in 1946. *How God Fix Jonah,* with an introduction by his future brother-in-law, W. E. B. Du Bois, is a collection of BIBLE stories told in West African idiom. Reissued in 2000, the book is newly illustrated by Ashley BRYAN with the original Du Bois and Effie Lee Morris forewords.

G. wanted his writing to bridge the gap between Americans' ideas about Africa and the Africa he knew. He included the social problems of his era in his writings and tried particularly to promote cross-cultural and inter-racial understanding and to allay the racial fears with which he grew up. G. was told by a publisher that his African American characters too closely resembled white people and would not be believed; this was exactly the kind of prejudice G. wanted to dispel. His writing portrayed people as individuals and as members of a distinctive culture. In *South Town* (1958), one of the four novels in his Town series, an African American boy struggles to find his rightful place in a frequently unjust society.

AWARDS: Thomas Alva Edison Foundation citation for G.'s edition of *The Ten Commandments* (adaptation). Association for Study of Negro Life and History Award. Child Study Association of America Award for *South Town* (1958)

FURTHER WORKS: In the Town series: *North Town,* 1965. *Whose Town?* 1969. *Return to South Town.* 1976. Biblical retellings: *A Road down in the Sea.* 1970. *Every Man Heart Lay Down.* 1970.

David He No Fear. 1971. *God Wash the World and Start Again.* 1971. *Hongry Catch the Foolish Boy.* 1973. *How God Fix Jonah.* 1946. Ashley Bryan, illus. 2000. Stories set in Africa: *Tales of Momolu.* 1947. *Song of the Boat.* 1975

BIBLIOGRAPHY: Graham, L. 1973. An author speaks. *Elementary English.* 50 (2), 185–88. Small, R. C. 1970. *South Town: A Junior Novel of Prejudice. Negro American Literature Forum.* 4 (4), 136–41

JANE WEST

GRAHAM, Margaret Bloy
Illustrator, author, b. 2 November 1920, Toronto, Ontario, Canada

G. was born and reared in Ontario, Canada, the daughter of a physician. A voracious reader as a child, she also acquired an early interest in art and majored in art history at the University of Toronto. After graduation she moved to New York City and worked at a variety of jobs including a ship's draftsman during World War II. The first children's book G. illustrated was Gene ZION's *All Falling Down* (1951). It is done in pastel colors reflecting the pensive thoughtful tone of the book. The following year, she illustrated Charlotte ZOLOTOW's *The Storm Book* with double-page spreads showing the sky darkening followed by the driving rain. She is perhaps most fondly regarded for the gently humorous ILLUSTRATIONS for Zion's series about Harry, an irascible dog, including *Harry the Dirty Dog* (1956), *No Roses for Harry!* (1958), and *Harry and the Lady Next Door* (1960). G. has also written and illustrated her own books, including *Be Nice to Spiders* (1968) and *Benjy and the Barking Bird* (1970). Her drawings possess a charming naive quality that is well-suited to the comic spirit of the texts she illustrates.

AWARDS: ALA CALDECOTT MEDAL Honor Book (1952) for *All Falling Down* (Gene Zion, author), and (1953) for *The Storm Book* (Charlotte Zolotow, author)

FURTHER WORKS: *Benjy's Dog House.* 1972. *The Meanest Squirrel I Ever Met.* (Gene Zion, author). 1962. *The Pack Rat's Day.* (Jack PRELUTSKY, author). 1974

BIBLIOGRAPHY: *Something about the Author.* vol. 11, 1977; *More Junior Authors.* 1963

DAVID L. RUSSELL

GRAHAME, Kenneth

Author, b. 8 March 1859, Edinburgh, Scotland;
d. 6 July 1932, Pangbourne, England

G., author of the classic children's FANTASY, *The Wind in the Willows* (1908), was the third of four children of a rather unsuccessful lawyer, reputedly descended from Robert the Bruce. When G. was five, his mother died suddenly of scarlet fever, and his father sent the children to the south of England to live with their maternal grandmother Ingles. She was a distant and domineering woman, undoubtedly distressed at having to rear four young children in her old age and on her modest means. Nevertheless, even these years were not unhappy for G., and fond memories of the peaceful rural landscape near the riverside would resurface in his writing. After a failed attempt to reunite the family, their father, a hopeless alcoholic, abandoned them and spent his remaining years in France, never seeing his children again. Educated at St. Edward's School, G. had dreamed of an Oxford education that he might become a writer or educator, but was sent by his unimaginative uncles to London to take a position as a clerk in the Bank of England.

Being deprived of Oxford was the great disappointment of his life, but G. made the most of his London experience and was rapidly promoted through the ranks. He met Frederick James Furnivall, the noted scholar, who introduced him to great literature and encouraged him to write. G. began by writing miscellaneous essays for journals, most notably for W. E. Henley's *National Observer*. Henley exerted great influence on G. and encouraged him in those romantic writings eulogizing the simple life, the lure of the open road, and condemning dehumanized modern industrial society.

His early essays were collected as *Pagan Papers* (1893), his first book. *The Golden Age* (1895) was the next accumulation of G.'s stories, romantic reveries of childhood that attacked adult pretensions and sentimentalities. He used the term "Olympians" to refer to the adults, a satiric reference not lost on his readers. This work was enormously popular and established G.'s international reputation. It was followed by *Dream Days*

(1898), a continuation of his story-essays; all three of his collections went into numerous editions and were admired by such luminaries as Algernon Swinburne, the prime minister of Australia, Kaiser Wilhelm II, and President Theodore Roosevelt, who repeatedly invited him to the White House, an invitation G. never accepted. In 1898, G. became one of the youngest men ever appointed Secretary of the Bank of England, one of the three highest-ranking posts in the institution.

G.'s only son, Alastair, nicknamed "Mouse," suffered from blinding cataracts in one eye and impaired vision in the other. G. records that on Mouse's fourth birthday, May 12, 1904, to assuage the boy's crying fit, he "had to tell him stories about moles, giraffes & water-rats." This, it is assumed, was the genesis of *The Wind in the Willows*. Also during this time, G. moved his family near the Thames to Cookham Dean, where he had spent much of his childhood. This environment likely inspired the direction of his writing. In 1907, Alastair spent the summer at the seaside with his mother and G. sent stories about Mr. Toad and his compatriots to him by mail. The result, *The Wind in the Willows,* was finally published in 1908, shortly after he had resigned from the Bank of England. It was his first work since before his marriage, and it would be his last work, save for his editing of *The Cambridge Book of Poetry for Children* in 1916.

The Wind in the Willows was originally titled *The Wind in the Reeds,* but W. B. Yeats's *The Wind among the Reeds* appeared shortly before. An anthropomorphic fantasy, it was widely misunderstood by the literary establishment of the day. The *Times Literary Supplement* reviewer, completely out of touch with the child mind, was thoroughly perplexed, complaining that the behavior of the animal characters was inconsistent with their animal natures and lamenting the book's lack of humor. He groused: "Grown up readers will find it monotonous and elusive; children will hope in vain for more fun." Time has proven otherwise.

The Wind in the Willows is a deeply personal statement, resulting from a lifetime of thought and experience. The three principal characters seem to reveal various facets of G.'s complex personality, and act out his own repressed fantasies. Its celebration of home, companionship, the good life is part of its nostalgic look backward, which captures the interest of many adults. Its appealing animal characters drawn from the least glamorous regions of the animal world—Toad, Mole, Water Rat, and Badger—appeal to young children who quickly identify with the affable creatures. The comical adventures, including some rather sharp satire directed toward Mr. Toad, reach audiences of all ages. The Edwardian flavor of the work is unmistakable, elevating as it does a very masculine world, but one softened by good manners, gracious living, and camaraderie. However, throughout the book a distinct longing for times past is evident, and an antagonism toward the trappings of modern industrialism, such as the motor car, which causes so much grief for poor Mr. Toad.

The work bears the literary influence of such authors as Homer, Shakespeare, Malory, Tennyson, Browning, and others. It is a very personal piece, hearkening back to G.'s romantic notions of his own childhood in an Arcadian setting by the River Thames. *The Wind in the Willows* is rescued from sentimentality by the charm and ingenuity of the characters and its pervasive wit. It remains one of the undisputed classics of children's literature, rich with subtle complexities that make it as appealing to adults as to children.

The remaining years of G.'s life were unproductive, punctuated in 1920 by the great tragedy of his life, the death of his unhappy son on a railroad track outside of Oxford. Although officially ruled an accident, the specter of suicide was never entirely vanquished. G. lived the life of an eccentric recluse following Alastair's death, finding at last some solace in the company of his equally eccentric wife. He died on July 6, 1932 and was buried in Oxford, the place that had so eluded him in his lifetime. The epitaph over his grave was written by his cousin, Anthony Hope, famed author of *The Prisoner of Zenda*, and it proclaimed that G. had left "childhood and literature through him the more blest for all time." It is indeed difficult to imagine children's literature without him.

AWARDS: Lewis CARROLL Shelf Award, 1958, for *The Wind in the Willows*, and 1963, for *The Reluctant Dragon*

BIBLIOGRAPHY: Carpenter, H., *Secret Gardens*, 1985; *The Oxford Companion to Children's Literature*, 1984; Cott, Jonathan, *Pipers at the Gates of Dawn*, 1981; *Dictionary of Literary Biography; British Novelist, 1890–1929: Traditionalists*, vol. 34; Green, Peter, *Kenneth G.: A Biography*, 1959; Hunt, Peter, ed., *Illustrated History of Children's Literature*, 1995; *Something about the Author*, vol. 100, 1999; "Review," *Times Literary Supplement*, October 22, 1908

DAVID L. RUSSELL

GRAMATKY, Hardie

Author, illustrator, animator, b. 12 April 1907, Dallas, Texas; d. 29 April 1979, Westport, Connecticut

G. began his career as an animator for DISNEY studios and later became a pictorial reporter for *Fortune* magazine. But G. is best known as the creator of the Little Toot books, a SERIES of self-illustrated stories about a naughty little tugboat. Although G. had difficulty selling the first *Little Toot* (1939) to a publisher, he finally persuaded G. P. Putnam's Sons to publish his work, and the story was immediately popular. Using watercolor separations, G. tells the story of a little tugboat that prefers play to work until it saves an ocean liner foundering in a fierce storm. The message about hard work and determination is told in an enduring positive story. Disney Studios made the book into a movie and Little Toot became a prize-winning float in the Tournament of Roses. The book also won the Lewis CARROLL Shelf Award in 1969. Following the first Little Toot book, Gramatky produced other books in the series, including *Little Toot on the Thames* (1964), *Little Toot on the Grand Canal* (1968), *Little Toot on the Mississippi* (1973), and *Little Toot through the Golden Gate* (1975).

FURTHER WORKS: *Hercules: The Story of an Old-Fashioned Fire Engine*. 1940; *Loopy*. 1941; *Creeper's Jeep*. 1948; *Sparky: The Story of a Little Trolley Car*. 1952; *Homer and the Circus Train*. 1957; *Bolivar*. 1961; *Nikos and the Sea God*. 1963; *Happy's Christmas*. 1970

BIBLIOGRAPHY: HOPKINS, Lee Bennett, *Pauses: Autobiographical Reflections of 101 Creators of Children's Books*, 1995

MARY ARIAIL BROUGHTON

GRAY, Elizabeth Janet Vining

Author, b. 6 October 1902, Philadelphia, Pennsylvania; d. 27 November 1999, Kennett Square, Pennsylvania

G. is best known for her historical fiction, most notably for the ALA NEWBERY MEDAL Book *Adam of the Road* (1942). It is a colorful story set in thirteenth-century England, telling the adventures of Adam and his trained dog as they travel in search of Adam's minstrel father. During her childhood G. attended the Germantown Friends School, and at the age of thirteen she published her first piece, that she described as a moral story for children. G. recounts with pleasure the fact that the publishers did not know she was a teenager. After earning degrees at Bryn Mawr and the Drexel Institute, G. worked at odd jobs tutoring and grading papers. She then accepted a teaching position in a New Jersey high school and continued her library work. G. published her first book, *Meredith's Ann* in 1929. In the midst of her writing career, G. tutored the Crown Prince of Japan with the hope that international service would add to peace and cooperation among nations. This experience led to G.'s writing *Windows for the Crown Prince* (1952). In addition to her award-winning historical fiction, G. has written in other genres including nonfiction and BIOGRAPHY. When asked why she writes for children, she responded, "I write because I can't help it."

AWARDS: ALA Newbery Medal (1943) for *Adam of the Road*. *Herald Tribune* Spring Festival award for *Sandy* (1945). American Woman's Eminent Achievement Award

FURTHER WORKS: *Young Walter Scott*. 1938. *Contributions of the Quakers*. 1939. *Friend of Life: The Biography of Rufus M. Jones*. 1958. *Return to Japan*. 1960. *Flora: A Biography*. 1966. *Quiet Pilgrimage*. 1970. *The Taken Girl*. 1972

BIBLIOGRAPHY: *Something about the Author*, vol. 6, 1974; *Junior Book of Authors and Illustrators*. 1934 and 1951

SANDRA IMDIEKE

GREEN, Roger Lancelyn

Author, compiler, b. 2 November 1918, Norwich, England; d. 8 October 1987, London, England

G. spent most of his early years growing up at Poulton Hall, the estate in Cheshire that had been in his family since at least 1093. This dark, old rambling home influenced many of G.'s early tales of ADVENTURE. He was often ill as a child and while kept at home was able to read a great deal. Among G.'s favorites were Rudyard KIPLING, Lewis CARROLL, Andrew LANG, and J. M. BARRIE. G. would later write biographies of these authors that had influenced him so greatly. He went to Oxford where he earned a B.A. degree in 1940 and four years later his Master's Degree. He worked for a time as a librarian, an actor, an antiquarian bookseller, and an educator. In 1950, G. returned to Poulton-Lancelyn while he held a two-year fellowship. G. wrote more than fifty books for children and adults. For adults, G. wrote mostly biographies and literary histories. In his original writing for children G. ranged from FANTASY like *The Land of the Lord High Tiger* (1958) to adventure like *The Theft of the Golden Cat* (1955). G. had a lifelong fascination with Ancient Greece and used it and Greek MYTHOLOGY as the inspiration for many works such as *The Luck of Troy* (1961). It is however, G.'s work as a compiler and reteller of tales for which he is best known. His collections were wide-ranging, including *Folk Tales of the World* (1966), *Stories of Ancient Greece* (1968), *A Cavalcade of Dragons* (1971), and *A Cavalcade of Magicians* (1973). G.'s enthusiasm for the tales he shared and his respect and admiration for the authors about whom he wrote illustrate how a good story can touch a life and how a good story is best when shared.

FURTHER WORKS: *The Story of King Arthur and His Knights of the Round Table*. 1953. *Old Greek FAIRY TALES*. 1958. *Jason and the Golden Fleece*. 1968

BIBLIOGRAPHY: Silvey, A., ed. *Children's Books and Their Creators*. 1995. *Something about the Author*. vol. 2, 1971 and vol. 53, 1988. *Third Book of Junior Authors and Illustrators*. 1972

DEDE SMALL

GREENAWAY, Kate

Illustrator, author, b. 17 March 1846, Hoxton, London, England; d. 6 November 1901, Hampstead, England

G., daughter of a woodblock engraver, grew up in both the country and the environs of London during the Victorian Age. A contemporary of Randolph CALDECOTT, G. was identified as a gifted artist at a very young age and sent for formal art instruction at age twelve. Having completed the National Course in Art Instruction, G. won the bronze medal of the National Medallion Award in 1864, and in 1868, at age twenty-two, G. first exhibited her work publicly at the Dudley Gallery, Egyptian Hall, London.

G.'s exhibited line drawings were purchased by *People's* magazine in 1868. Christmas and Valentine cards and calendars served as further sources for income, and some of her first illustrations expressly for children were published in children's magazines such as *Little Folks* in Great Britain and *St. Nicholas* in the United States. G. also illustrated many books for children anonymously such as *Diamonds and Toads* (1868) and *Bluebeard* (translated by Madame Comtesse d'Aulnoy). G. ended her anonymity in 1874 when her name appeared in *Fairy Gifts; or, A Wallet of Wonders* by Kathleen Knox.

Edmund Evans, a colleague of G.'s father, met with her in 1877 to evaluate her work. Unable to convince her to sell her illustrations without the verse she had written to accompany them, Evans arranged for the publication of *Under the Window* in 1878, to great success. *Kate Greenaway's Birthday Book for Children* (1880) with verse by Mrs. Sale Barker maintained G.'s popularity. MOTHER GOOSE soon followed in 1881, *Little Ann and Other Poems* (verse by Jane and Ann Taylor) in 1883, and *Marigold Garden* in 1885. G. quickly became associated with writing light verse accompanied with line drawings or color block illustrations of children at play, just being children. Her attention to children and their activities gave focus to her writing and her art.

G.'s sense of design for young Victorian children extended beyond their portrayal in books, however. She also designed clothes and costumes for children and wallpaper for nurseries. Her designs were so well liked but they were stolen for portrayal on china, fabrics, and stationery. Her books, still popular, are reprinted frequently and available to today's readers. In 1956, recognizing G.'s importance to the field of children's book ILLUSTRATION, the British Library Association designated the KATE GREENAWAY MEDAL. The Kate Greenaway Medal is awarded yearly to the most distinguished work in children's illustration published in the United Kingdom.

FURTHER WORKS: Illustrator: *A Day in a Child's Life.* (Music by Myles Foster). 1881. *The Pied Piper of Hamelin.* (Robert Browning). 1888. Author and Illustrator: *A Apple Pie.* 1886. *Kate Greenaway's Book of Games.* 1889. *Kate Greenaway's Almanacks.* 1883–95

BIBLIOGRAPHY: Holme, Bryan. *The Kate G. Book.* 1976. Spielmann, M. H. and G. S. Layard. *Kate G.* 1905. Taylor, Ina. *The Art of Kate G.: A Nostalgic Portrait of Childhood.* 1991

GWYNNE ELLEN ASH

GREENE, Bette
Author, b. 28 June 1934, Memphis, Tennessee

Like the alienated protagonist of her first and best-known novel, *Summer of My German Soldier* (1973), G. was reared Jewish in Bible Belt Arkansas during World War II, a white child in the AFRICAN AMERICAN community of the maid who largely reared her. In *Summer of My German Soldier* and later REALISTIC FICTION for middle graders and YOUNG ADULTS, the intensity of G.'s first-person stories plumbs issues ranging from alienation and discrimination to homophobia and violence. G. uses the voice of eleven-year-old Beth Lambert to discuss the hard decision of whether or not to let friendship influence choices she needs to make in *Philip Hall Likes Me, I Reckon Maybe* (1974).

AWARDS: Golden Kite Award, AMERICAN LIBRARY ASSOCIATION Notable Book, *New York Times* Notable Book, National Book Award finalist (1974) for *Summer of My German Soldier.* ALA NEWBERY MEDAL Honor Book, ALA Notable Book, *New York Times* Notable Book (1975) for *Philip Hall Likes Me, I Reckon Maybe.* Parents' Choice Award (1974) for *Them That Glitter and Them That Don't*

FURTHER WORKS: *Get on out of Here, Philip Hall.* 1981. *Summer of My German Soldier.* 1973. *Morning Is a Long Time Coming.* 1978. *Them That Glitters and Them That Don't.* 1983. *The Drowning of Stephan Jones.* 1991

BIBLIOGRAPHY: Silvey, Anita ed., *Children's Books and Their Creators,* 1995; *Something about the Author,* vol. 102, 1999

DIANE L. CHAPMAN

GREENE, Constance

Author, b. 27 October 1924, New York City

G. had a happy childhood growing up in Larchmont, New York. G.'s mother, father, and grandfather were all newspaper people and G. knew that she wanted a writing career from an early age. When she was fifteen, her father became the managing editor of the *Daily News* and the family moved into New York City. After high school, G. attended Skidmore College for two years. However, in 1944 G. left college determined to find work in the newspaper industry. After great difficulty G. was finally able to find work in the Associated Press mailroom. G. made rapid progress at the Associated Press and by 1945 was moved up to the City Desk. It was an exciting job, but G. left a year later to marry. Finding it difficult to write longer pieces in a busy household, G. wrote mostly short stories. Joining a short story writing group at the Darien Community Association, G. was encouraged to try the juvenile market. G.'s first book, *A Girl Called Al* (1968), was named an AMERICAN LIBRARY ASSOCIATION Notable Book. The title character, Al, is an intelligent and independent girl in her early teens and has appeared in a number of G.'s subsequent novels: *I Know You, Al* (1975); *Al(exandra) The Great* (1982); *Just Plain Al* (1986); and *Al's Blind Date* (1989). It is, however, a more serious work of fiction for which G. is best known. *Beat the Turtle Drum* (1976) was taken from G.'s own life and is the story of her older sister's death at the age of thirteen. G. wrote it in part to help her remember and piece together an event that happened when she was only eleven. *Beat the Turtle Drum* was named an American Library Association Notable Book and was adapted as "Very Good Friends" for an *ABC Afterschool Special.*

FURTHER WORKS: *Leo the Lioness.* 1970. *Unmaking of Rabbit.* 1972. *Getting Nowhere.* 1977. *Double Dare O'Toole.* 1981. *The Love Letters of J. Timothy Owen.* 1986. *Monday I Love You.* 1988. *Odds on Oliver.* 1992

BIBLIOGRAPHY: *Something about the Author,* vol. 11, 1977 and vol. 72, 1993, *Fourth Book of Junior Authors and Illustrators,* 1978

DEDE SMALL

GREENFIELD, Eloise

Author, poet, b. 17 May 1929, Parmele, North Carolina

G. has lived in Washington, D.C., since she was an infant. Her dad was a truck driver and her mother a clerk-typist and writer. When she was nine years old, her family moved to one of the first public housing projects. This move caused her family to live in a home without extended family members for the first time. G. loved the feeling of community in the neighborhood. Residents organized a council to confront problems. They participated in activities with choral groups, sports, and reading clubs. The library was nearby. The environment felt safe to G. and her community. A sense of belonging helped her family deal with the issues of racism that they knew existed in the outside world. Visits to her grandparents in the South frightened her and made a lasting impact. These early impressions and experiences provided her with the emotions and substance for later writings.

After attending Miner Teachers' College (now the University of the District of Columbia) for two years, G. became a clerk-typist. The boredom in this job provided the motivation to begin writing in the early 1960s. Her first published work was "To a Violin," an adult poem, which appeared in the *Hartford Times* in 1962. G. began to write for children only after she could not find works for her own children in which they could see themselves reflected. Her first children's book was *Bubbles,* a picture book, written in 1966, published in 1972, and reissued under the title of *Good News* in 1977. G. joined the staff of the District of Columbia Black Writers' Workshop. This organization was led by playwright Annie Crittenden for the purpose of bringing writers of all genres together to share and collaborate. Here G. met Sharon Bell MATHIS who encouraged her to write the much acclaimed *Rosa Parks* (1973). G. also credits her association with Mathis with confirming her opinion of the need to write to eradicate the dearth of quality black literature that then existed. G.'s publications include collections of poems, single poem PICTURE BOOKS, poetry board books, read-aloud books, picture books, biographies, and novels. *Honey, I Love*

40. WANDA GAG

41. JEAN CRAIGHEAD GEORGE

42. GAIL GIBBONS

43. JAMES CROSS GIBLIN

44. PATRICIA REILLY GIFF

45. NIKKI GIOVANNI

46. PAUL GOBLE

47. ELOISE GREENFIELD

and Other Poems (1978) was G.'s first collections of poems. She first wrote the title poem as a picture book but the publisher wanted her to write more poems to publish as a collection instead. Ironically, unaware of the poems' original beginnings, a publisher asked her to write *Honey I Love* as a picture book; therefore, it eventually became a Let's Read Aloud book (1995). An example of a single poem picture book is *Africa Dream* (1977). Illustrated by Jan Spivey GIL-CHRIST, poetry board books such as *Daddy and I* (1991) are written for very young children. G.'s mother, Lessie Jones Little, joined her in writing the picture book *I Can Do It by Myself* (1978). In addition to the award-winning *Rosa Parks* (1973) and *Paul Robeson* (1975), G. wrote *Mary McLeod Bethune* (1977). The author considers *Childtimes: A Three Generation Memoir* (1979), illustrated by Jerry PINKNEY, autobiographical. G.'s first novel for young people, *Sister* (1974), is an examination of life with its myriad emotions.

G. states that children are for loving and writing is her work. She has several "wants" for children evident in her writing: an appreciation for music, art, POETRY, and even mischief to develop creativity; encouragement for children to build self-confidence, self-respect, and self-love; exposure to avenues for coping with negativisms so that they might become problem solvers; appreciation for elders' wisdom; presentation of accurate black heritage so they can inform themselves for the future; development of love for black heroes and heroines through her stories; reinforcement of positive aspects of their lives; and sharing with young readers the feeling she has for words. G.'s works are full of emotion, strong rhythms with varying patterns, emittance of children's voices, and support for the journey through life. Love and support of family members for each other is evident in many of her books of poetry; between mother and child in *Night on Neighborhood Street* (1991) and within the family in *Honey, I Love and Other Poems* (1978).

AWARDS: NATIONAL COUNCIL OF TEACHERS OF ENGLISH Award for Excellence in Poetry for Children for entire body of work (1997). CORETTA SCOTT KING AWARD (1980) for *Childtimes: A Three-Generation Memoir* and (1978) for *Africa Dream.* Coretta Scott King Honor Award (1992) for *Night on Neighborhood Street,* (1990) for *Na-*

thaniel Talking, (1978) for *Mary McLeod Bethune,* and (1976) for *Paul Robeson.* Carter G. Woodson Award, National Council for Social Studies (1973) for *Rosa Parks.* Jane Addams Children's Book Award (1975) for *Paul Robeson.* ALA Notable Book for (1978) *Honey, I Love and Other Poems.* Carter G. Woodson Book Award for Outstanding Merit and New York Public Library's books for Teen Age (1979) for *Childtimes,* all for body of work: Citation from the District of Columbia Association of School Librarians (1977), National Black Child Development Institute Award (1981), and Mills College Award (1983)

FURTHER WORKS: *Me and Nessie.* 1975. *First Pink Light.* 1976. *Talk about Family.* 1978. *Daydreamers.* 1981. *Alesia.* 1981. *Night on Neighborhood Street.* 1991. *Aaron and Gayla's Counting Book.* 1992. *William and the Good Old Days.* 1993. *My Doll Keshia.* 1994. *For the Love of the Game: Michael Jordan and Me.* 1997. *Angels in the Trees.* 1998. Contributor to anthologies: *The Journey: Scholastic Black Literature.* 1970. *Love.* 1975. *Friends Are Like That.* 1979. *Listen, Children.* 1982

BIBLIOGRAPHY: Bishop, Rudine Sims. "Profile: Eloise Greenfield." *Language Arts.* December 1997, vol. 74 no. 8, pp. 630–34. Greenfield, Eloise. "Something to Shout About." *Horn Book* magazine. December 1975, vol. LI, no. 6, p. 624. Kiah, Rosalie Black. "Profile: Eloise Greenfield," *Language Arts.* September 1980, vol. 57 no. 6, pp. 653–59. "Meet the Author," *Ladybug.* June 1994, vol. 4 i. 10. *Major Authors and Illustrators for Children and YOUNG ADULTS: A Selection of Sketches from Something about the Author.* 1993. Silvey, Anita, ed. *Children's Books and Their Creators.* 1995. Ward, Martha E. *Authors of Books for Young People.* 1990

NANCY HORTON

GREENLAW, M. Jean
Author, b. 1 April 1941, St. Petersburg, Florida

Born in Florida, G. grew up in Pennsylvania and later received two degrees from Stetson University and her doctorate at Michigan State University. G.'s prolific career in both children's literature and reading includes receiving the Arbuthnot Award in 1992. She has taught in public schools and at the university level as well as has held many positions in literacy organizations. G. has used her expertise to create books about life in Texas, her adopted state. For *Ranch Dressing: The Story of Western Wear* (1997), G. researched people, museums, and libraries discovering information about the development of Western–style clothing. *Welcome to the Stock Show* (1997) shares, through a photographic essay, the story of children growing livestock to exhibit at State Fairs and stock shows. This "Kuraltian slice of Americana" as described by one reviewer, shares a bit of Texas lifestyle for readers everywhere. G. is presently researching the women in the National Cowgirl Hall of Fame and writing a book about an incident in Maine taken from her family's history.

BIBLIOGRAPHY: *Bulletin of the Center for Children's Books.* January, 1994. *Something about the Author,* vol. 107, 1999. Manning, Patricia, review of *Welcome to the Stock Show* in *School Library Journal.* September, 1997, p. 230

JANELLE B. MATHIS

GREENWALD, Sheila
Author, illustrator, b. 26 May 1934, New York City

G.'s style of illustrating was influenced by her childhood passion of reading COMIC BOOKS AND GRAPHIC NOVELS. She began drawing as a young child for recreational purposes and continued her formal education at the High School of Music and Art and Sarah Lawrence College. G. credits a professor, interested in her sketches in the margins of her papers, for encouraging her to acquaint publishers with her artwork. Thus began her professional career illustrating magazines, children's books, and collections of POETRY and HUMOR. After having children of her own who were searching for more involved and witty stories, G. began to write her own books for children. Although not autobiographical, her sensitive and humorous fiction for middle and young adult readers often focuses on situations that she herself has experienced.

G.'s fiction is marked with humorous situations and characters who accept themselves and the complications frequently found in their lives. Her books dip into contemporary issues and modern concerns that children, especially girls, face such as growing-up female, conforming to society's expectations, becoming involved in the community, anorexia, or divorce. She also encompasses themes that all children can relate to like school experiences, friendship, and relationships with the opposite sex. *Will the Real Gertrude Hollings Please Stand Up* (1983) focuses on learning DISABILITIES. G. has a knack for realistically portraying life's ups and downs for her mostly female protagonists who frequently attack them with spunk, humor, and success, amid a few bumps and bruises along the way.

G.'s ILLUSTRATIONS, usually pen and ink sketches are a worthy complement to her fiction, often portraying details that extend the text, giving the reader a more vivid portrayal of events and characters.

AWARDS: AMERICAN LIBRARY ASSOCIATION Notable Children's Book (1981) for *Give Us a Great Big Smile, Rosy Cole*

FURTHER WORKS: Written and illustrated by G.: *Mat Pit and the Tunnel Tenants.* 1972. *The Secret Museum.* 1974. *The Secret in Miranda's Closet.* 1977. *The Mariah Delany Lending Library Disaster.* 1977. *Blissful Joy and the SATs: A Multiple Choice Romance.* 1982. *Rosy's Romance.* 1989. *My Fabulous New Life.* 1993. *Rosy Cole: She Walks in Beauty.* 1994. *The Rose Grows.* 1996. Illustrated by G: *Pocketful of Poems.* (With Marie Allen). 1957. *Brave Betsy.* (With Miriam Dreifus). 1961. *Jump the Rope Jingles.* (With Emma Worstell). 1967. *Henny Youngman's Book of Jokes.* (With Henny Youngman). 1992

BIBLIOGRAPHY: Silvey, Anita, ed., *Children's Books and Their Creators,* 1995; *Something about the Author,* vol. 87, 1995

GERALYN A. CHESNER

GRIFALCONI, Ann
Author, illustrator, b. 22 September 1929, New York City

G. aspires to create books that help children develop awareness about the world, just as books did for her as she was growing up. As a child, she moved a lot with her brother and mother, a writer. Local libraries stocked with books became her friends and helped to expand her view of the world, along with exposing her to a wide variety of ILLUSTRATION styles, including COMIC BOOKS AND GRAPHIC NOVELS.

At ten, an art teacher encouraged her to practice drawing and painting. Her formal art education began in high school where she enjoyed creative writing and art classes and was educated by a number of nurturing teachers who helped her realize her talent. Upon receiving a scholarship to attend Cooper Union College in New York, G. was exposed to famous writers and artists who were a great inspiration to her. Graduating in 1950 with a certificate in advertising, she began a job that she did not enjoy. She decided to go back to school and earn a Bachelor's Degree in art history with a minor in history at New York University. Her desire to teach led her to the High School of Fashion Industry in New York where she taught fashion art and interior design.

G. began her illustrating career creating woodcuts that became her first book, *City Rhythms* (1965), which depicted a vibrant Harlem setting. In 1966 *The Jazz Man,* written by her mother Mary Hays Weik, and illustrated with woodcuts by G., was published. Realizing that publishing was her passion, she stopped teaching to work full-time writing and illustrating.

Deliberately choosing the medium that best suits the story, be it with the books she writes or those of others G. uses a variety of media, from pencil to watercolors to collage and woodcuts. Bold, dramatic, warm illustrations are her signature, portraying characters with precise detail and personality, inviting the reader to get acquainted intimately. Traveling extensively goes hand in hand with G.'s regard for history and research. Studying her subjects thoroughly, she writes and illustrates stories with characters from a variety of cultures such as *The Toy Trumpet* (1968) set in Mexico. *The Village of Round and Square Houses* (1986), illustrated in pastels, depicts the customs of a village in Cameroon, West AFRICA. G.'s illustrations for Lucille CLIFTON's CORETTA SCOTT KING AWARD–winning book, *Everett Anderson's Goodbye* (1983), are soft black-and-white drawings that deepen and extend the tone of sadness and grief without becoming sentimental or maudlin. G.'s drawings impart a sense of strength and family solidarity in the companion book *Everett Anderson's Friend* (1976).

AWARDS: ALA CALDECOTT MEDAL Honor Book (1987) for *The Village of Round and Square Houses. New York Times* Best Illustrated Children's Books of the Year (1966) for *The Jazz Man* (M. Weik, author)

FURTHER WORKS: *The Matter with Lucy.* 1973. *Darkness and the Butterfly.* 1987. *Osa's Pride.* 1989. *Flyaway Girl.* 1991. *Kinda Blue.* 1993. *The Bravest Flute: A Story of Courage in the Mayan Tradition.* 1994. *Tiny's Hat.* 1999. Illustrated by G.: *The Ballad of the Burglar of Babylon.* (Elizabeth Bishop). 1968. *Don't You Turn Back.* (Langston HUGHES). 1969. *Everett Anderson's Year.* (Lucille Clifton). 1974. *Don't Leave an Elephant and Go and Chase a Bird.* (James BERRY). 1996. *Tio Armando.* (Florence Parry HEIDE and Roxanne Heide Pierce). 1998

BIBLIOGRAPHY: HOPKINS, Lee Bennett, *Books Are by People,* 1969; Hopkins, Lee Bennett, *Pauses: Autobiographical Reflections of 101 Creators of Children's Books,* 1995; *Children's Literary Review,* vol. 35, 1995

GERALYN A. CHESNER

GRIFFITH, Helen V.
Author, b. 31 October 1934, Wilmington, Delaware

Writing POETRY as a child, usually about animals, marked the beginning of G.'s career. In tenth grade, with encouragement from a teacher, she submitted a poem to a magazine, which was published. Many years passed before her first published book for children in 1980, *"Mine Will,"* *Said John.* It was the first of several PICTURE BOOKS featuring G.'s love of animals, especially dogs and cats, and the environment. *Alex and the Cat* (Joseph Low, illus., 1982), a *School Library Journal* Best Book, *Alex Remembers* (1983) and *More Alex and the Cat* (1983), both illustrated by Donald CARRICK, depict loving relationships between pets and their owners. G. is also known for her poignant and respectful Grandaddy stories, illustrated by James STEVENSON. These stories portray the loving relationship between Janetta and her grandfather who lives on a farm. *Georgia Music* (1986) was the first in the beginning chapter book series.

G.'s work is marked by a sense of HUMOR and consideration for both the animal and human world as she gives a glimpse into relationships between young and old, strong and vulnerable. Writing with children in mind she helps them see the gentle side of things and gets into the minds of creatures by assuming realistic dreams and conversations among them, much as children do. Her picture books use little text, yet the careful choice of words give a complete picture of characters and settings.

G. also writes FANTASY stories with FAIRY TALE-like characters for young independent readers such as *Emily and the Enchanted Frog* (1989) and *Doll Trouble* (1993). *Journal of a Teenage Genius* (1987), a fantasy for older readers, is laden with humor.

AWARDS: Selection in 1987 as well as honored as an AMERICAN LIBRARY ASSOCIATION Notable Book. Two others were awarded ALA Notable Books as well, *Grandaddy's Place* (1987), and *Grandaddy and Janetta* (1993)

FURTHER WORKS: *Foxy.* 1984. *Nata.* (Nancy TA-FURI). 1985. *Caitlin's Holiday.* 1990. *Plunk's Dreams.* 1990. *Dream Meadow.* 1994. *Grandaddy's Stars.* (James STEVENSON). 1995

GERALYN A. CHESNER

GRIMES, Nikki
Author, poet, b. 20 October 1950, New York City

Writing books that include themes and events that she wanted to read about as a child, G. focuses emphatically on friendship and the trials of coming of age. Her love of words blossomed early and she wrote POETRY that her father set to music. Moving frequently as a child, G. read to escape the difficulties of starting over, but was disheartened when the faces looking out at her from books were not like her own. This has influenced the content and characters in her books, which often contain AFRICAN AMERICAN characters and urban settings. As a teenager, she made the decision to become a professional writer. After graduating from Rutgers University with a Bachelor of Arts degree in 1974, G. received a grant from the Ford Foundation to do research in Tanzania.

Growin', G.'s first novel (1977) focuses on the difficulties of a young girl growing up experiencing events similar to G.'s own life. *Meet Danitra Brown* (1994), illustrated by Floyd COOPER, is a collection of poems based on the theme of friendship and relationships between two young girls. G. enjoys creating new characters; she begins by choosing their names and then develops their biographies. Having her characters' voices speak for herself, protagonists like Danitra Brown possess characteristics similar to G. as a child, such as skinny legs and getting teased about wearing glasses but also being exuberant and self-assured and proud of being black. G. rhythmically introduces readers to her characters, often using lilting, rhyming poetry that she associates with music.

G.'s books and poetry exude a sense of community and strong settings. *C is for City* (Pat CUMMINGS, illus., 1994) describes the vibrancy and diversity of city life. *Jazmin's Notebook* (1998) combines prose and poetry in a coming-of-age novel presenting a lyrical portrait of a young teenager trying to cope with the death of her father and mental illness of her mother. Jazmin records her thoughts and anxieties in a journal, helping her to sort out her powerful emotions. G. has also written books for young adult readers such as *Malcolm X: A Force for Change* (1992), a biography of the African American leader.

AWARDS: CORETTA SCOTT KING AWARD Honor Book (1999) for *Jazmin's Notebook.* Coretta Scott King ILLUSTRATION Award Winner (1979) for *Something on My Mind* (Tom FEELINGS, illus.). Coretta Scott King Illustration Award Honor Book (1995) for *Meet Danitra Brown* (Floyd Cooper, illus.). ALA Notable Book (1979) for *Something on My Mind* and (1994) for *Meet Danitra Brown*

FURTHER WORKS: *From a Child's Head.* 1993. *Baby's Bedtime.* 1995. *Come Sunday.* 1996. *Wild, Wild Hair.* 1996. *It's Raining Laughter.* 1997. *Danitra Brown Leaves Town.* (Floyd Cooper, illus.). 1998. *My Man Blue.* 1999. *At Break of Day.* 2000

BIBLIOGRAPHY: Smith, Henrietta M. *The Coretta Scott King Awards Book, 1970–99.* 1999

GERALYN A. CHESNER

GRIMM, Jacob
Folklorist, philologist, b. 4 January 1785, Hanau, Hesse-Kassel, Germany; d. 20 September 1863, Berlin, Germany

GRIMM, Wilhelm
Folklorist, philologist, b. 24 February 1786, Hanau, Hesse-Kassel; d. 16 December 1859, Berlin, Germany

The brothers, J. and W. G., achieved lasting fame as pioneer collectors of German FOLKLORE and groundbreaking philologists. Two of six children of a lawyer, J.G. and W.G. were inseparable from their childhood. Their father's premature death left the family financially strained, and economic exigencies plagued them for many years. Both brothers studied law at Marburg University, but only W.G. passed his final examinations. J.G. became a protegé of the great jurist Friedrich Savigny, who aroused in both brothers a passion for cultural history. During the French occupation of Hesse-Kassel, J.G. was made librarian for Napoleon's brother, King Jerome of Westphalia. It was a well-paying sinecure that left him free to pursue his collection of folktales. The result was the two-volume, *Kinder-und Hausmarchen,* published in concert with W.G., 1812–15. The first volumes were illustrated by a younger brother, Ludwig Emil Grimm. "Little Red Cap," a version of "Little Red Riding-Hood." "Little Briar-Rose," a variant of "Sleeping Beauty," and "Hansel and Gretel" are among the stories in the first edition. The collection was an immediate success, and it soon became the second most widely read work in the world, superseded only by the Bible. The work was revised and continually enlarged seven times. The final edition appeared in 1857, containing some 200 tales. The second volume and the revisions were largely the work of W.G., J.G. having become absorbed in his philological studies and political pursuits (he had an official post at the Congress of Vienna in 1815 and in 1848 he was elected to the Frankfurt Parliament, which was charged with establishing a united constitutional government for Germany).

Between 1819 and 1837 J.G. published a comprehensive work on German law and the four volumes of his seminal history of German grammar, *Deutsche Grammatik.* As part of this latter achievement, J.G. formulated a theory that identified the corresponding consonant shifts in cognate words between related Indo-European languages. The theory, known as Grimm's Law, remains a tenet in the study of linguistic development to this day. From 1830–37 both J. and W. were professors at Gottingen University, but were dismissed along with five others for political reasons, having loudly protested the unilateral abrogation of the constitution by the new Elector of Hanover. Finally in 1840, J.G. and W.G. were invited to Berlin as members of the prestigious Academy of Sciences, the preferment the brothers had longed for, since it meant the end of their financial worries and the ability to concentrate on scholarly pursuits. J.G. and W.G. began to work in earnest on the monumental German dictionary, *Deutsches Worterbuch,* an ambitious work that sought to trace the complete history of the German language. The final volume was not published until 1961.

J.G. was more vigorous than W.G., whose chronic ill health (he suffered from asthma) restrained his activities. J. was a political activist who promoted German unity. His interest in German folklore was timely, for it meshed well with the emerging German nationalism as well as with the Romantic movement's interest in folk life and traditions. Their international fame will be forever linked to their folktale collections, which were soon translated into several languages. The first English TRANSLATION was Edgar Taylor's, 1823–26. The G.s themselves subscribed to the theory that the folktales were versions of Indo-European prototypes. Their work inspired others to search out their own native folklore, most notably the Norwegians, ASBJORNSEN and MOE. The first tales were thoroughly annotated, although the notes were eventually relegated to a separate volume. To the criticism that some of the tales seemed unsuitable for children, J.G. wrote, "The book of fairy is . . . not written for children at all, but is just what they like, and that pleases me." By his own admission J.G. left the later volumes up to W.G. Ostensibly tales gathered from the common folk of the German countryside, it is now known that many of the tales came from educated, middle-class Germans, most of whom were friends and relatives of the G.s. The retellings are not as artless as the G.s would like to have readers believe; they reflect the beliefs and mores of the retellers, not necessarily of the German peasant class. All this aside, the influence of the G.s was enormous and their efforts put folktales into the hands of countless children the world over and engendered the serious study of folklore.

J.G. never married and his domestic affairs were largely managed by his brother W.G. and his wife. The most congenial of collaborators, J.G. and W.G. were virtually inseparable throughout their lives, living in the same household and working in the same room. Yet they enjoyed distinctive personalities, J.G. being more solitary, exacting, and scientific; W.G. being more gregarious, sensitive, and poetic. J.G. became absorbed by grammar and lexicography, and W.G. continued to collect folktales throughout his life and gave literary form to the old stories. By the ends of their lives, they were widely celebrated throughout Europe, and they were buried, as they wished, side by side in Berlin.

AWARDS: Jacob—Orden pour le merite (1842)

BIBLIOGRAPHY: Cott, Jonathan, *Pipers at the Gates of Dawn: The Wisdom of Children's Literature,* 1981; Knoepflmacher, V. C., *Ventures into Childland,* 1998

DAVID L. RUSSELL

GRIPE, Maria
Author, b. 25 July 1923, Vaxholm, Sweden

G. is a Swedish author of fiction, FANTASY, and scripts. Listening continuously to the works of Hans Christian ANDERSEN as a child, G. was inspired to write stories that realistically and sensitively portray the joys and sorrows of childhood. Many of them evolved from requests for stories made by G.'s daughter and illustrated by G.'s artist husband. A trilogy of novels, *Hugo and Josephine* (1969), *Josephine* (1970), and *Hugo* (1970), are typical of the universal motifs that characterize her writing with melancholy, fantasy, and psychological inquiry. In these and other novels, her realistic and perceptive renderings of the anxieties and fantasies of childhood are a result of explicit memories of her own youth. G. has received numerous awards including the Lewis CARROLL Shelf Award for *Pappa Pellerin's Daughter* (1966), the Astrid LINDGRIN Prize in 1972, and the Hans Christian ANDERSEN International Children's Book Award in 1974.

FURTHER WORKS (TRANSLATED): *In the Time of the Bells.* 1976: *Elvis and His Secret.* 1976: *Agnes Cecilia.* 1990

BIBLIOGRAPHY: *Children's Literature Review.* 1983. Gripe, Maria. "A Word and a Shadow." *Bookbird.* March 15, 1974, pp. 4–10. *Something about the Author.* vol. 74, 1993

JANELLE B. MATHIS

GUNNING, Monica
Author, b. 5 January 1930, Jamaica, West Indies

G. emigrated from Jamaica to the United States at the age of seventeen. She received a B.A. from City University of New York, in 1957; continued with graduate study at the University of Guadalajara in 1971; and earned a M.S.Ed. from Mount St. Mary's College, Los Angeles, California, in 1971. She taught bilingual elementary school and English as a second language for over fifteen years in the Los Angeles School System. G.'s love for children's literature and a desire to write for children have manifested themselves in the creation of her children's books. G. studied with Myra Cohn LIVINGSTON in a master class for poets at UCLA.

Perico Bonito/Pretty Parrot (1976) and *The Two Georges/Los Dos Jorges* (1976) are bilingual books for children. *Not a Copper Penny in Me House: Poems from the Caribbean* (1993), illustrated by Frané LESSAC and *Under the Breadfruit Tree: Island Poems* (1998) illustrated by Fabrico Vanden Broeck, are collections of original poems reflective of G.'s childhood home in Jamaica. *Not a Copper Penny,* selected as a NATIONAL COUNCIL OF TEACHERS OF ENGLISH Notable Book, takes readers through a year in the life of a village child, from one Christmas to the next, with stops in between to swim in the sea, gaze at a hurricane, and observe adult behaviors. *Under the Breadfruit Tree* celebrates the resourcefulness, generosity, faults, foibles, and love a young girl perceives in people around her.

BIBLIOGRAPHY: *Contemporary Authors Online,* 1999

ELIZABETH A. POE

(See also CARIBBEAN LITERATURE)

GUY, Rosa
Author, b. 1 September 1925 [some sources give 1928], Diego Martin, Trinidad

Critically acclaimed for her novels about young black urban adolescents, G.'s work is informed by her experiences as an immigrant, orphan, and politically aware AFRICAN AMERICAN woman. She arrived in Harlem at the age of seven and quit school to earn a living at the age of fourteen. After marriage and motherhood, she continued her education as well as her factory work. In 1951, G. cofounded the Harlem Writer's Guild, publishing her first novel in 1966.

The Friends (1973), G.'s first novel for younger readers, about two West Indian families living in Harlem was hailed by Alice Walker as important for its depiction of growth through upheaval. *Ruby* (1976) and *Edith Jackson* (1978) complete the trilogy begun in *The Friends. The*

Disappearance (1979), *New Guys around the Block, And I Heard a Bird Sing* (1986) form a second Harlem trilogy, each involving a mystery. G.'s fiction enjoys international popularity. *Mother Crocodile: An Uncle Amadou Tale from Senegal* (John STEPTOE, illus., 1981), was translated and adapted by G. from a Senegalese folktale. G. tells a universal cautionary tale about averting a near tragedy when Mother Crocodile's children do not listen to her words of warning. Her political view of contemporary issues combines with her ability to create vital characters. She also writes fiction for adults.

AWARDS: AMERICAN LIBRARY ASSOCIATION Notable Book and CORETTA SCOTT KING ILLUSTRATOR Award winner (1982) for *Mother Crocodile* (John Steptoe, illus., 1981). Parents' Choice Award (1983) for *New Guys around the Block.* ALA Best Book for YOUNG ADULTS (1974) for *The Friends*

FURTHER WORKS: *Paris, Pee Wee, and Big Dog.* 1985. *The Ups and Downs of Carl Davis III.* 1989. *The Music of Summer.* 1992

BIBLIOGRAPHY: *American Women Writers.* vol. 5, Supplement, 1994. Norris, J. *Presenting Rosa Guy.* 1988. Silvey, Anita, ed. *Children's Books and Their Creators.* 1995. Smith, Henrietta. *The Coretta Scott King Awards Book, 1970–1999.* 1999. *Something about the Author.* vol. 62, 1990

FRANCISCA GOLDSMITH

HAAS, Irene
Author, illustrator, b. 5 June 1929, New York City

H. grew up in suburban New York where she had plenty of time to think and be lazy: to dream and to be alone. She spent much of her youth engaged in imaginative play, where she was often left to her own devices without adults directing her. She attributes much of the creative freedom of her childhood as providing the inspiration and experience that eventually led her to theater design, graphic arts, wallpaper design, and china design. After H.'s work was shown to an editor, she began her career creating books for children. H. has worked primarily doing ILLUSTRATIONS for children's books and found that when she decided to try writing one of her own that the writing required a different kind of involvement and concentration from that required in illustrating books. H. finds it more difficult to write than to illustrate books although she does both. Despite this, several books she has written or illustrated, including *Tatsinda,* written by Elizabeth ENRIGHT (1961) and *Emily's Voyage* (1967) have appeared on the *Horn Book*'s annual honor list. H.'s works have been exhibited by the American Institute of Graphic Art.

H. deems it important to provide children with a lifestyle that helps them discover their own special gifts as humans. She has never forgotten how important that gift was for her during her own childhood.

AWARDS: *New York Times* Best Illustrated Children's Books of the Year (1955) for *A Little House of Your Own* and (1956) for *Was It a Good Trade?*

FURTHER WORKS: *The Mysterious Leaf.* Richard Owen. 1954. *A Little House of Your Own.* Beatrice Schenk DE REGNIERS. 1956. *The Summertime Song.* 1997

BIBLIOGRAPHY: *Something about the Author.* vol. 17, 1979

MICHAEL O'LAUGHLIN

HADER, Berta
Author, illustrator, b. ca. 1891, San Pedro Coahuila, Mexico; d. 6 February 1976

HADER, Elmer (Stanley)
Author, illustrator, b. 9 September 1889, Pajaro, California; d. 7 September 1973, Willow Hill, Nyack, New York

E.H. and B.H. were both artists in their own right when they married in 1919. However, the marriage began their collaboration as writers and illustrators of children's books. B.H., born in Mexico, moved later to the United States and eventually to New York City. In New York B.H. began taking art classes with the encouragement of her mother. By the time she was eighteen, she was painting portraits, attending the Washington School of Journalism, and learning fashion design and ILLUSTRATION. In 1915, B.H. moved to San Francisco where she became the roommate of Rose Wilder Lane, helping her to publish her first Little House SERIES BOOKS. B.H.'s move to San Francisco also resulted in her attendance at the San Francisco School of Design where she

340

met E.H. The H.s were married on July 4, 1919, in New York City.

E.H. was a California native whose jobs included being a silversmith's assistant, and locomotive fireman before he became an artist. E.H. studied painting in Paris, working his way through school as a vaudevillian. E.H. later served in France during World War I. After the war E.H. returned to the United States where he and B.H. began their careers as writers and illustrators of children's books.

In the beginning of their marriage and careers, the H.'s illustrated children's sections of MAGAZINES, including *McCalls* and *Good Housekeeping.* Eventually they did a series of drawings that led to "The Happy Hours" picture-book collection. The H.s' art work was soon appearing in several books by various authors. By 1928 the H.s began writing and illustrating their own stories.

B.H. and E.H. chronicled the building of their home in Nyack, New York, in their 1944 book, *The Little Stone Bridge.* B.H. once commented that the story tended to tell the bright side of building one's own home and that in reality "there were many backaches." *The Big Snow* (1948), an account of animal SURVIVAL during one very fierce winter, features the author/illustrators as the human characters in the story.

The H.s were not only writers and illustrators but also conservationists and pacifists before it was fashionable. Their interest in nature and the environment is evident in many of their books including: *Lions and Tigers and Elephants Too* (1930), *Under the Pig-Nut Tree* (1930), *The Cat and the Kitten* (1940), and *The Runaways: A Tale of the Woodlands* (1956). Until their deaths in the 1970s both H.s worked for peace and the preservation of their beloved New York home.

AWARDS: ALA CALDECOTT MEDAL (1949) for *The Big Snow.* ALA Caldecott Medal Honor Book (1944) for *The Mighty Hunter* and (1940) for *Cock-a-Doodle-Doo*

FURTHER WORKS: *Chicken Little and Little Half Chick.* 1944. *The Little Red Hen.* 1994. *Humpty Dumpty and Other MOTHER GOOSE Rhymes.* 1994. *The Story of the Ugly Duckling.* 1994

BIBLIOGRAPHY: HOPKINS, Lee Bennett, *Pauses: Autobiographical Reflections of 101 Creators of Children's Books,* 1995; Silvey, Anita, ed. *Chil-*
dren's Books and Their Creators. 1995; *Something about the Author,* vol. 16, 1979

MICHAEL O'LAUGHLIN

HAFNER, Marilyn
Illustrator, b. 14 December 1925, Brooklyn, New York

H., illustrator of books for children and adolescents, has illustrated over forty books throughout her career. She creates illustrations that complement the author's text. In 1989, H. won the National Jewish Book Award for ILLUSTRATION for *Just Enough Is Plenty,* written by Barbara Goldin. Ritual celebrations, reflected in many of her books, play an important role in her family life. H. has moved from illustrating others' books to writing PICTURE BOOKS. H. uses humorous, watercolor line drawings to illustrate the mechanics of how clothes are put together in *Getting Dressed* (Vicki COBB, 1989). Her drawings of buttons, zippers, Velcro, and other materials clearly illustrate the function of each item. With cartoonlike watercolor illustrations H. tells the humorously exaggerated story of a child trying to help when her mother is sick but meeting with disaster in *Mommies Don't Get Sick!* (1995).

FURTHER WORKS: *Bonnie Bess: The Weathervane Horse.* 1949. *It's Christmas.* 1981. *Happy Mother's Day.* 1985. *Hanukkah.* 1990. *Show and Tell Bunnies.* 1998

BIBLIOGRAPHY: Cianciolo, P. *Picture Books for Children,* 4th ed. 1997. *Something about the Author.* vol. 7, 1975

JODI PILGRIM

HAGUE, Michael
Illustrator, b. 8 September 1948, Los Angeles, California

H. is best known as an illustrator of children's books. His carefully rendered and detailed depictions of characters in such classics as *The Wind in the Willows* (Kenneth GRAHAME, 1980 ed.), *The Lion, The Witch, and the Wardrobe* (C. S. LEWIS), *The Velveteen Rabbit* (Margery WILLIAMS, 1983 ed.), and *Peter Pan* (J. M. BARRIE) have received widespread critical acclaim. H. has also illustrated many FAIRY TALES and fables, including *Aesop's Fables* (1985) and *The Frog Princess* (1984). The artist has collaborated with his wife, Kathleen, to create several self-illustrated books, retelling such tales as *East of the Sun and West of the Moon* (1980) and *The Man Who Kept House* (1981). Among H.'s award-winning works is his self-illustrated book, *The Unicorn and the Lake* (1982), which received The Colorado Children's Book Award from the University of Colorado, as well as the Georgia Children's Picture Storybook Award from the University of Georgia. His book, *A Child's Book of Prayers* (1985) received the Graphic Arts Award for best juvenile book, Printing Industries Association.

FURTHER WORKS: *Dream Weaver.* 1979. *A Child's Book of Prayers.* 1995. *Michael Hague's Favorite Hans Christian ANDERSEN Fairy Tales.* 1981

BIBLIOGRAPHY: *Something about the Author.* vol. 80, 1995. A Profile of Michael Hague: http://208.240.91.202/Bios/HaugeBio.html. Accessed February 2, 1999

MARY ARIAIL BROUGHTON

HAHN, Mary Downing
Author, b. 9 December 1937, Washington, D.C.

Ironically, as a child H. disliked writing, yet was known as the class artist. Instead of using the written word, she told stories in pictures and illustrated her book reports and term papers with relish. After graduating from the University of Maryland at College Park in 1960 with a degree in fine arts and English, she taught art in a junior high school for one year. Reading to her daughters spurred her to cultivate her talent for writing. After a few rejected attempts at writing books, H. began doctoral work in English literature. Due to a disagreement regarding an appropriate dissertation topic, H. left graduate school and began working as a freelance artist for a children's reading program, "Cover to Cover." Her penchant for STORYTELLING ultimately led her to a job as a children's librarian in Maryland where telling stories with puppetry was part of her job description. Reading children's books on the job was the inspiration that brought her to write her first book, *The Sara Summer,* written and published in 1979. Ideas for this book, like much of her work, are drawn from her memories of being a young teenager and the enchantment and hardships involved.

When beginning a new book, H. usually starts with a character or a situation and lets the story build itself from there, spending a lot of time thinking and revising. According to H., writing is a journey of discovery, very much like the journey of the characters in her books. Her work skillfully includes realistic characters, contemporary themes, and often elements of mystery and suspense. Deliberately mirroring real life, H.'s books often end with not-so-happy endings, yet leave a glimmer of hope for the characters.

H.'s books have received numerous children's choice AWARDS and state honors. H. received an ALA Reviewer's Choice award for *Daphne's Book* (1983) as well as a NATIONAL COUNCIL OF TEACHERS OF ENGLISH Teacher's Choice (1984). *December Stillness,* which focuses on war and its effects, was a 1989 Jane Addams Peace Association Honor book.

AWARDS: ALA Book for the Reluctant Reader (1990) for *The Dead Man in Indian Creek.* Scott O'DELL Award for Historical Fiction (1992) for *Stepping on the Cracks*

FURTHER WORKS: *The Time of the Witch.* 1982. *Tallahassee Higgins.* 1987. *The Doll in the Garden.* 1989. *The Wind Blows Backward.* 1993. *Time for Andrew.* 1994. *Look for Me by Moonlight.* 1995. *The Gentleman Outlaw and Me, Eli.* 1996. *As Ever, Gordy.* 1998. Short Stories: "Give a Puppet a Hand," in *Bruce COVILLE's Book of Nightmares.* 1995. "Trouble Afoot," in *Bruce Coville's Book of Monsters.* 1996

GERALYN A. CHESNER

HALE, Lucretia Peabody
Author, educator, b. 2 September 1820, Boston, Massachusetts; d. 12 June 1900, Boston, Massachusetts

H. exemplified many of the creative traits of her literary and patriotic family. Daughter of a publisher, sister to several other writers and publishers, including short story writer Edward Everett Hale, H. began writing reviews and editorials, as well as providing translations, while still a schoolgirl. For the era, she received an excellent education, becoming close lifelong friends with several of her schoolmates. H.'s humorous stories about the Peterkin family developed during her years of entertaining first her friends and then their children, by whom she was recognized as an honorary aunt.

H. published stories in *The Atlantic Monthly* and *Our Young Folk* (which later became *St. Nicholas*). *The Peterkin Papers* (1880), brought together several Peterkin family stories in book form that had first appeared in these MAGAZINES. These nonsense stories about a bumblingly incompetent family, and their wise friend, the Lady from Philadelphia, are recognized as the first nonsense stories written and published for American children. The humorous book enjoyed national success and the fun provided by the characters' foolishness has kept it popular for more than a century. In 1989 a PICTURE BOOK version of a single Peterkin story, *The Lady Who Put Salt in Her Coffee* was adapted and illustrated by Amy SCHWARTZ.

In addition to writing, STORYTELLING and traveling, H. also was the first woman to serve on the Boston School Committee and was an early promoter of kindergarten education. She ran a dame school and wrote religious novels and domestic arts books for adults.

FURTHER WORKS: *The Last of the Peterkins with Others of Their Kin,* 1886

BIBLIOGRAPHY: *American Women Writers,* 1980; *Something about the Author,* vol. 26, 1982

FRANCISCA GOLDSMITH

HALE, Sara Josepha

Poet, b. 24 October 1788, Newport, New Hampshire; d. 30 April 1879

After becoming a widow with five children to support, H. had an illustrious career as the editor of *Godey's Lady's Book,* a prominent fashion and literary magazine and at *Boston Ladies' Magazine* where she was in charge of the children's section of the magazine. H. is best remembered for her popular children's rhyme "Mary Had a Little Lamb." As an editor, she was the first to print works by Frances Hodgson BURNETT. H. frequently wrote essays supporting women's causes, including the right of women to higher education, as well as novels and short stories. She was also instrumental in establishing Thanksgiving as a national holiday. Always a popular verse, controversy exists because many people have claimed to be the author of "Mary"; experts now

agree H. is indeed the author. The verse first appeared in an 1830 periodical and in H.'s *Poems for our Children* that same year. A 1984 edition with period ILLUSTRATIONS by Tomie DEPAOLA includes the score and details about H. and the authorship controversy. Another version of "Mary Had a Little Lamb" with winning photographs of a contemporary, AFRICAN AMERICAN Mary was created by Bruce MCMILLAN (1990).

BIBLIOGRAPHY: *The Oxford Companion to Children's Literature,* 1984; *Grolier International Encyclopedia,* 1993

REBECCA RAPPORT

HALEY, Gail E.

Author, illustrator, b. 4 November 1939, Charlotte, North Carolina

Nurtured and influenced by her family and experiences during childhood, H. engaged in the creative processes of writing, drawing, and puppetry. Living in rural North Carolina, H. explored the farms and woods and entertained her siblings as their storyteller, doll and puppet creator. Frequent visits to her father's place of employment, the *Charlotte Observer,* helped H. realize she wanted to communicate through the written word. After attending art school for two years studying graphics and painting, she took a job as a technical illustrator. Displeased with this employment she returned to college at the University of Virginia where, with encouragement from a professor, she began writing and illustrating children's books. Having difficulty getting published, she wrote *My Kingdom for a Dragon* (1962), an allegory of her desire to be published, and with the assistance of a local publisher, produced the book herself.

H. is also well known as a folklorist. After her year-long residence in the Caribbean she wrote and illustrated *A Story, A Story: An AFRICAN Tale* (1970). From this Ananse trickster tale she is credited as being the first children's author to introduce a black God. Believing the purpose of a picture book or folktale is to invite participation among author, reader, and child, H.'s books are enjoyable read-alouds that invite sharing.

Concerned with helping children grapple with important issues such as caring for the environment and avoiding the pressure coercion of mass media, H.'s work offers children an optimistic view of the world. Her vibrant ILLUSTRATION style is varied. Using woodcuts, watercolor, and pen and ink, H. captures the culture and authentic setting of her stories. Pattern and texture are evident to readers as washes of color over thickly formed lines depict objects and detail creating an opulent feast for the eyes such as in *The Post Office Cat* (1973).

AWARDS: ALA CALDECOTT MEDAL (1970) for *A Story, A Story.* KATE GREENAWAY MEDAL (1976) and Japan's Kadai Tosho award for *The Post Office Cat.* Kerlan Award from the University of Minnesota, THE KERLAN COLLECTION (1989), for lifetime achievement and contribution to children's literature, where a permanent collection of her work is housed

FURTHER WORKS: *Noah's Ark,* 1971; *Jack Joytt's Hide,* 1973; *The Post Office Cat,* 1973; *The Abominable Swampman,* 1975; *The Green Man,* 1979; *Birdsong,* 1984; *Jack and the Bean Tree,* 1986; *Sea Tale,* 1990; *Dream Peddler,* 1993; *Mountain Jack Tales,* 1993; *Two Bad Boys: A Very Old Cherokee Tale,* 1996

BIBLIOGRAPHY: Kingman, Lee, ed., *NEWBERY MEDAL and Caldecott Medal Books, 1966–76; Twentieth-Century Children's Writers,* 1978

GERALYN A. CHESNER

HALL, Donald

Author, poet, b. 20 September 1928, Danbury, New Hampshire

H. acknowledges his parents' modeling a love of reading and his grandmother and her home as inspiration for his work as a poet and writer. A voracious reader as a child, he devoured POETRY and literature. When, at age twelve, a neighbor turned him on to Edgar Allan Poe, H. claims his life was changed. Spending time after school, H. wrote volumes of poetry as a child, emulating the style of poets he admired. At age fourteen, he met an older boy who quit school to write poetry—H.'s dream. This began a friendship of discussions centered around poetry and critiquing each others' work. At sixteen, his first poem was published in a small magazine. H. received his Bachelor of Arts degree from Harvard University and met a myriad of poets including Robert Bly and Robert FROST. He attended Oxford University for two years, then received a grant for creative writing at Stanford University. Becoming a junior fellow in the Society of Fellows from 1954–57 he wrote his first book of poems for adults, *Exiles and Marriages* (1955).

H. began teaching composition at the University of Michigan, Ann Arbor, and published his second book of poems for adults, *The Dark Houses* (1958). In 1975 he took a year's leave from the university and moved into his grandmother's house in New Hampshire. After a short time he realized he would not be going back to Michigan, and he courageously began a career of writing.

Focused on the cyclical nature of farm life, *Ox-Cart Man* (1979) was first written as a poem for *The New Yorker* and is based on an oral retelling. Dedicated to the sound of poetry, H. feels it is necessary to write poetry that resonates in the listener's ear. He wants readers to be moved by the sound of the words in his writing and find delight in the images he creates.

Evident that his childhood and adolescence are the roots of his writing, his books for children include themes and experiences from the farm and visits with his grandparents. Often historical and loosely biographical in nature, his books such as *Ox-Cart Man, The Farm Summer 1942* (Barry MOSER, illus. 1994), *Old Home Day* (Emily Arnold MCCULLY, illus. 1996), and *The Milkman's Boy* (Greg Shed, illus. 1997) are set in the rural northeast. Genuinely capturing the time period and setting, H. uses gentle, poetic text to share homespun, nostalgic tales.

AWARDS: H. received the *New York Times* Notable Children's Book citation in 1979 for *Ox-Cart Man,* his most well known book for children. Illustrated by Barbara COONEY, it won the CALDECOTT MEDAL in 1980. He was also lauded on *Horn Book's* honor list in 1986 for editing the *The Oxford Book of Children's Verse in America*

FURTHER WORKS: *Andrew and the Lion Farmer.* (Jane Miller, illus). 1959. *Riddle Rat* (Mort Gerberg, illus). 1977. *I Am the Dog, I Am the Cat.* (Barry Moser, illus). 1994. *Lucy's Christmas.* (Michael McCurdy, illus). 1994. *When Willard Met Babe Ruth.* (Barry Moser, illus). 1996

BIBLIOGRAPHY: *Contemporary Authors Autobiography Series,* vol. 7, 1988; *Children's Literature Review,* vol. 1, 1973, vol. 37, 1986, vol. 59, 1990; *Dictionary of Literary Biography,* vol. 5, 1980; Silvey, Anita, ed., *Children's Books and*

Their Creators, 1995; *Something about the Author,* vol. 23, 1981, and vol. 97, 1998

GERALYN A. CHESNER

HALL, Lynn

Author, b. 9 November 1937, Lombard, Illinois

H. is the author of more than seventy books, half for YOUNG ADULTS and half for middle-grade readers. As a child she read any book she could find about animals, particularly horses. Her work reflects her love of animals and her stories often evolve from her own experiences with horses and dogs. While working as a copywriter she revered authors as "creative geniuses who sat at the right hand of God." H. quit her job and spent six months analyzing ANIMAL STORIES she brought home from the library; she sold her first book in a year. H. is praised for her work featuring teenage protagonists facing difficult situations.

FURTHER WORKS: *A Horse Called Dragon,* 1971; *Sticks and Stones,* 1972; *Barry, the Bravest St. Bernard,* 1973; *Tazo and Me,* 1985; *Danger Dog,* 1986; *The Secret Life of Dagmar Schultz,* 1988; *Here Comes Zelda Claus,* 1989

BIBLIOGRAPHY: Gallo, D. R., ed., *Speaking for Ourselves,* 1990; *Something about the Author,* vol. 79, 1995

JODI PILGRIM

HAMANAKA, Sheila

Author, illustrator, b. 1 August 1949, New York City

H. is a third generation Japanese American whose life as a Japanese American has influenced her work in many ways. As a youth growing up on New York's lower East Side in the 1950s, H.'s father played a pivotal role in her life. She has fond memories of the times she spent with her father and the places they both visited. Much of H.'s work is inspired by her experiences as a youth. One example is her memory of her father's folding paper cranes for children on New York City buses.

H.'s artistic talent was nurtured and cultivated at the New York City High School of Music and Art. However, she did not study art in college but majored in history instead. Her career as an author and illustrator began after her children were born. Along with her own childhood memories, her children also serve as fodder and inspiration

for H.'s work. *All the Colors of the Earth* (1994) is partially a celebration of her children's multi-ethnic heritage. She often uses her children, cats, and friends as the subjects in her ILLUSTRATIONS. Her work is marked by its focus on depicting character and personality through her illustrations done mostly in oils on canvas.

H.'s *The Journey: Japanese Americans, Racism, and Renewal* (1990) was awarded the Jane Addams Peace Award honor book. Her writing is featured in the introduction of the critically lauded *On the Wings of Peace: Writers and Illustrators Speak out for Peace, in Memory of Hiroshima and Nagasaki* (1995). *The Journey* is based on a mural that depicts H.'s life, the lives of her family who fought in World War II, and those who were confined to relocation camps. Her work was inspired by others who have contributed to the discovery as well as the telling, of their own remarkable histories as Japanese Americans.

FURTHER WORKS: *Peace Crane,* 1995; *I Look like a Girl,* (1999); *Bebop-a-Do-Walk,* 1995; *All the Colors of the Earth,* 1994

BIBLIOGRAPHY: Carney-Miller, http://www.house ofem.com/clrseath.htm; Cummings, Pat. *Talking with Artists,* 1995

MICHAEL O'LAUGHLIN

HAMILTON, Virginia

Author, b. 12 March 1936, Yellow Springs, Ohio

Unlike many writers, H. knew from an early age that she wanted to become a writer; she began writing stories as a child. She later studied at Antioch College, The Ohio State University, and The New School for Social Research in New York. H. has written some fifty books of contemporary fiction, historical fiction, FANTASY, retellings, and nonfiction for children and YOUNG ADULTS. Critics praise H.'s work for its creativity, imagery, form, and content. H. is a gifted storyteller who draws on her memories, experiences, and imagination to create time-honored books for children and young adults. Bishop (1996) writes that H.'s writing "is characterized in part by its uniqueness: a certain air of mystery or even a touch of the bizarre, a creative interweaving of symbolism and myth, a masterful use of language and imagery." Michael Patrick Hearne (1996) says that H. "has heightened the standards for children's literature as few other authors have.

345

She does not address children so much as she explores with them, sometimes ahead of them, the full possibilities of imagination."

The themes of identity and the need for others are apparent in works by H., such as *Plain City* (1993). In this work, Buhlaire, a twelve-year-old girl of mixed heritage, ponders her physical features of "blue-green" eyes, "carrot-honey" skin, and "Rasta" hair as she tries to fit in with her darker friends and relatives. After discovering that her father, whom she has been told died in Vietnam, is actually alive, she finds that he is homeless, unbalanced, and living in a cave under an interstate highway. One reviewer wrote "Through candid thoughts, realistic dialogue, and a symbolic blend of setting and self-discovery, H. has created a testimonial on the powerful bonds of blood and 'back-time,' or heritage."

Although she has been praised for her depiction of AFRICAN AMERICAN life and its historical heritage, H. insists that her chief goal is to tell a good story. When asked what she tries to accomplish with each book, she replied, "That's not how you write a book. You're not trying to 'accomplish' anything but tell a good story, and my books are full of good stories" ("A Visit with Virginia H.," 1999).

Many of H.'s tales were inspired by stories told to her by her parents and other relatives as she was growing up in Ohio. One of her most vivid memories is about Levi Perry, her grandfather, who escaped from slavery through the Underground Railroad. H. makes a significant contribution to children who have not had family storytellers to tell them of their rich ethnic culture. She combines her STORYTELLING talents with folktale motifs, elements of fantasy, and racial themes. These elements are combined with many FAMILY STORIES in H.'s trilogy: *The People Could Fly: American Black Folktales* (1985); *Many Thousands Gone: African Americans from Slavery to Freedom* (1993); *Her Stories: African-American Folktales,* FAIRY TALES, *and True Tales* (1995).

Like many of H.'s works, *M. C. Higgins, the Great* (1974), has a somewhat surreal quality and is crafted around the shapes, rhythms, and sounds of language. This novel, full of unabashed symbolism, tells of a boy finding a way to hold his family together while trying to save his ancestral home from destruction. A reviewer notes that the book is "H.'s most accessible as well as her most complex book . . . [It is] a touchstone . . . for it represents how complex and how profound apparently simple fictions can be." Although the character of M.C. copes with his awakening identity as an African American, the story itself addresses the universal condition of the struggle for survival enacted daily by all humanity.

One of the most celebrated authors of books for children today, H. has won almost every major award and honor in her field. H. was the first African American woman and writer to receive the NEWBERY MEDAL and have three Newbery Medal Honor Books. Her novel, *M. C. Higgins, the Great,* won the Newbery Medal, the *Boston Globe-Horn Book* Award, and the National Book Award.

AWARDS: AMERICAN LIBRARY ASSOCIATION Newbery Medal (1975) for *M. C. Higgins, the Great.* ALA Newbery Medal Honor titles (1989) for *In the Beginning: Creation Stories from around the World,* (1983) for *Sweet Whispers, Brother Rush,* and (1972) for *The Planet of Jr. Brown. Boston Globe–Horn Book* (1973) for *M. C. Higgins, the Great* and (1983) for *Sweet Whispers, Brother Rush.* CORETTA SCOTT KING AWARD (1996) for *Her Stories: African American Folktales, Fairy Tales and True Tales,* (1986) for *The People Could Fly: American Black Folktales,* (1983) for *Sweet Whispers, Brother Rush,* (1984) for *The Magical Adventures of Pretty Pearl,* Coretta Scott King Honor Award: (1990) for *The Bells of Christmas,* (1989) for *Anthony Burns: The Defeat and Triumph of a Fugitive Slave,* (1986) for *Junius over Far,* (1985) for *A Little Love,* (1979) for *Justice and her Brothers.* Edgar Allan Poe Award (1970) for *The House of Dies Drear.* American Book Award nomination (1982) for *Sweet Whispers, Brother Rush.* INTERNATIONAL BOARD ON BOOKS FOR YOUNG PEOPLE (1976) for *M. C. Higgins, the Great,* and (1984) for *Sweet Whispers, Brother Rush.* Hans Christian ANDERSEN (1992) and Laura Ingalls WILDER Medal (1995) for her body of work. In 1995, Hamilton became the first author of children's books to receive the prestigious John D. and Catherine C. MacArthur Fellowship

FURTHER WORKS: *Zeely,* 1967; *The Time-Ago Tales of Jahdu,* 1969; *The Planet of Junior Brown,* 1971; *W. E. B. Du Bois: A BIOGRAPHY,* 1972; *The Magical Adventures of Pretty Pearl,* 1983; *Anthony Burns: The Defeat and Triumph of a Fugitive Slave,* 1988; *Cousins,* 1990; *Drylongso,* 1992; *Bluish,* 1999

BIBLIOGRAPHY: *Children's Literature Review,* vol. 40, 1996; Demann, A., and Ramsey, I.; *Virginia H.,* 1999; HOPKINS, Lee Bennett, *Pauses: Autobiographical Reflections of 101 Creators of Children's Books,* 1995; http://falcon.jmu.edu/~ramseyil/hamilton.htm (accessed Sept. 19, 1999); McBimeel, S. L., *100 Most Popular Children's Authors,* 1999; "A Visit with Virginia Hamilton," http://www.virginiahamilton.com/pages/biostuff.htm (accessed July 29, 1999); Gallo, D., *Speaking for Ourselves,* 1990

MARY ARIAIL BROUGHTON

HANDFORTH, Thomas
Author, illustrator, b. 16 September 1897, Tacoma, Washington; d. 19 October 1948, Pasadena, California

H. was a world traveler who lived in Paris, Mexico, North Africa, INDIA, and China, studying art formally in the United States and in France at L'Ecole des Beaux Arts. He began his career in children's literature illustrating books for many of the famous picture-book authors of the 1920s and 1930s, including Elizabeth COATSWORTH (*Toutou in Bondage,* 1929). He was very impressed by the mythical qualities of Chinese scrolls and studied the artistic techniques of Chinese painters. *Mei Li* (1938), a book whose content and artistic style were greatly influenced by the seven years he spent in China, uses bold traditional brush strokes to illustrate his story. Text complements ILLUSTRATIONS in this story of bold Mei Li, a little girl who does not accept staying at home and goes off to see the New Year's Fair for herself.

AWARD: ALA CALDECOTT MEDAL, 1930, *Mei Li*

BIBLIOGRAPHY: *Something about the Author,* vol. 42, 1986

REBECCA RAPPORT

HANDLER, Daniel
(See SNICKET, Lemony)

HANSEN, Joyce
Author, b. 18 October 1942, the Bronx, New York

H. was born and reared in the Bronx, and for twenty-five years taught language arts to students with reading problems in the New York City school system. She received her Bachelor of Arts from Pace University and her Master's of Arts degree from New York University. As a child she read widely, but did not encounter AFRICAN AMERICAN characters whose lives reflected her own middle-class upbringing. She noticed this as a teacher as well. Her master's thesis was a children's novel about a fifth-grade girl much like herself. This story, published as *The Gift-Giver* (1980), started H.'s career as a writer for YOUNG ADULTS. Since then she has written two sequels to *The Gift-Giver* and one other novel set in the inner city. The rest of her work has been historical fiction or nonfiction and frequently deals with the Civil War and Reconstruction periods. In all her books, H. strives to portray the African American experience honestly while celebrating the strength of character revealed over and over in her research and her own experience.

H. explores the work of anthropologists and historians in revealing social conditions and traditions of African American slaves in colonial America in *Breaking Ground, Breaking Silence: The Story of New York's African Burial Ground* (with Gary McGowan, 1998). She creates a lively text that reads like a MYSTERY STORY but that is the historically accurate result of much scholarly research. In writing the text, H. shows how original source material, physical evidence, and disinterred personal effects are used to create an exciting narrative. Since retiring from teaching in 1996, H. devotes herself to writing full-time.

AWARDS: CORETTA SCOTT KING AWARD (1999) for *Breaking Ground, Breaking Silence: The Story of New York's African Burial Ground* (with Gary McGowan, (1998) for *I Thought My Soul Would Rise and Fly,* (1995) for *The Captive,* and (1987) for *Which Way Freedom?* National Council of Social Studies and CHILDREN'S BOOK COUNCIL Notable Children's Trade Book in the Field of Social Studies (1986) for *The Gift-Giver, Yellow Bird and Me,* (1986) for *Which Way Freedom?* (1988) for *Out From This Place,* (1993) for *Between Two Fires: Black Soldiers in the Civil War,* and (1998) for *Women of Hope: African Americans Who Made A Difference.* IRA YOUNG ADULTS' Choice Book (1999) for *I Thought My Soul Would Rise and Fly*

FURTHER WORKS: *Homeboy.* 1982. "The Tail," in *Funny You Should Ask: The Delacorte Book of Original Humorous Short Stories.* (David Gale, ed). 1992. *Women of Hope.* 1992. "Sweet Hour of Prayer," in *Don't Give up the Ghost: The Delacorte Book of Original Ghost Stories.* 1993.

"New Day Dawning," in *But That's Another Story*. (Sandy Asher, ed). 1996. *The Heart Calls Home*. 1999. *Bury Me Not in a Land of Slaves: African-Americans in the Time of Reconstruction*. 2000. *My Dear Amir*. 2000

BIBLIOGRAPHY: Brown, Jean E. and Elaine C. Stephens, eds., "MULTICULTURAL LITERATURE: A Story of Your Own." *United in Diversity: Using Multicultural Young Adult Literature in the Classroom*. 1998. H., Joyce. "Writing Breaking Ground, Breaking Silence." *SIGNAL Journal*, 1999. H., Joyce. "Young Adult Books." The *Horn Book* magazine. 1987. Melius, Maria. "On Writing for Young Adults: An Interview with Joyce H." *SIGNAL Journal*. 1999. Rinn, Miriam. "Joyce H." *Book Report*. 1997

ELIZABETH A. POE

HARNETT, Cynthia M.
Author, illustrator, b. 22 June 1893, London, England; d. 24 October 1981

H., remembered for her meticulous attention to the details of everyday life in medieval England, was a pioneer of modern historical novels for young people. H. believed every detail in her novels must be scrupulously accurate because teachers relied on these historical novels to supplement their textbooks. She also thought it was important to document the lives of ordinary people in history, rather than the extraordinary. In her first book, *The Great House* (1949), H. tells the story of children born to seventeenth century architects. In her last book, *The Writing on the Hearth* (1971), H. describes the destruction that results from the War of the Roses, by telling it through the words of a young school boy.

H.'s most prestigious book, *The Wool Pack*, also known as *Nicholas and the Woolpack* (1951), tells about the son of a wool merchant in fifteenth century England, who uncovers a plot to ruin his father's business. As part of H.'s effort to ensure historical accuracy and re-create authentic atmosphere, H. provided her own ILLUSTRATIONS for her historical novels showing minute details of dressing and eating, and aspects of daily life. H. studied at the Chelsea School of Art and early in her career produced a series of PICTURE BOOKS about life in the country. *David's New Life* (1937), about a boy and the animals he sees in the country, was produced with her artist cousin, Vernon Stokes.

AWARDS: CARNEGIE MEDAL (1951) for *The Wool-Pack*

FURTHER WORKS: *Ring out, Bow Bells!* 1953. *Stars of Fortune*. 1956. *The Lord of Unicorn*. 1959. *The Writing on the Hearth*. 1971

BIBLIOGRAPHY: Chevalier, Tracy, ed., *Twentieth Century Children's Writers*. 1989

DENISE P. BEASLEY

HARRIS, Joel Chandler
Author, journalist, b. 9 December 1848, Eatonton, Georgia; d. 3 July 1908, Atlanta, Georgia

H. was born in rural Georgia and reared by his unmarried mother. He spent much of his childhood engaging in practical jokes and pranks to amuse his friends. H. remembered his childhood favorably and often had kind remarks for the people of Eatonton who were good to him during his formative years. H. attributed his love of writing to his mother who read to him often. Even when H. was too young to appreciate the story his mother was reading, he was somehow aware of aspects of style or HUMOR that caught his fancy and stayed with him as he began to write. H. left school when he was thirteen and became an apprentice to the typesetter of a weekly publication. H. lived on a plantation and shared the owner's library, devouring everything he could find. During this period H. had some of his own short pieces published. After the Civil War, H. worked for numerous papers, finally ending up with the *Atlanta Constitution*. While H. was with the *Constitution* he created the character of Uncle Remus, who began as a philosopher and eventually evolved into a storyteller. His first Uncle Remus stories appeared in the newspaper and proved to be very popular. The popularity of the newspaper stories led to the 1880 publication of *Uncle Remus: His Songs and His Sayings*, H.'s first book.

The Uncle Remus stories were actually retellings of traditional AFRICAN AMERICAN tales that H. researched and collected. H. spent a good deal of time reading different versions of the same story before he would settle on his own retelling. H. retained the language of former African American slaves who told the stories believing that voice is an important component of the tale. Much of the original dialect H. used in his stories was prevalent among the former slaves who lived in Georgia during the time H. wrote his books.

Besides the Uncle Remus tales, many featuring the adventures of Brer Rabbit, H. also wrote several other books for children including: *Little Mr. Thimblefinger and His Queer Country: What the Children Saw and Heard There* (1894); *The Story of Aaron (So Called), the Son of Ben Ali, Told by His Friends and Acquaintances* (1895), and *Aaron in the Wildwoods* (1897).

Many of H.'s tales were adapted in the 1940s through the 1970s in movie and filmstrip form by DISNEY and other companies. With their humorous emphasis on small animals outwitting larger predators by any means including mischief, they have retained their popularity with readers of all ages. Today authors such as Julius LESTER are adapting H.'s work by incorporating authentic dialects and eliminating stereotypical and offensive characters. H.'s work to preserve the stories of the slaves is an important contribution to the documentation of the slave culture of the early American South.

SELECTED FURTHER WORKS: *Brer Rabbit and Boss Lion.* 1996. *Brer Rabbit and the Wonderful Tar Baby.* 1992. *The Classic Tales of Brer Rabbit.* 1995. *Complete Tales of Uncle Remus.* 1955. *Giant Treasure of Brer Rabbit.* 1991

BIBLIOGRAPHY: *Yesterday's Authors of Books for Children,* vol. 1; Silvey, Anita, ed., *Children's Books and Their Creators,* 1995

MICHAEL O'LAUGHLIN

HARRISON, David

Author, poet, b. 13 March 1937, Springfield, Missouri

H. grew up in a loving, supportive family that encouraged him to try new things, to imagine, and to learn all that he could. On a vacation trip with his parents, H. wanted to climb to the top of a mountain near their picnic spot. His parents said, "Go ahead." His mother challenged him to memorize the Gettysburg Address, which, of course, he did. H. earned a bachelor's degree in biology from Drury College (1959) and a master's degree in parasitology from Emory University (1960). H. has had experiences in many fields: as a professional musician, a music teacher, and a principal trombonist in a symphony orchestra. He has also worked as a pharmacologist, an editorial manager for a greeting-card company, and a businessman. He is the president and owner of a manufacturing and building-materials supply house in Missouri. H. gets up every morning at 6:00 A.M. to write; he says he does not like to get up that early but likes the communication with people who read his books.

H. is a service-oriented, community-minded person who contributes to its educational welfare. He served on the school board, he initiated a city-wide project for kids to write about what they have learned. He contributes to the Missouri Writer's Program and supports any good idea to help children learn to read, write, and love POETRY. H. spends most of his time composing poetry but also creates engaging PICTURE BOOK texts.

H. began his writing career with stories for adults. He wrote his first book for children in 1969. It was called *The Boy with a Drum* and sold two million copies. His fiftieth book, *Farmer's Garden: Rhymes for Two Voices,* was published in 2000. H. received the Christopher Medal (1973) for *The Book of Giant Stories. Somebody Catch My Homework* (1993) was chosen as the Bank Street College Children's Book of the Year. That book and several others have been chosen as Children's Choices for the INTERNATIONAL READING ASSOCIATION/CHILDREN'S BOOK COUNCIL list.

H. has an eclectic background to draw upon for his writing. He says that *The Purchase of Small Secrets* (1998) is a scrapbook of poems based upon defining moments in his life. H. has a wealth of materials to feed his imagination given his experiences as a child, the work he does in schools, and the interaction with other Missouri writers. Through the use of memorable imagery, *Wild Country: Outdoor Poems for Young People* (1999) expresses H.'s strong emotions for the outdoors, his respect for nature, and the universal connections between people and the environment. The free verse poems are arranged according to the natural landscape with a section on mountains, the sea, the forest, and the high country.

FURTHER WORKS: *When Cows Come Home,* 1994; *The Boy Who Counted Stars,* 1994; *A Thousand Cousins,* 1995; *The Animals' Song,* 1997

BIBLIOGRAPHY: http://redrival.com/mowrites4kids/
harrison; connections: "Book News for Teachers
and Librarians," 2000

BERNICE E. CULLINAN

HARRISON, Ted (Edward Hardy)
Illustrator, b. 28 August 1926, Wingate, Durham,
England

Born in a coal mining town in England, H. has
"sought color, fresh air and fantasy ever since."
He became interested in art while in an English
elementary school but attendance at a British
classical art school proved so rigorous and academic that he lost interest in painting for a time.
After receiving a Bachelor of Education degree
in 1977 he was interested in what motivated children to read and to learn. He considers "the education and the educators of youth as vital concerns for humanity and its future."

Settling in the Yukon in the 1960s, he took up
art again but found that academic art did not fit in
a Northern landscape; he developed a new artistic
response to his surroundings. Known for his surrealistic representation of his North, he presents
a unique view of that country to the world.

Children of the Yukon (1977) was named one
of Child Study Association of America's Best
Children's Books of the Year, a Choice Book by
the Children's Book Centre (Toronto) and one of
Eight CANADIAN Books for Choice List by the
International Youth Library for the Twenty-ninth
Annual International Exhibition. Including some
historical material, he presents life in the Yukon
today.

A Northern Alphabet: A Is for Arctic (1982)
received the Amelia Frances Howard-Gibbon
Award runner-up from the Canadian Association
of Children's Librarians, was designated a Choice
Book from the Children's Book Centre (Toronto)
and placed on the INTERNATIONAL BOARD OF
BOOKS FOR YOUNG PEOPLE Honor List for ILLUS-
TRATION (1984). The book depicts people, scenes,
and objects associated with the far North.

Combining Robert W. SERVICE's verse with
H.'s art resulted in publication of *The Cremation
of Sam McGee* (1986). It was selected as one of
the *New York Times* Best Illustrated Children's
Books and an American Library Association Notable Book. *The Shooting of Dan McGrew* (1987)
was equally well received.

In honor of Canada's one hundred and twenty-
fifth birthday in 1992, H. designed a book entitled
0 Canada! that interprets every province and territory through the format of the Canadian national anthem. It was short-listed for the Canadian Elizabeth Mrazik-Cleaver PICTURE BOOK
Award. His unusual world of pink ice, blue dogs,
orange rivers, and purple trees incorporates in a
surprising way many elements of the familiar.

Of his art H. says, "I enjoy illustrating in the
same bold vigorous style I have developed, and
constantly seek new themes to explore. I feel that
good illustrations should leave something to the
reader's imagination and increase their enjoyment of the text. It is through our imaginations
that life can become more interesting."

BIBLIOGRAPHY: Gillespie, J. T. and C. J. Naden,
eds., *Best Books for Children: Preschool through
Grade 6*, 1994; Silvey, A. ed., *Children's Books
and Their Creators*, 1995; *Something about the
Author*, vol. 56, 1989

IRVYN G. GILBERTSON

HARVEY, Brett
Author, b. 28 April 1936, New York City

H. credits the grandmother she never met as having inspired her to become a children's author.
Her grandmother's journals were the fodder H.
used to create her first story, the ALA Notable
Book: *My Prairie Year: Based on the Diary of
Elenore Plaisted* (1986). H. does careful research
using primary sources such as diaries, journals,
and letters for her historical stories for beginning
readers. H. is actively involved in the National
Writer's Union, fighting for the rights of authors
everywhere.

AWARDS: AMERICAN LIBRARY ASSOCIATION Notable Book (1986) for *My Prairie Year*

FURTHER WORKS: *Cassie's Journey: Going West
in the 1860s*, 1988; *Immigrant Girl: Becky of Eldridge Street*, 1987; *My Prairie Christmas*, 1990

BIBLIOGRAPHY: *Kliatt Young Adult Paperback
Guide*, Sept. 1994; *New York Times Book Review*,
Sept. 13, 1987; interview with author, 1986

MICHAEL O'LAUGHLIN

HASKINS, James
Author, b. 19 September 1941, Montgomery,
Alabama

Born in Alabama, H. attended high school in
Boston, and received college degrees from

Georgetown University, Alabama State University, and the University of New Mexico. While H., author of more than one hundred INFORMATION BOOKS and BIOGRAPHIES, writes mainly about AFRICAN AMERICANS and their achievements, his subjects cover a broad range of topics from the violence of the Vietnam War to that of street gangs, from MUSIC to SPORTS. Using a straightforward writing style, H. writes carefully researched stories about real people who represent the best in their respective fields: Martin Luther King, Jr., Ralph Bunch, Hank Aaron, Barbara Jordan, Dr. J, and Rosa Parks. Children who are only familiar with famous sports figures or Dr. King will learn about others, perhaps less well known, who were also heroes. He also has children counting their way through many countries and learning about their cultures and unique features in his Count Your Way series.

AWARDS: CORETTA SCOTT KING Honor Book (1998) for *Bayard Rustin: Behind the Scenes of the Civil Rights Movement,* (1991) for *Black Dance in America: A History Through Its People,* (1984) for *Lena Horne,* (1980) for *Andrew Young: Young Man with a Mission,* (1978) for *Barbara Jordan,* and (1977) for *The Story of Stevie Wonder.* Carter G. Woodson Book Award (1988) for *Black Music in America: A History through Its People*

BIBLIOGRAPHY: *Something about the Author,* vol. 69, 1992; Publishers' pamphlets; THE KERLAN COLLECTION vertical files

REBECCA RAPPORT

HAUGAARD, Erik Christian

Author, dramatist, poet, b. 13 April 1923, Frederiksberg, Denmark

In early adulthood, H. fled his homeland to escape the German invasion during World War II. That event has clearly contributed to H.'s prevalent theme, the triumph of an individual's shared humanity in the context of horrific circumstances, the theme of most of H.'s books for YOUNG ADULTS. H.'s novels present the reader with characters in wartime settings during different historical periods, who learn about themselves through the situations in which they are placed. *Hakon of Rogen's Saga* (1963) is the story of a teen tragically orphaned at the end of the Viking period. *The Little Fishes* (1967) looks at the lives of three

Italian orphans left to survive as beggars in the streets of Naples during World War II. H. attempts to show the horrors of war and the survival of the individual spirit through the character of Guido, one of the orphans.

AWARDS: *Boston Globe-Horn Book* Award (1967) for *The Little Fishes.* AMERICAN LIBRARY ASSOCIATION Notable Book Award (1963) for *Hakon of Rogen's Saga,* and (1965) for *The Untold Tale*

FURTHER WORKS: *A Slave's Tale,* 1965; *The Untold Tale,* 1971; *The Rider and His Horse,* 1968; *Orphans of the Wind,* 1966; *Chase Me, Catch Nobody,* 1980; *The Revenge of the Forty-seven Samurai,* 1995

BIBLIOGRAPHY: *Something about the Author,* vol. 4, 1973, and vol. 68, 1992

MICHAEL O'LAUGHLIN

HAUTZIG, Esther

Author, b. 18 October, 1930, Vilna, Poland

H.'s award-winning work, *The Endless Steppe: Growing up in Siberia* (1968), tells of her early life as the daughter of Polish Jews who were arrested by the Soviets and banished to Siberia for six years. *The Endless Steppe* won numerous AWARDS including the Lewis CARROLL Shelf Award (1971), and was listed as a National Book Award finalist in 1969. H. further discusses her life experiences in *Remember Who You Are: Stories about Being Jewish* (1990), a collection of short sketches of people who influenced her life. H. has collaborated with her daughter, Deborah, also an author.

H. also creates craft books that teach children how to make gifts or food without having prior experience or money. These books include: *Let's Cook without Cooking* (1955), *Let's Make Presents* (1962), *Christmas Goodies* (1981), and *Holiday Treats* (1983)

AWARDS: Sydney TAYLOR Book Award (1968) for *The Endless Steppe*

BIBLIOGRAPHY: HOPKINS, Lee Bennett, *Pauses: Autobiographical Reflections of 101 Creators of Children's Books,* 1995

DENISE P. BEASLEY

HAVILAND, Virginia

Author, b. 21 May 1911, Rochester, New York; d. 6 January 1988, Washington, D.C.

H. spent much of her life working toward the improvement and promotion of children's literature.

She began her career as a librarian at the Boston Public Library where she served in several capacities. During this period H. began writing articles and books to fulfill the demand for INFORMATIONAL texts that discussed children's books and their relation to reading. Her first publication, *Children and Their Friends the Authors* was published in the *Boston Public Library Quarterly* (1946). Subsequently she published *The Travelogue Storybook of the Nineteenth Century* (1950), *Children and Poetry* (1970), and *Children's Literature: A Guide to Reference Sources* (1966).

H.'s early works led her toward a deepening interest in early children's books and finally to FAIRY TALES that she often studied, compiled, and edited. Her interest in fairy tales led her to search for lesser known versions as she traveled abroad and investigated different cultures. Librarians and storytellers from countries she visited often shared with her. H. collected and edited sixteen titles in Little Brown's Favorite Fairy Tales series, several of which remain in print today.

H.'s work at the Boston Public Library led her to the Library of Congress where she was the director of the Children's Book Section. Under her leadership the Children's Section was completely reorganized into its present form and renamed the Children's Literature Center. In addition to her duties with the Library of Congress, H. also served as president of the Children's Services Division of the AMERICAN LIBRARY ASSOCIATION. H. also reviewed children's books for several periodicals including *The Horn Book.* For her overall contribution to children's literature H. received several awards including the Catholic Library Association's Regina Medal and an award from Grolier Publishing.

H. often felt that she was writing because she was asked to and not because she wanted to, but when she began to write and enjoy the topic at hand, she inevitably enjoyed the process. Before her death, H. stated that "research and writing has filled my life to the brim."

FURTHER WORKS: *Favorite Fairy Tales Told in Denmark.* 1996. *Favorite Fairy Tales Told in Greece.* 1996. *Favorite Fairy Tales Told in Ireland.* 1996

BIBLIOGRAPHY: Cott, Jonathan, *Pipers at the Gates of Dawn: The Wisdom of Children's Literature,* 1981; *Children's Literature: A Guide to Reference Sources.* 1966; *Something about the Author.* vol. 54, 1989

MICHAEL O'LAUGHLIN

HAVILL, Juanita
Author, b. 11 May 1949, Evansville, Indiana

Before learning to write for herself, H. dictated stories and poems to her mother, who wrote them down for her. In high school, H. worked for the school newspaper writing editorials, articles, and poems; later, after the birth of her children, she began to write professionally.

H. has written more than fifteen critically acclaimed books for children. *Jamaica's Find* (1986) won the Library of Congress's Children's Book of the Year, and H. won the Ezra Jack KEATS New Writer award for this book as well. In *Jamaica's Find,* the main character struggles over the moral dilemma of right vs. wrong. In its subsequent sequels, *Jamaica Tag-Along* (1989) and *Jamaica and Brianna* (1993), H. discusses other moral dilemmas of early childhood including jealousy and sibling rivalry.

H. has also written books for older readers that discuss similar issues including *It Always Happens to Leona* (1989), and *Leona and Ike* (1990).

BIBLIOGRAPHY: *Something about the Author.* vol. 74, 1993

DENISE P. BEASLEY

HAWTHORNE, Nathaniel
Author, b. 4 July 1804, Salem, Massachusetts; d. 19 May 1864, Plymouth, New Hampshire

At four years of age H.'s father, a sea captain, died leaving his mother to rear three children alone. H. lived what he called a lonely youth, spending a lot of solitary time thinking and writing. He graduated from Bowdoin College in 1825 with career aspirations of becoming a writer, despite his concern for the poor pay one received in this profession.

H.'s first attempt at publishing a novel failed, however, it did bring his talent to the attention of the publisher of *The Token,* a literary annual, in which he published several short stories. At this time he worked as a measurer of salt and coal in the Boston Custom House.

In 1842 H. married Sophia Peabody and moved to Brook Farm where he became acquainted with Emerson and Thoreau. H. took on the job of surveyor at the Salem Customhouse, which provided him with a regular salary until a change of management caused him to lose the job. This proved to be beneficial since his time was now spent completing the two books for which he is best known, *The Scarlet Letter* (1850) and *The House of the Seven Gables* (1851).

H. is credited with the first retelling of Greek myths for children with *A Wonder Book for Boys and Girls* (1852). The most popular of the stories in this book includes "The Golden Touch," based on the tale of King Midas. Another book, *Tanglewood Tales for Girls and Boys,* written in 1853, also embodies retold classic tales.

In 1853, he was appointed to the consulship at Liverpool, England, and during this time he met Elizabeth Barrett Browning and Alfred Lord Tennyson. H.'s family moved to Italy in 1858, then to England in 1859 and back to Boston in 1860, where he died in Plymouth, New Hampshire, in 1864. Many books have been written about H. and his works, for both adults and children.

FURTHER WORKS: *Peter Parley's Universal History.* 1837. *Grandfather's Chair: A History for Youth.* 1841. *Little Daffydowndilly and Other Stories.* 1887. *The Golden Touch.* (Valenti Angelo, illus., reissued 1927, Paul GALDONE, illus.), 1959. *Pandora's Box.* (Rafaello Busoni, illus., reissued 1951, Paul Galdone, illus.), 1967

GERALYN A. CHESNER

(For a fuller treatment of the life and career of H., see Steven R. Serafin, general editor, *The Continuum Encyclopedia of American Literature*, pp. 495–97)

HAYWOOD, Carolyn
Author, illustrator, b. 3 January 1898, Philadelphia, Pennsylvania; d. 11 January 1990, Philadelphia, Pennsylvania

Beginning at an early age, H. spent a lot of time painting and drawing and was determined to become an artist. After teaching for a year at Friends Central School in Philadelphia, she enrolled in Pennsylvania Academy of Fine Arts where among other things, she was a studio assistant to mural artist Violet Oakley. This experience encouraged her to paint a few of her own murals, which now grace local Philadelphia locations.

H.'s writing career began when she showed some of her ILLUSTRATIONS to a children's book editor who suggested she write a story. This suggestion resulted in *B Is for Betsy* (1939). Her first book began a long line of Betsy books, starring a typical young girl living a normal life sprinkled with excitement and HUMOR. Chronicling the adventures of Betsy's friend, Eddie Wilson, a series surrounding this character began with *Little Eddie* in 1947 and includes such titles as *Eddie and the Fire Engine* (1949), *Eddie's Green Thumb* (1964), and *Eddie's Happenings* (1971).

Sometimes considered ordinary yet entertaining, many of H.'s childhood experiences show up in her books. These include typical problems and adventures all children have, coupled with frequent action. She illustrated a large number of her own books utilizing detailed line drawings that exemplify her characters' personalities and experiences. H. wrote books with holiday themes such as *A Christmas FANTASY*, illustrated by Glenys and Victor Ambrus (1972), *Halloween Treats,* illustrated by Victoria de Larrea (1981), and *Happy Birthday from Carolyn Haywood,* illustrated by Wendy WATSON (1984). Haywood's final book, *Eddie's Friend Boodles,* illustrated by Catherine Stock, was published in 1991, a year after her death.

AWARDS: Boys Club of America Junior Book Award (1956) for *Eddie and His Big Deals.* Distinguished Daughter of Pennsylvania by the governor (1967) for her contribution to children's literature and for her skill as an artist

FURTHER WORKS: *Here's a Penny.* 1944. *Betsy and the Boys.* 1945. *Eddie and Gardenia.* 1951. *Eddie Makes Music.* 1957. *Snowbound with Betsy.* 1962. *Here Comes the Bus.* 1963. *Eddie, the Dog Holder.* 1966. *Away Went the Balloons.* 1973. *Summer Fun.* (With Julie Durrell). 1986. *Hello, Star.* (With Julie Durrell). 1987

BIBLIOGRAPHY: HOPKINS, Lee Bennett, *Pauses: Autobiographical Reflections of 101 Creators of Children's Books,* 1995; Silvey, Anita, ed., *Children's Books and Their Creators.* 1995

GERALYN A. CHESNER

HEARNE, Betsy Gould
Author, b. 6 October 1942, Wilsonville, Alabama

H. has worked as a librarian, editor, and professor of children's literature. She analyzes and critiques books for *Booklist* and the *Bulletin of the Center for Children's Books,* and has created numerous books for educators, librarians, and parents, including two volumes of *Choosing Books for Children: A Commonsense Guide* (1981, 1990), and *Evaluating Children's Books: A Critical Look* (1993).

H. has written several books for young readers. Her first book, *South Star* (1977), and its sequel, *Home* (1979), use FANTASY to convey the importance of family and home. *Eli's Ghost* (1987), a supernatural mystery, uses HUMOR and suspense to entice intermediate readers. H. discusses the responsibilities of being a pet owner in *Eliza's Dog* (1996). She created a children's collection of beauty and the beast folktales from different cultures and time periods in *Beauties and Beasts: The Oryx MULTICULTURAL Folktale Series* (1993). H. has also created two volumes of poetry for mature adolescents about family, friends, and love, called *Love Lines: Poetry in Person* (1987), and *Polaroid and Other Poems of View* (1991).

BIBLIOGRAPHY: *Something about the Author,* vol. 95, 1998

DENISE P. BEASLEY

HEIDE, Florence Parry
Author, b. 27 February 1919, Pittsburgh, Pennsylvania

While growing up, words were very important in H.'s life. Her widowed mother, a columnist for the *Pittsburgh Press* and a drama critic, was a strong influence, encouraging H. to use her creativity. For a time she lived with her grandparents where she was greatly loved and coddled, yet as a typical child she compared herself to her siblings while searching for her place in the world. Many of her books for children carry this theme, mirroring her own shyness while growing up. H. received a bachelor's degree in English at the University of California at Los Angeles in 1939. H.'s writing career began after her children were all in school; she collaborated with friend Sylvia Worth Van Chef and wrote children's songs and later PICTURE BOOKS and mysteries. After Chef's death she worked with her daughter Roxanne to complete the Spotlight Club Mystery SERIES.

Known for writing in many different genres, both serious and funny novels, mysteries, song

books and PICTURE BOOKS, H. admits to writing fiction because she is not a person who thrives on fact. Often humorous, her fiction for younger children amplifies the relationships between the serious world of adults and the lighthearted lives of children. *In Tales for the Perfect Child* (1985), illustrated by Victoria CHESS, children accomplish what they want to by acting perfectly awful, as adults stand by helplessly. H.'s fiction for older children often punctuates the pain and awkwardness—teenagers survive while trying to find their rightful place in the scheme of things.

Much of H.'s work has been done in collaboration with her children, including the picture books *The Day of Ahmed's Secret* (1990) and *Sami and the Time of Troubles* (1992), illustrated by Ted LEWIN. Both books are set in the Middle East where her daughter Judith Gilliland spent five years. It is evident that being surrounded with words during childhood was of great importance and an influence on H.'s writing career.

AWARDS: *New York Times* Best Illustrated Children's Books of the Year Award (1971) for *The Shrinking of Treehorn,* (Edward GOREY, illus.). CHILDREN'S BOOK COUNCIL and National Council of Social Studies (1975) for *When the Sad One Comes to Stay.* ALA Notable Book, *Booklist* Editors Choice, and *School Library Journal*'s Best Book (1990) for *The Day of Ahmed's Secret* (with Judith Heide Gilliland, Ted Lewin, illus.)

FURTHER WORKS: *Sound of Sunshine, Sound of Rain.* (Ken Longtemps). 1970. *The Mystery of the Missing Suitcase.* (with Sylvia Worth Van Chef, Seymour Fleishman, illus.) 1972. *Growing Anyway Up.* 1975. *Treehorn's Wish.* (Edward Gorey, illus.). 1984. *Oh, Grow Up!* (with Roxanne H. Pierce). 1996. *The House of Wisdom.* (with Judith Gilliland). 1998

BIBLIOGRAPHY: *Something about the Author,* vol. 6, 1988; *Twentieth-Century Children's Writers,* 4th ed., 1995; Ward, M. and D. Marquardt, *Authors of Books for Young People,* 1979

GERALYN A. CHESNER

HEINE, Helme
Author, illustrator, b. 4 April 1941, Berlin, Germany

The author and illustrator of numerous PICTURE BOOKS, including *Friends* (1983), H. is noted for his whimsical ILLUSTRATIONS and his unique ability to combine thought-provoking moral themes with sheer entertainment. His stories are often absurd (as when pigs paint formal attire on themselves in *The Pig's Wedding,* 1978) as well as imaginative (as when a man and his dog gradually switch places in *Mr. Miller the Dog,* 1980). His creative watercolor illustrations run the gamut from sketchy and lucid to outrageous and comical. In addition to his original stories, H.'s work includes several retellings of classic fables and FAIRY TALES infused with an offbeat touch of HUMOR that makes them uniquely his own. H.'s philosophy that "there are different layers in a book and it ought to grow with the child" often results in creations that can be enjoyed as much by adults as by children of many ages.

AWARDS: *New York Times* Best Illustrated Children's Books of the Year Award (1980) for *Mr. Miller the Dog,* and (1991) for *the Marvelous Journey through the Night.* European Prize for Children's Literature (1985) for *The Pearl*

FURTHER WORKS: *The Boxer and the Princess.* 1998. *Friends.* 1982. *Merry-Go-Round.* 1980. *The Most Wonderful Egg in the World.* 1983. *The Pearl.* 1988. *Prince Bear.* 1989. *Seven Wild Pigs: Eleven Picture Book Fantasies.* 1988

BIBLIOGRAPHY: Carter, M. *Books for Your Children.* Spring, 1985. *Children's Literature Review.* 1989. *Something about the Author.* vol. 67, 1992

JENNIFER E. DUNNE

HEINLEIN, Robert A(nson)

Author, b. 7 July 1907, Butler, Missouri; d. 8 May 1988, Carmel, California

H. is considered by many critics to be the father of modern SCIENCE FICTION, the author who raised the level of the genre from FANTASY to realistic and extrapolative science fiction. Born the third child of seven offspring, his interest in science, engineering, and literature developed early. In 1925, H. attended the University of Missouri. Following in his next older brother's footsteps, H. then attended the United States Naval Academy. After graduating and being commissioned, he served aboard the *Lexington* and later as a gunnery officer. He retired from the navy after contracting tuberculosis. H. tried several other occupations, including silver mining, politics, and selling real estate. He also furthered his education in engineering, doing graduate studies in physics

and math at the University of California at Los Angeles. But his life took a different turn when, needing money to pay off a mortgage, he became interested in writing science fiction for a magazine contest. Once he completed the story, he decided to send it to a magazine with higher standards than the one sponsoring the contest; he submitted "Life-Line" to *Astounding Science Fiction.* John W. Campbell, Jr., purchased the story for publication in the August 1939 issue, establishing a relationship between the two that would last, and whetting H.'s appetite to continue writing. In fact, Campbell chose so many of H.'s stories to publish, he asked the author to use pseudonyms to avoid multiple listings of his name as author in any single issue. During World War II, H. returned to the navy to work as an aviation engineer in Philadelphia for three years. During this time he was so confident space exploration was possible that he wrote two letters encouraging the navy to begin the endeavor. Although one letter reached the head of the Philadelphia Naval Air Experimental Station, and the other was reportedly considered by President Truman, no one would support the notion of the capability of a rocket being launched from the deck of a ship! Later, the author would be recognized for his vision of the future.

H.'s desire to write after the war expanded to wider interests. He was asked to write for juveniles and sold stories to the *Saturday Evening Post.* His work in the field of juvenile stories led to television and film work. H., himself, never saw a distinction between writing for youth and adults. He wanted to make the future believable for both audiences without "writing down" to children. Many of H.'s works contain plots strong enough to withstand becoming outdated. For example, *Rocket Ship Galileo,* published in 1947, tells of a trip to the moon. Years later, the book is still read with interest although the first (real) trip to the moon happened differently.

H.'s interests and talents exceeded writing for juveniles. His knowledge of every branch of science was near encyclopedic. He wrote nonfiction as well as fiction, and wanted his audience to include interested readers of all ages. He authored technical engineering reports, such as *Test Procedures for Plastic Materials Intended for Structural and Semi-Structural Aircraft Uses* (1944), contributed to the *Encyclopaedia Britannica,* and wrote over 150 stories for the *Saturday Evening Post, Analog, Galaxy,* and *Vertex,* in addition to his work for *Astounding Science Fiction.* Many of his works appeared under pseudonyms.

Some critics faulted H. for imposing his own beliefs, accused him of promoting fascism, and sending strong militaristic messages in his writings. H. argued that he encourages his readers to ask questions about life and to envision mankind's ability to see the future. *Space Cadet* (1948), *Farmer in the Sky* (1950), *Starman Jones* (1953), and *Tunnel in the Sky* (1955) are novels in which young protagonists mature into adulthood and include the conquest of space. H.'s popularity grew immensely during the 1950s when his work was introduced on television and in film. H.'s career took another turn in the late 1950s with the publication of *Starship Troopers* (1959). This novel initiated an exploration into future scientific changes and speculation about societal changes. Regardless of the criticism about H.'s representation of future societies, H. was catapulted into more intense fame. After publication of the classic, *Stranger in a Strange Land* (1961), the author became more controversial because it was perceived as a challenge to traditional ideas about religion and sex. In addition, H. was forced to build fences to keep from being harassed by his admirers. Many of his readers misunderstood the novel, thinking that H. was giving answers; the author felt the book's theme was to encourage readers to think for themselves, not for the author to give answers. Critics disagree on which works of H.'s are the best; however, the importance of his influence in the field of science fiction is recognized by all.

Fans of H. can find much personal information in *Requiem* (1992). Included in this volume are a biographical preface written by H.'s widow, many new works by H., and fourteen tributes to the author that include intriguing information about H., his life, and the relationships he formed with those giving tributes. Another biography of H. is written by his widow in *Grumbles from the Grave* (1989), a collection of correspondence between the author, his agent, and others.

AWARDS: World Science Fiction Convention's Guest of Honor in 1941, 1961, and 1976. Hugo Award, World Science Fiction Convention (1956)

for *Double Star,* (1960) for *Starship Troopers,* (1962) for *Stranger in a Strange Land,* and (1967) for *The Moon Is a Harsh Mistress.* Best all-time author, *Locus* magazine, 1973 and 1975. Science Fiction Writers of America, 1975. Inkspot Award, 1977. Distinguished Public Service Medal, National Aeronautics and Space Administration (NASA) posthumously (1988) "in recognition of his meritous service to the nation and mankind in advocating and promoting the exploration of space"

FURTHER WORKS: *Red Planet.* 1949. *Space Cadet.* 1948. *Between Planets.* 1951. *Methuselah's Children.* 1958. *Time Enough for Love: The Lives of Lazarus Long.* 1973. *The Cat Who Walks through Walls: A Comedy of Manners.* 1985. *To Sail beyond the Sunset: The Life and Loves of Maureen Johnson, Being the Memoirs of a Somewhat Irregular Lady.* 1987

BIBLIOGRAPHY: H., Robert A. with Virginia H. (ed.) *Grumbles from the Grave.* 1989. H., Robert with Kondo, Yoji (ed.) *Requiem: New Collected Works by Robert A. H. and Tributes to the Grand Master.* 1992

NANCY HORTON

HENKES, Kevin
Author, illustrator, b. 27 November 1960, Racine, Wisconsin

H.'s books provide children with accessible and appealing tales dramatizing the trials, tribulations and HUMOR involved in dealing with the ordinary emotions of childhood and its myriad interpersonal relationships.

During his own childhood, H. began to identify himself both as an artist and as a lover of books. Even as he became an independent reader, he made choices among the public library's collections based on favorite illustrators, including Garth WILLIAMS. His family, including several siblings, both supported his emerging self-image and provided the experiential grist for some of his future books. In high school, a teacher encouraged H. to develop his writing as well as his drawing; the two artistic expressions melded into a career choice when H. realized both talents are needed to create PICTURE BOOKS. After attending the University of Wisconsin in Madison for a year, he went to New York City, at nineteen, and signed a contract that began his successful career in children's publishing. His first book, *All Alone,* was published in 1981.

A Weekend with Wendell (1986), one of many picture books H. has populated with expressive mice, garnered the 1986 Children's Choice Award, sponsored by the CHILDREN'S BOOK COUNCIL and the INTERNATIONAL READING ASSOCIATION. *Chester's Way* (1988) was named an AMERICAN LIBRARY ASSOCIATION Notable Book of 1988. *Owen* (1993) was a 1994 ALA CALDECOTT MEDAL Honor Book and *Lilly's Purple Plastic Purse* (1996) earned the American Booksellers Book of the Year Award in 1997, as well as nomination as a favorite by several state reading associations. *Sun and Spoon* (1997), a novel for middle grade readers, was named an AMERICAN LIBRARY ASSOCIATION Notable Book of 1998.

H.'s early picture books featured human characters. In *Bailey Goes Camping* (1985), he offers viewers anthropomorphic mice, drawn in a style that seems deceptively simple. However, the elegant archness of the characters' facial expressions and accurately childlike physical activities come about through considerable reworking and attention to the details of lines and angles. By offering characters who are of no human ethnic group, H.'s books cut no child off from identifying with his protagonists.

H.'s picture-book plot lines devolve around issues both familiar and important to small children, including parental support, sibling rivalry, and expectations about school. *Chester* is the tale of how friendship is understood and explored by preschool-aged children. In *Julius, the Baby of the World* (1990), the introduction of a new baby into the family upsets his sister, Lilly. Her reactions to the attentions Julius reaps from family and friends are both credible and insightful, allowing both child and parent readers to view or remember their own similar circumstances with fresh humor.

One of H.'s most commercially popular picture books has been *Lilly's Purple Plastic Purse,* featuring the jealous sister of Julius. Here, Lilly must contend with the damage she does to her relationship with her teacher when she becomes impatient about showing off her new purse. The popularity of the book was augmented in the years immediately following its release by the production of Lilly dolls, child-sized purple plastic purses and even a stage version of the tale.

H.'s colorfully painted ILLUSTRATIONS delight because they are comical, but they also expand the emotional depth of his stories. A few of his picture book stories, including *Good-bye, Curtis* (1995, illustrated by Marisabina RUSSO) and *Circle Dogs* (1998, illustrated by Dan Yaccarino), have borne the work of other illustrators, demonstrating the strength of H.'s narrative even when visually conceived by another.

In his novels for middle grade readers, H. continues to work with the themes of children's emotions and family dynamics. *Two under Par* (1987) explores the emotional rough waters a child can experience when he becomes part of a blended family. *The Zebra Wall* (1988), like *Julius, the Baby of the World,* presents a situation in which a girl becomes an older sister. Here, however, it is having to share her room with a visiting relative that presages the protagonist's sense of losing her place in the family. Like Lilly in *Julius,* however, she comes to terms with how life has changed, and comes to see that the change isn't necessarily for the worse.

Other issues facing H.'s characters are sisterly devotion *(Sheila Rae, the Brave,* 1987), displeasure with a given name *(Chrysanthemum,* 1991), a grandparent's DEATH *(Sun and Spoon,* 1997), and forgiveness *(The Birthday Room,* 1999). H.'s talent, according to both critics and his young readers, is for giving common emotions credible and revealing contexts in which they become both clarified and are shown to be manageable.

FURTHER WORKS: *Clean Enough,* 1982; *Shhhh,* 1989; *Words of Stone,* 1992; *Protecting Marie,* 1995; *Biggest Boy,* 1995; *Wemberly Worried,* 2000

BIBLIOGRAPHY: *Sixth Book of Junior Authors and Illustrators,* 1989; *Something about the Author,* vol. 76, 1994; Silvey, Anita, ed., *Children's Books and Their Creators* 1995; Cooper, I., "Kevin H. [interview]," *Booklist,* Jan. 1997

FRANCISCA GOLDSMITH

HENRY, Marguerite
Author, b. 13 April 1902, Milwaukee, Wisconsin; d. 26 November 1997, Rancho Santa Fe, California

H. is among the most well-known writers of horse stories for children. She is the youngest of five children whose father owned a small publishing business. He read to his family frequently and provided early encouragement for H.'s writing career. She was only eleven when her first story was sold to a New York women's magazine, *Delineator*. She wrote throughout high school and during her two years at Milwaukee State Teachers College.

H. moved to Chicago where she did technical writing and published articles in journals, including *Forum* and *Nation's Business*. Between 1935 and 1939 H. wrote a series for the *Saturday Evening Post* entitled "Turning Points in the Lives of Famous Men." Little in these early years suggested that H. would turn to writing for children or about horses. Her first children's book, *Auno and Tauno* (1940), a fictionalized account of childhood in Finland, grew out of stories she heard from two Finnish household servants. This experience persuaded her that her true calling was writing for children, which is where she turned her efforts.

H. began writing INFORMATIONAL BOOKS for very young children, most notably two educational series, Pictured Geographies, for third- and fourth-graders, with books on such places as Alaska, AUSTRALIA, NEW ZEALAND, Latin America, and the West Indies. Both series enjoyed the distinction of being illustrated by Kurt WIESE. Two of her early biographies for older children were highly praised: *Robert Fulton, Boy Craftsman* (1945), *and Benjamin West and His Cat Grimalkin* (1947). Also at this time she wrote *Justin Morgan Had a Horse* (1945), a fictional account of the origin of the famed Morgan horses during and after the Revolutionary War. This was her first horse story and it earned H. her first NEWBERY MEDAL Honor citation. Its success encouraged H. to continue writing horse stories. To illustrate *Justin Morgan Had a Horse,* H. sought out Wesley Dennis whose work she had loved. Dennis was excited to illustrate H.'s book and this became the start of a long and happy collaboration.

Misty of Chincoteague (1947), one of her most popular books, brought her another Newbery Metal Honor citation. H. captures the thrill of the annual Pony Penning on Chincoteague Island, Virginia, when the wild ponies, who live on nearby Assateague Island, are driven across the shallow channel to be sold. This is the story, based largely on actual events, of two children

raising one of these wild ponies and her newborn foal. The foal, Misty, became a national celebrity; H. kept the filly at her Illinois home for several years.

H.'s next work, *King of the Wind* (1948), is the story of the Goldolphin Arabian, one of three progenitors of all modern thoroughbreds. Set in the early eighteenth century in Morocco, France, and finally England, this book required exhaustive research on H.'s part. And although the account is fictionalized, the fundamental facts are authentic. Praised for its vivid portrait of the period and its sensitive treatment of the characters, the book won the Newbery Medal. She continued to write ANIMAL STORIES, usually horse stories. Most notable were the several sequels to *Misty of Chincoteague,* including *Sea Star: Orphan of Chincoteague* (1949); *Misty, the Wonder Pony* (1956); *Stormy, Misty's Foal* (1963); and *Misty's Twilight* (1992), all of which were very popular.

H.'s horse stories are realistic, the horses are portrayed true to their animal nature, not anthropomorphized. Her human portraits are insightful, exciting scenes are created and atmosphere is authentically established. Perhaps a holdover for her days as a technical writer, her research was always painstakingly thorough and involved extensive travel, correspondence, and interviews with anyone who could enlighten her. Some critics find her style, at times, pedestrian and her tone occasionally sentimental, always a danger with animal stories, but her books are never preachy or maudlin, nor are they shallow. Many of H.'s works are enduringly popular with young readers, and her horse stories remain some of the finest ever written.

AWARDS: AMERICAN LIBRARY ASSOCIATION Newbery Medal (1949) for *King of the Wind.* ALA Newbery Medal Honor Book (1948) for *Misty of Chincoteague* and (1946) for *Justin Morgan Had a Horse.* Lewis CARROLL Shelf Award (1952) for *Misty of Chincoteague.* William Allen White Award (1956) for *Brighty of the Grand Canyon.* KERLAN Award, University of Minnesota (1975). Honorary Doctor of Letters, Hamilton College (1992)

FURTHER WORKS: *Album of Horses.* 1951. *Wagging Tails: An Album of Dogs.* 1955. *Cinnabar: The One O'Clock Fox.* 1956. *White Stallion of Lipizza.* 1964

BIBLIOGRAPHY: *Children's Literature Review.* vol. 4. 1982. *Dictionary of Literary Biography.* vol 22. 1983. *American Writers for Children: 1900–1960. Something about the Author,* vol. 100, 1999. Sutherland, Z. and M. H. Arbuthnot, *Children and Books,* 7th ed. 1986. Miller, Bertha Mahoney an Elinor Whitney Field, *Newbery Medal Books: 1922–1955 Acceptance Speeches*

DAVID L. RUSSELL

HENSTRA, Friso

Artist, illustrator, b. 9 February 1928, Amsterdam, Netherlands

H. was born and grew up in Amsterdam, a site of conflict during World War II. H.'s memories of the war influenced his style of art, which is often noted for its unconventional and grotesque images. His early work included comic strips, pictures for children's MAGAZINES, and ILLUSTRATIONS for books. In 1968, H. began collaborating with author Jay WILLIAMS, whose works often feature violent and disturbing subject matter. H.'s illustrations for Williams's *The Practical Princess and Other Liberating FAIRY TALES* (1978) received the Golden Apple Prize at the Bratislava Illustration Biennial in Czechoslovakia. H. has also written some books of his own, including *Wait and See, Mighty Mizzling Mouse* (1983), and *Mighty Mizzling Mouse and the Red Cabbage House* (1984).

FURTHER WORKS: Illustrations for books by Jay Williams: *The Round Sultan and the Straight Answer* (1970), *Stupid Marco* (1970), *Petronella* (1973), *The Little Spotted Fish, Space Cats* (Steven KROLL. author 1979). *Pig and Bear* (Vit Horejs. 1989). *Pedro and the Padre.* Verna AARDEMA. 1991), *The Last Snow Winter* (by Tony JOHNSTON, 1993)

BIBLIOGRAPHY: *Something about the Author,* vol. 73, 1993

MARY ARIAIL BROUGHTON

HENTOFF, Nat

Author, jazz critic, social activist, b. 10 June 1925, Boston, Massachusetts

As an undergraduate, H. edited the school newspaper; when it was censored his lifelong interest in First Amendment issues was born. While some literary critics find H.'s messages outstrip his STORYTELLING, they are impressed with the even-

handedness with which he presents characters along the political spectrum.

Graduating from Northeastern University (1946), H. pursued graduate studies in literature and Constitutional law at Harvard University and the Sorbonne. After a brief career as a radio producer and announcer, he began editing and writing for adult periodicals.

H.'s love of jazz, interest in civil liberties, and devotion to literature meld in his writing for children. *Jazz Country* (1965), written under the mentorship of Ursula Nordstrom, editor at Harper Publishers, portrays a young white musician's efforts to succeed in the jazz scene. *I'm Really Dragged but Nothing Gets Me Down* (1968) concerns compulsory military service. *The Day They Came to Arrest the Book* (1982) examines censorship. H.'s work has been the object of community-based challenges although he includes characters who provide well-considered reasons for their actions.

H. writes nonfiction for children. *Journey into Jazz* (1968) is a history of the black musicians who developed this American art form. *The First Freedom: The Tumultuous History of Free Speech in America* (1980) offers a readable account of CENSORSHIP.

H.'s adult books are concerned with jazz, social, and educational reform. H. has taught at several colleges, including New York University and New School for Social Research; he writes for the *Village Voice,* a liberal newspaper.

FURTHER WORKS: *Does This School Have Capital Punishment?* 1981. *American Heroes: In and Out of School.* 1987

BIBLIOGRAPHY: *Contemporary Authors, New Revision Series.* 1989 *Something about the Author.* vol. 69, 1992

FRANCISCA GOLDSMITH

HENTY, G. A.

Author, b. 8 December 1832, Trumpington, near Cambridge, England; d. 16 November 1902, Weymouth Harbor, Dorset, England

H. was born the son of a stockbroker–mine owner and became the author of some 80 popular, late-19th century adventures stories for boys. H. was a sickly boy and spent much of his childhood in bed where he read a great deal. He read natural history and took a special interest in poetry. H. attended Westminster School at age fourteen and learned boxing and wrestling as self-defense. H.

attended Cambridge University to read Classics. He also rowed and took training from professional boxers and wrestlers. H. left Cambridge after one year to work in his father's Welsh mine but returned to Cambridge and then left again when the Crimean War broke out. While in the war, H. wrote interesting letters home. His father took his letters to a daily newspaper and suggested that his son become their correspondent. The newspaper staff agreed and while H. remained in the army for five more years, he polished his skills as a journalist. In 1866, H. covered the Austro–Italian War as a correspondent. He wrote a series of dispatches as well as an adult novel. In 1870–71, H. reported on the Franco–Prussian War.

H. wanted to write more books for adults but his publisher urged him to write for a young audience. The first children's book was *Out on the Pampas; or, the Young Settlers* (1871) and the second *The Young Franc-Tireurs* (1872). H. continued as a correspondent in Russia, AFRICA, Spain, India, and the Balkans. After the Turkish–Serbian War of 1876, he came home exhausted and remained in England, except for one visit to the United States. In 1880, H. published *The Young Buglers: A Tale of the Peninsular War* and in 1881 he published *The Cornet of Horse: A Tale of Marlborough's Wars.* By this time he had worked out his formula: he ordered numerous reference books from the library and would write or dictate his own story with the reference books spread open in front of him.

H.'s writing gained prestige and his productivity increased. By 1886, he was producing four books a year. In 1880, he assumed editorship of a boys' newspaper called *Union Jack.* He moved to *Boys' Own* magazine when the first newspaper collapsed and collaborated on *Camps and Quarters,* which was produced annually. H. became the dominant figure in boys' fiction in the last two decades of the 1800s. There are several G. A. H. fan clubs. Approximately 30 million copies of his books have been sold across the English–speaking world.

H.'s formula centered on a boy of fifteen or sixteen years, physically fit, good-hearted and hot-headed. He would put the boy near a great historical moment, an insurrection, or a war. The experience allows the boy to rise to maturity,

show his intelligence and his good heart, and to conquer the situation. H. made a sizable income from his fast-paced adventure stories. His writing shows unabashed pride in late Victorian imperialism. He later began his books with a letter to readers "My Dear Lads" and drew attention to the heroic exploits within the story to follow. They helped to create the British Empire.

FURTHER WORKS (SELECT): *Facing Death: The Hero of the Vaughan Pit* (1883); *With Clive in India* (1884); *The Cat of Bubastes* (1889); *Beric the Briton* (1893); *A Soldier's Daughter* (1906).

BIBLIOGRAPHY: Arnold, Guy, *Held Fast for England,* 1979; Doyle, Brian, ed. *The Who's Who of Children's Literature,* 1968; Hunt, Peter, ed., *Children's Literature: An Illustrated History,* 1995; *The Oxford Companion to Children's Literature,* 1985

BERNICE E. CULLINAN

HERGÉ, (pseud. Georges Remi)

Belgian cartoonist, author, illustrator, b. 1907, Brussels, Belgium; d. ca. March 1983, Brussels, Belgium

H., who was born Georges Remi but always used the pseudonym of "Hergé," was born in Brussels, Belgium where he lived throughout his life. He devised the pseudonym of H. by inverting his initials to R.G.

H.'s began his career writing and illustrating comics. He is best known for his COMIC BOOK hero Tintin, a boy reporter who traveled throughout the world accompanied by his faithful dog Milou. Tintin's adventures included trips to the moon before Neil Armstrong, and outsmarting gunslingers and corrupt politicians and the nefarious Al Capone. Tintin first appeared in French in the January 10, 1929, edition of *Le Petit Vingtieme.* Twenty-three books featuring his famous Tintin character and seventy million copies of comics in thirty-two different languages are in print.

H.'s writing process required close attention to detail. Each Tintin book required months of study to guarantee authenticity. The background of each story and items that might appear in the story were meticulously researched by H.'s staff. H. himself was involved in the research process; he once embarked on a cargo boat voyage in order to assure the accuracy of detail when writing a Tintin adventure that was to take place on a similar cargo boat. H.'s writings are remarkably accurate due to his extensive research and eye for detail. Chang, a character rescued from the Yangtze River by Tintin, who first appeared in the *The Blue Lotus* (1935), was based on H.'s friendship with Chinese artist Chang Chong-Jen. The artist urged H. to avoid racial stereotypes and influenced his use of traditional Chinese pen and ink drawings in preparing his comic strip art. Chang appeared again in *Tintin in Tibet* (1960).

Some of H.'s Tintin books that were titled in English include: *Tintin in Tibet* (1965), *Flight 714* (1968), and *Tintin and the Picaros* (1975).

FURTHER WORKS: *The Land of the Black Gold,* 1972; *Tintin and the Broken Ear,* 1975; *Tintin and the Golden Fleece,* 1965

BIBLIOGRAPHY: *Something about the Author,* vol. 32, 1983

MICHAEL O'LAUGHLIN

HERMES, Patricia
Author, b. 21 February 1936, Brooklyn, New York

H., author of INFORMATION BOOKS, BIOGRAPHIES, and novels for middle-grade readers, writes about herself, "I spy on children, watching how they act, listening to their words, learning about their concerns and struggles and dreams." These are the hallmarks of H.'s books for children. H. remembers her own childhood vividly, and as the mother of five children and a former English teacher, knows the lives of children intimately. She knows that childhood is not always the paradise adults like to believe that it is. Children have very real problems: difficult relationships, the death of a parent or a sibling; conditions like epilepsy, which she struggled with as a child. But children also do eat dead flies and put snakes in brothers' beds, and so there are lighter moments in her realistic stories as well.

FURTHER WORKS: *Kevin Corbett Eats Flies,* 1986; *Heads, I Win,* 1989; *Mama, Let's Dance,* 1991; *Nothing but Trouble, Trouble, Trouble,* 1995

BIBLIOGRAPHY: Harcourt Brace Publisher's biographical pamphlet. *Something about the Author,* vol. 31, 1983, and vol. 78, 1994. THE KERLAN COLLECTION vertical files

REBECCA RAPPORT

HERRIOT, James (Alfred Wright)
Author, veterinarian, b. 3 October 1916, Sunderland County, Tyne and Werr, England; d. 23 February 1995, Yorkshire, England

With the publication of *All Creatures Great and Small* in 1973 and *All Things Bright and Beautiful* in 1974, H. became famous in England and the United States. Readers and critics appreciated the pleasure found in his work; they laughed at his humorous anecdotes and delighted in his vivid description of the local countryside. *All Creatures Great and Small* was dramatized on television in 1975, and in 1978 the BBC produced it as a TV series that was later shown on PBS in 1979; it was adapted as a musical on the BBC in 1979.

Beginning in 1984, to the delight of children and adults, H. transformed some of his most endearing tales into PICTURE BOOKS such as *Moses, the Kitten* (1984). Although these stories are short and uncomplicated, their emotional content is vintage H. They exude love, HUMOR, and often tears.

H. was reared in a small village near Glasgow. He spent much of his childhood walking and camping in the Highlands. Early on he developed a love of animals, reading, and the countryside. At age thirteen he decided to become a veterinarian. On completing his training he planned to work in the city, but it was the Depression and he took a position as a vet's assistant in northern Yorkshire and loved it. For years he told his family anecdotes about his experiences; they finally encouraged him to write them down. When he became a professional writer, he took a pseudonym since he did not want his new vocation to weaken his credibility as a vet. His first books, *If Only They Could Talk* (1970) and *It Shouldn't Happen to a Vet* (1972) sold fewer than 1,200 copies, but *All Creatures Great and Small* (1973) and *All Creatures Bright and Beautiful* (1974) were best-sellers. In 1992 his final work, *Every Living Thing,* was published.

FURTHER WORKS: *James Herriot's Dog Stories,* 1986; *James Herriot's Cat Stories,* 1994; *Blossom Comes Home,* 1988; *The Market Square Dog,* 1990; *Oscar, Cat about Town,* 1993

BIBLIOGRAPHY: Silvey, Anita, ed., *Children's Books and Their Creators,* 1995; *Something about the Author,* vol. 44, 1986 and vol. 86, 1996

JUDY LIPSITT

HESSE, Karen
Author, b. 29 August 1952, Baltimore, Maryland

H. grew up in Baltimore, Maryland, where she suffered through an often lonely childhood. Born prematurely, H. was ill frequently as a young girl and felt quite alone although she had an older brother and several neighborhood friends. Because she was often ill, she was, by her own admission, often whiny. Her mother created a system where H. got a gold star on days she was not whiny; those days were few and far between H. read a lot as a child, often reading her favorites over and over again. She recalls reading John Hersey's *Hiroshima* (1946) and the effect it had on her. The book changed her life and her reading habits and convinced her that writers for young people should address crucial issues of the times. H. believes that if more books for children that dealt with real issues had existed when she was a child, her own loneliness may have been less greatly felt. H. states that she wants to help children through hard times; she presents characters who survive difficult ordeals and grow as a result of them.

H. attended Towson State University and received a B.A. from the University of Maryland in 1975. During her college years, H. began writing poetry and has continued to write in that genre, winning AWARDS from *Writer's Digest* and the Poetry Society of Vermont. The majority of H.'s work can be categorized as realistic and historical fiction novels although she writes POETRY as well. Her books are memorable for strong characterization and an unforgettable sense of place. After writing several novels, H. returned to writing poetry in *Out of the Dust* (1997), a novel set during the Oklahoma dust bowl in 1934, written entirely in free verse. H. felt that the story demanded a style that uses an economy of words, captures the fragility of life, the hard work of farming, and the grimness of conditions during the dust bowl. The sensual writing leads readers to feel the taste of dust in their mouths. H. says the book took her back to her human roots. *Phoenix Rising* (1994) shows a strong love of the land

and a profound respect for it. *The Music of Dolphins* (1996) reveals her willingness to take chances. *Letters from Rifka* (1992) and *Poppy's Chair* (1993) reflect her Jewish heritage and love of family. Family is important in all of H.'s books just as it is in her own life. H.'s undeniable measure of emotional integrity shows in her work. Her characters live courageously and say valiant things in simple words. Their strength tears at readers' heartstrings. They know that they will inevitably go down under life's pressures if they do not stand up for themselves.

H. genuinely enjoys the hard work that writing entails and the months she spends researching in order to feel confident about what she is writing. H. works with other authors, sharing each others' work and acting as critical readers for one another. H. writes "for children like the child I was, to show young readers that they are not alone in this world."

AWARDS: ALA NEWBERY MEDAL (1998) for *Out of the Dust.* National Jewish Book Award (1993), Sydney TAYLOR Book Award (1992), and Christopher Medal (1993) for *Letters from Rifka*

FURTHER WORKS: *Wish on a Unicorn,* 1991; *Lavender,* 1993; *Sable,* 1994; *A Time of Angels,* 1995; *Come on, Rain,* 1997; *A Light in the Storm,* 1999

BIBLIOGRAPHY: Bowen, Brenda. "Karen H." The *Horn Book* magazine. vol. 74, no. 4, pp. 428–32. 1998. H., Karen. "Newbery Medal Acceptance Speech." The *Horn Book* magazine. vol. 74, no. 4, pp. 422–27. 1998. *Something about the Author,* vol. 25, 1998

MICHAEL O'LAUGHLIN

HEST, Amy
Author, b. 1950, New York City

Growing up in a suburb about an hour away from New York afforded H. the advantage of spending a lot of time in the city. Those city adventures influenced H. a great deal. By the time she was seven years old, she knew she would someday call New York City her home. After graduating from library school H. moved to the Upper East Side, fulfilling her childhood dream. H. did not start her career as a writer. After graduation from college H. worked as a librarian and in the children's department of several publishing companies before she began to write.

Many of H.'s stories take place in New York City and involve depictions of different family and friend relationships. *The Purple Coat* (1986), which describes a little girl and her mother's trip to the tailor, was featured on *READING RAINBOW* in 1988. *Jamaica Louise James* (1996), an intergenerational story about the loving bonds between a girl and her grandmother, takes place in a New York City–subway station. H. uses her own children's names for the main characters in many of her books. In her first published book entitled *Maybe Next Year* (1982), the main character is named Kate, after her own daughter.

H. not only tells the stories of typical nuclear and extended family relationships but also tells stories about different kinds of family and friendships. In *Where in the World Is the Perfect Family?* (1989) H. tells the story of young Cornie who is trying to come to terms with the shifting dynamics of her divorced family as her stepmother is about to have a new baby. The story of two friends who have to say goodbye to one another because one is moving away is explored in H.'s *The Best-Ever Good-bye Party* (1989).

A series of PICTURE BOOKS about Baby Duck explore events that loom as crises in young children's lives and show how loving family members unite to help young readers learn coping skills. H. explores topics such as the need to wear glasses in *Baby Duck and the Bad Eyeglases* (1996) and jealousy of a new new sibling in *You're the Boss, Baby Duck* (1997).

In *When Jessie Came across the Sea* (P. J. LYNCH, illus, 1997), winner of the KATE GREENAWAY MEDAL, H. shows the loving strength of family relationships over time and across oceans. When Jessie is chosen by the Rabbi in her village in Eastern Europe to come to America she has to leave her grandmother and all she loves. Jessie's tale reflects those of many young women who immigrated to America; it is a tale of hope and courage.

H. has been involved with children's books in one capacity or another since she graduated from college. During her time as a librarian and while working in publishing houses, H. dreamed of writing her own books but lacked confidence in her writing abilities. She did, however, know that she was a good observer of life and because of her keen skills of observation discovered she had

many stories to tell. Once she finally began to write, she has had no trouble finding topics to write about.

AWARDS: Kate Greenaway Medal, IBBY Award Honor Book, Parents' Choice Gold Award, Christopher Award, Sydney TAYLOR Award, Notable Children's Trade Book in the Field of Social Studies, and INTERNATIONAL READING ASSOCIATION Notable Book for a Global Society (1998) for *When Jessie Came across the Sea*. Christopher Award (1987) for *The Purple Coat*. AMERICAN LIBRARY ASSOCIATION Notable Children's Book and Child Study Association Children's Books of the Year (1986) for *Pete and Lily*

FURTHER WORKS: *Pete and Lily*. 1986. *Nana's Birthday Party*. 1993. *Party on Ice*. 1995. *In the Rain with Baby Duck*. 1995. *The Private Notebook of Katie Roberts, Age 11*. 1995. *How to Get Famous in Brooklyn*. 1994. *Rosie's Fishing Trip*. 1994. *Love You, Soldier*. 1991

BIBLIOGRAPHY: *Something about the Author,* vol. 82, 1995

MICHAEL O'LAUGHLIN

HEWITT, Kathryn

Illustrator, b. 24 May 1951, Santa Monica, California

A lifelong lover of art and books, H. decided to become a painter at the age of nine after watching a film biography about Toulouse-Lautrec. H. usually has live models pose for her ILLUSTRATIONS, which include works done in watercolor, gouache, colored pencil, and oil. H.'s oil paintings in *Flower Garden* (Eve BUNTING, 1994) portrays the excitement of urban gardening in a window box. In *Sunflower House* (Bunting, 1996), H. uses watercolor and colored pencils to capture the cheerful rhyming text. H. is best known for her caricature-style portraits that include humorous visual details and for a series of collective BIOGRAPHIES written by Kathleen KRULL beginning with *Lives of the Musicians: Good Times Bad Times (And What the Neighbors Thought)* (1993).

FURTHER WORKS: *King Midas and the Golden Touch*. 1986. *Lives of the Writers: Comedies, Tragedies (And What the Neighbors Thought)*. (Kathleen Krull). 1994. *Lives of the Artists: Masterpieces. Messes (And What the Neighbors Thought)*. (Kathleen Krull). 1995. *Sunflower House*. (Eve Bunting). 1996. *Marguerite Makes a Book*. (Bruce Robertson et al.). 1999

BIBLIOGRAPHY: Publisher's notes; "Marguerite Makes a Book: A Conversation with Illustrator Kathryn Hewitt."; http:I/www.geffy.edu/publications/titles/marg/ga.html

DENISE E. AGOSTO

HICKMAN, Janet (Gephart)
Author, b. 8 July 1940, Kilbourne, Ohio

H. was an avid reader who began writing in elementary school and high school. She attended Ohio State University where she earned a B.Sc, M.A., and Ph.D. She began publishing short stories in magazines very early. H. became a teacher who taught her students to write and did her own writing along with them. H. states, "When I was little, the stories that interested me were not the ones my parents read to me but the real-life ones I overheard in my grandparents' kitchen or on the front porch where personal crises and world disasters were discussed by great aunts and uncles, older cousins, and assorted friends and neighbors. In Kilbourne, the tiny Ohio town where I grew up, extended families kept in touch. The past survived very close to the present and I spent a lot of time listening to people talk. What I kept from that time in my childhood is a close allegiance to family, a sense of connections to other generations, and an ear for the language of everyday speech."

H. draws upon FAMILY STORIES, childhood memories, and characters from her village in the historical novels that she writes. *Susannah* (1998) is a fourteen-year-old girl who does not want to live in the Shaker community that her father joins after her mother's death. In *Jericho: A Novel* (1994), great-grandmother Grand Min and twelve-year-old Angela, her great granddaughter, view the world from different points of view. Grand Min does not easily recall recent events but she remembers events from fifty years ago with great clarity. *Zoar Blue* (1978), set during the Civil War, centers on two young Separatists who disobey their communities' strictures about war. *The Stones* (1976), set during World War II, focuses on children's fear that a village recluse is really Adolf Hitler hiding out in their village. *The Valley of the Shadow* (1974), based on historical diaries and documents, involves the massacre of the Moravian Indian tribes during the Revolutionary War.

H. has received numerous AWARDS for her novels including the Ohioana Award (1979) and (1995) and the Midland Author Award (1995). H. is a past president of the Children's Literature Assembly. She currently serves as professor of children's literature at Ohio State University, works actively in professional organizations, and co-chairs the annual children's literature conference at Ohio State each year.

FURTHER WORKS: *Thunder Pup,* 1980

BIBLIOGRAPHY: Hickman, J., and B. Cullinan, eds., *Children's Literature in the Classroom: Weaving Charlotte's Web,* 1989; Huck, C. S., S. Hepler, J. Hickman, and B. Z. Kiefer, *Children's Literature in the Elementary School,* Sixth Edition, 1997

BERNICE E. CULLINAN

HIGH INTEREST–EASY READING BOOK SERIES

Increasingly, reading educators are coming to appreciate fully the enormous importance of students doing a substantial amount of reading. The motivation for encouraging wide reading may be to build students' automaticity in recognizing words, to get students in the habit of reading, to build students' vocabulary and background knowledge, or simply to follow the commonsense notion that in order to get better at almost anything you have to practice it a lot. Whatever the reason, the interest in providing students with readable, enticing, and enjoyable reading material is keen. As Richard Allington (1977) remarked after observing that students in remedial reading classes do very little reading, "If they don't read much, how they ever gonna get good?" The answer, of course, is that they are not. High interest–easy reading series, or "high-lows" as they are often called, can provide substantial amounts of reading material for students who read less well than their age mates and who have difficulty reading materials written for their age level.

The genre of high interest–easy reading book series was created specifically for such students. It consists of sets of books on related topics and themes, similarly packaged, advertised, and sold as sets. The vast majority of these SERIES fall into four categories: original fiction, simplified classics, self-help/teenage problems or concerns, and other nonfiction. The nature of the first two categories is obvious. The third category includes a burgeoning array of titles dealing with problem issues such as coping with divorce, and a host of health-related topics. The last category includes all other nonfiction.

One sample series, Cover-to-Cover Novels (1966–98), consists of twenty original fiction ADVENTURE STORIES written at the second- to third-grade level and intended for students in grades four to eight. In *Don't Bug Me,* for example, Zack moves to a new school and is teased about his father's pest control business until his expertise in pest control helps him outwit the class bully and lead his English group to an exciting presentation. This eighty-page paperback includes no supplementary material.

The Pacemaker Classic series (1967–99) includes sixty-two classic novels abridged and simplified for students reading at a third-to fourth-grade level, yet interesting to students in grades six to twelve. In *The Adventures of Tom Sawyer,* the reader follows Tom as he tricks his friends into painting Aunt Polly's fence, develops a crush on Becky Thatcher, and eventually confronts Injun Joe for the murder of Dr. Robinson. This paperback is seventy-six pages long and is available on an audiocassette.

The Need-to-Know Library (1992–99), a third series illustrative of the self-help genre, is comprised of ten sets of eight or nine books each, written at the fourth- to sixth-grade level and intended for students in grades seven to twelve. *Everything You Need to Know about Stepfamilies,* explores divorce, death, stepsiblings, and other topics related to the joining of two families. This hardcover book is sixty-three pages long, and includes a glossary, addresses for additional help, and recommendations for further reading.

The Living History Series (1998) consists of four nonfiction titles written at the second-to third-grade level and intended for students in grades two to seven. For example, *Lighthouse: Living in a Great Lakes Lighthouse, 1910 to 1940,* explores the lives of lighthouse keepers and their families. Also included in this thirty-two page hardcover are a glossary, internet sites, recommended books, and suggestions for places to write and visit.

High interest–easy reading books are not considered fine literature but do have a role to play for children who find reading a challenge. If such children are to become truly able readers—and voluntarily seek out reading for pleasure—they need a great deal of practice in reading. They need materials that they can read fluently, understand fully, learn from, and enjoy.

The genre could be improved in several ways. Research indicates that writing according to the dictates of readability formulae may actually make texts more difficult to read. The books in these series are obviously written to score low on readability formulas. This results in the constant use of short, choppy sentences that do not sound natural and fail to signal important information such as causal connections. It also results in stilted dialogue, most notably dialogue without any contractions. Further, the inappropriate use of words occurs when a more frequent, but not-quite-right word is substituted for the word that really fits the context.

Another way to make the books more enticing to reluctant readers is to print them without including instructional material in them. The ancillary material almost screams "remedial material!" at the readers. Many books listed as high interest–easy reading contain so much ancillary material that they could be classified as workbooks.

Finally, the books could be improved through their content. The fiction could be diverse, more complex, with more adultlike stories. Fiction should be as diverse as IRA/ALA annual lists of books for children and young adults. Nonfiction and self-help books need to address positive issues and avoid an overemphasis on negative topics. Reluctant readers have problems, but not all of them deal with negative issues. Areas such as history, BIOGRAPHY, the natural world, and the world of invention provide informative and exciting paths for less skilled readers to explore.

BIBLIOGRAPHY: Allington, R. L. "If They Don't Read Much, How They Ever Gonna Get Good?" *Journal of Reading,* 21, 57–61. 1977. Chambliss, M. J., and R. C. Calfee. *Textbooks for Learning: Nurturing Children's Minds.* 1998. Davidson, A., and G. M. Green. *Linguistic Complexity and Text Comprehension: Readability Issues Reconsidered.* 1988. Graves, M. F., and B.B. Graves. *Scaffolding Reading Experiences: Designs for Student Success.* 1994. Ryder, R. J., B.B. Graves and

M.F. Graves. *Easy Reading: Book Series and Periodicals for Less Able Readers* (2nd ed.). 1989

MICHAEL GRAVES AND RAYMOND A. PHILIPPOT

(See also SERIES BOOKS)

HIGHWATER, Jamake (pseud. J. Marks)
Author, b. 14 February 1942, Glacier County, Montana

H. was born in Montana to Jamie and Amanda Highwater. H.'s parents, Blackfoot Indians, unable to take care of him, placed him in an orphanage where he was adopted by Alexander and Marcia Marks, an Anglo couple from California. H.'s upbringing between the two different cultures played an important role in his early writing and has continued to be an integral aspect of H.'s style and content choice. His academic training was in music, the arts and as a music critic. H.'s early books include: *Rock and Other Four Letter Words: Music of the Electric Generation* and *Europe under Twenty-five: A Young People's Guide* (1968), which were written under the name of J. Marks or J. Marks-Highwater. After the NATIVE AMERICAN takeover of Alcatraz in 1969, H. began to work on his first book that bore the name of Jamake Highwater—*Fodor's Indian America: A Cultural and Travel Guide* (1975).

H.'s name change marked a change in subject matter with most of his subsequent writings having Native American concepts and themes. H.'s 1974 book entitled *Song from the Earth: North American Painting* was a Literary Guild Book Club selection. H.'s interest in American Indian culture does not stop with writing. *Anpao: An American Indian Odyssey* (1977), tells the legend of Anpao and his twin brother's search for their origin and destiny. It reflects Native American legends and religious beliefs, as well as interpretation of historical events.

H. lectures on world cultures and Native Americans in particular. H.'s philanthropic endeavors include serving as a consultant on American Indians to the New York State Council on the Arts, the President's Commission on Mental Health and the New York Arts Council's American Indian Community House.

H.'s educational background is a combination of anthropology, MUSIC, FOLKLORE and art in university and traditional Indian cultural training. He

talks little about specifics of his education and other personal aspects of his life saying that "they have no relationship to my writing." He also declines talking about some aspects of his personal life in order to protect the privacy of his adoptive family. H. has said that his adoptive sister and a grammar school teacher were influential in his becoming a writer and the human he is. H. continues to write books but also writes on music, dance, art, and theater for magazines and newspapers. He has been involved in television by both producing and appearing in several series for PBS.

AWARDS: ALA NEWBERY MEDAL Honor Book and AMERICAN LIBRARY ASSOCIATION Best Books for YOUNG ADULTS Award (1978) for *Anpao: An American Indian Odyssey*

FURTHER WORKS: *Ghost Horse Trilogy: Legend Days.* 1984. *I Wear the Morning Star.* 1985. *Myth of Our Own: Adventures in World Religions.* 1996. *Songs for the Seasons.* 1995

BIBLIOGRAPHY: *Something about the Author.* vol. 32, 1983 and vol. 69, 1992. Silvey, Anita, ed. *Children's Books and Their Creators* 1995

MICHAEL O'LAUGHLIN

HILDICK, E. W. (Edmund Wallace)
Author, b. 29 December 1925, Bradford, England

From the time he was fifteen years old, H. knew that he wanted to be a writer. H. credits his own schooling in mathematics and science for giving him the ability to be precise in his writing. He worked at several jobs upon completion of public school before entering a teacher training program at Leeds Training College. H. taught underprivileged boys for several years before leaving the profession in 1954 with the intention of becoming a full-time writer. Finding a void in juvenile fiction representing working class children, H. wrote his first children's novel, *Jim Starling* (1958). This book led to the creation of the Starling series, which ultimately numbered over seven books. H. would eventually write several other juvenile SERIES.

H.'s AWARDS include the 1968 International Hans Christian ANDERSEN Honor Book award for *Louie's Lot (1965),* which later became a series. *Lucky Les* was named an Austrian Children and Youth Book Prize Award honor book in 1976. He also was awarded the Edgar Allan Poe honor as well as the Mystery Writers of America award in 1979. Along with his work in juvenile series, including *The Ghost Squad* and *McGurk* FANTASY books, H. also wrote several adult works under the name of Wallace Hildick. Some of H.'s works including *Jim Starling,* were adapted for the British Broadcasting Corporation Radio.

H.'s characters have evolved throughout the years with his McGurk books changing from a mystery to fantasy series that featured lead characters traveling in a time machine. After making his own move from Britain to the United States, H. also wrote books specifically for American audiences including *Manhattan Is Missing* (1969) and *Top Boy at Twisters Creek* (1970). Throughout his career H. has "received consistent praise for his knowledge of young people—a knowledge exhibited in his characterizations of children as well as his understanding of what interests them." This knowledge has led to a string of successful books both in Britain and the United States.

FURTHER WORKS: *The Famous Father.* 1966. *The Memory Tap.* 1990. *The Top-Flight Fully-Automated Junior High School Girl Detective.* 1977. Louie Juvenile Series. 1968–78. Lemon Kelly Juvenile Series. 1963–68. Birdy Jones Juvenile Series. 1963–74

BIBLIOGRAPHY: *Something about the Author.* vol. 68, 1992

MICHAEL O'LAUGHLIN

HILL, Eric
Author, b. 7 September 1927, London, England

H. is best known for his lift-the-flap books featuring Spot, a friendly, curious puppy. The first Spot book, *Where's Spot?,* published in 1980, became an immediate best-seller. H. has since written dozens of other books about Spot, and the SERIES has sold more than 28 million copies. In addition, he has illustrated books for several other authors, including June Dutton, Helen Hoke, and Allan AHLBERG. Prior to his career as an author and illustrator, H. worked as a freelance cartoonist, an art director for an advertising agency, and a freelance artist.

In 1978, while H. was making movable flaps for an advertising project, he noticed that his two-year-old son, Christopher, enjoyed lifting the flaps to see what was underneath. H. decided to create a children's book with flaps, cartoonlike ILLUSTRATIONS, and simple text for his young son. He chose to feature dogs because he loves dogs and it is easy to draw something he loves. Within six months, *Where's Spot?* became the number one best-seller in London and H. gave up his freelance work to write full-time. *Spot's First Walk* (1981) set the theme for all subsequent Spot books. In all the books, H. maintains a natural progression of events that young children can understand. Titles such as *Spot's Birthday Party* (1982), *Spot's First Christmas* (1983), *Spot Learns to Count* (1983), and *Spot Goes to School* (1984) indicate the chronological advancement of children through their early years.

H.'s illustrations reflect his concern for making the book accessible and appealing to very young readers. Recalling the difficulty of reading books to his son with small print and complex illustrations, H. designs his books with the youngest readers in mind. He begins each drawing with a black pen outline, then colors in with watercolor inks. Dipping his brush into the bottle, he achieves a constant, almost flat color, sometimes adding depth with a wash. The flaps are drawn separately. Most pages contain one large object with an animal concealed behind its lift-up flap. The author believes that his simple, uncluttered style contributes to their enduring appeal to small children. Critics praise his style for its clearly delineated illustrations and good HUMOR.

Early in his career, H. captured the imagination and enthusiasm of an international audience. Spot books have been translated into more than 60 languages, including American Sign Language. When the book is translated, H.'s drawings remain unaltered, but he allows some flexibility in the TRANSLATION of the text to allow for cultural differences. He also uses different names for the dog in various countries, choosing names that seem most common for a puppy in that country. For example, in Portuguese, Spot becomes Bolinha; in Swedish, he is Tippen; in Welsh, he is Smot; and in Japanese, he is Korochan. In addition to the Spot series, H. has also written and illustrated a Peek-a-Book series and a Baby Bear Storybook series. Books in the Peek-a-Book series include *Nursery Rhymes* (1982), *Opposites* (1982), *Baby Animals* (1984), and *FAIRY TALES*

(1985). Books in the Baby Bear Storybook series include *At Home* (1983), *My Pets* (1983), *Baby Bear's Bedtime* (1984), and *Good Morning, Baby Bear* (1984). In addition, he has written and illustrated FAIRY TALES, concept books about colors and shapes, and mix-or-match interactive books.

FURTHER WORKS: Self-illustrated: *Puppy Love,* 1982; *Spot Tells the Time,* 1983; *Spot's Toys,* 1984; *Spot Goes to the Beach,* 1985; *Spot Looks at Colors,* 1986; *Spot Goes to the Farm,* 1987; *Spot's Big Book of Words,* 1988; *Spot Looks at Opposites,* 1989; *Spot Sleeps Over,* 1990; *Spot Goes to the Park,* 1991; *Spot Goes to a Party,* 1997; *Spot's Favorite Words,* 1997; *Spot's Favorite Baby Animals,* 1997; *Spot Visits His Grandparents,* 1999; *Goodnight Spot,* 1999. Illustrator: *Smorgasbord,* (June Dutton), 1970; *Hoke's Jokes,* (Helen Hoke), 1973; *Poorly Pig.* (Allan Ahlberg), 1982

BIBLIOGRAPHY: Frith, M. Interview with Eric Hill. The *Horn Book* magazine. 63, 577–85. 1987. *Something about the Author,* vol. 66, 1991; *Children's Literature Review,* vol. 13, 1987

MARY ARIAIL BROUGHTON

HIMLER, Ronald

Author, illustrator, b. 16 November 1937, Cleveland, Ohio

H. was reared in Cleveland, Ohio, where much of his youth was spent engaged in drawing. His love of drawing eventually led him to study painting at the Cleveland Institute of Art and finally to graduate school at the Cranbrook Academy of Art. H. also studied at New York University and Hunter College. He worked for many years as a commercial artist, which included a stint as a technical sculptor for General Motors, before studying art abroad. There his investigation of art in the world's major museums influenced his own work. H. works in several artistic media, including watercolor, oils, gouache, and pencil.

Although H. is known primarily as an illustrator, he also has written books for children including *Little Owl, Keeper of the Trees* (1974); it was awarded the New Jersey Institute of Technology award. He also wrote *The Girl on the Yellow Giraffe* (1976), which was favorably reviewed by *Booklist,* and *Wake up, Jeremiah* (1979) whose ILLUSTRATIONS were deemed "his best, most colorful performance to date" by the *New York Times* Book Review. Several of his illustrated works won recognition. He was on the Pick of the

Lists from the American Booksellers for *Nettie's Trip South* (Ann TURNER, 1987), *The Wall* (Eve BUNTING, 1990), *I'm Going to Pet a Worm Today* (Constance Levy, 1991), *Fly Away Home* (Eve BUNTING, 1991) and *Katie's Trunk* (Ann Turner, 1992).

H.'s recent works have included collaborations with Eve Bunting on *Fly Away Home* and *The Wall.* The books feature watercolors reflecting the somber subject of both stories, homelessness and the Vietnam War Memorial. H. has also worked extensively in the area of Western art. Many of his paintings have been featured in magazine articles and television programs dealing with Western history. In 1992 H. was awarded the silver medal from the Society of Illustrators for best Western painting in book cover art. H.'s illustrations, both for children and adults, continue to inspire and captivate through the fine use of detail and color.

FURTHER WORKS: *After the Goat Man.* (Betsy BYARS). 1982. *Dakota Dugout.* (Ann Turner). 1985. *The Best Town in the World.* (Byrd BAYLOR). 1986. *Someday a Tree.* 1993. *The Log Cabin Quilt.* (Ellen Howard). 1996. *Desert Trip.* (Barbara Steiner). 1996. *Train to Somewhere.* (Eve Bunting). 1996. *The Cheyennes.* (Virginia Driving Hawk SNEVE). 1996

BIBLIOGRAPHY: *Something about the Author,* vol. 92, 1997

MICHAEL O'LAUGHLIN

HINES, Anna Grossnickle

Author, b. 13 July 1946, Cincinnati, Ohio

H. decided to become a writer of children's books at an early age because of her love of both the text and illustrations in books she read. She was the daughter of a mathematician and the oldest of seven children, which helped to provide her with ideas for future stories. She was born in Ohio but moved to Southern California as a youngster and studied art at what is now California State University, Northridge. She eventually obtained her bachelor's degree in 1974 from Pacific Oaks College and in 1979 received her master's degree from the same institution.

H. says that she was discouraged from studying the art in PICTURE BOOKS as children's book illustrations were not considered a worthy topic for study. She disagreed saying, "to me, the art of the picture book, which can be held in the hands, carried about, taken to bed, is much more personal and intimate than the art which hangs in galleries or museums."

H.'s love of children's stories continued throughout her career as a preschool and elementary school teacher. Besides using books with her school children, she shared books with her own two children and never lost her love for fine IL-LUSTRATION and story. Initially H. considered moving into the realm of illustrator but soon discovered that she had many stories to tell. Her first book, *Taste the Raindrops,* was published in 1983 after which she became a full-time author and illustrator.

H. was on the Children's Book of the Year list in 1985 for *All by Myself.* She also won the Children's Choice Award for *Grandma Gets Grumpy* (1990) and the Outstanding Science Book for Children from the National Science Teachers Association for *Remember the Butterflies* (1991). Many other titles by H. have been included in several book clubs including the Junior Literary Guild.

H.'s goal of becoming a children's writer has come true with several published works including collaborative works. H. continues to write and work toward perfecting her style "to do her best to make the books better and better."

FURTHER WORKS: *Gramma's Walk,* 1993; *Big Help!,* 1995; *When the Goblins Came Knocking,* 1995; *When We Married Gary,* 1996; *Miss Emma's Wild Garden,* 1997

BIBLIOGRAPHY: *Sixth Book of Junior Authors and Illustrators,* 1989; *Something about the Author,* vol. 77, 1994

MICHAEL O'LAUGHLIN

HINTON, S(usan) E(loise)
Author, b. 22 July 1948, Tulsa, Oklahoma

H. became a writer as soon as she began reading. In the early years of her literary endeavors—from mid-elementary through junior high school—she worked on stories about horses and cowboys, without producing anything she felt the need to publish. However, during high school she began writing *The Outsiders* (1967), which she completed in four drafts. During the writing of this book, her father died, a biographical fact that some critics regard as significant to all of her novels. *The Outsiders* was accepted for publication while H. was still a teenager, and she used the proceeds from the sale to pay for her college education at the University of Tulsa (1970).

The Outsiders received the AMERICAN LIBRARY ASSOCIATION's Best YOUNG ADULT Books citation in 1975. *That Was Then, This Is Now* (1971) received the same citation in 1971. *Rumble Fish* (1975) earned H. the third such citation, in 1975, and *Tex* (1979) brought another Best Young Adult Books citation, in 1979. In 1988, H. was honored with ALA's first Young Adult Services Division Margaret A. Edwards Award for a body of work.

H's precocious social awareness and her desire to show the teen reality of the class struggle—rather than to accept and perpetuate the standard adult-approved FANTASY of teen life as fun and carefree—invested her first published novel with grittiness that shocked some parents, roused some critics, and brought respect and enthusiasm from her peers. Through the eyes of a sympathetic greaser, *The Outsiders* features gang warfare and the individual's struggle for survival, portraying the working class "greasers" attempting to hold their own and gain respect from the middle-class "socials." H. chose to publish this first title using her first and middle initials, to conceal from male readers her gender identity. This foil has served her well, although she now sees the original need as growing from her time period, the generation before girls and women were viewed as knowledgeable about activities beyond home and hearth.

The settings of H.'s novels are based on details of life in Tulsa, although readers throughout the United States are able to identify with the surroundings. *That Was Then, This Is Now* combines H.'s lifelong interest in horses with her hallmark theme of a central character's discovery of his unexpected parentage. In *Tex* and *Taming the Star Runner* (1988), H. places a horse within the story as a central figure and literary device. In contrast to her earlier novels, *Taming the Star Runner* presents the teenage male protagonist as developing a relationship with a girl (as well as with the horse). Yet, H. has not written a teen romance, for the plot here incorporates a budding friendship that moves through an erotic period to emerge as one from which romantic interest has passed.

Each of H.'s Young Adult novels is written from the viewpoint of an intelligent male teenager, and each involves violent events that are the outgrowths of social stratification, economic imbalances, and inattentive (or completely absent) parents. The protagonist survives by choosing to take decisive action at each story's denouement, encouraging some critics to claim that H.'s novels are too much alike in structure. However, English teachers and librarians find H.'s work to be an excellent bridge for students and teen readers who have outgrown children's books (in which they may never have been interested when younger) and yet lack both the literary sophistication and mature outlook to broach adult works. Many aliterate teens who are stimulated to read because of H.'s books celebrate her incisive presentation of teen life as they have experienced it, rather than as the misremembered time of ease found in other novels for the age and interest group. H.'s characters transcend their own time and place because their emotions, not necessarily their situations, are realistic and readily identifiable by their reading peers.

Through the years and all of her novels, H. has not lost her sensitivity to and understanding of the issues with which teenagers grapple during high school. Her character-driven novels do not rely on period scenery or fads and thus gain new readers with each generation. Her audience has been expanded by the production of most of her novels as major motion pictures. Unlike many novelists, she was given the opportunity to provide on-the-set input in both the scripting and the casting of these films, working with directors like Francis Ford Coppola. *Rumble Fish* (Universal Pictures, 1983) utilizes the dialogue just as H. wrote it in her novel.

In recent years, H. has turned to writing for younger audiences. *The Puppy Sister* (1995) is a fantasy once again invested with emotional realism. Intended for early elementary readers, the story addresses a single-child family's desire for a second child. When they receive a puppy, she responds to that desire by slowly metamorphosizing into the little sister. The problems this fantastic change entail, including what the neighbors will think and what sort of medical advice to seek, become intrinsic to the plot's unfolding. For even younger children, *Big David, Little David*

(1994) explores a preschooler's confusion when faced by a peer who has the same name as his own father.

H.'s realism has become a tradition continued by other contemporary YA fiction writers. Some literary historians credit H. with beginning a new and important chapter in juvenile publishing, a few going even so far as to date the "YA novel" as a genre emerging with the appearance of *The Outsiders.*

BIBLIOGRAPHY: *Contemporary Authors, New Revision Series,* 1998. *Contemporary Literary Criticism,* 1999; Daly, J., *Presenting S. E. H.,* 1987; *Something about the Author,* vol. 58, 1990

FRANCISCA GOLDSMITH

HIRSCHI, Ron
Author, b. 18 May 1948, Bremerton, Washington

Children's author H. spent much of his youth outdoors investigating animals and their environments. This experience led him to pursue an education leading to graduate research in wildlife ecology. Along the way, H. worked as wildlife biologist and counselor in a NATIVE AMERICAN education program. When he was a student at the University of Washington, he and his family would often escape to the outdoors; those experiences were often the inspiration for stories that H. would create and tell his daughter. Later, H.'s work as a wildlife biologist often required investigation and writing. These school and work-related experiences proved helpful when H. created his first published work, *Headgear* (1986), a nonfiction piece about horns and antlers.

H. eventually created the Where Animals Live SERIES based on books he wrote for adults. His prose style was praised in the *Horn Book* as being "brief and expressive" while appealing to his young audience. H. has authored several other series for children in addition to the Where Animals Live series, including Discover My World, and How Animals Live. H.'s *Headgear* (1986) and *One Day on Pike's Peak* (1986) were each chosen as Children's Books of the Year by the Child Study Association in 1986. *Headgear* also won the Outstanding Science Trade Book for Children from the National Science Teachers Association in 1986. That same award was given to H. in 1987 for *City Geese* (1987), *Who Lives in . . . the Forest?* (1987), and *What Is a Bird?* (1987).

As in his youth H. still loves spending time in the mountains and at the beach. His job as a children's author affords him the opportunity to do just that. Because his books require a great deal of research, H. spends time traveling all over the country to investigate his topics. Although he still writes some fiction, his main focus is on nonfiction, which allows him communicate to children the need for all of us to become engaged with the animals and the land with which we coexist.

FURTHER WORKS: *People of Salmon and Cedar.* 1995. *When the Wolves Return.* 1995. *Dance with Me.* 1995. *Seya's Song.* 1992. *Loon Lake.* 1991. *Faces in the Mountains.* 1997. *Save Our Wetlands.* 1994. *Where Are My Puffins, Whales, and Seals?* 1992. *A Time for Singing.* 1994

BIBLIOGRAPHY: *Something about the Author.* vol. 95, 1995. The *Horn Book* magazine. May–June 1987

MICHAEL O'LAUGHLIN

HOBAN, Lillian
Author, illustrator, b. 18 May 1925, Philadelphia, Pennsylvania; d. 17 July 1998, New York City

H. was born in Philadelphia and enjoyed a childhood steeped in the arts. She came from a family of readers and museum-goers and spent much of her time drawing and reading. At an early age H. decided she wanted to become an illustrator of children's books. She attended the Philadelphia High School for Girls and was awarded a scholarship to the Philadelphia Museum School of Art, which she attended from 1942 to 1944. After studying with Martha Graham she danced professionally on television in the 1950s and taught modern dance in New York and Connecticut.

H. was self-taught as an illustrator and did not begin writing stories until after she had her own children, her work inspired by their daily adventures. Some of her most renowned drawings and books dealt with the difficulties of early childhood. H. is best known for her ILLUSTRATIONS in the PICTURE BOOK series by Russell HOBAN about the badger, Frances, very much a humanlike child who needs her parents' reassurance when she is jealous of her little sister, finds it difficult to share, and learns how to have a best friend. H. dealt with childhood traumas and everyday dilemmas with candor and HUMOR; her illustrations

are characterized by cheerful, rotund pencil-drawn figures in soft pastel colors. In 1972, she published the first Authur book, *Arthur's Christmas Cookies,* which was included in the Harper-Collins I Can Read series depicting the joys and concerns of early childhood. The series features Arthur, a chimpanzee. It was the first book that she wrote and illustrated by herself. The last book in the series, *Arthur's Birthday Party,* was published early in 1999, a few months after her death. Other self-illustrated books include *Stick-in-the-Mud Turtle* (1977), *The Case of the Two Masked Robbers* (1985), and *Silly Tilly and the Easter Bunny* (1987).

Two of H.'s most popular books that H. illustrated for Russell Hoban won AWARDS. *Charlie the Tramp* (1967) won the Boys Club Award and *Emmet Otter's Jug Band Christmas* (1971) won the Lewis CARROLL Shelf Award and the Christopher Award, Children's Book Category in 1972. H. was active in the National Arts Club creative writing program, in which she encouraged children to read and write. Most of her illustrations were done in pencil, which she used to illustrate several of the Frances books, or in pen and ink wash. In addition to illustrating books for Russell Hoban, she collaborated with Meindert DEJONG, Miriam COHEN, Johanna HURWITZ, Marjorie Weinman SHARMAT, Louise Borden, Tony JOHNSTON, and daughter Julia Hoban. She illustrated over one hundred books in her career.

FURTHER WORKS: Written by Russell Hoban: *Herman the Loser.* 1961. *Bread and Jam for Frances.* 1964. *Will I Have a Friend?* (Miriam Cohen). 1967. *See You in Second Grade!* (Cohen). 1989. *The Big Seed.* (Ellen Howard). 1993

BIBLIOGRAPHY: Children's book illustrator, author, Lillian H., at 73. Associated Press obituary. Lillian H. 1925–98. *Publishers Weekly.* 245, 31, p. 22. *Something about the Author.* vol. 69, 1992, and vol. 104, 1999; http://www.bergenrecord.com/obits/obhoban19980803e.htm (accessed September 26, 1999)

MARY ARIAIL BROUGHTON

HOBAN, Russell
Author, b. 4 February 1925, Lansdale, Pennsylvania

H. was good at drawing and writing when he was a child. His parents encouraged him, especially

371

in the area of art, thinking he had the potential to become a great painter. H. eventually became an illustrator but still found the freedom of expression that he sought in the area of writing. H. attended the Philadelphia Museum School of Industrial Art before becoming an illustrator for both magazines and an advertising studio. He also worked as a television art director as well as an art instructor and copywriter. H. began writing for children and adults in the late 1960s.

H. is the author of over sixty books, most of which have been for children. His writing has been praised for offering characters that children can relate to and adults can understand. H.'s characters, including Frances, are not one-dimensional; they are not all simply good or bad but offer surprisingly "real" personalities. In an essay that was featured in *The Thorny Paradise: Writers on Writing for Children* (1975), H. makes mention that his intent is to join his own thoughts and being with those of his collective readers. This is one underlying premise in both his works for children and those for adults.

Many of H.'s characters for children are famous in children's literature circles. H.'s Frances in *Bread and Jam for Frances* (1964) was selected as a Library of Congress Children's book. Frances has also been featured in recorded selections produced in 1977. *Charlie the Tramp* (1967) received a Boys' Club Junior Book Award. Several of H.'s works for children have been adapted for film. *The Mouse and His Child* (1967) was made into a feature film in 1977, while *The Marzipan Pig* (1986) was adapted as an animated feature in the early 1990s. His best known novel, *Riddley Walker* (1980), is set in the future in England, following a nuclear war.

AWARDS: AMERICAN LIBRARY ASSOCIATION Notable Book (1964) for *The Sorely Trying Day,* (1967) for *The Mouse and His Child,* (1974) for *How Tom Beat Captain Najork and His Hired Sportsmen,* (1975) for *Dinner at Albert's*

FURTHER WORKS: *M.O.L.E.* 1994. *Jim Hedgehog's Supernatural Christmas.* 1992. *Monsters.* 1989. *Ponders.* 1988. *The Rain Door.* 1986. *A Bargain for Frances.* 1979. *Best Friends for Frances.* 1969. *A Birthday for Frances.* 1968

BIBLIOGRAPHY: *The Thorny Paradise: Writers on Writing for Children,* 1975

MICHAEL O'LAUGHLIN

HOBAN, Tana
Author, photographer, b. Date unknown, Philadelphia, Pennsylvania

At a very early age, H., the daughter of Russian immigrants, was encouraged by her father to have her own career. H. started taking art classes as a young girl, where she was not only the youngest, but also the most praised student in these courses. She graduated from Moore College of Art in Philadelphia in 1938, and began painting in Europe on a fellowship. In 1939, H. received her first camera and in 1946 opened a photography studio. She then decided to focus her career on photography instead of painting.

By 1950, H.'s photography was included in New York City's Museum of Modern Art's permanent collection. In 1953, *Time* magazine featured her work in its collection called "Half a Century of U.S. Photography." She was the only woman whose talents were applauded and acknowledged by the magazine. By 1959, H. was named one of the Top Ten Women Photographers in the United States by the Professional Photographers of America.

Shapes and Things (1970), H.'s first book for children, derived from her interest in photographing children, as well as her fascination with childhood development. This led to creating books for children based on educational concepts such as shapes, sizes, numbers, and so on. Several of her books, including *Push/Pull, Empty/Full* (1972), *Big Ones, Little Ones* (1976), *Is It Rough? Is It Smooth? Is It Shiny?* (1984), *Is It Larger, Is it Smaller?* (1985), and *Exactly the Opposite* (1990), use photographs to help children make the connection between opposites. The clear visual images make these abstract concepts become more concrete for young readers.

H. believes her books are "about everyday things that are so ordinary that one tends to overlook them." For instance, she uses pictures of familiar signs seen everyday in the community to teach children the language of symbols. In *I Read Signs* (1983) and *I Read Symbols* (1983), H. incorporates vivid pictures of stop signs, traffic lights, and Do Not Enter signs in order to familiarize children with these symbols.

H.'s work received accolades for her use of color, balance, and texture in order to entice the young child to read further, and to encourage readers to use their imaginations. Books that focus attention on texture and shape include *Dots, Spots, Speckles and Stripes* (1987), *Of Colors and Things* (1989), *Shadows and Reflections* (1990), and *Spirals, Curves; Fanshapes, and Lines* (1992). In *Twenty-Six Letters and Ninety-Nine Cents* (1987), letters and numbers are revealed in large shiny primary colors accompanied by realistic photographs of corresponding symbols. For instance, the letter "U," shown in both upper and lower case, is complemented with a photo of a colorful umbrella. By flipping the book over, and starting from the back, the reader sees numbers, once again in primary colors, which are accompanied by the monetary value of that number in change. For instance, the number "9" is shown in two different ways: nine pennies, as well as one nickel and four pennies.

In her fascinating "textural" books, such as *Look Again!* (1971) and *Just Look* (1996), H. uses small cutouts for the reader to guess what is behind the window. The next page reveals what the object is, and on the third page the object is shown in its natural environment. H.'s objective is for readers to realize that "there are shapes here and everywhere, things to count, colors to see and always, surprises." Her work is praised for using everyday objects such as cups, spoons, and socks with which children can identify, as well as the uncommon, such as mechanical objects that can be found in *Dig/Drill, Dump/Fill* (1975) and *Construction Zone* (1977).

H.'s books use relatively little text. No text is included in *Count and See* (1972) and *Exactly the Opposite* (1990), which allows readers to draw their own conclusions and meanings from the book. Therefore, these books can be enjoyed by children of all ages. H. has also created several similar board books for infants and toddlers including *1, 2, 3* (1985), *Panda, Panda* (1986), *Red, Blue, Yellow Shoe* (1986), *White on Black* (1993), and *Black on White* (1993).

In addition to her books, H. has created several filmstrips, taught photography classes at New York University, and currently lectures teachers and school children in the United States and Europe.

AWARDS: *New York Times* Best Illustrated Children's Books of the Year (1971) for *Look Again,* (1972) for *Count and See!*, (1988) for *Look! Look! Look!* AMERICAN LIBRARY ASSOCIATION Notable Books (1979) for *Is It Red? Is It Yellow? Is It Blue?*, (1981) for *Take Another Look,* (1990) for *Shadows and Reflections*

FURTHER WORKS: *Over, under, and through, and Other Special Concepts.* 1973. *Where Is It?* 1974. *Circles, Triangles and Squares.* 1974. *One Little Kitten.* 1979. *More Than One.* 1981. *A, B, See.* 1982. *I Walk and Read.* 1984. *What Is It?* 1985; *A Children's Zoo.* 1985. *Shapes, Shapes, Shapes.* 1986. *All About Where.* 1991. *Look Up, Look Down.* 1992. *The Wonder of Hands.* 1992

BIBLIOGRAPHY: *Contemporary Authors, New Revision Series.* vol. 23. *Fourth Book of Junior Authors and Illustrators.* 1978. *Something about the Author.* vol. 22 and vol. 70, 1978, 1993

DENISE P. BEASLEY

HOBBS, Will

Author, b. 22 August 1947, Pittsburgh, Pennsylvania

H. spent a great deal of time outdoors as a youth. He enjoyed communing with nature and through his time outdoors learned a good deal about the environments that he visited. When H. was in the fourth grade he discovered his personal love for reading after being introduced to the NEWBERY MEDAL title *Call It Courage* (SPERRY, 1940). The reading and writing connection did not go unnoticed by H. It was his newfound love of reading and literature that would eventually lead him to become a writer himself. Through reading, H. "primed his own pump" and gained knowledge and insight that helped him with his own writing.

H. attended Stanford University where he received both his bachelor's and master's degrees. He became a high school reading and English teacher in Durango, Colorado, from 1973 to 1989. In 1988 H. published his first novel, *Changes in Latitudes* (1988), which told the story of a family of sea turtles. *Changes in Latitudes* would later be included as a runner-up for the 1990 Earthworm Children's Book Award.

Many of H.'s stories are set outdoors. His time spent with nature as a youth has served him well as he looks for topics and themes for his novels. H.'s love of the outdoors did not end when he became an adult. *Downriver* (1991) is set on the Colorado River in the Grand Canyon, a stretch of water that H. himself has rafted numerous times.

H. strives to write stories for young people to which they can relate. He helps connect readers with the natural world and environment to help them care about what is going on in the world around them and appreciate other creatures and living things that share their world.

AWARDS: AMERICAN LIBRARY ASSOCIATION Best Book for Young Adults Award (1989) for *Bearstone* and (1991) for *Downriver*. ALA Best Book for Reluctant Readers (1992) for *Downriver*

FURTHER WORKS: *Beardance.* 1995. *The Big Wander.* 1992. *Far North.* 1997. *Ghost Canoe.* 1997. *Kokopelli's Flute.* 1997. *River Thunder.* 1997. *Jason's Gold.* 1998

BIBLIOGRAPHY: *Something about the Author,* vol. 72, 1993

MICHAEL O'LAUGHLIN

HOBERMAN, Mary Ann
Author, poet, b. 12 August 1930, Stamford, Connecticut

H. knew from a very early age, in fact before she could write, that she wanted to be an author. She remembers when she made the connection that the words in the books she enjoyed were actually thought up by real people. The idea of being a person who had her words printed in books intrigued and delighted the young H. who spent her days singing and making up POETRY. As H. grew those songs and poems and daydreams were transferred to paper.

H. attended Smith College and graduated magna cum laude in 1951. She married and was soon caring for four small children. Her love of poetry and song came in handy as she made up new verse to entertain her little ones. On a whim she wrote down a collection of her poetry, her architect husband illustrated the work, and it was accepted by a publisher. H. was a published author with her first collection, *All My Shoes Come in Two's* (1957).

H.'s work has been praised by critics who find her verse effective for young children. Her poetry is amusing and joyous, often using subjects such as animals and insects. Her writing style seems especially suited toward the preschool and primary grade reader. H. was asked to write the Book Week Poem by the CHILDREN'S BOOK COUNCIL in 1976; she was also awarded the American Book Award in 1983 for *A House Is a House for Me*

(1978). Both *A House Is a House for Me* and *The Looking Book* (1973) were listed as selections of the Junior Literary Guild. H. has contributed her poetry to a variety of magazines including *Harper's* and *The Southern Poetry Review.*

H.'s writing process is interesting. A great deal of the actual creation of her verse is done in her head. She will hear a word, sound, or rhythm that she will work and rework. Often these thoughts and sounds come to her as she is walking in the woods or on the beach. H. told Junior Literary Guild that "not writing a poem would be more difficult" than writing one. For her, writing is an all important component of her life.

FURTHER WORKS: *Bugs. 1976. The Cozy Book.* 1982. *Mr. And Mrs. Muddle.* 1988. *Fathers, Mothers, Sisters, Brothers: A Collection of Family Poems.* 1991. *A Fine Fat Pig, and Other Animal Poems.* 1991. *One Hand Clapping.* 1997. *The Llama Who Had No Pajama: 100 Favorite Poems.* 1998. *Miss Mary Mack: A Hand-Clapping Rhyme.* 1998. *And to Think That I Thought We'd Never Be Friends.* 1999

BIBLIOGRAPHY: *Something about the Author.* vol. 72, 1993. *Junior Literary Guild.* 1973, 1978

MICHAEL O'LAUGHLIN

HODGES, Margaret Moore
Author, b. 26 July 1911, Indianapolis, Indiana

H. grew up in Indianapolis in a household that included her father, brother John, and cousin Margaret Carlisle, who was brought into the home to care for the children when H.'s mother died. H.'s home was literature-rich with books and stories playing an important role in her life. Her first published piece was titled "Miss Matty's Library and was published in H.'s elementary school magazine. She also contributed poetry to *St. Nicholas* magazine, a children's publication that invited readers to share their prose and poetry.

H. attended college at Vassar where she graduated with honors in 1932. She continued on to get her master's degree in Library Science from Carnegie Mellon University in 1958. H. worked as a children's librarian in Pittsburgh before becoming a story specialist in the Pittsburgh Public Schools. She later became a professor at the University of Pittsburgh where she taught courses in Library Science. Along the way, H. was a member of the NEWBERY and CALDECOTT MEDAL committees and acted as a storyteller on the television show *Tell Me a Story*. H.'s own distinguished career as a writer has earned her a good deal of recognition.

H.'s early books were often based, in part, on the real-life adventures of her own three sons as she told about the adventures of Joshua Cobb. Her later works concentrate more on her interest in history and historical folktales. Many of H.'s more recent works have been retellings of legends and stories across many cultures and throughout history. H.'s love of writing was partially due to the fact that her work served as inspiration for many youngsters to investigate literature and literacy. Her stories, whether told aloud, retold from history and legend, or set down from her own experience and that of her family, serve the same purpose of bringing the joy of reading to children and encouraging them to continue learning.

Among many of her AWARDS was a Caldecott Medal in 1965 for *The Wave* (1964). *Lady Queen Anne: A Biography of Queen Anne of England* (1968) was selected as one of the best books for children by an Indiana author in 1971. *St. George and the Dragon: A Golden Legend* (1984) won the *New York Times* Best Illustrated Children's Book Award as well as the *Horn Book* Honor Book Award and the Caldecott Medal in 1985. She was also awarded the 1991 Parents' Choice Honor for Story Books and the 1991 CHILDREN'S BOOK COUNCIL award for *Buried Moon* (1990).

AWARDS: AMERICAN LIBRARY ASSOCIATION Caldecott Medal (1985) for *St. George and the Dragon* (Trina Schart HYMAN, illus.); ALA Caldecott Medal Honor Book (1965) for *The Wave* (Blair LENT, illus.). *New York Times* Best Illustrated Children's Books of the Year (1984) for *St. George and the Dragon* and (1964) for *The Wave*

FURTHER WORKS: *The Freewheeling of Joshua Cobb.* 1974. *Knight Prisoner: The Tale of Sir Thomas Malory and His King Arthur.* 1976. *The High Riders.* 1980. *The Avenger.* 1982. *Making a Difference: The Story of an American Family.* 1989. *The Hero of Bremen.* 1993. *Saint Patrick and the Peddler.* 1993

BIBLIOGRAPHY: *Something about the Author.* vol. 75, 1993

MICHAEL O'LAUGHLIN

HOFF, Sydney (Syd)

Author, illustrator, b. 4 September 1912, New York City

As a youngster, H. was the family artist by proclamation of his mother. He was, in fact, a good artist and excelled especially in the area of cartooning. Some of his early artwork was hung on the family wall. However, H. was not academically inclined and dropped out of school when he was sixteen years old. From there he lied about his age to gain admission to the National Academy of Design in New York City. When H. was eighteen he sold his first cartoon to *The New Yorker* magazine and has contributed to that publication ever since.

In addition to his cartoons for *The New Yorker,* H. was the creator of two long-running comic strips, *Tuffy* and *Laugh It Off*. *Tuffy* was known as a trailblazer as its main character was a female and not stereotypical. Along with his cartooning, H. had his own television series on CBS called *Tales of Hoff*. His work has also been featured on numerous television commercials including those for Chevrolet and Maxwell House coffee.

One of H.'s most endearing children's characters originated from drawings he did for his daughter that would eventually become *Danny and the Dinosaur* (1958), a favorite the world round. *Danny the Dinosaur* has been made into a film strip distributed by Weston Woods. H.'s *Irving and Me* (1967) was selected as one of the year's best children's books by the *New York Times*. H. has also contributed to *Esquire, Look, Saturday Evening Post,* and other periodicals.

H.'s work is humorous, usually done in ink, washes, crayon, and watercolor. His inspiration was often derived from his native New York and the neighborhoods he was familiar with. H.'s text is usually done in an EASY-TO-READ format that lends itself well to beginning elementary readers. His characters are often likeable animals whose stories are told in a straightforward way that young children and adults alike appreciate. H. strives for humorous interpretations that people can relate to in his work, stating that "the best humor has to do with events that people can identify as having happened to them."

FURTHER WORKS: *Sammy, the Seal.* 1959. *Chester.* 1961. *Thunderhoof.* 1971. *Soft Skull Sam.*

1981. *Happy Birthday, Henrietta!* 1983. *Barney's Horse.* 1987. *Mrs. Brice's Mice.* 1988

BIBLIOGRAPHY: *Something about the Author.* vol. 72, 1993; *Something about the Author Autobiography Series,* vol. 4

MICHAEL O'LAUGHLIN

HOFFMAN, Mary

Author, journalist, b. 20 April 1945, Eastleigh, Hampshire, England

After graduating from Cambridge University and writing her first novel, *White Magic* (1975), H. decided to pursue her love of writing as a career. She taught for five years and then began to write children's books. During the 1980s H. published over thirty-five fiction and nonfiction books and articles. She addresses issues of racism, discrimination, positive coping with prejudice, and invites children to think beyond stereotypical roles in her writing. *Amazing Grace* (1991), which received a KATE GREENAWAY MEDAL commendation, *Boundless Grace* (1995) and *Starring Grace* (2000) illustrate the themes of MULTICULTURAL LITERATURE. Also within her work are themes of animal conservation as seen in Animals in the Wild SERIES (1983–87), a focus on ecology and culture as in *Earth, Fire, Water, and Air* (1995), and feminist insights leading to strong heroines found in *Beware, Princess!* (1985) and *My Grandma Has Black Hair* (1988). H. also focuses on family relationships and FANTASY in her books for preschool children.

FURTHER WORKS: *The Second Hand Ghost.* 1986. *Whales and Sharks.* 1986. *Dog Powder.* 1989. *Henry's Baby.* 1993. *Quantum Squeak.* 1996. *An Angel Just Like Me.* 1997. *Sun, Moon, and Stars.* 1998

BIBLIOGRAPHY: *Seventh Book of Junior Authors and Illustrators.* 1996; *Something about the Author,* vol. 97, 1998; *Something about the Author Autobiography Series,* vol. 24, 1997

JANELLE B. MATHIS

HOGROGIAN, Nonny

Author, illustrator, b. 7 May 1932, New York City

H.'s home in the Bronx was one where reading, art, and work were considered paramount. H.'s father was a photoengraver by profession but enjoyed the hobbies of painting and gardening while he was at home. H.'s mother was interested in sketching and the craft of needlework. Her grandfather also lived with the family and it was in his room that the family library was kept. H. would often sit in her grandfather's room and look through the beautiful books, "dreaming about the possibility of making such beautiful pictures" herself.

H. eventually attended Hunter College where she majored in art and history. Her schooling led to a job with the book publisher William Morrow, where she had the opportunity to work on dustjacket art. Sometimes she created her own art for dust jackets. H. became a production assistant at Crowell Publishers where she was given her first chance at ILLUSTRATION. Her subsequent work with author Sorche NIC LEODHAS, pseudonym for Leclaire Alger, resulted in the 1966 CALDECOTT MEDAL for *Always Room for One More.*

H. collaborated with poet David KHERDIAN on many books including *The Great Fishing Contest* (1991) and *The Cat's Midsummer Jamboree* (1990) where H. served as illustrator. She has also written and self-illustrated several volumes including *The Cat Who Loved to Sing* (1988) and *Carrot Cake* (1977). H. has received praise and accolades from readers and critics for both her illustrations and her writing. Often it is her attention to detail that is mentioned when listing H.'s talents. Still, H. strives to become better, saying that "I am always dissatisfied with my work"; her constant goal is to try harder and perfect her craft.

AWARDS: AMERICAN LIBRARY ASSOCIATION Caldecott Medal (1966) for *Always Room for One More* and (1972) for *One Fine Day.* ALA Caldecott Medal Honor Book (1977) for *The Contest.* *New York Times* Outstanding Books citation (1971) for *About Wise Men and Simpletons.*

FURTHER WORKS: *Favorite* FAIRY TALES *Told in Greece.* 1970. *Three Apples Fell from Heaven.* 1971. *Handmade Secret Hiding Places.* 1977. *Noah's Ark.* 1986. *By Myself.* 1993. *Juna's Journey.* 1993

BIBLIOGRAPHY: ALDERSON, Brian. *Children's Book Review,* 1973; *Children's Literature Review,* vol. 2, 1976; HOPKINS, Lee Bennett, *Pauses: Autobiographical Reflections of 101 Creators of Children's Books,* 1995

MICHAEL O'LAUGHLIN

HOLLAND, Isabelle

Author, b. 16 June 1920, Basel, Switzerland

Living abroad and moving frequently as a young child, H. relied on her mother to entertain her by telling stories. H. found herself listening to and enjoying her mother's stories of history, legend, MYTHOLOGY, the BIBLE, and FAMILY tales. She credits this early relationship with story as significant to her eventual success in writing. She writes with the same fervor with which her mother told stories. H. states that this "story-listening led to story-writing." When H. was thirteen she sold her first story to a children's magazine and was delighted to receive a book as her prize.

H. attended the University of Liverpool for two years and earned a B.A. from Tulane University of Louisiana in 1942. For more than twenty years H. held positions in the publicity department of magazine and book publishers including Crown, Lippincott, Dell, Putnam, and McCalls. She wrote all the time, creating many short stories. Her stories were rejected by publishing companies, but H. persisted and soon her novels became popular with YOUNG ADULT readers. H. began writing full-time in 1967; her first book, *Cecily,* a semiautobiographical novel, was published the same year.

In her writing, H. tackles contemporary problems of adolescents struggling to grow up and make sense of the world. *Heads You Win, Tails I Lose* (1973) deals sensitively with being overweight, a problem common among teenagers. H. has a keen insight into the challenge of relationships that are encountered all through life. Her strong characters are well-rounded and dynamically crafted with authentic dialogue and fully developed characterization. *The Man without a Face* (1972) is H.'s most controversial work; it remains an excellent example of how H. introduces characters that readers care deeply about. H. constructs a complex, multilayered friendship and exposes the human condition as Charles, a young fatherless boy, and his teacher, Justin, learn from each other. Despite controversy raised by critics concerning the brief and vague reference to a homosexual encounter, this book remains a popular young adult novel and successful Hollywood film.

Many readers and critics consider *Of Love and Death and Other Journeys* (1975) an outstanding work for young people. In this novel, Meg encounters numerous crises, the most difficult being the death of her mother. While some criticize H.

for psychologizing and moralizing, H. crafts entertaining stories that trust readers to make their own meanings. H. honestly and realistically creates characters that face problems directly; this aspect of her work compels readers to reflect upon their own lives and worlds. H. also writes for adults; many of these books have Gothic mystery themes and echo the same intense characterization as her works for young adults.

H. was nominated for a National Book Award in 1976 for *Of Love and Death and Other Journeys;* Church and Synagogue Library Association Ott Award for *Abbie's God Book* (1982) and *God, Mrs. Muskrat, and Aunt Dot* (1983).

FURTHER WORKS: *Summer of My First Love.* 1981. *Kevin's Hat.* 1984. *Henry and Grudge.* 1986. *The Unfrightened Dark.* 1989. *The Promised Land.* 1996

BIBLIOGRAPHY: Gallo, Donald, ed. *Speaking for Ourselves.* 1990. *Major Authors and Illustrators for Children and Young Adults,* vol. 3; *Something about the Author,* vol. 70, 1993

SHANE RAYBURN

HOLLING, Holling C.

Author, illustrator, b. 2 August 1900, Jackson County, Michigan; d. 7 September 1973, Pasadena, California

The themes of H.'s works echo his intense interest in nature as a young child. H. grew up in the woods of northern Michigan and enjoyed exploring the natural terrain of the land. At an early age, H. became an avid artist and set his goal on art as a career. After graduating high school, H. attended the Art Institute of Chicago, earning a diploma in 1923. H. then studied privately under Dr. Ralph Linton, an anthropologist at Yale University. Much of his early work was done in black and white. Through an opportunity to study art in New Mexico, H. discovered the power and glamour of color. Almost immediately, he began using color as an important element in his artistic creations. Prior to dedicating his life to producing children's books, H. spent a short time in advertising.

H. created several books on Indians and the West between 1926 and 1940, but H.'s *Paddle to the Sea* (1941), his most well-known book, clearly established H. as a prominent author/illustrator of geographic tales. In this book, H. weaves fact and fiction as the reader follows a miniature wooden canoe on a journey from the Great Lakes to the Atlantic Ocean. The journey accents the geographical and historical aspect of the region. Readers enjoy an exploration of the sea by following the adventures of a carved ivory seagull in *Seabird* (1943). In a similar ADVENTURE, H. introduces a snapping turtle, Minn, who journeys the length of the Mississippi in *Minn of the Mississippi* (1951). In *Pagoo* (1957), H., collaborating with Lucille Webster Holling, an artist, reveals the amazing life cycle of a hermit crab through pictures and text. While H. received most of the recognition and accolades for his work, it is worth noting that many of his works include his acknowledgment of Lucille's contributions to the work, ranging from ILLUSTRATIONS to research. H. masterfully accomplishes an educational journey through geography and STORYTELLING in his profusely illustrated books. Readers' imaginations are piqued as H. combines fact and fiction by illuminating the text with color illustrations, accented with black and white sketches.

AWARDS: ALA CALDECOTT MEDAL Honor Book (1942) for *Paddle-to-the-Sea*. ALA NEWBERY MEDAL Honor Book (1949) for *Seabird* and (1952) for *Minn of the Mississippi*

FURTHER WORKS: *Little Buffalo Boy,* 1939; *Tree in the Trail,* 1942

BIBLIOGRAPHY: *Major Authors and Illustrators for Children and Young Adults,* vol. 3, 1993; *Something about the Author,* vol. 26, 1982

SHANE RAYBURN

HOLM, Anne
Author, journalist, b. 10 September 1922, Aal, Jutland, Denmark

Of H.'s numerous books, this Danish author and journalist is best known for *David* (1963), upon which a television series and movie were based. Published first as *I Am David* in the United States and then as *Road to Freedom* (1965), this story is about a young boy who struggles as he flees north on a treacherous journey to Denmark after escaping from an Eastern European concentration camp. This coming of age story set in the era of Nazi Germany is a triumph of good over evil and has won H. a place in the hearts of young readers.

FURTHER WORKS: *Peter,* 1968

BIBLIOGRAPHY: *Something about the Author,* vol. 1, 1971

JANELLE B. MATHIS

HOLMAN, Felice
Author, poet, b. 24 October 1919 New York City

H. read a lot as a child and always knew she wanted to be a writer. She started her career writing advertising copy and, best of all, loves writing books and screenplays. H.'s works span several genres, including POETRY, FANTASY, mystery, REALISTIC FICTION, and historical fiction. Three of H.'s earliest books, the Elisabeth series, were inspired by experiences of her daughter, Nanine. The third book in the SERIES, *Elisabeth and the Marsh Mystery* (1966), features a theme of environmental awareness. H. has written several fantasy books, including *Professor Diggin's Dragons* (1965), *The Witch on the Corner* (1966), *The Cricket Winter* (1967), and *The Blackmail Machine* (1968). H.'s works for YOUNG ADULT readers include her novel, *Secret City, U.S.A.* (1990), about homeless children who fight for their survival and her most popular and acclaimed novel, *Slake's Limbo* (1974) about a teenager's struggle to survive, give voice to issues that H. cares deeply about. Like much of H.'s work, her collections of poetry, such as *At the Top of My Voice and Other Poems* (1970), are characterized by their upbeat and humorous approaches to life.

FURTHER WORKS: *Victoria's Castle.* 1966. *A Year to Grow.* 1968. *The Murderer.* 1978. *The Wild Children.* 1983. *Terrible Jane.* 1987

BIBLIOGRAPHY: Gallo, Donald, ed. *Speaking for Ourselves, Too.* 1993. *Something about the Author,* vol. 82, 1995

MARY ARIAIL BROUGHTON

THE HOLOCAUST

Any writer of children's books attempting to make sense out of an event as cataclysmic as the Holocaust faces a dilemma similar to the one that confronted Dr. Pangloss in Voltaire's *Candide*. How can one maintain a belief in the goodness and decency of humanity despite all evidence to the contrary?

This may be the reason why no juvenile author has yet attempted to penetrate the core of darkness as deeply as Primo Levi, Elie Wiesel, or the French filmmaker Claude Lanzmann in his film *Shoah,* in which a veteran of the Warsaw Ghetto uprising tells the interviewer, "If you could lick my heart, it would poison you."

Anne Frank's *The Diary of a Young Girl* (1952) is the best-known and most widely read Holocaust book. The recently published definitive edition of Anne's diary (Frank & Pressler, eds., 1995), in addition to autobiographies by her friends Miep Gies and Alison Gold, add revealing details to the portrait of Anne, her family, and the people who shared the Annex with her.

However, Anne's experience was atypical. She was sheltered and protected from the world outside by her family and their non–Jewish friends. What would Anne have written had she survived? Would she still maintain that people are basically good at heart after experiencing Auschwitz and Bergen-Belsen?

To balance the picture it is necessary to compare Anne's diary with autobiographies by authors who did survive the Nazi persecution. Two outstanding ones recounting the respective experiences of a Hungarian and Polish family are Aranka SIEGAL's *Upon the Head of a Goat* (1981) and Ruth Minsky Sender's *The Cage* (1986). Rose Zar's *In the Mouth of the Wolf* (1983) is a remarkable account of an indomitable teenager who escapes from a Polish ghetto and, with luck, courage, and a good set of false papers, ultimately becomes a nanny in the home of the SS commandant of Krakow. Ilse Koehn's *Mischling, Second Degree* (1977) portrays another girl with a secret; she has a Jewish grandmother, which classifies her as a semi–Jew under the Nuremburg Laws. Ilse wears her mask so well that she finds herself recommended for Hitler Youth leadership training even as her father is being taken to a labor camp and her grandmother deported to Terezin. The book has parallels with Roberto IN-NOCENTI's exquisitely illustrated *Rose Blanche* (1986), in which a German girl, much like Ilse, loses her life trying to help children in a camp during the war's last days.

In the area of nonfiction, there are many significant books to help children better understand the events of the Nazi period. *Hilde and Eli* (1994) and *Child of the Warsaw Ghetto* (1995), both written by David ADLER and illustrated by

Karen Ritz, focus on how the era's events affected the lives of real children. Chana Byers Abells's *The Children We Remember* (1986) does the same with a sparse text and unsettling photographs from the Yad Vashem archives. For older readers, Miriam CHAIKIN's *A Nightmare in History* (1987) and Barbara ROGASKY's *Smoke and Ashes* (1988) are both vividly written, well-illustrated accounts of the history of the Holocaust. So, too, is Susan Bachrach's *Tell Them We Remember* (1994), a companion volume for the exhibits in the United States Holocaust Memorial Museum. It punctuates its discussion of larger events by telling the stories of real individuals, mostly children, from different countries and backgrounds.

A noteworthy book in a category by itself is *I Never Saw Another Butterfly* (1978). This is a collection of poems and drawings written by children in the Terezein camp. Terezein was a show camp, created to "prove" to the Red Cross and other international organizations that Jewish deportees were being well treated. Most of the families in Terezen were eventually transported to the gas chambers. The fragments in the book are all that remain of most of these children. Inge Auerbacher's *I Am a Star* (1993) paints a poignant portrait of how children lived in that "privileged" camp.

Also in a class by itself is Art Spiegelman's *Maus: A Survivor's Tale* (1986). Spiegelman tells his father's story in a weird but fascinating cartoon where human beings appear as animals. Jews are mice. Germans are cats. These two brilliant images instantly encapsulate the entire history of the Holocaust.

Fiction pales when compared to the actual words of people who lived through these events. Three books, however, deserve to be mentioned for the vividness of the stories they tell and the quality of their writing. In Jane YOLEN's *The Devil's Arithmetic* (1988), self-centered Hannah finds herself transported across space and time to a small Eastern European village on the eve of a deportation. Lois LOWRY's masterful *Number the Stars,* the 1990 NEWBERY MEDAL book, portrays how Annemarie's loyalty to her Jewish friend involves her in the heroic rescue of the Jews of Denmark. Yuri Suhl's *Uncle Misha's Partisans* (1973) and Yuri Orlev's *Island on Bird Street*

(1983) are among the few early books presenting Jews as fighters, not victims.

This subject is so important that many Holocaust titles continue to be published each year. In an effort to reach and inform a younger audience, picture books such as David Adler's *The Number on My Grandfather's Arm* (photos by Rose Eichenbaum, 1987), Shulamith Levey OPPEN-HEIM's *The Lily Cupboard* (Ronald HIMLER, illus., 1995), and Steven Schnur's *The Tie Man's Miracle* (Steven Johnson, illus., 1993) continue to appear. Each book reveals an aspect of the Holocaust set within a reassuring context of hope and affirmation for young readers.

ERIC A. KIMMEL

HOOKS, William H.
Author, b. 14 November 1921, Whiteville, North Carolina

H. earned degrees from the University of North Carolina at Chapel Hill in 1948 (B.A.) and 1950 (M.A.). H. has had a varied career in education, arts, and media. He worked as a high school history teacher, an instructor of dance and history at Hampton Institute, a choreographer at Brooklyn's Opera Workshop, owned a dance studio, and was managing editor of the Bank Street reading series. H. was also involved in media production as a consultant for ABC-TV's "Afterschool Specials" and wrote scripts for CBS's *Captain Kangaroo*. This illustrates H.'s wide range of interests and commitment to varied forms of artistic expression. H. published his first work for young people, *The Seventeen Gerbils of Class 4A*, in 1976. H. has been quite prolific writing across genres on a variety of topics ranging from retellings of fables and folktales (*Moss Gown*, 1990) to historical fiction (*Maria's Cave*, 1977, and *Pioneer Cat*, 1988) to FANTASY stories for beginning readers (*A Dozen Dizzy Dogs*, 1990). The major thrust of his work is retellings of old tales. In *Freedom's Fruit* (1996) H. retells a conjure tale about Mama Marina, a slave, and her powerful spells. He creates a character with the ability to outwit those in power over her. James RANSOME's illustrations support and extend H.'s story of the reality of slavery. In *The Girl Who Could Fly* (1995), a fantasy about Tomasina, a girl alien who comes to the rescue of Adam Lee and his

hapless baseball team, H. again displays his ability to appeal to readers through HUMOR and zaniness. H. seeks just the right voice for telling the tale. His conscious effort at constructing this voice influences word choice, rhythm, dialogue, and imagery. H. states that "getting this voice" enables him to "reveal the wonder, mystery, adventure, and yes, even the magic that inhabit all good stories." H.'s works enable readers to enjoy a good story as well as participate in the distinctive culture from which the tale has evolved.

FURTHER WORKS: *Mean Jake and the Devils*, 1981; *A Flight of Dazzle Angels*, 1988; *The Legend of the White Doe*, 1988; *The Three Little Pigs and the Fox*, 1989; *The Ballad of Belle Dorcas*, 1990; *Freedom's Fruit*, 1990; *Legend of the Christmas Rose*, 1999

BIBLIOGRAPHY: H., W., "Searching for the Voice," 1996; In McClure, A. A., and Kristo, J. V., eds., *Books That Invite Talk, Wonder, and Play*, pp. 249–51; *Something about the Author*, vol. 94, 1998

SHANE RAYBURN

HOOVER, H. M. (Helen Mary)
Author, b. 5 April 1935, Stark County, Ohio

H. grew up in a rural town in Northeast Ohio in a household surrounded by literature. In high school, she found the sciences fascinating. Soon after graduation, H. and a friend ventured to New York City, where H. committed herself to a writing career. H. gained confidence when she sold two short stories to *Scholastic* magazine. While working many temporary jobs, H. began her first novel. After a few years, she submitted three novels under the name Helen Hoover, but soon discovered that another children's author wrote under the same name. She tried H. M. Hoover and noticed a much better reception to a "male" name. Finally, close to the fourth year of writing, *Children of Morrow* (1973) was accepted for publication. *Children of Morrow* and its sequel, *Treasures of Morrow* (1976), were the first of several books in which H. explored Earth's ecological future. Since these publications, H. has become well known for her SCIENCE FICTION works.

AWARDS: ALA Best Book for YOUNG ADULTS (1974) for *The Lion's Cub*, (1981) for *Another Heaven, Another Earth* and (1988) for *The Dawn Palace*. ALA Notable Book (1981) for *Another Heaven, Another Earth*

FURTHER WORKS: *The Bell Tree*. 1982. *Orvis*. 1987. *The Lion's Cub*. 1974. *The Shepherd Moon*. 1984. *The Dawn Palace: The Story of Medea*. 1988

BIBLIOGRAPHY: *Something about the Author*. vol. 83, 1996

JODI PILGRIM

HOPKINS, Lee Bennett

Poet, anthologist, educator, b. 13 April 1938, Scranton, Pennsylvania

H. writes in a variety of literary genres for young people and is best known for his POETRY and numerous anthologies based on specific themes. H. spent his first ten years in Scranton, Pennsylvania, with his parents, brother and sister. In the late 1940s, the family moved in with relatives in Newark, New Jersey. When H. was fourteen, his parents separated, and for a period of time he found himself disinterested in anything except surviving. Eventually, a teacher introduced him to the pleasures of reading and the theater, giving him hope and direction. Inspired by Mrs. McLaughlin, H. worked his way through college. All of this and much more is related in *Been to Yesterdays: Poems of a Life* (1995).

After graduation, H. became a sixth-grade teacher at a suburban school; while he was teaching there he developed the idea of using poetry to help children with reading problems. He reasoned that struggling readers could find more success with poetry than with prose because of the simple vocabulary, repetition of phrases, and condensed nature. In the late 1960s, H. became a consultant at Bank Street College of Education, using poetry to help disadvantaged children, especially minority youth in the area. While there, H. searched for poems by AFRICAN AMERICAN poet Langston HUGHES to share with his students. Finding only one outdated volume, with stereotyped illustrations, he compiled a new collection. In 1976, H. wrote a YOUNG ADULT novel, *Mama* (1977). His collection of poems from Langston Hughes, published in 1969, was called, *Don't You Turn Back: Poems by Langston Hughes*. This collection was well received and was named a 1969 AMERICAN LIBRARY ASSOCIATION Notable Book. A reviewer said that the poems H. selected were "brief, childlike in their simplicity, and timeless in their interpretation of Black dreams." The success of the Hughes anthology spawned the creation of dozens of further award-winning verse collections for children, including more ALA Notable Books, *Rainbows Are Made: Poems* by Carl SANDBURG (1982); *A Song in Stone: City Poems* (1983); and *Surprises* (1984), one of several I Can Read Books that he edited.

H. has many other AWARDS for his work, including the prestigious Christopher Award for *Been to Yesterdays: Poems of a Life* (1995), a collection of poems that chronicle his thirteenth year when his parents separated and his family moved. There is joy, too; it comes through a teacher. Three other volumes were chosen as American Booksellers Pick-of-the-List Books: *Side by Side: Poems to Read Together* (1988); *Voyages: Poems by Walt Whitman* (1988); and *On the Farm* (1991). In addition to the awards, H.'s works have earned extensive critical acclaim.

Literary critic Anthony Manna said that *Rainbows Are Made* has a tight thematic focus with variations that resonate like a satisfying musical score." Ellen Mandel said that *Side by Side: Poems to Read Together* has "rhythmic narrative verses with characters prancing across the pages." Ilene Cooper describes *More Surprises* (1987) as a compilation to teach the joys of poetry to very young children. Words and rhyme schemes are simple enough for beginning readers to handle themselves.

H. received the University of Southern Mississippi Medallion awarded through the DE GRUMMOND RESEARCH COLLECTION for lasting contributions to children's literature. He served on the board of directors of the NATIONAL COUNCIL OF TEACHERS OF ENGLISH, and has twice chaired the NCTE Poetry Award Committee. H. himself created and funded two major awards to encourage the recognition of poetry—the Lee Bennett H. Poetry Award, administered by the University of Pennsylvania, for a book of poetry and the Lee Bennett H.–INTERNATIONAL READING ASSOCIATION Promising Poet Award.

H.'s success as an anthologist is due, in part, to the meticulous care he takes in selecting works to include in his collections, as well as to his knowledge of what students understand and what teachers want to enrich the curriculum. H. acknowledges that the compilation of poems for an anthology is a lengthy and time-consuming process. He reads thousands of verses before selecting the ones to include in a particular volume. For example, H. spent over ten years collecting poems for *Dinosaurs* (1987). He strives for balance in his collections, rarely using more than three works by the same poet. He also likes to achieve a balance between well-known poets and new poets. In choosing the poems for his works, H. considers the flow of the language, often looking for poems where the last word of one poem leads to the next. He tries to envision each volume as a stage play, film, or story having a definite beginning, middle, and end.

FURTHER WORKS: *Happy Birthday to Me!*, 1972; *Charlie's World: A Book of Poems*, 1972; *A Haunting We Will Go: Ghostly Stories and Poems*, 1976; *How Do You Make an Elephant Float and Other Delicious Food Riddles*, 1983; *Good Books, Good Times*, 1990; Compiler: *Voyages: Poems by Walt Whitman*, 1988; *Ragged Shadows: Poems of Halloween Night*, 1993; *It's About Time*, 1993; *April, Bubbles, Chocolate: An ABC of Poetry*, 1994; Young Adult Novels: *Wonder Wheels*, 1979; *Mama and Her Boys*, 1981; *Pauses: Autobiographical Reflections of 101 Creators of Children's Books*, 1995; *My America: A Poetry Atlas of the United States*, 1999

BIBLIOGRAPHY: *Children's Literature Review*, vol. 44, 1997; *Major Authors and Illustrators Supplement*, 1998; McElmeel, S., *100 Most Popular Children's Authors*, 1999; L. B. H., *Pass the Poetry, Please!*, 3rd ed., 1998

MARY ARIAIL BROUGHTON

HOUSTON, Gloria
Author, b. 24 November 1942(?), Marion, North Carolina

H.'s work includes PICTURE BOOKS and novels set in the Appalachian Mountains of North Carolina where she was reared. She draws from events she encountered while growing up in North Carolina. H. captures the dialogue and the customs of the mountain people. She researches her historical fiction using a variety of resources, including interviews with people of the area creating an authentic setting and voice of a bygone era in the rural South. Set in Appalachia in the early 1900s, *My Great-Aunt Arizona* (1992) recalls the joys of attending a one-room schoolhouse and a teacher who inspires her students to dream of faraway places and read about them in books. *But No*

Candy (1992) re-creates the World War II era on the homefront and lets readers share in food rationing efforts with Lee who misses her favorite chocolate bar.

FURTHER WORKS: *My Brother Joey Died*. 1982; *The Year of the Perfect Christmas Tree*. 1988; *Littlejim*. 1990; *Young Will*. 1997

BIBLIOGRAPHY: *Something about the Author*. vol. 81, 1995

JODI PILGRIM

HOUSTON, James A.
Author, illustrator, b. 12 June 1921, Toronto, Ontario, Canada

As a child, H. longed to hear stories of ADVENTURE from his traveling-salesman father. Many of these stories recounted his father's interactions and trading with Inuits and NATIVE AMERICANS. While H. was quarantined with scarlet fever as a young boy, his mother played an instrumental role in developing a love of art and STORYTELLING in H.'s life. H. recalls his mother coming into his bedroom with a large hardcover book and how disappointed he was to find that it was a blank book with no words or pictures. His mother told him if he wanted a book he should write it himself. And so H.'s life as an adventurer, writer, and illustrator began. He studied at the Ontario College of Art, 1938–40, the Ecole Grand Chaumiere, Paris, 1947–48, Unichi-Hiratsuka, Tokyo, 1958–59, and Atelier 17, 1961.

In 1948, H. boarded a train for Moosonee, Ontario. H. began sketching the Cree Indians but longed for more. That same year, H. joined a doctor on a flight to the Arctic on a medical emergency, expecting to spend four days in the nearly uninhabited area. Those four days turned into fourteen years. As the plane departed. H. stood on the coast of Hudson Bay with a sleeping bag, a sketch pad, and a can of peaches. H. states, "At that moment, a great northern adventure was opening before me." He captures the essence of the Inuit people, reflecting a harmonious vision of nature and man in a "perpetual partnership." It was within this partnership that H. created characters and stories, drawing upon his direct experience and the mythical stories shared by the Inuit people. It is important to his integrity as an author and illustrator to have first-hand knowledge with the subject he is writing about, living among the people and sharing their lives with them. He cites the example of falling through the ice five times as the ultimate first-hand experience. H.'s stories appeal to readers of many ages in action-packed survival stories.

Readers share H.'s northern adventures through his books and ILLUSTRATIONS created with a distinctive black and white pencil sketching technique. Many Inuit artworks are on display in museums due to H.'s efforts. H. brought the Inuit art of soapstone carvings to the public; in turn, he helped the Inuit by teaching them printmaking. His other careers include first federal civil administrator of West Baffin Island and associate director of design for Stueben Glass in New York.

AWARDS: CANADIAN Library Association Book of the Year Award (1966) for *Tikta-Liktak: An Eskimo Legend,* (1968) for *The White Archer: An Eskimo Legend,* (1980) for *River Runners: A Tale of Hardship and Bravery.* AMERICAN LIBRARY ASSOCIATION Notable Books Award (1967) for *The White Archer,* (1968) for *Akavak,* and (1971) for *The White Dawn*

FURTHER WORKS: *Drifting Snow: An Arctic Search,* 1992

BIBLIOGRAPHY: *Something about the Author,* vol. 17, 1979
                                    SHANE RAYBURN

HOWE, James
Author, b. 2 August 1946, Oneida, New York

H. grew up in a family that loved words; jokes, riddles, and word games abounded in all forms in every room of the house. He says he "grew up in a house of words. . . . Words were playthings, balls bounced through the air in an endless game of verbal toss." H. draws upon his experiences as the youngest family member to create believable characters. He worked hard as a child to impress his other siblings and so do many of his characters. At age nine, H. self-published the official newspaper of his Vampire Club, *The Story Gazette,* and later, he wrote HUMOR columns for the high school newspaper. In 1968 H. received a B.F.A degree from Boston University, and in 1977 a M.A. from Hunter College of the City University of New York.

Upon the suggestion of Deborah Smith, H. and Smith collaborated on the creation of *Bunnicula: A Rabbit-Tale Mystery* (1979). This first book became popular instantly, winning more than ten children's choice AWARDS. The vampire bunny established H. firmly as a favorite author of elementary school children; it was followed by *Howliday Inn* (1982) and *The Celery Stalks at Midnight* (1983). H. is best known for this comic mystery series where fast-paced story lines and engaging dialogue invite readers to enjoy absurd fantasies of the most humorous kind. H. created two other series, the Pinky and Rex series (first book published in 1990) and the Sebastian Barth series (first book published in 1985). Pinky and Rex, two best friends, often find themselves in the midst of realistic childhood dilemmas. Sebastian Barth, a junior-high school sleuth, leads readers through mysterious, sometimes dangerous, and always humorous situations. H. takes his authorial responsibility seriously saying, "It is the writer's privilege and responsibility to give children a world they can enter, recognize, at times be frightened of, but which ultimately they can master and control."

H. also writes nonfiction books for beginning readers such as *When You Go to Kindergarten* (1986) and *The Hospital Book* (1981). In the latter book, a young child narrates details of hospital procedures. It is an accessible and reassuring book and the recipient of several nonfiction awards.

AWARDS: AMERICAN LIBRARY ASSOCIATION Notable Book Citation (1979) for *Bunnicula,* and (1981) for *Howliday Inn.* ALA Children's Book of the Year citation (1982) for *The Hospital Book*

FURTHER WORKS: *I Wish I Were a Butterfly.* 1987. *Dew Drop Dead.* 1990. *Playing with Words.* 1994. *The New Nick Kramer, or My Life as a Baby-sitter.* 1995. *The Watcher.* 1997

BIBLIOGRAPHY: H., J. 1996. "Starting with Celery; or, How to Toss a Verbal Salad." In McClure, A. A., and J. V. Kristo, (eds.). *Books That Invite Talk, Wonder, and Play. Something about the Author.* vol. 71, 1993
                                    SHANE RAYBURN

HOWKER, Janni
Author, b. 6 July 1957, Nicosia, Greece

Critics note with high regard YOUNG ADULT author H.'s ability to present serious issues in spare, evocative language. In both her short stories and novels, H. writes about adolescent struggles rife with social and economic issues. Her characters enjoy intergenerational relationships and suffer from the kinds of working-class problems endemic in depressed industrialized areas.

Born into a British military family, H. spent her early years abroad. When her family returned to England, she became intrigued with the natural world and then, as a teenager, with her extended family's history in the industrialized North. After graduating from Lancaster University (1980) she earned a masters in creative writing (1984).

Badger on the Barge and Other Stories (1984) earned the INTERNATIONAL READING ASSOCIATION's Children's Book Award (1985), and was named Best Book of the Year by the AMERICAN LIBRARY ASSOCIATION (ALA) (1984). *The Nature of the Beast* (1985) earned the Whitbread Literary Award in the children's fiction category (1985), the Silver Pencil Award (1987), and commendation as an ALA Notable Book (1985). *Isaac Campion* (1986) earned the 1987 Somerset Maugham award (1987) and was named a Best Book of the Year by ALA. Both *The Nature of the Beast* and *Isaac Campion* were highly commended by the CARNEGIE MEDAL Awards committee in the years of their publications.

H. began to write seriously as a teenager. Her first attempt at publication, when she was twenty-seven, was successful. "Jakey" became one of five stories comprising *Badger on the Barge*. The emotional lives of H.'s characters are invested with authenticity that comes from memories of her own youth and her family's experiences.

FURTHER WORKS: *Walk with a Wolf,* 1998

BIBLIOGRAPHY: *Contemporary Authors,* vol. 137, 1992; Silvey, Anita, ed., *Children's Books and Their Creators,* 1995

FRANCISCA GOLDSMITH

HOW-TO BOOKS

Books that invite children to participate actively and investigate are referred to as how-to books, a subcategory of INFORMATIONAL BOOKS. These books give children directions for various activities and include children's cookbooks, craft books, and science experiment books. Although how-to books have become increasingly popular

in recent years, they are not a new phenomenon in children's publishing. In 1911, the Boy Scouts of America authored *The Official Handbook for Boys* that provided instructions on how boys could fulfill the goals of scouting. *The Pinwheel Book* (Williams, 1910) and *The House That Glue Built* (Williams, 1910) have pictures that were intended to be cut out and assembled by children, the pinwheels on landscapes and the furnishings and people pasted onto pages of the house. *Shadowgraphs Anyone Can Make* by Phila Webb and Jane Corey in 1927 has recently been reissued; it gives children step-by-step verbal and visual instructions for making handshadows on the wall. Contemporary how-to books are available on a wide range of topics and in a variety of formats.

How-to books are identified by their unique characteristics. These include the presentation of information in distinctive visual formats such as lists, boxed information, sidebars, charts, and graphs. The language is usually presented in an identifiable format consisting of sets of directions for readers to follow and is presented in a specific sequence. In addition, how-to books generally include extensive graphics that illustrate the directions, show the final craft or food, or convey additional information visually. An example of these characteristics is seen in *Dazzling Disguises and Clever Costumes* (Wilkes, 1996). With the subtitle *More Than Fifty Step-by-Step Projects to Make, Paint, Sew, Prepare, and Wear,* the book guides young readers through the process of costume design and preparation. A table of contents and index provide children access to the specific costumes described such as "tunics" and "hats on parade." Color photographs illustrate both the needed materials and supplies and the directions that guide children step-by-step through the process of making the costume. These steps are numbered and bold headings designate different aspects of the process.

Many museums have authored how-to books to support children's curiosity, exploration, and investigation of topics. For instance, in 1993 the Smithsonian Institution authored a series of "Hands-On Science: Step-by-Step Science Activity Projects from the Smithsonian Institution." In one of these books, *Food and the Kitchen,* children can follow directions to make cheese, prepare ginger ale, and learn about yogurt. Boston

Children's Museum staff member Bernie Zubrowski has authored a series of "Activity Books" on such topics as balloons, mobiles, clocks, mirrors, and bubbles. Author Vicki COBB has written many science experiment books with HUMOR and unusual approaches such as *The Secret Life of Cosmetics: A Science Experiment Book* (1985) and *Science Experiments You Can Eat* (1994).

Children's cookbooks abound for children of all ages, often with unique themes. Cookbooks relate to children's literature such as *The Little House Cookbook* (Walker, 1979) with recipes for foods discussed in the books by Laura Ingalls WILDER. They also link to MULTICULTURALISM as in *Passport on a Plate: A Round-the-World Cookbook for Children* (Vezza, 1997).

Another kind of how-to book focuses on hobbies, crafts, and SPORTS. National Geographic Society's *A World of Things to Do* (1987) includes a variety of activities in such categories as "puzzlers," and "games to go." Diane Rhoades shares *Garden Crafts for Kids: 50 Great Reasons to Get Your Hands Dirty* (1995) and Dave Brown and Paul Reeve instruct would-be magicians in *Amazing Magic Tricks* (1995). How-to books even encourage children to engage in social action as with *I Can Save the Earth: A Kid's Handbook for Keeping Earth Healthy and Green* (Holmes, 1993). Lerner Publishing has a series of "Beginning Sports" books that include action color photographs and directions for students to learn skills in many sports such as *Beginning Karate* (Dallas, 1998) and *Beginning Mountain Biking* (King, 1997).

How-to books encourage children to become involved in a variety of activities that support their interests and favorite pastimes.

BIBLIOGRAPHY: Bamford, R. A. and J. V. Kristo, *Checking out Nonfiction K–8: Good Choices for Best Learning,* 2000.

EVELYN B. FREEMAN

(See also INFORMATIONAL BOOKS and INFORMATIONAL BOOKS, AN AUTHOR'S POINT OF VIEW)

HOYT-GOLDSMITH, Diane
Author, b. 1 July 1950, Peoria, Illinois

H-G. studied graphic design and typography at Brooklyn's Pratt Institute, earning a B.F.A. degree in 1973. She recalls early fascination with

fonts, letter forms, and type styles when she and her sister spent hours tracing capital letters in an encyclopedia. H-G. began as a book designer for Macmillan Publishing and Harcourt Brace and Jovanovich in New York, specializing in children's books. In 1979, H-G. and her husband started Square Moon Productions in the San Francisco Bay area. While designing book layouts for her company, H-G. had an idea for a book of her own. She was an avid collector of Northwest Coast native American art and knew a Tsimshian Indian carver. This friendship provided the inspiration for her book, *Totem Pole* (1989). Collaborating with photographer Lawrence MIGDALE, H-G. published *Totem Pole,* a photo essay narrated by a boy whose NATIVE AMERICAN father is carving a totem pole in the style of his Tsimshian tribe.

As part of a military family, H-G. experienced many new faces, places, and adventures as her family moved from base to base. During this period of her childhood, H-G. clung to books making them her "constant companion[s]." She writes, "books were my most dependable allies against loneliness. Books let me escape to their worlds and other times, visit exotic locations and meet the most interesting people." Through these experiences and travels on land and in books, H-G. marveled at new places and developed new friendships. In her many books, she shares the richness and diversity of our cultural heritage. With *Totem Pole,* she launched a prolific career creating authentic INFORMATIONAL BOOKS accompanied by photographic images that complement the story. Her books captivate readers, lead them to faraway places, and reveal the potential for diverse friendships. Each book contains a glossary and index of key terms and acknowledgments of cooperating families; many include special notes from the author. Contemporary young people narrate many of H-G.'s books, providing a current perspective on historical rituals and cultural events.

H-G. and her collaborator, Migdale, tell the story of lacrosse as a SPORT and an integral part of Iroquois Native American culture in *Lacrosse: The National Game of the Iroquois* (1998). In *Celebrating Chinese New Year* (1998), H-G. shares this colorful holiday tradition as it is celebrated in San Francisco; family customs and rituals are colorfully shown against a background of community celebration. Through H-G.'s works, readers celebrate the richness and diversity of cultures.

AWARDS: Notable Children's Trade Books in the Field of Social Studies (1990) for *Totem Pole,* (1991) for *Pueblo Storyteller,* and (1992) for *Hoang Anh: A Vietnamese–American Boy* and for *Arctic Hunter*

FURTHER WORKS: *Celebrating Kwanzaa.* 1993. *Cherokee Summer.* 1993. *Day of the Dead: A Mexican-American Celebration.* 1994. *Apache Rodeo.* 1995. *Mardi Gras: A Cajun Country Celebration.* 1995. *Potlatch: A Tsimshian Celebration.* 1997. *Buffalo Days.* 1997

BIBLIOGRAPHY: *Seventh Book of Junior Authors and Illustrators.* 1996

SHANE RAYBURN

HUGHES, Langston

Poet, author, b. 1 February 1902, Joplin, Missouri; d. 22 May 1967, New York City

H. lived much of his early life with his maternal grandmother while his mother traveled for work. His grandmother was influential in his life, telling him stories and taking him to hear famous speeches. His grandmother's words and the beautiful stories of his AFRICAN AMERICAN ancestors resound with magnificent display in his works. This early introduction to the power of words fueled H.'s subsequent endeavors. When H. was twelve, his grandmother died and he lived with family friends until his mother sent for him. In the eighth grade, H. was chosen class poet and began seriously thinking about writing in high school when he was elected yearbook editor. His first POETRY was written at Central High School in Cleveland, Ohio. H. wrote his first major poem, "The Negro Speaks of Rivers," as he crossed the Mississippi River in route to visit his father in Mexico. It was first published by the National Association for the Advancement of Colored People in 1921 in the *Crisis* and continues to be one of his most popular poems. He attended Columbia University in 1921–22 and received an A.B. degree in 1929 from Lincoln University. In 1935 H. received a Guggenheim fellowship for creative work; in 1960 he received a Springarn Medal.

H. soon became one of the leading figures of the Harlem Renaissance of the 1920s. Voices and images of the common people reverberate in all of his works. After extensive traveling, H. settled in Harlem in 1947 and resided there until his death. He continued his mission of sharing truth and honest depiction of black people through fiction, poetry, DRAMA, nonfiction, and juvenile works. His work invite readers to join him in what he calls home. While much of his work was not intended for children, *The Dream Keeper and Other Poems* (1932) was specifically organized and published for a juvenile audience as well as *Black Misery* (1969). Another powerful anthology of his work that is accessible to children is *Don't You Turn Back* (1969), edited by Lee Bennett HOPKINS. H. became known as the poet laureate of Harlem as he authentically captured the essence of life there. H. collaborated with Milton MELTZER and published *A Pictorial History of the Negro in America* (1956). He also authored several BIOGRAPHY collections for young people, seeking to reveal the rich and heroic history of black people. H. worked against injustice and sought to move people with words; he has deeply influenced literary history and his fight for equality continues through his legacy of words. He remains one of the most influential black American writers of all times.

FURTHER WORKS: (With Arna BONTEMPS): *Popo and Fifina: Children of Haiti.* 1932. *The First Book of Rhythms.* 1954. *Famous Negro Music Makers.* 1955. *Famous Negro Heroes of America.* 1958. *The Sweet and Sour Animal Book.* 1994

BIBLIOGRAPHY: Berry, Faith, *Langston Hughes; Before and Beyond Harlem,* 1983; *Major Authors and Illustrators,* vol. 3, 1993

SHANE RAYBURN

HUGHES, Monica (Lindsay)

Author, b. 3 November 1925, Liverpool, England

H. is the highly acclaimed author of more than thirty books for young people and is considered one of Canada's finest writers for children and YOUNG ADULTS. Although she is best known for SCIENCE FICTION novels, she also writes FANTASY, realism, and historical fiction. H. was born in England, but her family moved to Egypt shortly after her birth. She lived there until 1931 when she returned to England to attend school. She graduated from the Convent of the Holy Child Jesus in Yorkshire in 1942 and attended Edinburgh University from 1942 until 1943. H.'s parents shared their love of astronomy with young H., a subject that later became the nucleus of much of her writing. As an adult, she traveled and worked in several countries, eventually settling in Canada, where she became a naturalized CANADIAN citizen.

One of the author's most popular and critically acclaimed projects is her Isis trilogy. The three books, *The Keeper of the Isis Light* (1980), *The Guardian of Isis* (1981), and *The Isis Pedlar* (1982) feature Olwen Pendennis, a girl who is born to Earth parents while they work as research scientists on an isolated planet called Isis. Orphaned at the age of five, Olwen is rescued and cared for by an unusually intelligent robot. The books in the trilogy center on H.'s favorite themes, which include moral and personal growth, the integration of disparate cultures, isolation and the search for identity, and survival in challenging environments. *The Keeper of the Isis Light* was named a best book for young adults by the AMERICAN LIBRARY ASSOCIATION and was included on the INTERNATIONAL BOARD ON BOOKS FOR YOUNG PEOPLE's honor list. Other award-winning books by H. include *Hunter in the Dark* (1982), *The Guardian of Isis* (1981), and *Ring-Rise, Ring-Set* (1982).

Critics have noted that, unlike many writers, H. brings a gentleness to her books that is rare in science fiction. Her work is also recognized for its attention to moral issues, such as the tension between scientific progress and the health of the environment. Most of her writing is set in the near future and follows a logical projection of current events on earth.

FURTHER WORKS: *Goldfever Trail.* 1974. *Crisis on Conshelf Ten.* 1975. *Beckoning Lights.* 1982. *Invitation to the Game.* 1990. *The Golden Aquarians.* 1995. *A Handful of Seeds.* 1996. *The Faces of Fear.* 1997. *The Story Box.* 1998

BIBLIOGRAPHY: Drew, B. A. *The 100 Most Popular Young Adult Authors: Biographical Sketches and Bibliographies.* 1997. Gallo, Donald, ed. *Speaking for Ourselves, Too.* 1993. *Major Authors and Illustrators for Children and Young Adults: A Selection of Sketches from Something about the Author.* 1993. *Sixth Book of Junior Authors and Illustrators.* 1989

MARY ARIAL BROUGHTON

HUGHES, Richard (Arthur Warren)
Author, b. 19 April 1900, Weybridge, Surrey, England; d. 28 April 1976, Bangor, Wales

H. began writing when he was six and insisted his mother "write down his stories" before he was able to write. As a young man he was a vagabond and pavement artist in Europe but later became Gresham Professor of Rhetoric at the University of London.

H. is best known for his novel *The Innocent Voyage* (1929) published eight years later as *A High Wind in Jamaica*. His unforgiving story of the loss of innocence and morality when five children are kidnapped by pirates is relentless as the children adapt comfortably to shipboard cruelty. The book was awarded the Femina-Vie Heureuse prize and dramatized as a play on Broadway in 1943. The script was included in *The Best Plays of 1943–1944* and published in 1946. The novel, popular with YOUNG ADULT readers, was released as a film by 20th Century-Fox in 1965 under the title *High Wind in Jamaica*. H. considered himself a slow writer and considered writing "a race between the publisher and the undertaker." H. wrote several humorous short story collections beginning with *The Spider's Palace and Other Stories* in 1931.

FURTHER WORKS: *Don't Blame Me!* 1940. *Gertrude's Child.* 1966. *Gertrude and the Mermaid.* 1967. *The Wonder Dog: The Collected Children's Stories of Richard Hughes.* 1977

BIBLIOGRAPHY: *Fiction, FOLKLORE, FANTASY, and POETRY for Children, 1876–1985,* vol. 1 1986; *Something about the Author,* vol. 8, 1976, and vol. 25, 1981

IRVYN G. GILBERTSON

HUGHES, Shirley
Author, illustrator, b. 16 July 1927, Hoylake, England

One of England's most respected and popular authors, H. attended Liverpool Art School and Ruskin School of Drawing and Fine Arts, Oxford. She began her career illustrating Louisa May ALCOTT's *Little Women* (1869) in 1953 and has illustrated more than 200 works for additional authors since then. Her notable ILLUSTRATIONS reveal the beauty of everyday life. She wrote and illustrated her first book, *Lucy and Tom's Day* in 1960; several other Lucy and Tom books followed. In these books, as well as the Alfie series, H. presents real-life situations such as birthday parties, bathing rituals, and first days of school. Her no-nonsense approach reassures young readers and sets challenges and life's problems in hilarious contrast. Many of these first books were written with her own children as the primary audience. H. captures children and the joys of childhood in text and illustrations. She has also created several basic concept books for preschool children centered around topics such as counting, shapes, colors, and sounds.

H. says, "Like most illustrators, I think in pictures." She writes, "PICTURE BOOK ideas, like movies, are unthinkable without the visual element." H.'s ideas and pictures percolate as she observes children in natural settings; she combines colorful, whimsical, in-motion drawings with cheerful and delightful text. H. has compared designing a picture book to a theatrical production, playing the many various roles seeking unified narrative that engages young children and endures the test of repeated readings. H. notes, "pictures aren't just the icing on the cake, they are crucial to the way the reader perceives the story, a first introduction to fiction. The characterization, the setting of the scene and a lot of the HUMOR goes into the pictures." In her works, H. reveals not only the extraordinary but also the drama of the familiar in everyday life. Her universal themes have made her a favorite author of young and old.

AWARDS: KATE GREENAWAY MEDAL (1977) for *Dogger*

FURTHER WORKS: *When We Went to the Park*, 1985; *Bathwater's Hot*, 1985; *All Shapes and Sizes*, 1986; *Out and About*, 1988; *Angel Mae*, 1989

BIBLIOGRAPHY: *Children's Literature Review*, vol. 15, 1988; *Fifth Book of Junior Authors and Illustrators*, 1983; *Major Authors and Illustrators for Children and Young Adults*, vol. 3, 1993; Silvey, Anita, ed., *Children's Books and Their Creators*, 1995; *Something about the Author*, vol. 70, 1993 *Twentieth Century Children's Writers*, 4th ed., 1995

SHANE RAYBURN

HUGHES, Ted

Author, poet, playwright, b. 17 August 1930, Mytholmroyd, West Yorkshire, England; d. 29 October 1998, England

H., appointed England's Poet Laureate in 1984, grew up in the Yorkshire countryside and received a degree from Cambridge in archaeology and anthropology. Early on H. expressed a keen interest in animals and nature. These interests are echoed throughout his work for children and adults. H., at age fifteen, was disturbed by the relationship between humans, nature, and animals and began writing POETRY from the point of view of animals and nature. He perceives "poems as a sort of animal. They have their own life, like animals, by which I mean that they seem quite separate from any person, even from their author, and nothing can be added to them or taken away without maiming and perhaps even killing them. And they have a certain wisdom." H., one of the most significant poets of his time as well as the husband of Sylvia Plath, seeks to capture the essence of experiences and to learn from them. In *Poetry Is* (1967), H. writes, "It is when we set out to find words for some seemingly quite simple experience that we begin to realize what a huge gap there is between our understanding of what happens around us and inside us, and the words we have at our command to say something about it." This prolific writer spans many moods, myths, genres, and subjects. For example, in *Moon Whales and Other Poems* (1978), H. creates an image of a moon-whale "lifting the moon's skin/ like a muscle" and clearly opens our imagination to the events that occur "in the utter utter stillness" of the moon. H. invites readers into imaginative worlds. In his poetry, H. accomplishes this invitation to imagine. *Under the North Star* (1981) invites readers to meet the creatures of the Arctic region through imaginative portraits of animals such as a lynx, heron, and arctic fox.

AWARDS: Kurt Maschler *Emil* Award (1985) for *The Iron Man*. Signal Poetry Award (1979) for *Moon-Bells and Other Poems* and (1985) for *What Is the Truth?* Guardian Award (1985) for *What Is the Truth?*

FURTHER WORKS: *The Iron Man*. 1968. *Fangs the Vampire Bat and The Kiss of Truth*. 1986; *Moon-*

48. ROBERT A. HEINLEIN

49. KEVIN HENKES

50. S. E. HINTON

51. LILLIAN HOBAN

52. TANA HOBAN

53. LEE BENNETT HOPKINS

54. LANGSTON HUGHES

Whales. 1978. *Tales of the Early Worlds.* 1988. *The Dreamfighter and Other Creation Tales.* 1996

BIBLIOGRAPHY: H., Ted. *Poetry Is,* 1967

SHANE RAYBURN

HUMOR

H. is fundamental to our survival as a species; human beings, in fact, are the only animals that laugh. Laughter relieves the pain, doubt, and anxiety of daily life. It is a means of at least temporarily escaping from the oppressions of the world and is as essential for children as it is for grown-ups. Laughter releases tension and helps calm fears. It even heals emotional wounds. Children may not consciously understand that, but they intuitively look for books that will make them laugh.

In literature there are three basic types of humor. The first appears universally in literature across national boundaries using talking or otherwise anthropomorphized animals for humorous purpose. Tall tale and frontier humor, the second type, is singularly American as is the third, the domestic or family comedy. The tall tale is identified by its use of native–American humor, including the lampooning of authority, the enlivening of conversation with regional simile and metaphor, and the employment of comically exaggerated regional traits to define character. Initially, oral stories based on exaggerated legends of real people such as Davy Crockett and Mike Fink, the repertoire of tall stories expanded to contain mythical animals and people such as the Arkansas Big Bear, Paul Bunyan, and Pecos Bill. Glen ROUNDS and Steven KELLOGG have extended the popularity of tall tales among contemporary readers. Sid FLEISCHMAN extends the voice of the tall tale and use of hyperbole in original stories rooted in the reality of nineteenth-century American frontier history. He demonstrates over and over again the comic possibilities of the English language and the glorious fun that can be had with it. *Swamp Angel* (Anne Isaacs, Paul O. ZELINSKY, illus.), a 1995 CALDECOTT MEDAL Honor Book, spins an original tall tale of Swamp Angel, the greatest woodsman of Tennessee who swallows an entire lake and throws a tornado with absurd humor and farfetched exaggeration in her effort to catch Thundering Tarnation, a bear. Many

American authors choose to write in the style of the tall tale; Robert MCCLOSKEY's *Lentil* (1940), *Homer Price* (1943), and *Centerburg Tales* (1951) are each written in traditionally humorous tall-tale style. Each of these stories uses many of the myriad devices of humor: essential incongruity, frustration of expectation, wit, nonsense, wordplay, satire, slapstick and exaggeration of character and situation, the rude, the polished, the crude, and the polite.

The domestic or family comedy such as Beverly CLEARY's series about Ramona, Lois LOWRY's Anastasia Krupnik series and Eleanor ESTES's series about the Moffats is a celebration of family life and home. Such comedy has long been a staple of American children's literature and one of its significant contributions to the larger world of children's literature. Authors of PICTURE BOOKS from Judith VIORST in her SERIES about Alexander and his family to Cynthia RYLANT's series about Henry and Mudge are favorites of the read-aloud set precisely because they recognize their own siblings and families in these stories. Kevin HENKES picture book stories about a small mouse, Lili, or Lillian HOBAN's series of books about Francis and her badger family are representative domestic stories using anthropomorphized animals in humorous contexts. Betsy BYARS, Paula DANZIGER, Johanna HURWITZ and Judy BLUME offer older readers wit, humor, and emotional honesty using familiar comic elements. Abundant use of wordplay, funny names and the humor they inspire, forbidden words, repetition and anticipation, and superiority humor contribute to the success of these FAMILY STORIES. The inferred or naive pun—a child's too-literal misunderstanding of a word that has an implicit double meaning—is a reliable source of superiority humor in all of these series. For example, when Anastasia Krupnik wants to get her ears pierced, she tells her father she wants a "lobotomy."

A sense of humor is developmental as young children mature, moving from tickling and peek-a-boo to sophisticated considerations of incongruity, frustration of expectations, and inventive wordplay. An early theory about humor and the human condition attempted to explain humor as a response to situations that invoke feelings of superiority or degradation among listeners and readers. Readers feel superior to a storybook character whose exaggerated or grotesque behavior they interpret as humorous. The superiority theory of humor is invoked by Beverly Cleary when she says that she created the character of Ramona so that children could enjoy a book about a child younger than themselves and feel superior to that remembered younger self. Because they have grown and are more sure of themselves, they can laugh at and feel superior to the inexperienced child who now appears foolish. Another aspect of the superiority theory of humor is that it provides relief from tension, fear, or anxiety. Characters who are humorous because of their eccentricities or exaggerated characteristics include Harry ALLARD's Stupids, Helen CRESSWELL's Bagthorpes, Louis SACHAR's faculty at Wayside School, Morris GLEITZMAN's books, or Lucretia HALE's Peterkin stories. H. A. REY's little monkey, George, is beloved by young children because they can feel superior to him and his troublesome curiosity, a characteristic that they have learned to control but are able to enjoy as an eccentricity in a storybook character.

Humor, identified as the outrightly funny, zany, grotesque, and slapstick—all of which originate in a physical context—is the poor cousin of wit, which is clearly the more cerebral. Wit and humor coalesce in literature since reading is a cerebral activity. In Jon SCIESZKA and Lane SMITH's literary send-up of the traditional story of "The Three Little Pigs," wit and humor coalesce to create the hilarious retelling. The humor derives from A. Wolf's sneezing spells and their slapstick physical disasters; the wit originates in the wolf's language and point of view as he relates events to readers.

Incongruity, akin to surprise, as a type of humor refers to the matching of two generally accepted incompatibles (Walter R. BROOKS's Freddy the Pig riding a bicycle disguised in a dress as an Irish washerwoman or Arnold LOBEL's Toad dressed in an ill-fitting bathing suit being embarrassed lest the pond denizens laugh at his appearance), whereas the frustration of expectation requires an understanding of cause and effect so that readers can laugh at a character's frustration. Readers and viewers laugh when Bullwinkle the Moose reaches into a hat and pulls out not a rabbit but an angry tiger, instead. Children laugh, too, at the further incongruity of a moose as a

magician, and also because the cartoonist who has created Bullwinkle has, through exaggeration and caricature, made him funny-looking. Readers laugh at J. K. ROWLING's Harry Potter and his frustrated expectation when he misses his train back to school, and at the incongruity of the enormous train station with track 8½ invisible to all passengers except Potter and his wizard schoolmates. Both of these types of humor require a fairly sophisticated degree of maturity on the part of readers.

A practical joke involves an element of surprise. And surprising the mind seems to be at the heart of incongruous humor and frustrated expectation. When the element of anticipation is added to this, literary considerations of pacing and timing invoke the pleasurable mind-set children enjoy five minutes before recess. Pippi Longstocking in Astrid LINDGREN's series about an eccentric child and the penguins in *Mr. Popper's Penguins* (ATWATER, 1938) are examples of practical jokes, wordplay, and incongruous situations providing belly laugh humor.

Relief of tension, the third principal theory of humor, is defined by the use of the forbidden kind of dirty-word, scatological (bathroom), or sexual humor that is more likely to be greeted with a snigger than with a laugh. Roald DAHL is a master practitioner of this type of humor as is Gordon KORMAN in his Nose-Picker series and Dav PILKEY in his Captain Underpants series. Pilkey uses forbidden bathroom language in his titles: *Captain Underpants and the Attack of the Talking Toilets* (1999) and *Captain Underpants and the Perilous Plot of Professor Poopypants* (2000). Guaranteed to engender roars of laughter, the professor's full name is Pippy Pee-Pee Poopypants. Superiority humor is used by Pilkey in the ridiculous figure of Captain Underpants, a grown-up who appears in his underwear but is really the school principal in disguise. Pilkey's cartoon ILLUSTRATIONS emphasize the traditional slapstick humor of the text. Enduringly popular, Thomas ROCKWELL's *How to Eat Fried Worms* (1973) continues to be viewed as gross by adults and as a rite of passage among young readers. This type of humor is particularly popular with seven-to-ten-year-old boys.

As noted, laughter, as a means of temporary escape from tension and emotional wounds is essential for children, and they intuitively look for books that will make them laugh. Humorous books need to be taken seriously by critics and presenters of book AWARDS and prizes, if it is true that one of the functions of criticism and award-giving is to encourage the publication of good books, for more good humorous books for children are needed. The light-spirited in literature continues to be treated as if it were lightweight. It is wryly amusing to consider that the NEWBERY MEDAL each won by Betsy Byars, Beverly Cleary, Lois Lowry, and Louis Sachar, and Dav Pilkey's Newbery Medal Honor Book, acknowledge the "serious" work by these authors and not the kinds of humorous works that make them so enormously popular, which continue to command the love of their readers.

BIBLIOGRAPHY: This entry has been adapted from Michael Cart's *What's So Funny?*, 1995

MICHAEL CART

HUNT, Irene

Author, b. 18 May 1907, Pontiac, Illinois

After the early death of her father, H. spent much of her youth on her grandparents' farm in South-eastern Illinois, gathering life experiences that would later appear in her books. For example, her grandfather regaled her with tales of his child-hood, including his memoirs of the Civil War, from which she drew for her first novel, *Across Five Aprils* (1964). The first forty years of H.'s professional career were spent in the Illinois public school system, as a teacher of English and French, a consultant and a director of language arts, along with a brief period as a psychology instructor at the University of South Dakota. Having noted a dearth of good historical fiction for young people, H. began her career as a writer for children shortly before she retired as an educator in 1969.

A hallmark of H.'s novels is her ability to create sensitively drawn, believable characters struggling to cope with their interpersonal problems, often in dysfunctional, depleted, or nontraditional family units. Tackling social issues not commonly addressed in children's novels of the 1960s and 1970s, H. dared to write about children suffering from neglect or abuse by alcoholic or emotionally disturbed caregivers. Some of her child characters grapple with such harrowing issues as teenage pregnancy, rejection due to mental retardation, alienation or isolation from uncaring parents, or the death of a parent. Despite the seeming grimness of such topics, H. writes with insightful compassion and warmth about the courage and strength these young characters draw from their adversity, and the support they receive from sympathetic characters. The protagonists, predominantly young males, ultimately triumph and grow to wisdom and maturity, often forging strong family relationships along the way.

H. has written eight novels in just over twenty years; five of them have been historical novels, set variously in times ranging from the early 1800s frontier days, the Civil War, the early 1900s suffragette struggles, and the Depression years of the 1930s, in both city and mountain, Northern and Southern regions. Although these books are set against an authentically detailed historical backdrop, the main focus of these family-oriented stories is family relationships, initially strained by the turbulent times that divide family members, but usually resolved in uplifting and deeply moving ways. Her book about children who took to the road during the Great Depression, *No Promises in the Wind* (1970), has been optioned for film rights. H. has also been a contributor to the *Horn Book* magazine, and *The Writers' Handbook*.

AWARDS: ALA NEWBERY MEDAL (1967) for *Up a Road Slowly*. ALA Newbery Medal Honor Book (1965) for *Across Five Aprils*

FURTHER WORKS: *Trail of Apple Blossoms.* 1968. *The Lottery Rose* 1976. *William.* 1977. *Claws of a Young Century.* 1980. *The Everlasting Hills.* 1985

BIBLIOGRAPHY: THE KERLAN COLLECTION; *Children's Literature Review,* 1976; *Dictionary of Literary Biography,* vol. 52, 1986; HOPKINS, Lee Bennett, *More Books by More People,* 1974; Hopkins, Lee Bennett, *Pauses: Autobiographical Reflections of 101 Creators of Children's Books,* 1995; Silvey, Anita, ed., *Children's Books and Their Illustrators,* 1995

BARBARA TOBIN

HUNTER, Mollie (Maureen Mollie Hunter McIlwraith)

Author, b. 30 June 1922, Longniddy, East Lothian, Scotland

H. skillfully blends Scottish FOLKLORE, historical knowledge and a thorough understanding of children's psychology in the creation of her critically praised and popular novels for children. Her STORYTELLING displays a mastery of two genres, FANTASY and historical fiction, as well as it reveals avenues young readers can follow toward a mature understanding of the human condition.

H. was born into a working-class family for whom both literature and folklore were held in high esteem. She learned to read early and realized that a career as a writer was indeed an excellent fit for herself when it was foretold to her by a friendly teacher. H. left school in her early teens to go to work, but she was by then grounded solidly in Scottish history and an understanding of grammar that included reference points to the ancient Doric language of her birthplace. She continued her education independently, reading and researching her way through library books on history, religion, and other subjects of concern to her maturing intellect.

The Kelpie's Pearls (1964) features the distinctly Scottish folk creature of the kelpie, a species-changing sea animal; *The Ferlie* (1968), is another tale with folkloric roots. H.'s fantasies, including *The Walking Stones* (1970), *The Haunted Mountain* (1972), and *A Stranger Came Ashore* (1975), are not the retellings of folktales but rather original stories with their roots in Celtic lore. H.'s childhood memories of her great-grandmother's stories, augmented by her adult studies of folklorists' research, imbue these fantasies with insights that are accessible to children searching for the meanings behind their own fears, cultural superstitions, and false appearances within the natural everyday world. Witches, shape-changers, and other traditional Celtic folk beings populate these fantasies in which humans are the protagonists.

To write her historical novels, H. has relied upon considerable original research. Going beyond history books, she has consulted primary documents such as letters and diaries. Her own love of language has attuned her to the difference between storytelling aloud and writing a story, which must remain accessible to youth with age-limited vocabularies and grammatical knowledge, while maintaining a story-appropriate archaic vocabulary and diction. She has solved this issue gracefully by providing archaic flavorings,

using simplified grammar and well-selected phrases, rather than forcing her audience to learn the rudiments of Doric in order to enjoy the story. *The Spanish Letters* (1964), *The Thirteenth Member* (1971), and *The Stronghold* (1974) all developed from H.'s study of particular events in history, from the premillenial Roman attack on the Celts, in *The Stronghold*, through the sixteenth century. *A Pistol in Greenyards* (1965) brought to readers' attention the concept of class struggle, telling of an event in nineteenth century Scotland but clearly applicable to other times and places. *The King's Swift Rider: A Novel on Robert the Bruce* (1998) reaches back to the thirteenth century to present a character whose peace-loving nature is challenged by the need to fight for king and country. H. said, "We Scots live close to our history. I chat with my neighbors about Robert the Bruce on the way to pick up my mail." By offering young readers real history, clothed in real storytelling, H. gives children the opportunity to meet characters about whom they can also feel real emotions.

A Sound of Chariots (1972) is H.'s most autobiographical novel. The death of her father when she was nine left H. grief-stricken. In her protagonist, Bridie McShane, H. reveals how a child can find her way from grief back to life. Like H., Bridie is active, rather than passive, intent on working out her future. *Hold on to Love* (1983) continues Bridie's story as she develops into a writer.

Although the main body of H.'s work has been novels for children and YOUNG ADULTS, she has created plays and picture-book texts as well. *The Knight of the Golden Plain* (1983), *The Three-Day Enchantment* (1985), and *Day of the Unicorn* (1994) depict the chivalric daydreams of a modern little boy. *Gilly Martin the Fox* (1994) retells a Scottish FAIRY TALE for very young readers.

AWARDS: British Library Association CARNEGIE MEDAL (1974) for *The Stronghold*. Scottish Arts Council Award (1973) for *The Haunted Mountain*. AMERICAN LIBRARY ASSOCIATION Notable Book (1964) for *The Kelpie's Pearls,* (1972) for *A Sound of Chariots* and *The Haunted Mountain,* (1974) for *The Stronghold,* (1975) for *A Stranger Came Ashore,* and (1977) for *The Wicked One: A Story of Suspense*. ALA Best Books for Young Adults (1986) for *Cat Herself*. National Council of Social Studies and the CHILDREN'S BOOK

COUNCIL Notable Children's Trade Book in the Field of Social Studies (1982) for *You Never Knew Her as I Did!* ALA May Hill Arbuthnot Lecture award (1975). H. received the highest award Scotland gives: her portrait hangs in the Scottish National Portrait Gallery.

FURTHER WORKS: *Patrick Kentigern Keenan,* 1963. Published in the United States as *The Smartest Man in Ireland,* 1965; *Hi, Johnny,* 1963; *The Ghosts of Glencoe,* 1966; *Thomas and the Warlock,* 1967; *The Lothian Run,* 1970; *Talent Is Not Enough,* 1975; *A Furl of Fairy Wind: Four Stories,* 1977; *Cat Herself,* 1986. Published in the United Kingdom as *I'll Go My Own Way,* 1985; *The Mermaid Summer,* 1988

BIBLIOGRAPHY: Hunter, M. *Talent Is Not Enough: On Writing for Children,* 1976; Hunter, M., *"The Pied Piper Syndrome" and Other Essays,* 1993; Silvey, Anita, ed., *Children's Books and Their Creators,* 1995; *Something about the Author,* vol. 54, 1989; personal contact with the author

FRANCISCA GOLDSMITH

HURD, Clement

Author, illustrator, b. 12 January 1908, New York City; d. 5 February 1988, San Francisco, California

In response to H.'s creation of the mischievous bunny and magical bedroom in Margaret Wise BROWN's classic *Goodnight Moon* (1947), H. has become one of the best known American illustrators. H. was trained as a classical painter and entered the field of children's literature rather serendipitously after earning a Ph.D. degree from Yale University (1930) and studying painting in Paris with Fernand Leger from 1931 to 1933. The difficult economic conditions of the 1930s forced H., as a freelance designer, to accept odd jobs such as painting murals on bathroom walls, designing needlework charts, and rug designing. While painting a mural on a bathroom wall, H. met Margaret Wise BROWN and was invited to illustrate one of her books, *Bumble Bugs and Elephants* (1938). H. and his wife, Edith Thacher HURD, continued collaborating successfully with Brown through their membership in the Writer's Laboratory at the Bank Street College of Education.

H.'s most successful collaboration with Brown was on her classic *Goodnight Moon* (1947) in which a little bunny says good night to all the things in his room as bold colors and black-and-white ILLUSTRATIONS combine with intersecting lines and angles to calm and reassure young children in a predictable repetition of text and image. H. fondly recalled work sessions with Brown as intense, exciting, and stimulating. H. noted that "maybe collaboration on a creative level is always difficult, and maybe the more creative a person is, the more difficult he or she is to work with; but I do feel that all Margaret's main illustrators did their best work on her books. . . . Without doubt, my pictures for *The Runaway Bunny* (1942) and *Goodnight Moon* are considered my best work. . . . I do know that working with Margaret was difficult but at the same time stimulating and satisfying." And through such books, H.'s distinctive style of bold shapes, bright, flat colors, and the importance of line and perspective are best celebrated. His illustrations comfort readers and lend themselves well to memorable readings with young children. H. and Edith Thacher Hurd worked together on more than fifty books; this collaboration provided him space for experimentation with various media including prints and woodcuts. H. used linoleum-block prints on weathered wood for the illustrations of two flying fish in *Wingfin and Topple* (Edmund Valens, 1962). The illustrations have the look of being done under water and appear to flow from page to page. H. completed many of the illustrations for the I Can Read series published by Harper and Row.

At his funeral service, H.'s grandson read *Goodnight Moon.* More than two million copies of this book have been sold since 1947 and continue to find their way into the hearts of families each year. Readers continue to relive the legacy of H. through his powerfully engaging and distinctive illustrations.

FURTHER WORKS: (written by Edith Thacher H.) *Engine, Engine, No. 9.* 1940. *Christmas Eve.* 1962. *The So-So Cat.* 1965. *The Mother Beaver.* 1971. *Under the Lemon Tree.* 1980. Written by Margaret Wise Brown: *Runaway Bunny.* 1942. *The Little Brass Band.* 1955. *Diggers.* 1960

BIBLIOGRAPHY: MEIGS, C., Anne T. Eaton, Elizabeth NESBIT, Ruth Hill Viguers, eds. 1969. *A Crit-*

ical History of Children's Literature. Something About the Author. vol. 64, 1991

SHANE RAYBURN

HURD, Edith Thacher

Author, illustrator; b. 14 September 1910, Kansas City, Missouri; d. 25 January 1997, Walnut Creek, California

Having participated in the Bank Street College Writer's Laboratory where creativity and innovation were used to challenge conventional notions in education, H. began her writing career working for Young Scott Books, a company focusing on a new child-centered direction in children's books. Margaret Wise BROWN and Ruth KRAUSS were also among this group who began writing books from a child's point of view and exploring children's experiences through their senses as opposed to the predominant narrative form of folktales and ADVENTURE STORIES. Publishing more than seventy-five books for young readers, H. often published with her husband, Clement HURD, as illustrator. These books include *Engine, Engine, No. 9* (1940), *Mr. Charlie's Pet Shop* (1959), *The Day the Sun Danced* (1965), and *The Mother Kangaroo* (1976). *Five Little Firemen* (1948), *Two Little Gardners* (1951), and other titles were collaborations between H. and Margaret Wise Brown; they also wrote under the joint pseudonym of Juniper Sage. The H.'s son, Thacher HURD, is also an author and illustrator.

FURTHER WORKS: *The Wreck of the Wild Wave.* 1942. *Mr. Shortsleeve's Great Big Store.* 1952. *Come with Me to Nursery School.* 1970. *I Dance in My Red Pajamas.* 1982

BIBLIOGRAPHY: *Something about the Author,* vol. 64, 1991, and vol. 95, 1998; Fuller, Muriel, ed. *More Junior Authors,* 1963

JANELLE B. MATHIS

HURWITZ, Johanna

Author, b. 9 October 1937, New York City

H. is the author of many books for young readers and adolescents. Her novels present a light-hearted look into the world of childhood and the struggles of growing up. H. grew up in New York City, the daughter of a journalist and a librarian's assistant who met in a bookstore. Her parents passed on their love of books to H. At the age of

ten H. decided to become a writer and librarian. While in high school she worked in a branch of the New York Public Library. She attended Queens College and Columbia University. In 1959 H. became a children's librarian. Although she began writing at an early age H.'s first book, *Busybody Nora,* was not published until 1976.

This book like many of H.'s other novels is based on the author's experiences in rearing a family in a New York apartment. The novel is about the daily adventures of the seven-year-old protagonist living in a large New York City apartment building. H. has written many other books that are derived from her own experiences. *Baseball Fever* (1981) is about the author's love of baseball. *Once I Was a Plum Tree* (1980) reflects her experiences growing up in the post-World War II era. *The Rabbi's Girls* (1982) is about H.'s mother's childhood. *Yellow Blue Jay* (1986) is about a summer vacation in Vermont. *Hurricane Elaine* (1986) is derived from H.'s cat's experience with fleas.

H.'s books often involve recurring characters. A minor character in one book may appear to be a main character in another. For example, Aldo, a fourth grader, in *Aldo Ice Cream* (1981) and *Aldo Applesauce* (1979) has an older sister who becomes the focus of *Tough-Luck Karen* (1982). In another novel, *Hurricane Elaine* (1986), H. focuses on Elaine, another one of Aldo's older sisters. The recurring families are not limited to the Sousa family; they appear in her books about school. In *Class Clown* (1987), Lucas, a second grader, learns to control his behavior. A class member, Cricket Kaufman, is a minor antagonist in this novel. Yet in *Teacher's Pet* (1988) Cricket is the protagonist and Lucas appears as a minor character. The recurring characters often allow the reader to form a connection with H.'s books and to make friends with the characters.

H. presents the struggles of being a child with vivid realism. H.'s ability to show the growth of her characters through simple everyday events is evident in many of her books. For example in *Teacher's Pet* (1988) Cricket wants to impress her teacher; but a new student, Zoe, seems to keep showing her up. Cricket, a fourth grader, makes a personal discovery about being herself. In *The Hot and Cold Summer* (1984) Derek and Rory, best friends, are looking forward to fun during a summer together. A neighbor's niece comes to visit and they have to accept a change in their friendship. In *Even Stephen* (1996) Sunny learns how to help her "perfect" brother understand that he cannot fix everything; while she learns that she has as much potential as he. These novels present issues that children feel are important in their own lives. The realism becomes evident as the child reads. Hope for the future appears in H.'s novels as her main characters experience personal growth.

H.'s novels are not preachy; yet through the characters' actions readers can learn important lessons. In *Class Clown* (1987) Lucas shows the reader that it pays to try to behave in school. In *The Hot and Cold Summer* (1984) Derek and Rory learn to accept and make a new friend. In *Even Stephen* (1996) and *Teacher's Pet* (1988) the idea that no one can really be perfect is understood. In *Once I Was a Plum Tree* (1980) Geraldine learns that she can form her own sense of identity. In *Hurray for Ali Baba Bernstein* (1989) there are a combination of short stories that show the reason David chooses a unique name. H. does an excellent job of helping young children learn more about themselves and search for their own identity. Her books remain in print and appear frequently on children's choices lists in all states.

FURTHER WORKS: *Nora and Mrs. Mind Your Own Business.* 1977 and 1991. *What Goes up Must Come Down.* 1983. *Much Ado about Aldo.* 1978. *New Neighbors for Nora.* 1979 and 1991. *Superduper Teddy.* 1980 and 1990. *Rip-Roaring Russell.* 1983. *DeDe Takes Charge!* 1984. *The Adventures of Ali Baba Bernstein.* 1985. *Russell Rides Again.* 1985. *Russell Sprouts.* 1987. *The Cold and Hot Winter.* 1988. *Anne Frank: Life in Hiding.* 1988. *Astrid Lindgren: Storyteller to the World.* 1989. *Russell and Elisa.* 1989. *Class President.* 1990. *Aldo Peanut Butter.* 1990. *"E" is for Elisa.* 1991. *School's Out.* 1991. *Roz and Ozzie.* 1992. *Ali Baba Bernstein: Lost and Found.* 1992. *Faraway Summer.* 1998

BIBLIOGRAPHY: *Something about the Author,* vol. 71, 1993; *Sixth Book of Junior Authors and Illustrators,* 1989; *Twentieth Century Children's Writers,* 4th ed., 1995

NANCE S. WILSON

HUTCHINS, Pat

Author, illustrator, b. 18 June 1942, Yorkshire, England

An illustrator and author of over twenty-four books for young children, H. has written and illustrated ANIMAL STORIES, moral tales, concept books, and REALISTIC FICTION. H. was one of seven children. "Being born and brought up in the country affected my work enormously. We were surrounded by fields and woods full of wildlife, and spent many hours watching the animals and birds." Injured animals were taken home and cared for. H. began drawing pictures of the local countryside, Norman churches and stone cottages. She received a scholarship to Darlington School of Art at age sixteen. Two years later she won a scholarship to Leeds College of Art and studied ILLUSTRATION. She worked as an assistant art director at an advertising agency upon graduation and there met and married. Her husband was transferred to New York City and H. began showing her illustrations to New York publishers. Editor Susan Hirschman encouraged H. to illustrate and write her own books; *Rosie's Walk* (1968) was the result. H. says the original *Rosie's Walk* had a host of farm animals such as cows, sheep, and ducks but she decided it was "boring" and pared it down. *Rosie's Walk* is considered a picture-book classic. Rosie the Hen goes for a walk; in just thirty-two words and thirty-two pages a complete logical story is clearly and humorously presented and resolved. Rosie begins her walk with her beak in the air; she strides off oblivious to the fox stalking her. The patterned illustrations have the look of woodcuts. Very young children can follow the action and the HUMOR. In 1968 *Rosie's Walk* was named an American Library Association Notable Book and also received a *Boston Globe–Horn Book* illustration honor.

Simplicity is a dynamic aim for H. She believes young children can understand difficult concepts if they are presented simply and logically. In *Changes, Changes* (1971), a wordless PICTURE BOOK, two wooden figures arrange multicolored blocks and create recognizable forms that solve emergencies. Excellent for STORYTELLING, children look at the pictures and tell the story as elaborately as they choose, using pictures as clues. To H. the most difficult part of writing a book is to acquire an original basic idea. Once she has an idea she works out how to present it in book form. After that she writes the story and does the layout. "To a very small child an opened book is one page, not two—he doesn't see the gutter as a dividing line."

Titch (1971) was on the INTERNATIONAL BOARD ON BOOKS FOR YOUNG PEOPLE illustrations honor list in 1974. A straightforward tale of the third child who is youngest and smallest, Titch has his moment of victory. Making good use of white space, the large type size and colorful figures make this an appealing book. *One-Eyed Jake* (1979), a colorful repetitive story, is about a pirate captain and his crew who are out to rob everyone on the high seas until three of his crew decide they want to stop. One-Eyed Jake meets an untimely end and the bosun, cook and ship's cat are released from their imprisonment. *The Doorbell Rang* (1986) is an exuberant book with a busy background, a brief repetitive text and a math concept at the root. Children divide cookies grudgingly until Grandma arrives bringing dozens more cookies. H. says about her writing, "I think the most important thing is to entertain, but I also want to make a point that will make children think."

AWARDS: KATE GREENAWAY MEDAL (1974) for *The Wind Blew. New York Times* Best Illustrated Children's Books of the Year (1971), Spring Book Festival picture book (1971), Children's Book Showcase title (1972) and Brooklyn Art Books for Children Award (1973) for *Changes, Changes.* IBBY (1974) for *Titch*

FURTHER WORKS: *Happy Birthday, Sam,* 1978; *The Tale of Thomas Mead,* 1980; *One Hunter,* 1982; *Little Pink Pig,* 1994; *Shrinking Mouse,* 1997

BIBLIOGRAPHY: *Children's Literature Review,* vol. 20, 1990. *Fiction, FOLKLORE, FANTASY and POETRY for Children, 1876–1985,* vols. 1 and 2; Jones, Delores Blythe, ed., *Children's Literature AWARDS and Winners, Authors and Illustrators,* 3rd ed., 1994; Silvey, Anita, ed., *Children's Books and Their Creators,* 1995; *Something about the Author,* vol. 15, 1979, and vol. 70, 1993

IRVYN G. GILBERTSON

HUTTON, Warwick

Author, illustrator, b. 17 July 1939; d. 28 September 1994

A resident of Cambridge, England, H. was an illustrator, painter, and glass engraver. He also worked with woodcuts. In addition to his art, H. wrote, adapted and translated several self-illus-

trated children's books including *Adam and Eve: The BIBLE Story* (1987) and *The Tinderbox* (Hans Christian ANDERSEN, 1988). H. enjoyed writing his own texts and then "drawing and painting his way into the stories." He worked with real models such as objects and landscapes to inspire his work. His hope was that adults as well as children would appreciate his work. H.'s ILLUSTRATIONS, often done in pen and ink with full-color watercolors, are notable for their expressionistic style and placement on the page. In *Adam and Eve,* based on the opening chapters of Genesis, H. depicts Adam and Eve in the Garden of Eden; God is shown in rear view image only to appear less intimidating and leave young readers to their own imaginations.

AWARDS: *New York Times* Best Illustrated Children's Books of the Year (1981) for *the Nose Tree* and (1984) for *Jonah and the Great Fish,* and (1989) for *Theseus and the Minotaur. Boston Globe-Horn Book* Illustrator Award (1984) for *Jonah and the Great Fish*

FURTHER WORKS: Illus: *The Selkie Girl.* (Susan COOPER, reteller), 1986. *Tam Lin.* (S. Cooper, reteller). 1991. *Moses in the Bulrushes.* 1986. *Thesus and the Minotaur.* 1989

BIBLIOGRAPHY: Cianciolo, Patricia. *PICTURE BOOKS for Children.* 3rd ed. 1990. *Something about the Author.* vol. 20, 1980 and vol. 83, 1996

MICHAEL O'LAUGHLIN

HYMAN, Trina Schart

Author, illustrator, b. 8 April 1939, Philadelphia, Pennsylvania

The winner of the 1985 CALDECOTT MEDAL for *Saint George and the Dragon* and recipient of many honors, H. has been hailed as one of the great quintessentially romantic interpreters of FOLKLORE and myths. Her gloriously illustrated FAIRY TALES and legends, the best known of her many works, continue the classic traditions set by Arthur RACKHAM and Edmund DULAC.

Growing up in a rural area north of Philadelphia, H. and her sisters were deeply involved in imaginary play. The tales of the GRIMMS and ANDERSEN were completely familiar, and the sisters were encouraged to believe that supernatural beings hovered just beyond their vision. Early on, H. was able to visualize characters and settings and share them with others. She particularly enjoyed the magical tales her father invented on long walks they took on starry nights; she credits him for her love of myth and FANTASY.

H. studied at the Philadelphia College of Art, The Museum School of Fine Art in Boston, and at the School of Applied Art in Stockholm, Sweden. From 1971 to 1978 she worked as an art director at *Cricket* magazine where she created many of the "cricket" and "ladybug" characters. In 1961 she launched her highly successful career as an illustrator with the publication of a Swedish tale, *Toffe and the Little Car.* Since then she has illustrated over 130 books, four of which she has authored.

Although H.'s illustrations are extremely precise and technically skillful, always based on carefully rendered black-and-white drawing with acrylics laid on, her work is remarkable primarily for its realistic, romantic, and expressive qualities. The influence of gothic art and literature on her work is clearly evident. Settings are truly macabre, mysterious, violent, gloriously romantic, or exceedingly cozy, while princesses are most beautiful, princes most handsome, and the forces of evil incredibly ugly. This exaggerated expressive quality works well to clarify the meaning of her highly dramatic subject matter.

In many of her books H. uses an elaborate series of patterned or designed borders that enclose a page of text or illustration. The borders often contain charming pictorial elements that help to illuminate the text. Frequently, if without a designed border, H.'s illustrations create the illusion that the scene is being viewed through a window or framed by a forest. At times viewers have the sense of looking through a proscenium arch at a play about to unfold. This technique is particularly effective in *The Kitchen Knight* (1990) and *Saint George and the Dragon* (1984), Arthurian tales retold by Margaret HODGES.

Before beginning a project, H. becomes completely familiar with the story. She tries to gear the color, mood, energy of line, and atmosphere to the feelings and intent of the text. If there is a particular geographic, historical, or cultural framework, she does quantities of research to assure the credibility and integrity of the illustrations. Generally, she begins with a black and white line drawing, and gradually adds a palette of acrylics that are often basic or earth tones. This technique gives the pictures a rather moody and somber tone. However, on occasion she uses the bright rich colors typical of medieval egg tempera paintings. Although landscapes and architecture are important, it is her sensitive work on facial expression and body movement that allows the reader to feel the true meaning of her story. This attention to faces led her to illustrate *Little Red Riding Hood* (1983)—among the illustrations on the dustjacket of this book—her favorite childhood story, using herself, her mother and grandmother as lovingly remembered models. The magic and mystery of fairy tales and legends are completely captured by this gifted illustrator. However, even when illustrating more realistic subject matters of love and loss, H. has a great impact on her young audience.

AWARDS: AMERICAN LIBRARY ASSOCIATION Caldecott Medal (1985) for *Saint George and the Dragon* (Margaret Hodges, reteller). ALA Caldecott Medal Honor Book (1984) for *Little Red Riding Hood;* (1990) for *Hershel and the Hanukkah Goblins* (Eric KIMMEL, author), and (2000) for *A Child's Calendar* (John Updike, poet). *Boston Globe-Horn Book* Award for ILLUSTRATION (1973) for *King Stork* and (1993) for *The Fortune Tellers* (Lloyd ALEXANDER, author). Golden Kite Award (1983) for *Little Red Riding Hood. New York Times* Best Illustrated Children's Books of the Year (1984) for *Saint George and the Dragon* (Margaret Hodges, reteller) and (1992) for *The Fortune Tellers* (Lloyd Alexander, author)

FURTHER WORKS: *Self-Portrait: Trina Schart Hyman.* 1989. *A Little Alphabet.* 1993. *Canterbury Tales.* (Barbara COHEN, adapter). 1988. *Comus.* (John Milton, Margaret Hodges, adapter). 1996. *The Golem.* (Barbara ROGASKY, adapter). 1996. *Iron John: A Tale from the Brothers Grimm.* (Eric A. Kimmel, adapter). 1994. *Swan Lake.* (Retold by Margot Fonteyn). 1989. *Child's Christmas in Wales.* (Dylan Thomas). 1985. *Why Don't You Get a Horse, Sam Adams?* (Jean FRITZ). 1974

BIBLIOGRAPHY: *Children's Literature Review,* vol. 50, 1999. Cummins, J. *Children's Book Illustration and Design.* 1992. Evans, D. The Art of Trina Schart H. in *Comus* and *The Golem.* 1997. *Book Links,* vol. 6, no. 4, 27–29. Kovacs, D. and J. Preller. *Meet the Authors and Illustrators.* 1991. *Something about the Author,* vol. 46, 1987, and vol. 95, 1998

JUDITH LIPSITT

ILLUSTRATION

Illustration is the vigor and vitality of children's books. From Randolph CALDECOTT to Peggy RATHMANN, illustrators have played a significant role in children's books. One hundred years have passed from the late 1800s when Caldecott's energetic lines and careful compositions created lively action to the late 1990s when Rathmann's own energetic line and dramatic composition echoes the standards that Caldecott created. That liveliness of spirit and excitement has continued amid the changes that have taken place in illustration, and the measure of delight has increased as visual images depict, interpret, enliven, and enhance words on the pages of children's books.

A picture book is a unique art form; it is a unified blend of picture and books that together create a whole. The fusion of pictures and text is essential for the unity of presentation. In PICTURE BOOKS, the illustrations blend with the narrative to serve as one voice telling the story. History cites *Orbis Pictus* as the first picture book, produced in 1658 by COMENIUS, a Moravian educator and bishop. His purpose in adding pictures to an informational text was to "stir up attention." There is no question that today's state of children's book illustration is one that whirls with attention-getting pictures.

Children's books have always reflected attitudes of the times in which they originated. In the nineteenth century days of Randolph Caldecott, Walter CRANE, and Kate GREENAWAY, picture books depicted Victorian behavior, sentimental-ity and fashion. Today's picture books no longer treat children as miniature adults; instead they present all types of contemporary issues as well as simple entertainment, with respect for the child's feelings and intelligence. The stiffness of Victorian families has been set aside for realistic portrayals of modern times ranging from single parents in poverty settings to urban immigrant children to clever animal tales.

The production of book illustration has been revolutionized by technology. Gone are the days of labor intensive, four-color separations painted on overlays by hand; now they are camera separated and mechanically engineered. Computer generated art has become a commonly used method. The capability of technology has given a free hand to illustrators to create at will, with few limitations.

Techniques, styles, and choice of media are as varied as flavors of ice cream. No longer is there an "accustomed" proscribed look to picture books, in the way that books published in the 1930s, 1940s, and 1950s had a particularly distinctive style. There is no list of what is acceptable in the ways stories are presented. Imagination, creativity, child appeal, and adaptation of style to story are the key ingredients in the cornucopia of successful illustration.

From the dramatic black-and-white perspectives Chris Van ALLSBURG drew in *Jumanji* (1981) to the pulp paper paintings created by Denise FLEMING in *The Small, Small Pond* (1993) illustrators are using a multitude of paints, pencils, fabrics, and objects to create exciting, artistic works in children's books. Traditional techniques such as woodcuts and scratchboard are still in use with enhanced reproduction capabilities making them even more striking, while experimentation with mixed media substances are producing fresh, textural images crafted from clay, fabrics, and collages of paper and real objects. Humorous cartoonish styles are equally as appropriate as painterly, sophisticated oil renderings for all ages of children. What matters is that style and media choice are germane to the content presentation.

The burgeoning of the field has attracted artists from other art specialties, such as films, advertising, graphic design, and cartoon illustration. The works of Gerald MCDERMOTT, Peter SIS, David MACAULAY, Lane SMITH, and David Catrow are outstanding examples of how techniques applied from other artistic fields effectively modulate to children's book illustration. Bold, graphic designs, cinematic movement, sculptured perspectives, jaunty layouts that incorporate playfulness with typefaces and composition, and the exaggeration of political cartooning have manifested wonderful picture books.

The "white bread" look of children's illustration from decades past has faded away from depicting the perfect white family with cookie-baking mother and newspaper-reading father to the multicultural wholesomeness of diverse cultures and ethnically stylized illustrations. In the growing years of illustration patterns, there was a thrust toward an Americanized look. The peasant drawings of Wanda GAG and the folk art quality of the D'AULAIRES were among the few exceptions of ethnic style, but they quietly laid the groundwork for contemporary cross-cultural appreciation. With the styles of Patricia PALOCCO, Yumi Heo, Jerry PINKNEY, and Jean and Mousien Tseng reflecting their cultural heritages, these illustrators are contributing an essence of their origins to today's stories that lends a feeling of universality.

There are two illustrators whose inventiveness and individual style have forever influenced children's book illustration. They are the two "S's"—Dr. SEUSS and Maurice SENDAK. The images created by both men speak to the child, one in a whimsical, cartoonish fashion, the other in beautifully rendered, sophisticated fantasies.

Their readily identifiable styles are at opposite ends of the spectrum, yet each treats their audience with respect and without condescension, at one end providing silliness and comic relief and at the other, psychologically reaching the child within. As with any successful artists, there are imitators but the work of Seuss and Sendak have set milestones in the evolution of children's book illustration and creativity; their unique imprints are the apex.

Recognition of illustration in children's books has been elevated through numerous awards. The two most prestigious are the CALDECOTT MEDAL and the Kate GREENAWAY AWARD. Bestowed annually, the Caldecott Medal is presented to the artist of the most distinguished American picture book for children. The Kate Greenaway Award is the British counterpart that is awarded annually to an artist who has produced the most distinguished work in illustration of a children's book. Both medals are named after British artists who were instrumental in revolutionizing children's book illustration. Internationally, the Hans Christian ANDERSEN Medal is presented every two years for a body of work and the Biennale of Illustrations Bratislava is presented every two years for original art for individual books. The *New York Times*'s annual list of "10 Best Illustrated Books" cites excellence in illustration and adds to the stature of the field.

From the realism of Barry MOSER to the impressionistic images of Robert Andrew Parker; from the simple cut-out shapes of Leo LIONNI to the intricately detailed watercolors of Gennady Spirin; from the playfulness of Janet STEVENS to the elegance of Allan SAY; from the dramatically etched black-white scratchboards of Michael McCurdy to the brilliantly hued collages of Lois EHLERT; illustrations in children's picture books are alive and well. They are pulsing with vitality, creativity, and ingenuity as they depict the wonderment of childhood. Pictures are a child's introduction to the world of books. Visual images lead to visual literacy that leads to literacy. They serve a role as the first-step "eye-opener" to the enjoyment found in books that gradually becomes an experience with pictures that fill the eye with delight.

In the last ten years, more than twenty types of media have been used in the Caldecott Medal and Honor books. From the first Caldecott Medal in 1938 with black-white lithographs by Dorothy LATHROP in *Animals of the Bible* to sixty years later with the elegant, Renaissance-styled interpretation of *Rapunzel* by Paul O. ZELINSKY, illustration has attained the status of an art form. Standards of excellence have been rooted firmly by the early masters such as Marcia BROWN, Robert MCCLOSKEY, Wanda GAG, and Ludwig BEMELMANS, and they continue to bloom as new talents add their own creative touch.

Lewis CARROLL put it succinctly in *Alice in Wonderland:* "What is the use of a book," thought Alice, "without pictures or conversations?"

JULIE CUMMINS

(See also BOOK DESIGN; PICTURE BOOKS; VISUAL LITERACY)

INDIAN (EAST) LITERATURE

India is a geopolitical entity, but one cannot homogenize Indian children's literature into one tradition and one set of classics, any more than "European children's literature" can be seen as a seamless whole. Literacy is not universal in South Asia: more than half of India's population cannot read or write, and Indian literatures consist of oral materials in many languages (over 3,000 dialects under 105 languages), and writings primarily in the fourteen major languages recognized in the Constitution. The languages relate to different regions, ethnicities and cultures, and cross-various religious groups. In each major language, children's literature has its own points of origin, its own features, its own luminaries, its own often short-lived children's MAGAZINES, its own more stable children's sections in regional newspapers, its own scholarship, and its own sometimes very sophisticated critical interpretations of texts.

Accounts usually start by evoking materials of interest to children in classical tale collections in Sanskrit and Pali- Puranic Hindu religious tales, the witty fables of the *Panchatantra* (proudly assigned to ca. 600 C.E.) and the *Hitopadesha,* the birth stories of the Buddha in the *Jatakas* (including probably the earliest form of "The Tar Baby"), the exemplary Buddhist *Avadanas,* and the sometimes romantic novella-like tales of the *Brihat-Katha* and the *Katha-Sarit-Sagara.* The

classic compendia drew upon folk and oral materials (the *Katha-Sarit-Sagara* in the eleventh century), were themselves translated into the modern vernaculars over time, and these materials exist in live folk oral traditions and popular culture, including children's literature, to this day—in the 1960s, the *Panchatantra* was serialized in English for urban Indian Anglophone children in comic-strip form in the *Illustrated Weekly of India.* Apart from local folk nursery rhymes and lullabies, Indic folk tales themselves, many of them heard and read by children, are often pan–Indian as well as international, comprising the distinct genres of moral tales, beast fables, aetiologies, local legends, romances, Märchen, tales about tales, chain tales, formula tales, circular tales, riddle tales, numbskull tales, and nonsense tales. Children are usually familiar with some form of the classical epics the *Ramayana* and the *Mahabharata.*

On the whole, the nontraditional modern children's literature originated from the early or mid-nineteenth century and developed at different rates, often under the influence of Western notions of education and child development, sometimes under the aegis of enlightened royalty, as in Malayalam and Marathi, more often particularly as a result of Christian missionary literary and pedagogic activity, including the work of Indian converts. For example, the late eighteenth-century Italian Jesuit, Costantino Beschi, wrote numbskull tales in Tamil *(The Adventures of Guru Paramarthan),* which may have originated either locally or in Europe, and became part of both living folk and children's oral/literary traditions in Tamil, Telegu, and Kannada. The Baptist William Carey's *Itihas Mala* (1812), "history [= story] garland," a textbook, was the first book for children in Bengali, and stands at the head of what is arguably the richest Indian tradition of children's literature, some of it available in English translation. Missionaries published the first Assamese magazine, *Arunodaya,* "dawn," in 1836, and added a children's section to it early on. There are proud memories of completely indigenous traditional relations between pedagogy and art, as in the *chautisa* ("thirty-two") verse-form in Oriya, with sections in alphabetical sequence, and the subsequent Oriya adoption of folk meters and imagery in children's poetry, or the traditional Telegu form of the *sataka* ("hundred poem" collection) used for educational purposes.

Indian children's literature published in English parallels the colonial era. Mary Frere, daughter of the British Governor of Bombay, published a collection of Indian folktales in English titled *Old Deccan Days; or, Hindoo Fairy Legends* in 1868. These were stories told to Frere by her Indian nursemaid. It was followed by Flora Annie Steel's *Wide-Awake Stories* in 1884 and republished in 1894 as *Tales of the Punjab*. The FOLKLORE anthologist Joseph JACOBS used these two collections as well as Jataka and Bidpai tales to publish his classic collection of *Indian FAIRY TALES* in 1892, thereby bringing the rich stories of the Indian subcontinent to the English–speaking world. Bidpai fables were first translated into English from the Sanskrit and Hindu languages in 1570 by Sir Thomas North. The celebrated Indian poet, Rabindranath Tagore, wrote for children as well; his POETRY, *Paper Boats* (1992), is available today in an English–language edition. Dhan Gopal MUKERJI was born in Calcutta, worked in the U.S., and won a NEWBERY MEDAL in 1928 for *Gay Neck*. Several contemporary Indian authors are writing in English for today's young readers. Shirley Arora *(What Then, Ramon?* 1960), Anita Desai *(The Peacock Garden,* 1979; *The Village by the Sea,* 1982), Ruskin BOND, and Madhur Jaffray *(Seasons of Splendor; Tales, Myths, and Legends of India,* 1985) are bringing Indian literary traditions and sensibilities to English–speaking children.

Many of the children's literatures have long histories of translations from English—the major European folktales, ANDERSEN, La Fontaine, the European classics from Cervantes, SWIFT, Bunyan, DEFOE, Lewis CARROLL to Tolstoy, Jules VERNE, Mark TWAIN and Robert Louis STEVENSON. Yet there was and still is relatively little cross-translation between children's works in the Indian languages themselves, though some pan–Indian magazines are published in more than one language (e.g., *Chandamana,* "Uncle Moon").

Thus, most languages have independent and variegated children's literary traditions of lyric poetry, nonsense verse, DRAMA, farce, historical romance, ADVENTURE STORY, MYSTERY AND DE-TECTIVE STORY, ghost story, HUMOR, art-fairy tale, FANTASY fiction, and, more recently, SCHOOL STORY and SCIENCE FICTION. Today, about five

hundred titles in all languages are published annually, a relatively low figure that reflects economic constraints on publication, but belies the extremely high quality of both the older and newer classics in various genres.

Writings for children in a naturalized English are cross-regional and cross-cultural, but restricted to the upper classes (only two percent speak English, and only a few hundred thousand use it as a first language). This tradition grew out of retellings of folktales into a post-colonial movement of original writing about twenty-five years ago, and today forty percent of Indian children's books are in English. For socioeconomic reasons and possibly because of competition with imports, this work is often relatively more realistic and creative than Indian–language work, but it is also criticized as uneasy, culturally alien cloning of popular foreign genres.

Apart from the efforts of independent publishers, there is a great deal of good work from the Central Government's Publications Division, the Government's autonomous National Book Trust (NBT, 1957) and its "Nehru Bala Pustakalaya: (Nehru Children's Library) series in many Indian languages, from the National Council of Educational Research and Training and its textbooks (NCERT, 1961), from the Sahitya Akademi (Literary Academy), and the brainchild of K. Shankar Pillai, the independent Children's Book Trust (CBT, 1957) with its cross-translations, competitions, and AWARDS. There are also regional awards by state governments, and various associations that work to develop children's literature in some of the different languages.

BIBLIOGRAPHY: Dasgupta, Amit, ed., *Indian Horizons: Telling Tales,* 44: 2, 1995; Dey, Provash Ronjan, *Children's Literature of India,* 1977; Jamuna, K. A. *Children's Literature in Indian Languages,* 1982

SANJAY SIRCAR

INFORMATIONAL BOOKS

Orbis Sensualium Pictus (the visible world in pictures), written by Moravian Bishop John Amos COMENIUS in 1657, is considered the first informational book for children. This Latin picture dictionary is the precursor to informational books, a rapidly growing genre for children today. Informational books, often called the literature of fact, are classified as nonfiction within the Dewey Decimal Library system and receive a numerical call number indicating their subject matter. The primary purpose of informational books is to tell readers about the real world—its people, places, environment, history, concepts, events, and issues. In informational books, the treatment of content ranges from overviews of a large subject, such as *One World, Many Religions: The Ways We Worship* (1996), by Mary Pope OSBORNE, to in-depth examination of one particular topic such as Jim MURPHY's award-winning *The Great Fire* (1995), about Chicago's 1871 fire. Informational books, published for all age ranges and interest areas, include concept BOOKS FOR THE VERY YOUNG, craft and HOW-TO BOOKS, books about the arts and nature, books that revisit the past, and books about peoples and cultures across the globe. The challenge facing an author of informational books is to make concepts, often complex and abstract ones, clear to young readers without losing the subject's integrity. Authors must select material from a large body of knowledge and then organize it to craft an interesting, child-appealing book. Informational books relate a story—a story grounded in fact—and many contemporary authors adopt a narrative approach. Other writers use a variety of formats to present information such as an alphabetical arrangement, diaries, and postcards. Visual elements, the illustrations and graphics, are also important in creating interest and conveying knowledge.

This genre, often considered the stepchild to fiction and PICTURE BOOKS, has flourished in recent years. Its history in the United States can be traced back to 1922 when the first NEWBERY MEDAL was awarded to *The Story of Mankind,* by Hendrik Willem VAN LOON. The informational picture book was recognized in 1942 when *Paddle-to-the-Sea* by Holling C. HOLLING was named a CALDECOTT MEDAL Honor Book. Although this book was fictionalized, it provided a geographically accurate description of an expedition from the Great Lakes to the Atlantic Ocean. Then, several decades passed before informational books achieved national prominence. In the 1970s recognition of the informational picture book re-emerged with two works by David MACAULAY named Caldecott Medal Honor Books: *Cathedral* in 1974 and *Castle* in 1978. Informational books began to receive Newbery Honor status in 1983

with *Sugaring Time,* a photo-essay by Kathryn LASKY and photographer Christopher Knight. Then in 1988 the NEWBERY MEDAL was granted to *Lincoln: A Photobiography,* by Russell FREEDMAN. The AMERICAN LIBRARY ASSOCIATION next honored Freedman in 1998 with the Laura Ingalls WILDER Award given to an author for a body of work that makes a significant and lasting contribution to literature for children. The *Boston Globe–Horn Book* Award initiated a separate category for nonfiction in 1976 and the NATIONAL COUNCIL OF TEACHERS OF ENGLISH established the ORBIS PICTUS AWARD for Outstanding Nonfiction for Children in 1989.

Informational books have changed dramatically over the years with several current trends. First, today's informational books feature eye-catching, visually appealing designs like Seymour SIMON's *The Brain: Our Nervous System* (1997) in which large color photographs of the brain's interior and white ink printed against black paper are indeed striking. Second, effective graphics and illustrations are commonplace. *National Geographic* photographer Jim Brandenburg traveled to the Artic to take color photographs for *To the Top of the World: Adventures with Arctic Wolves* (1993). Other authors such as Russell Freedman, James Cross GIBLIN, and Rhoda BLUMBERG carefully select historical photographs, reprints, and other graphics to illustrate their works. Informational picture books mesh text and illustrations in a seamless whole to present facts and concepts. For example, in *Click: A Book about Cameras and Taking Pictures* (1997) author/illustrator Gail GIBBONS uses watercolor, colored pencil, and black pen to create pictures in a variety of sizes, shapes, and positions on the page with captions and labels, all of which convey information. A third trend is the proliferation of SERIES BOOKS, a group of books developed by a publisher on related topics or with a similar format. The *Eyewitness Books,* produced by Dorling Kindersley Publishing, have a distinctive format and are a popular example of series books. Another trend is the photo-essay, often written from the perspective of a child. Author/photographer George ANCONA introduces readers to Alicia who lives in the Acoma Pueblo of New Mexico in *Earth Daughter: Alicia of Acoma Pueblo* (1995). Author Diane HOYT-GOLDSMITH has teamed with photographer Lawrence MIGDALE to share cultures of the United States through the first person voice of children such as *Totem Pole* (1990), a photo esssay about the Pacific Northwest Tsimshian tribe, narrated by David, a young boy. Finally, informational books are not limited to serious treatment of topics. HUMOR has become an important element of many informational books, most notably the Magic School Bus books by Joanna COLE with humorous illustrations by Bruce DEGEN. These books follow Ms. Frizzle and her class as they have many adventures to learn about complex topics such as the waterworks, dinosaurs, and the human body.

How does one evaluate and select informational books to read? While the curiosity and interest of readers will always guide book choice, various literary criteria can also be applied in selection. Accuracy and a balanced approach to a topic are appropriate considerations. To determine if the book has been well researched, readers check for a reference list or acknowledgment of sources or experts. How the book is organized influences readers' ability to understand facts and concepts. Information should follow a logical sequence and may be arranged chronologically, from general ideas to more specific ones, or from known facts to new material. The book might offer readers helpful aids to locate and understand content, such as table of contents, index, headings, or glossary. Readers may also review the book's overall format and design. Although one cannot judge a book by its cover, for young readers raised in a visually oriented world, the book's look will affect their interest in it. One should also consider the author's writing style, how enthusiasm for the topic is generated and maintained, how technical terms are explained, and how language is used descriptively.

From a Latin picture dictionary to today's vast array of topics and formats, informational books continue to whet children's curiosity, arouse their interest, and satisfy their desire and need to know about the world around them.

BIBLIOGRAPHY: Bamford, Rosemary A., and Kristo, Janice V., *Making Facts Come Alive: Choosing Quality Nonfiction Literature K-8,* 1998; Freeman, Evelyn B., and Person, Diane Goetz, *Connecting Informational Children's Books with Content Area Learning,* 1998; Freeman, Evelyn

B., and Person, Diane Goetz, eds., *Using Nonfiction Trade Books in the Elementary Classroom: From Ants to Zeppelins,* 1992; Kobrin, Beverly, *Eyeopeners II,* 1995; Saul, Wendy, ed., *Nonfiction for the Classroom: Milton* MELTZER *on Writing, History, and Social Responsibility,* 1994

EVELYN B. FREEMAN

INFORMATIONAL BOOKS, AN AUTHOR'S POINT OF VIEW

Most authors I know save special letters from their readers. No letter has moved me more than the one from the mother of a young son who had died. She wrote, "Alan cherished your book, *Shark Lady: True Adventures of Eugenie Clark* (1978) rereading it many times over the years . . . While he delighted in stories I read to him as a small child, his own selection in books reflected an appetite for the 'truth' about things. . . . Later Alan enjoyed a wide variety of books but he always found nonfiction his most compelling reason to read. Our son had an inquiring mind and a zest for life. Your book about Eugenie Clark captured his imagination and, as the worn condition of his copy attests, gave him great pleasure. Your writing I'm sure has made a difference to others, but know that there was one very special child whose brief life was differentiated and enriched by your work."

I feel honored to have made a difference in Alan's short life. His reaction to the "truth about things" has helped define my appreciation of this genre and deepened my reasons for writing nonfiction. My goals have always been to tell a truth, to illuminate a few dark corners of knowledge, to reveal the spirit and purpose of an unexplored life, to reinforce the fact that learning is fulfilling and fun, to bring a dimension of good literature to homework and research assignments; above all, to write a book that will be eagerly reread.

My other reasons for writing nonfiction are more personal and stem from my desire to share with children the extraordinary ADVENTURES I have experienced traveling to all seven continents and scuba diving beneath the sea. I add to my bank of knowledge by researching and writing about subjects that catch and hold my interest. The BIOGRAPHIES increase my understanding and admiration for the varied lives I investigate.

What is nonfiction? My dictionary defines non as not. Not fiction. We know fiction to be imaginative, vibrant, stirring, evocative. Does nonfiction also posses all these qualities? Milton Meltzer stated in an essay about nonfiction in the *Horn Book* magazine: "If the subject is significant and the artist is up to it, then the book can enlarge, it can deepen, it can intensify the reader's experience of life."

I would add inspiring passion to the list. Nonfiction evokes passion and demands it. How else does a diligent author go through twenty-five rewrites and still be enthralled and enthralling at the end of the year or two that it takes to write the book?

When I was a child in the 1930s, history was taught dryly, by boring rote. I was totally turned off. Yet in my adulthood I could not get enough of what I had missed in elementary school. I vowed to make American history interesting and fun and to project my enthusiasm onto today's readers. I am proud that many of my history books in the If You Lived SERIES I inaugurated for *Scholastic* are being read these days by a second generation. *Playing with Penguins* (1994) and *Swimming with Sea Lions* (1992) were inspired by wondrous expeditions to Antarctica and the Galapagos Islands respectively, and are told in diary form. *Questions and Answers about Sharks* (1995) and *The Desert beneath the Sea* (1991) reflect my abiding interest and first-hand experiences in the sea and its inhabitants, including scuba diving down to a depth of one hundred feet or more to study sharks in their natural habitat. Because heroines did not get their fair share in the 1970s, I wrote *The Secret Soldier: The Story of Deborah Sampson* (1975, 1992) about a girl who disguised herself as a man and joined the Continental Army and *Wanted Dead or Alive: The True Story of Harriet Tubman* who led hundreds of slaves to freedom at the risk of her own life. There are many biographies today about women whose courage and dedication to ideals make them heroic role models. The gender scale is finally better balanced. There are now also many more good books about our varied cultures. Jim Haskins's books about AFRICAN AMERICANS and Virginia Driving Hawk SNEVE's books about NATIVE AMERICANS come to mind.

Today's nonfiction is a feast for the eyes and the range of subjects is seemingly inexhaustible. Reading a recent issue of the the *Horn Book* mag-

azine revealed nonfiction books that run the gamut from what it is like behind the scenes at a ballpark to Lou Gehrig, and from the story of Katherine Lee Bates who wrote "America the Beautiful," to John Stetson, the man whose name is best known for a hat.

Younger children find nonfiction as engrossing as fiction. Because of their limited experiences and innate sense of wonder, everything appears deliciously new. And there are enough good books about almost every subject to suit older children's overwhelming interests of the moment and provide them with enough knowledge to give them the heady feeling of becoming experts.

It wasn't too long ago that nonfiction authors were overlooked when children's literature prizes were handed out. But recent prizewinners include Jean FRITZ, Rhoda BLUMBERG, Kathryn LASKY, and Jean GEORGE among many others.

The "truth about things" is an exciting discovery. Beware of books that fictionalize scientific facts or distort historical accounts. How is the information portrayed? Are complicated ideas made clear and concise, stimulating and vivid? Is the book prosaic or does it have just enough of a creative twist that adds rather than confuses or detracts from its purpose? Are the ILLUSTRATIONS accurate and pertinent to the printed page? One does not have to be an expert to judge whether the book will lead a child to another and still another good book and provide the positive reading and thinking experiences that are the windows to a child's world.

To judge good biographies, check the author's bibliography. Note if there are primary original sources—documents, diaries, letters, newspapers, and the like. Does the dialogue ring true? In *Wanted Dead or Alive*, I chose to use Harriet Tubman's own words exclusively. In my research at the Schomburg Library I found a slim book written by a woman who knew her. Researching *The Secret Soldier*, I traveled to Sharon, Massachusetts, where Deborah Sampson lived with her family after the Revolutionary War. Her house was still standing and the present occupants invited me in. I walked down the street named for her and visited her grave. I found my prime source at Yale University's library in a magazine article written in 1797 by a man who knew Sampson. Bit by bit, facts emerged, including parts of her diary from the Library of Congress and her pension file in the National Archives in Washington.

These days, many children use the INTERNET for research, a fine tool but not exactly an experience in literature. Which is all the more reason to welcome the new, enriching nonfiction books that invite delighted reading and lead eventually to a worn copy of an old favorite, a fitting symbol of a child's dedication to "the truth about things."

BIBLIOGRAPHY—All books listed are by Ann Mc-Govern: *Shark Lady: True Adventures of Eugenie Clark* (1978); *If You Lived in Colonial Times* (1964; re-illus., 1992); *If You Sailed on the Mayflower* (1969; re-illus., 1992); *If You Lived with the Sioux Indians* (1974, re-illus., 1992); *If You Grew up with Abraham Lincoln* (1966; re-illus., 1992); *Playing with Penguins and Other Adventures in Antarctica* (1994); *Swimming with Sea Lions and Other Adventures in the Galapagos Islands* (1992); *Questions and Answers about Sharks* (1995); *The Desert beneath the Sea* (1991, with Eugenie Clark); *Adventures of the Shark Lady: Eugenie Clark around the World* (1998). *The Secret Soldier: The Story of Deborah Sampson* (1975; re-illus., 1992); *Wanted Dead or Alive: The True Story of Harriet Tubman* (1977)

ANN MCGOVERN

INGELOW, Jean

Author, b. 17 March 1820, Boston, Lincolnshire, England; d. 20 July 1897, Kensington, England

A thoughtful child, I. learned her letters by the age of three and retained her recollections of early childhood into adulthood. A writer of POETRY and novels, she began her writing career on the back of her room's white window shutters because her mother thought poetry was frivolous and would not provide her with writing paper. Following the discovery of the verses her mother relented and encouraged her poetry writing. Her first poems were printed in a little paper published weekly by her brother and his fellow pupils at St. Stephen's School.

In 1850 *Rhyming Chronicle of Incidents and Feelings* was published anonymously with the help of her friend, the Vicar of Tamworth. Only one edition was printed but Alfred Tennyson found some very charming things in her book. In 1860, at her own expense, she published a collection of children's short stories, *Tales of Orris,* originally written for *Youth* magazine.

Her most critically acclaimed volume was *Poems* (1863), published with the help of her brother. It went through thirty editions and it is estimated some 200,000 books were sold in the United States. A two-volume second collection of children's stories, *Studies for Stories from Girls' Lives* was published in 1864. In 1865 she met Christina Rossetti, a contemporary who became her good friend.

Mopsa the Fairy, published in 1869, is I.'s most famous children's story. It has been included in several SERIES: The Little Men series, The Wellesley series for Girls, The Cornell series, Classics of Children's Literature, Children's Classics, and The Macmillan Children's Classics to name a few. It is a Victorian FANTASY about a boy, Jack, who finds a nest of fairies in a hollow tree and is transported to fairyland. After waking Mopsa with a kiss, he has several adventures with Mopsa and the other fairies and then flies safely home. I. was strongly influenced in writing *Mopsa the Fairy* by Lewis CARROLL's Alice stories.

Off the Skelligs (1872) is a four-volume somewhat autobiographical novel. *POEMS*, second series, was published in 1874 followed by *Fated to Be Free* in 1875. I. wrote that she had "not aimed at producing a work of art at all, but a piece of nature. I have attempted to beguile my readers into something like a sense of reality."

One of I.'s dominant themes was love—love lost, earthly love, troubled love, newfound love, and religious love. Her language is simple and clear and she often used dialogue to create tension. Another theme was sailors. "Why sailors? Sailors touch everybody's heart. Sailors are ready made heroes of romance to English people, much more appealing and convincing than even soldiers." A third theme was water, whether rivers, streams, floods, or the sea.

I. was deeply concerned about Victorian social and political events. Concerning Women's Rights she wrote: "I don't approve of them at all. We cannot have rights and privileges and I prefer privileges." Of her writing she said, "If I had married, I should not have written books . . . I have suffered much from a feeling of shyness and reserve, and I have not been able to do things by trying to do them. What comes to me comes of its own accord, and almost in spite of me."

FURTHER WORKS: *Stories Told to a Child.* 1866. *The Little Wonder-Horn.* 1872

BIBLIOGRAPHY: *Dictionary of Literary Biography.* 1985. *Fiction, FOLKLORE, Fantasy and Poetry for Children, 1876–1985.* 1986. Hunt, P., ed. *Children's Literature, An Illustrated History.* 1995. *Something about the Author.* vol. 33, 1983. Knoepflmacher, U. C., *Ventures into Childhood.* 1998

IRVYN G. GILBERTSON

INGPEN, Robert
Author, illustrator, b. 1936, Geelong, Australia

I., one of AUSTRALIA's most popular authors and illustrators of children's books, focuses his writing on environmental themes as well as fables, FAIRY TALES, and other FANTASY literature. His books draw his readers in and make them think, which demonstrates why he received the Hans Christian ANDERSEN Medal for children's literature in 1986, and the Dromkeen Medal in 1989.

Colin THIELE's, *Storm Boy* (1963), which I. illustrated, marked his beginning as a children's picture-book illustrator. Since then, many of I.'s books have been included in collections, such as *The Mystery and Magic Series* (1996), which includes: ghouls and monsters, gods and goddesses, heroes and heroines, magicians and fairies. I.'s most famous ILLUSTRATIONS can be found in Michael Page's *Encyclopedia of Things That Never Were* (1985). This reference book consists of over 400 creatures, gods, settings, and objects from MYTHOLOGY, legends, and literature throughout the world. The encyclopedia includes such items as illustrated entries for Zeus, Atlantis, Wonderland, and Avalon. I.'s artwork has also been commissioned to commemorate Australian postage stamps, public buildings, murals, and flags.

FURTHER WORKS: *Peace Begins with You.* (K. Scholes, author). 1990. *Folk Tales and Fables of Asia and Australia.* 1994. *Folk Tales and Fables of the Americas and the Pacific.* 1994. *Folk Tales and Fables of the Middle East and Africa.* 1994

BIBLIOGRAPHY: National Library of Australia, "Papers of Robert Ingpen"; http://www.nla.gov.au/ms/findaids/9141.html

DENISE P. BEASLEY

INNOCENTI, Roberto
Illustrator, b. 1940, Bagno a Ripoli, Italy

Self-trained as an artist in his home country of Italy, I. has become an award-winning illustrator.

His style is realistic and highly detailed, and he demonstrates delicacy and refinement of palette in his beautiful depictions of characters in children's books. *Rose Blanche* (1985), written by I. and Christophe Gallaz and illustrated by I., has won several AWARDS, including Golden Apple, Biennale of Illustrators Bratislava; Notable Book citation, ALA Honor Book citation. The book, set during World War II, tells the story of a young German girl who is thrust into the horrors of the HOLOCAUST. I. has also illustrated several classic works, such as PERRAULT's *Cinderella* (1983), DICKEN's *A Christmas Carol* (1990), COLLODI's *Adventures of Pinocchio* (1944, 1988), and E.T.A. Hoffman's *Nutcracker* (1996).

AWARDS: ALA Mildred L. Batchelder Award (1986) for *Rose Blanche. New York Times* Best Illustrated Children's Books of the Year (1990) for *A Christmas Carol* (DICKENS)

FURTHER WORKS: Illustrator: *La Luna Nelle Baracche.* (Alberto Manzi) 1974: *The Adventures of Pinnochio.* (Carlo Collodi) 1944: *All Kinds of Planes* (Seymour Reit) 1978: 1978 *All Kinds of Trains* (Seymour Reit) 1978: *All Kinds of Ships* (Seymour Reit) 1978: *Snails, and Rails, and Wings.* (Seymour Reit) 1978

BIBLIOGRAPHY: *Something about the Author,* vol. 96, 1998

MARY ARIAIL BROUGHTON

INTERNATIONAL BOARD ON BOOKS FOR YOUNG PEOPLE

The International Board on Books for Young People is an international network of people from all over the world who are committed to bringing books and children together. It is a nonprofit organization founded in Zurich, Switzerland, in 1953. IBBY's stated missions are: to promote international understanding through children's books; to give children everywhere the opportunity to have access to books with high literary and artistic standards; to encourage the publication and distribution of children's books, especially in developing countries; to provide support and training for those involved with children's literature; and to stimulate research and scholarly works in the field of children's literature.

Every other year IBBY presents the Hans Christian ANDERSEN Awards to a living author and a living illustrator whose complete works have made an important contribution to children's literature. The Author's Award has been given since 1956, the Illustrator's Award since 1966. Recipients are selected by a distinguished international jury of children's literature specialists. AWARDS for writing have been given to Eleanor FARJEON, Great Britain; Astrid LINDGREN, Sweden; Eric KASTNER, Germany; Meindert DEJONG, U.S.; Rene Guillot, France; Tove JANSSON, Finland; James Kruess, Germany; Jose Maria Sanches-Silva, Spain; Gianni Rodari, Italy; Scott O'DELL, U.S.; Maria GRIPE, Sweden; Cecil Bodker; Denmark, Paula FOX, U.S.; Bohumil Riha, Czechoslovakia; Livia Bojunga Nunes, Brazil; Christine Noestlinger, Austria; Patricia WRIGHTSON, AUSTRALIA; Annie M.G. Schmidt, Netherlands; Tormod Haugen, Norway; Virginia HAMILTON, U.S.; Michio Mado, Japan; Uri ORLEV, Israel; and Katherine PATERSON, U.S. Awards for ILLUSTRATION have been presented to Alois Carigiet, Switzerland; Jiri Trnka, Czechoslovakia; Maurice SENDAK, U.S.; Ib Spang Olsen, Denmark; Farshid Mesghali, Iran; Tatjana Mawrina, the former U.S.S.R.; Otto S. Svend, Denmark; Suekichi Akaba, Japan; Sbigniews Rychlicki, Poland; Mitsumasa ANNO, Japan; Robert INGPEN, Australia; Dusan Kallay, Czechoslovakia; Lisbeth ZWERGER, Austria; Kveta Pacovska, Czech Republic; Jorg Mueller, Switzerland; and Klaus Ensikat, Germany.

Books chosen for the IBBY Honor List, presented biennially, are selected by the IBBY National Sections. Prizes honor authors, illustrators, and translators, and are presented by IBBY Congresses, as are the Hans Christian Andersen Awards. Since 1953, IBBY Congresses have been held every other year in a different country. They are attended by several hundred people involved in children's and YOUNG ADULT LITERATURE and reading development. Workshops and seminars on writing, illustrating, production, promotion, and distribution of children's books have been held around the world.

The IBBY-Asahi Award, endowed for one million Yen, is cosponsored by IBBY and the Japanese newspaper publisher Asahi Shinbun. Since 1988 it has been presented ever year to a group or institution that is making a significant contribution to book promotion programs for children and young adults. Prizes have been won by projects from Venezuela, Thailand, Zimbabwe, India, Mali, Spain, Lebanon, Colombia, South Africa, France, and other countries.

Established at the Norwegian Institute of Special Education in 1985, the Center for Books for DISABLED Children promotes international exhibits, seminars, and bibliographic surveys. Books for Language Delayed Children and Books for Disabled Young People, cosponsored by UNESCO, have been exhibited by IBBY worldwide. One of the major international magazines on children's literature, the quarterly journal *Bookbird* covers facets of books from many countries. It also contains news from IBBY and IBBY National Sections.

Each year, on or around Hans Christian Andersen's birthday, April 2, a special day is celebrated to inspire a love of reading and to call attention to children's books. IBBY initiated International Children's Book Day, and each National Section has the opportunity to sponsor it through a poster and a message to the children of the world. IBBY has operational relations with UNESCO, UNICEF, and is a member of the International Book Committee. IBBY works with the International Federation of Library Associations, INTERNATIONAL READING ASSOCIATION, the Biennial of Illustrations Bratislava, the Premi Catalonia d'Illustracio, the Centro Regional para el Fomento del Libro en América Latina y el Caribe, the Asian Cultural Center for UNESCO, and the International Youth Library. The founder of the International Youth Library, Jella Lepman, was also the Founder of IBBY.

RALPH STAIGER AND DAVID ROBERTS

(See also INTERNATIONAL LITERATURE and TRANSLATION)

INTERNATIONAL LITERATURE

International children's literature, for those who live in the United States, is that body of books originally published for children in a foreign country and later published in this country. These books can be subdivided into (1) books that were originally written in a language other than English and subsequently translated into English (e.g., *Heidi* [1881] by Johanna SPYRI, originally published in Switzerland in German); (2) books that were originally written in English, but in a country other than the United States (e.g., *Peter Pan* [1904] by Sir James BARRIE, originally published in England); and (3) books that were originally published in a country other than the United States in a language other than English and subsequently published in the United States in the original language (e.g., *The Little Prince* [1943] by Antoine de SAINT EXUPÉRY, originally published in French).

Formal international exchange of children's stories began several centuries ago. *Histoires du Temps Passés* (Stories of Times Past" [1698]), which we know as *Tales of MOTHER GOOSE*, written down by Charles PERRAULT in France at the end of the seventeenth century, and *Robinson Crusoe,* by the English Daniel DEFOE and published in 1719, are examples of early books enjoyed by children in many countries and in many different languages. Many of the classics of children's literature originated outside the United States.

Today, AUSTRALIA, CANADA, the European nations, Great Britain, Japan, NEW ZEALAND, and the United States have well-developed bodies of children's literature. Most children's books originate in these countries. Venezuela, Russia, China, South Africa, and India also actively publish children's books, though not in the variety or quality produced in the developed countries mentioned above. In China and India, while the numbers of children's books published are impressive, the quality and content of these books are less so, being didactic and obviously intended to teach moral values or to mold young readers' characters. (Louie, 1996, Khorana, 1993). Russia, still in a state of political flux at this writing, is making valiant efforts to establish a new, private publishing industry despite an unstable economy, huge inflation, and lack of booksellers. Many developing countries have yet to establish a children's book publishing industry, primarily due to economic constraints. In some countries of Africa, for instance, there are virtually no books for children. The oral tradition prevails in these countries, with ancient stories, rich in history and culture, passed along by word of mouth from generation to generation.

The international children's literature movement was founded primarily through the efforts of Jella Lepman of Germany. Determined to prevent the recurrence of the destruction of World War II, Ms. Lepman in 1946 organized a traveling exhibit of children's books from all European countries. These books, Ms. Lepman believed, would build bridges of understanding among the children who read them. In 1949, after a hugely successful tour, this exhibit became the foundation of the International Youth Library. In 1953, encouraged by this success, Ms. Lepman and others founded the INTERNATIONAL BOARD ON BOOKS FOR YOUNG PEOPLE, or IBBY. This nonprofit organization provides an international forum for those committed to bringing children and books together and is the centerpiece of the international children's literature movement. Its general mission is to promote international understanding and world peace through children's books.

All countries are eligible to join IBBY. Currently, there are sixty-two member nations, each of which has a national organization affiliated with IBBY. The organization is headquartered in Basel, Switzerland, and is supported through dues from the national sections and donations. Individuals join the organization through their national section. In the United States one joins the United States Board on Books for Young People (USBBY). IBBY's main activities are the administration and oversight of the Hans Christian ANDERSEN Award Program, IBBY's journal, *Bookbird: World of Children's Books,* the IBBY Honor List of Books, IBBY's biennial world congresses, the IBBY-UNESCO Workshops and Seminars for Developing Countries, and The IBBY Documentation Centre of Books for DISABLED Young People. Information about any of these projects can be found on the INTERNET at www.ibby.org.

The status of imported books in the United States is inexact, since no U.S. agency officially tracks such information. One must rely on the estimates of children's book experts. Horning, Kruse, and Schleisman (1996), giving an overview of books received at the Cooperative Children's Book Center in Madison, Wisconsin, estimated that in 1995 at least 4,500 new books were published for children and young adults in the United States and that of these, fifty-four—1.2 percent of the total—were translations. Moreover, they noted that only eight of the fifty-four were translations of books of "substantial length." By all estimates, the number of translated children's books brought to this country annually is a mere trickle. By contrast, according to Tomlinson, translated books account for as much as 50 percent of the total annual children's book production in many developed countries. Books originally written in English in other English-speaking countries and then published in the United States are more numerous than translations; but again, there are no exact figures for how many of these books are imported each year. It is safe to say, however, that the great majority of imported English-language books comes from Great Britain, Canada, and Australia.

The Mildred L. Batchelder Book Award Program and the United States Board on Books for Young People are the major promoters of international children's literature in the United States. The Batchelder Award Program, operating under the auspices of the AMERICAN LIBRARY ASSOCIATION, encourages the importation and translation of high quality children's books in the United States. This annual award is made to an American publisher for the most outstanding book originally published in a foreign language in a foreign country and subsequently translated into English and published in the United States during the previous calendar year. The award program honors its namesake, Mildred L. Batchelder, a children's librarian who was outspoken on the need for greater exchange of children's books around the world.

The United States Board on Books for Young People (USBBY) is the United States national section of IBBY. USBBY's purposes are to explore and promote excellent children's reading materials that have been created throughout the world; to cooperate with IBBY and with other groups whose goals are comparable to those of USBBY; to facilitate exchange of information about books of international interest; and to promote access to and reading of these books by children and young adults in the United States and elsewhere. Through its semiannual *USBBY Bulletin,* its publication, *Children's Books from Other Countries,* and its biennial national conferences, USBBY provides support for, and disseminates information to, those involved with children and children's literature and stimulates research and scholarship in the field of children's literature. More specific information about

USBBY is available on the Internet at www.usbby.org.

BIBLIOGRAPHY: Horning, K., Kruse, G. and Schleisman, M., *CCBC Choices 1995,* 1996; Khorana, M., *The Indian Subcontinent in Literature for Children and Young Adults,* 1993; Louie, B. Y., "Children's Literature in the People's Republic of China" in *The Reading Teacher, 49*(6), pp. 494–96, 1996; Tomlinson, C. M., ed., *Children's Books from Other Countries,* 1998 (Portions of this article were adapted from *Children's Books from Other Countries,* C. M. Tomlinson, editor, 1998

CARL M. TOMLINSON

(See also TRANSLATION)

INTERNATIONAL READING ASSOCIATION

The International Reading Association is a nonprofit service organization dedicated to the improvement of reading instruction and the promotion of the lifetime reading habit. Members include teachers, reading specialists, administrators, LIBRARIANS, authors, illustrators, publishers, parents, journalists, professors of reading, and others interested in reading instruction. The International Reading Association was formed in 1955 when two organizations (National Association of Remedial Teachers/Teaching and International Council for the Improvement of Reading Instruction) merged. Some of the founding members include William S. Gray and Nancy LARRICK (first president and president-elect). The first to serve on the Board of Directors were Albert J. Harris, Margaret Robinson, William Sheldon, Elizabeth Simpson, LaVerne Strong, and George Spache. Dues were set at $2.50. Early leaders include Nila Banton Smith, Russell Stauffer, and Ralph Staiger. People who served as Executive Secretary or Executive Director include: Donald Cleland (1955–57); James McAllister (1957–62); Ralph Staiger (1962–84); Ron Mitchell (1984–89); Peter Mitchell (1990–91); Alan Farstrup (1992 to present [2000]).

It publishes a variety of journals and newspapers appropriate for all levels of reading professionals. *The Reading Teacher* is directed toward preschool, primary, and elementary school educators. The journal regularly includes the review of children's books, the list of Children's Choices

(October) and the list of Teachers' Choices (November). *The Journal of Adolescent and Adult Literacy* is directed toward middle school, secondary, college, and adult educators. *JAAL* contains the list of Young Adult Choices (November). *Signal* is the journal of the IRA Special Interest Group on Literature for the Adolescent Reader. *Lectura y vida,* published in Spanish, contains articles and items of interest to professionals in the LATINA/O community. *Reading Today,* a newspaper, is mailed bimonthly to all Association members. It carries news and features about children's book authors and illustrators, reading materials, research, and issues that influence the field. The Association now publishes an electronic journal called *Reading Online.*

The IRA has its headquarters in Newark, Delaware, and maintains another office in Washington, D.C., to coordinate legislative activities and international affairs. Washington Representative Richard Long, and Director of International Development Scott Walker, work out of the Washington office.

Each year, the Arbuthnot Award honors an outstanding college or university teacher of children's and young adult literature. Nominees must be Association members, affiliated with a college or university, and engaged in teacher and/or librarian preparation at the undergraduate and/or graduate level. Recipients of the Arbuthnot Award include Norine Odland, Sam Sebesta, Charlotte S. Huck, Bernice E. Cullinan, Eileen D. Tway, M. Jerry Weiss, M. Jean GREENLAW, Dianne L. Monson, Eileen M. Burke, Patricia J. Cianciolo, Rudine Sims Bishop, Anthony L. Mana, and Ron Jobe.

Each year, the International Reading Association Children's Book Awards honor new authors who show exceptional promise for a career in children's literature. The AWARDS are given for an author's first or second published book in three categories: younger readers (ages four to ten); older readers (ten to sixteen plus); and INFORMATIONAL BOOK (ages four to sixteen plus). Books from any country and in any language copyrighted during the preceding calendar year are considered. Entries in a language other than English must include a one-page abstract in English and a TRANSLATION into English of one chapter or similar selection that in the submitter's estimation is representative of the book. Some previous winners include T. Degens, Laurence YEP, Nancy BOND, Lois LOWRY, Ouida SEBESTYEN, Michelle MAGORIAN, Meredith PIERCE, Clare Bell, Jannie HOWKER, Pan CONRAD, Margaret ROSTKOWSKI, Marisabina RUSSO, Philip PULLMAN, Leslie Baker, Patricia POLACCO, Virginia Euwer WOLFF, Anna Egan Smucker, Steve Johnson, Megan MCDONALD, Karen HESSE, and Deborah Hopkinson.

The Lee Bennett HOPKINS Promising Poet Award is given every three years for a book of poetry for children written by a promising new poet. Winners include Deborah Chandra and Kristine O'Connell George.

Begun in 1974, Children's Choices is an annual joint project of the CHILDREN'S BOOK COUNCIL and the International Reading Association. The Children's Choices project is directed toward these goals: to develop an annual annotated reading list of new books that will encourage young people to read, to help teachers, librarians, booksellers, parents, and others find books that young readers will enjoy, and to provide young readers with an opportunity to voice their opinions about books being written for them. Each year an average of 100 favorite books are chosen by approximately 10,000 children ages five to thirteen from different regions of the United States. Books are selected from new publications donated by publishers. Regional teams circulate the books to teachers and librarians who use them with students. Students rate the books according to their appeal. Regional ratings are tallied into cumulative reports of the top 100-plus favorite books. The list appears in the October issue of the *Reading Teacher.*

The goals of the Young Adults' Choices project are to encourage young people to read; to make teens, teachers, librarians, and parents aware of new literature for young adults; and to provide middle and secondary school students with an opportunity to voice their opinions about books being written for them. The project committee selects teams to field-test new books and to develop an annual annotated reading list. The project began in 1986, funded by a special grant and supervised by the Association's Literature for Adolescents Committee. The books selected each year are the result of voting by students in five different regions of the United States. Newly

MOTHER GOOSE, Cassell & Co., 1888. Mother Goose, in her pointed black hat, riding abroad with her mysterious paraphernalia, is typically portrayed as a wizened old woman full of mysterious knowledge-wielding power over the household, especially the children's nursery.

Lucy Fitch PERKINS, *Eskimo Twins,* 1914. Perkins's black-and-white line drawings capture the unique essence of traditional dress and living conditions in each of her books about fictional twins set in countries around the world. At the same time, her drawings manage to illustrate universal features of childhood that transcend national borders

Edmund DULAC, *The Princess and the Pea*, 1911. Dulac's pen defines figures and objects, drawing readers into a sumptuous, detailed feast of rich patterns and jewel-like enameled-watercolor painting, reminiscent of an exotic Persian miniature. It is an early example of an illustrator reaching out to the international community for artistic inspiration in children's illustration.

Eulalie (pseud.), *The Cock, the Mouse and the Little Red Hen,* 1925, by Watty Piper (pseud.). At a time when publishers were establishing children's departments, few people were writing and illustrating children's books. Publishers were eager to respond to the demands for children's books and encouraged their own staffs' creativity. Using new color-printing technology, a group of young editors prepared a set of inexpensive books featuring traditional stories and illustrations that appeared familiar and comforting.

E. H. SHEPARD, *When We Were Very Young,* 1924, by A. A. MILNE. Working in the style of the finest Victorian line-drawing illustrators, Shepard drew airy, unframed illustrations creating an informal effect that complemented the world of the children's nursery. Shepard used photographs of the real Christopher Robin and his toys to draw his illustrations—as can be seen in this drawing that has Winnie-the-Pooh lying near Christopher Robin, at the top of the stairs. (From *When We Were Very Young* by A. A. Milne, illustrations by E. H. Shepard, copyright 1924 by E. P, Dutton, renewed 1952 by A. A. Milne. Used by permission of Dutton Children's Books, an imprint of Penguin Putnam Books for Young Readers, a division of Penguin Putnam Inc.)

In the great forest
a little elephant is born.
His name is Babar.
His mother loves him very much.
She rocks him to sleep
with her trunk
while singing softly to him.

Jean DE BRUNHOFF, *The Story of Babar*, 1933. Using vivid primary colors and lots of white space on an oversized page, de Brunhoff's lithographs are accompanied by a handwritten text creating a unified effect of childlike innocence. (From *The Story of Babar* by Jean de Brunhoff, translated by Merle Haas, copyright © 1933, renewed 1961 by Random House, Inc. Used by permission of Random House Children's Books, a division of Random House, Inc. © Hachette Jeunesse, 43 quai de Grenell, Paris, CEDEX 15, France.)

Robert LAWSON, *The Story of Ferdinand,* 1936, by
Munro LEAF. In this story with a strong antiviolence
theme, Lawson uses bold black-and-white etchings to
show Ferdinand's strength but also the beauty of the
trees and flowers. Size and proportion are important
in the illustration as a way of contrasting the beauty
of a single flower against the powerful bulk of the
grown-up Ferdinand. (From *The Story of Ferdinand*
by Munro Leaf and Robert Lawson, copyright 1936 by
Munro Leaf and Robert Lawson, renewed © 1964 by
Munro Leaf and John W. Boyd. Used by permission of
Viking Penguin, an imprint of Penguin Putnam Books
for Young Readers, a division of Penguin Putnam Inc.)

Garth WILLIAMS, *Charlotte's Web,* 1952, by E. B. WHITE.
Using pen-and-ink drawings, Williams imbues his
animal characters, including the spider Charlotte, with
distinctive personalities, warmth, and vitality. He
captures the essence of White's unsentimental prose as
his drawing interpret the text and lend flavor to scenes
and personalities. (Illustration from *Charlotte's Web* by
E. B. White. Illustrated by Garth Williams. Copyright
1952 by E. B. White. Illustrations copyright renewed
1980 by Garth Williams. Reprinted by permission
of HarperCollins Publishers.)

Edward ARDIZZONE, *Tim's
Friend Towser,* 1962.
Watercolor drawing,
reproduced by offset lithography—which was a
new process at the time –
distinguish Ardizzone's
deceptively simple art, as
do frequent use of cross-
hatching drawings and
"word balloons." These
elements give Ardizzone's
books a child-friendly
format and familiar
cartoonlike appearance.
(Reprinted by permission
of HarperCollins
Publishers.)

Ezra Jack KEATS, *The Snowy Day,* 1962. Collage illustrations on board created with bits of paper and fabric as well as Keats's use of paint and gum-eraser stamps convey the joy and wonder of a small boy's anticipation of playing in the snow. The love and support of his mother are evident in the illustrator's use of rounded-human shapes and curving lines of the snow-laden trees and streets. (From *The Snowy Day* by Ezra Jack Keats with permission of the Ezra Jack Keats Foundation.)

Alice and Martin PROVENSEN, *A Visit to William Blake's Inn,* 1981, by Nancy WILLARD. Lighthearted whimsical illustrations done in acrylic and ink on illustration board lend a feeling of eighteenth-century England. Bathed in golden sunlight, cutaway drawings of the inn and its varied inhabitants show an assortment of people, animals, and mythical creatures living together as the poet and artist Blake may have imagined. (Illustration from *A Visit to William Blake's Inn* by Nancy Willard, illustration copyright © 1981 by Alice Provensen and Martin Provensen, reproduced by permission of Harcourt, Inc.)

Chris Van ALLSBURG, *The Polar Express,* 1985. Working in full-color oil pastels on pastel paper, Van Allsburg configures a gentle palette of soft nighttime colors to create a mood of the eternal mystery of night, when children wonder what happens in the world. Special nighttime events are highlighted by Van Allsburg's use of bright red in a repeated candy-cane effect befitting the holiday spirit. (From *The Polar Express* by Christopher Van Allsburg. Copyright © 1985 by Chris Van Allsburg. Reprinted by permission of Houghton Mifflin Company. All rights reserved.)

Ted HARRISON, *The Shooting of Dan McGrew,* 1988 edition, by Robert W. SERVICE. In keeping with Service's text, Harrison's abstract paintings create a mood that boldly visualizes the majesty, vastness, and stillness of the CANADIAN Yukon in contrast to a single human figure. His use of a warm palette is evocative of the sun's reflection on the unbroken panorama of snow and ice. (From *The Shooting of Dan McGrew* by Robert W. Service, Reprinted by permission of David R. Godine, Publisher, Inc. Illustrations Copyright © 1988 by Ted Harrison.)

David WIESNER, *Tuesday*, 1991. The wordless picture book, painted in luminous watercolor on watercolor paper, uses several double-page spreads to create a narrative effect. Viewers need to study the paintings of flying frogs on lily pads attentively to appreciate Wiesner's slapstick humor, sense of eerie mystery, and details that heighten the mood of anticipation. (From *Tuesday* by David Wiesner. Illustration Copyright © 1991 by David Wiesner. Reprinted by permission of Clarion Books, an imprint of Houghton Mifflin Company. All rights reserved.)

Leo LIONNI, *Little Blue and Little Yellow,* 1959. In this story of friendship and identity, Lionni uses color and form—in a modern, nonrepresentational way—to illustrate how children develop their own personalities while learning to share ideas and work together harmoniously. By the end of the book, the colored forms have learned how to cooperate yet maintain their own points of view as the forms blend to become a green shade. (Copyright © 1959, 1987 by Leo Lionni)

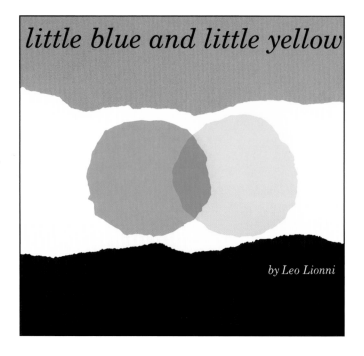

published trade books (not textbooks) are submitted by more than fifty publishers and field-tested with students in the five regions. Each book submitted must have at least two positive reviews from recognized professional REVIEW JOURNALS. Students in grades seven to twelve read the books submitted and rate them on ballots. The results are reported in the November issue of the *Journal of Adolescent and Adult Literacy.*

The Teachers' Choices project is directed toward these goals: to develop an annual annotated reading list of new books that will encourage young people to read; to help teachers, librarians, booksellers, parents, and others find books that young readers will enjoy; to help teachers find books that can be used across the curriculum; and to help young people find books they might not discover or fully appreciate without the help of a teacher, librarian, parent, or other adult. The Teachers' Choices project was initiated at IRA in 1989; it had been administered by NCTE from 1979 to 1988. The selection process is conducted through a national field test of several hundred newly published books submitted by United States trade book publishers. Seven teams, made up of a regional coordinator, field leaders, teacher reviewers, and trainees for the project, try out the books in classrooms and libraries to select those that meet the established criteria. Regional coordinators circulate copies of the books among teachers and librarians who use them with students. Project coordinators record educators' reactions to each book and tabulate their final ratings. Each book is read by a minimum of six teachers or librarians in each region, although some books are read by more than 200 people in a single region. Ratings from the seven regions are collated to produce the national list. Results are published in the November issue of *The Reading Teacher.*

JANET BUTLER, DEBORAH HOUSTON,
AND RALPH STAIGER

INTERNET RESOURCES FOR CHILDREN

In the last several years, use of the Internet, or World Wide Web, has exploded both as a source of information and entertainment. Although some may fear that this new TECHNOLOGY will sup-

plant reading, it can in fact enrich children's experiences with literature. Web sites can provide background information about books and authors, opportunities to interact directly with authors through online chats and bulletin boards, games and activities related to favorite books or characters, and avenues for publishing their own book reviews or literature responses. Teachers, librarians, and other adults will also find a wealth of resources and information ranging from ideas about teaching with literature to information on how to arrange author visits.

Many current children's authors maintain their own web sites, either on their own or hosted by their publishers. Most of these sites provide biographical information, photographs, descriptions, and sometimes excerpts from the author's books, and personal messages from the authors. Some, such as Jan BRETT's, also provide downloadable activities. Some provide an opportunity to send E-mail to the author as well.

Publishers also provide excellent information about their books and authors, frequently with special sections of their web sites devoted to children's books and authors. HarperCollins has a special web site just for children's and young adult literature. Children can learn how a book is made, read excerpts from recently published selections, and participate in a variety of online activities and contests. Random House has created a special site devoted exclusively to the works of Dr. SEUSS and Frederick Warne, a site devoted to the works of Beatrix POTTER, both with games and activities for young readers as well as information about the authors. Scholastic provides online areas for fans of its various SERIES BOOKS such as Magic School Bus, Animorphs, Goosebumps, Dear America and Harry Potter. Most other major publishers provide similar services. Some include scheduled live chats during which students can post questions directly to their favorite authors.

Fans are another source of online sites devoted to children's literature. Laura Ingalls WILDER and the Little House on the Prairie series have inspired a number of web sites, where readers will find photographs, information, and even audio clips of Pa's fiddle music. A site devoted to *Treasure Island* (1883) from the University of Bath in England provides lots of links to information about pirate life as well as about Robert Louis STEVENSON and the book itself. *Winnie-the-Pooh* (1926), *The Wonderful Wizard of Oz* (1900), *Alice in Wonderland* (1865), the Anne of Green Gables series by Lucy Maud MONTGOMERY, and dozens of other children's classics have been the beneficiaries of similar tributes on the World Wide Web. Most of these labors of love have an impressive depth and quality of information and resources. One of the unique features of the Internet is the ability to link directly to other related sites via hyperlinks, so discovering any one of these sites will often open the gateway to additional materials from other enthusiasts who have created their own online collections.

One of the most powerful ways to interact with books is to share your responses with other readers, and the Internet provides opportunities to do just that. The well-known online bookseller amazon.com invites readers to post their own responses to books, which are then available online along with the book description and official print reviews. A variety of other sites devoted to books and reading, such as World of Reading, or targeted to youth in general, such as A Girl's World, also have special sections devoted to book reviews from readers.

Larger libraries also frequently have web sites. An excellent one for young readers is the New York Public Library's "On-Lion" for Kids site, where children can find recommended reading lists as well as links to a variety of other resources. Another excellent online resource is the Internet Public Library's Reading Zone, featuring online stories, author interviews, and lots more links to related sites.

How can students find all these riches without getting lost in the vast disorganization of the Internet? Unlike print, the Internet is a very fluid medium, with resources appearing, disappearing, and moving constantly. Many sites do provide lists of links as one of their services to users, and make every effort to keep those lists up to date. As use of the Internet has grown, a number of search engines and directories just for young people have also become available. One of the best-known is the Internet directory site Yahooligans, where students can find literature-related resources under "Art Soup" by selecting Language

Arts, or can type in the exact term they are interested in, whether an author, book title, or genre. Another search engine designed for younger Internet users is Dig, the DISNEY Internet Guide, where students can browse under Stories and Comics or use the online search. While these have the advantage of being designed with young users in mind, a more targeted and valuable resource can be found in the Children's Literature Web Guide, maintained by a professor in Canada, which provides links to every conceivable resource related to children's literature available on the World Wide Web. Another excellent resource for teachers and librarians is Carol Hurst's Children's Literature Site, where this well-known educator provides reviews of great books for kids, ideas of ways to use them in the classroom, and collections of books and activities about particular subjects, curriculum areas, and themes.

INTERNET RESOURCES: Jan Brett—http://www.jan brett.com/; HarperCollins Children's Books—http://www.harperchildrens.com/; Seussville—http://www.randomhouse.com/seussville/; Beatrix Potter—http://www.peterrabbit.com/; Scholastic—http://www.scholastic.com/kids/;Treasure Island—http: / / www.ukoln.ac.uk / services / treasure /; amazon.com—http://www.amazon.com/; World of Reading—http://worldreading.org/; A Girl's World—http://www.agirlsworld.com/; "On-Lion" for Kids—http://www.nypl.org/branch/kids/; Internet Public Library Youth Division—http:// ipl.org/youth/; Yahooligans—http://www.yahoo ligans.com/; Dig—http://www.disney.com/dig/ today/; Children's Literature Web Guide—http:// www.acs.ucalgary.ca/~dkbrown/index.html; Carol Hurst's Children's Literature Site—http://www. carolhurst.com/index.html

CATHY VANDERHOOF

IPCAR, Dahlov

Author, illustrator, b. 12 November 1917, Windsor, Vermont

Daughter of artists William and Marguerite Zorach, I. was reared in a house with modern art painted on the walls. Encouraged by her parents to put her heart into her art, and supported through attendance at progressive schools, I. translated her love of animals and Maine farm life, replete with color and pattern, into paintings, murals, and thirty-eight children's books. Her animals are alive and running: they caper, hop, soar, vault, and frolic. Her sense of design, backgrounding the curves and arcs of animal bodies with sharp angular lines, animates her wonderful creatures, taking them down, around, across and off the pages. The lively, descriptive language of her texts doubles the joy of her visual feasts. Her art, which includes soft sculpture as well as paintings, has been displayed in more than fifty exhibitions and is included in upwards of two dozen public and private collections. Recognized as an artist, PICTURE BOOK illustrator, and YOUNG ADULT novelist, I. is the recipient of numerous AWARDS, including the coveted Kerlan Award (1998) for her lifelong contribution to children's literature. Original material is archived by the Children's Literature Research Collection (THE KERLAN COLLECTION) and the DE GRUMMOND COLLECTION (University of Southern Mississippi).

FURTHER WORKS: *Animal Hide and Seek.* 1947. *Brown Cow Farm.* 1959. *I Love My Anteater with an A.* 1964. *Bright Barnyard.* 1966. *Whisperings and Other Things.* 1967. *The Cat Came Back.* 1971. *A Flood of Creatures.* 1973. *The Queen of Spells.* 1973. *The Nightmare and Her Foal.* 1990

BIBLIOGRAPHY: Interviews and conversations: personal acquaintance since 1964; personal assessment of books; de Grummond website: http://avatar.lib.usm.edu/~degrum/findaids/ipcar.htm; Library of Congress website: http://lcweb.loc.gov/cgi-bin/zgate; Dahlov Ipcar website: http://www.exitfive.com/dahlov

MARGARET Y. PHINNEY

IRVING, Washington
Author, b. 3 April 1783, New York City; d. 28 November 1859, Irvington, New York

I., author of children's and adult novels, wrote under a variety of pseudonyms during his career. Besides being an author, I. was also a lawyer and served in the army, becoming a colonel in the War of 1812. I.'s best-known works read by children include "The Legend of Sleepy Hollow" (1820) and "Rip Van Winkle" (1820), both of which have been made into numerous movies and television shows. Both stories appear to be among the earliest instances of indigenous American folktales but were actually based on an ob-

scure German source that I. discovered and adapted for American readers. Full of sly HUMOR, intentional innuendo, and eerie details of dark moonlit nights along the Palisades cliffs with the fog rising from the Hudson River, I.'s stories have delighted generations of children. Numerous abridged retellings of these CLASSICS are available in print.

FURTHER WORKS: *A History of the Life and Voyages of Christopher Columbus.* 1928. *Tales of a Traveler.* 1824

MICHAEL O'LAUGHLIN

(For a fuller treatment of the life and career of I., see Steven R. Serafin, general editor, *The Continuum Encyclopedia of American Literature*, 1999, pp. 570–73.)

ISADORA, Rachel
Author, illustrator, b. 1953, New York City

After she retired from dancing in her early twenties, I. turned to a career in children's literature. She incorporates ballet, MUSIC, and art into many of her stories and ILLUSTRATIONS. Her scenes often contain black-and-white drawings, and feature people of various cultures and ages. I.'s best known work, *Ben's Trumpet* (1979), focuses on a young boy living in the ghetto who wants to play the trumpet. I.'s drawings pulsate with the jazz rhythms that Ben hears the musicians playing at a neighborhood nightclub. *At the Crossroads* (1991), set in contemporary South Africa, illustrates the pain of apartheid as suffered from the perspective of children. In glowing double-page spreads, I. shows the children waiting patiently for the return of their fathers from an enforced ten-month separation. I. has also illustrated popular books for other authors such as *Flossie and the Fox* (Patricia MCKISSACK, 1986) and *The White Stallion* (Elizabeth Shub, 1982).

AWARDS: ALA CALDECOTT MEDAL Honor Book (1980) for *Ben's Trumpet*

FURTHER WORKS: *Seeing Is Believing.* 1979. *A Little Interlude.* (R. Maiorano, author). 1980. *My Ballet Class.* 1980. *City Seen from A to Z.* 1983. *Cutlass in the Snow.* 1986. *Over the Green Hills.* 1992. *Lili at Ballet.* 1993. *Young Mozart.* 1997

BIBLIOGRAPHY: Rochman, Hazel. *Against Borders.* 1993. *Something about the Author*, vol. 79, 1995

JODI PILGRIM

ISH-KISHOR, Shulamith

Author, b. 1896, London, England; d. 23 June 1977

By the age of five I. was writing and by the time she was ten some of her poems had been published in literary magazines. In 1909 I. immigrated to the United States with her family. She attended Hunter College in New York City studying languages and history. I.'s first publications appeared in religious periodicals and her early nonfiction books were intended for a Jewish religious school population. *Children's History of Israel from the Creation to the Present* (1933), a three-volume set, and *American Promise: A History of Jews in the New World* (1947) were well-received in the religious school community.

In the 1960s, as publishers sought children's books with a MULTICULTURAL focus, I. brought her knowledge of Jewish history and personal experience as an immigrant to accommodate a wide reading audience. *A Boy of Old Prague* (1963), a National Jewish Book Award winner, brings together a Christian boy and a Jewish family against a background of medieval superstition.

Despite their friendship and growing understanding of each other's beliefs, the characters in the story are unable to avert the culminating event, a pogrom in the Prague ghetto. *Our Eddie* (1969), like immigrant stories from many cultures, is a story of a loving but difficult family relationship during the 1920s as the Old World culture of parents clashes with the culture of modern, secular American children.

The Carpet of Solomon (Uri SHULEVITZ, illus., 1966) retells a Hebrew legend as does *The Master of the Miracle: A New Novel of the Golem* (Arnold LOBEL, illus., 1971). Both books received critical praise.

AWARD: ALA NEWBERY MEDAL Honor Book (1970), and Sydney TAYLOR Book Award (1969) for *Our Eddie*. National Jewish Book Award (1964) for *A Boy of Old Prague*

BIBLIOGRAPHY: *Contemporary Authors.* vols. 73–76, 1978. *Fiction, FOLKLORE, FANTASY and POETRY for Children, 1876–1985.* vol. 1, 1986. Silvey, A. ed. *Children's Books and Their Creators.* 1995. *Something about the Author.* vol. 17, 1979

IRVYN G. GILBERTSON

JACOBS, Joseph

Folklorist, scholar, literary critic, historian, b. 29 August 1854, Sydney, Australia; d. 30 January 1916, Yonkers, New York

J. grew up in Australia but moved to Cambridge, England, to become a lawyer. While in Cambridge, J. became interested in literature and moved to London to become a writer. There, he served as president of the Folk Lore Society and as editor of its journal, *Folk-Lore*. In 1896, J. decided that he wanted his children to grow up in America, and in 1900, he moved his family to the United States where he became registrar and professor of English literature and rhetoric at the Jewish Theological Seminary of America and revising editor of the *Jewish Encyclopedia*.

J. is perhaps best known for his collections of traditional legends and FAIRY TALES, including *English Fairy Tales* (1890), *Celtic Fairy Tales* (1892), and *The Fables of Aesop* (1896). During his intensive study of FOLKLORE, J. discovered tales that had migrated for hundreds of years, leading him to compare tales from disparate regions of the world. His work encouraged other folklorists to recognize and emphasize the importance of diffusion and migration of folktales among cultures.

J., who loved to entertain children, was the first writer to prepare folk tales specifically for a juvenile audience. He often gathered children around and delighted them with the retelling of a tale such as "Tom Tit Tot" or "The King o' the Cats." He wanted to make children feel that literature was such great fun that they would develop the desire to read for themselves. Although his collections of fairy tales, folk tales, and fables were well received by the general public, they were sometimes criticized by folklore purists who charged that his written versions of the stories were not exactly as they had been told in the oral tradition. J. responded by pointing out that since multiple variants of the tales were common, he wished to present the stories in ways that children would enjoy them most. J. did, however, spend many years tracing the direct derivations of the tales, and he included any changes he had made in the appendices of his books. He prefaced the notes with illustrations by John D. Batten along with the whimsical warning, "Man or woman, boy or girl that reads what follows 3 times shall fall asleep an hundred years." J.'s notes are a valuable source of information for folklorists today.

FURTHER WORKS: *More English Fairy Tales*. 1894. *More Celtic Fairy Tales*. 1895. *Book of Wonder Voyages*. 1986. *Reynard the Fox*. 1900. *Indian Fairy Tales*. 1903. *Europa's Fairy Book*. 1916

BIBLIOGRAPHY: Hays, M. Memories of My Father, Joseph Jacobs. *The Horn Book*. 1952. vol. 28, 385–92. Leeming, D.A., and Sader, M. *STORYTELLING Encyclopedia: Historical, Cultural, and Multiethnic Approaches to Oral Traditions around the World*. 1997. *Major Authors and Illustrators for Children and Young Adults: A Selection of Sketches from Something about the Author*, vol. 3, 1993

MARY ARAIL BROUGHTON

JACOBS, William Jay
Author, b. 23 August 1933, Cincinnati, Ohio

J., author of children's history books and BIO-GRAPHIES, was a history teacher at both the high school and university levels as well as a Fulbright and a Taft fellow. His love for history stems from his family's immigrant status and his subsequent passion for the United States and what it means to be a citizen. He has worked and traveled all over the United States and abroad, which has helped him with his historical research and provided insight into the backgrounds of his subjects. J.'s *Ellis Island: New Hope in a New Land* (1990), a Notable Children's Book in Social Studies, presents the history of immigration in the United States with emphasis on the process of arrival at Ellis Island. *Mother, Aunt Susan and Me: The First Fight for Women's Rights* was a Best Children's Books of 1979 selection from the Child Study Association. *Great Lives: Human Rights* (1990) uses black and white photos and drawings to document a lively text about many of the people who have spoken up in loud clear voices for the human rights of all citizens since the founding of the United States.

FURTHER WORKS: *Dwight D. Eisenhower: Soldier and Statesman*, 1995; *They Shaped the Game: Ty Cobb, Babe Ruth, Jackie Robinson*, 1994; *Search for Peace: The Story of the United Nations*, 1994; *War with Mexico*, 1993; *Mother Teresa: Helping the Poor*, 1991; *Lincoln*, 1991; *Washington*, 1991; *LaSalle: A Life of Boundless Adventure*, 1994

BIBLIOGRAPHY: *Something about the Author*, vol. 89, 1997; *World Religions*, 1996

MICHAEL O'LAUGHLIN

JACQUES, Brian
Novelist, b. 15 June 1939, Liverpool, England

J. is the child of Irish Catholic parents who immigrated to England before he was born. His father, a truck driver, loved literature and taught J. to love the works of authors such as Sir Arthur Conan DOYLE, Zane Grey, Robert Louis STEVENSON, and Edgar Rice Burroughs. At age ten, J. wrote his first animal FANTASY in school; his teacher accused him of plagiarism because it was so well written.

Fortunately, a subsequent teacher recognized J.'s talent and encouraged him to read poetry and Greek literature. At age fifteen, J. left school and worked at a string of jobs including seaman, railway fireman, longshoreman, truck driver, docks representative, logger, bus driver, boxer, police officer, postmaster, stand-up comic, and folk singer. J. found his niche as a radio broadcaster for the BBC, where he hosts a variety of programs including music, school and movie quiz shows, and documentaries. J. is an opera fan and is most well known for his opera programs. He is also a popular humorous lecturer and has long been involved with a school for the blind in Liverpool. He began writing the Redwall stories to tell to the children at this school, not originally intending the stories for publication.

J.'s stories are about anthropomorphized animals, set in and around medieval Redwall Abbey. Traditional themes of good versus evil are strong, with brave, kind heroes and heroines, and wicked, depraved villains. He tries to tell a good story with clear moral values. J.'s books are often noted both for their detailed descriptions (especially of food and battles) and for their swashbuckling adventure.

AWARDS: Parents' Choice Honor Book, *Booklist* Editor's Choice, AMERICAN LIBRARY ASSOCIATION Best Book for YOUNG ADULTS, and *School Library Journal* Best Book (1987) all for *Redwall*. CARNEGIE MEDAL Nominations (1988) for *Redwall, Mossflower*, (1989) for *Mattimeo*, and (1992) for *Salamandastron*. Literary AWARDS in England and Australia and numerous awards for his radio programs

FURTHER WORKS: In the Redwall series: *Mariel of Redwall*. 1991. *Martin the Warrior*. 1993. *The Bellmaker*. 1994. *The Great Redwall Feast*. 1995. *The Outcasts of Redwall*. 1995. *Pearls of Lutra*. 1996. *The Long Patrol: A Tale from Redwall*. 1998. Other: *Seven Strange and Ghostly Tales*. 1991. Numerous plays and documentaries for radio, television, and theater

BIBLIOGRAPHY: Jacques, B. "Describing the Fantasy of My Own Life." 1995. In Lehr, S. (ed.). *Battling Dragons: Issues and Controversy in Children's Literature: Seventh Book of Junior Authors and Illustrators*. 1996: Silvey, A. (ed.). *Children's Books and Their Creators*. 1995

JANE WEST

JAMES, Will (J. E. N. Dufault)

Author, illustrator, b. 6 June 1892, Great Falls, Montana; d. 3 September 1942, Hollywood, California

J., author and illustrator of Western stories, was born in Montana and spent a great deal of his youth living and working on horse and cattle ranches. He began drawing during his youth, sometimes using a stick and making pictures in the dirt while he guarded the cattle. As a young adult J. worked rodeos and even spent time rounding up wild horses. These experiences inspired his work that J. described as nonfiction based on his own life experiences. J.'s *Smoky the Cowhorse* won the ALA NEWBERY MEDAL in 1927 and in 1946 was made into a movie starring Fred MacMurray. This story of a horse's harsh treatment on the rodeo circuit and rescue by a sympathetic cowboy reflects the attitudes of the era in which it was written. By contemporary standards it is considered excessively sentimental and conveying stereotyped portraits. Several other of J.'s works were also made into movies, including *Sand* (1929) and *Lone Cowboy* (1935), J.'s autobiography.

FURTHER WORKS: *Cowboys North and South*, 1924; *Drifting Cowboy*, 1925; *Smoky the Cowhorse*, 1926; *Lone Cowboy: My Life Story*, 1930; *Uncle Bill: A Tale of Two Kind Cowboys*, 1932; *Young Cowboy*, 1935; *The Will James Cowboy Book* (ed. Alice DALGLIESH), 1938; *Book of Cowboy Stories*, 1951; *The American Cowboy Horses I've Known*, 1942; *The Dark Horse*, 1939; *Home Ranch*, 1935; *Uncle Bill: A Tale of Two Kids and a Cowboy*, 1932

BIBLIOGRAPHY: *Something about the Author*, vol. 19, 1980

MICHAEL O'LAUGHLIN

JANECZKO, Paul

Poet, anthologist, b. 27 June 1945, Passaic, New Jersey

J. first started writing in grade school and continued writing in high school for the school newspaper. However, it was not until J. went to college at St. Francis College in Biddeford, Maine, and later to graduate school at John Carroll University, that he started writing POETRY. J. taught high school English but was never satisfied with the poetry he found in anthologies for YOUNG ADULTS. Using poems he felt spoke to his students, J. assembled his own collections. At the prompting of a colleague, J. put them together formally and published them as *The Crystal Image* (1977). That was the first of many anthologies J. produced to bring poetry to young adults.

J.'s compilations center on themes that resonate with young people. Each work is carefully selected and ordered so that readers are drawn in and invited to enjoy. *Don't Forget to Fly: A Cycle of Modern Poems* (1981), *Poetspeak: In Their Work, about Their Work* (1983), *Strings: A Gathering of Family Poems* (1984), *Pocket Poems: Selected for a Journey* (1985) and *The Place My Words Are Looking For* (1990) have all been named to the Best Books for Young Adults list by the AMERICAN LIBRARY ASSOCIATION. In 1989, J. published his first book of original poetry, *Brickyard Summer*. J. has also written fiction and nonfiction prose for young adults. Interested for a long time in codes and spycraft, J. wrote the nonfiction *Loads of Codes and Secret Ciphers* (1984). In the REALISTIC FICTION genre, J.'s first novel *Bridges to Cross* (1986), is based in part on his experiences in a Catholic High School in New Jersey. In 1990, after twenty-two years in the classroom, J. retired from teaching to devote more time to his own writing. He spends his time writing, conducting workshops, visiting classrooms, and serving as poetry editor for the *English Journal* and as poetry columnist for *Scholastic Instructor*.

J.'s original poetry is distinguished by his emphasis on character rather than the telling of events and his use of language in unusual contexts. He starts writing by developing a profile of a character's personality, then creates an exciting story about the character. "Everything in writing," he says, "begins with characterization." He first names his characters and then writes down a complete word picture on a legal pad. The words and sounds, and the images they create come next. J. never loses sight of the audience he is writing for and the things that interest children and adolescents.

FURTHER WORKS: *Postcard Poems: A Collection of Poetry for Sharing*. 1979. *It's Elementary*. 1981. *Going over to Your Place: Poems for Each Other*. 1987. *The Music of What Happens*. 1988.

The Place My Words Are Looking For: What Poets Say about and through Their Work. 1990. *Stardust Hotel.* 1993

BIBLIOGRAPHY: Copeland, J. and V. L. Copeland, eds. *Speaking of Poets 2: More Interviews with Poets Who Write for Children and Young Adults.* 1994. Silvey, A. ed. *Children's Books and Their Creators.* 1995. *Sixth Book of Junior Authors and Illustrators.* 1989. *Something about the Author.* vol. 53, 1988

DEDE SMALL

JANSSON, Tove

Author, illustrator, b. 9 August 1914, Helsinki, Finland

J. grew up in a large dilapidated studio with her father, Viktor Jansson, a sculptor, and her mother, Signe Hammarsten Jansson, a designer of book covers. In this wild exciting home J. was surrounded by artistic endeavors and a multitude of books. J. read endlessly unless it was a book her mother said was instructional and good for her. Each summer the family would go out to an island in the Finnish archipelago where they would sail and brave the elements. On one of these adventurous trips the inspiration for J.'s best known works occurred. Once the family was kept off the water by stormy seas and they had to spend the night on a small uninhabited island. J. imagined that she heard the scurrying of trolls. J.'s mother comforted her by telling her that trolls were nice creatures who merely were enjoying the storm.

The Story of the Moomins came from this memory. The Moomins are small, roundish, troll-like creatures drawn in pen and ink, with wild hair and big wide eyes, who do whatever they like. They always find adventure in their home in Moomin Valley where nobody is ever bored. The dominant theme in the Moomin books is showing consideration for others and understanding for those who are different. Initially the Moomins appeared in cartoon strips, but in 1945 the first children's book, *The Little Trolls and the Great Flood* was published. There are nine Moomin titles in all but it was the third in the SERIES, *Finn Family Moomintroll* (1950), that became the biggest success and established J.'s reputation as an author of children's books. J. is a member of the Swedish speaking minority in Finland and all her books have been written in Swedish. The Moo-

min books have been translated into thirty-three different languages including: Bulgarian, Chinese, English, French, German, Hebrew, Italian, and Persian. They have also appeared in other media: theater, opera, film, radio, and television.

J. is the author of the autobiographical novel *The Sculptor's Daughter* (1974). Before writing children's books, J. studied BOOK DESIGN in Stockholm (1930–33), painting in Helsinki, Finland (1933–36), Paris, France (1938), and Florence, Italy. Her oil paintings have been shown in several exhibitions. J. has received all the major Scandinavian AWARDS including the Great Prize of the Swedish Academy (1994). She received the international Hans Christian ANDERSEN Award in 1966.

FURTHER WORKS: *Comet in Moominland.* 1951. *Who Will Comfort Toffle?* 1961. *Tales from Moominvalley.* 1964. *Moominpapa at Sea.* 1967. *Moominvalley in November.* 1971

BIBLIOGRAPHY: Carpenter, H. and M. Prichard. *Oxford Companion to Children's Literature.* 1985. Promotional Material; Farrar, Staus, and Giroux. Silvey, A. (ed). *Children's Books and Their Creators.* 1995. *Something about the Author,* vol. 41, 1985. *Third Book of Junior Authors and Illustrators.* 1972

MICHAEL OPITZ AND DEDE SMALL

JARRELL, Randall

Author, poet, and critic, b. 6 May 1914, Nashville, Tennessee; d. 14 October 1965, Chapel Hill, North Carolina

When J., the distinguished poet and critic, began to write for children, he had already established himself as a major literary figure. In 1962, three years before his untimely death when struck by a car, J. concentrated much of his creative energy on his books for children, resulting in a significant contribution to the field. After graduating from Vanderbilt University in 1936, with membership in Phi Beta Kappa and a degree in psychology, J. completed his M.A. in English (1939). For much of his professional life (1947–65), J. was a professor at the Women's College of the University of North Carolina (UNC at Greensboro), in addition to holding several visiting appointments, including a year (1951–52) as a Visiting Fellow in Creative Writing at Princeton University. During his literary career, J. was also POETRY critic for *Parisian Review* and *Yale Re-*

view and a contributor to *New Republic* and *New York Times Book Review.*

The Bat-Poet (1964) and *The Animal Family* (1965), both illustrated by Maurice SENDAK, are among the notable works in his contribution to children's literature. Through the character of a small brown bat who becomes a poet, *The Bat-Poet* offers an insightful and revealing glimpse of the poet's life and soul, as well as the creative process. Unable to sleep during the day, the little bat discovers a bright and wonderful world, teeming with exciting new sights and sounds. Inspired and moved by life around him, he attempts to awaken the senses of his fellow forest creatures who fail to see or appreciate the wonders and beauty that surround them. Creating poems to reach his unwilling audience, the bat finally achieves success when a chipmunk hears not only the sound of the bat's poetry but also its sense. In *The Animal Family,* a boy and his parents find themselves shipwrecked. As the boy becomes a man, his parents die, leaving him lonely and empty. Seeking the warmth and friendship of others, he acquires an unusual family of a mermaid, lynx, bear, and a shipwrecked baby. The universal human need for love is a powerful and compelling theme in this FANTASY.

AWARDS: Guggenheim Fellowship in poetry (1946); Levinson prize (1948); Oscar Blumenthal prize (1951); National Institute of Arts and Letters Grant (1951); 1961 National Book Award for *The Woman at the Washington Zoo: Poems and Translations* (1960); O. Max Gardner Award (University of North Carolina, 1962); Ingram-Merrill Literary award (1965); AMERICAN LIBRARY ASSOCIATION Notable Book and Children's Book Showcase Title (1974) for *The Juniper Tree and Other Tales from GRIMM* (1973), translated by Lore SEGAL with illustrations by Maurice Sendak

FURTHER WORKS: *The Gingerbread Rabbit.* (Garth WILLIAMS, illus.) 1964. *Fly by Night.* (Maurice Sendak, illus.) 1976. *A Bat Is Born.* (John SCHOENHERR, illus.) 1978. TRANSLATIONS: *The Rabbit Catcher and Other FAIRY TALES* of Ludwig Bechstein. 1962. *The Golden Bird and Other Fairy Tales by the Brothers Grimm.* 1962. *Snow-White and the Seven Dwarfs: A Tale from the Brothers Grimm.* (Nancy Ekholm BURKERT, illus.) 1972. *The Fisherman and His Wife.* (Margot ZEMACH, illus.) 1980

BIBLIOGRAPHY: Cott, Jonathan, *Pipers at the Gates of Dawn: The Wisdom of Children's Literature,* 1981. *Dictionary of Literary Biography American Writers for Children Since 1960: Fiction.* vol. 52. Ferguson, Suzanne. 1983. *Critical Essays on Randall J.* 1983. Griswold, Jerry. 1984. *Randall J.'s Children's Books.* 1988. and *The Children's Books of Randall J.* Helbig, Althea and Agnes Regan Perkins. *Dictionary of American Children's Fiction 1960–1984. Twentieth-Century Children's Writers.* Huck, Charlotte, *Children's Literature in the Elementary School.* 1971. Lowell, Robert, Peter Taylor, and Robert Penn Warren, eds. *Randall J. 1914–1965.* 1967

ANDREW KANTAR

JEFFERS, Susan
Author, illustrator, b. 7 October 1942, New Jersey

Growing up in Oakland, California, J. discovered art at a young age. J. remembers being chosen to paint a history mural in school. Her mother showed her how to mix paint and how to make objects appear round or flat. Her mother's teaching and enthusiasm inspired her, and she pursued art studies at Brooklyn's Pratt Institute. After graduation in 1964, J. worked at publishing houses in New York City designing book jackets. Children's books intrigued her, so she began freelancing as a designer. She also operated a design studio with author/illustrator Rosemary WELLS. In 1997 J. and Wells collaborated on a SERIES of brightly colored PICTURE BOOKS about McDuff, a fluffy white Scotch terrier with lots of appeal to preschoolers. J.'s evocative illustrations in *Rachel Field's Hitty, Her First Hundred Years,* newly revised in 1999 by Wells, represents a new level of collaboration between author and illustrator as the two bring life to the 1930 NEWBERY MEDAL book.

J.'s first assignment was a children's book called *The Buried Moon* (Joseph JACOBS, 1969). Her next assignment, *Three Jovial Huntsmen* (1973), took three years to perfect. The story of hunters roaming for game was adapted from a MOTHER GOOSE rhyme and was an ALA CALDECOTT MEDAL Honor Book. J. has illustrated many retellings of classic FOLKLORE and POETRY. Primarily illustrating the work of others, she is best known for her pen-and-ink drawings using the crosshatch method of intersecting parallel lines with colors added afterwards. J. specializes in outdoor landscapes of country scenes and detailed animal drawings. She is praised for her detailed nature scenes.

J. is a major illustrator of contemporary American picture books and one of the few author/illustrators to have a picture book on the *New York Times* best-seller list. *Brother Eagle/Sister Sky* (1991) done in pen and colored ink is adapted from the words of NATIVE AMERICAN Chief Seattle. The chief's words are an eloquent reminder of the need to respect the environment and work to preserve ecological harmony.

AWARDS: AMERICAN LIBRARY ASSOCIATION Caldecott Medal Honor Award (1974) and Golden Apple award (1975) for *Three Jovial Huntsmen*. Golden Kite Award (1988) for *Forest of Dreams*. Society of Illustrators Citation of Merit (1985) for *Thumbelina* and (1980) for *Hansel and Gretel*. Bratislava Biennale of Illustrations (1985) for *Thumbelina* and (1983) for *Hiawatha*

FURTHER WORKS: *All the Pretty Horses*. 1974. *Close Your Eyes*. (Jean MARZOLLO). 1976. *Stopping by Woods on a Snowy Evening*. (Robert FROST). 1976. *Wild Robin*. 1976. *If Wishes Were Horses and Other Rhymes*. 1979. *Thumbelina*. (ANDERSEN). 1979. *Little People's Book of Baby Animals*. 1980. *Hansel and Gretel*. 1980. *Hiawatha*. (LONGFELLOW). 1983. *Forest of Dreams*. 1988. *McDuff Comes Home*. (Rosemary Wells, author). 1997

BIBLIOGRAPHY: *Children's Literature Review*. 1993. Cummins, J. *Children's Book ILLUSTRATION and Design*. 1992. *Something about the Author*. vol. 70, 1993

JODI PILGRIM

JENNINGS, Paul
Author, b. 30 April 1943, England

J.'s career as a writer stems from his work as a speech pathologist and teacher. Now living and writing in Australia since 1949, his books are specifically targeted for reluctant readers through J.'s use of vivid imagery and HUMOR that adults label disgusting. The humor is intended to appeal to readers who are most unlikely to pick up a book on their own. J.'s most popular books include collections of short stories such as *Unreal!* (1987), *Quirky Tails!* (1987), and *Uncovered!* (1995), that introduce readers to his imaginative fiction in small digestible chunks. These stories include surprise endings, and unbelievable settings such as haunted outhouses and piles of pig feces. J. believes in the importance of writing books that kids want to read, not books that adults

think kids should read. This explains J.'s use of rib-tickling humor, crazy characters, and disgusting descriptions that his young audiences relish. He says he tries to include at least three elements to delight readers in every short story: "a surprise ending, something yucky, weird happenings, a lot of laughs, spooky events."

Critics applaud J.'s efforts to provide nonreaders with books that appeal to them. *Unreal!* received the 1987 Young AUSTRALIAN Best Book Award, and J. consistently receives Australian child-selected AWARDS including the COOL, KOALA, KROC, and BILBY Awards.

BIBLIOGRAPHY: *Something about the Author*, vol. 88, 1997

DENISE P. BEASLEY

JOHNS, William Earl
Author, illustrator, b. 5 February 1893, Bengeo, Hertfordshire, England; d. 21 June 1968, Hampton Court Palace, Middlesex, England

Service for Great Britain during World War I became the core of experiences from which J. would draw much of his writing for children. During the war he began his service in the army, later becoming a pilot until shot down over Germany where he was held as a prisoner until the end of the war. He remained with the Royal Air Force for the next ten years. After his retirement from the Air Force, he began a career as an aviation illustrator. His early writing for *Popular Flying*, an aviation journal, gave rise to the character James Bigglesworth, a young pilot readers met in many of J.'s 100-plus works for children. J. used numerous pseudonyms but eventually settled on writing under the name Captain W. E. Johns. J. also wrote ADVENTURE STORIES, SCIENCE FICTION and nonfiction, and some of his "Biggies" stories became radio dramas on the BBC's *Children's Hour* on the subject of COMIC BOOKS AND GRAPHIC NOVELS.

J. acknowledged that his writing reflected the values and morals of his times. When criticized for portraying prejudice, sexism, and violence, J. responded, "I give boys what they want, not what their elders and betters think they ought to read . . . I teach sportsmanship under the British idea. One doesn't need blood and thunder to do that." Of Bigglesworth, J. wrote, "He could have been found in any RFC (Royal Flying Corps, now the Royal Air Force) mess during those great days of 1917 and 1918 when air combat had become the order of the day and air dueling was a fine art. He developed . . . into the sort of man most men would like to be: fearless but modest, efficient and resolute in what he undertook."

FURTHER WORKS: *The Camels Are Coming.* 1932. *Biggies of the Camel Squadron.* 1934. *Biggies in France.* 1935. *Biggies—Secret Agent.* 1940. *Worrals of the WAAF.* 1941. *Gimlet Goes Again.* 1944. *Biggies in the Orient.* 1945. *The Rustlers of Rattlesnake Valley.* 1948. *Return to Mars.* 1955. *Biggies on Mystery Island.* 1958. *Adventures of the Junior Detection Club.* 1960. *Biggies and the Plot that Failed.* 1965

BIBLIOGRAPHY: *Something about the Author.* vol. 55, 1989

SANDRA IMDIEKE

JOHNSON, Angela
Author, b. 18 June 1961, Tuskegee, Alabama

J., a former VISTA (Volunteers in Service to America) member and worker in a Head Start program, grew up in a multigenerational family where she heard stories all the time. STORYTELLING, J. says, is traditional in the AFRICAN AMERICAN community and "is art, dance, and music all rolled into one." She is praised frequently for the representation of African American family life in her books. J. has published at least one book a year since 1989, reaching a variety of readers, both young and old. Her books often feature young black protagonists narrating events universally familiar to all readers. In 1991 J. received the Ezra Jack KEATS New Writer Award "to a promising writer" for *Tell Me a Story, Mama.*

J. is only the second writer to win the CORETTA SCOTT KING AWARD for an Author and Author Honor Award in the same year. Her novel, *Heaven,* 1999 winner, is a coming-of-age story. It tells how Marley learns, with unconditional love from her family, to put her life back together and resolutely face the future. J. uses the rural landscape as a metaphor for the calm comfort Marley seeks. J.'s autobiographical book of poetry, *The Other Side: Shorter Poems,* about life in a rural southern community, is a 1999 King Honor Book. It affectionately recalls family and community from J.'s childhood without sentimentality or glossing over the hard times.

Following the selection of *When I Am Old with You* (1990), a PICTURE BOOK about the joyful activities a child and grandfather plan to enjoy together, as a Coretta Scott King Honor Book selection in 1991, J.'s *Toning the Sweep* was the Coretta Scott King Award winning title in 1994. Again, J. tells a young girl's coming-of-age story where several members of a cross-generational family support each other's decisions and share the intimacy of family secrets. In 1995 J. received a PEN award to an emerging author for her novel *Humming Whispers.*

FURTHER WORKS: *What Are You Figuring Now? A Story About Benjamin Banneker.* 1988. *One of Three.* 1991. *Joshua by the Sea.* 1994. *Joshua's Night Whispers.* 1994

BIBLIOGRAPHY: Smith, H., ed. *The Coretta Scott King Awards Book, 1970–1999.* 1999. *Something about the Author,* vol. 102, 1999

JODI PILGRIM

JOHNSON, Crockett (David Johnson Leisk)
Author, illustrator, b. 20 October 1906, New York City; d. 11 July 1975, Norwalk, Connecticut

J. is best known by his pseudonym, Crockett Johnson, under which he wrote and illustrated more than twenty books for children. His most famous creation was *Harold and the Purple Crayon* (1955). J. studied art in the 1920s at Cooper Union and New York University, played professional football, and was employed by the advertising department at Macy's. In 1940 he married Ruth KRAUSS, a children's author with whom he collaborated on books, such as *The Carrot Seed* (1945) and *Is This You?* (1955). Although J.'s career included work as an art editor for several magazines and as an artist whose oil paintings have been exhibited in New York galleries, his professional success is primarily linked to his children's books and his syndicated newspaper comic strip, "Barnaby," which ran in over fifty newspapers from 1941–62, reaching a readership of over five million readers.

J.'s popularity as a children's author and illustrator was assured with the publication of *Harold and the Purple Crayon.* Harold, the bald, nightshirted, wide-eyed protagonist, has become one of the most recognizable and beloved characters in modern children's literature. In this magical FANTASY, baby Harold uses a crayon to create whatever his imagination can dream—an ocean, a dragon, a building, a mountain, even his favorite pies. When Harold draws the ocean he realizes that he must draw a boat, so as not to drown, and when he craves something sweet he simply draws and then samples his nine favorite kinds of pie. He draws and then climbs a mountain but forgets to draw the other side, and as he falls "in thin air" he saves himself by drawing a giant balloon that gently floats him to safety. The simplicity of these imaginative ADVENTURES is conveyed by a world where everything is expressed in lines of purple. Following the release of *Harold and the Purple Crayon* several other Harold books were published, including *Harold's FAIRY TALE: Further Adventures with the Purple Crayon* (1956); *Harold's Trip to the Sky* (1957); *Harold at the North Pole: A Christmas Journey with the Purple Crayon* (1958); *Harold's Circus: An Astounding, Colossal Purple Crayon Event* (1959); and *A Picture for Harold's Room: A Purple Crayon Adventure* (1960). *Harold and the Purple Crayon, Harold's Fairy Tale, Harold's Circus,* and *A Picture for Harold's Room* were also made into motion pictures.

FURTHER WORKS: *Willie's Adventures.* (With Margaret Wise BROWN). 1954. *Mickey's Magnet.* (With Franklyn BRANLEY and Eleanor K. Vaughn). 1956. *Blue Ribbon Puppies.* 1958. *The Frowning Prince.* 1959. *Ellen's Lion.* 1959. *Will Spring Be Early? or Will Spring Be Late?* 1959. *Harold's ABC.* 1963. *The Lion's Own Story.* 1963. *We Wonder What Will Walter Be, when He Grows Up?* 1964. *The Emperor's Gifts.* 1965. *The Happy Egg.* (With Ruth Krauss). 1968

BIBLIOGRAPHY: MEIGS, Cornelia, et al., *A Critical History of Children's Literature,* 1969; *Something about the Author,* vol. 30, 1983

ANDREW KANTAR

JOHNSTON, Tony (Susan Taylor)
Author, b. 30 January 1942, Los Angeles, California

J., author of PICTURE BOOKS and easy readers, earned a B.A. and M.Ed from Stanford University. She uses southern California as the setting for many of her books such as *Iguana Brothers: A Tale of Two Lizards* (1995) and *Cowboy and*

the *Black-eyed Pea* (1992). J. taught briefly in California public elementary schools and worked in New York as an editing supervisor and copy editor for children's books. J. has written over eighty children's books since her first book, *The Adventures of Mole and Troll,* an easy reader, was published in 1972.

Seeking to entertain herself and her readers, J. writes stories that span a wide range of moods and genres, from the fanciful make-believe of *The Witch's Hat* (1984) and *The Soup Bone* (1990), both illustrated by Margot TOMES, to the REALISTIC FICTION of *Amber on the Mountain* (illus. by Robert Duncan, 1994), a tender story about a mountain child whose new friend gives her the twin gifts of literacy and determination during a brief, joyful friendship.

MULTICULTURAL LITERATURE interests inform much of J.'s work, notably the many books set in Mexico, where she lived for fifteen years. J.'s collaborations with Tomie DEPAOLA in *The Tale of Rabbit and Coyote* (1994), *Badger and the Magic Fan: A Japanese Folktale* (1990), *Alice Nizzy Nassy, the Witch of Santa Fe* (1995), *Quilt Story* (1985), and others as well as many other fine artists, have resulted in engaging books that appeal to children.

FURTHER WORKS: *Day of the Dead.* Jeanette WINTER, illus). 1987. *The Wagon.* (James B. RANSOME, illus). 1996. *Whale Song.* (Ed YOUNG). 1987. *Yonder.* (Lloyd Bloom, illus). 1988. *Sparky and Eddie: The First Day of School.* (Susannah Ryan, illus). 1997

BIBLIOGRAPHY: *Something about the Author.* vol. 83, 1996. pp. 96–100; *Contemporary Authors.* 1985; Internet resource: http://www.plcmc.lib. nc.us/find/biosljohnston.htm accessed November 20, 1998

KATHRIE KRIEGER CERRA

JONAS, Ann
Author, illustrator, b. 28 January 1932, Queens, New York

J. grew up in a borough of New York City spending a great deal of time outdoors with her brother. J.'s family felt it was important to be able to do a wide range of hands-on projects that stressed individual self-reliance. However, the skill of drawing was viewed as secondary, only one step in the planning and design process. After high school, J. worked in the advertising office of a department store but did not consider college until she recognized the need to build a career in art. J. attended Cooper Union for the Advancement of Science and Art where she met and married Donald CREWS, also an author and illustrator of children's books. Crews was inducted into the army and he and J. stayed together in Germany for eighteen months. Upon returning to the United States, J. and Crews started a freelance design business. Through her husband's publisher J. herself became involved with children's books. Encouraged by the publisher to try her hand at a children's book, J. produced *When You Were a Baby* in 1982. Writing and illustrating books for children has been a full-time occupation for J. ever since.

Because of J.'s design background she is able to approach each book differently. But while style and technique of J.'s works vary, each contains a type of visual game or challenge for the reader. J.'s third book was *Round Trip* (1983). This award winning black and white work can be read starting at the front, following a day trip to the city, and then turned upside down and read in reverse, returning to the country. In *The Trek* (1985) J. places hidden animals in the scenery for a young girl to discover and in *Splash* (1995) animals jump into and out of a pond in a clever counting book. In *Watch William Walk* (1997) the reader looks down on the scene as though from above as the entire book progresses using words that start only with the letter W.

J.'s books always challenge the reader's imagination and her graphic versatility offers new worlds for children to discover as well as new ways to look at the world we inhabit. Nina Crews, daughter of J. and Don Crews is now creating her OWN PICTURE BOOKS.

AWARDS: *New York Times* Best Illustrated Books of the Year and *Booklist*'s Children's Editors' Choice (1983) both for *Round Trip*. AMERICAN LIBRARY ASSOCIATION Notable Book (1985) for *The Trek*

FURTHER WORKS: *Two Bear Cubs*. 1982. *Holes and Peeks*. 1984. *The Quilt*. 1984. *Now We Can Go*. 1986. *Aardvarks, Disembark!* 1990

BIBLIOGRAPHY: *Seventh Book of Junior Authors and Illustrators*. 1996. Silvey, Anita, ed. *Children's Books and Their Creators*. 1995. *Some-*

thing about the Author, vol. 42, 1986, and vol. 50, 1988

DEDE SMALL

JONES, Elizabeth Orton

Author, illustrator, b. 1910, Highland Park, Illinois

J. was educated as an artist at the Art Institute of Chicago and at Fountainebleau, France. Early in her career, she illustrated works written by her mother, Jessie Orton Jones. Working together, their book *Small Rain: Verses from the Bible* was named an ALA CALDECOTT MEDAL Honor Book in 1944. Jessie Orton Jones selected verses from the King James Bible and J. illustrated them mostly in black-and-white with some pastels. In an unusually rare choice in the 1940s, J. portrays multiethnic children going through the ordinary events of daily activities.

In 1945, J. received the Caldecott Medal for her idealized portraits of children in *Prayer for a Child* with text by Rachel FIELD. Her gold tinged full-page pastel watercolor ILLUSTRATIONS depict familiar bedtime rituals of childhood. In *Big Susan* (1940) J. created dolls who came alive with all the emotions of real children. Her illustrations can be found in books by several other authors.

FURTHER WORKS: *Ragman of Paris and His Ragmuffins*. 1937. *Maminka's Children*. 1940. *Twig*. 1942. *A Prayer for Little Things*. (Eleanor FARJEON, author). 1945

BIBLIOGRAPHY: Ward, M.E., D.A. Marquardt, N. Dolan, and D. Eaton. (eds.). 1990. *Authors of Books for Young People*. 3rd ed.

MARY ARIAIL BROUGHTON

JORDAN, June

Poet, author, essayist, teacher, b. 9 July 1936, New York City

By the age of seven, J. was already writing. The daughter of Jamaican immigrants, she studied at Barnard College and the University of Chicago and has received several academic awards, including a Rockefeller Foundation grant in creative writing (1969) and a Poetry Fellowship from the National Endowment for the Arts (1982). Her works for children include free verse poetry of her own, editing POETRY anthologies, and writing novels for YOUNG ADULTS. Her teaching includes workshops for young writers on both coasts. J.'s literary work expresses a strong sense of AFRICAN AMERICAN identity as well as her feminism. *Who Look at Me* (1969), a booklength poem that recapitulates for children the African American history of repression, is one of her many texts using black English. *The Voice of Children* (1970, with Terri Bush) anthologizes poems by African American and Puerto Rican children whom J. invited to write about their impressions of ghetto life. J.'s deep love of language can be found in her fiction for children, including *Kimako's Story* (1981), in which the young protagonist plays with poetry. J. is best known for her poetry for adults and her political essays.

AWARDS: CORETTA SCOTT KING AWARD (1971) for *The Voice of the Children* (with Terri Bush). AMERICAN LIBRARY ASSOCIATION Notable Book (1969) for *Who Look at Me*

FURTHER WORKS: *His Own Where—*. 1971. *Fannie Lou Hamer*. 1972. *Dry Victories*. 1972

BIBLIOGRAPHY: *American Women Writers*. 1994. *Contemporary Poets*. 1991. *Contemporary Authors, New Revision Series*. 1989. Smith, Henrietta M., ed. *The Coretta Scott King Awards Book, 1970–99*. 1999

FRANCISCA GOLDSMITH

JOSLYN, Sesyle
Author, b. 30 August 1929, Providence, Rhode Island

J.'s best known work, *What Do You Say, Dear?* (Maurice SENDAK, illus., 1958), is both an ALA CALDECOTT MEDAL Honor book and AMERICAN LIBRARY ASSOCIATION Notable Children's book. This illustrated encyclopedia of manners uses humorously absurd hypothetical situations to model proper social behavior for young readers. Its sequel, *What Do You Do, Dear* (1961), also outlines good manners for all occasions. Another SERIES of books written by J. include: *Brave Baby Elephant* (1960), *Baby Elephant's Trunk* (1961), *Baby Elephant and the Secret Wishes* (1962). The series emphasizes young children's growing independence and mastery of simple tasks set within a context of good manners and proper behavior. J.'s other works include books written with French, Italian, and Spanish phrases. They include: *La Petite Famille* (1964), *La Fiesta*

(1967), and *Que se Dice, Nino* (1966) as do several of the Baby Elephant books.

She has also written several chapter books for older readers such as *Spy Lady and the Muffin Man* (1971). Another chapter book, *The Gentle Savages* (1979), recounts the story of two English children who flee their families when their cruise ship docks at a North African port as they embark on a new life full of independence, adventure, and danger.

FURTHER WORKS: *There Is a Dragon in My Bed* (Irene HAAS, au.), 1961

DENISE P. BEASLEY

JOYCE, William (Bill)
Author, illustrator, b. 11 December 1957, Shreveport, Louisiana

J. claims that growing up, his family was more eccentric than any SCIENCE FICTION movie or television program he was addicted to watching. He includes some memory of their eccentricities in each of the books he writes and illustrates. Always fascinated by STORYTELLING, ILLUSTRATION, and movies, J. decided to study filmmaking and illustration at Southern Methodist University. His first published self-illustrated book, *George Shrinks* (1985), is about a little boy who one night dreams he is small only to wake up the next morning to discover that he has indeed shrunk. The story's text is made up of a list of chores that George's parents have left for him to complete. Realizing the advantages that his new size affords him, George creatively finds ways to complete these mundane household tasks, such as using a "surfboard" sponge as a dish-washing technique and his crawling baby brother as a pack mule to whom he hitches a wagon of trash to be hauled away. He even finds time to fly around the room in his model airplane. George, in reverse, is based on J.'s memories of King Kong movies, *The Incredible Shrinking Man* (1957), and a favorite childhood book, *The Borrowers* (M. NORTON, 1952), all of which J. believed were true.

The theme of friendship is an important part of J.'s popular *Bently and Egg* (1992). Illustrated in watercolors, it depicts the relationship between a musical artistic frog, Bently Hopperton, and the egg a duck friend is waiting to hatch. Friendship also enters into *Santa Calls* (1993), J.'s picture storybook set in 1908 in Abilene, Texas. It is the story of three children: Art Atchinson Aimesworth, his sister Esther, and a friend named Spaulding, who find themselves in a full-blown North Pole FANTASY complete with Santa Claus, an evil queen, and her elves. It turns out that Esther's Christmas wish from Santa was for her brother, Art, to be her friend, a wish that is eventually fulfilled. J.'s early television watching led him to conclude that all stories have happy endings; he has made this a hallmark of his PICTURE BOOKS. The adventures of a baseball-playing dinosaur and his relationship with his adopted American family are the focus of J.'s popular *Dinosaur Bob and His Adventures with the Family Lazardo* (1988). Children enjoy following the mischievous exploits of the lovable, cheerful Bob in this humorous and entertaining story. J.'s off-the-wall, imaginative situations and playful characters coupled with his often bold use of color and creative exaggeration have earned him recognition from children and critics alike.

J. has an extensive book collection he uses when he needs a picture for his own drawing as well as models of objects such as dinosaurs and trains. He works in several art mediums to create his illustrations: acrylic paints, pen-and-ink, colored pencils, oil, and watercolors.

AWARDS: Christopher Award for picture book (1988) for *Humphrey's Bear* (Jan WAHL, author). *New York Times* Best Illustrated Children's Books of the Year (1989) for *Nicholas Cricket* (Joyce Maxner, author). Society of Illustrators Silver Medal (1992) for *Bently and Egg*. *School Library Journal*'s Best Book Award (1985) for *George Shrinks*

FURTHER WORKS: *A Day with Wilbur Robinson.* 1990. *The Leaf Men and the Brave Good Bugs.* 1996. *Buddy: Based on the True Story of Gertrude Lintz.* 1997. Illus. only: *Tammy and the Gigantic Fish.* (Catherine and James Gray). 1983. *My First Book of Nursery Tales: Five MOTHER GOOSE Stories.* (Marianna MAYER. 1983. *Waiting-for-Spring Stories.* (Bethany Roberts). 1984. *Shoes.* (Elizabeth Winthrop). 1986. *Humphrey's Bear.* (Jan Wahl). 1987. *Nicolas Cricket.* (Joyce Maxner). 1989. *Some of the Adventures of Rhode Island Red.* (Stephen Manes). 1990

BIBLIOGRAPHY: Cummings, P., ed. *Talking with Artists.* vol. 2. 1995. Cummins, J., ed. *Children's Book Illustration and Design.* 1992. Huck, C. *Children's Literature in the Elementary School.*

1971. Norton, D. *Through the Eyes of a Child. Something about the Author.* vol. 72. 1993

ANDREW KANTAR

JUKES, Mavis
Author, b. 3 May 1947, Nyack, New York

J. is an author adept in her ability to write about the life topics of children and YOUNG ADULTS. Her strong fictional characterizations engage readers as do the straightforward facts and advice in her informational titles. J. graduated with a B.A. in art from the University of California, Berkeley, and earned a Doctor of Jurisprudence degree from Golden Gate University. J. first realized she wanted to write when she wrote a story for her newborn daughter and was pleased with the results. Although she was in her third year of law school, she continued to write through law school. J.'s first publication was *No One Is Going to Nashville* (1983) in which she communicates her strengths in style, theme, and form. This first title along with her second book *Like Jake and Me* (1984), establishes J.'s deftness concerning children and their stepparents. Companion books, *Getting Even* (1988) and *Wild Iris Bloom* (1991), are written for intermediate readers and center on the middle-school experience as well as stepfamilies. Continuing with family themes, *Lights around the Palm* (1987), focuses on a brother-sister relationship. Grandparents and death are the issues in *Blackberries in the Dark* (1985) as a young boy continues the traditions of his recently deceased grandfather and forges new ground for the future with his grandmother. In addition to the young adult titles *Getting Even* and *Wild Iris Bloom,* J. has written *Expecting the Unexpected: Sex Ed with Mrs. Gladys B. Furley, R. N.* (1996); fiction; and *It's a Girl Thing: How to Stay Healthy, Safe, and in Charge* (1996); and nonfiction, in which the interests and concerns of female adolescents are addressed. In *Expecting,* J. displays HUMOR in a lighthearted novel whereas she provides straightforward information on the same issues as in *It's a Girl Thing.* Above all, J. succeeds in her attempts to be in tune with the concerns, thoughts, and interests of authentic lives of children and young people.

AWARDS: Bank Street College of Education's Irma Simonton Black Award, Parents' Choice Foundation Parents' Choice Award (1983) for *No One Is Going to Nashville*. ALA NEWBERY MEDAL Honor Book (1985) for *Like Jake and Me*. AMERICAN LIBRARY ASSOCIATION Notable Book and Notable Children's Trade Book in the Field of Social Studies (1985) for *Blackberries in the Dark*

FURTHER WORKS: *I'll See You in My Dreams.* 1992. *Losers Weepers.* 1997. *Growing Up: It's a Girl Thing.* 1998. *It's a Girl Thing: Dating.* 1998

BIBLIOGRAPHY: *Booklist,* April 1, 1988, vol. 84, no. 15, p. 1349. Cullinan, Bernice E. *Literature and the Child* (1989). *Newbery and CALDECOTT MEDAL Books* (1986). *Publishers Weekly,* April 1, 1996, vol. 243, no. 14, p. 78. *Publishers Weekly,* Aug. 26, 1996, vol. 243, no. 35, p. 98. *Twentieth-Century Children's Writers* (1995)

NANCY HORTON

JUSTER, Norton
Author, b. 2 June 1929, Brooklyn, New York

J., like his father, became an architect. After receiving his degree from the University of Pennsylvania, J. was awarded a Fulbright scholarship (1952–53) for graduate study at the University of Liverpool. Later, he was the recipient of a Ford Foundation Grant (1960), as well as a Guggenheim Fellowship (1967). As a practicing architect, J. also worked as an instructor of environmental design at Pratt Institute in Brooklyn. After moving to Massachusetts, he continued to combine his architectural career with a professorship of design at Hampshire College in Amherst. In 1961, J. published *The Phantom Tollbooth* (illustrated by Jules Feiffer), his most popular book for children. A humorous FANTASY journey in the tradition of Lewis CARROLL, *The Phantom Tollbooth* is about the adventures of Milo after discovering a large package in his apartment that contains a purple tollbooth, a map, and a set of instructions. Milo, who has been bored with school and learning in general, cannot resist the desire to explore the strange locations on the map, and, after climbing into a toy car and passing the tollbooth, he is transported to a world of eccentric characters with lessons to teach. Using his map as a guide, Milo finds himself in such strange places as the Doldrums, the boring home of the Lethargians who know only how to waste time; Dictionopolis, a city that claims to be the origin of all words (where "ragamuffins" and

"synonym buns" are foods); the ironically nonexistent City of Reality and silent Valley of Sound (to which Milo helps bring back sound). While locked in a dungeon in Dictionopolis for mixing up words, Milo learns about the tragic fate of the royal princesses, Rhyme and Reason, and agrees to free them from their imprisonment in the Castle in Air. Throughout his journey, Milo encounters a cast of Wonderland-like characters, such as Tock, a Watchdog whose body is a clock; Spelling Bee the pristine speller; the Humbug, whose words cannot be believed; Faintly Macabre, a mildly scary witch; a Mathemagician in the city of Digitopolis; and the Everpresent Wordsnatcher, who takes the words right out of your mouth. Milo learns and grows with each experience in this fast-paced adventure. Though thought by some to be overly didactic and moralistic, *The Phantom Tollbooth* is a magical allegory that possesses a good deal of creative energy and no shortage of comic characters, colorful dialogue and wordplay, and lively situations. *The Phantom Tollbooth* was made into a movie and released by MGM in 1970.

Speaking to a group of children, J. was asked by one child where his ideas for his stories came from. J. replied "From a post box in Poughkeepsie" in an effort to help the children understand that ideas come at us just from being alive, that ideas are all around us if we simply stop and think about what is surrounding us—but the most important part of his job is writing, putting his ideas down on paper.

AWARD: George C. Stone Center for Children's Books Seventh Recognition of Merit (1971)

FURTHER WORKS: *The Dot and the Line: A Romance in Lower Mathematics.* 1964; reissued 2000. *Alberic the Wise and Other Journeys.* (Domenico Gnoli, illus.). 1965. *Otter Nonsense.* (Eric CARLE, illus.). 1983. *As: A Surfteit of Similes.* (David Small, illus.). 1989

BIBLIOGRAPHY: Carpenter, H. and M. Prichard. *Oxford Companion of Children's Literature.* 1984. *Dictionary of American Children's Fiction, 1960–1984.* Helbig, A. and A. Perkins: *Twentieth-Century Children's Writers. Something about the Author.* vol. 3, 1972. YOLEN, Jane: *Discovering the Joy of Writing.* 1998. In Highlights Foundation, Inc.

ANDREW KANTAR

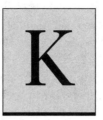

KALMAN, Maira
Author, illustrator, b. 1949, Tel Aviv, Israel

K.'s family moved to the United States from Israel when K. was four years old. She grew up in Riverdale, a section of the Bronx. K.'s family exposed her to the arts at an early age. She attended the High School of Music and Art and studied literature at New York University. She met her husband, Tibor Kalman, at college. K. concentrated on drawing for the next several years, helping her husband with graphic designs. K. finally made her writing a priority and combined it with her drawing—her first project was illustrating *Stay Up Late!*, which derives from lyrics written by David Byrne, a member of the musical group Talking Heads. From the beginning of her writing career, K. planned her books to be for children and adults. K. wrote and self-illustrated *Hey Willy, See the Pyramids* a year later. This book evolved around her son and daughter, Alexander and Lulu. Her next book, *Sayonara, Mrs. Kackleman,* continues Lulu and Alexander's adventures. K. has also written books based on a friendly beagle named Max. The theme in K.'s *Max* books is the lure of the exotic and the safety of home. They are enjoyed as well by young adults and college students who appreciate their sophisticated writing, outrageous humor, subtle word play, and sense of the ridiculous. In fact, they are being adapted as a Hollywood film.

K. received the Parents' Choice award for PICTURE BOOKS from the Parents' Choice Foundation in 1989 for *Hey Willy, See the Pyramids. Ooh-la-la (Max in Love)* earned a Best Illustrated Children's Books of the Year citation from the *New York Times* in 1991. K. is known for her animated ILLUSTRATIONS. Her books often contain dreamlike adventures of children and animals, which entertain both children and adults.

FURTHER WORKS: *Hey Willy, See the Pyramids,* 1988: *Sayonara, Mrs. Kackleman,* 1989; *Max Makes a Million,* 1990; *Ooh-la-la (Max In Love),* 1991; *Max in Hollywood,* 1992; *Chicken Soup, Boots,* 1993; *Swami on Rye: Max in India,* 1995; *Max Doll,* 1995; *Max Deluxe,* 1996

BIBLIOGRAPHY: *Something about the Author,* vol. 96, 1998

JODI PILGRIM

KASTNER, Erich
Author, b. 23 February 1899, Dresden, Germany; d. 29 July 1974, Munich, Germany

K. became one of the best-known international children's authors in the twentieth century. His first book *Emil und die Detektiv* (1929), published as *Emil and the Detectives* in the United States in 1929, won him fame across the globe for its criticism of contemporary issues. Set in Berlin, this is a MYSTERY AND DETECTIVE STORY in which Emil tracks down and pursues a thief who stole his money. Its enduring popularity is due to its themes of leadership, courage, and teamwork. His other books for children include *Das fliegende Klassenzimmer* (1933), *Punktchen und Anton* (1937), *Das doppelte Lottchen* (1949), *Let's Face It Poems* (1963), and *Little Man*

427

(1966). Both *Emil und die Detektiv* and *Punkt-chen und Anton* have been adapted into films. Because of his outspoken political convictions, K. was prohibited from publishing books in Germany from 1933 to 1945. He continued to live in Germany during this period, under Adolf Hitler's rule, but published his books in Switzerland.

AWARDS: AMERICAN LIBRARY ASSOCIATION Mildred L. BATCHELDER Award (1968) for *The Little Man:* Hans Christian ANDERSEN Award (1960)

BIBLIOGRAPHY: *Kuusankosken kaupunginkirjasto.* 1997; www.kirjasto.sci.fi/kastner.htm

DENISE P. BEASLEY

KASTNER, Jill
Illustrator, b. 30 April 1964, Elizabeth, New Jersey

K. has illustrated children's books for several authors, including Cynthia RYLANT, Will HOBBS, Russell Sanders, Phyllis Rose Eisenberg, Alice McLerran, and Elvira Woodruff. Her self-illustrated book, *Snake Hunt* (1993), is based on a true personal experience with her grandfather. K. lists David WIESNER and Troy Howell as artists whose work greatly affected her own.

FURTHER WORKS: Illustrator: *Aurora Means Dawn.* R. Sanders, author, 1989: *You're My Nikki* (P. R. Rosenberg, author, 1992); *I Want to Go Home* (A. McElerran, author, 1992); *Beardream* (W. Hobbs, author, 1997)

BIBLIOGRAPHY: *Something about the Author,* vol. 70, 1993

MARY ARIAIL BROUGHTON

KASZA, Keiko
Author, illustrator, b. 23 December 1951, Innoshima City, Japan

Although she grew up in Japan, K. left her native country to attend college at the California State University at Northridge, where she received a degree in graphic design. K. moved to the United States permanently when she married an American citizen. She currently lives in Bloomington, Indiana, with her husband and two sons. After the birth of her sons, K. concluded her career as a graphic designer and began writing and illustrating children's books full-time. Her work includes ILLUSTRATIONS done in gouache and pen, and features a generous use of white space. Most of

her tales involve anthropomorphic cartoon-style animals in simple, humorous stories. *The Wolf's Chicken Stew* (1987), winner of a Kentucky Bluegrass Award, tells a traditional cautionary story of greed with HUMOR and colorful watercolor illustrations.

FURTHER WORKS: *When the Elephant Walks.* 1990: *A Mother for Choco.* 1992: *Rat and the Tiger.* 1993: *Grandpa Toad's Secrets.* 1995: *Don't Laugh Joe!* 1997: *Dorothy & Mikey.* 2000

BIBLIOGRAPHY: Publisher's notes

DENISE E. AGOSTO

KATE GREENAWAY MEDAL

The Greenaway Medal is given for the most distinguished work in ILLUSTRATION of children's books first published in the United Kingdom in the preceding year. The Greenaway has been given annually by the British Library Association since 1955. The medal is given in the summer of the year following the book's publication. Since 1990, the Peters Library Service makes a substantial contribution, matched by the Business Sponsorship Incentive Scheme of the British government, to publicize the Greenaway and the CARNEGIE MEDALS. The Greenaway Medal is comparable to the U.S. CALDECOTT MEDAL. Winners are dated for the year in which the book was published. The Medal is announced during the summer of the following year.

1955: No Award; 1956–57: *Tim All Alone,* by Edward ARDIZZONE; 1957–56: *Mrs. Easter and the Storks,* by V. H. Drummond; 1958: No Award; 1959: *Kashtanka and a Bundle of Ballads,* William Stobbs; 1960: *Old Winkle and the Seagulls,* Elizabeth ROSE, ill. Gerald ROSE; 1961: *Mrs. Cockle's Cat,* Philippa PEARCE, ill. Antony MAITLAND; 1962: *Brian Wildsmith's A B C,* Brian WILDSMITH; 1963: *Borka,* by John BURNINGHAM; 1964: *Shakespeare's Theatre,* by C. W. Hodges; 1965: *Three Poor Tailors,* by Victor Ambrus; 1966: MOTHER GOOSE *Treasury,* by Raymond BRIGGS; 1967: *Charlie, Charlotte & the Golden Canary,* by Charles KEEPING; 1968: *Dictionary of Chivalry,* by Grant Uden, ill. by Pauline Baynes; 1969: *The Quangle-Wangle's Hat,* by Edward LEAR, ill. by Helen OXENBURY, *Dragon of an Ordinary Family,* by Margaret MAHY, ill. by Helen Oxenbury; 1970: *Mr. Gumpy's Outing,* by John

BURNINGHAM; 1971: *The Kingdom under the Sea,* by Jan PIENKOWSKI; 1972: *The Woodcutter's Duck,* by Krystyna Turska; 1973: *Father Christmas,* by Raymond BRIGGS; 1974: *The Wind Blew,* by Pat HUTCHINS; 1975: *Horses in Battle,* by Victor Ambrus, *Mishka,* by Victor Ambrus; 1976: *The Post Office Cat,* by Gail E. HALEY; 1977: *Dogger,* by Shirley HUGHES; 1978: *Each Peach Pear Plum,* Allan AHLBERG, ill. Janet AHLBERG; 1979: *The Haunted House,* Jan PIENKOWSKI; 1980: *Mr. Magnolia,* by Quentin BLAKE; 1981: *The Highwayman,* by Alfred Noyes, ill. Charles Keeping; 1982: *Long Neck and Thunder Foot,* by Helen Piers, ill. Michael FOREMAN, *Sleeping Beauty & Other Favourite* FAIRY TALES, chosen by Angela Carter, ill. Michael Foreman; 1983: *Gorilla,* by Anthony BROWNE; 1984: *Hiawatha's Childhood,* by Errol LE CAIN; 1985: *Sir Gawain and the Loathly Lady,* by Selina HASTINGS, ill. Juan Wijngaard; 1986: *Snow White in New York,* by Fiona French; 1987: *Crafty Chameleon,* by Mwenye Hadithi, ill. Adrienne Kennaway; 1988: *Can't You Sleep, Little Bear?,* Martin WADDELL, ill. Barbara Firth; 1989: *War Boy: A Country Childhood,* by Michael Foreman; 1990: *The Whale's Song,* by Dyan Sheldon, ill. Gary BLYTHE; 1991: *The Jolly Christmas Postman,* by Janet and Allan Ahlberg; 1992: *Zoo,* by Anthony Browne; 1993: *Black Ships before Troy,* by Rosemary SUTCLIFF, ill. Alan Lee; 1994: *Way Home,* by Libby Hawthorne, ill. Gregory Rogers; 1995: *The Christmas Miracle of Jonathan Toomey,* P. J. LYNCH; 1996: *The Baby Who Wouldn't Go To Bed,* Helen Cooper; 1997: *When Jessie Came across the Sea,* P. J. Lynch; 1998: *Pumpkin Soup,* Helen Cooper; 1999: *Alice's Adventures in Wonderland,* Helen Oxenbury

BERNICE E. CULLINAN

KEATS, Ezra Jack

Author, illustrator, b. 11 March 1916, Brooklyn, New York; d. 6 May 1983, Brooklyn, New York

K. was born Jacob Ezra Katz to Polish immigrant parents. He grew up in New York and lived there most of his life. He began his artistic efforts as a four-year-old, sketching pictures on his mother's enamel kitchen table. His mother displayed delight and boasted to neighbors at every opportunity; his father, having witnessed the poverty of some artists in the coffee shop in which he worked in Greenwich Village, discouraged his son. This division of encouragement from his mother and disdain from his father continued until young K., at the age of eight, was paid to paint a sign for a local candy store: only then could his father see that art could be a money-making career. This lack of support bothered K. up until the death of his father at which time, K. discovered well-worn newspaper clippings of the AWARDS he had won in his dad's wallet. K. won the National Scholastic Art Competition Award for one of his paintings in high school and several scholarships to further his education, but with no father, the family needed him to work to help support his mother and siblings. Fortunately he was able to continue working in the area of art. He worked for the Works Progress Administration painting murals and as a production assistant for the COMIC BOOK *Captain Marvel Adventures.*

During World War II, K. entered the service of the United States Army Air Corps and helped design camouflage patterns. In 1949, K. traveled to France where he studied painting and changed his name to Ezra Jack K. A year later he returned to New York to sell his paintings and to settle into a career. After leaving samples of his work with several publishers, a children's book editor asked him to illustrate *Jubilant for Sure* (1954), written by Elizabeth Hubbard Lansing. Thus his career as an illustrator began. For ten years K. illustrated other people's works, including covers and stories for magazines such as *Collier's* and *Reader's Digest.* Throughout this ten-year period, K. wanted to see two developments in children's literature: more of a sense of action in books along with less rigid structure and the presence of black characters. He created *The Snowy Day* (1962). It was the first full-color PICTURE BOOK to feature an AFRICAN AMERICAN child, his family and friends enjoying the wonder of a snowy day and the everyday activities of childhood. K. had saved pictures from magazines of children with intriguing expressions and strong character from *Life* magazine for over twenty years; these became models for the character Peter and his friends in *The Snowy Day* and later in *Whistle for Willie* (1964), *Peter's Chair* (1967), and *A Letter for Amy* (1968). K. prepared his own paper for the collage paintings. The snow against a blue sky was made by brushing white cotton across paste on blue paper. The contrast of light and dark acrylic colors and rich palette of collage textures capture the essence of life in an urban neighborhood as seen through the eyes of a young child. The use of plenty of white space on the page complements the serenity of the accompanying text.

K. pioneered MULTICULTURALISM in PICTURE BOOKS. His exceptional coupling of gentle, lyrical texts and premium use of gouache and collage rendered success for the author, delight for young readers, and satisfaction from adults. K. wrote his books by first creating characters with very typical problems, next he envisioned these happenings in his mind. Then he would display the pictures on his wall in sequence, feeling that he was writing a ballet. Finally, he would experiment with the art until it was mastered. He used myriad materials, tools, textures, and colors to create his collages. He referred to his work as an "unusual balance between illusion and reality."

K.'s emergence as an author and artist coincided with the civil rights movement, providing a much needed representation of black characters. As a white author, he felt that although his characters were of different colors, it was important to note that the experiences were universal ones in which all children could share. K.'s engaging style captures the child's perception.

K. believed that the character Peter and his friends were like his own children. He nurtured them through childhood concerns like learning to whistle, adjusting to a new sibling, and dealing with bullies. These happenings, as K. liked to refer to them, were also autobiographical. These occurrences and others in his life are reflected in *Ezra Jack Keats: A Biography with ILLUSTRATIONS* (1995).

K.'s widespread appeal is evidenced in the response to *Skates* (1973), a story of two dogs' escapades on skates. Children in Japan were so taken with the book that they began rollerskating all around Tokyo. After a petition from parents, a skating rink was built that bears a plaque with K.'s name in tribute to his influence.

K. felt most rewarded by the response he received from his readers, including poet Langston HUGHES, and a multitude of children, teachers, and parents. He kept all of the correspondence. These papers along with other professional correspondence, photographs, and childhood memorabilia, easel art, and works dating back to his high school are housed at the DE GRUMMOND REFERENCE COLLECTION at the University of Southern Mississippi; this is the sole repository for the Ezra Jack Keats Archive. The collection includes manuscripts, sketches, illustrations, and proofs for thirty-seven books written and or illustrated by the author. A statue of K.'s signature character Peter stands in Brooklyn's Prospect Park and an elementary school is named in his memory. An award, the Ezra Jack K. Award, is presented annually to an author/illustrator who works in the tradition of K. Numerous adaptations of K.'s works exist as films, cassettes, and plays. His works have been translated into sixteen languages.

AWARDS: CALDECOTT MEDAL, and Brooklyn Art Books for Children citation (1962) for *The Snowy Day:* Caldecott Honor Book (1969) for *Goggles! Boston Globe–Horn* Book Award for *Hi, Cat!* (1970): *School Library Journal's* Best Books for *Apt. 3* (1971). *The King's Fountain* (illustrator only 1971). Children's Choice from the INTERNATIONAL READING ASSOCIATION and the Children's Book Council for *The Trip* (1978): Silver Medallion from the University of Southern Mississippi, 1980, for Outstanding Service in the Field of Children's Literature

FURTHER WORKS: self-illustrated: (with Pat Cherr) *My Dog is Lost!* 1960: *Jennie's Hat.* 1966: *Goggles!* 1969: *Apt. 3.* 1971: *Psst! Doggie—.* 1973: *Dreams.* 1974: *Kitten for a Day.* 1974: *Louie.* 1975: *Maggie and the Pirate.* 1979: *Louie's Search.* 1980: *Regards to the Moon.* 1981: *Clementina's Cactus.* 1982: as illustrator only: *Chester.* 1954: *Danny Dunn and the Anti-Gravity Paint.* 1956: *The Indians Knew.* 1957: *Zoo, Where Are You?* 1964: *In a Spring Garden.* 1965: *How to Be a Nature Detective.* 1966 edition. *The Little Drummer Boy.* Davis, Onorati, Simeone. 1968: *The King's Fountain.* 1971

BIBLIOGRAPHY: Engel, Dean, and Florence B. Freedman. *Ezra Jack K.: A Biography with Illustrations.* 1995: HOPKINS, Lee Bennett, *Pauses: Autobiographical Reflections of 101 Creators of Children's Books,* 1995; K., Ezra Jack. "The Artist at Work: Collage," the *Horn Book* magazine, June 3, 1964; K., Ezra Jack, "Dear Mr. Keats . . . ," the *Horn Book* magazine, June 3, 1972; *Something about the Author.* vols. 57 and 34. *Children's Literature Review* vol. 35; http://www.lib.usm.edu/~degrum/keats/main.html

NANCY HORTON

KEENE, Carolyn
(See STRATEMEYER, Edward)

KEEPING, Charles
Illustrator, author, b. 22 September 1924, London, England; d. 16 May 1988, England

K. is regarded as one of the most brilliant and original children's illustrators of the twentieth century. K. started out in the printing business and then created wall murals, posters, and book jackets. His work has been shown in museums in England and the United States. Using a mixture of gouache, watercolor, tempera and ink, his drawings are either done in browns or blacks, or in contrasting bright splashy colors. His sophisticated quirky drawings portray the mood, tone, and emotions of the story rather than illustrate actual events. This is particularly evident in K.'s ILLUSTRATIONS for *Elidor* (Alan GARNER, 1965) and, in 1981, Alfred Noyes's narrative poem "The Highwayman."

K. authored and illustrated twenty-four of his own books including *Shaun and the Cart-Horse* (1966) and *Joseph's Yard* (1969) based on his childhood experiences living next door to a stable and watching the horses through a crack in the fence. K. said that this was akin to watching the action on a stage. *Richard* (1973) is about a London police horse. K. conceived and illustrated a single wordless PICTURE BOOK, *Inter-City* (1977), showing a child's view of the world from a moving train. He was nominated for the Hans Christian ANDERSEN Highly Commended Illustrator award in 1974, given for distinguished contributions to children's literature.

K. also illustrated many books for other authors, such as two retellings of Greek myths by Edward BLISHEN and Leon GARFIELD called *The God beneath the Sea* (1970) and *The Golden Shadow* (1973) as well as Philip Neil's *Tale of Sir Gawain* (1987). He also illustrated numerous adult titles.

AWARDS: KATE GREENAWAY MEDAL (1967) for *Charley, Charlotte and the Golden Canary* and (1981) for *The Highwayman* (Noyes). Kurt Maschler Award (1987) for *Jack the Treacle Eater* (Charles CAUSLEY). W. H. Smith Illustration Award (1988) for *Charles Keeping's Classic Tales of the Macabre*

FURTHER WORKS: Illustrator: *The Silver Branch* (Rosemary SUTCLIFF, 1957); *Beowulf* (Kevin CROSSLEY-HOLLAND, ed., 1982); *The Wedding Ghost* (Leon GARFIELD, 1985)

BIBLIOGRAPHY: *The Oxford Companion to Children's Literature*, 1984; *Someting about the Author*, vol. 56, 1989

                                    DENISE P. BEASLEY

KEITH, Harold
Author, b. 8 April 1903, Lambert, Oklahoma; d. 24 Feb. 1998, Norman, Oklahoma

K. is best known for his enduringly popular historical novel, *Rifles for Watie* (1957), a Civil War story about the tedium of war and a young spy for the Union Army trapped behind Confederate lines in the West. The book won the NEWBERY MEDAL in 1958 and the Lewis CARROLL Shelf Award in 1964. It is based on research K. did among surviving Cherokee Indians who fought under General Stand Watie. Other award-winning books include *The Runt of Rogers School* (1971); *Susy's Scoundrel* (1974); and *The Obstinate Land* (1977). K.'s works, which reflect his interests in history and sports, have been praised for their accuracy and attention to detail.

FURTHER WORKS: *Komantcia*. 1965: *Go, Red, Go!* 1972: *The Bluejay Boarders*. 1972: *The Sound of Strings: Sequel to Komantcia*. 1992: *Chico and Dan*. 1998

BIBLIOGRAPHY: Harold K. http:/Iinfoplease.lycos.com/ipa/A0763303.html. Accessed March 27, 1999. HOPKINS, Lee Bennett, *Pauses: Autobiographical Reflections of 101 Creators of Children's Literature*, 1995. Ward, M. E., D. A. Marquardt, N. Dolan and D. EATON. Eds. 1990. *Authors of Books for Young People*, 3rd ed.

                                    MARY ARIAIL BROUGHTON

KELLER, Holly
Author, illustrator, b. 11 February 1942, New York City

Children are first drawn to K.'s books because of her simple, whimsical, cartoon-style characters beckoning from the book jackets. They want to hear her books read again and again because she writes about young children's true feelings and the kinds of issues and problems they face: getting along with others, the death of a pet, or being the new kid at school. In most stories a loving adult eases the pain. Children like Geraldine in *Geraldine's Big Snow* (1988) and *Horace* (1991), a leopard "child" adopted by striped parents who struggles with the fact that he's different, and all of K.'s family of characters. They are glad when they encounter these sympathetic characters again, as in *Brave Horace* (1998) and other Geraldine books.

BIBLIOGRAPHY: *Something about the Author,* vol. 42, 1986, and vol. 76, 1994

REBECCA RAPPORT

KELLOGG, Steven

Author, illustrator, b. 26 October, 1941, Norwalk, Connecticut

K. was a storyteller/illustrator even as a child. He made up stories for his younger sisters and accompanied them with drawings as the stories progressed. He also loved PICTURE BOOKS, particularly the illustrations of Beatrix POTTER and N. C. WYETH. Influenced by his studies at the Rhode Island School of Design, including a year of study in Italy, he has turned this "telling stories on paper" into his lifework: he has illustrated over ninety books, many of which he has also written. K. draws most of his ideas from his childhood feelings and images, from his family life and from his keen observation of animals and people. The "stubborn unadaptability during puppyhood" of the family Great Dane inspired the Pinkerton collection. The family's "senior cat . . . an independent old grouch who . . . devoted her long life to harassing everyone in the world, including Pinkerton," was the model for "Rose" in *A Rose for Pinkerton* (1981).

K.'s goal is to "blend illustrations and words so that each book is a feast for the eye and ear." His artwork is flamboyant and colorful. His characters have expressive faces and body language, and action is portrayed in a grand, rambunctious style that carries the story's energy out of the book and into the reader's life. He even adds a sprinkling of abstract expression, as in some of the scenes in *Jack and the Beanstalk* (1991), in which Jack's earth and the giant's sky blend in tornadic swirls, and shadowy shapes are vaguely discernible in the clouds. Like a film, he says, a picture book should be a collection of "moving pictures: . . . the individual spreads are designed

so that they crackle with graphic vitality. The characters seem to speak, cavort, and leap from the page so energetically that their life and movement are totally convincing. The moving qualities of each picture are heightened by the placement of the turning pages within the unfolding narrative and by the conception of the book as a whole." Combined with the text, the book becomes a piece of music.

In addition to his own and others' fiction stories, K. illustrates traditional songs such as *A-Hunting We Will Go* (1998), retellings of traditional stories such as *Chicken Little* (1985), and tall tales. K.'s versions of tall tales provide him an outlet for his fondness for hyperbole. About *Pecos Bill* (1986), he says, "like other American tall tales, it takes delight in the concoction of epic challenges and in outrageous and energetic sense of HUMOR." In his Author's Note for *Johnny Appleseed* (1988), he explains his perspective: "When a folktale attains the status of a myth and embodies a cherished ideal of the people, then its true worth no longer lies merely in the dead facts that may have inspired it, but in the new, living, and creating force that it has become in the present." He extends his philosophy to his own liberal retellings of traditional tales, and to his interpretations of others' tall-tale creations. Although the plot of *The Three Little Pigs* (1997) is basically intact, his rewrite using waffle-making pigs and a gangster wolf who gets the meanness steamed out of him in a waffle iron gives the popular old tale a hilarious new slant.

The themes K. chooses for his own writing touch the child-heart. Pets, animals, and other creatures help children understand such topics as loneliness *(A Rose for Pinkerton; Can I Keep Him?* [1971]); accidentally getting into trouble (all the Pinkerton series); growing pains *(Much Bigger Than Martin* [1976]); and getting along with and understanding others *(The Orchard Cat* [1972]; *The Island of the Skog* [1973]).

K. builds in devices to keep his readers connected to the body of his work. One of these is to insert characters from previous books into later works. For example, Dr. Aleasha Kibble, the snobbish, rule-rigid canine "expert" that everyone dislikes, appears as the dog-school instructor in *Pinkerton, Behave!* (1979), the poodle judge in *A Rose for Pinkerton,* and the fox-hunting guide in *Tallyho, Pinkerton* (1982). Cameo appearances of earlier characters in the role of bystanders or secondary characters are another trademark. The madcap ballooning wizard from *How Much Is a Million* (1985) as well as Pinkerton and Rose, reappear, among other families, in *Jack and the Beanstalk*. Even the hide of the saber-toothed tiger on the ogre's back appears live in his version of the traditional song, *I Was Born about 10,000 Years Ago* (1996). He incorporates written references to other literature as well, as when he concludes the demise of Jack's giant with the words, "The ogre fell down and broke his crown and the beanstalk came tumbling after." Such continuations serve to draw children further into engagement with literature, providing the opportunity to make associations with language, themes, and ILLUSTRATION style.

Readers will also find jokes and bits of humorous absurdity secreted in the illustrations. In *Can I Keep Him* (1971), a train car carrying eleven animals has a sign on the side that reads, "CAR CAPACITY: 3 BEASTS" and a sign in *The Orchard Cat* (1972) reads, "LADIES COLLECTING MONEY FOR CHARITY WILL BE PROPERLY PUNCHED." In *Jack and the Beanstalk,* hanging on a wall in the sky castle, is a wedding portrait of the ogre and his wife. The ogre's belly button is showing. A trip to a pet show *(A Rose for Pinkerton)* shows monkeys selling balloons and ice cream, a statue in a public square of a dancing elephant, a matador taking his bull as a pet, and fruit displayed in the category of "SMALL, QUIET PETS." *The Island of the Skog* (1973) is especially replete with such opportunities for discovery.

If one word could characterize K.'s works, it would be "joyful." Every one of his books incorporates laugh-out-loud humor, intricate, action-filled visual detail, lively use of color and design, dramatic overstatement, imaginative interpretation, a healthy sense of the absurd, and, above all, child appeal. His contribution is jubilant entertainment for children of all ages.

AWARDS: Multiple awards, including: repeated appearances on *Book List*'s Reviewer's Choice list, American Booksellers Pick of the Lists and Children's Choice of the INTERNATIONAL READING ASSOCIATION: 1980 *Horn Book* Fanfare Honor List. *Book List* Reviewer's Choice. Junior Literary Guild Selection. American Book Award Finalist. 1981–82 Georgia Children's Picture Storybook Award for *Pinkerton, Behave!* 1981 *Learning*'s The Year's Ten Best. AIGA Book Show. Junior Literary Guild Selection. 1985 American Booksellers Pick of the Lists for *A Rose for Pinkerton. Horn Book* Honor Award for *How Much Is a Million* (Schwartz): Regina Medal (1989)

FURTHER WORKS: *The Mystery of the Missing Red Mitten.* 1974: *The Mysterious Tadpole.* 1977: *Best Friends.* 1986; *Prehistoric Pinkerton.* 1987: *The Christmas Witch.* 1992. Illustrated: *Granny and the Desperadoes.* (Parish) 1970: *The Day Jimmy's Boa Ate the Wash* (Noble) 1980: *Iva Dunnit and the Big Wind* (Purdy) 1985: *Adventures of Hucklebery Finn* (TWAIN) 1994: *The Rattlebang Picnic* (Mahy) 1994: *Snuffles and Snouts* (Robb) 1995: Tall Tales: *Paul Bunyan.* 1984: *Mike Fink* (1992): *Sally Ann Thunder Ann Whirlwind Crockett* 1995: Traditional tales and songs: *There Was an Old Woman.* 1974: *Yankee Doodle* (BANGS) 1976: *The Three Sillies.* 1999

BIBLIOGRAPHY: *Something about the Author* vol. 57, 1989; http://www.frend.ly.net/scoop/biographies/skellog.html; Library of Congress website www.lcweb.loc.gov; flyleaves of books; University of Georgia website: http://www.coe.uga.edu/gachildlit/awards/winners/html#storybook

MARGARET YATSEVITCH PHINNEY

KELLY, Eric Philbrook
Author, b. 16 March 1884, Amesbury, Massachusetts; d. 3 January 1960, Youngstown, Arizona

K. worked as a reporter and an instructor in English as well as a writer. His first book, *The Trumpeter of Krakow* (1928), a work of historical fiction set in fifteenth century Poland, received the NEWBERY MEDAL. It is a thrilling adventure tale that shows the suffering of ordinary people against a backdrop of superstition, political, social, and religious upheaval. K. had experience distributing relief supplies in Poland after World War I. During World War II, he was chosen by the United States Department of State to settle Polish refugees in Mexico. His sympathy toward Poland became the source for many of his books including *The Hand in the Picture: A Story of Poland* (1947). He also wrote children's stories for *St. Nicholas* magazine.

FURTHER WORKS: *The Trumpeter of Krakow: A Tale of the Fifteenth Century.* 1928: *The Christmas Nightingale: Three Christmas Stories from*

Poland. 1932: *Treasure Mountain.* 1937: *A Girl Who Would Be Queen: The Story and the Diary of the Young Countess Krasinska.* 1939

JODI PILGRIM

KENDALL, Carol
Author, b. 13 September 1917, Bucyrus, Ohio

K. is best known for her 1960 NEWBERY MEDAL Honor Book, *The Gammage Cup* (1959). The book tells the story of people known as Minnipins living in isolated villages who become divided when some of the population question their leaders. It was published in England as *The Minnipins* (1965). As in the best of FANTASY, K. creates an alternate, parallel world with its own history, customs, and inhabitants who save their world through their daring initiative. Its sequel, *The Whisper of Glocken* (1965), continues the heroic adventures of the Outlaw Heroes. K. has also worked with Yao-wen Li on translations of Chinese folktales in *Sweet and Sour* (1978) and has retold six stories of Japanese origin in *Haunting Tales from Japan* (1985).

FURTHER WORKS: *The Other Side of the Tunnel* 1957; *The Firelings,* 1982 (Mythopoeic Society Asian Award)

BIBLIOGRAPHY: *Something about the Author.* vol. 74, 1993

JODI PILGRIM

KENNEDY, (Jerome) Richard
Author, b. 23 December 1932, Jefferson City, Missouri

Before becoming a writer, K. served in the United States Air Force and was a fifth-grade teacher. Having received a B.S. degree at Portland State University and attended school at Oregon State University, K. resides in Oregon. Both fantasy and REALISTIC FICTION characterize his work as K., never talking down to children, tells stories of the triumph of the human spirit. Love and relationships with others are the focus of many of his stories such as *Oliver Hyde's Dishrag Concert* (1977) and *Crazy in Love* (1980). *The Blue Stone* (1976) and *The Porcelain Man* (1976) won the Pacific Northwest Bookseller's Award. His work has been illustrated by significant artists such as Ronald HIMLER and Uri SHULEVITZ.

AWARDS: AMERICAN LIBRARY ASSOCIATION Notable Book Award (1976) for *The Blue Stone* and (1978) for *The Dark Princess*

FURTHER WORKS: *The Mouse God,* 1979; *The Leprechaun's Story,* 1979; *The Story of a Giant,* 1979

BIBLIOGRAPHY: *Something about the Author,* vol. 22, 1981

JANELLE B. MATHIS

KENNEDY, X. J. (Joseph Charles)
Poet, b. 21 August 1929, Dover, New Jersey

Born of working-class parents and reared during the Great Depression, Joseph Charles Kennedy grew up in a home that valued literature. Writing under the pseudonym of X. J. Kennedy, he has created numerous award-winning books of POETRY for children and adults and edited several anthologies of prose and poetry. After graduating from Seton Hall University in 1950 and from Columbia University with a master's degree in 1951, K. was accepted as a teaching assistant in the doctoral program at the University of Michigan. After six years as a doctoral student, K. taught at universities around the country, from California to North Carolina, but spent most of his teaching career as a professor at Tufts University. Among his many literary honors, K. has been awarded a Guggenheim fellowship (1973), a Bruern fellowship in American Literature (University of Leeds, 1974–75), and a grant from the National Endowment for the Arts (1967). Since 1979, he has been a freelance writer, publishing nearly all of his works for children during this time.

The poetry that has endeared him to children in the middle grades is richly imaginative and often comical, a world of wonderfully bizzare images, like the dinner-plate war where a gravy boat (or navy goat) floods the mashed potatoes, releasing torpedoes that swim out and attack the "hunk of ham." A marvelously talented and resourceful poet, K. employs metaphor, alliteration, onomatopoeia, and wordplay to encourage readers to perceive the familiar in unusual and creative ways. His books of comic verse on the Brats (*Brats,* 1986; *Fresh Brats,* 1990; and *Drat These Brats!,* 1993; all illustrated by James Watts) show problems caused by unruly behavior. Taking readers in another, more serious, direction is *The Forgetful Wishing Well: Poems for Young People*

(1985), dealing with the issues of growing up and coping with loss.

Whether the verse is nonsense or serious, K.'s knowledge of poetry and classical literary grounding are apparent in his skillful application of meter and rhyme. Using traditional poetic form, K. enlists a cast of lively characters, including animals and supernatural creatures, as well as adults and children, to address familiar situations and childhood concerns with wit, originality, and sensitivity. One of his most popular books, *The Owlstone Crown* (1983), a FANTASY novel that took him ten years to write, depicts the classic struggle of good and evil and is played out in Owlstonia, an alternate world. It is the story of teenage twins' search for their grandparents who are held captive by the villainous Raoul Owlstone. With the help of various creatures, the twins eventually overcome the obstacles that confront them, winning the freedom of their grandparents and reuniting them with their mother who was also a prisoner of the evil dictator. K. has collaborated with his wife, Dorothy M. Kennedy, on two immensely successful and critically acclaimed anthologies of children's poetry, *Knock at a Star: A Child's Introduction to Poetry* (1982) and *Talking like the Rain: A First Book of Poems* (1992).

AWARDS: Outstanding Book of the Year citation, *New York Times Book Review* for *One Winter Night in August and Other Nonsense Jingles* (1975, illustrated by David MCPAHIL): Teachers' choice Book (NCTE) and *School Library Journal*'s Book of the Year citation for *Knock at a Star: A Child's Introduction to Poetry* (1982): Library of Congress Best Children's Books of the Year citation; AMERICAN LIBRARY ASSOCIATION Notable Book citation, Notable Children's Trade Book for the Language Arts (NCTE), and William Allen White nomination for *The Forgetful Wishing Well: Poems for Young People* (1985): Notable Children's Trade Book for the Language Arts (NTCE) for *Brats* (1986): *Booklist*'s Editors' Choice citation, New York Public Library's 100 Best Books of the Year citation, and Children's Choice citation (INTERNATIONAL READING ASSOCIATION and CHILDREN'S BOOK COUNCIL) for *Fresh Brats* (1990): Awards from *School Library Journal*, *New York Times Book Review*, *Horn Book* magazine, American Library Association, *Parenting* magazine, and New York Public Library for *Talking like the Rain: A First Book of Poems* (1992)

FURTHER WORKS: *The Phantom Ice Cream Man: More Nonsense Verse,* 1979 (illus. D. McPhail); *Did Adam Name the Vinegarroonn?,* 1982; *Ghastlies, Goops, and Pincushions: Nonsense Verse,* 1989; *The Beasts of Bethlehem,* 1993

BIBLIOGRAPHY: *Children's Literature Review,* vol. 27, 1992; *Contemporary Authors, Autobiography Series,* vol. 9, 1989. *Dictionary of Literary Biography,* vol. 5, 1980; *Something about the Author,* vol. 86, 1996; *Twentieth-Century Children's Writers,* 1983

ANDREW KANTAR

KENT, Jack (John Wellington)
Author, illustrator, b. 10 March 1920, Burlington, Iowa; d. 18 October 1985, San Antonio, Texas

K. worked as a commercial artist and cartoonist before becoming a writer and illustrator of children's books in the 1960s. His books used HUMOR as the medium to inspire young readers to want to read and to continue reading once they start. K.'s inspiration for his stories came from his interests, which included the arts, travel, and nature. His meetings with people and the sights and sounds around him often made their way into his stories. K. always felt fortunate to make his living in a field he really enjoyed.

FURTHER WORKS: *King Aroo,* 1953; *Just Only John,* 1968; *The Scribble Monster,* 1981; *The Biggest Shadow in the Zoo,* 1981; *Little Peep,* 1981; *Knee-High Nina,* 1981; *Caterpillar and the Polliwog,* 1982; illustrator: *Easy As Pie: A Guessing Game of Sayings* (M. Folson), 1985

BIBLIOGRAPHY: *Something about the Author.,* vol. 24, 1981, vol. 45, 1986, vol. 74, 1993

MIKE O'LAUGHLIN

THE KERLAN COLLECTION

The Kerlan Collection at the University of Minnesota acquires children's books and related materials for adult study. As one of the Children's Literature Research Collections, it holds manuscripts and original ILLUSTRATIONS for more than 8,700 titles along with 100,000 children's books. The year 1999 was a dual celebration time for the fiftieth anniversary of its founding and its move to the Elmer L. Andersen Library at the University of Minnesota.

Irvin Kerlan, M.D. (1912–63), collected children's books privately in the 1940s and in 1949 founded the collection at the University; and continued to contribute until his death. He corresponded with and befriended authors and illustrators and arranged for them to inscribe newly published titles. By the time of his death fourteen years later, he had transferred to the University a nucleus of 9,000 books with manuscripts and illustrations for many of them. By 1999, more than 1,800 authors, illustrators, and translators were represented in the collection by personal papers and original materials. These individuals are selected for their potential to be studied or exhibited. They include papers for CALDECOTT MEDAL and NEWBERY MEDAL as well as Honor Book and Mildred L. Batchelder Award recipients, AFRICAN AMERICANS and ASIAN AMERICANS, Scandinavian-Americans, immigrants, midwesterners, poets, and many other significant creators of children's books.

Numerous Caldecott and Newbery winners are represented in the collection by manuscripts or art respectively. Original ink studies for Emily Arnold MCCULLY's 1993 Caldecott Medal PICTURE BOOK, *Mirette on the High Wire,* are in the Kerlan Collection. Louis SACHAR donated drafts of his Wayside series before winning the Newbery Medal for *Holes* in 1999 and Karen HESSE placed her manuscripts there prior to *Out of the Dust* (1997). Marguerite HENRY, Katherine PATERSON, Lois LOWRY, and many others are available for study.

Books and manuscripts comprise a significant aspect of the collection relating to the Mildred L. Batchelder Award for the translation of a children's book originally published in a foreign language. Since this award was first established in 1966, the Kerlan Collection attempts to acquire the book in its original language and the American edition for each annual award along with the translator's manuscript. Astrid LINDGREN donated a handwritten shorthand version of her Swedish book, translated as *Ronia, the Robber's Daughter* (1983). For *Thanks to My Mother* (1998), author Schoschana Rabinovici provided the handwritten manuscript in the Hebrew language, James Skofield gave his English TRANSLATION from the German edition, and the publisher, Farrar, Straus and Giroux, donated both the Hebrew and English–language editions.

AFRICAN AMERICAN authors and illustrators included Mildred Pitts WALTER, Joyce HANSEN, Jacqueline WOODSON, Nikki GRIMES, and Synthia Saint James. The authors donated manuscripts for both historical and contemporary fiction and POETRY. Walter's *Lillie of Watts* (1969) provides current readers with information about the turmoil in the 1960s, while the Mariah series is current everyday life. Hansen conducts research in archives for her stories such as *The Captive* (1994) and *Bury Me Not in a Land of Slaves* (2000). The University's Archie Givens, Jr., Collection of African American and AFRICAN LITERATURE provides continuity in this area of study.

ASIAN AMERICAN authors with extensive work in the Kerlan Collection include Lensey NAMIOKA, Marie G. Lee, Mifong Ho, Taro YASHIMA, and Tony CHEN. Namioka, a Chinese-American living in Seattle and married to a Japanese-American, contributed manuscripts like *Yang the Second and Her Secret Admirers* (1998). Korean-American Marie G. Lee writes about a successful high-school soccer player who moves from Los Angeles to Northern Minnesota in *Necessary Roughness* (1996), a girl in *Finding My Way* (1992), and a Harvard University girl in *Saying Goodbye* (1994). Ho contributed titles such as the 1997 Caldecott Honor Book *Hush!: A Thai Lullaby.*

Midwesterners such as Marion Dane BAUER, Judy DELTON, and Jane Resh THOMAS are faithful donors of manuscripts. Likewise, Midwest artists such as Betsy Bowen, a Lake Superior North Shore dweller, placed studies for *Antler, Bear and Canoe* (1991) and *The Troll With No Heart in His Body* (1999) in the collection. Scandinavian Americans are well represented in the Kerlan Collection since this remains Minnesota's major immigrant group. The Kerlan possesses the art of Ib Ohlsson's Encyclopedia Brown series and Gustaf Tenggren's *Poky Little Puppy* (1942). Immigrants contributed enormously to twentieth-century AMERICAN children's books. Polish-American Janina DOMANSKA's art for books like the 1972 Caldecott Medal Honor Book, *If All the Seas Were One Sea,* incorporates tiny dummies donated by her editor Susan Hirschman.

Several poets honored by the NATIONAL COUNCIL OF TEACHERS OF ENGLISH with receipt of its Award for Poetry for Children placed their manuscripts in the Kerlan. Among them are Myra Cohn LIVINGSTON, Eve MERRIAM, and Barbara ESBENSEN and their families. More than fifty books by Livingston are represented with working drafts in the collection. Her correspondence with editor and friend Margaret McElderry spanning many years is included in Livingston's manuscripts.

Jane YOLEN placed sixty-two manuscripts in a wide range of genres, while Patricia LAUBER sent manuscripts for seventy-four nonfiction books such as *Alligators: A Success Story* (1993) and *You're Aboard Spaceship Earth* (1996); and Marilyn SACHS gave thirty-five REALISTIC FICTION manuscripts, for titles like *Thirteen, Going on Seven* (1993). Theodore TAYLOR, best known for *The Cay* (1969) and its prequel *Timothy of the Cay* (1993), donated manuscripts for titles published from 1971 to the present.

Illustrators well represented by original art are Glen ROUNDS and Charles MIKOLAYCAK, whose studies and art number in the hundreds. Rounds donated his manuscripts, too, while Mikolaycak left behind notes made about his dining companions and the subject of conversations on menus. The accompanying materials enhance an understanding of these lives.

Lectures, exhibits, and conferences comprise the Kerlan's program in conjunction with the collection. Children's Literature Summer Forums bring community and campus groups together. As Dr. Kerlan loaned exhibits internationally, current policy encourages the sharing of books, manuscripts, and art. They traveled to the Bologna Children's Book Fair in Italy in 1985, to Sweden, and to Japan. Conferences hosted by Tin Cities organizations frequently include a field trip to the Kerlan in the program. Among them are the Children's Literature Association, the Plains Regional INTERNATIONAL READING ASSOCIATION and AMERICAN LIBRARY ASSOCIATION School Librarian Association Division.

The Ezra Jack KEATS Foundation funds an annual Keats–Kerlan Memorial Fellowship for a published author or illustrator to study further using the materials. Ilse Plume, Ellen Stoll Walsh, Leslie Tryon, and David Pelletier are among the past recipients. The National Endowment to the Humanities funded grants to support the processing, preservation, and recording in electronic form of the holdings of many of the collections.

As noted, the year 1999 was the fiftieth anniversary of the Kerlan Collection's founding at the University of Minnesota as well as the twenty-fifth anniversary year of the Kerlan Award and the Kerlan Friends. The Kerlan Award was recently given to Phyllis Reynolds NAYLOR, Paul GALDONE (posthumous), Lois LENSKI (posthumous), and Eve BUNTING. Researchers range from parents with children who hope to gain insight into a favorite book to scholars writing journal articles and books.

Beginning in June 2000, the Kerlan has hosted the Naomi Chase Lecture at the Andersen Library. The Chase Lecture is sponsored by the University of Minnesota's College of Education and Human Development, and the Department of Curriculum and Instruction.

BIBLIOGRAPHY: *The K. Manuscripts and Illustrations for Children's Books: A Checklist,* 1985

KAREN NELSON HOYLE

KERR, M. E. (Marijane Agnes Meaker)
Author, b. 27 May 1927, Auburn, New York

Inspired by her father's appreciation for literature and her mother's flair for STORYTELLING and keen sense of ethnic and social differences, K. (Marijane Meaker's pseudonym) knew at a young age that she wanted to become a writer. After graduating from the University of Missouri (1949), K. took a job as a clerk with E. P. Dutton Publishing in New York City. Although she has penned more than two dozen adult novels including suspense and murder stories written under various pseudonyms (e.g., Vin Packer and Ann Aldrich), for the last twenty-five years, K.'s most devoted readers have been young adults. Her popularity is often linked to her ability to entertain her readers through adroitly crafted problem novels that deal with relationships, religion, and social issues. *Dinky Hocker Shoots Smack!* (1972), her first and arguably best-known young-adult novel, is just one of many award-winning titles. Dinky Hocker is not a heroin addict; she is an overweight, attention-starved high school teen. In a desperate attempt to embarrass her community-conscious and socially active mother into taking notice of her, she scrawls the book's self-incriminating title phrase as graffiti for all to see. The popularity of the book led to the 1978 release of *Dinky Hocker,* a television movie. Religious issues and spirituality have factored into novels like

Is That You, Miss Blue? (1975), *What I Really Think of You* (1981), and *Little Little* (1981).

Is That You, Miss Blue? set in an Episcopalian girls' school, juxtaposes the issues of conformity and peer pressure against cruel abuse and ridicule leading to the mental breakdown suffered by an exceptionally religious teacher at the hands of students and parents. As the novel progresses, Handers Brown demonstrates a burgeoning maturity, from her early conformity with attacks on Miss Blue to the cultivation of a newfound respect for her teacher. *What I Really Think of You* depicts the difficulties encountered by two ministers' children (narrated by Opal Ringer and Jesse Pegler) as they struggle with spiritual beliefs, social values, and religious hypocrisy. *Little Little,* another dually narrated problem novel, has a different twist—a forbidden romance between two teenage dwarfs, Little Little La Belle and Sydney Cinnamon. A fast-paced novel of courage, tolerance, and the universality of human needs, *Little Little* also tackles the issue of commercialized evangelical preaching. Internal character struggles continue in K.'s *Gentlehands* (1978), when young Buddy Boyle learns that his German grandfather is being hunted down as a Nazi war criminal. K.'s autobiography, *Me, Me, Me, Me, Me: Not a Novel* (1983), incorporates childhood and adolescent experiences, giving readers insight into the genesis of her story ideas, situations, and characters. Exhibiting a sensitivity to the frustrations, concerns, and problems faced by her young-adult audience, K.'s contemporary social realism is extraordinarily successful at entertaining readers with humor, lively plots, and intriguing characters.

AWARDS: *Dinky Hocker Shoots Smack!*, the *Media* and *Methods* Maxi Award (1974): *Gentlehands*, Christopher Award (1979): *Little Little,* Golden Kite Award for Fiction from the Society of Children's Book Writers (1981): Numerous other awards, including the New York Public Library's Books for the Teenager, *New York Times* Notable Books of the Year, *School Library Journal*'s Best Books of the Year, and the AMERICAN LIBRARY ASSOCIATION's Best Books for Young Adults

FURTHER WORKS: *If I Love You, Am I Trapped Forever?*, 1973; *The Son of Someone Famous,* 1974; *Love Is a Missing Person,* 1975; *I'll Love You When You're More Like Me,* 1977; *Him She Loves?*, 1984; *I Stay Near You,* 1985; *Night Kites,* 1986; *Linger,* 1993; *Deliver Us from Evie,* 1994; *Fell,* 1987; *Fell Back,* 1989; *Fell Down,* 1991

BIBLIOGRAPHY: *Children's Literature Review,* vol. 29, 1993; Drew, Bernard A., *The 100 Most Popular Young Adult Authors,* 1997; *Something about the Author,* vol. 61; *Twentieth-Century Children's Writers,* 1983

ANDREW KANTAR

KESSLER, Leonard P.
Author, illustrator, b. 28 October 1921, Ohio

K. began his career as a writer and illustrator of children's books in 1951, but his interest in ILLUSTRATION began when he was a child. He has written and illustrated several books that demonstrate the techniques of drawing and painting for young readers. These works include his first book, the humorous *What's in a Line* (1951), a rhyming text describing the things a line can be and do such as tell a story or turn into a picture of anything because "a line is only an idea caught and set down on paper." *Art Is Everywhere* (1958), and *Colors, Colors All Around* (1965) followed.

K.'s most popular stories, written in an easy "I Can Read Book" format, are those based on sports such as baseball, swimming, and football, and include simple rules and directions for play. *Here Comes the Strikeout* (1965) describes a young boy's perseverance as he overcomes being an "easy out" in baseball games. It has been translated into Spanish under the title *!Aqui viene el que se poncha!* (1995) as has K.'s SPORTS STORY written for young readers, *Last One in Is a Rotten Egg* (1969) published as *Ultimo en Tirarse es un Miedoso.*

FURTHER WORKS: *Kick, Pass and Run,* 1966; *Old Turtle's Baseball Stories,* 1988; *Stan the Hot Dog Man,* 1990; *Old Turtle's 90 Knock-knocks, Jokes, and Riddles,* 1991

BIBLIOGRAPHY: *Something about the Author,* vol. 13, 1978

DENISE P. BEASLEY

KHALSA, Dayal Kaur (Marcia Schoenfeld)
Author, illustrator, b. 17 April 1943, Queens, New York; d. 17 July 1989, Vancouver, British Columbia, Canada

K. grew up in Queens, New York, and moved to Canada in 1970. She was a self-taught artist whose PICTURE BOOKS for older readers portray her experiences as a child. *Tales of a Gambling Grandma* (1986) is based on K.'s eccentric grandmother. *My Family Vacation* (1988) tells of her holidays spent in Florida. K. believed it was vital for her books to teach important lessons. In *The Snow Cat* (1992), she relays the story of a young girl who receives a cat made of snow. The girl does not follow the directions to care for it, and thus learns the importance of taking responsibility. The belief in achieving aspirations is portrayed in *Cowboy Dreams* (1989) as it tells the story of a young city girl who dreams of becoming a cowboy. Her collection of twelve wordless *Baabee* books, written especially for babies, contains bright vivid colors, instead of pastels, to stimulate visual perception. *How Pizza Came to Queens* (1989), K.'s best-known book, tells how friends work together to help Mrs. Pellegrino, a visitor from Italy overcome her homesickness. Accompanied by brightly colored folk art, K. tells a cheerful story of cooperation and empathy.

AWARDS: AMERICAN LIBRARY ASSOCIATION Notable Book (1990) for *Cowboy Dreams*

BIBLIOGRAPHY: *Writing Stories, Making Pictures: Biographies of 150 Canadian Children's Authors and Illustrators,* 1994

DENISE P. BEASLEY

KHERDIAN, David

Author, poet, b. 17 December 1931, Racine, Wisconsin

Although formal education did not come easy to K., who at nineteen dropped out of high school, he earned a bachelor's degree in philosophy from the University of Wisconsin (1960). Holding a variety of jobs, including bookseller, editor, teacher, poet, bartender, factory worker, and shoe salesman, it was not until his marriage to noted children's illustrator and artist, Nonny HOGROGIAN, that he considered writing for children. In much of his writing, K. explores his unique family history and Armenian ethnic perspective. Nowhere is this more powerfully demonstrated than in the critically acclaimed biography of his mother, *The Road from Home: The Story of an Armenian Girl* (1979). A NEWBERY MEDAL Honor Book (1980), *The Road from Home* is a first-person narrative based upon his mother's

painful childhood memories while growing up amid the brutal persecution she and other Armenians endured in Turkey early in the twentieth century. Orphaned after losing her entire family at the hands of the Turks, she made her way to Greece and agreed, at the age of fifteen, to a matchmaker wedding with a total stranger. *The Road from Home* provides the reader with an understanding of and appreciation for Armenian culture, traditions, and family life. The human tragedy and brutal historical realities that are depicted also enable readers to recognize the universal pain of human suffering, regardless of the ethnicity. In *Finding Home* (1981) K. continues his mother's story as she makes a life for herself in America. Critics acknowledge that while this work does not express the same dramatic force and powerful imagery as *The Road from Home,* it possesses a toned-down stylistic subtlety that is appropriate to the characters and narrative, touching the heart in a different way. Both works celebrate the inner strength of a survivor, first in overcoming a harsh world of brutality and violence and, later, the immigrant's effort to make a better life for herself and her family. *Root River Run* (illustrated by Nonny Hogrogian, 1984), a memoir of K.'s childhood growing up in Racine, Wisconsin, represents the next generation of the Armenian community—American-born children who are very much aware of their ethnic heritage and roots. Self-discovery factors into two of K.'s works of fiction, *It Started with Old Man Bean* (1980) and *Beyond Two Rivers* (1981). In both, the best-friend protagonists, Ted and Joe, explore the Wisconsin wilderness of the 1940s and in so doing, learn about themselves. In addition to his nonfiction and fiction prose, K. is an accomplished poet, publishing numerous books of POETRY, including *Country Cat, City Cat* (illustrated by Hogrogian, 1978), a collection of poems for children.

AWARDS: *The Road from Home: The Story of An Armenian Girl* (1979), NEWBERY MEDAL Honor Book (1980), *Horn Book* Award (1979), Jane Addams Book Award, 1980: *Boston Globe–Horn Book* Award, 1979: Lewis CARROLL Shelf Award (1979). Banta Award. American Book Award nomination; *Beyond Two Rivers* (1981). Friends of American Writers Award (1982)

FURTHER WORKS: *Bridger: The Story of a Mountain Man.* 1987. *On a Spaceship with Beelzebub:*

By a Grandson of Gurdjieff. Autobiography, 1991: Illustrated by Nonny Hogrogian: *Right Now.* 1983. *The Animal.* 1984. *A Song for Uncle Harry.* 1989, fictionalized memoir. *A Cat's Midsummer Jamboree.* 1990. *The Great Fishing Contest.* 1991. *Feathers and Tails: Animal Fables from around the World.* 1992, retelling. *Juna's Journey.* 1993. *By Myself.* 1993

BIBLIOGRAPHY: *Children's Literature Review,* (1991), vol. 24; *Something about the Author.* vol. 74, 1993

ANDREW KANTAR

KIMMEL, Eric
Author, b. 30 October 1946, Brooklyn, New York

K. is a folklorist who adapts tales from various cultures and religious traditions, introducing contemporary children to the rich tapestry of human experience through story. Many of the motifs with which K. works emphasize the power of humor as well as the intrinsic dignity with which we need to regard others who share the world with us.

As a boy, K. lived in a MULTICULTURAL and multilingual neighborhood, eagerly listened to his Yiddish-speaking grandmother's many tales, and fed his appetite for stories by reading FAIRY TALES by the Brothers GRIMM. After graduating from Lafayette College (1967), he entered graduate school, earning a masters degree at New York University (1969) and a doctorate at the University of Illinois (1973). Until 1994, K. earned a living as a professor of education. Since then, he has written full-time.

K.'s first children's book, *The Tartar's Sword* (1974) earned the 1975 Friends of American Writers' Juvenile Book Merit Award. *Anansi and the Moss-Covered Rock* (1988) was named one of the 10 Best Books of 1989, by the Association of Booksellers for Children. *Hershel and the Hanukkah Goblins* (1989) merited awards from several groups, including the NATIONAL COUNCIL OF TEACHERS OF ENGLISH (1990). Trina Schart HYMAN's ILLUSTRATIONS for this book won the AMERICAN LIBRARY ASSOCIATION's recognition for it as a CALDECOTT MEDAL Honor Book (1990). *Four Dollars and Fifty Cents* (1990) earned the INTERNATIONAL READING ASSOCIATION's Paul A. Witty Short Story Award. *The Chanukkah Guest* (1990) won the Association for Jewish Libraries' 1990 Sydney TAYLOR Picture

Book Award and was nominated for the National Jewish Book Award. *The Greatest of All: A Japanese Folktale* (1991) and *Days of Awe: Stories for Rosh Hashanah and Yom Kippur* (1991) each received recognition as Notable by the CHILDREN'S BOOK COUNCIL—National Council of Teachers of Social Studies (1992 and 1993, respectively). *Days of Awe* also earned the Aesop Prize of the American FOLKLORE Society's Children's Folklore Section (1993). *The Spotted Pony: A Collection of Hanukkah Stories* (1992) was awarded the Anne Izard Storytellers' Choice Award. *The Three Princes: A Tale from the Middle East* (1994) merited the Parents' Choice Award (1994). Many of K.'s adaptions and retellings have earned local and professional awards.

In addition to writing, K. has worked extensively as a performing storyteller. As an adaptor and reteller of folktales, he uses his oral STORYTELLING rounds as opportunities to work out how best to commit a tale to written form. K. works from a vast amount of resource material, including traveling to neighborhoods around the world to listen to stories. He uses Biblical history to produce picture-book stories, such as *Nicanor's Gate* (1979), as well as memories of his own grandmother's tales, to give him inspiration as in *Nanny Goat and the Seven Little Kids* (1990).

K.'s writings for children had gained little popular notice until he was invited, in 1990 by the children's literary magazine *Cricket,* to provide a Hanukkah story in place of one Isaac Bashevis SINGER has been slated to write. *Hershel and the Hanukkah Goblins* reached the magazine's multiculturally attuned and literarily sophisticated subscribers who discovered a welcome storytelling voice and became promoters of K.'s subsequent books.

The story of *Hershel and the Hanukkah Goblins* is one originating within K.'s imagination, rather than a reworking of a folktale. Here, as in *The Magic Dreidels: A Hanukkah Story* (1996), K. combines elements of Jewish religious tradition with Native American trickster characterizations. *Four Dollars and Fifty Cents* is an original Wild West romp, while *Charlie Drives the Stage* (1989) retells the story of a young woman with an unusual job—and name; both are written with broad humor.

K.'s crafting of folkloric matter into clever and insightful retellings and adaptions is important to contemporary readers. By making the characterizations, themes, and plots of such traditional tales as *Baba Yaga: A Russian Folktale* (1991), *The Tale of Aladdin and the Wonderful Lamp* (1992), *The Witch's Face: A Mexican Tale* (1993), *Iron John: A Tale from the Brothers Grimm* (1994), and *Rimonah and the Flashing Sword: A North African Tale* (1995) accessible to modern children, K. ensures continuity of interest in the multidimensional nature of human experience and awareness of human history.

Although most of K.'s texts become PICTURE BOOKS for reading aloud to young children, he has written for independent readers as well. *Sword of the Sumurai: Adventure Stories from Japan* (1999) is a collection of tales suited to children in middle grades. K.'s sensitivity to cultural nuance and the spiritual basis for religious and ceremonial tenets provides these tales with grace as well as exciting storytelling. As in his picture book texts for younger readers, he provides clarification of cultural concepts necessary to the reader's understanding of the stories in the context of the tale, allowing readers to remain immersed in their literary experience without having to break for pedagogy.

Expanding on his interest in Jewish cultural and religious experience, K. has provided older readers with a compendium of stories, verse, and other narratives exploring *Bar Mitzvah: A Jewish Boy's Coming of Age* (1995). Here, in addition to explaining and storytelling, K. provides readers with some of the interviews he undertook as part of the process of creating the whole book.

K. provides children with windows into other places and other times. Using both canonical and original tales, his storyteller's voice imbues his books with a liveliness and, often, a HUMOR, that makes each one fresh.

FURTHER WORKS: *Mishka, Pishka, and Fishka, and Other Galician Tales.* 1976: *Hershel of Ostropol.* 1981: *I Took My Frog to the Library.* 1990: *Anansi Goes Fishing.* 1991: *Boots and His Brothers: A Norwegian Tale.* 1992: *Three Sacks of Truth: A Story from France.* 1993: *The Gingerbread Man.* 1993: *One Eye, Two Eyes, Three Eyes: A Hutzul Tale.* 1996: *The Tale of Ali Baba and the Forty Thieves: A Story from the Arabian Nights.* 1996

BIBLIOGRAPHY: Silvey, A. ed., *Children's Books and Their Creators,* 1995; *Something about the Author,* vol. 80, 1995

FRANCISCA GOLDSMITH

CORETTA SCOTT KING AWARDS

The Coretta Scott King Awards, administered by the Social Responsibilities Round Table with the cooperation of the Association for Library Service to Children of the AMERICAN LIBRARY ASSOCIATION, are designed to commemorate and foster the life, works, and dreams of Dr. Martin Luther King, Jr. They are also intended to honor his wife Coretta Scott King for her courage and determination to continue the work for peace and world fellowship. The recipients receive a citation, an honorarium, and an encyclopedia. The award is given annually to a black author and, since 1974, to a black illustrator whose books, published in the preceding year, are outstanding, inspirational and educational contributions to literature for children and young people.

Winners include Charlemae Rollins, Sharon Bell MATHIS, Pearl Bailey, James HASKINS, Eloise GREENFIELD, Carole BYARD, Ossie Davis, Nikki GRIMES, Tom FEELINGS, Camille YARBROUGH, Sidney Poitier, Ashley BRYAN, Mildred TAYLOR, John STEPTOE, Virginia HAMILTON, Lucile CLIFTON, Mildred Pitts WALTER, Pat CUMMINGS, Walter Dean MYERS, Valerie FLOURNOY, Jerry PINKNEY, Crescent DRAGONWAGON, Patricia MCKISSACK, Frederick MCKISSACK, Jan Spivey GILCHRIST, Leontyne Price, Leo and Diane DILLON, Faith RINGGOLD, Angela JOHNSON, James Weldon Johnson, James RANSOME, and others.

BERNICE E. CULLINAN

KINGSLEY, Charles

Author, clergyman, historian, b. 12 June 1819 near Dartmoore, Devonshire, England; d. 23 January 1875, Eversley, Hampshire, England

As a rector in the village of Eversley, K. worked to improve social conditions and collaborated with others, including Thomas Hughes, author of *Tom Brown's Schooldays* (1857), in publishing a periodical, *Politics for the People,* that addressed social and economic ills. K. was concerned with the education and welfare of the poor, and his early novels for adults address these issues.

K.'s best known works for children include three books that are still enjoyed: *The Heroes; or, Greek FAIRY TALES for My Children* (1856), *The Water-Babies* (1863), and *Westward Ho!* (1855), an adventure story set in Elizabethan times written for adults and later appropriated by older children. *The Heroes,* K.'s retelling of three Greek stories—Perseus, Jason and the Argonauts, and Theseus—is considered by critics to be the least didactic of the three. *Westward Ho!,* an ADVENTURE set in Elizabethan times, appeared in a new edition as recently as 1992, with original ILLUSTRATIONS by N. C. WYETH. A natural history, *Glaucus; or, the Wonders of the Shore* (1855), was written for his own children after a series of nature walks to the "miraculous and divine element underlying" nature. This theme is further developed in *The Water-Babies,* one of the great early English fantasies written for children, in context with K.'s Victorian moralizing and social criticism. The book rails against the conditions of the poor and the abuses of child labor. Through the character of Tom, K. exposes the plight of small boys used as chimney sweeps, allowed to contract tuberculosis and die. Tom is transported to the bottom of the sea to cleanse his sooty body and soul and anthropomorphized as an immortal waterbaby, pure of body and soul. K. created the memorable characters of Mrs. Bedonebyasyoudid, rewarder of good and bad behavior, and Mrs. Doasyouwouldbedoneby, the embodiment of unshakable motherly love. As much an attack on the evils of child labor, *The Water-Babies* is also a diatribe against the rejection of fairy tales for children so popular at the time.

A good friend of both Lewis CARROLL and George MACDONALD, author of *At the Back of the North Wind* (1871) and *The Light Princess* (1883), K. was influenced by both fantasists; they read and commented on each other's work before publication.

FURTHER WORKS: *Madam How and Lady Why.* 1870.

BIBLIOGRAPHY: *The Oxford Companion to Children's Literature.* 1984. *Yesterday's Authors of Books for Children: Facts and Pictures about Authors and Illustrators of Books for Young People, from Early Times to 1960,* vol. 2. 1978. Silvey, Anita, ed., *Children's Books and Their Creators.* 1995

KATHIE KRIEGER CERRA

KING-SMITH, Dick

Author, b. 27 March 1922, Bitton, Gloucestershire, England

A farmer for twenty years, an elementary school teacher, and a writer for the past twenty years, Dick K.-S. is the prolific author of more than thirty books for children. His humorous animal fantasies, told with warmth and sensitivity, have captivated children and adults for decades. K.-S.'s witty stories for juvenile readers utilize inventive plots, lively dialogue, and unlikely heroes who possess the inner strength to overcome significant obstacles. Upon graduating from Bristol University (1975) at the age of fifty-three, K.-S. accepted a teaching position at a primary school in Avon, near Bath, England. Three years later he embarked on a highly successful career, writing fiction and nonfiction for children and programs for children's television, including Yorkshire Television's *Tumbledown Farm* series beginning in 1983. One of his first books, the award-winning *Daggie Dogfoot* (1980, published in America as *Pigs Might Fly,* 1982), has as its protagonist a runt pig that critics have likened to E. B. WHITE's Wilbur (*Charlotte's Web,* 1952). Daggie watches the birds and wishes he, too, could fly, but learns that his deformed, webbed feet make him an excellent swimmer. The skill proves both valuable and rewarding as it enables this lovable hero to swim for help during a flood and rescue all the pigs on a farm from certain death. Also, on the subject of pigs, K.-S. has authored the critically praised *All Pigs Are Beautiful* (1993) and the exceedingly popular modern classic, *The Sheep-Pig* (1983). Released in America as *Babe: The Gallant Pig* (1985), *The Sheep-Pig* was later made into an Oscar-nominated movie (*Babe,* 1995). It is the action-filled story of Babe, a pig who averts the cruel fate that awaits him by demonstrating a talent for being a superb herder of sheep. Thematically, the book shows readers that adaptation is part of survival. Although K.-S.'s stories often convey a lesson, they are not presented in a heavy-handed, moralistic fashion. Rather, his characters endear themselves to readers, drawing them in to the plights and circumstances that must be overcome through courage, luck, and ingenuity. K.-S.'s poetry includes *Alphabeasts* (1992, illustrated by Quentin BLAKE), a humorous and amusing collection of nonsense poems that is an entertaining and light-hearted introduction to the alphabet.

AWARDS: *Daggie Dogfoot* (1980), *The Mouse Butcher* (1981), and *Magnus Powermouse* (1982) were all Guardian Award runners-up: *The Sheep-Pig* (1983) received the 1984 Guardian award and the 1985 *Boston Globe–Horn* Book Award for fiction (as *Babe: The Gallant Pig*): K.-S. was also the recipient of the British Book Award, Children's Author of the Year (1991)

FURTHER WORKS: *The Fox Busters,* 1978; *Harry's Mad,* 1984; *Saddlebottom,* 1985; *Town Watch,* 1987; *Country Watch: Animals to Look out for in the Countryside,* 1987; *Martin's Alice,* 1988; *Dodo Comes to Tumbledown Farm,* 1988; *Sophie's Snail,* 1989; *Paddy's Pot of Gold,* 1992; *The Animal Parade,* 1992; *The Invisible Dog,* 1993

BIBLIOGRAPHY: *Children's Literature Review.* vol. 40, 1996; Huck, Charlotte. *Children's Literature in the Elementary School; Something about the Author,* vol. 80, 1995; *Twentieth-Century Children's Writers,* 1983

ANDREW KANTAR

KIPLING, Rudyard

Author, b. 30 December 1865, Bombay, India; d. 18 January 1936, London, England

Son of an architect, teacher, and minister, K. was born in India, and with his sister returned to England to attend school and to avoid health problems. He was miserably unhappy in the rigid, Calvinist foster home he was sent to by his parents. K. was treated cruelly and remembers the only highlight of these years as holidays spent with his mother's family. After his parents removed him to a private school, although still teased, he learned to love literature and developed strong loyalties. *Stalky and Co.* (1899) reflects these times.

Returning to his parents in India at the age of seventeen, he became a journalist for newspapers and began writing stories and poems. By the time he returned to England, K.'s work was already well known. He was admired by many for his swinging verse written in Cockney dialect and the Imperialist sentiments they expressed. K. was thought of as the poet of British Imperialism as he presented India through the eyes of the common soldier trying to understand events. His

work was disliked by detractors for these same reasons. *Ballads and Barrack-Room Ballads* (1892) represents this type of writing. His genius at POETRY was nurtured by the sophistication of the Pre-Raphaelite movement with which he was familiar through his mother's family and his literary predecessors such as Swinburne and Browning. He was also influenced by musical forms of the day. Both his grandfathers were Methodist clergymen and he was affected by Protestant hymns. Likewise, in the secular world he was influenced by the songs of music halls. While he was not considered musical, he created poems that beg to be set to music. "Gentlemen Rankers" and "The Road to Mandalay" lend themselves to melody.

K. formed a friendship at this time with an American publisher, Wolcott Balestier, and went to America with him to collaborate on a novel, *The Naulahka,* which was not successful. Balestier died; K., however, married his sister and remained in the United States for several years until a family quarrel led to K., his wife, and two daughters to return to Britain. While in Vermont, K. wrote *The Jungle Books* (1894, 1895). The adventures of Mowgli, the child raised by wolves, constitute some of the most popular of all his works. Other stories from the collection include "Rikki-Tikki-Tavi" and "The White Seal." These stories are found in numerous media adaptations. The sources of these stories appear in a book of tales K. heard as a young child as well as in the *Jataka* tales of India that are over 2,000 years old and tell of the various births of Buddha. As India was Britain's most important colony at the end of the nineteenth century, English people had a keen curiosity about the country. *The Jungle Books* were considered a source of insight into the Indian environment.

K.'s life in New England is reflected in *Captains Courageous* (1897), which was written while K. lived near his parents' home in England. In 1899, while the family was visiting America, K.'s daughter Josephine died from pneumonia. Grief-stricken, K. buried himself in his work and in 1901 *Kim* was published. K. gives his father credit for the memories and descriptions that are part of what many consider to be his best novel due to the complexity and authenticity of the Indian setting, its land, people, social system, and culture. *Kim* represents K.'s sensitive approach to portraying the Indians with understanding.

Another outstanding work for children is K.'s *Just So Stories* (1902). Written for his own children, these stories are about the beginnings of things. The vivid imagery honors the sophistication of young readers, and the lyrical language asks to be read aloud. On the grounds of the seventeenth century home that K. and his family occupied since 1902 called Bateman, K. found inspiration for his last children's works. *Puck of Pook's Hill* (1907) and *Rewards and Fairies* (1910) both were created as a result of artifacts found on his property. Dan and Una in the stories meet Puck and learn about the history of Sussex.

K. continued writing into the twentieth century for thirty-six years, speaking out against Germany during World War I. His political views were not popular and the death of his son in the war contributed to the bitterness that is reflected in his later writing. With strong Imperialist sentiments, some said he lost touch with social reality in his later life. He had strong feelings concerning the common man yet was not trusting of democratic forms of government. Often considered the most popular British author since Charles DICKENS and the most quoted poet since Alfred, Lord Tennyson, K. is perhaps best known to present day readers for his contributions to children's literature. The richness of language and sophistication of story elements for the young denote the seriousness with which he created stories for young readers. K.'s life experiences and the impetus of various events are reflected in his writing for adults and children. He is buried in Westminster Abbey beside T. S. Eliot. His autobiography, *Something of Myself* (1937), was published the following year.

AWARDS: K. was named Poet Laureate in 1895 and received the British Order of Merit. He refused both these awards. K. was the first British author to be honored with the Nobel Prize for Literature in 1907. He was awarded the Gold Medal of the Royal Society of Literature in 1926

FURTHER WORKS: *"Wee Willie Winkie" and Other Child Stories*, 1888; *The Second Jungle Book*, 1895; *Collected Verse*, 1907; *Songs for Youth*, 1924; *Collected Dog Stories*, 1934; *Toomai of the Elephants*, 1937

BIBLIOGRAPHY: Amis, Kingsley. *Rudyard K. and His World.* 1975. *Children's Literature Review.*

1996. Harrison, James. *Rudyard K.* 1982. *Something about the Author.* vol. 100. 1998. "Rudyard K.: A Brief Biography." at http://www.stg.brown.edu/projects/ . . . andow/victorian/kipling/rkbio.html (accessed April 6, 1999)

JANELLE B. MATHIS

KJELGAARD, James Arthur
Author, b. 5 December 1910, New York City; d. 12 July 1959, Milwaukee, Wisconsin

The author of stories about ANIMAL heroes and historical fiction, K. was the son of a physician and one of six children. K. and his brothers spent hours roaming the Black Forest region of Pennsylvania. Times were hard and as a teenager K. contributed to the family income by digging ditches, running trap lines, pitching hay, and running transit for the county surveyor, all the while writing and sending out stories. His first "sale" was a story sold to a magazine in 1928, the year K. finished high school. His payment was a two-year subscription to the magazine. His first book, *Forest Patrol,* based on personal wilderness experiences, was published in 1941. *Rebel Siege,* a well-received work of historical fiction about the American Revolution in the South, was published in 1943 and his third book, *Big Red* (1945), about a champion Irish setter, made him famous. K. wrote more than forty books for children, several hundred articles and short stories and edited two books, *Wild Horse Roundup* (1957) and *Hound Dog and Others* (1958). His attention to detail and accurate portrayal of life in his writing stemmed from his belief that when writing for young people an author owes them "the best he can give."

Several of his books were adapted as movies and filmstrips. *Big Red* was released by DISNEY as a film in 1962 and as a filmstrip in 1971.

FURTHER WORKS: *Desert Dog,* 1950, 1981; *Wild Trek,* 1950, 1981; *Outlaw Red, Son of Big Red,* 1953; *The Explorations of Pere Marquette,* 1951

BIBLIOGRAPHY: *Fiction, FOLKLORE, FANTASY and Poetry for Children* 1986; *Holiday House News,* Feb. 1959; *Something about the Author,* vol. 17, 1979

IRVYN G. GILBERTSON

KLAUSE, Annette Curtis
Author, b. 20 June 1953, Bristol, England

K.'s FANTASY novels for YOUNG ADULTS feature vampires and other FANTASY beings. She became a devoted fantasy reader in early childhood, a time during which she also began writing. In her early teens, she discovered vampire books and, in response to her fascination with these romantic horror tales, K. wrote POETRY and short stories. Years later, she used her adolescent writings when she began work on her first novel.

Moving with her family to the United States during high school, K. attended college and then graduate school in library science. Since 1981, she has been a children's librarian in Maryland. After several years' hiatus from writing, K. again turned to developing her own fantasy stories. Her first novel, *The Silver Kiss* (1990), earned commendations from the AMERICAN LIBRARY ASSOCIATION as a Best Book for Young Adults and a Best Book for Reluctant Readers the same year. *Alien Secrets* (1993), an ALA Notable Book for Children, evokes reader appeal as a mystery rather than a horror story; it has been recognized by critics as trenchant to our society's struggle with race relations.

The Silver Kiss and *Blood and Chocolate* (1997) address themes unusual to contemporary children's literature. Both books feature heroines who become romantically entwined in situations inhabited by bloodthirsty creatures. While K.'s first novel depicts a young woman in love with a vampire, *Blood and Chocolate* tells the tale of a human boy and a female werewolf. K.'s research and well-honed STORYTELLING skills have brought her critical praise in spite of the grisly territory these books explore. Just as did K. in her own adolescence, the teen audience who enjoy her stories seek tales about issues foremost in their minds; being an outsider, metamorphosis, and the horrors with which the imagination can fill the unknown. Thus K. enjoys popularity as well as critical acclaim. K. also writes stories and poetry for adults.

BIBLIOGRAPHY: *Something about the Author,* vol. 80, 1995

FRANCISCA GOLDSMITH

KLEIN, Norma
Author, b. 13 May 1938, New York City; d. 25 April 1989, New York City

K., an author of YOUNG ADULT FICTION, lived in New York City and attended private schools there. She was reared as a strong, open-minded woman. After graduating from Barnard College, K. wrote over sixty short stories. Her first published book was *Mom, the Wolfman, and Me* (1972), about an eleven-year-old girl who lives with her mother who has never married. K. wrote over twenty-five young adult books dealing with once taboo topics such as sex, abortion, masturbation, and the human body. They also contain strong, intelligent, intellectual girls, and adults are portrayed with realistic flaws and faults. In her last book, *Just Friends* (1990), two teens in their final year of high school discover there is something deeper to their relationship than just friendship. It also details the pressures of making adult decisions, and shows teens beginning to analyze their relationships with their parents.

FURTHER WORKS: *It's Okay If You Don't Love Me,* 1977; *Love Is One of the Choices,* 1978

BIBLIOGRAPHY: *Something about the Author,* vol. 7, 1975

DENISE P. BEASLEY

KLEIN, Robin
Author, b. 28 February 1936, Kempsey, Australia

K. tried several careers before beginning to write for children. Since turning her innate sense of understanding of young people into stories for them, she has succeeded on an international level. A product of the AUSTRALIAN suburbs, her picture-book stories, novels for middle graders, and YOUNG ADULT BOOKS provide their characters with the opportunity to rebel against urban and suburban environments. *Thing* (1982), a PICTURE BOOK story about a baby stegosaurus, was named Australian Junior Book of the Year by the Children's Book Council of Australia. In 1984, CBCA awarded *Penny Pollard's Diary,* one in a series for middle grade readers, a Book of the Year Award Highly Commended Citation. The series, featuring Penny Pollard, is presented through documents, such as letters and diaries. *Came Back to Show You I Could Fly* (1990), a young adult novel, won CBCA's Australian Book of the Year Award for older readers. In 1989, K. earned the Australian Human Rights Award for Literature. Several of K.'s books have been adapted for television and stage. While much of what she has written for younger readers is humorous, her young adult novels have a dark side that has brought criticism as well as praise. K. experiments with style and viewpoints in her books. *Laurie Loved Me Best* (1988) is told by alternating teenaged narrators.

FURTHER WORKS: *The Giraffe of Pepperell Street.* 1978: *People Might Hear You.* 1984: *Hating Alison Ashley.* 1984: *Penny Pollard's Guide to Modern Manners.* 1989

BIBLIOGRAPHY: *Children's Literature Review,* vol. 23, 1991: *Something about the Author,* vol. 80, 1995

FRANCISCA GOLDSMITH

KLEVEN, Elisa
Author, illustrator, b. 14 October 1958, Los Angeles, California

Using mixed-media collage, K. has created characters and scenes for her own books, as well as those of other authors. Among K.'s books are *Ernst* (1979), *The Lion and the Little Red Bird* (1992), *The Paper Princess* (1994), *Hurray! A Piñata* (1996), and *The Puddle Pail* (1997). K. provided the illustrations for *Abuela* (Arthur DORROS, 1991), which was given the Parent's Choice Award for ILLUSTRATION. *Abuela* was also named a notable book by the AMERICAN LIBRARY ASSOCIATION and a Fanfare Book by *Horn Book.* More recently, K. has illustrated Dorros's *Isla* (1995), a companion title to *Abuela* and Karen E. Lotz's *Snow Song Whistling* (1993). K.'s illustrations are notable for their rich, jewel-like colors and exquisite collages created with gouache, watercolor, ink, pastel, lace, cloth, and cut paper.

FURTHER WORKS: Illustrator: *B Is for Bethlehem* (Isabel Wilner, 1990); *City by the Bay: A Magical Journey around San Francisco* (Tricia Brown, author, 1993); *A Monster in My House* (1998)

BIBLIOGRAPHY: *Something about the Author,* vol. 77, 1994

MARY ARIAIL BROUGHTON

KNIGHT, Eric Mowbray
Author, b. 10 April 1897, Menston, Yorkshire, England; d. 15 January 1943, Surinam

K., the author of *Lassie Come-Home* (1940), worked in mills and factories as a young boy until 1912. His widowed mother, who had moved to the United States earlier, then sent for him to join her and his brothers. K. studied at Cambridge Latin School, the Boston Museum of FINE ARTS, and the National Academy of Design in New York City where he was awarded the Elliott Silver Medal for drawing. K. joined the Canadian Light Infantry where he worked as a signaler in France during World War I. By the war's end, K. had lost his family; two brothers serving in the U.S. Army had been killed on the same June day in 1918, and his mother died shortly thereafter. His youngest brother had died in childhood.

Searching for a sense of direction, K. tried his hand at many vocations, including painter, cartoonist, drama critic, and columnist for the *Philadelphia Public Ledger,* and finally, short story writer and novelist. Though he lived in the United States, K. felt close ties to Yorkshire. Living on a farm near Valley Forge, Pennsylvania, he was able to merge his two worlds in a short story, "Lassie Come Home," that was published in the *Saturday Evening Post* on December 12, 1938. The story was later expanded into a novel that became a Junior Literary Guild selection. Set in Yorkshire, it is the moving and dramatic story of a collie that is sold and transported to the northern edge of Scotland. In a desire to be with the Yorkshire boy who loves her, the collie escapes; using her instinct, intelligence, and strong will, she overcomes many obstacles on the four hundred-mile journey home. On his farm, K. actually owned a collie named Toots, who became lost in the woods, and after enduring many hardships found her way home. K.'s novel was immensely popular and was quickly adapted as a Hollywood movie in 1943, costarring Elizabeth Taylor. Several sequels followed and with the beginning of television, a highly successful Lassie series was produced. Unfortunately, K. never fully realized the extent of the success and popularity of his much-loved dog story. He lost his life while serving as an officer in the United States Army in World War II when his plane crashed in the Surinam jungle (between Guyana and French Guiana). In addition to *Lassie,* K. wrote several novels for adults, including *This above All* (1941), a best-selling World War II novel that was also made into a movie and *You Play the Black and Red Comes Up* (1937), a satire on Hollywood written under the pseudonym Richard Hallas.

BIBLIOGRAPHY: *Oxford Companion to Children's Literature;* Helbig, A., and A. Perkins, *Dictionary of American Children's Fiction 1960–1984: Junior Authors and Illustrators,* 1978; *Twentieth-Century Children's Writers,* vol. 4, 1983

ANDREW KANTAR

KOERTGE, Ron

Author, poet, b. 22 April 1940, Olney, Illinois

K., author of YOUNG ADULT LITERATURE, discovered his interest and talent in writing while a high school student. He earned a masters degree from the University of Arizona (1965) and has been a professor of English at Pasadena City College since 1965. As a graduate student, he started writing poetry, which he began publishing in 1970. In 1986, he published his first young adult novel, *Where the Kissing Never Stops,* demonstrating both a sense of HUMOR and an honesty about what it feels like to be an adolescent boy. That first book, as well as *The Arizona Kid* (1988), *The Boy in the Moon* (1990), *The Harmony Arms* (1992), and *Tiger, Tiger Burning Bright* (1994) have all been honored as AMERICAN LIBRARY ASSOCIATION Best Books for Young Adults. While humorous, K.'s books treat serious subjects with appropriate respect. Some of these subjects have caused social critics to question the books' appropriateness for youthful readers while literary critics and those who work with teenagers applaud K.'s treatment of such topics as AIDS, homosexuality, losing one's virginity, and other hurdles of contemporary coming-of-age reality. K. ascribes his success as a young adult author to his clear memories of being a teen himself. He continues to write and publish poetry for adults.

FURTHER WORKS: *Mariposa Blues,* 1991; *Confess-O-Rama,* 1996

BIBLIOGRAPHY: Koertge, Ron. *"Sex and the Single Kid." Los Angeles Times* Book Review, March 21, 1993: *Something about the Author,* vol. 90. 1997: *Twentieth Century Young Adult Writers,* 1994

FRANCISCA GOLDSMITH

KOGAN, Deborah (Ray)

Artist, author, illustrator, b. 31 August 1940, Philadelphia, Pennsylvania

K. uses two other professional names, Deborah Ray and Deborah Kogan Ray. She writes and illustrates her own books, as well as illustrates books for other authors, such as Charlotte ZOLOTOW, Patricia MACLACHLAN, Crescent DRAGONWAGON, and e.e. cummings. Among the award-winning books illustrated by K. is Robert Welber's *The Winter Picnic* (1970), which was chosen one of American Institute of Graphic Arts Children's Books and Emily Herman's *Hubknuckles* (1985), which was selected one of Child Study Association of America's Children's Book of the Year. Although K. works primarily in watercolor and acrylics for her professional paintings, she prefers pencil for ILLUSTRATIONS of children's books.

FURTHER WORKS: Self-illustrated: *The Fair at Sorochintsi: A Nikolai Gogal Story Retold.* (as Deborah Ray). 1969: *Fog Drift Morning* (as Deborah Kogan Ray). 1983. Illustrator: *Through Grandpa's Eyes.* (MacLachan). 1980: *The White Marble.* (Zolotow). 1982: *Diana, Maybe.* (Dragonwagon). 1987: *Little Tree.* (e.e. cummings). 1987: *Chang's Paper Pony.* (COERR). 1988

BIBLIOGRAPHY: *Something about the Author,* vol. 51, 1988

MARY ARIAIL BROUGHTON

KONIGSBURG, E(laine) L(obl)

Author, b. 10 February 1930, New York City

K. grew up in Northwestern Pennsylvania, where her family moved when she was a small child. She became an inveterate reader early, consuming both classics and popular material, a range she credits with giving her the opportunity to hone her literary tastes. However, one disappointment pervaded these childhood readings: no matter what the book jacket promised, the characters in the stories seemed removed from her own Depression Era small town life experiences, leaving K. longing for books in which she could see herself. As an author, she is acclaimed for her creation of characters who are searching for their personal identities, as well as for her hallmark HUMOR. The settings of K.'s stories are largely middle class and suburban, sharing the context of her own children's world. During a brief teaching career, K. became interested in the fact that all children of certain years—those roughly associated with junior high school—are working through issues of identity. This realization underpins the creation of each of her self-conscious characters.

From the first, she has written for children who think and reflect and are looking for themselves when they read children's literature. K. was an excellent student who enjoyed art as well as reading. However, in college she majored in chemistry because such an education seemed vocationally sensible. After earning a bachelor's degree at the Carnegie Institute of Technology in 1952, she continued graduate studies at the University of Pittsburgh. Her inability to function agilely in a laboratory kept her from entering the chemical profession.

K. began to write after moving to suburban Port Chester, New York. As with all her future novels, the plot of her first novel, *Jennifer, Hecate, Macbeth, William McKinley, and Me, Elizabeth* (1967), was inspired by a simple incident in the life of someone she knew well; in this case, her own daughter's deliberate and dignified approach to making friends in a new place. K. has earned critical acclaim from the first. In the same year as her first novel, published in England as *Jennifer, Hecate, MacBeth, and Me,* in 1968, she also published *From the Mixed-up Files of Mrs. Basil E. Frankweiler* and both books were nominated for the ALA NEWBERY MEDAL. *From the Mixed-up Files of Mrs. Basil E. Frankweiler* won the 1968 NEWBERY MEDAL, and *Jennifer, Hecate, Macbeth, William McKinley, and Me, Elizabeth* was named a Newbery Medal Honor book. *From the Mixed-up Files of Mrs. Basil E. Frankweiler* also won the William Allen White Award (1970). *A Proud Taste of Scarlet and Miniver* (1973) was named an AMERICAN LIBRARY ASSOCIATION Notable Children's Book and was nominated for the National Book Award, both in 1974. *The Second Mrs. Giaconda* (1975) and *Father Arcane's Daughter* (1976) were named by ALA as Best Books for Young Adults. A collection of four short stories, *Throwing Shadows* (1979), was named an ALA Notable Children's Book and was nominated for the American Book Award, both in 1980. *Up from Jericho Tel* (1986) earned the Parents' Choice Award in 1987. *The View from Saturday* (1996) earned K. a second Newbery Medal (1997).

K. reasserts her childhood interest in art by illustrating some of her novels in pen and ink, but many of her stories gain narrative color from her interest and research in the Renaissance and art history. The *Second Mrs. Giaconda* is about Leonardo da Vinci, while *A Proud Taste of Scarlet and Miniver* grew from K.'s interest in Eleanor of Aquitaine. Critics note that K. portrays the latter as more of a feminist than seems likely for Eleanor's era. *From the Mixed-up Files of Mrs. Basil E. Frankweiler,* inspired by her children and set in New York City's Metropolitan Museum of Art, tells of two runaways who camp out at the Met, managing to avoid detection for several days (and nights). The runaways' highly civilized adventure becomes believable in K.'s hands. The truths K. incorporates in her stories are of her characters' interior changes, not the technicalities of their adventures.

K. also has written about DISABILITIES in various books. However, readers are not faced with any "problem novel" treatment of disability. Instead, the array of each novel's characters are just like real-world people, some of whom carry the baggage of mental and physical challenges. *(George)* (1970), published in England as *Benjamin Dickenson Carr and His (George),* 1974, concerns a twelve-year-old boy undergoing an identity crisis of such proportion that both other characters in the book and some adult readers label him psychotic. In fact, K. asserts, Ben's struggles to integrate his identity—including the alter ego he's dubbed George—make the boy vulnerable to misidentification as schizophrenic. *The View from Saturday,* in which a teacher must use a wheelchair to get around, also utilizes K.'s art and history research because the plot itself involves a quiz kid program. Told from multiple viewpoints, this novel is a refined expression of K.'s continuing concern with bright children's issues of identity.

In *TalkTalk: A Children's Book Author Speaks to Grown-ups* (1995) K. discusses her devotion to children and to creating excellent literature for them. K. is a witty, intelligent, and psychologically astute author who understands that praise from a child who lets her know how delightful the experience of reading a book by her has been is itself the best critical acclaim a children's author can earn.

FURTHER WORKS: *About the B'nai Bagels,* 1969; *Altogether, One at a Time,* 1971; *The Dragon in the Ghetto Caper,* 1974; *Journey to an 800 Number,* 1982; published in England as *Journey by First Class Camel,* 1983; *T-Backs, T-Shirts, COAT, and Suit,* 1993

BIBLIOGRAPHY: *American Writers for Children Since 1960: Fiction.* 1986: *Contemporary Authors,* New Revision Series. 1986: *Contemporary Authors,* New Revision Series. 1998. Hanks, Dorrel. *E.L. K.,* 1992: HOPKINS, Lee Bennett, *Pauses: Autobiographical Reflections of 101 Creators of Children's Books,* 1995; *Something about the Author,* vol. 4, 1973, and vol. 95, 1998

FRANCISCA GOLDSMITH

KORMAN, Gordon
Author, b. 23 October, 1963, Montreal, Quebec, Canada

K. is best known for his contemporary and humorous descriptions of the exploits of his adolescent literary characters. At the age of fourteen K. wrote his first book, *This Can't Be Happening at Macdonald Hall!* (1978), about grade ten boys Bruno Walter and Boots O'Neal. These characters would reappear in several of K.'s subsequent titles. Now writing as an adult, K. reflects that he has always written back a few years from his own age, and as a result, his books have changed and developed just as he has as a writer. He continues to write for children and YOUNG ADULTS, but his slapstick humorous style has become more satirical and he is exploring more serious social themes.

K. received the Air Canada Award for the Most Promising Writer under Thirty-five from the Canadian Authors Association in 1981 for his first five novels. In addition he received the Ontario Youth Medal from the Ontario Government in 1985, a prize given for his contribution to children's literature. He states that the "books I enjoy most are serious books that just happen to be hilarious." He has observed that although quite serious things can happen within the plot of a book, it is in the discussion of them, or the description of them, that funny things come out.

FURTHER WORKS: *Go Jump in the Pool!* 1979. *Beware the Fish!* 1980. *Who is Bugs Potter?* 1980. *I Want to Go Home!* 1981. *Our Man Weston.* 1982. *The War with Mr. Wizzle.* 1982. *Bugs Potter Lives at Nickaninny.* 1983. *No Coins, Please.* 1984. *Son of Interflux.* 1986. *A Semester in the Life of a Garbage Bag.* 1987. *Radio Fifth Grade.*

1989. *Losing Joe's Place.* 1990. *The Twinkie Squad.* 1992. *The Toilet Paper Tigers.* 1995. *The Last-Place Sports Poems of Jeremy Bloom.* 1996. *Liar, Liar, Pants on Fire.* 1997. *The Sixth Grade Nickname Game.* 1988

BIBLIOGRAPHY: *Children's Literature Review,* vol. 23, 1991

SANDRA IMDIEKE

KRASILOVSKY, Phyllis
Author, b. 28 August 1926, Brooklyn, New York

K.'s books have delighted young readers for many years. The author has been praised for her talent in describing the problems and feelings common to many children. She is best known for her series of books featuring a character known simply as "the man," a comical character who gets into humorous dilemmas. Three of K.'s books, *The Cow Who Fell in the Canal* (1957), *The Man Who Didn't Wash His Dishes* (1950), and *The Man Who Tried to Save Time* (1979) have been adapted for filmstrips. Many of K.'s books have been translated into other languages such as German, Swedish, and Japanese. In addition to writing books, K. has taught courses in children's literature and has spent much time speaking at schools, colleges, and libraries.

FURTHER WORKS: *Susan Sometimes,* 1962; *The Girl Who Was a Cowboy,* 1965; *The Very Tall Little Girl,* 1969; *The Popular Girls Club,* 1972; *The First Tulips in Holland,* 1982

BIBLIOGRAPHY: *Major Authors and Illustrators for Children and Young Adults: A Selection of Sketches from Something about the Author,* vol. 4, 1993

MARY ARIAIL BROUGHTON

KRAUS, Robert
Author, illustrator, b. 21 June 1925, Milwaukee, Wisconsin

K. began his career as a cartoonist early, selling his first cartoon at the age of ten to a local barbershop. Soon after, K.'s first published cartoon was featured on the children's page of the *Milwaukee Journal.* While still in high school K. sold cartoons to such magazines as the *Saturday Evening Post* and *Esquire* and after graduation headed for New York and the Art Student's League. K.'s big break came when he sold a cartoon to *The New Yorker* which he then contracted for fifty cartoons a year. K. worked at *The New Yorker* for fifteen years and during this time he had also began to write and illustrate children's books. His first work *Junior the Spoiled Cat* was published in 1955. K. left *The New Yorker* to try writing and drawing children's books on a full-time basis.

In 1965, feeling that there were many fine cartoonists who could make important contributions to the field of children's publishing, K. began a new publishing company, Windmill Books. In the beginning, K. wrote books that were then illustrated by artist friends Charles Addams and William STEIG, whom he knew from his days at *The New Yorker*. Windmill Books had a solid reputation and one of K.'s publishing innovations was Tubby Books, small waterproof books made with vinyl pages designed to be bathtub toys. In the early 1980s, Simon and Schuster assumed publication of the Windmill imprint and its publishing lists. Working with several publishers, K. is best known for his personable animal characters and for his collaborations with illustrators Jose ARUEGO and Ariane DEWEY.

Two of his best known characters are Leo and Owliver. *Leo the Late Bloomer* (1977) is the story of a late developing youngster and his parents, one fretful and the other patient, and *Owliver* (1974) is the story of an owl whose parents have their own designs for his future but ultimately see they must allow him to follow his own dreams. *Little Louie the Baby Bloomer* (1998) continues the story of Leo, the late blooming tiger. Here Leo becomes an older sibling impatiently determined to help baby Louie develop a variety of toddler skills, all with disastrous results. In recent years, K. has developed new characters like Daddy Long Ears and Little Louie while at the same time continuing with old favorites. K. has also turned to parodying and illustrating classic tales with *Fables Aesop Never Wrote* (1994) and *New Myths: Dug up and Dusted Off* (1996).

At various times K. has published under a variety of pseudonyms such as Eugene H. Hippopotamus, E. S. Silly and I. M. Tubby. Regardless of name, K.'s works are always a gently humorous look at life in which we can recognize ourselves and our loved ones.

FURTHER WORKS: *Harriet and the Promised Land.* 1968: *Whose Mouse Are You?* 1970: *Milton the Early Riser.* 1972: *Spider's First Day at School.* 1987: *Big Squeak, Little Squeak.* 1996: *The Making of Monkey King.* 1998.

BIBLIOGRAPHY: Silvey, Anita, ed., *Children's Books and Their Creators,* 1995; *Something about the Author.* vol. 4, 1973, vol. 65, 1991, vol. 93, 1997; *Third Book of Junior Authors and Illustrators,* 1972

DEDE SMALL

KRAUSS, Ruth

Author, b. 25 July 1911, Baltimore, Maryland; d. 10 July, 1993, Westport, Connecticut

K. was one of the first children's authors to collaborate with illustrators and create minimum text for PICTURE BOOKS representing a whimsical view of the world through a child's eyes. Her childhood interests in art, music, and reading culminated in a career as a children's book author. In addition to writing children's books, K. wrote plays and poetry for adults. Her poetry has been published in periodicals including *Harper's*. Theaters in New York, New Haven, and Boston are among the sites in which her plays have been produced. She married David Johnson Liesk (pen name of Crockett JOHNSON), writer–illustrator and comic-strip artist, in 1940. They worked together on several of K.'s books. K. studied at the Peabody Institute in Baltimore and New York City's Parsons School of Fine and Applied Art. She also studied anthropology at Columbia University and poetry at the New School of Social Research in New York.

K.'s studies at Columbia coupled with her experience at the Writers Laboratory at Bank Street School in Greenwich Village provided her the fodder and context to create books that she felt reflected the authentic language of the children's world. K. published her first book, *A Good Man and His Wife* in 1944. As an author, she was sensitive to gender stereotypes. For example, while writing *A Hole Is to Dig* (1952), she insisted that illustrator Maurice SENDAK include a girl on the last page to demonstrate both boys and girls as book lovers. Also in this book, girls as well as boys are illustrated playing in the mud, a boy is making his bed, and both boys and girls are doing dishes. K. worked with Sendak before either was well recognized. Sendak credits K. and her husband with shaping him as an artist. She and Sendak collaborated on eight books from 1952 to 1960. K.'s book writing slowed between the mid-1960s to the 1970s. She then published a few more including *Little Boat Lighter Than a Cork* (1976).

K. received the Spring Book Festival honor citation for *The Carrot Seed* in 1945 and *I Can Fly* in 1951. Her collaboration with illustrators Marc SIMONT and Maurice Sendak brought CALDECOTT MEDAL Honor designation for her books *The Happy Day* (1950) and *A Very Special House* (1954).

FURTHER WORKS: *The Great Duffy.* 1946: *The Growing Story.* 1947: *The Bundle Book.* 1951. Reissued as *You're Just What I Need.* 1998: *I'll Be You and You Be Me.* 1954: *How to Make an Earthquake.* 1954: *The Happy Egg.* 1967: *Big and Little.* 1987

BIBLIOGRAPHY: *Children's Literature Review.* vol. 42, 1997. HOPKINS, Lee Bennett, *Pauses: Autobiographical Reflections of 101 Creators of Children's Books,* 1995. *Publishers Weekly.* July 26, 1993, vol. 240 no. 30, p. 32. Sendak, Maurice. "Ruth K. and Me: A Very Special Partnership." *Horn Book.* May/June, 1994. *Twentieth Century Children's Writers.* 1978

NANCY HORTON

KREMENTZ, Jill
Photographer, author, b. 19 February 1940, New York City

K. is best known for her photographs that realistically portray the lives and stories of contemporary children and adults. Her photographic essays about young children show them at play pursuing their hobbies and interests. In describing her work, one critic wrote that K. "captures in text and picture the true person exposing his or her innermost feelings." She began her career as a freelance photographer but became the youngest full-time staff photographer at the *New York Herald Tribune.*

Her first book with a child as the main character, *Sweet Pea: A Black Girl Growing up in the Rural South* (1969), came from her year spent in Alabama living with a poor black family and documenting the life of the ten-year-old daughter. Known professionally for her photographs of literary figures, K. is also acclaimed for her books about young people faced with challenges, whether physically or emotionally. Her How It

Feels series of books focus on children as they cope with emotional challenges. In addition to her books for children, her photographic work is frequently exhibited and is in permanent collections at the Museum of Modern Art and Library of Congress. *A Very Young Dancer* was named to the American Institute of Graphic Artists Fifty Books of the Year List, *School Library Journal* Best Books of the Year List, and the *New York Times* Best Seller List of children's books, all in 1976; *A Very Young Rider* and *A Very Young Gymnast* were named to the School Library Journal Best Books of the Year List, 1978; K. won the Garden State Children's Book Award in 1980.

FURTHER WORKS: *A Very Young Circus Flyer,* 1979; *A Very Young Skater,* 1979; *How It Feels When a Parent Dies,* 1981; *How It Feels to Be Adopted,* 1982; *Benjy Goes to a Restaurant,* 1986; *Taryn Goes to the Dentist,* 1986; *Holly's Farm Animals,* 1986; *Zachary Goes to the Zoo,* 1986; *A Very Young Skier,* 1990; *A Very Young Actress,* 1991; *A Very Young Gardener,* 1991; *A Very Young Musician,* 1991; *How It Feels to Live with a Physical* DISABILITY, 1992; *A Storyteller's Story,* 1992

BIBLIOGRAPHY: *Contemporary Authors New Revision Series,* vol. 46, 1995

SANDRA IMDIEKE

KROEBER, Theodora
Author, b. 24 March 1897, Denver, Colorado; d. 4 July 1979, Berkeley, California

K. grew up and lived in Telluride, Colorado, before moving to Berkeley, California, where she attended the University of California earning a bachelor's degree in 1919 and a master's degree one year later. K.'s first work, a novel that was never published but which helped her to polish her writing talent, was written when she was in her fifties. At that time she was living on the campus of Stanford University with her husband, the noted anthropologist Alfred L. Kroeber. He was studying NATIVE AMERICAN culture through the accounts of Ishi, the last surviving member of the Yahi tribe of Native Americans. In 1964, K. wrote a fictionalized account of Ishi's life, *Ishi, Last of His Tribe.* Based on her husband and his colleagues' notes, K. was able to describe many details of Yahi culture not previously known to whites. This novel followed the publication in

1964 of K.'s first major work, a biography written for adults titled *Ishi in Two Worlds: A Biography of the Last Wild Indian in North America*. It was named an ALA Notable Book.

Drawing on her childhood memories, K. wrote a PICTURE BOOK, *A Green Christmas* (1967), the story of two young children who, after their move from Colorado to California, must face their first Christmas in a warm climate. K. also expanded into the FANTASY genre. In *Carrousel* (1977), a fantasy novella, the carousel animals come out for adventure when the keeper of the carousel forgets to close the door all the way one night.

K. was followed into writing for children by one of her own four children, Ursula LEGUIN, the acclaimed fantasy and SCIENCE FICTION author. In addition to writing for children, K. also collected folktales from California Native Americans and wrote a biography of her husband. While K. has displayed considerable range as an author, she continues to be best remembered for her two works regarding Ishi.

AWARDS: ALA Notable Book Award (1965) for *Ishi, Last of His People*

FURTHER WORKS: *The Inland Whale*, 1959; *Almost Ancestors: The First Californians* (with Robert Heizer), 1969

BIBLIOGRAPHY: Silvey, Anita. ed. *Children's Books and Their Creators:* 1995. *Something about the Author.* vol. 1, 1971

DEDE SMALL

KROLL, Steven
Author, b. 11 August 1941, New York City

As a youngster, K. studied sculpture at New York's Museum of Modern Art, but turned increasingly to writing as editor of his high school literary journal. After graduation from Harvard he worked in New York and London as an editor of trade books for adults, but began writing for children in the 1970s at the suggestion of a children's book editor. Author of more than seventy-five PICTURE BOOKS and chapter books for middle-grade readers, K. often draws on scenes and memories from his Manhattan childhood as background for his books. Recent titles by K. include an increasing number of history and BIOGRAPHY works for young readers.

FURTHER WORKS: *Is Milton Missing?*, 1975: *The Biggest Pumpkin Ever*, 1984: *The Hit and Run Gang*, (volumes 1–4 1992): *The Hit and Run Gang*, (volumes 5–8 1994): *Lewis and Clark: Explorers of the American West*, 1994: *Pony Express*, 1996: *Oh, Tucker!* 1998: *The Boston Tea Party*, 1998: *Robert Fulton: From Submarine to Steamboat*, 1999: *William Penn, Founder of Pennsylvania*, 2000

BIBLIOGRAPHY: *Contemporary Authors, New Revision Series*, 1996; *Something about the Author*, vol. 64, 1991

DIANE L. CHAPMAN

KROLL, Virginia
Author, b. 28 April 1948, Buffalo, New York

K. is a prolific author who is happiest when she is writing. She says that writing is a necessary part of her life, almost like breathing. She has composed novels, plays, poetry, short stories, nonfiction books, and articles. K. attended Canisius College and the State University of New York in Buffalo. She was a teacher and has been a full-time author since 1984. K. has published more than forty books and over one thousand six hundred items in juvenile magazines.

K. attributes a score of the wealth of her ideas to her six children and her innumerable pets. Her work conveys a joie de vivre and celebration of life. *New Friends, True Friends, Stuck like Glue Friends* (1994) sings of the joy of friendships. *Naomi Knows It's Springtime* (1993) shows a blind (see THE DISABLED IN CHILDREN'S AND YOUNG ADULT LITERATURE) girl discovering signs of the season. *Beginnings: How Families Come to Be* (1994) tells the stories of six children, one from a traditional birth family and the others from a variety of adoptive families. *Faraway Drums* (1998) shows a brave young girl who baby-sits her little sister while her mother works.

AWARDS: *Publishers Weekly* Best Book of the Year, American Booksellers Association Pick-of-the-Lists, Jane Addams Peace Association commendation (1992) for *Masai and I*. American Book Award (1994) for *Wood-Hoopoe Willie*. Notable Book in the Field of Social Studies (1996) for *Fireflies, Peace Pies, and Lillabies*. American Bookseller Pick-of-the-Lists (1994) for *The Seasons and Someone*, (1996) for *Can You Dance, Dalila?*, (1997) for *Butterfly Boy*, and (1999) for *Cat!*. Outstanding Book in the Field

55. MOLLIE HUNTER

56. JOHANNA HURWITZ

58. TRINA SCHART HYMAN

57. PAT HUTCHINS

59. EZRA JACK KEATS

60. ERIC A. KIMMEL

61. E. L. KONIGSBURG

62. KARLA KUSKIN

of Science and Skipping Stones MULTICULTURAL Book Award (1996) for *Sweet Magnolia*.

FURTHER WORKS (SELECT): *I Got a Family,* 1993; *Every Monday in the Mailbox,* 1995; *Shelter Folks,* 1995; *Hats off to Hair,* 1995; *Hands!,* 1997; *Faraway Drums,* 1998; *With Love, To Earth's Endangered Peoples,* 1998; *The Making of Angels,* 1998; *Pets,* 1998; *Kwanzaa,* 1999; *She Is Born!,* 2000; *Girl, You're Amazing,* 2001

BIBLIOGRAPHY: *School Library Journal,* 1992; *Contemporary Authors,* 1994; *Something about the Author,* 1994; *Publishers Weekly,* December 28, 1992; *Creative Classroom,* 1996; Book of Junior Authors and Illustrators, 1998

BERNICE E. CULLINAN

KRULL, Kathleen
Author, b. 29 July 1952, Ft. Leonard Wood, Missouri

As an eclectic author, K.'s works range from biographies to musical anthologies and appeal to many ages. In *Gonna Sing My Head!* (1992), K. takes readers on a journey of musical heritage. In *Lives of the Musicians: Good Times, Bad Times (and What the Neighbors Thought)* (1993), K. not only provides brief biographical sketches of twenty musicians but also tidbits of interesting, unusual details and humorous anecdotes of their lives. This work spawned other collective BIOGRAPHIES of writers, artists, and authors. Several other works explore the diversity of various lifestyles and cultures. K. spent time getting to know three Latino children living in California, balancing their lives between two cultures, American and Mexican. She crafted *The Other Side: How Kids Live in a California Latino Neighborhood* (1994) as a tribute. Engaging both in research and writing, her work blends the elements of everyday events and good STORYTELLING.

AWARDS: *Boston Globe–Horn Book* honor book (1994) for *Lives of the Musicians*

FURTHER WORKS: *Wilma Unlimited: How Wilma Rudolph Became the World's Fastest Woman.* 1996: *Wish You Were Here: Emily's Guide to the 50 States.* 1997: *Lives of the Writers: Comedies, Tragedies (and What the Neighbors Thought).* 1994

BIBLIOGRAPHY: Andres, Linda R. ed., *Children's Literature Review.* vol. 44, 1997: *Something About the Author.* vol. 80, 1995

SHANE RAYBURN

KRUMGOLD, Joseph
Author, b. 9 April 1908, Jersey City, New Jersey; d. 10 July, 1980, Hope, New Jersey

K. was the first recipient to be awarded two NEWBERY MEDALS despite his first career interest in the movies. He was reared in a movie-oriented family in the early 1900s. His father owned and operated movie houses and his brother was an organist accompanying silent pictures. K. received a bachelor's degree from New York University with majors in English and history. He became significantly involved in virtually all aspects of the movie production business as a screenwriter, producer, director, and owner of Joseph Krumgold Productions. As an established screenwriter of more than twenty works, many of which were documentaries, K. had created myriad works to his credit. In 1953 he was commissioned to adapt his film ". . . And Now Miguel" into a children's book. This coming of age story of young Miguel Chavez brought K. his first Newbery Medal in 1954. He wrote the book with a rhythm that mirrors the speech pattern of bilingual Spanish-Americans. The medal motivated him to pursue a second career in writing for children. The second Newbery Medal for *Onion John* only six years later validated this ambition. *Henry 3* (1967) completed the trilogy of man's journey to maturity. The last title in the trilogy does not quite match the excellence of the first two but is well written and perceptive in characterization. Although K. wrote only a few children's books, he was fittingly recognized for his efforts.

AWARDS: AMERICAN LIBRARY ASSOCIATION Newbery Award (1954) for . . . *And Now Miguel* and (1960) for *Onion John*. Both titles were awarded the Boy's Club Junior Book Award and the Freedom's Foundation Award for . . . *And Now Miguel*. The film . . . *And Now Miguel* received the Robert Flaherty Award honorable mention. *Onion John* received the Lewis CARROLL Shelf Award

FURTHER WORKS: *The Most Terrible Turk.* 1969: ". . . *And Now Miguel,*" (filmstrip with cassette), 1978: "*Onion John,*" (filmstrip with cassette) 1978

BIBLIOGRAPHY: *Children's Literature Review,* vol. 12, 1981: *Contemporary Authors, New Revised Series,* vol. 7: MEIGS, et al., *A Critical His-*

tory of Children's Literature, 1969: More Junior Authors. 1963: Peterson, L. K., and M. L. Solt. 1982. *Newbery and* CALDECOTT MEDAL *and Honor Books:* Sutherland, Z. "One World for Youth." *Saturday Review.* Sept. 16, 1967, p. 49: *School Library Journal,* October 1968 and January 1971

NANCY HORTON

KRUSH, Beth and Joe
Illustrators. b. Beth: 31 March 1918, Washington, D.C.; Joe: 18 May 1918, Camden, New Jersey

B. and J. K. have illustrated numerous books individually and as a team. They met at the Philadelphia Museum School of Art, where each won AWARDS in a variety of mediums. They married during World War II and J. served in the Office of Strategic Services as a graphic designer. J. attended the United Nations charter meeting in San Francisco and the war trials in Nuremberg for the OSS. Both have been instructors of ILLUSTRATION, B. at Moore College of Art and J. at the Philadelphia Museum School of Art. Creating illustrations that are realistic while at the same time reflect energy and whimsy, the K.'s are the original artists of the miniature world of Mary NORTON's *The Borrowers* (1952), a book that won the CARNEGIE MEDAL. Later they also illustrated *The Borrowers Afield* (1955), *The Borrowers Afloat* (1961), *The Borrowers Aloft* (1961), and *The Borrowers Avenged* (1982). Additionally their talents are seen in Virginia SORENSEN's *Miracles on Maple Hill* (1956), a NEWBERY MEDAL winner. In Beverly CLEARY's *Emily's Runaway Imagination* (1961) the K.s' illustrations support Cleary's imaginative yet realistic quality of writing. Elizabeth ENRIGHT's, *Gone Away Lake* (1990) displays the sprightly art of the K.'s as does the sequel to this well-loved book. The K.'s are illustrators for numerous other chapter books.

FURTHER WORKS: *Spring Comes Riding.* CAVANNA, 1950: *Golden Picture Dictionary.* Lilian MOORE, 1954: *Fifteen.* Cleary, 1956: *Jean and Johnny.* Cleary, 1959: *Sister of the Bride.* Cleary, 1963: *Ride a Wild Horse.* Carlsen, 1970: Florence and Roxanne HEIDE. *Brillstone Break-In,* HEIDE. F and R. 1977

BIBLIOGRAPHY: Kingman, L., *Illustrators of Children's Books, 1957–1966; More Junior Authors;* 1963; *Something about the Author,* vol. 18, 162–65, 1980

JANELLE B. MATHIS

454

KUSKIN, Karla
Poet, illustrator, author, b. 17 July, 1932, New York City

K. grew up as Karla Seidman on the East Coast, primarily in New York City, except for a few early years in an old house in Connecticut. She remembers composing poetry as a young child; her mother wrote the poems on paper for her before she could write. K.'s creative endeavors received much attention and encouragement. Her parents and her teachers read poetry to her, and served as an audience for her poetry. K. attributes her love of language, words, and books to these early experiences.

K. entered a work-study program at Antioch College (1950) in an effort to find her life's work. Her literary and artistic talents became apparent to her supervisor at a Chicago department store, where she began writing promotional copy and working on design projects. She developed an interest in graphic arts and transferred to Yale University's School of Fine Arts, where she earned a B.F.A. in 1955. K.'s first book, *Roar and More* (1956; rev. 1990) was developed as part of a degree requirement to design, create, and print a book on a small motorized printing press. The book, making clever use of typeface and ILLUSTRATION to portray animals and their noises, won an award from the American Institute of Graphic Arts.

In a career that spans forty-five years, K. has created over fifty books as artist, author, or artist and author combined. K.'s work in POETRY, prose, and art frequently derives from her life experiences. *James and the Rain* (1957; rev. 1995, illustrated by Reg Cartwright), uses verse to depict young James, who asks a series of animals, "What do you do in the rain?" The book was inspired by a stormy summer vacation on Cape Cod. K. created *The Bear Who Saw the Spring* (1961), *Alexander Soames, His Poems* (1961) and *The Philharmonic Gets Dressed* (1982), among others, in response to experiences with her family. K. describes her writing and illustrating process for young readers in two of her self-illustrated poetry collections, *Near the Window Tree: Poems and Notes* (1975), and *Dogs and Dragons, Trees and Dreams: A Collection of Poems* (1980); in these books, she identifies the sources of inspiration for particular poems, thereby guiding young readers who wish to try a similar process themselves. In *Thoughts, Pictures, and Words* (1995, photographs by Nicholas Kuskin), a children's book about herself that K. created for a "Meet the Author" series, she explains where she gets the idea for a poem by asking children about the sources of their ideas. "I suspect the answer is that you, like me, remembered something, saw something, felt something that started you thinking."

K.'s prolific work in poetry is characterized by strength of rhythm, internal and end rhymes that flow easily off the tongue and are never contrived, sprightly HUMOR and play with language, and fresh, clear images that are at the heart of a child's experience. *Soap Soup and Other Verses* (1992, illustrated by K.) engages beginning readers with humorous rhyming word play, frequently interspersing illustrations with the words and lines of a poem and addressing such diverse topics as ears, elbows, knees, feet, eating an egg, and the departure of summer. In *Something Sleeping in the Hall* (1985, illustrated by K.), another early reader, K. provides a very funny collection of poems and drawings about animals, frequently ending a poem with a surprise, which heightens the humor. With *James and the Rain* (1957), *Herbert Hated Being Small* (1979), about a boy troubled by his size who meets a girl with a similar but opposite problem, and *City Dog* (1994), about a city dog joyfully exploring the country, K. demonstrates her deft mastery of poems that tell a story. For *The Sky Is Always in the Sky* (1998, illustrated by Isabelle Dervaus) K. selected a collection of poems from her previously published works, plus one new poem. Many of these make use of the shape of a poem on a page, as well as employing K.'s other finely honed poetic techniques.

K.'s books written in prose savor language as fully as does her verse. *The Philharmonic Gets Dressed* (1982, illustrated by Marc SIMONT) is at once playful and informative, artful and funny.

The child reader enters into the life of professional musicians in a most intimate way, from witnessing bathing and the donning of underwear and formal wear, to the first notes of a symphony. *Jerusalem, Shining Still* (1987, illustrated by David FRAMPTON), inspired by a trip to Israel, presents a short history of that 4,000 year-old city, in stimulating prose interspersed with verse.

As an illustrator of her own work, and as an artist reflecting the writing of others, K. matches her writer's understanding of childhood through simplicity and ingenuity of design, expressed in pen and ink drawings or watercolor paintings. K.'s self-illustrated books, from her first book in 1956 to her recent work in the 1990s, celebrate imagination and humor through the interplay of her twin languages, verse and visual art.

AWARDS: Children's Book Award, INTERNATIONAL READING ASSOCIATION (1976) for *Near the Window Tree: Poems and Notes:* Children's Book Showcase selection, CHILDREN'S BOOK COUNCIL (1976) for *Near the Window Tree: Poems and Notes,* and for *A Boy Had a Mother Who Bought Him a Hat* (1976): Award for Excellence in Poetry for Children, NATIONAL COUNCIL OF TEACHERS OF ENGLISH (1979) for the body of her work: New York Academy of Sciences Children's Science Book Award (1980) for *A Space Story* (1978, illustrated by Marc Simont): ALA Notable Book Award (1982), Library of Congress Children's Book (1982) both for *The Philharmonic Gets Dressed*

FURTHER WORKS: *Any Me I Want to Be: Poems.* 1972: *A Boy Had a Mother Who Bought Him a Hat.* 1976: *The Dallas Titans Get Ready for Bed.* (Marc Simont, illus.) 1986: *A Great Miracle Happened There: A Chanukah Story* (Robert Andrew Parker, illus), 1993: *Paul.* Paintings by Milton Avery: 1994: *Patchwork Island* (Petra MATHERS, illus) 1994

BIBLIOGRAPHY: HOPKINS, Lee Bennett, *Pauses: Autobiographical Reflections of 101 Creators of Children's Books,* 1995. Kuskin, Karla. *Thoughts, Pictures, and Words.* 1995. Silvey, Anita. ed. 1995. *Children's Books and Their Creators. Something about the Author.* vol. 68. 1992

KATHIE KRIEGER CERRA

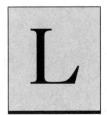

LACAPA, Michael
Author, b. 25 November 1955, Place unknown

L. is an Apache/Hopi/Tewa NATIVE AMERICAN. Reared on the Fort Apache Indian Reservation in Whiteriver, Arizona, L. earned a BA degree from Arizona State University and an M.F.A. from Northern Arizona University. He is the recipient of many regional AWARDS for his children's books and is a gifted storyteller and musician.

L.'s gouache ILLUSTRATIONS in *Less Than Half, More Than Whole* (1994), written with Kathleen Lacapa, authentically reflect Native American culture within a story that relates a young boy's emotional conflict as a member of two cultures.

FURTHER WORKS: *The Mouse Couple,* 1988; *The Flute Player,* 1990; *Antelope Woman,* 1992; *Flovtespilleren and Antilopekvinnen,* 1994; *The Magic Hummingbird,* 1996

AINE KYNE-NORRIS

LA FONTAINE, Jean de
Poet, author, b. 8 July 1621, Chateau Thierry, France; d. 13 April 1695, Paris, France

The son of a prosperous civil servant, L., a poet and author of fables, grew up relatively carefree. At age twenty he entered the Oratory in the Rue Saint-Honoré to study for the priesthood, but had to leave after he was found writing verses about the way prayer was conducted. A few years later, he studied in Paris and joined a literary group known as "the round table." His father arranged his marriage to Marie Hericart in 1647. In 1653, they had a son named Charles, to whom L. paid little attention. L. and his wife had separated by 1659.

In 1659, L. traveled to Paris to begin his literary career. He published his first book, *Contes et Nouvelles en Vers,* in 1664. L. had plenty of free time to write over the next several years while he worked as a gentleman-servant to the Duchese of Orleans. In 1668, six books of L.'s fables written in verse were issued. In 1693, his last collection of fables was published and dedicated to the eight-year-old grandson of Louis XIV. Many of L.'s fables have been translated, republished, and continue to be popular today. Some individual fables include "The Lion and the Rat;" "The North Wind and the Sun;" "The Rich Man and the Shoemaker;" "The Hare and the Tortoise;" "The Miller, the Boy, and the Donkey;" "The Town Mouse and the Country Mouse;" and "The Crow and the Fox." L. was elected to the French Academy in 1683.

FURTHER WORKS: *Fables,* Books I–VI, 1668; *Fables,* Books VII–XI, 1673–79; Book XII, 1694; *Contes et Nouvelles en Vers* (stories based on stories by Boccacio, Ariosto, and Rabelais), part I, 1664; part II, 1668; part III, 1671; part IV, 1674; *Les Amours de Psyche et de Cupidon,* 1669; *Adonis,* 1669; *Recueil de Poesies Chrestiennes et Diverses,* 1671–74; *Poeme de la Captivite de saint Malo,* 1673; *Epitrea Huet,* 1687

JODI PILGRIM

LAGERLOF, Selma
Author, adapter of folktales, b. 20 Nov. 1858, Maarbacka, Varmland, Sweden; d. 16 March, 1940, Maarbacka, Varmland, Sweden

L., author and adapter of Swedish folktales and legends, was the first woman to receive the Nobel Prize for Literature, awarded in 1909. Her first career was as a school mistress in Sweden for ten years, but eventually her writing, for children and adults, became her focus. She fondly remembered the impact of her grandmother who would sit in the corner of a couch telling story after story to entertain her. Nils, now a famous character in Swedish literature, first appeared in L.'s book *The Wonderful Adventures of Nils* (1906), written at the request of Swedish school authorities. In honor of this favorite character, the Nils Holgersson Award is now given annually to a Swedish children's author. Many of L.'s stories have elements of the supernatural interwoven with segments of timeless Swedish legends and FOLKLORE. Her books have been translated in several languages including English.

FURTHER WORKS: *Further Adventures of Nils,* 1911; *The Legend of the Christmas Rose,* 1914, 1942, reissued 1990 with illus. by Charles MIKO-LAYCAK, trans. E. Greene; *General's Ring,* 1928; *The Changeling,* reissued 1992 with illus. by Jeanette WINTER, trans. Susan Stevens

BIBLIOGRAPHY: Dust-jacket copy; *Something about the Author,* vol. 15, 1979

SANDRA IMDIEKE

LAMB, Charles and Mary
Charles: b. 10 February 1775, London, England; d. 27 December 1834, Edmonton, England; Mary: b. 3 December 1764, London, England; d. 20 May 1847, London, England

This brother-sister duo's most notable contribution to the children's literature field was *Tales from Shakespeare* (1807; reissued, 1976). Together, sitting across from each other at the same table, they adapted Shakespeare's plays into short stories for children. Shuffling drafts back and forth between each other, C. and M. became each others' greatest critics. While the Shakespearean tales are by far their most recognized work, C. and M. also engaged in other projects, both

joint and separate. Despite C.'s desperate loneliness and M.'s occasional commitment to asylums, C. and M. managed to sustain each other's creativity and devoted themselves to each other.

FURTHER WORKS: *POETRY for Children,* 1809; reprinted, 1970

BIBLIOGRAPHY: *Something about the Author,* vol. 17, 1979

SHANE RAYBURN

LAMPMAN, Evelyn Sibley (Lynn Bronson)
Author, b. 18 April 1907, Dallas, Oregon; d. 13 June 1980, Portland, Oregon

L., author of BIOGRAPHIES, historical fiction, and contemporary fiction, who also wrote under the pen name of Lynn Bronson, wrote more than thirty books for children. She often wrote stories about ethnic minorities, especially NATIVE AMERICANS. Her work has been praised for its balanced viewpoint as she depicts the complex relationships among disparate cultures. Representative of L.'s work are *White Captives* (1975), *The Potlatch Family* (1976), and *Cayuse Courage* (1970). L. received the Western Writers of America Spur Award in 1968 and 1971. Her *Popular Girl* was named a Junior Literary Guild Selection. In *The Bounces of Cynthiann* (1950), L. wrote about the plight of a self-reliant orphan family, their resilience and adventures.

FURTHER WORKS: *Elder Brother,* 1951; *Captain Apple's Ghost,* 1952; *The Shy Stegosaurus of Cricket Creek,* 1955; *Temple of the Sun,* 1964; *The Tilted Sombrero,* 1966; *Bargain Bride,* 1977; *Squaw Man's Son,* 1978; *Three Knocks on the Wall,* 1980

BIBLIOGRAPHY: *Something about the Author,* vol. 97, 1996; Ward, M. E., D. A. Marquardt, N. Dolan, and D. Eaton, eds., *Authors of Books for Young People,* 3rd ed., 1990

MARY ARIAIL BROUGHTON

LANG, Andrew
Author, b. 31 March, 1844, Selkirk, Scotland; d. 20 July 1912, Banshory, Aberdeenshire, Scotland

L. grew up in the border country of Scotland, where he spent much of his childhood outdoors fishing or playing cricket. He also spent time alone, immersed in books. L. was educated in St. Andrews University, the University of Glasgow, and Oxford where he earned a first in classics in 1868. Although his formal training was in classical literature, early in his career he pursued journalism, writing for the *Daily News,* the *Morning Post,* and *Longman's* magazine, as well as contributing entries for the *Encyclopaedia Britannica.* His interest in classic literature and the FAIRY TALES he remembered from his childhood in Scotland resulted in his first fairy-tale collection, *The Blue Fairy Book,* published in 1889. About this collection of traditional folktales and fairy tales he later wrote, "This collection, made for the pleasure of children and without scientific purpose, included nursery tales which have a purely literary origin." *The Blue Fairy Book* would be the first in a series of anthologies of folktales, each with a designating color in the title. L. was awarded an LL.D., St. Andrews University, 1888, and Oxford University, 1904. He was also elected a member of the Royal British Academy, the Athenaeum Club, and founder and president of the Society for Psychical Research.

As a critic and writer, he believed his role should be to focus on the classics rather than on contemporary literature. This philosophy was repeated in his remarks about writer's attempts to modernize fairy tales. He felt that the old tales were more human and not silly but full of unobtrusively taught "true" lessons, and, indeed, his collections of traditional tales have helped preserve these old tales for modern readers.

FURTHER WORKS: PERRAULT's *Popular Tales,* 1888; *The Red Fairy Book,* 1890; *The Blue Fairy Book,* 1891; *The Green Fairy Book,* 1892; *The True Story Book,* 1893; *The Yellow Fairy Book,* 1894; *The Nursery Rhyme Book,* 1897; *The Crimson Fairy Book,* 1903; *The Olive Fairy Book,* 1907; *Tales of a Fairy Court,* 1907; *Tales of Troy and Greece,* 1907

BIBLIOGRAPHY: *Something about the Author,* vol. 16, 1979

SANDRA IMDIEKE

LANGE, Dietrich

Author, educator, naturalist, b. 2 June 1863, Bonstorff, Kreis Celle, Germany; d. 18 November 1940, St. Paul, Minnesota

Author of numerous frontier novels, L. immigrated from Germany at age eighteen. He was a teacher, principal, and superintendent in the St. Paul public school system. His fifteen Indian ADVENTURE books for boys, published between 1912 and 1930, were set in different historical periods, such as the French and Indian War (*The Raid of the* Ottawa, 1921), the Civil War (*The Lure of the Mississippi,* 1917), and the time of Custer (*The Threat of Sitting Bull,* 1920). The collection was atypical of most SERIES in that the historical and regional variations did not carry over specific characters. The plots, however, were formulaic, commonly involving two boys in search of a third (often a kidnapped brother) with the assistance of a friendly, knowledgeable Indian (the Fenimore Cooper influence). As a naturalist, L. used his novels as a vehicle to instruct his readers on wilderness survival and regional flora and fauna. Although these instructional digressions slowed the narrative, the exciting action kept his readers loyal. L. also published wildlife articles and stories in many popular magazines as well as numerous ornithological guide books. Former U.S. Supreme Court Justice Harry Blackmun, a student of L.'s, recalled reading L.'s books as a boy and described him as "an old and valued friend as well as a remarkable character" from whom he learned "about the beauties of nature."

FURTHER WORKS: *On the Trail of the Sioux,* 1912; *Lost in the Fur Country,* 1914; *In the Great Wild North,* 1915; *The Gold Rock of the Chippewa,* 1925

ANDREW KANTAR

LANGSTAFF, John

Author, musician, b. 24 December 1920, Brooklyn, New York

L.'s childhood was surrounded with music and song starting with his birth on Christmas Eve after his parents had gone caroling through their Brooklyn Heights neighborhood. L. sang publicly in early childhood first as a soprano soloist at Manhattan's Grace Church and then with the Bretton Woods Boy Singers. After graduation from the Choate School, L. attended the Curtis Institute of Music for two years and later the Juilliard School of Music. L. became interested in traditional folk songs and studied briefly under the director of the English Folk Dance and Song Society. His interest in folk songs has been wide ranging, including Appalachian folk songs, Scottish ballads, and AFRICAN AMERICAN spirituals.

In 1953, L. began his professional career in music working with children as the director of the music department of the Potomac School in Washington, D.C. L. has also been an instructor at a number of colleges and universities and has been an artist-lecturer for the Association of American Colleges. As a musician L. has given concerts throughout the United States and abroad. In 1957, recognizing the need for communities to come together in celebration, L. organized the "Christmas Revels." This combination of singing and merrymaking traces back to ancient festivals that marked the solstice. These much anticipated events occur in a number of cities each winter and spring and emphasize audience participation to the delight of young children. In 1985, L. published *The Christmas Revels Songbook.*

L.'s strong connection to folk song brought him to writing for children. *Frog Went a Courting* (1955) was L.'s first retelling of a folk song in a PICTURE BOOK format. Feodor ROJANKOVSKY's humorous ILLUSTRATIONS earned this book the 1956 CALDECOTT MEDAL. L. did a number of other successful retellings including *Ol' Dan Tucker* (1963) and *Oh, a Hunting We Will Go* (1974) and *Over in the Meadow* (1957). L. has been praised for his choice of folk songs that work well in the picture-book format. Recognizing the strong folk culture of children, L. worked with his daughter Carol collecting material from playgrounds across the United States. Together they wrote *Shimmy Shimmy Coke-Ca-Pop!: A Collection of City Children's Street Games and Rhymes* (1973). Whether working as a teacher, a writer, or as a musician, L. has always encouraged participation and a sense of belonging with the audience. The building of community through song has been the hallmark of his life.

FURTHER WORKS: *The Swapping Boy,* 1960; *Jim Along Josie,* 1970; *St. George and the Dragon,* 1972; *Hot Cross Buns and Other Old Street Cries,* 1978; *What a Morning!: The Christmas Story in Black Spirituals,* 1987; *The Revels Garland of Song: In Celebration of Spring, Summer and Autumn,* 1996

BIBLIOGRAPHY: Silvey, Anita, ed., *Children's Books and Their Creators,* 1995; *Something about the Author,* vol. 6, and vol. 68; *Third Book of Jr. Authors and Illustrators,* 1972

DEDE SMALL

LANGTON, Jane
Author, b. 30 December 1922, Boston, Massachusetts

A YOUNG ADULT author, L. did not consider writing books for young adults until she began reading to her two sons. Since that time, she has become not only a writer, but a writing teacher as well. L.'s books have a distinctly American character, the majority take place in the town of Concord, Massachusetts, a place she knows well. One such book is the NEWBERY MEDAL Honor Book, *The Fledgling* (1980), which tells the story of a young girl who dreams of flying. The sequel, *The Fragile Flag* (1984) is based on L.'s own participation in war and nuclear weapons protests. *The Diamond in the Window* (1962) and *The Swing in the Summerhouse* (1967) feature time travel within the historic and symbolic Concord setting.

Her writing career also includes formerly serving as a *New York Times* book reviewer. L. spends time writing and illustrating adult mystery novels as well. These books include *Emily Dickinson Is Dead* (1984), and *The Dante Game* (1991). L. has also written one book for young children, *The Queen's Necklace* (1994), a FAIRY TALE about a prince searching for a princess to marry.

FURTHER WORKS: *Her Majesty, Grace Jones,* 1961; *The Astonishing Stereoscope,* 1971

BIBLIOGRAPHY: *Something about the Author,* vol. 68, 1992

DENISE P. BEASLEY

LARRICK, Nancy
Author, anthologist, b. 28 December 1910, Winchester, Virginia

L. is a major contributor to children's literature, POETRY, and the field of reading education. She received a B.A. from Goucher College in 1930, her M.A. from Columbia University in 1937, and her Ed.D. from New York University in 1955. L.'s career touched many aspects of the world of children and their literature. Her teaching experiences ranged from public schools to college. She also held numerous positions of leadership in education in the areas of U.S. government, publishing, and the INTERNATIONAL READING ASSOCIA-TION. L.'s works regarding children and their reading have been published in *Saturday Review, Parents'* magazine, and *Reading Teacher. A Parent's Guide to Children's Reading* (1958, revised 1982) served as a classic work of information to develop young children's reading ability and an appreciation of quality literature. Another classic of L.'s is an eye-opening study she conducted in the midsixties. Her findings, published in *Saturday Review's* "All-White World of Children's Books" (1965), revealed that in spite of the plea for representation of diverse races in children's books, they were almost nonexistent. As a noted anthologist, L. edited more than twenty titles of poetry for children and YOUNG ADULTS including the following books: *The Night of the Whippoorwill: Poems Selected by L.* (1992); *Mice Are Nice: Poems Compiled by Nancy L.* (1990); *Cats Are Cats* (1988); and *When the Dark Comes Dancing* (1983). L.'s direct experience with children gave her background to create authentic anthologies. For example, in *Green Is Like a Meadow of Grass,* she included children's reactions to nature. Her collection in *I Heard a Scream in the Street* came from teacher workshops, class magazines, student newspapers, and a college poetry-writing class. The poems reflect the high emotions and insight evident in the students' writings. *Piper, Pipe That Song Again* (1965) is an engaging title chosen by a group of second-and-third graders that L. asked to find an inviting title for the book. The children selected it from a lyric in William Blake's *Songs of Innocence.*

L. received the Founders Day Award at New York University in 1955, the certificate of merit from the International Reading Association, and the Drexel University certificate for contribution to children's literature in 1977. That same year she was named to the Reading Hall of Fame. L. was a founder and the second president of the International Reading Association.

FURTHER WORKS: *Poetry for Holidays,* 1966; *Piping Down the Valley Wild,* 1967; *The Wheels of the Bus Go round and Round,* 1972; *Bring Me All of Your Dreams,* 1980; *To Ride a Butterfly,* 1991

BIBLIOGRAPHY: *Contemporary Authors, New Revision Series,* vol. 1, 1981; Cullinan, B. E., *Literature and the Child,* 1989; L., Nancy, "The All-White World of Children's Books," *Saturday Review,* Sept. 11, 1965; *Saturday Review,* Jan. 24, 1970 book review, p. 68; Silvey, Anita, ed., *Children's Books and Their Creators,* 1995; Sutherland, Zena, "Children as Poets," *Saturday Review,* August 21, 1971

NANCY HORTON

LARSSON, Carl
Illustrator, b. 28 May 1853, Gamla Stan, Stockholm, Sweden; d. 22 January 1919, Falun, Sweden

Despite a childhood in poverty, this Swedish artist, muralist, and illustrator attended Stockholm's Royal Academy of Fine Arts where he was promoted within the academy to several schools during his years there. He was employed by various publications at this time and eventually illustrated Hans Christian ANDERSEN'S *FAIRY TALES* as well as a series of Finnish novels, Tales of an Army Doctor. He won a Royal Medal for his art at this time. After his marriage he turned to nature, home, and his large family for subject matter. *A Home* (1899), inspired by nature, family living, and a cottage the family inherited and *A Farm* (1906), honoring Swedish peasants' labor, were published and later translated into English. *A Home* was chosen as a 1974 *New York Times* Best Illustrated Children's Books of the Year, and *A Farm* was selected for the 1977 Children's Book Showcase. His self-illustrated books were nonfiction.

FURTHER WORKS: *De Mina, My Loved One,* 1895; *At Solsidan, House in the Sun,* 1910; *Andras Barn, Other People's Children,* 1913

BIBLIOGRAPHY: *Something About the Author,* vol. 35, 1985; Carl L., *Jag,* 1932; *The World of Carl L.,* transl. Allan Ladke Rice, 1982

JANELLE B. MATHIS

LASKER, Joe
Author, illustrator, b. 26 June 1919, Brooklyn, New York

L.'s subjects, both as writer and illustrator, depict the variety of possible worlds experienced by individuals throughout history. L. earned recognition for his art work in primary school, having spent his preschool years creating chalk sketches in his tenement neighborhood. Later, while still in high school, L. attended Cooper Union. After

World War II, he began his career as a painter, winning the Prix de Rome fellowship (1950, 1951), and a Guggenheim fellowship (1954).

L.'s first book of ILLUSTRATIONS were for Miriam Schlein's *The Sun, the Wind, the Sea, and the Rain* (1960). His first writing effort, *Mothers Can Do Anything* (1972) was in response to feminist criticism that PICTURE BOOKS help to instill sexism. *Merry Ever after: The Story of Two Medieval Weddings* (1976), an award winning book, is exemplary of L.'s work. This story of medieval nuptial celebrations by different classes—gentry and serfs—provides readers with excellent information and engrossing paintings. *The Boy Who Loved Music* (1979), written by his son, David Lasker, and illustrated by L., was an ALA Notable Book (1979). L.'s oil paintings are held in numerous permanent collections, including the Whitney Museum of American Art.

AWARDS: AMERICAN LIBRARY ASSOCIATION Notable Book Award (1977) for *Merry Ever After: The Story of Two Medieval Weddings*

FURTHER WORKS: *He's My Brother,* 1974; *The Strange Voyage of Neptune's Car,* 1977; *The Great Alexander the Great,* 1983; *A Tournament of Knights,* 1986

BIBLIOGRAPHY: *Something about the author Autobiography Series,* vol. 17, 1974, and vol. 83, 1996

FRANCISCA GOLDSMITH

LASKY, Kathryn
Author, b. 24 June, 1944, Indianapolis, Indiana

L., author of juvenile fiction and nonfiction, grew up creating stories. L. received her B.A. from the University of Michigan in 1966. In 1971, she married Christopher Knight, a photographer with whom she collaborates. L. then completed her M.A. at Wheelock College in 1977. Included among her PICTURE BOOKS is a photo essay called *A Baby for Max,* which documents her son, Maxwell's, reactions to his mother's pregnancy and the arrival of his sister, in real life Meribah.

L. is best known for her juvenile nonfiction books, many of which feature photographs by Knight. Many of her nonfiction works are how-to books dealing with arts and traditional crafts, such as doll making and weaving. L. received the *Boston Globe–Horn Book* Award for *The Weaver's Gift* in 1981. *The Weaver's Gift* also received

an AMERICAN LIBRARY ASSOCIATION (ALA) Notable Book Citation in 1981. Other citations include *The Night Journey* (1981), *Sugaring Time* (1984), and *Puppeteer* (1985). *The Night Journey,* which tells the story of a Jewish family's escape from Czarist Russia, won the National Jewish Book Award in 1982 from the Jewish Book Council and the Sydney TAYLOR Book Award in 1981. *Beyond the Divide* (1983), *Prank* (1984), and *Pageant* (1986) earned ALA Best Books for YOUNG ADULTS Citations. *Sugaring Time* became a NEW-BERY MEDAL Honor Book in 1984. L. won the Children's Book Guild Nonfiction Award in 1986 for a body of work. The Pratt Library's Young Adult Advisory Board awarded L. the Youth-to-Youth Books Award. She also received an Imagination and Survival Citation in 1988 for *The Bone Wars.*

L. does extensive research for her novels, which often contain ethnic, historical, or religious elements that inspire or challenge characters. Critics praise L. for her eloquent, clear style, well-developed characterizations, and use of vivid imagery. L. is also the author of a popular adult detective series featuring a children's award-winning book illustrator as the main character/detective, Calista Jacobs.

FURTHER WORKS: *Agatha's Alphabet,* 1975; *The Weaver's Gift,* 1981; *The Night Journey,* 1981; *Dollmaker,* 1981; *Sugaring Time,* 1983; *Beyond the Divide,* 1983; *A Baby for Max,* 1984; *Prank,* 1984; *Puppeteer,* 1985; *Pageant,* 1986; *The Bone Wars,* 1988; *Dinosaur Dig,* 1990; *Double Trouble Squared,* 1991; *Days of the Dead,* 1994; *Marven of the Great North Woods,* 1994; *Robin Hood,* 1998; *Baby Love,* 2001

BIBLIOGRAPHY: Brown, Joanne, *Presenting Kathryn L.* 1998; *Children's Literature Review,* vol. 11, 1986; *Something about the Author,* vol. 69, 1982

JODI PILGRIM

LATHAM, Jean Lee
Author, b. 19 April 1902, Buckhannon, West Virginia; d. 13 June 1995, Coral Gables, Florida

Even when she was young, L., author of biographies, novels, plays, and POETRY for children and adults, told stories to her brothers. Although she began writing radio plays in the 1920s and became editor-in-chief of Dramatic Publishing Company, she is best known for her children's biographies of American scientists and inventors. She was always curious about the people who were pioneers in the fields of science and technology and enjoyed researching their lives and understanding their passions. Her best known book, *Carry on, Mr. Bowditch* (1955) won the NEWBERY MEDAL. In this BIOGRAPHY of a young math genius who became a navigational genius as well, she was able to explain to children difficult scientific principles while keeping them entertained with a good story. In her Newbery Medal acceptance speech she said, "It seems to me a writer has a personal Geiger counter that, on occasions, says to him: Dig here for treasure." She found treasure in the lives of Nathaniel Bowditch, Eli Whitney, and others like them.

BIBLIOGRAPHY: HOPKINS, Lee Bennett, *Pauses: Autobiographical Reflections of 101 Creators of Children's Books,* 1995 *Something about the Author,* vol. 2., 1971, vol. 68, 1992; Newbery Medal speech, THE KERLAN COLLECTION

REBECCA RAPPORT

LATHROP, Dorothy P.

Author, illustrator, b. 16 April 1891, Albany, New York; d. 30 December 1980, Falls Village, Connecticut

L. was destined to have a career in art and literature; her grandfather owned a bookstore and her sister was a sculptor. At Teachers College, Columbia University, L. studied drawing, and wrote ANIMAL STORIES and FAIRY TALES. Her career began in 1918 when she worked as a writer and teacher in Albany, New York. Her first published work, which she illustrated and wrote, *The Fairy Circus* (1931), was a NEWBERY MEDAL Honor Book. Her beautiful paintings, and pen-and-ink drawings included in *Animals of the BIBLE* by Helen Dean Fish, are her greatest achievement; the book was awarded the very first CALDECOTT MEDAL in 1938. Before writing and illustrating her own works, L. illustrated several books for Walter DE LA MARE such as: The *Three Mulla-Mulgars* (1919), *Down-a-Down Derry* (1922), *Crossings* (1923), *Dutch Cheese* (1931), and *Mr. Bumps and His Monkey* (1942). Her last-known published work is *Follow the Brook* (1960).

BIBLIOGRAPHY: HOPKINS, Lee Bennett, *Pauses: Autobiographical Reflections of 101 Creators of Children's Books,* 1995; Viguers, Ruth Hill, comp., *Illustrators of Children's Books, 1946–56,* 1958

DENISE P. BEASLEY

LATINA/O LITERATURE

Among the early settlers to build their homes in what later became the United States were many who spoke Spanish. Along with their language, they brought with them a rich oral literature. As they established the cities of St. Augustine and Tampa in Florida, settled along the Mississippi or in the lands we know today as New Mexico, Arizona, Colorado, Texas, and California, some of their old legends and stories took on new settings and characters. And just as new children were born to these settlers, children who carried the blend of Indigenous, African, and Spanish roots in their blood, new tales were born as well.

La Edad de Oro (The golden age) published in 1898 was a literary magazine "for the boys and girls of the Americas," written solely by José Marti, Cuban poet and spiritual leader. Although only four issues were published, they were later reprinted as a book, which is still in print today. It is recognized as the beginning of Latin American children's literature. The body of literature written by Latinos, people of Spanish-speaking ancestry who live in the United States, is diverse and growing. It includes works written originally in Spanish and works written originally in English. Some works have been published simultaneously in both languages, or later translated, while others have not.

During the first seventy-five years of the twentieth century, literature about Latino themes was minimal. In 1966, Nancy LARRICK denounced the all-white world of American children's literature; Latinos were among those whose voices were absent. Latino themes are prevalent now although Latino voices seldom appear. A growing MULTICULTURAL awareness, the increasing number of Latinos, and the visibility that Latinos have achieved have all drawn a number of non–Latino writers to Latino themes.

In 1932, Pura BELPRÉ, a Puerto Rican librarian who spent many years as a storyteller at the New York Public Library, published *Perez and Martina: A Puerto Rican Folktale.* In California, in the early 1970s, the Mexican-American writer

Ernesto Galarza self-published *Colección Mini-libros,* a series of nearly hand-crafted books in English, Spanish, and bilingual editions. Of special interest is his MOTHER GOOSE *in the Rio Grande,* (1974) where the traditional nursery rhymes take on a Mexican character.

In 1976, a handful of enthusiasts founded the International Association for Children's Literature in Spanish. The Association's first project was to invite authors, illustrators, specialists, teachers, and librarians from the Spanish-speaking world to gather in San Francisco, California, for a conference where Pura Belpré was honored with an award for her pioneering contributions in the field.

In 1981, Sylvia Cavazos Pena, an active member of the IACLS, edited *Kikiri,* which was soon followed by *Cuenta-catón,* two bilingual anthologies of Latino writers published by Arte Público Press in Houston. This was a significant first attempt to gather together the writing of Latino authors of children's literature and to give recognition to their work.

In 1988, Alma Flor ADA initiated a summer course entitled "Children's Literature in Spanish for Bilingual Students" at the Universidad Complutense in Madrid; such courses have since proliferated. Presentations on Latino children's literature are becoming more frequent at regional and national conferences, and there is a Center for the Study of Books Written in Spanish at the California State University at Dominguez Hill. In 1995 the Reforma group of the AMERICAN LIBRARY ASSOCIATION established the Pura Belpré Biannual Award for children's books written and/or illustrated by Latinos. The cry for authenticity was heard and led to the demand for Spanish children's literature. Latino children, in turn, had the opportunity to see themselves portrayed in books they read. Their families were valued; their culture was praised, talked about, and "discovered." At this point in history, Latino literature for children is helping to shape a wider, shared history and experience among various cultural groups. It is helping create, through a common language, a sense of that "Patria Grande" of larger Latin American unity dreamed of by Marti.

Among the Latino authors publishing for children in the United States today are some authors of adult literature who occasionally write for children, like Sandra CISNEROS, author of *Woman Hollering Creek and Other Stories* (1990) and *The House on Mango Street* (1984). Others write for both adults and children, such as Rudolfo ANAYA (*Farolitos of Christmas,* 1995). Others have devoted most of their creative energy to writing for children. The wealth of writers published today represent the variety of Latino cultures: Mexican-American (Gary SOTO), Puerto Rican (Nicholasa MOHR and Piri Thomas), Cuban (Hilda Perera and Lucia M. Gonzales), Colombian (Leila Torres), Guatemalan (Omar Castaneda).

The themes portray the realities of Latino life and values. An abundance of legends and traditional tales keep traditions alive by sharing Latino heritage. Some books affirm daily experiences, and the way experiences shape identity, as evidenced in *Vejigante Masquerader* (1993) by Lulu DELACRE D. H. Figueredo's *When This World Was New* (1999) and George ANCONA's photographic journals *Charro* (1999) *Barrio* (1998), *The Pinata Maker* (1994) and *Pablo Remembers* (1993). A theme of racism and discrimination underlies the story of *Felita* (1979) by Nicholasa Mohr, a girl who does not feel fully at home in New York or Puerto Rico. Américo Saliz experiences racial prejudice at school until a Latino poet visits her school and inspires her with poems and stories in *America Is Her Home* by Luis J. Rodriguez (1998). The rivalry between the long-established Chicano and the recently arrived Mexican is shown in *Friends from the Other Side* (1993) by Gloria Anzaldua. The suffering created by the loss of one's identity, as expressed in one's name, is central to *My Name Is Maria Isabel* (1998), by Alma Flor Ada.

Hispanic literature has a long tradition of using memoirs to offer models to children and the need to explore their place in the world (for example, J. R. Jiménez, A. Zamora Vicente, T. de La Parra, N. Lange, R. Mendez Capote) make memoir a preferred genre among Latino writers. It is a genre whose audiences escape narrow boundaries, to reach readers of all ages. Contemporary examples include Julia Alvarez, *How the García Girls Lost their Accent* (1991); Sandra Cisneros, *The House on Mango Street* (1984); Judith Ortiz Cofer, *Silent Dancing* (1991); Nicholasa Mohr, *In My Own Words: Growing up inside the Sanctuary of My Imagination* (1994); Ernesto

Galarza, *Barrio Boy* (1971); Victor Martinez, *Parrot in the Oven: Mi Vida* (1996); Alma Flor Ada, *Where the Flame Trees Bloom* (1994) and *Under the Royal Palms* (1998) and Gary SOTO, *Too Many Tamales* (1993). Francisco Jiménez has recently published *La Mariposa* (1998), a set of stories about his own childhood in a migrant farmworker's family. Alma Flor Ada has published an ABC book of poems about the fields, *Gathering the Sun* (1997). Both have been illustrated by Simon Silva, using bold and powerful colors and drawing on the passion of his own experience as a migrant child.

The 1998 *Boston Globe–Horn Book* Award to Francisco Jiménez recognizes the author's sensitively evoked childhood experiences as a member of a Mexican migrant farmworking family. In his acceptance speech for *The Circuit: Stories from the Life of a Migrant Child* (1997/1999), Jiménez said that in his writing "I hope to give readers insight into the lives of migrant farmworker families and their children . . . their courage, their hopes and dreams for a better life for their children and their children's children, give meaning to the 'American dream.' Their story *is* the American story." The same year Juan Felipe Herrera was chosen to receive the Ezra Jack KEATS New Writer Award for his book, *Calling the Doves* (1997).

Art has always been a very important element of Latino culture. Some renowned artists are Antonio Martorell (Puerto Rican), Felipe Davalos (Mexican), Enrique Sanchez (Dominican), and Carmen Lomas Garza (Chicana). David DIAZ is a 1995 CALDECOTT MEDAL winner for his illustrations in Eve BUNTING's *Smoky Nights*. His illustration for Gary Soto's *Neighborhood Odes: Poems* (1992) universalizes the joys of childhood through experiences in the Hispanic community. In *Going Home* (Bunting, 1996), Diaz captures the joyous reunion of a migrant working family when they return to their Mexican village and the wrenching ambivalence of children living in two worlds.

Some well-known Latino poets are also writing for children: Pat MORA explores our relationship with nature in *The Desert Is My Mother* (1994), Gary Soto draws abundantly from his childhood experiences in Fresno, California, in *Neighborhood Odes* (illustrated by Diaz, 1992), and Francisco X. Alarcon shares the joy of daily

life in *Laughing Tomatoes*. Juan Felipe Herrera, noted Mexican-American poet, writes of his childhood feelings of alienation in *The Upside Down Boy/El Niño de Cabege* (2000), a bilingual memoir in poetry. Music has also contributed to bringing poetry to life for children: Jose Luis Orozco has collected traditional children's FOLKLORE, and Suni Paz has set the work of some of the best Latino poets to music through her original compositions.

Yet the richness of traditional Hispanic culture, with its blend of Indigenous, African, and Spanish cultural elements, and the complex reality of Latinos in the United States are only barely tapped by all of these excellent efforts. All children deserve literature that reflects the rich Hispanic tradition of stories and folklore, as well as exploring the multifaceted experience of Latinos in the United States.

ALMA FLOR ADA AND F. ISABEL CAMPOY

(See also MULTICULTURAL LITERATURE)

LATTIMORE, Deborah Nourse
Author, illustrator, b. 16 May 1949, Beverly Hills, California

L. was reared in an eccentric but culturally lively household in Beverly Hills. This environment sparked a lifelong fascination with ancient cultures that is reflected in her growing body of exquisitely illustrated PICTURE BOOKS. L., who has a degree in art history from UCLA where she also studied Egyptology, has done graduate work in pre–Columbian, Egyptian, and classical art. Typically, she chooses a different culture as the setting for each of her books: the Tokugawa era of Japan for The *Fool and the Phoenix* (1997), ancient Egypt for *The Winged Cat*, thirteenth century China for her PEN Award–winning title, *The Dragon's Robe* (1990). For each book, L. writes an original text and creates illustrations in the style of art that is the setting's hallmark. The illuminations for the ancient–Celtic *Book of Kells*, for example, provided the aesthetic inspiration for *The Sailor Who Captured the Sea*. L.'s robust sense of HUMOR is revealed in three of her books: a MOVABLE BOOKS history of underclothing *I Wonder What's under There?* (1998), *CinderHazel* (1997), a wacky retelling of the traditional Cinderella tale, and an antic story of eighteenth-century France, The *Lady with the Ship on Her Head* (1990), a READING RAINBOW selection.

FURTHER WORKS: *The Flame of Peace*, 1987; *Frida Maria*, 1994; *Arabian Nights*, 1995; *Medusa*, 2000

BIBLIOGRAPHY: Cart, Michael, Interview with the author, September 15, 1998; *Seventh Book of Junior Authors and Illustrators*, 1996; *Twentieth Century Children's Writers*, 1989

MICHAEL CART

LATTIMORE, Eleanor Frances
Author, illustrator, b. 1904, Shanghai, China; d. Date unknown 1986 Raleigh, North Carolina

L. moved to the United States at the age of sixteen. She studied art at the California School of Arts, the Art Students League, and the Grand Central School of Arts in New York. After her marriage to Robert Armstrong Andrews, she made her home in South Carolina. Her self-illustrated books include *The Bittern's Nest* (1962) and *The Two Helens* (1967). L.'s early books were set in China, based on her childhood memories, and presented realistic pictures of warm, loving families. *Little Pear* (1931) was the first of her many stories set in China about everyday events in a little boy's life for beginning readers. It presented a universal portrait of childhood within the context of an authentic Chinese setting.

FURTHER WORKS: *Bayou Boy*, 1946; *Bells for a Chinese Donkey*, 1951; *The Chinese Daughter*, 1960; *More about Little Pear*, 1971

BIBLIOGRAPHY: Ward, M. E., D. A. Marquardt, N. Dolan, and D. Eaton, eds., *Authors of Books for Young People*, 3rd ed., 1990

MARY ARIAIL BROUGHTON

LAUBER, Patricia
Author, b. 5 February 1924, New York City

L. became a writer as soon as she was able to make letters, having discovered that she could provide for her endless desire for stories by creating them herself. She pursues whatever topics pique her interest, many of which are in the areas of natural science and history. After graduating from Wellesley College (1945), L. worked as a writer and editor for both adult and juvenile magazines. She began her prolific career as a book author in 1954, when she published *Magic up

Your Sleeve. Seed: Pop, Stick, Glide (1981) and *Journey to the Planets* (1982) were nominated for the American Book Award in the category of children's nonfiction. *Tales Mummies Tell* (1985), *Volcano: The Eruption and Healing of Mount St. Helens* (1986), *From Flower to Flower* (1986), and *The News about Dinosaurs* (1989) received citations as a New York Academy of Sciences Honor Book (respectively in 1986, 1987, 1988, and 1990). *Volcano: The Eruption and Healing of Mount St. Helens* was also named a NEWBERY MEDAL Honor Book by the AMERICAN LIBRARY ASSOCIATION in 1987. In 1988, L. was cited by the American Nature Study Society, which granted her the Eva L. Gordon Children's Science Author Award. L. has also received two ORBIS PICTUS Honor Book citations from the NATIONAL COUNCIL OF TEACHERS OF ENGLISH: for *The News about Dinosaurs*, in 1989, and for *Seeing Earth from Space*, in 1990. In 1992, L. earned the Lifetime Achievement Commendation from the National Forum on Children's Science Books (Carnegie-Mellon University).

L.'s nonfiction broaches topics that range in scale from microscopic to gargantuan, from *Seeds: Pop, Stick, Glide* to *Dinosaurs Walked Here* (1987). In other dimensions, she takes up similar extremes: she moves through time, from antiquity with *Tales Mummies Tell* to the twentieth century with *Lost Star: The Story of Amelia Earhart* (1988); from our own interiors, in *Your Body and How It Works* (1962) to the outer realms of space in *Journey to the Planets* (fourth revised edition, 1993). Her nonfiction is richly illustrated, often with photographs, further impressing upon young readers the veracity and the detail of L.'s narrative.

L. maintains a fully engaged curiosity about the way the world—and the universe—works. Some of her books arise from current events, as when Yellowstone National Park burned (*A Summer of Fire*, 1988). Others develop from longtime personal interests, as did *Cowboys and Cattle Ranching* (1973). In all cases, L.'s enthusiasm for the subject is augmented by her diligence as a researcher and her skill as a writer. Her books are accessible and inviting to children in the elementary grades while providing credible information at a depth that can serve older readers who approach the topic with a little background information. L. mirrors nature's intrinsic orderliness—which presents itself exuberantly and dramatically at some intervals—with an orderly, but enthusiasic, detailing of nature's hows and whys.

When writing of historical people, as she has in *Lost Star* and in *Who Discovered America?: Settlers and Explorers of the New World before the Time of Columbus* (new edition, 1992), L. maintains a narrative voice that is both respectful and lively. Because she selects her own subjects based on what (and who) interests her, these are not formula BIOGRAPHIES, but unique approaches to each subject's experiences.

In addition to her many nonfiction books, L. writes well-regarded humorous novels for children. In a series of novels featuring a dog based on her own pet, L. gives middle-grade readers light entertainment that is well-written and free of trend-inspired backdrops. First introduced in *Clarence, the TV Dog* (1955), this version of the ubiquitous American household animal combines typical dog traits such as loyalty with exaggerated degrees of insight. As with L.'s enthusiasm for volcanoes and forests, her delight in Clarence is infectious for her readers.

L. writes short stories and humorous essays for adult audiences. She also has worked as an editor and consultant for publishers producing series science books for children. The quality of her nonfiction has earned it a place in curricula planned by grade school science teachers, both as primary source reading and as support material.

FURTHER WORKS: *Valiant Scots: People of the Highlands Today*, 1957; *Clarence Goes to Town*, 1957; *The Runaway Flea Circus*, 1958; *Penguins on Parade*, 1958; *Dust Bowl: The Story of Man on the Great Plains*, 1958; *The Quest of Galileo*, 1959; *Our Friend the Forest*, 1959; *Champ, Gallant Collie*, 1960; *The Story of Numbers*, 1961; *Famous Mysteries of the Sea*, 1962; *The Friendly Dolphins*, 1963; *Volcanoes*, 1965; *The Story of Dogs*, 1966; *The Look-It-up Book of Stars and Planets*, 1967; *Bats: Wings in the Night*, 1968; *This Restless Earth*, 1970; *Of Man and Mouse: How House Mice Became Laboratory Mice*, 1971; *Everglades: A Question of Life or Death*, 1973; *Clarence and the Burglar*, 1973; *Life on a Giant Cactus*, 1974; *Too Much Garbage*, 1974; *Great Whales*, 1975; *Tapping Earth's Heat*, 1978; *What's Hatching out of That Egg?* 1979; *Get Ready for Robots!*, 1986; *How We Learned the World Is Round*, 1990; *How Animals Live Where They Do*, 1994

BIBLIOGRAPHY: *Contemporary Authors, New Revision Series*, vol. 38, 1993; Silvey, A., ed., *Children's Books and Their Creators*. 1995; *Something about the Author*, vol 75, 1994

FRANCISCA GOLDSMITH

LAVIES, Bianca
Author, photographer, b. Date unknown, The Hague, Holland

L. is one of a very limited number of people who can claim to have survived two killer-bee attacks, to have slithered among thousands of snakes and to have served as a landing pad for hundreds of monarch butterflies. L. has done each of these things and used her experiences and dramatic photographs in her writing for children.

Born in Holland, L. emigrated to New Zealand as a teenager and worked as a farm hand for a few years. She set sail planning to return to Holland, but after a breakdown at sea and floating adrift for three days, she reached Durban, South Africa. L. entered an article in a writing contest there and after winning the contest was offered a position as yachting reporter for the *Natal Mercury*. L. spent the next seven years writing and taking pictures of yachting events. In 1969 L. set sail across the Atlantic with one American crew member and four cats. Their vessel, the *Apogee*, was a thirty-foot sailboat and was the first fiberglass boat to circumnavigate the world. The media attention greeting their arrival helped to establish a market for L.'s journalism in the U.S. and she was hired by *National Geographic*. L. spent eighteen years at *National Geographic*, first as a writer and then as staff photographer winning several major photographic awards. One of L.'s photographs is in the permanent collection of the International Center of Photography in New York. Many of the books L. later wrote for children had their origins in *National Geographic* articles.

L. left *National Geographic* in 1987 and two years later started writing children's books using her own photographs, which have been praised for their excellence and the unique perspectives they offer. *Tree Trunk Traffic* (1989), one of L.'s first works for children, was a New York Academy of Sciences Children's Book Science Award Honor Book as well as a Children's Choice Book.

Two others, *It's an Armadillo!* (1989) and *A Gathering of Garter Snakes* (1993) were named by the AMERICAN LIBRARY ASSOCIATION as Notable Books of the Year. Many of L.'s books have also been named Outstanding Science Trade Books for Children including *Backyard Hunter: The Praying Mantis* (1990) and *Compost Critters* (1993).

L. spends a great deal of time traveling to schools, talking with students and introducing them to the worlds of writing, photography and adventure.

FURTHER WORKS: *Lily Pad Pond,* 1989; *The Secretive Timber Rattlesnake,* 1990; *Wasps at Home,* 1991; *The Atlantic Salmon,* 1992; *Monarch Butterflies: Mysterious Travelers,* 1992; *Killer Bees,* 1994; *Tundra Swan,* 1994

BIBLIOGRAPHY: *Seventh Book of Junior Authors and Illustrators,* 1996; Source Material provided by Bianca L.

DEDE SMALL

LAWRENCE, Louise (pseud. Elizabeth Rhoda Holden Mace/Elizabeth Rhoda Wintle)

Author; b. 5 June 1943, Leatherhead, England

A popular author of FANTASY and SCIENCE FICTION for YOUNG ADULTS, L. began her career as a librarian. The mother of three children, she began writing in her early twenties as a hobby and a means of escaping the real world in favor of the imaginary worlds of fantasy. Though L.'s writing transports readers to fantastic worlds of the past and future, her characters and their struggles reflect the realities of growing up. L.'s work often features young female protagonists and is marked by strong characterization, rich imagery, and a unique narrative style.

FURTHER WORKS: *Calling B for Butterfly,* 1982; *Children of the Dust,* 1985; *Moonwind,* 1986; *The Warriors of Taan,* 1986, published in the U.S. in 1988; *Ben-Harran's Castle,* 1992, published in the U.S. as *Keeper of the Universe,* 1993; *Patchwork People,* 1994; *Dream-Weaver,* 1996

BIBLIOGRAPHY: *Something about the Author.* vol. 78, 1994; Sullivan, C. W., III., *Science Fiction for Young Readers,* 1993

JENNIFER E. DUNNE

LAWSON, Robert

Author, illustrator, b. 4 October 1892, New York City; d. 26 May 1957, Westport Connecticut

Considered one of the finest American authors and illustrators, L. is one of the few people to win both the NEWBERY MEDAL and the CALDECOTT MEDAL. He studied at the New York School of Fine and Applied Art and worked as a magazine illustrator, greeting card designer, scenery designer, and etcher. L.'s first ILLUSTRATIONS for children's books appeared in 1930 in *The Wee Men of Ballywooden* by Arthur Mason. In 1938 he wrote *Ben and Me,* his first book. This is one of four titles that tell the stories of notable American historical characters (i.e., Benjamin Franklin) through the eyes of their pets. He continued to illustrate and write from the 1930s to the 1950s, producing more than fifty books; many were award winners. L.'s diverse books include factual and fictional accounts of history, ANIMAL tales, American folktales, patriotic stories, and PICTURE BOOKS. The dissimilar temperaments of gentleness and rebellion that he observed in his mom and dad from his childhood are reflected in many of his writings. This theme is evident in the depiction of a pacifist bull in *The Story of Ferdinand* (Munro LEAF, 1936), which also gave L. wide recognition for his black-and-white illustrations. The Caldecott Medal winner *They Were Strong and Good* (1940) is a picture book BIOGRAPHY in which L. uses his ancestors as universal symbols of the people who helped to build America. Some criticism is noted for L.'s treatment of minorities but it is thought that this treatment was a reflection of the attitudes of the times. *At That Time* (1947), L.'s autobiography, was published ten years before his death. After his death, *The Great Wheel* (1957) was published, in which he portrays America as a land of unlimited opportunity. Married to Marie Adams, also an author and illustrator, they named their country home "Rabbit Hill" after L.'s 1944 Newbery Medal-winning title.

AWARDS: AMERICAN LIBRARY ASSOCIATION Caldecott Medal Honor Book (1938) for *Four and Twenty Blackbirds* (1939) for *Wee Gillis* (Helen Dean Fish and Munro Leaf). ALA Caldecott Medal (1941) for *They Were Strong and Good.* ALA Newbery Medal (1945) for *Rabbit Hill.* ALA Newbery Medal Honor Book (1958) for *The Great Wheel.* Lewis CARROLL Shelf Awards (1961) for *Ben and Me* and (1963) for *Rabbit Hill*

FURTHER WORKS: *I Discover Columbus,* 1941; *Mr. Twigg's Mistake,* 1947; *The Fabulous Flight,* 1949; *Smeller Martin,* 1950; *Mr. Revere and I,* 1953; *The Tough Winter,* 1954; *Captain Kidd's*

Cat, 1956; Illustrated only *The Story of Simpson and Sampson,* 1941; *Adam of the Road,* 1942

BIBLIOGRAPHY: *Contemporary Authors,* vol. 118, 1986; Peterson, L. and M. Solt, *Newbery and Caldecott Medal Honor Books,* 1982; *Twentieth Century Writers,* 1995; *Writers for Children,* 1988

NANCY HORTON

LEACH, Maria
Author, folklorist, b. 30 April 1892, Brooklyn, New York; d. 22 May 1977, Barrington, Nova Scotia, Canada

L. earned a B.A. in 1914 from Earlham College, her A.M. in 1917 from the University of Illinois, and studied further at Johns Hopkins University. Her greatest contributions center around her work with FOLKLORE. As one of America's best remembered folklorists, L. compiled and edited one of the first folklore dictionaries, *Funk and Wagnall's Standard Dictionary of Folklore, Mythology, and Legend* (1949; 1984). With her wit and folklike wisdom, she compiled and edited folklore for children including *Noodles, Nitwits, and Numbskulls* (1961), *Whistle in the Graveyard: Folktales to Chill Your Bones* (1974), and *The Lion Sneezed: Folktales and Myths of the Cat* (1977). Her retellings will continue to tickle funny bones and spark the imaginations of readers for many years.

FURTHER WORKS: *The Luck Book,* 1964; *Riddle Me, Riddle Me, Ree,* 1970

BIBLIOGRAPHY: *Something about the Author,* vol. 39, 1985

SHANE RAYBURN

LEAF, Munro
Author, illustrator, b. 4 December 1905, Baltimore, Maryland; d. 21 December 1976, Garrett Park, Maryland

Much of L.'s work was conceived with the intention of educating young people. Many of these books blended HUMOR with instruction, demystifying difficult subject matter, and teaching socially appropriate behavior in painless fashion. However, his reputation as a popular and beloved creator of children's literature rests on the 1936 publication of *The Story of Ferdinand* illustrated by Robert LAWSON's expressive black and white etchings. More than three million copies have

been sold worldwide and Ferdinand's story has been a perennial favorite for more than sixty years.

L. graduated from the University of Maryland in 1927 and received a master's degree from Harvard in 1931. While teaching high school L. was also a manuscript reader at Bobbs-Merrill publishers in New York City. From 1933 to 1939 he was an editor and director at F. A. Stokes, a New York City publisher. In 1934 he began writing both fiction and nonfiction children's books. As a teacher he felt that subject matter could be demystified if it was taught in a humorous manner, whether it was grammar or correct behavior. He also believed that the world would be a better place if young people learned how to act in a socially appropriate manner. Therefore, as an author he tried to educate. Even his fiction had a message.

In 1936, with his friend Robert Lawson, an illustrator, he wrote *Ferdinand,* the story of an introspective, flower-loving bull who refused to go against his nature and enter the bullring to fight. This book established his literary reputation. It tells the story of a gentle bull who prefers sitting by himself under a cork tree, rather than engage in the rough-and-tumble play of his fellow bulls. His loving mother acquiesces with a sigh. When he is bitten by a bee his fierce yelp is mistaken for bravado and he is carted off to the bull ring where he simply sits and smells the ladies' flowers. Although Ferdinand was not lacking in strength, he refused to fulfill his preordained role, to kill or be killed as the climax of an annual spectacle. Ferdinand could not go against his nature and like the Cowardly Lion in *The Wizard of Oz* (BAUM), he was different from the others of his species. *Ferdinand* reveals that it is socially acceptable not to be a fighter, and the age-old ritual of fighting is seen as pointless.

Unintentionally, L. had created what later became known as an antihero, for Ferdinand behaved like a flower child in a nonviolent-resistance movement. Although L. claimed to have only created Ferdinand as a vehicle to show how individuality can be respected, many groups believed otherwise. Freudian analysts saw the story as an attack on male aggressiveness. However, in 1936 many people in the U.S. supported "peace at any price" and they saw *Ferdinand* as a great antiwar book, but the liberals fighting the Franco fascists in Spain felt that in being antiwar, Ferdinand was fascist propaganda against their involvement in the war. In Nazi Germany, Hitler called *Ferdinand* "subversive" and had it publicly burned. In Stalin's Soviet Republic, it was the only noncommunist publication allowed to be read to children. In spite of its controversial nature, *The Story of Ferdinand* was soon published in sixty languages, and DISNEY made it the subject of an Oscar-winning film. Following the devastation of World War II, society's position on war changed and *Ferdinand* was recognized as an international symbol of peace. The names of L. and Lawson were put forward for the Nobel Peace Prize.

In 1938, again with Lawson, he created *Wee Gillis,* a CALDECOTT MEDAL Honor Book (1939), about a Scottish orphan who had to choose on which side of his family to make his home. Then, with Ludwig BEMELMANS, he wrote *Novelle* (1937), a story about a dachshund who learns to appreciate his unusual shape. In 1928, L. wrote *Listen Little Girl,* a handbook for women considering employment in New York City. The Can Be Fun SERIES was published beginning in 1934 with *Manners Can Be Fun,* followed in 1938 by *Safety Can Be Fun,* 1943 with *Health Can Be Fun,* 1949 with *Arithmetic Can Be Fun, History Can Be Fun* in 1950, *Reading Can Be Fun* in 1953, and *Science Can Be Fun* in 1958. The series was highly successful and praised for the clarity of writing as well as its sound principles. Other notable books of instruction were *Fair Play* (1939), describing what a democracy is; *A Wartime Handbook for Young Americans* (1942) and *Boo, Who Used to Be Scared of the Dark* (1948) a book that sympathetically attempted, using humor as a device, to reduce the anxiety connected to one of childhood's great terrors.

In 1941, L. wrote *Who Cares? I Do!,* a work that tried to improve children's ecological awareness. The book, though highly controversial, was an immediate success. Even Eleanor Roosevelt referred to it in her column. Within weeks it topped the best-seller list; L. was amazed at its success. He claimed to have written it in just forty minutes as a vehicle for Robert Lawson.

AWARDS: AMERICAN LIBRARY ASSOCIATION Caldecott Medal Honor Book (1939) for *Wee Gillis* (Robert Lawson, illus.)

FURTHER WORKS: Author and illustrator: *Grammar Can Be Fun,* 1934, reissued 1962; *Robert Francis Weatherbee,* 1935; *Fair Play,* 1937; *The Watchbirds,* 1939; *More Watchbirds,* 1940; *Gordon the Goat,* 1944; Author: *The Story of Ferdinand,* Robert Lawson, illus. 1936, reissued 1969; *Noodle,* Ludwig BEMELMANS, illus. 1937, reissued 1969; *Wee Gillis,* Robert Lawson, illus. 1938, reissued 1967; *Listen, Little Girl,* Dick Rese, illus. 1938; Aesop's *Fables,* Robert Lawson, illus. 1941; *Boo, Who Used to Be Scared of the Dark,* 1948

BIBLIOGRAPHY: *Children's Literature Review,* vol. 25, 1991; HOPKINS, Lee Bennett, *Pauses: Autobiographical Reflections of 101 Creators of Children's Books,* 1995; Schwarz, J. and C., *The Picture Book Comes of Age,* 1991; Silvey, Anita, ed., *Children's Books and Their Creators,* 1995; *Something about the Author,* vol. 20, 1980; *Twentieth Century Children's Writers,* 1978

JUDY LIPSITT

LEAR, Edward
Author, illustrator, b. 12 May 1812, Holloway, England; d. 29 January 1888, San Remo, Italy

L. was the twentieth of twenty-one children. When his father, a stockbroker, became bankrupt in 1816, L. lived with his sister Anne, who looked after him throughout his childhood. L. suffered epileptic symptoms and depression at age seven. Anne tutored L. at home until, at age eleven, he went to school. In 1827, L. began drawing for money and food. He earned his living at age fifteen with zoological ILLUSTRATIONS, landscapes, and travel books. Lord Stanley asked L. to draw for him at Knowsley, England, in 1832. In the earl's nursery, L. entertained children with his writings, which were the beginnings of *The Book of Nonsense,* the collection for which he is best remembered. Published in 1845, it was illustrated with L.'s own drawings as were all his children's books. A year later he published *Illustrated Excursions* in Italy, which resulted in a summons by Queen Victoria to give her drawing lessons. After traveling awhile, L. received an acceptance at the Royal Academy. He published *Journal of a Landscape Painter in Greece and Albania* as a result of his Mediterranean journey. Many of L.'s books were written under the pseudonym Derry Down Derry. L. is best remembered for popularizing the limerick form and nonsense verse such as "The Owl and the Pussycat." Many of his works have undergone numerous publishings and are still widely enjoyed by adults and children.

FURTHER WORKS: *A Book of Nonsense*, 1846; *Nonsense Songs, Stories, Botany, and Alphabets*, 1871; *More Nonsense Pictures, Rhymes, and Botany*, 1872; *Laughable Lyrics: A Fourth Book of Nonsense Poems, Songs, Botany, and Music*, 1877; *How Pleasant to Know Mr. L.*, 1882; *A Book of Limericks*, 1888; *Teapots and Quails, and Other New Nonsense*, 1953; *Penned and Illustrated by Edward L., Himself*, newly found manuscript—1965; other items illustrated by L. include *Illustrations for the Family of Psittacidae, or, Parrots*, 1832; *Gleanings from the Menagerie at Knowsley Hall*, 1846; *Tortoises, Terrapins, and Turtles*, 1912; *The Lear Colored Bird Book for Children*, 1912

BIBLIOGRAPHY: Cott, Jonathan, *Pipers at the Gates of Dawn: The Wisdom of Children's Literature*, 1981; Doyle, Brian, ed., *The Who's Who of Children's Literature*, 1968; *Something about the Author*, vol. 18, 1980

JODI PILGRIM

LEE, Dennis

Poet, b. 31 August 1939, Toronto, Ontario, Canada

Publishing his first poem at the age of four, L. is considered the most popular CANADIAN children's poet. He received his bachelor and masters degree from the University of Toronto and lectured for three years at Victoria College. In 1967 he founded the House of Anansi Press with Dave Godfrey and worked as chief editor until the early 1970s. L. was inspired to write POETRY for children and published *Wiggle to the Laundromat*, his first book of verse for children, in 1970. When asked to share his concept of the essence of children's poetry he stated, "I can't . . . The essence of children's poetry went clean out of my head about two years after I started writing those poems [nursery rhymes for my children]. All I recall is that I used to know what constitutes a good kid's poem and now that I write and read them aloud all the time, I don't. At least not the way I used to . . . . Something, I began to realize, was out of synch. There seemed to be no direct connection between knowing what a poem should be and being able to write it. The key to writing for children . . . is to get in touch with one of those children in myself and then follow his nose, going wherever the children's interests lead me. . . . That often leads to neat poems." His second

book, *Alligator Pie* (1974), won the Canadian Association of Children's Librarians Best Book Medal, English Medal, Canadian Library Association Award and was on the Hans Christian ANDERSEN Honor List. Using narrative poetry, poems based on literary characters such as Winnie-the-Pooh and Peter Rabbit, he makes use of Canadian place and street names.

He was awarded the Canadian Library Association Award, Ruth Schwartz Award and INTERNATIONAL BOARD ON BOOKS FOR YOUNG PEOPLE Honor Book for *Garbage Delight* (1977) a book of poetry for primary children. In 1983 he published *Jelly Belly*, a volume of original nursery rhymes for very young children and babies. Reminiscent of MOTHER GOOSE, the book contains lullabies, finger plays, activity poems and games that provide visual and verbal amusement.

The Ice Cream Store (1991), a second volume of verse for young children, won the Vicky Metcalf Award, Canadian Author's Association with Mr. Christie's Book Award. Critics have hailed *The Ice Cream Store* as a "brand new Canadian classic."

L. explains that "to write as an adult for children means reconnecting with the capacity to feel directly. It means experiencing a partial integration of the adult and the children in oneself." Poems are always waiting to be written and this compels him to write.

BIBLIOGRAPHY: *Dictionary of Literary Biography: Canadian Writers since 1960*, vol. 53, 1986; *Fiction, FOLKLORE, FANTASY and Poetry for Children, 1876–1985*, vol. 1, 1986; Senick, G. J. ed., *Children's Literature Review*, vol. 3, 1978; Silvey, A. ed., *Children's Books and Their Creators*, 1995; *Something about the Author*, vol. 14, 1978, and vol. 102, 1999

IRVYN G. GILBERTSON

LEE, Mildred

Author, b. 19 February 1908, Blockton, Alabama

L. grew up in small towns across the Southern U.S. and began writing as a young child. She notes that her characters come from the real people she knows as well as from her own imagination. *The Rock and the Willow* (1963) received the 1964 Child Study Association Children's Book Award.

FURTHER WORKS: *Honor Sands,* 1966; *The Skating Rink,* 1969; *Sycamore Year,* 1974

BIBLIOGRAPHY: *Something about the Author,* vol. 6, 1974; *Third Book of Junior Authors,* 1972

                                    SANDRA IMDIEKE

LEEDY, Loreen

Author, illustrator, b. 15 June 1959, Wilmington, Delaware

L.'s first career as an artist was as a jewelry designer, but after meeting an author/illustrator at the age of twenty-five, she decided that she would like to become one herself. Her first PICTURE BOOK, *A Number of Dragons,* was published in 1985. Since that time, L. has written more than twenty self-illustrated books. L.'s ILLUSTRATIONS are considered simple, yet entertaining, and her books often contain instructions on a variety of subjects. For example, *The Furry News,* winner of the Ezra Jack KEATS Award for excellence in the arts, teaches children the basics of journalism. Her science book, *Tracks in the Sand* (1993), was given an Outstanding Science Trade Book citation by the National Science Teachers Association and CHILDREN'S BOOK COUNCIL. L. has also illustrated books for other authors, including David A. ADLER's *The Dinosaur Princess and Other Prehistoric Riddles* (1988) and Tom Birdseye's *Waiting for Baby* (1991).

FURTHER WORKS: *Messages In the Mailbox: How to Write a Letter,* 1991; *The Monster Money Book,* 1992; *Blast off to Earth!: A Look at Geography,* 1992; *Postcards from Pluto: A Tour of the Solar System,* 1993; *Fraction Action,* 1994; *Who's Who in My Family,* 1995; *2X2 = Boo!: A Set of Spooky Multiplication Stories,* 1995; *Mission: Addition,* 1997; *Measuring Penny,* 1998

BIBLIOGRAPHY: *Something about the Author,* vol. 84, 1996; Internet Public Library Youth Division: Ask the Author (Loreen Leedy), http://www.ipl.org/youth/AskAuthor/leedy.html, accessed February 6, 1999

                              MARY ARIAIL BROUGHTON

LE GUIN, Ursula K(roeber)

Author, b. 21 October 1929, Berkeley, California

L.'s SCIENCE FICTION and FANTASY writings, for children and adults, are informed by a lifelong acquaintance with the power of cultural structures and mythologies, her knowledge of Jungian psychology and Taoism, and an emerging and maturing embrace of feminist politics. The alternative universe of her Earthsea novels has been favorably compared with J. R. R. TOLKIEN's complex and fully developed Middle Earth fantasy world.

Daughter of author Theodora KROEBER, L. grew up in a family where anthropology was both academic and social. L. listened to stories told by scientists as well as by California Indians whose personal repertoire predated contact with white settlers. L. was writing poetry by the age of five. She read widely from her parents' library and earned her first rejection slip at the age of twelve for a fantasy story she submitted to a pulp magazine.

After earning a bachelor's degree from Radcliffe College (1951) and a masters degree from Columbia University (1952), with Phi Beta Kappa honors, L. received a Fulbright fellowship in 1953. She left for France to continue her studies of Romance languages. Aboard ship, she met her future husband, married, and began a family instead of continuing her studies. For several years, she taught languages part-time. After establishing her career as an author, she taught writing workshops and acted as writer in residence at schools of higher education both in the U.S. and abroad.

A Wizard of Earthsea (1968) earned the Lewis CARROLL Shelf Award, in 1969, and the AMERICAN LIBRARY ASSOCIATION's Notable Book citation. Its sequel, *The Tombs of Atuan* (1971), was also an ALA Notable Book and became a NEWBERY MEDAL Honor Book (1972) and a finalist for the National Book Award for Children's Literature (1972). *The Farthest Shore* (1972), third in the Earthsea cycle, earned a 1972 Child Study Association of America's Children's Books of the Year citation (1972) and the National Book Award for Children's Books (1973). *The Dispossessed: An Ambiguous Utopia* (1974) was named a Best YOUNG ADULT Book by the American Library Association in 1974, and, in 1975, won the Hugo Award, the Nebula Award, the Jupiter Award and the Jules VERNE Award. *Very Far Away from Anywhere Else* (1976, published in England as *A Very Long Way from Anywhere Else*) was a National Book Award finalist that year and was cited by the ALA as a Best Young Adult Book as well as by the Child Study Association of America as one of the Children's Books of the Year; in 1987, this young adult novel received the Prix Lectures-Jeunesse. L. has received four honorary doctorates, awarded by Bucknell University (1978), Lawrence University (1979), Lewis and Clark College (1983), and Occidental College (1984). She has received national and international awards for her fantasy and science fiction writing for adults.

The Earthsea trilogy stands as L.'s best known work for young readers. L. presents three phases of life and three aspects of living in these tales. *A Wizard of Earthsea* introduces the hero Ged as a young wizard and follows him on an epic journey to manhood and individuality. *The Tombs of Atuan* revolves around Tenar, a girl priestess for whom the world of Earthsea is a social realization. *The Farthest Shore* finds Ged an old being and thematizes spiritual concerns. These three books were republished in one volume, *Earthsea* (1977, published in England as *The Earthsea Trilogy,* 1979). In 1990, L. published a sequel, *Tehanu: The Last Book of Earthsea*, in which the action coincides with events in *The Farthest Shore*. The plot and themes of *Tehanu*, however, are intended for an older readership than the one targeted by the original trilogy.

L. has converted her interest in anthropology into several highly acclaimed books with wide teen appeal. *The Disposessed* presents readers with the clash between a character who works to foster the spread of knowledge and his society's deeply held regard for isolationism. *The Disposessed* developed from L.'s study of feminist and anarchist politics. *Always Coming Home* (1985, published with audiocassette, 1987) presents a might-come-to-be matrilineal society through their artifacts, including poems, documents, and music (composed by Todd Barton). This multimedia fiction presents young adult— and adult—readers with a fantasy universe that seems to display itself rather than be codified into story.

Younger children, too, are supplied with fantasy literature by L. *Catwings* (1988), *Catwings Return* (1989), and *Wonderful Alexander and the Catwings* (1994) are adventures featuring bewinged kittens. *A Ride on the Red Mare's Back* (1992) offers a moral tale about responsibility, palatably clothed in the adventures of a girl who must retrieve her little brother from trolls.

L.'s political astuteness and sensitivity to cultural syntax are evident throughout her range of work. In addition to novels, short stories and poetry collections for adult readers, L. is widely published in fantasy and science fiction periodicals and writes essays that appear in a variety of media.

FURTHER WORKS: *Solomon Leviathan's Nine Hundred Thirty-First Trip around the World,* 1976; *Leese Webster,* 1979; *A Visit from Dr. Katz,* 1988, published in England as *Dr. Katz; Buffalo Gals, Won't You Come out Tonight?,* 1994

FRANCISCA GOLDSMITH

LEMONY SNICKET
(See SNICKET, Lemony)

L'ENGLE, Madeleine
Author, b. 29 November 1918, New York City

L.'s family, the Camps, moved to a Chateau in the French Alps when she was twelve years old. Her mother was a pianist, her father a foreign correspondent and writer. L. attended boarding school in Switzerland and graduated from Smith College in 1941. L. often reflects autobiographical hints as echoes in her writing. For example, she and her husband, Hugh Franklin, took a ten-week cross-country camping trip with their children before moving to New York from Crosswicks. The family from *Meet the Austins* (1960) takes a similar trip. L. says the book came directly from her life; it could easily have been called "Meet the Franklins." Orphaned Maria comes to live with L.'s family, orphaned Maggy comes to live with the Austins. Carole Chase, author of *Suncatcher: A Study of Madeleine L. and Her Writing* says that the root of L.'s interest in large and loving families lies in her lonely childhood years. L.'s parents were older and less child-centered than many parents. Her father returned from World War I with lungs damaged by mustard gas, requiring him to give up his work as a war correspondent. He wrote late each night and slept late in the mornings. L. spent a great deal of time alone in her room, often eating her meals there. L. read a great deal, kept a journal and, by age five, had written her first story. As a child she was so shy and quiet her teacher could not believe she wrote poetry that was awarded a first prize.

Her mother had to come to school with a portfolio full of her writing to prove she wrote the winning poem. L. created fictional families—such as the Murrys, Austins, and Davidsons—that resemble the family she and her husband created with their own children. They are always loving, caring families, deeply concerned about each other, with the emphasis on doing things together and sharing common joy with a mixed FANTASY and SCIENCE FICTION setting.

L. says that the families in her stories are family for her and the reason she follows them into more than one book is that she wants to find out what happens to them. During her own family's camping trip, L. got the idea for the three strange beings—Mrs. Who, Mrs. Whatsit, and Mrs. Which—who became the angelic beings in *A Wrinkle in Time* (1962). The angelic beings support Meg Murry as she struggles against the powers of evil to rescue first her father, an internationally recognized scientist, and then her precocious little brother, Charles Wallace. *Wind in the Door* (1978) and *A Swiftly Tilting Planet* (1978) follow the adventures of the Murrys in equally thrilling fantasy adventures as they continue to fight against the powers of evil. L. included characters from the Time Trilogy in other novels including *Many Waters* (1986). A measure of spirituality pervades L.'s writing. In fact, L. is an ecumenist who believes in the universal church where all can worship in differing ways and still be one.

L. expresses her opposition to sexism as vehemently as she opposes the evils of racism, war, and environmental destruction. L. makes strong declarations about gender equality through her characters, plots, and themes. It was uncommon to have a female protagonist for a science fiction novel in the 1960s when L. was writing what ultimately became *A Wrinkle in Time*. L. had a difficult time finding a publisher; some believe it was not only because Meg Murry was a female main character in a science fiction novel but she was also good at math and science. Both characteristics broke the stereotypic molds for females at the time.

L. is devoted to a daily discipline of prayer and contemplation. She lives life on a reflective, contemplative level; some of these patterns can be observed in characters she writes about. L. has been praised and criticized for being a boundary breaker and a universe disturber. She openly expresses her beliefs about good and evil, human freedom and responsibility, God and Scripture and community and family.

AWARDS: ALA NEWBERY MEDAL (1963) for *A Wrinkle in Time*. DE GRUMMOND REFERENCE COLLECTION, University of Southern Mississippi Medallion. 1978. AMERICAN LIBRARY ASSOCIATION Newbery Medal Honor Book (1980) for *A Ring of Endless Light* and (1981) for *A Swiftly Tilting Planet*. American Book Award for *A Swiftly Tilting Planet* (1980). Dorothy Canfield Fisher Children's Book Award (1981) for *A Ring of Endless Light*. California Young Reader Medal (1982) for *A Ring of Endless Light*. Colorado Children's Book Award (1983) for *A Ring of Endless Light*. Regina Medal (1985). ALAN Award, NCTE (1986). KERLAN Award (1990). Margaret A. Edwards Award (1998) for lifetime writing for teenagers

FURTHER WORKS: *And Both Were Young,* 1949; *Meet the Austins,* 1960; *The Moon by Night,* 1963; *The Arm of the Starfish,* 1965; *The Young Unicorns,* 1968; *Dragons in the Waters,* 1976; *A Ring of Endless Light,* 1980; *A House Like a Lotus,* 1984; *Troubling a Star,* 1994; *Dance in the Desert,* 1969; *A Circle of Quiet,* 1972; *The Summer of the Great-Grandmother,* 1974; *The Irrational Season,* 1977; *Walking on Water: Reflections on Faith and Art,* 1980; *The Sphinx at Dawn* 1982; *A Severed Wasp,* 1983; *Many Waters,* 1986; *An Acceptable Time,* 1989; *The Twenty-four Days before Christmas,* 1964; *The Anti-Muffins,* 1980; *Moses, Prince of Egypt,* 1998; POETRY: *Lines Scribbled on an Envelope,* 1969; *The Weather of the Heart,* 1978; *A Cry like a Bell,* 1987; autobiography: *Marriage: A Two-Part Invention,* 1998

BIBLIOGRAPHY: Chase, Carole F. *Glimpses of Grace: Daily Thoughts and Reflections.* 1996; Chase, Carole F. *Suncatcher: A Study of Madeleine L. and Her Writing.* 1998 2nd Ed.; Gallo, Donald R., ed. *Speaking for Ourselves.* 1990; Gonzales, Doreen. *Madeleine L.* 1991; HOPKINS, Lee Bennett, *Pauses: Autobiographical Reflections of 101 Creators of Children's Books,* 1995; L, Madeleine. *Trailing Clouds of Glory: Spiritual Values in Children's Books.* with Avery Brooks. 1985; L. *Friends for the Journey,* with Luci Shaw. 1997; Silvey, Anita, ed. *Children's Books and Their Creators.* 1995; Townsend, John Rowe, *A Sense of Story: Essays on Contemporary Writers for Children,* 1973

BERNICE E. CULLINAN

LENSKI, Lois

Author, illustrator, b. 14 October 1893, Springfield, Ohio; d. 11 September 1974, Tarpon Springs, Florida

L. authored and illustrated numerous works accredited as highly perceptive and authentic accounts of American childhood. These works include historical fiction, PICTURE BOOKS, POETRY, and nonfiction. She was the daughter of a Lutheran minister and was the fourth of five children. Growing up in the small farming town of Anna, Ohio, L.'s childhood was filled with art, books, games, and family activities. L.'s first success with words and art came early in her school career. Students at her school read the Baldwin Readers and she would complete her reader the first day or two of school and then become bored as the other students read the books page by page, day after day. She became interested in art in the third grade by tracing and painting, and won her first contest with prize money of three dollars from "Aunt Jane" of *Woman's Home Companion* in 1907.

She received a B.S. in Education in 1915 from Ohio State University before studying at the Art Student's League in New York from 1915 to 1920 and for a year in London afterwards. In 1921, L. married Arthur Covey, an artist and mural painter, and adjusted delightfully to being a wife and stepmother to twelve-year-old Margaret and two-year-old Laird. She kept the name Lenski professionally because she did not want to be confused with the other artists named Covey: all the Lenskis that she knew were preachers. Working as an artist, she showed and sold her work, never considering herself a writer. Editor after editor told her that her work did not fit their manuscripts. She was then asked to provide her own writing. Gradually, her mode of expression shifted from art to the written word. The first books that L. both wrote and illustrated were *Skipping Village* (1927) and *Little Girl of 1900* (1928). L. gave birth to a son Stephen in 1929. When he was four years old and curious about automobiles, trains, and airplanes, he became her inspiration and audience-reaction critic for the Mr. Small books. The attraction to young readers

of these books lies in L.'s ability to tell an everyday story with few words. Arbuthnot stated that with the Mr. Small books, L. "omitted nothing important; nothing trivial or extraneous is included."

In the 1940s L. was advised to spend winters in warmer climates for her health. Her move signaled the beginning of the regional books. She spent her first winter in New Orleans, Louisiana, and later ones in Florida. The first regional book was *Bayou Suzette* (1943) followed by *Strawberry Girl* (1945), which received the NEWBERY MEDAL. L.'s purpose for writing the regional books was to afford young readers the opportunity to experience the lives of children from other parts of the U.S. with similarities and differences; therefore, teaching them understanding and compassion. The author's commitment to authenticity of research was accomplished by traveling to the region of the book's setting; she lived with the people who became characters in her stories. L. felt that this enabled her to experience her characters' lives while sustaining objectivity: L.'s first-hand research provides depth and sensitivity to the characters and their lives with true-to-life plots, sometimes harsh details, but always with the values of hard work, education, and endurance. *Cotton in My Sack* (1941) about Arkansas sharecroppers, *Prairie School* (1951) about the harsh winters on the Dakota prairies, and *Blue Ridge Billy* (1946) set in Appalachia sympathetically capture the lives of residents in diverse communities at a time when regional differences were pronounced. L. wrote regional literature for twenty-five years in addition to writing poetry with city and country settings. L. received the Children's Book Award of the Child Study Association of America in 1947 for *Judy's Journey* for dealing realistically with contemporary problems. For her body of work, L. received the Regina Medal and the University of Southern Mississippi Medallion from the DE GRUMMOND REFERENCE COLLECTION in 1969.

As an illustrator, L. exhibited a variety of styles. Her line drawings portrayed action, character, and HUMOR with little detail. Two-color washes with line drawings illustrate the Mr. Small SERIES. Her regional books were illustrated with soft detailed pencil sketches. L exhibited oil and watercolor paintings in addition to her book ILLUSTRATIONS. L.'s autobiography, *Journey into Childhood* (1972) exhibits her talent for description of life as well as informing the reader of valuable information about the author herself. The book is a detailed descriptive account of the late eighteen- to early nineteen-hundreds. She reveals stories about her home life, including the house, town, community, and relationships. Organization by chapters and italicized subheadings and documentation including letters, diaries, and pictures make the work both entertaining and comprehensible.

AWARDS: Newbery Medal (1946) for *Strawberry Girl* (1937); Newbery Medal Honor Book for *Phebe Fairchild: Her Book* (1942); *Indian Captive: The Story of Mary Jemison;* KERLAN Award (1999)

FURTHER WORKS: Illustrator only: *The Golden Age*, 1921; *The Chimney Corner Stories*, 1925; *There Were Giants*, 1929; *The Twilight of Magic*, 1930; *Betsy Tacy*, 1940; *Read-to-Me Storybook*, 1947; Author and illustrator: *Two Brothers and Their Animal Friends*, 1929; *The Little Auto*, 1934; *Gooseberry Garden*, 1934; *Indian Captive: The Story of Mary Jemison*, 1941; *Spring Is Here*, 1945; *The Little Fire Engine*, 1946; *Judy's Journey*, 1947; *Ice Cream Is Good*, 1948; *Boom Town Boy*, 1948; *I Like Winter*, 1950; *We Live in the South*, 1952; *A Dog Came to School*, 1955; *We Live in the Country*, 1960; *Shoo-Fly Girl*, 1963; *The Life I Live: Collected Poems*, 1965; *Lois L.'s Christmas Stories*, 1968; *Deer Valley Girl*, 1968; *Debbie and Her Family*, 1969; *Lois L.'s Big Book of Mr. Small*, 1979

BIBLIOGRAPHY: Bader, Barbara, *American Picturebooks from "Noah's Ark" to "The Beast Within,"* 1972; *Children's Literature Review*, vol. 26, 1992; HOPKINS, Lee Bennett, *Pauses: Autobiographical Reflections of 101 Creators of Children's Books*, 1995; L., Lois. *Journey into Childhood: The Autobiography of Lois L.*, 1992

NANCY HORTON

LENT, Blair

Author, illustrator, b. 22 January 1930, Boston, Massachusetts

L. was an only child who grew up during the Great Depression. His friends were the imaginary characters from the second-hand books his father bought. L.'s favorite childhood memories are of the summers he spent with his parents in a New Hampshire cottage. L.'s parents encouraged his writing, and he remembers creating stories with his grandmother. He attended the Boston Museum of Fine Arts School of Art, graduating with honors in 1953. L. then won a Museum scholarship to pursue his art study in Switzerland and Italy before working in business and advertising. In 1968 L. used a second travel scholarship to go to the Soviet Union and sketch cities, villages, and landscapes and to study FOLKLORE.

L. has illustrated books for numerous others as well as authoring several of his own texts. L.'s earliest works were cardboard cuts (printed on his own printing press), then he moved to pen and ink and wash, and to full color acrylic painting. He has a keen interest in folklore and uses his art to elaborate on themes and images of the cultures from which the tales originate. L. tries to communicate his own feelings about the world through his work.

AWARDS: ALA CALDECOTT MEDAL (1973) for *The Funny Little Woman* (MOSEL, author). AMERICAN LIBRARY ASSOCIATION Caldecott Medal Honor Book (1965) for *The Wave* (HODGES, author). 1969 for *Why the Sun and Moon Live in the Sky* (Dayrell, author). (1971) for *The Angry Moon* (SLEATOR, author). The American Institute of Graphic Arts Best Children's Books for *Pistachio* (1964), *The Wave* (1968), *John Tabor's Ride* (1966), and *Why the Sun and Moon Live in the Sky* (1968, 1977). *New York Times* Best Children's Books for *Baba Yaga* (Small, 1966) and *John Tabor's Ride*. International AWARDS in Brazil, Czechoslovakia, and Japan. Travel fellowships from the Boston Museum of Fine Arts

FURTHER WORKS: Author and illustrator: *Pistachio*, 1964; *From King Boggen's Hall to Nothing-at-All*, 1967; *Bayberry Bluff*, 1987; *Molasses Flood*, 1992; Illustrator: *The Little Match Girl* (ANDERSEN) 1968; *Tikki Tikki Tembo* (Mosel) 1968; *Many Horses* (WAHL) 1969; *The Angry Moon* 1970 *Blackbriar* 1972. (both Sleator); *Favorite* FAIRY TALES *Told in India* (HAVILAND) 1973; *The Telephone* (Smith) 1977; *I Stood upon a Mountain* (FISHER) 1979; *The Beastly Feast* (Goldstone) 1995

BIBLIOGRAPHY: *Third Book of Junior Authors*. 1972; Hopkins, L. B. *Books Are by People*. 1969; HOPKINS, Lee Bennett, *Pauses: Autobiographical Reflections of 101 Creators of Children's Books*, 1995; Lent, B. Kingman, L., ed., NEWBERY *and*

Caldecott Medal Books: 1966–1975 1968, pp. 250–55
JANE WEST

LESIEG, Theo
(See SEUSS, Dr.)

LESSAC, Frané
Illustrator, b. 18 June 1954, Jersey City, New Jersey

L. is committed to illustrating and publishing books that portray a MULTICULTURAL society and are nonsexist. She seeks to address the importance of protecting the environment and natural resources. She accomplishes this through what critics describe as a folk-art style, frequently with vivid color and considerable detail. L. lived in the Caribbean for many years. Her portrayals of Caribbean and African communities have been described as vibrant and exuberant. She currently lives in Australia.

FURTHER WORKS: *Caribbean Canvas,* 1987; *The Chalk Doll* (illus.), 1989; *Turtle and the Island* (illus.), 1990; *Nine O'Clock Lullaby* (illus.), 1991; *The Fire Children* (illus.), 1993; *Not a Copper Penny in Me House* (illus.), 1994; *Caribbean Alphabet,* 1994; *Sleep Rhymes around the World: The Wonderful World of Watts* (illus.), 1994; *The Distant Talking Drum: Poems from Nigeria* (illus.), 1995; *Queen Esther Saves Her People,* 1998; *On the Same Day in March,* 2000
SANDRA IMDIEKE

LESTER, Julius
Author, b. 27 January 1939, St. Louis, Missouri

L. is the son and grandson of Methodist ministers. He grew up in Kansas City, Kansas, and Nashville, Tennessee where he received a B.A. from Fisk University in 1960. His first artistic expressions were as a folksinger associating with participants in the civil rights movement such as Tom Paxton, Pete Seeger, and Judy Collins. His interests and jobs before he began to write were in television and as the host of a political radio show. He was considered a political activist for black civil rights. After writing an adult book, he was introduced to children's editor Phyllis Fogelman who guided his interest in AFRICAN AMERICAN history preservation and his simple writing style into the NEWBERY MEDAL Honor Book *To*

Be a Slave (1969). L. credits Fogelman with clear direction that led to a fulfilling career and an avenue for his words. While discussing his book *John Henry* (1995), he told the *Horn Book* magazine that "words need to be presented in a way that is attractive and appealing and invites people into the worlds and emotions evoked by those words."

He wants his books to provide interaction between adults and children as they read his books together. L. is an author with fervent beliefs and the words to express them to diverse audiences. He grew up in a segregated South, which was rich in STORYTELLING, yet riddled with racial segregation and violence. This background provides him with a Southern voice and memories. His works provide valuable FOLKLORE and history from the black perspective with strong African American characters.

L.'s search into his own genealogy led to the discovery that his great-grandfather, Adolf Altschel, was a German Jew. This discovery led to L.'s interest in black–Jewish relations and his ultimate conversion to Judaism. His memoir, *Lovesong: Becoming a Jew* (1988), describes his experience. Since then, his writings and teachings include this interest and involvement. His published works include essays and reviews in publications such as the *New York Times Book Review,* the *New York Times* op-ed page, the *Boston Globe,* the *Village Voice,* the *New Republic, Forward,* and *Dissent.* His works have been translated into seven languages. His photographs of the civil rights movement are part of a permanent collection at Howard University. L. has taught at the University of Massachusetts for more than twenty-four years.

L.'s books appeal to children and YOUNG ADULTS for their strong authenticity to African American experiences; however, these experiences are universal and appreciated by readers of many cultures. L. wants his readers to understand slavery, from a slavery point of view as in *To Be a Slave* (1969), a Newbery Medal Honor Book that L. edited from first-person accounts. He discovered forgotten verbatim transcripts of actual accounts by former slaves recorded for the Federal Writers Project during the Great Depression and published them with an introduction for young people. In *Long Journey Home* (1972) L. again uses such primary sources as old letters, marriage records, and bills of sale for slaves to create a highly charged but factually accurate picture of slavery.

As a black youth in Nashville, L. was not allowed to enter the main library. He used a bookmobile that visited his neighborhood each Friday evening. L.'s love for books influenced him to be a writer. He reflects that the act of reading is paradoxical in that nothing is more solitary and yet through the act of reading one is able to rid himself of solitude and loneliness. Collaboration with illustrator Jerry PINKNEY resulted in several stories told in rich language and impressive ILLUSTRATIONS. L. used anthropomorphic images to exaggerate and embellish formerly plain events in the John Henry folktale: "What he saw was a mountain as big as hurt feelings." In *John Henry* (1994) the author merges his interests in black culture, folktales, and the language of storytelling. Other collaborations with Pinkney resulted in retellings of stories with roots in African folktales. *Tales of Uncle Remus: The Adventures of Brer Rabbit* (1987) and its companion volumes reflect L.'s attempt to keep cultural memory alive for children today through HUMOR, distinctive dialect, and unforgettable characters. Pinkney and L. collaborated on a new telling of Helen BANNERMAN's *Little Black Sambo* (1923) now titled *Sam and the Tigers* (1996). L.'s strengths are many, his illuminating themes are revealed in rhythmic and melodic style for which he credits his father's Southern cadence and use of language in storytelling.

AWARDS: AMERICAN LIBRARY ASSOCIATION Newbery Medal Honor Book (1969) for *To Be a Slave* and Lewis CARROLL Shelf Award; Lewis Carroll Shelf Award and National Book Award finalist for *The Long Journey Home: Stories from Black History.* 1972. Lewis Carroll Shelf Award for *The Knee-High Man and Other Tales.* 1972. CORETTA SCOTT KING AWARD honorable mention for both *This Strange New Feeling.* 1982 and *Tales of Uncle Remus: The Adventures of Brer Rabbit.* 1987. ALA CALDECOTT MEDAL Honor Book (1995) for *John Henry* and (1994) *Boston Globe–Horn Book* Award. Teaching honors include: Distinguished Teacher's Award. 1983–84. Faculty Fellowship Award for Distinguished Research and Scholarship. 1985. National Professor of the Year Silver Medal Award, Council for Advancement and Support of Education. 1985. Massachusetts State Professor of the Year and Gold Medal Award for National Professor of the Year from the Council for Advancement and Support of Education in 1986. Distinguished Faculty Lecturer, 1986–87

FURTHER WORKS: *Black Folktales,* 1969; *The Further Adventures of Brer Rabbit,* 1987; *The Misadventures of Brer Rabbit, Brer Fox, Brer Wolf, the Doodang, and Other Creatures,* 1990; *How Many Spots Does a Leopard Have: And Other Creatures,* 1990; *Falling Pieces of the Broken Sky,* 1990; *Othello,* 1998; *Black Cowboy, Wild Horses: A True Story,* 1998; *What a Truly Cool World,* 1999; *When the Beginning Began: Stories about God, the Creatures, and Us,* 1999

BIBLIOGRAPHY: *Children's Literature Review,* vol. 41; Del Negro, Janice, "The *Booklist* Interview," *Booklist.* February 15, 1995; L., *Lovesong,* 1988. L., "John Henry," *Horn Book* magazine. Jan./Feb. 1996, vol. 72, i. 1; "The Beechwood Staff," *Horn Book* magazine. April 1984, vol. 60, i. 2; Nikola-Lisa, W., "John Henry: Then and Now." *African American Review,* Spring 1998, vol. 32, i. 1

NANCY HORTON

LEVITIN, Sonia (Wolff)
Author, b. 18 August 1934, Berlin, Germany

L., a survivor of the HOLOCAUST, incorporates the importance of Jewish heritage as a theme in her work. As she turns increasingly to her own heritage and Holocaust experience for inspiration, L. says that, a creative element for her is discussing and writing about the conflicts we all face in life. An author of books for children and YOUNG ADULTS, L. based her first book, *Journey to America* (1970, 1993), on experiences her family encountered. Since then, L. has published a new book almost every year.

L. is also capable of writing HUMOR and historical fiction. In *The Mark of Conte* (1976) she describes a preteen who is registered as Mark Conte and also as Conte Mark because of a computer glitch. The boy tries to fulfill both schedules hoping to graduate early. *Roanoke: A Novel of the Lost Colony* (1973) explains many possible endings to the mysterious disappearance of the colony.

AWARDS: Edgar Allan Poe Awards (1989) for *Incident at Loring Groves.* National Jewish Book Award (1971) for *Journey to America* and (1988) *The Return*

FURTHER WORKS: *Who Owns the Moon?*, 1973; *The Return: Incident at Loring Groves*, 1987; *The Man Who Kept His Heart in a Bucket*, 1991; *Silver Days*, 1970, 1993; *The Golem and the Dragon Girl*, 1992; *Annie's Year*, 1993; *The Cure*, 1999

BIBLIOGRAPHY: Gallo, D., ed., *Speaking for Ourselves, Too*, 1993; *Something about the Author*, vol. 68, 1992

JODI PILGRIM

LEWIN, Ted and Betsy

Illustrators, authors, Ted: 12 May 1937, Clearfield, Pennsylvania. Betty: b. 6 May 1935, Buffalo, New York

T. and B. are the prolific producers of more than 200 children's works. The L.s married in 1963 after meeting at the Pratt Institute of Art where they received their Bachelor of Fine Art degrees. Both artists grew up drawing and painting and aspired to become professional artists. T. and B. do not usually publish as a team; however, they do advise one another while working in their home studio. T.'s books and ILLUSTRATIONS are generally for older children and more serious in nature. B.'s works are for the younger reader and are often described as whimsical. The L.s travel extensively as part of their research and keep journals to record observations and notes to use later as they write and paint. The L.s' appreciation and concern for the conservation of the world's environment is prevalent in their works. B. published *Walk a Green Path* (1995) and *Booby Hatch* (1995) and T. contributed *Amazon Boy* (1993), *When the Rivers Go Home* (1992), and *Cowboy Country* (1993). T.'s *Peppe the Lamplighter*, (Elisa Bartone, 1993) is an example of how the illustrator supports an author's story. T.'s luminous watercolors accurately complement this story in which light is important for the story, the illustrations, and Peppe, the lamplighter. B. uses her watercolors to exaggerate comically the text as in *What's Black and White and Came to Visit?* (1994) and *Mr. Turtle and Hip Hop Hare* (1995). Young readers are exposed to the world as the L.s share their talents in writing and art and their interests in ecology, travel and people.

AWARDS: T.: ALA CALDECOTT MEDAL Honor Book (1994) for *Peppe the Lamplighter*, by Elisa Bartone. B.: Pick of the List American Booksellers (1990) for *Araminta's Paintbox* and (1993) for *Ho! Ho! Ho! The Complete Book of Christmas Words*, by Lynda Graham Barber. Children's Choice (1994) for *Yo! Hungry Wolf* by David Vozar, and *Somebody Catch My Homework*, by David L. HARRISON. Best Books of the Year, *School Library Journal* (1995) for *Booby Hatch*

FURTHER WORKS: T.'s: author and illustrator: *World within a World*, 1976; *I Was a Teenage Professional Wrestler*, 1993; *Market!*, 1996; *Fair!*, 1997; *The Storytellers*, 1998; Illustrator only: *A Blind Man Can!*, 1968; *Island of the Blue Dolphin*, 1990; *Sacred River*, 1995; *Ali, Child of the Desert*, 1997; *The Originals*, 1998; B.: Author and Illustrator: *Animal Snackers*, 1980; *Cat Count*, 1981; Illustrator only: *Itchy, Itchy Chicken Pox*, 1992; *A Thousand Cousins: Poems of Family Life*, 1996; *The Gym Day Winner*, 1996; *Sharing Time Troubles* 1997; *Rapunzel: A Happenin' Rap*, 1998; *Snake Alley Band*, 1998

BIBLIOGRAPHY: "Author and Illustrator Profile," *Library Talk*. Mar./Apr. 1997, vol. 10, no. 2, p. 20; Silvey, A., ed., *Children's Books and Their Creators*, 1995

NANCY HORTON

LEWIS, C(live) S(taples)

Author, b. 29 November 1898, Dublin, Ireland; d. 22 November 1963, Oxford, England

Oxford scholar and Christian theologian, L. produced a seven-volume fantasy SERIES that quickly became a children's classic. The Chronicles of Narnia can be traced back to L.'s boyhood literary creations in which he peopled imaginary lands with powerful and courtly beasts.

L. studied classics and English at University College, Oxford, earning two A.B. degrees (1922 and 1923 respectively), each with first class honors. He tutored and lectured in philosophy and English literature at Oxford, from 1924 to 1954. For the remainder of his teaching career, he served as professor of Medieval and Renaissance English at Cambridge University. He wrote prodigiously, publishing SCIENCE FICTION novels, theological works, POETRY, literary criticism, autobiography and letters, as well as children's FANTASY books.

In addition to literary AWARDS earned for texts he published for adults, L. won the 1955 CARNEGIE MEDAL Commendation for *The Horse and His Boy* (1954), the 1957 Carnegie Medal for *The Last Battle* (1956), and the 1962 Lewis CARROLL

Shelf Award for *The Lion, the Witch, and the Wardrobe: A Story for Children* (1950). L. earned five honorary doctorates from British and European universities.

The Chronicles of Narnia books were not written, or published, in the chronological order of the imaginary land's history. First to appear was *The Lion, the Witch, and the Wardrobe,* an AD-VENTURE STORY populated by four children, who accidentally discover Narnia, and the variety of allegorical creatures whom they meet there. Set during World War II, the children's adventures seem to take them years, but when they return from Narnia, only a few minutes have passed. In *Prince Caspian* (1951), the same children return to Narnia. Again, the time difference in Narnia is dramatic: centuries have passed and the children immediately become active in the events at hand. *The Voyage of the "Dawn Treader"* (1952) features the younger of the original foursome, accompanied by a cousin. The cousin and a friend return to Narnia in *The Silver Chair* (1953). The original four children appear as Narnian rulers in *The Horse and His Boy.* It is in the sixth volume of the series, *The Magician's Nephew* (1955), that L. tells the story of Narnia's creation, a tale that provides readers with information about how evil came to paradisical Narnia. *The Last Battle* brings together all the children who have explored Narnia in the earlier books while ending the construct of Narnia itself through apocalypse and undisguised birth to a life beyond death.

L.'s Christianity pervades his children's books without didacticism. While a convinced believer, his construction of story is no thin device. Plot is indeed allegorical here: the ruler of Narnia, the regal lion Aslan, is Christ-like; good and evil are pitched in tumultuous and often repeated battle; the life beyond mortal death is a better one. But the stories do not require religious belief on the part of the reader, nor comprehension of any theological system on the part of the child. L.'s wordsmithing brings characters, setting, plot, and symbols to life independent of the religious subtext.

The Chronicles of Narnia, and books within the series, have received treatment by a variety of popular media, including public television presentations, film, and even the recasting of some of the stories by other children's authors and illustrators. L.'s rich use of language and sumptu-

ous imagery, however, stand above these reconceived—and flattening—treatments.

L.'s writings for adults include a trilogy of science fiction novels that have appeal to teen readers. *Out of the Silent Planet* (1938), *Perelandra* (1943), and *That Hideous Strength: A Modern Fairy-Tale for Grown-ups* (1945) are, like the Narnia novels, imbued with Christian symbolism. And, like the Narnia novels, the STORYTELLING is of such high literary caliber that the books are not theological tracts but critically acclaimed artwork. *The Screwtape Letters* (1942), an adult novel in which the Devil himself is a correspondent, is also easily accessible to readers in their middle teens. A recent adaptation by Charles E. Hall presents this witty satire in COMIC BOOK format (1994).

FURTHER WORKS: L., C. S., *Surprised by Joy: The Shape of My Early Life,* 1956; *Experiment in Criticism,* 1961; *Narrative Poems,* 1972

BIBLIOGRAPHY: *Dictionary of Literary Biography,* vol. 160: *British Children's Writers, 1914–1960.* 1996; *Contemporary Authors, New Revision Series,* volume 71. 1999; Hannay, Margaret Patterson, *C.S. L.,* 1980; Silvey, Anita, ed., *Children's Books and Their Creators.* 1995

FRANCISCA GOLDSMITH

LEWIS, J. Patrick
Poet, author, b. 5 May 1942, Gary, Indiana

L., poet and picture book author, had a normal, happy childhood, growing up with two brothers, one his twin. He attended St. Joseph's College in Rensselaer, Indiana, and earned a Ph.D. in Economics at Ohio State University in 1974. In 1972–73, L. and his family spent the academic year in the former USSR, where he completed his doctoral dissertation as an International Research and Exchanges (IREX) Fellow. L. returned to Moscow and other Soviet and Russian cities eight times.

L. has published extensively in the field of economics through professional journals and newspapers. In 1991, he was awarded an Ohio Arts Council Individual Artist Grant for his adult poetry. L. has published more than twenty-eight children's PICTURE BOOKS, nineteen of them POETRY. He has also published widely in children's MAGAZINES and in more than sixty anthologies. L. was commissioned to write the 1992 National Children's Book Week poem, which was printed on one million bookmarks and distributed nationally. He also reviews children's titles for the *New York Times.*

In 1990, L. published *Hippopotamusn't,* his first book for children. But it was not the first book he wrote. His first book, *The Moonbow of Mr. B. Jones,* was written during the 1970s but was not published until 1992. During the 1990s, L. published numerous books of poetry for children including *Two-Legged, Four-Legged, No-Legged Rhymes* (1991); *Earth Verses and Water Rhymes* (1991); *July Is a Mad Mosquito* (1994); *The Fat-Cats at Sea* (1994); *Ridicholas Nicholas* (1995); *Black Swan/White Crow* (1995); *Riddle-icious* (1996); *The La-di-da Hare* (1997); *The Little Buggers* (1998); *Boshblobberbosh: Runcible Poems for Edward* LEAR (1998); *Doodle Dandies* (1998); *Riddle-lightful* (1998); *The Bookworm's Feast* (1999); and *Isabella Abnormella and the Very, Very Finicky Queen of Trouble* (2000). In addition, he published numerous folktales and other picture books.

FURTHER WORKS: *The Tsar and the Amazing Cow,* 1988; *One Dog Day,* 1993; *The Christmas of the Reddle Moon,* 1994; *The Frog Princess,* 1994; *The Boat of Many Rooms,* 1997; *Long Was the Winter Road They Traveled,* 1997; *The House of Boo,* 1998; *Night of the Goat Children,* 1999; *At the Wish of the Fish,* 1999; *Earth & Sea and You & Me,* 1999; *Our Blue Balloon,* 2000; *Freedom like Sunlight for Black Americans,* 2000

BIBLIOGRAPHY: Personal correspondence with the author; website: www.jpatricklewis.com

BERNICE E. CULLINAN

LEXAU, Joan M. (Joan L. Nodset, Marie Seth)

Author, illustrator, b. Date unknown, St. Paul, Minnesota

L. has written books for young children, including *The Trouble with Terry,* winner of the Child Study Association of America, Children's Book Award and *Striped Ice Cream* (1968, reissued 1992) winner of the Charlie May Simon Children's Book Award. In some books L. used the pseudonyms of Joan L. Nodset and Marie Seth. In addition to her books, L. has contributed to MAGAZINES for children and adults, including *Cricket* and *Good Housekeeping.*

BIBLIOGRAPHY: *Something about the Author,* vol. 36, 1984

FURTHER WORKS: *Olaf Reads, 1961; Benjie,* 1964; *Every Day a Dragon,* 1967; *Finders Keepers, Losers Weepers* (Tomie DEPAOLA, illus.), 1967; *The Rooftop Mystery,* 1968; *Don't Be My Valentine: Go Away, Dog* (as Joan L. Nodset), *Emily and the Klunky Baby and the Next-Door Dog,* 1972; *The Poison Ivy Case,* 1983; *Benjie: Dog Food Capers,* 1985; *Trouble Will Find You* 1994

MARY ARIAIL BROUGHTON

LIBRARIANS AND PUBLISHING

Symbiotic relationships—best described as teamwork between two different species—have existed for more than eighty years between the Coordinators of Children's Services at the New York Public Library (NYPL) and the children's publishing world. The foundation for those relationships were set by Anne Carroll Moore, the pioneer in children's services who initiated and led children's work at the New York Public Library for thirty-five years, from 1906 until her retirement in 1941. She and the six women who followed her each contributed in her own distinctive style to the community of children's book publishing through a combination of personality, individual talent, and acute sensitivity to the times. As leaders of children's services at NYPL, they all commanded respect both within their profession and among children's book PUBLISHERS. And the simple fact of geography, of being located in the heart of the publishing world, in New York City, meant that they could readily know what was happening and could establish useful contacts and friendships in that world. Children's book publishing grew and flourished on an almost parallel track with children's services in public libraries, and the perspicacity, shared values, and mutual respect of leaders in both fields led them to support and confer with each other. The circle was small but strong, and the players were dedicated and passionate.

Chief among them was Anne Carroll Moore, a name associated with standards of excellence that she applied to children's books and reading and known as the grande dame who initiated children's services at NYPL. Moore's reign at NYPL was long, historic, and significant. The standards that she set for quality children's books became the underpinning for the newly developing field of children's librarianship and publishing, and her favor and blessing were sought by virtually everyone involved with children's books. She exerted her influence with characteristic decisiveness and enthusiastic energy in three major ways: as a critic of books written for children; as a mentor of authors, illustrators, and library staff who became authors and editors, and as an author herself. Moore had had little direct experience with children but she delved into the subject wholeheartedly. She observed children in many settings, explored educational and social service philosophy, and studied child psychology and behavior, all of which helped to give form to the standards she employed in her career. The standards are expressed in the "Four Respects" she emphasized in training children's librarians. They are respect for children, respect for children's books, respect for fellow workers, and respect for the professional standing of children's librarians.

The year 1918 was a watershed. Writer Sherwood Anderson, foreseeing a brilliant future for children's books and a need for book publishers and booksellers to inform themselves on the subject, asked Moore to deliver a series of eight lectures to a group of distinguished book people. Recognition of children's books as a publishing entity was solidified with the creation of the first separate children's publishing division at Macmillan, headed by Louise Seaman Bechtel, a close associate of Moore's. Doubleday, Scribner's, and other publishers soon followed Macmillan's example. Carnegie-funded library buildings with separate rooms for children and their books and specially trained staff appeared all over the country. Also in 1918, Children's Book Week was started. Franklin K. Mathiews, chief librarian for the Boy Scouts of America, had asked Frederic MELCHER, the newly appointed editor of *Publishers Weekly* and secretary of the American Booksellers Association, for help in improving the kinds of books boys were reading. The two men went to see Moore in her office at NYPL, known to be a hatching ground for good ideas. As a result of the collaboration of the three women experts, Children's Book Week was founded as an annual event in praise of books and reading. The first Book Week celebration took place in the Central Children's room in NYPL in

1919 with Kate Douglas WIGGIN, author of *Rebecca of Sunnybrook Farm* (1903) as the speaker. Melcher's involvement with children's books spurred him soon afterward to establish first the NEWBERY MEDAL (1922) and then the CALDECOTT MEDAL (1938), given annually by the AMERICAN LIBRARY ASSOCIATION for the most distinguished contribution to American literature for children and the most distinguished American picture book for children, respectively.

In 1941 when Moore retired, Frances Clarke Sayers who served 1941–52, a practicing librarian, became the second Coordinator of Children's Services. As Coordinator she brought her NYPL training, her crusading spirit, and a vision of a flourishing community of those interested in children's books—librarians, authors, editors, and illustrators. She was an eloquent advocate of quality in children's literature and its recognition as an important and legitimate field of study and collecting. During her eleven-year tenure as Coordinator, her exuberance as well as disapproval was voiced in numerous writings for a variety of publications and in speeches, lectures, and her own children's books. In 1952, The Library of Congress asked Sayers to recognize its extensive collection of domestic and foreign children's books, which she did on a two-months' leave from NYPL. Sayers published three children's books: *Bluebonnets for Lucinda* (Helen SEWELL, illustrator, 1934); *Mr. Tidy Paws* (Zhenya Gay, lithographer, 1935); and *Tag-Along Tooloo* (Helen SEWELL, illustrator, 1941).

Eulalie Steinmentz Ross (1952–53), a storyteller and writer, served a brief term as Acting Superintendent of Work with Children, sustaining the level of integrity of the office through her own writings and her advice to publishers. She wrote a biography of Bertha Mahony Miller, founder and editor of The *Horn Book,* and three collections of stories for children: *The Buried Treasure and Other Picture Tales,* illustrated by Josef Cellini (1958); *The Lost Half-Hour,* illustrated by Enrico Arno (1963); and *The Blue Rose,* illustrated by Enrico Arno (1966).

The next Coordinator of Work with Children, Frances Lander Spain, 1953–61 came to NYPL in 1953. A Fulbright scholarship took her to Thailand in 1952 where she established a library training program; this led to the creation of the

Thailand Library Association. She is credited with advancing librarianship in the rapidly growing country. A year after returning to the United States, Spain was offered the position as head of children's work at NYPL. Her intelligence, warmth, and humor endeared her to the staff, and her passion for books reached across the oceans to other countries. She also continued Moore's reviewing tradition by editing the "Books for Young People" section of the *Saturday Review,* then a leading popular literary journal. Outstanding and unique among Spain's achievements was her election as president of the AMERICAN LIBRARY ASSOCIATION, the first children's librarian to be so honored.

The next coordinator, Augusta Baker, 1961–74 came from the ranks of the Library. Baker had been hired by Moore in 1937 as an assistant children's librarian at the West 136th Street Branch in Harlem (later renamed the Countee Cullen Regional Branch Library). The branch housed a sizable collection of black history books, and Baker quickly engendered respect for her leadership abilities and judgment when she worked with a group of women from the community to collect worthwhile books for children that would instill pride in black culture. The landmark collection was named the James Weldon Johnson Memorial collection, a list of whose holdings Baker compiled in 1946. This was the first edition of *Books about Negro Life for Children,* a benchmark for the selection of materials on minorities. The eleventh edition of the bibliography, now entitled *The Black Experience in Children's Literature,* was published in 1994. Baker's credibility and credentials as a persistent and convincing spokesperson for the improvement of children's literature by and about black people was thus established early in her distinguished career. "She talked to editors, authors, and publishers about the need for better books about Black life, enlisting the help of interracial organizations in the cause. In so doing, Baker helped to advance the idea that books can help children of different cultures and traditions understand and respect one another while instilling pride in their own cultural traditions" (Darlene Clark Hine, ed., *Black Women in America: An Historical Encyclopedia,* 1993. p. 69).

She was followed by Barbara Rollock, also an African American, who served from 1974–87.

She first served as the Assistant Children's Coordinator with Augusta Baker. Rollock carried on Baker's advocacy through publications and dialogues with publishers, and she also shared with Baker a special interest in *The Black Experience in Children's Books.* She edited three editions of *The Black Experience,* which is still a highly respected guide and recommendation tool for librarians, the public, and publishers. Rollock contributed to the literature on AFRICAN AMERICAN children's authors and illustrators and thus continued the authorship tradition among the Children's coordinators. Her publications included *Black Authors and Illustrators of Children's Books* (1992) and *Public Library Services for Children* (1988). Both Baker and Rollock, particularly because one immediately succeeded the other in the Coordinator's position, were leaders among black women in the library field whose association with publishers, critics, authors, and illustrators helped powerfully to create a sensibility of black culture in children's literature. Their advocacy and personal contributions applied Moore's "Respects" and shaped the foundation for a new subgenre of children's literature. Both Baker and Rollock were involved with local universities in training grants to educate teachers and librarians about new theories of learning and new materials. They recognized the need to work with children at younger ages and were instrumental in establishing the Early Childhood Resource and Information Center (ECRIC).

The current Coordinator, Julie Cummins, 1987 to the present, came from an outstanding and distinguished career in upstate New York. She approaches her role as a nurturing, intelligent leader who respects children and her staff, and demands high quality in children's books. Cummins has served as chair of both the NEWBERY MEDAL Award Committee and the CALDECOTT MEDAL Award Committee and is currently teaching children's literature for Pratt Institute Library School. She served as a jurist for the Society of Illustrators, Original Art from Children's Books Exhibition, as a judge for the *Boston Globe-Horn Book* Awards, and on the jury for the *New York Times* Best Illustrated Books, 1996. She works closely with the Ezra Jack KEATS New Writer Award and the Early Childhood Resource and Information Center, ECRIC. Cummins is active in local, state, and national organizations. She is past president of the New York State Library Association, the only working children's specialist ever elected to that position. She chaired the 1991 American Library Association Nominating Committee. Her publications include *Children's Book Illustration and Design* vol. 1 (1992); *Children's Book Illustration and Design,* vol. 2 (1998); *The Inside-out Book of Libraries* (Roxie MUNRO, illus. 1996). *Choices, A Core Collection for Reluctant Readers* (1990).

JULIE CUMMINS AND BERNICE E. CULLINAN

(See also EDITORS OF NOTE and PUBLISHERS AND BOOK PUBLISHING IN THE UNITED STATES)

LIBRARIANS AND STORYTELLING

Librarians enjoy a proud heritage of STORYTELLING. The exact date of the first library story hour is uncertain, but librarians have been telling stories to children for over a century. As early as 1896, Anne Carroll Moore (1871–1961) had given storytelling a place in the children's room of the new Pratt Institute Free Library in Brooklyn, New York. By 1899 both the Carnegie Library of Pittsburgh and the Buffalo, New York, Public Library had established the story hour as a regular part of library service to children. Storytelling was already practiced in schools, hospitals, playgrounds, and settlement houses when librarians began to recognize its potential for introducing children to literature.

In 1900 Marie Shedlock (1854–1935) came to the United States from England to lecture on Hans Christian ANDERSEN and tell his tales. Shedlock was a teacher of young children for many years before becoming a professional storyteller in 1890. Her lectures on storytelling formed the basis of a book, *The Art of the Storyteller* (1951) which became a classic. Mary Wright Plummer, director of the School of Library Science at Pratt Institute in Brooklyn, heard Shedlock and invited her to tell stories to the trustees, directors, and faculty of Pratt. When Anne Carroll Moore, head of the children's room at Pratt, heard Shedlock she knew the children must hear her too. At the children's program, held on a snowy Saturday morning in January 1903, a little girl asked Miss Moore, "Is she a fairy, or just a lady?" In later years Moore wrote, "There

was never any doubt in my mind after that morning that a children's library should have a regular story hour."

It was Shedlock's inspiration, as she traveled around the United States telling stories and lecturing on storytelling, that gave impetus to the idea of storytelling as a true art. Shedlock emphasized simplicity, careful selection, and reliance on the human voice alone to convey the nuances of the story. Anna Cogswell Tyler (1859–1923), Moore's assistant at Pratt, was inspired by Shedlock to become a storyteller and later developed the storytelling program at the New York Public Library, following Moore's appointment as the first Supervisor of Work with Children at the New York Public Library in 1907. Others who fell under Shedlock's spell and became well-known library storytellers during the first half of the century included Mary and John Cronan and Ruth SAWYER.

Gudrun Thorne-Thomsen (1873–1956) also had a great influence on the development of library storytelling. Thorne-Thomsen was the daughter of the Norwegian actress Fredrikke Nielsen, known for her portrayal of the women in Henrik Ibsen's plays. She came to Chicago in 1888 at the age of fifteen to live with her mother's sister and to train as a teacher at Cook County Normal School. There she came under the influence of Colonel Francis W. Parker, whom John Dewey called "the father of progressive education." On completion of her studies, Thorne-Thomsen joined the faculty of the University of Chicago where she taught children's literature, storytelling, and reading.

Library storytelling has always been associated with books and reading, and it was Gudrun Thorne-Thomsen who early on recognized the connection between listening to stories and learning to read. Story listening is not a passive activity; listeners are required to create images or pictures in their minds from the words of the teller. Similarly, to comprehend the meaning of printed material, the child must understand the oral language patterns and see the images that the printed words represent.

The first library story hours were planned for children of age nine and older. By that age, children were expected to have mastered the mechanics of reading. Librarians thought of storytelling as a form of reading guidance. By telling a story and indicating the book from which it came and pointing out that hundreds of other wonderful tales could be found in books, the librarian was introducing reading as a source of enjoyment throughout life.

It is interesting to note that library storytelling developed during a period of heavy immigration. Approximately a million immigrants entered the United States each year from 1900 to 1913. Librarians looked on storytelling as a way of integrating many diverse heritages and of teaching English and the English language orally.

Attendance at library story hours for children of school age peaked in the 1920s. In 1920 Alice Jordan estimated that the Cronans were telling stories to 1,800 library listeners per week as well as to 4,000 classroom pupils in auditorium groups. At the Carnegie Library in Pittsburgh nearly 150,000 children attended story hours in 1924.

Picture-book hours for children ages five to seven began as early as 1902, but did not reach their peak in popularity until decades later following the influx of artists from Europe after World War I and improved methods of reproducing art in books; these set the stage for the flowering of the American picture book.

In 1935 the Detroit Public Library began picture-book hours for preschoolers three to five years old. Other libraries soon followed. Storytelling programs for school-age children were scheduled less frequently as organized activities competed for the children's attention and greater administrative demands on children's librarians left less time for story-hour preparation.

An even greater change in library storytelling programming occurred in the 1960s. Results from research demonstrate the importance of interaction between children and their caregivers during the first three years of life. That interaction impacts on language development, cognitive functioning, personality, and social behavior. In response to the growing evidence that young children were capable of responding to stories on a more sophisticated level than formerly thought, children's librarians began experimenting with storytelling programs designed for children from eighteen months to three years of age, accompanied by a caregiver. Today infant and toddler programs are offered by almost every library in the United States, often with long waiting lists.

Only a small number of libraries now offer story hours for children over eight years of age on a regularly scheduled (weekly, semimonthly, or monthly) basis. The tendency is to invite a professional storyteller to perform on a special-occasion basis. Librarians continue to use storytelling techniques in book talks, to tell stories during class visits, and to offer workshops on storytelling to older boys and girls, young adults, and teachers. The whole-language movement made teachers more aware of children's literature and eager to learn effective ways of sharing it with children.

Through the outstanding contributions of such librarians as Augusta Baker (1911–98) and Pura BELPRÉ librarians and teachers came to realize the power of storytelling in preserving the traditions of a culture for the foreign-born child and of building appreciation of one's own or another's culture for the native-born child. Enjoying a story together creates a sense of community. It draws people closer to one another, adult to child, child to child.

Storytelling continues to be a vital part of library work with children in the United States and librarian-storyteller ambassadors, such as Caroline Feller Bauer, Anne Pellowski, and Spencer Shaw, are spreading the library storytelling tradition all over the world.

BIBLIOGRAPHY: Alvey, Richard G. *The Historical Development of Organized Storytelling to Children*, p. 16, 1981. Bauer, Caroline Feller Bauer. *Caroline Feller Bauer's New Handbook for Storytellers*, 1993. Greene, Ellin. *Storytelling: Art and Technique,* 3rd ed., 1996. See "Festschrift for Augusta Baker," pp. 186–256. Hamilton, Martha, and Mitch Weiss. *Children Tell Stories: A Teaching Guide*, 1990. Hernandez-Delgado, Julio L. "Pura Teresa Belpré, Storyteller and Pioneer Puerto Rican Librarian." *The Library Quarterly* 62 (October 1992): 425–40. Jeffery, Debby Ann. *Literate Beginnings: Programs for Babies and Toddlers*, 1994. Jordan, Alice M. "The Cronan Story Hours in Boston." *The Horn Book Magazine* 26 (November–December 1950), pp. 460–64. Moore, Anne Carroll. *My Roads to Childhood: Views and Reviews of Children's Books*, 1939, p. 145. Pellowski, Anne. *The World of Storytelling*, 1990. Sawyer, Ruth. *The Way of the Storyteller,* rev. ed., 1977. Sayers, Frances Clarke. *Anne Carroll Moore: A Biography*, 1972.

Shedlock, Marie. *The Art of the Story-Teller,* 3rd ed., 1951

ELLIN GREENE

(See also STORYTELLING: A PROFESSIONAL POINT OF VIEW)

LIBRARIES AND CHILDREN'S READING PROGRAMS

Libraries have offered children's reading programs since the late nineteenth century, when consideration was first given to their needs. To complement children's collections, libraries offered programs to promote literacy. Programs such as book discussions, reading aloud, and STORYTELLING were as much a staple of early children's library services as they are now. Most libraries offer some kind of reading aloud program. Sometimes advertised as picture-book hour or story time, it typically consists of a LIBRARIAN, a paraprofessional, or volunteer, reading aloud PICTURE BOOKS to children who generally range in ages from three to eight. If done properly, the reader holds the book open for children to see the illustrations while he or she reads aloud. The reader reads in a normal voice; there is no need for acting out the story through exaggerated voices or gestures. In a library setting, the reader typically does not stop throughout the first reading of the story to ask questions. When reading to a group of children who vary widely in age, it is important to choose picture books of varying degrees of difficulty to engage both the younger and older audience members. A large group may become restless, so a reader may augment the readings with a brief stretch exercise or fingerplay to keep the children's attention. Although usually targeted to younger children, read-aloud programs may be tailored especially for older school-age children who will appreciate longer, more complicated stories.

Storytelling involves the telling, rather than the actual reading of a text. For older children, usually between the ages of eight and twelve, tales are told from fables, FOLKLORE, MYTHOLOGY, short stories, or excerpts from longer texts. Tellers "make stories their own" by embellishing them with certain details, but they must always stay true to the story. Stories may be told using a flannel board, in which felt cutouts of characters and other elements are used to help children visualize the story. Besides entertaining, storytelling can be used as a means of publicizing, promoting, or advertising a collection of folktales, myths, or short stories. Telling one tale often inspires children to read others in the collection.

Book talking is another method of recommending a book to readers. Instead of telling the whole story, book talkers tell enough of a story to entice a child to read the rest. Book talking is used with older children and teenagers who are ready to read novel-length fiction and longer nonfiction books. Book talking can also be used to tell short stories or POETRY. There are a number of different ways to approach book talking. Margaret A. Edwards, a leader of young adult library services, talks about using "cuttings": memorized excerpts of a book recited to grab the reader's attention. Another approach to book talking is to assume the persona of a main character in the story and tell part of it. The most widely used method is to introduce the characters and plot of a story and stop at a point where listeners are engaged enough to want to read to rest of the story on their own.

Recognizing the importance of early childhood education, libraries also offer reading programs for infants and toddlers. These programs are always intergenerational, with a parent or caregiver interacting with the child. Sometimes called "lapsit" programs because the child literally sits on the adult's lap, the program consists of a librarian leading the children and parents in a variety of activities, such as singing, rhymes, and fingerplays. The librarian reads one or two picture books to the crowd to model the process followed by the opportunity for parents to share a book with their children.

For older children, some libraries offer book discussion groups or book clubs. These groups can take on a variety of forms. They might be genre specific (e.g., FANTASY or MYSTERY), specific to a particular author or series, or they could involve every member reading and discussing the same book. Recently, parent–child book clubs have become popular programs in libraries, an opportunity for a parent and child to read the same book and discuss it together. Other special programs include author visits and reader's theater. Libraries sometimes have authors visit to speak to children about the books they have written. Children have the opportunity to ask questions about the books they have read and go away encouraged to read more. Reader's theater is a program in which a book or short story is adapted for dramatic reading. The text is not performed, and the words are not acted out. Children read aloud from a script. The point is to let the words speak for themselves.

Most libraries offer a summer reading program for children of all ages. Libraries sometimes create original programs, but they are typically adaptations of a program designed by a state library agency, which produces activities, guidelines, and promotional materials that can be adapted for use by libraries of all budgets and sizes. Programs are organized around a broad theme, so a wide range of activities and books can be related to it. Children who register for the program are usually offered some small token as an incentive for reading a set number of books or for reading a set amount of time per day. They keep track of what they read over the summer with a reading log. At the end of the summer, libraries usually have some kind of celebration, certificate, or party to reward children for their participation. Younger children not yet able to read can participate by having their parents read books to them. The fundamental point of summer reading programs is to keep children reading all year long, to avoid the typical regression children show on reading tests after summer vacation.

The variety and volume of reading programs a library offers to children is dependent upon a number of factors: its budget, size, and whether there is a children's librarian on staff among them. Whatever the type, the purpose of any library reading program is to promote lifelong literacy to children. The more a library can offer, the better.

BIBLIOGRAPHY: Bauer, Caroline Feller, *Presenting Reader's Theater,* 1987; Bodart, Joni, *Booktalk! Booktalking and School Visiting for Young Adult Audiences,* 1980; Greene, Ellin, *Storytelling: Art and Technique,* 1996; Sayers, Frances Clarke, "The American Origins of Public Library Work with Children" in *Library Trends,* 12 (July 1963), pp. 6–12; Trelease, Jim, *The New Read Aloud Handbook,* 1989; Ward, Caroline. "Having Their Say: How to Lead Great Book Discussions with Children," *School Library Journal* (April 1998), pp. 24–29

EDWARD T. SULLIVAN

(See also BOOK CLUBS FOR CHILDREN; BOOK CLUBS FOR TEACHERS; STORYTELLING; STORYTELLING: A PROFESSIONAL POINT OF VIEW)

LINDBERGH, Reeve
Author, b. 2 October 1945, Westport, Connecticut

L. writes for children across a wide span of ages and interests. Her PICTURE BOOK texts include pastoral and humorous tales as well as collections of POETRY and prayers. Among her books for YOUNG ADULTS, her nonfiction addresses historic moments in flight. L. was born the fourth of five children to the famous aviators, Charles and Anne Morrow L. Educated at Radcliffe College, she became a teacher.

Reviewers often praise L.'s language for its grace. Titles such as *The Midnight Farm* (1987) and *The Day the Goose Got Loose* (1990) well suit very young audiences as L. and her illustrators, Susan JEFFERS and Steven KELLOGG, portray domestic life with gentle intimacy and HUMOR. For older children, L. provides insight on her father's environmental concerns in *View from the Air: Charles L.'s Earth and Sky* (1992). She recounts the history of courageously breaking political and racial barriers in *Nobody Owns the Sky: The Story of Brave Bessie Coleman* (1996).

L. continues to create both serious reworkings of such historic texts as "The Prayer of St. Francis" and *The Circle of Days* (1998), and silly stories like *Awful Aardvarks Go to School* (2000). She also writes nonfiction, novels, and poetry for adults.

FURTHER WORKS: *Benjamin's Barn,* 1990; *If I'd Known What I Know Now,* 1994; *In Every Grain of Sand: A Child's Book of Prayers and Praise,* 2000

BIBLIOGRAPHY: Chin, Paula, "Lindy's Daughter," *People Weekly,* vol. 39, no. 3, Jan. 25, 1993, p. 63; Hertog, Susan. *Anne Morrow L.,* 1999

FRANCISCA GOLDSMITH

LINDGREN, Astrid
Author b. 14 November 1907, Vimmerby, Sweden

L. was born the daughter of a farmer in southeastern Sweden, the second of four children in a close and loving family. She developed an early love for nature as well as for books. A voracious reader, she remembers fondly the popular girls' books of the day: *Pollyanna, The Little Princess,* and, her favorite, *Anne of Green Gables.* After graduating from grade school, L. went to Stockholm where she became a secretary, married, and had two children. She had long told her children stories, but never thought to write them down until an injury confined her to bed in 1944. She wrote the manuscript of *Pippi Longstocking* as a birthday gift for her daughter. Her first attempt at publication failed, but her second manuscript, for a story entitled *Britt-Mari Opens Her Heart,* won second place in a publisher's competition in the autumn of 1944. And in 1945, the manuscript of *Pippi Longstocking* won first place in a similar contest. L. achieved almost instant success as an author and continues to write.

Pippi Longstocking, the adventures of a fiercely independent red-headed girl, shocked many adult readers when it appeared, because of the heroine's unrefined manners, her rejection of adult authority, and her irrepressible nature. Of course, she is every child's dream, growing up in a home of her own, with ample wealth, and without adult supervision or rules. She immediately became a childhood favorite and remains one. L's exaggerated HUMOR is akin to American tall tales, and it is possible to find beneath the surface of the delightful farce a gentle jab at society's rigid conformity. Through *Pippi Longstocking* and its two sequels, *Pippi Goes on Board* (1946) and *Pippi in the South Seas* (1948), L. gained international fame and won literary AWARDS around the world. But she also published dozens of other books, primarily for children. As a children's writer, L. exhibited an extremely broad range, from PICTURE BOOKS for the very young—her Bill Bergson series and *The Tomten,* for example—to books for adolescents such as the Kati books.

The struggle between good and evil is a recurring theme in much of L.'s work. *Niels, the Midget* (1949), a collection of original FAIRY TALES, and *Mio, My Son* (1954), a lyrical FANTASY, are two of L.'s most celebrated books, both presenting the conflict between good and evil in terms accessible to children.

The Brothers Lionheart (1973), on the other hand, is a serious tale of death and reincarnation that raised controversy at the time it was published. The book deals with the deaths of two brothers, eschews traditional religious teachings, and shows the brothers continuing to have heroic adventures in Nangilyala, an imaginary land. L. claims she wrote the book deliberately to offer comfort to young children, particularly to those who have not been reared with the conventional Christian belief in the afterlife.

Ronia, the Robber's Daughter (1983), also for older readers, is a bildungsroman of fairy-tale magic and adventure set in the Middle Ages. The story echoes Romeo and Juliet but with a happier ending, since two young lovers from opposing bands of robbers bring about a reconciliation among the factions. The book describes Ronia's growth and development, both physically and emotionally, and, in some ways, is a complement to the Pippi tales. In *Ronia* readers see the free-spirited protagonist grow into responsibility. L.'s books have been translated into more than fifty languages, and the character of Pippi Longstocking has become a cultural icon, at least in the English-speaking world, giving rise to films, dolls, and other memorabilia.

L. has received many honors. The Astrid L. Prize, named in her honor, is awarded annually in Sweden to honor an outstanding writer of children's books. Typically, L. writes her books out in shorthand while lying in bed; she frequently uses her childhood home and environs as the setting for her fiction. Indeed, L.'s own childhood was the source of her inspiration for all her children's books. She once wrote "there is no child that can inspire me but the child that I myself once was."

AWARDS: Swedish State Award. 1957. Hans Christian ANDERSEN Award. 1958. State Artist Award (Sweden). 1965. Literis et Artibus Medal from the King of Sweden. 1975. German Peace Prize. 1978. Mildred L. Batchelder Award for *Ronia, the Robber's Daughter* (1984)

FURTHER WORKS: *Kati in America,* 1950 (English 1964); *Bill Bergson Lives Dangerously,* 1951 (English 1954); *Erik and Karisson-on-the-Roof,* 1955 (English 1958); *The Children of Noisy Village,* 1961 (English 1962); *Emil in the Soup Tureen,* 1963 (English 1970); *Of Course Polly Can Do Almost Everything,* 1977 (English 1978)

BIBLIOGRAPHY: Cott, Jonathan, *Pipers at the Gates of Dawn: The Wisdom of Children's Liter-*

ature, 1983; *Children's Literature Review,* vol. 39; Metcalf, Eva-Maria. *Astrid L.,* 1995; *Something about the Author,* vol. 34, 1984

DAVID L. RUSSELL

LIONNI, Leo (Leonard)

Author, illustrator, b. 5 May 1910, Amsterdam, Holland; d. 10 October 1999, Chianti, Italy

L. has been a freelance writer, painter, pioneer in advertising art and design, art director, and author and illustrator of children's books. He states, "Among the varied things I have done in my life few have given me greater satisfaction than my children's books."

Reared in Amsterdam, L. knew at a young age he wanted to become an artist. Although he did not have formal art training he spent much of his adolescence at art museums teaching himself to draw. He studied at the University of Genoa and earned a doctorate in economics. Immigrating to the United States he became a naturalized citizen in 1945 and was recognized for his "dynamic talent in commercial design."

His first children's book was the result of a train trip with his grandchildren. To pass the time he created a story about two blobs of color who are good friends. Thus *Little Blue and Little Yellow* (1959) came into being. Considered a classic in children's literature, there was some controversy about it being a social commentary on race relations rather than a children's story. L. himself admits, "My books, like all fables, are about people. Worms don't measure, torn paper doesn't go to school, little fish don't organize, birds don't engage in philanthropy, and pebbles don't make words. My characters are humans in disguise and their little problems and situations are human problems, human situations."

Little Blue and Little Yellow was one of the *New York Times* Best Illustrated Children's Books (1959) and L. received the Art Books for Children Award in 1973, 1974, and 1975. *Inch by Inch* (1960), a CALDECOTT MEDAL Honor Book, won the Lewis CARROLL Shelf Award (1962) and was one of the *New York Times* Best Illustrated Children's Books (1960). Following a tiny inchworm through his grassy world as he measures everything in sight for thirty-two pages keeps the reader involved. Done in collage, the main char-

acter interacts with others of comparative gigantic size to create an original imaginative story.

Swimmy (1963) was a Caldecott Medal Honor Book, AMERICAN LIBRARY ASSOCIATION Notable Book, German Government Illustrated Book Award, and an Bratislava Biennale Golden Apple award-winner. Swimmy is black and different from his red-fish brothers and sisters. Swimmy encourages the school of red fish to band together to look like a big fish to save themselves from attack by larger fish. Swimmy uses his distinctive coloring to become the eye. Typical of L.'s books, being different is beneficial and small can triumph over large. Watercolor monoprint ILLUS-TRATIONS illuminate the shimmering underwater scenes.

Frederick (1967) was a Caldecott Medal Honor Book (1968) and a *New York Times* Best Illustrated Children's Book (1967). The first and last pages are covered with the name "Frederick" from top to bottom and side to side; of course Frederick is the most important character. Frederick does different kinds of work while his brothers are busy filling the storehouse with food. Frederick just sits—but he is gathering colors and words. The reader learns to distinguish between physical work and imaginative work: man does not live by bread alone. Done in collage using muted colors there is good use of white space in this excellent read-aloud story.

In *The Biggest House in the World* (1968) father snail teaches little snail that he should be content with what he has and that biggest is not always best. Father snail advises little snail to keep his house small because when the leaves are gone a small snail cannot move a big house but will slowly fade away. L. uses animals, birds, and fish for his fables but the application is readily transferred to people.

Alexander and the Windup Mouse (1969) is a Caldecott Medal Honor Book, ALA Notable Book, and received the Christopher Book Award (1970). Alexander decides it is better to be a live mouse rather than a cast-off toy mouse. L. uses patterns and textures of household items; he shows a lizard in the midst of translucent leaves. The colors overshadow the two plain gray mice who search for a happy ending.

An Extraordinary Egg (1994) is a fable about pebbles and a pebble collector named Jessica who finds a beautiful round stone that cracks and the creature that emerges is labeled "chicken." When "chicken" returns to its mother and the three frogs hear it was called a "sweet little alligator" they "couldn't stop laughing." This story has a convoluted theme. One meaning could be that, no matter what others call you it does not change who you are. Or, perhaps, it does not matter what you call me, we can be friends. Or, even if I do not know who I am I can still be me and like you. Or, if you laugh at me and I do not know it, it will not hurt me and we are still friends. This is a fable to ponder.

In 1976 L. was given the George G. Stone Center for Children's Books Recognition of Merit Award for his body of work.

BIBLIOGRAPHY: Bader, Barbara, *American PICTURE BOOKS: From Noah's Ark to the Beast Within,* 1976; *Children's Literature Research,* 1984; Cummins, Julie ed., *Children's Book Illustrations and Design,* 1992; *Fiction, FOLKLORE, FANTASY and POETRY for Children, 1876–1985,* 1986; HOPKINS, Lee Bennett, *Pauses: Autobiographical Reflections of 101 Creators of Children's Books,* 1995; Jones, Delores Blythe, ed., *Children's Literature AWARDS and Winners: A Directory of Prizes and Illustrators,* 3rd ed., 1994; Silvey, Anita, ed., *Children's Books and Their Creators,* 1995; *Something about the Author,* vol. 8, 1976, and vol. 72, 1993

IRVYN G. GILBERTSON

LIPSYTE, Robert Michael

Author, journalist, b. 16 January 1938, New York City

L. is a seminal figure in the evolution of YOUNG ADULT LITERATURE. *The Contender* (1967), his first novel, was a landmark title that, along with S. E. Hinton's *The Outsiders,* helped create a new, socially relevant literature of realism for teenage readers. The story of Alfred Brooks, an AFRICAN AMERICAN teenager living in Harlem, *The Contender* is notable for its grittily realistic setting and its ambitious theme of self-transformation. Though this was his first novel, L. was already an established writer. He was one of two internationally syndicated SPORTS columnists for the *New York Times* and was the coauthor of *Nigger,* the 1964 autobiography of comedian and political activist Dick Gregory. At age twenty-one L., a Columbia University graduate, became the

youngest reporter on the staff of the *Times.* A collection of his newspaper articles and columns, published in 1970 as *Assignment Sports,* became his second young adult book. L. left the *Times* in 1971 to become a freelance writer. Two adult novels followed in quick succession—*Something Going* (1973) and *Liberty Two* (1974). He subsequently returned to young adult fiction with *One Fat Summer* (1977). This semiautobiographical story about overweight, wisecracking teenager Bobby Marks is the first volume of a trilogy that also includes *Summer Rules* and *The Summerboy.* It is historically important in its groundbreaking narrative use of an urban, Jewish voice— arguably the first time this had been employed in young adult fiction. In the years since, L. has written four additional novels. One of these, *The Chemo Kid* (1992), which is about a teenage boy's battle with cancer, was inspired by the author's own bouts with the illness that he calls "the beast." In literary terms it is an interesting departure from his earlier REALISTIC FICTION. In form and style, it resembles both the cyberpunk SCIENCE FICTION of William Gibson and contemporary superhero comics. *The Brave* (1991) and *The Chief* (1993) are more traditional novels about a mixed-race teenage boxer named Sonny Bear, whose mother is a NATIVE AMERICAN. However, in the second of these related novels L. also experimented, this time with a literary form called "metafiction," i.e., fiction that is playfully aware of itself as a work of art. All of L.'s novels to date are distinguished not only by their innovative and experimental qualities but also by their social conscience and political awareness.

L.'s favorite novelist as a young reader was John Steinbeck and his own adult work confirms the lasting impact of such novels as *The Grapes of Wrath* and *East of Eden.* His BIOGRAPHIES of such sports figures as Muhammad Ali and Jim Thorpe are also notable for their psychological complexity and their thoughtful emphasis on their subjects' early "outsider" environments. In 1991 L., following his Emmy Award-winning stint as host of his own PBS-television program, "The Eleventh Hour," returned to the *New York Times* as a columnist.

BIBLIOGRAPHY: Cart, Michael, *Presenting Robert L.,* 1995; Chevalier, Tracy, ed., *Twentieth Century Children's Writers,* 3rd ed., 1989; *Children's*

Literature Review, vol. 23, 1991; *Fifth Book of Junior Authors and Illustrators,* 1983; *Something about the Author,* vol. 23, 1992

MICHAEL CART

LISLE, Janet Taylor

Author, b. 13 February 1947, Englewood, New Jersey

L. and her four younger brothers grew up in Farmington, Connecticut. Being the oldest and the only girl, L. often found herself being both an observer and the one who sought to establish a compromise between bickering siblings. L. went to a girls' boarding school and then to Smith College. After graduating in 1969, L. joined VISTA (Volunteers in Service to America) and moved to Atlanta, Georgia, to help set up food buying co-operatives in the city's public housing projects. In 1971, L. studied journalism at Georgia State University and went on to an internship at the *Atlanta Journal.* L. wrote for various newspapers for the next ten years. Wanting to write fiction, L. switched from news stories and focused instead on human interest features.

After the birth of her daughter, L. began to write for children. Her first book, *The Dancing Cats of Applesap* (1984), was a lively look at cats who become quite active after everyone else has gone to sleep. After her second book she felt that she had really hit upon something that she liked to do. *Sirens and Spies* (1985), a YOUNG ADULT spy mystery set in World War II, was named an AMERICAN LIBRARY ASSOCIATION Notable Book, as well as a Junior Literary Guide selection. L.'s selection of topics and themes show evidence of versatility as she turned to FANTASY for her next novel, *The Great Dimpole Oak* (1987), which was also an ALA Notable Book. L. continues writing well-plotted and imaginative fantasies. *Afternoon of the Elves* (1989), centers on a tiny magical kingdom that exists in the yard next door. It was named a 1990 NEWBERY MEDAL Honor Book. L. has more recently written a fantasy SERIES, Investigators of the Unknown, which follows a girl named Angela through many adventures. L.'s fantasies captivate readers with their sharp imagery.

FURTHER WORKS: *The Lampfish of Twill,* 1991; *Forest,* 1993; *Gold Dust Letters,* 1994; *Looking for Juliette,* 1994; *Message from the Match Girl,* 1995; *Angela's Aliens,* 1997

BIBLIOGRAPHY: Silvey, Anita, ed., *Children's Books and Their Creators,* 1995; *Sixth Book of Junior Authors and Illustrators,* 1989; *Something about the Author,* vol. 47, 1987, and vol. 59, 1990

DEDE SMALL

LITTLE, Jean

Author, b. 2 January 1932, Tai-nan, Formosa (Taiwan)

L. is one of Canada's best-loved writers for children. She is known for her honest and unsentimental portrayals of young people who face physical, mental, and emotional challenges. L.'s more than twenty books include characters concerned with problems such as cerebral palsy, blindness, mental retardation, compulsive lying, and other conditions of the DISABLED.

Soon after L.'s birth, doctors discovered that she had scarring of the corneas of her eyes and diagnosed her as legally blind. Also, because one of her pupils was higher than the other, she could only use one eye at a time, causing her to have "crossed-eyes." By the time she was two, the scars had shrunk a bit, giving her partial sight. In 1939, when her family moved to Toronto, Canada, L. attended a special class for children with vision problems. Fortunately, her parents (both of whom were physicians) strongly supported her attempts to read and write, and she decided to pursue a degree in English. After her first year in college, L. completed a novel called *Let Me Be Gentle.* Although this work about a mentally retarded six-year-old girl was not published, L. continued to write. Upon completing her bachelor's degree in 1955, she spent six years working with handicapped children at camps, special schools, and in children's homes. It was during this time that she decided to write books about children with handicaps.

In her 1990 autobiography, *Stars Come out Within,* L. recalled that during the years she taught school, she and her students found in almost every book that included children with disabilities, the "boys and girls who started out crippled invariably ended up either dying like Beth in *Little Women* (ALCOTT, 1868) or miraculously cured like Colin Craven in *The Secret Garden* (BURNETT, 1911). L. wanted to write stories featuring children who remain disabled, yet learn to lead full, joyful lives. Consequently, L. draws on her personal life, as well as her experience as a teacher of children with handicaps, as she writes stories inspiring young readers to look for strength within themselves to overcome adversity. She refuses to offer magical cures for her protagonists' problems; rather, she focuses on having characters draw on their inner reserves of strength to cope with the challenges they face.

As one reviewer writes, "That is the real thrust of L.'s novels—recognizing and mastering the enemy within rather than tilting at the one without." L.'s novels reflect her belief that books should enable readers to grow. Most of her characters are believable young people who confront problems through which they learn to draw on their personal strengths. Writing from the experience of living successfully with her own physical limitations, L.'s works show sensitivity and insight.

Several of L.'s books have won prestigious AWARDS. Her first published book, *Mine for Keeps* (1962), won the Little, Brown CANADIAN Children's Book Award. This story features Sally Copeland, a young girl with cerebral palsy who comes home after living for five years in a school for disabled children. Sally returns to find additional personal problems as she tries to adjust to her family and her new school. The book was praised for its realistic unsensationalized depiction of the situation. One reviewer wrote, "The handicap recedes into a background fact that simply gives validity to a lively and satisfying story."

L.'s *Listen for the Singing* (1977), which won the Governor General's Literary Award for Children's Literature, and an earlier work, *From Anna* (1972), both address the subject of blindness. These stories feature a young girl who moves with her family from Germany to Canada just before the start of World War II. Anna battles her own shyness and insecurities, as well as her physical handicap, but triumphs in the end when she comes to accept her disability and finds friends who are supportive. As with many of L.'s novels, reviewers were especially appreciative of L.'s character development. In a *New York Times* book review, Milton MELTZER wrote that the book was "exceptional not only for its subtle handling of the domestic tensions created by the war between the refugee family's new country and its old one, but also for the way this circumstance is used to

link together an array of remarkably well-realized characters."

The author has received other awards, including the Vicky Metcalf Award from the Canadian Authors Association for her body of work inspirational to Canadian boys and girls. L.'s *Mama's Going to Buy You a Mockingbird* (1984) won the Children's Book Award of the Canada Council, the Canadian Library Association's Children's Book of the Year Award, and the Ruth Schwartz Award. She has written two volumes of autobiography, *Little by Little: A Writer's Education* (1987), which won numerous awards, and *Stars Come out Within* (1990), which was nominated for a 1991 Governor General's Book Award. L. was also awarded The Order of Canada in 1991.

More recently, L. has written several books for younger readers, including *Gruntle Pig Takes Off* (1996), *Emma's Magic Winter* (1998), and *Emma's Yucky Brother* (2000).

FURTHER WORKS: *Home from Far*, 1965; *Spring Begins in March*, 1966; *When the Pie Was Opened*, 1968; *Take Wing*, 1968; *One to Grow On*, 1969; *Look through My Window*, 1970; *Stand in the Wind*, 1975; *Listen for the Singing*, 1977; *Lost and Found*, 1985; *Different Dragons*, 1986; *Hey World, Here I Am!*, 1986; *Once upon a Golden Apple*, 1991; *His Banner over Me*, 1995; *The Belonging Place*, 1997

BIBLIOGRAPHY: *Children's Literature Review*, vol. 4, 1982; Little, J. *Stars Come out Within*, 1990; *Major Authors and Illustrators for Children and Young Adults*, vol. 4 1993; Jean Little, http://www.macabees.ab.ca/little.html (accessed November 20, 1999); Jean Little, http://www.know tv.com/primetime/literature/readers/jeanlittle.html (accessed November 28, 1999)

MARY ARAIL BROUGHTON

LIVELY, Penelope
Author, b. 17 March 1933, Cairo, Egypt

L.'s intricate plots, engaging characters, and sense of place contribute to establish her as an impressive novelist for children. She received a B.A. in modern history from St. Anne's College in Oxford. In addition to writing for children and adults, L. has been a presenter of children's literature on BBC Radio and a reviewer for newspapers and magazines in England. L.'s first book was *Astercote* (1970). Although the themes in L.'s books vary greatly, they reflect events from her childhood. L. lived her first twelve years in Egypt, was schooled at home and reared with heavier British than Egyptian influences. When she was twelve she was sent to boarding school in England. Her childhood was pleasant but lonely, spending very little time with her parents and attempting to adjust to the situation or escape it through reading and writing poetry forbidden by school authorities. English landscapes, importance of memory, and historical continuity mirror these influences from her childhood. For example, *The Ghost of Thomas Kempe* (1973) is a light approach to a child's realization of the presence of memory. A more significant work, *The House in Norham Gardens* (1974) is about time and continuity and the relationship of possessions and the people who own them. Also, the straightforward nature of *A Stitch in Time* is centered in a place and all the memories living in the house through the years. And in *The Driftway,* a young boy attempts to escape his unhappy home. Two of L.'s later books are PICTURE BOOKS whose stories are tales of whimsical adventures inspired by the births of her grandchildren. *The Cat, the Crow, and the Banyon Tree* (1994) and *Good Night, Sleep Tight* (1994) are dedicated to her two granddaughters.

AWARDS: *Book World* Children's Spring Book Festival Honor Book (1972) for *The Driftway.* CARNEGIE MEDAL (1973) for *The Ghost of Thomas Kempe.* Hans Christian ANDERSEN Honor List (1976) for *The Ghost of Thomas Kempe.* AMERICAN LIBRARY ASSOCIATION Notable Children's Book (1974) for *The House of Norham Gardens.* Whitbread Book of the Year Award (1976) for *A Stitch in Time.* Booklist's Children Reviewer's Choices (1985) for *The Revenge of Samuel Stokes* (1981). INTERNATIONAL READING ASSOCIATION/CHILDREN'S BOOK COUNCIL Children's Choice (1985) for *Fanny's Sister*

FURTHER WORKS: *The Wild Hunt of Hagworthy,* 1971; *Going Back,* 1975; *Boy without a Name,* 1975; *The Voyage of QV66,* 1978; *A House Inside Out,* 1987

BIBLIOGRAPHY: *Current Biography Yearbook,* 1994; *Fourth Book of Junior Authors and Illustrators,* 1978., *Oleander, Jacaranda: A Childhood Perceived,* (1994); *Publishers Weekly,* March 14, 1994, and April 10, 1995; *Twentieth-Century Children's Writers,* 1995

NANCY HORTON

LIVINGSTON, Myra Cohn

Poet, anthologist, b. 17 August 1926, Omaha, Nebraska; d. 23 August 1996, Los Angeles, California

L. was a poet, anthologist, musician, and lover of nature and life, which is evident in her works for children through four decades. She grew up in Nebraska where she was inspired to love nature by her mother; astronomy and science by her father; and the love for books, writing, and learning from both parents. As a child, she loved to record her observations and emotions on big tablets of paper with her prized pens and pencils. Her childhood was extremely happy with only two factors of distress, which she feels eventually led her to an even happier existence. Because she wore glasses, many of her friends laughed and called her "Four Eyes" and she had a severe overbite of which she was self-conscious. (see THE DISABLED IN CHILDREN'S AND YOUNG ADULT LITERATURE). She viewed her poor eyesight as a blessing that enabled her to deal in metaphors more easily than normal visioned people: She could see bushes as animals. The answer to her overbite was the suggestion from her orthodontist that she begin playing a brass instrument: This practice led to an appreciation for music and a love that lasted a lifetime and enhanced her POETRY interests. Music and writing consumed much of her young life. She received a B.A. from Sarah Lawrence College in 1948 and began her adult life with a variety of careers: professional French horn musician, 1941–48; book reviewer for the *Los Angeles Daily News* and *Los Angeles Mirror;* personal secretary for singer Dinah Shore and violinist Jascha Heifetz; public and school librarian in Dallas, Texas; writing teacher; poet in residence; senior extension lecturer at UCLA; and poetry consultant. L. was the poet or anthologist of more than 80 books in her career. She loved the role of reader as much as that of author. In a profile L. penned, she emphasized her great love for her collection of personal books and over 8,000 bookmarks from all over the world.

L.'s career as a professional writer began after she and her accountant husband moved to Dallas. She was working in a book store when the owner suggested that she take her book *Whispers,* yet to

63. PATRICIA LAUBER

64. MADELEINE L'ENGLE

66. C. S. LEWIS

65. JULIUS LESTER

67. ASTRID LINDGREN

68. LEO LIONNI

69. JEAN LITTLE

70. MYRA COHN LIVINGSTON

be accepted for publication, to the Dallas Public Library children's librarian. The librarian advised L. to send it to Margaret McElderry, children's book editor at Harcourt, where it was published, twelve years after being written. L.'s works reflected her happiness and positive view of childhood. She strongly believed that poets must obey the rules of their craft and have insight about when to stray from them. Throughout her career as a poet, she continued to write about childhood, but as she matured, she added slight glimpses of the seriousness and darkness of humanity and world she had experienced.

In addition to her books of original poetry, L. published collections of poems by other poets. She also wrote picture books for read-alouds. These PICTURE BOOKS are stories written in verse with ILLUSTRATIONS. *I'm Hiding* (1961), *See What I Found* (1962), and *Come Away* (1974) are titles reviewers familiar with needs of younger readers and prereaders applauded for their repetition of language and universal themes.

L.'s poems represent a variety of poetic techniques: free verse, rhythmic prose, haiku, and cinquain. Their content covers subjects from everyday activities to holidays and social problems. Her HUMOR and ability to write in clear contemporary language reinforces the popularity of her work. As one of our most respected modern poets and anthologists, L. also served as a contributor to numerous publications for and about writing, poetry, and children's literature.

AWARDS: *New York Herald Tribune* Children's Spring Book Festival Honor Award (1958) for *Whispers, and Other Poems.* Texas Institute of Letters Award (1961) for *I'm Hiding* and (1979) for *No Way of Knowing: Dallas Poems.* Southern California Council on Literature for Children and Young People Award (1968) for her contributions, and (1972) for *The Malibu, and Other Poems;* (1989) for *Earth Songs, Sea Songs, Sky Songs, and Space Songs.* Golden Kite Honor Award, Society of Children's Book Writers (1974) for *The Way Things Are, and Other Poems.* NATIONAL COUNCIL OF TEACHERS OF ENGLISH Award (1980) for excellence in poetry. Parents' Choice Award (1982) for *Why Am I Grown So Cold?* and (1984) for *Sky Songs.* National Jewish Book Award (1987) for *Poems for Jewish Holidays*

FURTHER WORKS: *Wide Awake, and Other Poems,* 1959; *The Moon and a Star, and Other Poems,* 1965; *A Lollygag of Limericks,* 1978; *Celebra-*tions, 1985; *Worlds I Know, and Other Poems,* 1985; *Higgledy-Piggledy: Verses and Pictures,* 1986; *There Was a Place, and Other Poems,* 1988; *My Head Is Red, and Other Riddle Rhymes,* 1990; *Abraham Lincoln: A Man for All the People,* 1993; *Festivals,* 1996; *Cricket Never Does: A Collection of Haiku and Tanka,* 1997; *B Is for Baby: An Alphabet of Verses,* 1996; As editor: *A Tune beyond Us: A Collection of Poetry,* 1968; *Listen, Children, Listen: An Anthology of Poems for the Very Young,* 1972; *How Pleasant to Know Mr. Lear!,* 1982; *Cat Poems* 1987

BIBLIOGRAPHY: *Children's Literature Review,* vol. 7, 1984; HOPKINS, Lee Bennett, *Pauses: Autobiographical Reflections of 101 Creators of Children's Books,* 1995; L., "Meet the Poet," *Ladybug,* Nov. 1996, vol. 6, i. 15; L., *Poem Making: Ways to Begin Writing Poetry,* 1991; Obituaries, *Reading Today,* Dec. 1996/Jan. 1997, vol. 14, i. 3

NANCY HORTON

LOBEL, Anita
Author, illustrator, b. 1934, Krakow, Poland

L. is both an illustrator and an author. Born in 1934 to a Jewish family living in Krakow, Poland, she literally had no childhood or formal education until she was twelve. During World War II, her nanny, a devoted Roman Catholic, took L. and her younger brother from town to town, hiding in Catholic churches and convents, passing them off as her own children. On Christmas Day, during the Nazi invasion of Poland in World War II, they were captured and taken to a concentration camp. How they survived is told by L. in her book, *No Pretty Pictures: A Child of War* (1998). After the war, they were sent to Sweden to recover from tuberculosis. Through the auspices of the Red Cross, they were reunited with their parents.

In 1952, the family moved to the United States. L. won a scholarship to Pratt Institute where she met Arnold LOBEL. After marriage and rearing two small children, she worked as a textile designer. She gave Susan Hirschman, Arnold Lobel's editor, three scarves made from fabrics she had designed. Hirschman recognized her talent and encouraged L. to become an illustrator.

Her first PICTURE BOOK, *Sven's Bridge,* published in 1965, was reissued in 1992. L. has illustrated nearly forty books, some of them her own—such as the ALA Notable Book, *Alison's Zinnia* (1990), an alphabet book of flowers, and *On Market Street* (1981) written by Arnold

Lobel, which earned her a CALDECOTT MEDAL Honor for the illustrations. Other books include *The Dwarf Giant* (1991) and *Away from Home* (1994), an alphabet book of cities that reflects L.'s love of the theater. Each city in the alphabet is shown as a backdrop on a stage. She has illustrated books written by Charlotte ZOLOTOW, B. P. Nichol, Ethel Heins, Charlotte Huck, and Charlotte POMERANTZ.

L. is always aware of the way art can extend the narrative aspect of a story. For example in the Cinderella tale of *Princess Furball* (Huck, 1989), the king wore the same colors the Princess had worn at the previous ball. L. suggested the passage of time by showing the waxing moon shining in the windows. And she saw the journey of the Princess as one going from darkness to light. She began with a dark opening ILLUSTRATION of her mother's funeral and ending with her marriage to the king under an arbor open to the skies. Her careful research of the period shows in her costumes, the choice of colors, and setting. Her characters are real people. She conveyed her love for the Catholic nanny who saved her life in the expression of the Princess as she looks at the nurse on the title page of *Princess Furball*. This attention to detail and the thoughtful planning enables L. to get at the heart of each of the stories she illustrates.

FURTHER WORKS: Books written and illus. by L.: *The Troll Music*, 1966; *Birthday for a Princess*, 1973; *The Straw Maid*, 1983; *Potatoes, Potatoes*, 1984; *Alison's Zinnia*, 1990; *Away from Home*, 1994; *The Dwarf Giant*, 1991, reissued 1996

BOOKS ILLUSTRATED BY L.: DALGLIESH, Alice. *The Little Wooden Farmer*. 1988; Hart, Jane ed. *Singing Bee!: A Collection of Children's Favorite Songs*. 1982; Heins, Ethel. *The Cat and the Cook and Other Fables of Kiylov*. 1995; Huck, Charlotte. *Princess Furball*. 1989; Huck, Charlotte. *Toads and Diamonds*. 1996; KROLL, Steven. *Looking for Daniela: A Romantic Adventure*. 1988; L., Arnold. *How Rooster Saved the Day*. 1977; L., Arnold. *On Market Street*. 1981; L., Arnold. *A Treeful of Pigs*. 1979; L., Arnold. *The Rose in My Garden*. 1985; MONJO, F. N. *Indian Summer*. 1968; MOORE, Clement C. *The Night before Christmas*. 1984; Nichol, B. P. *Once; A Lullaby*. 1996; Penelope, L. C. *Fanny's Sister*. 1980; Pomerantz, Charlotte. *Mangaboom* 1997; Shub, Elizabeth. *Clever Kate*. 1973; ZEIFERT, Harriet. *A*

New Coat for Anna. 1986; Zolotow, Charlotte. *This Quiet Lady*. 1992

BIBLIOGRAPHY: HOPKINS, Lee Bennett, *Pauses: Autobiographical Reflections of 101 Creators of Children's Books*, 1995

CHARLOTTE S. HUCK

LOBEL, Arnold

Author, illustrator, b. 22 May 1933, Los Angeles, California; d. 4 December 1987, New York City

Known for his perceptive qualities as a writer and artist, L. is a favorite author for many children who find both meaning and enjoyment in his stories and pictures. Incorporating into his work a unique combination of warmth, HUMOR, and sensitivity, L. uses literature as a means to communicate the intrinsic value of friendship, compassion, and community.

Reared by grandparents in Schenectady, New York, L. early demonstrated an interest in STORY-TELLING and drawing, pursuing his education at Pratt Institute in Brooklyn, where he studied ILLUSTRATION. Shortly after graduating, L. married Anita Kempler, who became a well-known children's book illustrator in her own right; they collaborated on several projects. In 1958, L. embarked on his own career by providing the illustrations for three activity books by Sol Scharfstein. This was followed with the publication of his drawings in Fred Phleger's *Red Tag Comes Back* (1961), which initiated a long-standing relationship with Harper and Row. He subsequently wrote and illustrated his own work as well as numerous books by other authors, many of them in Harper and Row's I Can Read SERIES.

In 1962, L. published his first PICTURE BOOK for children, *A Zoo for Mister Muster*, followed by its sequel, *A Holiday for Mister Muster* (1963), named by the *New York Times* as one of the Best Illustrated Books of the year. The publication in that same year of the comical *Prince Bertram the Bad* was followed by *Lucille* (1964), an animal FANTASY and the first book for the I Can Read series that L. both wrote and illustrated. The humorous plot of *The Bears of the Air* (1965) turns again to fantasy as L. depicts the activities of four young bears who prove to their grandfather that having fun is an essential part of learning. With the publication of *Martha, the Movie Mouse* and *Oscar Otter* (both 1966), an I

Can Read book by Nathaniel BENCHLEY, L. entered a new stage of development by introducing distinct border lines as a means to define his illustrations, a pattern he would use extensively in a majority of his future work.

Following the publication of *The Great Blueness and Other Predicaments* (1968), an imaginary tale about the creation of color, and *Small Pig* (1969), the second of his I Can Read books, L. produced one of his most beloved and enduring works for children, *Frog and Toad Are Friends*. Published in 1970, the book consists of five stories that portray the value of friendship between the two main characters with a combination of simplicity and affection. The third of L.'s I Can Read books, *Frog and Toad Are Friends* was named a CALDECOTT MEDAL Honor Book in 1971. In that same year, L. published two works in verse, *The Ice-Cream Cone Coot and Other Rare Birds* and *On the Day Peter Stuyvesant Sailed into Town,* for which L. received the Christopher Award. This was followed by the publication in 1972 of a sequel to the first Frog and Toad book entitled *Frog and Toad Together,* which was named a NEWBERY MEDAL Honor Book for the following year, 1973. Other Frog and Toad books include *Frog and Toad All Year* (1976), which also received the Christopher Award, *Days with Frog and Toad* (1979), *The Frog and Toad POP-UP Book* (1986), and *Frog and Toad Coloring Book* (1986).

Throughout the 1970s, L. gained increasing popularity and critical recognition as an author-illustrator and further enhanced his reputation by providing illustrations for a variety of works by other authors, notably Miriam Young's *Miss Suzy* (1964), Maxine Kumin's *The Microscope* (1968), Edward LEAR's *The New Vestments* (1970), Shulamith ISH-KISHOR's *The Master of Miracles* (1971), Cheli Durán Ryan's *Hildilid's Night* (1971), named a Caldecott Medal Honor Book, Paula FOX's *Good Ethan* (1973), Jack PRELUTSKY's *Circus* (1974), Anne K. Rose's *As Right as Right Can Be* (1976), and Doris ORGEL's *Merry Merry February* (1977), both of which were named by the *New York Times* as among the Best Illustrated Children's Books of the year, and Jean VAN LEEUWEN's *Tales of Oliver Pig* (1979). During this same period, L. produced *Mouse Tales* (1972), a collection of bedtime stories told by a father mouse to each of his seven children; *The Man Who Took the Indoors Out* (1974), selected by the *New York Times* as one of the best illustrated books of the year; *Mouse Soup* (1977); and *Grasshopper on the Road* (1978). In addition, L. collaborated for the first time with Anita LOBEL, who provided the illustrations for *How the Rooster Saved the Day* (1977). Other works by L. illustrated by Anita L. include *A Treeful of Pigs* (1979), *On Market Street* (1981), and *The Rose in My Garden* (1984).

In 1980, L. provided illustrations for Jack Prelutsky's *The Headless Horseman Rides Tonight: More Poems to Trouble Your Sleep* and Carol Chapman's *The Tale of Meshka the Kvetch,* and in that same year published *Fables,* an inventive collection of modern tales with animal characters expounding the virtues and foibles of society. Highly praised for coordination of text and design, distinguished by colorful and exuberant drawings, *Fables* was honored with the Caldecott medal in 1981. L. earned additional praise for his illustrations for *The Random House Book of Poetry for Children* (1983) and *The Random House Book of MOTHER GOOSE* (1986). Prolific as well as selective, L. is among the most gifted author-illustrators in contemporary children's literature, whose attention to detail, expression, and use of color is pleasing and appealing to both young and old alike.

FURTHER WORKS: Author and illustrator: *Giant John,* 1964; *Gregory Griggs and Other Nursery Rhyme People,* 1978; *Uncle Elephant,* 1981; *Ming Lo Moves the Mountain,* 1982; *The Book of Pigericks,* 1983; *Whiskers and Rhymes,* 1985; *A Three Hat Day,* 1985, written by Laura Geringer; *Tyrannosaurus Was a Beast: Dinosaur Poems,* 1988; Illustrator only: *Something Old, Something New* (Susan Oneacre Rhinehart), 1961; *Let's Be Indians* (Peggy PARISH), 1962; *Terry and the Caterpillars* (Millicent E. SELSAM), 1962; *The Little Runner of the Longhouse* (Betty Baker), 1962; *Greg's Microscope* (Selsam), 1963; *The Quarreling Book* (Charlotte ZOLOTOW), 1963; *The Secret Three* (Mildred Myrick), 1963. *Dudley Pippin* (Phil Ressner), 1965; *Let's Get Turtles* (Selsam), 1965; *Someday* (Zolotow), 1965; *The Magic Spectacles and Other Stories* (Lilian MOORE), 1966; *The Witch on the Corner* (Felice HOLMAN), 1966; *The Star Thief* (Andrea DiNoto), 1967; *As I Was Crossing Boston Common* (Norma Farber), 1973

BIBLIOGRAPHY: HOPKINS, Lee Bennett, *Pauses: Autobiographical Reflections of 101 Creators of*

Children's Books, 1995; Kiefer, Barbara, selector, *Getting to Know You: Profiles of Children's Authors Featured in Language Arts, 1985–90,* 1991; Matthews, G. B. "Bravery and Philosophy in the Adventures of Frog and Toad," *Triumphs of the Spirit in Children's Literature,* ed. Butler, F., and R. Rotert. 1986; Carnes, P. "L.'s Fables and Traditional Fable Features." *Children's* FOLKLORE *Review,* Spring 1993, pp. 3–19; Stanton, J., "Straight Man and Clown in the Picture Books of L.," *Journal of American Culture,* Summer 1994, 75–84

STEVEN R. SERAFIN

LOCKER, Thomas
Author, illustrator, b. 26 June 1937, New York City

L. graduated from the University of Chicago with a B.A. in 1960 and from the American University in Washington, D.C., with an M.A. in 1963. While reading to one of his five sons L. discovered picture-book art. He published his first book, *Where the River Begins,* in 1984 and experienced immediate success as an illustrator. His themes include simple, gentle stories about relationships between children and their adult relatives, the joy in receiving an animal's trust, the passage of the seasons, and the impact of weather. His illustrations include panoramic landscapes and seascapes that reflect the terrain of the Eastern United States.

Where the River Begins earned numerous AWARDS in 1984 and 1985 including one of the *New York Times* Best Illustrated Children's Books of the Year, Parents' Choice Award for ILLUSTRATION from the Parents' Choice Foundation, Outstanding Science Trade Book for Children, *Booklist's* Children's Reviewer's Choice, American Bookseller Pick of the Lists, one of Child Study Association of America's Children's Books of the Year, and was included in the Biennale of Illustrations, Bratislava. The Bologna International Children's Book Fair exhibited *The Mare on the Hill* in 1985. In addition, it was listed as one of the Child Study Association of America's Children's Books of the Year in 1986, a Colorado Children's Book Award runner-up from the University of Colorado, and Critici in Erba Honorable Mention from the Bologna Biennale. L. is consistently praised for successfully reflecting the beauty of nature and for his attention to detail. His PICTURE BOOKS provide wonderful visual experiences for readers of all ages.

FURTHER WORKS: *Where the River Begins,* 1984; *The Mare on the Hill,* 1985; *Sailing with the Wind,* 1986; *Family Farm,* 1988; *Rip Van Winkle,* 1988; *The Young Artist,* 1988; in addition, L. illustrated: *The Ugly Duckling,* 1987; *The Boy Who Held Back the Sea,* 1987; *The Ice Horse* (C. Christiansen, author), 1993; *The First Thanksgiving* (Jean GEORGE), 1996; *Between Earth and Sky: Legends of NATIVE AMERICAN Sacred Places* (Joseph BRUCHAC, ed.), 1996; *Water Dance,* 1997; *Grandfather's Christmas Tree* (Keith Strand), 1999; *Cloud Dance,* 2000

BIBLIOGRAPHY: *Children's Literature Review,* vol. 14, 1988; *Something about the Author,* vol. 59, 1990

JODI PILGRIM

LOFTING, Hugh
Author, illustrator, b. 14 January 1886, Maidenhead, Berkshire, England; d. 26 September 1947, Santa Monica, California

What began as letters home to his children later became the stories of Doctor Dolittle. His children requested letters with ILLUSTRATIONS while he was away serving in World War I. Not wanting to portray the hardships of war, L. focused instead on the cats, horses, and other animals he saw around him, which were also affected by the war. Out of that environment came Doctor Dolittle, a character L. described as "an eccentric country physician with a bent for natural history and a great love of pets who finally decides to give up his human practice for the more difficult, more sincere and, for him, more attractive therapy of the animal kingdom."

L. wished for permanent peace, and believed that the education of children was the way to achieve this. Regarding his attitudes toward writing for children, L. felt that many writers "wrote down" to children. Instead, L. believed that the reverse was needed, and when writing for entertainment, no preaching should get in the way. He also noted that children's interests were wide, and their literature should be as varied as the demands of their interests. L.'s books contain highly inventive characters in fanciful situations enhanced by black and white line illustrations. Doctor Dolittle was first made into a motion picture in 1967.

The portrayal of Prince Bumpo and other AFRICAN characters has been criticized as racially objectionable, and later editions since 1988 have been revised and reissued. L. hoped that the lively characters and humorous adventures would appeal to young and old readers. "Whenever a book is a real success for children, it is also a success and an enjoyment for grown-ups. If writers would only get away from this classifying of children as a separate species, we would get very much better books for the younger generation."

AWARDS: NEWBERY MEDAL (1923) for *The Voyages of Doctor Dolittle; The Story of Doctor Dolittle* was given the Lewis CARROLL Shelf Award in 1958

FURTHER WORKS: *Doctor Dolittle's Post Office,* 1923; *The Story of Mrs. Tubbs,* 1923; *Doctor Dolittle's Circus,* 1924; *Doctor Dolittle's Caravan,* 1926; *Doctor Dolittle in the Moon,* 1928; *Noisy Nora,* 1929; *Twilight of Magic,* 1930; *Doctor Dolittle's Puddleby Adventures,* 1952; *Doctor Dolittle's Treasury,* 1967

BIBLIOGRAPHY: Kunitz, Stanley J., and Howard Haycraft, eds. *The Junior Book of Authors.* 1934; Fish, Helen Dean, "Hugh L. 1886–1947," Miller, B. M., and E. W. Field, eds., *Newbery Medal Books: 1922–1955,* 1955

SANDRA IMDIEKE

LONDON, Jack (John Griffith London)

Novelist, short story writer, political essayist, b. 12 January 1876, San Francisco, California; d. 22 November 1916, Santa Rosa, California

L. was a self-educated adventurer who held many jobs including ice delivery, setting pins in a bowling alley, oyster pirate, state fish patrolman, jute mill worker, coal shoveler and seal hunter. L. traveled vagabond style, joined in the Klondike gold rush and moved between civilization and the wilds. He also reported on slum conditions in England and on the Russo-Japanese War for the Hearst newspapers. A committed Socialist, L. ran for mayor of Oakland, California, in 1905. He was an inveterate reader although reading matter was scarce; he was grateful for whatever fell into his hands. For L., the one great advantage of writing as a means of livelihood was that it gave him freedom. The author's office and business could go anywhere and he could write about anything as the spirit moved him. L. wrote 1,000 words a day, even when he was in pain.

His most famous contribution to the genre of adventure writing was *Call of the Wild* (1903). It remains in print today in many different editions.

The Sea-Wolf (1904) and *White-Fang,* (1905) likewise remain popular choices among all AD-VENTURE STORY enthusiasts. L. also wrote two semiautobiographical works: *Martin Eden* (1909) and *John Barleycorn* (1913). His short story collection, *Lost Face,* published in 1910 includes *To Build a Fire. South Sea Tales;* a second short story collection, was published one year later. Many of L.'s books have been adapted and abridged for children including, most popularly *Call of the Wild* and *White-Fang.*

L.'s books continue to be successfully adapted as motion picture films: *John Barleycorn* (Bosworth, 1914); *Martin Eden* (Bosworth, 1914); *The Call of the Wild* (Pathé Exchange, 1923, Twentieth Century, starring Clark Gable and Loretta Young, 1935); *White Fang* (R-C Pictures, 1925, Twentieth Century-Fox, 1936); *Conflict,* a motion picture adaptation of *The Abysmal Brute,* starring John Wayne (Universal, 1936); *The Adventures of Martin Eden,* an adaptation of *Martin Eden,* starring Glenn Ford and Claire Trevor (Columbia Pictures, 1942); *Wolf Larsen* an adaptation of *The Sea-Wolf,* starring Peter Graves and Barry Sullivan (Allied Artists Pictures, 1958); *To Build a Fire* (Montana State College, 1963). Perhaps most notable is Edward G. Robinson starring in the first Hollywood adaptation, *The Sea Wolf,* in 1941.

BIBLIOGRAPHY: Lundquist, James, *Jack L.,* 1988

CRAIG M. LIEBERMAN

LONGFELLOW, Henry Wadsworth

Poet, b. 27 February 1807, Portland, Maine; d. 24 March 1882, Cambridge, Massachusetts

L. was the most popular American poet of his time and many of his works became staples in American schools for a century beyond his death. Born to a distinguished family, he had a college degree by the age of eighteen, was a professor of modern languages at Bowdoin College, Maine, by twenty-two, and a Harvard professor by twenty-nine. A prolific writer of both scholarly works and POETRY, L. was perhaps above all a man of his time, which made him enormously popular. He brought poetry to the masses through his anthologies, and his own works, inspired by Wordsworth, contain simple language, metrical regularity, and echoed the conventional Victorian sense of morality shared by most Americans. Poems such as "The Psalm of Life," "The Village Blacksmith," and "The Children's Hour" were popular fare for young readers. L.'s long narrative poems were highly admired in his day, particularly *Evangeline: A Tale of Arcadie* (1847) and *The Song of Hiawatha* (1855). *Tales of a Wayside Inn* (1863) is an eclectic collection of tales inspired by Chaucer and Boccaccio, its most famous selection being "Paul Revere's Ride," long a required poem to be studied and memorized by school children.

L. was the first commercially successful American poet and his celebrity during his lifetime can hardly be exaggerated; his reputation began to decline in the early twentieth century, his ballads and poems seldom read outside the schoolroom. But he remains a quintessential "Victorian American," whose work captures the predominant spirit of his era.

BIBLIOGRAPHY: Serafin, Steven R., general ed., *Encyclopedia of American Literature,* 1999; Wagenknecht, Edward, *Henry Wadsworth L.: His Poetry and Prose,* 1986

DAVID L. RUSSELL

LOPSHIRE, Robert Martin
Author, illustrator, b. Date unknown, Sarasota, Florida

L. studied at the Vesper George School of Art and the School of Practical Art in Boston, Massachusetts. He served as art director in New York and operated his own advertising agency. He is best known for his book for early readers, *Put Me in the Zoo* (1960), a story that features a polka-dotted leopard named Spot. *Put Me in the Zoo* was followed by two more books about Spot, *New Tricks I Can Do* and *I Want to be Somebody New.*

FURTHER WORKS: *Big Max,* 1965; *Pig War,* 1969; *Biggest, I Am Better Than You,* 1968; *How to Make Snop Snappers & Other Fine Things,* 1977; *Smallest, Fastest, Tallest Things You've Ever Heard Of,* 1980

BIBLIOGRAPHY: Ward, M. E., D. A. Marquardt, N. Dolan, and D. Eaton, eds.; *Authors of Books for Young People,* 3rd. ed., 1990

MARY ARIAIL BROUGHTON

LORD, Bette Bao
Author, b. 3 November 1938, Shanghai, China

L. came to the United States at eight years of age and became a teacher and modern dance performer, a naturalized United States citizen at the age of twenty-six, in 1964. She is an award-winning photographer as well as a lecturer and director of various programs. She also serves on literary committees. Becoming a novelist was not her ambition. Her first book, *Eighth Moon: The True Story of a Young Girl's Life in Communist China* (1964), was her Chinese speaking sister's story. When it was finally published it was praised and is on reading lists of many secondary schools. L.'s first novel, *Spring Moon: A Novel of China* (1982) is a FAMILY STORY that takes place during the cultural and political upheavals in China during the past century. She was inspired and driven to completion by the idea that China was underrepresented to a Western audience. L.'s most popular book, *In the Year of the Boar and Jackie Robinson* (illustrated by Marc SIMONT, 1984), was an AMERICAN LIBRARY ASSOCIATION Notable Book. Based on her own experiences, it recounts a young girl's first year experiences in Brooklyn and adjustment to cultural life in the United States.

BIBLIOGRAPHY: *Something about the Author,* vol. 58, 1990

CRAIG LIEBERMAN

LOUIE, Ai-Ling
Author, b. 18 July, 1949, New York City

After earning a B.A. at Sarah Lawrence College and an M.A. at Wheelock College, L. taught elementary school for six years. While teaching elementary school, she developed a desire to write and, in 1977, turned to full-time writing. She has published articles, reviews, and a PICTURE BOOK. L. wrote *Yeh-Shen: A Cinderella Story from China* (1982), selected as an ALA Notable Book, for her elementary school class.

The story of Yeh-Shen had been told in L.'s family for three generations. As an immigrant, her grandmother brought the story to the U.S. from southern China. L. has traced the story's written origins to a book from the time of the T'ang dynasty (618–907 C.E.), a thousand years before the Cinderella tale's appearance in the West. In L.'s straightforward, action-filled retelling, the poor orphan, Yeh-Shen, is befriended by the bones of a pet fish, who grants her golden slippers and beautiful clothing to wear to the spring festival. Illustrator Ed YOUNG portrays the story through panels of sweeping ILLUSTRATIONS rendered in watercolors and pastels.

KATHIE KRIEGER CERRA

LOVELACE, Maud Hart

Author, b. 25 April 1892, Mankato, Minnesota; d. 11 March 1980, Claremont, California

L. is best known for her Betsy-Tacy stories, set at the turn of the century, which were inspired by L.'s own childhood memories. Many of her characters are based on friends and relatives. The series of ten books, first published in 1940, follows the two friends from childhood to careers and marriage. The books are still widely read despite some occasionally dated stereotypes. They have inspired a loyal following including the formation of a national Betsy-Tacy fan club with chapters in major cities of the United States. They meet regularly to share memories of the Betsy-Tacy stories and their continued pertinence in readers' lives.

FURTHER WORKS: *Betsy-Tacy,* 1940; *Betsy-Tacy and Tib,* 1941; *The Golden Wedge,* 1942; *Downtown,* 1943; *Betsy and the Great World,* 1952; *Betsy's Wedding,* 1955; *The Valentine Box,* 1966

BIBLIOGRAPHY: *Something about the Author,* vol. 2, 1971

JODI PILGRIM

LOW, Alice

Author, b. 5 June, 1926, New York City

L. grew up amid a circle of artists, writers, editors, and musicians. Her mother, in fact, was a children's book author. L. attended Birch Wathen School, where she was recognized as talented in art. She created several books during her elementary school years, doing the writing, illustrating, and binding herself; she believed that she would become an artist. L. liked to memorize poems by A. A. MILNE as well as those by Rosemary and Stephen Vincent Benét. She enjoyed the Gilbert and Sullivan melodies that she can still recite and sing in their entirety. L. attended Smith College with a major in art and a minor in English. She graduated in 1947, continuing to become an artist and a lyricist.

L.'s first published book for children, *Opening up My Suitcase* (1950), was inspired by a nephew who repeatedly packed his suitcase. L. wrote rhyming lyrics with music to accompany the words and mailed the manuscript to Golden Records. The recording department, however, moved the manuscript over to their book department, where it was published. L.'s three children inspired many other books and helped her recall her own feelings as a child.

L. studied short-story writing at Columbia University where she learned to scribble a first draft from the subconscious, let the characters take over, and then follow their lead. This requires many drafts to find the buried story through writing, rewriting, and revision. In *Popcorn Shop* (1993), Nell's big popcorn machine refuses to stop popping, which leaves the townspeople wading in popcorn begging her to stop. The rhyming text is excellent for reading aloud or for independent reading. *Spooky Stories for a Dark and Stormy Night* (1994) chills the bones and delights readers who enjoy being scared.

AWARDS: A member of P.E.N. American Center, the Society of Children's Book Writers and Illustrators, the Authors Guild of Authors League of America, and the American Society of Composers, Authors, and Publishers. Literary Guild Selection and Notable Children's Trade Book in the Field of Social Studies (1985) for *The Book of Greek Gods and Heroes* and (1986) for *Herbert's Treasure.* The *New York Times* Best-Seller List (2000) for *The Witch Who Was Afraid of Witches*

FURTHER WORKS: *The Family Read-Aloud Christmas Treasury,* 1989; *Zene and the Witch Circus,* 1990; *A Young Painter, the Life and Paintings of Wang Yani,* 1991; *The Quilted Elephant and the Green Velvet Dragon,* 1991; *The Family Read-Aloud Holiday Treasury,* 1991; *Mommy's Briefcase,* 1995; *Stories to Tell a Six-Year-Old,* 1997; *Witches' Holiday,* 1998; *Summer,* 2001

BIBLIOGRAPHY: *Sixth Book of Junior Authors and Illustrators,* 1992; *Contemporary Authors,* vols. 61–64; *Something about the Author,* vol. 11; personal interview, 2000

BERNICE E. CULLINAN

LOWRY, Lois

Author, b. 20 March 1937, Honolulu, Hawaii

L. is a two-time NEWBERY MEDAL winner who writes fiction and nonfiction for children and YOUNG ADULTS. She has taken her stream of memories and shared them with readers through her fictional works. Born of a military family, she traveled and lived in different lands and cultures. L.'s father was a dentist and career army officer. During World War II, she lived with her mother's family in the Amish country of Pennsylvania. Postwar time was spent in Japan. L. attended Brown University from 1954 to 1956 and received a B.A. from the University of Southern Maine in 1972. She married in 1956, at the age of nineteen, and concentrated on rearing a family. While rearing her children, she managed to write textbooks and magazine articles, and was a photographer. An editor who had read her stories suggested that she write for children. In 1977, L. fulfilled a lifelong dream and published her first novel, *A Summer to Die*; it received the INTERNATIONAL READING ASSOCIATION Award for Promising New Writers. Although the story is fiction, the emotions of dealing with the death of a loved one stem from the author's loss of her older sister when she was in her twenties. As a writer, L. captures her audiences' attention with the astonishing ability to create two styles of works: the popular, delightfully entertaining Anastasia books and the thought-provoking, critically acclaimed books, including the two Newbery Medal winners, *Number the Stars* (1989) and *The Giver* (1993). On the light-hearted side, the character of Anastasia was introduced by L. in 1979 in *Anastasia Krupnick* at the age of ten. Throughout the following books in the SERIES, Anastasia ages from ten to her teenage years. Anastasia and her friends and family provide readers with humorous, yet realistic accounts of growing up. Her younger brother Sam is the focus of subsequent books from L. In these series, the reader is lured and entertained from the first pages. As an author, L. encourages readers to read her works through their own experiences, interpreting the story in a way that helps them grow as individuals. This wish for her readers holds true for her more serious works also. In her acceptance speech for the 1994 Newbery Medal for *The Giver,* she shares with the audience her utter delight at the myriad different responses from young readers, each imposing his own life interpretations.

L. clearly demonstrates the style of thought processes that led to the writing of her autobiography, *Looking Back: A Book of Memories* (1998). In this book, brimming with photos of her family, quotes from her books, and glimpses of her life, L. shows how her experiences transform to memories, and in turn become fodder for her stories. The format of the book enlightens L.'s readers and fans. Following an introduction entitled "How Do You Do," L. creates thirty-seven sections with titles reminiscent of key elements from her works. The first section is titled "Back and Back," in which she quotes from *The Giver* (1993): "There's much more. There's all that goes beyond—all that is Elsewhere—and all that goes back, and back, and back." The quote is followed by a 1910 photograph of her mother as a child with her family, and L.'s fictionalization as she imagines a story surrounding the picture. In this manner, L. shares with her readers, her past, and the origins of many of her ideas for her books, tying them together as a nice gift for her audience.

L. writes about day-to-day events in a way that appeals to a broad audience. With her ability to reach readers through light accounts or more serious ones, she is immensely popular with readers and critics. She states that although her books may recount large events such as the HOLOCAUST, she sees the event through the eyes of the ordinary person. In *Number the Stars,* she uses the "high shiny boots" of the soldiers over and again because that was the memory told to her by her friend Annelise, who recounted her childhood memories of the event. L. tells stories through small ordinary events and hopes that they evoke the larger events in the mind's eye of the reader. As an author, L. is a risk taker who dares to tell seemingly everyday tales in an extremely unordinary way. She feels that the 1990 Newbery Medal gave her the confidence to take risks with her writing, which in turn provides her audiences with more of her works, including another Newbery Medal. Her profession as a writer of children's books is important to her because she believes that books give children choices and freedom. L. lives in Massachusetts and continues to write, and speak to children and teachers about her writing.

AWARDS: International Reading Association Award, 1978, for *A Summer to Die;* ALA Notable Book Citation, 1980 for *Autumn Street.* American Book Award nomination, 1983, for *Anastasia Again!; Boston Globe–Horn Book* Award, Golden Kite Award, Society of Children's Book

Writers, and Child Study Award, Children's Book Committee of Bank Street College, all 1987 for *Rabble Starkey.* Christopher Award, 1988. The 1990 Newbery Medal, National Jewish Book Award, and the Sidney TAYLOR Award, National Jewish Libraries for *Number the Stars,* and the 1994 Newbery Medal for *The Giver*

FURTHER WORKS: *Find a Stranger, Say Goodbye,* 1978; *Autumn Street,* 1979; *One Hundredth Thing about Caroline,* 1985; *Switcharound,* 1985; *Rabble Starkey,* 1987; *All about Sam,* 1988; *Anastasia at This Address,* 1991; *Anastasia Absolutely,* 1995; *Stay: Keeper's Story,* 1997; *Zooman Sam,* 1999; *Gathering Blue,* 2000

BIBLIOGRAPHY: Haley-James, Shirley, "Lois L.," the *Horn Book* magazine, July/Aug. 94, vol. 66, i. 4; Lorraine, Walter, "Lois L.," the *Horn Book* magazine, July/Aug. 1994, vol. 70, i. 4; L., Lois, *Looking Back: A Book of Memories,* 1998; L., Lois, "Newbery Medal Acceptance," the *Horn Book* magazine, July/Aug. 1990, vol. 66, i. 4; *Something about the Author,* vol. 70, 1993

NANCY HORTON

LUNN, Janet
Author, b. 28 December 1928, Dallas, Texas

Born Janet Louise Swoboda, L. was reared in Vermont, New York, and New Jersey before moving to Ottawa, Ontario, Canada, in 1946 to complete her schooling. L. attended Queen's University in Kingston where she met and married Richard Lunn. In 1963, L. joined her husband and five children and became a Canadian citizen.

L. started writing in her early twenties working mostly on articles, short stories and reviews of children's books. For a number of years, L. was the primary reviewer of children's books who addressed the general public in several major Canadian newspapers bringing the voice of CANADIAN CHILDREN'S LITERATURE to a wide audience. L. wrote her first novel for children, *Double Spell,* in 1968. Published in the United States one year later as *Twin Spell,* this FANTASY novel follows a set of twins who become wrapped up in a mystery that connects them through unexplained memories to the Toronto of the 1840s. All of L.'s historical fiction for older children is marked by her firm belief in the healing powers of the supernatural. L. herself believes in ghosts and believes she shares her home in Hillier, Ontario, with a friendly female ghost. L. uses her home as the

setting for her award-winning book, *The Root Cellar* (1981). This time-shifting novel centers on an unhappy girl who finds she can somehow travel back and forth through time by way of the root cellar in her relatives' house. *The Root Cellar* was an INTERNATIONAL BOARD ON BOOKS FOR YOUNG PEOPLE Honor Book and was also the Canadian Library Association Book of the Year for Children Award. L.'s next novel, *Shadow in Hawthorn Bay* (1986), was also awarded the Book of the Year for Children Medal by the Canadian Library Association. L. has also written PICTURE BOOKS for younger children. They include *Amos's Sweater* (1988) and *Duck Cakes for Sale* (1989), as well as the nonfiction *The Story of Canada* (1992).

All of L.'s work is marked with a strong connection to her adopted land and she has done much to establish the reputation of Canadian children's writing. L. was recognized in 1982 with the Vicki Metcalf Award for her body of work by the Canadian Author's Association.

FURTHER WORKS: Adapter: *The Twelve Dancing Princesses,* 1979; *Larger Than Life: True Stories of Canadian Heroes,* 1979; *One Proud Summer,* 1988; *Come to the Fair,* 1997

BIBLIOGRAPHY: *Children's Books and Their Creators,* 1995; *Something about the Author,* vol. 68, 1992

DEDE SMALL

LYNCH, Chris
Author, b. 2 July 1962, Boston, Massachusetts

L., the fifth of seven children, was only five years old when his father died. He describes his family as a "free cheese family." His fiction for YOUNG ADULTS is often set in the tough neighborhoods of Boston, on the streets where young males have to prove themselves, and survive both physical and emotional violence, to become men. These are the city kids with whom he grew up; he knows how they speak; he knows the rivalries between brothers first hand; he is a careful observer of the life in urban areas and how it affects those who live there. His stories often use SPORTS as the major proving ground for male characters who are struggling with the concept of who they are, characters who discover and accept their identities. It is all right to be who you are, to be an outsider, to be unable to fit in. Enthusiastic male readers really identify with the characters and their situations and seek out the latest L. book. Some of their favorite titles include: *Shadow Boxer* (1993), *Iceman* (1994), and *Slot Machine* (1995).

BIBLIOGRAPHY: *Something about the Author,* vol. 95, 1998

REBECCA RAPPORT

LYNCH, P(atrick) J(ames)

Illustrator, b. Date unknown 1962, Belfast, Northern Ireland

The youngest of five children, L. began drawing as a child and because he was encouraged, he "kept at it, practiced and improved." Troubled by division in Northern Ireland, at eighteen he left Belfast and went to Brighton College of Art in England where no one was concerned about his Catholic background.

At Brighton one of his professors was Raymond BRIGGS who encouraged him to illustrate children's books. His first book, *A Bag of Moonshine* (Alan GARNER, 1986) won the MOTHER GOOSE Award. L. found *Melisande* (Edith NESBIT, 1989) in a collection of stories that had only been illustrated in black and white.

When doing Oscar Wilde's *Stories for Children* (1990) he visited Wilde's grave. Although the author is dead, L. feels there is a sort of collaboration going on and it is "nice to pay respects to the person whom you're, in effect, collaborating with." The Norwegian *East o' the Sun and West o' the Moon* (1991) was inspiration for a trip to Norway.

Illustrators that have influenced him include Arthur RACKHAM and Edmund DULAC of England and Norman Rockwell, Maxfield Parrish, and N. C. WYETH of America. He is also fond of Pre-Raphaelite painters such as John Everett Millais.

After reading the text L. spends the first two or three months doing research. From the text there are usually two or three scenes that inspire him the most and he generally starts painting those scenes. "As a general rule it (takes) about a year" to complete a book of ILLUSTRATIONS. Beginning with an inspired scene helps him keep his enthusiasm for the rest of the task. When painting, L. works on two, maybe three pictures at a time.

When Jessie Came across the Sea (Amy HEST, 1997) won the KATE GREENAWAY MEDAL, was an ABBY Award Honor Book, Parents' Choice Gold Award, Christopher Award, Sydney TAYLOR Award Honor Book, Notable Children's Trade Book in the Field of Social Studies, and IRA Notable Book for a Global Society. Jessie is chosen by the Rabbi in a village in Eastern Europe to come to America. Leaving her grandmother and all she loves, Jessie's tale reflects those of many young women who immigrated to America. It is a tale of hope and courage.

The Christmas Miracle of Jonathan Toomey (Susan WOJCIECHOWSKI, 1995) won the Kate Greenaway Medal, the Christopher Medal, Parents' Choice Honor Award, and was an AMERICAN LIBRARY ASSOCIATION Notable Children's Book. L. hesitated for almost a year before deciding to do the illustrations. A trip to Vermont and the Shelburne Museum of Early Americana gave him the atmosphere and inspiration he needed "to bring Jonathan Toomey to life in my mind."

FURTHER WORKS: *Grandad's Prayers of the Earth,* 1999

BIBLIOGRAPHY: Gillespie, J. T. and C. J. Naden, eds., *Best Books for Children: Preschool through Grade 6,* 5th ed., 1994; Candlewick Press promotional material; Interview with P. J. L. by borders. com; http:/www.borders.com/features/mmk98047. html; *Something about the Author,* vol. 79, 1995

IRVYN G. GILBERTSON

LYON, George Ella

Author, poet, b. 25 April 1949, Harlan, Kentucky

L. is an author who diversified her writings to appeal to children, young people, and adult new readers. A girl named George because the name George was a tradition in her family, L. has always been a lover of words. She remembers herself as a reading and writing child, someone who always had a story to tell. She continues to tell her stories, which usually have family roots. L. received a B.A. in English from Center College in 1971, an M.A. degree in English from the University of Arkansas in 1972 and a Ph.D. in English and creative writing from Indiana University, Bloomington, in 1978. L. has been an instructor of English and creative writing, a lecturer in humanities, and a visiting professor. L.'s words and ideas spring forth from two sources: deep connections to her strong Southern Appalachian past and new awakenings with the future through her sons. She grew up in a house her two grandfathers built with a library to house a multitude of books. Her love of reading and dreaming is apparent in her works. *A Sign* (1998) is an autobiographical poem in which L. revisits her childhood dreams and shares with the readers how they have come true for her. One example is her childhood wish to become a neon sign maker like her neighbor; she wanted to make words glow. Her realization of the dream comes as she makes words glow with emotion and meaning for her readers. Several of her ideas for books grew from the journals she had kept with her own sons' wonderings. *Father Time and the Day Boxes* (1985) and *Together* (1989), and *The Outside Inn* are examples of her responses to the catalyst of conversations with her sons.

AWARDS: Lamont Hall Award, Andrew Mountain Press (1983) for *Mountain.* Golden Kite Award (1989) for *Borrowed Children*

FURTHER WORKS: *A Regular Rolling Noah,* 1986; *A B Cedar: An Alphabet of Trees,* 1989; *Red Rover, Red Rover,* 1989; *Come a Tide,* 1990; *Basket,* 1990; *Cecil's Story,* 1991; *Mama Is a Miner,* 1994; *Here and There,* 1994; *Ada's Pal,* 1996; *A Day at Damp Camp,* 1996; *The Stranger I Left Behind,* 1997; *With a Hammer for My Heart,* 1997; *Counting on the Woods,* 1998; *Dreamplace,* 1998

BIBLIOGRAPHY: Bishop, Rudine Sims. "Profile: George Ella L.," *Language Arts,* vol. 67, Oct. 1990, p. 611; Cooper, Ilene, "A Sign," *Booklist,* Feb. 15, 1998, vol. 94, no. 12, p. 101; L., George Ella, *A Wordful Child,* 1996; Phelan, Carolyn, "A Wordful Child," *Booklist,* Sept. 1, 1996, vol. 93, no. 1, p. 121

NANCY HORTON

LYONS, Mary E(velyn)
Author, b. 28 November 1947, Place unknown

A writer of biographical and historical works for children, L.'s Southern style is enlivened by her experiences as a school librarian and reading teacher. They were the inspiration for her first book, *Sorrow's Kitchen: The Life and* FOLKLORE *of Zora Neale Hurston* (1990). As a response to a lack of published work on important AFRICAN AMERICAN figures it also led to her five titles in the African American Artists and Artisans series. Prior to *Sorrow's Kitchen* L. authored *A Story of Her Own: A Resource Guide to Teaching Literature* (National Women's History Project, 1985) for adults. An activist author, L. reflects on the value of underrepresented figures in American culture. Despite not being African American, L. considers that presumption praise toward her effectiveness as a writer. Recipient of a National Endowment for the Humanities Teacher Scholar Award as well as three fellowships from the Virginia Foundation for the Humanities, L. also plays Irish penny whistle and banjo, performing with the group Virgil and the Chicken Heads in Charlottesville, Virginia.

BIBLIOGRAPHY: *Something about the Author,* vol. 93, 1997

CRAIG LIEBERMAN

MACAULAY, David

Author, illustrator, b. 2 December 1946, Burton-on-Trent, England

M. best described his own work when he said, "I consider myself first and foremost an illustrator, in the broadest sense, someone who makes things clear through pictures and teaches through pictures." Readers recognize the quality of his work as they are invited to consider complex architectural structures and principles of engineering in both understandable and aesthetically intriguing pen-and-ink drawings. M.'s illustrations are characterized by closeups, cutaway sections, and double-paged spreads. "By using fictional story lines and characters to outline the development of such diverse structures as an ancient pyramid, a thirteenth-century cathedral, a Roman city, and the underground of a modern metropolis, he enlivens well-researched facts with HUMOR, DRAMA, and social commentary while portraying the political and economic climate of each period with authority." M. is the recipient of many AWARDS and honors, demonstrating the internationally high regard for his work from various scholarly groups.

Born in England, M. remembers a pleasant childhood with parents who were attuned to the value of showing processes to their children. In his CALDECOTT MEDAL acceptance speech, M. reflects on his parent's insistence that their children explore how things were put together, instilling the value of creativity through experiences with craftsmanship in their own kitchen. He also remembers his experiences walking to school alone

nurturing his imagination as his mind wandered. M. came to America when his father took a job here and later, in high school, discovered his talent for drawing. He entered Rhode Island School of Design to study architecture which he felt "teaches you how to devise a way of thinking that allows you to believe you can tackle any problem of any scale. . . . It fueled and educated my desire to understand how things work. Since then, I have realized that what I was learning in architecture—how to break down an immense problem into its smallest parts and put it back together logically with knowledge, expertise, and imagination—could also be applied to making books." M.'s first award-winning book was the result of his submission of the story of a gargoyle to a publisher. While the story was not necessarily desired, the drawing of a church within the manuscripts caught the publisher's attention. M. was sent to France to research what became *Cathedral* (1973). This book details from start to finish the construction of a Gothic Cathedral. The impressive actual architectural processes are represented in detail, as well as the daily life around them represents the social and historical influences on the construction. Following this book, *City* (1974), *Pyramid* (1975), *Castle* (1977), and *Mill* (1983) each combine M.'s talent for explaining architectural process through detailed ILLUSTRATION with his research of technological, historical, and social influences of each era represented.

Other works by M. take a different perspective as he looks beneath a city street to explain the ongoing processes in *Underground* (1976). *Un-*

building (1980) takes a reverse point of view on the construction of the Empire State Building as a fictional character purchases and decides to dismantle it. Maintaining his exquisite drawing style, M. creates a spoof of fact and FANTASY in a mood of satiric humor.

Using his STORYTELLING talents even further, M. created *Ship* (1993). The story begins with the discovery of a fifteenth-century wooden ship by divers, and as the ship owner's diary is discovered in Spain, the story switches to the past. Based on research, the story weaves the human element with the construction of the ship through M.'s detailed art, which, in this case, is somewhat muted with the use of color. M. also has extended his talents as a writer with *Motel of Mysteries* (1979) and *BAAA* (1985). With sophisticated humor, M. makes fun of our society as twentieth-century civilization is uncovered 2,000 years later in *Motel of Mysteries. BAAA* has been described as a tale of "modern materialism that pictures contemporary society as morally derelict and self-destructive," (Svirin, 1985, p. 53).

In *The Way Things Work* (1988) M. explains both how simple and complex everyday items work. His desire is to relate the simplicity behind much of technology. He communicates this through fictitious scientists and humorous text, describing the process behind many common items that are often taken for granted.

Black and White (1990), a CALDECOTT MEDAL winner, brings together what appears to be four separate stories in a collage format that supports the significance of illustration in telling the story of a book. The interplay between words and pictures as well as among the four stories combines to create a multilayered story that puts various points-of-view on a bigger picture. M. also combines multiple stories in *Shortcut* (1995) as he describes events and consequences in the humorous stories of six people whose paths cross and recross. Attention to carefully constructed clues is necessary as the reader connects the stories of several people through plot details. Enjoyed by children of all ages, M. "has made a distinctive contribution to children's literature by providing informative, entertaining, and thought-provoking books on buildings and the societies they illuminate." He creates an awareness of the interconnectedness of events, stories, and life across space, time, and perspective.

AWARDS: AMERICAN LIBRARY ASSOCIATION Caldecott Medal Honor (1974) for *Cathedral: The Story of Its Construction. New York Times* Ten Best Illustrated Books citation (1973) for *Cathedral.* American Institute of Graphic Arts Children's Book Show citation (1973–74) for *Cathedral.* Jugendbuchpreis (Germany). Children's Book Showcase title (1975) for *City: A Story of Roman Planning and Construction. New York Times* Outstanding Children's Book of the Year (1975) for *Pyramid; Boston Globe-Horn Book* Honor Book (1976) for *Pyramid; School Library Journal* Best of the Best Citation (1966–76) for *Underground;* AMERICAN LIBRARY ASSOCIATION Caldecott Medal Honor Book (1978) for *Castle.* ALA Best Books for YOUNG ADULTS (1980) for *Motel of the Mysteries.* Parents' Choice Award for Illustration in Children's Books (1980) for *Unbuilding. New York Times Book Review* Notable Book of the Year (1982) for *Help! Let Me Out!* School Library Journal's Best Books citation (1983) for *Mill.* M. was nominated for the Hans Christian ANDERSEN Illustrator Medal (1984). The Science Museum/Copus (London) (1989) for *The Way Things Work. Boston Globe-Horn Book* Award for Best Nonfiction Book (1989) for *The Way Things Work.* American Institute of Physics Best Science Book of the Year Award (1990) for *The Way Things Work.* ALA Caldecott Medal (1991) for *Black and White*

BIBLIOGRAPHY: *Children's Literature Review.* vol. 14, 1988; Holmes, J., "The Way David M. Works," *Publishers Weekly.* October 28, 1988, pp. 30–31. M., D., "Caldecott Medal Acceptance," *Horn Book* magazine. July/August 1991; McDonnell, C. Review of *Unbuilding,* in *Horn Book.* December 1980. p. 655; *Something about the Author,* vol. 72. 1993. Zvirin, S. Review of *"BAAA." Booklist.* September 1, 1985. p. 53

JANELLE B. MATHIS

MACDONALD, Betty

Author, b. 26 March 1908, Boulder, Colorado; d. 7 February 1958, Place unknown

M. is best known for creating the character Mrs. Piggle-Wiggle, an elderly widow with innovative solutions and magical cures for children with unmanageable behavior problems. With HUMOR and irony, M. captures the quirks and unique qualities of humans in her writing. Each chapter presents a story about a child who is cured as a crybaby, a tattle tale or show-off by Mrs. Piggle Wiggle.

Mrs. Piggle Wiggle's Farm (1954) is one of the finest books in the series because the children all use their own resources to solve their problems. One of her adult books, *The Egg and I*, about life on a chicken farm was made into a popular Hollywood film and spawned a whole Hollywood and television series. All of her books were based on real-life events, many of them autobiographical.

FURTHER WORKS: *Mrs. Piggle-Wiggle,* 1957; *Hello Mrs. Piggle-Wiggle,* 1957; *Mrs. Piggle-Wiggle's Magic,* 1957

BIBLIOGRAPHY: *Anybody Can Do Anything: The Autobiography of Betty M.,* 1950; *Yesterday's Authors of Books for Children,* vol. 1, 1977

SANDRA IMDIEKE

MACDONALD, George

Author, poet, b. 10 December 1824, Aberdeenshire, Scotland; d. 18 September 1905, Surrey, England

M. attended the University of Aberdeen. He left school for a year to earn money cataloging a private library. The books he discovered there influenced his later writing. In 1845, he received a master's degree in chemistry and physics. After completing his education, M. moved to London, where he met his future wife, Louisa Powell. They would eventually have eleven children together. M. worked as a tutor in London. In 1848, M. entered Highsbury College to become a minister. After graduation, he served as pastor of Trinity Congregational Church. M. later resigned because of his unconventional preaching methods. He worked as a part time preacher, lecturer, and journalist to support his family. In 1855, he published a book-length poem, "Within and Without." The poem caught Lady Byron's attention. He also befriended Lewis CARROLL, John RUSKIN, and other literary figures who eventually persuaded him to move to Algiers to recover from tuberculosis and to begin a literary career.

M. wrote original fairy tale ADVENTURE STORIES for children, notably "The Light Princess" and "The Golden Key," both of which were collected in *Dealings with the Fairies* (1867) *At the Back of the North Wind,* a sentimental FANTASY with evangelical allusions, was originally serialized in the magazine *Good Words for the Young* in 1868 and published as a novel in 1871. It is the

tale of gentle Diamond who goes to live with the North Wind in a lush pastoral place where life is serenely calm and the evils of the industrial age have not intruded. *The Princess and the Goblin* (1872), an adventure story with fairy characters, was also first serialized in the magazine. This story and its sequel, *The Princess and Curdie* (1883), feature the symbolic fight between good and evil, which is portrayed through the efforts of brave Curdie, a miner's son, who attempts to rescue Princess Irene trapped inside a mountain by terrifying goblins. M. served as *Words for the Young*'s editor for a brief period but gave it up to return to writing full-time. M. published books regularly, but with his large family he frequently faced financial difficulties. M.'s works have remained available in many editions since his death.

AWARDS: LL.D., Aberdeen University, 1869

FURTHER WORKS: *Dealings with the Fairies,* 1867; *Ranald Bannerman's Boyhood,* 1871; *The Princess and the Goblin,* 1872; *The Wise Woman: A Parable,* 1875

BIBLIOGRAPHY: Carpenter, H. *Secret Gardens,* 1981; Doyle, B., *The Who's Who of Children's Literature,* 1968; Knoepflmacher, U.C., *Ventures into Childland,* 1998; SENDAK, M., *CALDECOTT and Co.,* 1988

JODI PILGRIM

MACDONALD, Suse

Author, illustrator, b. 3 March 1940, Evanston, Illinois

Susan Kelsey (Suse) MacDonald is best known for her 1987 CALDECOTT MEDAL Honor Book, *Alphabatics;* it also won the Golden Kite Award for ILLUSTRATION and was named a Notable Trade Book by the NATIONAL COUNCIL OF TEACHERS OF ENGLISH. M. grew up in Glencoe, Illinois, earned a B.A. from the State University of Iowa, and studied at the New England School of Art and Design and the Radcliffe Seminar Program. Her early jobs included work as a textbook illustrator, draftsman, and designer.

Numbers (1988), a series of double-page spreads, shows magical transformations of the numbers one through ten. Each number shifts its shape into a familiar object allowing children to make connections between abstract numbers and concrete, familiar shapes based on the shape of the number. The book is a collaboration with Bill

71. ANITA LOBEL

73. LOIS LOWRY

72. ARNOLD LOBEL

74. DAVID MACAULAY

75. MARGARET MAHY

76. PATRICIA MACLACHLAN

Oakes, M.'s husband, with whom she frequently works on text and illustrations, often using paper collage. M. believes that children learn most effectively through discovery and that books should provide a format for learning through discovery. Her books feature colorful and playful shapes and figures.

FURTHER WORKS: *Space Spinners,* 1991; *Sea Shapes,* 1994; *Mentra's Lion: A Search-and-Find Adventure,* 1995; *Peck, Slither, and Slide,* 1997; *Elephants on Board,* 1999; *I Love You: A Rebus Poem,* 2000; with Bill Oakes: *Puzzlers, Numbers,* 1988; *Once upon Another,* 1990; illus. only: *Who Says a Dog Goes Bow-Wow?* (Hank de Zutter), 1993

BIBLIOGRAPHY: *Something about the Author,* vol. 54, 1989; *Sixth Book of Junior Authors and Illustrators,* 1989; "Suse Macdonald" http://www.create4kids.com/books.html (accessed February 5, 1999)

MARY ARIAIL BROUGHTON

MACLACHLAN, Patricia
Author, b. 3 March 1938, Cheyenne, Wyoming

M.'s childhood, family relationships, and places of home are reflected in her highly acclaimed PIC-TURE BOOKS and novels. Early in her life, she moved from Wyoming to Minnesota, where she was reared, then to New England where she continues to reside in Massachusetts. She enjoys reading, traveling, and playing the cello. After receiving a B.A. in 1962 from the University of Connecticut, she taught high school. M.'s childhood was filled with strong family attachments that influence her writing. She has always read to become a writer. Her mother urged her to read to get acquainted with herself. Although an avid reader as a child, successful early writing experiences were nonexistent. After an unpleasant experience with her teacher about a writing assignment, she noted in her diary that she would try not to be a writer. Her early adult life was spent rearing her family and volunteering in the Children's Aid Family Service Agency, working with foster mothers. It was only after her children started to school and she felt she needed a new direction that she considered writing. She participated in a writing class taught by Jane YOLEN. With Yolen's continued mentoring and encour-

agement, M. began writing. It changed her life. Her first publication was *The Sick Day* (1979).

All of her books are autobiographical to some degree. Her life is her research. M. states that she always starts her books with the characters and "lives" with them awhile before the plot evolves. The focus of her writings are questions and issues that confront her; therefore, it is easy to examine the author's experiences and thoughts through her books. Importance of place, transgenerational relationships, characters with artistic interests, and unusual realizations in ordinary families are constants throughout her writings. A strong sense of place is prevalent in most of her books whether the protagonist is coping with a move as in *Sarah, Plain and Tall* (1985) and *What You Know First* (1995) or treasuring the permanency of tradition and home place as in *All the Places to Love* (1994). Characters with relationships that span generations dominate M.'s writings. Virtually all of her books tell the stories of complex, but comforting relationships where characters are close to encounters with loneliness but through insightful reflection cling to roots of stability. The author is able to take readers on these journeys without overdoses of sentimental manipulation. Readers, musicians, painters, writers, and photographers exist in her family memories and experiences (as a child growing up and now as a parent); they are prolific as characters in her works such as *The Facts and Fictions of Minna Pratt* (1988). The battle of ordinary versus extraordinary is found in *Cassie Binegar* (1982) and *Unclaimed Treasures* (1984) when the characters learn to appreciate the qualities of their respective families.

There are many activities in which M. participates to motivate herself to write. She reads and listens to music when she wants to get into the writing mode. She likes direct contact with children and is impressed with their level of sophistication. While struggling with writer's block with the text of *What You Know First* (1995), she hesitantly fulfilled an obligation to speak to an elementary classroom of students. As she shared with them the story of her move as a child and the small bag of dirt she still possessed from that first home place she was touched by their comments and suggestions and together they generated not only the motivation to finish the book, but the perfectly appropriate title. M.'s works have resulted in filmstrip/cassettes, television productions, audio cassettes, and TRANSLATIONS into other languages. The author has great respect for illustrators and feels that some of the best art in America today is in children's picture books. Artists who have illustrated M.'s books include Deborah Ray KOGAN, Lloyd BLOOM, Ruth Lercher Bornstein, Maria Pia Marrella, Alexander Pertzoff, Barry MOSER, and Mike Wimmer. M.'s writings are lauded for their natural characters and the fluid language that make them successful as read-alouds for listeners of any age.

AWARDS: NEWBERY MEDAL (1986), Scott O'DELL Historical Fiction Award, Notable Children's Trade Book in the Field of Social Studies from NCCS, Christopher Award (1985) for *Sarah, Plain and Tall;* Golden Kite Award for Fiction from SCBWI (1980) for *Arthur, for the Very First Time;* CBC/NCSS (1980) for *Through Grandpa's Eyes* and (1982) for *Mama One, Mama Two* (1982); *Boston Globe–Horn Book* Award Honor Book for Fiction (1984) for *Unclaimed Treasures* (1984); Parents' Choice Foundation (1988) for *The Facts and Fictions of Minna Pratt*

FURTHER WORKS: *Moon, Stars, Frogs, and Friends,* 1980; *Tomorrow's Wizard,* 1982; *Seven Kisses in a Row,* 1983; *Three Names,* 1991; *Journey,* 1991; *Baby,* 1993; *Skylark,* 1994

BIBLIOGRAPHY: Broadwater, Lisa. "Remembering Her Roots," *Dallas Morning News,* Oct. 10, 1995, p. 4C; Silvey, Anita, ed., *Children's Literature Review,* vol. 14, 1988; *Children's Books and Their Creators,* 1995; *Something about the Author,* vol. 62, 1990

NANCY HORTON

MAESTRO, Betsy

Author, illustrator, b. 5 January 1944, New York City

As a kindergarten and first-grade teacher for eleven years, M. noticed how few nonfiction books were available for her students. As a child growing up in New York City, in addition to the many cultural opportunities she was able to experience, books had always been a part of her life. She was able to use her appreciation of children's books as an educator, and later as a writer. She noticed story elements young children enjoyed, and was able to incorporate those elements into her first book for children, *A Wise Monkey Tale* (1975). Her next book, *Where Is My Friend?*

(1976), introduced readers to Harriet the elephant, a character who would appear in many later concept books. Collaborating on books throughout her career with illustrator husband Giulio MAESTRO, M. attempts to help young children see their own life experiences through the story characters she creates. More recently M. has written nonfiction books about American history and government, among other topics.

AWARDS: Child Study Association of America's Children's Books of the Year (1976) for *Fat Polka-Dot Cat and Other Haiku;* (1987) for *The Story of the Statue of Liberty.* Notable Children's Trade Book in the Field of Social Studies by the National Council for Social Studies and the CHILDREN'S BOOK COUNCIL (1986) for *Ferryboat*

FURTHER WORKS: *Harriet Goes to the Circus: A Number Concept Book,* 1977; *Lambs for Dinner,* 1978; *Traffic: A Book of Opposites,* 1981; *Harriet at School,* 1984; *The Perfect Picnic,* 1987; *A More Perfect Union: The Story of Our Constitution,* 1987; *Snow Day,* 1989; *The Discovery of the Americas,* 1991; *The Story of Money,* 1993; *Why Do Leaves Change Color?* 1994; *Coming to America,* 1996; *The Voice of the People,* 1996; *A Sea Full of Sharks,* 1997

BIBLIOGRAPHY: *Something about the Author,* vol. 59, 1990

SANDRA IMDIEKE

MAESTRO, Giulio

Illustrator, b. 6 May 1942, New York City

M. has always been interested in art, inspired by Walt DISNEY and Walt Kelly as a young child. He pursued this interest at Cooper Union, majoring in art, and entered the field of children's literature as a book dust-jacket illustrator. His first illustrated book was *The Beginnings of the Armadillos,* published in 1970. Since that time he has illustrated over 100 books, frequently collaborating with his wife, Betsy M. He is noted for his use of a variety of techniques and mediums, and attributes his success to his flexibility in meeting the varied needs of publishers. The art for his popular elephant character, Harriet, is simple yet abstract; other design elements such as type face and border are planned with young readers in mind. Many of M.'s titles have received the Child Study Association of America's Children's Books of the Year Awards. *The Tortoise's Tug of War* (1971) and *Three Kittens* (1973), translated from the Russian of Vladimir Sudlev by Mirra GINSBURG, were included in the American Institute of Graphic Arts Children's Book Show, *Lambs for Dinner* (1978, by Betsy M.) was chosen as a Children's Choice Award winner in 1979, *Fish Facts and Bird Brains,* by Helen Roney SATTLER (1984), was selected as an Outstanding Science Trade Books for Children by the National Science Teachers Association in 1985. M. is known for his ILLUSTRATIONS for outstanding science books by authors that include Franklyn M. BRANLEY, Melvin BERGER, and Helen Roney Sattler.

M. believes that many writers and illustrators err in expecting too little from children. Therefore, M. strives to provide art of the highest quality. He credits Walt Kelly with the advice to: "Draw every day. Draw anything and everything you like. The important thing is to draw every day."

FURTHER WORKS: *Riddle Romp,* 1983; *Comets,* 1984; *Space Telescope: A Voyage into Space Book,* 1985; *Through the Year with Harriet,* 1985; *Dollars and Cents for Harriet,* 1988; *Guppies in Tuxedos,* 1988; *Halloween Howls: Riddles That Are a Scream,* 1992; *More Science Experiments You Can Eat,* 1994; *Exploration and Conquest: The Americas after Columbus: 1500–1620,* 1994; *Our Patchwork Planet: The Story of Plate Tectonics,* 1995; *What Do You Hear When Cows Sing?,* 1996; *The Story of Religion,* 1997; *The New Americans: Colonial Times, 1620–1689,* 1998

SANDRA IMDIEKE

MAGAZINES AND PERIODICALS

The phenomenal growth in number and the recent explosion in variety of children's magazines need hardly surprise the thoughtful person. Magazines possess the ability to speak to the specific needs of a group of readers, to bond these readers with common experiences, loyalties, and expectations, and to react with lightninglike speed to cultural trends. These qualities nicely suit the magazine format to children and young adults.

Magazines have been part of the American culture since the early eighteenth century. The first edited for children—*The Children's Magazine: Calculated for the Use of Families and Schools*—appeared in Hartford, Connecticut, in 1789 and lasted four issues. The idea caught on, however, and during the nineteenth century over

250 magazines were published including the two most widely known: *The Youth's Companion* (1827–1929), and *St. Nicholas* (1873–1943).

Twentieth century children's magazines focused their readership on young boys and girls with specific interests such as a love for scouting (*Boys Life,* 1911, *The American Girl,* 1917), religious teaching (*Young Judean,* 1910), and other interests and hobbies (*Youth's Musical Companion,* 1924, and *American Newspaperboy,* 1927). The organization that was to become Scholastic Inc. marketed to children in their classrooms and began publishing the *Western Pennsylvania Scholastic,* later known as *Senior Scholastic,* in 1920. Other publications, including *My Weekly Reader* (1929) followed suit.

Despite heated competition for the American child's attention, the children's magazine publishing industry first matured and flourished during the twentieth century, reinventing itself to meet new challenges brought by competition and technology. At the start of the twenty-first century, after some retrenchment, the industry appears healthy and robust.

So-called kid's magazines, like all media directed toward children, are fundamentally different from media directed at adult audiences. First, because children are impressionable, their magazines need to be carefully monitored so that they are not too propagandistic. Second, their ability to foster literacy at the same time as they entertain cause these periodicals to be welcome in the classroom and the home. Finally, their potential to inculcate knowledge and values—almost without the reader's awareness—makes them important to any organization focused on shaping values.

Children's magazines reach their readers in essentially two ways: in their institutions—schools, LIBRARIES, churches, and clubs—and in their homes. Only in the past few years have children's magazines started showing up on newsstands. Classroom magazines are largely treated as supplemental curriculum materials and are distributed in classroom-sized packets by such companies as Scholastic, Weekly Reader, and Time for Kids. Usually aimed at particular subjects and reading levels, some focus on current events while others offer classroom teachers timely curricular material in attractive, colorful formats on topics not included in less flexible textbooks.

Most relate closely to teacher needs. The American Chemical Society's *ChemMatters* treats the chemistry of consumer goods in a somewhat informal fashion, offering a relief from traditional chemistry textbooks. The whole language approach to teaching reading stimulated many teachers to populate their classrooms with kid's periodicals beyond those used as supplements to the curriculum. Teachers believe the motivational value of reading magazines for pleasure is an effective tool in stimulating reluctant readers and promoting literacy.

Most community and school libraries subscribe to a number of children's magazines. In addition to their entertainment value, the increasing emphasis on teaching research skills to fourth through eighth graders has made nonfiction children's magazines important research tools. Kid's magazines even have their own periodical guide, Children's Magazine Guide.

Periodicals also appear as part of religious education, many providing the curriculum and teaching materials. Others serve as benefits of club membership and feature reports on the club's national activities and other organizational information. But when most Americans think about children's magazines, they envision those that come into the home.

At-home magazines generally shape themselves to meet the tastes and interests of a more select group of readers, much as their adult-audience counterparts do. *Spider* (stories and poems), *Ranger Rick* (animals), *Chickadee* (natural history), and *Kid City* (science)—each narrow their potential audience by age group (ages six to nine), reading level (grades one to four) and interests. *Highlights for Children* and several other "general purpose" magazines are exceptions, following in the tradition of *St. Nicholas. Highlights* seeks to meet the language skills and interests of children two to twelve, aiming at multiple readers within the same household. In 1990, the parent corporation of *Highlights for Children* launched a children's book publishing company, Boyds Mills Press. The successful venture, built upon the "general purpose" approach of *Highlights,* includes *Wordsong,* an imprint devoted to children's POETRY.

As reader age reaches ten or eleven, publications distinguish themselves from their competi-

tion by aiming more specifically at particular subjects. *Zillions* focuses on consumerism, *Cobblestone* on social studies, *Cricket* on literature, and *Dolphin Log* on ocean life. This information is carefully tailored to the interests and sophistication of kids by editorial and art teams sensitive to the needs and capabilities of young people. The result is trusting and loyal readers.

Another difference between adult-audience magazines and those directed at kids involves the inclusion of advertising, the traditional means by which periodicals keep subscription costs down and generate profits. Many children's magazines aimed at ages two to nine do not accept outside advertising, both from a belief that children should be protected from the noise of the marketplace and from the fear of parental objections. (This is not true for most teen magazines and hobby magazines, those that reach readers aged nine to seventeen.) Despite the significant readership of children's magazines—in the neighborhood of 60 million readers—this segment of the publishing business is not highly profitable.

The limited profitability has a substantial impact on the children's magazine publishing industry. Quite a few are published as "labors of love." Others, such as *Sesame Street, Kid City,* and *3*2*1 Contact,* publications for the Children's Television Workshop, are supported by not-for-profit corporations as part of their mission and may operate at a loss. A few, like *InSights Magazine,* published by the National Rifle Association, seek to influence future beliefs and habits, finding support from their organization's other revenues. Others, such as the *Wall Street Journal: Classroom Edition* and *Guide Posts for Kids,* use children's magazines to feed readers into their adult publications.

Another area in which lack of advertising and low-profit margins impact on children's magazines lies in the paper and production quality of the finished publication. Quite a few children's magazines, such as *New Moon* and *The Goldfinch,* appear only in decidedly "unslick" one or two colors, many are printed on lower quality, uncoated paper. Were advertising included, such cost cutting would not be tolerated.

Further, because the readership changes every three or four years, marketing costs are a higher percentage of the magazine's budget than is the case with adult-audience publications. Start-up costs are also high, limiting the number of launches of new magazines and keeping those that have gained a foothold from growing rapidly.

The beginning of the 1990s marked a change in the children's magazine publishing industry. Larger publishing companies became interested in children. Most notable was Time Warner's (now AOL Time Warner) start-up of SPORTS *Illustrated for Kids* in 1991. The success of *SI for Kids,* which does carry advertising and features full-color, glossy paper, and the general high production standards of that company, stimulated a number of other publications including *Crayola Kids,* DISNEY Adventures, and *Nickelodeon* magazine. All of these also carry advertising and all appear to be more profitable than their advertising-less competition. The continuing likelihood of large circulation magazines turning their attention to kids seems certain.

While American publishing interests dominate English-language children's magazines, periodicals designed for young people appear across the globe. Many countries believe the propagandistic value of these publications requires governmental participation. Scholastic Inc. shares a major role in the world market with Bayard Presse, the French publishing giant; together they dominate the Western Europe market.

But the enduring quality of children's magazines is the fun they bring into the lives of readers. This hard work and dedication behind the fun is recognized in several AWARDS competitions. These include the Parents Choice Awards; the Paul A. Witte Short Story Award, presented by the INTERNATIONAL READING ASSOCIATION for the best original fiction appearing in a children's periodical; and the Educational Press Association of America (EdPress) Distinguished Achievement Awards including the Golden Lamp Award.

EdPress provides professional services to the publishers of children's magazines including publishing *Magazines for Kids and Teens,* a comprehensive listing of nearly 300 magazines published around the world. The guide provides descriptions written by the magazine editors themselves as well as ordering information, addresses, telephone numbers, and circulation figures. EdPress is housed at Rowan College in New Jersey.

DONALD R. STOLL, PH.D

(See also *READING RAINBOW* AND CHILDREN'S LITERATURE ON TELEVISION)

MAGORIAN, Michelle
Author, b. 6 November 1947, Portsmouth, England

M. is an author of POETRY, short fiction, and books for YOUNG ADULTS. She trained as an actress and dancer at the Bruford College of Speech and Drama, received a certificate in film studies from the University of London and attended Marcel Marceau's Ecole Internationale de Mime. M. began her literary career writing short stories in her spare time. Her main ambition was to perform and she studied subjects including mime, dance, voice, speech, verse speaking, and phonetics. While studying she wrote poetry as an extension of her reading and then began keeping a journal. During her intense reading of children's novels she realized that she wanted to write one. M.'s first book *Good Night, Mr. Tom* (1982) took her four years to write and received the INTERNATIONAL READING ASSOCIATION Promising New Writer Award. It took three years to write the first draft and one more to rewrite it. In this tender story, set during the bombing of London, Will, a pale frightened child, is evacuated from London and thrust on elderly Tom who lives alone quietly in his English village. It is obvious that Will has been abused and Tom patiently and lovingly nurses him back to health. When Will returns to London and disappears, Tom goes to search for him.

Inspiration for her second book came while performing research for her first book in repertory theater. *Back Home* (1984) was based on a photograph taken after World War II, the same period setting as *Good Night, Mr. Tom,* that she could not get out of her mind. Both books deal with social disorganization following World War II. *Back Home* was adapted as a successful television film. M. attributes her writing success to relying on imagination and persistence. *Not a Swan* (1992), set in a similar time and place, deals with seventeen-year-old Rose who befriends an unwed pregnant woman. Each of M.'s books portrays an older character who befriends a young person with artistic and theatrical talent.

BIBLIOGRAPHY: *Something about the Author,* vol. 67, 1992

CRAIG LIEBERMAN

MAHY, Margaret

Author, b. 21 March 1936, Whatatame, New Zealand

M. is the author of many acclaimed works with life-important themes and rich language including PICTURE BOOKS, short stories, fiction and nonfiction, POETRY, and scripts. She was born the daughter of Francis George, a builder, and May, a teacher. She obtained a B.A. degree from the University of New Zealand in 1958 and then attended the New Zealand Library School to become a librarian. The importance of reading and its connection to writing has been integral throughout M.'s life as a writer. As long as M. can remember she was read to and in response to that reading, loved making up rhymes, stories, and dramas in her mind. She always knew that she wanted to write a book, even before she was old enough to write. First, as an ardent young reader, she had to rely on books written by her fellow native New Zealanders, too young to realize her future contribution to NEW ZEALAND LITERATURE. Although pleased and eager to read these volumes, the numbers were limited since commercial trading with the United States was not widespread. Then, as she became the reader of books for her children, there existed a wider realm of authors from which to choose. The numbers and myriad genres of books continued to increase. More recently, reading to her grandchildren causes her to reflect on the act of reading. While reading her childhood favorites to them, she has realized the "accumulated power" of a book. She feels the bond with the books she read as a young reader: a well loved, many-times read, "favorite" takes on the power of all the voices of the people who shared the piece; therefore, creating experiences of individual consciousness.

M. began writing as a seven-year-old girl, but her recognition as a published writer came unexpectedly when Helen Hoke Watts of the Franklin Watts publishing house purchased virtually all of her existing works in 1968. M.'s first book, published in the United States by Watts, was *A Lion in the Meadow* (1969). This fable about learning and knowing the difference between FANTASY and reality was the beginning of M.'s writing trek that successfully captivates her readers. Her

themes are valued by critics for their base in family relationships and coming-of-age issues. The themes are then woven with language that is both whimsical and earnest, exact and imaginative, and engaging and thought provoking. M. has shared with audiences the process she uses while writing: she says the words aloud that she is thinking in her head until they sound right, then she writes them down. Although a seemingly confident, obviously successful writer, M. has to combat many ups and downs in her writing. She periodically feels a lack of confidence and writer's block. She continues to write throughout these hesitancies until she has completed the piece. This determination has helped M. as a prolific writer of award-winning literature for children. In 1989 she was chosen by the AMERICAN LIBRARY ASSOCIATION's Association of Library Service to Children as the May Hill Arbuthnot Lecturer.

M.'s enticing HUMOR is evident in *The Great White Man-eating Shark: A Cautionary Tale* (1990) as she spins the story of a greedy young man's consequences in trying selfishly to keep a cove to himself. *The Haunting* (1982), a middle-grade novel, reveals M.'s ability to intertwine everyday life situations, suspense, and the unexpected. Other examples of the combination of realism and supernatural of fantasy are found in the plots of *The Trickster* (1987) and *The Changeover: A Supernatural Romance* (1984). Both stories convince their readers of reality while surprising them with the unexpected. M.'s writings exemplify her belief about books and their owners: "Books are the signs, not only of their own power and content, but of the true reader's receptivity. It is a great partnership." Once a story has become a book, it belongs to the reader.

AWARDS: New Zealand Library Association's Esther Glen Award (1970) for *A Lion in the Meadow* (1973) and for *The First Margaret M. Story Book: Stories and Poems.* CARNEGIE MEDAL, British Library Association (1982) for *The Haunting* (1986), for *The Changeover: A Supernatural Romance* (1987), and for *Memory.* INTERNATIONAL BOARD ON BOOKS FOR YOUNG PEOPLE (1986) for *The Changeover;* ALA Notable Children's Book (1984) for *The Changeover.* ALA Best Books for YOUNG ADULTS (1986) for *The Changeover* (1987), for *The Tricksters* (1989), and for *Memory*

FURTHER WORKS: *The Dragon of an Ordinary Family*, 1969; *Mrs. Discombobulous*, 1969; *The Little Witch*, 1970; *17 Kings and 42 Elephants*, 1972; *The Boy with Two Shadows*, 1972; *The Man Whose Mother Was a Pirate*, 1972; *The Great Millionaire Kidnap*, 1975; *The Boy Who Was Followed Home*, 1976; *Trouble on the Bus*, 1986; *The Catalogue of the Universe*, 1986; *The Door in the Air and Other Stories*, 1988; *The Blood-and-Thunder Adventure on Hurricane Peak*, 1989; *Seven Chinese Brothers*, 1990; *Dangerous Spaces*, 1991; *The Pumpkin Man and the Crafty Creeper*, 1991; *The Other Side of Silence*, 1995; *A Summery Saturday Morning*, 1998; *A Horribly Haunted School*, 1998; *Simply Delicious*, 1999

BIBLIOGRAPHY: *Children's Literature Review*, vol. 7, M., "Accumulated Power," the *Horn Book* magazine, Mar./Apr. 1997, vol. 73, issue 2, p. 148; M., Margaret, "The Mysteries of Book Ownership," the *Horn Book* magazine, Nov./Dec. 1994, vol. 70, issue 6, p. 688; *Something about the Author*, vol. 69, 1992

NANCY HORTON

MANNING-SANDERS, Ruth
Author, b. 1895 (some sources claim 1888), Swansea, Wales; d. 12 October 1988, Penzance, Cornwall, England

M. began her writing career as a poet and adult novelist. She started writing children's books after her husband's death in 1952, publishing sixty titles during that time. M. is known for her stories of circus life, which reflect her own experience as a circus worker. M. also retold FAIRY TALES and wrote a SERIES of books with titles beginning "A Book of." The subjects for the series included dragons, wizards, trolls, and other supernatural creatures.

FURTHER WORKS: *Swan of Denmark: The Story of Hans Christian ANDERSEN*, 1949; *Circus Boy*, 1960; *A Book of Dragons*, 1964; *Tortoise Tales*, 1974; *Robin Hood and Little John*, 1977; *Folk and Fairy Tales*, 1978; *A Cauldron of Witches*, 1988

BIBLIOGRAPHY: *Something about the Author*, vol. 73, 1993

JODI PILGRIM

MANUSHKIN, Fran
Author, b. 2 November 1942, Chicago, Illinois

M. was the fifth of six children born to a family of Jewish immigrants living in Chicago. She was an avid reader as a child, but never dreamed that she would be a writer. M. came to New York in 1965 to work at the Illinois Pavilion at the World's Fair. She liked New York and stayed on, working at various jobs such as tour guide at Lincoln Center and book seller at Doubleday Book Store. She worked for ten years as an editor at Harper Junior Books, from 1968 to 1978, where she learned about editing from Ursula Nordstrom and Charlotte ZOLOTOW, whom she calls geniuses. While she worked there, she met authors like Maurice SENDAK, Arnold LOBEL, and Tomi UNGERER, whose books she admired, but could not imagine that she could ever write. M. had always thought that books emerged from authors fully formed, down to the last comma, with no effort whatsoever. It was Zolotow who encouraged M. to try writing her own books. Her first book was *Baby, Come Out!* (1972), which was translated into Dutch, French, Swedish, Danish, Japanese, Portuguese, Norwegian, and braille and won a Silver Pencil Award in the Netherlands. Many of M.'s books have traditional Jewish themes such as *The Matzah That Papa Brought Home* (1995), a cumulative verse retelling of the Passover story. She says about writing, "I still think writing is the best fun of all, on a par with eating chocolate."

FURTHER WORKS: *Latkes and Applesauce: A Hanukkah Story*, 1990; *Peeping and Sleeping*, 1994; *Starlight and Candles: The Joy of the Sabbath*, 1995; *Miriam's Cup: A Passover Story*, 1998; *Come Let Us Be Joyful: The Story of Hava Nagela*, 2000

HARA PERSON

MARCELLINO, Fred
Illustrator, b. 25 October 1939, New York City

M. knew at a young age that he was interested in art. Part of his early interest was motivated by having an older sister. If she was drawing, so was M. His early childhood was influenced by cartoon and COMIC BOOK art but once in high school M. discovered paintings and sculpture. He went to Bayside High, New York, where he was able to develop his talents in an exceptionally strong art department. Working with an outstanding teacher, M. was encouraged to attend Cooper Union. While at Cooper Union, M. was involved in designing sets for a theater group. He went on to study painting at Yale University where he received his bachelor of fine arts degree in 1962. After graduation, M. went to Venice for a year on a Fulbright Fellowship. Once back in New York, he started painting but soon turned to ILLUSTRATION and graphic design. M. switched to book covers after initially illustrating record album covers. M.'s first book cover of note was the one he created for William Wharton's *Birdy*. The book won the 1979 American Book Award for Best Cover Design, an award M. has now won three times. His other notable book covers include Tom Wolfe's *The Bonfire of the Vanities* and Judith Rossner's *August*.

M. enjoyed the idea of designing a children's book but his first effort was not accepted for publication. However, an editor liked M.'s illustrations and hired him to do book jacket designs. In 1986 M. illustrated his first children's book, *A Rat's Tale* written by Tor Seidler. Its black and white illustrations of a community of rats in New York City was well received. But it was M.'s next work that became the pivotal work in his career. *Puss in Boots* (1990) was M.'s first full-colored PICTURE BOOK. The colored pencil illustrations, which pay tribute to the work of Paul Gustave Dore who had illustrated the Perrault tale in the nineteenth century. *Puss in Boots* was named a CALDECOTT MEDAL Honor Book and earned M. the most promising new artist Cuffies award from *Publisher's Weekly*. This humorous work was marked by its originality of design with its unique and varied perspectives and its title and credits placed on the back cover instead of the front. M. said "The book is illustrated in colored pencils, a medium that is both intricate and crude allowing for richness in detail, without the option or danger of over-refinement."

M. followed this effort by designing and illustrating Tor Seidler's adaptation of Hans Christian ANDERSEN's *The Steadfast Tin Soldier* (1992). It won an honorable mention for the Critici in Erba prize at the 1993 Bologna Book Fair. M.'s brilliant illustrations and subtle HUMOR work well with new tales and bring a real spark to the tales of old.

FURTHER WORKS: *The Wainscott Weasel* (Tor Seidler). 1993. *The Pelican Chorus and Other Nonsense.* (Edward LEAR). 1995. *The Story of Little Babaji.* (Helen Bannerman). 1996

BIBLIOGRAPHY: Cummins, Julie, (1998). *Children's Book Illustration and Design,* vol. 2, 1998; *Publisher's Weekly,* July 1990, pp. 128–29; *Seventh Book of Junior Authors and Illustrators,* 1996; *Something about the Author,* vol. 68, 1992

DEDE SMALL

MARINO, Jan
Author, b. ca. 22 September 1936 (sources vary), Place unknown

M. writes REALISTIC FICTION for YOUNG ADULT readers. Her characters face challenging situations and problems, and M. is adept at bringing diverse characters and situations together. In her writing style, she sometimes uses repeated images throughout a book to help make complex issues more understandable for her audience. M. frequently visits classrooms to talk about her work; and she currently teaches creative writing at Long Island University.

FURTHER WORKS: *Searching for Atticus; The Day That Elvis Came to Town,* 1991; *Eighty-eight Steps to September,* 1989; *For the Love of Pete,* 1994; *Like Some Kind of Hero,* 1992; *The Mona Lisa of Salem Street,* 1995

SANDRA IMDIEKE

MARK, Jan
Author, b. 22 June 1943, Welwyn, Hertfordshire, England

A writer of YOUNG ADULT fiction, M. states, "I do not write specifically for children. . . . I tend rather to write about children. . . . Although I did not go to school until I was nearly eight I learned to read when I was three and to write when I was four. My educational career comprised fourteen glorious years of state-subsidized reading time. I cannot recall doing very much else—certainly not learning, since I reckoned, along with one of my fictional characters that anything I wanted to know would stick."

She wrote poems, plays, and stories with the idea of becoming a published author before finishing high school. In college she wrote parts of a novel. After graduation her job of teaching art and English left little time or energy to write.

M.'s first book *Thunder and Lightnings,* (1976) was submitted to a competition in the Guardian newspaper and won the CARNEGIE MEDAL, the Penguin/Guardian Award, and was an

AMERICAN LIBRARY ASSOCIATION Notable Book. She felt she was starting late as she was thirty-three at the time but "in retrospect [I am] glad of it, since I had by then developed a voice of my own." This is a story about moving to a new place, acceptance, loyalty, resistance to formal education versus out-of-school learning, genuine interests versus school projects and fear of changes. Centered around Lightning airplanes that have become obsolete, the main character, Andrew, a middle-class boy goes from being a car buff to an airplane buff after he meets Victor, the son of working-class parents. Life's injustices are also addressed. Andrew tells his mother about an unfair punishment Victor receives. His mother replies: "There's no such thing as fairness. It's a word made up to keep children quiet. When you discover it's a fraud then you're starting to grow up. The difference between you and Victor is that you're still finding out and he knows perfectly well already." Dissimilar in exposing their feelings but similar in loneliness, the boys encourage and support one another. M. admits "it's got no plot" but it is straightforward, uncomplicated and an easy read.

M. felt she "started well by winning a competition for new fiction but this has imposed on me the challenge to produce always something at least as good as the first book. I dare not fall below that standard."

Under the Autumn Garden (1977) is a story of relationships and school. Matthew has convinced himself there is something historical buried in his garden and he digs holes in the backyard to find a specimen for his school project on local history. Children of the contractor fixing the house tolerate Matthew, help dig, take away some old bottles that are found and refuse to give them back. Matthew's efforts provide the story framework. A ghost of a knight, Sir Oliver, walks about in November and Matthew is certain the ghost wants him to find something to ease his lonely ghost walk. It becomes apparent that while Matthew seemingly is digging a hole searching for a medieval priory, in actuality he is hiding from reality. After all his digging Matthew accidentally finds a token of Sir Oliver's.

Handles (1983) won a Carnegie Medal. To compensate for her brother's going to camp, eleven-year-old Erica goes on a summer visit to her mother's sister only to find she wants her for the help she can give. To add to her frustration, her Aunt's son is excused from any labor and sits around while Erica works. Desperate to go home she writes a letter to her mother but then is sent to town and finds a motorcycle shop run by Mr. Wainright, better known as "Elsie." Erica loves motorcycles and Elsie has "handles" (a descriptive nickname) for everyone, hence the name of the book. This story is about adjusting to your situation, perseverance, attitude, responsibility, finding where you fit and acceptance. There is a glossary of terms at the end to explain the British terminology.

A staunch opponent of CENSORSHIP, M. has been criticized for the despairing messages of *The Ennead* (1978), *Divide and Rule* (1980), and *Aquarius* (1982), books written for mature young adults. Defending her writing, M. believes she should write what she wants without pressure from reviewers. She says she "is setting up situations and inviting the reader to explore the situation along with the writer. They're for a sophisticated reader and they're deliberately written to discourage an unsophisticated reader. . . . I like to make the reader work hard." *The Ennead* is SCIENCE FICTION set in the future. The story zeros in on the problem of how much a person should compromise to be accepted and on the question of whether morality can ruin good people. In this tale the individual struggles to keep integrity intact and to stay alive in a hostile alien society that exploits people. Only those who conform survive.

M. much prefers writing short stories. "I have to explain this to school children. They think I like writing short stories because short stories are quickly done and therefore easy. . . . In fact, writing short stories is harder than writing novels. You can't get away with anything in a short story. . . . It is said that in a novel every chapter must count; in a short story every sentence must count." Following the title of her short-story collection, *Nothing to Be Afraid Of* (1980) M. wrote an article for the British education journal *English in Education* entitled, "Something to Be Afraid Of." The article emphasizes a recurring theme in her work; there is something to be afraid of for the isolated, unusual, or sensitive child who must come to terms with reality.

"My main aim always is to write about people
. . . A character must be the author of his own
misfortune and he is likely to be venal, amoral
or downright corrupt. He is not likely to prosper
thereby, however, since he is stimulated by a
flourishing and invariably misplaced faith in his
own faulty perceptions. If there are any villians
in my books they are the opportunists who have
been successful. M. has also written several PIC-
TURE BOOKS including *Fun* (1987) and *Silly
Tails* (1993).

FURTHER WORKS: Author: *Fur,* 1986; *In Black
and White and Other Stories,* 1992; *Fun with
Mrs. Thumb,* 1993; Editor: *The Oxford Book of
Children's Stories,* 1995

BIBLIOGRAPHY: *CHILDREN'S BOOK COUNCIL:
Children's Book AWARDS and Prizes,* 1985; Children's Literature Research, vol. 11, 1986; *Fiction,
FOLKLORE, FANTASY and POETRY for Children,
1876–1985,* vols. 1 and 2, 1986; Silvey, Anita,
ed., *Children's Books and Their Creators,* 1995;
Something about the Author, vol. 22, 1981, and
vol. 69, 1992
IRVYN G. GILBERTSON

MARK TWAIN
(See CLEMENS, Samuel Langhorne)

MARRIN, Albert
Author, b. 24 July 1936, New York City

M. is a respected author of historical nonfiction
who engages young readers with DRAMA and intriguing characters. He received a B.A. from The
City College (1958), an M.Ed. from Yeshiva University, M.A. (1961) and Ph.D. (1968) from Columbia University. M. has been a high-school
social studies teacher, college professor, and
chairperson of the history department.

M. recounts past major events, struggles, con-
quests, and wars in the United States and the
world. From *Overland: D-Day and the Invasion
of Europe* (1982) to *Commander in Chief Abraham Lincoln and the Civil War* (1997), M. is meticulous in his details and anecdotes; yet his stories are told with the personalities of the leaders
and tyrants during significant periods of time. In
*"Unconditional Surrender": U. S. Grant and the
Civil War,* (1994), M. exhibits his craft as a writer
to explicate Grant's role at one point in the Civil
War. It is also in this title that the reader sees

evidence of M.'s fairness in his presentation of
Grant's shortcomings and triumphs. One of the
best examples of M.'s talent for telling compelling anecdotes and conveying vivid descriptions
is in *Plains Warrior: Chief Quanah Parker and
the Commanches* (1996). An especially impressive title in M.'s later works is *Commander in
Chief Abraham Lincoln and the Civil War* (1997).
It intrigues the reader with new insights, a detailed depiction of slavery in America and documentation with more than 120 bibliographical titles.
Although some critics allude to M.'s biases and
oversimplification, more importantly he is known
for his well-documented, readable chronicles.

AWARDS: Notable Children's Trade Book selec-
tion, National Council for Social Studies and
CHILDREN'S BOOK COUNCIL and *Boston Globe–
Horn Book* Honor Book (1985) for *1812: The
War Nobody Won.* Western Heritage Award, Na-
tional Cowboy Hall of Fame, and Spur Award,
Western Writers of America (1993) for *Cowboys,
Indians, and Gunfighters: The Story of the Cattle
Kingdom. Boston Globe/Horn Book* Honor Book
(1994) and Dorothy Canfield Fisher Children's
Book Award (1995) for *"Unconditional Surren-
der": U.S. Grant and the Civil War.* Children's
Book Guild and the *Washington Post* Nonfiction
Award for contribution to children's literature
(1995)

FURTHER WORKS: *The Yanks Are Coming: The
United States in the First World War,* 1986; *Hitler,* 1987; *America and Vietnam: The Elephant
and the Tiger,* 1992; *Empires Lost and Won: The
Spanish Heritage in the Southwest,* 1996

BIBLIOGRAPHY: Burns, Mary M., *Horn Book* maga-
zine July–August 1994, vol. 70, no. 4, p. 473. Culli-
nan, Bernice E., *Literature and the Child,* 1989;
Lempke, Susan, *Booklist,* Dec. 15, 1997, p. 693;
Phelan, Carolyn. *Booklist,* April 1, 1994, p. 1440;
Sherman, Chris. *Booklist,* June 1, 1996, p. 1723
NANCY HORTON

MARSHAK, Samuel (Samuil)
Author, translator, editor, publisher, b. 3 November 1887, Voronezh, Russia; d. 4 July 1964, Moscow, Union of Soviet Socialist Republics
(U.S.S.R.)

An eminent children's poet and playwright, translator, editor, and publisher, M. began writing at a
very young age. Shaping children's literature of
the early Soviet period, M.'s education in En-

gland may have influenced his interest in the POETRY and FOLKORE (which he later translated) of that country as well as that of his own. M. is best known outside the former U.S.S.R. for his works of Russian and Slavic folklore, such as *The Month Brothers* (1967/1983). Within the former U.S.S.R., in addition to being one of the best-loved writers for children, he was also a respected satirist and lyrical poet.

FURTHER WORKS: *House in the Meadow,* 1971; *The Merry Starlings* (With David Harms), 1983; *The Pup Grew Up,* 1989; *The Postman,* 1948

BIBLIOGRAPHY: *Readers' Guide to Russian Literature,* 1998

GWYNNE ASH

MARSHALL, James

Author, illustrator, b. 10 October 1942, San Antonio, Texas; d. 13 October 1992, New York City

M. was a popular author and self-taught illustrator who created several SERIES of books featuring unforgettable characters such as Fox, the Cut-ups, and the ebullient hippopotamus team of George and Martha. M. was known for his ability to use understatement and irony as he created characters who deal with friendship, kindness, and other themes relevant to childhood. His cartoonlike line drawings and flat spaces filled with watercolor washes provide a suitable context for many delightfully zany characters. Young children laugh with superiority as they realize the folly of the characters' actions. For example, in *Yummers!* (1973) Emily Pig, recognizing that she is overweight, decides to solve her problem by getting more exercise. Emily manages to turn a walk with her friend Eugene Turtle into an eating orgy. She consumes enough goodies of every description to give her a stomachache and needs to take a taxi home. When Eugene checks in on her, Emily tells her friend that the reason she got sick "must have been all that walking."

M. grew up on a farm near San Antonio. Reared in a musical family, he planned to study viola and won a scholarship to the New England Conservatory of Music in Boston. Although he flourished as a musician, his career was cut short when he injured his hand as he was jerked out of his seat during an airplane trip. He returned to Texas where he attended San Antonio College

and Trinity College. In 1967, M. earned his B.A. from Southern Connecticut State College with a degree in history and French. After graduation, he taught French and Spanish at Cathedral High School in Boston.

Although M. never formally studied art, he loved to draw pictures as a hobby. One afternoon in 1971, Marshall was making sketches as he lay on a hammock outside his mother's house. From inside, he overheard Edward Albee's drama, *Who's Afraid of Virginia Woolf,* playing on the television. Taking inspiration (and first names) from the contentious protagonists, George and Martha, he created the hippopotamus duo that became one of his most popular self-illustrated series. Unlike Albee's George and Martha, M.'s characters are lovable, humorous, and childlike. Each of the seven books in the series finds George and Martha involved in good-natured pranks and outright nonsense, making them delightful reading for younger children. In a review of *George and Martha* (1972), one reviewer wrote, "M. has a gimlet eye for the small conflicts that lead to wounded feelings between friends, and for the affectionate honesty that can heal the hurt. The drawings amplify the plot with comic details."

In order to circumvent an exclusive contract with his publishing house, the author wrote several of his books for another company under a pseudonym. His EASY-TO-READ Fox series, penned under the name of Edward Marshall, features a devilish character who tries to outwit others but usually winds up getting outfoxed himself. This self-illustrated series includes *Three by the Sea* (1981), *Fox and His Friends* (1982), *Fox in Love* (1982), *Fox on Wheels* (1983), *Four on the Shore* (1985), *Fox Outfoxed* (1992), and *Fox on the Stage* (1993). Among the many positive reviews of the Fox books was critic Betsy HEARNE's discussion of *Fox on the Job* (1988): "The words are easy, the stories funny, the watercolor cartoons absurdly suited to Fox's antics, which are calculated (correctly) to appeal to youngsters who need all the HUMOR they can get for the serious business of decoding."

While in college, M. studied French under Harry ALLARD, with whom he eventually collaborated on several works, including the popular Miss Nelson books. In *Miss Nelson Is Missing!*

(1977), a nice teacher, who is having difficulty getting her students under control, disguises herself as the strict and intimidating Miss Viola Swamp. The students learn a lesson in behavior and are happy to get their "real" teacher back. The book received an Edgar Allan Poe Award nomination in 1978. Other Miss Nelson books include *Miss Nelson Is Back* (1982) and *Miss Nelson Has a Field Day* (1985). M.'s long and successful collaboration with Allard also produced the Stupids, a series of stories about the members of a family who are prone to mishaps and preposterous antics. Typical Stupids foolishness is contained in *The Stupids Die* (1981) in which the Stupids do not actually die, but they assume that they are dead when the lights go out and that they have arrived in heaven when the lights come back on.

M. illustrated humorous retellings of several children's classics, including *Red Riding Hood* (1987), *Hey, Diddle, Diddle* (1989), *The Three Little Pigs* (1989), *Hansel and Gretel* (1990), and *Goldilocks and the Three Bears* (1988), for which he received a CALDECOTT MEDAL Honor. A reviewer wrote that M.'s "wonderfully unique characters" in *Goldilocks* "are as offbeat and self-propelled as ever; the book boasts many jolly details and the pictures burst with color."

Many of M.'s works have been adapted for audio and video releases. Two books that M. created with Harry Allard, *It's So Nice to Have a Wolf around the House* (1977) and *Miss Nelson Is Missing!* (1977) were made into full-length television cartoon features. Numerous books of M.'s or of M./Allard collaborations have been made into filmstrip/cassette or book/cassette sets. In addition, M. illustrated many books for other authors, including Byrd BAYLOR, Jane YOLEN, Russell HOBAN, and Cynthia Jameson. *Swine Lake* (1999), a manuscript M. was working on at his death was illustrated by Maurice SENDAK. This comic tour de force introduces young readers to the ballet and the dangers of a wolf hungry for a delicious roast pig dinner.

AWARDS: ALA Caldecott Medal Honor Book (1989) for *Goldilocks and the Three Bears*. *New York Times* Best Illustrated Children's Books of the Year (1972) for *George and Martha* (1975), for *The Tutti-Frutti Case* (Harry Allard, author) (1991), for *Old Mother Hubbard and Her Wonderful Dog*. University of Southern Mississippi,

DE GRUMMOND REFERENCE Collection Silver Medallion, 1992

FURTHER WORKS: Self-illustrated: *What's the Matter with Carruthers?* 1972. *Portly McSwine.* 1979. *Rapscallion Jones.* 1983. *Wings: A Tale of Two Chickens.* 1986. *Rats on the Roof and Other Stories.* 1991. *Pocketful of Nonsense.* 1992. *Rats on the Range and Other Stories.* 1993. Illustrator: *Plink, Plink, Plink.* (Byrd Baylor). 1971. *A Day with Whisker Wickles.* (Cynthia Jameson). 1975. *Dinner at Alberta's.* (Russell Hoban), 1975. *How Beastly! A Menagerie of Nonsense.* (Jane Yolen). 1980

BIBLIOGRAPHY: *Children's Literature Review,* vol. 21, 1990; *Major Authors and Illustrators Supplement,* 1998; *Something about the Author,* vol 75, 1994

MARY ARIAIL BROUGHTON

MARTIN, Ann M.

Author, b. 12 August 1955, Princeton, New Jersey

M., the child of a preschool teacher mother and artist father, was very well read as a child. Her favorite stories were *Winnie-the-Pooh* (MILNE, 1926) and *The Wonderful Wizard of Oz* (BAUM, 1900). Before she was able to write books of her own she would spend time dictating stories to her mother. She and her best friend created their own clubs and businesses as children, such as generating a local neighborhood newsletter, founding their own library, and producing, writing, and performing their own plays for friends and family. Although these businesses were short-lived, M.'s business savvy formed the basis for her most popular book SERIES, The Babysitters Club, for which *Publishers Weekly* deemed M. "the queen of the children's best-sellers."

M. did not realize she wanted to be an author right away; she had a desperate desire to teach. She graduated from Smith College in 1977 with a teaching degree and taught school for one year. M. realized after that first year that she wanted to be in the children's book business and entered the field of publishing. Her first book, *Bummer Summer,* was published in 1983, along with two other books, *Just You and Me,* and *My Puppy Scrapbook.*

M. uses childhood memories and past experiences as starting points for her books, but relatively few are based on actual events in her life.

Inside Out (1984) uses scenarios from her work as a therapist to help her main character cope with an autistic sibling. After reading the book, many children write to her saying they feel she understands what it is like having a family member with a handicap. *Stage Fright* (1984) is more autobiographical, because like her main character M. was terrified to speak in front of a crowd when she was young.

M. believes her books are successful because she uses themes relevant to her readers' lives, and keeps her writing down to earth and realistic. In *With You or without You* (1986) she discusses the theme of DEATH. Her readers can identify with Liza, the main character, because she uses realistic dialogue and heartfelt description to portray Liza's pain. *Missing since Monday* (1986), a gripping, tense mystery, explores Maggie's guilt after her younger sister is found to be missing while under Maggie's supervision. Children often left to care for their younger siblings identify with Maggie's plight.

Alternatively, in *Ten Kids, No Pets* (1988) M. uses HUMOR to describe the Rosso family's move from the city to the country. The Rossos have ten children who all want to have a family pet, which is a forbidden family rule. Each child tries to break the rule one way or another by sneaking various sorts of pets into the house including rabbits, birds, and a turkey. Readers identify with the comical lengths to which these children go in order to accomplish their mission. The Rosso's story is continued in *Eleven Kids, One Summer* (1991) when the family goes to Fire Island on a vacation filled with chaos and confusion.

When M. was asked to create a miniseries about a babysitting club, she once again relied on her past experiences to help her create realistic characters. She needed someone shy and quiet, someone outgoing and energetic, etc. She decided to model her characters on people she knew, including herself. These fundamental character traits add to the appeal of her first, and most lasting, series of books known as the Babysitters Club, which began in 1986. After the first six books in the series hit number one on the B. Dalton Juvenile Best-seller list, the publishers realized M.'s popularity, and they asked her to produce more books. Since 1986, M. has created over one hundred stories in the Babysitters Club

series for girls ages eight to twelve. She also created a Little Sister companion series, in 1988, for girls aged seven to nine.

M.'s series, California Diaries, beginning in 1997, uses the diary platform for her characters to introduce themselves and their dilemmas. These books, intended for ages eleven to thirteen, deal with significantly more realistic issues than those for her younger audience. Each character in the series has some sort of problem readers may be able to identify with, including the search for perfection, pressure from parents, peer pressure, family relationships, romance, terminal illness, etc. In this series, M. supplies the reader with an honest view on modern teenage lifestyles and the hardships adolescence can bring. M. and Paula DANZIGER collaborated on *P.S. Longer Letter Later* (1998) by E-mail correspondence. *Snail Mail No More* (2000) continues the long-distance correspondence between friends.

Unlike most series writers, M. writes most of the books herself. She only takes two months off each year, while another writer takes her place, but M. still has input with those books she doesn't actually write. Her writing schedule demands a disciplined routine: She wakes at 5:30 A.M. every day and begins writing, producing at least two books a month on this timetable. In addition to her heavy workload, M. also heads the Ann M. Martin Foundation, founded in 1990, which provides financial support to causes benefiting children, education, and literacy in communities throughout the United States.

FURTHER WORKS: *Me and Katie (the Pest)*, 1985; *Just a Summer Romance*, 1987; *Slam Book*, 1987; *Yours Truly*, 1988; *Fancy Dance in Feather Town*, 1988; *Ma and Pa Dracula*, 1989; *Moving Day in Feather Town*, 1989; *Rachel Parker, Kindergarten Show-off*, 1992; *Leo the Magnificat*, 1996

BIBLIOGRAPHY: Becker, Margot R., *A.M.M.: The Story of the Author of the Baby-Sitters Club*, 1995. *Something about the Author*, vol. 70, 1993

DENISE P. BEASLEY

MARTIN, Bill (William), Jr.
Author, b. 20 March 1916, Hiawatha, Kansas

M. is recognized by all elementary-school teachers in the United States for his writings and recordings of PICTURE BOOKS and beginning readers. It is noteworthy that a man who is credited with creating and editing nearly two dozen SERIES of texts for children was himself uninterested in reading as a child. However, he enjoyed listening to FAMILY STORIES. Eventually, an elementary school teacher inspired him to discover the joys of reading—as well as listening to—stories. M.'s delight in the sound of language permeates his work as a children's author.

M. graduated from Kansas State Teachers College (now Emporia State University) in 1934, and began a career as a high school teacher. After taking a post as a school principal, M. continued his education, earning his master's (1957) and doctoral degrees (1961) at Northwestern University. In 1960, he began a seven-year stint as a children's textbook and picture-book editor for Holt, Rinehart and Winston. Since 1967, he has continued to edit as well as write, lecture, and produce audio and video recordings for children.

During World War II, M. served in the Air Force as a newspaper editor. He began writing for children during this time, his career given a jump start when Eleanor Roosevelt mentioned his first picture book (written with his brother), *The Little Squeegy Bug* (1945), during one of her radio talks. M. continued to write picture books with his brother for the next eight years. One, *The Brave Little Indian* (1951), originally was published with ILLUSTRATIONS by Charlene Bisch. In 1967, it was reissued with new illustrations by Eric CARLE, who also illustrated *Brown Bear, Brown Bear, What Do You See?* (1967). Carle illustrated M.'s *A Ghost Story* (1970) and *Polar Bear, Polar Bear, What Do You Hear?* (1991) as well.

Besides his brother, M. has worked with several coauthors. Peggy Brogan coauthored the volumes of M.'s Sounds of Language series, including *Sounds After Dark* (1970), *Sounds Freedom Ring* (1973), and *Sounds of Our Heritage* (1981). With John ARCHAMBAULT, M. has created some of his most critically acclaimed books, including *Knots on a Counting Rope* (1966; reissued 1987), *The Ghost-Eye Tree* (1985), *Barn Dance!* (1986), *Here Are My Hands* (1987), and *Chicka Chicka Boom Boom* (Lois EHLERT, illus., 1989). These particular titles maintain M.'s goal of providing young readers with simple stories while offering them a sensitive and revealing view of the world, which is not, in fact, a simple place. *Knots on a Counting Rope* presents readers with a blind boy

and his loving grandfather, as the latter helps the boy learn the stories of the past and how to approach the future. *Chicka Chicka Boom Boom* is an alphabet book which has enjoyed a renaissance by way of the recording made of it, under M.'s direction, with Ray Charles as the narrator. The book features bold graphic designs in bright primary colors and the rhythmic alphabet sequences invite audience participation by dancing and chanting along with the narrator.

In the early 1970s, many of M.'s books were created or repackaged to provide early grade textbook series in social studies and science. His longtime publisher, Holt, as well as the *Encyclopaedia Britannica* Educational Corporation, brought these series to market at a time when classroom teachers were becoming interested in providing students with literature-based texts.

Old Devil Wind (originally, 1970; reissued with new illustrations by Barry Root, 1993) and *The Maestro Plays* (originally, 1970; reissued with new illustrations by Vladimir Radunsky, 1995) are among several of M.'s picture books written without a coauthor. In the first, his text conveys the spookiness of a windy night while the latter allows readers to appreciate M.'s enthusiasm for MUSIC through his use of adjectives. In both books, the illustrations advance the text without outshining it, making the works excellent read-alouds and providing illustrators the opportunity to reenvision an older picture-book story. In addition to authoring original stories and present literary approaches to introductory science, M. also adapts and retells traditional tales. *Fire! Fire! Said Mrs. McGuire* (Schroeder, illus., 1970) tells of a house fire and subsequent professional flame suppression, here featuring a host of female barnyard animals. M.'s Wise Owl Books: Literature series includes *The Emperor's Nightingale, The Proud Peacock,* and *The Selfish Giant* (all 1971).

True to his original interest in STORYTELLING, M. records some of his books so that they can be heard in his personal voice. These tapes often include information about the work of storytelling and creating literature. He has also written a book for adults on the subject of storytelling, *The Human Connection: Language and Literature* (1967).

FURTHER WORKS: *Hook and Ladder* No. 3 (with Bernard Martin). 1948. *Christmas Puppy* (with

B. Martin). 1949. *The Eagle Has Landed.* 1970. *The Happy Hippopotami.* 1970. *King of the Mountain.* 1970. Wise Owl Books: Science series. 1971. Wise Owl Books: Social Studies series. 1971. Wise Owl Books: Arithmetic series. 1971. *White Dynamite and Curly Kidd.* (with Archambault). 1986

BIBLIOGRAPHY: *Contemporary Authors,* vol. 130, 1990; Silvey, Anita, ed., *Children's Books and Their Creators,* 1995; Martin, B., "A Visit with Bill M., Jr. (videotape), 1996

FRANCISCA GOLDSMITH

MARTIN, Patricia Miles (Miska Miles)

Author, b. 14, November 1899, Cherokee, Kansas; d. 2 January 1986, San Mateo, California

Reared in the midwest, M. created many of her stories from childhood memories of her grandfather's farm in Kansas. She began writing stories and poems at a very young age. M. attended the University of Wyoming and taught school for four years in Colorado and Wyoming. She moved to San Mateo, California, in 1942. Her career as a writer began by chance. M. had planned to take an upholstery class at the College of San Mateo. Due to full enrollment, she took creative writing instead. A year later, her first book, *Sylvester Jones and the Voice in the Forest,* was published.

M. wrote over eighty books in her lifetime. She wrote about things that held importance to her. Many of her best-known works were published under the pseudonym Miska Miles. M. also wrote under the pseudonym Jerry Lane.

AWARDS: ALA NEWBERY MEDAL Honor Book (1972), Christopher Medal (1972), Brooklyn Museum-Brooklyn Public Library art books for Children citation (1973) for *Annie and the Old One. New York Herald Tribune* Children's Spring Book Festival Honor Book (1959) for *The Pointed Brush.* New York Academy of Sciences Citation (1973) for *Wharf Rat.* In addition, thirteen of M.'s books were honored as Junior Literary Guild selections

FURTHER WORKS: *Happy Piper and the Goat,* 1960; *Kickapoo,* 1961; *Little Two and the Peach Tree,* 1963; *The Greedy One,* 1964, *Mississippi Possum,* 1965; *Jump, Frog, Jump,* 1965; *One Special Dog,* 1968; *See a White Horse,* 1963; *The Pieces of Home,* 1967; *Uncle Fonzo's Ford,* 1968; *Hoagie's Rifle-gun,* 1970; *Gertrude's Pocket,* 1970; *Annie and the Old One,* 1971; *Wharf Rat,* 1973; *Swim Little Duck,* 1976

BIBLIOGRAPHY: *Something about the Author,* vol. 43, 1986, and vol. 48, 1987

JODI PILGRIM

MARTIN, Rafe

Author, storyteller, b. 22 January 1946, Place unknown

M.'s childhood was influenced by the many Asian objects decorating his New York City home. His father returned from World War II with items from China and Japan, as well as the stories he had heard while overseas. M.'s interest in the tales of Asia continued, and he has studied the cultures of Asia for over thirty years. He has retold many of these stories in his books for children, winning international recognition as a writer and storyteller. He says that stories empower children's imaginations. He regards STORYTELLING, the "interrelation of all living things," as an opportunity to have his readers share both the personal and universal experiences of other cultures. "To tell a story is to reenter the primary territory of the imagination, a realm in which words actually live," says M. "Books, cultures, our own personalities all arise from and take root in this ancient, familiar, essentially mythic—in the sense of being more, not less, than true facts—realm. The delight of storytelling is to know it again as one's own."

Mysterious Tales of Japan (1996) is based on the Buddhist and Shinto principle of compassion referred to as "kindness repaid" and Japanese "fundamental respect for the Invisible." In *The Hungry Tigress: Buddhist Myths, Legends, and Jataka Tales* (paperback ed, 1999), M. focuses on ancient Buddhist fables with animal characters, stressing themes of wisdom, heroism, nonviolence, and caring.

His interest in stories from the oral tradition has led him to the stories of the Chinook and Inuit people of the American Northwest. In *The Eagle's Gift* (1997) and *The Boy Who Lived with the Seals* (David SHANNON, illus, 1993) M. relates northwestern legends. *The Rough-Face Girl* (1992) retells an Algonquin Indian version of Cinderella, emphasizing the virtues of inner beauty and strength. In retelling old tales, M. passes on native people's reverence for the sacredness of all life.

AWARDS: AMERICAN LIBRARY ASSOCIATION Notable Children's Book (1985) for *Foolish Rabbit's Big Mistake* (Ed YOUNG, illus.), and (1989) for *Will's Mammoth* (Stephen GAMMELL, illus.)

FURTHER WORKS: *Foolish Rabbit's Big Mistake,* 1985; *One Hand Clapping: Zen Stories for All Ages,* 1995; *The Boy Who Loved Mammoths,* 1996; *The Monkey's Bridge,* 1997; *The Brave Little Parrot,* 1998

SANDRA IMDIEKE

MARZOLLO, Jean

Author, b. 24 June 1942, Manchester, Connecticut

M. attended the University of Connecticut, receiving her B.A. degree in 1964. One year later, M. earned her M.A.T. degree from Harvard University. After teaching for a year in Arlington, Massachusetts, M. worked at Harvard's Project Upward Bound. It was at this point that she knew she wanted to enter the field of educational publishing. M. moved to New York in order to be closer to the publishing world, but her first job was as a preschool researcher in the late 1960s.

In 1972, M. coauthored her first book, a practical book for parents titled *Learning through Play.* The same year M. became editor of Scholastic's kindergarten magazine *Let's Find Out.* Enjoying writing in a variety of styles, M. has worked in a number of genres and has more than sixty books to her credit. Nonfiction for parents, YOUNG ADULT novels, early readers, and PICTURE BOOKS are all a part of M.'s portfolio. In the picture-book format, she is best known for the I Spy series, with Walter WICK, of the early 1990s. The brightly colored photographs and rhymed riddles that accompany them are often used by teachers and parents to promote skills such as observation. A more traditional picture book, *Close Your Eyes* (1978), looks in at a sleeping child and ponders in poetic text what he must be thinking. It was a Junior Literary Guild selection.

M. has written numerous books for early readers, both fiction and nonfiction. Young adults have enjoyed *Halfway down Paddy Lane* (1981), a time-warp novel that draws on M.'s Irish background. It was named a Best Book for Young Adults by the AMERICAN LIBRARY ASSOCIATION. M. views writing as an intriguing and enjoyable challenge. Whatever the genre, readers can always be sure that M.'s work is written with the goal of supporting children and families.

FURTHER WORKS: *The House That Dreams Painted,* 1975; *Up on Hollercat Hill,* 1980; *Soccer Sam,* 1987; *The Teddy Bear Book,* 1989; *I'm a Tyrannosaurus: A Book of Dinosaur Rhymes,* 1993; *In 1776,* 1994; *Home Sweet Home,* 1997

BIBLIOGRAPHY: *Sixth Book of Junior Authors and Illustrators,* 1989; *Something about the Author,* vol. 77, 1994

DEDE SMALL

MASEFIELD, John

Poet, author, b. 1 June 1878, Ledbury, Herefordshire, England; d. 12 May 1967, Berkshire, England

Although primarily known as an adult author and British Poet Laureate from 1930 until his death, M. also wrote for children. His mother died when he was six and M. was sent to live with relatives who later thought a naval career best suited the thirteen-year-old. M. suffered violently from seasickness and deserted ship in America. He worked at odd jobs for two years and returned to England, where he started writing. His first published book, *Salt-Water Ballads,* appeared in 1902 and contained his famous poem "Sea Fever" with the memorable line "I must go down to the sea again."

His first children's books, *A Book of Discoveries* and *Martin Hyde* and *The Duke's Messenger,* were published in 1910. *Martin Hyde* uses a first-person narrative to tell a traditional adventure story with a historical-fiction setting; there are plots, counterplots, and lots of political intrigue typical of ADVENTURE STORIES of that era. His next book, *Jim Davis* (1911), is a sea adventure again filled with mystery, suspense, smuggling, and galloping hoofbeats, which is set along the Devon coast. Other adventure novels followed but it is his POETRY for which M. is best remembered. *Reynard the Fox* (1919) is a narrative poem relating a fox hunt through the eyes of the fox. *The Midnight Folk* (1927) and its sequel, *The Box of Delights* (1935), are ethereal stories of talking animals, shape changers, adventurers and highwaymen, evil governesses, enchantress, grotesque characters, and thoroughly depraved villains—a combination of stories with traditional child appeal. With its Christmas setting, *The Box of Delights* recounts its characters' return home from school for their Christmas holidays when an old man entrusts them with the safekeeping of an enchanted box. The story was successfully adapted as a BBC Christmas special in 1985. In 1961 a John Masefield Story-Telling Festival was established in Toronto.

FURTHER WORKS: *King Cole,* 1921; *Bird of Dawning,* 1933; *Dead Ned,* 1938; *Live and Kicking Ned,* 1930

BIBLIOGRAPHY: Dwyer, June, *John M.,* 1987; Hunt, P. ed., *Children's Literature: An Illustrated History,* 1995; MEIGS, C., et al., *A Critical History of Children's Literature,* 1969

DIANE G. PERSON

MATHERS, Petra
Artist, illustrator, b. 1945, Black Forest, Germany

M. is a watercolor artist and author whose work is bold and clean with messages from the heart interspersed with HUMOR. M.'s childhood love for books resulted in an apprenticeship in the book business and employment in book stores. As a young adult, she moved to Oregon where she worked in restaurants to help support her family as she painted and exhibited her work in galleries. ILLUSTRATIONS for her first children's book, done in black and white, appeared in *How Yossi Beat the Evil Urge* by Miriam CHAIKIN (1983). Two years later, M. published *Maria Theresa* (1985) as both author and illustrator. M.'s career as a writer took root as a child who was in love with her books: she put her favorite books to bed instead of her dolls. Her artistic talents were awakened when she started making pictures with her small son's giant box of crayons. She had no formal training. As an artist, M. works only in watercolors. She focuses more on content than technique. The use of humor in her illustrations is visible as she personifies a swatch of quilt material in *Patchwork Island* by Karla KUSKIN (1995), paints the musical cat's tail to accompany piano students in *Mrs. Merriwether's Musical Cat* by Carol Purdy (1994) and produces amusing stick features in *Mommy Go Away!* by Lynne Jonell (1997). Examples of M.'s superb artistic collaboration with authors is unmistakable with Mary McKenna Siddals' in *Tell Me a Season* (1997) and with Jacqueline Briggs Martin in *Grandmother Bryant's Pocket* (1996). In one of her later works, *Kisses from Rosa* (1995), M. exhibits the culmination of her perceptive writing,

brilliant illustrations and a personal recollection. Like her own mother, Rosa's must leave for months at a time to stay in the hospital for the treatment of tuberculosis. The German countryside and the narration reconfirm M. as an impressive author and illustrator for children.

AWARDS: *Boston Globe/Horn Book* Award (1991) for *Sophie and Lou. New York Times* Best Illustrated Children's Books of the Year (1986) for *Molly's New Washing Machine* (Geringer, author), 1988 for *Theodor and Mr. Balbini,* 1990 for *I'm Flying!* (A. Wade, author)

FURTHER WORKS: (author and illustrator). *Aunt Elaine Does the Dance from Spain* 1992. *Victor and Christabel.* 1993. *Lottie's New Beach Towel.* 1998. (illustrator only). *Frannie's Fruit.* 1989. *The Block Book.* 1990. *Borrequita and the Coyote.* 1991. *Little Love Song.* 1991. *When It Snowed That Night.* 1993. *Tell Me a Season.* 1997. *I Need a Snake.* 1998. *On Ramon's Farm: Five Tales of Mexico.* 1998. *How Nanita Learns to Make a Flan.* 1999. *It's My Birthday, Too.* 1999

BIBLIOGRAPHY: Silvey, Anita, ed., *Children's Books and Their Creators.* 1995. "The Artist at Work." *Horn Book* magazine, March 1992, vol. 68, no. 2, p. 171. Lempke, Susan Dove. *Booklist* April 1997 vol. 93, no. 15, p. 1339. Salvadore, Maria B. *Horn Book* magazine Nov.–Dec. 1995 vol. 71 no. 6, p. 729. Zeiger, Hanna. *Horn Book* magazine July–Aug. 1996, vol. 72 no. 4, p. 460

NANCY HORTON

MATHIS, Sharon Bell
Author, b. 26 February 1937, Atlantic City, New Jersey

M.'s parents separated when she was a child, and she lived with her mother. The fire escape of their New York apartment became a place where M. read the works of AFRICAN AMERICAN authors, especially, and wrote. She spent the summer of 1952 in Baltimore with her godmother who encouraged her writing and eventually assisted her entering college. After graduating magna cum laude from Morgan State College in 1958, she attended D. C. Teachers College and earned an M.L.S. from Catholic University of America in 1975. M. worked as an interviewer in a children's hospital, a teacher, and a school librarian before returning to writing. She was a Bread Loaf Writers Conference Fellow in 1970 and a Writer-in-Residence at Howard University from 1972–74.

After publishing several books between 1970 and 1975, M. suffered an extended writer's block and did not publish again until 1991.

M. had her first children's story, "The Fire Escape," published in the May 1969 issue of *News Explorer.* It was soon followed by the publication of *Brooklyn Story,* a high-interest, easy-reading novel, and the inclusion of her POETRY in Nikki GIOVANNI's *Night Comes Softly: Anthology of Black Female Voices,* both in 1970. M.'s goals in her work for young people are to combat racism and to portray black children who are smart, real, capable human beings. Her work is noted for presenting African American life through a contemporary lens.

AWARDS: ALA NEWBERY MEDAL Honor Book (1976) for *The Hundred Penny Box. Boston Globe–Horn Book* Honor Club, Child Study Association's Children's Books of the Year list, Notable Children's Trade Book in the Field of Social Studies, *New York Times* Outstanding Books list (1975) for *The Hundred Penny Box.* The Council on Interracial Books for Children (1969) and Child Study Association of America (1971) for *Sidewalk Story.* Child Study Association of America's Best Books of the Year, *New York Times* Best Books of the Year, and AMERICAN LIBRARY ASSOCIATION Best Books for YOUNG ADULTS (1972) for *Teacup Full of Roses.* CORETTA SCOTT KING AWARD (1974) for *Ray Charles.* ALA Best Young Adult Books (1974) for *Listen for the Fig Tree*

FURTHER WORKS: *The Hundred Penny Box,* 1975; *Cartwheels,* 1977; *Red Dog Blue Fly: Football Poems,* 1991; *Running Girl: The Diary of Ebonee Rose,* 1997; monthly column in *Ebony Jr.,* 1972–85

BIBLIOGRAPHY: *Dictionary of Literary Biography,* vol. 33, "African American Fiction Writers after 1955," 1984; Gallo, D. R., *Speaking for Ourselves: Autobiographical Sketches by Notable Authors of Books for Young Adults,* 1990; Mathis, S. B., "True-False Messages for the Black Child: Racism in Children's Literature," *Black Books Bulletin,* 1974; Mathis, S. B., "Ten Pennies and Green Mold, *Horn Book* magazine, vol. 52, August 1976

JANE WEST

MATTHEWS, Downs
Author, b. 24 March 1925, Waco, Texas

M. has created INFORMATIONAL children's books with photographer Dan Guravice that employ a

narrative format and extraordinary photographs. With great interest in natural science, especially the wildlife of the Arctic, M. uses sound scientific resources and his own observations to describe the life cycles of polar animals, as in *Harp Seal Pups* (1997) or *Polar Bear Cubs* (1993). He emphasizes that his characters are not anthropomorphic, since he creates realistic pictures that he hopes will be a lesson in sensible environmental conservation. Using a crisp compelling essay style, M. describes physical characteristics, habitats, behaviors, and seasonal adaptations with up-close photographs to present information in a concise readable format.

FURTHER WORKS: *Wetlands,* 1994; *Arctic Foxes,* 1995

BIBLIOGRAPHY: *Something about the Author,* vol. 71, 1993

JANELLE B. MATHIS

MAY, Karl
Author, b. 25 February 1842, Hohenstein Ernstthal, Germany; d. 30 March 1912, Dresden, Germany

M. was born into a family of poor weavers and was blind for the first six years of his life. Despite early disabilities, he became a successful writer of popular fiction. M. wrote 82 books that have sold more than 100 million copies in 39 languages, including Chinese and Japanese.

M.'s novel *Winnetou* (1892) became his most famous book. It is the story of a young Apache chief told by his white friend and bloodbrother, Old Shatterhand. Set in the American Southwest, the Indian way of life is threatened by the construction of the first transcontinental railroad. Winnetou is the only Native American chief who could have united the various quarreling tribes and reached an equitable settlement with the settlers. Tragically, Winnetou is murdered by gold-seeking thugs. His death also foreshadows the death of his people.

It is unlikely that M. ever visited the United States, which nonetheless captured his imagination. Winnetou became the most beloved of all of M.'s heroes, and for more than thirty years (1875–1909) the author returned to him again and again, in various novels and short stories. M.'s interest in Native Americans (see NATIVE

AMERICAN LITERATURE) was prompted by his compassion for victims of violence and injustice. He admired Harriet Beecher STOWE (*Uncle Tom's Cabin,* 1852), and like her tried not to entertain but to inform his readers about justice.

M.'s stories left lasting impressions on their readers. Herman Hesse called M.'s stories fiction as wish fulfillment and described his work as mythical-allegorical daydreams of discovery, strife, and redemption. Ironically, M. was a favorite author of Adolf Hitler as well as Albert Einstein—such was M.'s universal appeal.

With the advent of films, M.'s popularity spread. Even today, modern scriptwriters use M.'s well-described characters and write new scripts for them. Many of M.'s stories transferred to film can still be viewed on late-night television. It is rare that a publishing company publishes only one author. The M. company, Karl-May-Verlag, has been maintained for three generations.

BIBLIOGRAPHY: Novak, Ben, "Cowboys and Indians: Karl M.'s Teutonic American West," *Weekly Standard,* December 25, 2000

BERNICE E. CULLINAN

MAYER, Marianna
Author, illustrator, b. 8 November 1945, New York City

M., a picture-book author, illustrator, and folklorist, was reared in New York City, in a home where reading and telling stories were a regular part of family life. Before she could read, M. began illustrating the stories her parents told her. M. was encouraged to pursue her art by an illustrator who was a family friend. After one year of college, M. enrolled in the Art Students League to continue her studies. Following her education, she worked in an advertising agency as a commercial artist and as a copywriter. M. co-authored several books for children with author–illustrator Mercer MAYER.

M. has written several original stories, but is best known for her retellings of folk tales and classic stories for children, notably those of Hans Christian ANDERSEN. Her versions are noted for their sense of optimism and romantic, poetic style. She often gives the tales an original twist, such as the dream sequences in *Beauty and the Beast* (1978), which reveal the Beast's true identity to the reader.

AWARDS: Bologna International Children's Book Fair Exhibit (1985) for *Aladdin and the En-*

chanted Lamp. Brooklyn Art Books for Children (1973) for *A Boy a Dog, a Frog and a Friend,* coauthored with Mercer Mayer.

FURTHER WORKS: With Mercer Mayer: *Mine.* 1970. *Me and My Flying Machine.* 1971. *One Frog Too Many.* 1975. Reteller/adapter: *Carlo Collodi's The Adventures of Pinocchio* (ill. MC-DERMOTT). 1981, *Aladdin and the Enchanted Lamp.* 1985. *The Sorcerer's Apprentice.* 1986. *My First Book of Nursery Tales: Five Favorite Bedtime Tales.* 1983. *The Little Jewel Box.* 1986. *Thumbelina.* 1986. *The Ugly Duckling.* 1981. *Iduna and the Magic Apples.* 1988. *The Twelve Dancing Princesses.* 1989. *The Spirit of the Blue Light.* 1990. *Noble-Hearted Kate: A Celtic Tale.* 1990. *Rapunzel.* 1991. *Baba Yaga and Vasilisa the Brave.* 1994. *Pegasus.* 1998. *Young Mary of Nazareth.* 1998. Original stories (illustrated by McDermott): *Alley Oop!* 1985. The Brambleberrys series, 1987–91. *Marcel the Pastry Chef.* 1991. *Marcel at War.* 1991

BIBLIOGRAPHY: "Marianna M.: Myths, Legends, and Folktales," Raymond, Allen, ed., *Teaching PreK–8,* vol. 21, pp. 42–44; 1991. *Fourth Book of Junior Authors and Illustrators,* 1978

JANE WEST

MAYER, Mercer
Author, illustrator, b. 30 December 1943, Little Rock, Arkansas

M. is considered one of the first creators of wordless PICTURE BOOKS. He entertains his audiences with funny, not-so-scary monsterlike creatures, and everyday critters. As a child M. moved often with his family because his father was in the navy. His family settled in Hawaii where M. attended high school and then the Honolulu Academy of Arts. He continued art studies in 1964 by moving to New York and attending the Art Student's League. Publishers declined his art portfolio, so M. began to improve his sketching technique in his spare time while working with an advertising agency; eventually he was able to obtain several ILLUSTRATION contracts. Throughout M.'s career, his art technique has varied. He began his publishing career with a SERIES of wordless picture books featuring a boy, his dog, and a frog, appropriately titled *A Boy, a Dog, and a Frog* in 1967. From this first effort with one-color illustrations, M. continued his works, including multicolored, detailed, extravagant paintings in his retold folktales including *East of the Sun, West of the Moon* (1980) and *The Sleeping*

Beauty (1984). Just as his artistic techniques are diverse, so is his use of language. His books range from wordless and simple to rich and elaborate.

Regardless of the style of language or art, M. invariably captures his audiences with his engaging ability to present characters with strong personalities and likable values. The range of emotions and reactions to fast action are always evident. One of M.'s most widely recognized books is *There's a Nightmare in My Closet* (1968), later published in England as *There's a Nightmare in My Cupboard* (1976). Readers respond favorably to M.'s handling of potentially scary creatures, where they are revealed as more like children than they are monsters and are either ignored or befriended. Other not-so-scary stories of funny potential monsters include *There's an Alligator under My Bed,* with Marianna MAYER (1987) and *There's Something in My Attic* (1988), in which he created a female protagonist at the insistence of his younger daughter who complained that M. always wrote about boys.

In addition to his numerous other books, M. writes books for three series that are extremely popular with his readers: The Little Monster series began with *Little Monster's Word Book* (1977); The Little Critter series started with *The New Baby* (1983); and *Tinka Bakes a Cake* (1984) initiated the Tink! Tonk! Tales series. In the more than one hundred books that M. has created, he has worked with other authors including Gina Mayer, Marianna MAYER, Steven KELLOGG, Jane YOLEN, and Jan WAHL. Extensive accessibility is made possible with many of the series books and collaboration with Golden Books, which is widely distributed through grocery stores and elsewhere; thus enabling a large population of children to discover M.'s works.

Although critics have noted that M.'s art is similar to Maurice SENDAK's, his genius at capturing the interest of preschoolers and young readers with his strong protagonists is unquestionable. His characters exhibit admirable attributes that enable them to conquer their fears, anxieties, and uncertainties.

AWARDS: Citation of Merit, Society of Illustrators Annual National Exhibit (1970) for *A Boy, a Dog, and a Frog,* (1975) for *What Do You Do with a Kangaroo?* (1976) for *Frog Goes to Dinner.* Children's Book Award, American Institute of Graphic Arts (1971) for *A Special Trick;* Brooklyn Art Books for Children citation (1973) for *A Boy, a Dog, and a Frog,* (1975) for *What Do You Do with a Kangaroo?* and (1977) for *Frog Goes to Dinner. New York Times* Best Illustrated Children's Books of the Year (1977) for *Everyone Knows What a Dragon Looks Like*

FURTHER WORKS: Self-illustrated: *Terrible Troll.* 1968: *If I Had. . . .* 1968: *Two Moral Tales.* 1974: *One Monster after Another.* 1974: *Professor Wormbog in Search of the Zipperump-a-Zoo.* 1976: *Liza Lou and the Great Yeller Belly Swamp.* 1976: *Just Me and My Dad.* 1977: *Possum Child Goes Shopping.* 1983: *Little Critter's Day at the Farm.* 1984: *Little Monster's Sports Fun.* 1984: *A Monster Followed Me to School.* 1991: *What a Bad Dream.* 1992: *Little Critter's Read It Yourself Storybook.* 1993: *Just an Easter Egg.* 1998: *Taking Care of Mom.* 1998: With Gina Mayer: *Rosie's Mouse.* 1992: *A Very Special Critter.* 1993: Illustrator only: *The Great Brain.* 1967: *The Bird of Time.* 1971: *Margaret's Birthday.* 1971: *Applelard and Liverwurst.* 1978

BIBLIOGRAPHY: Craig, Jason and Inez Ramsey. "Mercer Mayer," http://falcon.jmu.edu/~ramseyil/mayer.htm; Silvey, Anita, ed., *Children's Books and Their Creators.* 1995. *Children's Literature Review,* vol. 11, 1986. *Something about the Author,* vol. 73, 1993

NANCY HORTON

MAYNE, William

Author, b. 16 March 1928, Kingston upon Hill, Yorkshire, England

Son of a doctor, oldest of five children, M. attended Canterbury Cathedral Choir School from 1937 to 1942. By age sixteen M. had written his first novel. Writing for children became M.'s full time career with occasional side jobs as an announcer for the British Broadcasting Company (BBC) and a teacher.

M. has written more than eighty-five books for children. M.'s first two books (published in 1953, 1954) were conventional ADVENTURE STORIES set in Yorkshire; they reflected a life similar to his own in rural England. His next book, *A Swarm in May,* echoed his school days in both setting and subject matter. *A Swarm in May,* considered one of the century's outstanding English novels, established M. as a leading British author. M. used a treasure hunt vehicle similar to one he had employed earlier but this time the treasure was ancient beehives hidden in a cranny of a cathedral. He used the device to link the present and the past. M. followed the popular book with two sequels, *Choirister's Cake* (1956) and *The Member for the Marsh* (1956). These stories earned M. the label of "master in contemporary English writing for children—of setting."

The novels produced between 1956 and 1966 contained similar elements: they had treasure hunts, were usually set in the Yorkshire fells, and involved the resolution to a problem. The treasure in the book, *A Grass Rope* (1957) that received the CARNEGIE MEDAL, was a unicorn confined beneath the Yorkshire fells. M. continued writing for children producing a book every year with emphasis upon the geographical setting. His goal was not so much to describe a setting as it was to present the setting through the eyes of a child.

Critics say that there are no heroes or villains in M.'s books. Characters are revealed slowly through dialogue. In the 1960s, M. purposefully changed his approach to writing. In 1966 he published *Earthfasts,* a FANTASY about an eighteenth-century drummer boy who disappears underground and reemerges two centuries later. M. began a SERIES of short novels for younger children. In *No More School* a group of children keep their school open despite the illness of their teacher. M. is well known for his character Hob, an elflike creature invisible to adults. Hob is a key figure in M.'s PICTURE BOOKS.

AWARDS: Carnegie Medal (1957) for *A Grass Rope.* IBBY Honor recipient (1978) for *A Year and a Day* and (1984) for *All the King's Men*

FURTHER WORKS: *Hob and Goblins* (1994); *Hob and the Peddler* (1997); *Lady Much & Pandora* (n.d.); *Ghosts: An Anthology* (1971); *Low Tide* (1993); *The Jersey Shore* (1973); *Gideon Ahoy* (1987); *All the King's Men* (1982); *Antal and the Eagles* (1989); *Battlefield* (1967); *Blue Boat* (1957); The Changeling (1961); *Choirister's Cake* (1957); *Day without Wind* (1964); *Drift* (1985); *Earthfasts* (1966); *A Game of Dark* (1971); *Glass Bell* (1961); *Grass Rope* (1957); *Green Book of Hob Stories* (1984); *Over the Hill and Far Away* (1968); *House in Town* (1987); *House on Fairmont* (1968); *Max's Dream* (1977); *Whistling Rufus* (1964); *Underground Alley* (1958); *Pig in the Middle* (1965); *Ravensgill* (1970); *The Incline* (1972); *Royal Harry* (1972); *Red Book of Hob Stories* (1984); *Salt River Times* (1980); *Sand* (1964); *Skiffy* (1972); *A Swarm in May* (1955);

Winter Quarters (1989); *A Year and a Day* (1976); *Yellow Airplane* (1974); *Yellow Book of Hob Stories* (1984); *The Big Egg* (1967)

BIBLIOGRAPHY: *Third Book of Junior Authors,* 1972; *Something about the Author,* vol. 68, 1992; Cameron, E., *The Green and Burning Tree,* 1962

SANDRA IMDIEKE

MAZER, Harry
Author, b. 31 May 1925, New York City

M. is a prolific YOUNG ADULT novelist who has wanted to be an author since adolescence. After serving in the army where he received the purple heart, he worked at a variety of occupations, struggling to gain confidence as a writer. He and his wife, young adult novelist Norma Fox MAZER, with whom he has written several books, first tried writing for different media before they began writing literature for young adults. Themes of perseverance, self-discovery and moral crises with strong realistic adolescent characters predominate in M.'s novels. Whether the story is about the difficulties of having divorced parents, as in *Guy Lenny* (1971), a Jewish fifteen-year-old who joins the army to fight Hitler, as in *The Last Mission* (1979), or friendship between a Down's syndrome (see THE DISABLED IN CHILDREN'S AND YOUNG ADULT LITERATURE) youth and a teen on the run, as in *The Wild Kid* (1998), M.'s characters are credible and the situations he creates draw from the universal needs and experiences of all people. *Twelve Shots: Outstanding Short Stories about Guns* (1997), was edited by M. and provides thoughtful insights about the effects of guns in people's lives. M. has won numerous awards and his works have been translated into several languages.

FURTHER WORKS: with Norma Fox Mazer: *The Solid Gold Kid.* 1977. *Heartbeat.* 1989. *Bright Days and Stupid Nights.* 1993. *The Island Keeper: A Tale of Courage and Survival.* 1981. *Cave under the City.* 1986. *Who Is Eddie Leonard?* 1993

BIBLIOGRAPHY: *Children's Literature Review,* vol. 16, 1989; Reed, Arthea J. S., *Presenting Harry M.,* 1996; *Something about the Author,* vol. 105, 1999; *Twentieth-Century Young Adult Writers,* 1994

JANELLE B. MATHIS

MAZER, Norma Fox

Author, b. 15 May 1931, New York City

M. writes with great sensitivity about the problems, issues, and emotional highs and lows of adolescent life. She portrays outsiders well and treats young female protagonists effectively as in *Up in Seth's Room* (1979). In both *Babyface* (1990) and *Taking Terri Mueller* (1981), she deals with family secrets and unravels the threads of those hidden things that threaten her characters. *After the Rain* (1987), her poignant story of cancer and death, as well as several other of M.'s titles are frequent award winners. M. is married to young adult author Harry MAZER and acknowledges they discuss their stories with each other.

AWARDS: ALA NEWBERY MEDAL Honor Book (1988) for *After the Rain*. Edgar Allan Poe Award for Best Juvenile Mystery (1982) for *Taking Terri Mueller*. Lewis CARROLL Shelf Award (1976) for *Saturday, the Twelfth of October*. Christopher Award (1977) for *"Dear Bill, Remember Me?" and Other Stories*. National Book Award Finalist (1974) for *A Figure of Speech. New York Times* Notable Books (1976) for *"Dear Bill, Remember Me?" and Other Stories* and (1984) for *Downtown*

FURTHER WORKS: With Harry Mazer: *The Solid Gold Kid*. 1977. *Heartbeat*. 1989. *Bright Days and Stupid Nights*. 1993. As sole author: *Someone to Love*. 1983. *A, My Name is Ami*. 1986. *Out of Control*. 1993. *Missing Pieces*. 1995. *Crazy Fish*. 1998

BIBLIOGRAPHY: Holtze, Sally Holmes, *Presenting Norma Fox Mazer,* 1987

KAY E. VANDERGRIFT

MCCAFFREY, Anne

Author, b. 1 April 1926, Cambridge, Massachusetts

M.'s parents reared her to believe in herself and her capabilities. A SCIENCE FICTION novelist, she wrote her first novel to amuse herself during Latin class. M. graduated from Radcliffe College cum laude in 1947, then studied meteorology at the University of the City of Dublin. M. also studied voice for nine years, and has been involved in local theater and opera. She worked as a copywriter and Director of Fin Film Productions and Dragonhold, Ltd. M. has written several bestsellers; her works have inspired music, stage plays, board games, and computer games. Sometimes called the Dragon Lady because of the dragonlike creatures in her Pern SERIES, M. now resides in Ireland in her home, Dragonhold, where she raises horses, cooks, and knits.

M.'s work is enjoyed by teens and adults alike. Best known is her Pern series, set on a former Earth colony. Several of the Pern books (the Harper Hall series) were written specifically for younger readers, including *Dragonsong* (1976), *Dragonsinger* (1977), and *Dragondrums* (1979). Although M.'s work has elements of FANTASY, her stories are solidly based on scientific principles. M. does a great deal of research, studying the science and technology necessary for her books, but the emphasis remains on character. She wants to portray strong women and children, as well as others thought to be weak who struggle against injustice and societal conventions.

AWARDS: M.'s novella *Weyr Search* won the World Science Fiction Society's Hugo Award in 1967. Another novella, *Dragonrider,* earned the Nebula Award of the Science Fiction Writers of America in 1969. *Dragonsong* and *Dragonsinger* were AMERICAN LIBRARY ASSOCIATION Notable Books in 1976 and 1977, respectively. M. won Science Fiction Book Club Awards for *Killashandra* (1986), *Dragonsdawn* (1989), *The Renegades of Pern,* and *The Rowan* (both 1990)

FURTHER WORKS: In the Pern series: *Dragonflight*. 1969. *Dragonquest*. 1971. *The White Dragon*. 1978. *Moreta: Dragonlady of Pern*. 1983. *The Girl Who Heard Dragons*. 1985. *The Dragonriders of Pern*. 1986. *Nerlika's Story*. 1986. *All the Weyrs of Pern*. 1991. *The Dolphins of Pern*. 1994. *The MasterHarper of Pern*. 1998. Also among the more than ninety books M. has authored or coauthored: *The Ship Who Sang*. 1969. *The Ship Who Searched*. With Lackey. 1992. *The City Who Fought*. With Stirling. 1993. *The Ship Who Won*. With Nye. 1994. *Three Gothic Novels: Omnibus: Ring of Fear, Mark of Merlin, and The Kilternan Legacy*. 1990. *The Crystal Singer Trilogy*. 1996. *The Powers That Be*. With Scarborough. 1990. *Power Lines*. 1994. *Power Play*. With Scarborough. 1995. *Acorna the Unicorn Girl*. With Ball. 1997. *Acorna's Quest*. 1998. *Freedom's Landing*. 1995. *Freedom's Choice*. 1997. *Freedom's Challenge*. 1998

BIBLIOGRAPHY: Barr, M. (1982). *Science Fiction and the Fact of Women's Repressed Creativity: Anne M. Portrays a Female Artist. Extrapolation* 23(1). Bogle, L. C. 1981. Anne M. *Dictionary of Literary Biography,* vol. 8: *Twentieth-century American Science Fiction Writers* (pp. 14–19). Brizzi, M. T. 1986. *Anne M.* Gallo, D. R. *Speaking for Ourselves: Autiobiographical Sketches by Notable Authors of Books for YOUNG ADULTS.* 1990. Roberts, R. *Anne M.: A Critical Companion.* 1998

JANE WEST

MCCAUGHREAN, Geraldine
Author, b. 6 June 1951, Enfield, London, England

An author of fiction and retellings, M. has adapted Greek myths, *The Odyssey,* Chaucer, Shakespeare, the legends of El Cid and St. George and stories from *One Thousand and One Arabian Nights.* She graduated with honors from Christ Church, Oxford, and has worked as a staff writer and editor for a British publishing firm. She started writing for children by retelling thirty-three tales from *One Thousand and One Arabian Nights* using a variety of sources and recreated stories suitable to be read silently or aloud. *The Canterbury Tales* (1964) focuses on the pilgrimage itself and the thirteen stories are tales within tales that make the journey to Canterbury romantic, heroic, and frivolous.

A Little Lower Than the Angels (1987), her first novel for young people, won the Whitbread Award for Children's Literature. A medieval tale about the dramatization of a Miracle and Mystery Play traditionally performed by local craftsmen, the professional players are rogues and scoundrels. Gabriel, to escape a brutal master, joins the group and is featured as an angel and through deception is led to believe he is a miracle worker until the troupe performs for an audience of plague victims. Presenting history through dialogue and Gabriel's experience, the story is compelling and appealing.

A Pack of Lies: Twelve Stories in One won the 1988 CARNEGIE MEDAL and 1989 Guardian Children's Fiction Award. Twelve short stories of tragedy, comedy, adventure, romance, treachery, and horror, all lies, are woven into a web of intrigue. M.C.C. Berkshire, an accomplished liar, becomes part of Ailsa's household and tells a different story to each customer about the antique piece (of junk) they are interested in. After he sells the bed he is sleeping on, M.C.C. disappears. In the last tale Ailsa reads about herself

and M.C.C. and how he found his way into her shop leaving the reader to puzzle who is the liar and what is real. Also published in 1999 was her version of *Saint George and the Dragon.*

M. translated Daisaku Ikeda's *The Cherry Tree* (1992) and *Over the Deep Blue Sea* (1993). Several Wizziwig tales were published in 1995: *Wizziwig and the Crazy Cooker, Wizziwig and the Singing Chair, Wizziwig and the Sweet Machine,* and *Wizziwig and the Wacky Weather Machine. The Golden Hoard: Myths and Legends of the World* was published in 1996.

M. states, "I have now found that my true talent lies in writing for children . . . This pure luck of being in the right place at the right time has led to a remarkable good fortune of making a living from the thing I like doing best."

BIBLIOGRAPHY: *Children's Literature Research,* vol. 38, 1996; *Fiction, FOLKLORE, FANTASY and POETRY for Children, 1876–1985,* vol. 1, 1986; *Something about the Author,* vol. 43, 1986, and vol. 87, 1996

IRVYN G. GILBERTSON

MCCLOSKEY, Robert
Author, illustrator. b 15 September 1914, Hamilton, Ohio

M. is one of the seminal figures in children's literature loved by both adults and children. His PICTURE BOOKS, written more than fifty years ago, are still classics. Although he has only written and illustrated eight books, he has won the CALDECOTT MEDAL twice; once in 1942 for *Make Way for Ducklings* and in 1958 for *Time of Wonder.* He has been a Caldecott Medal Honor Book winner three times; once in 1948 for *Blueberries for Sal;* in 1953 for *One Morning in Maine;* and again in 1954 as the illustrator of Ruth SAWYER's *Journey Cake, Ho!* His work is characterized by authenticity, winsomeness, HUMOR, gentle satire, and a warm aesthetic vision that is strongly influenced by his own background. As a young boy his great passions were music, drawing, and inventing mechanical and electrical gadgets. All of these interests appear in his later work. After graduation from high school, he attended the Vesper George School in Boston. In 1935 M. presented his portfolio to May Massee, the children's editor at Viking Press. She persuaded M. to gather inspiration from his own experience rather than to produce the dragons and other examples of "great art" that he had shown her. Undaunted, he stayed in New York City for two years and studied at the National Academy of Design and then returned to Ohio and began drawing everyday life and scenes from his boyhood. The result of this work was his first book *Lentil* (1940). It was immediately considered a potential American-boy classic in the tradition of *Adventures of Huckleberry Finn* (Mark TWAIN, 1884). Using masterfully caricatured sepia-charcoal drawings, McCloskey told the humorous story of a carefree harmonica-playing American boy of 1914, living in Alto, Ohio. He gains the admiration of all when the town band is unable to welcome a dignitary and Lentil saves the day by playing his harmonica. When the book came out, M. traveled from school to school reading, drawing, and playing his harmonica just like Lentil.

Both *Homer Price* (1943) and *Centerburg Tales* (1951) are set in the same time and place as *Lentil.* Once again using spirited caricatured sepia-charcoal drawings, M. tells a humorous story. It concerns Homer's resolution of a crisis with a malfunctioning doughnut machine. *Centerburg Tales* continues the saga of Homer Price and describes the town's colorful residents, but here the stories are really tall tales, an exaggeration of the truth. As in American myths and legends and Mark Twain's tall tales they reveal a philosophic humor that appreciates the absurdities and rueful comedy of the human condition. In text and picture they are an authentic piece of Americana.

In 1942, M. won his first Caldecott Medal for *Make Way for Ducklings.* In a series of large richly detailed sepia lithographs he created a believable Boston and revealed his first-hand knowledge of ducks and their ways. The story, concerning the trials and tribulations of a mother and father mallard seeking a safe place to nest and nurture their ducklings, is told with great warmth and humor. It is one of the first M. stories to use the themes of family life and nurturing—themes so dear to children. It is reassuring for young readers to see how strong, loving parents care for their young and resolve their difficulties. The book has such credibility that families often visit Boston looking for the landmarks, bronze ducklings in the Boston Public Gardens, that appear in the story. M.'s last four books were inspired by his family life during their summers in Penobscot Bay, Maine. In *Blueberries for Sal,* a 1949 Caldecott Medal Honor Book, M. used large spirited blueberry colored lithograph drawings, his real family, and their home in Maine to tell the story of a blueberry-picking adventure in which Sal and her mother are mixed up with a blueberry eating bear and her cub. Small children can identify with Sal and find great humor in the mix-up. The limited number of words and the simplicity of the story in a parallel plot allows young listeners to "read" the pictures.

One Morning in Maine, a 1953 Caldecott Medal Honor book, uses a slightly older Sal and her little sister, Jane, to reveal the family's interactions over the course of a few hours, on the momentous occasion when Sal loses her first tooth. The accompanying anxiety, excitement, and anticipation of that event, are movingly captured. This event of childhood and the routine of a life spent near the water in the Maine woods are clearly described using expressive navy blue lithograph drawings.

Time of Wonder (1957), M.'s second Caldecott Medal book is entirely different from his other books. It is a kind of prose poem in full color. Here he has made his love of his Maine island most evident. As one looks at his softly colored sensitive watercolor ILLUSTRATIONS and listens to the poetic text that contains rich imagery, one feels that every day is a time of wonder. Children reading the book are taught to love and wonder at the world and simply to appreciate living in it.

Burt Dow: Deep Water Man (1963) is another full-color book, but it has highly caricatured painting done in posterlike lavish colors that seem appropriate for this tall tale of exaggerated nonsense. With much humor, the story is told of a Jonah-like fisherman, his kindness to a whale and how that is repaid.

Although M. thinks in pictures and considers himself primarily an artist, his texts are well regarded and as a writer he has shown an enormous versatility from the simplicity of *Make Way for Ducklings* and *Blueberries for Sal* to the inspired humor of the small-town books, the warmth and nurturance of *Make Way for Ducklings,* and the majestic yet touching beauty of *Time of Wonder.*

M.'s words and illustrations enhance each other and his illustrations clarify the story.

Annis Duff, a Viking editor, wrote that M.'s humor, kindness, compassion, and beauty have great appeal, but it is the integrity of his work that makes his books perennial favorites. There is an underlying truth communicated not only in the way that things "look right" but in the way that they "act right." There is a credibility in picture and word that children find most appealing.

AWARDS: Caldecott Medal Award (1942) for *Make Way for Ducklings,* (1958) for *Time of Wonder.* Caldecott Medal Honor Book (1949) for *Blueberries for Sal,* (1953) for *One Morning in Maine,* (1954) for *Journey Cake, Ho!* (Ruth SAW-YER; author). President's Award, National Academy, Tiffany Foundation, Prix de Rome (1939)

FURTHER WORKS: Illustrator. *Journey Cake, Ho!* (Ruth Sawyer). 1955. *Henry Reed, Inc.* (Keith ROBERTSON). 1958. *Henry Reed's Baby-sitting Service.* (Keith Robertson). 1966. *Henry Reed's Big Sister.* (Keith Robertson). 1970

BIBLIOGRAPHY: *Children's Literature Review,* vol. 7, 1984; HOPKINS, Lee Bennett, *Pauses: Autobiographical Reflections of 101 Creators of Children's Books,* 1995; Marcus, L., *A Caldecott Celebration,* 1998; Silvey, Anita, ed., *Children's Books and Their Creators,* 1995; *Twentieth Century Children's Writers,* 1978

JUDY LIPSITT

MCCORD, David

Author, b. 15 November 1897, New York City; d. 13 April 1997, Boston, Massachusetts

As a poet and educator, M. devoted himself late in his career to enriching the lives of children through POETRY, and in that capacity initiated a rigorous campaign to be a poet for children of all ages. Publishing his first book of poems for children while in his mid-fifties, M. became one of the most significant figures in children's poetry in the second half of the twentieth century.

Born David Thompson Watson McCord, at age twelve M. moved with his family to Oregon, where he attended Lincoln High School in Portland. Afterward, he enrolled at Harvard University, graduating in 1921 with a degree in physics. In the following year, he earned a master's degree in Romance languages and remained at Harvard in several capacities for his entire professional career, primarily as the executive director, from 1925 to 1963, of the Harvard Fund Council. He also served as the associate editor of the *Harvard Alumni Bulletin* from 1923 to 1925 and then as editor from 1940 to 1946. M.'s affiliation with Harvard was further enhanced by his special affinity for the Boston area, which inspired *About Boston: Sight, Sound, Flavor and Inflection* (1948). Honored by the city with the title Grand Bostonian, M. considered the award among his most cherished accomplishments.

Before writing for children, M. initially gained recognition as a writer of verse for adults. His first published work appeared in 1926, a collection of essays entitled *Oddly Enough,* followed by *Floodgate* (1927), his first book of verse. Other volumes of adult poetry included *Stirabout* (1928), *The Crows* (1934), *Bay Window Ballads* (illus. John Lavalle, 1935), *And What's More* (1941), and *A Star by Day* (1950). In 1945, M. edited *What Cheer: An Anthology of American and British Humorous and Witty Verse,* which was republished in 1946 as *The Pocket Book of Humorous Verse,* and again in 1951 as *The Modern Treasury of Humorous Verse.* Published in 1952, *Far and Few, Rhymes of the Never Was and Always Is,* illustrated by Henry B. Kane, was M.'s first collection of verse for children. Afterward, he wrote exclusively for children, while simultaneously bringing his message to children, teachers, and librarians by speaking and reading his poems in schools throughout the U.S.

The Old Bateau and Other Poems (1953) was followed the next year by *Odds without Ends.* Thereafter, M. continued to produce a steady stream of new works, often returning to the thematic format of his first book for children, exemplified by *Take Sky, More Rhymes of the Never Was and Always Is* (1962), *All Day Long: Fifty Rhymes of the Never Was and Always Is* (1966), and *For Me to Say: Rhymes of the Never Was and Always Is* (1970), all of which were illustrated by Kane, as well as *Away and Ago: Rhymes of the Never Was and Always Is* (1974), illustrated by Leslie Morrill, and *Speak Up: More Rhymes of the Never Was and Always Is* (1979), illustrated by Marc SIMONT.

Highly respected and praised for his devotion to children, M. was nominated for a National Book Award in 1975 for the publication of *The Star in the Pail,* illustrated by Simont, and again in 1977 for *One at a Time: His Collected Poems for the Young,* illustrated by Kane, which includes some 450 poems reprinted from five earlier volumes. In that same year, M. was named the first recipient of the Award for Excellence in Poetry for Children from the NATIONAL COUNCIL OF TEACHERS OF ENGLISH.

In his books of poetry for children, M. combined a sense of the comical and curious to produce works that emphasize, through meter and rhyme, the sound of language and expression. For many, M. was a great inspiration, the poet who delighted in the composition and craft of poetry as feeling and emotion.

FURTHER WORKS: *The Camp at Lockjaw,* 1952; *Every Time I Climb a Tree* (illus. by Marc Simont), 1967; *Notes from Four Cities, 1927–1953,* 1969; *Pen, Paper and Poem,* 1971; *Mr. Bidery's Spidery Garden,* 1972; *All Small,* 1986

BIBLIOGRAPHY: Hay, S. H. "Man, Poet and World." *Saturday Review of Literature.* November 18, 1950; Dillon, D. "Perspective: David M." *Language Arts.* March 1978, pp. 379–87; Livingston, M. C., "David M.: The Singer, the Song, and the Sung." *Horn Book* magazine. February 1979, pp. 1. 24–38; Kennedy, X. J., " 'Go and Get Your Candle Lit': An Approach to Poetry." *Horn Book* magazine, no. 57 June 1981, pp. 273–79; Livingston, M. C. "David M.'s Poems: Something behind the Door." In *Touchstones: Reflections on the Best in Children's Literature: FAIRY TALES,* Fables, Myths, Legends, and Poetry (1987). 157–72; HOPKINS, Lee Bennett, *Pauses: Autobiographical Reflections of 101 Creators of Children's Books,* 1995

STEVEN R. SERAFIN

MCCULLY, Emily Arnold

Illustrator, author, b. 1 July 1939, Galesburg, Illinois

Daughter of a writer and a teacher, M. exhibited a talent for drawing and writing early in her life. She was drawing by age three and later she created detailed art for school and community projects. By adolescence, she considered her drawing a performance, but she kept her writing a solitary activity. It would be decades before she would combine the two in a concerted effort to write and illustrate children's books. M. received a B.A. in 1961 from Brown University and an M.A. from Columbia University in 1964. In addition to art and writing, M.'s interests and career took her

to advertising, freelancing as a magazine artist, and acting in an Off-Broadway play. In the mid-sixties while doing an advertising campaign, an editor asked her to illustrate a children's book. She illustrated over a hundred children's books for other authors while keeping her writing to herself. Finally, her two major interests of writing and art coincided. Although the first children's book, *Picnic* (1984), was wordless, the story and ILLUSTRATIONS were highly acclaimed. M.'s writing for children continued with brilliant illustrations; some remained wordless and others contained intriguing text.

Readers welcome seeing recurring characters in several works, including the mouse family, the thespian bears, and the opposite grandmas. The mouse family members who are introduced in *Picnic* are revisited in other works such as *The First Snow* (1985), *School* (1987), and *New Baby* (1988). The mouse family delights readers with the adventures and emotions of its members experiencing everyday occurrences and adjustments. The paintings convey the story without the use of words. The theatrical bears are featured first in *The Show Must Go On* (1987), and the two grandmas with opposite personalities and routines are introduced in *The Grandma Mix-up* (1988). By using recurring characters, M. provides her readers with familiarity, yet new situations in which they recognize their own lives.

Period fiction is one of M.'s strongest showings. *Mirette on the High Wire* (1992) exudes emotion and feeling for the time and place of setting. In her acceptance speech for the CALDECOTT MEDAL, M. explains how many elements in her background and her readiness to make a giant artistic leap resulted in the award-winning work. The story itself mirrors aspects of her own feisty personality as a young girl and her dad's personality. The artwork was a transformation in that she had never worked without lines in her paintings and needed to do so to authenticate the post-impressionist period of the setting. She later reflected that she had been walking a tightrope of her own. M.'s superb ability to create a period of time with her historically sound text and water-color illustrations is evident in several works. *The Boston Coffee Party* (written by Doreen Rappaport) based on an episode described by Abigail Adams to her husband, recreates the revolutionary period through a child's point of view; *The Amazing Felix* (1993) takes readers to the elegant culture of the 1920s in Europe; *Little Kit; or, The Industrious Flea Circus Girl* (1995) revives the streets of nineteenth-century London with its mistreatment of the less fortunate; *The Pirate Queen* (1995) tells the story of a sixteenth-century female swashbuckler; and *Bobbin Girl* (1996) exhibits the industrial mills of the nineteenth century in Lowell, Massachusetts. M. has illustrated over a hundred books in addition to her own writings. Her watercolors are expressive and her stories capture audiences with their characters' struggles and triumphs.

AWARDS: ALA Caldecott Medal (1993) for *Mirette on the High Wire*. *New York Times* Best Illustrated Children's Book (1992) for *Mirette on the High Wire*. AMERICAN LIBRARY ASSOCIATION Notable Book Award (1984) for *Picnic;* Christopher Award (1985) for *Picnic*. Inclusion in International Biennale at Bratislava (1985) *Picnic*. "Art Books for Children" citation, Brooklyn Museum and New York Public Library, for *MA nDA LA* (Arnold ADOFF, 1971). Juvenile Award, Council of Wisconsin Writers (1979) for *Edward Troy and the Witch Cat*. National Endowment for the Arts grant in creative writing (1980). New York State Council on Arts fiction grant (1982)

FURTHER WORKS: Self-illustrated: *Christmas Gift.* 1988. *You Lucky Duck.* 1988. *Grandmas at the Lake.* 1990. *My Real Family.* 1994. *Popcorn at the Palace.* 1997. *An Outlaw Thanksgiving.* 1998. *Beautiful Warrior: The Legend of the Nun's Kung Fu.* 1998. *Hurry! a Fable for the Earth.* 1999. *Mouse Practice.* 1999. Illustrator: *Sea Beach Express.* 1966. *MA nDA LA.* 1971. *Hurray for Captain Jane!* 1971. *How to Eat Fried Worms.* 1973. *Black Is Brown Is Tan.* 1973. *What I Did Last Summer.* 1978. *The New Friend.* 1981. *The Take-along Dog.* 1989. *Dinah's Mad, Bad Wishes.* 1989. *Meatball.* 1991. *Amzat and His Brothers: Three Italian Folktales.* 1993

BIBLIOGRAPHY: "Caldecott Medal Acceptance," *Horn Book* magazine. July/Aug. 1993. "An Interview with Emily M., Caldecott Medal Winner." *Reading Teacher,* Feb. 1994, vol. 47, no. 5, p. 358; *Children's Literature Review,* vol. 46

NANCY HORTON

MCDERMOTT, Gerald

Illustrator, folklorist, b. 31 January 1941, Detroit, Michigan

M. developed an early interest in art. From age four through adolescence, he took Saturday classes at Detroit Institute of Arts. M. also acted in a local radio program that dramatized folktales. In high school he studied Bauhaus design principles with its emphasis on bold shapes and a limited range of color; both are evident in much of M.'s work. There he won a Scholastic scholarship to Pratt Institute in Brooklyn, where he earned a B.F.A. M.'s early career included work as a graphic designer for New York public television and travel to France where he studied European filmmaking. Before he began creating children's books, M. earned a reputation as an innovative filmmaker with his animated films. During his work as a filmmaker, M. became acquainted with Joseph Campbell, who consulted on some of M.'s films. M. later became the Primary Education Program Director for the Joseph Campbell Foundation. His films and PICTURE BOOKS have been shown at festivals and museums around the United States as well as abroad.

M. believes that picture books are the art form most accessible to children and that the art must be held to high standards. M. compares today's artist to the ancient shaman, whose job it was to interpret universal truths present in common images, and communicate them to others. M.'s first picture books were adapted from his films. The transition from film to book was difficult; he felt less control with books. Without the music and sound effects, he had to find other ways to guide the reader, to suggest pacing, and to provide continuity. M.'s ILLUSTRATIONS have a bold, distinctive style accompanied by clear, simple text. His work is known for vivid colors and highly stylized design.

AWARDS: ALA CALDECOTT MEDAL (1975) for *Arrow to the Sun;* Caldecott Medal Honor Book (1973) for *Anansi the Spider;* (1994) for *Raven: A Trickster Tale from the Pacific Northwest*. Boston Globe–Horn Book Honor; (1994) for *Raven: A Trickster Tale from the Pacific Northwest*. Boston Globe–Horn Book Honor (1973) for *The Magic Tree*. Film awards from Educational Film Library Association and American Film Festival

FURTHER WORKS: Folklore, mythology: *The Stonecutter: A Japanese Folk Tale.* 1975. *The Voyage of Osiris: A Myth of Ancient Egypt.* 1977. *The Knight of the Lion.* 1979. *Sun Flight.* 1980. *Daughter of Earth: A Roman Myth.* 1984. *Daniel O'Rourke: An Irish Tale.* 1986. *Tim O'Toole and the Wee Folk.* 1990. *Zomo the Rabbit: A Trickster Tale from West Africa.* 1992. *Coyote.* 1994. *Musi-*

cians of the Sun. 1994. *The Light of the World: The Story of the Nativity.* 1998. An original tale: *Papagavo: The Mischief Maker.* 1980. As illus., by Marianna MAYER. *Alley Oop!* 1985. *Marcel, the Pastry Chef.* 1991. Her Brambleberrys series and retellings of the stories of Pinocchio and Aladdin

BIBLIOGRAPHY: Lasser, M. *Teaching the Myth of the Hero: The Films of Gerald M.* 1974. *Independent School Bulletin* 34 (2), 58–62. M., G. Caldecott Award acceptance. *Horn Book* magazine, vol. 51, 349–54. 1975. M., G. (1975); "On the Rainbow Trail," *Horn Book* magazine, vol. 51, 121–31. Moulton, P. (1975); Gerald M. in L. Kingman (ed.), *Newbery and Caldecott Books 1966–1975* (pp. 272–75); Profile: Gerald M. *Language Arts* 59, (1982), 273–79

JANE WEST

MCDONALD, Megan
Author, b. 28 February 1959, Pittsburgh, Pennsylvania

M. provides young people who are new to reading and literature with involving and accessible stories. A 1981 graduate of Oberlin College, M. received a masters degree in library science at the University of Pittsburgh in 1986. Before becoming a published author, she developed her STORYTELLING voice in a variety of careers, including park ranger and children's librarian in several American urban areas.

Is This a House for Hermit Crab? (1990) was chosen as an INTERNATIONAL READING ASSOCIATION and CHILDREN'S BOOK COUNCIL's 1991 Children's Choice Book. *The Potato Man* (1991) was named Notable Children's Trade Book in the Field of Social Studies, by the National Council for Social Studies and Children's Book Council. M.'s first novel for YOUNG ADULTS, *The Bridge to Nowhere* (1993), earned the Judy BLUME Contemporary Fiction Award from the SOCIETY OF CHILDREN'S BOOK WRITERS AND ILLUSTRATORS.

M. has worked with several illustrators, including S. D. SCHINDLER *(Is This a House for Hermit Crab?),* Ted LEWIN *(The Potato Man; The Great Pumpkin Switch,* 1992), Peter CATALANOTTO *(My House Has Stars,* 1996) and Nancy Poydar *(Beezy,* 1997; *Beezy at Bat,* 1998). She brings to her writing a talent for understanding what makes engaging read-aloud material. Her PICTURE BOOKS include both fiction and nonfiction texts, but all call upon the listener to think and respond

to the narrative. Her autobiographical novel extends her graceful style into a realm of such complex issues as depression, economic uncertainty and the changing status of familial roles.

FURTHER WORKS: *Whoo-oo Is it?* 1992. *Insects Are My Life.* 1995. *Tundra Mouse: A Storyknife Book.* 1997. *Beezy Magic.* 1998

BIBLIOGRAPHY: *Contemporary Authors,* vol. 135, 1992; *Something about the Author,* vol. 99, 1999

FRANCISCA GOLDSMITH

MCGINLEY, Phyllis
Author, songwriter, b. 21 March 1905, Ontario, Oregon; d. 22 February 1978, New York City

M. grew up in Oregon, Colorado, and Utah, attending high school and college in Utah, although she spent some time in the University of California system. After graduating from the University of Utah, Salt Lake City, in 1927, she became a teacher and began writing poetry. When she was received successfully by several magazines in the New York area, she moved to New Rochelle, New York, where she continued teaching and writing. She eventually became a copywriter in an advertising firm in the 1930s. She continued to publish light verse for adults, often in *The New Yorker.*

M. was extremely successful in writing for adults, publishing *On the Contrary* (1934), *One More Manhattan* (1937), *A Pocketful of Wry* (1940), and *Husbands Are Difficult; or, The Book of Oliver Ames* (1941) before she began publishing for children in 1944. Her first book for children, *The Horse Who Lived Upstairs* (1944), was followed quickly by *The Plain Princess* (1945), and most notably the urban alphabet book *All around the Town* (1948), which established her influence in the field of children's POETRY and verse. M. received a CALDECOTT MEDAL Honor Award (1949) for *All Around Town* and a *New York Times* Best Illustrated Children's Book Award (1966) for *Wonderful Time.*

Also in 1948, M. wrote the lyrics for a musical *Small Wonder,* which was produced in New York City, but poetry continued to be the focus of her writing. She published *A Name for Kitty* for children later in 1948. M. was prolific in writing for both children and adults in the 1950s with three books of poetry for adults and six children's titles. *The Year without a Santa Claus* (1957) was adapted as a play and later a television special, foretelling her future subject matter with four later books on Christmas themes.

In 1960 she published an adult collection of poetry, *Times Three: Selected Verse from Three Decades with Seventy New Poems,* for which she won the Pulitzer Prize for poetry. She also received the National Association of Independent Schools Award in 1961. In 1966, her children's book, *Wonderful Time,* was named as one of the best children's books of the year by the *New York Times.* M. received several honorary degrees including ones from Dartmouth College (1961), Boston College (1962), and Smith College (1964). M. was a member of the National Institute of Arts and Letters, and continued writing for children into the late 1960s.

FURTHER WORKS: *Blunderbus,* 1953; *The Horse Who Had His Name in the Paper,* 1951; *How Mrs. Santa Claus Saved Christmas,* 1963; *The Most Wonderful Doll in the World,* 1951; *Mince Pie and Mistletoe,* 1961; *Sugar and Spice: The ABC of Being a Girl,* 1960; *A Wreath of Christmas Legends,* 1967

BIBLIOGRAPHY: HOPKINS, L. B., *Books Are by People,* 1969; Kirkpatrick, D. L., ed., *Twentieth-Century Children's Writers,* 1978; Wagner, L. M., *Phyllis M.,* 1971

GWYNNE ELLEN ASH

MCGOVERN, Ann
Author, editor, b. 25 May 1930, New York City

The versatile M. has written about sixty children's books ranging from PICTURE BOOKS and adaptations of folktales to original stories for young readers, from history and BIOGRAPHY to natural science. She traces her roots as a writer back to childhood, when reading and writing were a way to deal with the difficulty she had speaking due to a stutter. Hours spent in her local library reading or sitting in a favorite tree in Central Park writing her own stories and poems led to careers as an editor and then as a full-time writer. She began her career as an editor for companies like Scholastic, but later turned to writing books for children.

If You Lived in Colonial Times (1964), *If You Grew up with Abraham Lincoln* (1966), *If You Lived with the Circus* (1971), plus others using this format take the reader into the environment

and time frame of the subject. After early biographies focused on historical subjects (Christopher Columbus, Deborah Sampson, Abraham Lincoln, Harriet Tubman), M.'s 1978 story of the life of marine biologist Eugenie Clark won recognition from the National Science Teachers Association. M., herself a scuba diver since 1970, got to know Clark when she asked the scientist to read the manuscript for *Sharks* (1976). Their mutual interest in diving and undersea life led to friendship, and the two have dived together in the Red Sea, the Caribbean, Indonesia, and China. In 1991 they collaborated on *Desert beneath the Sea,* exploring the tiny creatures that live on the ocean floor. M.'s love of diving combined with her love of travel (she has visited all seven continents) to produce a number of other books, including *Night Dive* (1984), *Down under, Down under: Diving Adventures on the Great Barrier Reef* (1989), and *Swimming with Sea Lions and Other Adventures in the Galapagos Islands* (1992).

Swimming with Sea Lions and *Playing with Penguins and Other Adventures in Anarctica* (1993) are illustrated with photographs taken by the author. *Night Dive* (1984) and other underseas books are illustrated with photos taken by Martin Schemer and his son Jim Schemer. In her personal life, M. has traveled the world and experienced adventures on all seven continents. M.'s interests shine through her books: the past, both folkloric and historic; the world around us, especially endangered animals and environments; adventures through scuba diving and travel; and photography.

AWARDS: National Science Teachers Association Outstanding Science Trade Book (1974) for *Sharks,* (1977) for *Shark Lady: True Adventures of Eugenie Clark,* (1984) for *Night Dive* in 1984

FURTHER WORKS: *The Story of Christopher Columbus,* 1962; *Too Much Noise,* 1967; *Stone Soup,* 1968; *If You Lived with the Sioux Indians,* 1974; *Sharks,* 1976; *Wanted Dead or Alive: The True Story of Harriet Tubman,* 1977; *Secret Soldier: The Story of Deborah Sampson,* 1978; *Night Dive,* 1984; *Drop Everything: It's DEAR Time,* 1993; *Questions and Answers about Sharks,* 1995; *Lady in the Box,* 1997; *If You Lived 100 Years Ago,* 2000

BIBLIOGRAPHY: *Contemporary Authors, New Revision Series,* vol. 44, 1994; *Something about the Author,* vol. 70, 1993; interview with M. found at

www.amazon.com; McGovern webpage: http://
www.annmcgovern.com

DIANE L. CHAPMAN AND SANDRA IMDIEKE

MCGRAW, Eloise Jarvis

Author, b. 9 December 1915, Houston, Texas

Author of historical, MYSTERY, and FANTASY novels for children, M. writes because she likes telling stories. She thinks that if fiction writers will deal directly and honestly with the world's grim realities, young readers can learn to cope as they develop into adults. M.'s writing intricately incorporates detailed research, ingenuity, and imagination. Spanning several decades, M.'s works have received prestigious AWARDS. *The Moorchild* (1996), a fantasy, is an example of M.'s research (into early medieval life and beliefs), which resulted in recognition as a NEWBERY MEDAL Honor Book, *Boston Globe–Horn Book* Honor Book, Society of Children's Book Writers and Illustrators Golden Kite Award. In the 1950s, *Moccasin Trail* was named a Newbery Medal Honor Book, and Lewis CARROLL Shelf Award title.

AWARDS: AMERICAN LIBRARY ASSOCIATION Newbery Medal Honor Book (1953) for *Moccasin Trail*, (1962) for *The Golden Goblet*

FURTHER WORKS: *Crown Fire*, 1951; *Master Cornhill*, 1973; *A Really Weird Summer*, 1977; *The Money Room*, 1981

BIBLIOGRAPHY: M., Eloise, "A View from the Deck," *Writer*, March 1995, vol. 108, i. 3, p. 9; M., Eloise, "Some Clues to the Juvenile Mystery," *Writer*, July 1996, vol. 109, i. 7, p. 10; M., Eloise, "Hands-on Research: Finding a Bagpiper," *The Writer*, Oct. 1997, vol. 110, i. 10, p. 16

NANCY HORTON

MCKILLIP, Patricia

Author, b. 29 February 1948, Salem, Oregon

M. earned a B.A. and M.A. from San Jose State University. Her books resonate with eerie magic, FANTASY, and mythological possibilities. Working in the fantasy and SCIENCE FICTION genres, M. has captured the imaginations of her large audience of readers. She began her first novel, *The House on Parchment Street* (1973), as a fourteen-year-old experiencing the roller-coaster ride of adolescence. Her fantasy trilogies such as *Riddle-*

Master: The Complete Trilogy (1999) blend the best of magic, romance, ADVENTURE, and heroic feats. M. received a World Fantasy Award in 1975 for *The Forgotten Beasts of Eld* (1974), a Balrog Award (1979) and Hugo Award nomination (1979) for *Harpist in the Wind.*

FURTHER WORKS: *Winter Rose*, 1997

BIBLIOGRAPHY: *Something about the Author*, vol. 80, 1995

SHANE RAYBURN

MCKINLEY, Robin

Author, b. 16 November 1952, Warren, Ohio

M.'s family moved often due to her father's career in the navy. She was an enthusiastic reader, finding her friends in books, especially horse books. The CLASSIC fantasy literature she read, such as the work of BAUM, TOLKIEN, and KIPLING, would later influence her writing. M.'s family spent several years in Japan, then returned to Maine where she completed high school. She spent her adolescence riding horses and longing for what she thought of as the kinds of adventures boys had. To compensate she made up stories about girls having exciting escapades. M. attended Dickinson College until (coincidentally) she married author Peter DICKINSON and moved to Washington, D.C., and later to England. She returned to school at Bowdoin College in Maine, where she studied English literature, graduating Phi Beta Kappa and summa cum laude. She has worked as an editor and transcriber for a stenographic reporting firm, a bookstore clerk, a teacher, barn manager on a horse farm, and a reader and editorial assistant in the children's literature division of Little, Brown.

M.'s books set in the imaginary land of Damar, *The Blue Sword* and *The Hero and the Crown*, exemplify her desire to promote the rights and freedoms of women. Her realistic female characters are brave, intelligent women with both struggles and triumphs. For example, in *The Outlaws of Sherwood*, M. focuses on many of the characters surrounding her nontraditional Robin Hood. Maid Marian is both beautiful and courageous—and a superior archer. M.'s books are based on themes of hope and heroism: she wants to write about girls who take action, but without some inner conflict.

77. JAN MARK

78. JAMES MARSHALL

79. JOHN MARSDEN

80. ANN M. MARTIN

81. ROBERT MCCLOSKEY

82. BRUCE MCMILLAN

AWARDS: ALA NEWBERY MEDAL (1985) for *The Hero and the Crown, Horn Book* Honor Book (1985) for *The Hero and the Crown.* AMERICAN LIBRARY ASSOCIATION Newbery Medal Honor Book (1983) for *The Blue Sword* and ALA's Best Books for YOUNG ADULTS (1982) for *The Blue Sword. Horn Book* Honor List Book (1978) for *Beauty: A Retelling of the Story of Beauty and the Beast* (1988) for *The Outlaws of Sherwood* (1995) for *A Knot in the Grain and Other Stories.* ALA Best Books for the Teen Age and Best Adult Book for the Teen Age (1994) for *Deerskin.* World FANTASY Award (1986) for best anthology for *Imaginary Lands*

FURTHER WORKS: Sequel to *Beauty: Rose Daughter,* 1997; Original stories: *The Door in the Hedge,* 1981; *My Father Is in the Navy,* 1992; *Rowan,* 1992; *The Stone Fey,* 1996; Adaptations: Kipling's *Tales from the Jungle Book,* 1983; SEWELL's *Black Beauty,* 1986; MACDONALD's *The Light Princess,* 1988; *Spindle's Castle,* 2000; M. has contributed to several anthologies, written book reviews in various periodicals, and authored the "In the Country" column for *New England Monthly,* 1987–88

BIBLIOGRAPHY: HOPKINS, Lee Bennett, *Pauses: Autobiographical Relections of 101 Creators of Children's Books,* 1995; M., R., Newbery Medal acceptance, the *Horn Book* magazine, 6 (4), pp. 395–405; M., R., "On the School Assignment Letter," in K. L. Donelson and A. P. Nilsen, *Literature for Today's Young Adults,* pp. 285–86, 1997; Windling, T., "Robin M." *Horn Book* magazine, 61 (4), pp. 406–9, 1985; Woolsey, D. P., "The Realm of Fairy Story: J. R. R. Tolkien and Robin M.'s *Beauty,*" *Children's Literature in Education,* 22, 2, 1991

JANE WEST

MCKISSACK, Patricia

Author, B. 9 August 1944, Smyrna, Tennessee

M.'s parents moved to St. Louis when she was three, but after her parents' divorce, her mother and younger brother and sister moved to Nashville. M. stayed with her paternal grandparents in St. Louis for several years, but later joined her mother and maternal grandparents in Tennessee. Her maternal grandparents told her wonderful African American FAMILY STORIES and imaginative tales about children who could do amazing things. Her paternal grandparents taught her to love music and told her scary stories during the "dark thirty,"—the thirty minutes of twilight before dark. M. based *The Dark Thirty: Southern*

Tales of the Supernatural (1992), a collection of original stories with roots in AFRICAN AMERICAN oral STORYTELLING, on her memories. The eerie ghost stories depict episodes of hauntings, the effects of racism, and acts of vengeance from slavery to the civil-rights era. M. says that she had a wonderful childhood, being the oldest, and only, grandchild for seven years.

After graduating from Tennessee State University, M. married a classmate, Fredrick McKissack, with whom she has written several books. M. taught eighth grade English and found little time for her own writing although she always kept a journal. She completed a BIOGRAPHY of Paul Laurence Dunbar, her favorite American poet, in 1971. By 1980 M. had been a children's book editor, teacher, and author. She and her husband, who likes to do research while she likes to write, have written more than one hundred books. They work individually on some and collaboratively on others. *Let My People Go: BIBLE Stories Told by a Freeman of Color* (1998), with ILLUSTRATIONS by James RANSOME, is a book the M.s have done together. A former slave tells twelve Hebrew Bible stories to his daughter, revealing their significance for African American readers. M. abhors the Eurocentric definition of cultural literacy; she prefers MULTICULTURAL literacy. She draws comparisons between Peter Rabbit and Brer Rabbit and sees connections between *Flossie and the Fox* (1986) and *Little Red Riding Hood.*

M. is a natural-born storyteller who searches for rhythm in the language she uses to tell a tale. She responds to the rhythms of words often searching not only for the right word, but the best word—the one that catches the rhythm of what she wants to say. "Before I was a writer, I was a reader. And before I was a reader, I was a listener. My Grandma recited Paul Laurence Dunbar poetry and switched from standard English to dialect without passing judgment."

AWARDS: ALA CALDECOTT MEDAL Honor Book (1989) for *Mirandy and Brother Wind* (1971). CORETTA SCOTT KING AWARD (1988) and Jane Addams Children's Book Award (1988) for *A Long Hard Journey: The Story of the Pullman Porters* (1988). ALA NEWBERY MEDAL Honor Book (1993) for *The Dark Thirty: Southern Tales of the Supernatural.* Coretta Scott King Award (1993) for *The Dark Thirty: Southern Tales of the Supernatural*

FURTHER WORKS: *Martin Luther King, Jr.: A Man to Remember,* 1984; *Messy Bessey,* 1987; *Nettie Jo's Friends,* 1989; *Jesse Jackson: A Biography,* 1989; *Story of Booker T. Washington,* 1991; *Civil Rights Movement in America from 1865 to the Present,* 1991; *Marian Anderson: A Great Singer,* 1991; *Mary Church Terrell: Leader for Equality,* 1991; *Mary McLeod Bethune,* 1992; *Paul Robeson: A Voice to Remember,* 1992; *Satchel Paige: The Best Arm in Baseball,* 1992; *Sojourner Truth: Ain't I a Woman?* 1992; *African American Scientists,* 1994, *Black Diamond: The Story of the Negro Baseball Leagues,* 1994; *Christmas in the Big House, Christmas in the Quarters,* 1994; *Royal Kingdoms of Ghana, Mali, and Songhay: Life in Medieval* AFRICA, 1994; *Rebels against Slavery: American Slave Revolts,* 1996; *Ma Dear's Apron,* 1997; *A Picture of Freedom: The Diary of Clotee,* 1997; *Black Hands, White Sails: The Story of African-American Whalers,* 1999

BERNICE E. CULLINAN

MCMILLAN, Bruce

Author, illustrator, b. 10 May 1947, Boston, Massachusetts

M. is a noted children's author and photo-illustrator. He has created more than forty popular children's books, several of which have won prestigious AWARDS. M. was born in Boston and has spent most of his life in Maine. He credits his father for giving him his start in photography. When M. was five years old, his father gave him his first camera, and when he was nine, he gave him a professional camera, a Rolleicord. Even as a young photographer, M. demonstrated that he could use the camera in creative ways as when, to his father's dismay, he experimented with photographing a burning candle—from above! M. believes that he should always turn what seems a disadvantage into an advantage. For example, when he was a senior in high school, he could not afford to pay for professional school pictures, so he took self-portraits, in various costumes, to trade with his friends.

After high school, M. attended the University of Maine at Orono, majoring in biology and working at a local television station. He graduated in 1969 and continued at the station, working his way up to producer. In 1973 he retired from television to become caretaker of McGee Island off the coast of Maine and to improve his writing skills. At the end of two years on the island, M.

wrote and photographed his first book, *Finest Kind O'Day: Lobstering in Maine* (1977). The book features photographs of his young son, Brett, who rows his boat to Port Clyde to help his friend, Allison Wilson, haul in lobster traps. Allison proves to be a capable teacher for the young sternman (lobsterman's helper), explaining the skills of lobstering and showing him how to sort out the "keepers." The trip ends with the boy returning home to his dog, who is patiently waiting for him. The book was praised in *Publishers Weekly* as "the finest kind of photojournalism for boys and girls who like action-filled days of outdoor adventure and who don't mind learning, at the same time, the workings of the fishing trade."

M. has published more than forty photo-illustrated books, categorized as three types: nonfiction/documentary, fiction/FANTASY, and concept. In his documentaries, like *The Weather Sky* (1991), he captures and records events on camera in the sequence in which actual events occur. In his fantasy books, he tries to mix the reality of photo-illustration with a fantasylike story. His third book, *The Remarkable, Riderless, Runaway Tricycle* (1978), which M. claims is autobiographical, and his thirty-fifth book, *Grandfather's Trolley* (1995) are examples of M.'s fiction. Many of his books, however, are concept books. He explains that when a photographer writes a concept book, "the book starts as an idea, as a concept. It's this idea that is going to be photographed. It flows from his mind, and out to what he creates in front of him. Then it flows back through the camera, and finally onto the film." M.'s concept books include *Here a Chick, There a Chick* (1983), *Growing Colors* (1988), and *Jelly Beans for Sale* (1996). Many of his concept books are useful in the classroom as students learn about the world around them.

M. has earned numerous AWARDS for his work. His most honored book is *Nights of the Pufflings* (1995), which has received more than ten distinctions and awards. *Counting Wildflowers* (1986), *One Sun: A Book of Terse Verse* (1990), and *Eating Fractions* (1991) all received Notable Book Awards from the AMERICAN LIBRARY ASSOCIATION. In *Counting Wildflowers,* a math-concept book, the author skillfully uses text and photographs to teach children a lesson in taxonomy.

Becca Backward, Becca Frontward (1986), *One Sun: A Book of Terse Verse* (1990), *The Baby Zoo* (1992), *Going on a Whale Watch* (1992), *A Beach for the Birds* (1993), *Penguins at Home, Gentoose of Antarctica* (1993), *Puffins Climb, Puffins Rhyme* (1995), *Nights of the Pufflings* (1995), *Summer Ice, Life along the Antarctic Peninsula* (1995), and *Wild Flamingos* (1997) were all named Outstanding Science Trade Books for Children by the National Science Teachers Association between 1986 and 1997.

M. sees himself as a photo-illustrator rather than a photographer. In an article for *School Library Journal,* he explains that the difference starts with the artist's approach to his work. M. approaches his books from the standpoint of an illustrator. He explains that, given the option of choosing to identify with children's illustrators or a group of photographers, he would choose the illustrators because he believes he has more in common with them. While a photographed book is a collection of individual creations, the photos in a photo-illustrated book are all interrelated. As M. takes photos for his books, he looks beyond the individual images and tries to visualize the entire book. "I see what's happening in the preceding and succeeding pages. I see how this fits into the whole." He provides an ending.

FURTHER WORKS: *The Alphabet Symphony.* 1977. *Apples: How They Grow.* 1979. (With son, Brett) *Puniddles.* 1982. *Fire Engine Shapes.* 1988. *One, Two, One Pair.* 1991. *The Baby Zoo.* 1992. *Beach Ball—Left, Right.* 1992. *A Beach for the Birds.* 1993. *Mouse Views: What the Class Pet Saw.* 1993

BIBLIOGRAPHY: *Children's Literature Review,* vol. 47, 1998. *Sixth Book of Junior Authors and Illustrators.* 1989. *Something about the Author,* vol. 70, 1993

MARY ARIAIL BROUGHTON

MCPHAIL, David

Illustrator, author, b. 30 June 1940, Newburyport, Massachusetts

M., an illustrator and picture-book author, came from a modest family; his mother was a secretary, and his father held down several jobs. M. loved to draw and play guitar, but his family regarded art and music as frivolous. After high school, M. did factory work to support his first love, playing guitar in a rock band. M. attended

Vesper George University on an art scholarship but left after one year to pursue his music in California. He eventually enrolled in the Boston Museum of Fine Arts School. While a student, he worked part-time for a book wholesaler and found himself reading children's books on his lunch hours. He was particularly struck by the art of Maurice SENDAK. M. began his career as an illustrator by illustrating textbooks before moving on to illustrate the works of other authors and finally to illustrating his own stories.

M.'s ILLUSTRATIONS are vivid and lively, and his characters humorous and lovable. Although M. has authored many books, he does not consider himself a writer. He admits knowing little about writing as a craft and depends on editors to polish his work if needed. M. writes from inspiration and has said that stories come to him as if through a transistor radio that he can tune in. His texts are often done in one draft, while his art requires more effort and refinement. He works in a variety of media.

AWARDS: *Boston Globe–Horn Book* Honor Book citation (1975) for *The Bear's Bicycle* (McLeod). *New York Times* Outstanding Books of the Year (1975) for *One Winter Night in August and Other Nonsense Jingles* (KENNEDY). Child Study Association of America's Children's Books of the Year (1985) for *Farm Morning* and *The Dream Child.* Lewis CARROLL Shelf Award for *Sailing to Cythera* (1977) and (1979) for *The Island of the Grass King: The Further Adventures of Anatole* (1979), both by Nancy WILLARD. INTERNATIONAL READING ASSOCIATION/CHILDREN'S BOOK COUNCIL Children's Choices (1980) for *Pig Pig Grows Up; School Library Journal's* Best Books (1982) for *Pig Pig Rides*

FURTHER WORKS: Author and illustrator the Pig Pig series, as well as *Emma's Pet.* 1985. *Emma's Vacation.* 1987. *Henry Bear's Park.* 1976. *The Train.* 1977. *Those Terrible Toy Breakers.* 1980. *Lorenzo.* 1984. *Fix-It.* 1984. *First Flight.* 1986. *Goldilocks and the Three Bears.* 1989. *Lost!* 1990. *Farm Boy's Year.* 1992. *Pigs Aplenty, Pigs Galore.* 1993. *Mooney B. Finch, the Fastest Draw in the West.* 1994. *The Three Little Pigs,* 1995. *Tinker and Tom and the Star Baby.* 1998. *The Puddle.* 1998. M. has written and illustrated an autobiography, *In Flight with David M.,* 1996. Illustrator: *Uncle Terrible: More Adventures of Anatole.* (Willard), 1982. *The Nightgown of the Sullen Moon.* (Willard), 1987. *A Big Fat Enormous Lie.* (SHARMAT), 1978. *The Phantom Ice Cream Man: More Nonsense Verse.* (Kennedy),

1979. *The Tale of Peter Rabbit.* (POTTER), 1986. *Night Sounds, Morning Colors.* (WELLS), 1994. *On a Starry Night.* (Kinsey-Warnock), 1994

BIBLIOGRAPHY: Raymond, Allen, David M., "He Leaps over Chasms," *Teaching Pre-K–8,* 23, pp. 40–42

JANE WEST

MEANS, Florence Crannell
Author, b. 15 May 1891, Baldwinsville, New York; d. 19 November 1980, Boulder, Colorado

M., author of YOUNG ADULT and children's books, was a pioneer in writing MULTICULTURAL books for young people. Her books were grounded in the belief that young people have the potential to change the world. M. used her writing to introduce one group of people to another, in order to alleviate the prejudices and fears of the "unknown." She chose children as her audience, because it was easier to introduce these concepts to young adults who had fewer prejudices than adults did. It was a formula that seemed to work, since M. wrote over forty books about various cultures. *Our Cup Is Broken* (1969) describes the life of a Hopi girl who returns to her village after living in the white man's world. Her NEWBERY MEDAL Honor Book, *The Moved Outers* (1945), portrays a Japanese American family sent from their home in California, to a series of relocation camps during World War II. It was considered groundbreaking, because it was published when anti-Japanese sentiment was high.

DENISE P. BEASLEY

MEDDAUGH, Susan
Author, illustrator, b. 4 October 1944, Montclair, New Jersey

A shy child, M. loved to read MYSTERY STORIES and draw to amuse herself. Her mother and father were both dramatic and often entertained the children with funny stories and humorous "performances" around the house. M. pursued her interest in art and story in an integrated art/English class in high school. She attended Wheaton College where she studied French and art. She received her B.A. in 1966. Between 1968 and 1977, M. worked as a children's book designer and art director for Houghton Mifflin. During this time, she read some old favorites with a fresh eye and was par-

ticularly influenced by H. A. REY's Curious George books. M. learned a great deal about picture-book formatting and ILLUSTRATION techniques.

M. believes that theme must arise from story, not vice versa, and that the text and art in a PICTURE BOOK must work together, each making its own contribution. Her books are lighthearted and humorous, often inspired by people and events in her own life. For example, the idea of Martha the talking dog came from her young son who wondered whether a dog who ate alphabet soup would be able to construct words and talk. Many of M.'s books have animals as central characters, like the cat in her first book, *Too Short Fred* (1978), and the sibling foxes in *Maude and Claude Go Abroad* (1980). M. did her early work in colored pencil, but now prefers pen-and-ink or watercolor wash.

AWARDS: Parents Choice Literature Award (1985) for *Bimwili and the Zimwi: A Tale from Zanzibar* (AARDEMA, illus). *New York Times* Best Illustrated Books (1992) for *Martha Speaks.* Parents Choice Illustration Award and Oppenheim Toy Portfolio Platinum Award Best Book, (1994) *Martha Calling*

FURTHER WORKS: In the Martha series: *The Witches' Supermarket.* 1991. *Martha Blah Blah.* 1996. *Martha Walks the Dog.* 1998. Other books written and illustrated by M.: *Beast.* 1981. *Beast Pa.* 1985. *Too Many Monsters.* 1982. *Tree of Birds.* 1990. *Hog-Eye.* 1995. *Cinderella's Rat.* 1997. M. has illustrated the following works of other authors: *No Nap.* 1989. *In the Haunted House.* 1990. *A Perfect Father's Day.* 1991, all by Eve BUNTING; *Silver Bear.* (J. MARZOLLO). 1987, *Red Sun Girl.* 1983. *Blue Sun Ben.* 1984. *Ruthie's Rude Friends.* 1984. *Two Ways to Count to Ten.* (Dee). 1988. *The Way I Feel . . . Sometimes* (author, DE REGNIERS). 1988. *The Hopeful Trout and Other Limericks.* (John CIARDI). 1989. *Good Zap, Little Grog!* (Sarah Wilson). 1995. *The Most Beautiful Kid in the World.* (Jennifer Ericsson). 1996

BIBLIOGRAPHY: *Seventh Book of Junior Authors and Illustrators,* 1996

JANE WEST

MEDEARIS, Angela Shelf
Author, b. 16 November 1956, Hampton, Virginia

M. moved often as a youngster, following her father who was a successful Air Force recruiter.

In 1974, she settled in Texas, attending Southwest Texas State University in San Marcos from 1974–75. In 1975, she married Michael Medearis who would later become her coauthor. M. began her involvement in children's literature in Austin, Texas in 1989, with Book Boosters, a program for school-age literary development with a MULTICULTURAL emphasis.

M. began writing for children when she was thirty, and published *Picking Peas for a Penny* (1990). This success was quickly followed by *Dancing with the Indians* in 1991, which won a special citation in the Violet Crown Awards and was named a Notable Children's Social Studies Book by the AMERICAN LIBRARY ASSOCIATION in 1992. Her next book, *Zebra-riding Cowboy* (1992), was also well received and was named to the American Booksellers Association's Pick of the List. *Annie's Gift* (1992) was praised for its realistic portrayal of an AFRICAN AMERICAN family and their lives.

M. is recognized as a strong voice in multicultural children's literature. Her topics have ranged from the lives of famous African Americans, *Little Louis and the Jazz Band: The Story of Louis "Satchmo" Armstrong* (1994), *Dare to Dream: Coretta Scott King and the Civil Rights Movement*, and *Princess of the Press: The Story of Ida B. Wells-Barnett* (1997); to coauthoring *African American Arts* (1997), a special series for Henry Holt with her husband, Michael. Additionally, *Come This Far to Freedom: A History of African Americans* (1993) is highly regarded as a chronicle of African American culture in the United States. In *Treemonisha* (1995), M. brought to life the opera of American composer Scott Joplin, telling the story of the little daughter of Ned and Monisha in the piney woods of Arkansas, and her books *Too Much Talk* (1995) and *The Singing Man: Adapted from a West AFRICAN Folktale* (1994) were based on African FOLKLORE. Her contribution to the inspiration and education of young children through outstanding literature was recognized with the CORETTA SCOTT KING AWARD for *The Singing Man* in 1995.

Recently, M. has begun writing for older readers. *Skin Deep: And Other Teenage Reflections* (1995) connect her to YOUNG ADULT audiences. Likewise her cookbooks *A Kwanzaa Celebra-*

tion: Festive Recipes and Homemade Gifts from an African American Kitchen (1995) and *Ideas for Entertaining from the African-American Kitchen* (1997) have shown her to be a flexible and talented writer. In 1997, M. was named by *Texas Monthly* magazine as one of the *Texas Twenty,* one of the most intriguing and influential Texans of that year.

FURTHER WORKS: *The Adventures of Sugar and Junior,* 1995; *The Ghost of Sifty-Sifty Sam,* 1997; *The Seven Days of Kwanzaa,* 1994; *Spray Paint Mystery,* 1996; *Tailypo: A New Fangled Tall Tale,* 1996; *Eat, Babies, Eat!,* 1995; *Seeds Grow,* 1999; *Seven Spools of Thread,* 2000

BIBLIOGRAPHY: Dingus, A. Angela Shelf Medearis, *Texas Monthly,* September 1997, pp. 120–21; *Something about the Author,* vol. 72, 1993

GWYNNE ELLEN ASH

MEIGS, Cornelia

Author, b. 6 December 1884, Rock Island, Illinois; d. 10 September 1973, Place unknown

M., an author and scholar, wrote fiction, BIOGRAPHY, and scholarly works in the field of children's literature and was professor emerita at Bryn Mawr College. Her first book for children was a collection of stories titled *The Kingdom of the Winding Road* (1915). *Invincible Louisa: The Story of the Author of Little Women* (1933) is the biography of Louisa May ALCOTT. *Swift Rivers,* a 1933 NEWBERY MEDAL Honor Book, tells the story of a boy who attempts to float logs down the Mississippi. M.'s scholarly text *A Critical History of Children's Literature: A Survey of Children's Books in English* remains a classic resource for those studying the field of children's literature.

AWARDS: AMERICAN LIBRARY ASSOCIATION Newbery Medal (1934) for *Invincible Louisa;* ALA Newbery Honor Book (1933) for *Swift Rivers* and (1929) for *Clearing Weather*

FURTHER WORKS: *The Pirate of Jasper Park,* 1918; *The Pool of Stars,* 1919; *The New Moon,* 1924; *As the Crow Flies,* 1927; *The Crooked Apple Tree,* 1929; *Willow Whistle,* 1931; *Mounted Messenger,* 1943; *Fair Wind to Virginia,* 1955; *Mystery at the Red House,* 1961

BIBLIOGRAPHY: *Something about the Author,* vol. 6, 1974

SANDRA IMDIEKE

MELCHER, Frederic G.

Publisher, b. 12 April 1879, Malden, Massachusetts; d. 9 March 1963, Montclair, New Jersey

M. was a publisher, editor, bookseller, and activist who took great interest in literature for children. He was a bookseller in Boston and Indianapolis for twenty-three years and became co-editor of *Publishers Weekly* in 1918 and chairman of R. R. Bowker in 1958. Working with Franklin K. Mathiews, chief librarian of the Boy Scouts of America, in 1919, M. developed Children's Book Week, which is still celebrated today.

M. is recognized for establishing the NEW-BERY MEDAL, awarded annually for the most distinguished contribution to American literature for children. At the AMERICAN LIBRARY ASSOCIA-TION's meeting on June 21, 1921 in Swampscott, Massachusetts, M. proposed to the Children's Librarians Sections, that an "original and creative" work, written by a U.S. citizen or resident, not a reprint or compilation, and published in the preceding year, be recognized. M. thought this would encourage "good writing for children" and recognize the efforts of children's LIBRARIANS. He suggested the award by named for the eighteenth century British bookseller John NEWBERY.

M. also established the CALDECOTT MEDAL, named in honor of British illustrator Randolph J. CALDECOTT, in 1937, for the most distinguished American PICTURE BOOK for children published in the preceding year. M. was involved in numerous publishing organizations and was a founding member of the National Book Committee.

BIBLIOGRAPHY: *Current Biography,* 1945; *Dictionary of American Library Biography,* 1978; *Horn Book* magazine, June 1963; *Library Journal,* April 1, 1963; *New York Times,* March 11, 1963; *Who's Who in America,* 1968; *Wilson Library Bulletin,* April 1963

BERNICE E. CULLINAN

(See also AWARDS; CALDECOTT MEDAL; NEWBERY MEDAL)

MELTZER, Milton

Author, b. 8 May 1915, Worcester, Massachusetts

M. was reared by working class immigrant parents in an ethnically diverse neighborhood. The family placed a high value on assimilation, but from childhood M. developed a deep and abiding concern for history and social justice. His many books for children concern historic events, including those with which he had personal experience such as the Great Depression, the experiences of oppressed peoples, especially in America, and the exemplary lives of individuals working for social changes that benefit many.

In addition to discovering an affinity for scholarship early in his grade school career, M. also undertook his own education at the public library. He worked as well as studying through high school and entered Columbia University in 1932 on full scholarship. He worked between periods of university attendance until 1936, when he left Columbia in his senior year, to live on relief for a few months before being accepted as a writer in the Federal Theater Project, a program under the auspices of President Roosevelt's Works Progress Administration. During the next decade, M. married, was drafted into the Army Air Force for service during World War II, and then worked as a researcher and writer for CBS radio. He tasted politics firsthand working as publicist for Henry Wallace's Presidential campaign (1947–48).

In 1956, M. wrote his first book, *A Pictorial History of the Negro in America,* coauthored by a new friend, Langston HUGHES. Since 1968, M. has worked full-time as a writer, editor, and lecturer. *In Their Own Words: A History of the American Negro,* volume 2 (1965) was cited for special excellence in portraying America's past with the Thomas Alva Edison Mass Media Award (1966). *Brother, Can You Spare a Dime?* (1969) earned that year's Christopher Award. *The Eye of Conscience: Photographers and Social Change* (coauthored by Bernard Cole, 1974) was named the 1975 Honor Book for the Jane Addams Peace Association Children's Book Award. *Never to Forget: the Jews of the HOLOCAUST* (1976) won a number of AWARDS, including the Association of Jewish Libraries Book Award (1976), the Jane Addams Peace Association Children's Book Award (1977), the Charles and Bertie G. Schwartz Award for Jewish Juvenile Literature (1978), selection for the Hans Christian ANDER-SEN Honor List (1979) and selection for the AMERICAN LIBRARY ASSOCIATION's "Best of the Best Books 1970–83." M. earned another Christopher Medal, in 1980, for *All Times, All Peoples: A World History of Slavery* (1980). The National Council for Social Studies gave M. its 1981 Carter G. Woodson Book Award for *The Chinese Americans* (1980). *Ain't Gonna Study War No More* (1985) earned a special citation from the Child Study Children's Book Committee (1985), the Olive Branch Award from the Writers' and Publishers' Alliance for Nuclear Disarmament (1986), and the Jane Addams Peace Association Children's Book Award (1986). *Poverty in America* (1986) won the John Brubaker Memorial Award from the Catholic Library Association (1986) and the Society of Children's Book Writers' Golden Kite Award for nonfiction (1987). M.'s books have been nominated for the National Book Award and the American Book Award and have been cited as Notable by the American Library Association, the National Council for Social Studies, and other professional groups.

M.'s nonfiction not only provides young readers with information about important moments in history and aspects of social issues, but his style blends primary source material (in the forms of diaries, letters, archival photos, etc.) with easily accessible analysis. M.'s work has been recognized as an antidote to committee-authored textbooks in the social sciences while often supplying children with leisure reading beyond the requirements of school assignments. He has written biographies of individuals, including *Tongue of Flame: The Life of Lydia Maria Child* (1965), *Langston Hughes* (1968), and *Dorothea Lange: Life through the Camera* (1985); discussed political movements in such works as *Bread-and-Roses: The Struggle of American Labor, 1865–1915* (1967), and *Ain't Gonna Study War No More;* delved into monumental historic events with *Hunted Like a Wolf: The Story of the Seminole War* (1972), *Rescue: The Story of How Gentiles Saved Jews in the Holocaust* (1988), and *Voices from the Civil War* (1989). M.'s liberal politics are evident in many of his books. A characteristic of M.'s writing is his ability to present many points of view within a relatively brief text, giving young readers an understanding that history is as much a matter of interpretation as it is blunt facts. In particular, *Never to Forget: The Jews of the Holocaust* continues to be lauded as

an introduction for children to an event that must be taught and that is daunting to most teachers.

M. also brings attention to often overlooked parts of everyday life. *A Book about Names* (1984) discusses naming customs as well as the derivations of our monikers. *The Amazing Potato* (1992) traces this root's journey from pre-Conquest cultures to our daily helpings of fast foods. *Cheap Raw Material: How Our Youngest Workers Are Exploited and Abused* (1994) provides readers in the upper elementary grades with information about their peers and their society that most children's authors leave unexplored or present as fiction. By providing children with nonfiction treatments of his subjects, M. allows them to see both problems and solutions as affecting many and requiring action on the parts of individuals.

FURTHER WORKS: *Taking Root: Jewish Immigrants in America,* 1976; *The Black Americans: A History in Their Own Words, 1619–1983,* 1984; *Betty Friedan: A Voice for Women's Rights,* 1985; *Benjamin Franklin: The New American,* 1988; *Starting from Home: A Writer's Beginnings,* 1988; *Gold: The True Story of Why People Search for It, Mine It, Trade It, Steal It, Mint It, Hoard It, Shape It, Wear It, Fight and Kill for It,* 1993; *Ten Queens: Portraits of Women of Power,* 1998

BIBLIOGRAPHY: *Contemporary Authors, New Revision Series,* vol. 38, 1993; M., *The Landscape of Memory,* 1987; *Something about the Author,* vol. 50, 1988, and vol. 80, 1995

                                    FRANCISCA GOLDSMITH

MERRIAM, Eve

Author, b. 19 July 1916, Germantown, Philadelphia, Pennsylvania; d. 11 April 1992, New York City

A writer of remarkable breadth and versatility, M. brought to her work a passion for language and literature appreciated by readers of all ages. Spanning a career of over fifty years, M. authored more than sixty works for both children and adults, including fiction, nonfiction, plays, and POETRY. M. is perhaps best known as a poet, and her numerous volumes written for children earned popular and critical recognition in the United States and abroad. Appealing to the contemporary tastes of young readers, M. delighted in making poetry meaningful as well as enjoyable. For M., poetry serves as a means for children to better understand and appreciate the world in which they live, a lesson valued as well by parents and teachers.

As a child, M. was absorbed by learning that nourished her love of reading and affinity for poetry. She began writing as a teenager, publishing poems in her high school newspaper and literary magazine. M. received her undergraduate education at Cornell University and the University of Pennsylvania, and pursed graduate studies at the University of Wisconsin and Columbia. In 1939, she began her professional career as a copywriter for the Columbia Broadcasting System (CBS) in New York City and then worked in a series of editorial positions while simultaneously fashioning her first volume of adult poetry.

Selected by poet Archibald MacLeish for the Yale Younger Poets Prize, *Family Circle* with a foreword by MacLeish, was published by Yale University Press in 1946 and introduced M. as an emerging voice in American poetry. Her second collection, *Tomorrow Morning* (1953), followed *The Real Book about Franklin D. Roosevelt* (1952), a nonfiction book for young readers. Early in her career, M. established a pattern of alternating between genres including adult nonfiction: *Emma Lazarus: Woman with a Torch* (1956; republished as *Emma Lazarus Rediscovered,* 1998) and *Figleaf: The Business of Being in Fashion* (1960). M. also wrote adult poetry, *Montgomery, Alabama, Money, Mississippi, and Other Places* (1956) and *The Trouble with Love* (1960). She wrote additional works for young readers, *The Real Book about Amazing Birds* (1955), and *A Gaggle of Geese* (1960), illustrated by Paul GALDONE.

In 1962, M. published her first book of poetry for children, *There is No Rhyme for Silver,* and named a Junior Literary Guild selection. Noteworthy for her use of poetic elements to emphasize the musicality of poetry, the volume produced two related sequels, *It Doesn't* Always *Have to Rhyme* (1964), and *Catch a Little Rhyme* (1966). Although she continued to publish poetry and nonfiction for adults as well as a variety of juvenile books, M. earned increasing recognition throughout the 1960s and 1970s for her collections of children's verse, notably *Independent Voices* (1968), *Finding a Poem* (1970), illustrated by Seymour Chwast, *I Am a Man: Ode to Martin Luther King, Jr.* (1971), *Out Loud* (1973), and *Rainbow Writing* (1976). During this same period, M. extended into a new area of interest when the poems of her adult book *The Inner City* MOTHER GOOSE (1969, Lawrence Ratzkin, photographer), were adapted as lyrics for a 1971 Broadway musical entitled *Inner City.* Other plays published by M. include *Out of Our Father's House* (1975), *The Club* (1976), recipient of an Off-Broadway Obie Award, *At Her Age* (1979), *Dialogue for Lovers* (1981), and *And I Ain't Finished Yet* (1982).

Throughout the 1980s, M. continued to produce collections of children's poetry, among them, *A Word or Two with You: New Rhymes for Young Readers* (1981), *Jamboree: Rhymes for All Times* (1984), *Blackberry Ink* (1985), *A Sky Full of Poems* (1986), *Fresh Paint: New Poems* (1986, with woodcuts by David FRAMPTON), *You Be Good and I'll Be Night: Jump-on-the-Bed Poems* (1988), and *A Poem for a Pickle: Funnybone Verses* (1989, Sheila HAMANAKA, illus.). In 1991, M. published *Train Leaves the Station.* Completed shortly before her death, *Quiet, Please* was published posthumously in 1993, illustrated by Sheila Hamanaka. Also published posthumously were *The Singing Green: Selected Poems for All Seasons* (1992) and *Higgle Wiggle: Happy Rhymes* (1994).

Accomplished in several genres, M. was perhaps most influential as a writer for and about children. Her creativity invited children as well as adults to share and appreciate her experience as an individual and as a poet. Dedicated to helping others to understand and value the needs and expectations of young readers, M. was the recipient in 1981 of the National Council of Teachers Award for Excellence in Poetry for Children.

FURTHER WORKS: *The Voice of Liberty: The Story of Emma Lazarus,* 1959; *Mommies at Work,* 1961; (illus. Beni MONTRESOR); *Funny Town,* 1963, (illus. Evaline NESS); *What's in the Middle of a Riddle?,* 1963; *What Can You Do with a Pocket?,* 1964; *Small Fry,* 1965; *Don't Think about a White Bear,* 1965; *Do You Want to See Something?,* 1965; *Miss Tibbett's Typewriter,* 1966; *Andy All Year Round: A PICTURE BOOK of Four Seasons and Five Senses,* 1967; *Epaminondas,* 1968, illus. Trina Schart HYMAN, republished as *That Noodle-Head Epaminondas,* 1972; *Growing up Female in America: Ten Lives,* 1971; *Un-*

hurry Harry, 1978; *The Birthday Cow,* 1978; *A Book of Wishes for You,* 1985; *The Christmas Box,* 1985; *The Birthday Door,* 1986

BIBLIOGRAPHY: Bosworth, P. "She Ain't Finished Yet," *Working Woman,* March 1982, pp. 136–37; HOPKINS, L. B., "NATIONAL COUNCIL OF TEACHERS OF ENGLISH Poetry Award Winner on Nonprint Media," *Language Arts,* 59 September 1982, pp. 615–16; Hopkins, Lee Bennett, *Pauses: Autobiographical Reflections of 101 Creators of Children's Books,* 1995; Sloan, G. "Profile: Eve M.," *Language Arts,* 58 Nov./Dec. 1981, pp. 957–64; *Something about the Author,* vol. 40, 1985, and vol. 73, 1993

STEVEN R. SERAFIN

MERRILL, Jean
Author, b. 27 January 1923, Rochester, New York

M. attended Allegheny College and Wellesley College and worked as an editor in addition to being an author. Her successful works for children include participation in adaptations for TV, opera, stage, and radio. Her books engage the reader with characters who may be ordinary and small, but prevail against the powerful. With her capacity to present the reader with an engaging struggle, the author also provides information in a nonintrusive manner. Examples of this fusion of elements are *The Toothpaste Millionaire* (1972), a story of enterprise, complete with hero and money lessons, and *The Pushcart War* (1964), possibly M.'s most well-known work. The Lewis CARROLL Shelf Award and the Boys' Clubs of America Award are among M.'s honors, confirming her consistency as a quality writer.

FURTHER WORKS: *Henry, the Hand-painted Mouse,* 1951; *The Superlative Horse,* 1961; *The Girl Who Loved Caterpillars: A Twelfth Century Tale from Japan,* 1992

BIBLIOGRAPHY: *Something about the Author,* vol. 82, 1995

NANCY HORTON

MEYER, Carolyn
Author, b. 8 June 1935, Lewistown, Pennsylvania

M. studied English at Bucknell University and despite receiving high grades followed a traditional career path into her first job as a secretary. With long-standing aspirations toward becoming a radio script writer M. found herself trying without success to sell stories to prestigious maga-

zines. Finally, her first story was published in a secretarial magazine and printed in shorthand. She soon found success in numerous HOW-TO BOOKS for young people. Since then, M. has been recognized as a correspondent for young people, expanding her range of topics from "learn-to's" to documenting her encounters with little known cultures such as Eskimos, members of Amish religious groups, rock 'n' roll bands, the Northern Irish and Japanese. M. has also written YOUNG ADULT novels, including the Bantam Hotline series about high schoolers who staff a counseling hotline and deal with significant, sensitive issues such as teen suicide and drug abuse. M. has served as an instructor with the Institute of Children's Literature and as Lecturer at Bucknell University. She continues to conduct workshops in high schools and colleges. In 1990, M. was given the Author of the Year Award from Pennsylvania School Librarians Association.

AWARDS: AMERICAN LIBRARY ASSOCIATION Notable Book (1971) for *The Bread Book: All about Bread and How to Make It* (Trina Schart HYMAN, illus.); ALA Notable Book (1976) for *Amish People: Plain Living in a Complex World* (photographs by Michael Ramsey, Gerald Dodds, and the author,); ALA Notable Book (1979) for *C. C. Poindexter;* ALA Best Book for Young Adults (1987) for *Voices of South Africa: Growing up in a Troubled Land,* and (1989) *Denny's Tapes*

FURTHER WORKS: *A Voice from Japan: An Outsider Looks In,* 1988; *Japan: How Do Hands Make Peace?,* 1990; *The Two Faces of Adam,* 1991; *Where the Broken Heart Still Beats: The Story of Cynthia Ann Parker,* 1992

BIBLIOGRAPHY: *Something about the Author,* vol. 70, 1993; Gallo, Don, ed., *Speaking for Ourselves, Too,* 1993

CRAIG LIEBERMAN

MIDDLE-GRADE STORIES

Students in the fourth, fifth, and sixth grades are interested in a variety of stories, ranging from beginning chapter books, short stories, and magazine articles to complex novels often chosen by teenagers. During this period in their lives children become aware of authors and repeatedly choose familiar ones. Their preferences can make books in series very popular.

Nine-year olds like INFORMATIONAL BOOKS, prefer tall tales to FAIRY TALES, are fascinated by strange but true facts, like mysteries, and they like happy endings. They have a weird sense of humor and enjoy gross, corny jokes and poetry. Ten-year olds like adventures with real heroes. They like to read biographies about real people and prefer funny books like *How to Eat Fried Worms* (1973) by Thomas ROCKWELL. They also enjoy Choose Your Own Adventure type books. Eleven-year olds prefer horror stories and mysteries, they like series and read teenage magazines, preferring to read about people just a little older than they are. Middle-graders also like animals and ANIMAL STORIES, particularly horse stories. They like SURVIVAL STORIES and ADVENTURE STORIES, and are beginning to take an interest in SCIENCE FICTION. Generally, they prefer stories that have happy endings. Twelve-year olds like horror stories, HUMOR, FANTASY, and science fiction. They read fashion magazines and enjoy national histories in fact and fiction.

SERIES BOOKS have been popular for a long time with middle-grade students. There were the Bobbsey Twins, Nancy Drew, Hardy Boys, the Boxcar Children, books by Beverly CLEARY *(Ramona Forever,* 1984; *Beezus and Ramona,* 1955; and so forth) and the Encyclopedia Brown mysteries by Donald SOBOL. Then the Choose Your Own Adventure books started a new trend that was popular for a while and still attracts many. Students (especially girls) started reading the Baby Sitter's Club and Sweet Valley High. For several years the top seller was the Goosebumps series by R. L. STINE. More than sixty books were published appealing to young readers who liked horror stories that made your flesh creep. Another series on the bestseller list is Animorphs by K. A. Applegate. The Animorphs are children who have acquired the power to morph themselves into other creatures—birds, cats, etc.—and have to use the power frequently in order to save the world from body-snatching aliens. The books, besides being scary, contain information about the creatures.

Most NEWBERY MEDAL books can be read by students in the middle grades, especially fifth- and sixth-graders. A few of the selections may appeal more to seventh- and eight-grade students but these wonderful books can be introduced and enjoyed by middle-grade students.

Through realistic literature middle-grade students read how others have solved problems similar to the ones they face in their daily lives. Students of today are drawn to books that test the ability of a person close to their age, trying to survive, in a hostile or primitive environment. Books like Jean Craighead GEORGE's *My Side of the Mountain* (1959) and Gary PAULSEN's *Hatchet* (1987) are excellent examples that make a lasting impression.

Middle-grade students discover the joy of having history come alive for them in historical fiction novels written by authors who have researched the time and place and are able to share with the reader a special imaginative vision of history such as *Across Five Aprils* (Irene HUNT, 1964), *The Witch of Blackbird Pond* (Elizabeth George SPEARE, 1958), *Roll of Thunder, Hear My Cry* (Mildred TAYLOR, 1976) and *Dragonwings* (Laurence YEP, 1975). Through a book like Scott O'DELL's *Island of the Blue Dolphins* (1960) students have a window into another culture and a different lifestyle and learn to appreciate similarities and differences with the way they live.

Books of fantasy and science fiction take students into other times and places and help them to problem-solve in real life. Students use their imaginations and visualize make-believe worlds. A book like *Mrs. Frisby and the Rats of NIMH* (1971) by Robert O'BRIEN or *Tuck Everlasting* (1975) by Natalie BABBITT awaken a student to issues in the real world through the medium of fantasy.

Many children in the middle grades are fascinated with the lives of real people. They learn about them by reading biographies and autobiographies. Some find someone they want to read about from a class in school such as a scientist or explorer or they may hear a name on TV. Reading a BIOGRAPHY often leads to a student's desire to write about his or her own life. Jean FRITZ writes biographies that are interesting and readable such as *And Then What Happened, Paul Revere?* (1973), *The Double Life of Pocahontas* (1983), and *Make Way for Sam Houston* (1986).

Children also explore the rich heritage of FOLKLORE from around the world and learn lessons about honesty, integrity, a good work ethic, etc. In fact, the clear moral and ethical tone of myths and legends satisfies their developmental need to probe values. At the same time legends speak to their yearning for romance. Children at this age are drawn to the days of King Arthur and the Greek heroes and heroines.

Children enrich their lives by reading POETRY that reflects mood, tone, and feelings as well as enjoying the humorous rhymes of poets such as Shel SILVERSTEIN and Jack PRELUTSKY.

Middle graders need to explore a wide variety of genres. This is the time in their lives when reading is extremely important as they become increasingly better independent readers and study how authors use words to paint pictures, persuade, and make the text interesting. These ideas can later be adapted in their own writing. The benefits of reading are the acquisition of an expanded vocabulary and a love of reading that is carried into later life.

LORI MORGAN

MIGDALE, Lawrence
Illustrator, b. 21 November 1951, Johannesburg, South Africa

M. earned a B.A. in photojournalism from Central London Polytechnic in 1976; and currently resides in Orinda, California. He became a U.S. citizen in 1982 and brought his camera with him to his adopted country. Using photography as a medium for expression, M. captures the diverse backgrounds of children who inhabit the United States. In collaboration with Diane HOYT-GOLD-SMITH, M. has created a series of photo-essays exploring the dimensions of a MULTICULTURAL world. M. plans to continue creating similar photographic contributions to the field.

FURTHER WORKS: All with Hoyt-Goldsmith: *Totem Pole,* 1990; *Migrant Worker,* 1995; *Celebrating Chinese New Year,* 1998; *Las Posadas: An Hispanic Christmas Celebration,* 1999

SHANE RAYBURN

MIKOLAYCAK, Charles
Author, illustrator, b. 26 January 1937, Scranton, Pennsylvania; d. 23 June 1993, New York City

M. first became interested in creating artwork when he was in elementary school. His parents enrolled him in art classes when they realized his interest and talents in visual arts. As he became older, M.'s dedication to his craft continued and

he decided to pursue his artistic ability professionally. His first published illustrations appeared in MAGAZINES including *Seventeen* and *Datebook.*

The first PICTURE BOOK he illustrated was Helen HOOVER's *Great Wolf and the Good Woodsman* (1967). After this book, M. decided to make a career illustrating books for young people. The majority of M.'s illustrations were completed for other authors including Miriam CHAI-KIN's *Exodus* (1987), which won the National Jewish Book Award.

M. also created several books of his own by recreating folktales. His best known works include *Babushka: An Old Russian Folktale* (1984) and a dramatically illustrated picture book for older readers, *Orpheus* (1992). *Tiger Hunt* (1982) and *Juma and the Magic Jinn* (1986) are folktales with AFRICAN settings.

Working in paint, watercolor, or colored pencil, M.'s style of sequential ILLUSTRATION and frequent use of double-page spreads, was influenced by the movies he saw as a teenager. His illustrations are enriched by his attention to the details, colors, and patterns of the settings he creates. In 1987, M. received the KERLAN Award "in recognition of singular attainments in the creation of children's literature." His work was recognized by the Society of Book Illustrators, the American Institute of Graphic Arts, and the AMERICAN LIBRARY ASSOCIATION Notable Book Lists.

BIBLIOGRAPHY: *Something about the Author,* vol. 78, 1994

DENISE P. BEASLEY

MILES, Betty
Author, b. 16 May 1928, Chicago, Illinois

M., best known for her books for beginning readers, writes fiction and nonfiction for children of various ages. A former kindergarten teacher and associate editor for Bank Street Readers, M. is a frequent lecturer to teachers and parents on how to help young children learn to read. Her book, *Hey! I'm Reading!: How to Read—For Kids Who Want to Read* (1995), is a HOW-TO BOOK for children getting ready to read. M. also takes tales from traditional literature such as *The Three Little Pigs* (1998), *The Tortoise and the Hare* (1998), and *Goldilocks and the Three Bears* (1998), and adapts the text for beginning readers.

FURTHER WORKS: *A Day of Spring,* 1970; *Save the Earth!: An Ecology Handbook for Kids,* 1974; *The Real Me,* 1974; *All It Takes Is Practice,* 1976; *Trouble with Thirteen,* 1979; *Maudie and Me and the Dirty Book,* 1980; *The Secret Life of the Underwear Champ,* 1981; *Sink or Swim,* 1986; *Save the Earth: An Action Handbook for Kids,* 1991; *The Sky Is Falling,* 1998

BIBLIOGRAPHY: *Something about the Author,* vol. 78, 1994

SANDRA IMDIEKE

MILHOUS, Katherine
Author, illustrator, b. 27 November 1894, Philadelphia, Pennsylvania; d. 5 December 1977, Place unknown

Coming from an old Quaker family in Pennsylvania, it is not surprising that M. set most of her books in Pennsylvania. After attending art school in Philadelphia, she settled there and worked there for the remainder of her life. Her 1951 ALA CALDECOTT MEDAL, PICTURE BOOK, *The Egg Tree* (1950), describes a Pennsylvania Dutch family's Easter celebration and is a reflection of M.'s loving portrayal of her home state. Using tempera paints, M. created colorful pages, borders, and Hex designs in traditional Pennsylvania Dutch folk patterns.

FURTHER WORKS: *With Bells On,* 1955; *Through These Arches: The Story of Independence Hall,* 1964

BIBLIOGRAPHY: Bingham, Jane M., *Writers for Children: Critical Studies of the Major Authors since the Seventeenth Century,* 1988; *The Junior Book of Authors,* 2nd ed., 1951

GWYNNE ASH

MILNE, A(lan) A(lexander)
Author, poet, b. 18 January 1882, London, England; d. 31 January 1956, Hartfield, England

Although M. spent much of his writing career producing essays, plays, and novels for adults, he achieved lasting fame from the books and POETRY he wrote for children. M. turned a teddy bear known as Winnie-the-Pooh, a favorite toy of M.'s son Christopher Robin, into one of the most enduring characters in children's fiction. M.'s two books featuring Pooh, Christopher Robin, and their friends—the other stuffed animals from the nursery—continue to be best-sellers decades after their original publication.

M.'s self-educated father, a teacher and owner of a modest boys' school, wanted to prepare his son to move in higher social circles, so M. attended Westminster School and Trinity College, Cambridge, on scholarships. He tried his hand at writing at the age of nine, adapting a threepenny novel into a play with the help of his brother Ken, and at Cambridge he pursued his literary interests by editing the *Granta.* His degree was, however, in mathematics. After Cambridge, his father's plans paid off: M. found himself in great demand as a guest at the homes of aristocrats, and he thoroughly enjoyed the leisurely life at the country estates he visited.

M. returned to London to try to become a professional writer at the age of twenty-one. His early works, many of which dealt with the lives of the upper class, reflect the sometimes amused, sometimes awed reactions of a young man who was not quite an insider. Soon, he had perfected the genre he called the "light article" and was earning a living; by 1906 he had become assistant editor of *Punch.* He contributed weekly articles to the magazine until he went to war in 1914. After he returned, he upset his wife, Dorothy (Daphne) de Selincourt, whom he had married in 1913, with the news that he wanted to try a career as a playwright. Fortunately, his plays were wildly successful with audiences, if not always with critics.

In August of 1920, M.'s only child, Christopher Robin, was born, and with him the subject that would lay the cornerstone of M.'s literary immortality. M., who had been charged with excessive whimsy in previous writings, now found the perfect outlet for his whimsical bent: poems and stories about, and for, children. M. began with a single poem, "Vespers," which his wife immediately sent to *Vanity Fair,* where it was accepted. In 1924, M. published an entire collection of poems written for his three-year-old son, *When We Were Very Young.* M. noted in the book's introduction that "this is why these verses go about together, because they are all friends of Christopher Robin," as a way of explaining the diversity of the contents; the poems introduce subjects that would remain an important part of all of M.'s children's literature. Some, like "Daffodowndilly," "Summer Afternoon," and "The Invaders," deal with nature—particularly such romanticized, gentle aspects of country living as clouds, flowers, and sweet-breathed cows. Born and reared in the city, M. viewed rural life with childlike optimism and enjoyment. Other poems in M.'s first collection focus on the human world from a child's-eye perspective. These often use a child narrator: "Puppy and I" and "Nursery Chairs," ostensibly spoken by Christopher Robin, depict the world in the boy's imagination as it overlaps with, and seems as real as, the everyday world of adults. Other poems, such as "Disobedience" and "Rice Pudding," avoid the child narrator but still take a child's perspective by showing childish adults who misbehave or simply fail to understand what is obvious to the children in the poems. Finally, the poem "Teddy Bear" introduced the "short and stout" stuffed animal later known as Winnie-the-Pooh to the world. Throughout, M. plays with words in ways often reminiscent of children's language games. The book's charming ILLUSTRATIONS are by Ernest H. SHEPARD, whose work M. only gradually came to admire, and who would also illustrate the Winnie-the-Pooh stories. *When We Were Very Young* was a runaway success and has never been out of print.

M. next wrote *Winnie-the-Pooh* (1926), a collection of stories he had developed about Christopher Robin and his beloved stuffed friends. The stories begin with Christopher Robin's pleas to the author to tell Winnie-the-Pooh stories about himself "[b]ecause he's that sort of Bear" and conclude when Christopher Robin goes to take his bath, promising to ask for more stories the following day. In between, the author spins tales of the animals' adventures in the forest where they and Christopher Robin ostensibly live. M. addresses his son as "you" in the first story and includes the boy's responses, but thereafter the narrator is omniscient and there are few interruptions, so the forest world seems to be as self-contained as a child's imagination. Each animal character is developed carefully and shown to be a little flawed—Pooh is a glutton, Piglet is timid, Eeyore is gloomy, Owl is pompous. These characterizations allow Christopher Robin to play the "adult" role in this world, stepping in to calm fears and solve problems, while remaining

enough of a child to suggest games and enjoy parties. The same calm assurance found in M.'s poems that nothing really bad happens in the outdoors permeates the book, in which storms may come and bees occasionally sting, but everything ultimately works out for the best. Winnie-the-Pooh has been translated into many languages, including Latin.

Each of these remarkably successful volumes was followed by a sequel. M. first published a second collection of poetry, *Now We Are Six* (1927), containing one poem, "Us Two," specifically about Pooh. M. understood the tremendous popularity of his "Bear of Very Little Brain," and even when the poems are unrelated to the Winnie-the-Pooh characters, several of the Shepard illustrations prominently feature the rotund teddy bear. M.'s introduction claims that Pooh "walked through [the book] one day, looking for his friend Piglet, and sat down on some of the pages by mistake." In response to public demand—and perhaps the entreaties of Christopher Robin—M. completed *The House at Pooh Corner* in 1928. This volume continues the adventures of the forest's residents and introduces the irrepressible Tigger. As in the previous Winnie-the-Pooh book, M. uses the Pooh character to integrate a few poems in the whimsical M. style. After the series of escapades, however, the book concludes on a melancholy note with a story that begins, "Christopher Robin was going away." The boy, about to depart—presumably for school, but metaphorically for the mature world where he can no longer "do Nothing" with his imaginary friends—makes Pooh promise not to forget him. But M's recognition of the demands of adulthood does leave a glimmer of hope for those who, like M. himself, can still draw on the magic of imagination. At the end, M. tells us of Christopher Robin and Pooh, "They went off together. But wherever they go, and whatever happens to them on the way, in that enchanted place on the top of the Forest, a little boy and his Bear will always be playing."

FURTHER WORKS: *Once on a Time,* 1917; *A Gallery of Children,* 1925; *The Ivory Door* (play), 1929; *Toad of Toad Hall* (play), 1930

BIBLIOGRAPHY: Swann, T. B. *A. A. M.,* 1971

CAROLYN J. LENGEL

MINARIK, Else Holmelund
Author, b. 13 September 1920, Denmark

M., author of PICTURE BOOKS, came to the United States with her family at age four. She attended Queens College (now part of the City University of New York) and New Paltz College of the State University of New York. During World War II, M. worked as a newspaper reporter and a teacher in rural Long Island. During her years of teaching, she found a dearth of good books that her first-grade students and her young daughter could read on their own; she began writing children's books to fill this void. Her first book, *Little Bear* (1957) was the beginning of Harper and Row's I Can Read series. M.'s Little Bear books, illustrated by Maurice SENDAK, have won wide acclaim. *Little Bear's Visit* (1962) received a CALDECOTT MEDAL Honor Citation. *Father Bear Comes Home* was included in *New York Times* Best Illustrated Children's Books in 1959, as was *A Kiss for Little Bear* in 1968.

M.'s books are noted for being easy to read and engagingly written. She uses simple, vivid language to create a sense of warmth and HUMOR. Despite the spare text, the characters are well developed. In all her books, M. attempts to address issues that concern young children, such as the desire both for independence and security, learning to solve problems, and the boundaries between the real world and the imaginary.

FURTHER WORKS: *No Fighting, No Biting!*, 1958; *Cat and Dog,* 1960; *Little Bear's Friend,* 1960; *The Little Giant Girl and the Elf Boy,* 1963; *The Winds That Come from Far Away and Other Poems,* 1964; *What If?,* 1987; *It's Spring!,* 1989; *Percy and the Five Houses,* 1989; *The Little Girl and the Dragon,* 1991; *Am I Beautiful?,* 1992

JANE WEST

MINIATURE BOOKS

Books were scarce, expensive, owned by scholars and confined to monasteries even after printing was invented. The earliest books for children were small religious books, books of manners and morals, and lesson books like the hornbooks used to teach reading. The latter were paddle-shaped pieces of wood on which paper or vellum was fastened, and covered with a thin piece of transparent horn, to protect the text from being worn, dirtied or torn by little fingers.

During the seventeenth century English peddlers sold little penny pamphlets of eight or sixteen pages from door to door. They ranged across ABCs, nursery rhymes, hymn books and songs, FAIRY TALES, fables and histories. With titles like *The Death and Burial of Cock Robin* and *Jack Jingle and Sucky Shingle* these chapbooks popularized reading for children.

In 1740 Thomas Boreman published *The Gigantick History of the Two Famous Giants* and in 1745 NEWBERY produced ten volumes called *The Circle of Science* each measuring less than four by three inches. Children of wealthy parents had little libraries like Marshall's Wooden Box Library, circa 1800, a whole curriculum in fourteen matching books (which became a facsimile edition in 1980).

In the 1930s and 1940s, inexpensively printed and bound miniature books for children were very popular. Printed with cardboard covers on poor quality paper, these three and one-half inch by four and one-half inch books, primarily from Whitman Publishing, were called Big Little Books. Anywhere from 300 to 400 pages in length, they had black-and-white cartoons on the righthand (recto) page with the story on the facing (verso) page. They were primarily ADVENTURE, suspense, space, and cowboy stories or expanded COMIC BOOK character stories such as Little Lulu, Little Orphan Annie, and Dick Tracy. The formulaic stories, whether based on popular motion pictures, comic strips, or well-known books, emphasized lots of action, hair-raising adventures, and dramatic last-minute rescues. Other literary elements such as character development were not significant in the stories. Good characters were consistently heroic and evil characters were stock stereotypes beyond redemption, and easily identified by name: Doctor Doom in *International Spy, Doctor Doom Faces Death at Dawn* (1937), for example. And Killer Kane is identified as "arch criminal" in the first sentence of *Buck Rogers and the Depth Men of Jupiter* (1933). Many titles were abridged and illustrated versions of CLASSIC NOVELS like *Black Beauty* (A. SEWELL, 1877).

Yet, after Beatrix POTTER's Peter Rabbit series was launched in 1901 miniature books for children almost disappeared. Contemporary books are beautifully illustrated by famous artists and often published in oversized formats. The notion of small books for small hands was revived along with small-book series. Once books for babies became a popular idea, small-boxed libraries reappeared. In 1962, the Nutshell Library by Maurice SENDAK was published consisting of four miniature volumes of cautionary tales: *Pierre; One Was Johnny; Alligators All Around;* and *Chicken Soup with Rice.*

BIBLIOGRAPHY: Welsh, Doris V., *The History of Miniature Books,* 1987

MARIE CLAY

MOE, Jørgen Engebretsen

Folklorist, poet, b. 22 April 1813, near Christiania, Norway; d. 27 March 1882, Christiania (Oslo), Norway

(See ASBJORNSEN, Peter Christian; for A. dates)

The names of A. and M. will be forever linked as the pioneer Norwegian folklorists. A. was the son of a glazier and as a child lacked ambition, causing his father to send him to a preparatory school in Ringerike, where he met M., the son of a wealthy farmer. A. and M. became lifelong friends, and both entered the University of Christiania where A. studied the natural sciences and M. studied theology. Inspired by the Brothers GRIMM, the two decided to collect Norwegian folktales and, in 1837, published *Nor, en Billedbok for den Norske Ungdom* (Nor, a PICTURE BOOK for Norwegian youth), followed in 1840 by *Sange, Folkeviser og Stev i Norske Almuedialekter* (Poems, folk songs, and rhymes in Norwegian dialects).

In 1841, the first volume of their *Norske Folkeeventyr* (Norwegian Folktales) appeared, the first of four volumes. Between 1845–47, A.'s work took him throughout Norway, and on his travels, he collected and published tales on his own in an eclectic work entitled *Norske Huldreeventyr og Folkesagen* (Norwegian FAIRY TALES and folk legends). A. and M. then decided to rework their early collections entirely giving

the stories a uniform style and adopting the unaffected style of the Grimms as their model. This revised and enlarged edition of *Norske Folkeeventyr* was published in 1851, and subsequently had a tremendous influence on the development of Norwegian as a literary language. Their tales are generally concise and are characterized by vigor and HUMOR. As might be expected, many tales are variants of other Western European folktales, but they still carry a distinctly Norwegian stamp. Many were obviously derived from Norse MYTHOLOGY, especially Trolls, those disagreeable creatures who are the literary issue of the Giants of Norse myths. A. and M.'s tales were translated into English as early as 1859, and Andrew LANG used many of them in his *Fairy Books.*

Although they were close collaborators and their individual contributions to the folktales are virtually indistinguishable, A. and M. led quite different lives. A., friendly and outgoing, was a famed naturalist who introduced Darwin's *Origin of Species* to Norway. M., who was more introspective, was considered a leading Norwegian romantic poet and, following a religious crisis, he took holy orders and was eventually created bishop of Christiansand. M.'s son, Moltke, became one of Norway's leading FOLKLORE scholars.

Today the folktales that A. and M. wrote down have been translated into many languages and published in various collections of folktales. One popular collection, *Favorite Fairy Tales Told in Norway,* was edited by Virginia HAVILAND in 1961. Other TRANSLATIONS of single tales include *East o' the Sun and West o' the Moon* (1912) and *The Three Billy Goats Gruff* (1940). Many of these tales have since been adapted into English as filmstrips, illustrated books, music, and movies. A. helped introduce the folktales of Norway to the world.

FURTHER WORKS: (Translations) *Princess of Glass Hill, and Other Fairy Stories,* 1905; *Norwegian Folk Tales,* 1960; *The Cat on the Dovrefell,* 1979; *The Squire's Bride,* 1983; *The Man Who Kept House,* 1992

BIBLIOGRAPHY: *The Oxford Companion to Children's Literature,* 1984; Doyle, Brian, ed., *Who's Who of Children's Literature,* 1968; *Encyclopae-*

dia Britannica, 1971; *Something about the Author,* vol. 15, 1979

DAVID L. RUSSELL AND SANDRA IMDIEKE

MOHR, Nicholasa

Author, illustrator, b. 1 November 1935, New York City

M. spent her early years in El Barrio (Spanish Harlem), the oldest Spanish-speaking community in New York City. During her school years her family moved to the Bronx, where she grew up struggling with her Puerto Rican identity, a struggle that would later fill her art and her writing. M. began as an artist, painter and printmaker, and pursued that vocation for many years. She attended the Arts Students League in New York, 1953–56, where she discovered the art of Diego Rivera and then traveled to Mexico City. Upon her return to the United States, from 1959 to 1966 she attended the Brooklyn Museum of Art School and the Pratt Institute Center for Contemporary Printmaking, 1966–69.

In 1973, after having persuaded a publisher to let her write about her life, M. published *Nilda,* the story of three years in the life of a ten-year-old Puerto Rican girl growing up in Spanish Harlem. Written and illustrated by M., *Nilda* was awarded the Jane Addams Children's Book Award of the U.S. Women's International League for Peace and Freedom, named to the AMERICAN LIBRARY ASSOCIATION's Best Books List, and named a *New York Times* Outstanding Book of the Year.

El Bronx Remembered: A Novella and Stories (1975) quickly followed as did her third book, *In Nueva York* (1977), which was equally lauded by reviewers garnishing another Outstanding Book of the Year title from the *New York Times,* as well as an American Library Association Best Books citation, and recognition as a Notable Trade Book in the Field of Social Studies. This collection of stories revolves around the lives of Puerto Rican families on New York's Lower East Side and contributed to M.'s reputation as a distinguished writer of YOUNG ADULT fiction.

Felita (1979), which follows a young girl's move from New York to Puerto Rico, was also a Notable Children's Book in the Field of Social Studies. Felita's story continues in *Going Home*

(1986), also a Notable Trade Book in the Field of Social Studies. In addition to her well-respected literature for young adults, M. has also written fiction for adults: *Rituals of Survival: A Woman's Portfolio* (1985), *The Song of El Coqui and Other Tales of Puerto Rico* (1995), *A Matter of Pride and Other Stories* (1997), and *Untitled Nicholasa M.* (1998), as well as her autobiography, *Growing up inside the Sanctuary of My Imagination* (1994). In 1997, M. was a recipient of the Hispanic Heritage Award, presented by the Hispanic Heritage Awards Foundation.

FURTHER WORKS: *The Magic Shell,* 1995; *Old Letivia and the Mountain of Sorrows,* 1996

BIBLIOGRAPHY: Day, F. A. *MULTICULTURAL Voices in Contemporary Literature,* 1994; *The Fifth Book of Junior Authors and Illustrators,* 1983; M., N. *Growing up inside the Sanctuary of My Imagination,* 1994

GWYNNE ELLEN ASH

MOLESWORTH, Mary Louisa Stewart

Author, b. 29 May 1839, High Legh, Cheshire, England; d. 20 July 1921, London, England

M., conventionally known as Mrs. M., wrote just over one hundred books. About thirteen are novels and short stories for adults published under the name Ennis Graham; about the same number are significant children's fantasies. M.'s short Kunstmaerchen (art-fairytales) are heavily influenced by Hans Christian ANDERSEN. Important shorter FANTASY works, *Kunstmärchen* and fantasy short stories, appear in *Tell Me a Story* (1875), *Carrots* (1876), *An Enchanted Garden* (1892), *Fairies-of-Sorts* (1908), and *Fairies Afield* (1911).

M.'s fantasy novels, many of which were illustrated by Walter CRANE, seem to have taken their initial impetus from her personal childhood experiences and are influenced by E. T. A. Hoffmann, Andersen, Lewis CARROLL, and George MACDONALD. Her primary contribution to the juvenile fantasy novel is her investment of Carroll's dream convention with narrative ambiguity about whether the status of the fantasy adventures are "actual" or dream. *The Cuckoo Clock* (1877) exemplifies features within the fantasy novel, but *The Carved Lions* (1895), a similar, complementary work, has been seen both as a fantasy novel and as an unequivocally realistic one. M.'s major fantasy novels are *The Tapestry Room* (1879), *Christmas Tree Land* (1884), which Hugh Crago claims probably influenced Enid BLYTON's Faraway Tree series, *Four Winds Farm* (1887), *The Children of the Castle* (1890), *The Magic Nuts* (1898), *The Wood-Pigeons and Mary* (1901), and *The Ruby Ring* (1904).

M.'s realistic and largely secular work, which often draws upon the experience of her own children, is written about and for a very large age range. It goes from superb psychological explorations of the inner life of infants, as in *Carrots* (1876), and *Herr Baby* (1881), acccording to Gillian AVERY, through detailed, leisurely, valuable depictions of the ordinary daily life of children, as in *Jasper* (1906) and moral developmental issues such as temper, in *Rosy* (1882). M. also wrote "stories for (adolescent) girls" that would today be called YOUNG ADULT fiction. *Nurse Heatherdale's Story* (1891) and *The Old Pincushion* (1889) use melodramatic motifs such as hidden treasure and missing wills. Some of her juvenile MYSTERY stories, *The Palace in the Garden* (1887), *Greyling Towers* (1898), and *The Grim House* (1899), foreshadow conventions later used by Blyton.

M. has been criticized for snobbery, but Ruth Robertson, the primary source of all M. scholarship this century, feels that these charges sometimes unfairly "hound" her. It is not true, as has been claimed, that she pioneered the concept of addressing the child reader directly. However, in all her variety, she is a Victorian writer who can be enjoyed by contemporary juvenile readers and appreciated by scholars. Such features as notions of bibliotherapy, *A Christmas Child* (1880), and the positive presentation of soft, explicitly "girlish" boy characters, *Little Mother Bunch* (1890), *The Girls and I* (1892), *The Grim House* (1899), would be of particular interest to readers and scholars.

BIBLIOGRAPHY: GREEN, Roger Lancelyn. *Mrs Molesworth*. 1961. Robertson, Ruth. Molesworth-related papers, collected ca. 1938–86. and essays on M., now being drawn on for a BIOGRAPHY by Jane Cooper. Sircar, Sanjay. "Aspects of Victorian Didacticism: Mrs. Molesworth's 'Christmas Child.' 1880." *International Review of Children's Literature and Librarianship.* 1991. Sircar, Sanjay. "The Fantasy Fiction of Mrs. Molesworth: Family Resemblances." *Orana,* 28:2, Aug. 1992

SANJAY SIRCAR

MONJO, F(erdinand) N.
Author, editor, b. 1924, Stamford, Connecticut; d. 9 October 1978, New York City

M., an author and editor of biographical and history books for children, graduated from Columbia University and became a children's-book editor. He was editor-in-chief of the Junior Library at American Heritage and editor-in-chief of Golden Press. As an editor, M. realized that most of the fun of history lay in the details that most children's books omit. M. wrote his historical fiction books from a child's point of view in an effort to humanize historical figures. He presented glimpses of personalities, attempting to entice young reader to investigate further. M.'s early childhood love for playing piano inspired a book of hypothetical letters written by the Mozart family. His mother's FAMILY STORIES of antebellum Mississippi inspired books about Civil War figures.

M.'s first book for children, *Indian Summer* (illustrated by Anita LOBEL, 1968) related the excitement transmitted to him by his father's fur merchant family. He won a National Book Award in 1974 for *Poor Richard in France* (illustrated by Brinton TURKLE, 1973). *The Drinking Gourd,* an AMERICAN LIBRARY ASSOCIATION Notable Book, 1970, was an early I Can Read nonfiction book.

BIBLIOGRAPHY: *Something about the Author,* vol. 16, 1979; *Children's Literature Review,* vol. 2, 1976

CRAIG LIEBERMAN

MONTGOMERY, L. M. (Lucy Maud)
Author, b. 30 November 1874, Prince Edward Island, Canada; d. 24 April 1942, Toronto, Ontario, Canada

M. was a prolific enduring CANADIAN writer whose stories have been loved by readers of all generations since her first novel and best-seller, *Anne of Green Gables,* was published in 1908. She started writing as a young child and developed her persistence as early as nine years of age when she offered one of her first creations to her father for review. His response to her blank verse, that it was indeed very blank, did not discourage her. She continued writing as a student while she studied at Prince of Wales College and at Dalhousie University and while she was a teacher in the small country schools of Prince Edward Island. By the time her father died in 1900, she had published thirty-nine poems and thirty-five stories, and had begun a lifelong commitment to writing in ten volumes of personal journals, *The Selected Journals of L. M. M.,* edited by Mary Rubio and Elizabeth Waterston.

M. authored twenty-two novels and one book of POETRY, *The Watchman and Other Poems,* (1916) and wrote over 500 poems and 500 short stories. Since her death, a short autobiographical book, *The Alpine Path,* a collection of poetry, *The Poetry of L. M. M.,* (eds. Kevin McCabe and Jon Ferns), four of five editions of her selected journals, two books of her collected letters, *The Green Gables Letters,* ed. Wilfrid Egglestson, *My Dear Mr. M.* (eds. F. W. P. Bolger and Elizabeth Epperly), and ten collections of her short stories (edited by Rea Wilmshurst) have been published.

M. enjoyed and revered poetry, but she learned that poetry did not sell as well as stories, so she set aside time from her work days to turn out potboilers for magazines. When she finished a book-length story about a red-haired precocious and imaginative orphan named Anne, she discovered that publishers were not interested. She put the manuscript away for almost two years until she reread it and sent it to a company in Boston. The publisher, L. C. Page, asked her to begin a sequel even before *Anne* was published. The demand for more books about Anne never ended and M. continued Anne's story, sometimes reluctantly, until the end of her life.

M. wrote eight novels about Anne Shirley and her family: *Anne of Green Gables* (1908), *Anne of Avonlea* (1909), *Anne of the Island* (1915), *Anne of Windy Poplars* (1936), *Anne's House of Dreams* (1917), *Rainbow Valley* (1919), *Anne of Ingleside* (1939) and *Rilla of Ingleside* (1921). Two books were written out of order, in the 1930s, to capitalize on the popularity of the 1934 RKO film of *Anne of Green Gables.*

Like Anne, other M. heroines lacked mothers. *Emily of New Moon* (1923) was an orphan and mirrored M.'s literary ambitions. *Jane of Lantern Hill* (1937) and *Pat of Silver Bush* (1933) had sickly or absent mothers and loved their home places as passionately as M. loved her own homes. M.'s mother died when she was less than two years old and her father left her in the care of her grandparents on the farm where her mother grew up in Cavendish, Prince Edward Island.

Cavendish was a beautiful agricultural settlement by the Gulf of St. Lawrence. M. was deeply affected by her environs and embedded these sensitivities in her writing. The combination of female characters with grit and gumption, within the context of a harmonious and poetic natural world, resonated with thousands, if not millions, of readers.

M.'s books have been reprinted by many publishers and translated into more than fifteen non-English editions. It would be hard to estimate exactly how many copies of M.'s books have been sold worldwide since Mark TWAIN described Anne as "the dearest, most moving and most delightful child since the immortal Alice" in the autumn of 1908. By 1951, L. C. Page alone had printed 1,250,000 copies of *Anne of Green Gables.*

By 1911, M. achieved instant worldwide fame as an author of four popular books, but lived modestly as the caretaker of her grandmother on the family farm. She became engaged to a Presbyterian minister, Ewen Macdonald, but postponed their marriage until her grandmother died. She married when she was thirty-seven years old and moved to Ontario, Canada after a honeymoon trip to Scotland. She lived in the church manses in the villages of Leaksdale (1911–26) and Norval (1926–35) and wrote fifteen books. When Ewen retired, they bought their first home and moved to Toronto where her last three books were written.

All of M.'s stories took place on Prince Edward Island except for *The Blue Castle* (1926), which was inspired by the Macdonalds' trip to the lake resort area of Muskoka, near Bala, Ontario. M. wanted to write an adult novel and used the lyrical setting of Bala as the backdrop for a story about a single woman who breaks out from the stifling conventions of her family and community to find her own romantic Blue Castle home on an island.

The marriage of Maud and Ewen was not as idyllic as the matches she created in her stories. The life of a minister's wife was a demanding one and M. more than fulfilled her share of responsibilities in her communities as well as continuing her own literary work. She had two sons, Chester (b. 1912) and Stuart (b. 1915) and one who died at birth in 1914. Beginning in 1919, Ewen Macdonald suffered the first of many nervous breakdowns and depressions that endured until his death. M. herself struggled with depression and insomnia throughout her life. Over the years, her husband's health, lawsuits brought about by car accidents and a greedy publisher, deaths of close friends, the wars, and requests for financial support from family and friends sapped her formidable energies. At the end of her life, she was in despair.

M. has long been regarded as a successful author of juvenile fiction but recent scholarly attention has brought new insights into her role as a powerful voice making serious social criticism through HUMOR and irony, and revealing cultural oppression through women's eyes. Elizabeth Waterston renewed interest in M.'s writing in her essay in *The Clear Spirit: Twenty Canadian Women and Their Times* in 1966. Mollie Gillen contributed more information about the author's life with her 1975 biography *The Wheel of Things*. In the 1980s, the first of M.'s journals was published and scholars like Elizabeth Epperly, Gabriella Ahmansson, and Mary Rubio began a discussion that illuminated M. as much more than a writer of simple girls stories.

AWARDS: Fellow of the Royal Society of Arts (1923), Order of the British Empire (1935), Institut des Lettres et des Arts (France, 1935)

FURTHER WORKS: *Kilmeny of the Orchard*. 1910. *The Story Girl*. 1911. *Chronicles of Avonlea*. 1912. *The Golden Road*. 1913. *Further Chronicles of Avonlea*. 1920. *Emily Climbs*. 1925. *Emily's Quest*. 1927. *Magic for Marigold*. 1929. *A Tangled Web*. 1931. *Courageous Women*. (With Marian Keith and Mabel Burns McKinley). 1934. *Mistress Pat*. 1935. *The Road to Yesterday*. 1974. *The Doctor's Sweetheart and Other Stories*. 1979

BIBLIOGRAPHY: Ahmansson, G. *A Life and Its Mirrors*. 1991. Cott, Jonathan, *Pipers at the Gates of Dawn: The Wisdom of Children's Literature*, 1981. Epperly, E. *The Fragrance of Sweet Grass*. 1992. McCabe, K. and A. Heilbron. *The Lucy Maud M. Album*. 1999. Rubio, M., "Subverting the Trite: L. M. M.'s 'Room of Her Own.'" *Canadian Children's Literature*. 1992. Rubio, M. and E. Waterston. *Writing a Life: L. M. M.* 1995

BETH CAVERT

MONTRESOR, Beni

Illustrator, author, b. 31 March 1926, Bussolengo, Italy

M.'s interest in drawing began by age two or three; he remembers asking his grandfather to bring him art supplies rather than sweets when he visited. As a child, M. spent time in the churches and museums of Verona, enchanted by the stories told him in the frescoes and sculptures. Inspired by these images, M. designed sets and costumes for his puppets at home. He attended the High School of Arts in Verona, Liceo Artistico, 1942–45, Academia di Belle Arti, 1945–49, and then Centro Seprimentale di Cinematografia, 1950–52. M. worked as film critic for an Italian newspaper, wrote radio plays, and became well known as a set and costume designer for theater, opera, ballet, and film, working with directors such as Fellini and Rosselini. He also wrote and directed for stage and film. M. came to the United States in 1960 and soon began his career as an author and illustrator of children's books.

M. compares his work in PICTURE BOOKS to designing stages for the theater and to the sculpted stories he grew up "reading" on the walls of churches in Italy. He sees his role as an illustrator as provoking the child's imagination, so that the child's own ideas elaborate his work. His goal is to bring the enchantment of theater to the pages of his books.

AWARDS: ALA CALDECOTT MEDAL (1965) for *May I Bring a Friend?* (DE REGNIERS, author). NEWBERY MEDAL Honor Book (1962) for *Belling the Tiger* (Mary STOLZ, au.). *New York Times* Best Illustrated Children's Books of the Year (1966) for *The Magic Flute* and (1962) for *The Princesses: Sixteen Stories about Princesses*. American Society of Illustrators Gold Medal (1967) for *I Saw a Ship a-Sailing*. In addition to his literary honors, M. has won numerous awards for his opera and ballet designs, and radio plays. M. was knighted by the Italian government in 1966 for services to the arts

FURTHER WORKS: Author and illustrator: *House of Flowers, House of Stars*. 1962. *The Witches of Venice*. 1963. *Cinderella*. 1965, a version based on the Rossini opera. *A for Angel*. 1969. *Bedtime*. 1978. *The Dragon Drummer: A Story ABC*. 1993. Illustrator: *The Great Rebellion*. 1961. *Siri the Conquistador*. 1963, both by STOLZ. On *Christ-*

mas Eve. (BROWN). 1961. *Little Red Riding Hood.* (PERRAULT). 1965. *Willy O'Dwyer Jumped in the Fire: Variations on a Folk Rhyme.* (De Regniers). 1968. *The Birthday of the Infanta and Other Stories by Oscar Wilde.* 1982. *The Nightingale.* (ANDERSEN). 1985

BIBLIOGRAPHY: HOPKINS, L. B. *Books Are by People.* 1969. *Pauses: Autobiographical Reflections of 101 Creators of Children's Books,* 1995. Caldecott Award acceptance. 1965. In L. Kingman (Ed.). *NEWBERY and Caldecott Medal Books: 1956–1965,* pp. 259–65. Scherer, B. L., "Light on the Piazza," *Opera News,* 1992

JANE WEST

MOORE, Clement Clarke

Poet, b. 15 July, 1779, New York City; d 10 July, 1863, Newport, Rhode Island

As a writer in the early 1800s M., a poet, scholar, and educator, was a member of the Knickerbocker Society in New York City with other writers such as James Fenimore Cooper and Washington IRVING. M.'s famous Christmas poem, known today as "Twas the Night before Christmas," has become a classic frequently adapted and illustrated in many versions for children. M. first read this poem aloud to family and friends on Christmas Eve, 1822. A young relative sent the then-untitled poem to the *Troy Sentinel,* where it was first published on December 23, 1823, as "A Visit from St. Nicholas." M. later revealed that the physical features of St. Nicholas were modeled after a local workman. Recently, poet Henry Livingston has been suggested as the true "Christmas" author.

BIBLIOGRAPHY: Gardner, Martin, *The Annotated Night before Christmas,* 1991

SANDRA IMDIEKE

MOORE, Lilian

Author, editor, b. 17 March 1909, New York City

M. grew up in the bustle of New York City, graduating from Hunter College with a B.A. in English in 1930. After graduation she became a teacher working with struggling readers, and did graduate work at Columbia University. Because of this interest in children first grappling with print, she sought to write books that would be appropriate for new or struggling readers but also of high quality. She succeeded in combining her two goals; her first book, written with Leone Ad-

elson, *Old Rosie, the Horse Nobody Understood* (1952) was selected as one of the *New York Times* Best Books of the Year when it was reprinted in 1960. Likewise her other EASY-TO-READ BOOKS including *The Magic Spectacles, and Other Easy-to-Read Stories* (1966), *I'll Meet You at the Cucumbers* (1988), *Don't Be Afraid, Amanda* (1992), and *Adam Mouse's Book of Poems* (1992) were well written as well as accessible for young readers. M. also wrote many books under the pseudonym Sara Asheron. These texts, *Surprise in the Tree* (1962) for example, provided even more reading material for those becoming familiar with the written word.

Another influential role for M. was as an editor. Shaping other writers, she sought to clarify writing for children. She edited the Grosset and Dunlap Easy Reader series, and worked as a SERIES editor for Thomas Y. Crowell. M. was the founding editor of Scholastic's Arrow Book Club, providing children access to excellent literature through paperback-book orders at their schools.

Supplementing her stories for early readers and her editing, M. wrote and compiled POETRY. Her books of poetry such as *I Feel the Same Way* (1967), *I Thought I Heard the City* (1969), *Sam's Place: Poems for the Country* (1973), and *Think of Shadows* (1980) were tight with no wasted words. *Sam's Place* concisely told of her husband Sam's love of the land as a farmer. She also compiled several poetry collections: *Catch Your Breath: A Book of Shivery Poems* (compiled with Lawrence Webster, 1973), *To See the World Afresh* (compiled with Judith Thurman, 1974), and *Sunflakes: Poems for Children* (1992). *Think of Shadows* was cited as a Notable Book by the AMERICAN LIBRARY ASSOCIATION, and *Sunflakes* was a Notable Children's Book for the American Library Association. However, M.'s greatest honor for her poetry was bestowed by the NATIONAL COUNCIL OF TEACHERS OF ENGLISH in 1985, when she was given their Award for Excellence in Poetry for Children.

FURTHER WORKS: *The Terrible Mr. Twitmeyer.* (With Leone Adelson). 1952. *The Important Pockets of Paul.* 1954. *Wobbly Wheels.* 1956. *Junk Day on Juniper Street and Other Easy-to-Read Stories.* 1969. *Hooray for Me.* (with Remy CHARLIP). 1975

BIBLIOGRAPHY: *Fourth Book of Junior Authors and Illustrators.* 1978. HOPKINS, L. B. *Books Are *by People.* 1969. *Pauses: Autobiographical Reflections of 101 Creators of Children's Books,* 1995. Kiefer, Barbara, selector, *Getting to Know You: Profiles of Children's Authors Featured in Language Arts, 1985–90,* 1991. *Major Authors and Illustrators for Children and Young Adults.* 1993

GWYNNE ELLEN ASH

MORA, Pat
Author, poet. b. 19 January 1942, El Paso, Texas

M. earned her B.A. from Texas Western College in 1963 and M.A. from the University of Texas at El Paso in 1967. In addition to her teaching and other work in public schools and universities, M. has served as host of the radio show, *Voices: The Mexican American in Perspective,* on National Public Radio affiliate KTEP. She also gives presentations and POETRY readings in the United States and other countries. M. has won numerous AWARDS for her books and poetry, including the Skipping Stones Book Award for *The Desert Is My Mother* (1994).

M. is an advocate for increasing the awareness of Hispanic viewpoints of our literary heritage, as well as focusing attention on the native traditions of Hispanic Americans. Her writing often explores the identities of Hispanic women. She is sometimes referred to as a "regional writer" because much of her work celebrates life in the desert regions of the American Southwest. For example, her first two collections, *Chants* (1984) and *Borders* (1986), feature the desert landscape of the region as they explore the theme of the relation between women and the earth.

M.'s books and poetry for children, which often focus on Hispanic culture and family relationships, seek to establish pride in heritage for young Chicanos. Her books, *A Birthday Party for Tia* (1992) and *Pablo's Tree* (1994), are both warm, engaging stories that celebrate family. M. also uses FOLKLORE to introduce Hispanic heritage to young readers. Her book, *The Race of Toad and Deer* (1995), helps children develop bicultural understanding through traditional narrative. Many of M.'s writings are bilingual (written in both Spanish and English). Her counting book, *Uno, Dos, Tres: One, Two, Three* (1996), uses rhyme and repetition as it features folk art and culture in two languages.

FURTHER WORKS: *Listen to the Desert/Oye al Desierto,* 1994; *Agua, Agua Agua,* 1994; *Confetti: Poems for Children,* 1996; *Tomasy la Senora de la Biblioteca/Tomas and the Library Lady,* 1997; *This Big Sky,* 1998; *The Rainbow Tulip,* 1999

BIBLIOGRAPHY: *Contemporary Authors,* vol. 129; the *Horn Book* magazine, July–August 1990, Nov.–Dec. 1994; *School Library Journal,* October 1994; *Something about the Author,* vol. 92, 1997; publisher's notes

MARY ARIAIL BROUGHTON

MORDVINOFF, Nicholas
Illustrator, b. 27 September 1911, Leningrad, Russia; d. 5 May 1973, Hampton, New Jersey

"From the time I was three I always wanted to draw and paint, and I always drew horses. I love horses." At seven his family left Russia, fled to Finland to escape the revolution, and settled in Paris where he went to school. After graduating from the University of Paris he opted for the South Pacific where he spent thirteen years developing his own painting style. Illustrating three books successfully in Tahiti by William S. Stone inspired M. to come to the United States in 1946.

In 1950, *The Two Reds,* written by Will Lipkind, was published and designated a CALDECOTT MEDAL Honor Book. It is notable for M.'s quirky line drawings and bright red dashes of color. *Finders Keepers* (1952) done once again with Will Lipkind, won the Caldecott Medal. Here, M. uses bold splashes of color to highlight a simple classic story about sharing and cooperation. Somewhat somber, M. felt "fulfillment of a lasting desire very often comes too late or brings some sort of disillusionment." His outlook on winning the Caldecott Medal was, "I am very happy about it. This time there will be no disillusionment, I am sure."

Burma Boy, by Willis Lindquist, was an AMERICAN LIBRARY ASSOCIATION Notable Book. *Alphonse, That Bearded One* (1954) received the *New York Herald Tribune* award. The *New York Times* listed *Circus Ruckus* (1954), *Chaga* (1955), and *The Magic Feather* (1958) among the Best Children's Illustrated Books of the year. *The Little Tiny Rooster* (1960) was an ALA Notable Book. M. believed, "a PICTURE BOOK must have complete unity in text and pictures. . . . It is a work of love."

BIBLIOGRAPHY: *Fiction, FOLKLORE, FANTASY and POETRY for Children, 1876–1985,* vol. 1, 1986; HOPKINS, Lee Bennett, *Pauses: Autobiographical Reflections of 101 Creators of Children's Books,* 1995

IRVYN G. GILBERTSON

MOREY, Walt

Author, b. 3 February 1907, Hoquiam, Washington; d. 12 January 1992, Wilsonville, Oregon

M. is a noted writer of fiction about nature and animals. He began writing in the 1920s, selling short stories to popular magazines. In the 1960s, he shifted his writing to books for children. *Gentle Ben* is a story of friendship between a teenage boy and a brown bear he saves from abuse. An AMERICAN LIBRARY ASSOCIATION Notable Book, *Gentle Ben* was later made into a motion picture and television series. His popular ADVENTURE STORIES have been republished as "The Walt M. Adventure Library" starting in 1989 with the republication of *Run Far, Run Fast* (1973) and *Runaway Stallion* (1974) through recent titles including *Death Walk* in 1993, *Canyon Winter* (1972) in 1994, and *Gloomy Gus* (1970) in 1999.

FURTHER WORKS: *Kavik the Wolf Dog,* 1968; *Scrub Dog of Alaska,* 1971

BIBLIOGRAPHY: *Something about the Author,* vol. 70, 1993

SANDRA IMDIEKE

MORI, Kyoko

Author, b. 9 March 1957, Kobe, Japan

Author of nonfiction, POETRY, and novels for YOUNG ADULTS and adults, M. immigrated to the United States in 1977. She became a naturalized citizen in 1984. Her first novel, *Shizuko's Daughter* (1993), was critically acclaimed and was recognized by the AMERICAN LIBRARY ASSOCIATION, *New York Times, Publishers Weekly,* Council of Wisconsin, and Elizabeth Burr Award. Her mother's suicide in 1969 and her own reaction to the tragedy catapulted her into an independence for making changes that vastly influenced her future and served as the foundation for the later written *Shizuko's Daughter* (1993). The author became determined to adjust to her mother's death and become strong as a tribute to her memory. Her early life and relationships greatly influenced her writings. As a young child, she was surrounded by books, writing, and art. M. writes stories and poems that she likes to tell and hear.

FURTHER WORKS: *Fallout,* 1994; *One Bird,* 1995; *The Dream of Water: A Memoir* 1995; *Polite Lies,* 1997; *Stone, Field, True, Arrow,* 2000

BIBLIOGRAPHY: M. Kyoko, "Learning to Swim," *When I Was Your Age,* Amy Ehrlich, ed., 1999; *Something about the Author,* vol. 106, 1999

NANCY HORTON

MORRISON, Lillian

Poet, anthologist, b. 27 October 1917 Jersey City, New Jersey

M. is well known as a writer and anthologist of POETRY for young people. Among her award-winning works are *Sprints and Distances: Sports in Poetry and the Poetry in Sports* (1965, 1990), an AMERICAN LIBRARY ASSOCIATION Notable Book, *The Ghosts of Jersey City and Other Poems* (1967), an American Ambassador Book by the English Speaking Union, and *Rhythm Road,* an AMERICAN LIBRARY ASSOCIATION Notable Book (1988) and Best Book for YOUNG ADULTS (1988). Her classic *Yours 'til Niagara Falls* (1950, 1990), a collection of folk rhymes, was inspired by her work with youth at a library in New York. Many of M.'s collections, such as *Slam Dunk: Basketball Poems* (1994), feature poems related to sports; *At the Crack of the Bat* (1992) is her first sports anthology focusing on a single sport. Her books emphasize the sounds, cadences, and rhythms of language as well as vivid visual images and energetic physical activity. Her science collection, *Overheard in a Bubble Chamber and Other Science Poems* (1981) uses the language of science to relate the physical sciences to human scale.

FURTHER WORKS: *Remember Me When This You See,* 1961; *Best Wishes, Amen: A New Collection of Autograph Verses,* 1974; *The Sidewalk Racer and Other Poems of Sports and Motion,* 1977; *Who Would Marry a Mineral,* 1978; *The Break Dance Kids: Poems of Sport, Motion, and Locomotion,* 1985; *I Scream, You Scream: A Feast of Food Rhymes,* 1998

BIBLIOGRAPHY: *Sixth Book of Junior Authors and Illustrators,* 1989; http://www.ach.uams.edu/parenting/fall97/in_review.htm accessed February 5, 1999

MARY ARIAIL BROUGHTON

MOSEL, Arlene (Tichy)
Folklorist, b. 27 August 1921, Cleveland, Ohio

M. began her library career at the Enoch Pratt Free Library in Baltimore, as assistant in the children's department. She has served as associate professor of library science at Case Western Reserve University, Cleveland, where she received her M.S.L.S. in 1959. M. has also served as assistant coordinator of Children's Services, Cuyahoga County Public Library. M.'s retelling of *Tikki Tikki Tembo* (illustrated by Blair LENT, 1968) received considerable praise. For M., subtle humor, deftly delivered, surprises children and allows them opportunity to laugh. She takes great pleasure telling stories and planning story-hour programs. Pen-and-ink drawings with an acrylic glaze lend drama to M.'s humorous retelling of how a little old woman outwits a mischievous underworld sprite in *The Funny Little Woman* (Blair Lent, illus., 1972).

AWARDS: ALA CALDECOTT MEDAL 1973, and INTERNATIONAL BOARD ON BOOKS FOR YOUNG PEOPLE, Honor Book 1972, *The Funny Little Woman; Boston Globe–Horn Book,* 1968, for *Tikki Tikki Tembo*

FURTHER WORKS: *The Funny Little Woman* (illus. Lent), 1972

BIBLIOGRAPHY: *Something about the Author,* vol. 7, 1975

CRAIG LIEBERMAN

MOSER, Barry
Artist, illustrator, author, b. 15 October 1940 Chattanooga, Tennessee

M. was reared in Chattanooga, Tennessee. As a child, he distinguished himself in school as the boy who could draw. His realistic drawings were an escape from school, which was not his favorite place to be. After elementary school, M. was sent to a military school where he "more or less slept" through those years. The school still remains an influence, however, in M.'s dress, manners, and suspicion of authority.

M. entered Auburn University in Alabama to study industrial design. He was not able to complete his degree because of financial problems but his "talents" were appreciated and celebrated. An interesting encounter was with his fraternity housemother, "Miss Lillian" Carter, who would tell stories about her life in Plains, Georgia, and her sons, Jimmy and Billy. M. returned home to attend the University of Chattanooga, where he received a degree in art education. In 1962, he married and began his teaching career.

Five years later, M. moved his wife and three daughters to New England. He says, "Most of my personality developed in the South. . . . Yet, my artistic personality developed in New England." He took a job at a school that was known for its intellectual and artistic freedom, meeting several people there who have played important roles in his life. About this time, M. decided that "the book would become the same as my canvases had been before." He wanted to see a book cover with his name on it and his illustrations inside.

To pursue this dream, he opened Pennyroyal Press, a private press. M. initiated each project and was involved in every facet of printing each book. He attributes "this feeling for the whole book" as what sets his work apart from others. "Making pictures for books is important to me but only in that it contributes to the overall beauty of the book. I see illustrations as equal to, not superior to, text, typography and overall design." M. took on classic works, including those by Dante, Homer, and Virgil. He is noted as a book designer, painter, printer, printmaker, and illustrator who is frequently invited all over the country as a guest lecturer.

In 1978, M. illustrated *Moby-Dick* (Herman Melville, 1851) for a private press in California. The success of this book made it possible for M. to take on five more projects for Pennyroyal, including *Through the Looking Glass* (CARROLL, 1872) and *Frankenstein* (SHELLEY, 1818). All of these books were reprinted in trade editions. An editor who knew M.'s work from seeing the trade book editions asked him to illustrate a book for children, *Jump!: The Adventures of Brer Rabbit* by musician and lyricist Van Dyke PARKS. His first trade book for a major publisher, *Jump!,* done in watercolor, was named an AMERICAN LIBRARY ASSOCIATION Notable Book in 1986. *Jump, Again!,* M.'s second book for children, was also selected as an AMERICAN LIBRARY ASSOCIATION Notable Book and a *New York Times* Best Illustrated Book of the Year in 1987. Many awards have followed including a *Boston Globe–Horn*

Book Award for nonfiction and an INTERNA-
TIONAL BOARD ON BOOKS FOR YOUNG PEOPLE Il-
lustration Award in 1992 for *Little Tricker the
Squirrel Meets Big Trouble the Bear,* by Ken
Kesey. Done in watercolor, *In the Beginning*
(1988) by Virginia HAMILTON, was a NEWBERY
MEDAL Honor Book in 1989, as well as an ALA
Notable Book. In all, M. has won over eighty
American Book Awards citations for design and
illustration.

M.'s favorite media are wood engraving and
watercolor with decorations done in calligraphy.
Both are difficult to handle and "unforgiving."
M. considers himself a book illustrator though he
prefers "booksmith," a person who makes books.
As he did in his *Brer Rabbit* watercolors, M.
often focuses on single illustrations that emphasize a character's personality within the setting
of the story. He keeps an extensive collection of
illustrations and texts for ideas and inspiration in
his own work. He begins the illustrating process
by reading the text many times, letting the characters speak to him and the plot germinate telling
him what kind of images to paint. Each time he
makes a book it is for the same purpose, "to
make a beautiful book." Because M. illustrates
both adult and children's books, he has been
asked if the task is the same. He feels each has
its own requirements and demands but there is
a "difference in density" in working with adult
materials.

His most recent project, a twelve-year-long
undertaking to illustrate the King James BIBLE,
emphasizes the issue of density. Completed in the
fall of 1999, in time for the millennium, M.'s version was printed by hand and has 240 illustrations. It is the first Bible illustrated by a single
artist since 1865.

With about 200 book projects to his credit, M.
has worked with both CLASSIC titles and many
outstanding contemporary authors. He has even
collaborated with his children and grandchildren.
In his work for children, M. wants them to take
art seriously and appreciate it. He wants them to
have "richness, a full meal, not just icing and ice
cream. When kids sit down at my books, they're
sitting down at a Thanksgiving dinner."

FURTHER WORK: Illus.: *Appalachia: The Voices
of Sleeping Birds.* (RYLANT). *Adventures of Sherlock Holmes.* (DOYLE). 1992. *Bingleman's Mid-*

way. (ACKERMAN). 1995. *When Birds Could Talk
and Bats Could Sing.* (Hamilton). 1996. *When
Willard Met Babe Ruth.* (HALL). 1996. *On Call
Back Mountain.* (BUNTING). 1997

BIBLIOGRAPHY: *Book Page.* 1994. Interview by
Susie Wilde, 1998, Calgary Children's Literature
Website. A. Olswanger "Kaleidoscope 6 Present-
ers" in *Children's Literature Review,* vol. 49
(1998). Cummins, J. (Ed.). (1992). *Children's
Book Illustration and Design*

SHARON HARTMAN

MOTHER GOOSE

Known primarily in America as "Mother Goose
Rhymes" and in Britain as "Nursery Rhymes,"
the majority of these familiar verses were not
composed for children. Many began as ballads,
folk or tavern songs, love songs, peddlers' street
cries, or were derived from street plays. Before
1800, the only verses written expressly for the
nursery were rhyming alphabets, lullabies, or
game rhymes. Some verses such as "Thirty Days
Hath September," documented back to the thirteenth century, and "London Bridge" from the
fifteenth century, are documented, and probably
half of the rhymes are more than two hundred and
fifty years old. A few very well known rhymes
are as recent as the nineteenth century and American in origin. "Mary Had a Little Lamb" was
most likely written by Sara Josepha HALE for an
1830 children's periodical that she edited. "There
Was a Little Girl," which appeared before 1870,
is often said to be a verse that Henry Wadsworth
LONGFELLOW wrote about his daughter.

For hundreds of years the oral tradition kept
nursery rhymes alive before they were recorded
in print. Some rhymes that were documented in
the seventeenth or eighteenth centuries were not
mentioned in print again for several generations.
Many rhymes, such as "Humpty Dumpty" and
"Ladybird, Ladybird," find their equivalents all
across Europe, often with the same proper names
and verse patterns.

It was popular for many years to attach political significance to nursery rhymes and to connect
historical persons with nursery rhyme characters.
For the most part, these relationships have proven
to be unfounded. Some rhymes have even been
given three or four historical interpretations. John
Bellenden Ker, in *An Essay on the Archaeology*

of Popular English Phrases and Nursery Rhymes, published in 1834, and in two subsequent volumes, was one of the first to mix nursery rhyme fact and fiction. As recently as 1930 *The Real Personages of Mother Goose* by Katherine Elwes Thomas was entertaining and misleading readers. This is not to say that none of the nursery rhymes correlate to real people for many, such as "Charley over the Water," "Jack Sprat" and "The Brave Old Duke of York," do have documented historical connections.

At the beginning of the eighteenth century the first book containing traditional rhymes for children appeared. *A Little Book for Little Children* by "T. W." contained two verses and three riddle verses, none of which are well known to today's children. Also at around this same time three authors, Dr. William King, Henry Carey, and one unidentified, wrote satires for adults that made reference to "Good King Cole," "Jacky Horner," and "This Pig Went to Market," among others.

In 1744 two tiny volumes, only one and three-fourths inches by three inches, appeared entitled *Tommy Thumb's Pretty Song Book Vol. I and II* by N. Lovechild. Although only the second volume survives, the contents of thirty-nine verses would be familiar to many children of today as they include "Who Did Kill Cock Robin?" and "Bah, Bah Black Sheep." *The Famous Tommy Thumb's Little Storybook* was printed between 1754 and 1768. After a section on the adventures of the title character and some fables the volume closed with nine verses that included "This Pig Went to Market" and the first record of "Little Boy Blue." Around the same time *The Top Book of All for Little Masters and Misses* contained "The Three Jovial Welshmen" and "Jack Nory" among its eight rhymes.

It is generally acknowledged that the noted publisher John NEWBERY compiled the first book of rhymes with the inclusion of Mother Goose in the title: *Mother Goose's Melody; or, Sonnets for the Cradle.* It does not bear the J. NEWBERY imprint but was probably printed by him in the mid-1760s. It is also believed that Newbery's friend, Oliver Goldsmith, may have been responsible not only for the preface but for the inclusion of several of the rhymes. *Mother Goose's Melody* is notable for the many verses it contains and for the number of times it was reprinted. The volume was

very popular in America where Isaiah Thomas of Boston published it and its popularity continued into the nineteenth century. Newbery's *Mother Goose's Melody* inspired Joseph Riston, a collector of old songs, to gather more verses after he purchased a copy in 1781. By the turn of the century Riston had seventy-nine entries for his *Gammer Gurton's Garland, or the Nursery Parnassus* and in the next few years several publishers produced books of a similar nature.

Just as the FOLKLORE linking nursery rhymes to actual persons persists so does the identification of Mother Goose herself. In 1697 Charles PERRAULT, a French courtier, published *Histories; or, Tales of Past Times, with Morals.* An engraving at the beginning of the book showed a woman sitting in front of a fire and telling tales to an audience of three. A wall sign read "Contes de Ma Mère L'Oye," or translated into English, "Tales of Mother Goose." Although the stories in the volume included "Cinderella," "Red Riding Hood," and "Sleeping Beauty," and no nursery rhymes at all, the name "Mother Goose" appeared for probably the first time in print.

Some scholars maintain that Charlemagne's mother, Queen Bertha, nicknamed "Goose-Footed Bertha" because of the size or shape of her foot was the original Mother Goose. Others claim that Mother Goose has origins all the way back to the Biblical Queen of Sheba. Americans have proposed that Mother Goose was actually Elizabeth Goose (or Vergoose or Vertigoose) of Boston, Massachusetts. Supposedly, Mrs. Goose took care of several grandchildren and entertained them with songs and rhymes. Her son-in-law, the publisher Thomas Fleet, is said to have published these rhymes in 1719 as *Songs for the Nursery; or, Mother Goose's Melodies.* Most scholars are doubtful about the story because no copy of the book has ever been located.

Mother Goose is often depicted as an old lady with a strong chin, wearing a tall pointed hat, and riding a goose through the sky. Knowing her rhymes have stood the test of time she flies confidently into the future where she will undoubtedly be as popular as ever.

The twentieth century brought several social commentaries on the violence of nursery rhymes and many "politically correct" editions have been published but Walter de La Mare in his introduction to *Nursery Rhymes for Certain Times,* in 1956, said it best: the rhymes of Mother Goose "free the fancy, charm the tongue and ear, delight the inward eye, and many of them are tiny masterpieces of word craftsmanship, of the latest device in rhythm, indeed—the 'sprung'!"

DONARITA VOCCA

MOVABLE BOOKS (POP-UP BOOKS)

Books are by design two-dimensional. It might seem impossible for a page to add motion or depth other than through illustrations with perspective and illusion. And yet, for over 700 years, artists, philosophers, scientists, and book designers have tried to challenge the two-dimensional physical boundaries of the book. They have added flaps, revolving parts, and other movable pieces to enhance the text. Movable, or pop-up, books are miniature-paper models of the world that present three-dimensional images within the traditional two-dimensional world of books.

One of the earliest examples was produced in the thirteenth century by Ramon Llull of Majorca using a revolving disc or *volvelle.* Volvelles were used in books in the fourteenth century for fortune-telling and for creating secret codes. Anatomical illustrations as early as 1345 used layers of superimposed plates that could be lifted to reveal parts of the body. It was not until the eighteenth century that these techniques were applied to books that were designed for children.

Robert Sayer produced "metamorphoses" books in 1766. These books, also called "turn-up" books or "harlequinades," changed and kept pace with the story. They were composed of single, printed sheets folded perpendicularly into four. Hinged at the top and bottom of each fold, the picture was cut through horizontally across the center to make two flaps that could be opened up or down. When raised, the pages disclosed another hidden picture underneath, each having a few lines of verse.

Paper Doll Books, created around 1810 by S. and J. Fuller, had seven or eight faceless cut-out figures in different costumes. A removable head could be inserted into a paper pocket to show the character in alternative outfits. These small, expensive books usually contained moral tales with hand-colored illustrations.

The first true movable books for children were published by Dean and Son. By the 1860s, the company claimed to be the "originator of children's movable books in which characters can be made to move and act in accordance with the incidents described in each story." To produce movable books, skilled craftsmen prepared the hand-made mechanicals while designers used cut-out scenes aligned one behind the other to give a three-dimensional effect. Each layer was fixed to the next by a piece of ribbon that emerged behind the uppermost portion, and when this was pulled, the whole scene sprang up into perspective. Dean also introduced movable books with transformational plates based on the jalousie or venetian-blind principle. The illustrations in these books had either a square or an oblong picture divided into four or five equal sections by corresponding horizontal or vertical slits. When a tab at the side or bottom of the illustration is pulled, the picture is "transformed" into another. In 1870, Raphael Tuck and his sons published Father Tuck's "Mechanical" SERIES. This included stand-up items with three-dimensional effects as well as movable books.

Ernest Nister's works, in the 1890s, had illustrations that stood up automatically. The books contained figures that were die-cut and mounted within a three-dimensional peep-show framework. The figures were connected by paper guides so that when the pages were turned, the figures lifted away from the page within the perspective-like setting. Nister also produced movable books with "dissolving" and revolving transformational slats. He developed a distinctive house style of chubby-cheeked children usually depicted in idealized-rural settings. Both the charming illustrations and surprising mechanicals contributed to the success of these publications.

McLoughlin Brothers of New York produced the first movable books in the U.S. Innovators of printing techniques, McLoughlin issued two separate Little Showman's series in the 1880s, each containing three-dimensional scenes. These large, colorful plates unfolded into multilayered displays.

In 1929, a new series of movable books was initiated. British publisher S. Louis Giraud conceived, designed, and produced books with movable illustrations described as "living models." Although the term had yet to be used on them, these were authentic pop-up books. Each title contained at least five double-page spreads that sprang up automatically when the book was opened with illustrations that could be viewed from all four sides. Giraud's moderately priced books were produced on coarse, absorbent paper, employing crude photo-litho printing and color-reproduction techniques, and finished with inexpensive covers and bindings. Between 1929 and 1949, Giraud produced a series of sixteen annuals that included stories, verses, and illustrations as well as five or more pop-ups. Despite their flaws, Giraud's books explained things clearly and reached a wide audience. In the 1930s Blue Ribbon Publishing of New York animated Walt DIS-NEY characters and FAIRY TALES with pop-ups. Blue Ribbon, the first publisher to use the pop-up term to describe their movable illustrations, registered the word in 1933.

Random House published Walt Disney's *The Victory March* in 1942 and it sold over 50,000 copies. Readers pulled a tab to see Dumbo fly and turned a wheel to watch the Disney gang chase the enemy. A feature of this particular item was the insertion of a World War II savings stamp and album in each copy.

The Exciting Adventures of Finnie the Fiddler was the first of a series featuring the animation of Julian Wehr. The tab-operated mechanicals worked by means of partially concealed die-cut cards eyeletted between the double-thickness illustrated pages. The pages were slit at various points to permit arms, heads, legs, or other moving parts to protrude. By moving the tab, which extended through the side or lower edge of the illustrated page, the various parts of the animation were put into motion. McLoughlin Brothers reentered the movable-book market in 1939 with the publication of their first Jolly Jump-up title.

The pop-up business began to expand in the 1960s with significant contributions published by Random House and Hallmark Cards. *Bennett Cerf's Pop-up Riddles* (1965) was the first Random House entry into the field, followed by 45 other titles. Hallmark began producing pop-up books in 1966 and issued about seventy titles during the late 1960s and 1970s.

Since the 1970s, the publication of pop-up books has become a production involving the skills of a number of individuals. The creation of

the book begins with a concept, story line, and situation. Once the basics are worked out, the project goes to the professional called the paper engineer. The paper engineer takes the ideas of the author and the illustrator, and puts motion into the characters as well as action into the scenes. He or she may even add sound, as in a book where the opening and closing of the pages causes the teeth of a saw to run across a log with a very sawlike noise. The paper engineer's task is to be imaginative as well as practical. The designer determines how movable pieces attach to the page so that they will not break, which points need glue and how much, how long pull tabs should be, and how high a piece can pop up. The final step for the paper engineer is to lay out or "nest" all the pages and pieces so that they fit onto the size sheet that will be run through the printing press.

Pop-up books are assembled by hand, and nearly all of the books published since the 1970s have been produced in Asia and South America. After printing, the nesting pieces of a book are die-cut from the sheets and collated with their pages. Production lines are set up, with as many as sixty people are involved in the handwork needed to complete one book. These people fold, insert paper tabs into slits, connect paper pivots, glue, and tape. Alignment of tip-in pieces with the printed page must be exact; angles must be precise. The most complex books can require over 100 individual handwork procedures.

Contemporary pop-ups have gained not only popularity and success but respectability as well. Numerous titles have appeared on best-book recommendations, and in 1979 Jan PIENKOWSKI's *Haunted House* won the prestigious KATE GREEN-AWAY MEDAL. *The Wonderful Wizard of Oz: A Commemorative Pop-Up* (2000), with paper engineering by Robert SABUDA, celebrates the one-hundredth anniversary of L. Frank BAUM's fantasy with spectacular effects. These are accordion-folded insets with pop-up figures, a tornado that spins up across an opening double-page spread, a witch who melts, and a ball of flame that bursts upward. The movable books of the last two decades have become increasingly complex with sophisticated pop-up illustrations and intricate mechanical devices. The addition of lights and music in some titles contributes to the surprise of the mechanical illustrations.

Movable and pop-up books are not ordinary books. For over a hundred years, their ingenious mechanical devices have surprised and entertained readers of all ages.

ANN MONTANARO

MOWAT, Farley

Author, b. 12 May 1921, Belleville, Ontario, Canada

M. grew up in Ontario and Saskatchewan, living a largely isolated existence, a mode of life he preferred. He was a quiet child who spent much of his time writing and in libraries, while his uncle, Frank Farley, took him on some of his earliest forays into the wilderness. M. first saw the caribou migration with his Uncle Frank and accompanied him on bird-watching trips to the Arctic circle. These experiences, as well as his unusual family pets would provide much of the inspiration and material for his writing.

Primarily known as a writer of vehemently conservationist nonfiction for adults and YOUNG ADULTS, M. began his professional writing as a soldier in the CANADIAN Army during World War II. There he tried to write about his war experience, but was unsuccessful; instead he began *The Dog That Wouldn't Be* (1957) his first nonfiction book for children. He would later write several books about his war experience including *And No Birds Sang* (1979) and *The Great Betrayal* (1980). Upon returning from the war, M. studied caribou migration on a government grant and came to know the Ihalmiut or *People of the Deer* (1952). His book, which spoke of the end of the people's livelihood due to disastrous governmental policies, was decried by the government of Canada, but well received by readers and critics. *People of the Deer* was the book that began M.'s career as a speaker for those who do not have the power to speak out, a speaker who did not try to keep his outrage and indignation hidden.

Perhaps M.'s best known book for children, *Owls in the Family* (1961), like the *Dog That Wouldn't Be,* was based on his own experiences as a child and was named an AMERICAN LIBRARY ASSOCIATION Notable Book. However, it is *Never Cry Wolf* (1963), a book not intended for the juvenile market that has become well known through both its reading and its adaptation as a film by

DISNEY Studios in 1983. *Never Cry Wolf* followed a wolf couple, with M. acting as an ethnologist in debunking many human assumptions about wolves. M. proceeded to write several more books criticizing the ecological policies of the Canadian and United States Government (*A Whale for the Killing* [1972] and *Sea of Slaughter* [1985]).

Although M.'s writing expressly for juveniles has been limited, many of his ecological books for adults are widely read by adolescents. M. has been honored for his writing and his stances, having been on the Hans Christian ANDERSEN Honor List (1965), received the Leacock Medal (1970), Vicki Metcalf Award (1970), and won the Boys Club of America Award. M. has also received several honorary doctorates from Lethbridge University, the University of Toronto, and the University of Prince Edward Island.

AWARDS: Canadian Library Association Book of the Year for Children Award (1958) and INTERNATIONAL BOARD ON BOOKS FOR YOUNG PEOPLE Honor List (1958) for *Lost In the Barrens*

FURTHER WORKS: *Lost in the Barrens* (1956, republished as *Two against the North,* 1977); *The Black Joke,* 1962; *The Curse of the Viking Grave,* 1966

BIBLIOGRAPHY: *Authors and Artists for Young Adults,* vol. 1, 1989; Orange, J. *Farley Mowat: Writing the Squib,* 1993; *Third Book of Junior Authors,* 1972; Thomas, W. *A Farley Mowat Reader,* 1997; *Twentieth-Century Children's Writers,* 1978

GWYNNE ELLEN ASH

MUKERJI, Dhan Gopal

Author, b. 6 July 1890, near Calcutta, India, d. 14 July 1936, New York City

M. was an Indian-born American author of fiction and reteller of folktales for children. Born in a small village near the Indian jungle, M.'s family were Brahmins and had charge of the temple. As a small boy M. performed INDIAN (EAST) rituals and found the intricacies and subtleties of "faces" an early motif. He is credited as the first writer of Indian descent to present Hindu FOLKLORE, epic POETRY, and philosophy for English-speaking children, and is best known for his animal adventure *Gay Neck: The Story of a Pigeon* (illustrated by Boris ARTZYBASHEFF, 1927, 1968). M. received the NEWBERY MEDAL in 1928 for *Gay Neck.* It describes the travels of a carrier pigeon who experiences World War I and later flies to a lama's monastery to be cured of battle wounds and other war-related trauma. Thematically, M. is recognized for exploring the virtue of self-control and the bond between human beings and other living creatures. The healing power of prayer and meditation is conveyed by the directness of the Indian vernacular style in combination with his formal English prose. M. also published many nonfiction works for adults as well as poetry. He has been criticized for the subject matter presented to young readers; however, his sincerity and skill as a storyteller are acknowledged.

BIBLIOGRAPHY: *Something about the Author,* vol. 40, 1985; *Children's Literature Review,* vol. 10, 1986

CRAIG LIEBERMAN

MULTICULTURAL LITERATURE

Multicultural literature is defined as writing that reflects the "customs, beliefs, and experiences of differing nationalities and races" and reflects the "interests, vocabulary, and experiences of students from various cultural or ethnic backgrounds" (*The Literacy Dictionary: The Vocabulary of Reading and Writing,* 1995). Further, Multicultural literature is defined by the Cooperative Children's Book Center as reference to people of color, including AFRICAN AMERICANS, Native Americans, Asian-Americans, and Latina/os. The study of Multicultural literature includes not only the publication of children's books, but also how these books are perceived, promoted, and used by teachers and parents. Multicultural literature enables adults to foster cultural awareness and appreciation in children.

In addition to the four major parallel cultures designated above, there are six types of Multicultural literature. These types of Multicultural literature follow, with a couple of the most outstanding examples of each: folktales, *Mufaro's Beautiful Daughters: An AFRICAN Tale* (STEPTOE, 1987), and *Yeh-Shen: A Cinderella Story from China* (LOUIE, 1982); historical fiction, *Immigrant Girl: Becky of Eldridge Street* (HARVEY, 1987) and *Molly's Pilgrim* (COHEN, 1983); contemporary REALISTIC FICTION, *I Hate English!* (Levine, 1989) and *Hello, My Name Is Scrambled Eggs* (GILSON, 1985); BIOGRAPHIES, *Escape from Slavery: The Boyhood of Frederick Douglass in*

His Own Words (McCurdy, 1994), and *Connie Chung: Broadcast Journalist* (Malone, 1992); POETRY, *A Cry from the Earth: Music of the North American Indians* (1979) and *In for Winter, out for Spring* (ADOFF, 1991); and INFORMATIONAL BOOKS, *Hector Lives in the United States Now: The Story of a Mexican American Child* (HEWITT, 1990), and *The Mexicans in America* (Pinshot, 1989). The most accepted realms of this topic continue to be those of the cultures of color (African American, Asian-American, American Indian, and Latina/o); however, works that are representative of all cultural, regional, and religious groups (Jewish, Amish, Moslem, and Appalachian among others) should be included in children's exposure to literature through adults' encouragement and guidance.

Nancy LARRICK, in her study that appeared in the *Saturday Review* in 1965, reported that there was a lack of representation of African Americans in children's literature. This report brought to the publishing world's attention the need to focus on publications for, about, and by African Americans. Emphasis on other ethnic backgrounds would follow. The Council on Interracial Books for Children (CIBC) was founded in 1967 to encourage such publications. The CIBC, along with African American, American Indian, and Asian American authors had great impact on the otherwise all-white publishing world. Throughout the next few decades, publications would provide readers with a multitude of writings and critiques—some confusing—of the authenticity and quality of Multicultural literature Awards such as the CORETTA SCOTT KING AWARDS, established in 1969, would encourage continuance of efforts in the area.

In the 1930s, publication of African American authors was an exception, but authors such as Langston HUGHES, Arna BONTEMPS, and Ann PETRY prevailed. With backgrounds in countries and cultures such as Swahili, Mali, Zulu, and Ashanti, tales and variations were brought to America. These retellings comprised some of the first traditional tales of perseverance, beauty, and generosity. Prominent African American literature works include *Beat the Story Drum, Pum-Pum* (Ashley BRYAN, 1980), *Amazing Grace* (Mary HOFFMAN, 1991), and *The People Could Fly: American Black Folktales* (Virginia HAMIL-

TON, 1985). Other African American authors are Sharon Bell MATHIS, Mildred B. TAYLOR, Lucille CLIFTON, Eloise GREENFIELD, Walter Dean MYERS, Julius LESTER, Patricia MCKISSACK, Faith RINGGOLD, and John Steptoe.

American Indian or Native American culture present a diversity of their own with more than 300 different tribes in North America reflecting various landscapes and rituals. Common patterns do exist including myths of creation, family, heroes, and rites of passage. Examples of NATIVE AMERICAN LITERATURE include *Anpao: An American Indian Odyssey* (HIGHWATER, 1977), *Thirteen Moons on Turtle's Back* (BRUCHAC and LONDON), *When Clay Sings* (BAYLOR, 1972), Kathleen and Michael LA CAPA's *Less Than Half More Than Whole* (1994), *Rough Faced Girl* (Raffe, 1992), and *Brother Eagle, Sister Sky* (Seattle, 1991). Other authors of American Indian literature include Nanabush Chee Dodge and Virginia Driving Hawk SNEVE.

ASIAN AMERICAN LITERATURE has roots in Japan, Vietnam, China, the Philippines, and other Pacific countries. Works of folktales include *Yeh-Shen: A Cinderella Story from China* (Louie, 1982), *The Rainbow People* (YEP, 1992), and *Many Lands, Many Stories: Asian Folktales for Children* (Conger, 1987), *Grandfather's Journey* (SAY, 1993), and *A Jar of Dreams* (UCHIDA, 1981). Other authors include Minfong Ho, Betty Bao LORD, Taro YASHIMA, Paul YEE, and Ed YOUNG.

Prominence of LATINA/O LITERATURE developed later than other parallel cultures and is not as prolific though this is rapidly changing. There also appears to be confusion in the designation of cultural and geographic definitions. Typically, the culture includes Mexico, South America, Puerto Rico, and islands of the Caribbean. Diversity and the wide range of histories of the different ancient civilizations such as the Incas, Aztec, and Mayans add to the difficulty of using the one term *Latina/o* to encompass all; however, it is the term currently used along with the term *Hispanic*, and at the least gives recognition where none existed before. Noted works include *Abuela* (DORROS, 1991), *The House on Mango Street* (CISNEROS, 1983), *Where Angels Glide at Dawn: New Stories from Latin America* (CARLSON, L. and C. Ventura, 1990). Other writers of Latina/o literature include

Alma Flor ADA, Carmen Lomas Garza, Nicholosa MOHR, Gary SOTO, and Rudolfo ANAYA.

Changes in publishing expanded the range of multicultural literature. The 1990s brought new systems and packager services to target specific audiences. The increase in the publication of multicultural literature requires teachers to consider and make available to librarians certain criteria when selecting literature. Quality of plot and characterization should be upheld as well as other considerations: value of diversity with sensitive treatment of cultural assimilation; portrayals of empowered, rather than stereotypical, characters; representation of United States settings with the understanding that many of the members of parallel cultures are born in the U.S.; and accurate (not stereotypical) ILLUSTRATIONS of physical features, dress, and mannerisms.

Numerous works exist to help the reader who wants to be informed about the different cultures and their literature. A few of these include: *Multicultural Children's Literature: An Annotated Bibliography Grades K-8* (Lind, Beth Beutler, 1996); *Native American Children's Literature* (Jon C. Scott, 1995); *Black Authors and Illustrators of Children's Books* (Barbara Rollock, 1992); *Literature for Children about Asians and Asian Americans* (Jenkins and Austin, 1987).

BIBLIOGRAPHY: Cornett, Claudia E. *The Arts as Meaning Makers: Integrating Literature and the Arts throughout the Curriculum,* 1999; Cox, Carole, *Teaching Language Arts,* Third Edition, 1999; Lindgren, Merri V., ed., *The Multicultural Mirror,* (1991); *The Literacy Dictionary: The Vocabulary of Reading and Writing,* 1995; Tompkins, Gail and Kenneth Hoskisson, *Language Arts: Content and Teaching Strategies,* 1995

NANCY HORTON

MUNARI, Bruno
Illustrator, b. 1907, Milan, Italy

M. began his artistic career in Milan at age twenty as a member of the Italian Futurist Movement. He is an accomplished painter, sculptor, photographer, illustrator, and designer of books, toys, and mobiles. Having established a reputation in Europe as a versatile artist, in 1967 he was invited by Harvard to teach basic design and advanced exploration in visual communication.

His first published works for children, *The Lorrie Driver* (1945) and *Georgie Lost His Cap* (1945) were published in Italy sometime after the birth of his son. *Who's There?, Open the Door!* (1957); *The Elephant's Wish* (1959); and *Jimmy Has Lost His Cap* (1959), an American version of *Georgie,* were his first American publications. Critics immediately lavished praise on M. In 1960 *Bruno Munari's ABC* was published and was cited by the *New York Times* as one of the Best Illustrated Children's Books of the Year. It was described as "a light hearted alphabet book, full of surreal surprises. Each double page spread is an experience in color, texture and space." The *Horn Book* called it "a work of beauty, imagination and fun."

M.'s ILLUSTRATIONS are considered modern in style and innovative like the best work from the Bauhaus. There is a whimsy and innocent HUMOR that any child can relate to. Although the books might appear to be effortless improvisations they are very carefully designed. Some have perforated pages so the reader can see the next page, or have flaps that, when moved, change the progression of the story in content and design. M. has also published books without texts such as *In the Dark Night* (1962). Although he has been called "Libri Illegibili," M.'s ambiguity is understood by children.

FURTHER WORKS: *Circus in the Mist,* 1960; *Bruno Munari's Zoo,* 1963; *The Discovery of the Circle,* 1970

BIBLIOGRAPHY: *Children's Literature Review,* vol. 9, 1985; *Something about the Author,* vol. 15, 1980

JUDY LIPSITT

MUNRO, Roxie

Author, illustrator, b. 5 September 1945, Mineral Wells, Texas

In the field of children's literature, M. is best known for her self-illustrated nonfiction books that depict daily life in famous cities, such as the *Inside-Outside Book of Washington, D.C.* (1987), *Inside-Outside Book of London* (1989), and the *Inside-Outside Book of Paris* (1992). Her first book in the SERIES, *Inside-Outside New York City* (1985), was named one of the *New York Times* Best Illustrated Children's Books and one of *Time*'s Best Children's Books. M. has also col-laborated with her husband, Bo Zaunders on a book called *Crocodiles, Camels, and Dug-out Canoes* (1998), the adventures of eight travelers who are following their dreams. In addition to M.'s contributions to children's books, her artwork has appeared on the covers of several popular magazines, including *The New Yorker.*

FURTHER WORKS: Self-illustrated: *Architects Make Zigzags: Looking at Architecture from A to Z.* 1986. *Christmastime in New York City.* 1987. *Blimps.* 1989. Illus. only: *American Defenders of Land, Sea and Sky.* (K. Weeks). 1996. *The Inside-Outside Book of Libraries.* (J. Cummins). 1996

BIBLIOGRAPHY: *Something about the Author,* vol. 58, 1990. Ward, M. E., Marquardt, D. A., N., Dolan, and D. Eaton. (eds.). *Authors of Books for Young People.* 3rd ed. 1990

MARY ARIAIL BROUGHTON

MUNSCH, Robert

Author, storyteller, b. 11 June 1945, Pittsburgh, Pennsylvania

Although M. was born in the United States, he later immigrated to Canada and became a naturalized CANADIAN citizen. M. studied for the priesthood for several years before enrolling in Fordham University, where he earned a B.A. in history. He holds two master's degrees, an M.A. in anthropology from Boston University, and an M.Ed. in child studies from Tufts University.

M. is Canada's best-selling author of PICTURE BOOKS, but long before he became a published author, he entertained children with his stories in a day-care center. He found that the children loved his improvised tales and begged to hear them over and over. With encouragement from the director of his department, he began to put his stories into writing. At first, he attempted to change the stories into what he considered good writing; however, he soon found that the most successful written versions were the ones that closely reflected his oral style. Before writing down a story, he retells the story over and over, changing the wording until the children can easily participate. He believes that a good story takes at least three years of telling. As a result of his careful attention to the sounds of the narratives and the responses of the children, many of his picture books have become favorite read-alouds for children.

Many of M.'s stories are humorous, noisy, and entertaining. For example, M.'s earliest made-up story, *Mortimer* (1983), features a pesky little boy who, although he has been put to bed, repeatedly sings, "Bang-bang, raffle-ding-bang, goin' to make my noise all day!" His family becomes so disturbed and unnerved that they become involved in a big fight. Mortimer then peacefully falls asleep. Other popular titles for children include *The Paper Bag Princess* (1980), *Millicent and the Wind* (1984), and *Thomas's Snowsuit* (1985). His most commercially successful book, *Love You Forever* (1986), deviates from the more rollicking, humorous stories as it tells of a mother's unending love for her son. Although the book has enjoyed little critical acclaim, it has sold millions of copies, becoming a best-selling picture book in Canada and the United States. M. received the 1987 Vicki Metcalf Award to a Canadian Author "for his body of work with appeal to children." He maintains a website for children at http://www.robertmunsch.com/kids.cfm

FURTHER WORKS: *The Mud Puddle.* 1979: *The Dark.* 1979: *Murmel, Murmel, Murmel.* 1982: *David's Father.* (1983): *50 Below Zero.* 1985: *I Have to Go!* 1986: *Moira's Birthday.* 1987: *Stephanie's Ponytail.* 1996: *Alligator Baby.* 1997

BIBLIOGRAPHY: *Booklist.* March, 15, 1998, September 15, 1998, January 1, 1999. *Children's Literature Review.* vol. 19. *Contemporary Authors, New Revision Series.* vol. 37. *Horn Book,* May–June 1985. *Major Authors and Illustrators for Children and YOUNG ADULTS: A Selection of Sketches from Something about the Author* 1993; Tomlinson, Carl, *Children's Books from Other Countries,* 1998. *Twentieth Century Writers,* 4th ed., 1995

MARY ARIAIL BROUGHTON

MURPHY, Jim

Author, b. 25 September 1947, Newark, New Jersey

M.'s future as a writer of award-winning nonfiction might have been a surprise to many of his teachers; he did not read very much as a child. He grew up in Kearney, New Jersey, a suburb of Newark, just a train ride away from New York City. He was athletic, running track and working on several physically demanding jobs. M. received his bachelor's degree from Rutgers University in 1970, and did some graduate study at Radcliffe College the same year.

He left academia, however, to become an editorial secretary at Seabury Press. He worked his way up the ladder, eventually becoming a managing editor, and then freelance author and editor for the newly renamed Clarion Books. Primarily a nonfiction writer, his first book, *Weird and Wacky Inventions* (1978), was recognized by both critics and children, winning a *School Library Journal* Best Book of the Year nomination as well as being named an INTERNATIONAL READING ASSOCIATION Children's Book Choice. Likewise, later books such as *Tractors: From Yesterday's Steam Wagons to Today's Supercharged Giants* (1984), which was named a National Science Teachers Association Outstanding Trade Book for Children, *The Last Dinosaur* (1988) also selected as an IRA Children's Choice Book, and *Across America on an Immigrant Train* (1993), named a National Council of Teachers of English ORBIS PICTUS AWARD Winner for Outstanding Nonfiction, continued his success of critical acclaim and wide readership.

M. often writes his nonfiction paying careful attention to the roles of children in historical events, a commitment that explains his avid readers. *The Boys War: Confederate and Union Soldiers Talk about the Civil War* (1990), *The Long Road to Gettysburg* (1992), *The Great Fire* (1995), and *A Young Patriot: The American Revolution as Experienced by One Boy* (1996) all provide, within the intricately woven narratives, at least one child's voice. Both Civil War books were recognized with the Golden Kite Award presented by the SOCIETY OF CHILDREN'S WRITERS AND ILLUSTRATORS.

The Great Fire, which tells the story of the great fire of Chicago, is one of M.'s most lauded books. Winning the NCTE Orbis Pictus Award for Outstanding Nonfiction and the *Boston Globe–Horn Book* Outstanding Nonfiction Award, *The Great Fire* was also a NEWBERY MEDAL Honor Book for 1996. With *The Great Fire* on three AMERICAN LIBRARY ASSOCIATION recommended lists (Notable Children Books, Best Books for Young Readers, and Quick Picks for Reluctant Readers), M. was again recognized for his outstanding research and perfection in writing quality nonfiction for children. *The Great Fire* was also

83. EMILY ARNOLD MCCULLY

84. FREDRICK AND PATRICIA MCKISSACK

86. EVE MERRIAM

85. MILTON MELTZER

87. A. A. MILNE

88. JIM MURPHY

89. WALTER DEAN MYERS

named a Notable Children's Trade Book in the Field of Social Studies. M. writes nonfiction that involves and enthralls the reader, making the reader a part of the experience. *Across America on an Emigrant Train* was the 1994 Orbis Pictus Award–winning title.

FURTHER BOOKS: *The Indy 500,* 1983; *Two Hundred Years of Bicycles,* 1983; *Baseball's All-Time Stars,* 1984; *The Call of the Wolves,* 1989; *Night Terrors,* 1994; *Into the Deep Forest with Henry Thoreau,* 1995

BIBLIOGRAPHY: Bamford, R. A., and J. V. Kristo, *Making Facts Come Alive,* 1998; *The Seventh Book of Junior Authors and Illustrators,* 1996; *Something about the Author,* vol. 32, 1983, and vol. 37, 1989

GWYNNE ELLEN ASH

MURPHY, Shirley Rousseau

Author, illustrator, b. 20 May, 1928, Oakland, California

M. began her career in FINE ARTS after studying at the California School of Fine Arts. She shifted her creative talent to writing when she moved to Central America, where she found it too difficult to ship her art. M has been described as a writer of the "feline sleuth genre" with books such as *Cat in the Dark* (1999) and *Cat under Fire,* both featuring feline Joe Grey and his love Dulcie, a library cat. In these feline mysteries, the cats discover they have the astonishing ability to speak and read as they go about solving their cases. Other works are in more of a traditional FANTASY style such as *The Catswold Portal.* In all of her books, M. writes with HUMOR and clever dialogue, using detail and plot twists. She has received a Parents' Choice Award, and most recently the Cat Writers' Association's 1997 Muse Medallion Award for *Cat Raise the Dead.*

FURTHER WORKS: *Cat on the Edge,* 1996; *Wind Child,* 1999; *Castle of Hape,* 1980; *Dragonbards,* 1988; *The Ivory Lyre,* 1987; *Cat to the Dogs,* 2000

BIBLIOGRAPHY: Notes from an interview with the author found at www.amazon.com; *Something about the Author,* vol. 71, 1993

SANDRA IMDIEKE

MUSIC AND CHILDREN'S LITERATURE

Literature and music have in common the development of motifs as an organizational scheme and the use of rhythm in the movement of language and melody. Perhaps that is why literature and music have appeared together in combined art forms over the centuries. The stories behind operas often come from literature, particularly folk literature as in Wagner's *Ring of the Nibelungen* and Humperdinck's *Hansel* and *Gretel.* Ballets such as *The Firebird, Sleeping Beauty,* and *Cinderella* are also often based on folktales.

As the field of publishing for children has expanded, a good many books have been created that combine literature and music in ever new and interesting ways. Stories and poetry are meant to be read aloud; music is meant to be played or sung. Many of these musically related books are fine read-alouds and it is important to note that publishers have often printed the music so that oral sharing can include singing. Some notable books that include musical lines are Peter SPIER's *The Fox Went out on a Chilly Night,* a 1962 CALDECOTT MEDAL Honor Book; *Old MacDonald Had a Farm,* (1989, Glen ROUNDS, illus.); *Abiyoyo: Based on a South African Lullaby and Folk Story* with text by Pete Seeger and illustrations by Michael Hays (1986); *Go In and Out the Window: An Illustrated Songbook for Young* People, music arranged and edited by Dan Fox, commentary by Claude Marks, published by the Metropolitan Museum of Art in 1987; Jane YOLEN's *Mother Goose Songbook* (1992, arranged by Adam Stemple, illustrated by Rosekrans Hoffman) and *From Sea to Shining Sea: A Treasury of American FOLKLORE and Folk Songs,* compiled by Amy L. Cohn (1993).

Young readers are curious about people who make music and the instruments they play. Excellent biographies are available to whet their interest in famous musicians. *Duke Ellington: The Piano Prince and His Orchestra,* is a 1999 Caldecott Medal Honor book and CORETTA SCOTT KING Illustrator Award Honor book, by Andrea Davis PINKNEY and illustrated by Brian PINKNEY. It conveys the movement of the ragtime beat of Ellington's music through the illustrations as well as the text. *Satchmo's Blues* by Alan Schroeder, illustrated by Floyd COOPER, (1996) is a beautifully illustrated story about Louis Armstrong and his rise to fame as a jazz trumpeter. *What a Wonderful World* (George David Weiss and Bob Thiele, Ashley BRYAN, illustrator, 1995) uses

Armstrong's own words and music to depict an exuberant, MULTICULTURAL world. Schroeder's *Ragtime Tumpie*, illustrated by Bernie Fuchs, (1989) gives us a glimpse of the early life of Josephine Baker. *Charlie Parker Played Be Bop* (Chris RASCHKA, 1992), tells the life of the celebrated jazz saxophonist and composer with text and illustrations that joyfully capture the jazz idiom. *The Jazz Man* (1966, Mary Ann Weik, Ann GRIFALCONI, illus.), A Caldecott Honor Book, tells about Zeke's dreams as he listens night after night to a jazz pianist dreaming of a happier life and his mother's return. *Lives of the Musicians: Good Times, Bad Times (And What the Neighbors Thought)* by Kathleen KRULL, illustrated by Kathryn HEWITT (1993) relates many interesting anecdotes about the lives of famous composers and performers. A very different kind of informational book, *Music in the Wood* by Cornelia Cornelissen with photos by John MacLachlan (1995) explains the process of making a cello, from the beginning of choosing just the right pieces of wood to putting the final touches on the finished instrument. A CD of a Bach Suite for cello and a Boccherini Sonata is included.

There are fascinating pieces of fiction that explore the influence of music on the lives of people who make music and those who enjoy listening to it. The simplicity of Paul FLEISCHMAN's Rondo in C (Wentworth, illus., 1988) is profoundly moving. A young student plays Beethoven's Rondo in C during a piano recital, and the picture book reveals the responses of people in the audience as they reflect on the piece and its meaning in their personal lives. For older readers, *The Facts and Fictions of Minna Pratt* (Patricia MACLACHLAN, 1988) features a young cellist who loves Mozart. *Yolanda's Genius* (Turner, 1995), a NEWBERY MEDAL Honor Book, is an uplifting story of Yolanda's determination to help her young brother Andrew discover his musical gift as a fine harmonica player. In Paul FLEISCHMAN's *Saturnalia* (1990), set in the seventeenth century, a simple bone flute is the instrument that William plays as he seeks to find his brother and reclaim his Narraganset heritage. The stress of dealing with sudden fame and family pressure become unbearable for eleven-year-old bluegrass star James in *Come Sing, Jimmy Jo* (PATERSON, 1985), a novel

set against the backdrop of TV and personal singing appearances. Music is at the core of Bruce BROOKS's coming-of-age novel, *Midnight Hour Encores* (1986), as Sib, a renowned teenage cellist, searches for self-awareness and acceptance of her mother's disappearance from her life.

There is humorous fiction, too, that invites readers to enjoy the world of music. Karla KUSKIN's *The Philharmonic Gets Dressed* (1982, Marc SIMONT, illustrator) follows members of the Philharmonic Orchestra as they take their showers and dress for the concert, then make their various ways to the concert hall and finally, before the performance, don the special formal clothes worn by symphony musicians. *Berlioz the Bear* (Jan BRETT, 1991) is a light-hearted story for younger children in which Berlioz and his bass fiddle set off for a concert along with the other musicians, and barely make it in time. *Zin! Zin! Zin! A Violin* (Lloyd Moss, Marjorie PRICEMAN, illustrator, 1995), a Caldecott Honor Book, is a rhyming story with wonderfully rhythmic illustrations featuring ten instruments of the orchestra; a related title is *Meet the Orchestra* (Ann Hayes, 1991). *Yang the Youngest and His Terrible Ear* (NAMIOKA, de Kiefte, illus, 1992) is a very funny story about a family in which all are musically gifted except for Yang. His efforts to overcome and hide his problem result in many amusing episodes. Set in Brooklyn, *Music over Manhattan* (Karlins, Davis, illus., 1998) tells of the rivalry between two cousins as Bernie learns to compete through his trumpet playing and resolve the acrimony between the cousins. *Song and Dance Man* (Karen ACKERMAN, Stephen GAMMELL, illus., 1988), a Caldecott Medal book, captures the rhythm and mood of music as grandpa and the children reminisce about his days as a professional tapdancer who is still able to spin and leap into the air as he takes center stage. A familiar situation is hilariously captured in *Mama Don't Allow* (Thacher HURD, 1984) when Mama sends Miles and his noisy badger Swamp Band outdoors to play and they barely escape becoming stew for the alligators' dinner. The title song is included at the end for children able to read simple music. A thoughtful book, recalling the days of the segregated black baseball league, *The Batboy and His Violin* (Gavin Curtis, E. B. LEWIS, illus., 1998), a Coretta Scott King Illustrator

Award Honor book, tells the story of Reginald who would rather play his violin than play baseball to the dismay of this father, the team manager. As bat boy Reginald practices in the dugout where he soon has the team listening to Mozart and forgetting their losing streak. The classic picture book story for middle-grade readers, *Lentil* (MCCLOSKEY, 1940) is set in small town, pretechnology America when one small boy, Lentil, brings an overbearing, pompous adult to a stop with his harmonica playing and a few puckery lemons.

These books are examples of the many ways music and literature come together in children's books. In them, the power of literature allows us not only to be an audience of readers but also to enter into the musical experiences of the people involved, whether they are children such as Andrew, Yang, and Reginald, or professional musicians such as Duke Ellington and Louis Armstrong.

DIANNE MONSON

MYERS, Walter Dean

Author, b. 12 August 1937, Martinsburg, West Virginia

M. is an award-winning author of books for children and YOUNG ADULTS. His mother died when he was two years old and at three he was adopted by Herbert and Florence Dean. The Deans fostered a love of reading in M., and he learned to read at the age of four. Reading and writing became a tool for M. to overcome many difficulties. As a young child, he had a severe speech impediment. When he was in fifth grade he wrote poems about books he read, avoiding the speech patterns he found difficult. This made school a hard place for M., which, in turn, made his attendance sporadic. In tenth grade, his English teacher encouraged him to read the novels of the great European writers. This was when M. became inspired to imitate these writers. It was not until he read Langston HUGHES that he saw the value in writing about his own neighborhood. As a teenager, M. won contests for his writing. Despite his talent and love of writing, he never thought of writing as a career. His talent was not overlooked, but considered unimportant since his family could not afford to send him to college. At seventeen, M. joined the United States Army for three years.

After his discharge he worked numerous jobs until he decided that he wanted to be a writer.

M.'s professional writing career began in 1960 when he entered a contest sponsored by the Council on Interracial Books for Children. He won for *Where Does the Day Go?*, formally published in 1969. This accomplishment encouraged M. that writing could be a full-time career. He overcame his previous feeling that "writing is not work" by setting up goals for each day. To feel that he put in a good day's work, M. strives to write ten pages a day.

M. is best known for his young adult literature. His novels offer an optimistic, yet realistic look at life in an urban setting. He provides the realism of drugs and ghetto life with a hope for the future. His characters are often young adolescents in the search for self. His characters struggle against the pressures of the neighborhood while determining what is right. In *Hoops* (1981), *Scorpions* (1988), *Fast Sam, Cool Clyde, and Stuff* (1975), *Motown and Didi: A Love Story* (1984), *Darnell Rock Reporting* (1996), *Slam!* (1998), and *The Mouse Rap* (1990) the characters are struggling with the pressures of growing up in Harlem. In each book characters overcome a struggle with violence, drugs, and/or parents. The protagonists never allow themselves to be taken in by the perils of inner city life. M. helps readers see that although pressures are present and forceful, it is up to the individual to stand above temptations. In each of these novels M. does not present the protagonist as being alone. The role of the social group, or in some cases one friend, is a powerful force in aiding the protagonist. Friends often provide the voice of reason, which allows a character to take time to think about the situation.

Although the picture of Harlem presented in these novels is predominantly negative, *Fast Sam, Cool Clyde, and Stuff* and *The Mouse Rap* depict an optimistic view of Harlem. In both books M. presents a group of teenage girls and boys finding ways to spend their time. In these novels the characters struggle with problems such as acquaintances using drugs, and parents splitting up; but the atmosphere is not filled with turmoil. The novels present a calmer picture of life in Harlem; but still do not ignore the hardships.

These books present realistic dialogue in combination with strong characters to create vivid pictures. Part of that realism is developed through M.'s ability to integrate the language used by urban AFRICAN AMERICANS. In all of M.'s novels, the characters speak so that readers can easily picture them as a part of a movie. The characters are alive in front of the reader.

Mothers plays a strong role in many of these books; fathers are often working or have simply left. The mother is the force that holds the family together. She is often the primary caregiver and in many cases provides a conscience to the violent world of Harlem.

M., although well known for his young adult books, has written in many different genres. He has written many novels for young readers such as *Me, Mop and the Moondance Kid* (1991) and *Story of the Three Kingdoms* (1997). He has written PICTURE BOOKS narrated with POETRY: *Glorious Angels* (1997), *Brown Angels* (1993), and *Angel to Angel* (1998). His poem, "Harlem" (1997), illustrated by M.'s son Christopher, was a CALDECOTT MEDAL Honor Book in 1998. He has written a BIOGRAPHY, *Malcolm X: By Any Means Necessary* (1994). M. has also authored some historical fiction novels. *The Glory Field* (1996) follows a family from the coast of Africa through two hundred and fifty years of struggle in the United States. *Amistad: A Long Road to Freedom* (1998) is about the dramatic struggle for freedom on the slave ship *Amistad. Fallen Angels* (1991) is about a young soldier's tour of duty in Vietnam. He has also written nonfiction, SCIENCE FICTION, and FANTASY books.

M. says that he is always looking for subjects to write about that he feels have been neglected. He is a writer that readers connect with on many levels. He writes in order to reach out to readers and help them find strength and direction in this confusing world. His novels show that in a difficult world we can survive.

AWARDS: Council on Interracial Books for Children Award (1968) for *Where Does the Day Go?* Child Study Association of America's Children's Books of the Year (1972) for *The Dancers,* AMERICAN LIBRARY ASSOCIATION Notable Book Citations (1975) for *Fast Sam, Cool Clyde, and Stuff,* (1978) for *It Ain't All for Nothin',* (1979) for *The Young Landlords,* and (1988) for *Scorpions* and *Me, Mop, and the Moondance Kid.* ALA Best Books for Young Adults (1978) for *It Ain't All for Nothin'* (1979) for *The Young Landlords* (1981),

for *The Legend of Tarik* (1982), for *Hoops* (1988), for *Fallen Angels,* and *Scorpions.* CORETTA SCOTT KING AWARDS for Fiction (1980) for *The Young Landlords* (1985), for *Motown and Didi* (1989), for *Fallen Angels,* and for nonfiction (1992), for *Now Is Your Time: The African-American Struggle for Freedom.* Notable Children's Trade Book in the Field of Social Studies from the National Council for Social Studies and CHILDREN'S BOOK COUNCIL (1982) for *The Legend of Tarik,* for *Fallen Angels.* Child Study Association of America's Children's Books of the Year (1987) for *Adventure in Granada.* ALA NEWBERY MEDAL Honor Book (1989) for *Scorpions* and (1993) for *Somewhere in the Darkness. Boston Globe–Horn Book* Honor Book (1992) for *Somewhere in the Darkness.* ALA CALDECOTT MEDAL Honor Book (1998) for *Harlem* (Christopher M., illus.)

FURTHER WORKS: *The Dragon Takes a Wife.* 1972. *The Dancers.* 1972. *Fly! Jimmy, Fly!* 1974. *Brainstorm.* 1977. *Mojo and the Russians.* 1977. *Victory for Janie.* 1977. *The Black Pearl and the Ghost.* 1980. *The Golden Serpent.* 1980. *Won't Know Till I Get There.* 1982. *Tales of a Dead King.* 1983. *The Outside Shot.* 1984. *Mr. Monkey and the Gotcha Bird.* 1984. *Adventure in Granada.* 1985. *Sweet Illusions.* 1986. *Ambush in the Amazon.* 1986. *Crystal.* 1987. *Mop, Moondance and the Nagaski Knights.* 1992. *The Righteous Revenge of Artemis Bonner.* 1992

BIBLIOGRAPHY: Bishop. R. S. "Profile: Walter Dean M.," *Language Arts,* vol. 67, December 1990, pp. 862–66; *Children's Literature Review,* vol. 4, 1982, and vol. 35, 1995; *Contemporary Literary Criticism.* vol. 35, 1985; *Contemporary Authors, New Revision Series,* vol. 42; *Dictionary of Literary Biography,* vol. 33, 1984; The *Horn Book,* January–February, 1994, and March–April, 1995; Kiefer, Barbara, selector, *Getting to Know You: Profiles of Children's Authors Featured in Language Arts, 1985–90,* 1991; *School Literary Journal,* May 1996, and December 1995; *Something about the Author,* vol. 71, 1993

NANCE S. WILSON

MYSTERY AND DETECTIVE STORIES

Like their counterparts in adult fiction, mysteries for children rank among the most popular of juvenile genres. Mysteries have won more state children's choice AWARDS than any other type of literature for children.

SERIES BOOKS constitute a large share of the mystery market. Just as adult readers clamored for Arthur Conan DOYLE to resurrect Sherlock

Holmes after the great detective's untimely death, so young readers devour title after title featuring their favorite young sleuths. Series books satisfy young readers' needs for predictability. At every stage young readers respond to the familiar: pre-readers want their favorite stories read and reread; beginning readers gain confidence reading familiar text; and newly independent readers derive a sense of fluency from the predictability of familiar characters and repetitive plot construction in series books.

Edward STRATEMEYER recognized the potential for juvenile mysteries. Early series published by the Stratemeyer Literary Syndicate, including The Rover Boys series (1899–1926) and the Tom Swift series (1910–41), were primarily ADVENTURE STORIES but included elements of detective fiction. In 1927, the detective series The Hardy Boys appeared, followed by its female counterpart Nancy Drew in 1930. In the 1950s, Harriet Stratemeyer Adams added a junior-detective focus to The Bobbsey Twins series begun by her father in 1904, lending new life to the series for three more decades. At about the same time, Gertrude Chandler Warner expanded her Boxcar Children series (1924–) to include The Boxcar Children Mysteries (1953–). Though never renowned for literary quality, these early formulaic detective series established the mystery and detective genre in children's literature. Erich KASTNER's Emil and the Detectives (1930) and its sequels place solutions in the hands of boy detectives to the admiration of the Berlin police. The books are notable for their literary quality and popularity wherever they have been translated.

Today mystery series abound for young readers of every age. What the successful series share is a protagonist with whom readers can identify. Memorable protagonists in mystery series for younger readers include Crosby BONSALL's Wizard, Private Eye, and his clubhouse companions in the Case Mysteries (1963–), Marjorie Weinman SHARMAT's pancake-eating young detective in the Nate the Great books (1972–), Elizabeth Levy's Gwen and Jill in the Something Queer books (1973–), David A. ADLER's female sleuth in the Cam Jansen books (1980–) and Patricia Reilly GIFF's Polk Street School kids in the Polka Dot Private Eye series (1985–). The Basil of Baker Street stories (1958) by Eve Titus

feature a mouse detective who learned sleuthing skills from Holmes himself, and Robert QUACKENBUSH's detectives are animals in the Piet Potter books (1980–), the Sherlock Chick series (1986–) and others.

Two series for middle-grade readers also evoke Conan Doyle's Sherlock Holmes stories. Robert Newman's The Case of the Baker Street Irregular (1978) and its sequels are solved with the aid of the great detective himself. In Terrance Dicks's The Baker Street Irregulars series (1979), a group of London youngsters model Holmes's techniques to outwit villains.

Both realism and FANTASY are popular in mystery series for middle-grade readers. REALISTIC series include James HOWE's Sebastian Barth Mysteries (1985–), Phyllis Reynolds NAYLOR's Bernie Magruder Mysteries (1986–) and two series featuring strong female sleuths: Betsy BYAR's Herculeah Jones Mysteries (1994–), and Wendelin Van Draanen's Sammy Keyes Mysteries (1998–). Fantasy series for middle-graders include Howe's Bunnicula (1979–) books featuring the rabbit who may or may not be a vampire and Janet Taylor LISLE's Investigators of the Unknown books (1994–), in which three girl sleuths get help from a cat with supernatural powers.

Several middle-grade mystery series are interactive, stopping the story just short of a solution and challenging readers to beat the detective to the answers. Donald SOBOL's Encyclopedia Brown books (1963–) and Seymour SIMON's Einstein Anderson: Science Detective series (1980–) are examples. Edward Packard's Mystery of Chimney Rock (1979) is a Choose Your Own Adventure mystery that requires the reader to make choices that develop the plot and reveal solutions.

Even more challenging are Ellen RASKIN's puzzle mysteries for older readers, including The Mysterious Disappearance of Leon (I Mean Noel) (1971), Figgs and Phantoms (1974), and the award-winning The Westing Game (1978). Raskin's clever word plays provide clues to the solution of a puzzle or mystery at the heart of each book.

Like Raskin, many award-winning authors have produced outstanding mysteries for middle-grade and older readers. While the popularity of series mysteries ensures their continued success in the market, mystery and detective fiction for older children is enriched by the literary quality brought to the genre by writers like Vivien AL-COCK, Joan AIKEN, AVI, Natalie BABBITT, Eve BUNTING, Betsy BYARS, Pam CONRAD, Sid FLEISCHMAN, Leon GARFIELD, Mary Downing HAHN, E. W. HILDICK, Joan Lowery NIXON, Phillipa PEARCE, Richard PECK, Willo Davis Roberts, Nancy Springer, Zilpha Keatley SNYDER, Barbara Brooks Wallace, Betty Ren Wright, and others. Many of these writers have been recognized by the Mystery Writers of America's Edgar Allen Poe Awards. Since 1989 the Edgar Awards have recognized the best in juvenile as well as YOUNG ADULT mysteries.

A number of recognized children's authors blend mystery with their own special interests and unique perspectives. Jean Craighead GEORGE's commitment to the environment led her to create a new genre, the ecological mystery, including *Who Really Killed Cock Robin?* (1971), *The Missing Gator of Gumbo Limbo* (1992), *The Fire Bug Connection* (1993), and *The Case of the Missing Cutthroats* (1996). AFRICAN AMERICAN history comes to life in Virginia HAMILTON's Edgar-winning mysteries *The House of Dies Drear* (1968) and *The Mystery of Drear House* (1987) and in Eleanora TATE's *The Secret of Gumbo Grove* (1987). Avi's *The Man Who Was Poe* (1991) is biographical fiction in which Poe takes on the persona of his own character, *The Gold Bug* protagonist Auguste Dupin, to solve several mysterious disappearances.

Some mysteries employ tricks with time. Pamela Service's *The Reluctant God* (1988) is a time-warp story in which a boy king of ancient Egypt comes face-to-face with modern archaeological explorations; her *Storm at the Edge of Time* (1994) a tale of time travel back to the beginnings of a Neolithic stone circle. Eleanor CAMERON's *Court of the Stone Children* (1973), Mary Downing Hahn's *The Doll in the Garden* (1989) and *Time for Andrew* (1994) and Pam Conrad's *Stonewords* (1990) all revolve around modern-day youngsters who travel back in time to solve long-buried mysteries. Closely related whodunits include ghost stories such as Richard PECK's *The Ghost Belonged to Me* (1975), Avi's *Something Upstairs* (1988), and Betty Ren Wright's *The*

Ghost Comes Calling (1994). Gothic mysteries abound, including Natalie Babbitt's *Goody Hall* (1971) and *The Eyes of the Amaryllis* (1977), as well as John BELLAIR's *The Curse of the Blue Figurine* (1983) and other Johnny Dixon mysteries.

Mysteries cut across every genre, realistic and fantastic, contemporary and historical. Even a few picture-book mysteries are available, including Chris Van ALLSBURG's nearly wordless *The Mysteries of Harris Burdick* (1984), Jane YOLEN's English-mystery spoof, *Piggins* (1987), and—if the reader wants a mysterious puzzle to solve—David MACAULAY's four stories in one, *Black and White* (1990).

Author James Howe (1990) observed that the question in a mystery for children is less likely to be "Who done it?" than "What's going on here?" As long as young readers seek puzzles to solve, whether those puzzles are revealed in fast-paced stories that afford light entertainment or in more challenging titles of literary quality, juvenile mystery and detective fiction will remain a popular genre.

BIBLIOGRAPHY: Howe, James, "Writing Mysteries for Children," the *Horn Book* magazine, March–April 1990, pp. 178–83; Tomlinson, Carl, and Carol Lynch-Brown, *Essentials of Children's Literature*, 1996

DIANE L. CHAPMAN

MYTHOLOGY AND LEGEND

Myths are stories that arose and were passed down as people searched to explain the origins of earth, sky, humans, and human behaviors. In another sense, myths are also stories of humankind's search for meaning, truth, and significance. Most myths include both a continuing cast of characters known to the culture telling the stories and superhuman beings or a god or gods. Without this weight of importance, a story may more generally be classified as a folktale. However, the distinction between a folktale, a legend, and a myth is often not made in children's books so that many myths may be found in folktale collections as well. While we tend to think of myths as ancient products, there are also modern-day myth makers. John BIERHORST (1988) points out that in remote areas of South America, for instance, myths are still being created to explain recent contacts with civilization and other current phenomena.

The Pacific northwest native people knew the myth of the wily trickster Raven who stole light from the Sky People and brought it to humans, a CALDECOTT MEDAL Honor story vibrantly told and illustrated by Gerald MCDERMOTT (1993). One in a series of stories about Raven, this story explains a natural phenomenon as well as rejoices in the tricking of powerful gods by a small and seemingly insignificant being. The Greeks told of Pandora who in spite of warnings from Zeus opened a box out of which poured all the troubles of the world. Shown in the Ingri and Edgar D'AU-LAIRE's illustrations (1962) are Fibs, Lies, Envy, Old Age, Gossip, and Scheming, among others. But Pandora clapped the lid on so that Hope remained in the box. Thus not only does the myth explain why there is so much unhappiness in the world but it also conveys the messages both that "there is always hope," and that obeying the gods or heeding a warning is wise. The universality of this last message is echoed in Rosemary WELLS's humorously retold version for very young children, *Max and Ruby's First Greek Myth: Pandora's Box* (1993) to illustrate the meaning of "hands off."

Types of myths include creation myths, nature myths, and hero myths. Every culture has a story of how the world began, how earth and its people came to be, and how animals began. In her collection of creation myths from around the world, *In the Beginning* (1988), Virginia HAMILTON retells a Huron myth of how a turtle dived down into the endless waters and brought up a bit of earth on his back so that Divine Woman the Creator might have a place to give birth. To this day turtle still holds up the earth. Pacific Island people told a myth in which another turtle built an island and found the first humans to people it in Wilson's *The Turtle and the Island* (1990). In a story taken from the Mayan codices, Hunab Ku spits in a jar of rainwater and pours out the world. Then, gods compete to populate it and the Maize God finally wins. Deborah Nourse LATTIMORE's illustrations for this myth (*Why There Is No Arguing In Heaven,* 1989) feature patterns and motifs taken from Mayan stonework and other art found in Guatemala and parts of Mexico.

Nature myths explain seasonal changes, animal characteristics, earth formations, constellations, and the workings of celestial bodies. The Greek myth of Persephone and Demeter explains that because the girl Persephone had eaten four pomegranate seeds while she was in Hades, she must return for those four months. During that time, her mother Demeter is desolate and, as goddess of grain and plants, she neglects the wintry earth in *Persephone* (Warwick HUTTON, 1994). A Caribbean Taino native myth tells of how the oceans were formed when children accidentally dropped the magic gourd that held many-colored fish swimming in the water and the spill produced rivers, lakes, oceans, and seas in *Golden Tales* (Lulu DELACRE, 1996).

Hero myths do not attempt to explain anything but tell of an amazing mortal challenged by monsters, impossible tasks set by tyrants, or the doings of the gods. The Odyssey, retold in Rosemary SUTCLIFF's *The Wanderings of Odysseus* (1995) is one such STORYTELLING of a hero challenged by the gods' ill will following the Trojan War. He must defeat monsters, lose all of his men, and resist numerous temptations before he arrives home decades later.

While myths have long been available in collections published for children, a recent trend is the publishing of single stories complete with an introduction stating the myth's origins (or provenance), and often endnotes suggesting further connections with the culture from which the myth originates. Authors like Paul GOBLE (*Star Boy* 1991; *Remaking the Earth,* 1996) have contributed many scholarly yet accessible and authentically illustrated single-tale myths told for children. Gobel's introductory notes and back matter detail sources, where or from whom he received the story, and notes on the illustrative style he has chosen for his work. In addition, the sometimes fusty sound of the language of stories told over time has been replaced by the lively voice of storytellers such as Bernard EVSLIN (*Hercules,* 1984), Virginia Hamilton (1988), or Mary Pope OSBORNE (*Favorite Norse Myths,* 1996). In these contemporary tellings, the vibrant emotions and horror-producing events are not softened so that they often appeal to older children and are less appropriate for impressionable younger ones.

Along with these trends of lively tellings and authentic and well-researched stories comes artwork that accurately reflects the culture of origin of the myth. Gerald McDermott's stylized artwork for his retellings of NATIVE AMERICAN myths (1994) reflect his study of visual motifs found in the art and architecture of Southwest or Northwest tribes. Deborah Nourse Lattimore and Paul Goble are two more examples of illustrators who respect the visual cultural traditions from which a story springs. Reviewers of traditional literature are quick to criticize tales that do not list a provenance (Betsy Hearne, 1993) and so the quality of books in which myths are retold as well as that of traditional literature in general has been greatly improved in the last decades.

Finally, the field of children's literature has begun to tap world cultural traditions formerly ignored in books for children. Greek, Norse, and a few AFRICAN myths have been readily available in children's editions for many years but the arrival of immigrants to this country has produced a tremendous demand for the literature to reflect a more varied cultural background. Little by little, the myths of ASIAN cultures, individual African countries, South and Central American cultures, as well as those from the Pacific islands, India, and Arab culture are slowly coming to the attention of writers, illustrators, and publishers.

Popular culture, from music to movies, from advertising to COMIC BOOKS AND GRAPHIC NOVELS, is steeped in mythology. From heroes, mentors, and monsters to the themes, motifs, and language of story, children today experience myths on a daily basis. While popular culture may obscure its mythological roots, children's books offer myth straightforwardly, direct from its source, as a way for children to perceive, reflect on, or be moved by the meaning of human experience.

BIBLIOGRAPHY: Bierhorst, John. *The Mythology of South America,* 1988; D'Aulaire, Edgar Parrin and Ingri, "Pandora" in *The D'Aulaires' Book of Greek Myths,* 1962; Delacre, Lulu. *Golden Tales: Myths, Legends, and Folktales from Latin America,* 1996; Dooley, Patricia (1994). "Beyond Cultural Literacy: The Enduring Power of Myths." *School Library Journal,* June (40:6), p. 52. Hearne, Betsy (1993). "Cite the Source: Cultural Chaos in Picture Books, Part One." *School Library Journal,* July (39:2), p. 24; Evslin, Bernard. *Hercules* (illus. J. A. Smith) 1984; Gobel, Paul, *Star Boy,* 1991; *Remaking the Earth: A Creation Story from the Great Plains of North America,* 1996; Hamilton, Virginia. *In the Beginning: Creation Stories from around the World* (illus. Barry MOSER), 1988; Hutton, Warwick, *Persephone,* 1994; Lattimore, Barbara Nourse, *Why There Is No Arguing in Heaven: A Mayan Myth,* 1989. McDermott, Gerald. *Raven: A Trickster Tale from the Pacific Northwest,* 1994. Osborne, Mary Pope, *Favorite Norse Myths* (illus. Troy Howell), 1996. Sutcliff, Rosemary. *The Wanderings of Odysseus: The Story of the Odyssey* (illus. Alan Lee), 1995): Wells, Rosemary. *Max and Ruby's First Greek Myth,* 1993; Wilson, Barbara Ker, *The Turtle and the Island: A Folktale from Papua New Guinea* (illus. Frane LESSAC), 1990

SUSAN HEPLER

(See also FOLKLORE)

NAIDOO, Beverley
Author, b. 21 May 1943, Johannesburg, South Africa

"I was brought up with the usual conceptions most white South AFRICANS have, completely taking for granted the services of our cook-cum-nanny." At the age of eighteen N. underwent a profound change of attitude. N. became an activist writer as a result of her interest in children.

Journey to Jo'Burg: A South African Story (1984), her first work of fiction "was inspired by her work with the Education Group of the British Defense and Aid Fund for Southern Africa." It was written to "encourage all children to explore and help strengthen their responses to the injustice of racism." It received the Other Award in England, was a Parents' Choice Honor Book for paperback literature in the United States, and won the Award of the Child Study Children's Book Committee at Bank Street College.

Censoring Reality: An Examination of Books on South Africa (1985) was the result of a study of the image of South Africa presented in nonfiction books for British children. The study revealed that racist images were glossed over, sometimes totally ignored or even made to appear good. Glaring omissions surfaced where actual statistics had been omitted or falsified, half-truths included and documentation left out. Both books were placed on the list of banned books by the South African government (see CENSORSHIP).

In 1987, *Free as I Know* was published in the United Kingdom. It was the result of "a strong commitment to giving young people access to writing which would encourage them to ask fundamental questions. . . . Literature has the tremendous quality of allowing us to engage imaginatively in the lives of others."

Published in 1989, *Chain of Fire* reveals the black perspective throughout. The characters are believable and the cruelty of apartheid as experienced by children, haunting. Originally intended to be a sequel to *Journey to Jo'Burg* it became a YOUNG ADULT novel "dedicated to all those who have struggled to resist and I hope it will enable young people in various parts of the world to feel links of both heart and mind."

FURTHER WORKS: *No Turning Back: A Novel of South Africa*, 1997

BIBLIOGRAPHY: *Children's Literature Review*, vol. 29, 1993; *Fiction, FOLKLORE, FANTASY and POETRY for Children, 1876–1985*, vol. 1, 1986; *Something about the Author*, vol. 63, 1991

IRVYN C. GILBERTSON

NAMIOKA, Lensey
Author, b. 14 June 1929, Peking, China

N., author of children's mysteries, trained as a mathematician and was employed as an instructor before her career as a published writer in the mid-1970s. N.'s works are thematically inspired by her Chinese heritage and her husband's Japanese heritage. She is best known for her adventure-mystery books. The *Samurai and the Long-nosed Devils* (1976) features two young sixteenth-century freelance Japanese samurai warriors. The books include historical notes and bibliographies. N.'s humorous YOUNG ADULT novels about young Chinese immigrants living in Seattle include *April and the Dragon Lady* (1994). Written in first person narrative style, a girl comes to terms with her Chinese cultural heritage and contemporary American expectations; the story resembles N.'s own experiences. In *Yang the Youngest and His Terrible Ear* (1992), a family of Chinese musicians deal with a tone-deaf son who prefers baseball. N.'s hobbies include musical composition.

FURTHER WORKS: *Valley of the Broken Cherry Trees,* 1981; *Island of Ogres,* 1989; *Yang the Third and Her Impossible Family,* 1995

BIBLIOGRAPHY: *Something about the Author,* vols. 27, 1982, and vol. 89, 1997; *Children's Literature Review,* vol. 10, 1986

CRAIG M. LIEBERMAN

NASH, (Frederic) Ogden

Author, playwright, lecturer, b. 19 August 1902, Rye, New York; d. 19 May 1971, Baltimore, Maryland

Following his graduation from Harvard, N. began teaching at the St. George School. In 1925 he began writing light verses that he sent to *The New Yorker.* After several pieces were published, he became a staff member and eventually a full-time regular contributor of verses. From 1947 to 1971 he was a public lecturer and narrator of his work and of others.

N. is known for his unconventional rhymes and his mangled verse. For many years he was successfully involved in publishing articles, plays, and verse for adults. Initially to entertain his own children, N. began to read them his writings; he wrote some things specifically for this new audience. In 1951 he took many verses that he'd written years before, edited them, added new verses, and produced *Parents Keep Out: Elderly Poems for Youngerly Readers.* Children found them especially funny with their sense of absurdity and their own pleasure in mangling formal English. Following this great success N. subsequently published *The Christmas That Almost Wasn't* (1957), *Custard the Dragon* (1959), *Beastly POETRY* (1960), *The Wicked Night* (1961), and *Girls Are Silly* (1962).

FURTHER WORKS: *The Cruise of the Aardvark,* 1967; *The Scroobious Pip,* (Edward LEAR, author, with additions by N.), 1968; *The Old Dog Barks Backwards,* 1972; *The Carnival of the Animals* (video); 1990

BIBLIOGRAPHY: Serafin, S. R., ed., *Encyclopedia of American Literature,* 1999; Silvey, Anita, ed., *Children's Books and Their Creators,* 1995; *Something about the Author,* vol. 2, 1971, and vol. 46, 1987

JUDY LIPSITT

NATIONAL COUNCIL OF TEACHERS OF ENGLISH (NCTE)

The National Council of Teachers of English (NCTE) is a professional organization devoted to improving the teaching and learning of English and the English language arts at all levels of education. Since its founding in 1911, NCTE has provided a forum for the profession, an array of opportunities for teachers to continue their professional growth throughout their careers, and a framework for cooperation to deal with issues that affect the teaching of English.

NCTE publishes a member newspaper, *The Council Chronicle,* several journals including *Language Arts, Primary Voices K-6, Voices from the Middle, School Talk, Research in the Teaching of English, English Journal, College English, College Composition and Communication, English Education, English Leadership Quarterly, NOTES Plus, Teaching English in the Two-Year College, Talking Points, The Quarterly Review of Doublespeak, The Alan Review,* and newsletters, position papers, and pamphlets.

The Children's Literature Assembly is a working group of professionals within NCTE. Members with a personal and professional interest in promoting children's literature to children and adults shape CLA's programs. The assembly provides professional development programs, publications, and sessions directed to these interests. CLA members organize workshops, programs, and discussion groups at annual meetings. Twice a year CLA publishes the *Journal of Children's Literature.* A CLA selection committee chooses an annual list of Notable Children's Books in the Language Arts, K-8, published in *Language Arts.*

The NCTE ORBIS PICTUS AWARD for Outstanding Nonfiction for Children commemorates the work of John COMENIUS's, *Orbis Pictus: The*

World in Pictures, published in 1657. Historically this is considered the first book actually planned and published for children; its goal was to teach children about their world. The goal of the Orbis Pictus Award is to encourage the production of high quality nonfiction and to promote its use in the classroom. Some of the books selected for the award are *The Great Little Madison* (Jean FRITZ, 1989); *Franklin Delano Roosevelt* (Russell FREEDMAN, 1990); *Flight: The Journey of Charles Lindbergh* (Robert BURLEIGH, illustrated by Mike Wimmer, 1991); *Children of the Dust Bowl: The True Story of the School at Weedpatch Camp* (Jerry Stanley, 1992); *Across America on an Emigrant Train* (Jim MURPHY, 1993); *Safari beneath the Sea: The Wonder World of the North Pacific Coast* (Diane Swanson, 1994); *The Great Fire* (Jim Murphy, 1995); Leonardo da Vinci (Diane STANLEY, 1996); *An Extraordinary Life: The Story of a Monarch Butterfly* (Laurence PRINGLE, illustrated by Bob Marstall, 1997).

Established in 1977, the NCTE Award for Excellence in Poetry for Children is presented every three years to a living American poet for an aggregate body of work for children ages three to thirteen. The goal is to foster excellence in poetry for children by encouraging its publication and to explore ways to acquaint teachers and children with poetry through such means as publications, programs, and displays. Recipients include David MCCORD, Aileen FISHER, Karla KUSKIN, Myra Cohn LIVINGSTON, Eve MERRIAM, John CIARDI, Lilian MOORE, Arnold ADOFF, Valerie WORTH, Barbara ESBENSEN, and Eloise GREENFIELD. Educators who chaired the selection committees include Ann Terry, Lee Bennett HOPKINS, M. Jean GREENLAW, Glenna Sloan Davis, Michael Tunnell, Richard Ammon.

The NCTE/Children's Book Council Committee is established to develop cooperative activities that serve members of both organizations. Its activities include, but are not limited to, a series of articles on children's literature, and serving as a resource for both organizations in matters of common concern. The committee publicizes literature-related activities, publishes lists of effective trade books for language study, and coordinates author appearances at national conventions.

The Elementary Section is made up of people interested in the education of children from birth to age fourteen. The members elect officers who serve on an advisory board, develop programs, create publications, and see that the needs of their membership are served. Among other things, an Elementary Section Committee chooses an Outstanding Educator who has made a significant contribution in teaching the English Language Arts. Recipients include Donald Graves, Ken and Yetta Goodman, Charlotte S. Huck, Dorothy S. Strickland.

The Whole Language Umbrella is a confederation of whole language support groups and individual professionals interested in developing and implementing whole language in educational institutions. The WLU is based on a dynamic philosophy of education in preschool through college classrooms. *Talking Points,* a biannual publication of WLU, is a forum for the whole language community to reflect about literacy and learning. The editors of *Talking Points* welcome submissions from classroom teachers, researchers, authors, and parents who explore current issues in whole language instruction.

LORI BIANCHINI AND BERNICE E. CULLINAN

NATIVE AMERICAN LITERATURE

During the 1970s and 1980s, the Native American children's literature genre expanded and changed as more Native American authors began writing for younger children, often motivated by the need to provide more authentic information about themselves for their own children. Virginia Driving Hawk SNEVE (Lakota) and Joseph BRUCHAC (Abenaki) were the most prolific in the 1970s-to-mid-1980s. In *Jimmy Yellow Hawk* (1972), *When Thunder Spoke* (1974), and *Chichi Hoohoo Bogeyman* (1975), Sneve paints a contemporary picture of life on Native reservations. Her well-rounded characters face the problems all children face as they develop their own personalities, as well as the specific problems Native American children face when attempting to forge a cultural identity between two conflicting worlds. Bruchac, on the other hand, initially focuses more on Native American traditional stories to provide Native American children, especially those living in urban areas, with traditional information about their cultures. In *Turkey Brother and Other Tales* (1975) and *Iroquois Sto-*

ries: Heroes and Heroines, Monsters, and Magic (1985), he retells Native American stories and legends. Other Indian authors look to past historic events to create both fiction and nonfiction stories. Awiakta's (Cherokee) *Rising Fawn and the Fire Mystery* (1983) belongs in this category. It is one of the few stories about the historic Indian Removal told from the N. viewpoint and gives a balanced account of a historic event. Simon ORTIZ's (Acoma) *The People Shall Continue* (1987) is similar in that it provides a balanced account of the history of Native American people, and puts the Native American experience into a larger, contemporary context.

Much of what was published in the 1990s by Native American authors attempts to counter the stereotypical Hollywood-and-TV Indian image that had been reinforced in publications about Native American cultures. Native American authors try to create more authentic and contemporary characters and situations while providing books for N. children about their traditions and culture. For instance, LACAPA's (Apache/Hopi/Tewa) *The Flute Player* (1990), *The Antelope Woman* (1992), and *Less Than Half, More Than Whole* (1994) all successfully weave traditional and contemporary themes together by re-creating a traditional story, scene for scene, told in contemporary settings. Bruchac, ROSS, and Stroud (Cherokee) also use this technique successfully in *The Story of the Milky Way* (1995), and Stroud (Cherokee) in *Doesn't Fall off His Horse* (1994). With this technique, the emphasis is more on the traditional; in *Eagle Song* (1997) and *The Heart of a Chief* (1998), however, Bruchac accomplishes the same goal, but emphasizes the contemporary experience. Bruchac has published several books of legends popular with young children: *Gluskabe and the Four Wishes* (1995) and *Great Ball Game: A Muscogee Story* (1994). Like Bruchac, Monture (Mohawk) emphasizes the contemporary in *Cloudwalker* (1996), portraying children bridging the gap between their contemporary and traditional lives in six initiation stories. *Conley* (Cherokee) combines STORYTELLING tradition with history and fiction in his novel *Windsong: A Novel of the Trail of Tears* (1992), weaving it together so delicately that each of the segments complements the other. Power's (Lakota) *Grass Dancer* (1994) incorporates traditional beliefs and superstitions into an otherwise contemporary Indian experience.

Concerned with recording cultural information from the elders and teaching their children the values of their cultures, other Native American authors collect, translate, and retell Indian legends and stories for publication, usually with ILLUSTRATIONS. *Ktunaxa Legends* (1997) exemplifies this, in a collection of legends from the Kootenai people, featuring Coyote or other animals solving problems creatively, stories with strong moral lessons for the young. Ellen White's (Salish) *Kwulasulwul* (1992) and *Kwulasulwul II* (1997) accomplish the same goal with a collection of Salish legends that were passed on to her by her ancestors. Yamane's (Ohlone) *The Snake That Lived in the Santa Cruz Mountains and Other Ohlone Stories* (1998) is a retelling of Ohlone stories collected from elders about sixty years ago, and includes information about Ohlone languages with which the stories are identified. In *When the World Ended/How Hummingbird Got Fire/How People Were Made* (1995), she retells three Rumsien Ohlone stories collected from Rumsien elders, the late Isabelle Meadows, and Manuel Onesimo. Jimmy Santiago Baca, a Native American poet of Mayan and Navajo descent, combines several elements of his heritage to encourage readers to be proud of who they are and to have compassion for each other: to respect all people.

Bilingual texts are seen by many Native authors as an important way to expose Indian children today to the language of their cultural groups, thus ensuring continuance. During the 1990s, a substantive number have been published in PICTURE BOOK format by authors representing various language groups. *Coyote and Little Turtle* (1994), a shortened version of a traditional story told by Herschel Talashoerna, and illustrated by Hopi children, is a Hopi/English bilingual book for beginning readers. *How Eagle Got His Good Eyes* (1995) is a more advanced book in Cree/English, written by fifth-grade and illustrated by seventh-grade Cree students. Another Cree/English bilingual text, an autobiography, is Glecia Bear's *Two Little Girls Lost in the Bush* (1991), a suitable text for third and fourth grade children encouraging them to create stories. Keeshig-Tobias's (Obijway) *Emma amid the Trees* (1996) is an Obijway bilingual book for beginning readers.

A number of non–Native American authors have also written sensitively and authentically about Native people and cultures in recent years. GOBLE's *Buffalo Woman* (1984) retells a Plains Indian legend about the power of love and the unique relationship between the buffalo and Native American people. An author's note tells the reader that in the past, Buffalo stories were primarily told by Indians to celebrate their main source of sustenance. In *Death of the Iron Horse* (1987), Goble retells a story about a historic event, the derailment of the Union Pacific freight train in 1867 by Cheyennes. Goble describes it as merely a "moment of success" for the Indians in their long struggle for liberty and happiness. Norman's *Who Paddled Backward with Trout* (1997) retells a story told to the author by George Wesukmin (Sour Berry) a Cree elder about the Cree custom of "earning" one's name. The significance of this is stressed in a humorous way. In Collura's *Winners* (1986), an angry fifteen-year-old who has spent most of his life in foster homes returns to the Ash Creek reservation in Canada to the grandfather he scarcely knows. How they relate to one another paves the way for the boy's initiation into a new and responsible existence as Jordy Threebears. Charlotte and David Yue's *The Pueblo* (1986) provides a well-researched portrait of the Pueblos of the Southwest in an informative and objective tone, showing how the climate and vegetation of this region define its inhabitants. ASHABRANNER's *Children of the Maya* (1986), a nonfiction book illustrated with photographs, tells of the resilience of a group of Guatamalan Indians who managed to escape to Florida and of the people who are helping them rebuild their lives. Several non–Native authors, such as Russell FREEDMAN in *Buffalo Hunt* (1988), have tried to depict accurately the traditional lifestyles of Native Americans. Others have chosen to retell MYTHS AND LEGENDS for young readers as Gerald MCDERMOTT did first in his 1975 CALDECOTT MEDAL picture book *Arrow to the Sun*, then in *Raven* (Caldecott Medal Honor, 1994), as well as Barbara ESBENSEN's retelling of a Seneca legend in *Great Buffalo Race: How the Buffalo Got Its Hump*. In *The First Thanksgiving* (1993), Jean GEORGE retells the first Thanksgiving celebration as an Indian tradition and attributes the colonists' survival to the help they received from Squanto and tribe members.

Other non–Native American authors achieve this level of authenticity by portraying Native American people in a universal context. In many of these books the term N. is not used by the authors. Instead, the focus is entirely on the universality of the theme. In Peter Eyvindson's *Kyle's Bath* (1984), currently in its sixth reprint, a young boy devises an elaborate scheme to avoid having to take his daily bath, but is unsuccessful. Whereas every youngster will identify with Kyle's predicament in this book, N. children will recognize themselves in the authentic illustrations and feel validated. Brnjolson's *Foster Baby* (1996) and *Red Parka Mary* (1996) are similarly designed. *Foster Baby* is a reassuring text for any child who has been, or is, a foster child or orphan. In terms of setting and cultural details depicted in text and illustrations, *Red Parka Mary* is more clearly set in the Native American world. But, again, the author sees no need to name this world specifically. The emphasis is on the insights gained by the boy who befriends an old woman, and the important lesson he learns from this experience about friendship and giving. His concluding question, "Why did someone, somehow, sometime, tell me to be frightened of those twinkling brown eyes?" echoes long after one has finished reading this book.

BIBLIOGRAPHY: Bruchac, J., "Notes of a Translator's Son," in A. Wiget, ed., *I'll Tell You Now,* 1987; Fisher, D. "The Transformation of Tradition: A Study of Zitkala-Sa and Mourning Dove, Two Transitional American Indian Writers, in A. Wiget, ed., *Critical Essays in N. Literature,* 1985; Hirschfelder, A. B., *American Indian Stereotypes in the World of Children: A Reader and Bibliography,* 1982; Krupat, A., *For Those Who Come After: A study of N. Autobiography,* 1985; Larson, C. R., *American Indian Fiction,* 1978; Moore and Hirschfelder, A. B., "Feathers, Tomahawks, and Tipis: A study of Stereotyped 'Indian' Imagery in Children's Books," in A. B. Hirschfelder, *American Indian Stereotypes in the World of Children: A Reader and Bibliography,* 1977, 1982; Noll, F., "Accuracy and Authenticity in American Indian Children's Literature: The Social Responsibility of Authors and Illustrators," *New Advocate,* Winter 1995, pp. 29–43; Norris, A. J. Kyne, "The Unheard Voices on Turtle Island: The Voice of N. Authors in Children's Literature in the United States," unpublished doctoral dissertation, University of San Francisco, 1998; Ruoff, A. L. V. Brown, *American Indian Literatures,* 1990

AINE J. KYNE-NORRIS

NAYLOR, Phyllis Reynolds

Author, b. 4 January 1933, Anderson, Indiana

Having written almost one hundred books for young people, N. is one of the most prolific and well-loved children's authors of the twentieth century. Moving frequently as a young child, following the assignments of her traveling salesman father, books were very important in N.'s life. She began writing at an early age, making books from papers discarded in the trash. N. published her first stories as a teenager and was infected with the writing bug before earning her diploma from Joliet Junior College in 1953. N. resumed her education to become a clinical psychologist, earning her bachelors degree in psychology from the American University in 1963. However, rather than practicing as a psychologist, she pursued her writing full-time.

N.'s first novel for children, *What the Gulls Were Singing,* was published in 1967. Her writings have been as varied as her adult nonfiction (*Crazy Love: An Autobiographical Account of Marriage and Madness,* 1977) and children's mysteries (*Night Cry,* 1985, winner of the Edgar Allan Poe Award). N. also wrote her Golden Kite award-winning autobiography, *How I Became a Writer* in 1978 (revised 1987).

Some of her more lighthearted titles such as *Beetles Lightly Toasted* (1987) and *How Lazy Can You Get* (1979) tell the tales of children committing outrageous acts such as designing insect recipes and tricking their baby-sitter. However, N. has been most lauded for fiction exploring the troubles encountered by children growing up. The topics of her serious writing have ranged from the death of a parent (*The Agony of Alice,* 1985), to a crisis of faith (*A String of Chances,* 1982), to mental illness (*The Keeper,* 1986); she has excelled in all of these areas—an AMERICAN LIBRARY ASSOCIATION Notable Book for *The Agony of Alice,* Best Book for YOUNG ADULTS from ALA, Notable Children's Book in the Field of Social Studies from both the National Council for Social Studies and the CHILDREN'S BOOK

COUNCIL for *A String of Chances,* and a Best Book for Young Adults from ALA for *The Keeper.*

Shiloh, 1992 ALA NEWBERY MEDAL Award winner, exemplifies N.'s ability to use her personal experience in her writing (as in *The Keeper* where her first husband's mental illness was explored through a child's eyes). Spotting a stray dog on the roadside, N. took it home and began her story of a boy, a dog, moral courage, and inner turmoil. Following with *The Shiloh Season* (1996) and *Saving Shiloh* (1997), N. created another timeless trilogy like her Witch and York Trilogies, and her Alice and Bessledorf series.

FURTHER WORKS: *Alice in Rapture, Sort Of.* 1989. *Bodies in the Bessledorf Hotel.* 1986. *The Dark Side of the Moon.* 1969. *The Mad Gasser of Bessledorf Street.* 1983. *Reluctantly Alice.* 1991. *Send No Blessings.* 1990. *Witch's Sister.* 1975. *Witch's Water.* 1976. *The Witch Herself.* 1978. *The Year of the Gopher.* 1987

BIBLIOGRAPHY: Collier, L. and L. Nakamura. *Major Authors and Illustrators for Children and Young Adults.* 1993. Naylor, P. R. *How I Became a Writer.* 1978, rev. 1987. Naylor, P. R. The Writing of "Shiloh" *The Reading Teacher,* vol. 46, 1992. *The Seventh Book of Junior Authors and Illustrators.* 1996

GWYNNE ELLEN ASH

NESBIT, Edith

Author, b. 15 August 1858, Place unknown; d. 4 May 1924, Jesson St. Mary's, New Romney, Kent, England

Nicknamed "Daisy," N. was the youngest of six children (although one authority said she was the youngest of five). As a child she prayed "fervently, tearfully, that when I should be grown up I might never forget what I thought, felt, and suffered then." Her father died when she was almost four. She was a sensitive child, full of fears and terrors. "My nurse . . . never went downstairs to supper after she found out my terrors, which she very quickly did. She used to sit in the day nursery with the door open 'a tiny crack' and that light was company, because I knew I had only to call out and someone who loved me would come and banish fear."

At seven, N. was sent to a boarding school but was very unhappy there and stayed for only one term. At eight she was sent to a "select boarding establishment for young ladies and gentlemen at Stamford, and I venture to think that I should have preferred a penal settlement. Day after day, I sat lonely in the schoolroom . . . and ate my dry bread and milk and water in the depths of disgrace. . . . Night after night I cried myself to sleep in my bed . . . because I could not get the (long division) answers right."

In 1868, the family found a house at La Haye, near Dinan in Brittany. It had a large walled garden on one side and a farm on the other. N.'s mother expected the children to appear at mealtime but otherwise they were left on their own: "part of the infinite charm of those days lies in the fact that we were never bored, and children are bored."

N. attended an Ursuline Convent in Germany at eleven and ran away at least three times. The family finally settled at Halstead Hall in the Kentish village of Halstead, England. Nicknamed "The Hall," it was a low, long red-brick house with roses and ivy in front and heavy, rich jasmine covering the side. N. had her own little room that held an old mahogany bookcase with a deep top drawer that let down to form a writing table. Here she sat and wrote "verse, verse, always verse—and [I] dream of the days when I should be a great poet like Shakespeare, or Christina Rossetti." The house provided the setting for many of her later writings. At fifteen she showed some of the verses to her mother who in turn showed them to the editor of *Good Words* and the *Sunday* magazine. "By and by they were printed, and I got a check for a guinea, a whole guinea, think of it!"

At twenty-two, in 1880, she married Hubert Bland and within the year had a son, Paul. The same year her husband came down with smallpox. After recovering he discovered his investment partner had defrauded him and left him penniless. To support the family N. began writing more regularly with her husband at times collaborating with her. At the office of *Sylvia's Home Journal* she met Alice Hoatson who became a member of their household as a general aide and housekeeper. She stayed for over thirty years. Hoatson and N., a liberated woman who smoked in public, were members of the Fabian Society. Here N. met such notables as Bernard Shaw who later became a benefactor, and H. G. WELLS.

In 1892 her first children's book, *The Voyage of Columbus: Discovery of America,* was published. In 1899 *The Story of the Treasure Seekers: The Adventures of the Bastable Children in Search of a Fortune* was published and featured Oswald Bastable as the narrator. HUMOR and natural dialogue are some of the trademarks of N.'s writing. Her ability to make children seem alive and full of action yet childlike and believable sets her apart from many children's writers. N. published her books under the name of E. Nesbit, leading many to believe the author was a man; this suited N.'s visionary thinking.

The Book of Dragons was published in 1900. Eight unique stories about eight different dragons keep the reader apprehensive (Who can predict what a dragon will do?) yet intrigued. Although skillfully written, *The Book of Dragons* is not as lighthearted and sunny as *The Treasure Seekers.*

The Wouldbegoods, Being the Further Adventures of the Treasure Seekers, published in 1901, again involves the Bastable children after first being serialized in British MAGAZINES. The children, although physically small and weak, nonetheless are intelligent, humorous, kind, compassionate, and at times aggressive and careless. N. does not talk down to readers and does not overwhelm them with didacticism. Like all of N.'s writings it is characterized by a humorous blend of realism and magical FANTASY, creating the mold for future supernatural fairy characters.

The Five Children and It, published in 1902, hinges on the children uncovering a Sand Fairy (called a Psammead, pronounced Sammy-add) and the surprising discovery that he can grant them one wish a day. The book consists of chapters detailing the escapades that result from their wishes. Readers come to realize wishes are not the key to happiness.

In 1906 *The Story of the Amulet* was published. A time fantasy that uses half an Egyptian amulet as the vehicle for visiting the past or future, the reader is introduced to the history of ancient Egypt, Babylon, and Caesar's Britain. A glimpse of a Utopian future that is everything N. would long for is also included. N. was one of the first to use the idea that time progressing within the fantasy has taken up no real time at all upon the return to reality. *The Five Children* was published in 1930 and included "Five Children and

It," "The Phoenix and the Carpet," and "The Story of the Amulet." The children in the fantasies are realistic and the dialogue believable.

Also published in 1906 was *The Railway Children.* This is her only nonmagical children's novel. Drawn from her own life, there is the father who is taken away, the idealized mother who does endless writing so the family can have food, the children who try valiantly to help each other and their mother.

From N.'s viewpoint, "POETRY . . . is really what I should naturally have done, that and no prose, if I had not had to write for a living." From the reader's viewpoint we would have been deprived of all those glorious stories if she had written only poetry.

BIBLIOGRAPHY: Cameron, E. *The Green and Burning Tree: On the Writing and Enjoyment of Children's Books.* 1962. *Children's Literature Research,* vol. 3, 1978. *Fiction, FOLKLORE, Fantasy and Poetry for Children, 1876–1985.* 1986. Silvey, Anita, ed. 1995. *Children's Books and Their Creators. Something about the Author,* vol. 100, 1999. *Yesterday's Authors of Books for Children,* vol. 1, 1977

IRVYN G. GILBERTSON

NESS, Evaline

Illustrator, author, b. 24 April 1911, Union City, Ohio; d. 12 August 1987, Kingston, New York

Illustrator, writer, artist, and tapestry designer, N. is known primarily as a gifted illustrator of more than fifty children's books; some of which received both ALA NEWBERY MEDAL and CALDECOTT MEDAL honors. However, one of the sixteen books she both wrote and illustrated, *Sam, Bangs and Moonshine,* was the 1967 Caldecott Medal book. Born in Union City, Ohio, N. briefly attended the state teachers college. Shortly after, her art talent was recognized and she studied at The Art Institute of Chicago from 1933–35 and then at the Corcoran Gallery in Washington, D.C., 1933–35. There, N. met and married Eliot Ness, chief of the Federal Bureau of Investigation. In 1951, she went to Rome and attended the Academia della Belles Artes. Between her years of education, she worked as an artist's model and as a professional illustrator for fashion magazines and for ad agencies. It was not until the early 1960s that she began to work on children's books. Her

realistic ILLUSTRATIONS were admired for their freshness and versatility. She was considered a master craftsman who was expert at a variety of techniques such as woodcut, serigraph, ink wash, lithograph, and chalk; she often used traditional materials in nontraditional ways.

N.'s 1967 Caldecott Medal–winning book, *Sam, Bangs and Moonshine,* tells the story of a motherless little girl, Sam, who loved making up stories, which ultimately get her into trouble. Since most children typically invent tall tales, they could empathize with Sam. However, the sensitive, expressive illustrations of the sad, lonely girl truly helped readers to sympathize and to understand her real need to create other worlds.

N. was also a noted architectural designer who created a variety of paper houses for children.

AWARDS: AMERICAN LIBRARY ASSOCIATION Caldecott Medal (1967) for *Sam, Bangs and Moonshine.* ALA Caldecott Medal Honor Book (1964) for *All in the Morning Early* (Nic Sorche LEODHAS, author (1965) for *A Pocketful of Cricket* (Rebecca CAUDILL, author) (1966) for *Tom Tit Tot: An English Folk Tale* (Virginia HAVILAND, author). ALA Newbery Medal Honor Book (1963) for *Thistle and Thyme: Tales and Legends from Scotland* (Nic Sorche Leodhas, author)

FURTHER WORKS: Author and illus.: *A Gift for Sula, Sula.* 1963. *Josefina.* 1963. *Exactly Alike.* 1964. *Pavo and the Princess.* 1964. *A Double Discovery.* 1965. *The Girl and the Goatherd.* 1970. *Do You Have the Time, Lydia?* 1971. *Amelia Mixed the Mustard.* 1979. *Marcella's Guardian Angel.* 1979. *Fierce, the Lion.* 1980. Illus. only: *Where Did Josie Go?* (H. Buckley). 1962. *Funny Tom.* (Eve MERRIAM), 1963. *Some of the Days of Everett Anderson.* (Lucille CLIFTON). 1970

BIBLIOGRAPHY: *Children's Literature Review,* vol. 6, 1984; HOPKINS, Lee Bennett, *Pauses: Autobiographical Reflections of 101 Creators of Children's Books,* 1995; Silvey, Anita, ed., *Children's Books and Their Creators,* 1995

JUDY LIPSITT

NEUFELD, John

Author, b. 14 December 1938, Chicago, Illinois

N. might be called the father of the adolescent problem novel, a surprise for a man who never intended to write for children or young adults. He read widely and extensively as a child, and began writing while in middle school. He attended Philips Exeter Academy and received his B.A. from Yale University in 1960. N. then toured England, returning to a United States that drafted him into the army. There he taught English lessons for fellow draftees. This experience led him to a career in publishing.

In 1968, N. published his first novel, *Edgar Allan,* a controversial look at interracial adoption, based on true events. While telling the story of a family forced to give up their adopted African American child due to community demands, he focused on the point of view of the other children in the family. *Edgar Allan* was given a Notable Book Award from the AMERICAN LIBRARY ASSOCIATION, a Best Book Citation from the children's division of the *New York Times,* and a Book of the Year citation from *Time* magazine.

N.'s best known novel, however, was not published until the next year. In 1969, when *Lisa, Bright and Dark* premiered, mental illness had never before been a topic for YOUNG ADULT LITERATURE, but N.'s novel was well received by the critics. The story of a young girl aware of her growing insanity while the adults around her ignore it caught the attention of adolescents all too familiar with being told their problems are only a phase. *Lisa, Bright and Dark* was adapted as a *Hallmark Hall of Fame* television special, with the teleplay written by N. himself, further broadening its audience.

With the success of *Lisa, Bright and Dark,* N. became a full-time, freelance writer. While living in England he published *Touching* (1970, also published as *Twink,* 1971), the story of a young girl's battle with cerebral palsy (see THE DISABLED IN CHILDREN'S AND YOUNG ADULT LITERATURE). Also controversial were 1973's *Freddy's Book,* in which a young boy seeks the etymology of an obscenity he reads on a graffiti-laden wall, and *For All the Wrong Reasons* (1974), one of the first books to address teenage pregnancy and motherhood.

In the mid-1970s, N. wrote for adults under the pseudonym of Joan Lea, but returned to YA novels in the early 1980s with *A Small Civil War* (1982). The story of a town split over CENSORSHIP was extensively revised and republished under the same title in 1996. N. reappeared in the 1990s

with *Almost a Hero* (1995) and *Gaps in Stone Walls* (1996). *Gaps in Stone Walls* was a compelling mystery set among a primarily deaf community in Martha's Vineyard in the 1880s and was nominated for an Edgar Allan Poe Award.

FURTHER WORKS: *Sleep, Two, Three, Four!,* 1971. *Sunday Father,* 1975. *Sharell,* 1983

BIBLIOGRAPHY: Collier, L. and L. Nakamura. *Major Authors and Illustrators for Children and Young Adults,* 1993; *Something about the Author Autobiography Series,* vol. 3, 1986; Ward, M., D. A. Marquardt, N. Nolan, and D. Eaton, *Authors of Books for Young People,* 1990

GWYNNE ELLEN ASH

NEVILLE, Emily Cheney
Author, b. 28 December 1919, Manchester, Connecticut

N., grew up in a large New England family. She graduated from Bryn Mawr College in 1940 and from Albany Law School in 1976. Married to a newspaperman, she practiced law in New York City for many years in addition to writing books for children.

N. is best known for her first book, *It's like This, Cat,* a 1964 NEWBERY MEDAL–winning book. At the time of its publication, it was considered exceptionally innovative writing for children. Her realistic yet lighthearted depiction of a boy growing up in New York City delighted readers with its fresh approach to juvenile fiction. In the novel, fourteen-year-old Dave Mitchell struggles with the problems and pleasures of urban life, including his arguments with his father, his adventures with his cat, and a budding romance with a girl named Mary. One reviewer wrote, "*It's like This, Cat* is a far cry from the saccharine stories which flooded the children's book market for years about blonde white children who always lived in the suburbs, in pleasant houses, with idyllically married parents."

N.'s second novel, *Berries Goodman* (1965), won the Jane Addams Children's Book Award and was chosen as a 1965 AMERICAN LIBRARY ASSOCIATION Notable Children's Book. Like her first work, the story tackles difficult issues, including anti-Semitism and a family's adjustment to life in the suburbs. Her fictionalized autobiography, *Traveler from a Small Kingdom* (1968), is set in a small mill town, reminiscent of South Manchester, Connecticut, the town where Neville was born and reared. The author wrote one PICTURE BOOK, *The Bridge* (1988), which features an American girl visiting China during the demonstrations at Tiananmen Square.

FURTHER WORKS: *The Seventeenth-Street Gang,* 1966; *Fogarty,* 1969; *Garden of Broken Glass,* 1975; *The China Year,* 1991

BIBLIOGRAPHY: *Major Authors and Illustrators for Children and Young Adults: A Selection of Sketches from "Something about the Author,"* 1993; *Contemporary Authors, New Revision Series,* vol. 3; *Children's Writers,* p. 929; *Children's Literature Review,* vol. 12, 1980; *Horn Book,* August 1964; MEIGS, et al., *Critical History of Children's Literature,* 1969; *Something about the Author Autobiographical Series,* vol. 2, 1986; *Twentieth Century Young Adult Writers,* vol. 1, 1994; Ward, M. E., D. A. Marquardt. N. Dolan, and D. Eaton, eds., *Authors of Books for Young People,* 3rd edition, 1990

MARY ARIAIL BROUGHTON

NEWBERRY, Clare Turley

Author, illustrator, b. 10 April, 1903, Enterprise, Oregon; d. 12 February, 1970, San Diego, California

Known worldwide for her ILLUSTRATIONS of cats, N.'s daughter recounts her mother's method of painting her "furry" drawings by wetting the paper and quickly applying a brush. Her Japanese style of art was influenced by the work of Hokusai. Four of her books beginning with *Barkis* (1938, 1998), were named CALDECOTT MEDAL Honor Books, and *Smudge* (1948, 1998) was named one of the Fifty Books of the Year by the American Institute of Graphic Arts. All but three of her books feature cats.

AWARDS: AMERICAN LIBRARY ASSOCIATION Caldecott Medal Honor Book (1939) for *Barkis;* (1941) for *April's Kittens;* (1943) for *Marshmallow;* (1951) for *T-Bone, the Baby Sitter*

FURTHER WORKS: *Herbert the Lion,* 1931, 1998; *Kittens' ABC,* 1946; *Percy, Polly, and Pete,* 1952; *Widget,* 1958; *Frosty,* 1961; *Mittens,* reissued 1998

BIBLIOGRAPHY: Notes from N.'s daughter at www.amazon.com.; *Something about the Author,* vol. 26, 1982

SANDRA IMDIEKE

NEWBERY, John

Publisher, b. 1713, Waltham St. Lawrence, Berkshire, England; d. 22 December 1767, Islington, England

N. was a farmer's son who educated himself and, at the age of sixteen, was apprenticed to a newspaper printer, William Carnan, in Reading. In 1737, Carnan died, leaving half his property to N., who soon thereafter married Carnan's widow Mary. N. had acquired a passionate love for books and learned all he could about the book trade. In 1744, he set up a branch office in London and seeing the brighter prospects there soon moved permanently to the capital, establishing his business in St. Paul's Churchyard.

Also in 1744, N. published his first children's book, *A Little Pretty Pocket-Book,* the first of a planned SERIES of volumes for the amusement of young children. The book is a miscellany of illustrated verses, nursery rhymes, FABLES, and moral lessons, and much of it seems to have been written and compiled by N. himself. The book proved very popular and was reprinted several times during the eighteenth century. N. acknowledged his debt to John Locke in the preface along with his intention to offer "instruction with delight," and N.'s children's books were by and large books of moral instruction.

N. undertook a children's instructional series, The Circle of Sciences, between 1745 and 1748, including volumes on arithmetic, chronology, geography, grammar, logic, POETRY, and rhetoric, all rather lengthy volumes containing more instruction than delight. N. perhaps published the first children's periodical, *Lilliputian* magazine, which appeared between 1751 and 1752, a venture that may have been too far ahead of its time. This publication as well had a thinly disguised moral purpose. To what extent N. wrote the children's books he published is unclear; although some of his works probably appeared under pseudonyms (Abraham Aesop, Tom Telescope, and John-the-Giant Killer). He was frequently an adapter rather than a creative writer.

As his name became established, N. was able to commission writers such as Tobias George Smollett, Oliver Goldsmith, and Dr. Samuel Johnson to write for him. Goldsmith, grateful for

N.'s encouragement, praises N. in *The Vicar of Wakefield* (1765) as the "philanthropic bookseller in St. Paul's Churchyard . . . a friend of all mankind." Both Goldsmith and Johnson have left descriptions of N.'s peripatetic ways, for he was always on the move about some urgent business. In fact, N.'s true genius was as an entrepreneur. He made much of his fortune marketing Dr. James's Fever Powder, perhaps the most popular patent medicine of its day. He was also an inventive advertiser who early discovered the power of the press.

In 1765–66, one of his most famous children's books, *The History of Little Goody Two Shoes*, appeared. It is the story of an orphaned girl who overcomes dire circumstances to become a beloved teacher and eventually the wife of a wealthy lord. The purity of her character being her most prominent feature, the heroine enjoys the dubious distinction of inspiring the now disparaging epithet "Goody Two Shoes." The book was immensely popular and reprinted frequently. Its authorship is in question, with many reputable commentators attributing it to Goldsmith. Others believe N. himself had a hand in it, but the truth may never be known.

Although his children's publications actually constituted only a fraction of his printing business, N. clearly regarded this venture with a great deal of pride. He died in 1767, a wealthy man at the pinnacle of his success, and was buried beside his parents in the village of his birth, Waltham St. Lawrence. The inscription on his tombstone reads simply that he was a "writer of children's stories," a clear indication of his own sense of accomplishment. His publishing business was continued by his heirs until 1801 and by their successors for many more years. His influence extended to America where booksellers such as Isaiah Thomas of Worcester, Massachusetts, published pirated editions of his children's books.

Prior to N., no English book publisher pursued the children's market, a fact that would certainly discourage anyone with aspirations of writing exclusively for children. N.'s principal achievement was to prove that such a market existed and that it could be profitable. This, in turn, gave impetus to writers to write for children. And if most of the early authors were limited in scope and typically didactic and sentimental, they at least laid the

necessary groundwork for the emergence of a great body of literature in the late nineteenth century. It was N. who made all this possible, and for that reason he is regarded by many as the forebear of BRITISH and American children's literature.

It is fitting that N.'s name is perpetuated by a prestigious award in children's literature. In 1922, at the suggestion of Frederic MELCHER, Chairman of the American Booksellers' Association, the NEWBERY MEDAL was established as an annual award for "the most distinguished contribution to AMERICAN LITERATURE for children." Melcher donated the medal itself and selected the name Newbery, in honor of the great book publisher. The medal is administered by the AMERICAN LIBRARY ASSOCIATION and the first Medal was awarded to *The Story of Mankind* by Hendrik VAN LOON in 1922. One or more Honor Books are typically selected each year.

Despite the rise of a plethora of annual AWARDS for children's books, the Newbery Medal remains the most coveted American award in children's literature, and winning titles and authors are assured immediate celebrity in the world of children's books. The medal is a fitting tribute to the man whom the late Harvey Darton referred to as "Newbery the Conqueror."

FURTHER WORKS: *A Pretty Book of Pictures for Little Masters and Misses.* 1752. *Food for the Mind, or a New Riddle Book.* c. 1757. *Fables in Verse by Abraham Aesop, Esq.* 1757. *The Valentine's Gift.* 1763

BIBLIOGRAPHY: Cott, Jonathan, *Pipers at the Gates of Dawn: The Wisdom of Children's Literature,* 1981; *The Oxford Companion to Children's Literature,* 1984; *Something about the Author.* vol. 20, 1980; Townsend, John Rowe, *Written for Children,* 1987; MEIGS, C., et al., *Critical History of Children's Literature,* 1969; Doyle, Brian, *Who's Who of Children's Literature,* 1968

DAVID L. RUSSELL

NEWBERY MEDAL

Donated by the Frederic G. Melcher family, the Newbery Medal has been awarded annually since 1922 under the supervision of the Association for Library Service to Children of the AMERICAN LIBRARY ASSOCIATION (ALA). The Newbery Medal is given to the author of the most distinguished contribution to literature for children published in the U.S. during the preceding year. Announced in January, the award is limited to residents or citizens of the United States.

The ingredients to create an audience for children's books included the new Carnegie-endowed libraries with separate rooms for children's services, staffed by librarians trained to provide children's services, the establishment of separate children's publishing departments and a groundswell of children's book reviews by specialists in the field.

The ALA gave enthusiastic support for these efforts, especially in its Children's Librarians Section, now the Association for Library Service to Children. As advocates of good books for children, their gratitude and ours go to such catalysts as the post–World War I triumvirate of Franklin Mathiews, Frederic MELCHER, and Anne Carroll Moore. The two bookmen had approached Moore with a proposal for the establishment of a Children's Book Week in 1919 and then Melcher donated the money to create an award named after British children's book publisher John NEWBERY. It would be, however, the children's librarians who would choose the books to be honored.

It is a monumental task, one that is usually considered a pleasure and a privilege by those who are elected or appointed. It may have been easier in 1922, choosing that first Newbery winner. There were fewer books then. Between 1915 and 1945 the annual average of new titles was only 713. No doubt librarians felt, as we do now, the same sense of obligation to choose wisely. They must have hoped, as we do today, that children who read the award books would enjoy them. Almost certainly, they too were familiar with children's needs and reading interests. And surely, even with fewer eligible books, they were frustrated by the conflicting or competing virtues of fiction and nonfiction, realism and FANTASY, POETRY and prose.

There are other factors that influence the opinions and evaluations of committee members, and some of those factors may operate silently. We are all products of our time as well as of our heredity and our environment. We all have convictions about what children should know, or not know, and perhaps at what age. We each have a preference for some styles of writing and most of us have a desire to be objective and rational. We may unwittingly be swayed in individual establishment of priorities by sympathy for an author who has had many Honor Books but never won the medal. Most of us respond favorably to books that espouse a cause we hold dear, and we may differ in our opinions of whether a good novel with an important social message or a good novel with superb characterization is the more worthy.

It is true now, as it was true when John Newbery published children's books, that what is published for children reflects contemporary society's idea of what children should read, and that opinions about that idea change with time and place. Today our language has changed, our mores have changed, and our ideas about how children learn and what we want them to learn have shifted repeatedly and will surely continue to change in the future.

If we look at the Newbery Medal books as examples of their times (even as the best of their time) we will find influences of the periods from which they came. They have been worthy of the kudos they have received, even though there are many cases in which members of committees, or librarians not on committees, felt that an Honor Book was equally worthy (or even more worthy) of the medal.

The Newbery winners of the 1920s were, for the most part, not easy reading. Although *The Story of Mankind* (VAN LOON, 1921) has a flowing style and pervasive HUMOR, it is packed with facts and theories and covers a vast expanse of time. While Hugh LOFTING's *The Voyages of Doctor Dolittle* (1922) is a FANTASY with animal characters (always popular with children), there has been contemporary criticism about its depiction of native characters and the use of racial epithets. Although those depictions may not have raised objections at the time of publication, subsequent adverse criticism resulted in a partial revision in the 1980s. These two quite different books most surely would not be published today without major changes.

Despite the severe financial depression of the 1930s, children's book publishing flourished, as did circulation statistics in libraries. While there was an observable interest in books set outside the United States, this was the last decade in which four of the ten medal winners were so framed: *The Cat Who Went to Heaven* (COATS-WORTH, 1930), Japan; *Young Fu of the Upper Yangtze* (Lewis, 1932), China; *Dobry* (Shannon, 1934), Bulgaria; and *The White Stag* (SEREDY, 1937), Hungary.

Although there was an increasing interest in FOLKLORE and in modern FAIRY TALES, that trend may also have been caused by a combination of financial stress and the reinforced patriotism engendered by the recent war. Although *Caddie Woodlawn* (BRINK, 1935) was immediately popular as period fiction it was later criticized for its treatment of NATIVE AMERICANS, but at the time there were few voiced objections. "Sensitivity training" and "political correctness" were phrases of the future. However, both of those concepts were exemplified in Laura Armer's *Waterless Mountain* (1931), a dignified yet moving story of a Navajo boy.

In the next twenty years, the preference for books set in the United States continued, with only Armstrong SPERRY's *Call It Courage* (1940), Elizabeth Janet GRAY's *Adam of the Road* (1942), Marguerite DE ANGELI's *The Door in the Wall* (1949), Ann Nolan CLARK's *Secret of the Andes* (1952), and Meindert DEJONG's *The Wheel on the School* (1954) being set in other countries. Again, some of this focus on the home scene may have been due to the war in Europe.

There was little literary experimentation or boundary-crossing save for the yeasty mix of science, humor, and fantasy in *The Twenty-One Balloons* (William Pene DU BOIS, 1947), and in two books that were surely influenced by the growing emphasis on the representation of ethnic diversity in our world. One was *Amos Fortune, Free Man* (Elizabeth YATES, 1950), the true life story of a slave who became a free man, a landowner, and a valued member of a New Hampshire community. *Secret of the Andes,* with a Peruvian Indian boy as protagonist, is a bit heavy stylistically. With Lois LENSKI's *Strawberry Girl* (1945), the books above show a picture of economic as well as ethnic diversity.

It is not unusual for children's book publishing to show a time lag in depicting changes—a phenomenon that may indicate a reluctance to admit change, perhaps to take the chance, by publishing a taboo-breaking book—to seem to indicate approval of change. Whether books such as E. B.

WHITE's *Trumpet of the Swan* (1970) or *Stuart Little* (1945) were on the voting list for award consideration only the committee members for the years in which those books were eligible to know. It is certainly possible that they were considered daring and it is more than possible that Louise FITZHUGH's *Harriet the Spy* (1967) or *Ellen Grae* by Vera and Bill CLEAVER (1967) never even made it onto a preliminary list since both aroused some controversy.

In the 1960s, there was some indication that societal concerns affected what was published and what was applauded. It seems unlikely that an eccentric man who lives in a dilapidated shack and who has difficulty in communicating would have been deemed an appropriate protagonist for the prestigious Newbery Medal in earlier years, but Joseph KRUMGOLD's *Onion John* was the 1960 winner.

In truth, the Newbery Award winners and Honor Books are a small sampling of what is published each year. That perfect-parent image that was maintained for so long is missing from many contemporary books, some of which have had fine reviews—but no Newbery Awards. But changes creep in, as is evident in E. L. KONIGSBURG's *From the Mixed-up Files of Mrs. Basil E. Frankweiler* (1967), there are no parents to assess in a story in which two children run away—for a while—from home. In Irene HUNT's *Up a Road Slowly* (1966), there's an alcoholic uncle in a story about a child who is sent away to stay with kinfolk for ten years by her widowed father.

Perhaps the 1970s were the years in which there was clear evidence that Newbery committees were corroborating the fact that those children who were coping with real problems in books were a mirror of those who coped in real life. What is remarkable is that half of the Newbery Award books of this decade deal with children facing serious problems; would bereavement, THE DISABLED IN CHILDREN'S AND YOUNG ADULT LITERATURE, racial prejudice, and discrimination have been so honestly explored even a decade earlier?

In the 1980s and 1990s, there were some unusual choices: not one but two poetry books. In Nancy WILLARD's *A Visit to William Blake's Inn: Poems for Innocent and Experienced Travelers* (1981), a carousel of vitality in ebullient verse, an amazing cast of characters visit an inn whose host is William Blake. The book received the singular distinction of being named a CALDECOTT MEDAL Honor Book in the same year. Paul FLEISCH-MAN's *Joyful Noise: Poems for Two Voices* (1988) offers an elegant revival of the art of choral reading, with both the voices of each poem spoken by insects, alone or together.

Russell FREEDMAN, in *Lincoln, A Photobiography* (1987) shows his readers that nonfiction can be outstanding for its distinctive style and be "the most distinguished contribution of the year." A first in Newbery history, Beverly CLEARY's *Dear Mr. Henshaw* (1983) is a story effectively told in deftly sustained letters.

We cannot fail to recognize that for seventy-five years a great many people have created an impressive record of enlightened choice. Of course some books are dated, of course some fine books were missed, of course each of us has been disappointed at times. The list of winners and honor books is a testament to the democratic process.
(Excerpted by the author from "The Newbery at 75: Changing with the Times" in *American Libraries,* March 1997)

ZENA SUTHERLAND

NEW ZEALAND LITERATURE

Very few books were written, let alone published, for children in New Zealand prior to 1900. The early stories of the twentieth century mixed folktale and FANTASY with doses of didacticism such as *Fairyland in New Zealand, A Story of the Caves* (1909), by Mrs. Ambrose Moore.

Edith Howes wrote over twenty books in the early part of the century, including *Silver Island* (1925), one of the country's first ADVENTURE STORIES. Three children search for silver, which turns out to be ambergris, a valuable product at the time. This novel mixed adventure with didacticism about the flora and fauna. For instance, Jim tells the others the story of the kiwi losing its power to fly and about the harmless nature of the bush.

Isabel Maud Peacocke wrote FAMILY STORIES that reflected life between the two great wars. Her stories had a recognizable Auckland setting, such as Auckland harbor in *The Cruise of the Crazy*

Jane (1932). Meanwhile in the South Island Esther Glen made her mark upon children's literature. Her love of quality literature is remembered today with the Esther Glen Award for distinguished contribution to New Zealand literature for children. This award is New Zealand's oldest surviving literary award. Glen's best-known book is *Six Little New Zealanders* (1917), a title that alludes to *Seven Little Australians,* published earlier by Australian author Ethel TURNER. Glen's writing accurately captured the social hierarchies of the period, but her authorial intrusion into the narrative seems quaint today. For instance, Ngaire, the narrator, suggests that the reader ought to begin by looking up New Zealand in an atlas.

Mona Tracy explored the question of cultural identity between the European settlers (Pakeha) and the indigenous population (Maori) in *Rifle and Tomahawk* (1927). In 1945 the Esther Glen Award was given for the first time to Stella Morice for her novel *The Book of Wiremu* (1944). Although it was a landmark book at the time for its depiction of Maori rural life, it appears stilted today, given the ways in which society has progressed. The second recipient of the Esther Glen Award was A. W. Reed for *Myths and Legends of Maoriland* (1946). This SERIES of twenty-one tales about Maori mythology begins with the Maori story of creation. An early fantasy, *Falter Tom and the Water Boy* (Maurice Duggan, 1958), lacks the earnest morality of earlier stories. It tells of an old sea captain, Falter Tom, who gave up his life on the land for everlasting life at sea with the waterboy. This won the Esther Glen Award in 1959, which was given only thirteen times between 1945 and 1985—an indication of the variable quality of literature for children during this period.

The year 1969 was a major turning point in the growth of children's literature. Four women writers appeared on the literary landscape: Ruth Dallas with *The Children in the Bush*, Anne de Roo with *Moa Valley*, Joy COWLEY with *The Duck in the Gun*, and Margaret MAHY with *A Lion in the Meadow*, 1969. Both Cowley and Mahy continue to influence generations of New Zealand children with their picture books and novels that children read throughout their school years. Their brands of fantasy and social realism are unparalleled. *The Duck in the Gun* explored an alternative to conflict, while *A Lion in the Meadow* told how a young boy's imagination was allayed by his mother. This title won the Esther Glen Award; Mahy subsequently won the Esther Glen Award four more times.

Ron Bacon's picture book trilogy was influential; he was a Pakeha author creating Maori FOLK-LORE to explain the creation of a canoe and buildings. The first in the trilogy, *The House of the People* (1977), illustrated in traditional earthen colors by Robert Jahnke, received the New Zealand Library Association's inaugural Russell Clark Award for ILLUSTRATION.

In 1982 a new series of annual awards for children's literature was established. Sponsored initially by the Government Printing Office, the first recipients were Joy COWLEY for *The Silent One* (1981), the story of an albino turtle and a mute island boy, and a PICTURE BOOK, *The Kuia and the Spider* (1981), by the Maori duo of Patricia Grace and Robyn Kahukiwa. This story is about a spinning competition between an old woman and a spider. These awards are sponsored today by the *New Zealand Post.*

By the 1980s New Zealand children's literature was well established and flourishing. Solid foundations had been established by the Children's Literature Association in 1969, the Writers in Schools Scheme in 1977 and the New Zealand Literary Fund in 1978.

Using the work of New Zealand writers and illustrators created great interest in schools and readers. Colleges, too, began to conduct courses in children's literature. This growth was accompanied by scholarly works such as Diane Hebley's *Off the Shelf* (1980) and Betty Gilderdale's *A Sea Change: 145 Years of New Zealand Junior Fiction* (1982), a comprehensive chronicle of books between 1833–1978. New authors such as Lynley DODD, Tessa DUDER, William Taylor and Maurice Gee made their mark on the literary scene. The incredible success of Lynley Dodd's canine creation, *Hairy Maclary from Donaldson's Dairy* (1983), spawned a whole commercial industry. Dodd's ability to incorporate a lively rhythmical, repetitious text to accompany her illustrations established Hairy Maclary as one of this country's children's book icons. In the same year, *Greedy Cat* (1983) by Joy Cowley and Robyn BELTON appeared as an educational

reader. Greedy Cat is also readily identified by nearly all young children. Tessa Duder created a strong female protagonist, Alex Archer, in *Alex* (1987) which spanned a quartet of titles and was made into a movie.

William Taylor, another award-winning author, writes a distinctive brand of kiwi HUMOR with such titles as *The Worst Soccer Team Ever* (1987) and *Agnes the Sheep* (1990). He also writes more serious novels, such as *Possum Perkins* (1987), which is concerned with abuse, and *The Blue Lawn* (1994), which deals sensitively with a close relationship between two adolescent boys.

Margaret MAHY continued to demonstrate excellence in writing as evidenced by winning the CARNEGIE MEDAL twice, first for *The Haunting* (1982) and then for *The Changeover: A Supernatural Romance* (1984). Maurice Gee, also a strong fantasy writer, published *Under the Mountain* (1979), followed by a trilogy: *The Halfmen of O* (1982), *The Priests of Ferris* (1984) and *Motherstone* (1983), in which the balance between good and evil is threatened.

In recognition of their oustanding contribution to literature for children, Joy Cowley was awarded the Order of the British Empire in 1992 and Margaret Mahy the Order of New Zealand, the country's highest honor, in 1993. Only a few new authors surfaced in the 1990s. One is Paula Boock who won the *New Zealand Post* Senior Fiction Award for *Truth, Dare, or Promise* (1997), a tightly written novel about a loving relationship between two adolescent girls. Kate De Goldi is another new novelist who won both the Esther Glen and the *New Zealand Post* Senior Fiction Award for *Sanctuary* (1996), a gripping tale of a four-way relationship between a girl, two brothers and a black panther. These two titles caused concern in some quarters but they and others expanded the boundaries of fiction for children. Maurice Gee's *The Fat Man* (1994) and Kate De Goldi's *Closed, Stranger* (1999) are part of the expansion.

Significant picture books of the 1990s include *Lily and the Present* (1992) by Christine Ross, a tale about a gift for a baby brother; *Hinepau* (1993) by Gavin Bishop, the story of a young Maori woman ostracized from her tribe; *Kotuku: The Flight of the White Heron* (1994) by Philip Temple (Chris Gaskin, illus.) the story of the annual migration of the heron from New Zealand to Australia and *The Cheese Trap* (1995) by Joy Cowley (Linda McClelland, illus.), the tale of bold mice pilfering cheese from an old cat. *The Bantam and the Soldier* (1996) by Jennifer Beck (Robyn Belton, illus.) tells about World War I soldiers' suffering. Margaret Mahy and Selina Young (illus.) won the millennium's final *New Zealand Post* Picture Book Award for *A Summery Saturday Morning* (1998), a turn-tail-and-run story of a family out on an early morning stroll.

The end of the final decade in the twentieth century brought a leveling out in publishing children's literature in New Zealand. The New Zealand Library and Information Awards were not presented in 1999 for lack of a sponsor and grants to authors and illustrators were not abundant. Three new awards, however, were initiated by the New Zealand Children's Book Foundation, a new organization formed in 1990 to foster the growth of children's literature. The awards are the Margaret Mahy Medal 1991 for a substantial contribution to children's literature, the Tom Fitzgibbon Award (1994) for a previously unpublished children's novelist, and the Gaelyn Gordon Award (1999) for A Much-loved Book. Several courses in childrens' literature at a master's level were established in higher educational institutions and a national diploma course in children's literature was also established in 1992. The New Zealand Children's Book Foundation, the New Zealand Reading Association, and *The New Zealand Herald,* the leading newspaper, were responsible for the daily serialization of a children's book in the newspaper in late 1999. This move was designed to increase national awareness of children's literature and to improve literacy. The potential bright spots have yet to be formalized but they need to be nurtured carefully to ensure that the importance and position of children's literature and literacy is maintained. The growth of New Zealand literature for children in a hundred years has been phenomenal, and there is no reason to think this trend will not continue.

WAYNE MILLS

NICHOLSON, Sir William

Author, illustrator, b. 1872 Newark-on-Trent, England d. 1949, Place unknown

N.'s style was bold and graphic and exerted influence on a number of illustrators of children's literature. He changed the format of the children's book in *Clever Bill* (1929, reprinted 1961) where he used the oblong shape and also began the technique of breaking sentences to encourage the reader to turn the page. N. was the illustrator of the classic edition of *The Velveteen Rabbit* (Margery BIANCO, 1922) that has captured the hearts of children for many years.

FURTHER WORKS: *An Alphabet,* 1898; *The Square Book of Animals* (A. Waugh, author), 1900; *The Pirate Twins,* 1929

BIBLIOGRAPHY: Mahoney, Bertha E., et al., *"Illustrators of Children's Books 1744–1945,"* the *Horn Book* magazine, 1947. pp. 233–34, 342

KAY E. VANDERGRIFT

(NIC LEODHAS, Sorche) ALGER, Leclaire Gowens

Author, b. 20 May 1898, Youngstown, Ohio; d. 14 November 1969, Wilkensburg, Pennsylvania

"Sorche Nic Leodhas" was the pseudonym used by N. through the later part of her writing career. N. was said to have chosen the name because it means Claire, daughter of Louis in Gaelic. An avid and early reader, N. was often ill as a child and after missing so much school was tutored at home by her family. N. started writing at the age of six and wished to imitate her father and sister who did freelance writing for enjoyment. N.'s family was demanding as well as encouraging and at the age of twelve encouraged N. to send her writing to a publisher. The work was accepted and N.'s writing career began.

N. started her association with the CARNEGIE Library as a page in 1915. One year later she married and had a son but was widowed only two years later. N. returned to library work, first in New York and then again later in Pittsburgh as a student at the Carnegie Library School. Never having attended college, N. was admitted to the school through a special exam and graduated in 1929. N. continued her association with the Carnegie Library for the next thirty-seven years working in various branches as a librarian and children's librarian.

N. came from a family that had as a tradition collected old Scottish stories, superstitions, songs, and poems. The family prided itself on only collecting tales that had not previously been published and found much of the enjoyment in the gathering itself. This influence was strong on N.'s writing career. N.'s first three books, *Jan and the Wonderful Mouth Organ* (1939), *Dougal's Wish* (1942), and *The Golden Summer* (1942), were published in her own name. It was shortly before retiring from the library to work at writing full-time that N. began using the pseudonym Sorche Nic Leodhas. *Heather and Broom: Tales of the Scottish Highlands* (1961) was a collection of *seanichie* stories as was *Thistle and Thyme: Tales and Legends from Scotland* (1962). This title was a 1963 ALA NEWBERY MEDAL Honor Book selection. Both works, based on Scottish and Gaelic oral STORYTELLING traditions, were praised for N.'s ability to adapt the tales to English while at the same time honoring their roots and oral tradition.

N. also adapted tales to the picture-book format. *All in the Morning Early* (1963) was named an ALA CALDECOTT MEDAL Honor Book for Evaline NESS'S ILLUSTRATIONS, and Nonny HOGROGIAN's illustrations won the Caldecott Medal with *Always Room for One More* (1965).

N. was an accomplished storyteller and her collections and PICTURE BOOKS have done much to share the oral tradition of Scotland with children everywhere.

FURTHER WORKS: *Gaelic Ghosts,* 1963; *Ghosts Go Haunting,* editor, 1965; *Claymore and Kilt: Tales of Scottish Kings and Castles,* 1967; *Sea Spell and Moor Magic: Tales of the Western Isles,* 1968

BIBLIOGRAPHY: Silvey, Anita. ed., *Children's Books and Their Creators,* 1995; *Something about the Author,* vol. 15, 1979; *Third Book of Junior Authors and Illustrators,* 1972

DEDE SMALL

NIELSEN, Kay

Illustrator, b. 12 March 1886, Copenhagen, Denmark; d. 1957, Place unknown

After being reared in a home of artists, N. studied art in Paris at the Academic Julien, the Academic Collarossi, and with Lucien Simon. In 1915, N. showed his twenty-five art nouveau watercolors for *East of the Sun and West of the Moon* (1914), a Norwegian FOLKLORE collection retold by Peter Christian ASBJORSEN and Jorgen MOE. This set of ILLUSTRATIONS received wide recognition and is

considered his most complex and greatest work. As a noted artist of folktales and FAIRY TALES, he also illustrated *Fairy Tales by Hans Christian* ANDERSEN (1922) and *Hansel and Gretel: Stories from the Brothers* GRIMM (1925). In addition to his periods of illustrating, N. engaged in set design for theater productions. His unique illustrations add a new dimension to traditional fairy tales and require readers to read yet another level of the story.

FURTHER WORKS: *Red Magic: A Collection of the World's Best Fairy Tales from All Countries.* (R. Wilson, editor). 1936

BIBLIOGRAPHY: *Something about the Author,* vol. 16, 1979

SHANE RAYBURN

NIMMO, Jenny

Author, b. 15 January 1942, Windsor, Berkshire, England

N.'s childhood in a rural community in Wales provided her with the background for the authentic representations in her landscaped settings. She won the Tir Na n'Og Award given by the Welsh Books Council for best book with an authentic Welsh background for *The Snow Spider* (1986), the first in a trilogy. The book also won the 1986 Smarties Book Prize Grand Prize, an award in which children participate in the selection. Many of N.'s stories combine Welsh tradition with the supernatural. Her characters grow emotionally as they draw readers into their lives. Several of N.'s works have been adapted for British television.

FURTHER WORKS: *Emilyn's Moon,* 1987. *The Chestnut Soldier,* 1989. *Ultramarine,* 1990. *Delilah and the Dogspell,* 1991. *Ronnie and the Giant Millipede,* 1995

BIBLIOGRAPHY: *Something about the Author,* vol. 106, 1999

NANCY HORTON

NIXON, Joan Lowery

Author, b. 3 February 1927, Los Angeles, California

A prolific writer for children and adolescents, N.'s career began at the surprisingly young age of two when she dictated POETRY to her mother. Growing up in Los Angeles, N. was active in reading, writing, and performing. At school she did well in English, and majored in journalism at the University of Southern California, graduating in 1947. She was discouraged from pursuing a career as a writer by prospective employers because of her gender, and so quietly became certified in elementary education and began teaching school in California.

Later, N. moved to Texas, attended the Southwest Writers Conference, and came home with the idea that she should write for children. Her own children encouraged her to write a mystery with them as characters. She published *The Mystery of Hurricane Castle* (1964), recognized for its fast pacing and strong characterization. Her writing career took off and soon she was writing more books, teaching courses on creative writing, and writing a column for the *Houston Post.*

She has published well over fifty MYSTERIES. Many have been recognized as outstanding by the Mystery Writers of America. They have awarded her the Edgar Allan Poe Award three times for *The Kidnapping of Christina Lattimore* (1979), *The Seance* (1980), and *The Other Side of Dark* (1986). Two other books, *The Mysterious Red Tape Gang* (1974) and *The Ghosts of Now* (1984), were also nominated for the award.

N. has been lauded for more than her mysteries, however. Three books in her nonfiction series (coauthored by her husband) *Volcanoes: Nature's Fireworks* (1978), *Glaciers: Nature's Frozen Rivers* (1979), and *Earthquakes: Nature's Motion* (1980) were named Outstanding Science Trade Books for Children by the National Science Teachers Association and the CHILDREN'S BOOK COUNCIL Joint Committee. She has also been awarded the Golden Spur from the Western Writers of America for *A Family Apart* (1987) the first novel in the Orphan Train Quartet, a historical-fiction series. Many of her books have received numerous state honors including those in Maryland, Indiana, Colorado, Oklahoma, California, and Utah.

N.'s SERIES BOOKS have been popular with readers; they are based on a wide range of topics. Her First Read-Alone Mysteries for young readers are mysteries based around holiday settings (*The New Year's Mystery,* 1979; *The Christmas Eve Mystery,* 1981). *Kleep: Space Detective* books combine SCIENCE FICTION and mystery (*Kidnapped on Astarr,* 1981; *Mysterious Queen of Magic,* 1981; *Mystery Dolls from Planet Urd,*

1981). The Orphan Train Quartet books are well-researched historical fiction (*Caught in the Act,* 1988; *In the Face of Danger,* 1988; *A Place to Belong,* 1989), about six siblings sent West to escape poverty and learn a useful trade or farming skills. The Hollywood Daughters trilogy brings N.'s Los Angeles to life (*Star Baby,* 1989; *Overnight Sensation,* 1990; *Encore,* 1990).

FURTHER WORKS: *The Alligator under the Bed.* 1974. *If You Say So, Claude.* 1980. *The Mystery of the Hidden Cockatoo.* 1966. *Whispers from the Dead.* 1989

BIBLIOGRAPHY: Nixon, J. L. *Something about the Author Autobiography Series.* 1990. Nixon, J. L. *Writing Mysteries for Young People.* 1977

GWYNNE ELLEN ASH

NOLAN, Dennis

Author, illustrator, b. 19 October 1945, San Francisco, California

N. has written several award-winning self-illustrated books for children. *The Castle Builder* (1987) won several AWARDS, including American Bookseller's Pick of the List and the *Christian Science Monitor*'s Top Twelve Books Award. Other award-winning self-illustrated books include *Monster Bubbles: A Counting Book* (1976), *The Joy of Chickens* (1981), and *Dinosaur Dream* (1990). In 1995 *Fairy Wings* (Lauren Mills, author) was awarded the Golden Kite Award for excellence in picture ILLUSTRATION and appeal to children.

N. has also illustrated books for other notable authors such as Jane YOLEN, Joanne RYDER, William HOOKS, and Lauren Mills. His highly realistic and detailed illustrations are often done in acrylics, but he has also successfully used other media, such as watercolors, which he used in Nancy CARLSTOM's *No Nap for Benjamin Badger* (1991).

FURTHER WORKS: Self-Illustrated: *Big Pig.* 1976. *Alphabrutes.* 1976. *Witch Bazooza.* 1979. Illustrator: *The Legend of the White Doe.* (William Hooks). 1988. *Step into the Night.* (Joanne Ryder). 1988. *Dove Isabeau.* (Jane Yolen). 1989. *Wings.* (Jane Yolen), 1991

BIBLIOGRAPHY: *Something about the Author,* vol. 92, 1997

MARY ARIAIL BROUGHTON

NOLEN, Jerdine

Author, b. 4 June 1953, Crystal Springs, Mississippi

N. was reared in Chicago along with five sisters and two brothers. She attributes her rollicking sense of HUMOR to learning to navigate peacefully among so many siblings. Her mother insisted so many children could never be bored; they amused themselves telling stories, dressing up, and putting on plays. N. says she always wrote stories and played with the sounds of words, saying them over and over, chanting them, enjoying the emotions and feelings they conjured up for her.

N.'s name first appeared in print when a Thanksgiving poem she wrote in second grade was printed in her school newspaper and that excitement has never faded for her. *Harvey Potter's Balloon Farm* (1994), a picture-book FANTASY about a farmer whose mainstay crop is glossy, brightly colored balloons, combines traditional oral STORYTELLING techniques within a whimsical matrix of the ordinary and the bizarre. It has successfully been transferred to film and is fast becoming a classic in both formats. *In My Momma's Kitchen* (1999) is a quiet narrative of intergenerational connections with the kitchen at the center of family life, activities, and memories.

AWARDS: AMERICAN LIBRARY ASSOCIATION Notable Book (1995) for *Harvey Potter's Balloon Farm.* Christopher Award (1998) for *Raising Dragons*

FURTHER WORKS: *Big Jabe,* 2000

BIBLIOGRAPHY: Publisher's press release; interview with the author

DIANE G. PERSON

NORTH, Sterling

Author, b. 4 November 1906, Edgerton, Wisconsin; d. 22 December 1974, Morristown, New Jersey

N. grew up on a farm, and until the age of seven his literary development was nurtured by his well-educated mother. After she died, he was reared by his father and his sister, a poet. He attributed his ability to write well to a rewarding childhood at a time when values concerning living with others and with nature were in place in society. These values are seen in works such as *So Dear to My Heart* (1947), the story of a boy and a lamb in Indiana at the turn of the century.

After working for the *Chicago Daily News* as reporter and literary editor, he moved with his wife and two children to New Jersey. Following a position with the *New York Post* and an editorship with Houghton Mifflin's North Star Books, for which he wrote biographies of Edison, Thoreau, TWAIN, and Washington, N. became a full-time writer. *Rascal: A Memoir of a Better Era* (1962), which received numerous AWARDS, was the autobiographical story of a raccoon he adopted when he was a young boy. His works have been translated into more than fifty languages and have provided a glimpse of American culture to readers.

AWARDS: ALA NEWBERY MEDAL Honor Book (1964) for *Rascal*

FURTHER WORKS: *Midnight and Jeremiah,* 1943; *Hurry Spring,* 1966; *The Wolfling,* 1969

BIBLIOGRAPHY: *The Third Book of Junior Authors and Illustrators,* 1978; *Something about the Author,* vol. 45, 1986

JANELLE B. MATHIS

NORTON, Andre

Author, b. 17 February 1912, Cleveland, Ohio

Born Alice Mary Norton, N., author of SCIENCE FICTION and FANTASY, changed her name legally in 1934 to suit the male-dominated science-fiction genre. Beginning her career as a children's librarian at the Cleveland Public Library, N. began writing juvenile historical novels and ADVENTURES before turning to science fiction in the 1950s and to fantasy by the mid-1960s. Because of associations with juvenile literature her work was critically ignored although her writing appeals to all ages. N. is the author of over 150 books, many of which are categorized in SERIES editions with recurring villains and protagonists. N.'s career as a librarian ceased when she was diagnosed with agoraphobia. Her condition turned her to writing and editing. From 1950 onward, she developed a formula for her work that concerned the passage or initiation of a youthful protagonist, usually an outsider, coming to grips with his or her own identity while battling for justice.

N.'s early books were based on medieval legends. In a story rich with medieval flavor, *Huon of the Horn* (1951) retells the heroic legend of the duke of Bordeaux, a figure from the era of Charlemagne. She returned to this scene in 1965 with *Steel Magic,* a time warp fantasy in which modern children are transported back in time to search for Huon's talismans that give him the power to overcome evil. The children need to find Arthur's sword, Huon's horn, and Merlin's ring.

A series of galactic Star novels spans many years' publication. *Star Man's Son, 2250 A.D.* was the first title published in the series in 1952; it was followed by such titles as *Star Rangers* (1953), *Star Born* (1957), and *Star Gate* (1958). A more recent title, *Redline the Stars,* features Rael Cofort, a female main character, and was published in 1993. N.'s works have been translated into eighteen languages. *The Beast Master* was made into a film by MGM/UA in 1982.

FURTHER WORKS: *Star Man's Son,* 1952; *Galactic Derelict,* 1959; *Judgment on Janus,* 1963; *Fur Magic,* 1968; *Red Hart Magic,* 1976

BIBLIOGRAPHY: MEIGS, C., A. T. Eaton, E. NESBIT, and R. H. Viguers. *A Critical History of Children's Literature,* 1969; Townsend, John Rose, *A Sense of Story: Essays on Contemporary Writers for Children,* 1973

CRAIG LIEBERMAN

NORTON, Mary

Author, b. 10 December 1903, London, England; d. 29 August 1992, Hartland, Devonshire, England

N. grew up in Leighton Buzzard, England, loving the theater. She and her siblings would act out plays in their backyard, often scenes from their favorite books. Remotely related to the poet Edmund Spenser, N. attended convent schools for seven years before joining the Old Vic Theatre Company in London. She lived for a while in Portugal until the outbreak of World War II, when she and her family returned to England. While there, she worked for the War Office. After the war, she worked for a period of time in New York as an agent for the British Purchasing Committee and began writing.

Her first book, *The Magic Bed-Knob; or, How to Become a Witch in Ten Easy Lessons* (1943) was followed by *Bonfires and Broomsticks* (1947). Exploring a spinster with magical powers

and her ADVENTURES with three young children, the two books were published together in the United States as *Bed-Knobs and Broomsticks* (1957) and would later become a DISNEY live-action and animated film (1971). Although children's FANTASY was not yet a popular genre in the United States, but N. was on her way to becoming one of its leaders.

In 1952, N. published *The Borrowers* to much praise and accolade. For her story of miniature people who live behind the grandfather clock and survive on what they can steal or "borrow" from the house's human inhabitants, N. received the CARNEGIE MEDAL from the British Library Association in 1953, and the Lewis CARROLL Shelf Award for its reprint in 1960. *The Borrowers* was also named one of the most distinguished books of the year by the AMERICAN LIBRARY ASSOCIATION in 1953.

Because of their immense popularity, the Borrowers were brought back in several additional books, each with its own particular set of adventures. In *The Borrowers Afield* (1955) we find the Clock family, who have fled their home to avoid discovery, living in a shoe. *The Borrowers Afield* was named a Notable Book by the ALA. Later, *The Borrowers Afloat* (1959) follow adventures on water, and *The Borrowers Aloft* (1961), in a hot air balloon. All four novels were published as *The Borrowers Omnibus* (1966) and *The Complete Adventures of the Borrowers* (1967). However, in 1971 *Poor Stainless: A New Story about the Borrowers* emerged, adding a fifth to the series. In 1998, the Borrowers was turned into a live-action film by Polygram.

FURTHER WORKS: *Are All the Giants Dead?,* 1975

BIBLIOGRAPHY: Kirkpatrick, D. L., ed., *Twentieth-Century Children's Writers,* 1978; *Third Book of Junior Authors,* 1972

GWYNNE ELLEN ASH

NOURSE, Alan E. (a.k.a. Dr. X)

Author, b. 11 August 1928, Des Moines, Iowa

N. has been blessed to have two prolific careers as both a doctor and a writer. He began his medical career in 1955, and has also worked as a freelance writer. N.'s hobbies include fishing, hunting, and hiking. The majority of his books for a YOUNG ADULT audience focus on medicine and science, including N.'s nonfiction SERIES of books with titles such as *So You Want to Be a Doctor* (1957), *So You Want to Be a Chemist* (1964) and others. N. became the contributing editor of the "Family Doctor" column in *Good Housekeeping* magazine in 1976.

He based his adult book, *The Elk Hunt* (1986) on his own recovery from a severe heart attack.

The Elk Hunt is written in terms a lay person can understand and discusses what coronary artery disease is, as well as how to recover from it.

FURTHER WORKS: *Teen Guide to AIDS Prevention*, 1990; *Lumps, Bumps, and Rashes*, 1990

BIBLIOGRAPHY: *Something about the Author*, vol. 48, 1987

DENISE P. BEASLEY

OAKLEY, Graham

Author, illustrator, b. 27 August 1929, Shrewsbury, Shropshire, England

O. is well known for his heavily illustrated popular Church Mice series. These PICTURE BOOKS, first published in 1972, involve the adventures of two mice named Arthur and Humphrey, and the church cat named Sampson who takes a vow never to eat the mice. O. believes that the ILLUSTRATIONS are the most important part of a book. His work is widely praised for its rich detail. *The Church Mice Adrift* was a *New York Times* Best Illustrated Children's Book of the Year in 1977.

FURTHER WORKS: *The Church Mouse*, 1972; *Graham Oakley's Magical Changes*, 1980; *The Church Mice in Action*, 1983; *The Foxbury Force*, 1994

BIBLIOGRAPHY: *Something about the Author*, vol. 84, 1996

JODI PILGRIM

O'BRIEN, Robert C. (Conly, Robert Leslie)

Author, editor, b. ca. 1918; d. 5 March, 1973, Washington, D.C.

First an editor for *National Geographic* magazine and later a journalist for publications such as *Newsweek*, O. is best known for his NEWBERY MEDAL book *Mrs. Frisby and the Rats of NIMH* (1971), which also won the Lewis CARROLL Shelf Award in 1972. O. did not begin publishing his fantasies until he was in his forties; he recalls that the story of Mrs. Frisby came from questions he posed about who would take over the planet if the human race was extinguished. Another futuristic book, *Z for Zachariah,* received the Jane Addams Children's Book Award in 1976 and the Mystery Writers of America award for best juvenile novel in 1977.

AWARDS: AMERICAN LIBRARY ASSOCIATION Newbery Medal (1972) *Mrs. Frisby and the Rats of NIMH*

FURTHER WORKS: *The Secret of NIMH*, 1988; *The Silver Crown; A Report from Group 17*

BIBLIOGRAPHY: *Something about the Author*, vol. 23, 1981

SANDRA IMDIEKE

O'CONNOR, Jane

Author, b. 30 December 1947, New York City

In addition to a career in publishing, O. has written books including stories for beginning readers: the Here Come the Brownies series geared toward young Girl Scouts, and novels for YOUNG ADULTS. O.'s husband and her son, Robert, participated in the writing of several books including *The Magic Top Mystery* (1984) and *Super Cluck!* (1991).

FURTHER WORKS: *Yours 'til Niagara Falls, Abby,* 1979. *Magic in the Movies: The Story of Special Effects,* 1981. *Just Good Friends,* 1983. *Lulu and the Witch Baby,* 1986. *The Ghost in Tent Nineteen,* 1989. *Nina, Nina, Ballerina,* 1993. *Lauren and the New Baby,* 1994. *Comeback!: Four True Stories,* 1992

BIBLIOGRAPHY: *Something about the Author*, vol. 103, 1999

JODI PILGRIM

O'DELL, Scott

Author, b. 23 May 1898, Los Angeles, California; d. 5 October 1989, Mount Kisco, New York

O. is an award-winning author of more than two dozen books for children and YOUNG ADULTS. When he began his career as a writer of adult books in 1934, O. wrote primarily of his home, Southern California. O.'s step into children's literature was by accident. He was angered seeing the hunting of animals near his home. In his anger he decided to write about a girl, Karana, who learns to revere all living things. When *Island of the Blue Dolphins* (1960) was completed, O.'s publisher suggested that it was better suited for children. It was published in 1960 and won the ALA NEWBERY MEDAL in 1961.

After his success, O. continued writing award-winning books for children, many of which are historical fiction. Some of his books are set among Indian tribes, Spanish Conquistadors, and colonial settlers. In each setting O. provides the reader with a sense of time, place, and temperament, giving a focus to the novel. O. meticulously researched the setting providing accurate details that add credibility to his well-crafted stories. As a celebration of historical fiction for children, O. helped establish the Annual Scott O'Dell Award for Historical Fiction administered by the Bulletin of the Center for Children's Books. It carries a $5,000 prize designed to encourage authors to write historical fiction for children. The work must be published by a United States publisher and set in the New World.

In many of O.'s novels the wilderness comes alive as he creates images familiar to him during his childhood. Growing up on the Pacific coast, the sound of the ocean made a deep imprint on O. In several of his books: *Island of the Blue Dolphins* (1960); *The Black Pearl* (1968); *Streams to the River, River to the Sea* (1986); and *Zia* (1976), descriptions of the sounds of the ocean create vivid images for the reader. O. sets up visual images that are focused and sharp, easily transporting readers to his world. He uses short direct sentences compelling readers to participate in the reading. Readers can add their own imagery to O.'s scene using his sentences as a starting point. This style creates readers who are actively engaged with reading. His style sets the scene for readers to take the journey with the protagonist, filling in details as they read.

O.'s stories, although often set in the past, are not limited to history lessons. O. is didactic in his belief that readers should take something with them after reading. His novels deal with life lessons that are as poignant today as they were in the past. In his writing for children O. has not limited his lessons to historical fiction. His contemporary novels are rich in the same themes as his historical fiction. The themes that O. deals with most often are prejudice, greed, feminism, courage and isolation.

O.'s characters often struggle against an exterior force driven by hatred. In *Zia*, sequel to *Island of the Blue Dolphins,* the characters deal with life at a mission where their Indian culture is devalued for Western ways. In *Sing Down Moon,* 1970 AMERICAN LIBRARY ASSOCIATION Newbery Medal Honor book, Bright Morning and the Navajos are forced from their homeland to Fort Sumner. In *Streams to the River, River to the Sea* Sacagawea deals with prejudice against her tribe, considered inferior to Europeans. O.'s trilogy about the Spanish Conquistadors, *The Captive* (1979), *The Feathered Serpent* (1980), and *The Amethyst Ring* (1981), allows Escobar to confront his prejudice against the Mayans. In *Alexandra* (1984), a winner of the Florida State Historical Association Award in 1985, the protagonist deals with prejudice against women. As O. narrates conflict between people, readers get a taste of the world's injustice. From this they take away the idea that all people should be treated equally.

Greed is a powerful force in many of O.'s books. He portrays characters placed in crisis situations due to greed for riches or good fortune. *Island of the Blue Dolphins* presents Karana and her family's forced emigration because of seal hunters. In *The Black Pearl*, 1968 Newbery Medal Honor Book winner and ALA Notable Book, Ramon has to decide what to do when he finds a precious black pearl. In *The King's Fifth* (1966), Esteban is on a search for gold that motivates him to commit unspeakable acts against Native tribes. Greed is a force of evil and through his characters, O. portrays how greed can negatively affect lives.

Most of O.'s protagonists are strong females. O. stated in an interview that he used female characters to show that women and men have the same potential. In *Alexandra,* the protagonist takes on the difficult job of a sponge diver, a position traditionally reserved for men. Bright Dawn in *Black Star Bright Dawn* (1988) competes in the grueling Iditarod dog-sled race. As a woman she struggles to survive and complete the race. Karana, Sarah Bishop, and Kathleen are three other female characters O. writes about. Each character is a strong-willed individual who overcomes great odds. O. accomplishes his goal of creating strong female characters that girls can emulate.

O.'s characters also exhibit a great deal of courage. Bright Star and Alexandra have to overcome great odds to deal with the pressures of struggling to survive while living in male-dominated worlds. In O.'s historical fiction NATIVE AMERICAN tribes and colonial settlers must have courage to overcome the obstacles of isolation, greed and/or prejudice.

Many of O.'s characters are isolated. In *Island of the Blue Dolphins* Karana is isolated and learns to get along on her own. Bright Star is alone on the Alaskan frontier, and Alexandra has no one to turn to when she learns drugs are being smuggled on her ship. Bright Morning, although surrounded by family, is isolated in her hope to escape. Readers, who are at an age where they often feel alone, identify readily with these characters. They learn through their struggles that all people need to be loved, and in fact that is what they were searching for all along.

AWARDS: ALA Newbery Medal, Lewis CARROLL Shelf Award, and Southern California Council on Literature for Children and Young People (1961), Hans Christian ANDERSEN Award of Merit (1962) William Allen White Award, German Juvenile International Award (1963), OMAR Award 1985, Rupert Hughes Award (1960) all for *Island of the Blue Dolphins.* ALA Newbery Honor Book (1967), German Juvenile International Award (1968) for *The King's Fifth.* ALA Newbery Medal Honor Book (1968) for *The Black Pearl* and (1971) for *Sing Down Moon.* Hans Christian Andersen Medal (1972) for his body of work. Freedoms Foundation Award (1973) for *Sing Down Moon. New York Times* outstanding book (1974) for *Child of Fire.* University of Southern Mississippi Medallion DE GRUMMOND REFERENCE COLLECTION (1976). Regina Medal from the Catholic Library Association (1978) for his body of work. Parent's Choice award for Literature from the Parents Choice foundation, 1984, for *Alexandra,* and 1986, for *Streams to the River, River to the Sea.* Scott O'Dell Award for Historical Fiction and Child Study Association of America's Children's Books of the Year (1987) for *Streams to the River, River to the Sea*

FURTHER WORKS: *The Dark Canoe.* 1968. *Journey to Jericho.* 1969. *The Treasure of Topo-el-Bampo.* 1972. *The Cruise of Artic Star.* 1973. *Child of Fire.* 1974. *The Hawk That Dare Not Hunt by Day.* 1975. *The 290.* 1976. *Carlota.* 1977. *Kathleen, Please Come Home.* 1978. *Sarah Bishop.* 1980. *The Spanish Smile.* 1982. *The Castle in the Sea.* 1983. *The Road to Damietta.* 1985. *The Serpent Never Sleeps.* 1987. *My Name Is Not Angelica.* 1989

BIBLIOGRAPHY: *Contemporary Authors, New Revision Series.* vol. 30. *Contemporary Literary Criticism.* vol. 30, 1984. *Children's Literature Review,* vol. 1, 1976. *Dictionary of Literary Biography,* vol. 52, 1986; HOPKINS, Lee Bennett, *Pauses: Autobiographical Reflections of 101 Creators of Children's Books,* 1995; MEIGS, et al., *A Critical History of Children's Literature,* 1969. M. H. Lovelace, "Scott O." the *Horn Book* magazine, Aug. 1961, pp. 316–19; P. Roop, "Profile: Scott O.," *Language Arts,* vol. 61, no. 7, November 1984, pp. 750–52. Townsend, John Rowe, *Written for Children: An Outline of English Language Children's Literature,* 1965; *A Sense of Story: Essays on Contemporary Writers for Children,* 1973

NANCE S. WILSON

OLALEYE, Isaac
Author, b. 17 May 1941, Erin, Nigeria

Born in the small village of Erin in the Nigerian rain forest, O. was the fifth of seven children. From early childhood he knew he wanted to travel and see the world as much as he enjoyed life in his village and listening to communal STORYTELLING events that passed down the history of his people. He traveled to England to attend college and graduated from Thurrock Technical College in 1970 before moving to the United States in 1971. O. held many part-time jobs, continuously writing and revising stories based on the tales he heard as a boy back in Nigeria. He was determined to share the folktales and memories of life in the rain forest with Western readers.

O.'s first book, *Bitter Bananas* (1994), set in a rain-forest village, tells about Yusuf's attempt to outwit a band of baboons. They are stealing his palm sap, which Yusuf sells at the local market to help his family. Ed YOUNG's brightly colored cut-paper photographs help convey the sense of another culture. The book is based on stories O.'s father told him when he was a boy. O. uses POETRY in *The Distant Talking Drum* (1995), which is filled with HUMOR and affection, to paint dramatic word pictures of life as he remembers it back in his Nigerian village.

FURTHER WORKS: *Land of the Big Snake: An African Rain Forest Adventure*, 1998; *In the Rainfield*, 1999; *In the Rainfield: Who Is the Greatest?*, 2000; *Bikes for Rent*, 2001

DIANE G. PERSON

O'NEAL, Elizabeth (Zibby)
Author, b. 17 March 1934, Omaha, Nebraska

O., author of YOUNG ADULT novels, attended Stanford University and earned a B.A. from the University of Michigan. She embarked upon her writing career after the birth of her children when she began to write stories for them. Her first book, *War Work* (1971), a light, suspense tale about three children trying to do their part for the war effort during World War II, introduced her to the public as a competent writer. *War Work* won the Friends of American Writers Award for 1972. O. also wrote two PICTURE BOOKS for children, *The Improbable Adventures of Marvelous O'Hara Soapstone* (1972) and *Turtle and Snail* (1979).

O. claims that, as her own children grew into adolescence, so did her protagonists. *The Language of Goldfish* (1980), one of three contemporary novels for young adults, earned her critical acclaim as a novelist. *Goldfish* won AMERICAN LIBRARY ASSOCIATION "Notable Book" citations and "Best Book for Young Adults" citations. The story, which deals with the sensitive subject of a child's emotional breakdown, was described in the *Horn Book* (1980) as "carefully crafted with delicacy of control." Another reviewer wrote, "The story is believable and heartwarming. It offers reasonable hope, calm moments of joy, and the possibility of a future, without deviating from a serious appraisal of the problems today's young people face as they try to fit themselves into worlds they don't understand."

The Language of Goldfish was followed by two more award-winning young adult novels, *A Formal Feeling* (1982) and *In Summer Light* (1985), further establishing O. as an author of depth, clarity, and sensitivity. Her writing has been described as intellectual, literary, and cultured, especially in *A Formal Feeling* and *In Summer Light*. O. believes that adolescence is a special time of change in one's life when a person is in the process of becoming what he or she will be.

FURTHER WORKS: *Maude and Walter*, 1985; *Grandma Moses: Painter of Rural America*, 1986; *A Long Way to Go*, 1990

BIBLIOGRAPHY: Bloom, S. P., and C. M. Mercier, *Zibby O.*, 1991. *Children's Literature Review*. vol. 13, 1987. MacPike, L. Review of *The Language of Goldfish* in *Best Sellers*. vol. 40, 1980. McDonnell, C. Review of *The Language of Goldfish* in the *Horn Book* magazine. 1980. Small, R. C. Review of *A Formal Feeling* in *The ALAN Review*. 1983. *Something about the Author*, vol. 92, 1995

MARY ARIAIL BROUGHTON

O'NEILL, Mary L.
Author, poet, b. 16 February 1908, New York City; d. 2 January 1990, Yuma, Arizona

O. grew up in a large Victorian house in Berea, Ohio, where she wrote and directed plays for her brothers and sisters. She attended St. Joseph Academy in Cleveland, Cleveland College of the Western Reserve University, and the University of Michigan. O. worked as a copywriter for ten years, then became vice president of her own advertising agency. In 1970 she volunteered with the Peace Corps, teaching journalism and writing in Ghana. O. was interested in travel, opera, theater, and music.

O. is best known for her POETRY. Each of her poetry collections is thematic, often developing a concept such as color (*Hailstones and Halibut Bones*), community helpers (*People I'd Like to Keep*, 1964), or sound (*What Is That Sound?!*, 1966). O.'s nonfiction, some published posthumously, informs readers on topics ranging from dinosaurs to salmon to air pollution.

O. received an honorable mention, Foley anthology of best short stories. Her collection of color poems, *Hailstones and Halibut Bones*, was among the *New York Times Book Review*'s 100 Best Books for Children in 1961.

FURTHER WORKS: Poetry collections: *Fingers are Always Bringing Me News.* 1969. *Winds.* 1970. *The Sound of Day: The Sound of Night.* 1999. *What Is Orange?* 1993. Nonfiction: *Saints: Adventures of Courage.* 1963. *The White Palace.* 1966. *Take a Number.* 1968. *Dinosaur Mysteries.* 1989. *A Family of Dinosaurs.* 1989. *Life after the Dinosaurs.* 1989. *Water Squeeze.* 1989. *Where Are All the Dinosaurs?* 1989. *Air Scare.* 1991. *Nature in Danger.* 1991. *Power Failure.* 1991. Fiction: *Ali.* 1968. *Anna Amelia's Apteryx.* 1966. *Poor Merlo.* 1967. *The Boy.* 1970. *Big Red Hen.* 1971.

BIBLIOGRAPHY: Marquardt, D. A., and M. E. Ward. 1971. *Authors of Books for Young People.* 2nd ed.

JANE WEST

OPIE, Iona and Peter

Iona: Author, b. 13 October 1923, Colchester, England; Peter: Author, b. 25 November 1918, Cairo, Egypt; d. 5 February 1982, West Liss, Hampshire, England

Together the O.s' have shed considerable light on the methods of invention, contextual meanings, and muses that underlie the transmission of children's proverbial lore. While their copious and scholarly research was undertaken with British children, much of the body of nursery rhymes, informal games and related folk culture is shared by children in other English–speaking countries.

In childhood, Iona developed a love of books that went beyond simply reading them to collecting them. As a youth, Peter stepped into writing early. At the age of twenty, he published his autobiography, *I Want to Be a Success* (1939). The two met during World War II, brought together first through correspondence over Peter's book. Marrying in 1943, they began a lifelong exploration of nursery tales and children's games while awaiting the birth of their first child. Their approach to learning about the topics of concern to them showed the O.s to be diligent researchers, availing themselves of scholarly collections as well as performing broad and deep observations of children at play.

In 1960, they were jointly awarded the Coot Lake Research Medal and, in 1962, each was awarded an honorary master of arts degree by Oxford University. Cities in Europe and the United States awarded them recognition for their research and writing. *The Oxford Book of Children's Verse* (1973) was named one of the Child

Study Association's Children's Books of the Year (1973) as was *The Classic FAIRY TALES* (1974). Iona also has been awarded an honorary doctorate by Southampton University (1987). *Tail Feathers from MOTHER GOOSE: The Opie Rhyme Book* (1988), edited by Iona., was an AMERICAN LIBRARY ASSOCIATION Notable Book. She was further honored by ALA as the May Hill Arbuthnot Lecturer in 1991.

Whereas Peter wrote three books independent of his wife and Iona has continued to write and edit books since her husband's death, the great body of work attributed to either was undertaken together. Iona did much of the field research that went into *The Lore and Language of Schoolchildren* (1959); *Children's Games in Street and Playground: Chasing, Catching, Seeking, Hunting, Racing, Dueling, Exerting, Daring, Guessing, Acting, Pretending* (1969); and *The Singing Game* (1985)—listening to and interviewing tens of thousands of children at free play. Peter imbued the texts that were based in part on these field researches with the writer's voice that became emblematic of the O.s' work: clear, concise, replete with vivid but judiciously chosen detail, and never ponderous or overly analytic. Notes, which abound through the texts or are gathered at their ends, read like conversational comments, rather than authoritative citations.

In order to compose these texts about children's play, as well as in their work to compile nursery rhymes and fairy tales, the O.'s undertook considerable literary research. Their collaboration included the amassing of a vast home library but also took them on separate jaunts to the major academic libraries of Great Britain. In writing such texts as *I Saw Esau* (1947, 1992), *The Oxford Nursery Rhyme Book* (1955), and *The Classic Fairy Tales* (1974), they were concerned that their conversion of essentially oral literature to book form could damage the very artifacts they hoped to preserve for modern popular conveyance. However, their sensitivity to variation and restraint from pronouncement on canonical or noncanonical status for competing versions of similar ditties helped assuage their fears and those of their early critics.

Reviewers of *The Oxford Book of Children's Verse* voiced concern that such a historical approach to collecting rhymes could be intended for use only by adults. However, the O.s were not interested in limiting themselves to offering other scholars reference material but rather worked to organize and present their findings for parents and even children to use and read. *The Oxford Nursery Rhyme Book* is organized developmentally, with great attention paid to providing appropriate amounts of ILLUSTRATION, varying with audience age, to accompany its verses. Indicative of the care and precision the O.s invested in their presentation of the copious research they undertook is the concern with which they selected illustrators. Contemporary children are given new opportunities to respond to the riches mined by their efforts, as Iona enlisted Maurice SENDAK to refurbish *I Saw Esau* with his droll full-color illustrations (1992). She chose Rosemary WELLS to illustrate *My Very First Mother Goose* (1996) and its companion volume, *Here Comes Mother Goose* (1999).

In addition to writing about children's sayings, stories, and games, the O.s also collected children's toys. After Peter's death, Iona arranged with the University of Oxford to acquire the Opie Collection of Children's Literature for its Bodleian Library.

FURTHER WORKS: *Christmas Party Games,* 1957; *A Nursery Companion,* 1980; *The People in the Playground,* (Iona. ed.), 1993

BIBLIOGRAPHY: Cott, Jonathan, *Pipers at the Gates of Dawn: The Wisdom of Children's Literature,* 1983; *St. James Guide to Children's Writers,* 1999; *Children and Their Books: A Celebration of the Work of Iona and Peter O.* (G. AVERY, editor), 1990

FRANCISCA GOLDSMITH

ORBIS PICTUS AWARD

The Orbis Pictus Award for outstanding nonfiction for children was established in 1989 by the NATIONAL COUNCIL OF TEACHERS OF ENGLISH. The NCTE Orbis for Outstanding Nonfiction for Children commemorates the work of John Amos COMENIUS'S, *Orbis Pictus: The World Illustrated,* published in English in 1658. Historically, this is considered the first book actually planned and published for children, its goal was to teach children about their world. The goal of the Orbis is to encourage the production of high-quality nonfiction and to promote its use in the classroom.

The NCTE Committee on the Orbis Pictus Award for Outstanding Nonfiction for Children established the criteria of excellence and meets annually to select the winner and any Honor Books. The first award was presented in 1990 to *The Great Little Madison* by Jean FRITZ. This award recognizes excellence in writing INFORMATIONAL BOOKS for children. Other winners include Robert BURLEIGH, Jim MURPHY, Jerry Stanley, Diane Swanson, Russell FREEDMAN, Jean FRITZ, and Mike Wimmer.

1990: *The Great Little Madison,* Jean Fritz; 1991: *Franklin Delano Roosevelt,* Russell Freedman; 1992: *Flight: The Journey of Charles Lindberg,* Robert Burleigh, illus. Mike Wimmer; 1993: *Children of the Dustbowl: The True Story of the School at Weedpatch Camp,* Jerry Stanley; 1994: *Across America on an Emigrant Train,* Jim Murphy; 1995: *Safari beneath the Sea: The Wonder of the North Pacific Coast,* Diane Swanson; 1996: *The Great Fire,* Jim Murphy; 1997: *Leonardo Da Vinci,* Diane STANLEY; 1998: *An Extraordinary Life: The Story of a Monarch Butterfly,* Laurence PRINGLE; 1999: *Shipwreck at the Bottom of the World: The Extraordinary True Story of Schackleton and the Endurance,* Jennifer Armstrong; 2000: *Through My Eyes,* Ruby Bridges

DIANE G. PERSON

ORGEL, Doris
Author, translator, b. 15 February 1929, Vienna, Austria

Coming to writing from publishing, O. has been successful as both the author of original novels and the translator and adaptor of FOLKLORE. O. has won several AWARDS for her 1978 novel, *The Devil in Vienna,* a tale that mirrors her own experience as a Jewish teenager in Austria during World War II. She has also received awards for her TRANSLATIONS of German FAIRY TALES (*Dwarf Long-nose,* 1960) as well as her retellings and adaptations of such tales (*Little John,* 1972). Well known for the popular *Next Door Neighbors* (1979, previously published as *Next Door to Xanadu* 1969), and *Bartholomew, We Love You* (1973), O. also reviews children's books for the *New York Times.*

FURTHER WORKS: *Cindy's Snowdrops,* 1966; *Merry, Merry FIBruary,* 1977; *On the Sand Dune,*

1968; *Sarah's Room,* 1963; *The Tale of Gockel, Hinkel, and Gackelich* (By Clemens Brentano, retold, 1961)

GWYNNE ASH

ORMEROD, Jan

Author, illustrator, b. 23 September 1946, Bunbury, Western Australia

As an illustrator and author of PICTURE BOOKS for young children and the adults who read to them, O. captures the emotions and interactions of the lives of babies, toddlers, and their parents. Her paintings and books with few or no words succinctly express the delight of interaction between loved ones in settings of warm homes. O. was born in Australia and attended Western Australian Institute of Technology and Claremont Teachers College, where she received a teacher's certificate. She worked as an art teacher and lecturer, predominantly at the college level, in the sixties and seventies with the Western Australian Education Department, Bunbury; Mt. Lawley College of Advanced Education, Perth, Western Australia; and the Western Australian Institute of Technology, Perth. O. continued to teach art but became intrigued with children's books when her husband, who was a librarian, brought home books for their baby. She discovered picture books with her daughter Sophie and credits her involvement in the field with those times of sharing. Her focus on her infant daughter and her experimentation with her own ideas were fulfilling.

Once she and her husband felt that her work had promise, they made the decision to move from their somewhat isolated home in Australia to the more publishing-oriented London. There, O.'s talents and insights into the minds of young and old catapulted her career in the realm of children's literature. O. is a master observer of small children and their world. Her eye for detail and knowledge of the young's imagination, along with her talents as an artist make her one of the most prolific and successful producers of books for families. O.'s works convey a gentleness that is evident in many of her watercolors. Her works include picture books authored by others as well as those she authored. The self-authored books tell stories with little or no words. Her HUMOR engages adults while educating toddlers. The productive use of concepts such as numbers, adjec-

tives, and prepositions support the ILLUSTRATIONS, resulting in entertaining and informing with an appeal that is intergenerational.

Two SERIES that are self-illustrated are the Jan Ormerod Baby Book series and the Jan Ormerod New Baby Book series. Such titles, giving evidence of the topics within, for babies, toddlers, and their caregivers include *Sleeping* (1985), *Reading* (1985), *Dad's Back* (1985), and *Messy Baby* (1985). Examples of titles of interest to families with new arrivals or who are expecting new babies enjoy these titles: *Bend and Stretch* (1987), in which the expectant mom and her firstborn toddler do floor exercises together; and *This Little Nose* (1987) in which the expectant mom and her young child explore the noses of all his stuffed toys as he copes with his own uncomfortable nose, ill with a cold. Other titles in this series include *Making Friends* (1987) and *Mom's Home* (1987). As an illustrator, O. has worked with other authors including Margaret MAHY, Jan MARK, Pat Thompson, Karin Lorentzen, Sarah Hayes, J. M. BARRIE, Vivian French, Helen Elizabeth Buckley, Mary HOFFMAN, Charles KINGSLEY, and Penelope LIVELY.

O.'s intention of designing for adults as well as children has paid off with her ability to create the right balance and atmosphere for family reading. It is the product of this balance and enjoyment by all generations that motivates O. to continue writing. She has been published in numerous countries, and in many languages as diverse as Chinese and Hebrew. O. lives in Cambridge, England, and is considered to be a contemporary leader in board books.

AWARDS: KATE GREENAWAY MEDAL commendation (1981), MOTHER GOOSE Award, Australian Picture Book of the Year Award, Australian Children's Book Council (1982) for *Sunshine* (1981). AMERICAN LIBRARY ASSOCIATION Notable Book (1981) for *Sunshine,* (1982) for *Moonlight,* (1985) for *Dad's Back, Messy Baby, Sleeping,* and *Reading,* (1986) for *The Story of Chicken Licken,* (1987) for *Bend and Stretch, Making Friends, Mom's Home,* and *This Little Nose.* Kate Greenaway Medal commendation (1986) for *Happy Christmas, Gemma*

FURTHER WORKS: Self-illustrated: *Be Brave, Billy.* 1983. *Young Joe.* 1985. *Just Like Me.* 1986. *Kitten Day.* 1989. *The Frog Prince.* (Retold with David Lloyd). 1990. *When We Went to the Zoo.*

1991. *Midnight Pillow Fight.* 1993. *Ms. Mac-Donald Has a Class.* 1996. *Who's Whose?* 1998. *Peek-A-Boo.* 1998. *Rock-A-Baby.* 1998. As illustrator only: *Hairs in the Palm of the Hand.* 1981. *The Chewing Gum Rescue and Other Stories.* 1982. *Rhymes around the Day.* 1983. *Lanky Longlegs.* 1983. *Peter Pan.* 1987. *Eat up, Gemma.* 1988. *Ballerina Two.* 1991. *Sunflakes: Poems for Children.* 1992. *The Water Babies.* 1998. *A Twist in the Tail.* 1998. *One, Two, Three, Jump.* 1999. *Where Did Josie Go?* 1999

BIBLIOGRAPHY: Carter, Margaret. "Cover Artist-Jan Ormerod." *Books for Your Children.* 1983. Silvey, Anita. ed. 1995. *Children's Books and Their Creators.* Sutherland, Zena. *"Sunshine," Bulletin of the Center for Children's Books.* 1982

NANCY HORTON

ORTIZ, Simon
Author, poet, b. 21 May 1941, Albuquerque, New Mexico

While growing up in Pueblo of Acoma, near Albuquerque, New Mexico, O., an Acoma NATIVE AMERICAN, began writing POETRY and short stories in both Acoma and English. Since then, he has become a respected and widely read Native American poet and author.

O.'s writing acknowledges his connection to the land and the STORYTELLING culture in which he grew up. His effort to preserve Native American traditions and instill tribal pride in young readers predominates in O.'s writing. His thoughts on growing up with a dual Indian and American heritage are included in Joseph BRUCHAC's *Survival This Way: Interviews with American Indian Poets* (1990). In *The People Shall Continue* (Sharol Graves, illus, 1988), O. uses vivid poetic imagery and traditional oral storytelling rhythm to retell Native American history from ancient to modern times. Starting with creation myths, continuing with Indian habitation on the continent and eventual suffering at the hands of European settlers, O. presents history from a Native American point of view. He has also collaborated with Rudolfo ANAYA on *A Ceremony of Brotherhood, 1680–1980* (1980), a volume that celebrates ethnic heritage.

FURTHER WORKS: *A Good Journey,* 1977; *Howbah Indians,* 1978; *A Poem Is a Journey,* 1981; *Blue and Red,* 1982; *The Importance of Childhood,* 1982; *The People Shall Continue,* 1988; *Woven Stone,* 1991; *Speaking for the Generations,* 1998

BIBLIOGRAPHY: Bruchac, Joseph, *Survival This Way,* 1990; *Contemporary Literary Criticism,* vol. 45, 1987; *Dictionary of Literary Biography,* vol. 120, 1992

AINE KYNE-NORRIS

ORWELL, George (Eric Arthur Blair)
Author, essayist, critic, journalist, b. 25 June 1903, Bengal, India; d. 21 January 1950, London, England

O. was born to upper middle-class parents and attended Eton. After service with the Indian Imperial Police in Burma, he returned to Europe to attempt to earn his living by writing. He held a series of unpleasant working-class positions that later became material in his writings. O. was essentially a political writer who wrote either realistically or imaginatively about his own times. He was a man of intense feelings and fiery nature who despised totalitarianism and served with the loyalist forces in the Spanish Civil War in the late thirties. O. distrusted intellectuals although he became a literary critic. He hated cruelty in life and literature. Of particular interest to YOUNG ADULT readers were the books in which he created an imaginary environment of great credibility such as *1984* (1949), where he invented a totalitarian society of the future, and *Animal Farm* (1946), where he satirized a fascist state. In *Animal Farm,* there is a devastating attack on the pigheaded gluttonous rulers in which he exposed a range of human experiences from love to hate, from comedy to tragedy. Although the themes are profound, all was done with sensitivity and much HUMOR. O. died at forty-seven, leaving behind a substantial body of work and a growing reputation. His writings suggest that modern man is ill-equipped to deal with the demands of history.

FURTHER WORKS: *Down and Out in Paris,* 1933, 1969; *Burmese Days,* 1934, 1974; *A Clergyman's Daughter,* 1935; *Homage to Catalonia,* 1938

JUDY LIPSITT

OSBORNE, Mary Pope
Author, b. 20 May 1949, Fort Sill, Oklahoma

Because her family was in the military, O. lived on numerous United States army posts and in

Salzburg, Austria, as she was growing up. Her father retired when she was fifteen, and the family settled in North Carolina. In 1971, she earned a B.A. from the University of North Carolina at Chapel Hill and traveled extensively in Europe and Asia. When she returned to the United States, she worked in California, Washington, D.C., and New York City. She married actor Will Osborne on May 16, 1976, and the couple took off the next day on a theater tour. It was while traveling with her new husband that she began writing.

Her first novel, *Run, Run, as Fast as You Can,* was published in 1979. Reflecting her own experiences, the novel features a girl whose family retires from the military and settles in the South. The novel features an eleven-year-old girl who is faced with the impending death of her younger brother as well as rejection by her peers. Like O.'s first novel, her subsequent books have been acclaimed for their well-developed characters while focusing on the difficulties and conflicts of adolescence. For example, one reviewer commenting on the characters in O.'s *Last One Home* (1986), noted that the author's "finely crafted characterization enhances this affecting story about the difficulties of coping."

In the early 1990s, O. began a SERIES of books for younger children called the Magic Tree House featuring the adventures of Jack and Annie. The books in this collection, although fiction, contain a lot of factual information, making them useful and enjoyable supplements for thematic studies. The books contain large type and beautiful illustrations by Sal Murdocca. O. has also done several thematic collections of folktales.

FURTHER WORKS: *Love Always, Blue.* 1983. *Best Wishes, Joe Brady.* 1984. *Mo to the Rescue.* 1985. *Christopher Columbus: Admiral of the Sea.* 1987. *Pandora's Box.* 1987. *American Tall Tales.* 1991. *Spider Kane and the Mystery at Jumbo Nightcrawler's* (Victoria CHESS, illus). 1994. *One World, Many Religions: The Ways We Worship.* 1996. *Favorite Medieval Tales.* 1997. Selections from the Magic Tree House series: *Dinosaurs before Dark.* 1992. *The Knight at Dawn: A First Stepping Stone Book.* 1992. *Pirates Past Noon.* 1994. *Night of the Ninjas.* 1995. *Afternoon on the Amazon.* 1995. *Dolphins at Daybreak.* 1997. *Polar Bears Past Bedtime.* 1998. *Hour of the Olympics.* 1998. *Tonight on the Titanic.* 1999

BIBLIOGRAPHY: *Contemporary Authors—New Revision Series.* vol 29. Graves, P. In *School Library Journal,* May 1986. *Something about the Author,* vols. 41, 1985, and 55, 1989

MARY ARIAIL BROUGHTON

OXENBURY, Helen
Author, illustrator. b. 2 June 1938, Suffolk, England

O., author and illustrator of PICTURE BOOKS for the very young, is well known for her insights and humorous depictions of very young children and the adults who participate in their early experiences. Her work has been characterized as highly imaginative, capturing the expressions and explorations of babies and young children. Her illustrations are deceptively simple yet very detailed and are at their best when depicting quirks of human nature. Appealing to both adults and young children, O.'s sophisticated drawings are uncluttered, childlike but not at all childish. They are full of humorous details that are enjoyed by children and adults who read to them. O. is acknowledged for her singular contributions in creating the board book format for toddlers. Her titles are widely recognized and regularly sought after among board book collections.

Having attended Ipswich School of Art and Central School of Arts and Crafts in London, O.'s desire was to design sets for theater. While in college she met her future husband, John BURNINGHAM whose interest in ILLUSTRATION and graphic design led him to become a children's book illustrator. After marrying in 1964 and having a family, O. decided that book illustration might be something that she could do while at home. She illustrated Edward LEAR's *The Quangle Wangle Hat* (1969) and Lewis CARROLL's *The Hunting of the Snark* (1970), combining the appeal that HUMOR and FANTASY had for her.

Numbers of Things (1968), a fun-filled counting book with familiar, yet detailed and humorous pictures, was O.'s first self-authored book. A variety of animals and people in colorful detailed illustrations help a child learn to count from one to ten and then by tens to fifty. This established her particular style as a children's author and illustrator. Afterward, she wrote *Helen O.'s ABC of Things* (1971), which combines many unrelated items beginning with the same letter on one page. "Here, the work of unification is beautifully done in the pictures; the most incongruous associations are made in a perfectly matter-of-fact way, setting the mind off in pursuit of the stories that must lie behind them" according to a reviewer in the *Times Literary Supplement*. Some of O.'s best-known books, respectively, are in the SERIES that describes the young child at slightly different developmental stages. The round-faced baby who appears in these books appeals to adults as well as children. O.'s awareness of the actions and interests of young children is obvious in *Dressing, Family, Friends, Playing,* and *Working* (all 1981). In each of these books, seven nouns make up the text; the illustrations, line drawings washed in color, are full of subtle humor. Another series of books shows the child a bit older and experiencing such activities as *Beach Day; Good Night, Good Morning; Monkey, See, Monkey Do; Mother's Helper; Shopping Trip* (all 1982). Both of these series represent literature illustrated for the very young, literature created in board book format especially for this age group. Both her subjects and format for books were influenced greatly by her experiences with her own children. Another series shows the child even older and just as humorously, although not juvenile in tone, conveying such experiences as *The Car Trip, The Checkup,* and *The First Day of School* (all 1983). Three other books—*Grandma and Grandpa, Our Dog,* and *The Important Visitor* (all 1984), further extend a growing child's activities within the text.

O. again demonstrates her insights into the personalities of young children in the delightful Tom and Pippo series of stories. In 1988 and 1989, various adventures of a young boy and his toy monkey reflect the relationship a child has with a toy and the role this relationship plays in his everyday experiences. Here, too, with simple but realistic, expressive drawings, O. places much of the responsibility for telling the story within the illustrations. The expressions on both Tom and Pippo's faces catch the attention of adults and children as they embark on such adventures as *Tom and Pippo Go for a Walk* (1988), *Tom and Pippo Make a Mess* (1988), *Tom and Pippo Read a Story* (1988), *Pippo Gets Lost* (1989), *Tom and Pippo and the Bicycle* (1993), and *Tom and Pippo and the Dog* (1989). Both the joys and fears of daily life are reflected in the relationship between the boy and his monkey.

O. has also established herself as a versatile illustrator of various types of children's literature and has collaborated with authors such as Michael J. Rosen, *Going on a Bear Hunt* (1989), Eugene Trivizas, *The Three Little Wolves and the Big Bad Pig* (1993), and Martin WADDELL, *Farmer Duck* (1995), for which her illustrations received both a British Book Award for Illustration and a Smarties Award for Illustration. Her work is praised for its detail, vigor, and sly, lively humor. Additionally, she has retold through story and art various FAIRY TALES and nursery rhymes. O.'s goal as a children's book illustrator is to avoid creating "mediocre" children's books. An earlier comment by O., "I believe children to be very canny people who immediately sense if adults talk, write, or illustrate down to them, hence the unpopularity of self-conscious, child-like drawings that appear in some children's books," continues to be evident in her art, which speaks to the complexity of young readers' understandings.

AWARDS: KATE GREENAWAY MEDAL, British Library Association (1969) for Illustration for *The Dragon of an Ordinary Family* (Margaret MAHY, author) and *The Quangle Wangle Hat* (Edward Lear). Runner-up for the Kurt Maschler Award (1985) for *The Helen O. Nursery Story Book*

FURTHER WORKS: Author and illustrator: *I Can, I Hear, I See, I Touch*. 1986. *All Fall Down, Say Goodnight, Tickle, Tickle, Clap Hands, The Queen and Rosie Randall*. 1979. *The Helen O. Nursery Story Book*. 1985; Illustrator: Alexei Tolstoy. *The Great Big Enormous Turnip*. 1968. *The Helen O. Nursery Rhyme Book*. 1987.

BIBLIOGRAPHY: Field, Michele. "PW Interviews: John Burningham and Helen O." *Publishers Weekly,* July 24, 1987, pp. 168–69; "Good Enough to Keep," *Times Literary Supplement,* December 3, 1971, pp. 1514–15; *Children's Literature Review,* vol. 22, 1991; *Something about the Author,* vol. 68, 1992; O., Helen. "Drawing for Children," *The Junior Bookshelf,* vol. 34, no. 4, 1970, pp. 199–201

JANELLE B. MATHIS

P

PARISH, Peggy (Margaret Cecile)

Author, b. 14 July 1927, Manning, South Carolina; d. 19 November 1988, Manning, South Carolina

P. grew up in rural South Carolina. Educated at the University of South Carolina, she taught school for many years, including fifteen years in New York City's Dalton Elementary School. Her first published book was *My Golden Book of Manners,* illustrated by the noted artist Richard SCARRY (1962). She wrote a SERIES of books about Little Indian, beginning with *Good Hunting, Little Indian* (1962), but these are now discredited by many readers for their stereotyping of NATIVE AMERICANS.

P.'s reputation rests with *Amelia Bedelia* (1963) and its eleven sequels, the stories of an eccentric housekeeper who interprets language literally. Her naive misunderstandings result in outrageous antics—she adds dust to the furniture when she is told to dust it, clothes the turkey when she is told to dress it, sketches pictures of the drapes when she is told to draw them. Her job is spared by sympathetic employers and her lemon-meringue pie. The Amelia Bedelia books are written for beginning readers and bring great satisfaction to children in their early effort to learn the language; they have been selected as frequent children's choice winners by youngsters across the United States. The series is so very popular that new titles about Amelia Bedelia continue to be written by her nephew, Herman Parish.

P. created other bizarre, but lovable characters, such as the fiercely independent Granny Gruntry, in *Granny and the Indians* (1969). Granny is an absent-minded pioneer who, with cheerful aplomb, meets peril on her own terms and always wins.

A prolific writer, P. launched a series for older readers in 1968 with *Key to the Treasure* in which a sister and two brothers solve mysteries by puzzling out the clues. She also produced many nonfiction books on such diverse subjects as making costumes, creating games from old bedsheets, making holiday decorations. Her nonfiction work, *Dinosaur Time* (1974), received considerable praise including a 1974 School Library Journal Best Book of the Year citation.

FURTHER WORKS: *Thank You, Amelia Bedelia,* 1964; *Amelia Bedelia and the Surprise Shower,* 1966; *Granny and the Desperadoes,* 1970; *Haunted House,* 1971; *Amelia Bedelia Goes Camping,* 1985

BIBLIOGRAPHY: *Children's Writers; Contemporary Authors, New Revised Series,* vol. 38; *Major Authors and Illustrators* 1993; *Something about the Author,* vol. 73, 1993

DAVID L. RUSSELL

PARK, Barbara

Author, b. 21 April 1947, Mount Holly, New Jersey

Noted for her humorous writing for middle-school readers, P. has written several books beginning with *Skinnybones* (1982) featuring Alex "Skinnybones" Frankovitch, a small built middle-schooler. Her series featuring Junie B. Jones revolves around the world of the kindergartener. She is credited with honestly portraying children's lives through HUMOR.

FURTHER WORKS: *Almost Starring Skinnybones* (1988). *The Kid in the Red Jacket.* (1987). *Don't Make Me Smile* (1981). *Junie B. Jones and the Stupid Smelly Bus* (1992). *Psssst! It's Me . . . the Bogeyman* (1998). *Rosie Swanson: Fourth-grade Geek for President* (1991). *My Mother Got Married (and Other Disasters)* (1989). *Mick Harte Was Here* (1995)

BIBLIOGRAPHY: *Something about the Author,* vol. 78, 1994

SANDRA IMDIEKE

PARKER, Nancy Winslow
Author, illustrator, b. 18, October 1930, Maplewood, New Jersey

P.'s books for children often contain animals, which are her favorite subjects for characters. She self-illustrates her work, researching the accuracy of her drawings and facts. Her books sometimes mirror actual events in her life. For example, *Poofy Loves Company* (1980) was based on an incident where her dog ambushed a visiting youngster, messing up her clothes and stealing her cookie.

FURTHER WORKS: *Warm as Woof, Cool as Cotton: The Story of Natural Fibers,* 1975; *The Goat in the Rug,* 1976; *Willy Bear,* 1976; *My Mom Travels a Lot,* 1981; *The President's Car,* 1981; *The Christmas Camel,* 1983; *The United Nations from A to Z,* 1985

BIBLIOGRAPHY: *Something about the Author,* vol. 69, 1992

JODI PILGRIM

PARKS, Van Dyke
Lyricist, singer, folklorist, b. 3 January 1943, Hattiesburg, Mississippi

P.'s career in songwriting and production preceded his work in children's literature. He is best known for his work with Brian Wilson of The Beach Boys, The Mojo Men, and other popular musicians, as well as a few idiosyncratic solo recordings—including *Jump!* (1984). With an intense interest in the Brer Rabbit FOLKLORE, P.'s own retelling of certain tales led to a publisher's interest in creating a book of these retellings. As a result, *Jump!* (1986) was published containing

five of the best-known Brer Rabbit tales. Barry MOSER aptly illustrated these adaptations from the original Joel Chandler HARRIS Uncle Remus tales. *Jump Again!: More Adventures of Brer Rabbit* (1987) followed as well as a third group of five tales, *Jump on Over!: The Adventures of Brer Rabbit and His Family* (1990). Each is told with precisely enough dialect and lilting rhythm to preserve its authenticity, and capture the attention of readers and listeners.

AWARDS: AMERICAN LIBRARY ASSOCIATION Notable Children's Book Award (1987) for *Jump!*

JANELLE B. MATHIS

PARNALL, Peter
Illustrator, author, b. 23 May 1936, Syracuse, New York

P.'s early love for animals led him to enroll at Cornell University with the plan of becoming a veterinarian. He quickly realized a preference for drawing wildlife over science and left school to wander through the Southwest region of the U.S., developing his drawing style. Returning to New York, he enrolled in an advertising course at Pratt Institute, but left it to pursue a career as an art director and to do freelance design work. In 1967, he left advertising to become a full-time illustrator and author of children's books.

P.'s artistic approach to rendering animal and other outdoor life gives readers a clear and engaging view of the natural world and humanity's place in it. His images are composed of tiny lines and sweeping washes that capture realistic detail. In 1971, P. began to write as well as illustrate children's books. *A Dog's Book of Birds* (1977) and *The Woodpile* (1990) show children how engaging the simplest aspects of the natural world can be. P.'s concern for ecology is communicated quietly but concretely through his writing as well as through his pictures.

AWARDS: ALA Caldecott Medal Honor Book (1976) for *The Desert Is Theirs* (Byrd Baylor, author, 1977) for *Hawk, I'm Your Brother* (Byrd Baylor, author) and (1979) for *The Way to Start a Day* (Byrd Baylor, author). ALA NEWBERY MEDAL Honor Book (1972) for *Annie and the Old One* (Miska MILES, author). Christopher Medal (1972) for *Annie and the Old One* (Miska Miles, author). *Boston Globe-Horn Book* Award (1976) for *The Desert Is Theirs* (Byrd Baylor, author).

The New York Times Best Illustrated Book List (1967) for *A Dog's Book of Bugs* (E. Griffen, author) and *Knee-Deep in Thunder* (S. Moon, author), (1968) for *Malachi Mudge* (C. Maiden, author). Art Books for Children Award (1973) for *Annie and the Old One* (Miska MILES, author, 1976) for *Everybody Needs a Rock* (Byrd Baylor, author, 1974) and (1977) for *The Desert Is Theirs* (Byrd Baylor, author, 1975).

FURTHER WORKS: *The Mountain.* 1971. *The Great Fish.* 1973. *The Daywatchers.* 1975. *The Marsh Cat.* 1991. Illustrated by P.: *Kavik the Wolf Dog.* (Walt MOREY). 1968. *The Moon of the Wild Pigs.* (Jean Craighead GEORGE). 1968. *Underground Hideaway.* (Murray Goodwin). 1968. *A Beastly Circus.* (Peggy PARISH, 1969. *Doctor Rabbit.* (Jan WAHL). 1970. *A Little Book of Little Beasts.* (Mary Ann HOBERMAN). 1973. *Roadrunner.* (N. John). 1980. *Desert Voices.* (Byrd Baylor). 1981

BIBLIOGRAPHY: *Something about the Author, Autobiography Series,* vol. 11, 1991

FRANCISCA GOLDSMITH

PASCAL, Francine
Author, b. 13 May, 1938, New York City

P. was born in New York City. Her family moved from Manhattan to Jamaica, Queens, when she was five years old. Interested from an early age in writing poetry, P. was strongly influenced by her older brother Michael, who would later become a successful playwright *(Mack and Mabel).* P. did not receive a great deal of support for her writing from her parents but was encouraged by teachers and classmates with whom she shared her work. Shortly after graduating from New York University in 1958, P. met John Pascal, a journalist. He became her mentor and her writing partner. After developing her own writing first with magazines like *True Confessions, Modern Screen, Ladies' Home Journal* and *Cosmpolitan,* the Pascals began writing the soap opera *The Young Marrieds.* They also collaborated on the nonfiction work *The Strange Case of Patty Hearst* (1974) and with her brother Michael on the musical *George M!* P.'s first YOUNG ADULT novel *Hangin' out with CiCi* (1977) was quickly accepted for publication. The story, set in the Jamaica, Queens, neighborhood where P. grew up, is the story of a selfish young girl who believes that she time-travels back to 1944 where she unwittingly becomes friends with her own mother.

Hangin' out with Cici was praised for its HUMOR and REALISM, and was adapted as *My Mother Was Never a Kid* and aired as an ABC *Afterschool Special.* P.'s second novel for young adults, *My First Date and Other Disasters* (1979) was named a Best Book for Young Adults by the AMERICAN LIBRARY ASSOCIATION. P.'s next novel, *The Hand-Me-Down Kid* (1980), looked at the issue of sibling rivalry and was also adapted as an ABC *Afterschool Special.* P.'s popularity grew with her creation of the Sweet Valley High series featuring Jessica and Elizabeth, a set of beautiful and popular identical twins. There are more than one hundred titles in Sweet Valley High alone in addition to the series spin-offs Sweet Valley Twins and Sweet Valley Kids. With so many series in progress, it is impossible for P. to do all the writing herself. But she oversees a number of authors and maintains artistic control of each novel.

FURTHER WORKS: *Love and Betrayal and Hold the Mayo!* 1985; *If Wishes Were Horses,* 1994

BIBLIOGRAPHY: *Something about the Author.* vol. 51, 1988, and vol. 80, 1995; *Fifth Book of Junior Authors and Illustrators,* 1983

DEDE SMALL

PATENT, Dorothy Hinshaw
Author, b. 30 April 1940, Rochester, New York

P., author of INFORMATIONAL BOOKS for children and YOUNG ADULTS, received a B.A. from Stanford University, and an M.A. and Ph.D. from the University of California, Berkeley. From an early age, P. knew that she loved animals, but did not begin writing about them until she had children of her own. Her *Weasels, Otters, Skunks, and Their Families* (1973) was the first one of more than ninety informational books for children, particularly books about animals. This book was quickly followed by *Microscopic Animals and Plants* (1974), *Frogs, Toads, Salamanders, and How They Reproduce* (1975), *How Insects Communicate* (1975), and *Fish and How They Reproduce* (1976), as well as books about plants, evolution, reptiles, worms, butterflies and moths, and raccoons. In the early 1980s, P. began a collaboration with photographer William Muñoz, with whom she has written more than two dozen books. For example, in *The Sheep Book* (1985), P.'s descriptions of the world of lambs, ewes, and rams

90. SHELDON OBERMAN

91. SCOTT O'DELL

92. KATHERINE PATERSON

94. PHILIPPA PEARCE

93. GARY PAULSEN

are beautifully enhanced by Muñoz's striking black-and-white photographs. The team traveled to Alaska, New Mexico, Texas, and other states to gather material for books about cows, farm animals, eagles, horses, wolves, and other subjects.

P.'s work has received AWARDS from several organizations, including the Golden Kite Award for nonfiction, SOCIETY OF CHILDREN'S BOOK WRITERS, for *Evolution Goes on Every Day* (1977) and for *The Lives of Spiders* (1980). The National Science Teachers Association has named more than forty of her books as outstanding science trade books. And the AMERICAN LIBRARY ASSOCIATION cited *The Quest for Artificial Intelligence* (1986) as a Best Book for Young Adults. Many of P.'s books, especially those done with Muñoz, emphasize efforts to rescue endangered species and restore them to their natural habitats. P. often includes names and addresses of organizations children can contact to participate in conservation efforts.

FURTHER WORKS: Text by P. with photographs by Munoz: *A Picture Book of Cows*. 1982. *A Picture Book of Ponies*. 1983. *Farm Animals*. 1984. *Quarter Horses*. 1985. *Draft Horses*. 1986. *Buffalo: The American Bison Today*. 1986. *The Way of the Grizzly*. 1987. *The Whooping Crane: A Comeback Story*. 1988. *Nutrition: What's in the Food We Eat*. 1992. *Fire: Friend or Foe*. 1998. *Homesteading: Settling America's Heartland*. 1998. Other books by P.: *All about Whales*. 1987. *Dolphins and Porpoises*. 1987. *Christmas Trees*. 1987. *Looking at Ants*. 1989. *Seals, Sea Lions, and Walruses*. 1990. *How Smart Are Animals?* 1990. *Children Save the Rain Forest*. 1996

REFERENCES: *Children's Literature Review*, vol. 19, 1990; *Major Authors and Illustrators for Children and Young Adults: A Selection of Sketches from Something about the Author*, vol. 2, 1987; Ward, M. E., D. A. Marquardt, N. Dolan, and D. Eaton, eds., *Authors of Books for Young People* 3rd ed., 1990

MARY ARIAIL BROUGHTON

PATERSON, Katherine

Author, b. 31 October 1932, Qing Jiang, Jiangsu, China

Born in China to missionary parents from the American South, P.'s family fled to North Carolina at the outbreak of World War II. Her family moved eighteen times during her school years;

she attended thirteen different schools before she graduated. Repeatedly, she was the newcomer, the outsider, the one who did not fit in with the crowd. Her Southern classmates considered her strange because she spoke with a British accent, wore hand-me-down clothes salvaged from the missionary barrel, and acted differently from them. Like her classmate Eugene, she was an outcast and since no one would talk to either of them, Eugene and Katherine talked to each other. They called themselves "the weirdos." As an adult, P. says that no one bothered to tell her as a child that she would use those bitter experiences in her writing when she grew up. P. returned to missionary life after receiving her B.A. (1954) from King College and her master's degree in English Bible (1957) from the Presbyterian School of Christian Education. She worked as a teacher in the Far East and served as a missionary in Japan from 1957 to 1961. In Japan she studied at Naganuma School of the Japanese Language in Kobe. She returned to the United States to complete a fellowship and M.A. at Union Theological Seminary in 1962.

P.'s strong faith, religious belief, and spiritual values permeate her life and her work. Although not blatant or preachy, worthy themes of acceptance, abiding love, and courage are evident in her characters' lives and in her books. P. earned a reputation as an outstanding writer in her earliest books. Her first two novels, set in medieval Japan, *The Sign of the Chrysanthemum* (1973) and *Of Nightingales That Weep* (1974), were inspired by her work in Japan and her interest in the country's culture and history. *The Master Puppeteer* (1975) set in an eighteenth-century Japanese puppet theater, won a National Book Award. P. developed a strong personal voice in three contemporary books set in the United States: *Bridge to Terabithia* (1977 ALA NEWBERY MEDAL), *The Great Gilly Hopkins* (1978, National Book Award), *Jacob Have I Loved* (1980, Newbery Medal winner). P. has an ear for dialogue. She catches the authentic flavor of dialogue in historical periods in *Lyddie* (1991) and *Jip: His Story* (1996), regional dialects in *Come Sing, Jimmy, Jo* (1985) and *Flip-Flop Girl* (1994), and the multilayered sound of voices from Arthurian legends, a modern young boy, and a sassy girl learning English as a second language in *Park's Quest* (1988).

P. creates unique, memorable characters: Gilly Hopkins, Mame Trotter, Leslie, Jess, Louise, Lyddie, and Jip are ones readers do not forget. As P. writes, the characters become real to her; taking on a life of their own. P. is as protective of them as she is of her own children. She expresses fear that people may not be kind to them once she releases their book. When she wrote *Jip: His Story,* she said that characters from previous books "spoke" to her to help her resolve dilemmas in Jip's life.

The dominant idea in much of P.'s work is the need for self-acceptance amid strength in adversity, a situation she faced often as she was growing up. Her characters do not necessarily get what they think they want in life; instead they learn to want what they get. That strong belief pervades her work. P.'s books do not have "and they lived happily ever after" endings; they are far more RE-ALISTIC—often heart-wrenchingly so. In *Bridge to Terabithia,* Jess and Leslie create a magical, make-believe kingdom inspired by reading the Narnia books. Leslie dies in a tragic accident; Jess is left to deal with his loss and grief. The story grew from a similar tragedy in P.'s real world when her son's dear friend was struck by lightning and killed. *Jacob Have I Loved,* told from Louise's perspective, shows the resentment Louise feels because her family obviously favors her talented twin sister Caroline. Paterson weaves in a biblical story by having the grandmother quote, "Jacob have I loved but Esau have I hated," the story of the firstborn who is tricked into giving up his birthright to Jacob, the younger twin. The rivalry between twins on an isolated Chesapeake Bay island affects every turn of the plot.

Some readers, especially young ones still caught developmentally in a happiness-binding stage, express dissatisfaction with the endings of P.'s novels. In *The Great Gilly Hopkins,* Gilly leaves Mame Trotter, a foster mother she eventually learns to love, to live with a grandmother she does not know. In *Bridge to Terabithia,* Jess builds a bridge for his younger sister Maybeth to enter the magical kingdom of Terabithia he and Leslie created. Louise reflects on her life as an adult *In Jacob Have I Loved* while she fights as a midwife to save the life of a smaller twin during childbirth. Questioned about the endings of her stories, P. says the endings are inevitable, rooted

in this earth and ending the only way the stories can possibly end.

P. uses the settings she knows well. Her first three novels—*The Master Puppeteer* (1975, 1981), *The Sign of the Chrysanthemum* (1973, 1988), *Of Nightingales That Weep,* set in eighteenth-century and twelfth-century Japan—have a strong sense of place based on living in Japan and a studious pursuit of its history. Her next three novels—*Bridge* (1977), *Gilly* (1978), and *Jacob* (1980)—are set in the Chesapeake Bay area where she lived while she was writing them. Two novels, *Flip-Flop Girl* (1994) and *Come Sing, Jimmy Jo* (1985), are set in Appalachia, a region in which she lived as she was growing up. Since she moved to New England, her novels—*Lyddie* (1991), *Jip: His Story* (1996), and *Preacher's Boy* (1999)—are set in New England. P. uses the sense of place as an integral part of her stories; the place affects plot; her stories could only have happened in the settings she chooses.

AWARDS: ALA NEWBERY MEDAL (1978) for *Bridge to Terabithia,* (1981) for *Jacob Have I Loved.* National Book Award (1975) for *The Master Puppeteer,* (1978) for *The Great Gilly Hopkins.* Scott O'DELL Award (1996) for *Jip: His Story.* 1998 Hans Christian ANDERSEN Award

FURTHER WORKS: *Angels and Other Strangers: Family Christmas Stories,* 1979; *Rebels of the Heavenly Kingdom,* 1983; *The Tale of the Mandarin Ducks,* 1990; *The Smallest Cow in the World,* 1991; *The King's Equal,* 1992; *Who Am I?,* 1992; *A Midnight Clear: Twelve Family Stories for the Christmas Season,* 1995

BIBLIOGRAPHY: Paterson, Katherine. *The Secret Life of Katherine Clements Womeldorf,* 1986; In *Once upon a Time,* (pp. 18–19); Paterson, Katherine, *Gates of Excellence: On Reading and Writing Books for Children,* 1981. Paterson, Katherine, *The Spying Heart: More Thoughts on Reading and Writing Books for Children,* 1989

BERNICE E. CULLINAN

PATON WALSH, Jill
Author, b. 29 April 1939, London, England

Born Jill Bliss, the eldest of four children, she was encouraged, loved, and actively stimulated to enjoy learning. Her mother's stepfather moved the family to Cornwall as a means of protecting them during World War II. "For five crucial years of my childhood—from the year I was three to the year I was eight—the war dominated and shaped everything around me . . . and then for many years, until well into my teens, postwar hardships remained." P. says, "I left St. Ives when I was just eight, and I didn't go back there till I was thirty-six. A part of me is still rooted in that rocky shore, and it appears again and again in what I write."

"The children I talk to nowadays are very interested in the Second World War. They think it must have been a time of excitement and danger, whereas it was actually dreadfully boring. I remember, in short, a time of discomfort and gloom, and, above all, upheaval."

P. attended a Catholic girls' school in North Finchley and found school easy. She left school to go to Oxford University where she made friends, enjoyed herself, and sat in on lectures by C. S. LEWIS, and J. R. R. TOLKIEN. "The example [those great men] set by being both great and serious scholars, and writers of FANTASY and books for children was not lost on me."

After completing her degree she obtained a teaching position but disliked teaching. "I got married in my second year as a teacher, and eighteen months later was expecting a child." As a housewife "I was bored frantic. I went nearly crazy, locked up alone with a howling baby all day and all night . . . I needed something intellectual, cheap and quiet . . . [so] I began to write a book. It was a children's book. It never occurred to me to write another kind. Until the moment I began to write I did not know that I was a writer."

An editor with Macmillan, Kevin CROSSLEY-HOLLAND offered an option on her second book (the first one "was, unfortunately, a dreadfully bad book"). *Hengest's Tale* (1966), a story of vengeance and treachery pieced together from an episode in *Beowulf,* recounts loyalty and honor juxtaposed against deceit, cruelty, and fear.

Fireweed (1969) was an AMERICAN LIBRARY ASSOCIATION Notable Book, received the Book World Festival Award and was on the *Horn Book* Honor List. Named for a plant that grows from the scars of ruin and pain, the fireweed plant symbolizes two teenagers and their struggle to survive during the London Blitz of World War II. Familiar experiences that survive even in horror are related in this historical fiction story about class, survival, patience, HUMOR, and bravery with a bittersweet ending.

The Emperor's Winding Sheet (1974) received the Whitbread Prize. A novel with a historical background, the siege and fall of Constantinople in 1453 is depicted as seen through the eyes of an English boy, Piers Barber, a young shipwrecked seaman from Bristol. Piers finds his way into the Emperor's garden, climbs a tree and falls in a faint at the Emperor's feet. A prophecy is given the Emperor Constantine that as long as one person is at the Emperor's side who was there during the prophecy, the City of Constantinople will not perish. Piers is chosen to be that person and his name is changed to Vrethiki, meaning lucky find. Vrethiki observes intrigue, fear, loyalty, morbid details of invasion and battle and finally the fall of the City and the death of Constantine. A tale rich in the history of the Byzantine Empire and its demise in 1453, it won a Whitbread Book of the Year Award in 1974.

A Chance Child (1978) an ALA Notable Book, is a time fantasy of sorts. Creep, a severely neglected starving child is freed from his closet prison by a wrecking ball that knocks a hole in the wall. He slips back in time to Victorian England during the Industrial Revolution while his step brother and sister are searching for him in the current century. The gruesome details of child labor during the nineteenth century and the long hours to earn food are accurate but depressing. It is a tale of neglect, abuse, sibling devotion, courage and kindness that keeps echoing in the reader's mind long after the book is finished.

Gaffer Samson's Luck (1954), a tale about acceptance, friendship, bullies, fear, honor, responsibility and courage, was awarded the Smarties Prize Grand Prix. James struggles to fit into a new town and is accepted by the neighbor next door. Confronted by a bully and gang at school, he agrees to a dare to gain use of a boat to retrieve a good luck charm for the neighbor, Gaffer Samson, in a well-paced, intriguing read.

Matthew and the Sea Singer (1992) begins "Once there was a little girl named Birdy who paid a shilling for a living boy." His name is Matthew and he sings "as a bird sings, a song sound without words, a song shape without tunes and the sound wove in and out of the wind and waves, like a streamlet of water falling in a steep little valley." One day Matthew is missing and Birdy frets. Designated an ALA Notable Book and awarded the Parenting Reading Magic Award, this is a short chapter book of unique imagination.

When Grandma Came, 1992, is a PICTURE BOOK. Grandma comes to stay and although she has traveled extensively and witnessed marvelous places and things of interest, nothing compares to the miracle of her granddaughter. A gentle affirmation of love. *Thomas and the Tinners,* another book for young readers, won a Smarties Book Prize in 1995. P. says, "A writer is what I shall be as long as there is a daydream in my head, and I have strength to sit up and type."

AWARDS: *Boston Globe–Horn Book* Award (1976) for *Unlearning*

FURTHER WORKS: *Toolmaker,* 1973; *Unlearning,* 1976; *Children of the Fox,* 1978; *A Parcel of Patterns,* 1983; *Babylon,* 1982

BIBLIOGRAPHY: Gillespie, J., C. J. Naden, eds. *Best Books for Children: Preschool through Grade 6.* 5th ed. 1994. Silvey, Anita, ed. *Children's Books and Their Creators.* 1995. Riley, C. ed. *Children's Literature Research.* 1976. *Fiction, FOLKLORE, Fantasy and POETRY for Children, 1876–1985.* 1956. *Something about the Author.* vol. 4, 1973, and vol. 72, 1993

IRVYN. G. GILBERTSON

PAULSEN, Gary

Author, b. 17 May 1939, Minneapolis, Minnesota

P.'s popularity with YOUNG ADULT readers grows directly from his ability to provide a seemingly inexhaustible stream of ADVENTURE STORIES that he can create with authority. His prolific career as a writer, spanning more than three decades, has its roots in his youthful discovery of the riches he found at the public library. Although his childhood was marred by a disrupted family life, painful shyness, and a lack of popularity among both teachers and peers at school, P. has been able to provide contemporary youth with books that inspire readers to admire his customarily determined, brave, and often lonely heroes. P.'s corpus includes novels, stories, magazine articles and several autobiographical works.

P. earned his way through two years of Bimidji College, the first by working as a trapper for the State of Minnesota. This kind of solitary occupation finds its way into many of his books, as do his experiences camping, tracking, sailing, and working with sled dogs. After serving in the military and taking extension courses, P. became a technical writer. From there, he was inspired to enter a more creative arena of publishing: his first foray beyond technical writing was an editorial job he gained through submitting a fictitious resume. By 1977, P. had published a variety of novels, including his first children's book, *Mr. Tucket* (1968), as well as nonfiction adult and juvenile books. He put aside his writing career that year, after being sued for libel upon the publication of his young adult novel *Winterkill* (1977). P. won the suit but lost, for a time, his taste for publishing. Instead, he sought new challenges, including training for and participating in the Iditarod, the 1,200-mile Alaskan dogsled race. This experience inspired him to take up the challenge of writing once again.

Dancing Carl (1983) was named an AMERICAN LIBRARY ASSOCIATION Best Young Adult Book that year, as was *Tracker* (1984) the following year. *Dogsong* (1985) was a NEWBERY MEDAL Honor Book and earned the Child Study Association of America's Children's Books of the Year Award (both in 1986). *Hatchet* (1987) and *The Winter Room* (1991) were each named Newbery Medal Honor Books (1988 and 1990, respectively). *The Boy Who Owned the School* (1990) won the Parents' Choice Award. *Woodsong* (1990) won the 1991 Western Writers of America Spur Award. In 1991, P. also won the Award from the Adolescent Literature Award from the NATIONAL COUNCIL OF TEACHERS OF ENGLISH.

P.'s novels generally are brief, plot driven, and feature characters who must rely on their own wit and perseverance to see them through physical and emotional challenges. In addition to finding themselves in solitary situations, they often are in tune with nature and work to be at one with it rather than fight against it. P. sometimes presents one or another particular theme in multiple novels or stories, changing the viewpoint or altering the realities of the characters so that readers can more fully explore the issue at hand. *Hatchet, Brian's Winter* (1996) and *Brian's Return* (1999) tell three versions of one SURVIVAL STORY. After a plane crash in the far northern wilderness, only teenaged Brian survives. In the earliest novel, he is rescued during the summer, while in the second, his rescue does not come until he has passed a harrowing winter alone. In the third, the transformation he undergoes leaves Brian at a different point in his understanding of his experiences than did the previous versions. *Sisters/Hermanas* (1993) is a bilingual novel in which the separate stories of two teenaged girls unfold to a denouement in which they dramatically meet. *Nightjohn* (1993) recounts the grim realities faced by AFRICAN AMERICAN slaves who would dare to learn to read. *Sarny* (1997) continues the story of one such literate slave after emancipation and the close of the Civil War.

P.'s juvenile nonfiction includes a series of lighthearted SPORTS books, such as *Dribbling, Shooting, and Scoring—Sometimes* (1976), *Riding, Roping, and Bulldogging—Almost* (1977), and *Going Very Fast in a Circle—If You Don't Run out of Gas* (1979). His fiction for younger readers includes novels about ANIMALS, lonely children, and workaday life. P.'s poetic language lends delicacy to what, in less artful hands, could be maudlin, as when he combines a tale about a dying child with verification of Santa Claus's existence, in *A Christmas Sonata* (1992). The Culpepper Adventure series, comprising humorous tales such as *The Case of the Dirty Bird* (1992), *Dunc Gets Tweaked* (1992), and *Dunc and the Greased Sticks of Doom* (1994) forego message for rapid-fire wit. He has written PICTURE BOOKS as well, including *The Tortilla Factory* (1995) and *Worksong* (1997), in which a variety of occupations—several of which P. has himself pursued—are described in rhyme.

P.'s autobiographical work is sometimes lightly fictionalized, as in *Harris and Me: A Summer Remembered* (1993). Here he tells of one season in the life of an eleven-year-old boy whose experiences are much like those of his own dislocated boyhood. *Woodsong* (1990) is a factual account of his own adult experiences in the wilderness, including the time he spent preparing for and participating in the Iditarod. In *My Life in Dog Years* (1998), P. gives readers, from middle school through adult, an account of his youth and adulthood, with each phase organized around the dog with whom he shared the ups and downs of an era.

P. continues to enjoy critical success, both as a novelist for youth and a nonfiction writer for adults. He plans to continue to write especially for young adults, perceiving the audience of adolescent readers to be those who most welcome and best understand his writing.

FURTHER WORKS: *The Night the White Deer Died,* 1978; *Popcorn Days and Buttermilk Nights,* 1983; *Sentries,* 1986; *The Cookcamp,* 1991; *Monument,* 1991; *The Car,* 1994; *The Tent: A Tale in One Sitting,* 1995; *The Transall Saga,* 1998; *Alida's Song,* 1999

BIBLIOGRAPHY: *Contemporary Authors New Revision Series,* vol. 54, 1997; *Something about the Author,* vol. 79, 1995

FRANCISCA GOLDSMITH

PEARCE, Philippa

Author, b. 23 January 1920, Great Shelford, England

Known for her PICTURE BOOKS for children and her fiction designed for YOUNG ADULT readers, P. has produced a wide assortment of works ranging from light stories of ADVENTURE and FANTASY to darker images of secrecy, loss of innocence, and fear of the unknown. An imaginative and talented storyteller, P. perceives literature as a means to enter a fictional world to understand and appreciate our own better.

Born Ann Philippa Pearce, P. was educated at the Pearce Girls' School in Cambridge and then attended Girton College, Cambridge. From 1945 to 1958, she worked as a scriptwriter and producer for the School Broadcasting Department of the BBC. After a brief period at the Clarendon Press in Oxford, P. became a children's editor at the publishing house of André Deutsch in London and simultaneously began reviewing children's books for the *Guardian* and the *Times Literary Supplement.* After her husband's death in 1965, P. remained in London until moving back to Great Shelford with her daughter in 1973.

Her first published work, *Minnow on the Say,* illustrated by Edward ARDIZZONE, appeared in 1954 under her full name, as did *Tom's Midnight Garden* (1958). Named a runner-up for the prestigious CARNEGIE MEDAL, *Minnow on the Say* was published in the United States in 1958 as *The Minnow Leads to Treasure,* where it received the Lewis CARROLL Shelf Award in 1959; it was re-released in the U.S. in 2000 as *Minnow on the Say.* The novel was the first of P.'s works in which elements of her own upbringing in Great Shelford play a significant role in the development of the story. P. re-creates the house and garden on the banks of the River Cam of her childhood with intimate detail and care that is both supplemental to the plausibility of the plot and engaging for the reader.

The setting of the house and garden reappears in *Tom's Midnight Garden,* a modern fantasy in which the protagonist discovers a garden that only exists in the past but holds a secret linking it to the present. Visiting the garden at night, Tom enters a world of adventure and mystery from which the secret unfolds. The experience provides Tom with a renewed sense of his own self-worth and appreciation for the value of friendship and personal growth. Awarded the Carnegie Medal, the novel established P. as a significant voice among writers for young readers and a storyteller of extraordinary ability.

In 1961, P. published her first picture book, *Mrs. Cockle's Cat,* illustrated by Anthony Maitland, which earned the KATE GREENAWAY MEDAL followed by *A Dog So Small* (1962), the story of a young boy whose desire for an animal to love is finally realized when he is given a dog by his grandfather. In sharp contrast to the happy ending of *A Dog So Small, The Children of the House* (1968), coauthored by Brian Fairfax-Lucy and illustrated by John Sergeant, revealed a darker side of P.'s creativity. Denied love and affection from their parents, the four children of an aristocratic family come to depend on each other for companionship and survival. The book was republished in 1989 as *The Children of Charlecote,* with a new foreword by Alice Fairfax-Lucy, who credits P. with shaping what she claimed was an account based in part on her husband's life.

Following *The Elm Street Lot* (1969), a collection of stories all but one of which was originally written for the BBC and illustrated by Peter Rush, P. produced her second picture book, *The Squirrel Wife* (1971), illustrated by Derek Collard. In 1972, she published an adaption of *Beauty and the Beast* and also collected and edited *Stories from Hans Christian ANDERSEN.* That same year, she published *What the Neighbors Did and Other Stories,* illustrated by Faith Jaques, which was named a British honor book for the Hans Christian Andersen Award and earned recognition

from the INTERNATIONAL BOARD ON BOOKS FOR YOUNG PEOPLE.

Characteristic of her writing, P. continued throughout her career to alternate between fictional opposites: the dark stories collected in *The Shadow-Cage and Other Tales of the Supernatural* (1977, Ted LEWIN, illus), and awarded a Carnegie Medal commendation, was followed by *The Battle of Bubble and Squeak* (1978), in which two gerbils serve to bridge the void between a young boy and his mother. Illustrated by Alan Baker, the book was also awarded a Carnegie Medal commendation and received the Whitbread Award. Likewise, the dark secrets that permeate *The Way to Satin Shore* (1983 Charlotte Voake, illus), seem far removed from the SERIES of Bunnykins stories that followed, which P. intended for younger readers; and *Who's Afraid? and Other Strange Stories* (1986) seems an unlikely predecessor to works such as *The Tooth Ball* (1987), and *Emily's Own Elephant* (1987). P. nonetheless remained consistent in weaving a unifying theme through her body of work, from *Minnow in the Say* to *Here Comes Tod!* (1991), in which we once again encounter a young protagonist ready to step forward and discover the world.

FURTHER WORKS: *Still Jim and Silent Jim,* 1960; *The Strange Sunflower,* 1966; *A Picnic for Bunnykins,* 1984; *Two Bunnykins out for Tea,* 1984; *Bunnykins in the Snow,* 1985 (illus. Walter Hayward); *Lion at School and Other Stories,* 1985 (illus. Caroline Sharpe); *Freddy,* 1988 (illus. David Armitage); *Old Belle's Summer Holiday,* 1989 (illus. William Geldart); *In the Middle of the Night,* 1990

BIBLIOGRAPHY: R. E. Jones, "Philippa P.'s Tom's Midnight Garden: Finding and Losing Eden," *Touchstones: Reflections on the Best in Children's Literature* (edited by P. Nodelman) 1985, vol. 1: 212–21; D. Rees, "Achieving One's Heart's Desires," *The Marble in the Water: Essays on Contemporary Writers of Fiction for Children and Young Adults,* 1980: 36–55; J. R. Townsend, "Philippa P.," *A Sense of the Story: Essays on Contemporary Writers for Children* (1971), 163–71; John R. Townsend, *Written for Children: An Outline of English-Language Children's Literature* (1990), 236–37, 247–49; *A Sense of Story: Essays on Contemporary Writers for Children,* 1973

STEVEN R. SERAFIN

PEARE, Catherine Owens

Biographer, b. 4 February 1911, Perth Amboy, New Jersey

Author of twenty-four biographies including two on Mahatma Gandhi, P. received praise and the Sequoyah Award in 1962 for *The Helen Keller Story*. P. wrote the definitive life story of William Penn basing the book on hundreds of rare manuscripts never before investigated. The book was the result of three and a half years of writing and research in the United States, England, and Ireland. P. considers traveling to her subjects' places of origin and experience vital to her descriptive writings. P.'s subjects cover the arts (*Rosa Bonheur, Her Life,* 1956), science (*Albert Einstein,* 1949), and politics (*The FDR Story*, 1962). Her work as editor of her high school newspaper in Tenafly, New Jersey, and contributions of poetry and plays at New Jersey State Teachers College, provided background to enter the newly developing children's book field. P. is also the author of two works of fiction.

FURTHER WORKS: *John James Audubon*, 1953; *The Lost Lakes, a Story of the Texas Rangers,* 1953; *A Scientist of Two Worlds: Louis Agassiz,* 1958; *The Helen Keller Story,* 1959; *Mahatma Gandhi, Father of Nonviolence,* 1969

BIBLIOGRAPHY: *Something about the Author*, vol. 9, 1976

CRAIG LIEBERMAN

PEARSON, Kit

Author, b. 30 April, 1947, Edmonton, Alberta, Canada

Growing up in Edmonton and Vancouver, British Columbia, P. literally devoured books. Becoming so absorbed in her reading, P. would not notice that she was actually tearing off the corners of the pages and eating them. When P. was twelve-years old she read *Emily of New Moon* (1923) by CANADIAN author L. M. MONTGOMERY and she knew she would some day become a writer. P.'s entire life has revolved around literature and children's literature in particular. P. graduated with a bachelor of arts degree in English from the University of Alberta in 1969 and a master of library science degree from the University of British Columbia in 1976. Working as a children's librarian in On-

tario, P. found the audience she wanted to write for in children. Taking a year and a half off to earn her M.A. from the Simmons College Center for the Study of Children's Literature in Boston, P. met many children's authors and took writing courses. P.'s first book, *The Daring Game* (1986), is autobiographical and draws on P.'s own experience at a girls' boarding school in Vancouver. *A Handful of Time* (1987), P.'s second novel, also draws on P.'s memories for the setting of this time travel FANTASY. Taking place on the Alberta lake where her family had a cottage, Patricia, the twelve-year-old narrator, travels back in time using a magical watch and witnesses her mother's own twelfth summer at the cottage. Gaining a better understanding of how her mother has become the person she is, Patricia learns how the relationships of the past can affect the relationships of the present. *A Handful of Time* was named Book of the Year for Children by the Canadian Library Association. The first of a World War II trilogy, P.'s third novel *The Sky Is Falling* (1989) begins in the summer of 1940 in England but soon moves to Canada following the story of Norah and her brother Gavin who are war evacuees. They have been separated from their family and must adjust to their new situation with Mrs. Ogilvie who adores Gavin but has great difficulties with Norah who is the book's narrator. *The Sky Is Falling* won the Canadian Library Association Book of the Year for Children, the first Mr. Christie Book Award and the Geoffrey Bilson Award for Historical Fiction for Young People. Second in the trilogy, *Looking at the Moon* (1991) continues the story of Norah who is now thirteen and may be falling in love. It was given a Governor General's Award shortlist citation. The third and concluding novel in the trilogy, *The Lights Go on Again* (1993), is told this time from Gavin's point of view. The war over, Gavin must decide whether to stay with the Ogilvies and a country he has grown to love or return to England with his older sister. This novel earned P. her second Geoffrey Bilson Award. P.'s novels have been praised for their insight and sensitivity and her genuine love of children's literature is evident in the many references to classic works of children's literature that she sprinkles throughout her novels.

FURTHER WORKS: (Reteller) *The Singing Basket* (A. Blades, illus.), 1991; *Awake and Dreaming,* 1997

BIBLIOGRAPHY: *Seventh Book of Junior Authors and Illustrators,* 1996; Silvey, Anita, ed., *Children's Books and Their Creators,* 1995; *Something about the Author.* vol. 77, 1994

DEDE SMALL

PECK, Robert Newton
Author, b. 17 February 1928, Vermont

P., the son of a farmer, was reared with the staunch values of hard work and individualism traditionally associated with rural life. Although his parents were Plain People and did not read, P. was introduced to books very early by a dedicated teacher, Miss Kelly, who instilled in him a love for literature. Her influence on him was so profound he maintained a lifelong friendship with her and dedicated many of his books to her. P. eventually graduated from college and married a librarian with TV's Mr. Fred Rogers (see READING RAINBOW AND CHILDREN'S LITERATURE ON TELEVISION) standing for him as best man, but he never forgot those early roots. His first book was *A Day No Pigs Would Die* (1972), a partially autobiographical story set on a Shaker farm in Vermont in the 1930s. It is a coming-of-age story, dealing with the conflict between the simple Shaker life and the modern world. Although it contains warm HUMOR, the tone is essentially serious as the young protagonist, Rob, must come to terms first with the loss of his pet and then with the death of his father. It is with special poignancy that Rob realizes that he cannot follow in his father's footsteps and take up the Shaker life. *A Part of the Sky,* its sequel, was published in 1994.

This serious, almost tragic, tone and the father-son relationship is found in *Millie's Boy* (1973), *Hang for Treason* (1976), both for young readers, and *Fawn* (1975), an adult novel. As the author of more than sixty books, numerous poems and songs and several TV specials, P.'s writing style, tone, and literary standards have varied from *A Day No Pigs Would Die.* In his own words, P. states, "I don't write quality, I write quantity," but always with honesty, showing children life as it is and not as adults wish it to be. His *Clunie* (1979), the story of an intellectually challenged girl, is bold in its subject matter, but simple and straightforward in its treatment.

After *A Day No Pigs Would Die,* P.'s most memorable works are his Soup stories, humorous books for young readers, beginning with *Soup* (1974) and its many sequels, including *Soup and Me* (1975), *Soup on Wheels* (1981), *Soup on Ice* (1985), and *Soup's Hoop* (1989), to name only a few. They are immensely popular with children, who enjoy the antics of Soup, a figure out of the bad-boy tradition of literature. Some of the stories have been adapted for television. As with *A Day No Pigs Would Die,* the Soup stories often rely heavily on autobiographical material, the area in which P. works most comfortably and most successfully.

AWARDS: *New York Times* Outstanding Book for *Mille's Boy* (1973). AMERICAN LIBRARY ASSOCIATION Best Books for YOUNG ADULTS for *A Day No Pigs Would Die* (1975)

FURTHER WORKS: *Soup in the Saddle,* 1983; *Spanish Hoof,* 1985; *Arly,* 1989

BIBLIOGRAPHY: *Children's Literature Review,* vol. 45, 1998; *Contemporary Authors, New Revised Stories,* vol. 31; Gallo, Donald. *Speaking for Ourselves,* 1990; Kovacs, D., *Meet the Authors,* 1995; *Something about the Author,* vol. 62, 1990

DAVID L. RUSSELL

PEET, Bill
Illustrator, author, b. 29 January 1915, Grandview, Indiana

P., who altered his name from William Bartlett Peed around 1947 but never legally changed it, grew up in rural Indiana. He devoted his energy to drawing, often to the detriment of his schoolwork. High school art classes allowed him to discover the prospect of a future as a professional artist. After leaving Indianapolis's John Herron Art Institute in 1936, P. worked briefly designing greeting cards. In 1937, he was hired by Walt DISNEY Studios, where he worked his way up through the artistic ranks to become a screenwriter. While still working for Disney, P. began to explore a second career as picture-book illustrator. He left Disney in 1964, credited with bringing *One Hundred and One Dalmatians* (1961) and *The Sword in the Stone* (1963) to the screen.

P.'s PICTURE BOOKS are populated by friendly cartoonlike creatures ranging from the domestic to the fantastic. *The Wump World* (1970) exemplifies P.'s approach to presenting human problems—and possible solutions—through fables. Human beings appear in many of the stories, sometimes as problems, as in *Fly, Homer, Fly* (1969), sometimes as part of the scenery, as in *The Caboose Who Got Loose* (1971), and sometimes as sympathetic characters, such as the small boy who inspires generosity in the heart of *Kermit the Hermit Crab* (1965). P. sees himself in *Chester the Worldly Pig* (1965), a runt who leaves home and becomes a star.

P. writes some of his book in rhyme. *Bill P.: An Autobiography* (1988), written for school-aged readers, is appropriately illustrated as well as being comprehensive. P. discusses his growing dissatisfaction with the direction of Disney productions here in a way that creative children will grasp and appreciate. He enjoys meeting his readers and once incorporated a class's suggestions in the creation of a story, *The Whingdingdilly* (1970). P.'s enjoyment of drawing and of children's imaginative powers have helped him to maintain consistent freshness in his ILLUSTRATIONS and stories.

AWARDS: Box Office awarded P. Blue Ribbons for each of his screenplays. ALA CALDECOTT MEDAL Honor Book (1989) for *Bill P.: An Autobiography*. The George C. Stone Center bestowed a Recognition of Merit award (1985) for his body of work. P. has been voted a favorite author by children in several states across the decades. His books remain in print, many have been translated into other languages, and some have been produced in braille

FURTHER WORKS FOR CHILDREN: *The Pinkish, Purplish, Bluish Egg*, 1963; *Randy's Dandy Lions*, 1964; *Farewell to Shady Glade*, 1966; *Capyboppy*, 1966; *Buford, the Little Bighorn*, 1967; *Jennifer and Josephine*, 1967; *How Droofus the Dragon Lost His Head*, 1971; *Pamela Camel*, 1984; *Zella, Zack, and Zodiac*, 1986; *Cock-a-Doodle Dudley*, 1990

BIBLIOGRAPHY: Ingwerson, Marshall. "It's Just as if I Was Still Six—Drawing Lions in Books," *Christian Science Monitor*. Nov. 9, 1981; Oliver, Myrna, "For Bill P., Work Is a Flight of Fancy," *Los Angeles Times*, Dec. 23, 1990

FRANCISCA GOLDSMITH

PELLOWSKI, Anne

Author, storyteller, lecturer, b. 28 June 1933, Pine Creek, Wisconsin

P. is well known for her research and writings about the art of STORYTELLING. She collected stories from around the world based on plants and published her findings in *Hidden Stories in Plants* (1984). *The Family Storytelling Handbook* (1987) is a sourcebook of ways in which storytelling and stories are used in families around the world. Early in her career she was a children's librarian for the New York Public Library and later founded and directed the Information Center on Children's Cultures of the United States Committee for UNICEF. Three times a member of the Hans Christian ANDERSEN Award jury, she has received the Grolier Foundation Award of the AMERICAN LIBRARY ASSOCIATION and the Constance Lindsay Skinner Award of the Women's National Book Association. P. has recently begun to publish a SERIES of fiction about Polish-American girls.

FURTHER WORKS: *The Story Vine*, 1984; *World of Storytelling*, 1984; *World of Children's Stories*, 1993; *Betsy's up-and-down Year*, 1997; *First Farm in the Valley*, 1997

BIBLIOGRAPHY: *Something about the Author*, vol. 20, 1980

SANDRA IMDIEKE

PERKINS, Lucy Fitch

Author, illustrator, teacher, b. 12 July 1865, Maples, Indiana; d. 18 Mary 1937, Place unknown

P.'s fame rests on her extensive twin SERIES. During the prime years of the series there were more than twenty-four books. P. was educated at the Union school, Kalamazoo and attended the Museum of Fine Arts School in Boston. From 1886 to 1903 she worked as an illustrator for the Prang Educational Company in Boston; from 1887 to 1990 she taught ILLUSTRATION at Pratt Institute, Brooklyn.

Her initial inspiration to develop a series of books about young people from other countries came after visiting Ellis Island. There she became aware of the great diversity of people entering the U.S. and the need to make children aware of the differences and customs of all the people who were eventually to become part of their own country. Another experience that motivated her to write about other cultures was a visit to a Chicago school where twenty-seven different nations were represented in one classroom.

Beginning with the *Dutch Twins* in 1911, P. began a series for eight to ten year olds that simply and accurately told about life in another country. The fact that P. was able to maintain a freshness and vitality for twenty-four books used all over the United States and continued to be reissued is a credit to her writing ability. She also wrote twin books that were about historical times in the United States and other countries. The enduring vitality and usefulness of the series can be proven by the fact that at least ten or more have been reissued for contemporary children.

Some critics felt that the twins books tended to stereotype nationalities and overly emphasize differences. Her defenders, however, have said that this style has been a way to crystallize young reader's ideas of how others live and to show the values others may have contributed to American life within an atmosphere of respect for other cultures.

FURTHER WORKS: *Japanese Twins,* 1912; *Irish Twins,* 1922; *Eskimo Twins,* 1922; *Mexican Twins,* 1916, 1955; *Belgian Twins,* 1917, 1940; *French Twins,* 1918, 1939; *Spartan Twins,* 1918, 1936; *Italian Twins,* 1920, 1952; *Scotch Twins,* 1922; *Swiss Twins,* 1922, 1936; *Colonial Twins,* 1924, 1949

BIBLIOGRAPHY: Silvey, Anita, ed., *Children's Books and Their Creators,* 1995; *Something about the Author,* vol. 72, 1993; *Twentieth Century Children's Writers,* 1978

JUDY LIPSITT

PERL, Lila

Author, b. ca. 1936–38 (sources vary), New York City

P. never intended to become a writer; she believed she had nothing exciting to write about. Later, she realized she had a rich inner emotional life to draw from to create fiction for YOUNG ADULTS. P.'s four Fat Glenda books, including *Me and Fat Glenda* (1972) and *Fat Glenda Turns Fourteen* (1991), exemplify P.'s ability to empathize with the main character's insecurities and vulnerabilities using a humorous tone.

P.'s nonfiction for young adults is fueled by her desire to know more about the past. In *Mummies, Tombs, and Treasure* (1987), and *The Great Ancestor Hunt* (1989), P.'s descriptions of families from the ancient past, encourage readers to think about their own family histories. She has created several cookbooks based on America's heritage including the AMERICAN LIBRARY ASSOCIATION Nonfiction Notable Book, *Red-Flannel Hash and Shoo-Fly Pie* (1965), and the *Horn Book* magazine Nonfiction Honor Book *Junk Food, Fast Food, Health Food* (1980). P. continues her historical research and documentation in *Four Perfect Pebbles* (1996), which details the struggles of the Blumenthal family, HOLOCAUST survivors.

FURTHER WORKS: *America Goes to the Fair,* 1974; *Annabelle Starr, E.S.P.,* 1983; *Candles, Cakes and Donkey Tails: Birthday Symbols and Celebrations,* 1984; *It Happened in America,* 1992; *North across the Border,* 2000

BIBLIOGRAPHY: *Something about the Author,* vol. 72, 1993

DENISE P. BEASLEY

PERRAULT, Charles

Author, b. 13 January 1628, Paris, France; d. 16 May 1703, Paris, France

P. was a member of an influential family of intellectuals; his father was a lawyer and three brothers earned at least footnotes in history, one as an architect and scientist, another as a writer, and still another as a noted theologian. P. initially studied law, but early on turned to writing rather scandalous, popular verse, while employed by his brother in the civil service. He then held important government offices under Jean-Baptiste Colbert during the reign of Louis XIV, advancing the cause of literature and the arts. As assistant superintendent of public works he secured the gardens at Les Tuileries as a public space especially for children rather than royal use. For his efforts as a government official, he was elected to the Academie Francaise in 1671, where he gained celebrity for defending the "Moderns" against the "Ancients," promulgating a famous intellectual struggle. He advanced the controversial notion that, since civilization was constantly progressing, modern literature was more refined than ancient literature. It was a concept that shocked many of his contemporaries. P. retired in 1683 and devoted his time to rearing his children (he was now a widower) and to writing. His works of this later period consisted largely of devotional poetry, biographical works and memoirs.

P. is remembered today as the author of *Histoires ou contes du temps passé* (Stories from times past), or better known by its alternate title, *Contes de ma mere l'Oye* (Tales from MOTHER GOOSE). These were first published in 1697, under his son's name, and the authorship has never been conclusively proven. P. had, from time to time, published individual pieces, some in verse, based on the old folktales, but as a member of the prestigious Academie he was ridiculed for these works. This may explain his reluctance to acknowledge authorship of the collection. Further, his son was only eighteen when they were published, and they bear a great deal of sophistication for one so young. Still, some scholars believe that the tales may have been a collaborative effort between father and son. Certainly, neither P. nor his son ever dreamed these tales would rise to such prominence.

They were not the first FAIRY TALES to be written down, but they became the most popular, largely because of their accessible style and lack of affectation. They were first translated into English in 1729, and reprinted numerous times. It is because of P.'s work that such tales as "The Little Red Riding-Hood," "The Blue Beard," "Puss in Boots," "Sleeping Beauty," and "Cinderella" became childhood staples. Unlike modern editions of fairy tales, P.'s stories end with a moral in verse form. Whereas these literary tales possess an adult sophistication and attention to detail, they have become the standard version of many familiar fairy tales told around the world. P. invested his fairy tales with the actions of kings and queens, princes and princesses, living in courtly splendor in contrast to the *Märchen* collected by the Brothers GRIMM, which emphasize dwarfs and elves living mysteriously in darkness in the Black Forest of Germany. P.'s tales pleased the French court at Versailles where telling fairy tales for the court's amusement was fashionable. They can be traced to popular European oral traditional literature and Neapolitan fairy stories collected and published by Giambattista Basile in 1634–36.

P.'s fairy tales were the first such stories written down and published in England specifically for children. One particularly popular edition was later edited by Andrew Lang as *Perrault's Popular Tales* (1888). It is through P. that the term "Mother Goose" was introduced into English; in seventeenth-century France, folktales (or "old wive's tales") were popularly known as Mother Goose. In America, the term was eventually applied to nursery rhymes as well.

BIBLIOGRAPHY: Cullinan, B., *Literature and the Child,* 1981; Hunt, Peter, ed., *Children's Literature, an Illustrated History,* 1995; Johnson, A. E., trans., *Perrault's Fairy Tales,* 1969; Knoepflmacher, U. C., *Ventures into Childhood,* 1998; *The Oxford Companion to Children's Literature,* 1984

DAVID L. RUSSELL

PETERSHAM, Maud and Miska

Authors, illustrators. Maud: b. 5 August 1890, Kingston, New York; d. 29 November 1971. Miska: b. 20 September 1888, Toeroekszentimiklos, Hungary; d. 15 May 1960, Place unknown

Maud and her three sisters, daughters of a Baptist minister, moved around the country to New York, South Dakota, and Pennsylvania. Maud's interest in the Bible later evolved in works she composed. Miska grew up in Hungary—his given name was Petrezselyem Mikaly. At age seven, he saved money to buy a box of paints. From that point on, he wanted to become an artist. Both Maud and Miska attended art school. Maud graduated from Vassar College and studied art at the New York School of Fine and Applied Art. Miska attended the Art School in Budapest. Miska traveled to America in 1912 after having little luck as an artist in London. Maud and Miska met while working in an advertising firm, the International Art Service. They married and had one child, a son named Miki.

Maud and Miska began their career together as illustrators of fiction and anthologies written by other authors. Their first collaborative work together was *Miki* (1929). This book tells the personal story of an American boy who visits his grandparents in Budapest. Some people consider this book to be the first American PICTURE BOOK to be set in a foreign country. Two additional Miki books followed. Between 1933 and 1939, the P.s wrote six SERIES of nonfiction titles on topics such as food, clothing, homes, utensils, and transportation. During World War II, the P.s wrote patriotic books known collectively as This Is America series. *An American ABC* (1941) and *The Rooster Crows: A Book of American Rhymes and Jingles* (1945) were included in this series.

The P.s worked together on most of their books. Maud handled the rough dummies and the writing while Miska prepared the page layouts and finalized the illustrations. The two are often praised for introducing an international scope to the American picture book, for developing attractive INFORMATIONAL BOOKS, and for setting a standard in book ILLUSTRATION through their mastery of the lithographic method, experimentation with printing processes, and focus on total BOOK DESIGN.

AWARDS: ALA CALDECOTT MEDAL (1946) for *The Rooster Crows.* AMERICAN LIBRARY ASSOCIATION Caldecott Medal Honor Book (1942) for *An American ABC*

FURTHER WORKS: *The Art of Father Noah and Mother Noah.* 1930: *Auntie and Celia Jane and Miki.* 1932: *Miki and Mary: Their Search for Treasures.* 1934: *The Story Book of Transportation.* 1933: *The Story Book of Food.* 1933: *America's Stamps: The Story of One Hundred Years of U.S. Postage Stamps.* 1947

BIBLIOGRAPHY: *Children's Literature Review,* vol. 24, 1991. *Something about the Author,* vol. 17, 1979

JODI PILGRIM

PETRY, Ann Lane

Author, b. 12 October 1908, Old Saybrook, Connecticut; d. 28 April 1997, Old Saybrook, Connecticut

P. was born into a middle-class AFRICAN AMERICAN family in a largely white community. From early childhood, she was impressed by her immediate family's professional stature, the acceptance of racial prejudice by her teachers and peers, and her mother's devotion to language. Like her father and other relatives, she chose a career in pharmacology, graduating from the University of Connecticut in 1931, and establishing a practice in her family's drug stores. However, her true vocation was as a writer, a life for which she trained herself assiduously after moving to New York

City in 1938. There she found employment as a journalist with the *Amsterdam News* and the *People's Voice,* rival Harlem papers. She studied piano and creative writing, worked with children in a Harlem elementary school and acted in the American Negro Theater. She also organized political activists to empower African American women in Harlem, with the intent of seeing and understanding the Harlem community from the inside. After meeting critical success with her adult novels, and the birth of her daughter, she returned to Connecticut where she began writing books for children. Houghton Mifflin awarded P. a literary fellowship in 1946, allowing her to complete her first adult novel.

P.'s novels and stories for adults earned popular and critical acclaim. She has been likened to Richard Wright as a realist working within and presenting for readers everywhere the African American community. Her first book for children, *The Drugstore Cat* (1949), relied upon her experiences of witnessing small-town life from a pharmacist's vantage point. Her next two works for children emerged from a self-conscious desire to provide children with information about and inspiration from African American women. P.'s feminism and pride in her African American identity are evident in her compelling BIOGRAPHY *Harriet Tubman: Conductor on the Underground Railroad* (1955) (published 1960 in England as *A Girl Called Moses: The Story of Harriet Tubman*) and the fictional *Tituba of Salem Village* (1964), featuring an African American slave in a compelling and accessible account of the seventeenth century Witch Trials. *Tituba* was published to wide critical acclaim. The desire to provide role models and to expose young readers to spiritual inquiry led to her last work for children, *Legends of the Saints* (1970), a collection of ten biographical sketches.

P. developed as a professional writer by reading widely and attending to her surroundings with a writer's ear and eye. Her treatment of African American women characters in her work for children, as for adults, continues to engage and inspire readers of all races. She was awarded honorary academic titles by Suffolk University (1983), the University of Connecticut (1988) and Mount Holyoke College (1989).

BIBLIOGRAPHY: *Contemporary Authors Autobiography Series,* vol. 6, 1988; "The Common Ground," the *Horn Book,* 41:141–51, April 1965; Mobley, Marilyn Sanders, "Ann P.," *African American Writers,* 1991, pp. 347–59

FRANCISCA GOLDSMITH

PEVSNER, Stella
Author. b. Date unknown, Lincoln, Illinois

P. is an author of modern YOUNG ADULT fiction. She began writing as the result of a challenge from one of her children to "write a funny book that kids can enjoy." She believes writing a book is similar to making a collage: bits of this and pieces of that are woven together to make something familiar, yet new. When writing, her main purpose is to entertain and through this she wants readers to realize reading is an enjoyable activity that they can practice the rest of their lives. In 1977 *Keep Stompin' 'til the Music Stops* was listed as a Notable Children's Trade Book in the field of Social Studies. In 1978, she won the Golden Kite Award, Society of Children's Books Writers, Clara Ingram Judson Award, Society of Midland Authors, and Omar's Award for *And You Give Me a Pain, Elaine.* (1978). The Carl Sandburg Award and Friends of the Chicago Public Library Award were given in 1980 for *Cute Is a Four-Letter Word* (1980). *How Could You Do It, Diane?* (1989) was on the AMERICAN LIBRARY ASSOCIATION Best Books for Young Adults list in 1989. P. wants children "to know the world holds endless possibilities for them . . . to create . . . a life that will bring them joy, wonder and satisfaction."

BIBLIOGRAPHY: *Something about the Author,* vol. 77, 1994; *Fiction, FOLKLORE, FANTASY and POETRY for Children, 1876–1985,* vol. 1, 1986

IRVYN GILBERTSON

PEYTON, K. M. (Kathleen Wendy Peyton; Kathleen Herald)
Author, b. 2 August 1929, Birmingham, England

P. began writing book-length stories, in longhand, at the age of nine. She submitted a novel for publication at the age of fifteen and *Sabre, the Horse from the Sea* (1947) became the first of three juvenile novels published under her maiden name, Kathleen Herald. Instead of entering a career as an author immediately, P. trained as an artist and received an Art Teacher's Diploma, from Manchester Art School, in 1952. She married a fellow art student with whom she wrote her first juvenile novels, including *North to Adventure* (1959), under the name of K M. Peyton.

After a period of writing children's novels on themes and about subjects suggested by her husband, P. developed into an independent author. Details in her stories about such skills as horseback riding and barge sailing come from personal experience. P. participates in a wide field of adventuresome pastimes and has an active family life to take her where she might not have considered venturing. *Thunder in the Sky* (1966), while set during World War I, utilizes direct experience with barge life as well as her skills as a researcher. In several of her novels, including those of the Flambards trilogy, P. utilizes the literary device of orphaned children to allow her characters to solve their own problems. The trilogy of *Pennington's Last Term, The Beethoven Medal* (1971) and *Pennington's Heir* (1973) are self-illustrated. P. has also published novels for adults.

AWARDS: British Library Association CARNEGIE MEDAL (1969) for *The Edge of the Cloud* (the middle book of the Flambards trilogy). Carnegie Medal Commendation (1962) for *Windfall* (published in the U.S. as *Sea Fever,* an AMERICAN LIBRARY ASSOCIATION Notable Book (1963), (1965) for *The Maplin Bird, The Plan for Birdsmarsh* (1966), *The Thunder in the Sky* (1967), for *Flambards* (1969), for *Flambards in Summer,* and (1977) for *The Team* (1977). The *New York Herald Tribune* Spring Book Festival Honor Book (1965) for *The Maplin Bird. Boston Globe-Horn Book* Award Honor Book (1969) and The *Guardian* Award (1970) for *Flambards.* ALA Notable Books (1968) for *Flambards,* (1970) for *Flambards in Summer,* (1971) for *Pennington's Seventeenth Summer* (published in the U.S. as *Pennington's Last Term*), (1972) for *The Beethoven Medal,* (1973) for *A Pattern of Roses,* and *Pennington's Heir*

FURTHER WORKS: *Brownsea Silver,* 1964; *A Midsummer Night's Death,* 1979; *Flambards Divided,* 1982; *Going Home,* 1982; *Darkling,* 1989; *Who, Sir? Me, Sir?,* 1989

BIBLIOGRAPHY: Jones, Cornelia, and Olivia Way. *British Children's Authors: Interviews at Home,* 1976; Peyton, K. M., "On Not Writing the Proper Book," *The Thorny Paradise: Writers on Writing for Children,* 1975

FRANCISCA GOLDSMITH

PFISTER, Marcus

Author, illustrator, b. Date unknown, Berne, Switzerland

P. has worked as an artist in the fields of advertising, graphic design, photography, sculpting, and painting. It is no wonder that the accolades he receives from critics are more for his ILLUSTRATIONS than story lines. He is most noted for his signature holographic-foil stamping first used in *The Rainbow Fish* (1992), which has been translated into thirty languages. P.'s works employ animal characters who encounter emotional issues of friendship, sharing, loneliness, and other universal childhood challenges. P.'s books, with their intriguing illustrations, are immensely popular with the PICTURE BOOK reading audience.

FURTHER WORKS: *Where Is My Friend?*, 1986; *The Sleepy Owl*, 1986; *Penguin Pete*, 1987; *Hopper*, 1991; *Dazzle the Dinosaur*, 1994; *The Happy Hedgehog*, 2000

BIBLIOGRAPHY: *Something about the Author*, vol. 83, 1996

NANCY HORTON

PHIPSON, Joan (pseud. Joan M. Fitzardinge)

Author, b. 10 November 1912, Wanawee, New South Wales, Australia

P.'s stories for children and adolescents are recognized for their accurate depiction of the AUSTRALIAN countryside and its people. She attributes remembering her childhood feelings, emotions, and reactions to her ability to portray young people realistically, adjusting to demanding and often dangerous situations. Books such as *Good Luck to the Rider* (1952) and *The Watcher in the Garden* (1982) are about youths who develop confidence and begin to like themselves as a result of difficult real-life situations. Both characters and settings are realistic, even in her later books that show older children in FANTASY situations fraught with suspense. The setting is often urban rather than rural in her later books. She has won numerous AWARDS including the Children's Book Council of Australia Book of the Year and an INTERNATIONAL BOARD ON BOOKS FOR YOUNG PEOPLE Honor Book.

FURTHER WORKS: *Six and Silver*, 1954; *The Family Conspiracy*, 1962; *Threat to the Barkers*, 1963; *The Way Home*, 1973; *The Watcher in the Garden*, 1982; *The Shadow*, 1989

BIBLIOGRAPHY: *Children's Literature Review*, pp. 77–187, 1983; *Something about the Author*, vol. 73, 1993

JANELLE B. MATHIS

PICTURE BOOKS

The expertly crafted text evokes vivid images on the part of the reader. But a tremendous power in illustrations lies in the direct sensuous appeal of the pictures accompanying the text. For example, expertly crafted illustrations stimulate the reader to extract new, richer, and deeper meanings from a text and to recall particular passages. Visual artists can sharpen the eyes, mind, and feelings of those who view their pictures. Illustrations also contribute toward helping children and adults grow in their interest in reading, in appreciation of fine books, fine art, and graphic art.

To create a picture book, a unique form of literary genre in itself, two distinct forms of creative expression, words and pictures, are combined; each creates conditions of dependence and interdependence. The full meaning of any book ILLUSTRATION can only be revealed in the context of the old adage, "the whole is greater than the sum of the parts"; in other words, a book illustration amounts to far more when it is viewed in the context of the complete story and the other pictures in the book than when it is viewed as a single picture, even though it is beautiful and appears to be as complete and comprehensive a work of visual art as any gallery painting could be. Individual paintings and drawings are attractive but, when viewed as illustrations designed to depict the literary elements in a text, their perspective changes. When viewed as a whole each picture exudes greater depth and breadth in mood, rhythm, design, and meaning. Another phenomenon occurs when looking at any one picture in relation to all other pictures in the book. The way visual elements coalesce in relation to the literary elements in the text enables the viewer to see a complete and comprehensive work of art known as a picture book.

The text of a picture book must reflect accomplished writing. Theoretically, when one reads a picture book, the responsibility for developing the story is to be shared equally by the words and the pictures that comprise this unique kind of literature. When one sets out to critique a picture book, one must first focus on the manner and the quality of the author's use of language and what it has to offer in terms of the literary elements (if it is fiction or a narrative poem), or presenting facts or ideas, and to inform or teach and thus help the readers acquire knowledge or understanding. One can then examine the illustrations to determine more accurately the extent to which they not only support the text, but enhance and enrich it. Readers are provided with visual images they would never have created on their own, but still are in keeping with the content, setting, mood, and/or mood and tone of the text. Finally, one can then read the text and the illustrations together and thereby experience the gestalt, experience the picture book as it was actually intended to be. To separate reading the text and the illustrations that make up the picture book is no easy task. Very often the illustrations are not only large and colorful, but by their very nature tend to be more intriguing and dramatic graphically than the text. Note: this approach to reading a picture book works well for a critic, it is not to be used with children. Their first reading of all picture books should be a simultaneous exposure to the text and the pictures.

An illustration is more than a literal "translation" of the printed word. The combination of the verbal with the visual to create a picture book does not mean that the contents and meanings may be literally translated from one medium to another. No communication in any medium is ever literally translatable from one medium to any other. By its very nature and purpose an illustration must go well beyond the literal level of translation. A sensitive intertwining of the skills of the writer and visual artist is epitomized in Marcia BROWN's 1983 CALDECOTT MEDAL winner, *Shadow*. The text of this picture book, a portion of Blaise Cendrars's classic poem, was translated from the French and illustrated by Marcia Brown. It brings to life the many images of the haunting and enchanting "Shadow" described by shamans and storytellers around the fires in an Africa of long ago. Brown's superbly executed collage and gouache illustrations reflect the exotic atmosphere and the dramatic qualities of the text. The very essence of the climate and atmosphere in East Africa results from the inclusion of Brown's stylized illustrations of animals and vegetation common to various parts of this region of Africa and through her effective use of color and brush strokes. Traditionally, the lore of AFRICA tended to be expressed in music, dance, and wood sculpture. Interestingly, her paper cuttings of human figures and their shadows strongly suggest dance sequences and body movements to the music played during East Africa's tribal celebrations in times past. Wood carvings dominated the visual arts of old Africa and Brown pictures them in her wood block prints of the numerous ritual masks and dance masks. Cendrars's poems, whether in French or in Brown's translation, plus the professional and talented artistic elements incorporated in her accomplished illustrations constitute an artistic and authentic interpretation of traditional African beliefs, folk art, and literary heritage.

Illustrations should be examined in terms of artistic elements. The art critic E. H. Gombrich writes "There is no real distinction between 'art' and illustration. Thus one may rightly examine book illustrations in terms of their artistic elements and incorporate these elements into the criteria for evaluating the artistic excellence of illustrations in picture books and other illustrated books. The one significant point to consider when examining a book illustration pertains to the illusion in art. It is important to recognize that artistic excellence is not identical with mirror reflections of reality. What is expressed about some aspect of reality in handmade visual statements, in contrast with a mirror reflection, is the selective interpretation the artist has engaged in; it is an illusion rather than a miniature of the reality depicted in and associated with aspects of the story.

Most modern artists rebel against a mere transcript of nature, against something that suggests photographic accuracy. They do not try to transcribe what they see in reality itself or in the reality alluded to in the author's text, for the "essence of art is not imitation but expression" as Uri SHULEVITZ noted in his 1969 Caldecott Medal acceptance speech. The artist interprets the ideas and concepts through the media used and within the range of the tones the media will yield. The personal accent inherent in the style or the expression of these ideas and concepts is revealed in unique qualities of the distributions, sequence and relationships of the artist's movements and shapes.

This attitude about what constitutes artistic expressions explains quite clearly why we presently find such refreshing diversity in picture books. In fact, there seems to be a healthier variety and individuality in artists' interpretation of picture book stories than even a decade ago. The proliferation of art styles in picture books published currently, coupled with the fact that many artists are employing these styles in their individual ways, means that children must adjust to a different stylistic expression with almost every picture book they pick up. Experience has demonstrated that children tend to adapt to the variety of techniques and styles used in book illustrations and writing, too; they tend to be more flexible and respond to this diversity more easily than do adults. Furthermore, this diversity and proliferation in styles in illustration stimulates children's imagination and provides them with new ways of looking at life.

Picture books are no longer just for the preschool and early primary school child. Nor are they all EASY-TO-READ BOOKS; picture books are for readers of all ages. Admittedly, the majority of the picture books published each season are for the young reader, but there is a healthy percentage of them addressed directly to the older reader, whether adolescent or adult. A significant number of picture books are multilevel, which is to say that younger children will read them and get several layers of meaning from the illustrations and text; older readers will read the same book and get several more layers of meaning. Actually the levels of meaning and appreciation one gets from the illustrations and text is not so much dependent upon one's response to "the shape of the content" (the style of art) and the interpretation of individual words in the text so much as it is to the content or theme of the illustrations and nuances in the language of the text.

Among the many picture books published each year a gratifying number are well written and contain illustrations that are truly handsome and original; many reflect refined and sophisticated literary accomplishments. It is of great importance that the books given to children are artistic literary creations. The quality of a picture book, its unity and beauty influence a reader, especially a child, for these qualities tend to induce creative and critical

thinking. It is the literary and graphic perfection of a picture book that directs the child's eye to a new hunger and thirst after beauty and perfection. They function as his "mental and aesthetic food."

What we see in contemporary picture books reflects our attitudes about children and our concepts of childhood; it represents our literary tastes and our attitudes about the visual arts, especially book art. Some of the most accomplished artists of our times are devoting their talents to designing and illustrating picture books. The illustrations in many of these picture books are comprehensible, evoking emotional identification and intense emotional response; they provide the reader with new, wholesome, and vital ways of looking at the world and at life.

BIBLIOGRAPHY OF SOURCES CITED: Cendrars, Blaise. *Shadow.* Translated and illustrated by Marcia Brown, 1982; Gombrich, E. H. *Art and Illusion: A Study of the Psychology of Pictorial Representation,* 1969; Shulevitz, Uri. "Caldecott Award Acceptance." *The Horn Book,* 45: pp. 385–88, August 1969

PATRICIA J. CIANCIOLO

(See also BOOK DESIGN; ILLUSTRATION; VISUAL LITERACY)

PICTURE BOOKS FOR OLDER READERS

Quality PICTURE BOOKS are enjoyed by readers of all ages. Within the last two decades, however, some books have come to be classified as picture books for older readers where the themes or content are judged to be most suitable for the intellectual levels of older readers, generally defined as children ages ten and up. Picture books for older readers typically contain content of interest to an older audience as it relates to the life experiences of an older reader or as it relates to the types of topics typically studied in the upper grades. The combination of the familiar format of the picture book, when used to present new, stimulating content, serves both to capture and stretch the unique intellect of the older reader. As Kiefer notes, when introducing topics such as war or homelessness, the combined visual and textual impact possible in picture books may be stronger than text alone.

Examples of picture books for older readers can be found in every genre, covering many curricular areas or topics of interest to the older reader. Picture books on historical topics for older readers began to gain prominence in the 1980s. Toshi Maruki's *Hiroshima No Pika* (1982) introduced readers to the effects of the atomic bombing of Hiroshima through the eyes of a young girl; Christophe Gallaz and Roberto INNO-CENTI's *Rose Blanche* (1985) is set outside a concentration camp during World War II; *Faithful Elephants* (Yukio Tsuchiya, 1988) recounts the fate of zoo animals in Japan prior to the bomb; and *Let the Celebrations Begin* (Margaret Wild, 1991) tells of women in concentration camps sewing toys for children. American history through the middle of the nineteenth century is portrayed in books such as Patricia POLACCO's *Pink and Say* (1994), and Tom and Muriel FEEL-INGS' books *The Middle Passage* (1995) and *Soul Looks Back in Wonder* (1993). Ann TURNER provides a visual and textual introduction to a family settling in the midwest in *Dakota Dugout* (1985) and Jacob Lawrence's artwork visually traces AF-RICAN AMERICANS who moved to the northern industrial states seeking employment in *The Great Migration: An American Story* (1993). Children's experiences in the Japanese internment camps of World War II are portrayed in Yoshiko UCHIDA's *The Bracelet* (1993) and Ken Mochizuki's *Baseball Saved Us* (1993). More contemporary issues are the focus of BUNTING's 1995 CALDECOTT MEDAL Award winner, *Smoky Night*, a story of the Los Angeles riots, and *The Whispering Cloth* (Peggy Dietz Shea, 1995), the story of a young girl and her grandmother, both Hmong refugees. BIOGRAPHIES in picture book format offer older readers an introduction to famous persons they may choose to read more about. Biographical text plus illustrations in books such as Leontyne Price's *Aida* (1990), or Diane STANLEY and Peter VENNEMA's *The Bard of Avon: The Story of William Shakespeare* (1992) provide a rich context for learning about notable persons.

Many folktales enjoyed by older readers are complex and lengthy. Margaret HODGE's *Saint George and the Dragon* (1990) and Selina Hastings's *Sir Gawain and the Loathly Lady* (1985), may be less well known than many traditional tales enjoyed by younger readers, but these tales offer a more complex plot and detailed descriptions than what might hold the interest of a younger audience. Older readers are also ready to enjoy the satire found in retellings of familiar fairy tales, such as Jon SCIESZKA's and Lane SMITH's *The True Story of the Three Little Pigs* (1989). Other picture books containing abstract themes and fantastic events that suit the intellect of the older reader such as *The Tale I Told Sasha* (Nancy WILLARD, 1999), Maurice SENDAK's *Outside over There* (1981), and Chris VAN ALLS-BURG's books *The Wretched Stone* (1991) and *The Sweetest Fig* (1993).

Older readers also appreciate alphabet books that are more sophisticated in their content or delivery than the letter identification books typical for younger readers. Mitsomasa ANNO's *Anno's Alphabet* (1975) and Graeme BASE's *Animalia* (1986) are examples of picture books that extend the traditional letter recognition format. David Wiesner's 1992 Caldecott Medal winner, *Tuesday*, is a wordless picture book with wry HUMOR, sophisticated wit and a comic sense of irony that has great appeal among older readers.

The increasing use of literature in the curriculum has coincided with the publication of picture books for older readers. Teachers find a picture book with content relative to their curriculum a potentially rich resource for introducing a topic of study, for becoming a centerpiece for a thematic study, or for serving as a model for writing or illustration. Teachers have used students' familiarity with picture books as an avenue to enhance their instruction in literary and artistic elements. Students can study the plot, characterization, setting, and theme in folktales, for example, which in turn can be used as a framework for their own compositions. In *Valentine and Orson* (1989), Nancy Ekholm BURKERT's adaptation of the Renaissance story of twin brothers separated at birth, a surprising plot and many levels of historical details provide a rich context for the study of the writer's craft. Picture books also can be used to study the visual elements and the craft of the artist. Students can examine the design, layout, and media used in the creation of picture books. The paper-cut illustrations in David WIS-NIEWSKI's 1997 Caldecott Medal winner, *Golem*, portraying the good and evil in sixteenth century Prague will visually challenge students. Students can also compare and contrast the visual impact of illustrations in books on similar topics, such as the illustrations in *Rose Blanche* and *Let the Celebrations Begin.*

By examining the nature of the picture books for older readers, it becomes clear that what was the province of young readers at the beginning of this century is now of interest and value to older readers as well.

BIBLIOGRAPHY: Benedict, S. and Carlisle, L., *Beyond Words: Picture Books for Older Readers and Writers,* 1992. Kiefer, B., *The Potential of Picturebooks: From Visual Literacy to Aesthetic Understanding,* 1995
SANDRA IMDIEKE

(See also BOOK DESIGN; CROSSOVERS; ILLUSTRATION; PICTURE BOOKS; STORYOGRAPHIES; VISUAL LITERACY)

PIENKOWSKI, Jan
Author, illustrator, b. 8 August 1936, Warsaw, Poland

P. spent his childhood moving from country to country, from Poland, to Austria, to Germany, to Italy, and finally, to England. He did not receive any formal art training, but while he was attending Cambridge University, in England, he began designing posters and greeting cards for his friends. Because of the popularity of this artwork, P. created his own publishing company called Gallery Five. P.'s art includes bright vivid colors and realistic pictures. He has written and illustrated several different beautiful books based on stories from THE BIBLE including *Christmas: The King James Version* (1984), and *Easter: The King James Version* (1989), both of which contain elegant ornamentation. P. is probably best known for his development of several three-dimensional pop-up books such as *ABC Dinosaurs: And Other Prehistoric Creatures* (1993), and *La Casa Embrujada* (1992).

BIBLIOGRAPHY: Kingman, Lee, *Illustrators of Children's Books: 1967–1976,* 1978
DENISE P. BEASLEY

PIERCE, Meredith Ann
Author, b. 5 July 1958, Seattle, Washington

P. earned her B.A. (1978) and M.A. (1980) from University of Florida. As a prolific writer of high FANTASY, P. creates courageous and brave heroines who face dark, dangerous adventures. Her debut novel, *The Darkangel* (1982), received wide acclaim and attention. In this fantasy, P. invites readers to suspend reality and join Aerial, a servant girl, as she determines to rescue her mistress from an evil vampire. The following two novels in this trilogy are filled with a medieval ethos, surprising plots, magical beasts, enchantment, and believable physical descriptions. The Firebringer triology enchants readers with unicorns, MYTHOLOGY, and rituals. P.'s catalysts for writing are often personal life events. She writes for herself; she is her own audience.

AWARDS: INTERNATIONAL READING ASSOCIATION Children's Book Award (1983) and AMERICAN LIBRARY ASSOCIATION *Booklist* Best Books of the Decade (1980–1989) both for *The Darkangel* (1982) ALA Best Books citation (1991) and for *The Pearl of the Soul of the World*

FURTHER WORKS: *The Woman Who Loved Reindeer,* 1989

BIBLIOGRAPHY: *Children's Literature Review,* vol. 20, 1990; *Something about the Author,* vol. 67, 1992
SHANE RAYBURN

PIERCE, Tamora
Author, b. 13 December 1954, Connellsville, Pennsylvania

P., a writer of YOUNG ADULT fantasy, took only one writing course in college. She planned to go into social work but found that "stories were a wonderful way to escape the real world." P. studies the customs and chivalry of medieval life in order to create strong young female protagonists who deal with life head-on and shape their futures to fit their own needs and beliefs, characters with whom young readers can identify. P. has written three SERIES of books featuring young women who shed their conventional upbringing and enter the medieval world of adventure that was traditionally meant only for men.

Song of the Lioness (1983–88), P.'s first series, contains four books, beginning with *Alanna: The First Adventure.* (1983). This series follows the main character, Alanna, as she disguises herself as a young male knight in search of adventure. In her second series, The Immortals (1992–96) P.'s main character is a thirteen-year-old orphaned girl who has a heightened sense for danger and cares greatly for wild creatures. P.'s third series, The Circle of Magic, began in 1996. Her passion for Japanese, Arabic, and Asian history is evident as she brings together four culturally diverse young people who use their unusual backgrounds and talents to work together for a common purpose.

BIBLIOGRAPHY: *Something about the Author,* vol. 96, 1988; Gallo, Donald, ed., *Speaking for Ourselves, Too,* 1993

DENISE P. BEASLEY

PILKEY, Dav

Author, illustrator, b. 4 March 1966, Cleveland, Ohio

As far back as P. can remember he loved to draw and spent all his free time inside the house drawing animals, monsters, and superheroes. Television cartoons were his inspiration. In school, he remembers being unable to sit still and becoming the class clown. His teacher moved his desk into the hall allowing P. to spend his elementary school years creating cartoons and COMIC BOOKS. P. understood the HUMOR in his situation and bonded humor to literature to create an innovative, slapstick style of writing with enormous appeal to middle-grade boys. His hallway desk was well-stocked with paper and art supplies in hope that he would be quiet. Sitting there, P. created the humorous cartoon character of Captain Underpants to the delight of his classmates and the chagrin of the school principal. In 1984, while attending Kent State University, a professor encouraged P. to develop his writing skills. P. tried writing a children's book and submitted it to a contest for new writers and illustrators. He was amazed when he won and his entry, *World War Won,* was selected for publication. P. says it was the most exciting moment in his life and took all of his self-control "not to scream, jump up and down, and laugh hysterically. I was going to be an author!"

The popular Captain Underpants series, rich in puns and imaginative word play, is based on the cartoon stories he started writing back in elementary school, down to the character of a mean principal. With brief text and lots of black-and-white cartoon drawings (that some adults find repugnant), P. creates a world of super heroes with absurd names, using bathroom humor that young readers, boys especially, delight in. Captain Un-

derpants and Ricky Ricotta SERIES BOOKS are interactive with directions for flipping the pages to show the characters moving and with instructions for drawing cartoons. The colorful covers, always featuring a large, center ILLUSTRATION of the hero in his underpants on books like *Captain Underpants and the Incredibly Naughty Cafeteria Ladies from Outer Space* (1999) scream out at readers in lurid purple and fiery orange or similar colors. P. maintains a busy writing and illustrating schedule, and sometimes works with other authors or illustrators to keep pace with his creative ideas.

P. also writes and illustrates for younger children. In these series, his masterful use of bright colors and cartoon-style art appears deceptively childlike. P. works in a combination of art media, including watercolor, gouache, acrylics, pencil, and ink to create unusual-colorful illustrations. His board book series for preschoolers, Big Dog and Little Dog, uses simple language to describe events that relate to the everyday lives of very young children. P.'s EASY-TO-READ BOOKS for beginning readers, The Dragon Tale series or individual titles such as *Dog Breath: The Horrible Trouble with Hally Tosis* (1994) and *The Silly Gooses* (1998) emphasize the zany and ridiculous in text and illustrations. *The Dumb Bunnies* (Sue Denim, author, 1994), the first in a silly series of easy-to-read PICTURE BOOKS with P.'s signature-cartoon illustrations, presents a mixed-up version of verbal and visual puns based on familiar children's stories. The cover features the bunny family posed in a green bedroom reminiscent of *Good Night Moon* (Margaret Wise BROWN, author, Clement HURD, illus., 1947). They present responses to the world that appear reasonable to young children just starting to navigate social situations on their own.

Using acrylic and India ink in *The Paperboy* (1996), P. creates a gentle picture book story of a young boy dedicated to delivering his newspapers every morning while his family and the town sleep. The story's tone of quiet determination, following a routine, and the satisfaction of a job well done are matched by P.'s illustrations showing the boy's resolve at awakening in the dark, bundling his papers, and riding out with the first streaks of light in the sky.

AWARDS: ALA CALDECOTT MEDAL Honor Book (1997) for *The Paperboy*

FURTHER WORKS: Dumb Bunny series: *The Dumb Bunnies' Easter,* 1995; *Make Way for Dumb Bunnies,* 1996; *The Dumb Bunnies Go to the Zoo,* 1997; *The Hallo-wiener,* 1995; Captain Underpants series: *The Adventures of Captain Underpants,* 1997; *Captain Underpants and the Attack of the Talking Toilets,* 1997; *Captain Underpants and the Perilous Plot of Professor Poopypants,* 2000; *Ricky Ricotta's Giant Robot vs. the Mutant Mosquitoes from Mercury* (Martin Ontiveros, illus.), 2000

BIBLIOGRAPHY: Author's website: http://www.pilkey.com/abdavs.htm; publisher's notes; *Something about the Author,* vol. 68, 1992

MARY ARIAIL BROUGHTON

PINKNEY, Andrea Davis
Author, b. 25 September 1963, Washington, D.C.

P. was reared in a small town in Connecticut in a loving, literary, and supportive family. Her mother is a teacher who reads all the time and her father is a very good storyteller. She remembers writing her first story when she was in the second grade but her first book to be published was *Alvin Ailey* (1993). P. conducts thorough research on every book she writes; she spent a long time talking to Alvin Ailey's mother who told her that Alvin liked to sit in the front row at church. His favorite hymn was "Rock-a-My-Soul in the Bosom of Abraham." She started his BIOGRAPHY with that song.

Since Benjamin Banneker lived during the eighteenth century, it was impossible to meet him. P. and her husband, Brian PINKNEY who illustrated *Dear Benjamin Banneker* (1994), took a trip to the small town of Oella, Maryland, where Benjamin Banneker lived. There was a Benjamin Banneker museum with all kinds of books and information on him. P. even met and talked with one of Banneker's descendants. P. did a remarkable job on *Duke Ellington: The Piano Prince and His Orchestra,* a 1998 CALDECOTT MEDAL Honor Book. She captures in rhythmic prose the jazz beat of Ellington's music: Brian Pinkney matches the sounds with fluid rolling ILLUSTRATIONS. P. creates music with her words that makes you want to tap your feet as you read. She describes Ellington's blues music as deeper than the deep-blue sea or sassy-cool tones; it has notes that curl the tail of a kite in the wind. Brian Pinkney translated her words into scratchboard

gouache and oil paintings that swirl across double-page spreads in vibrant, breezy strokes to reflect the visual prose. The book beautifully evokes the mood and spirit of the jazz era.

P. earned her degree in journalism from Syracuse University in 1985. She served as an editor at *Essence* magazine, Simon and Schuster, and Scholastic for a number of years before moving to Hyperion Books for Children as senior editor and director of the Jump at the Sun imprint, which celebrates the beauty of black culture. P. has shaped many excellent books through this imprint.

AWARDS: Caldecott Medal Honor Book (1999) for *Duke Ellington: The Piano Prince and His Orchestra;* AMERICAN LIBRARY ASSOCIATION Notable Book (1996) for *Bill Pickett, Rodeo-ridin' Cowboy;* National Council of Social Studies–CHILDREN'S BOOK COUNCIL Notable book (1994) for *Dear Benjamin Banneker; Horn Book* Fanfare (1993) for *Alvin Ailey;* American Bookseller Pick of the List (1993) for *Seven Candles for Kwanzaa*

FURTHER WORKS: *Shake, Shake, Shake,* 1994, 1997; *I Smell Honey,* 1997; *Pretty Brown Face,* 1997; *Solo Girl,* 1997; *Watch Me Dance,* 1997; *Raven in a Dove House,* 1998; *Silent Thunder: A Civil War Story,* 1999; *Jump Back, Honey: The Poems of Paul Laurence Dunbar,* 1999; *Let It Shine: Stories of Black Women Freedom Fighters,* 2000; *Mim's Christmas Jam,* 2001

BIBLIOGRAPHY: Publisher's press releases, biographies; www.DISNEY.go.com/educational/feature_bio_adp.html

BERNICE E. CULLINAN

PINKNEY, Brian
Illustrator, author, b. 28 August 1961, Boston, Massachusetts

P. is the son of illustrator Jerry PINKNEY and author Gloria Jean P. His formal education continued to build on the influences of his early home life: he earned an undergraduate degree at Philadelphia College of Art in 1983 and a masters degree in fine arts from the School of Visual Arts (New York City) in 1990. In addition to working as an illustrator, P. has taught at the Children's Art Carnival, in Harlem, and at the School of Visual Arts; he has displayed work at shows organized by the Society of Illustrators.

In 1990, *The Boy and His Ghost* (1989) received the National Arts Club Award of Distinction, and the Parents' Choice Honor Award for ILLUSTRATION. That same year, he was awarded the Parents' Choice Honor Award for Story Books for *The Ballad of Belle Dorcas* (1990), in which P. and author William HOOKS recount the tale of a free-born AFRICAN AMERICAN woman using conjure magic to liberate the slave she loves. The following year, Parents' Choice PICTURE BOOK awards went to *Where Does This Trail Lead?* (1991), a picture book written by Burton Albert about a small boy and his family at the seashore, and to *A Wave in Her Pocket* (1991), stories from Trinidad collected and retold by Lynn Joseph. *Where Does This Trail Lead?* also won a Golden Kite Honor Award in 1991. In 1993, *Sukey and the Mermaid* (Robert SAN SOUCI, author) won the CORETTA SCOTT KING AWARD Honor Book for illustration.

P. employs the technique of scratchboard to illustrate works about African American life (both historic and contemporary), folktales (including *Wiley and the Hairy Man,* 1996), and Ethiopia's Jewish traditions (*Day of Delight,* and *When I Left My Village,* both by Maxine Rose Schnur, 1994 and 1996, respectively). Among the BIOGRAPHIES he has illustrated are those of *Harriet Tubman and Black History Month* (by Polly Carter, 1990) and *Alvin Ailey,* by P's wife, Andrea Davis PINKNEY (1993). P. researches his topics in depth, taking dance lessons, for instance, when working on Alvin Ailey. P. has also illustrated collections of children's poems by noted African Americans: *The Lost Zoo,* by Countee Cullen (1992) and *The Dream Keeper and Other Poems,* by Langston HUGHES (1994), bring these classics to modern children.

P. has also added writing to his career with children's books. *Max Found Two Sticks* (1994), *Jojo's Flying Sidekick* (1995), and *The Adventures of Sparrow Boy* (1997) feature contemporary African American children. He collaborates with Andrea PINKNEY on a SERIES of board books for babies, including *I Smell Honey* and *Pretty Brown Face* (both 1997).

AWARDS: ALA CALDECOTT MEDAL Honor Book (1999) for *Duke Ellington: The Piano Prince and His Orchestra* (Andrea Davis PINKNEY, author)

FURTHER WORKS: *Julie Brown: Racing against the World,* 1988; *The Dark Thirty: Southern Tales of the Supernatural,* 1992; *The Elephant's Wres-*

tling Match, 1992; *Seven Candles for Kwanzaa,* 1993; *Happy Birthday, Martin Luther King,* 1993; *Dear Benjamin Banneker,* 1994; *Bill Pickett, Rodeo-Ridin' Cowboy,* 1996; *Duke Ellington: The Piano Prince and His Orchestra,* 1998

BIBLIOGRAPHY: *Something about the Author,* vol. 73 1993

FRANCISCA GOLDSMITH

PINKNEY, Gloria Jean
Author, b. 5 September 1941, Lumberton, North Carolina

P.'s first books, *Back Home* (1992) and its prequel, *The Sunday Outing* (1994), evolved from childhood memories of a trip she took to North Carolina when she was eight years old. P.'s husband, illustrator Jerry PINKNEY, provided the ILLUSTRATIONS for the books. His illustrations portrayed a loving AFRICAN AMERICAN family. P.'s *The Sunday Outing* was named a *New York Times* Best Illustrated Book of the Year in 1994. P. often does research in connection with her husband's writing and illustrating efforts.

FURTHER WORKS: *The Grand Finale,* 1996

BIBLIOGRAPHY: *Something about the Author,* vol. 85, 1996

JODI PILGRIM

PINKNEY, Jerry
Illustrator, b. 22 December 1939, Philadelphia, Pennsylvania

P. is a popular and critically acclaimed picture-book illustrator, his range of artistic venues includes record jackets, greeting cards, china, and U.S.–postage stamps. His artistic career began early when he gained recognition from family, friends, and teachers for his talent for drawing. Reading was of little interest to him as a child, but P. won scholarships for art classes as a boy and attended a vocational secondary school that prepared him for a scholarship-supported higher education at the Philadelphia Museum College of Art (now University of the Arts).

P.'s career in book ILLUSTRATION developed from other pursuits in painting and commercial art. While working on textbook designs, he became involved in picture-book publishing, an arena that allows him to explore DESIGN, illustration, and STORYTELLING simultaneously.

P.'s PICTURE BOOKS have won many AWARDS. *Song of the Trees* (Mildred TAYLOR, 1975) earned him the Council on Interracial Books for Children Award (1973), was selected for the Children's Book Showcase (1976) and merited the Jane Addams Book Group Award (1976). Again working with Taylor, P. illustrated *Roll of Thunder, Hear My Cry* (1976), which earned the ALA NEWBERY MEDAL and the Jane Addams Book Group Award (both 1976), then became a National Book Award finalist (1977) and Young Readers' Choice Award winner (1979). *Childtimes: A Three-Generation Memoir* (Eloise GREENFIELD and Lessie Jones Little, 1979) and *Tonweya and the Eagles, and Other Lakota Indian Tales* (retold by Rosebud Yellow Robe, 1979) were selected for the American Institute of Graphics Arts Book Show (both 1980). *Childtimes* also won the Carter J. Woodson Award (1980). *Count on Your Fingers African Style* (Claudia Zaslavsky, 1980) earned the Outstanding Science Book Award from the National Association of Science Teachers and the Carter G. Woodson Award (both 1980), as well as runner-up for the CORETTA SCOTT KING AWARD that year.

The Patchwork Quilt (Valerie FLOURNOY, 1985) earned P. the Christopher Award and the Coretta Scott King Award (both 1986). He earned another Coretta Scott King Award in 1987, for *Half a Moon and One Whole Star* (Crescent DRAGONWAGON, 1986), and a third, in 1988, for *Mirandy and Brother Wind* (Patricia MCKISSACK, 1988). *Mirandy and Brother Wind* also was named a CALDECOTT MEDAL Honor Book in 1989. *The Talking Eggs* (Robert SAN SOUCI, 1989) is a Caldecott Medal Honor Book (1990), Coretta Scott King Honor Book (1990), and winner of the Golden Sower Award (1992). *Home Place* (Dragonwagon, 1990) won the SOCIETY OF CHILDREN'S BOOK WRITERS AND ILLUSTRATORS Golden Kite Award (1990). P. has been cited by Drexel University, the Philadelphia College of Art and Design Alumni, and Framingham State College for his work in the field of children's literature.

P., whose illustrative style is realistic and energetic, has worked with many well-known children's authors who address AFRICAN AMERICAN culture through contemporary stories, historical fiction, and folktales. He works with live models and undertakes large amounts of research to invest each project with cultural integrity as well as pleasing aesthetics. His favorite medium remains the pencil sketch and he continues to employ that alone in some illustrations. Much of his work is done with watercolor, the earmark pencil sketches underlying the brightness of the paints. Whether rendered in black and white or color, his scenes are generally presented close up and filled with action.

P. enjoys allowing animals to remain realistic in his illustrations, although certain stories require them to be humanized. In *Sam and the Tigers* (Julius LESTER, 1996), the title human character lives in a world where animals and humans talk to—and do business with—each other, but P.'s tigers remain untamed. Their costuming with Sam's elegant garments is but a momentary lapse in their ferocious projection of the jungle's wildness.

Many of P.'s picture books present readers with information about social and family life in the United States between the antebellum and the civil-rights eras. Working with, among others, Crescent Dragonwagon, Valerie Flournoy, Eloise Greenfield, Julius Lester, and San Souci, P. provides vivid imagery to expand upon the stories they tell of African American history. The stories include those of historical persons as well as tales that feature events that might have been. He has worked with Lester on many projects, including *The Tales of Uncle Remus* (1988), which have been controversial in the African American literary community due to the author's exploration of a racially charged FOLKLORE history. P. has illustrated Zora Neale HURSTON's *Their Eyes Were Watching God* (1991) and has worked with his wife, Gloria Jean PINKNEY, on several picture-book projects. P.'s interpretive concerns are not limited to the experiences and folklore of African Americans but also include illustrating tales from NATIVE AMERICA (*Tonweya and the Eagles,* and Cruz Martel's *Yagua Days,* 1976), THE BIBLE (Barbara Diamond Goldin's *Journeys with Elijah: Eight Tales of the Prophet,* 1999), and stories from other peoples and times.

In addition to book, commercial, and FINE ARTS projects, P. has provided illustration work for such periodicals as *National Geographic.* He has designed jackets for juvenile biographies and novels, including those by Virginia HAMILTON and Alice CHILDRESS. P. has been involved in the design of U.S. postage stamps, creating several in the Black Heritage series, and perceives this specialized but highly visible arena as one that allows him to share with the general public the importance of such African American heroes and heroines as Scott Joplin and Harriet Tubman. He has shown his paintings internationally for more than thirty years.

FURTHER WORKS: *The Adventures of Spider: West African Folk Tales.* (Retold by Joyce Cooper Arkhurst). 1964: *Babushka and the Pig* (Ann Trofimuk), 1969: *Kasho and the Twin Flutes.* (Adjai Robinson). 1973: *Jahdu.* (V. Hamilton). 1980: *Rabbit Makes a Monkey of Lion.* (Verna AARDEMA). 1989: *Back Home.* (G. Pinkney). 1992: *Drylongso.* (V. Hamilton). 1992: *The Last Tales of Uncle Remus.* (J. Lester). 1994: *Tanya's Reunion.* (V. Flournoy. 1995: *Black Cowboy, Wild Horses: A True Story.* (J. Lester). 1998: *The Little Match Girl.* (ANDERSEN). author. 1999

BIBLIOGRAPHY: Meglin, N. "The Strength of Weakness: A Profile of Illustrator Jerry Pinkney," *American Artist*, January 1982; Silvey, A. ed., *Children's Books and Their Creators*, 1995; *Something about the Author*, vols. 41, 1985, and 71, 1993

                                    FRANCISCA GOLDSMITH

PINKWATER, Daniel
Author, illustrator, b. 15 November 1941, Memphis, Tennessee

Although P. was born in Memphis, he grew up in Chicago and Los Angeles. P. went to Bard College in Annandale-on-Hudson, New York, where he graduated with a Bachelor of Arts degree in 1964. P. decided to study sculpture, believing it would make him a better writer, and for three years he apprenticed with David Nyvall. For a time, P. worked as a fine artist and taught art to children. When P. created a set of ILLUSTRATIONS that were later to become *The Terrible Roar* (1970), he realized that he did not want anyone else to write the text. P. then thought about doing books for children. P.'s work is often described as being FANTASY or SCIENCE FICTION but others contend that it is more the case of the extraordinary within the ordinary. Although some critics

call P.'s work nontraditional, all of P.'s books have a sense of adventure and a glorious sense of the absurd. Whether it contains a blue moose, the Frankenbagel Monster, a 266-pound chicken, or a free-spirited prep-school student, all of P.'s works are bursting with imagination. In *I Was a Second Grade Werewolf* (1983) a young boy becomes a werewolf only to become dismayed when no one notices. In *Blue Moose* (1975), a moose walks into a restaurant and ends up working as a waiter. With his wife Jill Pinkwater, a children's author and illustrator, P. has created an affable if opinionated polar bear named Larry who just happens to live in the pool of a nice hotel. In *At the Hotel Larry* (1998) you are welcome to swim, but only if Larry likes you.

P. also writes for YOUNG ADULTS; *The Education of Robert Nifkin* (1998) is a unique novel set in the 1950s written in the form of a college application essay. A number of P.'s works have been recognized. *Lizard Music* (1976) was named an AMERICAN LIBRARY ASSOCIATION Notable Book. *Fat Men from Space* (1977) was a 1977 Junior Literary Guild selection. *The Wuggie Norple Story* (1980) was selected as a Children's Choice and *Roger's Umbrella* (1982) received the Parents' Choice Award. While P. considers himself an author for children and others of good taste, his off-the-wall HUMOR and quick wit are not limited to print alone. P.'s humorous take on life can also be heard on National Public Radio's *All Things Considered.*

FURTHER WORKS: *Big Orange Splot*, 1977; *The Snarkout Boys and the Avocado of Death*, 1982; *Jolly Roger, a Dog of Hoboken*, 1985; *Doodle Flute*, 1991; *Author's Day*, 1993; *Bongo Larry*, 1998

BIBLIOGRAPHY: Silvey, Anita, ed., *Children's Books and Their Creators*, 1995; *Fifth Book of Junior Authors and Illustrators*, 1983; *Something about the Author*, vol. 76, 1994
                                    DEDE SMALL

PIPER, Watty
Collective pseudonym

P. is a pseudonym created by the Platt and Munk publishing house in the early 1920s and used through 1978. In 1978, Platt and Munk became a division of Grosset and Dunlap. While moving from their former offices to their new quarters, records of Platt and Munk's children's division were lost, making it impossible to substantiate which authors, illustrators, and editors were actually responsible for those works attributed to "Watty Piper." However, it seems that—in addition to MOTHER GOOSE—such identifiable children's artists and authors as Lois LENSKI, Mabel C. Bragg, George and Doris Hauman, Eulalie Banks, and Helen BANNERMAN contributed either inspiration for or the actual work published as Watty Piper's.

Adapted from a story by Bragg, *The Pony Engine,* P.'s most famous work, *The Little Engine That Could* (1930, 1945, 1954, 1957, 1961, 1976, and 1979), was awarded the Lewis CARROLL Shelf Award in 1959. Lois Lenski provided the ILLUSTRATIONS for the first edition, but it was the work of George and Doris Hauman that earned *The Little Engine* (1954 edition) the title of being worthy to sit on the same shelf as *Alice's Adventures in Wonderland.* Ruth Sanderson's illustrations, for the 1976 edition, received considerable critical attention at the time of its appearance, as did the fact that the engines in the story reflect the stereotypes of masculine strength and feminine weakness in vogue when it was written.

Most works attributed to P. are anthologies of nursery verses, simplistic stories of children in countries around the world, ANIMAL tales or retellings of folktales. However, P. is also credited with renditions of Carlo COLLODI's *Pinocchio* (1940) and Helen BANNERMAN's *Little Black Sambo* (1972). Although often unpopular with literary critics, P.'s work has been the object of affection for generations of very young readers. Many books by P., like *The Little Engine* with her refrain of "I think I can, I think I can," are simply so minimalist in plotting and theme that children in the early stages of literacy can readily comprehend the essential message.

FURTHER WORKS: *The Gateway to Storyland,* 1925; FAIRY TALES *That Never Grow Old,* 1927; *The Rooster, the Mouse, and the Little Red Hen,* 1928; *Little Folks of Other Lands,* 1929; *Folk Tales Children Love,* 1934; *The Three Little Pigs,* 1945; *Animal Stories,* 1954; *Mother Goose, a Treasury of Best Loved Rhymes,* 1972; *Watty Piper's Trucks,* 1978

BIBLIOGRAPHY: Ord, Priscilla, *American Writers for Children,* 1983

FRANCISCA GOLDSMITH

PLOTZ, Helen
Poet, anthologist, b. 20 March 1913, New York City; d. 3 March 2000, Brooklyn, New York

P. has always loved POETRY; she is interested in all its forms and in poets whose work appeals to children. Among her collections are the works of Emily Dickinson and Robert Louis STEVENSON. She also edited books of sonnets and ballads, both of which include poetry classics that capture children's interest. P. has published several collections of spiritual poetry, poetry from dance and music, art and architecture, and science and math. All the topics P. has anthologized impact the lives of children, allowing them to acquire imaginative perspective from their poetic treatment. Children especially enjoy her anthology of school poems, *Gladly Learn and Gladly Teach: Poems of the School Experience* (1982), which deals with all aspects of the place, outside the home, that has greatest influence on them.

FURTHER WORKS: *Imagination's Other Place: Poems of Science and Math,* 1955; *Eye's Delight: Poems of Art and Architecture,* 1983

REBECCA RAPPORT

POETRY IN CHILDREN'S LITERATURE

When Ralph Waldo Emerson said that poetry "teaches us the power of a few words" he pinpointed the gift that simple poetry gives to young readers. Verse—free or more formally constructed, including everything from couplets, cinquains, and quatrains to haiku or jump-rope jingles, limericks, and song lyrics—all can introduce young readers, and those who are not yet readers to the wonders of rhythmic language. It is language they can appreciate and respond to with ease.

There is probably no hard definition of poetry for children; one is not necessary. But in their introduction to *The Oxford Book of Children's Verse* (1973) Iona and Peter OPIE differentiated between poetry originally written for children and poetry that, like FAIRY TALES, became theirs through use and adoption. The Opies, renowned anthologists and literary historians, noted that before the mid-eighteenth century there was little written for children that was not exhortative; to be for a child poems had to be edifying. Writing that "verse for children tends to be intimately related to the period in which it was written" they added that "Wordsworth's ballads link the eighteenth century to the new awareness of children in the nineteenth century." As I reread those words the twenty-first century is upon us. Poetry for everyone, young and old, appears to be everywhere. Politicians use rhyming couplets, song lyrics are the lingua franca of the under-twenty crowd. A program called "Poetry in Motion," begun a few years in about half a dozen mass transit systems across the country, has used at least two poems for children on subways and buses so far, one by Shel SILVERSTEIN and one by me. Poetry is news now. Silverstein's recent death was marked on the evening report with a reading by the nation's poet laureate Robert Pinsky, a regular guest. There are poetry slams and jams, and conferences on poetry abound. Even the roll of paper towels sitting on my kitchen counter this morning has a short, haikulike verse about butterflies, printed on it, over and over.

Instead of an art that few practiced, and fewer enjoyed, poetry seems to be growing into a part and pillar of popular culture. Perhaps this is because it is particularly suited to those reared in an age of imagery. As television and film have continued breaking narrative into smaller sound bites and thinner slices of time, we have gotten used to absorbing information delivered in short forms, stories built of brief scenes intercut by briefer scenes. Poetry, which Matthew Arnold described as "thought and art in one," is very good at this kind of thing, at serving emotion and information in well-wrapped nutshells. We live with talking machines now, automated voices answer our phones, and call to sell us real estate at dinnertime. Maybe this partially explains why so many of us desire a kind of personal expression that affirms one as an "I" rather than as an automated "it." That I is the soul of a poem.

In the second half of the twentieth century, as the so-called inner child blossomed, self-expression bloomed. Slowly but surely some of the more complicated poetic forms were left to gather dust, and wise teachers, stressing word sounds, rhythm, and short simple verse, developed children's poetry as a multipurpose teaching tool useful for loosening writing skills, and helping the young read (rhyming texts it was discovered, give clues to novice readers). Dr. SEUSS dove into the rhythm and rhyme business with swinging ease, entrancing millions of young readers, and transformed the Pied Piper into a charismatic Cat . . . in a Hat. When Seuss needed syllables to stretch a line he just reached into his extraordinary bag of nonsense sounds and found them, much as Edward LEAR and Lewis CARROLL had done a hundred years before. Only now the sounds and the rhythms were different. At the same time the gradual entrance of haiku into classrooms helped discerning teachers understand that good poetry does not have to rhyme. An infinite variety of free verse forms reshaped the look of words on the page. But while many assumptions about poetry were discarded or readjusted in the last quarter of the twentieth century, rhyme, particularly in children's poetry, did not disappear. It is so satisfying to listen to rhyme. Maybe this has to do with the way those neat explosions marking the ends of lines resonate in our heads or echo our heartbeats.

Certainly children continue to respond with pleasure to rhyme. However, like many others, when I am given the opportunity I discourage young writers from reaching for rhymes. The young see with such fresh vision, such unfettered imagination that given a chance, they create splendid images. But their rhyming is usually borrowed, and therefore tired. David MCCORD labeled it "Doggerel." He wrote that poetry "like rain, should fall with elemental music." McCord was born in 1897 and died, poetically enough, in 1997. He wrote brisk, witty verse that often was both streamlined and intricate. You feel the classical foundation in his writing as you read his lines. McCord won the first award for children's poetry given by the NATIONAL COUNCIL OF TEACHERS OF ENGLISH. That was in 1977.

A short list of twentieth century poets writing for children must begin with four others who have died in the last few years: Eve MERRIAM, who wrote successfully in many areas, and whose smart, funny verse is well attuned to children's ears; Myra Cohn LIVINGSTON, a disciplined poet and thinker who was also an influential teacher of writers; Valerie WORTH, whose clear eyes and perceptive pen helped us see so much that is old in new ways; and Barbara Juster ESBENSEN, whose enthusiasm and talent as a teacher is very much alive in her books. Then there are many who, unaffected by so-called Y2K, will keep writing in the new century. Among them are: Charlotte ZOLOTOW who understands that good picture books and poetry are written with the same gifts for hearing and appreciating the subtleties of language; Nancy WILLARD who, with her magical imagination, won the first NEWBERY MEDAL awarded to a poetry book; multivoiced, ingenious Paul FLEISCHMAN who won the next; Eloise GREENFIELD whose pared-down lines rejoice, confront, and sing. And there is the energy and experimental spirit of Arnold ADOFF, that master of funny short forms X. J. Kennedy; Joyce Carol THOMAS, whose poetic voice is soft and compelling; lively versifier and anthologist Jack PRELUTSKY; and Lee Bennett HOPKINS who has worked hard and long as a missionary bringing poetry to teachers and children, and whose verse autobiography convinces through simplicity and strength.

David McCord insisted that poetry for children "should catch the eye as well the ear and the mind." There's the rub. If children come to poetry when they are very young, if they are introduced to it by good readers who love poetry, if they listen to it a lot, and read it often, they will very likely grow into committed poetry readers and even, as time goes by, poetry writers.

KARLA KUSKIN

POLACCO, Patricia

Author, illustrator, b. 11 July 1944, Lansing, Michigan

Combining her artistic talents and her gifts as a storyteller, P. draws upon both the stories told her by her grandparents and her own life experiences as she shares her rich cultural heritage with readers of all ages. Her books are noted for their family and MULTICULTURAL points of view, as she includes, in a naturally positive light, diverse ages, genders, and ethnicities that have shared her own life experiences.

Coming from a heritage that includes Russian–Ukranian, Irish, as well as Jewish and Christian backgrounds, P. credits her grandparents for much of her imaginative abilities, and she credits her imagination as the source of her creativity.

She has said on many occasions that her mother's parents—her Russian grandparents—were lyrical and turned ordinary happenings into extraordinary events. The oral tradition shared by her father's "shanty Irish" family gave her historical anecdotes and added to her sense of the significance of story. Her artistic ability was encouraged by all her family and was her strength in school. Since she unknowingly suffered from dyslexia, reading made school work stressful until a discerning teacher identified her situation and helped her adapt to the problem.

Not only did P. have an abundance of family resources to draw upon as she created books, but she also lived in a quite diverse community in California. Born in Michigan, P. lived with her maternal grandmother for almost three years after her parents' divorce at the age of three. After her grandmother died, she and her mother moved to Florida for a few years and then to California where P. lived for thirty-seven years. Her experiences and friendships here are found in many of her books, such as *Chicken Sunday* (1992) and *Mrs. Katz and Tush* (1992). However, during this time she spent summers in Michigan with her father and grandparents, so her family influence continued throughout her life as did her love of the farm land on which they lived.

After majoring in fine arts at Monash University, P. earned both a masters and doctorate degree in Australia at the University of Melborne in 1978 while her husband was working there. Initial work involved restoring Russian and Greek art for museums. P.'s writing career began when, at age forty-one, she retold through words and art the story of a meteor that fell in her family's yard. After *Meteor* (1987) was accepted for publication, recognition of her talents in terms of STORYTELLING and illustrating quickly grew.

FAMILY STORIES provide the basis for titles such as *The Keeping Quilt* (1988) and *Uncle Vova's Tree* (1989). *Pink and Say* (1994) was also a family story that was passed down by her great-great-grandfather who befriended a black soldier at Andersonville Prison during the Civil War. *Thunder Cake* (1990) continues this theme of family stories that show relationships between children and older adults. This books contains the momentum that one often feels in P.'s books as the grandmother and child quickly gather the ingredients that will resolve the child's fear of thunder.

Multicultural experiences are authentically embedded within the plots of *Chicken Sunday* and *Mrs. Katz and Tush;* however, P. extends her invitation to readers to experience other cultures in the pages of *Rechenka's Eggs* (1988) and *Just Plain Fancy* (1990). P. realizes that for many children their only exposure to other cultures is through literature. Her work emphasizes the commonalities and shared life experiences as well as shows the uniqueness of various ages, religions, gender, communities, and ethnicity.

Literacy events are often the topic of her books. *The Bee Tree* (1993) tells the story of a community chase after a bee to the honey that represents the sweetness of reading and knowledge. *Aunt Chip and the Great Triple Creek Dam Affair* (1996) humorously tells of a town that had forgotten the joys of reading and what the librarian did about the problem. *Thank You, Mr. Falker* (1998) is P.'s own story of a caring teacher who identified her reading disability and helped her learn to read. P.'s own love of reading is reflected in her texts and enthusiastically supports the significance of reading.

P.'s work extends across several genres—FOLKLORE, fiction, autobiography, and FANTASY. She has even adapted POETRY in a book, *Casey at the Bat* (1988). Each form of storytelling, however, is brought to life with colorful, intense, authentically detailed pictures. The process of elaborating on an idea and mentally creating a book has its roots in the many rocking chairs P. owns. Before the intricate process of actually creating illustrations and text, each story has been carefully considered to the rhythm of a rocker. When P. begins her work, she breaks only to eat until it is finished on paper. She uses markers, acrylic paint, pencils, and oil pastels to create her vibrant pictures. Occasionally she actually places a photograph of a particular real-life character within a drawn picture.

P. approaches with vitality and sensitivity topics concerning culture, literacy, and the value of family stories. Through both illustration and text many potential connections for readers lie within her books. The unique nature of her stories as well as the universal themes woven within draw a large audience to her books both for personal reading and classroom use.

AWARDS: INTERNATIONAL READING ASSOCIATION Best PICTURE BOOK Award (1988) for *Rechenka's Eggs;* Sydney TAYLOR Award (1988) for *The Keeping Quilt.* She received the Educators for Social Responsibility Award in 1991. Golden Kite Award for ILLUSTRATION (1992) for *Chicken Sunday. Applemando's Dreams* was a READING RAINBOW Book. Numerous books have been designated NATIONAL COUNCIL OF TEACHERS OF ENGLISH Notable Trade Books in the Language Arts and AMERICAN LIBRARY ASSOCIATION Notable Children's Books, including *Just Plain Fancy* (1990) and *Pink and Say* (1995)

FURTHER WORKS: *Babushka's Doll,* 1990; *Applemando's Dreams,* 1991; *Some Birthday!,* 1991; *Picnic at Mudsock Meadow,* 1992; *Babushka Baba Yaga,* 1993; *Tikvah Means Hope,* 1994; *My Rotten Redheaded Older Brother,* 1994; *I Can Hear the Sun: A Modern Myth,* 1996; *In Enzo's Splendid Gardens,* 1997; *Trees of the Dancing Goats,* 1996; *Mrs. Mack,* 1998

BIBLIOGRAPHY: Anhold, S. and I. Ramsey. "P.P." at <http://falcon.jmu.edu/ [Dec. 20, 1998]. Penguin/Putnam Publishers (1998), "P.P." at <http://www.penguinputnam.com//> [Dec. 20, 1998], P.P., *Fire Talking,* 1994; "P.P." at <http://www.patriciapolacco.com//> [Dec. 20, 1998]; *Seventh Book of Junior Authors and Illustrators,* 1996. *Something about the Author,* vol. 74, 1993

JANELLE B. MATHIS

POLITI, Leo

Author, illustrator, b. 21 November 1908, Fresno, California; d. 24 March 1996, Los Angeles, California

P. was born in the United States, but his family returned to Italy when he was seven, and P. remained there until his early twenties. While in Italy, and during a year that his family spent in London, P. enjoyed art both in museums and as he watched sidewalk chalk artists creating it. As a small child, P. demonstrated an interest in drawing and had an active imagination. His mother encouraged him to compete for an art school scholarship as a teenager. In 1923, P. won a scholarship to study at the Art Institute at the Royal Palace of Monza, near Milan, Italy. When P. returned to the United States in 1931, he became keenly interested in Mexican street life in Los Angeles, where he lived in the heart of the oldest part of that city. His first children's book was the self-illustrated *Little Pancho* (1938), which he wrote while supporting himself and his family as a muralist and sidewalk artist.

P.'s PICTURE BOOKS were often inspired by the people he really knew from the streets of Los Angeles or children he met in his travels. Simple Spanish and Italian phrases are included in some of his texts, as is music from the Mexican and Italian immigrant cultures he knew so well. In 1961, he published *Moy Moy,* a story about Chinese children in Los Angeles, again basing his work on daily experience with real children. In addition to writing his own picture books, he illustrated stories written by others, including Ruth SAWYER's *The Least One* (1941), Louis Perez's *El Coyote, the Rebel* (1947), and Elizabeth COATSWORTH's *The Noble Doll* (1961). P. worked largely in watercolor, sometimes mixing in white for a tempera-like appearance. In addition to his work for children, P. also published several books about Los Angeles for adults.

AWARDS: ALA CALDECOTT MEDAL (1950) for *Song of the Swallows.* AMERICAN LIBRARY ASSOCIATION Caldecott Medal Honor Book (1947) for *Pedro, the Angel of Olvera Street* and (1949) for *Juanita.* New York Herald Tribune's Spring Festival Honor Award (1948) for *Juanita,* (1949) for *At the Palace Gates* (H. R. Parish, author) and (1952) for *Looking-for-Something: The Story of a Stray Burro in Ecuador* (Ann Nolan CLARK, author.) Catholic Library Association Regina Medal (1966) for P.'s contribution to children's literature. ALA Notable Books (1946) for *Pedro,* (1950) for *Magic Money* (Ann Nolan Clark, author), (1955) for *The Columbus Story* (Alice DALGLIESH, author) and (1953) for *The Mission Bell*

FURTHER WORKS: *Little Leo,* 1951; *Saint Francis and the Animals,* 1959; *A Boat for Peppe,* 1960; *Rosa,* 1963; *Emmet,* 1971; *The Nicest Gift,* 1973; *Mr. Fong's Toy Shop,* 1978

BIBLIOGRAPHY: Arbuthnot, May Hill, *Children and Books,* 3rd ed., 1964; HOPKINS, Lee Bennett, *Books Are by People,* 1964; Hopkins, Lee Bennett, *Pauses: Autobiographical Reflections of 101 Creators of Children's Books,* 1995; P., Leo, *Reminiscences of Bygone Days,* 1964

FRANCISCA GOLDSMITH

POMERANTZ, Charlotte

Author, b. 24 July 1930, New York City

P. spent most of her childhood in New Rochelle, New York, but when sixteen, lived a year in Europe while her father was deputy chief counsel of the Nuremberg Trials. Living in Manhattan once they returned to the United States, P. graduated from the Walden School. P. attended Sarah Lawrence College and while there contributed to a campus literary magazine. After graduating with her B.A. degree in 1953, P. worked for a time as a salesperson, waitress, researcher, copy editor, and writer. While working as a salesperson, P. wrote a long children's story about the hierarchy of personnel in a zoo, which paralleled the department store in which she worked. Years later, a friend suggested that P. submit it to a publisher. After many revisions it was accepted and published. Encouraged by this success, P. wrote and submitted others.

One of P.'s early books, *The Day They Parachuted Cats into Borneo: A Drama of Ecology* (1971) told the true story of ecological near disaster. In order to kill malaria spreading mosquitoes, DDT was sprayed throughout the island. In addition to killing the mosquitoes, roaches ingested the DDT and in turn the geckos and the cats were affected. With the island's ecosystem in havoc, the rat population increased dramatically and cats literally had to be flown in to restore the balance. Written as a play, *The Day They Parachuted Cats into Borneo,* was given an Outstanding PICTURE BOOK of the Year citation by the *New York Times.* Always fresh, P's work is marked by its variety and originality. Another of P.'s well-known books, *The Princess and the Admiral* (1974), is an adaptation of a folktale set during Kublai Khan's invasion of Vietnam. Princess Mat Mat must use her clever wit to outsmart the warrior and ensure the Tiny Kingdom's celebration of one hundred years' peace.

The Chalk Doll (1989), a Parent's Choice selection, is the story of a Jamaican mother telling her daughter about her own childhood. P.'s work's also includes collections of POETRY. *The Tamarindo Puppy and Other Poems* (1980) combines Spanish and English together in lively poems. It was named an AMERICAN LIBRARY ASSOCIATION Notable Book of the Year. Also MULTICULTURAL in theme is *If I Had a Paka* (1982). Twelve poems feature words from eleven languages, including Dutch, Indonesian, Samoan, Swahili, and Vietnamese. Although P. has written for a number of years, she is still finding new material from her life.

FURTHER WORKS: *The Piggy in the Puddle.* (J. MARSHALL, illus). 1974: *The Mango Tooth.* (Marilyn HAFNER, illus). 1977: *The Half-Birthday Party* (DiSalvo-Ryan, illus). 1984: *Serena Katz.* (Alley, illus). 1992

BIBLIOGRAPHY: *Sixth Book of Junior Authors and Illustrators,* 1989; *Something about the Author,* vol. 80, 1995

DEDE SMALL

POPE, Elizabeth Marie
Author, b. 1 May 1917, Washington, D.C.

P. receives praise for her STORYTELLING ability and the subtle HUMOR in her two novels for children. Both FANTASY in nature, *The Sherwood Ring* (1958) and *The Perilous Gard* (1974), contain historical elements and details. *The Sherwood Ring* skillfully combines events from the American Revolutionary War and the twentieth century to create a fantasy setting for two love stories. *The Perilous Gard* was named an ALA NEWBERY MEDAL Honor Book in 1975. P. also contributed to periodicals such as *Shakespeare Quarterly.*

FURTHER WORKS: *Paradise Regained,* 1947; *The Sherwood Ring,* 1958

BIBLIOGRAPHY: *Something about the Author,* vol. 36, 1984

JODI PILGRIM

POP-UP BOOKS

(See Movable Books [Pop-up Books])

PORTE, Barbara Ann
Author, b. 18 May 1943, New York City

P. was head of Children's Services at Nassau County LIBRARIES on Long Island, New York, for many years. She served on numerous professional committees for AMERICAN LIBRARY ASSOCIATION, INTERNATIONAL READING ASSOCIATION, CHILDREN'S BOOK COUNCIL and others. She has a strong background in FOLKLORE and stories of cultural heritage.

P.'s first books contained a small-boy narrator who lives with his single parent dad. The Harry books are very popular. Although P. is best known for her Harry books for beginning readers,

she has also contributed a variety of books for middle graders and YOUNG ADULTS.

FURTHER WORKS: *Harry's Visit,* 1983. *Harry's Dog,* 1984. *Harry in Trouble,* 1985. *Harry's Mom,* 1985. *The Kidnapping of Aunt Elizabeth,* 1985. *Ruthann and Her Pig,* 1989. *Something Terrible Happened,* 1994. *Chickens! Chickens!* 1995

BIBLIOGRAPHY: *Something about the Author,* vol. 93, 1997

JODI PILGRIM

PORTER, Eleanor
Author, b. 19 December 1868, Littleton, New Hampshire; d. 21 May 1920, Cambridge, Massachusetts

P. was a writer of popular novels. Her first book, *Cross Currents,* was published in 1907. She wrote thirteen more novels in thirteen years. Best sellers were *Miss Billy* (1911) and *Just David* (1916). Her best remembered book that sold millions of copies is *Pollyanna* (1913), a story about an eternally optimistic orphan girl. Pollyanna retained her cheerful outlook with her "glad game," a game similar to the saying: "It could be worse; be glad you didn't need the crutches in the missionary barrel." The Pollyanna name remains in our vocabulary to signify an optimistic person. Due to the overwhelming popularity of *Pollyanna, The Pollyanna Annual,* the *Yearly Glad Book,* and a Pollyanna Calendar were published. *Pollyanna Grows Up* (1914) was a sequel set in Boston. *Pollyanna* was so popular, after the author's death other writers were commissioned to continue the stories. P.'s novels and short stories all emphasize a positive attitude toward life. No matter what the problem, cheerfulness, love, and self-sacrifice will see the reader through.

BIBLIOGRAPHY: *Contemporary Authors.* vol. 108, 1983. *Dictionary of Literary Biography,* vol. 9, 1982; *American Novelists: 1910–1945,* 1981; *Who Was Who in America,* vol. 1, 1897–1942, 1943

IRVYN G. GILBERTSON

POTTER, (Helen) Beatrix (Heelis)
Author, illustrator, b. 28 July 1866, Kensington, London, England; d. 22 December 1943, Near Sawrey, England

P. whose picture- and storybooks began to delight children in England, the United States, and Europe before World War I, remains one of the best-known authors and illustrators of children's books. Her Peter Rabbit SERIES features not only the world-famous Peter and his misadventures in Mr. McGregor's garden, but also the watercolor ILLUSTRATIONS of animals, simultaneously naturalistic and anthropomorphized, which continue to adorn merchandise.

By all accounts, P. passed a solitary childhood as the daughter of a wealthy London couple who expected nannies and governesses to ensure that their children were neither seen nor heard. Although P. had one sibling, a brother five years younger than herself, he was sent to boarding school when he turned seven. P. later recalled her childhood as isolated, but not unhappy. She was allowed to walk in the gardens at Kensington and sometimes to visit the Victoria and Albert Museum with her governesses. She was fond of sketching from early childhood, and these outings provided models for her drawings of flowers and costumes. In addition, every summer the family spent three or four months in the northern England Lake District or southern Scotland, where the children had the freedom to wander the rural neighborhood. The country vacations provided P. with the most enduring companions of her youth, the small animals she was able to capture and keep as pets, and whose portraits adorned her sketchbook.

By the age of eleven or twelve, P. was signing sketches she considered finished. She was allowed to take art lessons, and her father purchased some works by the famed children's illustrator Randolph CALDECOTT to display them in P.'s schoolroom.

At eighteen, P. was tutored by her last governess, Annie Carter, who was herself only twenty. The two young women soon became good friends, and when Carter left her post to marry, P.'s continuing friendship with the new Mrs. Moore and her growing family provided P. with her first real exposure to young children. Both she and the children seemed to delight in the entertainments P. concocted for their benefit. In 1893, Moore's oldest son, Noel, became ill, and P. sent him a letter containing the illustrated story of Peter Rabbit. The picture-letter was a huge success with Noel and the other Moore children, who begged for and received more illustrated stories from P.

Since 1890, P. had occasionally worked as an illustrator of greeting cards and children's literature. In 1900 she decided to put out a children's book of her own and borrowed the Peter Rabbit letter from the Moore children. Unable to find an interested publisher, she published *The Tale of Peter Rabbit* herself with the money she had earned from illustrations. After its appearance, she took the book to Frederick Warne and Company, a publisher she had previously approached, which agreed to bring out a second edition of the book. Between 1902 and 1930, Warne published all twenty-three of P.'s books.

P.'s simple, plain style uses the alliteration and short paragraphs that have come to be associated with much writing for young children. Still, P. was aware that "children like a fine word occasionally," and she liked to include surprisingly sophisticated vocabulary words as a treat. The laconic, impartial narrative voice in her books is unmistakably adult, but it never condescends to children or makes too many concessions to their supposedly delicate sensibilities.

P.'s "selective realism," as Graham Greene called it, also blurs the distinctions between human and animal. In her books, young animals behave (and frequently misbehave) much like human children, but they simultaneously face mortal danger from predators—a fact of life for the prey animals ("rubbish animals," in P.'s words), such as rabbits, squirrels, and mice, who are usually P.'s protagonists. The young animals' inability to resist the allure of the forbidden resonates with children; the moral endings and comeuppances also appeal to young readers for whom the restoration of order and adult control is reassuring. But the reality of death, which so often lies just around the corner, lends an air of potential tragedy to P.'s works. Her careful balancing of childlike human and naturalistic animal qualities carries over into the illustrations—the rabbits look like rabbits (P.'s years of sketching her pets stood her in good stead) but with added human clothing and expressions.

The Tale of Peter Rabbit, still the most famous of P.'s works, has a charm that transcends both time and place. It has remained continuously popular since its publication and has been translated into dozens of languages. Peter Rabbit is the quintessential naughty child whose misdeeds result in the loss of his jacket and shoes. At the end, having gotten lost, drenched, and thoroughly frightened, he becomes ill when he reaches home and so misses out on the treat his well-behaved sisters enjoy. But readers are always aware that Peter is a rabbit, doing what rabbits do—breaking into a garden and eating the vegetables there, an activity that his mother forbids because it cost his father his life—and that his misbehavior might have tragic consequences.

The great success of *Peter Rabbit* led P. to create sequels. The first, *The Tale of Benjamin Bunny* (1904) teams Peter with his intrepid cousin Benjamin who persuades a very reluctant Peter to return to the McGregor garden and rescue his clothing. This time, both little rabbits are saved from being a cat's dinner only by the timely intervention of Benjamin's father, who heroically attacks the cat, locks it in the shed, and then punishes the wayward boys. The setting echoes that of *Peter Rabbit,* with Benjamin playing the role of adventurer and Peter as an unwilling accomplice—a pairing of "two epic personalities," as Greene observed. Peter and Benjamin appear as adults in *The Tale of the Flopsy Bunnies* (1909), with Benjamin still carefree and Peter still the stolid, sensible rabbit-citizen he has apparently been since learning his lesson in the garden. Benjamin's children are trapped in a bag by Mr. McGregor after dozing off in the rubbish heap (because "the effect of eating too much lettuce is soporific," as P. drily observes) and are saved by a mouse, who chews a hole in the bag while all the adult rabbits despair. Peter and Benjamin's final appearance comes in *The Tale of Mr. Tod* (1912), one of the longest and most sophisticated books in the series, which Greene believes "would certainly have ended tragically" if children were not the audience. The book, in which another family of Benjamin's is threatened, contains passages of real horror in its descriptions of the fox's lair; Peter and Benjamin, almost overwhelmed by fear, manage to save the little rabbits through luck alone.

P.'s other memorable creations include the hedgehog-laundress in *The Tale of Mrs. Tiggy-Winkle* (1905), the fishing frog in *The Tale of Mr. Jeremy Fisher* (1906), the naive and careless duck in *The Tale of Jemima Puddle-Duck* (1908), and a host of mice, kittens, and other small animals. P. never had children of her own, but her words and pictures still fill the nurseries of young readers in many countries today.

FURTHER WORKS: *The Tailor of Gloucester,* 1903; *The Tale of Squirrel Nutkin,* 1903; *The Tale of Two Bad Mice,* 1904; *The Tale of the Pie and the Patty-Pan,* 1905; *The Tale of Tom Kitten,* 1907; *The Roly-Poly Pudding,* 1908; *Ginger and Pickles,* 1909; *The Tale of Pigling Bland,* 1913; *The Tale of Little Pig Robinson,* 1930

BIBLIOGRAPHY: Cott, Jonathan, *Pipers at the Gates of Dawn: The Wisdom of Children's Literature,* 1981; Greene, G., "B.P." *Collected Essays,* 1969; Linder, L., *A History of the Writings of B.P.,* 1971; R. K. MacDonald, *B.P.,* 1986

CAROLYN LENGEL

PRELUTSKY, Jack

Author, b. 8 September 1940, Brooklyn, New York

Possessed with a unique gift for entertaining readers of all ages, P. is known primarily as a writer who combines the nonsensical with the macabre most often in rhythmic, rhymed verse. Featuring an imaginative assortment of animals great and small and creatures both fantastic and horrific, P.'s POETRY for children illuminates the mystery as well as the wonderment of childhood. P. brings to his craft an eclectic background that incorporates a wide range of experiences and interests. After graduating from the High School of Music and Art in Manhattan, P. attended Hunter College, now part of the City University of New York. He then progressed through a series of occupations, from folk singer to furniture mover, before realizing his true potential as a writer, and more specifically as a children's poet.

P.'s first collection of verse, *A Gopher in the Garden and Other Animal Poems,* was published in 1967. Praised for its playful style and nonsensical theme, the volume was well received by readers and inspired P. to continue writing for children. His next collection appeared in 1969, *Lazy Blackbird and Other Verses,* followed in that same year by *Three Saxon Nobles and Other Verses,* and *The Terrible Tiger* (1970), illustrated by Arnold LOBEL. P. would collaborate with Lobel, the noted author-illustrator, on several works, including *Circus* (1974), *Nightmares: Poems to Trouble Your Sleep* (1976), *The Mean Old Hyena* (1978), *The Headless Horseman Rides Tonight: More Poems to Trouble Your Sleep* (1980), and *The Random House Book of Poetry for Children,* which P. edited in 1983. Both *Nightmares* and *The Headless Horseman Rides Tonight* are particularly noteworthy for P.'s ability to exaggerate the macabre to induce a mixture of fear and delight.

Throughout the 1970s and 1980s, P. gained increasing popularity as well as critical recognition both for his nonsencial verse and humorous depiction of childhood experience. Published in 1977, *"The Snopp on the Sidewalk" and Other Poems,* illustrated by Byron BARTON, was named a notable book by the AMERICAN LIBRARY ASSOCIATION, and in that same year, P. published *It's Halloween* (1977), illustrated by Marylin HAFNER, the first of a series of books about holidays. Other books in the series include *It's Christmas* (1981) and *It's Thanksgiving* (1982), also illustrated by Hafner, and *It's Valentine's Day* (1983), illustrated by Yossi ABOLAFIA. The publication in 1978 of *The Queen of Eene,* illustrated by Victoria CHESS, was also named a Notable Book by the ALA. In 1982, P. published the highly successful *The Sheriff of Rottenshot,* illustrated by Chess, and *Kermit's Garden of Verses,* illustrated by Bruce McNally, in which P. features Kermit the Frog and other Muppet characters created by Jim Henson. P. was also praised for the lighthearted verse of *The New Kid on the Block* (1984), illustrated by James STEVENSON, and *Ride a Purple Pelican* (1986), illustrated by Garth WILLIAMS. Notable collections published in the 1990s include *Beneath a Blue Umbrella* (1990), illustrated by Williams, *The Dragons Are Singing Tonight* (1993) and *Monday's Troll* (1996), both illustrated by Peter SIS, and *A Pizza the Size of the Sun* (1996), illustrated by Stevenson.

Supplementing the publication of his own poetry, P. has translated works by other writers and has also edited important collections of children's poetry. Notable among his TRANSLATIONS is Rudolf Neumann's *The Bad Bear,* published in 1967, in which the ferocious beast introduced at the beginning of the story is reformed into a playful, dancing creature of nature. Other translations include Heinrich Hoffman-Donner's *The Moun-*tain Bounder* (1967) as well as Barbro Lindgren's *The Wild Baby* (1981) and *The Wild Baby Goes to Sea* (1983), both illustrated by Eva Eriksson. In addition to *The Random House Book of Poetry for Children,* P.'s editions include *Read Aloud Rhymes for the Very Young* (1986), illustrated by Marc BROWN, *Poems of A. Nonny Mouse* (1989), illustrated by Henrik DRESCHER, *For Laughing out Loud: Poems to Tickle Your Funnybone* (1991), and *Beauty of the Beast: Poems from the Animal Kingdom* (1997).

FURTHER WORKS: *Toucans Two and Other Poems.* (José ARUEGO), 1970, republished as *"Zoo Doings" and Other Poems,* 1971; *"The Pack Rat's Day" and Other Poems* (Margaret Bloy GRAHAM) 1974; *Rainy, Rainy Saturday* (Marilyn Hafner), 1980; *Rolling Harvey down the Hill* (Victoria Chess), 1980; *The Baby Uggs Are Hatching* (James Stevenson), 1982; *Zoo Doings: Animal Poems* (Paul O. ZELINSKY), 1983; *What I Did Last Summer* (Yossi Abolafia), 1984; *It's Snowing! It's Snowing!* (Jeanne Titherington), 1984; *My Parents Think I'm Sleeping* (Abolafia), 1985; *Brave Little Pete of Geranium Street* (Eva Eriksson), 1986

BIBLIOGRAPHY: HOPKINS, Lee Bennett, *Pauses: Autobiographical Reflections of 101 Creators of Children's Books,* 1995; Trout, A. "Jack Prelutsky," *American Writers for Children since 1960: Poets, Illustrators, and Nonfiction Authors,* ed. G. E. Estes, 1987, 242–47

STEVEN R. SERAFIN

PREUSSLER, Otfried
Author, b. 1923, Reichenberg, Germany

P. has contributed greatly to the field as a writer of FANTASY. His entertaining, lighthearted ADVENTURES nearly all include a wayward, foolish character who becomes enchanted through magic and romance. While writing in German, he has had many of his works translated and marketed in the United States. His most popular and highly acclaimed works include *The Tale of the Unicorn* (1988; trans. 1989) and *The Satanic Mill* (1971; trans. 1973).

AWARDS: German Children's Book Prize for *Krabat* (1971) in 1972 [translated as *The Satanic Mill* (1973)]: this title also won the Premio Europeo di Letteratura Giovanile in 1973 for the best title published in Europe

FURTHER WORKS: *The Wise Men of Schilda* 1962, trans. 1962; *The Little Ghost* 1968, trans. 1970

95. JERRY PINKNEY

96. PATRICIA POLACCO

97. BEATRIX POTTER

98. JACK PRELUTSKY

BIBLIOGRAPHY: *Something about the Author,* vol. 24, 1981
                              SHANE RAYBURN

PRICEMAN, Marjorie
Author, illustrator b.

P., author and illustrator of children's PICTURE BOOKS, bases her stories on her own personal experiences. Her first book, *Friend or Frog?* (1989), stems from her love of frogs. She was reared by her parents to love and respect the green amphibians, and her humorous accounts in this book won *Redbook* magazine's Top Ten Picture Books of the Year (1989) award.

Emeline at the Circus (1999) highlights P.'s exuberant, zany text and lighthearted ILLUSTRATIONS about a class trip to the circus. A teacher intent on making the circus a learning experience reads scientific texts about the circus animals to the class while Emeline takes off to join the performance and cavort with abandon across madcap double-paged spreads painted cotton-candy colors.

P. has also illustrated books for other authors including the ALA CALDECOTT MEDAL Honor Book *Zin! Zin! Zin! A Violin* (1995), by Lloyd Moss. P. is well known for her jubilant, boldly colored folk art illustrations. This is exemplified in Elsa Okon Rael's two books *What Zeesie Saw on Delancey Street* (1996), and *When Zaydeh Danced on Eldridge Street* (1997), which P. illustrated as well.

FURTHER WORKS: *How to Make an Apple Pie and See the World,* 1989; Illus by P.; *A. Nonny Mouse Writes Again: Poems* (Jack PRELUTSKY, ed.), 1993; *For Laughing Out Loud: Poems to Tickle Your Funnybone* (Jack Prelutsky, ed.), 1991; *Tiny, Tiny Boy and the Big, Big Cow* (N. Van Laan), 1993; *Rachel Fister's Blister* (A. Macdonald), 1990
                              DENISE P. BEASLEY

PRINGLE, Laurence
Author, b. 26 November 1935, Rochester, New York

P. grew up in rural New York where he learned to hunt and fish. He received a Bachelor of Science degree from Cornell University in 1958, a Master of Science degree from the University of Massachusetts in 1960, majoring in wildlife biology, and did further graduate work at Syracuse University. He was a high school science teacher in Lima, New York, in 1961–62 and edited *Nature and Science,* a magazine published by the American Museum of Natural History from 1963 to 1970. P. has worked as a freelance writer, photographer, writer in residence at Kean College in Union, New Jersey, and a full-time writer. He is a member of the Faculty at the Chautauqua Writer's Workshop, 1984–present. His books feature science and nature topics, and issues.

P. established a high standard of excellence for writing nonfiction; his work serves as a model. A scientist and a science and writing teacher, he portrays qualities of scholarship in his own work. He supports ideas with facts, supports facts with documentation, and acknowledges his own bias. He writes clearly, conveys personal values, presents evidence to support opposing viewpoints, and appeals to reason rather than to emotions. For example, he presents both positive and negative effects on society in *Nuclear Power: From Physics to Politics* (1989). He says, "It is difficult to find a well-informed person who is also neutral [about nuclear power]. This book is not neutral either. However, I have tried to present views and arguments from both proponents and opponents of nuclear energy." P. presents arguments for and against nuclear power and says that in the end, it is people like ourselves who must assume the awesome responsibility for weighing the relative benefits and costs of nuclear energy in the future.

P. is a nonfiction writer who explores the relations between science and public policy. He identifies links between science and politics as he presents social and political ramifications of an issue. P. believes that understanding an environmental issue requires a knowledge of its context. P. describes the context of environmental issues so that readers can assess them more accurately. He courageously predicts possible outcomes, deduces principles, examines varied meanings, raises questions, and encourages observation. P. makes it possible for readers to find out for themselves. He frequently provides an excellent bibliography for further reading, an index, a comprehensive table of contents, and revealing photographs to convey information. He then urges readers to find better solutions to environmental problems than ones we have found.

Critics and reviewers say that P. presents ideas supported by facts, facts supported by documentation. P. acknowledges biases through writing that appeal more to reason than emotion. They believe that P. writes books that serve as models to demonstrate the delicate balance between conviction and objectivity. P. fulfills the necessity for documentation and declaring one's bias. He is recognized as an excellent writer of nonfiction on science, conservation, and ecology. He is credited with a lucid style, high standards of accuracy, readability, sensitivity to interrelationships, and a joyousness that invites children to become involved and develop their scientific literacy. He encourages readers to keep on asking questions since no aspect of nonfiction writing is more important.

P. likes the term *nonfiction* better than INFORMATIONAL to characterize his books. He thinks the term informational suggests cold facts standing alone. He rejects the notion that pure objectivity is essential or even desirable in nonfiction. He argues that his works are infused with his personal voice, his values, and his biases. He says, "If there is a single thread that runs through all of my books, I think it is a thread of hopefulness. It is important to offer children some hope for solving our problems."

AWARDS: AMERICAN LIBRARY ASSOCIATION Notable Book Awards 1976, 1977, 1978. National Wildlife Federation Special Award for commitment to conservation, 1978. Eva Gordon Award for Children's Science Literature from the American Nature Study Society, 1983

FURTHER WORKS: *Dinosaurs and Their World.* 1968: *Death Is Natural.* 1971: *Wild Foods: A Beginner's Guide.* 1978: *Restoring Our Earth.* 1985: *Rain of Troubles: Science and Politics of Acid Rain.* 1988: *Bearman: Exploring the World of Black Bears.* 1989: *Living in a Risky World.* 1989: *Nuclear Energy: Troubled Past, Uncertain Future.* 1989: *Global Warming.* 1990: *Killer Bees.* 1990: *Batman: Exploring the World of Bats.* 1991: *Living Treasure: Saving Earth's Threatened Biodiversity.* 1991: *Antarctica: The Last Unspoiled Continent.* 1992: *Oil Spills.* 1993: *Octopus Hug.* 1993: *Jackal Woman: Exploring the World of Jackals.* 1993: *Scorpion Man: Exploring the World of Scorpions.* 1994: *Coral Reefs: Earth's Undersea Treasures.* 1995. Contributor to MAGAZINES: *Highlights for Children, Audubon, Ranger Rick, Smithsonian*

BIBLIOGRAPHY: American Association for the Advancement of Science (1991); *The Best Science*

Books for Children. Carr, J. *Beyond Fact: Nonfiction for Children and Young People.* 1982. *Children's Literary Review,* vol. 4, 1984. Doll, C. A. 1990. *Nonfiction Books for Children: Activities for Thinking, Learning, and Doing.* Freeman, E. and D. Person. *Connecting Informational Children's Books with Content Area Learning.* 1998. Galda, L. 1991. "Saving Our Planet, Saving Ourselves." In the *Reading Teacher.* Dec. 1991. Hearne B., and H. Kaye, *Celebrating Children's Books,* 1981. Hearne, Betsy. *Choosing Books for Children.* 1990. Kobrin, Beverly. *Eye Openers! How to Choose and Use Children's Books about Real People, Places, and Things.* 1988. *Nonfiction for Young Adults,* 1990. *Something about the Author Autobiographical Series,* vol. 6, 1988

BERNICE E. CULLINAN

PROFESSORS OF CHILDREN'S LITERATURE

Professors of children's literature are deemed notable for exemplary teaching, communicating love of books to students, major contributions to the field through authorship of books, and for recognized leadership in professional organizations.

An early pioneer in the field, Eloise Ramsey, taught at Detroit Teachers College, later Wayne State University, published *A Handbook of Children's Literature* (1927). She left her collection of children's books to Wayne State, which formed the nucleus of their children's literature collection.

May Hill Arbuthnot was a noted pioneer whose well-known text, *Children and Books* (1947), continues to be published under the authorship of Zena Sutherland. Arbuthnot joined the faculty of Western Reserve University and helped to establish the first nursery schools there. The kindergarten-primary training school became the department of elementary education at Case Western Reserve University. Her publisher funded two AWARDS in honor of her work. The first was the May Hill Arbuthnot Honor Lecture given annually by the Association for Library Service (ALSC) of the AMERICAN LIBRARY ASSOCIATION to a distinguished author, critic, librarian, historian, or teacher of children's literature. The lecture is presented annually and published in ALSC's *Journal of Youth Service* and compiled in book form each decade. The Arbuthnot Award is given annually by the INTERNATIONAL READ-

ING ASSOCIATION (IRA) to an outstanding teacher of children's literature.

Zena Sutherland, a professor at the University of Chicago, continues to maintain and update *Children and Books,* now in its ninth edition. For many years she edited *The Bulletin of the Center for Children's Books* and wrote critical reviews of new books. She is active in NATIONAL COUNCIL OF TEACHERS OF ENGLISH, IRA, ALA where she chaired award committees and IBBY.

Other professors include Bess Porter Adams, author of a historical survey of children's books, *About Children and Books* (1953). Dora V. Smith, a past president of the National Council of Teachers of English (NCTE) and professor at the University of Minnesota, wrote *Fifty Years of Children's Books* (1963). During her tenure at the University of Minnesota THE KERLAN COLLECTION of books, ILLUSTRATIONS, and manuscripts was established. Leland B. Jacobs, a professor of children's literature at The Ohio State University, and later at Teacher's College, Columbia University. He coauthored *Using Literature with Young Children* (1965) and published numerous books for children, including several collections of his original POETRY. He was elected to the Reading Hall of Fame and invited to give the Arbuthnot Honor Lecture in 1983.

Nancy LARRICK, also a member of the Reading Hall of Fame, was a founder and second president of the International Reading Association. She received two Ph.D's, one in Education, and one in Literature. Her professional writing includes *A Teacher's Guide to Children's Books* (1972) and *A Parent's Guide to Children's Reading* (1975) now in its fifth edition. In 1965 she raised the consciousness level of the book community by writing an article for *The Saturday Evening Review,* titled "The All White World of Children's Books." Always interested in poetry, she edited many collections of poetry for children and young adults. Her most recent professional book is titled *Let's Do a Poem* (1991). Retired now, she serves on the Board of Trustees for Shenandoah University and participates in its annual Children's Literature Conference.

Charlotte Huck created a nationally recognized program offering specialization in children's literature at the masters and doctoral levels. Her text, *Children's Literature in the Elementary School* (1961), combined literature study and literature teaching. Huck's former students, Susan Hepler, Janet Hickman, and Barbara Kiefer continue to work on various editions of the text. She coedited *The Web* (Wonderfully Exciting Books), a review quarterly that focused on classroom uses of children's books. Huck was president of NCTE, chair of the CALDECOTT MEDAL Committee, chair of the Arbuthnot Lecture Committee and member of the NEWBERY MEDAL Committee. She received the Arbuthnot Award for outstanding teaching and was invited to give the 1992 May Hill Arbuthnot Honor Lecture. A member of the Reading Hall of Fame, she received the Outstanding Educator in Language Arts Award. The Ohio State University established the Charlotte S. Huck Children's Literature Professorship, the first children's literature endowed chair in the United States. The first recipient was Bernice Cullinan, Huck's first doctoral student. Huck has published four books for children and helped establish the first conference on children's literature in California.

Bernice E. Cullinan taught at New York University for thirty years. The most recent revision of her college text, *Literature and the Child* (1998), is coauthored with Lee Galda, a professor at the University of Minnesota. Cullinan is a prolific author, writing or editing over thirty books (including co-editorship of the present reference work), many of them for such professional organizations as NCTE and IRA. She is editor-in-chief of a children's poetry imprint Wordsong for Boyds Mills and helped establish the NCTE Award for Excellence in Poetry for Children. Her book, *A Jar of Tiny Stars,* includes children's choices from the award-winning poems. *Three Voices, an Invitation to Poetry across the Curriculum* (1995) was written with Marilyn Scala and Virginia Schroder and *Poetry Lessons that Dazzle and Delight* (1999) builds a love of poetry. Cullinan is former president of the International Reading Association, chair of the Ezra Jack KEATS New Writer Selection Committee, chair of the National Language Arts Conference for NCTE, and member of the Caldecott Medal Committee. She received the Arbuthnot Award and serves as President of the Reading Hall of Fame. In 1997, she was the first Charlotte Huck Professor of Children's Literature at Ohio State University.

Janet Hickman, a professor of children's literature at The Ohio State University, is a coauthor of several editions of *Children's Literature in the Elementary School.* She coedited *Children's Literature in the Classroom: Weaving Charlotte's Web* (1989) and *Children's Literature in the Classroom: Extending Charlotte's Web* (1994), and is the codirector of the annual Children's Literature Festival. She is noted for her research on children's responses to literature and has written numerous books of historical fiction for children.

Joan Glazer teaches children's literature at Rhode Island College and codirects a graduate program in children's literature. Her publications include *Introduction to Children's Literature* (1979) and *Literature for Young Children* (third edition, 1990). She was president of the Special Interest in Children's Literature group, past president of the United States Section of International Board of Books for Youth, and a member of the Executive Committee of IBBY.

Dorothy Strickland is the State of New Jersey Professor of Reading at Rutgers University and formerly Arthur I. Gates Professor of Education at Teachers College, Columbia University. Her publications include *Language Literacy and the Child* (1997), *Listen Children: An Anthology of Black Literature* (1982), and *Families: Poems Celebrating the AFRICAN AMERICAN Experience* (1995). Strickland is a past president of IRA and a member of the Reading Hall of Fame. She was recognized by NCTE as "The Outstanding Educator in Language Arts" for 1998.

Dianne Monson taught children's literature, language arts, and reading at the University of Minnesota. She wrote *Experiencing Children's Literature* (1986) and the last three chapters in Sutherland and Arbuthnot's text, *Children and Books* (1998). Monson chaired the Elementary Section Committee of NCTE, is a member of the Reading Hall of Fame, and is a recipient of the Arbuthnot Award.

Lee Galda is a professor of children's literature at the University of Minnesota. She is the coauthor of *Literature and the Child* (1998), *Language, Literacy and the Child* (1997), and *Looking Through the Faraway End* (2000). Her research interest is in children's response to literature. She chairs the Naomi Chase Lecture Series.

As the field of children's literature became larger, many professors began to specialize in a particular aspect or genre. Patricia Cianciolo, professor at Michigan State University, was one of the first with *PICTURE BOOKS for Children* (fourth edition, 1997). She served as the Chair of the Caldecott Medal Committee, a member of the Newbery Medal Committee and received the Arbuthnot Award.

Barbara Kiefer, a professor at Teachers College, Columbia University, conducted research on young children's response to picture books. Following this interest, she wrote *The Potential of Picturebooks: From Visual Literacy to Aesthetic Understanding* (1989) and is a coauthor of *Children's Literature in the Elementary Schools* (1998). She served as chair of the Elementary Section Committee, and was a member of the Executive Board of NCTE. She was a member of the Caldecott Committee (1988) and chair in 2000. She chaired the CBC/IRA joint committee for the Children's Choices project, and the NCTE/CLA Notable Trade Books.

Rudine Sims Bishop is a professor of children's literature at The Ohio State University. She served on NCTE's Editorial Board and was national program chair for its Conference on the Language Arts. Sims Bishop wrote *Shadow and Substance: Afro-American Experience in Contemporary Children's Fiction* (1982) and edited *Kaleidoscope: A MULTICULTURAL Booklist for Grades K–8* (1992) for NCTE and *Wonders: Poems of Effie Lee Newsome* (2000). She cochairs Ohio State's Festival of Books Conference. She was elected President of the U.S. section of IBBY in 1998.

Susan Lehr studied young children's ability to discern theme in stories. Her book *The Child's Developing Sense of Theme: A Response to Literature* (1991) includes her conclusions and implications for teaching. She edited the book, *Battling Dragons: Issues and Controversy in Children's Literature* (1995), which looks at censorship and criticisms of children's books. Lehr is chair of the education department and associate professor of reading and children's literature at Skidmore College.

Kathy Short is a professor at the University of Arizona. Much of her work focuses on teaching children's literature and reading and writing as authoring processes. She is a coauthor of *Creating Classrooms for Authors* (1994) and edited *Talking about Books* (1990). She has served as chair of the elementary section for NCTE and been a member of the NCTE Executive Board. She is editor of the *New Advocate.*

John STEWIG, professor of children's literature at the University of Wisconsin-Milwaukee, was president of NCTE. His publications include *Children and Literature, Read to Write* (1984), and *Using Literature in the Elementary Classroom* (1989). Stewig has also authored several retellings of folktales for children.

Barbara Elleman was the creator and editor-in-chief of *Book Links,* a monthly journal published by the ALA. She was the first Distinguished Scholar of Children's Literature at Marquette University in Milwaukee where she teaches children's literature, coordinates their literature collection, and organizes an annual Children's Literature Conference.

Children's literature is also taught in countries other than the United States. For many years, Sheila Egoff was a professor of librarianship in Canada. She wrote *The New Republic of Childhood* (1990), *Thursday's Child: Trends and Patterns in Contemporary Children's Literature* (1981), *Only Connect: Readings on Children's Literature* (1986), and *One Ocean Touching* (1979). Ronald Jobe teaches children's literature at the University of British Columbia and conducts an annual children's literature conference; he is a past president of IBBY. Perry Nodelman is a professor of English at the University of Winnipeg. He is the author of *Words about Pictures: The Narrative Art of Children's Picture Books* (1987), *The Pleasures of Children's Literature* (1996), and *Touchstones: Reflections on the Best in Children's Literature* volumes 1, 2 (1986).

Margaret Spencer Meek's studies and writings about ways children and young adults acquire literacy have had a tremendous impact in England and the United States. Now retired from the Department of English Media and Drama of the University of London Institute of Education, her point of view is expressed in her essays in *New Readings: Contributions to an Understanding of Literacy* (1983), *The Cool Web: The Pattern of Children's Reading* (1978) and *On Being Literate*

(1989). In 1970, she received the Eleanor FARJEON Award for her services to children and books.

Much of the writing about children's books in England is criticism or history of children's literature. Aidan CHAMBERS, a teacher of English and Drama before becoming a full-time writer, has been a visiting lecturer at Westminster College, Oxford, and is the author of four books for teenagers and younger children. His *Booktalk* (1986) or *Introducing Children to Books* (1983) explores the role of literature in children's lives. John Rowe TOWNSEND has lectured and taught in workshops and conferences in the U.S. and in England. *Written for Children* (1996) provides an account of the development of children's books in England. *A Sounding of Storytellers* (1979) expands essays on writers of children's fiction in the U.S. and England. Peter Hunt teaches English Literature at the University of Wales. He has written and edited books on the criticisms of children's literature including: *Criticism, Theory and Children's Literature* (1991); *Children's Literature: The Development of Criticisms* (1990), and *Literature for Children: Contemporary Criticism* (1993). He has also edited *Children's Literature: An Illustrated History* (1995).

Certainly, there is no dearth of persons teaching and writing about children's literature. Their approaches differ, however, and vary on a continuum from a historical, theoretical, and critical approach to a study of how children acquire literacy and develop a sense of story. Most textbooks inform teachers about books, children's responses, and ways to incorporate literature in the curriculum.

CHARLOTTE S. HUCK

PROVENSEN, Alice (Twitchell) and Martin

Authors, illustrators. Alice: b. 14 August 1918, Chicago, Illinois. Martin: b. 10 July 1916, Chicago, Illinois; d. 1987, New York City

For more than forty years, Alice and Martin Provensen were equal collaborators as they wrote and illustrated children's books. Both husband and wife were born in Chicago and grew up loving books and book illustrations. Each won a scholarship to the Art Institute of Chicago, and later transferred to the University of California. After graduation they both worked on animated films—Alice P. at the Walter Lang Studios, and Martin at Walt DISNEY. There he contributed to both full-length, animated feature films, *Fantasia* and *Dumbo.* They met in 1943 on a Universal Studio lot, and were married in Washington, D.C., where they were working on films for the Department of Strategic Services as part of the war effort. In 1945, the *Fireside Songbook,* their first collaboration as illustrators was published; its success was followed by several other Fireside Books and *Alice and Martin Provensen's The MOTHER GOOSE* Book (1976). They then went on a lengthy trip to Europe, which produced many sketches, photographs, prints, and engravings that later were used as reference materials for their illustrations. In 1952 they returned to the U.S. and bought a farmhouse in Staatsburg, New York, which provided frequent inspiration for both illustrations and stories.

From the early 1950s through the 1960s they continued illustrating many classic volumes of literature such as The New Testament, *The Iliad and The Odyssey, Aesop's Fables,* and *A Treasury of Myths and Legends.* In 1952, with the publication of the *Animal Fair,* they began their collaboration as author/illustrators. They won a 1982 ALA CALDECOTT MEDAL Honor Book award for their collaboration on Nancy WILLARD's *A Visit to William Blake's Inn* (1981), which also was the ALA NEWBERY MEDAL winner that year, a singular achievement for any book. They won the CALDECOTT MEDAL in 1984 for their joint effort on *The Glorious Flight: Across the Channel with Louis Blériot,* which they also wrote.

Critics have hailed the P.s' work for its charm, originality, diversity, and HUMOR. They are regarded as artists of great integrity who wrote succinct, informative stories that instructed without being didactic. Perhaps their experiences as animators gave them the skill to take a serious subject and give it warmth and humor, making it palatable to young readers. Their PICTURE BOOKS on nature, science, history, and literature generally featured realistically detailed, but stylized paintings in unusual compositions. The authenticity of detail is a result of careful research and, often, first-hand observation. Critics also applaud their unsentimental yet affectionate portrayal of animals. Their 1984 Caldecott Medal Award book, *The Glorious Flight,* wryly relates the adventures

of the pilot Louis Blériot and his successful solo crossing of the English Channel in 1909. The book was honored not only for its factual accuracy, but also for its witty, humorous reincarnation of Blériot's family, Blériot's obsession with flying machines, and his many aeronautical misadventures before his final success. In 1984 the *New York Times Book Review* wrote: "The story is as brief, graceful and direct as the course of a paper airplane across a living room. This spaciously crafted book is very much in the spirit of its subject. Fact is turned into magic."

Martin P. died in 1987; Alice P. has continued writing and illustrating her own books.

AWARDS: AMERICAN LIBRARY ASSOCIATION Newbery Medal and Caldecott Medal Honor Book (1982) for *A Visit to William Blake's Inn* (Nancy Willard, author). ALA Caldecott Medal Honor Book (1984) for *The Glorious Flight: Across the Channel with Louis Blériot*

FURTHER WORKS: As authors and illus: *The Animal Fair.* 1952, revised 1974. *Karen's Curiosity.* 1963. *Karen's Opposites.* 1963. *What Is a Color?* 1967. *Who's in the Egg?* 1968. *Provensen's Book of FAIRY TALES.* (Editors). 1971. *Play on Words.* 1972. *My Little Hen.* 1973. *Roses Are Red.* 1973. *Our Animal Friends at Maple Hill Farm.* 1974. *A Book of Seasons.* 1976. *Owl and Three Pussycats.* 1981, reissued 1994. *Leonardo da Vinci.* 1984. *Shaker Lane.* 1987. Illustrators only: *Fireside Book of Folksongs.* (M. B. Boni, ed). 1947. *Fireside Book of Lovesongs* (M. B. Boni, ed). 1954. *Fireside Cookbook.* (James A. Beard). 1949. *The Golden Mother Goose.* (Dorothy Bennett, ed.), 1948. *A Child's Garden of Verses.* (Robert Louis STEVENSON). 1951. *The Iliad and the Odyssey.* (Elsa Jane Watts, adapter). 1956. *The Golden Treasury of Myths and Legends.* 1959. *Shakespeare: Ten Great Plays.* 1962. *The Charge of the Light Brigade.* (Alfred, Lord Tennyson). 1964. *Aesop's Fables.* (Louis UNTERMEYER, adapter). 1965. *Fun and Nonsense.* (Louis Untermeyer, ed.). 1967. A. P. *The Buck Stops Here: The Presidents of the United States.* 1990. A. P. *Punch in New York City.* 1991

BIBLIOGRAPHY: *Children's Literature Review,* vol. 11, 1986; Cummins, J., *Children's Book ILLUSTRATION and DESIGN,* 1992; Silvey, Anita, ed., *Children's Books and Their Creators,* 1995; *Something about the Author,* vol. 9, 1976, and vol. 76, 1994; *Twentieth Century Children's Writers,* 1978

JUDY LIPSITT

PUBLISHERS AND BOOK PUBLISHING IN THE UNITED STATES

Publishing specifically for children in the United States can be traced to the early part of the twentieth century; pinpointed, some say, to the hiring of Louise Seaman (later Bechtel) in 1922 to head a new children's department at Macmillan. Through the efforts of Seaman and her highly talented colleagues, May Massee at Doubleday and Helen Dean Fish at Frederick A. Stokes, chronicled under EDITORS OF NOTE in this volume, children's publishing departments began producing high-quality literature for the young. The hope of these pioneers was to create books that children would enjoy, that would enrich their lives, and that would help them develop a lifelong love of reading. And, in many ways, these dedicated women succeeded. Improvements in bookmaking, experimentation in the illustrative process, and publication of more titles the year round increased interest in children's books. Children's Book Week was introduced in 1919 and the creation of the NEWBERY MEDAL followed in 1922 (the CALDECOTT MEDAL was established in 1938). Publishers sought the finest talent possible and picture books blossomed under the creative hands of Maud and Miska PETERSHAM, Wanda GAG, and William NICHOLSON, and novels by the likes of Rachel FIELD and Hugh LOFTING became readily available in public libraries and bookstores. Nevertheless, a continuing concern, then as now, was how to reach children through the everpresent, multilayers of adult filters.

Children's books continued to prosper during the money-tight Depression era of the 1930s and the wrenching World War II years of the 1940s. This somewhat surprising situation was due in part to reduced prices of books and somewhat to the development of photo-offset technology, which allowed the publishing of a greater number and variety of titles. As the field grew upward and outward, it attracted the diverse talents of authors Margaret Wise BROWN and Dr. SEUSS, illustrators James DAUGHERTY and Roger DUVOISIN, and stimulated the opening of children's-only publishing houses, such as Holiday House and William R. Scott, Inc. And for the first time, books were designed especially for the preschool child—opening up another new market. In the next decade, the 1950s, INFORMATIONAL BOOKS for children became the genre of note as publishers responded to the launching of Sputnik and the need for books on science and technology. Interestingly, this decade is also earmarked by a flush of FANTASY, a genre not heretofore given much recognition in America. Contributing to its popularity—and its success—was the release of E. B. WHITE's *Charlotte's Web* (1952) from Harper and Row, Eleanor CAMERON's *Mushroom Planet* stories from Little Brown, and Edward EAGER's time travel books from Harcourt Brace, where editor Margaret McElderry's early interest in this genre has had a long-lasting effect.

It is often said that children's books reflect the time in which they are published, and nowhere does this become clearer than when surveying the 1960s publishing trends. The upheaval of American society is strongly reflected in the kinds of books publishers released: Maurice SENDAK's *Where the Wild Things Are* (1963), Louise FITZHUGH's *Harriet the Spy* (1964), Ezra Jack KEATS's *Snowy Day* (1962), Emily NEVILLE's *It's like This, Cat* (1963), and S. E. HINTON's *The Outsiders* (1967) represent the beginnings of the new realism that has permeated the market—one that has escalated up through the children's book field in increasing proportions ever since.

The 1970s' novels and informational books openly discussed drugs, divorce, sexuality, mental illness, death, and abortion, spawning a new category of books labeled YOUNG ADULT. Judy BLUME, who addressed menstrual periods, masturbation, and sexual encounters in the guise of story, was the author of the decade. These (mostly) highly applauded new liberal leanings, however, also brought a rise in CENSORSHIP. The 1970s found an audience for MULTICULTURAL titles, and publishers looked for ethnic authors and illustrators to tell the stories of AFRICAN AMERICANS, NATIVE AMERICANS, ASIANS, and LATINA/OS. Folktales, in particular, were on every publisher's seasonal list. Although multiculturalism rode the publishing crest into the 1980s, the trend, unfortunately, abated just as children's books had started to reflect America's diverse population. With the exception of established writers such as Virginia HAMILTON, Diane and Leon DILLON, Ed YOUNG, Laurence YEP, and Jerry PINKNEY, the search for new talent among people of color lessened in the last half of the decade, slowed, in part, by the controversy of "political correctness."

The 1990s, however, re-energized the multicultural publishing emphasis. Strongly voiced concerns from teachers, via the whole language movement, and from parents, worried about reading scores, resulted in an array of books with diverse cultural focus. Small houses such as Lee and Low, with a stated multicultural mission, cropped up and older houses such as Children's Book Press gained momentum. But another voice was also heard—big business. Multinational companies with their eyes steadily on the bottom line had moved into the publishing world and had reared their heads in the children's book world. Suddenly, what would sell became the watchword, marketing departments became more important than editorial, and making a profit was essential.

Children's books as part of America's mainstream, a dream envisioned by the Bechtels and Massees during the early days of publishing literature for the young, was realized, but the price being paid—the presence of a corporate watchdog—has taken its toll. Recasting of familiar stories into alternative formats, gimmicks in the form of pop-ups and guessing games, and television and movie tie-ins not only top the best-seller lists, but often overshadow the well-researched informational book or biography, the imaginatively illustrated PICTURE BOOK, and the soul-stirring novel still being created today. The highly hyped consumer-targeted products released to satisfy budget lines are many; however, the mission to get good books into the hands of children is much the same as it was some seventy years ago. What is more questionable is how children's books will fare as technology becomes more entrenched in children's lives. The direct line from book to child, it seems, remains as elusive as ever.

REFERENCES: Allen, Marjorie N. *100 Years of Children's Books in America,* 1996; Bader, Barbara. *American* PICTURE BOOKS: *From Noah's Ark to the Beast Within,* 1969

BARBARA ELLEMAN

(See also EDITORS OF NOTE and LIBRARIANS AND PUBLISHING)

PUBLISHERS, INDEPENDENT

Growing up with a family business, Halle Brothers, a Cleveland department store founded by her grandfather, influenced independent children's book publisher Kate Briggs's decision to be active in a family business through her adult life. In March 1965 she and her husband, John Briggs, purchased Holiday House, a children's book publishing company, from Vernon and Helen Ives. As head of the marketing department for Holiday House, K. Briggs works in promotion to the institutional market—public and school libraries and media centers—and independent bookstores; she has developed an emphasis on promoting authors and illustrators through appearances and presentations.

The Briggses strive for and support quality in children's books and maintain close, long-term ties with authors and illustrators. Artist and author Glen ROUNDS, who published *Beavers* with Holiday House in 1999, has been on the list since 1936. Trina Schart HYMAN, an artist who has long collaborated with Holiday House, illustrated the 2000 CALDECOTT MEDAL Honor Book of John Updike's poetry, *A Child's Calendar.* Hyman's comments characterize the feeling of community that is the firm's hallmark: "They take a personal interest in you at Holiday House. You feel as though you're working with people who appreciate what you're doing. . . . They're one of the last remaining publishers in the old tradition—small, independent, personally owned, and caring."

Holiday House is the oldest house that publishes only children's literature, and it continues to flourish. In the fifteen years between 1985 and 2000, Holiday House published more books than it did in its first fifty years. Under the leadership of Kate and John Briggs, Holiday House celebrated its sixty-fifth anniversary in 2000.

BIBLIOGRAPHY: Personal interview with Kate Briggs, July 29, 1999; FREEDMAN, Russell, *Holiday House: The First Fifty Years,* 1985

KATHIE KRIEGER CERRA, PH.D.

PYLE, Howard

Author, illustrator, b. 5 March 1853, Wilmington, Delaware; d. 9 November 1911, Florence, Italy

P. remembered his early childhood as an idyllic one in which his mother's gardens, his father's house, and the family's library of FAIRY TALES and classics all influenced his career. While he listened avidly to stories and devoted himself to drawing, he did not develop into the scholar his parents hoped. After attending art school in Philadelphia, he moved to New York City and worked as a painter and magazine illustrator. Returning to Wilmington, he continued to paint and illustrate for magazines but began to write for children as well, retelling *The Merry Adventures of Robin Hood of Great Renown in Nottinghamshire* (1883), *The Story of King Arthur and His Knights* (1903), and *Adventures of Pirates and Sea-Rovers* (1908). He established his own art school in Wilmington where his students included Maxfield Parrish and N. C. WYETH.

P.'s stories, like his paintings, emphasized the dramatic elements of tales he had known from his own childhood. He cast King Arthur, Robin Hood, and other FOLKLORE heroes in tales where romanticism—but not sexuality—was given free reign. His pirate tales, like *Men of Iron* (1892), inspired movie adaptations years after his death. He instructed his art students to write stories to stimulate their artistic imaginations.

P. illustrated children's books by other writers, including *Lady of Shalott* (Alfred Lord Tennyson). (1881), *Illustrated Poems* (Oliver Wendell Holmes, 1885), *The Novels and Tales of Robert Louis STEVENSON* (1895), *Odysseus, the Hero of Ithaca* (Mary E. Burt, 1898), and *The Buccaneers* (Don Seitz, 1912). He also continued to illustrate for both general and children's MAGAZINES after he was well established as an artist, author, and teacher. He died while touring Europe.

Although P. used a rather difficult style to give the flavor of medieval speech to some of his characters, his ADVENTURE books continue to be enjoyed by new generations, introducing them to Anglo-Saxon mythology in both word and vision. His influence on graphic arts also continues to be seen in PICTURE BOOKS for children. Modern illustrators, including Trina Schart HYMAN, have traced elements of their own illustrating style to P.'s literature for children.

FURTHER WORKS: *Pepper and Salt; or, Seasoning for Young Folk,* 1885; *Otto of the Silver Hand,* 1888; *Book of Pirates,* 1891; *A Modern Aladdin; or, The Wonderful Adventures of Oliver Munier,* 1891; *The Story of the Holy Grail and the Passing of Arthur,* 1910

BIBLIOGRAPHY: Nesbitt, Elizabeth. *H.P.,* 1966: Pitz, Henry, *H.P.: Writer, Illustrator, Founder of the Brandywine School,* 1975

FRANCISCA GOLDSMITH

QUACKENBUSH, Robert M.

Author, illustrator, b. 23 July 1929, Hollywood, California

Q. has written and illustrated over 170 books for young readers. He is a three-time winner of the American Flag Institute Award for outstanding contributions to children's literature and winner of an Edgar Allan Poe Special Award for best juvenile mystery. In April 1998, at United Nations Headquarters, he received a Gradiva Award for *Bathaby,* voted Best Children's Book of the Year by the National Association for the Advancement of Psychoanalysis (NAAP). Q. is best known for his SERIES of humorous mysteries and biographies. His popular book characters include Detective Mole, Sherlock Chick, Miss Mallard, Henry the Duck, Pete Pack Rat, and Sheriff Sally Gopher. His visiting-author tours to schools and LIBRARIES have taken him all over the world, and his art is in major museums and private collections.

FURTHER WORKS (SELECT): *Where Did Your Family Come From?: A Book about Immigrants,* 1993; *Whole World in Your Hands: Looking at Maps,* 1993; *Arthur Ashe and His Match with History,* 1994; *Daughter of Liberty,* 1999

BIBLIOGRAPHY: *Major Authors and Illustrators for Children and YOUNG ADULTS: A Selection of Sketches from Something about the Author,* 1993; "Welcome to the Woild [sic] of Robert Quackenbush." httpcflwwwrquackenbush.com accessed March 21, 1999

MARY ARIAIL BROUGHTON

QUILLER-COUCH, Sir Arthur

Author, literary critic, anthologist, b. 21 November 1863, Bodmin, Cornwall, England; d. 12 May 1944, Fowey, Cornwall

Even before graduating from Trinity College, Oxford (1896), Q. began his career as an author and editor. His editorial work earned him a reputation as a scholar while his fiction enjoyed both critical and popular reception. He edited the first edition of *The Oxford Book of English Verse, 1250–1900* (1900) as well as other anthologies of verse, FAIRY TALES, and stories for family reading. His anthologies continue to give children and students well-ordered access to imaginary worlds. Q. was knighted in 1910, his literary efforts cited as contributing to this distinction.

Q. completed Robert Louis STEVENSON's novel *St. Ives* (1897); subsequent fiction by Q. reminded readers of Stevenson's romantic ADVENTURE tales with memorable characters. At his death, Q. left a romance, *Castle Dor,* unfinished. His friend Daphne DuMaurier agreed to complete this recasting of the Tristan and Iseult legend, which was published in 1962.

The pseudonym "Q" was used from the time he wrote parodies as an undergraduate.

FURTHER WORKS: *Fairy Tales Far and Near,* 1895; *The Black Adventure Book,* 1905; *The Sleeping Beauty and Other Fairy Tales from the Old French,* 1910

BIBLIOGRAPHY: *Contemporary Authors,* vol. 118, 1986; *Twentieth Century Literary Criticism,* vol. 53, 1994; *World Authors, 1900–1950,* 1996

FRANCISCA GOLDSMITH

RACKHAM, Arthur

Artist, illustrator, b. 19 September 1867, London, England; d. 6 September 1939, Hampstead, London, England

R. was the fourth of twelve children born to a middle-class Victorian family in London, England. He showed a talent for art as a youngster and began by drawing outlandish caricatures. R. studied art in night school while working in an insurance office. He went on to work as a staff artist for the *Westminster Budget,* a newspaper, and eventually became a freelance illustrator until his death.

R. won several AWARDS as an artist including Master of the Art Worker's Guild and gold medals at several exhibitions in Italy and Spain. His drawings are exhibited in public collections in Barcelona, Melbourne, Paris, Vienna, and London. R.'s fame as an illustrator was established with the publication of FAIRY TALES *of the Brothers* GRIMM (1900). In 1909 a reworked edition of the stories was published with new ILLUSTRATIONS by R.; almost half were in color and this became a standard for R. By 1910, R. was considered a leading illustrator and worked on books for adults as well as children. R.'s work includes illustrations for *The Pied Piper of Hamelin* (1934) and *Tales of Mystery and Imagination* (1935). He also contributed drawings to numerous periodicals including the *Westminster Gazette, Scraps, Illustrated Bits, Daily Graphic* and *St. Nicholas* magazine.

R. traveled extensively including trips to the United States, where he advised aspiring high school students to aim for the highest quality work they could possibly muster and never to be satisfied. Always a perfectionist, he traveled through Denmark to work on illustrations for AN-DERSEN's *Fairy Tales* (1932). R. died after finishing the illustrations for an American edition of *The Wind in the Willows* (1940). He had been asked to illustrate the book originally but had declined because of prior illustrating commitments. R.'s illustrations are characterized by the fairies, gnomes, and elves he drew with imaginative details in soft, misty colors that emphasize the FAN-TASY elements in children's stories so popular early in the twentieth century.

FURTHER WORKS: *Tales from Shakespeare.* (LAMB). 1899. *Gulliver's Travels.* (SWIFT). 1900. *Rip van Winkle.* (IRVING). 1905. *Peter Pan in Kensington Gardens.* (BARRIE). 1906. *Alice in Wonderland.* (CARROLL). 1907. *The Night before Christmas.* (MOORE). 1931. *Goblin Market.* (ROSETTI). 1933. *The Wind in the Willows.* (GRAHAME). 1940

BIBLIOGRAPHY: Doyle, Brian, *The Who's Who of Children's Literature* 1968; Egoff, Sheila, *Thursday's Child* 1981; *Something about the Author,* vol. 15, 1979

MICHAEL O'LAUGHLIN

RAFFI (Raffi Cavoukian)

Singer, songwriter, b. 8 July, 1948, Cairo, Egypt

Known professionally only by his first name, R. was born to Armenian parents and spent his early years in Egypt. When he was ten years old, the family moved to Canada. R. attended the University of Toronto where he sang in coffee houses and clubs.

R. began playing the guitar at age sixteen and performing publicly in the late 1960s. In the early years of his career, he played mostly folk songs for adults. He eventually became interested in music for children through the influence of his wife, a kindergarten teacher who had been his high school sweetheart. Concerned with the lack of quality music for children, R. began to write songs and perform for a younger audience. He soon produced and distributed his first recording, *Singable Songs for the Very Young* (1976), which was an immediate success. Since that time, he has produced and sold millions of record albums, performed in hundreds of sold-out concerts, and had concert videos broadcast on the DISNEY Channel.

Since his early recordings, R. has been one of the most popular children's recording artists in Canada and the United States. His many AWARDS and honors include two Grammy Award nominations for *Everything Grows* (1987) and *Raffi in Concert with the Rise and Shine Band* (1989), the AYA Award, Canadian Institute of the Arts for Young Audiences, 1988; and the Recording Industry Association of America's Gold Award for the album, *Singable Songs for the Very Young* (1976).

Incorporating a wide range of musical styles and subject matter, R.'s music delights both children and parents. His musical style includes jazz, reggae, waltz, folk-rock, country, and ragtime. His musical topics include common elements of children's everyday lives, such as taking baths, eating peanut butter sandwiches, and loving animals. Although much of R.'s music appears light and humorous, he often incorporates serious themes such as world peace and concern for the environment. He insists that children deserve respect as an audience and he conscientiously avoids stereotypes, violence, and negativity.

R. often uses music as a means of educating children and adults. He believes "The repetition and predictable pattern of my songs make them 'singable' and easy for children to remember. The same qualities make them readable, too." In the early 1990s, R. shifted his educational emphasis to an older audience. His first album aimed at grown-ups, *Evergreen Blue* (1990), empha-

sizes ecological problems and encourages adults to take action.

FURTHER WORKS: *Baby Beluga,* 1980; *Down by the Bay,* 1987; *The Raffi Singable Songbook,* 1987; *The Raffi Christmas Treasure: Fourteen Illustrated Songs and Musical Arrangements,* 1988; *Shake My Sillies Out,* 1988; *The Wheels on the Bus.* 1988

BIBLIOGRAPHY: *Sixth Book of Junior Authors and Illustrators,* 1989; *Something about the Author,* vol. 68, 1992

MARY ARIAIL BROUGHTON

RAND, Gloria
Author, Date of birth and place unknown

Collaborating with her husband, illustrator Ted RAND, R. writes PICTURE BOOKS based on actual events about which she has heard or read. There are important insights in each of her stories dealing with community, SURVIVAL, trust, and kindness told in straightforward, nondidactic writing. Extensive research on the Pacific Northwest provided authentic contexts for *Salty Dog* (1989) and two sequels based on a dog's real experiences. This research was also evident in *Prince William* (1992). After visiting Prince William Sound, R. was inspired to write this fictional story that describes the volunteer efforts to save land and animals following an oil spill. *Baby in a Basket* (1997) is about a true event in the Alaskan wilderness. *Spooky* (1998), a REALISTIC story compassionately told about a stray dog, is also based on a true story.

FURTHER WORKS: *Salty Sails North,* 1990; *Aloha, Salty,* 1996; *The Cabin Key,* 1994; *Willie Takes a Hike,* 1996

BIBLIOGRAPHY: *Booklist,* March 1, 1989, March 1, 1990, April 1, 1998, and September 1, 1998; *School Library Journal,* March 1990, April 1991, and June 1996; *Something about the Author,* vol. 101, 1999

JANELLE B. MATHIS

RAND, Ted
Illustrator, b. 27 December 1915, Mercer Island, Washington

R. was born on Mercer Island in Washington and still lives there. He remembers the first time he felt the urge to draw what happened when he was a youngster, delving into the family Bible. The dramatic depictions of biblical verse inspired R.

to pick up a pencil and from that time on he has been drawing. Because of his love of art, R. was often enlisted to do the holiday decorations for his grammar school and soon learned that he could avoid academics by getting dismissed to do art work.

After leaving high school, R. took a job as an illustrator for a department store, designing its newspaper advertisements. This job led to R.'s becoming a freelance illustrator, a job that was interrupted by his service in World War II. During R.'s freelance years he also worked as an instructor at the University of Washington. After creating illustrations from a pack trip with conservationist and U.S. Supreme Court Justice William O. Douglas, R.'s works were shown in the New York Society of Illustrators Annual Exhibit. As a result, he was hired to do textbook and encyclopedia illustrations. R.'s work as an illustrator of children's books began in the early 1980s with his illustrations for Bill MARTIN Jr. and John ARCHAMBAULT's *The Ghost-Eye Tree* (1985). His love for illustrating children's books led him to discontinue portrait commissions and painting for exhibitions.

R.'s work in *The Ghost-Eye Tree* was named an Irma Simonton Black Award Honor Book for 1985. It was also named a 1986 Children's Choice Book. Both *Knots on a Counting Rope* (1987) and *Barn Dance!* (1986) have been featured on public television's READING RAINBOW. *Knots on a Counting Rope* was also named a Notable Trade Book in the Field of Social Studies by the National Council on the Social Studies in 1997.

R. spends a lot of time in LIBRARIES researching his projects. When he is working on a picture book, research takes a good chunk of the time involved in getting to the final product. R.'s work is notable for his efforts at creating a seamless unity between the text and illustrations. He frequently works in traditional watercolors, often combining them with other compatible media.

R. enjoys spending time in schools visiting with students, teachers, and librarians. He enjoys the freedom he has in the creation of his illustrations and the knowledge that what he is doing leads to children reading. He frequently collaborates with his wife, illustrator Gloria RAND.

AWARDS: Christopher Award (1991) for *Paul Revere's Ride* (LONGFELLOW)

FURTHER WORKS: *Up and Down on the Merry-Go-Round.* 1988. *The Sun, the Wind and the Rain.* 1988. *Once When I Was Scared.* 1988. *The Hornbeam Tree and Other Poems.* 1988. *Salty Dog.* 1989. *A Little Excitement.* 1989. *The Jumblies.* 1989

BIBLIOGRAPHY: *Sixth Book of Junior Authors and Illustrators,* 1989; Cummins, Julie, ed., *Children's Book ILLUSTRATION and Design,* 1992

MICHAEL O'LAUGHLIN

RANSOME, Arthur M.

Writer, critic, journalist, b. 18 January 1884, Leeds, Yorkshire, England; d. 3 June, 1967, Lake Windermere, Lake District, England

R. grew up in Leeds, England, and spent his early years fishing, sailing, and reading—pastimes that were encouraged by his parents. The British author is best known for his ADVENTURE BOOKS for children and for his collections and TRANSLATIONS of Russian folktales. His novel, *Pigeon Post* (1936), was the first book to be awarded the CARNEGIE MEDAL, the English equivalent of the NEWBERY MEDAL in the United States. He also earned the AMERICAN LIBRARY ASSOCIATION Notable Book citation and *Boston Globe–Horn Book* honor list citation, for *The Fool of the World and the Flying Ship* (1968), a translation of an old Russian folktale. Another novel, *Great Northern?* (1947), was one of the earliest books for children that raised the issue of the environment as a social concern. It also demonstrated R.'s ability to write vividly about the English countryside.

R. wrote that his father "was a fisherman who was a professor of history in his spare time." From his father, the younger R. learned to love and respect the hills and lakes of the lake district resort, Coniston, where the family often spent long vacations. After his education at Rugby (1897–1901) and a brief stay at Yorkshire College, R. went to London and worked as an office boy in a publishing firm. Whenever possible, he returned to his boyhood vacation home, and it was there that he met the Collingwood family who would profoundly influence his writing. The picnics, explorations, and sailing trips he made with the Collingwoods were revived later in some of the most enduring literature that has been written for children. His memories of those days came to life some twenty-five years later in his Swallows and Amazon books and his other books about children who sailed and explored the lakes and hills of England.

The Arthur R. Society (TARS) was established in June 1990 and is based in Kendal, England. Much memorabilia, given by R.'s widow, Eugenia, may be seen there at the Abbot Hall Museum. The society seeks to "celebrate the life, promote the works, and diffuse the ideas of Arthur R." (The Arthur R. Society, 1998).

FURTHER WORKS: *The Soldier and Death: A Russian Folk Tale in English.* 1920. *Swallows and Amazons.* 1930. *Swallowdale.* 1931. *Peter Duck.* 1932. *We Didn't Mean to Go to Sea.* 1938. *Missee Lee.* 1942

BIBLIOGRAPHY: *Major Authors and Illustrators for Children and YOUNG ADULTS,* vol. 5, 1993. *The Junior Book of Authors,* 2nd ed., 1951. The Arthur R. Society. 1998. Available online http://www.arthur ransome.org/ar/tars.html (accessed July 23, 1998)

MARY ARIAIL BROUGHTON

RANSOME, James
Illustrator, b. 25 September 1961, Rich Square, North Carolina

R.'s interest in art began at an early age and continued through his college career where he received a Bachelor of FINE ARTS from Pratt Institute. R. was influenced by television cartoons, superhero COMIC BOOKS, and *Mad* magazine. As R. grew older he became interested in the areas of film and photography. He also developed an appreciation for the works of such artists as Mary Cassatt and Winslow Homer. These artists among others influenced his own style of ILLUSTRATION for children's books.

R.'s AWARDS for his illustrations include the *Parenting* magazine Reading Magic Award, for *Do Like Kyla* (Angela JOHNSON, 1990), Parent's Choice Foundation's Annual Award for *Aunt Flossie's Hats (and Crab Cakes Later)* (Elizabeth F. Howard, au., 1991), and 1994, INTERNATIONAL READING ASSOCIATION Award for *Sweet Clara and the Freedom Quilt* (HOPKINSON). R. has illustrated several books including Angela Johnson's *All the Lights in the Night* (1991) and Lenny Hort's *How Many Stars in the Sky?* (1991). R. has also been the illustrator for several book jack-

ets for young adult works including, *The Middle of Somewhere* (1990) and *Children of the Fire* (1991).

R. considers himself a visual storyteller. He sees each book as having a special voice and therefore makes every illustration different to convey the differences in voice. R. likes to experiment with palette, design, and perspective to achieve a unique look for each book that he illustrates. He describes his work by saying that he hopes he is "conveying to young readers the individual traits of characters" that in turn will help readers see the diverse and unique qualities of people.

R. works in oil paint using bold colors that radiate a rich stateliness, giving his illustrations a sense of lush density. This is evident in books as disparate in subject as *Satchel Paige* (Lesa Cline-Ransome, 2000), a biography of the first black baseball player admitted to the Hall of Fame, and *Uncle Jed's Barbershop* (Margaree King Mitchell, 1993), about a family in the segregated south of the 1920s. In the latter book R.'s brightly colored oil paintings show a warm, loving family and their emotions as they struggle to help make Uncle Jed's dream a reality despite social and economic obstacles. R. establishes a clearly visualized sense of time and place through his realistic illustrations.

AWARDS: IBBY Honor book (1996) for *The Creation* (James Weldon Johnson); CORETTA SCOTT KING AWARD (1995) for Illustration for *The Creation* (1994), for *Uncle Jed's Barbershop.*

FURTHER WORKS: *All the Lights in the Night.* (A. Levine), 1991. *Red Dancing Shoes.* (Denise Patrick). 1993. *The Creation.* (James Johnson). 1994. *Freedom's Fruit.* (William H. HOOKS). 1995. *I Am the Darker Brother.* (Arnold ADOFF). 1997, rev. ed. *The Jukebox Man.* (J. Ogburn). 1998

BIBLIOGRAPHY: *Something about the Author,* vol. 76, 1994

MICHAEL O'LAUGHLIN

RASCHKA, Chris
Author, illustrator, b. 6 March 1959, Huntington, Pennsylvania

R. is the son of an American father and an Austrian mother, and claims a bit of both nationalities. Although born in Pennsylvania, R. spent many of his early years in Europe and grew up speaking both German and English. He recalls that his earliest stories were Viennese FAIRY TALES and sagas of Vienna told by his mother. He believes that the PICTURE BOOKS, such as *Die Kleine Hexe* (*The Little Witch*, 1972) by Otto PREUSSLER, and other works from his mother's part of the world have had a great influence on his own work.

Although R. gained early success as a freelance artist, he decided to go to medical school after working as an intern in a children's orthopedic clinic in Germany. He passed the entrance tests and was admitted to medical school, but changed his mind just before classes began and decided to continue working as an artist. He worked as an illustrator for various regional newspapers and periodicals and eventually decided to write a children's book. His first self-illustrated book, *R and R: A Story about Two Alphabets,* was published in 1990.

The creator of some of the most sophisticated and intelligent of today's picture books, R.'s seemingly simple stories and illustrations are actually carefully crafted visual and aural elements in beautifully constructed compositions that appeal to both children and adults. R.'s deep connection to music is clear. In ILLUSTRATION, his bold and fluid lines carry the reader through the melody of a page, and his colors often function symbolically and musically. His subjects have been musicians including *Charlie Parker Played Be-Bop* (1992) about the jazz saxophone player, and *Mysterious Thelonious* (1997) about the jazz pianist and composer. He has illustrated song, *Simple Gifts* (1998); and his poetic sensibility has made him a successful collaborator, as illustrator, with Nikki GIOVANNI in *Genie in a Jar* (1996) and bell hooks's *Happy to be Nappy* (1999). Often provocative, R.'s work has addressed issues such as race relations, *Yo! Yes?* (1993), child abuse, *Elizabeth Imagined an Iceberg* (1994), and death, in the much discussed *Arlene Sardine* (1998).

Yo! Yes? (1993), R.'s third book, containing just thirty-four words, tells a story of friendship between an outgoing AFRICAN AMERICAN boy and a lonely white boy. Like most of R.'s works, the book contains a rhythmic text and jaunty illustra-

tions. In addition to his self-illustrated books, R. has illustrated books for other well-known authors including Margaret Wise BROWN and Sharon CREECH.

AWARDS: ALA CALDECOTT MEDAL Honor Book (1994) for *Yo! Yes?* ALA Notable Book (1993) for *Charlie Parker Played Be-Bop*

FURTHER WORKS: Self-illustrated: *Elizabeth Imagined an Iceberg.* 1994. *Can't Sleep.* 1995. *Blushful Hippopotamus.* 1995. *Like Likes Like.* 1999. Illustrator: *The Genie in the Jar.* (Nikki Giovanni). 1998. *Another Important Book.* (Margaret Wise Brown). 1999. *Happy to Be Nappy.* (bell hooks). 1999. *Fishing in the Air.* (Sharon Creech). 2000

BIBLIOGRAPHY: Richardson, F., *Children' Book Page,* 1999; http://www.bookpage.com/9902bp/childrens/like_likes_like.html (accessed October 24, 1999); *Seventh Book of Junior Authors and Illustrators,* 1996. *Something about the Author,* vol. 80, 1995

MARY ARIAIL BROUGHTON AND

REBECCA PLATZNER

RASKIN, Ellen

Author, illustrator, b. 13 March 1928, Milwaukee, Wisconsin; d. 8 August 1984, New York City

R. began her career as a commercial illustrator and designer. She drew more than 5,000 ILLUSTRATIONS and designed over 1,000 dust jackets. In 1966, R. changed to a career as an author, self-illustrating her books; she was immediately successful. R. is best known for *The Westing Game* (1978), a compelling NEWBERY MEDAL winning MYSTERY in which readers try to figure out which of the heirs to Sam Westing's fortune is his murderer.

AWARDS: AMERICAN LIBRARY ASSOCIATION Newbery Medal Award (1979) for *The Westing Game;* ALA Newbery Medal Honor Book (1975) for *Figgs and Phantoms*

FURTHER WORKS: *Nothing Ever Happens on My Block.* 1966: *Spectacles.* 1968: *Ghost in a Four-Room Apartment.* 1969: *And It Rained.* 1969: *The Mysterious Disappearance of Leon (I Mean Noel).* 1972: *Franklin Stein.* 1972: *Who, Said Sue, Said Whoo?* 1973: *Moose, Goose and Little Nobody.* 1974: *The Tattooed Potato and Other Clues.* 1975

BIBLIOGRAPHY: HOPKINS, Lee Bennett, *Pauses: Autobiographical Reflections of 101 Creators of Children's Books,* 1995

JODI PILGRIM

RATHMANN, Peggy (Margaret Crosby)

Author, illustrator, b. 4 March 1953, St. Paul, Minnesota

R. earned a B.A. in psychology from the University of Minnesota, and studied children's book writing and ILLUSTRATION at the Otis Parson's School of Design in Los Angeles. R. works in San Francisco and travels to speak at schools and bookstores, explaining her process of book creation.

R. develops children's books that draw upon funny and embarassing experiences in her own life. Action and HUMOR in vibrant illustrations, and a good sense of story, join to create books of high quality that appeal to children. *Ruby the Copycat* (1991), which R. both wrote and illustrated, was cited in *Publishers Weekly* as a Cuffie Award title for a "Most Promising New Author." Illustrations in *Good Night, Gorilla* (1994), combined with only a few repeated words of text, convey the clever story of a gorilla who follows the zookeeper on his nighttime rounds. *Officer Buckle and Gloria* (1995) is the hilarious account of a school safety officer who is secretly upstaged by his dog, Gloria. Detail, humor, and hidden parallel stories in R.'s illustrations invite repeated listening and reading by children.

AWARDS: ALA CALDECOTT MEDAL (1996) for *Officer Buckle and Gloria.* AMERICAN LIBRARY ASSOCIATION Notable Children's Book Award (1995) for *Good Night, Gorilla*

FURTHER WORKS: *Bootsie Barker Bites.* (Barbara Bottner). 1992. *10 Minutes Till Bedtime.* 2000

BIBLIOGRAPHY: *Something about the Author.* vol. 94, 1998. R., Peggy. "Caldecott Medal Acceptance." The *Horn Book* magazine. July–Aug. 1996. pp. 424–27. R.-Noonan, Robin. "Aunt Peggy." *Horn Book.* July–Aug. 1996. pp. 428–29. "Peggy R." (brochure). G. P. Putnam's Sons. INTERNET resources: www.peggyrathmann.com/links.html (accessed November 17, 1998); www.ala.org/alsclrathman.html (accessed November 17, 1998)

KATHIE KRIEGER CERRA

RAWLINGS, Marjorie Kinnan

Author, b. 8 August 1896, Washington, D.C.; d. 14 December 1953, St. Augustine, Florida

After graduating from the University of Wisconsin in 1918, W. spent most of her years living in isolation on a seventy-two-acre orange grove in Cross Creek, Florida. The rural life and landscape inspired R. to write about what she saw right before her eyes: nature and beauty, children and small communities. Her collection of short stories, *Jacob's Ladder,* won second place in Scribner's Prize contest in 1931 and *Gal Young Un* won the O. Henry Memorial Award in 1933. She published her first novel in 1933, *South Moon Under.*

She is best known for her CLASSIC NOVELS, *The Yearling* (1938) and *The Secret River* (1955). *The Yearling* was not published specifically for children; it has long been loved and read by children and is considered a children's classic novel today. Although it is a story of a boy and his pet deer, it is also the story of passage from boyhood to adulthood. R. expressed her deepest sentiments in her autobiographical memoir, *Cross Creek* (1942).

It is important to situate R.'s works historically since many of the ethnic characterizations continue to cause heated debates among scholars about the meaningfulness and intent of her work. A resurgence of reprintings and continued interest in R.'s works assures that children and adults are afforded the opportunity to delve into these significant and timeless contributions to the field.

AWARDS: Pulitzer Prize for fiction (1939) for *the Yearling.* Lewis CARROLL Shelf Award (1963) for *The Yearling.* ALA NEWBERY MEDAL Award Honor Book (1956) for *The Secret River*

BIBLIOGRAPHY: Silvey, Anita, ed., *Children's Books and Their Creators,* 1995; *The Oxford Encyclopedia of Children's Literature,* 1984; *Something about the Author,* vol. 100, 1999

SHANE RAYBURN AND IRVYN G. GILBERTSON

RAWLS, Wilson

Author, b. 24 September 1913, Scraper, Oklahoma; d. 16 December 1984

R. was reared in rural Oklahoma and was taught at home by his mother, though he had some formal education through the eighth grade. He had to leave his Ozarks home when he was young to go to work during the Great Depression. Eventually, he decided to write about his early years in *Where the Red Fern Grows* (1961), the emotional story of the mutual devotion of a boy and his two hunting dogs, which often moves readers to tears. Young readers in many states selected it as their favorite book of the year soon after its publication. He also wrote more lightheartedly about the relationship of people and animals in *Summer of the Monkeys* (1976). In a letter written to THE KERLAN COLLECTION, University of Minnesota, after his death, his wife said that his papers were donated to The Cherokee National Historical Society in Tahlequah, Oklahoma "because he was always proud to be part Cherokee."

BIBLIOGRAPHY: *Something about the Author,* vol. 22, 1981

REBECCA RAPPORT

RAYNER, Mary

Author, illustrator, b. 30 December 1933, Mandalay, Burma

R., now residing in Wiltshire, England, entertains her audiences with whimsical tales of ANIMAL characters who provide domestic views of family life, most notably the Mr. and Mrs. Pig books. She has the talent to engage young readers with her tales of family stories and ILLUSTRATIONS that delight her audience. Her three children, now grown, provided the motivation to write episodes that allow the young reader to examine everyday common childhood fears at a safe distance. In *Mr. and Mrs. Pig's Evening Out* (1976), the ten piglet children devise a plan to cope with the wolf-in-disguise babysitter. Her illustrations in Dick KING-SMITH's *Babe: The Gallant Pig* (1985) precede the popular Academy Award nominated movie. R.'s first published book was *The Witch-Finder* in 1975.

FURTHER WORKS: *Crocodarling.* 1985. *Mrs. Pig Gets Cress and Other Stories.* 1986. *Reilly.* 1987. *Marathon and Steve.* 1989. *Garth Pig Steals the Show.* 1993

BIBLIOGRAPHY: *Children's Literature Review,* vol. 41, 1997. *Something about the Author,* vol. 87, 1996

NANCY HORTON

READING RAINBOW AND CHILDREN'S LITERATURE ON TELEVISION

(This article has been prepared by Twila Liggett, who is Senior Vice President for Education and Special Projects and Executive Producer of PBS Television's Reading Rainbow *series. She has been with the program since its inception and first airing, and shares her experience translating books into another medium from an insider's point of view.)*

Without a doubt, *Reading Rainbow*'s tenure on public television has established that TV is a successful ally in encouraging, even compelling, children to read. *Reading Rainbow* is a well-established PBS children's series designed to bring the fun of wonderful children's literature, reading, and learning for the sheer joy of the experience to young viewers (targeting five- to eight-year-olds). Centering each theme on a featured book, the programs use on-location segments to engage children in enriching adventures related to the book's theme. Three additional books are reviewed and promoted by young readers who entice the viewers with more book choices. Hosted by LeVar Burton, the series first aired in 1983. In the early days of *Reading Rainbow* it was difficult to convince authors and publishers that putting their books on television was advantageous. In fact, there were a number of people who felt that television was the enemy to literature and to reading. Within two years, most publishers were promoting their titles for selection. There are two key issues that relate to children's literature on *Reading Rainbow*—choosing the books and adapting the books to television.

The primary or "featured" PICTURE BOOK is the backbone of each show. Thus, our review and selection of exceptional children's literature is an essential first step in the production process. The selection process is straightforward. We find books through recommendations by our viewers, with the advice of professionals in children's literature and by looking everywhere and reading everything we can. We have a special interest in good stories featuring protagonists who represent a cross section of cultures, e.g., AFRICAN AMERICAN, LATINA/O, ASIAN, NATIVE AMERICAN and so forth. We also search for stories with female protagonists in positive and active roles. As we read books, the qualities we look for in *Reading Rainbow* titles are (1) literary merit, (2) visual impact and artistic achievement, (3) adaptability to the television format, and (4) ability to interest children. We consider a number of factors in determining literary merit. AWARDS and other acknowledgments of literary achievement are important to us. Not only new titles, but books that have stood the test of time, interest us. We look for diverse literary styles. A book must be appealing as a read-aloud. We are also interested in awards and other distinctions given to PICTURE BOOKS in evaluating a title for visual impact and artistic achievement. Books with strong, vivid, colorful graphics and artistic HUMOR are often selected as feature books.

Adaptability refers to the way the book will translate from print to television. There must be a strong relationship between story and art, and the art must be graphically suited to television. Stories with too much graphic detail may get lost, as may those with too little. On TV, action in picture books works better than atmosphere or mood. Occasionally we ask the original illustrator to "colorize" a black-and-white book to enhance the impact of the art. Once books meet our criteria, they are tested with children. *Reading Rainbow* researchers visit schools in New York City and suburban areas and read stories to groups of beginning readers who represent a range of cultures and socioeconomic levels. Questions are asked to determine children's reactions, opinions, and recall of the story. The story session is considered one of the most vital aspects of the selection process. If children do not respond enthusiastically to a book, it is not used. With the list narrowed down, proposed titles are sent to education and literary consultants. In-house we discuss each book's potential for a *Reading Rainbow* show. We agonize over decisions, make them, and contact the publishers for permission to use the books in the series. *Reading Rainbow* books must be available in bookstores and libraries nationwide. Publishers are also encouraged to put *Reading Rainbow* books into paperback, and many do. We now are approaching 600 titles in the Reading Rainbow booklist. Each book has been through the process of evaluating, testing,

brainstorming, and adapting, and has finally reached our viewers. Over the sixteen years that *Reading Rainbow* has been on PBS, librarians, booksellers, parents, and teachers have reported a stunning increase in requests for books seen on the show. Sales of these books have dramatically increased, with some jumping as high as 600 percent. This impact has convinced the children's book and television community that *Reading Rainbow* is successful in motivating children to seek out good books. It is vitally important to our *Reading Rainbow* team to ensure that child viewers do not mistake the featured book for a cartoon, but understand that what they are seeing is a "real" book—a concept we have come to call the "bookness" of a book. We implement the bookness, in part, by beginning each presentation with the title page, using actual illustrations with slight camera movement, iconographic animation, and superimposing the words "The End" at the book's conclusion. In iconographic animation, an approach we feel is most compatible with picture books, the camera (controlled by a computer) performs a series of strategically planned moves on each ILLUSTRATION. Thus, as the story is read, the camera focuses on appropriate parts of the illustration—for instance, a particular character that is speaking is highlighted even though there are other people in the picture. At some point, each illustration is shown in full zoom out. The end result approximates the way a child might look at an illustration in order to extract meaning from the story. While the visuals are in production, the narrator, often but not always a celebrity voice, records the story. The audio is then carefully mixed to include sound effects and original music sweetening.

Simultaneously, the rest of the creative process is also under way. First, the production team extrapolates thematic ideas from the book and works together to brainstorm extensions of those themes. The primary challenge for the team is how best to treat the topic so that kids will be so excited that they clamor for the featured books. These field segments have run the gamut from inside the earth in the California Caverns, outside of San Francisco, to a Native American powwow at the Crow Fair in Crow Agency, Montana, to the Vietnam War Memorial in Washington, D.C.

The final element, produced for each show is the segment called "book reviews" in which children recommend three more picture books that emphasize or amplify the show's theme. Our feedback from publishers and authors alike is that they love *Reading Rainbow*'s qualitative adaptation of their books and that the surrounding program material sends a message of respect and delight about children's literature. And best of all, children demand and read the books.

TWILA LIGGETT

(See also TECHNOLOGY AND COMMUNICATION)

REALISTIC FICTION

Children frequently describe realistic fiction as "real stories about real people." In essence, this description is fairly accurate. Realistic fiction is the term used to describe stories that could have actually occurred to people or animals. The possibility exists that the events or similar events could have taken place. Fictional characters react to a situation in the same manner that real people might react.

Realistic fiction can be divided into four categories: factual, situational, emotional, and social. In factual realism, facts describing actual persons, places, and events are accurately recorded; it is often a main characteristic of historical fiction. Situational realism occurs when a situation is not only possible, but probable. The author identifies both location and characters by place, age, and social class and treats them in a believable manner. The SURVIVAL STORY is one example of this type of realism. Emotional realism, often a major element in the coming-of-age story, has believable feelings and relationships between characters. Social realism provides an honest portrait of society, both the good and the bad. A work of realistic fiction will include some or all of these categories.

The contemporary realistic novel, also called contemporary realism, describes stories that take place in the present with accurately portrayed attitudes and social mores. Frequently this type of story is considered a "problem novel" in that the plot emphasizes social or personal issues such as child abuse, alcoholism, divorce, teenage pregnancy, or suicide. Examples of problem novels include the NEWBERY MEDAL books *Holes* (SA-CHAR, 1998), *Walk Two Moons* (CREECH, 1994), and the Honor Title *What Jamie Saw* (1995, Coman). The problem of the protagonist becomes the source of the plot as in Newbery Medal title *Maniac Magee* (SPINELLI, 1990). True-to-life portrayals of minority and MULTICULTURAL characters and situations has become another aspect of the genre. Walter Dean MYER's *Scorpions,* 1989, Newbery Medal Honor Book, and *Somewhere in the Darkness,* his 1993 Newbery Medal Honor Book, are examples. Realistic fiction does not have to be contemporary. Historical fiction or historical realism places the plot and characters in the past with verifiable details as to dress, food, and life. Characters and plot may be based on historical figures, may be just "pretend" and placed in a historical setting (*The Midwife's Apprentice,* CUSHMAN, 1996 Newbery Medal Award), or may be a combination of both as in the 1990 Newbery Medal Award title *Number the Stars* (LOWRY). Animal realism adds a story dimension to accurate details about the animal as in Phyllis Reynolds NAYLOR's 1992 Newbery Medal dog story, *Shiloh.* An objective point of view is necessary in order for the animals to act like animals and not be given human characteristics. SPORTS STORIES, MYSTERIES, and romances may be considered types of realistic fiction, but are also considered separate genres.

The content of children's literature, while it has always contained elements of realism, has changed markedly as society's view of children has changed. In the seventeenth century, children were seen as being in need of salvation and most children's literature was instructional, didactic, and of a religious nature. During the eighteenth century, the trend towards instruction continued, but some literature was written strictly for entertainment. By the nineteenth century, children's literature became less moralistic and folktales and FANTASY became important genres. An early type of realistic fiction that reflected this decline in didacticism was the ADVENTURE novel, exemplified by *Swiss Family Robinson* (1816) by Johann WYSS and *Kidnapped* (1886), as well as *Treasure Island* (1883) by Robert Louis STEVENSON. Realistic ANIMAL STORIES like Anna SEWELL's *Black Beauty* (1877) also became popular during the latter half of the nineteenth century. A more modern kind of realism became popular with the publication of the dime novels, Mark TWAIN's *The Adventures of Tom Sawyer* (1876) and *Adventures of Huckleberry Finn* (1884), the Horatio Alger novels, and FAMILY STORIES such as Louisa May ALCOTT's *Little Women* (1868) and Margaret SYDNEY's (pseud. Harriet M. Lothrop) Five Little Peppers and How They Grew series (1881). During the twentieth century, childhood came to be considered a "golden age" and the attention paid to children's literature grew markedly. Early realistic novels of the century included books such as Lucy Maud MONT-GOMERY's Anne of Green Gables series, Kate Douglas WIGGIN's *Rebecca of Sunnybrook Farm* (1903), and Frances Hodgson BURNETT's *The Secret Garden* (1911). The NEWBERY MEDAL (1922) and CALDECOTT (1938) MEDAL AWARDS, that recognized outstanding quality in children's literature, began during the early part of the century. Realism in children's fiction grew as a major genre, with dime novels and SERIES BOOKS important early examples of the trend. *Harriet the Spy* by Louise FITZHUGH, published in 1964, is considered the benchmark novel for modern realism with its graphic and truthful depiction of an unhappy, unpleasant child. Children's literature in the 1960s and 1970s focused on intellectual freedom, relevance, and realism, supporting the trend toward the "problem novel." Unlike the realistic novels of earlier periods that emphasized happy, mostly middle-class families and few controversial issues, today's realistic fiction speaks openly of current societal issues such as divorce, child abuse, drug addiction, and alcoholism, poverty, racism, and homelessness. Also, prior to 1950, few books for children and YOUNG ADULTS portraying any culture other than the white middle class were available. According to Kay Vandergrift, "Young Americans could more easily read about cultures of those in different lands than they could about various racial, ethnic, class, or religious differences within their own neighborhoods or nation."

Plot, character, setting, and theme remain the standard elements for evaluating realistic fiction. Well-developed, dynamic characters who show growth or change and a well-structured, believable plot are essential. The setting should be suitable for the story line and the theme should not be didactic or overtly moralistic. Also, in contemporary fiction of the problem novel type, the character's situation should not overwhelm the plot or characterization nor should the book become a soapbox for the author.

As the popularity of realistic fiction continues to grow, so do the issues concerning its subject matter; contemporary realistic fiction has become a major area for book challenges and CENSORSHIP attempts. To help avoid such challenges, five values of realistic fiction are identified as: (1) The stories are easy for children to relate to and enjoy because they can often see their own lives or lives much like their own. (2) Realistic fiction permits children to see how other people live their lives and solve their problems. (3) Children can explore the many commonalities in basic human values across cultures. (4) Children can become aware that other children have lives that are much different from their own. (5) Bibliotherapy, using selected to books to help children deal with social and emotional problems, often draws books from this genre.

BIBLIOGRAPHY: Glazer, J., *Introduction to Children's Literature.* 2nd ed., 1997; Lukens, R., *A Critical Handbook of Children's Literature,* 1994; Lynch-Brown, C., and C. Tomlinson. *Essentials of Children's Literature,* 1993; Vandergrift, K., *A Feminist Perspective on Multicultural Children's Literature in the Middle Years of the Twentieth Century,* 1993

JANET HILBUN

REID, Barbara
Illustrator, author, b. 16 November 1957, Toronto, Ontario, Canada

A 1980 graduate of the Ontario College of Art, R. loved to play with plasticine, a colorful moldable clay as a child. On rainy days or days when she was home sick from school, she would fill the hours creating animals, people, and other worlds. In school, she often volunteered for special projects in which she could practice her art and avoid the montony of the classroom. As R. grew older, she continued to enjoy working with plasticine and found a way to turn her pastime into a profession. The first three books she illustrated, Betty Waterton's *Mustard* (1983), Mary Blakeslee's *It's Tough to Be a Kid* (1983) and Mary Alice Downie's *Jenny Greenteeth* (1984) were done without plasticine, but her fourth book, Edith

Newlin Chase's *The New Baby Calf* (1984), introduced her signature style of ILLUSTRATION—realistically detailed plasticine representations.

In addition to illustrating works for other authors, R. has written and illustrated several books of her own, including *Playing with Plasticine* (1988), *Two by Two* (1992), and *The Party* (1997). She has also published a SERIES of textless picture-board books. *Zoe's Rainy Day, Zoe's Sunny Day, Zoe's Snowy Day,* and *Zoe's Windy Day* (all 1991) featuring the adventures of a little girl in each kind of weather. In 1997, she published a second series called First Look Board Books.

Critics have praised R. for her artistic interpretations of text as well as the rich colors, textures, and creative detail that enhance the realistic three-dimensional quality of her work. Her illustrations, particularly for *The New Baby Calf* (1984) and *Have You Seen Birds?* (1986) have won many AWARDS and honors in Canada, Germany, and the United States. Her self-illustrated books, notably *Playing with Plasticine,* the Zoe series, and *Two by Two* have also earned critical acclaim.

Before planning the illustrations for an author's story, R. first reads the text repeatedly until she feels familiar with it. To construct the illustrations, she sketches the scenes in pencil, then applies the flat plasticine background to rough cardboard, building layer upon layer of plasticine to achieve the desired effect. To shape and texture the work, R. says she uses common materials—her fingers and fingernails, sticks, pins, combs, wires, cloth, and other items. R. works with her husband, Ian, a photographer.

FURTHER WORKS: *First Look Board Books: Acorn to Oak Tree. Seed to Flower. Caterpillar to Butterfly. Tadpole to Frog.* All 1997. Self-illustrated: *Have You Seen Birds?* (J. Oppenheim). 1986. *How to Make Pop-Ups.* (J. Irvine). 1987. *Effie* (B. Allinson). 1990. *Gifts.* (J. E. Bogart). 1994

BIBLIOGRAPHY: http://www.nlc-bnc.ca/events/illustra/stylist/ereid2.htm#top (accessed July 22, 1998); *Something about the Author,* vol. 93, 1997

MARY ARIAIL BROUGHTON

REISS, Johanna De Leeuw

Author, b. 4 April, 1932, Winterswijk, Holland

The youngest of three sisters, R. was born and grew up in a town near the Holland-German border. R.'s mother was frequently ill and found it difficult to care for the three girls. The Nazi occupation of the Netherlands during World War II forced R. to become separated from her family when she was ten years old. In 1942 R.'s father hid her and her sister Sini for almost three years in the attic of a sympathetic Christian couple, Johan and Dientje Oosterveld, to escape the horrors of a concentration camp. The few weeks they expected to stay in hiding on the farm near Usselo turned into more than two years of hiding. Following the war, R. was educated in Holland where she taught for several years, and later moved to America in 1955 where she first found odd jobs such as a baby-sitter and a cheese cutter.

Nearly thirty years after the war, R. put into words her experiences in hiding on the small farm in the award-winning book, *The Upstairs Room* (1972). In sparse prose this fictional account vividly recalls the despair of being hidden and the slowly growing awareness of the events of the HOLOCAUST through the eyes of a ten-year-old child. In 1976 *The Upstairs Room* received the Buxtehuder Bulle, a German children's book award "as an outstanding book promoting peace." A critic for the *New York Times* wrote about *The Upstairs Room:* "This admirable account is as important in every aspect as the one bequeathed to us by Anne Frank. In the end, we are grateful to fate for having spared a child who can reminisce with neither hate nor bitterness but a kind of gentleness that leaves us with a lump in our throats." A decade later R. published a sequel that encompasses the aftermath of war, a time of rebuilding for the family and for the community.

AWARDS: ALA NEWBERY MEDAL Honor Book (1973) for *The Upstairs Room.* National Jewish Book Award (1973) for *The Upstairs Room*

FURTHER WORKS: *The Journey Back,* 1987

BIBLIOGRAPHY: *Fifth Book of Junior Authors,* 1983

SANDRA IMDIEKE

RESEARCH ON CHILDREN'S LITERATURE

Research on children's literature is a systematic inquiry into the nature of children's literature, the developing interests and literary understandings of its readers, or the implications of literary study in the classroom. This research reflects the vastness and diversity of the field, as it ranges from close textual analysis to large reading interest surveys, from statistical studies with literature as a treatment variable to case studies of individual readers. It also overlaps with research on reading, early literacy, literacy instruction, and reader response.

Scholars have been conducting research on children's literature for over a century, but this research has flourished especially since the 1980s when the literature-based curriculum movement sparked increased interest in children's literature. From early to current studies there is a developing sense of the complexity of the constructs of literature, readers, and contexts for reading, as well as the interaction among these readers, texts, and contexts. What initially seemed simple and straightforward is now understood as multifaceted and complex as our understanding of the transactional nature of literary response; reading and learning, and the influence of context have complicated our ideas about children's literature. The questions, methodologies, and theoretical bases of research today reflect this complexity.

Research on children's literature texts can be divided into literary and content analyses, with each containing considerable variation. Literary analyses examine individual texts or genres to describe what authors do, looking at narrative patterns, character development, metaphor, intertextuality, and so on. These studies may be historical, focus on one or several texts, encompass one or several genres, or examine the work of one particular author. Literary analyses treat children's literature as an object of literary criticism and analysis, just as adult literature is treated. This research has been increasing steadily since 1970 and the founding of the International Research Society for Children's Literature. Current literary analyses often explore texts and illustrations from a postmodern point of view.

Content analyses, on the other hand, examine texts to determine what they are about, usually considering the content from a particular perspective, such as gender or ethnicity, cultural, or thematic studies. Many early content analyses were simplistic, being counts of content markers such as race, gender, or occupations. The content focus of these studies reflects the interests of the

times, with many researchers, for example, exploring the presence and image of African Americans in children's literature in the 1960s and 1970s. These early content analyses rarely considered the social and cultural forces that shaped the content, or the possible implications of the consideration of that content by child readers. However, most contemporary content analyses are based on an understanding of texts as influenced by the social, cultural, and political contexts in which they are created.

Today, many content analyses focus on gender and ethnicity; some explore the history and development of culturally diverse literature. A current issue is authorial authenticity—considering the consequences of writing from inside or outside a particular culture. Unfortunately, in many of these studies the role of the reader in the creation of meaning is ignored as the researcher's own particular reading becomes the only reading considered.

There are many studies that fall into the second major strand of research on children's literature—research on the readers of children's literature. Early research in this area consisted of preference and interest studies, with research on children's responses to literature beginning in the 1980s. Across studies of preference and interest and of response, findings reveal a pattern of broad consistencies and marked individual differences. Preference and interest studies over the years point to broad patterns that relate especially to age and gender. Contemporary studies seek to understand these patterns by viewing them through the lens of critical theory and social constructivism, seeing preferences and interests as something that cultures and readers do, something that is influenced by our social lives.

Studies of children responding to literature also reflect a greater complexity. They have evolved from exploring how children's preferences, cognitive development, and life experiences shape their responses to an examination of how culture influences reading and responding to literature. Several recent studies look at the responses of readers to literature that challenges their cultural assumptions, that presents values and experiences that differ from the values and experiences operating in the reader's life. Many researchers find that students "resist" these texts, and are not able to enter into the virtual experience that a literary text can provide. Other studies indicate that children do use literature to explore themselves and their worlds, and to think about both personal and social issues.

Research on the contexts that support children's engagement with literature are the third major strand of research on children's literature. These studies focus on literary studies in the classroom, effects of teachers' reading aloud, and teacher beliefs and practices regarding children's literature. Much of the research on literary studies looks at children's ability to recognize literary elements or to use those elements in their own writing. Researchers have discovered that even primary grade children can and do recognize and use literary elements, and that the way a teacher encourages students to approach a text makes a huge difference in what they are able and willing to do with it. Asking students to approach a literary text aesthetically, for the experience, has vastly different results from asking students to approach a literary text for information. Hearing literature read aloud also affects children as readers. Results from current research indicate, however, that not all read-alouds are alike, and the books teachers choose, how often they read, where they read, and how they read all influence the effects of reading aloud. Likewise, the way children discuss the books they read impacts their understanding of those books. At their best, discussions can help increase children's literary understanding, allow them to explore issues and meaning, and socialize them into ways of talking about books. Further, teachers' beliefs about using children's literature and their practices as enacted in selection and curriculum development also influence how children read that literature. Often practices belie beliefs, and thus what may be admirable goals are not realized in practice.

Both interest in and scope of research in children's literature has grown over the century, spanning many disciplines, methodologies, and theoretical perspectives. Literature for children has spilled into the greater body of reading research as well. The richness and diversity of these studies are welcome, for taken as a whole, they reflect the complexity of what it means to read and write children's literature. It is the research that explores particular readers and particular texts in particular contexts that is the most enlightening and exciting. Studies grounded in theory, that use articulated strategies for close and careful analysis, inform us all. Today we have many ways of looking at the complex issues that surround children's literature, and our scholarship can only benefit.

LEE GALDA

(See also CRITICAL THEORISTS)

REVIEW JOURNALS

Children's book reviewing has had a long, rich history in the United States. In his landmark study, *The Rise of Children's Book Reviewing in America, 1865–1881,* Richard L. Darling found that children's books were regularly reviewed in mid- to-late-nineteenth century literary monthlies and popular magazines by reviewers who showed a considerable understanding of children and their books. More than one hundred years later, this sort of understanding continues to play a crucial role in children's book reviewing. Then, as now, the function of reviews appearing in the popular press was to call new books to the attention of potential readers, or, as Virginia Woolf succinctly described it: "partly to sort current literature; partly to advertise the author; partly to inform the public." This attention to new children's books in general periodical literature was carried well into the twentieth century with regular children's book review columns appearing in publications such as the *New York Herald Tribune, New York Times Book Review, Chicago Tribune* and *Saturday Review of Literature.*

With the development of children's library services in the early twentieth century, reviewing began to serve another function: to provide children's librarians with a guide for selecting books. *Booklist,* a professional library journal consisting of reviews of new titles recommended for purchase, has included a children's books section since its inception in 1905. Other general library periodicals, such as *Kirkus Reviews* and *Library Journal,* included children's book reviews as well. The *Horn Book* magazine, founded in 1924 by Bertha Mahony Miller and Elinor Whitney Field, was entirely devoted to articles and reviews of children's books and throughout much of the twentieth century was very influential in setting contemporary standards for excellence in children's books. Unlike other review journals, the *Horn Book* has always enjoyed a wide general readership that extends far beyond the library profession, largely due to its emphasis on the literary aspects of children's books, rather than the library profession.

In 1954, the children's book section of *Library Journal* broke off to establish its own publication, *School Library Journal,* which strives to review every book published for children whether it is recommended for purchase or not. At the University of Chicago, *the Bulletin of the Center for Children's Books* was established in 1945; it remains the only national journal to consist entirely of children's book reviews. Taken as a whole, these five journals *(Booklist, Bulletin of the Center for Children's Books,* the *Horn Book, Kirkus Reviews,* and *School Library Journal)* comprise the basis for most school and public library book selection in the United States.

In response to the growing emphasis on adolescent and young adult literature in the mid-twentieth century, *Voice of Youth Advocates (VOYA)* was established in 1977 by Dorothy Broderick and Mary K. Chelton to address the specific needs of librarians and allied professionals who work with teenagers. With an emphasis on responding to, rather than shaping, the reading tastes of teen readers, *VOYA* gives special attention to popular appeal when recommending newly published books.

Although the critical mission and editorial stance may vary slightly in the professional journals cited above, all follow the same basic guidelines in their approach to evaluation: a good review will briefly describe the contents, scope, and style of a book; critically assess its quality; and suggest its potential audience. In her study of fiction reviews, Phyllis K. Kennemer categorized these three types of statements and labeled them *descriptive, analytical,* and *sociological.* She defined them as follows: *descriptive* statements provide objective observations about the characters, plot, theme, or ILLUSTRATIONS; *analytical* statements focus on literary and artistic elements, and include evaluation, comparison, and mention of contributions to the field; and *sociological* statements provide judgments based on nonliterary considerations, such as potential controversial elements or predictions about popularity.

One of the most common complaints about children's book reviews today is that they rely heavily on description and offer very little in the way of critical analysis. This is most likely due to the fact that the children's book review industry primarily functions as a buying guide for librarians, rather than offering serious literary criticism.

Although the words *review* and *criticism* are often used interchangeably, most experts differentiate between the two by pointing out that reviews are limited by time and space; that is, a review is published as closely as possible to the publication date of the book under consideration and the reviewer is generally limited to a set number of words, typically 100 to 400 per review.

In an eloquent essay entitled "Out on a Limb with the Critics: Some Random Thoughts on the Present State of the Criticism of Children's Literature," former editor of the *Horn Book,* Paul Heins, drew the following distinction: "Reviewing . . . is only concerned with what is imminent in publishing, with what is being produced at the present time; and does its job well by selecting, classifying, and evaluating—evaluating for the time being. Criticism deals with literature in perspective and places a book in a larger context."

This is not to say that criticism should not enter into reviewing. In fact, Heins makes the point in the same article that it would be virtually impossible to keep criticism out of a review: "Any form of literary classification, comparison, or evaluation must also be considered a form of criticism."

Because reviewers do not have the advantage of time, it is to their advantage to have a broad knowledge of contemporary children's literature as a context for "selecting, classifying, and evaluating." A solid literature background helps the reviewer put a book into some context in order to answer the questions: Are there other books like this one? If so, how does it compare to them? What does it offer that is unique?

BIBLIOGRAPHY: Darling, Richard L. *The Rise of Children's Book Reviewing in America, 1865–1881,* 1968; Heins, Paul. "Out on a Limb with the Critics: Some Random Thoughts on the Present State of the Criticism of Children's Literature," *Horn Book* 46:3, pp. 264–73, June 1970; Kennemer, Phyllis K. "Reviews of Fiction Books: How They Differ" in *Top of the News* 40:4, pp. 419–22, Summer 1984; Woolf, Virginia. "Reviewing" in *The Captain's Death Bed, and Other Essay,* pp. 127–42, 1950

KATHLEEN T. HORNING

REY, H(ans) A(ugusto)

Author, illustrator, b. 16 September 1898, Hamburg, Germany; d. 26 August 1977, Boston, Massachusetts

R. began displaying an aptitude for drawing at the age of two. He attended the University of Munich and the University of Hamburg, 1919–23 and served in the army during World War I. Although he continued his interest in art, his adult career began in the family import/export business in Rio de Janeiro since he could not afford tuition to an art school. While in Brazil, he met Margret Elizabeth Waldstein, his future wife, who was also interested in art. They married and moved to Paris. In 1940 they were forced to flee Paris and Nazi invasion. Their flight was by bicycle in the dark and gray of early morning since cars were often detained. They took with them only a small amount of food and previously written but unsold manuscripts. Somehow they knew that the manuscripts would be more important than any other possessions. One of the manuscripts, later developed as the popular *Curious George* (1941), was first published in Denmark with the main character called Peter Pedal. The R.s traveled to the Spanish border, sleeping in barns along the way and selling their bicycles to get train fare to Lisbon. Eventually they moved to New York City and then to Cambridge, Massachusetts. R.'s wife is credited as cocreator of the character George and many of the books authored by R.

R.'s numerous animal characters originated from his early childhood as he often visited a nearby zoo. He states that he was much more familiar with zoo animals than farm animals. These close relationships resulted in the delightful characters of his books. R.'s first book in the U.S., *Raffy and Nine Monkeys,* 1939 (*Cecily G. and Nine Monkeys,* 1942, in the U.S.) introduced a "clever and curious" monkey named George. Whence, subsequently, the ever-popular George met his audience. This "good little monkey" who was "always curious" was the center of an entire book and eventually many more.

Preliminary reader approval came when the R.s were detained prior to their flight from Paris. The French police suspected them of being spies and arrested them. But as the officer read the confiscated manuscript, he realized that no author of this little monkey story could be a spy and the R.s were released.

The popularity of the Curious George books is the enticement for young readers and listeners to live vicariously through George who does all the things in the name of curiosity that they dare not. Although he is known as Peter Pedal in Denmark, Zozo in England, and Fifi in France, his antics are enjoyed by all. There are TRANSLATIONS into more than a dozen languages. George misbehaves but does not receive punitive consequences. The fact that the disobedient character is a monkey helps young children distinguish between the fictional life of George and the reality of their own world. The illustrations are as captivating as comic strips and slapstick HUMOR for children. R.'s ability to tell an interesting story with detail, yet simplicity of style and ILLUSTRATION, adds to the success of the Curious George stories. Although most of the stories provide pure entertainment, he did work on two titles before his death in which he added educational elements: *Curious George Learns the Alphabet* (1963) and *Curious George Goes to the Hospital* (1966).

R. also illustrated books that his wife wrote about other animal characters who had problems to solve. *Pretzel* (1944), about an extra long dachshund, and *Spotty* (1945), a different colored bunny, are self-conscious about their looks. R. entertained children during the late thirties and early forties with small flap books in which they had to look under flaps to find the answers to the questions asked in *Is Anybody Home?* (1939), *How Do You Get There?* (1941), and *Where's My Buddy?* (1943). Writing for entertainment was not R.'s only interest. He was a scientist who reveled in sharing knowledge in an understandable manner. In *Find the Constellations* (1954), he illustrates the constellations by using displays of star patterns and stick figures that relate to the names and themes to aid the reader in identification.

After R.'s death, his wife devoted herself to continuing Curious George's popularity as a token of her affection for her late husband. She collaborated with Alan Shelleck to increase the total of seven Curious George books to thirty-five. Numerous works of R.'s have been adapted to films, movies, and recordings. In 2000, *Whiteblack the Penguin Sees the World,* a precursor to the Curious George books, was published. This significant new title was uncovered by Anita Silvey at the DE GRUMMOND REFERENCE COLLECTION, under the direction of Dee Jones. *Whiteblack* manifests similarities in artistic style, and the "curiosity factor," to R.'s celebrated SERIES.

AWARDS: Lewis CARROLL Shelf Award (1960) for *Curious George Takes a Job* (1947). Children's Book Award, Child Study Association of America (1966) for *Curious George Goes to the Hospital. Curious George* (1941) was named best picture book in the 1987 Children's Choice AWARDS held by *School Library Journal* and a notable book by the AMERICAN LIBRARY ASSOCIATION

FURTHER WORKS: *Zebrology.* 1937. Under pseudonym Uncle Gus: *Christmas Manger. Uncle Gus's Circus. Uncle Gus's Farm.* all 1942. *Elizabite: The Adventures of a Carnivorous Plant.* 1942. *Curious George Takes a Job.* 1947. *Curious George Gets a Medal.* 1957. As illustrator: *The Polite Penguin.* 1941. *Katy No-Pocket.* 1944

BIBLIOGRAPHY: *Children's Literature Review.* vol. 5; Silvey, Anita, ed., *Children's Books and Their Creators,* 1995; *Christian Science Monitor,* vol. 88, i. 125, p. B3, May 23, 1996; HOPKINS, Lee Bennett, *Pauses: Autobiographical Reflections of 101 Creators of Children's Books,* 1995; *People,* vol. 47 i. 1, p. 74, May 13, 1997; *People,* vol. 46, i. 5, p. 28, July 29, 1996; *Time for Kids,* vol. 2, i. 13, p. 8; www.lib.usm.edu/~degrum

NANCY HORTON

RICE, Eve
Author, illustrator, b. 2 February 1951, New York City

An author and illustrator of children's books for toddlers to teenagers, R. was busy drawing at the age of three. Her mother kept her well supplied with art materials. While in middle school she made her decision to illustrate children's books. At Yale University she "discovered the great joys of reading" and has since combined artistic talent with creative writing. R. graduated from medical school in 1989. *Oh Lewis* (1974), her first book, was followed by *New Blue Shoes* (1975). *What Sadie Sang* (1976) received the Children's Book Showcase designation and was a Junior Literary Guild selection. Her ILLUSTRATIONS are done using line drawings and filled with detail. *Good-*

night, Goodnight (1980) and *Benny Bakes a Cake,* (1981) received positive reviews. R. likes to create PICTURE BOOKS for very young children, books that draw on family ties and the wonder of daily life.

BIBLIOGRAPHY: Silvey, Anita, ed. *Children's Books and Their Creators.* 1995. FICTION, FOLKLORE, FANTASY and POETRY *for Children, 1876–1985.* 1986. *Something about the Author.* vol. 34, 1984, and vol. 91, 1997

IRVYN GILBERTSON

RICHARDS, Laura E.
Author, b. 27 February 1850, Boston, Massachusetts; d. 14 January 1943, Gardner, Maine

Reared on the nonsense verse of Edward LEAR, R. began writing jingles and nonsense verses she had made up for her own children. She was the daughter of Julia Ward Howe, author of "The Battle Hymn of the Republic." As her seven children grew up, she wrote more stories and poems that appeared in *St. Nicholas* magazine, as well as stories for older children. R.'s verses reflect a strong and distinctive sense of HUMOR, flowing rhythm, and alliterative language. Her nonsense verse, such as *Eletelephony,* and humorous jingles are frequently anthologized. *Tirra Lirra: Rhymes Old and New* (1932) was published when R. was eighty-one; she continued writing into her nineties. Her book, *Captain January* (1890), a sentimental story about an orphan was filmed twice, once starring Shirley Temple (1936).

R. also wrote BIOGRAPHIES featuring strong female characters distinguished for their notable achievements. Each of her subjects is placed within the historical context of her era and is made memorable by R.'s enthusiasm for her subject and attention to authentic historical details. Her biographies are among the earliest to use extensive quotes from letters, journals, and diaries. R. also wrote two SERIES about happy families and events familiar to young readers; the Queen Hildegarde series first appeared in 1889 and Three Margarets in 1897.

FURTHER WORKS: *The Joyous Story of Toto.* 1885. *In My Nursery.* 1890. *When I Was Your Age.* 1894. *The Hurdy Gurdy.* 1902. *Florence Nightingale; the Angel of the Crimea.* 1909. *Abigail Adams and Her Times.* 1917. *Tirra Lirra.* 1932

BIBLIOGRAPHY: Kunitz, S. and H. Haycraft, (eds.) *Twentieth Century Authors.* 1942. MEIGS, C., A. T. Eaton, E. NESBIT and R. H. Viguers. *A Critical History of Children's Literature.* 1969

JODI PILGRIM

RICHTER, Conrad
Author, b. October 13, 1890 Pine Grove, Pennsylvania; d. 1968

Pulitzer Prize–winning novelist, R. grew up as the son and grandson of preachers in central Pennsylvania. During this time, he met the descendants of many pioneers, and listened to their ancestors' stories. These tales became the basis for his writing, which detailed American frontier life. His first novel, *Sea of Grass* (1937) was made into a movie in 1947 starring Katharine Hepburn. After this book he wrote a trilogy: *The Trees* (1940), *The Fields* (1946), and *The Town* (1950). R. was awarded the 1951 Pulitzer Prize for *The Town.* These books contain the legends, FOLKLORE, and vernacular of the age, which truly gives the reader the essence of that era in American history. R.'s best known work is *The Light in the Forest* (1953), which depicts a fifteen-year-old boy's quest for his true identity. It was made into a DISNEY film in 1958.

FURTHER WORKS: *Tracey Cromwell.* 1942. *The Waters of Kronos.* 1960. *A Simple Honorable Man.* 1962. *The Awakening Land.* 1966

BIBLIOGRAPHY: *The Columbia Encyclopedia.* 1993

DENISE P. BEASLEY

RILEY, James Whitcomb
Poet, b. 7 October 1849, Greenfield, Indiana; d. 22 July 1916, Indianapolis, Indiana

R. was born and reared in a small town in Indiana. Judging by contemporary standards he was not a great poet, but he was extremely successful and popular, very much in tune with his times. He had a gift for writing fluent rhythmical verse using broad HUMOR and regional dialect to chronicle the ways of nineteenth century small-town America. While working as the editor of the *Greenfield News* in 1877, R. began publishing verse. In 1883 *The Old Swimmin'-Hole and 'leven More Poems* was published, followed by *The Boss Girl: A Christmas Story and Other Sketches* in 1886. In 1897 R. became a member of the American Academy of Arts and Letters and received an honorary degree from Yale University in 1902. R. was elected to the National Institute of Arts and Letters in 1908. He was considered so popular by his home state that Riley Day was observed by the Indiana school system in 1910.

The last decade of the nineteenth century was a time that celebrated the common man. This was the hero who had pushed his way westward in midcentury and whose descendants on the farm and in the small towns and villages of the midwest formed the backbone of America. R. understood and wrote about this man with his shrewdness, homely wisdom, humor, sentimentality, humanity, and appreciation of America's folk heroes. His verses reflected locality in incident, character, and time. R. was well acquainted with rural America's love of gossip and celebration of everyday events. However, his reverence for his own childhood is that of an adult looking back on his past in a romantic, sentimental way that often obscured the deeper significance of an event. Selections of R.'s verses frequently appear in children's poetry anthologies, especially "Little Orphant Annie" (closer to a Raggedy Ann doll than to Harold Gray's Little Orphan Annie) and "The Raggedy Man."

FURTHER WORKS: *The Days Gone By.* 1893. *A Tinkle of Bells.* 1895. *The Book of Joyous Children.* 1902. *The Best Loved Poems of James Whitcomb Riley.* 1934. *The Gobble-Uns 'll Git You If You Don't Watch Out.*" 1975

BIBLIOGRAPHY: MEIGS, C. et al. *A Critical History of Children's Literature.* 1969. Serafin, Steven R., ed., *Encyclopedia of American Literature.* 1999. *Something about the Author.* vol. 17, 1979

JUDY LIPSITT

RINALDI, Ann
Author, b. 27 August 1934, New York City

Although she was not encouraged to write as a child, R. has become well known for her young adult historical fiction. Her early career began in journalism, first as a columnist for the *Somerset Messenger Gazette* in New Jersey, and later a *Trentonian* columnist, feature writer, and editorial writer from 1970–91. She credits her children's keen interest in history as the impetus for her interest in writing historical fiction, as well as her perception that YOUNG ADULTS would enjoy books set in the early days of America's history. R. recalls her difficulty persuading publishers that young adults would enjoy historical fiction. Her extensive research and her portrayal of the young adult coming of age within the genre of historical fiction shows her respect for the young adult audience.

Critically acclaimed for her research for her books set in the colonial time period, R. was quoted as saying "I don't write for young people. I just write. I have an aim to write good stuff for them, to treat them as people, not write down to them with stories about romance and acne and the spring dance. Real life, as I know it, as I've learned it to be from my newspaper experience and own past, goes into my books. I draw all my characters fully, give my adults as many problems and as much dimension as the young protagonist. I give them good literary writing."

AWARDS: ALA Best Books for Young Adults (1986) for *Time Enough for Drums;* (1987) for *The Last Silk Dress;* (1991) for *Wolf by the Ears;* (1992) for *A Break with Charity*

FURTHER WORKS: *The Fifth of March: The Story of the Boston Massacre,* 1993; *A Stitch in Time,* 1994; *Hang a Thousand Trees with Ribbons: The Story of Phillis Wheatly,* 1996

BIBLIOGRAPHY: *Contemporary Authors* 1984

SANDRA IMDIEKE

RINGGOLD, Faith
Author, illustrator, b. October 8, 1930, New York City

R., the youngest of three children, grew up in New York City during the Great Depression. Having asthma her entire life, she missed quite a bit of school. Instead of going to school when she was sick, she would visit museums, or stay home and work on her own artistic skills. Her mother, a fashion designer, would give R. scraps of fabric, crayons, paper, etc., and she would create her own artistic masterpieces. This sparked her interest in art, and she continued to use and refine her talents by becoming the "class artist" throughout her school years.

R. attended The City College of the City University of New York, where she continued her studies in art, graduating in 1955. While attending college, her talents intensified and her interest in AFRICAN AMERICAN art was aroused. After graduation, she became an art teacher in the New York public school system. She continued to work on her own art projects while she taught. Her early pieces were traditional oil paintings. But in the early 1960s, she began to focus her work on her passion for AFRICAN political, racial, and social issues. In 1972, R. began painting on a quiltlike canvas, which was easy to transport from city to city as she displayed her work. These early quilts became her signature work—story quilts—for which she is internationally famous.

R.'s first PICTURE BOOK *Tar Beach* (1991) evolved from the paintings of one of her story quilts. After being approached by Andrea Cascardi, an editor, about making the story quilt "Tar Beach" into a picture book for children, R. elaborated on the story of eight-year-old Cassie Lightfoot, the main character on her quilt as well as in her book. *Tar Beach* tells Cassie's story of flying above her New York City apartment rooftop as she looks down on Harlem in 1939. While she is flying, Cassie claims objects such as the George Washington Bridge, and the Union Building (which her father helped build) as her own. *Tar Beach* is part autobiography, part fiction, and part black history; it won the CORETTA SCOTT KING AWARD, the Ezra Jack KEATS Award, and was named a CALDECOTT MEDAL Honor Book, all in 1992, for its stunning and beautiful full color illustrations. *Tar Beach* was also chosen as a *New York Times* Best Illustrated Children's Book (1992).

After the success of *Tar Beach,* R. realized how important writing children's books was to her, and it became a second career. Her second book, *Aunt Harriet's Underground Railroad in the Sky* (1992), continues Cassie's flying dream and introduces the reader to her younger brother BeBe. BeBe and Cassie meet a train full of people, and before she knows it, BeBe has boarded the train and is whisked away before Cassie can save him. As her dream continues, she meets Harriet Tubman who tells Cassie the stories of slavery and the escape to freedom. This historical picture book, which also contains biographical notes, a map, and a bibliography, is an excellent tool to spark discussion about slavery, and to help explain the trials and tribulations of the African American's struggle for freedom.

R. bases her book *Dinner at Aunt Connie's House* (1993) on another one of her story quilts called "The Dinner Quilt," which she painted in 1986. Again, this book focuses on R.'s African American heritage. Lonnie, the main character, rummages through his Aunt Connie's attic to find portraits of twelve famous African American women including Rosa Parks, Zora Neale Hurston, Mary McCleod Bethune, and Marion Anderson. As the story unfolds, so does the history of these famous women. The book emphasizes messages of family tradition, strength, and self-esteem. R. continues Lonnie's story in *Bonjour, Lonnie* (1996) as he begins to trace his own multiracial heritage. In this book, Lonnie, who is an orphan, travels back in time to meet his grandparents and parents in order to learn about his family's past. Lonnie learns about his black grandfather who married his white grandmother, as well as about his Jewish mother who was taken by the Nazis, and his father who was killed in World War II.

R. continues her dream metaphors and historical approach to African American literature for children with her book *My Dream of Martin Luther King* (1995). The narrator in this book dreams of Martin Luther King's life as a child, attending segregated schools, and witnessing violent civil rights protests. The dream continues showing Martin Luther King as he gives his famous "I Have a Dream" speech, and is ultimately assassinated. In this book, R. has captured the spirit and the history of this important man who sacrificed his life for the civil rights cause.

All of R.'s books resonate with African American history and beautiful artwork. Her artwork has been praised for its strong, powerful, and striking images, as well as for the bold and vibrant colors she incorporates. Her picture books serve as wonderful historical references, as well as poignant stories for children of all ages.

FURTHER WORKS: *The Invisible Princess*, 1998; *Cassie's Colorful Day*, 1999; *If a Bus Could Talk: The Story of Rosa Parks*, 1999

BIBLIOGRAPHY: *Booklist* (September, 1993; February, 1996; October, 1996); Gouma-Peterson, Thalia, *Faith Ringgold Change: Painted Story Quilts*. 1989; *Horn Book* magazine (1991, 1993,

1994, 1996); *Kirkus Reviews* (December, 1992; September, 1993; August, 1996; November, 1998); Ringgold, Faith, *Talking to Faith Ringgold*. 1996; *Something about the Author*, vol. 71, 1993

DENISE P. BEASLEY

RITZ, Karen
Illustrator, b. 6 January 1967, Hudson, New York

R., an illustrator of over twenty-five children's books, had her artistic talents recognized early by her kindergarten teacher who predicted that she would be an artist when she grew up. As a high school student, R. studied drawing, entered art contests, and did portraits for hire. She also developed an interest in history. These interests are reflected in her sensitive portrayal of children's faces and her attention to accuracy in historical detail. *Kate Shelley and the Midnight Express* by Margaret Wetterer appeared as an animated feature on public television's READING RAINBOW, in 1991, using R.'s ILLUSTRATIONS, and was chosen as a Notable Children's Trade Book in Social Studies in 1990. Also receiving the notable trade book award were three PICTURE BOOKS about the Holocaust authored by David ADLER: A *Picture Book of Anne Frank* (1993), *Hilde and Eli: Children of the Holocaust* (1994), and *Child of the Warsaw Ghetto* (1995). The latter title was also selected for the Society of Illustrator's Show in 1995 as was *The Country Artist: A Story about Beatrix POTTER* by David Collins in 1990. *Ellis Island: Doorway to Freedom* by Steven KROLL was a winner of the 1994 Minnesota Book Award. R. has also done numerous illustrations for children's magazines including *Cricket* and *Ladybug*.

FURTHER WORKS: *Sisters against Slavery*, 1999; *Seneca Chief, Army General*, 2001

ADELE GREENLEE

ROBERTSON, Keith (Carlton) (pseud. Keith Carlton)
Author, b. 9 May 1914, Dows, Iowa; d. 23 September 1991, Hopewell, New Jersey

R. was born in Iowa and spent much of his youth living throughout the United States. Because R.'s father moved around a lot, R. never spent more than two years at any one school. He started writing as young boy and was often discouraged saying "Oddly, people will encourage a boy if he wants to be a doctor, engineer, or scientist but will tell him he is being impractical if he says he wants to write books." Because he was often discouraged he abandoned his writing for several years before deciding to try again.

After a stint in the army, R. once again set about writing and soon published his first book, *Ticktock and Jim* (1950). He followed this book with several more, many of which were set in the New Jersey area where he lived with his wife and children. R. reported that his children frequently served as fodder for his writing. He would often combine the adventures he remembered as a child with those of this own children to develop themes for his stories. Perhaps R.'s best known books chronicle the adventures of Henry Reed. Henry is the featured character in *Henry Reed's Journey* (1963), *Henry Reed, Inc.* (1958), and *Henry Reed's Baby-Sitting Service* (1966). Henry turned up again in R.'s *Henry Reed's Think Tank*, which was published in 1986. Other titles by R. include *Tales of Myrtle the Turtle* (1974) and *In Search of a Sandhill Crane* (1973). R. also wrote adult fiction under the name of Keith Carlton.

R. received several AWARDS during his writing career including the Spring Book Festival Award in 1956 for *The Pilgrim Goose,* and the Young Reader's Choice Award and Nene Award for *Henry Reed's Baby-Sitting Service* (1966).

R.'s books were geared toward ten- to fifteen-year-olds. R. reported that there were many advantages to writing for this age group citing that "Young people are essentially old-fashioned or square in their approach to literature." This suited R. who said he felt both old-fashioned and square in his approach to writing for them.

FURTHER WORKS: *Mascot of the Melroy.* 1953. *The Dog Next Door.* 1950. *The Wreck of the Saginaw.* 1950

BIBLIOGRAPHY: *Something about the Author.* vol. 85, 1996

MICHAEL O'LAUGHLIN

ROBINSON, Barbara

Author, b. 24 October 1927, Portsmouth, Ohio

R.'s best known and most loved book is *The Best Christmas Pageant Ever* (1972). A combination of hilarious, absurd characters and situations full of mayhem, the story of the Herdman family and their involvement in a Christmas pageant bring laughter to the pages of this novel. This favorite boasts a sequel, *The Best School Year Ever* (1994), that continues to entertain readers two decades later. With an education in theater, R. naturally focuses on character, and frequently preposterous ones, within her writing. These characters, she says, become real enough to her to show her what is happening next as she writes the story. R. has lived in various states and she has received reading and children's book AWARDS from Georgia, Indiana, Alabama, Minnesota, and Pennsylvania. She has also spoken at several writer's conferences. *The Best Christmas Pageant Ever* has been published in play form, adapted by R.

FURTHER WORKS: *Across from Indian Shore.* 1962. *Trace through the Forest.* 1966. *The Fattest Bear in the First Grade.* 1969. *Temporary Times, Temporary Places.* 1982. *My Brother Louis Measures Worms.* 1988

BIBLIOGRAPHY: *The Fifth Book of Junior Authors and Illustrators.* 1983. *Something about the Author.* vol. 84, 1996

JANELLE B. MATHIS

ROBINSON, Charles

Illustrator, b. 22 October 1870, Islington, London, England; d. 13 March 1937

R. was the second of three famous artist brothers (Thomas Heath and William Heath ROBINSON) who made their mark at the beginning of the twentieth century; their father was also an artist and engraver. R. studied art from childhood and briefly attended the Royal Academy. At twenty-five he was contracted to illustrate R. L. STEVENSON's *A Child's Garden of Verses* (1895), which is often considered his most successful work. He collaborated with his brothers in illustrating FAIRY TALES from Hans Christian ANDERSEN (1899). Their collaboration earned them the epithet, "The Three Musketeers."

R. illustrated many gift books for children, and worked on more than twenty books written by his close friend, Walter C. Jerrold (who wrote under the pseudonym of W. Copeland). He is also remembered for his illustrations in Frances Hodgson BURNETT's *The Secret Garden* (1911) and Oscar Wilde's *The Happy Prince* (1913).

R.'s chief artistic influences were William Morris and Walter CRANE, and his ILLUSTRATIONS are noted for their graceful figures, delicate lines, and decorative borders. One of his hallmarks was the lavish chapter heading, with intricately woven floral designs, and the books he illustrated were widely regarded as striking works of art.

FURTHER WORKS: Lewis CARROLL's *Alice's Adventures in Wonderland,* 1907; PERRAULT's *Fairy Tales,* 1913; A. A. MILNE's *Once upon a Time,* 1925; MOTHER GOOSE *Nursery Rhymes,* 1928

BIBLIOGRAPHY: *Something about the Author,* vol. 1979; *The Golden Age of Children's Book Illustration,* 1991

DAVID L. RUSSELL

ROBINSON, William Heath
Author, illustrator, b. 31 May 1872, Hornsey, North London, England; d: 13 September 1944, Highgate, London, England

Raised in an era without TV, electric lights or electronic games, R. and his brothers (naming themselves The Three Musketeers) used their imaginations to amuse themselves. They drew stories on slates and created model theaters with their own stages, lighting, characters and plays. At fifteen R. left school to pursue a career in art.

For several years he concentrated on ILLUSTRATIONS exclusively (usually humorous ones) but in 1902 he wrote and illustrated his first book, *Uncle Lubin.* His humorous cartoons and oddball mechanical contraptions are evident here as R. depicts Uncle Lubin searching for the nephew he is minding; the uncle designs and constructs an airship, a submarine and a seaworthy sailboat before rescuing his nephew. In 1903 he illustrated *The Works of Mr. Francis Rabelais* and in 1908 Shakespeare's *Twelfth Night* and KIPLING's *A Song of the English.* In 1942 R. authored and illustrated *Bill the Minder,* targeted for older children than *The Adventures of Uncle Lubin* but equally zany. He illustrated Hans Christian ANDERSEN stories three times, in 1897, in 1899 with his brothers Thomas H. and Charles, and in 1913 by himself.

He felt his life had been uneventful but stated "Each of us is given a bag of treasures, and it is up to us to make the best of it. If we don't we have only ourselves to blame."

BIBLIOGRAPHY: *Fiction, FOLKLORE, FANTASY, and POETRY for Children, 1876–1985,* vol. 1 1986; *Something about the Author,* vol. 17, 1979

IRVYN GILBERTSON

ROCKWELL, Ann
Author, illustrator, b. 8 February 1934, Memphis, Tennessee

R. is a prolific author and illustrator of more than a hundred books for young children. Many of her books are her own creation, but over thirty books are the result of the collaboration with her husband Harlow ROCKWELL. Growing up, R. lived in many different places including New Mexico, Arizona, Ohio, and New York, including some time going to school on an Indian reservation. She recalls that her closest friends were the characters in the books that she read, and art and writing were favorite pastimes. Mainly a self-taught artist, R. attended the Sculpture Center and the Pratt Institute Graphic Arts Center. Her publications include folktales and INFORMATIONAL BOOKS on subjects of interest to very young readers such as transportation, weather, and familiar objects, and several of her titles are classified as EASY-TO-READ BOOKS.

R. first wrote for middle graders but she is now best known for her concept and board books for the young child. Her books, whether written and illustrated by her or illustrated by Harlow ROCKWELL, use a spare simple text and bright primary colored illustrations. They depict familiar objects and scenes, such as a visit to the emergency room in *The Emergency Room* (Harlow Rockwell, illus. 1985). Her Ready to Read books and early concept books evolved from her interest in her own children's language development. She believes that for very young readers pictures can communicate better than words. Her pictures use a combination of pen and ink and watercolor, and she makes extensive use of carefully researched, detailed backgrounds and animated animals.

AWARDS: American Institute of Graphic Arts selection for children's book show; (1971–72) for *The Toolbox;* (1973–74) for *Head to Toe, Games (and How to Play Them), The Awful Mess,* and *Paul and Arthur and the Little Explorer.* Child Study Association children's books of the year (1976) for *No More Work* and *Poor Goose: A French Folktale*

FURTHER WORKS: *Befana: A Christmas Story.* 1974. *A Bump in the Night.* 1980. *Fire Engines.* 1986. *Apples and Pumpkins.* 1989. *At the Beach.* 1991. *The First Snowfall.* 1992. *Boats.* 1993. *Trains.* 1993. *Ducklings and Pollywogs.* 1994. *The Storm.* 1994. *The Acorn Tree and Other Folktales.* 1995. *My Spring Robin.* 1996. *The One-Eyed Giant and Other Monsters from the Greek Myths.* 1996. *I Fly.* 1997. *Once upon a Time This Morning.* 1997. *Show and Tell Day.* 1997

BIBLIOGRAPHY: *Fifth Book of Junior Authors.* 1983

SANDRA IMDIEKE

ROCKWELL, Harlow

Author, illustrator, b. 1910; d. 7 April 1988

R. pursued several jobs in the field of art. He published his first self-illustrated story, *ABC Book,* in 1961. R. worked in a studio with his wife, Anne, author and picture book illustrator, in Greenwich, Connecticut, where they collectively wrote and illustrated many books for children, including two award-winning books, *Toad* (1972) and *Head to Toe* (1973). Many titles, such as *The Emergency Room* (1985), help young children anticipate events in a young child's world in a reassuring, nonthreatening atmosphere illustrated in clear graphic detail. *I Did It* (1974), an EASY-TO-READ BOOK with vivid ILLUSTRATIONS, provides young children with clear directions for simple craft projects they can make on their own with minimal adult supervision.

AWARDS: American Institute of Graphic Arts Children's Books Show; (1971) for *The Toolbox;* (1971) for *Head to Toe,* (1973) for *Toad.* NSSC Notable Children's Trade Book in the field of Social Studies (1975) for *My Dentist*

FURTHER WORKS: *My Doctor.* 1973. *My Nursery School.* 1976. *Our Garage Sale.* 1981. *The Supermarket.* 1979

BIBLIOGRAPHY: *Something about the Author.* vol. 33, 1983

JODI PILGRIM

ROCKWELL, Thomas

Author, b. 13 March 1933, New Rochelle, New York

R., the son of artist Norman Rockwell, is known for his outlandishly humorous books for young readers like *How to Eat Fried Worms* (1973), with ILLUSTRATIONS by Emily Arnold MCCULLY,

where a young boy actually eats worms to win a bet. Billy wins his one hundred fifty dollar bet with the help of his parents and friends despite efforts by his opponents. The book remains a favorite of middle-grade boys and reluctant readers. R.'s books are perennially popular among all children, having received twelve Children's Choice Awards (INTERNATIONAL READING ASSOCIATION).

FURTHER WORKS: *Rackety-Bang and Other Verses,* 1969; *Norman Rockwell's Hometown,* 1970; *Humpf!,* 1971; *Squawwwk!,* 1972; *Tin Cans,* 1975; *How to Fight a Girl,* 1987

BIBLIOGRAPHY: *Something about the Author,* vol. 70, 1993

JODI PILGRIM

RODGERS, Mary

Author, b. 11 January 1931, New York City

Multitalented novelist, screenwriter, composer, lyricist, and columnist, R. is the daughter of Broadway composer Richard Rodgers. After studying music privately and at Wellesley College, R. worked in the 1950s–60s as a composer and lyricist. During this time, she assisted conductor Leonard Bernstein in producing the *New York Philharmonic Young People's Concerts.* R. gained recognition in her own right as the composer of scores for Broadway and off-Broadway musicals including *Once upon a Mattress* and children's musicals.

R.'s first book for children was *The Rotten Book* (1969), a picture book illustrated by Steven KELLOGG. A switch to intermediate fiction produced her best-known book, *Freaky Friday* (1972), its sequel, *A Billion for Boris* (1974), and the sequel to *Boris, Summer Switch* (1982). All three novels are distinguished by R.'s gifts for authentic-sounding dialogue and HUMOR. All three are cautionary tales in which the child protagonists suddenly find themselves in adultlike roles. In *Freaky Friday* and *Summer Switch* a child metamorphosizes into a parent; in *A Billion for Boris* a child mysteriously acquires precognition via a run-amuck television that airs the next day's news in advance. Despite the early 1970s flavor of the stories, textured with the language style and events of the period, R.'s stories reflect traditional values. Her protagonists emerge from humorously frustrating experiences in adultlike roles with new insights about the responsibilities of the adult world. R. wrote the screenplay for the DISNEY production of *Freaky Friday* in 1977 and followed it in 1981 with the screenplay for a second popular Disney comedy, *The Devil and Max Devlin.*

In 1970 R. and her mother, Dorothy Feiner Rodgers, coauthored *A Word to the Wives.* In this conversational book for adults, mother and daughter each bring their own perspectives to exploring the pros and cons of living in New York City, the older Rodgers focusing on urban lifestyle from her experience as an interior designer and her daughter exploring what life in the city means to a mother of five. Publication of the book led to the monthly column "Of Two Minds," which appeared in *McCall's* magazine from 1971 to 1978. As a children's author, R. is recognized for imaginative plots that explore adult-child relationships with convincing dialogue, HUMOR, and lots of New York City local color.

AWARDS: AMERICAN LIBRARY ASSOCIATION Notable Book Award (1973) for *Freaky Friday.* Christopher Award (1973) for *Freaky Friday;* (1975) for *A Billion for Boris. Book World* Spring Book Festival Award (1972) for *Freaky Friday*

BIBLIOGRAPHY: *Children's Literature Review.* 1990. *Contemporary Authors, New Revision Series.* vol. 55. 1997. *Contemporary Literary Criticism.* vol. 12. 1980. HOPKINS, Lee Bennett, *Pauses: Autobiographical Reflections of 101 Creators of Children's Books,* 1995. Silvey, Anita, ed. *Children's Books and Their Creators.* 1995

DIANE L. CHAPMAN

ROGASKY, Barbara
Author, b. 9 April, 1933, Wilmington, Delaware

A skilled writer and reteller of historical fiction, folktales, and work in other genres, R. gives her older sister much of the credit for introducing her to literature. She also remembers a few great teachers who encouraged her early writing. R. moved to New York City right after college; in her early career she freelanced as an editor and held editorial positions with Macmillan Publishing, Harcourt Brace Jovanovich, and Pyramid Books. Critically acclaimed *Smoke and Ashes: The Story of the HOLOCAUST* (1988), one of her earliest books, uses photographs taken by Nazi SS and German newspaper photographers to re-

veal the human story of World War II through language that reaches YOUNG ADULTS.

R.'s interests in children's literature include history, POETRY, and FAIRY TALES. Her retellings of fairy tales are often illustrated by Trina Shart HYMAN. In commenting on her writing, R. states, "*Smoke and Ashes* will arguably remain the most lasting books of my career." It was selected as a best nonfiction book for young adults by *Publisher's Weekly,* one of the best books of the year by *School Library Journal* and the AMERICAN LIBRARY ASSOCIATION Young Adult Services Division, and the most outstanding book in secondary social studies by the Society of School Librarians International. She connects the language in the poems in her *Winter Poems* collection with the musical nature of language, a language that is "used to convey images that can be revealed in no other way."

AWARDS: American Library Association Notable Children's Book 1989 for *Smoke and Ashes: The Story of the Holocaust,* and 1994 for *Winter Poems*

FURTHER WORKS: Reteller: *Rapunzel.* 1982. *The Water of Life.* 1986. Photographer: *Light and Shadow.* 1992. *The Golem: A Version.* 1996

BIBLIOGRAPHY: *Something about the Author.* vol. 86, 1996

SANDRA IMDIEKE

ROJANKOVSKY, Feodor (Stepphanovich) (pseud. Rojan)
Author, illustrator, b. 24 December 1891, Mitava, Russia; d. 12 October 1970, Bronxville, New York

Born in Russia to a high school teacher and administrator, R. came from a family that valued education. Even though art was not viewed as a suitable profession for men during R.'s childhood, he dabbled in it anyway. A trip to the zoo inspired him to begin drawing and his love for art did not dissipate. His other great love was for books, of which the family had plenty, even in hard times. By 1912, R. had entered the Moscow FINE ARTS Academy. His schooling was cut short by a stint in the army but R. continued illustrating during the Russian Revolution. He also served as an art director for both a fashion magazine and a book publishing company. R. eventually immmigrated to the United States where he resided in New York. His illustrations were highly acclaimed by Anne Carroll Moore and Ursula Nordstrom.

Several of R.'s writings were self-illustrated and are notable for their bold, vivacious ILLUSTRATIONS. They include *The Great Big Animal Book* (1950), and *Animals in the Zoo* (1962). Although R. wrote and illustrated many books he is best known for his art. He won the Art Directors Club Gold Medal for *Frog Went a-Courtin'* (1955). Other books illustrated by R. include Aileen FISHER's *A Cricket in a Thicket* (1973) and Jeanette Krinsley's *The Cow Went over the Mountain* (1963). R. also illustrated under the pseudonym of Rojan. Some of those works include *The Kingfisher* (1940) and *Cuckoo* (1942).

R.'s love of nature inspired many of his illustrations. His last book for children was *F. Rojankovsky's ABC: An Alphabet of Many Things* (1970). R. hoped that "children who like my books feel instinctively that I see nature with the same wonder and thrill that they do."

AWARDS: ALA CALDECOTT MEDAL (1956) for *Frog Went a-Courtin'* (John LANGSTAFF, adaptor)

FURTHER WORKS: *Tall Book of MOTHER GOOSE,* 1942; *The Great Big Wild Animal Book,* 1951; *Animals on the Farm,* 1967

BIBLIOGRAPHY: HOPKINS, Lee Bennett, *Pauses: Autobiographical Reflections of 101 Creators of Children's Books,* 1995; MEIGS, C. et al. *A Critical History of Children's Literature,* 1969

MICHAEL O'LAUGHLIN

ROOP, Peter and Connie

Connie: b. 18 June, 1951, Elkhorn, Wisconsin; Peter: b. 8 March, 1951, Winchester, Massachusetts

Husband and wife team P. and C.R. are best known for their nonfiction writing for children. Both received degrees from Lawrence University and teach in Appleton, Wisconsin. C. is a science teacher and educational consultant, and a member of numerous science-related professional organizations. She attributes her interest in science to her active and outdoor childhood experiences; a geological area of study in college confirmed her interest in science. While her husband was earning his master's degree in children's literature, C.

read the science trade books he was bringing home, and realized she might be able to do this type of writing. P. began his writing career writing plays, articles, and stories for MAGAZINES and newspapers for children and adults. P. has also taught workshops at universities, served as a consultant for educational publishers, and is a member of professional organizations such as the Children's Literature Association and the Society of Children's Book Writers and Illustrators. As a member of NATIONAL COUNCIL OF TEACHERS OF ENGLISH, P. served on the committee that established the ORBIS PICTUS AWARD given annually for a children's INFORMATIONAL BOOK. Both P. and C. taught in England for a year under the Fulbright Exchange Program.

P. and C. write in a variety of genres including historical fiction, science, mysteries, and joke and riddle books on many different topics. Several of their books such as *Keep the Lights Burning, Abbie* (1985) and *Going Buggy! Jokes about Insescts* were READING RAINBOW selections. *Keep the Lights Burning, Abbie* was named a 1986 NCTE Outstanding Trade Book in the Language Arts. *Out to Lunch* (1989) was an INTERNATIONAL READING ASSOCIATION Children's Choice Award in 1984. *Buttons for General Washington* (1986) was selected as an Outstanding Trade Book in the Field of Social Studies from the National Council of Social Studies and the CHILDREN'S BOOK COUNCIL in 1986.

P. wrote alone the first six years of publishing, then the husband and wife collaboration began. Their current classroom teaching is the impetus for much of their writing. P. notes that "the easy appearance of any children's books hides the hours of hard work involved in creating a worthwhile book for young readers." He likes to write stories about children who are, like Abbie, what he describes as children who are the "footnotes of history."

FURTHER WORKS: *Space Out.* 1984. *Go Hog Wild!* 1984. *Out to Lunch.* 1984. *Stick Out Your Tongue: Jokes About Drs. and Patients.* 1989. *Columbus: My Journal, 1492–3.* 1990. *Ahyoka and the Talking Leaves.* 1992. *Capturing Nature: The Writings and Art of John James Audubon.* 1993. *Off the Map: The Journals of Lewis and Clark.* 1993. *Martin Luther King Jr.* 1997. *Pilgrim Voices: Our First Year in the New World.*

1997. *Susan B. Anthony.* 1997. *Walk on the Wild Side!* 1997

BIBLIOGRAPHY: *Contemporary Authors New Revision.* 1995

SANDRA IMDIEKE

ROOT, Kimberly Bulcken
Illustrator, b. Date unknown, Pennsylania

R. grew up in New York, Connecticut and South Carolina. Earlier in her life she wanted to be a veterinarian, however an illustrator friend persuaded her to show her art to the director of the Parsons School of Design. She ultimately graduated from Parsons and has since illustrated books by children's authors such as Margaret HODGES' *The True Tale of Johnny Appleseed* (1997) and Eric KIMMEL, *Boots and His Brothers: A Norwegian Tale* (1992). Expressive use of color and lifelike figures and settings characterize her pen and watercolor ILLUSTRATIONS. *Boots and His Brothers* was included on *Parenting* magazine's list of top titles for 1992. *Gulliver in Lilliput* was a School Library Journal's Best Book of 1995. R. has also illustrated for several MAGAZINES. She received the *New York Times* Best Illustrated Award for *When the Whippoorwill Calls* in 1995.

FURTHER WORKS: *Hugh Can Do.* (Jennifer Armstrong). 1992. *In a Creepy, Creepy Place and Other Scary Stories.* (Judith Gorig). 1996. *The Year of the Ranch.* (Alice McLarren). 1996. *Birdie's Lighthouse.* (Deborah HOPKINSON). 1997

BIBLIOGRAPHY: Kimberly Bulcken Root (author/illustrator biographical information) by Holiday House. *Kirkus Reviews,* "Boots and His Brothers," May 1, 1992; Lempke, D., review of *The Year of the Ranch, Booklist,* July 19, 1996

JANELLE B. MATHIS

ROSS, Gayle
Author, b. 3 October 1951

A Cherokee NATIVE AMERICAN, R. is a descendent of John Ross, Principal Chief of the Cherokee Nation during the Trail of Tears. She has become a much-loved and respected storyteller and had won awards for her audio collections before coauthoring her first children's book, *The Girl Who Married the Moon* (1994) with Joseph BRUCHAC. The book won a Skipping Stone Award in 1994 for promoting MULTICULTURAL awareness. Both *How Rabbit Tricked Otter and Other Cherokee*

Trickster Tales (1994) and *How Turtle's Back Was Cracked: A Traditional Cherokee Tale* (1995) are retellings of traditional Cherokee *pourquoi* FOLKLORE stories.

FURTHER WORKS: *The Story of the Milky Way* (with Joseph Bruchac). 1995: *The Legend of Windigo.* 1996

AINE KYNE-NORRIS

ROSSETTI, Christina (Georgina)
Poet, b. 5 December 1830, London, England; d. 29 December 1894, Place unknown

R. was born in London to Gabriele and Frances (Polidori) Rossetti, her brother was the poet Dante Gabriel Rossetti. The Rossetti family was artistic by nature and R. was no exception, beginning to write POETRY as a child. She developed into a poet while dealing with the other artistic, sometimes temperamental and essentially religious members of her family.

When her father became ill she and her mother began a day school in an attempt to support the family financially. Her own health was never good and she was often sick with illnesses that have been diagnosed as being everything from angina to tuberculosis. R. fell in love with Charles Cayley but refused to marry him because she determined he was not a Christian.

R.'s first volume of poetry, *Goblin Market and Other Poems* (1862), marked the first literary success of the Pre-Raphaelites. This was a form of poetry that had no lack of readers. R.'s work includes four published volumes of poetry. Along with *Goblin Market and Other Poems,* her work includes *The Prince's Progress and Other Poems* (1866) and *Commonplace and Other Stories* (1870). *A Pageant and Other Poems* was published in 1871 and, after her death, *New Poems* was published in 1896. Her first book of poetry specifically for children, *Sing-Song: A Nursery Rhyme Book* was published in 1872. *Speaking Likenesses,* a story loosely based on Lewis CARROLL's *Alice's Adventures in Wonderland,* appeared in 1874.

R. spent a lot of time with her grandfather as she was growing up. They often were together in the country, which afforded R. exposure to nature and the wilderness. Her time spent in the outdoors is seen in much of her children's poetry. Political and religious themes as influenced by the Victorian era and Pre-Raphaelite movement are also present in much of R.'s work. Her poems still appear frequently in poetry anthologies for children. Toward the end of her writing career she began research for a biography of Elizabeth Barrett Browning who was one of her own inspirational sources and mentors. She was unable to continue this project because of lack of available material.

FURTHER WORKS: *Maude: A Story for Girls,* 1897

BIBLIOGRAPHY: "The Life of Christina Rossetti," http://www.stg.brown.edu/projects

MICHAEL O'LAUGHLIN

ROSTKOWSKI, Margaret
Author, b. 12 January 1945, Little Rock, Arkansas

R., author of YOUNG ADULT novels, believes everything that has occurred in her life has been in preparation to be a writer. Many of her books contain family stories. In addition, R. uses the woods in which she grew up as the setting for much of her writing. R.'s high-school students give her ideas, models, and language for her books as well as help her know which issues are important to young adults. *After the Dancing Days* (1986) tells the story of a young girl who befriends a wounded soldier during World War I. It won several AWARDS including selection as an AMERICAN LIBRARY ASSOCIATION Notable Book, a Golden Kite Award, and was given a Children's Editor's Choice award by *Booklist.*

FURTHER WORKS: *The Best of Friends,* 1989; *Moon Dancer,* 1995

JODI PILGRIM

ROUNDS, Glen (Harold)
Author, illustrator, b. 4 April 1906, near Wall, South Dakota

R., son of a Montana rancher, learned to draw the animals and workers that were part of his formative environment. After a stint at the Kansas City Art Institute he wandered the western United States taking on odd jobs including mule skinner, cowboy, sign painter, railroad section hand, baker, carnival medicine man, and textile designer. At thirty-six, he began a four-year tenure in the United States Army, rising to staff sergeant.

Determined to make his living as an artist, R. eventually traveled to New York City hoping to sell his pictures. Believing stories should be told instead of written and using his abilities to gain the interest of editors, R. was soon convinced that the best way to get his drawings published would be to write text to accompany them. *Ol' Paul, the Mighty Logger* (1936) was published using unorthodox compilation methods and R. was on his way to writing and illustrating nearly fifty books and providing the artwork for more than sixty others. His direct writing style and clear, often humorous, brush-line drawings are the hallmark of his tall tales and cowboy adventures. His work is characterized by text and ILLUSTRATIONS that capture the outlandish HUMOR and exaggerated characteristics of American FOLKLORE heroes. A member of the Authors Guild, his works have been translated into Spanish, Dutch, and German and have received numerous awards.

AWARDS: Lewis CARROLL Shelf Award (1958) for *Ol' Paul, the Mighty Logger,* revised edition (1949); KERLAN Award from University of Minnesota (1980)

FURTHER WORKS: *I Know an Old Lady Who Swallowed a Fly,* 1990; *Cowboys,* 1991; *Three Billy Goats Gruff,* 1993; *Witcracks: Jokes and Jests from American Folklore* (Alvin SCHWARTZ, author), 1973, 1993; *Beavers,* 1999

BIBLIOGRAPHY: *Something about the Author,* vol. 70, 1993

CRAIG LIEBERMAN

ROWLING, J(oanne) K.
Author, b. 31 July 1965, Bristol, England

R. wrote her first story at age six about a rabbit she called Rabbit and has considered herself a writer ever since. She did not think specifically about writing for children saying that "children's books chose me." Her next two novels, which she never submitted for publication, were intended for adults. R. regards being able to say she is a published author as "the fulfillment of a dream I had had since I was a very small child." R. read widely as a child, and can still remember many books and authors vividly: C. S. LEWIS, E. NESBIT and especially Elizabeth Goudge's *The Little White Horse* (1946) and Paul Gallico's *Manxmouse* (1940) as wonderful stories that were influential in her life. As an adult her favorite authors are Roddy Doyle and Jane Austen, all of whose books she has reread many times. Although she seems to write knowledgeably about boarding school life, R. was educated in Scotland at "what we call state school, a day school that you would call public school," graduated from Exeter University and later taught elementary school. As a divorced single mother she was despondent over her living conditions and was casting about for a challenge, the need to achieve something. Five years in the writing, the idea for the character of Harry Potter came to her while riding on a train and she immediately planned for seven books, each one to correspond to one year at a British boarding school.

Writing in longhand, as she continues to do, with her infant daughter napping in a carriage by her side, R. was noticed sitting alone at an Edinburgh cafe. She was writing the first draft of *Harry Potter and the Sorcerer's Stone* (1998, first published in Great Britain as *Harry Potter and the Philosopher's Stone* in 1997). The Scottish Arts Council gave her a grant to finish the book and afterwards she edited it by typing it onto her computer. Immediately upon publication in 1997 *Harry Potter* received starred reviews in both British and American REVIEW JOURNALS. Word of mouth among children further enhanced the popularity of the books but their popularity among adults has propelled them to the top of best-seller lists such as the *New York Times* and *Publishers Weekly*. The CROSSOVER appeal between child and adult audiences has established R.'s reputation. *Harry Potter and the Chamber of Secrets* (1999) was released soon after the first Harry Potter book because readers were begging for a sequel. The books have been published in one-hundred-fifteen countries, in twenty-five languages and at this writing have sold two million-plus copies. Further ensuring the books' success has been the purchase of film and merchandising rights. The SERIES is considered a publishing phenomenon, attracting a large adult readership as well as young boys, including those classified as so-called reluctant readers.

Along with the third title, *Harry Potter and the Prisoner of Azkaban* (1999), and the fourth, *Harry Potter and the Goblet of Fire* (2000), all of R.'s books are traditional British fantasies replete with wizards, witches, magic spells, and broom-

sticks leavened by R.'s HUMOR and memories of what it felt like to be a kid. She says that her books are "about the power of the imagination. What Harry is learning to do is to develop his full potential. Wizardry is just the analogy." As much as the books are about Harry Potter learning to deal with the loss of his parents and discovery of his special magical powers, they are also humorous and imaginative in R.'s creation of a consistent but parallel world. As part of Harry's life at Hogwarts, boarding school for training future wizards, R. invented a sport called Quidditch; she made up the rules, created diagrams for playing, and named the balls Snitch, Bludgers, and Quaffle. She lets her sense of humor reign when inventing words but borrows many others from old myths, tales, and the Bible (Hedwig), placenames (Snape), and obsolete words (Dumbledore), very much in the British tradition.

AWARDS: British Book Awards Children's Books of the Year for *Harry Potter and the Philosopher's Stone,* and *Harry Potter and the Chamber of Secrets,* Smarties Prize for *Harry Potter and the Philosopher's Stone,* 1997

BIBLIOGRAPHY: O'Malley, Judith, 1999, "Talking with J. K. R.," *Book Links,* vol 8, no. 6, pp. 32–36; Maughan, S., "The Race for Harry Potter," *Publishers Weekly,* February 15, 1999, pp. 33–34; Lipson, E. "Books' Hero Wins Young Minds" *New York Times,* July 12, 1999, section C, pp. 1, 6

DIANE G. PERSON

RUBEL, Nicole
Author, illustrator, b. 29 April 1953, Miami, Florida

R.'s energetic ILLUSTRATIONS capture the attention of primary readers. Best known for her colorful illustrations of the Rotten Ralph (1979) SERIES, authored by Jack GANTOS, R.'s brightly colored pictures furnish the reader with engaging details. R.'s illustrations inspired Gantos to put words to the sibling rivalry of the cats Sarah and Ralph. R.'s characters sometimes act reproachfully, being mischievous and silly; yet children learn the lessons of love and acceptance through their actions. R.'s childhood in Miami, Florida, encouraged her use of sunshine bright colors; her vivid characters are reminiscent of the colors of the art deco buildings. Her own twin sister, Bonnie, has added to her writing inspiration; *Sam and Violet Are Twins* (1981) is the first in a series about twin cats. This series of books takes the twin cats through many exciting adventures. R.'s cartoonlike characters are not limited to illustrations of cats as in *Rotten Ralph* (1979) and *Sam and Violet* (1981); in *Goldie* (1989) and *The Ghost Family Meets Its Match* (1992) a mischievous chick is featured. Crocodiles and alligators play a major role in *Uncle Henry and Aunt Henrietta's Honeymoon* (1986) and *It Comes from the Swamp* (1988), which appear to be inspired by R.'s childhood in Florida. Through illustrations and playful words R.'s books engage young readers in thoughtful and exciting adventures.

AWARDS: Children's Book Award for Outstanding Graphic Design (1977) for *Rotten Ralph;* American Book Association and American Institute of Graphic Arts (1979); American Bookseller's "pick of the lists" (1984) for *Rotten Ralph* and (1992) for *It Came from the Swamp* and *Grizzly Riddles*

FURTHER WORKS: *Pete Apatosaurus.* 1991. *Me and My Kitty.* 1993. *I Can Get Dressed.* 1984. *Bernie and the Bulldog.* 1984. *Pirate Jupiter and the Moondogs.* 1985. *Uncle Henry and Aunt Henrietta's Honeymoon.* 1986. *Goldie's Nap.* 1991. *Conga Crocodile.* 1993. *Cyrano the Bear.* 1995. *A Cowboy Called Ernestine.* 2000. Illustrator: *Fairweather Friends.* (Gantos). 1977. *Aunt Vernice* (Gantos). 1982. *Woof! Woof!* (KROLL). 1982. *The House That Bear Built.* (Muntean). 1984. *Little Lamb Bakes a Cake.* (Muntean). 1984. *Monkey's Marching Band.* (Muntean). 1984. *Rhia Is Weird.* (Wolcott). 1986. *When Someone in the Family Drinks Too Much* (Langsen). 1996

BIBLIOGRAPHY: *Something about the Author.* vol. 95, 1998

NANCE S. WILSON

RUBINSTEIN, Gillian
Author, b. 29 August 1942, Berkhamstead, England

R. has used her inventive imagination to create exciting, award-winning books for YOUNG ADULTS. Her first and most prestigious book, *Space Demons* (1986), won the Children's Literature Peace Prize and Australia's Best Book Award. Both *Space Demons* and its sequel, *Skymaze* (1989), portray characters caught up in computer games, and show how manipulative friendships and sibling rivalries can become. Several of her other novels are also SCIENCE FICTION, such as *Galax-Arena* (1994), and *Under the Cat's Eye: A Tale of Morph and Mystery* (1998). In R.'s novel *Foxspell* (1996), the main character, Tod, must face the decision of leaving his life as a human or taking on the spirit of a fox. This novel shows the theme R. tries to portray in each of her novels, "if we love and respect the planet we live on, the other species we share it with, and each other, then our lives won't have been wasted." R. has also written several PICTURE BOOKS including *The Fairy's Wings* (1998) and *The Giant's Tooth* (1995).

BIBLIOGRAPHY: *Something about the Author,* vol. 68, 1992

DENISE P. BEASLEY

RUFFINS, Reynold
Author, illustrator, graphic artist, teacher, b. 5 August 1930, New York City

R. has been a professional author and illustrator for more than thirty years. Before graduating from Cooper Union, he and his fellow students, Milton Glazer and Seymour Chwast, formed Push Pin Studios in Manhattan, where they produced high quality cutting-edge graphic designs. Between 1963 and 1971, R. and Simms TABACK, another artist colleague formed Ruffins Taback, a design studio where they both create many varieties of graphic arts and books. In 1970 R. and Taback illustrated *The Amazing Maze* by Harry Hartwick. In 1973, R. met Jane Sarnoff, a writer, who became his collaborator on many science and riddle books. In 1973 their book, *The Chess Book,* received an award from the American Institute of Graphic Arts. In 1976 the INTERNATIONAL READING ASSOCIATION gave a prize to *Codes and Ciphers. The Monster Riddle Book* (1978) was adapted as a film strip in 1981. R. has been an instructor of visual arts at Parsons School of Design in New York City, and a visiting professor at Syracuse University.

AWARDS: CORETTA SCOTT KING Illustrator Honor Book Award (1997) for *Running the Road to ABC*

FURTHER WORKS: Author and illustrator: *Light and Darkness.* 1975. *My Brother Never Feeds the Cat.* 1979. *About the Origins of Everyday Words and Phrases.* 1980. With Jane Sarnoff: *Giants!: A Riddle Book.* 1977. *Space: A Fact and Riddle*

Book. 1978. *If You Were Really Superstitious.* 1981

BIBLIOGRAPHY: *Something about the Author,* vol. 41, 1985; publisher materials; personal contact on Ezra Jack KEATS Selection Committee

JUDY LIPSITT

RUSKIN, John
Author, b. 8 February 1819, London, England; d. 20 January 1900, Coniston, England

Although a prolific author, R. wrote very little for young people except *The King of the Golden River* (1841). Still, through his critical writings in the area of children's education and literature and his associations with authors, editors, and illustrators such as Kate GREENAWAY, R. established an enduring influence on children's literature. A teacher, lecturer, artist, and critic, R.'s nonfiction work for an adult audience covers a wide range of topics including labor and economics, drawing, and the relationship of art and architecture to morality. *The King of the Golden River* is a literary fairy tale in which good triumphs over evil. It incorporates elements from German FAIRY TALES, Charles DICKENS, and the Arabian Nights. Like R.'s critical writings concerning education, *The King of the Golden River* emphasizes the importance of moral virtues such as kindness and charity.

FURTHER WORKS: *The King of the Golden River; or, The Black Brothers: A Legend of Stiria.* 1851, 1860

BIBLIOGRAPHY: Abse, J., *John R.: The Passionate Moralist,* 1981: Evans, J., *John R.,* 1954: Hunt, J. D., *The Wider Sea: A Life of John R.,* 1982: Rhodes, R., and D. I. Janick, eds., *Studies in R.,* 1982: Spear, J. L., *The Dreams of an English Eden: R. and His Tradition in Social Criticism,* 1984: *Dictionary of Literary Biography,* vol. 163: *British Children's Writers, 1800–1880,* 1996: MEIGS, et al., *A Critical History of Children's Literature,* 1953, 1969

JENNIFER DUNNE

RUSSO, Marisabina
Author, illustrator, b. 1 May, 1950, New York City

R. grew up in a family rich in culture and language. She was the first person in her family to be born in the United States; the rest of her family had immigrated following World War II. An Italian father and relatives who spoke German and Yiddish, as well as English, provided many language experiences. Her early memories are of starting nursery school when she was two years old and of beginning to draw as soon as she could hold a pencil. R. first attended a strict Catholic school, but later transferred to a public school after the family moved. She has been described as a shy child until she discovered that writing was a good way to express herself and her emotions. Art was a favorite subject of study in high school and college, and following graduation from Mt. Holyoke College in 1971 she freelanced for magazines and newspapers. From the beginning she knew she wanted to write and illustrate children's books, but her first published books were cookbooks. In addition, she illustrated five covers for *The New Yorker,* as well as some drawings within the magazine.

Her first book for children, *The Line up Book* (1987), was published when the youngest of her three children was a baby. Although she enjoys making up the characters in her books and designing the pages and layout, R. notes that painting the pictures is the best part of the process. *Easy to Make Space Ships That Really Fly* (1985) was a 1987 *READING RAINBOW* selection.

AWARDS: INTERNATIONAL READING ASSOCIATION Children's Book Award (1987) for *The Line up Book*

FURTHER WORKS: *A Week of Lullabies.* 1988. *Where Is Ben?* 1990. *Goodbye, House.* 1991. *Visit to Oma.* 1991. *Alex Is My Friend.* 1992. *It Begins with an A.* 1993. *Trade-In Mother.* 1993. *I Don't Want to Go Back to School.* 1994. *Time to Wake Up!* 1994. *Bear E. Bear.* 1995. *Good-Bye, Curtis.* 1995. *Grandpa Abe.* 1996. *Swim!* 1996. *Under the Table.* 1997. *Only Six More Days.* 1988. *When Mama Gets Home.* 1998

BIBLIOGRAPHY: *Reading Teacher,* February 1988. *Teaching Pre-K to 8,* March 1988

SANDRA IMDIEKE

RYDER, Joanne
Author, b. 16 September 1946, Lake Hiawatha, New Jersey

R., who has written more than forty books for young readers, is known for her books about nature. Weaving fiction and nonfiction together, R.

681

takes the reader into the world of snails, spiders, fireflies, bears, whales, and other living creatures. R. has won many awards and honors for her books. Two of her works, *Inside Turtle's Shell, and Other Poems of the Field* (1985) and *Where Butterflies Grow* (1989) were each named Outstanding Book of the Year for Children by the NATIONAL COUNCIL OF TEACHERS OF ENGLISH. *The Snail's Spell* (1982) was named a Parents Choice Book by *Parents'* magazine and received the New York Academy of Sciences Children's Science Book Award in the younger category. In 1995 R. was awarded the Eva L. Gordon Award for Children's Science Literature for her books' consistent high standards of accuracy, readability, and enthusiasm for science among children. R. is married to renowned children's author, Lawrence YEP.

FURTHER WORKS: *Simon Underground,* 1976; *Fireflies,* 1977; *Fog in the Meadow,* 1979; *Chipmunk Song,* 1987; *Step into the Night,* 1988; *Lizard in the Sun,* 1990; *Earthdance,* 1999

BIBLIOGRAPHY: http://www.henryholt.comlbyr/99s/ earthdance.htm, accessed March 28, 1999; *Something about the Author,* vol. 65, 1991

MARY ARIAIL BROUGHTON

RYLANT, Cynthia

Author, b. 6 June 1954, Hopewell, Virginia

NEWBERY MEDAL-winner R. writes with emotion, insight, and conveyance of the importance of family and intergenerational relationships. Her straightforward approach appears in the forms of poems, PICTURE BOOKS, nonfiction, and novels. Reared in the Appalachian mountains, the author relates her connection and pride in that upbringing to many of her books. R. lived with her grandparents in Cool Ridge, a coal-mining town in West Virginia, most of her childhood until she was eight years old. They had no running water and depended on their own gardening and hunting skills for nourishment. At eight, she went to live with her mother in an apartment in a tiny town called Beaver. Here she remembers loving her life: going to school with friends, drinking Nehi Grape pop, reading Archie COMIC BOOKS and riding bikes through the community. She went to college in Charleston, West Virginia, where she developd a love for books. R. received

a B.A. in 1975, an M.A. from Marshall University in 1976, and M.L.S. from Kent State University in 1982.

After receiving her degree, R. searched for a teaching job with no luck, and she eventually got a job as a clerk in the children's section of the public library. There she discovered the genre she would learn to love and eventually write! R. was greatly influenced to write by reading her favorite authors who include Randall JARRELL, Donald HALL, and E. B. WHITE. As a young child growing up, she had never been to a library. Even the elementary school in Beaver that she loved so, did not have a library.

R. is one of the few writers who did not know anything about the writing business before she began her effort to be published. In 1978, she purchased a copy of *The Writer's Market* and sent stories to the publishers listed in New York. A couple of months later, an agent called her in West Virginia to say that they would publish *When I Was Young in the Mountains.* This work and several others, including *Appalachia: The Voices of Sleeping Birds* (1991) and the poetry collection *Waiting to Waltz: A Childhood* (1984) depict life as she and family and friends lived in the mountains.

R. is well known and recognized for her Henry and Mudge SERIES. *Henry and Mudge: The First Book of Their Adventures* (1987) introduces the small boy Henry and his large dog Mudge. The series, with its more than fifteen volumes, is easy to read and a necessary addition to young readers' lists. Another series of R.'s is The Everyday Books, published in 1993. In 1998, R. published the first in a series about three creative young cousins who live with their Aunt Lucy while their parents travel in a ballet group. The Cobble Street Cousins series, beginning with *In Aunt Lucy's Kitchen* (1998), support young readers in creative efforts and positive pastimes for energetic readers. Readers also enjoy R.'s Mr. Putter and Tabby and Poppleton series.

R. states that she writes when she "senses" a story. She observes what surrounds her and imagines a story that accompanies the images: While driving through stark isolation in the mountains, she imagined a lonely trailer with two people missing someone they loved. From this process of imagination sprang *Missing May* (1992), for which R. received the NEWBERY MEDAL. R. writes what she sees and feels, without consideration for the age of her audience; she does not target children, but is pleased that her audiences are children. The only exception is her autobiography, *But I'll Be Back Again* (1989). She decided to write this autobiographical piece when she tired of traveling and felt it was too emotionally draining. In the book, she answers many questions that children often ask, along with photographs and information about her own childhood. Another autobiographical work is *Best Wishes* (1992), with color photographs by Carlo Ontal. This work focuses more on the interweaving of her life and the writing process.

AWARDS: ALA CALDECOTT MEDAL Honor Book (1983) for *When I Was Young in the Mountains* (Diane GOODE, illus); (1986) for *The Relatives Came* (Stephen GAMMELL, illus). AMERICAN LIBRARY ASSOCIATION Newbery Medal Honor Book (1986) for *A Fine White Dust*. ALA Newbery Medal (1993) for *Missing May*. American Book Award nominee (1982) for *When I Was Young in the Mountains*. AMERICAN LIBRARY ASSOCIATION Notable Book, School Library Journal Best Book (1984), National Council for Social Studies Best Book (1984) all for *Waiting to Waltz: A Childhood*. *New York Times* Best Illustrated Book, *Horn Book* Honor Book (1985) for *The Relatives Came*. Boston Globe–Horn Book Award (1991) for *Appalachia: The Voices of Sleeping Birds* (1992) for *Missing May*. ALA Best Book for Young Adult citation (1990) for *A Couple of Kooks and Other Stories about Love*. *School Library Journal* Best Book of the Year citation (1987) for *Children of Christmas*

FURTHER WORKS: *Miss Maggie.* 1983: *This Year's Garden.* 1984: *A Blue-eyed Daisy.* 1985: *Every Living Thing.* 1985: *Night in the Country.* 1986: *Birthday Presents.* 1987: *Children of Christmas: Stories for the Season.* 1987: *All I See.* 1988: *An Angel for Solomon Singer.* 1992: *The Dreamer.* 1993: *Margaret, Frank, and Andy: Three Writers' Stories.* 1996: *A Little Shopping.* 1998: *Bear Day.* 1998: *Bless Us All: A Child's Yearbook of Blessings.* 1998: *Cookie-Store Cat.* 1999: *Special Gifts.* 1999: *Some Good News.* 1999

BIBLIOGRAPHY: http://www.rylant.com/Welcome. htm; Antonucci, Ron. "R. on Writing," *School Library Journal.* May 1993, vol. 39, 5; R., Cynthia. *But I'll Be Back Again.* 1989; R., Cynthia. *Best Wishes.* 1992; R., Cynthia. *Appalachia; the Horn Book* magazine. Jan. 1992. v.68. i.1; R., Cynthia. *Missing May,* the *Horn Book* magazine, Jan./Feb. 1993, v.69, i.1; R., Cynthia. "Newbery Acceptance," the *Horn Book* magazine, Jul./Aug. 1993, v.69, i.4; Ward, Diane, "Cynthia R." the *Horn Book* magazine, Jul./Aug. 1993, v.69, i.4; *Children's Literature Review,* v.15 (1988)

NANCY HORTON

S

SABUDA, Robert
Author, illustrator, b. 8 March, 1965, Michigan

S. knew he would be an illustrator early in his childhood when he made his first pop-up book, a book portraying *The Wizard of Oz*. He remembers giving it as a gift to his mother; that project and others that always left his bedroom a mess were the initial endeavors of the young artist. He received a Bachelor of Fine Arts degree from Pratt Institute in 1987 and is a member of the Society of Children's Book Writers and Illustrators and the New York Genealogical and Biographical Society.

The artwork in his early books has been recognized as contributing significantly to children's understanding of the world and society, particularly in *Walden* (1990) and *Saint Valentine* (1992). Although his more recent works fall into the category of MOVABLE BOOKS (POP-UP BOOKS), S.'s ILLUSTRATIONS, such as those found in *Saint Valentine*, have been described as a works of art because of the mosaics created from color and the marbleized-paper effects S. designs. Creativity and experimentation that began as a young child in a messy bedroom have grown into FINE ART that characterizes his work today.

AWARDS: CHILDREN'S BOOK COUNCIL Notable Children's Trade Book in the Field of Social Studies (1990) and New York Public Library Best Children's Book of the Year (1990) for *Walden;* *Parenting* magazine (1992) for *Saint Valentine;* *Boston Globe–Horn Book* Honor Award (1994) for *A Tree Place;* Gold Medal winner, Dimension Illustration Awards (1994) for *A Christmas Alphabet*

FURTHER WORKS: *I Hear America Singing.* 1991. *The Mummy's Tomb: A Pop-up Book.* 1994. *Help the Animals of Africa.* (A Pop-up Book). 1995. *Help the Animals of Asia.* (A Pop-up Book). 1995. *Help the Animals of North America.* (A Pop-up Book). 1995. *Help the Animals of South America.* (A Pop-up Book). 1995. *Kwanzaa Celebration: Pop-up Book.* 1995. *Cookie Count: A Tasty Pop-up.* 1997

BIBLIOGRAPHY: *Something about the Author,* vol. 81, 1995

SANDRA IMDIEKE

SACHAR, Louis
Author, b. 20 March, 1954, East Meadow, New York

S. enjoyed school as a child and earned good grades in East Meadow, Long Island, New York, and later in Tustin, California where his family moved when he was nine years old. S. began to love reading in high school. After high school S. attended Antioch College in Ohio, but the unfortunate and untimely death of his father brought him back to California to be near his mother. Taking time off from school, S. worked as a Fuller Brush salesman with great success. However, S. returned to college to major in economics. S. also took creative writing classes and developed a strong interest in Russian literature. Once when S. dropped a class, he found himself in need of credits. While walking across campus he met an elementary schoolgirl handing out fliers. The grade school needed teachers' aides and offered three credits for the position. This turned out to be the most important class of S.'s life. Part of his assignment included supervising lunch and recess period where S. became known as Louis the Yard Teacher. This experience became the subject for his first book, *Sideways Stories from Wayside School* (1978), the story of several unique children and a few unusual teachers at a very strange school. The book was named a 1979 Children's Choice selection.

While working on this first novel, S. also worked as a shipping manager for a sweater factory in Connecticut. S. felt, however, that he should return to school and sent out his manuscript to different publishers at the same time he sent out applications to law schools. During S.'s first week as a law student his first manuscript was accepted. S. continued to write children's books. He finished law school and passed the bar but his heart was not in practicing law. S. worked part-time as a lawyer in order to have time to write. He had written *There's a Boy in the Girls' Bathroom* (1987) but had been unable to place it with a publisher until starting work on a second Wayside School book. S. enjoyed math as a student and wanted *Sideways Arithmetic from Wayside School* (1989) to help children discover that math could be fun.

S.'s work has been influenced by his daughter. The character of Marvin's little sister in S.'s Marvin Redpost early reader is based on his daughter. S. has long been a favorite of children. His recent work *Holes,* the 1999 NEWBERY MEDAL winner, is praised for its complex plot, suspense, and expert character deployment. It brought S. a new level of attention, the 1998 National Book Award and the Newbery Medal. The plot for *Holes* is more complex than any of his earlier books. Stanley Yelnats (a palindrome) is sent to a juvenile detention center and ordered to dig a series of large holes in the ground. The seemingly nonsensical punishment leads to Stanley's great-grandfather, a family curse, and a notorious outlaw. S. says "I never intended to write a grim story. I wanted it to be fun and adventurous. I like the idea that the boys were digging holes ostenisbly to build character while the camp warden was really looking for buried treasure."

S. explains the way he writes: "I try to write so it can be understood by a ten- or eleven-year-old kid, but at the same time I'm writing to please myself. It is a story that I enjoy reading and writing. I just have to make it simple enough for younger people to read." *Holes* has become a CROSSOVER book read by adults and children.

AWARDS: AMERICAN LIBRARY ASSOCIATION Newbery Medal (1999), *Boston Globe–Horn Book Award* (1999), National Book Award (1999) all for *Holes*

FURTHER WORKS: *Johnny's in the Basement.* 1981. *Someday Angeline.* 1983. *The Boy Who Lost His Face.* 1989. *Wayside School Is Falling Down.* 1989. *Dogs Don't Tell Jokes.* 1991. *Marvin Redpost: Kidnapped at Birth.* 1992. *Wayside School Gets a Little Stranger.* 1995

BIBLIOGRAPHY: "Digging for Victory," *Bookseller,* October 29, 1999; Morrow Junior Books promotional material; *Seventh Book of Junior Authors and Illustrators,* 1996; *Something about the Author,* vol. 63, 1991

DEDE SMALL

SACHS, Marilyn (Stickle)

Author, b. 18 December 1927, the Bronx, New York

S. remembers being a skinny little girl who was a bit of a coward and who was called a liar. All of these attributes would serve her well as a writer for young adults. Because of her cowardliness, S. spent a great deal of time in her neighborhood library in order to avoid being the victim of neighborhood bullies. This time allowed her to immerse herself in books of all sorts and her love for reading was established. Her talent for rearranging the truth and developing her own life seemed to be inherited; her father was also a teller of tales. S.'s childhood was a fairly happy one marred only by the death of her mother, which left a huge void in the family. After an adolescence with the typical problems of young love and pimples, S. attended college, and went to work as a children's librarian. She eventually received her master's degree in library science. Through her work with children and books S. decided that she wanted to write books for adolescents. S.'s first book *Amy Moves In* was not published for ten years after its completion in 1954. Publishers saw the book as being too negative and asked that S. give the story a happy ending. S. refused and in 1964 finally saw the book published. S. would later say that *Amy Moves In* probably best described her life as a young girl more than any of her subsequent books.

S. acknowledges that her own childhood shapes her books: not the shortcomings of growing up in a poor, crowded urban neighborhood with no open fields and babbling brooks but the variety of people there. She remembers the "fat ones, skinny ones, mean ones, friendly ones, smart ones, scared ones. . . . They all lived on my block, and they are with me when I write my books. They push and shove each other and shout, "I'm next! Look at me! I doubt if I will ever in one lifetime get around to all of them."

S. received the 1971 Outstanding Book of the Year Award from the *New York Times* and *School Library Journal*'s book of the year award for *The Bears' House,* a sensitive portrayal of a girl bereft of parental attention who escapes to a FANTASY world to find the emotional support she so desperately seeks.

S. has been hailed by critics for taking pertinent social issues and offering believable protagonists. She has been credited for being a leader in the field of REALISTIC FICTION for YOUNG ADULTS. S. has been delighted with the way her life has gone saying, "Each book I write is a new territory for me, new research, new thoughts, and new daydreams."

AWARDS: AMERICAN LIBRARY ASSOCIATION Notable Book (1968) for *Veronica Ganz,* and (1991) for *The Big Book for Peace;* Christopher Award (1986) for *Underdog*

FURTHER WORKS: *Fran Ellen's House,* 1987; *Just like a Friend,* 1989; *At the Sound of the Beep,* 1990; *What My Sister Remembered,* 1992

BIBLIOGRAPHY: *Something about the Author,* vol. 68, 1992

MICHAEL O'LAUGHLIN

SAINT-EXUPÉRY, Antoine de
Author, b. 29 June 1900, Lyons, France; d. 9 August 1944, near Corsica

Pilot and writer S. was born into an aristocratic French family. From the time he was a child he had a fascination for flying, which would lead him to his career as an airmail pilot. He moved to America in the 1940s to flee the Nazi invasion of France. The majority of S.'s writing stems from his experiences as an aviator, such as *Southern Mail* (1933); *Night Flight* (1932); and *Wind, Sand and Stars* (1939). His best known work, though, is *The Little Prince* (1943), in French called *Le Petit Prince.* He wrote and illustrated this book as a children's fable intended for adults (CROSSOVERS: CHILDREN'S BOOKS FOR ADULT READERS). In it, S.'s prose is often exalted as POETRY. The language in *The Little Prince* is rich in imagery and symbolism, and he uses satire to portray the bureaucratic world of adulthood. S. made his last flight over the fields of France during World War II, and disappeared on August 9, 1944.

DENISE P. BEASLEY

ST. GEORGE, Judith
Author, b. 26 February 1931, Westfield, New Jersey

A writer of both historical fiction and nonfiction, S. has incorporated personal experiences and real-life material into her stories. Once she learned to read, "reading became a permanent habit." A move to Millington, New Jersey, near Morristown where George Washington once wintered his troops, triggered research on the Revolutionary War. *Turncoat Winter: Rebel Spring* was published in 1970. S. writes to inspire her readers "to care . . . about the outcome of historical events. I want the people in my books to come alive for my readers the way they come alive for me." In *Crazy Horse* (1994) S. portrays the NATIVE AMERICAN chief within the context of the existing historical era, trying to lead his people through a time of displacement and upheaval, struggling to provide a home and food for a desperate nation. For her BIOGRAPHY of Sitting Bull, *To See with the Heart: The Life of Sitting Bull* (1996), S. traveled to significant locations and examined original source materials to present an accurate picture of Sitting Bull and people and events prominent in his life. S. received the Christopher Award in 1986 for *The Mount Rushmore Story.*

The Brooklyn Bridge: They Said It Couldn't Be Built (1982) was named an AMERICAN LIBRARY ASSOCIATION Notable Book, American Book Award Honor Book winner, a Golden Kite Honor Book, a *New York Times* Notable Book, and winner of the New York Academy of Sciences Award. *Panama Canal: Gateway to The World* (1989) received the New Jersey Institute of Technology Children's Literature Award, Golden Kite Nonfiction Award, and ALA Notable Book designation. *Dear Dr. Bell—Your Friend Helen Keller* (1992) won the Young Hoosier Award, Notable Book in Social Studies and William Allen White Award. *Betsy Ross: Patriot of Philadelphia* (1993) was cited with a New York State Book Award and Sons of the American Revolution.

BIBLIOGRAPHY: *Something about the Author,* vol. 13, 1978, and vol. 99, 1999; *Fiction, FOLKLORE, FANTASY and Poetry 1876–1985,* 1986

IRVYN GILBERTSON

SALINGER, J(erome) D(David)
Author, b. 1 January 1919, New York City

Since the publication of *The Catcher in the Rye* in 1951, S. has been recognized as a brilliant writer, as well as a spokesman for disenchanted youth. Young people could identify with the character of Holden Caulfield, the innocent protagonist, struggling to grow up, to find his identity in what he perceives as an evil corrupt adult world. Although more than 10 million copies have been sold and it has been translated into many languages, *The Catcher in the Rye* is controversial. S. continued to write after he retreated to rural New Hampshire a few years after the book's publication.

Before writing *The Catcher in the Rye,* S. had published stories in magazines such as *Saturday Evening Post* and *Good Housekeeping.* In 1946 he began publishing in *The New Yorker;* by 1948 he published exclusively in that magazine.

Many YOUNG ADULTS find that *The Catcher in the Rye* is an honest and humorous story about a character they recognize in themselves. Holden Caulfield, the protagonist, is in a psychiatric hospital recovering from a breakdown. Written in the first person, the story describes two days Holden spends in New York City after being expelled from his third prep school. Holden's age dictates the language, the slang, and the four-letter words that caused the book to be widely banned (see CENSORSHIP). To this day, some librarians keep a copy on a restricted shelf. In the story, S. describes the difficulties of this innocent young character's metamorphosis from childhood to adulthood. Clearly, to mature and survive Holden must acquire a sense of humor and a sense of proportion. He must learn compassion for the pompous, the phony, and the perverse to survive his move to adulthood.

FURTHER WORKS: *Nine Stories,* 1953; *Franny and Zooey,* 1961; *Raise High the Roof Beam, Carpenter,* 1959; *The Complete Uncollected Short Stories,* 1974

BIBLIOGRAPHY: Lundquist, James, *J. D. S.,* 1979; *Children's Literature Review,* vol. 18, 1989; *Something about the Author,* vol. 67, 1992

JUDY LIPSITT

SALISBURY, Graham
Author, b. 11 April 1944, Philadelphia, Pennsylvania

S. earned a B.A. from California State University and an M.F.A. from Vermont College of Norwich University. S. grew up in the Hawaiian Islands; many of his childhood experiences occurred without a father. He uses the Islands as the setting for many of his works and fills what he calls the holes in his life with words, words that explore the wide range of human emotions as adolescents struggle with family relationships. He started writing later in his life after encountering a love of reading in his thirties. S. began writing from memories and found himself stretching the truth, creating fantastical worlds of fiction. He creates authentic characters engaged in universal struggles for understanding the world, relationships, and themselves. He received a Parents Choice Award and citations as one of the best books for young adults from the AMERICAN LIBRARY ASSOCIATION, and best books of the year from *School Library Journal,* all 1992, for *Blue Skin of the Sea* (1992).

FURTHER WORKS: *Shark Bait,* 1997; *Under the Blood-Red Sun,* 1994

BIBLIOGRAPHY: *Something about the Author,* vol. 67, 1992

SHANE RAYBURN

SALTEN, Felix (pseud. Siegmund Salzmann)
Novelist, b. 6 September 1869, Budapest, Hungary; d. 8 October 1945, Zurich, Switzerland

S. began writing at age seventeen and became accepted as a journalist in literary magazines. He wrote under the pseudonyms Felix Salten and Martin Finder. Under the pseudonym Felix Salten he created the well-known story of *Bambi,* which was translated and published in English in 1928 and adapted as an animated film by Walt DISNEY in 1942. S. loved animals and wrote many stories depicting animal characters. Many of his works were translated into English and made into motion pictures. *The Shaggy Dog,* a 1959 Disney film, was adapted from S.'s 1923 story *The Hound of Florence.*

FURTHER WORKS: *Perri: The Youth of a Squirrel.* (Walt Disney's "Perri and Her Friends"). *Florian. Bambi's Children,* 1939

BIBLIOGRAPHY: *Something about the Author,* vol. 25, 1981

JODI PILGRIM

SANCHA, Sheila
Author, illustrator, b. 27 November 1924, Grimsby, England

S. attended the Byam Shaw School of Drawing and Painting. After working as an illustrator for the *Shell-B.P. News* in London, she decided to write a book about knights. Realizing her lack of knowledge about life in those times, she researched this era intensely; her success is evident in meticulous, verifiable attention to authentic details of the era. As a result, *Knight after Knight* (1974), *The Castle Story* (1979), and *The Luttrell Village: Country Life in the Middle Ages* (1982) are all firmly grounded in historical and archaeological research. S. stated that she enjoyed all aspects of this research, much of it from primary sources, as well as learning about the setting in which she placed her characters.

FURTHER WORKS: *Walter Dragon's Town: Crafts and Trade in the Middle Ages,* 1987

BIBLIOGRAPHY: *Something about the Author,* vol. 38, 1985

JANELLE B. MATHIS

SANDBURG, Carl (August)
Author, b. 6 January 1878, Galesburg, Illinois; d. 22 July 1967, Flat Rock, North Carolina

S. was born in Illinois to Swedish immigrant parents. He worked before and after school from the time he was eleven and finished elementary school at fourteen. S. served in the Spanish-American War and later entered Lombard College in Galesburg, Illinois, where he worked his way through school. S. worked a variety of jobs including work for several newspapers and magazines including the *Milwaukee Sentinel* and *The Magazine of Business.* Other jobs included working as a fireman, a department store manager and secretary to the Mayor of Milwaukee. In 1914 S. was still an unknown in the literary world when his work appeared in *Poetry.* Soon thereafter his first book, *Chicago Poems* was published.

S. received numerous AWARDS for his works including the 1939 Pulitzer Prize in history for his work on Abraham Lincoln and the 1951 Pulitzer Prize for poetry. He also received honorary doctorates from several universities including Yale and Harvard. S. was also given the National Association for the Advancement of Colored People Award in 1965. S.'s writing for children includes the humorous *Rootabaga Stories* part one and part two which were originally published in 1922 and were republished in 1990 with new ILLUSTRATIONS by Michael HAGUE. The charm of *Rootabaga Stories* is its quintessentially American character, celebrating America's rise to prominence as an industrial power, builder of skyscrapers and settlement of the vast prairie. *The Wedding Procession of the Rag Doll and the Broom Handle, and Who Was in It* (Harriet Pineus, illus., 1967) and *The Huckabuck Family and How They Raised Popcorn in Nebraska and Quit, and Came Back* (David Small, illus., 1999) are individual Rootabaga Stories published in a colorful picture-book format. Several books of poetry for children include *Poems for Children Nowhere* (1998) and *Rainbows Are Made: Poems by Carl Sandburg,* edited by Lee Bennett HOPKINS (1982).

S., who also used the pseudonym Jack Phillips Militant, remained unassuming despite his fame. During his lifetime he saw several schools named for him and received up to 400 letters per week from admirers. Still his goals were to "stay out of jail, to eat regular, and to get what I want printed."

FURTHER WORKS: *Rootabaga Pigeons,* 1923; *Potato Face,* 1930; *Abe Lincoln Grows Up,* 1975; *Carl S.,* 1995; *Not Everyday an Aurora Borealis,* 1998

BIBLIOGRAPHY: *Something about the Author,* vol. 8, 1976; *Children's Books in Print,* 1998

MICHAEL O'LAUGHLIN

SAN SOUCI, Robert D.

Author, reteller, b. 10 October, 1946, San Francisco, California

S. is best known for retellings of folktales from all parts of the world. During his childhood S. remembers listening to stories told by others, but he also remembers embellishing them himself, with his brothers and sisters as the audience. His early writing experiences stem from writing for his high school yearbook; after graduate school he worked in a book store, for Harper and Row, as a journalist and theater critic and consultant for Walt DISNEY Feature Animation. Today, in addition to his work as a children's writer, S. is also a freelance writer, and he frequently lectures to children and educators in schools and at professional conferences. His memberships include professional organizations like the SOCIETY OF CHILDREN'S BOOK WRITERS AND ILLUSTRATORS.

S. frequently collaborates with illustrators Daniel San Souci, his brother, and Brian PINKNEY or Jerry PINKNEY. His folktales portray male and female characters from many cultures and ethnicities, inside and outside the U.S. His extensive research into different versions of less well known tales results in stories that reflect the original oral quality, making many of his books excellent for reading out loud to children.

AWARDS: ALA CALDECOTT MEDAL Honor Book (1990) for *The Talking Eggs: A Folktale from the American South* (Jerry Pinkney, illus.) and (1996) for *The Faithful Friend* (Brian Pinkney, illus.). *The Legend of Scarface: A Blackfeet Indian Tale* (1996) was selected as one of the Ten Best Illustrated Children's Books of the Year by the *New York Times,* Notable Children's Trade Book in Social Studies, National Council for Social Studies and the CHILDREN'S BOOK COUNCIL. Notable Children's Trade Book in the Social Studies, National Council for Social Studies and the Children's Book Council for *Song of Sedna: Sea-Goddess of the North;* (1981); *Legend of Sleepy Hollow: Retold from Washington* IRVING; (1986); *The Enchanted Tapestry: A Chinese Folktale* (1990) and *The Samurai's Daughter* (1992). S. received the Irma Simonton Black Book Award, Bank Street College of Education, 1989, AMERICAN LIBRARY ASSOCIATION Notable Book citation

(1989) for *The Talking Eggs.* ALA Notable Book citation for *Sukey and the Mermaid* (1992) Aesop Award, Children's FOLKLORE Section, American FOLKLORE Society (1993) for *Cut from the Same Cloth: American Women in Myth, Legend, and Tall Tale* (Brian Pinkney, illus.)

FURTHER WORKS: *The Boy and the Ghost.* 1989. *Short and Shivery: Thirty Chilling Tales.* 1989. *The Samurai's Daughter: A Japanese Legend.* 1992. *The Snow Wife.* 1993. *The Brave Little Tailor.* 1994. *Sootface: An Ojibwa Cinderella Story.* 1994. *Kate Shelley: Bound for Legend.* 1995. *The Hobyahs.* 1996. *Even More Short and Shivery: Thirty Spine-Tingling Stories.* 1997. *The Hired Hand: An* AFRICAN AMERICAN *Folktale.* 1997. *Fa Mulan: The Story of a Woman Warrior.* 1998

BIBLIOGRAPHY: *Children's Literary Review,* vol. 43, 1996; the *Horn Book* magazine, Jan./Feb. 1996, Jan./Feb. 1997, Sept./Oct. 1992; *New York Times Review of Books,* Jan. 28, 1990; *Publishers Weekly,* July 19, 1993; *Something about the Author,* vol. 81, 1995

SANDRA IMDIEKE

SASEK, Miroslav

Czech author, illustrator, b. 18 November 1916, Prague, Czechoslovakia; d. May, 1980

S. was born in Czechoslovakia and moved to Paris after the communists invaded his country in the 1940s. During his time in Paris, S. studied at l'Ecole des Beaux Arts. It was during a three-week vacation to Paris that S. found his inspiration to write travel books for children. His first, *This Is Paris* (1959), was eventually followed by several other books that featured both European and American cities. S.'s work was selected as a *New York Times* Best Illustrated Children's book of the year in 1959 for *This Is London* and in 1960 for *This Is New York* which was also produced as a filmstrip by Weston Woods.

FURTHER WORKS: *This Is the United Nations,* (1968) *This Is Washington, D.C.,* 1969; *This Is* AUSTRALIA, 1970; *This Is Historic Britain,* 1974

BIBLIOGRAPHY: *Contemporary Authors Online:* www.galenet.com/servelet/GLD; *New York Times Book Review,* Jan. 28, 1990; *Publishers Weekly,* June 27, 1980

MICHAEL O'LAUGHLIN

SATTLER, Helen Roney

Author, illustrator, b. 2 March 1921, Newton, Iowa

S. is widely known for her writing and ILLUSTRATION of nonfiction, particularly nonfiction books that show the reader how to do or make something. In her early years, S. was an elementary school teacher and children's librarian. Her later volunteer work as a Scout leader helped her to realize that children need reference sources for ideas and information on how to make things from objects readily available. She is also known for her extensive expertise and research regarding dinosaurs that have been discovered and identified. Her dinosaur books, which were written at the request of her grandson, contain references for over 300 dinosaurs. In addition to her nonfiction writing, she has worked as a journalist and writer of fiction. She is widely known for books such as *Recipes for Art and Craft Material* (1973), *Dinosaurs of North America* (1981), *The Illustrated Dinosaur Dictionary* (1983), and *Sharks, the Super Fish* (1986).

S. believes that things made for and by children are more valuable than things that are bought. Her books give directions for making crafts and toys and games, and her simple black and white illustrations and figures guide the child's creative process. Her nonfiction is noteworthy for its accuracy, clarity, and detailed support information such as graphs, indexes, charts, and maps.

AWARDS: *Illustrated Dinosaur Dictionary* received the Golden Kite Award for nonfiction in 1983; *Dinosaurs of North America* was named a Nonfiction Honor Book by the committees for both the Golden Kite Award in 1981 and the *Boston Globe–Horn Book* Award in 1982. Eight books have been named Notable Books of the Year by the AMERICAN LIBRARIAN ASSOCIATION

FURTHER WORKS: *Kitchen Carton Crafts.* 1970. *Holiday Gifts, Favors and Decorations That You Can Make.* 1971. *Sock Craft: Toys, Gifts, and Other Things to Make.* 1972. *Jewelry from Junk.* 1973. *No Place for a Goat.* 1981. *Smallest Witch.* 1981. *Fish Facts and Bird Brains: Animal Intelligence.* 1984. *Pterosaurs, the Flying Reptiles.* 1985. *Hominids: A Look Back at Our Ancestors.* 1985. *Whales, the Nomads of the Sea.* 1987. *The Book of Eagles.* 1989. *Tyrannosaurus Rex and Its Kin: The Mesozoic Monsters.* 1989. *Giraffes, the Sentinels of the Savannas.* 1990. *The New Illustrated Dinosaur Dictionary.* 1990. *The Earliest Americans.* 1993. *Stegosaurus: The Solar-Powered Dinosaurs.* 1992. *The Book of North American Owls.* 1995. *Our Patchwork Planet: The Story of Plate Tectonics.* 1995

BIBLIOGRAPHY: *Contemporary Authors Online* www.galenet.com/servelet/GLD; *New York Times Book Review,* May 10, 1959, Nov. 13, 1983; publication notes; *Something about the Author,* vol. 74 1993; *Children's Literature Review,* vol. 224, 1991

SANDRA IMDIEKE

SAWYER, Ruth

Author, b. 5 August 1880, Boston, Massachusetts; d. 3 June 1970, Hancock, Maine

S., a storyteller and author of books and short stories, contributed over 200 articles, stories, poems, and periodicals to the field of children's literature. In addition, she started the first STORYTELLING program for children at the New York Public Library. S. spent time in Ireland and Spain gathering folktales for articles and books. *Roller Skates,* the 1937 ALA NEWBERY MEDAL Award title, still widely read by children, is a fictionalized account of a year she spent with two spinster aunts in upstate New York. *The Christmas Anna Angel* (Kate SEREDY, illus., 1944) and *Journey Cake, Ho!* (1953), illustrated by Robert MCCLOSKEY, were both ALA CALDECOTT MEDAL Honor Books. S. received the Laura Ingalls WILDER Award in 1965. Robert MCCLOSKEY was married to S.'s daughter.

FURTHER WORKS: *This Way to Christmas,* 1916; *Picture Tales from Spain,* 1936; *The Long Christmas,* 1941; *The Least One,* 1941; *The Way of the Storyteller,* 1942; *Joy to the World.* 1966

BIBLIOGRAPHY: MEIGS, C., A. T. Eaton, E. NESBIT, R. H. Viguers, *A Critical History of Children's Literature.* 1969; *Something about the Author,* vol. 15, 1979

JODI PILGRIM

SAY, Allen

Author, illustrator, b. 28 August 1937, Yokohama, Japan

Although most of his work features Japanese and Japanese American characters, S. perceives himself not as an ethnic or MULTICULTURAL artist but as an artist who is uniquely American. Both his illustrations and his stories often relate to his personal experiences as an immigrant and as a person who must continue to work through his transplanted cultural identity.

S. was born of a Japanese American mother, whose family had returned to Japan so that she would have training appropriate to that of a Samurai family's daughter, and a Korean father. His parents divorced when he was twelve and, like the protagonist in his autobiographical novel *The Ink-Keeper's Apprentice* (1979), S. went to Tokyo, first to live with his grandmother and then to live on his own. Both his father and his grandmother are objects of disdain to S., in life as well as in fiction. Also in life, as in the novel, S. apprenticed himself as a young teenager to Noro Shinpei, a popular cartoonist in postwar Japan. Shinpei guided S.'s early art education and became a father figure to whom S. continued to turn to show off his adult artistic successes. Mining his own early life creatively, S. wrote and illustrated the picture book, *The Bicycle Man* (1982), in which he tells about his experience as a schoolboy enjoying the presence of young American soldiers in occupied Japan. In spite of the military implications of the situation, both the narrative and the images are happy, depicting a kind of cross-cultural discovery of boisterous good nature. A later picture book also is based explicitly on S.'s childhood experiences. *Tree of Cranes* (1991) recounts how his Japanese-American mother introduced him to Christmas when he was a small boy in Japan.

S. immigrated to the United States as a sixteen-year-old knowing no English. He returned to Japan after graduating from high school and studied for three years at Aoyama Gakuin. He then spent a year at the Chouinard Art Institute, followed by studies at the Los Angeles Art Center School, then the University of California (Berkeley) and San Francisco Art Institute. He earned his living as a commercial photographer for twenty years.

S.'s early critical successes were largely for his line illustrations of PICTURE BOOKS written by others. However, *The Ink-Keeper's Apprentice* was named both an AMERICAN LIBRARY ASSOCIATION Notable Book and Best Book for Young Adults (1979). *How My Parents Learned to Eat* (1984), written by Ina Friedman and illustrated by S., earned the Christopher Award (1985). *The Boy of the Three-Year Nap* (1988), authored by Dianne Snyder and illustrated by S., was named an ALA Notable Children's Book that year and an ALA CALDECOTT MEDAL Honor Book in 1989. S.'s painterly style was beginning to evolve from the flat but engaging cartoon drawings of his early illustrations. *The Boy of the Three-Year Nap,* while still comically rounded, presents images in deeply hued and luminous watercolors.

In 1993, S. published *Grandfather's Journey,* a picture book depicting his family's and his own immigration and bicultural experiences. This 1994 Caldecott Medal winner is a portfolio of sophisticated landscapes and portraits. Like *The Ink-Keeper's Apprentice, Grandfather's Journey* is both largely autobiographical and aesthetically refined. The stately paintings derive their character from S.'s vast experience as a photographer, as well as his own sense of insight on himself, other people and the very landscapes he had inhabited. A companion picture book, *Tea with Milk* (1999) tells how S.'s parents met and learned to live with two cultures, recognizing that home is wherever the heart is.

In both his ILLUSTRATION work and his writing, S. explores the nature of identity, particularly his own, and human relationships both within the family and between cultures. In *A River Dream* (1988) and *The Lost Lake* (1989), he presents readers with stories about the stresses and joys of parent and child relations while also giving readers a view on outdoor environments which few can visit in person. The landscapes are dramatic, realistic and would be endangered if populated by many more than the characters in the story. *El Chino* (1990) depicts the self-realization of Billy Wong, a Chinese matador in Spain. Billy was a real person, of whom S. had only read, but in writing the story, S. came to identify with him just as S. would later identify with the character of his grandfather in *Grandfather's Journey.* More recently, with *Stranger in the Mirror* (1995) and *Allison* (1997), S. explores the awakening of identity, separation and the anxieties that accompany these realizations in small children. *Allison,* a picture book treatment of adoption, places the title character in the sensitive, age-appropriate and compelling situation of comparing herself to the kitten for which she cares. *Emma's Rug* (1996) explores the nature of creativity and one young artist's apprehension of its loss.

S.'s picture books have enjoyed both critical acclaim and popularity among young readers. He has made several existential realities accessible in content and beautiful in depiction, giving children the opportunity to find words and images that do justice to their own awakening individuality and sense of worldly connectedness.

FURTHER WORKS: *Once under the Cherry Blossom Tree: An Old Japanese Tale.* 1974. *The Feast of Lanterns.* 1976. *Magic and the Night River.* (Eve BUNTING, author). 1978. *The Lucky Yak.* (Annetta Lawson, author). 1980

BIBLIOGRAPHY: *Contemporary Authors.* 1972–78. *Contemporary Authors,* New Revision Series. vol. 30. 1990. *Notable ASIAN AMERICANS.* 1995. Rochman, H., "The Booklist Interview: Allen Say." *Booklist.* October 1993. *Something about the Author.* vol. 69. 1992

FRANCISCA GOLDSMITH

SCARRY, Richard (McLure)
Author, illustrator, b. 5 June 1919, Boston, Massachusetts; d. 30 April 1994, Gstaad, Switzerland

In a career that spanned more than forty years, S. produced over 250 titles that have sold over 100 million copies in thirty different languages, and include seven of the fifty top-selling children's books of all time. His early studies at the Boston Museum School of Fine Arts were interrupted by his wartime service in North Africa and Italy, where he served as an art director in the Morale Services Section from 1941–46. Initially seeking a career as a commercial artist after his discharge, S. began illustrating other authors' children's books in 1946, before turning to producing his own. His breakthrough came with his still-popular *Richard Scarry's Best Word Book Ever* (1963).

Although S. insisted that he wrote with no age range in mind, his books seem designed to entertain and instruct preschoolers about the bustling world in which they live. His counting books, alphabet books, picture dictionaries, beginning readers, and more advanced storybooks are crammed full with his trademark busy details of cartoonlike, anthropomorphic animals. S. believed that children can more readily identify with pictures of animals than those of children, who may look different from them. In this way, he also hoped to avoid racial conflict. S. took great pride in helping young children to discover the joy of learning. He used labeled drawings to explain objects and concepts, letters and numbers; to celebrate the familiar happenings of their daily life; and to help them understand how the

larger world around them is organized as in *Richard Scarry's What Do People Do All Day?* (1968). Purposeful messages playfully offer instruction on such issues as manners, safety, sharing, and sportsmanship.

His books that tell stories also contain overt messages of traditional family values, both in his gentler tales of domestic life, and his more exotic tales of slapstick adventure. In these, his broad cast of pigs, cats, owls, and the like, frenetically dash through farcical plots, notably in the detective chase scenes of his mystery SERIES (e.g., *The Great Pie Robbery,* 1969), and the fast-paced international romp of *Busy, Busy World* (1965). S. brushed aside criticisms of the accident-prone antics of these madcap characters, by insisting that the "violence" is gently tempered, and no one ever actually gets hurt. Nevertheless, he was aware of his responsibilities in influencing millions of children, and in later works, he bowed to feminist criticism of his stereotyped "happy housewives," and began introducing more female characters in traditionally male roles.

It is the chaotic, yet benign, clutter of S.'s miniature humanized animal world that keeps young readers engaged for long periods. To them, the plain language, simple plots, and clichéd characterizations are peripheral to the intricately detailed pictures that are the real source of fascination for them, and the device that entices their repeated browsing that reinforces learning. They eagerly search for the recurring characters of Busyland, especially the Tyrolean-hatted Lowly Worm. Many of the books invite reader participation, like scratch-and-sniff, coloring, and pop-up books. S.'s animated Busytown characters have become a top-rated television series, *The Busy World of Richard Scarry,* and also appear in video and CD-ROM adaptations. S.'s works have suffered a lack of critical acclaim, attributable largely to his staggering productivity and highly commercialized marketing, that matches the frenetically overcrowded pages of his books. Nevertheless his books remain overwhelmingly popular with preschoolers and their parents.

FURTHER WORKS: *Storybook Dictionary,* 1966. *ABC Word Book,* 1971. *Richard Scarry's Great Steamboat Mystery,* an Edgar Allan Poe nomination for children's mystery, 1976

99. MARGRET AND H. A. REY

100. FAITH RINGGOLD

101. J. K. ROWLING

102. CYNTHIA RYLANT

103. ALLEN SAY

104. JON SCIESZKA

105. LANE SMITH AND JON SCIESZKA

106. MAURICE SENDAK

BIBLIOGRAPHY: *Children's Literature Review,* vol. 41, 1997; *Something about the Author,* vol. 75, 1994, and vol. 90, 1997
BARBARA TOBIN

SCHERTLE, Alice
Author, poet, b. 7 April, 1941, Los Angeles, California

S., author of more than thirty books for young children, spends much of her time traveling around the United States making school visits. She loves to read her stories and POETRY to children, both to gauge its effect on them, and to inspire them to become avid readers and writers themselves. After a childhood spent immersed in reading and writing stories, and a short, early career as an elementary-school teacher, S. took up full-time writing for children after the births of her three children. Before she wrote her first book (*The Gorilla in the Hall,* 1975), she spent three years studying children's books at her local library, shaping her own unique vision of what she wanted to create for children. S. studied with Myra Cohn LIVINGSTON in a masters class at UCLA.

S.'s PICTURE BOOKS frequently deal with themes of love, friendship, and family relationships, and are sometimes based on her personal experiences. *William and Grandpa* (1989) celebrates the gentle warmth of intergenerational relationships, as does *Maisie* (1995). This was inspired by memories of her mother, and documents the life of a vibrant matriarch, from her birth on a farm at the turn of the century to her ninetieth birthday, where her thirty great-grandchildren help her blow out the candles on her cake. *Down the Road* (1994) shows S.'s continuing exploration of family nurturing and closeness with its tender demonstration of parental understanding that supports a young child's growth toward independence.

S. has a great love of poetry and urges parents to teach this same love to their children by reading poetry aloud to them. Her lively contributions to this end include her original collections *How Now Brown Cow* (1994), *Advice for a Frog* (1995), and *Keepers* (1996). At times thoughtful, and often lighthearted, S.'s verse is always fun to read aloud. S.'s AWARDS include Parents' Choice Picture Book awards for *William and Grandpa*

and *Witch Hazel* (1991); and ALA Notable Children's Books citations for *Advice for a Frog* and *Down the Road.*

FURTHER WORKS: Cathy and Company series, 1980; *In My Treehouse,* 1983; *Jeremy Bean's St. Patrick's Day,* 1987; *Little Frog's Song,* 1992

BIBLIOGRAPHY: *Something about the Author,* vol. 90, 1997; *Booklist,* September 15, 1995; Fern, Ong Sor, *Children Love Poetry but Parents Must Get the Book,* March 14, 1998; The *Straits Times Interactive Books* (on-line), available: http://web3.asial.com. sg/archive/st/31pages/b031 411.html
BARBARA TOBIN

SCHICK, Eleanor
Author, illustrator, b. 15 April 1942, New York City

S. has illustrated nearly twenty children's books. Her philosophy regarding books for children is that literature should encompass the human experience and should reflect its culture. She also believes that children are important human beings who need to be recognized and respected. S.'s characters are realistic, and her ILLUSTRATIONS represent the emotions and feelings of her characters. In *Home Alone* (1980), Andy must deal with the loneliness of returning home from school to an empty house, while his mother is at work. *City in the Summer* (1969), portrays a young boy who goes to the roof of his apartment to escape the commotion of the big city. *City in the Winter* (1970) follows Jimmy through a day at home when a blizzard forces his school to close.

S. has written, coauthored, and illustrated several books with NATIVE AMERICAN settings. *My Navajo Sister* (1996), an autobiographical book written and illustrated by S., depicts a young girl who recalls her days spent on a Navajo reservation with her Navajo friend. She also coauthored and illustrated *Navajo ABC: A Dine Alphabet Book* (1995), which pairs Navajo words with their corresponding pictures.

BIBLIOGRAPHY: Kingman, Lee, *Illustrators of Children's Books: 1967–1976,* 1978
DENISE P. BEASLEY

SCHINDLER, S. D.
Illustrator, b. 27 September 1952, Kenosha, Wisconsin

S.'s diverse styles and his ability to represent accurately myriad text genres result in the frequent appearances of his ILLUSTRATIONS in children's books. S. graduated with a degree in biology from the University of Pennsylvania. Although he has no formal instruction in art, he has been an artist since he was very young. All through his early school years he loved to copy, draw, and color. He earned money to attend college by selling his art at exhibits. At his parents urging, S. earned a degree as a pre-med student, but pursued a career in art. His professional publishing career took off only when agents involved him in the illustration of textbooks and children's books. S.'s success lies in his talent of interpreting text accurately in pictures, regardless of genre.

He illustrates for many well-known authors in fiction and nonfiction, from science to folktales and rhymes. In *Every Living Thing* (1985), S. and Cynthia RYLANT, one of his favorite authors, create stories in which people's lives are greatly improved by animals. Also, the duo entertain their readers with *Children of Christmas: Stories for the Season* (1987). S. has illustrated books authored by current and classic writers including Ursula K. LE GUIN, Virginia HAVILAND, and Steven KROLL. Illustration for SERIES includes the SCIENCE FICTION books about Einstein Anderson, by Seymour SIMON, in which a boy science detective tackles the puzzles of science and the "Lottery Luck" ADVENTURE fiction series authored by Judy DELTON where readers follow the adventures of the Green family members who have won the lottery. S. examines the text he is to portray in detail before he begins his illustrations. For example, in *The First Tulips in Holland* (1982), the reader experiences S.'s depiction of Dutch art and accurate details of architecture, costume, and the coloring of the tulips. He received the Parents Choice Award for Children's Books for his illustrations in *The First Tulips in Holland*. In *Catwings* (1988), S.'s pen-and-ink finely drawn illustrations match the delicacy of the tabby kittens.

AWARDS: INTERNATIONAL READING ASSOCIATION CHILDREN'S Book Award (1991) for *Is This a House for Hermit Crab? School Library Journal* Best Book Award (1985) for *Every Living Thing. Parenting* magazine's Reading Magic Award (1988) and Carolyn W. Field Award (1989) for *Catwings*

FURTHER WORKS: *Favorite FAIRY TALES Told around the World.* 1985: *Oh, What a Thanksgiving!* 1988: *Catwings Return.* 1989: *Big Pumpkin.* 1992: *Charlie Malarkey and the Singing Moose.* 1994: *Those Amazing Ants.* 1994: *Winning Ticket!* 1995: *Eency Weency Spider.* 1997: *Whuppity Stoorie: A Scottish Folktale.* 1997: *Bat: In the Dining Room.* 1997: *Betcha! A Mathstart Book.* 1997: *The Mysterious Lights.* 1998: *Clever Crow.* 1998: *The Liberty Tree: The Beginning of the American Revolution.* 1998

BIBLIOGRAPHY: *Children's Literature AWARDS and Winners.* 1994. The *Horn Book* magazine, March/April 1989

NANCY HORTON

SCHOENHERR, John

Author, illustrator, wildlife artist, b. 5 July 1935, New York City

S. has enjoyed a successful career painting and illustrating wild animals in over forty children's books and nationally exhibited artworks. He uses art as a means of communicating the respectful awe he feels for these animals. Growing up in cosmopolitan Queens, New York, this son of European immigrants quickly realized the communicative value of drawing. He used the daily comics to master English at an early age, and later spent hours drawing animals at the Bronx Zoo, and exploring New York's art and natural history museums.

Drawn almost mystically to nature's rugged beauty, S. regularly planned backpacking and spelunking expeditions. His love of the wilderness became the focal point for applying the art skills he acquired at Brooklyn's Pratt Institute, but not before he had illustrated hundreds of SCIENCE FICTION books and magazines. Turning to book ILLUSTRATION for the income that was not forthcoming from FINE ARTS, S. later stumbled into children's book illustrating with little interest in this genre. However, immediate success with his raccoons in Sterling NORTH's *Rascal* (1963), precipitated regular commissions to illustrate animals like otters, bears, skunks, and eagles in books by many children's authors, including ten by Miska Miles.

S. has roamed as far afield as Alaska, Puerto Rico, and Iran to study animals in their natural habitats, gathering materials for his books and paintings, and finding new artistic directions. His travels through undeveloped areas of Arizona, the Dakotas, and Montana produced a deep appreciation of the structure of earth and stone, more readily visible in these massive sweeps of landscape than the densely vegetated East Coast. His frequent depiction of landscape vistas and fascination with the tactile feel of stone appear most recently in *Bear* (1991).

S. became disenchanted with illustration's technical restrictions, having worked mainly in scratchboard and acrylics for the sake of speed and sharpness of detail. For seven years he painted full-time, relishing the rich texture and range of impasto oils. Without constant deadlines, he could focus total energy into one picture, reworking it to his satisfaction, concentrating on the inner life of his subjects. He was enticed back to illustrating by Jane YOLEN's *Owl Moon* (1987), the quiet, sensitive story of a father taking his daughter owling for the first time. S.'s intimate knowledge of the owls in his own woods, and an opportunity to use full color for the first time, enabled him to weave his soft watercolor images seamlessly with Yolen's spare, poetic text, evoking a profound sense of the wonderment of a child meeting the wildness. The book's success and his editor's urging to write more stories of his own resulted in *Bear and Rebel* (1995), each of which tell, in plain text, watercolors, and shifting visual perspectives, of a young animal striking out on its own.

AWARDS: ALA CALDECOTT MEDAL (1988) and an INTERNATIONAL BOARD ON BOOKS FOR YOUNG PEOPLE Illustration Award (1990) for *Owl Moon*

FURTHER WORKS: *Gentle Ben* (Walt MOREY, author), 1963; *Julie of the Wolves* (Jean Craighead GEORGE, author), 1971; *Dune* (Frank Herbert, author), 1977

REFERENCES: *Something about the Author,* vol. 66, 1991; *Something about the Author Autobiography Series,* vol. 13, 1992

BARBARA TOBIN

SCHOOL STORIES

School stories—that is, stories whose primary setting is school—comprise a large percentage of the children's books currently on bookstore and library shelves. The fact that there is such a vast number of children's books with school settings is hardly surprising since children between the ages six and eighteen spend on average thirty hours a week in the classroom. Add to that the time spent in school-related activities such as SPORTS, DRAMA, MUSIC, clubs, and so on; and you get a hefty portion of most American youngster's lives revolving around the community we call school. Interests are born at school, friendships are made and broken, goals achieved and not achieved. School is the childhood's world, or at least a significant part of it. No wonder children want stories that reflect and illuminate that world.

Because children are so familiar with the school setting, the people there, and the problems they face, school stories are highly appealing and accessible to most young readers. Youngsters' schema for school life is well established. They know what schools look like, sound like, smell like, and feel like; and they know what you do there. The characters they meet in school stories sound and look familiar because they have met them in their classrooms, on playgrounds, and in locker rooms.

School stories have been around for about as long as there have been schools and stories for children. Some of the earliest works with school settings are Thomas Hughes's *Tom Brown's Schooldays* (1857) and Frances Hodgson BURNETT's *Little Princess,* which was first published in 1888 as *Sara Crewe; or, What Happened at Miss Minchin's.* Hughes's book depicts English public school life in the Victorian era and Burnett's life in a London boarding school. Much of the drama in Laura Ingalls WILDER's Little House books, first published in 1932, takes place in one-room prairie schools, while Lucy Maud MONTGOMERY's books about the redheaded orphan, Anne, who first appeared in *Anne of Green Gables* (1908), depict the one-room schools of Prince Edward Island.

Not surprisingly perhaps, the greatest proliferation of contemporary school stories appears to be for the elementary grade reader in the form of CHAPTER BOOKS FOR BEGINNING READERS as well as middle-grade novels. Authors of these school stories, many of them teachers or former teachers, have a special knack for creating vivid classroom portraits, stories full of memorable classroom characters, and told with HUMOR and pathos. Among these are writers who have produced series of books about classroom life, such as Patricia Reilly GIFF (Polk Street School Series); Suzy Kline (Horrible Harry, Herbie Jones, and Mary Marony series); Louis SACHAR (the Wayside School and Marvin Redpost series); and Joanna COLE's The Magic School Bus series, in which the zany Ms. Frizzle takes her students via the magic school bus to explore the various wonders of science, from inside the human body—*The Magic School Bus Inside the Human Body* (1989)—to the depths of the sea—*The Magic School Bus on the Ocean Floor* (1992). Then there is Beverly CLEARY's *Muggie Maggie* (1990) and her many stories of Ramona Quimby and Otis Spofford. Other notable chapter books and middle-grade novels include Judy BLUME's *Tales of a Fourth-Grade Nothing* (1972) and *Blubber* (Bradbury, 1974); Bruce COVILLE's *The Teacher Fried My Brains* (1991); Johanna HURWITZ's *Class Clown* (1987); Gordon KORMAN's *This Can't Be Happening at MacDonald Hall* (1978) and *The Twinkie Squad* (1992); and Barthe DE-CLEMENT's *Liar, Liar* (1998).

Since stories with school settings are highly accessible, they make excellent choices for students who struggle with reading. For example, Margo Sorenson's high-interest easy reading novel, *Don't Bug Me* (1996), and her many time-travel adventure biographies feature middle-school kids dealing with issues such as friendships and peer pressure while juggling school assignments, responsibilities, and teacher-parent expectations, all situations that reluctant readers can identify with.

There are also many excellent PICTURE BOOKS and young adult novels with school settings. Kevin HENKES's *Lily's Purple Plastic Purse* (1996) is a wonderful example of a picture book school story. Lily, whom Henkes portrays as a mouse, adores school and her teacher until he makes her wait before showing off her new purse. Other fine picture books with school settings are Martha ALEXANDER's *Move Over Twerp* (1989), James HOWES's *The Day the Teacher Went Bananas* (1984), Harry ALLARD and James MAR-SHALL's *Miss Nelson Has a Field Day* (1985), Rosemary WELLS's *Timothy Goes to School* (1981), Amy SCHWARTZ's *Annabelle Swift, Kindergartner* (1988), Miriam COHEN's *First Grade Takes a Test* (1980), and Bruce MCMILLAN's *Mouse Views: What the Class Pet Saw* (1993)

where, with the use of photographs, McMillan shows common school items from an escaped mouse's perspective. At the other end of the spectrum, young adult novels, are John Knowles' *A Separate Peace* (1959) and Robert CORMIER's landmark *The Chocolate War* (1974). Other young adult authors and titles include Paula DAN-ZIGER's *The Cat Ate My Gymsuit* (1974), Norma Fox MAZER's *Mrs. Fish, Ape, and Me, The Dump Queen* (1980), Nat HENTOFF's *The Day They Came to Arrest the Book* (1982), Richard PECK's *Remembering the Good Times* (1985), AVI's *Nothing but the Truth* (1991), Robert Thomas's *Slave Day* (1997), and Daniel PINKWATER's *The Education of Robert Rifkin* (1998) in which the narrator, Robert Rifkin, in the form of a college essay, tells about his unorthodox experiences in high school during the 1950s.

There are also many outstanding books with school settings that portray MULTICULTURAL settings and themes. Two of these books with foreign settings include the 1955 NEWBERY MEDAL winner, *The Wheel on the School* (1954) by Meindert DEJONG, which features the students in a Dutch fishing village school, and 1956 CALDE-COTT MEDAL Honor book, *Crow Boy* (1955) by Taro YASHIMA, which depicts young Chibi and his school experiences in Japan. Multicultural books set in the United States include Barbara COHEN's *Molly's Pilgrim* (1983) in which the concept of pilgrim is expanded to include third-grader Molly's mother, a Russian Jewish immigrant; Gary SOTO's *Off and Running* (1996) in which two fifth-grade Chicana girls run against the class clowns in student elections; and Jaqueline WOOD-SON's *Maizon at Blue Hill* (1992), in which the academically talented Maizon finds herself one of only five black students at a Connecticut boarding school and wonders if she will fit in.

The best school series, only a fraction of which have been mentioned here, not only mirror the child's world at school—the delights, disappointments, disasters, and the challenges—but, like the best teachers and the best schools, with empathy and often with great good humor, give the child something to think about and on which to grow.

BONNIE GRAVES

SCHULZ, Charles M(onroe)

Author, cartoonist, b. 26 November 1922, St. Paul, Minnesota; d. 12 February 2000, Santa Rosa, California

The first syndicated *Peanuts* comic strip appeared on October 2, 1950; it is now read in more than 2,600 newspapers in seventy-five countries. Following S.'s death, only *Classic Peanuts* appears in syndication.

Universally enjoyed by children and adults, *Peanuts* has since appeared in book format, as a successful Broadway play twice, frequently as an animated television show, and has been TRANS-LATED into several languages. S. got his start in ILLUSTRATION when he responded to an advertisement asking readers if they like to draw. After serving in the Army during World War II S. taught art and sold cartoons to the *Saturday Evening Post*. He first created the "Lil Folks" feature cartoon, forerunner of *Peanuts,* for the *St. Paul Pioneer Press* in 1947. S. was not pleased when its name was changed to *Peanuts* reflecting the gang's response to the DRAMA of daily life. He wrote and drew the comic strip by himself without support staff, saying that cartooning was "his life."

The appeal of *Peanuts* to people of all ages and backgrounds lies in the comic strip's representation of universal sentiments of unflagging hope, frequent frustration, and a belief that we can succeed. Each familiar character has a distinctive personality. Charlie Brown with his stoic expression "Good Grief" when faced with adversity, Schroeder with dreams of fame as a concert pianist, Linus dragging his security blanket, and Lucy at her lemonade stand dispensing advice illuminate the human condition recognized by children and adults. Snoopy, Charlie Brown's intrepid beagle who fantasizes himself as the Red Baron of World War I fame symbolizes the hero we all long to be.

S. received cartooning's highest award, the Reuben Award, in 1955 and 1964. Comic-strip artists from around the world chose S. as International Cartoonist of the Year (1978). He was designated to receive a lifetime achievement award from the National Cartoonists Society before his death. The annual Modern Language Association convention held a special session devoted to *Peanuts* and S. in 2000.

BIBLIOGRAPHY: www.peanuts.com

DIANE G. PERSON

SCHWARTZ, Alvin

Folklorist, author, b. 25 April, 1927, Brooklyn, New York; d. 14 March, 1992, Princeton, New Jersey

S., compiler, reteller of FOLKLORE for young readers, and author of nonfiction for adults and children, was a newspaper reporter and professional writer before turning to freelance writing in the 1960s. He produced a small body of adult nonfiction (e.g., *A Parent's Guide to Children's Play and Recreation,* 1963), as well as a series of children's nonfiction books that explored the same issues of contemporary life that he had pursued less intensively as a journalist: urban problems, trade unions, public opinion, and public institutions. *The Night Workers* (1966) was his first children's book.

S. is best remembered for his comprehensive exploration of American folklore. Growing up in an extended family of Hungarian and Russian heritage, S. was delighted to discover American folklore as an adult. Beginning with *A Twister of Twists, A Tangler of Tongues* (1972), S. systematically researched many folklore genres, compiling separate collections for each: tongue-twisters, riddles, superstitions, hoaxes, folk POETRY, ghost stories, tall tales, noodle tales, and so on. Besides searching archival materials, S. collected from primary sources, particularly children and old people, the most enthusiastic carriers and transmitters of traditional folklore. Guidance from eminent folklorists strengthened the scholarship of his work, as evidenced in his meticulous citation of sources, bibliographies, and detailed notes explaining the oral development of the material he liberally embellished. This information is simplified in his books for younger readers, namely his I Can Read titles (e.g., *Ten Copycats in a Boat and Other Riddles,* 1980).

S. sought not just to entertain his readers, but to help them recognize their role in a living tradition that anchors them to the roots of humanity.

He believed that the erosion of the extended family has alienated us from our traditions, diminishing our sense of place and self. His books invite young people to laugh while they can, to share his fascination with the colorful imagery and sheer absurdity of the wordplay inherent in folklore, and to keep it alive.

S.'s most popular books are his collections of stories about witches, ghosts, and other fearful creatures (e.g., *In a Dark, Dark Room and Other Scary Stories*, 1984, *Scary Stories 3: More Tales to Chill Your Bones*, 1991). Although criticized for being too frightening for children, these books have consistently polled high in children's choice AWARDS. Many of his titles have been the target of CENSORSHIP efforts precisely because of S.'s efforts to transmit the folklore of superstition. S.'s books have also garnered many adult bestowed awards, including NCSS/CBC Notable Children's Trade Book in the Field of Social Studies citations for *Central City/Spread City* (1973); *Cross Your Fingers, Spit in Your Hat: Superstitions and Other Beliefs* (1974); and *Whoppers: Tall Tales and Other Lies* (1975)

FURTHER WORKS: *Kickle Snifters and Other Fearsome Critters* (*School Library Journal* Best Book, 1976; INTERNATIONAL READING ASSOCIATION/CHILDREN'S BOOK COUNCIL Children's Choices). 1975; *And the Green Grass Grew All around: Folk Poetry from Everywhere*, 1992

BIBLIOGRAPHY: Kiefer, Barbara, selector, *Getting to Know You: Profile of Children's Authors Featured in Language Arts*, 1985–90, 1991; *Children's Literature Review*. vol. 3, 1978; *Something about the Author*, vol. 56, 1989, and vol. 71, 1993; *Fifth Book of Junior Authors and Illustrators*, 1983

BARBARA TOBIN

SCHWARTZ, Amy

Author, illustration, b. 2 April, 1954, San Diego, California

S. is well known for accurately capturing childhood experiences from a child's perspective through her stories of everyday events. Whether in her first book, *Bea and Mr. Jones* (1982), set in a kindergarten, or in later books such as *Oma and Bob* (1987), portraying an extended family, S. uses gentle HUMOR to portray the honest feelings of children. As an illustrator, she is known for using pen and ink and watercolor to re-create

the child's world for the reader. Both *Bea and Mr. Jones* (1982, 1994) and *The Purple Coat* (1986) have been highlighted on READING RAINBOW. About her work, S. comments that after reading her stories, she wants children "to have laughed and to have felt that they've heard a really good story."

AWARDS: Numerous, including Best Children's Books of 1982 citation, *School Library Journal*, and 100 Best Children's Books citation, New York Public Library, 1982, for *Bea and Mr. Jones;* Parents' Choice Award and Children's Choice Award for *The Crack-of-Dawn Walkers* (1984); Parents' Choice Award for *The Lady Who Put Salt in Her Coffee* (1989); *New York Times* Best Illustrated Children's Book for *A Teeny Tiny Baby* (1994)

FURTHER WORKS: *Mrs. Moskowitz and the Sabbath Candlesticks*, 1983; *The Purple Coat*, 1986; *Annabelle Swift, Kindergartner*, 1988; *My Island Grandma*, 1993; *Gabby Growing Up*, 1988; *Old McDonald*, 1999

BIBLIOGRAPHY: *Something about the Author*, vol. 83, 1996

SANDRA IMDIEKE

SCIENCE FICTION

Now into the twenty-first century and a new millennium, the media are filled with speculation of what will come in the twenty-first century. Pundits write articles and speak on news shows; the possibilities are both intriguing and frightening. What is occurring is similar to what science fiction writers have been writing about for most of the twentieth century.

Science fiction is a literature of the imagination. It is *not* FANTASY, in that good science fiction depicts plausible events based in the reality of the universe as we know it. These events might not happen in our time or in our world, but they are logical extrapolations of known facts. Science fiction writers take what is known and interpolate into the future to explore what is unknown.

Science fiction is one of the newest literary genres, as the term was not coined until 1926. H. G. WELLS, Jules VERNE, and others had written several books of speculative fiction before this time, but it was not until a sufficient body of literature had been produced that a term defining the genre was created. The term was coined by Hugo Gernsback, who founded the pulp magazine

Amazing Stories in 1926. Considered the father of science fiction, Gernsback reprinted much of the writing of Verne and Wells in serial form. The Hugo Awards, given for science fiction writing, are named in his honor.

It was John Campbell, Jr., the founder in 1938 of a magazine known as *Astounding Science Fiction,* who truly developed the form of literature and introduced many new writers to the medium. When he began his magazine, he went far beyond reprints of Wells and Verne. He was an exacting editor who demanded that his writers show sophistication in both their literary work and their knowledge of the science upon which their stories were based. In addition, he encouraged writers to explore the social consequences of scientific development. Early science fiction had a "gee whiz" quality that focused on the wonders of emerging technology and science. World War II was a watershed for both science and science fiction. The awful consequences of the explosion of the atomic bomb, and the implications for the future, caused many to begin to question the "rightness" of unfettered scientific exploration. Campbell encouraged his writers to examine moral dilemmas, the social impact of TECHNOLOGY AND COMMUNICATION on society, and the value systems of society. The writers in Campbell's stable influenced the course of science fiction for the balance of the century. Among these writers were Isaac ASIMOV, Robert HEINLEIN, Lester del Rey, L. Sprague DeCamp, and A. E. van Vogt.

The line between juvenile and adult science fiction is very hard to draw, because many writers write for both levels, and because books intended for adults have been read avidly by juveniles. However, the first science fiction book written specifically for children was *The Angry Planet,* by BRITISH writer John Kier Cross in 1946. Noted American science fiction author Robert Heinlein entered the children's publishing realm with *Rocket Ship Galileo,* in 1947. He continued to write what were known as junior novels, completing twelve in as many years. Not only do the books reflect the nature of science of the day, but they show what was happening in the world in general. For example, in *Rocket Ship Galileo,* there is a struggle between good and evil, with evil personified as Nazi forces. *Space Cadet*

(1948) presents the complicated training necessary for space travel, while extolling the value of individualism and the development of a code to protect men from their proclivity for war.

A brief overview of the decades between 1950 and 1990 documents changes in society and technology. In the 1950s, our concern with Communism was at the forefront and Lester del Rey's *Step to the Stars* (1954) and Arthur C. CLARKE's *Childhood's End* (1953) were among the best to examine the dangers of a mass society. In response to the advent of racial equality as a major force in the United States, authors changed their subtle pleas via interaction with aliens, to more direct presentations of the need for all races to get along. Both Heinlein in *The Last Planet* (1953) and Asimov in *Pebble in the Sky* (1950) examine this theme. The 1960s was a decade of upheaval. For the first time, a book of science fiction received the NEWBERY MEDAL, given to Madeleine L'ENGLE for *A Wrinkle in Time* (1962). As with many fine books that demand much of the reader, the book remains both popular and controversial. In the 1970s, a concern for ecology entered the spectrum, as well as many "isms." Robert C. O'BRIEN won the NEWBERY MEDAL for his thought-provoking *Mrs. Frisby and the Rats of NIMH* (1971). During this decade, many women began publishing science fiction. Andre NORTON, who began writing for children in 1952 and remains a prolific author, adopted an androgynous pseudonym so she could get her works published and read. In the 1970s she was joined by other fine writers who no longer felt the need to disguise their gender. Kate Wilhelm, Vonda McInytre, H. M. HOOVER, Louise LAWRENCE, Pamela Sargent, Pamela Service, Wilanne Belden, and Anne MCCAFFREY all became productive. The 1980s was a period of bleak books that looked at nuclear holocausts, genetic mutations, nuclear winter, and the very survival of the species.

Very few science fiction works for youth were published in the 1990s. A notable exception is *The Giver* (1993), by Lois LOWRY, which received the Newbery Medal. The book opens in a utopia, where all are provided for and there are few worries. But what is the price of such an existence? The inexorable revelation of what is truly a dystopia challenges the reader. Others include

New World (1994) by Gillian CROSS, that explores the dangers of virtual reality games that take over the life of the players; Sonia LEVITIN's *The Cure* (1999), which depicts our world in 2407 when all individuality has been erased; and Kathryn LASKY's *Star Split* (1999), in which the protagonist discovers an underground movement to save the human race from the consequences of rampant genetic manipulation that has become commonplace in 3038.

An interesting paradox emerges when considering the decade of the 1990s. There is an explosion of technological development with the attendant concerns that people have about the impact on society. Science fiction is hugely popular in the media, with movies such as the latest segments of *Star Wars* and *Star Trek* and television programs, such as *The X-Files*. Yet there is a noticeable dearth of science fiction being written for youth. When editors are asked why there are so few books being published, they say there is no market! Perhaps few editors today are willing to take a chance on speculative fiction, or perhaps they have little knowledge of the genre. It is hoped that there will be a resurgence of this field in the twenty-first century.

M. JEAN GREENLAW

SCIESZKA, Jon
Author, b. 8 September 1954, Flint, Michigan

S. has come into prominence during the 1990s as a popular author of both PICTURE BOOKS and simply constructed read-alone stories. He grew up enjoying books and his own cadre of brothers. After graduating from Albion College (1976), he moved to New York City and earned a master of fine arts degree in writing at Columbia University (1980), supposing that he would become the author of the Great American Novel. His plans to write with such serious focus were set aside as he entered a teaching career, where he discovered an enjoyment of and devotion to children as an audience in want of stories that engage them through narrative HUMOR.

S.'s professional relationship with illustrator Lane SMITH has been the catalyst for a stream of humorous books that appeal to young children, beginning readers and adults. S.'s belief that parody is within the scope of a seven-year-old's

comprehension was substantiated with the popular reception of *The True Story of the Three Little Pigs* (1989), in which the titular folktale is retold from the putatively innocent wolf's viewpoint. The *Frog Prince, Continued* (1991) again uses a familiar FAIRY TALE as the basis for a mind bending, side-splitting, reexploration of possible outcomes. S. questions the original's anthropocentrism: in his version, the frog wants to be a frog, not a prince! *The Stinky Cheese Man and Other Fairly Stupid Tales* (1992) presents an array of reimagined stories that are familiar to young readers. Here, for instance, *Little Red Riding Hood* is revivified as *Little Red Running Shorts*. *The Stinky Cheese Man* was named by the AMERICAN LIBRARY ASSOCIATION as a CALDECOTT MEDAL Honor Book (Lane Smith, illus., 1993).

S.'s pedagogical concern for children in the beginning grades, who have difficulty finding reading matter that is both accessible to their meager skills and engaging of their sophisticated tastes, has led him to create a series called The Time Warp Trio. Specifically targeting little boys who need to practice reading without compromising perceived threats to their social status as bright, this series provides emerging readers with glibly fractured tales they can and will read. The *Not-So-Jolly Roger* (1991), *The Good, the Bad, and the Goofy* (1992), and *Your Mother Is a Neanderthal* (1993) are among the exploits through times and cultures on which the three small boy heroes embark for silly adventures, almost gross jokes and similarly age-appealing capers. These books work precisely because S. trusts readers to bring cultural understanding, and a schoolboy's funny bone, rather than well-honed reading skills, to the process of becoming literate.

S. and Smith's picture books for school-age readers concern schoolhouse topics. *Math Curse* (1995) plays on many children's anxieties about numeracy. *Squids Will Be Squids: Fresh Morals, Beastly Fables* (1998) skewers such issues as the impact of television commercials and homework assignments on their daily lives.

S.'s work has been well received by critics and by adults who select books to read to their children, although there was initial concern expressed about his choice of narrative angle being one of parody. This concern focused on critical doubt that children would be able to differentiate between the traditional story and a parody of it. S. maintained belief in the abilities of young school-aged children to appreciate such a difference and was well supported in his contention by his editor. Experience proved his assertion correct and reviews of more recent books by him have not met with such doubt, but with unabashed praise. It is likely, too, that the books' appeal to adult readers' own sense of the absurd give younger children better access to these books through having them read aloud, as adult readers are inclined to share their own finds of entertainment with the children in their lives.

S.'s work provides everyone who reads it with slick but relatively undemanding fun. This experience readily predisposes children to look for enjoyment through books and is a further, more serious, benefit S. provides his readers.

FURTHER WORKS: *The Book That Jack Wrote*, 1994; *Tut, Tut*, 1996; *Knights of the Kitchen Table*, 1991; *2095*, 1995

BIBLIOGRAPHY: *St. James Guide to Children's Writers*, 1999; Silvey, Anita, ed., *Children's Books and Their Creators*, 1995; *Something about the Author*, vol. 68, 1992. *Contemporary Authors*, vol. 135, 1992; Smith, A. "Jon S. and Lane Smith," *Publishers Weekly*, July 26, 1991

FRANCISCA GOLDSMITH

SCOTT, Ann Herbert
Author, b. 19 November 1926, Germantown, Pennsylvania

S., author of PICTURE BOOKS for children, uses simple narrative and realistic dialogue to write stories with universal themes such as a mother's love or the longing to become important. Her books typically feature Western, ethnic, or rural settings. Among her award-winning books are *Sam* (1967), *Not Just One* (1968), *On Mother's Lap* (1972), *A Brand Is Forever* (1993), *Cowboy Country* (1993), and *Brave as a Mountain Lion* (1996). S. lives in Nevada and is cofounder of the Annual Art of the Children's Book Festival.

FURTHER WORKS: *Big Cowboy Western*. 1965. *Let's Catch a Monster*. 1967. *Someday Rider*. 1989. *One Good Horse: A Cowpuncher's Counting Book*. 1990. *Grandmother's Chair*. 1990. *Hi*. 1994

BIBLIOGRAPHY: *Something about the Author*, vol. 94, 1998; Ann Herbert Scott: Friends of the Uni-

versity Libraries, last modified November 14, 1997; http://www.library.unr.edu/scott.html (accessed March 30, 1999)

MARY ARIAIL BROUGHTON

SEBESTYEN, Ouida
Author, b. 13 February 1924, Vernon, Texas

S. lives in Colorado and writes REALISTIC FICTION for YOUNG ADULTS. Growing up in a small town as a lonely, shy, only child of two teachers, S. came to love learning and reading, and, as an adult, wanted to repay some of the pleasure that books had brought her. Yet success was slow coming to this aspiring writer, who sent off her first adult novel to a publisher at the age of twenty. Despite hundreds of rejections of her works for adults (four novels, countless short stories, poems, plays), S. managed to sell just enough short stories to keep her dream alive. One of her published short stories was based on an incident from her aunt's childhood, and was later refashioned to form the introduction of *Words by Heart* (1979), her first novel for young people, and her first published book at age fifty-five. *Words by Heart* was an instant success, receiving many literary AWARDS. Despite wide critical acclaim, however, the book was attacked by some as sending a regressive, racist message and perpetuating negative stereotypes. These flaws were seen to emanate from the books "ethnocentric outsider's viewpoint" of a passive black family facing the prejudice and bigotry of an all-white town in the early 1900s. Such critics perceived an implied intent to raise the social conscience of white readers, while masking deeply entrenched racism and obscuring the truth of the black experience. Its sequel, *On Fire* (1985), told now from the perspective of one of the poor, white antagonists of the earlier story, instead of the young black protagonist, does not explore racial issues. Like some of S.'s later works, e.g., *The Girl in the Box*, (1988), this book requires a more mature reader to access the nuances of meaning folded into its finely crafted layers.

S.'s body of work reflects the big themes that she finds most compelling: love, acceptance, and belonging as human needs; and the connectedness that comes through forging family ties. Her robust, yet sensitively drawn characters are spirited, independent twelve to thirteen-year-olds, forced to mature quickly through the harsh circumstances of their lives. Often misfits in society because of their class, age, or race, they battle against poverty, hatred, injustice, and their own fears and insecurities. They wrestle with moral dilemmas and confront the pain of loss of family members through death, divorce, or desertion. Yet these are survivors, who emerge strenghtened by a new, optimistic sense of identity and self-worth. S. lightens the oppressive tones with tenderness, HUMOR, a sense of hope, and a celebration of family.

AWARDS: AMERICAN LIBRARY ASSOCIATION Best Book for Young Adults, 1979; INTERNATIONAL READING ASSOCIATION Children's Book Award, 1980, for *Words by Heart;* ALA Best Book for Young Adults, 1980; Silver Pencil Award, Netherlands, for best TRANSLATION of a children's book, 1984 for *Far from Home;* ALA Best Book for Young Adults, 1982

FURTHER WORKS: *On Fire,* 1985; *The Girl in the Box,* 1988; *Out of Nowhere,* 1994

BIBLIOGRAPHY: *Children's Literature Review,* vol. 8, 1985; *Something about the Author,* vol. 63, 1991, and vol. 73, 1993

BARBARA TOBIN

SEGAL, Lore (Groszmann)
Author, professor, b. 8 March 1928, Vienna, Austria

S. received her education at the University of London. In 1951, she came to America via the Dominican Republic where she worked as a writer and teacher. Between 1967 and 1978 she was an English professor at Columbia University. More recently she taught creative writing at the University of Illinois, Princeton, and Sarah Lawrence. In 1965 she received a Guggenheim Fellowship.

Since 1964 S. has produced several well-received adult novels. Lester Goran, a critic for the *Chicago Tribune* has said "to read Lore Segal's prose is to sit at a table with one of those rare people who combine art, eccentricity, honesty and wisdom." Her way into children's writing was the result of STORYTELLING to her own children. *Tell Me a Mitzi* (1970), a charming book, about the escapades of a loving urban family has Mitzi, a little girl, asking her mother to tell a Mitzi, a story about herself. In 1970 S. and Har-

riet Pincus, illustrator of *Tell Me a Mitzi* won an ALA Notable Book Award. Many of S.'s books have received praise. *The Juniper Tree and Other Tales from GRIMM* (Maurice SENDAK, illus., 1973) was included in the Children's Book showcase in 1974. The books, *Mrs. Lovewright and Purrless Her Cat* (1985) and *The Book of Adam to Moses* (1987) were both cited by the *New York Times* as outstanding children's literature.

S. has been a regular contributor to the *New Yorker, New Republic, Commentary, New York Times Book Review* and *Partisan Review.*

BIBLIOGRAPHY: Cott, Jonathan, *Pipers at the Gates of Dawn: The Wisdom of Children's Literature,* 1981; *Something about the Author,* vol. 66, 1991

JUDY LIPSITT

SELDEN (THOMPSON), George
Author, playwright, screenwriter, b. 14 May 1929, Hartford, Connecticut; d. 5 December 1989, New York City

Thompson wrote under the name of George S., producing almost twenty children's books between 1956 and 1987. Growing up in Connecticut, he developed a love of nature, archaeology, music, and opera, and felt an early calling to be a writer. As an adult resident of New York City, his initial unsuccessful attempts to launch a career as a playwright led him to children's literature, a genre he had always enjoyed. On his third try, he produced the most successful book of his writing career, both in terms of critical acclaim and enduring popularity. *The Cricket in Times Square* (1960) tells the story of Chester, a displaced rural Connecticut cricket befriended by a streetwise mouse and kindly cat in a subway station, where his nightly concert recitals save the newsstand business of his human benefactors.

Over the span of several decades, S. produced six subsequent stories featuring the same lovable, unlikely menage of animal friends, in alternating urban and rural settings. *Harry Kitten and Tucker Mouse* (1985) is a prequel set in the streets and subways of New York before Chester's arrival. It was in the first of this SERIES, however, that S. best developed the original, imaginative plots for which he is noted. Breaking new ground for the animal FANTASY genre with its inner city setting, *The Cricket in Times Square* is often considered an urban parallel to such modern classics as *Charlotte's Web* and *The Wind in the Willows*. Commended for its witty dialogue and unforgettable characters, it was produced as a dramatized recording in 1972 and an animated television show in 1973. The great majority of S.'s books are innovative, amusing animal fantasies, and many have an urban New York City setting and a recurring theme of loyalty among friends. Behind the breezy pace and whimsical charm of the protagonists and their anthropomorphic concerns, such as conservation of natural resources, there is a gentle compassion and satire, an echoing commentary on human foibles and problems. Although some of S.'s books are less successful than others, his works of fiction are distinctive for their fresh, inventive plots, warmly endearing characters, and exuberant entertainment. S.'s lifelong interest in archaeology is reflected in his BIOGRAPHIES of two famous archaeologists, *Heinrich Schliemann, Discoverer of Buried Treasure* (1964) and *Sir Arthur Evans, Discoverer of Knossos* (1964).

AWARDS: ALA NEWBERY MEDAL Honor Book (1961) and Lewis CARROLL Shelf Award (1963) for *The Cricket in Times Square*. *School Library Journal* Best Book of the Year (1969) and *New York Times* Outstanding Book of the Year (1969) for *Tucker's Countryside*. AMERICAN LIBRARY ASSOCIATION Notable Book (1974) and William White Children's Book Award (1974) for *Harry Cat's Pet Puppy*

FURTHER WORKS: *Sparrow Socks*, 1965; *The Children's Story* (play, 1996, based on a novel by James Clavell), 1969; *The Genie of Sutton Place* (adapted from his television play), 1973

BIBLIOGRAPHY: *Children's Literature Review*, vol. 8, 1985; *Something about the Author*, vol. 63, 1991, and vol. 73, 1993

BARBARA TOBIN

SELSAM, Millicent E.

Author, b. 30 May 1912, Brooklyn, New York; d. 12 October 1996, New York City

S. was a prolific writer of more than a hundred books for inquisitive children and YOUNG ADULTS to help them understand the concepts of the physical world. S. studied biology at Brooklyn College and received a master's degree in botany from Columbia University. She married author Howard B. Selsam in 1936. After teaching, S.

converted her skills in teaching, science, and writing and her own lifelong curiosity to creating entertaining and understandable science books for the beginning reader. She published her first book *Egg to Chick* in 1946. S. also contributed to the I Can Read Books for Harper and Row and the First Look at . . . SERIES for Walker and Company. Both series' goals are to help young readers develop powers of observation and understand scientific classification. *Benny's Animals and How He Put Them in Order* (1966) is an excellent example of the author's ability to incorporate methodology and basic science principles. The clear format, continuous text, large print, and abundant space between lines presents the content of animal classification clearly for beginning readers.

S. was the first recipient of the Eva L. Gordon Award of the American Nature Study Society in 1964 for her many contributions to the literature of natural history. *Biography of an Atom* (1965) won the Thomas A. Edison Award for best juvenile science book. *Benny's Animals and How He Put Them in Order* was awarded the Boys Club certificate, 1966–67. The Garden State Children's nonfiction award went to *How Kittens Grow* in 1978 and *Tyrannosaurus Rex* in 1981. In 1977, S. received the *Washington Post/Children's Book Guild* award for her body of work.

FURTHER WORKS: *Play with Plants*, 1948; *Microbes at Work*, 1953; *Language of Animals*, 1962; *Stars, Mosquitoes, and Crocodiles: The American Travels of Alexander Von Humboldt*, 1962; *A First Look at Leaves*, 1972; *The Apple and Other Fruits*, 1973; *All about Eggs*, 1952, 1980; *A First Look at Cats*, 1981; *Backyard Insects*, 1991; *How to Be a Nature Detective*, 1995

BIBLIOGRAPHY: *Children's Book Council, Children's Books: AWARDS and Prizes*, 1996 edition; *New York Times*, October 15, 1996, vol. 146, i. 50, 581, p. B10; *Publishers Weekly*, October 28, 1996, vol. 243, i. 44, p. 34; Sutherland, Zena, and May Hill Arbuthnot, *Children and Books*, 8th ed., 1991

NANCY HORTON

SENDAK, Maurice (Bernard)

Author, illustrator, b. 10 June 1928, Brooklyn, New York

S. was the youngest of three children born to Polish immigrants who had come to New York prior to World War I. Despite his close family, S.'s childhood was marked by illness, overprotective parents, and economic hardships. He had few books, chiefly COMIC BOOKS and cheap paperbacks. From early childhood, S.'s artistic influences were the popular media, especially the cartoons of Walt DISNEY, but also the monster movies and similar popular fare of the Depression Era. His sister gave him a finely bound volume of Mark TWAIN's *The Prince and the Pauper,* from which he first learned to love books for their physical beauty, and which aroused his passion to create beautiful books.

Formal school was not a positive influence on S. and he would later complain school was where he was taught to disavow DISNEY. Only as an adult did he again begin to trust his own instincts and return to an appreciation for the animator's art. Mickey Mouse—coincidentally created in the year of S.'s birth—would be especially influential in his artistic work. Echoes of Mickey and his comfortably proportioned rounded shapes can be seen in many S. characters. His first illustrating job was for a comic-book publisher, drawing backgrounds for the "Mutt and Jeff" comic strip.

Immediately following high school S. illustrated an adult work, *Atomies for the Millions* (1947), written by one of his high school teachers, but he paid his bills by decorating windows for F. A. O. Schwarz, the famed toy store. His first break came in 1950, when he met the Harper and Brothers children's editor Ursula Nordstrom, who commissioned him to illustrate Marcel Ayme's children's story *The Wonderful Farm* (1951). This was the beginning of a happy professional relationship between S. and Nordstrom; she was responsible for his collaboration with Ruth KRAUSS on *A Hole Is to Dig* (1952). Among the artists who most strongly influenced S.'s style were several nineteenth-century figures: the French illustrator of the *Fables* of La Fontaine, Maurice Boutet DE MONVEL; the pioneer English illustrator, George Cruikshank; and the German poet and artist, Wilhelm Busch, best remembered for *Max and Moritz, a Boy's Story in Seven Pranks* (1865). The influence of the great English illustrator Randolph CALDECOTT is unquestionable. Many critics have commented on the heavy European flavor in S.'s work. Indeed, S.'s children's faces have been characterized as Euro-

pean; however, S. has noted that his children's faces are really caricatures of his own face, which is consistent with the intensely personal quality of his art. Additionally, the European flavor of S.'s art is tempered by the influence of American comic-strip art and American popular art in general, giving S.'s work its unmistakable individual stamp.

Following *A Hole Is to Dig,* S. illustrated several of Krauss's stories, including *A Very Special House* (1953), which earned him his first ALA CALDECOTT MEDAL Honor Book award in 1954. Between 1959 and 1963, S. would win no fewer than four Caldecott Metal Honor Book Awards. But perhaps the most enduring of S.'s work from this early period are his beloved illustrations for Else Holmelund MINARIK's Little Bear books, now an animated television program.

He first tried his hand at writing in 1956 with *Kenny's Window,* a work he himself would describe as "overwritten." *Very Far Away* (1957) was his second attempt, but this time the result seemed too sparse. Both books reveal S.'s interest in the dreamworld of the child and the relationship of FANTASY to reality. In his book, *The Sign on Rosie's Door* (1960), he would create one of his favorite characters, the audacious and imaginative Rosie, based on a girl he had once observed in his old neighborhood.

Rosie would continue to be S.'s inspiration for many of his child protagonists of both sexes, including Max, the hero of *Where the Wild Things Are* (1963), a book he both wrote and illustrated. This, S.'s most celebrated work explores the child's psyche through a dream sequence. The book was initially quite controversial—it features a naughty boy and an assemblage of monsters that many adults were sure would frighten children. The children themselves put these fears to rest, for the book remains today one of the most popular picture books of all time and appropriately won the Caldecott Medal in 1964. *Where the Wild Things Are* is a triumph of BOOK DESIGN, effectively unified by visual symbols throughout, and the whole reinforcing the story's dream psychology.

S.'s next major work was *Higglety Pigglety Pop!; or, There Must Be More to Life* (1967), a melancholy FAIRY TALE intended as a tribute to his dog Jennie. This work has proven to be as popular with adults as with children. Its publication was followed by a series of personal crises for S., including a major heart attack when he was only thirty-nine, the death of his dog, and the death of his mother, all of which seemed only to make him more devoted to his art and more determined to celebrate childhood.

His next great success, *In the Night Kitchen* (1970) is the story of a little boy, Mickey, who becomes a hero by ensuring that fresh-baked bread is ready for the world by morning. Inspired by the advertisements of Sunshine bread proclaiming that it is baked "while you sleep," S. wrote this story to fulfill the fantasies of all children who resent established bedtimes and who possess a driving curiosity to know what happens when they sleep. The book's layout reveals the influence of comic strips, with each ILLUSTRATION distinctly framed and with the characteristic dialogue bubbles projecting from the characters' mouths. S. once again found himself the center of controversy for depicting male frontal nudity.

During the 1960s and 1970s, S. illustrated many works by classic and celebrated writers, including Randall JARRELL's *The Animal Family* (1965), Isaac Bashevis SINGER's *"Zlateh the Goat" and Other Stories* (1966), George MACDONALD's *The Light Princess* (1969), the Brothers GRIMM *"The Juniper Tree" and Other Tales from Grimm* (1973). S. began to venture into a new medium when he adapted *The Sign on Rosie's Door* for television as *Really Rosie,* an animated film that he wrote and directed with music by Carole King in 1975. He eventually designed opera sets for a production of *Where the Wild Things Are* (1980) with music by Oliver Knussen, and also designed the set and costumes for productions of Mozart's *The Magic Flute* (1980) and Leon Janacek's opera *The Cunning Little Vixen* (1981). In 1981, the third book in his trilogy of the world of children's dream fantasy, *Outside over There,* was published. *Where the Wild Things Are* is exciting, *In the Night Kitchen* is joyous, but *Outside over There* is enchanting. This book contains some of S.'s most beautiful and mysterious illustrations, quite suited to its tone, which is darker than its predecessors. The illustrations are rich in symbolism, the most compelling symbol being the omnipresent moon, that most magical of celestial objects (which, not by

chance is found throughout the trilogy). Also more serious are its plot and theme, for it is the story of a baby's kidnapping by goblins while in the charge of her older sister, Ida, who sets out to recover the baby. *Outside over There* recalls S.'s own childhood when his older sister Natalie cared for him, and he has said that this book gave him the greatest inner peace. S. has always acknowledged that he writes for himself, happily children have enjoyed the products.

In the 1990s S. has largely turned to illustrating traditional works or the texts of other writers, including a newly discovered tale by Wilhelm Grimm, *Dear Mili* (1995), and Edward LEAR's *The Owl and the Pussycat* (1998). His most recent collaboration is *Swine Lake* (1999) by James MARSHALL, a humorous interpretation of the classic ballet featuring the "Boarshoi Ballet" dance company. S. is widely regarded as one of the great twentieth-century children's illustrators and authors.

AWARDS: ALA Caldecott Medal (1964) and INTERNATIONAL BOARD ON BOOKS FOR YOUNG PEOPLE Honor List (1966) for *Where the Wild Things Are.* Caldecott Medal Honor Book Award (1954) for *A Very Special House* (Ruth Krauss, author), (1959) for *What Do You Say, Dear? A Book of Manners for All Occasions* (Sesyle JOSLIN, author), (1960) for *The Moon Jumpers* (Janice May UDRY, author), (1962) for *Little Bear's Visit* (Else Homelund Minarik, author), (1963) for *Mr. Rabbit and the Lovely Present* (Charlotte ZOLOTOW, author), (1971) for *In the Night Kitchen,* and (1982) for *Outside over There* (1982). Hans Christian ANDERSEN Illustrator Medal (1970). University of Southern Mississippi Medallion of the DE GRUMMOND RESEARCH COLLECTION (1981). Laura Ingalls WILDER Award (1983). National Medal of Arts (1966) in recognition of S.'s contribution to the arts in America

FURTHER WORKS: *What Can You Do with a Shoe?* (Beatrice Schenk DE REGNIERS, author). 1955. *The Nutshell Library.* 1962. *The Bat-Poet* (story by Randall JARRELL). 1964. *Hector Protector and As I Went over the Water.* 1965. *The Juniper Tree and Other Tales from Grimm.* 1973. *The Nutcracker* (story by E. T. A. Hoffmann, tr. by Ralph Manheim). 1984. *The Miami Giant* (story by Arthur YORINKS). 1995

BIBLIOGRAPHY: Basbanes, N. "Call of the Wild:, *Civilization,* Dec. 1997/Jan. 1998. *The Oxford Companion to Children's Literature.* 1984. *Children's Literature Review.* vol. 17. Cott, Jonathan,

Pipers at the Gates of Dawn: The Wisdom of Children's Literature, HOPKINS, Lee Bennett, *Pauses: Autobiographical Reflections of 101 Creator of Children's Books,* 1995. Lanes, S., *The Art of Maurice Sendak.* 1980. Spitz, Ellen Handler, Inside Picture Books. 1999

DAVID L. RUSSELL

SEREDY, Kate

Author, illustrator, b. 10 November 1899, Budapest, Hungary; d. 7 March 1975, Middletown, New York

S.'s books are characterized by strong narrative and positive, sometimes sentimental, values. *The White Stag* (1937), an acclaimed novel based on Hungarian legend, is a rhythmic prose retelling of the epic story of Attila the Hun. S. attended the Academy of Arts in Budapest and received an art teacher's diploma. Prior to writing, she was a nurse in World War I. In 1922, she moved to the U.S. and worked designing greeting cards and book jackets. Eventually she illustrated textbooks and children's books. At the suggestion of her editor, S. wrote her first book based on her childhood memories growing up on a ranch in Hungary, *The Good Master* (1935).

AWARDS: ALA NEWBERRY MEDAL (1938) for *The White Stag.* ALA Newberry Medal Honor Book (1936) for *The Good Master* and (1940) for *The Singing Tree.* ALA CALDECOTT MEDAL Honor Book (1945) for *The Christmas Anna Angel* (Ruth SAWYER, author)

FURTHER WORKS: *Listening.* 1936. *A Tree for Peter,* 1940; *The Chestry Oak.* 1948; *Gypsy.* 1951; *Philomena.* 1955; *The Tenement Tree.* 1959; As illus: *Caddie Woodlawn.* (Carol Ryrie BRINK, author); *The Wonderful Year* (Nancy Barnes, 1946)

BIBLIOGRAPHY: *Children's Literature Review.* vol. 10, 1986

NANCY HORTON

SERIES BOOKS

Any novel that has several sequels could be called a series book. Many well-loved children's stories have had continuing volumes. Children who loved Lucy Maud MONTGOMERY's *Anne of Green Gables* (1908) could read about her as she attended school, taught school, married, and became a mother. Readers could follow Laura and her family in their pioneer travels in Laura Ingalls

WILDER's Little House series. Gary PAULSEN's survival story, *Hatchet,* has had several popular sequels. J. K. ROWLING's *Harry Potter and the Sorcerer's Stone* (1998), and the following three sequels at this writing (seven books are planned), have occupied the top spots on the *New York Times* Bestseller List. But the term *series books* is most often used to describe a book written to a formula. PUBLISHERS take a story that meets the emotional needs of a targeted audience and use the same plot structure and the same underlying values to create new events for succeeding volumes. The books are marketed in numbered series with the title of the series often more prominent on the cover than the title of the volume. Formula series books have not been recognized by literary critics as legitimate literature, but they have had an enduring popularity with children and have played a major role in the children's publishing market.

The person who most influenced the early series book publishing market in the United States was Edward STRATEMEYER. In 1906 he formed the Stratemeyer Syndicate, which created over 100 different series including the Rover Boys, Tom Swift, Honey Bunch, the Bobbsey Twins, The Hardy Boys, and Nancy Drew. Stratemeyer wrote detailed plot outlines and gave them to freelance writers to flesh out. He kept control over his writing projects, editing and rewriting as needed.

His final creation was the Nancy Drew series for which he completed the outlines for the first three volumes. After his death in 1930, his daughter, Harriet Adams, oversaw their publication. The books follow a formula with a mystery quickly introduced on the first pages usually centering on some unjust and puzzling situation. Later, Nancy discovers a second mystery, amazingly interconnected to the first. The capable and independent Nancy locates lost wills, restores fortunes to their rightful owners, and uncovers spy rings with courage, cleverness, persistence, and modesty in her unfailing successes. Nancy Drew, and the similar Hardy Boys, are the most enduring MYSTERY series. New volumes continue to be written in slightly revised formats and the older ones revised to eliminate racial and gender stereotypes and to maintain a contemporary setting.

The multiple-storyline series feature adventure in a gamelike format. Bantam's Choose Your Own ADVENTURE series began in 1979. After a few pages in which the adventure is introduced, "you" as the main character, are asked to make a choice that will determine the outcome of the story. Should "you" go the right or the left? Should you fight the enemy, flee, or do nothing? Page numbers are given for the choice taken. The main challenge is often to see how long "you" can stay alive. The settings are those of high adventure where the reader takes the role of a pirate, archaeologist, or galaxy explorer.

The friendship and FAMILY series are quieter stories and are often referred to as girls' series books. The Elsie Dinsmore series, first written by Martha Finley and published in 1867, features a beautiful, motherless child who is mistreated by her father's relatives who care for her. Her strong Christian faith and strength of character eventually wins the family's respect. An early Stratemeyer series, Dorothy Dale, first published in 1908, has Dorothy managing the town newspaper for her father during his illness, working in the temperance league, teaching values to her friends, and helping the disadvantaged in her community.

Some of the girls' series books focus on romance. The most enduring has been the Sweet Valley series, first published in 1983, featuring beautiful identical twin sisters. Elizabeth is serious and virtuous while Jessica experiments with the wilder side. The books were "created by" Francine PASCAL, written by various authors, packaged by Cloverdale Press, and published by Bantam. Packagers come up with the idea for a series, write a proposal for the publisher, hire the authors, and edit the manuscript. The publisher prints, promotes, and sells the books with some assistance from the packager in marketing strategy.

Scholastic's Baby-Sitters Club by Ann MARTIN, first published in 1986, had record-breaking sales during its early years. The top-selling Baby-Sitters Club volume sometimes outsold the adult bestsellers and dominated the *Publishers Weekly* list of bestsellers for middle readers with multiple volumes on a single list. There are over 100 volumes in the series, some written by Martin herself and others by authors who wrote from detailed plot outlines that Martin provided. The Baby-Sitters Club focuses on a group of young adolescent girls from a middle-class suburban New England community. They form a club to increase their opportunities for baby-sitting jobs. They also have sleep-overs and pizza parties, visit New York City, enter art contests, organize softball teams for younger girls, and have crushes on boys. The books end happily with projects completed, struggles overcome, and friendships maintained.

Scholastic had even more dramatic sales with R. L. STINE's mildly scary Goosebumps series and his Fear Street series for teens. At its peak in the mid-1990s, R. L. Stine wrote two books a month. One million copies of each title were printed and some titles sold out in two weeks. The Goosebumps series shows ordinary children encountering the strange and the supernatural: a girl discovers that she cannot pull off her Halloween mask and is losing her identity; a family comes across a quiet amusement park that turns out to be a horror land: a botanist father seems to be turning into an evil plant.

Sales figures for popular series books are especially dramatic when compared to sales for a typical children's best-seller which might be in the range of 100,000–150,000 copies. Volumes from Nancy Drew, the Hardy Boys, Sweet Valley, Baby-Sitters Club, and Goosebumps series appear on *Publishers Weekly* All-time Bestselling Paperback Children's Books with sales of over a million copies.

Children's enthusiasm for series books has not been shared by literary critics who find the awkward writing, stock characters, and unrealistic and formulaic plots distasteful. The Nancy Drew and Hardy Boys series had several decades of popularity before they were purchased by most public LIBRARIES. Book review sources generally ignore series books or review them in a special section. Other adults object to the message of the books. The romances have been criticized for depicting a patriarchal society where young women find their identity through beauty and romance. Romances have been criticized for being too sexually explicit. Some object to horror stories for children. The contemporary stories have been criticized for depiction of life as comfortable, white, and affluent. Children, however, keep on choosing the series books, and some teachers and parents welcome them as an entry into the world of reading.

BIBLIOGRAPHY: Billman, Carol, *The Secret of the Stratemeyer Syndicate: Nancy Drew, The Hardy Boys, and the Million Dollar Fiction Factory*, 1986; O'Keefe, Deborah, *Good Girl Messages: How Young Women Were Misled by Their Favorite Books*, 2000

ADELE GREENLEE

SERRAILLIER, Ian
Author, b. 24 September, 1912, London, England; d. 28 November 1994

S. attended boarding schools in England and spent vacations in Switzerland visiting his sick mother. His education instilled in him a passion for classic literature. S. worked as a teacher for twenty-five years, and worried about what children read, which energized his enthusiasm for classic literature. After leaving teaching, in 1948, S. and his wife, Anne, edited and rewrote more than 350 classic FAIRY TALES, folktales and legends, bringing them to life for young readers. Several of these titles include: *Heracles the Strong* (1970), *The Road to Canterbury* (1979), and *Beowulf the Warrior* (1954). He initially retold *Beowulf* in his first published book, *The Windmill Book of Ballads* (1962). His narrative poems, retelling ancient legends, retain the epic majesty of the traditional literature. *The Tale of Three Landlubbers* (1970) is a humorous poem illustrated by Raymond BRIGGS.

S.'s nonfiction YOUNG ADULT BOOK *The Silver Sword* (1956)—also known as *Escape from Warsaw* (1963)—realistically portrays a group of Polish children who travel across Europe during World War II, searching for their parents. While their sufferings are dramatically recounted, S. leavens the story with flashes of HUMOR and reminders of their courage. *The Silver Sword* has been translated into twelve different languages. S. spent five years carefully researching *The Silver Sword*, the most well-known of his books.

FURTHER WORKS: *They Raced for Treasure*. 1946. *There's No Escape*. 1950. *The Cave of Death*. 1965. *The Windmill Book of Ballads*. 1962. *The Challenge of the Green Knight*. 1967.

BIBLIOGRAPHY: Carpenter, H. and M. Prichard, eds. *The Oxford Companion to Children's Litera-* *ture*. 1984. *Something about the Author*. vol. 74. 1993

DENISE P. BEASLEY

SERVICE, Robert W.
Author, poet, b. 16 January 1874, Lancashire, England; d. 11 September 1958; Brittany, France

S. remembered always having a fondness for POETRY. He began experimenting with writing and poetry in 1889 while apprenticing in a bank. S. emigrated to Canada in 1895, just about the time of the Yukon gold rush, which greatly impacted his writing. *Songs of a Sourdough* was published in 1907, commemorating the gold rush. It contained the ballad poems "The Shooting of Dan McGrew" and "The Cremation of Sam McGee" about events in the Yukon territory and for which S. is best remembered. It was published in the U.S. as *The Spell of the Yukon and Other Verses (1915)*. The book became a movie, as did many of S.'s pieces including *The Shooting of Dan McGrew* and *Poisoned Paradise*.

FURTHER WORKS: *Ballad of a Cheechako*. 1909. *Rhymes of a Rolling Stone*. 1912. *Rhymes of a Red Cross Man*. 1916. *The Trail of '98*. 1911. *Cremation of Sam McGee* (Ted HARRISON, illus.). 1987 ed. *The Poisoned Paradise; The Shooting of Dan McGrew* (Ted Harrison, illus.). 1988 ed. *Rhymes of a Roughneck; The Cremation of Sam McGee*. Issued in a single volume, Ted Harrison, illus. 1986.

BIBLIOGRAPHY: *Something about the Author*, vol. 20, 1980; Kunitz, S., ed., *Twentieth Century Authors*, 1955

JODI PILGRIM

SETON, Ernest Thompson
Author, b. 14 August 1860, Durham, England; d. 23 October 1946, Santa Fe, New Mexico

Artist, author/illustrator, and naturalist, S. grew up in Canada, but studied art in his native England and in Paris. Popularity of the Impressionists limited acceptance of his realistic wildlife drawings in Europe, and failing eyesight made painting difficult, so he returned to North America and turned to writing, publishing more than twenty self-illustrated books he called "animal biography." While his wild creatures were more realistically portrayed than those of earlier writers whose animals behaved like humans, S. gave them powers of thought and speech that make them seem quaintly romanticized today. Nevertheless, S. is credited with establishing the true-ANIMAL STORY genre. His earliest writings appeared in *St. Nicholas* magazine; his full-length books were about animals, nature, and woodcraft. S. is also remembered as the founder of the Woodcraft Indians, an organization that lead to the founding of the Boy Scouts of America in 1910.

AWARDS: 1909 Camp Fire Gold Medal for *Life Histories of Northern Animals: An Account of the Mammals of Manitoba;* 1928 Daniel Girard Elliot Gold Medal for *Game Animals and the Lives They Live*

FURTHER WORKS: *Wild Animals I Have Known,* 1898. *Johnny Lobo and Other Stories,* 1935. Adapted as a film by Walt DISNEY in 1962

BIBLIOGRAPHY: *Contemporary Authors.* 1983. Silvey, Anita, ed. *Children's Books and Their Creators.* 1995. *Something about the Author,* vol. 20. 1980

DIANE L. CHAPMAN

SEUSS, Dr. (Theodore Seuss Geisel)

Author, b. 2 March 1904, Springfield, Massachusetts; d. 21 September 1991, La Jolla, California

Theodore Seuss Geisel, known to generations as Dr. S. is a legend among children. Since 1937 "Dr. S." created literature for children that encourages reading as well as imagination. S. won the hearts of children by making them laugh. In 1984, he won the Pulitzer Prize "for his contribution over nearly half a century to the education and enjoyment of America's children and their parents." But the most important praise comes from the children who read and enjoy his books. An eight-year-old wrote: "Dear Dr. S., you sure thunk up a lot of funny books. You sure thunk up a million funny animals. . . . Who thunk you up Dr. S.?"

S. recalled that his own love for reading and doodling began almost simultaneously in his life at a very young age. S. never had formal art training. He sat for one art lesson in high school but never took another because he felt that it did not fit his style. S. was influenced by his father, Big Ted, who taught S. that one must never give up, and must always leave his mark on the world.

S. attended Dartmouth College, graduating in 1925. There he contributed to the college HUMOR

magazine, writing essays and comics. In 1925, S. went to Oxford to receive his doctorate in literature with the goal of becoming a college professor. Instead, he dropped out to tour Europe.

S.'s writing career took many turns before he encountered the world of children's literature. He worked as a commercial cartoonist, writer of military films, political cartoonist, foreign correspondent, and documentary writer. His first book for children was written after traveling on an ocean liner in 1937. S. could not get the sound of the waves out of his mind, so instead of ignoring the rhythm he wrote his first children's book, the strongly cadenced *And to Think That I Saw It on Mulberry Street* (1937). Although this book did not bring him the fame he enjoys today, it was the beginning of a philosophy that would change the way that people think of children's literature. S. not only introduced a new view of children and their books; he made reading fun for them.

In the late 1950s a plethora of publicity dealt with problems of literacy among American children. In 1954 an article in *Life* magazine by John Hersey complained that literacy problems stemmed from the sorry state of children's primers, such as the *Dick and Jane* readers. S. was encouraged to write a book that would inspire children to read. Thus came *The Cat in the Hat* (1957), the start of S.'s books for beginning readers and a new philosophy of how to encourage children to read.

S. demonstrated a high regard for children that he carried out in the philosophy for Beginner Books, a division of Random House. S. wrote with the assumption that a child can understand anything that is read to him if the writer states the story simply and clearly. S. helped teachers and children to view learning to read as a pleasurable event.

S.'s books have several factors that help a child to love reading. The words and stories are exciting, encouraging a child to read on. Make-believe is played in all cultures, S. puts it into his books. Words spoken by the characters in S.'s books are in rhyme. This makes the books fun. Children thrive on fun, making it easier to teach something when children enjoy what they are doing. The ILLUSTRATIONS in S.'s books are colorful and creative, and so are the ideas. Children express joy when reading one of his books.

S.'s books are predictable—another way he helps children to love words. This gives children the opportunity to use the context and illustrations to predict what the text says. In many of S.'s books not only does he begin with a familiar word; but he uses rhythm and rhyme to help children predict words. S. uses his illustrations to engage the reader and to give clues about the text. Pictures help children learn to read. When children get stuck on a word they are able to look at the picture for a clue.

Beyond the literary and fanciful messages of his books, S. often gives children a view of serious concerns. In *The Sneetches and Other Stories* (1961) and *The Lorax* (1971) children learn about equality and conservation. In the *Butter Battle Book* (1984) and *Yertle the Turtle* (1958) they see issues about fascism and the cold war. In 2000, *How the Grinch Stole Christmas* (1957) was made into a hit motion picture. This further attests to Dr. S.'s ongoing influence, as does the 2000 Broadway production *Seussical*. S. gave to the world books with lovable characters, predictable text, imaginative illustrations, and themes that help generations of children learn to read and learn to love reading.

AWARDS: Academy Award (1946) for "Hitler Lives," (1947) for "Design for Death," and (1951) for "Gerald McBoing-Boing." ALA CALDECOTT MEDAL Honor Book (1948) for *McElligot's Pool*, (1950) for *Bartholomew and the Oobleck*, and (1951) for *If I Ran the Zoo*. Lewis CARROLL Shelf Award (1958) for *Horton Hatches the Egg*, and (1961) for *And to Think That I Saw It on Mulberry Street*. Peabody Award (1971) for animated cartoons "How the Grinch Stole Christmas" and "Horton Hears a Who." Critics Award from International Animated Cartoon Festival and Silver Medal from International Film and Television Festival of New York (1972) for "The Lorax." Emmy Award (1977) for "Halloween is Grinch Night." AMERICAN LIBRARY ASSOCIATION Laura Ingalls WILDER Award (1980). "Dr. S. Week" proclaimed by State Governors, March 2–7, 1981. Regina Medal, Catholic Library Association (1982) National Association of Elementary School Principals special award, (1982) for distinguished service to children. Pulitzer Prize (1984) for his "special contribution to over nearly half a century to the education and enjoyment of America's children and their parents." PEN Los Angeles Center Award for Children's Literature (1985) for *The Butter Battle Book*

FURTHER WORKS: *The 500 Hats of Bartholomew Cubbins*. 1938. *The Seven Lady Godivas*. 1939. *The King Stilts*. 1939. *Horton Hatches the Egg*. 1940. *Thudwick, the Big Hearted Moose*. 1949. *McElligot's Pool*. 1947. *Bartholomew and the Oobleck*. 1949. *If I Ran the Zoo*. 1950. *Scrambled Eggs Super!* 1953. *Horton Hears a Who!* 1954. *On beyond Zebra*. 1955. *Signs of Civilization*. 1956. *If I Ran the Circus*. 1956. *The Cat in the Hat Comes Back!* 1958. *Yertle the Turtle and Other Stories*. 1958. *Happy Birthday to You!* 1959. *One Fish, Two Fish, Red Fish, Blue Fish*. 1960. *Green Eggs and Ham*. 1960. *The Sneetches and Other Stories*. 1961. *Dr. S. Sleep Book*. 1962. *Hop on Pop*. 1963. *Dr. S.s' ABC*. 1963. *The Cat in the Hat Dictionary*. (With Philip EASTMAN). 1964. *Fox in Sox*. 1965. *I Had Trouble in Getting to Solla Sollew*. 1965. *The Cat in the Hat Songbook*. 1967. *Dr. S.s' Lost World Revisited: A Forward Looking Backward Glance*. 1967. *The Foot Book*. 1968. *I Can Lick 30 Tigers Today and Other Stories*. 1969. *I Can Draw It Myself*. 1970. *Mr. Brown Can Moo! Can You?* 1970. *The Lorax*. 1971. *Marvin K. Mooney, Will You Please Go Now?* 1972. *Did I Ever Tell You How Lucky You Are?* 1973. *The Shape of Me and Other Stuff*. 1973. *There's a Wocket in My Pocket!* 1974. *Oh, the Thinks You Can Think!* 1975. *The Cat's Quizzer*. 1975. *I Can Read with My Eyes Shut!* 1978. *The Dr. Seuss Storybook*. 1979. *Hunches in Bunches*. 1982. *You're Only Old Once*. 1986. *The Tough Coughs as He Ploughs the Dough: Early Writings and Cartoons by Dr. S.* (Edited by R. Marschall). 1986. *Oh, The Places You'll Go!* 1990. *Six by S.: A Treasury of Dr. S. Classics*. 1991. Under the Pseudonym Theo. LESIEG: *Ten Apples up on Top!* 1961. *I Wish That I Had Duck Feet*. 1965. *Come over to My House*. 1966. *The Eye Book*. 1968. *I Can Write—By Me, Myself*. 1971. *In a People House*. 1972. *The Many Mice of Mr. Brice*. 1973. *Wacky Wednesday*. 1974. *Would You Rather Be a Bullfrog?* 1975. *Hooper Humperdink. . . ? Not Him!* 1976. *Please Try and Remember the First of Octember!* 1977. *Maybe You Should Fly a Jet! You Should Be a Vet*. 1980. *The Tooth Book*. 1981. Other Books: *Boners*. 1931. *More Boners*. 1931. *My Book about Me, by Me Myself: I Wrote It! I Drew It!* 1969. *Great Day for Up!* 1974. *Dr. S. from Then to Now*. 1987. *I Am Not Going to Get up Today*. 1987. *Hooray for Diffendoofer Day*. 1998. *Oh, the Places You'll Go*. 1999

BIBLIOGRAPHY: Cott, Jonathan. *Pipers at the Gates of Dawn: The Wisdom of Children's Literature*, 1983; Hoffman, M. and E. Samuels. *Authors and Illustrators of Children's Books*. 1972; HOPKINS, Lee Bennett. *Pauses: Autobiographical Reflections of 101 Creators of Children's Books*, 1995; Kahn, E.J. "Profiles: Children's Friend." *The New Yorker*. December 17, 1960. MacDonald, R. K., *Dr. S.* 1988: Pace, E. "Dr. S., Modern MOTHER GOOSE, Dies at 87." *New York Times.* September 26, 1991. *Contemporary Authors New Revision Series,* vol. 32, 1990

NANCE S. WILSON

SEWALL, Marcia

Author, illustrator, b. 5 November 1935, Providence, Rhode Island

S. was an art major at Brown University's Pembroke College and attended the Rhode Island School of Design. Before becoming an illustrator, she worked as a staff artist at the Children's Museum in Boston and taught high school art. The more than thirty books she has illustrated for other authors include Paul FLEISCHMAN's *The Birthday Tree* (1979) and *Finzel the Farsighted* (1983), John Reynolds GARDINER's *The Stone Fox* (1980), Nancy WILLARD's *The Marzipan Moon* (1981), as well as books by Clyde Robert BULLA and eight books for Richard KENNEDY. S. has also written or adapted and illustrated eight books of her own. Her books have been designated as Outstanding Books by *The New York Times,* selected as ALA notable books and for Parent's Choice AWARDS for ILLUSTRATIONS. *The Pilgrims of Plimoth,* published in 1986, won the *Boston Globe–Horn Book* award for nonfiction in 1987.

AWARDS: For illustrations: *New York Times* Outstanding Book (1976) for *Come Again in the Spring* (1978), for *The Nutcrackers and the Sugar Tongs* (1980), for *The Stone Fox* (1981), for *The Story of Old Mrs. Brubeck and How She Looked for Trouble and How She Found Him and The Marzipan Moon.* ALA Notable Book (1978) for *Little Things,* (1981) for *The Song of the Horse.* Parent's Choice Award (1980) for *Crazy in Love*

FURTHER WORKS: *Animal Song,* 1988; *People of the Breaking Day,* 1990

BIBLIOGRAPHY: *Something about the Author,* vol. 68, 1992

JANET HILBUN

SEWELL, Anna

Author, b. 30 March 1820, Great Yarmouth, Norfolk, England; d. 25 April 1878, Old Catton near Norwich, England

Born into a strict Quaker home, S. was educated at home. She assisted with the household duties

and acted as the family housekeeper while her mother wrote children's books. At fourteen she was injured in a fall that left her crippled for life. Although unable to walk far, she could drive her parents' carriage; in her thirties and forties she established a Working Man's Evening Institute to teach local miners and laborers.

Her only book, *Black Beauty: An Autobiography of a Horse,* was published in 1877, a year before she died. *Black Beauty* was adapted by The Society for the Prevention of Cruelty to Animals and accomplished the purpose for which the book was written, to improve conditions for horses. S. wrote *Black Beauty* to "induce kindness, sympathy and an understanding treatment of horses." The book also highlights the cruel treatment of working-class people at the time through its dramatic presentation of widespread social problems such as poverty and alcoholism.

BIBLIOGRAPHY: *Something about the Author,* vol. 23. 1981; Silvey, Anita, ed. *Children's Books and Their Creator.* 1995. *Fiction, FOLKLORE, FANTASY and POETRY for Children, 1876–1985.* 1986

IRVYN GILBERTSON

SEWELL, Helen M.

Author, illustrator, b. 1896, Mare Island Navy Yard, California; d. 24 February 1957, New York City

S. was born in California and soon afterwards her family moved to Guam where she spent her childhood. S. was a prominent children's book illustrator during the Golden Age of ILLUSTRATION. She wrote and illustrated her own PICTURE BOOK *Blue Barns* (1933), which depicted beautiful farm animals. During this age, S. also did the illustrations for other authors' works including Carol Ryrie BRINK's *Baby Island* (1937) and Thomas Bulfinch's *Book of Myths* (1942). S. was known for her realistic style. Using strong stylized drawings, she was the original illustrator of the first three Laura Ingalls WILDER Little House books that went out of print in 1953. S. collaborated with Mildred Boyle on the others. Alice DALGLIESH's *The Thanksgiving Story* (1954) was illustrated by S., and was named an ALA CALDECOTT MEDAL Honor Book for its beautiful full color pictures.

FURTHER WORKS: As illus: *Ten Saints.* (E. FARJEON). 1936. *The Bears on Hemlock Mountain.*

(A. Dalgliesh). 1952. As author and illus: *A Head for Happy.* 1931. *Three Tall Tales.* 1947

BIBLIOGRAPHY: Irby, LeeAnne and Phil Greetham. *Helen Sewell.* 1996. MEIGS, C., A. T. Eaton, E. NESBITT, and R. H. Viguers. *A Critical History of Children's Literature,* rev. ed. 1969. Laura Ingalls Wilder, Frontier Girl. http://webpages.marshall.edu/~irby1/laura/

DENISE P. BEASLEY

SHANNON, David

Author, illustrator, b. 5 October 1959, Spokane, Washington

Following his education at Art Center College of Design, S. began his career by illustrating stories by Isaac ASIMOV. He caught the attention of readers with the rich images and warm colors that characterized the art in many books of FOLKLORE. Beginning with Julius LESTER's *"How Many Spots Does a Leopard Have?" and Other Tales* (1989), S. also created the ILLUSTRATIONS for Rafe MARTIN's retelling of *The Rough Face Girl* (1992), an Algonquin Cinderella story, and *The Boy Who Lived with the Seals* (1993), a Chinook legend about a boy who leaves his parents to find a home among the seals. In each book, S.'s art captures the tone of the story as well as the characterization and conflict. His research is reflected in the authenticity of people and landscapes. In *Encounter* (Jane YOLEN, 1992), S. captures the dramatic intent of this account of Columbus's landing on San Salvador. S. also illustrated other folklore retellings by Audrey WOOD in *The Bunyan's* (1996) and Robert D. SAN SOUCI in *Nicholas Pipe* (1997) with bold colors and strong figures. He collaborated with his brother Mark on *Gawain and the Green Knight* (1994).

S., also author and illustrator of nonsense PICTURE BOOKS, uses colors and details to create books that invite multiple readings. In *A Bad Case of Stripes* (1998), S. deals with the topic of being oneself. *The Amazing Christmas Extravaganza* (1995) stresses family love. *How Georgie Radbourn Saved Baseball* (1994), a picture book for older readers encourages discussion among middle-grade students. S. received accolades for his CALDECOTT MEDAL Honor Book, *No David!* (1999), that tells about the frustrating life of a young child trying to explore his world. *No David!* filled with childlike illustrations show

David as a wooden doll with oddly proportioned body parts. David's antics are amusing as he runs down the street, floods the bathroom, and writes on the wall. *No David!* allows readers to feel sorry for David while laughing at his actions. A sequel, *David Goes to School* (1999), continues David's further misguided adventures when he starts school and tries to interpret his teacher's instructions about school behavior.

S.'s work represents diversity in visually representing the elements of story as well as excellence in research resulting in illustrations that authentically help tell the story. His use of color and dramatic effects both in character and setting help draw readers of all ages into the story.

AWARDS: *New York Times* Best Illustrated Children's Book (1994) for *How Georgie Radbourn Saved Baseball.* American Bookseller Pick of the Lists (1995) for *The Amazing Christmas Extravaganza.* AMERICAN LIBRARY ASSOCIATION Notable Book (1989) for *How Many Spots Does a Leopard Have?* (Julius Lester, reteller). ALA Caldecott Medal Honor Book (1999) for *No, David!*

FURTHER WORKS: Illus.: *The Ballad of the Pirate Queens* (Yolen). 1995; *Sacred Places* (Yolen). 1996; *The Acrobat and the Angel* 1999; *Encounter* 1992

BIBLIOGRAPHY: Cianciolo, Patricia. *Picture Books for Children.* 4th ed. 1997; Drennan, M. "Back to School with David Shannon;" "Book Page First Person"; Publishers Notes; *Something about the Author,* vol. 107, 1999

JANELLE B. MATHIS AND NANCE S. WILSON

SHANNON, George

Author, b. 14 February 1952, Caldwell, Kansas

S.'s career in professional STORYTELLING has influenced his writing for children and young adults. Several of his books have developed from stories he has performed in public. S. is known for his series of popular retellings of folktales— *Stories to Solve* (1985). Using characters and customs from all over the world, S. creates short stories that require the reader or listener to use logic in solving the puzzles. In addition to his fiction works, he has written several nonfiction titles and a young adult novel. Relationships between family members are vital to many of S.'s stories. *Knock at the Door* (1992) is a collection of thirty-five folktales from around the world in which S. identifies additional variations for most of the tales.

FURTHER WORKS: *The Piney Woods Peddler,* 1987 (Nancy TAFURI, illus.); *Unlived Affections.* 1989. (Friends of American Writers Award). *Lizard's Song* 1992; *The Gang and Mrs. Higgins; Stories to Solve: Folktales from around the World.* 1985; *More Stories to Solve: Fifteen Folktales from around the World.* 1991; *Still More Stories to Solve: Fourteen Folktales from around the World.* 1985; *Dance Away* 1991; *Climbing Kansas Mountains* 1996; *April Showers.* 1995

BIBLIOGRAPHY: *Something about the Author,* vol. 96, 1998

JODI PILGRIM

SHANNON, Monica
Author, b. Belleville, Ontario, Canada; d. 13 August 1965

S. came to the U.S. with her family when she was about six months old and spent her childhood on a thoroughbred stock ranch in the Bitter Root Valley of the Rocky Mountains. Here she developed an appreciation for nature and respect for people as she daily observed the beauty of the Rocky Mountains, played with a bear cub, and learned about life on the ranch. Her children's books reflect these experiences. *Dobry* (1934), a story of Bulgarian peasant life told with reverence for the land and the wrenching upheavals when Dobry wishes to leave the farm and become an artist was awarded the ALA NEWBERRY MEDAL in 1935. Other books also share her insights into the natural world; in particular, *California FAIRY TALES* (1946) shows S.'s delight in the colors and terrain of California through her use of poetic, rhythmic language. After spending nine years as a librarian, S. devoted her life to writing and adapting stories for children.

FURTHER WORKS: *Eyes for the Dark,* 1928; *Ungar,* 1975; *Goose Grass Rhymes,* 1930; *Tawnymore,* 1931

BIBLIOGRAPHY: *Something about the Author,* vol. 28, 1982; *Twentieth-Century Children's Writers,* 1995

JANELLE B. MATHIS

SHARMAT, Marjorie Weinman
Author, b. 12 November, 1928, Portland, Maine

S. is the author of PICTURE BOOKS, beginner reader books, and romance novels for young adults. Her lifelong relentless compulsion to write has resulted in the production of about 140 books for young people. As an introverted child she spent much of her time writing diaries, poems, newspapers, and stories, which her parents encouraged her to submit for publication. Her earliest effort, at age eight, was a newspaper, *The Snoopers' Gazette,* for which she and a friend spied on adults to generate articles for their detective agency. MYSTERY AND DETECTIVE STORIES have been one of S.'s favorite genres ever since. Her first jobs were in marketing and library management, during which time she had her first works published, a few adult short stories and some nonfiction. After the birth of her two sons, she became interested in children's books, and since 1967, when her first book, *Rex,* was published, she has written only for children, often drawing on her sons' experiences. The continued popularity of her stories for young readers can be largely attributed to her endearing characters. Whether in the guise of animals or depicted as cartoonlike children, her characters grapple with the common anxieties of childhood, such as moving to a new house, and making and losing friends. Young readers can identify with Mitchell, the dragon, when he is parted from his best friend in *Mitchell Is Moving* (1996), and can laugh at the absurd stereotypes a young boy from New York harbors about his imminent new life "out west" in *Gila Monsters Meet You at the Airport* (1980). Based on her own family's parallel move and the perceptions of real children, stories like this resonate for young readers because of the authentic child concerns undergirding the lighthearted fun.

S.'s prolific, ongoing production of SERIES BOOKS for beginning readers is perhaps her greatest contribution. She is best known for her mystery series about the pancake munching boy detective Nate the Great. In recent years S. has collaborated on this popular series with family members, son, Craig, and sister, Rosalind, to help extend and perpetuate a cycle that now has young children sharing the same books that delighted their parents some twenty years ago. S. has also coauthored books with her husband, Mitchell (e.g., *The Day I Was Born,* 1980; *The Green Toenails Gang,* 1991; the Sly Spy series) and her son, Andrew (Kids on the Bus series). After initially writing only for young readers, S. has also been writing for young adults since 1982 (e.g., *How to Meet a Gorgeous Guy*; Sorority Sisters series). Some of S.'s books have been made into television films, such as *I'm Not Oscar's Friend Any More* (1984), *Gila Monsters Meet You at the Airport* (1980), Nate the Great series, (1986) and stage productions such as *The Adventures of Nate the Great* (1996).

AWARDS: Notable Children's Trade Book in the Field of Social Studies (1976) for *Edgemont*

FURTHER WORKS: *Maggie Marmelstein for President*, 1971; *Genghis Khan: A Dog Star Is Born*; 1994

REFERENCES: *Fifth Book of Junior Authors and Illustrators*. 1983. *Something about the Author*, vol. 33, 1983, and vol. 74, 1993

BARBARA TOBIN

SHARP, Margery

Author, dramatist, b. 25 January 1905 on the island of Maka; d. 14 March 1991, London, England

S. wrote many books, plays, and short stories for children and adults during her life, but she is best remembered by young readers for her Miss Bianca series featuring an animal organization, the Mouse Prisoner Aid Society, that helps people in distress. Miss Bianca, a petite but intrepid white mouse with her constant companion, Bernard, grows from reluctant heroine to indefatigable president of the MPA Society. Two books from the series of nine fantasies, *The Rescuers* (1959) and *Miss Bianca* (1962), were adapted by Walt DISNEY Productions to produce the animated film, *The Rescuers* (1977). A later film, *The Rescuers down Under* (1991) also featured characters inspired by the series. In addition to her SERIES BOOKS, S. wrote other juvenile fiction. Her book, *Something Light* (1960), was named to the *Horn Book* honor list.

FURTHER WORKS: *Miss Bianca in the Salt Mines*, 1966. *Miss Bianca in the Orient*, 1970. *Melisande*, 1960. *Lost at the Fair*, 1965. *The Children Next Door*, 1974. *The Magical Cockatoo*, 1974

BIBLIOGRAPHY: *Major Authors and Illustrators for Children and Young Adults: A Selection of Sketches from Something about the Author*, vol. 5. 1993. *Something about the author*, vol. 68. 1992

MARY ARIAIL BROUGHTON

SHELLEY, Mary Wollstonecraft *née* Godwin

Author, b. 30 August 1797, London, England; d. 1 February 1851, London, England

Since her mother died ten days after she was born, S. was reared by her father, a philosopher. He provided S. with an education that was typically only available for boys at that time. While she was still quite young, S. eloped and in 1816 married the poet Percy Bysshe Shelley. Living in Switzerland, the S.'s were neighbors of Lord George Gordon Byron, who encouraged them to tell ghost stories. After many of these stories and discussions with the men, S. had the basis for her most famous piece of literature, *Frankenstein* (1831). She wrote the suspenseful and thrilling masterpiece when she was only eighteen years old. The novel is known for its ability to force the reader to ask the question: how far should science go in altering the way human beings lead their life on earth? Although she would write several more pieces of literature, none was as well received as *Frankenstein*.

FURTHER WORKS: *The Last Man*, 1826

BIBLIOGRAPHY: Kiely, Robert. *The Romantic Novel in England*, 1972

DENISE P. BEASLEY

SHEPARD, Ernest Howard

Author, illustrator, b. 10 December 1879, St. John's Wood, London, England; d. 24 March 1976, Lodsworth, England

A prolific illustrator of fiction and nonfiction for children and adults, S. is best known for his detailed pen-and-ink drawings for volumes of children's stories and poems written by a variety of authors. Yet despite the versatility of his creative endeavors, S. is remembered primarily in connection with author A. A. MILNE, most notably for illustrating the timeless *Winnie-the-Pooh*, published in 1926. Their successful collaboration also included *When We Were Very Young* (1924) and *Now We Are Six* (1927), both collections of verse, and the sequel to *Winnie-the-Pooh* entitled *The House at Pooh Corner* (1928).

    Born into an artistic family, S. lived for part of his childhood in an artists' colony, where he moved with his father and siblings after the death of his mother. He attended preparatory school and then St. Paul's, continuing his studies at Heatherley's Art School. In July 1897, he entered the Royal Academy, where he came under the influence of noted artists Frank Dicksee and Edwain A. "Need" Abbey.

S. first established himself as a book illustrator with the Partridge Publishing house in London in the early part of the twentieth century, providing drawings for literary works by authors such as Thomas Hughes, Harold Avery, Charles DICKENS, and Evelyn Everett Green. During this same time, he initiated what would develop into a long-standing association with *Punch,* eventually becoming a principal cartoonist and member of the editorial board. In 1924, S. was invited by author and editor E. V. Lucas to illustrate the first of his collaborations with Milne, and the success of the relationship produced, in addition to the major works, numerous supplemental volumes, such as *Fourteen Songs from "When We Were Very Young"* (1925), *Songs from "Now We Are Six"* (1927), *The Christopher Robin Story Book* (1929), *The Very Young Calendar* (1929), *Tales of Pooh* (1930), *The Christopher Robin Birthday Book* (1930), and *The Hums of Pooh* (1937). Following Milne's death in 1956, the publishing industry continued to capitalize on the popularity of the Pooh phenomenon with additional works illustrated by S.: *The World of Pooh* (1957), *The World of Christopher Robin* (1958), *The Pooh Song Book* (1961), *Pooh's Birthday Book* (1963), *The Pooh Story Book* (1965), *The Christopher Robin Verse Book* (1967), *Pooh's Pot O'Honey* (1968), and *Pooh's Alphabet Book* (1975), among others.

Although he is most often associated with Milne, S. created memorable ILLUSTRATIONS for other children's authors, ranging from Hans Christian ANDERSEN to Richard Jeffries. In particular, S. received high praise for his editions of Kenneth GRAHAME's *The Wind in the Willows* (1931), Frances Hodgson BURNETT's *The Secret Garden* (1956), and Andersen's *FAIRY TALES* (1961), translated by L. W. Kingsland. During his lifetime, S. also published two volumes of his memoirs, *Drawn from Memory* (1957), a detailed account of early childhood, and *Drawn from Life* (1961), in which S. recounts the period from the

death of his mother to his first marriage. For readers, however, the legacy left by S. is found in the world of FANTASY brought to life in the characterization of Christopher Robin and his friends.

FURTHER WORKS: Illus. by S.: *Jeremy.* 1919. Henry Walpole. *Playtime and Company.* 1925. E. V. Lucas. *The Holly-Tree and Other Christmas Stories.* 1926. Charles Dickens. *Fun and Fantasy: Punch Anthology.* 1927. *The Little One's Log.* 1927. Eva Violet Isaacs Erleigh. *Let's Pretend.* 1927. Georgette Agnew. *The Golden Age.* 1928. Kenneth Grahame. *Christmas Poems.* 1931. John Drinkwater. *The Cricket in the Cage.* 1933. Patrick Chalmers. *The Goblin Market.* 1933. Laurence Housman. *Perfume Provence.* 1935. Winifred Fortescue. *Cheddar Gorge.* 1937. John Collings Squire. *The Islanders.* 1950. Roland Pertwee. *Enter David Garrick.* 1951. Anna B. Stewart. *The Silver Curlew.* 1953. Eleanor FARJEON. *Susan, Bill, and the Wolf-Dog.* 1954. Malcolm Saville. *The Brownies and Other Stories.* 1954. Juliana EWING. *The Cuckoo Clock.* 1954. Mary Louisa MOLESWORTH. *Frogmorton.* 1955. Susan Colling. *The Crystal Mountain.* 1956. B. C. Rugh. *Royal Reflections.* 1956. George MACDONALD. *At the Back of the North Wind.* 1956 edition. *Pooh: His Art Gallery: Anthology of Drawings.* 1962. *The Flattered Flying Fish.* 1962. E. V. Rieu. *Ben and Brock.* 1965. *Betsy and Joe.* 1966. *The Pooh Craftbook.* 1976. Carol S. Friedrichsen. *Modern Fairy Tales.* 1955. (Roger Lancelyn GREEN ed.)

BIBLIOGRAPHY: Knox, R., ed., *The Work of E. H. Shepard,* 1979; *Something about the Author,* vol. 32, 1983, and vol. 105, 1999

STEVEN R. SERAFIN

SHIMIN, Symeon

Illustrator, author, b. 1 November 1902, Astrakhan, Russia

Coming to the United States as an infant, S. began drawing as a youth and was apprenticed to a commercial artist. Becoming a naturalized citizen in 1927, he then spent time in France and Spain studying the old masters and other artists. S. uses watercolor and acrylics as he creates book illustrations from live models. Dividing his time between book ILLUSTRATION and painting, S. has illustrated numerous books by significant children's writers, such as Virginia HAMILTON, *Zeely* (1967) and *M. C. Higgins, the Great* (1989); Aline Glasgow, *Pair of Shoes* (1970); Bill MARTIN, Jr., *I Am Freedom's Child* (1970); Isaac Bashevis SINGER, *Joseph and Koza* (1970); Isaac ASIMOV, *Best New Thing* (1971); and Byrd BAYLOR, *Coyote Cry* (1972). Additionally, he has written as well as illustrated *I Wish There Were Two of Me* (1976) and *A Special Birthday* (1976).

FURTHER WORKS: Illus.: *Young Kangaroo,* Margaret Wise BROWN, 1953; *Onion John,* Joseph KRUMGOLD, 1959; *One Small Blue Bead,* Schweitzer, 1965; *All Kinds of Babies,* SELSAM, 1967; *Lighthouse Island,* COATSWORTH, 1968; *Sing, Little Mouse,* Aileen FISHER, 1969; *Grandpa and Me,* Patricia L. GAUCH, 1969; *Dance in a Desert,* L'ENGLE, 1969; *Petey,* Tobias, 1978; *Sam,* Ann Herbert SCOTT, 1967; reissued 1996

BIBLIOGRAPHY: HOPKINS, Lee B. *Books Are by People,* 1969; Hopkins, Lee Bennett, *Pauses: Autobiographical Reflections of 101 Creators of Children's Books,* 1995

JANELLE B. MATHIS

SHULEVITZ, Uri
Author, illustrator, b. 27 February 1935, Warsaw, Poland

An ALA CALDECOTT MEDAL winner, S. writes and illustrates folktales and fantasies set in diverse lands encompassing the earth. He grew up in Poland, France, and Israel. While in Tel Aviv, he studied at the Art Institute and Teacher's Institute. He moved to New York City as an adult and studied at the Brooklyn Museum Art School. He has directed workshops in writing and illustrating children's books and wrote *Writing with Pictures: How to Write and Illustrate Children's Books* (1985). This explicit 271-page guide is complete with ILLUSTRATIONS (his own and other well-known illustrators'), appendices, and a comprehensive index. S. details step-by-step information to take the aspiring author-illustrator from the initial stages of thought collection and storyboards to a publisher search, and the finishing touches of reproduction preparation. S. published his first book, *The Moon in My Room* (1963) under the guidance of editor Susan Hirschman who encouraged him to visualize the language of stories he wanted to share. S.'s material is the culmination of his learning and experiences in literature and art. For example, *Dawn* (1974) was inspired by a brief poem by Liu Chung-yuan. S. rewrote the poem, which tells of an elderly man and his grandson on the lake before dawn. With

his soft colors, S. creates a pastoral setting with paintings that accurately depict the silent darkness of night as it is transformed into the wakening of the early day's brightness. Also, *One Monday Morning* (1967) is based on a French song with S.'s playful interpretation of a deck of cards as the characters. S.'s books encourage young readers to integrate the pictures and text for full understanding and invites them to add their own imagination. S.'s most recent Caldecott Medal Honor Book, *Snow* (1998), depicts an East European village scene, reminiscent of many of S.'s illustrations but done in soft muted grays and whites of a snowy day rather than the usual glowing colors of so many of his other PICTURE BOOKS with similar settings.

AWARDS: AMERICAN LIBRARY ASSOCIATION Caldecott Medal (1969) for *The Fool of the World and the Flying Ship* (Arthur RANSOME, reteller). ALA Caldecott Medal Honor Book (1980) for *The Treasure* and (1999) for *Snow.* Child Study Association of America's Children's Books of the Year (1969) for *Rain Rain Rivers.* Christopher Award (1974) for *Dawn.* New York Times Outstanding Book of the Year (1982) and *School Library Journal*'s Best Children's Books (1982) for *The Golem.* New York Times Outstanding Books of the Year and *Horn Book*'s Honor List for *The Secret Room* (1993)

FURTHER WORKS: Author and illus. *The Magician.* 1973. *The Treasure.* 1979. *The Golden Goose.* 1995. Illus. only: *The Mystery of the Woods.* 1964. *Charley Sang a Song.* 1964. *Maximilian's World.* 1966. *Soldier and Tsar in the Forest.* 1972. *Hanukah Money.* 1978. *Lilith's Cave: Jewish Tales of the Supernatural.* 1990. *Toddlecreek Post Office.* 1991. *The Diamond Tree: Jewish Folktales from around the World.* 1991. *Hosni the Dreamer: An Arabian Tale.* 1997

BIBLIOGRAPHY: HOPKINS, Lee Bennett. *Pauses: Autobiographical Reflection of 101 Creators of Children's Books,* 1995. *Illustrators of Children's Books: 1957–1966.* 1968. Shulevitz, Uri. *Writing with Pictures.* 1985

NANCY HORTON

SIDJAKOV, Nicolas
Illustrator, b. 1924, Riga, Lativia

At a time when PICTURE BOOK art flourished because of new technology that allowed reasonably priced color reproductions, S. gained an estimable reputation for his artistic style, use of color, and recall of European folk-art illustration. Several of his own books and those he illustrated for other authors had European settings and were retellings of traditional folktales. *The Emperor and the Drummer Boy* (1962) by Ruth Robbins with whom S. frequently collaborated, is about the French emperor Napoleon and his little drummer boy.

S.'s most widely known picture book, for which he won the CALDECOTT MEDAL in 1961, is *Baboushka and the Three Kings* (Ruth Robbins, reteller). Drawing on his own European background and traditions, S. captures the essence of Russian iconic art to portray the familiar legend of the invitations that the Three Wise Men extend to an old peasant woman to go with them in search of the infant Jesus. Old Baboushka refuses because she must stay at home and finish her chores. Later on, she regrets her choice, prepares gifts for the Holy Baby, and goes in search of the Wise Men. Following the traditional folktale, Baboushka does not find them but each year at the holiday season wanders the landscape distributing gifts to children. A beloved figure in Russian FOLKLORE, Baboushka's essence is captured in S.'s ILLUSTRATIONS. His rich reds, blues, and yellows are reminiscent of old illuminated manuscripts and his angular, vertical figures affect a primitive folk-art style. Using tempera paint and felt-tipped pens to capture the rhythm of the story, S. portrays a sense of believing and faith typical of a similar era in which the story takes place.

AWARDS: AMERICAN LIBRARY ASSOCIATION Caldecott Medal (1961) for *Baboushka and the Three Kings* (Ruth Robbins, reteller); *New York Times* Best Illustrated Children's Books of the Year (1957) for *The Friendly Beasts* (Laura Baker, author); (1960) for *Baboushka and the Three Kings* (Ruth Robbins, reteller); (1962) *The Emperor and the Drummer Boy* (Ruth Robbins, author)

FURTHER WORKS: *A Lodestone and a Toadstone* (Irene Elmer, author), 1969; *Stoffan: An old Christian Folk Song* (Ross Shideler, trans.), 1970

BIBLIOGRAPHY: Association for Library Service to Children, *The NEWBERY and Caldecott Awards,* 2000; MEIGS, C., et al., *A Critical History of Children's Literature,* 1969

DIANE G. PERSON

SIDNEY, Margaret (a.k.a. Harriet Lothrop)

Author, b. 22 June, 1844, New Haven, Connecticut; d. 2 August 1924, San Francisco, California

Harriet Lothrop's penname derived from a name she always admired, 'Margaret,' and her father's first name, 'Sidney.' She was the child of one of Connecticut's most famous architects, and her best playmates growing up were those she created in her imagination.

The first two chapters of *Five Little Peppers and How They Grew* appeared in the magazine *Wide Awake* in 1880, published by Daniel Lothrop, S.'s husband. The children's magazine, which later merged with *St. Nicholas* magazine, its popular appeal significantly enhanced by the installments about the Pepper family. The stories about the poor, fatherless Peppers were enormously popular and were published in book form in 1881. It was such a success that S. was asked to write more, which led to the publication of twelve more books about the Pepper family. S. created the Peppers and their adventures from her own childhood imaginings, and based the Pepper characters on people she knew. Without melodramatic actions and life-threatening events, the stories' popularity rests on the accounts of everyday events in a large, loving family.

S. also wrote many other stories for children including *A Little Maid of Boston Town* (1910), based on the house she lived in that had once been owned by Nathaniel HAWTHORNE, and Louisa May ALCOTT's family.

FURTHER WORKS: *Five Little Peppers Midway,* 1893; *Five Little Peppers Grown-Up,* 1892; *Phronsie Pepper,* 1897

BIBLIOGRAPHY: Meigg, E., et al., *A Critical History of Children's Literature,* 1969; *Something about the Author,* vol. 20, 1980

DENISE P. BEASLEY

SIEBERT, Diane

Author, b. 18 March 1948, Chicago, Illinois

S. grew up in the midwest, and now lives in central Oregon, where she and her husband have created a wildlife habitat on their property, so that they may enjoy frequent visits by local wildlife. S. has written six PICTURE BOOKS that are poetic responses to the musical pulse she feels through living in such close contact with the land. Extensive travel around the United States and Mexico fuelled her passion for the environment. Breaking free from the demands of a registered nurse's schedule shortly after graduation, she and her husband took off on a ten-year motorcycle journey. The natural rhythms she felt for the land, as she traversed it as both a long distance runner and a motorcyclist, started to emerge in POETRY, prose, and song. Some of her poems initially appeared in magazines for both adults and children. Although she really does not see herself as writing specifically for children, she began to translate the land songs that filtered through her mind into the wider showcase of picture-book format. Her first book, *Truck Song* (1984), evokes the rhythms of a trucker's endless cross-country journeys. *Train Song* (1990) is based on an old poem published nine years earlier in *Cricket* magazine, and transforms her long hours of training runs alongside railway tracks into an onomatopoeic lullaby of a transcontinental train. *Plane Song* (1993) continues her celebration of the diverse modes of transportation that move readers rhythmically across the vast expanses of our land.

In direct contrast to the sometimes squealing, strident cacophony of these man-made machines, S.'s environmentally sensitive trilogy (*Mohave,* 1988; *Heartland,* 1989; *Sierra,* 1991) projects a more majestic, serene harmony of the living land. S.'s deep respect for the environment and keen awareness of the need to preserve its wildlife and natural resources, coupled with Wendell MINOR's striking illustrations, have elicited a sense of wonder and homage in readers of many ages, although the books are marketed mainly for younger readers. S.'s lyrical poetry is rich with imagery and seems both spiritual and scientifically grounded. The scrupulously observed factual details are presented through the resonating voices of the central characters, the mountain itself, in Sierra, and the desert, in Mohave. These personified sirens lure us to clamber over them, alongside their creatures. "I am the mountain/Tall and grand/And like a sentinel I stand," proclaims the wise Sierra Nevada mountain, inviting us to learn of her geological evolution, her role in supporting the delicate ecological balance of life,

and her own susceptibility to the erosive ravages of both time, and, more significantly, man.

AWARDS: *Sierra* was named a Notable Children's Trade Book in the Field of Social Studies (NCSS–CBC), as were *Truck Song, Mohave, Heartland,* and *Train Song. Sierra, Train Song,* and *Plane Song* were all named Outstanding Science Trade Books (NSTA–CBC)

REFERENCES: *Seventh Book of Junior Authors and Illustrators,* 1996

BARBARA TOBIN

SIEGAL, Aranka (Davidowitz)

Author, b. 10 June, 1930, Beregszasz, Czechoslovakia

Although S.'s two books have earned several prominent AWARDS, she is relatively unknown in the world of YOUNG ADULT LITERATURE; but the subject matter about which she writes is so important and so personal, her books deserve careful attention. *Upon the Head of a Goat* (1981), her first book, is an autobiography in which she recalls her childhood growing up Jewish in Europe during World War II. She begins the book at the turning point of her life, when she is witness to the Hungarian invasion of her idyllic summer retreat in the Ukraine, and ends it as she and her family board a "cattle car" bound for Auschwitz. She describes the events and the emotions of the downward journey to the ghetto and then to the camps in which she eventually loses everything except for the lives of her sister and herself. Her second book, *Grace in the Wilderness* (1985), is a sequel that recounts their life after the liberation of the concentration camps and her emigration to the United States. S. is currently working on a novel about several generations of a family that live in the Europe of her childhood.

BIBLIOGRAPHY: *Something about the Author,* vol. 88, 1997; various reviews and notes

BARBARA L. BATTLES

SILVERSTEIN, Alvin and Virginia

Authors. Alvin: b. 30 December 1933, New York City. Virginia: b. April 1937, Philadelphia, Pennsylvania

As a husband and wife science writing team that frequently receives AWARDS, the S.s have produced over a hundred INFORMATIONAL BOOKS for all ages. A.S.'s education includes a B.A. from Brooklyn College in 1955, an M.S. from the University of Pennsylvania in 1959, and a Ph.D. from New York University in 1962. V.S. obtained an A.B. from the University of Pennsylvania in 1958. They married in 1958 after meeting while working together in a chemistry lab. One of their six children, Robert, joined them in some of their publications. As young children, both A.S. and V.S. were avid readers with great thirsts for knowledge. V.S. was also involved in languages, which led to her accompanying interest of translating Russian scientific works. Each has worked in diversified areas of related fields. Their first publication as a team was *Life in the Universe* (1967). The S.s have written SERIES BOOKS such as Systems of the Body series and Story of Your. . . . series. They have also collaborated on college texts, nonfiction for adults, and a novel. In addition to explaining topics as varied as pets to diseases, the authors extend their expository passages with supporting features. In *Smell, the Subtle Sense* (1992) the S.s not only discuss how smell is the least understood sense, they provide Ann Neumann's drawings and diagrams as well as a bibliography and index. In *Steroids: Big Muscles, Big Problems* (1992), the S.s use terminology easily understood by teenagers supplemented with chapter references, illustrations, and a glossary. Reading audiences find the S.s' treatment of complex, scientific information to be clear, concise, and comprehensible.

AWARDS: Children's Book of the Year citations, Child Study Association of America, (1969) for *A World in a Drop of Water,* and (1972) for *The Code of Life, Nature's Defenses,* and *Nature's Pincushion. Circulatory Systems* was named a Science Educators' Book Society Selection. The Outstanding Science Books for Children citation from the National Science Teachers Association and CHILDREN'S BOOK COUNCIL (1972) for *The Long Voyage, The Muscular System, The Skeleton System, Cancer, Nature's Pincushion,* and *Life in a Bucket of Soil,* (1973) for *Rabbits,* (1974) for *Animal Invaders* and *Hamsters,* (1976) for *Potatoes* and *Gerbils,* (1983) for *Heartbeats,* (1987) for *The Story of Your Foot,* (1988) for *Wonders of Speech* and *Nature's Living Lights,* and (1990) for *Overcoming Acne.* Notable Trade Book, National Council for Social Studies and Children's Book Council (1975) for *Alcoholism*

FURTHER WORKS: *Rabies.* 1994. *Chicken Pox and Shingles.* 1997. *Evolution.* 1998. *Food Chains.* 1998. *The California Condor.* 1998. *Cycles and Rhythms.* 1998

BIBLIOGRAPHY: Bush, Margaret, "Booklist: Nonfiction." The *Horn Book* magazine, Sep. 92, vol. 68, i5, p. 602; *Fifth Book of Junior Authors and Illustrators* (1983); Sutherland, Zena and May Hill Arbuthnot, (1991), *Children and Books;* Whitson, Joyce. "Reviews: Nonfiction," *Book Report,* March/April 93, vol. 11, i 5, p. 50

NANCY HORTON

SILVERSTEIN, Shel(by)

Cartoonist, songwriter, recording artist, writer, illustrator, poet, b. 18 October 1932, Chicago, Illinois; d. 10 May 1999, Key West, Florida

Known to his many admirers by his pseudonym, Uncle Shelby, S. has produced a variety of creative works over more than three decades. His offbeat HUMOR, ranging from nonsensical and outrageous to philosophical and tender, has endeared him to a wide audience of all ages. Young children relate to his lack of respect for parental authority, his keen insights into their pet peeves and fears, and his sense of silliness, that is reminiscent of SEUSS and LEAR. His irreverent, satirical outlook on life has earned him cult figure status with many college students. Despite the enduring popularity of his best-selling children's books, S. shunned publicity, rarely granting interviews.

S. began his writing career as a cartoonist for adult magazines. During his service in the United States armed forces during the Korean War in the 1950s, he was a cartoonist for *Pacific Stars and Stripes.* He was a contributor of cartoons to *Playboy* magazine since 1956. In the 1960s, through the coaxing of his friend, fellow illustrator Tomi UNGERER, S. came under the nurturing genius of children's book editor Ursula Nordstrom. His successful debut in this field was his self-illustrated *Lafcadio, the Lion Who Shot Back* (1963), followed by *The Giving Tree* (1964). The *Giving Tree* is a deceptively simple parable that has been enormously popular across generations, yet is controversial in its interpretation. Revered by many for its religious message of selfless giving, it has also been condemned for its concealed glorification of male selfishness and exploitation.

S.'s *The Missing Piece* (1976) and *The Missing Piece Meets the Big O* (1981) are also often read as allegories, with widely varied interpretations and mixed reviews. The latter was an INTERNATIONAL READING ASSOCIATION Children's Choice in 1982.

S. is perhaps best loved by young readers for his poetry trilogy (*Where the Sidewalk Ends,* 1974; *A Light in the Attic,* 1981; *Falling Up,* 1996). These collections of lighthearted, rollicking verse are illustrated by his simple, yet expressive black-and-white line drawings. In several states these best-selling volumes have provoked the ire of some adults, who have challenged the books' use in schools on the grounds that they undermine parental and religious authority, and promote violence and horror. Nevertheless, the books have received notable designations from such sources as *School Library Journal* (*A Light in the Attic*) and the *New York Times* (*Where the Sidewalk Ends*). They have also sold millions of copies.

S. has also had a respectable career as a songwriter since the 1960s, producing folk and country songs for such artists as Johnny Cash ("A Boy Named Sue"), The Irish Rovers ("The Unicorn Song"), Jerry Lee Lewis, and Dr. Hook. In 1980 he recorded his own country music album, *The Great Conch Train Robbery.* He has composed music for a number of movies (e.g., *Ned Kelly,* 1970; *Thieves,* 1977), winning an Academy Award nomination for his song, "I'm Checking Out," in *Postcards from the Edge.*

During the 1980s and 1990s, S. wrote a number of plays for adults that have been successfully staged in his hometown of New York (e.g., *The Lady or The Tiger Show*). He collaborated with David Mamet on his play *Oh, Hell!,* and his screenplay *Things Change* (1988).

FURTHER WORKS: *A Giraffe and a Half,* 1964

REFERENCES: *Children's Literature Review.* 1983. Ramsey, Inez. (accessed May 7, 1997), Shel Silverstein. [online], available: http://falcon.jmu.edu/~ramseyil/silverstein.htm. *Something about the Author,* vol. 92, 1997

BARBARA TOBIN

SIMON, Seymour

Author, b. 9 August 1931, New York City

It was clear early on that science would be an integral part of S.'s life. An avid reader of SCI-

ENCE FICTION magazines since childhood, S.'s fascination with science, particularly astronomy and zoology, can be traced back to his school days. He attended the Bronx High School of Science and served as president of the Junior Astronomy Club at the American Museum of Natural History. After receiving his B.A. at City College of New York (now City College of CUNY) in 1953, S. began two years of service in the army. Upon his discharge in 1955, S. returned to City College where he pursued graduate studies in animal behavior while teaching science in the New York City public schools. His career as a science teacher spanned more than twenty years, but this scientist is also a writer. Teaching mainly junior high school children gave S. the perspective he needed to write for children. In 1968, S. completed his first work, *Animals in Field and Laboratory: Science Projects in Animal Behavior,* which was originally written for S.'s ninth-grade students but adopted at high schools and even colleges. It marked the career beginning of one of the most prolific writers of children's science books. Within two years of publication of his first book, S. was writing a remarkable four to six books a year, working on several projects concurrently. To date, S. has published more than ninety books.

S.'s teaching experience served him in good stead when it came to writing for children. Stylistically, he is able to capture his readers' attention by imparting interesting facts or developing stories. S. uses literature as a vehicle to provide answers to questions about scientific subjects. His "hands-on" emphasis on experimentation encourages children to explore the scientific method from inquiry to discovery. The presentations are neither bland nor didactic, two pitfalls frequently found in INFORMATIONAL BOOKS. Rather, S.'s success can best be attributed to his superb scientific knowledge base, his creativity and skill as a teacher, and a writing talent that enables him to fulfill the Horatian charge to instruct and delight. Because of his extensive background in zoology, many of S.'s books often focus on animals. These books grab a reader's attention simply by offering up an original perspective. For example, *Life in the Dark: How Animals Survive at Night* (1974) and *Life and Death in Nature* (1976), give readers a glimpse of a world they rarely encounter. Books such as *Birds on Your Street* (1974),

Pets in a Jar: Collecting and Caring for Small Wild Animals (1975), and *Animals in Your Neighborhood* (1976) all acquaint children with new ways of examining and appreciating the environment that they share with sometimes unseen creatures or those they may have otherwise taken for granted. In the Discovering series, S. takes a closer look at the behavior and care of distinct species that one might find as classroom pets, such as earthworms (1968), frogs (1969), goldfish (1970), gerbils (1971), crickets (1973), and garter snakes (1975). To S., no life forms are too small to excite a child's imagination, as evidenced by one of his earliest titles, *Exploring with a Microscope* (1969).

Although he frequently writes about animals, S.'s scientific repertoire extends well beyond that domain, including such diverse topics as meteorology (*Storms,* 1989), geology (*The Rock-Hound's Book,* 1973), chemistry (*Chemistry in the Kitchen,* 1971), astronomy (*Comets, Meteors, and Asteroids,* 1994), ecology and the environment (*Science Projects in Ecology,* 1972), aerodynamics (*The Paper Airplane Book,* 1971), physics (*The Optical Illusion Book,* 1976), oceanography (*From Shore to Ocean Floor: How Life Survives in the Sea,* 1973), and computer technology (*Your First Home Computer,* 1985).

S. has done an acclaimed series on the solar system using photographs startling in their precise details of the planets. Along with his customary focused, precise writing each title features photographs taken in space and sent back to earth by the Mariner and Viking spacecrafts. The satellite photography provides colorful, breathtaking details that are complemented by up-to-date, clearly explained information in nontechnical language that young readers can easily understand. Some of S.'s most visually spectacular titles are *Mars* (1987), *Venus* (1992), and *Mercury* (1992).

S. has also written works of fiction, but even these books deal with science and technology. His Einstein Anderson series, for example, is a collection of mysteries (ten in each book) that are eventually solved by the intelligent, humorous boy detective Einstein Anderson. Using scientific clues, readers venture into the world of science, applying their knowledge without fear or frustration. S.'s learn-by-doing philosophy is evident in the effort he makes to involve his readers. His

approach is not to lecture, but rather to engage his readers. He accomplishes this by sustaining reader interest through unusual facts, thought-provoking questions, and experimental projects and activities. His efforts have been recognized by the National Science Teachers Association who have named more than thirty of S.'s books to their list of Outstanding Science and Trade Books for Children.

AWARDS: Children's Book Showcase Award, CHILDREN'S BOOK COUNCIL (1972) for *The Paper Airplane Book.* More than thirty books have been designated Outstanding Science and Trade Books for Children by the National Science Teachers Association. *School Library Journal* Best Books of 1975 for *Pets in a Jar*

FURTHER WORKS: *The Look-It-Up Book of Earth.* 1968. *Motion.* 1968. *Weather and Climate.* 1969. *Let's Try It Out: Wet and Dry.* 1969. *Handful of Soil.* 1970. *Science in a Vacant Lot.* 1970. *Let's Try It Out: Light and Dark.* 1970. *Science at Work: Projects in Space Science.* 1971. *Science at Work: Easy Models You Can Make.* 1971. *Let's Try It Out: Finding out about Your Senses.* 1971. *Let's Try It Out: Hot and Cold.* 1972. *Science Projects in Pollution.* 1972. *Science at Work: Projects in Oceanography.* 1972. *Projects with Plants.* 1973. *Let's Try It Out: About Your Heart.* 1974. *Life on Ice.* 1976. *Ghosts.* 1976. *The Saltwater Aquarium Book: How to Set Them up and Keep Them Going.* 1976. *The Long View into Space.* 1979. *The Long Journey from Space.* 1982. *The Moon.* 1984. *Earth: Our Planet in Space.* 1984. *Computer Sense, Computer Nonsense.* 1984. *Soap Bubble Magic.* 1985. *Galaxies.* 1988. *Spring across America.* 1996

BIBLIOGRAPHY: *Children's Literature Review.* vol. 9, 1985; *Contemporary Authors,* vols. 25–28. Huck, C., (1996); *Children's Literature in the Elementary School; Something about the Author,* vol. 4, 1973; Sutherland, Zena, Arbuthnot, May Hill and Dianne Monson, 1997, *Children and Books*

ANDREW KANTAR

SIMONT, Marc
Illustrator, author, b. 23 November 1915, Paris, France

S.'s ILLUSTRATIONS expand the narratives of FAIRY TALES, picture-book stories, and beginning readers. Growing up in France, the United States, and Spain, among a family of artists, S. became fascinated as a child with the details of faces, postures, activities, and objects in his daily life. S. attended art schools in Paris and New York City and has lived in the United States since 1936.

S.'s expressive watercolor illustrations for *A Tree Is Nice* by Janice UDRY won the 1957 ALA CALDECOTT MEDAL. *The Happy Day* (Ruth KRAUSS, 1949) was named an AMERICAN LIBRARY ASSOCIATION 1950 Caldecott Medal Honor Book winner. Black-and-white drawings capture several animals celebrating a joyous summer day, dancing around a single bright yellow flower, the only color used in the book. *Jareb* (Miriam Powell, 1952) won the Child Study Association Book Award. *The Star in the Pail* (David MC-CORD, 1975) was a National Book Award finalist in 1976. The 1986 Parents' Choice Award went to *The Dallas Titans Get Ready for Bed* (Karla KUSKIN, 1986).

S.'s illustrations are rendered in black and white and in full spectrum watercolors. They offer the viewer charming detail of expressions, background scenes and interactions among the characters depicted. In a series of beginning readers by Marjorie Weinman SHARMAT, "Nate the Great," S.'s depictions of the boy detective keep the story moving and accessible as well as does Sharmat's plotting.

S. has worked with a wide range of authors, including Margaret Wise BROWN (*The First Story,* 1947), Charlotte ZOLOTOW (*If You Listen,* 1980) and Mollie HUNTER (*The Knight of the Golden Plain,* 1983). He has provided new illustrations for works by Andrew LANG (*The Red Fairy Book,* 1948) and James THURBER (*Many Moons,* 1990) and has authored several self-illustrated books as well.

FURTHER WORKS: *The Pirate of Chatham Square: A Story of Old New York.* Emma Sterne. 1939. *Fish Head.* Jean FRITZ. 1954. *The Wonderful "O."* Thurber. 1957. *Nate the Great.* Sharmat. 1972. *How to Dig a Hole to the Other Side of the World.* Faith McNulty. 1979. *The Philharmonic Gets Dressed.* Kuskin. 1982. *In the Year of the Boar and Jackie Robinson.* Betty Bao LORD. 1984. *Journey into a Black Hole.* Franklyn BRANLEY. 1986. *Nate the Great and the Stolen Base.* Sharmat. 1992

BIBLIOGRAPHY: HOPKINS, Lee Bennett, *Pauses: Autobiographical Reflections of 101 Creators of Children's Literature,* 1995; Silvey, A. ed., *Children's Books and Their Creators.* 1995; *Something about the Author,* vol. 74, 1993

FRANCISCA GOLDSMITH

SINGER, Isaac Bashevis, (pseud. Warshofky)

Author, journalist, essayist, b. 14 July 1904, Leoncin, Poland; d. 24 July 1991, Surfside, Florida

Born Icek-Hersz Zynger in the small town of Leoncin, Poland, S. came from a devout Hasidic family. In 1908 his father became the supervisor of a rabbinical court in Warsaw. As a boy, young S. used his vivid imagination to spin visions and dreams instead of playing with toys. He attained proficiency in Yiddish and Aramaic texts, which subsequently served him in his teaching and writing.

At the age of twenty S. worked as a proofreader for the Literasche Bleter, edited by his brother, Israel Joshua, also a noted author and novelist. It was then that S. wrote his first stories about the Jewish occult, including witches, demons, and other supernatural phenomena. His first novel was *Satan in Goray (Der Sotin in Goray),* which was published in 1932 and established S.'s distinctive style of presenting his characters as people tormented by demons of their own imaginations. It was written in a style reminiscent of medieval Yiddish chronicles, and described events connected to the seventeenth century false Messiah, Shabbatai Tzvi. In 1935, S. was appointed foreign correspondent for the *Jewish Daily Forward* in New York City. Fleeing the impending threat of anti-Semitism, S. emigrated to the United States. He settled in New York and became a U.S. citizen. S. became an exuberant and prolific writer of timeless tales based on Jewish culture, FOLKLORE, and mysticism that appealed to people of all ages. Many of his children's stories transpire in a daydream of FANTASY, evocative of the bright colors and simple plots of childhood, where every story has a happy ending. These stories read like FAIRY TALES, inhabited by fairies, devils and angels.

In *A Day of Pleasure: Stories of a Boy Growing up in Warsaw* (1969), S. describes some autobiographical aspects of his own childhood experiences with exhilarating and evocative tales that are considered an important part of world folk literature. Events from S.'s childhood are retold and mixed with fancifully inspired events and improbably exaggerated characters yet do manage to impart an authentic flavor of prewar Poland in the Jewish ghetto. In his stories rabbis, thieves, and demons interact in mystical sequences that are presented as everyday events and illustrate the best of human nature as well as its darker side. He was awarded the Nobel Prize for literature in 1978. S. died in 1991 and is buried in Beth-El Cemetery, Oradell, New Jersey.

Additional children's literature by S. includes *Zlateh the Goat and Other Stories* (1966), *The Topsy-Turvy Emperor of China* (1971), and in 1984, *Stories for Children,* containing thirty-six of his most popular short stories, was published. *The Fools of Chelm and Their History* (1973) is an exuberant, humorous retelling of traditional Yiddish/Polish folktales about an inept community of fools who invariably find the most difficult solutions to their problems without the intervention of S.'s usual assortment of demons and witches.

AWARDS: ALA NEWBERY MEDAL Honor Book (1967) for *Zlateh the Goat and Other Stories* (Maurice SENDAK, illus.), (1968) for *The Fearsome Inn* (Nonny HOGROGIAN, illus.), (1969) for *"When Shlemiel Went to Warsaw" and Other Stories* (Margot ZEMACH, illus.). The Sydney TAYLOR Book Award (1971) for S.'s body of work. The Nobel Prize for Literature, 1978. National Book Award (1969) for *A Day of Pleasure*

FURTHER WORKS: *Mazel and Shlimazel; or, The Milk of a Lioness,* 1967; *Alone in the Wild Forest,* 1971, *Naftali the Storyteller and His Horse, Sus,* 1973; *The Power of Light,* 1980; *The Golem,* 1982

ELANA RECHTMAN

SINGER, Marilyn

Author, b. 3 October 1948, New York City

S., author of over fifty books for children and YOUNG ADULTS, writes across a wide spectrum of genres, including PICTURE BOOKS, short stories, POETRY, nonfiction, MYSTERY series, FANTASY and realistic fiction. S. grew up in the Bronx and on suburban Long Island. Her studies at Queens College included a year abroad at Reading University. She taught high school English literature, resigning after four years, disillusioned and struggling to get a writing career started. After an unsatisfying attempt at magazine writing and producing teacher's film guides, she discovered the joy of writing for children while sitting in the Brooklyn Botanic Gardens, bringing to life insect characters she had created as a teenager. Encouraged to continue writing by positive critiques from a writers' workshop, she soon had her first book, *The Dog Who Insisted He Wasn't* (1976), published and selected as an INTERNATIONAL READING ASSOCIATION Children's Choice.

S.'s childhood immersion in stories, both the homespun tales of her Rumanian grandmother, with whom she shared a bed, and the wealth of FAIRY TALES provided by her parents, created in her a lifelong passion for creating and sharing her own fantasies. These influences are seen in her picture-book series of her own fairy tales (e.g., *The Golden Heart of Winter,* 1991). Her fantasy novels often explore the supernatural (e.g., *Storm Rising,* 1989), occasionally originating in haunting dreams she weaves into her stories (e.g., *Horsemaster,* 1985). S.'s life experiences permeate her books. Her dogs, for example, inspired her mystery parody series of doggy detective, Samantha Spayed. Several of her REALISTIC FICTION novels are strongly autobiographical. *It Can't Hurt Forever* (1978) was written to heal the lingering emotional trauma she experienced as a child undergoing heart surgery. *The First Few Friends* (1981) mirrors her experiences in the sixties, returning from her junior year abroad to find life in New York radically changed, and her friends absorbed in rock music, free love, and drugs.

S.'s favorite writing genre since the first grade has been poetry. Her collections of poems reflect her enduring interest in the warm, funny antics of families and their pets (e.g., *Family Reunion,* 1994; *Please Don't Squeeze Your Boa, Noah,* 1995), and her sense of wonder about the natural world in *Sky Words* (1994). Her nonfiction books explore unusual plant and animal characteristics (e.g., *Prairie Dogs Kiss and Lobsters Wave,* 1995).

S. has had varied experiences writing for film and television, including guides for PBS's *Nova* series, scripts for the *Electric Company*, and an introduction to *A History of the American Avant-Garde Cinema.* She was curator of a traveling children's avant-garde film exhibition, and hosted an internet chatroom for children's writers.

FURTHER WORKS: *The Fido Frame-Up.* 1983 Parents' Choice. *Several Kinds of Silence.* 1988 ALA best books for young adults. *Turtle in July.* 1989. NCTE Notable Book. *Time Magazine's* Best Children's Books. *Stay True: Short Stories for Strong Girls.* 1988

BIBLIOGRAPHY: *Something about the Author Autobiography Series.* vol. 68. 1992 and vol. 81. 1995. Lori Soard, an exclusive interview with S. http://www.wordmuseum.com/C101.htm (accessed June 27, 1998)

BARBARA TOBIN

SIS, Peter

Author, illustrator, b. 11 May 1949, Brno, Moravia, Czechoslovakia

S.'s father was a filmmaker and explorer, his mother an artist. S. began drawing at age four or five and was soon a serious student of art. His parents encouraged his creativity and gave him illustration assignments, complete with deadlines. This parental influence helped insure what S. remembers as a wonderful childhood, despite the dreary political times in Czechoslovakia. He earned an M.A. (1974) from the Academy of Applied Arts in Prague, then attended the Royal College of Art in London (1977–79). The artistic freedom he enjoyed as a child caused some tension when he began his more strictly guided formal training. When his teachers ranked their students' work, S.'s was always among the lowest in his class. After art school, S. worked as a graphic designer for the Czech army's symphony orchestra. By the early 1980s, he had become a popular filmmaker in Europe. S. came to the U.S. in 1982 to work on a film project connected to the 1984 Los Angeles Olympics. Although Czechoslovakia and other Soviet nations withdrew from Olympic competition, S. remained in Los Angeles to pursue his art. Because of his unique style, he had difficulty getting work as an artist. Instead, he taught art classes and painted decorative eggs that were commissioned by a Swiss woman. S. sent samples of his work to artist Maurice SENDAK, who arranged for S. to meet the art director of Greenwillow Books. On the spot, S. agreed to illustrate George SHANNON's *Bean Boy* (1984). In 1989, S. became a United States citizen.

S. believes that the illustrator's job is to complement the text, and his work is noted for effectively capturing the feeling and intent of other writers' words. His ILLUSTRATIONS for *Starry Messenger* (1996), a so-called storyography (see STORYOGRAPHIES: PICTURE-BOOK BIOGRAPHIES) of Galileo, reflect the Renaissance in art and architecture. Through brief excerpts from Galileo's journals and diaries S. evokes the excitement of the Renaissance and the fear of the Inquisition. In *Tibet through the Red Box* (1998) he captures the downward spiral of chaos during the Communist takeover of Tibet and the disappearance of his father, there to report on events. S. won an ALA CALDECOTT MEDAL Honor Book citations for both books.

S. prefers to illustrate his own work, where he has artistic control. He gleans story ideas from new, unfamiliar experiences and surroundings. For example, *Waving* (1988) grew from S.'s observations of how people hail cabs in New York. One of his best known books, *Follow the Dream* (1991), is the story of Columbus's voyage. The book was inspired by S.'s father's explorations and his own immigration to the U.S. S. wants his work to nurture children's creativity and freedom of thought, to challenge the imagination.

AWARDS: AMERICAN LIBRARY ASSOCIATION Caldecott Medal Honor Book (1997) for *Starry Messenger: Galileo and Galilei* and (1999) for *Tibet through the Red Box.* ALA Notable Book (1997) for *Starry Messenger. Boston Globe–Horn Book* Honor Book (1994) for *A Small, Tall Tale from the Far, Far North. New York Times* Best Illustrated Children's Books (1987) for *Rainbow Rhino* and (1990) for *Beach Ball.* He has also won several AWARDS for his films

FURTHER WORKS: Self-illustrated: *Going Up!: A Color Counting Book.* 1989. *An Ocean World.* 1992. *Komodo!* 1993. *A Small, Tall Tale from the Far, Far North.* 1993. *The Three Golden Keys.* 1994. *Fire Truck.* 1998. *Trucks, Trucks, Trucks.* 1999. Illus.: *Oaf.* (Cunningham). 1986, *The Whipping Boy.* (FLEISCHMAN). 1986. *Jed and the Space Bandits.* (Marzollo and Marzollo), 1987. *The Scarebird.* (Fleischman). 1988. *The Ghost in the Noonday Sun.* (Fleischman). 1989. *Halloween Stories and Poems.* (Bauer). 1989. *The Midnight Horse.* (Fleischman). 1990. *The Dragons Are Singing Tonight.* (PRELUTSKY). 1993. *Rumpelstiltskin.* (Noel). 1993. *The 13th Floor: A Ghost Story.* 1995. *Monday's Troll.* (Prelutsky). 1996. *Sleep Safe, Little Whale: A Lullaby.* (Schlein).

1997. *Many Waters.* (L'ENGLE). 1998. Three "Stories to Solve" folktale collections. (George Shannon). 1985, 1990, 1994

BIBLIOGRAPHY: Silvey, A. ed. *Children's Books and their Creators.* 1995

JANE WEST

SKURZYNSKI, Gloria (Jean)

Author, b. 6 July, 1930, Duquesne, Pennsylvania

S. is the daughter of a steel-mill worker and a telegraph operator. She grew up in the multiethnic mill town of Duquesne during the Great Depression and loved to escape to the world of romance through books and movies. She attended Mount Mercy College for two years, then worked at a steel company.

Encouraged by the influence of writer Phyllis MCGINLEY, S. began to write stories after her children were in school. Her first publication was a story for *Teen* magazine. Since that time, S. has written stories and books for children in several genres. Her nonfiction books have earned acclaim from literary critics as well as scientific organizations. Her book, *Bionic Parts for People: The Real Story of Artificial Organs and Replacement Parts* (1978), won a Golden Kite Honor Book Award, and *Almost the Real Thing: Simulation in Your High-Tech World* (1991) was both praised by a reviewer for *School Library Journal* and won the Science Writing Award from the American Institute of Physics. S. has also written SCIENCE FICTION, such as *Virtual War* (1997), which was listed in Best Books for YOUNG ADULTS by the AMERICAN LIBRARY ASSOCIATION, and historical fiction, such as *Goodbye, Billy Radish* (1992), listed in Best Books of the Year by *School Library Journal.* Another historic fiction novel, *What Happened in Hamelin* (1979), received a Christopher Award and was adapted by the Columbia Broadcasting system and featured on "Storybreak" in 1987.

Delighting in what has come before as well as what promises to be, S. enjoys exploring the worlds of the past and the future. She writes, "I'm greedy. I want to write about all of it—the history, the grief, joy, and excitement of being human in times past; the cutting-edge inventions of times almost here."

Recently, S. and her daughter, Alane Ferguson, have collaborated on a series of mysteries.

Their novel, *Wolf Stalker* (1997), is the first novel published by the century-old National Geographic Society.

FURTHER WORKS: *Manwolf.* 1981. *The Tempering.* 1983. *Trapped in the Slickrock Canyon.* 1984. *Lost in the Devil's Desert.* 1993. *Zero Gravity.* 1994. *Cyberstorm.* 1995. *Waves: The Electromagnetic Universe.* 1996

BIBLIOGRAPHY: S.'s biography—[online] available: http://redhawknorth.com/gloria/bio.html [June 25, 1998]. S.'s AWARDS. [online] Available: http://redhawknorth.com/gloria/awards.html (accessed July 20, 1998); *Something about the Author,* vol. 74, 1993

MARY ARIAIL BROUGHTON

SLEATOR, William B.

Author, b. 13 February 1945 Havre de Grace, Maryland

S. is a SCIENCE FICTION writer whose fantasies embody time travel, aliens, and journeys to the scary and unknown. He spent his childhood in Missouri, visited Thailand as an adult and later chose to live there. S.'s family greatly valued music, reading, and writing, which later proved to be cornerstones for his careers. Graduating from Harvard with a B.A. in English in 1967, he then studied musical composition in London and worked as a ballet pianist. When almost forty he discontinued his work in music to concentrate on his writing. His first book was *The Angry Moon* (1970). S. attracts readers by propelling ordinary characters with typical problems into extremely unusual plots. For example, in *House of Stairs* (1974), six teenagers are unknowingly being watched by experimenters. Twins Barry and Harry in *Singularity* (1985) experience common sibling rivalry until one twin enters a universe where time is fast forwarded and he becomes a year older than his twin.

Some of S.'s works mirror either his current state of mind while writing the book or a past unpleasantry. The setting in *Blackbriar* (1972) is reminiscent of a past residence of S.'s, a 200-year-old cottage that had previously served as a quarantine for diseased people. Additionally, the bitter tone noted in *Fingers* (1983) is a reflection of the confinement and resentment he experienced in his role as a ballet pianist. After writing *Duplicate* (1988) in which a boy copies himself both to fulfill his obligations and still be free to do whatever he wants, S. realized his yearning to be in Thailand instead of the U.S. S. proudly shares fictionalized versions of autobiographical stories in *Oddballs* (1993) where, much like his own upbringing, children are encouraged to cultivate their individual interests.

AWARDS: ALA CALDECOTT MEDAL Honor Book and *Boston Globe–Horn* Book ILLUSTRATION honor book (1971) for *The Angry Moon*. AMERICAN LIBRARY ASSOCIATION Best Books for Young Adults (1974) for *House of Stairs*, (1984) for *Interstellar Pig*, (1985) for *Singularity*, (1987) for *The Boy Who Reserved Himself*. IRA Children's Choice (1984) for *Into the Dream*. *School Library Journal*'s Best Books of the Year (1981) for *The Green Futures of Tycho*. (1983) for *Fingers* and (1984) for *Interstellar Pig*

FURTHER WORKS: *Run*. 1973. *That's Silly*. 1981. *Strange Attractors*. 1990. *Others See Us*. 1993. *Dangerous Wishes*. 1995. *The Night the Heads Came*. 1996. *The Beasties*. 1997. and *The Boxes*. 1998

BIBLIOGRAPHY: Davis, J. E., and H. K. Davis. *Presenting William Sleator*. 1992; Jenkinson, Dave. "Portraits: William Sleator: Stellar Science Fiction Author;" *Emergency Librarian*, Jan./Feb. 1990, vol. 17 i3, p. 67. Thorson, A. S. "An Interview with William Sleator;" *Book Report*, May 1992, vol. 1, i.1, p. 26

NANCY HORTON

SLEPIAN, Jan
Author, b. 2 January 1921, New York City

S., author of books for children and young adults, grew up in Manhattan, the Bronx, and Brooklyn. She received a psychology degree from Brooklyn College and pursued a career in speech pathology. As a speech therapist, she began writing articles for a newspaper column about common speech problems. These articles led to her first set of PICTURE BOOKS she coauthored with Dr. Ann Seidler, known as The Listen-Hear Books, including the titles *The Hungry Thing* (1967), and *The Hungry Thing Returns* (1990). These books dealt with speech problems. S. took a children's literature course that piqued her interest in writing adolescent novels. Based on her own experiences dealing with a disabled brother, she wrote *The Alfred Summer* (1990), which received an American Book Award nomination, and became a *Horn Book* Honor Book (see THE DISABLED IN

CHILDREN'S AND YOUNG ADULT LITERATURE). *Back to Before* (1993), Slepian's novel about death and time travel, won the William Allen White Book Award. Her psychological thriller, *Pinocchio's Sister* (1995), is full of complex characters who struggle with the emotions of anger, jealousy, and love.

BIBLIOGRAPHY: "Jan Slepian." Penguin Putnam Catalog: Young Readers Catalog. http://www2. penguinputnam.com/catalog/yreader/authors/714_ biography.html

DENISE P. BEASLEY

SLOBODKIN, Louis
Illustrator, sculptor, author, b. 19 February 1903, Albany, New York; d. 8 May 1975, Bar Harbor Islands, Miami Beach, Florida

S., whose father was an inventor, was given some modeling clay at age thirteen. He began reading about sculpture and studying examples of sculptures. In high school he drew cartoons for the school paper. At age fifteen he quit school to study art. S. attended the Beaux Arts Institute of Design in New York (1918–22). He supported himself as a factory hand, waiter, and dishwasher. After art school, S. worked in a commercial architectural modeling studio. He was also a sculptor in several U.S. and European studios, head of the sculpture department at the Roerich Museum, and instructor at the Art Student's League (1931–37). However, believing that sculpture should be part of a particular place, S. wanted to be an architectural sculptor. He created statues and panels for buildings in Washington, D.C., New York, and elsewhere. His statue of Abraham Lincoln created for the New York World's Fair is permanently located at the Interior Department in Washington. S. began illustrating when his friend Eleanor ESTES asked him to illustrate her first book, *The Moffats* (1941). Within a short time, S. had shifted his attention from sculpture to illustrating and writing children's books, where it remained until his death in 1975.

S.'s experience as a sculptor influenced his drawing. His illustrations were whimsical, simple and sketchy. S. got ideas for many of his self-illustrated books from his sons and grandchildren. S.'s work, usually written to appeal to readers under ten, is sometimes didactic as in *Thank You, You're Welcome* (1957) and *Excuse Me!*

Certainly! (1959). Among S.'s better known works is his humorous SCIENCE FICTION Space Ship series about the friendship between an eleven-year-old boy and an alien. He collaborated on several books with his wife, Florence Slobodkin, is the author of more than forty self-illustrated books, and illustrated Eleanor Estes's *Moffat* series, as well as classic stories by authors such as Mark TWAIN and Charles DICKENS.

AWARDS: S.'s illustrations for *Many Moons* by James THURBER received the ALA CALDECOTT MEDAL in 1943. He also won numerous sculpture competitions

FURTHER WORKS: *Friendly Animals.* 1944. *Fo'-Castle Waltz.* 1945. *Bixby and the Secret Message.* 1948. *Mr. Mushroom.* 1950. *Dinny and Danny.* 1951. *Our Friendly Friends.* 1951. *Mr. Petersham's Cats.* 1954. *The Horse with the High-Heeled Shoes.* 1954. *The Amiable Giant.* 1955. *The Mermaid Who Could Not Sing.* 1956. *The Little Owl Who Could Not Sleep.* 1958. *The First Book of Drawing.* 1958. *Gogo the French Seagull.* 1960. *Moon Blossom and the Golden Penny.* 1963. *Read about the Policeman.* 1966. *Read about the Postman.* 1966. *Read about the Fireman.* 1967. *Read about the Busman.* 1967. *Wilbur the Warrior.* 1972. In the Space Ship series: *The Space Ship under the Apple Tree.* 1952. *The Space Ship Returns to the Apple Tree.* 1958. *The Three-Seated Space Ship.* 1962. *Round-Trip Space Ship.* 1968. *The Space Ship in the Park.* 1972. Books by Eleanor Estes: *The Middle Moffat.* 1943. *Rufus M.* 1943. *The Sun and the Wind and Mr. Todd.* 1943. *The Hundred Dresses.* 1944

BIBLIOGRAPHY: Berger, L. S. *Twentieth-Century Children's Writers.* 1995. HOPKINS, L. B. *Books Are by People.* 1969. Hopkins, Lee Bennett, *Pauses: Autobiographical Reflections of 101 Creators of Children's Books,* 1995. Silvey, A., ed. *Children's Books and Their Creators* 1995.

JANE WEST

SLOBODKINA, Esphyr

Illustrator, author, painter, sculptor, textile designer, b. 22 September 1908, Siberia, Russia

S. is a Russian-American artist who began illustrating and writing children's books in the late 1930s as a means of financial support. She is the creator of the beloved classic *Caps for Sale,* first published in 1940 and reissued many times. S. was born in prerevolutionary Siberia where her father was the manager of an oil yard. At home she and her brothers and sisters led a comfortable upper-middle-class life. There they were surrounded with books, art, and music. As politics in the country became more erratic, and war appeared imminent, the family fled to Manchuria, where her father found a position with an oil company. In Manchuria S. continued her education and began developing as an artist. After graduating from high school in 1927, she was able to travel to the United States on a student visa. She had asked her brother who had emigrated to New York City to enroll her in The National Academy of Design. However, he inadvertently enrolled her at the national Academy, a school for missionaries. By day, she attended missionary school, and at night she went to the Academy of Design, where she continued to develop her art. There she became acquainted with other modern artists like Ilya Bolotowsky, a well-known abstract expressionist. In the early 1930s, she married Bolotowsky, but they divorced in 1936. In 1931, her father had reluctantly left Manchuria for New York, where he lived for several years, until he was killed in a car accident in 1937.

By the late thirties, her personal losses, and the depressed economy made it very difficult to find work. Previously she had supported herself by working on Seventh Avenue as a design assistant, and as a textile designer in an experimental printing shop in New Jersey. A friend suggested that she might earn money by making children's books. Since she had never studied writing or attempted to write for children, she borrowed a young friend's story, which she illustrated with very bold, bright flat collages. She then took her book to Margaret Wise BROWN, a well-known creator of children's literature, who worked with Lucy Sprague Mitchell at Bank Street Teachers College. S. had a most productive interview. Brown loved her collages, and although S.'s book was never published, the women became good friends, and Brown gave her three books to illustrate: *The Little Fireman, The Little Cowboy,* and *The Sleepy ABC Book.* After several more jobs as an illustrator, S. created her own first book—the delightful *Caps for Sale.* Based on a folk tale, this is a story about a peddler who carries all his merchandise on his head (a novel idea to American children) until his caps are mysteriously stolen by a pack of monkeys, and the delightful way that the peddler manages to get them back. Children love the idea of the little monkeys outsmarting the peddler and they often take the roles of the monkey/thieves as they imitate the angry peddler. After the success of *Caps for Sale,* S. wrote and illustrated many books, but none have been as unique as her first.

As World War II progressed many European artists arrived in New York City and S., who was very social, hosted parties to help them become acquainted with other artists. At one of the social events, she met William Urquhart, the principal of a business school who asked her to work for him. She learned to type and take dictation and became his office manager; in 1960 they were married.

S. is a founding member of the Federation of Modern Painters and Sculptors, and the Federation of Abstract Expressionists. Her paintings are in the permanent collection of the Whitney Museum in New York City, the Corcoran Gallery in Washington, D.C., and in the Philadelphia Museum of Art.

FURTHER WORKS: Illustrator/Author: *Caps for Sale.* 1940, reissued, 1947. *The Wonderful Feast.* 1955. *Little Dog Lost, Little Dog Found.* 1956. *The Clock.* 1956. *Pinky and the Petunias.* 1959. *Moving Day for the Middlemans,* date unknown; *The Little Ducklings.* 1961. *Pezzo the Peddler.* 1968. Illus.: *The Little Fireman.* Margaret Wise Brown. 1938, reissued, 1952. *Hiding Place.* Louis Woodcock. 1943. *The Little Cowboy.* Margaret Wise Brown. 1938, reissued, 1948. *The Sleepy ABC.* Margaret Wise Brown, reissued 1953

BIBLIOGRAPHY: *Something about the Author,* vol. 1, 1971; *Twentieth Century Children's Writers,* 1978

JUDY LIPSITT

SLOTE, Alfred
Author, b. 11 September 1926, New York City

S. is best known for his SPORTS STORIES. S. loves sports, and his son John first suggested he write about children's sports. Most of S.'s stories take place in his own Ann Arbor, Michigan, "Arborville." Although his books involve sports, especially baseball, the characters' relationships at home and at school remain the focus of his stories. *Hang Tough, Paul Mather* (1973), typically uses baseball as a setting for the action, portraying a child whose focus on the game allows him to maintain an optimistic outlook in the face of life-threatening medical problems. In addition to sports stories, S. also writes SCIENCE FICTION novels that follow the adventures of the futuristic Jameson family.

FURTHER WORKS: *C.O.L.A.R.* 1978. *Finding Buck McHenry.* 1991. *A Friend like That.* 1988. *Make-believe Ball Player.* 1989. *Moving In.* 1988. *My Robot Buddy.* 1978. *My Trip to Alpha.* 1978. *Omega Station.* 1983. *Rabbit Ears.* 1982. *Trouble on Janus.* 1978

BIBLIOGRAPHY: *Something about the Author,* vol. 72, 1993

JODI PILGRIM

SMITH, Doris Buchanan
Author, b. 1 June 1934, Washington, D.C.

A gifted writer of realistic YOUNG ADULT NOVELS, S. began to create stories of her own when only a small child. A move to Atlanta, Georgia, when she was nine left her withdrawn and shy until a sixth grade teacher noticed she had a talent for writing. One summer she wrote an ADVENTURE novel with her children and while waiting to hear from the publishers wrote *A Taste of Blackberries.* Published in 1973, this novel addressed the topic of the death of a child's playmate. It won an AMERICAN LIBRARY ASSOCIATION Notable Book Citation, Child Study Association Book of the Year Award, Georgia Children's Book Author of the Year and Georgia General Author of the Year Award, Dixie Council of Authors and Journalists, Sue Hafner Award and Kinderbook Award. *The First Hard Times* (1983) won an ALA notable book citation. *Kelly's Creek* (1975) was awarded Georgia Children's Book Author of the Year Award and the National Council for Social Studies notable book citation. *Last Was Lloyd* (1981) received the Georgia Children's Book Author of the Year Award and *School Library Journal* best book of the year citation. *Return to Bitter Creek* (1986) received the Parent's Choice Literature Award. S. creates believable characters that grow and change. In her words, "The most wonderful thing in the world to me is doing what I love to do and earning my living at it."

BIBLIOGRAPHY: *Fiction, FOLKLORE, FANTASY and POETRY for Children, 1876–1985,* 1995. Silvey,

Anita, ed., *Children's Books and Their Creators.
Something about the Author,* vol. 28, 1982, and
vol. 78, 1994

IRVYN GILBERTSON

SMITH, Jessie Willcox

Illustrator, artist, b. 8 September, 1863, Philadelphia, Pennsylvania; d. 3 May 1935, Philadelphia, Pennsylvania

Born into an educated family, but expected to make her own living, S.'s interest in children directed her at first toward teaching kindergarten. However, a chance discovery of her artistic talents set her to painting children instead of teaching them. Although Howard PYLE was her mentor, she followed her own course as a mature painter. With posterlike borders and balanced designs, Maxfield Parrish–like light and shadow, soft facial expressions, and relaxed, natural body language, her paintings give a sense of gentle harmony and comfort. She was able to blend superb realism with FANTASY: detailed and accurate lobsters, toads, and fish in clear converse with *The Water Babies* (1907) (Kingsley, 1863), or Mistress Mary, a perfectly attired and composed little girl watering her garden of "pretty maids" emerging, sunlit, from a bed of tulip blooms in *The Jessie Willcox Smith MOTHER GOOSE* (1912). Movement, expression, and sensuousness through color and billowing folds of cloth bring her paintings alive. Roger Reed writes in his website about S., "Jessie Willcox Smith (1863–1935) was among the most gifted of the students of Howard Pyle, and she took to heart his precept of . . . studying a particular subject thoroughly, and conversely, painting what one knows best in order to bring the subject alive. Quite early, she settled on exploring the universe of the child, and did so with great sensitivity and tenderness over the first thirty years of this century."

S.'s cherubic, pink-cheeked, white-skinned children are often portrayed in acts of curiosity and deep concentration as they explore their world and engage in the typical activities of childhood. Often, too, there is an element of mystery or anticipation in her paintings as children sit on a wall staring down at something concealed, look through a door with intense interest at an unseen curiosity, or peer into the depths of poppies in search of a hidden secret. Children

cannot help but be drawn into her world as they look at her illustrations. Concerned by what she perceived as the neglect of children, she wanted to honor and celebrate their lives and their childhood interests. As Reed notes, "Smith changed and enlarged the appreciation of children in American popular culture by her enormously sympathetic portrayals."

AWARDS: Bronze Medal, Charleston Exposition (1902). Mary Smith Prize, Pennsylvania Academy of the FINE ARTS (1903). Silver Medal, St. Louis Exposition (1904). Beck Prize of the Philadelphia Water Color Club (1911). Silver Medal, Panama-Pacific Exposition (1915)

FURTHER WORKS: *Evangeline.* (LONGFELLOW; with Oakley), 1897. *Rhymes of Real Children.* (Sage). 1903. *In the Closed Room.* (BURNETT). 1904. *A Child's Garden of Verses.* (STEVENSON). 1905. *The Everyday Fairy Book.* (Chapin). 1907. *Seven Ages of Childhood.* (Wells). 1908/9. *The Now-a-Days Fairy Book.* (Chapin). 1911. *Dickens's Children: Ten Drawings by Jessie Willcox Smith.* 1912. *Little Women.* (ALCOTT). 1915. *The Water Babies.* (KINGSLEY). 1916. *Heidi.* (SPYRI). 1922. *A Child's Book of Country Stories.* (Skinner and Skinner). 1925

BIBLIOGRAPHY: Contributor's assessment. THE KERLAN COLLECTION. Reed, Roger T. "Artists' Biographies" at http://www.illustration-house.com/bios/smith_bio.html. *Something about the Author,* vol. 21, 1980

MARGARET YATSEVITCH PHINNEY

SMITH, Lane

Illustrator, author, b. 25 August 1959, Tulsa, Oklahoma

When S. was three, his family moved to California where he and his brother Shane spent much of their after-school time exploring the nearby foothills. Some of S.'s writing, such as *The Big Pets* (1991), evolved from his memories of those experiences. S. worked for five years as a janitor at Disneyland to earn money for his education at the California Art Center College of Design, from which he graduated in 1983 with a B.F.A. in ILLUSTRATION.

In 1984, S. moved to New York where he began his career as a freelance illustrator. He soon became interested in children's books and began a series of paintings of the letters of the alphabet, which he submitted to Macmillan. The

729

company liked his work so much that they asked children's author Eve MERRIAM to write poems to go with his illustrations. The resulting book, *Halloween ABC* (1987) claimed the *New York Times* Ten Best Illustrated Children's Books of the Year citation, *School Library Journal* Best Book of the Year citation, the *Horn Book* Honor List, and other AWARDS. Nevertheless, S. notes that the book was quickly banned in several places amid charges that it was "satanic" (Smith, 1993). Although challenges to the book were countered by vigorous support from editorial writers, S. believes that the publicity ultimately hurt the book. In an interview with Jessica Ferguson of the *Horn Book* magazine, S. said, "If you're an adult writer like Salman Rushdie and you do that controversial book, it stirs up interest, and everybody buys the book. If you're a children's book person, they stay away. There *is* a definite dark side to my work" (p. 66).

In addition to the Halloween book, S.'s self-illustrated books have won many other awards. For example, his book *The Big Pets* (1990) won the Golden Apple Award, Bratislava International Biennial of Illustrations; Silver Medal, Society of Illustrators; and first place, New York Book Show. His third book, *Glasses—Who Needs 'em?* (1991), won Parent's Choice Award for Illustration, *New York Times* Best Book of the Year citation, and ALA Notable Children's Book citation.

S.'s work is decidedly unconventional as he breaks most prevailing standards for illustrations of children's books. His paintings have been described as "goofy," "macabre," "surreal," and "strange." Although S. gets his ideas for his illustrations from various places (including many hours watching cartoons), he claims that his exaggerated style of illustration is directly influenced by an animation director from the forties, Tex Avery, whose work was the antithesis of the DISNEY style. He has also been influenced by illustrators like N. C. WYETH, Maurice SENDAK, Athur RACKHAM, and Edward LEAR. He credits his father for his dry sense of humor and his mother's interest in antiques for his "sense of decay and crackle." His work appeals strongly to adults, children, and reviewers. In a review in *School Library Journal,* the writer noted that S.'s illustrations of the wolf's sneezes in *The True*

Story of the 3 Little Pigs (1989) "tear like thunderbolts through a dim, grainy world."

S. works mostly in oil paints and occasionally uses collage. Using an unusual palette of colors, he often creates his characters and scenes by applying paint on a board, building up several glazes of the oil. He then seals the layers between coats with acrylic spray varnish. The application of acrylic against oil causes a chemical reaction, creating a visual effect similar to airbrushing. He continues with the layers until he is satisfied with the results. Later, he uses a fine brush to add details.

In 1986, S. met author Jon SCIESZKA through his friend, Molly Leach. S. and Scieszka teamed up to write *The True Story of the 3 Little Pigs* (1989). Although originally rejected by several publishers, Viking eventually accepted the book, which sold out in the first few weeks after publication. The retelling of the classic Three Little Pigs story, told from the wolf's point of view, has since sold over a million copies and has been translated into ten languages.

The Smith/Scieszka team has continued to collaborate on other successful books, most notably, an ALA CALDECOTT MEDAL Honor Book, *The Stinky Cheese Man and Other Fairly Stupid Tales* (1992). S. says that the book plays with all the conventions of traditional stories and turns them upside down. For example, the zany character spoofs in the book include Chicken Licken, a parody of Chicken Little, who tells everyone the sky is falling, only to get crushed by the book's falling table of contents. Titles of stories are also rewritten—Little Red Riding Hood becomes "Little Red Running Shorts" and "The Princess and the Pea" becomes "The Princess and the Bowling Ball." Like their first book, *The Stinky Cheese Man* was an immediate success. S. told *New York* magazine's Barbara Ensor (1996), "Kind of overnight, we were legitimate children's books guys."

Later works by the successful duo include *Math Curse* (1995), the mathematical adventures of a hapless student whose teacher tells the students that they can think of almost everything as a math problem, and *Squids Will Be Squids* (1998), a book of contemporary fables. S. and Scieszka have also written a series of CHAPTER BOOKS for early or reluctant readers called The

Time Warp Trio. The series features three boys who experience various misadventures while traveling back in time.

In addition to his self-illustrated books for children and his collaborations with Scieszka, S. has made many other contributions to the world of children's literature. He provided artistic support for the 1996 animated film version of Roald DAHL's *James and the Giant Peach*, designing several of the animated characters and painting some of the pivotal moments in the story. He has also collaborated with Jack PRELUTSKY on the completion of a book begun by Theodore Geisel (Dr. SEUSS) called *Hooray for Diffendoofer Day!* (1998), the story of a teacher named "Miss Bonkers."

FURTHER WORKS: Self-illustrated: *Flying Jake,* 1989; *The Happy Hocky Family,* 1993; With Jon Scieszka: *The Good, the Bad, and the Goofy,* 1992; *Summer Reading Is Killing Me,* 1998; *Knights of the Kitchen Table,* 1991; *Tut, Tut!* 1998; *Your Mother Was a Neanderthal,* 1993; *2095,* 1995

REFERENCES: Ensor, B.; *Mr. Smith Goes to Hollywood.* New York, April 8, 1996, pp.50–53; "Lane Smith" Penguin Putnam Catalog web site. Accessed 4/7/99 (no author given); http://www. penguinputnam.com/catalog/yreader/authors/2783 _biography.html; Smith, L., 1993, "The Artist at Work," *The Horn Book* magazine, 69, pp. 65–70; *Something about the Author,* vol. 76, 1994

MARY ARIAIL BROUGHTON

SMITH, Robert Kimmel

Author, playwright, b. 31 July 1930, Brooklyn, New York

When he was eight years old, S. was confined to bed for months with rheumatic fever, with nothing to do but read. When the book *Toby Tyler; or, Ten Weeks with a Circus* (James Otis, 1881) made him cry, he started to dream of being a writer. The dream was reinforced when, at age ten, he had a joke published in a national magazine. "Seeing my name in print just made all kinds of things for me. Getting published jolted me." But it was not until age forty, after leaving a career in advertising, that S. embarked on writing full-time. His first book took shape when a bedtime story for his daughter developed into the novel that eventually became *Chocolate Fever* (1972).

S. gets his ideas from his own personal experiences. His process is not to make an outline, but rather to start with a hero and a general idea, then let the story unfold. "I don't want to know everything; that would be too boring for me. So in a sense, I am discovering the story along with my characters."

S. addresses the troubling issues that plague preadolescents: pressures of academics and competition, sibling irritations, difficult family relations, being overweight, and divorce. Both HUMOR and seriousness are important elements of his writing. In a publisher's biography, he says humor is "part of my character and part of my life. My father came home with new jokes every single day." Light, humorous banter, funny situations, original turns of phrase ("out of the corner of his ear") and comic word combinations ("Little pops and bigger pops and poppity-pop-pops kept popping") pepper his stories to keep his readers engaged.

"There are so many terrible things that happen every single day in the world. If you don't try to look on the funny side of life, it can be very grim." He incorporates underlying messages, such as the notion of "too much of a good thing," but without preaching to his readers. His message to children is, "Get the most out of yourself, enjoy life, and be good to people along the way." Love and compassion are the most important things in the world to him. "How we love and how we get along is what I'm usually writing about." Ultimately, he says, "My secret agenda is to create books so entertaining that the kids get hooked on reading, particularly boys, who need help."

AWARDS: Nene Award (1985) for *Jelly Belly.* Massachusetts Children's Book Award (1980) for *Chocolate Fever.* AMERICAN LIBRARY ASSOCIATION Best Book Award (1983) for *Jane's House.* Mark TWAIN Award (1987) Georgia Children's Book Award (1988–89) and ten additional state AWARDS for *The War with Grandpa.* Parents' Choice Award for Story Books (1992) for *The Squeaky Wheel*

FURTHER WORKS: *Ransom,* 1971; *Sadie Shapiro Trilogy,* 1973–79; *Jelly Belly,* 1981; *The War with Grandpa,* 1984; *Mostly Michael,* 1987; *Bobby Baseball,* 1989; *The Squeaky Wheel,* 1990

BIBLIOGRAPHY: *Something about the Author,* vol. 77, 1994. Young Hoosier award site: http://ideanet. doe.state.in.us/aime/yhbawinn; Georgia Awards list: http://www.mindspring.com/~mcarswell/win1.htm; http://library.cwu.edu/search/aCoville+Katherine/-5,-1,0,B/frameset&a+coville+ka;therine&1,1. Nene Awards: http://www.hcc.hawaii.edu/hspls/nene.html; Mark Twain Awards: http://www.mcpl.lib.mo.us/ch/mt.htm; BDD Books for Young Readers Teacher's Resource Center; http://www.bdd.com/bin/forums/teachers/smit.html; Library of Congress Website

MARGARET YATSEVITCH PHINNEY

SMITH, William Jay

Poet, translator, b. 22 April 1918, Winnfield, Louisiana

S. has distinguished himself as a creative and skilled poet whose love of language emanates from his POETRY. S.'s love of language stems from the guidance provided by a high school teacher and study abroad. S. is fluent in French and Italian and able to read Spanish and Russian; which allows him to see the nuances in language that create engaging poetry. As a translator, S. has introduced English speaking audiences to poetry from France and Eastern Europe. His own poems for children are full of imagery with lyric-like verse allowing readers to be swept up in fun. His wonderfully imaginative use of language creates an unforgettable experience for the reader. S.'s use of imagery in his children's poems creates a sophisticated result. His *Boy Blue's Book of Beasts* (1957), *Puptents and Pebbles: A Nonsense ABC* (1959), *Laughing Time: Nonsense Poems* (1980) and *Behind the King's Kitchen,* 1993, are examples of vibrant use of language that allows the reader to think, laugh, and imagine. S.'s rhythms capture the reader as well as the listener. *Birds and Beasts* (1990) is a spectacularly cadenced and visually imaginative book of poems to read aloud. S.'s poems for children are whimsical and often use nonsense verse that allows the reader's imagination to soar.

AWARDS: Young Poets Prize, *Poetry* magazine (1945). Alumni citation, Washington University (1963). Ford Fellowship for DRAMA (1964). Henry Bellamann Major Award (1970). Loines Award (1972). National Endowment for the Arts grant (1972). D. Litt, New England College (1973). National Endowment for the Humanities grant (1975). Gold Medal of Labor (Hungary, 1978). New England Poetry Club Golden Rose (1980). California Children's Book and Video Awards for recognition for excellence (1990) for

Ho for a Hat! Medal for service to the French language, French Academy (1991)

FURTHER WORKS: *Laughing Time,* 1955; *Typewriter Town,* 1960; *What Did I See?,* 1962; *My Little Book of Big and Little,* 1963; *If I Had a Boat,* 1966; *Mr. Smith and Other Nonsense,* 1968; *Around My Room and Other Poems,* 1969; *Grandmother Ostrich and Other Poems,* 1969; *Laughing Time and Other Poems,* 1969; *The Key,* 1982; *Laughing Time: Collected Nonsense,* 1990

BIBLIOGRAPHY: *Something about the Author,* vol. 68, 1992

NANCE S. WILSON

SNEVE, Virginia Driving Hawk

Author, anthologist, b. 21 February 1933, Rosebud, South Dakota

A Brule Sioux and enrolled member of the Rosebud Sioux Tribe, S. received her precollegiate education in Bureau of Indian Affairs and Catholic schools before completing B.S. and M.Ed. degrees at South Dakota State College. She holds an honorary doctorate from Dakota Wesleyan University. She has worked as a high school English teacher and counselor and an associate instructor in English at Oglala-Lakota College. She lectures and writes on Indian affairs. Dramatic dialogue and suspenseful STORYTELLING characterize her intermediate novels (e.g., *Betrayed,* 1974; *The Chichi Hoohoo Bogeyman,* 1975) at the same time that they acknowledge the blend of historical and contemporary Indian culture. Her First American SERIES (e.g., *The Navajos,* 1993; *The Cherokees,* 1996), written in a direct, instructive style, locate each tribe geographically, trace history, and describe customs, culture, government, social roles, games, the tribe's creation story, and the influence of the continent's newcomers. As a series, the books point out that this continent was inhabited by many cultures, illuminating the uniqueness of each tribe, and dispelling the stereotype of NATIVE AMERICANS as one culture. Without preaching, they implicitly show the endurance, adaptability, and resiliency of America's original peoples.

S.'s aim is to describe and portray her native heritage thoroughly and accurately. It was her daughter's interest in family stories that prompted her to write for children. An investigation of representations of Native Americans in written histories compelled her to dispel the stereotypes she found. She did not approve of the violent demonstrations by the American Indian Movement, which she sees as leaving local residents to deal with the backlash that such efforts precipitate. Instead, she quietly presents the facts, allowing her readers to discover for themselves the inequities of historical and current events. *Betrayed* (1974), for example, is the painful story of the broken promises by whites resulting in the desperate 1862 Minnesota uprising by the Santee Sioux. More so, she celebrates her heritage and its value to her people: *High Elk's Treasure* (1972) emphasizes the preciousness of artifacts of historical significance to a tribe. A particular strength of her fiction writing is her portrayal of modern, everyday Native American life on a reservation. S.'s clear, honest, and noneditorial presentation of facts serves to credibly clarify and reorient history and to dispel stereotypes.

AWARDS: Writer of the Year Award from the Western Heritage Hall of Fame (1984). North American Indian Prose Award (1991). Author-Illustrator Human and Civil Rights Award from the National Education Association (1996). South Dakota State Counselors' Association 1996 Human Rights Award. Spirit of Crazy Horse Award from Black Hills Seminars' Youth at Risk (1996). Living Indian Artist Treasure Award presented by Northern Plains Tribal Arts and South Dakotans for the Arts (1997)

FURTHER WORKS: *Jimmy Yellow Hawk,* 1972; *When Thunder Spoke,* 1974; *The Twelve Moons,* 1977; *Dancing TeePees: Poems of American Indian Youth,* 1989; First American series. 1993–97

BIBLIOGRAPHY: http://www.nativeauthors.com/search/bio/biosneve.html; http://www.nativeauthors.com/search/title/3842.html; *Institute of American Indian Studies,* Annual Joseph Harper Cash Memorial Lecture, Fall, 1997; Introduction: http://www.usd.edu/iais/iais/people/cashlecture 3.html; http://www.usd.edu/iais/iais/people/cash lecture.html; North American Indian Prose Award Entries: http://hanksville.phast.umass.edu/misc/announce/UNP.html; Author paper: "Women of the Circle": http://www.usd.edu/iais/iais/people/WOC~1.HTM; *Seventh Book of Junior Authors,* 1996; *Something about the Author,* vol. 95, 1998; Library of Congress web site. Contributor's assessment

MARGARET YATSEVITCH PHINNEY

SNICKET, Lemony (Daniel Handler)

Author, b. 1969, San Francisco, California

Lemony Snicket is the pseudonym of Daniel Handler, author of adult novels *The Basic Eight* (1999) and *Watch Your Mouth* (2000) under his own name. A 1992 graduate of Wesleyan University in Massachusetts, S. received an Academy of American Poets Prize in 1990 and an Olin Fellowship in 1992, which enabled him to write full-time. The son of an accountant and a college dean, S. first wrote poetry and then switched to fiction as he noticed his poetry become increasingly proselike. He also wrote comedy material for a syndicated radio program called *The House of Blues Radio Hour* in his native San Francisco.

"If you are interested in stories with happy endings, you would be better off reading some other book." So begins *The Bad Beginning* (1999), the first in a projected SERIES of thirteen gothic-style melodramatic novels under the collective name A Series of Unfortunate Events. S. is a master of the morose description, the gloomy, bleak archaic phrase and literary send-up, striking an even balance of delight and despair. He writes in the tradition of Charles DICKENS, Roald DAHL, and Edward GOREY. Working in a serio-comic Victorian–gothic style, S. presents the evil Count Olaf, so thoroughly evil that he has no redeeming or virtuous characteristics. He is single-mindedly determined to get his hands on the Baudelaire orphans' fortune by any means available. His relentless pursuit follows Violet, Klaus, and baby Sunny through shade and darkness; the three being pursued all the time retaining their positive outlook on life, certain that good will triumph over evil despite the series' opening sentence and the hapless efforts of a series of inept guardians, one of whom is eaten by monster-sized leeches in *The Wide Window* (2000), while the others are similarly dispatched to comically grotesque violent ends.

S.'s series of novels intended for middle-grade readers, four of which appeared at the same time on the extended *New York Times* list of best-selling Children's Novels on July 23, 2000, make consistent use of wordplay, literary allusions, and stock characters from gothic novels. The young heroes are good, pure of heart, ever cheerful, and hopeful despite the number of unrelenting obstacles put in their path. Count Olaf is unrelentingly evil, a composite of all such dreary characters from every second-rate grade–B movie. He appears at each opportune moment that catastrophe overtakes the ever-happy orphans.

S.'s sophisticated HUMOR is repeatedly dispensed as he interrupts the stories to define words and expressions: "Uncle Monty would often segue—a word which here means 'let the conversation veer off.' " (*The Reptile Room,* 1999). Even the author's name is an allusion to the sly, suppressed laughter that fill the pages of each book. Sinister puns and literary allusions abound. One of their custodians, Uncle Monty, advises them about handling toads and snakes "to never, under any circumstances, let the Virginia Wolfsnake near a typewriter." The orphans, inveterate readers, find a library available to them at each macabre place they are sent to live.

Television, film, and audio rights to S.'s work have been purchased, and foreign-publishing rights have been sold in many countries.

FURTHER WORKS: *The Miserable Mill,* 2000; *The Austere Academy,* 2000; *The Ersatz Elevator,* 2001

BIBLIOGRAPHY: *New York Times* Book Review, October 14, 2000; publisher's press release

DIANE G. PERSON

SNYDER, Zilpha Keatley

Author, teacher, lecturer, b. 11 May 1927, Lemoore, California

S. spent the early years of her life in rural southern California. After graduation from Whittier College, S. taught school for nine years, three of them as a master teacher for the University of California at Berkeley.

S.'s books, most of which are written for children and young adults, have won numerous literary awards, including three ALA NEWBERY MEDAL Honor Book AWARDS for *The Egypt Game* (1967), *The Headless Cupid* (1971), and *The Witches of Worm* (1972). *The Witches of Worm* also received a nomination for the National Book Award. Other books have received honors from the AMERICAN LIBRARY ASSOCIATION, the Christopher Medal, *School Library Journal,* and the American Library Guild. Her works have been included on several state book master lists. In addition, her books have been published in eleven foreign countries, and five have been recorded on audiocassettes. The SCIENCE FICTION "Green-sky trilogy" *Below the Root* (1975), *And All Between* (1976), and *Until the Celebration* (1977) has been recast as a computer game.

Although S. claims that she decided to become a writer at the age of eight, it was not until she was an adult that she found time to write books for publication. S. claims, "All of my books are fiction—for me writing anything else is simply a chore—and many of my stories have a touch of the fantastical." Most of her early works were inspired by memories from her childhood. She recalls that, as a child, she constantly invented games and fantasies that enlivened her ordinary environment. Her critically acclaimed book, *The Egypt Game,* came from a period of her youth that she called the "Egyptian period," a year during which she was fascinated by the life and times of ancient Egyptian culture. Most of S.'s books have a strong, powerful element of FANTASY regardless of setting.

S. often speaks to groups of children and adults about her writing. To the popular question, Why do you write? she replies, "The maximum reward is simply—joy; the storyteller's joy in creating a story and sharing it with an audience."

FURTHER WORKS: *Libby on Wednesday,* 1990; *Cat Running,* 1994; *Fool's Gold,* 1994; *Song of the Gargoyle,* 1994; *The Trespassers,* 1996; *The Gypsy Game,* 1997; *Gib Rides Home,* 1998

BIBLIOGRAPHY: HOPKINS, Lee Bennett, *Pauses: Autobiographical Reflections of 101 Creators of Children's Books,* 1995. Gallo, D. R. ed. *Speaking for Ourselves.* 1990. Snyder, Z. K. 1998. [online]. Available: http://www~microweb.com~lsnyder/Autobiography.html [June 25, 1998]; 25

MARY ANAIL BROUGHTON

SOBOL, Donald

Author, b. 4 October 1924, New York City

S. grew up in New York City. He was in the U.S. Army Corps of Engineers from 1943 to 1946, serving in the Pacific Theater during World War II. He then worked as a copyboy and later reporter for the *New York Sun* and *Long Island Daily Press,* 1946–52. S. received a B.A. from Oberlin College in 1948, and attended the New

School for Social Research from 1949 to 1951. At age thirty, S. began writing, inspired by a short-story writing course he had taken in college years earlier. He wrote under various pen names in pulp magazines while working as a reporter. S., the author of numerous MYSTERY AND DETECTIVE STORIES, has many interests, including restoring antique cars, boating, fishing, and gardening.

S.'s first books were nonfiction, generally historical in nature, ranging from *The First Book of Barbarian Invaders, A.D. 375–511* (1962) to *Two Flags Flying* (BIOGRAPHIES of Civil War leaders, 1960). He is best known, however, for his Encyclopedia Brown books. The first of these, *Encyclopedia Brown: Boy Detective*, was published in 1963 after twenty-six rejections. Each of the hugely popular Encyclopedia Brown books contains ten short mysteries for readers to solve (with solutions provided in the back of the book). The books are plot-driven, with minimal characterization, and full of puns and jokes. The uniform design of each short mystery makes the books easy for young children to read. Sobol's foremost goal as a writer for children is to entertain. His Encyclopedia Brown books have been translated into thirteen languages and Braille and have made their way into film, television shows, films, and comic strips.

AWARDS: S. won the Mystery Writers of America's Edgar Allan Poe Award in 1975 for his body of work. In addition, S.'s Encyclopedia Brown books have won many state and regional awards, including the Young Readers Choice Award of the Pacific Northwest Library Association, the Garden State Children's Book Award, a Buckeye honor citation, and the Aiken County, South Carolina Children's Book Award

FURTHER WORKS: Among the many titles in the Encyclopedia Brown series: *Encyclopedia Brown and the Case of the Secret Pitch*. 1965. *Encyclopedia Brown Saves the Day*. 1970. *Encyclopedia Brown Takes the Cake*. 1973. *Encyclopedia Brown Lends a Hand*. 1974. *Encyclopedia Brown and the Case of the Midnight Visitor*. 1977. *Encyclopedia Brown Carries On*. 1980. *Encyclopedia Brown and the Case of the Mysterious Handprints*. 1985. *Encyclopedia Brown and the Case of the Treasure Hunt*. 1988. *Encyclopedia Brown and the Case of the Two Spies*. 1994. *Encyclopedia Brown and the Case of Pablo's Nose*. 1996. *Encyclopedia Brown and the Case of the Sleep-*

ing Dog. 1998. Other fiction: *Secret Agents Four*. 1967. *Milton, the Model A*. 1970. *Angie's First Case*. 1981. *The Amazing Power of Ashur Fine*. 1986. *My Name Is Amelia*. 1994. Three books in the Two-Minute Mysteries series, based on S.'s 1959–68 internationally syndicated newspaper feature. History and biography: *The Double Quest*. 1957. *First Book of Medieval Man*. 1959. *The Wright Brothers at Kitty Hawk*. 1961. *The First Book of Stocks and Bonds*. (with wife Rose Sobol). 1963. *Lock, Stock, and Barrel*. 1965. *The Amazons of Greek Mythology*. 1972. *Great Sea Stories*. 1975. *True Sea Adventures*. 1975. *Greta the Strong*. 1979. Two edited history collections—*A Civil War Sampler*. 1961. And *An American Revolutionary War Reader*. 1964

BIBLIOGRAPHY: Berger, L. S. *Twentieth-Century Children's Writers*. 1995. *Fourth Book of Junior Authors and Illustrators*. 1978. Silvey, Anita, ed. *Children's Books and Their Creators*. 1995

JANE WEST

SOCIETY OF CHILDREN'S BOOK WRITERS AND ILLUSTRATORS

Founded in 1971, The Society of Children's Book Writers and Illustrators (SCBWI), located in Beverly Hills, California, is an organization of 11,500 people working in the areas of children's books, multimedia, magazines, film, and television. Writers or illustrators new to the field are welcomed as associate members. Professionals working in the children's field are welcomed as full members. SCBWI serves as a unified voice for professional writers and illustrators across the country to take positions and effect important changes within the field of children's literature. Membership in the SCBWI is open to anyone with an active interest in children's literature. Full membership is open to those whose work for children—books, ILLUSTRATIONS, photographs, films, television, electronic media, articles, poems or stories—has been published or produced. Professional EDITORS, agents, and PUBLISHERS are included in this category. Associate membership is open to all those with an interest in children's literature or media, whether or not they have been published or produced.

SCBWI members have successfully lobbied for new copyright legislation, equitable treatment of authors and artists, and fair contract terms. SCBWI is a national guild with regional activities that offers maximum opportunities for member participation on a one-to-one basis. It provides individual advice, information, and counsel. The organization prides itself on taking a personal interest in the careers of its members. There are more than fifty regional advisors in every state and several countries who organize regular writing and illustrating meetings, critique groups, and workshops for new and published authors.

A four-day National Conference, held each summer, is devoted entirely to writing and illustrating literature for children. Notable award-winning authors, illustrators, editors, agents, and publishers present lectures, workshops, and individual manuscript and art consultation. Regional conferences, workshops, and critique groups, sponsored by SCBWI, provide members the opportunity to share writing and illustrating experiences. They meet well-known writers, illustrators, editors and publishers of children's literature.

The *SCBWI Bulletin* is published bimonthly and contains current and comprehensive information in the field of children's literature. The *Bulletin* features the latest market reports, articles on issues in writing, illustrating, and publishing, information of contests and awards, news of SCBWI members, changes in publishing programs and staff as well as ongoing SCBWI activities throughout the country. New members receive a bound book containing over twenty separate publications including guides to agents; foreign, magazine, and religious markets; contracts, small press markets, work-in-progress grants, multimedia producers, critique groups, frequently asked questions, and market surveys. These materials are frequently updated. They are available only to SCBWI members. New members also receive a bound roster that includes the names and addresses of members and regional advisors in the United States and foreign countries.

The Golden Kite Awards are given annually to SCBWI members for outstanding work in fiction, nonfiction, illustration and picture-book text. These AWARDS are among the most prestigious national honors in children's literature. Recipients receive a Golden Kite statue or an Honor book plaque. Awards are also given for outstanding original magazine work for young people, written or illustrated by SCBWI members. Four plaques and Honor certificates are awarded annu-

ally for fiction, nonfiction, poetry, and illustration in the magazine category. Financial grants are available each year to full and associate SCBWI members. Four work-in-progress grants are awarded annually to assit individual members to complete specific projects. The grants made include General, Contemporary Novel, Nonfiction Research, and Previously Unpublished Author. The Don FREEMAN Memorial Grant-in-Aid stipend in honor of an outstanding artist is given to SCBWI artists working in the picture-book field. The stipend memorializes the life of Don Freeman, creator of the Corduroy PICTURE BOOK titles. The Barbara Karlin Grant is an annual grant to encourage the work of aspiring picture-book writers. The recipient of the annual Sue ALEXANDER Grant, awarded annually for an outstanding manuscript, receives an expense-paid trip to New York and private meetings with three editors.

LIN OLIVER AND BERNICE E. CULLINAN

SOENTPIET, Chris
Author, illustrator, b. 3 January 1970, Seoul, South Korea

S.'s illustrations are characterized as lively and detailed as well as expressive, emotional and warm. *Around Town* (1994) written and illustrated by S. celebrates life in the city with an appropriate vitality of illustrations and text. The expressive faces in *Peacebound Train* (1996), a chapter book with pictures, and the richly illuminated, warm illustrations of *More Than Anything Else* (1995) show another aspect of S.'s art. The illustrations greatly contribute to the authenticity and the cultural portrayal within each book. S. has received many AWARDS including Notable Children's Trade Books in the Field of Social Studies by NCSS, the INTERNATIONAL READING ASSOCIATION Teacher Choices Recognition, and American Booksellers Award.

FURTHER WORKS: Illustrator: *The Last Dragon* (S. Nunes), 1995; *Silver Packages* (H. Balgassi, C. RYLANT), 1997; *A Sign* (George Ella LYON) 1998, *So Far from the Sea* (Eve BUNTING), 1998

BIBLIOGRAPHY: *Something about the Author*, vol. 96, 1998; the *Horn Book* magazine, pp. 586–87, Sept./Oct., 1995

JANELLE B. MATHIS

SORENSEN, Virginia

Author, b. 17 February 1912, Provo, Utah; d. 24 December 1991, Hendersonville, North Carolina

S. was well known for both her children's and adult books. Of Danish ancestry, S. said that she was devoted to the United States, Denmark, and Morocco, where her husband chose to live and write, since all three countries represent her life experiences. (She was married to Alec Waugh.) Her adult novels were noted for simple, direct prose with characters that were realistic and convincing. Her books for adults represented a variety of interests such as Mormon women and Yaqui Indians. S. began to focus on writing children's books in the mid-1950s.

Miracles on Maple Hill (1957), the story of an adventurous family and the miracles they discover around them, received the ALA NEWBERY MEDAL. Set in rural Pennsylvania, this story of growth and renewal tells the tale of how two city children learn about the pleasures of life in a rural setting, after their father returns from a prisoner-of-war camp. *Plain Girl* (1955) winner of the Children's Book Award of the Child Study Association of America, presents a sympathetic portrait of the Amish people in Pennsylvania. In *Lotte's Locket* (1964), S. sensitively portrays the difficulty of moving to a new country as Lotte prepares to leave the home her family has lived in for generations and move to the United States, always a wrenching prospect for a child.

FURTHER WORKS: *Curious Missie,* 1953; *The House Next Door,* 1954; *Around the Corner,* 1971

BIBLIOGRAPHY: HOPKINS, Lee Bennett, *Pauses: Autobiographical Reflections of 101 Creators of Children's Books*, 1995; *Something about the Author,* vol. 1, 1972, and vol. 68, 1992

JANELLE B. MATHIS

SOTO, Gary

Poet, essayist, children's fiction writer, filmmaker, b. 12 April 1952, Fresno, California

Growing up poor, S. learned the meaning of hard work in the truck farms and factories of California's San Joaquin Central Valley. From experiences picking grapes, melons, and cotton, painting houses, and washing cars, Soto came to realize the only way he would escape a life of hard labor was to go on with his education. In 1974 he graduated magna cum laude with an English degree from California State University, Fresno, and later earned a Master of Fine Arts in Creative Writing from the University of California, Irvine.

Influenced by his love of POETRY, particularly the beat poets, S.'s books for children and young adults, set in the family-oriented barrio communities where he grew up, are imbued with "a poet's eye for detail and a poet's love of language." Lines like, "two pairs of shoes moored under my bed," and "I let the dirt pour like time from my palm," (*Jesse,* 1994) are subtle reinforcement of his comment that he is "a poet first. But prose pays the bills." He is a master at unobtrusively embedding descriptions of both the beauty and chaos of the barrio without distracting from the central story thread he is building. His plots are low-key, quiet, allowing his reader to focus on the theme and the personalities of his central characters and their relationships. His protagonists, young Mexican-Americans, are neither villains nor Pollyannas, but complex human beings trying to find their way as they balance a sense of morality with a need to explore themselves and their place in the multiple worlds of family, peers, school culture, Mexican culture, and the sometimes confusing and contradictory larger society.

S. recognizes and celebrates the pleasures, dilemmas, and issues of childhood and coming of age as a Mexican-American in America. He writes, "My mission of portraying Mexican-Americans is a continual worry and one I take seriously. . . . I am accountable to my people; for me, there is no place to hide if I make a mistake."

AWARDS: Numerous AWARDS, including: U.S. Award for International Poetry Forum (1977) for *The Elements of San Joaquin.* Before Columbus Foundation American Book Award (1985) for *Living up the Street.* AMERICAN LIBRARY ASSOCIATION's Best Book for YOUNG ADULTS (1990), Beatty Award from California Library Association, and Reading Magic Award from *Parenting* magazine (1991) and for *Baseball in April and Other Stories.* CARNEGIE MEDAL for Excellence in Children's Video for *Pool Party* (1993), ALA Booklist Books for Young Editors' Choices (1993) for *Too Many Tamales.* ALA Notable Book and Parenting Reading Magic Award

(1995) for *Chato's Kitchen.* Bank Street College Child Study Children's Books of the Year (1997) for *The Old Man and His Door* (1996)

FURTHER WORKS: *Cat's Meow,* 1987; *Taking Sides.* 1991; *Neighborhood Odes,* 1992; *Too Many Tamales,* 1993; *Snapshots from the Wedding,* 1997; *Buried Onions,* 1997; *Chato and the Party Animals,* 1998; *Petty Crimes,* 1998

BIBLIOGRAPHY: Bremner, B. "Exalting the Everyday: An Interview with Gary Soto." *Hungry Mind Review.* Fall, 1992; contributor's assessment, http://www.penguinputnam.com/catalog/ yreader/authors/ 199_biography.html; Library of Congress website; *Something about the Author,* vol. 80, 1995; Soto, G., (January 1996), "Chato's Kitchen;" Booklinks, p. 54

MARGARET YATSEVITCH PHINNEY

SORCHE NIC LEODHAS
(See NIC LEODHAS, Sorche)

SOUTHALL, Ivan
Author, b. 8 June 1921, Melbourne, Victoria, Australia

S. was reared in a devoutly religious Methodist family, which he remembers with fondness and gratitude; he credits his literary foundation to the influence of the King James version of the Bible. His writing career began during adolescence when he entered and won a short story competition. His parents had little money or education, but they supported their son's decision to become a writer. However, the family's lack of resources and the early death of his father forced S. to abandon his studies shortly after he completed the ninth grade. In 1941, he joined the Royal Australian Air Force, during which he kept a diary that later served as a basis for his book, *The Long Night Watch* (1983). After a distinguished career in the military, S. worked briefly as a photoengraver, but resigned in 1947 in order to devote more time to writing.

S. is a prolific writer who has written fiction and nonfiction for both adults and children. Despite his limited formal schooling, he has become one of Australia's most celebrated children's authors, winning such prestigious AWARDS as the Australian Children's Book of the Year Award: *Ash Road* (1965), *To the Wild Sky* (1967), *Bread and Honey* (1970), and *Fly West* (1975); the Australian PICTURE BOOK of the Year Award for *Sly*

Old Wardrobe (1968), and the CARNEGIE MEDAL, Library Association (England) for *Josh* (1971). His novels often feature ordinary children coping with extraordinary circumstances through which they learn, grow, and change. Although some critics have challenged S.'s characteristically mature and potentially frightening subject matter, he maintains his technique because he respects children as intellectuals. The endings of his books are often ambiguous, leaving the reader to fill in the gaps. In an essay for *Something about the Author Autobiography Series,* S. wrote, "One of my objectives as a writer primarily for the young has been to 'protect' the great moments of live [sic], not to spoil them or 'give them away.' It's why so many of my ending [sic] are open and why I've brought the reader to bridges over which imagination has to cross."

FURTHER WORKS: *Hill's End,* 1962; *The Curse of Cain: Bible Stories Retold,* 1968; *A City Out of Sight,* 1984; *Rachel,* 1986; *Blackbird,* 1988; *The Mysterious World of Marcus Leadbeater,* 1990

BIBLIOGRAPHY: *Major Authors and Illustrators for Children and YOUNG ADULTS: A Selection of Sketches from "Something about the Author."* vol. 5. 1993. Schmidt, M., and P. Schmidt. 1996. Ivan Southall. (online available: http://dargo.vicnet. net.au/ozlit/writers.cfin?id=520.0 (accessed July 24, 1988)

MARY ARIAIL BROUGHTON

(See AUSTRALIAN LITERATURE)

SPEARE, Elizabeth George
Author, b. 21 November 1908, Melrose, Massachusetts; d. 15 November 1994, Tucson, Arizona

Ever since she was a child, S. knew that she wanted to write. It was not unusual to see her at a family reunion, huddled with her favorite cousin, excitedly sharing stories they had written. A native New Englander, S. felt comfortable writing about the Colonial Period in American history, believing that, in many ways, very little had changed in the people and the countryside during the past three hundred years. S. attended Smith College (1926–27) and received her B.A. (1930) and M.A. (1932) from Boston University. For the next four years, S. taught high school English in Rockland and Auburn, Massachusetts. Although her attempts to teach Shakespeare and Browning were not fully embraced by the students, S. discovered that she enjoyed teaching. In 1936, she married an industrial engineer. She did not return to her lifelong dream of being a writer until her children were in junior high school.

Publishing only five books for children, S.'s recognition and place in children's literature comes from the literary quality of her work, rather than the quantity. S. admitted that it took a year or more to gather material for a book, culling through library and museum records and producing copious notes. Though not a prolific writer, her literature has endured four decades of critical scrutiny, twice receiving the NEWBERY MEDAL. Primarily regarded as an author of historical fiction, S. has established herself as a meticulous researcher who can recreate settings and convincingly place readers in periods as diverse as the time of Jesus (*The Bronze Bow*) and colonial America (*Calico Captive, The Witch of Blackbird Pond,* and *The Sign of the Beaver*). *Calico Captive* (1957), S.'s first book, is a fictionalized adaptation of a true story based on a pre–Revolutionary War journal published in 1807. Intended for teenage girls, the story's protagonist is Miriam Willard, a New England girl who, along with her family, is held captive by Indians. Readers accompany Miriam and her family on a forced march to Canada (eventually Montreal) where they are sold by the Indians to the French, with whom the English are in conflict. Although sometimes criticized for its 1957 viewpoint and lack of attention to NATIVE AMERICANS, this novel proved to be a worthy first work, showcasing S.'s considerable research skill, an indefatigable attention to detail, and a talent for developing believable characters through situation and dialogue.

In *The Witch of Blackbird Pond* (1958), her writing skills became even more apparent. Set during seventeenth century Puritan times in Wethersfield, Connecticut, it is the story of Kit, a young, impulsive, outgoing girl who has just arrived at her relatives' home in a small, dour New England community from her carefree existence in Barbados. In tackling the bigotry and persecution that surrounded the witch trials, S. balances the narrative with characters and relationships that convey compassion, friendship, and courage. Young Kit befriends Hannah Tupper, an old Quaker woman who is believed to be a witch and is, therefore, something of a town pariah. When

the community is struck by illness, Hannah is targeted as the scapegoat, and the vibrant Kit, in an attempt to help Hannah, is also labeled a witch and put on trial. The dramatic use of contrast in character and setting enlivens the tale, as S. juxtaposes the effervescent, carefree Kit with the stodgy, rigid Puritan community and the sunny skies and exotic island of Barbados with the damp, grayness of New England. Though some critics have complained that Kit's character is diminished because her main concerns revolve around marriage, S.'s characterization of Kit has been defended precisely in terms of its historical accuracy. Kit's perspective reflects the limited choices available to young women during the seventeenth century. To deny this would do a disservice to the genre of historical fiction and taint the author's credibility.

After being awarded the 1959 ALA NEWBERY MEDAL for *The Witch of Blackbird Pond,* S. published her third work of historical fiction, *The Bronze Bow* and it, too, would receive the Newbery Medal in 1962. For this novel, S. departed from Colonial times in New England, yet pursued the issue of religious persecution. Set during the time of Jesus, it is the story of Daniel of Galilee who joins the Rosh, a mountain group that is determined to resist the Romans. Consumed with hatred for the people who crucified his parents and seeing the pain it has caused his sister Leah, Daniel accepts the sometimes cruel methods employed by the underground resistance. His dynamic character evolves upon an encounter with Jesus, whose teachings of love soothe his hatred and enable Daniel to turn from the violence of the Rosh. In *The Bronze Bow,* S. effectively unites character and setting with a style that has been praised as both restrained and compassionate.

If *Calico Captive* lacked a balanced point of view, S.'s *The Sign of the Beaver* (1983) certainly achieves this balance by way of a meaningful relationship between two characters and two cultures. An ALA Newbery Medal Honor Book (1984) and winner of the Scott O'DELL Award for Historical Fiction (1983), *The Sign of the Beaver* is arguably S.'s best work. Set in the eighteenth century, this novel combines historical fiction with wilderness SURVIVAL STORIES. It is the story of thirteen-year-old Matt, who must try to survive while his father leaves to bring his mother and sister to their new cabin in the Maine woods. Near death from an attack of angry bees, Matt is rescued by an old Indian, Saknis, and his grandson, Attean. From this modest premise, S. develops a relationship between Matt and Attean that becomes almost symbiotic, where the boys and the reader can appreciate the strengths of each culture. Using *Robinson Crusoe,* Matt teaches Attean how to read, and Attean passes on to Matt the secrets and wonders of the forest, giving him a greater appreciation of NATIVE AMERICAN culture. Mutual respect grows and Matt begins to recognize that the ways of the Indian are being threatened by the encroachment of the white man, and, most importantly, that the white man's ways are not necessarily better. S.'s narrative is exquisitely written, accurately and poetically conveying the forest setting through the colors, sounds, and activity of regional flora and fauna. Through his relationship with Attean, Matt acquires an inner strength and self-confidence that is genuine, not contrived. These characters, as in all of S.'s novels, are believable because S. allows them to evolve with the narrative. In 1989, S. was given the Laura Ingalls WILDER Award for her substantial and lasting contribution to children's literature.

AWARDS: ALA Newbery Medal (1959) for *The Witch of Blackbird Pond* and (1962) for *The Bronze Bow.* ALA Newbery Medal Honor Book (1984), Scott O'Dell Award (1983), Christopher Award (1984), and Child Study Committee Award (1983) all for *The Sign of the Beaver* (1983) and Laura Ingalls Wilder Award (1989)

FURTHER WORKS: *Life in Colonial America,* 1963

BIBLIOGRAPHY: HOPKINS, Lee Bennett, *Pauses: Autobiographical Reflections of 101 Creators of Children's Books,* 1995; *Children's Literature Review,* vol. 8, 1984

ANDREW KANTAR

SPENCE, Eleanor R.

Australian author, b. 21 October 1928, Sydney, New South Wales, Australia

S.'s former occupations led to her career as a fiction writer. During her days working as a librarian, she realized that relatively little literature was available for children of families intending to move to Australia. This led her to write books such as *Patterson's Track* (1958), *Lillypilly Hill* (1961), and *Green Laurel* (1963). Other S. books

are based on the journals she kept while working with autistic and handicapped children. In *The Nothing Place* (1972), she describes a boy who must learn to accept his partial deafness, while he adjusts to living in a new neighborhood. *The October Child,* a.k.a. *The Devil Hole* (1976), portrays a family dealing with the birth of a child with autism.

Green Laurel, The October Child, and *Deezle Boy* (1987) received the Family Award, given to those books that present families coping with challenges in a realistic fashion, and show believable difficulties that can be overcome. Both *Green Laurel* and *The October Child* also won the AUSTRALIAN Children's Book of the Year Award.

BIBLIOGRAPHY: *Contemporary Authors,* vol. 3, 1981

DENISE P. BEASLEY

SPERRY, Armstrong W.

Author, b. 7 November 1897, New Haven, Connecticut; d. 28 April 1976, Hanover, New Hampshire

Intrigued as a boy by his grandfather's tales of the South Sea Islands, in later years S. explored the South Sea Islands, Europe, the West Indies, and the United States. A writer of ADVENTURE fiction, REALISTIC FICTION, biography and INFORMATIONAL BOOKS, he began his career as an illustrator, tried writing and then became a writer/illustrator of children's books. He spent two years in the South Pacific French-owned islands and many of his story themes have come from this. *Call It Courage,* winner of the 1941 ALA NEWBERY MEDAL, is one such book. *Storm Canvas* (1944) won the *New York Herald Tribune* Children's Spring Book Festival award and *The Rain Forest* (1947) won the Boy's Clubs of America Junior Book Award in 1949.

Set Sail (1935) was named an ALA Newbery Medal Honor Book and concerns an actual 1840s ship, *The Flying Cloud.* He wrote young adult novels with main characters that faced adult situations causing them to grow and mature. His conviction was that "No writer should ever write down to children. He should tell his story clearly . . . presented to them honestly."

BIBLIOGRAPHY: *Something about the Author,* vol. 27, 1982; Silvey, Anita, ed., *Children's Books*

107. DR. SEUSS (THEODOR GEISEL)

108. ERNEST H. SHEPARD

109. SEYMOUR SIMON

110. ISAAC BASHEVIS SINGER

111. ELIZABETH GEORGE SPEARE

and Their Creators 1995; *Fiction, FOLKLORE, FANTASY and Poetry for Children, 1876–1985,* 1986

IRVYN GILBERTSON

SPIER, Peter
Author, illustrator, b. 6 June 1927, Amsterdam, Netherlands

Illustrator of dozens of titles, including more than forty he has authored, S. is one of the most widely acclaimed and talented author-illustrators in the field. S. was reared in the birthplace of the legendary Hans Brinker, the small farming village of Broek in Waterland. After graduating from an Amsterdam art school, serving in the Dutch navy, and working for Holland's largest magazine as a reporter, S. came to New York City in 1958 to sell his art work. His career in children's literature started with a project focused on goats, and he has been writing and illustrating children's books ever since. S.'s books help us know the everyday lives of all kinds of people engaged in a wide variety of activities in different parts of the world, and in different times in history. Through his careful research, he satisfies our curiosity about what life was really like "back then" or "over there." He makes us comfortable with differences through intimate details, color, humor, and a delightful gaiety that seems to permeate every page. About his process, he writes, "Since most of the PICTURE BOOKS I have done had some sort of historical background . . . I first try to find out as much as possible about subject or region. Then I go there . . . to collect the hundreds of details . . . that go into the making of a book . . . [There] you find the things one's imagination cannot supply and which one needs to give the very essence of the subject."

"I have come to the conclusion that a good children's book is child-like, and a bad one is childish. After the books reach their young hands, it is up to the children to decide whether a book will live or die. It's a good thing, too, for I have always found them pretty shrewd and reliable judges!" S.'s books deliver subtle, positive, nonpreachy messages about life and living to his readers. On the title page of *People* (1980), he quotes fourth century Greek poet Menander: "In many ways the saying, 'Know thyself' is not well said. / It were more practical to say, 'Know other people!' "

AWARDS: ALA CALDECOTT MEDAL Honor Book (1962) for *The Fox Went out on a Chilly Night.* New York Academy of Science's Children's Science Book Award for *Gobble, Growl, Grunt* (1972). AMERICAN LIBRARY ASSOCIATION Caldecott Medal (1978) for *Noah's Ark.* National Conference of Christians' and Jews' National Mass Media Award (1980) for *People.* Christopher Medal (1971) for *The Erie Canal,* (1978) for *Noah's Ark,* (1981) for *People.* American Book Award (1980) for *People. Horn Book–Boston Globe* Award (1967) for *London Bridge Is Falling Down.* University of Southern Mississippi Silver Medallion/DE GRUMMOND COLLECTION (1984) for his overall career work in children's literature

FURTHER WORKS: *The Star Spangled Banner.* 1974. *Oh, Were They Ever Happy!* 1978. *Food Market.* 1981. *Peter Spier's Christmas!* 1983. *The Book of Jonah.* 1985. *Dreams.* 1986. *Circus.* 1992

BIBLIOGRAPHY: HOPKINS, Lee Bennett, *Pauses: Autobiographical Reflections of 101 Creators of Children's Books,* 1995; Contributor's assessment. The Kerlan Archive material. Release (in THE KERLAN COLLECTION). www.asc.ucalgary.ca/~dkbrown/christopher.html; letter from Peter Spier to the *Juvenile Book Fair Newsletter,* v. xiii, November 1969, pp. 2–3

MARGARET YATSEVITCH PHINNEY

SPINELLI, Jerry
Author, b. 1 February 1941, Norristown, Pennsylvania

Author of children's and young adult books, S. spent most of his childhood in the West End of Norristown, Pennsylvania. He earned an A.B. from Gettysburg College in 1963 and an M.A. from Johns Hopkins University in 1964. He also attended Temple University in 1964.

S. is best known for his contemporary tall tale, *Maniac Magee* (1990), which won the NEWBERY MEDAL. Like most of S.'s work, *Maniac Magee* is characterized by its HUMOR, appeal to early adolescents, and imaginative characters. The hero is a boy who, after running away from his foster home, continues to run—right through the racially divided town of Two Mills and into the hearts of its citizens. Initially, S. struggled to find a way to speak for the character but eventually he decided to tell the tale through the voice of its legend. He says of the character, "Now I understood where Maniac had been running. He had

741

been heading for that repository in our collective memory, to the attic treasures in our heads, where today spills into yesterday and all becomes believable. . . . Maniac Magee is us."

Many of the characters and events in S.'s books are drawn from his experiences with his children and from memories of his own adolescence. For example, the inspiration for *Space Station Seventh Grade* (1982) resulted from an incident when he went to the refrigerator to retrieve some leftover fried chicken for his lunch but found that one of his children had left only chicken bones. He was angry about having to go to work "chickenless." He decided to write about the incident from the kid's point of view and continued to write his first novel. He notes, "A lot of folks would have seen a bag of chicken bones. I saw a career." Although some of S.'s work has been criticized for its "ribald jokes and risqué topics of conversation" and for its irreverent treatment of serious issues such as racism, S.'s books continue to be enormously popular with young readers.

AWARDS: ALA Newbery Medal Award (1991) for *Maniac Magee. Boston Globe–Horn Book* Award (1990) for *Maniac Magee.* AMERICAN LIBRARY ASSOCIATION Newbery Medal Honor Award (1998) for *Wringer*

FURTHER WORKS: *Who Put That Hair in My Toothbrush?* 1984. *Jason and Marceline.* 1986. *Do the Funky Pickle.* 1992. *Who Ran My Under-Wear up the Flagpole?* 1992. *Crash.* 1996. *Wringer.* 1997. *Blue Ribbon Blues: A Tooter Tale.* 1998

BIBLIOGRAPHY: Gallo, D. R., ed. *Speaking for Ourselves.* 1990. *Major Authors and Illustrators for Children and Young Adults.* 1993. Kovacs, D. and J. Preller. *Meet the Authors and Illustrators.* 1993. Spinelli, J. "Catching Maniac Magee." *The Reading Teacher* 1991

MARY ARIAIL BROUGHTON

SPORTS STORIES

Sports stories have been a significant and popular segment of children's literature since the early days of children's book publishing. They combine elements of playing a specific sport with themes about fair play, ethics, and morality on an individual basis or as part of a team. Bullies, slackers, and cheaters get their comeuppance and virtue triumphs consistently. Stories about sports have traditionally served as metaphors for living one's life. Sports stories reflect the values of the era in which they are written. Early sports stories promoted team spirit and cooperation, whereas contemporary stories focus on individual efforts and frequently noncompetitive sports where children and teens compete as individuals rather than as members of a team. Whereas games and sports events are described in exciting detail, overall, these stories attempt to inculcate the values that adults want to instill in children.

The earliest sports stories emanate from the traditions of the British public-school system. The duke of Wellington said, "The Battle of Waterloo was won on the playing fields of Eton," and stories from the mid-nineteenth century to World War II reflect the prevailing attitude that winning is the only thing that matters. Harold Avery's school stories *Won for the School, Not Cricket!* and *Play the Game,* as well as Talbot Reed's *Parkhurst Sketches* (1899), including "My First Football Match," were typical of the genre. Both authors also wrote sports stories for the *Boys' Own Paper* with a sports story by Reed appearing in the 1878 first edition of the magazine. Boys who excelled on the playing fields of British public schools were prepared to lead the Empire and become captains of industry. In a send-up of this lofty British ideal, J. K. ROWLING's contemporary Harry Potter SERIES, set at the Hogwarts School for training future wizards, has teams of students—boys and girls—playing the author-created sport of *quidditch.* In the best tradition of public-school rugby and cricket teams, quidditch is played with balls and a fierce determination to win at all costs. Except quidditch is played in the air with the team members perched on broomsticks with balls named Snitch, Bludgers, and Quaffle. To help readers follow the sport, Rowling provides playing rules and diagrams.

In contrast, in the United States the first popular sports book was by a woman, Mary Mapes DODGE, who began the tradition of combining social themes in a sports setting. *Hans Brinker; or, The Silver Skates* (1865) is set in Holland and tells of a brother's and sister's efforts to enter a skating competition and win the silver skates while they are trying to get a noted doctor to treat their DISABLED father. The story has been translated into many languages, received a prize from the French Academy, and remains in print.

John R. TUNIS told exciting sports stories starting in 1938 with *Iron Duke*, which is about college-level athletics. He provided dramatic play-by-play descriptions of major-league sports. But his reputation rests on his baseball novels centering around a fictional group of players for the Brooklyn Dodgers. *The Kid from Tompkinsville* (1940) follows a rookie's first season. In spite of Tunis's details about the game, the real emphasis is on Roy Tucker's strong character and emergence as a hero because of his code of ethics, and moral values. All of Tunis's heroes are outstanding examples of athletes who play by the rules, believe in teamwork over the cult of the individual, and follow the rules of good sportsmanship. At a time when it was not popular, Tunis wrote about social and moral responsibility, social justice, the ideals of a democratic society, and the inclusion of all qualified players without racial and religious restrictions. Other authors, like Tex Maule *(The Receiver,* 1968), wrote similar stories but none captured Tunis's passion and enthusiasm, and their books are no longer in print.

The intensity and emphasis in sports stories shifted in the 1960s with the publication of stories that depicted dual themes of sports and social issues. Beginning in 1967 with Robert LIPSYTE's *The Contender,* the sports novel, according to Bruce BROOKS, let "kids play the sport across the pages, are likely to be written in a way that lets readers play with the words: and with the ideas and feelings that come from them. Respect for play often equates with respect for young readers, and for kids in general." Lipsyte is a sports columnist for the *New York Times,* covering professional sports events, and writes the sports novel with a jabbing, staccato voice in which the event is the matrix for social issues. Alfred Brooks, an AFRICAN AMERICAN teenager, becomes a contender in the boxing ring and in the events of his own life through devotion to his chosen sport and long hours of practice at the gym. Several books about Alfred highlight the altered focus in sports novels: emphasis on the social issues of the sport and the individual competing against himself. In *The Runner* (1985), Cynthia VOIGT relates the story of Bullet, using the metaphor of running to describe how Bullet runs away from his emotions and the people who care most deeply about him.

Girls appear as main characters in today's sports novels. Voigt uses volleyball as the vehicle to tell the story of three college students who view life from very different points of view until tragedy strikes. R. R. Knudson focuses on character in her stories about Suzanne (Zan) Hagen competing in several different sports. The most successful of all female sports stories is Tessa DUDER's series about Alex Archer, a teenage swimmer who represents NEW ZEALAND in international competitions. Striving to win a place on the 1960 Olympics team, Alex almost loses sight of her goal until she learns to believe in herself in the novel *In Lane Three, Alex Archer* (1989). Winner of New Zealand's Esther Glen Award, the book was adapted as a Hollywood film.

The abiding friendship between two middle-schools boys, one black and one white, is related in Bruce Brook's 1985 NEWBERY MEDAL Honor Book *The Moves Make the Man.* Although the basketball court is the setting for the story and myriad details of how to play the game are provided, the real story is the emotional support the boys provide one another and lasting lessons they learn from one another. Others soon wrote with the intensity of emotion expressed by Brooks, most notably Chris CRUTCHER in several sports novels including *Stotan!* (1986), *Crazy Horse Electric Game* (1987), *Athletic Shorts* (1991), and *Ironman* (1995). Walter Dean MYERS writes fast-paced sports stories about African American athletes in *Hoops* (1981), *The Outside Shot* (1984), and *The Glory Field* (1995), or in his books for younger readers like *Mop, Moondance, and the Nagasaki Knights* (1992).

Sports stories for younger readers are featured in several more recent novels by Matt CHRISTOPHER *(The Hit-Away Kid,* 1988 and *Pressure Play,* 1993), Thomas DYGARD *(Rebound Caper,* 1983), and Chris LYNCH *(Gold Dust,* 2000). Though they did not write sports stories, their books are straightforward and easy to read; there is usually an off-the-field problem involving family, health, or friendship; and games become critical win-or-lose moments resolved in the last few pages. Good sportsmanship and grace in winning are essential as triumph is achieved over nearly impossible odds. The series sports story became popular for younger readers as many noted authors created stories featuring the members of a single team such as Bruce Brooks in his many titles about the Wolfbay Wings, a Peewee League ice-hockey team made up of boys and girls.

Books with a sports theme remain popular in other genres as well. Biographies of sports heroes are perennial favorites as are PICTURE BOOKS with a sports theme. Karla KUSKIN's *The Dallas Titans Get Ready for Bed* (Marc SIMONT, illus., 1986) describes what a professional football team does off the field in preparation for the next big game. Many POETRY anthologies are available, either about a single sport such as Lee Bennett HOPKINS's *Extra Innings: Baseball Poems* (1993) and Lillian MORRISON's *Slam Dunk: Basketball Poems* (1995), or about sports in general as in Hopkins's *Opening Days: Sports Poems* (1996), Morrison's *Sprints & Distances: Sports in Poetry and Poetry in Sport* (1965, 1990), a collection ranging from Pindar to today's poets, or her *The Break Dance Kids: Poems of Sport, Motion, and Locomotion* (1985), as well as Arnold ADOFF's *Sports Pages* (1986). However children choose to read about sports, there is a genre available to match their interests, even songbooks such as *Take Me Out to the Ball Game* (Norworth, Gillman, 1993) and numerous editions of Ernest THAYER's ever-popular "Casey at the Bat."

DIANE G. PERSON

SPYRI, Johanna (Heusser)
Author, b. 12 July 1827, Hirzel, Switzerland; d. 7 July 1901, Zurich, Switzerland

S. is the author of the classic children's novel *Heidi* (1890). She attended a village school and grew up in Zurich with the kind of people and environment that she would later incorporate into her stories. S.'s description of snow-capped mountains, stately pines, and fields of wild flowers give readers of *Heidi* a most positive and vivid picture of nature. One of S.'s accomplishments was that she made a usually wild and hostile landscape not only familiar, but beloved by readers. In the opening chapter, readers are presented with a small child being led up into the mountain wilderness to stay with her antisocial grandfather. Within the next few chapters readers

see what a nurturing place it really is. S. had great insight into the needs of children and understood how well-meaning adults might unintentionally bring about unhappiness. The reader vicariously shares in Heidi's pleasure in her grandfather's simple cottage, her mattress of straw, the open wooden shutters facing snow-covered mountains, and her simple diet of fresh milk, bread, and cheese. Generations of children have enjoyed how this charming, wide-eyed child brings happiness into the old grandfather's life.

The book remains steadily in print with many new editions appearing frequently and TRANSLATIONS into many languages. It was made into a full-length movie in 1937 and again in 1968, as a telemovie on NBC, which became famous for having preempted a football game that is even to this day referred to as "The Heidi Game." In 1955, PBS made it into a televised play. More recently in 1978 it was produced as a TV musical.

FURTHER WORKS: *Red-Letter Stories*. 1884. *Uncle Titus*. 1886. *Gritl's Children*. 1887

BIBLIOGRAPHY: Doyle, Brian. *The Who's Who of Children's Literature*, 1968; Silvey, Anita, ed., *Children's Books and Their Creators; Something about the Author*, vol. 19, 1980 and vol. 100, 1999

JUDY LIPSITT

STANLEY, Diane (Diane Zuromskis)
Author, illustrator, b. 27 December 1943, Abilene, Texas

S. says that she grew up with a mother who was a writer and was reared with a love of rich language and good stories. As her mother read aloud, she emphasized the power and beauty of "good" words, words to be savored. S. had no siblings; reading was her "best companion." S. also loved to draw; the margins of her school notebooks were crammed with her drawings. During her senior year in college, an art teacher convinced her she had talent; this led her to take a job as a medical illustrator. She learned the basics of printing and book making by writing, illustrating, and hand-printing a book of her own design. She later became art director in the children's book department of a major publisher. Her interest in creating children's books was piqued when she started reading PICTURE BOOKS to her own children. Her ILLUSTRATION style varies as her subjects vary; she matches art with content. For example, she can create a fanciful *Little Mouse Nibbling,* (JOHNSTON, 1979), the cultural styles of Renaissance Italy *(Leonardo da Vinci,* 1996), old Bohemia *(The Month-Brothers,* Marshak, 1983), or Elizabethan England *(Good Queen Bess: The Story of Elizabeth I of England,* with Peter VENNEMA, 1990). S.'s BIOGRAPHIES are carefully detailed. Not only does she research the subject's life, but the architecture and clothing of the period in her quest to find a design theme she can use throughout the book. S. uses acrylic paints to create the look of an authentic, hand-illuminated, gilded medieval manuscript in *Joan of Arc* (1998). Actual quotes from the transcripts of Joan's heresy trial are used to enhance the effect of the book as a text from the Middle Ages.

Many of her self-authored stories celebrate strong-minded women. S. says that she has come full circle, by reading aloud and sharing her love of books with her own children. She says that was the greatest gift she received as a child, and with abundant joy passes it on to her children.

AWARDS: *New York Times* Best Illustrated Children's Books of the Year (1988) and ALA Booklist Children's Editors' Choice (1988) for *Shaka, King of the Zulus* (S. and Peter Vennema, S., illus.). AMERICAN LIBRARY ASSOCIATION Notable Book, *Booklist* Top of the List, Youth Nonfiction, *Horn Book* Fanfare Book, and a *Parenting* magazine Reading Magic Award's Ten Best Books (all 1992) for *Bard of Avon: The Story of William Shakespeare* (S. and Peter Vennema). American Bookseller Pick of the Lists, *Parenting* magazine's Best Books (1993) for *Charles Dickens: The Man Who Had Great Expectations.* ALA Notable Book, ALA Booklist Children's Editors' Choice, *Publishers Weekly*'s Best Books, and *Parenting* magazine's Best Books (1994) for *Cleopatra* (S. with Peter Vennema)

FURTHER WORKS: *The Farmer in the Dell* 1978; *Half-a-Ball-of Kenki: An Ashanti Tale Retold* (AARDEMA) 1979; *Fiddle-i-fee: A Traditional American Chant* 1979; *Petrosinella, a Neapolitan Rapunzel* (Basile/Taylor) 1981; *Sleeping Ugly* (YOLEN). 1981; *Little Orphant Annie* (RILEY). 1983; *Peter the Great* 1986; *Cleopatra* (With Vennema) 1994; *Woe Is Moe* 1995; *Saving Sweetness* 1996; *Elena* 1996; *Raising Sweetness* 1999

BIBLIOGRAPHY: Contributor's assessment; Autobiography in a Four Winds Press flier (1993); THE KERLAN COLLECTION files. Flyleaves of books;

Library of Congress website; *Something about the Author,* vol. 80, 1995

MARGARET YATSEVITCH PHINNEY

STAPLES, Suzanne Fisher
Author, b. 27 August 1945, Philadelphia, Pennsylvania

S. grew up in rural Pennsylvania, where, like her character Shabanu, she felt a great attachment to the land on which she lived. S. attended Cedar Crest College, earning a B.A. in 1967. She became Asian Marketing director for Business International Corporation and then worked as a news editor and correspondent for United Press International in New York, Washington, D.C., Hong Kong, and India. Her travels for UPI and later the *Washington Post* honed her skills of cultural observation that she would draw on later as an author. When her husband accepted a position in the diplomatic corps in Pakistan, S. quit journalism and began work on *Shabanu: Daughter of the Wind* (1989). In addition to her writing, she now lectures on the role of women in Pakistani culture.

During her travels, S. became intrigued with the lives of women in Pakistan. She found that terrorism has resulted in narrow Western views of Islamic society, and there were few Islamic writers who attempted to portray their culture to Western audiences. S. left journalism and began writing fiction because she wanted to express her strong feelings for Pakistan and its people and to show the universality between Islamic and Western peoples. Her first novel *Shabanu, Daughter of the Wind* (1989) tells the story of a spirited girl growing up in the Pakistani desert who is forced to choose between an arranged marriage to a wealthy older landowner (a choice that would save her family) and her own independence. S.'s work is marked by vivid depictions of both culture and place.

AWARDS: ALA NEWBERY MEDAL Honor Book, *New York Times* Notable Book of the Year and ALA Notable Book (1990) all for *Shabanu: Daughter of the Wind*

FURTHER WORKS: *Haveli.* 1993. *Dangerous Skies.* 1996

BIBLIOGRAPHY: Sawyer, W. E., and J. C. Sawyer. "A Discussion with Suzanne Fisher Staples: The

Author as Writer and Cultural Observer." *The New Advocate.* 6(3). 159–69. 1993. Silvey, A. ed. *Children's Books and Their Creators.* 1995. Staples, S. F. "Different Is Just Different." *ALAN Review.* 22(2). 44–45. 1995. Staples, S. F. "Why Johnny Can't Read: Censorship in American Libraries." (See INDIAN [EAST] LITERATURE) *ALAN Review. 23(2).* 49–50. 1996

JANE WEST

STEELE, Mary Q. (Wilson Gage)
Author, b. 8 May 1922, Chattanooga, Tennessee

S. has written many books, most of which were published under her pen name, Wilson Gage. The first book written under her own name, *Journey Outside* (1969), was selected as an ALA NEWBERY MEDAL Honor Book. An allegorical novel for mature readers, it tells of a boy's search for knowledge and his effort to bring enlightenment to his people. The author collaborated with her husband, William O. STEELE, on another award-winning book, *The Eye in the Forest* (1975). S.'s books often use natural history as a theme, with a particular emphasis on birds. The author has explored many topics, including magic, witchcraft, death, and suicide. In all her books, S. tries to stress the acceptability and desirability of being different.

FURTHER WORKS: (Written under pen name Wilson Gage): *The Secret of Fiery George,* 1960; *Big Blue Island,* 1964; *Mrs. Gaddy and the Ghost,* 1979

BIBLIOGRAPHY: *Major Authors and Illustrators for Children and Young Adults: A Selection of Sketches from "Something about the Author,"* vol. 5, 1993

MARY ARIAIL BROUGHTON

STEELE, William O(wen)
Author, b. 22 December 1917, Franklin, Tennessee; d. 25 June 1979, Chattanooga, Tennessee

S. is best known for his carefully researched historical fiction. His interest in historical fiction stemmed from his boyhood of hunting fields for Indian arrowheads and exploring log cabins in Tennessee. Reading stories about the Old Southwest to his daughter prompted him to write his first children's book, *The Buffalo Knife* (1990). S. retold stories based on legendary American folk heroes as humorous tall tales. He published thirty-nine books during his lifetime.

AWARDS: (1958) ALA NEWBERY MEDAL Honor Book for *The Perilous Road* and (1958) Jane Addams Book Award

FURTHER WORKS: *The Golden Root* (1950), *Winter Danger* (1954), *Davy Crockett's Earthquake* (1956), *The Lone Hunt* (1956), *Daniel Boone's Echo* (1957), *Flaming Arrows* (1957), *Bloody Sevens* (1963), *Westward Adventure* (1965), *The Eye In the Forest* (1975)

BIBLIOGRAPHY: *Something about the Author,* vol. 52, 1988

JODI PILGRIM

STEIG, William
Author, illustrator, b. 14 November 1907, New York City

Equipped with a unique ability to merge the traditional with the modern, S. is recognized as one of the prominent figures in twentieth century children's literature. Having enjoyed a remarkably successful career as a cartoonist, S. began writing and illustrating books for children when he was already in his early sixties, embarking on what he fondly refers to as his second profession. He has since authored over thirty children's books of extraordinary versatility and stature. Engaging as well as energetic, S. is possessed with a keen sense of HUMOR and vibrant imagination, whose sensitivity and demeanor underscore his STORYTELLING. For S. the world is at once magical and mysterious, full of wonderment, joy, and adventure.

Artistically inclined even as a young child, S. attended public school in the Bronx and then studied at the National Academy of Design. In 1930, at age twenty-three, he began contributing cartoons to *The New Yorker,* gradually earning a reputation as one of the magazine's most popular cartoonists. Late in his career, S. was encouraged by publisher Robert KRAUS to attempt a children's book, and following the suggestion he wrote and illustrated *Roland, the Minstrel Pig* (1968). For his first work of children's fiction, S. presents a humorous tale of a wanderlust pig seeking fame and fortune whose innocence leads instead to his near demise in the form of a sly fox. Rescued by the king, a magnanimous lion who then rewards his newfound friend, Roland serves as a prototype for many of S.'s characters whose curiosity about the world serves as a means to provide them with understanding and meaning.

With his next work, *Sylvester and the Magic Pebble* (1969), S. gained increasing popularity as well as critical recognition. Similar to Roland, the innocent Sylvester must also be rescued when he finds a magic pebble that turns him from a donkey into a rock. The whimsical tale illustrated with exceptional care and inventiveness was nominated for a National Book Award and earned for S. the prestigious ALA CALDECOTT MEDAL in 1970. Published in 1971, *Amos and Boris* was also nominated for a National Book Award and was listed by the *New York Times* as one of the best illustrated children's books of the year. Turning to the novel form, S. next published *Dominic* (1972), illustrated with black-and-white drawings, in which the illustrious protagonist, a dog named Dominic, sets off like the earlier Roland seeking adventure and encounters instead a series of arduous mishaps before finding solace and romance with his canine counterpart, the beautiful Evelyn. Named an AMERICAN LIBRARY ASSOCIATION Notable Book, the novel was also nominated for a National Book Award and received the Christopher Award in 1973.

Following the publication of *The Real Thief* (1973) and *Farmer Palmer's Wagon Ride* (1974), both named notable books by the ALA, S. established himself as a masterful storyteller with *Abel's Island* (1976), cited as an ALA NEWBERY MEDAL Honor Book in the following year. The tale unfolds as the unsuspecting mouse named Abelard, while chasing after his wife's scarf during a storm, is catastrophically swept away by a tumultuous river. Finding himself alone on an island, Abel survives hardship and near death while discovering in himself the true measure of his ability to persist and endure. When he is finally reunited with his wife and family, Abel returns with a renewed sense of self and purpose.

In *The Amazing Bone* (1976), an ALA Caldecott Metal Honor Book, S. for the first time introduces a female protagonist, a pig named Pearl whose harmonious world is invaded by the advances of a lecherous fox. Pearl is saved from harm by her magical protector, the "amazing" bone she discovered that can speak in any language. S. next introduced human characters into his work with the publication of *Caleb and Kate* (1977), in which the quarrelsome Caleb is turned into a dog by a witch and then magically returned to his former self while defending his wife from would-be robbers. Typical of S., the joyful reunion at the end of the story restores both harmony and attentiveness. Likewise, in *Gorky Rises,* published in 1980 and listed as one of the best illustrated books of the year by the *New York Times,* a philosophical frog who concocts a magic potion that enables him to fly returns from flight to a jubilant family reception.

Active as an author and illustrator throughout the 1980s and 1990s, S. received the American Book Award for a children's PICTURE BOOK for the highly acclaimed *Doctor De Soto* (1982), in which the affable Dr. De Soto, a mouse dentist, and his inventive wife outsmart a cunning fox intent on their demise. Other notable works include *Solomon and the Rusty Nail* (1985), *Spinky Sulks* (1988), *Grown-ups Get to Do All the Driving* (1995), a humorous look at adult behavior from a child's point of view, *The Toy Brother* (1996), and *Pete's a Pizza* (1998). Prolific as well as versatile, S. remains an author who combines warmth, compassion, and humor into works of enduring value and popularity.

FURTHER WORKS: *The Rejected Lovers,* 1951; *Continuous Performance,* 1963; *CDB!,* 1968; *The Bad Island,* 1969; republished as *Rotten Island,* 1984; *The Bad Speller,* 1970; *The Lonely Ones,* 1970; *An Eye for Elephants,* 1970; *Male/Female,* 1971; *Tiffky Doofky,* 1978; *Drawing,* 1979; *CDC?,* 1984; *Ruminations,* 1984; *Yellow and Pink,* 1984; *Brave Irene,* 1986; *Strutters and Fretters; or, The Inescapable Self,* 1992; *Zeke Pippin,* 1994; *A Handful of Beans: Six FAIRY TALES,* 1998, retold by Jeanne S.

BIBLIOGRAPHY: Angell, R. "The Minstrel Steig." *The New Yorker.* 71 (February 20–27, 1995): 252–56. *Children's Literature,* 18 (1990): 31–41, 125–26. Cott, Jonathan, *Piper at the Gates of Dawn: The Wisdom of Children's Literature,* 1983. Jones, M., "The King of Cartoons." *Newsweek,* 125 (May 15, 1995): 60–62. Kroll, S., "Steig: Nobody Is Grown-Up." *New York Times Book Review,* 92 (June 28, 1987): 26. Lanes, S. G., *Down the Rabbit Hole: Adventures and Misadventures in the Realm of Children's Literature*

(1971). Wilner, A., " 'Unlocked by Love': William Steig's Tales of Transformation and Magic"

STEVEN R. SERAFIN

STEPTOE, John

Author, illustrator, b. 14 September 1950, Brooklyn, New York; d. 28 August 1989, New York City

S. is recognized as the first children's author to present universal themes to young children from the authentic perspective of an AFRICAN AMERICAN. *Stevie* (1969), which was written when S. was only seventeen, is about a young boy who has to deal with jealousy when his mother takes care of a younger child. With illustrations, language, setting, and tone to which most African American children could relate, *Stevie* was the beginning of S.'s career in children's literature that was praised for optimism in addressing topics and versatility in artistic style.

S. grew up in Brooklyn where as a young boy he enjoyed staying home and drawing. He was a senior at the High School of Art and Design when John Torres recognized his talents and invited him to participate in a summer program for minority artists at the Vermont Academy. Realizing the quality of his work, Torres provided his own studio for S. to use, and an instructor at the program provided S. with an apartment to continue his work after the summer. It was here that *Stevie,* a 1969 Lewis CARROLL Shelf Award was written. S.'s intent was to create a book that would reflect what the black child would know and ultimately create a pride in their cultural experiences. Editor Ursula Nordstrom at Harper and Row recognized S.'s early talent.

S. has been recognized for the diversity in his work. He explained this as a reflection of what was missing for him as a child and his efforts as an adult to fill these gaps. He sought answers to and for the problems, questions, and angers he had as a child. Remembering that not everyone has the same problems and fears, S. said that if he reached deep enough inside himself, he would come up with universal ideas. Following *Stevie,* S. wrote *Uptown* (1970) and *Train Ride* (1971), which focused even more sharply on the African American experience and celebrated city life.

S. said that there are many different ways to portray what the author/illustrator is trying to say

and different artistic forms and elements recreate the complexity of ways to see the world. Within his own work, one observes a diversity of ways to represent the messages within each book. Line, light and dark, color, and drawings in black, white, and shades of gray each distinctively characterize his artistic style, which extends from expressionistic art to Surrealism. In *Stevie* he uses bold lines and colors while in *The Story of Jumping Mouse* (1984), a Native American legend about a selfless mouse who is eventually transferred into an eagle, he uses detailed black and white pencil sketches. S. found that although he did not set out to do a black and white book, as he worked his understanding of black and white grew more distinct. He continued to develop these insights as he added them to color in *Mufaro's Beautiful Daughters* (1987).

Besides addressing the issues that were problematic for him as a child, some of S.'s work is more directly autobiographical. In *Daddy Is a Monster . . . Sometimes* (1980) S. uses his own children as the main characters and himself as the father. He also used his own family members as models for the characters in *Mufaro's Beautiful Daughters.*

One of S.'s most significant works, *Mufaro's Beautiful Daughters,* a Notable Children's Trade Book in the Field of Social Studies, reflected ongoing investigation of his African heritage as well as the origins of Cinderella stories. The outcome of this extended writing project was manifold. S. learned more about his culture and the misconceptions about the origins of African communities, such as that Zimbabwe is now known to be of African origin rather than European. The productive society of the ancient city reminded him of the universality of people's behavior and emotions, and he created strong characters with dignity and grace for this book. Also, by receiving an ALA CALDECOTT MEDAL Honor Book award and CORETTA SCOTT KING AWARD, S. realized that he was able to convey to others the messages he wanted to create. He said in the *Horn Book* that receiving these awards gave him hope that "children who are still caught in the frustration of being black and poor in America will be encouraged to love themselves enough to accomplish the dreams I know are in their hearts."

In addition to various PICTURE BOOKS, S. wrote one novel, *Marcia* (1976), for young adults, which addresses the issues surrounding a sexual relationship. Additionally, he illustrated many books with African American subjects by noted authors.

With great respect for childhood and the character development that these years hold, S. created books that he hoped would assure visibility for the ghetto child. In so doing, his contributions to children's literature provide shared experiences for all readers.

AWARDS: AMERICAN LIBRARY ASSOCIATION Caldecott Medal Honor Book (1985) for *The Story of Jumping Mouse* and (1988) for *Mufaro's Beautiful Daughters*. Coretta Scott King Award for Illustration (1982) for *Mother Crocodile* and (1988) for *Mufaro's Beautiful Daughters*. Boston Globe-Horn Book Award for Illustration (1987) for *Mufaro's Beautiful Daughters*

FURTHER WORKS: *Uptown,* 1970; *Train Ride,* 1971; *Birthday,* 1972; *My Special Best Words,* 1974; *Jeffrey Bear Cleans up His Act,* 1983; *Baby Says,* 1988; as illus.: *All Us Come Cross the Water.* (Lucille B. CLIFTON). 1972. *OUTside/INside: Poems.* (Arnold ADOFF). 1981. *All the Colors of the Race: Poems.* (Arnold ADOFF. 1982)

BIBLIOGRAPHY: Berg, Julie. *John Steptoe,* 1994; *Children's Literature Review,* vol. 12, 1976; Cummins, Julie, ed., *Children's Book Illustration and Design,* 1992; *Something about the Author,* vol. 63, 1991; Steptoe, John. *Mufaro's Beautiful Daughters. Horn Book* magazine (January/February 1988)

JANELLE B. MATHIS

STEVENS, Janet

Author, illustrator, reteller, b. 17 January 1953, Dallas, Texas

About her background in art, S. says, "I have been drawing as long as I can remember. In school I drew pictures for my book reports, on math assignments, on anything I could find." Although she was not as good at reading and math, her parents recognized and encouraged her artistic talent. She studied art at the University of Colorado, and after graduation, had "pictures of bears in sneakers, rhinos in ties, and walruses in Hawaiian shirts." After an inspiring seminar with Tomie DEPAOLA, who advised her to try children's book illustrating, she landed a contract and found that "creating children's books was a perfect fit."

The anthropomorphic illustrations in her forty-plus books are characterized by exaggeration, expressiveness, and ebullient HUMOR. Anansi's bulbous body and angular legs in each of the Eric KIMMEL folktales S. illustrated emphasize his pointy personality. The lazy, bejeweled bear in *Tops and Bottoms* (1995) fills the page as he drapes himself limply, bottom-side-up in his lawn chair. Fabulously funny, bigger than life, her rhino in a belly dance outfit with a diamond ring on her toe, her camel with sunglasses wearing sandals, and an elephant in a tutu, all from *Animal Fair* (1981), typify the kind of joyful ridiculousness that children appreciate so much. Her use of perspective, such as drawing a page-sized warthog with its snout foremost, puts this "tuskiest" of creatures right in the reader's face. As one review stated, "Her characters are imbued with distinctive and unmistakable personalities . . . showing a sense of movement, composition, and drama."

Influenced by her own children's suggestions and responses, S.'s goal is "to create books that children want to read. This," she says, "is the real joy of bookmaking. . . . The world of children's books gives me an outlet for my zany pictures . . . and a way to reach children and excite them about reading."

AWARDS: ALA CALDECOTT MEDAL Honor (1996) and Booklist Editors' Choice (1996) for *Tops and Bottoms*. ALA Notable Book, Golden Kite Honor Book, and American Booksellers Honor Book (1997) for *To Market, To Market. Booklist* starred review and READING RAINBOW Feature Book (1987) for *The Town Mouse and the Country Mouse*. Reading Rainbow Feature Book (1984) for *The Tortoise and the Hare*. INTERNATIONAL READING ASSOCIATION's Readers' Choice Award (1982) for *The Princess and the Pea*

FURTHER WORKS: *The Owl and the Pussy-cat.* (LEAR). 1983. *The House That Jack Built.* 1985. *The Three Billy Goats Gruff.* 1987. *Anansi and the Moss-Covered Rock.* (Kimmel). 1988. *The Quangle Wangle's Hat.* (LEAR). 1988. *Anansi and the Talking Melon.* (Kimmel). 1994. *From Pictures to Words: A Book about Making a Book.* 1995. *Old Bag of Bones.* 1996. *Shoe Town.* (with Crummel). 1999. *My Big Dog.* 1999

REFERENCES: Janet Stevens's web site: http:// www.janetstevens.com/ Library of Congress web site; *Booklist* review on flyleaf of The Town Mouse and the City Mouse. Harcourt Brace publicity brochure. *Something about the Author.* vol. 92, 1997. Contributor's assessment

MARGARET YATSEVITCH PHINNEY

STERLING, Dorothy

Author, b. 23 November 1913, New York City

S., author of fiction and nonfiction for children and adolescents, uses a clear style to write about well-researched topics usually dealing with science and AFRICAN AMERICAN history. Working for Roosevelt's Federal Writers Project and as a researcher for *Life* magazine provided a basis for S.'s approach to writing. Her first book was a photo essay for children, *Sophie and Her Puppies* (1951), followed by *Billy Goes Exploring* (1953), and *Trees and Their Story* (1953). While doing research for *Freedom Train: The Story of Harriet Tubman* (1954), she discovered the wealth of history and untold stories about African American people. Other significant, well-received biographies followed, such as *Captain of the Planter: The Story of Robert Smalls* (1958) and *Lucretia Mott: Gentle Warrior* (1964). S.'s only novel, *Mary Jane* (1959), addresses segregation in the South. Her works have been praised for their perception, objectivity, compassion, and skillfully accurate retellings of history.

FURTHER WORKS: *The Silver Spoon Mystery.* 1958. *The Story of Mosses, Ferns, and Mushrooms.* 1955. *Caterpillars.* 1961. *It Started in Montgomery: A Picture History of the Civil Rights Movement.* 1972. *The Making of an Afro-American: Martin Robison Delany 1812–1885.* 1971. *Speak Out in Thunder Tones: Letters and Other Writings by Black Northerners, 1787–1865.* 1973. *We Are Your Sisters: Black Women in the Nineteenth Century.* 1984

BIBLIOGRAPHY: *Something about the Author,* vol. 10, 1976; 1966. *Children's Literature Review,* vol. 2, 1976

JANELLE B. MATHIS

STEVENSON, James

Author, illustrator, b. 11 July 1929, New York City

S. has gained critical and popular recognition on several literary fronts. He is a popular *New Yorker* magazine cartoonist, writes articles and books for adults, and writes and illustrates books for chil-

dren of a wide age range. As early as elementary school, S. was introduced to the idea of social and political commentary. His father, a painter, encouraged S.'s interest in art. Inspired by his teachers to try doing whatever interested him, S. decided to become a writer. He continued his education at Yale University, graduating in 1951, having already had some cartoon idea sales to *The New Yorker.* After serving in the U. S. Marine Corps, S. became a reporter, working first for *Life* and later for *The New Yorker.* He became the art editor at *The New Yorker,* a position that gave him an opportunity to create the ideas with which the magazine's cartoonists worked to create published cartoons. He published a volume of social and political cartoons of his own, in 1963, and, during the same decade, produced several novels for adults. *If I Owned a Candy Factory* (1968), S.'s first book for children, was authored by his son, James, and published with S.'s cartoon illustrations.

S.'s first popular success in the world of children's books was *Could Be Worse!* (1977), the first of an informal series featuring a tall-tale-telling grandpa. The AMERICAN LIBRARY ASSOCIATION awarded Notable Book status to *The Sea View Hotel* (1978), *Fast Friends: Two Stories* (1979), *That Terrible Halloween Night* (1980), *What's Under My Bed?* (1983), and *When I Was Nine* (1986). In 1979, the INTERNATIONAL READING ASSOCIATION's Children's Choice Award went to *The Worst Person in the World* (1978); *That Terrible Halloween Night* won the same award the following year. *The Night After Christmas* (1981), *The Supreme Souvenir Factory* (1988), and *Oh No, It's Waylon's Birthday!* (1989) were selected as Children's Choices as well, each in the year following that title's publication. *We Can't Sleep* (1982) won the Christopher Award in 1982. The 1982 Parents' Choice Award went to *Oliver, Clarence, and Violet* (1982). S. has received additional literary AWARDS from periodicals and state library associations.

S. has published many PICTURE BOOKS as well as novels for older children. His plot devices are simple without being simplistic, drawing in their intended audiences because they address familiar emotions. Often, S. has used his own life as inspiration for specific stories, recounting his autobiography across five picture books: *When I Was Nine* (1986), *Higher on the Door* (1987), *July*

(1990), *Don't You Know There's a War On?* (1992), and *Fun No Fun* (1994). Picture books featuring Grandpa, including *What's under My Bed?* and *Brrr!* (1991), feature, according to S., his alter ego in the persona of the wise, caring, slightly tart Grandpa.

Other characters S. has developed from his imagination are familiar types without being stereotypical. The Worst, a misanthropic but evidently lonely old guy appears in *The Worst Person in the World* (1978), *The Worst Person in the World at Crab Beach* (1988), *The Worst Person's Christmas* (1991), *Worse Than the Worst* (1994), and *The Worst Goes South* (1995). Another SERIES features Emma, a good little witch who is up against less well-intentioned folks in such titles as *Emma* (1985) and *Emma at the Beach* (1990). More recently, S. has begun a new series of picture books with text that is accessible to beginning independent readers: *The Mud Flat Olympics* (1994), *Heat Wave at Mud Flat* (1997), *Mystery at Mud Flat* (1997), and *Mud Flat April Fool* (1998) feature a cast of Wild Westernized anthropomorphic animals who combine witty words with deeds of civilized derring-do.

S.'s cartoon approach to ILLUSTRATION brings a lively and loose aspect to his illustrations. Often, supplementary text is presented directly from the characters' mouths, in the requisite COMIC BOOKS AND GRAPHIC NOVELS–style balloon. However, S.'s expertise as a storyteller and adult in the life of his child reader prevents him from producing illustrations that are stylistically similar even when the mood and tone of the specific story differs from his usual fare. His autobiographical picture books, for instance, are illustrated more sedately, almost abstractly, as befits memorializing events and emotions that have mellowed through the years.

S. has written a few books for older children, reaching an audience beyond the PICTURE BOOKS years. *The Bones in the Cliff* (1995) and *The Unprotected Witness* (1997) feature the son of an assassinated criminal. These literary thrillers are appropriate for and appeal to young adolescents. Several collections of S.'s poems, including *Popcorn* (1998), are appropriate for children of all ages but especially appealing to independent readers.

In addition to illustrating his own texts, S. has worked as illustrator for such authors as Charlotte ZOLOTOW (*Say It!*, 1980), Jack PRELUTSKY (*The New Kid on the Block,* 1984), Cynthia RYLANT (*Henry and Mudge,* 1987), and Dr. SEUSS (*I Am Not Going to Get up Today,* 1987). S.'s own text for *Sam the Zamboni Man* (1998) is illustrated by his son, Harvey.

FURTHER WORKS: *Clams Can't Sing.* 1980. *Grandpa's Great City Tour.* 1983. *Are We Almost There?* 1985. *No Friends.* 1986. *Happy Valentine's Day, Emma!* 1987. *National Worm Day.* 1990. *That's Exactly the Way It Wasn't.* 1991. *Sweet Corn: Poems.* 1995

BIBLIOGRAPHY: Cart, M. "How Memory Looks." *Booklist.* Jan. 15, 1995. *St. James Guide to Children's Writers.* 1999. Silvey, A. ed., *Children's Books and Their Creators.* 1995. *Something about the Author.* vol. 71. 1993

FRANCISCA GOLDSMITH

STEVENSON, Robert Louis (a.k.a. Chief Tusitala)

Author, b. 13 November 1850, Edinburgh, Scotland; d. 12 March 1894, Samoa

S. had poor health and spent much of his childhood confined indoors. Even as a child, he wanted to write. S. attended prep school, then Edinburgh Academy and finally Edinburgh University. When it became apparent that S. did not have the inclination to become a lighthouse engineer, following the family tradition and his father's wishes, his father urged him to study law. S. became a barrister, but never pursued an active law practice. Instead, he wrote, publishing numerous essays and articles. Despite his continuing ill health, he enjoyed traveling, and his first book, *An Inland Voyage* (1878) described a canoe trip S. took through France and Belgium. S. eventually settled in Samoa in 1890, where the climate was better for his health. He was known by the Samoans as *Tusitala,* or Teller of Tales. S. died in Samoa in 1894 and was buried there under a gravestone, which is inscribed with these lines from S.'s "Requiem": "Here he lies where he longed to be, Home is the sailor, home from the sea, And the hunter home from the hill."

S. wrote numerous essays, poems, and travel journals before becoming a novelist. He wrote the adventure novel *Treasure Island* to entertain his stepson Lloyd Osbourne; the two spent a rainy afternoon creating a treasure map, and S. wrote the first chapter that night. After that, he did a new chapter daily, reading each to the boy upon its completion. The story was serialized in *Young Folks* in 1881–82 under the pen name Captain George North and received little notice until its publication in book form in 1883, when critics predicted *Treasure Island* would revitalize the genre of ADVENTURE STORIES. Other S. novels which were first serialized in *Young Folks* include *Kidnapped* (1886) and *The Black Arrow* (1888). S.'s stories are noted for their vivid description, fast pacing, carefully constructed plots, and lively, memorable characters. His best-known poems for children are collected in *A Child's Garden of Verses* (1885), which S. dedicated to the nurse who cared for him as a child. It is still widely available and editions with new illustrations are very popular.

FURTHER WORKS: Among S.'s other works read by young people are *Dr. Jekyll and Mr. Hyde* (1886), *The Master of Ballantrae* (1889), and *Catriona* (1898, after serialization in a magazine for girls). S. wrote two books with his stepson Lloyd Osbourne, *The Wrong Box* (1889) and *The Wrecker* (1892)

BIBLIOGRAPHY: Carpenter, A. S., *Robert Louis Stevenson: Finding Treasure Island.* 1997. Doyle, B. *The Who's Who of Children's Literature.* 1968. Proudfit, I. *The Treasure Hunter: The Story of Robert Louis Stevenson.* 1939. Silvey, Anita, ed., *Children's Books and Their Creators.* 1995. Wilkie, K. E. *Robert Louis Stevenson: Storyteller and Adventurer.* 1961

JANE WEST

STEWART, Mary
Author, b. 17 September 1916, Sunderland, Durham, England

An author of FANTASY for children, S. is best known for her suspense and romance adult novels. She began writing fiction in her midthirties following a career at the University of Durham where she lectured for several years. Her first book, *Madam Will You Talk,* was published in 1953. In 1956 she gave up university work to write full time. Her first children's book, *The Little Broomstick,* was published in 1971. *The Crystal Cave* (1970), the first book in an Arthurian Trilogy, won the Frederick Neven award. This

was followed by *The Hollow Hills* (1973). *The Last Enchantment* (1979) completed the trilogy. Her second children's book, a fantasy, *Ludo and the Star Horse,* (1974) won the Scottish Arts Council Award and a place on the AMERICAN LIBRARY ASSOCIATION Best YOUNG ADULT books list. STORYTELLING comes as naturally to her "as leaves to a tree."

BIBLIOGRAPHY: *Something about the Author,* vol. 12, 1977. Silvey, Anita, ed., *Children's Books and Their Creators,* 1995; *Fiction, FOLKLORE, Fantasy and Poetry for Children, 1876–1985,* vol. 1, 1986

IRVYN GILBERTSON

STINE, R(obert) L(awrence)
Author, b. 8 October 1943, Columbus, Ohio

S. began his writing career early when he discovered an old typewriter in the family attic. Wasting no time, S. started typing up stories and little joke books. Although at first shy about showing others his work, S. later began publishing and passing them out at school. His writing was influenced by his interest in radio shows. *The Shadow, Suspense,* and *Inner Sanctum* were his favorites. After high school, S. attended Ohio State University. While there he spent three years as editor of the campus HUMOR magazine. After graduating with a B.A. in English, S. spent one year teaching social studies in junior high school. He then moved to New York City, believing that was where all writers lived. His first MAGAZINES AND PERIODICALS job was with a publisher of fan and movie magazines. The work was good training as was his next magazine work with a trade publication. Both taught S. to write creatively and prodigiously. S. spent sixteen years working on different *Scholastic* magazines. In 1968 S. became assistant editor for *Junior Scholastic* magazine and four years later he was named editor of a new social studies magazine, *Search.* S. next worked on a humor magazine for older readers called *Bananas.* This fulfilled one of S.'s lifelong ambitions of editing a national humor magazine. He would also later create and edit a humor magazine called *Maniac.*

S.'s first book for children was *How to Be Funny* (1978). It was published along with several other humorous books for children under the name Jovial Bob Stine. S. also published under the pseudonyms Eric Affabee and Zachary Blue. S. was approached by an editorial director at *Scholastic* about doing a scary book for children. He was given a suggested title and the resulting novel *Blind Date* (1985) was a big seller. The horror genre was growing in the YOUNG ADULT market and S., now writing as R. L. Stine, agreed to do other novels. *Twisted* (1986) and *The Baby-sitter* (1989) soon followed and his prominence in the genre was firmly established. With his wife Jane, S. created two horror series for children, *Fear Street* for young adult readers and *Goose-bumps* for younger readers. S. and his wife also wrote *The Sick of Being Sick Book* (1980), which was named a Children's Choice Book. S. has written over one hundred books for children and his quick-paced stories and contemporary characters have made his books very popular. Although some of his work has been denigrated by critics, S. aims and succeeds in writing books that children enjoy reading. In addition to his novels, S. is also head writer for *Eureeka's Castle,* a television show on the Nickelodeon cable network.

FURTHER WORKS: *Attack on the King.* 1986. *Bozos on Patrol.* 1992. *The Boyfriend.* 1990. *Silent Night.* 1991. *Halloween Night.* 1993. *Bad Hare Day.* 1997

BIBLIOGRAPHY: *Seventh Book of Junior Authors and Illustrators.* 1996. *Something about the Author.* vol. 76, 1994

DEDE SMALL

STOCKTON, Francis Richard (Frank R. Stockton, Paul Fort, John Lewees)

Author, b. 5 April 1834, Blockley, Pennsylvania; d. 20 April 1902, Washington, D.C.

S., whose father was a writer and mother a school administrator, initially took up wood engraving and drafting, but in his thirties became a freelance writer. He eventually worked with several notable journals, including *Hearth and Home* (where he assisted Mary Mapes DODGE), *Scribner's Monthly* (later *Century*), and *St. Nicholas,* of which he was assistant editor from 1873–81. During this period he wrote many brief fantasies and humorous tales for children. In 1879, S. published his comic novel for adults, *Rudder Grange,* one of the first American novels set in the suburbs. Its success lured him away from writing for children and he spent much of the remainder of

his career as a popular humorist and writer of adult fiction.

S. is perhaps best remembered today for a story that brought him great celebrity in his own lifetime, "The Lady, or the Tiger?" published in 1882. Its open-ended conclusion tantalized the entire country and to this day the story is widely anthologized in school texts. S.'s *A Storyteller's Pack* (1897), a collection of his most popular short stories, is reprinted from time to time. In 1963 Maurice SENDAK illustrated S.'s *The Griffin and the Minor Canon* and in 1964 he illustrated *The Bee-Man of Orn.*

BIBLIOGRAPHY: Carpenter, H. and M. Prichard, *The Oxford Companion to Children's Literature.* 1984, *Dictionary of Literary Biography,* vol. 1; Spiller, R. E., and others, *Literary History of the United States.* 3rd ed., 1968

DAVID L. RUSSELL

STOLZ, Mary (Slattery)

Author, b. 24 March 1920, Boston, Massachusetts

S., author of children's and adolescent literature, grew up in New York City with her sister and cousin. She loved to read, which eventually led to her desire to write. S. always wanted to be a writer—she wrote often while a student at Birch Wathen School in New York City. S. continued her studies at Columbia University Teacher's College and at Katharine Gibbs School. S. began writing in 1950 while recovering from surgery. *To Tell Your Love* was published that year.

S. initially wrote for adolescent girls, but changed her audience as her son became old enough for children's books. He wanted his mother to write stories that he would enjoy. S. published her first book for young children, *The Leftover Elf,* in 1952. Several books for children followed. S. used personal experiences from her own life in her writing. Her books for teenage girls were among the first to be recognized for their accurate representation of the emotional issues of adolescence. S. is praised for her portrayal of female protagonists.

Over the years several of S.'s books have received many AWARDS. S. received a Notable Book citation from ALA for *The Sea Gulls Woke Me* (1951). *In a Mirror* won a Children's Book Award from the Child Study Children's Book Committee at Bank Street College in 1953. The *New York Herald Tribune* awarded *Ready or Not* (1953), *The Day and the Way We Met* (1956), and *Because of Madeline* (1957) the Spring Book Festival Older Honor Award. *Belling the Tiger* earned an ALA Notable Book citation (1961) as well as ALA NEWBERY MEDAL Honor Book (1962). *The Noonday Friends* was also named an AMERICAN LIBRARY ASSOCIATION Newbery Medal Honor Book in 1966. *The Bully of Barkham Street* received a Junior Book award (1964) while *The Edge of Next Year* earned an Honor List citation from *Boston Globe–Horn Book* and became a National Book Award finalist, all in 1975. S. earned the Recognition of Merit award from the George G. Stone Center for Children's Books in 1982. S. received an ALA Notable Book citation in 1985 for *Quentin Corn*. In addition, *Night of Ghosts and Hermits: Nocturnal Life on the Seashore* won the Children's Science Book Younger Honor Award in 1986. Finally, *Storm in the Night* earned several AWARDS including German Youth Festival Award (1988), ALA Notable Book citation (1988), Notable Children's Trade Books in Social Studies (1988), and Teacher's Choice citation (1989).

FURTHER WORKS: *To Tell Your Love*. 1950. *The Sea Gulls Woke Me*. 1951. *In a Mirror*. 1953. *Because of Madeline*. 1957. *Emmett's Pig*. 1959. *The Bully of Barkham Street*. 1963. *The Edge of Next Year*. 1974. *Storm in the Night*. 1988. *King Emmett the Second*. 1991

BIBLIOGRAPHY: HOPKINS, Lee Bennett, *Pauses: Autobiographical Reflections of 101 Creators of Children's Books*, 1995; *Something about the Author*, vol. 1993

JODI PILGRIM

STORYOGRAPHIES: PICTURE-BOOK BIOGRAPHIES

Trends appear and disappear in children's books and sometimes they linger and last. Frequently children's books zoom in on a "hot topic"; often several titles are published within the same year with similar themes or about the same person or event. What is published reflects social interests and can provide perspective. So it is natural that children's books can and do evolve into new genres. One such case is the growth of picture-book biographies. In recent years there has been a surge of books of this type.

It is the picture-book format that shapes and defines this new species. In the way that Truman Capote essentially created the so-called nonfiction novel or *faction* with *In Cold Blood* (1966), these picture-book biographies have generated a new children's genre categorized as "storyographies." The best of them are interesting, lively, and fill a niche in children's literature collections.

A *storyography* is first, a story, and second, a BIOGRAPHY. It is not just a simplified description of a person's life, written at a young reading level and encased within a picture-book framework. Instead, it uses an incident in a person's life and builds a narrative around it. The book does not necessarily relate everything about the individual. It is a "story presentation" rather than a factual recounting of the person's whole life, and contains the dramatic tension of a well-constructed plot. Sometimes dialogue or fictional characters are created to add to the flow of the narrative. A definitive storyography must retain the spirit, the format, and the liveliness of a PICTURE BOOK. The 1999 CALDECOTT MEDAL winner, *Snowflake Bentley,* with text by Jacqueline Briggs Martin and hand-tinted watercolor woodcuts by Mary Azarian fits the description of "storyography." A single aspect of Wilson Bentley's life, his study of snowflakes, is narrated in the book along with informational sidebars of scientific interest.

When did this genre begin? One could point back as far as Maurice BOUTET DE MONVEL's *Joan of Arc*, first published in French in 1896. With his luminous illustrations on every double spread in a picture-book format, the book partially fills the definition. However, the fifty-five pages contain a sizable amount of text and the book itself was mostly a vehicle for Boutet de Monvel's stunning art work.

When citing forerunners of this new category, one must mention the D'AULAIRES. Ingri and Edgar Parrin d'Aulaire established the concept of picture biographies for younger children as having a valid role in library collections. From 1938 to 1955 they wrote and illustrated seven such picture biographies with large-size formats, color or black-and-white lithographs on every spread, and a simplicity of text intended to appeal to young readers. The length of the biographies was longer than picture books, running to forty and fifty-plus pages and their hours of research were not documented in any way. From *Abraham Lincoln* (1939), which won the Caldecott Medal to *Columbus* (1955) their biographies reflected the times in which they were written.

Certainly, Jean FRITZ was pivotal in paving the way for this new genre. She deserves credit for breathing life into historical figures in children's books. Her question biographies, *And Then What Happened, Paul Revere?* (1973), *Will You Sign Here, John Hancock?* (1976), etc., published in the 1970s, were a refreshingly new approach to regenerating history with dimensional characters and their accompanying foibles. The short texts were a boon for younger readers at that time. Though the framework of these books extends beyond the picture-book format, they demonstrated that biographies could be readable and history could be fun.

It is more likely that the prototype that set a standard for storyographies was a title published in 1983: *The Glorious Flight: Across the Channel with Louis Bleriot*. Coincidentally, Alice and Martin PROVENSEN's book also was selected for the Caldecott Medal. Their *Flight* "gloriously" positioned the parameters for this new category, though no one viewed the book as the start of a new genre at the time.

The next book creator who was influential in shaping this style of biography is Diane STANLEY. Though most of her biographical titles portray the entire life of the individual, the page design and the structuring of information convey a picture book perspective. From *Shaka, King of the Zulus* (1988), she has written and/or illustrated numerous picture-book biographies including *Leonardo da Vinci* (1992), *Good Queen Bess* (1990), and *Bard of Avon* (1992). Her luxuriant illustrations accurately reflect time and place and her selection of information for children's interests depict fascinating portraits of historical figures.

An interesting example of the statement made in the first paragraph of this entry, is two storyographies of Joan of Arc published in the same season. Diane Stanley's sumptuous, gilded illustrations of *Joan of Arc* (1998) were inspired by the illuminated manuscripts of that time as she portrays the peasant girl who became the savior of France. Josephine Poole brings her *Joan of Arc*

(1998) to life with evocative language while Angela Barrett's illustrations evoke the drama and tragedy of the life of this revered saint. Stanley's book has a lengthy text that is contoured by her research, bibliography included, which relied on the transcript of Joan's trial. Poole's version is more story with simpler narrative and an energetic composition of page. Each is different in approach but together these books stunningly give life to legend.

One of the most recent pacesetters who has put the finishing touches on the standards for storyographies is Don Brown. *Alice Ramsey's Grand Adventure* (1997), *Ruth Law Thrills a Nation* (1993), and *One Giant Leap: The Story of Neil Armstrong* (1998) cast the mold for what a "good" storyography should be. First of all, they tell a good story, they convey a sense of that moment in time, they relate a specific achievement of the individuals that contributed to history, and the illustrations provide a stereoptic view of their landscapes and adventures.

Storyographies have blossomed from all types of biographical subjects, from SPORTS to arts to inventors. Robert BURLEIGH's *Home Run: The Story of Babe Ruth* (1998) is written from the viewpoint of this American hero at bat. Jeanette WINTER captures the unique personality and vision of Georgia O'Keeffe in *My Name Is Georgia* (1998). In *Boss to the Plains* (1998) Laurie Carlson relates how John Stetson created the most popular hat west of the Mississippi.

A criterion for storyographies should apply the following considerations: does it have a picture book format of thirty-two to forty pages with a small amount of text and an abundance of ILLUSTRATION; is it written with a focus on an incident, episode, ambition or event rather than a straightforward accounting of a person's life; is the telling of the event shaped by traditional story components including dramatic tension; does it have child appeal and provide a child's perspective; do the illustrations depict the person within a setting; is it an individual publication and not part of an identified series; what is the overall effect of the book and how well does it convey a lasting impression of the individual person?

The research that is necessary for storyographies should have a presence in the book itself, such as author's notes, chronologies, or reference to sources. The research should be evident, part of the design of the book, but not be intrusive of the narrative.

In her afterword for *Joan of Arc,* Diane Stanley makes this observation: "Sometimes, in studying history, we have to accept what we know and let the rest remain a mystery." Story-ographies underscore her point, yet convey the essence of the person in a meaningful way for young readers.

(Adapted from an article in School Library Journal, *August 1998, by the author.)*

JULIE CUMMINS

STORYTELLING

Storytelling includes telling stories as part of everyday conversation, such as relating first- or second-hand life experiences, as well as telling prepared stories to audiences, a great deal of which is based on oral or written literature. Almost as long as there has been human language, people have engaged in storytelling. It is likely that the earliest prepared stories were chants created to praise nature or to recount events of tribal heroism. The finest storytellers became community historians, passing ancestral lore from generation to generation, century to century.

Nearly all cultures had storytelling performers, although storytelling played especially significant roles in certain civilizations. Storytelling, particularly tales of MYTHOLOGY and heroism, has long been central in NATIVE AMERICAN and Eskimo cultures. Many African cultures south of the Sahara have powerful poetic and narrative oral traditions, in which storytelling is usually combined with musical performance. Before it was finally written down in the eighth century, Arab *rawis* (oral poets) recited pre–Islamic POETRY, successfully preserving this body of literature for many generations. In China during the Middle Ages, storytellers performed in public places, often telling lengthy and involved tales of historical fiction.

In medieval Europe, storytelling became the prevailing form of popular entertainment. Traveling storytellers, known as bards, skalds, troubadours, and minstrels, entertained both the wealthy and working classes in royal courts and public marketplaces. In Wales and Ireland, highly trained bards recited heroic poetry, wrote eulo-

gies and satires, composed and sang music, and preserved oral history. From the ninth to the thirteenth century, Norwegian skalds recited court poetry, often praising kings and reciting epitaphs of royal personages. During the twelfth and thirteenth centuries, troubadours, or lyric poets, traveled Provence, northern Italy, and northern Spain, and from the twelfth to seventeenth centuries, minstrels across Europe played instruments, sang songs, told stories, and performed acrobatic tricks.

The travels of these various storytellers helped spread stories across cultural boundaries, leading to the multitude of cultural variants of folk and FAIRY TALES that survive today. With the invention of movable type in Europe ca. 1440, the medieval heyday of storytelling dwindled as the popularity and availability of printed stories, news, and other texts grew and literacy increased.

The late seventeenth through nineteenth centuries produced heightened scholarly interest in folk literature, much of which had previously existed exclusively in oral form. Scholars across Europe recorded many of the oral tales that had survived the primacy of the printed word, publishing anthologies and indexes of folk and fairy tales. French writer Charles PERRAULT recorded popular fairy tales from the oral tradition, such as "Cinderella" and "Sleeping Beauty," in *Stories; or, Tales from Olden Times* (1697; trans. 1729). The GRIMM Brothers, Jacob Ludwig Karl Grimm and Wilhelm Karl Grimm, collected German folktales in *Household Tales* (2 vol., 1812–15; trans. 1884). Now known as *Grimm's Fairy Tales,* the stories included many modern favorites, such as "Hansel and Gretel," "Snow White and the Seven Dwarfs," and "Rapunzel." Peter Christen ASBJORNSEN and Jørgen Engebretsen MOE (see ASBJORNSEN) preserved stories from Norwegian folklore in *Norske folkeeventyr (Norwegian Folktales,* 1841). In Finland, Elias Lonnrot gathered folk poetry, which he melded into his own poetry in *The Kalevala* (1849). Australian-born Joseph JACOBS collected fairy tales popular in England, publishing them in various volumes, including *The Fables of Aesop* (1894), *English Fairy Tales* (1890), *Celtic Fairy Tales* (1892), and *Indian Fairy Tales* (1892).

It was not until the early twentieth century that European interest in folk literature ripened into a dynamic flourish of storytelling in the United

States, resulting in the formaiton of the still-extant National Story League in 1903. During the ensuing century, storytelling became principally associated with children and children's literature, due in part to British storyteller Marie Shedlock's many lectures about storytelling as a method of introducing children to literature. Her lectures, delivered during her travels across the United States, were gathered into a book and published as *The Art of the Story-teller* (1915). Another influential storytelling proponent and performer was Ruth SAWYER (1880–1970), whose *The Way of the Storyteller* (1942), a mixture of scholarly history, personal anecdotes, storytelling instruction, and story anthology, remains in print today. The use of storytelling in schools and public libraries flourished until the middle of the century, when picture-book publication increased and began to dominate school reading programs and library story times.

Interest in storytelling swelled again in the 1970s. The National Association for the Preservation and Perpetuation of Storytelling (now The National Storytelling Association) was formed in 1974. The Association continues to hold an annual storytelling festival in Jonesborough, Tennessee. During the storytelling revival of the 1970s, a new class of traveling storytellers began charging fees for their art. Many of these professional performers employed more dramatic gestures, used more radically distinct characters' voices, wore more theatrical costumes, and used more props, such as puppets, flannel boards, and stuffed animals than had previously been common in performance storytelling. Several nonprofessional storytellers, such as New York Public Library storytellers Augusta Baker and Ellin Greene, authors of *Storytelling: Art and Technique* (1996), rejected these techniques as creative dramatics, not storytelling. For her part, Baker has had a significant influence on the development of storytelling programs in United States public libraries, serving as the storytelling specialist and coordinator of children's services at the New York Public Library. Reflecting a renaissance in the art, many universities and colleges in the United States soon began offering formal instruction in storytelling. East Tennessee State University created the country's first gradu-

ate degree program in storytelling, granting its first master's degree in 1989.

With the advent of the World Wide Web (WWW) and other electronic information technologies, a new manifestation of storytelling gained popularity in the last years of the twentieth century: digital storytelling, or telling tales with the aid of electronic media. Digital storytelling can take many forms, from stories typed into the WWW in text-only format, to the posting of oral stories in audio or video format on the WWW, to digital performance storytelling in which the teller presents a story with the aid of audio and video equipment in person to an audience.

Today, storytellers tell many types of stories, including folktales, fairy tales, literary fairy tales, myths, legends, fables, and self-authored autobiographical tales. Folktales are stories by unknown authors handed down through oral tradition, such as "The Three Little Pigs" and "Juan Bobo." Fairy tales, or folktales with an element of magic, include stories such as "Jack and the Beanstalk" and "Urashima Taro." Hans Christian ANDERSEN is perhaps the best-known author of literary fairy tales, or modern stories written in the style of fairy tales. Andersen published six volumes of original fairy tales between 1835 and 1842, including beloved classics such as "The Emperor's New Clothes" (1837), "The Little Mermaid" (1837), and "The Ugly Duckling" (1843). Among the huge body of existing myths, or stories that explain the natural or supernatural world, Greek, Roman, Norse, and Native American myths are some of the most frequently told today. Also prevalent are legends, which combine fact and fiction to immortalize great or unusual deeds or events. Examples include the tales of King Arthur and modern urban legends. Aesop's fables are also still popular storytelling material, as are more recent fables, usually involving animals as the main characters. Short stories, poetry, and PICTURE BOOKS also provide a wealth of material for contemporary storytellers.

Modern storytelling techniques vary widely. Some storytellers memorize their tales, but most merely memorize the order of the stories' events and verbalize them uniquely with each telling. Regardless of the methods storytellers choose to learn their stories, every story performance is unique. No two storytellers use exactly the same vocal inflection, timing, facial expressions, etc., and no storyteller tells the same story exactly the same way twice, making every story a singular contribution to the history of oral literature.

DENISE E. AGOSTO

(See also LIBRARIES AND CHILDREN'S READING PROGRAMS and STORYTELLING: A PROFESSIONAL POINT OF VIEW)

STORYTELLING: A PROFESSIONAL POINT OF VIEW

(Jeslyn Wheeless, the author of this essay, is a professional storyteller participating in the current storytelling renaissance. She appears in various venues and accompanies herself on guitar, dulcimer, and autoharp.)

Storytelling is the art of sharing aloud MYTHOLOGY AND LEGEND, fables, folk- and FAIRY TALES, family stories, and original tales in the oral tradition. From prehistoric ancestors recounting stories of the hunt by the fire, to twenty-first century professional storytellers recording ancient myths on compact discs, the art of storytelling has survived as an enduring means of sharing the human spirit.

Storytelling today takes many forms. A grandfather regales his grandsons with original adventure stories; a Scout leader repeats the spooky tale, "Wiley and the Hairy Man," to young insomniacs around the campfire. Many classroom teachers stretch the imaginations of their students, enriching the curriculum with folktales from around the world, encouraging the acceptance of diversity with such stories as "The Legend of Lucia Zenteno." As has been the tradition in America, children's librarians keep the listening candle burning, sharing with children in story hours the best of folk- and fairy tales, legends, myths, and literary tales.

The current renaissance of storytelling in America is perhaps best exemplified by the professional storyteller who researches and identifies treasures of FOLKLORE from many cultures, learns to tell the tales, narrating by memory without the use of a book, and hones the technique of presentation that brings each story to life in a captivating way when shared with listeners. Storytellers perform in many settings such as schools, librar-

ies, museums, book stores, parks, churches and synagogues, festivals, and hospitals.

As the value of this folk art has become recognized, the number of storytellers has grown significantly over the last three decades. The values to listeners, especially children, are as follows: providing an enjoyable group experience, instilling an appreciation for literature and a love of reading, developing empathy for the characters, sharpening listening skills, stimulating creativity and the imagination, increasing vocabulary, learning the sequencing of events in a plot, and, indirectly, improving writing skills.

Many storytellers teach courses in which children learn to tell stories themselves. Besides providing an enjoyable method of learning public speaking, such courses also sharpen memory skills and build confidence. Students are taught to read many stories before choosing a special one from a preselected list of well-written, short folktales. Next, techniques for learning the story are presented, such as reading it aloud many times, making a cartoon sequence of events, and using a cassette tape recorder. The art of storytelling is taught so that young tellers can capture an audience with an interestingly modulated tone, volume, and pitch, appropriate gestures, confident stance, and eye to eye contact. Culminating in a school-wide festival, each storyteller tells his special tale to an audience of eager listeners.

Historically, storytelling dates back to the earliest times, when people informed and entertained each other by telling tales, handing down memories of family history, and teaching the cultural and religious mythology of the tribe. The power of the oral tradition, listening, remembering, retelling, preserved such treasures as Greek mythology, the Bible, and ancient epics like *Beowulf* for centuries before these stories were ever written down.

Throughout the ages children have been warned against danger in cautionary tales, and inspired by stories of bravery, told to them by parents, grandparents, and teachers. "Little Red Riding Hood" cautions against speaking to strangers, and the English folktale "Tamlane" presents a heroine of breathtaking courage. Imaginations of listeners young and old have been stimulated by creative stories that explain the origins of natural phenomena, such as "Why the Sun and Moon Live in the Sky," a *pourquoi* tale from AFRICA.

Besides the family story sharers in past centuries there were individuals who became highly skilled at the art of storytelling, learning and remembering many stories, myths, and legends, and bringing them to life with a winning style, often accompanied by music. Many of these master storytellers remained within one village, serving the ruler as historian, poet, and entertainer. Relieved of other duties and supported by the court, in return for their talents, such bards as the Greek minstrel, Icelandic skald, and Irish *seanachie*, were able to refine and develop the art of storytelling to a higher level.

During the Middle Ages, storytellers reached the height of esteem as many troubadours traveled from village to village, castle to castle, welcomed by listeners who longed to hear heroic tales and romances as well as history and news of wars and rulers. These artists were well trained and highly skilled, playing at least two musical instruments and knowing hundreds of stories that they told to mesmerized audiences. During this period such riches of literature as the legends of King Arthur were remembered, further developed, and refined by the traveling storytellers.

With the development of printing in the fifteenth century, many of the old tales were recorded, and the troubadours began to lose status, eventually becoming obsolete. Still, storytelling continued to exist in the folktales handed down in families from generation to generation, just as it had before the days of the professional artists.

In the nineteenth and twentieth centuries, many scholars researched and published collections of authentic folktales gleaned from family and community tellers. Quite popular among those published are *Household Tales,* German folktales collected by Jakob and Wilhelm GRIMM in the early 1800s; *Jack Tales* and *Grandfather Tales,* Appalachian stories collected by Richard CHASE in the 1940s; and *The Magic Orange Tree and Other Haitian Folktales* recorded by Diane WOLKSTEIN in the early 1970s. These scholars have preserved not only the authenticity of the stories, but also the form and flavor of the storytellers.

The twentieth century has seen a renaissance in the art of storytelling, beginning with French storyteller Marie Shedlock's visit to New York City in the early 1900s. Her teaching of the storytelling art to teachers and LIBRARIANS marked the beginning of storytelling as an important tradition in American libraries. Ruth SAWYER furthered the concept of storytelling as a profession with her outstanding performances, research, and writing in midcentury.

In 1977 the renowned storytellers Augusta Baker and Ellin Greene published *Storytelling: Art and Technique,* a most comprehensive and useful guide, based on their own experiences as tellers and teachers of storytelling in the New York Public Library system and on their extensive knowledge of children's literature and folktales. Courses in storytelling were taught by Baker and Greene at Columbia and Rutgers Universities respectively, and similar courses were offered at most Graduate Schools of Library Science in American universities. Other outstanding names among many fine artists in the field today are Diane WOLKSTEIN, Laura Sims, Jackie Torrence, David Holt, Carol Birch, Jay O'Callahan, and Elizabeth Ellis.

The National Association for the Preservation and Perpetuation of Storytelling, or NAPPS, was founded in Jonesboro, Tennessee, in 1975, "to encourage the practice and application of the storytelling art." This organization, now renamed the National Storytelling Network, provides an annual national storytelling festival, professional conferences and workshops, a national directory, monthly publication, and archives. Local storytelling organizations, such as the New Jersey Storytellers Circle, and the New York Storytelling Center, also provide monthly meetings, statewide festivals, and professional seminars for artists in these areas.

As did their predecessors, the troubadours of the Middle Ages, today's storytellers often travel from place to place, sharing the wonder and joy of the special tales they have collected. Some incorporate MUSIC, accompanying themselves on guitar, dulcimer, or banjo, to enhance the mood of the tale, or simply engage the audience in singing. And all of these artists strive to emulate Ruth Sawyer's "Peddler of Ballaghadereen" who "knew how to tell the stories in such a way that the children would keep them close in their hearts until they were old."

BIBLIOGRAPHY: Baker, A. and E. Greene, *Story-telling: Art and Technique*. 1977, 1987. Barton, B. *Tell Me Another: Storytelling and Reading Aloud at Home, at School and in the Community*. 1986. Holt, D. and B. Mooney. eds. *Ready-To-Tell Tales: Sure-Fire Stories from America's Favorite Storytellers*. 1994. A. Silvey, ed., *The Horn Book Magazine:* Storytelling Issue. June, 1983. Kardaleff, S., exec. ed. *Storytelling Magazine*. Reed, B. "Storytelling: What It Can Teach." *School Library Journal*. October 1987, pp. 35–39. Sawyer, Ruth. *The Way of the Storyteller*. 1942. Shedlock, Marie. *The Art of the Story-Teller*. 1951. Wolkstein, D. *The Magic Orange Tree and Other Haitian Folktales*. 1978

JESLYN WHEELESS

(See also LIBRARIES AND CHILDREN'S READING PROGRAMS and STORYTELLING)

STOUTENBURG, Adrien
Author, poet, b. 1 December 1916, Darfur, Minnesota

Having always wanted to be a poet, S. has not only published poetry but also has written books for young readers in the PICTURE BOOKS, MYSTERY, BIOGRAPHY, and folk-tale genres, and INFORMATIONAL BOOKS on the conservation of wildlife. The need for income was her first impetus for writing commercially, as she finished school during the Depression. Although she attended Minneapolis School of the Arts, she attributes her interest and success in writing to being an avid reader. S. has won numerous AWARDS for her POETRY and has also published in MAGAZINES AND PERIODICALS under pseudonyms such as Barbie Arden, Lace Kendall, and Nelson Minier. *American Tall Tales* (1966) and *American Tall Tale Animals* (1968) were both issued as recordings.

FURTHER WORKS: *Timberline Treasure*, 1951; *The Silver Trap*, 1954; *Snowshoe Thompson*, 1957; *Wild Animals of the Far West*, 1958; *A Time for Dreaming*, 1963; *The Crocodile's Mouth*, 1966; *Listen America: A Life of Walt Whitman*, 1968; *Out There*, 1971

BIBLIOGRAPHY: *Something about the Author,* vol. 3, 1972, *Third Book of Junior Authors,* 1972

JANELLE B. MATHIS

STOWE, Harriet Beecher
Author, b. 14 June 1811, Litchfield, Connecticut; d. 1 July 1896, Hartford, Connecticut

Although S. wrote many books and was one of the most influential women of the Victorian pe-riod, she is best known as the author of the classic novel, *Uncle Tom's Cabin; or, The Man That Was a Thing* (1852). The book, which S. originally wrote in weekly installments for an antislavery newspaper, the *National Era,* echoed the concerns of many who opposed the institution. *Uncle Tom's Cabin* quickly became popular, selling over half a million copies in the United States in five years and three million copies before the Civil War began. S. worked vigorously after the controversial book's publication to defend her work against commentators. S.'s work has been criticized as being uneven but has also been lauded as a good example of effective realism. She also worked tirelessly to further the temperance and women's suffrage movements.

Uncle Tom's Cabin is still widely read in classrooms. In addition to *Uncle Tom's Cabin* and other novels, S. also wrote studies of social life, essays, and a small volume of religious poems.

FURTHER WORKS: *A Key to Uncle Tom's Cabin: Presenting the Original Facts and Documents upon which the Story Is Founded,* 1853; *Uncle Sam's Emancipation,* 1854; *Dred: A Tale of the Great Dismal Swamp,* 1856; *The Minister's Wooing,* 1859

BIBLIOGRAPHY: *Major Authors and Illustrators for Children and Young Adults: A Selection of Sketches From Something about the Author.* vol. 5, 1993; "Harriet Beecher Stowe," http://www.kirjasto.seLfi/hbstowe.htm web sites: www.cs.smu.edu/People. = /mmbt/women/StoweHB.html; www.lonestar.texas.net/~kwells/stowebib.htm

MARY ARIAIL BROUGHTON
AND MICHAEL O'LAUGHLIN

STRATEMEYER, Edward
Author, operator of writing syndicate, b. 1861, Elizabeth, New Jersey; d. 1930, Newark, New Jersey

S. created a large and prolific syndicate in which he sketched plot lines and assigned them to writers. His writing career began one day while he was working in his brother's tobacco store in Elizabeth, New Jersey. S. took a piece of wrapping paper, sat down and wrote a story. That was the beginning of a lifelong writing career that led to more than a thousand books written under a hundred pseudonyms and translated into twenty-six languages. He mailed his first story to a Philadelphia weekly for boys and received $75 in return, a remarkable sum for the time. His father was impressed and advised him to write some more. Instead, S. invested the $75 and saved enough to open a stationery store in Newark, New Jersey.

S. admired the Horatio Alger, Jr., and the Oliver Optic stories that had a work hard, persevere, and you will succeed morality. He began his career by writing stories for MAGAZINES AND PERIODICALS (*Golden Days, Golden Argosy*) and assumed the editorship of *Good News,* a weekly magazine for boys published by Street and Smith. He was working at Street and Smith when Horatio Alger and William T. Adams died; S. subsequently completed eleven books under Alger's name and three as Oliver Optic. The idea of writing books under a pseudonym became obvious.

S. continued to write books with similar "be brave, work hard" themes including war stories. One of his early manuscripts featured two boys on a battleship just about the same time that Admiral Dewey declared victory at Manila Bay. His publisher asked if he could revise his manuscript to parallel the major event of the day. He certainly could and *Under Dewey at Manila* was published in 1899. It was a financial success, called the Old Glory Series, and sequels followed in quick order. Other publishing houses offered S. contracts to initiate series with them. A series about the boyhood of U.S. Presidents never caught on, but the Dave Porter Series, the Lakeport Series, and the Putnam Hall Series showed that S. had found a successful formula. In 1899 S. released The Rover Boy Series for Young Americans Series; this became his personal favorite and a tremendous financial success. Later came The Motor Boys Series, The Racer Boys Series, The Jack Ranger Series, and The Movie Boys Series. S. wrote under the pseudonym, Victor Appleton, for some of these series and again for The Tom Swift Series.

S. was a business man as well as a prolific writer. He knew that half of the reading population was female, so he initiated The Barton Books for Girls Series, The Nan Sherwood Series, The Betty Gordon Series and The Ruth Fielding Series. As Laura Lee Hope he began The Moving Picture Girls Series, The Outdoor Girls Series,

The Six Little Bunkers Series and The Bunny Brown Series. As Helen Louise Thorndike, he created The Honey Bunch Series. In 1904, S. made financial gains while using the pseudonym Laura Lee Hope for the author of The Bobbsey Twins Series. The Bobbsey Twins Series sold and continues to sell millions of copies annually. By 1926, the AMERICAN LIBRARY ASSOCIATION sponsored a national survey of juvenile reading. The study asked 36,000 children in thirty-four cities to identify their favorite book. More than 98 percent of the group responded with a Stratemeyer title.

In 1927, S. supervised the creation of two new series, The Nancy Drew Series, written under the name Carolyn Keene, and The Hardy Boys Series, written under the name of Franklin S. Dixon; these eventually outsold all other series except the Bobbsey Twins. After S. died (1930), his daughter, Harriet Stratemeyer Adams, took over responsibility for the series and produced a new Nancy Drew book each year. She also continued her father's practice of issuing plot outlines to writers on contract. Writers hired by the Stratemeyer Syndicate rewrote the older books; they continue to sell today in revised formats more consistent with current gender and ethnic sensibilities. Harriet Stratemeyer Adams continued to ghost write The Bobbsey Twins, The Nancy Drew, and The Hardy Boys Series. Harriet S. Adams died, March 28, 1982 in Maplewood, New Jersey. Book series, ghost writing and use of pseudonyms continues today.

BIBLIOGRAPHY: Billman, C., *The Secret of the Stratemeyer Syndicate,* 1986; Hunt, Peter, ed., *Children's Literature: An Illustrated History,* 1995; Serafin, Steven R., ed., *Encyclopedia of American Literature,* 1999

BERNICE E. CULLINAN

(See also SERIES BOOKS and MYSTERY AND DETECTIVE STORIES)

STREATFEILD, Noel

Author, b. 24 December 1897, Amberley, Sussex, England; d. 11 September 1986, London

Author of fiction and nonfiction books for children, S. began an acting career after studying at the Royal Academy of Dramatic Art. Following the writing of several adult novels, she began her career as a children's author with *Ballet Shoes: A*

Story of Three Children on the Stage (1936). S. won the CARNEGIE MEDAL for *The Circus Is Coming* (1938), about two runaway orphans and their uncle, a circus clown. She continued a prolific career, writing over fifty children's books, mostly theater-related career stories. Her books focused on a variety of topics such as *Tennis Shoes* (1937), *Party Frock* (1946), *The Painted Garden* (1949), and *When the Sirens Wailed* (1974), a book about World War II. Over many years she wrote a series of books on shoes and another series of Baby Books. Her Gemma series is about a child movie star. Each of the varied titles reflected aspects of her life and many have been adapted for radio and television.

FURTHER WORKS: *Thursday's Child.* Junior Literary Guild Selection. 1971. *A Young Person's Guide to the Ballet.* Children's Book of the Year by the Child Study Association. 1975

BIBLIOGRAPHY: *Something about the Author,* vol. 20, 1980, and vol. 48, 1987

JANELLE B. MATHIS

STRICKLAND, Michael R.

Author, b. 8 June 1965, Orange, New Jersey

S., a poet and anthologist, graduated with a bachelor of arts degree from Cornell University in 1987 and with a masters degree from Seton Hall University in New Jersey in 1993. He currently teaches writing at Jersey City State College. S., whose mother is noted educator Dorothy S., grew up as the youngest of three very close-knit brothers who went to school together and played together. Those shared memories of life in a small town and times the brothers spent at their grandparent's home are influential in everything S. writes. *Families: Poems Celebrating the AFRICAN AMERICAN Experience* (1994) selected by S. and Dorothy S., reflect those days of being a little boy in the loving embrace of a warm African American family.

Other POETRY anthologies edited by S. include *Poems That Sing to You* (1993) and *My Own Song: And Other Poems to Groove To* (1997). Both anthologies span a broad geographic vista and timespan, and are intended to be enjoyed as musical performances. They emphasize the beat, rhythm, and music that is inherent in poetry and is recognized as universal in all cultures. There

are poems young people know as classic rock-'n'-roll lyrics, such as the song "Dancing in the Street" and poems by authors like William Blake. In S.'s first PICTURE BOOK, *Haircuts at Sleepy Sam's* (1998), he revisits scenes of his boyhood. S. says he wanted to write a book that would specifically "speak to and about African American boys" while, at the same time, speak to children of all cultures. Since the barbershop is often the nerve center of the community where people come together to talk, joke, and debate, and since he has fond memories of trips to the barber with his brothers on Saturday mornings, this was the perfect setting for S.'s first picture book. He completes the scene with memorable, yet universal, small-town characters. School District 22 in Brooklyn, New York, recognized S.'s emphasis on African American boys by giving him their Role Model of the Year award in 1999.

AWARDS: Fordham University Poetry Award

FURTHER WORKS: *African-American Poets,* 1996; *A-to-Z of African-American History,* 2000; *African-American Writers: A Dictionary* (with Shari Hatch), 2000

BIBLIOGRAPHY: Boyds Mills Publisher's press release; interview with author

DIANE G. PERSON

SURVIVAL STORIES

Survival stories are often set in a natural setting. The genre presents opportunities for readers to experience vicarious independence and to examine survival as a literary theme. Readers identify with characters who struggle for survival without adult help. Their interest relates to "reality orientation," which psychosocial theorist Erik H. Erikson attributes to children between seven and twelve years of age; an orientation toward handling situations independently and toward being able to assess their own ability to cope. Erikson suggests this age group has a growing "sense of industry and task orientation," a theme found in survival stories. Some include *Hatchet* (Gary PAULSEN, 1987), *My Side of the Mountain* (Jean GEORGE, 1959) and *From the Mixed-up Files of Mrs. Basil E. Frankweiler* (E. L. KONIGSBERG, 1970)—NEWBERY MEDAL and Honor Book titles.

Four major themes appear: survival stories set in a historical context; survival while assisting a dependent child, adult, or animal; characters working together to survive; survival in the wild after an accident.

Survival stories set in a historical context include *Save Queen of Sheba* (Louise Moeri, 1981) and *Sarah Bishop* (Scott O'DELL, 1980). In *Save Queen of Sheba,* twelve-year-old King David, named from the biblical figure, and his sister, Queen of Sheba, are the only survivors of an Indian attack on their wagon train. David is frustrated at first by the lack of adult intervention and by the burden of caring for his six-year-old sister as they attempt to cross the Prairie alone. David is tempted to go on alone because of Sheba's stubborn independence.

Sarah Bishop is set at the beginning of the American Revolutionary War. Sarah's father, a British sympathizer, is murdered by men claiming to be patriots. Sarah then learns her older brother, who has left the family to join the patriots in battle, has died as a prisoner of war. Now orphaned, and labeled a Tory, she is arrested on a false pretense. Convinced a fair trial is impossible, Sarah escapes and flees to the countryside to live her life as a fugitive. She takes residence in a cave where she spends a winter using her skills to gather and preserve food, reinforce her shelter, and meet the challenges necessary for survival.

The main character assisting a dependent child, adult, or animal is another theme used in survival tales. *Rescue Josh McGuire* (Ben Mikaelsen, 1991) focuses on the story of Josh, who runs away from home with a young bear cub in order to save the cub's life. Josh must provide for himself, the cub, and his dog while in the wilderness. Unseasonable storms, wild animals, and hiding from human trackers are some of the unexpected challenges.

Kirkpatrick Hill's *Toughboy and Sister* (1990) is the prequel to *Winter Camp* (1993). In this book the unexpected death of their father forces ten-year-old Toughboy, and his younger sister, to survive alone in the isolated wilderness along Alaska's Yukon River. They begin their ordeal with a supply of food and a simple cabin for shelter, but struggle to meet the challenge of wilderness living and the fact that both their parents are dead. The story revolves around life in a NATIVE AMERICAN village and a fishing camp in Alaska.

The book combines a MULTICULTURAL point of view with a survival tale.

In *Winter Camp,* Toughboy and Sister are taken to winter camp by Natasha, an Athabascan Native woman, who cares for the children after their parents' death. Natasha teaches the children how to trap animals as well as how to use native methods to survive in the Alaskan wilderness at temperatures of 20 degrees below zero. Unexpectedly, Toughboy and Sister must use Natasha's teachings when they are forced to survive in the wilderness on their own as they care for Natasha's injured friend.

The Cay, by Theodore TAYLOR (1969), is an unusual twist on the typical survival format. Phillip, an eleven-year-old now blinded as a result of injuries, is rescued by Timothy, a West Indian fisherman, after being shipwrecked. *The Cay* and *Timothy of the Cay* (1993), its prequel, provide exciting survival stories emphasizing mutual human interdependence in a multicultural setting.

Armstrong SPERRY's 1941 NEWBERY MEDAL book, *Call It Courage* relates how Mafatu, a Polynesian boy, is taunted by his tribe because of his fear of the sea, a fear developed after witnessing his mother's drowning. He realizes he must overcome this fear if he is to survive in a culture that lives by fishing. Mafatu decides to leave his native island and seek courage while he survives elsewhere, alone, in the Pacific. He is forced to confront his fear many times as he struggles alone to survive.

Many survival stories involve characters working cooperatively. *Frozen Fire* (James HOUSTON, 1977) relates the experiences of a young boy, aided by his Eskimo friend, as they search for the boy's father who is lost in a CANADIAN–Arctic storm. The youngsters must survive the challenges of storms, starvation, and wild animals, as well as human enemies, while on their quest.

A classic, *The Incredible Journey* (Sheila BURNFORD, 1961), is a variation on the theme of a vicarious experience through reading about survival of young adolescents since its main characters are all animals. This book relates the tale of three family pets—an old English bull terrier, a young Labrador, and a Siamese cat—as they set out to cross two hundred fifty miles of wilderness in an attempt to return home. Incredibly, these house pets demonstrate a remarkable ability to adapt to their new wilderness existence. Their acts of courage, love, and loyalty to each other, as well as to humans, make this story noteworthy.

Gary Paulsen is known for using wilderness-survival themes resulting from an accident or other, unplanned, circumstance. In *Hatchet* (1986), Brian miraculously lands a small plane alone after the pilot suffers a fatal heart attack. He then must learn how to survive in the Canadian Wilderness with only the clothes on his back, a small hatchet, and his wits. Paulsen wrote *Brian's Winter* (1996) as a response to readers' comments on the earlier novel, *Hatchet*. It is a variation on the plot of *Hatchet*: the main character from *Hatchet* is not rescued at the end of the summer. Instead, thirteen-year-old Brian must face the rigors of a cold Canadian winter in the wilderness with the benefit of only a few items retrieved from a survival kit found aboard his crashed plane and the lessons he has learned from summer months alone in the wilderness. This book begins where *Hatchet* ends, but can also be read alone.

The Voyage of the Frog (1989), also by Paulsen, begins when fourteen-year-old David has been given his uncle's sailboat after his uncle's death. David decides to head to the open sea off the coast of California to disperse his uncle's ashes. He is unexpectedly caught in high winds and forced to survive for weeks on the ocean with meager supplies. David learns about the world of the sea as well as his own ability to solve problems.

Readers identify with the characters portrayed and, vicariously, share the character's trials and tribulations. In addition, S. provide an opportunity for children to develop independence as they consider their own abilities to "survive" without adult assistance.

BIBLIOGRAPHY: Moss, J., *Focus Units in Literature: A Handbook for School Teachers*, 1984

PENNY G. BRIGHT

SUTCLIFF, Rosemary
Author, b. 14 December 1920, East Clanden, Surrey, England; d. 23 July 1992, Walburton, West Sussex, England

S.'s fiction grew from her own abiding interest in British history and traditional epics. Working from period to plot, her stories include palpable period detail and engage the reader's sense of his-

toric consciousness. Because of her thorough grasp of historical nuance and detail, S. has been able to put the factual aspects of her stories to service as artistic elements in her STORYTELLING. Politics and cultures come to life through the adventures S. creates with her characters.

S.'s own childhood was both exotic and constricted. The daughter of a naval officer, she and her family lived abroad in her early years, a time when she first manifested rheumatoid arthritis. Her mother read to her from such British classics as the Anglo-Saxon epic *Beowulf*, but hampered her daughter's own progress as an independent reader by providing her with unliterary phonetic material. Although S. learned to read after entering a neighborhood school upon the family's return to England, her lack of interest in scholarship led to the end of her academic education at age fourteen. She spent three years in art school training as a miniature portraitist. Shortly after the close of World War II, S. turned to writing and discovered her true vocation.

The Eagle and the Ninth (1954) earned the CARNEGIE MEDAL commendation (1955); as did *The Shield Ring* (1956), in 1957; *The Silver Branch* (1957), in 1958; and *Warrior Scarlet* (1958), in 1959. *Warrior Scarlet* earned citation as an honor book for the Hans Christian ANDERSEN Award (1959), ranked on the honor list of the INTERNATIONAL BOARD ON BOOKS FOR YOUNG PEOPLE (1960), and earned S. the title of Highly Commended Author (1974). *The Lantern Bearers* (1959) received the 1960 Carnegie Medal. *Knight's Fee* (1960) was cited by the AMERICAN LIBRARY ASSOCIATION as a notable book (1960), as were, upon their publication in the United States, *Beowulf* (1962, published in England as *Dragon Slayer*, 1961), *The Hound of Ulster* (1963), *The Mark of the Horse Lord* (1965), and *The Road to Camlann: The Death of King Arthur* (1982; published in England, 1981). *The Witch's Brat* (1970) received the 1971 Lewis CARROLL Shelf Award and was an ALA Notable Book. *Tristan and Iseult* (1971) was a runner up for the 1972 Carnegie Medal as well as being an ALA notable book. The Child Study Association's 1972 list of Children's Books of the Year included *Heather, Oak, and Olive: Three Stories* (1972), and *The Capricorn Bracelet* (1973) was cited for the 1973 list. *Song for a Dark Queen*

(1978) received the Other Award, in 1978, from the Children's Book Bulletin. The 1985 Phoenix Award, presented by the Children's Literature Association, went to *The Mark of the Horse Lord*. S. was cited by the Children's Rights Workshop with their 1978 Award. She became a fellow of the Royal Society of Literature in 1982. In 1975, S. was awarded the title of Officer, Order of the British Empire; in 1992, she became Commander, Order of the British Empire.

S. researched historic periods in great depth and developed political story lines that manifested humanitarian themes. From childhood she had great familiarity with British legends, many of which she revivified in her novels, including *The Chronicles of Robin Hood* (1950), *Dragon Slayer* (republished as *Dragon Slayer: The Story of Beowulf*, in 1980), *The High Deeds of Finn MacCool* (1967) and *Tristan and Iseult*. Many of her original novels for children are set during the Roman period of British history. Her Roman Trilogy comprises the story of a second-century centurion in Britain, in *The Eagle and the Ninth*; some third century military youth who perceive the need to unify Britain, in *The Silver Branch*; and the desertion of a Roman soldier as the Empire loses its hold on Britain, in *The Lantern Bearers*. Several independently standing novels also delve into the politics and society of Roman Britain, including *Outcast* (1955), *The Capricorn Bracelet*, *Song for a Dark Queen* and *Frontier Wolf* (1980).

Warrior Scarlet takes readers even further back in time as S. explores life in Britain during the Bronze Age. *Sun Horse, Moon Horse* (1977) is set during the period just preceding Rome's conquest of Britain. Chronologically following the Roman era, *Dawn Wind* (1961) is set at the time of the Saxon invasion of Britain. *Bonnie Dundee* (1983) and *Flame-Coloured Taffeta* (1985, published in the U.S. as *Flame-Colored Taffeta*, 1986) bring to life Jacobite intrigues of the seventeenth and eighteenth century.

S.'s later works include a second trilogy for young readers, the Arthurian Knights, comprising *The Light beyond the Forest: The Quest for the Holy Grail* (1980), *The Sword and the Circle: King Arthur and the Knights of the Round Table* (1981), and *The Road to Camlann: The Death of King Arthur*. *The Shining Company* (1990), the

last of her books published during S.'s lifetime, gives her readers a reconstituted *Y Gododdin*, the Welsh epic poem.

Several books completed by S. have been published since her death. *Black Ships before Troy: The Story of the Iliad* (1993) and its sequel, *The Wanderings of Odysseus: The Story of the Odyssey* (1995), take readers back to the ancient Mediterranean. *The Minstrel and the Dragon Pup* (1993) reaches younger audiences than S.'s novels, telling an original tale about a wanderer, his pet dragon, and their rescue of a prince.

In addition to her many novels for children, S. published historical fiction for adults throughout her writing career.

FURTHER WORKS: *The Chief Daughter*, 1967; *The Truce of the Games*, 1971; *Eagle's Egg*, 1981; *Blue Remembered Hills*. 1983

BIBLIOGRAPHY: *Contemporary Authors, New Revision Series*, 1992; *Something about the Author*, vol. 44, 1986, and vol. 78, 1994; Jones, R. "Pilgrimage to Swallowshaw," *Horn Book* magazine, May 1999; Townsend, John Ruse, *A Sense of Story: Essays on Contemporary Writers for Children*, 1973

FRANCISCA GOLDSMITH

SWIFT, Hildegard Hoyt

Author, b. 1890, Clinton, New York; d. 1 January 1977, Redlands, California

S.'s background included work with children in the Union Settlement in New York City after studying at The New School for Social Research. She indicated that it was this interface with children from which she learned a great deal that went into her children's stories. Her *Little Red Lighthouse and the Great Gray Bridge* (1942), one of her books illustrated by Lynd WARD, was a classic tale based on a lighthouse at the foot of the George Washington Bridge on the New York City side. Her *Little Blacknose* (1929) told the fanciful story of De Witt Clinton's steam engine expressing interest in the new mechanical inventions. Although fictional, S.'s account of Harriet Tubman's life, *The Railroad to Freedom: A Story of the Civil War* (James DAUGHERTY, illus., 1932) was entirely factual and true to the spirit of Tubman's life. S. was one of the first authors to write about AFRICAN AMERICAN heroes for children. In *North Star Shining* (1947), S. with illustrator

Lynd Ward presented a rhythmic, dramatic interpretation of African American history.

FURTHER WORKS: *From the Eagle's Wing: A Biography of John Muir.* (Lynd WARD). Illus., 1962. *House by the Sea.* (Lynd Ward). Illus., 1938. *The Railroad to Freedom: A Story of Harriet Tubman.* 1932

BIBLIOGRAPHY: MEIGS, C. et al., *A Critical History of Children's Literature,* 1969; "Power of a Children's Book." *Saturday Review of Literature,* vol. 46, May 11, 1963, 43

JANE ANNE HANNIGAN

SWIFT, Jonathan
Author, b. 30 November 1667, Dublin, Ireland; d. 19 October 1745, Dublin, Ireland

A novelist, poet, satirist, and pamphleteer, S. was born in Hoey's Court in Dublin. His nurse took him in infancy to Whitehaven across the Irish Channel where they stayed for three years. When he was returned to his family at age three he could spell and "read any chapter in the Bible." He studied poetry for some years in England and when he was twenty-eight returned to Ireland to be ordained as an Anglican priest. He defended the Church in Ireland against English injustices and in his writings attacked the clergy, literary critics, philosophers, and people in positions of power. He loved the individual but despised "all nations, professions and communities."

A *Tale of a Tub* was published in 1704, written while S. was in England settling the estate of Sir William Temple. In 1720 he began writing *Gulliver's Travels* and finished it in 1725. He believed Gulliver's story would "wonderfully mend the world" and was amazed at the acquiescence and laughter that accompanied the tale. Although originally published for adults it quickly became a children's classic in abridged form. It has been made into a film several times, possibly most notably for children in animated form in 1939, which features the singing talents of Lanny Ross and Jessica Dragonette. Arthur RACKHAM is one of several well-known illustrators who have published notable editions. S. suffered a stroke in 1742 and died three years later.

IRVYN GILBERTSON

SZEKERES, Cyndy
Author, illustrator, b. 31 October 1933, Bridgeport, Connecticut

An artist, S.'s interest in children's books began with ILLUSTRATION. After sixteen years of illustrating, S. wrote her first book, *My Workbook Diary* (1963). She has produced many Golden Books including the Tiny Paw SERIES. Her illustrations consist mostly of animals, which are anthropomorphic. She uses nature to enhance her work; for example, she collects details for her backgrounds from the woods near her house.

FURTHER WORKS: Author: My *Workbook Diary* 1963. *Cyndy Szekeres's Animal Calendar* 1992. *Baby Bear's Surprise* 8. Illus.: *New Shoes* 9. *Mrs. Updaisy* 10. *Happy Birthday Mole and Troll* 1964 *and Pippa Pops Out!* 1966 *Walter the Lazy Mouse.* (Margery FLACK, au.). 1963. *Bedtime for Bears.* (A. Holl, au.). 1973; *C.S.'s ABC,* (1983) *C.S.'s Counting Book 1 to 10* (1984); *Scaredy Cat* (1984); *Puppy Lost* (1986); *C.S.'s Baby Animals* (1994); *The Mouse That Jack Built* (1997); *A Small Child's Book of Cozy Poems* (1999) *Christmas Mouse,* 1995

BIBLIOGRAPHY: *Something about the Author,* vol. 60, 1990

JODI PILGRIM

TABACK, Simms
Author, illustrator, graphic artist, b. 13 February 1932, New York City

T. has had a successful career as an illustrator and author of children's books for thirty years, receiving the ALA CALDECOTT MEDAL in 2000. As a graduate of Cooper Union he initially worked as an advertising designer and graphic artist; by the mid-1960s he began making his humorous stylized line and watercolor drawings for children's books. Between 1963 and 1971 he and a colleague, Reynold RUFFINS, formed Ruffins Taback Design Studio where they each created their own successful graphics and illustrations.

T.'s line drawings clearly express the absurdity and HUMOR in situations and in characters. Although his drawings are not cartoons in the literal sense, they are highly expressive and can be understood without text. Collaborating with author Sesyle JOSLIN, their book *Please Share That Peanut: A Preposterous Pageant in 14 Acts* was named one of the *New York Times* Best Illustrated Books in 1965. *There's Motion Everywhere* (John Moore, 1970), *Joseph Had a Little Overcoat* (1970) and *Laughing Together* (1980) were listed as outstanding works by the American Institute of Graphic Arts. Between 1961 and 1983, T. received many certificates of merit from the Society of Illustrators.

Both of T.'s award-winning PICTURE BOOKS, *Joseph Had a Little Overcoat* (1999 edition) and *There Was an Old Lady Who Swallowed a Fly* (1996) are distinguished by T.'s signature die-cut illustrations in vibrantly rich watercolors, gouache, pencil, ink, and collage. The die-cut peepholes in *There Was an Old Lady* allow readers to peek inside and watch the old lady's girth increase with each succeeding morsel she swallows; in *Joseph Had a Little Overcoat* the peepholes follow the progression from overcoat to button to loving memory.

AWARDS: ALA Caldecott Medal (2000) for *Joseph Had a Little Overcoat*. ALA Caldecott Medal Honor Book (1997) for *There Was an Old Lady Who Swallowed a Fly*. *New York Times* Outstanding Book of the Year (1997) for *There Was an Old Lady Who Swallowed a Fly*

FURTHER WORKS: *Jabberwocky and Other Favorites*. (Lewis CARROLL). 1966. *Too Much Noise*. (Ann MCGOVERN). 1967. *Two Little Witches*. (Harriet ZIEFERT). 1996. *Buggy Riddles*. 1986; *Fishy Riddles*. 1983. *Spacey Riddles*. 1992. *Snakey Riddles*. 1990

BIBLIOGRAPHY: *Something about the Author*, vol. 36, 1984, vol. 40, 1985, and vol. 104, 1999

JUDITH LIPSITT

TAFURI, Nancy
Author, illustrator, b. 14 November 1946, Brooklyn, New York

A graduate of New York's School of Visual Arts and co-owner of a graphic design studio, T.'s illustrations reflect her training and experience in graphics, type, and painting. Effective use of white space, and borders that frame, but do not contain, over which her characters caper or dangle their legs, is reminiscent of Art Deco compositions. Large, simple, stylized figures outlined lightly in black, bright splashes of color, gentle humor, and curious details to discover speak to the preschool and primary children who make up her audience. Always, her illustrations complement and support the text. In *If I had a Paka: Poems in Eleven Languages* by Charlotte POMERANTZ (1982), for example, T.'s versatility is reflected not only in the different meanings, but the different cultures each poem represents. Her topics are relevant to young children—dreams, family, animals, everyday objects and events, presented through gentle expression and minimal, quietly lyrical texts. They provide comfort as they assure children that the world is both interesting and safe. *Junglewalk* (1988) is the story of a child's dream in which his room becomes a jungle. Unlike the "wild things" in Maurice SENDAK's *Where the Wild Things Are,* this book's animals, although large, mind their own business as the child journeys through their habitat, neither threatening to, nor threatened by, the small observer in their midst. The boy's cat, which changes to a tiger in the dream, provides implicit protection, as well as being the guide who brings him safely home again. T.'s stories help children see that it is possible to explore the world and still feel secure and loved. *Have You Seen My Duckling?* shows an adventurous duckling exploring his world and returning to the safety of mother duckling's protective wing.

T.'s early experiences with books have inspired her work: "I adored snuggling up to my mother while she would read . . . the same favorites over and over. Maybe that, coupled with crayons and endless hours of coloring and the love of nature, has helped form my destined fate. I couldn't be happier drawing ducks, rabbits, mice, and fairies and making children smile! To know that youngsters will be eager to turn the pages of a book that I have helped form gives me a strong sense of accomplishment and pleasure." T. understands the importance of getting appealing books into the hands of small children.

AWARDS: Children's Choice, INTERNATIONAL READING ASSOCIATION, and AMERICAN LIBRARY ASSOCIATION Notable Book (1982) for *The Piney Woods Peddler.* ALA Best Books, and ALA Notable Book (1983) for *Across the Stream* (GINSBURG, 1982). *School Library Journal* for *Early Morning in the Barn.* Jane Addams Honor Book (1983) for *If I Had a Paka: Poems in Eleven Languages.* ALA CALDECOTT MEDAL Honor Book (1985) for *Have You Seen My Duckling?*

FURTHER WORKS: *All Year Long.* 1983. *Early Morning in the Barn.* 1983. *Nata* (GRIFFITH). 1985. *Who's Counting?* 1986. *Four Brave Sailors.* (Ginsburg). 1987. *Where We Sleep.* 1987. *Spots, Feathers, and Curly Tails.* 1988. *Flap Your Wings and Try.* (Pomerantz). 1989. *The Barn Party.* 1995. *I Love You, Little One.* 1998. *Counting to Christmas.* 1998

BIBLIOGRAPHY: *Something about the Author,* vol. 75, 1993; *Piney Woods* flyleaf; Greenwillow autobiographical flier; Library of Congress website

MARGARET YATSEVITCH PHINNEY

TARKINGTON, (Newton) Booth
Author, b. 29 July 1869, Indianapolis, Indiana; d. 19 May 1946, Indianapolis, Indiana

A novelist, playwright, illustrator, and author of books for young readers, T. began talking at the age of seven months and at the age of three had a family of imagined companions, the Munchbergs. He talked with them whether he was with people or alone and played with their dog, Simpledoria. At age seven he produced modernistic drawings and watercolors on rainy days. Later he attended business college and art school and then went on to attend Princeton University. After graduation he took up writing and drawing and when *Life* magazine accepted a drawing and paid him $20 he felt his usefulness had been established. His first *Penrod* story (1914) was an instant success. It glorifies the antics of Penrod Schofield who has the reputation of being the naughtiest boy in his small Midwestern town. This was followed by *Penrod and Sam* (1916), *Seventeen* (1916), and *Penrod Jashber* (1929). T. received the Pulitzer Prize for fiction in 1919 for *The Magnificent Ambersons* and in 1922 for *Alice Adams.* To write he said, "A writer must go into training . . . just as an athlete does. You have to make your mind do its calisthenics."

IRVYN GILBERTSON

TATE, Eleanora
Author, b. 16 April 1948, Canton, Missouri

T., author of children's novels and short stories, lives in North Carolina and writes for upper elementary and middle-school readers. She edits adult POETRY and short story collections for which she also writes. T. uses local Southern AFRICAN AMERICAN settings that emphasize loving family relationships, family values, and the importance of community in building a positive self-image. Her intention is to encourage children to understand the contributions of African Americans to our nation's history and development and to appreciate unique aspects of Southern black culture. Her book, *Just an Overnight Guest,* was adapted as an AMERICAN LIBRARY ASSOCIATION Young Adult prize-winning film in 1985 and shown on PBS Wonderworks and Nickelodeon.

AWARDS: NCSS-CBC Notable Children's Book (1997) for *Thank You, Dr. Martin Luther King, Jr.!*

FURTHER WORKS: *Secret of Gumbo Grove,* 1987; *Retold African Myths,* 1992; *Front Porch Stories at the One-Room School,* 1992; *A Blessing in Disguise,* 1995; *Don't Split the Pole: Tales of Down Home Folk Wisdom,* 1997

BIBLIOGRAPHY: *Children's Literary Review,* vol. 37, 1996; publisher's publicity fliers

DIANE G. PERSON

TAYLOR, Mildred D.
Author, b. 13 September 1943, Jackson, Mississippi

T., author of young adult fiction, is well recognized and respected for her novels that authentically portray for all readers the pride, family love and support, and rich historical and societal traditions of AFRICAN AMERICAN LITERATURE and people. Additionally, her books sensitively describe the tragedy of racism. Inspired by the rich oral history of her family as shared by her father, T. began her writing career with *Song of the Trees,* a book about life in rural Mississippi as seen through the eyes of Cassie Logan. A vibrant young African American child, Cassie is shown within the context of the Depression era when racism was woven in the fiber of daily life in the South. Thus begins a trilogy of novels, including *Roll of Thunder, Hear My Cry* (1976), and *Let the Circle Be Unbroken* (1981), which focus on Cassie's family and their community. T.'s writings are described as filling a void that bridges all

generations' understandings of how we got where we are.

As a young person, T. realized that the family and community contexts in which she was living were not the same world that was being described in history books and that contributed to the misconceptions of other students. She felt this contradiction between what was in the text and what she learned at home presented a "lackluster history devoid of pride or heroic qualities." As she entered high school, T. knew that she wanted to write about the world in which black children were reared—its values, principles, and teachings. She wanted to present the heroic aspects of her people missing from the schoolbooks of her childhood—black men, women, and children of whom young readers could be proud. After attending the University of Toledo, T. served in the Peace Corps in Ethiopia for two years following which she returned to the United States to teach and recruit for the Peace Corps. While attending the University of Colorado to study journalism, T. was active in the black student alliance to create a black studies program. It was not until 1973 that she wrote *Song of the Trees* (1975), incorporating her father's teachings and stories with actual historical incidents. Writing about life in the mid-twentieth century, her books emphasize the importance of this era preceding the civil rights movement through the experiences of the Logan family. "In *Roll of Thunder, Hear My Cry* (1976), I included the teachings of my own childhood, the values and principles by which I and so many other Black children were reared, for I wanted to show a different kind of Black world from the one so often seen. I wanted to show a family united in love and self-respect, and parents, strong and sensitive, attempting to guide their children successfully, without harming their spirits, through the hazardous maze of living in a discriminatory society." (Taylor, 1998)

T.'s characters reflect humor, pathos, and frequently tragedy, but they always mirror a simple heroic dignity throughout their daily life experiences. According to one reviewer, "Her themes—self-respect, integrity, independence, strong family bonds, and love of nature and the land—underscore works that powerfully express the indomitableness of the human spirit in lyrical prose and vivid dialogue." T. portrays the ongoing struggle of her people following the abolition of slavery as they face oppression with endurance and imagination. As the characters remain true to themselves, an emotional story with significant insights into the tapestry of human experiences is woven for young readers of all races. Just as T.'s father modeled for her both awareness of discrimination and wisdom that constrains anger, so her characters represent discernment in destroying the bigotry that manifested itself in both daily petty nuisances and events of horror. T. comments that her books, "one of the first chronicles to mirror a Black child's hopes and fears from childhood innocence to awareness to bitterness and disillusionment, will one day be instrumental in teaching children of all colors the tremendous influence that Cassie's generation—my father's generation—had in bringing about the great Civil Rights movement of the fifties and sixties. Without understanding that generation and what it and the generations before it endured, children of today and of the future cannot understand or cherish the precious rights of equality which they now possess."

T.'s unique characters also come to life in her stories that followed the trilogy of books on the Logans. Clear, smooth, and graceful language bring to life characters in *The Friendship* (1987), *The Gold Cadillac* (1987), *The Road to Memphis* (1988), and *Mississippi Bridge* (1990). Both emotion and humor are found in her descriptions as each of these stories relate poignant incidents concerning relationships and interactions among people in the struggle to overcome racism in the South. Besides outstanding characterizations, T.'s work is also noted for its lush descriptions of nature that help relieve the tensions of this particular era in society.

AWARDS: ALA NEWBERY MEDAL (1977) for *Roll of Thunder, Hear My Cry*. AMERICAN LIBRARY ASSOCIATION Notable Book, National Book Award finalist, and *Boston Globe-Horn Book* Honor Book, (1976) for *Roll of Thunder, Hear My Cry*. The Council on Interracial Books for Children first prize in African American category. *New York Times* outstanding book of the year (1975) for *Song of the Trees. New York Times* Outstanding Book of the Year (1981), Jane Addams Award (1982), America Book Award nomination (1982), and CORETTA SCOTT KING AWARD (1982) all for *Let the Circle Be Unbroken*. Coretta Scott King

Award (1987) for *The Friendship. New York Times* Notable Book and Christopher Award (1987) for *The Gold Cadillac*. Coretta Scott King Book Award (1990) for *The Road to Memphis*

FURTHER WORKS: *The Well: David's Story*, 1995

BIBLIOGRAPHY: Hobbs, M. review of "Let the Circle Be Unbroken," in *The Junior Bookshelf*, June 1982, p. 112. *Children's Literature Review*, vol. 9, 1985; *Something about the Author*, vol. 70, 1992; "Mildred D. Taylor," (1998) http://penguinputnam.com/catalog/yreader/authors/2104_; biography.html> (accessed Dec. 26, 1998). Taylor, M. Newbery Medal acceptance speech, *Horn Book* magazine, August 1977, pp. 401–9

JANELLE B. MATHIS

TAYLOR, Sydney

Author, b. ca. 1904, New York City; d. 12 February 1978, Queens, New York

T.'s works include novels and PICTURE BOOKS about children, their families, and communities. T. studied drama at New York University and studied with the Martha Graham Dance Studio. She began writing for her daughter, an only child, stories of first generation American Jewish families living on New York's Lower East Side in the early part of the twentieth century. Her husband submitted the stories to a publisher without her knowledge. *All-of-a-Kind Family* (1951), the first in a series of five, received the Follett Award and recognition from the Jewish Book Council, and encouraged her to continue writing for children. The Association of Jewish Libraries established the annual "Sydney Taylor Body-of-Work" award in 1979 for "outstanding contribution to the field of Jewish literature for children" and recognized T. as its first recipient a year after her death.

AWARDS: National Jewish Book Award (1952) for *All-of-a-Kind Family*

FURTHER WORKS: *The Holiday Story Book*, 1953; *Mr. Barney's Beard*, 1961; *Now That You Are Eight*, 1963; *Papa like Everyone Else*, 1966; *The Dog Who Came to Dinner*, 1968; *Danny Loves a Holiday*, 1980

NANCY HORTON

TAYLOR, Theodore

Author, screenwriter, journalist, b. 23 June 1921, Statesville, North Carolina

When he was a child, T.'s father suggested that T. should make a career of being a monkey, he loved trees so much. He was an avid explorer of the natural world that surrounded him. As a teenager during the Great Depression, he worked at many jobs, earning small amounts here and there, including writing sports copy for a newspaper. Later, the sea called on his adventuresome spirit; he served both in the Merchant Marines and the Navy during World War II. The Caribbean held particular appeal for him, and later became the setting for several of his stories. He was also deeply affected by the contamination of Bikini Atoll, the island used to test the atomic bomb, and the tragic consequences for the inhabitants. While he was in the navy, he was a member of the team that prepared the atoll for the tests, and his haunting book, *The Bomb* (1995), is his effort to deal with his troubled feelings about that government action. "Not realizing it," he writes about his varied life experiences, "I was training to become a writer, a worker in words. I tell aspiring young writers to do diverse things, to go to as many places as possible, to watch and listen." T. is a superb storyteller, weaving history into his adventurous, REALISTIC FICTION. Survival under adverse conditions, a theme that runs through several of T.'s most popular books such as *The Cay* (1969), *Sweet Friday Island* (1994), and *The Sniper* (1989), is a notion that particularly intrigues his juvenile and YOUNG ADULT audiences.

Writing for youth in grades five and up, T. embeds subtle, relevant messages about environmental responsibility and self-reliance in his stories. He presents honest characters who not only become self-determined, but are able to grow beyond their prejudices and come to appreciate other people for their inner strength and beauty. One teenage reader, objecting to an effort to ban T.'s most popular, although controversial book, *The Cay,* sees the message that "brotherhood can, and should exist between men, regardless of race." Writing about why he chose to return the Jane Addams Book Award for *The Cay* in 1975, T. defended his author's right to describe his characters as he imagined them wrestling with concepts of racism, bigotry, and human equality. *The Cay,* also a successful made-for-TV movie, has become part of the canon of young adult novels and was followed by a prequel (*Timothy of the Cay,* 1993). Striving for authenticity in his work, T. achieves credibility by basing his characters on

people he knows. He writes, "I hope that they'll say, 'This feels real, it sounds real, the people are real, the places are real.' "

AWARDS: Lewis CARROLL Shelf Award, Jane Addams Peace Prize and twelve other AWARDS for *The Cay* (1970). AMERICAN LIBRARY ASSOCIATION Best Book for Young Adults (1989) for *The Sniper.* Edgar Allan Poe Award for Best Young Adult Mystery (1991) for *The Weirdo.* ALA Best Book for Young Adults (1993) for *Timothy of the Cay.* ALA Best Book for Young Adults (1996), and Scott O'DELL Award for Best Historical Fiction for *The Bomb* (1995)

FURTHER WORKS: *The Children's War.* 1971. *Teetoncey.* 1974. *Teetoncey and Ben O'Neal.* 1975. *The Trouble with Tuck.* 1981. *The Stalker.* 1987. *The Weirdo.* 1991. *The Flight of Jesse Leroy Brown.* 1998

BIBLIOGRAPHY: Avon Books biography flier (undated). The *Baltimore Sun,* Friday, March 17, 1995. The Children's Book Council, Inc (1996); *Children's Books Awards and Prizes.* Contributor's assessment. Harcourt Brace publicity flyer. Library of Congress website catalogue. Moon, Travis (1993). "Youth Opinion: The 'Challenged' Isn't Being Met but Avoided." The *Los Angeles Times,* Monday, March 8, 1993, p. B8. Powder, Jackie (1995). "A Lifetime of Diverse Experiences Contributes to Author's Success," *Publishers Weekly* review, September 18, 1995. Roginski, Jim. Interview with Theodore Taylor. *Behind the Covers,* vol. 2, Spring, 1990. Sassone, Sharon (1992). "Writing with Young Readers in Mind." *St. Paul Pioneer Press,* April 15, 1992, p. D11, D16. *Something about the Author,* vol. 83, 1996. Taylor, Theodore (1975) *Top of the News,* April, 1975, pp. 284–8. Taylor, T. (1995). *On Writing the Bomb.* Taylor, T. (1996) Harcourt Brace and Company "Author at a Glance" autobiography

MARGARET YATSEVITCH PHINNEY

TECHNOLOGY AND COMMUNICATION

Before the era of electronic media, the communication technology that a child encountered was writing—which is hardly thought of as a technology today. Writing was however a technology and had been restricted to those who had the power to access it and the leisure time to learn. Writing technology did not become popular with ordinary people until the invention of print technology. Learning how to command and communicate using another sign system—written words rather than uttered words—has been a major technology taught to children since the nineteenth century. The concept of educating children in a formal school setting and learning to read and write was demanded by the rise of a middle class. Writing technology was no longer in the hands of just the privileged, but also of the public.

Radio, more flexible to use and timely as an information source, is the most available medium globally. Since its inception in the 1920s, later challenged by TV in the 1950s, radio has evolved in the world of media technology. Many radio stations now serve as voices for minority, special interest, and social groups. Radio as a background media is little used by children until they reach preadolescence when radio becomes an influential part of adolescent and young adult culture.

Although experimental TV sets existed in the late 1930s, television was sparse among the general public at the end of World War II. Only .02 percent of the U.S. homes owned a TV set in 1946; the figure rose to 9 percent by 1950. By 1962, the penetration rate was about 90 percent. In the 1980s, televisions were in about 98 percent of U.S. households; and the figure has remained constant since that time. The amount of TV viewing varies throughout the life span. In general, children under twelve spend about three hours every day in front of the set. The viewing time decreases during high school, college years, and young adulthood because of other social activities and responsibilities. Older adults, women, and lower socioeconomic groups are some of the heaviest viewers of TV.

The communication technology landscape was transformed toward the end of the 20th century. Video cassette recorders (VCR) were introduced in 1970, and gained popularity over the next ten years. By 1997, 96 percent of U.S. homes were equipped with a VCR. Today more then 40 percent of American households own personal computers. Children from ten to fourteen are the greatest users of computer games. TVs and personal computers (PCs) are inseparable; and many parents see the home computer as a powerful educational tool, which not only entertains but also helps their children learn. The continued rapid increase of information technology at home is to be expected.

The popularity of the INTERNET is also increasing rapidly. Children are reported to spend hours in front of this new screen-based communication technology, encountering age-inappropriate content, such as sexually explicit materials, violence, advertising, or extremist views. A critical issue is how to provide parents with more control over the information available on line to their children, especially to protect children from age-inappropriate content. The Internet market offers various software tools and services to block out various categories of objectionable content or to limit children's access to inappropriate content. In 1995, Internet filtering software became available, often at no charge from websites, installed on the computer or bundled with a variety of software.

Many people hold that media content is responsible for related consequential behaviors, such as violence in society. This belief is controversial and unproven, and some are skeptical. However, just like a school's choice of books in a classroom or a parent's decision to take a child to certain social events, the TV or online/Internet diet a child consumes affects his or her taste of visual arts and value systems to some extent.

Pervasive media messages model how we dress, what we eat, and where we go for fun. They also demonstrate how men and women interact, and portray relationships among young, workplace colleagues, and different generations. The emotional sides of media experiences including identification, empathy, suspense, and HUMOR are compelling forces in children's understanding of the adult world. There is little doubt that media messages ultimately influence a child's worldview.

Among many possible media effects on children, televised violence, as a product of market-driven forces, concerns parents, educators, and society as a whole. Broadcasters and cable channels often air violence to attract young adult viewers, and children aged two to eleven are a by-product audience of such programming strategies. Many researchers of children and their use of media have been concentrating on time spent watching, analyzing the content of mediated messages, and the possible effect of such consumption. Some research suggests that children can become addicted to the pleasure of TV viewing as well as computer game playing. Some statistics suggest that children watch about 8,000 murders and 100,000 other acts of violence by the time they finish elementary school. It is also reported that more than half of all leading characters on TV programs are involved in violence. In addition to TV violence, about 85 percent of video games contain violence as a major theme.

Advertisements in print and more so on electronic media have a tremendous impact on children's consumption behavior and as a result, according to some of the consumer research, are the root of their materially oriented value system. Related issues include medical concerns about eating disorders and psychological and moral concerns regarding young children's immaturity in decoding persuasive, saturated visual and audio effects of commercials. There is also the social impact of a distorted portrayal of different groups. In general, women are more likely to be represented in the media for their physical appearance. Staying young and attractive is more often valued in a female character's appearance. Women in the media are also expected to be homemakers and mothers, as sole caregivers in domestic affairs on media, yet their professional and community roles are underrepresented. On the other hand, men are usually represented as emotionless, and their physical appearances are different from women. It is more acceptable for a man to be older than a woman, all other considerations being equal.

The introduction of the V-chip has been debated for some time, the controversy being whether broadcasters should comply in rating their programs and controlling access to children. With the pervasive representation of violence, sexual scenes, coarse language, and suggestive dialogues on TV programs, age-based and/or content-based rating systems are in demand. The United States Telecommunication Act of 1996 requires all television sets over thirteen inches to include a "V-chip." As a result, an industry-sponsored rating system for the V-chip was introduced and implemented. Later in 1997, major American networks agreed to supplement the age-based rating by adding codes for violence (V), sexual situations (S), coarse language (L), suggestive dialogue (D), and FANTASY violence (FV).

Although many TV programs, video games, and computer games seem problematic, there is much prosocial learning software available. These programs include educational and informational TV shows such as *Sesame Street, READING RAINBOW,* and other similar programs targeted to complement subjects taught in school and to teach strong social values such as sharing, cooperation, helping, persistence, empathy, and gender balance.

The general belief that children should not be the victims of unsuitable communication technology has led to the need for media education to empower children with critical thinking and viewing skills. Canada, Australia, the United Kingdom, and other countries throughout the globe have recognized the importance of media literacy for citizens in the information age. Media-literate individuals, while enjoying the pleasures of media entertainment, should understand how media affects audiences as consumers, be able to differentiate between fact and opinion, be sensitive to media stereotypes, identify persuasive intentions of televised messages, and most importantly, voice their concerns.

SOPHIA WU

(See also BOOKS AS FILM; INTERNET RESOURCES FOR CHILDREN; *READING RAINBOW* AND CHILDREN'S LITERATURE ON TELEVISION)

TEMPLE, Frances Nolting
Author, b. 15 August 1945, Washington, D.C.; d. 5 July 1995, Geneva, New York

T., elementary school teacher and mother of three, wrote fiction only the last eight years of her life, completing just five novels before her death at fifty. Her award-winning stories chronicle political events, viewed through the lives and actions of young adults. She draws on her extensive life and travel experiences and her stories reflect her beliefs about justice and integrity, without lecturing or moralizing. Coming of age in the 1960s, T. acted on her convictions, volunteering for humanitarian causes throughout her life. Her widely acclaimed *Taste of Salt: A Story of Modern Haiti* (1992), and a later novel *Tonight, by Sea* (1995) were inspired while volunteering in the Dominican Republic. Her involvement with the Sanctuary movement prompted *Grab Hands and Run* (1993), about a young boy who leads his family to refuge in Canada. *The Ramsay Scallop*

(1994) and its sequel *Bedouin's Gazelle* (1996), are set in Medieval Europe and Africa and, through the story of a young couple making a pilgrimage, T. imparts extensive Christian and Islamic history. Another sequel, portraying AFRICAN culture before slave trading, was not completed. She also authored and illustrated a PICTURE BOOK, *Tiger Soup: An Anansi Story* from Jamaica (1994), an adapted folktale.

FURTHER WORKS: *Classroom Strategies That Work.* 1989; with Ruth Nathan, *The Beginnings of Writing;* with husband Charles Temple, 1992

BIBLIOGRAPHY: *Something about the Author.* vol. 85, 1996. Silvey, Anita. "The Intelligent, the Witty, the Brave." *Horn Book* magazine. Sept.–Oct. 1995, p. 518

BARBARA L. BATTLES

TENNIEL, Sir John

Illustrator, b. 28 February 1820, Kensington, London, England; d. 25 February 1914, Kensington, London, England

T. was, in his day, a celebrated cartoonist for *Punch,* although his lasting fame derives from his illustrations for Lewis CARROLL's *Alice's Adventures in Wonderland* (1865) and *Through the Looking-Glass* (1871). His father was a dancing and fencing master, and when T. was twenty he lost his right eye, accidentally, in a fencing match with his father, but how this affected his work remains pure speculation. Always interested in art, he studied briefly at Royal Academy Schools, but he left in disappointment and proceeded to teach himself. He worked in sculpture, oils, and fresco painting, and was commissioned to do a fresco for the new Houses of Parliament on the subject of British poetry, specifically Dryden's St. Cecilia, although the work no longer exists.

T. eventually turned to book ILLUSTRATION, which had, in fact, been an early interest, and he abandoned all aspirations for "High Art." In 1848, his illustrations for Thomas James's version of *Aesop's Fables,* brought him considerable fame and, two years later, he accepted a position with *Punch* magazine. He remained at *Punch* for over half a century, and was, from 1864 until 1901, the publication's chief artist. T. deserves recognition for elevating political cartoons to an art form, combining artistic skill with impartiality and clever wit. His work was further blessed in that many of his illustrations were engraved by the celebrated Dalziel brothers and by Joseph Swain, themselves artists at the top of their profession.

Carroll likely chose T. to illustrate *Alice's Adventures in Wonderland* in part because he believed the illustrator's fame would bring notice to the book. And, indeed, when the first reviews appeared, it was T. whose name received the most attention. Carroll, who had initially wished to illustrate the book himself, and T. endured a strained relationship. Each believed the other to be stubborn, egotistical, and temperamental. Carroll initially rejected most of T.'s drawings, and T., a perfectionist, insisted that the first printing be withdrawn because the drawings were too faint. The volumes were eventually sent to America and published as the first American edition by Appleton.

Carroll, despite his personal antagonism, recognized the genius of T.'s work and insisted that he illustrate the sequel, *Through the Looking-Glass,* which T. reluctantly agreed to do. This proved an even more exasperating experience. Carroll was constantly sending suggestions to T., and T. referred to Carroll as "that conceited old Don." Carroll recommended not only subjects for the illustrations, but even the sizes and positions on the page, which advice T. promptly ignored. And T. also had the temerity to suggest textual changes to Carroll, including the deletion of whole passages. On a few occasions he succeeded, most notably when Carroll agreed to cut an entire episode featuring a yellow-wigged wasp, which T. thought "beyond the appliances of art." So harrowing was the whole experience that following *Through the Looking-Glass,* T. vowed never to illustrate another book—and he never did.

Like any good illustrator, T. enriches the text with his own interpretations. Many of the same qualities that made T. a first-rate political cartoonist contributed to his success with the *Alice* books with their underlying social commentary and subtle wit. His most famous portraits—the Duchess, the Mad Hatter, the Cheshire Cat, Tweedledum and Tweedledee, and Alice herself—attest to his cartoonist's skill at revealing character traits through exaggerated physical features. And all is imbued with a wry HUMOR that is ideally suited to the text. Many have seen in the drawing of the White Knight T.'s self-portrait. And, ironically, the White Knight is widely believed to be Carroll's caricature of himself. T.'s influences are thought to have included Thackeray, particularly his illustrations for *The Rose and the Ring,* Richard DOYLE, a one-time *Punch* illustrator known for his work on Ruskin's *The King of the Golden River,* and the influential French artist, J.-J. Grandville, illustrator of a collection of nonsense drawings, *Un Autre Monde.* An examination of his political cartoons reveals both foreshadowings and echoes of the *Alice* illustrations. T.'s private life was uneventful. He married Julia Giani in 1854, but was widowed two years later and thereafter led a quiet domestic existence, first with his mother-in-law and then his sister. He was knighted in 1893 and died three days before his ninety-fourth birthday in 1914. The poet Austin Dobson characterized T.'s lasting fame in verse: *Enchanting Alice! Black-and-white / Has made your charm perennial; / And nought save "Chaos and Old Night" / Can part you now from Tenniel.*

AWARDS: Knight of the British Empire, 1893

BIBLIOGRAPHY: Gardner, Martin, *The Annotated Alice,* 1970; Hancher, Michael, *The Tenniel Illustrations to the "Alice" Books,* 1985; Knoepflmacher, U. C., *U. C. Ventures Into Childhood,* 1998; *Something about the Author.* vol. 74, 1993; *Children's Literature Review,* vol. 18, 1989; Carpenter and Prichard, *The Oxford Companion to Children's Literature* 1984

DAVID L. RUSSELL

TERBAN, Marvin
Author, teacher, speaker, b. 28 April 1940, Chelsea, Massachusetts

T. received a B.A. from Tufts University in 1961 and an M.F.A. in communications from Columbia University in 1963. He has taught English, Latin, drama, and public speaking at Columbia Grammar and Preparatory School in New York City since 1963. Terban has also directed plays at summer camp, organized a tutoring service, produced educational media at CBS and New York City's public television station, and acted in community theater productions and feature films (several by Woody Allen).

T. is well known for his wordplay books, which began as teaching games for his students. Using riddles, rhymes, and jokes, he helps chil-

dren realize that learning about the English language can be fun. For example, his first book, *Eight Ate: A Feast of Homonym Riddles* (1982), asks questions such as "How does Moose begin a letter to his cousin? Dear Deer." Other books focus on idioms, homonyms, homographs, irregular nouns and verbs, palindromes, eponyms, rhymes, grammar, spelling, and punctuation. T. hopes that his books will help children "unconfuse" the often complicated English language. His books are used in bilingual and ESL classes in schools around the world as well as by native English speakers.

T.'s books have been chosen as Children's Choice (The Reading Teacher), Pick of the List (American Bookseller), and the New York Public Library for its "One Hundred Titles for Reading and Sharing" list. *Checking Your Grammar* (1993) was selected by the Association of Library Services for Children and Association of Booksellers to Children as one of fifteen books every family should have.

T. especially enjoys visiting schools where he can meet his readers in person and get ideas for future books. He has spoken at schools across the United States and around the world.

FURTHER WORKS: *In a Pickle and Other Funny Idioms.* 1983. *I Think I Thought and Other Tricky Verbs.* 1984. *Too Hot to Hoot: Funny Palindrome Riddles.* 1985. *Your Foot's on My Feet! And Other Tricky Nouns.* 1986. *Mad as a Wet Hen and Other Funny Idioms.* 1987. *Guppies in Tuxedos: Funny Eponyms.* 1988. *The Dove Dove: Funny Homograph Riddles.* 1988. *Superdupers! Really Funny Real Words.* 1989. *Punching the Clock: Funny Action Idioms.* 1990. *Hey, Hay! A Wagonful of Funny Homonym Riddles.* 1991. *Funny You Should Ask: How to Make up Jokes and Riddles with Wordplay.* 1992. *It Figures! Fun Figures of Speech.* 1993. *Time to Rhyme: A Rhyming Dictionary.* 1994. *Dictionary of Idioms.* 1996. *Dictionary of Spelling.* 1998. *Punctuation Power!* 2000

BIBLIOGRAPHY: Interview with author

MARY ARIAIL BROUGHTON

TERHUNE, Albert Payson
Author, b. 21 December 1872, Newark, New Jersey; d. 18 February 1942, Pompton Lakes, New Jersey

T., an author of children's and adult books, motion picture scripts, and a journalist, was a prolific writer of sports events, travel accounts, history, fiction, and verse. Although he did not plan to be a children's writer, the popularity of his dog stories determined he would combine his love of raising collies with writing their stories for others to enjoy. His many dog books began with *Lad: A Dog* (1919) followed by *Bruce* (1920), *Buff: A Collie and Other Dog Stories* (1921), *The Heart of a Dog* (1925), and others. The protagonists, all collies, display significant human values of understanding, determination, and loyalty in a context that is often highly sentimental. Several of T.'s books have been adapted for film.

FURTHER WORKS: *Real Tales of Real Dogs,* 1935; *True Dog Stories,* 1936

BIBLIOGRAPHY: *Twentieth Century Children's Writers,* 1989; *Something about the Author,* vol. 15, 1979

KNOWLEDGE   JANELLE B. MATHIS

THACKERAY, William Makepeace

Author, illustrator, b. 18 July 1811, Calcutta, India; d. 24 December 1863, London, England

Although primarily writing for adults, *The Rose and the Ring; or, The History of Prince Giglio and Prince Bulbo: A Fireside Pantomime for Great and Small Children* (the manuscript with original illustrations is in the Pierpont Morgan Library) (1855) is an extraordinary work that draws on traditional FAIRY TALES, adding T.'s own sense of magic and delighting the reader with hilarious names for characters. Many consider this work, the sixth in his Christmas stories, to be an outstanding contribution to children's literature in the pantomime mode. T.'s own illustrations add to the nonsense and absurdity of this tale.

FURTHER WORKS: *Mrs. Perkins' Ball,* 1846

BIBLIOGRAPHY: McMaster, Juliet. "The Rose and the Ring: Quintessential Thackeray." *Mosaic.* Summer 1976. 157–65; Monsarrat, Ann. *An Uneasy Victorian: Thackeray the Man.* 1980

KAY E. VANDERGRIFT

THAYER, Ernest Lawrence

Author; b. 14 August 1863, Lawrence, Massachusetts; d. 21 August 1940, Santa Barbara, California

A journalist and poet, T. graduated from Harvard University Phi Beta Kappa and moved to San

Francisco where he wrote editorials, special stories, and reported for the *Examiner*. He began reading W. S. Gilbert's *Bab Ballads* and decided he should write something similar, so he wrote a poem for each *Examiner* Sunday issue. "Casey at the Bat" was printed in the *San Francisco Examiner* on June 3, 1858. Actor DeWolf Hopper recited "Casey" between performances at Wallack's Theater in New York City and the ballad was immortalized. DeWolf claimed to have recited the ballad over 10,000 times in forty-seven years. Many claimed to be the author of "Casey" and at one time T. hired a detective to expose some of the impostors. He worked for his family's textile mills and traveled overseas for a few years. Friends urged him to write but his reply was, "I have nothing to say" and he did no more literary work after "Casey" until 1896 when he wrote four ballads that sank into oblivion. Shortly before his death T. attempted to write again but commented, "Now I have something to say, and I am too weak to say it." "Casey" had gained recognition as an authentic American masterpiece by the time T. died in 1940. Many editions of the poem are in print today, illustrated by such distinguished artists as Leonard Everett FISHER and Patricia POLACCO.

IRVYN GILBERTSON

THESMAN, Jean

Author, b. Date and place unknown

T.'s YOUNG ADULT novels focus on issues teenagers face such as romance, suicide, dysfunctional families, and more. T. published three novels in 1987, which established her career as a writer. T.'s work includes books in The Whitney Cousins SERIES and The Birthday Girl series.

AWARDS: SOCIETY OF CHILDREN'S BOOK WRITERS AND ILLUSTRATORS Golden Kite Award (1991) for *The Rain Catchers* (1991)

FURTHER WORKS: *Who Said Life is Fair?,* 1987; *Running Scared,* 1987; *The Last April Dancers,* 1987; *Was It Something I Said?,* 1988; *Appointment with a Stranger,* 1989; *Rachel Chance,* 1990; *Erin,* 1990; *When the Road Ends,* 1992; *Nothing Grows Here,* 1994

BIBLIOGRAPHY: *Something about the Author,* vol. 74, 1993

JODI PILGRIM

THIELE, Colin
Author, b. 15 November 1920, Eudunda, South Australia, Australia

T., considered one of AUSTRALIA's outstanding authors for children, has written over eighty books for all age groups in various fields, including: POETRY, prose, fiction, DRAMA, history, criticism, and BIOGRAPHY. T. believes in writing about what one knows best, which explains why many of his books are set in Southern Australia. He also believes books should discuss the "universal things that live in people from generation to generation: happiness and sadness, wisdom and folly, avarice and generosity, cruelty and compassion." His novels are characterized by themes of hopefulness and stories with HUMOR and caring families even while dangerous events are occurring.

Many of T.'s works discuss environmental or conservation issues. For example, *Blue Fin* (1972), which was placed on the Hans Christian ANDERSEN International Honors List, tells the story of Steve, who helps save his family while they are out at sea during a violent storm. *Storm Boy* (1963), his most popular conservationist novel, portrays a young boy who endures the shooting and eventual death of his pet pelican, whereas another novel, *Albatross Two* (1974), discusses the dangers of offshore drilling.

Farmer Schulz's Ducks (1986) presents a conservation issue in PICTURE-BOOK format. When Farmer Schulz's beautiful prized ducks need to cross the road to get to the river they are threatened by oncoming traffic. A satisfying solution is provided for very young readers.

AWARDS: IBBY Honor List (1972) for *Blue Fin.* Australian Children's Book of the Year Award (1982) for *The Valley Between*

FURTHER WORKS: *The Sun on the Stubble,* 1961; *The Fire in the Stone,* 1973; *The Valley Between,* 1981; *Shadow Shark,* 1985; *Jodie's Journey, 1988*

BIBLIOGRAPHY: *Something about the Author,* vol. 72, 1993; Tomlinson, Carl, *Children's Books from Other Countries,* 1998

DENISE P. BEASLEY

THOMAS, Jane Resh
Author, b. 15 August 1936, Kalamazoo, Michigan

T. believes that one should write from one's own experiences. This belief is evident in the fiction she has written for children, such as her memories of migrant workers near her Michigan home, which were woven into *Lights on the River* (1994), or her fishing experiences from which her first book, *Elizabeth Catches a Fish* (1977), was drawn. In addition to writing for children, T. is a frequent reviewer of children's books for the *Minneapolis Tribune,* contributes articles and reviews to MAGAZINES AND PERIODICALS such as the *Horn Book* and the *New Advocate,* and conducts and teaches writing workshops. Commentators frequently commend T.'s honest, sensitively written books that capture children's inner feelings and emotions.

AWARDS: Parents' Choice Award for fiction (1984) for *Courage at Indian Deep.* AMERICAN LIBRARY ASSOCIATION Notable Book citation (1988) for *Saying Good-bye to Grandma.* British Children's Book Award Runner-up (1989) for *The Princess in the Pigpen*

FURTHER WORKS: *The Comeback Dog.* 1981. *Fox in a Trap.* 1987. *Daddy Doesn't Have to Be a Giant Anymore.* 1996. *Scaredy Dog.* 1996. *Celebration!* 1997. *Behind the Mask: The Life of Queen Elizabeth I.* 1998

BIBLIOGRAPHY: *Contemporary Authors,* 1998

SANDRA IMDIEKE

THOMAS, Joyce Carol
Author, poet, b. 25 May 1938, Ponca, Oklahoma

Fifth of nine children, T. took pleasure in hiding under the house where she made up songs, poems, and plays. In kindergarten the librarian and her teachers encouraged her reading and writing, and church nurtured her love of joyful music. At ten, her family moved to California, where she spent summers helping support the family working the fruit and vegetable harvests. After receiving an M.A. at Stanford, and teaching for many years, she retired to write full-time, "finding through her POETRY, PICTURE BOOKS, novels for children and YOUNG ADULTS, and short stories yet another joyous, creative way to teach and to learn."

T. writes in gentle, almost poetic prose that keeps a story moving like a ship on a gentle sea. Drawing on her own childhood settings and experiences for inspiration, her themes are positive, incorporating plot elements that border on the mystical, as she shows that life, though often agonizing, is also full of cause for celebration. Her protagonists are strong, courageous, and thoughtful. They do not allow themselves to be victimized by difficult circumstances and they do not do it alone, but with the support of the "warm rooms of patience" provided by loving friends and family. Her poetry, descriptive and metaphorical, paints the contrasts of human life and relationships sometimes wistful with yearning, sometimes quietly bitter, but ultimately hopeful and courageous.

To her readers, T. writes, "On my writing journeys I meet characters who speak with colorful language. I hear rhythms that make me laugh. I feel a young girl's hope, a young boy's mischief, and a teenager's despair. Reading, too, can be a splendid adventure. I hope my books will sometimes make you bounce with laughter, will often make you stop and think, and will open up many new pathways to joy."

AWARDS: AMERICAN LIBRARY ASSOCIATION Best Book for Young Adults and American Book Award (1982) for *Marked by Fire*. National Book Award, and the *New York Times* Outstanding Book of the Year (1983) for *Bright Shadow*. CORETTA SCOTT KING Honor Award Book (1984) for *The Golden Pasture*. 1986 American Booksellers Pick of the List (1986) for *A Gathering of Flowers*. 1991 University of Tennessee Chancellor's Award for Research and Creativity. National Conference of Christians and Jews Selected Title for Children and Young Adults (1991) for *Brown Honey in Broomwheat Tea*. Coretta Scott King Honor Award Book, ALA Notable Children's Book, NATIONAL COUNCIL OF TEACHERS OF ENGLISH (1992) for *When the Nightingale Sings*. 1996 Poet Laureate for Life Award, University of Oklahoma Center for Poets and Writers at the University of Oklahoma at Norman

FURTHER WORKS: *Bittersweet,* 1973; *Journey,* 1988; *Gingerbread Days,* 1995. *I Have Heard of a Land,* 1997. *Cherish Me,* 1998; *You Are My Perfect Baby,* 1999

REFERENCES: Contributor's assessment; Joyce Carol Thomas website: www.joycecarolthomas. com/bio.htm; Library of Congress web catalog; *Something about the Author.* vol. 40, 1985, and vol. 78, 1994

MARGARET YATSEVITCH PHINNEY

THURBER, James (Grover)

Author, playwright, illustrator, cartoonist, b. 8 December 1894, Columbus, Ohio; d. 2 November 1961, New York City

T., internationally acclaimed adult humorist, writer, artist, and playwright wrote only five stories specifically for children. However, his first juvenile book, *Many Moons* (1943, reissued 1973) illustrated by Louis SLOBODKIN, won the ALA CALDECOTT MEDAL in 1944. After graduating from Ohio State University in 1919, he worked as a reporter for various newspapers. He began his lifetime association with *The New Yorker* magazine in 1927, first as a managing editor, and then as a staff writer chiefly for the "Talk of the Town" column. Beginning in 1933 he became a contributing writer. During his lifetime he wrote and illustrated many sophisticated adult books and plays. Using his satirical HUMOR in both text and cartoon-style illustrations, he revealed the absurdities and ironies of society. In the thirties and early forties T. was a prominent member of the New York City literary set and had a loyal audience that admired his perspective. His children's stories, written as humorous fantasies, often in a subtle way, revealed his view of society. Frequently his heroes and heroines were ineffective and the weak or humble were triumphant. In *Many Moons,* a sick princess refused to recuperate without receiving a gift of the moon. The impossible task of procuring the moon was resolved not by the most powerful grown-ups, but the seemingly powerless court jester and the little princess. Both adults and children enjoy the irony of the weakest outsmarting the strongest, and, unquestionably this perspective empowers children.

FURTHER WORKS: *The Great Quillow.* (Doris Lee, illus.). 1944. *The White Deer.* (T. and Don FREEMAN, illus.). 1945, reissued 1968. *The Thirteen Clocks.* (Marc SIMONT, illus.). 1950. *The Wonderful O.* (Marc Simont, illus.). 1957

BIBLIOGRAPHY: MEIGS, C. et al., *A Critical History of Children's Literature* (1969); Serafin, Steven R., general editor, *The Continuum Encyclopedia of American Literature*, 1999; Silvey, Anita, ed., *Children's Books and Their Creators*, 1995; *Something about the Author*, vol. 13, 1978; *Twentieth Century Children's Writers*, 1978

JUDITH LIPSITT

TOLAN, Stephanie S.
Author, b. 25 October 1942, Canton, Ohio

T. grew up reading. She knew from age nine that she wanted to be a writer. She wrote through high school, then studied education at Purdue University. She received her bachelor's degree in 1964 and received her master's degree in 1967. T. taught for a while, but became a full-time writer by 1976. Her first play was *The Ledge* in 1968. She published her first book, *Grandpa—and Me*, in 1978.

T. is concerned about social issues that children encounter; she and Katherine PATERSON have taken leadership positions in activist programs for children's rights. Further, she has approached poverty, education, housing, and abuse in several of her books. Even her humorous Skinner Series books involve issues about making a living that many middle-class people face in times of changing technology.

T. received artist fellowships from the Ohio Arts Council in 1978 and 1981. In addition, she was a Post-Corbett award finalist in 1981. T. also earned the *Ohioana* Book Award for juvenile fiction in 1981 for *The Liberation of Tansy Warner* and the Bread Loaf Writers' Conference fellowship in 1981. T. received the APA media award for best book of 1983 for *Guiding the Gifted Child. A Good Courage* was named Best Book of 1988 by *School Library Journal*, and *Grandpa—and Me* was nominated for the Sequoyah Children's Book Award and for the Georgia Children's Book Award.

FURTHER WORKS: *The Liberation of Tansy Warner*. 1980. *The Great Skinner Strike*. 1983. *Pride of the Peacock*. 1986. *A Good Courage*. 1988. *Plague Year*. 1991. *Sophie and the Sidewalk Man*. 1992. *The Witch of Maple Park*. 1992

BIBLIOGRAPHY: *Something about the Author*, vol. 78, 1994

JODI PILGRIM

TOLKIEN, J(ohn) R(onald) R(euel)
Author, b. 3 January 1892, Bloemfontein, South Africa; d. 3 September 1973, Bournemouth, England

That which fascinated T. from early childhood he turned into the substance of his famous books: dragons and other mythic creatures, the complexity and magic of language, and an abiding concern for differentiating between good and evil. In addition to a childhood devotion to legend, T. at an early age became aware of and deeply interested in the workings of language's rules, a concern that he carried into his adult life as an Oxford scholar specializing in the study of the English language and its antecedents.

T.'s traditionally English family was living in South Africa at the time of his birth but they relocated "home" to Great Britain when he was quite young (1895). His father died the following year and his mother died when he was twelve, but T. remembered his youth as one of literary, linguistic, and intellectual explorations, rather than one of familial deprivation. Not only did he write from childhood on, but he remembered into adulthood the experience of learning that linguistic rules apply to how specific words are conjoined. This early introduction to philology was enhanced by T.'s accidental discovery, early in his formal education, of Gothic, as well as the curriculum's inclusion of Anglo-Saxon and Greek. T. began inventing languages at this point, before his teens, an interest that carried into his mythically couched novels.

After he became orphaned, his guardian provided care and attention to both his spiritual and scholastic growth, earning so much respect from T. that, when his guardian forbid the continuation of a love affair until T. became of age, T. broke off with the young lady who later would become his wife.

After earning his B.A. at Exeter College, Oxford, in 1915, T. joined the service during World War I. Already married when he was mustered out, he completed his M.A. in 1919. From 1918 to 1920, he worked on *The Oxford English Dictionary*, earning high praise for his knowledge of Anglo-Saxon from older scholars. Beginning with a post as reader in English, at the University of Leeds, in 1920, and advancing to rank of professor, in 1924, T. pursued academic life at Oxford University and guest lectureships elsewhere in Great Britain for the next forty years. His first book has proved to be of timeless appeal to both children and adults. *The Hobbit; or, There and Back Again,* was first published in a self-illustrated edition in 1937.

The Lord of the Rings (1954, 1955) earned the International FANTASY Award in 1957. T. earned the Royal Society of Literature's Benson Award in 1966. In 1972, he was named Commander, Order of the British Empire. The Gandalf Award went to T. in 1974. He received honorary degrees from University College, Dublin, and the University of Liège, both in 1954. He received his third honorary doctorate from the University of Nottingham in 1970.

The species invented for *The Hobbit* is human-like in many of its physical, psychological, and moral characteristics. In correspondence with his first American publisher, in 1938, T. wrote quite explicitly of how he—the hobbit's creator—imagined the species to look, even to the level of detail of the color and texture of the clothing worn by Bilbo Baggins (the titular hobbit). Because of the long-standing popularity of T.'s major works, with waves of cult attention occurring in the history of his readership, T.'s creatures have endured many subsequent illustrative treatments and critical descriptions, often not to the author's satisfaction.

In addition to creating a species, T. created languages in his fantasy novels, basing the linguistics on Gothic, Greek, Anglo-Saxon, and Finnish. Often, his personal use of MYTHOLOGY AND LEGEND was worked around the contrivances of the invented languages, the latter driving the former. It is essential to note as well that a Christian ethos pervades his STORYTELLING. *The Lord of the Rings,* comprising *The Fellowship of the Ring, The Two Towers,* and *The Return of the King,* certainly devolves on issues of magic and wizardry, but allegorical interpretations of this quest tale reasonably associate elements of the action and characteristics of the protagonist and antagonist with the Christian quest for sanctity and spiritual unification with the Good. T. himself, in the decade following publication of *The Lord of the Rings,* identified its chief figure, Gandalf, as an angel. However, T. decried critical association of his embodiments of good and evil with white and black, maintaining that his fantasy worlds were both more complex than such bifurcation implies and that they were, really, fantasy worlds. Filmed versions are scheduled for 2001–3.

The Silmarillion, not published until 1977, four years after T.'s death, was begun by T. even before the Great War. Its tales, peopled by elves, elaborate a mythology that is both Christian and Anglo-Saxon. *The Silmarillion* is an extreme example of T.'s propensity for working and reworking his tales, devising POETRY from which stories grow and songs that grow from his further reflection on characters in completed books.

In addition to his creative writing and his teaching, T. was a prolific letter writer, discussing works in progress and reviewers' opinions with many of his correspondents, including his friend C. S. LEWIS and T.'s own son, Christopher, has been responsible for editing and bringing into print several volumes of T.'s stories and poems that remained unpublished at his death.

SELECT FURTHER WORKS: *Farmer Giles of Ham,* 1949; *The Adventures of Tom Bombadil and Other Verses from the Red Book,* 1962; *Smith of Wootton Major,* 1967; *The Father Christmas Letters,* 1976

BIBLIOGRAPHY: Carpenter, Humphrey, *Tolkien: A Biography,* 1977; Cott, Jonathan, *Pipers at the Gates of Dawn: The Wisdom of Children's Literature,* 1981; Crabbe, Kathryn W., *J. R. R. Tolkien,* 1981, 1988; Neimark, Anne. *Myth Maker: J. R. R. Tolkien,* 1996

FRANCISCA GOLDSMITH

TOMES, Margot (Ladd)

Illustrator, b. 10 August 1917, Yonkers, New York; d. 25 June 1991, New York City

T. was unhappy as a child, but she and her family loved to read books. As an adult she worked as a fabric designer. Her illustrating career began in 1963 with Barbara WERSBA's book, *Brave Balloon of Benjamin Burkley.* T. and Wersba were at Martha's Vineyard on vacation when Wersba urged T. to try illustrating one of her books. Eventually, T. left fabric designing to work full-time as an illustrator. She admitted that illustrating was not easy or fun for her, but she hoped children would like her illustrations.

AWARDS: T. illustrated many books that received honors. *Little Sister and the Month Brothers* was

112. JOHN STEPTOE

113. JAMES STEVENSON

114. MILDRED TAYLOR

115. J. R. R. TOLKIEN

116. MICHAEL O. TUNNELL

included in Children's Book Showcase in 1977. *Jack and the Wonder Beans* was recognized as a *New York Times* Ten Best Illustrated Children's Books of the Year in 1977 and was chosen one of the New York Public Library's 100 Books of the Year in 1980. T. received the Society of Illustrators Certificate of Merit in 1979 for *The Sorcerer's Apprentice. Homesick: My Own Story* (by Jean FRITZ) was an ALA NEWBERY MEDAL Honor Book and an American Book Award (1983). *Chimney Sweeps: Yesterday and Today* (by James Cross GIBLIN) also received an American Book Award in 1983 while *If There Were Dreams to Sell* (B. Lalicki, comp.) was among the *New York Times* Ten Best Illustrated Children's Books of the Year in 1984

FURTHER WORKS: *The Secret of the Sachem's Tree.* 1972. *And Then What Happened, Paul Revere?* (Fritz). 1973. *Where Was Patrick Henry on the 29th of May?* (Fritz). 1975. *By George, Bloomers!* 1976. 1982. *Snowy Day: Stories and Poems.* (Caroline Feller Bauer). 1986. *Stone Soup* (John STEWIG). 1991

BIBLIOGRAPHY: *Something about the Author,* vol. 70, 1993

JODI PILGRIM

TOWNSEND, John Rowe

Author, b. 10 May 1922, Leeds, England

T. knew from the age of five that he wanted to be an author. By the time he was eight years old he had written his first ADVENTURE novel, which was titled "The Crew's Boat." T. came from a poor family but because of his aptitude he won a scholarship to Leeds Grammar School that was attended by children from families wealthier than his own. He did a good job in school but found that many of the books that he was assigned to read really did not capture his interest or imagination. He wanted to write to improve upon the literature that he was presented to read. T. served in World War II and subsequently enrolled at Cambridge University. T.'s love of writing continued after he graduated from Cambridge; he worked as an editor for the *Manchester Guardian.* T. began writing reviews of books for young children and discovered a gap in works that portrayed children from lower-class families. T.'s first novel, *Hell's Kitchen,* an attempt to fill this gap, was published in 1963.

Several of T.'s books including *A Sense of Story* (1971), a professional reference for librari-

ans, teachers, and scholars in children's literature, appeared on the *Horn Book* Honor List. *Grumble's Yard* (1961), *The Intruder,* and *Noah's Castle* were all adapted for television in the late 1970s.

T. summed up his career by saying "Professionally, I'm one of the world's lucky ones. I am what I always wanted to be, a writer. I am very happy to write for children and young people who seem to me to be an ideal audience, receptive, and constantly renewed." T. is a highly respected literary critic who has written several scholarly texts.

AWARDS: AMERICAN LIBRARY ASSOCIATION Notable Book (1968) for *Pirate's Island,* (1970) *Good-Night Prof. Dear,* (1972) *The Summer People* and *The Intruder,* and (1975) for *Noah's Castle; Boston Globe-Horn Book* Award (1970) for *The Intruder;* CARNEGIE MEDAL honorable mention (1964) for *Hell's Kitchen;* Christopher Award (1982) for *The Islanders;* Edgar Allan Poe Award (1972) for *The Intruder*

FURTHER WORKS: *The Golden Journey,* 1989; *Rob's Place,* 1988; *Downstream,* 1987; *The Persuading Stick,* 1986

BIBLIOGRAPHY: *Something about the Author,* vol. 68, 1992; *Something about the Author Autobiographies Series,* vol. 2

MICHAEL O'LAUGHLIN

TRANSLATION

Over the generations, the lives of children and young people have been enriched by the translation of books from other cultures. We have all benefited from translated editions of *The Bible, The Iliad* and *The Odyssey, The Ramayana,* and *Aesop's Fables,* as well as folktales and legends from many lands.

Looking back, there are many classic titles that have become a major part of the literary heritage of our young people: *The Arabian Nights* (Arabic, 1712); Johann David WYSS's *Swiss Family Robinson* (German, 1814); Hans Christian ANDERSEN's *Fairy Tales* (Danish, 1846), Johanna SPYRI's *Heidi* (German, 1884), Jules VERNE's *Twenty Thousand Leagues under the Sea* (French, 1870), Carlo COLLODI's *Pinocchio* (Italian, 1891), Felix SALTEN's *Bambi* (German, 1929), and Jean and Laurent DE BRUNHOFF's *The Story of Babar* (French, 1935). Books in translation are a window to the world, providing a sensitive glimpse into the minds and actions of people in other countries. Through their stories, we gain a sense of another culture, another landscape and another set of expectations. Children's lives would be definitely poorer if they could not reflect on the humor of Pippi Longstocking, on the beauty of the Alps at sunset along with Heidi, or laugh at the foibles of Mrs. Pepperpot.

Translations have been a way of life in European countries for generations; 30 percent to 70 percent of their publishing for young people is translated from other languages. By reading books in translation young people develop an appreciation of the universality of humanity. This is increasingly important, what with the shrinking of our world via the media and the ease of transport as well as the dramatic rise in immigration. These result in our need to be more aware of the lives and cultures of others.

Translating a work of literature is much more than just a word-for-word exchange from one language to another. A translator must faithfully capture the spirit of the story as if the author was originally writing in English. This is no small task and requires hours of intense scrutiny: hence the translator must be an accomplished linguist in both languages, sensitive to recognizing the importance of words to convey meaning and culture. Not only must the individual know the language of the text extensively, the translator must be faithful to the style of the author, and in addition must be a discriminating reader to recognize the literary merits of the work for young people. Relating to the translation process, BRITISH translator Patricia Crampton often refers to a musical metaphor with the translator as the performer trying to do the best to allow the audience to understand what the composer meant in the composition. Another British translator, Anthea Bell, perceives herself to be an actor on paper, yet strives to keep herself as a clear piece of glass, so that her self does not show through. It is what the author wrote not what the translator thinks that must come across.

PICTURE BOOKS present a different challenge to publishers. When a publishing company tries to sell the rights to a picture book, perhaps at the Bologna Children's Book Fair, it presents a "raw" English version to give the general idea of the story. Too frequently, to save translator fees,

this copy is taken by an editor who, after looking at the illustrations revises it to make a new edition. Tragically much of the original insight, wit, HUMOR, and beauty of language is lost in one quick cut. Luckily, some editors request a professional translator and the result is quite wonderful: e.g., Michio Mado's *The Animals: Selected Poems* (Japanese, 1992), which was translated by the Empress Michiko.

After World War II, during a period of intense upheaval and inward-focused reconstruction policies, there was little literary communication between countries. Interest grew in translated books to provide an opportunity to look out from our situation and to be able to laugh at life. Thus a powerful impact was made by *Anne Frank: The Diary of a Young Girl* (German, 1953) and the introduction of Astrid LINDGREN's *Pippi Longstocking* (Swedish, 1950) series.

From the 1960s through the 1980s, the relative calm in international affairs led individuals to reflect on past events, to become curious about others, and to long for adventure. Thus the golden age of books translated into English began: war novels were first to come: Anne HOLM's *I Am David* (Danish, 1965); Hans Peter RICHTER's *Friedrich* (German, 1970), and *I Was There* (German, 1972); Jap teer Haar's *Boris* (Dutch, 1970); Vasil Bykov's *Pack of Wolves* (Russian, 1981); and Else Pelgrom's *The Winter When Time Was Frozen* (Dutch, 1980). ADVENTURE STORIES with powerful plots quickly followed: Siny Rose van Iterson's *Pulga* (Dutch, 1971); Hanelore Valenacak's *When Half-Gods Go* (German, 1976); and Ottfried PREUSSLER's *The Satanic Mill* (German, 1973). Novels featuring interesting characters soon followed: Elfie Donnelly's *Offbeat Friends* (German, 1982); Anatoli Aleksin's *A Late-born Child* (Russian, 1971); and Christine Nostlinger's *Konrad* (German, 1977). Since the mid-1980s there has been a sense of isolation within the English speaking countries. The importance of having books from other cultures and language groups is simply not valued in the current economic climate—all judgments of a book's value are based on its sales. Fewer titles were produced but a larger number of them were INFORMATIONAL BOOKS with a natural history focus: Christina Björk's *Linnea in Monet's Garden* (Swedish, 1987) and *Linnea's Almanac* (Swedish, 1989);

Heiderose and Andreas Fischer-Nagel's *Birth of Hamsters* (German, 1985); and *The Housefly* (German, 1990); Hans-Heinrich Isenbart's *Birth of a Foal* (German, 1986); and Rosabianca Skira-Venturi's *A Weekend with Leonardo da Vinci* (French, 1993). Novels included Tamar Bergman's *Along the Tracks* (Hebrew, 1991); Peter Härtling's *Crutches* (German, 1988); Uri ORLEV's *Lydia, Queen of Palestine* (Hebrew, 1993); and Marethia Maaratens's *Paper Bird* (Afrikan, 1991). Noteworthy PICTURE BOOKS included Takaaki Nomura's *Grandpa's Town* (Japanese, 1991); Harutaka Nakawatari's *The Sea and I* (Japanese, 1992); Max Velthuijs's *Frog in Love* (Dutch, 1989); and Monica Zak's *Save My Rain Forest* (Spanish, 1992).

In the English–speaking world, there has been precious little attention given to recognizing the quality of translations for children and young people. The only award for translation is the Mildred L. Batchelder Award. This is given by the AMERICAN LIBRARY ASSOCIATION to the American publisher of a children's book considered to be the most outstanding of those published abroad in a foreign language and later published in the United States. Recent winners include: (1994) *The Apprentice* by Pilar Molina Llorente, translated from the Spanish by Robin Longshaw; (1995) *The Boys from St. Petri* by Bjarne Reuter, translated from the Danish by Anthea Bell; (1996) *The Lady with the Hat* by Uri Orlev, translated from the Hebrew by Hillel Halkin; (1997) *The Friends* by Kasum Yumoto, translated from the Japanese by Cathy Hirano; (1998) *The Robber and Me* by Josef Holub, translated from the German by Elizabeth D. Crawford.

This is a time in our world's history when young people have to be aware of and have a greater sensitivity to the lives of others living on this planet. We need to meet them within their own language environs, and if we cannot, then we need to be able to read their books in translation. Unfortunately, the English-speaking world is notorious for the low numbers of translations present on publisher lists. Why? Many British publishers maintain that they have the greatest children's literature in the world. Why would they need to bring other literatures in? United States, Canadian, and AUSTRALIAN publishers say that translations do not sell, and sales are the bot-

tom line. Fortunately, there are dedicated editors and publishers who believe in the value of quality translations and strive to bring them to English-speaking youngsters. There is hope as a few titles get translated each year. Where there is a trickle or a stream, can perhaps a flood be far behind?

RONALD JOBE

(See also INTERNATIONAL LITERATURE)

TRAVERS, P(amela) L(yndon)

Author, b. 9 August 1906, Queensland, Australia; d. 23 April 1996, London, England

T. grew up in Queensland and Sydney, Australia. An avid reader, she especially enjoyed FAIRY TALES and myths, which later influenced her writing. She remembers buying "penny" books as a child, which were fairy tales for a penny. T. began to write poems and stories at age seven. In addition to writing, T. enjoyed acting. As a teenager, she worked as an actress while writing. She began to publish articles and poems after showing some of her writing to a man from a newspaper. T. spent time visiting and writing in England, Ireland, and the United States. During World War II she stayed on a NATIVE AMERICAN Reservation.

T. is best known for her popular book, *Mary Poppins* (1934) that she wrote while recovering from an illness. Mary Poppins portrays a magical governess who blows into the lives of the Banks' family on the wind. T. feels that one of Mary Poppins's chief characteristics is that she never explains anything, which was also a characteristic of T.'s father, who died when she was young. Mary Poppins's character also resembles T.'s Aunt Christina, who came to live with the family after her father's death. T. preferred to remain anonymous as a writer and uses her initials on her books. By using initials only, readers cannot distinguish whether a man or woman wrote the book. Several Mary Poppins books followed the first. In 1963, DISNEY produced the very successful film *Mary Poppins.*

The illustrator of *Mary Poppins,* Mary Shepard, died on September 4, 2000, in London, England.

AWARDS: *Mary Poppins Opens the Door* won the AMERICAN LIBRARY ASSOCIATION Notable Books in 1943. T. received the Nene Award from the Hawaii Association of School LIBRARIANS and the Hawaii Library Association for *Mary Poppins* in

1965. *Friend Monkey* (1971) and *About the Sleeping Beauty* (1975) were selected as Child Study Association of America's Children's Books of the Year. T. received an honorary doctorate from Chatham College in 1978

FURTHER WORKS: *Mary Poppins.* 1934. *Mary Poppins Comes Back.* 1935. *I Go by Sea, I Go by Land.* 1941. *Mary Poppins Opens the Door.* 1943. *Mary Poppins in the Park.* 1952. *The Fox at the Manger.* 1962. *Mary Poppins from A to Z.* 1962. *Friend Monkey.* 1971. *Mary Poppins in the Kitchen: A Cookery Book with a Story.* 1975. *The Complete Mary Poppins.* 1976. *Two Pairs of Shoes.* 1980. *Mary Poppins in the Cherry Tree Lane.* 1982

BIBLIOGRAPHY: Cott, Jonathan, *Pipers at the Gates of Dawn: The Wisdom of Children's Literature,* 1981; *Something about the Author,* vol. 54, 1989

JODI PILGRIM

TREASE, (Robert) Geoffrey

Author, b. 11 August 1909, Nottingham, England; d. 27 January 1998, England

From earliest childhood, T. pursued a STORY-TELLING career; he was a voracious reader and writer. He made up his own stories before he could write them down but by age thirteen he was using his own typewriter. Events during boyhood such as World War I and winning a Classics scholarship provided grist for his imagination. T. spent a year at Oxford but left to teach at a prep school before his career as an author gained momentum, allowing him to earn a living by writing. Besides writing historical fiction for children, T. wrote juvenile plays and histories, and fiction and nonfiction for adults.

He wrote mostly MYSTERIES and historical fiction filled with action, suspense, and excitement relying on language to tell the story. His first book published in the U.S. was *Cue for Treason* (1941) set in the Elizabethan era about a group of strolling actors. T. later wrote *Seven Stages* (1965), a collected BIOGRAPHY of seven performers and authors from the theater. *Victory at Valmy* (1960), set during the French Revolution, told about the events through the eyes of a young boy. T. won the *New York Herald Tribune* Award for *This Is Your Century* (1965).

Bows against the Barons (1934) developed from his boyhood interest in the local hero, Robin Hood. Subsequent historical novels were based on less well-known persons and events, requiring T. to research intensively. *No Boats on the Bannermere* (1949) involves discovery of a Viking-era skeleton. *The Red Towers of Grenada* (1966) concerns the expulsion of the Jews from England. Nineteen-fifties' standards for juvenile publishing, which discouraged the portrayal of heavy drinking and children swearing, forced the prolific T. to work within restrictions that annoyed him. Later editorial standards also irritated him as he sought to portray historical epochs accurately, with currently impolitic "isms" included. Nonetheless, T.'s historical fiction remains both academically accurate and artistically engaging.

FURTHER WORKS: *Comrades for the Charter.* 1934. *A Cue for Treason.* 1940. *Trumpets in the West.* 1947. *Under the Black Banner.* 1950. *Message to Hadrian.* 1956. *Bent Is the Bow.* 1965. *A Masque for the Queen.* 1970. *A Voice in the Night.* 1973. *Hidden Treasure.* 1989

BIBLIOGRAPHY: Meek, Margaret. *Geoffrey Trease,* 1960. *Something about the Author,* vol. 60, 1990

FRANCISCA GOLDSMITH AND
MICHAEL O'LAUGHLIN

TREECE, Henry

Author, b. 1911, Wednesbury, Staffordshire, England (exact date uncertain); d. 10 June 1966, Place unknown

T., author of twenty-five historical children's novels, was given historical books to read at an early age and credits this influence with his desire to present active historical characters in his teaching and writings. T. wrote POETRY, short stories, and historical plays before turning to children's books. His first juvenile title, *Legions of the Eagle* (1954) was about Celtic/Roman history; many of his books were about Scandinavian/British history. His often repeated themes include growth through voyaging, the meeting of two cultures, and the search for a father. He also wrote books about what he called "crossroads," eras of significant change, in European history, but he always returned repeatedly to the clash of Rome and Britain and the Viking way of life.

His finest book about the Vikings, *The Last of the Vikings* (1964), the third in a trilogy of the Viking King Harald, tells the story of a hero as he comes to understand that his world and his values are changing. T.'s books have great appeal for readers who enjoy ADVENTURE STORIES and although reprints are few, LIBRARY circulation records show children still read and enjoy his stories.

FURTHER WORKS: *The Eagles Have Flown*. 1954. *Hounds of the King*. 1955. *The Road to Miklagard*. 1957. *Man with a Sword*. 1962. *The Dream-Time*. 1967

BIBLIOGRAPHY: *Children's Literature Review*. 1976. *Fiction*, FOLKLORE, FANTASY *and Poetry for Children, 1876–1985*. 1986. *The Oxford Companion to Children's Literature*. 1984. Silvey, A., ed. *Children's Books and Their Creators*. 1995. Literature Resource Center; The Gale Group, 1999; http://www.galenet.com/servlet/LitRC/hi...Henry + Treece&PX = 0000099 717&DT = Biography

IRVYN G. GILBERTSON

TRELEASE, James

Author, lecturer, b. 23 March 1941, Orange, New Jersey

T. is best known in the field of children's literature for his advocacy of the importance of reading aloud to children. He has used his writing and speaking skills to promote parent and teacher involvement in children's literacy development from children's earliest years. T. credits his father for fostering an early love and appreciation for words. He later made use of that appreciation when he became an award-winning journalist. He worked for the *Springfield Daily News* in Massachusetts for twenty years, first as a writer, later as an artist and sports cartoonist. T. spoke to children in schools about his career as a journalist, visiting classrooms about once a week for fifteen years. During one of these visits the focus of his talk began to change. As he was leaving a classroom, he saw a book he was reading to his daughter sitting on the teacher's desk. T. asked the class about it, began telling an animated portrayal of the story, and hooked the students' interest. As he went to other classrooms, he continued to ask students about their reading. These conversations convinced T. that parents and teachers might want a pamphlet about reading aloud, and he used his summer vacation money to self-publish a small brochure. With the help of a literary agent, this brochure would later become the *New York Times* bestseller, *The Read-Aloud Handbook* (1979). T. continues to write and lecture, wanting educators

and parents not only to teach children to read but to instill in them the desire to read. He states that "readers aren't born, they're made" and "one person can make a lasting difference in children's lives."

FURTHER WORKS: *Reading Aloud: Motivating Children to Make Books into Friends, Not Enemies*. Video. 1983. *The New Read-Aloud Handbook*. 1989. *Hey! Listen to This: Stories to Read Aloud*. 1992. *Read All About It! : Great Read-Aloud Stories, Poems, and Newspaper Pieces for Preteens and Teens*. 1993

BIBLIOGRAPHY: *Contemporary Authors,* vol. 112, 1985; Raymond, Allen. "Meet Jim Trelease: He Made 'Reading Aloud' a Priority," *Early Years,* vol. 15, pp. 23–25

SANDRA IMDIEKE

TRESSELT, Alvin R.

Author, editor, teacher, b. 30 September 1916, Passaic, New Jersey; d. 24 July 2000, Burlington, Vermont

From 1946 to 1952 T. worked at B. Altman's, a New York City department store, as a display designer and copywriter. Between 1952 and 1956 he became the editor of *Humpty Dumpty*, a children's magazine. From 1967 to 1974 he was the editor and the executive vice president of *Parent's* magazine. In 1974 he became an instructor and dean of faculty at The Institute of Children's Literature at Redding Ridge, Connecticut.

Along with Margaret Wise BROWN, T. helped to pioneer the design of the "mood" PICTURE BOOK. These books sought to catch and hold the attention of young readers by projecting the poetic essence of a familiar experience in nature using vivid yet simple descriptive language. With illustrator Roger DUVOISIN, S. won the 1948 ALA CALDECOTT MEDAL for *White Snow, Bright Snow*. This book is an example of a mood story, having no plot, no central character—only a poetic essence that creates a mood. T. could take the most mundane material from nature and shape it into something fresh and vivid just for children. In *White Snow, Bright Snow* he structured the text in a dramatic way, starting with a gray sky that presages a snowstorm and ending with the first robin that signals the beginning of spring. These simple descriptive nature books spawned a whole series of imitations.

FURTHER WORKS: *Rain Drop Splash.* 1946. *Hi, Mr. Robin.* 1950. *Wake up Farm.* 1966. *Hide and Seek Fog.* 1965. *The Dead Tree.* 1970. *The Beaver Pond.* 1970. *The Gift of the Tree.* 1992

BIBLIOGRAPHY: *Children's Literature Review,* vol. 30, 1993; Silvey, Anita, ed., *Children's Books and Their Creators,* 1995; *Something about the Author,* vol. 30, 1983; *Twentieth Century Children's Writers,* 1983

JUDY LIPSITT

TRIMMER, Sarah (Mrs.)
Author, b. 6 January 1741, Ipswich, England; d. 15 December 1810, England

In 1802, T. founded *The Guardian of Education,* a periodical devoted to assessing the quality and appropriateness of children's literature, approving only the most religious and carefully constructed texts while consistently and vigorously condemning FAIRY TALES. Her books were models of support for middle- and upper-class values. Even her most popular work, *Fabulous Histories* (1786), also known as the *History of Robins* (1855), upheld class consciousness and accepting one's lot in life through the comparison of two households, a middle-class family and a nest of robins. She was also involved in the Sunday School movement, writing prescriptive moral commentaries on Biblical stories.

FURTHER WORKS: *A Concise History of England: Comprised in a Set of Easy Lessons for Children.* 1829. *Fabulous Histories: Designed for the Instruction of Children, Respecting Their Treatment of Animals.* 1786. *The History of Robins: For the Instruction for Children on Their Treatment of Animals.* 1855

BIBLIOGRAPHY: "Some Account of the Life and Writings of Mrs. Trimmer" (microform): with *Original Letters, and Mediations, and Prayers, Selected from Her Journal,* 3rd ed., London: Printed for C. and J. Rivington (1825). Yarde, Doris M., *Sarah Trimmer of Bretford and Her Children: With Some of Her Early Writings 1780–86,* Heston: Hounslow and District History Society (1990). F. J. Harvey Darton. *Children's Books in England: Five Centuries of Social Life* (1970)

KAY E. VANDERGRIFT

TRIPP, Wallace
Author, illustrator, b. 26 June 1940, Boston, Massachusetts

T. began working as an English teacher and became an author and illustrator of children's books

in 1965. As a young boy, T. always loved drawing pictures and reading books about MYTHOLOGY, knighthood, chivalry, and ANIMALS. This explains why several of his books, including *Sir Toby Jingle's Beastly Journey* (1976), combine these elements. T. is known for the mythological ILLUSTRATIONS he created for other writers including several he illustrated for Hamish Hamilton, such as *The Hamish Hamilton Book of Witches* (1966), *Ellen and the Queen* (1971), and *The Hamish Hamilton Book of Sea Legends* (1971).

T. is best known for the illustrations he created for Peggy PARISH's Amelia Bedelia series including, *Come Back, Amelia Bedelia* (1971), and *Play Ball, Amelia Bedelia* (1972). Both of these books have been adapted as filmstrips. T.'s cartoon-style illustrations for Ernest THAYER's *Casey at the Bat* (1978), rendered in full color and black and white, is a humorous retelling of the classic verse with animals as the ballplayers.

BIBLIOGRAPHY: Cianciolo, P. PICTURE BOOKS *for Children,* 1990; *Something about the Author,* vol. 31, 1983

DENISE P. BEASLEY

TUDOR, Tasha
Author, illustrator, b. 28 August 1915, Boston, Massachusetts

T.'s wish to exemplify the life of the nineteenth century is evident in her lifestyle and in the children's books she writes and illustrates. Although her earliest years were spent in metropolitan Boston, in a life of formality and tradition, she attributes her later childhood in rural Connecticut for fostering her creativity. T. was sent to live with her aunt following her parent's divorce, since her mother believed that New York City, where her mother now worked as a painter, would not be a good environment for a young girl. In Connecticut T. thrived on country living, presenting plays, enjoying dance and nature, and dreaming of the farm she one day hoped to own. T.'s choice to become an illustrator began after she read Oliver Goldsmith's *The Vicar of Wakefield* (1766). She wrote stories to have something to illustrate, and her husband helped her find a publisher for her first book, *Pumpkin Moonshine* (1938). While living on her farm and rearing her family, T. continued to write and illustrate over sixty books for children.

T.'s ILLUSTRATIONS are notable for capturing the lives and lifestyles of a time now past. Her finely detailed illustrations portray a simpler time and her characters are often dressed in Victorian costume. Watercolor and pen and ink evoke an old-fashioned gentility and a lifestyle that T. incorporated into her life.

AWARDS: ALA CALDECOTT MEDAL Honor Book (1945) for MOTHER GOOSE and (1957) for *I Is One*. Regina Medal, Catholic Library Association, Child Study Association's Children's Book of the Year (1975) for *The Night before Christmas*

FURTHER WORKS: *Alexander the Gander*. 1939. *A Tale for Easter*. 1941. *A Child's Garden of Verses*. 1947. *Thistle B.* 1949. *The Doll's Christmas*. 1950. *Becky's Birthday*. 1960. *A Time to Keep: The Tasha Tudor Book of Holidays*. 1977. *A Book of Christmas*. 1987. *First Delights: A Book about the Five Senses*. 1988. *First Graces*. 1989. *The Christmas Cat*. 1989. *Jenny Wren Book of Valentines*. 1989. *Becky's Christmas*. 1991. *The Night before Christmas*. 1997

BIBLIOGRAPHY: *Something about the Author*, vol. 69, 1992

SANDRA IMDIEKE

TUNIS, Edwin

Illustrator, social historian, b. 8 December 1897, Cold Spring Harbor, New York; d. 7 August 1973, Baltimore, Maryland

After graduating from high school, T. enrolled at the Maryland Institute of Art and Design but left to join the service at the outbreak of World War I. Returning to civilian life, he undertook commercial art projects including book ILLUSTRATION. In 1952, he was commissioned to paint a mural. His research for that project led to his first book, *Oars, Sails, and Steam* (1952), depicting the development of maritime transportation. T.'s illustrated nonfiction provides clear and concise understanding of the history of material culture. *Wheels* (1955) won the Boys' Club of America Junior Book Award. He won the Thomas A. Edison Foundation Award for *Colonial Living* (1957) and an ALA NEWBERY MEDAL Honor Book (1962) for *Frontier Living. The Young United States, 1783 to 1830* (1969) was nominated for the National Book Award. Besides a visual ac-

count of American history, T. communicates the shared humanity of NATIVE AMERICANS and settlers in each of these how-it-was books about pioneer life. T.'s illustration work was done largely in ink. He was meticulous in his research as he was in his drawings, brooking romanticism in neither.

FURTHER WORKS: *Weapons*. 1954. *Indians*. 1959. *Colonial Craftsmen*. 1965. *Shaw's Fortune: The Picture Story of a Colonial Plantation*. 1966. *Chipmunks on My Doorstep*. 1971. *The Tavern at the Ferry*. 1973

BIBLIOGRAPHY: *Something about the Author*, vol. 28, 1982; *Publishers Weekly*, August 27, 1973

FRANCISCA GOLDSMITH

TUNIS, John R(oberts)

Author, b. 7 December 1889, Boston, Massachusetts; d. 4, February 1975, Essex, Connecticut

As a youngster, T., author of children's and young adults' SPORTS STORIES, knew that education was valued in his home. He was encouraged by his parents, especially his mother, to excel in his schooling. T. eventually attended Harvard where he flourished in two areas that had always been encouraged by his mother, athletics and theater. After World War I, T. began writing and was published in magazines. He became a sports writer and radio commentator. This was the beginning of a career that would eventually lead to writing for children. While his stories for older children always had sports-centered plots, their themes dealt with issues of social and racial injustice. T. won the Junior Book Award from the Boys' Club of America for *Highpockets* (1948) and the Child Study Children's Book Award for *Keystone Kids* (1943). *Hard, Fast and Beautiful* was made into a movie by RKO in 1951.

T.'s most well-known sports novel, *The Kid from Tompkinsville* (1940, reissued 1987) is a widely read perennial favorite. It features the ordeal of Ray Tucker, a new recruit for the Brooklyn Dodgers who pulls his team out of a losing streak. A freak accident ends his playing career but the young pitcher finds a way to stay on the team, much to the delight of generations of young readers.

FURTHER WORKS: *The Duke Decides*, 1939; *Champions Choice*, 1940; *Kid From Tompkins-*

ville, 1940; *Democracy and Spirit,* 1941; *Go, Team, Go,* 1954; *All-American,* 1942; *The Kid Comes Back,* 1946; *Young Razzle,* 1949; *The American Way of Sport,* 1958; *His Enemy, His Friend,* 1967; *Grand National,* 1973

BIBLIOGRAPHY: *Children's Literature Review,* vol. 12, 1980; *Dictionary of Literary Biography,* vol. 22, 1983; *Horn Book,* December 1977; MEIGS, et al., *A Critical History of Children's Literature,* 1969

MICHAEL O'LAUGHLIN

TURKLE, Brinton
Author, illustrator, b. 15 August 1915, Alliance, Ohio

T. has produced outstanding examples of PICTURE BOOKS where words and pictures are interdependent. As a child he received little encouragement for his artistic drawings, so after high school he majored in drama at the Carnegie Institute of Technology. Deciding his opportunities in theater would be limited, he pursued drawing at the Museum of Fine Arts School in Boston. His first book, *Obadiah the Bold* (1965), a gentle story about a Quaker boy and his family, was the forerunner of several Obadiah books. *Thy Friend, Obadiah* (1969), featuring T.'s characteristic quiet, gentle drawings, was an ALA CALDECOTT MEDAL Honor Book and *The Adventures of Obadiah* (1972) won the Christopher Award. Wordless books, *Deep in the Forest* (1976) and *Do Not Open* (1981), both won AWARDS from the AMERICAN LIBRARY ASSOCIATION. T. explains that he deliberately writes to offset materialism, hypocrisy, and brutality in society by presenting children with "integrity, mutual respect, kindness, and reverence for life."

BIBLIOGRAPHY: *Fiction, FOLKLORE, FANTASY and POETRY for Children, 1876–1985,* vol. 1, 1986; HOPKINS, Lee Bennett, *Pauses: Autobiographical Reflections of 101 Creators of Children's Books,* 1995; Silvey, Anita, ed., *Children's Books and Their Creators,* 1995

IRVYN GILBERTSON

TURNER, Ann
Author, b. 10 December 1945, Northampton, Massachusetts

Through story and verse T. combines a love of reading and writing with an artist's eye for beauty in the common place as she creates in-

sights to both the past and present. Although T. claims writing POETRY to be her first love, her books include fiction, FANTASY, and nonfiction as well. Rich imagery can be found in both literature that entertains, such as *Tickle a Pickle* (1986), or that sensitively describes the struggles and emotions of individuals in past historical eras, as in *Nettie's Trip South* (1987), an IRA/CBC Children's Choice Award winner. Whether drawing from FAMILY STORIES, historical events, or natural occurrences, T. uses language sensitively to create connections to times past through universal emotions, relationships, and everyday situations.

AWARDS: AMERICAN LIBRARY ASSOCIATION Notable Book (1989) *Dakota Dugout.* NCSS Notable Book citation (1989) for *Heron Street*

FURTHER WORKS: *Katie's Trunk,* 1992; *Grass Songs: Poems,* 1993; *Rosemary's Witch,* 1994; *Shaker Hearts,* 1997; *Angel Hide and Seek,* 1998; *Drummer Boy: Marching to the Civil War,* 1998

BIBLIOGRAPHY: *Seventh Book of Junior Authors and Illustrators,* 1996; *Something about the Author,* vol. 77, 1994

JANELLE B. MATHIS

TURNER, Ethel Sibyl Mary Burwell
Author, b. 24 January 1870, Doncaster, Yorkshire, England; d. Date unknown 1958, Mosman, Sydney, Australia

T.'s twice widowed mother emigrated with her daughters to Australia in 1880, where she married again. T. and her sister Lillian, who took their first stepfather's surname, attended Sydney Girls High School, where today a library is named after T. They edited and virtually co-wrote the school magazines. Lillian later wrote over twenty novels for YOUNG ADULTS. T., novelist and short story writer, poet, and anthologist, contributed to *Windsor Magazine* (U.K.), the *Australian Bulletin* and *Daily Telegraph.* As "Dame Durden" she edited the children's section of the *Illustrated Sydney News.* Her first children's book, *Seven Little Australians* (1894), starts by avowedly rejecting older European literary models and model child characters. She did not let her publishers place it in an English series; the format in which it finally appeared was then used for an Australian series including other authors. It is the only AUSTRALIAN juvenile novel to be almost continuously in print for a century, has been translated into ten languages, made into a play (1915), a film (1939), a British television series (BBC, 1953), an Australian Broadcasting Corporation series (1973), and a stage musical (1988). Its sequels include *The Family at Misrule* (1895), *Little Mother Meg* (1902), and *Judy and Punch* (1928). These, along with the early *The Little Larrikin* (1896) and *Miss Bobbie* (1897) are perhaps the most popular works in T.'s large oeuvre.

T.'s juvenile novels are in the tradition of the late nineteenth century episodic middle-class FAMILY STORY with comic and melodramatic incidents, like Susan COOLIDGE's Katy books. They draw on the post–1880s literary image of naughty "pickles" and "scamps"—mischievous but always good-hearted, fun-loving, adventurous children. They examine family solidarity, the relationships between siblings and parents in a background of suburban Sydney life, moving away from the more usual Australian bush setting. They include such period motifs as infant death (though T. is unusual in that she also includes the death of a previously healthy central character), the father as unquestionable and punitive paterfamilias, complete endorsement of British Empire values, and sometimes a rather rigid attitude toward social class (in *The Family at Misrule* [1895], a daughter is severely condemned for associating with a nouveau riche family, and a son's romantic attachment to a shop girl is ridiculed and vetoed). Despite an occasional lack of continuity, the emotional lives of T.'s child characters, who mature and evolve, and the realism of her social settings, remain credible and are much beloved today. The New South Wales Premier's Literary Awards include an Ethel Turner Award for Young People's Literature.

BIBLIOGRAPHY: Niall, Brenda. *Seven Little Billabongs: The World of Ethel Turner and Mary Grant Bruce.* 1979, 1982. Phelan, Nancy. *The Romantic Lives of Louise Mack.* 1991. Poole, Philippa, ed. *Selections from Ethel Turner's Diaries 1889–1930.* 1979. Yarwood, A. T. *From a Chair in the Sun: The Life of Ethel Turner.* 1994; online: Schmidt, Mareya & Peter. (accessed October 26, 1998); Turner, Ethel Mary Burwell (1870–1958); online. Available at: http://dargo.vicnet. net.au/ozlit/writers.cfm?id=924; Tipper, John. (accessed January 27, 1999); Ethel Turner, Lillian Turner, and Jean Curlewis, (online). http://www. penrithcity.nsw.gov.au/usrpages/Collect/ethel.htm Ferguson, Sandra. (accessed April 8, 1996); "My Oath! 102 Years Of Seven Little Australians!"; (online, contains relevant links) available http:// www.slv.vic.gov.au/slv/children/seven/

SANJAY SIRCAR

TWAIN, Mark
(See CLEMENS, Samuel Langhorne)

UCHIDA, Yoshiko

Author, illustrator, b. 24 November 1921, Alameda, California; d. 21 June 1992, Berkeley, California

U. is best known for helping readers appreciate Japanese culture and the Japanese American experience through the books she wrote and illustrated. U. and her family were interned in a Utah relocation camp for Japanese Americans during World War II, where she was an elementary school teacher. Her award-winning book, *Journey to Topaz* (1971), and other writings are based on that experience. U. earned degrees from the University of California at Berkeley and Smith College. She continued to teach after World War II, trying to write in the evenings, but eventually she switched to writing full time. She received a grant from the Ford Foundation to visit Japan to study art and collect folktales. Over her forty-five year career, U. retold folktales and wrote PICTURE BOOKS, historical as well as REALISTIC FICTION. Sumi, a contemporary Japanese character found in several of her books, portrays children's universal concerns and experiences. One of her last books, *The Bracelet* (1993), returns in picture book format to the earlier themes of *Journey to Topaz*.

U. described her purpose for writing as her desire to "give young ASIAN AMERICANS a sense of their past and to reinforce their self-esteem and self-knowledge." For all readers, she hoped to "write to celebrate our common humanity."

AWARDS: AMERICAN LIBRARY ASSOCIATION Notable Book citation (1972) for *Journey to Topaz*. Citation, Contra Costa chapter of Japanese American Citizens League (1976) for outstanding contribution to the cultural development of society. *School Library Journal* Best Book of the Year citation (1983) for *The Best Bad Thing*. Child Study Association of America, Children's Book of the Year citation (1985) for *The Happiest Ending*. Friends of Children and Literature award (1987) for *A Jar of Dreams*. Japanese American of the Biennium award, Japanese American Citizens Leagues, 1988, for outstanding achievement

FURTHER WORKS: *The Dancing Kettle, and Other Japanese Folk Tales*. 1949. *Takao and Grandfather's Sword*. 1958. *Sumi's Prize*. 1964. *Samurai of Gold Hill*. 1972. *The Rooster Who Understood Japanese*. 1976. *Journey Home*. 1978. *A Jar of Dreams*. 1981. *The Magic Purse*. 1993. *The Wise Old Woman*. 1994. *The Invisible Thread* (an autobiography). 1991

BIBLIOGRAPHY: *Children's Literary Review*, vol. 6, 1984; *Contemporary Authors New Revision Series*, vol. 61, 1998

SANDRA IMDIEKE

UDRY, Janice May

Author, b. 14 June 1928, Jacksonville, Illinois

U. was reared as an only child in the rural town of Jacksonville, Illinois. As soon as she learned to read and write, reading, making up stories and poems, and drawing pictures became favorite pastimes. Playing on hot summer nights in Illinois later inspired U. to write *The Moon Jumpers* (Maurice SENDAK, illus; 1959). While attending Northwestern University, U. worked part time in a library. She graduated from the University in 1950. As an assistant in a Chicago nursery school, U. became interested in new PICTURE BOOKS for small children. When U. moved to Southern California, she noticed beautiful trees being cut down for housing developments. This destruction inspired her to write *A Tree Is Nice* (Marc SIMONT, illus; 1956) for children.

The ideas for many of U.'s books evolved from actions or words of her two daughters. For example, *"The Mean Mouse" and Other Mean Stories* (1962) is a collection written for one of her daughters when she was a small child.

AWARDS: ALA CALDECOTT MEDAL (1957) for *A Tree Is Nice.* AMERICAN LIBRARY ASSOCIATION Caldecott Medal Honor Book (1960) for *The Moon Jumpers. New York Herald Tribune* Children's Spring Book Festival Honor Book (1961) for *Let's Be Enemies* (1961)

FURTHER WORKS: *Theodore's Parents.* 1958. *Danny's Pig.* 1960. *Alfred.* 1960. *Is Susan Here?* 1962. *"The Mean Mouse," and Other Mean Stories.* 1962. *The End of the Line.* 1962. *Betsy-Back-in-Bed.* 1963. *Next Door to Laura Linda.* 1965. *What Mary Jo Shared.* 1966. *If You're a Bear.* 1967. *Mary Ann's Mud Day.* 1967. *What Mary Jo Wanted.* 1968. *Glenda.* 1969. *The Sunflower Garden.* 1969. *Emily's Autumn.* 1969. *Mary Jo's Grandmother.* 1971

BIBLIOGRAPHY: HOPKINS, Lee Bennett, *Pauses: Autobiographical Reflections of 101 Creators of Children's Books,* 1995; *Third Book of Junior Authors,* 1972

JODI PILGRIM

UNGERER, Tomi

Author, illustrator, b. 28 November 1931, Strasbourg, France

U. is a brilliant painter, cartoonist, graphic designer, and a writer and illustrator of both adult and children's books. He is known for his bitingly satirical drawings of men and animals. Using the sickest, blackest HUMOR, he reveals a most corrupt and decadent society. He has been called the "enfant terrible" of children's books since he refuses to present a sugar-coated version of the world. His work at times has been accused of perpetuating violence and vulgarity. However, although his stories may not be for the faint-hearted, as in good FAIRY TALES, his fantasies often have some blood and gore, and tell of a world beset with evils that are ultimately overcome by goodness. Using humorous, wry drawings, and a

very euphonious and unique vocabulary, he creates entertaining and original morality tales.

U.'s particular consciousness of society's fluctuating morality may be the result of a childhood spent in occupied France during World War II. He was born into a middle-class family of watchmakers in the city of Strasbourg, in Alsace-Lorraine. His family consisted of his parents, two older sisters and an older brother. His father died before he was ten; shortly after the Nazis came and occupied Alsace-Lorraine and U. was sent to school in Germany. The experience of being a sheltered, well-loved younger son of a bourgeois family, attending a rigid German school that taught Nazi philosophy and witnessing the hypocrisies and horrors of war had a profound effect on his concept of society. After the war he studied at the Art Decoratif in Strasbourg and in Paris. Although his art was influenced by the work of Gruewall, Durer, Schongauer, and turn-of-the-century illustrators Hansi and Schnugg, he felt that his greatest education came from hitch-hiking around Europe, doing odd jobs, and of course continuing to draw, paint, and design.

In 1956 he came to the United States, and in 1957 his first book, *The Mellops Go Flying,* was published. Besides children's books, he has published several sophisticated collections of posters. His work has been featured in many worldwide exhibitions.

In his earliest books he exploited the comic potential of civilizing farm or wild animals as DE-BRUNHOFF did in his Babar books. U.'s Mellops (possibly a name composed of mellow and slop) were a sensitive, gentle, ingenious middle-class family who, incidentally, were pigs. Their clever adventures lead to near disasters, brilliantly averted so that they returned unscathed to their loving home. In *Crictor* (1969), a boa constrictor, instead of being a killer, incongruously becomes a student as he is taught the alphabet by an old lady. In *Orlando the Brave Vulture* (1966), a vulture is not a carnivorous beast, but a courageous hero. U.'s life has perhaps taught him that experience does not necessarily match expectations. Beasts are not always wild nor are children always innocent. In the *Moon Man* (1967) the gentle rotund moon is eager to come down to earth and experience the exciting parties earthlings seem to be having, but when he does actually visit, he finds a wild revel and a cruel militaristic society that jails him for his unconventional appearance. Finally he escapes by "waning," and an understanding scientist sends him home. U. is not romantic in his depiction of children. They are often either angry, destructive, overindulged pests as Peter Paw in *No Kiss for Mother* (1973) or as in *Zeralda's Ogre* (1967) and *The Three Robbers* (1962). They are strong children who miraculously convert evil into goodness. By 1967 as the United States experienced more national violence, U.'s work began to show a darker strain. Not only was the text more violent, but the ILLUSTRATIONS were bolder. His line-and-monochromatic-watercolor drawings were replaced with black-ink drawings that used bold flat shapes of bright color. The grotesque and macabre imagery, always present, was used more frequently and caused some negative reactions. The prevalence of comic illustrations of improbably violent acts, pictures of the lower body and digestive functions can be defended as being part of an ancient tradition in folk humor and are generally subjects of children's verbal humor. *The Three Robbers* was a gentle poke at the thoughtless, greedy society that robbed the unsuspecting. In less than three hundred words U. tells how an innocent child's goodness reforms the robbers. In *Zeralda's Ogre* a town is held hostage by an ogre's appetite for little children. The ogre's evil is assaulted by domestic comfort in the form of Zeralda's gourmet cooking, which gives the ogre an appetite for haute cuisine instead of kids. In *The Beast of Monsieur Racine* (1971) a reclusive selfish retired tax collector is charmed by a mysterious beast whom he befriends and who ultimately outsmarts him and the French Academy. Again, as in other U. tales, the beast turns out to be genuine. When at last the two mischievous children are exposed as "the beast," they are not punished, but returned home to continue their friendship with the newly generous and fun-loving M. Racine. In later books, U. again reveals a world of unremitting evil that is occasionally redeemed by unusual virtue.

Tomi: A Childhood under the Nazis (1998) contrasts U.'s childhood experiences with his adult perspective of the world revealing the forces that shape his writing. U.'s vivid memories along with drawings saved from his childhood, documents, and old photos enable readers to understand a child's view of the Nazi occupation. In 1970, U. moved from New York City to a farm in Nova Scotia. Since 1975, he has lived with his family on a 200-acre farm in Southwestern Ireland.

AWARDS: Hans Christian ANDERSEN Award (1998) for lifetime achievement as illustrator. Children's Spring Book Award (1958) for *Crictor* and (1967) for *Moon Man.* Society of Illustrators Gold Medal (1960). Children's Book of the Year (1962) for *The Three Robbers* and (1971) for *The Beast of M. Racine.* American Institute of Graphic Arts (1969) for *The Hat.* Children's Book Showcase (1972) for *The Beast of M. Racine*

FURTHER WORKS: As illus: *Seeds and More Seeds* (M. SELSAM). 1959. *Fredow* (Mary STOLZ). 1962. *Flat Stanley.* (Jeff Brown). 1964. *Warwick's Three Bottles.* (Andre Hodeir). 1966. *Oh What Nonsense.* (William COLE). 1966. *Nonsense Verses.* (Edward LEAR). 1966. *Cleopatra Goes Sledding.* (Hodeir). 1968. *That Pest Jonathan.* (Cole). 1970. *Oh How Silly.* (Cole). 1970. *The Book of Giggles.* (Cole). 1970. *Beastly Boys and Ghastly Girls.* (Cole). 1964. As author/illus.: *The Mellops Go Flying.* 1957. *Mellops Diving for Treasure.* 1958. *The Mellops Strike Oil.* 1958. *Adelaide.* 1959. *Emile.* 1959. *Christmas Eve at the Mellops.* 1960. *Snail Where Are You?* 1962. *The Mellops Go Spelunking.* 1963. *One, Two, Where's My Shoe?* 1964. *The Hat.* 1970. *I Am Papa Snap.* 1972. *A Storybook from Tomi Ungerer.* 1974. *Allumette.* 1974

BIBLIOGRAPHY: U., Tomi, *Tomi: A Childhood Under the Nazis,* 1998; *Children's Literature Review,* vol. 3; *Something about the Author,* vol. 5, 1974, and vol. 33, 1983, vol. 106, 1999; *Twentieth Century Children's Writers,* 1983

JUDITH LIPSITT

UNTERMEYER, Louis

Poet, anthologist, b. 1 October 1885, New York City; d. 18 December, 1977, Newtown, Connecticut

U. and his younger sister Pauline were reared in New York City by a governess and a seamstress. U. also had a brother named Martin, who listened to his stories as a child. U. was an avid reader, but he bored easily with school. He left high school before graduating, and tried to get accepted into Columbia University without a high school degree. His math scores prevented him from being accepted. U. began working in his father's jewelry business in 1901. He considered becoming a musician. It was not until he was eighteen that he thought about becoming a writer. He then experimented composing lyrics and verse.

He began publishing POETRY, at first without pay. Eventually, his poems began to appear in *The Forum*. His first volume of verse, *First Love,* was published in 1911. Working in several genres, U. edited numerous books, wrote poetry, and retold stories such as *The Fat of the Cat,* a 1925 retelling of Gottfried Keller's Swiss FAIRY TALES. His poetry anthologies included a wide variety of poets and writing styles. *This Singing World* (1923) included works of living poets who were familiar to young readers, an innovation in children's anthologies at the time. U. served in prestigious roles including consultant in poetry for the Library of Congress and chairman of the Pulitzer Prize Poetry Jury. In 1956 U. received a Gold Medal from the Poetry Society of America for services to poetry. He was also selected Phi Beta Kappa poet at Harvard in 1956. U. earned the Sarah Josepha HALE Award in 1965 and the Golden Rose from the New England Poetry Society in 1966.

FURTHER WORKS: *The Forms of Poetry: A Pocket Dictionary of Verse.* 1926. *The Donkey of God.* 1932. *Chip: My Life and Times, as Overheard by Louis Untermeyer.* 1933. *The Last Pirate: Tales from the Gilbert and Sullivan Operas.* 1934. *Songs to Sing to Children.* 1935. *The Wonderful Adventures of Paul Bunyan.* Retold, 1945. *French Fairy Tales.* Retold, 1945. *The Golden Treasury of Poetry.* Editor, 1959. *The Kitten Who Barked.* 1962. *The World's Great Stories: Fifty-Five Legends That Live Forever.* 1968. *Plants of the Bible.* 1970. *Cat o'Nine Tales.* 1971

BIBLIOGRAPHY: MEIGS, C. et al. *A Critical History of Children's Literature.* 1969; *Something about the Author,* vol. 37, 1985

JODI PILGRIM

UTTLEY, Alison Jane (Taylor) (a.k.a. Alison Uttley)

Author, b. 17 December 1884, Cromford, Derbyshire, England; d. 7 May 1976, High Wycombe, England

U. was a prolific writer of more than ninety books for children as well as plays for children and several novels for adults. She grew up in the English countryside on a farm that had been in her family for over 200 years, surrounded by nature and ani-

mals. Later she wrote about her childhood in *A Country Child* (1931). She earned a Bachelor of Science Degree from Manchester University and pursued graduate study at Cambridge University. Her writing career would not begin, however, until her young son John went away to school and she began to write her stories down. She recalls that as a young child she never wrote stories but she "could always tell stories, so why write them?" Her early childhood experiences would become the familiar elements in so many of her books for children. The character of Little Grey Rabbit is probably her most famous, first appearing in her book *The Squirrel, the Hare and the Little Grey Rabbit* (1929). Each of her animal characters exhibit a distinct personality, from the mothering nature of Little Grey Rabbit to the self-absorbed Squirrel. One biographer pointed out the close connection between the personalities of U.'s characters and the aspects of human nature they mirror. Stories about Little Grey Rabbit would later be compiled in the collection, *Tales of Little Grey Rabbit* 1930. Her other popular SERIES, originated in 1940 with *Tales of the Four Pigs and Brock the Badger,* about a character named Sam Pig.

U. also wrote FAIRY TALES that incorporated elements of nature familiar to the author, such as the lives of village people in *Fairy Tales* (1975). Even time travel in the Derbyshire countryside became the basis of a book for older readers, *A Traveler in Time* (1939). This time-warp FANTASY, grounded in historical events, involves a modern girl and a sixteenth century plot to rescue Mary, Queen of Scots. For all of her stories, U. strongly believed that each should be firmly grounded in truth from which imaginative situations could spring. In his biography of U., Peter du Sautoy quotes U. as saying: "So each and every tale holds everyday magic, and each is connected with awareness of everyday life, where reality is made visible, and one sees what goes on with new eyes." Uttley's manuscript collection is housed in THE KERLAN COLLECTION at the University of Minnesota, Minneapolis.

FURTHER WORKS: *How Little Grey Rabbit Got Her Tail Back.* 1930. *The Great Adventure of Hare.* 1931. *Little Grey Rabbit's Christmas.* 1939. *Little Grey Rabbit's Washing-Day.* 1942. *Water-Rat's Picnic.* 1943. *Hare Goes Shopping.*

1965. *Stories for Christmas.* 1977. *From Spring to Spring.* 1978. *Foxglove Tales.* 1984

BIBLIOGRAPHY: Du Sautoy, Peter. *Twentieth-Century Children's Writers.* 1995. Hunt, Peter. *Children's Literature: An Illustrated History.* 1995. *Something about the Author*, vol. 88, 1997

SANDRA IMDIEKE

V

VAN ALLSBURG, Chris
Author, b. 18 June 1949, Grand Rapids, Michigan

V. grew up in Grand Rapids, Michigan during the 1950s. His childhood included catching tadpoles, sledding on nearby slopes, riding his bike to school, and playing baseball. During third grade he read a BIOGRAPHY about Babe Ruth nonstop from beginning to end. His enthusiasm for reading Babe Ruth's biography was not totally derived from interest in the story or baseball, but rather from completing an entire book. The summer following third grade he borrowed a collection of Walt DISNEY comic books from a neighbor. He loaded them in his red wagon, hauled them home to his bedroom and started reading. It took him one week to read them all, cover to cover. He grew fond of the lively characters and discovered after returning them that he missed his newly acquainted literary friends. Strong imaginative seeds were planted in the act of reading as well as a commitment to completing a task. Putting aside an uncompleted book was never an option for V.; this type of obsessive reading behavior, has followed him into adulthood.

He rediscovered his love for art at the University of Michigan. He earned an undergraduate degree there in fine arts and continued at Rhode Island School of Design to earn a Master's Degree in sculpture. V. worked diligently at sculpting and drawing while affiliated with RISD. His wife connected V. to the world of children's literature when she showed his works to David MACAULAY. Macaulay persuaded V. to submit his drawings to Macaulay's editor, resulting in a relationship with Walter Lorraine at Houghton Mifflin.

From the beginning of V.'s career his unique artistic style, point of view, and use of light combine with the text to tell an engaging story. These qualities called attention to V.'s work with his first publication, *The Garden of Abdul Gasazi* (1979). In this book the world of illusion fuses with reality enticing readers to wonder whether a bull terrier has turned into a duck. The same mischievous bull terrier appears mysteriously in each of V.'s future PICTURE BOOKS.

V. won the CALDECOTT MEDAL with his second book, *Jumanji* (1981). This story is rooted in V.'s childhood memories of board games. *Ben's Dream* (1982) is a story of a young boy's dream seeing ten famous landmarks around the world. *The Wreck of the Zephyr* (1983) soars high in the sky in a boat with a boy and a mysterious tale. *The Mystery of Harris Burdick* (1984) is a collection of fourteen separate drawings and captions that invite readers to solve the mysteries.

V. won his second Caldecott Medal with *The Polar Express* (1985). On the tenth anniversary of the book's publication V. revealed the origin of the story. One snowy evening V. encountered a young red-haired, blue-eyed boy selling matches and trinkets in the street. Among the items for sale was a small bell. The boy told V. a magical story about the bell and offered to sell it to him for five dollars. When V. discovered that the bell did not ring he tried to return it, only to be met with sadness in the young boy's eyes. V. then reached into his wallet and offered the boy all of the cash he had. The young boy took the cash and only then did the bell begin to ring. But when V. turned to thank the boy, he had vanished like a heavenly angel. V. went home to record the young boy's story.

The Stranger (1986) changes seasons from winter to autumn. Since they contain several layers of meaning in text and illustrations, V.'s books appeal to children and adults alike. *The Z Was Zapped* (1987) is set in Alphabet Theater where words, letters, and action-packed illustrations become a play. *Two Bad Ants* (1988) venture into a cartoon FANTASY with red-hot dangers and bluish purple delights. Their adventure is short-lived because the ants learn that they need to be faithful to their nature to survive; they rejoin their colony.

Famous artists' techniques, such as Vermeer's use of light and Degas's craft of composition, are reflected in V. books. In *Just a Dream* (1990) V. uses light and composition to send a warning about our fragile environment. He sounds an alarm about the perils of watching too much television in *The Wretched Stone* (1991).

The Widow's Broom (1992) is a haunting story about a widow and a witch's broom that has lost its flying power. Good wins over evil when the kind, innocent widow and the broom trick their prejudiced, narrow-minded neighbors. Another struggle between good and evil appears in *The Sweetest Fig* (1993) in which a cruel dentist receives two magical figs as payment from one of his patients. The dentist soon realizes that eating the figs can make his dreams come true.

Bad Day at Riverbend (1995) appears to be a child's coloring book. The story takes the reader to a peaceful Western outpost called Riverbend. Suddenly a stagecoach arrives with its horses covered with "great stripes of some kind of shiny, greasy slime." An outside influence is involved and V.'s young daughter, Sophia, seems to be responsible.

AWARDS: AMERICAN LIBRARY ASSOCIATION Caldecott Medal Honor Book (1980) for *The Garden of Abdul Gasazi;* ALA Caldecott Medal (1982) for *Jumanji* and (1986) *The Polar Express; Boston Globe–Horn Book* Award for ILLUSTRATION for *The Garden of Abdul Gasazi* (1980); Awarded the Regina Medal for lifetime achievement in children's literature

FURTHER WORKS: *The Mystery of Harris Burdick,* 1984; *The Polar Express,* 1985; *The Stranger,* 1986; *Swan Lake* (illustrations), 1989; *The Widow's Broom,* 1992; *The Sweetest Fig,* 1993; *Bad Day at Riverbend,* 1995

BIBLIOGRAPHY: Kiefer, Barbara, selector, *Getting to Know You: Profiles of Children's Authors Featured in Language Arts, 1985–90,* 1991

DEBORAH W. WOOTEN

VAN LEEUWEN, Jean
Author, b. 26 December 1937, Glen Ridge, New Jersey

V. writes fiction and historical fiction in PICTURE BOOKS, easy readers, and middle-grade books with perception and HUMOR. She received a BA from Syracuse University in 1959 and started her writing and publishing career with *TV Guide.* Many of her books are based on her children; her husband served as technical consultant. V.'s first book was *Timothy's Flower* (1967). Her imaginative ANIMAL ADVENTURES include the exaggerated mice personalities in *The Great Cheese Conspiracy* (1969) and its sequels and the Oliver and Amanda EASY-TO-READ SERIES. Oliver and Amanda behave like small children, baking cookies, going to school, being read bedtime stories. It is in historical fiction for beginning readers that V. re-creates authentic scenes meaningful to very young children. *Fourth of July on the Plains* (1997), based on an actual diary account, conveys the danger and excitement of a wagon train on the Oregon Trail.

FURTHER WORKS: *I Was a 98-Pound Duckling.* 1972. *Too Hot for Ice Cream.* 1974. *Tales of Oliver Pig.* 1979. *Tales of Amanda Pig.* 1983. *Dear Mom, You're Ruining My Life.* 1989. *Going West.* 1992. *Bound for Oregon.* 1994. *Amanda Pig, Schoolgirl.* 1997

BIBLIOGRAPHY: Robb, Laura. "The Books of Jean Van Leeuwen." *Book Links.* March, 1995. *Something about the Author.* vols. 26 and 28

NANCY HORTON

VAN LOON, Hendrik Willem
Author, b. 14 January 1882, Rotterdam, Holland; d. 11 March 1944, Old Greenwich, Connecticut

V., a historian, journalist, and illustrator, was reared in Holland in a home that he remembered as somber. He was however, close to his mother who encouraged his drawing and sent him to art school. V. came to the U.S. in 1903 and studied at Harvard and Cornell Universities, then worked as a writer, illustrator, and lecturer in Europe and the United States. His works for children include *The Story of Mankind* (1921), a history of the world from prehistoric times to the early twentieth century. It was the first recipient of the newly created NEWBERY MEDAL in 1922. It is significant that the first book to receive the Newbery Medal was an INFORMATIONAL BOOK that revolutionized the way authors wrote for children. Without condescension V. brought a creative human voice to children's literature by introducing historical characters as real-life people; he presented history as more than a set of accumulated facts and dates of wars and kings' reigns. The book was made into a movie in 1957. Other works for children include *An Elephant up a Tree* (1933) and *Around the World with the Alphabet* (1935), which were both self-illustrated.

FURTHER WORKS: *History with a Match: Being an Account of the Earliest Navigators,* 1917; *The Story of THE BIBLE,* 1923; *The Story of Wilbur the Hat,* 1925; *America: Van Loon's Geography,* 1932; *The Life and Times of Simón Bolivar,* 1943

BIBLIOGRAPHY: *Dictionary of American Biography,* supp. 3: 1941–1945, 1973; MEIGS, C. et al., *A Critical History of Children's Literature,* 1969; *The Newbery and CALDECOTT Awards,* 2000; *Something about the Author,* vol. 115, 2000

MICHAEL O'LAUGHLIN

VENNEMA, Peter
Author, b. Date and place unknown

V. and his wife, Diane STANLEY, have collaborated on highly acclaimed picture-book biographies, STORYOGRAPHIES, such as *Shaka, King of the Zulus* (1988), Texas Bluebonnet Award Master List, *Bard of Avon: The Story of William Shakespeare* (1992), an AMERICAN LIBRARY ASSOCIATION Notable Book for that year as well as *Booklist's* 1992 Top of the List winner for nonfiction, and *Cleopatra* (1994). In each book, the team combines detailed research about the person and the period in which the subject lived in an incisively written text that has aesthetic appeal as well as interesting information for the reader. In each biography they go beyond the popularly held beliefs regarding the historical figure to reveal authentic personalities and life experiences,

making the character come alive for the reader. Illuminating gouache drawings created by Stanley are characterized by attention to period detail. The rich details support the factual, succinct, and yet dramatic biographies for which this team is well known.

FURTHER WORKS: *Good Queen Bess: The Story of Elizabeth I of England,* 1990; *Charles DICKENS: The Man Who Had Great Expectations,* 1993; *Shaka, King of the Zulus,* 1988

JANELLE B. MATHIS

VENTURA, Piero
Author, illustrator, b. 3 December 1937, Milan, Italy

V. enjoys traveling; his first book, *Piero Ventura's Book of Cities* (1975) presents well-known cities and towns around the world. He describes the book as a re-creation of scenes from cities he has visited and tried to describe to his sons in words and with sketches that are unique to his experiences and impressions. V. writes nonfiction, which includes BIOGRAPHIES of popular figures, famous archaeologists and their discoveries, and historical looks at cities, architecture, and Western civilization. V. is praised for his accurate and detailed illustrations.

V.'s art work has won numerous AWARDS. *Piero Ventura's Book of Cities* received several honors including the award of excellence from the Society of Illustrators (1976), inclusion in the American Institute of Graphic Arts Book show in 1976, book of the year by the American Institute of Graphic Arts (1977), and an Art Books for Children Citation from the Brooklyn Museum and the Brooklyn Public Library (1977, 1978, 1979). *Christopher Columbus* was selected as one of *School Library Journal's* Best Books for Spring (1979). V. received the Prix de Treize from the Office Chretien du Livre in 1979 and the Award from Ministero Spagnolo della Cultura in 1980 for *I Viaggi al Polo Nord. Pompei* received an Honorable Mention from the Biennale of ILLUSTRATION Bratislava (1983). *School Library Journal* (1983) chose *Grand Constructions* as a Best Book. *Venice* and *Anna dei porci* won the Pier Paolo Vergerio Honor Prize in 1989.

FURTHER WORKS: *Piero Ventura's Book of Cities.* 1975. *The Magic Well.* 1976. *The Painter's Trick.*

1977. *Anna dei porci.* 1987. *Venice: Birth of a City.* 1988. *Michelangelo's World.* 1989. *Great Composers.* 1988. Illus. only: *Christopher Columbus.* 1978. *I viaggi al Polo Nord.* 1979. *Houses: Structures, Methods, and Ways of Living.* 1993

BIBLIOGRAPHY: *Something about the Author,* vol. 61, 1990

JODI PILGRIM

VERNE, Jules

Author, b. 8 February 1828, Nantes, France; d. 24 March 1905, Amiens, France

V. promised his mother that he would travel "only in the imagination" when he returned home after running away to sea at the age of eleven. His promise came true as he became renowned for his SCIENCE FICTION writing. He first pursued a career in law, as his father, a lawyer, had hoped. But once V. moved to Paris he began to write, first plays and stories, a few of which were published or produced. Because of his limited success as a writer, and in order to support his family, he took a job at the Stock Exchange in Paris. He continued writing, but became frustrated with no success until he adapted a nonfiction piece on ballooning into his famed ADVENTURE STORY, *Five Weeks in a Balloon* (1863). His publisher offered V. a contract for future stories of adventure to be published serially in a new magazine. Over the next forty years he wrote over sixty books and short pieces, many of which were later to be categorized under the new term *science fiction.*

V. was thorough in his research on the many scientific and technical subjects he included in his novels. Even scientists were eager to read his new novels to learn of V.'s predictions for the future. He took what was known to be possible and let his imagination move forward in time, actually predicting later inventions such as the submarine and the radio. He is considered the originator of the science fiction genre; all of his stories had the possibility of actually happening in an era of scientific invention at the end of the nineteenth century. V. received the Legion of Honor from the French Academy.

FURTHER WORKS: *A Journey to the Center of the Earth,* 1864; *From the Earth to the Moon,* 1865;

Twenty Thousand Leagues under the Sea, 1870; *Around the World in Eighty Days,* 1873

SANDRA IMDIEKE

VIORST, Judith

Author, b. 2 February 1933, Newark, New Jersey

V. received a B.A. from Rutgers University in 1952. She is well known for her humorous children's books based on her own children, Anthony, Nicholas, and Alexander. However, her first published books consisted of nonfiction for children. V. presents her young characters realistically, including their shortcomings. Her SERIES of books about two brothers, Alexander and Anthony, capture the essence of sibling love and rivalry in humorous, everyday situations that young children gleefully recognize.

V. is praised for tackling difficult subjects, challenging sexist stereotypes, and presenting both children and their parents realistically. *The Tenth Good Thing about Barney* (1971), about the death of a child's beloved pet cat, is widely acknowledged as a helpful addition to the literature of death and grieving for children. Absorbed in his grief, a little boy cannot think of anything else until his mother gently encourages him to think of ten good things he remembers about Barney. V. is also a prominent adult author.

AWARDS: Christopher Award (1989) for *The Good-bye Book. New York Times* Best Illustrated Children's Books of the Year 1974 for *Rosie and Michael* (L. Tomei, illus). V. received the New Jersey Institute of Technology Award (1969) for *Sunday Morning* (1970) for *I'll Fix Anthony.* She was one of several to win an Emmy Award in 1970 for poetic monologues written for the television special, *Annie: The Women in the Life of a Man. School Library Journal* best books of the year (1972) for *Alexander and the Terrible, Horrible, No Good, Very Bad Day.* U. won the Silver Pencil Award (1973) for *The Tenth Good Thing about Barney.* In addition to these AWARDS for children's books, V. earned several awards for contributions to the magazine *Redbook*

FURTHER WORKS: *The Changing Earth,* 1967; *Sunday Morning,* 1968; *If I Were in Charge of the World and Other Worries: Poems for Children and Their Parents,* 1981; *I'll Fix Anthony,* 1969; *The Tenth Good Thing about Barney,* 1971; *Alexander and the Terrible, Horrible, No Good, Very Bad Day,* 1972; *Alexander, Who Used to Be Rich*

Last Sunday, 1978; *The Good-bye Book,* 1988; *Earrings!,* 1990

BIBLIOGRAPHY: *Children's Literature Review,* vol. 63, 1978; *Something about the Author,* vol. 70, 1993

JODI PILGRIM

VISUAL LITERACY

What is visual literacy, and why should those interested in children's literature be concerned about the topic? For a long time literacy was defined simply as the ability to process, decode, and respond to print. Later, writing literacy expanded the definition. Now, we can add yet a third component: visual literacy. This means the ability to receive, process, interact with, and respond to visual messages.

Awareness of the importance of this process is not new. J. J. Debes (1970) first estimated that over 80 percent of the information we receive comes to us visually. A wide variety of people in disparate but related fields have investigated various aspects of how viewers become more discriminating receivers of visual messages. Scholars often study moving images in film and video, and new interests in the visual nature of IN-TERNET RESOURCES have also emerged and are being researched and reported.

The illustrative art in PICTURE BOOKS and the nature of the book itself as a physical object with visual qualities is the focus of visual literacy for young literacy learners. Experts writing about picture books make much of the necessary integral relation between words and pictures in this medium, though indeed writing about the art in picture books has until recently been relatively unsophisticated, focusing more on describing what is in the pictures than on describing the artistic styles evident and mediums used. Attention to the physical nature of the book (i.e., such elements as size, vertical or horizontal orientation, binding, paper quality, type face, and other elements) has been largely ignored in the writing about picture books. Recent writing has become much more helpful in describing what viewers ought to see in picture books.

More information about the art in picture books has become available: publishers have begun including in the books notes about the art, though the practice is far from universal; review-ers devote increased attention to describing the art; and periodicals (like *Booklinks,* with a series of articles by Dilys Evans) have begun publishing serious articles about the topic of ILLUSTRATION.

Two kinds of writing are becoming available. One, there is more descriptive writing about the visual elements apparent in picture-book art, for example, see B. Z. Kiefer, 1995, or J. W. STEWIG, 1995. Two, we are beginning to get research reports about how children respond to the art in picture books and about the nature of planned programs to encourage children to interact with picture-book illustration. Some of this research comes from art educators, who are providing research data that suggest children can profitably be engaged in looking at, thinking about, and responding to the art in museums because it will affect their response to the art in books, as well. This comes as a result of the important pioneering work of the Getty Foundation, which was the major influence in promulgating the idea that children could study and respond critically to visuals. To support this effort, there are now fine children's books that explore the art of contemporary painters who are not book illustrators.

We know that adults can develop more sophisticated descriptions of the style of the art in picture books, and that we can help children learn something of this. We can describe illustration in terms of what styles it represents, for example, the realism of Gennady Spirin, the impressionism of Neil Waldman, the expressionism of Katya Arnold, or the abstraction of Synthia Saint James. We can describe and help children study what visual elements are apparent and which are most important in any given set of pictures. We could compare the line of Hans FISCHER with that of Pat CUMMINGS, the hard-edged shapes of Vladimir Radunsky with the softly focused shapes of Sandra Speidel, or the muted colors of Catherine Stock with the intense, highly saturated colors of Lois EHLERT. We can do the same sort of comparing and contrasting with such compositional principles as balance, repetition, and opposition. To help children begin to understand some of these ideas we can use the superb Looking at Paintings series. Ten volumes, arranged topically, present artists from many different periods, with ample opportunities to develop visual awareness.

Authors of reviews, longer articles, and books are now aware of the necessity of describing accurately and fully the nature of the art. More authors are beginning to be aware of the truth in J. Doonan's comments on the value of close, repeated looking, because "every mark matters." Some are extending this into recommendations about how much of this children should encounter and at what ages.

Children's response is much more fully understood now, and we know that even preschool children are (1) interested in talking about the art in picture books; and (2) much more capable of doing so than we thought was the case even a decade ago. What has become increasingly clear is the relation between visual perception and language: children seem better able to understand complex art in picture books as they use language to describe what they are seeing (Stewig, 1992).

We also know much more about how we structure individual experiences and entire sequential programs to maximize the increased awareness of and ability to describe art in books, which is children's potential. We are beginning to have descriptions of what has been done in classrooms with children and what the effects have been. For instance, we have learned that when kindergarten teachers talk about aesthetic qualities, similar increases in children's talk occurs. Some school districts, like Tucson, have begun implementing these programs in many classrooms to test their effectiveness.

So in just a decade of increased interest in the art of picture books, we have come a long way in refining our knowledge and expanding our ideas about what aspects of visual literacy can and should be studied. The result is that teachers and librarians have far clearer directions to pursue as they help children to develop deeper understanding of how to receive and respond to visuals.

Note: to learn more about this topic, contact the International Visual Literacy Association, at www.ivla.org: or contact the National Telemedia Council at Ntelemedia@aol.com.

BIBLIOGRAPHY: Braden, R. A. (1996). "Visual literacy, and Addendum to visual literacy." *Journal of Visual Literacy,* 16(2), 9–84. Debes, J. J., (1970). "The Loom of Visual Literacy—An Overview." In C. M. Williams and J. L. Debes (eds.), *Proceedings of the First National Conference on Visual Literacy.* Doonan, J. (1993). *Looking at Pictures in Picture Books.* Kiefer, B. Z. (1988). "Picture Books as Contexts for Literacy." *Language Arts; 65,* 260–71. Kiefer, B. Z. (1995). *The Potential of Picturebooks: From Visual Literacy to Aesthetic Understanding.* Rush, J. C., Greer, W. D., and Feinstein, H. (1986). "The Getty Institute: Putting Educational Theory into Practice." *Journal of Aesthetic Education,* 20(1), 85–95. Stewig, J. W. (1992). "Reading Pictures, Reading Text: Some Similarities." *The New Advocate,* S(1), 11–22. Stewig, J. W. (1994). "First Graders Talk about Painting." *The Journal of Educational Research,* 87(5), 309–16. Stewig, J. W. (1995). *Looking at Picture Books.* Stewig, J. W. (1997). Talking and Writing about Noah Variants. *Journal of Children's Literature,* 23(1), 54–61. Taunton M., and Colbert, C. (1984). "Artistic and Aesthetic Development: Considerations for Early Childhood Educators." *Childhood Education,* 61(1), 55–63

JOHN W. STEWIG

VIVAS, Julie
Illustrator, b. 1947, Adelaide, Australia

After receiving a diploma in Interior Design, V. worked for several years as an animator. Later she worked as a portrait artist in Spain until she returned to her native Australia. She continued as an artist, first entering the children's literature field in 1978. Her first successes came in partnership with Mem FOX, illustrating *Hush the Invisible Mouse.* In 1981 V. published her first written and illustrated book, *The Tram to Bondi Beach,* which was named a Highly Commended PICTURE BOOK of the Year by the AUSTRALIAN Children's Book Council.

V.'s watercolors are typified by their rounded shapes and soft edges, often using pastel tones. Her watercolor paintings visually capture her character's HUMOR and personality. One reviewer described her as having great "comic flair."

AWARDS: Australia Children's Book of the Year, picture book category (1990) for *The Very Best of Friends* (M. Wild, author). Highly Commended Picture Book of the Year by the Australian Children's Book Council, INTERNATIONAL BOARD ON BOOKS FOR YOUNG PEOPLE Honor Diploma for ILLUSTRATION (1986), and Australian Koala Award (1987) for *Possum Magic* (Mem Fox, author). AMERICAN LIBRARY ASSOCIATION Notable Book for *Wilfrid Gordon McDonald Partridge* (1985). *Boston Globe–Horn Book* Honor Book, Italy Bologna Children's Book Fair Commendation Premio Grafico Award, and ALA Notable Book of the Year for *The Nativity* (1986); The Dromkeen Award (1992)

FURTHER WORKS: *Stories from Our House.* 1987. *Stories from Our Street.* 1989. *I Went Walking.* 1990. *The Very Best of Friends.* 1990. *Let the Celebrations Begin!* 1991. *Our Granny.* 1994. *Let's Eat.* 1997

BIBLIOGRAPHY: *Seventh Book of Junior Authors and Illustrators.* 1996. *Something about the Author*, vol. 96, 1998

SANDRA IMDIEKE

VOIGT, Cynthia

Author, b. 25 February 1942, Boston, Massachusetts

V. grew up in southern Connecticut and graduated from Smith College in 1963. She became an English teacher more by happy accident than by design and as such discovered children's literature, a world of books she could read and recommend to and enjoy with her students. She is noted for her clear characterizations, skillful plotting and propensity for placing the children in her stories in hostile circumstances. Most of her books are deemed appropriate to YOUNG ADULT, rather than to juvenile, audiences.

Her first novel, *Homecoming* (1981), was nominated for the American Book Award. *Tell Me If All the Lovers Are Losers* (1982) was cited as a Best Young Adult Book that year by the AMERICAN LIBRARY ASSOCIATION. *Dicey's Song* (1982) won the ALA NEWBERY MEDAL in 1983, as well as a citation as a Best Children's Book. *A Solitary Blue* (1983) was named an ALA Best Young Adult Book in 1983, and a Newbery Honor book in 1984. Also in 1984, *The Calendar Papers* (1983) earned the Mystery Writers of America's Edgar Allen Poe Award in the juvenile category. *The Runner* (1985) earned both the Dutch Silver Pencil Award (1988) and the German Jungensbuchpreis (1989). In 1989, V. earned the ALAN Award for achievement in young adult literature.

Homecoming, Dicey's Song, A Solitary Blue, The Runner, Come a Stranger, (all 1986), *Sons from Afar* (1987), and *Seventeen against the Dealer* (1989) comprise a saga about the Tillerman family. With their father dead and their mother so mentally ill that she cannot care for them, the four Tillerman children, ranging from six to thirteen years old, leave home to travel to Maryland where they hope to be taken in by their grandmother. As in many of V.'s books, not only are the circumstances that set the plot in motion dire, but children and older adults work to achieve communication across a generation and experience gap. Some books in this saga diverge from focusing directly on the Tillermans to tell the stories of supporting characters. In *The Runner* and *Come a Stranger*, V. addresses racial prejudice. Critics disagree on the degree of success she has in her efforts to provide readers with a cogent understanding of this social issue, but her individual characters remain realistic and engaging.

Building Blocks (1984), intended for younger readers, was V.'s first foray into FANTASY. This is a brief and satisfying story of a boy's discovery that his father's own boyhood experiences shaped him into the grim man he has become. *Jackaroo* (1985), a Robin Hood–type story with a female protagonist, is set in the Middle Ages, incorporates some of the elements V. most enjoys in her own casual reading: romance and gothic ADVENTURE. *Wings of a Falcon* (1993) also employs fantasy while presenting readers with a substantive tale about slavery during the Middle Ages.

While the Tillerman saga relates the trials of characters who lack economic backing and social standing, as well as facing acute personal problems, V. also writes about middle-class teenagers facing perilous circumstances. In *Izzy, Willy-Nilly* (1986), she gives young adult readers a clear-eyed understanding of the title character, a girl who must learn to live without the leg she lost in a car accident (see THE DISABLED IN CHILDREN'S AND YOUNG ADULT LITERATURE). In *David and Jonathan* (1992) she incorporates two major and compelling issues, the HOLOCAUST and homosexuality. Less critically successful is *Orfe* (1993), which features the grimmer aspects of rock band life. *When She Hollers* (1994) is staged in a world lacking most trappings of ordinary family security. Here, V. offers a reality that is so harrowing that a lesser heroine than hers would fail not only herself but also young adult readers. However, the story of teenage Tess's dramatic response to years of sexual abuse by her stepfather, told in compact sentences and within the time frame of a single day, instead is inspiring. Written for young readers, *Bad Girls* (1996) and its less critically successful sequel, *Bad, Badder, Baddest* (1997) address concerns that border on the mundane. However, in V.'s hands the rebellious middle-grade girls who unite forces in spite of their initial enmity ring true and engaging.

V.'s years of teaching English clearly inform her fiction on two levels. First, she has excellent technical control of the craft of writing, a skill she worked to transmit to students in more than twenty years in the classroom. But it is her connection to young people—her own children, her students, and children she sees as she goes about her daily errands—on which she builds tales both dramatic and mundane that are accessible to and long remembered by her readers. The parameters within which many of her characters must cope have been cited as harsh and overloaded with negative adult roles. But her books attract young readers because they portray events young adolescents find credible even in—and often because of—the plots' starkness and because of the presence of compelling characters who act and change their unpromising circumstances.

FURTHER WORKS: *Tree by Leaf,* 1988; *On Fortune's Wheel,* 1990; *The Vandemark Mummy,* 1991

BIBLIOGRAPHY: *Contemporary Authors, New Revision Series,* vol. 18, 1986; Kiefer, Barbara, selector, *Getting to Know You: Profiles of Children's Authors Featured in Language Arts, 1985–90,* 1991; *Publishers Weekly,* July 18, 1994, pp. 225–26

FRANCISCA GOLDSMITH

WABER, Bernard

Author, illustrator, b. 27 September 1908, Philadelphia, Pennsylvania

In his more than twenty-four PICTURE BOOKS W. exhibits a thorough and compassionate understanding of the traumas of childhood and writes about them sympathetically from a child's perspective. In *Ira Sleeps Over* (1972), Ira worries that he will be teased about his attachment to a stuffed bear if he takes the bear to his friend's house. Likewise, Ira represents the confused emotions of many young children in *Ira Says Goodbye* (1988) when forced to say good-bye to a neighbor who is moving. *Gina* (1995) represents the transitions a child must make when moving and adopting a new group of playmates. In this case, Gina finds her new apartment building has many boys and no girls, so she must prove her ability to participate in boys' activities. Each story reflects W.'s childhood of frequently moving and subsequently relying on movies and the library to provide companionship during these times of transition. His imaginative talents, he has said, were probably nurtured by an after-school job in which he frequently saw the endings of movies and had to create his own beginnings and plot conflicts. Using FANTASY in text and illustrations, W. also realistically portrays the various feelings of childhood through imaginary characters such as Lyle, the Crocodile; or Shirley, the Lion.

W.'s rhyme and wordplay are most recognized in the character of Lyle. Lyle, the Crocodile, is a charming crocodile found in the bathtub of a family's new home in *The House on East 88th Street* (1962). Five following books about Lyle and his adopted family present a series of FANTASY situations with realistic, emotional, and humorous insights.

The interactive nature of *Do You See a Mouse?* (1955) delights many as characters in the text cannot see what the reader can see. Likewise, the humorous involvement with the story and illustrations in *A Lion Named Shirley Williamson* (1996) holds the reader's attention.

AWARDS: In 1962 W. received the *New York Tribune*'s Children's Spring Book Festival picture book honor, for *The House on East 88th Street*. *An Anteater Named Arthur* (1967) was selected one of the American Institute of Graphic Arts Children's Books for 1967–68. In 1971, *A Firefly Named Torchy* received the *Boston Globe-Horn Book* Honor Book for ILLUSTRATION. *Ira Sleeps Over* was included in the Children's Book Showcase of the CHILDREN'S BOOK COUNCIL, 1973; *But Names Will Never Hurt Me* was selected one of the Child Study Association's Children's Books of the Year in 1976. He was awarded the Lewis CARROLL Shelf Award in 1979 for *Lyle, Lyle, Crocodile*. *The Snake: A Very Long Story* was selected one of the INTERNATIONAL READING ASSOCIATION's Children's Choices in 1979. In addition to these AWARDS he has been honored by having his manuscripts included in THE KERLAN COLLECTION, University of Minnesota

FURTHER WORKS: *Lorenzo.* 1961. *How to Go about Laying an Egg.* 1963. *Rich Cat, Poor Cat.* 1963. *Just Like Abraham Lincoln.* 1965. *Lyle and the Birthday Party.* 1966. *An Anteater Named Arthur.* 1967. *Loveable Lyle.* 1969. *Lyle Finds His Mother.* 1974. *Bernard.* 1982. *Funny, Funny Lyle.*

1987. *Lyle at the Office.* 1994. *Bearsie Bear and the Surprise Sleepover Party.* 1997

BIBLIOGRAPHY: Silvey, A. ed. *Children's Books and Their Creators.* 1995. *Something about the Author,* vol. 95, 1998
JANELLE B. MATHIS

WADDELL, Martin (a.k.a. Catherine Sefton)

Author, b. 10 April 1941, Belfast, Northern Ireland

W., born in Belfast, Northern Ireland during an attack by Germany in World War II, was whisked away to the tranquil countryside of Newcastle in County Down where he spent his childhood days. While living in Newcastle, W. formed his love of literature. As a child, he loved to have people read to him. His favorites included works by Hans Christian ANDERSEN and the Brothers GRIMM. His life as a reader led him naturally to his life as a writer.

W. quit school before his sixteenth birthday and worked as an apprentice in a print shop. While there, he cherished the opportunity to work on his writing, but the required machinery work befuddled him. W., also an accomplished soccer player, left his apprentice position to play with a prestigious London soccer club. When that did not work out, he fell back on his writing. After creating many unsuccessful novels, W. had his first book, *Otley* (1966) published, which was an adult spy thriller. The book was adapted into a movie, and he continued writing novels for adults. He realized after publishing his first YOUNG ADULT novel, *In a Blue Velvet Dress: Almost a Ghost Story* (1972), that his writing is actually better when he uses fewer words. This book led him to write over 100 books for children and young adults.

W.'s books for children and young adults have been honored and applauded in various countries around the world. *Can't You Sleep, Little Bear?* (1989) won Belgium's Le Prix des Critiques de Livres pour Enfantes, as well as the Kate GREENAWAY MEDAL from the British Library Association (1988). *Island of the Strangers* was nominated for the CARNEGIE MEDAL in 1984, and also won the Smarties Grand Prize. *Rosie's Babies* was awarded the Best Book for Babies in 1990.

W.'s work is well known because he uses a light and entertaining tone to discuss topics such as family relationships, getting lost, overcoming fear of the dark, and not taking yourself too seriously. Children gain valuable life lessons from his literature, and learn how to reflect on what is important to them as they grow older, and how to learn from their experiences. In *The Big Big Sea* (1994), a young girl and her mother go on an adventure by sea one moonlit night. Together they discover the magic of the ocean at nighttime, and the majesty of their mother-daughter relationship. In *When the Teddy Bears Came* (1995) a young boy shows concern when his mother brings home a new baby, and all the focus turns to the new child. The boy begins to think there is no room left for him, until his mother makes room on her lap for both her children, which provides reassurance for big brothers and big sisters that there is room enough for everyone. Other books that focus on familial concerns include *Sam Vole and His Brothers* (1992), dealing with sibling rivalry; *Once There Were Giants* (1989) concerning growing up; *Sailor Bear* (1992) and its sequel *Small Bear Lost* (1996) discussing getting lost or losing something.

Many of W.'s books use animal characters to convey human characteristics and traits. W. employs this technique to see the "text as a patented 'script' that leaves room for interaction." Children find it easier to share their own fears and apprehensions by vicariously discussing what happens to the characters in his books. In W.'s well-known books about a little bear, including *Can't You Sleep, Little Bear* (1988), *Let's Go Home, Little Bear* (1991), *You and Me, Little Bear* (1996), and *Good Job, Little Bear* (1998), W. uses the bear family to discuss relationships between a young bear and his parents. W.'s other stories about ANIMALS with human qualities include: *Farmer Duck* (1991), *The Happy Hedgehog Band* (1991), *Owl Babies* (1992), and *Little Mo* (1993).

W. began writing longer books and SERIES BOOKS in 1978. The first series, his Napper books, brings the game of soccer to life for readers. Other series include Mystery Squad detective books, Harriet stories about an accident-prone child, and Little Dracula books about a young vampire and his family.

W. chose to use the pseudonym Catherine Sefton for his young adult works because he did not want these books to be confused with those he intended for adults. His young adult novels have received critical praise for examining the problems of Northern Ireland. *Island of the Strangers* (1983) has been commended for its powerful prose, portraying a busload of Belfast children who cause prejudice and violence to erupt when they enter a remote village. His Irish political trilogy *Starry Night* (1986), *Frankie's Story* (1988), and *The Beat of the Drum* (1989) helps teenagers understand the tragedies of Northern Ireland which W. believes will "one day bring that suffering to an end." Several of his young adult books including *In a Blue Velvet Dress* (1972), *The Sleepers on the Hill* (1973), and *Island of the Strangers* (1983) have become television movie productions.

W. takes several weeks every year to visit the schools of Northern Ireland to teach workshops to young writers. He teaches them the basics of a good plot and encourages them to use their imaginations to create their own stories. W. has clearly done this in his own writing for readers of all ages, which has made this Irish writer successful around the world.

FURTHER WORKS: *The Great Green Mouse Disaster.* 1981. *Going West.* 1983. *The Tough Princess.* 1987. *The Park in the Dark.* 1989. *Who Do You Love?* 1999

BIBLIOGRAPHY: *Booklist* (September, 1994; September, 1996; October, 1996), *Children's Literature Review,* vol. 31 (1993); *Horn Book* (1992, 1993, 1994, 1995, 1998, 1999); *Kirkus Reviews* (January, 1992; April, 1992; May, 1992; October, 1992; April, 1993; October, 1993; August, 1994; July, 1996; March, 1999); *Something about the Author,* vol. 81, 1995

DENISE P. BEASLEY

WAHL, Jan
Author, b. 1 April 1933, Columbus, Ohio

In early childhood W. discovered his desire to tell stories and to connect pictures with stories. He has created more than seventy-five picture-book stories, usually featuring animals, which give young readers truths they can understand. W.'s interest in animated film informs his STORYTELLING technique, allowing dozens of illustrators to work with him to produce critically acclaimed books. After graduating from Cornell University (1953), W. won a Fulbright Scholarship. He returned from Denmark to a scholarship at the University of Michigan, where he earned an M.A. (1958). The *Woman with the Eggs* (1974) received an AMERICAN LIBRARY ASSOCIATION Notable Book citation. *Tiger Watch* (1982) won a Parents' Choice literary award.

Maurice SENDAK illustrated W.'s first successful book, *Pleasant Fieldmouse* (1964). Pleasant returns in several books, variously illustrated by Peter PARNALL, Wallace TRIPP and Erik BLEGVAD. W. also has worked with Edward GOREY (*Cobweb Castle,* 1968), Steven KELLOGG (*Crabapple Night,* 1971), Cyndy SZEKERES (*Doctor Rabbit's Lost Scout* 1979) and William JOYCE (*Humphrey's Bear,* 1987).

W. bases some of his stories on European and AFRICAN AMERICAN folklore as well as on THE BIBLE. His rollicking adaptation of *Little Eight John* (Wil Clay, illus. 1992), based on a well-known character in African American FOLKLORE, is a CORETTA SCOTT KING Illustrator Honor Book. In 1969, he worked with Norman Rockwell to produce *The Norman Rockwell Storybook,* comprising the painter's famous ILLUSTRATIONS accompanied by W.'s stories of the characters they depict. W. has published one volume of children's verse, *The Beast Book* (1964), and has written short stories for YOUNG ADULTS.

FURTHER WORKS: The *Muffletumps.* 1966. *Pocahontas in London.* 1967. *The Furious Flycycle.* 1968. *How the Children Stopped the Wars.* 1969. *Magic Heart.* 1972. *Dracula's Cat.* 1977. *The Teeny Tiny Witches.* 1979. *The Little Blind Goat.* 1981. *Once When the World Was Green.* 1996. *The Singing Geese.* 1998

BIBLIOGRAPHY: *Something about the Author*, vol. 73, 1993. *Something about the Author Autobiography Series*, vol. 3, 1986

FRANCISCA GOLDSMITH

WALLACE, Ian
Author, illustrator, b. 31 March 1950, Niagara Falls, Ontario, Canada

Growing up, W. spent weekends exploring the Canadian countryside with his family. At the age of thirteen he announced he was going to be an artist. His goal in creating children's fiction is to intrigue, inspire, and touch young readers: "Everything creative must have a purpose and a reason for its expression."

Chin Chiang and the Dragon's Dance (1984) took six years to create and was inspired by seeing a New Year's celebration that included the dragon's dance. W.'s full-page watercolor paintings capture Chin Chiang's nervousness, his grandfather's love and encouragement and the excitement of the performance as well. The book received the Amelia Frances Howard-Gibbon Medal for ILLUSTRATION from the Canadian Library Association and was included on the INTERNATIONAL BOARD ON BOOKS FOR YOUNG PEOPLE Honor List.

Working mostly in pencil, watercolor, and gouache, many of W.'s books are published simultaneously in the United States and Canada. *The Very Last First Time* (Andrews, 1985), exhibited at the Bologna International Children's Book Fair, is one example. In this title as well as in Valgardson's *Sarah and the People of the River* (1996), W.'s illustrations create a realistic picture of the NATIVE AMERICAN Inuit population. Illustrated with W.'s pastel prints, *The Name of the Tree: A Bantu Folktale* (1989), retold by Celia Lottridge, garnered the Mr. Christie's Book Award for English Illustration, the Elizabeth Mrazik-Cleaver Canadian PICTURE BOOK Award and was second runner-up for the Amelia Francis Howard-Gibbon Illustrator Award.

FURTHER WORKS: *The Sparrow's Song*, 1986; *Morgan the Magnificent*, 1987

BIBLIOGRAPHY: *Children's Literature Review*, vol. 37, 1996; *Fiction, FOLKLORE, FANTASY and POETRY for Children, 1876–1985*, 1986; *Something about the Author*, vol. 56, 1989

IRVYN G. GILBERTSON

WALTER, Mildred Pitts

Author, b. 9 September 1922, De Ridder, Louisiana

W. began to write for children in 1969 after seventeen years of teaching. She incorporated her principles of community, family, and hard work in the plots and characters of her fiction. As a teacher, she had noticed that few books portrayed contemporary AFRICAN AMERICAN children. W. was encouraged to write them herself, and her award-winning career as an author began. W. was the seventh child of a hardworking Louisiana family, growing up in a time and location where racism was common. Her African American community and family provided a solid foundation of values, and her childhood memories of racism, as well as her participation in the civil rights movement contribute to the themes found in her books. For example, the main character in W.'s first book, *Lillie of Watts: A Birthday Surprise* (1969), learns that the strength of family can overcome any other troubles.

Regarding the craft of writing, W. notes that the author must have a love for the story and a love for the words in that story. The basic skills of writing must first be learned before one can become the artist. W. began to write novels in the early 1980s after struggling through the 1970s, a time when literature portraying African American children was less in demand. W. states that the theme in many of her books "is the dynamics of choice, courage, and change." She believes that today's children are presented with particular challenges as they make choices since the guidance of community and family are absent for many children.

AWARDS: Irma Simonton Black Award Honor book (1981) for *Ty's One Man Band*. CORETTA SCOTT KING Author Honor Book (1993) for *Mississippi Challenge*, (1984) for *Because We Are* and (1986), for *Trouble's Child* and winner (1987), for *Justin and the Best Biscuits in the World*. Coretta Scott King Illustrator Award winner (1984) for *My Mama Needs Me* (Pat CUMMINGS, illus.)

FURTHER WORKS: *Lillie of Watts Takes a Giant Step*. 1971. *The Girl on the Outside*. 1982. *Brother to the Wind*. 1985. *Have a Happy*. 1989. *Mariah Keeps Cool*. 1990. *Mississippi Challenge*. 1992. *Darkness*. 1995. *Kwanzaa: A Family Affair*. 1995. *Second Daughter: The Story of a Slave Girl*. 1996

BIBLIOGRAPHY: *Something about the Author*, vol. 69, 1992

SANDRA IMDIEKE

WATERS, Kate

Author, photographer, editor, b. 4 September 1951, Rochester, New York

W.'s mother read to the six Waters children every day and W. started keeping a diary in second grade, writing poems and stories. After college W. attended library school and worked as a children's and YOUNG ADULT librarian. As a LIBRARIAN, she would act out books with children during story hour and give book talks. The first book she wrote, *Sarah Morton's Day: A Day in the Life of a Pilgrim Girl* (1989) evolved from a trip to Plimoth Plantation where she took photographs from the Plantation's living history museum in costumes re-creating the era for visitors. That was the beginning of the Plimoth Plantation series based on real people of the time. *Sarah Morton's Day,* an INTERNATIONAL READING ASSOCIATION Teachers Choice and Notable Children's Trade Book in the Field of Social Studies winner, re-creates in a simple-story context a typical day in the life of a nine-year-old in 1627: doing her chores, learning to read, having a friend. Its companion volume, *Samuel Eaton's Day: A Day in the Life of a Pilgrim Boy* (1993), is an American Bookseller Pick of the Lists title. Also included in the series are *On the Mayflower: Voyage of the Ship's Apprentice and a Passenger Girl* (1996) and *Tapenum's Day: A Wampanoag Indian Boy in Pilgrim Times* (1996). W.'s photographs provide an abundance of authentic detail while evoking a sense of looking back in time. W. says, "I love writing. It combines the things that were so important to me growing up—STORYTELLING and immersing myself in another time and place."

Lion Dancer: Ernie Wan's Chinese New Year (1990), a READING RAINBOW selection and Notable Children's Trade Book in the Field of Social Studies, is a photo essay of a boy's first participation in his community's annual New Year celebration. W.'s photos are bright, vivid, crackling with the excitement of a Chinese New Year community celebration. *The Story of the White House* (1991) is also an American Bookseller Pick of the Lists and a Notable Children's Trade Book in the Field of Social Studies.

BIBLIOGRAPHY: Biographical information from *Scholastic,* 1999, courtesy of Stephanie Wimmer

IRVYN G. GILBERTSON

WARD, Lynd

Illustrator, b. 26 June 1905, Chicago, Illinois; d. 28 June 1985, Reston, Virginia

W., a graphic artist and illustrator, grew up in Chicago as well as in the Canadian wilderness where his parents had built a cabin. W.'s father was involved with the movement sparked by Jane Addams to improve conditions of those who lived around Chicago's stockyards; his father's influence was reflected in his work that showed a profound respect for the dignity of the human spirit in all peoples. Summers spent on Lonely Lake in Canada gave W. a closeness with the strength of the wilderness. His early experiences with books resulted in great interest in the form of literature and its accompanying art. He graduated from Columbia University with a major in fine arts in 1926 where his interest in children's books developed. Later, he studied at the National Academy for Graphic Arts in Leipzig, Germany. Upon return to the United States, his wife May McNeer began writing children's books and W. wrote *God's Man* (1929), his first novel illustrated with woodcut engravings. A totally wordless book, the graphics depicted the notion that man bargains for creative talents in exchange for a shortened life. After creating five more books with wood engraving, W.'s reputation was established as the first American creator of wordless novels.

W.'s interest in the craftsmanship of book making and the interrelated style of type and picture established him as one of the first artists to express a philosophy of illustrating children's books. The unity of text and pictures that both tell the story in a PICTURE BOOK was enhanced by his unique understandings and skill as a graphic artist. His own first authored and illustrated children's book was *The Biggest Bear* (1952), which won the ALA CALDECOTT MEDAL in 1953.

He also illustrated several NEWBERY MEDAL winners. The research and collaboration of W. and his wife, May McNeer, when writing *Lincoln* exemplified the magnitude of research necessary on both the subject and the material in the political, social, and cultural era in which he lived. W.'s collaborative efforts made him aware of the necessity of working together at all stages of the creative effort. He considered McNeer the writer and said that he told stories through his art that sometimes needed words. The significance of his work is seen in its inclusion in THE KERLAN COLLECTION at the University of Minnesota.

AWARDS: As illustrator of AMERICAN LIBRARY ASSOCIATION Newbery Medal Honor Books (1930) for *Little Blacknose* (Hildegarde SWIFT), (1931)

for *Spice and the Devil's Cave* (A. Hewes), (1938) for *Bright Island* (Mabel Robinson), (1940) for *Runner of the Mountain Tops* (Mabel Robinson), (1944) for *Fog Magic* (Julia Sauer). As illustrator of AMERICAN LIBRARY ASSOCIATION Newbery Medal Books (1931) for *The Cat Who Went to Heaven* (E. COATSWORTH), (1944) for *Johnny Tremain* (Kathryn FORBES). *New York Herald Tribune* Spring Book Festival Award Honor book, 1937, 1947, 1953, 1955. Library of Congress award for wood engraving, 1948. National Academy of Design print award, 1949. ALA Caldecott Honor Book (1950) for *America's Ethan Allen* (Stewart Holbrook, author). ALA Caldecott Medal (1953) for *The Biggest Bear*. Samuel F. B. Morse Medal (1966) Rutgers University Award (1969) for "a distinguished contribution to literature for children and young people." Silver medallion from the DE GRUMMOND REFERENCE COLLECTION, University of Southern Mississippi (1973) "for distinguished service to children's literature." Lewis CARROLL Shelf Award and *New York Times* Best Illustrated Children's ILLUSTRATION (1973) for *The Silver Pony*

FURTHER WORKS: *Bright Island,* 1937; *North Star Shining,* 1947; *Martin Luther,* 1953; *Santiago,* 1955

BIBLIOGRAPHY: HOPKINS, Lee Bennett, *Pauses: Autobiographical Reflections of 101 Creators of Children's Books,* 1995; MEIGS, C. et al., *A Critical History of Children's Literature,* 1969

JANELLE B. MATHIS

WATSON, Clyde
Author, b. 25 July 1947, New York City

WATSON, Wendy
Illustrator, b. 7 July 1942, Paterson New Jersey

Two sisters, Clyde (C.W.) and Wendy (W.W.), work as an author-illustrator team. W.W. is most often recognized for her illustrations; C.W. is most often recognized as a writer. The two sisters received much support and training from their parents in drawing and reading. Scenes from their childhood appear in both their texts and illustrations. Their award-winning collaboration, *Father Fox's Pennyrhymes* (1971) was widely praised by critics and was called an American original by a *New York Times* critic. As other of their books, there is a distinct early American perspective in their works. They depict childhood in rural Vermont throughout their work with one-room

schoolhouses, maple sugar, country fairs, apple cider, and colorful autumn leaves. The illustrations reflect a New England country charm with authentic color and attention to small eye-catching details. C.W., composer of music and a professional violinist, wrote some of the original lyrics to *Father Fox's Pennyrhymes* as songs played on a guitar. She has also played violin professionally. C.W. said, "Ideas for stories are everywhere—all around me. The hard part is putting them on paper so that they come out the way I want them to. I like reading to people—children and grown-ups too—and I often read out loud to myself when I'm working on a new story." C.W. also plays with POETRY, as seen in her book for young children, *Catch Me and Kiss Me and Say It Again* (1992).

W.W. fills her cartoonlike drawings with minute details of early American FOLKLORE. Her watercolor and pen-and-ink illustrations, with their rural New England settings, remind readers of an earlier, slower time when families collected and prepared their own maple syrup and went to country fairs. Her characters are animal or human families who enjoy closely knit family activities and reflect the warmth of C.W.'s traditionally American MOTHER GOOSE-style verses. As she did in *Tales for a Winter's Eve* (1988) W.W. occasionally writes her own PICTURE BOOKS.

AWARDS: *New York Times* Outstanding Book citation (1971), Children's Book Showcase Award of the CHILDREN'S BOOK COUNCIL (1972), *School Library Journal* Best Book (1971), and Association of American Publishers National Book Award finalist citation (1972) all for *Father Fox's Pennyrhymes.* American Institute of Graphic Arts Children's Book Show (1972) and the Biennial of Illustrations (1973) for *Father Fox's Pennyrhymes.* Wendy has received several AWARDS for ILLUSTRATION such as the inclusion of *Fisherman Lullabies* in the American Institue of Graphic Arts children's books show 1967–68 and the inclusion of *When Noodlehead Went to the Fair* in the Printing Industries of America Graphic Arts Awards Competition (1969)

FURTHER WORKS: *Tom Fox and the Apple Pie,* 1972; *Binary Numbers,* 1977; *Hickory Stick Rag,* 1976; *Valentine Foxes,* 1981

BIBLIOGRAPHY: *Children's Literature Review,* vol. 74, pp. 241–42; *Something about the Author,* vol. 74 (1993); *Something about the Author,* vol. 68 (1992)

JANELLE B. MATHIS

WEBSTER, Jean
Author, b. 24 July 1876, Fredonia, New York; d. 11 June 1916, New York City

Jane Chandler, the grandniece of Mark TWAIN, wrote under the pen name of Jean Webster. She received a B.A. from Vassar in 1901. While studying at Vassar, she visited institutions for the destitute and delinquent, which helped her form her belief that underprivileged children could succeed in life. This belief led to the story of the delightful orphan character Jerusha in *Daddy-Long-Legs* (1912) and the humorous account that began as a novel but eventually became a four-act play and popular movie.

FURTHER WORKS: *When Patty Went to College,* 1903; *Much Ado about Peter,* 1909; *Dear Enemy,* 1915

BIBLIOGRAPHY: *Something about the Author,* vol. 17, 1979

NANCY HORTON

WEIL, Lisl
Author, illustrator, b. 1910, Vienna, Austria

W. was educated in Vienna, came to the United States in 1939, and became a naturalized citizen in 1944. Having both written and illustrated books for children, her love of drawing and MUSIC came together as she illustrated the music being played on stage at children's concerts of The Little Orchestra Society at New York's Carnegie Hall and Philharmonic Hall. Creating life-size figures in perfect rhythm to the music also included choreographed movements that W. referred to as "real picture ballet." Her goal was to make "audiences listen with their eyes as well as their ears." She hopes young readers will find her stories humorous and yet still provide thoughtful situations, as in *Foolish King* (1982) or *Melissa* (1969). Her books represent several genres including BIBLE STORIES, historical interpretations, and adaptations of operas and musical scores. W. has also illustrated for authors like Marjorie Wienman SHARMAT in *51 Sycamore Lane* and for major publishing companies of children's reading SERIES.

FURTHER WORKS: *Fat Ernest,* 1973; *Foolish King,* 1982; *Let's Go to the Museum,* 1989; *The Magic of Music,* 1989; *Wolfer,* 1991

BIBLIOGRAPHY: *Something about the Author,* vol. 10, 1975

JANELLE B. MATHIS

WEISGARD, Leonard
Author, illustrator, b. 13 December 1916, New Haven, Connecticut; d. 14 January 2000, Copenhagen Denmark

W., the author and illustrator of more than 180 books for children, had a career that spanned over fifty years. W. moved frequently during his childhood and became a resident of Denmark in 1970. As a child he moved from the United States to his father's homeland and then to England where he met many people in many different contexts. The family returned to America while W. was still a child, and a teacher in New York nurtured his drawing and painting abilities. As a young person, he often read and felt that books, especially those used as text books, were dreary. After graduating from high school, W. studied graphic arts at Brooklyn's Pratt Institute and the New School for Social Research in New York. W. and his friends felt that they could contribute to creating better books to which children could relate. His first book was *Suki the Siamese Pussy* (1937).

Margaret Wise BROWN was influential in W.'s artistic studies; he collaborated with her on more than twenty-five books—the first one was *The Noisy Book* (1939). His art consisted of a variety of media—water color, gouache, poster paint, crayon, chalk, ink, or whatever the story itself suggests. He also emphasized the importance of experiencing the subject. To prepare for illustrating *The Little Island* (1946), W. spent time on the actual island off the coast of Maine. He collected impressions of the constantly changing environment that are reflected in the ILLUSTRATIONS. The subjects for his many books come from a variety of emotional impressions and sensory experiences.

AWARDS: ALA CALDECOTT MEDAL (1947) for *The Little Island.* ALA Caldecott Medal Honor Book (1946) for *Little Lost Lamb,* (1947) for *Rain Drop Splash,* (1955) for *The Secret River,* and (1956) for *Treasures to See. New York Herald Tribune* Spring Book Festival Award (1944) for *Dorinda.* The Spring Book Festival AWARDS, Middle Honor (1952) for *Indian, Indian,* and (1954) for *The Courage of Sarah Noble.* Lewis CARROLL Shelf Award (1959) for *The Courage of Sarah Noble* (Alice DALGLIESH, author), and George G. Stone

Center for Children's Books Recognition of Merit Award (1968) for *White Bird*

FURTHER WORKS: Self-illustrated, some under the pseudonym Adam Green: *Whose Little Bird Am I?* 1944. *The Plymouth Thanksgiving.* 1967. *The Funny Bunny Factory.* 1950. *Silly Willy Nilly.* 1953. *The Most Beautiful Tree in the World.* 1956. *Treasure to See, A Museum* PICTURE BOOK. 1956. Illustrator: *The Indoor Noisy Book* (M. W. Brown). 1942. *Night and Day.* 1942. *The Noisy Bird Book.* (M. W. Brown). 1943. *Heidi* (SPYRI). 1946. *Rain Drop Splash.* (Alvin TRESSELT). 1946. *The Important Book.* 1949. *Whistle for the Train.* 1956. *Favorite Poems Old and New.* (Helen FERRIS). 1957. *Baby Elephant's Trunk.* (Sesyle JOSLIN). 1961. *Hailstones and Halibut Bones.* (M. O'NEILL). 1961. *See along the Shore.* (Millicent SELSAM). 1961. *Like Nothing at All.* (Aileen FISHER). 1962. *The Lost Prince.* 1967. *Wake up and Good Night.* 1971

BIBLIOGRAPHY: HOPKINS, Lee Bennett, *Pauses: Autobiographical Reflections of 101 Creators of Children's Books,* 1995; *Something about the Author,* vol. 85, 1996

JANELLE B. MATHIS

WELLS, H(erbert) G(eorge)
Author, b. 21 September 1866, Bromley, Kent, England; d. 13 August 1946, London, England

W. is most famous as a writer of SCIENCE FICTION and a social critic. Although not intended for children, many of his science fiction novels have been read and enjoyed particularly by YOUNG ADULTS. His childhood was spent in poverty, which undoubtedly influenced his fascination with socialism. He turned to books early and studied at London University. W. became friends with Hubert Bland and his wife, Edith NESBIT, who is said to have been influenced in her time-travel FANTASY writing by W. His first great success was *The Time Machine* (1895), followed by, among others, *The Island of Doctor Moreau* (1896), *The Invisible Man* (1897), and *The War of the Worlds* (1898). The only true children's story he wrote is an inconsequential piece, *The Adventures of Tommy* (written 1898, published 1929).

W. quickly gained celebrity status and, partly because of the social views expressed in his writings, was invited by Bernard Shaw to join the Fabian Society in 1903. Although known as a science fiction writer, his books are, in fact, thinly

veiled social commentary. His writing, colored by a pervasive pessimism, is filled with forebodings about the future of humankind. Unlike Jules VERNE, W. had little real interest in scientific matters and called his works "social fables," unabashedly using his creative talents to political ends. Critics see his penchant for propagandizing as the fundamental flaw in his art, and the principal reason his reputation has declined since his death.

BIBLIOGRAPHY: *The Oxford Companion to Children's Literature,* 1984; Costa, R. H., *H. G. W.,* 1967; Murray, Brian. *H. G. W.,* 1990; *Something about the Author,* vol. 20, 1980

DAVID L. RUSSELL

WELLS, Rosemary
Author, illustrator, b. 29 January 1943, New York City

W. has earned popular and critical acclaim in two markedly different venues of children's literature. Her psychological thrillers for YOUNG ADULTS and her expressively anthropomorphic PICTURE BOOKS address opposite ends of the juvenile book spectrum, but through each she provides young readers with emotionally satisfying characterizations and plots.

W. finalized her indifferent career as a student with studies at Boston's Museum School. Theater, rather than representational art, stimulated her imagination, and she has applied her understanding of comedy, character, and setting to both her narrative and her ILLUSTRATION work. W. entered the world of children's publishing, first as an editor, then as a picture book illustrator, and finally as an author/illustrator. In all these fields she has been successful and innovative. Her first published illustration work was Gilbert and Sullivan's lyrics from *The Yeoman of the Guard* in *"A Song to Sing, O!"* (1968). She has illustrated writings by other authors in the years since, including those of Robert W. SERVICE, Rudyard KIPLING, Paula FOX, and Ellen CONFORD.

In 1974, the CHILDREN'S BOOK COUNCIL honored her self-illustrated picture book, *Noisy Nora* (1973) with the Book Showcase Award. *Benjamin and Tulip* (1973) earned a Citation of Merit in 1974 from the Society of Illustrators. Both of these picture books earned Notable Book citations from the AMERICAN LIBRARY ASSOCIATION, as did *Morris's Disappearing Bag: A Christmas Story* (1975), *Max's Breakfast* (1985), *Max's Christmas* (1986), *Max's Chocolate Chicken* (1989), and *Max's Dragon Shirt* (1991). *Morris's Disappearing Bag* (1992) and *Don't Spill It Again, James* (1977) were cited by the Child Study Association as Children's Books of the Year. *Max's Chocolate Chicken, Timothy Goes to School* (1981), *A Lion for Lewis* (1982) and *Peabody* (1983) each merited the INTERNATIONAL READING ASSOCIATION Children's Choices citation. In 1981, her fourth young adult novel, *When No One Was Looking* (1980), earned the Mystery Writers of America's Edgar Allan Poe Special Award. *Through the Hidden Door* (1987), her sixth young adult novel, was cited by ALA as a Best Book for Young Adults. *Shy Charles* (1988) earned the Parents' Choice Award. *Forest of Dreams* (1988), authored by W. and illustrated by Susan JEFFERS, earned the SOCIETY OF CHILDREN'S BOOK WRITERS AND ILLUSTRATORS Golden Kite Award. *The Little Lame Prince* (1990), self-illustrated by W., won the Blue Ribbon from the Bulletin for the Center for Children's Books.

The creatures who inhabit W.'s picture books are mice, rabbits, and other small woodland mammals who are, indisputably to even the youngest reader, human children. The dramas in which Noisy Nora, Max, and his sister Ruby, and the array of other engagingly fuzzy and cutely dressed beings disport, revolve around sibling rivalry issues and other dilemmas of very early childhood. W. supports her claim to be a storyteller first and an illustrator next, for the narrative flow within the briefest of her books—some of which are board book length at sixteen pages—is cogent. She bases the plotlines of these toddler stories on her observations of her own children's early struggles with family and social dynamics. The words of the texts are rhythmic and easy for the (adult) reader to replay with the intense frequency often demanded from the target audience. Although the images are cute, the narratives are not saccharine.

The psychologically astute MYSTERIES W. writes for young teens, on the other hand, are based on memories of her own youth. Her youthful characters are well rounded, realistic in their flawed viewpoints, appropriately mature—as well

as being fully human, not anthropomorphized!—and caught in both physical and emotional dangers. In *The Man in the Woods* (1984), the action is oriented around both contemporary and historical events as a ninth-grade girl, accompanied by a newly made male friend, works to solve a problem in which authorities seem to lack sufficient interest. The main characters in *Through the Hidden Door* are both male and, like protagonists in several other novels by W., boarding school students. In all these young adult stories, the protagonists are thoughtful as well as actively engaged in events which have ethical and moral issues to be confronted and resolved. The relative flatness of the adult characters complements W.'s arrangement of her picture-book stories to render small children central and their parents, or other significant adults, on the periphery. (One exception is *Shy Charles,* where the eponymous child is taken by his mother from adult encounter to adult encounter.)

In 1992, W. published three small volumes as the Voyage to the Bunny Planet series. *First Tomato, The Island Light,* and *Moss Pillows* each present a child for whom things are not going well, due to illness, accident or other misfortune. Janet, of the Bunny Planet, is the proposed alternative made by the invisible narrator. Unlike books in the Max series, the Bunny Planet books sound repetitious and are too tiny to be handled by toddlers. Max himself reappears in two picture books, *Bunny Cakes* and *Bunny Money* (both 1997).

Also in 1997, W. published a re-illustrated *Noisy Nora,* offering readers a brasher and bigger little rodent girl in need of attentions lost to her baby brother. This new version is satisfying to both those familiar with the old Noisy Nora and to new W. readers. *Yoko* (1998) presents picturebook readers with a MULTICULTURAL experience in a story about a Japanese American primary school girl (kitten) who is teased for bringing sushi for lunch. W. demonstrates her ability to work through this sort of childhood crisis that, heretofore, has been absent in not only her writings but in the vast majority of works for preschoolers.

W.'s recent collaborations include a new edition titled *Rachel FIELD's Hitty: Her First Hundred Years* (1999) with Susan Jeffers. Field's novel, winner of the 1930 NEWBERY MEDAL, has been edited for today's readers accustomed to briefer texts with lush full-color illustrations on every page. As illustrator she has also collaborated with Iona OPIE on two classic nursery rhyme collections: *My Very First MOTHER GOOSE* (1996) and *Here Comes Mother Goose* (1999).

FURTHER WORKS: *Martha's Birthday.* 1970. *The Fog Comes on Little Pig Feet.* 1972. *None of the Above.* 1974. *Abdul.* 1975. *Leave Well Enough Alone.* 1977. *Stanley and Rhoda.* 1978. *Max's First Word.* 1979. *Max's New Suit.* 1979. *Max's Bath.* 1985. *Hazel's Amazing Mother.* 1985. *Fritz and the Mess Fairy.* 1991. *Max and Ruby's First Greek Myth: Pandora's Box.* 1993. *The Fisherman and His Wife.* 1998. *Emily's First 100 Days of School.* 2000

BIBLIOGRAPHY: *Contemporary Authors, New Revision Series,* vol. 48, 1995; Long, J., *"How They've Grown! Nora and Tommy Try on New Sizes," Horn Book,* September–October 1998; *Something About the Author,* vol. 18, 1980, and vol. 69, 1992
                                    FRANCISCA GOLDSMITH

WERSBA, Barbara
Author, b. 19 August 1932, Chicago, Illinois

W. lived in suburban San Francisco until age eleven, moving with her mother to New York City following her parents' divorce. She studied acting at Bard College but recognized that she did not like to act and turned to writing in her twenties. W. has published nine books for children, including two books of POETRY, and more than a dozen YOUNG ADULT novels.

AWARDS: Deutscher Jugend Buchpreis (1973) for *Run Softly, Go Fast.* ALA Best Book for Young Adults (1976), Notable Children's Book (1976), and National Book Award nomination (1977) for *Tunes for a Small Harmonica.* ALA Best Book for Young Adults (1982) for *The Carnival in My Mind*

FURTHER WORKS: Fiction for children: *The Boy who Loved the Sea,* 1961; *The Brave Balloon of Benjamin Buckley,* 1963; *The Legend of Forgotten Beasts,* 1964; *A Song for Clowns,* 1965; *Let Me Fall before I Fly,* 1971; *Amanda, Dreaming,* 1973; *The Crystal Child,* 1982; poetry for children: *Do Tigers Ever Bite Kings?,* 1966; *Twenty-six Starlings Will Fly through Your Mind,* 1980; *Beautiful Losers,* 1988; *The Best Place to Live Is the Ceiling,* 1990; *Whistle Me Home,* 1997

BIBLIOGRAPHY: *Contemporary Authors, New Revision Series,* 1993; *Something about the Author,* vol. 103, 1999, and vol. 58, 1990
                                    DIANE L. CHAPMAN

WESTALL, Robert
Author, b. 7 October 1929, Tynemouth, England; d. 15 April 1993, Cheshire, England

W., considered one of the best writers for YOUNG ADULTS, writes REALISTIC FICTION, historical fiction, supernatural and ghost stories, time travel, and SCIENCE FICTION. W. credited his father's influence on his writing through his own creativity reflected in the things he made for his home and the self-reliance with which he controlled his own life. His self-confidence in school supported his early desire and attempts to write, although none of the efforts went beyond drafts until after he finished college at the University of Durham.

W. wrote his first book, *The Machine Gunners* (1975), to share with his twelve-year-old son about how it had felt to be twelve. The book was awarded the CARNEGIE MEDAL. When the story was published, it was praised and criticized for its realistic events, language, and violence. In the story a young man finds a machine gun during World War II, and with friends decides to use it to threaten enemy bombers. The novel shows people's weariness with the war, destruction of towns, and the actions of the desperate, cowardly, and courageous. The authentic context helps support W.'s theme that violence does not pay. Young people and war are also the focus of *Children of the Blitz: Memories of Wartime Childhood* (1985), *Blitzcat* (1989), and *The Kingdom by the Sea* (1991).

W.'s other works include *The Devil on the Road* (1978), a novel whose main character travels through time; it was based on W.'s own son who was killed in an accident at age eighteen. *The Scarecrows* (1980), which won a second Carnegie Medal for W., deals with the psychological and supernatural complexities of a young man distraught by his mother's remarriage.

W. is praised for his characterizations, especially the keen insights into adolescent protagonists caught in personal struggles. He also is commended for his strength of narrative writing, originality, and emotional quality. He is criticized

117. CHRIS VAN ALLSBURG

118. JULES VERNE

119. CYNTHIA VOIGT

120. MARTIN WADDELL

121. ROSEMARY WELLS

for his extensive use of violence, demeaning portrayal of women, and sexual references.

AWARDS: Library Association of Great Britain Carnegie Medal (1976) for *The Machine Gunners* and (1982) for *The Scarecrows. Boston Globe–Horn Book* Honor Books (1978), (1982), and (1983). Carnegie Medal nomination (1978) and AMERICAN LIBRARY ASSOCIATION Best Book for Young Adults (1979) for *The Devil on the Road.* W. received the German Lese. Prize in 1988, 1990, and 1991. In 1991, he received other Carnegie Award commendations and runner-up AWARDS as well as various other notable recognitions

FURTHER WORKS FOR YOUNG ADULTS: *The Wind Eye.* 1976. *The Watch House.* 1977. *Break of Day.* 1981. *The Haunting of Chas McGill, and Other Stories.* 1983. *The Cats of Seroster.* 1984. *Urn Burial.* 1988. *Blitzcat 5.* 1989. *Ghost Abbey.* 1990. *Echoes of War.* 1991. *The Kingdom by the Sea.* 1991. *Gulf.* 1993. *The Promise.* 1993. *A Place to Hide.* 1994

BIBLIOGRAPHY: Drew, Bernard S. *The 100 Most Popular Young Adult Authors,* 1997; *Something about the Author,* vol. 69, 1992

JANELLE B. MATHIS

WHEATLEY, Nadia
Author, b. 1949, Sydney, Australia

W., author of children's and YOUNG ADULT novels, short stories, and PICTURE BOOKS, grew up in Sydney and always wanted to write. After postgraduate studies in AUSTRALIAN history, she went to Greece in 1976, and wrote *Five Times Dizzy* (1982) in her three years there. Its Greek-Australian subject suited the changing mindset of the early 1980s; it was probably the first Australian children's book with a MULTICULTURAL subject to enter the mainstream. It received the New South Wales Premier's Special Children's Book Award, and was made into a TV series (1986).

W.'s longer-than-usual picture book, *My Place* (1987), in collaboration with Donna Rawlins, was the CHILDREN'S BOOK COUNCIL of Australia's Book of the Year for Younger Readers (1988) and won the Eve Pownall Award for nonfiction. Framed by the Australian aboriginal flag, its panorama of images delineates how the same small area in Sydney changed over 200 years of white Australian history (the United States edition includes a glossary). Schools often use the book to awaken interest in local history. A sense of place is central to W.'s books. Many have inner-city settings, and draw on her own youth in the Sydney Newtown area. This is the specific setting of the antieviction battles in *The House That Was Eureka* (1985), which received the Premier's Children's Book Prize. *The Blooding* (1987) conveys a quintessential sense of its remote, unnamed coastal setting. It weaves factual information on "preferential voting" into a plot about a "swinging seat" in an election. Similarly, astronomy is woven into *Lucy and the Leap Year* (1993), on a parent's death. W.'s own childhood experience within a dysfunctional family gives credence to her treatment of death and divorce.

W.'s work is informed by her commitment to such social justice issues as conservation and unemployment. She draws strong female characters, and is not afraid to present sensitive male ones, e.g., Nobby and Noel in *Eureka,* Colum in *The Blooding.* Her work sometimes has a marked whimsical quality—*1 for One* (Helen Leitch, illus., 1985). *Darius Detwiler* (1996) is a postmodernist counting book, in which three volumes nest inside each other.

W. feels the reading levels of her books often correspond approximately with the age of her protagonists, who range from eight to seventeen years old. W. also writes historical articles, conducts workshops for young people of all ages in schools throughout Australia, and works toward dismantling the "ghetto" to which children's literature is often consigned. She recommends a disciplined organized approach to writing, with a strict routine.

FURTHER WORK: *Dancing in the Anzac Deli.* 1984. *The Greatest Treasure of Charlemagne the King.* 1997. *Highway.* 1998. *The Night TOLKIEN Died.* 1994. Radio Feature: (Biography with Gary Kinnane.) *George Johnston and Charmian Clift.* 1986. *Radio Helicon.* Australian Broadcasting Corporation. Editor, *Landmarks* (1991)

BIBLIOGRAPHY: Nieuwenhuizen, Agnes (interview with W.) "No Kidding: Top Writers for Young People Talk about Their Work," 1991; anon, 1998; online at http://www.scholastic.com.au/bookstore/profiles/bs nadia_wheat_html; http://webfronds.com.au.b2wheat.html

SANJAY SIRCAR

WHITE, E(lwyn) B(rooks)

Author, b. 11 July 1899, Mount Vernon, New York; d. 1 October 1985, North Brooklin, Maine

W. is noted as a classic stylist who worked successfully in a variety of literary venues, ranging from POETRY and satiric essays for sophisticated adults to a trio of novels for children. He remembered his own childhood as touched by pervasive melancholy and shyness that remained with him throughout his life. This somber side, in childhood and in adulthood, as well as in his children's novels, was counterbalanced by witty good HUMOR and willingness to try the unexpected.

After attending public schools through secondary graduation, W. entered Cornell University, absenting himself for a year during World War I, and then returning to complete his Bachelor's Degree in 1921. He worked on the college newspaper and, after graduation, briefly worked as a reporter. During his—and the century's—early twenties, he undertook a cross-country automobile trip and then worked aboard a trade ship headed for the Arctic. He returned to New York City, working on and off as a writer for an advertising agency. In 1925, W. began contributing to the newly formed *New Yorker* magazine, becoming one of the authorial and editorial presences that helped to make the weekly's identity as a publication in which long essays, well-shaped verbal riposte, and cartoons shared space and avid readership.

In the following decades, W. authored pamphlets, compilations of essays and poetry. As early as 1936, he began to work on his first children's book, *Stuart Little* (1945), a project that emerged from his desire to create it rather than any need or wish to derive recompense for his effort.

In addition to a variety of literary AWARDS for his work targeting adult audiences, W. received a number of literary citations for his second children's novel, *Charlotte's Web* (1952): it was an ALA NEWBERY MEDAL Honor Book (1953), winner of the Lewis CARROLL Shelf Award (1958) and earned the George C. Stone Center for Children's Books Recognition of Merit Award (1970). Also in 1970, W. was recognized for his lasting contribution to children's literature with the AMERICAN LIBRARY ASSOCIATION's Laura Ingalls

WILDER Award. *The Trumpet of the Swan* (1970) was nominated for the National Book Award in 1971, and was among the titles on the INTERNATIONAL BOARD ON BOOKS FOR YOUNG PEOPLE Honor List in 1972. In 1978, W. received a special Pulitzer prize for the body of his work. During his lifetime, W. received six honorary doctorates from various American universities, including Yale (1948) and Harvard (1954).

W. retired to his Maine farm before he began publishing for children. Each of his three juvenile novels was sparked by his interest in the lives of the farm animals with whom his days were shared but the plot of each springs from an initial fantastic element. In *Stuart Little,* the title character is a mouse boy, born into a family of humans. His physical limitations require considerable familial support but the adventures upon which Stuart embarks are realistic—if romanticized—once the reader has made the initial leap of credulity in regard to his species. The titular character in *Charlotte's Web* is a spider who can spell and the story devolves on her rescuing a farm pig bound for slaughter. Although the farm animals in this second novel are anthropomorphized in a number of trenchant ways—they talk to each other, reason, plan—they are bound by certain realities of their species. One example is that Charlotte herself must die after laying her eggs. *The Trumpet of the Swan* posits a voiceless swan whose human friend makes sure he has the opportunity to learn to communicate—through learning to read and write. The gift of a trumpet allows Louis the swan to learn his species customary method of communication—sort of—and to woo a female swan.

Because of W.'s reputation as an essayist, through his *New Yorker* writings and beyond, he had no difficulty finding ready acceptance by the publishing world for his children's work. Initial response from LIBRARIANS, however, included some cold criticism of his mixing FANTASY with fact. Ever since the popular reception of *Charlotte's Web*, W. has gained high regard from both literary critics and children. Among his three novels for children, this one has earned the most popular acclaim, but all three remain continuously in print since their first publication.

Although it was not conceived or published with a secondary school audience in mind, one nonfiction work to which W. contributed has become a staple of many high school students and their teachers. *The Elements of Style* (1995), originally authored by W.'s former college professor, William Strunk, was edited by W. in its second and third editions (1959 and 1979). Known popularly as "Strunk and White" this guidebook to appropriate use of language in its formal written presentation is accessible to those new to expository writing and clarifying to those occasionally stumped by an unwieldly construction. Teen writers, as well as beginning college students, are introduced to this aid by many teachers and librarians who take the opportunity to note that the "Strunk and White" is the same White who authored *Charlotte's Web.*

BIBLIOGRAPHY: HOPKINS, Lee Bennett, *Pauses: Autobiographical Reflections of 101 Creators of Children's Books,* 1995; Keifer, Barbara, selector, *Getting to Know You: Profiles of Children's Authors Featured in Language Arts, 1985–90,* 1991

FRANCISCA GOLDSMITH

WHITE, T(erence) H(anbury)

Author, b. 29 May 1906, Bombay, India; d. 17 January 1964, Piraeus, Greece

W. began his career as a teacher, but quit at the age of thirty to devote his time to writing. He adored hunting, fishing, and studying Arthurian legends. W.'s most notable work is a quartet of novels known as *The Once and Future King* (1962), which includes: *The Sword in the Stone* (1938), *The Witch in the Wood* (1939), *The Ill-Made Knight* (1940), and *The Candle in the Wind* (1958). In this collection, W. tells the stories of Arthur, Sir Gawain, Sir Lancelot, and Queen Guinevere, based on Sir Thomas Malory's fifteenth century romance, *Morte d'Arthur. The Once and Future King* has been adapted as the Broadway musical *Camelot* (1960), and the Walt DISNEY movie, *The Sword in the Stone* (1963).

W. also published several detective novels, ADVENTURE books, short stories, and poems. His first critical success, *England Have My Bones* (1936), was an autobiographical account of his life.

BIBLIOGRAPHY: *Something about the Author,* vol. 12, 1977

DENISE P. BEASLEY

WIBBERLEY, Leonard (Patrick O'Connor)

Author, b. 9 April 1915, Dublin, Ireland; d. 23 November 1983, Santa Monica, California

W., a prolific writer, authored many juvenile fiction and INFORMATIONAL BOOKS under his own name but also used the pseudonyms Leonard Holden, Patrick O'Connor, and Christopher Web. An immigrant himself, it became evident to him that the American Revolution was the most important struggle in the history of mankind. "It was a war for the rights of all men." His first book, *Kings Beard,* was published in 1952 but he is known for his four historical fiction Treegate books on the Revolutionary War and his Thomas Jefferson BIOGRAPHY series, *Young Man from Piedmont: The Youth of Thomas Jefferson* (1963); *A Dawn in the Trees: Thomas Jefferson, the Years 1776–1789* (1964); *The Gales of Spring: Thomas Jefferson, the Years from 1789–1801* (1965), and *The Time of Harvest: Thomas Jefferson, the Years 1801–1826* (1966). *Sea Captain from Salem* (1961) was an AMERICAN LIBRARY ASSOCIATION Notable Book. He was staunch in his belief that it takes just as much skill and talent to write a good book for children as it does to write a good novel for adults, and perhaps a bit more. W. credits a carefree childhood for his ability to write. "We are eternally children. . . . we must nourish the innocent and hopeful child inside us."

BIBLIOGRAPHY: *Fiction, FOLKLORE, FANTASY and POETRY for Children, 1876–1985,* vol. 1, 1986; *Something about the Author,* vol. 36, 1984, and vol. 45, 1986

IRVYN GILBERTSON

WICK, Walter

Illustrator, photographer, b. 23 February 1953, Hartford, Connecticut

W., an illustrator/photographer, engages the attention of young readers by appealing to their imaginations and intellect. W. and Jean MARZOLLO have collaborated on a series of I Spy books. W. studied photojournalism and landscape photography at Paier College. He also frequently collaborates with his wife, a photo stylist. W. took photographs for over 300 magazine covers including *Games, Psychology Today, Discover,* and *Newsweek* before he began his work for children. W.'s first venture in children's publishing began with photographs for book posters (Scholastic). He also began his initial collaboration with the I Spy author, Marzollo. W. and Marzollo have published more than ten I Spy books with sales of more than two million copies, attesting to the popularity of the SERIES. The I Spy series turns the childhood game of I Spy into books brimming with optical games, visual puzzles, and photographic special effects. The original volume, *I Spy* (1992), features thirteen unrelated still lifes; however subsequent volumes follow engaging themes such as Christmas, spooky nights, fun house thrills, and mystery. *Walter Wick's Optical Tricks* (1998) follows the I Spy pattern; it encourages readers to observe carefully and to think critically about objects they discuss.

In an acceptance speech for the *Boston Globe-Horn Book* Award for *A Drop of Water* (1997) W. admitted that he had been a poor student and a reluctant reader. His role as a photographer for children's books is both reflective and rewarding for him. He finds that books with photographs appeal to students who are visual learners. W. wanted to make a science book from the perspective he knows best, "direct observations of science phenomena through photographs." This goal resulted in *A Drop of Water: A Book of Science and Wonder*.

AWARDS: *Boston Globe–Horn Book* Award for nonfiction (1997) for *A Drop of Water*

FURTHER WORKS: *I Spy Christmas,* 1992; *I Spy Funhouse,* 1993; *I Spy Mystery,* 1993; *I Spy FANTASY,* 1994; *I Spy School Days,* 1995; *I Spy Spooky Night,* 1996; *I Spy Super Challenger!* 1997; *I Spy Little Animals,* 1998; *I Spy Gold Challenger,* 1998; *Illusions,* 1998; *I Spy Extreme Challenger,* 2000; *I Spy Little Letters,* 2000

BIBLIOGRAPHY: Wick, Walter. *"Boston Globe–Horn Book* Award Acceptance," *Horn Book,* Jan.–Feb. 1998, vol. 74; Wignell, Jeff, "The Secret Worlds of Walter Wick," *Photo District News,* June 1997, vol. 17, p. 43

NANCY HORTON

WIESE, Kurt
Author, illustrator, b. 22 April 1887, Minden, Germany; d. 27 May 1974, Frenchtown, New Jersey

Trained in the export trade, W. lived and worked in China from 1909–14. Traveling throughout the country, he became conversant with its culture and fluent in its language. The eruption of World War I interrupted his commercial career and the years 1914 to 1919 were spent as a British prisoner of war in Hong Kong and later in Australia where, by observing the animal life and natural scenery, he discovered his true vocation: art. Returning to Germany at the war's end, he worked for three years creating children's books and designing motion picture sets. In 1923 anxious, as he later put it, "to live under a warm sun again," he set sail for Brazil where he spent a year traveling and three as an illustrator of textbooks and children's books.

In 1927, he immigrated to the United States, married and bought a small farm on the banks of the Delaware River twenty-five miles north of Trenton, New Jersey. Here he began a career as one of America's most productive and accomplished children's book illustrators. His working life spanned forty-four years, during which time he illustrated more than 400 books, nineteen of which he wrote. Though he had no formal training in art, W. was a master of lithography and line drawing. He also worked in a broad variety of other media and styles often calling on memories of his earlier life for inspiration. In illustrating the first American edition of Felix SALTEN's *Bambi* (1929), for example, he visually re-created the German forests of his childhood. It was, however, the years in China that provided the most fertile mine for memory; most notably in the pictures he produced for such modern classics as *The Story about Ping* (1933) by Marjorie FLACK and *The Five Chinese Brothers* (1938) by Claire Huchet BISHOP, and three titles for which he provided ILLUSTRATIONS and text: *The Chinese Ink Stick* (1929), *You Can Write Chinese* (1945), and *Fish in the Air* (1948).

W. demonstrated his mastery of the American milieu and his particular affinity for drawing animals in his illustrations for Walter R. BROOKS's series of domestic fantasies, the Freddy the Pig books, and in the pictures he produced of the Midwest for a series of titles by Iowan Phil Stong, including the NEWBERY Honor title, *Honk the Story of a Moose* (1935). W. continued his prodigious output until late in his career, illustrating thirteen books in 1950 alone.

AWARDS: ALA CALDECOTT MEDAL Honor Books (1949) for *Fish in the Air* and (1946) for *You Can Write Chinese*. ALA NEWBERY MEDAL (1933) for *Young Fu of the Upper Yangtze* (E. Lewis, author). AMERICAN LIBRARY ASSOCIATION Newbery Medal Honor Book (1936) for *Honk the Moose* (P. Stong, author), (1948) for *Li Lun, Lad of Courage* (C. Treffinger, author) and (1949) for *Daughter of the Mountain* (L. Rankin, author)

FURTHER WORKS: (By W.) *Kanoo, the Kangaroo*, 1929; *Liang and Lo*, 1930; *Joe Buys Nails*, 1931; *Buddy, the Bear*, 1936; *The Cunning Turtle*, 1956; *The Groundhog and His Shadow*, 1959

BIBLIOGRAPHY: Kunitz, Stanley J., and Howard Haycraft, eds., *The Junior Book of Authors*, 2nd ed., rev. 1951; *Something about the Author*, vol. 36, 1984

MICHAEL CART

WIESNER, David

Author, illustrator, b. 5 February 1956, Bridgewater, New Jersey

W.'s career as an award-winning author and illustrator can be traced back to many childhood events and influences. He recalls his early love of drawing, which was influenced by watching Jon Gnagy's television drawing show. His creativity was evident in his imaginative play; he had a love for the fantastic and was drawn to the surrealism of artists he learned about in school. W. graduated with a degree from the Rhode Island School of Design where he utilized his interest in FANTASY. He created short, wordless sequences in art that told a story, similar to the format he would later use in his wordless books for children. Artist Trina Schart HYMAN helped W. break into the children's publishing field by hiring him to illustrate a cover for *Cricket* magazine. He soon began to illustrate covers and other writings for children. *Free Fall* (1988) is the first book he published. The wordless story of a young boy's dream where objects change shape then revert to their original shapes fit the fantasy style W. has developed. The premise for *Tuesday* (1991), another wordless PICTURE BOOK, came from a *Cricket* cover, this time of frogs flying through the air on lily pads. W. developed the idea by considering what frogs would actually do if they could fly.

W. generally uses watercolors to express ideas and stories in visual form. His desire is to help

children have fun when they read his books. And although there may be no words, W. believes that reading a picture is just as challenging for the reader. He says, "It's exciting for me to develop that VISUAL LITERACY."

AWARDS: ALA CALDECOTT MEDAL (1992) for *Tuesday*. AMERICAN LIBRARY ASSOCIATION Caldecott Medal Honor Book (2000) for *Sector 7* and (1989) for *Free Fall*. *Redbook* magazine Children's Picturebook Award (1987) for *The Loathsome Dragon*. *American Bookseller* "Pick of the List" for *Hurricane*. Parents' Choice Citation (1992) for June 29, 1999

FURTHER WORKS: *Man from the Sky*, 1980; *Owly*, 1982; *Kite Flier*, 1986; *Rainbow Children*, 1989; *Tongues of Jade*, 1991; *Night of the Gargoyles*, 1994

BIBLIOGRAPHY: Caroff, Susan F., and Moje, Elizabeth B. "A Conversation with W.: 1992 Caldecott Medal winner"; the *Reading Teacher*, vol. 46, pp. 284–89; Cummins, Julie, ed., *Children's Book ILLUSTRATION and Design*, 1992; *Something about the Author*, vol. 72, 1993

SANDRA IMDIEKE

WIGGIN, Kate Douglas

Author, b. 28 September 1856, Philadelphia, Pennsylvania; d. 24 August 1923, Place unknown

After the death of her father and her mother's remarriage to a country doctor, W. moved to the small village of Hollis, Maine, which she later used as a setting for many of her stories. A highlight of her childhood was a train ride where she met her favorite author, Charles DICKENS. W. delighted Dickens by retelling his stories. She admonished him to remove the long and tedious descriptive passages that she confessed omitting as she read. Trained as a teacher, she opened the first free kindergarten on the west coast in San Francisco in 1878 and with her sister, Norah Smith, established a school to train kindergarten teachers. To help raise money for her kindergarten she wrote *The Story of Patsy* (1883) and the popular *The Birds' Christmas Carol* (1887). Frequent writing collaborations with her sister resulted in a five-volume collection of FAIRY TALES, *The Library of Fairy Literature*, published between 1906 and 1911.

Rebecca of Sunnybrook Farm (1903), a perennial best-seller, is typical of the sentimental, romanticized novels of that era in which an ever-cheerful young girl from a fatherless family is forced to face hardship and deprivation in order to triumph over adversity, rescue her family from poverty, and secure their future. It was twice released as a film, starring Mary Pickford in 1917 and Shirley Temple in 1937. A sequel, *More about Rebecca of Sunnybrook Farm,* was published in 1907.

FURTHER WORKS: *Timothy's Quest,* 1890; *Mother Carey's Chickens,* 1911

BIBLIOGRAPHY: Doyle, Brian, *The Who's Who of Children's Literature,* 1968; Pool, Daniel, *Dickens' Fur Coat and Charlotte's Unanswered Letters,* 1998

DIANE G. PERSON

WILDER, Laura Ingalls

Author, b. 7 February 1867, Pepin, Wisconsin; d. 10 February 1957, Mansfield, Missouri

The Little House SERIES consists of eight books written by W. with some assistance from her daughter, Rose: *Little House in the Big Woods* (1932), *Farmer Boy* (1933), *Little House on the Prairie* (1935), *On the Banks of Plum Creek* (1937), *By the Shores of Silver Lake* (1939), *The Long Winter* (1940), *Little Town on the Prairie* (1941), and *These Happy Golden Years* (1943). They were supplemented by the posthumous, unedited *The First Four Years* (1971), and a volume of letters from Laura to her husband Manly, describing a visit to San Francisco in 1915, *West from Home* (1974). A series of sequels, beginning with *Little House on Rocky Ridge* (1993), describing the childhood of Rose Wilder, has been produced by Roger Lea MacBride, Laura's executor. Attempts to exploit the popularity of the books, such as *Little House in Brookfield* (1996)—which describes the childhood of Laura's Mother, Caroline Quiner, as well as a television series (see below)—failed to capture the authenticity of the originals.

With the exception of *Farmer Boy,* the books describe (in slightly edited and politicized form) the travels of Charles Ingalls and his family around the Midwest between 1868 and the early 1890s. Together, they are a tribute to the pioneering spirit, a detailed documentary account of social and domestic conditions, and a gripping story of the growth of a sensitive, tough, intelligent

young child. It has been suggested that some of the gaps between reality and fiction—notably the idea that Laura's father was a victim of incompetent government, rather than simply not a very good farmer—may have stemmed from Laura's and Rose's disapproval of the interventionist New Deal in the 1930s.

W. was born in Wisconsin, near the town of Pepin; her father, Charles Ingalls (Pa) sold his farm, and the family's journey westwards to Kansas is described in *Little House on the Prairie.* The book relates how they inadvertently settled in Indian Reserve country, and the realistic, but sympathetic treatment of NATIVE AMERICANS gives considerable depth and understanding to the book. The themes of Pa's competence and independence are also balanced by Ma's homemaking capabilities under difficult circumstances. When W. was four, they returned to the "big woods" of Wisconsin, and their life at that period (1871–73) is described in the first of the novels, *Little House in the Big Woods.* The book has a tight, unified structure—covering one year—and centers on Pa, an idealized version of Charles Ingalls.

The next installment, *On the Banks of Plum Creek,* moves the family onwards to the Minnesota prairies, near Walnut Grove, and sees Laura and her sisters having their first social encounters. It also sees Pa leaving the family to find work elsewhere on three occasions, after a natural disaster (grasshoppers) destroyed the crops. The book can be seen as an exploration of modes of independence. In real life, the Wilders hung on until 1876, when they drove south and east to South Troy, Minnesota, to stay with Peter Ingalls (Charles's brother) and his wife Eliza (Caroline's sister). Laura's nine-month-old brother Freddie died, and the family moved on to Burr Oak, Iowa, where they helped to run a hotel for a period.

Fiction and fact resume their correspondence with *On the Shores of Silver Lake.* In 1879 Laura's sister Mary was blinded by spinal meningitis (scarlet fever in the book), and Charles became paymaster and timekeeper for the new railroad companies. The family moved to the new town of de Smet, and the book provides a remarkable picture of people moving across the plains; at the end, the Ingalls family settle in a claim shanty.

The harshness of the environment is arguably best shown in *The Long Winter,* which accurately describes the events of 1880. The Ingalls moved into town, but still come close to starvation before the first rescue trains arrived in April 1881. There is a strong element of cautious romance in this book, as Almanzo Wilder braves the snow to bring grain back to the town and impresses the young Laura.

It seems, with *Little Town on the Prairie,* that nature has done its worst, and the family now lived half of the year in the town; pioneering was over. Mary left the family to attend the school for the blind at Vinton, Iowa, and this book expands the social side of Laura's life (the character of Laura's rival, Nellie Oleson, is developed), including her first courtship (in several very charming episodes). At the end of the book (December 1882), she gets her first teaching job, even though she was still only fifteen.

The account of her first teaching (at the Bouchie School), with its harsh conditions, loneliness, and isolation, shown in *These Happy Golden Years* is for many readers one of the most affecting parts of the saga. It makes her "rescue" by Almanzo, all the more striking. Their marriage, on August 25, 1884, forms a natural conclusion to the story.

The other book in the group, *Farmer Boy,* is a tightly written account of Almanzo's childhood, and provides an interesting contrast in terms of affluence and a settled environment, to Laura's life.

After their marriage, Laura and Almanzo remained in de Smet until July 1894. Rose was born in December 1886, but they lost a baby son in 1889, and suffered illness (Almanzo was disabled by diphtheria), crop failure, and a house fire. They moved to Almanzo's family in Minnesota, to Florida, and eventually settled in Mansfield, Missouri. They lived a happy and successful life, Almanzo dying in 1949 when he was 92, and Laura just over seven years later. Rocky Ridge Farmhouse is now open to the public, and the exhibits include Pa's famous violin. It was left to Laura's daughter, Rose, and her executor to collect material that describes this period. *The First Four Years* was printed from an unedited manuscript found among Laura's papers after her death, and *On the Way Home* was edited from her diaries.

The series is one of the high points of twentieth-century American children's literature: it is a chronicle of a massive change in society, written at a time when other unusual changes were taking place. In the fictionalized Laura and Almanzo and Ma and Pa, W. created major characters who speak to both adults and children. The 1953 series edition with ILLUSTRATIONS by Garth WILLIAMS is recognized everywhere; it has been translated into several languages and was the basis for a very successful American television series.

AWARDS: ALA NEWBERY MEDAL Honor Book (1938) for *On the Banks of Plum Creek,* (1940) for *By the Shores of Silver Lake,* (1941) for *The Long Winter,* (1942) for *Little Town on the Prairie,* (1944) for *These Happy Golden Years.* The Laura Ingalls W. Award, administered by the Association for Library Service to Children of the AMERICAN LIBRARY ASSOCIATION, was established in 1954 and is now given every three years to an author or illustrator whose body of work has made a lasting contribution to literature for children. W. was the first recipient of the award in 1954

BIBLIOGRAPHY: Bosmajian, H. "Vastness and Contraction of Space in *Little House on the Prairie." Children's Literature.* 11, 49–63 (1983). Moore, R. A. "Laura Ingalls W.'s Orange Notebooks and the Art of the Little House Books." *Children's Literature.* 4, 105–119. (1975) Moore, R. A. "The Little House Books: Rose Colored Classics." *Children's Literature.* 7, 7–16. (1978) Moore, R. A. "Laura Ingalls W. and Rose W." 11, 3, 101–109. (1980) Segal, Elizabeth. "Laura Ingalls W.'s America: An Unflinching Assessment." *Children's Literature in Education.* 8, 63–70. (1977) Spaeth, J. *Laura Ingalls W.* (1987) Zochert, D. *The Life of Laura Ingalls W.* (1976)

SARAH AND PETER HUNT

WILDSMITH, Brian

Artist, illustrator, b. 22 January 1930, Penistone, Yorkshire, England

W. is well known for his exuberant pictures and fine style of painting in children's PICTURE BOOKS. Growing up in Yorkshire England, W. was interested in sports, cricket, and science, but at age sixteen he decided to focus on art. He was supported by both parents in his endeavors. He received a degree from the Slade School of Art in London, served in England's military service, and taught art before making it his full-time career. His belief in creating fine ILLUSTRATIONS for children's books began with his initial work at Oxford University Press where he created both black and white and colored illustrations for books. When requested to do an alphabet book, the result, *ABC* (1962), was the winner of the KATE GREENAWAY MEDAL in 1962.

W.'s fascination with language is seen in *Birds* (1967) and in *Wild Animals* (1967). His illustrations of the bird or animal, its group term, such as "wedge of swans," "siege of bitterns," "sloth of bears," or "ambush of tigers," combine with exquisite settings in colorful and humorously depicted scenes. Each book broadens readers' vocabularies as well as provides outstanding illustrations. During the 1960s he also illustrated fables and MOTHER GOOSE rhymes. With *Owl and Woodpecker* (1971), W. focused on creating story lines as well as colorful images. Following a move from England to southern France, he received much inspiration from the countryside. Among his many productive efforts was that of designing sets and costumes for children's film. W. is also well-known for his ANIMAL books, such as *Hunter and His Dog* (1979) and *Bear's Adventure* (1981).

Employing various forms and subjects in his books, W.'s art reflects vibrancy in color and DESIGN as well as sophistication. His books support VISUAL LITERACY, language learning, and provide story lines with humanitarian principles. He also illustrates for other authors.

AWARDS: Kate Greenaway Medal (1962) for *ABC;* Kate Greenaway commendations (1963) for *The Lion and the Rat* and *The Oxford Book of POETRY for Children,* (1967) for *Birds,* and (1971) for *The Owl and the Woodpecker.* Hans Christian ANDERSEN Award runner-up (1966) and (1968). Art Books for Children citation (1965) for *Brian Wildsmith's 1,2,3. New York Times* Best Illustrated Children's Books of the Year (1967) for *Birds.* Brooklyn Art Books for Children Citation, Parent's Choice citation for illustration, and American Bookseller's Spring Children's "Pick of the Lists."

FURTHER WORKS: *The Circus.* 1970. *The Little Wood Duck.* 1972. *The Lazy Bear.* 1973. *What the Moon Saw.* 1978. *Animal Games.* 1980. *Animal Homes.* 1980. *Pelican.* 1972. *The Island.* 1983. *Whose Shoes?* 1984. *My Dream.* 1986. *If I Were You.* 1987. *Carousel.* 1988. *A Christmas Story.* 1989. *The Creation: A Pop-up Book.* 1996. *Saint Francis.* 1996. *Joseph.* 1997

BIBLIOGRAPHY: *Children's Literary Review,* vol. 2, 1976; Cianciolo, Patricia, *Picture Books for Children,* 3d ed., 1990; Doyle, Brian, *The Who's Who of Children's Literature,* 1968; Riley, Carolyn, ed., "Brian W.," *British Children's Authors,* 1976, pp. 155–66; *Something about the Author,* vol. 69, 1992; *Something about the Author Autobiographical Series,* vol. 5, 1998; Townsend, John Rose, *Written for Children: An Outline of English Language Children's Literature,* 1974

JANELLE B. MATHIS

WILLARD, Barbara

Author, b. 1909, Hove, Sussex, England; d. 24 February 1994

W. was an acclaimed writer of historical fiction, primarily noted for her Mantlemass series of books. Influenced at an early age by her actor father, W. remembered touring with him and playing parts in the theater herself. Of that time she said that "it remains for me the root of all experience." Indeed, that experience was later woven into one of her books titled *Summer Season* (1981). She credited her eventual success as a writer for children to the times when she would tell stories to her younger brother. He died as a serviceman in the Royal Air Force but she remembered entertaining him with stories she read or made up.

W.'s formal schooling took place in London where she also benefited from the impact of the theater and the strong English curriculum of her convent school. Although her first book was turned down by over fifty publishers, she eventually found success with *The House with Roots,* published in 1959. A key turning point in her career occurred when she moved to Ashdown Forest, a setting that inspired much of her historical fiction writing. Later, she began to write her best known Mantlemass series, which takes place between the fifteenth and eighteenth centuries, tracing the lives of two families. Critics acclaim W.'s fine character development, and her ability to describe in vivid detail a time long past.

AWARDS: Guardian Awards for children's fiction (1972) for *The Sprig of Broom,* (1973) for *A Cold Wind Blowing,* and (1974) for *The Iron Lily.* AMERICAN LIBRARY ASSOCIATION Notable Book (1974) for *The Iron Lily.* Whitbread Award (1984) for *The Queen of the Pharisees' Children*

FURTHER WORKS: *A Dog and a Half,* 1964; *Surprise Island,* 1969; *The Lark and the Laurel,* 1970; *A Cold Wind Blowing,* 1973; *Harrow and Harvest,* 1974; *The Country Maid,* 1978; *The Keys of Mantlemass,* 1981; *Famous Rowena Lamont,* 1983; *The Magic Cornfield,* 1997; *Son of Charlemagne,* 1998

BIBLIOGRAPHY: Fisher, Margery, "Barbara Willard," *School Librarian.* December 1969, pp. 343–48; *Something about the Author,* vol. 74, 1993

SANDRA IMDIEKE

WILLARD, Nancy

Author, poet, b. 26 June 1936, Ann Arbor, Michigan

As an engaging storyteller and poet, W. is the author of the first book of POETRY to win the NEWBERY MEDAL. W. received a B.A. from University of Michigan, M.A. in medieval literature from Stanford, and Ph.D. in modern literature from University of Michigan. She also studied art in Paris, France, and Oslo, Norway. W. has written for adults and young people, taught at Vassar, conducted workshops at the Breadloaf Writer's conferences, and been a visiting poet at Oberlin College. W. was encouraged by her parents to draw and write, which she did from an early age, publishing her first poem at age seven. While in high school she wrote *A Child Star* published in *Horn Book.* Continuing as a prolific award-winning writer, W. wrote several volumes of poetry before writing her first children's book *The Merry History of a Christmas Pie* (1974). Three years later W. wrote the award-winning *Sailing to Cythera and Other Anatole Stories* (1974) in which her son James Anatole was the model for the hero and was the first of a trilogy of FANTASY books. W.'s own childhood and extended family members, many of whom lived with her are fodder for many of her works. As a child she learned from her mother that an "inn" is a resting place with cracks in the plaster for interesting people. She thought to herself that she had been living in an inn without knowing it! It is no coincidence that she would later produce a multiaward–winning children's book that featured an inn and one of her favorite poets, William Blake in *A Visit to William Blake's Inn: Poems for Innocent and Experienced Travelers* (1981).

AWARDS: Lewis CARROLL Shelf Award (1977) for *Sailing to Cythera and Other Anatole Stories* and (1979) for *The Island of the Grass King: The Further Adventures of Anatole.* Art Books for Children award (1978) for *Simple Pictures Are Best* (Tomie DE PAOLA, illus.). *Boston Globe–Horn Book* Award (1982), Golden Kite (1981), ALA CALDECOTT MEDAL Honor Book (1982), and AMERICAN LIBRARY ASSOCIATION Newbery Medal (1982) all for *A Visit to William Blake's Inn: Poems for Innocent and Experienced Travelers.* It is the only book ever to win both categories of award in the same year

FURTHER WORKS: *The Snow Rabbit.* 1975. *The Marzipan Moon.* 1981. *Uncle Terrible: More Adventures of Anatole.* 1982. *The Mountains of Quilt.* 1987. *Firebrat.* 1988. Poetry: *In His Country: Poems.* 1966. *All on a May Morning.* 1975. *Night Story.* 1986. *The Voyage of the Ludgate Hill: A Journey with Robert Louis STEVENSON.* 1987. *The Ballad of Biddy Early.* 1989.

BIBLIOGRAPHY: *Fifth Book of Junior Authors and Illustrators,* 1983; Lucas, Barbara, "Nancy Willard," the *Horn Book,* August 1982, vol. 58, no. 4, p. 374; Willard, Nancy, "Newbery Medal Acceptance," the *Horn Book* magazine, August 1982, vol. 58, no. 4, p. 369

NANCY HORTON

WILLIAMS, Garth

Illustrator, b. 16 April 1912, New York City; d. 8 May 1996, Guanajuato, Mexico

The son of two English artists, his father a political cartoonist and his mother a landscape painter, W. spent his childhood variously in the United States, France, Canada, and, from the age of ten, England. He originally wanted to be an architect, but won a scholarship to the Royal College of Art. W. soon established himself as a sculptor, winning the prestigious British Prix de Rome, allowing him to study on the Continent for two years then returned to England. During the war W. moved to the United States where, in 1943, he began working for *The New Yorker* magazine. There he met E. B. WHITE, who arranged for W. to illustrate his new children's book *Stuart Little* (1945). This launched his career as a children's illustrator and he was soon illustrating works by various authors, notably Margaret Wise BROWN including *Little Fur Family* (1946), *Wait Till the Moon Is Full* (1948), and *Mister Dog, The Dog Who Belonged to Himself* (1952). His ILLUSTRATIONS for White's classic, *Charlotte's Web*

(1952) will be forever associated with that work, as are TENNIEL's with Lewis CARROLL's Alice books, and SHEPARD's with *Winnie-the-Pooh.* His fame was further augmented when he was chosen to illustrate the republished editions of Laura Ingalls WILDER's Little House books, beginning with *The Little House in the Big Woods* (1953). For this assignment, he researched his subject meticulously, visiting all the places identified in the books and consulted freely with Wilder herself.

He occasionally wrote his own texts, the best known being his series on animals for Simon and Schuster—*Baby Animals* (1952) and others. The most well known of his own books is undoubtedly *The Rabbit's Wedding* (1958), which created considerable controversy in the South because it depicts the marriage of two rabbits, one black and one white. The book was banned in some parts of the South and one politician even called for its burning. W. himself was astonished by the uproar and claimed never to have intended any social message. Of course, the notoriety made the book one of W.'s best-selling titles.

W., a prolific artist, turned almost exclusively to illustrating the works of others. In addition to the Little House series, he worked on such acclaimed books as Margery SHARP's *The Rescuers* (1959) and its sequels, George SELDEN's *The Cricket in Times Square* (1960) and its sequels, Russell HOBAN's *Bedtime for Frances* (1960), Randall JARRELL's *The Gingerbread Rabbit* (1964), Jan WAHL's *Push Kitty* (1968), and Jack PRELUTSKY's *Ride a Purple Pelican* (1986).

W. is particularly noted for his illustrations of ANIMAL STORIES and his ability to imbue his animal characters with distinctive personalities. His pictures convey warmth and vitality and at the same time avoid sentimentality. His PICTURE BOOKS for younger children generally contain illustrations in ink and full-color wash; the illustrated books for older readers are more commonly done in simple pen and ink. W.'s particular gift was in interpreting the texts he illustrated, conveying in his illustrations the very essence of the scene and nature of the characters. It is difficult to imagine *Charlotte's Web* or *The Little House in the Big Woods* without W.'s illustrations.

AWARDS: British Prix de Rome for sculpture (1936), American Institute of Graphic Arts Chil-

dren's books selection (1958–60) for *The Rescuers. New York Times* Ten Best Illustrated Books (1990) for *Beneath a Blue Umbrella* (Jack Prelutsky, poet)

FURTHER WORKS: As illus.: *The Golden Name Day.* (Jennie D. Lindquist). 1955. *Do You Know What I'll Do?* (Charlotte ZOLOTOW). 1958. *Miss Bianca.* (Margery Sharp). 1962. *Tucker's Countryside.* (George SELDEN). 1969. *Beneath a Blue Umbrella.* (Jack Prelutsky). 1990

BIBLIOGRAPHY: *Dictionary of Literary Biography,* vol. 22; HOPKINS, Lee Bennett, *Pauses: Autobiographical Reflections of 101 Creators of Children's Books,* 1995

DAVID L. RUSSELL

WILLIAMS, Jay

Author, b. 31 May 1914, Buffalo, New York; d. 12 July 1978, London, England

A writer of SCIENCE FICTION, W. is best known for his Danny Dunn series, written with Raymond Abrashkin from 1956 to 1977. An original ghost story told around a campfire in a boys camp brought a prize when he was twelve. He claims this was the catalyst that propelled him into STORYTELLING and writing. His first book was a historical mystery novel, *The Stolen Oracle* (1943). Science fiction stories based on scientific fact, *Danny Dunn and the Homework Machine* (1958) and *Danny Dunn on the Ocean Floor* (1960) received The Young Readers Choice Award. *Danny Dunn and the Scientific Detective* (1975) was a Junior Literary Guild selection. The stories ask questions about the universe and aid in developing critical thinking skills. *Everyone Knows What a Dragon Looks Like* (1976) was a Junior Literary Guild selection and a *New York Times* Best Illustrated Book of the Year; it was included in the American Institute of Graphic Arts Book Show. *The Practical Princess and Other Liberating FAIRY TALES* (1978) was one of *School Library Journal's* best books. He stated, "Most of all, I like writing stories for children, who seem to have as much fun reading them as I have writing them."

BIBLIOGRAPHY: *Fiction, FOLKLORE, FANTASY and POETRY for Children, 1876–1985,* vol. 1, 1986; *Something about the Author,* vol. 36, 1984, and vol. 45, 1986

IRVYN GILBERTSON

WILLIAMS, Margery

Author, b. 22 July 1881, London, England; d. 4 September 1944, New York City

W. entertained children by making toys and pets come alive in the fictional ADVENTURES of her children's books. She moved to the United States at age nine, two years after her father's death. With little formal education, W. spent two years at the Convent School, Sharon Hill, Pennsylvania, (1896–98). She married Captain Francesco Bianco, an authority on rare books and printing. While living in London, she and her husband had a son, Cecco, in 1905 and a daughter, Pamela, in 1906, who became a children's author and illustrator. The family lived in Paris, London, Italy, and in 1921 returned to New York City. W.'s childhood set the stage for many of her children's books. Although her father did not believe in much formal education, he did believe that she should learn to read early. W. did read early and having no playmates close by, she spent much of her time reading the three-volume *Wood's Natural History,* learning about the reptiles, birds, and other animals. This interest led to her own creations and play with paper dolls, pet mice, toys, and games evident in later writings for children. Her first published children's book and possibly the most familiar is *The Velveteen Rabbit; or, How Toys Become Real* (1922), a classic that W. felt was the beginning of all her stories since it stimulated her memories. *The Skin Horse* (1927) was given the title because W. remembered Dobbin, her brother's skin horse toy that had to be left behind when they moved to America as children. *The Little Wooden Doll* (1925), illustrated by daughter Pamela, is the story of a group of compassionate mice who, with the help of other creatures from the woods and meadow, help a worn, discarded doll from the attic by redressing and updating her. Then they find her a new home with a well deserving, lonely little girl. W. has encouraged countless young imaginations to develop through her heartfelt and compelling literary adventures.

AWARDS: ALA NEWBERY MEDAL Honor Book (1937) for *Winterbound*

FURTHER WORKS: *Poor Cecco,* 1925; *The Apple Tree,* 1926; *The Adventure of Andy,* 1927; *All about Pete,* 1929; *Green Grows the Garden,* 1936; *Other People's Houses,* 1939; *Penny and the White Horse,* 1942

BIBLIOGRAPHY: *Junior Book of Authors,* 1951

NANCY HORTON

WILLIAMS, Vera B.

Author, illustrator, b. 28 January 1927, Hollywood, California

W. grew up in an orthodox Jewish family. Her mother, active in the community and school, worked to improve the living situation of children who were part of her Bronx neighborhood. Her family struggled like many others during the Depression to stay together, pay rent, and meanwhile encourage a cultural upbringing including music and art for their children. W. attended special art classes because of the promise that her school found in her work. She attended the High School of Music and Art, followed by college at Black Mountain, North Carolina, and later continued her education at Boston Museum School. Together with friends from Black Mountain College, W. founded a community of artists, musicians, writers, and crafts people. After teaching art at a small independent school, W. went to Canada in 1970. Here she took a long Yukon trip, the basis for her book *Three Days on a River in a Red Canoe* (1981). This book contained journal-style entries and soft crayola-colored ILLUSTRATIONS dealing with the practicalities of putting up a tent, cooking, catching fish, telling stories, and weathering a storm. She returned to New York to write in 1979.

W. is perhaps best known for her series about Rosa; the stories exemplify the warmth of family love and the importance of shared family, generational, and community experiences. *A Chair for My Mother* (1982), autobiographical in nature, is the story of saving money to buy a chair for Rosa's mother; it celebrates the joy when the time finally comes to select one. *Something Special for Me* (1983) describes Rosa's joy and discernment in selecting a personal gift that would be for everyone. Predictably, the third book in the series focuses on the joy of MUSIC—Rosa's accordion—and other authentic aspects of life in *Music,*

Music for Everyone (1984). All three books communicate the struggles dealing with economic limitations while also focusing on life's inherent riches. The characters are strong, caring women who overcome odds to accomplish goals. The illustrations, using primitive folk art technique, bright colors, childlike watercolors, and cheerful borders with motifs, are as emotional as the text.

"More, More, More," Said the Baby (1990) tells the stories of three toddlers in MULTICULTURAL families sharing the bond between babies and their closest caregivers. As with her other works, simplicity, spontaneity, depth of feeling, and positive messages pervade. W.'s natural, sensitive, and objective presentation of family life has been acclaimed. Universal values are presented in an exuberant way as she focuses on children, women, nonviolence, community cooperation, interracial friendships, and the environment.

AWARDS: Parents' Choice Award for illustrations (1981). Jane Addams Honor Book Award (1985) for *Music, Music for Everyone*. Parents' Choice Award in Literature Notable Book, Child Study Association of America's Children's Books of the Year, and *New York Times* Best Illustrated Children's Books of the Year (1986) and *Boston Globe–Horn Book* Award Honor Book for illustration (1987) all for *Cherries and Cherry Pits*. ALA CALDECOTT MEDAL Honor Book and *Boston Globe–Horn Book* Award for illustration (1983), *A Chair for My Mother;* AMERICAN LIBRARY ASSOCIATION Caldecott Medal Honor Book (1991), *"More, More, More," Said the Baby: Three Love Stories; Boston Globe–Horn Book* Award for fiction (1994) for *Scooter*

FURTHER WORKS: *It's a Gingerbread House: Bake It! Eat It!* 1978. *The Great Watermelon Birthday.* 1980. *Cherries and Cherry Pits.* 1986. *Stringbean's Trip to the Shining Sea.* (With Jennifer Williams), 1988. *Scooter.* 1993

BIBLIOGRAPHY: *Boston Globe–Horn Book* Award acceptance speech, *Horn Book* magazine, vol. 60, 1984; *Children's Literary Review,* vol. 9, 1985; Holtze, Sally Holmes, ed., *Fifth Book of Junior Authors and Illustrators,* 1983; *Something about the Author,* vol. 53, 1988, vol. 61, 1990, and vol. 102, 1999; *Twentieth Century Children's Writers,* 1989

JANELLE B. MATHIS

WILSON, Jacqueline
Author, b. 17 December 1945, Bath, England

In both her REALISTIC FICTION and FANTASY writing, W. often finds characters and situations in real life that become the basis of her stories for children and YOUNG ADULTS. W. remembers her first attempts at writing—at nine years of age—a novel about a large family and other early attempts at CHAPTER BOOKS. She successfully published short stories for teenage MAGAZINES when she was seventeen, but resisted the stereotypical portrayal of characters sought by publishers. She says about her writing for children that "I wanted to write about young people and their problems but I didn't want to pretend there were the easy solutions offered in the magazine stories." A brief period of crime novel writing convinced her that she most wanted to write about and for children. Her first book, *Nobody's Perfect* (1984), was inspired by a newspaper article she read about adopted children searching for their parents. Watching a group of "hippy" young people inspired *Amber* (1987), a novel in which W. explores what would happen if such a child wanted to pursue a more traditional lifestyle. In addition to realistic fiction, W. wrote a series of detective stories for younger readers, as well as a time warp story that returns to the Victorian period. W. is an avid reader herself who admits to owning over ten thousand books.

AWARDS: Young Observer/Rank Organization Fiction Prize Runner-up (1982) for *Nobody's Perfect* and (1984) for *The Other Side*

FURTHER WORKS: *Waiting for the Sky to Fall,* 1983; *The School Trip,* 1984; *How to Survive Summer Camp,* 1985; *The Monster in the Cupboard,* 1986; *Supersleuth,* 1987; *This Girl,* 1988; *Is There Anybody There?,* 1990; *Double Act,* 1995; *Elisa, Star of the Shelter,* 1995; *The Suitcase Kid,* 1997; *Bad Girls,* 1997

BIBLIOGRAPHY: *Something about the Author,* vol. 61, 1991

SANDRA IMDIEKE

WINTER, Jeanette
Author, illustrator, b. 6 October 1939, Chicago, Illinois

Born in Chicago to Swedish immigrant parents, W. says that she always loved to draw. W. studied at the Art Institute of Chicago and the University of Iowa, where she earned a bachelor of Fine Arts degree. W. used pen and ink drawings in her first book, *The Christmas Visitors: A Norwegian Folktale* (1968), and in other early works. Since then, however, W. has illustrated most of her more than twenty-seven PICTURE BOOKS with acrylic paintings, a medium that she says allows her to make changes easily and to concentrate fully on telling stories with image and color. The rich colors and distinctive characters within her books are warm and well suited to the many genres and cultural events represented. W. also illustrates for other authors. Her award-winning picture books display a diversity of well-researched topics, such as *Diego* (1991), a Notable Children's Trade Book in the Field of Social Studies published in English and Spanish, *Follow the Drinking Gourd* (1988), an AMERICAN LIBRARY ASSOCIATION Notable Book, and *Klara's New World* (1992).

Among the ten picture books W. has written as well as illustrated are several fine biographical portraits of artists: *Cowboy Charlie* (1995), the story of the cowboy artist Charles M. Russell; *Josefina* (1996), inspired by the Mexican folk artist Josefina Aguilar; and *My Name is Georgia: A Portrait* (1998), about Georgia O'Keeffe. In these books, using strength of detail and color to define mood, W. effectively captures the spirit of the artist's experience and work, making them accessible and engaging for children.

AWARDS: American Illustrators Guild Award Children's Book (1968) for *The Christmas Visitors: A Norwegian Folktale. New York Times* Best Illustrated Book of the Year (1991) for *Diego* (1991)

FURTHER WORKS: *Day of the Dead* (Tony JOHNSTON, 1997; *Sebastian: A Book About Bach,* 1999

BIBLIOGRAPHY: Cummins, Julie, ed., *Children's Book Illustrations and Design,* vol. 11, 1998; copy on book flaps from several books by Jeanette Winter

KATHIE KRIEGER CERRA AND JANELLE B. MATHIS

WISNIEWSKI, David

Author, illustrator, b. 21 March 1953, South Ruislip Air Force Base, Middlesex, England

W.'s cut-paper-illustrated PICTURE BOOKS portray elegant folktales and sophisticated romps, meeting with critical acclaim and popularity among readers in the middle grades. An American citizen born overseas, W. grew up in the American Midwest and Middle Atlantic states. Entering the University of Maryland at College Park, he soon

left to attend Ringling Brothers and Barnum and Bailey Clown College instead. From 1973 to 1976, he traveled first with Ringling Brothers and Barnum and Bailey and then with Circus Vargas. Resettling in Maryland, W. learned puppetry and then graphic design. In all these media, he works to acquaint audiences with other cultures and universal moral issues.

W. received grants from the Henson foundation for his puppetry in 1983 and in 1985; he was cited by the International Puppeteers Union for excellence in 1984. *Elfwyn's Saga* (1990) was named a Notable Children's Trade Book in the Field of Social Studies, by the National Council for the Social Studies and Children's Book Council. *Golem* (1996) was the ALA CALDECOTT MEDAL winner (1997).

W.'s first half dozen self-illustrated books form a cycle of culture-specific moral tales. *The Warrior and the Wise Man* (1989) depicts the alternative values of force and wisdom in an ancient Japanese setting. *Elfwyn's Saga,* set in a Viking milieu, explores the power of metaphysical insight. The Mayan-situated *Rain Player* (1991) presents readers not only with the devastating fear of drought but also with the universal enjoyment of sports well played. *Sundiata: Lion King of Mali* (1992) is recounted in a tone appropriate to oral STORYTELLING. *The Wave of the Sea-Wolf* (1994), set in the Pacific Northwest, shows the meeting between white Europeans and the native Tlingit from the latter's viewpoint. *Golem* (1996) presents the sixth-century legend of the clay man without a brain who is brought to life to help the Polish Jews ward off their anti-Semitic neighbors. W. researches the cultures he depicts so thoroughly that the tales unfold as though from within the community he is representing.

More recently, W. has produced witty tales that are no less intellectually engaging and visually attractive. *The Secret Knowledge of Grownups* (1998) stands several parental exhortations on their heads, while *Tough Cookie* (1999) offers up the eponymous character as a detective.

W.'s ILLUSTRATION work involves an elaborate process of sketching, selecting a color palette, cutting paper and layering it to form images that, under the lights of photographic equipment, show depth and shadow. In addition to his own stories, W. has illustrated picture books for others, including Eve BUNTING (*Ducky,* 1998) and Andrew Clements (*Workshop,* 1999).

W.'s picture books are emblematic of a current trend toward publishing illustrated stories that have cultural integrity and are intended for older children rather than pre-readers.

FURTHER WORKS: *Amanda Joins the Circus,* 1999; *Keep Your Eyes on Amanda,* 1999

BIBLIOGRAPHY: Evans, D. "David Wisniewski, the *Horn Book* magazine, July–August 1997; Op de Beeck, N., "David Wisniewski: Crafting Serious Entertainment," *Publishers Weekly,* February 16, 1998; *Something about the Author,* vol. 95, 1998

FRANCISCA GOLDSMITH

WOJCIECHOWSKA, Maja (Maia Larkin, Maia Rodman)
Author, b. 7 August 1927, Warsaw, Poland

As a young child, W.'s family fled from war-torn Poland to France, traveling some of the way on foot. They settled permanently in the U.S. in 1942. After graduating from high school in California, W. attended Immaculate Heart College for a year. She published her first book, *Market Day for Ti Andre* (1952), under the name Maia Rodman.

Most of W.'s books portray YOUNG ADULTS struggling with a major life decision while seeking to discover their true identity, as in *Shadow of a Bull,* winner of the 1965 ALA NEWBERY MEDAL. In this book Manolo, a Spanish youth, must decide whether to follow his father as a bullfighter or become a doctor. She was also awarded the German Jungensbuchpreis (1968), the German children's book award. Although her career has been as a children's and young adult author, poet, and translator, W. has also held myriad other jobs, from professional tennis player to undercover detective.

FURTHER WORKS: *The Hollywood Kid,* 1966; *A Single Light,* 1968; *Tuned Out,* 1968; *Don't Play Dead before You Have To,* 1970; *The Rotten Years,* 1971; *Till the Break of Day,* 1972; *The People in His Life,* 1980; *Dreams of Golf,* 1993

BIBLIOGRAPHY: *Children's Literary Review,* vol. 20, 1990; HOPKINS, Lee Bennett, *More Books by More People,* 1974; Kingman, Lee, *Newbery and CALDECOTT Awards,* 1965, W., M., *Till the Break of Day: Memories 1939–1942,* 1973

DENISE E. AGOSTO

WOLFF, (Jenifer) Ashley
Author, illustrator, muralist, b. 26 January 1956, Boston, Massachusetts

W. grew up in Middlebury, Vermont, graduated from the Rhode Island School of Design, where she studied ILLUSTRATION, and moved to San Francisco. Settings in her PICTURE BOOK illustrations frequently reflect the cities and beaches of Northern California.

W.'s illustrations are distinctive in their use of linoleum block prints and watercolor, as in *Little Donkey Close Your Eyes* (1995) by Margaret Wise BROWN and *Stella and Roy* (1993), written by W. and chosen as an American Booksellers Association Pick of the Lists and a *School Library Journal* Best Book of the Year. The latter, a contemporary story about two young siblings racing in a park, is a clever adaptation of the fable of the tortoise and the hare. W. has used other techniques in books she wrote, including acrylic and gouache in *Only the Cat Saw* (1985) and watercolor in *Come with Me* (1990), a Child Study Association Book of the Year.

Illustrations for titles as diverse as *Doctor Bird: Three Looking up Tales from Jamaica* (1998) by Gerald Hausman and *How Chipmunk Got Tiny Feet: NATIVE AMERICAN Animal Origin Stories* (1995) also by Hausman, demonstrate W.'s versatility and her careful research. In an engaging role reversal for preschoolers, W. uses double-page spreads to illustrate the teacher preparing for the first day of school in *Miss Bindergarten Gets Ready for Kindergarten* (Joseph Slate, 1996), an ABA Pick of the Lists title.

W. both reflects and engages the eye and spirit of the young child in her artwork and writing. Her playful, detailed, and well-designed paintings and block prints appeal to children in ways that stimulate language and repeated involvement.

FURTHER WORKS: Illus. only: *Miss Bindergarten Celebrates the 100th Day of Kindergarten.* (Slate). 1998. *Home Sweet Home.* (Jean MARZOLLO). 1997. *Goody O'Grumpity.* (Carol Ryrie BRINK). 1994

BIBLIOGRAPHY: *Something about the Author,* vol. 81, 1995; online, http//208.204.91/Bios/WolffBio.html

KATHIE KRIEGER CERRA

WOLFF, Virginia Euwer
Author, b. 25 August 1937, Portland, Oregon

W.'s award-winning titles with their unique characters and recognizable problems appeal to young readers. W. grew up in a wooded area of Oregon with few modern conveniences but with many values and much literature. W. received a B.A. from Smith College in 1959 and taught elementary school and high school English before she became a writer. W. brings a perceptive sensitivity to her YOUNG ADULT novels with issues of adolescence, special problems, and young people with learning differences. *Probably Still Nick Swansen* (1988) received the PEN-West Book Award and the INTERNATIONAL READING ASSOCIATION Children's Book Award, Young Adult division. The Child Study Children's Book Committee at Bank Street College recognized *Make Lemonade* (1993). W.'s experience as a violin student is evident in *The Mozart Season* (1991); she writes that MUSIC is "the most profound healer of human pain." If it were not for music rehearsals, she says, she might never have learned to accept criticism as constructive advice.

AWARDS: Golden Kite Award (1993) for *Make Lemonade*

FURTHER WORKS: *Bat 6,* 1998

BIBLIOGRAPHY: Gallo, Donald, ed. *Speaking for Ourselves, Too.* 1993. *Something about the Author.* vol. 78, 1994. W., Virginia. "If I Was Doing It Proper, What Was You Laughing At?: Some Notes on the Language of Community." *Horn Book* magazine. May–June 1998, vol. 74, i. 3 pp. 297–300

NANCY HORTON

WOLITZER, Hilma
Author, b. 25 January 1930, Brooklyn, New York

A writer of adult and juvenile fiction, W. remembers having a poem about winter published in *The Junior Inspectors' Club Journal* and going downtown along streets lined with garbage trucks to get a certificate for winning the contest sponsored by The New York City Department of Sanitation. Her first juvenile book, *Introducing Shirley Braverman,* was published in 1975 and her second, *Out of Love,* in 1976. *Toby Lived Here* followed in 1978. She not only writes but has taught writ-

ing workshops at the Bread Loaf Writers' Conference at Middlebury College in Vermont and at Columbia University and the University of Iowa. Her fiction is a mixture of reality and imagination. She "tries to be working on something all the time, even if it's only in my head."

FURTHER WORKS: *Wish You Were Here,* 1984

BIBLIOGRAPHY: *Fiction, FOLKLORE, FANTASY and POETRY for Children, 1876–1985,* vol. 1, 1986; *Something about the Author,* vol. 31, 1983

IRVYN GILBERTSON

WOLKSTEIN, Diane
Author, storyteller, b. 11 November 1942, New York City

W. is a storyteller of oral and written original and adapted tales from many cultures. W. received a B.A. in drama in 1964 from Smith College and an M.A. from the Bank Street College of Education in 1967. She also studied pantomime in Paris in the years between her undergraduate and graduate work. After graduation, W. decided that what she loved to do most is tell stories, just as she had loved to listen to stories as a child. Her mother told her entertaining bedtime stories and her neighborhood rabbi told her short, dramatic stories. These experiences coupled with her inquisitive nature gave W. the passion to share the spirit of story. She has served as a radio host for weekly STORYTELLING, told stories around the world, and taught storytelling to novice tellers. W. travels to absorb the authenticity of gestures and the culture of her tales. *The Magic Orange Tree and Other Haitian Tales* (1978) and *The Banza: A Haitian Tale* (1980) were the culmination of seven visits to the Caribbean and Haiti. In her introduction to *The Magic Orange Tree,* W. shares that the Haitian storyteller solicits cooperation from the listeners by asking "Cric?" (pronounced "creek") when he or she has a story to tell. The audience answers "Crac!" *if* they want the storyteller to begin. This type of interaction exemplifies the intensity and camaraderie W. feels is a necessity between a teller and audience. Although a story is told and retold numerous times, W. feels that each new experience is a recreation of the spirit of a new story.

AWARDS: New York Academy of Sciences Children's Science Book honorable mention (1973) for *8,000 Stories: A Chinese Folktale* (1972). Lithgow-Osborne fellowship (1976, 1977) and American Institute of Graphic Arts award (1977) for *The Red Lion: A Persian Sufi Tale*. ALA notable book citation (1978) for *The Magic Orange Tree and Other Haitian Folk Tales* and (1979) for *White Wave: A Tao Tale*

FURTHER WORKS: Adapted folktales: *The Cool Ride in the Sky.* 1973. *Squirrel's Song: A Hopi-Indian Story.* 1975. *Lazy Stories.* 1976. *The Magic Wings.* 1983. *The Legend of Sleepy Hollow.* 1987. *Oom Razoom; or, I Know Not Where, Bring Back I Know Not What: A Russian Tale.* 1991. *Bouki Dances the Kokioko: A Comical Tale from Haiti.* 1997. Other works: *The Visit.* 1977. *Little Mouse's Painting.* 1991. *Dream Songs: Abulafia, Part of My Heart.* 1992. *Step by Step.* 1994

BIBLIOGRAPHY: *Fifth Book of Junior Authors and Illustrators.* 1983. Wolkstein, Diane and James Wiggins. "On Story and Storytelling: A Conversation." *Horn Book.* June 1983, vol. 59, no. 3, pp. 350–57. Wolkstein, Diane. "Twenty-Five Years of Storytelling: The Spirit of the Art." *Horn Book.* November–December 1992, pp. 702–8

NANCY HORTON

WOOD, Audrey
Author, illustrator, b. 1948, Little Rock, Arkansas

WOOD, Don
Illustrator, author, b. 4 May 1945, Atwater, California

A.W. and D.W. write and illustrate PICTURE BOOKS, producing literature rooted in theatrical performance as the STORYTELLING medium. A.W. works with several illustrators, including her husband D.W., and also illustrates many of her own texts. D.W. illustrates texts exclusively for A.W., or for those he co-writes with her.

While A.W.'s childhood was rich with travel and art experiences ranging from her father's mural painting to her mother's antique restoring, D.W. grew up on a California farm where his labors were required in the field. A.W. learned to read by age three, and grew up bilingual due to her family's sojourn in Mexico during her preschool years. As a boy, D.W. nurtured an appreciation for COMIC BOOKS AND GRAPHIC NOVELS' expression of narrative through pictures. Both received encouragement in childhood artistic pursuits, D.W. from his teachers and A.W. from her family. D.W. continued his formal education at

the University of California, Santa Barbara, graduating with a bachelor's degree in 1967. He moved to Northern California and earned a Master of Fine Arts Degree from the California College of Arts and Crafts (1969).

A.W. moved from Arkansas to Berkeley, California, and was working as an independent artist when the two met in 1968. Marrying the following year, they traveled to Central America, operated an antiques store in Arkansas, and settled in California to work as artists. A.W. realized her childhood decision to pursue a career as a children's book writer, self-illustrating her first published works, including *Twenty-four Robbers* (1980) and *Scaredy-Cats* (1980). She then encouraged her husband to illustrate a book she was writing; *Moonflute* (1980) became their first joint work.

The *Napping House* (1984), their fourth collaboration, earned the Society of Children's Book Writers' Golden Kite Award, the AMERICAN LIBRARY ASSOCIATION's Notable Book designation, and a place on the list of the INTERNATIONAL READING ASSOCIATION/CHILDREN'S BOOK COUNCIL's Children's Choices, all 1984. In 1985, it earned a Certificate of Merit from the Society of Illustrators. *King Bidgood's in the Bathtub* (1985), was an ALA Notable Book, a Child Study Association of America Children's Books of the Year, a Parents' Choice Award selection, and a Society of Illustrators Certificate of Merit choice, all in 1985. In 1986, it was named an ALA CALDECOTT MEDAL Honor Book.

Most of A.W.'s narratives and D.W.'s illustrations rely on cumulative plotlines or echoes of nursery games, served up with gentle HUMOR that speaks well to preschoolers. For *Elbert's Bad Word* (1988), the story of a little boy getting the best of his would-be social betters, D.W. depicts a Roaring Twenties world in which A.W.'s satire unfolds. Among their co-authored texts, *Piggies* (1991), a counting book, shows D.W.'s illustrations providing narrative flow in addition to offering static portraits of the porcine personifications of a child's digits.

D.W. prefers oil paint as his ILLUSTRATION medium, enjoying the ease with which it permits changes in line and light while he is working on a picture. Several of his books echo work by sixteenth century Lowland painters. In *Heckedy Peg* (by A.W., 1987), the artwork has a period glow

123. LAURA INGALLS WILDER

122. E. B. WHITE

124. GARTH WILLIAMS

125. DON AND AUDREY WOOD

126. LAURENCE YEP

that complements the story of a mother whose seven children have been cast under a spell. Like *King Bidgood's in the Bathtub, Heckedy Peg* both reads and looks theatrical, in keeping with the fact that A.W. and D.W. often perform their stories before putting them down on paper.

A.W.'s illustrations for children are comical and often declared with word balloons. Dialogue is presented literally from the mouths of the characters, as in *The Princess and the Dragon* (1981), a tale about the title characters' desire to exchange places. This type of FANTASY wish, familiar to many children, has become a hallmark of D.W. and A.W.'s storytelling: she gives dreams a narrative coherence and they both provide carefully composed, visible expressions of flights of fancy.

In addition to books illustrated by herself or D.W., A.W. works with other artists, including Rosenkranz Hoffman, who created the illustrations for *The Three Sisters* (1986), and Mark Teague, who illustrated *The Flying Dragon Room* (1996) and *Sweet Dream Pie* (1988). A.W. has authored some stories that derive from FOLKLORE. *The Bunyans* (illustrated by David SHANNON, 1996) recounts a series of adventures undertaken by the American tall tale family of giants. *The Rainbow Bridge: Inspired by a Chumash Tale* (illustrated by Robert Florczak, 1995) recounts a California NATIVE AMERICAN legend about dolphins.

In a move away from the traditional, both A.W. and D.W. have created illustrations on the computer. D.W.'s artwork for A.W.'s fantasy *Bright and Early Thursday Evening: A Tangled Tale* (1996), and A.W.'s self-illustrated *The Red Racer* (1996), about a little girl's longing for a shiny new bicycle, were accomplished through the use of a variety of painting software programs. A.W. quickly adopted this new tool; she has composed an aesthetically pleasing interactive website as well as book illustrations. D.W., too, continues to explore the aesthetic frontiers offered by digital art but finds that the expansive opportunities offered by the computer threaten to overwhelm the production of a finished illustration project.

FURTHER WORKS: *Balloonia.* 1981. *Detective Valentine.* 1987. *Little Penguin's Tale.* 1989. *Rude Giants.* 1993. *The Christmas Adventure of Space Elf Sam.* 1998. All self-illustrated by A.W.: *Quick as a Cricket.* (A.W., illus, by D.W.). 1982. *The*

Big Hungry Bear. (A.W. and D.W., illus. by D.W.). 1984. *The Tickleoctopus.* (A.W., illus. by B. Morrison; 1980, reissued 1994, illus. by D.W.). *Jubal's Wish.* 2000

BIBLIOGRAPHY: Lodge, S. "Don and Audrey Go Digital." *Publishers Weekly,* September 2, 1996; Silvey, A., ed., *Children's Books and Their Creators,* 1995; *Something about the Author,* vol. 50, 1988, and vol. 81, 1995

FRANCISCA GOLDSMITH

WOODSON, Jacqueline
Author, b. 12 February 1964, Columbus, Ohio

W., a children's and YOUNG ADULT author, grew up in Greenville, South Carolina, and New York City, and recalls a turbulent and abusive childhood. Her interest in writing began early with W. focusing on experiences she feels were missing from the literature she read growing up. She writes to bring hope to abused young people and works with children in shelters and homes as a DRAMA therapist.

Portraying truths about life in modern American society, W. does not shy away from controversial subjects. She is also acclaimed for her books about friendship and daily life that deal with safe acceptable topics. However, while not forcing an ideology on readers, she reflects a genuine concern for all types of people. Controversy surrounds some of her writings as they focus on issues such as alcoholism, teen pregnancy, and homosexuality.

A touching portrayal of friendship among positive female characters characterize a trilogy of books by W. In *Last Summer with Maizon* (1990) Margaret and Maizon deal with issues of friendship as well as the loss of Margaret's father. *Blue Hill* (1992) reveals Maizon's unpleasant experiences with snobbery and racism at an exclusive all-white boarding school where she must deal with issues of self-esteem and identity. In *Between Madison and Palmetto* (1993) the eighth-graders confront issues such as bulimia, integration, and the unavoidable testing of friendship.

A novel that spans race and class, *I Hadn't Meant to Tell You This* (1994), has aroused controversy. Marie befriends Lena, whom Marie's family thinks is "white trash." Both girls are dealing with problems. Marie's mother has abandoned her family and Lena is victim of her father's sexual molestation.

Although she deals with provocative topics, such as homosexuality and biracialism, as in *The Dear One* (1991), *From the Notebooks of Melanin Sun* (1995), and *The House You Pass on the Way* (1997), W. displays sensitivity and skill in addressing these topics. W. says that she writes about the people who exist on the margins— young girls, minorities, homosexuals, the poor. W. knows well the struggle of finding individual value, and rather than positioning herself as an advocate of merely one community, she addresses all of her own identities as she opposes stereotypes in her novels.

AWARDS: W. received the Kenyon Review Award for Literary Excellence in Fiction (1992). AMERICAN LIBRARY ASSOCIATION's Best Books for Young Adults (1993) for *Maizon at Blue Hill.* CORETTA SCOTT KING Honor Book (1995) for *I Hadn't Meant to Tell You This,* and (1996) for *From the Notebooks of Melanin Sun*

FURTHER WRITING: *Martin Luther King, Jr., and His Birthday.* 1990. *Book Chase.* 1994. *We Had a Picnic This Sunday Past.* 1997. *If You Come Softly.* 1998

BIBLIOGRAPHY: W., Jacqueline. "A Sign of Having Been Here." *Horn Book.* November–December, 1995. 711–15. W., Jacqueline. "Who Can Tell My Story?" *Horn Book.* January–February, 1998, pp. 34–38. *Something about the Author,* vol. 94, 1998

JANELLE B. MATHIS

WORTH, Valerie
Poet, b. 29 October 1933, Philadelphia, Pennsylvania; d. 31 July 1994, Clinton, New York

Remembered for her POETRY, W.'s childhood memories and loves are imbedded in her poems. She was the smallest child in her class and felt an affinity for small things. She loved to explore the nearby woods watching insects, wildlife, and flowers. W. was in a writer's group with author Natalie BABBITT, who first encouraged her to submit her poetry to an editor for publication.

Small Poems (1972) contains two dozen free-verse poems describing animals and small everyday common objects. *More Small Poems* (1976) and *Still More Small Poems* (1978) won Notable Book Citations from the AMERICAN LIBRARY ASSOCIATION. Natalie Babbitt illustrated W.'s

books. *Small Poems Again* (1986) has the same format and vivid precise language as all the Small Poems books. W. was named the Book Week Poet, CHILDREN'S BOOK COUNCIL (1991), and received the Award for Excellence in Poetry for Children, NATIONAL COUNCIL OF TEACHERS OF ENGLISH (1991). She attempts to "express the essential qualities of an object or an experience . . . especially for children. For me . . . childhood and poetry are profoundly connected."

BIBLIOGRAPHY: *Fiction, FOLKLORE, FANTASY and Poetry for Children, 1876–1985.* vol. 1. 1986. HOPKINS, Lee Bennett, *Pauses: Autobiographical Reflections of 101 Creators of Children's Books,* 1995. The *New York Times.* August 1994, p. 1162. Silvey, Anita, ed. *Children's Books and Their Creators.* 1995

IRVYN GILBERTSON

WRIGHTSON, Patricia
Author, b. 19 June 1921 Lismore, New South Wales, Australia

A popular and well-recognized author, W. writes fantasies based on ancient AUSTRALIAN myths. She attended St. Catherine's College in 1932 and State Correspondence School in 1933–34. Before becoming an author, W. worked as a hospital administrator for twenty years and as an editor for the Sydney *School Magazine* for ten years. Many of her books reached the final competition for Australia's Book of the Year award given by the CHILDREN'S BOOK COUNCIL of Australia. W.'s first publication, *The Crooked Snake* (1955), won this prestigious award. She began writing for her own two children. As they listened to her stories, their facial reactions gave her the feedback she needed for revision. W.'s recognition extended worldwide with her publication of *A Racecourse for Andy* (1968). The title character is a retarded boy whose portrayal by W. is realistic and sensitive. W. engages readers in fantasies in which familiar, believable characters interact with characters drawn from ancient legends. For example, in *A Little Fear* (1983), elderly Mrs. Tucker must confront the Njimbin, an ancient gnome. Also, in *Baylet* (1989), fourteen-year-old Jo comes to know and pity the title character, which in turn leads her to imminent danger. Australia plays an important role as the setting in W.'s books. In *Moon Dark* (1987) the author exhibits her deep knowledge of the land of Australia and its animals of the wild. In all of her books W. likes to choose themes that require readers to explore their minds and stretch their understanding.

AWARDS: Children's Book Council of Australia's Book of the Year (1956) for *The Crooked Snake,* (1974) for *The Nargun and the Stars,* (1978) for *The Ice Is Coming,* and (1984) for *A Little Fear. Boston Globe–Horn Book* Award (1984) for *A Little Fear.* Hans Christian ANDERSEN Award (1986), Dromkeen (1984), Golden Cat (1986), New South Wales State Literary Special Award (1988)

FURTHER WORKS: *The Feather Star.* 1963. *Down to Earth.* 1965. *An Older Kind of Magic.* 1972. *The Dark Bright Water.* 1978. *Night Outside.* 1985. *The Sugar-Gum Tree.* 1992. *Shadows of Time.* 1994

BIBLIOGRAPHY: *Children's Literature* AWARDS *and Winners.* 1994. *Dictionary of* BRITISH *Children's Fiction: Books of Recognized Merit.* 1989. *Fourth Book of Junior Authors and Illustrators.* 1978

NANCY HORTON

WYETH, N(ewell) C(onvers)

Painter, illustrator, b. 22 October 1882, Needham, Massachusetts; d. 19 October 1945, Chadds Ford, Pennsylvania

W.'s career illustrating children's books began with Scribner's Illustrated Classics. A student of illustrator Howard PYLE, W. created pictures that captured dramatic, emotional incidents and consistently carry out the theme of the work. He enthusiastically illustrated such stories as *Treasure Island* (STEVENSON, 1911), *Kidnapped* (Stevenson, 1913), and *The Last of the Mohicans* (James Fenimore Cooper, 1919). He later illustrated other works like Marjorie Kinnan RAWLINGS, *The Yearling* (1939). In 1940, the Metropolitan Life Insurance Company commissioned him to paint a series of murals that are used as the ILLUSTRATIONS for a book by Robert SAN SOUCI, *N. C. Wyeth's Pilgrims* (1991). A commentary in this book states, "In these murals, Wyeth challenged the existing notions of Pilgrim society as unremittingly severe by depicting the pleasures and beauty of the colony. The paintings reveal the romantic vision and lyricism that were the hallmarks of Wyeth's style." Of his five children, Andrew became a painter as did Andrew's son, James Wyeth.

FURTHER WORKS: *Rip Van Winkle.* (Washington IRVING). 1921. *The Odyssey.* 1929. *Hans Brinker.* (Mary Mapes DODGE). 1932. *Drums.* James Boyd. 1928

BIBLIOGRAPHY: *Something about the Author,* vol. 17, 1979. Michaelis, Davis. *N. C. Wyeth: A Biography.* 1998. San Souci, Robert. *N. C. Wyeth's Pilgrims.* 1991

JANNELLE B. MATHIS

WYNNE JONES, Diana

Author, b. 16 August 1934, London, England

The daughter of two educators, W.J., an award-winning and highly prolific author of magical fantasies, graduated from St. Anne's College, Oxford (1956) where she was influenced by C. S. LEWIS and J. R. R. TOLKIEN. Her many young-adult novels (including more than thirty titles), unveil a panoply of mysterious and intriguing supernatural characters—witches, ghosts, futuristic time travelers, genies, and wizards. Frequently utilizing theme and character in a creative mix of MYTHOLOGY and FAIRY TALES as well as SCIENCE FICTION and romance novels, W.J. has successfully developed an innovative style that has earned her considerable critical acclaim. Her work, described by critics as sophisticated, inventive, and distinctive, deals with thematic issues of good and evil, use of power, discovery of one's inner strength, and the virtues of loyalty and courage. One of her best-known works, *Charmed Life* (1977) is the first in the Chrestomanci Cycle, a SERIES of four novels. Set in mythical Europe and contemporary England, these stories depict a world where magic is legal under the watchful eye of Chrestomanci, a mysterious sorcerer. In *Charmed Life,* Cat, a young boy who possesses remarkable magical powers, struggles with his cruel, controlling sister who wishes to misuse his power to satisfy her own desire to rule the world. In *The Homeward Bounders* (1981), W.J. juxtaposes a teenage character from nineteeth-century Victorian England with superhuman beings and alternate worlds. The protagonist, a thirteen-year-old named Jamie, stumbles upon a multiple-world war game that is controlled by mysterious, faceless beings, referred to as "Them." Jamie learns that this game affects the destinies of several worlds. In his effort to find his way home, a task that must be accomplished accidentally if it is to be successful, Jamie befriends several imaginative characters.

W.J. also published the Dalemark Cycle, a trilogy set in an imaginary world that chronicles the medieval history of a country torn by war. Although most of W.J.'s books are written for a middle-grade audience, she has also published books for younger readers, including *The Ogre Downstairs* (1974), *Fire and Hemlock* (1985), and *Chair Person* (1989). W.J.'s literature is the creative amalgamation of richly imaginative plots and settings, dynamic protagonists, and intriguing supernatural characters, expressed through universally human themes.

AWARDS: CARNEGIE MEDAL commendation (1975) for *Dogsbody* and (1977) for *Charmed Life.* Guardian commendation (1977) for *Power of Three.* Guardian Award (1978) for *Charmed Life.* Boston Globe–Horn Book Honor Book Award (1984) for *Archer's Goon. Horn Book* Honor List (1984) for *Fire and Hemlock. Horn Book* Fanfare List (1978) for *Howl's Moving Castle*

FURTHER WORKS: *Wilkin's Tooth.* 1973. *Eight Days of Luke.* 1974. *The Homeward Bounders.* 1981. *The Time of the Ghost.* 1981. *Warlock at the Wheel and Other Stories.* 1984. *A Tale of Time City.* 1987. *Aunt Maria.* 1991. The Dalemark Cycle: *Cart and Cwidder.* 1975. *Drowned Ammet.* 1977. *The Spellcoats.* 1979. The Chrestomanci Cycle: *Charmed Life.* 1977. *Magicians of Caprona.* 1980. *Witch Week.* 1982. *The Lives of Christopher Chant.* 1988. YOUNG ADULT plays: *The Batterpool Business.* 1968. *The King's Things.* 1970. *The Terrible Fisk Machine.* 1971

BIBLIOGRAPHY: *Children's Literature Review.* vol. 23. Drew, Bernard A. *The 100 Most Popular Young Adult Authors. Something about the Author.* vol. 70, 1993

ANDREW KANTAR

WYNNE-JONES, Tim

Author, b. 12 August 1948, Bromborough, Cheshire, England

As a writer for young children, W.J. is perhaps best known for his Zoom series: *Zoom at Sea* (1983), *Zoom Away* (1985), and *Zoom Upstream* (1994). Each furthers the adventures of a small white cat and his friend Maria. Zoom loves adventure and the world he explores in Maria's house. Besides the Zoom books, W.J. uses the FANTASY and wonder of childhood as he develops themes of conquering personal fears and developing relationships with parents. The idea of huge adults and how threatening they might seem in appearance to small children is seen in *I'll Make You Small* and *Mischief City,* both published in 1986. The latter consists of twenty-five poems in which six-year-old Winchell shares his thoughts and those of an imaginary friend.

In his books for adolescents, W.J. uses eccentric but believable characters in plots that involve fantasy to help explain the truth. *Some of the Kinder Planets* (1995) is a collection of nine short stories that introduces ordinary boys and girls in realistic situations. Each character, however, enters the world of fantasy to resolve the rather mundane problem that confronts him. W.J. uses his dry HUMOR and perceptive insight in these highly imaginative stories. In *The Book of Changes: Stories* (1995), universal situations of the middle-school student are humorously described. As these characters work through their dilemmas, W.J. reminds the reader that the power to make the most of a situation lies within the self.

W.J.'s works are recognized by characters who show strength of mind and body as they are involved in complex situations. *The Maestro* (1996) combines strong characterization with the unpredictable plot of a compelling ADVENTURE STORY as Burl, fourteen, runs away into the Canadian wilderness to escape an abusive father. He meets a reclusive musician who provides shelter and companionship. Burl must survive using his understanding of the woods, adult manipulative strategies, and compassion, as well as brutality in this coming-of-age story. *Stephen Fair: A Novel* (1997) for YOUNG ADULTS opens with a mood of confusion and fear as Stephen tries to find the meaning of a troubling dream. W.J. uses rich imagery in this novel that focuses on truth and the meaning of family.

AWARDS: Seal First Novel Award, Bantam/Seal Books (1980) for *Odd's End.* IODE Award (1983) and Ruth Schwartz Children's Book Award (1984) for *Zoom at Sea.* Also, Author's Award, The Foundation for the Advancement of Canadian Letter (1990) for *Fastyngange* (1988). Governor General's Award in Canada (1993) for *Some of the Kinder Planets*

FURTHER WORKS: *Architect of the Moon,* 1988; *Madeline and Ermadello,* 1977; *Mischief City,* 1986; *Odds End,* 1980; *Rosie Backstage,* 1997

BIBLIOGRAPHY: *Children's Literature Review,* vol. 21, 1984

JANELLE B. MATHIS

WYSS, Johann David

Author, b. 1743, Berne, Switzerland; d. 1818, Berne, Switzerland

W., a Swiss pastor, never actually worked as a writer. His most famous work, *Der schweize- rische Robinson* (1812), derived from stories he told his four young sons for their instruction and amusement. Every day he would commence tell- ing the story from where he left off the previous day. At some point, W. wrote down his story. His son, Johann Rudolf, later located the manuscript, revised it, and sent it off to a publisher. After the story's acceptance, it was translated into English as *The Swiss Family Robinson; or, The Shipwreck of the Swiss Minister and His Family* (1812). This story details the daily trials of a shipwrecked pas- tor, his wife, and four young sons as they struggle to survive. It painstakingly details the flora, fauna, history, and geography of their fictional island. Since its original publication, over two hundred versions of this classic story have been published in England and America, and was adapted for the big screen three times: 1940, 1960, and 1975.

DENISE P. BEASLEY

YARBROUGH, Camille

Author, b. 8 January 1934, Chicago, Illinois

Y.'s career spans the arts of DRAMA and dance as well as writing. As a result, her stories encourage self-expression, creativity, and pride in children. *Corn Rows* (1979) richly describes the AFRICAN AMERICAN culture of hair braiding while also using story and song to share other aspects of culture. Drawing on her performance background, the text of this book is POETRY in story form, in the tradition of a griot as Y. herself has said. *Corn Rows* shows pride in one's heritage, respect for elders, and a rich cultural experience for readers of all ethnicities. *The ShimmerShine Queens* (1989) uses African American dialect interwoven with proverbs to tell a story of the trouble in inner city schools. A message throughout is to respect others, school, and achievement. Additionally, *The Little Tree Growin' in the Shade* (1985) weaves, in story and poetry, the rich threads that make up the culture of AFRICANS who came to the United States as slaves.

AWARDS: CORETTA SCOTT KING Illustrators Award Honor Book (1980) for *Cornrows* (Carole BYARD, illus.)

FURTHER WORKS: *Tamika and the Wisdom Rings.* 1994

BIBLIOGRAPHY: *Children's Literature Review,* 1993. *Something about the Author,* vol. 80, 1995

JANNELLE B. MATHIS

YASHIMA, Taro (Jun Atsushi Iwamatusu)

Author, illustrator, b. 21 September 1908, Kagoshima, Japan; d. 30 June 1994, exact place in the United States unknown

Y. came to America in 1939 to study Western art. While here, war between the United States and Japan began, and he joined the U.S. Office of Strategic Services and the U.S. Army Office of War Information to fight for Japanese democracy. The name Taro Yashima was a pseudonym he adopted when he began writing two politically autobiographical works. He continued using his pen name while writing for children as the name itself was symbolic of his childhood in Kyushu. Although he remained in the United States, his books reflected his longing for his village. His delicate impressionistic illustrations sensitively represented the culture and lifestyle of Kyushu.

Y. regarded highly the innocence, resilience, and imagination of children. It seemed only natural that he create books that reflected these characteristics. *The Village Tree* (1953) was created as a gift for his daughter to share his memories of childhood in Japan. It portrays simply a child's sense of wonder, innocence, and fun. The book has been said to reflect the universality of play as well as the love and respect Y. had for children. *Crow Boy* (1956) also reflects his childhood as it is based on the school experiences of a classmate in grade school. Said to be his most beloved work, it tells the story of a shy and lonely boy whose understanding teacher sees his potential and helps him develop it. The artistry of his colorful yet subtle pictures lies both in simplicity of form and in fine use of blank spaces. One critic said that Y. combined the bright light of the Impressionists with a refined elegance reminiscent of Japanese paintings.

Y. is also noted for his special attention to the small incidents of life that make up a child's world. With charm and delicacy *Umbrella* (1959) was created as a gift for Y.'s daughter on her eighth birthday. It tenderly conveys the excitement and pleasure of a small child using her first umbrella and boots.

AWARDS: ALA CALDECOTT MEDAL Honor Book (1956) for *Crow Boy,* (1959) for *Umbrella,* and (1968) for *Seashore Story. New York Times* Best Illustrated Children's Books of the Year (1967) for *Seashore Story.* Southern California Council on Literature of Children and Young People Award for significant contribution in the field of ILLUSTRATION (1968). Y.'s paintings are on display in permanent collections in museums. His artistry was also seen in one-man shows in Los Angeles and New York and in his dedicated work directing and teaching in the Yashima Art Institute

FURTHER WORKS: *Plenty to Watch,* 1954; *Momo's Kitten,* (collaborated with wife, Mitsu). 1961; *Youngest One,* 1962; *Seashore Story,* 1967

BIBLIOGRAPHY: *Children's Literature Review,* vol. 4, 1982; HOPKINS, Lee Bennett, *Pauses: Autobiographical Reflections of 101 Creators of Children's Books,* 1995

JANELLE B. MATHIS

YATES, Elizabeth
Author, b. 6 December 1905, Buffalo, New York

A writer of fictional BIOGRAPHY, an editor and contributor to magazines and journals, Y. spent her most memorable childhood days on her father's farm south of Buffalo, New York. She would go off riding on her horse, Bluemouse, and write stories in her head. When a rainy day came she would write down the stories she had been creating. When one of her poems was published, Y. knew she wanted to be a writer. Her first book, *High Holiday* (1938), a novel based on mountain climbing experiences in the Swiss Alps, was published in England. *Mountain Born* (1943), an ALA NEWBERY MEDAL Honor Book, is about a

real sheep who became a pet. *Amos Fortune, Free Man,* about a black man who was a prince in Africa, was brought to America as a slave and later purchased his freedom and became a farmer, won the 1951 Newbery Medal. *Rainbow 'Round the World: A Story of UNICEF* (1954) won the Jane Addams Children's Book Award from the U.S. section of the Women's International League for Peace and Freedom. *Carolina's Courage* (1964) received an AMERICAN LIBRARY ASSOCIATION Notable Book award. Y. professes "a deep and ever deepening conviction of the enduring nature of good . . . in people and in situations. As a person, I want to put myself on the side of good . . . and so make my life count in the sum total."

BIBLIOGRAPHY: *Fiction, FOLKLORE, FANTASY and POETRY for Children, 1876–1985,* vol. 1, 1986; HOPKINS, Lee Bennett, *Pauses: Autobiographical Reflections of 101 Creators of Children's Books,* 1995; Silvey, Anita, ed., *Children's Books and Their Creators,* 1995

IRVYN GILBERTSON

YEE, Paul
Author, b. 1 October 1958, Saskatchewan, Canada

Y. is a third generation Chinese Canadian whose writing for children has been informed by his career as an archivist. Although Y. has taught occasionally since earning both his masters and bachelor degrees at the University of British Columbia, he sees himself primarily as an archivist and policy analyst. Y.'s first children's book, *Teach Me to Fly, Skyfighter!* (1983), a collection of short stories about what life was like growing up in Vancouver's immigrant community, was the result of an invitation from a Canadian publisher. His subsequent children's books have derived their plots from Chinese Canadian history. However, Y. has provided readers with heroines as well as male characters, in an effort to counter the male-dominated history of the immigrant Chinese. *Tales from Gold Mountain* (1989) (1990 in the United States) won critical acclaim, including the Parents' Choice Honor, for its use of traditional Chinese story elements in an accessible story collection for children. *Roses Sing on New Snow: A Delicious Tale* (1992) has been identified as frankly feminist. In all his writing for children, Y. is conscious of history and optimistic about current changes in attitudes toward immigration and diversity.

FURTHER WORKS: *The Curses of Third Uncle,* 1986; *Ghost Train,* 1996

BIBLIOGRAPHY: *Something about the Author,* vol. 96, 1998; *Seventh Book of Junior Authors and Illustrators,* 1996

FRANCISCA GOLDSMITH

YEP, Laurence

Author, b. 14 June 1968, San Francisco, California

Y.'s childhood was marked by positive influence from his family. His parents ran a grocery where Y. learned the value of hard work. He spent time restocking shelves, washing vegetables, cleaning, and doing the many chores that come with running a grocery store. These early experiences with hard work and routine taught Y. that success comes from putting forth effort each and every day. Y.'s parents played a valuable part in helping him become a dedicated successful author.

Y.'s parents also encouraged his love of reading. Both parents were avid readers who read four newspapers daily. They read to him with the understanding that for every story they read to him, he would read one to them. His mother also read to Y. to help calm him during asthma attacks. For instance, she read *The Pirates of Oz* (1931) by Ruth Plumy Thompson, to him during a particularly bad attack, inspiring Y.'s love of FANTASY. He continued to read all of the Oz books and then turned to SCIENCE FICTION.

As a writer, imagination is Y.'s primary tool. Throughout his childhood Y. created adventures in his mind based on the family car. The car, Jezebel, had a running board. In his imagination, Y. leaped onto the running board and traveled in vehicles ranging from stage coaches to space ships.

Imaginative worlds became the place where Y. searched to find himself. His love for science fiction was stimulated by his search for self. In his autobiography he says he writes about alienated people and science fiction aliens, but in reality he is writing about himself as a Chinese American. He grew up in a predominantly black neighborhood. His parents sent Y. to a Chinese school in Chinatown to help him learn his own culture. He did not belong to his own neighborhood and yet was too different from his Chinese classmates to belong there. He did not speak Chinese; he was often left out of jokes. As a writer he uses his novels to understand his own culture.

In *Child of the Owl* (1977), Y. shares bits of his childhood through the main character Casey. When Casey's father is unable to care for her she goes to live with her grandmother in Chinatown. Like Y., Casey found Chinatown an alien place from the world in which she grew up. Y.'s search for identity is apparent in other novels. He captures the reader's sense of loneliness by alerting students to the protagonists' struggles. In *Dragonwings* (1975) Moon Shadow searches for his identity in America as a Chinese American whose father dreams of flight. This search for self is a powerful theme for adolescent readers; Y. captures their attention by creating characters to whom readers can relate.

The search for identity as an individual is a strong force in Y.'s novels, yet he also stresses the importance of family. In *Dragonwings* the extended family support of the men at the company becomes an important focus. Even though Wind Rider had moved out of the city and reduced his contact with the company, the family comes to his aid on the day of his flight. In the end it is the importance of family that survives in the thoughts of Wind Rider.

Y. creates strong characters in his novels. As he writes he assumes the personality of the character in order truly to understand its motives. His own interaction with characters creates novels that help adolescents connect with his books. He presents a taste of his own life within a story that relates to the concerns of adolescent readers.

AWARDS: *New York Times* Outstanding Book of the Year (1975), ALA NEWBERY MEDAL Honor Book, ALA Children's Book Award, INTERNATIONAL READING ASSOCIATION Children's Book Award, Carter G. WOODSON Book Award, Lewis CARROLL Shelf Award (all 1976) all for *Dragonwings. Boston Globe–Horn Book* Award for fiction (1977) and Jane Addams Children's Book Award (1978) for *Child of the Owl.* AMERICAN LIBRARY ASSOCIATION Newbery Medal Honor Book (1994) for *Dragon's Gate*

FURTHER WORKS: *American Dragons.* 1995. *The Butterfly Boy.* 1993. *The Care of the Goblin Pearls.* 1997. *The Case of the Lion Dance.* 1998. *The Cook's Family.* 1998. *Dragon Cauldron.*

1994. *The Dragon Prince.* 1997. *Dragon Steel.* 1993. *Dragon War.* 1994. *Dragon's Gate.* 1993. *The Ghost Fox.* 1997. *Hiroshima.* 1995. *The Imp That Ate My Homework.* 1998. *The Junior Thunder Lord.* 1994. *The Khan's Daughter.* 1997. *The Lost Garden.* 1996. *The Man Who Touched the Ghost.* 1993. *Mountain Light.* 1997. *The Rainbow People.* 1992. *Ribbons.* 1996. *The Serpent's Children.* 1996. *Thief of Hearts.* 1995. *Tiger Woman.* 1995. *Tree of Dreams.* 1995. *City of Dragons.* 1997. *The Shell Woman and the King.* 1993. *The Curse of the Squirrel.* 1989. *The Tom Sawyer Fires.* 1984

BIBLIOGRAPHY: Burnson, P. "In the Studio with Laurence Y." *Publishers Weekly.* May 16, 1994. *Children's Literary Review,* vol. 35, 1995. *Contemporary Literary Criticism.* vol. 35. Dinchak, M. "Recommended: Laurence Y." *English Journal.* vol. 71 no. 3, March 1982. HOPKINS, Lee Bennett, *Pauses: Autobiographical Reflections of 101 Creators of Children's Books,* 1995. Y., L. *The Lost Garden.* 1991

NANCE S. WILSON

YOLEN, Jane

Author, b. 11 February 1939, New York City

Y. identifies herself as a storyteller, a literary practitioner who is more interested in metaphor and plot than in portraying facts. Her STORYTELLING is realized through POETRY, DRAMA, PICTURE BOOKS, FOLKLORE, short stories, and novels for children, teenagers, and adults. Y.'s language is varied, in elegantly simple syntax and rich vocabulary, through more than 200 books.

As a child in New York City, Y. played imaginative games throughout the city's landscape. In first grade her class performed a play she composed. In junior high school, she completed a nonfiction book about pirates as well as a brief novel. She sold poems to magazines and presented one as a term paper while a student at Smith College (B.A., 1960). From college, Y. entered the field of publishing. In 1965, she became a professional writer on a full-time basis. She earned a Master's Degree in education at the University of Massachusetts (1976).

Y. believes the reader is necessary to storytelling; the writer presents material that is brought to life by its audience. Her FANTASY stories are metaphoric, the most dramatic one being her novel about the HOLOCAUST. In *The Devil's Arithmetic* (1988) which won the National Jewish

Book Award, Y. presents both her protagonist and the contemporary reader with an unexpected and intimate view of Nazi concentration-camp existence. Published at a time when children's fiction about the Holocaust had not allowed readers to view camp life directly, Y. was both criticized and praised for her openness on the subject. The book continues to be popular, both among fantasy readers and as curriculum support material where the Holocaust is taught in the middle grades.

Less daring but just as strong are Y.'s many collections of literary FAIRY TALES. In the tradition of Oscar Wilde, Y. creates her own folklorically charged stories. One of her collections, *Dream Weaver* (1979), offers a series of tales about what the future might hold for each of a bevy of characters according to a seer. The setting is both timeless and exotic, made even more dramatic by Michael HAGUE's ILLUSTRATIONS.

Y. frequently works with critically acclaimed illustrators. In addition to Hague, Ed YOUNG (*The Emperor and the Kite,* 1967), Remy CHARLIP (*The Seeing Stick,* 1977), Tomie DEPAOLA (*The Giants' Farm,* 1977), James MARSHALL (*How Beastly! A Menagerie of Nonsense Poems,* 1980), David WIESNER (*The Boy Who Spoke Chimp,* 1981), Barry MOSER (*Sky Dogs,* 1990), Ted LEWIN (*The Originals,* 1996), and dozens of others have given image to her narratives.

Y. writes SERIES books, for readers of widely varying ages and interests. EASY-TO-READ Commander Toad appears in *Commander Toad in Space* (1980), *Commander Toad and the Planet of the Grapes* (1982), and *Commander Toad and the Space Pirates* (1987), as well as several other pun-filled adventures, all illustrated by Bruce DEGEN. Sophisticated picture-book readers enjoy *Piggins* (1987), a porcine butler in an Edwardian home, who subsequently appears in *Picnic with Piggins* (1988) and *Piggins and the Royal Wedding* (1988), all illustrated by Jane Dyer. Children in the middle grades turn to The Young Merlin Trilogy: *Passager* (1966), *Hobby* (1996), and *Merlin* (1997) take the reader into a world of traditional literary magic. The fantasy trilogy of a dragon-keeping youth, *Dragon's Blood* (1982), *Heart's Blood* (1984), and *A Sending of Dragons* (1987), appeals to young teen readers.

Y.'s nonfiction for children addresses subjects that she finds personally compelling. *Pirates in Petticoats* (1963) and *World on a String: The Story of Kites* (1968) reflect her own youthful interests. *Friend: The Story of George Fox and the Quakers* (1972) and *Simple Gifts: The Story of the Shakers* (1976) developed from her spiritual and ethical investigations. Her many collections of original poems voice the silly, the serious and the engagingly simple, including *An Invitation to the Butterfly Ball: A Counting Rhyme* (1976), *Best Witches: Poems for Halloween* (1989), *Once upon Ice and Other Frozen Poems* (1997), *Snow, Snow* (1998), and *Mother–Daughter,* 2000.

Y. continues to write widely and prodigiously. In 1999, she published eight new books, including *Fairies' Ring: A Book of Fairy Stories and Poems; Gray Heroes: Elder Tales from Around the World;* and the first book in a new fantasy series, *The Wizard's Map: Tartan Magic.* Using alternating voices and opposing perspectives, Y. and Bruce COVILLE wrote *Armageddon Summer* (1998) about two teenagers facing a cult's cataclysmic expectations for the end of the world. The successful novel garnered many YOUNG ADULT awards. She has selected and edited many collections of traditional and contemporary fantasy stories for readers of all ages. Y. takes especial pride in the fact that *How Do Dragons Say Goodnight?* was a *New York Times* best-seller in 2000.

AWARDS: Boys Clubs America Junior Book Award (1968) for *The Minstrel and the Mountain.* ALA CALDECOTT MEDAL Honor Book, Lewis CARROLL Shelf Award, and AMERICAN LIBRARY ASSOCIATION Notable Book (1968) all for *The Emperor and the Kite* (Ed Young, illus.). Lewis Carroll Shelf Award (1973) for *The Girl Who Loved the Wind.* SOCIETY OF CHILDREN'S BOOK WRITERS AND ILLUSTRATORS Golden Kite Award (1974) for *The Girl Who Cried Flowers and Other Tales.* Christopher Medal (1978) for *The Seeing Stick.* World Fantasy Award (1988) for *Favorite Folktales from around the World* (Y. ed.). ALA Caldecott Medal (1988) for *Owl Moon* (John Schoenherr, illus.) 1989, Jewish Book Council Award, the Sydney J. TAYLOR Award from the Association of the Jewish Libraries, and the Judy Lopez Award (all 1989) for *The Devil's Arithmetic.* Y. has won several AWARDS for her fantasy novels and poems for adults. The College of Our Lady of the Elms awarded her an honorary

doctorate (1981). Catholic Library Association's Regina Medal (1992) for her body of work

FURTHER WORKS (SELECT): *Greyling: A Picture Story from the Islands of Shetland,* 1968; *The Bird of Time,* 1971; *Mice on Ice,* 1980; *Letting Swift River Go,* 1992; *Animal Fare: Poems,* 1994; *Here There Be Angels,* 1996; *King Long Shanks,* 1998

BIBLIOGRAPHY: Y., J., *Touch Magic: Fantasy, Faerie and Folklore in the Literature of Childhood,* 1981

FRANCISCA GOLDSMITH

YONGE, Charlotte

Author, b. 11 August 1823, Otterbourne, Hampshire, England; d. 24 March 1901, Elderfield, England

Y. was educated at home by her mother and father. She was a prolific writer of fiction, nonfiction, and history. Many of her works are categorized as promoting the idealized Victorian Christian family. In addition to writing hundreds of works, Y. was the editor of a periodical for young people, *The Monthly Packet.* Her life in the church was paramount in her career and inspired much of her writings. Y.'s first book *Abbey Church* was published in 1844. *The Daisy Chain* (1856), first serialized in *The Monthly Packet,* is credited with establishing the FAMILY centered story as a distinct category. Her Victorian families were often involved in church and missionary work as was typical in novels of that era. Much discussion with her family preceded permission to publish: all revenues were to be given to charity. This charitable practice persisted as she continued to write. *Heir of Redclyffe* (1853), a historic romance, brought Y. considerable popularity. She is considered a serious researcher and published an average of three books per year between 1850 and 1900 in addition to her church work and other writings.

FURTHER WORKS: *Henrietta's Wish,* 1850; *The Daisy Chain,* 1856; *History of Christian Names,* 1862; *The Clever Woman of the Family,* 1865

BIBLIOGRAPHY: Knoepflmacher, U. C., *Ventures into Childhood,* 1998; *Something about the Author.* vol. 17, 1979; *The Oxford Companion to Children's Literature,* 1984

NANCY HORTON

YORINKS, Arthur
Author, b. 21 August 1953, Roslyn, New York

Y. credits his aesthetically rich childhood, where he was surrounded by many forms of art, for his adult sensibilities to the world around him. His mother was a fashion illustrator, his aunt a piano teacher, and a friend was a young illustrator. Involved in art himself, he took piano lessons, wrote stories and poems and mimicked his mother's work drawing and painting. In high school, Y. worked with a friend creating COMIC BOOKS. At sixteen, he bravely knocked on the studio door of Maurice SENDAK, whose work he greatly admired, and asked for advice on his stories. That began a friendship between the two, some book collaborations and the founding of a national children's theater together. After high school, Y. studied acting and ballet, wrote plays, performed and taught at the American Mime Theater. Through Sendak, Y. was introduced to Richard EGIELSKI, an illustrator, and the two soon became a successful collaborative team.

Believing PICTURE BOOKS work on many levels, Y.'s often outlandish stories include irony and dry HUMOR, which he defends as appropriate for children because of their youthful perception of the world. The plots of his stories often focus on desiring something other than what one has, and are peppered with magical FANTASY that in the end helps the protagonist live "well his whole life," as in *Sid and Sol* (1977), happy to be oneself as in *It Happened in Pinsk* (1983), and finally satisfied with one's lot in life as in *Hey, Al* (1986): all illustrated by Egielski. Many of their collaborations have been recognized as award-winning books.

Y. utilizes varied sentence length and clear, staccato-like language that adds impact, information, and importance to his stories. The urban setting in many of Y.'s books such as *Hey, Al* depict cities as comfortable and vibrant places to take up residence and are based on his own experiences and appreciation of cities.

Contending that children's books are works of art rather than simply teaching tools, Y.'s stories speak of the human condition and offer a view into individual and worldly aspirations.

AWARDS: ALA CALDECOTT MEDAL (1987) for *Hey, Al* (Egielski, illus). *School Library Journal* best books of the year (1980) for *Louis the Fish,* (1988) for *Bravo Minski,* (1989) for *Oh, Brother,* and (1990) for *Ugh. Booklist's* Children's Editor's Choice (1984) for *It Happened in Pinsk*

FURTHER WORKS: With Richard Egielski: *Christmas in July.* 1991. With Maurice Sendak: *The Miami Giant.* 1995. *Frank and Joey Eat Lunch.* 1996. *Frank and Joey Go to Work.* 1996. *The Magic Meatballs.* (Under the pseudonym Alan Yaffe with Karen B. Anderson.) 1979. *Company's Coming.* (With David Small). 1988. *Whitefish Will Rides Again.* (With Mort Drucker). 1994

BIBLIOGRAPHY: *Children's Literary Review,* vol. 9, 1990; *Horn Book,* January–February 1996; Silvey, Anita, ed., *Children's Books and Their Creators,* 1995; *Sixth Book of Junior Authors and Illustrators,* 1989; *Something about the Author,* vol. 33, 1983, vol. 49, 1987, and vol. 85, 1996; *Teaching Pre–K-8,* November–December 1991; *Twentieth Century Children's Writers,* 4th ed., 1995

GERALYN A. CHESNER

YOUNG ADULT LITERATURE

Young Adult Literature, typically regarded as REALISTIC FICTION for readers aged twelve through eighteen, is an American contribution to world literature that emerged during the 1940s when adolescence—the period between childhood and early adulthood—came to be regarded as a separate stage of human development.

Many observers cite Maureen Daly's influential romance, *Seventeenth Summer* (1942), as the first young adult novel. Though actually published for adults, its enormous popularity with teenage readers inspired countless other romance novels by such authentic young adult authors as Betty CAVANNA, Janet Lambert, Rosamund DUJARDIN, Anne Emery, James L. Summers, Mary STOLZ, and others. Indeed, the 1940s, in retrospect, may be dubbed the "decade of romance."

The most significant title of the 1950s was J. D. SALINGER's *The Catcher in the Rye* (1951). Like *Seventeenth Summer* it was originally published for adults but was quickly embraced by teenagers. *Catcher* introduced important themes of adolescent angst, anomie, and alienation that, however, did not become staples of young adult fiction until nearly two decades later. In the meantime while romance remained popular, a number of other genres flourished, including SPORTS

STORIES (John R. TUNIS), ADVENTURE (Howard Pease, Robb White, Paul Annixter), and car stories (Henry Gregor Felsen) for boys. For readers of both sexes there was SCIENCE FICTION (Robert HEINLEIN, Andre NORTON), career novels (Stephen W. Meader, Helen Wells), and ANIMAL STORIES (Walter FARLEY, Fred GIPSON, Marguerite HENRY).

Although topically diverse, these books had in common their depiction of a world that looked like a *Saturday Evening Post* cover—a small-town, middle-American world populated by characters with faces as white as the picket fences that surrounded the comfortable, two-story houses in which they lived. The most serious problems that seemed to confront their protagonists were falling in love for the first time and finding a date for the senior prom.

All of this changed abruptly in 1967 with the publication of two landmark novels: *The Outsiders* by S. E. HINTON and *The Contenders* by Robert LIPSYTE. The former dealt with gang and class warfare on the mean streets of Tulsa, while the latter—set on the even meaner streets of New York City's Harlem—was an acutely observed novel about the self-transformation of a black teenager from high school dropout in a dead-end job into a contender, in the boxing ring and in life.

By focusing on the often unpleasant, life-and-death realities of adolescent life in America, these two authors pushed back the boundaries of what had previously been deemed "acceptable" in books for young readers, ushering in an era of realistic fiction that engaged—in its themes, characters, and settings—the authentic lives of American teenagers.

Thanks in large part to Hinton and Lipsyte's liberating example, the 1970s became a golden age of young adult literature, a period when such modern masters as Robert CORMIER, John DONOVAN, Richard PECK, M. E. KERR, Walter Dean MYERS, Harry MAZER, and Norma Fox MAZER began publishing. Of these, Cormier is indisputably the most important and arguably the first writer who dared to introduce determinism into young adult fiction, demonstrating that hope may be fugitive and evil might prevail.

Unfortunately innovation quickly bred less talented imitation and the seventies are, thus, also remembered as the decade of the problem novel, i.e., the work of social realism in which character,

setting, and style are sacrificed to an almost expository treatment of a single social problem: e.g., drugs, alcohol abuse, parental divorce, and so forth. The formerly taboo topic of sex also became a staple of the problem novel, though the act itself was almost never discussed; instead, its consequences (inevitably depicted as unhappy) became the topic *du jour*. One of these, abortion, was first dealt with in Paul ZINDEL's *My Darling, My Hamburger* (1969) and a second, rape, in Richard Peck's *Are You in the House Alone?* (1976). However, it was not until 1975 that the sexual act itself would be celebrated as normal and healthy in Judy BLUME's frequently banned *Forever* (1975). Perhaps in reaction to the plethora of problem novels, the 1980s became a period defined by a return of bland romances, usually published in paperback series with names like "Wildfire," "Sweet Dreams," "Caprice," "First Love," and so forth.

Also responsible for the 1980s explosion of paperbacks was the dwindling of resources available to public libraries and schools, the institutions that had been the traditional market for YA books. Now the teenagers themselves became the consumers targeted by publishers; their point of purchase was the chain bookstore, a fixture of the omnipresent shopping malls that had begun appearing in the 1970s.

By the end of the eighties, horror had replaced romance in the genre lists and the novels of Christopher Pike and R. L. STINE seemed poised to pound the final nail in the coffin of traditional hardover young adult publishing.

Predictions of the death of the young adult novel were premature, however, for by the mid-nineties, a revival was under way. In part this was due to publishers' rediscovering older teen readers, a market segment they had abandoned in the early nineties when young adult literature had turned into "middle-school literature" with protagonists as young as twelve and seldom older then fourteen. Today, however, authors like Francesca Lia BLOCK, Chris LYNCH, Rob Thomas, and Brock COLE are writing books with intrinsic appeal to high school age readers and even those in their early twenties. Protagonists have begun to grow up and their creators have begun dealing realistically, and, artfully with the complexities of their postmodern, at-risk lives. REALISTIC FICTION has taken on a harder edge and the last taboos have begun falling, including themes of child abuse and incest, which have been addressed by major writers such as Francesca Lia Block, Carolyn Coman, Cynthia VOIGT, Jacqueline WOODSON, and Brock Cole. Homosexuality has also begun emerging from publishing's closet, though cautiously. Some fifty novels with homosexual themes and characters have appeared in the first eight years of the 1990s, as many as were published altogether in the twenty years between 1969, when John Donovan first addressed the topic in *I'll Get There, It Better Be Worth the Trip,* and 1990.

Another reason for the recent revival is that, in counterpoint to the huge entertainment conglomerates that own most major American publishers today, a number of independent so-called niche PUBLISHERS have emerged. Some like Front Street and Milkweed specialize in risk-taking "literary" fiction, while others like Arte Publico, Clear Light and Lee and Low reflect the interest in MULTICULTURAL publishing that has emerged in the wake of the 1980s' surge in immigration.

For young adult literature the nineties, a decade that began with a near-death experience, is ending with a return to robust publishing activity and a rebirth of artistic viability.

MICHAEL CART

(See also CROSSOVERS: CHILDREN'S BOOKS FOR ADULT READERS.)

YOUNG, Ed (Tse-chun)

Illustrator, author, b. 28 November 1931, Tientsin, China

Y. spent his earliest years in Shanghai. He was a disinterested student even after moving to Hong Kong to attend high school. Inexplicably, he claims, he was offered a college education in the United States. After a year at City College of San Francisco, he continued his studies at the University of Illinois at the Champaign-Urbana campus and the Art Center College of Design in Los Angeles. He began his college career studying architecture but switched to commercial art. After graduation Y. went to New York where he found a job in commercial art and began graduate studies at Pratt Institute. In 1961, he was invited to illustrate a children's book when sketches he had

made at Central Park Zoo were seen by friends. Ursula Nordstrom, a children's book editor at Harper's, provided his first ILLUSTRATION assignment, *The Mean Mouse and Other Mean Stories* by Janice UDRY (1962).

Y.'s subjects, both as an illustrator and a storyteller, are usually folkloric, deriving from Chinese, Persian, and other cultures. He has illustrated Aesop (*The Lion and the Mouse,* 1979), Oscar Wilde (*The Happy Prince,* 1989) and Lafcadio Hearn (*The Voice of the Great Bell,* 1989). In addition to FOLKLORE, history has been a source of inspiration for Y. One of his favorite projects was working with Jean FRITZ illustrating *The Double Life of Pocahontas* (1985). Y. does considerable research on his projects to insure their accuracy. He has illustrated POETRY, too, including Robert FROST's *Birches* (1988).

Y. relearned traditional Chinese brush stroking as an adult and the technique informs many of his books. For *The Girl Who Loved the Wind* by Jane YOLEN (1972) he used illlustrations reminiscent of traditional Indian style; sharp delineation of miniature objects is highlighted by the dramatic use of gold. *Up a Tree* (1983) and *The Other Bone* (1984) are wordless stories in which the soft-toned illustrations focus on details of expression and motion. Extrapolating from the tones created by ink absorbed by soft paper, he has made extensive use of soft pastel and wash illustrations as well. *Foolish Rabbit's Big Mistake* (Rafe MARTIN, 1985) and *Lon Po Po* (1989) exemplify Y.'s use of broad sweeping strokes, smudging and enlarged detail to convey both mood and movement. The seeming explosion of image from the page is sometimes enhanced by presenting the illustration in panels, each extending the otherwise static surface of the picture.

Cat and Rat: The Legend of the Chinese Zodiac (1995) and *The Lost Horse: a Chinese Folktale* (1998) provide readers with insight on traditional Chinese tales through their evocative illustrations with simple texts. Both of these books display a hardening of the pastels' application to form a denser and more stylized image. *Night Visitors* (1995), which follows one small boy's exploration of the world of ants, is rendered in Y.'s early preference for soft darkness highlighted with color setting each scene ablaze.

Y. has enjoyed critical success throughout his children's book career and continues to work on his own and other writers' projects. Along with his prolific publishing, he has taught for many years at Pratt, the Naropa Institute, University of California (Santa Cruz) and Yale University.

AWARDS: American Institute of Graphic Arts Award (1962) for *The Mean Mouse and Other Stories.* ALA CALDECOTT MEDAL Honor Book (1968) for *The Emperor and the Kite* (Jane YOLEN, ed.) AMERICAN LIBRARY ASSOCIATION Notable Children's Book (1981) for *Bo Rabbit Smart for True: Folktales from the Gullah* (Priscilla Jaquith, author). ALA Caldecott Medal (1990) for *Lon Po Po: A Red Riding Hood Story from China.* ALA Caldecott Medal Honor Book (1992) for *Seven Blind Mice*

FURTHER WORKS: *Chinese MOTHER GOOSE Rhymes* (Robert Wyndham, editor), 1968; *Cricket Boy* (Feenie Ziner), 1977; *The Terrible Nung Gwama: A Chinese Folktale,* 1978; *High on a Hill: A Book of Chinese Riddles,* 1980; *Yeh-Shen: A Cinderella Story from China* (Ai-Ling Louie, reteller), 1982; *Moon Tiger* (Phyllis Root), 1985; *Eyes of the Dragon.* (Margaret Leaf), 1987; *Red Thread,* 1993; *Little Plum,* 1994; *Donkey Trouble,* 1995

BIBLIOGRAPHY: *Something about the Author,* vol. 74, 1993; *Contemporary Authors,* vol. 130, 1990; Silvey, Anita, ed., *Children's Books and Their Creators,* 1995

FRANCISCA GOLDSMITH

ZALBEN, Jane Breskin

Author, illustrator, b. 21 April 1950, New York City

Z. grew up in New York City and currently lives on Long Island with her family. She remembers drawing as something that was always a part of her life. Her mother arranged weekly art lessons at the Metropolitan Museum of Art that started when she was five years old. By second grade, Z. was writing poems for her school newspaper. Z. was also studying piano and had to decide whether to pursue music or painting. Because performing made her nervous, this gifted artist chose to study art at Queens College where she received her B.A.

After graduation, Z. worked in the art department of a New York publisher. Her job was part-time so she was able to work on her own projects while learning all aspects of BOOK DESIGN. This knowledge allowed Z. to make decisions about her books, not only writing and illustrating, but making all choices that go into book making.

Before she worked a year, Z. had a book published. In *Cecilia's Older Brother* (1973) and her next two books, Z. described her painting style as "a modern flat graphic Matisse kind of thing." Her later books became "more old-fashioned." Most critics comment on the delicacy of her water color and pencil drawings, which are described as "whimsical," "warm," and "exquisite." Z.'s sensitive paintings illuminate *Inner Chimes* (1992), POETRY collected by Bobbye Goldstein.

In ten years, Z. wrote and/or illustrated thirteen PICTURE BOOKS. Z. decided it was time to write a novel after an editor suggested that perhaps she had more to say than she could fit in a picture book. *Maybe It Will Rain Tomorrow* (1982) was the first title about common problems teens face. *Unfinished Dreams* (1996) deals with AIDS and was on several Best Books lists.

Z.'s picture book production came to a halt while she wrote the early novels but an incident about a Christmas tree with one of her children prompted Z. to write a Chanukah book. *Beni's First Chanukah* (1988) began an ongoing series of Jewish holiday stories. A new character joined Beni in 1995 when *Pearl Plants a Tree* was published. The Beni books and the Pearl books have been on the American Bookseller Pick of the List, Sidney TAYLOR Honor Books, INTERNATIONAL READING ASSOCIATION Teachers' Choice Award and *Parents'* magazine award. Z. is best known for these books that have universal appeal and help Jewish children celebrate their heritage.

FURTHER WORKS: *All in the Woodland Early,* 1979, 1991; *The Fortuneteller in 5B,* 1991; *Happy New Year, Beni,* 1988; *Leo and Blossom's Sukkah,* 1988; illus.: *Inner Chimes: Poems on Poetry* (B. Goldstein, ed.), 1992

BIBLIOGRAPHY: *Fifth Book of Junior Authors and Illustrators,* 1983; The Official Homepage of Jane Breskin Zalben, janebreskinzalben.com/library4.html; *School Library Journal,* vol. 26, 6, February 1980; *Something about the Author,* vol. 7, 1975, and vol. 79, 1995

SHARON HARTMAN

ZELINSKY, Paul O.
Author, illustrator, b. 14 February 1948, Evanston, Illinois

In 1998, Z. was awarded the CALDECOTT MEDAL for his lavish retelling of *Rapunzel* (1997), a book that took him several years to complete. Previously his books *Hansel and Gretel* (Rika Lesser, author, 1984), *Rumpelstiltskin* (1986), and *Swamp Angel* (Anne Isaacs, author, 1994) had all been named Caldcott Medal Honor Books. *The Maid and the Mouse and the Odd-Shaped House* (1981) and *The Story of Mrs. Lovewright and Purrless Her Cat* (SEGAL, 1985), along with *Swamp Angel,* had been named *New York Times* Best Illustrated Books of the Year. Unlike other illustrators with very recognizable, distinctive styles, Z. intentionally adapts his artistic style to suit the story being told; he says that his illustrations can be "recognized by their unrecognizability" and diversity of style. "I want the pictures to speak the same language as the words. This desire has led me to try various kinds of drawings in different books. I have used quite a wide stretch of styles, and I'm fortunate to have been asked to illustrate such a range of stories." However, there are some similarities among his works and certain influences can be seen in much of the art Z. has created. The faces of his characters have a distinctive wide-eyed look and architectural details are given close attention. There is clever wit even in the books that are more serious in their overall intent. *Rapunzel,* with its Renaissance Old Master influences, may represent the zenith of Z.'s style.

Z. began drawing as a very young boy, his first obsession being the geishas he admired after moving with his family to Japan at the age of two. *Highlights* magazine (1957) published his drawing of a delicate geisha in a kimono he had created before he was four years old. Young Z. moved from Japan back to Princeton, New Jersey, across the street from a construction site. He became fascinated with the big machines he saw each day digging holes and moving earth. In his drawings all the machines were being operated by geishas. By the time he was fourteen, Z. and a friend wrote and illustrated a book about a monkey astronaut who saves the world from aggressive gorillas. Several years ago, in his friend's scrapbook, Z. discovered a rejection letter from a publisher. His friend's father had unsuccessfully submitted the book to an editor Z. now considers a good friend who has published some of his adult work.

Z., though interested in science, always knew that art would be a part of his world. He did not really consider the possibilities of a career in illustrating until he took a course in the history and making of children's books at Yale University with Maurice SENDAK, his first and only illustration teacher. Sendak was the first person he mentioned in his Caldecott Medal acceptance speech when talking about the people who had influenced him, acknowledging that Sendak "raised a curtain for me on the workings of the PICTURE BOOK when he applied the word rhythm to it." Z. has always been concerned with form and its inherent beauty when it works well. He notes, "When shapes perform dances with other shapes, when colors play up and down scales, when they fall into chords, when lines move in patterns that look inevitably right, we will all feel it." He masters form to tell a vivid story, always the ultimate intent of his carefully crafted, rhythmic work.

Z. has illustrated books for many authors, giving form to their words, enhancing the feelings in their stories with his illustrations. He creates a hushed tone for Mirra GINSBURG's *The Sun's Asleep behind the Hill* (1982). The stillness of the language is repeated in the stillness of the art, beginning with long shadows washed with the soft peach and lilac light of the sunset and ending with a landscape bathed in the silver light of the moon. In novels by AVI and Beverly CLEARY, children see the emotional impact of each story in Z.'s pen and ink line drawings of the characters' faces. They are given information about the Victorian era through Z.'s research and reproduction of the time period for Avi's *How Deadwood Dick Saved the Banker's Niece: A Massachusetts Adventure.* Readers of Cleary's books see how ingenious Leigh's lunch box alarm is in *Dear Mr. Henshaw* (1983) or the intricacies of the maze Ralph must negotiate in *Ralph S. Mouse* (1982). The fine line between comedy and tragedy is reflected in his comic illustrations of poor, skinny,

127. JANE YOLEN

128. ED YOUNG

129. PAUL O. ZELINSKY

130. PAUL ZINDEL

frustrated Mrs. Lovewright as she is abused by her large, nonpurring cat (*The Story of Mrs. Lovewright and Purrless Her Cat*). Angelica Longrider, also known as Swamp Angel, looks directly at the reader from her prim Early American portrait on the title page. While the style of the art may be reminiscent of the static portraiture of a much earlier time, Z.'s illustrations capture the tall-tale HUMOR and sweep of Swamp Angel's remarkable feats. Swamp Angel and Tarnation, the giant bear, wrestle across the pages with Herculean effort, and readers tumble headlong through the book, anxious to see the outcome of the fight.

In his adaptation of a children's favorite traditional song, *The Wheels on the Bus* (1990), Z.'s clever comic exuberance perfectly suits the rollicking lyrics. Everything is in motion at once, and not just because it is "a book with parts that move." On the first double page spread, a dog leaps at a boy carrying a box that observant readers soon realize is full of kittens while racing after the zooming bus. The illustrations are done in bright rainbow colors touched with a rainbow iridescence. Purple tree trunks and pigeons with hot pink feet stand in front of turquoise and orange houses. Young children love the pictures of bus riders lurching "all over town."

With delicate pastels, comic Early American primitive style and MOTHER GOOSE–inspired characters, Z. tells the harrowing story of a maid and her plump mouse who are threatened by a hungry cat of their own unintentional creation in *The Maid and the Mouse and the Odd-shaped House,* an adaptation of an 1897 rhyming "tell and draw" story. The whimsical illustrations are a contrast to the dangerous surprise that is foreshadowed in the background action.

Of all his books, Z. is probably best known for his retelling of two folktales, *Rumpelstiltskin* and *Rapunzel,* both illustrated in a style influenced by the Old Masters. His research and attention to detail, from correct costuming and architecture to the comb Rapunzel uses or the spinning wheel used by Rumpelstiltskin, is vital in retelling stories set in the time periods and locations he envisions. When Z. decided that *Rapunzel* needed to be told as an Italian story with the young woman living in a marble Tuscan tower, he worked at re-creating the beauty he admired in art by Renais-

sance painters Raphael and Rembrandt. His pictures look as if they were created hundreds of years ago in Europe; they are perfectly suited to his vision of the story he tells.

Z. wrote, "What the children reading my books make me out to be, if anything, I can't guess. But it really doesn't matter: it's not the authors they should remember, it's the books. (Or maybe, for the most part, the pictures!)"

FURTHER WORKS: As illustrator: *The Sun's Asleep behind the Hill.* (GINSBURG), 1982; *Emily Uphan's Revenge* (AVI), 1978; *More Rootabagas.* (SANDBURG), 1993; *Random House Book of Humor for Children* (Pollack), 1988; *The Enchanted Castle* (E. NESBIT), 1992; *Strider* (Cleary. 1991)

BIBLIOGRAPHY: Brooks, Donna. "Paul O. Z.: Geishas on Tractors." *Horn Book* magazine, July/August, 1998. pps. 442–49. Dutton Children's Books, pamphlet on Paul O. Z. Peck, Jackie and Judy Hendershot. "Release from 'GRIMM' Captivity: Paul O. Z; Talks about the Making of *Rapunzel,* the 1998 Caldecott Medal Winner," *The Reading Teacher.* March, 1999, pps. 570–75. *Something about the Author.* vol. 102, 1999. STEWIG, John Warren. "A Caldecott Committee at Work." *Book Links.* March 1999. pps. 15–18; Z., Paul O. "Caldecott Medal Acceptance." *Horn Book* magazine. July/August 1998, pps. 433–41

REBECCA RAPPORT

ZEMACH, Harve

Author, educator, b. 5 December 1933, Newark, New Jersey; d. 2 November, 1974, London, England

Z. was born Harvey Fischtrom. He graduated from Wesleyan University in Middletown, Connecticut, and won a Fulbright Scholarship to continue his studies at the University of Vienna, Austria. There he met and married another Fulbright scholar, illustrator Margot ZEMACH, with whom he collaborated writing children's books.

During the early years of their marriage, the Z.s stayed in Europe and began their joint effort writing children's books. Z. decided to use the pseudonym, Harve Zemach, for all professional collaborations with his wife. This left their name, Mrs. and Mrs. Harvey Fischtrom, to use for their private life, a very clear distinction for them.

A Small Boy Is Listening (1959), an original story by Z. about MUSIC in Vienna, was their first book. Living in Italy, Denmark, and England sparked an interest in folktales from cultures all over the world. This interest definitely influenced the books that were to follow. The couple returned to the United States in 1961 for Z. to teach history and social science at Boston University while continuing to search folk literature collections for book ideas. An important find were the verses for *Mommy, Buy Me a China Doll* (1966), an Ozark Mountain children's song that was a perfect fit for the PICTURE BOOK format; it became their first AMERICAN LIBRARY ASSOCIATION Notable Children's Book.

A few years later, Z. used cumulative verse in folktale style to narrate *The Judge: An Untrue Tale* (1969), one of his most humorous efforts. This refreshing book was both an ALA Notable Book and a 1970 ALA CALDECOTT MEDAL Honor book. Z. continued retelling folktales when he wrote *Duffy and the Devil: A Cornish Tale,* winner of the 1974 Caldecott Medal. This Rumpelstiltskin variant involves spinning, sewing, and knitting clothing instead of gold. Everything Tarraway, the Rumpelstiltskin character, knitted for the young maiden, Duffy, turns to ashes when she guesses his name. The squire returns home wearing nothing but his hat and his shoes. Children love the rollicking good HUMOR of the text and the ILLUSTRATIONS.

Z.'s last book, *The Princess and the Froggie* (1975), expanded the family collaboration. Margot illustrated the book, as she did all of his texts, but their daughter, Kaethe, helped her father write this final manuscript. The dozen books that Z. produced following his first story were all retellings or written in the style of folk literature, confirming the influence folk literature had on his writing.

FURTHER WORKS: All with Margot Zemach: *Nail Soup: A Swedish Folk Tale Retold,* 1964; *Salt: A Russian Tale,* 1965; *Too Much Noise: An Italian Tale,* 1967; *Judge, an Untrue Tale,* 1969; *Penny a Look.* 1971

BIBLIOGRAPHY: Bader, Barbara. *American Picturebooks from Noah's Ark to The Beast Within,* 1976; Huck, Charlotte, *Children's Literature in the Elementary School,* 1979; *Something about the Author,* vol. 3, 1972

SHARON HARTMAN

ZEMACH, Margot

Author, illustrator, b. 30 November 1931, Los Angeles, California; d. 21 May 1989, Berkeley, California

Z. grew up in California. Both her parents were in show business and this early influence led to her theatrical metaphor about books. She once said that "when the book closes, the curtain comes down," explaining how her books are like a play.

From an early age, Z. was determined to be an artist. She studied art in Los Angeles and won a Fulbright Scholarship to continue her education at the Vienna Academy of Fine Arts. While there she met another Fulbright Scholar, Harvey Fischstrom. The two married and began a lifetime of collaboration on children's books. For this union, Fischstrom took the pseudonym of Harve ZEMACH. He wrote and Z. illustrated a total of thirteen books together. She illustrated works of her own and of others, as well. During the early years of their marriage they lived in Europe where they became interested in folktales and their variants. This was a natural extension of Z.'s early drawings. As a child, she illustrated her favorite FAIRY TALES.

A Small Boy Is Listening (1959), a story about MUSIC in Vienna, was their first collaboration. Z. is best remembered for the books that followed. Her line drawings with color wash are known for their HUMOR and for incredible detail. Z. said, "Children need detail, color, excellence—the best a person can do." She often drew the same page thirty to forty times to meet that standard.

Z.'s books have won many major AWARDS. Harve's adaptation and Z.'s ILLUSTRATIONS for *Mommy, Buy Me a China Doll* (1966) was the first of their several AMERICAN LIBRARY ASSOCIATION Notable Children's Book awards. Z.'s illustrations for *Duffy and the Devil, a Cornish Tale* received the 1974 ALA CALDECOTT MEDAL and the second Lewis CARROLL Bookshelf Award. *The Just, An Untrue Tale* (1969) and *It Could Always Be Worse* (1976) were Caldecott Medal Honor books. *Hush, Little Baby* (1976) was chosen to represent the United States by the INTERNATIONAL BOARD ON BOOKS FOR YOUNG PEOPLE. Z. was nominated twice as the U.S. candidate for the Hans Christian ANDERSEN Award, an international award given to honor an illustrator's total body of work. Several of her titles were listed on the *New York Times* Best Illustrated Books list. *Self-Portrait: Margot Z.* (1978) was an Honor Book for the *Boston Globe–Horn Book* Award.

Z. has been hailed in the United States as "a national treasure." Her peers regard her with utmost respect. William STEIG summed it up best when he proclaimed her "the consummate illustrator for children's literature. There's no doubt her work will endure."

FURTHER WORKS: Author: *Little Red Hen, An Old Story.* 1983. *Three Wishes: An Old Story.* 1986. Illustrator: *Mazel and Shlimazel: Or, The Milk of a Lioness.* (I.B. SINGER). 1967. *Naftali the Storyteller and His Horse Sus.* (I. B. Singer). 1987

BIBLIOGRAPHY: Bader, Barbara. *American Picturebooks from Noah's Ark to The Beast Within.* 1976. Silvey, Anita, ed. *Children's Books and Their Creators.* 1995. *Something about the Author,* vol. 21, 1980, vol. 59, 1990, and vol. 70, 1993. *Third Book of Junior Authors.* 1972

SHARON HARTMAN

ZIEFERT, Harriet
Author, b. July 7, 1941, North Bergen, New Jersey

Z., originally an elementary school teacher, creates and packages large quantities of EASY-TO-READ PICTURE BOOKS for young readers that help them learn the skills needed during the early elementary years. For instance, Z.'s concept books, including *Bear All Year* (1986), *Bear Gets Dressed* (1986), and *Bear Goes Shopping* (1986), help beginning readers learn the concepts of time, sequencing, and days of the week. Z. depicts activities such as getting dressed and doing chores in her books *So Big! So Busy! So Clean! So Hungry!* and *So Little!* (1987), and *My Clothes and My Food* (1996). Other concepts Z. conveys in her books include counting, the alphabet, and rhyming.

Z. has published over one hundred books in twenty years. It takes her about twelve hours to produce the text of a book, because she tells a single story in fifty to seventy-five words. After completing the text, she finds an illustrator and printer. She then takes the completed package to the publisher, which allows her to have control over her work, something she believes is extremely important.

FURTHER WORKS: *A New Coat for Anna* (Anita Lobel, illus.), 1989; *Baby Buggy, Buggy Baby,* 1997; *April Fool,* 2000

BIBLIOGRAPHY: *Something about the Author,* vol. 101, 1999

DENISE P. BEASLEY

ZIM, Herbert
Author, teacher, editor, b. 12 July 1909, New York City; d. 5 December 1994, Plantation, Florida

Z. was surprised to find himself an author. It was never something he aspired to be and he never took any writing courses beyond what was required. In school, he wrote for the newspaper and won some writing awards but from a very young age he wanted to be a scientist. Z. spent his youth collecting specimens and doing experiments; any spare time was spent in the science lab. At seventeen, before graduating from high school, he was hired as a science teacher for elementary students. For the next thirty years, he taught science at various levels, even while he was in school himself, earning a B.S., M.A., and a Ph.D., all from Columbia University. Z. influenced how science is now taught in the early grades by developing the first elementary science laboratories. He said he began writing in response to the questions and needs of young readers. His first book, *Mice, Men, and Elephants* (1942), about reproduction and intelligence, was written for students age twelve and up. He continued writing books about why and how things happen for this age group until an editor approached him about writing for a younger audience. *Elephants* (1946), the first single-species book, was his answer to this request. In it Z. was able to pare down the material by selecting key essential data and connecting it to the child's world. This worked so well he wrote fifty titles following this format and is credited with having a major impact on other writers of nonfiction for children. Z.'s success is attributed to his passion for being clear, up to date and accurate and for his knowledge of what children want to know. He noted that many of his students not only liked INFORMATIONAL BOOKS, but many of them preferred this long-neglected genre.

While continuing to write books, Z. also began editing the Golden Guides. *American Birds and Wildflowers* (1949) was the first of these enormously popular self-teaching nature books. The publisher was so pleased, Z. was given a staff of six and an office in the Florida Keys to continue producing the guides. By 1986, over a dozen titles had sold well over a million copies each and *Birds of the World* (1961) had been translated into five languages.

At the time of his death, Z. had written over one hundred books for young people. His work had taken him all over the world and he had changed that world—at least in the way science is taught and children's information books are written.

FURTHER WORKS: *Our Wonderful World,* 1955–60; *The Golden Book Encyclopedia of Natural Science,* 1962

BIBLIOGRAPHY: Bader, Barbara, *American PICTURE BOOKS from Noah's Ark to The Beast Within,* 1976; *Junior Book of Authors,* 1951; Silvey, Anita, ed., *Children's Books and Their Creators,* 1995; *Something about the Author,* vol. 1, 1971, and vol. 30, 1983; *Something about the Author Autobiographical Series,* vol. 2, 1986

SHARON HARTMAN

ZINDEL, Paul
Author, b. 15 May 1936, Staten Island, New York

Z. lived a turbulent childhood. His family, headed by his mother, moved frequently. The lack of continuity of homes and friends helped him develop a powerful imagination. He never left Staten Island, but he saw the world. In one significant move he met his "Pigman," the adult who helped him sort out the dilemmas of adolescence. Z. recounts this experience in his autobiography *The Pigman and Me* (1991).

While he lived in Staten Island, Z. realized that writing might be in his future. When asking his "Pigman" for advice, he was encouraged to write. He wrote his first play in high school. Z. entered the play in a contest sponsored by the American Cancer Society and won a fountain pen. Z. attended Wagner College on Staten Island majoring in chemistry. During this time, he took a creative writing class with playwright Edward Albee who became his mentor and encouraged him to pursue writing.

Z.'s first career was an attempt to combine his two loves, writing and chemistry. He became a technical writer at a chemical company. After just a few months, Z. returned to Wagner to earn an

M.S. in Education. For ten years, 1959–69, Z. taught high school chemistry. His experience with teenagers and his willingness to listen, proved an invaluable resource for his writing. While teaching, Z. continued to write plays. In 1963 he wrote *The Effect of Gamma Rays on Man-in-the-Moon Marigolds.* In 1965 the play was produced on stage, and in 1966, produced for television. In 1971, Z. was awarded a Pulitzer Prize for *Marigolds.*

The television version of *Marigolds* led to Z.'s dual career as a dramatist and YOUNG ADULT author. Charlotte ZOLOTOW, children's book editor for Harper and Row, was moved by the realistic dialogue and depictions of teenagers in *Marigolds,* and asked Z. if he would be interested in writing for young adults. After a look at the existing literature for this age group, Z. decided to do so. The result was *The Pigman* (1969), a story about two teenagers, Lorraine and John, who tell the tale of their relationship with a lonely old man. In its departure from traditional books for young adults, *The Pigman* is considered a trail blazer in the young adult literary genre.

The characters in Z.'s books are believable; they encounter emotions similar to young adults who read them. Z. addresses basic themes of loneliness, self-deprecation, and parental resentment. When he taught, he took time to listen and learn about his students. He saw they often felt alone in the world; Z.'s characters often speak of their feelings of isolation. In *The Amazing and Death Defying Diary of Eugene Dingman* (1987) Eugene struggles with feeling different from his peers. Z.'s characters exhibit real emotions of adolescents who feel they are alone in struggling to sort out the confusing world.

As teenagers struggle for an understanding of the world, they often have a negative view of themselves. Z.'s readers relate to his characters easily; they question their physical appearance and mental capacities. Liz, Sean, Maggie, and Dennis, the characters in *My Darling, My Hamburger* (1969), are constantly evaluating their physical and mental worth. In *A Begonia for Miss Applebaum* (1989) Henry and Zelda question their actions and analyze each other. Feelings of insecurity are common among Z.'s characters. The parents in Z.'s novels are incompetent or people to be loathed. As children become teenagers they begin to see their parents' faults. In *The Pigman,* John and Lorraine's parents each have their faults. In *My Darling, My Hamburger,* Liz acts out against her parents' wishes and makes the mistake of a lifetime.

Z. does not limit his writing to young adults; he writes books for middle-grade readers such as *The Wacky Facts Lunch Bunch* (1994) and *Doom Stone* (1995), and he continues to write plays. These include *Ladies at the Alamo* (1977), *And Miss Reardon Drinks a Little* (1967), and *The Secret Affairs of Mildred Wild* (1972).

AWARDS: Ford Foundation Grant (1967) for DRAMA. Child Study Association of America's Children's Books of the Year (1968) for *The Pigman. New York Times* Outstanding Children's Books of the Year (1969) for *My Darling, My Hamburger,* (1970) for *I Never Loved Your Mind,* (1976) for *Pardon Me, You're Stepping on My Eyeball!* (1976) for *The Undertaker's Gone Bananas,* and (1980) for *The Pigman's Legacy.* Obie Award for Best American Play, New York Drama Critics Vernon Rice Drama Desk Award for the Most Promising Playwright, and New York Drama Critics Circle Award for Best American Play of the Year (all 1970), Pulitzer Prize in Drama and New York Critics Award (both 1971) all for *The Effect of Gamma Rays on Man-in-the-Moon Marigolds.* Honorary Doctorate of Humanities from Wagner College (1971) AMERICAN LIBRARY ASSOCIATION Best Young Adult Books (1971) for *The Effect of Gamma Rays on Man-in-the-Moon Marigolds,* (1975) for *The Pigman,* (1976) for *Pardon Me, You're Stepping on My Eyeball!* (1977) for *Confessions of a Teenage Baboon,* (1980) for *The Pigman's Legacy,* and (1982) for *To Take a Dare*

FURTHER WORKS: *I Never Loved Your Mind,* 1970; *I Love My Mother,* 1975; *The Girl Who Wanted a Boy,* 1981; *Let Me Hear You Whisper* (play), 1966

BIBLIOGRAPHY: *Children's Literary Review,* vol. 3, 1978, and vol. 45, 1998; *Contemporary Authors, New Revision Series,* vol. 31; *Contemporary Literary Criticism,* vol. 26; *Dictionary of Literary Biography,* vol. 7, 1981, and vol. 52, 1986; L. L. Harris, "Paul Z.," *Biography Today, Author Series,* vol. 1, 1995; *Something about the Author,* vol. 58, 1990; Rees, David, *The Marble in the Water: Essays on Contemporary Writers of Fiction for Children and Young Adults,* 1980; D. L. Winarski, "Paul Z.: Flirting with the Bizarre," *Teaching K-8,* vol. 25, no. 3, pp. 47–49

NANCE S. WILSON

ZION, Gene

Author, b. 1913, New York City; d. 5 December, 1975, New York City

Z. said he knew he was an artist when his kindergarten teacher praised one of his drawings. His first paid job was painting pictures on the back of his classmates' raincoats. Eventually this talent led to an art degree from Brooklyn's Pratt Institute. In 1936, Z. won a national travel poster contest. The prize was a trip to Europe. While there, he became interested in the design and printing of books after visiting printing plants. During World War II, Z. served in the army, designing training manuals and filmstrips. When the war was over, Z. worked in television and magazine art departments before working independently as a designer and art director.

Z. credited his wife, children's illustrator Margaret Bloy GRAHAM, and editor Ursula Nordstrom with convincing him to write children's books for Graham to illustrate. Z.'s first book, *All Falling Down* (1951) was inspired by a drawing of children picking apples that Graham had done many years earlier. The simple story of objects that fall, except for a falling baby who is rescued, was well received and honored for its ILLUSTRATIONS.

Harry, a white dog with black spots, is Z.'s most beloved character. In *Harry the Dirty Dog* (1956), Harry, like many children who read the book, hates to take baths. The gentle HUMOR and the theme strike a familiar chord with children today, just as they did more than fifty years ago when the book was published. The New York Public Library has this book on its list of one hundred PICTURE BOOKS Everyone Should Know. In fact, most suggested-reading lists for young children include the Harry books. Z. took Harry on three more adventures. *No Roses for Harry* (1958), *Harry and the Lady Next Door* (1960), and *Harry by the Sea* (1965) make up the set.

The idea for *The Plant Sitter* (1959) came from an ongoing problem for Z. Who waters the plants when you are out of town? Tommy solves this dilemma for his neighbors when he decides to take care of plants one summer. The plants eventually take over the house but Tommy knows just what to do. He goes to the library looking for a book to help solve his problem. The story is a great commercial for where to get information when you need it and goes back to Z.'s love of books and libraries when he was a child.

In all, Z. and Graham collaborated on thirteen books, he as writer and she as illustrator. When his publishing career ended in 1968, Z. evaluated his experience by noting that no creative effort had been more gratifying than writing books for children.

FURTHER WORKS: *Dear Garbage Man,* 1957

BIBLIOGRAPHY: *More Junior Authors,* 1963; Silvey, Anita, ed., *Children's Books and Their Creators,* 1995; *Something about the Author,* vol. 18, 1980

SHARON HARTMAN

ZOLOTOW, Charlotte S.
Author, editor, b. 26 June 1915, Norfolk, Virginia

Z., distinguished both as a writer and an influential book editor, developed an early love for writing, which was nurtured by Ursula Nordstrom, the famed children's book editor at Harper's. Z. held numerous positions at Harper's over several decades; Harper's has published many of her books, beginning with her first, *The Park Book* (1944). Z.'s PICTURE BOOKS have been illustrated by some of the finest artists in the field, including Leonard WEISGARD, Garth WILLIAMS, Roger DU-VOISIN, Uri SHULEVITZ, and Maurice SENDAK. *Mr. Rabbit and the Lovely Present* (1962) illustrated by Sendak, has the distinction of being both a CALDECOTT MEDAL and a NEWBERY MEDAL Honor Book. *William's Doll* (1972), illustrated by William Pene DU BOIS, about a boy with an attachment to a doll, was an early children's book attempting to break down gender stereotypes. In *My Grandson Lew* (1974), Z. broaches the delicate subject of a child's dealing with the death of a grandparent. In addition to her writing, Z.'s influence in children's book publishing has been considerable; she acquired her own imprint from HarperCollins. Z. has also published books under the pseudonyms Charlotte Bookman and Sarah Abbott.

AWARDS: AMERICAN LIBRARY ASSOCIATION Newbery Medal Honor Book (1962) for *Mr. Rabbit and the Lovely Present.* ALA Caldecott Medal Honor Book (1953) for *The Storm Book* (Margaret Bloy GRAHAM, illus), (1962) for *Mr. Rabbit and the Lovely Present* (Maurice Sendak, illus.). *New York Times* Outstanding Book of the Year

and *School Library Journal* Best Book of the Year (1972) for *William's Doll.* Christopher Award (1974) for *My Grandson Lew*

FURTHER WORKS: *A Father like That* (Ben Schecter, illus.), 1971; *Someone New* (Erik BLEG-VAD, illus.), 1978; *The Song* (Nancy TAFURI, illus.), 1982

BIBLIOGRAPHY: HOPKINS, Lee Bennett, *Pauses: Autobiographical Reflections of 101 Creators of Children's Books,* 1995; *Something about the Author,* vol. 35, 1984

DAVID L. RUSSELL

ZWERGER, Lisbeth
Illustrator, b. 26 May 1965, Vienna, Austria

As a child, growing up with a father who was a graphic artist, Z. was encouraged to draw by her parents but school was a different matter. She "was a problem child," interested in illustrating, not in academics. Her teachers were "antiillustration." Eventually she lost interest in drawing altogether until she met John Rowe, an English artist. He brought her a book by Arthur RACKHAM and that book "Was to change my whole outlook if not my life!" As Z. looked through the book, "My love for illustrating returned there and then." The ILLUSTRATIONS for her first book, *The Strange Child* (1984), took a year to finish and were honored for graphic excellence at the Bologna International Book Fair. Accuracy of detail is important to her and over the years her art has evolved to include more color. Z.'s eloquent watercolors often accompany traditional tales such as Hans Christian ANDERSEN's *Swineherd* (1995) and *The Nightingale* (1984, 1999). The *New York Times* chose *The Gift of the Magi* (1982) and *Little Red Cap* (1983) as among the Best Illustrated Books of the year. In 1990 she was awarded the Hans Christian Andersen Medal for lifetime achievement and contribution to the field of children's literature. Her never-ending search is to find a story she likes to illustrate. "When I look for a story, it has to contain all the right ingredients. . . . It has to be the sort of story that my type of illustrations fit."

BIBLIOGRAPHY: *Fiction, FOLKLORE, FANTASY and POETRY for Children, 1876–1985,* vol. 1, 1986; Silvey, Anita, ed., *Children's Books and Their Creators,* 1995; *Something about the Author,* vol. 66, 1991

IRVYN GILBERTSON

Index

L'Engle, Madeleine, 10, 82, 260, 276,
    472–73, 699
Lenski, Lois, 128, 437, 474, 589, 634
Lent, Blair, 139, 475, 559
Lepman, Jella, 407, 408
Leprince de Beaumont, Marie, 272
Lesnik-Oberstein, Karin, 207
Lessac, Frane, 338, 476
Lester, Julius, 63, 82, 260, 296, 349,
    476–77, 712
Le Tord, Bijou, 81
Levi, Primo, 379
Levinson, Riki, 325
Levitin, Sonia, 477, 700
Levitt, Sidney, 258
Levy, Constance, 368
Levy, Elizabeth, 160, 312
Lewin, Betsy, 478
Lewin, Ted, 354, 478, 534, 616
Lewis, Claudia, 86
Lewis, C. S., 10, 82, 135, 197, 237, 276,
    341, 478–79, 613, 678, 780, 831
Lewis, David, 207
Lewis, E. B., 12
Lewis, J. Patrick, 163, 479–80
Lexau, Joan M., 480
Li, Yao-wen, 434
Liddell, Alice, 152
Liggett, Twila, 659
Lincoln, Abraham, 84, 298
Lind, Jenny, 34
Lindbergh, Charles and Anne Morrow,
    486
Lindbergh, Reeve, 486
Lindgren, Astrid, 390, 436, 486–87, 782
Lindquist, Willis, 557
Linton, Ralph, 377
Linton, W. J., 203
Lionni, Leo, 30, 38, 399, 488–89
Lipkind, William, 260, 557
Lipsyte, Robert, 489, 743, 840
Lisle, Janet Taylor, 490
Little, Jean, 144, 490–91
Little, Lessie Jones, 317, 333
Lively, Penelope, 491–92
Livingston, Henry, 556
Livingston, Myra Cohn, 38, 86, 288,
    338, 436–37, 492–93, 635, 693
Llull, Ramon, 562
Lobel, Anita, 210, 493, 495, 553
Lobel, Arnold, 38, 139, 258, 390, 414,
    493–95, 513, 641
Locke, John, 272, 586
Locker, Thomas, 126, 496
Lockwood, Nancy Harris, 158
Lofting, Hugh, 10, 118, 171, 496–97,
    588, 649
London, Jack, 497
Long, Richard, 410
Longfellow, Henry Wadsworth, 497,
    560
Lonnrot, Elias, 756
Lopshire, Robert Martin, 498
Lord, Betty Bao, 498
Lorenzini, Carlo. *See* Collodi, Carlo
Lorraine, Walter, 260, 795
Lothrop, Harriet, 662, 717
Louie, Ai-Ling, 498
Louie, B. Y., 408
Lovechild, N., 561

Lovelace, Maud Hart, 499
Low, Alice, 282, 290, 499
Low, Joseph, 260
Lowry, Lois, 10, 80, 273, 379, 389, 391,
    436, 499–500, 661, 699
Lucado, Max, 82
Lucas, E. V., 715
Lunn, Janet, 143, 144, 501
Lynch, Chris, 501–2, 743, 840
Lynch, P. J., 363, 502
Lyon, George Ella, 502–3
Lyons, Mary E., 503

M

Macaulay, David, 140, 260, 402, 504–5,
    795
MacDonald, Betty, 505–6
Macdonald, Ewen, 554–55
MacDonald, George, xix, 114, 226, 276,
    442, 506, 552, 705
MacDonald, Golden, 138
MacDonald, Suse, 506
Macey, Barry, 94
Mackay, Claire, 144
MacLachlan, Patricia, 88, 159, 273, 447,
    507–8
MacLeish, Archibald, 544
MacMurray, Fred, 417
Madhubuti, Haki, 13
Mado, Michio, 782
Maestro, Betsy, 508–9
Maestro, Giulio, 508–9
Maggio, Viqui, 83
Magorian, Michelle, 511
Mahy, Margaret, 512, 590–92
Maitland, Anthony, 616
Major, Kevin, 144
Malmkjaer, Kirsten, 207
Mamet, David, 720
Mandel, Ellen, 381
Mandela, Nelson, 14
Manna, Anthony, 381
Manning-Sanders, Ruth, 513
Manushkin, Fran, 513
Marcellino, Fred, 63, 513–14
Marchetta, Melina, 48
Marino, Jan, 514
Mark, Jan, 514–16
Marks, J., 366
Mark Twain. See Twain, Mark; Clem-
    ens, Samuel L.
Marrella, Maria Pia, 508
Marrin, Albert, 56, 516
Marryat, Captain, 113
Marsden, John, 48
Marshak, Samuel, 516–17
Marshall, James, 23, 260, 517–18, 705
Martchenko, Michael, 144
Marti, Jose, 462, 463
Martin, Ann, 219, 518–19, 707
Martin, Bill, Jr., 39–40, 147, 519–20,
    655
Martin, Jacqueline Briggs, 523, 754
Martin, Patricia, 521
Martin, Rafe, 521, 712, 841
Martinez, Victor, 211
Martorell, Antonio, 464
Maruki, Toshi, 627
Marzollo, Jean, 522, 815–16
Masefield, John, 298, 522

Mason, Arthur, 467
Massee, May, 75, 76, 259, 529, 649
Mathers, Petra, 238, 523
Mathiews, Franklin K., 481, 542, 588
Mathis, Sharon Bell, 12, 237, 239, 317,
    332, 523–24
Matthews, Downs, 524
Maule, Tex, 743
May, Karl, 524–25
Mayer, Gina, 526
Mayer, Marianna, 525, 526
Mayer, Mercer, 525–26
Mayne, William, 114, 308, 526–27
Mays, Osceola, 55
Mazer, Harry, 527, 528
Mazer, Norma Fox, 527, 528
Mazzola, Anthony, 76
McBride, Roger Lea, 818
McCabe, Kevin, 554
McCaffrey, Anne, 10, 528, 699
McCampbell, Darlene, 210
McCaughrean, Geraldine, 529
McCauley, David, 399
McClelland, Linda, 592
McCloskey, Robert, 27, 102, 138, 259,
    275, 389, 400, 529–31, 571, 690
McCloud, Scott, 190
McCord, David, 29, 531–32, 635, 636,
    722
McCracken, Harold, 37
McCullers, Carson, 237
McCully, Emily Arnold, 8, 106, 344,
    436, 532–33, 674
McCurdy, Michael, 399
McDermott, Gerald, 139, 399, 533, 575,
    576, 581
McDonald, Alan, 82
McDonald, Megan, 259, 534
McElderry, Margaret, 197, 260, 437,
    493, 649
McGillis, Roderick, 206
McGinley, Phyllis, 534–35, 725
McGovern, Ann, 85, 535
McGowan, Gary, 347
McGraw, Eloise Jarvis, 536
McIntyre, Vonda, 699
McKee, David, 94
McKillip, Patricia, 536
McKinley, Robin, 10, 276, 536
McKissack, Frederick L., 249–50, 537
McKissack, Patricia C., 12, 249–50,
    257, 413, 537
McLerran, Alice, 428
McMillan, Bruce, 106, 343–44, 538–59
McNally, Bruce, 642
McNeer, May, 807
McPhail, David, 38, 539
Meadows, Isabelle, 580
Meaker, Marijane Agnes, 437
Means, Florence Crannell, 540
Meddaugh, Susan, 540
Medearis, Angela Shelf, 540–41
Medearis, Michael, 541
Meek, Margaret, 207, 647
Meigs, Cornelia, 84, 171, 541
Melcher, Frederic, 141, 481, 542, 587,
    588
Mellonie, Bryan, 222
Meltzer, Milton, 386, 404, 491, 542–43
Melville, Herman, 559